German Technical Dictionary

Universal-Wörterbuch der Technik Englisch

Routledge
German Technical Dictionary
Universal-Wörterbuch der Technik Englisch

Volume/Band
1

GERMAN – ENGLISH
DEUTSCH – ENGLISCH

London and New York

First published 1996
by Routledge
11 New Fetter Lane, London EC4P 4EE

A division of International Thomson Publishing Inc.
The ITP is a trademark under licence.

Simultaneously published in the USA and Canada
by Routledge
29 West 35th Street, New York, NY 10001

© 1996 Routledge

Conversion tables adapted from *Dictionary of Scientific Units*, H. G. Jerrard and
D. B. McNeill, London: Chapman & Hall, 1992

Typeset in Monotype Times, Helvetica 55 and Bauer Bodoni
by Routledge

Printed in Great Britain by TJ Press (Padstow), Cornwall

Printed on acid-free paper

British Library Cataloguing-in-Publication Data
A catalogue record for this book is available from the British Library

Library of Congress Cataloging-in-Publication Data
Applied for

ISBNs:
Vol 1 German–English 0–415–11209–5
Vol 2 English–German 0–415–11210–9
2-volume set 0–415–09392–9

Contents/Inhalt

German Technical Dictionary
Universal-Wörterbuch der Technik Englisch

Project Manager/Projektmanagement

Susanne Jordans

Programme Manager/ Programmleitung

Elizabeth White

Managing Editor/Redaktionsleitung

Sinda López

Editorial/Lektorat

Martin Barr   Gemma Marren
Lisa Carden

Marketing

Rachel Miller   Judith Watts

Systems/Datenbanksystem

Simon Thompson

Administration/Verwaltung

Kristoffer Blegvad   Jessica Ramage
Amanda Brindley

Production/Herstellung

Abigail Carter   Maureen James
Susan Hayes   Nigel Marsh

Contributors/Mitarbeit

Gerta K. Badde
Prof. Klaus Bethge
Hans Bokx
Dr. Jan C. Bongaerts
Martina Ebeling
Claus Eberhard
Dr G. M. Ettinger
Thomas D. Feise
Henry Freeman
Sabine Gerwin
Günter Glass
Prof. L. Göttsching
Rosemarie Hagenkordt-Hafner
Prof. Helmut Herminghaus
Annegret Hoyer
Dr. Hans-Dieter Junge
Barbara Ketzer
Dagmar Kiefer
Dr. Thomas B. Koch
Dr. Armin Kohl
Dr. Harald Krüger
Verena Krüpe
Petra Labonte

Dr. Erich Lück
Dr. Klaus Magdlung
Astrid I. Mangold
Bärbel McCloskey
Günter Merboth
Marion Meunier-Geske
Amy Newland
Karl Heinz Peters
Frank Petzold
Dr. Jens Peter Rehahn
Prof. Karl G. Roesner
Margit Röntgen-Bick
Peter A.W. Rosenthal
Petra Schaaf
Christian Schmidt
Renate Schreiber
Ulrike Seeberger
H.J. Stellbrink
Dorothy Thierstein
Günter Thierstein
Klaus G. Viermann
Otto Vollnhals

The English term list is based on our database of terminology first published in the *Routledge French Technical Dictionary*, 1994. We gratefully acknowledge the original contribution of the following:

Die englische Stichwortliste folgt inhaltlich der bereits für das *Routledge French Technical Dictionary* zusammengetragenen Datenbank (1994). Für diese englische Ursprungsterminologie danken wir:

Yves Arden, Réjane Amery, Josephine Bacon, John P. Bryon, Michael Carpenter, Anna Cordon, Maguy Couette, Elisabeth Coyne, P.J. Doyle, J.V. Drazil, Bill Duffin, James Dunster, Christopher Freeland, Crispin Geoghegan, Susan Green, Freda Klipstein, C.A. Lagall, David Larcher, Virginia Lester, Pamela Mayorcas, James Millard, Charles Polley, Michael Rawson, Louis Rioual, Tom Williams, Stephen Wilson, Stewart Wittering

Lexicographers/Lexikographie

Stephen Curtis	Amy Newland
Charles Denroche	Ute Reusch
Monika Lee	Robin Sawers

Proofreaders/Korrekturlesung

Jane Bainbridge	Anke Kornmüller
Marilyn Cameron	Gunhild Prowe
Patrick Cunningham	Frances Reynolds
Yvonne Dixon	Christine Shuttleworth
Susanne Dunsmore	Mary Starkey
Keith Hammond	Miranda Timewell
Julia Harding	Daphne Williams
Petra Kopp	Rita Winter

Keyboarders/Datenerfassung

Katrin Bohl	Susannah Kingston
Matthew Darlison	Marianne Pendray
Suzanne Dent	Alisa Salamon
Carole Duell	Bettina Schmitt
Sara Fenby	Silke Strickrodt
Uli Greco	Meike Ziervogel

Faraz Kermani

Acknowledgements/Danksagung

We also wish to acknowledge the valuable contribution of Flavia Hodges and Wendy Morris during the early stages of the project.

Wir möchten ebenfalls Flavia Hodges und Wendy Morris unseren Dank für ihren wertvollen Beitrag in der Frühphase des Projektes ausdrücken.

We are also particularly grateful to Henry Freeman for providing us with the German subject-area names; Ulrike Seeberger for supplying the German front and back matter; and Thomas D. Feise for continual feedback on terminology queries throughout the project.

Wir bedanken uns besonders bei Henry Freeman, der die deutschen Fachgebietsnamen auswählte, Ulrike Seeberger, die Titelei und Anhang Deutsch erarbeitete und Thomas D. Feise, der in allen Stadien des Projektes die Redaktion bei Terminologiefragen unterstützte.

American terms supplied by Frank Abate and his team.

Einträge in amerikanischem Englisch stammen von Frank Abate und seinem Team.

Preface/Vorwort

This is the second dictionary to be published from Routledge's new programme of bilingual specialist and technical dictionaries: the first was the *French Technical Dictionary* in October 1994.

The two factors that have enabled us to create such completely new bilingual technical dictionaries that set new standards in their field are the database system and the method of compilation.

It would not have been possible to compile this dictionary within a realistic timescale, and to the standard achieved, without the use of a highly sophisticated, custom-designed database.

The database's most significant feature is that it is designed as a relational database: term records for each language are held in separate files, with further files consisting only of link records. Links between terms in different language files represent translations which enable us to handle, in a complex way, various types of one-to-many and many-to-one translation equivalences. Links between terms within a single language file represent cross-references, themselves of a wide variety of types: synonyms, spelling variants, geographical variants and abbreviations.

The content of the database for this dictionary was created in three principal phases. A considerable proportion of the English term list was already available following the publication of our *French Technical Dictionary*. The German terminology was then solicited from specialist translators with current practical experience of a narrowly defined specialist subject area and an interest in the collection and dissemination of technology. The specialist translators targeted the coverage to the German market. The terms in each language were then vetted by native-speaker subject specialists working at the leading edge of the respective technology in order to ensure their currency, the accuracy of explanations, and the adequacy of coverage. Finally, each language file was reviewed by editors to ensure coverage of North-American terms and spelling variants; these are clearly labelled and distinguished.

Dieses Wörterbuch ist nach dem *French Technical Dictionary,* das im Oktober 1994 erschien, das zweite im Rahmen des neuen zweisprachigen Fachwörterbuchprogramms von Routledge.

Zwei Faktoren haben es uns ermöglicht, ein völlig neues zweisprachiges Technikwörterbuch zu schaffen, das für sein Feld neue Maßstäbe setzt: die Benutzung eines Datenbanksystems und eine neuartige Methode bei der Zusammenstellung der Wortliste.

Es wäre ohne den Einsatz einer hochkomplexen und für unsere Bedürfnisse speziell zugeschnittenen Datenbank unmöglich gewesen, dieses Wörterbuch innerhalb einer realistischen Zeitspanne und in der vorliegenden Qualität zusammenzustellen.

Die herausragendste Eigenschaft der Datenbank ist, daß sie als relationale Datenbank konzipiert wurde: die Datensätze zu den einzelnen Stichwörtern sind für jede Sprache in einer separaten Datei untergebracht, während gesonderte Dateien nur Datensätze enthalten, die die Verbindungen zwischen Ausgangs- und Zielsprache herstellen. Diese Verbindungen zwischen den Sprachen stellen die Übersetzungen dar, sie schaffen die Möglichkeit, komplexe und sehr unterschiedliche Verknüpfungen herzustellen: von einem Ausgangswort zu mehreren Übersetzungen oder auch von mehreren Ausgangswörtern zu einer gemeinsamen Übersetzung. Innerhalb der einsprachigen Dateien lassen sich ebenfalls Verknüpfungen schaffen, nämlich Querverweise verschiedener Art wie auf Synonyme, abweichende Schreibweisen, geographische Varianten und Abkürzungen.

Der Inhalt der Datenbank für dieses Wörterbuch wurde in drei Stufen zusammengestellt. Nach der Veröffentlichung des *French Technical Dictionary* konnten wir bereits auf eine erhebliche Anzahl von englischen Stichwörtern zurückgreifen. Eine Gruppe von Berufsübersetzern, die über praktische Erfahrung in eng umrissenen technischen Teilgebieten verfügt und ein ausgeprägtes Interesse an Fachterminologie und ihrer Verbreitung zeigt, wurde dann um die deutschen Übersetzungen gebeten. Auf diese Weise wurde die Terminologie den Erwar-

The creation and editing of the database of terms was, however, only the first stage in the making of the dictionary. Within the database the distinction between source and target languages is not meaningful, but for this printed dictionary it has been necessary to format the data to produce separate German–English and English–German volumes. The data was processed by a further software module to produce two alphabetic sequences, of German headwords with English translations and vice versa, each displaying the nesting of compounds, ordering of translations, style for cross-references of different types, and other features according to a complex algorithm.

At this stage the formatted text was edited by a team of experienced German and English lexicographers whose task it was to eliminate duplication or inconsistency; edit the contextual information and explanations; and remove terms that were on the one hand too general, or on the other, too specialized for inclusion in a general technical dictionary. This phased method of working has enabled us to set extremely high standards of quality control.

The editorial team

tungen des deutschsprachigen Marktes angeglichen. Die Wortlisten in den einzelnen Sprachen wurden dann von Muttersprachlern überprüft, die als Fachleute in den jeweiligen Gebieten arbeiten und auf dem technisch neuesten Stand sind. So wurde sichergestellt, daß die Wortliste höchste Aktualität hat, daß die Worterklärungen präzise sind und daß wirklich das in Fachkreisen geläufigste Vokabular behandelt wird. Schließlich wurde noch jede Sprachdatei von Redakteuren überprüft, um eine internationale Terminologieabdeckung zu gewährleisten. Varianten in britischem und nordamerikanischem Englisch werden so unterschieden und sind entsprechend gekennzeichnet.

Die Erstellung der Datenbankgrundlage war jedoch nur der erste Schritt bei der Herstellung dieses Wörterbuches. Innerhalb einer Datenbank erübrigt sich die Unterscheidung zwischen Ausgangs- und Zielsprache im Grunde, aber für das vorliegende Wörterbuch mußten natürlich die Daten so bearbeitet werden, daß separate Bände für Deutsch–Englisch und Englisch–Deutsch entstehen konnten. Mit Hilfe eines weiteren Softwaremoduls wurden zwei alphabetische Listen erstellt, eine deutsche Stichwortliste mit englischen Übersetzungen und umgekehrt. Dabei wurden mit Hilfe eines komplexen Algorithmus zusammengesetzte Begriffe in Blöcken aufgeführt, Übersetzungen in sinnvoller Reihenfolge angeordnet und verschiedene Arten von Querverweisen hergestellt.

Dann wurde der formatierte Text von einem Team erfahrener deutscher und englischer Lexikographen redigiert; ihre Aufgabe war es, Doppelnennungen und Unstimmigkeiten auszumerzen, die zum Wortzusammenhang gegebenen Informationen zu bearbeiten und all die Stichwörter zu streichen, die zu allgemeinsprachlich oder zu speziell für ein allgemein technisches Wörterbuch sind. Diese stufenweise Arbeitsmethode gab uns die Möglichkeit, äußerst hohe Qualitätsmaßstäbe zu setzen.

Das Redaktionsteam

Features of the dictionary/
Aufbau und Anordnung der Einträge

The main features of the dictionary are high-lighted in the text extracts on the opposite page. For a more detailed explanation of each of these features and information on how to get the most out of the dictionary, see pages xv-xvii.

Das folgende Textbeispiel illustriert Aufbau und Anordnung der Einträge. Weitere Erläuterungen und Hinweise zur Benutzung des Wörterbuches befinden sich auf den Seiten xix–xxii.

Base form of adjective is replaced by a swung dash in adjective noun combinations

British-English and American-English spelling variants are given in full and are labelled accordingly

German dummy entries in italics indicate the continuation of an earlier nest of compounds

Cross-references to abbreviations are shown for both the German and the English translation

Genders are indicated at German nouns

Subject-area labels given in alphabetical order show appropriate translation

Contexts give supplementary information to help locate the right translation

German terms are ordered in strict letter-by-letter order

komplementär: **~es Paar** *nt* ELEKTRONIK *Transistoren* complementary pair

Komplementär- *pref* FOTO, PHYS complementary; **Komplementärausgaben** *f pl* ELEKTRONIK complementary outputs; **Komplementärfarbe** *f* FOTO, PHYS complementary color (AmE), complementary colour (BrE)

Komplementarität *f* PHYS, TEILPHYS complementarity; **Komplementaritätsprinzip** *nt* PHYS principle of complementarity

Komplementär-: **Komplementär-Metalloxid-Halbleiter** *m* *(CMOS)* COMP & DV, ELEKTRONIK complementary metal oxide semiconductor *(CMOS)*; **Komplementär-Symmetrischer Metalloxid-Halbleiter** *m* *(COSMOS)* ELEKTRONIK complementary-symmetrical metal oxide semiconductor *(COSMOS)*; **Komplementärtransistoren** *m pl* ELEKTRONIK complementary transistors; **Komplementärwinkel** *m* GEOM complementary angles

Komplementmenge *f* MATH complementary set

komplett: **~e Bremse** *f* KFZTECH brake assembly

Komplettierung *f* ERDÖL *Bohrtechnik* completion

Komplettschnitt *m* MASCHINEN combination die, compound die

komplex[1] *adj* COMP & DV, ELEKTRIZ, ELEKTROTECH, GEOM, KONTROLL, PHYS complex

komplex:[2] **~e Admittanz** *f* ELEKTRIZ complex admittance; **~er Brechungsindex** *m* PHYS complex refractive index; **~e Impedanz** *f* ELEKTRIZ complex impedance; **~e Kreisverstärkung** *f* REGELUNG complex loop chain; **~e Leistung** *f* ELEKTRIZ *AC-Leistungsberechnung* complex power; **~e Permeabilität** *f* ELEKTRIZ complex permeability; **~er Regelfaktor** *m* REGELUNG complex control factor; **~er Scheinwiderstand** *m* ELEKTROTECH complex impedance; **~es Signal** *nt* ELEKTRONIK complex signal; **~e Variable** *f* COMP & DV complex variable; **~e Wellenform** *f* ELEKTRIZ complex waveform; **~er Widerstand** *m* PHYS complex impedance; **~er Wirkleitwert** *m* PHYS complex admittance; **~e Zahl** *f* COMP & DV, MATH complex number

Komplexbildner m CHEMIE chelating agent, complexing agent; KERNTECH complexing agent

Komplexbildung *f* CHEMIE chelation, complexing

Komplexerz *nt* KOHLEN complex ore

Komplexität *f* CHEMIE, COMP & DV complexity

Komponente *f* ELEKTRIZ, ELEKTRONIK *Funktionselement*, KERNTECH, KOHLEN, MASCHINEN, MATH *eines Vektors*, MECHAN, TELEKOM *physikalisch* component

Kompost *m* ABFALL compost; **Kompostaufbereitungsanlage** *f* ABFALL composting plant; **Kompostaufbetrieb** *m* ABFALL composting plant; **Kompostbelüftung** *f* ABFALL compost aeration; **Kompostbereitung** *f* ABFALL composting

kompostierbar: **~er Abfall** *m* ABFALL compostable waste; **nicht ~er Abfall** *m* ABFALL noncompostable waste

Kompostierung *f* ABFALL *von Hausmüll* composting; **Kompostierungsanlage** *f* ABFALL composting plant; **Kompostierungsrückstand** *m* ABFALL composting residue; **Kompostierungstechnik** *f* ABFALL composting technique

Kompost: **Kompostreifung** *f* ABFALL compost maturing, compost ripening; **Kompostwerk** *nt* ABFALL composting plant

Kompoundierung *f* ELEKTROTECH compounding

Kompoundmotor *m* ELEKTRIZ, ELEKTROTECH compound motor

Kompressibilität *f* LUFTTRANS, METALL, PAPIER, PHYS, STRÖMPHYS, THERMOD *Gas* compressibility; **Kompressibilitätseffekte** *m pl* LUFTTRANS compressibility effects;

Grundform des Adjektivs wird in flektierten Formen durch die Tilde ersetzt

Britische und amerikanische Übersetzungsvarianten werden voll ausgeschrieben und entsprechend gekennzeichnet

Deutscher Blindeintrag in Kursivschrift zeigt die Fortsetzung eines vorhergehenden Blocks mit zusammengesetzten Formen an

Sowohl für den deutschen Eintrag wie für die englische Übersetzung werden Querverweise auf Abkürzungen gegeben

Bei deutschen Substantiven wird das grammatikalische Geschlecht angegeben

Sachgebietskürzel in alphabetischer Reihenfolge helfen beim Finden der korrekten Übersetzung

Die Angabe von Zusammenhängen ergänzt die gegebenen Informationen und unterstützt die Suche nach dem passenden Übersetzungsäquivalent

Deutsche Einträge sind streng alphabetisch geordnet

Using the dictionary

Range of coverage

This is one volume (the German–English volume) of a general technical dictionary that covers the whole range of modern technology and the scientific knowledge that underlies it. It contains a broad base of terminology drawn from traditional areas of technology such as mechanical engineering, construction industry, electrical engineering and electronics, but also includes the vocabulary of newly prominent subject areas such as fuelless energy sources, safety engineering and quality assurance.

Selection of terms

We have aimed to include the essential vocabulary of each subject area, and the material has been checked by leading subject experts to ensure that both the English and the German terms are accurate and current, that the translations are valid equivalents, and that there are no gaps in coverage.

We have been careful about including only genuine technical terms and not allowing general vocabulary with no technical value. At the same time, we have entered the core vocabulary of technical discourse in its totality, although some of these items may also be found in general dictionaries. Although other variant translations would often be permissible in a particular subject area, we have given the term most widely preferred by specialists in the area.

Coverage of the subject areas is given proportionally so that an established and wide-ranging area such as mechanical engineering has a count of around 8,000 terms whereas a new area in which terminology is still developing, such as fuelless energy sources, will have considerably fewer terms.

Placement of terms

All terms are ordered alphabetically at their first element. This is also the policy for hyphenated compounds.

Stoplists

Terms in German are not entered under the following elements:

aber, alle, allein, alleine, alleinig, alleinige, alleinigem, alleinigen, alleiniger, alleiniges, allem, allen, aller, alles, allgemein, allgemeine, allgemeinen, allgemeiner, allgemeines, als, am, an, andere, anderem, anderen, anderer, anderes, ans, auch, auf, aufeinander, aus, außen, außer, äußere, äußeres, äußerem, äußeren, bei, beim, das, dasselbe, dem, demselben, den, denselben, der, derselbe, derselben, des, desselben, die, dies, diese, dieselbe, dieselben, diesem, diesen, dieser, dieses, durch, ein, eine, einem, einen, einer, eines, es, etwas, für, im, in, ins, kein, keine, keinem, keinen, keiner, keines, mit, miteinander, nach, neu, nicht, nur, ob, sehr, sein, seine, seinem, seinen, seiner, seines, selber, selbst, sich, über, um, ums, und, vom, von, vor, wenig, wenigem, wenigen, weniger, wenigst, wenigste, wenigstem, wenigsten, wenigster, wenigstes, wieder, zu, zum, zur, zwischen

Compound terms are listed at their first element. When this first element is itself a headword with a technical sense of its own, compound forms follow the simple form. In the case of noun nests, open forms are listed first with the headword replaced by a swung dash. Compounds are spelt out in full and directly follow the nest of open forms. For example:

Kabel[1] *nt* AUFNAHME, COMP & DV, ELEKTRIZ cable, ELEKTROTECH cable, lead, FERNSEH, FERTIG, KFZTECH, KUNSTSTOFF, MASCHINEN, MECHAN cable, OPTIK cable assembly, RADIO, TELEKOM, TRANS, VERPACK, WASSERTRANS cable; **~ mit abgestufter Koppeldämpfung** *nt* TELEKOM grading coupling loss cable; **~ zwischen Eingabegerät und Computer** *nt* COMP & DV input lead; **~ mit losem Aufbau** *nt* OPTIK loose construction cable; **~ mit metallischen Leitern** *nt* TELEKOM metal conductor cable; **~ mit Nutenstruktur** *nt* TELEKOM grooved cable; **~ mit separater Bleiumhüllung** *nt* ELEKTRIZ separately lead-sheathed cable; **~ mit separater Bleiummantelung** *nt* ELEKTRIZ separately lead-sheathed cable; **~ mit symmetrischen Adernpaaren** *nt* TELEKOM symmetrical pair cable
Kabel:[2] **~ verlegen** *vi* AUFNAHME lay tracks
Kabel: **Kabelabschluß** *m* ELEKTRIZ cable termination, ELEKTROTECH cable head; **Kabelabschnitt** *m* ELEKTROTECH cable section; **Kabelabzweigdose** *f* ELEKTRIZ cable junction box; **Kabelabzweigkasten** *m* ELEKTRIZ cable junction box; **Kabelader** *f* ELEKTROTECH cable core; **Kabeladernpaar** *nt* ELEKTROTECH cable pair; **Kabelarmatur** *f* ELEKTROTECH cable fit-

ting; **Kabelaufhängung** *f* ELEKTROTECH, KFZTECH cable support; **Kabelaufhängungsdraht** *m* ELEKTROTECH cable suspension wire; **Kabelausziehvorrichtung** *f* ELEKTRIZ pull box; **Kabelbahn** *f* TRANS cable railroad (AmE), cable railway (BrE);

If the first element is not itself a headword with a technical sense, compounds formed from that element are entered as headwords:

Wägefläschen *nt* LABOR density bottle, *Dichtemessung* pycnometer
Wägeglas *nt* CHEMIE, LABOR weighing bottle
Wägemaschine *f* VERPACK checkweighing machine

Compounds are entered in alphabetical sequence. When a nest is interrupted by other entries, the run of compounds is picked up again later in the correct alphabetical sequence. A dummy headword in bold italics indicates the continuation of a run of compounds. For example:

Fächer *m* HEIZ & KÄLTE fan, ventilator
fächerförmig: ~**es Lichtbündel** *nt* ELEKTRONIK *Beleuchtungstechnik* fan beam
Fächer: **Fächerfunkfeuer** *nt* WASSERTRANS *Seezeichen* fan marker beacon; **Fächerkasten** *f* VERPACK compartment case; **Fächerkeule** *f* ELEKTRONIK *Antennentechnik* fan beam; **Fächermaschine** *f* PAPIER harper machine; **Fächermethode** *f* ABFALL cell method; **Fächerplatte** *f* WASSERTRANS *Schiffbau* gusset plate; **Fächerscheibe** *f* MASCHINEN serrated lock washer; **Fächerwand** *f* VERPACK partition wall

Adjective-noun combinations are entered at the base form of the adjective. In the nest, the base form is replaced by a swung dash and followed by the relevant inflection. For example:

radioaktiv:[2] ~**er Abfall** *m* ABFALL nuclear waste, radioactive waste, radwaste, KERNTECH effluent, nuclear waste, radioactive waste, STRAHLPHYS radioactive waste; ~**e Altersbestimmung** *f* KERNTECH, STRAHLPHYS radioactive dating; ~**es Cobalt** *nt* CHEMIE radiocobalt; ~**es Element** *nt* KERNTECH, STRAHLPHYS radioactive element; ~**es Gleichgewicht** *nt* KERNTECH, STRAHLPHYS radioactive equilibrium; ~**e Halbwertszeit** *f* KERNTECH, STRAHLPHYS radioactive lifetime; ~**es Isotop** *nt* CHEMIE radioisotope, KERNTECH radioactive isotope, PHYS radioisotope, STRAHLPHYS radioactive isotope, TEILPHYS radioisotope; ~**er Kern** *m* PHYS radionuclide; ~**er Kohlenstoff** *m* PHYS radiocarbon; ~ **kontaminiertes Wasser** *nt* UMWELTSCHMUTZ contaminated water; ~**e Kontaminierung** *f* KERNTECH, STRAHLPHYS radioactive contamination; ~**er Körper** *m* KERNTECH, STRAHLPHYS radioactive body; ~**es Log** *nt* ERDÖL radioactive log;

Definite and indefinite articles (*der, die, das, ein, eine, einer*), their inflected forms (*dem, den, des, einem, einen, einer, eines*), demonstrative pronouns (*dasselbe, derselbe, dieselbe, selbst*), their inflected forms (*demselben, denselben, derselben, desselben, dieselben, selber*), and possessive pronouns (*sein, seine, seiner*), their inflected forms (*seinem, seinen, seines*), the pronoun/adverb *etwa*, prepositions (*bei, für, im, in, ins, mit, um, von, vor, zu, zwischen*), their inflected forms (*beim, ums, vom, zum, zur*), conjunctions (*als, und*), pronouns (*dies, diese, dieser, dieses, es*), their inflected forms (*diesem, diesen*), and the reflexive pronoun *sich* are ignored in determining the sequence of nested open forms. For example:

Kurve:[2] **in ~ legen** *vt* RAUMFAHRT bank; **als ~ zeichnen** *vt* math graph
Kurve:[3] **eine ~ zeichnen** *vi* MATH plot a curve

Abbreviations and acronyms written in upper case appear separately from vocabulary words of the same form written in lower case:

C[2] *(Kohlenstoff)* CHEMIE C *(carbon)*
c *abbr* ELECTRONIK *(Konzentration)*, ELEKTRIZ *(Konzentration)* c *(concentration)*, HYDRAUL *(Wellenausbreitungsgeschwindigkeit)* c *(wave celerity)*, KOHLEN *(Konzentration)*, KUNSTSTOFF

Terms containing figures and symbols are alphabetized according to the usual expansion when written out in full:

Neukalibrierung *f* STRAHLPHYS recalibration; **Neukonditionierung** *f* RAUMFAHRT *Raumschiff* reconditioning; **Neulackieren** *nt* KUNSTOFF refinishing
Neuneck *nt* MATH nonagon
Neunerkomplement *nt* COMP&DV nine's complement
90: um ~ Grad phasenverschoben *adj* PHYS in quadrature
90°: ~ Verschiebung *f* ELEKTRONIK *Phasenverschiebung* quadrature

Homographs

Every term is accompanied by a label indicating its part of speech. For a complete list of these labels and their expansions, please see page xxiii.

When terms beginning with the same element fall into two or more part-of-speech categories, the different nests will be distinguished by a raised number immediately following the head of that nest, whether the head has technical senses of its own or is a dummy. The sequence is abbreviation, adjective, adverb, noun and verb followed by less frequent parts of speech. For example:

abgehend[1] *adj* TELEKOM outgoing
abgehend:[2] ~**er Anruf** *m* TELEKOM outgoing call; ~**es Bündel** *nt* TELEKOM outgoing group; ~**e Leitung** *f* TELEKOM outgoing circuit, outgoing line; ~**e Verbin-**

dung *f* TELEKOM outgoing call; **~er Verkehr** *m* TELEKOM outgoing traffic

abgehend:[3] **~e Rufe gesperrt** *phr* TELEKOM outgoing calls barred

Ordering of translations

Every term is accompanied by one or more labels indicating the technological area in which it is used. For a complete list of these labels and their expansions, please see pages xxiii–xxiv.

Where the same term is used in more than one technological area, multiple labels are given as appropriate. These labels appear in alphabetical order.

Where a term has the same translation in more than one technological area, this translation is given after the sequence of labels. For example:

Bändchen *nt* AKUSTIK, AUFNAHME, OPTIK ribbon

When a term has different translations according to the technological area in which it is used, the appropriate translation is given after each label or set of labels. For example:

Mundstück *nt* BAU nozzle, KER & GLAS die, TELEKOM mouthpiece

Supplementary information

In many cases additional data is given about a term in order to show how it is used. Such contextual information can be:

(a) the typical subject or object of a verb, for example:

abbiegen *vt* BAU *Bewehrungsstahl* bend down

(b) typical nouns used with an adjective, for example:

orthogonal[1] *adj* MATH *Vektoren* orthogonal

(c) words indicating the reference of a noun, for example:

Mantel *m* ELEKTROTECH jacket, HYDRAUL cladding, KERNTECH shell casing, *Umhüllung* shell, *zum Kühlen, Erwärmen* jacket, KFZTECH *amerikanischer Reifentyp* cover, LABOR *Glasartikel* jacket, MASCHINEN jacket, skirt, MECHAN jacket, OPTIK *Lichtleiter* cladding, RAUMFAHRT *Kabel* shielding, TELEKOM cladding

(d) information which supplements the subject-area label, for example:

Laufschiene *f* EISENBAHN running rail, slide rail, *der Einschienenbahn* monorail, MACHINEN runner, running rail

(e) a paraphrase or broad equivalent, for example:

Aerometer *nt* METROL, PAPIER *Luftdichtemesser*, PHYSIK aerometer

When various different translations apply in the same subject area, contextual information is also used to show which translation is appropriate in different circumstances. For example:

Zylinder *m* COMP&DV *Festplatte*, DRUCK cylinder, ELEKTROTECH *Spule* solenoid, FERTIG drum, *Extruder, Plastherstellung* barrel, GEOM cylinder HYDRAUL *Dampfmaschine* barrel, *Dampfdruckindikator* drum, KER&GLAS *zur Produktion von gewalztem Flachglas*, KFZTECH, *Motor* cylinder, KUNSTOFF, MASCHINEN, MECHAN, PAPIER cylinder, VERPACK drum, WASSERTRANS *Motor* cylinder

Cross-references

Geographical variants, both spelling and lexical, are given in full when they are translations:

Kofferraum *m* KFZTECH boot (BrE), rear boot (BrE), rear trunk (AmE), trunk (AmE), receiving boot (BrE), receiving trunk (AmE)

Both abbreviations and their full forms are entered in the main body of the dictionary in alphabetical sequence. Full information – including translations and cross-references to the full form or abbreviation as appropriate – is given at each entry. For example:

Q-Bit *nt* (*Unterscheidungsbit*) TELEKOM Q bit (*qualifier bit*)

QCD *abbr* (*Quantenchromodynamik*) TEILPHYS QCD (*quantum chromodynamics*)

Abbreviations are also listed in a separate alphabetical sequence at the back of this volume to allow browsing in cases where the exact form of the abbreviation is not known.

Hinweise für die Benutzung des Wörterbuches

Umfang des Wörterbuches

Sie haben einen Band (Deutsch–Englisch) eines allgemeinen Technikwörterbuches vor sich, das alle Bereiche der modernen Technik und des zugrundeliegenden naturwissenschaftlichen Wissens abdeckt. Zusätzlich zu einer breiten Grundlage technischer Ausdrücke aus traditionellen Bereichen wie etwa Maschinenbau, Bauindustrie, Elektrotechnik und Elektronik enthält dieses Wörterbuch auch Vokabular aus neuen und hochaktuellen Sachgebieten wie etwa nichtfossile Energiequellen, Sicherheitstechnik und Qualitätssicherung.

Auswahl der Stichwörter

Wir haben uns das Ziel gesetzt, aus jedem Fachgebiet das Basisvokabular aufzunehmen; hierzu wurde die Stichwortliste sowohl im Englischen wie im Deutschen von führenden Experten in den einzelnen Fachgebieten auf Genauigkeit, Richtigkeit und Vollständigkeit überprüft.

Es wurde sorgfältig darauf geachtet, daß nur echtes technisches Vokabular und kein Allgemeinvokabular ohne technisches Interesse aufgenommen wurde. Gleichzeitig waren wir aber auch darauf bedacht, das wichtigste technische Grundvokabular vollständig aufzunehmen, auch wenn einige Einträge bereits in allgemeinsprachlichen Wörterbüchern zu finden sind. Obwohl manchmal in bestimmten Fachgebieten auch andere Übersetzungsvarianten möglich wären, haben wir stets den in der Fachwelt gängigsten Terminus angegeben.

Die einzelnen Fachgebiete sind proportional zu ihrer Anwendungshäufigkeit vertreten, so daß also ein etabliertes und umfangreiches Gebiet wie der Maschinenbau mit etwa 8 000 Stichwörtern vertreten ist, während ein Gebiet, in dem sich das Vokabular im Augenblick noch stark in der Entwicklung befindet, wie etwa nichtfossile Energiequellen, dagegen deutlich weniger Stichwörter aufweist.

Reihenfolge der Anordnung

Alle Einträge sind alphabetisch angeordnet. Zusammengesetzte Einträge erscheinen unter ihrem Basiswort. Dies gilt auch für Komposita mit Bindestrich.

Stoppliste

Deutsche zusammengesetzte Stichwörter sind nicht unter den folgenden Wörtern aufgeführt:

aber, alle, allein, alleine, alleinig, alleinige, alleinigem, alleinigen, alleiniger, alleiniges, allem, allen, aller, alles, allgemein, allgemeine, allgemeinen, allgemeiner, allgemeines, als, am, an, andere, anderem, anderen, anderer, anderes, ans, auch, auf, aufeinander, aus, außen, außer, äußere, äußeres, äußerem, äußeren, bei, beim, das, dasselbe, dem, demselben, den, denselben, der, derselbe, derselben, des, desselben, die, dies, diese, dieselbe, dieselben, diesem, diesen, dieser, dieses, durch, ein, eine, einem, einen, einer, eines, es, etwas, für, im, in, ins, kein, keine, keinem, keinen, keiner, keines, mit, miteinander, nach, neu, nicht, nur, ob, sehr, sein, seine, seinem, seinen, seiner, seines, selber, selbst, sich, über, um, ums, und, vom, von, vor, wenig, wenigem, wenigen, weniger, wenigst, wenigste, wenigstem, wenigsten, wenigster, wenigstes, wieder, zu, zum, zur, zwischen

Zusammengesetzte Einträge sind in Nestform unter ihrem Basiswort aufgeführt. Wenn das Basiswort ein eigenes Stichwort mit einer technischen Bedeutung darstellt, folgen alle weiteren Zusammensetzungen diesem Stichwort. Hier ersetzt die Tilde das gleiche Stichwort. Komposita werden voll ausgeschrieben und folgen auf zusammengesetzte Stichwörter. Zum Beispiel:

Kabel[1] *nt* AUFNAHME, COMP & DV, ELEKTRIZ cable, ELEKTROTECH cable, lead, FERNSEH, FERTIG, KFZTECH, KUNSTSTOFF, MASCHINEN, MECHAN cable, OPTIK cable assembly, RADIO, TELEKOM, TRANS, VERPACK, WASSERTRANS cable; **~ mit abgestufter Koppeldämpfung** *nt* TELEKOM grading coupling loss cable; **~ zwischen Eingabegerät und Computer** *nt* COMP & DV input lead; **~ mit losem Aufbau** *nt* OPTIK loose construction cable; **~ mit metallischen Leitern** *nt* TELEKOM metal conductor cable; **~ mit Nutenstruktur** *nt* TELEKOM grooved cable; **~ mit separater Bleium-**

hüllung *nt* ELEKTRIZ separately lead-sheathed cable; ~ **mit separater Bleiummantelung** *nt* ELEKTRIZ separately lead-sheathed cable; ~ **mit symmetrischen Adernpaaren** *nt* TELEKOM symmetrical pair cable; **Kabel:**[2] ~ **verlegen** *vi* AUFNAHME lay tracks

Kabel: **Kabelabschluß** *m* ELEKTRIZ cable termination, ELEKTROTECH cable head; **Kabelabschnitt** *m* ELEKTROTECH cable section; **Kabelabzweigdose** *f* ELEKTRIZ cable junction box; **Kabelabzweigkasten** *m* ELEKTRIZ cable junction box; **Kabelader** *f* ELEKTROTECH cable core; **Kabeladernpaar** *nt* ELEKTROTECH cable pair; **Kabelarmatur** *f* ELEKTROTECH cable fitting; **Kabelaufhängung** *f* ELEKTROTECH, KFZTECH cable support; **Kabelaufhängungsdraht** *m* ELEKTROTECH cable suspension wire; **Kabelausziehvorrichtung** *f* ELEKTRIZ pull box; **Kabelbahn** *f* TRANS cable railroad (AmE), cable railway (BrE);

Komposita, deren Basiswort kein eigenes Stichwort mit einer technischen Bedeutung darstellt, sind nicht in Nestform aufgeführt, sondern erscheinen als separate Einträge.
Zum Beispiel:

Wägefläschen *nt* LABOR density bottle, *Dichtemessung* pycnometer
Wägeglas *nt* CHEMIE, LABOR weighing bottle
Wägemaschine *f* VERPACK checkweighing machine

Komposita sind in alphabetischer Reihenfolge angeordnet. Nester, die aufgrund anderer Stichwörter unterbrochen werden, werden bei der nächsten alphabetisch adäquaten Möglichkeit wieder aufgenommen. Das Basiswort als Blindeintrag in Fettkursivdruck weist auf die Fortführung des Artikels hin.
Zum Beispiel:

Fächer *m* HEIZ & KÄLTE fan, ventilator
fächerförmig: ~**es Lichtbündel** *nt* ELEKTRONIK *Beleuchtungstechnik* fan beam
Fächer: **Fächerfunkfeuer** *nt* WASSERTRANS *Seezeichen* fan marker beacon; **Fächerkasten** *m* VERPACK compartment case; **Fächerkeule** *f* ELEKTRONIK *Antennentechnik* fan beam; **Fächermaschine** *f* PAPIER harper machine; **Fächermethode** *f* ABFALL cell method; **Fächerplatte** *f* WASSERTRANS *Schiffbau* gusset plate; **Fächerscheibe** *f* MASCHINEN serrated lock washer; **Fächerwand** *f* VERPACK partition wall

Zusammensetzungen aus Adjektiv und Substantiv sind unter der Grundform des Adjektives aufgeführt. Im sich anschließenden Artikel wird die Grundform des Adjektives durch die Tilde ersetzt. Die entsprechende Adjektivendung schließt sich der Tilde an.
Zum Beispiel:

radioaktiv:[2] ~**er Abfall** *m* ABFALL nuclear waste, radioactive waste, radwaste, KERNTECH effluent, nuclear waste, radioactive waste, STRAHLPHYS radioactive waste; ~**e Altersbestimmung** *f* KERNTECH, STRAHLPHYS radioactive dating; ~**es Cobalt** *nt* CHE-

MIE radiocobalt; ~**es Element** *nt* KERNTECH, STRAHLPHYS radioactive element; ~**es Gleichgewicht** *nt* KERNTECH, STRAHLPHYS radioactive equilibrium; ~**e Halbwertszeit** *f* KERNTECH, STRAHLPHYS radioactive lifetime; ~**es Isotop** *nt* CHEMIE radioisotope, KERNTECH radioactive isotope, PHYS radioisotope, STRAHLPHYS radioactive isotope, TEILPHYS radioisotope; ~**er Kern** *m* PHYS radionuclide; ~**er Kohlenstoff** *m* PHYS radiocarbon; ~ **kontaminiertes Wasser** *nt* UMWELTSCHMUTZ contaminated water; ~**e Kontaminierung** *f* KERNTECH, STRAHLPHYS radioactive contamination; ~**er Körper** *m* KERNTECH, STRAHLPHYS radioactive body; ~**es Log** *nt* ERDÖL radioactive log;

Folgende Wörter werden bei der alphabetischen Reihenfolge ignoriert: bestimmte und unbestimmte Artikel (*der, die, das, ein, eine, einer*), deren gebeugte Formen (*dem, den, des, einem, einen, einer, eines*), Demonstrativpronomen (*dasselbe, derselbe, dieselbe, selbst*), deren gebeugte Formen (*demselben, denselben, derselben, desselben, dieselben, selber*), Possessivpronomen (*sein, seine, seiner*), deren gebeugte Formen (*seinem, seinen, seines*), das Pronomen/Adverb *etwa*, Präpositionen (*bei, für, im, in, ins, mit, um, von, vor, zu, zum, zur, zwischen*), deren gebeugte Formen (*beim, ums, vom, zum, zur*), Konjunktionen (*als, und*), Pronomen (*dies, diese, dieser, dieses, es*), deren gebeugte Formen (*diesem, diesen*) sowie das Reflexivpronomen *sich*.
Zum Beispiel:

Kurve:[2] **in** ~ **legen** *vt* RAUMFAHRT bank; **als** ~ **zeichnen** *vt* math graph
Kurve:[3] **eine** ~ **zeichnen** *vi* MATH plot a curve

Kleingeschriebene Abkürzungen und großgeschriebene Abkürzungen werden separat aufgelistet.
Zum Beispiel:

C[2] *(Kohlenstoff)* CHEMIE C *(carbon)*
c *abbr* ELEKTRONIK *(Konzentration)*, ELEKTRIZ *(Konzentration)* c *(concentration)*, HYDRAUL *(Wellenausbreitungsgeschwindigkeit)* c *(wave celerity)*, KOHLEN *(Konzentration)*, KUNSTSTOFF

Einträge, die Zahlen oder Symbole beinhalten, werden an der Stelle angeführt, an der die ausgeschriebene Variante der entsprechenden Zahlen oder Symbole erscheinen würde.
Zum Beispiel:

Neukalibrierung *f* STRAHLPHYS recalibration; **Neukonditionierung** f RAUMFAHRT *Raumschiff* reconditioning; **Neulackieren** *nt* KUNSTOFF refinishing
Neuneck *nt* MATH nonagon
Neunerkomplement *nt* COMP&DV nine's complement
90: um ~ **Grad phasenverschoben** *adj* PHYS in quadrature

90°: ~ Verschiebung *f* ELEKTRONIK *Phasenverschie-bung* quadrature

Homographen

Alle Einträge sind mit einem Label versehen, das die grammatikalische Bezeichnung angibt. Eine vollständige Liste dieser Labels befindet sich auf Seite xxiii.

Einträge mit gemeinsamem Basiswort jedoch unterschiedlicher Wortklassenzugehörigkeit erhalten für jede Wortklasse einen eigenen Eintrag. Eine unmittelbar dem Eintrag folgende hochgestellte Zahl verweist auf die unterschiedliche Wortklasse. Dies gilt auch für Zusammensetzungen mit Basiswort als Blindeintrag. Die Einträge sind in der Reihenfolge Adjektiv, Adverb, Substantiv, Verb aufgeführt. Dem schließen sich weniger häufig vorkommende grammatikalische Einheiten an. Zum Beispiel:

anlegen[1] *vt* COMP & DV create, ELEKTROTECH *Spannung*, FERTIG *Spannung* feed
anlegen[2] *vi* WASSERTRANS berth, land

Reihenfolge der Übersetzungen

Auf jedes Stichwort der Ausgangssprache folgen ein oder mehrere Labels, die das technische Fachgebiet angeben, in dem das Wort benutzt wird. Eine vollständige Liste dieser Labels mit Erklärungen befindet sich auf den Seiten xxiii–xxiv.

Wenn dasselbe Stichwort in mehr als einem technischen Fachgebiet benutzt wird, so werden entsprechend mehrere Labels angegeben. Sie werden stets in alphabetischer Reihenfolge aufgeführt.

Falls die angegebene Übersetzung in mehr als einem Fachgebiet benutzt wird, so folgt die Übersetzung jeweils im Anschluß an die entsprechenden Labels. Zum Beispiel:

Bändchen *nt* AKUSTIK, AUFNAHME, OPTIK ribbon

Hat ein Stichwort verschiedene, von seinen jeweiligen Fachgebieten abhängige Übersetzungen, so ist die zutreffende Übersetzung jeweils nach dem entsprechenden Kürzel zu finden. Zum Beispiel:

Mundstück *nt* BAU nozzle, KER & GLAS die, TELEKOM mouthpiece

Zusatzinformationen

Deutsche Substantive sind mit Geschlechtsangabe versehen. In vielen Fällen wird über das Stichwort noch zusätzliche Information gegeben, die über die Benutzung des Wortes Aufschluß gibt. Solche Informationen zum Benutzungszusammenhang können verschiedene Formen annehmen:

(a) bei einem Verb ein typisches Subjekt oder Objekt:

abbiegen *vt* BAU *Bewehrungsstahl* bend down

(b) typische Substantive, die mit einem bestimmten Adjektiv verwendet werden:

orthogonal[1] *adj* MATH *Vektoren* orthogonal

(c) Wörter, die für Substantive einen typischen Bezug erläutern:

Mantel *m* ELEKTROTECH jacket, HYDRAUL cladding, KERNTECH shell casing, *Umhüllung* shell, *zum Kühlen, Erwärmen* jacket, KFZTECH *amerikanischer Reifentyp* cover, LABOR *Glasartikel* jacket, MASCHINEN jacket, skirt, MECHAN jacket, OPTIK *Lichtleiter* cladding, RAUMFAHRT *Kabel* shielding, TELEKOM cladding

(d) Informationen, die das Fachgebiet noch weiter eingrenzen:

Laufschiene *f* EISENBAHN running rail, slide rail, *der Einschienenbahn* monorail, MASCHINEN runner, running rail

(e) Umschreibungen oder ungefähre Äquivalente:

Aerometer *nt* METROL, PAPIER *Luftdichtemesser*, PHYSIK aerometer

Wenn in einem Fachgebiet verschiedene Übersetzungen für ein Stichwort möglich sind, so soll hier die zusätzliche Information anzeigen, welches im jeweiligen Zusammenhang die korrekte Übersetzung ist. Zum Beispiel:

Zylinder *m* COMP&DV *Festplatte*, DRUCK cylinder, ELEKTROTECH *Spule* solenoid, FERTIG drum, *Extruder, Plastherstellung* barrel, GEOM cylinder HYDRAUL *Dampfmaschine* barrel, *Dampfdruckindikator* drum, KER&GLAS *zur Produktion von gewalztem Flachglas*, KFZTECH *Motor* cylinder, KUNSTOFF, MASCHINEN, MECHAN, PAPIER cylinder, VERPACK drum, WASSERTRANS *Motor* cylinder

Querverweise

Geographische Varianten der Übersetzungen, sowohl orthographischer als auch lexikalischer Art, werden immer angegeben und voll ausgeschrieben.

Zum Beispiel:

Kofferraum *m* KFZTECH boot (BrE), rear boot (BrE), rear trunk (AmE), trunk (AmE), receiving boot (BrE), receiving trunk (AmE)

Im Hauptteil des Wörterbuches sind auch Abkürzungen und ihre ausgeschriebenen Formen in streng alphabetischer Reihenfolge angeordnet. Bei jedem Eintrag wird die vollständige Information – inklusive Übersetzungen und Querverweisen zur Vollform respektive Abkür-

zung – aufgeführt.

Also:

Q-Bit *nt (Unterscheidungsbit)* TELEKOM Q bit *(qualifier bit)*

QCD *abbr (Quantenchromodynamik)* TEILPHYS QCD *(quantum chromodynamics)*

Außerdem sind Abkürzungen im Anhang des Bandes als separate Liste aufgeführt. Dies erleichtert die Suche, wenn die genaue Form einer Abkürzung nicht bekannt ist.

Abbreviations used in this dictionary/
Im Wörterbuch verwendete Abkürzungen

Parts of speech/Wortarten

abbr	Abkürzung	abbreviation
adj	Adjektiv	adjective
adv	Adverb	adverb
f	Femininum	feminine
f pl	Femininum Plural	feminine plural
m	Maskulinum	masculine
m pl	Maskulinum Plural	masculine plural
n	Substantiv	noun
n pl	Substantiv Plural	noun plural
nt	Neutrum	neuter
nt pl	Neutrum Plural	neuter plural
phr	fachsprachliche Redewendung	phrase
pref	Präfix; Grundwort bei Komposita	prefix; base form in compounds
prep	Präposition	preposition
vi	intransitives Verb	intransitive verb
v refl	reflexives Verb	reflexive verb
vt	transitives Verb	transitive verb
vti	transitives und intransitives Verb	transitive and intransitive verb

Geographic codes/Geographische Kürzel

AmE	Amerikanisches Englisch	American English
BrE	Britisches Englisch	British English

Subject-area labels/Fachgebietskürzel

ABFALL	Abfallwirtschaft	Waste Management
AKUSTIK	Akustik	Acoustics
ANSTRICH	Anstrichtechnik	Coatings Technology
AUFNAHME	Aufnahmetechnik	Recording Engineering
BAU	Bauwesen	Construction
CHEMIE	Chemie	Chemistry
CHEMTECH	Chemotechnik	Chemical Engineering
COMP & DV	Computertechnik & Datenverarbeitung	Computer Technology & Data Processing
DRUCK	Druckereiwesen	Printing

EISENBAHN	Eisenbahnbau	Railway Engineering
ELEKTRIZ	Elektrizität	Electricity
ELEKTRONIK	Elektronik	Electronics
ELEKTROTECH	Elektrotechnik	Electrical Engineering
ERDÖL	Erdöltechnologie	Petroleum Technology
ERGON	Ergonomie	Ergonomics
FERNSEH	Fernsehtechnik	Television
FERTIG	Fertigungstechnik	Production Engineering
FOTO	Fotografie	Photography
GEOM	Geometrie	Geometry
GERÄT	Geräte & Instrumente	Instrumentation
HEIZ & KÄLTE	Heizungs- & Kältetechnik	Heating & Refrigeration
HYDRAUL	Hydraulische Anlagen	Hydraulic Equipment
KER & GLAS	Keramik & Glas	Ceramics & Glass
KERNTECH	Kerntechnik	Nuclear Technology
KOHLEN	Kohlentechnik	Coal Technology
KONSTZEICH	Konstruktionszeichnung	Engineering Drawing
KONTROLL	Kontrolltechnik	Control Technology
KFZTECH	Kraftfahrzeugtechnik	Automotive Engineering
KÜNSTL INT	Künstliche Intelligenz	Artificial Intelligence
KUNSTSTOFF	Kunststoffindustrie	Plastics
LABOR	Laboreinrichtungen	Laboratory Equipment
LEBENSMITTEL	Lebensmitteltechnik	Food Technology
LUFTTRANS	Lufttransport	Air Transportation
MASCHINEN	Maschinenbau	Mechanical Engineering
MATH	Mathematik	Mathematics
MECHAN	Mechanik	Mechanics
MEERSCHMUTZ	Meeresverschmutzung	Marine Pollution
METALL	Metallurgie	Metallurgy
METROL	Metrologie	Metrology
NICHTFOSS ENERG	Nichtfossile Energiequellen	Fuelless Energy Sources
OPTIK	Optik	Optics
PAPIER	Papier & Pappe	Paper & Board
PATENT	Patente & Warenzeichen	Patents & Trademarks
PHYS	Physik	Physics
QUAL	Qualitätssicherung	Quality Assurance
RADIO	Radiotechnik & Radar	Radio Technology & Radar
RAUMFAHRT	Raumfahrttechnik	Space Technology
REGELUNG	Regelungs- & Steuerungstechnik	Industrial Process Measurement & Control
SICHERHEIT	Sicherheitstechnik	Safety Engineering
STRAHLPHYS	Strahlenphysik	Radiation Physics
STRÖMPHYS	Strömungsphysik	Fluid Physics
TEILPHYS	Teilchenphysik	Particle Physics
TELEKOM	Telekommunikation	Telecommunications
TEXTIL	Textiltechnik	Textiles
THERMOD	Thermodynamik	Thermodynamics
TRANS	Transportwesen	Transportation
UMWELTSCHMUTZ	Umweltverschmutzung	Pollution
VERPACK	Verpackungstechnik	Packaging
WASSERTRANS	Wassertransport	Water Transportation
WASSERVERSORG	Wasserversorgungstechnik	Water Supply Engineering
WELLPHYS	Wellenphysik	Wave Physics
WERKPRÜF	Werkstoffprüfung	Testing of Materials

Trademarks

Every effort has been made to label terms which we believe constitute trademarks. These are designated by the symbol ®. The legal status of these, however, remains unchanged by the presence or absence of any such symbol.

Warenzeichen

Bei der Kennzeichnung von Wörtern, die nach Kenntnis der Redaktion eingetragene Warenzeichen darstellen, wurde mit größter Sorgfalt verfahren. Diese Wörter sind mit ® gekennzeichnet. Weder das Vorhandensein noch das Fehlen solcher Kennzeichnungen berührt die Rechtslage hinsichtlich eingetragener Warenzeichen.

A

A *abbr* AKUSTIK *(Amplitude)*, AUFNAHME *(Amplitude)* A *(amplitude)*, CHEMIE *(Affinität)* A *(affinity)*, COMP & DV *(Amplitude)* A *(amplitude)*, ELEKTRIZ *(Ampere)* A *(ampere)*, ELEKTRIZ *(Amplitude)* A *(amplitude)*, ELEKTRIZ *(lineare Stromdichte)* A *(linear current density)*, ELEKTRONIK *(Amplitude)* A *(amplitude)*, ELEKTROTECH *(Ampere)* A *(ampere)*, ELEKTROTECH *(Anode)*, FERNSEH *(Anode)* A *(anode)*, FERTIG *(Ampere)* A *(ampere)*, KERNTECH *(Aktivität)* A *(activity)*, KERNTECH *(Massenzahl)* A *(mass number)*, METROL *(Ampere)* A *(ampere)*, PHYS *(Aktivität, Schallstärke)* A *(activity)*, PHYS *(Ampere)* A *(ampere)*, PHYS *(Amplitude)* A *(amplitude)*, PHYS *(Anode)* A *(anode)*, PHYS *(Isotopenmasse, Massenzahl)* A *(mass number)*, RADIO *(Ampere)* A *(ampere)*, RADIO *(Amplitude)* A *(amplitude)*, RADIO *(Anode)* A *(anode)*, TEILPHYS *(Massenzahl, Nukleonenzahl)* A *(mass number)*, WASSERTRANS *(Amplitude)* A *(amplitude)*, WASSERTRANS *(Anode)* A *(anode)*, WELLPHYS *(Amplitude)* A *(amplitude)*

a *abbr* AKUSTIK *(akustische Absorption)* a *(total acoustic absorption)*, METROL *(Ar)* a *(are)*

Å *abbr (Angström)* METROL Å *(angstrom)*

a_0 *abbr (Bohrscher Radius)* PHYS a_0 *(Bohr radius)*

AACS *abbr (Luftfahrtfunkdienst)* RAUMFAHRT AACS *(airways and air communications service)*

AADT *abbr (durchschnittliches Tagesverkehrsaufkommen pro Jahr)* TRANS AADT *(annual average daily traffic)*

AAP *abbr (akustischer Akzeptanzpegel)* AKUSTIK ACI *(acoustic comfort index)*

AB *abbr (akustischer Blindleitwert)* AKUSTIK BA *(acoustic susceptance)*

abätzen *vt* FERTIG etch

Abbau *m* CHEMIE breakdown, decomposition, KUNSTSTOFF degradation, mastication, TEXTIL breakdown

abbaubar *adj* ABFALL degradable

abbauen *vt* BAU dismantle, MASCHINEN dismount, MEERSCHMUTZ foul, TELEKOM clear

abbauend: **~er Mikroorganismus** *m* CHEMIE reducer

Abbau: **Abbauförderstrecke** *f* KOHLEN gate road; **Abbaumittel** *nt* KUNSTSTOFF peptizer; **Abbauprozeß** *m* VERPACK destruction process; **Abbaurate** *f* ERDÖL *Lagerstättenkunde* depletion rate; **Abbaustrecke** *f* KOHLEN coal drift, gate road; **Abbaustufe** *f* ABFALL stage of decomposition

Abbe: **~sches Refraktometer** *nt* PHYS Abbe refractometer; **~sche Theorie** *f* PHYS Abbe theory; **~sche Zahl** *f* KER & GLAS Abbe coefficient, PHYS *Dispersion* Abbe number

Abbeizbehälter *m* ANSTRICH strip tank

Abbeizen *nt* BAU, WASSERTRANS *Schiffinstandhaltung* pickling

abbeizen *vt* ANSTRICH strip, BAU scour, FERTIG pickle

Abbeizer *m* BAU paint stripper, *Farbe* remover

Abbeizmittel *nt* CHEMIE scouring agent

AB-Betrieb *m* ELEKTRONIK class AB mode

Abbiege- *pref* TRANS turning

abbiegen *vt* BAU *Bewehrungsstahl* bend down

abbiegend: **~er Verkehr** *m* TRANS turning traffic

Abbiege-: **Abbiegespur** *f* TRANS turning; **Abbiegeströme** *m pl* TRANS turning movements

Abbild[1] *nt* COMP & DV image, map, *virtuelle Nachbildung eines Körpers* instance, ERGON image

Abbild:[2] **~ wiedergeben** *vt* COMP & DV image

Abbild: **Abbild-Aktualisierung** *f* COMP & DV image refreshing; **Abbildbereich** *m* COMP & DV image area

Abbilden *nt* COMP & DV mapping

abbilden *vt* COMP & DV image, *Speicher* map

Abbildträger *m* COMP & DV image carrier

Abbildung *f* BAU projection, COMP & DV image, picture, *des Speichers* map, DRUCK figure, illustration, MATH, PATENT *einer Zeichnung* figure; **Abbildungsfehler** *m* PHYS aberration; **Abbildungsmaßstab** *m* KONSTZEICH reproduction scale; **Abbildungsmechanismus** *m* OPTIK imaging mechanism; **Abbildungssystem** *nt* OPTIK imaging system

Abbildverarbeitung *f* COMP & DV image processing

Abbild-Wiederherstellung *f* COMP & DV image restoration

Abbindebeschleuniger *m* BAU *Beton*, CHEMTECH *Zement* accelerator

Abbindefaden *m* LUFTTRANS lacing cord

Abbinden *nt* BAU setting, *Emulsion* breakdown, CHEMTECH *Zement* setting, FERTIG *Kleber* hardening

abbinden[1] *vt* BAU break, condition, *Kleber* cure, FERTIG *Kleber* harden, RADIO *Kabelbäume* lace

abbinden[2] *vi* BAU set

Abbindzeit *f* ABFALL setting time, BAU cure period, FERTIG *Kleber* pot life

abblasen *vt* KERNTECH blow off

Abblasventil *nt* FERTIG bleeder, HYDRAUL blow valve

Abblättern *nt* FERTIG scaling, TEXTIL peeling

abblättern[1] *vt* FERTIG scale

abblättern[2] *vi* BAU chip, peel, spall

Abblend- *pref* ELEKTROTECH, KFZTECH dimmed, dipped

abblenden[1] *vt* FOTO stop down

abblenden[2] *vi* ELEKTROTECH dim

Abblend-: **Abblendlicht** *nt* KFZTECH dimmed headlight (BrE), dipped beam, dipped headlight (AmE), passing light (AmE); **Abblendschalter** *m* ELEKTROTECH dimmer switch

abböschen *vt* BAU batter, slant, slope

Abbrand *m* KERNTECH burnout

Abbrechen *nt* CHEMTECH breaking; **~ des Flaschenbodens** *nt* KER & GLAS breaking-off of base

abbrechen *vt* BAU *Gebäude* demolish, COMP & DV abort, cancel, KER & GLAS break off (BrE), cap, KONTROLL, RAUMFAHRT abort, TELEKOM *Programm* terminate

Abbrems- *pref* RAUMFAHRT retardation, retrograde

abbremsen[1] *vt* CHEMIE *Elektronen*, RAUMFAHRT *Raumschiff* retard

abbremsen[2] *vi* PHYS decelerate

abbremsend *adj* PHYS decelerated, RAUMFAHRT retrograde

Abbrems-: **Abbremsorbit** *m* RAUMFAHRT retrograde or-

bit; **Abbremsrakete** f RAUMFAHRT retardation rocket
Abbremsung f MECHAN, PHYS deceleration
Abbremszeit f COMP & DV stop time
Abbrennbürste f BAU breaker point
abbrennen vt CHEMIE explosionsfrei deflagrate
Abbrennschweißen nt BAU flash welding
abbröckeln vti BAU crumble away
Abbruch m COMP & DV abort, hang-up, termination, cancel, TELEKOM disconnection; **Abbruchabfall** m ABFALL demolition waste, rubble, BAU demolition waste; **Abbruchbedingung** f KONTROLL truncation condition; **Abbruchfehler** m COMP & DV truncation error; **Abbruchhöhe** f LUFTTRANS critical altitude; **Abbruchkolonne** f BAU breakdown gang; **Abbruchmaterial** nt ABFALL demolition waste, rubble, BAU demolition waste; **Abbruchzustand** m KONTROLL truncation condition
abbrühen vt THERMOD scald
ABC abbr (automatische Helligkeitsregelung) FERNSEH ABC (automatic brightness control)
ABC-Hubschrauber m LUFTTRANS ABC helicopter, advanced blade concept helicopter
Abdachen nt FERTIG Zahnräder pointing
abdachen vt FERTIG Zahnräder point
abdämmen vt WASSERVERSORG gegen Wasser block off
Abdampf m HYDRAUL, LEBENSMITTEL, MASCHINEN dead steam, exhaust steam, waste steam; **Abdampfapparat** m CHEMTECH evaporator
Abdampfen nt CHEMTECH Lösemittel vaporization
abdampfen[1] vt CHEMTECH vaporize, Flüssigkeiten evaporate
abdampfen[2] vi THERMOD boil away
Abdampf: **Abdampfgefäß** nt CHEMTECH evaporating vessel; **Abdampfkasserolle** f CHEMTECH evaporating pan; **Abdampfkessel** m CHEMTECH evaporating boiler, HEIZ & KÄLTE exhaust steam boiler; **Abdampfschale** f CHEMTECH evaporating dish, evaporating pan, evaporating basin, LABOR evaporating basin, evaporating dish, evaporating pan; **Abdampfturbine** f HEIZ & KÄLTE exhaust steam turbine; **Abdampfventil** nt HYDRAUL exhaust valve
Abdeck- pref DRUCK, ELEKTRONIK, VERPACK masking; **Abdeckband** nt DRUCK masking paper, VERPACK masking tape, surface protection tape; **Abdeckbanddichtung** f VERPACK band sealing; **Abdeckblech** nt BAU flashing, MECHAN base plate; **Abdeckblende** f ELEKTRONIK mask
Abdecken nt BAU coping
abdecken vt BAU Böschung, Fundament revet, Träger cope, KERNTECH blanket
Abdecker m LEBENSMITTEL knacker
Abdeck-: **Abdeckhaube** f LUFTTRANS Motor cowl; **Abdeckmaterial** nt ABFALL covering material, DRUCK resist; **Abdeckplatte** f BAU cap, FERTIG Bettbahn cover, Walzen apron, KER & GLAS cover tile (BrE), KERNTECH cover gas discharge line, cover slab, LUFTTRANS access panel; **Abdeckscheibe** f FERTIG Kunststoffinstallationen sealing plug; **Abdeckschicht** f KUNSTSTOFF resist coating; **Abdeckstein** m BAU capstone
Abdeckung f BAU cover, covering, ERDÖL cap rock, KERNTECH cover cap, KFZTECH Kühler blind, MECHAN guard, SICHERHEIT cover WASSERVERSORG coping; **~ einer Hemisphäre** f TELEKOM hemispherical coverage; **~ für Schaftrippe** f LUFTTRANS cover strip of root rib
abdestillieren[1] vt THERMOD distil
abdestillieren[2] vi CHEMTECH, THERMOD distil off

Abdicht- pref BAU, CHEMIE, MECHAN sealing
Abdichten nt BAU sealing
abdichten vt ABFALL line, Deponie seal, BAU caulk, make impermeable, proof, seal, MECHAN pack, PAPIER, WASSERTRANS Schiffbau seal
Abdicht-: **Abdichtleiste** f BAU window bar; **Abdichtmittel** nt CHEMIE sealant
Abdichtung f BAU packing, ERDÖL, FERTIG Kunststoffinstallationen, MASCHINEN sealing, MECHAN seal; **Abdichtungslage** f BAU barrier; **Abdichtungsmasse** f BAU sealing agent, VERPACK lining compound; **Abdichtungsmittel** nt BAU sealant
Abdrehen nt FERTIG Schleifscheibe dressing, truing
abdrehen vt FERTIG Schleifkörper dress, Schleifscheibe true, WASSERVERSORG Hahn turn off
Abdrehvorrichtung f MASCHINEN truing attachment, turning attachment
Abdrift f LUFTTRANS Seitwärtsbewegung des Flugzeugs, MEERSCHMUTZ, RAUMFAHRT Raumschiff drift; **Abdriftbereich** m ELEKTRONIK drift region; **Abdriftwinkel** m LUFTTRANS drift angle, WASSERTRANS leeway angle
Abdrosselung f LUFTTRANS Kompressor, Turbomotor stall
Abdruck m DRUCK impression, FERTIG mold (AmE), mould (BrE)
abdruckbar: **~es Zeichen** nt DRUCK printing character
Abdruck: **Abdruckbarkeit** f DRUCK printability
Abdrücksignal nt EISENBAHN backing signal
Abdrückversuch m MASCHINEN hydraulic test
Abduktion f ERGON abduction
Aberration f METALL, OPTIK, WELLPHYS aberration; **Aberrationskreis** m OPTIK circle of aberration
Abfackeln nt ERDÖL Verbrennung flaring
abfackeln vt THERMOD burn off
Abfall[1] m ABFALL junk, BAU tailings, ELEKTRONIK der Spannung fall-off, ELEKTROTECH der Spannung drop, HYDRAUL Niveau fall, MECHAN junk, scrap, PAPIER waste, QUAL scrap, VERPACK garbage (AmE), rubbish (BrE), WASSERVERSORG refuse, spillage
Abfall[2] **als ~ zurückhalten** vt BAU throw back to waste
Abfall: **Abfallablauf** m KERNTECH waste outlet; **Abfallagerung** f ABFALL waste storage
abfallarm: **~e Technologie** f ABFALL clean technology, low-waste technolgy
Abfall: **Abfallaufbereitung** f ABFALL, UMWELTSCHMUTZ waste recovery; **Abfallausgrabung** f KERNTECH disinternment of waste; **Abfallbecken der Sortiermaschine** nt KER & GLAS grader waste pond; **Abfallbehälter** m ABFALL garbage can (AmE), rubbish bin (BrE), waste container, KERNTECH für Endlagerung waste canister; **Abfallbehandlung** f ABFALL waste processing, waste treatment; **Abfallbeseitigung** f ABFALL refuse disposal, waste disposal, WASSERVERSORG waste disposal; **Abfallbeseitigungsunternehmen** nt ABFALL waste disposal company; **Abfallbörse** f ABFALL waste exchange market; **Abfallbrennstoff** m ABFALL waste fuel; **Abfallcontainer** m ABFALL caster-equipped container; **Abfalldeponie** f WASSERVERSORG refuse dump; **Abfalldesinfektion** f ABFALL waste disinfection
Abfallen nt ELEKTROTECH drop-out, FERNSEH decay
abfallen vi BAU sink, Gelände slope, COMP & DV decay, WASSERTRANS bear away, vom Wind beim Segeln fall off
abfallend: **~er Bogen** m BAU rising arch; **~e Flanke** f ELEKTRONIK eines Impulses trailing edge; **~e Schneide** f FERTIG leading tool edge (AmE)

Abfall: **Abfallentsorgung** *f* ABFALL waste disposal; **Abfallentsorgung vor Ort** *f* KERNTECH on-site waste disposal; **Abfallerzeuger** *m* ABFALL waste generator, waste producer; **Abfallerzeugung** *f* ABFALL waste formation, waste generation, waste production, waste stream; **Abfallextraktionssystem** *nt* VERPACK waste extraction system; **Abfallfluß** *m* ABFALL flow of waste
abfallfrei: **~e Technologie** *f* ABFALL NWT, nonwaste technology
Abfall: **Abfallgärung** *f* ABFALL fermentation of refuse; **Abfallgesetz** *nt* (*AbfG*) ABFALL Waste Avoidance and Management Act, Waste Disposal Act; **Abfallhaufen** *m* BAU waste heap; **Abfallkompensation** *f* FERNSEH dropout compensator; **Abfallkondensatpumpe** *f* KERNTECH waste condensate pump; **Abfallkonzentration** *f* KERNTECH waste concentration; **Abfallmaterial** *nt* VERPACK scrap material; **Abfallneutralisation** *f* ABFALL waste neutralization; **Abfallprodukt** *nt* MASCHINEN by-product, UMWELTSCHMUTZ *unverwertbar* waste product; **Abfallrate** *f* FERNSEH decay rate; **Abfallrelais** *nt* ELEKTRIZ release relay; **Abfallrückholung** *f* KERNTECH disinternment of waste; **Abfallsäure** *f* ABFALL waste acid, TEXTIL spent acid; **Abfallschaltsignal** *nt* FERNSEH dropout switch signal; **Abfallschicht** *f* ABFALL waste layer; **Abfallsortieranlage** *f* ABFALL refuse separation plant, sorting plant, waste sorting plant; **Abfallsortierung am Anfallsort** *f* ABFALL source separation; **Abfallspannung** *f* ELEKTROTECH drop-out voltage; **Abfallstoff** *m* ABFALL junk; **Abfallstreifen** *m* FERTIG *Ausschneiden* skeleton; **Abfallstrom** *m* ABFALL flow of waste, ELEKTRIZ, ELEKTROTECH drop-out current; **Abfallverbrennungsanlage** *f* ABFALL refuse incinerator; **Abfallverbrennungsofen** *m* UMWELTSCHMUTZ incinerator; **Abfallvermeidung** *f* ABFALL waste avoidance; **Abfallverursacher** *m* ABFALL waste producer; **Abfallverwertung** *f* ABFALL waste processing, waste treatment; **Abfallverwertungsanlage** *f* ABFALL waste treatment plant, UMWELTSCHMUTZ waste utilization plant
abfallwirtschaftlich: **~e Planung** *f* UMWELTSCHMUTZ waste-economical planning
Abfall: **Abfallzeit** *f* ELEKTRIZ drop-out time, ELEKTRONIK decay time, *Transistor* fall time, ELEKTROTECH decay time, LUFTTRANS *Verkehr* release time, PHYS *Impuls*, RADIO fall time; **Abfallzellstoff** *m* ABFALL waste pulp; **Abfallzerkleinerer** *m* ABFALL waste crusher, waste disintegrator; **Abfallzeugung** *f* ABFALL waste generation
Abfang *m* RAUMFAHRT intercept, TRANS safety stop; **Abfangbogen** *m* TRANS flare-out; **Abfangen** *nt* CHEMIE scavenging, LUFTTRANS *Flugmanöver* recovery, RAUMFAHRT intercept, WASSERTRANS recovery
Abfangen: **~ eines Flugzeugs** *nt* LUFTTRANS aircraft interception
abfangen: **~ und Höhe halten** *vt* LUFTTRANS level out
Abfang: **Abfangkeil** *m* ERDÖL *Bohrtechnik* slip; **Abfangpunkt** *m* RAUMFAHRT intercept point; **Abfangseil** *nt* TRANS safety stop cable
Abfärben *nt* DRUCK set-off
Abfasen *nt* BAU beveling (AmE), bevelling (BrE)
abfasen *vt* BAU, MASCHINEN chamfer
Abfasung *f* MASCHINEN bevel; **Abfasungswinkel** *m* MASCHINEN angle of bevel
Abfederung *f* KERNTECH whipping
abfeilen *vt* MASCHINEN file
Abfeim- *pref* KER & GLAS skimming; **Abfeimen** *nt* KER & GLAS skimming

abfeimen *vt* KER & GLAS skim
Abfeim-: **Abfeimnische** *f* KER & GLAS skimming pocket; **Abfeimstange** *f* KER & GLAS skimming rod
abfendern *vt* WASSERTRANS fend off
Abfertigung *f* LUFTTRANS check-in, handling; **Abfertigungsgebäude** *nt* LUFTTRANS passenger terminal; **Abfertigungsterminal** *nt* LUFTTRANS cargo terminal
AbfG *abbr* (*Abfallgesetz*) ABFALL Waste Avoidance and Management Act, Waste Disposal Act
abfiltrieren *vt* CHEMTECH filter out
Abflachen *nt* ELEKTRONIK *Kurvenverlauf* leveling (AmE), levelling (BrE)
Abflachung *f* KFZTECH *eines Reifens* flattening
Abflammen *nt* TEXTIL singeing
abflammen *vt* TEXTIL gas, singe
abflanschen *vt* FERTIG *Werkstofftrennen* notch
abflauen *vi* WASSERTRANS *Wind* calm down
abfließen *vt* BAU outflow
Abflug *m* LUFTTRANS departure; **Abflugflughafen** *m* LUFTTRANS airport of departure; **Abflugleitstrahl** *m* LUFTTRANS *Navigation* outbound beam; **Abflugstation** *f* LUFTTRANS departure terminal; **Abflugsteuerkurs** *m* LUFTTRANS *Navigation* outbound heading
Abfluß *m* ABFALL effluent, ELEKTROTECH leakage, HYDRAUL sink, MASCHINEN drain, MEERSCHMUTZ, NICHTFOSS ENERG, UMWELTSCHMUTZ runoff, WASSERVERSORG discharge; **~ im Oberflächenbereich** *m* ABFALL surface runoff; **Abflußbecken** *nt* HYDRAUL, LABOR sink; **Abflußgraben** *m* LUFTTRANS gutter; **Abflußkanal** *m* WASSERVERSORG distributing canal, effluent channel, tailrace, tailrace tunnel; **Abflußkoeffizient** *m* WASSERVERSORG runoff coefficient
abflußlos: **~es Einzugsgebiet** *nt* WASSERVERSORG blind drainage area
Abfluß: **Abflußmenge** *f* WASSERVERSORG discharge, rate of flow; **Abflußregler** *m* NICHTFOSS ENERG discharge regulator; **Abflußrinne** *f* LUFTTRANS guttering, MECHAN gutter, WASSERVERSORG flume, sluice box; **Abflußrohr** *nt* BAU drainpipe, HYDRAUL flow pipe, WASSERVERSORG downpipe, *einer Pumpe* discharge lift, discharge pipe; **Abflußschleuse** *f* HYDRAUL sink; **Abflußventil** *nt* HYDRAUL escape valve; **Abflußvorrichtung** *f* WASSERTRANS drain
Abfolge *f* KONTROLL sequence
abfördern *vt* HEIZ & KÄLTE discharge
Abfrage *f* COMP & DV inquiry, query, request, GERÄT, REGELUNG scan, TELEKOM polling, scan; **Abfragebearbeitung** *f* COMP & DV query processing; **Abfragecode** *m* COMP & DV inquiry character; **Abfragedienst** *m* TELEKOM answering service; **Abfrageklinke** *f* TELEKOM jack; **Abfragemethode** *f* COMP & DV lookup; **Abfragemodus** *m* ELEKTRONIK interrogation mode
abfragen *vt* COMP & DV interrogate, query, poll
Abfrage: **Abfragerate** *f* REGELUNG revisit rate; **Abfrageschalter** *m* COMP & DV sampler; **Abfragesprache** *f* COMP & DV QL, query language; **Abfragestation** *f* COMP & DV inquiry station; **Abfragesteuerung** *f* COMP & DV inquiry control; **Abfragesystem** *nt* TELEKOM polling system; **Abfrageverarbeitung** *f* COMP & DV inquiry processing, query processing
Abfühlen *nt* COMP & DV sensing
Abfuhr *f* ABFALL collection; **~ der Nachwärme** *f* KERNTECH afterheat release
abführen *vt* BAU *Wasser* carry off
Abführmechanismus *m* TEXTIL take-away mechanism

Abführung *f* FERTIG *Späne* clearance, HEIZ & KÄLTE eduction

Abfuhrwagen *m* ABFALL skip, tipper truck

Abfüll- *pref* VERPACK filling; **Abfüll- und Dosierautomat** *m* VERPACK filling and dosing machine; **Abfüll- und Kappenaufsetzmaschine** *f* VERPACK filling and capping machine; **Abfüll- und Siegelmaschine** *f* VERPACK filling and sealing machine; **Abfüll- und Versiegelungseinheit für Beutel** *f* VERPACK sachet form fill seal unit; **Abfüllanlage** *f* VERPACK filling machine; **Abfüllautomat** *m* VERPACK bottling machine; **Abfüllbehälter** *m* LEBENSMITTEL bottling tank

Abfüllen *nt* LEBENSMITTEL *von Getränken* racking; ~ **auf Flaschen** *nt* LEBENSMITTEL filling bottles

Abfüll-: **Abfüllgerät** *nt* MASCHINEN filler, filling machine; **Abfülllinie** *f* VERPACK filling line; **Abfüllpackung** *f* VERPACK dosing packing

Abfüllung: ~ **in Kartons** *f* VERPACK bag-in-a-box packaging; ~ **in Säcke von Hand** *f* VERPACK hand bagging

Abfüll-: **Abfüllvorrichtung** *f* LEBENSMITTEL dispenser; **Abfüllwaage** *f* GERÄT bag-filling scale, dispensing scale, VERPACK checkweighing machine

Abgabeseite *f* MASCHINEN discharge side

Abgang *m* KFZTECH, TELEKOM, TRANS originating, outgoing, output; **Abgangsverkehr** *m* TELEKOM originating traffic, outgoing traffic, TRANS originating traffic; **Abgangswelle** *f* KFZTECH output shaft

Abgas *nt* FERTIG waste gas, HEIZ & KÄLTE flue gas, KERNTECH off-gas, waste gas, KFZTECH emission, exhaust gas, LUFTTRANS emission, *Triebwerk, Motor* exhaust, MECHAN exhaust, PHYS flue gas, THERMOD exhaust gas, flue gas, UMWELTSCHMUTZ exhaust gas, waste gas; **Abgasanlage** *f* KFZTECH exhaust system

abgasarm: ~**es Gemisch** *nt* KFZTECH lean mixture

Abgas: **Abgasausströmöffnung** *f* MECHAN exhaust gate

abgasbeheizt *adj* MECHAN exhaust-operated

Abgas: **Abgasdüse** *f* LUFTTRANS exhaust nozzle; **Abgasdüsenverschlußstücke** *nt pl* LUFTTRANS exhaust nozzle breeches; **Abgasentschwefelung** *f* ABFALL waste gas desulfurization (AmE), waste gas desulphurization (BrE); **Abgasfilterung** *f* THERMOD exhaust gas cleaning; **Abgasgehäuse** *nt* LUFTTRANS exhaust case

abgasgetrieben *adj* MECHAN exhaust-operated

Abgas: **Abgasgewicht** *nt* MECHAN exhaust weight; **Abgaskatalysator** *m* KFZTECH catalytic converter (BrE), catalytic muffler (AmE), catalytic silencer (BrE); **Abgaskondensator** *m* KERNTECH off-gas condenser; **Abgaskonus** *m* LUFTTRANS exhaust cone; **Abgaskrümmer** *m* MECHAN exhaust manifold; **Abgasleitung** *f* FERTIG exhaust duct, KFZTECH, LUFTTRANS exhaust pipe, MECHAN exhaust conduit, exhaust pipe, THERMOD, WASSERTRANS exhaust pipe; **Abgasmeßgerät** *nt* GERÄT waste gas meter; **Abgasmeßstrecke** *f* HEIZ & KÄLTE flue gas test section; **Abgasprüfgerät** *nt* MECHAN exhaust gas analyser (BrE), exhaust analyzer (AmE); **Abgasreinigung** *f* ABFALL waste gas cleaning, THERMOD exhaust gas cleaning; **Abgasreinigungsanlage** *f* SICHERHEIT flue gas cleaning installation; **Abgasrohr** *nt* KERNTECH flue tube, KFZTECH *Motor* exhaust pipe, tail pipe, LUFTTRANS, MECHAN, THERMOD, WASSERTRANS exhaust pipe; **Abgasrohrkrümmer** *m* KFZTECH, LUFTTRANS exhaust manifold; **Abgasrückführung** *f* KFZTECH exhaust gas recirculation; **Abgasrückführung mit Lufteinblasung** *f* KFZTECH exhaust gas recirculation with air injection;

Abgassammler *m* KFZTECH, LUFTTRANS, THERMOD exhaust manifold; **Abgasschalldämpfer** *m* KFZTECH exhaust muffler (AmE), exhaust silencer (BrE), exhaust nozzle; **Abgasschubrahmen** *m* LUFTTRANS exhaust nozzle; **Abgassensor** *m* KFZTECH lambda probe; **Abgasstutzen** *m* MECHAN exhaust stack; - **Abgastemperatur** *f* KFZTECH exhaust gas temperature, LUFTTRANS exhaust gas temperature, jet pipe temperature; **Abgastemperaturanzeige** *f* KFZTECH, LUFTTRANS exhaust gas temperature indicator; **Abgasturbine** *f* LUFTTRANS exhaust gas turbine, MECHAN exhaust-driven turbine; **Abgasturbolader** *m* KFZTECH exhaust turbocharger, turbosupercharger, MECHAN exhaust-turbine supercharger; **Abgasventil** *nt* KFZTECH exhaust valve; **Abgasverbrennung** *f* KFZTECH exhaust gas combustion; **Abgaswärme** *f* THERMOD waste gas heat; **Abgaswärmerückgewinnung** *f* THERMOD waste gas heat recovery; **Abgaswiederverwertung** *f* KFZTECH exhaust recycling

abgebaut *adj* BAU struck

Abgeben *nt* CHEMIE *Verbindungen* liberation

abgeben *vt* THERMOD emit, give off

abgeblättert *adj* FERTIG scaled

abgeblendet: ~**er Scheinwerfer** *m* KFZTECH dipped headlight (AmE)

abgebrochen:[1] ~**er Anflug** *m* LUFTTRANS discontinued approach; ~**e Prüfung** *f* QUAL curtailed inspection

abgebrochen:[2] ~ **darstellen** *vt* KONSTZEICH represent broken

abgebunden *adj* FERTIG *Kleber* hardened

abgedacht *adj* FERTIG *Zahnrad* pointed

abgedichtet *adj* FERTIG gasketed

abgefahren: ~**er Reifen** *m* KFZTECH bald tire (AmE), bald tyre (BrE)

abgefangen: ~**e Landung** *f* LUFTTRANS flared landing

abgefast: ~**e Kante** *f* MASCHINEN bevel edge, beveled edge (AmE), bevelled edge (BrE), chamfered edge; ~**e Scheibe** *f* MASCHINEN beveled washer (AmE), bevelled washer (BrE)

abgeführt: ~**e Wärme** *f* HEIZ & KÄLTE heat removed

abgegeben: ~**e Leistung** *f* MASCHINEN power output; ~**e Strahlungsmenge** *f* STRAHLPHYS radiated output; ~**e Wärmedichte** *f* KERNTECH heat output density

abgeglichen: ~**e Leitung** *f* ELEKTRIZ balanced line, balancing coil

abgehängt: ~**e Decke** *f* BAU suspended ceiling

abgehend[1] *adj* TELEKOM outgoing

abgehend:[2] ~**er Anruf** *m* TELEKOM outgoing call; ~**es Bündel** *nt* TELEKOM outgoing group; ~**e Leitung** *f* TELEKOM outgoing circuit, outgoing line; ~**e Verbindung** *f* TELEKOM outgoing call; ~**er Verkehr** *m* TELEKOM outgoing traffic

abgehend:[3] ~**e Rufe gesperrt** *phr* TELEKOM outgoing calls barred

abgehoben *adj* TELEKOM off hook, off the hook

abgeklungen: ~**e Radioaktivität** *f* STRAHLPHYS cooled-down radioactivity

abgekühlt: ~**e Radioaktivität** *f* STRAHLPHYS cooled-down radioactivity

abgelagert: ~**es Holz** *nt* WASSERTRANS *Schiffbaumaterial* seasoned timber, seasoned wood

abgelaufen: ~**e Zeit** *f* COMP & DV elapsed time

abgelegt: ~**er Satz** *m* DRUCK dead matter, dead type

abgeleitet: ~**e Anströmgeschwindigkeit** *f* LUFTTRANS derived gust velocity; ~**e Einheit** *f* MASCHINEN, PHYS derived unit; ~**e Schaltung** *f* ELEKTRIZ derived circuit;

~er **Strom** *m* ELEKTRIZ derived current

abgelenkt: ~es **Bohren** *nt* ERDÖL *Bohrtechnik* deviated drilling; ~e **Bohrung** *f* ERDÖL *Bohrtechnik* deviated well

abgelesen: ~er **Meßwert** *m* GERÄT reading; ~er **Wert** *m* GERÄT reading

abgenommen *adj* TELEKOM off hook, off the hook

abgenutzt[1] *adj* MECHAN worn, TEXTIL worn out

abgenutzt:[2] ~es **Werkzeug** *nt* SICHERHEIT *Unfallursache* worn tool

abgeplattet[1] *adj* GEOM oblate

abgeplattet:[2] ~es **Ellipsoid** *nt* GEOM, PHYS oblate ellipsoid; ~er **Kern** *m* KERNTECH oblate nucleus; ~es **Sphäroid** *nt* GEOM oblate spheroid

abgeplatzt: ~e **Ecke** *f* KER & GLAS chipped corner; ~e **Kante** *f* KER & GLAS chipped edge

abgereichert: ~er **Kernbrennstoff** *m* KERNTECH depleted nuclear fuel

abgerundet: ~e **Anfahrdüse** *f* HYDRAUL *Steuerung* rounded approach orifice; ~e **Kante** *f* KER & GLAS rounded edge

abgeschaltet[1] *adj* ELEKTROTECH off, TELEKOM *Gerät* disabled

abgeschaltet:[2] ~er **Thyristor** *m* ELEKTRONIK off thyristor; ~er **Transistor** *m* ELEKTRONIK off transistor

abgeschert *adj* FERTIG sheared

abgeschirmt: ~e **Ader** *f* ELEKTRIZ screened core; ~e **Antenne** *f* FERNSEH screened aerial; ~er **Ausgang** *m* ELEKTROTECH guarded output; ~er **Draht** *m* ELEKTROTECH shielded wire; ~er **Eingang** *m* ELEKTROTECH guarded input; ~es **Gehäuse** *nt* ELEKTROTECH shielded enclosure; ~es **Kabel** *nt* AUFNAHME, COMP & DV, ELEKTRIZ, ELEKTROTECH, FERNSEH, PHYS screened cable, shielded cable; **nicht** ~e **Strahlungsquelle** *f* KERNTECH unshielded source; ~e **symmetrische Leitung** *f* ELEKTROTECH shielded pair; ~er **Transformator** *m* ELEKTROTECH shielded transformer; ~e **Übertragung** *f* ELEKTROTECH shielded transmission

abgeschlagen: ~es **Garn** *nt* KER & GLAS sloughed yarn

abgeschliffen *adj* FERTIG attrite

abgeschlossen[1] *adj* MEERSCHMUTZ sealed, PHYS self-contained; **in sich** ~ *adj* HEIZ & KÄLTE self-contained

abgeschlossen:[2] ~er **Behälter** *m* LABOR closed vessel; ~e **Deponie** *f* ABFALL complete fill; ~er **Innenraum** *m* PHYS enclosure; ~es **Intervall** *nt* MATH closed interval; ~e **Schale** *f* KERNTECH *Atom* closed shell; ~es **System** *nt* PHYS isolated system

abgeschnitten[1] *adj* FERTIG sheared

abgeschnitten:[2] ~er **Kegel** *m* GEOM truncated cone; ~e **Pyramide** *f* GEOM truncated pyramid

abgeschrägt[1] *adj* BAU *Zimmerhandwerk* splayed; **nicht** ~ *adj* FERTIG unbeveled (AmE), unbevelled (BrE)

abgeschrägt:[2] ~e **Gehrungsfuge** *f* BAU splayed mitre joint; ~e **Kante** *f* MASCHINEN bevel edge, beveled edge (AmE), bevelled edge (BrE); ~er **Meißel** *m* MASCHINEN beveled chisel (AmE), bevelled chisel (BrE); ~er **Stein** *m* KER & GLAS skew block

abgeschreckt: ~e **Scherben** *f pl* KER & GLAS quenched cullet

abgesetzt: ~es **Abwasser** *nt* WASSERVERSORG settled sewage; ~es **Betriebs-Terminal** *nt* TELEKOM remote operating terminal; ~e **Bohrung** *f* FERTIG shouldered hole; ~er **Konzentrator** *m* TELEKOM remote concentrator, remote line concentrator; **nicht** ~er **Konzentrator** *m* TELEKOM co-located concentrator; ~e **Konzentratoreinheit** *f* TELEKOM RCU, remote concentration

unit; ~es **Luftschraubenblatt** *nt* LUFTTRANS *Hubschrauber* offset blade; ~er **Meißel** *m* FERTIG offset cutting tool; ~es **Schlaggelenk** *nt* LUFTTRANS *Hubschrauber* offset flapping hinge; ~e **Vermittlung** *f* TELEKOM stand-alone exchange

abgesichert[1] *adj* ELEKTROTECH fuse-protected

abgesichert:[2] ~es **Gerät** *nt* SICHERHEIT fail-safe device

abgesoffen: ~e **Turbine** *f* HYDRAUL drowned turbine

abgesteift: ~er **Schacht** *m* BAU timbered shaft

abgestimmt: ~es **Filter** *nt* ELEKTRONIK tuned filter; ~e **Leitung** *f* ELEKTRONIK resonant line; ~e **Pistenlänge** *f* LUFTTRANS balanced field length; ~es **Reed-Relais** *nt* ELEKTROTECH resonant reed relay; ~er **Schwingkreis** *m* WELLPHYS tuned circuit

abgestrahlt: ~e **Leistung** *f* TELEKOM radiated power

abgestuft[1] *adj* BAU stepped, *Körnung* screened

abgestuft:[2] ~er **Grenzwert** *m* QUAL stepped limiting value; ~er **Höchstwert** *m* QUAL stepped upper limiting value; ~er **Mindestwert** *m* QUAL stepped lower limiting value; ~er **Steigflug** *m* LUFTTRANS stepped climb; ~e **Toleranz** *f* QUAL stepped tolerance

abgestumpft[1] *adj* MECHAN dull

abgestumpft:[2] ~e **Pyramide** *f* GEOM truncated pyramid

abgetastet: ~es **Signal** *nt* TELEKOM sampled signal

abgetragen *adj* TEXTIL worn out

abgetreppt *adj* BAU benched, stepped

abgewalmt: ~es **Mansardendach** *nt* BAU double pitch roof

abgewickelt: ~er **Verkehr** *m* TELEKOM handled traffic

abgewinkelt: ~er **Schraubenzieher** *m* MASCHINEN offset screwdriver

Abgießen *nt* CHEMTECH, LEBENSMITTEL decantation

abgießen *vt* CHEMIE decant

Abgleich *m* FERNSEH *der Videoköpfe* alignment, GERÄT *Meßbereich* trimming, MECHAN equalization, PHYS *Brückenabgleich* balancing, TELEKOM *Frequenzempfänger* tuning; **Abgleicharbeiten** *f pl* QUAL adjusting operations; **Abgleichband** *nt* FERNSEH alignment tape; **Abgleichbesteck** *nt* GERÄT alignment tool set, trimming kit; **Abgleicheinrichtung** *f* GERÄT calibration equipment; **Abgleichelement** *nt* GERÄT adjusting element, trimming element

Abgleichen *nt* RADIO alignment, TELEKOM balancing

abgleichen *vt* BAU trim, *Mauern* level, FERTIG parfolicalize, MECHAN trim, RADIO align, TELEKOM *Frequenz* tune

abgleichen: **neu** ~ *vt* GERÄT rebalance

Abgleich: **Abgleichfehler** *m* TELEKOM alignment fault; **Abgleichfrequenz** *f* ELEKTRONIK *bei Überlagerungsempfänger* tie-down point; **Abgleichmechanismus** *m* GERÄT balancing mechanism; **Abgleichpunkt** *m* GERÄT *Brücke* balance point; **Abgleichverstärker** *m* ELEKTRONIK leveling amplifier (AmE), levelling amplifier (BrE); **Abgleichwiderstand** *m* ELEKTRIZ balancing resistor, ELEKTROTECH adjustable resistor, GERÄT trimming resistor, *Bauelement* balancing resistor

Abgleisen *nt* EISENBAHN derailing

Abgleitung *f* ELEKTROTECH slip

Abgraten: ~ **in Trommelmaschine** *nt* FERTIG barrel deburring

abgraten *vt* BAU chip, FERTIG clip, snag

Abgratfehler:[1] **mit** ~ *adj* FERTIG mistrimmed

Abgratfehler[2] *m* FERTIG mistrimming

Abgratpresse *f* FERTIG stripping press, MASCHINEN trimming machine

Abgreifen *nt* MASCHINEN calipering (AmE), callipering (BrE)

abgreifen *vt* MASCHINEN caliper (AmE), calliper (BrE)

Abgreifpunkt *m* ELEKTROTECH tapping point

abgrenzen *vt* ELEKTROTECH locate

Abgriff *m* PHYS tapping

Abguß *m* FERTIG pouring, METALL casting

abhalten *vt* COMP & DV hold

Abhämmern *nt* FERTIG peening

Abhang *m* BAU downhill slope, slope

abhängig[1] *adj* PATENT dependent

abhängig:[2] **~er Datensatz** *m* COMP & DV member set; **~e Gleichungen** *f pl* MATH dependent equations; **~es Patent** *nt* PATENT dependent patent; **~er Patentanspruch** *m* PATENT dependent claim; **~e Variable** *f* MATH dependent variable

Abhängigkeit *f* FERTIG, SICHERHEIT interlock, interlocking; **Abhängigkeitsschaltung** *f* FERTIG interlock; **Abhängigkeitsschutz** *m* SICHERHEIT interlocking guard

Abhaspelmaschine *f* KUNSTSTOFF reeling machine

Abhebebewegung *f* FERTIG *Hobelmeißel* relief motion

Abhebegeschwindigkeit *f* LUFTTRANS liftoff speed, unstick speed

Abhebegewicht *nt* RAUMFAHRT liftoff weight

Abheben *nt* FERTIG skimming, *Hobelmeißel* relieving, RAUMFAHRT lift-off

abheben[1] *vt* FERTIG skim, *Späne* cut off, *Werkzeug* clear, TELEKOM *Hörer* lift

abheben[2] *vi* LUFTTRANS lift off

Abhebeöse *f* FERTIG *Gießen* lifting lug

Abhilfe *f* PATENT interlocutory revision, QUAL remedy, TELEKOM corrective measure; **Abhilfemaßnahme** *f* QUAL corrective action, remedy

Abhitze *f* HEIZ & KÄLTE, MASCHINEN, THERMOD waste heat; **Abhitzekessel** *m* HEIZ & KÄLTE, THERMOD waste heat boiler; **Abhitzerückgewinnung** *f* THERMOD waste heat recovery; **Abhitzeverwerter** *m* METALL regenerator

Abholen *nt* ABFALL collection

Abhör- *pref* AUFNAHME control; **Abhörkabine** *f* AUFNAHME control cubicle; **Abhörlautsprecher** *m* AUFNAHME control loudspeaker; **Abhörsicherheit** *f* TELEKOM safety from interception

Abietan *nt* CHEMIE abietate

Abietin *nt* CHEMIE coniferin; **Abietinsäure** *f* PAPIER abietic acid

abisolierbar *adj* FERTIG strippable

abisolieren *vt* KFZTECH strip

Abkant- *pref* FERTIG, MASCHINEN edging, folding; **Abkanten** *nt* FERTIG, MASCHINEN edging, folding

abkanten *vt* BAU bend at right angles, FERTIG *Blech* fold

Abkant-: **Abkantmaschine** *f* FERTIG, MASCHINEN edging machine, folding machine; **Abkantpresse** *f* FERTIG brake, press brake

Abkantung *f* BAU chamfer

Abkant-: **Abkantwinkel** *m* FERTIG *Blechabkantmaschine*, MASCHINEN *Blechabkantmaschine* angle of bend

abkapseln *vt* ANSTRICH encapsule

Abkipp- *pref* BAU dumping, LUFTTRANS dive; **Abkippen** *nt* LUFTTRANS *des Flugzeugs nach vorne* dive, dumping

abkippen *vt* BAU shoot, tip

Abkipp-: **Abkippförderkorb** *m* BAU dump skip; **Abkipptrudelverhalten** *nt* LUFTTRANS stall spin characteristics

abklären *vt* CHEMIE clarify, CHEMTECH clarify, elutriate

Abklärgefäß *nt* CHEMTECH decantation vessel, decanter, decanting glass, UMWELTSCHMUTZ decanter

Abklärung *f* CHEMIE clarification

abklemmen *vt* ELEKTROTECH, KONTROLL, TELEKOM *Draht* disconnect

Abkling- *pref* KERNTECH decay; **Abklingbecken** *nt* KERNTECH neutralization pond; **Abklingcharakteristik** *f* ELEKTROTECH decay characteristic

Abklingen *nt* ELEKTROTECH decay, FERNSEH damping, decay, KERNTECH decay, neutralization, *Reaktor* cooling, STRAHLPHYS decay; **~ des angeregten Zustandes** *nt* KERNTECH, STRAHLPHYS excited-state deactivation

abklingen *vi* STRAHLPHYS decay

abklingend: **~es Feld** *nt* OPTIK, TELEKOM evanescent field; **~e Schwingung** *f* TELEKOM *Oszillation* ringing; **~e Welle** *f* PHYS decaying wave

Abkling-: **Abklingfaktor** *m* ELEKTROTECH decay factor; **Abklingkonstante** *f* PHYS, STRAHLPHYS, TEILPHYS decay constant; **Abklingrate** *f* AKUSTIK decay rate; **Abklingteich** *m* KERNTECH *für verbrauchte Brennelemente* discharge pond; **Abklingzeit** *f* ELEKTRONIK, ELEKTROTECH decay time, KERNTECH *von radioaktivem Material* cooling-down period, OPTIK settling time, PHYS *Impuls* decay time; **Abklingzeitkonstante** *f* GERÄT damping time constant

Abklopfen *nt* BAU picking

abklopfen *vt* FERTIG rap

Abklopfer *m* FERTIG *Gießen* rapper

Abknallen *nt* HEIZ & KÄLTE *Brenner* backfiring

abknallen *vt* FERTIG *Flamme* pop

Abknickung *f* KONSTZEICH offset, zigzag

Abkochmittel *nt* CHEMIE *Rohseide* scouring agent

Abkochung *f* LEBENSMITTEL decoction

abkohlen *vi* KOHLEN break coal

abkoppeln *vt* KONTROLL disconnect

Abkopplung *f* KERNTECH *für Abschaltstab* disconnect rod

Abkreiden *nt* KUNSTSTOFF chalking

Abkühlen *nt* KUNSTSTOFF chilling

abkühlen[1] *vt* HEIZ & KÄLTE chill, MECHAN chill, quench, TEXTIL cool, THERMOD chill

abkühlen[2] *vi* KER & GLAS cool down

Abkühlphase *f* KER & GLAS cooling-down period

Abkühlung *f* HEIZ & KÄLTE chilling, TEXTIL, VERPACK cooling; **Abkühlungsgeschwindigkeit** *f* HEIZ & KÄLTE cooling rate, THERMOD rate of cooling; **Abkühlungskurve** *f* METALL cooling curve

Abkühlzeit *f* KERNTECH cooling-down period

abkuppeln *vt* MASCHINEN throw out, MECHAN disengage

Abkürzung *f* TRANS shortcut

Abladestation *f* BAU dumping station

Ablage *f* COMP & DV filing, VERPACK deposit

Ablagern *nt* VERPACK *von Karton* deposition

ablagern *vt* ABFALL *Müll* tip

Ablagerung *f* BAU alluviation, deposit, CHEMIE deposit, CHEMTECH sediment, *Holz* desiccation, FERTIG deposit, UMWELTSCHMUTZ *Bergbau* deposition, WASSERVERSORG accretion, deposit, sediment; **Ablagerungsbecken** *nt* WASSERVERSORG settling basin; **Ablagerungsgeschwindigkeit** *f* UMWELTSCHMUTZ *radioaktive Partikel* deposition velocity; **Ablagerungsplatz** *m* ABFALL storage area; **Ablagerungswert** *m* UMWELTSCHMUTZ deposition value

ablandig[1] *adj* WASSERTRANS offshore

ablandig:[2] **~er Wind** *m* WASSERTRANS offshore wind

Ablaß *m* BAU *eines Ausgußbeckens* bibcock, KOHLEN blow-off, MASCHINEN drain, WASSERVERSORG outlet

ablaßbar: ~er unnutzbarer Treibstoff *m* LUFTTRANS drainable unusable fuel

Ablassen *nt* KERNTECH, MECHAN bleeding; ~ der Luft *nt* KFZTECH *Reifen* deflation

ablassen *vt* FERTIG *Flüssigkeit* bleed, MASCHINEN *Flüssigkeit* bleed, drain, *Luft aus Reifen* deflate, RAUMFAHRT *Raumschiff* jettison, SICHERHEIT lower, UMWELTSCHMUTZ *Wasser* discharge

Ablaß: **Ablaßgraben** *m* WASSERVERSORG outlet channel; **Ablaßhahn** *m* BAU, FERTIG, KFZTECH *Kühler* drain cock, MASCHINEN drain cock, draw-off tap; **Ablaßkühlung** *f* RAUMFAHRT *Raumschiff* dump cooling; **Ablaßrohr** *nt* WASSERVERSORG outlet pipe; **Ablaßstollen** *m* WASSERVERSORG tailrace tunnel; **Ablaßventil** *nt* EISENBAHN overflow valve, HYDRAUL discharge valve, poppet valve, MASCHINEN drain valve, RAUMFAHRT *Raumschiff* jettison valve, WASSERTRANS drain valve; **Ablaßventilsteuerung** *f* HYDRAUL *Dampfmaschine* poppet valve gear

Ablation *f* COMP & DV, KERNTECH ablation; **Ablationsimpuls** *m* KERNTECH ablating momentum; **Ablationsion** *nt* KERNTECH ablated ion; **Ablationskühlung** *f* RAUMFAHRT *Raumschiff* ablative cooling; **Ablationsschild** *m* RAUMFAHRT *Raumschiff* ablation shield

ablativ *adj* RAUMFAHRT *Raumschiff* ablative

Ablauf *m* COMP & DV flow, run, FERTIG operating sequence, work cycle, KERNTECH outlet, KONTROLL routine, MEERSCHMUTZ, NICHTFOSS ENERG runoff, PHYS *Experiment* course, WASSERVERSORG outflow; ~ des Zeitgebers *m* TELEKOM expiry of timer; **Ablaufbacke** *f* KFZTECH *Bremse* trailing shoe; **Ablaufbahnhof** *m* EISENBAHN classification yard with hump; **Ablaufbogen** *m* BAU arch of discharge; **Ablaufdiagramm** *nt* COMP & DV flow diagram, flowchart

Ablaufen *nt* KUNSTSTOFF curtaining

ablaufen[1] *vt* FERTIG, WASSERVERSORG run off; ~ lassen *vt* COMP & DV *Programm* run

ablaufen[2] *vi* COMP & DV pass

ablaufend: ~e Bandspule *f* FERNSEH supply reel; ~e Filmrolle *f* FERNSEH supply roll; ~es Wasser *nt* WASSERTRANS *Gezeiten* falling tide

Ablauf: **Ablauffolge** *f* KONTROLL sequence; **Ablaufgerinne** *nt* WASSERVERSORG *eines Wasserrads* tail race; **Ablaufhaspel** *f* FERTIG pay-off reel; **Ablaufkanal** *m* NICHTFOSS ENERG, WASSERVERSORG flume; **Ablaufplansymbol** *nt* COMP & DV flowchart symbol; **Ablauframpe** *f* BAU *Eisenbahn* gravity incline; **Ablaufrangierbetrieb** *m* EISENBAHN hump shunting; **Ablaufrichtung** *f* COMP & DV flow direction; **Ablaufrohr** *nt* FERTIG *Kunststoffinstallationen* outlet pipe, WASSERVERSORG delivery pipe; **Ablaufschritt** *m* COMP & DV step; **Ablaufsteuerung** *f* COMP & DV sequencer, sequencing

ablaufsynchron: ~er Betrieb *m* COMP & DV real-time operation

Ablauf: **Ablaufüberwachungssystem** *nt* KONTROLL supervising system; **Ablaufverfolgung** *f* COMP & DV trace; **Ablaufverfolgungsprogramm** *nt* COMP & DV trace program

Ablauge *f* ABFALL waste lye

Ablauger *m* BAU paint stripper

Abläutesignal *nt* EISENBAHN train-announcing signal

Ablegen: ~ auf Gips *nt* KER & GLAS laying on plaster; ~ auf Stoff *nt* KER & GLAS laying on cloth; ~ von Rohglas

nt KER & GLAS *zum Schleifer* laying

ablegen[1] *vt* ERDÖL *Leitung vom Verlegeschiff* lay down

ablegen[2] *vi* WASSERTRANS *festmachen* cast off

Ablegeplatz *m* KER & GLAS laying yard

Ablegesatz *m* DRUCK dead matter, dead type

Ablehngrenze *f* QUAL limiting quality

ableichtern *vt* MEERSCHMUTZ lighten

ableiten *vt* BAU *Wärme* carry off, FERTIG leak

Ableitstrom *m* ELEKTROTECH leakage current

Ableitung *f* ELEKTROTECH dissipation, leakage, GEOM *trigonometrischer Funktionen* differentiation, MATH derivative, differential coefficient, differential derivative, *einer Funktion* derivative, RADIO leak, TELEKOM leakage, WASSERVERSORG offtake, *eines Flusses* diverting; ~ trigonometrischer Funktionen *f* GEOM differentiation of trigonometrical functions; **Ableitungskanal** *m* WASSERVERSORG discharge canal; **Ableitungsverlust** *m* ELEKTROTECH dissipative loss

Ableitvorrichtung *f* ELEKTROTECH sink

Ableitwiderstand *m* ELEKTROTECH bleeder, bleeder resistor

Ablenk- *pref* BAU baffle, GERÄT deflecting, deflection; **Ablenkamplitude** *f* GERÄT amplitude of deflection; **Ablenkblech** *nt* BAU baffle plate, CHEMTECH deflector, HEIZ & KÄLTE deflector plate, KER & GLAS *Ofen*, KFZTECH *Auspufftopf* baffle, LUFTTRANS deflector, MASCHINEN baffle, deflector plate; **Ablenkbohren** *nt* ERDÖL sidetrack drilling; **Ablenkeinrichtung** *f* FERNSEH scan registration; **Ablenkelektrode** *f* ELEKTROTECH, GERÄT, KERNTECH deflecting electrode, deflection electrode; **Ablenkempfindlichkeit** *f* ELEKTRONIK deflection sensitivity

ablenken *vt* FERNSEH, GERÄT *Elektronenstrahl*, MASCHINEN deflect

Ablenker *m* FERTIG deflector

Ablenk-: **Ablenkfaktor** *m* ELEKTRONIK deflection factor; **Ablenkjoch** *nt* ELEKTRONIK *Kathodenstrahlröhre* deflection yoke, FERNSEH deflection yoke, scanning yoke; **Ablenkkeil** *m* ERDÖL whipstock; **Ablenkmagnet** *m* FERNSEH deflection magnet, TEILPHYS deflecting magnet; **Ablenknormen** *f pl* FERNSEH scanning standards; **Ablenkplatte** *f* CHEMTECH baffle, ELEKTRONIK *Ionenfalle*, FERNSEH deflection plate, FERTIG baffle board, GERÄT deflecting electrode, HEIZ & KÄLTE deflector plate, KER & GLAS baffle plate, MASCHINEN baffle, RAUMFAHRT *Raumschiff*, STRAHLPHYS deflection plate; **Ablenkrohr** *nt* STRAHLPHYS deflection tube; **Ablenksieb** *nt* PAPIER baffle wire; **Ablenkspule** *f* ELEKTROTECH deflection coil, FERNSEH scanning coil, KERNTECH, PHYS deflecting coil; **Ablenkstrahl** *m* FERNSEH scanning beam; **Ablenkstromgenerator** *m* FERNSEH scan current generator; **Ablenksystem** *nt* FERNSEH deflection system

Ablenkung *f* ERDÖL *Tiefbohrtechnik* sidetracking, GERÄT *Oszilloskop* scan, MASCHINEN, MECHAN, OPTIK deflection, PHYS *Lichtstrahlen* deviation, RAUMFAHRT, STRAHLPHYS *elektrisches oder magnetisches Feld* deflection, TELEKOM *eines Strahls*, WASSERTRANS *Kompaß* deviation; ~ im Magnetfeld *f* KERNTECH magnetic deflection

Ablenk-: **Ablenkventil** *nt* HYDRAUL deflecting valve; **Ablenkverstärker** *m* ELEKTRONIK deflection amplifier, GERÄT *Oszilloskop* sweep deflection amplifier; **Ablenkvorrichtung** *f* MASCHINEN, TELEKOM deflector; **Ablenkweite** *f* FERNSEH trace interval; **Ablenkwinkel** *m* FERNSEH deflection angle, PHYS angle of deviation

Ablesen *nt* BAU reading
ablesen *vt* GERÄT *Meßergebnis* read
Ablesesystem *nt* MASCHINEN read-out system
Ablesewert *m* GERÄT reading
Ablesung *f* GERÄT reading, TELEKOM readout
Ablieferung *f* QUAL delivery
Ablieferungsprüfung *f* QUAL user's inspection
Ablieferungszeichnung *f* QUAL as-delivered condition
abliegend: ~**e Zunge** *f* EISENBAHN open point, open switch
ablöhnen *vt* WASSERTRANS *Besatzung* pay off
Ablösbarkeit *f* PAPIER release
ablöschen *vt* CHEMIE *Kalk* slake
Ablöseschaltung *f* TELEKOM combining circuit
Ablösung *f* MASCHINEN parting; ~ **der Verdichterströmung** *f* LUFTTRANS *Turbinenmotoren* compressor stall; **Ablösungsmannschaft** *f* LUFTTRANS relief crew
Abluft *f* ABFALL cleaned gas, scrubbed gas, HEIZ & KÄLTE vitiated air, PAPIER exhaust; **Abluftleistung** *f* HEIZ & KÄLTE extracted-air flow rate; **Abluftreiniger** *m* TEXTIL exhaust cleaning installation; **Abluftstrom** *m* HEIZ & KÄLTE exhaust airstream; **Abluftsystem** *nt* SICHERHEIT exhaust vent installation; **Abluftventilator** *m* PAPIER exhaust fan; **Abluftvolumenstrom** *m* HEIZ & KÄLTE extracted-air flow rate
Abmaß *nt* MASCHINEN deviation, permissible allowance, QUAL deviation, TEXTIL tolerance
Abmelden *nt* COMP & DV logoff, logout
abmelden: **sich ~** *v refl* COMP & DV log off, log out, *vom System* sign off
Abmeßeinheit *f* VERPACK volumetric filling unit
abmessen *vt* KONTROLL, TEXTIL, WASSERVERSORG gage (AmE), gauge (BrE)
Abmeßpumpe *f* VERPACK dosing pump
Abmessung *f* COMP & DV physical dimension, DRUCK dimension, ELEKTRONIK measurement; ~ **von Hand** *f* VERPACK hand dosing; **Abmessungskompatibilität** *f* TELEKOM dimensional compatibility
abmustern *vt* WASSERTRANS *Schiffbesatzung* discharge
Abmusterung *f* WASSERTRANS *Besatzung* paying-off
Abnahme *f* MASCHINEN inspection, MECHAN acceptance; **Abnahmebeamter** *m* QUAL inspector; **Abnahmebeauftragter** *m* QUAL inspector; **Abnahmebericht** *m* MECHAN acceptance report; **Abnahmebescheinigung** *f* QUAL acceptance certificate; **Abnahmegesellschaft** *f* QUAL authorized inspection agency; **Abnahmekriterium** *nt* RAUMFAHRT *Raumschiff* acceptance criterion; **Abnahmelehre** *f* MASCHINEN inspection gage (AmE), inspection gauge (BrE); **Abnahmemodell** *nt* RAUMFAHRT qualification model; **Abnahmeprobebrand** *m* RAUMFAHRT acceptance firing test; **Abnahmeprobeflug** *m* LUFTTRANS acceptance flight; **Abnahmeprotokoll** *nt* QUAL acceptance certificate, acceptance report; **Abnahmeprüfprotokoll** *nt* QUAL certificate of acceptance; **Abnahmeprüfung** *f* COMP & DV acceptance test, FERTIG receiving inspection, KOHLEN acceptance test, QUAL acceptance inspection, TELEKOM acceptance test; **Abnahmeprüfungen** *f pl* WASSERTRANS acceptance trials; **Abnahmeprüfzeugnis** *nt* QUAL acceptance test certificate, inspection report; **Abnahmepunkt** *m* QUAL witness point; **Abnahmetest** *m* MASCHINEN acceptance inspection, MECHAN acceptance testing, TELEKOM acceptance test; **Abnahmeverfahren** *nt* QUAL acceptance procedure; **Abnahmeverweigerung** *f* ELEKTRONIK *Computertechnik* rejection; **Abnahme-**

vorschriften *f pl* TELEKOM acceptance test specification; **Abnahmewalze** *f* PAPIER pick-up roll; **Abnahmezeichnung** *f* HEIZ & KÄLTE, QUAL acceptance drawing
abnehmbar[1] *adj* FOTO, MASCHINEN, OPTIK detachable, removable
abnehmbar:[2] ~**e Andruckplatte** *f* FOTO detachable pressure plate; ~**e Backen** *f pl* MASCHINEN detachable jaws; ~**er Griff** *m* MASCHINEN detachable handle; ~**e Kupplungslasche** *f* EISENBAHN removable coupling link; ~**e Rückwand** *f* FOTO removable back; ~**e Tastatur** *f* COMP & DV detachable keyboard
Abnehmen *nt* KER & GLAS take-down, PAPIER pick-up
abnehmen[1] *vt* QUAL accept, TELEKOM unhook
abnehmen[2] *vi* COMP & DV decay
Abnehmer *m* KER & GLAS doff; **Abnehmerleitung** *f* TELEKOM outgoing trunk circuit; **Abnehmerrisiko** *nt* QUAL consumer's risk; **Abnehmerzähler** *m* GERÄT *für Energieverbrauch* consumer meter
abnormal: ~**e Beendigung** *f* COMP & DV abnormal termination
abnutzen *vt* ANSTRICH erode, *durch Korrosion oder Reiben* fret, TEXTIL wear out
Abnutzung *f* ANSTRICH erosion, ELEKTRIZ wearout, KERNTECH wastage, MASCHINEN wear, MECHAN abrasion, fretting, wear, MEERSCHMUTZ, TEXTIL wear; **Abnutzungsausgleich** *m* FERTIG wear compensation; **Abnutzungsfaktor** *m* MECHAN abrasion factor; **Abnutzungsfläche** *f* MASCHINEN, TEXTIL wearing surface; **Abnutzungsgrenze** *f* FERTIG wear limit
Abpackung: ~ **in Steigen** *f* VERPACK tray packing
abpausen *vt* MASCHINEN trace
Abplatzen *nt* ANSTRICH, BAU spalling, KER & GLAS chipping
abplatzen *vi* BAU spall, KER & GLAS chip
Abprall *m* FERTIG ricochet
abprallen *vi* FERTIG ricochet
abpumpen *vt* MASCHINEN, WASSERTRANS pump off, pump out
abputzen *vt* FERTIG scour
Abquetsch- *pref* KUNSTSTOFF flash, TEXTIL quetsch
abquetschen *vt* FOTO squeegee
Abquetschfläche: **mit ~** *adj* FERTIG landed
Abquetsch-: **Abquetschgrat** *m* KUNSTSTOFF flash; **Abquetschvorrichtung** *f* TEXTIL quetsch unit (AmE); **Abquetschwalze** *f* PAPIER squeeze roll, TEXTIL quetsch roller (AmE); **Abquetschwerkzeug** *nt* KUNSTSTOFF flash mold (AmE), flash mould (BrE)
Abraham: ~**scher Impuls** *m* KERNTECH Abraham momentum
Abrasion *f* ANSTRICH, KOHLEN abrasion; **Abrasionswiderstand** *m* ANSTRICH abrasion resistance
abrasiv: ~**er Verschleiß** *m* MASCHINEN abrasive wear
Abraum- *pref* KOHLEN overburden; **Abraumbau** *m* COAL open-pit mining; **Abraumbohrer** *m* KOHLEN overburden drill; **Abraumdruck** *m* KOHLEN overburden pressure
Abräumen *nt* KOHLEN stripping
abräumen *vt* BAU clear
Abraum-: **Abraumkippe** *f* BAU spoil area; **Abraumschicht** *f* KOHLEN overburden
Abrechnung *f* COMP & DV accounting; **Abrechnungsdatei** *f* COMP & DV accounting file
abreiben *vt* BAU *Putz* rub, FERTIG waste, *Werkzeug* grind, MASCHINEN, MECHAN, PAPIER abrade, abrase
abreibend *adj* PAPIER abradant

abreichern *vt* KERNTECH deplete

Abreicherung *f* KERNTECH depletion

Abreißen *nt* FERTIG *Lichtbogen* interruption, RADIO *Verbindung* loss

abreißen *vt* BAU break down, *Gebäude* demolish, FERTIG *Lichtbogen* interrupt, MASCHINEN tear down

Abreißstab: ~ **für Schreiberstreifen** *m* GERÄT chart paper tear-off bar

Abreißstartstrom *m* ELEKTRIZ breakaway starting current

Abreißverschluß *m* VERPACK snap-off closure, tear-off closure

Abreißzündung *f* KFZTECH make-and-break ignition

Abrichtdiamant *m* FERTIG diamond dresser

Abrichten *nt* KER & GLAS planing, MASCHINEN dressing, truing; ~ **durch Profilrolle** *nt* FERTIG crush dressing

abrichten *vt* MASCHINEN dress, true, true up

Abrichter *m* FERTIG truer, *für Schleifscheibe* dresser

Abrichtgerät *nt* MASCHINEN dressing device

Abrichthobeln *nt* MASCHINEN surface planing, surfacing

abrichthobeln *vt* MASCHINEN surface

Abrichtrolle *f* FERTIG block truer

Abrichtscheibe *f* MASCHINEN truing wheel

Abrichtvorrichtung *f* MASCHINEN dressing equipment; ~ **für Schleifscheiben** *f* MASCHINEN grinding wheel dressing equipment

Abrieb *m* ANSTRICH abrasion, BAU attrition, DRUCK, FERTIG *spanende Bearbeitung* abrasion, KER & GLAS attrition, KERNTECH galling, KOHLEN fines, KUNSTSTOFF abrasion, MASCHINEN abrasion, attrition, MECHAN, PAPIER abrasion; **Abriebbeständigkeit** *f* PAPIER abrasion resistance; **Abriebeigenschaften** *f pl* PAPIER abrasiveness

abriebfest *adj* DRUCK abrasion-resistant, MECHAN abrasion-proof

Abrieb: **Abriebfestigkeit** *f* ANSTRICH, BAU, KUNSTSTOFF, MASCHINEN, MECHAN abrasion resistance; **Abriebkorrosion** *f* CHEMIE fretting corrosion; **Abriebmarkierung** *f* KER & GLAS scuff mark; **Abriebprüfmaschine** *f* KUNSTSTOFF abrasion tester, PAPIER abrasion tester, adrader; **Abriebprüfung** *f* MASCHINEN abrasion test; **Abriebsprotektor** *m* LUFTTRANS certification weight, chafing strip; **Abriebtest** *m* MASCHINEN attrition test; **Abriebverschleiß** *m* BAU abrasive wear

Abriegelung *f* WASSERVERSORG blocking

Abriß: ~ **der Verdichterströmung** *m* LUFTTRANS *Turbinenmotor* compressor stall; **Abrißhäufigkeit** *f* PAPIER breakage rate

Abrollabrichten *nt* FERTIG *Schleifscheibe* crushing

Abrollen *nt* PAPIER reeling off

abrollen *vt* AUFNAHME roll off, COMP & DV scroll

Abrollhaspel *f* FERTIG uncoiler

Abruf *m* COMP & DV fetch, KER & GLAS call down, QUAL requisition, TELEKOM polling; ~ **auf Aufforderung** *m* COMP & DV demand fetching; **Abrufanweisung** *f* COMP & DV fetch instruction; **Abrufbefehl** *m* COMP & DV fetch instruction; **Abrufbusdienst** *m* TRANS demand-scheduled bus service

Abrufen: ~ **von Nachrichten** *nt* COMP & DV message retrieval; ~ **von Systemmeldungen** *nt* COMP & DV message retrieval; ~ **von Text** *nt* COMP & DV text retrieval

abrufen *vt* COMP & DV fetch, request, retrieve

Abruf: **Abrufphase** *f* COMP & DV fetch phase; **Abrufsignal** *nt* COMP & DV fetch signal; **Abruftaste** *f* COMP & DV attention key; **Abruftechnik** *f* COMP & DV polling mode; **Abrufunterbrechung** *f* COMP & DV attention interrupt;

Abrufzyklus *m* COMP & DV fetch cycle

Abrunden *nt* FERTIG *Spanung* radii-forming, MATH rounding

abrunden *vt* COMP & DV round down, round off, MATH round

Abrundung *f* MATH truncation

abrüsten *vt* BAU dismantle

Abrutschen *nt* KER & GLAS slough

ABS *abbr* KFZTECH *(Antiblockiersystem)* ABS *(antiblocking system)*, KUNSTSTOFF *(Acrylnitril-Butadien-Styrol) Copolymer* ABS *(acrylonitrile butadiene styrene)*

Absacken *nt* BAU subsidence

Absacklinie *f* VERPACK sack-filling line

Absackung *f* BAU slump

Absackwaage *f* GERÄT sacking balance

Absatz *m* BAU bench, berm, COMP & DV paragraph, DRUCK break, MECHAN offset; **Absatzdrehen** *nt* FERTIG shoulder turning

absatzfähig *adj* TEXTIL marketable

Absatz: **Absatzmaß** *nt* KONSTZEICH stepped dimension; **Absatzwechsel** *m* DRUCK new paragraph

absaufen *vi* KFZTECH flood

Absaug- *pref* CHEMTECH filtering, HEIZ & KÄLTE extract, SICHERHEIT suction; **Absaug- und Filtervorrichtung** *f* SICHERHEIT *für Staub und Späne* suction and filter installation; **Absauganlage** *f* LEBENSMITTEL exhauster

absaugbar: **~er unnutzbarer Treibstoff** *m* LUFTTRANS drainable unusable fuel

Absaug-: **Absaugbehälter** *m* LEBENSMITTEL exhaustion box

absaugen *vt* HEIZ & KÄLTE extract

Absauger *m* LABOR aspirator, MECHAN exhaust pump

Absaug-: **Absaugeschweißtisch** *m* SICHERHEIT welding table; **Absaugflasche** *f* CHEMTECH filtering flask; **Absauggebläse** *nt* HEIZ & KÄLTE extract fan; **Absaugmittel** *nt* MECHAN absorbent; **Absaugpumpe** *f* HYDRAUL aspiration pump, aspiring pump

Absaugung *f* FERTIG *Kunststoffinstallationen* extraction, SICHERHEIT welding, TEXTIL suction

Absaug-: **Absaugventil** *nt* LABOR exhaust valve

Abschäler *m* BAU scarifier

Abschalt- *pref* MASCHINEN shut-off, RAUMFAHRT shutdown; **Abschaltanweisung** *f* RAUMFAHRT *Raumschiff* shutdown procedure; **Abschaltdruck** *m* MASCHINEN shut-off pressure

Abschalten *nt* RAUMFAHRT *Raumschiff* shutdown procedure

abschalten *vt* COMP & DV disconnect, ELEKTROTECH de-energize, disable, disconnect, isolate, power down, switch off, *Stromversorgung abstellen* turn off, KONTROLL switch off, MASCHINEN stop, RAUMFAHRT shut down, shut off, TELEKOM *Gerät* disconnect

abschaltend: **~er Kreis** *m* ELEKTROTECH opening circuit

Abschalt-: **Abschaltfühler** *m* RAUMFAHRT *Raumschiff* shutdown sensor; **Abschaltimpuls** *m* ELEKTRONIK turn-off pulse; **Abschaltkreis** *m* REGELUNG de-energizing circuit; **Abschaltrelais** *nt* ELEKTRIZ cutoff relay; **Abschaltschütz** *nt* ELEKTRIZ cutoff relay; **Abschaltspannung** *f* ELEKTROTECH interrupting voltage; **Abschaltstrom** *m* ELEKTRIZ breaking capacity, breaking current, cutoff current; **Abschaltstromkreis** *m* ELEKTROTECH shutdown circuit; **Abschaltung** *f* ELEKTROTECH cutoff, de-energization, disconnection, power down, *Stromversorgung* turn-off, FERNSEH, HYDRAUL *Dampfzufuhr* cutoff, KERNTECH *Reaktor*,

RAUMFAHRT *Raumschiff* shutdown; **Abschaltverzöge-rung** *f* KERNTECH scram delay, KONTROLL turn-off delay; **Abschaltvorgang** *m* ELEKTROTECH power down; **Abschaltvorrichtung** *f* ELEKTROTECH *Halblei-terspeichertechnik* power-down feature, HYDRAUL *Dampfzufuhr* cutoff device; **Abschaltzeit** *f* ELEKTRIZ opening time, ELEKTROTECH turn-off time, KERN-TECH disable time, switched-off time, *bei Reinigung* turnaround time (AmE), turnround time (BrE), *einer Wiederaufbereitungsanlage* turnaround time (AmE), turnround time (BrE), KONTROLL turn-off time, ME-CHAN downtime

Abschattung *f* FERNSEH shadowing, KERNTECH *Bild-schirm* corner cutting, TELEKOM shadowing

abschätzen *vt* BAU rate

Abschätzung *f* MASCHINEN assessment

Abschäum- *pref* KER & GLAS skim, skimming; **Ab-schäumbalken** *m* KER & GLAS skim bar

abschäumen *vt* KER & GLAS skim

Abschäumer *m* KER & GLAS skimmer

Abschäum-: **Abschäumloch** *nt* KER & GLAS skimming hole; **Abschäumvorbau** *m* KER & GLAS skim pocket

Abscheide- *pref* CHEMTECH separation

Abscheiden *nt* CHEMTECH *Komponenten* separation

abscheiden *vt* ABFALL segregate, CHEMTECH separate, settle

Abscheider *m* CHEMTECH separator, settling tank, trap, ERDÖL *Rohrleitungen* catchpot, FERTIG *Kunststoffin-stallationen* strainer, HEIZ & KÄLTE trap, MASCHINEN, MEERSCHMUTZ separator; **Abscheiderzyklon** *m* LE-BENSMITTEL *Fliehkraftscheider* cyclone

Abscheide-: **Abscheidevorrichtung** *f* CHEMTECH separa-tor; **Abscheidewirkung** *f* CHEMTECH separation effect

Abscheidung *f* ABFALL segregation, CHEMIE deposit

Abscherbolzen *m* FERTIG, MASCHINEN shear pin

Abscheren *nt* KER & GLAS shearing-off

abscheren[1] *vt* BAU shear

abscheren[2] *vi* FERTIG *Kunststoffinstallationen* shear off, WASSERTRANS *Navigation* sheer off

Abscherfestigkeit *f* MASCHINEN shearing tenacity, ME-CHAN shear strength

Abscherstift *m* MASCHINEN shear pin

Abscherung *f* MASCHINEN shearing

Abscherversuch *m* MASCHINEN shear test, *Nieten* shear test

abscheuern *vt* WASSERTRANS hog

abschießen *vt* RAUMFAHRT launch

Abschilferung *f* MECHAN scale

Abschirm- *pref* ELEKTRIZ shielding, LUFTTRANS deflec-tor; **Abschirmblech** *nt* LUFTTRANS deflector; **Abschirmeffekt** *m* ELEKTRIZ shielding effect

Abschirmen *nt* FERNSEH screening

abschirmen *vt* BAU shield, CHEMTECH baffle, RADIO, RAUMFAHRT shield

Abschirm-: **Abschirmfaktor** *m* KERNTECH screen factor; **Abschirmkabel** *nt* ELEKTROTECH shielded cable; **Ab-schirmkonstante** *f* KERNTECH screening constant; **Abschirmleiter** *m* ELEKTRIZ shielding conductor; **Ab-schirmplatte** *f* KERNTECH screen plate; **Abschirmrelais** *nt* ELEKTROTECH guarding relay

Abschirmung *f* AUFNAHME, COMP & DV *Schutz*, ELEK-TRIZ, ELEKTROTECH *eines Netzwerkes*, FERNSEH, KERNTECH, PHYS, RADIO, RAUMFAHRT screening, shielding, SICHERHEIT shield, STRAHLPHYS screen-ing, shielding; **Abschirmungseffekt** *m* TELEKOM screen effect; **Abschirmungszahl** *f* KERNTECH screening

number

Abschlacken *nt* FERTIG deslagging

abschlacken *vt* FERTIG flush

Abschlagen *nt* BAU spalling

Abschlämmen *nt* CHEMIE clarification, CHEMTECH elu-triation, WASSERVERSORG blowdown

abschlämmen *vt* CHEMIE clarify, CHEMTECH elutriate, WASSERVERSORG blow down

Abschlämmer *m* ERDÖL *Bohrtechnik* desilter

Abschleifen *nt* FERTIG abrading, MASCHINEN grinding-off; **~ von Porzellanemail** *nt* KER & GLAS stoning

abschleifen *vt* BAU *mit Sandpapier* sand, KER & GLAS *der Glaskanten* cut off, MASCHINEN, MECHAN, PAPIER abrade, abrase

abschleifend *adj* MECHAN abrasive

Abschlepp- *pref* TRANS towing

Abschleppen *nt* TRANS *eines Fahrzeuges aus Schlamm* debogging

abschleppen *vt* TRANS tow

Abschlepp-: **Abschlepphaken** *m* KFZTECH *für Anhänger* tow hook; **Abschleppöse** *f* KFZTECH towing bracket; **Abschleppstange** *f* KFZTECH bullbar; **Abschleppwa-gen** *m* KFZTECH salvage car (AmE), salvage lorry (BrE), towing vehicle, wrecker (AmE)

abschleudern *vt* CHEMTECH centrifuge

Abschließen *nt* ELEKTROTECH terminating

abschließen *vt* TELEKOM *Kabel* terminate

Abschluß *m* COMP & DV *des aktiven Betriebszustandes* closedown, KONTROLL *eines Prozesses* termination; **Abschlußanweisung** *f* COMP & DV close statement; **Abschlußblende** *f* FOTO front diaphragm; **Abschluß-block** *m* KONTROLL terminal block; **Abschlußcheck** *m* LUFTTRANS postflying check; **Abschlußdeckel** *m* FER-TIG end plate; **Abschlußelement** *nt* ELEKTROTECH terminating element; **Abschlußelement für Lichtleitfa-sern** *nt* OPTIK optical fiber pigtail (AmE), optical fibre pigtail (BrE); **Abschlußflansch** *m* MASCHINEN blank flange, blind flange; **Abschlußimpedanz** *f* ELEKTRO-TECH terminating impedance; **Abschlußkappe** *f* ELEKTROTECH end cap; **Abschlußmast** *m* ELEKTRIZ terminal tower; **Abschlußmauer** *f* BAU head wall; **Ab-schlußplatte** *f* FOTO stop plate; **Abschlußprozedur** *f* KONTROLL termination procedure; **Abschlußseite** *f* COMP & DV trailer page; **Abschlußstecker** *m* COMP & DV terminator; **Abschlußstein** *m* KER & GLAS seal block, tuckstone; **Abschlußstopfen** *m* FERTIG *Kunststoffin-stallationen* end plug; **Abschlußstück für Lichtleitfasern** *nt* OPTIK optical fiber pigtail (AmE), optical fibre pigtail (BrE); **Abschlußwiderstand** *m* COMP & DV terminator, ELEKTROTECH terminating re-sistor; **Abschlußzeichen** *nt* COMP & DV terminator

Abschmelzbug *m* RAUMFAHRT *Raumschiff* ablating cone

Abschmelzen *nt* PHYS ablating

abschmelzend: **~e Schweißelektrode** *f* BAU consumable welding

Abschmelzleistung *f* FERTIG *Schweißen*, UMWELT-SCHMUTZ deposition rate

Abschmelzung *f* ELEKTROTECH smelting

Abschmier- *pref* MASCHINEN grease, lubrication; **Ab-schmierfett** *nt* MASCHINEN lubricating grease; **Abschmiergrube** *f* MASCHINEN grease pit, greasing pit

Abschnappkupplung *f* MASCHINEN impulse coupling

Abschneide- *pref* COMP & DV truncation, TELEKOM cut-back; **Abschneidefehler** *m* COMP & DV truncation error; **Abschneidemethode** *f* TELEKOM cutback technique

Abschneiden *nt* BAU cutting-off, COMP & DV clipping, scissoring, truncation, FERTIG cropping, GEOM truncating, KER & GLAS *Kanten* cutting-off, KÜNSTL INT pruning

abschneiden *vt* COMP & DV truncate, FERTIG *Eisen* draw, GEOM subtend, truncate, KER & GLAS break off (BrE), cap, MASCHINEN shear

Abschnellen *nt* TEXTIL picking

Abschnitt *m* COMP & DV, DRUCK, EISENBAHN section, GEOM intercept, segment, KERNTECH *Rohr* leg, KOHLEN cuttings, MASCHINEN, TELEKOM section, TEXTIL cutting; **~ auf Geraden** *m* GEOM line segment

abschnittsweise: **~ Beladung** *f* KERNTECH *Reaktor* zoned fuel loading; **~ Leitweglenkung** *f* TELEKOM link-by-link traffic routing

Abschöpf- *pref*-MEERSCHMUTZ skimming; **Abschöpfbarke** *f* MEERSCHMUTZ skimming barge; **Abschöpfeinrichtung** *f* MEERSCHMUTZ skimmer

abschöpfen *vt* FERTIG, UMWELTSCHMUTZ skim off

Abschöpf-: **Abschöpfkopf** *m* MEERSCHMUTZ skimming head; **Abschöpfölsperre** *f* MEERSCHMUTZ skimming barrier

Abschrägen *nt* BAU beveling (AmE), bevelling (BrE), KER & GLAS beveling (AmE), bevelling (BrE), siding

abschrägen *vt* BAU bevel, slope, splay, FERTIG, MASCHINEN chamfer

Abschrägung *f* BAU bevel, cant, chamfer, ELEKTROTECH ramp, FERTIG bevel, splay, KER & GLAS, MASCHINEN bevel

Abschraubbohrrohr *nt* ERDÖL *Bohrtechnik* unscrewing pipe

Abschrauben *nt* MASCHINEN unscrewing

abschrauben *vt* MASCHINEN unscrew, MECHAN loosen

Abschraubrohr *nt* ERDÖL *Bohrtechnik* unscrewing pipe

Abschreck- *pref* KERNTECH quench, METALL quench, quenching; **Abschreckalterung** *f* KERNTECH, METALL quench ageing (BrE), quench aging (AmE); **Abschreckbad** *nt* METALL quenching bath

Abschrecken *nt* KER & GLAS chilling, METALL quench

abschrecken *vt* BAU quench, HEIZ & KÄLTE chill, MECHAN chill, quench, METALL quench, THERMOD chill, *Stahl* quench

Abschreck-: **Abschreckflüssigkeit** *f* MECHAN quenchant, quenching liquor; **Abschreckhärten** *nt* KERNTECH, METALL quench hardening; **Abschreckmittel** *nt* FERTIG, MECHAN quenchant; **Abschreckprüfung** *f* WERKPRÜF *Glas* thermal shock test; **Abschreckrißempfindlichkeit** *f* THERMOD heat treatment crack sensitivity; **Abschreckversuch** *m* MASCHINEN quench hardening test

Abschreibung *f* FERTIG depreciation

Abschrot *m* FERTIG anvil cutter, hardie, MASCHINEN anvil chisel, anvil cutter, hardie

abschroten *vt* FERTIG chop

abschwächen *vt* ELEKTRIZ damp, ERGON attenuate, FOTO reduce, MASCHINEN deaden

Abschwächer *m* FOTO reducer

Abschwächung *f* COMP & DV damping attenuation, PHYS attenuation, RAUMFAHRT *Weltraumfunk* de-emphasis, WELLPHYS attenuation; **Abschwächungsmittel** *nt* CHEMIE diluent

abschwefeln *vt* CHEMIE desulfurize (AmE), desulphurize (BrE)

Abschwefelung *f* CHEMIE desulfurization (AmE), desulphurization (BrE)

ABS-Copolymer *nt* ELEKTRIZ ABS copolymer

abseihen *vt* CHEMTECH filter

Absender *m* TELEKOM sender

absenkbar: **~e Rumpfnase** *f* LUFTTRANS *Concorde* droop nose

Absenken *nt* FERTIG driving

absenken[1] *vt* BAU sink, KOHLEN depress, SICHERHEIT lower

absenken[2] *vi* BAU *Bohrloch* sink

Absenkung *f* ERDÖL subsidence, *Bohrtechnik* drawdown

Absetz- *pref* ABFALL sedimentation, settling, CHEMTECH precipitation, sedimentation, settling, WASSERVERSORG sedimentation, settling; **Absetzbecken** *nt* ABFALL, CHEMTECH, WASSERVERSORG sedimentation basin, settling basin; **Absetzbehälter** *m* CHEMTECH precipitation tank, sedimentation tank; **Absetzbottich** *m* CHEMTECH settling tub, settling vat; **Absetzdauer** *f* CHEMTECH settling time

Absetzen *nt* KUNSTSTOFF sedimentation, PHYS settling

absetzen *vt* CHEMTECH settle, FERTIG shoulder, *Schneidmeißel* offset, KOHLEN retreat, WASSERTRANS *Peilung* plot

Absetz-: **Absetzgefäß** *nt* ABFALL settling vessel, CHEMTECH *Elektrochemie* thickener; **Absetzgeschwindigkeit** *f* ABFALL settling velocity, CHEMTECH settling speed; **Absetzgrube** *f* WASSERVERSORG cess pit, cess pool; **Absetzkammer** *f* ABFALL settling chamber; **Absetzklärung** *f* ABFALL decantation, settling; **Absetzkonus** *m* CHEMTECH settling cone; **Absetzprobe** *f* BAU sedimentation test; **Absetztank** *m* CHEMTECH settling reservoir, ERDÖL *Bohrtechnik* settling tank; **Absetzzisterne** *f* CHEMTECH settling cistern

Absieben *nt* CHEMTECH sieving

absieben *vt* MEERSCHMUTZ sift, *Öl* screen

Absinken *nt* ERDÖL *Geologie* subduction, THERMOD fall, WASSERVERSORG drawdown

absinken[1] *vt* WASSERVERSORG draw down

absinken[2] *vi* CHEMTECH settle

Absinkzone *f* ERDÖL *Geologie* subduction zone

ABS-Kunststoff *m* VERPACK ABS plastic

Absolut- *pref* GERÄT, MATH, PHYS absolute

absolut[1] *adj* COMP & DV absolute

absolut:[2] **~e Adresse** *f* COMP & DV absolute address, direct address, specific address; **~er Betrag** *m* MATH *komplexe Zahl* absolute value; **~er Brechungsindex** *m* STRAHLPHYS absolute refractive index; **~er Code** *m* COMP & DV absolute code, specific code; **~e Dielektrizitätskonstante** *f* ELEKTRIZ absolute permittivity, ELEKTROTECH absolute permittivity, dielectric constant; **~er Druck** *m* HEIZ & KÄLTE absolute pressure; **~er Fehler** *m* COMP & DV absolute error; **~e Feuchte** *f* HEIZ & KÄLTE, PHYS absolute humidity; **~e Geschwindigkeitsänderung** *f* ELEKTRIZ absolute speed variation; **~er Helligkeitsschwellwert** *m* FERNSEH absolute threshold of luminance; **~e Instruktion** *f* COMP & DV absolute instruction; **~e Kapazität** *f* TRANS absolute capacity; **~e Konstanz** *f* TELEKOM absolute stability; **~es Maßsystem** *nt* WERKPRÜF absolute system; **~er Nullpunkt** *m* HEIZ & KÄLTE, PHYS, THERMOD absolute zero; **~e Permeabilität** *f* ELEKTRIZ, ELEKTROTECH absolute permeability; **~e Spannungsänderung** *f* ELEKTROTECH regulation; **~e Temperatur** *f* HEIZ & KÄLTE absolute temperature, HYDRAUL (θ) absolute temperature, LABOR *(T)* absolute temperature *(T)*, LEBENSMITTEL, PHYS absolute temperature, RAUMFAHRT, THERMOD Kelvin temperature, THER-

MOD (θ) absolute temperature, thermodynamic temperature; **~e Temperaturskale** *f* PHYS perfect gas scale of temperature; **~es Vakuum** *nt* HEIZ & KÄLTE absolute vacuum; **~er wasserfreier Alkohol** *m* LEBENSMITTEL dehydrated alcohol; **~er Wert** *m* COMP & DV absolute value

Absolut-: Absolutbetrag *m* MATH *einer komplexen Zahl* modulus; **Absolutbewegung** *f* PHYS absolute motion; **Absolutdruck** *m* HEIZ & KÄLTE absolute pressure; **Absolutdruck-Manometer** *nt* GERÄT absolute pressure gage (AmE), absolute pressure gauge (BrE)

Absolutierung *f* CHEMTECH dehydration

Absolut-: Absolutmaßsystem *nt* GERÄT *bei numerischer Steuerung* absolute measure system; **Absolutmeßsystem** *nt* ELEKTRONIK absolute measuring system; **Absolutwert** *m* HEIZ & KÄLTE absolute value, MATH *komplexe Zahlen* modulus, *reelle Zahl* absolute value

Absondern *nt* CHEMTECH *Komponenten* separation

absondern[1] *vt* CHEMIE abstract, *Harz* exude, THERMOD emit, give off

absondern:[2] **sich ~** *v refl* CHEMIE exude

Absorber *m* HEIZ & KÄLTE absorber; **Absorberelement** *nt* HEIZ & KÄLTE, KERNTECH absorber element; **Absorberelement mit Gelenkverbindung** *nt* KERNTECH articulated absorber; **Absorberglied** *nt* KERNTECH absorber member; **Absorberplatte** *f* KERNTECH absorber plate; **Absorberschalldämpfer** *m* SICHERHEIT absorption muffler (AmE), absorption silencer (BrE)

absorbierbar *adj* PAPIER absorbable

absorbieren *vt* KOHLEN, MASCHINEN, PAPIER, SICHERHEIT absorb

absorbierend: ~es Förderband *nt* UMWELTSCHMUTZ *zur Ölaufnahme* absorbent belt skimmer

absorbiert: ~e Dosis *f (D)* STRAHLPHYS absorbed dose *(D)*; **~e Dosisrate** *f* STRAHLPHYS absorbed dose rate; **~e Energie** *f* METALL, STRAHLPHYS absorbed energy

Absorption *f* ELEKTROTECH *von Leistung, Energie, Kraft* absorption, ERDÖL *trockene Gasreinigung* gas absorption, HEIZ & KÄLTE, KOHLEN, KUNSTSTOFF, LEBENSMITTEL, OPTIK, PAPIER, RADIO, STRAHLPHYS, THERMOD, WASSERVERSORG absorption; **~ ionisierender Strahlung** *f* STRAHLPHYS absorption of ionizing radiation; **~ von Röntgenstrahlen** *f* STRAHLPHYS X-ray absorption; **Absorptionsabschwächer** *m* TELEKOM absorptive attenuator; **Absorptionsanlage** *f* ERDÖL *Raffinerie* absorption plant; **Absorptionsband** *nt* PHYS, STRAHLPHYS absorption band; **Absorptionsbehälter** *m* CHEMTECH absorption cell; **Absorptionsdämpfungsglied** *nt* ELEKTRONIK absorptive attenuator; **Absorptionsdosis** *f (D)* KERNTECH absorbed dose *(D)*; **Absorptions-Dynamometer** *nt* GERÄT absorption dynamometer; **Absorptionseinrichtung** *f* SICHERHEIT absorption plant

absorptionsfähig *adj* CHEMIE absorbent

Absorption: Absorptionsfähigkeit *f* VERPACK absorbency; **Absorptionsfaktor** *m (α)* OPTIK absorption factor *(α)*; **Absorptionsfalle** *f* CHEMTECH absorber trap; **Absorptionsfiltern** *nt* AUFNAHME absorption filtering; **Absorptionsfrequenzmeßgerät** *nt* GERÄT absorption frequency meter; **Absorptionsgefäß** *nt* CHEMTECH absorption vessel, PAPIER absorber; **Absorptionsgeometrie** *f* STRAHLPHYS geometry of absorption; **Absorptionsgrad** *m* OPTIK absorption capacity, PAPIER absorption factor, PHYS coefficient of absorption, TELEKOM absorption factor; **Absorptions-Hygrometer** *nt* GERÄT absorption hygrometer;

Absorptionskälteanlage *f* HEIZ & KÄLTE absorption refrigeration system; **Absorptionskältekreislauf** *m* HEIZ & KÄLTE absorption refrigerating cycle; **Absorptionskältemaschine** *f* HEIZ & KÄLTE absorption refrigeration machine, THERMOD absorption type refrigerator; **Absorptionskante** *f* KERNTECH, STRAHLPHYS absorption edge; **Absorptionskoeffizient** *m (α)* AKUSTIK, PHYS, RADIO, STRAHLPHYS absorption coefficient *(α)*; **Absorptionskolonne** *f* CHEMTECH absorber column, ERDÖL *Raffinerie* absorption column; **Absorptionskühlschrank** *m* HEIZ & KÄLTE absorption refrigerator; **Absorptionskühlung** *f* NICHTFOSS ENERG absorption cooling; **Absorptionsküvette** *f* CHEMTECH *analytische Chemie* absorption cell; **Absorptionslinie** *f* PHYS absorption line; **Absorptionsmaximum** *nt* ELEKTROTECH absorption peak; **Absorptionsmeßgerät** *nt* PAPIER absorptionmeter; **Absorptionsmeßtechnik** *f* GERÄT absorptiometry; **Absorptionsmessung** *f* KERNTECH absorptiometry; **Absorptionsmittel** *nt* CHEMTECH absorber, KOHLEN, PAPIER, UMWELTSCHMUTZ absorbent; **Absorptionsmodulator** *m* ELEKTRONIK absorptive modulator; **Absorptionsplatte** *f* NICHTFOSS ENERG absorption plate; **Absorptionspumpe** *f* PHYS absorption pump; **Absorptionsquerschnitt** *m* KERNTECH, STRAHLPHYS absorption cross-section; **Absorptionsrate** *f* WASSERVERSORG rate of absorption; **Absorptionsrohr** *nt* CHEMTECH absorber tube, LABOR absorption tube; **Absorptionsröhrchen** *nt* LABOR absorption tube; **Absorptionssäule** *f* CHEMTECH absorber column, KOHLEN absorption tower, PAPIER absorption column; **Absorptionsschaltung** *f* ELEKTRIZ absorption circuit; **Absorptions-Spektralanalyse** *f* STRAHLPHYS absorption spectroanalysis; **Absorptions-Spektrofotometer** *nt* STRAHLPHYS absorption spectrophotometer; **Absorptions-Spektrometer** *nt* LABOR absorption spectrometer; **Absorptions-Spektrometrie** *f* TELEKOM absorption spectrometry; **Absorptions-Spektroskopie** *f* PHYS, STRAHLPHYS absorption spectroscopy; **Absorptionsspektrum** *nt* OPTIK, PAPIER, PHYS, RAUMFAHRT, STRAHLPHYS absorption spectrum; **Absorptionsstrom** *m* ELEKTRIZ absorption current; **Absorptionsturm** *m* CHEMTECH, ERDÖL *Raffinerie*, KOHLEN, LEBENSMITTEL absorption tower; **Absorptionsverlust** *m* ELEKTROTECH, FERNSEH, RADIO absorption loss; **Absorptionsvermögen** *nt* HEIZ & KÄLTE absorptivity, OPTIK absorptance, PAPIER absorbency, PHYS absorptance, WASSERVERSORG absorption capacity; **Absorptionswärme** *f* THERMOD heat of absorption; **Absorptionswert** *m* MECHAN absorbing capacity; **Absorptionszahl** *f* FERNSEH absorptivity, MASCHINEN absorption coefficient

Abspann- *pref* BAU, ELEKTROTECH, ERDÖL guy; **Abspannanker** *m* ERDÖL guy anchor; **Abspanndraht** *m* BAU stay wire

Abspannen *nt* BAU *Mast* anchoring

abspannen *vt* BAU *Mast* anchor, WASSERTRANS rig

Abspann-: Abspannisolator *m* ELEKTROTECH shackle insulator, *bei Abspanndraht* guy insulator; **Abspannmast** *m* ELEKTRIZ dead-end tower, span pole; **Abspannring** *m* ERDÖL guy ring; **Abspannseil** *nt* BAU guy rope, ERDÖL guy anchor, FERTIG guy, RADIO guy wire; **Abspanntransformator** *m* ELEKTROTECH step-down transformer

Abspannung *f* BAU guy, guying, FERTIG, MECHAN, RADIO guy; **Abspannungs-Unterwerk** *nt* ELEKTRIZ step-down

station

Abspeer- *pref* BAU cutoff, MASCHINEN shut-off; **Abspeerarmatur** *f* MASCHINEN shut-off valve

Absperr- *pref* BAU, LABOR, MASCHINEN cutoff

Absperren *nt* BAU stopping

absperren *vt* BAU close, shut, stop, FERTIG *Kunststoffinstallationen* shut off, HYDRAUL *Dampfzufuhr* cut off, WASSERTRANS block off, WASSERVERSORG *des Wassers* shut off

Absperr-: **Absperrhahn** *m* BAU cutoff cock, faucet (AmE), stopcock, LABOR, MASCHINEN stopcock; **Absperrklappe** *f* BAU flap, FERTIG *Kunststoffinstallationen* butterfly valve, HEIZ & KÄLTE butterfly damper, MASCHINEN, WASSERVERSORG shutoff valve; **Absperrorgan** *nt* FERTIG cock, *Kunststoffinstallationen* valve, HEIZ & KÄLTE obturator, HYDRAUL *von Rohrleitungen* valve, MASCHINEN obturator; **Absperrplatte** *f* HYDRAUL *Dampfzufuhr* cutoff plate; **Absperrschieber** *m* MASCHINEN shut-off slide

Absperrung *f* BAU *Straße* barrier, HYDRAUL *Dampfzufuhr* cutoff, cutting-off, SICHERHEIT barricade, crush barrier

Absperr-: **Absperrventil** *nt* BAU check valve, stop valve, FERTIG check valve, stop valve, *Kunststoffinstallationen* check valve, stop valve, MASCHINEN, MECHAN, NICHTFOSS ENERG, PAPIER, RAUMFAHRT *Raumschiff*, WASSERTRANS *Motor*, WASSERVERSORG check valve, stop valve; **Absperrvorrichtung** *f* HEIZ & KÄLTE *gegen Brandübertragung* barrier, HYDRAUL *Dampfzufuhr* cutoff device, KER & GLAS shut-off

Abspiel- *pref* AUFNAHME replay

Abspielen *nt* AUFNAHME playback

abspielen *vt* AUFNAHME replay

Abspiel-: **Abspielgerät** *nt* AUFNAHME play-only recorder; **Abspielgeräusch** *nt* AUFNAHME needle noise, surface noise; **Abspielkopf** *m* AUFNAHME replay head; **Abspielnadel** *f* AUFNAHME needle; **Abspielzeit** *f* AUFNAHME *einer CD, Kassette oder Schallplatte* playing time

Abspitzen *nt* BAU *von Stein* picking

absplitten *vt* BAU gravel

Absplittern *nt* BAU spalling

Abspreng- *pref* KER & GLAS crack-off, wetting-off; **Abspreng- und Kantenschmelzmaschine** *f* KER & GLAS burning-off and edge-melting machine (BrE), remelting machine (AmE)

Absprengen *nt* KER & GLAS burning-off, cracking-off

Abspreng-: **Absprenghaken** *m* KER & GLAS crack-off iron (AmE), wetting-off iron (BrE); **Absprengkappe** *f* KER & GLAS moil; **Absprengring** *m* KER & GLAS cracking ring; **Absprengverschluß** *m* KER & GLAS pry-off finish; **Absprengwerkzeug** *nt* KER & GLAS cracking tool

absprießen *vt* BAU *Rahmen* brace

abspringen[1] *vt* RAUMFAHRT bail out

abspringen[2] *vi* FERTIG rebound

Abspulen *nt* MASCHINEN unwinding

abspulen *vt* FERTIG run off, FOTO unspool

Abstand *m* COMP & DV gap, ELEKTRIZ pitch, ELEKTROTECH clearance, *bei Relais* gap, GERÄT range, HYDRAUL *Kolben, Zylinderwand* space, KERNTECH clearance, LUFTTRANS spacing, *Propeller, Flügel clearance*, MASCHINEN, MECHAN clearance, RAUMFAHRT *Raumschiff* separation, TRANS spacing, WASSERTRANS clearance, spacing; **~ zwischen Brenn-**

stoff und Hülse *m* KERNTECH clad-fuel clearance; **~ zwischen Energiebändern** *m* KERNTECH energy band gap; **Abstandscheibe** *f* MASCHINEN shim; **Abstandsensor** *m* GERÄT proximity sensor

abstandsgleich *adj* MASCHINEN equally-spaced

Abstand: **Abstandshalter** *m* BAU distance piece, spacer block; **Abstandskontrolle** *f* TRANS headway control; **Abstandsleiste** *f* MASCHINEN bumper rod; **Abstandsmaske** *f* ELEKTRONIK proximity mask; **Abstandsmesser** *m* METROL gap gage (AmE), gap gauge (BrE); **Abstandsring** *m* FERTIG spacer, WASSERTRANS *Radar* calibration ring; **Abstandsstange** *f* MASCHINEN distance bar; **Abstandsstück** *nt* KER & GLAS spacer, MASCHINEN distance piece; **Abstandsverlust** *m* AUFNAHME, FERNSEH spacing loss; **Abstandswarnanzeiger** *m* LUFTTRANS proximity warning indicator; **Abstandswarnvorrichtung** *f* TRANS headway warning device

Abstapeln *nt* VERPACK *von Paletten* destacking

Abstech- *pref* MASCHINEN cutoff, cutting-off; **Abstech- und Formdrehmaschine** *f* MASCHINEN cutting-off and forming lathe; **Abstechdrehmaschine** *f* MASCHINEN cutoff machine, cutting-off lathe

Abstechen *nt* FERTIG *Spanung* parting, LEBENSMITTEL racking, MASCHINEN parting-off

abstechen *vt* FERTIG truncate

Abstech-: **Abstechmaschine** *f* MASCHINEN cutting-off machine; **Abstechmeißel** *m* MASCHINEN cutting-off tool; **Abstechmeißelhalter** *m* MASCHINEN cutting-off tool holder; **Abstechschlitten** *m* MASCHINEN cutting-off slide; **Abstechstahl** *m* MASCHINEN parting tool; **Abstechwerkzeug** *nt* MASCHINEN cutting-off tool, parting tool

Abstecken *nt* BAU *Vermessung* setting out, staking

abstecken *vt* BAU *Vermessung* peg out, set out

Absteckkette *f* BAU surveyor's chain

Absteckpfahl *m* BAU peg, surveyor's staff, *Vermessung* picket, stake

Absteh- *pref* KER & GLAS conditioning, soaking

Abstehen *nt* KER & GLAS conditioning

Absteh-: **Abstehofen** *m* KER & GLAS *Guß und optisches Glas* soaking pit; **Abstehzone** *f* KER & GLAS conditioning zone

Absteifen *nt* BAU shoring

absteifen *vt* BAU brace, prop, shore, FERTIG truss, TEXTIL stiffen

Absteifung *f* BAU sheeting, FERTIG stiffening

absteigend: **~er Ast** *m* COMP & DV descendant

Abstell- *pref* EISENBAHN storage, LUFTTRANS parking

Abstellen *nt* EISENBAHN stabling

abstellen *vt* BAU stock, LUFTTRANS *Motor und Triebwerk* shut down, TEXTIL stop

Absteller *m* BAU *Schloß* deadbolt

Abstell-: **Abstellfläche** *f* LUFTTRANS parking area; **Abstellgleis** *nt* EISENBAHN storage siding

absteppen *vt* TEXTIL quilt, stitch down

Absterben *nt* KFZTECH *Motor* stall

Abstich *m* FERTIG, KER & GLAS tapping, LEBENSMITTEL racking; **Abstichgraben** *m* FERTIG sow; **Abstichloch** *nt* FERTIG taphole, METALL notch; **Abstichpfanne** *f* FERTIG tap ladle, tapping ladle

Abstieg *m* RAUMFAHRT descent; **Abstiegstriebwerk** *nt* RAUMFAHRT *Raumschiff* descent engine

Abstimm- *pref* ELEKTRONIK tuning; **Abstimmanzeige** *f* ELEKTRONIK tuning indicator, RADIO zero beat indicator; **Abstimmauge** *nt* ELEKTRONIK magic eye

abstimmbar: ~**er Breitband-Oszillator** *m* ELEKTRONIK wideband tunable oscillator; ~**er Klystron** *m* RAUMFAHRT tunable klystron; ~**es Magnetron** *nt* ELEKTRONIK tunable magnetron; ~**er Oszillator** *m* ELEKTRONIK tunable oscillator; ~**er Schwingungskreis** *m* ELEKTRONIK tuned circuit; ~**es Voltmeter** *nt* ELEKTRIZ selective voltmeter

Abstimm-: **Abstimmbereich** *m* STRAHLPHYS tuning range; **Abstimmeigenschaften** *f pl* STRAHLPHYS tuning characteristics

Abstimmen *nt* ELEKTRONIK tuning

abstimmen *vt* ELEKTRONIK tune, PAPIER *Farbton* adjust, RADIO *Frequenz*, TELEKOM *Empfänger*, WELLPHYS *auf eine Frequenz* tune

Abstimm-: **Abstimmkondensator** *m* ELEKTROTECH tuning capacitor; **Abstimmkreis** *m* ELEKTROTECH, TELEKOM tuning circuit; **Abstimmschaltung** *f* ELEKTRONIK tuning circuit; **Abstimmschraube** *f* ELEKTROTECH, PHYS tuning screw; **Abstimmschraubendreher** *m* RADIO alignment tool

Abstimmung *f* ELEKTROTECH slug tuning, RADIO, TELEKOM *Empfänger* tuning; ~ **des Durchlaßbereichs** *f* RADIO passband tuning

abstoppen *vt* WASSERTRANS *Tauwerk* check, stopper

Abstoß *m* ELEKTRIZ, PHYS repulsion

abstoßend: ~**e Kraft** *f* PHYS force of repulsion, repulsive force

Abstoß: **Abstoßkraft** *f* ELEKTRIZ repulsive force; **Abstoßrangierbetrieb** *m* EISENBAHN fly shunting

Abstoßung *f* PHYS repulsion; **Abstoßungskraft** *f* ELEKTROTECH repulsive force

Abstrahlen *nt* FERTIG release

abstrahlend: ~**es Kabel** *nt* TELEKOM radiating cable

Abstrahlkeulenbreite *f* RADIO *Richtantenne* beamwidth

Abstrahlung *f* ELEKTRONIK radiation, OPTIK radiant emittance

abstrakt[1] *adj* COMP & DV abstract

abstrakt:[2] ~**es Symbol** *nt* COMP & DV abstract symbol

Abstraktion *f* COMP & DV abstraction

abstreichen *vt* FERTIG strickle, *Gießen* level

Abstreichlineal *nt* FERTIG strike

Abstreichplatte *f* BAU strickle board

Abstreichvorrichtung *f* LEBENSMITTEL scraper

abstreifen *vt* BAU wipe, COMP & DV truncate, METALL strip

Abstreifer *m* BAU wiper, KER & GLAS *zum Emaillieren* squeegee, KOHLEN stripper, MASCHINEN scraper, stripper plate, MECHAN, PAPIER scraper

Abstreifmesser *nt* TEXTIL knife

Abstreifring *m* KFZTECH *Kolben* oil control ring

Abstreusplitt *m* BAU blotter material

Abstrich *m* FERTIG scum

Abström- *pref* LUFTTRANS trailing; **Abströmkante** *f* LUFTTRANS *Flügel* trailing edge; **Abströmkante des Leitwerks** *f* LUFTTRANS fin leading edge; **Abströmkegel** *m* HEIZ & KÄLTE diffuser cone

Abstufen *nt* COMP & DV staging

abstufen *vt* BAU grade, graduate

Abstufung *f* DRUCK graduation

abstumpfen[1] *vt* DRUCK, MASCHINEN blunt

abstumpfen[2] *vi* MASCHINEN blunt

Absturz *m* COMP & DV crash

abstürzen *vi* COMP & DV crash

Abstützbohle *f* BAU raking shore

abstützen *vt* BAU prop, strut

Abstützstrebe *f* LUFTTRANS brace

Absuchen *nt* TELEKOM *Radar* scanning

Abszisse *f* COMP & DV, ELEKTRIZ, FERTIG, MATH abscissa

abtakeln *vt* WASSERTRANS *Segeln* unrig

Abtast- *pref* ELEKTRIZ, GERÄT scanning; **Abtast- und Haltekreis** *m* ELEKTROTECH sample-and-hold circuit; **Abtastbereich** *m* COMP & DV scan area, GERÄT scanning range; **Abtasteinrichtung** *f* FERNSEH scanning device; **Abtastelektrode** *f* ELEKTROTECH sensing electrode; **Abtastelektronenmikroskop** *nt* ELEKTRIZ, PHYS scanning electron microscope; **Abtastelement** *nt* GERÄT sampling element, KERNTECH sensing element

Abtasten *nt* COMP & DV sampling, scanning, sensing, FERNSEH scanning, GERÄT scanning, *von Daten* data sampling, *von Meßdaten* measuring data sampling, measuring data scanning, KERNTECH sensing, MASCHINEN calipering (AmE), callipering (BrE), PHYS, STRAHLPHYS scanning

abtasten *vt* COMP & DV read, sample, sense, scan, ELEKTRONIK sample, FERNSEH, FERTIG, LUFTTRANS *Radar* scan, MASCHINEN caliper (AmE), calliper (BrE), TELEKOM sample, WASSERTRANS *Radar*, WELLPHYS *Radar* scan

Abtaster *m* AKUSTIK pick-up, COMP & DV sampler, scanner, ELEKTRIZ, ELEKTRONIK scanner, FERNSEH sampler, GERÄT, KONTROLL, STRAHLPHYS scanner, TELEKOM sampler, scanner

Abtast-: **Abtastfehler** *m* AUFNAHME tracking error, COMP & DV, FERNSEH scanning error; **Abtastfilterung** *f* ELEKTRONIK sampled data filtering; **Abtastfläche** *f* FERNSEH scanning area, RAUMFAHRT *Raumschiff* scan platform; **Abtastfrequenz** *f* ELEKTRONIK digitizing rate, sampling rate, TELEKOM sampling frequency; **Abtastgerät** *nt* COMP & DV scanner, scanning device, WELLPHYS *medizinisch* scanner; **Abtastgeschwindigkeit** *f* COMP & DV sampling rate, scanning rate, scanning speed, FERNSEH scanning speed, LUFTTRANS, WASSERTRANS *Radar* scanning rate, scanning speed; **Abtastglied** *nt* GERÄT sampling element, scanner; **Abtastimpuls** *m* GERÄT sample pulse; **Abtastintervall** *nt* COMP & DV sampling interval, GERÄT scan interval; **Abtastkopf** *m* FERNSEH scanning head, GERÄT, OPTIK pick-up head; **Abtastlaser** *m* OPTIK read laser, scanning laser; **Abtastlaserstrahl** *m* OPTIK scanning laser beam; **Abtastlichtstrahl** *m* AUFNAHME *für optische Aufzeichnung auf Film* scanning light beam; **Abtastlücke** *f* FERNSEH scanning gap; **Abtastoszilloskop** *nt* GERÄT sampling oscilloscope; **Abtastpunkt** *m* COMP & DV scanning spot, FERNSEH scanning dot; **Abtastpunktsteuerung** *f* FERNSEH scanning spot control; **Abtastrate** *f* COMP & DV scan rate; **Abtastregelung** *f* REGELUNG sampling control; **Abtastregler** *m* REGELUNG sampling controller; **Abtastschalter** *m* ELEKTROTECH scanning switch; **Abtastschaltung** *f* TELEKOM sampler; **Abtastschlitz** *m* AUFNAHME *für optische Tonspur auf Film* scanning slit; **Abtastsignal** *nt* ELEKTRONIK sampled signal; **Abtast-Spektralanalysator** *m* ELEKTRONIK sampling spectrum analyser (BrE), sampling spectrum analyzer (AmE); **Abtastspektrometer** *nt* STRAHLPHYS scanning spectrometer; **Abtaststrahl** *m* ELEKTRONIK, FERNSEH scanning beam; **Abtastsystem** *nt* GERÄT sampled data system; **Abtasttheorem** *nt* COMP & DV, GERÄT sampling theorem; **Abtasttrommel** *f* FERNSEH scanning drum; **Abtastumfang** *m* ELEKTRONIK sampled data size; **Abtastumsetzer** *m* ELEKTRONIK scan converter

Abtastung *f* COMP & DV sampling, scanning, ELEKTRO-

NIK, FERNSEH, FERTIG, GERÄT, LUFTTRANS, TELEKOM, WASSERTRANS, WELLPHYS sampling, scan, scanning; ~ **im Gegentakt** *f* OPTIK push-pull scanning; **~ mit variabler Geschwindigkeit** *f* FERNSEH variable-speed scanning

Abtast-: **Abtastverfahren** *nt* FERNSEH scanning process; **Abtastverhalten** *nt* REGELUNG sampling action; **Abtastvertikalverstärker** *m* ELEKTRONIK sampling vertical amplifier; **Abtastverzerrung** *f* AUFNAHME tracking distortion; **Abtastwert** *m* ELEKTRONIK sample, sampled value, TELEKOM sample; **Abtastzeile** *f* COMP & DV, ELEKTRONIK, FERNSEH scanning line; **Abtastzyklus** *m* FERNSEH scanning cycle, GERÄT sampling cycle

Abtauen *nt* LEBENSMITTEL defrosting

abtauen *vt* HEIZ & KÄLTE thaw, LEBENSMITTEL defrost

Abteilung *f* BAU *Werkstatt*, MECHAN *Laden* bay

abteilungsübergreifend: **~es Qualitätssicherungssystem** *nt* *(TQMS)* QUAL Total Quality Management System *(TQMS)*

Abteilventil *nt* FERTIG *Kunststoffinstallationen* block valve

abteufen *vt* BAU bore

Abteufgerüst *nt* KOHLEN sinking trestle

Abteufpumpe *f* WASSERVERSORG borehole pump

Abtönen *nt* KUNSTSTOFF shading, tinting

abtönen *vt* BAU tint

Abtönung *f* KUNSTSTOFF shading, tinting

Abtrag *m* BAU *Erdreich* cut, EISENBAHN excavated material; **Abtragemethode** *f* OPTIK ablative method

Abtragen *nt* MASCHINEN removal, PHYS ablating

abtragen *vt* ANSTRICH erode, BAU skim, wreck, *Erdreich* clear out, cut, *Lasten* transfer, FERTIG *Zerspanung* erode

abtragend: **~es Mittel** *nt* ANSTRICH abrasive surface; **~e Oberfläche** *f* ANSTRICH abrasive surface

Abtragung *f* ANSTRICH, FERTIG *Zerspanung* erosion, MEERSCHMUTZ wear; **Abtragungsrate** *f* RAUMFAHRT *Raumschiff* erosion rate

Abtransport *m* BAU removal; **~ von Korrosionsprodukten** *m* KERNTECH carry-off of corrosion products

abtrennbar: **~es Düsenaggregat** *nt* LUFTTRANS *Hubschrauber* detachable pod; **~er Nasenkegel** *m* LUFTTRANS detachable nose cone

Abtrennen *nt* FERTIG *Stoffteilchen* separating; **~ der Blaskappe** *nt* KER & GLAS bursting-off; **~ des Nietkopfes** *nt* FERTIG rivet washing

abtrennen[1] *vt* BAU partition, CHEMIE isolate, KONTROLL disconnect, STRÖMPHYS bail out

abtrennen:[2] **sich ~** *v refl* CHEMTECH separate out

Abtrennende *nt* FERTIG crop end

Abtrennung *f* ABFALL separation, BAU *durch Trennwände* partitioning, CHEMIE dissociation, PHYS, RAUMFAHRT *Raumschiff* separation

abtreppen *vt* BAU bench

Abtretender *m* PATENT assignor

Abtretungsempfänger *m* PATENT assignee

Abtrieb *m* MASCHINEN output, power takeoff; **Abtriebsdrehmoment** *nt* FERTIG output torque; **Abtriebsdrehzahl** *f* MASCHINEN output speed; **Abtriebsglied** *nt* MASCHINEN output link; **Abtriebskupplung** *f* MASCHINEN output drive clutch; **Abtriebsrad** *nt* MASCHINEN following gear; **Abtriebsseite** *f* MASCHINEN output end, power takeoff side; **Abtriebsteilchen** *nt* FERTIG abraded particle; **Abtriebswelle** *f* KFZTECH, output shaft, third motion shaft, MASCHINEN output shaft

Abtriftmesser *m* LUFTTRANS driftmeter

Abtropf- *pref* LABOR draining, dripping, MASCHINEN drip; **Abtropfblech** *nt* MASCHINEN drain pan, drip plate; **Abtropfflüssigkeit** *f* LEBENSMITTEL drip; **Abtropfgestell** *nt* LABOR, LEBENSMITTEL draining rack; **Abtropfröhrchen** *nt* LABOR dripping tube; **Abtropfschale** *f* MASCHINEN drip pan, drip tray

Abtrudeln *nt* RAUMFAHRT *Raumschiff* spin-down

abvieren *vt* BAU *Holz* timber

Abwälzfräsen *nt* MASCHINEN gear hobbing, hob cutting, hobbing

Abwälzfräser *m* MASCHINEN gear hob, generating cutter, hob

Abwälzfräsmaschine *f* MASCHINEN hob, hobber, hobbing machine

Abwärme *f* ABFALL thermal discharge, waste heat, HEIZ & KÄLTE, KERNTECH waste heat, THERMOD off-heat, waste heat, UMWELTSCHMUTZ waste heat

Abwärts- *pref* MECHAN downstroke; **Abwärtsbewegung** *f* MECHAN downstroke

abwärtsgehend: **~e Destillation** *f* THERMOD distillation by descent; **~er Kolbenhub** *m* KFZTECH *Motor* downstroke

Abwärts-: **Abwärtshub** *m* FERTIG downstroke, HYDRAUL instroke, KFZTECH *Motor*, MASCHINEN downstroke

abwärtskompatibel *adj* COMP & DV downward compatible

Abwärts-: **Abwärtskompatibilität** *f* COMP & DV downward compatibility; **Abwärtsmischer** *m* TELEKOM *Frequenzwechselschalter* down-converter; **Abwärtsmodulation** *f* ELEKTRONIK downward modulation; **Abwärtsstrecke** *f* RADIO *Satellitenfunk* downlink, TELEKOM downlink feeder link; **Abwärtstaster** *m* FERNSEH downstream keyer; **Abwärtstransformator** *m* ELEKTRIZ, PHYS step-down transformer; **Abwärtsumsetzer** *m* TELEKOM downconverter; **Abwärtsunterwerk** *nt* ELEKTRIZ step-down station; **Abwärtsverbindung** *f* TELEKOM downlink feeder link; **Abwärtswandler** *m* PHYS step-down transformer

abwaschbar *adj* PAPIER washable

Abwaschfestigkeit *f* KONSTZEICH resistance to washing

Abwasser *nt* ABFALL drain water, effluent, wastewater, ERDÖL effluent, WASSERVERSORG sewage, sewage wastewater; **~ aus Sanitäranlagen** *nt* WASSERVERSORG sanitary wastewater; **Abwasserablauf** *m* WASSERVERSORG sewage effluent; **Abwasseranalyse** *f* ABFALL wastewater analysis, WASSERVERSORG sewage analysis; **Abwasseranfall** *m* ABFALL sewage flow, volume of sewage; **Abwasseraufbereitung** *f* ABFALL sewage treatment, UMWELTSCHMUTZ wastewater treatment; **Abwasserbecken** *m* ABFALL stabilization pond; **Abwasserbehandlung** *f* ABFALL sewage treatment, WASSERVERSORG wastewater purification; **Abwasserbehandlung mittels aerober Reinigung** *f* ABFALL aerobic sewage treatment; **Abwasserbehandlungsanlage** *f* ABFALL clarification plant, sewage treatment plant; **Abwasserbehandlungsverfahren** *nt* ABFALL sewage treatment process; **Abwasserbeseitigung** *f* ABFALL sewage disposal, sewage water disposal, UMWELTSCHMUTZ wastewater disposal; **Abwassereinlauf** *m* WASSERVERSORG wastewater outfall; **Abwassereinleitung** *f* ABFALL sewage discharge, MEERSCHMUTZ *ins Meer* marine sewage disposal, UMWELTSCHMUTZ wastewater discharge, WASSERVERSORG

sewage effluent, *in den Untergrund* underground wastewater disposal; **Abwassereinleitung ins Meer** *f* ABFALL marine sewage disposal; **Abwassereinleitungsstelle** *f* ABFALL sewage outfall; **Abwasserfaulraum** *m* ABFALL hydrolizing tank, privy tank, septic tank; **Abwasserfischteich** *m* ABFALL wastewater fishpond; **Abwasserkanal** *m* BAU, WASSERVERSORG sewer; **Abwasserkanalisation** *f* WASSERVERSORG sewerage; **Abwasserkanalreinigung** *f* WASSERVERSORG sewer cleaning; **Abwasserkläranlage** *f* ABFALL clarification plant, sewage treatment plant, WASSERVERSORG sewage disposal plant; **Abwasserklärung** *f* ABFALL sewage purification, sewage treatment; **Abwasserkontrolle** *f* UMWELTSCHMUTZ wastewater control; **Abwasserleitung** *f* BAU sewer, WASSERVERSORG canalization; **Abwassermenge** *f* ABFALL sewage flow, volume of sewage; **Abwasserpilz** *m* ABFALL sewage fungus; **Abwasserreinigung** *f* ABFALL sewage purification, sewage treatment, WASSERVERSORG wastewater purification; **Abwasserreinigungsanlage** *f* ABFALL sewage treatment works; **Abwasserrohr** *nt* BAU drainpipe, waste pipe; **Abwasserrückführung** *f* KERNTECH wastewater recycling operation; **Abwassersammeltank** *m* ABFALL wastewater collection tank; **Abwassersammler** *m* ABFALL interceptor sewer; **Abwassersanierung** *f* ABFALL wastewater renovation; **Abwasserschlamm** *m* ABFALL effluent sludge, *von Haushalten* sewage sludge, CHEMIE digested sludge; **Abwasserstripper** *m* ABFALL wastewater stripper; **Abwasserverrieselung** *f* WASSERVERSORG broad irrigation; **Abwasserversenkung** *f* WASSERVERSORG underground wastewater disposal; **Abwasserzusammensetzung** *f* UMWELTSCHMUTZ sewage composition
abwechselnd *adj* MASCHINEN alternating
abwedeln *vt* FOTO dodge
Abwehrring *m* ELEKTRIZ guard ring
abweichen *vi* ELEKTRIZ fluctuate
Abweichung *f* COMP & DV variance, *eines Übertragungssignals* jitter, ELEKTRIZ fluctuation, FERNSEH deviation, MASCHINEN deviation, variation, MATH deviation, NICHTFOSS ENERG, PHYS declination, QUAL deviation, discrepancy, RADIO deviation, RAUMFAHRT *Raumschiff* drift, *Weltraumfunk* deviation, TELEKOM deviation, drift, WASSERTRANS *astronomische Navigation* declination; **Abweichungsanalyse** *f* COMP & DV analysis of variance; **Abweichungsanzeige** *f* GERÄT deviation indication, error indication; **Abweichungsbericht** *m* QUAL nonconformance report
abweichungsfrei: **~e Stirnräder** *nt pl* FERTIG zero-deviation cylindrical gears
Abweichung: **Abweichungskreis** *m* OPTIK circle of declination; **Abweichungswinkel** *m* LUFTTRANS *Navigation* declination angle
Abweiseplatte *f* CHEMTECH deflector plate
Abweiser *m* RAUMFAHRT *Raumschiff* jet deflector
Abweisstein *m* BAU baffle brick
abwerfbar *adj* LUFTTRANS jettisonable
Abwerfen *nt* RAUMFAHRT *Raumschiff* drop
abwerfen *vt* RAUMFAHRT *Raumschiff* jettison
Abwickel- *pref* FERTIG, MASCHINEN decoiling, unwinding; **Abwickeleinrichtung** *f* FERTIG decoiler
Abwickeln *nt* FERNSEH batting down, MASCHINEN unwinding
abwickeln *vt* FOTO unwind, GEOM develop, TELEKOM carry
Abwickel-: **Abwickelspule** *f* GERÄT *Bandregistriergerät*

supply reel; **Abwickelvorrichtung** *f* TEXTIL unwinder
Abwicklung *f* BAU, GEOM development, TELEKOM *Verkehr* handling
Abwind *m* LUFTTRANS downdraft (AmE), downdraught (BrE), downwash, downwind
abwischen *vt* BAU wipe
Abwracken *nt* WASSERTRANS ship breaking
Abwurf *m* RAUMFAHRT *Raumschiff* drop; **Abwurfbremsschirm** *m* LUFTTRANS *Hubschrauber* message chute; **Abwurfeinrichtung** *f* MASCHINEN tripper; **Abwurfgebiet** *nt* RAUMFAHRT *Raumschiff* drop zone; **Abwurfhöhe** *f* LUFTTRANS free drop height; **Abwurfkapsel** *f* RAUMFAHRT *Raumschiff* ejectable capsule; **Abwurfschacht** *m* BAU chute; **Abwurfspitze** *f* RAUMFAHRT *Raumschiff* ejectable nose cone
Abwürgen *nt* KFZTECH *des Motors*, LUFTTRANS *des Kompressors, des Turbomotors* stall
abwürgen *vt* KFZTECH *Motor* stall
Abzapf- *pref* ELEKTRIZ tapping; **Abzapfbreite** *f* ELEKTRIZ tapping range
abzapfen *vt* FERTIG *Flüssigkeit*, MASCHINEN *Flüssigkeit* bleed
Abzapf-: **Abzapfintervall** *nt* ELEKTRIZ tapping step; **Abzapfpunkt** *m* ELEKTRIZ tapping; **Abzapfpunkt für reduzierte Leistung** *m* ELEKTRIZ reduced power tapping; **Abzapfstrom aus einer Wicklung** *m* ELEKTRIZ tapping current of winding
abzapfungslos *adj* ELEKTRIZ *Transformator* untapped
Abzapf-: **Abzapfwechsel bei Last** *m* ELEKTRIZ load-tap-changer; **Abzapfwechsler unter Last** *m* ELEKTRIZ on-load tap-changer
Abzieh- *pref* BAU screed, KER & GLAS transfer (BrE); **Abziehapparate** *m pl* TEXTIL doffing devices
abziehbar: **~e Kupplung** *f* ELEKTRIZ pull-off coupling; **~er Schutzbelag** *m* VERPACK peelable protective coating
Abzieh-: **Abziehbild** *nt* KER & GLAS decal (AmE), transfer (BrE); **Abziehbohle** *f* BAU screed board
Abziehen *nt* FERTIG *Kokille* stripping, FOTO printing, LEBENSMITTEL racking; **~ von Schlacke** *f* METALL skimming off the dross
abziehen[1] *vt* BAU rub, smooth, *Beton* finish, *Mauern* level, *Oberfläche* strike off, COMP & DV *Stecker, Kabel* disconnect, FERTIG hone, FOTO print, LEBENSMITTEL *Haut, Fell* skin, MASCHINEN hone, withdraw, MATH subtract, MECHAN hone
abziehen[2] *vi* BAU draw
Abzieher *m* KFZTECH *Werkzeug* gear puller
Abzieh-: **Abziehfestigkeit** *f* WERKPRÜF peel strength; **Abziehfilmverpackung** *f* VERPACK peel-off wrapping; **Abziehhülse** *f* MASCHINEN withdrawal sleeve; **Abziehstein** *m* FERTIG oilstone, MECHAN honing stone; **Abziehsystem** *nt* VERPACK peelable system; **Abziehvorrichtung** *f* MASCHINEN extractor, withdrawal tool
Abzisse *f* MATH horizontal axis, x-axis, PHYS x-coordinate
abzuführend: **~e Verlustleistung** *f* HEIZ & KÄLTE amount of heat to be dissipated; **~e Wärmemenge** *f* HEIZ & KÄLTE amount of heat to be dissipated
Abzug *m* COMP & DV, FOTO *eines Negativs* print, HEIZ & KÄLTE eduction, LABOR fume hood, MECHAN vent, PAPIER exhaust, QUAL *bei Folgestichprobenprüfung* penalty
Abzüge: **~ machen** *vt* DRUCK pull proofs, FOTO print
Abzug: **Abzugsgas** *nt* MECHAN exhaust gas, PHYS flue gas; **Abzugsgraben** *m* WASSERVERSORG drainage ditch;

Abzugshaube *f* BAU hood; **Abzugskanal** *m* WASSERVERSORG delivery channel; **Abzugsleine** *f* WASSERTRANS tripping line

abzugslos *adj* HEIZ & KÄLTE, MASCHINEN flueless

Abzug: **Abzugsöse** *f* FERTIG *Kunststoffinstallationen* withdrawal eye; **Abzugsrohr** *nt* BAU, HEIZ & KÄLTE, KER & GLAS, KERNTECH, KUNSTSTOFF, LABOR, MASCHINEN, MECHAN vent pipe; **Abzugsschrank** *m* LABOR fume cupboard

Abzweig *m* ELEKTRIZ branch, ELEKTROTECH stub, tapping, MECHAN, PHYS branch; **Abzweigdose** *f* BAU joint box, ELEKTRIZ branch box, ELEKTROTECH conduit box, distribution box, junction box, HEIZ & KÄLTE junction box; **Abzweigelement** *nt* OPTIK branching device

abzweigen[1] *vt* BAU branch, branch off

abzweigen[2] *vi* BAU branch off

Abzweig: **Abzweigfilter** *nt* ELEKTRONIK ladder filter; **Abzweigkasten** *m* BAU, ELEKTRIZ branch box, ELEKTROTECH junction box; **Abzweigklemme** *f* ELEKTRIZ branch terminal; **Abzweigkreis** *m* ELEKTROTECH derived circuit; **Abzweigleitung** *f* COMP & DV *Schaltung* branch, ELEKTRIZ branch line, FERTIG shunt line; **Abzweigmuffe** *f* FERTIG Y-joint, branch tee, parallel-joint sleeve; **Abzweigpunkt** *m* ELEKTRONIK *in einer Schaltung* branch point; **Abzweigregler** *m* ELEKTROTECH tapped control; **Abzweigrohr** *nt* BAU branch pipe, FERTIG branch, MASCHINEN, MECHAN, WASSERVERSORG *zur Feuerlöschung* branch pipe; **Abzweigspule** *f* ELEKTROTECH tapped coil; **Abzweigstromkreis** *m* ELEKTROTECH derived circuit; **Abzweigstück** *nt* BAU Y-branch

Abzweigung *f* BAU junction, turnout, *Sanitärbereich* branch, ELEKTRIZ branch, spur, ELEKTRONIK *einer Schaltung* branch, ELEKTROTECH tapping, MECHAN, PHYS branch, TELEKOM *Kabel* leg, WASSERVERSORG branching

AC *abbr* ELEKTROTECH *(Wechselstrom)* AC *(alternating current)*, FERTIG *(Adaptivsteuerung)* AC *(adaptive control)*

AC: **AC-Adapter** *m* ELEKTROTECH AC adaptor; **AC-Animeter** *nt* ELEKTROTECH AC animeter; **AC-Ausgang** *m* ELEKTROTECH AC output; **AC-Beschichten** *nt* CHEMTECH AC bed coating; **AC-Betrieb** *m* ELEKTROTECH AC operation; **AC-Brücke** *f* ELEKTROTECH AC bridge

ACC *abbr* *(automatische Chrominanzregelung)* FERNSEH ACC *(automatic chrominance control)*

AC: **AC-Dickfilm-Elektrolumineszenzanzeige** *f* ELEKTRONIK AC thick-film electroluminescent display; **AC-Eingang** *m* ELEKTROTECH AC input; **AC-Entladung** *f* ELEKTROTECH AC discharge; **AC-Erregung** *f* ELEKTROTECH AC excitation; **AC-Erzeugung** *f* ELEKTROTECH AC current generation, AC generation

Acetal *nt* KUNSTSTOFF, LEBENSMITTEL acetal; **Acetaldehyd** *m* CHEMIE ethanal, LEBENSMITTEL acetaldehyde; **Acetaldol** *nt* CHEMIE acetaldol, LEBENSMITTEL aldol

Acetanhydrid *nt* LEBENSMITTEL acetic anhydride

Acetat *nt* CHEMIE, LEBENSMITTEL acetate, TEXTIL acetate, cellulose acetate; **Acetatfaser** *f* TEXTIL acetate, cellulose acetate; **Acetatfaserstoff** *m* TEXTIL acetate, cellulose acetate; **Acetatfolie** *f* VERPACK acetate film; **Acetatkleber** *m* VERPACK acetate adhesive, acetate glue; **Acetatlaminat** *nt* VERPACK acetate laminate; **Acetatseide** *f* KUNSTSTOFF rayon; **Acetatverbundmaterial** *nt* VERPACK acetate laminate

Acetessig- *pref* CHEMIE diacetic

Acetin *nt* LEBENSMITTEL acetin

Acetoglycerid *nt* LEBENSMITTEL acetoglyceride

Acetolyse *f* LEBENSMITTEL acetolysis

Aceton *nt* CHEMIE acetone, propanone, DRUCK, KUNSTSTOFF acetone; **Acetonextraktion** *f* KUNSTSTOFF acetone extraction; **Acetonharz** *nt* FERTIG, KUNSTSTOFF, VERPACK acetone resin

Acetonitril *nt* CHEMIE acetonitrile, ethanenitrile

Acetophenon *nt* CHEMIE acetophenone

Acetoxygruppe *f* LEBENSMITTEL acetoxy group

Acetyl: **Acetylcellulose** *f* KUNSTSTOFF acetate, cellulose acetate

AC: **AC-Feld** *nt* ELEKTRIZ AC field

AC-gekoppelt *adj* KONTROLL AC-coupled

AC: **AC-Generator** *m* ELEKTRIZ, PHYS AC generator

AC-GS[1] *abbr* *(Wechselstrom-Gleichstrom)* ELEKTROTECH AC-DC

AC-GS[2]: **AC-GS-Umsetzer** *m* ELEKTROTECH AC-DC converter; **AC-GS-Umsetzung** *f* ELEKTROTECH AC-DC conversion; **AC-GS-Wandler** *m* ELEKTROTECH AC-DC converter; **AC-GS-Wandlung** *f* ELEKTROTECH AC-DC conversion

Achat *m* KER & GLAS agate; **Achatsteingut** *nt* KER & GLAS agate ware

Achromat *m* DRUCK, FOTO, OPTIK achromatic lens

achromatisch[1] *adj* ERGON, OPTIK, PHYS achromatic

achromatisch[2]: **~es Dublett** *nt* PHYS achromatic doublet; **~e Linse** *f* DRUCK, FOTO achromatic lens; **~es Objektiv** *nt* OPTIK achromatic lens; **~e Ringe** *m pl* PHYS achromatic fringes; **~e Streifen** *m pl* PHYS achromatic fringes

achromatisieren *vt* OPTIK achromatize

Achromatisierung *f* OPTIK achromatization

Achromatismus *m* OPTIK achromatism

Achs-[1] in Achsrichtung *adj* FERTIG endwise

Achs-[2] *pref* BAU, KFZTECH axle; **Achsabstand** *m* FERTIG, KFZTECH, MASCHINEN center distance (AmE), centre distance (BrE); **Achsaggregat** *nt* EISENBAHN bogie (BrE); **Achsantrieb** *m* KFZTECH final drive, wheel and axle drive; **Achsbaum** *m* KFZTECH axletree; **Achsbolzen** *m* KFZTECH axle pin; **Achsbuchsenführung** *f* KFZTECH axle box guide, axle guide; **Achsdichtung** *f* FERTIG *Kunststoffinstallationen* axial seal; **Achsdruck** *m* BAU axle load; **Achsdrucklager** *nt* MASCHINEN axial thrust bearing

Achse[1]: **von ~ zu Achse** *adv* MASCHINEN from center to center (AmE), from centre to centre (BrE)

Achse[2] *f* BAU axle, GEOM axis, KFZTECH, MASCHINEN axle, MECHAN trunnion, *einer Riemenscheibe oder eines Kräftepaars* axis, PAPIER, PHYS axis; **~ des Zugsattelzapfens** *f* KFZTECH *bei Sattelschlepper* fifth-wheel kingpin axis; **um die ~ rotierende Körper** *m pl* STRÖMPHYS *Untersuchung von Fluiden* spinning bodies

Achse[3]: **~ verschieben** *vi* BAU move the center line (AmE), move the centre line (BrE)

Achselhöhe *f* DRUCK shoulder height

Achsen- *pref* GEOM axial

Achse: **Achsenabstand** *m* MASCHINEN distance between axles; **Achsendrehmaschine** *f* MASCHINEN axle lathe

achsenparallel: **~er Strahl** *m* OPTIK paraxial ray

Achse: **Achsenschenkel** *m* FERTIG spindle; **Achsensymmetrie** *f* GEOM axial symmetry; **Achsensystem** *nt* GEOM system of coordinates; **Achsenwinkel** *m* FERTIG *Kegelräder* shaft angle

achsfern *adj* FERTIG abaxial

Achs-: **Achsflansch** *m* KFZTECH *Räder* axle flange;

Achsführung *f* EISENBAHN cylindrical axle guide; **Achsgabel** *f* EISENBAHN pedestal, KFZTECH axle guard, TRANS pedestal; **Achsgehäuse** *nt* KFZTECH axle casing; **Achsgehäusedeckel** *m* KFZTECH axle box cover, axle box lid; **Achsgehäuse-Entwässerungsbehälter** *m* KFZTECH axle box cellar, axle box sponge-box
achsgerade: ~ **einstellen** *vt* FERTIG align
Achs-: Achshaltersteg *m* KFZTECH axle guide stay; **Achskappe** *f* KFZTECH axle cap; **Achslagefehler** *m* FERTIG *Zahnrad* error of alignment caused by deflection of the shafts; **Achslager** *nt* EISENBAHN axle box (BrE), journal box (AmE), KERNTECH journal bearing, KFZTECH axle box bearing, TRANS *Wagen, Fahrgestell* axle box (BrE), journal box (AmE); **Achslagergehäuse** *nt* MASCHINEN journal box; **Achslast** *f* BAU axle load, MASCHINEN axle weight; **Achslaufbuchse** *f* KFZTECH axle bush, axle bushing; **Achslenker** *m* KFZTECH axle guide; **Achsmitte** *f* KFZTECH axle center (AmE), axle centre (BrE); **Achsmutter** *f* KFZTECH axle nut; **Achsparallelität** *f* KFZTECH tracking; **Achsrichtung** *f* FERTIG end; **Achsschälmaschine** *f* FERTIG axle peeling lathe; **Achsscheibe** *f* BAU *Beschläge* axle pulley; **Achsschenkel** *m* KFZTECH *Federung, Aufhängung* control arm, *Lenkung* steering knuckle, *Rad* stub axle; **Achsschenkelbolzen** *m* MASCHINEN, MECHAN kingbolt (AmE), kingpin (BrE); **Achsschenkelbolzenspreizung** *f* KFZTECH kingbolt inclination (AmE), kingpin inclination (BrE), steering axis inclination; **Achsschenkelfederbein** *nt* KFZTECH McPherson strut; **Achssitz** *m* MASCHINEN axle seat; **Achsstand** *m* EISENBAHN, KFZTECH wheelbase; **Achssturzwinkel** *m* LUFTTRANS *Fahrwerk* angle of wing setting, toe-in angle; **Achsübersetzungsverhältnis** *nt* KFZTECH axle ratio; **Achswelle** *f* KFZTECH axle shaft; **Achswellenkegelrad** *nt* KFZTECH differential side gear; **Achszapfen** *m* KFZTECH journal, *Rad* spindle
Acht *f* MATH eight; **aus 8 Bits bestehendes Byte** *nt* ELEKTRONIK eight-bit byte
achtbindig *adj* CHEMIE octavalent
Acht-Bit: *pref* COMP & DV, ELEKTRONIK eight-bits; **Acht-Bit-Byte** *nt* COMP & DV eight-bit byte; **Acht-Bit-Genauigkeit** *f* ELEKTRONIK eight-bit accuracy; **Acht-Bit-Umsetzer** *m* ELEKTRONIK eight-bit converter; **Acht-Bit-Umsetzung** *f* ELEKTRONIK eight-bit conversion
Achteck *nt* GEOM, METALL octagon; **Achteck-Antenne** *f* RADIO octagon antenna
achteckig[1] *adj* GEOM octagonal
achteckig:[2] ~**e Mutter** *f* MASCHINEN octagonal nut; ~**e Reibahle** *f* MASCHINEN octagonal reamer
Achtelmeile *f* METROL furlong
Achter- *pref* ELEKTRONIK eight-, MATH octa-, WASSERTRANS aft, stern; **Achteralphabet** *nt* ELEKTRONIK eight-level code
achteraus[1] *adv* WASSERTRANS astern, *hinter dem Schiff* abaft
achteraus:[2] ~ **laufen** *vi* WASSERTRANS go astern
Achter-: Achterdeck *nt* WASSERTRANS afterdeck; **Achtergruppe** *f* CHEMIE octet
achterlastig[1] *adj* WASSERTRANS trimmed by the stern
achterlastig[2] *adv* WASSERTRANS *Schiff* down by the stern
achterlich[1] *adj* WASSERTRANS abaft
achterlich:[2] ~**er Wind** *m* WASSERTRANS following wind
achtern *adv* RAUMFAHRT aft, WASSERTRANS astern, *hinter mittschiffs* abaft; **nach** ~ *adv* WASSERTRANS aft

Achter-: Achterschiff *nt* WASSERTRANS aft section; **Achterstag** *nt* WASSERTRANS *Tauwerk* aft stay; **Achtersteven** *m* WASSERTRANS *Schiffbau* stern frame, sternpost
achtflächig *adj* CHEMIE, GEOM octahedral
Achtflächner *m* GEOM octahedron
achtförmig: ~ **verbogenes Rad** *nt* TRANS buckled wheel
Acht: Achtkanteisen *nt* METALL octagon iron; **Achtkantstahl** *m* METALL octagon bar; **Achtknoten** *m* WASSERTRANS figure-of-eight knot; **Achtpol** *m* ELEKTROTECH octupole; **Achtpolröhre** *f* ELEKTRONIK octode; **Achtspur-Recorder** *m* AUFNAHME eight-track recorder
Achtungssignal *nt* AUFNAHME *Tonstudio* audio cue
achtzig: ~ **Spalten breite Anzeige** *f* COMP & DV eighty-column screen
Achtzylinder-V-Motor *m* KFZTECH V-eight engine
ACIA *abbr* (*Asynchron-Übertragungs-Schnittstellenanpasser, asynchronischer Übertragungs-Schnittstellenanpasser*) KONTROLL ACIA (*asynchronous communications interface adaptor*)
ACIA-Schaltkreis *m* KONTROLL ACIA switching circuit
Acidimeter *nt* CHEMIE acidimeter, acidometer, CHEMTECH, LEBENSMITTEL acidimeter
Acidimetrie *f* CHEMIE, CHEMTECH, LEBENSMITTEL, PAPIER acidimetry
acidimetrisch *adj* CHEMIE, PAPIER acidimetric
Acidität *f* CHEMIE acidity
Acidolyse *f* LEBENSMITTEL acidolysis
Acidometer *nt* CHEMIE acidimeter, acidometer, CHEMTECH acidimeter
aci-Form *f* CHEMIE aci-form
AC: AC-Josephson-Effekt *m* ELEKTRONIK AC Josephson effect; **AC-Kompensator** *m* ELEKTRIZ AC potentiometer; **AC-Komponente** *f* ELEKTRIZ AC component; **AC-Kondensator** *m* ELEKTROTECH AC capacitor; **AC-Koppler** *m* TELEKOM AC coupler; **AC-Kraft** *f* ELEKTROTECH AC electromotive force; **AC-Kreis** *m* ELEKTRIZ AC circuit, AC network; **AC-Last** *f* ELEKTROTECH AC load; **AC-Leistung** *f* ELEKTROTECH AC power; **AC-Leitung** *f* ELEKTROTECH AC line; **AC-Lichtbogen** *m* ELEKTROTECH AC arc; **AC-Lichtbogenschweißen** *nt* ELEKTROTECH AC arc welding; **AC-Marker** *m* WASSERTRANS *Radar* AC marker; **AC-Maschine** *f* ELEKTROTECH AC machine; **AC-Meßbrücke** *f* ELEKTRIZ AC bridge; **AC-Meßinstrument** *nt* ELEKTRIZ AC meter
Acmetrapezgewinde *nt* FERTIG acme standard screw thread, MASCHINEN trapezoidal thread
AC: AC-Motor *m* ELEKTRIZ, ELEKTROTECH, FERTIG, PHYS AC motor
ACN *abbr* (*automatische Himmelsnavigation*) RAUMFAHRT ACN (*automatic celestial navigation*)
ACNA *abbr* (*Analogrechner für Netzabgleich*) COMP & DV ACNA (*analog computer for net adjustment*)
AC: AC-Netz *nt* ELEKTRIZ AC network, ELEKTROTECH AC network, AC power line; **AC-Netzausfall** *m* ELEKTROTECH AC power failure; **AC-Netzleitung** *f* ELEKTROTECH AC power line
ACO *abbr* (*Anpassungssteuerung mit Optimierung*) LABOR ACO (*adaptive control optimization*)
Aconit- *pref* CHEMIE aconitic; **Aconitase** *f* CHEMIE aconitase; **Aconitat** *nt* CHEMIE aconitate; **Aconitin** *nt* LEBENSMITTEL aconitine
AC: AC-Quelle *f* ELEKTROTECH AC current source; **AC-Relais** *nt* ELEKTRIZ AC relay, ELEKTROTECH AC

armature relay, AC relay

ACR *abbr (Anflugradar)* RAUMFAHRT ACR *(approach control radar)*

Acryl- *pref* ANSTRICH acrylic

Acrylat *nt* KUNSTSTOFF acrylate

Acryl-: **Acrylfarbe** *f* BAU acrylic paint; **Acrylfaserstoff** *m* TEXTIL acrylic; **Acrylgewebe** *nt* TEXTIL acrylic; **Acrylglas** *nt* VERPACK acrylic plastic; **Acrylharz** *nt* FERTIG, KUNSTSTOFF, MECHAN, VERPACK acrylic resin; **Acrylkautschuk** *m* VERPACK acrylic rubber; **Acrylkunststoff** *m* FERTIG acrylic plastic; **Acryllack** *m* KUNSTSTOFF acrylic paint; **Acrylnitril-Butatien-Styrol** *nt* ELEKTRIZ acrylonitrile butadiene styrene, KUNSTSTOFF *Copolymer* acrylonitrile butadiene styrene; **Acrylnitrilgummi** *m* MECHAN acrylonitrile rubber; **Acrylnitrilkautschuk** *m* KUNSTSTOFF acrylonitrile rubber; **Acrylschlichte** *f* TEXTIL acrylic size; **Acrylstoff** *m* TEXTIL acrylic

AC: **AC-Schaltkreis** *m* ELEKTROTECH AC circuit; **AC-Schaltung** *f* ELEKTROTECH AC switching; **AC-Schweißlichtbogen** *m* FERTIG AC welding arc; **AC-Servomotor** *m* ELEKTROTECH AC servomotor; **AC-Spannung** *f* ELEKTRIZ AC voltage

ACSR *abbr (Einseitenband mit kompandierter Amplitude)* RADIO ACSS *(amplitude-compandered single sideband)*

AC: **AC-Stellmotor** *m* ELEKTROTECH AC servomotor

Actin *nt* LEBENSMITTEL actin

Actinidenelement *nt* PHYS actinide, STRAHLPHYS actinide element, actinoid

Actinidenreihe *f* STRAHLPHYS actinide series, actinium series

Actomyosin *nt* LEBENSMITTEL actomyosin

ACU *abbr (automatisches Rufgerät)* RAUMFAHRT, TELEKOM ACU *(automatic calling unit)*

AC: **AC-Übertragungsleitung** *f* ELEKTRIZ AC transmission line; **AC-Versorgung** *f* ELEKTRIZ AC supply, ELEKTROTECH AC current source; **AC-Versorgungssystem** *nt* RAUMFAHRT *Raumschiff* AC power system; **AC-Verstärker** *m* ELEKTROTECH AC amplifier; **AC-Voltmeter** *nt* ELEKTRIZ, ELEKTROTECH AC voltmeter; **AC-Vorspannung** *f* AUFNAHME AC bias; **AC-Widerstand** *m* ELEKTROTECH AC resistance

acyclisch[1] *adj* CHEMIE acyclic

acyclisch:[2] **~es Diacylamin** *nt* CHEMIE imide; **~es Säureamid** *nt* CHEMIE imide

Acyl *nt* CHEMIE acyl

acylieren *vt* CHEMIE acylate

A/D *abbr (Analog-Digital-)* ELECTRONIC, FERNSEH, FERTIG A/D *(analog-digital)*

A/D: **A/D-Umsetzer** *m* COMP & DV, ELEKTRIZ, ELEKTRONIK, FERTIG, GERÄT, PHYS, TELEKOM A/D converter; **A/D-Umsetzung** *f* AUFNAHME, COMP & DV, ELEKTRIZ, ELEKTRONIK, FERTIG A/D conversion; **A/D-Wandler** *m* COMP & DV, ELEKTRIZ, ELEKTRONIK, FERTIG, LABOR, PHYS, TELEKOM A/D converter; **A/D-Wandlung** *f* AUFNAHME, COMP & DV, ELEKTRIZ, ELEKTRONIK, FERTIG A/D conversion

Adaptationsniveau *nt* ERGON adaptation level

Adapter *m* COMP & DV, ELEKTRIZ, ELEKTROTECH adaptor, FERTIG adaptor, *Kunststoffinstallationen* adaptor, LABOR, MASCHINEN, MECHAN, PHYS, RADIO, TELEKOM, TEXTIL adaptor; **Adapterplatte** *f* MASCHINEN adaptor plate

Adaption *f* ERGON adaptation

adaptiv[1] *adj* COMP & DV, KÜNSTL INT *Programm, System*, MECHAN, PHYS adaptive

adaptiv:[2] **~e Abstimmung** *f* ELEKTRONIK adaptive tuning; **~e Abtastung** *f* GERÄT adaptive sampling; **~e Antenne** *f* TELEKOM adaptive antenna; **~e Codierung** *f* TELEKOM adaptive coding; **~e Differenz-Pulscodemodulation** *f* *(ADPCM)* TELEKOM adaptive differential pulse code modulation *(ADPCM)*; **~er Entzerrer** *m* ELEKTRONIK *Übertragungstechnik* adaptive equalizer; **~e Entzerrung** *f* ELEKTROTECH adaptive equalization; **~es Filter** *nt* ELEKTRONIK, TELEKOM adaptive filter; **~es Filtern** *nt* COMP & DV adaptive filtering; **~e Kanalzuordnung** *f* COMP & DV adaptive channel allocation; **~es Kippen** *nt* ELEKTRONIK *Kathodenstrahlröhren* adaptive sweep; **~er Prozeß** *m* COMP & DV adaptive process; **~es Regelungssystem** *nt* ELEKTROTECH, MECHAN, PHYS adaptive control system; **~e Signalverarbeitung** *f* ELEKTRONIK adaptive signal processing

Adaptivsteuerung *f* ELEKTROTECH AC, adaptive control, FERTIG *Spannung* adaptive control

Adcock-Peiler *m* RADIO Adcock direction finder

Addendum *nt* DRUCK addendum

Adder *m* MATH adder

Addier- *pref* COMP & DV, ELEKTRIZ, MATH adding; **Addiereinrichtung** *f* COMP & DV adder

Addierer *m* MATH adder, *Rechenmaschine* adding machine; **~ mit Parallelübertrag** *m* COMP & DV lookahead

Addier-: **Addiermaschine** *f* COMP & DV, MATH adding machine; **Addierschaltkreis** *m* MATH adder; **Addierschaltung** *f* ELEKTRIZ adding network, ELEKTRONIK *Schaltkreistechnik* adder; **Addierzähler** *m* ELEKTRONIK adding counter

Addition *f* MATH addition; **Additionspolymer** *nt* KUNSTSTOFF addition polymer; **Additionspolymerisat** *nt* KUNSTSTOFF addition polymer; **Additionspolymerisation** *f* KUNSTSTOFF addition polymerization; **Additionsstelle** *f* REGELUNG summing point; **Additionsvorgang** *m* ELEKTRONIK additive process; **Additionszähler** *m* GERÄT accumulating counter

Additiv *nt* ABFALL additive, CHEMIE *Mineralöl* dope, DRUCK, KUNSTSTOFF, MASCHINEN additive

additiv[1] *adj* MATH *Term* additive

additiv:[2] **~e Mischung** *f* ELEKTRONIK *Hochfrequenztechnik* additive mixing; **~es Rauschen** *nt* TELEKOM additive noise

Additiv: **Additivsynthese** *f* FOTO additive synthesis

Adduktion *f* CHEMIE, ERGON adduction

Adenin *nt* CHEMIE adenine, aminopurine, LEBENSMITTEL adenine

Adenosin *nt* CHEMIE adenosine; **Adenosintriphosphat** *nt* *(ATP)* LEBENSMITTEL adenosine triphosphate *(ATP)*

Ader *f* ELEKTRIZ conductor, core, ELEKTROTECH conductor, wire, *eines Drahtseils oder elektrischen Kabels* core, KOHLEN seam, PHYS conductor, TELEKOM *Kabel* core; **~ zum Stöpselhals** *f* TELEKOM R-wire, ring wire; **~ zur Stöpselspitze** *f* TELEKOM tip wire; **Adernabschirmung** *f* ELEKTRIZ core screen

ADF *abbr (Funkpeilgerät, automatischer Funkkompaß)* LUFTTRANS, RADIO, TELEKOM ADF *(automatic direction finder)*

Adhäsiometer *nt* KUNSTSTOFF adherometer

Adhäsion *f* KUNSTSTOFF adhesion; **Adhäsionseisenbahn** *f* EISENBAHN adhesion railroad (AmE), adhesion railway (BrE); **Adhäsionsfestigkeit** *f* KUNSTSTOFF adhesive strength; **Adhäsionskraft** *f* VERPACK adherence; **Adhäsionsmesser** *m* KUNSTSTOFF adherometer; **Adhäsionssystem** *nt* TRANS adhesion system; **Adhäsionsverbesserer** *m* KUNSTSTOFF adhesion promoter; **Adhäsionszug** *m* EISENBAHN total adherence train

ADI *abbr (duldbare tägliche Aufnahmemenge)* LEBENSMITTEL ADI *(acceptable daily intake)*

adiabatisch[1] *adj* MECHAN, PHYS, STRÖMPHYS, THERMOD adiabatic

adiabatisch[2] *adv* STRÖMPHYS, THERMOD adiabatically

adiabatisch:[3] **~e Änderung** *f* STRÖMPHYS, THERMOD adiabatic change; **~e Ausdehnung** *f* STRÖMPHYS, THERMOD adiabatic expansion; **~er Beiwert** *m* STRÖMPHYS, THERMOD adiabatic coefficient, adiabatic curve; **~er Druckabfall** *m* STRÖMPHYS, THERMOD adiabatic pressure drop; **~e Entmagnetisierung** *f* STRÖMPHYS, THERMOD adiabatic demagnetization; **~e Invariante** *f* STRÖMPHYS, THERMOD adiabatic invariant; **~e Kompressibilität** *f* PHYS isentropic compressibility; **~e Kompression** *f* STRÖMPHYS, THERMOD adiabatic compression; **~er Prozeß** *m* STRÖMPHYS, THERMOD adiabatic process; **~e Schallwellen** *f pl* STRÖMPHYS, THERMOD adiabatic sound waves; **~e Stoßwelle** *f* STRÖMPHYS, THERMOD adiabatic shock wave; **~es System** *nt* STRÖMPHYS, THERMOD adiabatic system; **~es Temperaturgefälle** *nt* THERMOD adiabatic lapse rate; **~er Temperaturgradient** *m* STRÖMPHYS, THERMOD adiabatic temperature gradient; **~e Transformation** *f* STRÖMPHYS, THERMOD adiabatic transformation; **~es Verhalten** *nt* STRÖMPHYS, THERMOD adiabatism; **~er vertikaler Gradient** *m* THERMOD adiabatic lapse rate; **~e Wand** *f* STRÖMPHYS, THERMOD adiabatic wall; **~er Wirkungsgrad** *m* STRÖMPHYS, THERMOD adiabatic efficiency; **~e Zustandsänderung** *f* STRÖMPHYS, THERMOD adiabatic change

Adipinsäureester *m* KUNSTSTOFF adipic ester

Adiuretin *nt* CHEMIE vasopressin

Adjazenz *f* GEOM adjacency

Admittanz *f* AKUSTIK, ELEKTROTECH, PHYS admittance

ADPCM *abbr (adaptive Differenz-Pulscodemodulation)* TELEKOM ADPCM *(adaptive differential pulse code modulation)*

Adrenocorticotropin *nt* CHEMIE corticotrophin

Adreß- *pref* COMP & DV address, sequence; **Adreßabbildung** *f* COMP & DV address mapping

Adressat *m* TRANS consignee

Adreß-: Adreßbus *m* COMP & DV address bus

Adresse *f* COMP & DV, RADIO address; **Adressendatei** *f* TELEKOM address file; **Adressenende** *nt* COMP & DV end of address; **Adressenformat** *nt* COMP & DV address format; **Adressengenerierung** *f* COMP & DV address generation; **Adressenmatrize** *f* VERPACK address stencil; **Adressenregister** *nt* COMP & DV address register; **Adressenschild** *nt* VERPACK address label; **Adressenvielfachleitung** *f* COMP & DV address highway

Adreß-: Adreßfolgeregister *nt* COMP & DV sequence control register, sequence counter, sequence register

adressierbar[1] *adj* COMP & DV addressable

adressierbar:[2] **~e Speicherstelle** *f* COMP & DV addressable location

adressieren *vt* COMP & DV address

Adressiersystem *nt* COMP & DV addressing system

Adressierung *f* COMP & DV, TELEKOM addressing; **~ über Basisadresse** *f* COMP & DV base displacement address; **Adressierungsart** *f* COMP & DV addressing mode

Adreß-: Adreßliste *f* COMP & DV mailing list; **Adreßmodi-** fikation *f* COMP & DV address modification; **Adreßposition** *f* COMP & DV address position; **Adreßraum** *m* COMP & DV address space

Adsorbens *nt* CHEMIE adsorbent

adsorbierbar *adj* CHEMIE adsorbable

adsorbieren *vt* KOHLEN adsorb

Adsorption *f* KOHLEN, KUNSTSTOFF, LEBENSMITTEL adsorption; **Adsorptionsfalle** *f* KERNTECH adsorption trap; **Adsorptionsisotherme** *f* KERNTECH adsorption isotherm; **Adsorptionskohle** *f* CHEMIE active carbon; **Adsorptionsmittel** *nt* LEBENSMITTEL adsorbent; **Adsorptionswärme** *f* KERNTECH adsorption heat; **Adsorptionswirkung** *f* ABFALL adsorption efficiency

ADU *abbr (Analog-Digital-Umsetzer)* COMP & DV, ELEKTRONIK, FERNSEH, FERTIG ADC *(analog-digital converter)*

ADV *abbr (automatische Datenverarbeitung)* COMP & DV ADP *(automatic data processing)*

Advektion *f* PHYS, STRÖMPHYS advection

AE *abbr (astronomische Einheit)* LABOR AU *(astronomical unit)*

AEC *abbr (Amerikanischer Atomenergieverband)* KERNTECH AEC *(Atomic Energy Commission)*

aerob[1] *adj* ERGON, LEBENSMITTEL aerobic

aerob:[2] **~er Abbau** *m* ABFALL aerobic degradation; **~e Bakterien** *f pl* ABFALL aerobic bacteria; **~es Behandlungsverfahren** *nt* ABFALL aerobic treatment process; **~e Gärung** *f* ABFALL, LEBENSMITTEL aerobic fermentation; **~er Metabolismus** *m* ERGON aerobic metabolism; **~e Schlammfaulung** *f* WASSERVERSORG aerobic sludge digestion; **~e Schlammstabilisierung** *f* ABFALL aerobic sludge stabilization; **~ stabilisierter Schlamm** *m* ABFALL aerobically digested sludge; **~e Zersetzung** *f* ABFALL aerobic decomposition

Aerobier *m* LEBENSMITTEL aerobe

Aerobus *m* LUFTTRANS aerobus

Aerodynamik *f* MASCHINEN, PHYS, TRANS aerodynamics; **Aerodynamikkoeffizient** *m* RAUMFAHRT aerodynamic coefficient

aerodynamisch[1] *adj* MASCHINEN, PHYS, TRANS aerodynamic

aerodynamisch:[2] **~er Auftrieb** *m* LUFTTRANS aerodynamic lift; **~es Bremsen** *nt* RAUMFAHRT *Raumschiff* aerodynamic braking; **~er Druck** *m* LUFTTRANS aerodynamic pressure; **~er Faktor** *m* LUFTTRANS aerodynamic factor; **~e Form** *f* KFZTECH *Karosserie* aerodynamic shape; **~e Geräusche** *nt pl* LUFTTRANS aerodynamic noise, airframe noise; **~e Kraft** *f* NICHTFOSS ENERG aerodynamic power; **~e Last** *f* LUFTTRANS aerodynamic load; **~es Luftkissenfahrzeug** *nt* TRANS aerodynamic-type air cushion vehicle; **~er Mittelpunkt** *m* LUFTTRANS aerodynamic center (AmE), aerodynamic centre (BrE); **~er Mittelpunkt des Blattes** *m* LUFTTRANS blade aerodynamic center (AmE), blade aerodynamic centre (BrE); **~es Schweben** *nt* TRANS aerodynamic levitation; **~e Stabilisierungsflosse** *f* RAUMFAHRT aerodynamic stabilizing fin; **~er Übergang** *m* LUFTTRANS *Flugzeug* fairing, *Flugwerk* fillet; **~e Verwindung** *f* LUFTTRANS aerodynamic twist; **~e Verzögerung** *f* LUFTTRANS aerodynamic lag; **~e Waage** *f* LUFTTRANS aerodynamic balance, wind tunnel balance, WASSERTRANS wind tunnel balance; **~er Windkanal** *m* LUFTTRANS, WASSERTRANS wind tunnel; **~er Wirkungsgrad** *m* LUFTTRANS aerodynamic efficiency

Aeroelastizität *f* KERNTECH, NICHTFOSS ENERG

aeroelasticity

Aerograph *m* DRUCK, KER & GLAS aerograph; **Aerographie** *f* DRUCK, KER & GLAS aerography

aeromagnetisch: ~**er Zug** *m* EISENBAHN aeromagnetic train

Aerometer *nt* METROL, PAPIER *Luftdichtemesser*, PHYS aerometer

Aerometrie *f* PAPIER, PHYS aerometry

aerometrisch *adj* PAPIER aerometric

aeronautisch: ~**er Informationsdienst** *m* (*AIS*) RAUMFAHRT aeronautical information service (*AIS*); ~**e Werkstoffnorm** *f* (*AMS*) RAUMFAHRT aeronautical material standard (*AMS*)

Aerosol *nt* PHYS, SICHERHEIT, UMWELTSCHMUTZ *schwebestoffhaltige Luft*, VERPACK aerosol; **Aerosolbehälter** *m* MASCHINEN aerosol container; **Aerosoldose** *f* VERPACK aerosol container; **Aerosolpackung** *f* ABFALL aerosol dispenser; **Aerosolsprühdose** *f* MASCHINEN aerosol spray container; **Aerosoltreibgas** *nt* ERDÖL *Petrochemie* aerosol propellant; **Aerosolventil** *nt* VERPACK aerosol valve; **Aerosolverschluß** *m* VERPACK aerosol cap

Aerostatik *f* MASCHINEN aerostatics

aerostatisch: ~**es Luftkissenfahrzeug** *nt* TRANS aerostatic-type air cushion vehicle

AES *abbr* (*Augersche Elektronenspektroskopie*) PHYS, STRAHLPHYS AES (*Auger electron spectroscopy*)

Aesculin *nt* CHEMIE aesculin

afferent: ~**er Nerv** *m* ERGON afferent nerve

affin: ~**e Geometrie** *f* GEOM affine geometry

Affinität *f* (*A*) CHEMIE affinity (*A*)

Affintransformation *f* METALL affine transformation

AFGC *abbr* (*automatische Frequenz- und Verstärkungsregelung*) ELEKTRONIK, FERNSEH, RADIO AFGC (*automatic frequency and gain control*)

AFI *abbr* (*automatische Fahrzeugidentifikation*) TRANS AVI (*automatic vehicle identification*)

Aflatoxin *nt* LEBENSMITTEL *Toxikologie* aflatoxin

AFO *abbr* (*automatische Fahrzeugortung*) TRANS AVL (*automatic vehicle location*)

AFR *abbr* (*automatische Frequenzregelung*) ELEKTRONIK, FERNSEH, RADIO AFC (*automatic frequency control*)

AFS *abbr* (*fester Flugfunkdienst*) LUFTTRANS AFS (*aeronautical-fixed service*)

AFT *abbr* (*automatische Scharfabstimmung*) RADIO AFT (*automatic fine tuning*)

AFTN *abbr* (*festes Flugfunknetz*) LUFTTRANS AFTN (*aeronautical-fixed telecommunication network*)

AG *abbr* (*amerikanisches Maß*) MASCHINEN AG (*American gage*)

Ag (*Silber*) CHEMIE Ag (*silver*)

Agar *nt* LEBENSMITTEL *aus Polysacchariden bestehender Rotalgenextrakt* agar; **--Agar** *nt* LEBENSMITTEL *aus Polysacchariden bestehender Rotalgenextrakt* agar-agar

Agatlinie *f* DRUCK agate line

AGCA *abbr* (*automatische Anflugsteuerung vom Boden*) RAUMFAHRT AGCA (*automatic ground-controlled approach*)

AGCL *abbr* (*automatische Landesteuerung vom Boden*) RAUMFAHRT AGCL (*automatic ground-controlled landing*)

AGE *abbr* (*Allylglycidether*) KUNSTSTOFF AGE (*allyl glycidyl ether*)

Agene *nt* LEBENSMITTEL agene

Agens *nt* CHEMIE agent

Agglomerat *nt* FERTIG agglomerate; **Agglomeratbildung** *f* CHEMTECH agglomeration

Agglomeration *f* CHEMTECH, KUNSTSTOFF agglomeration

agglomerieren *vi* CHEMTECH agglomerate

Agglutination *f* CHEMTECH, LEBENSMITTEL agglutination

agglutinierend *adj* CHEMIE agglutinant

Agglutinin *nt* LEBENSMITTEL *spezifischer Antikörper* agglutinin

Aggradation *f* WASSERVERSORG aggradation

Aggragat *nt* FERTIG bank

Aggregat *nt* BAU set, COMP & DV unit, FERTIG aggregate, unit, KFZTECH unit, KOHLEN aggregate, MASCHINEN assembly, unit, METALL aggregate; **Aggregatkratzer** *m* TRANS aggregate scraper; **Aggregatschrappförderer** *m* TRANS aggregate scraper; **Aggregatzustand** *m* MASCHINEN state of aggregation

aggressiv[1] *adj* FERTIG *Kunststoffinstallationen* corrosive

aggressiv:[2] ~**e Mittel** *nt pl* HEIZ & KÄLTE corrosive media; ~**es Wasser** *nt* WASSERVERSORG aggressive water

AGR *abbr* (*fortgeschrittener Gas-Graphit-Reaktor*) KERNTECH AGR (*advanced gas-cooled reactor*)

Agrobusiness *nt* LEBENSMITTEL agrobusiness

Ahle *f* DRUCK bodkin

Ahminges *f pl* WASSERTRANS *Schiffkonstruktion* draft marks (AmE), draught marks (BrE)

ähnlich: ~**e Figuren** *f pl* GEOM similar figures; ~**e Ladungsmengen** *f pl* ELEKTRIZ like charges; ~**e Pole** *m pl* ELEKTRIZ like poles

Ähnlichkeitsverhältnis *nt* GEOM similarity relation

AI *abbr* (*Schallimpedanz, Schallwellenwiderstand, akustische Impedanz, akustischer Scheinwiderstand*) AKUSTIK ZA (*acoustic impedance*)

AIA *abbr* (*Amerikanischer Luft- und Raumfahrtverband*) RAUMFAHRT AIA (*Aerospace Industries Association*)

A-Index *m* RADIO A-index

Airbag *m* KFZTECH air bag; **Airbag-Haltesystem** *nt* KFZTECH air bag restraint system

Airbus *m* LUFTTRANS airbus

Air-Terminal *m* LUFTTRANS airways terminal; ~ **für Frachtflugzeuge** *m* LUFTTRANS freight terminal

Airy-Scheibchen *nt* PHYS Airy disc (BrE), Airy disk (AmE)

AIS *abbr* (*aeronautischer Informationsdienst*) RAUMFAHRT AIS (*aeronautical information service*)

AK *abbr* (*akustische Kapazität*) AKUSTIK AC (*acoustic capacitance*)

Akklimatisation *f* ERGON acclimatization

Akkomodation *f* ERGON accommodation

Akkord *m* AKUSTIK chord; **Akkordarbeit** *f* BAU job work

Akku *m* (*Akkumulator*) COMP & DV, ELEKTRIZ, ELEKTROTECH, FERNSEH, HEIZ & KÄLTE, HYDRAUL, KFZTECH, PAPIER, PHYS, RADIO *wiederaufladbare Batterie* accumulator, rechargeable battery, storage battery; **Akkubatterie** *f* COMP & DV, ELEKTRIZ, ELEKTROTECH, FERNSEH, HEIZ & KÄLTE, HYDRAUL, PAPIER, PHYS, RADIO accumulator, rechargeable battery, storage battery

Akku: **Akkuladeschaltung** *f* ELEKTRIZ charging circuit

Akkumulator *m* (*Akku*) COMP & DV, ELEKTRIZ, ELEKTROTECH, FERNSEH, HEIZ & KÄLTE, HYDRAUL, KFZTECH, PAPIER, PHYS, RADIO *wiederaufladbare Batterie* accumulator, rechargeable battery, storage battery; **Akkumulatorbatterie** _f_ ELEKTROTECH, KFZTECH, TELEKOM accumulator battery, rechargeable battery, storage battery; **Akkumulatorelektrode** _f_ ELEKTRIZ battery electrode; **Akkumulatorentladung** _f_ ELEKTRIZ accumulator discharge; **Akkumulatorfahrzeug** _nt_ TRANS accumulator vehicle; **Akkumulatorkasten** _m_ PAPIER accumulator box; **Akkumulatorladung** _f_ ELEKTRIZ accumulator charge; **Akkumulatorleistungsanzeige** _f_ PAPIER accumulator capacity indicator; **Akkumulatorplatte** _f_ ELEKTRIZ accumulator plate, battery plate; **Akkumulatorregister** _nt_ COMP & DV accumulator register; **Akkumulatorsäure** _f_ CHEMIE, ELEKTRIZ electrolyte, ELEKTROTECH battery acid; **Akkumulatortriebwagen** _m_ TRANS accumulator railcar; **Akkumulatorzelle** _f_ ELEKTRIZ accumulator cell, ELEKTROTECH storage cell

akkumuliert: **~e Energiedosis** _f_ KERNTECH accumulated dose, cumulative dose; **~er Fehler** _m_ GERÄT accumulated error

Akku: **Akkuplatte** _f_ ELEKTRIZ accumulator plate

A-Kohle _f (Aktivkohle)_ CHEMIE, KOHLEN, KUNSTSTOFF, LEBENSMITTEL, PAPIER, WASSERVERSORG activated carbon, activated charcoal, active carbon

Akquisition _f_ KÜNSTL INT _des Wissens_ acquisition

Akronym _nt_ COMP & DV acronym

Akteneinsicht _f_ PATENT inspection of files

Aktentaschencomputer _m_ COMP & DV laptop computer, portable

aktinisch[1] _adj_ FOTO actinic

aktinisch:[2] **~e Strahlen** _m pl_ FOTO actinic rays

Aktinität _f_ DRUCK actinic effect

Aktiniumemanation _f_ STRAHLPHYS actinium emanation

Aktinometrie _f_ PHYS, STRAHLPHYS _hauptsächlich Licht_ actinometry

Aktion _f_ COMP & DV, ERGON, KFZTECH action

Aktions- _pref_ COMP & DV action, drop-down, TRANS working; **Aktionseintrag** _m_ COMP & DV action entry; **Aktionsfenster** _nt_ COMP & DV drop-down menu, pulldown menu; **Aktionspotential** _nt_ ERGON action potential; **Aktionsradius** _m_ KFZTECH _Elektrofahrzeuge_ cruising range, TRANS useful working range; **Aktionsturbine** _f_ HYDRAUL action turbine, NICHTFOSS ENERG impulse turbine

Aktiv- _pref_ COMP & DV, ELEKTROTECH, FERTIG active; **Aktivabfallverdampfer** _m_ KERNTECH radioactive waste evaporator

aktiv[1] _adj_ COMP & DV, ELEKTROTECH, FERTIG active; **nicht ~** _adj_ COMP & DV, WASSERTRANS inactive

aktiv:[2] **~es Anfahren eines Reaktors** _nt_ KERNTECH _Atomkraftwerk_ energetic start-up; **~er Bandpaß** _m_ ELEKTRONIK active band-pass filter; **~es Bandpaßfilter** _nt_ ELEKTRONIK active band-pass filter, active notch filter; **~es Bauelement** _nt_ ELEKTRIZ, ELEKTROTECH active component; **~er Bereich** _m_ ELEKTRONIK _Halbleitersubstrat_ active region; **~e Datei** _f_ COMP & DV active file; **~er Dipol** _m_ ELEKTROTECH active dipole; **~es Element** _nt_ ELEKTROTECH active element; **~e Emanation** _f_ KERNTECH active emanation; **~er Equalizer** _m_ AUFNAHME _Entzerrer_ active equalizer; **~er Erddruck** _m_ KOHLEN active earth pressure; **~e Fahrzeugsicherheit** _f_ TRANS active motor vehicle safety; **~e Feldzeit** _f_ FERNSEH active field period; **~es Filter** _nt_ ELEKTRONIK, TELEKOM active filter; **~es Filter dritter Ordnung** _nt_ ELEKTRONIK third order active filter; **~es Filtern** _nt_ ELEKTRONIK active filtering; **~e Flanke** _f_ FERTIG _Getriebelehre_ active profile; **~e Führung** _f_ RAUMFAHRT

Raumschiff active guidance; **~er Füllstoff** _m_ KUNSTSTOFF _verstärkend wirkend_ active filler; **~es Glied** _nt_ REGELUNG active element, final controlling element; **~es I-Element** _nt_ ELEKTRONIK _Automatisierungstechnik_ active integrator; **~er Infrarotdetektor** _m_ TRANS active infrared detector; **~es Integrierglied** _nt_ ELEKTRONIK active integrator; **~e integrierte Mikrowellenschaltung** _f_ ELEKTRONIK active microwave integrated circuit; **~e Kamera** _f_ FERNSEH hot camera; **~er Kreislauftest** _m_ KERNTECH active test loop; **~e Länge** _f_ KERNTECH _eines Brennelementes_ active length; **~es Lasermedium** _nt_ OPTIK, TELEKOM active laser medium; **~e Leitung** _f_ ELEKTRONIK, FERNSEH active line; **~es Leuchtfeuer-Kollisionswarnsystem** _nt_ LUFTTRANS active beacon collision avoidance system; **~es Lösemittel** _nt_ KUNSTSTOFF active solvent, true solvent; **~es Lösungsmittel** _nt_ VERPACK active solvent; **~es Netzwerk** _nt_ ELEKTROTECH active network; **~er Prozessor** _m_ TELEKOM active processor; **~er Richtstollen** _m_ KOHLEN active mine heading; **~er Schaltkreis** _m_ PHYS active circuit; **~e Schicht** _f_ ELEKTRONIK active layer; **~es Sonnensystem** _nt_ NICHTFOSS ENERG active solar system; **~er Spiegel** _m_ KERNTECH active mirror; **~e Spiegelmaschine** _f_ KERNTECH active mirror; **~e Steuerung** _f_ RAUMFAHRT _Raumschiff_ active control; **~es System** _nt_ AKUSTIK active system; **~er Transducer** _m_ ELEKTRIZ, ELEKTROTECH active transducer; **~er Vierpol** _m_ ELEKTROTECH active quadripole; **~er Wandler** _m_ ELEKTRIZ, ELEKTROTECH active transducer; **~es Wasser** _nt_ WASSERVERSORG active water; **~e Zielsuchlenkung** _f_ LUFTTRANS homing active guidance

Aktivation _f_ KÜNSTL INT _von Neuronen_ activation

Aktivator _m_ ELEKTROTECH activator, KOHLEN activating agent, activator, KUNSTSTOFF activator

aktivieren _vt_ COMP & DV _Rechner_ enable, execute, KOHLEN, KONTROLL, PAPIER activate, TEXTIL boost

aktiviert[1] _adj_ ELEKTROTECH on active

aktiviert:[2] **~es Aluminiumoxid** _nt_ LEBENSMITTEL activated alumina; **~e Holzkohle** _f_ LEBENSMITTEL activated charcoal; **~e Kohle** _f_ LEBENSMITTEL activated carbon, active carbon; **~er Komplex** _m_ METALL activated complex; **~es Molekül** _nt_ STRAHLPHYS activated molecule; **~e Tonerde** _f_ LEBENSMITTEL activated alumina; **~er Zustand** _m_ METALL activated state

Aktivierung _f_ KERNTECH, KOHLEN, KÜNSTL INT _von Neuronen_, METALL, PAPIER, STRAHLPHYS, TELEKOM activation; **~ durch Gammastrahlen** _f_ STRAHLPHYS, TEILPHYS, WELLPHYS gamma photon activation; **Aktivierungsanalyse** _f_ PHYS activation analysis, STRAHLPHYS activation analysis, radioactivation analysis; **Aktivierungsanalyse mit Hilfe geladener Teilchen** _f_ KERNTECH, STRAHLPHYS, TEILPHYS charged-particle activation analysis; **Aktivierungsbereich** _m_ METALL activation area; **Aktivierungsenergie** _f_ KERNTECH activation, METALL, STRAHLPHYS activation energy; **Aktivierungsentropie** _f_ METALL activation entropy; **Aktivierungslog** _nt_ ERDÖL _Bohrlochmessung_ activation log; **Aktivierungsmittel** _nt_ PAPIER activator; **Aktivierungsparameter** _nt_ METALL activation parameter; **Aktivierungswärme** _f_ THERMOD heat of activation

Aktivität _f_ COMP & DV activity, KERNTECH _(A)_, PHYS _(A)_ activity _(A)_; **~ eines Atomkerns** _f_ STRAHLPHYS nuclear activity; **Aktivitätsbeiwert** _m_ RAUMFAHRT _Weltraumfunk_ activity factor; **Aktivitätsgrenzwerte** _m pl_ KERNTECH activity threshold; **Aktivitätskoeffizient**

m PHYS activity coefficient; **Aktivitätsüberspannung** *f* RAUMFAHRT *Raumschiff* activity overvoltage; **Aktivitätsverzeichnis** *nt* KERNTECH activity inventory

Aktiv-: **Aktivkohle** *f* *(A-Kohle)* CHEMIE, KOHLEN, KUNSTSTOFF, LEBENSMITTEL, PAPIER, WASSERVERSORG activated carbon, activated charcoal, active carbon; **Aktivkohle-Absorption** *f* UMWELTSCHMUTZ active carbon absorption; **Aktivkohlebehandlung** *f* ABFALL activated carbon treatment; **Aktivkohlebett** *nt* KERNTECH activated charcoal bed; **Aktivkohlefilter** *nt* KERNTECH activated carbon filter; **Aktivruß** *m* KUNSTSTOFF activated carbon black

Aktor *m* COMP & DV actuator, KÜNSTL INT actor

aktualisieren *vt* COMP & DV refresh, update, MASCHINEN bring up to date, update

aktualisiert: ~ **anzeigen** *vt* COMP & DV refresh

Aktualisierung *f* COMP & DV refresh, update, TELEKOM updating; **Aktualisierungsdatei** *f* COMP & DV update file; **Aktualisierungslauf** *m* COMP & DV update run; **Aktualisierungsmodus** *f* COMP & DV update mode; **Aktualisierungsrate** *f* COMP & DV refresh rate; **Aktualisierungsspeicher** *m* COMP & DV refresh memory; **Aktualisierungszyklus** *m* COMP & DV refresh cycle

Aktuator *m* ELEKTRIZ *Stellglied* actuator

aktuell: ~**er Adreßschlüssel** *m* COMP & DV *Programmiersprache* actual key; ~**e Datei** *f* COMP & DV update

Akuphonie *f* AKUSTIK acouphony

Akustik *f* AUFNAHME *Lautlehre*, ERGON, PHYS, RADIO acoustics; **Akustikentwurf** *m* AUFNAHME acoustical design; **Akustikkoppler** *m* COMP & DV, ELEKTRONIK *Peripheriegerät* acoustic coupler; **Akustiklog** *nt* ERDÖL *Bohrlochmessung* acoustic log, *Meßtechnik* sonic log; **Akustikprozessor** *m* KÜNSTL INT acoustic processor; **Akustikspektrum** *nt* AUFNAHME acoustic spectrum; **Akustiktest** *m* SICHERHEIT acoustical test; **Akustiktrauma** *nt* AKUSTIK acoustic trauma; **Akustikverstärker** *m* AUFNAHME acoustic amplifier

akustisch[1] *adj* AUFNAHME, ERDÖL, PHYS acoustic, sonic

akustisch:[2] ~**e Abschirmung** *f* AUFNAHME acoustic screen, acoustic shielding; ~**e Absorption** *f* AKUSTIK *(a)* total acoustic absorption *(a)*, AUFNAHME *Schallschlucken* acoustic absorption; ~**er Absorptionskoeffizient** *m* PHYS acoustic absorption coefficient; ~**er Absorptionsverlust** *m* AUFNAHME acoustic absorption loss; ~**e Admittanz** *f* *(YA)* AKUSTIK, ELEKTROTECH acoustic admittance *(YA)*; ~**er Akzeptanzpegel** *m* *(AAP)* AKUSTIK acoustic comfort index *(ACI)*; ~**er Alarm** *m* TELEKOM audible alarm; ~**er Anrufmelder** *m* TELEKOM tone pager; ~**e Ausbreitungskonstante** *f* AKUSTIK acoustic propagation constant; ~**e Beugung** *f* AKUSTIK acoustic diffraction; ~**e Blendung** *f* AKUSTIK aural dazzling; ~**er Blindleitwert** *m* *(AB)* AKUSTIK acoustic susceptance *(BA)*; ~**er Blindwiderstand** *m* AKUSTIK, ELEKTROTECH, PHYS acoustic reactance; ~**e Dämpfung** *f* ELEKTRONIK acoustic damping; ~**e Diffraktion** *f* AKUSTIK acoustic diffraction; ~**e Dispersion** *f* AKUSTIK acoustic dispersion; ~**e Emission** *f* KERNTECH acoustic emission; ~**e Energie** *f* ELEKTROTECH acoustic energy; ~**e Federung** *f* AUFNAHME acoustic compliance; ~**es Filter** *nt* AKUSTIK, AUFNAHME acoustic filter, ELEKTRONIK acoustic filter, acoustic-wave filter, MASCHINEN acoustic filter; ~**er Frequenzbereich** *m* STRAHLPHYS audio range; ~**e Impedanz** *f* AKUSTIK *(AI)*, AUFNAHME *(ZA)*, ELEKTROTECH *(ZA)*, PHYS *(ZA)* acoustic impedance *(ZA)*; ~**es Interferometer** *nt* AKUSTIK acoustic inter-

ferometer; ~**e Kapazität** *f* *(AK)* AKUSTIK acoustic capacitance *(AC)*; ~**e Kernimpedanz** *f* AKUSTIK transfer acoustic impedance; ~**e Kopplung** *f* ELEKTRONIK acoustic coupling; ~**er Leitwert** *m* *(AL)* AKUSTIK acoustic conductance *(GA)*; ~**e Masse** *f* AKUSTIK inertance, AKUSTIK *(AM)* acoustic mass *(AM)*, PHYS acoustic inertance; ~**e Mobilität** *f* AKUSTIK acoustic mobility; ~**e Oberflächenwelle** *f* *(AOW)* ELEKTRONIK, TELEKOM surface acoustic wave *(SAW)*; ~**er Oszillator** *m* STRAHLPHYS audio oscillator; ~**e Perspektive** *f* AUFNAHME acoustic perspective; ~**es Radiometer** *nt* AKUSTIK acoustic radiometer; ~**e Reaktanz** *f* AKUSTIK, ELEKTROTECH acoustic reactance; ~**e Resistanz** *f* AKUSTIK acoustic resistance; ~**er Resonator** *m* ELEKTRONIK acoustic resonator; ~**e Rückkopplung** *f* AUFNAHME acoustic feedback; ~**es Rufzeichen** *nt* TELEKOM audible signal; ~**er Scheinwiderstand** *m* AKUSTIK *(AI)*, AUFNAHME *(ZA)*, ELEKTROTECH *(ZA)*, PHYS *(ZA)* acoustic impedance *(ZA)*; ~**es Signal** *nt* EISENBAHN sound signal, ELEKTRONIK, MASCHINEN acoustic signal, TELEKOM *Telefon* sound signal; ~**er Speicher** *m* COMP & DV acoustic memory, acoustic store, ELEKTRONIK acoustic delay line; ~**e Steifheit** *f* AKUSTIK, PHYS acoustic stiffness; ~**e Streuung** *f* AKUSTIK acoustic dispersion, AUFNAHME acoustic scattering; ~**e Suszeptanz** *f* AKUSTIK acoustic susceptance; ~**es System** *nt* AKUSTIK acoustic system; ~**er Tonabnehmer** *m* AUFNAHME acoustic pick-up; ~**er Träger** *m* ELEKTRONIK acoustic carrier; ~**e Trägheitsmasse** *f* AKUSTIK inertance; ~**e Übertragungslinie** *f* ELEKTROTECH acoustic transmission line; ~**e Verzögerungsleitung** *f* COMP & DV acoustic delay line; ~**e Verzögerungsstrecke** *f* ELEKTRONIK acoustic delay line; ~**e Warnanlage** *f* GERÄT audio alarm system; ~**er Widerstand** *m* AKUSTIK acoustic resistance; ~**er Wirkungsgrad** *m* AUFNAHME acoustic efficiency; ~**es Zentrum** *nt* AKUSTIK effective acoustic center (AmE), effective acoustic centre (BrE); ~**er Zweig** *m* PHYS *Festkörperphysik* acoustic branch

akustooptisch: ~**er Effekt** *m* OPTIK acousto-optic effect; ~**e Modulation** *f* ELEKTRONIK acousto-optic modulation; ~**er Modulator** *m* ELEKTRONIK, OPTIK acousto-optic modulator; ~**er Prozessor** *m* ELEKTRONIK acousto-optic processor

Akut *m* DRUCK acute accent

akut: ~**e Wirkung** *f* UMWELTSCHMUTZ acute effect

Akzent *m* DRUCK accent; **Akzentbuchstabe** *m* DRUCK accented letter

akzeptabler: ~ **Qualitätspegel** *m* *(AQL)* QUAL acceptable quality level *(AQL)*; ~ **Zuverlässigkeitspegel** *m* *(ARL)* QUAL acceptable reliability level *(ARL)*

Akzeptanz *f* RAUMFAHRT, TELEKOM acceptance; **Akzeptanzkriterium** *nt* RAUMFAHRT *Raumschiff* acceptance criterion; **Akzeptanzwinkel** *m* TELEKOM acceptance angle

Akzeptor *m* COMP & DV *Halbleiter*, ELEKTRONIK *Halbleiter* acceptor; **Akzeptoratom** *nt* ELEKTRONIK, PHYS acceptor atom; **Akzeptorniveau** *nt* ELEKTRONIK *Halbleiter* acceptor level; **Akzeptorverunreinigung** *f* ELEKTRONIK acceptor impurity

Akzidenz *f* DRUCK job, jobbing; **Akzidenzsatz** *m* DRUCK job composition; **Akzidenzschriften** *f pl* DRUCK jobbing types

AL *abbr* AKUSTIK *(akustischer Leitwert)* GA *(acoustic conductance)*, TELEKOM *(Anschlußleitung)*

subscriber's line

Al *(Aluminium)* CHEMIE Al *(aluminium)*

Alabasterglas *nt* KER & GLAS alabaster glass

Alanin *nt* CHEMIE alanine

Alantin *nt* CHEMIE alantin, dahlin, helenin, inulin, sinistrin

Alantstärke *f* CHEMIE alant starch, alantin, inulin

Alarm[1] *m* KERNTECH, MASCHINEN, SICHERHEIT alarm

Alarm:[2] **~ auslösen** *vi* SICHERHEIT give the alarm, TELEKOM trigger an alarm; **~ geben** *vi* SICHERHEIT give the alarm

Alarm: **Alarmblinker** *m* SICHERHEIT alarm flashing light; **Alarmdrucker** *m* TELEKOM alarm print-out facility; **Alarmeinstellung** *f* TELEKOM alarm setting; **Alarmglas** *nt* KER & GLAS signal glass; **Alarmglocke** *f* ELEKTRIZ, PAPIER alarm bell, SICHERHEIT alarm bell, warning bell

Alarmierung *f* TELEKOM alerting

Alarm: **Alarmleitung** *f* TELEKOM alarm circuit; **Alarmmeldelampe** *f* TELEKOM alarm indication lamp; **Alarmmelder** *m* GERÄT alarm annunciator; **Alarmmeldesignal** *nt* ELEKTRONIK *Nachrichtenübertragungstechnik* blue signal; **Alarmpatrone** *f* EISENBAHN torpedo; **Alarmrelais** *nt* ELEKTRIZ alarm relay; **Alarmruf** *m* TELEKOM alarm call; **Alarmschalter** *m* GERÄT alarm switch; **Alarmschaltungskarte** *f* TELEKOM alarm card; **Alarmschütz** *nt* ELEKTRIZ alarm relay; **Alarmschwimmer** *m* PAPIER alarm float; **Alarmsicherung** *f* ELEKTRIZ alarm fuse; **Alarmsignal** *nt* EISENBAHN danger signal, KERNTECH alarm, MASCHINEN, WASSERTRANS alarm signal; **Alarmsirene** *f* SICHERHEIT auditory signal; **Alarmsystem** *nt* SICHERHEIT alarm system; **Alarmtafel** *f* LUFTTRANS, SICHERHEIT general warning panel

Alaun *m* CHEMIE, LEBENSMITTEL, PAPIER alum

alaunen *vt* CHEMIE aluminate

Alaunerde *f* CHEMIE alumina

alaunhaltig *adj* CHEMIE aluminiferous

Alban *nt* CHEMIE alban

Albedo *f* CHEMIE pith, RAUMFAHRT albedo

Albit *m* KER & GLAS albite

Albumin *nt* LEBENSMITTEL albumin

albuminartig *adj* CHEMIE albuminoid, albuminous

Albuminat *nt* CHEMIE, LEBENSMITTEL albuminate

Albumin: **Albuminpapier** *nt* DRUCK, PAPIER albumenized paper; **Albuminverfahren** *nt* FOTO albumen process

Albumose *f* LEBENSMITTEL albumose

ALC *abbr* KFZTECH *(automatischer Niveauausgleich)*, RADIO *(automatische Pegelregelung)* ALC *(automatic level control)*

. **Älchen** *nt* LEBENSMITTEL *Phytopathologie* eelworm

Aldehyd *m* CHEMIE, KUNSTSTOFF, LEBENSMITTEL aldehyde

aldehydhaltig *adj* CHEMIE aldehydic

aldehydisch *adj* CHEMIE aldehydic

Aldehydsäure *f* LEBENSMITTEL aldehyde acid

Aldohexose *f* CHEMIE, LEBENSMITTEL aldohexose

Aldol *nt* CHEMIE acetaldol, LEBENSMITTEL aldol

Aldose *f* LEBENSMITTEL aldose

Aldosteron *nt* LEBENSMITTEL aldosterone

aleatorisch[1] *adj* MATH aleatoric, aleatory

aleatorisch:[2] **~e Reihe** *f* MATH aleatory series

Alfapapier *nt* DRUCK esparto paper

Algebra *f* COMP & DV, MATH algebra

algebraisch[1] *adj* MATH algebraic

algebraisch:[2] **~er Ausdruck** *m* MATH algebraic expression; **~e Geometrie** *f* GEOM algebraic geometry; **~e Gleichung** *f* MATH literal equation; **~es Symbol** *nt* MATH algebraic symbol; **~e Zahl** *f* MATH algebraic number; **~es Zeichen** *nt* MATH algebraic symbol

Algen *f pl* MEERSCHMUTZ seaweed

Alginat *nt* KUNSTSTOFF alginate

Alginsäure *f* LEBENSMITTEL alginic acid

Algorithmik *f* COMP & DV algorithmics

algorithmisch[1] *adj* COMP & DV algorithmic

algorithmisch:[2] **~e Sprache** *f* COMP & DV algorithmic language

Algorithmus *m* COMP & DV, ERGON, MATH algorithm

Alhidade *f* EISENBAHN, KFZTECH, LUFTTRANS, TRANS sight rule, WASSERTRANS alidade, index bar, sight rule

Alias *m* COMP & DV alias; **Alias-Effekt** *m* ELEKTRONIK aliasing; **Aliasing-Frequenz** *f* ELEKTRONIK aliased frequency

aliphatisch[1] *adj* CHEMIE acyclic, aliphatic, ERDÖL *Petrochemie* aliphatic

aliphatisch:[2] **~er Kohlenwasserstoff** *m* KUNSTSTOFF aliphatic hydrocarbon; **~es Lösungsmittel** *nt* ERDÖL *Raffinerie* aliphatic solvent; **~es Polyamin** *nt* KUNSTSTOFF aliphatic polyamine; **~es Solvent** *nt* ERDÖL aliphatic solvent

Alitieren *nt* FERTIG aluminizing, calorizing, *Stahl* alitizing

alitieren *vt* FERTIG aluminize, *Stahl* alitize

Alizarinviolett *nt* CHEMIE gallein

Alkali *nt* CHEMIE, ERDÖL *Petrochemie*, KOHLEN, PAPIER, TEXTIL alkali; **Alkali-Akkumulator** *m* PAPIER alkaline accumulator; **Alkalibatterie** *f* FOTO alkaline cell

alkalibeständig[1] *adj* PAPIER alkali-proof

alkalibeständig:[2] **~es Papier** *nt* VERPACK alkali-proof paper

Alkali: **Alkalibeständigkeit** *f* KUNSTSTOFF alkali resistance; **Alkalicellulose** *f* PAPIER alkali cellulose; **Alkaligehalt** *m* CHEMIE alkalinity

alkalihaltig *adj* CHEMIE alkaline

Alkali: **Alkalimesser** *m* LEBENSMITTEL alkalimeter; **Alkalimessung** *f* CHEMIE alkalimetry; **Alkalimetall** *nt* FERTIG, METALL alkali metal; **Alkalimeter** *nt* PAPIER *Laugenmesser* alkalimeter; **Alkalimetrie** *f* CHEMIE alkalimetry

Alkalinität *f* CHEMIE alkalescence, alkalinity

alkalisch[1] *adj* ANSTRICH, CHEMIE, RADIO alkaline

alkalisch:[2] **~er Akkumulator** *m* ELEKTRIZ, ELEKTROTECH alkaline storage battery; **~e Batterie** *f* ELEKTROTECH alkaline battery; **~er Sammler** *m* ELEKTROTECH alkaline storage battery; **~e Zelle** *f* ELEKTROTECH alkaline cell, alkaline storage battery

Alkalisierung *f* CHEMIE alkalization

Alkalität *f* LEBENSMITTEL, UMWELTSCHMUTZ *Laugengrad* alkalinity; **~ vor der Ansäuerung** *f* UMWELTSCHMUTZ preacidification alkalinity

Alkali: **Alkalizelle** *f* FOTO alkaline cell

Alkaloid *nt* CHEMIE alkaloid

Alkan *nt* CHEMIE alkane, methane series, ERDÖL *Petrochemie* alkane

Alkaptonurie *f* CHEMIE alkaptonuria

Alken *nt* CHEMIE alkene, olefin, olefine, ERDÖL *Petrochemie* alkene; **Alken-** *pref* CHEMIE olefinic; **Alkengehalt** *m* CHEMIE olefinic content

Alkine *nt pl* ERDÖL *Petrochemie* alkynes

Alkohol *m* CHEMIE, LEBENSMITTEL alcohol

Alkoholat *nt* CHEMIE, LEBENSMITTEL alcoholate

Alkohol: **Alkoholbrenner** *m* CHEMIE, LEBENSMITTEL

distiller

alkoholisch[1] *adj* CHEMIE, LEBENSMITTEL alcoholic

alkoholisch:[2] **~e Gärung** *f* CHEMIE, LEBENSMITTEL alcoholic fermentation

Alkohol: **Alkoholthermometer** *nt* HEIZ & KÄLTE alcohol thermometer

Alkyd *nt* CHEMIE alkyd, alkyd resin; **Alkydharz** *nt* CHEMIE alkyd, alkyd resin, FERTIG, KUNSTSTOFF alkyd resin

Alkyl *nt* CHEMIE, ERDÖL *Petrochemie* alkyl; **Alkylaromaten** *nt pl* ERDÖL *Petrochemie* alkyl aromatics; **Alkylenimin** *nt* CHEMIE imine

Allanit *m* KERNTECH orthite

Allantoin *nt* CHEMIE allantoin

Alleinflugzeit *f* LUFTTRANS solo time

allelotrop *adj* CHEMIE allelotropic

Allen *nt* CHEMIE allene, propadiene; **~sche Schleifenmethode** *f* ELEKTRIZ *Kabelwiderstandsmessung* Allen's loop test; **~sche Stromschlingenprüfung** *f* ELEKTRIZ *Kabelwiderstandsmessung* Allen's loop test

Alleskleber *m* VERPACK all-purpose adhesive

Alles-oder-Nichts-Reaktion *f* ERGON all-or-none response, all-or-nothing response

Allgeschwindigkeitsquerruder *nt* TRANS all-speed aileron

Allglasfaser *f* ELEKTROTECH all-glass optical fiber (AmE), all-glass optical fibre (BrE), OPTIK all-glass fiber (AmE), all-glass fibre (BrE)

Alligator- *pref* ELEKTRIZ crocodile, MASCHINEN alligator; **Alligatorklemme** *f* ELEKTRIZ crocodile clip; **Alligatorschere** *f* MASCHINEN alligator shears

Allmenge *f* MATH universal set

Allomorphie *f* CHEMIE allotropism

allotriomorph *adj* FERTIG *Kristall* allotriomorphic

Allotropie *f* CHEMIE allotropism, allotropy, FERTIG allotropy

allotropisch *adj* CHEMIE, FERTIG allotropic

Allpaß *m* ELEKTRONIK all-pass filter; **Allpaßfilter** *nt* ELEKTRONIK all-pass filter

Allplastfaser *f* OPTIK all-plastic fiber (AmE), all-plastic fibre (BrE)

Allradantrieb *m* KFZTECH four-wheel drive

Allrichtungsmikrofon *nt* AKUSTIK omnidirectional microphone, AUFNAHME astatic microphone

Allroundterminal *nt* WASSERTRANS multipurpose terminal

allseitig: ~ bearbeitet *adj* MECHAN machined all over

Allstrommotor *m* ELEKTRIZ all-current motor (AmE), all-mains motor (BrE)

All-Tantal-Kondensator *m* ELEKTROTECH all-tantalum capacitor

Allterrain-Reifen *m* KFZTECH town-and-country tire (AmE), town-and-country tyre (BrE)

Alluvialschicht *f* WASSERVERSORG alluvial bed

Alluvium *nt* BAU alluvium, WASSERVERSORG alluvial deposit

Allwellenantenne *f* PHYS multiband antenna

Allwetter- *pref* LUFTTRANS all-weather; **Allwetterflüge** *m pl* LUFTTRANS all-weather operations; **Allwetterhubschrauber** *m* LUFTTRANS all-weather helicopter

Allyl *nt* CHEMIE allyl; **Allylalkohol** *m* CHEMIE allyl alcohol

Allylen *nt* CHEMIE allylene, methylacetylene, propyne

Allylglycidether *m (AGE)* KUNSTSTOFF allyl glycidyl ether *(AGE)*

Allylmethylendioxybenzen *nt* CHEMIE allylmethylenedioxybenzene, safrole

Allzweck- *pref* ELEKTROTECH GP, general-purpose; **Allzweck-Laminat** *nt* ELEKTRONIK general-purpose laminate

Aloebitter *m* CHEMIE aloetic gum, aloin; **Aloebitterstoff** *m* CHEMIE aloetic gum, aloin

ALOHA-Verfahren *nt* TELEKOM ALOHA system; **ALOHA-Zugriffssystem mit festen Zeitschlitzen** *nt* TELEKOM slotted ALOHA system

Aloin *nt* CHEMIE aloin, barbaloin

Alpha *nt* (α) GEOM alpha (α); **Alphaablauf** *m* FERNSEH alpha wrap

α *abbr* AKUSTIK *(Absorptionskoeffizient)* α *(absorption coefficient)*, GEOM *(Alpha)* α *(alpha)*, MECHAN *(Winkelbeschleunigung)* α *(angular acceleration)*, OPTIK *(Absorptionsfaktor)* α *(absorption factor)*, OPTIK *(optischer Drehwinkel)* α *(angle of optical rotation)*, PHYS *(Absorptionskoeffizient)*, RADIO *(Absorptionskoeffizient)*, STRAHLPHYS *(Absorptionskoeffizient)* α *(absorption coefficient)*

Alphabet *nt* COMP & DV alphabet

alphabetisch[1] *adj* COMP & DV alphabetic

alphabetisch:[2] **~er Code** *m* COMP & DV alphabetic code; **~er Schlüssel** *m* COMP & DV alphabetic code

Alpha: **Alpha-Cellulose** *f* PAPIER alpha cellulose

alphageometrisch: ~e Anzeige *f* TELEKOM alphageometric display; **~es Bildschirmgerät** *nt* TELEKOM alphageometric display

Alpha: **Alpha-Ionisierungsgasanalyse** *f* KERNTECH alpha ionization gas analysis; **Alphamosaik-Verfahren** *nt* COMP & DV alphamosaic mode

alphanumerisch[1] *adj* COMP & DV alphanumeric

alphanumerisch:[2] **~e Anzeige** *f* TELEKOM alphanumeric display; **~es Bildschirmgerät** *nt* TELEKOM alphanumeric display; **~er Code** *m* COMP & DV alphanumeric code; **~e Sortierung** *f* COMP & DV alphanumeric sort; **~es Zeichen** *nt* COMP & DV alphanumeric character

Alpha: **Alpha-Profil** *nt* OPTIK alpha profile; **Alpha-Rhythmus** *m* ERGON alpha rhythm; **Alpha-Spektrometrie** *f* PHYS, STRAHLPHYS, TEILPHYS alpha ray spectrometry; **Alpha-Strahlen** *m pl* ELEKTRIZ, OPTIK, PHYS, STRAHLPHYS, TEILPHYS alpha rays; **Alpha-Strahler** *m* KERNTECH, PHYS, STRAHLPHYS, TEILPHYS alpha emitter; **Alpha-Teilchen** *nt* ELEKTRIZ, PHYS, STRAHLPHYS, TEILPHYS alpha particle; **Alpha-Zerfall** *m* KERNTECH, PHYS, STRAHLPHYS, TEILPHYS alpha decay, radioactive transmutation; **Alpha-Zerfallsenergie** *f* PHYS, STRAHLPHYS, TEILPHYS alpha disintegration energy

ALR *abbr (automatische Lautstärkeregelung)* ELEKTROTECH, FERNSEH, MECHAN, RADIO AVC *(automatic volume control)*

Alt- *pref* ABFALL, MASCHINEN waste; **Altablagerung** *f* UMWELTSCHMUTZ old deposit; **Altbackenwerden** *nt* LEBENSMITTEL *Brot* staling; **Altblei** *nt* ABFALL scrap lead

Altern *nt* ANSTRICH curing, BAU *Farbe, Bitumen, Beton* maturing, FERTIG *Leichtmetalle* age hardening

altern[1] *vt* FERTIG *Leichtmetalle* age-harden

altern[2] *vi* ANSTRICH cure, BAU weather, *Farbe, Bitumen, Beton* mature, PAPIER age

Alternativ- *pref* MASCHINEN, TELEKOM alternative

alternativ: ~e Betriebsart *f* ELEKTRONIK alternate mode; **~e Leitweglenkung** *f* TELEKOM alternative routing; **~e Prüfmethode** *f* TELEKOM alternative test method; **~e Verkehrslenkung** *f* TELEKOM alternative routing

Alternativ-: **Alternativmaterial** *nt* MASCHINEN alternative material; **Alternativname** *m* COMP & DV alias

Alternator *m* ELEKTRIZ alternating-current generator, alternator, ELEKTROTECH, PHYS alternator; **Alternatorfeldspannung** *f* ELEKTRIZ alternator field voltage
Alternieren *nt* MASCHINEN alternation
alternierend[1] *adj* ELEKTRIZ *Strom*, MASCHINEN alternating
alternierend:[2] ~**e Bewegung** *f* MASCHINEN alternating motion, alternation of a movement; ~**er Fluß** *m* ELEKTRIZ alternating flux; ~**e Komponente** *f* ELEKTRIZ alternating component; ~**e Reihe** *f* MATH alternating series
Altersbestimmung: ~ **mit Hilfe von Urantochternukliden** *f* KERNTECH dating by uranium daughters; ~ **mittels Radiokohlenstoff** *f* PHYS radiocarbon dating
Altersschwerhörigkeit *f* AKUSTIK presbyacusis
Alterung *f* ELEKTRIZ intentional accelerated component ageing (BrE), intentional accelerated component aging (AmE), intentional component ageing (BrE), intentional component aging (AmE), intentional normal component ageing (BrE), intentional normal component aging (AmE), FERTIG *Leichtmetalle* age hardening, KUNSTSTOFF, LEBENSMITTEL, PAPIER, TELEKOM, VERPACK ageing (BrE), aging (AmE); **Alterungsausfall** *m* KONTROLL wearout failure
alterungsbeständig *adj* VERPACK ageing-resistant (BrE), aging-resistant (AmE)
alterungsfähig *adj* FERTIG *Leichtmetalle* age-hardenable
Alterung: **Alterungsfähigkeit** *f* FERTIG *Leichtmetalle* age hardenability; **Alterungshärtung** *f* ELEKTRIZ intentional accelerated curing, intentional component curing, intentional normal curing; **Alterungstest** *m* VERPACK ageing test (BrE), aging test (AmE); **Alterungsuntersuchung** *f* RAUMFAHRT ageing studies (BrE), aging studies (AmE)
Alt-: **Altfahrzeug** *nt* ABFALL end-of-life vehicle; **Altgerät** *nt* ELEKTRIZ second-hand appliance; **Altglas** *nt* ABFALL waste glass; **Altglasbehälter** *m* ABFALL waste glass container; **Altglascontainer** *m* ABFALL bottle bank; **Altglasscherben** *f pl* KER & GLAS ecology cullet; **Altglasverwertung** *f* ABFALL glass recycling
Altimeter *nt* TRANS altimeter
Alt-: **Altlast** *f* ABFALL problem site, SICHERHEIT pollutant; **Altlastaufarbeitung** *f* UMWELTSCHMUTZ processing of an old site; **Altmaterial** *nt* FERTIG, TEXTIL junk
Altmaterial: **aus** ~ **gewinnen** *vt* UMWELTSCHMUTZ recover
Alt-: **Altmedikamente** *nt pl* ABFALL pharmaceutical waste; **Altmetall** *nt* ABFALL scrap metal
Altocumulus *m* LUFTTRANS *Meteorologie* altocumulus
Alt-: **Altöl** *nt* ABFALL residual oil, UMWELTSCHMUTZ used oil, waste oil; **Altölaufbereitung** *f* ABFALL waste oil preparation; **Altölaufbereitungsbetrieb** *m* ABFALL oil regeneration plant; **Altölgesetz** *nt* ABFALL Waste Oil Act; **Altölrückgewinnung** *f* ABFALL waste oil recovery; **Altölschmierung** *f* MASCHINEN waste oil lubrication; **Altöltank** *m* ABFALL slop tank; **Altölwiederverwertung** *f* ABFALL waste oil recovery
Altostratus *m* LUFTTRANS *Meteorologie* altostratus
Alt-: **Altpapier** *nt* ABFALL, PAPIER waste paper; **Altpapieraufbereitung** *f* ABFALL waste paper preparation; **Altpapierkompressor** *m* ABFALL waste paper compressing press; **Altpapierrecycling** *nt* ABFALL waste paper recycling; **Altpapiersammlung** *f* ABFALL collection of waste paper, paper collection, waste paper collection; **Altreifen** *m* ABFALL scrap tire (AmE), scrap tyre (BrE);

Altsand *m* FERTIG *Gießen* floor sand, used foundry sand
Altweiberknoten *m* WASSERTRANS granny knot
Alufolie *f (Aluminiumfolie)* LEBENSMITTEL aluminium foil (BrE), aluminum foil (AmE)
Alumetieren *nt* FERTIG aluminium coating by spraying (BrE), aluminum coating by spraying (AmE)
Alumetierung *f* FERTIG alumetizing
Aluminat *nt* CHEMIE aluminate
Aluminieren *nt* FERTIG aluminizing
aluminieren *vt* FERTIG aluminium-coat (BrE), aluminum-coat (AmE), aluminium-plate (BrE), aluminum-plate (AmE), aluminize, METALL aluminize, PAPIER aluminate
Aluminierung *f* PAPIER alumination
Aluminisieren *nt* METALL aluminization
aluminisieren *vt* KÜNSTL INT, METALL aluminize
Aluminium *nt (Al)* CHEMIE aluminium (BrE), aluminum (AmE) *(Al)*; **Aluminiumammoniumsulfat** *nt* CHEMIE ammonia alum
aluminiumangereichert[1] *adj* ANSTRICH aluminium-filled (BrE), aluminum-filled (AmE)
aluminiumangereichert:[2] ~**e Chromat-Phosphat-Beschichtung** *f* ANSTRICH aluminium-filled chromate/phosphate coat (BrE), aluminum-filled chromate/phosphate coat (AmE)
Aluminium: **Aluminiumanode** *f* ELEKTROTECH aluminium anode (BrE), aluminum anode (AmE)
aluminiumbehandelt *adj* FERTIG aluminium-killed (BrE), aluminum-killed (AmE)
Aluminium: **Aluminiumblech** *nt* FERTIG aluminium sheet (BrE), aluminum sheet (AmE); **Aluminiumbronze** *f* MECHAN, METALL aluminium bronze (BrE), aluminum bronze (AmE); **Aluminiumdose** *m* VERPACK *Getränke* metal can; **Aluminiumelektrolytkondensator** *m* ELEKTROTECH aluminium electrolytic capacitor (BrE), aluminum electrolytic capacitor (AmE); **Aluminiumfolie** *f* LEBENSMITTEL *(Alufolie)*, METALL aluminium foil (BrE), aluminum foil (AmE); **Aluminiumgatter** *nt* ELEKTRONIK aluminium gate (BrE), aluminum gate (AmE)
aluminiumhaltig[1] *adj* CHEMIE aluminiferous
aluminiumhaltig:[2] ~**er Uranbrennstoff** *m* KERNTECH uranium aluminide fuel
Aluminium: **Aluminiumhülse** *f* KERNTECH *Brennelement* aluminium can (BrE), aluminum can (AmE); **Aluminiumhydroxid** *nt* KUNSTSTOFF aluminium hydroxide (BrE), aluminum hydroxide (AmE); **Aluminium-Keramik** *f* ANSTRICH aluminium ceramic (BrE), aluminum ceramic (AmE); **Aluminiumkondensator mit Festelektrolyt** *m* ELEKTROTECH solid aluminium capacitor (BrE), solid aluminum capacitor (AmE); **Aluminiumlegierung** *f* MASCHINEN aluminium alloy (BrE), aluminum alloy (AmE); **Aluminiumleiter** *m* ELEKTRIZ aluminium conductor (BrE), aluminum conductor (AmE); **Aluminiumlot** *nt* METALL aluminium solder (BrE); **Aluminiummessing** *nt* METALL aluminium brass (BrE), aluminum brass (AmE); **Aluminiumoxid** *nt* CHEMIE, FERTIG alumina, aluminium oxide (BrE), aluminum oxide (AmE), PAPIER alumina; **Aluminiumoxidgehalt** *m* KOHLEN alumina content; **Aluminiumoxidschneide** *f* FERTIG aluminium oxide tool tip (BrE), aluminum oxide tool tip (AmE); **Aluminiumpellet** *nt* KERNTECH aluminium pellet (BrE), aluminum pellet (AmE); **Aluminiumschrott** *m* ABFALL aluminium scrap (BrE), aluminum scrap (AmE); **Alu-**

miniumsilikatfaser *f* HEIZ & KÄLTE aluminium silicate fibre (BrE), aluminum silicate fiber (AmE); **Aluminiumstahl** *m* METALL aluminium steel (BrE), aluminum steel (AmE); **Aluminiumsulfat** *nt* LEBENSMITTEL, PAPIER alum

aluminiumüberzogen: ~es Teflon ® *nt* RAUMFAHRT aluminized Teflon ®

aluminiumverspiegelt: ~er Bildschirm *m* ELEKTRONIK aluminized screen

Alumino- *pref* CHEMIE aluminic, alumino

aluminothermisch[1] *adj* FERTIG aluminothermic

aluminothermisch:[2] **~es Schweißen** *nt* BAU thermit welding, FERTIG *(AT-Schweißen)* aluminothermic welding *(AT welding)*

AM *abbr* AKUSTIK *(akustische Masse)* AM *(acoustic mass)*, AUFNAHME *(Amplitudenmodulation)*, DV *(Amplitudenmodulation)*, ELEKTRIZ *(Amplitudenmodulation)*, ELEKTRONIK *(Amplitudenmodulation)*, FERNSEH *(Amplitudenmodulation)*, PHYS *(Amplitudenmodulation)*, RADIO *(Amplitudenmodulation)*, TELEKOM *(Amplitudenmodulation)*, WELLPHYS *(Amplitudenmodulation)* AM *(amplitude modulation)*

Amalgam *nt* FERTIG, KOHLEN, METALL amalgam; **Amalgamation** *f* FERTIG amalgamation; **Amalgamationsplatte** *f* KOHLEN amalgamation plate; **Amalgamator** *m* MASCHINEN amalgamator; **Amalgambildung** *f* CHEMIE amalgamation, mercurification

amalgamieren *vt* FERTIG, KOHLEN amalgamate

Amalgam: **Amalgamierplatte** *f* METALL amalgamation plate; **Amalgamiertisch** *m* KOHLEN amalgamating table; **Amalgamierung** *f* KOHLEN, METALL amalgamation

Amarin *nt* CHEMIE amarine

Amateur *m* FERNSEH, TELEKOM amateur; **Amateurfunkdienst** *m* TELEKOM amateur radio service; **Amateurfunker** *m* TELEKOM radio amateur; **Amateurfernsehen** *nt* *(ATV)* FERNSEH amateur television *(ATV)*

Amboß *m* FERTIG *Blech* stake, MASCHINEN, MECHAN anvil; **Amboßbett** *nt* MASCHINEN anvil bed; **Amboßblock** *m* MASCHINEN anvil block, block of an anvil; **Amboßeinsatz** *m* FERTIG holdfast; **Amboßhahn** *m* FERTIG anvil pallet face; **Amboßhorn** *nt* MASCHINEN beak iron; **Amboßschlacke** *f* METALL anvil dross; **Amboßvierkantloch** *nt* FERTIG anvil hardie hole, hardie hole

Ambulanzwagen *m* TRANS ambulance

AME *abbr* *(Atommasseneinheit)* KERNTECH AWU *(atomic weight unit)*

Ameisensäure *f* FERTIG *Kunststoffinstallationen,* LEBENSMITTEL *Konservierungstoff* formic acid; **Ameisensäure-** *f* CHEMIE formic; **Ameisensäurealdehyd** *nt* CHEMIE formaldehyde; **Ameisensäureamid** *nt* CHEMIE formamide, methanamide

Amerikanisch: ~er Amateurdachverband *m* *(ARRL)* RADIO American Radio Relay League *(ARRL)*; **~er Atomenergieverband** *m* *(AEC)* KERNTECH Atomic Energy Commission *(AEC)*; **~e Datenübertragungs-Codenorm** *f* *(ASCII)* COMP & DV, DRUCK American Standard Code for Information Interchange *(ASCII)*; **~e Einheit für Drahtmesser** *f* *(AWG)* LABOR American wire gage (AmE), American wire gauge (BrE) *(AWG)*; **~es Erdölinstitut** *nt* *(API)* ERDÖL American Petroleum Institute *(API)*; **~er Fernsehnormungsausschuß** *m* *(NTSC)* FERNSEH National Television Standards Committee *(NTSC)*; **~e Gesellschaft der Maschinenbau-Ingenieure** *f*

(ASME) QUAL American Society of Mechanical Engineers *(ASME)*; **~e Gesellschaft für Werkstoffprüfung** *f* *(ASTM)* MASCHINEN, QUAL American Society for Testing Materials *(ASTM)*; **~er Luft- und Raumfahrtverband** *m* *(AIA)* RAUMFAHRT Aerospace Industries Association *(AIA)*; **~es NPT-Rohrgewinde** *nt* MASCHINEN *Faden* American NPT, American National Pipe Taper

amerikanisch: ~er Bushel *m* LEBENSMITTEL bushel; **~e Holzvolumeneinheit** *f* METROL cord (AmE); **~es Maß** *nt* *(AG)* MASCHINEN *Drahtdurchmesser, Gewinde* American gage (AmE), American gauge (BrE) *(American gage)*; **~e Projektion** *f* FERTIG third angle system

AM-Gang *m* ELEKTRONIK AM response

AMI *abbr* *(bipolare Schrittinversion)* TELEKOM AMI *(alternate mark inversion)*

Amici-Prisma *nt* PHYS Amici prism, direct-vision prism, roof prism

Amid *nt* KUNSTSTOFF amide

amidisch: ~er Härter *m* KUNSTSTOFF amide hardener

Amidogen *nt* CHEMIE amidogen

Amidogruppe *f* CHEMIE amido group

Amidoschwefel *m* CHEMIE *Säure* amido-sulfuric (AmE), amido-sulphuric (BrE), sulfamic (AmE), sulphamic (BrE)

Amin *nt* KUNSTSTOFF amine

Aminierung *f* CHEMIE amination

aminisch: ~ gehärtetes Epoxidharz *nt* KUNSTSTOFF amine cured epoxy; **~er Härter** *m* KUNSTSTOFF amine curing agent

Amino- *pref* CHEMIE amino; **Aminoanisol** *nt* CHEMIE anisidine; **Aminoazo-** *pref* CHEMIE aminoazo; **Aminobenzensulfonamido-Pyridin** *nt* CHEMIE *Pharmazie* aminobenzenesulfamidopyridine (AmE), sulfapyridine (AmE), sulphapyridine (BrE); **Aminobenzol** *nt* CHEMIE aminobenzene, aniline, phenylamine; **Aminocarbonsäure** *f* CHEMIE amino acid; **Aminodimethylbenzol** *nt* CHEMIE aminodimethylbenzene, dimethylaniline; **Aminoessigsäure** *f* LEBENSMITTEL glycine; **Aminoethan** *nt* CHEMIE aminoethane, ethylamine; **Aminoethanol** *nt* CHEMIE ethanolamine; **Aminoharz** *nt* KUNSTSTOFF amino resin; **Aminomethan** *nt* CHEMIE aminomethane, methylamine; **Aminomethanamidin** *nt* CHEMIE guanidine; **Aminonaphthalin** *nt* CHEMIE naphthylamine; **Aminonitrobenzol** *nt* CHEMIE nitroaniline; **Aminophenetol** *nt* CHEMIE ethoxyaniline, phenetidine; **Aminophenolethylether** *m* CHEMIE ethoxyaniline, phenetidine; **Aminophenylmethylether** *m* CHEMIE anisidine; **Aminophenylsulfonamid** *nt* CHEMIE *Pharmazie* sulfanilamide (AmE), sulphanilamide (BrE) **Aminoplast** *m* FERTIG amino-plast, amino-plastic; **Aminopurin** *nt* CHEMIE adenine, aminopurine; **Aminosäure** *f* CHEMIE, LEBENSMITTEL amino acid; **Aminotoluol** *nt* CHEMIE aminotoluene, toluidine

Amin: **Aminoxylen** *nt* CHEMIE xylidine; **Aminoxylol** *nt* CHEMIE dimethylaniline

Ammin *nt* CHEMIE ammine; **Amminverbindung** *f* CHEMIE ammine

Ammonal *nt* CHEMIE ammonal; **Ammonalaun** *m* PAPIER ammonial alum

Ammoniak *nt* CHEMIE, ELEKTRONIK *flüssig*, FERTIG, PAPIER, RAUMFAHRT, UMWELTSCHMUTZ ammonia

ammoniakalisch *adj* CHEMIE ammoniacal

ammoniakhaltig *adj* CHEMIE ammoniacal

Ammoniak: **Ammoniak-Maser** *f* ELEKTRONIK ammonia maser; **Ammoniakwasser** *nt* PAPIER ammonia liquor
Ammonit *nt* CHEMIE ammonia dynamite, ammonite
Ammonium *nt* CHEMIE ammonium; **Ammoniumchlorid** *nt* CHEMIE, LEBENSMITTEL ammonium chloride; **Ammoniumgruppe** *f* CHEMIE ammonium, ammonium radical, ammonium residue; **Ammoniumhexachlorostannat** *nt* CHEMIE ammonium hexachlorostannate; **Ammoniumhydrat** *nt* PAPIER ammonia hydrate; **Ammoniumhydroxid** *nt* ERDÖL *Petrochemie* ammonium hydroxide; **Ammoniumperchlorat** *nt* RAUMFAHRT *Raumschiff* ammonium perchlorate
amorph[1] *adj* ANSTRICH, FERTIG, KOHLEN amorphous
amorph:[2] **~es Gefüge** *nt* KUNSTSTOFF amorphous structure; **~er Halbleiter** *m* ELEKTRONIK amorphous semiconductor; **~e Schicht** *f* ELEKTRONIK amorphous layer; **~es Silizium** *nt* ELEKTRONIK amorphous silicon; **~es Trägermaterial** *nt* ELEKTRONIK amorphous substrate
Ampere *nt* (*A*) ELEKTRIZ, ELEKTROTECH, FERTIG, METROL, PHYS, RADIO ampere (*A*); **~sches Gesetz** *nt* ELEKTRIZ Ampere's law, Ampere's theorem, PHYS Ampere's law; **Ampere-Laplace-Satz** *m* ELEKTRIZ Ampere-Laplace theorem; **Amperemeter** *nt* ELEKTRIZ, ELEKTROTECH ammeter, amperemeter, FERNSEH ammeter, GERÄT ammeter, amperemeter, KFZTECH, LABOR, PHYS, RADIO ammeter; **~sche Molekularströme** *m pl* PHYS amperian currents; **~sche Schwimmerregel** *f* ELEKTRIZ Ampere's rule, amplitude modulation; **Amperesekunde** *f* ELEKTRIZ *Einheit* ampere-second; **Amperestunde** *f* ELEKTRIZ *Einheit der Ladung*, METROL, PHYS ampere-hour; **Amperestundenzähler** *m* GERÄT ampere-hour meter; **Amperewindung** *f* ELEKTRIZ, PHYS ampere-turn; **Amperewindungszahl** *f* ELEKTRIZ ampere-turn; **Amperezahl** *f* ELEKTRIZ, ELEKTROTECH amperage
Amphibien- *pref* WASSERTRANS amphibian; **Amphibienfahrzeug** *nt* WASSERTRANS amphibian vehicle
amphibisch[1] *adj* WASSERTRANS amphibian
amphibisch:[2] **nicht ~es Luftkissenfahrzeug** *nt* WASSERTRANS nonamphibious hovercraft
Amphibolasbest *m* FERTIG amphibole
Amplidyne *f* ELEKTRONIK, ELEKTROTECH amplidyne
Amplitron *nt* ELEKTRONIK, PHYS amplitron
Amplitude *f* (*A*) AKUSTIK, AUFNAHME, COMP & DV, ELEKTRIZ, ELEKTRONIK, PHYS, RADIO, WASSERTRANS *eines Himmelskörpers*, WELLPHYS amplitude (*A*)
amplitudenabhängig: **~e Folgesteuerung** *f* REGELUNG signal amplitude sequencing control
Amplitude: **Amplituden-Amplitudengang** *m* ELEKTRONIK amplitude-amplitude response; **Amplituden-Amplitudengangkurve** *f* ELEKTRONIK amplitude-amplitude response curve; **Amplituden-Amplituden-Verzerrung** *f* ELEKTRONIK amplitude-amplitude distortion; **Amplitudenbegrenzer** *m* ELEKTRONIK amplitude limiter; **Amplitudenbegrenzerschaltung** *f* FERNSEH amplitude limiter circuit; **Amplitudendemodulation** *f* ELEKTRONIK amplitude demodulation; **Amplitudeneichung** *f* ELEKTRONIK amplitude calibration; **Amplitudenentzerrer** *m* TELEKOM amplitude equalizer; **Amplitudenfilter** *nt* ELEKTRONIK amplitude filter; **Amplitudenfrequenzgang** *m* ELEKTRONIK amplitude-frequency response; **Amplitudenfrequenzgangkurve** *f* ELEKTRONIK amplitude-frequency response curve; **Amplitudenfrequenzverzerrung** *f*

ELEKTRONIK, TELEKOM amplitude-frequency distortion; **Amplitudengang** *m* ELEKTRONIK amplitude response; **Amplitudeninformation** *f* ELEKTRONIK amplitude information; **Amplitudenjustierung** *f* ELEKTRONIK amplitude adjustment; **Amplitudenkorrigierung** *f* FERNSEH amplitude corrector; **Amplitudenmodulation** *f* (*AM*) AUFNAHME, COMP & DV, ELEKTRIZ, ELEKTRONIK, FERNSEH, PHYS, RADIO, TELEKOM, WELLPHYS amplitude modulation (*AM*); **Amplitudenmodulationsgang** *m* ELEKTRONIK amplitude modulation response; **Amplitudenmodulationsrauschen** *nt* AUFNAHME, ELEKTRONIK amplitude modulation noise; **Amplitudenmodulationsträger** *m* ELEKTRONIK amplitude modulation carrier; **Amplitudenmodulator** *m* ELEKTRONIK amplitude modulator
amplitudenmoduliert[1] *adj* ELEKTRONIK amplitude-modulated
amplitudenmoduliert:[2] **~es Signal** *nt* ELEKTRONIK amplitude modulation signal; **~er Träger** *m* ELEKTRONIK amplitude-modulated carrier
Amplitude: **Amplitudenraster** *m* ELEKTRONIK amplitude grid; **Amplitudenresonanz** *f* PHYS, WELLPHYS amplitude resonance; **Amplitudenschrift** *f* AKUSTIK variable area recording; **Amplitudenschwelle** *f* ELEKTRONIK amplitude threshold; **Amplitudensieb** *nt* AUFNAHME *Video* clipper; **Amplitudenspektrum** *nt* PHYS, WELLPHYS amplitude spectrum; **Amplitudenspitze** *f* ELEKTRONIK peak amplitude; **Amplitudensteuerung** *f* PHYS, WELLPHYS amplitude control; **Amplitudentastung** *f* TELEKOM amplitude keying; **Amplitudenteilung** *f* PHYS amplitude division; **Amplitudenumtastung** *f* (*ASK*) ELEKTRONIK amplitude-shift keying (*ASK*); **Amplitudenverzerrung** *f* ELEKTRONIK amplitude distortion, amplitude filter, PHYS, TELEKOM, WELLPHYS amplitude distortion; **Amplitudenwahrscheinlichkeitsverteilung** *f* TELEKOM amplitude probability distribution
AM-PM: **~ Übertragungskoeffizient** *m* RAUMFAHRT AM-PM transfer coefficient; **~ Umwandlungskoeffizient** *m* RAUMFAHRT AM-PM conversion coefficient
Ampulle *f* KER & GLAS ampoule (BrE), ampule (AmE), LABOR ampoule (BrE), ampule (AmE), phial (BrE), VERPACK ampoule (BrE), ampule (AmE)
AM-Rauschen *nt* AUFNAHME, ELEKTRONIK AM noise
AMS *abbr* (*aeronautische Werkstoffnorm*) RAUMFAHRT AMS (*aeronautical material standard*)
AM-Signal *nt* ELEKTRONIK AM signal
Amt *nt* TELEKOM exchange; **~ mit Leitungsvermittlung** *nt* TELEKOM circuit-switched exchange; **~ zweiter Ordnung** *nt* TELEKOM secondary center (AmE), secondary centre (BrE)
Ämter: **zwischen ~n** *adj* TELEKOM interoffice; **zwischen ~n verlaufend** *adj* TELEKOM interoffice
amtlich: **nicht ~ geeichte Eigengeschwindigkeit** *f* LUFTTRANS calibrated airspeed; **~ gemessene Tonne** *f* WASSERTRANS measured ton; **~e Güteprüfung** *f* QUAL government inspection; **~er Inspektor** *m* BAU surveyor; **~e Qualitätssicherung** *f* QUAL government quality assurance
AM-Träger *m* ELEKTRONIK AM carrier
amtsberechtigt:[1] **nicht ~** *adj* TELEKOM fully restricted
amtsberechtigt:[2] **nicht ~e Nebenstelle** *f* TELEKOM completely restricted extension
Amt: **Amtsklappenschrank** *m* TELEKOM exchange switchboard; **Amtsleitung** *f* TELEKOM central exchan-

ge trunk (BrE), central office trunk (AmE), exchange line, trunk; **Amtsverbindungsleitung** *f* TELEKOM trunk

amu *abbr (atomare Masseneinheit)* KERNTECH amu *(atomic mass unit)*

Amygdalose *f* CHEMIE amygdalose, gentiobiose, isomaltose

Amyl *nt* PAPIER amyl; **Amylacetat** *nt* KUNSTSTOFF, PAPIER amyl acetate; **Amylalkohol** *m* CHEMIE amyl alcohol, pentanol, pentyl alcohol, PAPIER amyl alcohol

Amylase *f* CHEMIE amylase, diastase

Amylen *nt* CHEMIE amylene, pentene

Amylin *nt* CHEMIE amylin

Amylopektin *nt* TEXTIL amylopectin

an *adj* ELEKTROTECH *Motor* on

An- und Abfuhr *f* TRANS conveying

anachromatisch: **~es Objektiv** *nt* FOTO anachromatic lens

anaerob[1] *adj* ERGON, LEBENSMITTEL anaerobic

anaerob:[2] **~e Faulung** *f* ABFALL anaerobic digestion; **~e Gärung** *f* ABFALL anaerobic digestion, anaerobic fermentation; **~ härtender Klebstoff** *m* KUNSTSTOFF anaerobic adhesive; **~er Teich** *m* ABFALL anaerobic lagoon

Anaerobier *m* LEBENSMITTEL anaerobe

anakustisch: **~e Zone** *f* AUFNAHME anacoustic zone

anallaktisch *adj* OPTIK anallactic

Anallaktismus *m* OPTIK anallactism

Analog- *pref* COMP & DV, ELEKTRONIK, GERÄT analog

analog[1] *adj* COMP & DV analog ELEKTRONIK, RADIO, TELEKOM analog (AmE), analogue (BrE)

analog:[2] **~e Anzeige** *f* GERÄT analog read-out; **~ arbeitendes Meßgerät** *nt* GERÄT analog instrument; **~e Bipolarschaltung** *f* ELEKTRONIK analog bipolar integrated circuit; **~es Filter** *nt* ELEKTRONIK analog filter; **~es Filtern** *nt* ELEKTRONIK analog filtering; **~es Gatter** *nt* ELEKTRONIK analog gate; **~e integrierte Schaltung** *f* ELEKTRONIK analog integrated circuit; **~er Leitungsverstärker** *m* COMP & DV analog line driver; **~e Mietleitung** *f* TELEKOM analog private wire; **~es Schieberegister** *nt* COMP & DV analog shift register; **~es Trägerfrequenzsystem** *nt* COMP & DV analog carrier system; **~er Vergleicher** *m* ELEKTRONIK analog comparator; **~er Vermittlungsprozessor** *m* TELEKOM analog call processor; **~es Vermittlungssystem** *nt* TELEKOM analog switching system; **~e Verzögerungsleitung** *f* FERNSEH analog delay line; **~er Wert** *m* COMP & DV analog quantity

Analog-: **Analog-Amperemeter** *nt* ELEKTROTECH analog ammeter; **Analoganzeige** *f* GERÄT analog read-out; **Analogaufzeichnung** *f* TELEKOM analog recording; **Analogchip** *m* ELEKTRONIK analog chip; **Analogdaten** *nt pl* ELEKTRONIK analog data

Analog-Digital- *pref (A/D)* ELEKTRONIK, FERNSEH, FERTIG analog-digital *(A/D)*; **Analog-Digital-Parallelumsetzer** *m* ELEKTRONIK flash analog-digital converter; **Analog-Digital-Umsetzer** *m (ADU)* COMP & DV analog-digital converter *(ADC)*, ELEKTRONIK, FERNSEH, FERTIG analog-digital converter *(ADC)*; **Analog-Digital-Umsetzerausrüstung** *f* FERTIG analog-digital conversion equipment; **Analog-Digital-Wandler** *m* COMP & DV analog-digital converter, ELEKTRONIK, FERNSEH, FERTIG analog-digital converter; **Analog-Digital-Wandlerausrüstung** *f* FERTIG analog-digital conversion equipment; **Analog-Digital-Wandlung** *f* AUFNAHME analog-digital

conversion, COMP & DV analog-digital conversion, ELEKTRIZ, ELEKTRONIK, FERTIG analog-digital conversion

Analog-: **Analoggerät** *nt* TELEKOM analog device; **Analoginstrument** *nt* GERÄT analog instrument; **Analogkanal** *m* COMP & DV analog channel; **Analogkarte** *f* ELEKTRONIK analog board; **Analogkreis** *m* ELEKTROTECH analog circuit; **Analogleitung** *f* TELEKOM analog circuit; **Analogmenge** *f* COMP & DV analog quantity; **Analogmeßgerät** *nt* ELEKTROTECH analog meter, GERÄT analog instrument, analog measuring instrument; **Analogmeßinstrument** *nt* ELEKTRIZ, METROL analog measuring instrument; **Analogmeßsystem** *nt* COMP & DV analog measuring system; **Analogmodulation** *f* ELEKTRONIK, PHYS analog modulation; **Analogrechner** *m* COMP & DV analog computer; **Analogrechner für Netzabgleich** *m (ACNA)* COMP & DV analog computer for net adjustment *(ACNA)*; **Analogrechnung** *f* COMP & DV analog calculation; **Analogschaltung** *f* ELEKTRONIK, TELEKOM analog circuit; **Analogschnittstelle** *f* TELEKOM analog interface; **Analogschreiber** *m* GERÄT analog data recorder; **Analogsignal** *nt* COMP & DV analog signal, ELEKTRONIK, PHYS, TELEKOM analog signal; **Analogsignalgenerator** *m* ELEKTRONIK analog signal generator; **Analogsignalverarbeitung** *f* ELEKTRONIK analog signal processing; **Analogspannungsmeßgerät** *nt* ELEKTROTECH analog voltmeter; **Analogstellglied** *nt* ELEKTROTECH analog actuator; **Analogstromkreis** *m* ELEKTROTECH equivalent circuit; **Analogstrommesser** *m* ELEKTROTECH analog ammeter; **Analogsystem** *nt* TELEKOM analog system; **Analogübertragung** *f* TELEKOM analog transmission; **Analogverbindung** *f* TELEKOM analog circuit; **Analogvoltmeter** *nt* ELEKTROTECH analog voltmeter; **Analogwert** *m* COMP & DV analog quantity; **Analogwertschreiber** *m* GERÄT analog data recorder

Analysator *m* COMP & DV, ELEKTRIZ, ELEKTRONIK, METALL, PHYS, TELEKOM analyser (BrE), analyzer (AmE); **~ für Einschwingungsvorgänge** *m* ELEKTRONIK *Netzwerke* transient network analyser (BrE), transient network analyzer (AmE); **Analysatorschaltung** *f* ELEKTRONIK analyser circuit (BrE), analyzer circuit (AmE)

Analyse *f* ANSTRICH, KÜNSTL INT *von Bildern*, MASCHINEN, TEXTIL, WASSERVERSORG analysis; **~ von Einschwingvorgängen** *f* ELEKTRONIK transient analysis; **Analyseausrüstung** *f* LABOR analytical kit; **Analyseautomat** *m* GERÄT autoanalyser (BrE), autoanalyzer (AmE); **Analysefehler** *m* KOHLEN analysis error; **Analysegerät** *nt* GERÄT analytical instrument, TELEKOM analyser (BrE), analyzer (AmE); **Analysemeßeinrichtung** *f* GERÄT analysis measuring equipment; **Analysemeßgerät** *nt* GERÄT analyser (BrE), analyzer (AmE), analytical instrument; **Analysemessung** *f* GERÄT analytical measurement; **Analyseprobe** *f* KOHLEN, QUAL analysis sample; **Analysewaage** *f* GERÄT analytical balance, LABOR chemical balance, PHYS analytical balance

Analysis *f* MATH calculus

analytisch: **~e Geometrie** *f* GEOM, MATH analytical geometry; **~e Mechanik** *f* MECHAN, PHYS analytical mechanics

anamorphotisch: **~es Verfahren** *nt* TELEKOM anamorphosis

Anastigmat *m* FOTO, PHYS anastigmat

anastigmatisch: ~e Einschlaglupe *f* FERTIG anastigmatic folding magnifier; ~es **Objektiv** *nt* FOTO anastigmatic lens

Anastigmatlinse *f* FOTO anastigmat lens, anastigmatic lens

anatomisch:[1] ~ gestaltet *adj* FERTIG *Kunststoffinstallationen* contoured

anatomisch:[2] ~e Achsen *f pl* ERGON anatomical axes

Anattofarbstoff *m* LEBENSMITTEL anatto, bixin

An-/Ausschalter *m* ELEKTROTECH on-off switch

anbändseln *vt* WASSERTRANS seize

Anbau *m* BAU *Gebäude* extension

anbauen *vt* WASSERTRANS *Schiffteile* fit

Anbau: **Anbaurakete** *f* RAUMFAHRT *Raumschiff* kick rocket; **Anbauteil** *nt* MASCHINEN attaching part

Anbieten *nt* TELEKOM offer

anbieten *vt* BAU tender

anbinden *vt* AUFNAHME lace up

Anblaskühlung *f* HEIZ & KÄLTE air blast cooling

Anblaswinkel *m* PHYS angle of attack

Anblatten *nt* FERTIG halving

anblatten *vt* BAU, FERTIG halve

Anbohren *nt* MASCHINEN spot drilling

anbohren *vt* BAU tap

Anbohrer *m* FERTIG, MASCHINEN spotting drill

Anbohrschelle *f* FERTIG *Kunststoffinstallationen* tapping saddle, tapping tee

Anbohrung *f* FERTIG dimple, MASCHINEN dimpled hole

Anbordnahme *f* WASSERTRANS shipping, *Ladung* boarding

Anböschung *f* ABFALL ramp landfill, slope landfill, slope method

anbringen *vt* BAU fix, COMP & DV mount, MASCHINEN attach

ANC *abbr* (*Luftfahrt-Navigationsausschuß*) LUFTTRANS ICAO (*International Civil Aviation Organization*)

andämmen *vt* BAU bank up

andauernd: ~er Fehler *m* COMP & DV hard error

anderes: ~ in Frage kommenden Funkzonen *f pl* TELEKOM candidate cells

ändern *vt* COMP & DV modify, MASCHINEN amend

Anderson: ~sche Meßbrücke *f* ELEKTRIZ Anderson Bridge

Änderung *f* AKUSTIK alteration, MASCHINEN, PATENT amendment, QUAL change; ~ der Betrachtungsweise *f* COMP & DV viewing transformation; ~ der Induktanz *f* ELEKTRIZ self-inductance variation; **Änderungsanweisung** *f* COMP & DV update statement; **Änderungsdatei** *f* COMP & DV amendment file, change file, movement file, transaction file; **Änderungsnachweis** *m* QUAL record of changes; **Änderungssatz** *m* COMP & DV amendment record, change record; **Änderungsvermerk** *m* KONSTZEICH modification note; **Änderungsverzeichnis** *nt* QUAL table of revision; **Änderungszustand** *m* KONSTZEICH modification status

Andock- *pref* RAUMFAHRT docking

Andocken *nt* RAUMFAHRT *Raumschiff* docking

andocken *vi* RAUMFAHRT *Raumschiff* dock

Andock-: **Andocköffnung** *f* RAUMFAHRT docking port; **Andockzwischenstück** *nt* RAUMFAHRT docking piece

Andrehkurbel *f* MASCHINEN starting handle

Andruck *m* AUFNAHME, FOTO pressure

Andrückdeckel *m* VERPACK snap cap

Andrucke *m pl* DRUCK press proofs

Andrücketikette *f* VERPACK self-adhesive label

Andruck: **Andruckfenster** *nt* FOTO pressure gate; **Andruckplatte** *f* FOTO pressure plate; **Andruckrolle** *f* AUFNAHME pressure roller, FERNSEH tape roller; **Andruckwalze** *f* KER & GLAS backup roll

aneinanderfügen *vt* MASCHINEN join

Anelastizität *f* PHYS anelasticity

Anemometer *nt* GERÄT, LABOR anemometer, LUFTTRANS impeller, NICHTFOSS ENERG, PAPIER, WASSERTRANS anemometer

anemometrisch *adj* PAPIER anemometric

Anerkennung *f* QUAL approval

Aneroidbarometer *nt* GERÄT bellows gage (AmE), bellows gauge (BrE), LABOR, PHYS aneroid barometer

Anethol *nt* CHEMIE anethole

Aneurin *nt* CHEMIE aneurin, thiamin

Anfahrbrenner *m* KER & GLAS start-up burner

Anfahren *nt* KER & GLAS starting, MASCHINEN start-up, starting; ~ mit reduzierter Spannung *nt* ELEKTRIZ partial voltage starting

anfahren *vti* COMP & DV start, KONTROLL, MASCHINEN start, start up

Anfahrtransformator *m* ELEKTROTECH starting transformer

Anfahrvorgang *m* MASCHINEN start-up procedure

Anfall *m* FERTIG yield; ~ von Abfällen *m* ABFALL waste formation, waste production, waste stream

anfällig *adj* ANSTRICH prone

Anfang: ~ der Nachricht *m* (*SOM*) COMP & DV start of message (*SOM*)

anfangen[1] *vt* COMP & DV start

anfangen[2] *vi* COMP & DV log in, log on, sign on, start

anfänglich: ~e Rißausbreitung *f* KERNTECH initial crack growth; ~e Rückspannung *f* ELEKTRIZ initial inverse voltage; ~e Überschußreaktivität *f* KERNTECH built-in reactivity

Anfangs- *pref* COMP & DV, LUFTTRANS initial; **Anfangsadresse** *f* COMP & DV initial address; **Anfangsanflug** *m* LUFTTRANS initial approach; **Anfangsanweisung** *f* COMP & DV header statement; **Anfangsbeladung mit spaltbarem Material** *f* KERNTECH initial fissile charge; **Anfangsbestand** *m* QUAL initials; **Anfangsbit** *nt* COMP & DV start bit; **Anfangsbruttogewicht** *nt* LUFTTRANS initial gross weight; **Anfangsdruck** *m* MASCHINEN initial pressure; **Anfangsempfindlichkeit** *f* GERÄT minimum scale sensitivity; **Anfangsfehler** *m* COMP & DV initial error; **Anfangsflugbahn** *f* LUFTTRANS initial approach path; **Anfangsflugposition** *f* LUFTTRANS initial approach fix; **Anfangsgeschwindigkeit** *f* RAUMFAHRT initial velocity; **Anfangskapazität** *f* ELEKTRIZ initial capacity; **Anfangskennsatz** *m* COMP & DV header label; **Anfangskrängungswinkel** *m* WASSERTRANS *Schiffkonstruktion* angle of loll; **Anfangskritikalität** *f* KERNTECH initial criticality; **Anfangsladung** *f* LUFTTRANS initial forming charge; **Anfangsmagnetisierung** *f* PHYS initial magnetization curve; **Anfangsmodus** *m* RAUMFAHRT *Raumschiff* fundamental mode; **Anfangssetzung** *f* KOHLEN initial settlement; **Anfangsspannung** *f* MASCHINEN initial tension; **Anfangsstabilität** *f* WASSERTRANS *Schiffbau* initial stability; **Anfangsstadium** *nt* METALL initial stage; **Anfangsstatus** *m* COMP & DV initial state; **Anfangsstrom** *m* ELEKTRIZ, ELEKTROTECH initial current; **Anfangstemperatur** *f* HEIZ & KÄLTE initial temperature; **Anfangstest ohne Last** *m* KERNTECH start-up zero power test; **Anfangsvorzündung** *f* LUFTTRANS initial advance

Anfärben *nt* TEXTIL dyeing

anfärben *vt* TEXTIL dye
Anfärbung *f* TEXTIL dyeing
anfasen *vt* MASCHINEN chamfer
Anfaswerkzeug *nt* MASCHINEN chamfering tool
Anfertigung: ~ **von Probedrucken** *f* DRUCK proof printing
Anfeuchten *nt* PAPIER dampening; ~ **des Gemenges** *nt* KER & GLAS batch wetting; ~ **von Ton** *nt* KER & GLAS clay wetting
anfeuchten *vt* BAU damp, dampen, moisten, temper, wet, *Sand* temper, FERTIG *Sand* temper, LEBENSMITTEL, THERMOD moisten
Anfeuchter *m* FERTIG damper, PAPIER moistener
Anflanschen *nt* MASCHINEN flanging, flanging-on
anflanschen *vt* MASCHINEN flange
anfliegen *vi* KOHLEN settle
Anflug *m* LUFTTRANS approach; ~ **auf Startbahnende** *m* LUFTTRANS approach end of runway; ~ **ohne Verfahrenskurve** *m* LUFTTRANS straight-in approach; **Anflugbahn** *f* LUFTTRANS approach path; **Anflugbefeuerung** *f* LUFTTRANS approach lighting system; **Anflugende der Landebahn** *nt* LUFTTRANS approach end of runway; **Anflugfeuer** *nt* LUFTTRANS homing beacon; **Anflugfolge** *f* LUFTTRANS approach sequence; **Anflugfreigabe** *f* LUFTTRANS approach clearance; **Anflugführung** *f* RAUMFAHRT approach guidance; **Anflugführungssender** *m* LUFTTRANS radio homing beacon; **Anflugfunkfeuer** *nt* LUFTTRANS homing beacon, radio marker; **Anfluggeschwindigkeit** *f* LUFTTRANS, RAUMFAHRT approach speed; **Anfluggleitwinkel** *m* LUFTTRANS approach path; **Anflugkontrolldienst** *m* LUFTTRANS approach control service; **Anflugkontrolle** *f* LUFTTRANS approach control; **Anflugkontrollstelle** *f* LUFTTRANS approach control office; **Anflugkontrollstufe** *f* LUFTTRANS approach control rating; **Anfluglärmmeßpunkt** *m* LUFTTRANS approach noise measurement point; **Anflugleitstrahl** *m* LUFTTRANS approach light beacon; **Anflugnavigationskarte** *f* LUFTTRANS approach chart; **Anflugphase** *f* LUFTTRANS approach phase; **Anflugposition** *f* LUFTTRANS approach fix; **Anflugpräzisionsradarstufe** *f* LUFTTRANS approach surveillance radar rating; **Anflugradar** *m (ACR)* RAUMFAHRT approach control radar *(ACR)*; **Anflugradaranlage** *f* RADIO radar approach control equipment; **Anflugradareinstufung** *f* LUFTTRANS approach radar rating; **Anflugradarstufe** *f* LUFTTRANS approach radar rating, precision radar rating; **Anflugschneise** *f* LUFTTRANS landing lane; **Anflugstraße** *f* RAUMFAHRT *Raumschiff* descent path; **Anflugüberwachungsradareinstufung** *f* LUFTTRANS approach surveillance radar rating; **Anflugverfahren** *nt* RAUMFAHRT approach procedure; **Anflugzeit** *f* LUFTTRANS approach time
anfordern *vt* COMP & DV query, request
Anforderung *f* COMP & DV demand, enquiry, query, request; ~ **nach Datentransfer** *f* TELEKOM data transfer request; **Anforderungskanal** *m* RAUMFAHRT *Weltraumfunk* request channel; **Anforderungsstapel** *m* COMP & DV request stack; **Anforderungszuverlässigkeit** *f* QUAL demand reliability
Anfrage *f* COMP & DV inquiry, request
Anfressen: **vor** ~ **schützend** *adj* MECHAN antiseize
anfressen *vt* FERTIG pit
Angabenliste *f* COMP & DV option list
angeben *vt* COMP & DV identify

angeblasen: ~**e Klappe** *f* LUFTTRANS *Grenzschichtsteuerung* blown flap
Angebot *nt* MECHAN bid
angeboten: ~**e Belegung** *f* TELEKOM offered call
Angebotsbürgschaft *f* BAU bid bond
angefacht: ~**e aperiodische Seitenbewegung** *f* LUFTTRANS lateral divergence
angeflanscht *adj* MECHAN flanged
angefressen *adj* FERTIG pitted
angegeben: ~**e Flugbahn** *f* LUFTTRANS indicated flight path
angegossen[1] *adj* MECHAN integrally cast
angegossen:[2] ~**er Steckverbinder** *m* ELEKTROTECH one-piece connector
angehren *vt* FERTIG miter (AmE), mitre (BrE)
angeklammert: ~**e Halterung** *f* VERPACK clip-on carrier
angekoppelt: ~**e Stromkreise** *m pl* ELEKTROTECH coupled circuits
angekräuselt: ~**es Garn** *nt* TEXTIL abraded yarn
Angel *f* FERTIG *Gattersäge* buckle, MASCHINEN fang, tang, MECHAN hinge
angelaufen *adj* BAU struck
angelegt: ~**e Druckgradienten** *m pl* STRÖMPHYS *Strömungen* imposed pressure gradients; ~**e EMK** *f* PHYS applied emf; ~**e Spannung** *f* ELEKTRIZ impressed voltage
angelenkt[1] *adj* MECHAN articulated
angelenkt:[2] ~**e Hinterkantenklappe** *f* LUFTTRANS trailing edge flap; ~**er Strahl** *m* FERNSEH deflected beam
Angel: **Angelwurzel** *f* FERTIG heel, *Feile* shoulder
angemacht *adj* LEBENSMITTEL *Salat* dressed
angenähert: ~**er Knotenpunkt** *m* AKUSTIK partial node
angenommen: ~**er Schiffsort** *m* WASSERTRANS *Navigation* estimated position
angepaßt[1] *adj* PHYS matched
angepaßt:[2] ~**es Filter** *nt* ELEKTRONIK matched filter; ~**es Filtern** *nt* ELEKTRONIK matched filtering; ~**e Impedanz** *f* ELEKTROTECH matched impedance; ~**e Last** *f* ELEKTROTECH, PHYS matched load; ~**er Mantel** *m* TELEKOM matched cladding; ~**er Scheinwiderstand** *m* ELEKTROTECH matched impedance; ~**e Ummantelung** *f* OPTIK matched cladding; ~**er Wellenleiter** *m* ELEKTROTECH matched waveguide; ~**e Widerstände** *m pl* ELEKTROTECH matched resistors
angeregt[1] *adj* KERNTECH *Atomkern, Molekül* excited
angeregt:[2] ~**es Atom** *nt* KERNTECH excited atom; ~**er Zustand** *m* KERNTECH excited state
angereichert[1] *adj* LEBENSMITTEL fortified
angereichert:[2] ~**er Brennstoff** *m* KERNTECH enriched fuel; ~**er Kernbrennstoff** *m* KERNTECH enriched nuclear fuel; ~**es Material** *nt* STRAHLPHYS enriched material; ~**er Reaktor** *m* KERNTECH enriched reactor; ~**es Uran** *nt* STRAHLPHYS enriched uranium; **nicht** ~**es Uran** *nt* KERNTECH unenriched uranium
angerieben: ~**es Garn** *nt* TEXTIL abraded yarn
angesäuert[1] *adj* CHEMIE acidulous, sourish
angesäuert:[2] ~**e Bodenfläche** *f* UMWELTSCHMUTZ acidic area
angeschlämmt *adj* ANSTRICH slurried
angeschliffen: ~**er Grat** *m* FERTIG shoulder
angeschlossen: **nicht** ~ *adj* TELEKOM off-line
angeschuht: ~**e Stange** *f* BAU shoed bar
angesetzt: ~**es Holz** *nt* BAU pieced wood
angestoßen: ~**es Atom** *nt* KERNTECH knocked-on atom; ~**es Teilchen** *nt* KERNTECH knock-on
angetrieben: ~**es Element** *nt* MASCHINEN driven ele-

ment; ~**es Rad** *nt* MASCHINEN driven wheel; ~**e Scheibe** *f* MASCHINEN follower; ~**e Spindel** *f* FERTIG *Schraubenpumpe* idler impeller; ~**e Welle** *f* MASCHINEN driven shaft; ~**es Werkzeug** *nt* MECHAN power tool; ~**es Zahnrad** *nt* MASCHINEN follower

angewandt: ~**e Mathematik** *f* MATH applied mathematics; ~**e Thermodynamik** *f* MASCHINEN applied thermodynamics

angezapft: ~**er Fluß** *m* WASSERVERSORG beheaded river

angezeigt[1] *adj* MASCHINEN indicated

angezeigt:[2] ~**er Anstellwinkel** *m* LUFTTRANS *Hubschrauber* indicated pitch angle; ~**e Eigengeschwindigkeit** *f* LUFTTRANS indicated airspeed; ~**e Fluggeschwindigkeit** *f* LUFTTRANS IAS, indicated airspeed; ~**er Meßwert** *m* GERÄT indicated value, reading; ~**er Steigungswinkel** *m* LUFTTRANS *Hubschrauber* indicated pitch angle; ~**er Wert** *m* GERÄT reading, KERNTECH indicated value

Angießkanal *m* KUNSTSTOFF feed

angleichen *vt* BAU match

Angleichung *f* REGELUNG *Regelgrößen* adaptation

angreifend *adj* FERTIG *Kraft* active

Angrenzen *nt* GEOM adjacency, *zweier Seiten* adjacency

angrenzen *vt* BAU abut

angrenzend[1] *adj* COMP & DV contiguous, GEOM adjacent

angrenzend:[2] ~**e Dateien** *f pl* COMP & DV contiguous files; ~**e Winkel** *m pl* GEOM contiguous angles

Angriff *m* KOHLEN attack; **Angriffspunkt** *m* MASCHINEN contact point

Angström *nt* (*Å*) METROL angstrom (*Å*); **Angström-Einheit** *f* LEBENSMITTEL angstrom unit

Anguß *m* KUNSTSTOFF gate, sprue, MASCHINEN sprue; **Angußbuchse** *f* MASCHINEN feed bush, sprue bush; **Angußdruckstift** *m* MASCHINEN sprue ejector pin; **Angußfarbe** *f* KER & GLAS colored clay (AmE), coloured clay (BrE); **Angußkanal** *m* FERTIG *Plaste* runner; **Angußkegel** *m* KUNSTSTOFF feed

angußlos: ~**e Form** *f* MASCHINEN runnerless mold (AmE), runnerless mould (BrE)

Anguß: Angußöffnung *f* KUNSTSTOFF gate, sprue opening; **Angußzieher** *m* MASCHINEN sprue puller

Anhall *m* AKUSTIK attack

Anhalten *nt* NICHTFOSS ENERG stall, TEXTIL stop

anhalten *vti* COMP & DV hold, stop, TEXTIL stop

Anhaltestift *m* EISENBAHN catch pin

Anhaltleistung *f* (*S*) KERNTECH stopping power (*S*)

Anhang *m* DRUCK appendix

Anhängelast *f* TRANS trailing load

anhängen *vt* DRUCK run on, MASCHINEN attach

Anhänger *m* BAU, EISENBAHN bogie (BrE), trailer (AmE), KFZTECH bogie (BrE), lorry (BrE), trailer (AmE), truck (AmE), trail car, TEXTIL tag, TRANS trailer wagon, VERPACK hangtag, label; **Anhängerbremse** *f* KFZTECH trailer brake

Anhängsel *nt* VERPACK swing ticket

Anhäufung *f* BAU aggregate

Anhebeeinrichtung *f* FERTIG *Räumen* elevator

Anheben *nt* SICHERHEIT lifting

anheben *vt* BAU hoist, FERTIG jack, MECHAN lift

Anhebeschlitten *m* FERTIG broach-handling slide, *Räumen* elevating slide

Anhebung *f* BAU elevation

Anheizen *nt* EISENBAHN preheating

anheizen *vt* THERMOD heat up

Anheizklappe *f* HEIZ & KÄLTE start-up flap

anholen *vt* WASSERTRANS *Tauwerk* haul

Anholtau *nt* WASSERTRANS *Tauwerk* messenger

Anhub *m* KERNTECH lift; **Anhubstange** *f* MECHAN push rod

Anhydrid *nt* CHEMIE, PAPIER anhydride

anhydridisch: ~**e Härter** *m* KUNSTSTOFF anhydride hardener

anhydrisch *adj* ERDÖL *Mineral* anhydrous

Anhydrit *nt* ERDÖL *Mineral* anhydrite, LEBENSMITTEL calcium sulfate (AmE), calcium sulphate (BrE)

Anilin *nt* CHEMIE aminobenzene, aniline, phenylamine, PAPIER aniline; **Anilinfarbe** *f* DRUCK aniline ink; **Anilinfarbstoff** *m* CHEMIE aniline color (AmE), aniline colour (BrE), coal-tar dye, FOTO aniline dye; **Anilinformaldehydharz** *nt* FERTIG aniline formaldehyde resin, aniline resin; **Anilingummidruck** *m* DRUCK aniline rubber-plate printing; **Anilinharz** *nt* FERTIG aniline formaldehyde resin, aniline resin; **Anilinpunkt** *m* KUNSTSTOFF aniline point

Anion *nt* ELEKTRIZ, ELEKTROTECH, ERDÖL, KOHLEN, LEBENSMITTEL, PHYS, STRAHLPHYS anion; **Anionenaustauscher** *m* KOHLEN anion exchanger

anionisch *adj* KOHLEN anionic

Anionotropie *f* CHEMIE anionotropy

Anisaldehyd *nt* CHEMIE anisaldehyde, methoxybenzaldehyde

anisentropisch *adj* THERMOD anisentropic

Anisidin *nt* CHEMIE anisidine

anisochron[1] *adj* COMP & DV anisochronous

anisochron:[2] ~**e Übertragung** *f* COMP & DV anisochronous transmission

anisoelastisch[1] *adj* RAUMFAHRT *Gyroskop* anisoelastic

anisoelastisch:[2] ~**e Verschiebung** *f* RAUMFAHRT *Gyroskop* anisoelastic drift

Anisoelastizitätsfaktor *m* RAUMFAHRT *Gyroskop* anisoelasticity factor

Anisol *nt* CHEMIE anisole, methoxybenzene, LEBENSMITTEL anisole

anisotherm *adj* CHEMIE athermal

anisotrop *adj* KUNSTSTOFF, MECHAN, OPTIK, TELEKOM anisotropic

Anisotropie *f* FERTIG directionality, KUNSTSTOFF anisotropy; ~ **der Turbulenz** *f* STRÖMPHYS anisotropy of turbulence

Anker:[1] **vor dem** ~ **aufgedreht** *adj* WASSERTRANS *Festmachen des Schiffes* wind-rode

Anker[2] *m* COMP & DV member set, ELEKTRIZ, ELEKTROTECH *Dynamo, Wechselstromgenerator* armature, FERTIG stay, tie rod, *Gießen* belt, *Magnet* keeper, MECHAN anchor, guy, PHYS armature, WASSERTRANS anchor; ~ **mit geschlossenen Nuten** *m* ELEKTRIZ closed slot armature; **vor** ~ **treibendes Schiff** *nt* WASSERTRANS dragging ship

Anker:[3] **vor** ~ **legen** *vt* WASSERTRANS anchor, *des Schiffes* bring up to anchor

Anker:[4] **den** ~ **fallen lassen** *vi* WASSERTRANS *Festmachen* cast anchor, drop anchor; **vor** ~ **gehen** *vi* WASSERTRANS anchor; ~ **vom Grund lösen** *vi* WASSERTRANS trip anchor; ~ **lichten** *vi* WASSERTRANS weigh anchor; **vor** ~ **liegen** *vi* WASSERTRANS ride at anchor, *Festmachen* lie at anchor; ~ **schlippen** *vi* WASSERTRANS trip anchor; **vor** ~ **treiben** *vi* WASSERTRANS *Festmachen* drag the anchor; ~ **über Grund schleifen** *vi* WASSERTRANS club

Anker: Ankerarm *m* WASSERTRANS anchor arm; **Ankerblechpaket** *nt* ELEKTRIZ armature core; **Ankerblindwiderstand** *f* ELEKTRIZ armature reactance; **Ankerboje** *f* MEERSCHMUTZ mooring buoy, WASSERTRANS anchor buoy; **Ankerbolzen** *m* BAU lag screw, rockbolt, MASCHINEN tie bolt, MECHAN anchor bolt, tie rod; **Ankerbuchse** *f* ELEKTRIZ armature spider; **Ankerdeck** *nt* WASSERTRANS *Schiff* anchor deck; **Ankereisen** *nt* BAU *Klammer* tie bar, *Werksteinarbeiten* T-cramp, ELEKTROTECH armature iron; **Ankerfeld** *nt* ELEKTRIZ armature field; **Ankerflügel** *m* WASSERTRANS anchor fluke; **Ankerflügelspitze** *f* WASSERTRANS anchor bill; **Ankerflunke** *f* WASSERTRANS anchor fluke, *Festmachen* fluke; **Ankerfußschuh** *m* LABOR *Mikroskop* horseshoe foot; **Ankergegenwirkung** *f* ELEKTRIZ, ELEKTROTECH armature reaction

ankergegenwirkungserregt: ~e **Maschine** *f* ELEKTRIZ armature-reaction-excited machine

Anker: **Ankergehäuse** *nt* ELEKTROTECH armature casing; **Ankergeschirr** *nt* WASSERTRANS *Festmachen* ground tackle

ankergesteuert: ~er **Motor** *m* ELEKTRIZ armature-controlled motor

Anker: **Ankergrund** *m* WASSERTRANS anchoring ground; **Ankerhals** *m* WASSERTRANS anchor crown; **Ankerhand** *f* WASSERTRANS *Festmachen* fluke; **Ankerhub** *m* FERTIG escapement; **Ankerinduktion** *f* ELEKTRIZ armature induction; **Ankerkern** *m* ELEKTRIZ, ELEKTROTECH armature core; **Ankerkette** *f* WASSERTRANS anchor chain, cable, chain cable, *Festmachen* cable chain; **Ankerkettenbefestigung** *f* WASSERTRANS anchor cable attachment; **Ankerkettenschlipper** *m* WASSERTRANS *Decksausrüstung* senhouse slip; **Ankerklüse** *f* WASSERTRANS *Schiffbau* hawse pipe; **Ankerkreis** *m* ELEKTRIZ armature circuit; **Ankerkrone** *f* WASSERTRANS anchor crown; **Ankerlaterne** *f* WASSERTRANS *Signal* anchor light, riding light; **Ankerleiter** *m* ELEKTRIZ armature conductor; **Ankerlicht** *nt* WASSERTRANS *Signal* anchor light, riding light

ankern[1] *vt* WASSERTRANS anchor

ankern[2] *vi* WASSERTRANS drop anchor

Anker: **Ankerpeilung** *f* WASSERTRANS anchor bearing; **Ankerplatte** *f* BAU anchoring plate, *Spannbeton* bearing plate, FERTIG foundation plate, KOHLEN anchor plate; **Ankerplatz** *m* WASSERTRANS anchorage; **Ankerprüfgerät** *nt* ELEKTRIZ armature tester; **Ankerreaktanz** *f* ELEKTRIZ armature reactance; **Ankerregelung** *f* ELEKTRIZ armature control; **Ankerrelais** *nt* ELEKTROTECH armature relay; **Ankerring** *m* WASSERTRANS anchor ring; **Ankerrückwirkung** *f* ELEKTRIZ, ELEKTROTECH armature reaction; **Ankerrückwirkungsausgleich** *m* ELEKTROTECH armature reaction compensation; **Ankersäule** *f* KER & GLAS buckstay; **Ankerschall** *m* AKUSTIK reference sound; **Ankerschallbeschleunigung** *f* AKUSTIK reference sound acceleration; **Ankerschild** *m* ELEKTRIZ armature end plate; **Ankerschildanschlüsse** *m pl* ELEKTRIZ armature end connections; **Ankerschildklemmen** *f pl* ELEKTRIZ armature end connections; **Ankerschraube** *f* BAU anchor bolt, lag screw, MASCHINEN anchor bolt; **Ankerschraubenrohr** *nt* FERTIG anchor bolt tube; **Ankerspule** *f* ELEKTRIZ armature winding, ELEKTROTECH armature coil; **Ankerstab** *m* BAU anchor bar, stay rod, ELEKTRIZ, ELEKTROTECH armature bar, KOHLEN anchor rod; **Ankerstange** *f* ELEKTRIZ armature bar, LUFTTRANS *Hubschrauber* dog bone, tie bar; **Ankerstern** *m* ELEKTRIZ, ELEKTROTECH armature spider; **Ankerstich** *m* WASSERTRANS *Festmachen* cable clinch, *Knoten* clinch

Ankerstich: mit ~ **befestigen** *vt* WASSERTRANS *Tauwerk* clinch

Anker: **Ankerstock** *m* WASSERTRANS anchor stock; **Ankerstrom** *m* ELEKTRIZ, ELEKTROTECH armature current; **Ankertasche** *f* WASSERTRANS anchor pocket; **Ankervorrichtung** *f* BAU anchorage; **Ankerwelle** *f* ELEKTRIZ armature shaft; **Ankerwicklung** *f* ELEKTRIZ armature coil, armature winding, ELEKTROTECH armature winding; **Ankerwiderstand** *m* ELEKTRIZ, ELEKTROTECH armature resistance; **Ankerwinde** *f* BAU windlass, MECHAN capstan, WASSERTRANS *Deckausrüstung* windlass; **Ankerwulst** *m* WASSERTRANS anchor boss; **Ankerzahn** *m* ELEKTRIZ armature tooth; **Ankerzweig** *m* ELEKTROTECH path

anklammern *vt* MASCHINEN cramp, VERPACK clip to

Anklang *m* AKUSTIK concord

ankleben *vt* FERTIG freeze

Anklopf- *pref* TELEKOM call waiting; **Anklopfanzeige** *f* TELEKOM call waiting indication; **Anklopfzeichen** *nt* TELEKOM call waiting signal

ankochen *vt* LEBENSMITTEL parboil

ankommend[1] *adj* TELEKOM incoming

ankommend:[2] ~er **Anruf** *m* TELEKOM incoming call; ~es **Bündel** *nt* TELEKOM incoming group; ~e **Fernleitung** *f* TELEKOM incoming trunk circuit; ~e **Leitung** *f* TELEKOM incoming circuit, incoming line; ~er **Ruf** *m* TELEKOM *Signal* incoming call; ~es **Signal** *nt* ELEKTRONIK incoming signal; ~er **Verkehr** *m* TELEKOM incoming traffic, TRANS incoming traffic (AmE), inward traffic (BrE)

ankommend:[3] ~e **Anrufe gesperrt** *phr* TELEKOM ICB, incoming-calls-barred; ~er **Zugang verhindert** *phr* TELEKOM *Benutzerservice* ICB, incoming-calls-barred

Ankoppelschaltung *f* GERÄT coupling network

Ankoppelung *f* ELEKTROTECH coupling; **Ankoppelungsführung** *f* LUFTTRANS docking guidance system; **Ankoppelungsverlust** *m* OPTIK coupling loss; **Ankoppelungswirkungsgrad** *m* OPTIK coupling efficiency

Ankörnen *nt* FERTIG marking, punching

ankörnen *vt* FERTIG mark

Ankörner *m* MASCHINEN center punch (AmE), centre punch (BrE), prick punch, punch, MECHAN center punch (AmE), centre punch (BrE)

Ankörnmaschine *f* MASCHINEN centering machine (AmE), centring machine (BrE)

Ankörnung *f* FERTIG mark

Ankreis *m* FERTIG, GEOM escribed circle

Ankündigungssignal *nt* EISENBAHN distant caution signal, distant signal

Ankunftsflughafen *m* LUFTTRANS airport of arrival

Ankuppeln *nt* KFZTECH hitching

ankuppeln *vt* EISENBAHN couple, hook, KFZTECH hitch, hook, MASCHINEN attach

ankurbeln *vt* FERTIG, LUFTTRANS crank

Anlage *f* BAU equipment, plant, set, COMP & DV station (BrE), DRUCK lay, FERTIG *Werkstückaufspannung* abutting piece, block, MASCHINEN installation, unit, MECHAN layout, TELEKOM installation, *Gerät* system; ~ **zur Flugerprobung** *f* LUFTTRANS flying test bench; ~ **zur Schwefelrückgewinnung** *f* ABFALL sulfur recovery plant (AmE), sulphur recovery plant (BrE); ~ **zur Trennung von Uranisotopen** *f* KERNTECH uranium isotope separation plant; **Anlagenbau** *m* FERTIG *Kunststoffinstallationen* plant manufacturing; **Anlagenberechtigung** *f* TELEKOM installation barring level; **Anlagenleistung** *f* KERNTECH unit output; **Anla-**

gentechnik *f* COMP & DV systems engineering

anlagern *vt* FERTIG age

Anlagerung *f* FERTIG ageing (BrE), aging (AmE)

Anlandung *f* WASSERVERSORG alluvial deposit

Anlaß- *pref* ELEKTRIZ starting, LUFTTRANS primer, MASCHINEN starting, METALL tempering; **Anlaßbad** *nt* METALL tempering bath; **Anlaßdrehmoment** *nt* MASCHINEN starting torque; **Anlaßeinrichtung** *f* ELEKTRIZ starting device; **Anlaßeinspritzpumpe** *f* LUFTTRANS primer pump

Anlassen *nt* COMP & DV start, FERTIG *Wärmebehandlung von Stahl* drawing, temper, LUFTTRANS *Kolbenmotor* cranking

anlassen *vt* FERTIG temper, *Stahl* draw, LUFTTRANS crank, MASCHINEN start, start up, METALL temper

Anlasser *m* ELEKTRIZ starter, ELEKTROTECH motor starter, starter, KFZTECH, KONTROLL starter, MASCHINEN starter motor, starting motor; **~ mit Verzögerung** *m* ELEKTRIZ time delay starter; **Anlasserantriebseinheit** *f* KFZTECH starter drive assembly; **Anlasserbatterie** *f* ELEKTRIZ, ELEKTROTECH starter battery; **Anlasserdüse** *f* KFZTECH starter jet; **Anlasserelektrode** *f* ELEKTROTECH starter electrode; **Anlasserfeldspule** *f* KFZTECH starter field coil; **Anlasserfeldwicklung** *f* KFZTECH starter field winding; **Anlasserkabel** *nt* KFZTECH starter cable; **Anlasserknopf** *m* KFZTECH starter button; **Anlasserkohlebürste** *f* KFZTECH starter brush; **Anlasserkollektor** *m* KFZTECH starter commutator; **Anlasserkurbel** *f* KFZTECH starting crank, LUFTTRANS crank switch; **Anlassermotor** *m* ELEKTROTECH, KFZTECH starter motor; **Anlasserpolschuh** *m* KFZTECH starter pole shoe; **Anlasserrheostat** *m* ELEKTRIZ starting rheostat; **Anlasserritzel** *nt* KFZTECH drive pinion, *Motor* starter motor pinion, MASCHINEN starting gear; **Anlasserritzelwelle** *f* KFZTECH drive pinion shaft; **Anlasserschalter** *m* ELEKTRIZ starter; **Anlasserschleifring** *m* KFZTECH starter collector ring, starter slip ring; **Anlasserstarterzug** *m* KFZTECH starter control; **Anlasserzahnkranz** *m* KFZTECH *Motor* starter ring gear

Anlaß-: **Anlaßfarbe** *f* METALL tempering color (AmE), tempering colour (BrE); **Anlaßhebel** *m* MASCHINEN starting handle, starting lever; **Anlaßkondensator** *m* ELEKTRIZ starting capacitor; **Anlaßkraftstoffdüse** *f* KFZTECH starting jet; **Anlaßmotor** *m* ELEKTRIZ starting motor, KFZTECH starter; **Anlaßofen** *m* METALL tempering furnace; **Anlaßprobe** *f* METALL temper test; **Anlaßschalter** *m* ELEKTROTECH starter; **Anlaßschaltung** *f* TELEKOM start-up circuit; **Anlaßspartransformator** *m* ELEKTRIZ autotransformer starter; **Anlaßsprödigkeit** *f* METALL temper brittleness; **Anlaßspule** *f* KFZTECH booster coil; **Anlaßumschalter** *m* ELEKTRIZ starting changeover switch; **Anlaßwiderstand** *m* ELEKTRIZ starting rheostat; **Anlaßzahnkranz** *m* KFZTECH *Motor* flywheel starter ring gear

Anlauf *m* MASCHINEN starting; **Anlaufdrehmoment** *nt* FERTIG starting torque, *Kunststoffinstallationen* starting torque, HEIZ & KÄLTE starting torque

Anlaufen *nt* KUNSTSTOFF blushing, MASCHINEN start-up

anlaufen:[1] **~ lassen** *vt* MASCHINEN start, start up

anlaufen[2] *vi* FERTIG *Metallflächen* tarnish, KONTROLL start up

Anlauf-: **Anlaufflanke** *f* FERTIG *Kurve* lifting flank; **Anlaufhafen** *m* WASSERTRANS port of call; **Anlaufkupplung** *f* MASCHINEN centrifugal clutch; **An-**

laufmoment *nt* HEIZ & KÄLTE starting torque; **Anlaufprozedur** *f* COMP & DV initialization; **Anlaufreibung** *f* MASCHINEN starting friction; **Anlaufscheibe** *f* MASCHINEN thrust washer; **Anlaufstrom** *m* HEIZ & KÄLTE starting current; **Anlaufwert** *m* REGELUNG *einer Strecke* reaction value, transition value; **Anlaufzeit** *f* COMP & DV rise time, start time, MASCHINEN response time, PAPIER start-up

Anlege- *pref* WASSERTRANS docking, landing; **Anlegebrücke** *f* BAU jetty, WASSERTRANS landing pier; **Anlegekante** *f* DRUCK lay edge; **Anlegemanöver** *nt* WASSERTRANS *Hafen* docking maneuver (AmE), docking manoeuvre (BrE)

Anlegen: ~ an die Wand *nt* STRÖMPHYS wall attachment

anlegen[1] *vt* COMP & DV create, ELEKTROTECH *Spannung*, FERTIG *Spannung* feed

anlegen[2] *vi* WASSERTRANS berth, land

Anlege-: **Anlegeplatte** *f* DRUCK feed board; **Anlegeplatz** *m* WASSERTRANS landing place, landing; **Anlegesteg** *m* WASSERTRANS jetty, *Hafen* pier; **Anlegestelle** *f* WASSERTRANS landing place; **Anlegethermometer** *nt* GERÄT contact thermometer, surface temperature sensor; **Anlegewinkel** *m* METROL square; **Anlegewinkelmesser** *m* METROL bevel protractor

Anleimen *nt* VERPACK sizing

Anleimmaschine *f* VERPACK gluing machine

Anlieferungszustand *m* QUAL as-received condition

anliegend[1] *adj* GEOM adjacent

anliegend:[2] **~e Seiten** *f pl* GEOM adjacent sides; **~e Wirbel** *m pl* STRÖMPHYS attached eddies

Anliegestrich *m* LUFTTRANS *Kompaß* lubber's line

anlösen *vt* FERTIG *Plaste* bite

Anmachen *nt* BAU mixing

anmachen *vt* BAU temper, *Beton* mix, *Mörtel* temper

Anmelden *nt* COMP & DV login, logon

anmelden[1] *vt* MECHAN *zum Patent* apply for

anmelden[2] *vi* COMP & DV log in, log on, sign on

anmelden:[3] **sich ~** *v refl* COMP & DV *in einem System* log in, log on

Anmelder *m* PATENT applicant

Anmeldetag *m* PATENT date of filing, date of registration

Anmeldung[1] *f* PATENT application

Anmeldung:[2] **~ einreichen** *vi* PATENT file an application

Anmeldung:[3] **~ ist anhängig** *phr* PATENT application is pending

Anmerkung *f* COMP & DV annotation

annähern *vt* KONTROLL approximate

Annäherung *f* WASSERTRANS approach; **~ auf geringsten Abstand** *f* WASSERTRANS *Navigation* closest approach; **Annäherungsbahn** *f* RAUMFAHRT rendezvous trajectory; **Annäherungsgeschwindigkeit** *f* TRANS approach speed, WASSERTRANS *Navigation* closing speed; **Annäherungslog** *nt* ERDÖL proximity log; **Annäherungsradar** *m* RAUMFAHRT rendezvous radar; **Annäherungsschalter** *m* GERÄT approximating pickup; **Annäherungssensor** *m* GERÄT proximity sensor; **Annäherungsverfahren** *nt* RAUMFAHRT rendezvous procedure; **Annäherungsverschluß** *m* LUFTTRANS approach locking

Annahme *f* MECHAN, QUAL acceptance; **~ von Langadressen** *f* TELEKOM long-address acceptance; **Annahme- und Rückweisungskriterien** *nt pl* QUAL acceptance and rejection criteria; **Annahmekennlinie** *f* QUAL operating characteristic curve; **Annahmeprüfprotokoll** *nt* QUAL inspection certificate;

Annahmeprüfung *f* GERÄT acceptance inspection, QUAL acceptance test; **Annahmestichprobenplan** *m* QUAL acceptance sampling plan; **Annahmestichprobenprüfung** *f* QUAL acceptance sampling inspection

annahmetauglich *adj* QUAL acceptable

Annahme: **Annahmetauglichkeit** *f* QUAL acceptability; **Annahmeverfahren** *nt* QUAL acceptance procedure; **Annahmezahl** *f* QUAL acceptance number

annässen *vt* BAU wet

Annattofarbstoff *m* LEBENSMITTEL annatto

annehmbar: **~e Qualitätsgrenzlage** *f* *(AQL)* QUAL acceptable quality level *(AQL)*; **~e Qualitätslage** *f* *(AQL)* QUAL acceptable quality level *(AQL)*

Annehmbarkeitsnachweis *m* QUAL evidence of acceptability

annehmen *vt* QUAL accept

Annihilation *f* TEILPHYS annihilation

Annonce *f* *(cf Anzeige)* DRUCK advertisement

Anode *f* ELEKTROTECH drain, *Elektroplattierung, Galvanisierung* plate, ELEKTROTECH, FERNSEH, PHYS, RADIO, WASSERTRANS *Elektrik* anode; **Anodenbasisschaltung** *f* ELEKTROTECH cathode follower; **Anodenbasisverstärker** *m* ELEKTROTECH cathode follower; **Anodenkennlinie** *f* ELEKTROTECH anode characteristic; **Anodenkreis** *m* ELEKTROTECH anode circuit, plate circuit; **Anodenmodulation** *f* ELEKTRONIK anode modulation; **Anodensättigung** *f* ELEKTROTECH anode saturation; **Anodenspannung** *f* ELEKTROTECH anode voltage; **Anodenstrahlen** *m pl* ELEKTROTECH, STRAHLPHYS anode rays; **Anodenstrom** *m* ELEKTROTECH anode current

anodisch[1] *adj* ELEKTRIZ anodic

anodisch:[2] **~es Polieren** *nt* METALL electropolishing

Anodisieren *nt* METALL anodizing

anodisieren *vt* CHEMIE anodize

anomal: **~e Dispersion** *f* PHYS anomalous dispersion; **~er Zeeman-Effekt** *m* PHYS anomalous Zeeman effect

Anomalie *f* THERMOD *des Wassers* anomaly

anordnen *vt* BAU locate, COMP & DV order, set-up, ELEKTROTECH locate

Anordnung *f* COMP & DV array, layout, setup, ELEKTRIZ layout, ELEKTROTECH arrangement, grouping, MASCHINEN arrangement, layout, MECHAN layout, TELEKOM array; **Anordnungszeichnung** *f* KONSTZEICH arrangement drawing

anorganisch[1] *adj* ANSTRICH anorganic, inorganic

anorganisch:[2] **~er Flüssigkeitslaser** *m* ELEKTRONIK inorganic liquid laser

anormal: **~e Struktur** *f* METALL abnormal structure

Anorthit *m* KER & GLAS anorthite

Anpassen: **~ einer Kurve** *nt* MATH *an gegebene Datenwerte* curve fitting

anpassen[1] *vt* FERNSEH match, MECHAN adjust, RADIO match, RAUMFAHRT adapt

anpassen:[2] **sich ~** *v refl* RAUMFAHRT *den Weltraumbedingungen* adapt

Anpaßglied *nt* ELEKTROTECH pad

Anpassung *f* ERGON adaptation, adjustment, HEIZ & KÄLTE acclimatization, METROL, RADIO adjustment; **Anpassungsdämpfung** *f* ELEKTRONIK matching attenuation

anpassungsfähig[1] *adj* KÜNSTL INT *Programm, System* adaptive, MECHAN adjustable

anpassungsfähig:[2] **~es System** *nt* COMP & DV adaptive system

Anpassung: **Anpassungsfähigkeit** *f* WASSERTRANS flexibility; **Anpassungsimpedanz** *f* RADIO matching impedance; **Anpassungssteuerung mit Optimierung** *f* *(ACO)* LABOR adaptive control optimization *(ACO)*; **Anpassungstransformator** *m* ELEKTRIZ matching transformer, ELEKTROTECH impedance matching transformer; **Anpassungsunterbrechung** *f* FERNSEH match cut; **Anpassungsverfall** *m* FERNSEH match dissolve; **Anpassungsverstärker** *m* ELEKTRONIK matching amplifier

anpeilen *vt* WASSERTRANS *Schiff, Seezeichen* locate

ANPN-System *nt* TRANS *Brennstoff-Oktanzahl* Army Navy Performance Number System

Anprall *m* CHEMIE impingement

Anpreßdruck *m* MASCHINEN contact pressure; **~ des Stromabnehmers** *m* EISENBAHN pantograph pressure

Anquellen *nt* TEXTIL swelling

anquellen *vi* TEXTIL swell

Anrauhen *nt* BAU deadening

Anregelzeit *f* COMP & DV rise time

anregen *vt* MECHAN actuate, PHYS actuate, energize

Anregung *f* AKUSTIK incitation, ELEKTRIZ, KERNTECH excitation, STRAHLPHYS excitation, *Atomkern, Atom* energization, TELEKOM excitation; **Anregungsenergie** *f* KERNTECH, STRAHLPHYS excitation energy; **Anregungsfunktion** *f* KERNTECH, STRAHLPHYS excitation function; **Anregungspegel** *m* AKUSTIK critical band level; **Anregungsquelle** *f* KERNTECH, STRAHLPHYS excitation source; **Anregungszustand** *m* METALL excited state

Anreichern *nt* KOHLEN enrichment

anreichern *vt* CHEMTECH concentrate, KOHLEN, LEBENSMITTEL enrich

Anreicherung *f* ELEKTRONIK, KOHLEN enrichment, LEBENSMITTEL enrichment, fortification, PHYS *von Uran* enrichment, TELEKOM *Halbleiter* enhancement; **~ mit Leuchtstoff** *f* ELEKTRONIK phosphorus doping; **~ mit Sauerstoff** *f* CHEMIE aeration; **Anreicherungsabfall** *m* KERNTECH enrichment tails; **Anreicherungsanlage mit Ultrazentrifuge** *f* KERNTECH ultracentrifuge enrichment plant; **Anreicherungsbecken** *nt* ABFALL infiltration basin; **Anreicherungs-Isolierschicht-Feldeffekttransistor** *m* ELEKTRONIK enhancement-mode FET; **Anreicherungstyp** *m* ELEKTRONIK enhancement mode

Anreiß- *pref* BAU plotting, FERTIG marking

Anreißen *nt* ELEKTRONIK *mit Lasern* scribing, FERTIG layout, marking, KUNSTSTOFF tear initiation

anreißen *vt* BAU plot, score, scribe, FERTIG mark, snap, whitewash

Anreißer *m* ELEKTRONIK *mit Lasern*, MASCHINEN scriber

Anreiß-: **Anreißkasten** *m* FERTIG box angle plate; **Anreißkörner** *nt pl* FERTIG prick punch; **Anreißplatte** *f* MASCHINEN marking-out table, surface plate, MECHAN surface plate; **Anreißschritt** *m* ELEKTRONIK *mit Lasern* scribing step

Anreiz *m* ERGON incentive, TELEKOM *eines Kontrollverfahrens* event

Anreizen *nt* COMP & DV start

Anreizverarbeitung *f* TELEKOM event processing

Anriß *m* FERTIG initial cracking, *Dauerbruchzone* incipient crack, KERNTECH, LUFTTRANS incipient crack, MECHAN cracking, flaw

Anruf *m* TELEKOM call, ringing, telephone call; **~ in Warteschleife** *m* TELEKOM call queue; **Anrufbeantworter** *m* TELEKOM answering machine

anrufen[1] *vt* COMP & DV poll

anrufen² *vti* TELEKOM make a call, ring

Anrufer *m* TELEKOM caller

Anruf: **Anrufglocke** *f* ELEKTROTECH call bell; **Anrufmelder** *m* TELEKOM pager; **Anrufsignal** *nt* TELEKOM calling signal; **Anrufsperreinrichtung** *f* TELEKOM call barring equipment; **Anrufsucher** *m* ELEKTRONIK, TELEKOM line finder; **Anruftaste** *f* ELEKTROTECH *elektrische Klingel* call button; **Anrufumleiter** *m* TELEKOM call diverter; **Anrufumleitung** *f* TELEKOM call diversion; **Anrufverarbeitung** *f* TELEKOM call processing; **Anrufversuch** *m* TELEKOM call attempt; **Anrufversuche zur Hauptverkehrsstunde** *m pl* TELEKOM BHCA, busy hour call attempts; **Anrufverteiler** *m* TELEKOM call distributor; **Anrufwarteschleife** *f* TELEKOM call hold; **Anrufweiterschaltung** *f* TELEKOM call transfer, terminal call forwarding

Anrundung *f* FERTIG initial curvature

Ansage *f* LUFTTRANS PA, public address, TELEKOM announcement; **Ansageanlage** *f* LUFTTRANS PA system, public address system; **Ansagemaschine** *f* TELEKOM announcement machine, recorded announcement machine

Ansammlung *f* ELEKTROTECH *Elektronen, Strom* collection

Ansatz *m* BAU deposit, FERTIG lug, KFZTECH neck, KUNSTSTOFF mix, MASCHINEN lug, nose, shoulder, MECHAN batch, neck; **Ansatzbohrung** *f* FERTIG hole with shoulder, stepped hole; **Ansatzdrehen** *nt* FERTIG shoulder turning; **Ansatzflansch** *m* MASCHINEN neck flange; **Ansatzrahmen** *m* KFZTECH *Karosserie* stub frame

Ansatzrohr: mit ~ *adj* MASCHINEN tubulated

Ansatz: **Ansatzsäge** *f* BAU tenon saw; **Ansatzstück** *nt* FERTIG lateral

ansäuerbar *adj* CHEMIE acidifiable

ansäuern *vt* ANSTRICH, CHEMIE acidify, LEBENSMITTEL acidify, acidulate, PAPIER, TEXTIL, UMWELTSCHMUTZ acidify

ansäuernd *adj* UMWELTSCHMUTZ acidifying

Ansäuerung *f* UMWELTSCHMUTZ acidification

Ansaug- *pref* HYDRAUL suction, KOHLEN inlet; **Ansaugbehälter** *m* HYDRAUL suction tank; **Ansaugdruck** *m* KOHLEN inlet pressure, MASCHINEN inlet pressure, intake pressure

Ansaugen *nt* ELEKTROTECH *von Elektronen, Gasen* absorption, HEIZ & KÄLTE suction, KFZTECH *Luft-Kraftstoff-Gemisch* inlet, MECHAN intake, suction; **Ansaugenlassen** *nt* MASCHINEN, WASSERVERSORG *Pumpe* priming

ansaugen *vt* FERTIG prime, *Vorschub* take, HEIZ & KÄLTE aspirate; **~ lassen** *vt* WASSERVERSORG *Pumpe* prime

Ansaug-: **Ansauggrube** *f* ERDÖL suction pit; **Ansaughöhe** *f* HEIZ & KÄLTE suction head; **Ansaughub** *m* KFZTECH induction stroke; **Ansaugkanal** *m* KFZTECH inlet port; **Ansaugkrümmer** *m* KFZTECH *Motor* induction manifold, inlet manifold, LUFTTRANS *Motor, Triebwerk* intake manifold; **Ansaugleistung** *f* HEIZ & KÄLTE suction capacity; **Ansaugluftkammer** *f* LUFTTRANS plenum chamber; **Ansaugmenge** *f* MASCHINEN intake capacity; **Ansaugöffnung** *f* LUFTTRANS *Motor, Triebwerk* intake; **Ansaugpumpe** *f* HYDRAUL suction pump; **Ansaugring am Flugzeugrumpf** *m* LUFTTRANS nacelle intake ring; **Ansaugrohr** *nt* HYDRAUL induction pipe, KFZTECH suction pipe, *Motor* induction manifold, LUFTTRANS *Triebwerk* intake manifold, WASSERTRANS suction pipe, WASSERVERSORG *Pumpe*

priming pipe; **Ansaugschlitz** *m* KFZTECH *Motor* port; **Ansaugseite** *f* MASCHINEN intake side; **Ansaugspinne** *f* KFZTECH *Motor* induction manifold; **Ansaugstutzen** *m* MASCHINEN inlet manifold; **Ansaugtank** *m* HYDRAUL suction tank

Ansaugung *f* KFZTECH induction, MASCHINEN indraught, intake, suction, PAPIER aspiration, suction

Ansaug-: **Ansaugventil** *nt* FERTIG intake valve, HEIZ & KÄLTE, HYDRAUL suction valve, MASCHINEN priming valve

anschäkeln *vt* WASSERTRANS shackle on

Anschaltekoppler *m* TELEKOM access matrix

Anschalten *nt* ELEKTROTECH *Stromversorgung* turn-on, *Übergang in den An-Zustand* turn-on

anschalten *vt* ELEKTROTECH power up, *Stromversorgung* turn on

Anschellen *nt* MECHAN clamping

Anschlag *m* AKUSTIK attack, BAU back stop, stop, *Fenster, Tür* rabbet, FERTIG cupping operation, *Kunststoffinstallationen* end stop, KFZTECH stop, MASCHINEN end stop, stop, MECHAN dog, lug, snubber, stop; **Anschlagbolzen** *m* FERTIG T-slot bolt, MASCHINEN trip dog; **Anschlagbund** *m* MASCHINEN stop collar; **Anschlagdrehen** *nt* FERTIG tripping

anschlagdrehen *vt* FERTIG trip

anschlagen *vt* COMP & DV *Taste* hit, WASSERTRANS bend, WASSERVERSORG meet

anschlagfrei: ~er Drucker *m* COMP & DV *Laserdrucker* nonimpact printer

Anschlag: **Anschlagplatte** *f* FERTIG *Kunststoffinstallationen* stop plate; **Anschlagschleifen** *nt* FERTIG shoulder grinding; **Anschlagschraube** *f* FOTO stop screw; **Anschlagstift** *m* FERTIG pilot, FOTO stop pin; **Anschlagwinkel** *m* MASCHINEN try square

anschleifen *vi* KER & GLAS start a cut

Anschließbarkeit *f* TELEKOM connectivity

anschließen *vt* BAU connect, COMP & DV attach, connect, ELEKTROTECH connect, connect up, plug in, *Komponenten* connect, TELEKOM connect, connect up, plug in

Anschluß *m* BAU connection, joint, COMP & DV attachment, connector, input port, port, DRUCK port, EISENBAHN junction, ELEKTRIZ connection, ELEKTROTECH contact, *von Stromleitern* connection, FERTIG connection, *Kunststoffinstallationen* coupling, TELEKOM port, *Ausrüstung* access, *Telefon* line; **~ zum Grundtarif** *m* TELEKOM BRA, basic rate access; **~ integrierter Schaltungen** *m* ELEKTROTECH integrated-circuit connection; **~ der Saugleitung** *m* FERTIG *Pumpe* inlet; **Anschlußbewehrungsstab** *m* BAU starter bar; **Anschlußbuchse** *f* COMP & DV connector, port, ELEKTRIZ *Anhängerwagen*, ELEKTROTECH connector socket; **Anschlußchip** *m* ELEKTRONIK companion chip; **Anschlußdose** *f* ELEKTROTECH connection box, jack, HEIZ & KÄLTE junction box; **Anschlußdraht** *m* ELEKTRONIK lead, ELEKTROTECH pigtail; **Anschlußeinheit** *f* COMP & DV interface unit; **Anschlußerweiterung** *f* COMP & DV terminal extension; **Anschlußfaser** *f* TELEKOM optical fiber pigtail (AmE), optical fibre pigtail (BrE), *Lichtwellenleiter* pigtail; **Anschlußfeld** *nt* ELEKTROTECH pad; **Anschlußflansch** *m* MASCHINEN connecting flange, MECHAN, PHYS coupling flange; **Anschlußfleck** *m* ELEKTRONIK metallisiert* bonding pad; **Anschlußgas** *nt* ERDÖL *Förderung* connection gas; **Anschlußgerät** *nt* COMP & DV peripheral equipment, peripheral, peripheral unit;

Anschlußgleis *nt* BAU siding; **Anschlußhahn** *m* BAU union cock; **Anschlußkabel** *nt* ELEKTROTECH connecting cable; **Anschlußkasten** *m* ELEKTRIZ joint box (BrE), traveling waveguide (AmE), junction box, terminal box; **Anschlußklemme** *f* ELEKTRIZ connecting terminal, ELEKTROTECH binding post, terminal, KFZTECH terminal, TELEKOM block terminal; **Anschlußkontaktstelle** *f* KONTROLL terminal pad; **Anschlußleiste** *f* ELEKTROTECH terminal block, TELEKOM connection strip; **Anschlußleitung** *f* ELEKTROTECH connecting lead, service line, TELEKOM subscriber's line; **Anschlußlinie** *f* EISENBAHN branch line, feeder line; **Anschlußlitze** *f* KERNTECH pigtail; **Anschlußmaß** *nt* FERTIG mounting dimension, MASCHINEN connecting dimension, fitting dimension, mating dimension; **Anschlußmodul** *nt* COMP & DV input/output switching module; **Anschlußmöglichkeit** *f* TELEKOM connectivity; **Anschlußplatte** *f* ELEKTROTECH socket board; **Anschlußpunkt** *m* ELEKTROTECH junction point; **Anschlußspannung** *f* GERÄT connection voltage; **Anschlußspeicher** *m* TELEKOM subscriber's store; **Anschlußstecker** *m* COMP & DV connector, ELEKTRIZ coupler connector; **Anschlußstelle** *f* BAU *Autobahn* interchange (AmE), junction (BrE), COMP & DV port, EISENBAHN rail junction point; **Anschlußstift** *m* KONTROLL terminal pin; **Anschlußstück** *nt* BAU nipple, union, ELEKTROTECH connector, coupling, MECHAN gooseneck; **Anschluß-Stutzen** *m* FERTIG *Kunststoffinstallationen* spigot; **Anschlußteil** *nt* ELEKTROTECH, RADIO *Stecker* connector; **Anschlußverriegelung** *f* FERNSEH slavelock; **Anschlußweiche** *f* EISENBAHN junction points; **Anschlußwert** *m* FERTIG input power; **Anschlußwiderstand** *m* ELEKTROTECH ferrule resistor; **Anschlußwinkel** *m* BAU angle bracket; **Anschlußzug** *m* EISENBAHN connecting train, feeder train

Anschnitt *m* FERTIG chamfer edge, ingate, *Plaste* gate, KUNSTSTOFF gate; **Anschnittstechnik** *f* FERTIG gating; **Anschnittwinkel** *m* FERTIG *Spiralbohrer* angle of chamfer

Anschrägen *nt* FERTIG *Kunststoffinstallationen* chamfer

Anschrauben *nt* MASCHINEN bolting, screwing

anschrauben *vt* MASCHINEN screw

anschreiben *vt* FERTIG escribe

anschütten *vt* BAU bank up, slope

Anschüttung *f* KOHLEN backfill

Anschwänzen *nt* CHEMIE *Brauwesen* sparging

Anschweiß- *pref* MASCHINEN weld-on; **Anschweißmutter** *f* MASCHINEN weld nut, welding nut

anschwellen[1] *vt* BAU belly out

anschwellen[2] *vi* BAU bulge, PHYS swell

Anschwemmung *f* BAU alluviation

ansenken *vt* MASCHINEN spot-face, MECHAN countersink

Ansetzen: ~ **von Bädern** *nt* FOTO making-up of baths

Anspannung *f* FERTIG stretch

Ansprache *f* AKUSTIK designation

Ansprech- *pref* AUFNAHME, ELEKTRIZ, ELEKTROTECH, GERÄT, TELEKOM threshold; **Ansprecheigenschaft** *f* FERNSEH response characteristic; **Ansprechempfindlichkeit** *f* AUFNAHME, ELEKTROTECH sensitivity, OPTIK, TELEKOM responsiveness; **Ansprechgrenze** *f* ELEKTRONIK threshold, GERÄT threshold limit; **Ansprechleistung** *f* ELEKTRIZ pull-in power; **Ansprechrelais** *nt* ELEKTROTECH operate relay; **Ansprechschwelle** *f* GERÄT threshold limit; **Ansprech-**

signal *nt* GERÄT threshold signal; **Ansprechspannung** *f* ELEKTROTECH operate voltage; **Ansprechstrom** *m* ELEKTROTECH operate current, operating current; **Ansprechtemperatur** *f* HEIZ & KÄLTE critical temperature; **Ansprechverhalten** *nt* AUFNAHME, ELEKTRONIK response; **Ansprechvermögen** *nt* ELEKTRONIK sensitivity; **Ansprechverzögerung** *f* ELEKTROTECH operate lag; **Ansprechwert** *m* GERÄT threshold limit; **Ansprechzeit** *f* AUFNAHME *eines Begrenzers* attack time, ELEKTRONIK response time, ELEKTROTECH operate time, GERÄT *Meßgerät* answering time, METROL, TELEKOM response time

ansprengen *vt* MEERSCHMUTZ wring

Anspruch[1] *m* PATENT claim

Anspruch:[2] **in ~ nehmen** *vt* PATENT claim, take advantage of

Ansprüche: ~ **der gleichen Kategorie** *m pl* PATENT claims in the same category; ~ **verschiedener Kategorien** *m pl* PATENT claims in different categories

Anspruchsniveau *nt* ERGON level of aspiration, QUAL grade

Anstauchen *nt* FERTIG *Köpfe*, MASCHINEN heading

anstauchen *vt* FERTIG squeeze, *Köpfe* head

Anstauchwerkzeug *nt* MASCHINEN heading tool

anstechen *vt* LEBENSMITTEL *Faß* tap

Ansteckteil *nt* FERTIG *Gießen* looping piece

anstehend: ~**e Ader** *f* KOHLEN apex

Ansteigen *nt* ERDÖL rising, STRÖMPHYS surge

ansteigen *vi* BAU rise

ansteigend *adj* BAU uphill

Anstellen *nt* CHEMTECH *Gärung* setting

Anstellwinkel *m* LUFTTRANS attack angle, blade angle, MASCHINEN setting angle; ~ **des Luftschraubenblattes** *m* LUFTTRANS blade attack angle; ~ **für Nullauftrieb** *m* LUFTTRANS zero-lift angle; **Anstellwinkelanschlag** *m* LUFTTRANS *Hubschrauber* pitch stop; **Anstellwinkelanzeiger** *m* LUFTTRANS angle of attack indicator

Ansteuern *nt* COMP & DV gating

ansteuern *vt* COMP & DV select, WASSERTRANS *Navigation* approach, steer for

Ansteuerung *f* COMP & DV selection, ELEKTRONIK *eines Geräts* control, TELEKOM *eines Transmitters* excitation, WASSERTRANS approach; ~ **eines Leitstrahls** *f* LUFTTRANS beam interception; **Ansteuerungssignal** *nt* ELEKTRONIK gating signal; **Ansteuerungstonne** *f* WASSERTRANS sea buoy

Anstich: **den ~ machen** *vi* KER & GLAS *am Glasschmelzofen* tap

Anstieg *m* BAU *Wasser* elevation, ERDÖL *Ölspiegel in Bohrung* rising, PHYS slope; **Anstiegsrate** *f* ELEKTROTECH rate of rise; **Anstiegszeit** *f* AUFNAHME rise time, *eines Verstärkers* attack time, COMP & DV, PHYS rise time, REGELUNG ramp response

Anstoß *m* ANSTRICH impact, MECHAN impulse, RAUMFAHRT nudging

anstoßen *vt* BAU abut

anstoßend[1] *adj* GEOM contiguous

anstoßend:[2] ~**e Winkel** *m pl* GEOM adjacent angles

Anstoßmechanismus *m* RAUMFAHRT kick-off mechanism

Anstrich *m* ANSTRICH paint, PAPIER coat; **Anstrichmittelwanne** *f* LABOR sump; **Anstrichstoff zum Spritzen** *m* KUNSTSTOFF spraying paint; **Anstrichsystem** *nt* ANSTRICH paint system

Anström- *pref* LUFTTRANS leading; **Anströmgeschwindigkeit an der Rotorspitze** *f* LUFTTRANS *Hubschrauber*

rotor tip velocity; **Anströmkante** f LUFTTRANS leading edge; **Anströmkantenrippe** f LUFTTRANS leading-edge rib; **Anströmwinkel** m LUFTTRANS angle of incidence

Anteil m ELEKTRIZ component, KUNSTSTOFF content, MECHAN component, METROL *verhältnismäßig* rate; ~ **von Ausgangsatomen** m KERNTECH parent fraction; ~ **erfolgreich abgewickelter Anrufe** m TELEKOM call success rate; ~ **fehlerhafter Einheiten** m QUAL fraction defective, fraction nonconforming; ~ **fehlerhafter Einheiten in der Stichprobe** m QUAL sample fraction defective

Antenne f ELEKTROTECH, FERNSEH, KFZTECH *Zubehör*, PHYS, RADIO, RAUMFAHRT, TELEKOM aerial, antenna; ~ **mit periodischer Strahlschwenkung** f TELEKOM sweep antenna; ~ **mit Reflektor** f RAUMFAHRT *Weltraumfunk* reflector antenna; ~ **mit Richtwirkung** f RADIO directive array; ~ **mit schwenkbarer Charakteristik** f TELEKOM steerable antenna; ~ **für Schwerewellen** f STRAHLPHYS gravitational wave aerial; **Antennenabstimmspule** f *(ATI)* RADIO aerial-tuning inductance, antenna-tuning inductance *(ATI)*; **Antennenanpaßgerät** nt RADIO aerial-tuning unit; **Antennenanpassung** f RADIO *Gerät* antenna matching device, RADIO *(ATU)* aerial-tuning unit *(ATU)*, TELEKOM aerial matching; **Antennenanschluß** m FERNSEH aerial terminal; **Antennenaufzug** m LUFTTRANS halyard; **Antennenaufzugseil** nt LUFTTRANS halyard; **Antennengewinn** m AUFNAHME, ELEKTRONIK power gain, FERNSEH, PHYS, RADIO aerial gain, RAUMFAHRT antenna gain; **Antennengewinnfunktion** f ELEKTRONIK gain function; **Antennenkabel** nt ELEKTROTECH aerial cable; **Antennenkuppel** f LUFTTRANS *Hubschrauber* blister, RAUMFAHRT, TELEKOM radome; **Antennenleitung** f ELEKTRIZ aerial line; **Antennenmast** m FERNSEH, TELEKOM, WASSERTRANS *Funk* aerial mast; **Antennenrelaissystem ohne Verstärkung** nt TELEKOM nonboosted antenna repeater system; **Antennenrichtwirkung** f FERNSEH aerial directivity; **Antennenschüssel** f RAUMFAHRT dish antenna; **Antennenstrahlungswiderstand** m RADIO aerial radiation resistance; **Antennensystem** nt RAUMFAHRT antenna system; **Antennenverlängerungsspule** f RADIO aerial loading coil; **Antennenverstärker** m ELEKTRONIK antenna booster, booster; **Antennenverstärkung** f PHYS aerial gain; **Antennenweiche** f FERNSEH combiner; **Antennenwirkfläche** f ELEKTRONIK *Antennentechnik* capture area; **Antennenwirkungsgrad** m FERNSEH aerial efficiency; **Antennenwirkwiderstand** m PHYS aerial resistance; **Antennenzuleitung** f FERNSEH aerial lead

Anthracen nt CHEMIE anthracene; **Anthracenfarbstoff** m CHEMIE anthracene dye; **Anthracenöl** nt CHEMIE anthracene oil

Anthragallol nt CHEMIE anthragallol

Anthrazit m KOHLEN anthracite, hard coal; **Anthrazitkohle** f KOHLEN anthracite coal

anthropogen: ~e **bedingte Übersäuerung** f UMWELTSCHMUTZ anthropogenic acidification; ~ **verursachte Bodenerschütterung** f UMWELTSCHMUTZ man-made earth tremor; ~ **verursachtes Erdbeben** nt UMWELTSCHMUTZ man-made earthquake

Anthropologie f ERGON anthropology

Anthropometrie f ERGON anthropometry

anthropomorph: ~er **Roboter** m KÜNSTL INT anthropomorphic robot

anthropotechnisch adj ERGON anthropotechnical

Anti- pref CHEMIE, KFZTECH, KUNSTSTOFF, LEBENSMITTEL, LUFTTRANS, MASCHINEN, PHYS, STRAHLPHYS anti-; **Antialbumose** f LEBENSMITTEL anti-albumose

Antialiasing f ELEKTRONIK anti-aliasing; **Antialiasing-Filter** nt ELEKTRONIK anti-aliasing filter; **Antialiasing-Filterung** f ELEKTRONIK anti-aliasing filtering

Anti-: **Antiausschwimmmittel** nt KUNSTSTOFF antiflooding agent; **Antibackmittel** nt LEBENSMITTEL anticaking agent; **Antibaryon** nt TEILPHYS antibaryon

Antibindung f STRAHLPHYS antibonding; **Antibindungsbahn** f STRAHLPHYS antibonding atomic orbital; **Antibindungselektronen** nt pl STRAHLPHYS antibonding electrons

Anti-: **Antiblockiersystem** nt KFZTECH *(ABS)* antiblocking system, antilock system, antiskid braking system *(ALS)*, LUFTTRANS antiskid unit; **Antiblockmittel** nt KUNSTSTOFF antiblocking agent; **Antichlor** nt CHEMIE, PAPIER antichlor; **Antidot** nt CHEMIE antidote; **Antienzym** nt LEBENSMITTEL anti-enzyme

antiferromagnetisch adj PHYS antiferromagnetic

Anti-: **Antiferromagnetismus** m ELEKTRIZ, PHYS antiferromagnetism; **Antifouling-Anstrichfarbe** nt KUNSTSTOFF antifouling paint; **Antifriktionsmittel** nt PAPIER antifriction; **Antigen** nt CHEMIE antigen; **Antihautmittel** nt KUNSTSTOFF antiskinning agent; **Antikathode** f ELEKTRIZ, PHYS anticathode

Antikglas nt KER & GLAS antique glass;

antiklinal: ~e **Falle** f ERDÖL *Geologie* anticlinal trap

Anti-: **Antiklinale** f ERDÖL *Geologie* anticline; **Antiklopfmittel** nt ERDÖL *Raffinerie* antiknock, KFZTECH antiknock additive, *Kraftstoff* antiknock agent, UMWELTSCHMUTZ antiknock additive

Antikoinzidenz f GERÄT, STRAHLPHYS anticoincidence; **Antikoinzidenzschaltung** f PHYS anticoincidence circuit; **Antikoinzidenzzähler** m GERÄT anticoincidence counter

Anti-: **Antikollisionslicht** nt LUFTTRANS anticollision light; **Antikondensationsbeutel** m VERPACK desiccant bag; **Antilichthofbelag** m FOTO antihalation backing

antimagnetisch adj CHEMIE antimagnetic, nonmagnetic

Anti-: **Antimaterie** f PHYS antimatter

Antimon nt *(Sb)* CHEMIE antimonic, antimonous, antimony, stibic, stibium

antimonartig adj CHEMIE antimonial

Antimonat nt CHEMIE antimoniate, stibate, antimonite

Antimon: **Antimonglanz** m CHEMIE antimonite, antimony glance, stibnite

antimonhaltig adj CHEMIE antimonial

Antimonid nt CHEMIE antimonide, stabide

antimonig adj CHEMIE stibious

Antimonit m CHEMIE antimonite, antimony glance, stibnite

Antimon: **Antimontetroxid** nt CHEMIE antimony tetroxide

Antimykotikum nt CHEMIE *pilztötendes Mittel* fungicide

Anti-: **Antineutrino** nt PHYS antineutrino; **Antineutron** nt PHYS antineutron

Antioxidans nt KUNSTSTOFF, LEBENSMITTEL antioxidant; **Antioxidationsmittel** nt KUNSTSTOFF, LEBENSMITTEL antioxidant; **Antioxidationswirkstoff** m KUNSTSTOFF antioxidant

Antiparallel- pref ELEKTROTECH, GEOM antiparallel

antiparallel[1] adj GEOM antiparallel

antiparallel[2] ~e **Anordnung** f ELEKTROTECH antiparallel arrangement, *Kondensatoren* back-to-back arrangement

Antiparallel-: **Antiparallelgelenkviereck** *nt* FERTIG *Verbindungen* anti-ager-parallel four-bar

Anti-: **Antipassat** *m* WASSERTRANS *Windart* antitrades; **Antipodenpunkte** *m pl* GEOM antipodal points

antippen *vt* COMP & DV *Auswahl auf Tablett* identify

Antiproton *nt* PHYS, TEILPHYS antiproton; **Antiprotonenring mit geringer Energie** *m (LEAR)* TEILPHYS Low-Energy Antiproton Ring *(LEAR)*

Anti-: **Antiquark** *nt* PHYS, TEILPHYS antiquark; **Antiquaschrift** *f* DRUCK Roman type; **Antireaktivität** *f* KERNTECH antireactivity; **Antireflexbelag** *m* KER & GLAS, TELEKOM antireflection coating; **Antireflexionsüberzug** *m* OPTIK antireflection coating; **Antiresonanz** *f* AKUSTIK, ELEKTRONIK antiresonance; **Antiresonanzfrequenz** *f (fA)* AKUSTIK, ELEKTRONIK antiresonant frequency *(fA)*; **Antiresonanzkreis** *m* RADIO antiresonant circuit; **Antirutschsohle** *f* SICHERHEIT *Sicherheitsschuhwerk* slip-resistant sole; **Antisatellit-Laser** *m* ELEKTRONIK antisatellite laser *m* PAPIER anti froth; **Antischaummittel** *nt* CHEMIE defoaming agent, ERDÖL antifoam agent, KOHLEN, KUNSTSTOFF, MASCHINEN antifoaming agent, PAPIER antifoam, antifroth; **Antischleiermittel** *nt* FOTO antifogging agent; **Antischrumpfbehandlung** *f* TEXTIL antishrink treatment; **Antischwappdämpfer** *m pl* RAUMFAHRT *Einbauten* antislosh baffles; **Antischwerkraft** *f* RAUMFAHRT antigravity; **Antiskidsystem** *nt* LUFTTRANS antiskid unit; **Antispritzmittel** *nt* LEBENSMITTEL antispattering agent

Antistatik *f* FERTIG, MASCHINEN, TEXTIL antistatic; **Antistatikausrüstung** *f* MASCHINEN antistatic protection; **Antistatikgerät** *nt* TEXTIL static eliminator; **Antistatikmittel** *nt* FERTIG, TEXTIL antistatic agent; **Antistatikschuhe** *m pl* SICHERHEIT antistatic footwear; **Antistatikspray** *nt* COMP & DV antistatic spray

Antistatikum *nt* KUNSTSTOFF, TEXTIL antistatic agent

antistatisch[1] *adj* ELEKTRIZ, FOTO, MASCHINEN antistatic

antistatisch:[2] *~er* **Belag** *m* FOTO antistatic backing; *~es* **Material** *nt* SICHERHEIT antistatic material; *~e* **Matte** *f* COMP & DV antistatic mat; *~e* **Schutzkleidung** *f* SICHERHEIT antistatic protective clothing

antisymmetrisch: *~er* **Tensor** *m* STRÖMPHYS antisymmetric tensor; *~e* **Wellenfunktion** *f* PHYS antisymmetric wave function

Anti:- **Antiteilchen** *nt* PHYS, TEILPHYS antiparticle

Antivalenz *f* COMP & DV symmetric difference, ELEKTRONIK *Exklusiv-ODER-Verknüpfung* anticoincidence; **Antivalenzfunktion** *f* COMP & DV nonequivalence function; **Antivalenzglied** *nt* COMP & DV nonequivalence gate; **Antivalenztor** *nt* COMP & DV nonequivalence gate; **Antivalenzverknüpfung** *f* COMP & DV nonequivalence operation

Anti:- **Antivereisungsschieber** *m* LUFTTRANS engine anti-icing gate valve

antizyklonal: *~e* **Generation** *f* METROL anticyclonic generation

Anti:- **Antizyklone** *f* WASSERTRANS anticyclone

Antonit *m* KERNTECH antonite

Antrag *m* PATENT request

antreiben *vt* MASCHINEN drive, MECHAN actuate, drive, PAPIER drive, PHYS actuate, RAUMFAHRT *Raumschiff*, TEXTIL drive

Antrieb *m* ERGON incentive, FERNSEH transport mechanism, FERTIG actuation, KFZTECH propulsion, *Triebstrang* drive, KONTROLL *Plattenspielwerk* drive,

MASCHINEN drive, impulsion, propulsion, MECHAN actuator, drive, PAPIER drive, RAUMFAHRT *Raumschiff* propulsion, TEXTIL drive, WASSERTRANS *Schiffantrieb* propulsion; **~ durch feste Antriebsräder** *m* KFZTECH, WASSERTRANS propulsion by stationary drive wheels; **~ mit konstanter Drehzahl** *m* MASCHINEN constant-speed drive; **~ durch Luftdruck** *m* KFZTECH, WASSERTRANS propulsion by air pressure; **~ ohne Nachbrenner** *m* LUFTTRANS *Triebwerk, Motor* dry power; **~ ohne Rutschkupplung** *m* FERTIG *Gewindebohrer* positive drive; **~ mit Ritzel und Zahnstange** *m* KERNTECH rack-and-pinion drive gear; **~ durch Spiralantrieb mit wechselnder Steigung** *m* KFZTECH, WASSERTRANS propulsion by spiral drive with varying pitch; **Antriebsachse** *f* FERTIG *Kunststoffinstallationen* actuator shaft, KFZTECH *Triebstrang*, MASCHINEN driving axle, live axle; **Antriebsaggregat** *nt* FERTIG driving package, MASCHINEN drive unit, mover, power unit, prime mover; **Antriebsbatterie** *f* KFZTECH drive battery; **Antriebsdrehzahl** *f* KFZTECH *Motor* engine speed; **Antriebseinheit** *f* RAUMFAHRT *Raumschiff* propulsion unit; **Antriebselement** *nt* MASCHINEN driving element; **Antriebsgehäuse** *nt* FERTIG *Kunststoffinstallationen* actuator housing; **Antriebsglied** *nt* FERTIG *Getriebelehre* driving link, follower, input member, MASCHINEN driving member; **Antriebskegelrad** *nt* KFZTECH drive pinion, pinion gear; **Antriebskette** *f* KFZTECH *Motor, Triebstrang* drive chain, MASCHINEN driving chain, transmission chain; **Antriebskette der Nockenwelle** *f* KFZTECH camshaft drive chain; **Antriebskettenrad** *nt* FERTIG driving sprocket, KFZTECH *Motorradgetriebe* sprocket; **Antriebskraft** *f* MASCHINEN drive power, propulsive force, WASSERTRANS *Schiffkonstruktion* motive force; **Antriebskurbel** *f* FERTIG driving crank; **Antriebsleistung** *f* MASCHINEN driving power; **Antriebsmagnet** *m* KFZTECH, WASSERTRANS propulsion magnet; **Antriebsmaschine** *f* KFZTECH motor, LUFTTRANS, MASCHINEN prime mover; **Antriebsmechanismus** *m* KONTROLL drive mechanism; **Antriebsmotor** *m* AUFNAHME, ELEKTRIZ drive motor, FERTIG mover, FOTO drive motor, KFZTECH propulsion engine, propulsion motor, KONTROLL driving motor, WASSERTRANS *Schiffantrieb* propulsion engine, propulsion motor; **Antriebspotential** *nt* ELEKTROTECH driving potential; **Antriebspropeller** *m* LUFTTRANS driving propeller; **Antriebsrad** *nt* FERTIG impeller, KFZTECH driving wheel, *Rad, Kraftübertragung* drive wheel, MASCHINEN driver, driving gear, driving wheel, leader, PAPIER leader; **Antriebsriemen** *m* FERTIG driving belt, MASCHINEN belt, driving belt, transmission belt; **Antriebsriemenscheibe** *f* KFZTECH *Drehstromlichtmaschine* drive pulley; **Antriebsritzel** *nt* KFZTECH drive pinion, pinion gear, MASCHINEN driving pinion; **Antriebsritzelwelle** *f* KFZTECH drive pinion shaft; **Antriebsrolle** *f* COMP & DV capstan, FERNSEH drive sprocket, MASCHINEN driving pulley; **Antriebsschale** *f* KFZTECH input shell; **Antriebsscheibe** *f* FERTIG driver pulley, MASCHINEN driving disc (BrE), driving disk (AmE); **Antriebsseite** *f* ELEKTROTECH drive end, MASCHINEN driving end, PAPIER drive side; **Antriebsspindel** *f* MASCHINEN drive spindle; **Antriebsspule** *f* ELEKTROTECH drive coil; **Antriebsstange** *f* MECHAN push rod; **Antriebssystem** *nt* MASCHINEN drive system, transmission system, RAUMFAHRT *Raumschiff* propulsion system, TEXTIL drive system;

Antriebstrommel f KFZTECH driving drum; **Antriebswelle** f ELEKTROTECH capstan, FERTIG drive, driver, *Kunststoffinstallationen* drive shaft, KFZTECH axle shaft, *Kupplung, Getriebe* input shaft, *Triebstrang* drive shaft, half shaft, MASCHINEN drive shaft, driving shaft, engine shaft, transmission shaft, WASSERTRANS *Motor* driving shaft; **Antriebszahnrad der Antriebswelle** nt KFZTECH clutch gear

Antrocknungszeit f KUNSTSTOFF tack free time

Antwortt f COMP & DV response, ELEKTRONIK reply, ERGON response

antwortabhängig: ~e Nachricht f COMP & DV response message

Antwort: **Antwortfunkfeuer** nt LUFTTRANS responder beacon; **Antwortmodus** m COMP & DV response mode; **Antwortsender** m LUFTTRANS *Kommunikationswesen* responder, PHYS transponder; **Antwortsignal** nt TELEKOM answer signal; **Antwortwimpel** m WASSERTRANS *Signal* answering pennant; **Antwortzeit** f COMP & DV, ERGON response time

Anvisieren nt BAU sighting

anvisiert: ~e Dioptrie f BAU sighted alidade; **~e Höhe** f BAU sighted level

Anvulkanisation f KUNSTSTOFF scorch; **Anvulkanisationsverhinderer** m KUNSTSTOFF antiscorching agent

anvulkanisieren vt THERMOD scorch

Anwärm- pref BAU heating, THERMOD warm-up; **Anwärmbrenner** m BAU heating blowpipe

anwärmen vt THERMOD heat up, warm up

Anwärm-: **Anwärmloch** nt KER & GLAS glory hole; **Anwärmzeit** f THERMOD warm-up time

anweisen vt COMP & DV order

Anweisung f COMP & DV directive, instruction, order, *in Programm* statement, KONTROLL instruction; **Anweisungskennsatz** m COMP & DV statement label; **Anweisungsnummer** f COMP & DV statement number

anwenden vt MECHAN apply

Anwender m TELEKOM user; **Anwender-Betriebsumgebung** f COMP & DV user-operating environment; **Anwenderkollektiv** nt ERGON collective of users

Anwendung f ANSTRICH, COMP & DV *Software*, MECHAN application

anwendungsbezogen: ~e Sprache f COMP & DV application-oriented language

Anwendung: **Anwendungseinheit** f FERTIG *Kunststoffinstallationen* unit; **Anwendungshandbuch** nt COMP & DV application manual; **Anwendungsinstanz** f TELEKOM application entity; **Anwendungsprogramm** nt COMP & DV application, application program, application software; **Anwendungsprogrammpaket** nt COMP & DV application package; **Anwendungsschicht** f COMP & DV *ISO-Referenzmodell*, TELEKOM application layer

Anwerfen: ~ des Außenputzes nt BAU rendering

Anwurf m BAU roughcast

Anzahl f GERÄT count, METROL rate; **~ der Arbeitsgänge** f BAU number of passes; **~ der Proben** f WERKPRÜF number of specimens; **~ der Prüflinge** f WERKPRÜF number of specimens

Anzahlung f VERPACK deposit

anzapfen vt BAU blend, FERTIG *Punktschweißen*, PHYS tap, RADIO bug

Anzapftransformator m ELEKTROTECH tapped transformer

Anzapfung f ELEKTRIZ tap, ELEKTROTECH, PHYS tapping; **Anzapfungsanzeige** f ELEKTRIZ tap position indicator; **Anzapfungswähler** m ELEKTRIZ tap selector, tap switch; **Anzapfungswechsel** m ELEKTRIZ tap change operation; **Anzapfungswechsler** m ELEKTRIZ tap changer

Anzapfwiderstand m ELEKTROTECH tapped resistor

Anzeichen: ~ von Kohlenwasserstoffen nt ERDÖL *Bohrtechnik* show

anzeichnen vt BAU, FERTIG scribe

Anzeige f COMP & DV display, readout, DRUCK display, DRUCK advertisement, ELEKTRIZ display, readout, GERÄT reading, HYDRAUL indicator, KONTROLL display, MASCHINEN telltale, RAUMFAHRT *Bildschirm*, TELEKOM display; **~ des Blatteinstellwinkels** f LUFTTRANS *Hubschrauber* blade angle check gage (AmE), blade angle check gauge (BrE); **~ der gerufenen Nummer** f TELEKOM called number display; **~ der Grenzwertüberschreitung** f GERÄT out-of-limits indication; **~ der Nummer des gerufenen Teilnehmers** f TELEKOM connected-line identification presentation; **~ der Nummer des rufenden Teilnehmers** f TELEKOM CLIP, calling line identification presentation; **~ der rufenden Leitung** f TELEKOM CLID, calling line identification display; **~ über sichere Last** f SICHERHEIT safe load indicator; **Anzeigebereich** m GERÄT indicating range, indication range; **Anzeigeeinheit** f GERÄT display device; **Anzeigeeinrichtung** f GERÄT read-out device, MASCHINEN telltale; **Anzeigeformat** nt COMP & DV, KERNTECH display format; **Anzeigegenauigkeit** f GERÄT accuracy of indication; **Anzeigegerät** nt COMP & DV display device, GERÄT display device, read-out meter, KONTROLL display unit, monitor; **Anzeigegerät mit Kreisskale** nt GERÄT round scale indicator; **Anzeigehintergrund** m COMP & DV background display; **Anzeigelampe** f ELEKTRIZ indicator lamp; **Anzeigeleuchte** f KFZTECH *Zubehör* pilot light; **Anzeigemeßgerät** nt HYDRAUL indicator; **Anzeigemittel** nt FERTIG detecting agent; **Anzeigemodus** m COMP & DV display mode

anzeigen vt COMP & DV, DRUCK, ELEKTRONIK, KONTROLL display, METROL read, RAUMFAHRT *Bildschirm* display

Anzeige: **Anzeigenabbild** nt COMP & DV screen image; **Anzeigenabteilung** f DRUCK advertising department; **Anzeigenadel** f FOTO indicator needle

anzeigend: ~es Meßgerät nt GERÄT read-out meter

Anzeige: **Anzeigenfahne** f DRUCK ad galley; **Anzeigenlayout** nt DRUCK advertisement layout; **Anzeigenschrift** f DRUCK ad face; **Anzeigenseite** f DRUCK advertisement page; **Anzeigensetzer** m DRUCK advertisement setter; **Anzeigensetzerei** f DRUCK advertisement composing room

anzeigepflichtig adj QUAL notifiable

Anzeiger m COMP & DV flag, indicator, KFZTECH gage (AmE), gauge (BrE), MASCHINEN indicator; **~ für spannungstragende Leitung** m ELEKTRIZ, SICHERHEIT live line indicator

Anzeige: **Anzeigeregister** nt COMP & DV display register; **Anzeigeröhre** f ELEKTRONIK indicator tube; **Anzeigesäule** f LABOR *eines Barometers* cup; **Anzeigeskale** f GERÄT indicating scale; **Anzeigestelle** f KERNTECH *eines Massenspektrometers* indicator bay; **Anzeigetafel** f MECHAN index table; **Anzeigethermometer** nt HEIZ & KÄLTE indicating thermometer; **Anzeigewert** m GERÄT indicated value, reading; **Anzeigezeit** f GERÄT display time

Anziehdrehmoment nt MASCHINEN tightening torque

Anziehen nt EISENBAHN, MASCHINEN tightening

anziehen:[1] anziehend adj PHYS attractive

anziehen[2] *vt* MASCHINEN fasten, tighten, PHYS attract

Anziehung *f* PHYS attraction; **Anziehungseffekt** *m* TRANS attractive effect; **Anziehungskraft** *f* ELEKTRIZ attractive force, PHYS attractive force, force of attraction, gravitation, RAUMFAHRT pull

Anzug *m* ELEKTROTECH pick-up, MASCHINEN tightening; **Anzugmutter** *f* MASCHINEN tightening nut; **Anzugschraube** *f* FERTIG *Frässpindel* draw-in bolt; **Anzugsmoment** *nt* KFZTECH pick-up; **Anzugsspannung** *f* ELEKTROTECH pick-up voltage; **Anzugstoff** *m* TEXTIL suiting

anzünden *vt* THERMOD kindle

Anzünder *m* HEIZ & KÄLTE lighter

AOCS *abbr (Fluglage- und Umlaufbahnkontrollsystem)* RAUMFAHRT AOCS *(attitude and orbit control system)*

AOQ *abbr (durchschnittliche Fertigproduktqualität)* QUAL AOQ *(average outgoing quality)*

AOQL *abbr (durchschnittlicher Fertigproduktqualitätsgrenzwert)* QUAL AOQL *(average outgoing quality limit)*

AOS *abbr (automatisches Signal zur Mikrofonübergabe)* TELEKOM AOS *(automatic over signal)*

AOW[1] *abbr (akustische Oberflächenwelle)* ELEKTRONIK, TELEKOM SAW *(surface acoustic wave)*

AOW:[2] **AOW-Bauelement** *nt* ELEKTRONIK, TELEKOM SAW device; **AOW-Expansionsfilter** *nt* ELEKTRONIK SAW expansion filter; **AOW-Filterung** *f* ELEKTRONIK SAW filtering; **AOW-Kompressionsfilter** *nt* ELEKTRONIK SAW compression filter; **AOW-Laufzeitleitung** *f* ELEKTRONIK SAW delay line

Apatit *m* CHEMIE apatite, phosphate of lime

APD *abbr (Avalanchefotodiode)* ELEKTRONIK, OPTIK APD *(avalanche photodiode)*

aperiodisch[1] *adj* FERTIG *Schwingung* dead, PHYS aperiodic; **~ gedämpft** *adj* AUFNAHME dead beat

aperiodisch:[2] **~es Filter** *nt* RADIO aperiodic filter; **~es Galvanometer** *nt* ELEKTRIZ aperiodic galvanometer; **~ gedämpftes Galvanometer** *nt* ELEKTRIZ dead beat galvanometer; **~ gedämpftes Instrument** *nt* METROL aperiodic instrument; **~e Leitung** *f* ELEKTRONIK nonresonant line; **~e Schaltung** *f* ELEKTRONIK *frequenzunabhängig* aperiodic circuit; **~er Stromkreis** *m* COMP & DV aperiodic circuit

Apertur *f* COMP & DV, MECHAN, TELEKOM *Antenne* aperture; **Aperturantenne** *f* TELEKOM aperture antenna; **Aperturblende** *f* METALL aperture diaphragm, PHYS aperture stop; **Aperturgitter** *nt* ELEKTRONIK aperture grill; **Aperturverzerrung** *f* TELEKOM aperture distortion

APEX *abbr (im voraus bezahlter Sondertarif)* LUFTTRANS APEX *(advance purchase excursion fare)*

Apfelsäure *f* LEBENSMITTEL malic acid

Apfelsinenschale *f* KER & GLAS orange peel; **Apfelsinenschaleneffekt** *m* KUNSTSTOFF orange peel

Aphel *nt* PHYS aphelion

Aphongetriebe *nt* KFZTECH helical gear

API *abbr (Amerikanisches Erdölinstitut)* ERDÖL API *(American Petroleum Institute)*

API-Dichte *f* ERDÖL *Öl* API gravity

Apionol *nt* CHEMIE apionol, phenetrol

Aplanasie *f* OPTIK aplanatism

Aplanat *m* FOTO aplanatic lens, OPTIK aplanat

Apochromasie *f* OPTIK apochromatism

Apochromat *m* FERTIG, FOTO apochromatic lens

apochromatisch[1] *adj* OPTIK apochromatic

apochromatisch:[2] **~e Korrektur** *f* FOTO apochromatic correction

Apogäum *nt* PHYS, RAUMFAHRT apogee; **Apogäumsmanöver** *nt* RAUMFAHRT apogee maneuver (AmE), apogee manoeuvre (BrE); **Apogäumstriebwerk** *nt* RAUMFAHRT *Raumschiff* apogee motor

Apostilb *nt (asb)* OPTIK apostilb *(asb)*

Apothekerunze *f* METROL ounce, ounce troy

Apparat[1] *m* LABOR, MASCHINEN, PAPIER apparatus

Apparat:[2] **am ~ bleiben** *vi* TELEKOM hold the line

Apparate *m pl* FERTIG *Kunststoffinstallationen* equipment; **Apparatesatz** *m* ELEKTROTECH *Gruppe elektrischer Geräte* set; **Apparateschnur** *f* TELEKOM instrument cord

Appleton-Schicht *f* PHYS Appleton layer, F layer

Appret *nt* TEXTIL finish

Appreteur *m* TEXTIL finisher

Appretieren *nt* TEXTIL sizing

appretieren *vt* TEXTIL size

Appretur *f* TEXTIL *Baumwolle* finish

Approximation *f* MATH approximation; **Approximationsfehler** *m* GERÄT approximation error

APR *abbr* ELEKTRONIK *(automatische Phasenregelung)*, FERNSEH *(automatische Phasensteuerung)* APC *(automatic phase control)*

aprotisch: **~es Lösemittel** *nt* CHEMIE aprotic solvent

APT *abbr (programmierte Werkzeuge)* COMP & DV APT *(automatically programmed tools)*

apyrisch *adj* CHEMIE apyrous

AQL *abbr (akzeptabler Qualitätspegel, annehmbare Qualitätsgrenzlage, annehmbare Qualitätslage)* QUAL AQL *(acceptable quality level)*

Aquädukt *m* BAU, NICHTFOSS ENERG, WASSERVERSORG aqueduct

Aquakultur *f* WASSERVERSORG aquiculture

Aquaplaning *nt* KFZTECH aquaplaning

aquatisch: **~es System** *nt* WASSERVERSORG aquatic system

Äquator *m* WASSERTRANS *Geographie* equator

äquatorial: **~e Brennlinie** *f* PHYS sagittal focal line; **~e Fokuslinie** *f* PHYS sagittal focal line; **~e Umlaufbahn** *f* RAUMFAHRT equatorial orbit

Äquator: **Äquatortaufe** *f* WASSERTRANS crossing the line ceremony; **Äquatorüberflug** *m* RAUMFAHRT equatorial crossing; **Äquatorüberquerung** *f* WASSERTRANS crossing the line

Aquiclude *f* WASSERVERSORG aquiclude

äquidistant *adj* BAU, GEOM equidistant

Äquidistanzlinie *f* ERDÖL *Seekartierung* median line

Aquifer *m* NICHTFOSS ENERG, WASSERVERSORG aquifer

äquimolar *adj* CHEMIE equimolecular

Äquinoktialgezeit *f* NICHTFOSS ENERG equinoctial tide

äquipotential *adj* ELEKTRIZ, ELEKTROTECH equipotential

Äquipotential *nt* PHYS equipotential; **Äquipotentialfläche** *f* ELEKTRIZ, ELEKTROTECH, PHYS, RADIO, RAUMFAHRT equipotential surface; **Äquipotentialkathode** *f* ELEKTROTECH unipotential cathode; **Äquipotentiallinie** *f* RAUMFAHRT equipotential line

äquivalent[1] *adj* MATH equivalent

äquivalent:[2] **~e Absorptionsfläche** *f* AKUSTIK equivalent absorption area; **~es Bohrschlammgewicht** *nt* ERDÖL *Bohrtechnik* EMW, equivalent mud weight; **~e Dichte** *f* ERDÖL *Bohrtechnik* equivalent density; **~e Fluggeschwindigkeit** *f (EAS)* LUFTTRANS equivalent airspeed *(EAS)*; **~e Isotropenstrahlungsleistung** *f*

(EIRP) RADIO, RAUMFAHRT *Weltraumfunk* effective isotropically-radiated power *(EIRP)*; **~e Rauschleistung** *f* OPTIK, TELEKOM NEP, noise equivalent power; **~e Rauschtemperatur** *f* RAUMFAHRT *Weltraumfunk* equivalent noise temperature; **~e Rauschzahl** *f* RAUMFAHRT *Weltraumfunk* equivalent noise temperature; **~e Steigbögeschwindigkeit** *f* LUFTTRANS equivalent vertical gust speed; **~e Strahlungsleistung** *f* TELEKOM equivalent radiated power; **~er Stufenindex** *m* TELEKOM ESI, equivalent step index; **~e Stufenindex-Brechzahldifferenz** *f* TELEKOM ESI refractive index difference; **~es Stufenprofil** *nt* TELEKOM ESI profile, equivalent step index profile; **~e Tiefe** *f* ERDÖL *Bohrtechnik* equivalent depth; **~e Zirkulationsdichte** *f* ERDÖL *Bohrtechnik* ECD, equivalent circulating density; **~er Zufallsverkehrswert** *m* TELEKOM equivalent random traffic intensity

Äquivalent *nt* MATH equivalent; **~ je Million** *nt (EPM)* UMWELTSCHMUTZ equivalent per million *(EPM)*; **Äquivalentdosis** *f* PHYS dose equivalent; **Äquivalentleitwert** *m* THERMOD equivalent conductance; **Äquivalentschaltung** *f* ELEKTRIZ equivalent circuit; **Äquivalentvolumen** *nt* KERNTECH, PHYS, STRAHLPHYS atomic volume; **Äquivalentwiderstand** *m* ELEKTRIZ equivalent resistance

Äquivalenz *f* COMP & DV equivalence; **Äquivalenzfunktion** *f* COMP & DV equivalence function, equivalence operation; **Äquivalenzglied** *nt* COMP & DV equivalence gate, ELEKTRONIK exclusive NOR gate; **Äquivalenznormalruß** *m* UMWELTSCHMUTZ equivalent standard smoke; **Äquivalenzprinzip** *nt* PHYS principle of equivalence; **Äquivalenzverknüpfung** *f* COMP & DV equivalence operation, ELEKTRONIK exclusive NOR circuit

AR *abbr (Ausgangsregister)* TELEKOM HLR *(home location register)*

Ar¹ *nt (a)* METROL are *(a)*

Ar² *(Argon)* CHEMIE Ar *(argon)*

Arabinose *f* CHEMIE arabinose

arabisch: ~e Zahl *f* MATH *Ziffer* cipher; **~e Zahlen** *f pl* MATH arabic numerals; **~e Ziffern** *f pl* MATH arabic numerals

Arabit *m* CHEMIE arabitol

Arabitol *f* CHEMIE arabitol

Arachidonsäure *f* LEBENSMITTEL arachidonic acid

Arachin- *pref* CHEMIE arachic; **Arachinalkohol** *m* CHEMIE arachic alcohol, eicosyl alcohol

A-Rahmen *m* BAU *Dach* A-frame

Aramid *nt* KUNSTSTOFF aramid

Aräometer *nt* ERDÖL hydrometer, GERÄT areometer, LABOR hydrometer, LEBENSMITTEL densimeter, hydrometer, PHYS areometer

Aräometrie *f* PHYS araeometry

Arbeit *f* ELEKTRIZ energy, MASCHINEN work; **~ mit Gefahrstoffen** *f* SICHERHEIT handling of dangerous materials

Arbeiten *nt* MASCHINEN working

arbeiten *vi* MASCHINEN operate

arbeitend: ~es Teil *nt* MASCHINEN working part

Arbeit: Arbeitsablauf *m* FERTIG machining cycle, operating cycle; **Arbeitsabschnitt** *m* COMP & DV session; **Arbeitsakt** *m* FERTIG machining cycle; **Arbeitsanforderung** *f* ERGON job demand; **Arbeitsaufgabe** *f* ERGON work task; **Arbeitsauftrag** *m* COMP & DV job; **Arbeitsband** *nt* COMP & DV scratch tape; **Arbeitsbedingungen** *f pl* SICHERHEIT working conditions; **Arbeitsbegleitpa-**

pier *nt* QUAL process sheet; **Arbeitsbegleitpapiere** *nt pl* QUAL accompanying papers; **Arbeitsbelastung** *f* COMP & DV, ERGON workload; **Arbeitsbereich** *m* COMP & DV work area, working area, workspace, KERNTECH operation area; **Arbeitsbereicherung** *f* ERGON job enrichment; **Arbeitsbeschreibung** *f* ERGON job description, job specification; **Arbeitsbewertung** *f* ERGON job evaluation; **Arbeitsbrücke** *f* BAU staging; **Arbeitsbühne** *f* BAU platform, stage, working platform, ERDÖL *Bohrtechnik* drill floor, KER & GLAS working platform; **Arbeitsdatei** *f* COMP & DV scratch file, work file; **Arbeitsdatensatz** *m* COMP & DV work record; **Arbeitsdatenträger** *m* COMP & DV work volume; **Arbeitsdruck** *m* HEIZ & KÄLTE operating pressure, MASCHINEN operating pressure, working pressure; **Arbeitsebene** *f* FERTIG working plane; **Arbeitseingriff** *m* FERTIG working engagement; **Arbeitselement** *nt* COMP & DV work item; **Arbeitsende** *nt* KER & GLAS *des Wannenofens* working end; **Arbeitsenergieumsatz** *m* ERGON work energy expenditure; **Arbeitserweiterung** *f* ERGON job enlargement; **Arbeitsfläche** *f* ERGON work surface, FERTIG machined surface, working surface, MASCHINEN face; **Arbeitsfolgeregler** *m* ELEKTROTECH sequencer; **Arbeitsfrequenz** *f* MASCHINEN operating frequency; **Arbeitsfuge** *f* BAU *Beton* construction joint; **Arbeitsfunktion** *f* ELEKTROTECH work function; **Arbeitsgang** *m* COMP & DV operation, pass, transaction, FERTIG working traverse, MASCHINEN cutting stroke; **Arbeitsgemeinschaft** *f* ERDÖL *Unternehmenszusammenschluß* joint venture; **Arbeitsgeschwindigkeit** *f* MASCHINEN working speed; **Arbeitsgestalter** *m* ERGON job designer; **Arbeitsgestaltung** *f* ERGON job design, work design; **Arbeitshandschuhe** *m pl* SICHERHEIT working gloves; **Arbeitshub** *m* FERTIG working stroke, KFZTECH power stroke, MASCHINEN working stroke; **Arbeitsinformationsmittel** *nt* ERGON job aid; **Arbeitsinhalt** *m* ERGON job content, work content; **Arbeitskanal** *m* TELEKOM working channel; **Arbeitskarte** *f* ERGON instruction card, QUAL job card, *Laufkarte* work card; **Arbeitskleidung** *f* TEXTIL working clothes; **Arbeitskontakt** *m* ELEKTRIZ normally open contact, ELEKTROTECH make contact, normally open contact; **Arbeitsleben** *nt* ELEKTROTECH service life; **Arbeitslehre** *f* MASCHINEN manufacturing gage (AmE), manufacturing gauge (BrE), PHYS work standard; **Arbeitsleistung** *f* COMP & DV performance, FERTIG output; **Arbeitsmaschine** *f* MASCHINEN machine; **Arbeitsmechanismus** *m* MASCHINEN working mechanism; **Arbeitsmittel** *nt pl* ERGON work equipment; **Arbeitsmodus** *m* COMP & DV work mode; **Arbeitsnorm** *f* FERTIG output quota; **Arbeitsnormal** *nt* QUAL working standard; **Arbeitsphysiologie** *f* ERGON human factors engineering; **Arbeitsplan** *m* PHYS flowchart; **Arbeitsplatte** *f* COMP & DV work disk; **Arbeitsplatz** *m* COMP & DV workplace, *vom Netzwerk abhängiger Rechner* workstation, ERGON job, workplace, MASCHINEN work station, TELEKOM operating position; **Arbeitsplatzanalyse** *f* ERGON job analysis; **Arbeitsplatzbeschreibung** *f* ERGON job description; **Arbeitsplatzrechner** *m* COMP & DV work station; **Arbeitsplatzringtausch** *m* ERGON job rotation; **Arbeitsplatztausch** *m* ERGON job rotation; **Arbeitsplatzüberprüfung** *f* SICHERHEIT inspection of the workplace; **Arbeitsplatzvorschriften** *f pl* SICHERHEIT workplace regulations; **Arbeitsprüfung** *f* QUAL operating duty test; **Arbeitspuffer** *m* COMP & DV scratch pad; **Arbeitspunkt** *m* ELEKTROTECH operating point; **Arbeitspunkt-Drift** *f* REGELUNG point drift; **Arbeitsraum** *m* ERGON workspace, FERTIG driving free length, driving side, MECHAN workshop; **Arbeitsschiff** *nt* ERDÖL *Offshore-Arbeiten* work barge; **Arbeitsschuh** *m* SICHERHEIT work shoe; **Arbeitsschutzbrille** *f* SICHERHEIT protective goggles; **Arbeitsschutzkleidung** *f* SICHERHEIT workers' protective clothing; **Arbeitsschutzzelt** *nt* SICHERHEIT workers' protective tent

Arbeitssicherheit *f* ERGON occupational safety, SICHERHEIT occupational safety, work safety; **~ in der Industrie** *f* SICHERHEIT industrial safety; **Arbeitssicherheitseinrichtung** *f* SICHERHEIT safety device; **Arbeitssicherheitsgerät** *nt* SICHERHEIT safety device; **Arbeitssicherheitstechnik** *f* SICHERHEIT safety engineering

Arbeit: **Arbeitssitzung** *f* COMP & DV work session; **Arbeitsspannung** *f* ELEKTRIZ working voltage, ELEKTROTECH closed-circuit voltage, operating voltage; **Arbeitsspeicher** *m* COMP & DV working memory, working storage; **Arbeitsspeicherbank** *f* COMP & DV memory bank; **Arbeitsspeicherbereich** *m* COMP & DV partition; **Arbeitsspiel** *nt* KFZTECH working cycle, MASCHINEN cycle, working cycle, MECHAN duty cycle; **Arbeitsstation** *f* VERPACK work station; **Arbeitsstelle** *f* FERTIG *Maschine* work station; **Arbeitsstiefel** *m* SICHERHEIT work boot; **Arbeitsstrom** *m* ELEKTROTECH operating current; **Arbeitsstromrelais** *nt* ELEKTRIZ working current relay; **Arbeitsstück** *nt* MECHAN workpiece; **Arbeitsstunde** *f* BAU manhour; **Arbeitsstundenzähler** *m* SICHERHEIT working hours counter; **Arbeitssystem** *nt* ERGON work system

arbeitstäglich: **~e Abdeckung** *f* ABFALL *einer Deponie* daily cover

Arbeit: **Arbeitstakt** *m* FERTIG work cycle, HYDRAUL stroke, KFZTECH power stroke; **Arbeitstemperatur** *f* HEIZ & KÄLTE operating temperature; **Arbeitstisch** *m* FERTIG workholding table, *Walzen* live pass, MASCHINEN workbench; **Arbeitsturbine** *f* LUFTTRANS free turbine; **Arbeitsumgebung** *f* ERGON work environment; **Arbeitsunfall** *m* BAU accident at work; **Arbeitsvergütung** *f* SICHERHEIT workmen's compensation; **Arbeitsvermögen** *nt* MASCHINEN working capacity, NICHTFOSS ENERG available power; **Arbeitsverwaltung** *f* VERPACK *verschiedener Aufgaben* work handling; **Arbeitsvorgang** *m* MASCHINEN operation; **Arbeitsvorschub** *m* FERTIG working feed; **Arbeitswechsel** *m* ERGON job rotation; **Arbeitsweise** *f* ELEKTROTECH operation; **Arbeitswissenschaft** *f* COMP & DV ergonomics, ERGON ergonomics, human engineering, MASCHINEN, SICHERHEIT ergonomics; **Arbeitszufriedenheit** *f* ERGON job satisfaction; **Arbeitszyklus** *m* MASCHINEN duty cycle, working cycle, TRANS operating cycle; **Arbeitszylinder** *m* KFZTECH power cylinder

Arcatomschweißen *nt* FERTIG hydrogen arc-welding

Archimedes: **~scher Körper** *m* GEOM Archimedean solid; **~sches Prinzip** *nt* PHYS Archimedes' principle; **~sche Schraube** *f* HYDRAUL *Fördertechnik* Archimedean screw

Archipel *m* WASSERTRANS *Geographie* archipelago

Architektur *f* COMP & DV *Hardware* architecture; **~ offener Systeme** *f* TELEKOM OSA, open systems architecture

Archiv *nt* COMP & DV archive; **Archivbild** *nt* FOTO file

picture; **Archivdatei** *f* COMP & DV archived file

Archivieren *nt* COMP & DV archiving

archivieren *vt* COMP & DV archive

Archivton *m* AUFNAHME stock sound

Arecain *nt* CHEMIE arecaine

Argentan *nt* METALL argentan

Argentit *m* CHEMIE argentite

Arginase *f* CHEMIE arginase

Arginin *nt* CHEMIE arginine

Argon *nt* *(Ar)* CHEMIE argon *(Ar)*; **Argongaslaser** *m* STRAHLPHYS argon gas laser; **Argonlaser** *m* ELEKTRONIK argon laser; **Argonschutzgas** *nt* KERNTECH argon gas blanket

ARGOS *abbr (automatische Satellitenerfassung von geomagnetischen Daten)* WASSERTRANS ARGOS *(Automatic Remote Geomagnetic Observatory System)*

Argument *nt* COMP & DV, MATH *Funktion* argument

Argyrit *m* CHEMIE argentite

Arithmetik *f* COMP & DV, MATH arithmetic

arithmetisch[1] *adj* MATH arithmetic

arithmetisch:[2] **~e Folge** *f* FERTIG arithmetic progression; **~es Mittel** *nt* COMP & DV, MATH, QUAL arithmetic mean; **~er Mittelrauhwert** *m* MASCHINEN CLA height, arithmetic average height, center line average height (AmE), centre line average height (BrE); **~er Mittelwert** *m* MATH, QUAL arithmetic mean; **~e Operationen** *f pl* MATH arithmetic operations; **~er Operator** *m* COMP & DV *Programmiersprache* arithmetic operator; **~e Reihe** *f* MATH arithmetic progression, arithmetic series; **~e Stellenverschiebung** *f* COMP & DV arithmetic shift

Arkade *f* BAU arcade

Arkansas- *pref* BAU Arkansas; **Arkansas-Abziehstein** *m* BAU Arkansas oilstone; **Arkansas-Polierstein** *m* BAU Arkansas oilstone

Arkose *f* KER & GLAS arkose

ARL *abbr (akzeptabler Zuverlässigkeitspegel)* QUAL ARL *(acceptable reliability level)*

Arm *m* ELEKTROTECH *von elektrischer Leuchte* bracket, FERTIG arm, *Umlaufgetriebe* bracket, MASCHINEN bracket, PAPIER arm

Armatur *f* ERDÖL *Absperrung, Regelorgan*, FERTIG *Kunststoffinstallationen* valve

Armaturen *f pl* MASCHINEN fittings; **Armaturenbrett** *nt* KFZTECH dash, dashboard, *Zubehör* instrument panel

Arm: **Armauflage** *f* BAU elbow rail; **Armausladung** *f* FERTIG *Punktschweißmaschine* throat

armiert[1] *adj* ELEKTRIZ, TELEKOM armored (AmE), armoured (BrE)

armiert:[2] **~es Kabel** *nt* ELEKTRIZ, ELEKTROTECH, MASCHINEN, TELEKOM armored cable (AmE), armoured cable (BrE); **~er Kunststoff** *m* VERPACK reinforced plastic; **~er Schlauch** *m* BAU armored hose (AmE), armoured hose (BrE)

Armierung *f* BAU reinforcement, ELEKTRIZ armor (AmE), armour (BrE), reinforcement, sheath, ELEKTROTECH *Kabel* armor (AmE), armour (BrE); **Armierungsschelle** *f* ELEKTRIZ armor clamp (AmE), armour clamp (BrE)

Arm: **Armkreuzring** *m* PAPIER backing wire; **Armlehne** *f* KER & GLAS chair arm, KFZTECH *Fahrzeuginnenausstattung* armrest; **Armleuchter** *m* ELEKTRIZ chandelier

Aroma *nt* LEBENSMITTEL flavor (AmE), flavour (BrE); **Aromaten** *nt pl* CHEMIE aromatic compounds, aromatics

aromatisch: **~er Kohlenwasserstoff** *m* CHEMIE, KUNSTSTOFF aromatic hydrocarbon; **~e Verbindung** *f* LEBENSMITTEL aromatic compound

ARPA *abbr (automatische Radaraufnahmehilfe)* WASSERTRANS ARPA *(automatic radar plotting aid)*

ARQ *abbr (automatische Wiederholanforderung)* RADIO, TELEKOM ARQ *(automatic repeat request)*

Arrest *m* WASSERTRANS arrest

Arretier- *pref* FERTIG lock, FOTO locating; **Arretierfeder** *f* FERTIG check; **Arretierhebel** *m* FERTIG catch, lock lever; **Arretierschraube** *f* BAU stop screw; **Arretierstift** *m* FERTIG location pin, FOTO locating pin; **Arretierung** *f* COMP & DV latch, FERTIG detent, MASCHINEN detent, lock, stop

ARRL *abbr (Amerikanischer Amateurdachverband)* RADIO ARRL *(American Radio Relay League)*

Arrowrootstärke *f* LEBENSMITTEL arrowroot

Arsen *nt (As)* CHEMIE arsenic *(As)*

Arsenat *nt* CHEMIE arsenate, arsenite

Arsenid *nt* CHEMIE arsenide

Arsenigsäureanhydrid *nt* CHEMIE arsenic oxide, arsenic trioxide

Arsen: **Arsen-Implantation** *f* ELEKTRONIK arsenic implantation

Arsenosulfid *nt* CHEMIE sulfarsenide (AmE), sulpharsenide (BrE)

Arsen: **Arsen-Oxid** *nt* CHEMIE arsenic oxide, arsenic trioxide; **Arsentrioxid** *nt* CHEMIE arsenic oxide, arsenic trioxide

Arsin *nt* CHEMIE arsane

Arsonval-Galvanometer: **d'~** *nt* ELEKTROTECH d'Arsonval galvanometer

Arsphenamin *nt* CHEMIE arsphenamine, salvarsan

ARSR *abbr (Flugüberwachungsradar)* RAUMFAHRT ARSR *(air route surveillance radar)*

Art *f* COMP & DV type

Art.: **~ Nr.** *f (Artikelnummer)* VERPACK part number

Artefakt *nt* ERGON artifact

artesisch[1] *adj* ERDÖL *Brunnen,* WASSERVERSORG artesian

artesisch:[2] **~er Brunnen** *m* WASSERVERSORG artesian well; **~e Quelle** *f* WASSERVERSORG artesian spring; **~es Wasser** *nt* KOHLEN artesian water

Artikel *m* MASCHINEN item; **Artikelnummer** *f* MASCHINEN item number, VERPACK *(Art. Nr.)* part number

Artikulation *f* ERGON articulation

ARU *abbr* COMP & DV *(Sprachausgabe-Einheit)* ARU *(audio response unit)*, RADIO *(automatische Rauschunterdrückung)* ANL *(automatic noise limiter)*

Aryl- *pref* CHEMIE aryl

Arylamin *nt* CHEMIE aminoarene, arylamine

As *(Arsen)* CHEMIE As *(arsenic)*

asb *abbr (Apostilb)* OPTIK asb *(apostilb)*

Asbest *m* FERTIG asbestos, *Kunststoffinstallationen* asbestos, KER & GLAS, KUNSTSTOFF, MECHAN, PAPIER, SICHERHEIT, TEXTIL asbestos; **Asbestbelastungsgrenzwert** *m* SICHERHEIT asbestos exposure limit; **Asbestdichtung** *f* FERTIG asbestos gasket; **Asbesteinlage** *f* BAU asbestos-plaited packing; **Asbestfaser** *f* BAU asbestos thread, KERNTECH asbestos wool

asbestfrei: **~e Isolierplatte** *f* SICHERHEIT asbestos-free insulating plate; **~e Schutzkleidung** *f* SICHERHEIT asbestos-free protective clothing

Asbestin *nt* PAPIER asbestine

Asbest: **Asbestpappe** *f* BAU asbestos millboard; **Asbestplatte** *f* FERTIG, PAPIER asbestos sheet; **Asbestscheibe** *f* MASCHINEN asbestos washer; **Asbestschnur** *f* BAU

asbestos string; **Asbestschürze** *f* FERTIG *Schweißen* asbestos apron; **Asbestwalzenscheibe** *f* KER & GLAS asbestos roll disc (BrE), asbestos roll disk (AmE); **Asbestzement** *m* BAU, PAPIER asbestos cement; **Asbestzementplatten** *f pl* BAU asbestos cement sheeting; **Asbestzwirn** *m* BAU asbestos twine

Asche *f* KUNSTSTOFF, PAPIER ash, THERMOD ashes, UMWELTSCHMUTZ ash; **Asche- und Verbrennungsrückstand** *m* UMWELTSCHMUTZ ash and combustion residue

aschearm: **~es Filterpapier** *nt* LABOR ashless filter paper

Aschebrei *f* MASCHINEN slurry

aschefrei[1] *adj* PAPIER ashless, UMWELTSCHMUTZ ash-free

aschefrei:[2] **~es Filterpapier** *nt* LEBENSMITTEL ashless filter paper

Asche: **Aschegehalt** *m* LEBENSMITTEL, PAPIER ash content; **Aschenkasten** *m* HEIZ & KÄLTE ash box; **Ascherückstand** *m* MASCHINEN ash residue

ASCII *abbr (Amerikanische Datenübertragungs-Codenorm)* COMP & DV, DRUCK ASCII *(American Standard Code for Information Interchange)*

Ascorbin- *pref* CHEMIE ascorbic

ASD *abbr (Rutschsicherung)* KFZTECH ASD *(antiskid device)*

ASE *abbr* KÜNSTL INT *(automatische Spracherkennung)* ASR *(automatic speech recognition)*, TRANS *(Selbststabilisierungsgerät)* ASE *(automatic stabilizing equipment)*

ase *abbr (Flugnormwirkungsgrad)* RAUMFAHRT ase *(air standard efficiency)*

aseptisch[1] *adj* LEBENSMITTEL, VERPACK aseptic

aseptisch:[2] **~e Abfüllung** *f* LEBENSMITTEL aseptic filling

ASG *abbr (Flugnormengruppe)* RAUMFAHRT ASG *(aeronautical standards group)*

ASI *abbr* LUFTTRANS *(Eigengeschwindigkeitsanzeiger, Geschwindigkeitsmesser)*, RAUMFAHRT *(Geschwindigkeitsanzeiger)* ASI *(airspeed indicator)*

ASK *abbr (Amplitudenumtastung)* ELEKTRONIK ASK *(amplitude-shift keying)*

Askarel *nt* ELEKTROTECH *Isolieröl* Askarel

Äskulin *nt* CHEMIE esculin

ASL *abbr (atomare Sicherheitslinie)* KERNTECH ASL *(atomic safety line)*

ASLT *abbr (fortschrittliche Festkörperlogik)* ELEKTRONIK ASLT *(advanced solid logic technology)*

ASME *abbr (Amerikanische Gesellschaft der Maschinenbau-Ingenieure)* QUAL ASME *(American Society of Mechanical Engineers)*

ASME-Code *m* MECHAN ASME code

Asparagin- *pref* CHEMIE aspartic; **Asparaginsäure** *f* LEBENSMITTEL aspartic acid

Aspartam *nt* LEBENSMITTEL *Süßstoff* aspartame

Aspektverhältnis *nt* PHYS aspect ratio

Asphalt *m* BAU asphalt, bitumen; **Asphaltbeton** *m* BAU asphalt concrete; **Asphaltbinderschicht** *f* BAU binder course; **Asphaltdecke** *f* BAU asphalt surfacing; **Asphaltemulsion** *f* MASCHINEN bitumen emulsion

Asphaltieren *nt* BAU asphalting, bituminization

asphaltieren *vt* BAU asphalt, bituminize

asphaltiert *adj* BAU bituminized

Asphalt: **Asphaltkaltgemisch** *nt* BAU cold mix; **Asphaltkocher** *m* BAU asphalt boiler; **Asphalttragschicht** *f* BAU bituminous base course; **Asphaltwerk** *nt* BAU *Tiefbau* asphalt plant

asphärisch: **~e Korrekturplatte** *f* FERNSEH aspheric corrector plate

Aspiration *f* HYDRAUL, PAPIER aspiration; **Aspirations-Porosimeter** *nt* PAPIER aspiration porosimeter; **Aspirationsporositätsprüfer** *m* PAPIER aspiration porosity tester; **Aspirations-Psychrometer** *nt* GERÄT Assmann psychrometer, GERÄT PAPIER *Feuchtigkeitsmesser* aspiration psychrometer; **Aspirationspumpe** *f* HYDRAUL aspiration pump

Aspirator *m* LABOR aspirator

ASR *abbr* COMP & DV *(automatischer Sender-Empfänger)* ASR *(automatic send-receive)*, LUFTTRANS *(Flughafen-Überwachungsradar)* ASR *(airport surveillance radar)*

Assembler *m* COMP & DV *Programmiersprache* assembler; **Assemblerinstruktion** *f* COMP & DV assembler directive, assembler instruction; **Assemblerprogramm** *nt* COMP & DV assembler; **Assemblersprache** *f* COMP & DV assembly language

Assemblier: ~er *m* COMP & DV assembler

Aßmann: ~sches Psychrometer *nt* GERÄT *(Aspirations-Psychrometer)* Assmann psychrometer, GERÄT aspiration psychrometer

Assoziation *f* ERGON association; **Assoziationsliste** *f* KÜNSTL INT association list

Assoziativ- *pref* COMP & DV, MATH associative; **Assoziativadressierung** *f* COMP & DV associative addressing; **Assoziativdatei** *f* COMP & DV content-addressable file

assoziativ [1] *adj* KÜNSTL INT *Suche* associative

assoziativ: [2] ~e Zentraleinheit *f* TELEKOM associative processor

Assoziativ-: **Assoziativgesetz** *nt* MATH associative law; **Assoziativspeicher** *m* *(CAM)* COMP & DV associative memory, associative storage (AmE), associative store (BrE), content-addressable memory, content-addressable storage (AmE), content-addressable store (BrE) *(content-addressable storage)*, KÜNSTL INT associative memory, content-addressable memory *(AM)*

assoziiert: ~e Zeichengabe *f* TELEKOM associated signaling (AmE), associated signalling (BrE)

Ast *m* GEOM branch

astabil: ~e Kippschaltung *f* ELEKTRONIK astable multivibrator; ~e Schaltung *f* ELEKTRONIK astable circuit

astatisch [1] *adj* ELEKTRIZ, PHYS astatic

astatisch: [2] ~es Amperemeter *nt* ELEKTRIZ astatic ammeter; ~es Galvanometer *nt* ELEKTROTECH, PHYS astatic galvanometer; ~er Kreisel *m* RAUMFAHRT free gyroscope; ~es Spannungsmeßgerät *nt* ELEKTRIZ astatic voltmeter

Asteroid *m* RAUMFAHRT asteroid

Asthma-Papier *nt* PAPIER asthma paper

astigmatisch *adj* FERTIG, OPTIK, PHYS astigmatic

Astigmatismus *m* FERNSEH, OPTIK, PHYS astigmatism

ASTM *abbr* *(Amerikanische Gesellschaft für Werkstoffprüfung)* MASCHINEN, QUAL ASTM *(American Society for Testing Materials)*

Astro- *pref* RAUMFAHRT astro-; **Astrodynamik** *f* RAUMFAHRT astrodynamics; **Astrofixierung** *f* RAUMFAHRT astro fix; **Astroführung** *f* RAUMFAHRT stellar guidance; **Astrokompaß** *m* RAUMFAHRT astrocompass; **Astrolenkung** *f* RAUMFAHRT celestial guidance; **Astromechanik** *f* RAUMFAHRT celestial mechanics; **Astrometrie** *f* RAUMFAHRT astrometry; **Astronavigation** *f* WASSERTRANS astronavigation, astronomical navigation

astronomisch: ~es Besteck *nt* WASSERTRANS astronomical position; ~e Einheit *f* *(AE)* METROL astronomical unit *(AU)*; ~es Fernrohr *nt* PHYS astro-

nomical telescope; ~e Kamera *f* FOTO astronomical camera; ~e Navigation *f* LUFTTRANS celestial navigation, WASSERTRANS astronavigation, astronomical navigation, celestial navigation

Astro-: **Astrophysik** *f* RAUMFAHRT astrophysics

Asymmetrie *f* MATH asymmetry; **Asymmetriefehler** *m* PHYS coma

asymmetrisch [1] *adj* COMP & DV asymmetric, GEOM, MATH asymmetrical, asymmetric

asymmetrisch: [2] ~e Ablenkung *f* FERNSEH asymmetric deflection; ~e Doppelleiterspeisung *f* RADIO asymmetric twin feed; ~er Fehlerbereich *m* ELEKTROTECH bias; ~es Gewinde *nt* MASCHINEN asymmetric thread; ~e Schaltung *f* ELEKTRIZ asymmetric circuit; ~es Trapezgewinde *nt* MASCHINEN asymmetric trapezoidal screwthread

Asymptote *f* MATH asymptote

asymptotisch [1] *adj* GEOM asymptotic

asymptotisch: [2] ~e Näherung *f* TELEKOM asymptomatic approximation; ~es Verhalten *nt* GERÄT asymptotic behavior (AmE), asymptotic behaviour (BrE)

Asynchron- *pref* COMP & DV, ELEKTRIZ, TELEKOM asynchronous; **Asynchronbetrieb** *m* TELEKOM asynchronous mode; **Asynchrongenerator** *m* ELEKTRIZ asynchronous generator, ELEKTROTECH asynchronous alternator

asynchron [1] *adj* COMP & DV, EISENBAHN, ELEKTRIZ, FERNSEH, PHYS, RADIO *Satelliten, Umlaufbahnen* asynchronous

asynchron: [2] ~er Betrieb *m* ELEKTRIZ asynchronous running, *Energienetz* asynchronous operation; ~es Netz *nt* TELEKOM asynchronous network; ~e Schaltung *f* COMP & DV asynchronous circuit; ~e Übertragung *f* COMP & DV asynchronous communication, asynchronous transmission, asynchronous mode, TELEKOM asynchronous transmission; ~e Verbindung *f* ELEKTRIZ *Leitungsnetze* asynchronous link; ~es Zeitmultiplexverfahren *nt* TELEKOM ATDM, asynchronous time-division multiplexing

asynchronischer: ~ Übertragungsschnittstellenanpasser *m* *(ACIA)* KONTROLL asynchronous communications interface adaptor *(ACIA)*

Asynchron-: **Asynchronlinearmotor** *m* TRANS asynchronous linear induction motor; **Asynchronmaschine** *f* ELEKTROTECH asynchronous machine; **Asynchronmodem** *nt* ELEKTRONIK asynchronous modem; **Asynchronmotor** *m* ELEKTRIZ asynchronous motor, induction motor, ELEKTROTECH asynchronous motor, FERTIG induction motor, TRANS asynchronous motor; **Asynchronmotor mit Kompensationswicklung** *m* ELEKTRIZ compensated induction motor; **Asynchron-Übertragungsschnittstellenanpasser** *m* *(ACIA)* KONTROLL asynchronous communications interface adaptor *(ACIA)*

Aszension *f* FERTIG *Kapillar* elevating

AT *abbr* *(fortschrittliche Technologie)* COMP & DV AT *(advanced technology)*

aT *abbr* *(Thermodiffusionskonstante)* PHYS aT *(thermal diffusion constant)*

ataktisch: ~es Polymer *nt* KUNSTSTOFF atactic polymer

ATC *abbr* EISENBAHN *(automatische Zugsteuerung)* ATC, ATO *(automatic train operation)*, METALL *(automatischer Werkzeugwechsler)* ATC *(automatic tool changer)*, RADIO *(kapazitive Antennenanpassung)* ATC *(aerial-tuning capacitor)*

ATE *abbr* *(automatische Prüfeinrichtung)* COMP & DV

ATE *(automatic test equipment)*

Atebrin *nt* CHEMIE atebrin, quinacrine

Atelier *nt* FOTO studio; **Atelierarbeit** *f* FOTO studio work; **Atelierkamera** *f* FOTO studio camera

Atem *m* SICHERHEIT, UMWELTSCHUTZ breathing; **Atemgerät** *nt* SICHERHEIT breathing apparatus; **Atemgerät mit externer Luftversorgung** *nt* SICHERHEIT supplied air breathing apparatus; **Atemgrenzwert** *m* UMWELTSCHUTZ breathing capacity; **Atemluft** *f* SICHERHEIT breathable air

Atemschutz *m* SICHERHEIT respiratory protection; ~ **gegen Staub und Gase** *m* SICHERHEIT respirator against harmful dust and gases; **Atemschutzbereich** *m* SICHERHEIT respiratory protection workshop; **Atemschutzfilter** *nt* SICHERHEIT respiratory filter; **Atemschutzgerät** *nt* SICHERHEIT respiratory protective equipment, UMWELTSCHUTZ respiratory protection apparatus; **Atemschutzsystem** *nt* UMWELTSCHUTZ breathing protection system

Atemventil *nt* MASCHINEN breather

Atemzwecken: zu ~ ungeeignet *adj* SICHERHEIT *Luft* unfit for respiration

ATF *abbr (Automatikgetriebeöl)* KFZTECH ATF *(automatic transmission fluid)*

ätherisch[1] *adj* CHEMIE volatile

ätherisch:[2] ~**es Öl** *nt* LEBENSMITTEL essential oil

athermisch *adj* CHEMIE athermal

Athodyd *nt* LUFTTRANS *Staustrahltriebwerk* athodyd

ATI *abbr (Antennenabstimmspule)* RADIO ATI *(aerial-tuning inductance)*

ATM *abbr (Azimutal-Transversal-Mode)* OPTIK *optische Fasern* ATM *(azimuthal transversal mode)*

Atmolyse *f* CHEMIE atmolysis

Atmosphäre *f* PHYS atmosphere

atmosphärisch[1] *adj* PHYS atmospheric

atmosphärisch:[2] ~**e Absorption** *f* STRAHLPHYS atmospheric absorption; ~**er Auswaschvorgang** *m* UMWELTSCHUTZ atmospheric scrubbing; ~ **bedingte Spektrallinie** *f* PHYS atmospheric line; ~**er Druck** *m* WASSERTRANS atmospheric pressure; ~**e Entladung** *f* ELEKTROTECH lightning discharge; ~**e Erscheinung** *f* UMWELTSCHUTZ atmospheric phenomenon; ~**e Luftbelastung** *f* UMWELTSCHUTZ atmospheric loading; ~**e Masse** *f* NICHTFOSS ENERG air mass; ~**er Niederschlag** *m* UMWELTSCHUTZ atmospheric fallout, atmospheric precipitation, precipitation; ~**es Rauschen** *nt* AUFNAHME atmospheric noise, ELEKTROTECH atmospherics; ~**e Säurekapazität** *f* UMWELTSCHUTZ atmospheric acidity; ~**er Schwefel** *m* UMWELTSCHUTZ atmospheric sulfur (AmE), atmospheric sulphur (BrE); ~**e Störung** *f* AUFNAHME, ELEKTRONIK atmospheric noise, ELEKTROTECH atmospherics, WASSERTRANS atmospheric disturbance; ~**e Verdunklung** *f* UMWELTSCHUTZ atmospheric obscurity; ~**e Welle** *f* PHYS sky wave

ATMOS-Spur *f* AUFNAHME atmos track

Atmung:[1] **die ~ betreffend** *adj* SICHERHEIT respiratory

atmungsaktiv *adj* KUNSTSTOFF breathable

Atmung:[2] **Atmungsaktivität** *f* KUNSTSTOFF breathability; **Atmungsapparat** *m* KOHLEN breathing apparatus; **Atmungsferment** *nt* CHEMIE *Biochemie* oxygenase

Atoll *nt* WASSERTRANS *Geographie* atoll

Atom *nt* COMP & DV, PHYS, TEILPHYS atom; **Atomabfallbeseitigung durch Kernumwandlung** *f* KERNTECH waste disposal by nuclear transmutation; **Atomabsorptions-Spektrometer** *nt* LABOR atomic absorption

spectrometer; **Atomabsorptions-Spektroskopie** *f* KERNTECH, PHYS, STRAHLPHYS atomic absorption spectroscopy; **Atomanlage** *f* ELEKTROTECH, KERNTECH nuclear power plant

Atomantrieb: mit ~ *adj* KERNTECH, WASSERTRANS *Schiff, U-Boot* nuclear-powered

atomar[1] *adj* PHYS, TEILPHYS atomic

atomar:[2] ~**e Absorptionsanalyse** *f* KERNTECH, PHYS, STRAHLPHYS atomic absorption analysis; ~**es Absorptions-Spektrofotometer** *nt* KERNTECH, PHYS, STRAHLPHYS atomic absorption spectrophotometer; ~**e Elektronenumlaufbahn** *f* KERNTECH, PHYS, STRAHLPHYS atomic orbital; ~**es Energieniveau** *nt* KERNTECH, PHYS, STRAHLPHYS atomic energy level; ~**e Fluoreszenzanalyse** *f* KERNTECH *Spektrometrie*, PHYS *Spektrometrie*, STRAHLPHYS *Spektrometrie* atomic fluorescence analysis; ~**e Masseneinheit** *f (amu)* KERNTECH atomic mass unit *(amu)*; ~**e Polarisation** *f* KERNTECH, PHYS, STRAHLPHYS atomic polarization; ~**er Querschnitt** *m* KERNTECH, PHYS, STRAHLPHYS atomic cross-section; ~**e Sicherheitslinie** *f (ASL)* KERNTECH atomic safety line *(ASL)*; ~**e Strahlung** *f* KERNTECH, PHYS, STRAHLPHYS atomic radiation; ~**e Streuung** *f* KERNTECH, PHYS, STRAHLPHYS atomic scattering; ~**e Struktur** *f* KERNTECH atomistic structure; ~**er Urandampf** *m* KERNTECH atomic uranium vapor (AmE), atomic uranium vapour (BrE); ~**e Wärmekapazität** *f* KERNTECH, PHYS, STRAHLPHYS atomic heat capacity; ~**er Wasserstoffmaser** *m* ELEKTRONIK atomic hydrogen maser; ~**er Zwischenraum** *m* KERNTECH, PHYS, STRAHLPHYS atomic interspace

Atom: Atomforschung *f* KERNTECH atomic research; **Atomgas-Laser** *m* ELEKTRONIK atomic gas laser

atomgetrieben *adj* KERNTECH, WASSERTRANS *Schiff, U-Boot* nuclear-powered

Atom: Atomgewicht *nt* KERNTECH, MASCHINEN atomic weight, PHYS, STRAHLPHYS atomic mass, atomic weight; **Atomgewichtseinheit** *f* KERNTECH atomic weight unit; **Atomhülle** *f* KERNTECH, PHYS, STRAHLPHYS atomic electron shell

Atomisator *m* CHEMTECH atomizer

Atomistik *f* PHYS atomicity

Atomizität *f* COMP & DV atomicity

Atom: Atomkern *m* KERNTECH, PHYS, STRAHLPHYS atomic core, atomic nucleus, TEILPHYS nucleus; **Atomkraftwerk** *nt* ELEKTROTECH nuclear power station; **Atommasse** *f (Ma)* KERNTECH atomic mass *(Ma)*; **Atommasseneinheit** *f (AME)* KERNTECH atomic weight unit *(AWU)*; **Atommassenkonstante** *f (mu)* KERNTECH unified atomic mass constant *(mu)*; **Atommeiler** *m* KERNTECH pile; **Atommüll** *m* ABFALL, KERNTECH, STRAHLPHYS radioactive waste; **Atommüll mit langer Halbwertzeit** *m* ABFALL, KERNTECH long-life radioactive waste; **Atomphysik** *f* PHYS atomic physics; **Atomradius** *m* KERNTECH, PHYS, STRAHLPHYS atomic radius; **Atomradiustheorie** *f* KERNTECH theory of effective radius; **Atomrakete** *f* KERNTECH, RAUMFAHRT atomic rocket; **Atomspektroskopie** *f* KERNTECH, PHYS, STRAHLPHYS atomic spectroscopy; **Atomspektrum** *nt* KERNTECH, PHYS, STRAHLPHYS atomic spectrum; **Atomstrahl** *m* KERNTECH, PHYS, STRAHLPHYS atomic beam; **Atomstruktur** *f* KERNTECH atomic structure, PHYS atomic structure, structure of the atom, STRAHLPHYS atomic structure; **Atomtest** *m* KERNTECH, WERKPRÜF nuclear test

Atom-U-Boot *nt* WASSERTRANS *Marine* nuclear-powered submarine

Atom: **Atomuhr** *f* KERNTECH, PHYS, STRAHLPHYS, TELE-KOM atomic clock; **Atomumordnen** *nt* METALL atomic shuffling; **Atomverschiebung** *f* METALL atomic displacement; **Atomversuch** *m* KERNTECH, WERKPRÜF nuclear test; **Atomvolumen** *nt* KERNTECH, PHYS, STRAHLPHYS atomic volume; **Atomwärme** *f* KERNTECH, PHYS, STRAHLPHYS atomic heat capacity, THERMOD atomic heat; **Atomzahl** *f* (*Z*) KERNTECH atomic number (*Z*)

ATP *abbr* (*Adenosintriphosphat*) LEBENSMITTEL ATP (*adenosine triphosphate*)

Atropa- *pref* CHEMIE atropic

AT-Schweißen *nt* (*aluminothermisches Schweißen*) FER-TIG AT welding (*aluminothermic welding*)

Attapulgit *nt* ERDÖL *Adsorptionsmittel* attapulgite

Atterberg: **~sche Konsistenzgrenzen** *f pl* BAU *Tiefbau* Atterberg limits

Attrappe *f* WASSERTRANS *Schiffkonstruktion* mock-up

Attribut *nt* COMP & DV, KÜNSTL INT *eines Objekts*, QUAL attribute; **Attributprüfung** *f* GERÄT acceptance inspection, QUAL inspection by attributes

ATU *abbr* (*Antennenanpassung*) RADIO ATU (*aerial-tuning unit*)

ATV *abbr* (*Amateurfernsehen*) FERNSEH ATV (*amateur television*)

Atwater: **Atwater-Faktoren** *m pl* LEBENSMITTEL Atwater factors; **Atwater-Tabelle** *f* LEBENSMITTEL Atwater table

Atwood: **~sche Fallmaschine** *f* PHYS Atwood's machine

Ätz- *pref* CHEMIE caustic, FERTIG etching; **Ätzbad** *nt* FERTIG etching bath; **Ätzdruck** *m* TEXTIL discharge printing

ätzen *vt* BAU bite, etch, CHEMIE attack, etch, METALL, RADIO *Platinen* etch

Ätzen *nt* BAU pickling, CHEMIE attack, etching, DRUCK etching

Ätz-: **Ätzfigur** *f* FERTIG etch figure; **Ätzflüssigkeit** *f* MET-ALL etching solution; **Ätzgrube** *f* FERTIG etching pit; **Ätzkali** *nt* CHEMIE potassium hydroxide; **Ätzkalk** *m* CHEMIE, MEERSCHMUTZ quicklime; **Ätzkraft** *f* CHEMIE causticity, corrosiveness; **Ätzmaschine** *f* DRUCK etching machine; **Ätzmittel** *nt* FERTIG etchant; **Ätznatron** *nt* CHEMIE caustic soda, sodium hydrate, sodium hydroxide

ätzpolieren *vt* METALL attack-polish

Ätz-: **Ätzung** *f* DRUCK, ELEKTRONIK etching, FERTIG bite; **Ätzwasser** *nt* CHEMIE caustic water, nitric acid

Audio- *pref* AKUSTIK, AUFNAHME audio; **Audio-CD** *f* OPTIK audio compact disc (BrE), audio compact disk (AmE); **Audio-CD-Spieler** *m* OPTIK audio compact disc player (BrE), audio compact disk player (AmE); **Audio-Eingang** *m* AUFNAHME audio input; **Audiofrequenzbereich** *m* STRAHLPHYS audio range; **Audiogramm** *nt* AKUSTIK, ERGON audiogram; **Audiogramm-Maskierung** *f* AKUSTIK audiogram masking; **Audiokonferenz** *f* TELEKOM telephone conference; **Audiometer** *nt* AKUSTIK, ERGON, GERÄT audiometer; **Audiometrie** *f* AKUSTIK, AUFNAHME, ERGON audiometry; **Audiometrie evozierter Reaktionen** *f* ERGON evoked response audiometry

audiometrisch: **~e Kabine** *f* AUFNAHME audiometric booth

Audiosignal *nt* ELEKTRONIK audio signal

Audio-Videotext *m* TELEKOM audio videotex

Audit *nt* QUAL audit

auditieren *vti* QUAL audit

Auditor *m* QUAL auditor

Auditplan *m* QUAL audit plan

Auf- und Abbewegung *f* MASCHINEN reciprocating motion, up-and-down motion

auf- und abgehend *adj* MASCHINEN reciprocating

Auf- und Abwickelmaschine *f* VERPACK unwinding machine

Auf- und Abwickelvorrichtungen *f pl* VERPACK wind/unwind equipment

Auf- und Niedergang *m* MASCHINEN up-and-down motion

Aufarbeitung *f* KERNTECH reprocessing, MASCHINEN regeneration; **Aufarbeitungsvorrichtung** *f* UMWELT-SCHMUTZ recovery device; **Aufarbeitungszentrum für wiederverwertbare feste Abfallmaterialien** *nt* UMWELT-SCHMUTZ processing center for recyclable solid waste materials (AmE), processing centre for recyclable solid waste materials (BrE)

Aufbau *m* BAU assembly, erection, COMP & DV architecture, layout, setup, ERDÖL *Bohrtechnik* rigging up, FERTIG *Kunststoffinstallationen* assembly, KONTROLL structure, MECHAN assembly, PAPIER erection, WASSER-TRANS superstructure; **~ einer Nachricht** *m* COMP & DV message structure

aufbauen *vt* BAU build up, set up, COMP & DV set-up, KONTROLL configure, MASCHINEN, MECHAN erect; **neu ~** *vt* ELEKTRONIK *des Bildschirminhalts* refresh

Aufbau: **Aufbauenergie** *f* METALL formation energy; **Aufbaufaktor** *m* KERNTECH build-up factor; **Aufbaufeld** *nt* KONSTZEICH add-on block

Aufbäumung *f* TEXTIL beaming

Aufbau: **Aufbauorganisation** *f* QUAL organizational structure; **Aufbauschneide** *f* MASCHINEN built-up edge

Aufbereiten *nt* KOHLEN milling

aufbereiten *vt* ABFALL treat, BAU prepare, CHEMTECH *Erz* concentrate, FERTIG *Erz* dress, KOHLEN condition, table

Aufbereitung *f* CHEMTECH *Hadern* breaking, ERDÖL *Erdgas* treatment, FERTIG *Erz* dressing, KER & GLAS beneficiation, KOHLEN conditioning, processing, WAS-SERVERSORG make-up; **~ des Eingangssignals** *f* ELEKTRONIK input signal conditioning; **Aufbereitungsanlage** *f* ABFALL preparation plant, processing plant; **Aufbereitungsbehälter** *m* KOHLEN conditioning tank; **Aufbereitungsprodukt** *nt* LEBENSMITTEL concentrate; **Aufbereitungsverfahren** *nt* ABFALL conditioning process, preparation process, treatment process

aufbewahren *vt* BAU keep

Aufbewahrung *f* KERNTECH storage, QUAL filing, retention; **Aufbewahrungsfrist** *f* QUAL filing period, retention period; **Aufbewahrungskanister** *m* KERN-TECH storage canister

aufbiegen *vt* BAU *Bewehrungsstahl* bend up

Aufbiegung *f* BAU bend

Aufblasanschluß *m* MEERSCHMUTZ *einer Ölsperre* inflation cuff

aufblasbar[1] *adj* MEERSCHMUTZ inflatable

aufblasbar:[2] **~es Boot** *nt* WASSERTRANS inflatable dinghy; **~e Dichtung** *f* KERNTECH inflatable seal; **~e Pontons** *m pl* LUFTTRANS, WASSERTRANS inflatable pontoons; **~e Seenotrutsche** *f* LUFTTRANS inflatable slide

Aufblasen *nt* MEERSCHMUTZ inflation

aufblasen *vt* PHYS inflate
Aufblättern *nt* PHYS exfoliation
Aufblitzen *nt* ELEKTROTECH, FOTO flashing, METALL fulguration
Aufbocken *nt* MASCHINEN jacking
aufbocken *vt* KFZTECH *Verwendung von Werkzeug, Karosserie* jack
Aufbohren *nt* MASCHINEN boring, counterboring, reboring; ~ **tiefer Bohrungen** *nt* FERTIG deep-hole boring
aufbohren *vt* KFZTECH *Motor, Zylinder* rebore, MASCHINEN counterbore, rebore
Aufbohrer: ~ **für vorgegossene Löcher** *m* FERTIG *Spanung* core drill
Aufbohrmeißel *m* ERDÖL *Bohrtechnik* borer bit
Aufbohrung *f* MASCHINEN counterbore
Aufbrauch *m* METALL exhaustion
Aufbrechen *nt* MECHAN breaking up
aufbrechen *vt* BAU break, *eine Tür* break open, SICHERHEIT break open
Aufbringen *nt* ELEKTRONIK *Leiterplatte* deposition, WASSERTRANS *Schiff* seizure; ~ **einer neuen Schotterschicht** *nt* BAU *Straßenbau* remetaling (AmE), remetalling (BrE); ~ **von Schotter** *nt* BAU, TRANS macadamization
aufbringen *vt* ANSTRICH apply, WASSERTRANS *Schiffinstandhaltung* fit
Aufbringung *f* WASSERTRANS *Schiff* seizure
Aufbuchtung *f* WASSERTRANS hog
aufdämmen *vt* BAU bank up
Aufdampfen *nt* FERTIG vapor depositing (AmE), vapour depositing (BrE), THERMOD vapor deposition (AmE), vapour deposition (BrE)
aufdampfen *vt* FERTIG vapor-deposit (AmE), vapour-deposit (BrE)
Aufdampfverfahren *nt* CHEMTECH vapor deposition technique (AmE), vapour deposition technique (BrE)
Auf-den-Kopf-Stellen *nt* SICHERHEIT overturning
Aufdornen *nt* FERTIG piercing, MASCHINEN drifting
aufdornen *vt* FERTIG drift, pierce, MECHAN ream
Aufdorner *m* MECHAN reamer
Aufdornversuch *m* FERTIG expanding test
Aufdrehen *nt* MASCHINEN untwisting
aufdrehen *vt* WASSERVERSORG turn on, *einen Hahn* turn on
Aufdruck *m* TEXTIL impression
aufeinanderfolgend: ~ **er Fehlerblock** *m* TELEKOM CEB, consecutive error block
Aufenthalt *m* TRANS *Eisenbahn* halt; **Aufenthaltsmodul** *nt* RAUMFAHRT *bemannte Raumstation* habitation module; **Aufenthaltswahrscheinlichkeit** *f* STRAHLPHYS *eines Teilchens* probability of presence
Auffächern *nt* KERNTECH *eines Spektrums* unfolding
Auffächerung *f* ELEKTROTECH fan
Auffahren: ~ **der Weiche** *nt* EISENBAHN forcing the points
Auffahrunfall *m* TRANS rear end collision
Auffang *m* ANSTRICH strip, HEIZ & KÄLTE drip, MEERSCHMUTZ collection, interception; **Auffangbecken** *nt* BAU catchpit; **Auffangbehälter** *m* ERDÖL receiver; **Auffangeinrichtung** *f* MEERSCHMUTZ *für Öl* collection device
Auffangen *nt* MEERSCHMUTZ *von Öl* collection; ~ **eines Leitstrahls** *nt* LUFTTRANS beam interception
auffangen *vt* MEERSCHMUTZ *Öl* collect, TELEKOM *Signal* pick up

Auffang: **Auffangschale** *f* HEIZ & KÄLTE drip tray; **Auffangtank** *m* ANSTRICH strip tank; **Auffangtank für Reaktorkühlmittel** *m* KERNTECH reactor coolant drain tank; **Auffangwanne** *f* ANSTRICH strip tank
aufflammen: ~ **lassen** *vt* THERMOD flare up
aufflanschen *vt* ERDÖL flange up
auffordern *vt* COMP & DV prompt, request
Aufforderung *f* COMP & DV demand, enquiry, query
Aufformziehen *nt* TEXTIL boarding
auffrischen *vt* ELEKTRONIK *Daten* refresh, FERTIG recuperate, WASSERTRANS *Wind* rise
Auffrischung *f* AKUSTIK recruitment
aufführen *vt* COMP & DV list
Auffülladung *f* ELEKTROTECH topping charge
Auffüllen *nt* COMP & DV padding, KER & GLAS making-up
auffüllen *vt* BAU *Graben* fill up, COMP & DV pad
Auffüllung *f* BAU *Erdreich* made ground, *zur Schalldämmung* pugging, UMWELTSCHMUTZ backfill
Aufgabe *f* COMP & DV task, PATENT *technische Aufgabe in Erfindungsbeschreibung* problem; **Aufgabenanalyse** *f* ERGON task analysis; **Aufgabenbereich** *m* REGELUNG range of desired variable; **Aufgabenbeschreibung** *f* ERGON task description; **Aufgabenerfüllung** *f* ERGON accomplishment of task; **Aufgabengröße** *f* REGELUNG indirectly controlled variable; **Aufgabenhierarchie** *f* ERGON task hierarchy; **Aufgabensteuerung** *f* COMP & DV task management; **Aufgabetrichter** *m* BAU feed hopper; **Aufgabevorrichtung** *f* MASCHINEN feeder, feeding device
Aufgangszeit *f* LUFTTRANS *Schallknall* rise time
aufgearbeitet *adj* ELEKTRONIK regenerated
aufgeblasen: **nicht** ~ *adj* KER & GLAS not blown up
aufgebracht: ~ **e Schicht** *f* ELEKTRONIK deposited layer
aufgedampft: ~ **e Schicht** *f* CHEMTECH vapor-deposited layer (AmE), vapour-deposited layer (BrE), ELEKTRONIK evaporated layer
aufgedrückt: ~ **e Spannung** *f* METALL applied stress
aufgeführt: **in** ~ **er Reihenfolge** *adj* PATENT in the order specified
aufgegeben: ~ **Bohrung** *f* ERDÖL *Bohrtechnik* lost hole
aufgehängt: ~ **e Bedienung** *f* SICHERHEIT pendant switch control; ~ **e Steuerung** *f* SICHERHEIT pendant switch control
aufgeheizt *adj* KER & GLAS fired-on
aufgeklebt: ~ **e Dichtung** *f* VERPACK bonded seal, glued seal
aufgeladen: ~ **er Motor** *m* EISENBAHN supercharged engine
aufgelaufen[1] *adj* WASSERTRANS *Schiff* aground
aufgelaufen:[2] ~ **er Fehler** *m* GERÄT accumulated error
aufgelegt[1] *adj* WASSERTRANS *Schiff* laid-up
aufgelegt:[2] ~ **e elektromotorische Kraft** *f* ELEKTRIZ *EMK* impressed electromotive force; ~ **e Spannung** *f* ELEKTRIZ impressed voltage; ~ **e Tonnage** *f* WASSERTRANS *Seehandel* idle shipping
aufgelöst[1] *adj* CHEMTECH dissolved
aufgelöst:[2] ~ **e Scherspannung** *f* METALL resolved shear stress; ~ **er Stoff** *m* LEBENSMITTEL solute
aufgerahmt: ~ **er Latex** *m* KUNSTSTOFF creamed latex
aufgesattelt: ~ **e Treppe** *f* BAU cutstring staircase, open string stairs
aufgeschrumpft *adj* THERMOD heat-shrunk
aufgeschüttet *adj* BAU heaped, *Erdreich* made-up
aufgesetzt: ~ **er spannungsgeregelter Oszillator** *m* ELEKTRONIK set-on voltage-controlled oscillator
aufgespannt *adj* FERTIG *Werkzeug* set-up

aufgeständert: ~**e Fahrbahn** *f* EISENBAHN elevated track beam

aufgesteckt: ~**es Filter** *nt* FOTO mounted filter

aufgeteilt *adj* COMP & DV partitioned

aufgetrieben: ~**es Ende** *nt* KER & GLAS flared end; ~**er Flaschenhals** *m* KER & GLAS flared neck

aufgewickelt: ~**es Garn** *nt* KER & GLAS beamed yarn

aufgezeichnet: ~**e Dosis** *f* STRAHLPHYS dose recorded; ~**e Wellenlänge** *f* AKUSTIK recorded wavelength

Aufglasur *f* KER & GLAS overglazing

Aufgliederung *f* BAU breakdown

aufglühen *vt* TEXTIL blaze

Aufgrundlaufen *nt* WASSERTRANS *eines Schiffes* earthing (BrE), grounding (AmE)

Aufguß *m* LEBENSMITTEL infusion

aufhalden *vt* KOHLEN stockpile

Aufhängehaken *m* MASCHINEN suspension hook

Aufhänger *m* MASCHINEN hanger

Aufhängung *f* ELEKTROTECH *in Meßwerken,* MASCHINEN, PHYS *Montage* suspension; ~ **eines Trimm-Abschaltstabes** *f* KERNTECH shim safety rod suspension

Aufhängungen *f pl* MASCHINEN hanger fixtures

Aufhängungsteile *nt pl* MASCHINEN hanger fixtures

Aufhäufen *nt* BAU piling up

aufhäufen *vt* BAU bank

Aufheben *nt* TRANS lifting

aufheben *vt* TELEKOM *Alarm* set off

Aufhebungszeichen *nt* AKUSTIK natural

Aufheiz- *pref* KUNSTSTOFF, THERMOD heating

Aufheizen *nt* KER & GLAS firing-on, heating-up

aufheizen *vt* KER & GLAS, TEXTIL, THERMOD heat, heat up

aufheizend: ~**e und enthärtende Schadstoffe** *m pl* ABFALL thermosoftening contaminants

Aufheiz-: **Aufheizkurve** *f* KUNSTSTOFF heating curve, THERMOD heating-up curve; **Aufheiztiefe** *f* THERMOD heating depth; **Aufheizzeit** *f* THERMOD heating-up time

Aufhell- *pref* FOTO fill-in; **Aufhellblitz** *m* FOTO fill-in flash; **Aufhellungsschirm** *m* FOTO reflecting screen

aufhellen *vt* BAU tint, TEXTIL *Färben* raise

Aufhell-: **Aufhellicht** *nt* FOTO fill-in light; **Aufhellschirm** *m* FOTO reflecting screen

aufheulen: ~ **lassen** *vt* KFZTECH *Motor* rev up

Aufhöhung *f* BAU *einer Mauer* raising

Aufkimmung *f* WASSERTRANS *Schiffskonstruktion* deadrise, *Schiffkonstruktion* rise of floor

Aufklappmenü *nt* COMP & DV drop-down menu, pop-up menu

Aufklärungssatellit *m* RAUMFAHRT observation satellite

Aufkleber *m* COMP & DV external label, PAPIER paster

Aufklebezettel *m* QUAL sticker

aufklotzen *vt* TEXTIL *Färben* pad

Aufklotzung *f* WASSERTRANS *Schiffbau* chock

Aufkochen *nt* CHEMTECH boiling

Aufkochneigung *f* KER & GLAS tendency to reboil

Aufkohlen *nt* FERTIG *Stahl* acierage, MASCHINEN carburizing, METALL cementation

aufkohlen *vt* FERTIG carburize, cementite, METALL cement

Aufkohlung *f* FERTIG, RADIO carburization; **Aufkohlungsmittel** *nt* FERTIG carburizer

aufkommen *vi* WASSERTRANS *Sturm* rise

aufkratzen *vt* BAU scratch

aufladbar: ~**e Zelle** *f* PHYS rechargable cell

Auflade- *pref* ELEKTROTECH charging; **Aufladegebläse** *nt* FERTIG booster, KFZTECH supercharger

aufladen *vt* BAU recharge, *Last* saddle, ELEKTROTECH *Batterie* boost

Auflader *m* MECHAN supercharger

Auflade-: **Aufladestelle** *f* TRANS charging point; **Aufladevorrichtung** *f* TRANS charger; **Aufladezeit** *f* FOTO recharge time

Aufladung *f* ELEKTROTECH charge, charging, KFZTECH supercharging, LUFTTRANS supercharge; ~ **unter Last** *f* KERNTECH on-load refueling (AmE), on-load refuelling (BrE)

Auflage *f* BAU seat, FERTIG heel, MASCHINEN rest; **Auflagefläche** *f* BAU bearing area, seat, MASCHINEN bearing surface, seat, seating, TRANS bearing surface; **Auflageholz** *nt* BAU pole plate; **Auflagekonsole** *f* MECHAN bearing pad; **Auflagennummer** *f* VERPACK batch number; **Auflageplatte** *f* MASCHINEN base plate; **Auflageplattieren** *nt* MECHAN overlay cladding; **Auflagepuffer** *m* MECHAN bearing pad; **Auflagepunkt** *m* MASCHINEN point of support

Auflager *m* BAU bearing, saddle, support, COMP & DV, MASCHINEN support, TRANS bearing; **Auflagerfläche** *f* BAU bedding surface

auflagern *vt* BAU rest

Auflagerplatte *f* BAU bearing plate, bed plate, FERTIG *Spanung* bed plate

Auflagerung *f* BAU support

Auflageschiene *f* TRANS bearing rail; ~ **für das Werkstück** *f* MASCHINEN work plate

auflandig: ~**er Wind** *m* WASSERTRANS onshore wind

Auflaufbremsbacke *f* KFZTECH primary shoe

auflaufen *vi* WASSERTRANS *absichtlich, auf den Strand* beach

auflaufend: ~**es Wasser** *nt* WASSERTRANS *Gezeiten* rising tide

auflegen *vt* WASSERTRANS *Schiff* lay up

Auflicht *nt* FERTIG incident light, FOTO reflected light; **Auflichtmikroskop** *nt* METROL microscope for reflected light

aufliegen¹ *vt* BAU rest

aufliegen² *vi* BAU seat

auflisten *vt* COMP & DV list

Auflistung *f* COMP & DV listing

Auflockern *nt* FERTIG *Formsand* opening

auflockern *vt* FERTIG open, *Formsand* aerate

auflodern *vi* THERMOD blaze up

Auflösbarkeit *f* CHEMIE dissolubility

Auflösebehälter *m* CHEMTECH dissolver

Auflösen *nt* CHEMTECH *Vorgang* dissolution

auflösen *vt* MEERSCHMUTZ foul

Auflösung *f* AKUSTIK resolution, CHEMIE decomposition, dissolution, COMP & DV, ELEKTRIZ definition, resolution, FERNSEH *Grafik,* resolution, MATH solution, PATENT *eines Vertrages* cancellation, PHYS suspension; ~ **der Verzahnung** *f* ELEKTRONIK de-interleaving; **Auflösungsmittel** *nt* CHEMIE dissolvent; **Auflösungsvermögen** *nt* COMP & DV resolution, ELEKTRONIK resolving power, *Funkortung* discrimination, FOTO, METALL, PHYS resolving power; **Auflösungsvermögen des Ohres** *nt* AKUSTIK aural resolving power

Aufmachung *f* WASSERVERSORG make-up

Aufmaß *nt* HEIZ & KÄLTE allowance; ~**e** *nt pl* WASSERTRANS *Schiffbau* offsets

Aufmauern *nt* BAU coping

aufmauern *vt* BAU brick up, cope, mason

Aufmerksamkeit *f* ERGON asymmetry, SICHERHEIT care
Aufnahme *f* AKUSTIK detection, record, recording, AUF-
NAHME recording, *mit konstanter Geschwindigkeit*
constant-velocity recording, BAU *Gebäude, Bausub-
stanz* survey, ELEKTROTECH *von Leistung, Energie,
Kraft* absorption, FERTIG seat, FOTO shot, HYDRAUL
IP, input, LEBENSMITTEL absorption, MASCHINEN accommodation, TELEKOM *Akustik* recording, *Karte*
slot; ~ **aus der Froschperspektive** *f* FOTO low-angle
shot; ~ **des Imprägniermittels** *f* TEXTIL dip pick-up; ~
und Orientierung *f* FERTIG mounting and location; ~
zum sofortigen Abspielen *f* AKUSTIK, AUFNAHME instantaneous recording; ~ **von Streuspannungen** *f* GERÄT
stray signal pick-up; ~ **von unten** *f* FOTO low-angle
shot; ~ **für Werkstücke** *f* FERTIG workholder; **Aufnah-
me-/Abspielgerät** *nt* AUFNAHME recorder-player;
Aufnahme-/Speicherröhre *f* ELEKTRONIK recording
storage tube; **Aufnahme/Wiedergabe-Magnetkopf** *m*
AKUSTIK recording/reproducing magnetic head; **Auf-
nahmeabstellknopf** *m* AUFNAHME record defeat tab;
Aufnahmebandspule *f* FERNSEH take-up spool; **Auf-
nahmebehälter** *m* KERNTECH receiving assembly;
Aufnahmeblase *f* KER & GLAS gathering bubble; **Auf-
nahmebühne** *f* AUFNAHME recording stage;
Aufnahmebunker *m* ABFALL receiving bunker; **Aufnah-
mecharakteristik** *f* AUFNAHME *des Mikrofons*
directional characteristic; **Aufnahmeeigenschaft** *f*
FERNSEH recording characteristic; **Aufnahmeeisen** *nt*
KER & GLAS gathering iron; **Aufnahmeende** *nt* KER &
GLAS gathering end; **Aufnahmeentfernung** *f* FOTO
shooting distance; **Aufnahmeentzerrung** *f* AUFNAHME
pre-equalization; **Aufnahmefähigkeit** *f* PAPIER absorp-
tiveness, VERPACK holding capacity, WASSERVERSORG
absorption capacity; **Aufnahmegerät** *nt* AUFNAHME,
COMP & DV, TELEKOM recorder; **Aufnahmegeräusch** *nt*
AUFNAHME recording noise; **Aufnahmekabine** *f* AUF-
NAHME recording booth; **Aufnahmekanal** *m*
AUFNAHME recording channel; **Aufnahmekette** *f*
FERNSEH recording chain; **Aufnahmeknopf** *m* FERN-
SEH record button; **Aufnahmekopf** *m* FERNSEH
recording head; **Aufnahmeloch** *nt* KER & GLAS gathering hole; **Aufnahmemagnetkopf** *m* AKUSTIK recording
magnetic head; **Aufnahmenzähler** *m* FOTO exposure
counter; **Aufnahmeobjektiv** *nt* FOTO taking lens; **Auf-
nahmepegel** *m* AUFNAHME recording level;
Aufnahmepunkt *m* KONSTZEICH location point; **Auf-
nahmeraum** *m* AUFNAHME recording room; **Aufnahme-
rohr** *nt* MASCHINEN pilot hole; **Aufnahme-
röhre** *f* FERNSEH pick-up tube; **Aufnahmeschuh** *m* KER
& GLAS gathering shoe; **Aufnahmesender** *m* FERNSEH
pick-up transmitter; **Aufnahmesession** *f* AUFNAHME
recording session; **Aufnahmespitze** *f* FERTIG work
center (AmE), work centre (BrE); **Aufnahmespur** *f*
AKUSTIK recording track; **Aufnahmestrom** *m* FERNSEH
record current; **Aufnahmestudio** *nt* AUFNAHME recording studio; **Aufnahmetaste** *f* AUFNAHME record
button; **Aufnahmetemperatur** *f* KER & GLAS gathering
temperature; **Aufnahmetreiber** *m* FERNSEH record
driver; **Aufnahmevorgang** *m* AUFNAHME recording
process; **Aufnahmevorrichtung** *f* FERTIG workholding
device, workholding fixture
Aufnehmen *nt* FERNSEH recording, KER & GLAS gathering; ~ **von geformtem Glas zur Endbearbeitung** *nt* KER
& GLAS snapping; ~ **von Glas mit dem Hefteisen** *nt* KER
& GLAS puntying
aufnehmen[1] *vt* AUFNAHME record, BAU house, CHEMIE

Flüssigkeiten imbibe, FERNSEH record, KER & GLAS
gather, SICHERHEIT absorb, TELEKOM *Ton* pick up,
UMWELTSCHMUTZ *Biologie* ingest
aufnehmen[2] *vi* BAU *Vermessung* conduct a survey
aufnehmend: ~**es Außenteil** *nt* FERTIG female part
Aufnehmer *m* ELEKTRONIK *für Meßwerte* sensor, ERGON,
KERNTECH, MASCHINEN, TRANS pick-up; **Aufnehmer-
signal** *nt* ELEKTRONIK sensor signal
Aufprall *m* KOHLEN impact, MASCHINEN impact,
impingement, MECHAN impact, METALL impingement; **Aufprallbruchstelle** *f* KERNTECH impact
fracture
aufprallend: ~**es Teilchen** *nt* KERNTECH impinging
particle
Aufprallfestigkeit *f* KERNTECH impact strength
aufprallsicher: ~**e Motorhaube** *f* KFZTECH crush-proof
safety bonnet (BrE), crush-proof safety hood (AmE)
Aufprall: **Aufpralltest** *m* KERNTECH impact check; **Auf-
prallversuch** *m* KFZTECH collision test, impact test
aufpressen *vt* MASCHINEN force on
Aufpumpen *nt* MEERSCHMUTZ inflation
Aufputzmontage *f* COMP & DV surface mounting
Aufquellen *nt* KUNSTSTOFF swelling
aufquellend: ~**er Boden** *m* KOHLEN swelling soil
Aufrahmen *nt* KUNSTSTOFF creaming
Aufrahmmittel *nt* KUNSTSTOFF creaming agent
Aufrahmung *f* KUNSTSTOFF creaming
Aufrauhen *nt* BAU scarification, FERTIG ragging, TEXTIL
napping, *Tuch* raising
aufrauhen *vt* BAU scarify, score, FERTIG rag, *Schleifschei-
be* sharpen, *Walzen* boss, MASCHINEN roughen,
TEXTIL nap, *Tuch* raise
Aufrauhungszone: **mit** ~ *adj* FERTIG *Getriebelehre,
Zahnflanke* scuffed
aufrecht:[1] ~ **gehaltener Diamant** *m* KER & GLAS diamond
held upright
aufrecht:[2] ~ **transportieren** *vt* VERPACK keep upright
Aufrechterhaltung: ~ **eines Patents** *f* PATENT maintenance of a patent
Aufreibdorn *m* BAU reaming iron
Aufreiben *nt* MASCHINEN reaming, reaming-out
Aufreiß- *pref* VERPACK pull-off, tear-off; **Aufreißdeckel**
m VERPACK tear tab lid
Aufreißen *nt* BAU *Straßen* scarification
aufreißen *vt* BAU break open, rip, scarify, *Straße* break
open
Aufreißer *m* BAU scarifier, *Straßenbau* ripper, TRANS
scarifier
Aufreiß-: **Aufreißlasche** *f* VERPACK pull-off closure; **Auf-
reißpackung** *f* VERPACK tear-off pack; **Aufreißstreifen**
m VERPACK tear strip
aufrichten *vt* VERPACK erect
aufrichtend: ~**er Hebelarm** *m* WASSERTRANS *Schiffbau*
righting lever arm; ~**es Moment** *nt* WASSERTRANS
Schiffbau righting moment
Aufrichter *m* KER & GLAS uprighter
Aufrichtungsmarkierung *f* LUFTTRANS leveling mark
(AmE), levelling mark (BrE)
Aufriß *m* BAU *eines Gebäudes* elevation, FERTIG *Zeich-
nung* shear draft, MASCHINEN front elevation,
MECHAN, WASSERTRANS *Schiffkonstruktion* elevation
Aufroll- *pref* FOTO winder, PAPIER wind-up
Aufrollen *nt* PAPIER reeling
aufrollen *vt* COMP & DV scroll, MASCHINEN roll, roll up
Aufroll-: **Aufrollmaschine** *f* PAPIER winder; **Aufrollvor-
richtung** *f* FOTO rewinder, PAPIER wind-up stand

Aufruf *m* COMP & DV call, polling; **Aufrufantwortmodus** *m* COMP & DV normal response mode; **Aufrufbefehl** *m* COMP & DV call instruction; **Aufrufbetrieb** *m* COMP & DV polling selection

aufrufen *vt* COMP & DV poll

Aufrufliste *f* COMP & DV polling list

aufrühren *vt* CHEMTECH agitate

aufrunden *vt* COMP & DV round off, round up, MATH round

aufrüsten *vt* COMP & DV upgrade

Aufrüstposition *f* LUFTTRANS *Luftfahrzeug* rigging position

Aufrüstung *f* COMP & DV *Hardware* upgrade

aufsatteln *vt* BAU *Stufen* saddle

Aufsatz *m* MECHAN cowl; **Aufsatzkranz** *m* BAU curb (AmE), kerb (BrE); **Aufsatzventil** *nt* MASCHINEN yoke valve; **Aufsatzzusammenbau** *m* NICHTFOSS ENERG top assembly

Aufsaugen *nt* CHEMIE occlusion, ELEKTROTECH *von Elektronen, Gasen*, LEBENSMITTEL absorption

aufsaugen *vt* HEIZ & KÄLTE aspirate

Aufschalten *nt* TELEKOM trunk offer

aufschalten *vt* MECHAN, PHYS actuate

Aufschaltwert *m* PHYS modulation factor

Aufschäumblasen *f pl* KER & GLAS reboil bubbles

Aufschäumen *nt* KER & GLAS reboil, KUNSTSTOFF frothing

aufschäumen[1] *vt* FERTIG froth

aufschäumen[2] *vi* CHEMTECH foam

Aufschäumung *f* FERTIG *Plaste* expansion

aufschichten *vt* BAU pile, stack

aufschießen *vt* WASSERTRANS *Tauwerk* coil up

Aufschlag *m* ANSTRICH impact, BAU *Preis* surcharge, FERTIG deposit, MASCHINEN impact

Aufschlagen *nt* WASSERTRANS *Schiffbewegung* slamming

Aufschlag: **Aufschlagkrater** *m* RAUMFAHRT impact crater; **Aufschlagleuchten** *nt* FERNSEH impact fluorescence

aufschlämmen *vt* ANSTRICH suspend

Aufschlämmung *f* FERTIG, KOHLEN, LEBENSMITTEL slurry

Aufschließen *nt* ABFALL digestion, fouling, CHEMIE *Pflanzenteile* maceration

aufschließen *vt* CHEMIE *Pflanzenteile*, LEBENSMITTEL *Nahrungsmittel* macerate

aufschlitzen *vt* TEXTIL split

Aufschluß *m* ABFALL digestion, fouling, CHEMIE *Mineralerze* dissociation, *chemisch* pulping, PAPIER digestion; **Aufschlußapparat** *m* LABOR digestion apparatus; **Aufschlußbohren** *nt* ERDÖL exploration drilling, exploratory drilling; **Aufschlußbohrung** *f* ERDÖL exploration well, wildcat drilling

Aufschrauben *nt* MASCHINEN unscrewing

aufschrauben *vt* KERNTECH unbolt, unscrew, MASCHINEN unscrew

Aufschraubfräser *m* FERTIG screw-on cutter

aufschrumpfbar *adj* THERMOD heat-shrinkable

Aufschrumpfen *nt* FERTIG shrinking-on, MASCHINEN shrinkage, shrinking-on, THERMOD heat shrink fitting, heat shrinking

aufschütten *vt* BAU bank up, raise

Aufschüttung *f* KOHLEN fill, METALL debris

aufschweißen *vt* FERTIG *Schweißen* deposit

Aufschweißlegierung *f* FERTIG hard-facing alloy, surfacing alloy

Aufschweißung *f* FERTIG deposition

aufschwemmen *vt* ANSTRICH suspend

Aufschwimmen *nt* KFZTECH aquaplaning, KUNSTSTOFF *von Farbstoffen* flooding

aufschwimmen: ~ **lassen** *vt* WASSERTRANS *gestrandetes Schiff* float off

Aufsetz- *pref* LUFTTRANS, RAUMFAHRT touchdown; **Aufsetzbauelement** *nt* (*SMC*) TELEKOM surface-mounted component (*SMC*)

Aufsetzen *nt* LUFTTRANS touchdown

Aufsetzen: ~ **von Flicken** *nt* FERTIG *Kessel* patching; ~ **von Verschlußkappen** *nt* VERPACK capping

aufsetzen *vi* RAUMFAHRT *Raumschiff* touch down

Aufsetz-: **Aufsetzgeschwindigkeit** *f* LUFTTRANS touchdown speed; **Aufsetzpunkt** *m* RAUMFAHRT *Raumschiff* touchdown point; **Aufsetzzone** *f* LUFTTRANS touchdown zone; **Aufsetzzonenbefeuerung** *f* LUFTTRANS runway touch-down zone

Aufsicht *f* PAPIER lookdown, TELEKOM *Telefon* supervision; **Aufsichtsbehörde** *f* QUAL regulatory authority; **Aufsichtsbüro** *nt* TELEKOM observation office; **Aufsichtsorgan** *nt* MEERSCHMUTZ supervisor; **Aufsichtsperson** *f* COMP & DV supervisor; **Aufsichtssucher mit Mattscheibe** *m* FOTO reflex viewfinder

aufslippen *vt* WASSERTRANS haul up

Aufspalten *nt* MECHAN cracking

aufspalten *vt* BAU split

Aufspaltung *f* ANSTRICH analysis, BAU splitting, CHEMIE breakdown; ~ **eines Multipletts** *f* PHYS splitting of multiplet

Aufspann- *pref* FERTIG setting, MASCHINEN chucking, clamping

Aufspannen *nt* TEXTIL tentering; ~ **der Werkzeuge** *nt* FERTIG tooling

aufspannen *vt* FERTIG *Werkzeug* set, MASCHINEN chuck

Aufspann-: **Aufspannfläche** *f* MASCHINEN clamping surface; **Aufspannplatte** *f* FERTIG bolster, MASCHINEN adaptor plate, backing plate; **Aufspanntisch** *m* FERTIG worktable; **Aufspanntransformator** *m* FERNSEH step-up transformer

Aufspannung *f* FERTIG *Werkzeug* setting

Aufspann-: **Aufspannvorrichtung** *f* MASCHINEN chuck, chucking device, fixture; **Aufspannwinkel** *m* MASCHINEN, METROL angle plate

aufsplittern *vi* BAU split

Aufspringbildwand *f* FOTO self-erecting screen

Aufspritzung *f* PHYS metalization (AmE), metallization (BrE)

aufspröden *vt* ANSTRICH, FERTIG embrittle

Aufsprödung *f* ANSTRICH embrittlement

Aufspulen *nt* PHYS winding

aufspulen *vt* PHYS wind

Aufstampfen *nt* FERTIG *Formen* tamping

aufstapeln *vt* VERPACK stack up

Aufstäuben *nt* FERTIG deposition by sputtering

Aufsteck- *pref* FOTO push, GERÄT clip, MASCHINEN shell; **Aufsteckfassung** *f* FOTO push-on mount, slip-on sleeve; **Aufsteckfräser** *m* FERTIG arbor cutter, arbor-type mill, hole-type cutter, MASCHINEN shell mill; **Aufsteckgatter** *nt* TEXTIL creel; **Aufsteckreibahle** *f* MASCHINEN shell reamer; **Aufsteckschlüssel** *m* MECHAN socket spanner (BrE), socket wrench; **Aufstecksenker** *m* MASCHINEN arbor-mounted counterbore, shell drill; **Aufsteckskale** *f* GERÄT clip-on scale; **Aufsteckwerkzeug** *nt* FERTIG shell tool

aufsteigend: ~**e Destillation** *f* THERMOD distillation by ascent; **~e Sortierung** *f* COMP & DV ascending sort

Aufstell- und Abstellgleis *nt* EISENBAHN siding

aufstellen *vt* FERNSEH set up, FERTIG install, rig, MASCHINEN erect, WASSERTRANS *Technik* install

Aufstellung *f* COMP & DV installation, FERNSEH setup, KONTROLL positioning, PATENT drawing-up, TELEKOM installation; **Aufstellungsplan** *m* FERNSEH set-up diagram; **Aufstellungszeichnung** *f* HEIZ & KÄLTE installation drawing

Aufsticken *nt* CHEMIE nitridation

Aufstieg *m* ERDÖL rising, LUFTTRANS lift; **Aufstiegsmodus** *m* RAUMFAHRT ascending mode; **Aufstiegsstufe** *f* RAUMFAHRT *Raumschiff* ascent stage

Aufstoß *m* CHEMIE impingement

aufstoßen *vt* DRUCK jog

aufstreichbar: **~e Schlämmbeschichtung** *f* ANSTRICH paint-on slurry coating

aufstreichen *vt* ANSTRICH apply

Aufstreichmaschine *f* FERTIG spreader

Aufstreuen *nt* FERTIG dusting

Aufstrich *m* ANSTRICH application

Aufströmung *f* LUFTTRANS *Lufttüchtigkeit* upwash

Aufstromvergaser *m* KFZTECH updraft carburetor (AmE), updraught carburettor (BrE)

Aufstützring *m* FERTIG *Kunststoffinstallationen* seal support ring

Aufsuchung *f* ERDÖL exploration

Aufsummierzähler *m* GERÄT totalizing counter

auftakeln *vt* WASSERTRANS rig

Auftanken *nt* MASCHINEN, MEERSCHMUTZ refueling (AmE), refuelling (BrE); **~ in der Luft** *nt* LUFTTRANS refueling in flight (AmE), refuelling in flight (BrE)

auftanken *vt* KFZTECH, LUFTTRANS, WASSERTRANS refuel

Auftankfahrzeug *nt* LUFTTRANS refueling tanker (AmE), refuelling tanker (BrE)

auftasten *vt* KONTROLL strobe

auftauchen *vi* WASSERTRANS *U-Boot* surface

Auftauen *nt* LEBENSMITTEL defrosting

auftauen[1] *vt* HEIZ & KÄLTE defrost, LEBENSMITTEL thaw

auftauen[2] *vi* LEBENSMITTEL thaw

Auftauversuch *m* HEIZ & KÄLTE, MASCHINEN defrosting test

aufteilen *vt* BAU split into, COMP & DV partition

Aufteilung *f* BAU division, CHEMIE partitioning

Auftrag *m* RAUMFAHRT *Weltraumfunk* assignment; **~ im Erdumlauf** *m* RAUMFAHRT earth-orbiting mission; **Auftragefläche** *f* FERTIG *Meißelschaft* base

Auftragen *nt* KUNSTSTOFF coating

auftragen *vt* ANSTRICH apply, BAU deposit, plot, spread, *Farbe* distribute, KUNSTSTOFF coat

Auftrag: **Auftragmenge** *f* BAU application rate; **Auftragnehmer** *m* BAU contractor; **Auftragschweißung** *f* MASCHINEN build-up welding

auftragsgebunden *adj* KONSTZEICH *Zeichnungen, Bestelliste* order-tied

Auftrag: **Auftragslinie** *f* FERTIG abscissa; **Auftragsmaschine** *f* KUNSTSTOFF, VERPACK coating machine; **Auftragsmetall** *nt* FERTIG deposited metal; **Auftragsschreiben** *nt* BAU notice of award; **Auftragsschweißen** *nt* FERTIG hard-facing by welding

auftragsschweißen *vt* FERTIG pad

Auftrag: **Auftragswalze** *f* PAPIER applicator roll, spread roll; **Auftragswerkstatt** *f* FERTIG job shop

Auftragung *f* ANSTRICH application

Auftrag: **Auftragwalze** *f* METALL spreader roll; **Auftrag-**

walze für Klebstoff *f* VERPACK adhesive applicator

Auftreff- *pref* LUFTTRANS ram, METALL impact

auftreffen *vt* MECHAN impinge on

auftreffend: **~er Strahl** *m* PHYS, WELLPHYS incident beam, incident ray; **~es Teilchen** *nt* KERNTECH incident particle; **~e Welle** *f* PHYS, WELLPHYS incident wave

Auftreff-: **Auftreffenergie** *f* METALL impact energy; **Auftreffgeschwindigkeit** *f* METALL impact velocity; **Auftreffwucht** *f* LUFTTRANS *Aerodynamik* ram effect

Auftreiben *nt* KER & GLAS flaring, LEBENSMITTEL swell

Auftreiber *m* KER & GLAS reamer

Auftrennen: **~ des Zylinders in Längsrichtung** *nt* KER & GLAS splitting of the cylinder

Auftrieb *m* FERTIG *Gießen* lifting pressure, HYDRAUL buoyancy, LUFTTRANS buoyancy, lifting, lift, NICHTFOSS ENERG *Aerodynamik* lift, PHYS upthrust, *Flüssigkeit* buoyancy, STRÖMPHYS buoyancy, uplift, WASSERTRANS *Schiff, U-Boot* buoyancy; **~ am Luftschraubenblatt** *m* LUFTTRANS *Hubschrauber* blade lift; **Auftriebsbeiwert** *m* HYDRAUL *(CL)* lift coefficient *(CL)*, LUFTTRANS lift coefficient, NICHTFOSS ENERG *(CL)*, PHYS *(CL)*, WASSERTRANS *(CL)* *Schiffbau* lift coefficient *(CL)*

auftriebserhöhend: **~e Vorrichtungen** *f pl* LUFTTRANS high-lift devices

Auftrieb: **Auftriebskomponente** *f* LUFTTRANS lift component; **Auftriebskraft** *f* PHYS, STRÖMPHYS buoyancy force; **Auftriebskurve** *f* WASSERTRANS *Schiffskonstruktion* buoyancy curve; **Auftriebsmittelpunkt** *m* LUFTTRANS lift center (AmE), lift centre (BrE); **Auftriebsparameter** *m* PHYS, STRÖMPHYS buoyancy parameter; **Auftriebsreserve** *f* WASSERTRANS reserve buoyancy; **Auftriebssteigung** *f* LUFTTRANS lift curve slope; **Auftriebsverteilung** *f* LUFTTRANS lift distribution; **Auftriebszahl** *f* *(CL)* HYDRAUL, NICHTFOSS ENERG, PHYS, WASSERTRANS *Schiffbau* lift coefficient *(CL)*

Auftrittsbreite *f* BAU foothold

Auftrudeln *nt* RAUMFAHRT *Raumschiff* spin-up

auftuchen *vt* WASSERTRANS *Segeln* furl

Aufwachsen *nt* ELEKTRONIK *von Kristallen* epitaxial growth

Aufwallen *nt* CHEMTECH boiling

Aufwallung *f* PHYS bubbling

Aufwältigung *f* ERDÖL *Bohrtechnik* workover

Aufwärmloch *nt* KER & GLAS warming-in hole

Aufwärts- *pref* COMP & DV upward, ELEKTRIZ, ELEKTROTECH step-up, KFZTECH upward, MASCHINEN upstroke; **Aufwärtsblock** *m* TELEKOM uplink block; **Aufwärtsbohren** *nt* KER & GLAS upward drilling; **Aufwärtsgang** *m* KFZTECH upstroke; **Aufwärtshub** *m* HYDRAUL *Kolben* outstroke, KFZTECH upstroke, *Motor, Kolben* upstroke, MASCHINEN upstroke

aufwärtskompatibel *adj* COMP & DV upward compatible

Aufwärts-: **Aufwärtskompatibilität** *f* COMP & DV upward compatibility; **Aufwärtsströmung** *f* KERNTECH upflow, upward flow; **Aufwärtstakt** *m* MASCHINEN upstroke; **Aufwärtstransformator** *m* ELEKTRIZ, ELEKTROTECH, PHYS step-up transformer; **Aufwärtsverdampfung** *f* HEIZ & KÄLTE vertical evaporation; **Aufwärtswandler** *m* PHYS step-up transformer; **Aufwärtszähler** *m* ELEKTRONIK up counter

Aufweichen *nt* ABFALL maceration

Aufweite- *pref* MASCHINEN sizing, METALL expanding

Aufweiten *nt* FERTIG flaring

aufweiten *vt* BAU bulge, expand

Aufweite-: **Aufweitewalzwerk** *nt* METALL expanding mill; **Aufweitewerkzeug** *nt* MASCHINEN sizing tool

Aufwerfen *nt* FOTO *Emulsion* buckling

aufwerten *vt* BAU *Gebäude* grade up

Aufwickel- *pref* FOTO take-up; **Aufwickelkassette** *f* FOTO take-up cassette, take-up spool; **Aufwickelmaschine** *f* FOTO film winder, VERPACK rewind machine, winding machine, winding-on machine

aufwickeln *vt* MASCHINEN roll, roll up, wind, wind up, PAPIER wind

Aufwickel-: **Aufwickelspule** *f* AUFNAHME take-up spool, COMP & DV take-up reel

Aufwind *m* LUFTTRANS *Lufttüchtigkeit* upwash

Aufwinde- *pref* TEXTIL take-up

aufwinden *vt* MASCHINEN jack up

Aufwinde-: **Aufwindesystem** *nt* TEXTIL take-up system; **Aufwindevorrichtung** *f* TEXTIL take-up motion

Aufwölbung *f* BAU camber

Aufzählung *f* COMP & DV enumeration; **Aufzählungstyp** *m* COMP & DV enumeration type

Aufzeichnen *nt* COMP & DV logging, recording; **~ mit doppelter Schreibdichte** *nt* COMP & DV double-density recording

aufzeichnen *vt* AUFNAHME record, BAU plot, COMP & DV record, register, DRUCK record, FOTO register, KONTROLL, PHYS record

aufzeichnend: **~er Oszillograph** *m* AKUSTIK, PHYS, TELEKOM recording oscillograph

Aufzeichnung *f* AKUSTIK recording, PHYS record, TELEKOM recording; **der Flugerprobungsdaten** *f* LUFTTRANS flight test recorder; **~ mittels Elektronenstrahl** *f* ELEKTRONIK *direkt auf Mikrofilm* electron beam recording; **~ ohne Rückkehr zu Null** *f* *(NRZ-Aufzeichnung)* COMP & DV *Wechselschrift* nonreturn-to-zero recording *(NRZ recording)*; **~ auf Videomagnetband** *f* FERNSEH videotaping; **~ Aufzeichnungscharakteristik** *f* AKUSTIK recording characteristic; **Aufzeichnungsdichte** *f* COMP & DV recording density, storage density

aufzeichnungsfähig: **~e CD** *f* OPTIK recordable optical disc (BrE), recordable optical disk (AmE)

Aufzeichnung: **Aufzeichnungsfrequenzkurve** *f* AUFNAHME recording characteristic; **Aufzeichnungsgerät** *nt* COMP & DV recording instrument; **Aufzeichnungsmedium** *nt* COMP & DV recording medium; **Aufzeichnungsmodus** *m* COMP & DV recording mode; **Aufzeichnungsoberfläche** *f* COMP & DV *eines Datenträgers* recording surface; **Aufzeichnungsspur** *f* COMP & DV recording track; **Aufzeichnungsstromoptimierer** *m* FERNSEH record current optimizer; **Aufzeichnungsstufe** *f* COMP & DV recording level; **Aufzeichnungsverlust** *m* AUFNAHME recording loss

Aufziehen *nt* CHEMTECH *Farbstoffe* absorption, TEXTIL *Farbstoffe* attachment

aufziehen *vt* TEXTIL handle, WASSERTRANS *Segel, Flagge* hoist; **neu ~** *vt* KFZTECH *Bremsanlage* reline

Aufziehkarton *m* FOTO *zum Aufziehen eines Fotos* mount

Aufzug *m* BAU escalator, MASCHINEN elevator (AmE), lift (BrE), MECHAN elevation, TRANS elevator (AmE), lift (BrE); **Aufzuggewinde** *nt* LUFTTRANS elevator hoist (AmE), lift hoist (BrE); **Aufzugkolben** *m* LUFTTRANS hoisting block; **Aufzugmaschine** *f* LUFTTRANS engine hoist; **Aufzugring** *m* LUFTTRANS hoisting ring

Auf-Zu-Klappe *f* HEIZ & KÄLTE on/off butterfly valve

Aufzupfen *nt* TEXTIL *Wolle* picking

Auge *nt* MASCHINEN, WASSERTRANS eye; **Augenabstand** *m* ERGON interocular distance

Augenblick *m* ELEKTRONIK instant

augenblicklich: **~es elektrisches Dipolmoment** *nt* STRAHLPHYS instantaneous electric dipole moment; **~er Stand der Technik** *m* TELEKOM current state of the art

Augenblicks- *pref* GERÄT, TRANS instant; **Augenblicksbelastung** *f* WERKPRÜF instantaneous load; **Augenblicksfrequenz** *f* ELEKTRONIK instantaneous frequency; **Augenblicksfrequenzmessung** *f* ELEKTRONIK instantaneous frequency measurement; **Augenblickskapazität** *f* TRANS momentary capacity; **Augenblickswert** *m* GERÄT instantaneous value

Auge: **Augenbolzen** *m* MECHAN eyebolt; **Augendiagramm** *nt* TELEKOM eye diagram, eye-shape pattern; **Augenfilter** *nt* SICHERHEIT *gegen Laserstrahlen* eye filter; **Augenhöhe** *f* BAU eye level; **Augenkreis** *m* OPTIK eye ring; **Augenlinse** *f* FOTO eyepiece lens; **Augenmuschel** *f* FOTO eyecup; **Augenreizstoff** *m* CHEMIE lachrymator (BrE), lacrimator (AmE); **Augenscheinprüfung** *f* QUAL visual examination; **Augenschraube** *f* FERTIG, KFZTECH *Kupplung*, MASCHINEN eyebolt; **Augenschutz** *m* RAUMFAHRT eyepiece, SICHERHEIT eye protector, *für Schweißarbeiten* personal eye protector; **Augenschutz für Industrieeinsätze** *m* SICHERHEIT industrial eye protector; **Augenspülmittelflasche** *f* SICHERHEIT eye-rinse bottle; **Augenspülung** *f* SICHERHEIT eyewash; **Augenträgheit** *f* OPTIK persistence of vision; **Augentropfflasche** *f* KER & GLAS eye-drop bottle; **Augenverletzung** *f* SICHERHEIT eye injury

Augenverletzungen: **~ verursachend** *adj* SICHERHEIT injurious to the eyes

Auger: **Auger-Ausbeute** *f* PHYS, STRAHLPHYS Auger yield; **Auger-Effekt** *m* PHYS, STRAHLPHYS Auger effect; **Auger-Elektron** *nt* PHYS, STRAHLPHYS Auger electron; **~sche Elektronenspektroskopie** *f* *(AES)* PHYS, STRAHLPHYS Auger electron spectroscopy *(AES)*

Augplatte *f* WASSERTRANS *Deckbeschläge* eye plate; **Augspleiß** *m* WASSERTRANS *Tauwerk* eye splice; **Augspliß** *m* MASCHINEN eye splice

Aurantiin *nt* CHEMIE naringin

Aurichlorid *nt* CHEMIE auric chloride, gold chloride, gold trichloride

aus *adv* MASCHINEN off

Ausbaggern *nt* BAU digging, WASSERTRANS dredging

ausbaggern *vt* WASSERTRANS dredge

ausbalancieren *vt* MECHAN trim

Ausbau *m* BAU completion, development; **Ausbauchung** *f* BAU belly, bulge, MECHAN expansion; **Ausbauen** *nt* BAU removing

ausbauen *vt* FERTIG *Kunststoffinstallationen* dismantle

ausbäumen *vt* WASSERTRANS *Segeln* boom out

Ausbessern *nt* DRUCK touching-up, TEXTIL mending

Ausbeulen *nt* BAU, FERTIG, MASCHINEN buckling, crippling, planishing

ausbeulen *vt* BAU, FERTIG, MASCHINEN buckle, bulge, cripple, flatten, planish

Ausbeulhammer *m* MASCHINEN planisher, planishing hammer

Ausbeulung *f* KERNTECH *in einem Brennelement* buckling, MASCHINEN bulge

Ausbeute *f* CHEMIE *Reaktion*, COMP & DV, ELEKTRONIK, ERDÖL, FERTIG, KERNTECH, PAPIER, TEXTIL yield; **~ an Thermoionen** *f* KERNTECH thermal neutron yield

Ausbeutefaktor *m* ERDÖL *Förderung* recovery factor

Ausbeutung: ~ der geothermalen Energie *f* UMWELT-SCHMUTZ geothermal energy exploitation

Ausbilder *m* ELEKTRONIK trainer

Ausbildung *f* KERNTECH, MASCHINEN, WASSERTRANS training; **~ einer Grenzschicht** *f* STRÖMPHYS boundary layer formation; **~ durch Lernmaschine** *f* COMP & DV machine learning; **Ausbildungsplan** *m* MASCHINEN training scheme; **Ausbildungsreaktor** *m* KERNTECH training reactor; **Ausbildungsschiff** *nt* WASSERTRANS *Marine* training ship

Ausbinden *nt* AUFNAHME *eines Kabelstrangs* lacing

Ausbißbelastung *f* KOHLEN crop load

Ausblaseleitung *f* MECHAN exhaust line

Ausblasen *nt* ELEKTRIZ, HEIZ & KÄLTE blowing down, blowing out

ausblasen *vt* ELEKTRIZ, HEIZ & KÄLTE blow down, blow out

Ausblaseventil *nt* HYDRAUL blow valve

ausbleichen *vt* FOTO bleach out

Ausblenden *nt* AUFNAHME fading down, fading out, COMP & DV gating, reverse clipping, *von Programmen* masking, ELEKTRONIK gating; **~ der Bildspur** *nt* ELEKTRONIK trace blanking

ausblenden *vti* AUFNAHME fade down, fade out

Ausblühen *nt* KUNSTSTOFF blooming

Ausblühung *f* KER & GLAS scum, *durch Sulfatbildung während Kühlung* bloom

ausbluten *vi* KUNSTSTOFF bleed, TEXTIL bleed off

Ausbohr- und Stirnmaschine *f* FERTIG boring and facing mill

Ausbohren *nt* MASCHINEN boring, counterboring, reboring

ausbohren *vt* FERTIG enlarge, KFZTECH *Motor, Zylinder* rebore, MASCHINEN counterbore, rebore

Ausbohrmeißel *m* MASCHINEN boring tool

Ausbrechen *nt* KFZTECH *Lastwagen* breakaway, THERMOD outbreak; **~ der Ladung** *nt* LUFTTRANS *Hubschrauber* cargo swing; **~ der Schneide** *nt* FERTIG edge chipping

ausbrechen[1] *vt* FERTIG *Schneide bei Spannung* chip

ausbrechen[2] *vi* ERDÖL *Öl aus Bohrung* gush, KFZTECH break away, SICHERHEIT break out

Ausbreiten *nt* FERTIG hammering

ausbreiten: sich ~ *v refl* MEERSCHMUTZ spread, WELLPHYS propagate

ausbreitend: sich ~er Riß *m* KOHLEN progressive failure

Ausbreiteprobe *f* PHYS flattening test

Ausbreiter *m* TEXTIL stretcher

Ausbreitmaß *nt* BAU *Beton* slump; **Ausbreitmaßprüfung** *f* BAU slump test

Ausbreitung *f* BAU diffusion, COMP & DV, KÜNSTL INT, RADIO propagation, RAUMFAHRT spread, TELEKOM propagation, UMWELTSCHMUTZ diffusion; **~ der Emission** *f* PHYS evolution; **~ von Funkwellen** *f* STRAHLPHYS radio-wave propagation; **~ über Meteorschweife** *f* RADIO meteor trail propagation; **~ von Schallwellen** *f* ELEKTROTECH acoustic-wave propagation; **~ über sporadische E-Schicht-Reflektionen** *f* RADIO sporadic E; **Ausbreitungsanomalien in der Ionosphäre** *f pl* RADIO ionospheric propagation anomalies

ausbreitungsbedingt: ~e Verzögerung *f* RAUMFAHRT *Weltraumfunk* propagation delay

Ausbreitung: **Ausbreitungsfunktion** *f* PHYS propagator; **Ausbreitungsgeschwindigkeit** *f* BAU rate of spread, TELEKOM propagation velocity, WELLPHYS speed of propagation; **Ausbreitungskoeffizient** *m* OPTIK propagation coefficient; **Ausbreitungskonstante** *f* OPTIK, PHYS propagation constant; **Ausbreitungsmode** *f* OPTIK *elektromagnetische Welle* propagation mode; **Ausbreitungsschlauch** *m* RAUMFAHRT *Führung* heat pipe; **Ausbreitungsschlauch in der Atmosphäre** *m* RADIO atmospheric duct; **Ausbreitungsverluste** *m pl* PHYS propagation losses; **Ausbreitungsweg** *m* RADIO path

Ausbringen *nt* DRUCK quad, FERTIG output

ausbringen *vt* WASSERVERSORG *Fender* put out

Ausbruch *m* BAU outpouring, ERDÖL blowout, *Bohrtechnik, Fördertechnik* breakout, *plötzlicher Ölausbruch aus Bohrung* gush, FERTIG *Schneide* chip, KFZTECH *bei Reifen* deflection, KONSTZEICH auxiliary section, THERMOD outbreak; **Ausbruchsicherung** *f* ERDÖL blowout preventer

Ausbüchsen *nt* MASCHINEN bushing

ausbuchsen *vt* FERTIG *Schleifscheibe*, MASCHINEN bush

ausbüchsen *vt* FERTIG rebush

Ausbuchten *nt* KERNTECH ballooning

Ausbuchtung: ~ des Kötzers *f* TEXTIL bulge

Ausdauer *f* FERTIG stamina

ausdehnen *vt* BAU expand, FERTIG flare

Ausdehnung *f* GEOM dilation, HEIZ & KÄLTE, KUNSTSTOFF, MASCHINEN, MECHAN, METALL expansion, PHYS extension, RAUMFAHRT *Raumschiff*, THERMOD expansion; **Ausdehnungsbogen** *m* HEIZ & KÄLTE expansion bend; **Ausdehnungsgefäß** *nt* HEIZ & KÄLTE expansion tank, MASCHINEN expansion vessel; **Ausdehnungshub** *m* THERMOD expansion stroke; **Ausdehnungsknie** *nt* MECHAN expansion bend; **Ausdehnungskoeffizient** *m* KUNSTSTOFF coefficient of expansion, MECHAN expansion coefficient; **Ausdehnungskupplung** *f* MASCHINEN expansion coupling, slip joint; **Ausdehnungsnocke** *f* MECHAN expansion cam; **Ausdehnungsrohrverbindungen** *f pl* MASCHINEN bellow expansion joints; **Ausdehnungsstoß** *m* BAU expansion joint; **Ausdehnungsvermögen der Gase** *f* THERMOD expansibility of gases; **Ausdehnungswärme** *f* THERMOD heat of expansion; **Ausdehnungszahl** *f* BAU coefficient of expansion

Ausdreh- *pref* MASCHINEN boring; **Ausdrehen** *nt* MASCHINEN boring; **Ausdrehmeißel** *m* MASCHINEN boring tool; **Ausdrehschneidstahl** *m* MASCHINEN boring cutter

Ausdruck *m* COMP & DV, TELEKOM hard copy, printout

ausdrücken *vt* PAPIER squeeze

Ausdünstung *f* SICHERHEIT fume; **Ausdünstungsventil** *nt* LUFTTRANS exhalation valve

Ausecken *nt* FERTIG notching

auseinanderbrechen *vt* BAU break up

auseinandergezogen: ~e Darstellung *f* MECHAN exploded view

auseinanderlaufend *adj* GEOM divergent

auseinanderliegend: ~e Maße *nt pl* KONSTZEICH dimensions at different locations

Auseinanderspreizen: ~ der Ziehschleifsteine *nt* FERTIG expansion of honing stones

Ausfächerung *f* ELEKTROTECH fan-out

Ausfachung *f* BAU nogging

Ausfädeln *nt* TRANS leaving a traffic stream

ausfahrbar[1] *adj* FERTIG retractable

ausfahrbar[2]: **~e Antenne** *f* PHYS periscope aerial, periscope antenna; **~e Hilfsstütze** *f* LUFTTRANS outrigger; **~es Langsieb** *nt* PAPIER roll-out Fourdrinier

ausfahren *vi* BAU ride
ausfahrend: ~er Verkehr *m* TRANS outbound traffic, outward traffic
Ausfall *m* BAU, COMP & DV, ELEKTRIZ breakdown, failure, ELEKTROTECH breakdown, failure, *Stromnetz* drop-out, FERNSEH, KERNTECH, MASCHINEN, MECHAN, RADIO breakdown, failure, RAUMFAHRT blackout, SICHERHEIT *einer Maschine*, TELEKOM *Netz* breakdown, failure, WASSERTRANS *Schiffkonstruktion* flare; **~ mit Datenverlust** *m* MASCHINEN gang tuning capacitor; **~ des Vorstevens** *m* WASSERTRANS *Schiffkonstruktion* stem rake; **~ mit Zerstörung** *m* ELEKTRONIK destructive breakdown; **Ausfallart** *f* QUAL failure mode; **Ausfallart-, Ausfallauswirkungs- und Ausfallbedeutungsanalyse** *f* QUAL failure mode, effects and criticality analysis; **Ausfallbild** *nt* FERNSEH early-finish video; **Ausfalldatenkarte** *f* LUFTTRANS failure data card; **Ausfalldauer** *f* KERNTECH outage time, QUAL outage duration; **Ausfalldichte** *f* QUAL failure density; **Ausfalldichteverteilung** *f* QUAL failure density distribution
ausfallen *vi* CHEMTECH precipitate
ausfällen *vt* ABFALL precipitate
Ausfall: **Ausfallerkennung des Datenträgers** *f* TELEKOM data carrier failure detector; **Ausfallhäufigkeit** *f* QUAL failure frequency; **Ausfallhäufigkeitsdichte** *f* QUAL failure density; **Ausfallkriterium** *nt* QUAL failure criterion; **Ausfallmodus** *m* QUAL failure mode; **Ausfallmuster** *nt* QUAL sample, type sample; **Ausfallmuster-Prüfbericht** *m* QUAL type sample inspection and test report; **Ausfallquote** *f* MASCHINEN failure rate, QUAL failure quota, RAUMFAHRT *Raumschiff* failure rate; **Ausfallrate** *f* COMP & DV, ELEKTROTECH, QUAL, TELEKOM failure rate; **Ausfallratengewichtung** *f* QUAL failure rate weighting; **Ausfallratenniveau** *nt* QUAL failure rate level
ausfallsanft *adj* KONTROLL fail-soft
ausfallsicher[1] *adj* COMP & DV, ELEKTROTECH, KONTROLL, MECHAN, QUAL, RAUMFAHRT, TELEKOM fail-safe
ausfallsicher:[2] **~er Betrieb** *m* COMP & DV fail-safe operation; **~es System** *nt* COMP & DV fail-safe system
ausfalltolerierend *adj* KONTROLL fail-soft
Ausfall: **Ausfallton** *m* FERNSEH early-finish audio
Ausfällung *f* ABFALL coagulation, precipitation
Ausfall: **Ausfallursache** *f* QUAL failure cause; **Ausfallverhalten** *nt* QUAL failure mode; **Ausfallwahrscheinlichkeit** *f* QUAL failure probability; **Ausfallwahrscheinlichkeitsdichte** *f* QUAL failure probability density; **Ausfallwahrscheinlichkeitsverteilung** *f* QUAL failure probability distribution; **Ausfallwinkel** *m* PHYS, WELLPHYS angle of reflection; **Ausfallwirkungsanalyse** *f* QUAL failure mode and effects analysis; **Ausfallzeit** *f* COMP & DV downtime, fault time, ERDÖL *einer Anlage*, FERNSEH downtime, KERNTECH oscillating electron, unavailability time, LUFTTRANS downtime, TELEKOM out-of-service time, *Versagen* downtime
ausfaltbar: ~e Antenne *f* TELEKOM unfurlable aerial, unfurlable antenna
Ausfiltern *nt* COMP & DV gating
Ausflanschen *nt* FERTIG *Werkstofftrennen* notching
Ausflecken *nt* FOTO spotting
ausflecken *vt* FOTO spot
Ausfließen *nt* WASSERVERSORG efflux
ausflocken *vi* CHEMIE clot, flocculate, CHEMTECH coagulate, flocculate

Ausflockung[1] *f* ABFALL flocculation, CHEMIE flocculation, *Mineralaufbereitung* scavenging, CHEMTECH, ERDÖL, KOHLEN, KUNSTSTOFF, LEBENSMITTEL flocculation
Ausflockung:[2] **zur ~ bringen** *vt* CHEMTECH coagulate
Ausflockung: **Ausflockungsmittel** *nt* CHEMTECH coagulator; **Ausflockungspunkt** *m* CHEMTECH flocculation point
ausfluchten *vt* BAU *Linie* line out
Ausfluchtung *f* BAU alignment
Ausflugsdampfer *m* WASSERTRANS excursion steamer, *Boottyp* pleasure boat
Ausfluß *m* KERNTECH issue, MEERSCHMUTZ *Vorgang* runoff, PHYS effusion, outward flux, WASSERVERSORG outflow, *Fluβ*, Wehr discharge; **Ausflußkoeffizient** *m* HYDRAUL coefficient of efflux, HYDRAUL *(C)* discharge coefficient *(C)*; **Ausflußmenge** *f* KERNTECH issue; **Ausflußseite** *f* KERNTECH outlet side, *einer Pumpe* delivery side, *einer Turbine* outlet edge; **Ausflußstrahl** *m* FERTIG issuing jet; **Ausflußventil** *nt* HYDRAUL discharge valve; **Ausflußwehr für Aktivabfall** *nt* KERNTECH effluent weir
ausfugen *vt* BAU joint
Ausfugung *f* CONST *Aktion* pointing
Ausfuhr *f* WASSERTRANS export
ausführbar: ~e Anweisung *f* COMP & DV executable statement; **nicht ~e Anweisung** *f* COMP & DV nonoperable instruction; **~er Befehl** *m* COMP & DV executable instruction
ausführen *vt* COMP & DV *Programm* execute, run, PATENT carry out
Ausfuhr: **Ausfuhrgenehmigung** *f* WASSERTRANS *Dokumente* export licence (BrE), export license (AmE); **Ausfuhrhafen** *m* WASSERTRANS *Hafen* shipping port
ausführlich: ~e Darstellung *f* KONSTZEICH detailed representation
Ausführung *f* BAU design, workmanship, COMP & DV execution, running, DRUCK finish, FERTIG *Kunststoffinstallationen* model, KONTROLL execution, MASCHINEN version, PATENT carrying out; **~ für Fahrzeugeinbau** *f* TELEKOM car mounting version; **~ links** *f* KONSTZEICH left-hand version; **~ rechts** *f* KONSTZEICH right-hand version; **Ausführungsanweisung** *f* COMP & DV execute statement; **Ausführungseinheit** *f* COMP & DV run unit; **Ausführungsform** *f* PATENT *einer Erfindung* embodiment; **Ausführungsmodus** *m* COMP & DV execute mode; **Ausführungsphase** *f* COMP & DV execute phase, execution phase; **Ausführungssignal** *nt* COMP & DV execute signal; **Ausführungszeichnung** *f* HEIZ & KÄLTE, QUAL as-built drawing; **Ausführungszeit** *f* COMP & DV execution time
Ausfüllungsgrad *m* LUFTTRANS *Propeller* solidity
Ausgabe *f* COMP & DV output, output data, DRUCK, KONTROLL, RADIO output; **Ausgabeanschluß** *m* COMP & DV output port; **Ausgabeanschlußpunkt** *m* COMP & DV output port; **Ausgabeanzeige** *f* COMP & DV output display; **Ausgabebereich** *m* COMP & DV output area; **Ausgabeblock** *m* COMP & DV output block; **Ausgabedatei** *f* COMP & DV, DRUCK output file; **Ausgabedaten** *nt pl* COMP & DV output data; **Ausgabedrucker** *m* COMP & DV terminal printer; **Ausgabeeinheit** *f* DRUCK output device; **Ausgabeeinspeisung** *f* FERNSEH outgoing feed; **Ausgabeelement** *nt* COMP & DV output element
ausgabegebunden[1] *adj* COMP & DV output-limited
ausgabegebunden:[2] **~er Prozeß** *m* COMP & DV output-limited process

Ausgabe: **Ausgabegerät** *nt* COMP & DV, DRUCK output device; **Ausgabegeschwindigkeit** *f* COMP & DV output rate; **Ausgabegröße** *f* ELEKTROTECH output quantity; **Ausgabekanal** *m* COMP & DV output channel, FERNSEH outgoing channel; **Ausgabekapazität** *f* COMP & DV output capacity; **Ausgabekennsatz** *m* COMP & DV output label; **Ausgabeklasse** *f* COMP & DV output class; **Ausgabekonfiguration** *f* COMP & DV output configuration; **Ausgabeleistung** *f* ELEKTRIZ output; **Ausgabeleitung** *f* FERNSEH outgoing line; **Ausgabemedium** *nt* COMP & DV output medium; **Ausgabeöffnung** *f* COMP & DV gate; **Ausgabepuffer** *m* COMP & DV output buffer; **Ausgaberücksetzung** *f* RAUMFAHRT *Weltraumfunk* output backoff; **Ausgabesatz** *m* COMP & DV output record; **Ausgabesteuerzeichen** *nt* COMP & DV output control character; **Ausgabewarteschlange** *f* COMP & DV output queue

Ausgang *m* COMP & DV exit, output, outlet, FERNSEH output, KERNTECH issue, KONTROLL, RADIO output, TELEKOM outlet; **Ausgangsadmittanz** *f* ELEKTROTECH output admittance; **Ausgangsbelastbarkeit** *f* ELEKTROTECH fan-out; **Ausgangscode** *m* COMP & DV source code; **Ausgangsdämpfung** *f* ELEKTRONIK output attenuation; **Ausgangsdaten** *nt pl* COMP & DV raw data; **Ausgangsdose** *f* ELEKTRIZ outlet box; **Ausgangsdraht** *m* ELEKTRIZ leading-out wire; **Ausgangselektrode** *f* ELEKTROTECH output electrode; **Ausgangsfeld** *nt* COMP & DV parent field; **Ausgangsformat** *nt* KONSTZEICH starting size; **Ausgangsgleichstrom** *m* ELEKTROTECH DC output, direct current output; **Ausgangsgröße** *f* ELEKTROTECH output quantity; **Ausgangsimpedanz** *f* ELEKTRIZ, ELEKTROTECH, FERNSEH, TELEKOM output impedance; **Ausgangskammer** *f* ELEKTRONIK output cavity; **Ausgangskapazität** *f* ELEKTROTECH output capacitance; **Ausgangskasten** *m* ELEKTRIZ outlet box; **Ausgangsklemme** *f* ELEKTRIZ *Kontakt*, ELEKTROTECH output terminal; **Ausgangskondensator** *m* ELEKTROTECH output capacitor; **Ausgangskreis** *m* ELEKTROTECH, TELEKOM output circuit; **Ausgangsladung** *f* ELEKTROTECH output charge; **Ausgangsleistung** *f* ELEKTRIZ output power, ELEKTROTECH output power, output, power output, TELEKOM output power; **Ausgangsleitung** *f* AUFNAHME line out, ELEKTRIZ outgoing circuit, FERNSEH line out; **Ausgangsleitwert** *m* ELEKTROTECH output admittance; **Ausgangsmaterial** *nt* KOHLEN raw material; **Ausgangsmonitor** *m* FERNSEH output monitor; **Ausgangsnuklid** *nt* KERNTECH parent nuclide; **Ausgangspegel** *m* AUFNAHME, FERNSEH, TELEKOM output level; **Ausgangsphase** *f* METALL parent phase; **Ausgangspunkt** *m* TELEKOM output port; **Ausgangsregister** *nt (AR)* TELEKOM home location register *(HLR)*; **Ausgangsregler** *m* FERNSEH output control; **Ausgangsschaltung** *f* ELEKTROTECH output circuit; **Ausgangsseite** *f* FERTIG *Kunststoffinstallationen* outlet side; **Ausgangssignal** *nt* ELEKTROTECH, FERNSEH, TELEKOM output signal; **Ausgangsspalte** *f* DRUCK last column; **Ausgangsspannung** *f* ELEKTRIZ, ELEKTROTECH, FERNSEH, TELEKOM output voltage; **Ausgangssprache** *f* COMP & DV source language; **Ausgangsstecker** *m* ELEKTRIZ plug-type outlet; **Ausgangssteckverbinder** *m* TELEKOM outconnector; **Ausgangsstelle** *f* COMP & DV outconnector

Ausgangsstellung: in ~ bringen *vt* COMP & DV restore

Ausgang: **Ausgangsstoff einer Reaktion** *m* CHEMIE reactant; **Ausgangsstrahl** *m* KERNTECH ejected beam; **Ausgangsstrom** *m* ELEKTRIZ output current; **Ausgangsstufe ohne Transformator** *f* AUFNAHME transformerless output stage; **Ausgangsteilchen** *nt* KERNTECH initiating particle; **Ausgangsteiler** *m* ELEKTRONIK output attenuator; **Ausgangstemperatur** *f* HEIZ & KÄLTE initial temperature; **Ausgangstext** *m* COMP & DV corpus; **Ausgangstransformator** *m* AUFNAHME, ELEKTRIZ, ELEKTROTECH, PHYS output transformer; **Ausgangsübertrager** *m* PHYS output transformer; **Ausgangsverstärker** *m* ELEKTRONIK output amplifier; **Ausgangsverzeichnis** *nt* COMP & DV root directory; **Ausgangsverzweigung** *f* ELEKTROTECH fan-out; **Ausgangswandler** *m* ELEKTROTECH output transducer; **Ausgangswerte** *m pl* QUAL benchmarks; **Ausgangswicklung** *f* ELEKTRIZ output winding; **Ausgangszeile** *f* DRUCK break line

Ausgasung *f* KOHLEN *Bergbau* degasifying

ausgeblendet: ~es Signal *nt* ELEKTRONIK gated signal

ausgebrochen: ~e Bohrung *f* ERDÖL *Förderung von Erdöl und Erdgas* wild well

ausgebunden: ~er Kabelfächer *m* ELEKTROTECH laced cablefan

ausgedehnt *adj* RAUMFAHRT *Raumschiff* expanded

ausgefächert: ~es Kabel *nt* ELEKTROTECH fanned cable

ausgefahren: ~e Straße *f* BAU heavy road

ausgefallen *adj* TELEKOM out of order

ausgeflossen: ~es Öl *nt* MEERSCHMUTZ spill

ausgeformt: ~es Kabelende *nt* ELEKTROTECH cable form

ausgefräst *adj* MECHAN milled

ausgeführt: auf dem Chip ~e A/D-Wandlung *f* ELEKTRONIK on-chip analog-to-digital conversion; **auf dem Chip ~e D/A-Wandlung** *f* ELEKTRONIK on-chip digital-to-analog conversion

ausgefüllt *adj* BAU filled

ausgeglichen: ~es Querruder *nt* LUFTTRANS balanced aileron; **nicht ~es Ruder** *nt* WASSERTRANS unbalanced rudder; **~e Trittstufenfläche** *f* BAU balance step

ausgeheilt *adj* THERMOD *Halbleiter* annealed

ausgehen *vt* ELEKTROTECH *Licht* go out

ausgekehlt *adj* FERTIG recessed

ausgekolkt *adj* FERTIG grooved

ausgelaufen[1] *adj* FERTIG attrite; **nicht ~** *adj* FERTIG *Guß* misrun

ausgelaufen:[2] **~er Block** *m* METALL bled ingot; **~es Pleuellager** *nt* KFZTECH run bearing

ausgelaugt[1] *adj* KOHLEN *Erz* barren

ausgelaugt:[2] **~es Gangerz** *nt* KOHLEN barren gangue

ausgenutzt: ~er Entwickler *m* FOTO exhausted developer

ausgeprägt: ~er Pol *m* ELEKTRIZ, ELEKTROTECH salient pole; **~e Seitenkeulen** *f pl* ELEKTRONIK *Antenne* high sidelobes

ausgerückt *adj* MASCHINEN out of gear

ausgeschaltet: ~e Stellung *f* MASCHINEN off position

ausgeschlossen[1] *adj* DRUCK justified

ausgeschlossen:[2] **~er Text** *m* DRUCK justified text

ausgesetzt[1] *adj* ANSTRICH exposed, COMP & DV suspended

ausgesetzt:[2] **~e Adressierung** *f* COMP & DV deferred addressing

ausgespitzt *adj* FERTIG *Bohrer* pointed

ausgestellt[1] *adj* TEXTIL flared

ausgestellt:[2] **~er Abschnitt** *m* RAUMFAHRT *Raumschiff* flared section

ausgewählt: ~es Amt *nt* PATENT elected office; **~er optischer Rohling** *m* KER & GLAS selected chunk

ausgewalzt *adj* FERTIG sheeted
Ausgewogenheit *f* AUFNAHME balance
ausgewuchtet *adj* FERTIG balanced; **nicht ~** *adj* MASCHI-NEN unbalanced
ausgezogen *adj* ANSTRICH exposed
ausgießen *vt* FERTIG, MASCHINEN bush
Ausgießverschluß *m* VERPACK pour spout closure, pour spout seal
Ausgleich *m* ELEKTRIZ balance, ELEKTRONIK, ELEKTRO-TECH compensation, MASCHINEN make-up, MECHAN equalization, PHYS compensation; **~ des Parallaxen-fehlers** *m* GERÄT *Ablesefehler* compensation of parallax; **Ausgleichbecken** *nt* NICHTFOSS ENERG surge tank, WASSERVERSORG equalizing tank; **Ausgleichbe-hälter** *m* BAU make-up tank, HEIZ & KÄLTE equalizer tank, KFZTECH expansion tank, *Motor* header tank, MECHAN expansion tank, WASSERVERSORG compen-sator reservoir; **Ausgleichbereich** *m* KERNTECH range of compensation; **Ausgleicheinrichtung** *f* PHYS com-pensator
Ausgleichen *nt* PAPIER balancing; **~ mit Scheiben** *nt* MASCHINEN shimming
ausgleichen *vt* BAU average out, *Straße* trim, KOHLEN compensate, PAPIER balance, PHYS compensate
Ausgleicher *m* HEIZ & KÄLTE equalizer
Ausgleich: **Ausgleichfläche am Ruder** *f* LUFTTRANS ba-lance tab; **Ausgleichgetriebe** *nt* FERTIG, KFZTECH differential, MASCHINEN balance gear, differential gear, equalizing gear; **Ausgleichgewicht** *nt* BAU coun-terweight, MASCHINEN balance weight; **Aus-gleichhebel** *m* MASCHINEN balance lever; **Aus-gleichhorn** *nt* LUFTTRANS horn balance; **Ausgleichimpulse** *m pl* FERNSEH equalizing pulses; **Ausgleichkegelrad** *nt* KFZTECH differential pinion, differential spider pinion, *Teil des Ausgleichsgetriebes* pinion gear, *Triebstrang* differential bevel gear; **Aus-gleichkolben** *m* FERTIG dummy piston, HYDRAUL balancing piston, MASCHINEN balance piston; **Aus-gleichkraft** *f* LUFTTRANS equalizing; **Ausgleichkupplung** *f* MASCHINEN compensating coupling, flexible coupling, resilient coupling; **Aus-gleichkurve** *f* ELEKTRONIK equalization curve; **Ausgleichluftdüse** *f* KFZTECH air correction jet; **Aus-gleichmagnetstreifen** *m* FERNSEH balancing magnetic stripe; **Ausgleichpunkt** *m* LUFTTRANS balance point; **Ausgleichrad** *nt* MASCHINEN compensating gear; **Aus-gleichriet** *nt* TEXTIL spacing reed; **Ausgleichritzel** *nt* KFZTECH differential pinion, pinion gear; **Ausgleich-ruder** *nt* LUFTTRANS balance tab, balanced control surface; **Ausgleichschacht** *m* NICHTFOSS ENERG surge shaft; **Ausgleichschaltung** *f* FERNSEH shaping net-work, GERÄT compensating circuit; **Ausgleichscheibe** *f* MASCHINEN shim; **Ausgleichscheibenventil** *nt* NICHT-FOSS ENERG balanced disc valve (BrE), balanced disk valve (AmE); **Ausgleichschiene** *f* KFZTECH equalizer bar; **Ausgleichschwingung** *f* PHYS transient oscilla-tion; **Ausgleichsdüse** *f* KFZTECH *Vergaser* compensating jet; **Ausgleichstellerventil** *nt* NICHTFOSS ENERG balanced disc valve (BrE), balanced disk valve (AmE); **Ausgleichstern** *m* KFZTECH differential spi-der; **Ausgleichstromversorgungsleitung** *f* ELEKTRIZ equalizing feeder; **Ausgleichsystem** *nt* ELEKTROTECH balancer; **Ausgleichträger** *m* KFZTECH differential ca-sing; **Ausgleichunterlegscheibe** *f* LUFTTRANS balance washer; **Ausgleichventil** *nt* FERTIG pressure-main-taining valve; **Ausgleichverhalten** *nt* GERÄT transient

behavior (AmE), transient behaviour (BrE); **Aus-gleichwert** *m* REGELUNG compensation value; **Ausgleichzeit** *f* GERÄT settling time, REGELUNG com-pensation time
Ausglühen *nt* ELEKTRONIK, HEIZ & KÄLTE, METALL an-nealing, THERMOD annealing, *Stahl* anneal
ausglühen *vt* MECHAN anneal, METALL anneal, temper, PHYS, THERMOD *Stahl* anneal
ausgrenzen *vt* RADIO null
Ausguck[1] *m* WASSERTRANS *bei Navigation für Person* lookout
Ausguck:[2] **~ halten** *vi* WASSERTRANS keep a lookout
Ausguß *m* BAU lip, sewer, FERTIG lining, KER & GLAS lip, LABOR spout, MASCHINEN antifriction lining, nozzle, UMWELTSCHMUTZ sink, VERPACK pour spout, WASSER-VERSORG *Pumpe* spout; **Ausgußmetall** *nt* MASCHINEN bush metal, bushing metal; **Ausgußröhre** *f* WASSER-VERSORG delivery pipe; **Ausgußstutzen** *m* MASCHINEN pouring sleeve
Aushaken *nt* MASCHINEN unhooking
aushämmern *vt* FERTIG pane, MASCHINEN batter
aushärtbar *adj* MECHAN, THERMOD thermosetting
Aushärten *nt* ANSTRICH curing, KUNSTSTOFF hardening, METALL age hardening
aushärten[1] *vt* ANSTRICH cure, BAU *Mörtel, Beton* mature, KUNSTSTOFF cure, METALL temper
aushärten[2] *vi* BAU *Mörtel, Beton* mature
Aushärtung *f* FERTIG quench ageing (BrE), quench aging (AmE), METALL dispersion hardening, precip-itation hardening, WASSERTRANS *Schiffbau* curing
aushärtungsfähig *adj* FERTIG *Stahl* age-hardenable
Aushärtung: **Aushärtungsfähigkeit** *f* FERTIG *Stahl* age hardenability; **Aushärtungstemperatur** *f* ANSTRICH cure temperature
Ausheben *nt* BAU digging, FERTIG withdrawing, *Gießen* drawing
ausheben *vt* BAU cut, *Baugrube* sink, FERTIG draw, *Mo-dell* lift
Aushebestift *m* MECHAN ejector pin
Ausheilen *nt* THERMOD annealing
ausheilen *vt* MECHAN, PHYS anneal
Ausheizofen *m* THERMOD firebox
aushöhlen *vt* BAU hollow out, hollow
Aushöhlung *f* BAU hollow
Ausholer *m* WASSERTRANS *Segeln* outhaul
Aushub *m* BAU excavation, FERTIG *Tieflochbohren* relief motion, *Tieflochbohrer* retraction; **Aushubboden** *m* BAU spoil
auskehlen *vt* BAU channel, *Holz* hollow, FERTIG hollow, hollow out, mold (AmE), mould (BrE), MASCHINEN recess
Auskehlung *f* BAU hollowing, FERTIG channelling (BrE), MASCHINEN recess, MECHAN flute
Auskippen *nt* BAU dumping
auskippen *vt* TRANS dump
auskitten *vt* BAU stop with putty
auskleiden *vt* BAU line
Auskleidung *f* BAU coating, lining, METALL, PAPIER, WAS-SERVERSORG *einer Pumpe* lining; **~ des Fahrzeughimmels** *f* KFZTECH *Innenausstattung* head lining
Ausklink- *pref* BAU release, MASCHINEN trip
Ausklinken *nt* FERTIG *eines Trägers* coping, KERNTECH *eines Brennelementes* uncoupling, *eines Elementes bei Schnellabschaltung* unlatching, RAUMFAHRT *Weltraumfunk* decoupling; **~ der Ladung**

nt LUFTTRANS *Flugwesen* load release

ausklinken *vt* BAU notch, *Träger* cope, FERTIG *Gewindebohrer* interrupt, *Träger* cope, MASCHINEN release, throw out, MECHAN disengage, RAUMFAHRT *Raumschiff* drop

Ausklink-: **Ausklinkhaken** *m* BAU releasing hook; **Ausklinkmechanismus** *m* MASCHINEN trip, trip gear; **Ausklinkstelle** *f* LUFTTRANS knock-out station

Ausknicken *nt* FERTIG crippling

ausknicken *vt* FERTIG buckle (AmE), collapse (BrE)

auskohlen *vt* FERTIG *Spanung* crater

Auskohlung *f* FERTIG *Spanung* crater

Auskolken *nt* FERTIG cupping, MASCHINEN pitting

auskolken *vt* FERTIG pit, *Spanfläche* erode

Auskolkung *f* FERTIG crater wear, *Spanfläche* erosion, *Spanung* pit, MASCHINEN crater

Auskopier- *pref* DRUCK, FOTO printing-out; **Auskopieremulsion** *f* FOTO printing-out emulsion; **Auskopierpapier** *nt* DRUCK printing-out paper

Auskoppel- *pref* ELEKTRONIK catcher; **Auskoppelraum** *m* ELEKTRONIK *Klystron* catcher cavity; **Auskoppelspalt** *m* ELEKTRONIK catcher space

Auskopplung *f* EISENBAHN uncoupling

auskragen *vi* BAU project

auskragend *adj* BAU overhanging

Auskragung *f* BAU cantilever, overhang, projection

Auskreiden *nt* KUNSTSTOFF chalking

Auskreidung *f* KUNSTSTOFF chalking

Auskristallisieren *nt* KER & GLAS sulfuring (AmE), sulphuring (BrE)

auskristallisieren *vi* CHEMTECH crystallize out

Auskunftsdienste *m pl* TELEKOM directory enquiries

Auskuppeln *nt* KFZTECH clutch throwout, declutching, disengagement, MASCHINEN unclutching

auskuppeln[1] *vt* EISENBAHN uncouple, KFZTECH put out of gear, unclutch, MASCHINEN declutch, unclutch

auskuppeln[2] *vi* KFZTECH declutch

auskurbelbar: **~es Mittelrohr** *nt* FOTO *Stativ* geared center column (AmE), geared centre column (BrE)

Ausladen *nt* WASSERTRANS landing

ausladen *vt* COMP & DV roll out, WASSERTRANS *Ladung* unship

ausladend *adj* BAU overhanging, MECHAN flared

Ausladung *f* BAU *eines Kranes* radius, FERTIG overhang, throat distance, MASCHINEN overhang

Auslagern *nt* COMP & DV swap-out

auslagern *vt* COMP & DV roll out, swap

Auslagerungsfunktion *f* COMP & DV swapping

Auslands- *pref* TELEKOM international; **Auslandsfernwahl** *f* TELEKOM IDD, IDDD, international direct dialing (AmE), international direct dialling (BrE), international direct distance dialing (AmE), international direct distance dialling (BrE); **Auslands-Kopfvermittlungsstelle** *f* TELEKOM IGN, international gateway node; **Auslandsvermittlungsstelle** *f* TELEKOM international gateway exchange

Auslängung *f* KUNSTSTOFF sag

Auslaß *m* HEIZ & KÄLTE discharge, HYDRAUL gating, KERNTECH, KFZTECH, MASCHINEN, WASSERVERSORG outlet; **Auslaßdampf** *m* HYDRAUL exhaust steam; **Auslaßdeckung** *f* HYDRAUL *Steuerschieber* exhaust cover, exhaust lap; **Auslaßdurchflußregelung** *f* WASSERVERSORG outlet flow control

auslassen *vt* HYDRAUL gate

Auslaß: **Auslaßhub** *m* KFZTECH exhaust stroke; **Auslaßkanal** *m* HYDRAUL exhaust port, KFZTECH exhaust passage, *Viertaktmotor* exhaust port; **Auslaßkante** *f* HYDRAUL *Steuerschieber* exhaust edge; **Auslaßnocken** *m* MECHAN exhaust cam; **Auslaßöffnung** *f* HYDRAUL exhaust port, KER & GLAS outlet port, KFZTECH *Motor, Auspuff* exhaust port, MASCHINEN outlet; **Auslaßschlitz** *m* HYDRAUL *Zweitakt- und Kreiskolbenmotor*, KFZTECH *Zweitakt- und Kreiskolbenmotor* exhaust port; **Auslaßtemperatur** *f* HEIZ & KÄLTE, PHYS, THERMOD discharge temperature; **Auslaßüberdeckung** *f* HYDRAUL *Steuerschieber* exhaust cover, exhaust lap

Auslassung *f* COMP & DV skip, DRUCK ellipsis, out; **Auslassungszeichen** *nt* DRUCK caret

Auslaßventil *nt* HEIZ & KÄLTE discharge valve, HYDRAUL delivery valve, exhaust valve, outlet valve, KFZTECH outlet valve, MASCHINEN discharge valve, MECHAN, PAPIER exhaust valve

Auslastung *f* HEIZ & KÄLTE capacity utilization

Auslauf *m* BAU mouth, FERTIG *Kunststoffinstallationen* drainage, KER & GLAS *beim Walzverfahren* spout, MASCHINEN run-out, runout; **Auslaufabdeckung** *f* KER & GLAS spout cover (AmE); **Auslaufanschluß** *m* PAPIER outlet; **Auslaufbecher** *m* KUNSTSTOFF cup, flow cup; **Auslaufen** *nt* MEERSCHMUTZ leakage, WASSERTRANS sailing

auslaufen:[1] **auslaufend** *adj* WASSERTRANS *Schiff* outward bound

auslaufen[2] *vt* BAU leak, KOHLEN bleed off, WASSERVERSORG run out

auslaufen[3] *vi* KUNSTSTOFF bleed, TEXTIL *Farbe* bleed off, WASSERTRANS get under way, put to sea, sail away, *Schiff* set out

Auslauf: **Auslaufrille** *f* AKUSTIK lead-out groove, AUFNAHME concentric groove, lead-out groove, MASCHINEN undercut; **Auslaufrückstand** *m* KER & GLAS spout; **Auslaufschacht** *m* KER & GLAS running-out pit; **Auslaufstein** *m* KER & GLAS tap out block; **Auslaufventil** *nt* FERTIG *Kunststoffinstallationen* outlet valve, MASCHINEN plug cock, plug valve; **Auslaufzähler** *m* GERÄT outflow meter

Auslaug- *pref* ABFALL, KERNTECH leaching

Auslaugen *nt* ABFALL leaching, CHEMIE extraction, leaching, KOHLEN, LEBENSMITTEL, UMWELTSCHMUTZ leaching

auslaugen *vt* ABFALL lixiviate, CHEMIE extract, leach, FERTIG lixiviate, MEERSCHMUTZ leach

Auslaug-: **Auslaugkoeffizient** *m* KERNTECH leaching coefficient; **Auslaugmittel** *nt* KERNTECH leachant, leaching agent; **Auslaugtest** *m* ABFALL leachability test, leaching test

Auslaugung *f* ABFALL elutriation, lixiviation, FERTIG lixiviation, KER & GLAS dealkalization; **Auslaugungsgraben** *m* WASSERVERSORG leaching trench

Auslaugverfahren *nt* ABFALL leaching property

Auslegearm *m* EISENBAHN post bracket

Auslegen *nt* **~ von Seezeichen** *nt* WASSERTRANS seamarking

auslegen *vt* BAU *mit Parkett* inlay, MECHAN design

Ausleger *m* BAU cantilever, flange, *Kran* boom, EISENBAHN cantilever, ERDÖL *Kran* boom, FERTIG boom, jib, radial arm, *Kran* outrigger, *Radialbohrer* arm, KERNTECH *Kran*, LUFTTRANS *Hubschrauber* jib, MASCHINEN boom, cantilever, jib, outrigger, radial arm, PAPIER beam, cantilever, PHYS cantilever, RAUMFAHRT *Raumschiff* boom; **Auslegerarm** *m* BAU, FERTIG jib; **Auslegerbalken** *m* BAU, PHYS cantilever beam; **Auslegerbrücke** *f* BAU cantilever bridge;

Auslegerklemmung *f* FERTIG arm clamping, *Radialbohrer* arm-clamping mechanism; **Auslegerkran** *m* BAU, KERNTECH jib crane, LUFTTRANS *eines Hubschraubers* jib, MASCHINEN jib crane, MECHAN derrick

Auslegung *f* MASCHINEN design; **~ einer Analogschaltung** *f* ELEKTRONIK analog circuit design (AmE), analogue circuit design (BrE); **~ als integrierte Schaltung** *f* ELEKTRONIK integrated-circuit design; **~ einer integrierten Schaltung** *f* ELEKTRONIK integrated-circuit layout; **Auslegungsabbrand** *m* KERNTECH design burnup; **Auslegungsbeben** *nt* KERNTECH *größtes verzeichnetes Erdbeben* safe shutdown earthquake; **Auslegungsbericht** *m* QUAL design report; **Auslegungsbestimmungen** *f pl* QUAL design specifications; **Auslegungsdruck** *m* HEIZ & KÄLTE, QUAL design pressure; **Auslegungsgeschwindigkeit** *f* TRANS design speed; **Auslegungsgrenzen** *f pl* QUAL design limits; **Auslegungskriterium** *nt* KERNTECH design criterion; **Auslegungsleistungsabgabe** *f* KERNTECH designed power required output; **Auslegungsstörfall** *m* KERNTECH design basis accident, design basis event; **Auslegungsstrahlenpegel** *m* KERNTECH design irradiation level

Auslenkung *f* KFZTECH *bei einem Reifen* deflection

Auslesen *nt* COMP & DV readout

auslesen *vt* COMP & DV *Informationen* read out, KOHLEN cull

Ausleuchtung *f* ELEKTROTECH *Ziel* illumination, RAUMFAHRT *Weltraumfunk* luminance; **~ einer Hemisphäre** *f* TELEKOM hemispherical coverage; **Ausleuchtungswirkungsgrad** *m* RAUMFAHRT *Weltraumfunk* illumination efficiency

auslöschen *vt* THERMOD *Feuer* quench

Auslöschung *f* PHYS extinction

Auslöse- *pref* AUFNAHME, BAU, COMP & DV, TELEKOM release; **Auslöseanforderung** *f* COMP & DV clear request; **Auslöseanschlag** *m* FERTIG trip dog; **Auslösedauer** *f* AUFNAHME release time; **Auslösehandgriff mit Verschlußauslöser** *m* FOTO pistol grip with shutter release; **Auslösehebel** *m* BAU trip lever; **Auslöseimpuls** *m* COMP & DV trigger, TELEKOM triggering lead pulse; **Auslöseknopf** *m* FOTO shutter release button; **Auslösekontakte** *m pl* KFZTECH trigger contacts

Auslösen *nt* COMP & DV triggering, ELEKTRIZ tripping, TELEKOM *Telefon* release

auslösen *vt* COMP & DV, ELEKTRIZ trigger, MECHAN release, PHYS trigger, trip

auslösend: **~es Teilchen** *nt* KERNTECH initiating particle

Auslöse-: **Auslöseprozedur** *f* TELEKOM clearing procedure

Auslöser *m* ELEKTRIZ shutter release, trigger, ELEKTROTECH release, FERTIG detent, tripper, FOTO *Kameraverschluß*, MASCHINEN release, trigger, SICHERHEIT trip device; **Auslöserrelais** *nt* ELEKTRIZ tripping relay, FOTO trigger relay; **Auslöserstromkreis** *m* FOTO triggering circuit

Auslöse-: **Auslöseschaltung** *f* ELEKTRIZ tripping circuit; **Auslösesignal** *nt* KERNTECH *in automatischer Steuerung* actuating signal; **Auslösespule** *f* ELEKTRIZ tripping coil; **Auslösestrom** *m* ELEKTROTECH *bei Schalter* release current; **Auslöseverzögerung** *f* ELEKTROTECH release lag; **Auslösevorrichtung** *f* ELEKTRIZ trip gear, MASCHINEN tripper, tripping device, tripping mechanism; **Auslösezeit** *f* ELEKTROTECH release time

Auslösung *f* ELEKTROTECH firing, MASCHINEN *durch Nocken* release, TELEKOM cleardown; **Auslösungsanforderungspaket** *nt* TELEKOM clear-request packet

auslösungsfrei: **~es Abschalten** *nt* ELEKTRIZ trip-free release

ausloten *vt* BAU lead

Ausmahlungsgrad *m* LEBENSMITTEL *bei Getreide* extraction rate

Ausmauerung *f* BAU nogging

Ausmeißeln *nt* FERTIG gouging

Ausmeßgerät *nt* BAU measuring apparatus

Ausmündung *f* HYDRAUL *in Trennwand, Platte* opening

Ausnadeln *nt* METALL unpinning

Ausnahme *f* COMP & DV exception; **Ausnahmebedingung** *f* COMP & DV exception; **Ausnahmebehandlungsroutine** *f* COMP & DV exception handler

ausnehmen *vt* MASCHINEN recess

Ausnutzung *f* MECHAN efficiency; **Ausnutzungsfaktor** *m* MASCHINEN utilization factor; **Ausnutzungskurve** *f* NICHTFOSS ENERG utilization curve

auspacken *vt* COMP & DV unpack

auspflanzen *vt* BAU bed out

auspolstern *vt* TEXTIL pad

Ausprägung *f* KÜNSTL INT instance

auspressen *vt* BAU *Spannbeton* grout

ausprobieren *vt* BAU try

Ausprüfen *nt* KERNTECH checkout

Auspuff *m* KFZTECH exhaust, exhaust system, LUFTTRANS *Triebwerk, Motor* exhaust, MECHAN exhaust, muffler (AmE), silencer (BrE); **Auspuffanlage** *f* KFZTECH exhaust system; **Auspuffdampf** *m* THERMOD dead steam; **Auspuffgas** *nt* KFZTECH, MECHAN exhaust gas; **Auspuffgegendruck** *m* LUFTTRANS, MECHAN exhaust backpressure; **Auspuffgehäuse** *nt* KFZTECH muffler shell (AmE), silencer shell (BrE); **Auspuffhub** *m* KFZTECH, MECHAN exhaust stroke; **Auspuffkrümmer** *m* KFZTECH exhaust manifold; **Auspuffrohr** *nt* KFZTECH, LUFTTRANS, MECHAN, THERMOD, TRANS, WASSERTRANS exhaust pipe; **Auspuffsammelleitung** *f* MECHAN exhaust manifold; **Auspuffsammler** *m* MECHAN exhaust collector, exhaust manifold; **Auspuffstutzen** *m* MECHAN exhaust stack; **Auspuffsystem** *nt* MECHAN exhaust arrangement; **Auspufftopf** *m* KFZTECH exhaust muffler (AmE), exhaust silencer (BrE), *Auspuffanlage* muffler (AmE), silencer (BrE), MECHAN exhaust muffler (AmE), exhaust silencer (BrE); **Auspuffummantelung** *f* KFZTECH muffler jacket (AmE), silencer jacket (BrE); **Auspuffventil** *nt* MECHAN exhaust valve; **Auspuffverkleidung** *f* LUFTTRANS exhaust case

Auspumpen *nt* WASSERVERSORG pumping-out

auspumpen *vt* ELEKTRONIK *Röhren*, WASSERTRANS *Schiff* evacuate, WASSERVERSORG pump out

ausrechnen *vt* MATH calculate

Ausregelzeit *f* GERÄT transient time

Ausreiben: **~ fluchtender Bohrungen** *nt* FERTIG line reaming; **~ von Grundbohrungen** *nt* FERTIG blind-hole reaming

ausreichend *adj* KONTROLL satisfactory

Ausreißer *m* GERÄT *Meßwert im unnormalem Streubereich* outlier, QUAL maverick, outlier

Ausrichten *nt* BAU boning, FERTIG lining-up, KERNTECH deconvolution, RAUMFAHRT *Weltraumfunk* pointing

ausrichten *vt* BAU align, take out of wind, *Instrument* orient, FOTO *Kamera* sight, *Projektor* align, KER &

GLAS true up, MASCHINEN align
Ausrichtepaßstift *m* FERTIG location dowel
Ausrichtung *f* BAU, DRUCK alignment, MASCHINEN lining-in, location, MECHAN alignment, leveling (AmE), levelling (BrE), METALL *Moleküle* ordering; **~ magnetischer Teilchen** *f* FERNSEH magnetic particle orientation; **~ am Rand** *f* COMP & DV justification; **Ausrichtungsfehler** *m* RAUMFAHRT *Weltraumfunk* pointing error, TELEKOM *Antenne* alignment fault; **Ausrichtungsgenauigkeit** *f* RAUMFAHRT *Weltraumfunk* pointing accuracy; **Ausrichtungsverlust** *m* RAUMFAHRT *Weltraumfunk* pointing loss
Ausrück- *pref* KFZTECH clutch, MASCHINEN clutch, disengaging, release
Ausrücken *nt* TRANS disconnecting; **~ der Kupplung** *nt* KFZTECH declutching
ausrücken *vt* FERTIG demesh, *Kupplung* unclutch, MASCHINEN throw out of action, throw out of gear, MECHAN disengage
Ausrücker *m* MASCHINEN release, stop motion
Ausrück-: **Ausrückfeder** *f* MASCHINEN clutch spring; **Ausrückgabel** *f* KFZTECH *Kupplung* clutch release fork, MASCHINEN clutch fork, fork; **Ausrückhebel** *m* MASCHINEN disengaging lever, release lever; **Ausrücklager** *nt* KFZTECH *Kupplung* clutch release bearing
Ausrundung *f* FERTIG internal radius; **Ausrundungshalbmesser** *m* BAU vertical curve radius
Ausrüsten *nt* BAU fitting-out, WASSERTRANS *Schiff* fitting out
ausrüsten *vt* BAU fit, outfit, MASCHINEN fit out, TELEKOM equip, TEXTIL finish, WASSERTRANS *Schiff* equip, fit out; **neu ~** *vt* BAU re-equip, WASSERTRANS *schiff* refit
Ausrüstung *f* BAU plant, FERTIG outfit, FOTO apparatus, KERNTECH kit, MASCHINEN equipment, gear, outfit, PAPIER finishing, TEXTIL finish; **~ zur Probenentnahme** *f* WERKPRÜF sampling equipment; **Ausrüstungsbecken** *nt* WASSERTRANS fitting-out berth; **Ausrüstungshersteller** *m* WASSERTRANS equipment manufacturer
Aussägen *nt* KER & GLAS sawing out
Aussagenlogik *f* KÜNSTL INT propositional logic
Ausschachtbarkeit *f* KOHLEN excavatability
Ausschachten *nt* BAU digging
Ausschachtung *f* BAU, KOHLEN excavation
ausschalen[1] *vt* BAU strike, strip, *Beton* strike
ausschalen[2] *vi* BAU strip formwork
Ausschalt- *pref* ELEKTROTECH cutoff, KONTROLL turn-off
Ausschalten *nt* ELEKTROTECH *Lampe* turn-off
ausschalten *vt* COMP & DV disable, disconnect, ELEKTROTECH disconnect, *Lampe* turn off, FERNSEH, KONTROLL switch off, MASCHINEN stop
ausschaltend: **~e Windgeschwindigkeit** *f* NICHTFOSS ENERG cutout wind speed
Ausschalter *m* ELEKTROTECH cutout, interrupter, PHYS single throw switch
Ausschalt-: **Ausschaltrille** *f* AKUSTIK, AUFNAHME lead-out groove
Ausschaltung *f* ELEKTROTECH cutoff, disconnection
ausschaltverzögert: **~es Relais** *nt* ELEKTROTECH off-delay relay
Ausschalt-: **Ausschaltverzögerung** *f* KONTROLL turn-off delay; **Ausschaltverzug** *m* ELEKTROTECH opening time; **Ausschaltzeit** *f* ELEKTROTECH *Schaltung* off period, KONTROLL turn-off time; **Ausschaltzustand** *m* ELEKTROTECH off-state

Ausschankgerät *nt* VERPACK dispenser
Ausschärfung *f* FERTIG scarfing, *Blech* bevel
Ausschäumen *nt* CHEMTECH *Hohlräume* foaming
Ausscheidung *f* CHEMIE exudation, CHEMTECH sediment, METALL precipitation; **Ausscheidungsglühen** *nt* THERMOD precipitation anneal; **Ausscheidungshärten** *nt* FERTIG ageing (BrE), aging (AmE), *Stahl* age hardening, METALL age hardening
ausscheidungshärten *vt* THERMOD precipitation-harden
Ausscheidung: **Ausscheidungshärtung** *f* ELEKTRIZ intentional accelerated curing, intentional component curing, intentional normal curing, FERTIG, THERMOD precipitation hardening; **Ausscheidungsmittel** *nt* CHEMTECH separating agent
Ausscheren *nt* FERTIG crippling, TRANS leaving a line of traffic
ausscheren *vt* TEXTIL nap the pile
ausschieben *vt* FERTIG *Motor* exhaust
Ausschießen *nt* DRUCK imposition
ausschießen *vt* DRUCK impose
ausschiffen *vt* WASSERTRANS *Passagiere* disembark, land, put ashore
Ausschiffung *f* WASSERTRANS landing, *Passagiere* disembarkation
Ausschlachten *nt* KFZTECH *Autoverwertung* cannibalizing
ausschlacken *vt* FERTIG slag
Ausschlag- *pref* GERÄT deflection; **Ausschlagbecken** *nt* KOHLEN slurry pond
Ausschlagen *nt* FERTIG stuffing
ausschlagen:[1] **~ lassen** *vt* MASCHINEN *Zeigernadel* deflect
ausschlagen[2] *vi* GERÄT *Zeiger* deflect
Ausschläger *m* TEXTIL finisher scutcher
Ausschlag-: **Ausschlagmethode** *f* GERÄT deflection method; **Ausschlagwinkel** *m* GERÄT *Zeiger* deflection angle
ausschlämmen *vt* WASSERVERSORG cleanse
Ausschleifen *nt* KFZTECH reboring
Ausschleudermaschine *f* CHEMTECH centrifuge
ausschleudern *vt* CHEMTECH centrifuge
Ausschließen *nt* DRUCK justification
ausschließen *vt* DRUCK justify
ausschließlich:[1] **~ zugeordnet** *adj* COMP & DV dedicated
ausschließlich:[2] **~e Lizenz** *f* PATENT exclusive licence (BrE), exclusive license (AmE); **~es Recht** *nt* PATENT exclusive right
Ausschlußtaste *f* DRUCK justification key
Ausschlußtrommel *f* DRUCK justifying scale
Ausschmelzmodell *nt* FERTIG *Gießen* investment pattern
Ausschmelzverfahren:[1] **im ~ genauigkeitsgegossen** *adj* FERTIG investment-cast
Ausschmelzverfahren[2] *nt* MASCHINEN investment casting
Ausschmieden *nt* FERTIG drawing-out
ausschmieden *vt* FERTIG draw out
Ausschneiden *nt* FERTIG routing
ausschneiden *vt* FERTIG rout, MASCHINEN cut out
Ausschnitt *m* COMP & DV window, ELEKTROTECH cutout, FERTIG blanking, KER & GLAS cutout, MASCHINEN blank, blanking, cutout, MECHAN cutout, PHYS aperture; **Ausschnittsvergrößerung** *f* FOTO cutout photograph, section enlargement
ausschöpfen *vt* WASSERTRANS bail

Ausschreibung *f* BAU bidding; **Ausschreibungsbedingungen** *f pl* BAU conditions of the bid; **Ausschreibungsunterlagen** *f pl* BAU bidding documents

Ausschuß *m* DRUCK broke, FERTIG refuse, rejects, KOHLEN scrap, MECHAN discard, scrap, PAPIER broke, QUAL scrap, waste; **Ausschuß-** *pref* FERTIG, MASCHINEN no-go; **Ausschußgrenze** *f* QUAL limiting quality, limiting quality level, lot tolerance percentage of defectives, rejectable quality level; **Ausschußlehre** *f* MASCHINEN no-go gage (AmE), no-go gauge (BrE); **Ausschußpapier** *nt* PAPIER refuse; **Ausschußporzellan** *nt* KER & GLAS outshot of porcelain; **Ausschußseite** *f* MASCHINEN no-go end; **Ausschußteil** *nt* QUAL reject, rejected item

Ausschütten *nt* BAU dumping

ausschütten *vt* BAU tip

Ausschwefeln *nt* KUNSTSTOFF sulfur blooming (AmE), sulphur blooming (BrE)

Ausschweifung *f* FERTIG flaring

Ausschwimmen *nt* KUNSTSTOFF *von Farbstoffen* floating; **~ des Pigments** *nt* KUNSTSTOFF pigment floating

Ausschwing- *pref* AUFNAHME, ELEKTROTECH decay; **Ausschwingen** *nt* AUFNAHME decay; **Ausschwingkurve** *f* AUFNAHME decay curve; **Ausschwingzeit** *f* ELEKTROTECH *Meßanzeige* decay time

Ausschwitzen *nt* CHEMIE, KUNSTSTOFF exudation

ausschwitzen[1] *vt* CHEMIE exude, LEBENSMITTEL *Gießerei*, METALL sweat

ausschwitzen[2] *vi* LEBENSMITTEL *Ofen* sweat

Aussehen *nt* TEXTIL look, WERKPRÜF appearance, visual appearance

ausseigern *vt* FERTIG liquate

Außen- *pref* ELEKTRIZ exterior, external, ELEKTRONIK external, VERPACK exterior, outside; **Außen- und Innentaster** *m* MASCHINEN outside-and-inside calipers (AmE), outside-and-inside callipers (BrE); **Außenabmessungen** *f pl* MASCHINEN outside dimensions; **Außenabnahme beim Zulieferanten** *m* QUAL subcontractor source inspection; **Außenantrieb** *m* LUFTTRANS power takeoff; **Außenaufnahme** *f* FERNSEH field pick-up; **Außenbord** *nt* MASCHINEN, WASSERTRANS outboard; **Außenborder** *m* WASSERTRANS outboard motorboat; **Außenbord-:** **Außenborderschlauchboot** *nt* WASSERTRANS outboard inflatable; **Außenbordmotor** *m* WASSERTRANS outboard motor; **außenbords** *adv* WASSERTRANS outboard; **Außenbord-:** **Außenbordschnellboot** *nt* WASSERTRANS outboard speedboat; **aussenden** *vt* COMP & DV emit; **Außen-:** **Außendrehen** *nt* FERTIG external turning, outside turning; **Außendurchmesser** *m* FERTIG *Kunststoffinstallationen*, MASCHINEN, MECHAN OD, outside diameter; **Außenfläche** *f* GEOM outside face, VERPACK exterior surface; **Außenflächenräumen** *nt* FERTIG surface broaching; **Außenflächenräummaschine** *f* FERTIG surface broaching machine; **außengekühlt** *adj* KERNTECH externally cooled; **Außengewinde** *nt* MASCHINEN external screw thread, male thread, outside screw thread; **Außengewindeschneiden** *nt* FERTIG, MASCHINEN external threading; **Außengewindeschneider** *m* MASCHINEN outside-threading tool; **Außengewindeschneidmaschine** *f* FERTIG bolt cutter; **Außengewindeschraube** *f* MASCHINEN male screw; **Außen-:** **Außenhafen** *m* WASSERTRANS outer harbor (AmE), outer harbour (BrE); **Außenhaut** *f* LUFTTRANS *Luftfahrzeug* skin, WASSER-

TRANS *Schiffbau* outer hull, *Schiffbau* outer skin, *Schiffbau* shell, *Schiffbau* skin; **Außenhautbeplattung** *f* WASSERTRANS *Schiffbau* shell plating; **Außenhautplan** *m* WASSERTRANS *Schiffkonstruktion* drawing of shell expansion; **Außen-:** **Außenkegel** *m* FERTIG external taper

Aussenken *nt* FERTIG spotting

aussenken *vt* FERTIG *Naben* boss

Außen-: **Außenkühlung** *f* HEIZ & KÄLTE surface cooling; **Außenlastträger** *m* LUFTTRANS pylon; **Außenläufermotor** *m* ELEKTRIZ external rotor motor; **Außenleiter** *m* TELEKOM outer conductor; **Außenlinie** *f* FERTIG contour; **Außenluft** *f* HEIZ & KÄLTE outdoor air, outside air; **Außenlufttemperaturanzeige** *f* LUFTTRANS *Flugwesen* outside air temperature indicator; **Außenlufttemperaturfühler** *m* LUFTTRANS *Flugwesen* outside air temperature probe; **Außenmaße** *nt pl* VERPACK outside dimensions; **Außenmikrometer** *nt* MASCHINEN external micrometer; **Außenpackmaschine** *f* VERPACK exterior packaging machine; **Außenplanetenmission** *f* RAUMFAHRT outer planet mission; **Außenpolgenerator** *m* ELEKTRIZ exterior pole generator, external pole generator; **Außenrad** *nt* KFZTECH annulus; **Außenraster** *nt* ELEKTRONIK external grid; **Außenräummaschine** *f* MASCHINEN external broaching machine; **Außenräumwerkzeug** *nt* FERTIG surface broach, MASCHINEN external broach; **Außenreportage** *f* FERNSEH OB, outside broadcast; **Außenring** *m* *Kegelrollenlager* cup, *Kugellager* outer race, MASCHINEN outer race; **Außenrundschleifen** *nt* MASCHINEN cylindrical grinding, external cylindrical grinding; **Außenschleifen** *nt* FERTIG surface grinding

außenschleifen *vt* FERTIG surface grind

Außen-: **Außenschürze** *f* WASSERTRANS peripheral skirt; **Außenseite** *f* BAU face, VERPACK exterior surface

außenseitig: ~e elektrische Einrichtung *f* ELEKTRIZ outdoor electrical installation

Außen-: **Außenspiegel** *m* KFZTECH *Zubehör* side mirror

außenstehend: ~er Pfeil *m* KONSTZEICH outward-positioned arrowhead

Außen-: **Außenströmung** *f* STRÖMPHYS free stream; **Außentaster** *m* MASCHINEN outside calipers; **Außenteil** *nt* MASCHINEN outer member; **Außentreppe** *f* BAU fliers; **Außenübertragung** *f* FERNSEH OB, outside broadcast; **Außenübertragungsgruppe** *f* FERNSEH OB unit; **Außenübertragungskabel** *nt* FERNSEH outside plant cable; **Außenverpackung** *f* VERPACK outer case

außenverzahnt: ~es Rad *nt* MASCHINEN external gear; **~e Zahnscheibe** *f* FERTIG external tooth lock washer

Außen-: **Außenverzahnung** *f* MASCHINEN external toothing, outside gearing; **Außenvoreinströmung** *f* HYDRAUL outside lead; **Außenwand** *f* BAU enclosing wall; **Außenwiderstand** *m* ELEKTROTECH external resistor; **Außenwinkel** *m* GEOM exterior angle, outward angle

Außerband- *pref* ELEKTRONIK, TELEKOM out-of-band; **Außerbandfilterung** *f* ELEKTRONIK out-of-band filtering; **Außerband-Zeichengabe** *f* TELEKOM out-band signaling (AmE), out-band signalling (BrE)

äußere: mit äußerer Beaufschlagung *adj* FERTIG inward flow

außerhalb: ~ des Chips gelegen *adj* ELEKTRONIK off chip; **~ der Leiterplatte gelegen** *adj* ELEKTRONIK off board

außerirdisch: ~es Leben *nt* RAUMFAHRT extra-terrestrial

life
äußerlich *adj* UMWELTSCHMUTZ external
außermittig[1] *adj* MASCHINEN off-center (AmE), off-centre (BrE)
außermittig:[2] ~e Bohrung *f* FERTIG eccentric bore; ~es Spannen *nt* FERTIG eccentric chucking
Außermittigdrehen *nt* FERTIG, MASCHINEN eccentric turning
Außermittigkeit *f* PAPIER off-center (AmE), off-centre (BrE)
außerordentlich: ~er Strahl *m* PHYS extraordinary ray
außerphasig *adj* ELEKTRONIK out-of-phase
außerplanmäßig: ~es Ausfahren *nt* KERNTECH *eines Steuerstabes* unscheduled withdrawal
äußerst:[1] ~e Kraft voraus *adv* WASSERTRANS *Motor* full ahead; ~e Kraft zurück *adv* WASSERTRANS *Motor* full astern
äußerst:[2] das ~e Ende *nt* WASSERTRANS *Tauwerk* bitter end; ~ starkes Licht *nt* WELLPHYS intense light
aussetzbar: ~e Antenne *f* RAUMFAHRT *Weltraumfunk* deployable aerial, deployable antenna
Aussetzen *nt* FERNSEH dropout, RAUMFAHRT *Raumschiff* drop, WASSERTRANS *Boot* launching; ~ gegen saure Halogenide *nt* ANSTRICH acid halide exposure
aussetzen[1] *vt* ANSTRICH expose
aussetzen[2] *vi* PHYS break down
aussetzend: ~e Belastung *f* ELEKTRIZ, FERTIG intermittent load; ~er Betrieb *m* ELEKTRIZ intermittent duty
Aussickern *nt* MEERSCHMUTZ seepage
aussieben *vt* MEERSCHMUTZ *Öl* screen
aussondern *vt* QUAL segregate
Aussonderung *f* QUAL *von fehlerhaften Einheiten* segregation
ausspachteln *vt* BAU grout, smooth
ausspannen *vt* MASCHINEN unclamp
Aussparen *nt* BAU, MASCHINEN recessing
aussparen *vt* BAU block out, box out, recess, FERTIG recess, MASCHINEN relieve
Aussparung *f* BAU notch, pocket, recess, FERTIG pocket, recess, MASCHINEN clearance, recess, relief, MECHAN clearance, relief
ausspeichern *vt* COMP & DV roll out
Ausspeicherung *f* COMP & DV roll out
Aussperrung *f* COMP & DV lockout
Ausspitzen *nt* FERTIG *Bohrer* pointing, *Spiralbohrer* thinning
ausspitzen *vt* FERTIG *Spiralbohrer* thin
Ausspülen *nt* MECHAN flushing, WASSERVERSORG cleaning out
ausspülen *vt* NICHTFOSS ENERG scour, WASSERVERSORG *mit Wasser* flush
Ausspülung *f* CHEMTECH washing out, PAPIER baring
ausstanzen *vt* FERTIG blank, MECHAN punch out
ausstatten *vt* BAU furnish, MASCHINEN fit out, TELEKOM equip
Ausstattung *f* BAU equipment, set, MASCHINEN equipment; ~ mit Geräten *f* GERÄT instrumentation
aussteifen *vt* BAU buttress, MASCHINEN brace, buttress, MECHAN buttress
Aussteifung *f* BAU stiffening
ausstellen *vt* TEXTIL flare
Aus-Stellung *f* MASCHINEN off position
ausstemmen *vt* BAU mortice, mortise
Aussteuerung *f* COMP & DV, ELEKTRONIK *Radio* modulation, ELEKTROTECH excitation; Aussteuerungsanzeige *f* AUFNAHME level indicator, FERNSEH

VI meter; Aussteuerungsbereich des Vertikalverstärkers *m* ELEKTRONIK vertical-amplifier dynamic range; Aussteuerungsgrenze *f* AKUSTIK maximum recording level, AUFNAHME, ELEKTROTECH overload level; Aussteuerungsmesser *m* AUFNAHME peak program meter (AmE), peak programme meter (BrE); Aussteuerungsmeßgerät *nt* GERÄT volume unit meter
ausstöpseln *vt* BAU unstop, FERNSEH *Stecker* unplug
Ausstoß *m* ERDÖL *Kapillarwasser in Schieferschichten* expulsion, KERNTECH discharge, KFZTECH, LUFTTRANS emission, MASCHINEN output, production, MECHAN ejection, RADIO emission; ~ von Auspuffgasen *m* KFZTECH exhaust gas emission; Ausstoßdüse *f* KERNTECH discharge nozzle; Ausstoßung *f* CHEMIE *Gase, Flüssigkeiten* expulsion
ausstoßen *vt* FERTIG knock out, STRÖMPHYS jet, THERMOD give off
Ausstoßer *m* FERTIG lifter
Ausstoß: Ausstoßrate *f* ERDÖL *Kapillarwasser in Schieferschichten* expulsion rate; Ausstoßvorrichtung *f* KUNSTSTOFF, MASCHINEN ejector
ausstrahlen *vt* COMP & DV emit, THERMOD radiate
Ausstrahlung *f* CHEMIE emanation
Ausstrippen: ~ mit Dampf *nt* ABFALL *Sickerwasserbehandlung* steam stripping; ~ mit Luft *nt* ABFALL air stripping
Ausström- *pref* HEIZ & KÄLTE discharge, PHYS stream; Ausströmdruck *m* HEIZ & KÄLTE discharge pressure; Ausströme *nt* HEIZ & KÄLTE discharges WASSERVERSORG ELEKTROTECH leakage, efflux
ausströmen *vt* THERMOD emit; ~ lassen *vt* HEIZ & KÄLTE discharge
Ausström-: Ausströmgeschwindigkeit *f* PHYS free stream velocity; Ausströmraum *m* WASSERVERSORG *einer Kreisel- oder Zentrifugalpumpe* volute chamber
Ausströmung *f* MECHAN exhaust; Ausströmungsaushöhlung *f* HYDRAUL *Abdampfkavitation* exhaust cavity
Ausström-: Ausströmvorgang *m* MECHAN exhaust process
Austast- *pref* ELEKTRONIK, FERNSEH blanking; Austast- und Synchronisiersignal *nt* FERNSEH blanking and sync signal; Austast- und Synchronisiersignalmischer *m* FERNSEH blanking and sync signal mixer
Austasten *nt* COMP & DV, ELEKTRONIK, FERNSEH gating, GERÄT blanking
austastend: nicht ~e Impulse *m pl* FERNSEH unblanking pulses
Austast-: Austastgenerator *m* ELEKTRONIK blanking generator; Austastimpuls *m* FERNSEH blanking pulse; Austastkreis *m* FERNSEH blanking circuit; Austastlücke *f* FERNSEH blanking interval; Austastpegel *m* FERNSEH blanking level; Austastsignal *nt* ELEKTRONIK, FERNSEH blanking signal; Austastspannung *f* FERNSEH blanking voltage
Austastung *f* FERNSEH blanking
Austast-: Austastverstärker *m* ELEKTRONIK *Fernsehtechnik* blanking amplifier
Austausch *m* COMP & DV, MASCHINEN, TELEKOM exchange
austauschbar[1] *adj* FOTO, MASCHINEN interchangeable
austauschbar:[2] ~e Logik *f* ELEKTRONIK compatible logic; ~es optisches Medium *nt* OPTIK alterable optical medium; ~es Teil *nt* MASCHINEN interchangeable part
Austauschbarkeit *f* MASCHINEN interchangeability
austauschen *vt* COMP & DV swap

Austausch: **Austauschenergie** *f* METALL exchange energy; **Austauschsprungbefehl** *m* COMP & DV exchange jump; **Austauschwerkstoff** *m* MASCHINEN alternative material

Austenit *m* FERTIG, METALL austenite

austenitisch[1] *adj* FERTIG, MECHAN austenitic

austenitisch:[2] **~er Stahl** *m* MECHAN austenitic steel

austenitisieren *vt* FERTIG austenitize

Austenitisierung *f* FERTIG austenizing

Austenit: **Austenitstahl** *m* METALL austenic steel; **Austenitstahlrohr** *nt* MASCHINEN austenitic stainless steel tube

Austernbagger *m* WASSERTRANS *Schifftyp* oyster dredge, oyster dredger

Austrag *m* KOHLEN discharge

Austreiben *nt* DRUCK quad

Austreiber *m* FERTIG taper key, MASCHINEN center key (AmE), centre key (BrE), drift bolt, pin punch

Austreiberlappen: mit ~ *adj* FERTIG tanged

Austreibung *f* CHEMIE *Gase, Flüssigkeiten* expulsion

austreiben:[1] **~ lassen** *vt* HEIZ & KÄLTE discharge

austreten[2] *vi* HEIZ & KÄLTE discharge

austretend: ~er Fluß *m* PHYS outward flux; **~es Teilchen** *nt* KERNTECH outcoming particle; **~es Tragflächenboot** *nt* WASSERTRANS emerging foil craft

Austrieb *m* ERDÖL expulsion, KUNSTSTOFF flash; **Austriebrate** *f* ERDÖL expulsion rate

Austritt *m* ELEKTROTECH *elektrische Schwingungen* outlet, ERDÖL *Öl* spillage, HEIZ & KÄLTE discharge, MASCHINEN outlet; **Austrittsarbeit** *f* ELEKTROTECH *bei elektrischen Röhren*, PHYS *des Elektrons* work function; **Austrittsdivergenz** *f* TELEKOM output divergence; **Austrittsfläche** *f* MECHAN exhaust area; **Austrittsgeschwindigkeit** *f* FERTIG, HYDRAUL exit velocity; **Austrittshöhe** *f* KERNTECH *einer Pumpe* discharge head; **Austrittskonus** *m* LUFTTRANS exhaust cone; **Austrittskonus einer Düse** *m* PHYS exit cone of nozzle; **Austrittsluke** *f* OPTIK exit port; **Austrittsöffnung** *f* MASCHINEN outlet; **Austrittspfosten** *m* BAU newel; **Austrittspupille** *f* OPTIK eye ring, PHYS exit pupil; **Austrittsschaufelrad** *nt* WASSERTRANS exducer; **Austrittsseite** *f* TEXTIL downstream; **Austrittstemperatur** *f* UMWELTSCHMUTZ outlet temperature; **Austrittsventil** *nt* HYDRAUL escape valve; **Austrittsverlust** *m* MECHAN exhaust loss; **Austrittswinkel** *m* HYDRAUL exit angle, OPTIK, TELEKOM output angle

Austrocknen *nt* THERMOD drying-out

austrocknen *vti* BAU, THERMOD dry out

Austrocknung *f* CHEMIE desiccation

austrommeln *vt* MEERSCHMUTZ *Sperre* reel out

ausüben *vt* FERTIG *Druck* impart, PHYS *Kraft* exert

Auswahl *f* COMP & DV menu selection, selection, MATH sampling, QUAL applicability; **~ der Prüfschärfe** *f* QUAL procedure for normal, tightened and reduced inspection

auswählbar: ~er Name *m* COMP & DV generic name

Auswahl: **Auswahlcode** *m* COMP & DV option code; **Auswahleinheit** *f* QUAL sampling unit

auswählen *vt* COMP & DV select

Auswahl: **Auswahlmenü** *nt* COMP & DV menu; **Auswahlmethode** *f* ERGON selection method; **Auswahlmöglichkeit** *f* COMP & DV available choice, option; **Auswahlregel** *f* KERNTECH, PHYS, STRAHLPHYS selection rule; **Auswahlsortierung** *f* COMP & DV selective sort; **Auswahlverfahren** *nt* ERGON selection method

Auswalzen *nt* FERTIG *im Blockwalzwerk* blooming-down

auswalzen *vt* BAU *Tiefbau* sheet out, FERTIG *Luppen* bloom, *Walzen* get down

Auswanderung *f* TELEKOM *auf Null* drift

Auswärtsdrehung *f* ERGON eversion

Auswaschen *nt* CHEMTECH washing out

auswaschen *vt* BAU erode, leach, TEXTIL launder

Auswaschung *f* BAU erosion, LEBENSMITTEL elutriation, UMWELTSCHMUTZ washout

auswattieren *vt* TEXTIL pad

auswechselbar[1] *adj* FOTO interchangeable, MASCHINEN interchangeable, removable

auswechselbar:[2] **~e Amboßbahn** *f* FERTIG anvil pallet; **~er Aufsichtsucher** *m* FOTO interchangeable waist-level finder; **~er Einsatz** *m* MASCHINEN removable insert; **~es Kation** *nt* UMWELTSCHMUTZ exchangeable cation; **~e Mattscheibe** *f* FOTO interchangeable focusing screen; **~e Platte** *f* COMP & DV removable disk

Auswechselbarkeit *f* MASCHINEN interchangeability

Auswechselbeutel *m* VERPACK liner bag

auswechseln *vt* BAU trim

Ausweich- *pref* EISENBAHN, LUFTTRANS, RAUMFAHRT, WASSERTRANS alternate

ausweichen *vi* WASSERTRANS *Navigation* give way

Ausweich-: **Ausweichflughafen** *m* LUFTTRANS alternate airport; **Ausweichgleis** *nt* EISENBAHN passing track, siding, turnout; **Ausweichlandung** *f* RAUMFAHRT alternate landing; **Ausweichmanöver** *nt* WASSERTRANS emergency turn; **Ausweichrangiergleis** *nt* EISENBAHN classification siding; **Ausweichstelle** *f* BAU turnout, EISENBAHN passing point, shunt, turnout

Ausweis *m* COMP & DV badge; **Ausweisanhänger** *m* SICHERHEIT sling identification tag; **Ausweiskontrolle** *f* TRANS passport check; **Ausweisleser** *m* COMP & DV badge reader

Ausweitdorn *m* FERTIG drift

auswerfen *vt* FERTIG spew

Auswerfer *m* KUNSTSTOFF, MECHAN ejector; **Auswerferbolzen** *m* MECHAN ejector pin; **Auswerferbuchse** *f* MASCHINEN ejector sleeve; **Auswerferplatte** *f* MASCHINEN ejector plate; **Auswerferstift** *m* MASCHINEN ejection pin, ejector pin, knock-out pin

Auswerfvorrichtung *f* MASCHINEN ejector

auswerten *vt* COMP & DV interpret, MATH evaluate

Auswertung *f* COMP & DV interpretation, MATH evaluation; **~ von Prüfergebnissen** *f* QUAL evaluation of test results; **Auswertungs-Session** *f* AUFNAHME scoring session

auswiegen *vt* FERTIG poise

Auswirkung *f* MECHAN effect

auswölben *vt* BAU vault

Auswucht- *pref* LUFTTRANS, MASCHINEN balancing

Auswuchten *nt* FERTIG truing, MASCHINEN balancing, counterbalancing

auswuchten *vt* FERTIG balance, true, HEIZ & KÄLTE balance

Auswucht-: **Auswuchtgewicht** *nt* LUFTTRANS balance weight; **Auswuchtmaschine** *f* MASCHINEN balancing machine

Auswuchtung *f* FERTIG balance

Auswurf *m* KERNTECH washback, METALL spittings; **Auswurfkraft** *f* RAUMFAHRT *Raumschiff* ejection force

Auszeichnung *f* VERPACK labeling (AmE), labelling (BrE); **Auszeichnungsschrift** *f* DRUCK display face, display type

ausziehbar[1] *adj* MASCHINEN telescopic, telescoping

ausziehbar:[2] ~**er Bohrmeißel** *m* ERDÖL *Bohrtechnik* collapsible bit; ~**e Leitung** *f* PHYS line stretcher

ausziehen *vt* ANSTRICH expose

Auszieher *m* BAU extractor

Ausziehleiter *f* BAU extension

Auszug *m* FOTO *Balg* extension; **Auszugsfilter** *nt* FOTO color separation filter (AmE), colour separation filter (BrE); **Auszugsring** *m* FOTO extension ring

Autarkie *f* ERDÖL self-sufficiency

Authentifizierung *f* COMP & DV authentication; **Authentifizierungsprozedur** *f* TELEKOM authentication procedure

Auto *nt* *(Automobil)* KFZTECH *Fahrzeugart* auto, car, passenger car *(automobile)*

Autobahn *f* TRANS expressway (AmE), motorway (BrE), superhighway (AmE); **Autobahnparkplatz** *m* TRANS lay-by; **Autobahnzubringerkontrolle** *f* TRANS slip road control (BrE); **Autobahnzubringerverkehrszählung** *f* TRANS slip road census (BrE), slip road count (BrE), slip road metering (BrE)

Auto-: **Autobandspanner** *m* FERNSEH autotension; **Autocue** *nt* FERNSEH autocue; **Autodyn** *nt* ELEKTRONIK autodyne; **Autoedieren** *nt* FERNSEH autoediting; **Autoedit** *nt* FERNSEH automatic editing; **Autoequalizer** *m* FERNSEH autoequalization; **Autofähre** *f* WASSERTRANS ferry; **Autofrettage** *f* MECHAN cold drawing; **Autofriedhof** *m* ABFALL used car dump

Autogen- *pref* BAU oxyacetylene, KOHLEN, MASCHINEN autogenous; **Autogenbrenner** *m* BAU oxyacetylene blowpipe

autogen[1] *adj* KOHLEN, MASCHINEN autogenous

autogen:[2] ~**es Brennschneiden** *nt* THERMOD flame cutting; ~**es Mahlen** *nt* KOHLEN autogenous milling; ~**e Schweißung** *f* MASCHINEN autogenous welding

Autogen-: **Autogenhärten** *nt* FERTIG flame hardening; **Autogenmühle** *f* KOHLEN autogenous mill; **Autogenschweißbrenner** *m* MECHAN acetylene-oxygen torch; **Autogenschweißen** *nt* BAU oxyacetylene welding, MASCHINEN autogenous welding, gas welding, MECHAN oxyacetylene welding, THERMOD gas welding

Auto: **Autogiro** *nt* LUFTTRANS autogyro; **Autoheizung** *f* HEIZ & KÄLTE car heater; **Autoionisation** *f* PHYS, STRAHLPHYS autoionization

autokatalytisch[1] *adj* KERNTECH autocatalytic

autokatalytisch:[2] ~**e Wirkung** *f* METALL autocatalytic effect

Auto: **Autokinese** *f* ERGON autokinesis; **Autoklav** *m* CHEMIE, KER & GLAS, KOHLEN, LEBENSMITTEL autoclave, THERMOD digester; **Autoklavieren** *nt* CHEMIE retorting; **Autokollimationsfernrohr** *nt* METROL autocollimator; **Autokompensator** *m* GERÄT auto-matic potentiometer; **Autokorrelation** *f* ELEKTRONIK, TELEKOM autocorrelation; **Autokorrelationsanalyse** *f* GERÄT autocorrelation analysis; **Autokran** *m* BAU mobile crane; **Autolock** *nt* FERNSEH automatic lock

Autolyse *f* LEBENSMITTEL *Biochemie* autolysis

Automat *m* ELEKTRIZ automaton, MASCHINEN automatic, VERPACK *für Getränke, Snacks* dispensing machine; **Automatenmessing** *nt* MASCHINEN free-cutting brass; **Automatenpackung** *f* VERPACK package for vending machine; **Automatenstahl** *m* FERTIG free machine steel, MASCHINEN free-cutting steel, machining steel, METALL free-cutting steel

Automatik *f* VERPACK automatic control; **Automatikgetriebe** *nt* KFZTECH automatic transmission; **Automatikgetriebeöl** *nt* *(ATF)* KFZTECH automatic transmission fluid *(ATF)*; **Automatikmeißel** *m* BAU *Holzbau* self-coring chisel; **Automatikschalter** *m* REGELUNG automatic control switch; **Automatikschalthebel** *m* KFZTECH *Getriebe* selector lever; **Automatiksystem** *nt* RAUMFAHRT automatic system; **Automatiktür** *f* BAU self-closing door

Automation *f* BAU, COMP & DV, ERGON, MASCHINEN, RAUMFAHRT automation

automatisch[1] *adj* COMP & DV automatic, MASCHINEN self-acting, MECHAN, RADIO automatic; **mit ~er Zuführung** *adj* MASCHINEN self-feeding

automatisch:[2] ~**es Abfangen** *nt* TELEKOM automatic intercept system; ~**e Abgriffverbindung** *f* ELEKTROTECH automated tap bonding; ~**er Abruf** *m* TELEKOM automatic recall; ~**er Abspanntransformator** *m* ELEKTROTECH step-down autotransformer; ~**e Absperrarmatur** *f* ERDÖL *Rohrleitungen* automatic shutoff valve; ~**e Abstandskontrolle** *f* KFZTECH automatic control of headway; ~**e Amplitudenregelung** *f* ELEKTRONIK, RADIO, TELEKOM automatic gain control; ~**er Analog-Digital-Wandler** *m* TELEKOM automatic ADC; ~**e Anflugkontrolle** *f* LUFTTRANS *Navigation* automatic approach control; ~**e Anflugsteuerung vom Boden** *f* *(AGCA)* RAUMFAHRT automatic ground-controlled approach *(AGCA)*; ~**e Anlagen** *f* LEBENSMITTEL CIP; ~**e Anlagenreinigung** *f* LEBENSMITTEL cleaning in place; ~**e Anrufumlegung** *f* TELEKOM automatic call transfer; ~**er Anrufverteiler** *m* TELEKOM ACD, automatic call distributor; ~ **arbeitende Armatur** *f* ERDÖL *Rohrleitungen* automatic valve; ~**er Aufwärtstransformator** *m* ELEKTROTECH step-up autotransformer; ~**e Auslösung** *f* KERNTECH automatic release; ~**es Ausrücken** *nt* MASCHINEN automatic throwing out of action; ~**er Ausschalter** *m* ELEKTRIZ automatic switch, cutout switch; ~**e Ausschaltung** *f* AUFNAHME automatic stop; ~**e Autobahn** *f* TRANS automatic highway (AmE), automatic motorway (BrE); ~**er Azimutanzeiger** *m* LUFTTRANS OBI, omnibearing indicator; ~**er Betrieb** *m* BAU automatic operation, COMP & DV hands-off operation, unattended operation; ~**e Brandmeldeanlage** *f* BAU automatic fire alarm; ~**e Bremse** *f* KFZTECH automatic brake; ~**e Bürette** *f* LABOR automatic burette; ~**e Chrominanzsteuerung** *f* FERNSEH automatic chrominance control; ~**e Datenkonvertierung** *f* COMP & DV automatic data conversion; ~**e Datenumwandlung** *f* COMP & DV automatic data conversion; ~**e Datenverarbeitung** *f* *(ADV)* COMP & DV automatic data processing *(ADP)*; ~**e Diagnose** *f* KÜNSTL INT automatic diagnosis; ~**er Diawechsler** *m* FOTO automatic slide changer; ~**e Drehbank** *f* MECHAN automatic lathe; ~**e Drehzahlregelung** *f* KFZTECH automatic speed control; ~**e Dynamikdrängung** *f* AUFNAHME automatic volume compression; ~**e Erfassung der Ortsveränderungen** *f* TELEKOM automatic roaming; ~**e Ersatzschaltung** *f* TELEKOM *Standby-Betätigung* automatic changeover; ~**e Expansionsvorrichtung** *f* MASCHINEN automatic expansion gear; ~**e Fahr- und Bremssteuerung** *f* TRANS automatic running and braking control, automatic speed control; ~**e Fahrzeugidentifikation** *f* *(AFI)* TRANS automatic vehicle identification *(AVI)*; ~**e Fahrzeugortung** *f* *(AFO)* TRANS automatic vehicle location *(AVL)*; ~**e Fehlerberichtigung** *f* LUFTTRANS automatic error correction; ~**e Fehlererkennung** *f* COMP & DV automatic error detection; ~**e Fehlerkor-**

rektur *f* TELEKOM automatic error correction; ~er
Fernbetrieb *m* TELEKOM automatic trunk working; ~e
Fernwahl *f* TELEKOM automatic trunk dialing (AmE),
automatic trunk dialling (BrE); ~er Feueralarm *m*
SICHERHEIT automatic fire alarm; ~er Feuermelder *m*
SICHERHEIT automatic fire detection system; ~er Film-
druck *m* TEXTIL automatic screen printing; ~er
Fliehkraftregler *m* NICHTFOSS ENERG automatic gover-
nor; ~es Formen *nt* KER & GLAS automatic forming; ~e
Frequenz- und Verstärkungsregelung *f* *(AFGC)*
ELEKTRONIK, FERNSEH, RADIO automatic frequency
and gain control *(AFGC)*; ~e Frequenzregelung *f*
(AFR) ELEKTRONIK, FERNSEH, RADIO automatic fre-
quency control *(AFC)*; ~e Frequenzumtastung *f*
ELEKTRONIK, FERNSEH, RADIO *Fernschreiben* automatic frequency shift keying; ~er Funkkompaß *m*
(ADF) LUFTTRANS, RAUMFAHRT, TELEKOM automatic direction finder *(ADF)*; ~e
Geschwindigkeitssteuerung *f* TRANS automatic speed
control; ~e Gesprächsumlegung *f* TELEKOM automatic call transfer; ~ getaktete Farbkorrekturschaltung *f*
FERNSEH color automatic time-base corrector
(AmE), colour automatic time-base corrector (BrE);
~es Getriebe *nt* MASCHINEN automatic transmission;
~e Gittervorspannung *f* ELEKTROTECH self-bias; ~e
Haltlichtanlage *f* EISENBAHN automatic flashing light
signals; ~e Handschrifterkennung *f* KÜNSTL INT automatic handwriting recognition; ~e
Helligkeitsregelung *f* *(ABC)* FERNSEH auto-matic brightness control *(ABC)*; ~e
Helligkeitssteuerung *f* FERNSEH automatic brightness
control; ~ herabfallende Sauerstoffmaske *f* LUFT-
TRANS quick-downing oxygen mask; ~e
Himmelsnavigation *f* *(ACN)* RAUMFAHRT automatic
celestial navigation *(ACN)*; ~e KFZ-Identifizierung *f*
(automatische Kraftfahrzeug-Identifizierung)
KFZTECH ACI *(automatic car identification)*; ~er
Kompensator *m* GERÄT automatic potentiometer; ~e
Kopierdrehmaschine *f* MASCHINEN automatic copying lathe; ~e Kopiermaschine *f* FOTO automatic
printer; ~e Kraftfahrzeug-Identifizierung *f* *(automatische KFZ-Identifizierung)* KFZTECH automatic car
identification (AmE), automatic wagon identification (BrE) *(automatic car identification)*; ~e
Kraftübertragung *f* MECHAN automatic transmission;
~er Kreditkartendienst *m* TELEKOM automatic credit
card service; ~es Kurssteuerungssystem *nt* LUFT-
TRANS automatic flight-control system; ~es Laden *nt*
COMP & DV autoload; ~es Ladesystem *nt* FOTO automatic loading system; ~e Landesteuerung vom Boden
f *(AGCL)* RAUMFAHRT automatic ground-controlled
landing *(AGCL)*; ~e Lasttraverse *f* TRANS spreader;
~e Lastübergabe *f* ELEKTRIZ automatic load transfer;
~e Lautstärkeregelung *f* *(ALR)* ELEKTROTECH, FERN-
SEH, MECHAN, RADIO automatic volume control
(AVC); ~es Leitsystem *nt* ELEKTROTECH automatic
guidance system; ~e Lochung *f* COMP & DV automatic
punch, automatic tape; ~es Lösen *nt* MASCHINEN
automatic release; ~e Meßbereichsumschaltung *f* GE-
RÄT automatic ranging; ~e Müllsortierung *f* ABFALL
mechanical separation; ~e Nachformdrehmaschine *f*
MASCHINEN automatic copying lathe; ~e Nachführung
f RAUMFAHRT autotracking; ~e Nachrichten-Spei-
chervermittlungsstelle *f* TELEKOM automatic message
switching center (AmE), automatic message switching centre (BrE); ~e Nebenstellenanlage *f* TELEKOM

private branch exchange; ~er Niveauausgleich *m*
(ALC) KFZTECH automatic level control *(ALC)*; ~e
Nullstellung *f* KONTROLL *Rückstellung* automatic re-
set; ~e Ortung und Registrierung *f* TELEKOM *von
Schiffen* automatic location-registration; ~es Palet-
tenstapel- und Strecksystem *nt* VERPACK robotic
palletizing and stretch system; ~e Papierzuführung *f*
COMP & DV *Drucker* feeder; ~e Pegelregelung *f* *(ALC)*
RADIO automatic level control *(ALC)*; ~er Peilempfänger *m* LUFTTRANS automatic direction finder; ~er
Personenschnellverkehr *m* TRANS automated personal rapid transit; ~e Phasenregelung *f* *(APR)*
ELEKTRONIK automatic phase control *(APC)*; ~e
Phasensteuerung *f* *(APR)* FERNSEH automatic phase
control *(APC)*; ~es Pressen *nt* KER & GLAS automatic
pressing; ~e Probeentnahmevorrichtung *f* LABOR
automatic sampling device; ~er Prober *m* KOHLEN
automatic sampler; ~es Programmentwicklungssy-
stem *nt* COMP & DV automatic programming tool; ~er
Prüfcode *m* COMP & DV self-checking code; ~e Prüfeinrichtung *f* *(ATE)* COMP & DV automatic test
equipment *(ATE)*; ~e Prüfung *f* COMP & DV automatic
check; ~e Querbewegung *f* MASCHINEN *des Werkzeugs* automatic transverse movement; ~e
Radaraufnahmehilfe *f* *(ARPA)* WASSERTRANS automatic radar plotting aid *(ARPA)*; ~er Radiokompaß
m LUFTTRANS automatic direction finder; ~er
Rauschbegrenzer *m* *(ANL)* RADIO automatic noise
limiter *(ANL)*; ~e Rauschunterdrückung *f* *(ARU)*
RADIO automatic noise limiter *(ANL)*; ~e Regelung *f*
ELEKTRIZ automatic control; ~er Regler *m* MASCHI-
NEN automatic regulator; ~e Reparatur *f* TEXTIL
automatic repair; ~er Richtungsfinder *m* LUFTTRANS
automatic direction finder; ~es Rohrventil *nt* BAU self-
closing cock; ~e Rückspulvorrichtung *f* FOTO
automatic rewinder; ~e Rückstellung *f* ELEKTRIZ
automatic reset; ~es Rufgerät *nt* *(ACU)* RAUMFAHRT,
TELEKOM automatic calling unit *(ACU)*; ~e Satellitenerfassung von geomagnetischen Daten *f* *(AR-
GOS)* WASSERTRANS Automatic Remote
Geomagnetic Observatory System *(ARGOS)*; ~es
Schalten *nt* TRANS automatic switching; ~er Schalter
m ELEKTROTECH automatic switch, self-acting switch;
~e Scharfabstimmung *f* ELEKTRONIK, FERNSEH *Empfänger*, RADIO automatic frequency control, RADIO
(AFT) automatic fine tuning *(AFT)*; ~e Scharfeinstellung *f* FOTO automatic focusing; ~e
Schlauchbeutelfüllanlage *f* VERPACK automatic flexi-
ble-bag-filling machine; ~e Schneidvorrichtung *f* KER
& GLAS automatic cutter; ~er Schnellverkehr *m* TRANS
rapid automatic transport; ~e Schraubendrehbank *f*
MASCHINEN, MECHAN automatic screw machine; ~e
Schrifterkennung *f* KÜNSTL INT automatic writing recognition; ~e Schubsteuerung *f* LUFTTRANS
autothrottle; ~er Schußspulenwechsel *m* TEXTIL
automatic pirn change; ~e Schweißung *f* MASCHINEN
automatic welding; ~e Seitennumerierung *f* COMP &
DV automatic page numbering; ~es Senden-Empfan-
gen *nt* COMP & DV automatic send-receive; ~er
Sender-Empfänger *m* *(ASR)* COMP & DV automatic
send-receive *(ASR)*; ~es Signal zur Mikrofonübergabe
nt *(AOS)* TELEKOM automatic over signal *(AOS)*;
~e Silbentrennung *f* DRUCK automatic hyphenation;
~e Spannungsregelung *f* ELEKTRIZ automatic voltage
control; ~es Speisen *nt* KER & GLAS automatic feeding; ~er Spitzenbegrenzer *m* FERNSEH automatic

peak limiter; ~e **Spracherkennung** *f (ASE)* KÜNSTL INT automatic speech recognition *(ASR)*; ~e **Sprachverarbeitung** *f* KÜNSTL INT automatic speech processing; ~e **Standorterfassung** *f* TELEKOM self-location; ~e **Starrkupplung** *f* TRANS rigid automatic coupling; ~es **Steuerelement** *nt* KERNTECH automatic control assembly; ~er **Steuerschalter** *m* ELEKTRIZ automatic control switch; ~e **Steuerung** *f* BAU, ELEKTRIZ, ERDÖL, MASCHINEN, VERPACK automatic control; ~e **Stirnradfräsmaschine** *f* MASCHINEN automatic spur-gear-cutting machine; ~er **Stromregler** *m* ELEKTRIZ automatic current controller; ~er **Telefonumschalter** *m* ELEKTROTECH automatic telephone switch; ~e **Telefonzentrale** *f* TELEKOM automatic telephone exchange; ~e **Thermoformung** *f* VERPACK *von aufgerolltem Material* automatic thermoforming; ~e **Titration** *f* LABOR automatic titration; ~es **Tonsignal** *nt* RADIO *zur Mikrofonübergabe, Sprechfunk* automatic over signal; ~er **Transformator zur Spannungserhöhung** *m* ELEKTROTECH step-up autotransformer; ~es **Transportsystem** *nt* TRANS automatic transportation system; ~es **Trennen** *nt* MASCHINEN automatic release; ~er **Trennschalter** *m* ELEKTRIZ automatic cut-off switch; ~e **Umschaltung** *f* ELEKTRIZ automatic change-over switching, TELEKOM automatic change-over; ~e **Vakuumbremse** *f* MASCHINEN automatic vacuum brake; ~er **Vergrößerer** *m* FOTO automatic enlarger; ~e **Verkehrsumschaltung** *f* TELEKOM automatic change-over; ~e **Vermittlungsstelle** *f* TELEKOM automatic switchboard; ~e **Verstärkungsregelung** *f (AVR)* ELEKTRONIK, RADIO, TELEKOM automatic gain control *(AGC)*; ~e **Verstellung** *f* LUFTTRANS *Propeller* autofeathering; ~e **Vorrichtung** *f* TELEKOM automatic device; ~er **Vorschub** *m* MASCHINEN power feed; ~e **Waggonidentifikation** *f* TRANS ACI, automatic car identification (AmE), automatic wagon identification (BrE); ~er **Wassersprühnebel-Neuerlöscher** *m* SICHERHEIT automatic fire-fighting system; nicht ~er **Webstuhl** *m* TEXTIL nonautomatic loom; ~er **Weißabgleich** *m* FERNSEH automatic white balance; ~e **Werkzeugmaschine** *f* MASCHINEN automatic machine tool; ~er **Werkzeugwechsler** *m (ATC)* METALL automatic tool changer *(ATC)*; ~e **Wetterstation** *f* WASSERTRANS automatic weather station; ~e **Wiederholanforderung** *f (ARQ)* RADIO, TELEKOM automatic repeat request *(ARQ)*; ~er **Zentrifugalregler** *m* NICHTFOSS ENERG automatic governor; ~e **Zielaufschaltung** *f* LUFTTRANS *Flugwesen* lock-on; ~es **Zielfluggerät** *nt* LUFTTRANS automatic direction finder; ~e **Zielverfolgung** *f* WASSERTRANS *Radar* automatic tracking; ~e **Zuführung** *f* ERDÖL *Bohrtechnik* automatic feed, MASCHINEN automatic feed, power feed, VERPACK automatic feeding system; ~e **Zugdeckung** *f* EISENBAHN ATP (BrE), automatic train protection; ~e **Zugsteuerung** *f (ATC)* EISENBAHN automatic train control, automatic train operation *(ATO)*; ~e **Zugsteuerung per Minicomputer** *f* EISENBAHN automatic train operation by mini computer, TRANS ATOMIC; ~e **Zugüberwachung** *f* EISENBAHN automatic train monitoring; ~e **Zündung** *f* LUFTTRANS autoignition; ~es **Zurückklappen der Luftschraubenblätter** *nt* LUFTTRANS *Hubschrauber* automatic blade-folding system; ~e **Zurückstellung** *f* ELEKTRIZ automatic reset; ~e **Zusammentragung** *f* VERPACK automatic collation; ~e **Zustellung** *f* MASCHINEN automatic down-feed, automatic feed

automatisieren *vt* BAU automate, automatize, COMP & DV automate

automatisiert: ~es **Entscheiden** *nt* KÜNSTL INT automated decision-making; ~er **Kugelhahn** *m* FERTIG *Kunststoffinstallationen* actuated ball valve; ~e **Maschinenwerkzeugprogrammierung** *f (AUTOPROMT)* FERTIG automated programming of machine tools *(AUTOPROMT)*; ~e **Werkzeugpositionierung** *f (AUTOSPOT)* FERTIG automated system for positioning tools *(AUTOSPOT)*

Automatisierung *f* BAU, COMP & DV, ERGON, MASCHINEN, RAUMFAHRT automation

Automatverschluß *m* FOTO self-cocking shutter

Autometamorphismus *m* NICHTFOSS ENERG autometamorphism

Automobil *nt (Auto)* KFZTECH automobile, car

autonom[1] *adj* COMP & DV stand-alone, KONTROLL autonomous, RAUMFAHRT *Raumschiff* self-contained

autonom:[2] ~e **Arbeitsgruppe** *f* ERGON autonomous work group; ~e **Aufzeichnung** *f* NICHTFOSS ENERG spontaneous log; ~e **Navigationshilfe** *f* LUFTTRANS selfcontained navigational aid; ~es **System** *nt* RAUMFAHRT *Weltraumfunk* stand-alone system

autoorthogonal: ~e **Faltungscodierung** *f* TELEKOM self-orthogonal convolutional coding

Autopilot *m* LUFTTRANS automatic pilot, gyropilot, autopilot, RAUMFAHRT autopilot, WASSERTRANS autopilot, gyropilot; **Autopilot-Drehknopf** *m* LUFTTRANS autopilot turn knob; **Autopilot-Steigungsfeineinstellung** *f* LUFTTRANS autopilot pitch sensitivity system

AUTOPROMT *abbr (automatisierte Maschinenwerkzeugprogrammierung)* FERTIG AUTOPROMT *(automated programming of machine tools)*

Auto: **Autoradiographie** *f* PHYS, STRAHLPHYS autoradiography; **Autoradiolyse** *f* PHYS, STRAHLPHYS autoradiolysis; **Autoreisezug** *m* EISENBAHN car sleeper train, motorail; **Autorenkorrektur** *f* DRUCK AA, author's alterations; **Autorotationsflug** *m* LUFTTRANS autorotation flight, *Hubschrauber* autorotative flight; **Autorotationsübergangszeit** *f* LUFTTRANS autorotation transition time; **Autoservobetrieb** *m* FERNSEH autoservo mode

AUTOSPOT *abbr (automatisierte Werkzeugpositionierung)* FERTIG AUTOSPOT *(automated system for positioning tools)*

Auto: **Autospurlageeinstellung** *f* FERNSEH autotracking; **Autostraße** *f* TRANS expressway (AmE), motorway (BrE), superhighway (AmE); **Autotelefon** *nt* TELEKOM car phone, in-car telephone, TRANS car telephone; **Autothermikkolben** *m* KFZTECH autothermic piston; **Autotransformator** *m* ELEKTROTECH autotransformer

autotroph: ~e **Ernährung** *f* LEBENSMITTEL autotrophy; ~er **Mikroorganismus** *m* LEBENSMITTEL autotroph

Autotrophie *f* LEBENSMITTEL *Biochemie* autotrophy

Autotypie *f* DRUCK halftone process; **Autotypieraster** *nt* DRUCK halftone screen

Auto: **Autoverschrottungsanlage** *f* ABFALL car fragmentation plant; **Autowerkstatt** *f* TRANS garage; **Autowrack** *nt* ABFALL scrap motorcar; **Autoxidation** *f* LEBENSMITTEL autoxidation; **Autozubehör** *nt* KFZTECH car accessories

Auxochrom *nt* CHEMIE auxochrome

auxochrome: ~ **Gruppe** *f* CHEMIE auxochrome

AV *abbr (Säurewert)* CHEMIE AV *(acid value)*

Avalanche- *pref* ELEKTRIZ, PHYS avalanche; **Avalanchediode** *f* PHYS avalanche diode; **Avalanchedurchbruch**

m ELEKTRIZ avalanche breakdown; **Avalanchedurch-bruchspannung** *f* ELEKTRIZ avalanche voltage; **Avalanchefotodiode** *f (APD)* ELEKTRONIK, OPTIK avalanche photodiode *(APD)*

Avenin *nt* CHEMIE avenin

Aventurin *m* KER & GLAS aventurine

A-Verstärker *m* PHYS class A amplifier

A4-Format *nt* PAPIER *internationale Papiergröße* A4 size

Avionik *f* LUFTTRANS avionics; **Avionikkonsole** *f* RAUMFAHRT avionics console

Avogadro: ~ **sches Gesetz** *nt* PHYS, THERMOD Avogadro's hypothesis; **~sche Konstante** *f* PHYS, THERMOD Avogadro's constant; **~sche Zahl** *f (NA)* PHYS, THERMOD Avogadro's number *(NA)*

Avoirdupois-Gewicht *nt* METROL avoirdupois weight

AVR *abbr (automatische Verstärkungsregelung)* ELEKTRONIK, RADIO, TELEKOM AGC *(automatic gain control)*

AWACS *abbr (Überwachungs- und Leitsystem im Flugzeug)* LUFTTRANS AWACS *(airborne warning and control system)*

AWG *abbr (Amerikanische Einheit für Drahtdurchmesser)* METROL AWG *(American wire gage)*

Axial- *pref* ELEKTRIZ, FERTIG, KER & GLAS, MASCHINEN, OPTIK, TELEKOM axial; **Axialablagerung** *f* KER & GLAS axial deposition; **Axialabscheideverfahren aus Dampfphase** *nt (VAD)* OPTIK vapor phase axial deposition technique (AmE), vapour phase axial deposition technique (BrE) *(VAD)*, TELEKOM vapor phase axial deposition technique (AmE), vapour-phase axial deposition technique (BrE) *(VAD)*; **Axialabschirmung** *f* KERNTECH axial shield; **Axialanker** *m* ELEKTRIZ axial armature; **Axialbeanspruchung** *f* FERTIG thrust load, MASCHINEN axial load, axial strain; **Axialdauer** *f* RAUMFAHRT axial period; **Axialdruck** *m* FERTIG axial thrust; **Axialdrucklager** *nt* MASCHINEN axial thrust bearing, end-thrust bearing, thrust bearing, MECHAN thrust bearing

axial[1] *adj* GEOM, PAPIER axial

axial:[2] **~e Abtastung** *f* OPTIK axial scanning; **~er Ausbreitungskoeffizient** *m* OPTIK axial propagation coefficient; **~e Ausbreitungskonstante** *f* TELEKOM axial propagation coefficient; **~es Austauschen** *nt* KERNTECH *Brennelementen* axial shuffling; **~es Flächenträgheitsmoment** *nt* FERTIG geometrical moment; **~e Interferenzmikroskopie** *f* TELEKOM axial interference microscopy; **~es Plasma-Abscheideverfahren** *nt* TELEKOM axial plasma deposition; **~e Platteninterferometrie** *f* OPTIK axial slab interferometry; **~er Strahl** *m* OPTIK, TELEKOM axial ray; **~e Temperaturverteilung** *f* KERNTECH axial temperature distribution; **~er Tischvorschub** *m* FERTIG table feed; **~er Turboverdichter** *m* LUFTTRANS axial compressor; **~er Vorschub** *m* MASCHINEN axial feed; **~ zusammenschiebbare Lenksäule** *f* TRANS axially collapsing steering column

Axial-: **Axialempfindlichkeit** *f* AKUSTIK axial sensitivity; **Axialgebläse** *nt* MASCHINEN axial fan, propeller fan; **Axialgeschwindigkeit** *f* NICHTFOSS ENERG axial velocity; **Axialgeschwindigkeitsmelder** *m* RAUMFAHRT axial velocity sensor; **Axialinterferenzmikroskopie** *f* OPTIK axial interference microscopy

Axialität *f* FERTIG alignment

Axial-: **Axialkolbenpumpe** *f* MECHAN axial piston pump

Axialkompressor *m* MECHAN axial compressor; **Axialkompressortriebwerk** *nt* LUFTTRANS gas turbine engine

Axial-: **Axialkugellager** *nt* MASCHINEN thrust ball-bearing; **Axiallager** *nt* MASCHINEN, NICHTFOSS ENERG thrust bearing; **Axiallast** *f* METALL axial load; **Axiallüfter** *m* HEIZ & KÄLTE axial flow fan, SICHERHEIT axial blower; **Axialpendelrollenlager** *nt* MASCHINEN self-aligning roller thrust bearing; **Axialpumpe** *f* MASCHINEN axial flow pump, axial pump; **Axialrad** *nt* MASCHINEN axial flow wheel; **Axial-Radial-Verdichter** *m* MASCHINEN axial centrifugal compressor; **Axialrillenkugellager** *nt* MASCHINEN deep-groove ball thrust bearing; **Axialrollenlager** *nt* MASCHINEN thrust roller bearing; **Axialschlag** *m* MASCHINEN axial eccentricity; **Axialschub** *m* FERTIG, MASCHINEN axial thrust; **Axialspiel** *nt* FERTIG amount of axial freedom, end play, MECHAN axial clearance, end play; **Axialstellglied** *nt* RAUMFAHRT *Raumschiff* axial actuator; **Axialstrahl** *m* OPTIK axial ray; **Axialstrom** *m* LUFTTRANS axial flow; **Axialströmung** *f* KFZTECH *Motor*, MASCHINEN axial flow; **Axialströmungshubgebläse** *nt* LUFTTRANS axial flow lift fan; **Axialteilung** *f* MASCHINEN axial pitch; **Axialturbine** *f* HYDRAUL axial flow turbine; **Axialventilator** *m* ELEKTRIZ axial fan, SICHERHEIT axial ventilator; **Axialvergrößerung** *f* MECHAN axial magnification; **Axialverhältnis** *nt* RAUMFAHRT axial ratio; **Axialversatz** *m* FERNSEH axial displacement; **Axialvorschub** *m* MASCHINEN axial feed; **Axialzylinderrollenlager** *nt* MASCHINEN axial cylindrical roller bearing, thrust cylindrical roller bearing

Axiom *nt* GEOM, MATH axiom

axiomatisch *adj* GEOM axiomatic

Axonometrie *f* GEOM axonometry

axonometrisch: **~e Projektion** *f* KONSTZEICH axonometric projection

Axt *f* BAU ax (AmE), axe (BrE)

Azelain- *pref* CHEMIE azelaic

Azeotrop *nt* CHEMIE azeotrope

azeotrop[1] *adj* CHEMIE azeotropic

azeotrop:[2] **~e Destillation** *f* LEBENSMITTEL azeotropic distillation; **~es Gemisch** *nt* CHEMIE azeotrope, LEBENSMITTEL azeotropic mixture

Azetozon *nt* LEBENSMITTEL acetyl benzoyl peroxide

Azetyl *nt* PAPIER acetyl

Azetylen *nt* BAU acetylene, CHEMIE acetylene, ethine, ethyne, FERTIG acetylene, acetylene gas, MECHAN acetylene; **Azetylenbrenner** *m* BAU acetylene blowpipe; **Azetylenbrennschneiden** *nt* FERTIG acetylene cutting; **Azetylenbrennschneider** *m* FERTIG acetylene cutter; **Azetylendruck** *m* FERTIG acetylene pressure; **Azetylendruckminderer** *m* FERTIG acetylene pressure regulator, acetylene regulator; **Azetylenentwickler** *m* BAU, CHEMTECH, FERTIG, MASCHINEN acetylene generator; **Azetylenerzeuger** *m* CHEMTECH acetylene generator; **Azetylenerzeugung** *f* FERTIG acetylene generation; **Azetylenerzeugungsanlage** *f* FERTIG acetylene gas generating plant, acetylene generator station, acetylene producing plant; **Azetylenflamme** *f* FERTIG acetylene flame; **Azetylenflasche** *f* FERTIG, MASCHINEN, MECHAN, SICHERHEIT acetylene cylinder; **Azetylengas** *nt* CHEMIE acetylene gas

azetylenisch *adj* CHEMIE acetylenic

Azetylen: **Azetylenleitung** *f* FERTIG acetylene line; **Azetylensauerstoffbrenner** *m* BAU oxyacetylene blowpipe; **Azetylensauerstoffschweißen** *nt* FERTIG oxyacetylene welding; **Azetylenschlauch** *m* FERTIG acetylene hose; **Azetylenschweißbrenner** *m* BAU acetylene blowpipe;

Azetylenschweißen *nt* FERTIG acetylene welding, oxyacetylene welding; **Azetylenstahlflasche** *f* FERTIG acetylene cylinder; **Azetylenüberschuß** *m* FERTIG acetylene excess; **Azetylenventil** *nt* FERTIG acetylene valve;

Azetyl: Azetylgruppe *f* LEBENSMITTEL acetyl group

Azetylid *nt* CHEMIE acetylide

azetylieren *vt* PAPIER acetylate

Azetylierung *f* LEBENSMITTEL, PAPIER acetylation

Azetylsalicyl- *pref* CHEMIE acetylsalicylic

Azetylzahl *f* KUNSTSTOFF acetyl value

Azetylzellulosefilm *m* VERPACK cellulose acetate film

Azid *nt* CHEMIE azide, hydrazoate

azid *adj* CHEMIE acidic

Azidität *f* DRUCK acidity

Azimino- *pref* CHEMIE azimino; **Aziminoverbindung** *f* CHEMIE azimino compound

Azimut *m* BAU, FERNSEH, PHYS, RADIO, RAUMFAHRT, WASSERTRANS *Navigation* azimuth; **Azimutabweichung** *f* AUFNAHME azimuth deviation; **Azimutalbefestigung** *f* RAUMFAHRT Az-El mount

azimutal: **~e Führung** *f* LUFTTRANS *Navigation* back azimuth guidance; **~er Kurvenanflug** *m* LUFTTRANS *Mikrowellenlandesystem* curved azimuth approach path; **~e Quantenzahl** *f* PHYS azimuthal quantum number; **~es Steuerwerk** *nt* LUFTTRANS azimuthal control

Azimut: Azimutalschub *m* RAUMFAHRT azimuth thrust; **Azimutal-Transversal-Mode** *f (ATM)* OPTIK azimuthal transversal mode *(ATM)*; **Azimutalverlust** *m* FERNSEH azimuth loss; **Azimutalverzeichnung** *f* FERNSEH azimuth distortion; **Azimuteinstellung** *f* FERNSEH azimuth adjustment; **Azimutkreisel** *m* RAUMFAHRT azimuth gyro

Azobenzol *nt* CHEMIE azobenzene

Azofarbstoff *m* TEXTIL azoic dye

Azophenylen *nt* CHEMIE azophenylene, phenazine

Azotometer *nt* CHEMIE azotometer, nitrometer

Azoverbindung *f* CHEMIE azo compound, azo derivative

Azulen *nt* CHEMIE azulene

Azulminsäure *f* CHEMIE azulmin

Azurit *nt* CHEMIE azurite, chessylite

B

B[1] *abbr* AKUSTIK *(Bel)* B *(bel)*, AUFNAHME *(magnetischer Scheinwiderstand)*, ELEKTRIZ *(Magnetinduktion)* B *(magnetic induction)*, ELEKTROTECH *(Bel)* B *(bel)*, ELEKTROTECH *(Magnetinduktion)* B *(magnetic induction)*, KERNTECH *(Bindungsenergie)* B *(binding energy)*, PHYS *(Bel)* B *(bel)*, PHYS *(Magnetinduktion)* B *(magnetic induction)*, STRAHLPHYS, TEILPHYS *(Bindungsenergie, Kernbindungsenergie)* B *(binding energy)*, TELEKOM *(Magnetinduktion)* B *(magnetic induction)*, THERMOD *(Volumenelastizitätsmodul)* B *(modulus of volume elasticity)*

B[2] *(Bor)* CHEMIE B *(boron)*

b *abbr* KOHLEN *(Bar)*, LABOR *(Bar)* Luftdruckeinheit b *(bar)*, RAUMFAHRT *(Raumbreite)* b *(galactic latitude)*

Ba *(Barium)* CHEMIE Ba *(barium)*

Babbitmetall *nt* FERTIG babbitt

Babinet: ~scher Kompensator *m* PHYS Babinet compensator; ~sches Prinzip *nt* PHYS Babinet's principle; ~sches Theorem *nt* PHYS Babinet's principle

Back *f* WASSERTRANS *Schiffbau* forecastle

Backbord- *pref* WASSERTRANS port

Backbord *nt* LUFTTRANS port

backbord *adv* RAUMFAHRT *Raumschiff*, WASSERTRANS *Schiff* port

Back: Backdeck *nt* WASSERTRANS *Schiff* raised deck;

Backe *f* KERNTECH, KOHLEN jaw, MASCHINEN cheek, jaw, MECHAN jaw, WASSERTRANS *Deckausrüstung* cheek;

Backeigenschaft *f* LEBENSMITTEL baking quality

Backen *nt* FERTIG caking, KFZTECH *Bohrtechnik*, MASCHINEN *Bohrtechnik*, METALL baking

backen *vt* KOHLEN, LEBENSMITTEL bake

Backe: Backenbohrmeißel *m* ERDÖL *Bohrtechnik* Mother Hubbard bit; **Backenbrecher** *m* KOHLEN jaw crusher, MASCHINEN jaw breaker, jaw crusher; **Backenbremse** *f* KFZTECH, MASCHINEN shoe brake

backend[1] *adj* CHEMTECH agglutinative, KOHLEN caking; nicht ~ *adj* KOHLEN free-burning (AmE), nonbaking, noncaking

backend:[2] ~e Kohle *f* KOHLEN caking coal; nicht ~e Kohle *f* KOHLEN nonbaking coal

Backe: Backenfänger *m* BAU casing spears; **Backenfutter** *nt* MASCHINEN dog chuck, jaw chuck; **Backenklemme** *f* TRANS clip with jaws; **Backenklemmvorrichtung** *f* LABOR clamp with jaws; **Backenwerkzeug** *nt* KUNSTSTOFF split mold (AmE), split mould (BrE)

backholen *vt* WASSERTRANS *Segel* back

backlegen *vt* WASSERTRANS *Segel* lay aback

Backscatter-Peak *m* STRAHLPHYS backscatter peak

Backstagswind *m* WASSERTRANS quarter wind

backstehen *vi* WASSERTRANS *Segeln* aback

Backup *nt* ELEKTROTECH backup

Bad[1] *nt* METALL bath, TEXTIL bath, dip

Bad:[2] ~ reduzieren *vi* METALL reduce the bath

Badeanzugstoff *m* TEXTIL swimsuit fabric

Bad: Badthermometer *nt* FOTO tray thermometer

Baffle *nt* CHEMTECH *Vakuuumtechnik* baffle

Bagassenwalze *f* LEBENSMITTEL bagasse roller

BA-Gewinde *nt* MASCHINEN British Association screw thread

Bagger *m* BAU, KFZTECH excavator, KOHLEN digger; **Baggerarbeiten** *f pl* WASSERTRANS dredging operations; **Baggereimer** *m* TRANS digging bucket, WASSERTRANS dredge bucket; **Baggereimerzähne** *m pl* TRANS digging bucket teeth; **Baggerkette** *f* BAU bucket chain, MASCHINEN excavator chain; **Baggerkorb** *m* BAU grab

Baggern *nt* KOHLEN digging

Bagger: Baggerpumpe *f* WASSERTRANS dredge pump; **Baggersand** *m* BAU dredging sand; **Baggerschaufel** *f* BAU bucket; **Baggersumpf** *m* KOHLEN sedimentation pond

Bahn:[1] mit der ~ *adv* EISENBAHN by rail

Bahn[2] *f* PHYS orbit, path, trajectory, RAUMFAHRT path, trajectory, TELEKOM *Elektronen* path, TEXTIL sheeting, width, WASSERTRANS path; ~ eines Teilchens *f* PHYS path of a particle; **Bahnanlage** *f* EISENBAHN railroad system (AmE), railway system (BrE); **Bahnaufzeichnung** *f* STRAHLPHYS trajectography; **Bahnbenutzer** *m* EISENBAHN railroad user (AmE), railway user (BrE); **Bahnbetrieb** *m* EISENBAHN service; **Bahnbildung** *f* PAPIER web formation; **Bahnbreite** *f* DRUCK web width; **Bahndrehimpuls** *m* PHYS, STRAHLPHYS orbital angular momentum; **Bahndrehimpulsquantenzahl** *f* PHYS orbital angular momentum quantum number; **Bahneigenschaften** *f pl* ELEKTRONIK *Mikroelektronik* bulk properties; **Bahnelektronen** *nt pl* STRAHLPHYS orbital electrons; **Bahngeschwindigkeit** *f* PHYS *Umlaufbahn* orbital velocity; **Bahn-Halbleiter** *m* ELEKTRONIK bulk semiconductor

Bahnhof *m* EISENBAHN railroad depot (AmE), railway depot (BrE), railroad station (AmE), railway station (BrE), station; **Bahnhofsanlage** *f* EISENBAHN station area; **Bahnhofswagen** *m* EISENBAHN wagon

Bahn: Bahnimpuls *m* STRAHLPHYS orbital momentum; **Bahnkorrektur** *f* RAUMFAHRT path correction; **Bahnmotor** *m* EISENBAHN traction motor; **Bahnnetz** *nt* EISENBAHN railroad system (AmE), railway system (BrE); **Bahnoberbau** *m* EISENBAHN permanent way; **Bahnpostwagen** *m* EISENBAHN mail car (AmE), mail van (AmE), mailcoach (BrE), post wagon (BrE); **Bahnquantenzahl** *f* PHYS, STRAHLPHYS orbital quantum number; **Bahnrakete** *f* RAUMFAHRT orbital rocket; **Bahnrendezvous** *nt* RAUMFAHRT *im Erdorbit* earth orbit rendezvous; **Bahnriß in der Naßpartie** *m* PAPIER wet break; **Bahnsatellit** *m* RAUMFAHRT orbiting satellite; **Bahnsatellit für Amateurfunkzwecke** *m (OSCAR)* RADIO, RAUMFAHRT *Weltraumfunk* Orbiting Satellite Carrying Amateur Radio *(OSCAR)*; **Bahnscheibe** *f* ELEKTRONIK bulk wafer; **Bahnschranke** *f* EISENBAHN railroad gate (AmE), railway gate (BrE); **Bahnschreibung** *f* RAUMFAHRT trajectography;

Bahnstation f RAUMFAHRT orbiting station; **Bahnsteig** m EISENBAHN platform; **Bahnsteigkarte** f EISENBAHN platform ticket; **Bahnstromnetz** nt EISENBAHN traction network; **Bahnstromsystem** nt EISENBAHN traction network; **Bahnstromversorgung** f EISENBAHN traction power supply; **Bahntransport** m EISENBAHN rail transport, railroad transport (AmE), railway transport (BrE); **Bahnüberführung** f EISENBAHN bridge, road over railroad (AmE), road over railway (BrE); **Bahnübergangsfahrzeug** nt RAUMFAHRT orbital transfer vehicle; **Bahnverfolgung** f PHYS ray tracing, RADIO *Satelliten* tracking; **Bahnverkehr** m EISENBAHN service; **Bahnvermessung** f RAUMFAHRT *Raumschiff* tracking; **Bahnwärter** m EISENBAHN lineman

Bai f NICHTFOSS ENERG *Geographie* bay

Bailey-Behelfsbrücke f BAU Bailey bridge

Bainit m FERTIG, METALL bainite; **Bainitferrit** m METALL bainitic ferrite

Bajonett nt ELEKTROTECH bayonet; **Bajonettfassung** f BAU bayonet fitting, ELEKTRIZ bayonet socket, *für Leuchtstofflampe* bayonet holder, bayonet socket, FOTO bayonet socket, MASCHINEN bayonet socket; **Bajonettkupplung** f ELEKTROTECH bayonet coupling; **Bajonett-Lampenfassung** f ELEKTRIZ bayonet lamp holder; **Bajonettsockel** m ELEKTRIZ bayonet cap, *Leuchtstofflampe* bayonet cap, ELEKTROTECH, FOTO bayonet base; **Bajonettsteckverbinder mit Überwurfmutter** m *(BNC-Stecker)* ELEKTRONIK bayonet nut connector *(BNC)*; **Bajonettverbindung** f ELEKTRIZ bayonet joint; **Bajonettverschluß** m FERTIG *Kunststoffinstallationen* bayonet fastening, FOTO bayonet socket (BrE), quarter-turn fastener (AmE), KER & GLAS bayonet cap finish, KERNTECH bayonet closure, MECHAN bayonet locking, VERPACK bayonet catch

Bake f RADIO beacon, RAUMFAHRT beacon, *Raumschiff* beacon generator, WASSERTRANS *Seezeichen* beacon

Bakelit nt FERTIG bakelite

Bakensignal nt RAUMFAHRT *Weltraumfunk* beacon

Bakterien f pl CHEMIE, LEBENSMITTEL, UMWELTSCHMUTZ bacteria; **Bakterientoxin** nt CHEMIE bacterial toxin, bacteriotoxin; **Bakterienvermehrungsgefäß** nt LEBENSMITTEL bacteria propagation tank; **Bakterienverseuchung** f UMWELTSCHMUTZ bacterial contamination; **Bakterienzahl** f WASSERVERSORG *im Wasser* bacterial count; **Bakterienzuchtbehälter** m LEBENSMITTEL bacteria propagation tank

bakteriologisch: **~e Reinigung** f ABFALL bacteriological treatment, bacteriological purification; **~er Trockenschrank** m LABOR bacteriological oven

Bakteriolyse f LEBENSMITTEL bacteriolysis

Bakteriophage m LEBENSMITTEL bacteriophage

Bakteriostatikum nt LEBENSMITTEL bacteriostat

bakteriostatisch: **~es Mittel** nt LEBENSMITTEL bacteriostat

Bakterizid nt CHEMIE, LEBENSMITTEL *Bakteriengift* bactericide

Balance f AUFNAHME balance; **Balancefeder** f MASCHINEN equalizer spring; **Balanceregelung** f AUFNAHME balance control; **Balanceruder** nt WASSERTRANS balanced rudder

Balanciermaschine f MASCHINEN beam engine

Balata f FERTIG, KUNSTSTOFF balata; **Balatariemen** m MASCHINEN balata belt

Balg m MASCHINEN bellows

Balgen m FOTO, MASCHINEN bellows; **Balgenansatz** m FOTO bellows attachment; **Balgenauszug** m FOTO bellows extension; **Balgendichtung** f FOTO bellows covering; **Balgenkamera** f FOTO bellows camera; **Balgenklappkamera** f FOTO bellows-type folding camera; **Balgenrahmen** m FOTO bellows frame; **Balgenverschluß** m FOTO bellows shutter

Balgfeder f KFZTECH *Kupplung* cushion spring; **Balgfederdurchflußmeßgerät** nt GERÄT bellows flowmeter; **Balgfedermanometer** nt GERÄT bellows gage (AmE), bellows gauge (BrE)

Balken m BAU baulk (BrE), summer, MECHAN girder; **Balkenanzeige** f GERÄT bar graph display; **Balkenauflage** f METROL *Waage* beam support; **Balkenauflagerplatte** f BAU wall plate; **Balkenaussparung** f BAU wall box; **Balkenbiegung** f BAU beam bending; **Balkenbrücke** f BAU girder bridge; **Balkenbucht** f WASSERTRANS round of beam, *Schiffbau* camber; **Balkencode** m KONTROLL bar code; **Balkendiagramm** nt COMP & DV bar chart, bar graph, GERÄT, MATH bar chart; **Balkengenerator** m FERNSEH bar generator; **Balkenknie** nt WASSERTRANS *Schiffbau* beam knee; **Balkenlehre** f METROL beam caliper (AmE), beam caliper gage (AmE), beam calliper (BrE), beam calliper gauge (BrE); **Balkenleiter** m ELEKTRONIK *Mikroelektronik* beam lead; **Balkenleitergerät** nt ELEKTRONIK beam lead device; **Balkenleitertechnik** f ELEKTRONIK beam lead technique; **Balkenmuster** nt FERNSEH bar pattern; **Balkenträger** m BAU beam; **Balkenwaage** f GERÄT beam-type scale, METROL beam and scales, beam balance, beam scales; **Balkenwerk** nt BAU framework

Ball m LABOR *Kamera* ball

Ballast:[1] **in ~** adv WASSERTRANS *Schiff* in ballast

Ballast[2] m ELEKTROTECH ballast, MECHAN load, TRANS *Schiff* ballast

Ballast:[3] **in ~ fahren** vi WASSERTRANS sail in ballast

Ballast: **Ballastkiel** m WASSERTRANS *Schiffbau* ballast keel; **Ballastkreis** m ELEKTROTECH ballasting circuit; **Ballaststoffe** m pl LEBENSMITTEL crude fiber (AmE), crude fibre (BrE), dietary fiber (AmE), dietary fibre (BrE), roughage

ballaststoffreich adj LEBENSMITTEL high-fiber (AmE), high-fibre (BrE)

Ballast: **Ballasttank** m WASSERTRANS *Schiff* ballast tank; **Ballastwiderstand** m ELEKTRIZ ballast resistor, barretter, ELEKTROTECH ballast resistor; **Ballastzustand** m WASSERTRANS ballast condition

Ballen[1] m FERTIG *Walze* body, pack, PAPIER bale, TEXTIL bale, packet, VERPACK bale

Ballen:[2] **in ~ verpacken** vt VERPACK bale

ballen vt KOHLEN ball, VERPACK bale

Ballen: **Ballengriff** m MASCHINEN ball knob; **Ballenlader** m TRANS bale loader; **Ballenlänge** f FERTIG barrel length, body length, *Walze* surface length; **Ballenpresse** f PAPIER, VERPACK baling press; **Ballen-Pulper** m PAPIER bale pulper; **Ballenumreifung** f VERPACK bale hoop

ballig:[1] **~e Fläche** f FERTIG spherical surface; **~e Riemenscheibe** f FERTIG crown-face pulley

ballig:[2] **~ bearbeiten** vt FERTIG crown

Balligkeit f FERTIG *Zahnrad* crowning, MASCHINEN camber

balligtragend: **~es Zahnrad** nt FERTIG gear with localized tooth bearing

ballistisch[1] adj RAUMFAHRT ballistic

ballistisch:[2] **~e Auslesevorrichtung** f ABFALL ballistic sorter; **~e Bahn** *f* RAUMFAHRT ballistic path; **~e Flug-bahn** *f* RAUMFAHRT ballistic trajectory; **~es Galvanometer** *nt* ELEKTRIZ, GERÄT, PHYS ballistic galvanometer; **~e Rakete** *f* RAUMFAHRT ballistic missile; **~e Sichtung** *f* ABFALL ballistic separation; **~e Sortierung** *f* ABFALL *von Müll* ballistic sorting

Ballon *m* LABOR *Gebläseballon* bulb, LEBENSMITTEL carboy; **Ballonkorb** *m* MECHAN car; **Ballonreifen** *m* KFZTECH balloon tire (AmE), balloon tyre (BrE)

Ballung *f* ELEKTRONIK *Klystron*, LUFTTRANS bunching; **Ballungsraum** *m* ELEKTRONIK *Klystron* bunching space

Balmer: **~sche Gleichung** *f* PHYS Balmer's formula; **~sche Serie** *f* PHYS, TEILPHYS Balmer series

Balun *m* RADIO balun

Baluster *m* BAU baluster

Bambus *m* KER & GLAS bamboo; **Bambuseffekt** *m* KERNTECH bamboo effect

Bananen- *pref* ELEKTROTECH, KERNTECH banana; **Bananenbahn** *f* KERNTECH banana trajectory; **Bananenbuchse** *f* ELEKTROTECH banana jack; **Bananenstecker** *m* ELEKTROTECH, FOTO banana plug; **Bananenumlaufbahn** *f* KERNTECH banana orbit

Banbury-Innenmischer *m* KUNSTSTOFF Banbury mixer

Band[1] *nt* AKUSTIK band, BAU band, *Baubeschlag* hinge, COMP & DV band, ribbon, tape, ELEKTRIZ *zum Isolieren* tape, KER & GLAS ribbon, KONTROLL line, KUNSTSTOFF tape, MASCHINEN band, hoop, METROL ribbon, tape line, PAPIER strap, PHYS *Frequenz*, RADIO *Frequenz* band

Band:[2] **auf ~ aufnehmen** *vt* AUFNAHME tape; **auf ~ aufzeichnen** *vt* FERNSEH tape

Band:[3] **~ begrenzen** *vi* ELEKTRONIK band-limit

Band: **Bandabdichtung** *f* VERPACK tape sealer; **Bandabschöpfgerät** *nt* MEERSCHMUTZ rope skimmer; **Bandabspielgerät** *nt* AUFNAHME tape player; **Bandanfang** *m (BOT)* COMP & DV beginning of tape *(BOT)*; **Bandanfangsmarke** *f* COMP & DV BOT marker, tape mark, beginning-of-tape marker; **Bandantrieb** *m* AUFNAHME capstan drive, capstan servo, tape drive, COMP & DV capstan, tape transport, FERNSEH tape drive; **Bandantriebsachse** *f* AUFNAHME, ELEKTROTECH *Tonbandgerät* capstan; **Bandantriebswelle** *f* AKUSTIK, FERNSEH capstan; **Bandaufnahme** *f* AUFNAHME tape recording; **Bandaufnahmegerät** *nt* AUFNAHME tape recorder; **Bandausnutzung** *f* TELEKOM band efficiency; **Bandauszug** *m* COMP & DV tape dump; **Bandbasis** *f* AUFNAHME tape base; **Bandbefeuchtungsvorrichtung** *f* VERPACK tape-moistening device

bandbegrenzt: **~es Signal** *nt* ELEKTRONIK band-limited signal

Band: **Bandbelag** *m* AUFNAHME tape backing; **Bandbeschichtungsmaterial** *nt* AUFNAHME tape-coating material; **Bandbibliothek** *f* COMP & DV tape library; **Bandbiegung** *f* FERNSEH tape curvature; **Bandbreite** *f* AKUSTIK *(BW)* band, AUFNAHME *(BW)*, COMP & DV *(BW)*, ELEKTRONIK, FERNSEH *(BW)*, OPTIK *(BW)* Wellenlänge, RADIO *(BW)*, TELEKOM *(BW)* bandwidth *(BW)*; **Bandbreite nach Carson** *f* RAUMFAHRT *Weltraumfunk* Carson's rule bandwidth; **Bandbreite des Vertikalverstärkers** *f* ELEKTRONIK vertical-amplifier bandwidth

bandbreitenbegrenzt: **~er Betrieb** *m* TELEKOM bandwidth-limited operation; **~er Vorgang** *m* OPTIK bandwidth-limited operation

Band: **Bandbreitenbegrenzung** *f* ELEKTRONIK band-

width compression; **Bandbreitenreduzierung** *f* FERNSEH bandwidth compression; **Bandbremse** *f* MASCHINEN band brake, strap brake, MECHAN band brake

Bändchen *nt* AKUSTIK, AUFNAHME, OPTIK ribbon; **Bändchenkabel** *nt* OPTIK ribbon cable; **Bändchenlautsprecher** *m* AKUSTIK, AUFNAHME ribbon loudspeaker; **Bändchenmikrofon** *nt* AKUSTIK, AUFNAHME ribbon microphone

Band: **Banddatei** *f* COMP & DV tape file; **Banddatenauszug** *m* COMP & DV tape dump; **Banddehnung** *f* ELEKTRONIK bandwidth expansion; **Banddiagramm** *nt* QUAL band chart; **Banddrucker** *m* COMP & DV band printer, belt printer; **Banddurchlauf-Geschwindigkeit** *f* AKUSTIK tape speed

Bande *f* PHYS *Spektrum* band, TEXTIL stripe

Band: **Bandeinführung** *f* AUFNAHME tape threading; **Bandeinführungsstift** *m* FERNSEH tape input guide; **Bandeinheit** *f* COMP & DV tape unit; **Bandeisen** *nt* FERTIG hoop, MASCHINEN, VERPACK band iron; **Bandende** *nt* COMP & DV end of reel, COMP & DV end of tape; **Bandendemarke** *f* COMP & DV EOT marker, end-of-tape marker; **Bandenspektrum** *nt* PHYS, STRAHLPHYS band spectrum

Bänder *nt pl* WELLPHYS *aufgrund von Interferenz* bands; **Bändermodell** *nt* PHYS, STRAHLPHYS band theory, band theory of solids

Banderole *f* VERPACK band label, banderole; **Banderolendruck- und Klebemaschine** *f* VERPACK print and apply labeling machine (AmE), print and apply labelling machine (BrE)

Banderolieren *nt* VERPACK banding

Banderoliermaschine *f* VERPACK labeling machine (AmE), labelling machine (BrE), strapping machine

Band: **Bandetikett** *nt* COMP & DV tape label; **Bandfahrsteig** *m* TRANS belt-type moving pavement (BrE), belt-type moving sidewalk (AmE); **Bandfahrung** *f* BAU man-riding; **Bandfeder** *f* MASCHINEN volute spring; **Band-Film-Übertragung** *f* FERNSEH tape-to-film transfer; **Bandfluß-Frequenzgang** *m* AKUSTIK recording characteristic; **Bandförderer** *m* FERTIG belt conveyor, MASCHINEN band conveyor, PAPIER belt conveyor; **Bandförderer mit Zugseil** *m* PAPIER cable conveyor; **Bandformat** *nt* COMP & DV tape format; **Bandführung** *f* AUFNAHME, COMP & DV tape guide, FERNSEH ribbon guide, tape alignment guide, tape leader, tape output guide; **Bandführungslineal** *nt* FERNSEH tape guide; **Bandführungssystem** *nt* AUFNAHME vacuum guide system; **Bandgerät** *nt* AKUSTIK tape recorder, COMP & DV tape unit; **Bandgeschwindigkeit** *f* AUFNAHME, FERNSEH tape speed; **Bandgeschwindigkeitsregelung** *f* FERNSEH tape speed control

bandgesteuert: **~er Zeilenguß** *m* DRUCK tape-controlled linecasting

bandgewickelt: **~er Kern** *m* ELEKTROTECH tape-wound core

Band: **Bandhaspel** *f* AUFNAHME tape reel; **Bandheber** *m* AUFNAHME, FERNSEH tape lifter; **Bandholzschleifmaschine** *f* FERTIG band sander

Bandiermaschine *f* VERPACK paper-banding machine

Band: **Bandkabel** *nt* ELEKTROTECH flat cable, TELEKOM ribbon cable; **Bandkassette** *f* AUFNAHME tape cassette; **Bandkennsatz** *m* COMP & DV tape label; **Bandkennzeichnung** *f* COMP & DV tape label; **Bandkühlofen** *m* KER & GLAS conveyor belt lehr;

Bandkupplung f MASCHINEN band clutch, band coupling; **Bandlängenanzeige** f FERNSEH tape length indicator; **Bandlängsschlupf** m FERNSEH cinching; **Bandlauf** m AUFNAHME, FERNSEH tape run; **Bandlaufwerk** nt COMP & DV tape deck, tape drive; **Bandleiter** m ELEKTROTECH, PHYS strip line; **Bandleitung** f ELEKTROTECH, PHYS strip line; **Bandlineal** nt FERNSEH tape neutral plane; **Bandlochung** f FOTO *Film* perforation; **Bandlücke** f PHYS gap; **Bandmarke** f COMP & DV tape mark; **Bandmaschine** f KER & GLAS ribbon machine; **Bandmaß** nt MECHAN tape measure, METROL tape, tape measure; **Bandmechanismus mit Servosteuerung** m FERNSEH servo-controlled tape mechanism; **Bandmittenfrequenz** f ELEKTRONIK, RADIO, TELEKOM midband frequency; **Bandmittenverstärkung** f ELEKTRONIK midband gain; **Bandmodell** nt PHYS, STRAHLPHYS band theory of solids

bandoliert: ~**e Bauteile** nt pl ELEKTROTECH bandoliered components; ~**e Komponenten** f pl ELEKTROTECH bandoliered components

Band: **Bandoxidschicht** f FERNSEH tape oxide layer; **Bandpaß** m RADIO band-pass; **Bandpaßfilter** nt *(BPF)* AUFNAHME, ELEKTRONIK, FERNSEH, PHYS, RADIO, TELEKOM band-pass filter *(BPF)*; **Bandpaßfilter dritter Ordnung** nt ELEKTRONIK third order band-pass filter; **Bandpaßfilter zweiter Ordnung** nt ELEKTRONIK second order band-pass filter; **Bandpaßformung** f ELEKTRONIK band-pass filter shaping; **Bandpaßverstärker** m AUFNAHME, ELEKTRONIK band-pass amplifier; **Bandplan** m RADIO *Frequenzzuweisung* bandplan; **Bandring** m VERPACK coil; **Bandrolle** f AUFNAHME tape roller; **Bandrückseite** f AUFNAHME tape backing; **Bandsäge** f MASCHINEN band saw; **Bandsägemaschine** f MASCHINEN band-sawing machine; **Bandsägengefahr** f SICHERHEIT narrow bandsaw hazard; **Bandsalat** m AUFNAHME tape spill; **Bandschaben** nt AUFNAHME tape scrape; **Bandschalldruckpegel** m AUFNAHME band pressure level; **Bandscharnier** nt BAU strap hinge; **Bandscheibe** f MASCHINEN band wheel; **Bandscheider** m KOHLEN belt separator; **Bandschlaufe** f FERNSEH tape loop; **Bandschlaufencassette** f FERNSEH tape loop cassette; **Bandschleife** f AUFNAHME *Endlosband* tape loop; **Bandschleifen** nt MASCHINEN belt grinding; **Bandschleifmaschine** f FERTIG abrasive band grinding machine, MASCHINEN abrasive belt grinder, belt grinder; **Bandschlupf** m FERNSEH tape slippage; **Bandschräglauf** m AUFNAHME tape skew, FERNSEH skew; **Bandschreiber** m LABOR chart recorder, LUFTTRANS continuous chart recorder; **Bandseil** nt MASCHINEN flat rope

Bändsel: ~ **aufsetzen** vi WASSERTRANS seize

Band: **Bandsortieren** nt COMP & DV tape sorting; **Bandspannarm** m AUFNAHME tape tension arm; **Bandspannung** f AUFNAHME, FERNSEH tape tension, FERTIG *Schleifband* belt tension; **Bandspannungsregelung** f AUFNAHME, FERNSEH tape tension control; **Bandspannungsregler** m AUFNAHME, FERNSEH tape tension control; **Bandsperre** f ELEKTRONIK active band-stop filter, ELEKTROTECH blocking network; **Bandsperrfilter** nt AUFNAHME band-stop filter, COMP & DV band-rejection filter, band-stop filter, ELEKTRONIK active band-stop filter, band-stop filter, RAUMFAHRT *Weltraumfunk* band-rejection filter; **Bandsperrfilter dritter Ordnung** nt ELEKTRONIK third order band-stop filter; **Bandsperrfilter zweiter Ordnung** nt ELEKTRONIK second order band-stop filter; **Bandsperrfilterung** f ELEKTRONIK band-stop filtering; **Bandspleißer** m AUFNAHME tape splicer; **Bandspreizung** f PHYS, RADIO, STRAHLPHYS bandspread; **Bandspreizverfahren** nt WASSERTRANS *Elektronik* spread spectrum technique; **Bandsprosse** f ELEKTRONIK *Platz, den Zeichen auf Magnetband einnimmt* frame; **Bandspule** f AUFNAHME reel spindle, COMP & DV tape reel, FERNSEH spool; **Bandstahl** m FERTIG strip, METALL hoops; **Bandstahlbeschichtung** f KUNSTSTOFF coil coating; **Bandstreifigkeit** f TEXTIL barriness in the weft; **Bandströmung** f HEIZ & KÄLTE laminar flow; **Bandtransport** m AUFNAHME, COMP & DV tape transport; **Bandtransportgeometrie** f AUFNAHME tape transport geometry; **Bandtransportrolle** f AUFNAHME, ELEKTROTECH capstan; **Bandtrieb** m MASCHINEN belt drive; **Bandtrockner** m CHEMTECH belt drier, belt dryer; **Bandumwickelung** f OPTIK tape wrap; **Bandverdehnung** f AUFNAHME tape curvature; **Bandverformung** f FERNSEH tape curling; **Bandverspleißung** f AUFNAHME tape splice; **Bandvorschub** m AUFNAHME tape advance, COMP & DV tape skip; **Bandwalze** f FERTIG *Bandschleifen* belt drum; **Bandware** f TEXTIL narrow fabric; **Bandweite** f *(BW)* AUFNAHME *eines aufgezeichneten Signals*, COMP & DV, ELEKTRONIK, FERNSEH, OPTIK, RADIO, TELEKOM bandwidth *(BW)*; **Bandwickeln** nt FERTIG taping; **Bandwölbung** f AUFNAHME tape cupping; **Bandzählwerk** nt AUFNAHME, FERNSEH tape counter; **Bandzuführer** m CHEMTECH belt feed; **Bandzugempfindlichkeit** f AKUSTIK tension sensitivity; **Bandzugregler** m FERNSEH tension servo

Banjogehäuse nt KFZTECH *Hinterachse* banjo-type housing

Bank f BAU *Sand, Fels* bank, ELEKTROTECH *Gruppe von Kondensatoren* bank, *Tasten, Kontakte* bank, LABOR bench, MASCHINEN table, WASSERTRANS *Geographie* bank

Bankett nt BAU banquette, bench, berm, *einer Straße* flank

Bank: **Banknotenpapier** nt PAPIER banknote paper (BrE), onionskin paper (AmE); **Bankplatte** f KER & GLAS seat; **Bankpostpapier** nt DRUCK bank paper; **Bankschraube** f BAU bench screw; **Bankschraubstock** m BAU bench vice (BrE), bench vise (AmE), MASCHINEN *höhenverstellbarer Tisch* table vice (BrE), table vise (AmE)

Bar nt *(b)* KOHLEN, METROL *Luftdruckeinheit* bar *(b)*

Bär m FERTIG hammer head, *Gießen* salamander

Baracke f BAU barrack

Barbaloin nt CHEMIE aloin, barbaloin

Barbitur- pref CHEMIE barbituric

Barbiturat nt CHEMIE barbiturate

Barcode m VERPACK bar code; **Barcodelesegerät** nt VERPACK bar code reader; **Barcodeleser** m COMP & DV bar code reader; **Barcode-Scanner- und Decoder-Logik** f VERPACK bar code scanner and decoder logic

Bardeen-Cooper-Schrieffer-Theorie f *(BCS-Theorie)* PHYS Bardeen-Cooper-Schrieffer-Theory *(BCS theory)*

Bareboat-Charter f WASSERTRANS bareboat charter

barettförmig: ~**e Feile** f MASCHINEN barrette file

BARITT-Diode f PHYS BARITT diode, barrier injection transit-time diode

Barium nt *(Ba)* CHEMIE barium *(Ba)*; **Bariummonosulfid** nt DRUCK barium monosulfide (AmE), barium monosulphide (BrE); **Bariumoxid** nt CHEMIE bariumoxide, baryta

Barkhausen-Effekt *m* PHYS Barkhausen effect

Barlow-Rad *nt* PHYS Barlow's wheel

Barn *nt* PHYS *Einheit des Wirkungsquerschnittes,* TEIL-PHYS *Einheit des Wirkungsquerschnittes* barn

Barnett-Effekt *m* PHYS Barnett effect

Barodiffusion *f* KERNTECH barodiffusion

Barograph *m* GERÄT, LABOR *Luftdruck* barograph, PHYS barograph, recording barometer, WASSERTRANS *Wetterkunde* barograph

Barometer *nt* LABOR, PHYS, WASSERTRANS *Wetterkunde* barometer; **Barometerstand** *m* GERÄT, WASSERTRANS barometer reading

barometrisch[1] *adj* PHYS barometric

barometrisch:[2] **~er Druckhöhenregler** *m* LUFTTRANS barometric altitude controller; **~er Höhenmesser** *m* LUFTTRANS pressure altimeter; **~e Steuerung** *f* LUFTTRANS barometric controller

Baroskop *nt* PHYS baroscope

Barotrauma *nt* AKUSTIK barotrauma

barotrop: ~e Flüssigkeit *f* STRÖMPHYS barotropic fluid

Barovakuum-Meter *nt* GERÄT compound pressure-and-vacuum gauge

Barre *f* WASSERTRANS *Geographie* bar

Barrel: ~ pro Tag *nt pl (B/d)* ERDÖL *Fördermenge Öl* barrels per calendar day *(BCD)*

Barren *m* KER & GLAS bullion, KOHLEN ingot, MASCHINEN bullion, MECHAN ingot; **Barreneisen** *nt* METALL bar iron; **Barrenzinn** *nt* METALL bar tin

Barretter *m* ELEKTRIZ *(cf Ballastwiderstand)* ballast resistor, barretter, ELEKTROTECH *Stabilisatorröhre,* PHYS barretter

Barrierewirkung *f* KUNSTSTOFF hold-out

Barrikade *f* BAU, SICHERHEIT barricade

Bartlett-Kraft *f* KERNTECH Bartlett force

Barwagen *m* EISENBAHN bar coach (BrE)

Baryon *nt* PHYS, TEILPHYS baryon; **Baryonenzahl** *f* PHYS, TEILPHYS baryon number

Baryt *m* KER & GLAS, KUNSTSTOFF baryte; **Baryterde** *f* CHEMIE baryta

Baryzentrum *nt* RAUMFAHRT *Raumschiff* barycenter (AmE), barycentre (BrE)

Basalt *m* BAU, NICHTFOSS ENERG basalt

Base *f* CHEMIE base; **Base-Coat** *f* KUNSTSTOFF base coat; **Basengehalt** *m* CHEMIE *Boden* alkalinity; **Basenkation** *nt* UMWELTSCHMUTZ base cation

BASIC *abbr (Beginner's All-purpose Symbolic Instruction Code)* DRUCK *Programmiersprache* BASIC *(beginner's all-purpose symbolic instruction code)*

Basic: ~ Input/Output System *nt (BIOS)* COMP & DV Basic Input/Output System *(BIOS)*

Basis *f* AUFNAHME *Tonband* base, CHEMIE base, basis, COMP & DV base, radix, ELEKTRONIK, ELEKTROTECH, GEOM *einer geometrischen Figur,* MASCHINEN, RADIO *Transistor,* TELEKOM base; **~ des Transistors** *f* TELEKOM transistor base; **Basisabdichtung** *f* ABFALL bottom sealing, *einer Deponie* base sealing; **Basisadresse** *f* COMP & DV base address; **Basisadressenregister** *nt* COMP & DV base address register; **Basisanschluß** *m* ELEKTROTECH *Transistor* base contact; **Basisband** *nt* COMP & DV, TELEKOM, ELEKTROTECH *(BB)* baseband *(BB),* FERNSEH base band, **Basisbandcharakteristik** *f* TELEKOM baseband response function; **Basisbandmodem** *nt* TELEKOM baseband modem; **Basisbandsignal** *nt* ELEKTRONIK baseband signal; **Basisbandübertragungsfunktion** *f* TELEKOM baseband transfer function; **Basisbereich** *m*

ELEKTRONIK base region; **Basisbreite** *f* ELEKTRONIK base thickness one, base zone thickness

basisch[1] *adj* CHEMIE alkaline, basic

basisch:[2] **~ stellen** *vt* CHEMIE basify

basisch: ~es Acetat *nt* CHEMIE basic acetate; **~ Bleicarbonat** *nt* CHEMIE basic lead carbonate, ceruse, cerussa; **~ Carbonat** *nt* CHEMIE basic carbonate, subcarbonate; **~ Chlorid** *nt* CHEMIE basic chloride, subchloride; **~ Erz** *nt* METALL basic ore; **~ Farbstoff** *m* TEXTIL basic dye; **~ er Martinofen** *m* KER & GLAS basic openhearth furnace; **~ Nitrat** *nt* CHEMIE basic nitrate, subnitrate; **~ Salz** *nt* CHEMIE basic salt, subsalt; **~ er Stahl** *m* METALL basic steel

Basis: Basisdiffusion *f* ELEKTRONIK *Transistortechnik* base diffusion; **Basis-Dotierung** *f* ELEKTRONIK *Transistortechnik* base doping; **Basiseinheit** *f* COMP & DV *primitive,* TELEKOM *(BE)* base unit *(BU);* **Basiselektrode** *f* ELEKTROTECH base electrode; **Basiserweiterung** *f* ELEKTRONIK base widening; **Basisformat** *nt* COMP & DV native format; **Basiskanal** *m* TELEKOM basic access, basic channel; **Basiskomplement** *nt* COMP & DV radix complement; **Basiskreis** *m* GEOM base circle; **Basislinie** *f* WASSERTRANS *Navigation* base line; **Basismodulation** *f* ELEKTRONIK base modulation; **Basismodus** *m* COMP & DV native mode; **Basisraum** *m* ELEKTRONIK base region; **Basisregister** *nt* COMP & DV *CPU* base register; **Basisschaltung** *f* ELEKTROTECH earthed-base connection (BrE), grounded-base connection (AmE), *bei Transistoren* common-base connection; **Basisschicht** *f* FERNSEH base film; **Basisstation** *f* TELEKOM base station; **Basisstationssteuerung** *f* TELEKOM base station controller; **Basisstörstelle** *f* ELEKTRONIK base impurities; **Basisvektor** *m* PHYS basis vector; **Basisvolumen** *nt* TRANS base volume; **Basisweite** *f* ELEKTRONIK base thickness two, base width; **Basiswiderstand** *m* ELEKTROTECH base resistance; **Basiswissen** *nt* KÜNSTL INT basic knowledge

Baskerville *f* DRUCK Baskerville

Basov-Diagramm *nt* KERNTECH Basov diagram

Baß *m* AKUSTIK bass; **Baßanhebung** *f* AUFNAHME bass compensation, ELEKTRONIK *Radiotechnik* bass boost; **Baßfilter** *nt* AUFNAHME bass-cut filter; **Baßreflexgehäuse** *nt* AUFNAHME bass-reflex enclosure; **Baßregelung** *f* AUFNAHME bass control; **Baßstimme** *f* AKUSTIK bass; **Baßwiedergabe** *f* AUFNAHME bass response

Bastard- *pref* MASCHINEN, MECHAN bastard; **Bastardfeile** *f* MASCHINEN bastard file, bastard-cut file, MECHAN bastard file; **Bastardhieb** *m* MASCHINEN bastard cut

Batch *nt* KUNSTSTOFF batch; **Batchdestillation** *f* KERNTECH batch distillation

Bathymetrie *f* NICHTFOSS ENERG bathymetry

Batterie *f* ELEKTRIZ battery, ELEKTROTECH *Monozelle* battery, *Speicherzelle* battery, FERTIG group, FOTO, KFZTECH, MASCHINEN, PHYS, RADIO, TELEKOM, WASSERTRANS battery; **~ von Meßkondensatoren** *f* ELEKTROTECH *im geschlossenen Gehäuse* capacitance box; **Batterieanschluß** *m* ELEKTRIZ, ELEKTROTECH battery terminal; **Batterieanschlußklemme** *f* KFZTECH battery terminal; **Batterieantrieb** *m* FERTIG accumulator driver; **Batteriebetrieb** *m* ELEKTROTECH battery operation

batteriebetrieben[1] *adj* ELEKTROTECH battery-powered, self-powered

batteriebetrieben:[2] **~er Diabetrachter** *m* FOTO battery viewer; **~es Elektrofahrzeug** *nt* TRANS battery-powered electric vehicle; **~er Lastkraftwagen** *m* TRANS battery truck

Batterie: **Batterieblitzlicht** *nt* FOTO battery-powered flash unit; **Batterieelektrode** *f* ELEKTRIZ battery electrode; **Batterieelement** *nt* ELEKTRIZ battery cell; **Batteriefach** *nt* FOTO battery chamber; **Batteriefahrzeug** *nt* ELEKTROTECH battery vehicle; **Batteriegehäuse** *nt* KFZTECH battery box

batteriegepuffert: **~er Transferbus** *m* RAUMFAHRT *Raumschiff* battery transfer bus

batteriegespeist *adj* ELEKTROTECH battery-powered

Batterie: **Batteriegestell** *nt* ELEKTRIZ battery frame, battery framework, KFZTECH battery cradle

batteriegestützt: **~e Reservestromversorgung** *f* KONTROLL stand-by battery power supply

Batterie: **Batterieglas** *nt* KER & GLAS battery jar; **Batteriehauptschalter** *m* KFZTECH battery master switch; **Batteriekammer** *f* FOTO battery chamber; **Batteriekasten** *m* ELEKTRIZ, KFZTECH battery box; **Batterieklemme** *f* ELEKTRIZ battery terminal, ELEKTROTECH *federnd* battery clip, FOTO battery grip; **Batteriekontakt** *m* FOTO battery terminal; **Batterieladegerät** *nt* ELEKTROTECH battery charger; **Batterieladestelle** *f* KFZTECH battery loading point; **Batterieladung** *f* ELEKTROTECH battery charge; **Batterienotstromversorgung** *f* KONTROLL stand-by battery power supply; **Batteriepack** *m* FOTO powerpack unit; **Batteriepackung** *f* RADIO battery pack; **Batterieplatte** *f* ELEKTROTECH, KFZTECH battery plate; **Batteriepol** *m* ELEKTROTECH, KFZTECH battery terminal; **Batteriesammelschiene** *f* RAUMFAHRT *Raumschiff* battery transfer bus; **Batteriesäure** *f* CHEMIE battery acid, electrolyte; **Batteriesäuredichte** *f* KFZTECH acid; **Batterieschutzschalter** *m* FOTO battery switch; **Batterieteil** *nt* FOTO *Blitzlicht* battery pack; **Batterieumschaltrelais** *nt* KFZTECH battery change-over relay; **Batteriewechselstelle** *f* KFZTECH battery exchange point; **Batteriezelle** *f* ELEKTROTECH battery cell, KFZTECH accumulator cell, RAUMFAHRT *Raumschiff* battery cell; **Batteriezündung** *f* KFZTECH battery ignition; **Batteriezündunterbrecher** *m* KFZTECH breaker; **Batteriezustand** *m* TELEKOM battery condition

Bau *m* BAU construction; **Bauablaufgeschwindigkeit** *f* BAU rate of progress; **Bauablaufplan** *m* BAU construction schedule, progress chart; **Bauabschlagszahlung** *f* BAU progress payment; **Bauabschnitt** *m* BAU stage; **Bauangebot** *nt* BAU bid; **Bauarbeiten** *f pl* BAU construction work; **Bauarbeiten an der öffentlichen Hand** *f pl* BAU public works; **Bauaufsicht** *f* WASSERTRANS *Schiffbau* survey; **Bauaufsichtsbeauftragter** *m* BAU building inspector; **Bauausführung** *f* BAU building construction, construction; **Baubedingungen** *f pl* BAU specifications; **Baubeschläge** *m pl* BAU builder's hardware; **Baubeschränkung** *f* BAU building restriction; **Baubeschreibung** *f* BAU specification

Bauch *m* AKUSTIK antinode, FERTIG *Welle, Schwingung* loop, WASSERTRANS *eines Segels* belly, WELLPHYS antinode; **Bauchigkeit** *f* WASSERTRANS *eines Bootes* belly; **Bauchlandung** *f* LUFTTRANS belly landing

bauchen: **sich ~** *v refl* MASCHINEN bulge

Baud *nt* COMP & DV, DRUCK baud

Bau: **Baudienst** *m* TRANS Way and Structures Department

Baudot *m* RADIO Baudot; **Baudot-Code** *m* RADIO Bau-

dot Code, international telegraph alphabet number 2

Baudrate *f* COMP & DV baud rate

Bau: **Baueinheit** *f* ELEKTRIZ assembly; **Baueisen** *nt* BAU structural iron; **Bauelement** *nt* TELEKOM *elektrisches Bauelement* component; **Bauelement einer integrierten Schaltung** *nt* ELEKTRONIK integrated-circuit element; **Bauelementebene** *f* ELEKTRONIK component level; **Bauelementeseite** *f* TELEKOM component side

bauen *vt* BAU construct

Bau: **Bauentwurf** *m* BAU construction plan; **Baufachmann** *m* BAU builder; **Bauflucht** *f* BAU alignment; **Bauform** *f* MASCHINEN design, version; **Baufortschrittsbericht** *m* BAU progress report; **Baugenehmigung** *f* BAU building permit, planning permission; **Baugenossenschaft** *f* BAU benefit building society; **Baugewerbe** *nt* BAU trade; **Bauglas** *nt* KER & GLAS structural glass; **Baugrenzlinie** *f* BAU building line; **Baugrube** *f* BAU pit, trench, KOHLEN excavation; **Baugrund** *m* BAU site; **Baugruppe** *f* BAU, ELEKTRIZ assembly, KFZTECH unit, MECHAN, QUAL, RADIO assembly; **Baugruppe zur Peilung und Kraftübertragung** *f* RAUMFAHRT BAPTA, bearing and power transfer assembly; **Baugutachten** *nt* BAU survey; **Bauhandwerk** *nt* BAU building trade; **Bauhauptvertrag** *m* BAU general contract; **Bauhof** *m* BAU timber yard; **Bauholz** *nt* BAU builder's timber, timber; **Bauingenieur** *m* BAU civil engineer

Baukasten *m* COMP & DV modular; **Baukastenbauweise** *f* FERTIG modular construction, unit construction; **Baukastenprinzip** *nt* FERTIG building-block construction (AmE), *Kunststoffinstallationen* assembly of unit parts; **Baukastensystem** *nt* FERTIG unit assembly system, MASCHINEN modular system

Bau: **Baukonstruktion** *f* BAU building construction; **Baulänge** *f* FERTIG *Kunststoffinstallationen* length; **Bauleitplan** *m* BAU land use plan

Baum *m* FERTIG boom, KÜNSTL INT tree, RAUMFAHRT boom, TEXTIL beam, WASSERTRANS boom

Bau: **Baumangel** *m* BAU constructional defect; **Baumaß** *nt* FERTIG *Kunststoffinstallationen* dimension

Bäumen *nt* TEXTIL beaming

Baumé-Skale *f* LEBENSMITTEL Baumé scale

Baum: **Baumfärbeapparat** *m* TEXTIL beam-dyeing machine; **Baumfärben** *nt* TEXTIL beam dyeing; **Baumfärbung** *f* TEXTIL beam dyeing; **Baumgei** *f* WASSERTRANS boom guy

baumkantig *adj* BAU rough-hewn

Bäummaschine *f* TEXTIL beamer

Baum: **Baumnetz** *nt* TELEKOM tree network; **Baumnetzwerk** *nt* COMP & DV tree network; **Baumniederhalter** *m* WASSERTRANS *Segeln* boom vang, kicking strap; **Baumstruktur** *f* COMP & DV tree, tree structure, TELEKOM tree structure; **Baumstumpf** *m* BAU stub, stump; **Baumtopologie** *f* COMP & DV tree topology

Bau: **Baumusterprüfung** *f* QUAL prototype test

Baumwoll- *pref* ELEKTROTECH, TEXTIL cotton; **Baumwollatlas** *m* TEXTIL satin

Baumwolle *f* TEXTIL cotton

Baumwoll-: **Baumwollgarn** *nt* TEXTIL cotton; **Baumwollgeflecht** *nt* ELEKTROTECH cotton braid

baumwollisoliert[1] *adj* ELEKTROTECH *Stromdraht* cotton-covered

baumwollisoliert:[2] **~er Draht** *m* ELEKTRIZ double-covered cotton wire

Baumwoll-: **Baumwollisolierung** *f* ELEKTRIZ cotton insulation; **Baumwollnumerierung** *f* TEXTIL cotton count; **Baumwollöffner** *m* TEXTIL opener; **Baumwoll-saatöl** *nt* LEBENSMITTEL cottonseed oil; **Baumwollsatin** *m* TEXTIL satin; **Baumwollspinnerei** *f* TEXTIL cotton spinning

Bau: **Baupappe** *f* PAPIER felt; **Bauplan** *m* BAU construction plan, KERNTECH assembly plan; **Bauplatz** *m* BAU construction site, job site; **Bauprogramm** *nt* BAU construction program (AmE), construction programme (BrE); **Baureihe** *f* MASCHINEN series, TELEKOM *Herstellung* range; **Bausachverständiger** *m* BAU building expert; **Bausatz** *m* KERNTECH, RADIO kit

Bausch *m* TEXTIL *Faser* bulk

Bau: **Bauschreiner** *m* BAU joiner; **Bauschreinerei** *f* BAU joinery; **Bauschutt** *m* ABFALL construction waste, demolition waste, BAU demolition waste, waste

Bauschvermögen *nt* TEXTIL bulk

Bau: **Bauspantenriß** *m* WASSERTRANS *Schiffkonstruktion* frame plan

Bau: **Baustahl** *m* BAU structural steel, FERTIG mild steel; **Baustatistik** *f* BAU structural engineering; **Baustein** *m* COMP & DV module, unit, ELEKTRONIK, FERTIG, HYDRAUL module; **Bausteinsystem** *nt* COMP & DV modularity; **Bausteintechnik** *f* FERTIG packaging technique; **Baustelle** *f* BAU construction site, field, job site, site

Baustelle: **auf der ~** *adv* BAU on site

Bau: **Baustellenabfall** *m* ABFALL construction waste; **Baustellenbesprechung** *f* BAU site meeting; **Baustelleneinrichtung** *f* BAU job site installations, site installations; **Baustelleningenieur** *m* MECHAN field engineer; **Baustellenschweißen** *nt* KERNTECH field weld; **Bautafel** *f* BAU *Putzträger* lath; **Bautagebuch** *nt* BAU builder's diary; **Bautechniker** *m* BAU builder

bautechnisch: **~e Richtlinien** *f pl* BAU code of practice

Bauteil *nt* BAU member, ELEKTRIZ, HYDRAUL element, KFZTECH part, MASCHINEN component, member, TELEKOM component; **Bauteilauswahl** *f* RAUMFAHRT *Raumschiff* component selection; **Bauteilbeschaffung** *f* RAUMFAHRT *Raumschiff* component procurement; **Bauteileprüfung** *f* WERKPRÜF component testing; **Bauteilfarbe** *f* RADIO component color (AmE), component colour (BrE)

Bau: **Bautischler** *m* BAU joiner; **Bautischlerei** *f* BAU joinery; **Bauunternehmer** *m* BAU builder, building contractor, contractor; **Bauvorhaben** *nt* BAU construction project; **Bauvorrichtung** *f* MECHAN jig, WASSERTRANS *Schiffbau* erection jig; **Bauvorschriften** *f pl* BAU building regulations; **Bauweise** *f* BAU construction, design; **neue österreichische ~** *f* BAU new Austrian tunnelling method; **Bauwerft** *f* WASSERTRANS *Schiffbau* construction yard; **Bauwerk** *nt* BAU construction, structure

Bauxit *m* FERTIG, KER & GLAS bauxite

Bau: **Bauzeichnung** *f* MECHAN layout drawing; **Bauzeit** *f* BAU construction time

Bazin: **~sche Formel** *f* HYDRAUL Bazin's formula

Bazooka-Balun *m* RADIO *Antennen* bazooka balun

BB *abbr* (*Basisband*) ELEKTROTECH BB (*baseband*)

BBD *abbr* ELEKTROTECH (*Eimerkettenspeicher*), TELEKOM (*Eimerkettenschaltung*) BBD (*bucket brigade device*)

BBL *abbr* (*Blindlandung mit Bakeunterstützung*) RAUMFAHRT BBL (*beacons and blind landing*)

BBV *abbr* (*Breitbandverstärker*) ELEKTRONIK wideband amplifier

BCC *abbr* (*Blockprüfzeichen*) TELEKOM BCC (*block check character*)

BCD *abbr* COMP & DV (*binärcodierte Dezimalzahl, binärcodierte Drehzahl*), RADIO (*binärcodierte Dezimalzahl*) BCD (*binary-coded decimal*)

BCI *abbr* (*Rundfunkstörung*) RADIO BCI (*broadcast interference*)

BCS *abbr* (*Bardeen-Cooper-Schrieffer*) COMP & DV BCS (*Bardeen-Cooper-Schrieffer*)

BCS-Theorie *f* PHYS *Supraleitung* BCS theory

B/d *abbr* (*Barrel pro Tag*) ERDÖL BCD (*barrels per calendar day*)

BDP *abbr* (*Verbundpapier*) PAPIER BDP (*bonded double paper*)

BE *abbr* ELEKTRIZ (*elektrischer Blindleitwert*) BE (*electric susceptance*), TELEKOM (*Basiseinheit*) BU (*base unit*)

Be (*Beryllium*) CHEMIE Be (*beryllium*)

beabsichtigt: **~e Flugbahn** *f* LUFTTRANS intended flight path; **~e Störung** *f* TELEKOM jamming

Beachtung *f* SICHERHEIT care

Beam-Lead *pref* ELEKTRONIK beam lead; **Beam-Lead-Chip** *m* ELEKTRONIK *Mikroelektronik* beam lead chip; **Beam-Lead-Technik** *f* ELEKTRONIK beam lead technique

beanspruchen *vt* BAU load, strain, MASCHINEN stress, PATENT claim

Beanspruchung *f* ERGON, KER & GLAS strain, KOHLEN stress, MECHAN strain, stress, MEERSCHMUTZ, METALL stress, PHYS strain, WASSERTRANS *Werkstoff*, WERKPRÜF stress; **äußere ~** *f* WERKPRÜF external strain; **Beanspruchungsbeginn** *m* QUAL beginning of stress; **Beanspruchungskombination** *f* QUAL load combination; **Beanspruchungsschwankung** *f* METALL fluctuating stress

beanstandet *adj* QUAL nonconforming

Beanstandung *f* QUAL objection

beantragen *vt* MECHAN apply for

Bearbeitbarkeit *f* KUNSTSTOFF, MASCHINEN machinability

bearbeiten *vt* BAU handle, COMP & DV edit, MASCHINEN work, MECHAN machine; **neu ~** *vt* DRUCK revise

bearbeitet[1] *adj* MASCHINEN, MECHAN machined

bearbeitet:[2] **~e Oberfläche** *f* MECHAN machined surface

Bearbeitung *f* DRUCK adaptation, MASCHINEN, MECHAN machining; **~ des geblasenen Glaspostens** *f* KER & GLAS working on blown post; **Bearbeitungsfehler** *m* MASCHINEN machining defect; **Bearbeitungsmaschinen im Serienbetrieb** *f pl* VERPACK in-line finishing equipment; **Bearbeitungsspuren** *f pl* FERTIG lay; **Bearbeitungstoleranz** *f* MASCHINEN machining allowance; **Bearbeitungsvorschub** *m* FERTIG *beim Bohren* drilling feed; **Bearbeitungszeit** *f* COMP & DV productive time, target phase, run time; **Bearbeitungszugabe** *f* FERTIG allowance for machining, tooling allowance; **Bearbeitungszyklus** *m* MASCHINEN machining cycle, working cycle

Beatmungsgerät *nt* ERDÖL *Sicherheitsausrüstung* breathing apparatus, SICHERHEIT respirator

Beaufort-Skale *f* WASSERTRANS Beaufort scale

Beaufschlagung *f* FERTIG discharge

beauftragen *vt* QUAL appoint; **~ mit** *vt* QUAL entrust with

Beauftragung *f* SICHERHEIT care

Beaumé-Skale *f* PHYS *Aräometrie* Beaume scale

bebaut: **~e Fläche** *f* BAU building area

bebildern *vt* DRUCK illustrate

bebunkern *vt* WASSERTRANS bunker

Becher *m* LABOR, LEBENSMITTEL *Laborgerät* beaker; ~ mit Schnabel *m* LABOR beaker with spout; Becherbruch *m* METALL cup and cone fracture; Becherglas *nt* KER & GLAS beaker; Becherhalter *m* LABOR beaker holder; Becherleiter *f* BAU bucket ladder; Becherrelais *nt* ELEKTRIZ sealed relay; Becherschließzeit *f* KUNSTSTOFF cup-closing time; Becherschöpfrad *nt* HYDRAUL tympanus; Becherwerk *nt* BAU bucket elevator

Becken *nt* ERDÖL *Geologie*, KOHLEN, LABOR basin, PAPIER pond, WASSERVERSORG basin, lagoon; ~ für Rückstände *nt* ABFALL tailings pond; Beckenauskleidung *f* WASSERVERSORG reservoir lining; Beckenplatte *f* KER & GLAS pool tablet; Beckenstein *m* KER & GLAS pool block; Beckentiefe *f* PAPIER pond depth

Beckmann: ~sches Flüssigkeitsthermometer *nt* PHYS Beckmann thermometer

Beckschicht *f* WASSERVERSORG capping

Becquerel *nt* (*Bq*) METROL, PHYS becquerel (*Bq*); Becquereleffekt *m* ELEKTRIZ Becquerel effect; Becquerelzelle *f* ELEKTRIZ Becquerel cell

bedachen *vt* BAU roof

bedarfsgesteuert[1] *adj* COMP & DV demand-responsive

bedarfsgesteuert:[2] ~es System *nt* TRANS demand-responsive system; ~er Vielfachzugriff *m* (*DAMA*) TELEKOM demand-assigned multiple access (*DAMA*)

bedarfsmäßig: ~es Einspeichern *nt* COMP & DV demand staging

Bedarfswartung *f* COMP & DV remedial maintenance, TELEKOM corrective maintenance

Bedecken *nt* FERTIG coping

bedecken *vt* BAU cope, put under cover, top, FERTIG cope

bedeckt *adj* ELEKTRIZ covered

Bedeckung *f* RADIO, TELEKOM coverage

Bedielung *f* BAU deck

Bedienelement *nt* LUFTTRANS actuator

bedienen *vt* BAU attend to, MECHAN handle

Bediener *m* COMP & DV, DRUCK, MASCHINEN operator, TELEKOM server; Bedienerantwort *f* COMP & DV operator response; Bedienerbefehl *m* COMP & DV operator command; Bedienerkonsole *f* COMP & DV control panel, operator console; Bedienermeldung *f* COMP & DV operator message; Bedienernachricht *f* COMP & DV operator message; Bedienerstation *f* COMP & DV operator terminal

Bedienhebel *m* LUFTTRANS control lever

Bedienpodest *nt* LUFTTRANS control pedestal

Bedienpult *nt* GERÄT, LUFTTRANS console

Bedienteil *nt* ERGON control element

Bedienung *f* ELEKTROTECH operation, FERTIG operating, MASCHINEN control, operating, operation, PAPIER operating, RAUMFAHRT *des Raumschiffs* handling, TELEKOM control, operation; ~ am Gerät *f* MECHAN local control; Bedienungsanleitung *f* FERTIG operating instructions, MASCHINEN instruction book, operating instructions; Bedienungsfehler *m* KOHLEN operating error; Bedienungsfreundlichkeit *f* MECHAN ease of operation; Bedienungsgang *m* KERNTECH gangway; Bedienungsgleis *nt* EISENBAHN line serving a siding; Bedienungshandbuch *nt* MASCHINEN instruction book; Bedienungshandgriff *m* LUFTTRANS box-type stiffener; Bedienungshebel *m* MASCHINEN operating lever; Bedienungsknopf *m* ELEKTROTECH knob; Bedienungsperson *f* ERGON human operator; Bedienungspersonal *nt* KERNTECH service staff; Be-

dienungspult *nt* COMP & DV system control panel, EISENBAHN control desk, GERÄT console, MECHAN control panel, TELEKOM operating console, operator's console; Bedienungsreep *nt* WASSERTRANS lanyard; Bedienungsschalter *m* ELEKTRIZ operating switch; Bedienungsspannung *f* FERTIG operating voltage; Bedienungsstand *m* FERTIG platform; Bedienungssystem *nt* TELEKOM operator system; Bedienungstafel *f* ELEKTRIZ control board, WASSERTRANS *Elektrik* control panel; Bedienungszeit *f* FERTIG machine-handling time

bedingt[1] *adj* COMP & DV, KONTROLL conditional

bedingt:[2] ~e Anweisung *f* COMP & DV conditional instruction; ~er Befehl *m* COMP & DV conditional instruction; ~e Löslichkeit *f* METALL restricted solubility; ~er Programmstopp *m* COMP & DV checkpoint; ~er Schutz *m* PATENT conditional protection; ~er Sprungbefehl *m* COMP & DV conditional jump; ~e Verzweigung *f* COMP & DV conditional branch

Bedingung *f* COMP & DV condition, constraint; ~ für gleichbleibenden Zustand *f* ELEKTROTECH steady state condition; Bedingungsausdruck *m* COMP & DV conditional expression; Bedingungsbühne *f* LABOR bench

Bedruckbarkeit *f* PAPIER printability

Bedrucken *nt* TEXTIL printing

bedrucken *vt* TEXTIL impress, print

bedruckt: ~es Etikett *nt* VERPACK printed label; ~e Faltschachtel *f* VERPACK printed folding carton; ~e Seite *f* DRUCK printed sheet; ~er Stoff *m* TEXTIL printed fabric

beenden[1] *vt* COMP & DV exit

beenden[2] *vi* COMP & DV sign off

Befehl *m* COMP & DV command, instruction, order, KONTROLL command; ~ zur Speicherung nach der LIFO-Methode *m* COMP & DV push instruction, push operation; Befehls- und Steuersystem *nt* COMP & DV command-and-control system; Befehlsablauf *m* COMP & DV instruction cycle; Befehlsabruf *m* COMP & DV instruction fetching; Befehlsadreßregister *nt* COMP & DV IAR, instruction address register; Befehlsausführung *f* COMP & DV instruction execution; Befehlscode *m* COMP & DV instruction code, order code, program counter; Befehlscodeprozessor *m* COMP & DV OCP, order code processor; Befehlsdecodierer *m* COMP & DV instruction decoder; Befehlsfolge *f* COMP & DV instruction stream, sequence of instructions; Befehlsfolgeregister *nt* COMP & DV sequence control register, sequence counter, sequence register; Befehlsformat *nt* COMP & DV instruction format

befehlsgesteuert: ~e Schnittstelle *f* COMP & DV command-driven interface

Befehl: Befehlskette *f* COMP & DV pipeline; Befehlslänge *f* COMP & DV instruction length; Befehlsparameter *m* COMP & DV switch; Befehlsprozessor *m* COMP & DV instruction processor; Befehlsregister *nt* COMP & DV instruction register; Befehlsschlüssel *m* COMP & DV program counter; Befehlsspeicherbereich *m* COMP & DV instruction area; Befehlssprache *f* (*CL*) COMP & DV command language (*CL*); Befehlssystem *nt* COMP & DV command system; Befehlsvorrat *m* COMP & DV instruction repertoire, instruction set; Befehlswort *nt* COMP & DV instruction word; Befehlszähler *m* COMP & DV program counter; Befehlszeile *f* COMP & DV command line; Befehlszwischenspeicher *m* COMP & DV instruction cache; Befehlszyklus *m* COMP & DV instruction cycle

befeilen *vt* MASCHINEN file
Befestigen *nt* BAU sealing, MASCHINEN, MECHAN fastening
befestigen *vt* BAU fasten, mount, pave, secure, tack, tail, *mit Latten* batten, MECHAN fasten, MEERSCHMUTZ moor, PAPIER attach, VERPACK clip to, WASSERTRANS secure
Befestigung *f* BAU fastening, *Ufer* revetment, *von Wegen oder Straßen* pavement (BrE), sidewalk (AmE), KFZTECH *für Karosserieblech* panel mounting, MASCHINEN attachment, fixing, fastening, MECHAN clamping, fastening, PAPIER attachment, RAUMFAHRT *Raumschiff* fastener; **Befestigungsband** *nt* VERPACK clip band; **Befestigungsbügel** *m* FOTO *Blitzlicht*, MASCHINEN mounting bracket; **Befestigungsfeder** *f* MASCHINEN mounting spring; **Befestigungsfläche** *f* KERNTECH seating, MASCHINEN seat; **Befestigungsfuß** *m* FOTO mounting foot; **Befestigungsgeschirr** *nt* MEERSCHMUTZ mooring bracket; **Befestigungsglied** *nt* MASCHINEN attachment link; **Befestigungsmittel** *nt* MASCHINEN fastener, fastening device; **Befestigungsschraube** *f* BAU fixing screw, FERTIG holding-down bolt, MASCHINEN attaching screw, fixing bolt; **Befestigungsschrauben** *f pl* MASCHINEN threaded fasteners; **Befestigungsstück** *nt* MASCHINEN attachment fitting; **Befestigungssystem** *nt* RAUMFAHRT *Raumschiff* strapdown system; **Befestigungswinkel** *m* BAU angle bracket, MASCHINEN angle bracket, mounting bracket
befeuchten *vt* BAU moisten, water, HEIZ & KÄLTE humidify, LEBENSMITTEL moisten, PAPIER humidify, PHYS wet, THERMOD humidify, moisten
Befeuchter *m* HEIZ & KÄLTE, LUFTTRANS, PAPIER, THERMOD humidifier, VERPACK moistening device
Befeuchtung *f* HEIZ & KÄLTE, THERMOD humidification; **Befeuchtungsvorrichtung** *f* VERPACK moistening equipment
Befeuerung *f* WASSERTRANS light
befinden: **sich ~ in** *v refl* COMP & DV reside
befindlich: **auf dem Chip ~er Transistor** *m* ELEKTRONIK on-chip transistor; **auf dem Chip ~es Filter** *nt* ELEKTRONIK on-chip filter
Beflechtung *f* FERTIG braiding
Befolgungsgrad *m* TRANS obedience level
Beförderer *m* TRANS conveyor
befördern *vt* BAU haul, TEXTIL, TRANS carry, WASSERTRANS ship
Beförderung *f* TRANS carriage, conveyance, transport; **~ von Handelsgütern** *f* TRANS merchant haulage
Befrachter *m* WASSERTRANS *Seehandel* charterer
Befrachtung *f* WASSERTRANS *Seehandel* charterage, chartering; **Befrachtungsagent** *m* TRANS freight agent; **Befrachtungsmakler** *m* WASSERTRANS *Seehandel* chartering broker
Befragung *f* ERGON, KÜNSTL INT interview; **Befragungstechniken** *f pl* ERGON interview techniques; **Befragungswerkzeug** *nt* KÜNSTL INT consultation tool
Befüllung *f* ABFALL *einer Kaverne* waste injection
Befund *m* QUAL findings; **äußerer ~** *m* QUAL visual inspection result; **Befundbericht** *m* QUAL report of findings; **Befundprüfung** *f* QUAL as-found test
BEG *abbr* (*Bodeneffektgerät*) KFZTECH GEM (*ground effect machine*)
begast *adj* VERPACK gas-flushed
Begasungsextruder *m* KUNSTSTOFF gas injection extruder
begehbar: **~e Gefrieranlage** *f* HEIZ & KÄLTE walk-in

freezer; **~er Gitterrost** *m* HEIZ & KÄLTE step-on grille
begichten *vt* FERTIG *Hochofen* fill
Beginn *m* COMP & DV start; **~ des Sinkflugs** *m* LUFTTRANS top of descent
beginnen: **neu ~** *vt* TELEKOM restart
beginnend: **~er Ermüdungsbruch** *m* LUFTTRANS incipient fatigue failure; **~e kritische Wärmestromdichte** *f* KERNTECH departure from nuclear boiling
Beginner's: **~ All-purpose Symbolic Instruction Code** *m* (*BASIC*) DRUCK beginner's all-purpose symbolic instruction code (*BASIC*)
Beginnzeichen *nt* TELEKOM answer signal
Beglaubigung *f* QUAL certificate; **Beglaubigungsschein** *m* QUAL certificate of approval; **Beglaubigungszeichen** *nt* QUAL certification mark
Begleit- *pref* KONSTZEICH, RAUMFAHRT track; **Begleitkarte** *f* QUAL job card; **Begleitlinie** *f* KONSTZEICH tracer line; **Begleitradar** *m* RAUMFAHRT tracking radar; **Begleittextdatei** *f* COMP & DV narrative file
Begleitung *f* LUFTTRANS tracking
begradigen *vt* BAU rectify, straighten, *Straßenbau* level
begrenzen *vt* BAU border, ELEKTRONIK limit, ELEKTROTECH clip
Begrenzer *m* AUFNAHME, ELEKTRONIK, ELEKTROTECH, KONTROLL, MASCHINEN limiter, RADIO *Sprechfunk* clipper, limiter, RAUMFAHRT *Weltraumfunk*, TELEKOM limiter; **~ für Integralanteil** *m* REGELUNG integral action limiter; **Begrenzerdiode** *f* ELEKTRONIK clipper diode, limiter diode, FERNSEH limiter diode; **Begrenzerschaltung** *f* ELEKTRONIK clipper, clipper circuit, limiter, ELEKTROTECH limiter
begrenzt: **~es Ansprechen auf einen Impuls** *nt* (*FIR*) ELEKTRONIK finite impulse response (*FIR*); **~er Fluß durch einen Leiter** *m* PHYS flux cut by a conductor; **~er Fluß durch ein Schaltelement** *m* PHYS flux cut by a circuit element; **~e Sichtweite** *f* TRANS limit of visibility; **~e Warteschlange** *f* TELEKOM limited waiting queue
Begrenzung *f* AUFNAHME, ELEKTRONIK limiting, ERDÖL confinement, GEOM boundary; **~ des Schadstoffausstoßes** *f* MASCHINEN emission control; **Begrenzungslinie** *f* BAU boundary line; **Begrenzungsregelung** *f* REGELUNG limiting control; **Begrenzungsregelung nach oben** *f* REGELUNG high-limiting control; **Begrenzungsregelung nach unten** *f* REGELUNG low-limiting control; **Begrenzungsschalter** *m* ELEKTRIZ, ELEKTROTECH, KONTROLL, MECHAN limit switch; **Begrenzungsschaltkreis** *m* FERNSEH, TELEKOM limiter; **Begrenzungssymbol** *nt* COMP & DV delimiter, separator symbol; **Begrenzungsverstärker** *m* AUFNAHME limiter amplifier, ELEKTRONIK limiting amplifier; **Begrenzungswert** *m* ELEKTRONIK clipping level; **Begrenzungszeichen** *nt* COMP & DV delimiter, separator
Begriffsabhängigkeit *f* KÜNSTL INT CD, conceptual dependency, CD
begutachten *vti* QUAL *Lieferanten* evaluate
Begutachtung *f* QUAL survey
Behaglichkeit *f* ERGON comfort
Behälter *m* ERDÖL tank, FERTIG receiver, *Kunststoffinstallationen* tank, HEIZ & KÄLTE tank, HYDRAUL drum, KER & GLAS chest, KFZTECH *Öl, Kraftstoff* reservoir, KOHLEN container, KONTROLL enclosure, LABOR basin, bucket, vessel, MECHAN case, tank, MEERSCHMUTZ scoop, RADIO receptacle, TEXTIL vessel, UMWELTSCHMUTZ tank; **~ für Meßeinheit** *m* VERPACK

unit dose container; ~ **mit Plane** *m* TRANS tarpaulin-covered container; **Behälteranschluß** *m* FERTIG *Kunststoffinstallationen* tank adaptor; **Behälterbau** *m* FERTIG pressure vessel construction; **Behälterglas** *nt* KER & GLAS container glass; **Behälterkammer** *f* WASSERVERSORG *einer Kanalschleuse* chamber; **Behältermeßanlage** *f* GERÄT tank gaging system (AmE), tank gauging system (BrE); **Behältermeßsystem** *nt* GERÄT tank gaging system (AmE), tank gauging system (BrE); **Behälterwagen** *m* EISENBAHN tank car (AmE), tank wagon (BrE); **Behälterwand** *f* FERTIG *Kunststoffinstallationen* tank wall

behandeln *vt* LEBENSMITTEL process

Behandlung *f* TEXTIL treatment; ~ **der Anmeldung** *f* PATENT processing of an application; ~ **fehlerhafter Einheiten** *f* QUAL control of non-conforming items; ~ **von Klärschlamm** *f* ABFALL treatment of sewage sludge

Beharrung *f* HEIZ & KÄLTE, MASCHINEN inertia; **Beharrungsgesetz** *nt* MASCHINEN law of inertia; **Beharrungsmoment** *nt* MASCHINEN rotational inertia; **Beharrungsregler** *m* MASCHINEN inertia governor; **Beharrungsvermögen** *nt* HEIZ & KÄLTE, MASCHINEN, MECHAN, PHYS, UMWELTSCHMUTZ inertia; **Beharrungszustand** *m* ELEKTROTECH steady state, steady state condition

Behauen *nt* BAU *von Stein* dressing

behauen:[1] ~**er Naturstein** *m* BAU dressed stone

behauen[2] *vt* BAU axe, mill, *Holzbau* adze, *Stein* square, FERTIG *Feile* cut

behebbar: ~**er Fehler** *m* COMP & DV recoverable error; **nicht** ~**er Fehler** *m* COMP & DV irrecoverable error

beheben *vt* QUAL *Fehler* remedy, *Mängel* correct, TELEKOM *Fehler* recover

beheizt: ~**er Container** *m* TRANS heated container; ~**e Windschutzscheibe** *f* LUFTTRANS heated windscreen pane (BrE), heated windshield pane (AmE)

Behelfs- *pref* FERTIG makeshift, temporary; **Behelfsbau** *m* BAU temporary structure; **Behelfsbrücke** *f* BAU temporary bridge; **Behelfsruder** *nt* WASSERTRANS jury rudder

Behen- *pref* CHEMIE behenic

beherrscht: ~**er Prozeß** *m* QUAL controlled process, process in control; **nicht** ~**er Prozeß** *m* QUAL uncontrolled process, process out of control

Behinderung *f* SICHERHEIT hindrance

Behörde *f* PATENT authority; ~ **für internationale Vorprüfungen** *f* PATENT international preliminary examining authority

beibehalten *vt* MECHAN *Werkzeuge, Geräte* maintain

Beibehaltung *f* CHEMIE retention, OPTIK conservation; ~ **der Helligkeit** *f* OPTIK conservation of brightness; ~ **der Strahlungsintensität** *f* OPTIK conservation of radiance

Beiboot *nt* WASSERTRANS ship's boat

beidäugig *adj* OPTIK, PHYS binocular

beiderseitig: ~**e Belüftung** *f* HEIZ & KÄLTE double-ended ventilation

Beidhändigkeit *f* ERGON ambidexterity

beidohrig *adj* AKUSTIK binaural

beidrehen *vi* WASSERTRANS *Schiff* heave to

beidseitig:[1] ~ **beschreibbarer Datenträger** *m* COMP & DV double-sided disk; ~**er Gehrungswinkel** *m* KER & GLAS miter bevel both sides (AmE), mitre bevel both sides (BrE)

beidseitig:[2] ~ **bedrucken** *vt* DRUCK perfect

Beifahrer *m* TRANS *Automobil* passenger; **Beifahrerseite** *f* KFZTECH near side

beigedreht[1] *adj* WASSERTRANS *Schiff* ahull

beigedreht:[2] ~ **legen** *vt* WASSERTRANS *Schiff* lay ahull

Beijing: ~ **Electron Positron Collider** *m* (*BEPC*) TEILPHYS Beijing Electron Positron Collider (*BEPC*)

Beil *nt* BAU ax (AmE), axe (BrE)

Beilage *f* FERTIG shim; **Beilageblatt** *nt* VERPACK *Druckschrift als Anlage* leaflet insert; **Beilagefolie** *f* MECHAN shim

Beilagscheibe *f* MASCHINEN shim

Beilegering *m* FERTIG *Nutenfräser* packing

Beimengung *f* CHEMIE impurity, KER & GLAS admix, KUNSTSTOFF admixture

Beimischung *f* BAU admixture, CHEMIE impurity, KUNSTSTOFF, TEXTIL admixture

Bein- *pref* ERGON, KFZTECH leg

Beinahezusammenstoß *m* LUFTTRANS, RAUMFAHRT near miss

Bein-: **Beinfreiheit** *f* KFZTECH legroom; **Beinfreiraum** *m* ERGON legroom; **Beinraum** *m* ERGON legroom

Beispiel *nt* COMP & DV instance, sample

beißend: ~**er Geruch** *m* UMWELTSCHMUTZ acrid odor (AmE), acrid odour (BrE)

Beißzange *f* ELEKTRIZ pliers, MASCHINEN pincers, pliers, tongs

Beitel *m* MECHAN chisel

Beiwagen *m* KFZTECH side car; **Beiwagendrehgestell** *nt* EISENBAHN trailer bogie

Beizbrüchigkeit *f* FERTIG acid brittleness

Beize *f* CHEMIE caustic, FERTIG etchant, mordant, pickle, stain

Beizen *nt* FERTIG pickling

beizen *vt* BAU etch, FERTIG etch, mordant

beizend *adj* CHEMIE caustic

Beizfärben *nt* FOTO mordant dyeing

Beizkraft *f* CHEMIE causticity

bekannt: ~**es Kohlenvorkommen** *nt* KOHLEN known coal deposit

bekiesen *vt* BAU grit

Bekleidung *f* HYDRAUL clothing, TEXTIL apparel

bekohlen *vt* KOHLEN coal

Bekohlungsvorrichtung *f* KOHLEN coal-handling plant

Bel *nt* (*B*) AKUSTIK, ELEKTROTECH, PHYS bel (*B*)

Belademaschine *f* KERNTECH fuel-charging machine

Beladen *nt* TRANS stuffing; ~ **eines Schiffs** *nt* WASSERTRANS *Ladung* ship loading

beladen[1] *adj* ELEKTROTECH loaded; **nicht** ~ *adj* MEERSCHMUTZ unladen

beladen[2] *vt* MECHAN load, THERMOD *Brennofen, Hochofen* charge, TRANS stuff, WASSERTRANS *Schiff* load

Beladerohr *nt* KERNTECH feeder pipe

Beladeseite *f* KERNTECH charge face

Beladezone *f* KERNTECH charge area

Beladung *f* ELEKTROTECH, MASCHINEN, RAUMFAHRT *Raumschiff*, TRANS loading; ~ **bei abgeschalteter Last** *f* KERNTECH off-load charging; ~ **mit Brennmaterial** *f* KERNTECH fuel charge; ~ **unter Last** *f* KERNTECH on-load charging, on-load fueling (AmE), on-load fuelling (BrE)

Belag *m* BAU cover, overlay, overlaying, paving, KFZTECH pad, *Bremse, Kupplung* lining, LEBENSMITTEL *auf Früchten* bloom, MASCHINEN facing, MECHAN lining; **Belagverschleiß** *m* KFZTECH lining wear

Belassung *f* QUAL accept as is, use as is

Belastbarkeit *f* MASCHINEN load rating, loading capaci-

ty; ~ im Gebrauch *f* METALL working stress
belasten *vt* BAU load, PHYS stress, SICHERHEIT pollute
belastend: ~es Mittel *nt* SICHERHEIT polluting agent
belastet[1] *adj* ELEKTROTECH loaded
belastet:[2] ~es Kabel *nt* ELEKTROTECH loaded cable
Belastung *f* AUFNAHME *eines Lautsprechers* loading, COMP & DV load, ELEKTROTECH loading, ERGON stress, FERTIG load, loading, HYDRAUL *Ventil* load, KERNTECH exposure, KOHLEN stress, MASCHINEN, MECHAN, METALL, PAPIER, RADIO load, RAUMFAHRT *Raumschiff* battery drain, loading, TELEKOM load; ~ an Drittperson *f* TELEKOM third party charging; ~ außerhalb der Spitzenzeit *f* ELEKTROTECH off-peak load; ~ durch Dämpfe *f* SICHERHEIT exposure to fumes; ~ des Menschen *f* SICHERHEIT *durch mechanische Vibration* human exposure; ~ mit Spulen *f* ELEKTROTECH coil loading; ~ durch Widerstand *f* ELEKTROTECH resistive load; **Belastungsanalyse** *f* RAUMFAHRT *Raumschiff* stress analysis; **Belastungsbild einer Verbindung** *nt* TRANS desire line; **Belastungscharakteristik** *f* LUFTTRANS load characteristic; **Belastungsdiagramm** *nt* ELEKTROTECH load curve, MECHAN load diagram; **Belastungsfähigkeit** *f* MECHAN carrying capacity, WASSERVERSORG rated capacity, rated load; **Belastungsfaktor** *m* MECHAN load factor, RAUMFAHRT *Weltraumfunk* loading factor
belastungsfrei: ~es Anfahren *nt* ELEKTRIZ no-load start
Belastung: **Belastungsfunktion** *f* METALL loading function; **Belastungsgeschwindigkeit** *f* METALL rate of loading; **Belastungsgrenze** *f* MASCHINEN load limit; **Belastungskapazität** *f* ELEKTRIZ peaking capacity, ELEKTROTECH *bei Voltmetern* input capacitance; **Belastungskennlinie** *f* ELEKTROTECH load line; **Belastungskoeffizient** *m* ELEKTROTECH load factor; **Belastungskraft** *f* FERTIG active force; **Belastungskurve** *f* ELEKTROTECH load curve; **Belastungslinie** *f* MASCHINEN load line; **Belastungsprüfung** *f* BAU loading test; **Belastungsregelung** *f* ELEKTROTECH load regulation; **Belastungsregler** *m* PAPIER load governor; **Belastungsschaubild** *nt* MECHAN load diagram; **Belastungsspannung** *f* ELEKTROTECH on-load voltage; **Belastungsspitze** *f* ELEKTROTECH peak load; **Belastungsspule** *f* PHYS loading coil; **Belastungstal** *nt* ELEKTROTECH off-peak load; **Belastungsveränderungsmuster** *nt* RAUMFAHRT *Raumschiff* load fluctuation pattern; **Belastungswert** *m* ANSTRICH strain rate; **Belastungswiderstand** *m* ELEKTROTECH, PHYS load resistance, TELEKOM load impedance
belatten *vt* BAU *Wand* lath
Belebtschlamm *m* ABFALL, UMWELTSCHMUTZ activated sludge, WASSERVERSORG mixed liquor; **Belebtschlammanlage** *f* ABFALL activated sludge plant; **Belebtschlammbecken** *nt* ABFALL activated sludge tank, aeration tank; **Belebtschlammverfahren** *nt* ABFALL activated sludge process
Belebungsbecken *nt* WASSERVERSORG aeration basin
Beleg *m* COMP & DV document; **Belegbearbeitung** *f* COMP & DV document processing
belegen *vt* BAU *Gebäude* occupy, *mit Fliesen* tile, FERTIG *Schleifmittel* charge, coat, WASSERTRANS *Tauwerk* belay
Beleg: **Belegklampe** *f* WASSERTRANS *Deckausrüstung* belaying cleat, cleat; **Beleglesen** *nt* COMP & DV document reading; **Belegleser** *m* COMP & DV document reader, mark reader; **Belegmuster** *nt* QUAL known-good device; **Belegnagel** *m* WASSERTRANS *Deckausrüstung* belaying pin; **Belegsortierer** *m* COMP & DV document sorter
Belegung *f* COMP & DV load, FERTIG *Schleifscheibe* charging, KÜNSTL INT *einer Variablen* binding, TELEKOM seizure; ~ des Spektrums *f* TELEKOM spectral occupancy; **Belegungsdauer** *f* TELEKOM holding time; **Belegungsdetektor** *m* TRANS occupancy detector; **Belegungsrate** *f* TRANS occupancy rate; **Belegungsschleife** *f* TRANS presence loop; **Belegungsversuch** *m* TELEKOM bid; **Belegungszeit** *f* TELEKOM holding time
Beleg: **Belegwiederherstellung** *f* COMP & DV document recovery
beleuchtet[1] *adj* PHYS irradiated
beleuchtet:[2] ~e Einstellscheibe *f* FOTO illuminated dial
Beleuchtung *f* KFZTECH light, METALL illumination, PHYS illuminance, irradiance; **Beleuchtungs- und Bildregieraum** *m* FERNSEH lighting and vision control room; **Beleuchtungsanlage** *f* ELEKTROTECH lighting system; **Beleuchtungsausrüstung** *f* FOTO lighting equipment; **Beleuchtungsdämpferabdeckung** *f* LUFTTRANS dimmer cap; **Beleuchtungsglas** *nt* KER & GLAS lighting glass; **Beleuchtungskabel** *nt* ELEKTROTECH light cable; **Beleuchtungskörper** *m* ELEKTROTECH light fitting, HEIZ & KÄLTE light fitting, light fixture; **Beleuchtungsnetzschaltung** *f* ELEKTRIZ lighting circuit; **Beleuchtungsöffnung** *f* MECHAN lightening hole; **Beleuchtungsstärke** *f* ELEKTRIZ illumination, intensity of illumination, ELEKTROTECH *Lichtstromstärke* illumination, ERGON illuminance, illumination, PHYS brightness, TELEKOM *Quotient* irradiance; **Beleuchtungsstärkemesser** *m* METROL footcandle meter; **Beleuchtungsstärkemeßgerät** *nt* GERÄT luxmeter; **Beleuchtungsstativ** *nt* FOTO lighting stand; **Beleuchtungstärke** *f* STRAHLPHYS brightness
belichten *vt* FOTO *Emulsion* expose
Belichtung *f* DRUCK exposure, PHYS exposure, light exposure; **Belichtungsanlage** *f* DRUCK exposure unit; **Belichtungsapparat** *m* LABOR illuminating apparatus; **Belichtungsautomat** *m* GERÄT automatic exposure timer; **Belichtungsautomatik** *f* FOTO automatic exposure, automatic timer, exposure timer; **Belichtungsfaktor** *m* FOTO exposure factor; **Belichtungsmesser** *m* FOTO light meter, *mit Nachführsystem* exposure meter, PHYS exposure meter, light meter; **Belichtungsmesserskale** *f* FOTO light meter scale; **Belichtungsmessersonde** *f* FOTO light meter probe; **Belichtungsmeßzelle** *f* FOTO light meter cell; **Belichtungsschaltuhr** *f* FOTO darkroom timer; **Belichtungsspielraum** *m* FOTO exposure latitude; **Belichtungsstärke** *f* PHYS exposure rate; **Belichtungstabelle** *f* FOTO exposure-calculating chart, *am Apparat* exposure scale; **Belichtungszeit** *f* FOTO exposure time; **Belichtungszeitautomat** *m* GERÄT automatic exposure timer
beliebig: ~ verstellbar *adj* MASCHINEN adjustable at will
Belleville-Feder *f* MASCHINEN Belleville spring
Belsazzar *m* KER & GLAS belshazzar
Beltramiströmungen *f pl* STRÖMPHYS Beltrami flows
belüften *vt* BAU aerate, ventilate, vent, HEIZ & KÄLTE ventilate, MASCHINEN vent, SICHERHEIT *Werkstatt* air, THERMOD ventilate
Belüfter *m* ABFALL aerator, CHEMTECH *Druckbelüftung* diffuser
belüftet[1] *adj* HEIZ & KÄLTE, THERMOD ventilated
belüftet:[2] ~er Bohrschlamm *m* ERDÖL *Bohrtechnik* aera-

ted mud; **~er Propeller** *m* LUFTTRANS, WASSERTRANS ventilated propeller; **~e Wasserlamelle** *f* WASSERVERSORG ventilated nappe

Belüftung *f* ABFALL bio-aeration, BAU aeration, airing, HEIZ & KÄLTE, KFZTECH, MASCHINEN, THERMOD ventilation, VERPACK aeration, WASSERTRANS ventilation; **Belüftungsart** *f* HEIZ & KÄLTE method of ventilation; **Belüftungsbecken** *nt* ABFALL activated sludge tank, aeration tank, WASSERVERSORG aeration basin; **Belüftungsbehälter** *m* WASSERVERSORG aeration basin; **Belüftungseinrichtung** *f* LUFTTRANS aerator; **Belüftungshaube** *f* LUFTTRANS air scoop; **Belüftungshaubenabdeckung für Seitenflosse** *f* LUFTTRANS blanking cover for fin air scoop; **Belüftungsklappe** *f* MASCHINEN louver (AmE), louvre (BrE); **Belüftungsloch** *nt* MASCHINEN vent hole; **Belüftungsstörung** *f* HEIZ & KÄLTE ventilation breakdown; **Belüftungsventil** *nt* HEIZ & KÄLTE, MASCHINEN ventilation valve; **Belüftungsweg** *m* HEIZ & KÄLTE ventilating passage

bemannen *vt* WASSERTRANS *Besatzung* man

bemannt: **~es Amt** *nt* TELEKOM manned exchange; **~e Arbeitsstation** *f* RAUMFAHRT manned workshop; **~es Fahrzeug** *nt* RAUMFAHRT manned maneuvering unit (AmE), manned manoeuvring unit (BrE); **~er Flug** *m* RAUMFAHRT manned flight; **~er Hubschrauber** *m* LUFTTRANS manned helicopter; **~er Orbitalflug** *m* RAUMFAHRT *auf Umlaufbahnen* manned orbital space flight; **~es Orbitallabor** *nt* RAUMFAHRT MOL, manned orbiting laboratory; **~e Weltraumforschung** *f* RAUMFAHRT manned space research

Bemannung *f* WASSERTRANS manning

Bemaßen *nt* COMP & DV *CAD* dimensioning

bemaßen *f* COMP & DV *Konstruktionszeichnung mit Bemaßungen versehen* dimension

bemaßt: **~e Darstellung** *f* KONSTZEICH dimension representation, dimensioned representation

Bemaßung *f* MASCHINEN dimensioning

Bemerkung *f* COMP & DV comment

bemessen *vt* BAU batch, design, rate, size

Bemessung *f* HEIZ & KÄLTE design; **Bemessungsdaten für Wasserkühlung** *nt pl* HEIZ & KÄLTE water-cooled rating; **Bemessungstemperatur** *f* HEIZ & KÄLTE design temperature; **Bemessungsverkehrsstärke** *f* TRANS design volume

Bemusterung *f* FERTIG *Kunststoffinstallationen* sample molding (AmE), sample moulding (BrE)

benachbart: **~e Schicht** *f* METALL neighboring layer (AmE), neighbouring layer (BrE), neighboring stratum (AmE), neighbouring stratum

Benachrichtigung *f* MEERSCHMUTZ notification

Benadelung *f* METALL pinning

Bendix-® *pref* KFZTECH Bendix®, Bendix-type; **Bendixanlasser** *m* KFZTECH Bendix-type starter, *Motor* Bendix starter; **Bendixantrieb** *m* KFZTECH Bendixtype starter

benennen *vt* COMP & DV declare

Benennung *f* PATENT *eines Vertragsstaates* designation

benetzbar: **nicht ~** *adj* CHEMIE hydrophobic

Benetzbarkeit *f* KUNSTSTOFF wettability

Benetzen *nt* MASCHINEN wetting

benetzen *vt* PHYS, THERMOD wet

benetzt: **~e Oberfläche** *f* WASSERTRANS *Schiffkonstruktion* wetted surface

Benetzungsmittel *nt* ANSTRICH surfactant, KER & GLAS, KUNSTSTOFF, MASCHINEN, MEERSCHMUTZ wetting

agent

Benioff-Zone *f* NICHTFOSS ENERG Benioff zone

benötigt: **~e Startabbruchstrecke** *f* LUFTTRANS accelerate-stop distance required; **~e Startstrecke** *f* LUFTTRANS takeoff distance required; **~e Zeit von einem Gate zum anderen** *f* LUFTTRANS ramp-to-ramp time

Bentonit *m* ERDÖL *Bohrtechnik*, FERTIG, KOHLEN bentonite

Benummerung *f* DRUCK numbering

Benutzen *nt* COMP & DV use

benutzen *vt* COMP & DV use

Benutzer *m* COMP & DV user, KONTROLL operator, TELEKOM user; **Benutzerabfrage** *f* COMP & DV user query; **Benutzerattribut** *nt* COMP & DV user attribute; **Benutzerberechtigung** *f* COMP & DV user authorization; **Benutzerbereich** *m* COMP & DV user area; **Benutzerdaten** *nt pl* COMP & DV user data

benutzerdefiniert[1] *adj* COMP & DV user-defined

benutzerdefiniert:[2] **~e Systemumgebung** *f* COMP & DV user environment, user-operating environment

benutzerfreundlich *adj* COMP & DV user-friendly

Benutzer: **Benutzerführung** *f* COMP & DV prompt, TELEKOM user guide; **Benutzerführung mittels Hinweiszeichen an Promptausgabe** *f* KONTROLL prompting; **Benutzergruppe** *f* COMP & DV user group; **Benutzerhandbuch** *nt* COMP & DV user manual; **Benutzerkennzeichen** *nt* COMP & DV user ID; **Benutzerklasse** *f* COMP & DV access category, TELEKOM class of service; **Benutzermenü** *nt* COMP & DV user menu; **Benutzername** *m* COMP & DV user name; **Benutzeroberfläche** *f* COMP & DV user interface; **Benutzerprogramm** *nt* COMP & DV user program; **Benutzerschnittstelle** *f* COMP & DV, TELEKOM user interface; **Benutzerzugang** *m* TELEKOM user access; **Benutzerzugriffsmodus** *m* COMP & DV user access mode

Benutzung: **~ von Schutzgas** *f* KERNTECH inert gas blanketing; **Benutzungsbeweis** *m* PATENT evidence of use; **Benutzungsdauer** *f* QUAL operating time; **Benutzungsgrad** *m* TRANS degree of utilization

Benzal *nt* CHEMIE benzal; **Benzalacetophenon** *nt* CHEMIE chalcone; **Benzaldehyd** *m* CHEMIE benzaldehyde; **Benzaldoxim** *nt* CHEMIE benzaldehyde oxime, benzaldoxime

Benzamid *nt* CHEMIE benzamide

Benzanilid *nt* CHEMIE benzanilide

Benzen *nt* CHEMIE benzene

Benzidin *nt* CHEMIE benzidine

Benzil *nt* CHEMIE benzil

Benzin *nt* CHEMIE *für technische Zwecke oder als Reformingstock* benzin, naphtha, ERDÖL *Destillationsprodukt* gas (AmE), gasoline (AmE), petrol (BrE), KFZTECH fuel, gas (AmE), gasoline (AmE), petrol (BrE), THERMOD gas (AmE), gasoline (AmE), petrol (BrE), TRANS motor spirit; **~ mit geringem Bleigehalt** *nt* KFZTECH low-lead gasoline (AmE), low-lead petrol (BrE)

benzin- und ölbeständiger Schlauch *m* KUNSTSTOFF gas-and-oil-resisting hose (AmE), gasoline-and-oil-resisting hose (AmE), petrol-and-oil-resisting hose (BrE)

Benzin: **Benzinbeständigkeit** *f* KUNSTSTOFF gas resistance (AmE), gasoline resistance (AmE), petrol resistance (BrE); **Benzindampfrückgewinnungsanlage** *f* UMWELTSCHMUTZ gas vapor recovery plant (AmE), gasoline vapor recovery plant (AmE), petrol vapour recovery plant (BrE); **Benzinfilter** *nt* KFZTECH *Kraftstoff* gas filter (AmE), gasoline filter (AmE), petrol filter (BrE); **Benzingemisch** *nt* KFZTECH *Zweitaktmotor* gas mixture (AmE), gasoline mixture (AmE), petrol mixture (BrE); **Benzingewinnung** *f* ERDÖL *aus Raffinerierohgas, Erdgas* recovery of gasoline (AmE), recovery of petrol (BrE); **Benzingsicherung** *f* MASCHINEN circlip; **Benzingsicherungsring** *m* MASCHINEN circlip; **Benzinkanister** *m* TRANS jerry can; **Benzinleitung** *f* KFZTECH *Kraftstoff* fuel line; **Benzinmotor** *m* KFZTECH gas motor (AmE), gasoline motor (AmE), petrol motor (BrE), *Motor* gas engine (AmE), gasoline engine (AmE), petrol engine (BrE), THERMOD, WASSERTRANS *Verbrennungsmotor* gas engine (AmE), gasoline engine (AmE), petrol engine (BrE); **Benzinpumpe** *f* KFZTECH *Kraftstoff* fuel pump, gas pump (AmE), gasoline pump (AmE), petrol pump (BrE); **Benzinschlauch** *m* KFZTECH, KUNSTSTOFF gas hose (AmE), gasoline hose (AmE), petrol hose (BrE); **Benzintank** *m* KFZTECH fuel tank, *Kraftstoff* gas tank (AmE), gasoline tank (AmE), petrol tank (BrE); **Benzinuhr** *f* KFZTECH fuel gage (AmE), fuel gauge (BrE), fuel indicator; **Benzinverbrauch** *m* KFZTECH *Motor* gas consumption (AmE), gasoline consumption (AmE), petrol consumption (BrE)

Benzo- *pref* CHEMIE benzo-; **Benzoat** *nt* CHEMIE benzoate; **Benzocarbonitril** *nt* CHEMIE benzocarbonitrile, benzonitrile; **Benzochinolin** *nt* CHEMIE phenanthridine; **Benzochinon** *nt* CHEMIE benzoquinone, quinone; **Benzocyclopentadien** *nt* CHEMIE indene; **benzoehaltig** *adj* CHEMIE benzoic; **Benzoesäure** *f* LEBENSMITTEL benzoic acid; **Benzoesäuresalz** *nt* CHEMIE benzoate; **benzoid** *adj* CHEMIE benzenoid; **Benzoin** *nt* CHEMIE benzoin; **Benzol** *nt* CHEMIE, ERDÖL *Petrochemie*, FERTIG benzene; **Benzolhexachlorid** *nt* LEBENSMITTEL benzene hexachloride; **Benzoldiol** *nt* CHEMIE hydroquinone, quinol; **Benzo-**: **Benzonaphthol** *nt* CHEMIE benzonaphthol; **Benzonitril** *nt* CHEMIE benzonitrile; **Benzophenanthren** *nt* CHEMIE chrysene; **Benzophenon** *nt* CHEMIE benzophenone; **Benzopyrazin** *nt* CHEMIE quinoxaline; **Benzopyren** *nt* CHEMIE benzopyrene; **Benzopyridin** *nt* CHEMIE benzopyridine, quinoline; **Benzothiophen** *nt* CHEMIE benzothiophene, thionaphthene; **Benzoylbenzol** *nt* CHEMIE benzophenone; **Benzoylperoxid** *nt* KUNSTSTOFF, LEBENSMITTEL benzoyl peroxide; **Benzoylsalicin** *nt* CHEMIE benzoylsalicin, populin; **Benzoylsulfonimid** *nt* CHEMIE saccharin

Benzyl *nt* CHEMIE benzyl; **Benzylalkohol** *m* CHEMIE benzyl alcohol, phenylcarbinol; **Benzylcinnamat** *nt* LEBENSMITTEL benzyl cinnamate; **Benzyliden** *nt* CHEMIE benzylidene; **Benzylzellulose** *f* FERTIG benzyl cellulose

Beobachterfehler *m* GERÄT personal error

beobachtet: **~e Bestandsperzentile** *f* QUAL observed percentile life; **~e Schwelle** *f* KERNTECH *einer Kernreaktion* observed threshold; **~er Standort** *m* WASSERTRANS *Navigation* observed position

Beobachtung *f* QUAL surveillance; **~ durch Radarsonde** *f* LUFTTRANS radarsonde observation; **Beobachtungsbrunnen** *m* ABFALL monitoring well, observation well, WASSERVERSORG observation well; **Beobachtungsgröße** *f* ELEKTRONIK measurand; **Beobachtungskammer** *f* ERDÖL *Tauchtechnik* obser-

vation chamber; **Beobachtungspunkt** *m* ERGON point of observation; **Beobachtungsraster** *m* KERNTECH observation grid; **Beobachtungssatellit** *m* RAUMFAHRT observation satellite; **Beobachtungswert** *m* GERÄT, QUAL observed value

BEPC *abbr* (*Beijing Electron Positron Collider*) TEILPHYS BEPC (*Beijing Electron Positron Collider*)

Beplankung *f* BAU veneering

beplatten *vt* WASSERTRANS *Schiffbau* plate

Beplattung *f* WASSERTRANS *Schiffbau* plating

Beprobung *f* WASSERVERSORG sampling

BER *abbr* (*Bitfehlerquote, Bitfehlerrate*) COMP & DV BER (*bit error rate*)

Berandung *f* STRÖMPHYS boundary wall

Beratungssystem *nt* KÜNSTL INT advisory system

berechenbar: **~er Kondensator** *m* PHYS calculable capacitor

berechnen *vt* BAU design, MATH calculate, MECHAN design

Berechnung *f* BAU design, COMP & DV, LUFTTRANS *Schwerpunkt* computation, MATH calculation, computation; **Berechnungsdruck** *m* HEIZ & KÄLTE design pressure; **Berechnungstemperatur** *f* HEIZ & KÄLTE design temperature

Berechtigung *f* COMP & DV authorization, clearance, privilege; **~ zu IFR-Flügen** *f* LUFTTRANS instrument rating; **Berechtigungsebene** *f* COMP & DV clearance level

Bereich *m* AKUSTIK band, ANSTRICH, BAU area, COMP & DV area, range, array, ELEKTRONIK domain, range, GERÄT range, KÜNSTL INT *des Wissens* domain, PAPIER range, PHYS domain, RADIO, WASSERTRANS range; **~ mit angehobenem Nullpunkt** *m* REGELUNG elevated-zero range; **~ eines Fernamts** *m* TELEKOM trunk switching exchange area; **~ niedriger Ausbeute** *m* ELEKTRONIK low-yield region; **~ der Nockenbahn ohne Berühren des Stößels** *m* MECHAN dwell; **~ der Überstreichung** *m* FERTIG coverage; **Bereichsänderung** *f* GERÄT change in range; **Bereichsaufspaltung** *f* REGELUNG signal amplitude sequencing control, split ranging; **Bereichschalter** *m* ELEKTRIZ scale switch, ELEKTROTECH selector switch; **Bereichsentstörungsfilter** *nt* COMP & DV band-rejection filter; **Bereichskennzahl** *f* TELEKOM area code; **Bereichsmodell** *nt* TELEKOM compartmental model; **Bereichssperrfilter** *nt* COMP & DV band-stop filter; **Bereichsstruktur** *f* METALL domain structure; **Bereichsumschaltung** *f* FERNSEH waveband switching, GERÄT automatic ranging; **Bereichsunterdrückung** *f* GERÄT suppression of range; **Bereichsunterschreitung** *f* COMP & DV underflow; **Bereichsverhältnis** *nt* REGELUNG rangeability; **Bereichswahl** *f* GERÄT automatic ranging; **Bereichswähler** *m* GERÄT range selector

bereifen *vt* MECHAN hoop

bereinigen *vt* COMP & DV debug

bereit *adj* COMP & DV ready

Bereitschaft *f* COMP & DV, MEERSCHMUTZ stand-by, RAUMFAHRT availability; **Bereitschaftsaggregat** *nt* ELEKTROTECH stand-by set; **Bereitschaftsbetrieb** *m* KONTROLL stand-by, stand-by mode, TELEKOM stand-by working; **Bereitschaftsdienst** *m* MEERSCHMUTZ stand-by; **Bereitschaftsgerät** *nt* ELEKTROTECH stand-by unit; **Bereitschaftsstellung** *f* ELEKTROTECH on position; **Bereitschaftszeit** *f* COMP & DV stand-by time

Bereitstellung *f* TELEKOM provision

Bereitzustand *m* COMP & DV ready state

Berg *m* KOHLEN hill; **Bergarbeiter** *m* KOHLEN miner; **Bergbau** *m* KOHLEN mining; **Bergbauberechtigung** *f* ERDÖL *Recht* mineral rights; **Bergbauproduktion** *f* KOHLEN mine yield

Bergelohn *m* TRANS salvage money

bergen *vt* WASSERTRANS salvage

Berg: **Bergklein** *nt* KOHLEN refuse; **Berglandwirtschaft** *f* LEBENSMITTEL hill farming

bergmännisch: ~ **hergestellter Hohlraum** *m* ABFALL mined space

Berg: **Bergmittel** *nt* KOHLEN stone band; **Bergreinigerzelle** *f* KOHLEN scavenger cell; **Bergrutsch** *m* TRANS landslide, landslip; **Bergteich** *m* KOHLEN tailing pond

Bergung *f* LUFTTRANS *Flugmanöver* recovery, rescue, RAUMFAHRT *Raumschiff* recovery, WASSERTRANS recovery, salvage, *Notfall* rescue; **Bergungskran** *m* KFZTECH salvage crane; **Bergungspaket** *nt* RAUMFAHRT *Raumschiff* recovery package; **Bergungsschiff** *nt* WASSERTRANS salvage vessel, wrecker; **Bergungsschlepper** *m* TRANS, WASSERTRANS salvage tug

Beriberi *f* LEBENSMITTEL beriberi

Bericht *m* COMP & DV report

berichtigt: ~**e angezeigte Eigengeschwindigkeit** *f* LUFTTRANS *Flugwesen* calibrated airspeed; ~**e angezeigte Flugmindestgeschwindigkeit** *f* LUFTTRANS *bei normaler Luftströmung* minimum calibrated speed in flight time; **nicht** ~**e Eigengeschwindigkeit** *f* LUFTTRANS indicated airspeed

Bericht: **Berichtigung** *f* COMP & DV upgrade, PATENT correction; **Berichtigung der Anzeige der rufenden Nummer** *f* TELEKOM CLIR, calling line identification rectification; **Berichtigungsfaktor** *m* LUFTTRANS *Auftriebswiderstand* correction factor; **Berichterstellung** *f* COMP & DV report generation

Berieselung *f* CHEMTECH scrubbing, WASSERVERSORG border irrigation, irrigation; **Berieselungskanal** *m* WASSERVERSORG catch-feeder; **Berieselungskanone** *f* ELEKTRONIK flooding gun; **Berieselungskühler** *m* HEIZ & KÄLTE spray cooler; **Berieselungsturm** *m* CHEMTECH scrubber, washing column

Berkelium *nt (Bk)* CHEMIE berkelium *(Bk)*

Berme *f* ABFALL segregation berm, BAU berm, EISENBAHN bank, KOHLEN berm, WASSERVERSORG offset

Bern: ~**er Vierkantschlüssel** *m* EISENBAHN Berne key

Bernoulli: ~**sche Gleichung** *f* PHYS *Geschwindigkeits-und Druckänderungen entlang Stromlinie*, STRÖMPHYS Bernoulli's equation; ~**sches Theorem** *f* PHYS, STRÖMPHYS Bernoulli's theorem

Berst- *pref* KUNSTSTOFF, PAPIER, TEXTIL, VERPACK bursting; **Berstdruck** *m* FERTIG *Kunststoffinstallationen*, KER & GLAS, PAPIER, VERPACK bursting pressure

Bersten *nt* PAPIER burst

bersten *vt* BAU, PAPIER burst, THERMOD detonate

Berst-: **Berstfestigkeit** *f* KUNSTSTOFF, PAPIER, TEXTIL, VERPACK bursting strength; **Berstfestigkeitsprüfer** *m* PAPIER bursting-strength tester; **Berstindex** *m* PAPIER burst ratio; **Berstscheibe** *f* MASCHINEN, MECHAN bursting disc (BrE), bursting disk (AmE)

Beruf *m* ERGON vocation, TRANS business

berufen *vt* QUAL appoint

berufsbedingt: ~**e Belastungsgrenzen** *f pl* SICHERHEIT *Gesundheitsgefährdung* occupational exposure limits; ~**e Lärmbelastung** *f* SICHERHEIT occupational noise exposure; ~**e Taubheit** *f* AKUSTIK professional deafness

Beruf: **Berufseignungstest** *m* ERGON vocational aptitude test; **Berufsverkehr** *m* TRANS business traffic, home-to-work traffic

beruhigen *vt* FERTIG *Stahl* quiet, *Walzen* kill, METALL kill

beruhigt[1] *adj* FERTIG *Stahl* dead, *Walzen* killed; ~ **vergossen** *adj* FERTIG *Stahl* solid

beruhigt:[2] ~**er Stahl** *m* METALL killed steel

Beruhigung *f* FERTIG *Stahl* quieting; **Beruhigungskammer** *f* ABFALL settling chamber; **Beruhigungszeit** *f* GERÄT damping period, transient time, transition time, METROL *Meßinstrument* response time

berührend: ~**er Fühler** *m* GERÄT contact sensor; ~**er Sensor** *m* GERÄT contact sensor

Berührung *f* GEOM tangency; **Berührungsbogen** *m* FERTIG *Schleifscheibe* arc of conduct; **Berührungseingabe** *f* KONTROLL touch input

berührungsempfindlich: ~**er Bildschirm** *m* COMP & DV touch screen, touch-sensitive screen; ~**er Klebstoff mit hoher Klebfestigkeit** *m* VERPACK high-tack pressure-sensitive adhesive

Berührung: **Berührungsfläche** *f* MASCHINEN contact area, surface of contact

berührungsfrei[1] *adj* ELEKTRIZ contactless, noncontact

berührungsfrei:[2] ~**er Abnehmer** *m* ELEKTRIZ contactless pick-up; ~**e Dichtung** *f* MASCHINEN noncontacting seal; ~**es Trägerfahrzeug** *nt* KFZTECH contactless support vehicle

Berührung: **Berührungsfühler** *m* GERÄT contact sensor; **Berührungslinie** *f* GEOM tangent, MASCHINEN line of contact, MATH tangent

berührungslos: ~**es Oberflächenthermometer** *nt* GERÄT contactless surface thermometer

Berührung: **Berührungsmeßgerät** *nt* GERÄT contact-measuring instrument; **Berührungsmeßkopf** *m* GERÄT contact head; **Berührungspunkt** *m* GEOM point of tangency, PHYS point of contact; **Berührungsschalter** *m* ELEKTRIZ touch contact switch, ELEKTROTECH, KONTROLL touch switch; **Berührungssensor** *m* GERÄT tactile sensor, touch sensor, GERÄT contact sensor

berührungssicher: ~**e Buchse** *f* ELEKTRIZ shockproof socket; ~**e Steckverbindung** *f* ELEKTRIZ shockproof socket

Berührung: **Berührungsspannung** *f* ELEKTRIZ shock hazard voltage; **Berührungstaste** *f* GERÄT touching key; **Berührungsthermometer** *nt* GERÄT contact thermometer, surface temperature sensor

Beryll *m* KER & GLAS beryl; **Beryllerde** *f* KER & GLAS beryllia

Beryllium *nt (Be)* CHEMIE beryllium *(Be)*

berylliummoderiert: ~**er Reaktor** *m* KERNTECH beryllium-moderated reactor

Besan *m* WASSERTRANS *Segeln* mizzen

Besanden *nt* KER & GLAS sanding

besänftigen *vt* ANSTRICH *Legierungen* temper

Besanmast *m* WASSERTRANS *Segeln* mizzen mast

Besatz *m* LEBENSMITTEL dockage, TEXTIL trimming; **Besatztuch** *nt* TEXTIL facing

Besatzung *f* LUFTTRANS, WASSERTRANS crew; **Besatzungskabine** *f* LUFTTRANS crew compartment, flight deck; **Besatzungsraum** *m* LUFTTRANS cockpit

Besäum- *pref* BAU, FERTIG edging, squaring

Besäumen *nt* BAU *Holz* squaring, FERTIG *Holz* edging

besäumen *vt* BAU *Holz* trim

Besäum-: **Besäumkreissäge** *f* FERTIG edger; **Besäummaschine** *f* MASCHINEN trimmer

besäumt *adj* BAU *Holz* square-edged

beschädigt[1] *adj* KERNTECH *Brennstab* defective, TELE-KOM damaged

beschädigt:[2] **~es Brennelement** *nt* KERNTECH damaged fuel assembly; **~es Garn** *nt* KER & GLAS damaged yarn; **~er Wagen** *m* EISENBAHN damaged car (AmE), damaged wagon (BrE)

Beschädigung *f* FERTIG scoring

Beschaffung *f* BAU procurement; **Beschaffungsspezifikation** *f* RAUMFAHRT *Raumschiff* procurement specifications

Beschaufelung *f* MASCHINEN blades, MECHAN blading

Bescheid *m* TELEKOM interception; **Bescheidansage** *f* TELEKOM intercept announcer; **Bescheiddienst** *m* TELEKOM changed-number interception

bescheinigt: ~er Werkstoff-Prüfbericht *m* QUAL CMTR, certified material test report

Bescheinigung *f* PATENT certificate

Beschichten *nt* ANSTRICH plating, KUNSTSTOFF coating, PHYS cladding, VERPACK *mit Kunststoff* coating

beschichten *vt* BAU coat, overcoat, *Material* surface, KUNSTSTOFF, LEBENSMITTEL coat; **neu ~** *vt* ANSTRICH recoat

beschichtet[1] *adj* FERTIG *Kunststoffinstallationen* coated

beschichtet:[2] **~es Band** *nt* ANSTRICH film; **nicht ~es Brennstoffteilchen** *nt* KERNTECH uncoated fuel particle; **~es Gewebe** *nt* KUNSTSTOFF coated fabric; **~es Klebeband** *nt* VERPACK self-adhesive laminated tape; **~es Kunstdruckpapier** *nt* VERPACK coated synthetic paper; **~e Packung** *f* VERPACK laminated pack

Beschichtung *f* BAU coating, OPTIK sheath, PHYS, TEXTIL coating, VERPACK enameling (AmE), enamelling (BrE); **Beschichtungsmaschine** *f* KUNSTSTOFF coating machine; **Beschichtungssystem** *nt* ANSTRICH coating system; **Beschichtungsverfahren** *nt* ANSTRICH coating process

Beschicken *nt* KER & GLAS *mit einem Löffel* ladling, TEXTIL feeding

beschicken *vt* TRANS fill

Beschicktür *f* FERTIG charging door

Beschickung *f* FERTIG *Hochofen* round, KERNTECH *während des Betriebs* supply, MASCHINEN loading, TEXTIL batch; **~ bei abgeschalteter Last** *f* KERNTECH off-load charging; **~ unter Last** *f* KERNTECH on-load charging, on-load fueling (AmE), on-load fuelling (BrE), on-load refueling (AmE), on-load refuelling (BrE); **Beschickungsarmatur** *f* ERDÖL feed tank; **Beschickungseinrichtung** *f* ABFALL charging facility, loading mechanism, FERTIG loading device; **Beschickungskammer** *f* ABFALL *Atommüllagerung* charging chamber; **Beschickungskopf** *m* KERNTECH feeder head; **Beschickungsmaschine** *f* VERPACK *für Kästen* case loader; **Beschickungsrohr** *nt* KERNTECH feeder pipe; **Beschickungsseite** *f* KERNTECH *eines Reaktors* reactor charging face; **Beschickungstisch** *m* VERPACK feeding table; **Beschickungstrichter** *m* FERTIG hopper, MECHAN feed hopper; **Beschickungstür** *f* FERTIG charging door; **Beschickungsventil** *nt* ERDÖL feed valve; **Beschickungsverfahren** *nt* KERNTECH feeding process; **Beschickungsverriegelung** *f* KERNTECH *bei kugelförmigen Brennelementen* feeder lock; **Beschickungszone** *f* KERNTECH charge area

Beschlag *m* KER & GLAS *Fleck* bloom, MECHAN ferrule, plate

beschlagen *vt* FERTIG clout

Beschlagnahme *f* WASSERTRANS arrest

beschleunigen *vti* PAPIER, PHYS accelerate, speed up

beschleunigend[1] *adj* PAPIER accelerant, accelerative

beschleunigend:[2] **~e Kraft** *f* PHYS accelerating force

Beschleuniger *m* BAU, CHEMTECH accelerator, ELEKTROTECH accelerator, activator, KUNSTSTOFF, LEBENSMITTEL, MECHAN, PAPIER, TEILPHYS accelerator, WASSERTRANS *Bootbau* accelerator, *im Kunststoffbootbau* catalyst; **Beschleunigerdüse** *f* KFZTECH *Vergaser* accelerator jet; **Beschleuniger-Hohlraumresonator** *m* TEILPHYS accelerator cavity; **Beschleunigerpumpe** *f* KFZTECH accelerating pump, *Vergaser* accelerator pump

beschleunigt[1] *adj* PHYS accelerated

beschleunigt:[2] **~er Abschaltstab** *m* KERNTECH accelerated scram rod; **~e Bewegung** *f* MECHAN accelerated motion; **~e Filtration** *f* CHEMTECH accelerated filtration; **~e Kommutation** *f* ELEKTRIZ accelerated commutation; **~e Kompostierung** *f* ABFALL accelerated composting, mechanical composting, rapid fermentation; **~es Kriechen** *nt* METALL accelerated creep; **~e Lebensdauerprüfung** *f* GERÄT accelerated life test; **~er Leichtwasserreaktor** *m* KERNTECH accelerator-driven light-water reactor; **~e Leitwegumlenkung** *f* TELEKOM forced rerouting; **~e Prüfung** *f* QUAL accelerated test, WERKPRÜF accelerated testing; **~er Salzschmelzenbrüter** *m* KERNTECH accelerator molten-salt breeder; **~er Test** *m* MASCHINEN accelerated test

Beschleunigung *f* KFZTECH acceleration, KONTROLL speed-up, PAPIER acceleration; **Beschleunigungsabbruch** *m* KFZTECH acceleration stop; **Beschleunigungsabbruchstrecke** *f* KFZTECH accelerate-stop distance; **Beschleunigungsanode** *f* ELEKTROTECH accelerating anode, second anode, STRAHLPHYS accelerating anode; **Beschleunigungsanzeiger** *m* LUFTTRANS acceleration detector; **Beschleunigungsaufnehmer** *m* ERGON acceleration pick-up, HEIZ & KÄLTE acceleration sensor; **Beschleunigungsbelastung** *f* RAUMFAHRT *Raumschiff* G-force; **Beschleunigungsdüse** *f* KFZTECH acceleration jet; **Beschleunigungselektrode** *f* KERNTECH, STRAHLPHYS accelerating electrode, TELEKOM accelerator; **Beschleunigungskammer** *f* KERNTECH accelerating chamber; **Beschleunigungskraft** *f* ERGON acceleration force; **Beschleunigungsleistung** *f* KFZTECH accelerating power; **Beschleunigungsmesser** *m* ELEKTROTECH, ERGON, LUFTTRANS, MECHAN accelerometer; **Beschleunigungsmeßgerät** *nt* GERÄT, PAPIER, PHYS accelerometer; **Beschleunigungsrakete** *f* RAUMFAHRT *zum Treibstoffsammeln* acceleration rocket; **Beschleunigungsreiais** *nt* ELEKTRIZ acceleration relay; **Beschleunigungsröhre** *f* CHEMTECH accelerating tube; **Beschleunigungsschreiber** *m* GERÄT accelerograph; **Beschleunigungssensor** *m* GERÄT acceleration pick-up; **Beschleunigungsspannung** *f* ELEKTRIZ, ELEKTROTECH accelerating voltage; **Beschleunigungsspur** *f* TRANS acceleration lane; **Beschleunigungssteuereinheit** *f* LUFTTRANS acceleration control unit; **Beschleunigungsvermögen** *nt* KFZTECH pick-up; **Beschleunigungsvorrichtung** *f* TRANS acceleration device; **Beschleunigungsweg** *m* KFZTECH acceleration distance; **Beschleunigungszeit** *f* COMP & DV, PAPIER acceleration time

Beschneidemaschine *f* MASCHINEN trimmer, trimming machine

Beschneiden *nt* FERNSEH cropping

beschneiden vt DRUCK cut, trim, ELEKTROTECH clip, PAPIER trim

Beschnitt m DRUCK trimming edge; **Beschnittbreite** f DRUCK trim width

beschnitten: ~es **Format** nt DRUCK trim size, trimmed size, VERPACK *Papier* trimmed size; ~e **Lichtpause** f KONSTZEICH trimmed blueprint sheet; ~e **Zeichnung** f KONSTZEICH trimmed drawing sheet

Beschnitt: **Beschnittmarken** f pl DRUCK trim marks; **Beschnittrand** m DRUCK trimmed edges, KONSTZEICH trimming edge

Beschottern nt BAU, TRANS macadamization

beschottern vt BAU gravel, *Tiefbau* metal

Beschränker m KONTROLL limiter

beschränkt[1] adj MATH limited

beschränkt:[2] ~**er Informationsübermittlungsdienst** m TELEKOM restricted information transfer service; ~**er Platz** m SICHERHEIT confined space; ~**er Übermittlungsdienst mit 64 kbit/s** m TELEKOM *ISDN* sixty-four kbps restricted bearer service

Beschränkung f KÜNSTL INT constraint, PHYS constringence; ~ **der Dämpfe** f SICHERHEIT control of exposure to fumes; ~ **der Giftigkeit** f SICHERHEIT *am Arbeitsplatz* control of toxicity

beschreibbar: ~e **CD** f OPTIK writable optical disk, OPTIK compact disc-interactive (BrE), compact disk-interactive (AmE); ~e **Scheibe** f OPTIK writable disk

beschreibend[1] adj PATENT descriptive

beschreibend:[2] ~es **Modell** nt ERGON descriptive model

Beschreiber m COMP & DV descriptor

Beschreibung f PATENT description; ~ **und Messung von Umweltlärm** f SICHERHEIT description and measurement of environmental noise

Beschreibzeit f ELEKTRONIK *Fotolack* writing time

beschrieben[1] adj ELEKTRONIK written-state

beschrieben:[2] ~e **Oberfläche** f COMP & DV *eines Datenträgers* recorded surface

Beschriften nt COMP & DV labeling (AmE), labelling (BrE)

Beschriftung f COMP & DV annotation, DRUCK, KER & GLAS *auf Gefäßboden* lettering, KONSTZEICH inscription, lettering; **Beschriftungsanlage** f VERPACK marking equipment; **Beschriftungsfeld** nt AKUSTIK label area; **Beschriftungsmaschine** f VERPACK marking machine

Beschwerde f PATENT appeal; **Beschwerdeschrift** f PATENT notice of appeal

Beseitigen nt MEERSCHMUTZ *von Öl* removal

beseitigen vt BAU *Mängel* cure

Beseitigung f BAU removal, KERNTECH *einer Reaktoranlage* decommissioning, MEERSCHMUTZ disposal, UMWELTSCHUTZ *von organischen Bestandteilen* removal, *von Schwebstoffen durch Sedimentablagerung* removal

besetzen vt TEXTIL face

Besetzt- pref COMP & DV, TELEKOM busy

besetzt: ~es **Band** nt PHYS *Festkörpermaterial* full band; ~e **Leitung** f KONTROLL busy line (AmE), engaged line (BrE); ~e **Rufnummer** f TELEKOM busy number (AmE), engaged tone (BrE); ~e **Signalleitung** f KONTROLL busy line (AmE), engaged line (BrE)

Besetzt-: **Besetztstatus** m TELEKOM busy status; **Besetztzeichen** nt COMP & DV busy signal (AmE), engaged signal (BrE); **Besetztzustand** m TELEKOM busy state

Besetzung f PHYS, STRAHLPHYS population; **Besetzungsdichte angeregter Atome** f STRAHLPHYS population density of excited atoms; **Besetzungsinversion** f PHYS population inversion; **Besetzungsumkehr** f STRAHLPHYS population inversion

Besichtigung f BAU surveying, MECHAN inspection, RAUMFAHRT *Raumschiff* walkaround inspection

besonder: ~e **Anforderungen** f pl MASCHINEN special requirements

Bespannung f PAPIER clothing

bespanten vt WASSERTRANS *Schiffbau* frame

Bespantung f WASSERTRANS *Schiffbau* timber

bespielt: ~es **Band** nt FERNSEH prerecorded tape

Besprechung f DRUCK review

Besprengen nt WASSERVERSORG sprinkling

besprengen vt WASSERVERSORG sprinkle

besprühen vt MEERSCHMUTZ, PAPIER spray

bespult: ~es **Kabel** nt TELEKOM loaded cable

Bespulung f ELEKTROTECH coil loading

Bessemer: **Bessemerbirne** f FERTIG acid Bessemer converter, acid converter, MASCHINEN Bessemer converter; **Bessemerroheisen** nt FERTIG acid Bessemer pig, acid pig; **Bessemerstahl** m FERTIG acid Bessemer steel, acid converter steel, MASCHINEN *(BS)* Bessemer steel *(BS)*, METALL basic Bessemer steel; **Bessemerverfahren** nt FERTIG acid Bessemer process, acid converter process

bessern: sich ~ v refl WASSERTRANS *Wetter* abate

Bestand m ANSTRICH residue, QUAL survivals

beständig adj KUNSTSTOFF lasting, resistant

Beständigkeit f ANSTRICH durability, KUNSTSTOFF durability, resistance, MASCHINEN durability, TEXTIL resistance; ~ **gegen Sonnenlicht** f KUNSTSTOFF sunlight resistance

Bestandteil m ANSTRICH component, KUNSTSTOFF, LEBENSMITTEL ingredient, MECHAN component

bestätigen vt COMP & DV, KERNTECH *Notabschaltung* acknowledge, RAUMFAHRT validate

Bestätigung f COMP & DV ACK, acknowledgement, authentication, verification, KONTROLL, MASCHINEN verification, QUAL certification, verification, TELEKOM ACK, acknowledgement

Bestäuben nt KER & GLAS dry spray

bestäuben vt LEBENSMITTEL dust, PAPIER powder

Besteck[1] nt BAU set of instruments

Besteck:[2] ~ **absetzen** vi WASSERTRANS *Navigation* plot the position

Besteckabsetzen nt WASSERTRANS *Navigation* plotting

Bestellerrisiko nt QUAL consumer's risk

Bestellung: auf ~ **angefertigt** adj VERPACK custom-made

Bestensuche f KÜNSTL INT best-first search

Best-First-Suche f KÜNSTL INT best-first search

bestimmt: ~es **Integral** nt MATH definite integral

Bestimmung f SICHERHEIT, THERMOD *des Wärmewertes* determination; ~ **über Höhenstaffelung in bestimmten Quadranten** f LUFTTRANS quadrantal height rule; **Bestimmungsamt** nt PATENT designated office; **Bestimmungspunkte** m pl GEOM control points

Bestmarke f COMP & DV benchmark

bestrahlt adj PHYS irradiated

Bestrahlung[1] f KUNSTSTOFF exposure to radiation, STRAHLPHYS, TEILPHYS irradiation, UMWELTSCHUTZ irradiation, radiation; ~ **mit Kobalt 60** f KERNTECH cobalt 60 gamma irradiation

Bestrahlung:[2] **etwas einer** ~ **aussetzen** vt PHYS expose to

radiation
Bestrahlung: Bestrahlungsdichte *f* NICHTFOSS ENERG irradiance; **Bestrahlungsdosis** *f* STRAHLPHYS *gemessen in Röntgen* exposure dose; **Bestrahlungsfolie** *f* STRAHLPHYS beam foil; **Bestrahlungsgeometrie** *f* KERNTECH geometry of irradiation; **Bestrahlungshärten** *nt* METALL irradiation hardening; **Bestrahlungskammer** *f* KERNTECH radiation chamber, STRAHLPHYS irradiation chamber; **Bestrahlungsreaktor** *m* KERNTECH radiation reactor; **Bestrahlungsrisiken** *nt pl* STRAHLPHYS exposure risks; **Bestrahlungsschaden** *m* KERNTECH radiation damage; **Bestrahlungsstärke** *f* OPTIK *(H)* irradiance *(H)*, PHYS exposure rate; **Bestrahlungsversuch innerhalb des Reaktors** *m* KERNTECH in-pile test
bestreichen *vt* ANSTRICH paint
Bestücken *nt* KERNTECH hard-facing
bestücken *vt* FERTIG *Spanung* tip, MASCHINEN hardface
bestückt *adj* MASCHINEN hard-faced
Bestückung *f* FERTIG tip, tooling; **Bestückungsdichte** *f* ELEKTRONIK *bei ICs* packing density
Bestwertsteuerung *f* ELEKTROTECH AC, adaptive control, FERTIG adaptive control
Bestzeit- *pref* COMP & DV minimum-access, minimum-delay; **Bestzeitcode** *m* COMP & DV minimum-access code, minimum-delay code; **Bestzeitprogramm** *nt* COMP & DV minimum-access routine; **Bestzeitprogrammierung** *f* COMP & DV minimum-access programming
Beta *nt* (β) GEOM beta *(β)*; **Betaabsorptionsanalyse** *f* PHYS, STRAHLPHYS, TEILPHYS beta particle absorption analysis; **Betaamylase** *f* LEBENSMITTEL beta-amylase; **Betadichtemesser** *m* KERNTECH beta density gage (AmE), beta density gauge (BrE)
β *abbr* (Phasenkonstante) AKUSTIK, ELEKTRIZ β *(phase constant)*
betakeln *vt* WASSERTRANS rig
Beta: **Betamessing** *nt* FERTIG beta brass
Betanken *nt* KFZTECH, LUFTTRANS fueling (AmE), fuelling (BrE)
Betankung *f* LUFTTRANS fuel transfer, refueling (AmE), refuelling (BrE); **Betankungsausleger** *m* LUFTTRANS refueling boom (AmE), refuelling boom (BrE)
Beta: **Betarückstreuanalyse** *f* PHYS, STRAHLPHYS, TEILPHYS beta particle backscattering analysis; **Betarückstreumesser** *m* KERNTECH beta backscatter gage (AmE), beta backscatter gauge (BrE); **Betaspektrum** *nt* STRAHLPHYS, TEILPHYS beta ray spectrum; **Betastabilitätsinsel** *f* KERNTECH beta stability island; **Betastrahlen** *m pl* ELEKTRIZ beta rays, PHYS, STRAHLPHYS, TEILPHYS beta radiation, beta rays; **Betastrahlenspektrum** *nt* PHYS, STRAHLPHYS, TEILPHYS beta ray spectrum; **Betastrahler** *m* PHYS, STRAHLPHYS, TEILPHYS beta emitter; **Betastrahlung** *f* PHYS, STRAHLPHYS, TEILPHYS beta emission, beta radiation; **Betateilchen** *nt* ELEKTRIZ, PHYS *Elektron*, STRAHLPHYS, TEILPHYS beta particle; **Betatest** *m* COMP & DV beta test
betätigen *vt* MASCHINEN actuate
Betätigung *f* MASCHINEN actuation, control, operation; **Betätigungsbügel** *m* FERTIG *Kunststoffinstallationen* actuator; **Betätigungseinrichtung** *f* MASCHINEN actuator attachment; **Betätigungselement** *nt* COMP & DV, ELEKTROTECH *(cf Betätigungsglied)*, MASCHINEN actuator; **Betätigungsglied** *nt (cf Betätigungselement)*

ELEKTROTECH actuator; **Betätigungsknopf** *m* GERÄT control button; **Betätigungsplatte** *f* LUFTTRANS actuating plate; **Betätigungsspannung** *f* ELEKTRIZ actuating voltage; **Betätigungsspindel** *f* FERTIG actuating screw; **Betätigungsstange** *f* LUFTTRANS actuating rod; **Betätigungsstrom** *m* ELEKTRIZ operating current; **Betätigungstaste** *f* GERÄT operating key
Betatron *nt* PHYS, STRAHLPHYS betatron; **Betatronbewegung** *f* PHYS betatron motion
Betazerfall *m* PHYS, STRAHLPHYS, TEILPHYS beta decay; **Betazerfallsenergie** *f* PHYS, STRAHLPHYS, TEILPHYS beta disintegration energy
Bethe-Goldstone-Gleichung *f* KERNTECH Bethe-Goldstone equation
Beton[1] *m* BAU, KER & GLAS concrete; **~ mit Steineinlagen** *m* BAU cyclopean concrete
Beton:[2] **~ einbringen** *vi* BAU pour concrete
Beton: **Betonarbeiten** *f pl* BAU concrete work; **Betonaufbruchhammer** *m* BAU concrete breaker; **Betonauskleidung** *f* BAU concrete lining; **Betonbau** *m* BAU concrete structure; **Betonblockstein** *m* BAU concrete block; **Betondachziegel** *m* BAU concrete roofing tile; **Betondecke** *f* BAU *Straße* concrete pavement (BrE), concrete sidewalk (AmE); **Betondosieranlage** *f* BAU concrete-batching plant; **Betoneisen** *nt* BAU reinforcing bar; **Betonfertigteilwerk** *nt* BAU precasting plant; **Betonhaltbarkeit** *f* BAU concrete durability
Betonieren *nt* BAU concreting
betonieren[1] *vt* BAU concrete
betonieren[2] *vi* BAU *Beton* pour concrete
Beton: **Betonkern** *m* BAU core; **Betonmauerwerk** *nt* BAU concrete masonry; **Betonmischanlage** *f* BAU batch plant, concrete mixing plant; **Betonmischer** *m* BAU batch mixer, concrete mixer
betonnen *vt* WASSERTRANS *Seezeichen* buoy
Beton: **Betonnest** *nt* BAU honeycomb
Betonnung *f* WASSERTRANS *Navigation* buoyage
Beton: **Betonpfahl** *m* KOHLEN concrete pile; **Betonplattform** *f* ERDÖL *Offshore-Technik* concrete platform; **Betonring** *m* BAU concrete ring; **Betonrippenkonstruktion** *f* HEIZ & KÄLTE waffle slab; **Betonrohr** *nt* BAU concrete pipe; **Betonsäge** *f* BAU concrete saw; **Betonschrapper** *m* TRANS concrete scraper; **Betonschutt** *m* TRANS concrete scrap; **Betonschwelle** *f* BAU *Eisenbahn* concrete sleeper (BrE), concrete tie (AmE); **Betonschwellenverlegegerät** *nt* BAU concrete sleeper layer (BrE), concrete tie layer (AmE); **Betonschwellenvorspannung** *f* BAU concrete sleeper prestressing (BrE), concrete tie prestressing (AmE); **Betonsohle** *f* HEIZ & KÄLTE concrete floor; **Betonstein** *m* KER & GLAS concrete block
betonummantelt *adj* BAU haunched
Beton: **Betonverflüssiger** *m* BAU plastifying admixture
Betrachtung *f* FOTO viewing; **Betrachtungseinheit** *f* QUAL item; **Betrachtungsobjektiv** *nt* FOTO viewing lens; **Betrachtungsvergrößerer** *m* FOTO viewing magnifier
Betrag *m* COMP & DV sum; **~ eines Vektors** *m* PHYS magnitude of vector, modulus of vector
betrauen: **~ mit** *vt* QUAL entrust with
betreiben *vt* KERNTECH operate, MASCHINEN operate, work
Betreiber *m* TELEKOM operator
Betreuung *f* TELEKOM serving
Betrieb:[1] **außer ~** *adj* ELEKTRIZ out of operation, ELEKTROTECH off, KONTROLL inoperative, MASCHINEN out

of action, TELEKOM *Gerät* disabled; **außer ~befindlich** *adj* LUFTTRANS rest period; **in ~ befindlich** *adj* ELEKTROTECH active

Betrieb[2] *m* COMP & DV operation, *von Software* running, ELEKTROTECH *einer Maschine*, FERTIG *Kunststoffinstallationen* operation, MASCHINEN mill, operation, working, MECHAN shop, UMWELTSCHMUTZ existing plant; **~ auf einer Frequenz** *m* ELEKTRONIK, FERNSEH, RADIO, TELEKOM single frequency operation; **~ auf zwei Ebenen** *m* ELEKTROTECH bilevel operation; **~ bei konstantem Druck** *m* RAUMFAHRT *Raumschiff* constant-pressure operation; **~ mit Ersatzschaltung** *m* TELEKOM *Übertragung* stand-by working; **~ mit passivem Gitter** *m* RADIO *Röhrenschaltung* passive-grid operation

Betrieb:[3] **außer ~nehmen** *vt* BAU take out of service; **außer ~ setzen** *vt* BAU put out of service, LUFTTRANS *Motor, Triebwerk* shut down; **in ~ setzen** *vt* KONTROLL activate

Betrieb:[4] **in ~ sein** *vi* COMP & DV run

Betrieb: Betriebmeßbrücke *f* GERÄT field bridge

Betriebs- *pref* MASCHINEN operating; **Betriebs- und Datenserver** *m* TELEKOM administration and data server; **Betriebs- und Wartungszentrum** *nt* TELEKOM OMC, operations and maintenance center (AmE), operations and maintenance centre (BrE); **Betriebsablauf** *m* UMWELTSCHMUTZ industrial process

Betriebsanlage: neue ~ UMWELTSCHMUTZ new plant

Betriebs-: Betriebsanleitung *f* FERTIG, MASCHINEN operating instructions; **Betriebsanleitung für die Besatzung** *f* LUFTTRANS crew operating manual

Betriebsart *f* COMP & DV mode, mode of operation, ELEKTRONIK mode, ELEKTROTECH operating mode, TELEKOM mode of operation; **Betriebsartbefehlsformat** *nt* COMP & DV mode instruction code; **Betriebsartenextraktor** *m* RAUMFAHRT *Weltraumfunk* mode extractor; **Betriebsartenschalter** *m* ELEKTROTECH selector switch; **Betriebsartenwahlschalter** *m* LUFTTRANS mode selector switch; **Betriebsartregister** *nt* COMP & DV mode register; **Betriebsartwechsel** *m* COMP & DV mode change

Betriebs-: Betriebsaufnahme *f* KONTROLL initial operation phase; **Betriebsausfall** *m* ELEKTROTECH failure; **Betriebsbeauftragter für Abfall** *m* *(BfA)* ABFALL Waste Management Officer

betriebsbedingt: ~er Defekt *m* KERNTECH operations-related defect; **~er Fehler** *m* UMWELTSCHMUTZ operational error; **~e Verzögerung** *f* TRANS operational delay

Betriebs-: Betriebsbedingungen *f pl* ELEKTRIZ, ELEKTROTECH, METROL operating conditions

betriebsbereit *adj* COMP & DV online, ready for operation, ready, MASCHINEN in working order; **nicht ~** *adj* COMP & DV off-line

Betriebs-: Betriebsbereitschaftssignal *nt* COMP & DV enabling signal; **Betriebsbremse** *f* KFZTECH, MASCHINEN service brake; **Betriebsdaten** *nt pl* ELEKTROTECH, PHYS rating; **Betriebsdauer** *f* KERNTECH operating lifetime; **Betriebsdrehzahl** *f* MASCHINEN operating speed; **Betriebsdruck** *m* FERTIG *Kunststoffinstallationen* working pressure, MASCHINEN operating pressure, working pressure, RAUMFAHRT *Raumschiff* operating pressure; **~ im Durchlaßbereich** *m* ELEKTRONIK composite passband

betriebseigen: ~er Standard *m* KERNTECH in-house standard

Betriebs-: Betriebserlaubnis *f* KFZTECH *Rechtsvorschriften* certification, LUFTTRANS operating permit; **Betriebserwartung** *f* ELEKTROTECH service life; **Betriebsflughöhe** *f* RAUMFAHRT operating altitude; **Betriebsfrequenz** *f* ELEKTRIZ power frequency; **Betriebsführung** *f* KERNTECH operative management; **Betriebsgeschwindigkeit** *f* LUFTTRANS operating speed; **Betriebsgewicht** *nt* RAUMFAHRT operating weight; **Betriebsgipfelhöhe** *f* LUFTTRANS operating ceiling, service ceiling; **Betriebshandbuch** *nt* KONTROLL manual, LUFTTRANS operational manual, MASCHINEN operations manual; **Betriebshandrad** *nt* MASCHINEN operating hand-wheel; **Betriebsinstrument** *nt* GERÄT plant instrument

betriebsintern: ~e Software *f* COMP & DV in-house software

Betriebs-: Betriebskontrolle *f* ELEKTROTECH process control; **Betriebskosten** *f pl* TEXTIL running costs; **Betriebslast** *f* BAU rolling load, MASCHINEN working load; **Betriebslasten-Simulation** *f* WERKPRÜF testing under service loading conditions; **Betriebslebensdauer** *f* ELEKTROTECH service life; **Betriebsmeßgerät** *nt* GERÄT field instrument, plant instrument; **Betriebsmeßinstrument** *nt* GERÄT field instrument; **Betriebsmittel** *nt pl* COMP & DV resource, ERGON work equipment; **Betriebsmittelzuteilung** *f* COMP & DV resource allocation; **Betriebsmittelzuweisung** *f* COMP & DV resource allocation; **Betriebsmodus** *m* COMP & DV, TELEKOM mode of operation; **Betriebspausenzeit** *f* QUAL nonrequired time; **Betriebsprüfung** *f* QUAL functional test, in-service test, WERKPRÜF functional test; **Betriebsraum** *m* TELEKOM operations room; **Betriebsrechner** *m* COMP & DV scheduling computer; **Betriebssaal** *m* TELEKOM *Telefon* operations room

betriebssicher *adj* ELEKTROTECH, KFZTECH fail-safe

Betriebs-: Betriebssicherheit *f* ELEKTROTECH reliability, FERTIG operational safety; **Betriebsspannung** *f* ELEKTRIZ *eines Systems*, ELEKTROTECH operating voltage, FERTIG *Kunststoffinstallationen* voltage, KONTROLL operating voltage; **Betriebssprache** *f (CL)* COMP & DV command language *(CL)*; **Betriebssteuerung** *f* ELEKTROTECH process control; **Betriebsstörung** *f* ELEKTROTECH interruption; **Betriebsstrom** *m* ELEKTRIZ, ELEKTROTECH operating current; **Betriebsstundenanzeiger** *m* WASSERTRANS *Motor* operating hours indicator; **Betriebsstundenzähler** *m* GERÄT operating hour meter, time meter, MECHAN elapsed time counter, SICHERHEIT working hours counter; **Betriebssystem** *nt* COMP & DV OS, operating system, operation system, TELEKOM OS, operating system; **Betriebssystemkern** *m* COMP & DV kernel, operating system kernel; **Betriebssystemplatte** *f* COMP & DV master disk; **Betriebstemperatur** *f* HEIZ & KÄLTE, KFZTECH, KONTROLL, LUFTTRANS, RAUMFAHRT operating temperature

Betriebstemperatur: auf ~ aufheizen *vt* KER & GLAS *Schmelzofen in Leerzustand* fire over

Betriebs-: Betriebstest *m* METROL operational test; **Betriebsüberwachung** *f (ISM)* TELEKOM in-service monitoring *(ISM)*; **Betriebsverbot** *nt* SICHERHEIT prohibition notice; **Betriebsverhalten** *nt* COMP & DV performance, MASCHINEN operating characteristic; **Betriebsverwaltung** *f* KERNTECH operative management; **Betriebswasser** *nt* WASSERVERSORG industrial water, process water; **Betriebsweise** *f* COMP & DV mode of operation, MASCHINEN operation, TELEKOM mode of operation; **Betriebszeit** *f* COMP & DV operating time, uptime; **Betriebszentrale** *f* RAUMFAHRT operation center (AmE), operation centre (BrE); **Betriebszentrum** *nt (BZ)* TELEKOM operations center (AmE), operations centre (BrE); **Betriebszustand** *m* ELEKTROTECH operating conditions, FERTIG working order; **Betriebszustandsanzeiger** *m* COMP & DV mode indicator; **Betriebszuverlässigkeit** *f* ELEKTROTECH, MEERSCHMUTZ reliability; **Betriebszyklus** *m* KONTROLL duty cycle

betrügerisch: ~e Nutzung *f* TELEKOM fraudulent use

Bett *nt* MASCHINEN, *einer Drehmaschine* bed; ~ mit **Einsatzbrücke** *nt* MASCHINEN gap bed; **Bettdecke** *f* TEXTIL bedspread, blanket; **Bettführung** *f* MASCHINEN ways; **Bettführungsbahn** *f* MASCHINEN ways; **Bettschlitten** *m* MASCHINEN bed carriage, bed slide

Bettuchstoff *m* TEXTIL sheeting

Bettung *f* BAU ballast, *Mörtel* bed, TRANS ballast

bettungslos: ~e Schiene *f* EISENBAHN ballastless track

Bettung: **Bettungsmörtel** *m* BAU bedding mortar; **Bettungsmörtelschicht** *f* BAU bedding course; **Bettungsreinigung** *f* EISENBAHN ballast screening; **Bettungsrückstand** *m* EISENBAHN ballast residue

Beuchfaß *nt* TEXTIL kier

beugen *vt* FERTIG diffract

Beugung *f* ELEKTROTECH diffraction, ERGON flexion, FERTIG, FOTO, OPTIK, RADIO, TELEKOM, WELLPHYS diffraction; ~ von **Atomstrahlen** *f* KERNTECH, PHYS, STRAHLPHYS atomic beam diffraction; **Beugungsbild** *nt* METALL diffraction pattern; **Beugungsgitter** *nt* OPTIK, PHYS, TELEKOM, WELLPHYS diffraction grating; **Beugungsspektrum** *nt* OPTIK, STRAHLPHYS diffraction spectrum; **Beugungswinkel** *m* FERTIG angle of deflection

Beule *f* MASCHINEN bulge, MECHAN dent

Beulen *nt* MASCHINEN buckling

beulen[1] *vi* MECHAN buckle

beulen:[2] sich ~ *v refl* MASCHINEN bulge

Beullast *f* MECHAN buckling load

Beurteilung *f* ERGON rating; **Beurteilungsfehler** *m* QUAL error

Beutel *m* VERPACK bin liner, pouch, sachet; ~ mit **Innenausfütterung** *m* VERPACK lined bag; ~ mit **Reißverschluß** *m* VERPACK zip lock bag; ~ von der **Rolle** *m pl* VERPACK reel feed bags; ~ mit **Seitenfalten** *m* VERPACK square bag with gussets; **Beutelabfüllanlage** *f* VERPACK bag-filling machine

Beutelchen: ~ für **Maßeinheit** *nt* VERPACK unit dose sachet

Beutel: **Beutelfilter** *nt* KOHLEN bag filter; **Beutelhalter** *m* VERPACK bag holder; **Beutelhersteller** *m* VERPACK bagmaker; **Beutelherstellungsmaschine** *f* VERPACK pouch-making machine; **Beutelöffnungsmaschine** *f* VERPACK bag opener; **Beutelpackmaschine** *f* VERPACK bag-loading machine; **Beutelpapier** *nt* VERPACK bag paper; **Beutelpositioniersystem** *nt* VERPACK bag-placing system; **Beutelrollenhülse** *f* VERPACK bag reel; **Beutelverpackung** *f* VERPACK bag packaging; **Beutelverschließmaschine** *f* VERPACK bag-sealing equipment, sack-closing machine

Beverage: ~ Antenne® *f* RADIO Beverage aerial®

Bevölkerung *f* UMWELTSCHUTZ population; **Bevölkerungsgesamtdosis** *f* UMWELTSCHUTZ population dose; **Bevölkerungsteildosis** *f* UMWELTSCHUTZ subpopulation collective dose

bevollmächtigt: ~er gesetzlicher **Vertreter** *m* QUAL authorized jurisdictional inspector

bevorrechtigt: ~er **Befehl** *m* COMP & DV privileged instruction; ~er **Bereich** *m* COMP & DV privileged account; ~e **Operation** *f* COMP & DV privileged operation

bevorzugt: ~e **Annahmegrenzen** *f pl* QUAL preferred acceptable quality levels

bewachsen:[1] ~er **Schiffsboden** *m* WASSERTRANS foul bottom

bewachsen[2] *vt* WASSERTRANS *Schiff* foul

Bewaffnung *f* WASSERTRANS *Marine* armament

bewährt *adj* FERTIG *Kunststoffinstallationen* proven

Bewässerung *f* FERTIG *Kunststoffinstallationen*, WASSERVERSORG irrigation; **Bewässerungsgraben** *m* WASSERVERSORG catch-feeder; **Bewässerungskanal** *m* WASSERVERSORG irrigation canal

beweglich[1] *adj* TELEKOM mobile

beweglich:[2] ~er **Anschlag** *m* MASCHINEN movable stop; ~e **Arbeitsbühne** *f* BAU moving platform; ~e **Backe** *f* MASCHINEN chop, movable jaw; ~er **Backen** *m* FERTIG *Stauchen* movable die; ~es **Brechwerk** *nt* KOHLEN mobile crusher; ~e **Brücke** *f* WASSERTRANS *Schleusen, Binnenwasserstraßen* movable bridge; ~e **Druckgießformhälfte** *f* FERTIG ejector die; ~e **Einrichtung** *f* TELEKOM mobile installation; ~er **Flugfunkdienst über Satelliten** *m* TELEKOM aeronautical mobile satellite service; ~er **Flugfunksatellitendienst** *m* RAUMFAHRT *Weltraumfunk* aeronautical mobile satellite service; ~e **Funkstelle** *f* TELEKOM mobile station; ~es **Gelenk** *nt* MECHAN flexible drive; ~es **Herzstück** *nt* EISENBAHN switch diamond; ~er **Kern** *m* ELEKTRIZ movable core; ~e **Komponente** *f* UMWELTSCHUTZ mobile component; ~er **Kontakt** *m* ELEKTROTECH moving contact; ~e **Kraftübertragung** *f* MECHAN flexible drive; ~e **Ladung** *f* ELEKTROTECH moving charge; ~er **Landfunkdienst** *m* TELEKOM land mobile radio service; ~e **Last** *f* BAU moving load; ~e **Rolle** *f* MASCHINEN idle pulley; ~er **Rost** *m* HEIZ & KÄLTE moving grate; ~es **Rotorblatt** *nt* LUFTTRANS *Hubschrauber* movable rotor blade; ~er **Satellitenfunkdienst** *m* RAUMFAHRT *Weltraumfunk* mobile satellite service; ~er **Satelliten-Seefunkdienst** *m* TELEKOM *Satellitenfunk*, WASSERTRANS *Satellitenfunk* maritime mobile satellite service; ~es **Schaltstück** *nt* ELEKTROTECH moving contact; ~er **Seefunkdienst** *m* TELEKOM, WASSERTRANS maritime mobile service; ~er **Sitz** *m* HYDRAUL dancing seat; ~er **Spindelstock** *m* MASCHINEN sliding headstock, sliding poppet; ~es **Teil** *nt* MASCHINEN moving part; ~er **Tisch** *m* KER & GLAS moving table; ~es **Wehr** *nt* WASSERVERSORG bar weir

Beweglichkeit *f* PHYS mobility; **Beweglichkeitsgrad** *m* MASCHINEN degree of mobility

Bewegtbild-Videokonferenz *f* TELEKOM full-motion videoconferencing

Bewegung[1] *f* MASCHINEN motion, movement, MECHAN motion

Bewegung:[2] in ~ halten *vt* FOTO *Bad* agitate; in ~ versetzen *vt* MASCHINEN impart motion to, set in motion

Bewegung:[3] die ~ umkehren *vi* MASCHINEN reverse the motion

Bewegung: **Bewegungsablaufdetektor** *m* TRANS motion detector; **Bewegungsamplitude** *f* GERÄT *Meßgerät* amplitude of movement; **Bewegungsbedienteil** *nt* ERGON displacement control; **Bewegungsbereich** *m* ERGON random observation method, KERNTECH limit of travel; **Bewegungsdatei** *f*

COMP & DV movement file, transaction file; **Bewegungsenergie** *f* MASCHINEN energy of motion, MECHAN, PHYS kinetic energy; **Bewegungsgeschwindigkeit** *f* KERNTECH *eines Steuerstabs* rate of travel; **Bewegungsgleichung** *f* MASCHINEN motion equation; **Bewegungsgröße** *f* MASCHINEN kinetic quantity, PHYS momentum; **Bewegungsimpedanz** *f* AKUSTIK motional impedance; **Bewegungslehre** *f* MECHAN kinematics, kinetics, METALL, PHYS kinetics; **Bewegungsmittelpunkt** *m* MECHAN, PHYS center of motion (AmE), centre of motion (BrE); **Bewegungsrichtung** *f* MASCHINEN direction of motion; **Bewegungssatz** *m* COMP & DV transaction record; **Bewegungsschaufel** *f* LUFTTRANS *Turbomotor* impeller; **Bewegungssteuerung** *f* KONTROLL motion control; **Bewegungsstudie** *f* ERGON motion study; **Bewegungsumkehr** *f* MASCHINEN reversing the motion; **Bewegungsunschärfe** *f* FOTO motion blur

Bewehren *nt* BAU reinforcing

bewehrt[1] *adj* ELEKTROTECH armored clad (AmE), armoured clad (BrE), TELEKOM armored (AmE), armoured (BrE)

bewehrt:[2] **~er Beton** *m* BAU reinforced concrete; **~es Kabel** *nt* ELEKTROTECH armored cable (AmE), armoured cable (BrE), sheathed cable, MASCHINEN, TELEKOM armored cable (AmE), armoured cable (BrE)

Bewehrung *f* BAU reinforcement, ELEKTROTECH *Kabel* armor (AmE), armour (BrE); **Bewehrungsarbeiten** *f pl* BAU steel fixing; **Bewehrungsdraht** *m* OPTIK *Lichtleitkabel* armor wire (AmE), armour wire (BrE); **Bewehrungsmatte** *f* BAU mattress, wire mesh reinforcement; **Bewehrungsnetz** *nt* BAU mat reinforcement; **Bewehrungsstahl** *m* BAU reinforcing bar

Beweis *m* KÜNSTL INT, MATH proof

beweisen *vt* MATH prove, QUAL verify

Beweis: Beweisfindungsstrategie *f* KÜNSTL INT proof strategy; **Beweistheorie** *f* KÜNSTL INT proof theory

bewerten[1] *vt* LEBENSMITTEL grade, QUAL, SICHERHEIT evaluate, TEXTIL assess

bewerten[2] *vti* ERGON weight

bewertet: ~er Schalldruckpegel *m* AKUSTIK weighted sound level

Bewertung *f* KÜNSTL INT evaluation, MASCHINEN assessment; **Bewertungsgröße** *f* FERTIG quantity of assessment; **Bewertungsprogramm** *nt* COMP & DV benchmark program

bewettern *vt* KOHLEN aerate

Bewetterung *f* KOHLEN aeration

Bewicklung *f* PHYS winding; **Bewicklungsbreite** *f* TEXTIL dressed width of warp

Bewilligung *f* ERDÖL production licence (BrE), TRANS approval

Bewitterung *f* KUNSTSTOFF, TEXTIL weathering; **Bewitterungsbeanspruchung** *f* KUNSTSTOFF exposure to weather; **Bewitterungshaut** *f* KUNSTSTOFF alligatoring, crazing

bewuchsverhindernd: ~e Farbe *f* WASSERTRANS *Schiffinstandhaltung* antifouling paint

bezeichnen *vt* COMP & DV identify, label

Bezeichner *m* COMP & DV identifier

bezeichnet: ~e Frequenz *f* TELEKOM designated frequency

Bezeichnung *f* AKUSTIK designation, COMP & DV label, PATENT *des Gegenstandes der Erfindung* designation; **~ der Erfindung** *f* PATENT title of the invention

beziehen: sich ~ auf *v refl* PATENT *Patentanspruch* reduce to, refer to

Beziehung *f* MATH relation; **Beziehungsgraph** *m* KÜNSTL INT relation graph; **Beziehungssymbol** *nt* KÜNSTL INT relation symbol, relational operator

bezogen: ~e Anstiegsantwort *f* REGELUNG referenced ramp

Bezug *m* DRUCK blanket; **Bezugsadresse** *f* COMP & DV base address, reference address; **Bezugsatmosphäre** *f* RAUMFAHRT reference atmosphere; **Bezugsband** *nt* AKUSTIK reference tape, AUFNAHME standard play tape; **Bezugsbedingungen** *f pl* METROL reference conditions; **Bezugsbemaßung** *f* KONSTZEICH reference dimensioning; **Bezugsebene** *f* BAU datum plane; **Bezugselektrode** *f* LABOR *Elektrochemie* reference electrode; **Bezugsempfindlichkeit** *f* TELEKOM reference sensibility; **Bezugsenergie** *f* AKUSTIK reference energy; **Bezugsfrequenz** *f* TELEKOM reference frequency; **Bezugsgerät** *nt* QUAL known-good device; **Bezugsgeräuschquelle** *f* AUFNAHME reference noise source; **Bezugsgesamtheit** *f* QUAL standard population; **Bezugsgröße** *f* COMP & DV datum; **Bezugshaken** *m* KONSTZEICH tick; **Bezugshöhe** *f* BAU datum level; **Bezugshorizont** *m* MECHAN datum line; **Bezugskante** *f* FERTIG datum edge; **Bezugsklotz** *m* FERTIG datum block; **Bezugskopplung** *f* ELEKTROTECH reference coupling; **Bezugskreis** *m* MASCHINEN reference circle; **Bezugslandeanfluggeschwindigkeit** *f* LUFTTRANS reference landing approach speed, *ein Triebwerk außer Kraft* reference landing approach speed; **Bezugslautstärke** *f* AUFNAHME reference volume; **Bezugslinie** *f* BAU datum line, GEOM reference line, MASCHINEN datum line, leader line, reference line; **Bezugsmarkensensor** *m* KFZTECH reference sensor; **Bezugsmaß** *nt* KONSTZEICH datum dimension, MASCHINEN reference dimension; **Bezugsmaßsystem** *nt* GERÄT *bei numerischer Steuerung* absolute measure system; **Bezugsmenge** *f* QUAL basic size; **Bezugsmeßmethode** *f* TELEKOM reference test method; **Bezugsnormal** *nt* METROL reference standards, QUAL reference standard; **Bezugspegel** *m* AKUSTIK reference volume; **Bezugspotential** *nt* REGELUNG signal common; **Bezugsprofil** *nt* MASCHINEN reference profile; **Bezugspunkt** *m* AKUSTIK reference point, BAU datum point, *Vermessung* reference mark, COMP & DV datum, reference mark, reference, GEOM, MASCHINEN reference point; **Bezugspunkt für die Messung des Anfluglärms** *m* LUFTTRANS approach reference noise measurement point; **Bezugsrauschwert** *m* ELEKTRONIK reference noise; **Bezugsreaktor** *m* KERNTECH reference reactor; **Bezugsreibungsbedingungen** *f pl* LUFTTRANS *Start- und Landebahn* reference friction condition; **Bezugsschall** *m* AKUSTIK reference sound; **Bezugsschalldruck** *m* AKUSTIK, UMWELTSCHMUTZ reference sound pressure; **Bezugsschalleistung** *f* AKUSTIK reference sound power; **Bezugsschallgeschwindigkeit** *f* AKUSTIK reference sound velocity; **Bezugsschallintensität** *f* AKUSTIK reference sound intensity; **Bezugssignal** *nt* ELEKTRONIK reference signal; **Bezugssignaleingang** *m* ELEKTRONIK reference signal input; **Bezugssignalphase** *f* ELEKTRONIK reference signal phase; **Bezugsspannung** *f* ELEKTROTECH reference voltage; **Bezugsstation** *f* RAUMFAHRT *Weltraumfunk* reference station; **Bezugssteigung** *f* LUFTTRANS *Propeller* standard pitch; **Bezugsstück** *nt* MASCHINEN reference piece; **Bezugs-**

system *nt* ERGON benchmark system, MASCHINEN reference system, PHYS frame of reference, standard; **Bezugstabelle** *f* COMP & DV reference table; **Bezugstaktgeber** *m* TELEKOM reference clock; **Bezugstemperatur** *f* HEIZ & KÄLTE reference temperature, standard temperature, METROL reference temperature; **Bezugston** *m* AKUSTIK reference tone; **Bezugstonpegel** *m* AUFNAHME reference audio level; **Bezugsverbindung** *f* TELEKOM HRC, hypothetical reference connection; **Bezugswerkstück** *nt* MASCHINEN master piece; **Bezugszahnstange** *f* MASCHINEN basic rack; **Bezugszeichen** *nt* PATENT reference sign; **Bezugszeit** *f* COMP & DV reference time

BfA *m* (*Betriebsbeauftragter für Abfall*) ABFALL *Berufsbezeichnung* Waste Management Officer

BFO *abbr* (*Schwebungsfrequenzoszillator*) ELEKTRONIK, PHYS, RADIO BFO (*beat frequency oscillator*)

B-Format: ~ **Videorecorder** *m* FERNSEH B-format video recorder

Bg *abbr* (*geometrisches Buckling*) KERNTECH Bg (*geometric buckling*)

B/H: ~ **Schleife** *f* ELEKTRIZ B/H loop

BHA *abbr* (*Butylhydroxyanisol*) LEBENSMITTEL BHA (*butylated hydroxyanisole*)

BHT *abbr* (*Butylhydroxytoluol*) LEBENSMITTEL BHT (*butylated hydroxytoluene*)

Bi (*Bismut*) CHEMIE Bi (*bismuth*)

biaxial[1] *adj* METALL biaxial

biaxial:[2] ~**e Belastung** *f* METALL biaxial loading; ~ **orientierte Folie** *f* KUNSTSTOFF biaxially oriented film; ~**e Orientierung** *f* KUNSTSTOFF biaxial orientation

Bibeldruckpapier *nt* DRUCK thin paper

Biberschwanz *m* BAU plain tile

Bibliothek *f* COMP & DV library; **Bibliotheksautomation** *f* COMP & DV library automation; **Bibliotheksfunktion** *f* COMP & DV library function; **Bibliotheksmusik** *f* AUFNAHME library music; **Bibliotheksprogramm** *nt* COMP & DV library program; **Bibliotheksroutine** *f* COMP & DV library routine; **Bibliotheksverwaltungsprogramm** *nt* COMP & DV librarian program

Bi-CMOS-Transistor *m* COMP & DV BiCMOS transistor

Bicyclo-Decan *nt* CHEMIE biclodecane, decahydronaphthalene

bidirektional[1] *adj* COMP & DV, TELEKOM bidirectional

bidirektional:[2] ~**er Datenfluß** *m* COMP & DV bidirectional flow; ~**er Koppler** *m* ELEKTROTECH bidirectional coupler; ~**es Mikrofon** *nt* AKUSTIK bidirectional microphone; ~**es Netzwerk** *nt* ELEKTROTECH bidirectional network; ~**er Schalter** *m* ELEKTROTECH bidirectional switch; ~**e Suche** *f* KÜNSTL INT bidirectional search; ~**er Transducer** *m* ELEKTROTECH bidirectional transducer; ~**e Triggerdiode** *f* (*Diac*) ELEKTRONIK, RADIO *Zweiweg-Schaltdiode* diode alternating-current switch (*diac*); ~**er Übertragungsweg** *m* COMP & DV bidirectional bus; ~**er Wandler** *m* ELEKTROTECH bidirectional transducer

Biege- *pref* KUNSTSTOFF, METALL, WASSERTRANS bending, flexural; **Biegebeanspruchung** *f* KUNSTSTOFF, METALL, WASSERTRANS bending stress, WERKPRÜF flexural stress; **Biegebelastung** *f* MECHAN bending stress; **Biegedorn** *m* FERTIG internal mandrel; **Biegeeigenschaft** *f* MASCHINEN bending property; **Biege-Elastizitätsmodul** *m* (*Biege-E-Modul*) KUNSTSTOFF flexural modulus of elasticity; **Biege-E-Modul** *m* (*Biege-Elastizitätsmodul*) KUNSTSTOFF flexural modulus of elasticity; **Biegefeder** *f* MASCHINEN fle-

xion spring, spring subjected to bending; **Biegefestigkeit** *f* KERNTECH, KUNSTSTOFF flexural strength, MASCHINEN resistance to bending, ultimate bending strength, MECHAN fatigue strength, PAPIER bending strength, PHYS flexural rigidity, TELEKOM flexibility strength, WERKPRÜF flexural strength; **Biegeform** *f* KER & GLAS bending mold (AmE), bending mould (BrE), MASCHINEN former; **Biegekante** *f* FERTIG forming edge; **Biegemaschine** *f* MASCHINEN bending machine, bending press, machine for bending, MECHAN bending machine; **Biegemodul** *nt* WERKPRÜF flexural modulus; **Biegemoment** *nt* MASCHINEN, MECHAN, WASSERTRANS *Schiffkonstruktion* bending moment

Biegen *nt* BAU bending, KER & GLAS bend, *Flachglas* bending, *von Glasrohren* bending, *von Rohren* twisting, METALL bending

biegen *vt* BAU bend, camber, inflect, MASCHINEN fold, METALL, PAPIER bend

Biege-: **Biegepresse** *f* FERTIG bending press; **Biegeprisma** *nt* FERTIG vee die; **Biegeprobe** *f* METALL bend test piece; **Biegeprüfgerät** *nt* KUNSTSTOFF bending tester; **Biegeprüfmaschine** *f* GERÄT bending tester; **Biegeprüfstab** *m* METALL bend test piece; **Biegeradius** *m* MASCHINEN bend radius, MECHAN bending radius; **Biegerichten** *nt* MASCHINEN straightening by bending; **Biegeriß** *m* FERTIG flexural crack; **Biegeschablone** *f* FERTIG form (AmE); **Biegeschenkel** *m* FERTIG *Kunststoffinstallationen* flexible section; **Biegeschwellspannung** *f* FERTIG fluctuating bending, fluctuating bending stress; **Biegeschwinger** *m* ELEKTRONIK flexure-mode resonator; **Biegeschwingung** *f* MASCHINEN flexure; **Biegespannung** *f* KUNSTSTOFF, MASCHINEN, WASSERTRANS bending stress; **Biegesteifigkeit** *f* MASCHINEN bending strength, MECHAN flexural strength; **Biegesteifigkeitsprüfer** *m* PAPIER bending stiffness tester; **Biegestempel** *m* MASCHINEN bending die; **Biegeverschluß** *m* KER & GLAS bent finish; **Biegeversuch** *m* FERTIG beam test, MASCHINEN bend test, bending test, METALL bend test, WERKPRÜF bending test; **Biegewalze** *f* MASCHINEN bending roll, bending rollers; **Biegewalzmaschine** *f* MASCHINEN bending rollers; **Biegewerkzeug** *nt* MASCHINEN bending tool; **Biegewinkel** *m* FERTIG, MASCHINEN angle of bend; **Biegezange** *f* FERTIG bending pliers, claw; **Biegezugfestigkeit** *f* ANSTRICH tensile bond strength

biegsam[1] *adj* TEXTIL flexible

biegsam:[2] ~**er Hohlleiter** *m* ELEKTROTECH flexible waveguide; ~**es Kabel** *nt* ELEKTROTECH flexible cable; ~**er Leiter** *m* ELEKTROTECH flexible conductor; ~**e Leitung** *f* ELEKTROTECH flexible wire; ~**e Metallrohrleitung** *f* MASCHINEN flexible metal conduit; ~**es Rohr** *nt* BAU flexible hose; ~**er Schlauch** *m* MASCHINEN hose pipe; ~**e Verbindung** *f* MASCHINEN flexible joint; ~**e Welle** *f* MASCHINEN flexible shaft

Biegsamkeit *f* KUNSTSTOFF, TEXTIL, WASSERTRANS *Material* flexibility

Biegung *f* EISENBAHN flexion, ELEKTROTECH *Glasfaseroptik* bend, *Wellenleiter* bend, KERNTECH *eines Brennelementes* deflection, MASCHINEN, MECHAN bend, METALL deflection, WASSERTRANS bend; **Biegungsverlust** *m* ELEKTROTECH bending loss

Bienenkorbkühler *m* KFZTECH honeycomb radiator

Bi-Ergol-Technologie *f* RAUMFAHRT bi-ergol technology

Biertreber *m pl* LEBENSMITTEL brewer's grain; **Bierwürze** *f* LEBENSMITTEL *Brauerei* wort

Bifilar- *pref* ELEKTRIZ bifilar; **Bifilardrahtwicklung** *f* ELEKTRIZ bifilar winding; **Bifilarwicklung** *f* ELEKTRIZ bifilar winding

bifilar[1] *adj* ELEKTRIZ, PHYS, RADIO bifilar

bifilar:[2] ~ **gewickelter Transformator** *m* ELEKTROTECH double-wound transformer

Bifokalglas *nt* KER & GLAS bifocal lens

Bifokuslinse *f* OPTIK *mit runder Einfügung* bifocal lens

BIGFET *abbr* (*Feldeffekttransistor mit bipolarisoliertem Gatter*) ELEKTRONIK BIGFET (*bipolar-insulated gate field-effect transistor*)

Biguanid *nt* CHEMIE biguanide

bijektiv *adj* GEOM bijective

bikonkav *adj* OPTIK biconcave

Bikonkavlinse *f* OPTIK, PHYS biconcave lens

bikonvex *adj* OPTIK biconvex, convexo-convex

Bikonvexlinse *f* OPTIK, PHYS biconvex lens

bikubisch *adj* GEOM bicubic

bilateral: ~**er Transducer** *m* ELEKTROTECH bilateral transducer; ~**er Wandler** *m* ELEKTROTECH bilateral transducer

Bild *nt* COMP & DV picture, DRUCK face, figure, image, ERGON image, FERNSEH frame, picture, video, FERTIG pattern, FOTO image, picture, KER & GLAS, PHYS, RADIO image; **Bildablenkung** *f* FERNSEH vertical sweep; **Bildabtaster** *m* COMP & DV scanner, TELEKOM image analyser (BrE), image analyzer (AmE), scanner; **Bildabtastgerät** *nt* KONTROLL scanner; **Bildabtastung** *f* TELEKOM image analysis, scanning; **Bildanalyse** *f* KÜNSTL INT image analysis; **Bildanpassung** *f* FERNSEH picture match; **Bildauflösung** *f* TELEKOM picture definition; **Bildaufnahmemodul** *m* KONTROLL vision input module; **Bildaufnahmeröhre** *f* ELEKTRONIK pick-up tube, vidicon tube, TV camera tube; **Bildaufnehmer** *m* TELEKOM image sensor; **Bildaufzeichnungsstrom** *m* FERNSEH video record current; **Bildausfall** *m* FERNSEH picture failure; **Bildbreitendrossel** *f* FERNSEH width choke; **Bildbreiteschrumpfung** *f* FERNSEH underlap; **Bilddarstellung** *f* MATH pictogram, RADIO image display; **Bilddatei** *f* COMP & DV, ELEKTRONIK image file; **Bilddigitalisierer** *m* ELEKTRONIK image digitizer; **Bilddigitalisierung** *f* ELEKTRONIK image digitization; **Bilddrift** *f* FERNSEH picture drift; **Bildelement** *nt* COMP & DV pixel, COMP & DV picture element

Bilden: ~ **einer Fahrgemeinschaft** *m* TRANS car pooling

Bild: **Bilderbuch** *nt* DRUCK picture book; **Bilderfassung** *f* ELEKTRONIK image digitization; **Bilderglas** *nt* KER & GLAS picture glass; **Bilderkennen** *nt* KÜNSTL INT image recognition; **Bildfängerröhre** *f* TV camera tube; **Bildfernsprecher** *m* FERNSEH videophone; **Bildfläche** *f* FERNSEH scanning field; **Bildflackern** *nt* FERNSEH image flicker, picture flutter; **Bildflattern** *nt* FERNSEH fluttering video level; **Bildfolge** *f* TELEKOM image sequence; **Bildformat** *nt* PHYS aspect ratio; **Bildfreiraum** *m* DRUCK placeholder; **Bildfrequenz** *f* ELEKTRONIK *Faksimile* image frequency, FERNSEH frame frequency, image frequency; **Bildgröße** *f* FOTO picture size; **Bildinstabilität** *f* TV jitter; **Bildinversion** *f* FERNSEH inversion of image; **Bildkanal** *m* FERNSEH video channel; **Bildkonservierung** *f* FERNSEH image retention; **Bildlaufregler** *m* FERNSEH hold control, vertical hold control; **Bildlegende** *f* DRUCK caption; **Bildleuchtdichte** *f* ELEKTRONIK, STRAHLPHYS luminance

bildlich: ~ **anzeigen** *vt* TELEKOM display

Bild: **Bildmaske** *f* FERNSEH framing mask, FOTO mask; **Bildmaßstab** *m* FOTO scale of image; **Bildmischer** *m* FERNSEH vision mixer; **Bildmonitor** *m* FERNSEH picture monitor; **Bildmustererkennung** *f* ELEKTRONIK pattern recognition; **Bildnachlauf** *m* FERNSEH image lag; **Bildnormkonverter** *m* FERNSEH standards converter; **Bildpegelanzeige** *f* FERNSEH video level indicator; **Bildphasenumkehr** *f* FERNSEH video phase reversal; **Bildphasenwinkel-Koeffizient** *m* ELEKTRONIK image phase-change coefficient; **Bildplatte** *f* AUFNAHME, COMP & DV optical disk, FERNSEH videodisc (BrE), videodisk (AmE); **Bildplattenaufzeichnung** *f* FERNSEH videodisc recording (BrE), videodisk recording (AmE); **Bildplattenspieler** *m* FERNSEH videodisc player (BrE), videodisk player (AmE); **Bildprojektion** *f* ELEKTRONIK *Lithografie* image projection; **Bildprojektor** *m* FERNSEH video projector; **Bildpunkt** *m* COMP & DV pixel, COMP & DV picture element; **Bildraster** *m* ELEKTRONIK raster; **Bildrasterabtastung** *f* ELEKTRONIK raster scanning; **Bildrasterscannen** *nt* ELEKTRONIK raster scanning; **Bildrasterwandler** *m* FERNSEH scan converter; **Bildreaktor** *m* KERNTECH image reactor; **Bildregieraum** *m* FERNSEH video control room, vision control room; **Bildröhre** *f* ELEKTRONIK metal-cone tube, picture tube, TV kinescope

bildsam *adj* METALL ductile

Bild: **Bildscanner** *m* FERNSEH image scanner; **Bildschaltmatrix** *f* FERNSEH video switching matrix; **Bildschärfe** *f* FOTO definition, OPTIK sharpness

Bildschirm *m* COMP & DV display screen, display, monitor, screen, ELEKTRONIK display screen, screen, FERNSEH monitor, scope, screen, RADIO screen, TELEKOM display screen; ~ **mit starker Grundhelligkeit** *m* ELEKTRONIK high-brightness screen; **Bildschirmadapter** *m* COMP & DV display adaptor, monitor adaptor; **Bildschirmanschluß** *m* COMP & DV display adaptor; **Bildschirmanzeige** *f* COMP & DV panel, TELEKOM display, visual display unit; **Bildschirmanzeigeformat** *nt* COMP & DV screen format; **Bildschirmauflösung** *f* COMP & DV display resolution; **Bildschirmausdruck** *m* COMP & DV screen dump; **Bildschirmausgabe** *f* COMP & DV soft copy; **Bildschirmausgabegerät** *nt* GERÄT output display terminal; **Bildschirmauszug** *m* COMP & DV screen dump; **Bildschirmblättern** *nt* COMP & DV scrolling; **Bildschirmcontroller** *m* COMP & DV display controller; **Bildschirmdarstellung** *f* COMP & DV soft copy; **Bildschirmeditor** *m* COMP & DV screen editor; **Bildschirmeinstellung** *f* COMP & DV display setting; **Bildschirmendgerät** *nt* TELEKOM screen terminal; **Bildschirmgerät** *nt* COMP & DV VDU, visual display unit, FERNSEH VDU, video display unit, KONTROLL, PHYS, TELEKOM VDU; **Bildschirmgröße** *f* COMP & DV display size; **Bildschirmhelligkeit** *f* WASSERTRANS *Radar* display brilliance; **Bildschirminhalt** *m* COMP & DV screenful

Bildschirminhalt: ~ **löschen** *vi* COMP & DV clear screen

Bildschirm: **Bildschirmkarte** *f* COMP & DV video card; **Bildschirmkonsole** *f* COMP & DV display console; **Bildschirmmenü** *nt* COMP & DV display menu; **Bildschirmprozessor** *m* COMP & DV display processor; **Bildschirmregler** *m* ELEKTRONIK CRT controller; **Bildschirmspeicher** *m* COMP & DV screen memory; **Bildschirmsteuereinheit** *f* COMP & DV display controller; **Bildschirmtext** *m* (*Btx*) FERNSEH teletex, Videotex®, TELEKOM Teletext® (*Btx*) interactive videotex; **Bildschirmtreiber** *m* COMP & DV display driver; **Bildschirmtyp** *f* COMP & DV monitor type

Bild: **Bildschlupf** *m* FERNSEH picture slip; **Bildschwankungen** *f* *pl* FERNSEH jitter; **Bildseitenverhältniseinstellung** *f* FERNSEH aspect-ratio adjustment

bildseitig: **~er Brennpunkt** *m* FOTO rear focus

Bild: **Bildsequenz** *f* TELEKOM image sequence; **Bildsignal** *nt* ELEKTRONIK image signal, picture signal, FERNSEH, PHYS video signal, TELEKOM picture signal; **Bildsignal mit Austastung** *nt* FERNSEH video signal with blanking; **Bildsignalcodierung** *f* TELEKOM composite signal coding; **Bildsignalimpuls** *m* FERNSEH video signal pulse; **Bildsondenröhre** *f* TV image dissector; **Bildspeicher** *m* ELEKTRONIK image storage, FERNSEH frame store; **Bildspeicherröhre** *f* ELEKTRONIK image storage tube, storage tube; **Bildspeicherung** *f* ELEKTROTECH image storage; **Bildspur** *f* ELEKTRONIK trace; **Bildspur-Integration** *f* ELEKTRONIK trace integration; **Bildspur-Intensivierung** *f* ELEKTRONIK trace intensification; **Bildsteuerspule** *f* FERNSEH image control coil; **Bildsteuerung** *f* FERNSEH framing control; **Bildstörung** *f* ELEKTRONIK long-line effect, FERNSEH image interference; **Bildstrich** *m* FERNSEH frame line; **Bildstricheinstellung** *f* FERNSEH framing; **Bildsynchronisierung** *f* FERNSEH frame synchronization control; **Bildsynthese** *f* ELEKTRONIK imaging, KÜNSTL INT image synthesis; **Bildsynthese-Anordnung** *f* ELEKTRONIK imaging array; **Bildsynthese-Chip** *m* ELEKTRONIK imaging chip; **Bildsynthesizer** *m* FERNSEH video synthesizer; **Bildtelefon** *nt* FERNSEH videophone; **Bildtelefonvermittlungssystem** *nt* FERNSEH videophone switching system; **Bildtext** *m* DRUCK caption; **Bildtiefe** *f* FERNSEH depth of field; **Bildträger** *m* ELEKTRONIK picture carrier, FERNSEH image carrier, video carrier, vision carrier; **Bildtransfer** *m* TELEKOM image transfer; **Bildüberschrift** *f* VERPACK caption; **Bildübertragung** *f* COMP & DV picture transmission, TELEKOM image transmission; **Bildumlauf** *m* COMP & DV wraparound; **Bildumsetzung** *f* ELEKTRONIK image conversion

Bildung *f* AKUSTIK, MECHAN, PHYS, THERMOD formation; **~ der Lautheit** *f* AKUSTIK formation of loudness; **~ von Oberflächenerhebungen** *f* PAPIER *Fehler im Papier* blistering; **Bildungsenthalpie** *f* MECHAN, PHYS, THERMOD enthalpy of formation; **Bildungswärme** *f* THERMOD heat of formation

Bild: **Bildunterdrückung** *f* FERNSEH picture compression; **Bildunterschrift** *f* DRUCK VERPACK caption; **Bildverarbeitung** *f* COMP & DV picture processing, ELEKTRONIK, KÜNSTL INT, RADIO, TELEKOM image processing; **Bildverbesserung** *f* FERNSEH image enhancement; **Bildverdichtung** *f* ELEKTRONIK image compression; **Bildverlustsynchronisation** *f* FERNSEH loss of picture lock; **Bildverriegelung** *f* FERNSEH picture lock, pixlock; **Bildverschiebung** *f* FERNSEH picture shift; **Bildversetzung** *f* METALL image dislocation; **Bildverständnis** *nt* (*BV*) KÜNSTL INT image comprehension, image understanding; **Bildverstärker** *m* ELEKTRONIK image intensifier, *Röntgenstrahlen* image intensifier, FERNSEH image enhancer, image intensifier, video amplifier; **Bildverstärkerröhre** *f* ELEKTRONIK image enhancement tube, FERNSEH image intensifier tube; **Bildverstärkung** *f* ELEKTRONIK image enhancement; **Bildverstehen** *nt* (*BV*) KÜNSTL INT image comprehension, image understanding; **Bildverteilerverstärker** *m* FERNSEH video distribution amplifier; **Bildvervielfachung** *f* FERNSEH split image;

Bildvorlage *f* KONSTZEICH master illustration; **Bildvorverstärkung** *f* FERNSEH video pre-emphasis; **Bildwandler** *m* COMP & DV imager, ELEKTRONIK image converter; **Bildwandlerröhre** *f* ELEKTRONIK image converter tube; **Bildwandlung** *f* TELEKOM image conversion; **Bildwechselfrequenz** *f* FERNSEH field frequency, frame rate; **Bildwechselfrequenzabweichung** *f* FERNSEH frame slip; **Bildwechselimpuls** *m* FERNSEH frame pulse; **Bildwechselneutralisierungsmagnet** *m* FERNSEH field-neutralizing magnet; **Bildwechselschalter** *m* FERNSEH field shift switch; **Bildwechselsynchronisierung** *f* FERNSEH field sync alignment; **Bildwechsel-Synchronisierungsimpuls** *m* FERNSEH frame sync pulse; **Bildwiederholfrequenz** *f* COMP & DV refresh rate; **Bildwiederholmodus** *m* ELEKTRONIK refresh mode; **Bildwiederholsignal** *nt* ELEKTRONIK refresh signal; **Bildwiederholung** *f* TV refresh; **Bildzähler** *m* FOTO frame counter; **Bildzeichen** *nt* KONSTZEICH pictorial symbol, PATENT figurative mark; **Bildzeile** *f* COMP & DV display line; **Bildzentrierung** *f* FERNSEH shift control; **Bildzerfall** *m* FERNSEH picture breakup; **Bildzerleger** *m* FERNSEH dissector tube; **Bildzerlegung** *f* TELEKOM scanning; **Bildzusammenziehung** *f* FERNSEH image contraction; **Bildzwischenfrequenzfilter** *nt* ELEKTRONIK picture carrier filter

Bilge *f* WASSERTRANS *Schiffbau* bilge; **Bilgegebläse** *nt* WASSERTRANS bilge blower; **Bilgenpumpe** *f* MEERSCHMUTZ gulley sucker; **Bilgewasser** *nt* WASSERTRANS bilge water

Bilirubin *nt* CHEMIE bilirubin

Billet: **~sche Halblinse** *f* PHYS Billet's split lens

billig: **~stes Angebot** *nt* BAU lowest bid

Billigflagge *f* WASSERTRANS *Seehandel* flag of convenience

Billion *f* MATH billion (BrE), trillion (AmE)

Bimetall *nt* FERTIG bimetal; **Bimetall-** *pref* METALL bimetallic; **Bimetalldraht** *m* ELEKTROTECH bimetallic wire; **Bimetallinstrument** *nt* GERÄT bimetallic instrument

bimetallisch *adj* METALL bimetallic

Bimetall: **Bimetallkolben** *m* KFZTECH bimetal piston; **Bimetallkontakt** *m* ELEKTROTECH bimetallic contact; **Bimetallschalter** *m* ELEKTRIZ bimetallic switch; **Bimetallstreifen** *m* ELEKTRIZ bimetallic strip, bimetallic switch, METALL, PHYS, THERMOD bimetallic strip; **Bimetallthermometer** *nt* GERÄT bimetallic thermometer, THERMOD bimetallic strip thermometer

bimodal: **~er Bus** *m* KFZTECH dual-mode bus; **~e Wahrscheinlichkeitsverteilung** *f* QUAL bimodal probability distribution

bimolekular *adj* CHEMIE bimolecular

Bimsstein *m* FERTIG, KER & GLAS pumice

Binaphthalin *nt* CHEMIE binaphthyl

Binär- *pref* COMP & DV, ELEKTRONIK binary

binär[1] *adj* CHEMIE, COMP & DV, ELEKTRIZ, MATH, METALL binary

binär[2] **~er Abschaltkreis** *m* REGELUNG binary de-energizing circuit; **~e Addition** *f* ELEKTRONIK binary addition; **~er Baum** *m* COMP & DV binary tree, heap, tree; **nicht ~er Code** *m* TELEKOM nonbinary code; **~e Division** *f* ELEKTRONIK binary division; **~es Ladeprogramm** *nt* COMP & DV binary loader; **~e Legierung** *f* ELEKTRIZ binary; **~e Multiplikation** *f* ELEKTRONIK binary multiplication; **~e Phasenumtastung** *f* (*BPSK*) TELEKOM binary phase shift keying (*BPSK*); **~e**

Schaltkette *f* REGELUNG binary switching chain; **~es Signal** *nt* COMP & DV, ELEKTRONIK binary signal; **~es Sortieren** *nt* COMP & DV binary sort; **~er Speicherauszug** *m* COMP & DV binary dump; **~e Subtraktion** *f* ELEKTRONIK binary subtraction; **~er Suchbaum** *m* KÜNSTL INT binary search tree; **~e Suche** *f* COMP & DV binary search; **~es Suchen** *nt* COMP & DV dichotomizing search; **~es Verknüpfungsglied** *nt* REGELUNG binary combinational element; **~e Verzögerungsleitung** *f* FERNSEH binary delay line; **~e Wasserstoffverbindung** *f* CHEMIE hydride

Binär-: **Binäraddierer** *m* ELEKTRONIK binary adder; **Binärarithmetik** *f* COMP & DV, ELEKTRONIK binary arithmetic; **Binärcode** *m* COMP & DV binary code

binärcodiert: **~e Dezimalzahl** *f* (*BCD*) COMP & DV, RADIO binary-coded decimal (*BCD*); **~e Drehzahl** *f* (*BCD*) COMP & DV binary-coded decimal (*BCD*); **~es Signal** *nt* ELEKTRONIK binary-coded signal

Binär-: **Binärcodierung** *f* TELEKOM binary coding; **Binärdividierer** *m* ELEKTRONIK binary divider; **Binärexponent** *m* COMP & DV binary exponent; **Binärfolge** *f* TELEKOM binary sequence; **Binärlogik** *f* COMP & DV binary logic; **Binärmuster** *nt* COMP & DV bit pattern; **Binäroperation** *f* COMP & DV binary operation; **Binärpunkt** *m* COMP & DV binary point; **Binärschreibweise** *f* COMP & DV binary notation, binary representation; **Binärsequenz** *f* COMP & DV binary sequence; **Binärsignal** *nt* COMP & DV, TELEKOM binary signal; **Binärspalte** *f* COMP & DV binary column; **Binärspeicherelement** *nt* TELEKOM two-state register

binärsynchron: **~e Übertragung** *f* (*BSC-Übertragung*) COMP & DV binary synchronous communication (*BSC*)

Binär-: **Binärsystem** *nt* COMP & DV binary system; **Binäruntersetzer** *m* ELEKTRONIK binary scaler; **Binärzahl** *f* COMP & DV binary number, MATH binary; **Binärzähler** *m* COMP & DV, ELEKTRONIK binary counter, GERÄT binary counter, dual counter; **Binärzeichen** *nt* COMP & DV binary character, bit; **Binärzeichenfolge** *f* TELEKOM binary sequence; **Binärziffer** *f* COMP & DV binary digit

binaural *adj* ERGON binaural

Binde- *pref* BAU cementing, COMP & DV link, linking, MASCHINEN link, METALL binding; **Bindedraht** *m* ELEKTROTECH tie wire; **Bindeeisen** *nt* KER & GLAS stowing tool

bindefest *adj* ANSTRICH well-bonded

Binde-: **Bindeglied** *nt* MASCHINEN link; **Bindelader** *m* COMP & DV link loader, linking loader; **Bindemaschine** *f* VERPACK bundle-tying machine; **Bindemittel** *nt* ABFALL binder, binding agent, AUFNAHME binder, BAU binder, cement, cementing material, CHEMIE agglutinant, FERTIG agglomerant, agglutinant, KER & GLAS, KUNSTSTOFF binder, LEBENSMITTEL, MEERSCHMUTZ binding agent, METALL binding agent, cement, PAPIER fixing agent; **Bindemittelemulsion** *f* CHEMTECH emulsion binder

Binden *nt* DRUCK bookbinding, KOHLEN, KÜNSTL INT *einer Variablen* binding

binden *vt* BAU *Zement*, DRUCK *Bücher* bind

Binder *m* ANSTRICH binder, BAU binder, girder, COMP & DV link editor, linker, FERTIG matrix, MEERSCHMUTZ binding agent; **Binderbalken** *m* BAU binding beam, main girder; **Binderei** *f* DRUCK bindery; **Binderfarbe** *f* BAU water-based paint; **Binderlage** *f* BAU base course, header course

binderlos: **~e Dachkonstruktion** *f* BAU untrussed roof

Binder: **Binderprogramm** *nt* COMP & DV linkage editor; **Binderschicht** *f* BAU binder; **Bindersparren** *m* BAU common rafter, principal rafter; **Binderstein** *m* BAU header, *Mauerwerk* binding stone, *in Wandstärke* through stone; **Binderziegel** *m* BAU bonder, bondstone

Binde-: **Bindeschicht** *f* ANSTRICH tie coat, BAU *Straßenbau* tack coat; **Bindestrich** *m* DRUCK hyphen; **Bindeton** *m* BAU pipe clay; **Bindewort** *nt* COMP & DV connective

Bindfaden *m* TEXTIL cord, twine

bindig[1] *adj* BAU cohesive

bindig:[2] **~er Boden** *m* KOHLEN cohesive soil; **nicht ~er Boden** *m* KOHLEN noncohesive soil; **~es Erdmaterial** *nt* BAU binder soil

Bindigkeit *f* BAU cohesion, KOHLEN cohesion, cohesion strength

Bindung *f* ERDÖL *Petrochemie*, KER & GLAS bond, KUNSTSTOFF linkage, KÜNSTL INT *einer Variablen* binding, MASCHINEN bond; **Bindungsenergie** *f* (*B*) KERNTECH, STRAHLPHYS, TEILPHYS binding energy (*B*); **Bindungsenergiekurve** *f* KERNTECH binding energy curve; **Bindungsmuster** *nt* TEXTIL weave; **Bindungswärme** *f* THERMOD heat of absorption; **Bindungswertigkeit** *f* KERNTECH covalence

Binnen- *pref* WASSERTRANS, WASSERVERSORG home, inland, river; **Binnenflotte** *f* WASSERTRANS river fleet; **Binnengewässer** *nt pl* WASSERVERSORG inland waters; **Binnenhafen** *m* WASSERTRANS inner port; **Binnenhandel** *m* WASSERTRANS home trade; **Binnenquelle** *f* UMWELTSCHMUTZ internal source; **Binnenschiff** *nt* WASSERTRANS *Schifftyp* canal boat; **Binnenschiffahrt** *f* WASSERTRANS inland navigation, inland water transport; **Binnenschiffahrtsstraße** *f* WASSERTRANS inland waterway; **Binnenstrecke** *f* WASSERTRANS inland haulage; **Binnenvorsteven** *m* WASSERTRANS *Schiffbau* apron; **Binnenwasserstraße** *f* WASSERTRANS inland waterway

binokular[1] *adj* ERGON, OPTIK, PHYS binocular

binokular:[2] **~e Konkurrenz** *f* ERGON binocular rivalry; **~e Rivalität** *f* ERGON binocular rivalry

Binokular-Mikroskop *nt* LABOR binocular microscope

Binom *nt* MATH binomial

Binomial- *pref* PHYS, QUAL binominal; **Binomialverteilung** *f* PHYS binomial distribution

binominal: **~e Grundgesamtheit** *f* QUAL binominal population

Binominal- *pref* QUAL binominal; **Binominalverteilung** *f* QUAL binominal distribution; **Binominalwahrscheinlichkeit** *f* QUAL binominal probability

binomisch: **~er Lehrsatz** *m* MATH binomial theorem

Bio- *pref* UMWELTSCHMUTZ biological; **Bioabbaubarkeit** *f* VERPACK biodegradation; **Bioabfall** *m* UMWELTSCHMUTZ biological waste

biochemisch: **~er Indikator** *m* UMWELTSCHMUTZ biochemical tracer

Bio-: **Biodynamik** *f* ERGON biodynamics; **Bioengineering** *nt* ERGON bioengineering; **Biofilter** *nt* CHEMTECH biological filter, UMWELTSCHMUTZ biofilter; **Biogas** *nt* ABFALL biogas, digester gas, fermentation gas, manure gas, UMWELTSCHMUTZ fermentation gas

biogen *adj* ERDÖL biogenic

biogenetisch *adj* ERDÖL *Kohlenwasserstoff-Formation* biogenic

Bio-: **Bioglas** *nt* KER & GLAS bioglass; **Bioindikator** *m* UMWELTSCHMUTZ bioindicator, biological indicator

biologisch:[1] **~ abbaubar** *adj* ANSTRICH, UMWELTSCHMUTZ biodegradable

biologisch:[2] **~er Abbau** *m* MEERSCHMUTZ, UMWELT-SCHMUTZ biodegradation, biological degradation, VERPACK biodegradation; **~ abbaubare Substanz** *f* UMWELTSCHMUTZ biodegradable substance; **~ abbaubarer Abfall** *m* ABFALL biodegradable waste; **~ nicht abbaubarer Abfall** *m* ABFALL nonbiodegradable waste; **~e Abbaubarkeit** *f* UMWELTSCHMUTZ biodegradability; **~e Abschirmung** *f* KERNTECH biological shield; **~e Abwasserreinigung** *f* WASSERVERSORG biological water treatment; **~e Affinität** *f* KERNTECH *von Radioisotopen* biological affinity; **~es Agens** *nt* UMWELTSCHMUTZ biological agent; **~e Behandlung** *f* UMWELTSCHMUTZ biological treatment; **~er Effekt ionisierender Strahlung** *m* STRAHLPHYS biological effect of ionizing radiation; **~es Filter** *nt* ABFALL biological filter; **~e Gefahr** *f* SICHERHEIT biological hazard; **~es Gleichgewicht** *nt* UMWELTSCHMUTZ biological equilibrium; **~e Kläranlage** *f* UMWELTSCHMUTZ biological clarification plant; **~er Körper** *m* CHEMTECH biological filter; **~e Kriegsführung** *f* UMWELTSCHMUTZ biological warfare; **~e Nachreinigung** *f* ABFALL secondary sewage treatment; **~er Rasen** *m* CHEMTECH biological filter, WASSERVERSORG bacteria bed; **~er Sauerstoffbedarf** *m (BSB)* ABFALL, LEBENSMITTEL, UMWELTSCHMUTZ biological oxygen demand *(BOD)*; **~er Schild** *m* KERNTECH biological shield; **-schützendes Kühlsystem** *nt* KERNTECH biological protection cooling system; **~e Umwandlung** *f* ABFALL biological energy conversion; **~e Zersetzung** *f* MEERSCHMUTZ biodegradation, biological degradation

Bio-: **Biomasse** *f* NICHTFOSS ENERG biomass; **Biomechanik** *f* ERGON biomechanics; **Biometrie** *f* ERGON biometry; **Biomüllkompost** *m* UMWELTSCHMUTZ biowaste compost; **Biomüllkompostierung** *f* UMWELTSCHMUTZ biological waste composting; **Biophysik** *f* PHYS biophysics

biorientiert: **~e Folie** *f* KUNSTSTOFF biaxially oriented film

Biose *f* CHEMIE biose

biosozial *adj* ERGON biosocial

Bio-: **Biosphäre** *f* UMWELTSCHMUTZ biosphere; **Biostabilisator** *m* ABFALL biostabilizer; **Biotechnologie** *f* LEBENSMITTEL, CHEM biotechnology

Biotin *nt* LEBENSMITTEL biotin

Biotit *m* KER & GLAS biotite

Biot-Savart: **~sches Gesetz** *nt* PHYS Biot-Savart law, Laplace's law

Biozönose *f* UMWELTSCHMUTZ biocoenosis

Biphenyl *nt* CHEMIE biphenyl, phenylbenzene

Bipolar- *pref* COMP & DV, ELEKTRONIK, PHYS, RADIO bipolar; **Bipolarcode** *m* TELEKOM bipolar code; **Bipolar-Mischtechnik** *f* ELEKTRONIK merged bipolar technology; **Bipolar-Technologie** *f* ELEKTRONIK bipolar technology

bipolar[1] *adj* COMP & DV, PHYS, RADIO bipolar

bipolar:[2] **~e Diode** *f* ELEKTRONIK bipolar diode; **~ integrierte Schaltung** *f* COMP & DV bipolar integrated circuit; **~e integrierte Siliziumschaltung** *f* ELEKTRONIK silicon bipolar integrated circuit; **~er Leistungstransistor** *m* ELEKTRONIK bipolar power transistor; **~e Logik** *f* ELEKTRONIK bipolar logic; **~e Schrittinversion** *f* *(AMI)* TELEKOM alternate mark inversion *(AMI)*; **~es Signal** *nt* TELEKOM bipolar signal; **~e Stromversorgung** *f* ELEKTROTECH bipolar power supply

Bipolar-: **Bipolartransistor** *m* ELEKTRONIK *mit P- und mit N-Halbleitern aufgebaut* bipolar transistor, PHYS bipolar transistor, junction transistor, TELEKOM bipolar transistor

Biprisma *nt* FERTIG, OPTIK biprism

biquinär[1] *adj* COMP & DV biquinary

biquinär:[2] **~e Zahl** *f* COMP & DV biquinary number

Biquinärcode *m* COMP & DV biquinary code

Birne *f* FERTIG Bessemer converter, METALL converter; **Birnenblitz** *m* FOTO flash bulb

birnenförmig: **~es Gefäß** *nt* LABOR pear-shaped vessel

Bisazimethylen *nt* CHEMIE ketazine

Bisazofarbstoff *m* CHEMIE bis-azo dye

B-ISDN-Dienst *m* TELEKOM broadband ISDN service

bisherig: **~er Stand der Technik** *m* PATENT background art

Biskuit- *pref* KER & GLAS biscuit; **Biskuiteintauchvorrichtung** *f* KER & GLAS biscuit dipper; **Biskuitporzellan** *nt* KER & GLAS biscuit-baked porcelain; **Biskuitware** *f* KER & GLAS *Keramik* biscuit ware

Bismut *nt (Bi)* CHEMIE bismuth *(Bi)*

Bisphenol: **~ A** *nt* KUNSTSTOFF bisphenol A

Bißwinkel *m* KOHLEN angle of nip

bistabil[1] *adj* COMP & DV, ELEKTRONIK, RADIO bistable

bistabil:[2] **~es Kippglied** *nt* ELEKTRONIK bistable circuit; **~e Kippschaltung** *f* ELEKTRONIK *mit zwei stabilen Ausgangszuständen* flip-flop; **~e Kippschaltung** *f* PHYS flip-flop; **~er Multivibrator** *m* ELEKTRONIK bistable multivibrator, scaling circuit; **~es Relais** *nt* ELEKTROTECH bistable relay; **~e Schaltung** *f* COMP & DV flip-flop

Bistabilität *f* TELEKOM bistability

Bisulfit *nt* CHEMIE bisulfite (AmE), bisulphite (BrE)

Bit *nt* COMP & DV binary digit, bit, ELEKTRONIK *Binärziffer*, FERTIG, TELEKOM bit; **~ mit höchster Wertigkeit** *nt* COMP & DV high-order bit; **Bitabbildung** *f* COMP & DV bitmap; **Bitbearbeitung** *f* COMP & DV bit handling; **Bitebene** *f* COMP & DV bit plane; **Bitelement** *nt* ELEKTRONIK bit slice; **Bitfehlerquote** *f (BER)* COMP & DV binary error rate, bit error rate *(BER)*; **Bitfehlerrate** *f (BER)* COMP & DV binary error rate, bit error rate *(BER)*; **Bitfolgefrequenz** *f* TELEKOM bit rate; **Bit-für-Bit-Codierung** *f* TELEKOM bit-by-bit encoding; **Bitgruppe** *f* COMP & DV byte, TELEKOM bit group; **Bitkette** *f* COMP & DV, ELEKTRONIK bit string; **Bitmap** *f* COMP & DV *Dateiformat* bitmap, paper feed, paper throw; **Bitmapping** *nt* ELEKTRONIK *Speicherung als digitales Muster* bit mapping; **Bitmuster** *nt* COMP & DV, KONTROLL bit pattern

bitorientiert: **~e Datenübertragungssteuerung** *f (cf bitorientiertes Übertragungssteuerungsverfahren)* COMP & DV, TELEKOM high-level data link control; **~es Übertragungssteuerungsverfahren** *nt (cf bitorientierte Datenübertragungssteuerung)* COMP & DV, TELEKOM high-level data link control

bitparallel: **~e Übertragung** *f* COMP & DV bit-parallel transfer

Bit: **Bitrate** *f* TELEKOM bit rate; **Bitratenumschalter** *m* TELEKOM bit switch; **Bitreihe** *f* COMP & DV bit stream

Bits: **~ pro Sekunde** *nt pl (bps)* COMP & DV *Maß für die Datenübertragungsgeschwindigkeit* bits per second *(bps)*; **~ pro Zoll** *nt pl (bpi)* COMP & DV *Maß für die Aufzeichnungsdichte* bits per inch *(bpi)*

bit-seriell: **~e Übertragung** *f* COMP & DV bit-serial transfer

Bit-Slice *m* ELEKTRONIK *Prozessorelement* bit slice; **Bit-Slice-Prozessor** *m* ELEKTRONIK *Prozessor zur Erzielung bestimmter Wortlängen* bit slice processor

Bitter-Magnet *m* PHYS Bitter magnet

Bitterstoff *m* CHEMIE bittern
Bitter-Streifen *m* PHYS Bitter pattern
Bitterwert *m* LEBENSMITTEL bittering value
Bit: Bitübertragungsschicht *f* COMP & DV, TELEKOM *OSI* physical layer
Bitumen *nt* BAU bitumen, ERDÖL *Destillationsprodukt* bitumen, *Raffinerie* asphalt, KUNSTSTOFF bitumen; **Bitumenanstrich** *f* FERTIG bituminous paint; **Bitumenanstrichfarbe** *f* KUNSTSTOFF bituminous paint; **Bitumenbeton** *m* BAU asphalt concrete; **Bitumenemulsion** *f* BAU bitumen emulsion; **Bitumenfolie** *f* BAU bituminous membrane
bitumenhaltig *adj* BAU bituminous
Bitumen: **Bitumenlack** *m* FERTIG bitumen varnish; **Bitumenmembran** *f* BAU bituminous membrane; **Bitumenpapier** *nt* PAPIER tarred brown paper; **Bitumenpappe** *f* BAU bitumen board
Bituminieren *nt* BAU bituminization
bituminieren *vt* BAU bituminize
bituminiert: **~es Papier** *nt* VERPACK bitumen-coated paper
bituminös *adj* BAU bituminous
Bit: Bitverarbeitung *f* COMP & DV bit manipulation; **Bitvollgruppe** *f* TELEKOM *Datenvermittlung* envelope
bivalent[1] *adj* CHEMIE bivalent, divalent
bivalent:[2] **~es Heizsystem** *nt* HEIZ & KÄLTE fuel/electric heating system
Bivalenz *f* CHEMIE bivalence, divalence
Bivinyl *nt* CHEMIE bivinyl, divinyl
Bixin *nt* LEBENSMITTEL anatto, annatto, bixin
Bk *(Berkelium)* CHEMIE Bk *(berkelium)*
B-Kanal *m* TELEKOM B-channel
Blachenstoff *m* TEXTIL canvas
Blackboard *nt* KÜNSTL INT blackboard
Blackbox *f* COMP & DV, LUFTTRANS black box
Blähmittel *nt* CHEMTECH foaming agent
blanchieren *vt* LEBENSMITTEL blanch
Blank- *pref* FERTIG bright, *Draht* bare
blank[1] *adj* BAU bare, sound, ELEKTROTECH bare, FERTIG bright-finished, *Draht* bare, MASCHINEN bright, plain
blank:[2] **~er Aluminiumdraht** *m* ELEKTROTECH BAW, bare aluminium wire (BrE), bare aluminum wire (AmE); **~er Draht** *m* TELEKOM bare wire; **~e Kette** *f* METALL bright chain; **~er Leitungsdraht** *m* ELEKTROTECH bare wire; **~e Schraube** *f* MASCHINEN bright bolt; **~er Stahl** *m* METALL bright steel; **~er Stahldraht** *m* METALL bright steel wire
blank:[3] **~ reiben** *vt* BAU scour
Blank-: **Blankätzbad** *nt* KER & GLAS clear etching bath; **Blankätzen** *nt* KER & GLAS clear etching; **Blankbrennen** *nt* FERTIG bright dip finishing; **Blankdraht** *m* FERTIG naked wire, METALL bright wire, TELEKOM bare wire
Blanket *nt* KERNTECH breeding blanket
blankgeglüht[1] *adj* FERTIG bright-annealed
blankgeglüht:[2] **~er Draht** *m* MASCHINEN bright-annealed wire
Blank-: **Blankglühen** *nt* METALL bright annealing; **Blankschleifen** *nt* KER & GLAS smooth grinding, *von Spiegelglas* smoothing; **Blankziehen** *nt* FERTIG bright-drawing
Blas- *pref* KER & GLAS, VERPACK blow; **~-, Abfüll- und Verschließsystem** *nt* VERPACK blow fill seal system; **Blas-Blas-Verfahren** *nt* KER & GLAS blow-and-blow process
Bläschen *nt* KER & GLAS seed, OPTIK bubble; **Bläschenbildungspotential** *nt* KER & GLAS seeding potential

bläschenfrei *adj* KER & GLAS seed-free
Blase *f* CHEMIE void, CHEMTECH bubble, FERTIG *Guß* flaw, KOHLEN bubble, KUNSTSTOFF blister, bubble, METALL blister, blow hole, PAPIER, PHYS bubble, WASSERTRANS, WERKPRÜF blister; **~ mit eingeschlossenem Fremdkörper** *f* KER & GLAS cat's eye; **Blasebalg** *m* FERTIG bellows, smith's bellows, MECHAN bellows; **Blasebalgpumpe** *f* LABOR bellows pump
Blasen *nt* FERTIG air blasting; **~ im Konverter** *nt* FERTIG Bessemer blow
Blasen: **~ bilden** *vi* PAPIER bubble; **~ werfen** *vi* WERKPRÜF blister
blasen *vi* ELEKTRIZ, PAPIER, RAUMFAHRT *Raumschiff* blow
Blase: **Blasenauftrieb** *m* KER & GLAS train of bubbles; **Blasenbildung** *f* PAPIER bubbling; **Blasendestillation** *f* KERNTECH batch distillation; **Blasendestillationsanlage** *f* ERDÖL *Raffinerie* batch still; **Blasenfolie** *f* VERPACK bubble film; **Blasenglocke** *f* LEBENSMITTEL *einer Glockenbodenkolonne* bubble cap; **Blasenkammer** *f* KERNTECH, PHYS, STRAHLPHYS, TEILPHYS bubble chamber; **Blasenloch** *nt* FERTIG pit hole; **Blasenmodell** *nt* METALL bubble model; **Blasenprobe** *f* PAPIER bubble test
blasenreich: **~es Glas** *nt* KER & GLAS very seedy glass
Blase: **Blasenschleier** *m* KER & GLAS feather; **Blasensieden** *nt* HEIZ & KÄLTE nucleate boiling; **Blasenspeicher** *m* COMP & DV bubble memory, magnetic bubble memory; **Blasenstahl** *m* METALL blister steel; **Blasenverpackung** *f* VERPACK air bubble wrap, bubble pack; **Blasenzähler** *m* CHEMTECH bubble gage (AmE), bubble gauge (BrE)
Blas-: **Blasflasche** *f* VERPACK blown bottle; **Blasfolie** *f* KUNSTSTOFF blown film; **Blasform** *f* FERTIG *Plaste* blow die, MASCHINEN blow mold (AmE), blow mould (BrE); **Blasformen** *nt* KUNSTSTOFF blow molding (AmE), blow moulding (BrE); **Blasformverfahren** *nt* VERPACK blow-molding process (AmE), blow-moulding process (BrE); **Blaskopf** *m* KER & GLAS blow head, KUNSTSTOFF parison die; **Blasloch** *nt* FERTIG *Thermitschweißen* heating gate; **Blasmagnet** *m* ELEKTROTECH magnetic blowout; **Blasöl** *nt* MASCHINEN blown oil; **Blasring** *m* KER & GLAS blowing ring; **Blasrotor** *m* LUFTTRANS *eines Hubschraubers* jet-flapped rotor; **Blasspule** *f* ELEKTROTECH blowout coil; **Blastisch** *m* KER & GLAS blow table; **Blaswalze** *f* PAPIER blow roll; **Blaswirkung** *f* FERTIG arc blow, *Lichtbogenschweißen* magnetic arc blow
Blatt *nt* BAU blade, COMP & DV leaf, DRUCK leaf, sheet, FERTIG band, *einer Säge* blade, KÜNSTL INT *eines Baumes* end node, terminal node, MASCHINEN blade, leaf, TEXTIL reed; **~ der Luftschraube** *nt* LUFTTRANS *Hubschrauber* blade; **~ einer Metallbandsäge** *nt* MASCHINEN metal-cutting bandsaw blade; **~ Papier** *nt* PAPIER slip; **Blattanstellwinkel** *m* LUFTTRANS *Hubschrauber* blade pitch angle; **Blattanstellwinkel-Übertragungsgerät** *nt* LUFTTRANS *Hubschrauber* blade pitch transmitter; **Blattbelastung** *f* LUFTTRANS *Hubschrauber* blade loading; **Blattbildungseinheit** *f* PAPIER *Maschine* former; **Blattbohrmeißel** *m* ERDÖL *Bohrtechnik* drag bit, *Flachbohrtechnik* spudding bit; **Blattbreite** *f* TEXTIL width of reed
Blättchen *nt* KUNSTSTOFF platelet
Blatter *f* KER & GLAS blister
Blätter *nt pl* KOHLEN pieces of paper; **Blätteranker** *m* ELEKTRIZ laminated armature; **Blätterbürste** *f* ELEK-

TRIZ laminated brush; **Blättergips** *m* CHEMIE selenite; **Blätterkern** *m* ELEKTRIZ laminated core; **Blätterknauf** *m* BAU finial; **Blätterkohle** *f* KOHLEN paper coal, papyraceous lignite, slate-foliated lignite; **Blätterlack** *m* FERTIG shellac; **Blätterleiste** *f* COMP & DV scroll bar; **Blättermagnet** *m* ELEKTRIZ laminated magnet, PHYS compound magnet; **Blättermodus** *m* COMP & DV scroll mode

Blättern *nt* COMP & DV browsing, scrolling, scroll

blättern *vi* COMP & DV browse, scroll

Blatt: **Blattfeder** *f* KFZTECH *Motor* leaf spring, MASCHINEN laminated spring, leaf spring, plate spring; **Blattfederstarrachse** *f* KFZTECH *Triebstrang* Hotchkiss drive; **Blattfilm** *m* FOTO sheet film; **Blattindex** *m* UMWELTSCHMUTZ leaf-area index; **Blattkante** *f* KONSTZEICH sheet border, sheet edge; **Blattkräuselkrankheit** *f* LEBENSMITTEL *Pflanzenkrankheitslehre* leaf-curl; **Blattoberfläche** *f* UMWELTSCHMUTZ foliar surface; **Blattroller** *m* LEBENSMITTEL *Pflanzenkrankheitslehre* leaf-roller; **Blattspitzengeräusch** *nt* LUFTTRANS *Hubschrauber* blade slap; **Blattspitzen-Geschwindigkeitsverhältnis** *nt* NICHTFOSS ENERG tip speed ratio; **Blattspitzenverlustfaktor** *m* LUFTTRANS *Hubschrauber* blade tip loss factor; **Blattspurprüfung** *f* LUFTTRANS *Hubschrauber* blade tracking; **Blattsteigung beim Propeller** *f* LUFTTRANS *Lage eines Flugzeugs oder Schiffs* pitch; **Blattsteigungs-Synchronismusanzeiger** *m* LUFTTRANS pitch throttle synchronizer; **Blattsteigungsverriegelung** *f* LUFTTRANS *Hubschrauber* pitch locking system

Blattung *f* BAU splice joint, *Holzbau* halved joint

Blatt: **Blattwerkstoffe** *m pl* NICHTFOSS ENERG *Propeller* blade materials; **Blattwespe** *f* LEBENSMITTEL *Schädlingsbekämpfung* sawfly; **Blattwinkelanzeigersynchro** *f* LUFTTRANS pitch detector synchro; **Blattwinkelradius** *m* LUFTTRANS pitch radius; **Blattwinkelverstellung** *f* LUFTTRANS *Hubschrauber* pitch control; **Blattwinkelverstellungsarm** *m* LUFTTRANS *Hubschrauber* pitch control arm; **Blattwinkelverstellungsbelastung** *f* LUFTTRANS *Hubschrauber* pitch control load; **Blattwinkelverstellungshebel** *m* LUFTTRANS *Hubschrauber* pitch control lever; **Blattwinkelverstellungs-Stangenwinkel** *m* LUFTTRANS pitch control rod angle; **Blattziffer** *f* DRUCK folio

Blau- *pref* FERNSEH, FERTIG, METALL blue

blau: ~**es Kieselgel** *nt* VERPACK blue silica gel; ~**er Peter** *m* WASSERTRANS *Flaggen* blue peter; ~**es Vitriol** *nt* CHEMIE copper sulfate (AmE), copper sulphate (BrE)

Blau: **Blaubruchgebiet** *nt* FERTIG blue-brittle range

blaubrüchig *adj* FERTIG blue-brittle

Blau-: **Blaubrüchigkeit** *f* METALL blue-brittleness; **Blaudruck** *m* TEXTIL blueprint

blau: **blaugeglüht** *adj* FERTIG open-annealed

Blau-: **Blaugitter** *nt* FERNSEH blue screen-grid; **Blauglasquarz** *nt* CHEMIE blue hyaline-quartz; **Blauglühen** *nt* METALL blue annealing, open annealing

blauglühen *vt* FERTIG open-anneal

Blau-: **Blauglühung** *f* FERTIG open annealing

blaugrün: ~**er Laser** *m* ELEKTRONIK blue-green laser

Blau-: **Blaugrünfiltereinstellung** *f* FOTO minus red filter adjustment; **Blaukanone** *f* FERNSEH blue gun; **Blaumischer** *m* FERNSEH blue adder; **Blaupause** *f* BAU, DRUCK, MASCHINEN blueprint; **Blau-Schwarz-Pegel** *m* FERNSEH blue-black level

blauspröde *adj* FERTIG blue-short

Blau-: **Blausprödigkeit** *f* FERTIG blue-shortness, METALL

blue-brittleness; **Blaustein** *m* CHEMIE blue vitriol, copper vitriol, bluestone; **Blaustrahl** *m* FERNSEH blue beam; **Blaustrahlmagnet** *m* FERNSEH blue-beam magnet; **Blauton** *m* KER & GLAS blue clay; **Blauvitriol** *nt* CHEMIE blue vitriol, copper sulfate (AmE), copper sulphate (BrE); **Blauwärme** *f* FERTIG blue heat; **Blauwertspitze** *f* FERNSEH blue peak level

Blech *nt* FERTIG metal sheet, sheet metal, KERNTECH sheet, KFZTECH *Karosserieteil* panel, MECHAN sheet, METALL plate, sheet, WASSERTRANS *Metall* sheet; **Blechbiegemaschine** *f* FERTIG plate-bending rolls, sheet metal-bending machine, sheet-bending machine, MASCHINEN plate-bending press; **Blechbiegen** *nt* FERTIG sheet bending, MASCHINEN plate bending; **Blechbiegewalzen** *f pl* MASCHINEN plate-bending rollers, plate-bending rolls; **Blechbohrer** *m* FERTIG hole cutter, sheet drill; **Blechbördelmaschine** *f* FERTIG sheet-bordering machine

Blechen *nt* ELEKTROTECH *von Eisenkernen* lamination

Blech: **Blechfalz- und Biegemaschine** *f* MASCHINEN plate folding and bending machine; **Blechhalter** *m* FERTIG blank holder; **Blechkantenhobelmaschine** *f* FERTIG plate planer; **Blechkantennachformen** *nt* FERTIG plate-edge profiling; **Blechlehre** *f* FERTIG plate gage (AmE), plate gauge (BrE), sheet gage (AmE), sheet gauge (BrE), MASCHINEN plate gage (AmE), plate gauge (BrE), sheet gage (AmE), sheet gauge (BrE), sheet iron gage (AmE), sheet iron gauge (BrE), METROL plate gage (AmE), plate gauge (BrE); **Blechmaterial** *nt* FERTIG sheet stock; **Blechpaket** *nt* FERTIG packet, stacked sheets; **Blechpaketbohren** *nt* FERTIG packet drilling; **Blechrichtmaschine** *f* EISENBAHN, FERTIG plate-straightening machine; **Blechrohr** *nt* BAU sheet iron pipe; **Blechrundbiegemaschine** *f* FERTIG sheet metal-bending roll, sheet metal-bending rolls; **Blechschablone** *f* KONSTZEICH sheet metal stencil; **Blechschere** *f* FERTIG tinman's shear, MASCHINEN metal shears; **Blechschornstein** *m* BAU steel chimney; **Blechschraube** *f* MASCHINEN self-tapping screw, sheet metal screw, tapping screw; **Blechschraubengewinde** *nt* MASCHINEN tapping screw thread; **Blechschrott** *m* FERTIG sheet scrap; **Blechstegträger** *m* BAU plate web girder; **Blechtafelschere** *f* FERTIG plate shear; **Blechträger** *m* FERTIG plate girder; **Blechtrommel** *f* VERPACK metal drum; **Blechwalze** *f* MASCHINEN plate roll; **Blechwalzen** *nt* FERTIG plate rolling; **Blechwalzwerk** *nt* MASCHINEN plate mill; **Blechzange** *f* FERTIG dog; **Blechzuschnitt** *m* FERTIG blank

Blei[1] *nt (Pb)* CHEMIE lead

Blei:[2] ~ **und Zinnlegierungen** *phr* MASCHINEN lead and tin alloys

Blei: **Bleiakkumulator** *m* ELEKTRIZ, PHYS lead accumulator; **Bleiansatzstück** *nt* LABOR extension lead

bleiarm: ~**es Benzin** *nt* KFZTECH low-lead gasoline (AmE), low-lead petrol (BrE)

Blei: **Bleibatterie** *f* ELEKTRIZ lead accumulator

bleibend: ~**e Dehnung** *f* KUNSTSTOFF tension set; ~**er Fehler** *m* COMP & DV solid error; ~**e Regeldifferenz** *f* REGELUNG steady state deviation from the desired value; ~**e Verformung** *f* KUNSTSTOFF permanent set, set, MASCHINEN permanent set, METALL permanent deformation

Blei: **Bleiblech** *nt* BAU sheet lead

Bleich- *pref* FOTO bleach, KER & GLAS, PAPIER bleaching; **Bleichbad** *nt* FOTO bleach bath; **Bleichbütte** *f* PAPIER bleaching chest

Bleichen *nt* LEBENSMITTEL bleaching
bleichen *vt* LEBENSMITTEL, PAPIER, TEXTIL bleach
Bleich-: **Bleicherde** *f* KER & GLAS bleaching clay; **Bleichholländer** *m* PAPIER bleaching engine; **Bleichkalk** *m* TEXTIL bleaching powder; **Bleichlösung** *f* PAPIER bleaching liquor; **Bleichmittel** *nt* LEBENSMITTEL bleaching agent; **Bleichpulver** *nt* LEBENSMITTEL bleaching powder, chlorinated lime, PAPIER, TEXTIL bleaching powder; **Bleichturm** *m* PAPIER bleaching tower; **Bleichverfahren** *nt* PAPIER bleaching
Blei-: **Bleidichtung** *f* BAU lead joint, FERTIG lead packing; **Bleifarbe** *f* BAU lead paint; **Bleifeile** *f* BAU shave hook; **Bleifilter** *nt* KFZTECH lead filter
bleifrei[1] *adj* ERDÖL *Vergaserkraftstoffe* lead-free
bleifrei:[2] **~es Benzin** *nt* KFZTECH lead-free gasoline (AmE), lead-free petrol (BrE), unleaded gasoline (AmE), unleaded petrol (BrE), UMWELTSCHMUTZ lead-free gasoline (AmE), lead-free petrol (BrE)
Blei-: **Bleiglaszähler** *m* STRAHLPHYS lead glass counter; **Bleiglätte** *f* KUNSTSTOFF lead oxide, litharge
bleihaltig *adj* CHEMIE plumbic, plumbous
Blei-: **Bleikammerkristalle** *m pl* CHEMTECH chamber crystals; **Bleikammerverfahren** *nt* CHEMTECH chamber process; **Bleikristallglas** *nt* KER & GLAS lead crystal glass, *mit 30% Bleigehalt* full lead crystal glass; **Bleilot** *nt* ELEKTRIZ, MASCHINEN soft solder; **Bleimantel** *m* ELEKTRIZ, ELEKTROTECH *bei Kabel* lead sheath; **Bleimantelkabel** *nt* ELEKTROTECH lead-covered cable, lead-sheathed cable; **Bleimennige** *f* KER & GLAS, KUNSTSTOFF red lead; **Bleinaphthenat** *nt* KUNSTSTOFF lead naphthenate; **Blei-Orthoplumbat** *nt* CHEMIE lead tetroxide; **Bleioxid** *nt* CHEMIE lead dioxide, lead oxide, litharge; **Bleisatz** *m* DRUCK hot-metal typesetting; **Bleischwamm** *m* KFZTECH sponge lead; **Bleisicherung an der Fahrwerksfelge** *f* LUFTTRANS landing-gear wheel rim fusible plug; **Bleisilikat** *nt* KER & GLAS lead silicate; **Bleisulfat** *nt* CHEMIE lead sulfate (AmE), lead sulphate (BrE); **Bleisulfid** *nt* CHEMIE lead sulfide (AmE), lead sulphide (BrE); **Bleitetraethyl** *nt* CHEMIE lead tetraethyl, tetraethyl lead, tetraethylplumbane, KFZTECH tetraethyl lead; **Bleitype** *f* DRUCK lead printing letter
bleiumhüllt: **~es Kabel** *nt* ELEKTRIZ lead-covered cable, lead-sheathed cable
bleiverglast: **~es Fenster** *nt* KER & GLAS leaded light
Blei-: **Bleiversiegelung** *f* VERPACK lead seal; **Bleizucker** *m* LEBENSMITTEL sugar of lead; **Bleizusatzstoffe** *m pl* UMWELTSCHMUTZ lead additives
Blende[1] *f* AUFNAHME diaphragm, FERNSEH aperture, FERTIG shutter, slit, FOTO F stop, aperture, diaphragm, GERÄT *Pneumatik, Optik* measuring orifice, MECHAN diaphragm, PHYS aperture
Blende:[2] **~ schließen** *vi* FOTO stop down
Blende: **Blendeneinstellknopf** *m* FOTO aperture setting knob; **Blendeneinstellring** *m* FOTO aperture setting ring; **Blendeneinstellung** *f* FOTO aperture stop, stop; **Blendenöffnung** *f* COMP & DV aperture, FOTO focal aperture; **Blendenrevolver** *m* OPTIK revolving diaphragm; **Blendenring** *m* FOTO aperture ring; **Blendenrotor** *m* KFZTECH *mit gleicher Anzahl von Blenden wie Zylinder am Motor* trigger wheel; **Blendenskale** *f* FOTO aperture scale; **Blendensteuerung** *f* FERNSEH iris control button; **Blendenvorwähler** *m* FOTO aperture priority camera; **Blendenwert** *m* FOTO f-number, lens stop
Blendlicht *nt* SICHERHEIT glare

Blendmauer *f* BAU screen wall
Blendschutz *m* LUFTTRANS *gegen heiße Abgase* glare shield; **Blendschutzanstrich** *m* KUNSTSTOFF shading paint; **Blendschutzglas** *nt* KER & GLAS antidazzle glass; **Blendschutzschicht** *f* TELEKOM antiglare coating; **Blendschutzvisier** *nt* KFZTECH *Motorradhelm* antidazzle visor
Blendung *f* OPTIK glare
blendungsfrei *adj* SICHERHEIT glare-free, TRANS antidazzling
Blendziegel *m* BAU facing brick
blicken *vt* METALL brighten
Blickfeldblende *f* PHYS field stop
Blind- *pref* BAU blank, blind, ELEKTRIZ reactive, LUFTTRANS blind, MASCHINEN blank
blind[1] *adj* FERTIG *Walzen, Kaliber* false
blind:[2] **~er Gewindebolzen** *m* MASCHINEN blind stud bolt
Blind-: **Blindachse** *f* EISENBAHN blind axle; **Blindband** *m* DRUCK mock-up; **Blindboden** *m* FERTIG false bottom; **Blindbohrung** *f* BAU blind hole; **Blindelement** *nt* ELEKTROTECH reac-tive element; **Blindenergie** *f* ELEKTRIZ reactive energy; **Blindfarben** *f pl* DRUCK dropout colours; **Blindfehler** *m* FERNSEH quadrature error; **Blindfenster** *nt* BAU blank window, blind window; **Blindflansch** *m* MASCHINEN blank flange, blind flange; **Blindflug** *m* LUFTTRANS blind flight, RAUMFAHRT blind navigation; **Blindfluglandesystem durch Eigenpeilung** *nt (ILS)* LUFTTRANS, RAUMFAHRT instrument landing system *(ILS)*; **Blindfluglandung** *f* LUFTTRANS blind landing
blindgebohrt: **~e Welze** *f* PAPIER blind-drill roll
Blind-: **Blindkaliber** *nt* FERTIG *Walzen* dummy pass; **Blindkomponente** *f* ELEKTRIZ wattless component, ELEKTRONIK quadrature component, ELEKTROTECH idle component, reactive component; **Blindlandung mit Bakeunterstützung** *f (BBL)* RAUMFAHRT beacons and blind landing *(BBL)*; **Blindlast** *f* ELEKTROTECH, PHYS, TELEKOM reactive load, TRANS dummy load; **Blindleistung** *f* ELEKTRIZ, ELEKTROTECH, PHYS reactive power; **Blindleistungseinheit** *f (var)* LABOR volt-amperes reactive *(var)*; **Blindleistungskomponente** *f* ELEKTRIZ quadrature power; **Blindleistungsverbesserung** *f* ELEKTROTECH power factor correction; **Blindleistungsverbrauch** *m* ELEKTRIZ reactive energy; **Blindleitung** *f* ELEKTROTECH adjustable short, stub; **Blindleitwert** *m* ELEKTROTECH, PHYS susceptance; **Blindniet** *m* MASCHINEN blind rivet; **Blindphasen-Nebenträgersignal** *nt* FERNSEH quadrature phase subcarrier signal; **Blindprägung** *f* DRUCK blind blocking, blind embossing; **Blindschacht** *m* BAU blind shaft, *Bergbau* blind pit; **Blindschaltkreis** *m* ELEKTROTECH reactive circuit; **Blindspannung** *f* ELEKTRIZ, PHYS reactive voltage; **Blindspannungskomponente** *f* ELEKTRIZ quadrature voltage; **Blindstich** *m* FERTIG blind pass, *Walzen* dead pass, dummy pass; **Blindstrom** *m* ELEKTRIZ idle current, reactive current, wattless current, ELEKTROTECH reactive current, wattless current; **Blindstromkomponente** *f* ELEKTRIZ quadrature component; **Blindstrommaschine** *f* ELEKTRIZ compensator; **Blindtür** *f* BAU blank door, blind door; **Blindverbrauchszähler** *m* GERÄT var-hour meter; **Blindverlagerung** *f* FERNSEH quadrature displacement; **Blindwiderstand** *m* ELEKTRIZ *(X)* reactance *(X)*, ELEKTROTECH reactance, PHYS inductive reactance, RADIO reactance;

Blindwiderstandsrelais *nt* ELEKTROTECH reactance relay; **Blindwiderstandsschaltung** *f* ELEKTRIZ reactance circuit

Blink- *pref* ELEKTRIZ, VERPACK, WASSERTRANS flashing

Blinken *nt* COMP & DV blinking

blinken[1] *vt* METALL brighten

blinken[2] *vi* COMP & DV blink

Blinker *m* KFZTECH direction indicator, *Zubehör* flasher, indicator

Blink-: **Blinkfeuer** *nt* WASSERTRANS *Seezeichen* flashing light; **Blinklampe** *f* ELEKTRIZ *Morselampe* flashlight; **Blinkleuchte** *f* KFZTECH flashing light; **Blinklicht** *nt* SICHERHEIT flashing light; **Blinkzeichen** *nt* WASSERTRANS *Signal* flashing signal

Blip *m* WASSERTRANS *Radar* radar blip

Blister- *pref* VERPACK blister; **Blisterkarte** *f* VERPACK blister card; **Blisterkarte für Sicherungen** *f* VERPACK fuse seal sheet; **Blisterpack** *nt* VERPACK shrink pack; **Blisterpackautomat** *m* VERPACK blister packaging machine; **Blisterpackung** *f* VERPACK blister pack; **Blisterrand- und Klarsichtfolienverpackungsmaschine** *f* VERPACK blister edge and foil machine

Blitz *m* ELEKTROTECH lightning, FOTO flash; **Blitzableiter** *m* ELEKTRIZ lightning arrester, ELEKTROTECH arrester, lightning rod, lightning conductor, lightning arrester, surge arrester, SICHERHEIT lightning conductor, lightning rod, WASSERTRANS lightning arrester; **Blitzableitermaterial** *nt* SICHERHEIT lightning conductor material; **Blitzableiterstab** *m* ELEKTROTECH lightning rod; **Blitzableiterstange** *f* ELEKTRIZ lightning rod; **Blitzdauer** *f* FOTO flash duration; **Blitzeinschlag** *m* ELEKTRIZ lightning stroke; **Blitzeinschlagstelle** *f* ELEKTRIZ lightning strike position

Blitzen *nt* ELEKTRIZ lightning, FOTO flashing

Blitz: **Blitzentladung** *f* ELEKTRIZ, ELEKTROTECH lightning discharge; **Blitzfeuer** *nt* RAUMFAHRT blinking light; **Blitzfolgezeit** *f* FOTO recycle time, recycling time

blitzgeschützt[1] *adj* ELEKTROTECH lightning-resistant

blitzgeschützt:[2] **~e Starkstromleitung** *f* ELEKTRIZ lightning-resistant power line; **~er Transformator** *m* ELEKTRIZ lightning-proof transformer

Blitz: **Blitzkontakt** *m* FOTO hot-shoe flash contact; **Blitzleiste** *f* FOTO flash bar; **Blitzlicht** *nt* ELEKTROTECH, FOTO, MECHAN flashlight; **Blitzlichtaufnahme** *f* FOTO flash picture; **Blitzlichtkontakt** *m* FOTO flash contact; **Blitzlicht-Steckverbindung** *f* FOTO flash socket; **Blitzröhre** *f* ELEKTRONIK flash tube; **Blitzrohrzange** *f* MASCHINEN grip pipe-wrench; **Blitzschalter** *m* FOTO flash switch; **Blitzschlag** *m* ELEKTRIZ lightning strike, ELEKTROTECH lightning discharge, PHYS stroke; **Blitzschuh** *m* FOTO flash shoe; **Blitzschutz** *m* ELEKTRIZ lightning protection, lightning arrester, ELEKTROTECH arrester, lightning arrester, lightning protection, RADIO lightning protection, RAUMFAHRT lightning arrester, SICHERHEIT lightning protection, lightning protector, WASSERTRANS lightning arrester; **Blitzschutz mittels Luftstrecke** *m* ELEKTRIZ air gap protector; **Blitzstoß** *m* ELEKTRIZ lightning surge; **Blitzstrecke** *f* ELEKTRIZ lightning path; **Blitzstrom** *m* ELEKTROTECH lightning current; **Blitzwürfel** *m* FOTO flash cube

Block *m* COMP & DV block, pad, ERDÖL *Aufsuchen; Gewinnung* block, *Recht* licence block (BrE), license block (AmE), FERTIG ingot, pad, KOHLEN ingot, MASCHINEN bar, block, ingot, MECHAN ingot, WASSERTRANS block; **~ mit fester Länge** *m* COMP & DV

fixed-length block

Blockade *f* WASSERTRANS blockade

Block: **Blockanweisung** *m* COMP & DV block statement; **Block-Copolymer** *nt* KUNSTSTOFF block copolymer; **Blockdiagramm** *nt* COMP & DV, ELEKTROTECH, MASCHINEN, MATH block diagram; **Blockdruck** *m* TEXTIL block printing; **Blockeisen** *nt* METALL ingot iron

Blocken *nt* KUNSTSTOFF, TELEKOM *OSI* blocking

Block: **Blockende** *nt* (*EOB*) COMP & DV end of block (*EOB*); **Blockfehlerrate** *f* COMP & DV block error rate; **Blockform** *f* FERTIG ingot mold (AmE), ingot mould (BrE); **Blockgerüst** *nt* FERTIG blooming stand; **Blockgeschwindigkeit** *f* LUFTTRANS, TRANS block speed; **Blockgröße** *f* COMP & DV block size

Blockieren *nt* LUFTTRANS *Kompressor, Turbomotor* stall, MASCHINEN blocking, jam, jamming

blockieren[1] *vt* ELEKTROTECH interlock, HYDRAUL *Dampfmaschine* bar, *Ventil* jam, KFZTECH *Bremse*, MASCHINEN jam, WASSERTRANS *Schiffahrt, Hafen* block off, blockade

blockieren[2] *vi* MASCHINEN lock

Blockierregler *m* KFZTECH antiblocking system, antiskid braking system

blockiert[1] *adj* MASCHINEN blocked

blockiert:[2] **~e Tragschere** *f* KER & GLAS stuck shank

Blockierung *f* ELEKTROTECH interlock, *der Leitfähigkeit* blocking, LUFTTRANS interlock, METALL locking, TELEKOM blocking; **Blockierungseffekte** *m pl* TELEKOM blockage effects

blockierungsfrei: **~es Netz** *nt* TELEKOM nonblocking network

Blockierverhinderer *m* LUFTTRANS antiskid unit

Blockierzustand *m* ELEKTROTECH *von Thyristoren* off-state

Blocking *nt* KUNSTSTOFF blocking; **Blockingeffekt** *m* PHYS blocking effect

Block: **Blockkaliber** *nt* FERTIG blooming pass, cogging pass; **Blockkette** *f* MASCHINEN block chain; **Blockkokille** *f* FERTIG ingot mold (AmE), ingot mould (BrE); **Blockkondensator** *m* ELEKTROTECH blocking capacitor; **Blocklänge** *f* COMP & DV block length, block size; **Blocklehm** *m* KOHLEN till; **Blocklöscher** *m* FERNSEH bulk eraser; **Blockmeißelhalter** *m* FERTIG multiple-tool block; **Blockmetall** *nt* METALL ingot metal; **Blocknummer** *f* ERDÖL block number; **Blockparität** *f* COMP & DV horizontal parity; **Blockprüfung** *f* COMP & DV LRC, longitudinal redundancy check; **Blockprüfzeichen** *nt* (*BCC*) TELEKOM block check character (*BCC*); **Blockprüfzeichenfolge** *f* TELEKOM FCS, frame-checking sequence; **Blockquantisierung** *f* TELEKOM block quantization; **Blockreaktanz** *f* ELEKTROTECH block reactance; **Blockrolle** *f* WASSERTRANS pulley; **Blocksatz** *m* COMP & DV justification

Blocksatz: **im ~ setzen** *vt* DRUCK block; **Blockschaltbild** *nt* COMP & DV, ELEKTROTECH block diagram, KONTROLL schematic unit diagram, MASCHINEN block diagram, kinematic diagram, mimic diagram, TELEKOM block diagram; **Blockscheibe** *f* MASCHINEN sheave, sheave block, WASSERTRANS pulley; **Blockschema** *nt* TELEKOM block diagram; **Blockschere** *f* FERTIG bloom shears, MASCHINEN billet shears, bloom shears; **Blocksortierung** *f* COMP & DV block sort; **Blockstahl** *m* METALL ingot steel; **Blockstein** *m* BAU block; **Blockstraße** *f* FERTIG cogging train; **Blockstruktur** *f* COMP & DV block structure; **Blockstufe** *f* BAU flyer; **Blockübertragung** *f* COMP & DV block transfer, TELE-

KOM block transmission

Blockungsfaktor *m* COMP & DV blocking factor

Block: **Blockverband** *m* BAU *Mauerwerk* old English bond; **Blockverdichtung** *f* COMP & DV block compaction; **Blockverschluß** *m* EISENBAHN block signal interlocking; **Blockwagen** *m* MASCHINEN block carriage; **Blockwalze** *f* FERTIG blooming roll, cogging roll; **Blockwalzgerüst** *nt* FERTIG cogging stand; **Blockwalzwerk** *nt* FERTIG blooming mill, cogging mill; **Blockzugriff** *m* COMP & DV block retrieval; **Blockzwischenraum** *m* COMP & DV IBG, interblock gap

Bloop-Lampe *f* AUFNAHME bloop lamp

Blow-Down: **~ Druckbeaufschlagung** *f* RAUMFAHRT blow-down pressurization

Blowout *m* ERDÖL, UMWELTSCHMUTZ blowout

Blowout-Preventer *m* (*BOP*) ERDÖL *Bohrtechnik, Fördertechnik* blowout preventer (*BOP*)

Blubberstörung *f* RAD motorboating

Blut- *pref* GERÄT, LEBENSMITTEL blood, haemo- (BrE), hemo- (AmE); **Blutdruckmeßgerät** *nt* GERÄT blood pressure meter; **Blutgift** *nt* CHEMIE haemotoxin (BrE), hemotoxin (AmE); **Blutschwarz** *nt* LEBENSMITTEL blood black; **Blutserumalbumin** *nt* LEBENSMITTEL blood albumin; **Bluttransfusionsgerät** *nt* SICHERHEIT blood transfusion equipment

B-Modulation *f* ELEKTRONIK B-modulation

BMOSFET *abbr* (*Halbleiter-Feldeffekttransistor mit Rückgatter*) ELEKTRONIK BMOSFET (*back-gate metal-oxide semiconductor field-effect transistor*)

BNC-Stecker *m* (*Bajonettsteckverbinder mit Überwurfmutter*) ELEKTRONIK BNC (*bayonet nut connector*)

Bö *f* WASSERTRANS gust, squall

Bobine *f* TEXTIL bobbin

Bock *m* FERTIG trestle, *Auswuchten* stand; **Bockbrücke** *f* BAU trestle bridge; **Bockkran** *m* EISENBAHN gantry crane; **Bocklager** *nt* FERTIG pedestal bearing; **Bockschere** *f* BAU bench shears; **Bocksprungtest** *m* COMP & DV leapfrog test; **Bockstütze** *f* BAU trestle shore; **Bockwalzen** *nt* FERTIG roll cogging

Boden:[1] **vom ~ gesteuert** *adj* RAUMFAHRT ground-controlled

Boden[2] *m* KOHLEN earth (BrE), ground (AmE), soil, TEXTIL *Textildruck* blotch; **Boden- und Seitenbeladungsanlage** *f* VERPACK automatic side and bottom loading machine; **Bodenabfertigung** *f* LUFTTRANS ground handling services; **Bodenabstand** *m* KFZTECH road clearance; **Bodenabzugskanal** *m* WASSERVERSORG bottom culvert; **Bodenadresse** *f* TELEKOM earth address (BrE), ground address (AmE); **Bodenart** *f* KOHLEN type of soil; **Bodenaushub** *m* ABFALL excavation; **Bodenbefeuerung** *f* LUFTTRANS ground lighting; **Bodenbelag** *m* BAU decking, KER & GLAS bottom paving, SICHERHEIT flooring; **Bodenbelastung** *f* UMWELTSCHMUTZ impact of soil; **Bodenbeplattung** *f* WASSERTRANS bottom plating; **Bodenbetrieb** *m* LUFTTRANS *Flughafen*, RAUMFAHRT *Raumschiff* ground operation; **Bodenbewegung** *f* BAU earthwork, LUFTTRANS ground maneuver (AmE), ground manoeuvre (BrE); **Bodenbewegung nach oben** *f* KERNTECH upward heave of ground; **Bodenblech** *nt* LUFTTRANS floor panel; **Bodenbohranlage** *f* ERDÖL *Bohrtechnik* ground rig; **Boden-Bord Funkverkehr** *m* LUFTTRANS ground-to-air communication; **Bodencodierer** *m* VERPACK bottom coder; **Bodendichte** *f* KOHLEN bulk density; **Bodendiffusion** *f* ELEKTRONIK top-bottom diffusion; **Bodendruck** *m* BAU bearing load, EISEN-BAHN ground pressure, KOHLEN earth pressure; **Bodeneffekt** *m* LUFTTRANS ground effect; **Bodeneffektfahrzeug** *nt* KFZTECH surface effect vehicle; **Bodeneffektgerät** *nt* (*BEG*) KFZTECH ground effect machine (*GEM*); **Bodeneinfluß** *m* LUFTTRANS ground effect; **Bodeneinrichtungen** *f pl* LUFTTRANS ground installations, RAUMFAHRT ground facilities; **Bodenenergieversorgung** *f* RAUMFAHRT ground power system; **Bodenentleererkübel** *m* BAU drop-bottom bucket; **Bodenfalz** *m* VERPACK bottom fold; **Bodenfalz- und Nähmaschine** *f* VERPACK bottom folding and seaming machine; **Bodenfilter** *nt* ABFALL soil filter; **Bodenfräse** *f* TRANS pulvimixer; **Bodenfreiheit** *f* FERTIG underclearance, KFZTECH ground clearance, to ground clearance, *Karosserie* road clearance

bodenfremd: **~e Substanz** *f* UMWELTSCHMUTZ allochthonous matter

Boden: **Bodenfüllung** *f* VERPACK bottom filling; **Bodenfunkstation** *f* LUFTTRANS ground radio station; **Bodengang neben dem Kiel** *m* WASSERTRANS keel strake

bodengebunden: **~er Hochgeschwindgkeitstransport** *m* TRANS high-speed ground transportation

bodengeleitet: **~er Anflug** *m* LUFTTRANS ground-controlled approach

Boden: **Bodenglas** *nt* KER & GLAS bottom glass; **Bodenhaftung** *f* KFZTECH road adhesion; **Bodenkippe** *f* BAU tip; **Bodenklappe** *f* HEIZ & KÄLTE floor damper, KFZTECH drop bottom, VERPACK bottom flap; **Bodenkolonne** *f* ERDÖL *Destillationstechnik* plate column; **Bodenkunde** *f* KOHLEN pedology, soil science, WASSERVERSORG soil science; **Bodenluftkonzentration** *f* UMWELTSCHMUTZ soil atmosphere concentration; **Bodenluke** *f* BAU trap door, LUFTTRANS floor hatch; **Bodenmechanik** *f* BAU, KOHLEN soil mechanics; **Bodenniveau** *nt* KERNTECH ground level; **Bodenplatte** *f* BAU bed plate, bottom, tile, ELEKTRONIK *des Quarzhalters* base, FERTIG loam plate, MECHAN floor plate, RAUMFAHRT *Raumschiff* sole plate; **Bodenpressung** *f* BAU bearing load; **Bodenprobe** *f* KOHLEN core sample; **Bodenprüfung** *f* LUFTTRANS ground test; **Bodenpunkt** *m* MECHAN benchmark; **Bodenresonanz** *f* LUFTTRANS ground resonance; **Bodenriß** *m* KER & GLAS bottom tear; **Bodenrückstand** *m* CHEMIE *Öltank* residue; **Bodensatz** *m* BAU deposit, CHEMTECH precipitate, LEBENSMITTEL sludge, VERPACK deposit; **Bodensau** *f* FERTIG *Gießen* salamander; **Bodensäulen-Abscheider** *m* UMWELTSCHMUTZ plate column scrubber; **Bodenschicht** *f* WASSERVERSORG bottom deposit; **Bodensenkung** *f* BAU subsidence, KOHLEN settlement; **Bodensetzung** *f* ABFALL settlement, settling; **Bodensicht** *f* LUFTTRANS ground visibility; **Bodenstabilisierung** *f* BAU cementation; **Bodenstation** *f* FERNSEH earth station, RAUMFAHRT *Weltraumfunk* earth station, land station, WASSERTRANS (*LUT*) local user terminal (*LUT*); **Bodenstation für Satellitenempfang** *f* FERNSEH receiving earth station; **Bodenstein** *m* FERTIG hearth bottom, KER & GLAS bottom block; **Bodenstoß** *m* BAU thrust; **Bodenströmung** *f* WASSERVERSORG bottom current, bottom flow; **Bodenstromversorgung** *f* LUFTTRANS ground power supply; **Bodentasse** *f* VERPACK base cup; **Bodenuntersuchung** *f* BAU subsoil exploration, KOHLEN soil exploration; **Bodenventil** *nt* MASCHINEN bottom valve, foot valve; **Bodenverdichtungsmesser** *m* KOHLEN settlement gage (AmE), settlement gauge (BrE);

Bodenvermörtelung *f* BAU soil stabilization

bodenverschmutzend: **~er Stoff** *m* UMWELTSCHUTZ soil pollutant

bodenverunreinigend: **~er Stoff** *m* UMWELTSCHUTZ land pollutant

Boden: **Bodenverunreinigung** *f* UMWELTSCHUTZ land pollution, soil pollution; **Bodenwanne** *f* KFZTECH *Karosserie* floor pan; **Bodenwasser** *nt* WASSERVERSORG soil water; **Bodenwelle** *f* RADIO, TELEKOM, WASSERTRANS *Funk* ground wave; **Bodenwellenausbreitung** *f* RADIO ground wave propagation; **Bodenwrange** *f* WASSERTRANS *Schiffbau* floor, floor plate

Böen *f pl* LUFTTRANS gust; **Böenabminderungsfaktor** *m* LUFTTRANS gust alleviation factor; **Böenbelastungsgrenze** *f* LUFTTRANS gust load limit; **Böenbildungszeit** *f* LUFTTRANS gust formation time; **Böenlastvielfaches** *nt* LUFTTRANS gust load factor; **Böennenngeschwindigkeit** *f* LUFTTRANS nominal gust velocity; **Böentiefe** *f* LUFTTRANS gust gradient distance; **Böenverriegelung** *f* LUFTTRANS gust lock; **Böen-V-n Diagramm** *nt* LUFTTRANS gust V-n diagram, gust envelope

Bogen *m* BAU arch, bow, DRUCK sheet, signature, KÜNSTL INT *Graph* arc, *zwischen Knoten in einem Graph* edge, link, MASCHINEN bend, bow, RAUMFAHRT *Raumschiff* flute; **Bogenanfang** *m* BAU springing

Bogenanlage: **mit ~** *adj* DRUCK sheet-fed

Bogen: **Bogenbildung** *f* FERTIG arcing; **Bogenblende** *f* BAU *Architektur* blind arch; **Bogenbrücke** *f* BAU arched beam bridge; **Bogenbrücke mit Zugband** *f* BAU bowstring bridge; **Bogendickenmesser** *m* BAU bow calipers (AmE), bow callipers (BrE); **Bogenentladung** *f* ELEKTRIZ arc discharge; **Bogenentladungsröhre** *f* ELEKTROTECH arc discharge tube; **Bogenfeder** *f* MASCHINEN bow spring; **Bogenfederzirkel** *m* BAU bow spring compasses

bogenförmig: **~er Anschnitt** *m* KER & GLAS scalloped bevel

Bogen: **Bogengang** *m* BAU arcade; **Bogengewölbe** *nt* BAU arched vault; **Bogenherzstück** *nt* EISENBAHN curved common crossing; **Bogenkalender** *m* PAPIER sheet calender; **Bogenlampe** *f* ELEKTRIZ arc lamp; **Bogenlampenkohle** *f* MASCHINEN arc lamp carbon; **Bogenleibung** *f* BAU intrados; **Bogenlicht** *nt* ELEKTRIZ arc light; **Bogenlinie** *f* KONSTZEICH curved line; **Bogenmaß** *nt* GEOM circular measure, MASCHINEN radian measure; **Bogenmauer** *f* WASSERVERSORG arch dam; **Bogenminute** *f* PHYS arc minute; **Bogenpresse** *f* DRUCK sheet-fed machine; **Bogenrückschlag** *m* ELEKTROTECH arc back; **Bogensäge** *f* BAU backsaw, MASCHINEN bow saw; **Bogenschenkel** *m* BAU haunch; **Bogenschneider** *m* VERPACK sheet-cutting machine; **Bogenschweißen** *nt* MECHAN arc welding; **Bogensekunde** *f* METROL second, PHYS arc second, *Winkelmaß* second of arc; **Bogensignatur** *f* DRUCK signature number; **Bogenspektrum** *nt* PHYS arc spectrum; **Bogenspitzzirkel** *m* METROL dividers with quadrant; **Bogenstaumauer** *f* BAU, WASSERVERSORG arch dam; **Bogenstein** *m* BAU arched tile; **Bogenträger mit Zugband** *m* BAU bowstring girder; **Bogenverband** *m* BAU arch bond; **Bogenverzahnung** *f* FERTIG hyphoid teeth; **Bogenzahnkupplung** *f* MASCHINEN curved-tooth gear coupling; **Bogenziegel** *m* BAU arch brick, gage brick (AmE), gauge brick (BrE), voussoir

bogenziehend: **~e Kontakte** *m pl* ELEKTRIZ arcing contacts

Bogen: **Bogenzirkel** *m* BAU bow compass, MASCHINEN wing compasses; **Bogenzuführmaschine** *f* VERPACK sheet machine; **Bogenzuführungsapparat** *m* DRUCK sheet feeder

Bogheadkohle *f* KOHLEN boghead coal

Bogie *m* EISENBAHN bogie (BrE), trailer (AmE), KFZTECH *Anhänger* bogie (BrE)

Bohle *f* BAU batten, board, deal, plank; **Bohlenbelag** *m* BAU planking; **Bohlengang** *m* BAU duck board

Bohlen: **~ hochkant verlegen** *vi* BAU set boards edgewise

Bohlwand *f* MECHAN bulkhead

Böhmit *nt* KER & GLAS boehmite

Bohr- *pref* ERDÖL drilling, FERTIG boring, drilling, MECHAN drill; **~ und Drehwerk** *nt* MASCHINEN boring and turning mill; **~ und Fräsmaschine** *f* MASCHINEN boring and milling machine; **~ und Plandrehmaschine** *f* FERTIG boring and facing lathe

Bohr: **~sches Magneton** *nt* PHYS Bohr magneton; **~scher Radius** *m (a0)* PHYS Bohr radius *(a0)*

Bohr-: **~ und Schrämmaschine** *f* KOHLEN holing and shearing machine; **Bohranlage** *f* ERDÖL drilling rig, rig; **Bohranlagenetage** *f* ERDÖL *Bohrtechnik* rig floor; **Bohransatzpunkt** *m* BAU boring site; **Bohrarbeiter** *m* ERDÖL floorman, toolpusher, *Bohrtechnik* driller, *Tiefbohrtechnik* derrick man; **Bohrarm** *m* KOHLEN cutter arm; **Bohrausschuß** *m* FERTIG drilling rejects; **Bohrbank** *f* MASCHINEN boring bench, MECHAN drill press

bohrbar: **~er Stopfen** *m* ERDÖL drillable plug

Bohr-: **Bohrbarkeit** *f* ERDÖL drillability; **Bohrbedingungen** *f pl* ERDÖL drilling conditions; **Bohrbetrieb** *m* ERDÖL *Tiefbohrtechnik* drilling operations; **Bohrbrunnen** *m* WASSERVERSORG bored well; **Bohrbuchse** *f* MASCHINEN drill bushing; **Bohrbüchse** *f* MASCHINEN jig bush; **Bohreinrichtung** *f* MASCHINEN drilling attachment; **Bohreinsatz** *m* MASCHINEN drill

Bohren *nt* BAU boring, drilling, ERDÖL boring, MASCHINEN, MECHAN boring, drilling, PAPIER drilling; **~ ohne Bohrlochverrohrung** *nt* ERDÖL *Bohrtechnik* open-hole drilling; **~ von Rohknüppeln** *nt* FERTIG billet drilling; **~ von Sprenglöchern** *nt* KOHLEN drilling of blast holes

bohren *vt* BAU bore, drill, ERDÖL bore, MASCHINEN, MECHAN bore, drill, PAPIER drill

Bohrer[1] *m* BAU bit, ERDÖL driller, KOHLEN borer, MASCHINEN drill; **~ für Bohrwinden** *m* MASCHINEN brace bit; **~ mit geraden Nuten** *m* MASCHINEN straight-fluted drill; **~ mit Tiefenanschlag** *m* MASCHINEN stop drill; **~ mit Vierkantschaft** *m* MASCHINEN square shank drill

Bohrer:[2] **~ betreiben** *vi* MASCHINEN *mit Druckluft* run a drill

Bohrer: **Bohrereinsatz** *m* BAU bit; **Bohrerfutter** *nt* MASCHINEN drill socket; **Bohrergrößen** *f pl* MASCHINEN gage numbers (AmE), gauge numbers (BrE); **Bohrerhalter** *m* MASCHINEN drill holder; **Bohrerlehre** *f* MASCHINEN drill gage (AmE), drill gauge (BrE); **Bohrerschleifgerät** *nt* MASCHINEN drill sharpener; **Bohrerschleifmaschine** *f* MASCHINEN drill grinder

Bohr-: **Bohrfortschritt** *m* ERDÖL rate of penetration, *Bohrtechnik* drilling rate; **Bohrfutter** *nt* FERTIG drill chuck, MASCHINEN drill chuck, drill head, MECHAN drill bushing, jig, pad; **Bohrgarnitur** *f* ERDÖL *Bohrtechnik* drill string; **Bohrgeschwindigkeit** *f* BAU drilling rate, ERDÖL *Bohrtechnik* rotation rate, *Tiefbohrtechnik* rate of penetration; **Bohrgestängeeinbau** *m* ERDÖL *Bohrtechnik* snubbing; **Bohrgestell** *nt* NICHTFOSS ENERG drilling rig; **Bohrgut** *nt* ERDÖL cuttings, drill cuttings; **Bohrhammer** *m* BAU rock drill; **Bohr-**

hilfsarbeiter *m* ERDÖL roustabout; **Bohrhubinsel** *f* ERDÖL *Offshore-Technik* jack-up rig; **Bohrhülse** *f* MASCHINEN boring sleeve; **Bohringenieur** *m* ERDÖL drilling engineer; **Bohrinsel** *f* WASSERTRANS drilling platform, oil rig; **Bohrinselversorgungsschiff** *nt* WASSERTRANS offshore drilling rig supply vessel; **Bohrkäfer** *m* LEBENSMITTEL *Pflanzenschädlinge* borer; **Bohrkasten** *m* FERTIG box drill jig; **Bohrkern** *m* BAU, ERDÖL core, FERTIG *Hohlbohren* core, pin, plug; **Bohrkernanalyse** *f* ERDÖL core analysis; **Bohrkernrohr** *nt* ERDÖL core barrel; **Bohrkette** *f* KOHLEN cutter chain; **Bohrklein** *nt* ERDÖL cuttings, *Bohrtechnik* drill cuttings; **Bohrkleinausfall** *m* ERDÖL cuttings dropping out; **Bohrkleingas** *nt* ERDÖL *Tiefbohrtechnik* cuttings gas; **Bohrknarre** *f* MASCHINEN ratchet, ratchet brace, ratchet drill; **Bohrkopf** *m* MASCHINEN boring head, cutter head; **Bohrkopf mit verstellbarem Bohrbild** *m* FERTIG adjustable centre head; **Bohrkratzer** *m* KOHLEN scraper, WASSERVERSORG cleaner-up; **Bohrkrone** *f* KOHLEN drill bit; **Bohrkronenbolzen** *m pl* ERDÖL drill bit studs; **Bohrkronenzähne** *m pl* ERDÖL *Tiefbohrtechnik* drill bit studs; **Bohrkurbel** *f* MASCHINEN bit brace, bit stock, breast drill brace, crank brace; **Bohrleier** *f* FERTIG hand brace
Bohrloch *nt* BAU borehole, hole, ERDÖL well, KOHLEN borehole, MASCHINEN, WASSERVERSORG bore, borehole
Bohrloch: aus dem ~ fahren *vi* ERDÖL *Bohrwerkzeug* coming out of hole
Bohrloch-: **Bohrlochkopf** *m* ERDÖL wellhead; **Bohrlochmessung** *f* ERDÖL *Bohrtechnik* downhole measurements, *Meßtechnik* well logging; **Bohrlochproduktivitätstest** *m* ERDÖL drill stem test; **Bohrlochpumpe** *f* BAU, WASSERVERSORG borehole pump; **Bohrlochsohle** *f* ERDÖL *Bohrtechnik* bottom hole; **Bohrlochsohlenausrüstung** *f (BSA)* ERDÖL bottom hole assembly *(BHA)*; **Bohrlochsohlenbedingungen** *f pl* ERDÖL bottom hole conditions; **Bohrlochsohlen-Zementstopfen** *m* ERDÖL bottom cementing plug; **Bohrlochtemperatur-Logging** *nt* ERDÖL temperature well logging; **Bohrlochtemperatur-Meßverfahren** *nt* ERDÖL temperature well logging; **Bohrlochvermessung** *f* ERDÖL logging; **Bohrlochwandung** *f* WASSERVERSORG casing
Bohr-: **Bohrmannschaft** *f* ERDÖL drilling crew; **Bohrmaschine** *f* KOHLEN drill, MASCHINEN boring machine, drill, drill press, drilling machine, MECHAN boring machine, drill, drilling machine; **Bohrmaschine mit Hebelvorschub** *f* MASCHINEN lever feed drilling machine; **Bohrmaschinenfutter** *nt* MECHAN chuck
Bohrmeißel *m* BAU bore bit, boring bit, jumper, ERDÖL *Bohrtechnik* bit, *Tiefbohrtechnik* drill bit, FERTIG drill bit, single point boring tool, KOHLEN cutting bit, MASCHINEN boring tool; **Bohrmeißelabnutzung** *f* ERDÖL bit wear; **Bohrmeißelauflast** *f (WOB)* ERDÖL weight on bit *(WOB)*; **Bohrmeißelbrecher** *m* ERDÖL bit breaker; **Bohrmeißelverschleiß** *m* ERDÖL bit wear; **Bohrmeißelwechsel** *m* ERDÖL BC, bit change
Bohr-: **Bohrmesser** *nt* FERTIG bit; **Bohrplattform** *f* ERDÖL *Bohrtechnik* drilling platform; **Bohrprogramm** *nt* ERDÖL *Tiefbohrtechnik* drilling program (AmE), drilling programme (BrE); **Bohrrechteck** *nt* FERTIG area of drilling; **Bohrrohr** *nt* ERDÖL drill pipe, WASSERVERSORG casing pipe; **Bohrsäule** *f* MASCHINEN drilling pillar; **Bohrschablone** *f* FERTIG jig, MASCHINEN drill template, drilling jig, drilling template; **Bohrschacht**

m KOHLEN pit; **Bohrschachthebeschwinge** *f* ERDÖL *Getriebe* pit lever; **Bohrschiff** *nt* ERDÖL *Bohrtechnik* drill barge, *Tiefbohrtechnik* drill ship, WASSERTRANS drill ship; **Bohrschlamm auf Ölbasis** *m* ERDÖL *Tiefbohrtechnik* oil-base mud; **Bohrschlamm auf Wasserbasis** *m* ERDÖL water-based mud; **Bohrschlammpumpe** *f* ERDÖL slush pump; **Bohrschlitten** *m* FERTIG headstock, *Radialbohrer* drilling head; **Bohrschrappe** *f* KOHLEN spoon sampler
Bohr-Sommerfeld-Modell *nt* PHYS Bohr-Sommerfeld model
Bohr-: **Bohrspan** *m* FERTIG drill chip; **Bohrspindel** *f* FERTIG drill spindle, MASCHINEN boring spindle, drill spindle, drilling spindle, MECHAN boring spindle; **Bohrspindelkopf** *m* FERTIG drilling head; **Bohrspitzenhalter** *m* MASCHINEN bit holder; **Bohrstahl** *m* MASCHINEN drill steel; **Bohrstange** *f* BAU bore rod, boring rod, MASCHINEN boring bar; **Bohrstangenführungslager** *nt* FERTIG steady bearing; **Bohrstelle** *f* BAU boring site; **Bohrstift** *m* BAU drill pin; **Bohrstrang** *m* ERDÖL *Tiefbohrtechnik* drilling line; **Bohrtiefe** *f* MASCHINEN drill depth, drilling depth; **Bohrtiefenbegrenzung** *f* FERTIG depth control; **Bohrtisch** *m* ERDÖL *Tiefbohrtechnik* drilling table, KERNTECH jig table, MASCHINEN drilling table; **Bohrtour** *f* ERDÖL *Bohrtechnik* trip; **Bohrturm** *m* BAU, ERDÖL *Bohrtechnik*, MECHAN derrick, NICHTFOSS ENERG drilling rig
Bohrturm: den ~ auf Schlitten versetzen *vi* ERDÖL *Bohrtechnik* skid the rig
Bohr-: **Bohrturmkeller** *m* ERDÖL derrick cellar; **Bohrturmkopf** *m* ERDÖL crown, derrick crown; **Bohrturmkran** *m* ERDÖL derrick crane; **Bohrturmsohle** *f* ERDÖL *Bohrtechnik* derrick floor
Bohrung[1] *f* ERDÖL well, FERTIG *Kunststoffinstallationen* hole, HYDRAUL *in Trennwand, Platte* opening, KER & GLAS bore (BrE), corkage (AmE), KFZTECH *Motor, Zylinder* bore, KOHLEN drilling, MASCHINEN bore, borehole, passage, port, NICHTFOSS ENERG, RAUMFAHRT bore; **~ mit Gewinde** *f* KERNTECH threaded hole
Bohrung:[2] **~ vorgießen** *vi* FERTIG core
Bohrung: **Bohrungsdurchmesser** *m* ERDÖL *Bohrtechnik* well bore, MASCHINEN bore, size of bore; **Bohrungslehre** *f* MASCHINEN caliper gage (AmE), calliper gauge (BrE), internal cylindrical gage (AmE), internal cylindrical gauge (BrE); **Bohrungsmeßgerät** *nt* METROL bore gage (AmE), bore gauge (BrE)
Bohr-: **Bohrunternehmer** *m* BAU boring contractor; **Bohrvormann** *m* ERDÖL toolpusher; **Bohrvorrichtung** *f* MASCHINEN drilling jig; **Bohrvorschacht** *m* ERDÖL derrick cellar; **Bohrvorschub** *m* FERTIG drilling feed; **Bohrwelle** *f* MASCHINEN boring bar; **Bohrwerk** *nt* MASCHINEN, MECHAN boring mill; **Bohrwerkständer** *m* MASCHINEN boring-mill column; **Bohrwerkzeug** *nt* BAU drilling tool, MASCHINEN drill; **Bohrwinde** *f* BAU brace, FERTIG bit brace
Boiler *m* HEIZ & KÄLTE hot-water tank, MASCHINEN hot-water heater, water heater, MECHAN, THERMOD boiler
Boje[1] *f* WASSERTRANS *Seezeichen* buoy
Boje:[2] **an die ~ gehen** *vi* WASSERTRANS pick up moorings
Bojenreep *nt* WASSERTRANS *Tauwerk* buoy rope
Bolometer *nt* ELEKTRIZ, ELEKTROTECH, FERTIG bolometer, GERÄT bolometric instrument, HEIZ & KÄLTE, PHYS, RAUMFAHRT, THERMOD bolometer
bolometrisch[1] *adj* FERTIG bolometric

bolometrisch:[2] **~es Meßinstrument** nt GERÄT bolometric instrument

Boltzmann: ~sche Funktion f PHYS, THERMOD Boltzmann function; **~sche Gleichung** f PHYS, THERMOD Boltzmann equation of particle conservation, Boltzmann equation; **~sche Konstante** f PHYS (k), THERMOD (*Boltzmannsche Zahl, k*) Boltzmann constant (k); **~sche Zahl** f PHYS (k), THERMOD (*Boltzmannsche Konstante, k*) Boltzmann constant (k)

Bolzen m BAU fang bolt, pintle, pin, screw, stay, FERTIG bolt, *Kette* pin, KFZTECH, MASCHINEN bolt, MECHAN hob; **~ mit Splint** m FERTIG cotter bolt; **~ mit versenktem Kopf** m BAU countersunk head-bolt; **Bolzenanker** m BAU rag bolt; **Bolzenaufschweißen** nt FERTIG stud welding; **Bolzenkopf** m MASCHINEN bolt head; **Bolzenkupplung** f MASCHINEN bolt coupling, pin coupling; **Bolzenloch** nt MASCHINEN bolt hole; **Bolzenlochbohrmaschine** f FERTIG stud-inserting machine; **Bolzenschere** f MASCHINEN bolt clipper; **Bolzenschneider** m KFZTECH bolt cutter, MASCHINEN bolt cropper, bolt cutter, MECHAN bolt cutter; **Bolzenschraube** f MASCHINEN bolt; **Bolzenschweißen** nt BAU stud welding; **Bolzenschweißpistole** f BAU stud welding gun; **Bolzentreiber** m MASCHINEN pin drift; **Bolzenverbindung** f BAU *für Rohre* nose, FERTIG bolted union, MASCHINEN bolt fastening, RAUMFAHRT bolted connection

Bombage f LEBENSMITTEL swell

Bombenkalorimeter nt GERÄT, PHYS bomb calorimeter

Bombieren nt FERTIG *Walzen* crowning, LEBENSMITTEL *Konservendosen* blowing

bombiert: ~er Siebsauger m PAPIER cambered suction box

Bombierung f PAPIER camber; **Bombierungsstange** f PAPIER camber bar

Boole: ~sche Algebra f COMP & DV Boolean algebra, Boolean logic, MATH Boolean algebra; **~scher Datentyp** m COMP & DV logical-type; **~sche Komplementierung** f COMP & DV NOT operation; **~scher Operator** m COMP & DV Boolean operator; **~scher Primärausdruck** m COMP & DV Boolean primary; **~scher Ring** m COMP & DV Boolean ring; **~scher Sekundärausdruck** m COMP & DV Boolean secondary; **~sche Variable** f COMP & DV Boolean variable; **~sche Verknüpfung** f REGELUNG Boolean term **~scher Wert** m COMP & DV Boolean value, logical value;

Booster m MASCHINEN booster; **Boosterpumpe** f MASCHINEN booster pump

Boot nt WASSERTRANS boat; **Bootcharter** f ERDÖL *Schifffahrt* bareboat charter

Boote: ~ aussetzen vi WASSERTRANS *Notfall* lower the boats

Booten nt COMP & DV boot-up; **Bootsanhänger** m WASSERTRANS boat trailer; **Bootsdeck** nt WASSERTRANS boat deck; **Bootsführer** m WASSERTRANS boatsman, waterman, *Besatzung* coxswain; **Bootshaken** m WASSERTRANS boathook; **Bootshaus** nt TRANS boat house; **Bootshißstropp** m WASSERTRANS boat sling; **Bootsklampe** f WASSERTRANS *Decksausrüstung* boat chock; **Bootskörper** m WASSERTRANS hull; **Bootskurs** m WASSERTRANS boat's heading; **Bootsladung** f WASSERTRANS boat load; **Bootslagerung** f WASSERTRANS cradle; **Bootslift** m WASSERTRANS boat elevator, boat lift; **Bootsmann** m WASSERTRANS boat-swain; **Bootsmannsstuhl** m WASSERTRANS boatswain's chair;

Bootsrolle f WASSERTRANS *Notfall* boat stations bill; **Bootstaljenläufer** m WASSERTRANS *Decksausrüstung* boat fall; **Bootstank** m WASSERTRANS boat tank; **Bootstransport** m WASSERTRANS boat carriage

Bootstrap m FERNSEH bootstrap

Boot: Bootsverdeck nt WASSERTRANS canopy

BOP abbr (*Blowout-Preventer*) ERDÖL BOP (*blowout preventer*)

Bor nt (B) CHEMIE boron (B); **Bor-** pref CHEMIE boracic, boric

Boral nt KERNTECH boral

Boran nt CHEMIE borane

borartig adj CHEMIE boric

Borat nt CHEMIE borate

Borax m CHEMIE borax, disodium tetraborate decahydrate, KER & GLAS borax; **Boraxperle** f BAU borax bead; **Boraxperlenversuch** m CHEMIE borax bead test; **Boraxperlprüfung** f METALL borax bead test

Bord:[1] **über ~** adj WASSERTRANS overboard; **an ~ befindlich** adj LUFTTRANS inboard, WASSERTRANS aboard, on board

Bord[2] m WASSERTRANS *Schiff* board

Bord:[3] **an ~ bringen** vt WASSERTRANS put on board; **an ~ nehmen** vt WASSERTRANS *Passagiere, Ladung* embark, *Passagiere* ship; **über ~ spülen** vt WASSERTRANS wash overboard; **über ~ werfen** vt WASSERTRANS jettison

Bord:[4] **über ~ fallen** vi WASSERTRANS fall overboard; **an ~ gehen** vi WASSERTRANS board; **von ~ gehen** vi WASSERTRANS *Passagiere* disembark

Bord: Bordabstandswarnanzeiger m LUFTTRANS airborne proximity warning indicator

Borda: Borda-Mundstück nt HYDRAUL Borda mouthpiece; **Borda-Mündung** f HYDRAUL Borda mouthpiece

Bord: Bord-Bord-Alarmierung f TELEKOM ship-to-ship alerting; **Bordcomputer** m RAUMFAHRT *Raumschiff* on-board computer

Borde f TEXTIL trimming

Bördel- pref BAU flanged, FERTIG flanging, MASCHINEN crimping, TEXTIL flanging; **Bördelblech** nt BAU flanged plate; **Bördeleisen** nt FERTIG bordering tool; **Bördelmaschine** f FERTIG flanging machine, MASCHINEN seaming machine, VERPACK flanging machine

Bördeln nt FERTIG flanging, MASCHINEN crimping

bördeln vt FERTIG border, clinch, MASCHINEN seam, MECHAN crimp, VERPACK falten

Bördel-: Bördelpresse f MASCHINEN crimping machine, flanging press; **Bördelrand** m MECHAN bead; **Bördelversuch** m FERTIG flanging test; **Bördelwerkzeug** nt MASCHINEN crimping tool; **Bördelzange** f MASCHINEN crimping pliers

Bord: Bordempfangsschein m WASSERTRANS *Handelsmarine* mate's receipt; **Bordkollisionswarnsystem** nt LUFTTRANS airborne collision avoidance system; **Bordkommunikationsstation** f TELEKOM on-board communication station; **Bordküche** f LUFTTRANS galley; **Bord-Land-Alarmierung** f TELEKOM ship-to-shore alerting; **Bord-Land-Funkverbindung** f WASSERTRANS *Funk* ship-to-shore radio communication; **Bordpapiere** nt pl WASSERTRANS ship's books; **Bordradar** nt ELEKTRONIK *Cockpit* airborne radar; **Bordrand** m FERTIG *Riemenscheibe*, MASCHINEN flange; **Bordrechner** m WASSERTRANS computer; **Bordschaltung** f RAUMFAHRT *Weltraumfunk* on-board switching; **Bordsprechanlage** f AUFNAHME intercom; **Bordstein** m BAU curb (AmE), kerb (BrE), curbstone (AmE), kerb (BrE), kerbstone (BrE), KER & GLAS fluxline block; **Bordsysteme** nt pl RAUMFAHRT Raumschiff on-board systems; **Bordterminal für Satellitenfunk** m (SES) WASSERTRANS ship earth station (SES); **Bord-uhrrücksetzung** f RAUMFAHRT Weltraumfunk clock recovery

Bordüre f DRUCK border

Bord: **Bordverarbeitung** f RAUMFAHRT Weltraumfunk onboard processing

Bore f WASSERTRANS Fluß bore

Bor: **Borhydrid** nt CHEMIE borane

Borid nt CHEMIE boride

Borneocampher m CHEMIE borneol

Borneol nt CHEMIE borneol, camphol; **Borneolacetat** nt CHEMIE bornyl acetate

Bornyl- pref CHEMIE bornyl; **Bornylacetat** nt CHEMIE bornyl acetate; **Bornylalkohol** m CHEMIE borneol, bornyl alcohol

Borosilikat nt CHEMIE borosilicate; **Borosilikatglas** nt KER & GLAS, LABOR borosilicate glass

Borsäure f CHEMIE boric acid, orthoboric acid, KER & GLAS boric acid; **Borsäuremischpumpe** f KERNTECH boric acid blender

Borstahl m METALL boron steel; **Borstahlabsorber** m KERNTECH boronated steel absorber

Bort m FERTIG bort

Borte f KER & GLAS braid, TEXTIL braid, braiding; ~ **der Glasscheibe** f KER & GLAS edge of the sheet; **Borten-führungen** f pl KER & GLAS edge guides; **Bortenhalter** m KER & GLAS edge holder

Bor: **Bortrioxid** nt KER & GLAS boric oxide

Böschung f BAU bank, slope, KOHLEN slope; **Bö-schungsabdeckung** f BAU facing; **Böschungsabsatz** m WASSERVERSORG offset; **Böschungserdhobel** m BAU angledozer; **Böschungsfuß** m KOHLEN slope toe; **Bö-schungskrone** f KOHLEN slope top; **Böschungsmauer** f BAU retaining wall; **Böschungsneigung** f BAU batter; **Böschungssicherung** f BAU slope protection; **Bö-schungsstandfestigkeit** f KOHLEN slope stability; **Böschungsversagen** nt KOHLEN slope failure

Bose-Einstein: ~**sche Kondensation** f PHYS Bose-Ein-stein condensation; ~**sche Statistik** f PHYS Bose-Einstein statistics; ~**sche Verteilung** f PHYS Bose-Einstein distribution

Boson nt PHYS, TEILPHYS boson

Bosse f MASCHINEN boss

Bossieren nt KER & GLAS palleting

Bossierholz nt KER & GLAS pallet

BOT abbr (Bandanfang) COMP & DV BOT (beginning of tape)

Bote m TRANS carrier

Bottich m FERTIG vat, LABOR trough, LEBENSMITTEL vat, METALL pot, TEXTIL vat, VERPACK für Papierbeleimung tub

Bottomonium nt TEILPHYS bottomonium

Bottom-Up-Strategie f TEILPHYS bottom-up strategy

Botulinus m LEBENSMITTEL botulinus

Botulismus m LEBENSMITTEL botulism

Bouilleurkessel m HYDRAUL elephant boiler

Bourdon: ~**sches Manometer** nt GERÄT Bourdon tube gage (AmE), Bourdon tube gauge (BrE), boundary tube gage (AmE), boundary tube gauge (BrE), PHYS Bourdon gage (AmE), Bourdon gauge (BrE); ~**sche Röhre** f ERDÖL Bourdon gage (AmE), Bourdon gauge (BrE); ~**sches-Rohr** nt PHYS Bourdon gage (AmE), Bourdon gauge (BrE)

Bowdenzug m KFZTECH Kupplung, Bremse, MECHAN

Bowden cable

Box f FOTO, VERPACK box

Boxcar-Oszilloskop nt GERÄT Sampling-Oszilloskop boxcar oscilloscope

Boxermotor m KFZTECH flat engine

Box-: **Boxkamera** f FOTO box camera; **Boxpalette** f VER-PACK box pallet with sidewalls

Boyle: ~**sche Temperatur** f PHYS Boyle temperature

Boyle-Mariotte: ~**sches Gesetz** nt PHYS Boyle's law, THERMOD Boyle's law, Mariotte's law

B-Papierformat nt DRUCK B-size

BPF abbr (Bandpaßfilter) AUFNAHME, ELEKTRONIK, FERNSEH, PHYS, RADIO, TELEKOM BPF (band-pass filter)

bpi abbr (Bits pro Zoll) COMP & DV bpi (bits per inch)

BPS abbr (Bremspferdestärke) FERTIG, KFZTECH, ME-CHAN BHP (brake horsepower)

bps abbr (Bits pro Sekunde) COMP & DV bps (bits per second)

BPSK abbr (Zweiphasenumtastung, binäre Phasenumta-stung) TELEKOM BPSK (binary phase shift keying)

Bq abbr (Becquerel) METROL, PHYS Bq (becquerel)

Br (Brom) CHEMIE Br (bromine)

Brackett: ~**sche Serie** f PHYS Atomphysik Brackett series

brackig adj LEBENSMITTEL brackish

Brackwasser nt BAU, WASSERVERSORG brackish water; **Brackwassermoor** nt WASSERVERSORG salt swamp

Bradford-Brecher m KOHLEN Bradford breaker

Bragg: ~**scher Winkel** m PHYS Bragg angle; ~**sche Regel** f PHYS Bragg rule; ~**sche Zelle** f ELEKTROTECH Bragg cell

Brailtau nt WASSERTRANS bow line

Brain-Drain m TRANS brain drain

Bramme f FERTIG plate slab, Halbzeug slab, METALL slab; **Brammenherstellung** f FERTIG slabbing; **Bram-menschere** f FERTIG slab shears; **Brammenwalzwerk** nt FERTIG slabbing mill

Brand[1] m KER & GLAS baking, burning, LEBENSMITTEL rust, am Getreide mildew, SICHERHEIT fire

Brand:[2] **in ~ setzen** vt THERMOD set fire to

Brand: **Brandabschnitt** m THERMOD fire lobby; **Brand-ausbreitungsverhütung** f SICHERHEIT fire spread prevention; **Brandbekämpfung** f BAU, LUFTTRANS, SI-CHERHEIT, WASSERTRANS Notfall firefighting; **Brandende** nt RAUMFAHRT Raumschiff flameout

Brandfall: **im ~ Glas einschlagen** phr SICHERHEIT Feuer-melder in case of fire, break the glass

Brand: **Brandfleck** m FERTIG Schleifen burning; **Brand-gefahr** f LUFTTRANS, SICHERHEIT, WASSERTRANS fire hazard; **Brandlast** f THERMOD fire load; **Brandmarke** f KER & GLAS burn mark; **Brandmauer** f BAU party wall, SICHERHEIT fireproof wall; **Brandriß** m FERTIG Krokil-le crazing; **Brandschott** nt LUFTTRANS fire wall, WAS-SERTRANS Schiffkonstruktion fire bulkhead; **Brandschottring** m LUFTTRANS fireseal

Brandschutz m SICHERHEIT fire protection, THERMOD fire prevention, fireproofing; **Brandschutz- und Ret-tungsgerät** nt SICHERHEIT firefighting and rescue equipment; **Brandschutzbeschichtung** f KUNSTSTOFF fireproof coating; **Brandschutzhinweisschild** nt SI-CHERHEIT fire safety sign; **Brandschutzkabel** nt LUFTTRANS fire wire; **Brandschutzleitung** f LUFT-TRANS fire wire; **Brandschutztür** f SICHERHEIT fire door, fireproof door; **Brandschutzübung** f SICHER-HEIT fire drill; **Brandschutzvorschrift** f SICHERHEIT fire regulation; **Brandschutzvorsorge** f SICHERHEIT fire precautions; **Brandschutzvorsorgemaßnahmen** *f pl* SICHERHEIT fire precautions

Brand: **Brandstiftung** *f* THERMOD arson

Brandung *f* WASSERTRANS *Meer* breakers

Brand: **Brandverhalten** *nt* HEIZ & KÄLTE fire behavior (AmE), fire behaviour (BrE), SICHERHEIT *von Textilprodukten* burning behavior (AmE), burning behaviour (BrE); **Brandverhütung** *f* SICHERHEIT preventive fire protection; **Brandwache** *f* THERMOD fire station

Branntkalk *m* CHEMIE, KER & GLAS, MEERSCHMUTZ quicklime

Braß *f* WASSERTRANS brace

Brasse *f* WASSERTRANS *Tauwerk* brace

Brau- *pref* LEBENSMITTEL brewing, malting

brauchbar: **~es Bildfeld** *nt* FOTO effective image field

Brauchwasser *nt* WASSERVERSORG process water; **Brauchwassererwärmer** *m* HEIZ & KÄLTE service water calorifier

Brauen *nt* LEBENSMITTEL brewing

Brau-: **Braugerste** *f* LEBENSMITTEL malting barley; **Brauindustrie** *f* LEBENSMITTEL brewing industry

Braun- *pref* CHEMIE, KOHLEN brown; **Braunbeizen** *nt* METALL bluing of iron; **Brauneisen** *nt* CHEMIE brown haematite (BrE), brown hematite (AmE), brown iron ore; **Braunfleckigkeit** *f* LEBENSMITTEL *an Obst* scald mark; **Braunkohle** *f* KOHLEN brown coal, THERMOD brown coal, lignite

Braun: **~sche Röhre** *f* COMP & DV DRUCK, ELEKTRIZ, ELEKTRONIK, FERNSEH, RADIO cathode-ray tube

Braun-: **Braunschliffpappe** *f* PAPIER brown mechanical pulp board

Bräunung *f* LEBENSMITTEL *Brot* bloom

Brausesieb *nt* KOHLEN spraying screen

Brau-: **Brauwasser** *nt* LEBENSMITTEL brewing liquor

Breadth-First-Suchverfahren *nt* KÜNSTL INT breadth-first search

Breakpoint *m* KONTROLL breakpoint; **Breakpointbetrieb** *m* KONTROLL breakpoint operation; **Breakpointschalter** *m* KONTROLL breakpoint switch

Brech- *pref* CHEMIE, KOHLEN crushing; **Brechanlage** *f* CHEMTECH, KOHLEN crushing plant; **Brechbacke** *f* CHEMTECH crusher jaw, FERTIG breaker jaw, LABOR *Präparierung* jaw crusher; **Brechberge** *m pl* KOHLEN broken rocks; **Brecheisen** *nt* BAU crowbar, pinch bar, ELEKTROTECH crowbar, FERTIG crowbar, pry, MASCHINEN jimmy bar

Brechen *nt* CHEMTECH *Erz* milling, KOHLEN crushing; **~ in einem Durchgang** *nt* KOHLEN open circuit crushing

brechen[1] *vt* BAU break, CHEMTECH *Emulsion* separate out, FERTIG *Schall, Licht* refract, PAPIER break, PHYS *Lichtstrahl* refract, WASSERTRANS break

brechen[2] *vi* WASSERTRANS break

brechend[1] *adj* RAUMFAHRT *Raumschiff* refractory

brechend:[2] **~er Winkel** *m* PHYS *Prisma* angle of a prism

Brecher *m* CHEMTECH crushing machine, FERTIG crusher, KOHLEN crusher, crushing mill, grinding mill, *Bergbau* breaker, MASCHINEN breaker, crusher, WASSERTRANS *Seezustand* breaker; **Brecherplatte** *f* KOHLEN jaw plate

Brech-: **Brechgut** *nt* BAU crushed material; **Brechkraft** *f* PHYS *Linse* converging power, power, WELLPHYS *Linse* converging power; **Brechprisma** *nt* OPTIK refracting prism; **Brechpunkt** *m* BAU breakpoint, break; **Brechstange** *f* BAU pinch bar, *mit Finne* claw bar, ELEKTROTECH crowbar, FERTIG wrecking bar, MASCHI-

NEN handspike, jim crow, MECHAN crowbar

Brechung *f* FERTIG *Schall, Licht* refraction, OPTIK refraction, refringency, *Strahlen* refringence, PHYS refraction, RAUMFAHRT *Weltraumfunk* refractivity, WELLPHYS *Lichtwelle* refraction; **Brechungsachse** *f* OPTIK axis of refraction; **Brechungsbrennkurve** *f* OPTIK caustic by refraction; **Brechungsebene** *f* OPTIK plane of refraction; **Brechungsgesetze** *nt pl* PHYS laws of refraction

Brechungsindex *m* FOTO refractive index, OPTIK index of refraction, *eines Mediums* refractive index, PHYS, RAUMFAHRT *Weltraumfunk*, WELLPHYS refractive index; **~ der Luft** *m* MECHAN, PHYS air refractive index; **Brechungsindexkontrast** *m* OPTIK refractive index contrast; **Brechungsindexprofil** *nt* OPTIK refractive index profile

Brechung: **Brechungskoeffizient** *m* FOTO refractive index, OPTIK relative refractive index, TELEKOM refractive index; **Brechungsmesser** *m* LABOR refractometer; **Brechungsverlust** *m* AUFNAHME refraction loss; **Brechungsvermögen** *nt* RADIO refractivity; **Brechungswinkel** *m (r)* OPTIK, PHYS angle of refraction *(r)*; **Brechungszahl** *f* OPTIK relative refractive index

Brech-: **Brechvermögen** *nt* PHYS refractivity; **Brechwalze** *f* KOHLEN cracker, crusher roll, crushing roll; **Brechwalzwerk** *nt* KOHLEN breaker, crushing mill, MASCHINEN crushing roll; **Brechwerk** *nt* KOHLEN crusher, stamp mill; **Brechwerkzeuge** *nt pl* KER & GLAS pinching tools; **Brechwirkungsgrad** *m* KOHLEN crushing efficiency

Brechwurz *f* LEBENSMITTEL *Pharmakologie* ipecac, ipecacuanha

Brechzahl *f* FERTIG index of refraction, OPTIK relative refractive index, TELEKOM refractive index; **Brechzahleinbruch** *m* TELEKOM index dip; **Brechzahlprofil** *nt* TELEKOM index profile; **Brechzahlunterschied** *m* TELEKOM refractive index contrast

Brei *m* ABFALL, FERTIG, KOHLEN, LEBENSMITTEL pulp, slurry

Breit- *pref* BAU broad, FERTIG broad, wide

breit: **~es Bereichsnetzwerk** *nt* TELEKOM, *WAN* wide area network; **~er Drehmeißel** *m* FERTIG wide-face square-nose tool; **~ hergestellter Teppich** *m* TEXTIL broadloom carpet

Breitband *nt* COMP & DV broadband, wideband, FERNSEH broadband, FERTIG wide strip, TELEKOM broadband, wideband; **Breitbandachse** *f* FERNSEH wideband axis; **Breitbandantenne** *f* FERNSEH broadband aerial, RAUMFAHRT wideband antenna; **Breitband-Bandpaßfilter** *nt* ELEKTRONIK wideband band-pass filter; **Breitbandempfänger** *m* TELEKOM wideband receiver; **Breitbandfernsehen** *nt (FSTV)* FERNSEH fast-scan television *(FSTV)*; **Breitbandfilter** *nt* ELEKTRONIK wideband filter; **Breitbandfiltern** *nt* ELEKTRONIK wideband filtering; **Breitband-Hochpaßfilter** *nt* ELEKTRONIK wideband high-pass filter

breitbandig[1] *adj* TELEKOM broadband, wideband

breitbandig:[2] **~es Rauschen** *nt* TELEKOM broadband noise, wideband noise

Breitband: **Breitbandimpuls** *m* FERNSEH broad pulse; **Breitband-ISDN** *nt* TELEKOM broadband ISDN, wideband ISDN; **Breitband-ISDN-Dienst** *m* TELEKOM broadband ISDN service; **Breitbandkoppelfeld** *nt* TELEKOM broadband switching network; **Breitbandkoppelnetz** *nt* TELEKOM wideband switching network; **Breitbandkoppelpunkt** *m* TELEKOM broadband crosspoint; **Breitbandkoppler** *m* TELEKOM broadband switch; **Breitband-Leistungsverstärker** *m* ELEKTRONIK wideband power amplifier; **Breitbandmehrfachzugriff** *m (SSMA)* RAUMFAHRT *Weltraumfunk* spread spectrum multiple access *(SSMA)*; **Breitbandmessung** *f* ELEKTRONIK wideband measurement; **Breitbandmodem** *nt* ELEKTRONIK, TELEKOM wideband modem; **Breitband-Modulation** *f* ELEKTRONIK wideband modulation; **Breitbandrauschen** *nt* AUFNAHME broadband noise, ELEKTRONIK wideband noise; **Breitbandröhre** *f* ELEKTRONIK wideband tube; **Breitband-Schaltkreis** *m* TELEKOM *Komponente* wideband circuit; **Breitbandsignal** *nt* ELEKTRONIK, TELEKOM wideband signal; **Breitbandstahl** *m* FERTIG wide strip; **Breitbandstörung** *f* ELEKTRONIK wideband interference; **Breitbandstrahlen** *m pl* STRAHLPHYS wideband beams; **Breitband-Tiefpaßfilter** *nt* ELEKTRONIK wideband lowpass filter; **Breitbandübertragung** *f* TELEKOM wideband transmission; **Breitbandverbindung** *f* TELEKOM wideband circuit; **Breitbandverstärker** *m* ELEKTRONIK broadband amplifier, ELEKTRONIK *(BBV)* wideband amplifier; **Breitbandwalzwerk** *nt* FERTIG wide-strip mill; **Breitbeil** *nt* BAU *Holzverarbeitung* adz (AmE), adze (BrE); **Breitbrenner** *m* LABOR flat-flame burner

Breite *f* COMP & DV, DRUCK, GEOM width, PAPIER breadth, width; **~ des Bandes** *f* AUFNAHME tape width; **~ der reduzierten Spanfläche** *f* FERTIG width of reduced face; **~ über alles** *f* MASCHINEN overall width; **Breitenausdehnung** *f* KER & GLAS spread; **Breitende** *nt* BAU *eines Hammers* poll; **Breitengrad** *m* WASSERTRANS *Navigation* latitude; **Breitenjitter** *m* ELEKTRONIK width jitter; **Breitenmetazentrum** *nt* WASSERTRANS *Schiffskonstruktion* transverse metacenter (AmE), transverse metacentre (BrE)

breitenmoduliert: ~es Impulssignal *nt* REGELUNG width-modulated pulse signal

Breite: Breitensuche *f* KÜNSTL INT breadth-first search

breitenvariable: ~ Tonspur *f* AUFNAHME variable-width sound track

Breit-: Breitflansch-Scharnierband *nt* BAU H hinge; **Breitflanschträger** *m* BAU H-beam, H-girder, broad-flange girder; **Breitfußfahrbalken** *m* TRANS *Hängebahn* inverted-T-shaped track girder; **Breithacke** *f* BAU mattock; **Breithalter** *m* TEXTIL stretcher, temple

breitkantig: ~es Wehr *nt* WASSERVERSORG broad-crested weir

Breit-: Breitschlichten *nt* FERTIG wide finishing; **Breitschlichtmaschine** *f* FERTIG broad-nose machine; **Breitschlichtmeißel** *m* FERTIG broad-finishing tool, wide-finishing tool; **Breitschlitzdüse** *f* KUNSTSTOFF sheet die; **Breitschrift** *f* DRUCK expanded type, extended type; **Breitspur** *f* EISENBAHN broadgage (AmE), broadgauge (BrE); **Breitstrahler** *m* RADIO broadside array; **Breitstuhlteppich** *m* TEXTIL broadloom carpet

Breit-Wigner-Resonanz *f* KERNTECH Breit-Wigner resonance

Brems- *pref* FERTIG, KFZTECH, MECHAN brake; **Bremsaggregat** *nt* MECHAN brake load; **Bremsankerplatte** *f* KFZTECH brake anchor plate, brake carrier plate, brake shield; **Bremsanlage** *f* KFZTECH brake system; **Bremsausgleichgestänge** *nt* KFZTECH brake compensator

Bremsbacke *f* FERTIG brake shoe, KFZTECH brake shoe, *Bremse* shoe, MASCHINEN brake jaw, brake shoe, ME-

CHAN brake shoe; **Bremsbacken-Bremsweg** *m* TRANS braking distance less brake lag distance; **Bremsbackenrückzugfeder** *f* KFZTECH brake release spring

Brems-: Bremsband *nt* KFZTECH *Kupplung*, MECHAN brake band; **Bremsbaugruppe** *f* KFZTECH brake assembly; **Bremsbelag** *m* KER & GLAS brake lining, KFZTECH brake friction pad, brake lining, *Bremsanlage* brake lining, *der Scheibenbremse* brake pad, MASCHINEN, MECHAN brake lining

Bremsbeläge: ~ erneuern *vi* KFZTECH reline the brakes

Brems-: Bremsbelagverschleißanzeige *f* KFZTECH brake lining wear indicator; **Bremsbelastung** *f* MECHAN brake load; **Bremsbereich** *m* KFZTECH brake area; **Bremsberg** *m* KOHLEN running jig; **Bremsbetätigung** *f* KFZTECH brake application; **Bremsbetätigungshebel** *m* EISENBAHN brake lever; **Bremsdichte** *f* KERNTECH slowing-down density; **Bremsdrehkraft** *f* KFZTECH brake torque; **Bremsdrehmoment** *nt* KFZTECH brake torque; **Bremsdruck** *m* KFZTECH brake pressure; **Bremsdruckregler** *m* MASCHINEN brake pressure regulator; **Bremsdüse** *f* RAUMFAHRT *Raumschiff* resistojet; **Bremsdynamo** *m* ELEKTRIZ brake dynamo, dynamometer, dynamometric dynamo; **Bremsdynamometer** *nt* GERÄT, MASCHINEN absorption dynamometer

Bremse[1] *f* KFZTECH, MASCHINEN, MECHAN brake; **~ mit Bremskraftverstärker** *f* MASCHINEN power brake

Bremse:[2] **die ~ anziehen** *vi* KFZTECH put on the brake; **die ~ fest anziehen** *vi* KFZTECH put the brakes on hard; **die ~ ganz durchtreten** *vi* KFZTECH put the brakes on full

Brems-: Bremselektrode *f* ELEKTROTECH reflecting electrode

Bremsen *nt* MASCHINEN, TRANS braking

bremsen *vi* KFZTECH apply the brake, brake, put on the brake, MECHAN decelerate

Brems-: Bremsentlüftungsgerät *nt* KFZTECH brake bleeder unit; **Bremsfading** *nt* KFZTECH *Bremsklötze, Bremsbeläge* brake fade; **Bremsfallschirm** *m* LUFTTRANS brake parachute, deceleration parachute, drag chute, drag parachute, RAUMFAHRT *Raumschiff* drag chute; **Bremsfallschirmhülle** *f* LUFTTRANS drag chute cover; **Bremsfläche** *f* KERNTECH slowing-down area; **Bremsflüssigkeit** *f* KFZTECH *Bremsanlage*, MASCHINEN brake fluid; **Bremsflüssigkeitsbehälter** *m* KFZTECH brake-fluid reservoir, MASCHINEN brake-fluid tank; **Bremsfutter** *nt* MECHAN brake lining; **Bremsgestänge** *nt* EISENBAHN brake rigging, KFZTECH *Bremsanlage*, MASCHINEN brake linkage; **Bremsgewicht** *nt* MECHAN counterbalance; **Bremsgitter** *nt* ELEKTRONIK *Elektronenröhren* suppressor grid, ELEKTROTECH suppression grid; **Bremshebel** *m* MASCHINEN brake lever; **Bremskeil** *m* KFZTECH brake wedge; **Bremskette** *f* MASCHINEN braking chain; **Bremskissen** *nt* MECHAN brake pad; **Bremsklotz** *m* EISENBAHN brake block, KFZTECH *Bremsanlage* brake pad, *Scheibenbremse* pad, MASCHINEN brake block, MECHAN chock; **Bremskombination** *f* EISENBAHN brake · blending; **Bremskontrolleuchte** *f* KFZTECH *Bremsanlage* brake-warning light

Bremskraft *f* KFZTECH brake effort, MASCHINEN brake power, TRANS braking power; **Bremskraftregler** *m* MASCHINEN brake-power control facility; **Bremskraftverstärker** *m* KFZTECH *Bremsanlage* brake servo; **Bremskraftverteiler** *m* KFZTECH brake-power distributor

Brems-: Bremskreisaufteilung *f* KFZTECH L-split system; **Bremskupplung** *f* MECHAN brake coupling; **Bremslänge** *f* KERNTECH slowing-down length; **Bremslauf** *m* LUFTTRANS *Motor und Triebwerk* run-up; **Bremsleistung** *f* FERTIG, KFZTECH, MECHAN brake horsepower, TRANS braking power; **Bremsleitung** *f* KFZTECH brake line; **Bremsleitungsverbindung** *f* EISENBAHN brake-pipe connection; **Bremsleuchte** *f* KFZTECH stop lamp; **Bremslicht** *nt* KFZTECH stop lamp; **Bremslüfter** *m* MASCHINEN brake motor; **Bremsluftschraube** *f* TRANS braking airscrew; **Bremsmaschine** *f* ELEKTRIZ brake motor; **Bremsmasse** *f* EISENBAHN brake weight; **Bremsmoment** *nt* MASCHINEN brake torque, braking moment; **Bremsmotor** *m* ELEKTRIZ, MASCHINEN brake motor; **Bremsnocken** *m* KFZTECH brake bar, brake cam, MECHAN brake cam; **Bremsnutzung** *f* KERNTECH resonance escape probability; **Bremspedal** *nt* KFZTECH brake pedal; **Bremspferdestärke** *f (BPS)* FERTIG, KFZTECH, MECHAN brake horsepower *(BHP)*; **Bremspotential** *nt* PHYS stopping potential; **Bremsprobe** *f* BAU brake testing; **Bremspropeller** *m* WASSERTRANS reversible pitch propeller; **Bremsprozent** *nt* EISENBAHN percentage of brake power; **Bremsprüfstand** *m* MECHAN brake-test stand; **Bremsrad** *nt* MECHAN brake wheel; **Bremsrakete** *f* RAUMFAHRT retro rocket; **Bremsreaktion** *f* TRANS brake reaction; **Bremsregler** *m* TRANS braking governor; **Bremsring** *m* KFZTECH *Automatikgetriebe* brake plate, MASCHINEN brake ring; **Bremssattel** *m* KFZTECH brake caliper (AmE), brake calliper (BrE), caliper (AmE), calliper (BrE); **Bremssattel der Scheibenbremse** *m* KFZTECH caliper (AmE), calliper (BrE); **Bremsscheibe** *f* KFZTECH, MASCHINEN, MECHAN brake disc (BrE), brake disk (AmE); **Bremsscheibenzentriervorrichtung** *f* KFZTECH brake disc alignment jig (BrE), brake disk alignment jig (AmE); **Bremsschild** *nt* KFZTECH brake carrier plate, brake shield; **Bremsschirm** *m* LUFTTRANS brake parachute; **Bremsschlauch** *m* KFZTECH brake hose; **Bremsschlauch der Druckluftbremse** *m* MASCHINEN air brake hose; **Bremsschub** *m* LUFTTRANS reverse thrust; **Bremsschuh** *m* KFZTECH shoe, MECHAN brake shoe; **Bremsschwund** *m* KFZTECH braking fading, *Bremsklötze, Bremsbeläge* brake fade; **Bremsseil** *nt* KFZTECH, MASCHINEN brake cable; **Bremssichtweite** *f* TRANS stopping sight distance; **Bremsspiel** *nt* KFZTECH brake clearance; **Bremsspindelstütze** *f* EISENBAHN brakescrew support; **Bremsspurkranz** *m* EISENBAHN brake flange; **Bremsstange** *f* KFZTECH brake rod; **Bremsstellung** *f* LUFTTRANS brake pitch, *Hubschrauber* braking pitch; **Bremssteuerung** *f* MECHAN brake control; **Bremsstrahlung** *f* PHYS, STRAHLPHYS, TEILPHYS bremsstrahlung; **Bremsstrahlungsquelle** *f* KERNTECH bremsstrahlung source; **Bremsstrecke** *f* KFZTECH braking distance; **Bremssubstanz** *f* KERNTECH moderator; **Bremssystem** *nt* MASCHINEN brake system, braking system, MECHAN brake system; **Bremstest** *m* MASCHINEN brake test; **Bremsträger** *m* KFZTECH brake anchor plate, brake shield; **Bremsträgerplatte** *f* KFZTECH brake carrier plate; **Bremstrommel** *f* KFZTECH brake drum, *Bremsanlage* brake drum, MECHAN brake drum

Bremsung *f* ERGON deceleration, MECHAN braking, deceleration, TRANS braking; **~ auf Halt** *f* EISENBAHN braking to a stop

Brems-: **Bremsventil** *nt* EISENBAHN, KFZTECH brake valve; **Bremsvermögen** *nt* KERNTECH slowing-down power, PHYS stopping power; **Bremsversagen** *nt* KFZTECH brake failure; **Bremsversuch** *m* MASCHINEN brake test; **Bremsverzögerung** *f* TRANS braking deceleration; **Bremsvorrichtung** *f* TRANS deceleration device; **Bremswagen** *m* EISENBAHN brake van, brake wagon

Bremsweg *m* KFZTECH braking distance, TRANS stopping distance; **~ ohne Bremsverzögerungsabstand** *m* TRANS braking distance less brake lag distance

Brems-: **Bremswelle** *f* KFZTECH, MASCHINEN brake shaft; **Bremswiderstand** *m* TRANS braking resistance; **Bremswirkungsverlust** *m* KFZTECH braking fading; **Bremszeit** *f* TRANS braking time; **Bremszugstange** *f* KFZTECH brake connecting rod; **Bremszustand** *m* MECHAN brake state; **Bremszylinder** *m* FERTIG dashpot, KFZTECH, MASCHINEN brake cylinder

Brenn- *pref* CHEMTECH distilling, ELEKTRONIK focal, PHYS caustic, focal; **Brennapparat** *m* CHEMTECH distilling apparatus

brennbar[1] *adj* CHEMIE, FERTIG combustible, KUNSTSTOFF flammable, THERMOD combustible; **nicht ~** *adj* ABFALL, VERPACK incombustible, WERKPRÜF nonflammable

brennbar:[2] **~er Abfall** *m* UMWELTSCHMUTZ combustible waste; **~es Material** *nt* UMWELTSCHMUTZ combustible material; **~er Stoff** *m* SICHERHEIT combustible material

Brennbarkeit *f* KUNSTSTOFF flammability, SICHERHEIT, THERMOD, VERPACK combustibility; **Brennbarkeitstest** *m* SICHERHEIT *für Möbel* fire test

Brenn-: **Brennbohren** *nt* BAU oxygen lancing; **Brennebene** *f* ELEKTRONIK focal plane, PHYS caustic, focal plane; **Brenneisen** *nt* VERPACK branding iron; **Brennelement in Rasterbauweise** *nt* KERNTECH grid-spaced fuel assembly; **neues Brennelement** *nt* KERNTECH new fuel assembly, new fuel element; **Brennelementhülse** *f* KERNTECH fuel cladding; **Brennelementüberprüfung mit Gammastrahlen** *f* KERNTECH gamma heating

Brennen *nt* FERNSEH burn, KOHLEN calcination, roasting

brennen *vt* KER & GLAS *von Ton*, TEXTIL *Textildruck*, THERMOD *Keramik* bake

brennend[1] *adj* HEIZ & KÄLTE, KER & GLAS, METALL, THERMOD burning

brennend:[2] **~e Kohle** *f* KOHLEN burning coal

Brenner *m* BAU blowpipe, burner, torch, FERTIG blowpipe, torch, MASCHINEN, MECHAN blowpipe, burner, torch, TELEKOM, THERMOD *Bunsenbrenner, von Gasherd* burner; **Brennerdüse** *f* FERTIG blowpipe nozzle, HEIZ & KÄLTE burner head, burner mouth, MASCHINEN burner nozzle; **Brennerei** *f* LEBENSMITTEL distillery; **Brennereinsatz** *m* FERTIG torch head; **Brennerflamme** *f* FERTIG torch flame; **Brennerkopf** *m* HEIZ & KÄLTE burner head; **Brennerlöten** *nt* BAU torch brazing; **Brennermaul** *nt* KER & GLAS port mouth; **Brennermaulwange** *f* KER & GLAS port side wall; **Brennermundstück** *nt* BAU tip, FERTIG burner head; **Brenneröffnung** *f* KER & GLAS *des Hafenofens* eye; **Brennerschlauch** *m* FERTIG torch hose; **Brennerspitze** *f* BAU tip

Brenn-: **Brennfläche** *f* OPTIK caustic; **Brennfleck** *m* ELEKTRONIK focal spot, FERTIG arcing end; **Brenngasflasche** *f* FERTIG fuel-gas cylinder

brenngeschnitten *adj* FERTIG gas-cut

Brenn-: **Brenngut** *nt* ABFALL incinerator charge; **Brenn-**

härtemaschine *f* FERTIG flame-hardening machine
brennhärten *vt* THERMOD flame-harden
brennhobeln *vt* FERTIG *Stahlblöcke* hog
Brenn-: **Brennintervall** *nt* KER & GLAS firing range;
Brennkammer *f* HEIZ & KÄLTE fire box, RAUMFAHRT
Raumschiff combustion chamber, combustor, THER-
MOD firebox; **Brennkammerauskleidung** *f* HEIZ &
KÄLTE burner liner; **Brennkapsel** *f* KER & GLAS sagger;
Brennkapselstapel *m* KER & GLAS bung of saggers;
Brennkraftmaschine *f* KFZTECH combustion engine,
explosion engine, explosion motor, LUFTTRANS com-
bustion engine, MASCHINEN internal combustion
engine, TRANS, WASSERTRANS combustion engine;
Brennkurve *f* OPTIK caustic; **Brennlinie** *f* OPTIK caustic;
Brennofen *m* BAU, FERTIG, LEBENSMITTEL, METALL,
THERMOD kiln; **Brennpunkt** *m* FOTO focal point, GEOM
focus, HEIZ & KÄLTE fire point, PHYS focus, SICHERHEIT
fire point; **Brennputzen** *nt* FERTIG flame chipping,
flame descaling, flame deseaming, flame scarfing
brennputzen *vt* FERTIG torch-deseam
Brenn-: **Brennraum** *m* KFZTECH, LUFTTRANS, THERMOD,
WASSERTRANS combustion chamber; **Brennschluß** *m*
RAUMFAHRT flameout, *Raumschiff* burnout; **Brennschneiden** *nt* FERTIG gas cutting, oxycutting, oxygen
cutting, MASCHINEN, MECHAN acetylene cutting,
flame cutting, METALL flame cutting, THERMOD gas
cutting
brennschneiden *vt* FERTIG oxygen-cut, torch-cut
Brenn-: **Brennstab** *m* KERNTECH fuel rod; **Brennstempel**
m VERPACK branding iron
Brennstoff *m* HEIZ & KÄLTE, MASCHINEN, THERMOD fuel;
Brennstoffanreicherung *f* KERNTECH feed enrichment; **Brennstoffaufbereitung** *f* KERNTECH make-up
fuel; **Brennstoffaufbereitung durch Wäsche** *f* KERN-
TECH scrubbing; **Brennstoffauffrischung** *f* KERNTECH
fuel regeneration; **Brennstoffdichte** *f* KERNTECH fuel
density; **Brennstoffdosierung** *f* GERÄT fuel metering;
Brennstoffelement *nt* MASCHINEN fuel element, THER-
MOD fuel cell; **Brennstoffersparnis** *f* THERMOD fuel
economy; **Brennstoff-Fördertisch** *m* KERNTECH fuel
transfer table; **Brennstoffhülse** *f* KERNTECH fuel cladding; **Brennstoffinventar** *nt* KERNTECH activity
inventory, fuel inventory; **Brennstoffkanal** *m* KERN-
TECH fuel channel; **Brennstoffkreislauf im
Reaktorkern** *m* KERNTECH in-core fuel cycle; **Brenn-
stoffkühlung** *f* THERMOD fuel cooling;
Brennstofflebensdauer *f* KERNTECH fuel life; **Brenn-
stoffmatrix** *f* KERNTECH matrix fuel; **Brennstoff-Pellet
mit Uranoxid** *nt* KERNTECH uranium oxide pellet;
Brennstoffraster *m* KERNTECH grid-spaced fuel assembly; **Brennstoffschäden** *m pl* KERNTECH *Wachsen,
Beulenbildung, Risse* fuel detriment
brennstoffsparend *adj* THERMOD fuel-efficient
Brennstoff: **Brennstoffzelle** *f* ELEKTRIZ fuel cell; **Brenn-
stoffzinsen** *m pl* KERNTECH fuel rates
Brenn-: **Brennstumpfschweißen** *nt* FERTIG flash welding; **Brennstütze** *f* KER & GLAS buck (AmE), dot (BrE),
point bar (BrE); **Brenntemperatur** *f* KER & GLAS firing
temperature; **Brennverhalten** *nt* KUNSTSTOFF flammability; **Brennweite** *f* FOTO, PHYS focal length;
Brennweitenbereich *m* FOTO focusing range; **Brenn-
wert** *m* HEIZ & KÄLTE gross calorific value, useful heat,
LEBENSMITTEL, PHYS, THERMOD calorific value;
Brennzeit *f* FERNSEH focal time
Brenzcatechin-Monomethylether *m* CHEMIE guaiacol
Brenztraubensäure *f* CHEMIE pyruvic acid

Brett *nt* BAU board; **Bretterverkleidung** *f* BAU boarding,
KOHLEN planking; **Brettschaltungsmodell** *nt* ELEK-
TROTECH *Versuchsschaltung* breadboard model
Brewster: **~scher Effekt** *m* RADIO *Polarisationsdrehung*
Brewster effect; **~scher Einfallswinkel** *m* PHYS
Brewster incidence; **~scher Winkel** *m* OPTIK, PHYS
Brewster angle
Bride *f* MASCHINEN buckle
Bridge *f* TELEKOM bridge
Brief *m* COMP & DV letter, *E-Mail* mail message, DRUCK
letter; **Briefkopf** *m* DRUCK letterhead; **Briefqualität** *f*
COMP & DV letter-quality
Briggs-Gewinde *nt* MASCHINEN Brigg's pipe thread
Brikett *nt* KOHLEN briquette; **Brikettfett** *nt* MASCHINEN
block grease
brikettiert: **~es Karbid** *nt* FERTIG cake of carbide
Brillantschliff *m* KER & GLAS brilliant cutting
Brillantsucher *m* FOTO reflecting viewfinder
Brillanz *f* ELEKTRONIK *Fernsehtechnik*, METALL brillian-
ce, brilliancy
Brille *f* FERTIG *Stopfbuchse*, MASCHINEN gland; **~ mit
Sicherheitsglas** *f* SICHERHEIT safety spectacles
Brillenglas: **~ mit 3¹/₂" Wölbungsradius** *nt* KER & GLAS
coquille; **~ mit 7" Wölbungsradius** *nt* KER & GLAS
micoquille
Brillouin: **~sche Zone** *f* PHYS *Festkörperphysik* Brillouin
zone
Brinell- *pref* FERTIG, MASCHINEN Brinell; **Brinelleffekt** *m*
MASCHINEN Brinell effect; **Brinellhärte** *f* FERTIG Bri-
nell hardness, Brinell hardness number, MASCHINEN
BHN, Brinell hardness number, MECHAN Brinell
hardness; **Brinellhärteprüfung** *f* FERTIG ball indenta-
tion test; **Brinellhärtetest** *m* MASCHINEN Brinell
hardness testing machine
Brinellieren *nt* MASCHINEN brinelling
Brinell-: **Brinellkugel** *f* FERTIG ball penetrator; **Brinellku-
gelprüfung** *f* MASCHINEN Brinell ball test;
Brinellprüfung *f* MASCHINEN Brinell test
Britanniametall *nt* METALL Britannia, Britannia metal
Britisch: **~es BA-Gewinde** *nt* MASCHINEN BA screw thre-
ad; **~er Bushel** *m* LEBENSMITTEL bushel; **~er
Computerverband** *m* COMP & DV British Computer
Society; **~e Normenspezifikation** *f (BSS)* MASCHINEN
British Standard Specification *(BSS)*; **~e Normvor-
schrift** *f (BSS)* MASCHINEN British Standard
Specification *(BSS)*; **~es SF-Gewinde** *nt* MASCHINEN
British Standard fine thread; **~er Viertelacker** *m*
METROL rood; **~e Wärmeeinheit** *f (BTU, BThU)* LA-
BOR British Thermal unit *(BThU)*, MASCHINEN
British Thermal unit *(BTU)*
Brix-Skala *f* LEBENSMITTEL *für Zucker* Brix scale
bröckelig *adj* CHEMTECH pulverulent, KUNSTSTOFF fri-
able
Brodeln *nt* PHYS bubbling
Brokat *m* TEXTIL brocade; **Brokatgewebe** *nt* TEXTIL
brocade
Brom *nt (Br)* CHEMIE bromine *(Br)*; **Brom-** *pref* CHE-
MIE bromic; **Bromaceton** *nt* CHEMIE bromoacetone
Bromal *nt* CHEMIE bromal
Bromat *nt* CHEMIE trioxobromate
Brom: **Brombenzol** *nt* CHEMIE bromobenzene
Bromelin *nt* LEBENSMITTEL bromelin
Bromgelatine-Verfahren *nt* FOTO gelatino-bromide pro-
cess
Bromid *nt* CHEMIE bromide
Brom: **Bromoform** *nt* CHEMIE bromoform; **Bromölab-**

zug *m* FOTO bromoil print; **Bromphenol** *nt* CHEMIE bromophenol; **Bromsalz** *nt* CHEMIE bromide; **Bromsilberdruck** *m* DRUCK bromide, bromide print; **Bromsilberkollodiumplatte** *f* FOTO silver-bromide collodion plate; **Bromsilberpapier** *nt* DRUCK, FOTO bromide paper

Bronze *f* MECHAN gunmetal; **Bronzebüchse** *f* MASCHINEN gunmetal bush; **Bronzeführungsbuchse** *f* MASCHINEN bronze guide bush; **Bronzelager** *nt* MASCHINEN gunmetal bearing; **Bronzeschweißen** *nt* BAU bronze welding

Bronzierung *f* METALL bronzing

Brookfield-Viskosität *f* KUNSTSTOFF Brookfield viscosity

broschiert *adj* DRUCK stitched

Brot *nt* LEBENSMITTEL bread; **Brotgärung** *f* LEBENSMITTEL panary fermentation

Brotschrift *f* DRUCK body type

Brown: **~sche Molekularbewegung** *f* PHYS, STRAHLPHYS, THERMOD Brownian molecular movement, Brownian motion, Brownian movement; **~-und-Sharpe-Kegel** *m* FERTIG BS taper, Brown and Sharpe taper

Bruch *m* DRUCK fraction, ERDÖL fault, FERTIG crushing, KOHLEN break, crack, MASCHINEN fracture, MATH fraction, MECHAN crack, fracture, METALL crack, failure, fracture, rupture, PAPIER break, TEXTIL breakage, break, burst; **Bruchbeanspruchung** *f* MASCHINEN, MECHAN breaking stress; **Bruchbelastung** *f* PAPIER, VERPACK breaking load; **Bruchbild** *nt* MECHAN breaking pattern; **Bruchbildung** *f* ERDÖL *Geologie* fracturing; **Bruchdehnung** *f* BAU flexural strength, FERTIG elongation, KUNSTSTOFF elongation at break, ultimate elongation, MECHAN flexural strength, PAPIER stretch at breaking point, WERKPRÜF elongation at break; **Bruchdruck** *m* ERDÖL *Geologie* fracture pressure; **Bruchelement** *nt* HEIZ & KÄLTE rupture member; **Bruchfestigkeit** *f* BAU ultimate strength, FERTIG *Kunststoffinstallationen* breaking strain, KUNSTSTOFF breaking strength, MASCHINEN ultimate breaking strength, MECHAN breaking strength, METALL rupture strength, TEXTIL breaking strength, WERKPRÜF fracture strength; **Bruchglas** *nt* SICHERHEIT *an Feuermeldern* firebreak glass; **Bruchgradient** *m* ERDÖL *Geologie* fracture gradient; **Bruchgrenze** *f* MASCHINEN breaking point, ultimate breaking strength, WASSERTRANS breaking strain; **Bruchhefe** *f* LEBENSMITTEL *Brauerei* flocculating yeast

brüchig[1] *adj* ANSTRICH brittle, CHEMTECH pulverulent, KUNSTSTOFF brittle, friable, MECHAN brittle

brüchig:[2] **~e Kreide** *f* BAU fractured chalk

Brüchigkeit *f* KUNSTSTOFF brittleness

Bruch: **Bruchkanten** *f pl* MECHAN break edges; **Bruchkegel** *m* KER & GLAS fracture cone; **Bruchkreis** *m* BAU slip circle; **Bruchkriterium** *nt* METALL fracture criterion; **Bruchkriterium nach Griffith** *nt* KERNTECH Griffith's fracture criterion; **Bruchlast** *f* BAU breaking load, FERTIG collapse load, KOHLEN, KUNSTSTOFF breaking load, MASCHINEN breaking load, rupture load, MECHAN, VERPACK, WASSERTRANS breaking load; **Bruchlinie** *f* KONSTZEICH break line; **Bruchlochwicklung** *f* ELEKTROTECH fractional slot winding; **Bruchmechanik** *f* MECHAN fracture mechanics; **Bruchmechanikversuch** *m* WERKPRÜF fracture mechanics test; **Bruchmuster** *nt* KER & GLAS fracture pattern; **Bruchplatte** *f* MECHAN bursting disc (BrE), bursting disk (AmE); **Bruchpunkt** *m* PHYS yield point;

Bruchrechnen *nt* MATH fractional arithmetic; **Bruchreis** *m* LEBENSMITTEL broken rice

bruchsicher *adj* VERPACK shockproof

Bruch: **Bruchsicherheit** *f* WERKPRÜF fracture strength; **Bruchspannung** *f* BAU, MASCHINEN, MECHAN breaking stress; **Bruchspiegel** *m* KER & GLAS fracture mirror; **Bruchstein** *m* BAU broken stone, rubblestone; **Bruchsteinmauerwerk** *nt* BAU rubble masonry; **Bruchstelle** *f* NICHTFOSS ENERG fracture; **Bruchstrich** *m* MATH bar; **Bruchstück** *nt* SICHERHEIT *von abgenutztem Werkzeug* fragment; **Bruchteil** *m* COMP & DV fractional part, MATH fraction

bruchteilig: **~e Frequenzabweichung** *f* ELEKTRONIK fractional frequency deviation

Bruch: **Bruchtest** *m* MECHAN breaking test; **Bruchursprung** *m* WERKPRÜF fracture origin; **Bruchverhalten** *nt* METALL fracture behavior (AmE), fracture behaviour (BrE); **Bruchversuch** *m* BAU breaking test, MASCHINEN fracture test; **Bruchwertdesign** *nt* RAUMFAHRT *konstruiert bis zur Beulgrenze* design to buckling strength; **Bruchzähigkeit** *f* KUNSTSTOFF fracture toughness; **Bruchzähigkeitsfaktor** *m* WERKPRÜF fracture toughness factor; **Bruchzahl** *f* MATH fractional; **Bruchzeit** *f* METALL time to rupture; **Bruchzone** *f* KOHLEN *über dem Abbau* mat; **Bruchzugkraft** *f* BAU ultimate strength

Brucin *nt* LEBENSMITTEL brucine

Brücke[1] *f* BAU bridge, *eines Laufkranes* bridge, COMP & DV bridge, ELEKTRIZ jumper, ELEKTROTECH, GERÄT, KER & GLAS bridge, MASCHINEN bridge, runner, traveler (AmE), traveller (BrE), RADIO *Schaltung* bridge, WASSERTRANS *Handelsmarine* navigation bridge, *Schiff* bridge; **~ mit Gleitkontakt** *f* ELEKTROTECH slide bridge; **~ mit obenliegender Fahrbahn** *f* BAU deck bridge

Brücke:[2] **~ über einen Fluß schlagen** *vi* BAU throw a bridge over river

Brücke: **Brückenabgleich** *m* ELEKTROTECH bridge balancing; **Brückenarm** *m* ELEKTRIZ *Brückenzweig* bridge arm; **Brückenaufbau** *m* WASSERTRANS *Schiffbau* bridge superstructure; **Brückenaufnahme** *f* EISENBAHN bridge survey; **Brückenausgleich** *m* GERÄT bridge balance; **Brückenblech** *nt* BAU bridge plate; **Brückenbogen** *m* BAU arch; **Brückendeck** *nt* WASSERTRANS *Schiffbau* bridge deck; **Brückendiagonalspannung** *f* GERÄT *Meßbrücke* unbalance voltage; **Brückendrehkran** *m* BAU jib crane; **Brückendurchfahrtshöhe** *f* WASSERTRANS *Schiffkonstruktion* air draught; **Brückenfachwerkträger** *m* BAU bridge truss; **Brückenfahrbahn** *f* BAU bridge deck; **Brückenfilter** *nt* ELEKTRONIK, TELEKOM lattice filter; **Brückengeländer** *nt* BAU bridge railing; **Brückengleichgewicht** *nt* GERÄT bridge balance; **Brückengleichrichter** *m* ELEKTRIZ, ELEKTROTECH bridge rectifier; **Brückenhaus** *nt* WASSERTRANS *Schiffbau* bridge house; **Brückenkahn** *m* WASSERTRANS pontoon; **Brückenkran** *m* BAU bridge crane, overhead crane, MASCHINEN overhead crane

brückenlos: **~e Kontakte** *m pl* ELEKTROTECH non-bridging contacts

Brücke: **Brückenmessung** *f* GERÄT bridge measurement; **Brückenmischer** *m* ELEKTRONIK push-pull mixer, ELEKTROTECH balanced mixer; **Brückenpfeiler** *m* BAU pylon; **Brückenschaltung** *f* ELEKTRIZ bridge circuit, bridge connection, ELEKTROTECH bridge circuit; **Brückenschaltung aus Ohmschen Elementen** *f* GERÄT resistive bridge; **Brückenstecker** *m* KONTROLL strapping plug; **Brückenüberbau** *m* BAU bridge deck; **Brückenverhältnisarm** *m* ELEKTRIZ ratio arm; **Brückenverstärker** *m* ELEKTRONIK bridge amplifier; **Brückenwaage** *f* BAU weighbridge; **Brückenwärter** *m* WASSERTRANS *Fluß* bridge keeper; **Brückenwiderstand** *m* ELEKTRIZ *Bauelement* bridge resistor, *physikalische Größe* bridge resistance; **Brückenzweig** *m* GERÄT *Brückenschaltung* ratio arm

Brüdenverdichtung *f* CHEMTECH vapor compression (AmE), vapour compression (BrE)

brühen *vt* LEBENSMITTEL, THERMOD scald

brühend: ~ **heiß** *adj* THERMOD scalding

Brumm *m* AKUSTIK hum, ripple; **Brummabstand** *m* ELEKTRONIK signal-to-hum ratio; **Brummbalken** *m pl* FERNSEH hum bars; **Brummeinkopplung** *f* AUFNAHME hum pickup

Brummen *nt* AKUSTIK, ELEKTROTECH, RADIO hum

brummen *vi* RADIO hum

Brumm: **Brummfaktor** *m* ELEKTRONIK ripple factor; **Brummfilter** *nt* STRAHLPHYS ripple filter; **Brummfrequenz** *f* STRAHLPHYS ripple frequency; **Brummkompensationsspule** *f* ELEKTROTECH humbucking coil; **Brummspannung** *f* ELEKTRONIK ripple voltage, ELEKTROTECH hum voltage

Brünieren *nt* FERTIG *Stahl* black finishing, blackening, METALL *Stahl* bronzing

brünieren *vt* FERTIG black-finish, brown, *Stahl* blue

Brunnen *m* BAU spring, well; ~ **vom Beobachtungsnetz** *m* WASSERVERSORG observation well; **Brunnenbau** *m* NICHTFOSS ENERG well sinking; **Brunnenkopf** *m* NICHTFOSS ENERG well head; **Brunnenkopfdruck** *m* NICHTFOSS ENERG wellhead pressure; **Brunnenkopftemperatur** *f* NICHTFOSS ENERG wellhead temperature; **Brunnenkopfventil** *nt* NICHTFOSS ENERG wellhead valve; **Brunnenring** *m* KOHLEN, NICHTFOSS ENERG well casing; **Brunnensatz** *m* WASSERVERSORG set of wells

Brust *f* FERTIG breast, MASCHINEN breast, chest; **Brustbohrer** *m* MASCHINEN breast drill, chest drill; **Brustbohrmaschine** *f* MASCHINEN breast drill, chest drill; **Brusthölzer** *nt pl* BAU walings; **Brustleier** *f* FERTIG breast drill, MASCHINEN breast drill, chest drill; **Brustplatte** *f* MASCHINEN breast plate

Brüstung *f* BAU balustrade, parapet, railing; **Brüstungsgeländer** *nt* HYDRAUL breasting parapet; **Brüstungsmauer** *f* BAU *brusthoch* breast wall

Brust: **Brustwalze** *f* PAPIER breast roll; **Brustzapfenaufwölbung** *f* BAU tusk; **Brustzapfenverbindung** *f* BAU tusk tenon joint

Brut *f* KERNTECH breeding; **Brutabschnitt** *m* KERNTECH *eines Brennstabes* breeding section

Brüter *m* KERNTECH breeding reactor; **Brüterreaktor** *m* KERNTECH, PHYS breeder reactor

Brut: **Brutgewinn** *m* ELEKTRONIK *Atomphysik* conversion gain, KERNTECH breeding gain; **Brutkreislauf** *m* KERNTECH breeding cycle; **Brutmantel** *m* KERNTECH breeding blanket; **Brutreaktor** *m* KERNTECH breeding reactor; **Brutschrank** *m* LABOR *Mikrobiologie* incubator

Brutto- *pref* METROL gross; **Bruttogewicht** *nt* METROL, VERPACK gross weight; **Bruttoleistung** *f* KERNTECH gross installed capacity; **Bruttoraumgehalt** *m* WASSERTRANS gross registered tonnage, gross tonnage; **Bruttoregistertonne** *f* METROL displacement ton, WASSERTRANS gross ton; **Bruttotonnage** *f* ERDÖL *Schiffahrt* gross tonnage; **Bruttovolumen** *nt* VERPACK gross volume; **Bruttowärmeverlust** *m* HEIZ & KÄLTE gross heat loss

Brut: **Brutverfahren** *nt* KERNTECH breeding process; **Brutvorgang** *m* KERNTECH breeding process; **Brutvorgangswirkungsgrad** *m* KERNTECH breeding process efficiency; **Brutzyklus** *m* KERNTECH breeding cycle

BS *abbr* FERTIG *(Windfrischstahl)*, MASCHINEN *(Bessemerstahl)* BS *(Bessemer steel)*

BSA *abbr (Bohrlochsohlenausrüstung)* ERDÖL BHA *(bottom hole assembly)*

BSB *abbr (biologischer Sauerstoffbedarf)* ABFALL, LEBENSMITTEL, UMWELTSCHMUTZ BOD *(biological oxygen demand)*

BSC-Übertragung *f (binärsynchrone Übertragung)* COMP & DV BSC *(binary synchronous communication)*

BSF-Gewinde *nt (Gewinde nach britischem Standard)* MASCHINEN BSF *(British standard fine screw thread)*

BSP-Gewinde *nt (Gewinde nach britischem Standard)* MASCHINEN BSP *(British standard pipe thread)*

BSS *abbr (Britische Normenspezifikation, Britische Normvorschrift)* MASCHINEN BSS *(British Standard Specification)*

BThU *abbr (Britische Wärmeeinheit)* MASCHINEN, METROL *Energie* BThU *(British Thermal unit)*

BTU *abbr (Britische Wärmeeinheit)* LABOR BThU *(British Thermal unit)*, MASCHINEN BTU (AmE) *(British Thermal unit)*

Btx *abbr (Bildschirmtext)* FERNSEH Videotex®, TELEKOM Teletext®

Btx-Anbieter *m* FERNSEH videotex information provider

Bubble: ~ **Jet Drucker** *m* DRUCK bubble-jet printer; **Bubblesort** *nt* COMP & DV *einfaches Sortierverfahren* bubble sort

Bubbling *nt* KER & GLAS bubbling

Buch *nt* DRUCK book; ~ **mit festem Einband** *nt* DRUCK casebound book, cased book; **Buchbinden** *nt* DRUCK bookbinding

Buchbinder *m* DRUCK bookbinder; **Buchbinderei** *f* DRUCK bindery, bookbinding; **Buchbindernadel** *f* DRUCK bookbinder's needle; **Buchbinderpappe** *f* DRUCK millboard; **Buchbinderstempel** *m* DRUCK bookbinder's brass

Buch: **Buchdecke** *f* DRUCK book case, case; **Buchdruck** *m* DRUCK letterpress, letterpress printing; **Buchdruckmaschine** *f* DRUCK letterpress-printing machine; **Buchdruckpresse** *f* DRUCK letterpress-printing machine; **Buchführung** *f* MECHAN audit

Büchner: ~**scher Kolben** *m* LABOR *Filtrieren* Büchner flask; ~**scher Trichter** *m* LABOR *Filtrieren* Büchner funnel; ~**sche Nutsche** *f* LABOR *Filtrieren* Büchner funnel

Buch: **Buchrücken** *m* DRUCK shelfback; **Buchsatz** *m* DRUCK book composition

Buchse:[1] **mit** ~ **versehen** *adj* ELEKTROTECH jacked

Buchse[2] *f* AUFNAHME, COMP & DV jack; ELEKTRIZ bearing, female connector, ELEKTROTECH jack, FERNSEH *Stecker* socket, MASCHINEN bush, bushing, liner, sleeve, bushing, MECHAN bushing, sleeve, RADIO jack, receptacle, TELEKOM jack; ~ **aus Kupferlegierung** *f* MASCHINEN copper alloy bush; ~ **mit berührungsgeschützten Kontakten** *f* ELEKTRIZ socket with shrouded contacts

Büchse *f* FERTIG liner, MASCHINEN bushing, liner, VERPACK can (AmE), tin (BrE)

Büchsen: **in** ~ *adj* LEBENSMITTEL canned (AmE), tinned (BrE)

Buchse: **Buchsenfeld** *nt* AUFNAHME jack panel (BrE),

patch panel (AmE); **Buchsenkette** *f* MASCHINEN bush chain; **Buchsenkontakt** *m* ELEKTROTECH socket contact; **Buchsenleiste** *f* ELEKTROTECH socket board; **Buchsenstecker** *m* ELEKTRIZ socket plug; **Buchsensteckverbinder** *m* ELEKTROTECH female connector; **Buchsenteil** *m* ELEKTROTECH female contact; **Buchsenverbindung** *f* ELEKTRIZ socket coupler; **Buchsenzieher** *m* MASCHINEN bush extractor

Buchstabe *m* COMP & DV, DRUCK letter; ~ **mit Oberlänge** *m* DRUCK ascending letter; ~ **ohne Ober- und Unterlängen** *m* DRUCK short letter; **Buchstabenalgebra** *f* MATH literal algebra; **Buchstabenbezeichnung** *f* MASCHINEN *für Stahldraht* letter gage (AmE), letter gauge (BrE); **Buchstabencode** *m* COMP & DV *Kurzbefehl* mnemonic code; **Buchstabenfehler** *m* DRUCK literal error; **Buchstabengenerator** *m* FERNSEH character generator; **Buchstabengleichung** *f* MATH literal equation; **Buchstabenkennung** *f* KONSTZEICH letter code; **Buchstabenumschaltung** *f* COMP & DV, TELEKOM letter shift

Buchstabieralphabet *nt* RADIO phonetic alphabet

Bucht *f* WASSERTRANS *Geographie* bay, *Tauwerk* bight

Buch: **Buchzeichen** *nt* DRUCK bookmark

Buckel *m* MASCHINEN boss

buckelgeschweißt *adj* FERTIG projection-welded

Buckelschweißen *nt* MASCHINEN projection welding

buckelschweißen *vt* FERTIG projection-weld

Buckelschweißung *f* BAU, FERTIG projection welding

Buckram *m* DRUCK buckram

Bufotoxin *nt* CHEMIE bufotoxine

Bug:[1] **vor dem ~** *adv* WASSERTRANS across the bow

Bug[2] *m* BAU strut, RAUMFAHRT *Raumschiff* nose cone, WASSERTRANS bow, prow

Bug:[3] **mit ~ voran sinken** *vi* WASSERTRANS *Schiff* go down by the bows

Bug: **Buganker** *m* WASSERTRANS bow anchor, bower anchor; **Bugaufklotzung** *f* WASSERTRANS bow chock; **Bugdruckwelle** *f* RAUMFAHRT bow shock

Bügel *m* BAU bow, fastening, shackle, stirrup, FERTIG stirrup, *Kunststoffinstallationen* pin, *Meßschraube* C-frame, MASCHINEN bow, shackle, strap, yoke, MECHAN clevis, yoke, MEERSCHMUTZ shackle; **Bügelbolzen** *m* BAU U-bolt

bügelfrei *adj* TEXTIL drip-dry

Bügel: **Bügelmeßschraube** *f* FERTIG outside micrometer; **Bügelsäge** *f* FERTIG, MASCHINEN, MECHAN hacksaw; **Bügelschraube** *f* BAU U-bolt, BAU strap bolt

Bug: **Bugfahrwerk** *nt* LUFTTRANS nose gear; **Bugfahrwerksbein** *nt* LUFTTRANS nose gear leg; **Bugfahrwerksklappe** *f* LUFTTRANS nose gear door; **Bugfahrwerkslenkung** *f* LUFTTRANS nose gear steering; **Bugfahrwerkssattel** *m* LUFTTRANS nose gear saddle; **Bugfahrwerks-Steuerungsverriegelung** *f* LUFTTRANS nose gear steer lock; **Bugfender** *m* WASSERTRANS noseband, *Deckausrüstung* bow fender; **Bugholz** *nt* BAU angle tie, *Holzbau* angle brace; **Bugkettenstopper** *m* WASSERTRANS *Deckausrüstung* bow stopper; **Bugklappe** *f* WASSERTRANS bow door; **Bugpforte** *f* WASSERTRANS bow door; **Bugradfahrwerkszahnrad** *nt* LUFTTRANS nose gear wheel; **Bugradlenkstange** *f* LUFTTRANS nose wheel steering bar; **Bugradsteuerrad** *nt* LUFTTRANS nose wheel steering control wheel; **Bugradsteuerung** *f* LUFTTRANS nose wheel steering; **Bugsee** *f* WASSERTRANS bow wave

Bugsieren *nt* WASSERTRANS *Schiff* towage

bugsieren *vt* WASSERTRANS *Schiff* tow

Bug: **Bugspriet** *nt* WASSERTRANS *Schiffbau* bowsprit; **Bugstrahlruder** *nt* WASSERTRANS *Schiffantrieb* bow thruster; **Bugverdichtungsstoß** *m* RAUMFAHRT bow shock; **Bugwelle** *f* LUFTTRANS, WASSERTRANS bow wave

Buhne *f* WASSERTRANS groin (AmE), groyne (BrE), WASSERVERSORG breakwater, groin (AmE), groyne (BrE)

Buline *f* WASSERTRANS *Tauwerk* bowline

Bullauge *nt* RAUMFAHRT *Raumschiff* viewing port, WASSERTRANS porthole

Bulldozer *m* BAU, TRANS bulldozer

Bullentalje *f* WASSERTRANS *Segeln* boom vang, kicking strap

Bumerang *m* STRÖMPHYS boomerang

Bund *m* DRUCK gutter, FERTIG rap, *Walze* barrel, MASCHINEN collar, flange, set collar, MECHAN collar, flange, TEXTIL waist band; **Bundbolzen** *m* MASCHINEN flanged bolt; **Bundbuchse** *f* FERTIG *Kunststoffinstallationen* flange adaptor

Bündel *nt* KER & GLAS, PAPIER bundle, PHYS bunch, TELEKOM bundle, group, TV *Fibern, Fehlern* burst, VERPACK bundle; ~ **von Absorberelementen** *nt* KERNTECH absorber element bundle; **Bündelanordnung** *f* KERNTECH *von Brennelementen* banked configuration; **Bündelbreite** *f* OPTIK *Strahlen* beamwidth; **Bündelelement** *nt* KERNTECH block-shaped fuel element; **Bündelentkopplung** *f* PHYS bunch decoupling

Bündeler *m* PHYS collimator

Bündel: **Bündelfunk** *m* TELEKOM *Mobilradio* trunking; **Bündelkabel** *nt* ELEKTROTECH bunched cable (BrE), bundled cable (AmE); **Bündelknoten** *m* FERNSEH crossover; **Bündelmaschine** *f* VERPACK bundle-tying machine

bündeln *vt* COMP & DV multiplex, PAPIER bundle

Bündelung *f* EISENBAHN grouping, ELEKTRONIK collimation, LUFTTRANS bunching, METALL clustering; **Bündelungselektrode** *f* FERNSEH beam-forming plate, focusing electrode; **Bündelungsfaktor** *m* NICHTFOSS ENERG directionality factor; **Bündelungsgrad** *m* AKUSTIK sound power concentration; **Bündelungsmagnet** *m* FERNSEH focusing magnet; **Bündelungsspule** *f* FERNSEH focusing coil

Bundes-Immissionsschutzgesetz *nt* ABFALL *in Deutschland* Federal Clean Air Act (AmE)

Bundesmarine *f* WASSERTRANS *Marine* Federal Navy

Bundesstraße *f* TRANS trunk road (BrE)

Bund: **Bundfalz** *m* DRUCK back fold

bündig[1] *adj* BAU, DRUCK, MASCHINEN flush

bündig:[2] **~er Stoß** *m* FERTIG flushing; **~e Überlappverbindung** *f* FERTIG flush joint

bündig:[3] **~ machen** *vt* FERTIG flush, MASCHINEN make flush

Bund: **Bundlager** *nt* MASCHINEN flange bearing; **Bundmutter** *f* MASCHINEN collar nut, flanged nut; **Bundschraube** *f* MASCHINEN collar screw; **Bundsteg** *m* DRUCK gutter

Bunker *m* BAU, ERDÖL *Produktlagerung*, LUFTTRANS, WASSERTRANS bunker; **Bunkerfüllstandsmesser** *m* GERÄT bin level meter; **Bunkerkohle** *f* KOHLEN bunker coal; **Bunkeröle** *nt pl* LUFTTRANS, WASSERTRANS bunker oil; **Bunkertank** *m* UMWELTSCHMUTZ bunker tank

Bunsen: **Bunsenbrenner** *m* LABOR Bunsen burner; **Bunsenelement** *nt* ELEKTRIZ Bunsen cell

Bunt- *pref* KER & GLAS stained, KUNSTSTOFF colored (AmE), coloured (BrE)

Buntbartschloß *nt* BAU warded lock

Buntglas *nt* KER & GLAS tinted glass; **Buntglasfenster** *nt* KER & GLAS stained glass window

buntglasiert: ~e Kachel *f* KER & GLAS encaustic tile

Bunt-: **Buntpapier** *nt* KER & GLAS paper stain; **Buntpigment** *nt* KUNSTSTOFF colored pigment (AmE), coloured pigment (BrE); **Buntsandstein** *m* ERDÖL *Formation des Trias* bunter

Bürette *f* LABOR burette; **Bürettenständer** *m* LABOR burette stand

Bürgersteig *m* BAU pavement (BrE), sidewalk (AmE)

Burgunderflasche *f* KER & GLAS burgundy bottle

Büro *nt* COMP & DV, TELEKOM office; **Büroabfall** *m* ABFALL office waste; **Büroautomatisierung** *f* COMP & DV OA, office automation; **Bürodruckmaschine** *f* DRUCK office printing machine; **Bürofernschreiben** *nt* COMP & DV teletext; **Bürokommunikation** *f* TELEKOM office communication; **Bürokommunikationsprotokoll** *nt* *(TOP)* TELEKOM technical and office protocol *(TOP)*

Burrus-Diode *f* OPTIK, TELEKOM Burrus diode

Burst *m* ELEKTRIZ, FERNSEH, TV *Übertragung, Fehler* burst

Bürste *f* BAU wiper, ELEKTRIZ, MECHAN, PAPIER brush

Bürsten *nt* ELEKTROTECH, KER & GLAS, KFZTECH, TEXTIL brushing

Bürste: **Bürstenabheber** *m* ELEKTRIZ brush lifting device; **Bürstenbrücke** *f* ELEKTROTECH brush rocker; **Bürstenentladung** *f* ELEKTRIZ brush discharge; **Bürstenfeuer** *nt* ELEKTROTECH brown-out, brush discharge, sparking, PHYS brush discharge; **Bürstenglättmaschine** *f* PAPIER brush polishing machine; **Bürstenhalter** *m* ELEKTRIZ, ELEKTROTECH brush holder; **Bürstenhalterarm** *m* ELEKTROTECH brush rod; **Bürstenjoch** *nt* ELEKTRIZ brush yoke; **Bürstenkontaktwiderstand** *m* ELEKTRIZ brush contact resistance

bürstenlos: ~er Generator *m* ELEKTRIZ brushless generator motor; ~er Motor *m* ELEKTRIZ brushless generator motor

Bürste: **Bürstennacheilwinkel** *m* ELEKTRIZ angle of brush lag; **Bürstensatinage** *f* PAPIER brush glazing; **Bürstensprühen** *nt* ELEKTRIZ brush sparking; **Bürstenstellung** *f* ELEKTROTECH brush position; **Bürstenstreichverfahren** *nt* PAPIER brush coating; **Bürstenstriche** *m pl* KER & GLAS brush lines; **Bürstenträger** *m* ELEKTRIZ brush holder; **Bürstenverlustwiderstand** *m* ELEKTRIZ brush contact resistance; **Bürstenvoreilung** *f* ELEKTRIZ angle of lead of brushes; **Bürstenvoreilwinkel** *m* ELEKTRIZ angle of lead of brushes; **Bürstenwähler** *m* ELEKTRIZ brush selector; **Bürstenwalze** *f* PAPIER brush roller; **Bürstenwaschmaschine** *f* TEXTIL brush washer; **Bürstenwinkel** *m* ELEKTRIZ brush angle

Burst: **Burstoszillator** *m* FERNSEH burst-locked oscillator; **Burstverstärker** *m* FERNSEH burst amplifier

Bus *m* COMP & DV bus (BrE), highway, trunk (AmE), ELEKTROTECH bus; ~ auf Eisenbahngleisen *m* TRANS bus on railroad tracks (AmE), bus on railway tracks (BrE); ~ auf Eisenbahnwaggon *m* TRANS bus on railroad wagon (AmE), bus on railway wagon (BrE); **Busabschlußstecker** *m* COMP & DV bus terminator

Büschel *nt* METALL pencil, OPTIK bundle, TEXTIL cluster; **Büschelentladung** *f* ELEKTRIZ brush discharge, ELEKTROTECH brown-out, brush discharge, PHYS brush discharge

Büschungsmauer *f* BAU toe wall

Bushel *nt* METROL bushel

Bus: **Buskollision** *f* COMP & DV bus collision; **Buskonfiguration** *f* TELEKOM bus configuration; **Busleitung** *f* TELEKOM highway; **Buslinie** *f* TRANS bus line; **Bus-Master** *m* COMP & DV bus master; **Bus-Maus-Adapter** *m* COMP & DV bus-mouse adaptor; **Busnetz** *nt* COMP & DV bus network; **Busnetzwerk** *nt* COMP & DV bus network; **Busplatine** *f* COMP & DV bus board; **Busschnittstelle** *f* COMP & DV bus interface

Bussolenlinse *f* KER & GLAS compass lens

Bus: **Busspur** *f* TRANS bus lane; **Busspur mit Leitsystem** *f* TRANS bus lane equipped with guiding device; **Bustaxidienst** *m* TRANS on-call bus system; **Bustopologie** *f* COMP & DV bus topology; **Buszuteiler** *m* TELEKOM bus arbitrator

Butadien *nt* CHEMIE, ERDÖL *Petrochemie* butadiene; **Butadien-Acrylnitril-Kautschuk** *m* KUNSTSTOFF butadiene acrylonitrile rubber; **Butadienkautschuk** *m* FERTIG bivinyl rubber, KUNSTSTOFF butadiene rubber; **Butadien-Styrol-Copolymerisat** *nt* ERDÖL *Petrochemie* butadiene-styrene copolymer

Butan *nt* ERDÖL *Petrochemie* butane; **Butandion** *nt* CHEMIE butanedione, diacetyl; **Butangastanker** *m* WASSERTRANS butane carrier, *Schifftyp* butane gas tanker; **Butan-Tanker** *m* ERDÖL butane tanker; **Butan-Tankschiff** *nt* ERDÖL *Schiffahrt* butane tanker; **Butan-Tankwagen** *m* ERDÖL *Eisenbahn, Straße* butane carrier

Butenluv *m* WASSERTRANS *Schiffbau* bumpkin

Butler-Oszillator *m* RADIO Butler oscillator

Bütte *f* PAPIER chest; **Büttenofen** *m* KER & GLAS Butten . furnace

Büttenrand[1] *m* PAPIER deckle edge

Büttenrand:[2] mit ~ versehen *vt* VERPACK deckle

Büttenrandschneider *m* FOTO jagged edge trimmer

Butter- *pref* CHEMIE butyric; **Butterfaß** *nt* LEBENSMITTEL firkin; **Butterherstellung** *f* LEBENSMITTEL churning

Buttern *nt* LEBENSMITTEL churning

buttern *vt* LEBENSMITTEL churn

Buttersäure *f* CHEMIE butyric, LEBENSMITTEL butyric acid

Butterworth-Filter *nt* ELEKTRONIK Butterworth filter

Butyl- *pref* KUNSTSTOFF, LEBENSMITTEL butyl, butylated; **Butylacetat** *nt* KUNSTSTOFF butyl acetate; **Butylether** *nt* LEBENSMITTEL butyl ether; **Butylhydroxyanisol** *nt* *(BHA)* LEBENSMITTEL *Antioxidans* butylated hydroxyanisole *(BHA)*; **Butylhydroxytoluol** *nt* *(BHT)* LEBENSMITTEL butylated hydroxytoluene *(BHT)*; **Butylkautschuk** *m* FERTIG *Kunststoffinstallationen*, KUNSTSTOFF butyl rubber; **Butylkresol** *nt* LEBENSMITTEL BHT, butylated hydroxytoluene; **Butylphthalat** *nt* KUNSTSTOFF butyl phthalate

Butyrat *nt* CHEMIE butyrate

Butyrin *nt* CHEMIE butyrin

Butzen *m* FERTIG *Lochen* sludge, KUNSTSTOFF flash

BV *abbr* *(Bildverstehen, Bildverständnis)* KÜNSTL INT IU *(image understanding)*

BW *abbr* *(Bandbreite, Bandweite)* AUFNAHME, COMP & DV, ELEKTRONIK, FERNSEH, OPTIK, RADIO, TELEKOM BW *(bandwidth)*

B-Y: ~ Achse *f* FERNSEH B-Y axis; ~ Signal *nt* FERNSEH B-Y signal

Bypass *m* ERDÖL *Rohrleitungsbau*, HYDRAUL bypass; **Bypass-Bohrung** *f* KFZTECH bypass bore; **Bypass-Filter** *nt* MASCHINEN bypass filter; **Bypass-Luftstrom im Triebwerk** *m* LUFTTRANS engine bypass air; **Bypass-Schalter** *m* ELEKTRIZ bypass switch;

Bypass-Triebwerk *nt* LUFTTRANS bypass engine, ducted fan, THERMOD bypass engine; **Bypass-Turbinensystem** *nt* KERNTECH turbine bypass system; **Bypass-Verhältnis** *nt* LUFTTRANS *Turbolüfter, Turbojet* bypass ratio
Byte *nt* COMP & DV byte; **Byte-Umschalter** *m* TELEKOM byte switch
byteweise *adj* TELEKOM byte-by-byte
byzantinisch: **~er Bogen** *m* BAU stilted arch
BZ *abbr (Betriebszentrum)* TELEKOM operations center (AmE), operations centre (BrE) *(operations center)*
B-Zeit *f* KUNSTSTOFF B-stage time

C

C[1] *abbr* BAU *(Kapazität)*, ELEKTRIZ *(Kapazität)* C *(capacity)*, ELEKTRIZ *(Coulomb)* C *(coulomb)*, ELEKTROTECH *(Kapazität)* C *(capacity)*, ELEKTROTECH *(Coulomb)* C *(coulomb)*, ERDÖL *(Kapazität)*, HEIZ & KÄLTE *(Kapazität)* C *(capacity)*, HYDRAUL *(Cauchysche Zahl)* C *(Cauchy coefficient)*, HYDRAUL *(Chezy-Koeffizient)* C *(Chezy coefficient)*, HYDRAUL *(Ausflußkoeffizient, Durchflußkoeffizient)* C *(discharge coefficient)*, LABOR *(Celsius)* C *(centigrade)*, METROL *(Coulomb)* C *(coulomb)*, NICHTFOSS ENERG *(Schüttkoeffizient)* C *(discharge coefficient)*, PHYS *(Kapazität)* C *(capacitance)*, PHYS *(Coulomb)* C *(coulomb)*, RADIO *(Kapazität)*, TELEKOM *(Kapazität)* C *(capacitance)*

C[2] *(Kohlenstoff)* CHEMIE C *(carbon)*

c *abbr* ELECTRONIK *(Konzentration)*, ELEKTRIZ *(Konzentration)* c *(concentration)*, HYDRAUL *(Wellenausbreitungsgeschwindigkeit)* c *(wave celerity)*, KOHLEN *(Konzentration)*, KUNSTSTOFF *(Konzentration)* c *(concentration)*, METROL *(Zenti-)* c *(centi)*, METROL *(Lichtgeschwindigkeit)* c *(velocity of light)*, OPTIK *(Lichtgeschwindigkeit)* c *(speed of light in empty space)*, PHYS *(spezifische Wärme)* c *(specific heat capacity)*, PHYS *(Schallgeschwindigkeit)* c *(speed of sound)*, TELEKOM *(Konzentration)* c *(concentration)*, THERMOD *(spezifische Wärmekapazität)* c *(specific heat capacity)*, UMWELTSCHMUTZ *(Konzentration)* c *(concentration)*

CA *abbr* HEIZ & KÄLTE *(kontrollierte Atmosphäre)* CA *(controlled atmosphere)*, KUNSTSTOFF *(Celluloseacetat)*, TEXTIL *(Celluloseacetat)* CA *(cellulose acetate)*

Ca *(Calcium)* CHEMIE, LEBENSMITTEL Ca *(calcium)*

Cabalglas *nt* KER & GLAS cabal glass

Cabrio *nt* KFZTECH cabriolet, convertible

Cache *m* COMP & DV cache; **Cache-Speicher** *m* COMP & DV cache memory

Cachia-Dämpfungsschaltung *f* RADIO Cachia attenuator

CAD *abbr (computergestützte Konstruktion, computergestützter Entwurf)* COMP & DV, ELEKTRIZ, KONTROLL, MECHAN, TELEKOM, TRANS CAD *(computer-aided design)*

Cadaverin *nt* CHEMIE cadaverin, pentamethylenediamine

CADCAM *abbr (computergestützte Konstruktion und Anfertigung)* COMP & DV CADCAM *(computer-aided design and manufacturing)*

Caisson *m* WASSERTRANS caisson; **Caissonkrankheit** *f* WASSERTRANS caisson disease

CAL *abbr* COMP & DV *(computergestützter Unterricht)* CAI *(computer-aided instruction)*, COMP & DV *(computergestütztes Lernen)* CAL *(computer-aided learning)*

Calabarin *nt* CHEMIE *ein Alkaloid* calabarine, eserine, physostigmine

CA-Lagerung *f* LEBENSMITTEL controlled-atmosphere storage

Calciferol *nt* CHEMIE calciferol

calcifizieren *vt* CHEMIE calcify

calcinieren *vi* CHEMIE calcine

Calcium[1] *nt (Ca)* CHEMIE, LEBENSMITTEL calcium *(Ca)*

Calcium:[2] **~ entziehen** *vt* CHEMIE *Medizin* decalcify

Calcium: **Calciumacetylid** *nt* CHEMIE calcium acetylide, calcium carbide; **Calciumcarbid** *nt* CHEMIE calcium acetylide, calcium carbide; **Calciumcarbonat** *nt* LEBENSMITTEL calcium carbonate; **Calciumchlorid** *nt* CHEMIE, LEBENSMITTEL calcium chloride; **Calciumcyanamid** *nt* CHEMIE calcium carbide, calcium cyanamide; **Calciumhydroxid** *nt* CHEMIE, LEBENSMITTEL calcium hydroxide; **Calciumnaphthenat** *nt* KUNSTSTOFF calcium naphthenate; **Calciumpantothenat** *nt* LEBENSMITTEL calcium pantothenate; **Calciumphosphat** *nt* LEBENSMITTEL calcium phosphate; **Calciumsulfat** *nt* LEBENSMITTEL calcium sulfate (AmE), calcium sulphate (BrE)

Californium *nt (Cf)* CHEMIE californium *(Cf)*

CAM *abbr* COMP & DV *(computergestützte Fertigung, computergestützte Produktion)* CAM *(computer-aided manufacturing)*, COMP & DV *(Assoziativspeicher, inhaltsadressierbarer Speicher)* CAM *(content-addressable memory)*, ELEKTRIZ *(computergestützte Fertigung, computergestützte Produktion)* CAM *(computer-aided manufacturing)*, KÜNSTL INT *(Assoziativspeicher, inhaltsadressierbarer Speicher)* CAM *(content-addressable memory)*

Camcorder *m* FERNSEH camcorder

Camera-Lucida *f* FOTO camera lucida

Campbell-Stokes-Aufzeichner *m* NICHTFOSS ENERG Campbell-Stokes recorder

Camper *m* KFZTECH camper (AmE), caravan (BrE)

Camphen *nt* CHEMIE camphene

Camphorat *nt* CHEMIE camphorate

Candela *f (cd)* ELEKTROTECH, METROL, OPTIK, PHYS candela *(cd)*

Cantharidin *nt* CHEMIE cantharidine

Cantilever-Langsieb *nt* PAPIER cantilever foudrinier

CAP *abbr (computergestütztes Publizieren)* DRUCK CAP *(computer-aided publishing)*

Caproin *nt* CHEMIE caproin

Caprolactam *nt* CHEMIE caprolactam

Caproyl- *pref* CHEMIE octanoyl

Capryl- *pref* CHEMIE hexyl; **Capryliden** *nt* CHEMIE caprylidene, octyne

Capsaicin *nt* CHEMIE capsaicin

Capsicin *nt* CHEMIE capsicin

Capture-Effekt *m* TELEKOM capture effect

CAR *abbr (Zivilflugvorschriften)* RAUMFAHRT CAR *(Civil Air Regulations)*

Caravan *m* KFZTECH camper (AmE), caravan (BrE), trailer (AmE)

Carbamat *nt* CHEMIE carbamate

Carbamid *nt* CHEMIE carbamide, urea; **Carbamid-** *pref* CHEMIE carbamic; **Carbamidsäurehydrazid** *nt* CHEMIE semicarbazide

Carbamoyl *nt* CHEMIE carbamoyl

Carbanil *nt* CHEMIE carbanil, phenyl isocyanate; **Carba-**

nilid *nt* CHEMIE carbanilide
Carbanion *nt* CHEMIE carbanion
Carbazid *nt* CHEMIE carbazide
Carbazol *nt* CHEMIE carbazole, dibenzopyrrole
Carben *nt* CHEMIE carbene
Carbeniat-Anion *nt* CHEMIE carbanion
Carbid *nt* CHEMIE carbide; **Carbidkohle** *f* CHEMIE carbide carbon
carbocyclisch *adj* CHEMIE carbocyclic, homocyclic, isocyclic
Carbohydrase *f* LEBENSMITTEL carbohydrase
Carbol- *pref* CHEMIE carbolic; **Carbolyase** *f* CHEMIE decarboxylase
Carbonatation *f* CHEMIE *Entkalkung des Zuckerrübensaftes* carbonation
carbonisieren *vt* LEBENSMITTEL *Getränke mit Kohlensäure sättigen* aerate
Carbonisierung *f* CHEMIE *Brennverhalten von Textilien* charring
Carbonohydrazid *nt* CHEMIE carbazide, carbonohydrazide
Carbonylchlorid *nt* CHEMIE carbonyl dichloride, phosgene
Carbonylsulfid *nt* UMWELTSCHMUTZ carbonyl sulfide (AmE), carbonyl sulphide (BrE)
Carborundum® *nt* CHEMIE Carborundum®, silicon carbide
Carbostyril *nt* CHEMIE carbostyril
Carboxyl *nt* CHEMIE carboxyl
Carboxylation *f* CHEMIE *Entkalkung des Zuckerrübensaftes* carbonation
carboxyliert: ~**es Polymer** *nt* KUNSTSTOFF carboxylated polymer
Carboxymethylcellulose *f* *(CMC)* KUNSTSTOFF, LEBENSMITTEL *Verdickungsmittel, Emulgator* carboxymethylcellulose *(CMC)*
Carbroabzug *m* FOTO carbro color print (AmE), carbro colour print (BrE)
Carbrodrucken *nt* FOTO carbro printing
Cardew-Spannungsmeßgerät *nt* ELEKTRIZ Cardew voltmeter
Cargo *m* LUFTTRANS cargo
Carmin *nt* CHEMIE carmine; **Carminfarbe** *f* LEBENSMITTEL carmine
Carnitin *nt* CHEMIE carnitine, novain
Carnot: ~**scher Kreisprozeß** *m* PHYS, THERMOD Carnot cycle; ~**sche Maschine** *f* PHYS, THERMOD Carnot engine; ~**sches Theorem** *nt* PHYS *Wärmekraftmaschine* Carnot's theorem
Caron *nt* CHEMIE carone
Caroten *nt* CHEMIE carotene
Carotin *nt* LEBENSMITTEL carotene
Carrageen *nt* LEBENSMITTEL carrageen
Carrier *m* TEXTIL *Färberei* carrier
CASE *abbr* *(computergestützte Softwareentwicklung)* COMP & DV CASE *(computer-aided software engineering)*
Casein *nt* KUNSTSTOFF casein
Cashewnußschalenöl *nt* KUNSTSTOFF cashew-nut shell oil
Cashey-Kasten *m* KER & GLAS cashey box
Casing *nt* ERDÖL *Bohrtechnik* casing
Cäsium *nt* *(Cs)* CHEMIE caesium (BrE), cesium (AmE) *(Cs)*
Cassegrain: ~**sche Antenne** *f* PHYS Cassegrain aerial, Cassegrain antenna, RAUMFAHRT *Weltraumfunk* Cas-

segrain aerial (BrE), Cassegrain antenna (AmE); ~**sches Teleskop** *nt* PHYS Cassegrain telescope
Cassettenradio *nt* KFZTECH *Zubehör* radio-cassette
Castorin *nt* CHEMIE castorin
CAT *abbr* COMP & DV *(computerunterstützte Übersetzung)* CAT *(computer-assisted translation)*, ELEKTRONIK *(Senderöhre mit gekühlter Anode)* CAT *(cooled-anode transmitting valve)*, LUFTTRANS *(Kaltlufturbulenzen)* CAT *(cold air turbulence)*
Cat-Cracker *m* ERDÖL *Raffinerie* cat cracker
Catechin *nt* CHEMIE catechinic acid
Catecholamin *nt* CHEMIE catecholamine
Catechugerb- *pref* CHEMIE catechutannic
Caterpillar-Planierraupe *m* TRANS caterpillar bulldozer
Catforming *nt* CHEMIE catforming
CATV *abbr* *(Fernsehen über Gemeinschaftsantenne)* FERNSEH CATV *(community antenna television system)*
CATVI *abbr* FERNSEH *(Kabelfernsehstörung)*, RADIO *(störende Beeinflussung des Kabelfernsehdienstes)* CATVI *(cable television interference)*
Cauchy: ~**sche Zahl** *f* *(C)* HYDRAUL Cauchy coefficient *(C)*
Cauchy-Greenscher: ~ **Verzerrungstensor** *m* STRÖMPHYS Cauchy-Green strain tensor
Cauer-Filter *nt* PHYS Cauer filter
CAV *abbr* *(computerunterstütztes Sehen)* KÜNSTL INT CAV *(computer-aided vision)*
Cavendish-Experiment *nt* PHYS Cavendish experiment
CA-Verpackung *f* *(Verpackung in geregelter Atmosphäre)* VERPACK CAP *(controlled-atmosphere packaging)*
CB-Funk *m* RADIO, TELEKOM CB, CB radio, citizen's band radio
CBR-Wert *m* BAU California Bearing Ratio
CCD[1] *abbr* *(Ladungsverschiebeelement, Ladungsgekoppeltes Bauelement)* ELEKTRONIK, PHYS, TELEKOM CCD *(charge-coupled device)*
CCD[2]: **CCD-Bildwandler** *m* FERNSEH CCD imager; **CCD-Filter** *nt* ELEKTRONIK CCD filter; **CCD-Signalverarbeitung** *f* ELEKTRONIK CCD signal processing
CCITT *abbr* *(Internationaler Fernmeldeberatungsausschuß)* TELEKOM CCITT *(International Telegraph and Telephone Consultative Committee)*
C-Compiler *m* COMP & DV C-compiler
CCTV *abbr* *(Kabelfernsehen zu Überwachungszwecken)* FERNSEH CCTV *(closed-circuit television)*
CD[1] *abbr* COMP & DV *(Trägerdetektion, Trägererkennung)* CD *(carrier detection)*, COMP & DV *(Kollisionserkennung)* CD *(collision detection)*, COMP & DV *(Compact-Disk)* CD *(compact disk)*, ELEKTRONIK *(Trägerdetektion, Trägererkennung)* CD *(carrier detection)*, OPTIK *(Compact-Disk)* CD *(compact disk)*, TELEKOM *(Trägerdetektion, Trägererkennung)* CD *(carrier detection)*, TELEKOM *(Kollisionserkennung)* CD *(collision detection)*
Cd *(Kadmium)* CHEMIE Cd *(cadmium)*
cd *abbr* *(Candela)* ELEKTROTECH, METROL, OPTIK, PHYS cd *(candela)*
CD: **CD-Archivierungssystem** *nt* COMP & DV, OPTIK optical disk filing system; **CD-Bibliothek** *f* COMP & DV, OPTIK optical disk library; **CD-Festwertspeicher** *m* COMP & DV, OPTIK optical disk read-only memory
CD-i *abbr* *(beschreibbare CD)* OPTIK CD-I *(compact disk-interactive)*
CD: **CD-Kassette** *f* COMP & DV, OPTIK optical disk cassette; **CD-Laufwerk** *nt* COMP & DV optical disk drive,

OPTIK optical disk drive, optical drive; **CD-Leser** *m* COMP & DV, OPTIK optical disk reader

CDM *abbr (kompandierte Deltamodulation)* TELEKOM CDM *(companded delta modulation)*

CD: **CD-Platte** *f* OPTIK disk platter (AmE)

CD-ROM[1] *abbr* COMP & DV *(Compact-Disk ohne Schreibmöglichkeit)*, OPTIK *(Compact-Disk-Speicher ohne Schreibmöglichkeit)* CD-ROM *(compact disk readonly memory)*

CD-ROM:[2] **CD-ROM-Diskettenlaufwerk** *nt* COMP & DV CD-ROM disk drive; **CD-ROM-Festplattenlaufwerk** *nt* COMP & DV CD-ROM hard disk drive; **CD-ROM-Spieler** *m* OPTIK CD-ROM player

CD: **CD-Spieler** *m* COMP & DV optical disk player, OPTIK CD player, optical disk player; **CD-Spieler für Ton** *m* OPTIK audio CD player; **CD-Wechsler** *m* COMP & DV, OPTIK optical disk exchanger

CE *abbr (elektrische Kapazität)* AKUSTIK CE *(electric capacitance)*

Ce *(Cerium)* CHEMIE Ce *(cerium)*

CEBAF *abbr (Gleichstromelektronenbeschleuniger)* TEILPHYS CEBAF *(continuous electron beam facility)*

Cedren *nt* CHEMIE cedrene

Cedrol *nt* CHEMIE cedrol

Ceiling-Temperatur *f* KUNSTSTOFF ceiling temperature

Celluloid *nt* CHEMIE celluloid, KUNSTSTOFF xylonite

Cellulose *f* KUNSTSTOFF, LEBENSMITTEL cellulose; **Celluloseacetat** *nt (CA)* KUNSTSTOFF, TEXTIL acetate, cellulose acetate *(CA)*; **Celluloseacetobutyrat** *nt* KUNSTSTOFF cellulose acetobutyrate; **Celluloseanstrichfarbe** *f* KUNSTSTOFF cellulose paint; **Celluloseglykolsäure** *f* LEBENSMITTEL carboxymethylcellulose; **Cellulosenitrat** *nt* CHEMIE, KUNSTSTOFF cellulose nitrate; **Celluloseproprionat** *nt* KUNSTSTOFF CP, cellulose proprionate; **Cellulosetriacetat** *nt (CTA)* KUNSTSTOFF cellulose triacetate *(CTA)*

Celsius *nt (C)* METROL centigrade *(C)*; **Celsius-Grad** *m* PHYS, THERMOD centigrade; **Celsius-Temperaturskale** *f* PHYS centigrade

Centrex-Vermittlung® *f* TELEKOM Centrex system®

Centronics-Schnittstelle® *f* DRUCK Centronics interface®

Cephalosporin *nt* CHEMIE cephalosporin

Cer- *pref* CHEMIE ceric, cerium

Ceran *nt* CHEMIE cerane, hexacosane

Cerenkov: **~scher Detektor** *m* STRAHLPHYS, TEILPHYS Cerenkov detector; **~scher Effekt** *m* STRAHLPHYS, TEILPHYS Cerenkov effect; **~sche Strahlung** *f* STRAHLPHYS, TEILPHYS Cerenkov radiation; **~scher Zähler** *m* STRAHLPHYS, TEILPHYS Cerenkov counter

Cerfluorit *m* CHEMIE yttrocerite

Cerium *nt (Ce)* CHEMIE cerium *(Ce)*

Cermet *nt* KERNTECH *Metallkeramik-Werkstoff für Brennelemente* cermet

CERN *abbr (Europäisches Kernforschungszentrum)* TEILPHYS CERN *(European Organization for Nuclear Research)*

Cerussa *nt* CHEMIE ceruse, cerussa

Ceten *nt* CHEMIE hexadecanol

Cetylalkohol *m* CHEMIE ethal, hexadecanol

Cevadin *nt* CHEMIE cevadine

Cevin *nt* CHEMIE cevine

Cf *(Californium)* CHEMIE Cf *(californium)*

C-Feder *f* MASCHINEN C spring

C-Format-Videorecorder *m* FERNSEH C format videotape recorder

C-förmig: **~es Gestell** *nt* FERTIG *Presse* C-frame

CGA *abbr (Farbgrafikadapter)* COMP & DV CGA *(colour graphics adaptor)*

CGS-System *nt (Zentimeter-Gramm-Sekunde-System)* METROL CGS system *(centimetre-gramme-second system)*

Chalcon *nt* CHEMIE chalcone

Chalkanthit *m* CHEMIE blue vitriol, bluestone, chalcanthite

Chalkogenidglas *nt* KER & GLAS chalcogenide glass

Chambray *m* TEXTIL chambray

Chaos *nt* STRÖMPHYS *Stabilität* chaos

chaotisch: **~e Bewegung** *f* STRÖMPHYS chaotic motion

Chapman-Schicht *f* RADIO Chapman layer

Chaptalisierung *f* LEBENSMITTEL chaptalization

Charakteristik *f* ELEKTRIZ, MASCHINEN, MATH characteristic

charakteristisch[1] *adj* RADIO characteristic

charakteristisch:[2] **~e Empfindlichkeit** *f* AKUSTIK characteristic sensitivity; **~e Frequenz** *f* ELEKTRONIK, FERNSEH, RADIO characteristic frequency; **~e Impedanz** *f* ELEKTRIZ surge impedance; **~er Leitungswiderstand** *m* ELEKTROTECH, PHYS characteristic impedance; **~es Röntgenspektrum** *nt* STRAHLPHYS characteristic X-ray spectrum

Charge *f* ANSTRICH batch, ELEKTROTECH charge, FERTIG melt, LEBENSMITTEL, PAPIER *Verarbeitung*, TELEKOM, TEXTIL batch; **Chargecard** *f* TELEKOM *Handelsname* chargecard; **Chargenbeschickung** *f* KERNTECH batch fuel loading; **Chargenbetrieb** *m* CHEMTECH batch processing; **Chargenentladung** *f* KERNTECH batch extraction; **Chargenmischer** *m* CHEMTECH, KER & GLAS, LEBENSMITTEL batch mixer; **Chargenmischung** *f* BAU batch mix; **Chargenofen** *m* CHEMTECH batch furnace; **Chargenstreuung** *f* QUAL batch variation; **Chargenumfang** *m* QUAL batch size; **Chargenverarbeitung** *f* PAPIER batch processing

Charles-Gesetz *nt* PHYS Charles's law

Charm *m* PHYS, TEILPHYS charm

Charmeuse *f* TEXTIL charmeuse, locknit

Charmonium *nt* PHYS charmonium

Charpy: **~scher Kerbschlagbiegeversuch** *m* METALL Charpy impact test; **~scher Kerbschlagversuch** *m* PHYS Charpy test, WERKPRÜF Charpy impact test; **~scher Pendelschlagversuch** *m* ANSTRICH Charpy impact test; **~scher Rundkerbversuch** *m* MECHAN Charpy V-notch test, Charpy impact test; **~sches Schlagzähigkeitsprüfgerät** *nt* KUNSTSTOFF Charpy impact tester; **~sche Spitzkerbprobe** *f* KERNTECH Charpy V-notch test; **~scher V-Kerbtest** *m* MECHAN Charpy V-notch test

Charter *f* WASSERTRANS *Schiff* charter; **~ eines bloßen Schiffes** *f* WASSERTRANS bareboat charter; **Charterbuchung im voraus** *f* LUFTTRANS advance booking charter

Charterer *m* WASSERTRANS *Seehandel* charterer

chartern *vt* WASSERTRANS *Schiff* charter

Charter: **Charterpartie** *f* ERDÖL *Schiffahrt*, WASSERTRANS *Seehandel, Dokumente* charter party; **Chartertüchtigkeit** *f* LUFTTRANS charterworthiness;

Charterung *f* WASSERTRANS *Seehandel* chartering

Charter: **Chartervertrag** *m* ERDÖL charter party

Chassis *nt* KFZTECH *Karosserie* chassis; **Chassislängsträger** *m* KFZTECH *Karosserie* chassis member

Chaulmoograöl *nt* CHEMIE chaulmoogra oil

Chavibetol *nt* CHEMIE chavibetol

Chavicol *nt* CHEMIE chavicol

Checkliste *f* QUAL check list

Check-out *nt* KERNTECH checkout

Chef-Sekretär-Anlage *f* TELEKOM manager/secretary station

Chelat¹ *nt* CHEMIE chelate

Chelat:² ~e bilden *vi* CHEMIE chelate

Chelat: Chelatbildner *m* CHEMIE chelating agent; Chelatbildung *f* CHEMIE, KERNTECH chelation

chelatisieren *vi* CHEMIE chelate

CHEMFIX-Verfahren *nt* ABFALL CHEMFIX process

chemiebeständig *adj* VERPACK chemically resistant

Chemiereaktor *m* KERNTECH chemonuclear fuel reactor

Chemiezellstoff *m* PAPIER dissolving pulp

Chemigraph *m* DRUCK process engraver

Chemikalien *f pl* PAPIER chemicals

Chemilumineszenz *f* PHYS, STRAHLPHYS chemiluminescence

chemisch¹ *adj* TEXTIL chemical; ~ resistent *adj* VERPACK chemically resistant; ~ träge *adj* ANSTRICH chemically inert; ~ wirksam *adj* PHYS actinic

chemisch:² ~e Abfälle *m* ABFALL chemical waste; ~e Abscheidung aus der Dampfphase *f* TELEKOM chemical vapor deposition technique (AmE), chemical vapour deposition technique (BrE), vapor phase chemical deposition (AmE), vapour phase chemical deposition (BrE); ~e Abwasserreinigung *f* WASSERVERSORG chemical water treatment; ~e Analyse *f* KOHLEN chemical analysis; ~-atomare Masseneinheit *f* KERNTECH chemical atomic mass unit; ~e Aufbereitung *f* KOHLEN chemical treatment; ~es Bedampfungsverfahren *nt* ELEKTRONIK chemical vapor deposition technique (AmE), chemical vapour deposition technique (BrE); ~e Behandlung *f* KOHLEN chemical treatment; ~e Beschichtung *f* KERNTECH chemical coating; ~e Beständigkeit *f* KER & GLAS chemical durability, KOHLEN chemical stability, KUNSTSTOFF chemical resistance; ~e Bindung *f* ERDÖL *Petrochemie* chemical bond; ~e Dosimetrie *f* STRAHLPHYS *Radioaktivität* chemical dosimetry; ~es Enthülsen *nt* KERNTECH *von Brennmaterial* chemical decanning, chemical decladding; ~e Entwicklung *f* FOTO chemical development; ~e Fällung *f* ABFALL chemical precipitation; ~ gebundenes Wasser *nt* WASSERVERSORG combined water; ~e Gefahr *f* SICHERHEIT chemical hazard; ~es Gleichgewicht *nt* PHYS chemical balance; ~es Härten *nt* METALL chemical hardening; ~er Kampfstoff *m* UMWELTSCHMUTZ *Militär* toxic agent; ~e Kohlereinigung *f* UMWELTSCHMUTZ chemical coal cleaning; ~er Laser *m* ELEKTRONIK chemical laser; ~es Nachweismittel *nt* CHEMIE *anorganische Chemie* reagent; ~ neutrales Öl *nt* ERDÖL chemically neutral oil; ~e Oberflächenbearbeitung *f* MECHAN chemical machining; ~es Polieren *nt* METALL chemical polishing; ~es Potential *nt* PHYS chemical potential; ~er Prozeß in der Atmosphäre *m* UMWELTSCHMUTZ atmospheric chemical process; ~e Pulpe *f* ABFALL chemical pulp; ~es Raketentriebwerk *nt* MASCHINEN chemical rocket engine; ~e Reaktion *f* ANSTRICH reaction; ~e Rückstände *m pl* KERNTECH chemical drains; ~er Sauerstoffbedarf *m* (*CSB*) UMWELTSCHMUTZ chemical oxygen demand (*COD*); ~es Treibmittel *nt* LEBENSMITTEL chemical leavening; ~e Trimmung *f* KERNTECH chemical shimming; ~e Verstärkung *f* FOTO chemical intensification; ~e Waage *f* LABOR chemical balance; ~e Wechselwirkung zwi-

schen Pellet und Hülse *f* KERNTECH pellet-clad chemical interaction; ~ widerstandsfähiges Glas *nt* KER & GLAS chemically-resistant glass; ~e Wiederaufbereitungsanlage *f* KERNTECH chemical reprocessing plant; ~er Wirkstoff *m* UMWELTSCHMUTZ chemical agent

chemisch:³ ~ reinigen *vt* TEXTIL dry-clean

Chemorezeptoren *m pl* ERGON chemoreceptors

Chenillegarn *nt* TEXTIL chenille yarn

Chessylith *m* CHEMIE chessylite

Chezy-Koeffizient *m* (*C*) HYDRAUL Chezy coefficient (*C*)

Chiffrierschlüssel *m* TELEKOM key

Chill-Roll-Coextrusion *f* KUNSTSTOFF chill roll coextrusion

Chill-Roll-Extrusion *f* KUNSTSTOFF chill roll extrusion

China- *pref* CHEMIE quinic; China-Blau *nt* KER & GLAS China blue

Chinacrin *nt* CHEMIE atebrin, quinacrine

Chinaldin *nt* CHEMIE methylquinoline, quinaldine

Chinalizarin *nt* CHEMIE quinalizarin

Chinamin *nt* CHEMIE quinamine

Chinarinde *f* CHEMIE cinchona bark

Chinazin *nt* CHEMIE quinoxaline

Chinhydron *nt* CHEMIE quinhydrone

Chinicin *nt* CHEMIE chinicine, quinicine

Chinidin *nt* CHEMIE conchinine, quinidine

Chinin *nt* CHEMIE quinine

Chininum *nt* CHEMIE *Pharmazie* quinine

Chinit *m* CHEMIE cyclohexanediol, quinitol

chinoid *adj* CHEMIE quinoid

Chinolin *nt* CHEMIE quinoline

Chinolyl- *pref* CHEMIE quinolyl

Chinon *nt* CHEMIE quinone

Chinonphenolimin *nt* CHEMIE indophenol

Chinovabitter *nt* CHEMIE chinovin, quinova bitter, quinovin

Chinovin *nt* CHEMIE chinovin, quinova bitter, quinovin

Chinoxalin *nt* CHEMIE quinoxaline

Chinoyl- *pref* CHEMIE quinolyl

Chip:¹ nicht auf dem ~ befindlich *adj* ELEKTRONIK off chip; auf ~ generiert *adj* ELEKTRONIK generated on chip

Chip² *m* AKUSTIK chip, COMP & DV chip, wafer, ELEKTRIZ chip, ELEKTRONIK wafer, FERNSEH, TELEKOM *Signal, Halbleiter* chip; Chipauslegung *f* ELEKTRONIK chip layout; Chipentwurf *m* ELEKTRONIK chip design; Chip-Fläche *f* ELEKTRONIK chip area; Chipkarte *f* COMP & DV chip card, smart card; Chipkartenleser *m* TELEKOM chip-card reader, smart card reader; Chipkomplexität *f* ELEKTRONIK chip complexity; Chipkondensator *m* ELEKTROTECH on-chip capacitor; Chiprate *f* TELEKOM chip rate; Chipsatz *m* ELEKTRONIK chip set; Chipträger *m* ELEKTRONIK chip carrier

Chirpen *nt* TELEKOM chirping

Chirping *nt* TELEKOM chirping

Chitosamin *nt* CHEMIE chitosamine, glucosamine

Chlor *nt* (*Cl*) CHEMIE chlorine (*Cl*); Chloracetat *nt* CHEMIE chloroacetate

Chloral- *pref* CHEMIE chloral; Chloralformamid *nt* CHEMIE chloral formamide; Chloralose *f* CHEMIE chloralose

Chloranil *nt* CHEMIE chloranil

Chlorat *nt* CHEMIE chlorate

chloren *vi* CHEMIE chlorinate

Chlor-: Chloressig- *pref* CHEMIE chloracetic; Chlorfasern *f pl* TEXTIL chlorofibers (AmE), chlorofibres (BrE); **Chlorhydrat** *nt* CHEMIE chlorine hydrate; **Chlorhydrin** *nt* CHEMIE chlorohydrin

Chlorid *nt* CHEMIE chloride; **Chloridglas** *nt* KER & GLAS chloride glass; **Chloridpapier** *nt* FOTO chloride paper

chlorieren *vi* CHEMIE chlorinate

chloriert: **~es Polyethylen** *nt (PE-C)* KUNSTSTOFF chlorinated polyethylene *(CPE)*; **~es Polyvinylchlorid** *nt (PVC-C)* KUNSTSTOFF chlorinated polyvinyl chloride *(CPVC)*

Chlorierung *f* ABFALL, CHEMIE chlorination

chlorig *adj* CHEMIE chlorous

Chlorit *nt* CHEMIE, ERDÖL *Mineral*, KOHLEN chlorite

Chlor-: **Chlorkalk** *m* LEBENSMITTEL bleaching powder, chlorinated lime, TEXTIL bleaching powder; **Chlorkautschuk** *m* KUNSTSTOFF chlorinated rubber; **Chloroplatinat** *nt* CHEMIE tetrachloroplatinate

Chloropren: *nt* CHEMIE chloroprene; **Chloroprenkautschuk** *m (CPK)* KUNSTSTOFF chloroprene rubber *(CR)*

Chlor-: **Chlorphenol** *nt* CHEMIE chlorophenol; **Chlorpikrin** *nt* CHEMIE aquinite, nitrochloroform

chlorsauer *adj* CHEMIE chloric

Chlor-: **Chlorsäure** *f* LEBENSMITTEL chloric acid; **Chlorschwefelisocyanat** *nt (CSI)* UMWELTSCHMUTZ chlorosulfonyl isocyanate *(CSI)*

Chlorung *f* CHEMIE chlorination

Choke *m* KFZTECH, MECHAN choke

Chol- *pref* CHEMIE cholic; **Cholesten** *nt* CHEMIE cholestene, cholesterol; **Cholesterin** *nt* CHEMIE cholestene, cholesterol, LEBENSMITTEL cholesterol

Cholin *nt* LEBENSMITTEL choline; **Cholinesterase** *f* CHEMIE cholesterase, choline esterase

Chol-: **Cholsäureester** *m* CHEMIE cholate

Chondrin *nt* CHEMIE chondrin

chopperstabilisiert: **~er Verstärker** *m* ELEKTRONIK chopper stabilized amplifier

Chopper-Verstärker *m* ELEKTRONIK chopper amplifier

Chrom *nt (Cr)* CHEMIE chromium *(Cr)*

Chromalaun *m* CHEMIE ammonium chromic sulfate (AmE), ammonium chromic sulphate (BrE)

Chromat *nt* CHEMIE chromate

chromatieren *vt* METALL chromate

chromatisch[1] *adj* OPTIK chromatic

chromatisch:[2] **~er Abbildungsfehler** *m* FERNSEH chromatic aberration; **~e Aberration** *f* OPTIK, STRAHLPHYS chromatic aberration; **~e Aberration längs der optischen Achse** *f* PHYS longitudinal chromatic aberration; **~e Abweichung** *f* FOTO chromatic aberration; **~e Dispersion** *f* OPTIK chromatic dispersion; **~er Fehler** *m* OPTIK chromatic distortion; **~er Halbton** *m* AKUSTIK chromatic semitone; **~e Tonleiter** *f* AKUSTIK chromatic scale; **~e Verzeichnung** *f* OPTIK chromatic distortion; **~e Verzerrung** *f* TELEKOM chromatic distortion; **~e Zerlegung** *f* OPTIK *Licht* chromatic dispersion

Chromatograph *m* GERÄT chromatograph

Chromatographie *f* CHEMIE chromatography; **Chromatographiepapiere** *nt pl* LABOR chromatography papers; **Chromatographiesäule** *f* LABOR chromatography column

Chromat: **Chromattank** *m* LABOR chromatography tank

Chrom: **Chromdioxidband** *nt* FERNSEH chrome dioxide tape; **Chromel** *nt* METALL chromel; **Chromerz** *nt* KER & GLAS chrome ore

chromgrün *adj* KER & GLAS chrome green

Chrominanz *f* ELEKTRONIK *Fernsehtechnik* chrominance; **Chrominanzbandbreite** *f* FERNSEH chrominance bandwidth; **Chrominanzdemodulator** *m* FERNSEH chrominance demodulator; **Chrominanzhilfsträgersignal** *nt* FERNSEH chrominance subcarrier signal; **Chrominanzsignal** *nt* ELEKTRONIK, FERNSEH, RAUMFAHRT *Weltraumfunk* chrominance signal; **Chrominanzträger** *m* TV chrominance subcarrier; **Chrominanzträgerleistung** *f* FERNSEH chrominance carrier output; **Chrominanzunterträger** *m* FERNSEH chrominance subcarrier; **Chrominanzverstärker** *m* ELEKTRONIK chrominance amplifier

Chromit *m* KER & GLAS chromite

Chromium *nt (Cr)* CHEMIE chromium *(Cr)*

Chrom: **Chromnickelstahl** *m* METALL nickel chrome steel, nickel chromium steel

Chromodynamik *f* TEILPHYS chromodynamics

Chromogen *nt* CHEMIE chromogen

Chromosphäre *f* RADIO, RAUMFAHRT chromosphere;

Chromotrop- *pref* CHEMIE chromotropic

Chrom: **Chromoxid** *nt* KER & GLAS chromic oxide; **Chromsäuresalz** *nt* CHEMIE chromate; **Chromstahl** *m* METALL chrome steel, chromium steel; **Chromvanadiumstahl** *m* METALL chrome vanadium steel; **Chromverstärker** *m* FOTO chrome intensifier

chronisch: **~e Wirkung** *f* UMWELTSCHMUTZ chronic effect

Chronometer *nt* GERÄT, PHYS, WASSERTRANS *Navigation* chronometer; **Chronometergang** *m* WASSERTRANS *Navigation* chronometer rate

Chrysen *nt* CHEMIE chrysene

Chrysoidin *nt* CHEMIE chrysoidine, diaminoazobenzene

Chrysophan- *pref* CHEMIE chrysophanic

Ci *abbr (Curie)* PHYS, STRAHLPHYS Ci *(curie)*

CIM *abbr* COMP & DV *(CompuServe® Information Manager)* CIM *(CompuServe® Information manager)*, COMP & DV *(computerintegrierte Fertigung)* CIM *(computer-integrated manufacture)*

cim *abbr (Kubikzoll pro Minute)* LABOR cim *(cubic inches per minute)*

Ciminit *nt* ERDÖL *Mineral* ciminite

Cinchonidin *nt* CHEMIE chinidine, cinchonidine

Cinchonin *nt* CHEMIE cinchonine

Cinch-Stecker *m* FERNSEH cinch

Cineol *nt* CHEMIE cineole; **Cineol-** *pref* CHEMIE cineolic

Cinnamyl- *pref* CHEMIE cinnamyl

Cinnolin *nt* CHEMIE cinnoline

Circular-Pitch *m* MASCHINEN CP, circular pitch

CISC *abbr (Prozessor mit komplettem Befehlssatz, konventioneller Rechner)* COMP & DV CISC *(complex instruction set computer)*

cis-ständig *adj* CHEMIE cis

Cis-Trans-: *pref* CHEMIE cis-trans

Citral *nt* CHEMIE citral

Citrat *nt* CHEMIE citrate

Citronell *nt* LEBENSMITTEL citronella; **Citronellal** *nt* CHEMIE citronellal, dimethyloctenal; **Citronellaldehyd** *m* CHEMIE citronellal, dimethyloctenal; **Citronellaöl** *nt* CHEMIE citronella oil, citronyl; **Citronellöl** *nt* LEBENSMITTEL *Bestandteil von Lebensmittelaromen* citronella oil

Citrullin *nt* CHEMIE aminoureidovaleric acid, citrulline

CL *abbr* COMP & DV *(Befehlssprache, Betriebssprache)* CL *(command language)*, HYDRAUL *(Auftriebsbeiwert, Auftriebszahl)*, LUFTTRANS *(Auftriebszahl)*, NICHTFOSS ENERG *(Auftriebsbeiwert, Auftriebszahl)*,

PHYS *(Auftriebsbeiwert, Auftriebszahl)*, WASSER-
TRANS *(Auftriebsbeiwert, Auftriebszahl)* CL *(lift
coefficient)*

Cl *(Chlor)* CHEMIE Cl *(chlorine)*

cl *abbr (Geschwindigkeit von Längswellen)* AKUSTIK cl
(velocity of longitudinal waves)

Claisen-Destillierkolben *m* CHEMTECH Claisen flask

Claisen-Kolben *m* CHEMTECH Claisen flask

Clause *f* KÜNSTL INT clause

Clausius: ~**sche Formulierung** *f* PHYS *des zweiten Haupt-
satzes der Thermodynamik* Clausius statement

Clausius-Clapeyron: ~**sche Gleichung** *f* PHYS Clapey-
ron's equation

Clausius-Mosotti: ~**sche Gleichung** *f* PHYS *Lichtbrechung* Clausius-Mosotti formula

Clausius-Rankine-Prozeß-Motor *m* KFZTECH Rankine
cycle engine

Clearscan-Verfahren *nt* WASSERTRANS *Radar* clearscan

Cleveit *m* KERNTECH *Pechblendeart* cleveite

Client/Server-System *nt* COMP & DV client-server system

Clip-On-Kältesatz *m* HEIZ & KÄLTE clip-on refrigerating
machine

Clip-On-Meßinstrument *nt* ELEKTRIZ clip-on instrument

Clipper *m* ELEKTRONIK, LUFTTRANS, TELEKOM clipper;
Clipperverstärker *m* ELEKTRONIK clipper amplifier

Clon *m* COMP & DV clone

Closed-Loop-Verkehrsregelung *f* LUFTTRANS closed-
loop traffic control system

Closed-Shop-Betrieb *m* COMP & DV hands-off operation

Clupein *nt* CHEMIE clupein

Cluster *m* COMP & DV, KERNTECH, KONTROLL cluster;
Clustermodell *nt* KERNTECH *Atomkern* cluster model

CM *abbr (mechanische Auslenkung)* AKUSTIK CM *(mechanical compliance)*

Cm *(Curium)* CHEMIE Cm *(curium)*

CMC *abbr (Carboxymethylcellulose)* KUNSTSTOFF, LE-
BENSMITTEL CMC *(carboxymethylcellulose)*

CM-Cellulose *f* LEBENSMITTEL carboxymethylcellulose

CMD-Spieler *m* OPTIK CMD player

CMOS[1] *abbr* ELEKTRONIK *(Komplementär-Metalloxid-
Halbleiter)* CMOS *(complementary metal oxide
semiconductor)*

CMOS:[2] **CMOS-Halbleiterelement** *nt* COMP & DV CMOS
semiconductor; **CMOS-Koppelpunkt** *m* TELEKOM
CMOS crosspoint; **CMOS-Logik** *f* ELEKTRONIK
CMOS logic; **CMOS-Transistoren** *m pl* ELEKTRONIK
CMOS transistors

C-Multiplex *m (Codemultiplex)* TELEKOM CDM *(code-
division multiplexing)*

CNC *abbr (computernumerische Steuerung)* MASCHI-
NEN CNC *(computerized numeric control)*

Co *(Kobalt)* CHEMIE Co *(cobalt)*

Coanda: ~**scher Effekt** *m* STRÖMPHYS *Strömungsverhal-
ten* Coanda effect

coax *abbr (koaxial)* RADIO coax *(coaxial)*

Cobalamin *nt* CHEMIE cobalamin

Cobalt *nt* CHEMIE cobalt; **Cobaltammin** *nt* CHEMIE cobaltammine; **Cobaltiak** *nt* CHEMIE cobaltammine;
Cobaltnaphthenat *nt* KUNSTSTOFF cobalt naphthenate; **Cobalt-60** *nt* CHEMIE cobalt-60, radiocobalt

COBOL *abbr (problemorientierte Programmiersprache
für Geschäftsbetrieb)* COMP & DV COBOL *(common
business oriented language)*

Cochenille *m* LEBENSMITTEL cochineal

Cockpit *nt* KFZTECH cockpit, LUFTTRANS cockpit, flight

deck, WASSERTRANS *Schiff* cockpit

Code *m* COMP & DV code, ELEKTRONIK *Nachrichtentechnik* code, *Regelwerk zur Darstellung von
Informationen* code, TELEKOM *Übergang* code; ~ **der
Zielvermittlungsstelle** *m* TELEKOM destination point
code; **Codeausgaben** *f pl* QUAL code editions; **Code-
bereich** *m* COMP & DV code area

Codec *m (Codierer-Decodierer)* COMP & DV, ELEKTRO-
NIK, TELEKOM codec *(coder-decoder)*

Code: **Code-Element** *nt* COMP & DV code element

Codein *nt* CHEMIE codeine, methylmorphine

Code: **Codeklasse** *f* QUAL code class; **Codekonverter** *m*
ELEKTROTECH code converter; **Codemultiplex** *m (C-
Multiplex)* TELEKOM code-division multiplexing
(CDM); **Codeschlüssel** *m* ELEKTROTECH code key; **Code-
stempel** *m* QUAL code symbol stamp;
Codesteuerzeichen *nt* COMP & DV code extension char-
acter; **Codetaste** *f* COMP & DV code key

Codethylin *nt* CHEMIE ethylmorphine

codetransparent *adj* TELEKOM code-transparent

Code: **Codeumsetzer** *m* COMP & DV encoder, ELEKTRO-
TECH code converter; **Codeumsetzung** *f* COMP & DV
code conversion, TELEKOM transcoding

codeunabhängig: ~**es Steuerungsverfahren** *nt* COMP &
DV, TELEKOM high-level data link control

Code: **Codewandler** *m* ELEKTROTECH code converter,
TELEKOM transcoder

Codier- *pref* ELEKTRONIK, FERNSEH, KONTROLL, TELE-
KOM coding, encoding; **Codierblatt** *nt* COMP & DV
coding sheet

Codieren *nt* COMP & DV coding, ELEKTRONIK, TELEKOM
coding, encoding

codieren *vt* ELEKTRONIK encode, FERNSEH code, encode, TELEKOM encode

Codierer *m* ELEKTRONIK, FERNSEH coder, encoder, KON-
TROLL encoder, TELEKOM coder, encoder, TRANS
coding device; **Codierer-Decodierer** *m (Codec)* COMP
& DV, ELEKTRONIK, TELEKOM coder-decoder *(codec)*

Codier-: **Codierfehler** *m* COMP & DV, ELEKTRONIK coding
error; **Codierhöhenmesser** *m* LUFTTRANS encoding
altimeter; **Codiersystem** *nt* TRANS code-decode system; **Codiersystem mit Einzelkopf** *nt* VERPACK
single-head coding system; **Codiersystem mit vier
Köpfen** *nt* VERPACK four-head coding system

codiert[1] *adj* TELEKOM coded

codiert:[2] ~**er Exponent** *m* COMP & DV biased exponent; ~**e
Impulse** *m pl* FERNSEH encoded pulses; ~**e Kennzei-
chenübersicht** *f* TRANS precoded tag survey; ~**es
Signal** *nt* ELEKTRONIK encoded signal; ~**e Stereopho-
nie** *f* AUFNAHME coded stereo; ~**e Übertragung** *f*
TELEKOM coded transmission

Codier-: **Codiertabelle** *f* COMP & DV coding table; **Codier-
theorie** *f* COMP & DV coding theory

Codierung *f* ELEKTRONIK coding, encoding, RADIO encoding, TELEKOM coding, encoding, VERPACK
encoding; **Codierungsfeld** *nt* COMP & DV code field;
Codierungspotentiometer *nt* RAUMFAHRT *Weltraumfunk* encoding potentiometer

Coenzym *nt* LEBENSMITTEL coenzyme

Coeruleum *nt* CHEMIE ceruleum

Coil *nt* VERPACK coil; **Coil-Coating** *nt* KUNSTSTOFF coil
coating

CO₂-Laser *m (Kohlendioxidlaser)* ELEKTRONIK CO_2
laser *(carbon dioxide laser)*

Colchicin *nt* CHEMIE colchicine

Colcothar *m* CHEMIE colcothar

Coliforme *nt pl* LEBENSMITTEL coliform bacteria
Collargol *nt* CHEMIE collargol
Collider *m* TEILPHYS collider
Collodinlösung *f* CHEMIE colloxylin
Collodium *nt* CHEMIE collodion, nitrated cellulose
Colloxylin *nt* CHEMIE colloxylin
Colophen *nt* CHEMIE colophene
Colophonium *nt* CHEMIE colophony, rosin
colorieren *vt* DRUCK color (AmE), colour (BrE)
Colpitts-Oszillator *m* ELEKTRONIK Colpitts oscillator
Columbit *m* CHEMIE columbite
Comen- *pref* CHEMIE comenic
Compact: **~-Disk** *f (CD)* COMP & DV compact disk
(CD), OPTIK compact disc (BrE), compact disk
(AmE) *(CD)*; **Compact-Disk ohne Schreibmöglich-
keit** *m (CD-ROM)* COMP & DV compact disk
read-only memory *(CD-ROM)*; **Compact-Disk-
Speicher**: **~ ohne Schreibmöglichkeit** *m (CD-ROM)*
OPTIK compact disc read-only memory (BrE), com-
pact disk read-only memory (AmE) *(CD-ROM)*
Compound *nt* KUNSTSTOFF compound; **Compoundkern**
m KERNTECH, PHYS, STRAHLPHYS compound nucleus;
Compound-Zustand *m* KERNTECH compound state
Compton: **~scher Effekt** *m* PHYS, STRAHLPHYS, TEILPHYS
Compton effect; **~sches Kontinuum** *nt* PHYS, STRAHL-
PHYS, TEILPHYS Compton continuum; **~sches
Spektrometer** *nt* PHYS, STRAHLPHYS, TEILPHYS Comp-
ton spectrometer; **~sche Streuung** *f* PHYS,
STRAHLPHYS, TEILPHYS Compton scattering; **~sche
Wellenlänge** *f* KERNTECH, PHYS, STRAHLPHYS, TEIL-
PHYS Compton wavelength
Compurverschluß *m* FOTO Compur shutter
CompuServe®: **~ Information Manager** *m (CIM)* COMP
& DV CompuServe® Information Manager *(CIM)*
Computer *m* COMP & DV computer, machine, ELEKTRIZ,
WASSERTRANS computer; **~ der dritten Generation** *m*
COMP & DV third generation computer; **~ der ersten
Generation** *m* COMP & DV first generation computer; **~
der fünften Generation** *m* COMP & DV, KÜNSTL INT
FGC, fifth generation computer; **~ mit reduziertem
Befehlsvorrat** *m* COMP & DV RISC, reduced instruction
set computer; **~ mit seriellem Anschluß** *m* COMP & DV
serial computer; **~ mit variabler Wortlänge** *m* COMP &
DV variable-word-length computer; **~ der vierten Generation** *m* COMP & DV fourth generation computer; **~
der zweiten Generation** *m* COMP & DV second generation computer
computerabhängig *adj* COMP & DV machine-dependent
Computer: **Computeranimation** *f* COMP & DV, FERNSEH
computer animation; **Computerbediener** *m* COMP &
DV computer operator; **Computerfachkenntnis** *f* COMP
& DV computer literacy
computergesteuert *adj* TELEKOM computer-controlled
computergestützt[1] *adj* COMP & DV computer-aided,
computer-assisted, KONTROLL computer-aided
computergestützt:[2] **~e Abwicklung** *f* RAUMFAHRT *Welt-
raumfunk* computerized management; **~er Entwurf** *m
(CAD)* COMP & DV, ELEKTRIZ, KONTROLL, MECHAN,
TELEKOM, TRANS computer-aided design *(CAD)*; **~e
Fertigung** *f (CAM)* COMP & DV, ELEKTRIZ computer-
aided manufacturing *(CAM)*; **~e Konstruktion** *f
(CAD)* COMP & DV, ELEKTRIZ, KONTROLL, MECHAN,
TELEKOM, TRANS computer-aided design *(CAD)*; **~e
Konstruktion und Anfertigung** *f (CADCAM)* COMP &
DV computer-aided design and manufacturing
(CADCAM); **~es Lernen** *nt (CAL)* COMP & DV com-

puter-aided learning, computer-assisted learning
(CAL); **~e Produktion** *f (CAM)* COMP & DV, ELEK-
TRIZ computer-aided manufacturing *(CAM)*; **~es
Publizieren** *nt (CAP)* DRUCK computer-aided publis-
hing *(CAP)*; **~e Softwareentwicklung** *f (CASE)*
COMP & DV computer-aided software engineering
(CASE); **~es Training** *nt* TELEKOM computer-based
training; **~er Unterricht** *m (CAL)* COMP & DV computer-aided instruction, computer-assisted instruction
(CAI)
Computer: **Computergrafik** *f* COMP & DV, FERNSEH computer graphics
computerintegrierte: **~ Fertigung** *f (CIM)* COMP & DV
computer-integrated manufacture *(CIM)*
Computer: **Computerkenntnisse** *f pl* COMP & DV computer literacy; **Computerkunst** *f* COMP & DV computer
art; **Computerlauf** *m* COMP & DV machine run
computerlesbar[1] *adj* COMP & DV machine-readable
computerlesbar:[2] **~e Daten** *nt pl* COMP & DV machine-
readable data
Computer: **Computerlogik** *f* COMP & DV computer logic;
Computernetz *nt* COMP & DV, TELEKOM computer network; **Computernetzarchitektur** *f* COMP & DV
computer network architecture
computernumerisch: **~e Steuerung** *f (CNC)* MASCHI-
NEN computerized numeric control *(CNC)*
Computer: **Computerpapier** *nt* DRUCK printout paper;
Computerraum *m* AUFNAHME machine room; **Com-
putersatz** *m* COMP & DV computer setting;
Computerschnittstelle *f* TELEKOM computer interface; **Computersicherheit** *f* COMP & DV computer
security; **Computersystem** *nt* COMP & DV, ELEKTRIZ
computer system; **Computersystem mit Haupt- und
Nebenrechner** *nt* COMP & DV master-slave system;
Computertechnik *f* COMP & DV computer technology
computerunabhängig *adj* COMP & DV machine-independent
computerunterstützt: **~es Problemlösen** *nt* KÜNSTL INT
computer-aided problem solving; **~es Sehen** *nt
(CAV)* KÜNSTL INT computer-aided vision *(CAV)*;
~e Übersetzung *f (CAT)* COMP & DV computer-
assisted translation *(CAT)*
Computer: **Computervision** *f* KÜNSTL INT artificial vi-
sion, computer vision; **Computerwesen** *nt* COMP & DV
computing
ComSat *m* RAUMFAHRT *(Nachrichtensatellit)*, WASSER-
TRANS *(Fernmeldesatellit)* comsat *(communication
satellite)*
Conche *f* LEBENSMITTEL *Schokoladenfabrikation* con-
che
conchieren *vt* LEBENSMITTEL conche
Conchinin *nt* CHEMIE conchinine, quinidine
Cone *f* TEXTIL cone
Confinement *nt* PHYS, TEILPHYS confinement
Coniferin *nt* CHEMIE coniferin
Constraint *nt* KÜNSTL INT constraint
Container *m* KOHLEN container, MEERSCHMUTZ scoop,
TRANS, VERPACK *Entsorgung* container; **~ mit festen
Rädern** *m* TRANS container with fixed wheels; **~ für
den kombinierten Verkehr** *m* TRANS intermodal container; **~ mit zu öffnender Oberseite** *m* TRANS
container with opening top; **~ mit Seitenwandvorhang**
m EISENBAHN curtain-sided container; **Containerauf-
stellfläche** *f* TRANS marshaling area (AmE),
marshalling area (BrE); **Containerentladung** *f* TRANS
container destuffing, container stripping, container

unpacking

containerisieren *vt* TRANS containerize

Containerisierung *f* TRANS, VERPACK containerization

Container: **Containerkai** *m* WASSERTRANS container wharf; **Containerkapsel** *f* TRANS container capsule; **Containerleichter** *m* WASSERTRANS container lighter; **Containerleichter-Mutterschiff-System** *nt* TRANS CLASS, containerized lighter aboard ship system; **Container-LKW** *m* TRANS container carrier lorry (BrE), container carrier truck (AmE) **Containerschiff** *nt (CTS)* WASSERTRANS container ship *(CTS)*; **Containerspülanlage** *f* VERPACK container rinsing equipment; **Containerstandplatz** *m* TRANS container berth; **Containerstation** *f* TRANS container terminal; **Containertragwagen** *m* EISENBAHN container car (BrE), container truck (AmE); **Containertransportschiff** *nt* WASSERTRANS container transport ship; **Containerumschlagkran** *m* TRANS transtainer crane; **Containerumschlagplatz** *m* TRANS container station; **Containerwagen** *m* TRANS container car (BrE), container truck (AmE); **Containerzug** *m* EISENBAHN freightliner train

Controller *m* COMP & DV controller

Convolver *m* ELEKTRONIK *miltärische Nachrichtentechnik* convolver

Convolvulin *nt* CHEMIE convolvulin, rhodeorhetin

Cooper-Paare *nt pl* PHYS *Supraleitung* Cooper pairs

Copolymer *nt* CHEMIE, ERDÖL, KUNSTSTOFF, TEXTIL copolymer

Copolymerisat *nt* CHEMIE, ERDÖL, KUNSTSTOFF, TEXTIL copolymer

Copolymerisation *f* KUNSTSTOFF copolymerization

Coprozessor *m* COMP & DV coprocessor

Copyright-Vermerk *m* DRUCK copyright notice

COR *abbr (Druckausgabeverkleinerung)* COMP & DV COR *(character output reduction)*

Coracit *m* KERNTECH coracite

Cordierit *m* KER & GLAS cordierite

Coriandrol *nt* CHEMIE linalool

Coriolis-Beschleunigung *f* MECHAN, RAUMFAHRT Coriolis acceleration

Coriolis-Kraft *f* PHYS, RAUMFAHRT, STRÖMPHYS Coriolis force

Coronen *nt* CHEMIE coronene

Corticoid *nt* CHEMIE corticoid, corticosteroid

Corticosteroid *nt* CHEMIE corticoid, corticosteroid

Corticosteron *nt* CHEMIE corticosterone

Corticotropin *nt* CHEMIE corticotrophin

Cos-Austrittsgesetz *nt* OPTIK cosine emission law

COSMOS *abbr (Komplementär-Symmetrischer Metalloxid-Halbleiter)* ELEKTRONIK COSMOS *(complementary-symmetrical metal oxide semiconductor)*

Costas-Schleife *f* TELEKOM Costas loop

cot *abbr (Kotangens)* GEOM cot *(cotangent)*

Cotton: **~sche Waage** *f* PHYS *Magnetismus* Cotton balance

Cotton-Mouton: **~scher Effekt** *m* PHYS Cotton-Mouton effect

Couette: **~sche Strömung** *f* STRÖMPHYS Couette flow

Coulomb *nt (C)* ELEKTRIZ, ELEKTROTECH, METROL, PHYS coulomb *(C)*; **~sche Abstoßung** *f* PHYS Coulomb repulsion; **~sche Barriere** *f* STRAHLPHYS Coulomb barrier; **~sche Energie** *f* STRAHLPHYS Coulomb energy; **~sche Fließbedingung** *f* PHYS Coulomb's theorem; **~sches Gesetz** *nt* ELEKTRIZ, PHYS Cou-

lomb's law; **~sche Torsionswaage** *f* PHYS Coulomb's torsion balance; **~sche Waage** *f* PHYS Coulomb gage (AmE), Coulomb gauge (BrE)

Coulometer *nt* CHEMIE, ELEKTROTECH, PHYS coulometer, voltameter

Coumaronharz *nt* KUNSTSTOFF coumarone resin

Countdown *m* RAUMFAHRT *Rückwärtszählung zum Startzeitpunkt* countdown

Cowper: **~scher Winderhitzer** *m* KER & GLAS Cowper stove

Cp *abbr (Wärmekapazität bei konstantem Druck)* LABOR Cp *(heat capacity at constant pressure)*

CPFSK *abbr (phasenkontinuierliche Frequenzumtastung)* ELEKTRONIK, RADIO, TELEKOM CPFSK *(continuous phase frequency shift keying)*

CPK *abbr (Chloroprenkautschuk)* KUNSTSTOFF CR *(chloroprene rubber)*

CPM *abbr (Methode des kritischen Weges)* COMP & DV CPM *(critical path method)*

CPT-Theorem *nt* PHYS *Elementarteilchenphysik* CPT theorem, charge conjugation parity operation time reversal theorem

CPU *abbr (Zentraleinheit, zentrale Rechnereinheit)* COMP & DV, TELEKOM CPU *(central processing unit)*

CQR-Anker *nt (Danford-Anker)* WASSERTRANS CQR anchor *(coastal quick release anchor)*

CR *abbr (Rotationsauslenkung)* AKUSTIK CR *(rotational compliance)*

Cr *(Chrom, Chromium)* CHEMIE Cr *(chromium)*

Cracken *nt* ERDÖL *Raffinerie* cracking

Craqueléeglas *nt* KER & GLAS crackled glass

Craze-Bildung *f* KUNSTSTOFF crazing

Crazing-Effekt *m* KUNSTSTOFF crazing

CRC *abbr (zyklische Blockprüfung, zyklische Blocksicherung)* COMP & DV, ELEKTRONIK, LABOR, TELEKOM CRC *(cyclic redundancy check)*

CRCA *abbr (kalt gewalzt und ausgeglüht)* METALL CRCA *(cold-rolled and annealed)*

Crêpe *m* TEXTIL crepe; **Crêpe-Kautschuk** *m* KUNSTSTOFF crepe rubber

Cresolharz *nt* KUNSTSTOFF cresol resin

Crestfaktor *m* ELEKTROTECH crest factor

Crocein- *pref* CHEMIE crocein

Crocin *nt* CHEMIE crocin

Crookes: **~scher Dunkelraum** *m* PHYS Crookes dark space; **~sche Röhre** *f* ELEKTRONIK Crookes tube

Crookesglas *nt* KER & GLAS Crookes glass

Crossbar: **Crossbar-Selektor** *m* ELEKTROTECH cross coupling, crossbar selector; **Crossbar-System** *nt* TELEKOM crossbar system

Cross-Track-Error *m* WASSERTRANS *Satellitennavigation* cross-track error

Croton- *pref* CHEMIE crotonic

Crotonaldehyd *m* CHEMIE crotonaldehyde, methylacrolein

Crotyl *nt* CHEMIE butenyl, crotyl

Crown *nt* PAPIER crown

Crusher *m* KOHLEN crusher

Cryotron *nt s. Kryotron*

CS *abbr (Durchschaltevermittlung)* COMP & DV, TELEKOM CS *(circuit switching)*

Cs *(Cäsium)* CHEMIE Cs *(caesium)*

CSB *abbr (chemischer Sauerstoffbedarf)* UMWELTSCHMUTZ COD *(chemical oxygen demand)*

CSI *abbr (Chlorschwefelisocyanat)* UMWELTSCHMUTZ CSI *(chlorosulfonyl isocyanate)*

CSM *abbr (Kommando- und Servicemodul)* RAUMFAHRT *Raumschiff* CSM *(command and service module)*

CSMA *abbr (Mehrfachzugriff durch Trägerprüfung)* COMP & DV CSMA *(carrier sense multiple access)*

CSMA/CD[1] *abbr (CSMA/CD-Verfahren)* COMP & DV CSMA/CD *(carrier sense multiple access with collision detection)*

CSMA/CD:[2] **CSMA/CD-Verfahren** *nt (CSMA/CD)* COMP & DV carrier sense multiple access with collision detection *(CSMA/CD)*

CSN *abbr (Durchschalte-Vermittlungsnetz)* COMP & DV, TELEKOM CSN *(circuit-switched network)*

CSPDN *abbr (öffentliches Datenpaketvermittlungsnetz)* TELEKOM CSPDN *(circuit-switched public data network)*

C-Stahl *m* ANSTRICH carbon steel

ct *abbr (Geschwindigkeit von Transversalwellen)* LABOR ct *(velocity of transversal waves)*

CTA *abbr (Cellulosetriacetat)* KUNSTSTOFF CTA *(cellulose triacetate)*

CTCSS *abbr (Hilfsträgergeräuschsperre)* RADIO CTCSS *(continuous tone-coded squelch system)*

CTD *abbr* ELEKTROTECH *(Ladungsverschiebeschaltung)* Halbleiter, PHYS *(ladungsgekoppeltes Bauelement)*, RAUMFAHRT *(Ladungsübertragungsgerät)*, TELEKOM *(Ladungstransferelement)* CTD *(charge transfer device)*

CTOL-Flugzeug *nt (konventionell startendes und landendes Flugzeug)* LUFTTRANS CTOL ˙ aircraft *(conventional takeoff and landing aircraft)*

CTS *abbr (Containerschiff)* WASSERTRANS CTS *(container ship)*

Cu *(Kupfer)* CHEMIE, METALL Cu *(copper)*

Cubebin *nt* CHEMIE cubebin

CUG *abbr (geschlossene Benutzergruppe, geschlossener Benutzerkreis)* COMP & DV, TELEKOM CUG *(closed user group)*

Cumalin *nt* CHEMIE coumalin; **Cumalin-** *pref* CHEMIE coumalic

Cumar- *pref* CHEMIE coumaric

Cumaran *nt* CHEMIE coumaran

Cumarin *nt* CHEMIE benzopyrone, coumarin, cumarin; **Cumarinsäureanhydrid** *nt* CHEMIE benzopyrone, coumarin, cumarin

Cumin- *pref* CHEMIE cumic

Cuminaldehyd *m* CHEMIE cumic aldehyde

Cumol *nt* CHEMIE cumene, cumol, isopropylbenzene

Cumyl- *pref* CHEMIE cumyl

Cuprat *nt* CHEMIE cuprate

Cuprit *m* CHEMIE cuprite, red copper ore

Cupromangan *nt* CHEMIE cupromanganese, manganese copper

Curcuma *f* CHEMIE turmeric

Curcumin *nt* CHEMIE curcumin

Curie *nt (Ci)* PHYS, STRAHLPHYS *alte Einheit der Radioaktivität* curie *(Ci)*; **~sches Gesetz** *nt* PHYS, STRAHLPHYS Curie's law; **~sche Konstante** *f* PHYS, STRAHLPHYS Curie constant; **~scher Punkt** *m* ELEKTRIZ Curie point, PHYS, STRAHLPHYS Curie point, Curie temperature; **~sche Temperatur** *f* PHYS, STRAHLPHYS Curie point, Curie temperature

Curie-Weiss: **~-Gesetz** *nt* PHYS, STRAHLPHYS Curie-Weiss law

Curium *nt (Cm)* CHEMIE curium *(Cm)*; **Curium-Reihe** *f* STRAHLPHYS curium series

Curryklemme *f* WASSERTRANS *Beschläge* cam cleat

Cursor *m* COMP & DV, DRUCK cursor; **Cursorausgangsstellung** *f* COMP & DV cursor home; **Cursorsteuerungsfeld** *nt* COMP & DV touchpad; **Cursortaste** *f* COMP & DV cursor key

Curtain-Coater *m* KUNSTSTOFF curtain coater

CVD *abbr (Gasphasenabscheidung)* ELEKTRONIK, TELEKOM CVD *(chemical vapour deposition)*

C-Verstärker *m* ELEKTRONIK amplifier class C

CVS *abbr (Teilstromentnahme nach Verdünnung)* UMWELTSCHMUTZ CVS *(constant volume sampling)*

CW[1] *abbr (Dauerstrich, ungedämpfte Welle)* AUFNAHME, ELEKTRONIK, ELEKTROTECH, FERNSEH CW *(continuous wave)*

CW:[2] **CW-Betrieb** *m* TEILPHYS CW mode; **CW-Radar** *nt* WASSERTRANS CW radar; **CW-Wert** *m* KFZTECH drag coefficient

Cyan- *pref* CHEMIE cyanic; **Cyanamid** *nt* CHEMIE cyanamide

Cyanat *nt* CHEMIE cyanate

Cyan-: **Cyaneinstellung** *f* FOTO cyan filter adjustment; **Cyanhärtung** *f* METALL cyanide hardening

Cyanid *nt* CHEMIE cyanide; **Cyanidlaugerei** *f* CHEMIE *Gold- und Silbergewinnung* cyanide lixiviation process

Cyanisierung *f* CHEMIE cyanidation

Cyanoaurat *nt* CHEMIE dicyanoaurate

Cyanoferrat *nt* CHEMIE hexacyanoferrate

Cyan-: **Cyantoluol** *nt* CHEMIE cyanotoluene, tolunitrile; **Cyanwasserstoff** *m* CHEMIE hydrocyanic

cyclisch[1] *adj* ERDÖL cyclic

cyclisch:[2] **~e Kette** *f* CHEMIE closed chain

cycloaliphatisch: **~es Amin** *nt* KUNSTSTOFF cycloaliphatic amine

Cycloalkan *nt* CHEMIE cyclane, cycloalkane, naphthene, ERDÖL *Petrochemie* cycloalkane

Cyclobutan *nt* CHEMIE cyclobutane, tetramethylene

Cycloheptadecenon *nt* CHEMIE civetone, cycloheptadecenone

Cycloheptanon *nt* CHEMIE cycloheptanone, suberone

Cyclohexadien *nt* CHEMIE cyclohexadiene, dihydrobenzene

Cyclohexan *nt* CHEMIE cyclohexane, hexahydrobenzene, ERDÖL *Petrochemie* cyclohexane; **Cyclohexancarbonsäure** *f* CHEMIE hexahydrobenzoic acid; **Cyclohexandiol** *nt* CHEMIE cyclohexanediol, quinitol

Cyclokautschuk *m* KUNSTSTOFF cyclized rubber

Cyclonit *nt* CHEMIE cyclonite, hexogen

Cycloolefin *nt* ERDÖL *Petrochemie* cycloolefin

Cycloparaffin *nt* ERDÖL *Petrochemie* cycloparaffin

Cyclopentan *nt* CHEMIE cyclopentane, pentamethylene

Cyclopropan *nt* CHEMIE cyclopropane, trimethylene

D

D^1 *abbr* AKUSTIK *(Schwärzung)* D *(optical density)*, ELEKTRIZ *(Verschiebung)* D *(displacement)*, ELEKTRONIK *(Diffusionskoeffizient)* D *(diffusion coefficient)*, FERTIG *(Durchmesser)* D *(diameter)*, FERTIG *(Versetzung)* D *(displacement)*, GEOM *(Durchmesser)* D *(diameter)*, KERNTECH *(Absorptionsdosis)* D *(absorbed dose)*, MASCHINEN *(Durchmesser)* D *(diameter)*, OPTIK *(optische Dichte)* D *(optical density)*, PHYS *(Diffusionskoeffizient)* D *(diffusion coefficient)*, PHYS *(Versetzung)* D *(displacement)*, RADIO *(Diffusionskoeffizient)* D *(diffusion coefficient)*, STRAHLPHYS *(absorbierte Dosis)* D *(absorbed dose)*, THERMOD *(vierter Virialkoeffizient)* D *(fourth virial coefficient)*

D^2 *(Deuterium)* CHEMIE D *(deuterium)*

d *abbr* CHEMIE *(Deuteron)* d *(deuteron)*, LABOR *(Dezi)* d *(deci-)*, PHYS *(Deuteron)* d *(deuteron)*, TEILPHYS *(Deuteron)* d *(deuteron)*

D/A *abbr (Digital-Analog-)* AUFNAHME, COMP & DV, ELEKTRONIK, FERNSEH, LABOR, TELEKOM D/A *(digital-analog)*

DA *abbr (direkter Zugriff)* COMP & DV DA *(direct access)*

da *abbr (Deka-)* LABOR da *(deca-)*

Dach *nt* BAU, EISENBAHN, KFZTECH, KOHLEN roof; **Dachbinder** *m* BAU roof frame, roof truss, truss; **Dachdecker** *m* BAU roofer, slater; **Dachdeckung** *f* BAU roofing; **Dachfenster** *nt* BAU skylight, KER & GLAS roof light; **Dachfirst** *m* BAU crest; **Dachgepäckträger** *m* KFZTECH roof rack; **Dachhammer** *m* BAU roofer's hammer, slate axe (BrE), slate knife; **Dachkehle** *f* BAU valley, valley gutter; **Dachknick** *m* BAU break, curb (AmE), kerb (BrE), *eines Mansardendaches* breakpoint; **Dachlandeplatz für Hubschrauber** *m* LUFTTRANS rooftop heliport; **Dachlatte** *f* BAU batten; **Dachmanschette** *f* FERTIG *Kunststoffinstallationen* gland, seal; **Dachneigung** *f* BAU roof pitch; **Dachpappe** *f* BAU roofing felt; **Dachpappenrandstreifen** *m* BAU selvage; **Dachpfanne** *f* BAU pantile, roofing tile; **Dachprisma** *nt* PHYS Amici prism, roof prism; **Dachrahmen** *m* BAU purlin; **Dachrinne** *f* BAU eaves gutter, eaves trough, gutter; **Dachrinne hinter einer Brüstungsmauer** *f* BAU parapet gutter; **Dachrinnenhalter** *m* BAU gutter bracket; **Dachschalung** *f* BAU roofing; **Dachschieferlatte** *f* BAU slate ax (AmE), slate axe (BrE); **Dachschirmplatte** *f* KERNTECH roof shielding plate; **Dachschräge** *f* BAU roof pitch, ELEKTRONIK pulse tilt

dachstabilisiert: **~es Schnellverkehrssystem** *nt* TRANS top-stabilized rapid transit system

Dach: **Dachstein** *m* BAU roofing tiles, saddle stone; **Dachstuhl** *m* BAU principal, roof truss, truss; **Dachstuhl-Auflageplatte** *f* BAU roof plate; **Dachziegel** *m* BAU tile; **Dachziegelende** *nt* BAU tail; **Dachzierleiste** *f* KFZTECH *Karosserie* drip molding (AmE), drip moulding (BrE)

Dacron® *nt* WASSERTRANS *Segeln* Dacron® (AmE), Terylene® (BrE)

Daguerreotypie *f* FOTO daguerreotype

Dahlin *nt* CHEMIE dahlin, helenin, inulin, sinistrin

Dalbe *f* WASSERTRANS *Festmachen* dolphin

Dalton: **~sches Partialdruckgesetz** *nt* PHYS, THERMOD Dalton's law

DAMA *abbr (bedarfsgesteuerter Vielfachzugriff)* TELEKOM DAMA *(demand-assigned multiple access)*

Damköhlerzahlen *f pl* STRÖMPHYS Damköhler numbers

Damm *m* WASSERVERSORG dike (AmE), dyke (BrE), weir

Dämm- *pref* AUFNAHME, HEIZ & KÄLTE, VERPACK insulating

Damm: **Dammausspülung** *f* EISENBAHN embankment erosion, embankment washout; **Dammbalkenwehr** *nt* WASSERVERSORG stoplog weir

dämmen *vt* BAU insulate, WASSERVERSORG dam

Damm: **Dammkrone** *f* BAU, WASSERVERSORG crest

Dämm-: **Dämmplatte** *f* AUFNAHME acoustic tile, HEIZ & KÄLTE, VERPACK insulating board; **Dämmschicht** *f* ELEKTROTECH *bei Akustik* insulating layer

Damm: **Dammschüttung** *f* EISENBAHN embanking; **Dammstein** *m* KER & GLAS skimmer block

Dämm-: **Dämmstein** *m* HEIZ & KÄLTE insulating brick; **Dämmstoff** *m* BAU insulating material, insulator, CHEMIE insulator, ELEKTROTECH *bei Akustik* insulating material, FERTIG *Wärmeisolierung* lag, HEIZ & KÄLTE insulant, insulator

Damm: **Dammstraße** *f* BAU causeway

Dämmung *f* BAU insulation, ERDÖL *von Rohren, Behältern* lagging, KUNSTSTOFF, TELEKOM, WASSERTRANS insulation; **Dämmungswert** *m* AKUSTIK SRI, Sound Reduction Index, TL, transmission loss

Dämm-: **Dämmzahl** *f* AKUSTIK SRI, Sound Reduction Index, TL, transmission loss

Dampf^1 *m* CHEMIE, CHEMTECH steam, vapor (AmE), vapour (BrE), ELEKTRONIK, ERDÖL vapor (AmE), vapour (BrE), HYDRAUL steam, KER & GLAS vapor (AmE), vapour (BrE), KERNTECH steam, vapor (AmE), vapour (BrE), KFZTECH vapor (AmE), vapour (BrE), MASCHINEN steam, vapor (AmE), vapour (BrE), METALL vapor (AmE), vapour (BrE), NICHTFOSS ENERG, PAPIER steam, PHYS steam, vapor (AmE), vapour (BrE), TEXTIL steam, THERMOD vapor (AmE), vapour (BrE)

Dampf:^{2} **mit ~ behandeln** *vt* TEXTIL steam; **mit ~ entfetten** *vt* ANSTRICH vapor-degrease (AmE), vapour-degrease (BrE)

Dampf: **Dampfabblaseventil** *nt* HYDRAUL steam relief valve; **Dampfabgabesystem** *nt* KERNTECH steam dumping system; **Dampfabscheider** *m* HYDRAUL, MASCHINEN steam separator; **Dampfabscheidung** *f* ELEKTRONIK vapor deposition (AmE), vapour deposition (BrE); **Dampfabschrecken** *nt* METALL vapor quenching (AmE), vapour quenching (BrE); **Dampfabsperrventil** *nt* HYDRAUL steam stop valve; **Dampfaufmachen** *nt* HYDRAUL steam raising; **Dampfaufsaugzeit** *f* BAU *Autoklav* soaking period; **Dampfausdehnungszeit** *f* HYDRAUL duration of steam, expansion; **Dampfausgleich** *m* HYDRAUL steam balance; **Dampfauslaß** *m* HYDRAUL, MASCHI-

NEN steam outlet; **Dampfauslaßöffnung** *f* HYDRAUL steam port; **Dampfaustritt** *m* HYDRAUL, MASCHINEN steam outlet; **Dampfaustrittsöffnung** *f* HYDRAUL *Dampfzylinder* eduction port; **Dampfbad** *nt* CHEMTECH vapor bath (AmE), vapour bath (BrE); **Dampfbehälter** *m* HYDRAUL steam case; **Dampfbehandlung** *f* PAPIER, TEXTIL steaming; **Dampfblase** *f* CHEMTECH· vapor bubble (AmE), vapour bubble (BrE); **Dampfblasen** *nt* KER & GLAS steam blowing; **Dampfblasenbildung** *f* KFZTECH *Störung des Flüssigkeitszuflusses* vapor lock (AmE), vapour lock (BrE); **Dampfboiler** *m* HYDRAUL steam boiler; **Dampfbremse** *f* HYDRAUL steam brake; **Dampfbüchse** *f* HYDRAUL steam chest; **Dampfdestillation** *f* CHEMTECH steam distillation

dampfdicht *adj* HEIZ & KÄLTE, HYDRAUL, MASCHINEN steamtight

Dampf: **Dampfdichte** *f* CHEMIE, PHYS, THERMOD vapor density (AmE), vapour density (BrE); **Dampfdichteschreiber** *m* GERÄT vapor density recorder (AmE), vapour density recorder (BrE); **Dampfdichtung** *f* HYDRAUL steam packing; **Dampfdom** *m* HYDRAUL dome, steam dome; **Dampfdomnieter** *m* HYDRAUL dome riveter; **Dampfdruck** *m* ERDÖL vapor pressure (AmE), vapour pressure (BrE), MASCHINEN steam pressure, PHYS vapor pressure (AmE), vapour pressure (BrE), THERMOD steam pressure, vapor pressure (AmE), vapour pressure (BrE); **Dampfdruckkurve** *f* THERMOD vapor pressure diagram (AmE), vapour pressure diagram (BrE); **Dampfdruckmanometer** *nt* PHYS steam gage (AmE), steam gauge (BrE); **Dampfdrucksterilisator** *m* LABOR autoclave; **Dampfdruckthermometer** *nt* HEIZ & KÄLTE vapor pressure thermometer (AmE), vapour pressure thermometer (BrE); **Dampfdurchflußmesser** *m* PAPIER steam flowmeter; **Dampfdurchlässigkeit** *f* HEIZ & KÄLTE, THERMOD vapor permeability (AmE), vapour permeability (BrE); **Dampfdüse** *f* HYDRAUL steam jet, MASCHINEN steam nozzle; **Dampfeinlaß** *m* HYDRAUL, MASCHINEN steam inlet; **Dampfeinlaßöffnung** *f* HYDRAUL steam port; **Dampfeinlaßventil** *nt* MASCHINEN steam throttle; **Dampfeintritt** *m* HYDRAUL, MASCHINEN steam inlet; **Dampfeintrittskanal** *m* HYDRAUL steam admission port; **Dampfeintrittsventil** *nt* HYDRAUL eduction valve; **Dampfemissionen** *f pl* UMWELTSCHMUTZ steam-laden emissions

dämpfen *vt* AUFNAHME attenuate, BAU *Schall* damp, muffle, ELEKTRIZ, ELEKTRONIK damp, ERGON attenuate, HYDRAUL cushion, LEBENSMITTEL *Speisen* steam, MASCHINEN absorb, cushion, deaden, SICHERHEIT absorb, TEXTIL steam

dämpfend: **~es Element** *nt* ELEKTRONIK attenuating element; **~e Zwischenschicht** *f* FERTIG dolly

Dampf: **Dampfentladungslampe** *f* ELEKTROTECH, THERMOD vapor discharge lamp (AmE), vapour discharge lamp (BrE); **Dampfentlastungsventil** *nt* HYDRAUL steam relief valve; **Dampfentspannungszeit** *f* HYDRAUL duration of steam expansion

Dampfer *m* WASSERTRANS steamer, *Schifftyp* steamboat

Dämpfer *m* AKUSTIK damper, EISENBAHN bumper (BrE), damper, fender (AmE), ELEKTROTECH damper, HEIZ & KÄLTE attenuator, HYDRAUL cushion, MECHAN dashpot; **Dämpferspule** *f* ELEKTROTECH damping coil

Dampf: **Dampferzeuger** *m* HEIZ & KÄLTE steam generator, HYDRAUL boiler, KERNTECH vapor generator (AmE), vapour generator (BrE), MECHAN, THERMOD

boiler; **Dampferzeugung** *f* HYDRAUL steam raising, WASSERTRANS *Motor* steam generation, steam raising; **Dampfextraktion** *f* LEBENSMITTEL steam extraction; **Dampffahne** *f* ABFALL vapor plume (AmE), vapour plume (BrE)

dampffixieren *vt* TEXTIL steam-set

dampfförmig[1] *adj* CHEMIE vaporous (AmE), vapourous (BrE)

dampfförmig:[2] **~e Phase** *f* THERMOD vapor phase (AmE), vapour phase (BrE)

Dampf: **Dampfgenerator** *m* HEIZ & KÄLTE, KERNTECH steam generator; **Dampfhahn** *m* HYDRAUL steam cock

dampfhaltig *adj* THERMOD humid

Dampf: **Dampfhammer** *m* MASCHINEN steam hammer; **Dampfheizschlange** *f* HEIZ & KÄLTE steam coil; **Dampfheizung** *f* HEIZ & KÄLTE steam heating; **Dampfheizungsanlage** *f* HEIZ & KÄLTE steam heating

Dämpfkalander *m* TEXTIL steam calender

Dampf: **Dampfkammer** *f* HYDRAUL steam chamber; **Dampfkanal** *m* HYDRAUL steam port; **Dampfkante** *f* HYDRAUL steam edge; **Dampfkasten** *m* HYDRAUL steam box, steam case, steam chest; **Dampfkessel** *m* HEIZ & KÄLTE, HYDRAUL, LABOR, MASCHINEN, THERMOD steam boiler; **Dampfkesselanlage** *f* MASCHINEN steam boiler plant; **Dampfkesselmanometer** *nt* GERÄT boiler gage (AmE), boiler gauge (BrE); **Dampfkesselspeisung** *f* HEIZ & KÄLTE boiler feed; **Dampfkochtopf** *m* THERMOD digester; **Dampfkolben** *m* HYDRAUL steam piston; **Dampfkondensierung** *f* KERNTECH valve off; **Dampfkraft** *f* HYDRAUL steam power; **Dampfkraftgenerator** *m* ELEKTROTECH steam electric generating set; **Dampfkraftwerk** *nt* ELEKTROTECH steam electric power plant, steam electric power station; **Dampfkreis** *m* HYDRAUL steam loop; **Dampflampe** *f* ELEKTROTECH, THERMOD vapor discharge lamp (AmE), vapour discharge lamp (BrE); **Dampfmantel** *m* HEIZ & KÄLTE, HYDRAUL steam jacket; **Dampfmaschine** *f* HYDRAUL, KFZTECH, MASCHINEN, PHYS, THERMOD steam engine; **Dampfmaschinenanzeigegerät** *nt* HYDRAUL steam engine indicator; **Dampfmaschinenanzeiger** *m* HYDRAUL steam engine indicator; **Dampfmaschinenindikator** *m* HYDRAUL *Druckverlaufaufzeichnungsgerät in Kolbenmaschinenzylindern* steam engine indicator; **Dampfmeßgerät** *nt* HYDRAUL steam gage (AmE), steam gauge (BrE); **Dampföffnungen** *f pl* MASCHINEN steam ports; **Dampfomnibus** *m* KFZTECH steambus; **Dampfpackung** *f* HYDRAUL steam packing; **Dampfphase** *f* CHEMTECH, ELEKTRONIK vapor phase (AmE), vapour phase (BrE)

Dampfphase: mit ~ aufgebrachte Epitaxialschicht *f* ELEKTRONIK vapor phase grown epitaxial layer (AmE), vapour phase grown epitaxial layer (BrE)

Dampf: **Dampfphasenepitaxie** *f* CHEMTECH, ELEKTRONIK vapor phase epitaxy (AmE), vapour phase epitaxy (BrE); **Dampfphasennitrierung** *f* CHEMTECH vapor phase nitration (AmE), vapour phase nitration (BrE); **Dampfphasenreaktion** *f* ELEKTRONIK vapor phase reaction (AmE), vapour-phase reaction (BrE); **Dampfpipeline** *f* HYDRAUL steam pipeline; **Dampfpunkt** *m* MASCHINEN steam point; **Dampfraum** *m* ERDÖL *in Tank* ullage, HYDRAUL steam space; **Dampfregler** *m* HYDRAUL steam governor; **Dampfregulator** *m* HYDRAUL steam governor; **Dampfrohr** *nt* HYDRAUL, MASCHINEN steam pipe; **Dampfrohrleitung** *f* HYDRAUL steam pipeline; **Dampfrückleitung** *f* KFZTECH vapor return line (AmE), vapour return line (BrE); **Dampf-**

sammler *m* HYDRAUL steam accumulator; **Dampf-schiff** *nt* WASSERTRANS steamer, steamship; **Dampfschlange** *f* HEIZ & KÄLTE steam coil; **Dampf-schlauch** *m* HYDRAUL steam hose; **Dampfseparator** *m* HYDRAUL steam separator; **Dampfspannung** *f* HEIZ & KÄLTE steam pressure, MASCHINEN steam tension; **Dampfspeicher** *m* HYDRAUL, PAPIER steam accumulator; **Dampfsperre** *f* KFZTECH vapor lock (AmE), vapour lock (BrE); **Dampfstabilität** *f* HYDRAUL steam balance; **Dampfstrahl** *m* MASCHINEN, UMWELT-SCHMUTZ steam jet; **Dampfstrahlbrenner** *m* HEIZ & KÄLTE steam jet burner; **Dampfstrahlen** *nt* MEER-SCHMUTZ steam jet cleaning; **Dampfstrahlpumpe** *f* HYDRAUL injector, steam ejector, MASCHINEN steam jet pump; **Dampfstrahlverdichter** *m* HYDRAUL ejector condenser; **Dampfstutzen** *m* HYDRAUL steam nozzle; **Dampftechnik** *f* MASCHINEN steam engineering; **Dampftopf** *m* HYDRAUL steam trap; **Dampftrockner** *m* HYDRAUL steam drier, steam dryer; **Dampfturbine** *f* HYDRAUL, MASCHINEN, THERMOD, WASSERTRANS *Motor* steam turbine; **Dampfüberdeckung** *f* HYDRAUL steam lap; **Dampfüberhitzer** *m* HEIZ & KÄLTE steam superheater; **Dampfüberlappung** *f* HYDRAUL steam lap

Dämpfung *f* AUFNAHME attenuation, BAU *Stößen* absorption, COMP & DV damping, damping attenuation, ELEKTRIZ damping attenuation, ELEKTRONIK attenuation, ELEKTROTECH damping, *bei Stoß* absorption, ERGON damping, FERNSEH attenuation, GERÄT damping, MASCHINEN absorption, METALL damping, OPTIK attenuation, PHYS attenuation, damping, RADIO absorption, attenuation, dissipation, RAUMFAHRT *Weltraumfunk* attenuation, TELEKOM attenuation, loss, WELLPHYS attenuation; **~ an einer Kante** *f* TELE-KOM loss around a corner; **~ durch Ausrichtfehler** *f* TELEKOM pointing loss; **~ durch Ausrichtungsfehler** *f* TELEKOM angular misalignment loss, misalignment loss; **~ durch Längsversatz** *f* TELEKOM gap loss; **~ durch Makrobiegungen** *f* TELEKOM macrobend loss; **~ durch Mikrokrümmungen** *f* TELEKOM microbend loss; **~ durch seitlichen Versatz** *f* TELEKOM lateral offset loss, transverse offset loss; **Dämpfungsband** *nt* ELEK-TRONIK *Filter* attenuation band

dämpfungsbegrenzt: ~er Betrieb *m* TELEKOM attenuation-limited operation; **~er Vorgang** *m* OPTIK attenuation-limited operation

Dämpfung: **Dämpfungsbelag** *m* TELEKOM *Kabel* attenuation coefficient; **Dämpfungsdiode** *f* ELEKTRONIK *Mikrowellentechnik* attenuator diode; **Dämpfungsein-richtung** *f* ELEKTROTECH damper; **Dämpfungselement** *nt* GERÄT attenuating element; **Dämpfungsfähigkeit** *f* FERTIG *Stoß* absorbability; **Dämpfungsfaktor** *m* AUF-NAHME attenuation factor, ELEKTRIZ damping factor, ELEKTROTECH decay factor, PHYS damping factor; **Dämpfungsfilter** *nt* AUFNAHME attenuating filter; **Dämpfungsglied** *nt* AKUSTIK attenuator, pad, ELEK-TRONIK attenuator, pad, *Automatisierungstechnik* absorptive attenuator, ELEKTROTECH pad, ERGON attenuator, GERÄT attenuating element, attenuator pad, RADIO *Schaltkreis, Baugruppe*, TELEKOM attenuator; **Dämpfungsglied aus Ohmschen Widerständen** *nt* TE-LEKOM resistive attenuator; **Dämpfungsgrad** *m* GERÄT attenuation ratio; **Dämpfungskoeffizient** *m* AKUSTIK attenuation coefficient, KERNTECH linear attenuation coefficient, OPTIK attenuation coefficient, PHYS damping coefficient, RADIO dissipation coefficient,

TELEKOM linear attenuation coefficient; **Dämpfungs-kondensator** *m* ELEKTROTECH damping capacitor; **Dämpfungskonstante** *f* AUFNAHME decay factor, ELEKTRONIK, PHYS attenuation constant, TELEKOM attenuation coefficient, attenuation constant; **Dämpf-fungskontur** *f* ELEKTRONIK attenuation contour; **Dämpfungsmaß** *nt* GERÄT attenuation ratio; **Dämpf-fungsmesser** *m* ELEKTROTECH decremeter; **Dämpfungsmeßgerät** *nt* GERÄT decibel meter; **Dämpf-fungsmoment** *nt* LUFTTRANS damping moment; **Dämpfungsnetzwerk** *nt* ELEKTRIZ damping resistor; **Dämpfungsregler** *m* LUFTTRANS control damper; **Dämpfungssystem** *nt* RAUMFAHRT *Raumschiff* surge baffle system; **Dämpfungsventil** *nt* MASCHINEN dashpot valve; **Dämpfungsverhältnis** *nt* ERGON damping ratio, PHYS decrement; **Dämpfungsverlauf** *m* AUFNAHME, ELEKTRONIK response curve; **Dämpf-ungsverzerrung** *f* AUFNAHME, PHYS attenuation distortion; **Dämpfungsvorrichtung** *f* MASCHINEN damping device; **Dämpfungswicklung** *f* ELEKTRIZ damping coil; **Dämpfungswiderstand** *m* ELEKTRIZ damping resistor, damping resistance, PHYS damping resistance; **Dämpfungswinkel** *m* PHYS loss angle; **Dämpfungszeitkonstante** *f* GERÄT damping time constant; **Dämpfungsziffer** *f* AKUSTIK attenuation coefficient

Dampf: **Dampfventil** *nt* HYDRAUL, MASCHINEN steam valve; **Dampfverbindung** *f* PAPIER steam joint; **Dampf-verbrauchszähler** *m* GERÄT steam consumption meter; **Dampfverteiler** *m* PAPIER steam header; **Dampf-wagen** *m* KFZTECH steam car; **Dampfweg** *m* HYDRAUL steam way; **Dampfzufuhrrohr** *nt* HYDRAUL steam supply pipe; **Dampfzustand** *m* THERMOD vapor phase (AmE), vapour phase (BrE); **Dampfzylinder** *m* HY-DRAUL steam cylinder

Danait *nt* HYDRAUL danaide

Dandyroller *m* VERPACK dandy roll

Danford-Anker *m* (*CQR-Anker*) WASSERTRANS Danford anchor, coastal quick release anchor (*CQR anchor*)

Danksagung *f* DRUCK ACK, acknowledgement

Dano-Biostabilisator-Verfahren *nt* ABFALL Dano biosta-bilization process

Daphnetin *nt* CHEMIE daphnetin

Daphnin *nt* CHEMIE daphnin

dargestellt: ~e Wellenform *f* ELEKTRONIK *auf dem Oszil-loskop* displayed waveform

Darm *m* LEBENSMITTEL gut

darren *vt* FERTIG dry, kiln-dry, LEBENSMITTEL *Brauerei* cure, kiln-dry

Darrmalz *nt* LEBENSMITTEL *Brauereiwesen* kiln malt, *Destillation, Gärung* cured malt, kiln-dried malt

Darrofen *m* LEBENSMITTEL drying kiln, drying oven, kiln

Darrschrank *m* LEBENSMITTEL drying cupboard

darstellbar: nicht ~es Zeichen *nt* COMP & DV idle character

darstellen *vt* BAU plot, ELEKTRONIK display, TELEKOM display, *auf dem Bildschirm* display

darstellend: ~e Geometrie *f* GEOM descriptive geometry

Darstellung *f* BAU plot, COMP & DV representation, KONSTZEICH display, presentation, TELEKOM display; **~ der Erfindung** *f* PATENT *in der Beschreibung* disclosure of the invention; **Darstellungsfeld** *nt* KONSTZEICH display area, presentation area; **Darstellungsfläche** *f* COMP & DV display space; **Darstellungsgrafik** *f* COMP &

DV presentation graphics; **Darstellungsschicht** *f* COMP & DV presentation layer

Darstellzeit *f* GERÄT display time

Dasermantel *m* OPTIK fiber coating (AmE), fibre coating (BrE)

DAT *abbr (Digital-Audio-Tape)* AUFNAHME DAT *(digital audio tape)*

Datagramm *nt* COMP & DV, TELEKOM datagram

Datarom® *nt* OPTIK Datarom®

DAT-Cassette *f* AUFNAHME DAT cassette

Datei *f* COMP & DV data file, data set document, file, TELEKOM file; ~ **für den Direktzugriff** *f* COMP & DV direct file; ~ **für wahlfreien Zugriff** *f* COMP & DV random file; **Dateiabfrage** *f* COMP & DV file interrogation; **Dateiaktualisierung** *f* COMP & DV file updating; **Dateiaufbau** *m* COMP & DV file layout; **Dateibediener** *m* TELEKOM file server; **Dateibeschreibung** *f* COMP & DV file description; **Dateidefinition** *f* COMP & DV data set definition; **Dateiende** *nt (EOF)* COMP & DV end of document, end of file; **Dateiendekennsatz** *m* COMP & DV trailer; **Dateieröffnungsroutine** *f* COMP & DV open routine; **Dateierstellung** *f* COMP & DV file creation, file preparation; **Dateigeneration** *f* COMP & DV generation data set; **Dateigenerierung** *f* COMP & DV generation data set; **Dateigröße** *f* COMP & DV file size; **Dateigruppe** *f* COMP & DV file set; **Dateiindex** *m* COMP & DV file index; **Dateikennsatz** *m* COMP & DV file label; **Dateikennung** *f* COMP & DV file identifier, file name; **Dateilöschung** *f* COMP & DV file deletion, file purge; **Dateiname** *m* COMP & DV file identification, file name; **Dateinamenerweiterung** *f* COMP & DV file extension, file name extension; **Dateiorganisation** *f* COMP & DV file organization; **Dateipflege** *f* COMP & DV file maintenance; **Dateiprüfung** *f* COMP & DV file validation; **Dateisäuberung** *f* COMP & DV file cleanup; **Dateischutz** *m* COMP & DV file protection, file security; **Datei-Server** *m* COMP & DV file server; **Dateispeicherung** *f* COMP & DV file storage; **Dateistruktur** *f* COMP & DV file organization, file structure; **Dateitransfer** *m* COMP & DV file transfer; **Dateiübertragung** *f* COMP & DV file transfer; **Dateiumfang** *m* COMP & DV file extent; **Dateiumwandlung** *f* COMP & DV file conversion; **Dateiverarbeitung** *f* COMP & DV file processing; **Dateiverwaltung** *f* COMP & DV file handling, file management; **Dateiverwaltungsroutine** *f* COMP & DV file-handling routine; **Dateiverzeichnis** *nt* COMP & DV file directory; **Dateivorbereitung** *f* COMP & DV file preparation; **Dateiwiederherstellung** *f* COMP & DV file restore; **Dateizugriff** *m* COMP & DV file access; **Dateizuordnung** *f* COMP & DV file allocation

Daten[1] *nt pl* COMP & DV, ELEKTRONIK, ELEKTROTECH, KERNTECH, LABOR, QUAL, RADIO, RAUMFAHRT *Weltraumfunk*, TELEKOM data; ~ **in maschinenlesbarer Form** *nt pl* COMP & DV script

Daten:[2] ~ **aus Rechner aufrufen** *vi* KONTROLL download; ~ **aus Speicher aufrufen** *vi* KONTROLL download; ~ **eingeben** *vi* ELEKTRONIK enter data

Daten: **Datenabfrage** *f* COMP & DV data query, data retrieval; **Datenabfrageschlüssel** *m* TELEKOM polling key; **Datenabruf** *m* COMP & DV data retrieval; **Datenabstraktion** *f* COMP & DV data abstraction; **Datenadressenkettung** *f* COMP & DV data chaining; **Datenaggregat** *nt* COMP & DV data aggregate; **Datenanzeigestation** *f* RAUMFAHRT *Weltraumfunk* display terminal; **Datenauflösung** *f* COMP & DV data resolution; **Datenaufnehmer** *m* ELEKTRIZ logger, recorder; **Datenaufzeichnung** *f* COMP & DV data recording,

KERNTECH data logging, TELEKOM data recording; **Datenaufzeichnungsgerät** *nt* COMP & DV data recorder; **Datenaufzeichnungsmedium** *nt* GERÄT data recording medium; **Datenausgabe auf Mikrofilm** *f* COMP & DV computer output on microfilm; **Datenaustausch** *m* COMP & DV, ELEKTRONIK, RADIO, TELEKOM data communication; **Datenaustauschvermittlung** *f* COMP & DV DSE, data switching exchange; **Datenautobahn** *f* COMP & DV information super-highway

Datenbank *f* COMP & DV computer data base, data bank, database, ELEKTRONIK data bank, database, *strukturiertes System sachbezogener Dateien* database; **Datenbankabfrage** *f* COMP & DV database query; **Datenbankabfragesprache** *f* COMP & DV database query language; **Datenbankadministrator** *m (DBA)* COMP & DV database administrator *(DBA)*; **Datenbankaufgliederung** *f* COMP & DV database mapping; **Datenbankbetreiber** *m* COMP & DV host; **Datenbanknetz** *nt* COMP & DV database network; **Datenbankservice** *m* COMP & DV database services; **Datenbanksprache** *f* COMP & DV QL, query language, database language; **Datenbankverwalter** *m (DBA)* COMP & DV database administrator *(DBA)*; **Datenbankverwaltung** *nt* COMP & DV DBM, database management; **Datenbankverwaltungssystem** *nt* COMP & DV database management system

Daten: **Datenbasis** *f* TELEKOM database; **Datenbasisverwaltungssystem** *nt* TELEKOM database management system; **Datenbehandlungssprache** *f* COMP & DV data manipulation language; **Datenbereich** *m* ELEKTRONIK data domain; **Datenbericht** *m* QUAL data report; **Datenbeschreibung** *f* COMP & DV data description; **Datenbeschreibungssprache** *f* COMP & DV data description language; **Datenbetrieb** *m* COMP & DV data mode; **Datenbewegung** *f* COMP & DV data transaction; **Datenblatt** *nt* COMP & DV, TRANS data sheet; **Datenbus** *m* COMP & DV data bus, KONTROLL bus, data highway, RAUMFAHRT *Raumschiff* bus, data bus; **Datendarstellung** *f* COMP & DV data representation; **Datendefinition** *f* COMP & DV data definition; **Datendurchlauf** *m* COMP & DV throughput (BrE), thruput (AmE); **Datendurchsatz** *m* COMP & DV throughput (BrE), thruput (AmE); **Dateneingabe** *f* COMP & DV data entry, data input; **Dateneingabe über Tastatur** *f* COMP & DV keyboarding; **Dateneinheit** *f* COMP & DV entity; **Dateneintrag** *m* ELEKTRONIK data entry; **Datenelement** *nt* COMP & DV data element, data item, ELEKTRONIK data element; **Datenempfänger** *m* ELEKTROTECH data sink; **Datenende** *nt (EOD)* COMP & DV end of data *(EOD)*; **Datenendeinrichtung** *f (DEE)* COMP & DV, TELEKOM data terminal equipment *(DTE)*; **Datenendgerät** *nt* TELEKOM data terminal; **Datenerfassung** *f* COMP & DV data acquisition, data capture, data collection, data entry, data gathering, data logging, ELEKTRONIK, GERÄT data acquisition, KERNTECH data logging, TELEKOM data collection; **Datenerfassungsstation** *f* COMP & DV data collection platform; **Datenerfassungssystem** *nt* COMP & DV data logger; **Datenerstellung** *f* COMP & DV data origination; **Datenextraktion** *f* ELEKTRONIK data extraction; **Datenfehler** *m* COMP & DV data error; **Datenfeld** *nt* COMP & DV data field, data item, item; **Datenfeld mit konstanter Länge** *nt* COMP & DV constant length field; **Datenfernsprecher** *m* COMP & DV data phone; **Datenfernübertragung** *f* COMP & DV, ELEKTRONIK data communication, RADIO data communication, digital communication, TELECOM data communication; **Datenfernverarbeitung** *f* COMP & DV remote data processing, teleprocessing, TELEKOM teleinformatics; **Datenfernverarbeitung-sverbindung** *f* COMP & DV teleprocessing connection; **Datenfestnetz** *nt* TELEKOM dedicated circuit data network; **Datenfluß** *m* COMP & DV data flow, ELEKTROTECH data stream; **Datenfluß in Rückwärtsrichtung** *m* COMP & DV reverse direction flow; **Datenflußdiagramm** *nt* COMP & DV data flow diagram; **Datenflußplan** *m* COMP & DV data flow chart; **Datenformat** *nt* COMP & DV data format; **Datenfunk** *m* TELEKOM radio data transmission

datengesteuert: **~es System** *nt* KÜNSTL INT data-driven system

datengetrieben: **~es System** *nt* KÜNSTL INT data-driven system

Daten: **Datengruppierung** *f* COMP & DV data aggregate; **Datenhierarchie** *f* COMP & DV data hierarchy; **Datenintegrität** *f* COMP & DV data integrity; **Datenkanal** *m* COMP & DV data channel, TELEKOM information channel; **Datenkanalverteiler** *m* COMP & DV data channel multiplexer; **Datenkasse** *f* (*POS-Terminal*) COMP & DV, VERPACK point of sale terminal *(POS terminal)*; **Datenkassette** *f* COMP & DV data cartridge; **Datenkommunikation** *f* COMP & DV, ELEKTRONIK, RADIO, TELEKOM data communication; **Datenkommunikationsnetz** *nt* COMP & DV data communication network; **Datenkommunikationsstation** *f* COMP & DV data communication terminal; **Datenkompression** *f* COMP & DV data compaction, data compression, data reduction; **Datenkonverter** *m* ELEKTRONIK *Hardware oder Software zur Datenumsetzung* data converter; **Datenkonvertierung** *f* ELEKTRONIK *des Datenformats*, GERÄT data conversion; **Datenkonzentrator** *m* COMP & DV data concentrator; **Datenkorrektur** *f* COMP & DV data cleaning; **Datenleitung** *f* LUFTTRANS data link; **Datenleitungssteuerung** *f* COMP & DV data link control; **Datenleitungs-Steuerungsprotokoll** *nt* COMP & DV data link control protocol; **Datenmigration** *f* COMP & DV data migration; **Datenmodell** *nt* COMP & DV data model; **Datenmodulation** *f* TELEKOM data modulation; **Datenmodus** *m* COMP & DV data mode; **Datenmonitor** *m* FERNSEH viewdata terminal; **Datenmultiplexer** *m* COMP & DV, ELEKTRONIK, TELEKOM, TRANS data multiplexer; **Datenmultiplexing** *nt* ELEKTRONIK data multiplexing; **Datenmultiplexor** *m* COMP & DV, ELEKTRONIK, TELEKOM, TRANS data multiplexer; **Datenname** *m* COMP & DV data name; **Datennetz** *nt* COMP & DV, TELEKOM data network; **Datennetzkennzahl** *f* TELEKOM DNIC, data network identification code; **Datenpaket** *nt* ELEKTROTECH data packet, TELEKOM data packet, packet; **Datenpaketübertragung** *f* COMP & DV packet transmission; **Datenpaketvermittlung** *f* COMP & DV, ELEKTROTECH, TELEKOM packet switching; **Datenpfad** *m* COMP & DV data path; **Datenpflege** *f* COMP & DV data management; **Datenphase** *f* TELEKOM data phase; **Datenprotokollfunktion** *f* COMP & DV data logger; **Datenprotokollierung** *f* COMP & DV data logging; **Datenprüfung** *f* COMP & DV, GERÄT data check, data validation, data verification; **Datenquelle** *f* COMP & DV, ELEKTROTECH data source; **Datenrate** *f* TELEKOM bit rate; **Datenrecorder** *m* ELEKTRIZ, LABOR data recorder; **Datenregister** *nt* COMP & DV data register; **Datenregistriergerät** *nt* GERÄT data recorder; **Datenreihe** *f* COMP & DV stream; **Datenrückwand** *f* FOTO data back; **Datensammlung** *f* COMP & DV data gathering

Datensatz *m* COMP & DV data set, *Datenelement* data record, record, KONTROLL data set, record; **Datensatzaktualisierung** *f* COMP & DV record updating; **Datensatzbereich** *m* COMP & DV record area; **Datensatzdefinition** *f* COMP & DV data set definition; **Datensatzerstellung** *f* COMP & DV record creation; **Datensatzformat** *nt* COMP & DV record format, record layout; **Datensatzklasse** *f* COMP & DV record class; **Datensatzkopf** *m* COMP & DV record head; **Datensatzlänge** *f* COMP & DV record length

Daten: **einmal beschreibbare Datenscheibe** *f* OPTIK write-once data disk; **Datenschub** *m* RAUMFAHRT *Weltraumfunk* data burst; **Datenschutz** *m* COMP & DV data privacy (BrE), data security (AmE), data protection, privacy; **Datensender** *m* ELEKTROTECH data source; **Datensenke** *f* ELEKTROTECH, TELEKOM *Empfangsstelle* data sink; **Datensicherheit** *f* COMP & DV data privacy (BrE), data security (AmE), data reliability, security; **Datensicherung** *f* COMP & DV backup, data protection, ELEKTROTECH backup; **Datensicherungsschicht** *f* COMP & DV, TELEKOM data link layer, link layer; **Datensichtgerät** *nt* COMP & DV VDU, display, visual display unit, FERNSEH VDU, data display terminal, video terminal, GERÄT data display unit, KONTROLL, PHYS, TELEKOM VDU; **Datenspeicher** *m* COMP & DV data memory, data storage, memory, store, ELEKTROTECH data storage, FERNSEH information storage; **Datenspeicherkarte** *f* COMP & DV memory card; **Datenspeichern** *nt* TELEKOM data recording; **Datenspeicherung** *f* KERNTECH data storage; **Datensperre** *f* COMP & DV lock; **Datenspur** *f* COMP & DV data track

Datenstation *f* COMP & DV data station, data terminal, terminal, work station; **Datenstation für Datenpaketbetrieb** *f* COMP & DV packet mode terminal; **Datenstationsadapter** *m* COMP & DV terminal adaptor; **Datenstationsanschluß** *m* COMP & DV terminal port; **Datenstationsjob** *m* COMP & DV terminal job; **Datenstationskomponente** *f* COMP & DV terminal component; **Datenstationsmodus** *m* COMP & DV terminal mode; **Datenstationsprotokoll** *nt* COMP & DV terminal log; **Datenstationsserver** *m* COMP & DV terminal server; **Datenstationssteuerung** *f* COMP & DV terminal control

Daten: **Datenstelle** *f* REGELUNG data position; **Datenstrom** *m* COMP & DV data stream, stream, ELEKTROTECH, TELEKOM data stream; **Datenstrombandlaufwerk** *nt* COMP & DV streaming tape drive; **Datenstromeinheit** *f* COMP & DV streamer; **Datenstruktur** *f* COMP & DV data structure; **Datenteil** *nt* COMP & DV data division; **Datentelefon** *nt* ELEKTRONIK *mit Modem, Netzwerk* data phone

Datenträger *m* AUFNAHME recording medium, COMP & DV data carrier, data medium, disk (AmE), recording medium, storage medium, volume; **Datenträgerdetektor** *m* (*DCD*) TELEKOM data carrier detector (*DCD*); **Datenträgerende** *nt* COMP & DV end of medium; **Datenträgerkennsatz** *m* COMP & DV header label, volume label; **Datenträgeroberfläche** *f* COMP & DV data surface

Daten: **Datentransfergeschwindigkeit** *f* TELEKOM data transfer rate, information transfer rate; **Datentransfersystem** *nt* TELEKOM data transfer system; **Datentransportnetz** *nt* TELEKOM data transport network; **Datentyp** *m* COMP & DV data type;

Datenübermittlung *f* COMP & DV, ELEKTRONIK, RADIO, TELEKOM data communication; **Datenübermittlungsabschnitt** *m* COMP & DV, ELEKTRONIK data communication link; **Datenübermittlungskanal** *m* *(DCC)* TELEKOM data communication channel *(DCC)*

Datenübertragung *f* COMP & DV communication, data communication, data transfer, data transmission, ELEKTRONIK communication, data communication, LABOR data transmission, RADIO data communication, TELEKOM data communication, data transmission; **Datenübertragungsabschnitt** *m* COMP & DV, ELEKTRONIK data communication link; **Datenübertragungsblock** *m* COMP & DV *Datenfernverarbeitung* frame; **Datenübertragungsebene** *f* COMP & DV data link level; **Datenübertragungseinrichtung** *f (DÜE)* COMP & DV data communication terminating equipment *(DCE)*, TELEKOM data circuit terminating equipment *(DCE)*; **Datenübertragungsgeschwindigkeit** *f* COMP & DV baud rate, bit rate, data rate, data transfer rate, OPTIK data transfer rate; **Datenübertragungskanal** *m* COMP & DV data transmission channel, KONTROLL data highway; **Datenübertragungsleitung** *f* COMP & DV scheduled circuit; **Datenübertragungsphase** *f* TELEKOM data phase; **Datenübertragungssignal** *nt* ELEKTRONIK communications signal; **Datenübertragungssteuereinheit** *f* COMP & DV, ELEKTRONIK multiplexer; **Datenübertragungssteuerung** *f* COMP & DV data link control, line control; **Datenübertragungssystem** *nt* GERÄT data transmission system; **Datenübertragungssystemsteuerung** *f* LUFTTRANS data link; **Datenübertragungsumschaltung** *f* COMP & DV data link escape; **Datenübertragungsverbindung** *f* RAUMFAHRT *Weltraumfunk* data link; **Datenübertragungsvorrechner** *m* TELEKOM front-end processor; **Datenübertragungsweg** *m* COMP & DV data bus, data highway

Daten: **Datenumlagerung** *f* COMP & DV data migration; **Datenumsetzung** *f* ELEKTRONIK data conversion; **Datenunabhängigkeit** *f* COMP & DV data independence; **Datenunterbrechung** *f* COMP & DV data break; **Datenursprung** *m* COMP & DV data origin; **Datenverarbeitung** *f (DV)* COMP & DV, ELEKTRONIK *Verarbeitung analoger oder digitaler Daten*, KONTROLL, TELEKOM data processing *(DP)*; **Datenverarbeitung an Bord** *f* RAUMFAHRT *Weltraumfunk* on-board processing; **Datenverarbeitungssystem** *nt* COMP & DV, KERNTECH, TELEKOM dataprocessing system; **Datenverdichter** *m* TELEKOM compressor; **Datenverdichtung** *f* COMP & DV data compaction, data compression, data reduction; **Datenvereinbarung** *f* COMP & DV data declaration; **Datenverkehr** *m* COMP & DV traffic; **Datenverlust durch Überlauf** *m* DRUCK overrun; **Datenverlustausfall** *m* ELEKTROTECH overrun; **Datenvermittlung** *f* TELEKOM data switching; **Datenvermittlungsstelle** *f* TELEKOM DSE, data switch, data switching exchange; **Datenverschlüsselung** *f* COMP & DV data encryption; **Datenverstärker** *m* ELEKTRONIK data amplifier; **Datenverwaltung** *f* COMP & DV data control, data management; **Datenverzeichnis** *nt* COMP & DV data dictionary, data directory; **Datenvielfachleitung** *f* COMP & DV data highway; **Datenvorbereitung** *f* COMP & DV data preparation, preprocessing; **Datenwandler** *m* GERÄT data converter; **Datenwandlung** *f* ELEKTRONIK data conversion; **Datenwarteschlange** *f* COMP & DV data queue; **Datenweg** *m* ELEKTRONIK data path; **Datenwiederauffindesystem** *nt* STRAHLPHYS data recovery system; **Datenwort** *nt* COMP & DV data word; **Datenwörterbuch** *nt* COMP & DV data dictionary

Datexnetz *nt* TELEKOM datex network

Datierung *f* PHYS dating

Datiscagelb *nt* CHEMIE datiscin, datisosid

Datiscin *nt* CHEMIE datiscin

Datum *nt* MATH datum; **Datumscodierung** *f* VERPACK date code; **Datumsgrenze** *f* RAUMFAHRT datum line, WASSERTRANS date line; **Datumsstempel** *m* VERPACK date code

DAU *abbr (Digital-Analog-Umsetzer)* COMP & DV DAC *(digital-analog converter)*, ELEKTRONIK, FERNSEH, TELEKOM DAC *(digital-analog converter)*

Daube *f* FERTIG stave, MECHAN hoop

Dauer: **~ der Überfahrt** *f* WASSERTRANS crossing time; **Dauerablauf** *m* FERTIG continuous cycling; **Dauerbeanspruchung** *f* ELEKTRIZ continuous duty, uninterrupted duty; **Dauerbelastung** *f* KOHLEN, MASCHINEN permanent load, METALL repeated loading; **Dauerbetrieb** *m* COMP & DV steady state, ELEKTRIZ uninterrupted duty, ELEKTROTECH steady state, RAUMFAHRT continuous spectrum; **Dauerbetriebsbedingung** *f* ELEKTROTECH steady state condition; **Dauerbiegefestigkeit** *f* KUNSTSTOFF flexing endurance; **Dauerbruch** *m* FERTIG fatigue durability, fatigue fracture, progressive fracture; **Dauerbruchbeginn** *m* LUFTTRANS incipient crack; **Dauerbruchrastlinie** *f* FERTIG fatigue crescent; **Dauerbruchzone** *f* FERTIG fatigue nucleus; **Dauerdehngrenze** *f* METALL creep strength; **Dauerdrehzahl** *f* MASCHINEN continuous speed; **Dauereingriff** *m* FERTIG *Getriebelehre* permanent mesh; **Dauerelektrode** *f* BAU nonconsumable electrode, permanent electrode; **Dauererhitzung** *f* LEBENSMITTEL *Molkereiwesen* batch-type pasteurization; **Dauerfestigkeit** *f* FERTIG fatigue strength, *im Schwellbereich* fatigue limit, KUNSTSTOFF durability, LUFTTRANS, MECHAN, METALL fatigue strength; **Dauerfestigkeitsdiagramm** *nt* PHYS Smith chart; **Dauerfestigkeitsprüfmaschine** *f* FERTIG alternate strength testing machine; **Dauerfettschmierung** *f* FERTIG *Kunststoffinstallationen* permanent lubrication; **Dauerfeuerbeständigkeit** *f* FERTIG refractoriness under load; **Dauerfluß** *m* PHYS steady flow; **Dauerform** *f* FERTIG permanent mold (AmE), permanent mould (BrE); **Dauerfrost** *m* ERDÖL, KOHLEN permafrost; **Dauergießform** *f* FERTIG permanent mold (AmE), permanent mould (BrE); **Dauergleichgewicht** *nt* PHYS secular equilibrium

dauerhaft *adj* BAU permanent

Dauer: **Dauerhaftigkeit** *f* ANSTRICH, KUNSTSTOFF, METROL, TEXTIL durability; **Dauerhaltbarkeit** *f* FERTIG fatigue, fatigue durability; **Dauerhub** *m* FERTIG continuous stroking; **Dauerinspektion** *f* LUFTTRANS fatigue inspection; **Dauerlast** *f* ELEKTRIZ constant load, continuous load; **Dauerleistung** *f* AUFNAHME continuous power output, ELEKTRIZ constant duty, continuous output, KONTROLL continuous duty; **Dauerleistungsgrenze** *f* ERGON permanent performance limit; **Dauermagnet** *m* ELEKTRIZ, ELEKTROTECH, MASCHINEN, PHYS, TELEKOM, TRANS permanent magnet; **Dauermagnet-Generator** *m* NICHTFOSS ENERG permanent magnet generator

dauermagnetisch: **~e Substanz** *f* PHYS hard magnetic material

Dauer: **Dauermagnetlöschung** *f* AUFNAHME permanent magnet erasing; **Dauermagnetrelais** *nt* ELEKTRIZ permanent magnet relay; **Dauermessung** *f* GERÄT long-term measurement

dauernd[1] *adj* KONTROLL continuous, PHYS steady-state

dauernd:[2] **~e Magnetzentrierung** *f* FERNSEH permanent magnet centering (AmE), permanent magnet centring (BrE)

Dauer: **Dauer-Nennleistung** *f* ELEKTRIZ continuous rating

dauerplissiert *adj* TEXTIL permanently pleated

Dauer: **Dauerprüfung** *f* LUFTTRANS, WERKPRÜF fatigue test; **Dauerruf** *m* ELEKTROTECH *Telefonklingel* continuous ringing; **Dauerschwingbeanspruchung** *f* FERTIG cycling, fatigue, fatigue loading; **Dauerschwingfestigkeit** *f* FERTIG endurance limit, endurance, fatigue limit, MASCHINEN fatigue limit, WERKPRÜF fatigue strength

dauerschwingungsbeansprucht *adj* FERTIG fatigue-loaded

Dauer: **Dauersignal** *nt* ELEKTRONIK continuous signal; **Dauerspannung** *f* ELEKTROTECH constant voltage, KER & GLAS permanent stress; **Dauerspeicher** *m* COMP & DV permanent memory, permanent storage, ELEKTROTECH permanent memory; **Dauerstandfestigkeit** *f* FERTIG limiting creep stress; **Dauerstandkriechgrenze** *f* KOHLEN, METALL creep strength; **Dauerstrahl** *m* ELEKTRONIK continuous beam; **Dauerstreckgrenze** *f* METALL repeated yield point

Dauerstrich *m* (*CW*) AUFNAHME, ELEKTRONIK, ELEKTROTECH, FERNSEH continuous wave (*CW*); **Dauerstrichbetrieb** *m* TEILPHYS continuous-wave mode; **Dauerstrichgaslaser** *m* ELEKTRONIK CW gas laser, continuous-wave laser; **Dauerstrichlaser** *m* ELEKTRONIK CW laser, WELLPHYS CW laser, continuous-wave laser; **Dauerstrichlaserstrahl** *m* ELEKTRONIK CW laser beam, continuous-wave laser beam; **Dauerstrichradar** *nt* WASSERTRANS continuous wave radar; **Dauerstrichradardetektor** *m* TRANS CW radar detector, continuous-wave radar detector; **Dauerstrichultraschalldetektor** *m* TRANS CW ultrasonic detector, continuous-wave ultrasonic detector

Dauer: **Dauerstrom** *m* ELEKTROTECH constant current, contactor, continuous current, PHYS steady current; **Dauertauchen** *nt* ERDÖL *Tauchtechnik* saturation diving; **Dauertaucher** *m* ERDÖL *Tauchtechnik* saturation diver; **Dauerumschaltung** *f* COMP & DV SO, shift out; **Dauerversuch** *m* MASCHINEN endurance test, fatigue test, METROL, WERKPRÜF endurance test; **Dauerversuchmaschine** *f* MASCHINEN fatigue-testing machine; **Dauerversuchsprobe** *f* FERTIG fatigue specimen; **Dauerwärmebeständigkeit** *f* KUNSTSTOFF heat stability, THERMOD thermal stability; **Dauerwerbung** *f* FERNSEH back-to-back commercials; **Dauerzählstelle** *f* TRANS continuous counting station; **Dauerzugfestigkeit** *f* MASCHINEN endurance tensile strength; **Dauerzustand** *m* ELEKTROTECH steady state condition, PHYS steady state, steady state condition

Daumen *m* FERTIG, MASCHINEN cog; **Daumeneinschnitt** *m* DRUCK side index; **Daumenglashals** *m* KER & GLAS danny neck; **Daumenindex** *m* DRUCK thumb index; **Daumenregister** *nt* DRUCK thumb index; **Daumensteuerung** *f* FERTIG cam gear

D/A: **D/A-Umsetzer** *m* COMP & DV, ELEKTRONIK, TELEKOM D/A converter; **D/A-Umsetzung** *f* AUFNAHME, COMP & DV, ELEKTRONIK, TELEKOM D/A conversion

Davit *m* MECHAN, WASSERTRANS davit

D/A: **D/A-Wandler** *m* COMP & DV, ELEKTRONIK, TELEKOM D/A converter; **D/A-Wandlung** *f* AUFNAHME, COMP & DV, ELEKTRONIK, TELEKOM D/A conversion

Daycruiser *m* WASSERTRANS *Schifftyp* day cruiser

dB *abbr* (*Dezibel*) AKUSTIK, AUFNAHME, ELEKTRONIK, PHYS, RADIO, STRAHLPHYS, UMWELTSCHMUTZ dB (*decibel*)

DBA *abbr* (*Datenbankadministrator, Datenbankverwalter*) COMP & DV DBA (*database administrator*)

DBCS-Endezeichen *nt* COMP & DV SI character, shift-in character

DBCS-Startzeichen *nt* COMP & DV SO character, shift-out character

D-Beiwert *m* REGELUNG derivative action coefficient

dBi *abbr* (*Dezibel über Isotropstrahler*) STRAHLPHYS dBi (*decibels over isotropic*)

DC-AC-Spannungswandler *m* ELEKTROTECH DC-AC converter

DC-AC-Spannungswandlung *f* ELEKTROTECH DC-AC conversion

DCC *abbr* (*Datenübermittlungskanal*) TELEKOM DCC (*data communication channel*)

DCD *abbr* (*Datenträgerdetektor*) TELEKOM DCD (*data carrier detector*)

DC-Josephson-Effekt *m* ELEKTROTECH DC Josephson effect

DCTL *abbr* (*direktgekoppelte Transistorlogik*) ELEKTRONIK DCTL (*direct-coupled transistor logic*)

DC-Transducer *m* ELEKTROTECH DC transducer

DD *abbr* HYDRAUL (*Strömungswiderstand*), NICHTFOSS ENERG (*Luftwiderstandsbeiwert, Widerstandsbeiwert*) DD (*coefficient of drag*)

DDE *abbr* (*direkte Dateneingabe, direkter Dateneintrag*) COMP & DV DDE (*direct data entry*)

DDP *abbr* (*Doppeldiodenpentode*) ELEKTRONIK DDP (*double diode pentode*)

DDT *abbr* (*Dichlordiphenyltrichlorproäthan*) CHEMIE DDT (*dichlordiphenyltrichlorproethane*)

de: **~ Brogliesche Welle** *f* ELEKTROTECH, PHYS, STRAHLPHYS de Broglie wave; **~ Dion-Achse** *f* KFZTECH de Dion axle

deaktivieren *vt* MASCHINEN deactivate, RAUMFAHRT *Raumschiff* passivate

Deaktivierung *f* CHEMIE deactivation, inactivation; **~ des angeregten Zustandes** *f* KERNTECH, STRAHLPHYS excited-state deactivation

Dean: **~ und Stark-Apparat** *m* LABOR Dean and Stark apparatus

Debricin *nt* CHEMIE *Milchsaft in Ficusarten* ficin

Debugger *m* COMP & DV debugger

Debye: **~sches Modell** *nt* PHYS Debye model; **~sche Frequenz** *f* PHYS Debye frequency; **~sche Temperatur** *f* (θD) PHYS, THERMOD Debye temperature (θD)

Decahydronaphthalin *nt* CHEMIE decahydronaphthalene, decalin, naphthane

Decalin *nt* CHEMIE decahydronaphthalene, decalin, naphthane

Decan *nt* CHEMIE decane; **Decan-** *pref* CHEMIE capric

Decanol *nt* CHEMIE decanol

Decarbonisierung *f* CHEMIE decarbonization

Decarboxylase *f* CHEMIE decarboxylase

Dechiffrieren *nt* RAUMFAHRT *Weltraumfunk* descrambling

dechiffrieren *vt* ELEKTRONIK *Nachrichtentechnik* decipher

Dechiffriervorrichtung *f* TRANS decoding device
Dechsel *f* BAU *Holzbau* adz (AmE), EISENBAHN adz, adze
Deck *nt* WASSERTRANS *Schiffbau* deck; ~ **mit Decksbelag** *nt* WASSERTRANS sheathed deck; **Deckanstrich** *m* BAU, KUNSTSTOFF finishing coat, top coat
Deckanstrich: mit ~ versehen *vt* BAU finish
Deck: **Deckasphaltschicht** *f* BAU asphalt surfacing; **Deckbalken** *m* WASSERTRANS *Schiffbau* beam; **Deckbalkenknieblech** *nt* WASSERTRANS *Schiffbau* beam bracket; **Deckbogen** *m* DRUCK top blanket
Decke[1] *f* BAU roof, *Straße* paving, veneer, FERTIG *Schmelzherd*, KOHLEN roof, TEXTIL blanket, WASSERTRANS deckhead
Decke:[2] ~ **einziehen** *vi* BAU ceil
Deckel *m* DRUCK tympan, ELEKTROTECH cap, FERTIG *Lichtbogenofen* roof, HYDRAUL *Dampfbüchse* cap, *Dampfzylinder* cover, LABOR lid, MASCHINEN flap, head, lid, VERPACK *Verschlußkappe* lid; **Deckellager** *nt* MASCHINEN cap bearing; **Deckelpackstoff** *m* VERPACK cap-sealing compound; **Deckelring** *m* VERPACK lever ring; **Deckelsiegelmasse** *f* VERPACK lid sealing compound; **Deckelstanze** *f* VERPACK capping press; **Deckelversiegelung** *f* VERPACK cap sealing
decken *vt* BAU *Dach* tile
Decke: **Deckenbalken** *m* BAU ceiling joist; **Deckenbemessung** *f* BAU *Straßenbau* pavement design (BrE), sidewalk design (AmE); **Deckengeräte** *nt pl* HEIZ & KÄLTE ceiling-hung equipment; **Deckenkanalsystem** *nt* HEIZ & KÄLTE ceiling-mounted ducting; **Deckenkran** *m* MECHAN overhead crane, VERPACK overhead traveling crane (AmE), overhead travelling crane (BrE); **Deckenkühlschlange** *f* HEIZ & KÄLTE ceiling coil; **Deckenleuchte** *f* ELEKTRIZ *Hängelampe* ceiling fitting, WASSERTRANS deckhead light; **Deckenoberlicht** *nt* LUFTTRANS overhead light; **Deckenpapier** *nt* PAPIER liner; **Deckenrose** *f* ELEKTROTECH *elektrische Leuchte* ceiling rose; **Deckenschallplatte** *f* AUFNAHME ceiling baffle; **Deckenschalttafel** *f* LUFTTRANS overhead panel; **Deckenträger** *m* BAU joist; **Deckentransportband** *nt* VERPACK overhead conveyor; **Deckenunterzug** *m* BAU floor joist; **Deckenventilator** *m* MASCHINEN ceiling fan; **Deckenvorgelegewelle** *f* MASCHINEN ceiling countershaft
Deck: **Deckfähigkeit** *f* CHEMIE opacity; **Deckfarbe** *f* KUNSTSTOFF covering paint; **Deckgebirge** *nt* ERDÖL *Geologie* overburden, NICHTFOSS ENERG cap rock; **Deckgestein** *nt* NICHTFOSS ENERG cap rock; **Deckglas** *nt* KER & GLAS cover glass, LABOR cover glass, cover slip; **Deckhubschrauber** *m* LUFTTRANS carrier-borne helicopter; **Deckkraft** *f* KUNSTSTOFF covering power, hiding power; **Decklage** *f* BAU decking, FERTIG *Getriebelehre* coincidence; **Deckleiste** *f* BAU batten, fillet, MASCHINEN cover strip; **Deckmasse** *f* KER & GLAS cover coat; **Deckmeßglas** *nt* KER & GLAS cover glass gage (AmE), cover glass gauge (BrE); **Deckmetall** *nt* FERTIG deposited metal; **Deckpeilung** *f* WASSERTRANS alignment bearing; **Deckplatte** *f* BAU flange tile, FERTIG coping, METROL surface plate, PAPIER crown; **Deckplatte mit Rand** *f* KER & GLAS lipped cover tile; **Deckplatte der Wannensteine** *f* KER & GLAS top course of tank blocks; **Deckring** *m* KER & GLAS plunger ring; **Decksaufbau** *m* WASSERTRANS superstructure, *Schiffbau* deck superstructure; **Decksbalken** *m* WASSERTRANS *Schiffbau* deck beam, transverse beam; **Decksbelag** *m* WASSERTRANS *Schiffbau* decking;

Decksbeplattung *f* WASSERTRANS *Schiffbau* deck plating; **Decksbeschläge** *m pl* WASSERTRANS *Ausrüstung* deck fittings; **Decksbucht** *f* WASSERTRANS *Schiffbau* camber; **Deckschicht** *f* ABFALL *einer Deponie* covering layer, ANSTRICH top coat, BAU covering, *Straße* wearing course, ERDÖL *Geologie* cap rock, KUNSTSTOFF finishing coat, VERPACK paper liner; **Decksfracht** *f* WASSERTRANS *Ladung* deck cargo; **Deckskran** *m* WASSERTRANS *Ladung* deck crane; **Decksladung** *f* WASSERTRANS *Ladung* deck cargo; **Deckslängsbalken** *m* WASSERTRANS *Schiffbau* deck longitudinal; **Decksmann** *m* WASSERTRANS *Besatzung* deck hand; **Decksmannschaft** *f* WASSERTRANS *Besatzung* deck hands; **Decksoffizier** *m* WASSERTRANS *Besatzung* deck officer; **Decksplan** *m* WASSERTRANS *Schiffbau* deck plan; **Decksplatte** *f* WASSERTRANS *Ausrüstung* deck plate; **Decksplitt** *m* BAU blotter material; **Decksquerverband** *m* WASSERTRANS *Schiffbau* deck transverse structure; **Decksstütze** *f* WASSERTRANS *Schiffbau* deck pillar; **Decksträger** *m* WASSERTRANS *Schiffbau* deck girder; **Deckstrak** *m* WASSERTRANS *Schiffbau* deck line, sheer line; **Deckstütze** *f* WASSERTRANS stanchion; **Decksunterzug** *m* WASSERTRANS *Schiffbau* deck girder
deckungsgleich: **-e Dreiecke** *nt pl* GEOM congruent triangles
Deckungsgleichheit *f* GEOM congruence
Deck: **Deckvermögen** *nt* KUNSTSTOFF covering power, hiding power; **Deckziegel** *m* KER & GLAS cover tile
Decoder *m* COMP & DV, ELEKTRONIK, FERNSEH, KONTROLL, TELEKOM decoder
Decodieren *nt* ELEKTRONIK decoding
decodieren *vt* ELEKTRONIK, TELEKOM decode
decodieren-codieren *vt* FERNSEH decode-encode
Decodierer *m* COMP & DV, ELEKTRONIK, FERNSEH, KONTROLL, TELEKOM decoder
Decodiermatrix *f* FERNSEH decoding matrix
Decodierung *f* FERNSEH, RADIO, RAUMFAHRT, TELEKOM decoding; ~ **mit harter Entscheidung** *f* TELEKOM hard decision decoding; ~ **mit weicher Entscheidung** *f* TELEKOM soft decision decoding
Decodiervorrichtung *f* TRANS decoding device
Deconfinement-Impuls *m* KERNTECH deconfining momentum
Decyl- *pref* CHEMIE decyl; **Decylalkohol** *m* CHEMIE decanol
dediziert[1] *adj* COMP & DV dedicated
dediziert:[2] **-er Computer** *m* COMP & DV dedicated computer; **-er Kanal** *m* COMP & DV dedicated channel; **-er Modus** *m* COMP & DV dedicated mode; **-e Umgebung** *f* COMP & DV dedicated environment
Deduktion *f* COMP & DV inference, MATH deductive reasoning
deduktiv: **-e Argumentationsführung** *f* MATH deductive reasoning
DEE *abbr* (*Datenendeinrichtung*) COMP & DV, TELEKOM DTE (*data terminal equipment*)
Default-Reasoning *nt* KÜNSTL INT default reasoning
Defekt *m* ELEKTROTECH, KERNTECH, METALL defect, flaw
defekt: **-e Lettern** *f pl* DRUCK broken types
Defekt: **Defektbogenausstoß** *m* VERPACK faulty sheet ejection; **Defektelektron** *nt* FERTIG hole; **Defektstruktur** *f* METALL defect structure
definieren *vt* COMP & DV set, set up, MATH define
definiert: **-e Frequenz** *f* ELEKTRONIK discrete frequency; **nicht -e Taste** *f* COMP & DV undefined key

Definition *f* COMP & DV setup, ELEKTRONIK *Anzahl der pro Fläche unterscheidbaren Bildpunkte* definition, *Datenverarbeitung* definition, MATH definition; **Definitionstestbild** *nt* FERNSEH definition test pattern

deflagrieren *vi* CHEMIE deflagrate

Deflektor *m* CHEMTECH deflector, LUFTTRANS deflector, load hook up, NICHTFOSS ENERG deflector, RAUMFAHRT *Raumschiff* jet deflector, TELEKOM deflector; **Deflektorplatte** *f* LUFTTRANS deflector plate

Defokussierung *f* ELEKTRONIK defocusing

Defoliationsmittel *nt* CHEMIE defoliant

Defoliator *m* CHEMIE defoliant

Deformation *f* KERNTECH, KUNSTSTOFF, MASCHINEN, MECHAN, PHYS, STRAHLPHYS deformation; **Deformationsgradient** *m* PHYS deformation gradient; **Deformationsmesser** *m* MECHAN extensometer

dehnbar *adj* KUNSTSTOFF extensible, MASCHINEN tensile, MECHAN elastic, METALL ductile, PAPIER stretchable, TEXTIL stretchy

Dehnbarkeit *f* KUNSTSTOFF extensibility, MECHAN elasticity, METALL ductility, PAPIER elasticity, TEXTIL stretch

dehnen *vt* BAU strain, stretch, PAPIER stretch

Dehnfähigkeit *f* WERKPRÜF high elongation

Dehnfuge *f* BAU contraction joint, expansion joint, HEIZ & KÄLTE expansion joint

Dehngrenze *f* FERTIG proof stress, MASCHINEN limit of elasticity

Dehnschlupf *m* FERTIG *Riemen* creep

Dehnung *f* ELEKTRONIK expansion, KUNSTSTOFF elongation, strain, stretch, LABOR strain, MASCHINEN expansion, extension, MECHAN expansion, METALL elongation, strain, PAPIER elongation, stretch, PHYS elongation, strain, TELEKOM extension, WASSERTRANS strain, WERKPRÜF expansion; **Dehnungsangleicher** *m* ERDÖL *Formstück für Rohrleitungsbau* compensator; **Dehnungsausgleich** *m* MASCHINEN expansion compensation; **Dehnungsausgleicher** *m* HYDRAUL expansion joint; **Dehnungsausgleichskupplung** *f* HYDRAUL expansion coupling; **Dehnungsband** *nt* HEIZ & KÄLTE expansion loop; **Dehnungsbeanspruchung** *f* METALL tensile stress; **Dehnungsbogen** *m* HEIZ & KÄLTE expansion bend, expansion loop; **Dehnungsfilter** *nt* ELEKTRONIK expansion filter; **Dehnungsfuge** *f* BAU *Straßenbau* running joint, MASCHINEN, MECHAN expansion joint; **Dehnungsgrenze** *f* MECHAN elastic limit; **Dehnungskoeffizient** *m* BAU strain modulus, MASCHINEN expansion coefficient; **Dehnungsmeßbrücke** *f* ELEKTROTECH strain gage bridge (AmE), strain gauge bridge (BrE); **Dehnungsmesser** *m* BAU, ELEKTROTECH strain gage (AmE), strain gauge (BrE), FERTIG extensometer, GERÄT dilatometer, KUNSTSTOFF, MASCHINEN strain gage (AmE), strain gauge (BrE), MECHAN, METROL *Materialprüfung*, PAPIER extensometer, PHYS dilatometer; **Dehnungsmeßfühler** *m* ELEKTRONIK, GERÄT strain gage (AmE), strain gauge (BrE); **Dehnungsmeßstreifen** *m* ELEKTROTECH, KUNSTSTOFF, MECHAN, METROL strain gage (AmE), strain gauge (BrE); **Dehnungsrest** *m* FERTIG set; **Dehnungsriß** *m* MASCHINEN, MECHAN, WERKPRÜF expansion crack; **Dehnungsspannungsmeßgerät** *nt* PHYS strain gage (AmE), strain gauge (BrE); **Dehnungsstreifenbrücke** *f* GERÄT strain gage bridge (AmE), strain gauge bridge (BrE); **Dehnungstensor** *m* PHYS strain tensor; **Dehnungstest** *m* PHYS tensile test; **Dehnungsverbindung** *f* MECHAN expansion joint

Dehnvermögen *nt* FERTIG ductility

Dehnwechselprüfanlage *f* WERKPRÜF dynamic strain testing system

Dehydratation *f* CHEMIE, CHEMTECH dehydration

dehydratisieren *vt* CHEMIE desiccate, *einer Verbindung* dehydrate, HEIZ & KÄLTE, LEBENSMITTEL dehydrate

Dehydratisierung *f* CHEMIE, CHEMTECH, HEIZ & KÄLTE dehydration

dehydrieren *vt* CHEMIE dehydrogenate, dehydrogenize

dehydriert *adj* CHEMIE dehydrated

Dehydro-Gefrieren *nt* HEIZ & KÄLTE dehydrofreezing

Dehydrogenase *f* LEBENSMITTEL *dehydrierendes Enzym* dehydrogenase

Deich *m* BAU, NICHTFOSS ENERG, WASSERVERSORG dike (AmE), dyke (BrE)

Deichsel *f* KFZTECH *Anhänger* drawbar; **Deichselbolzen** *m* KFZTECH *Anhänger* drawbar bolt

Deinking *nt* PAPIER de-inking; ~ **durch Flotation** *m* ABFALL de-inking by flotation; **Deinkinganlage** *f* ABFALL de-inking unit

deinkt: ~**er Faserstoff** *m* PAPIER de-inked paper stock

Deiodothyroxin *nt* CHEMIE thyronine

Deka- *pref (da)* METROL deca- *(da)*

Dekadendämpfer *m* ELEKTRONIK decade attenuator; **Dekadengehäuse** *nt* LUFTTRANS decade box

Dekadenkasten *m* LUFTTRANS decade box

dekadisch: ~ **einstellbarer Kondensator** *m* ELEKTROTECH decade capacitor; ~ **einstellbarer Widerstand** *m* ELEKTROTECH decade resistor; ~ **einstellbare Selbstinduktivität** *f* ELEKTROTECH decade inductance box; ~**e Einstellung** *f* ELEKTROTECH decade box; ~**e Extinktion** *f* PHYS, STRAHLPHYS absorbance; ~**er Oszillator** *m* ELEKTRONIK decade oscillator

Deka-: **Dekaeder** *nt* GEOM decahedron; **Dekagon** *nt* GEOM decagon

dekagonal *adj* GEOM decagonal

Deka-: **Dekagramm** *nt* METROL decagram; **Dekaliter** *m* METROL decaliter (AmE), decalitre (BrE); **Dekameter** *m* METROL decameter (AmE), decametre (BrE)

Dekanter *m* CHEMTECH, UMWELTSCHMUTZ decanter

Dekantieren *nt* CHEMTECH *Vorgang*, ERDÖL, LEBENSMITTEL decantation

dekantieren *vt* CHEMIE, CHEMTECH, UMWELTSCHMUTZ decant

Dekantiergefäß *nt* CHEMTECH decantation glass, decantation vessel

Dekantierglas *nt* CHEMTECH decanting glass, *Labor* precipitation vessel

Dekapieren *nt* FERTIG pickling

dekatieren *vt* TEXTIL decatize, steam

Dekatiermaschine *f* TEXTIL decatizing machine

Dekatur *f* TEXTIL decatizing

deklarativ: ~**es Wissen** *nt* KÜNSTL INT declarative knowledge

deklarieren *vt* COMP & DV declare

Deklination *f* LUFTTRANS, NICHTFOSS ENERG, PHYS, WASSERTRANS *astronomische Navigation* declination; **Deklinationsabweichung** *f* PHYS angle of magnetic declination; **Deklinationskreis** *m* PHYS declination circle; **Deklinationsmesser** *m* PHYS declinometer; **Deklinationswinkel** *m* LUFTTRANS *Navigation* declination angle

Dekommutation *f* ELEKTRONIK *Prüfung und Entschlüsselung* decommutation

Dekommutator *m* ELEKTRONIK decommutator

Dekompressionskammer *f* ERDÖL *Tieftauchtechnik*,

WASSERTRANS decompression chamber

Dekompressionsunfall *m* KERNTECH depressurization accident

Dekontamination *f* CHEMIE, CHEMTECH decontamination; **Dekontaminationsfaktor** *m* STRAHLPHYS decontamination factor

dekontaminieren *vt* KERNTECH decontaminate

Dekontaminierung *f* CHEMIE, KERNTECH, STRAHLPHYS, UMWELTSCHUTZ decontamination; **Dekontaminierungssystem** *nt* KERNTECH decontamination system

Dekoration: ~ **bei Herstellung** *f* KER & GLAS decoration during production; **Dekorationsflachglas** *nt* KER & GLAS spandrel glass; **Dekorationslack** *m* KUNSTSTOFF decorative varnish; **Dekorationsstoff** *m* TEXTIL furnishing fabric

Dekorrelation *f* TELEKOM decorrelation

Dekorschliff *m* KER & GLAS decorative cutting

Dekrement *nt* PHYS decrement

Dekrepitationsprüfung *f* KER & GLAS decrepitation test

delaminieren *vti* KUNSTSTOFF delaminate

Delaminierung *f* KUNSTSTOFF delamination

Deleaturzeichen *nt* DRUCK deletion mark

D-Elektrode *f* PHYS *beim Zyklotron* dee

Dellinger-Schwund *m* RADIO Dellinger fade out

Delorenzit *m* KERNTECH delorenzite

Delphi-Detektor *m* TEILPHYS Delphi detector

Delphinin *nt* CHEMIE delphinin

Delta *nt* ELEKTROTECH, ERDÖL delta; ~ **x** *nt* MATH delta x; **Delta-Anpassung** *f* RADIO *Antennenanpassung* delta match; **Delta-Dreieck-Schaltung** *f* ELEKTRIZ mesh connection; **Delta-Eisen** *nt* METALL delta iron; **Deltaflügel** *m* LUFTTRANS delta wing

deltaförmig *adj* ERDÖL deltaic

Delta: **Deltametall** *nt* METALL delta metal; **Deltamodulation** *f* *(DM)* ELEKTRONIK, RAUMFAHRT *Weltraumfunk*, TELEKOM delta modulation *(DM)*; **Deltamodulation mit variablen Flanken** *f* RAUMFAHRT *Weltraumfunk* variable-slope delta modulation; **Deltaschaltung** *f* ELEKTRIZ delta connection; **Deltaschleife** *f* RADIO *Antenne* delta loop; **Delta-Sternschaltung** *f* ELEKTRIZ delta star connection; **Delta-Sternumformung** *f* ELEKTRIZ delta-to-star conversion; **Deltastrahlen** *m pl* STRAHLPHYS delta rays; **Deltastrahlung** *f* STRAHLPHYS delta rays

Demethylation *f* CHEMIE demethylation

demethylieren *vt* CHEMIE demethylate

Demineralisierung *f* CHEMTECH demineralizing

Demister *m* LUFTTRANS demister

Demodulation *f* AKUSTIK detection, COMP & DV, ELEKTRONIK, FERNSEH, PHYS, RADIO demodulation, RAUMFAHRT *Weltraumfunk* demodulation, detection, TELEKOM demodulation

Demodulator *m* AKUSTIK, COMP & DV, ELEKTRONIK, FERNSEH, PHYS, RADIO, RAUMFAHRT *Weltraumfunk*, TELEKOM demodulator; ~ **mit Bestimmung momentaner Frequenz** *m* RAUMFAHRT instantaneous frequency estimation demodulator; ~ **mit einspeisungsstabilisiertem Oszillator** *m* RAUMFAHRT *Weltraumfunk* injection-locked oscillator demodulator; ~ **mit Schwellwerterhöhung** *m* RAUMFAHRT *Weltraumfunk* threshold extension demodulator

demodulieren *vt* ELEKTRONIK, FERNSEH, RADIO, TELEKOM demodulate

demoduliert: ~**es Signal** *nt* ELEKTRONIK demodulated signal

Demontage *f* MASCHINEN disassembly, dismantling

demontierbar *adj* BAU collapsible

demontieren *vt* BAU dismantle, KERNTECH strip, MASCHINEN disassemble, dismantle, dismount, take down

Demulgator *m* MEERSCHMUTZ demulsifier, emulsion breaker, UMWELTSCHMUTZ emulsion breaker

Demulgierprodukt *nt* UMWELTSCHMUTZ demulsifying product

Demulgierung *f* CHEMTECH breaking

Demultiplexen *nt* ELEKTRONIK demultiplexing

demultiplexen *vt* ELEKTRONIK demultiplex

Demultiplexer *m* COMP & DV, ELEKTRONIK demultiplexer, TELEKOM demultiplexer, demux

Demultiplexieren *nt* TELEKOM demultiplexing

demultiplexieren *vt* TELEKOM demultiplex

Demultiplexing *nt* COMP & DV demultiplexing

Demux *m* TELEKOM demux

denaturiert: ~**er Alkohol** *m* CHEMIE denatured alcohol, methylated spirit, LEBENSMITTEL denatured alcohol

Dendrit *m* FERTIG fir tree crystal, pine crystal, *Gefüge* dendrite, METALL *Gefüge* dendrite

dendritisch *adj* FERTIG *Gefüge*, METALL dendritic

Denier *nt* TEXTIL denier

Denitrierung: ~ **des Abfalls** *f* ABFALL waste denitrification

Denitrifikation *f* UMWELTSCHMUTZ denitrification

Densimeter *nt* LABOR hydrometer

Densitometer *nt* FOTO, GERÄT, LABOR, OPTIK, PHYS densitometer

Densitometrie *f* FOTO, LABOR, OPTIK, PHYS densitometry

Dentalkeramik *f* KER & GLAS dental ceramic

Denudation *f* METALL denudation

denudiert: ~**e Zone** *f* METALL denuded zone

Depaketierer *m* TELEKOM depacketizer

Depesche *f* ELEKTROTECH cablegram

Dephlegmator[1] *m* CHEMIE *Destillation* dephlegmator

Dephlegmator:[2] **mit** ~ **behandeln** *vt* CHEMIE dephlegmate

Dephlegmiersäule *f* CHEMIE dephlegmator

Deplacement *nt* WASSERTRANS *Schiffskonstruktion* displacement

Depolarisation *f* CHEMIE, ELEKTROTECH depolarization; **Depolarisationsfeld** *nt* AUFNAHME depolarizing field

Depolarisator *m* CHEMIE depolarizer

depolarisieren *vt* CHEMIE, ELEKTROTECH, RAUMFAHRT depolarize

depolarisierend: ~**es Feld** *nt* PHYS depolarizing field

Depolarisierer *m* CHEMIE depolarizer

Depolarisierung *f* RAUMFAHRT *Weltraumfunk* depolarization; **Depolarisierungsmittel** *nt* ELEKTRIZ depolarizing agent

Depolymerisation *f* CHEMIE, KUNSTSTOFF depolymerization

Depolymerisierung *f* CHEMIE depolymerization

Deponie *f* ABFALL landfill, waste dump, waste tip, storage site, waste, KOHLEN landfill, UMWELTSCHMUTZ landfill, repository; **Deponiebetrieb** *m* ABFALL waste site operation; **Deponiegelände** *nt* ABFALL tipping site; **Deponiegut** *nt* ABFALL fill mass, waste mass; **Deponieoberfläche** *f* ABFALL operating face, working face; **Deponieschluß** *m* ABFALL waste site closure; **Deponiesickerwasserbehandlung** *f* ABFALL leachate treatment; **Deponiestandort** *m* ABFALL, MEERSCHMUTZ landfill site; **Deponietyp** *m* ABFALL landfill design, landfill type

Depression *f* WASSERTRANS *Tiefdruckgebiet* depression

Depth-First-Suchverfahren *nt* KÜNSTL INT depth-first search

Derating *nt* ELEKTROTECH derating

Derrick *m* BAU derrick; **Derrickkran** *m* BAU derrick crane, derrick, LUFTTRANS *Hubschrauber* derrick; **Derrickmast** *m* BAU derrick post

Derrin *nt* CHEMIE derrin, rotenone

Derriswurzelextrakt *m* CHEMIE derrin, rotenone

Desaminase *f* CHEMIE desaminase

desaxiert: **~e Pleuelstange** *f* KFZTECH offset connecting rod

Descrambler *m* TELEKOM descrambler

Desensibilisator *m* FOTO desensitizer

Desensibilisierung *f* FOTO, TELEKOM desensitization; **Desensibilisierungsbad** *nt* FOTO desensitizing bath

Design *nt* DRUCK, MASCHINEN design

Desinfektion *f* WASSERVERSORG disinfection; **Desinfektionsmittel** *nt* SICHERHEIT disinfectant

desinfizieren *vt* SICHERHEIT disinfect

Desintegratormühle *f* LEBENSMITTEL disintegrator

deskriptiv: **~es Modell** *nt* ERGON descriptive model

Deskriptor *m* COMP & DV descriptor

Desktop-Publishing *nt (DTP)* COMP & DV, DRUCK desktop publishing *(DTP)*

Desmotropie *f* CHEMIE desmotropy

Desodoriermittel *nt* KUNSTSTOFF deodorant

desorbieren *vt* CHEMIE desorb

Desorientiertheit *f* ERGON, METALL disorientation

Desorientierung *f* ERGON disorientation

Desorption *f* CHEMIE desorption

Desoxidation *f* CHEMIE deoxidization; **Desoxidationsmittel** *nt* CHEMIE deoxidizer, reducing agent, FERTIG scavenger

Desoxidieren *nt* CHEMIE deoxidization

Destillat *nt* ERDÖL *Raffinerie, Destillationsprodukt*, THERMOD distillate

Destillation *f* ERDÖL *Raffinerietechnik*, THERMOD distillation; **~ mittels Sonnenenergie** *f* NICHTFOSS ENERG solar distillation; **~ im Vakuum** *f* CHEMTECH vacuum distillation; **Destillationsanlage** *f* CHEMTECH still; **Destillationsapparat** *m* CHEMTECH distiller, distilling apparatus, still, LABOR still; **Destillationsbereich** *m* THERMOD distillation range; **Destillationsbetrieb** *m* CHEMTECH distillery; **Destillationsgas** *nt* CHEMTECH, THERMOD distillation gas; **Destillationsgerät** *nt* CHEMTECH distiller, distilling apparatus, still; **Destillationskolben** *m* CHEMTECH, LABOR distilling flask; **Destillationskolonne** *f* CHEMTECH distillation column, distilling column, ERDÖL *Raffinerie* distillation tower, fractionating tower, THERMOD distillation tower; **Destillationsrohr** *nt* CHEMTECH distilling tube; **Destillationsrückstand** *m* LEBENSMITTEL distillery residue; **Destillationsturm** *m* CHEMTECH distilling tower

Destillieranlage *f* CHEMTECH distillery, LABOR still, LEBENSMITTEL distillery; **Destillierapparat** *m* LABOR distillation apparatus

Destillieren *nt* THERMOD distillation

destillieren *vt* THERMOD distil

Destillierkolben *m* CHEMTECH distilling flask, THERMOD distillation flask

Destillierkolonne *f* CHEMTECH distilling tower

destilliert: **~es Wasser** *nt* KFZTECH *Batterie* distilled water

destruktiv: **~e Interferenz** *f* PHYS, WELLPHYS destructive interference

Desulfonierung *f* CHEMIE desulfonation (AmE), desulphonation (BrE)

Desulfurierung *f* CHEMIE desulfurization (AmE), desulphurization (BrE)

DESY *abbr (Deutsches Elektronensynchroton)* TEILPHYS DESY

Detail *nt* DRUCK, FERNSEH detail

detailliert: **~e Gebührenberechnung** *f* TELEKOM detailed billing

Detail: **Detailmontage** *f* DRUCK separate make-up; **Detailwiedergabe** *f* FERNSEH detail rendition

Detektion *f* TELEKOM detection; **Detektionsempfindlichkeit** *f* TELEKOM *Empfänger* detectivity; **Detektionsschwelle** *f* TELEKOM detection threshold

Detektor *m* ELEKTRIZ, ELEKTRONIK, ELEKTROTECH, KER & GLAS, KERNTECH, OPTIK, PHYS, RADIO, TELEKOM, TRANS detector; **~ für dünne Stellen** *m* KER & GLAS thin spot detector; **~ für Fahrzeugeigenschaften** *m* TRANS vehicle characteristic detector; **~ für ungeladene Teilchen** *m* KERNTECH neutral particle detector; **Detektordiode** *f* ELEKTRONIK detector diode; **Detektordiode für Schottky-Barriere** *f* ELEKTRONIK Schottky barrier detector diode; **Detektorröhre für Kurzzeitprobenentnahme** *f* SICHERHEIT detector tube for short-term sampling; **Detektorschaltung** *f* ELEKTRONIK detector circuit; **Detektorschleife** *f* TRANS detection loop; **Detektorsignal** *nt* ELEKTRONIK detector signal

Detergens *nt* ERDÖL detergent, MEERSCHMUTZ surface active agent, surfactant; **Detergensöl** *nt* KFZTECH *Schmierung* detergent oil

Detergentzusatz *m* MASCHINEN detergent additive

Determinante *f* COMP & DV, MATH determinant

deterministisch *adj* KÜNSTL INT deterministic

Detonation *f* THERMOD detonation; **Detonationsknall** *m* RAUMFAHRT *Raumschiff* boom

Detonator *m* EISENBAHN detonator

detonieren *vt* THERMOD detonate

Deuterium *nt (D)* CHEMIE deuterium *(D)*; **Deuteriumoxid** *nt (D₂O)* CHEMIE deuterium oxide *(D_2O)*

Deuteron *nt (d)* CHEMIE, PHYS, TEILPHYS deuteron *(d)*

Deutlichkeit *f* TELEKOM clarity

Deutsch: **~es Elektronensynchroton** *nt (DESY)* TEILPHYS DESY; **~es Institut für Normung** *nt (DIN)* MASCHINEN German Standards Institution; **~e Norm** *f* MASCHINEN German standard

Devastierung *f* UMWELTSCHMUTZ land degradation, land disturbance

Deviation *f* LUFTTRANS, WASSERTRANS *Kompaß* deviation; **Deviationsanzeige** *f* LUFTTRANS deviation indicator; **Deviationsgeber** *m* LUFTTRANS deviation detector; **Deviationssignal** *nt* LUFTTRANS deviation signal

Dewar-Gefäß *nt* CHEMTECH, LABOR *Isolierung* Dewar flask, THERMOD Dewar flask, Dewar vessel

Dextran *nt* CHEMIE dextran

Dextrin *nt* CHEMIE amylin, dextrin, KUNSTSTOFF, LEBENSMITTEL *Stärkeabbauprodukt* dextrin

Dextrose *f* LEBENSMITTEL dextrose, grape sugar

dezentral[1] *adj* COMP & DV distributed, TELEKOM decentralized

dezentral:[2] **~er Aufbau** *m* COMP & DV distributed architecture; **~e Datenbank** *f* COMP & DV distributed database; **~es Informationssystem** *nt* COMP & DV distributed information system; **~es Netz** *nt* COMP & DV distributed network; **~e Prozesse** *m pl* COMP & DV distributed processes; **~es System** *nt* TELEKOM decentralized system; **~er Vektorenrechner** *m* COMP & DV distributed array processor

dezentralisiert *adj* COMP & DV decentralized

Dezi- *pref (d)* METROL deci- *(d)*; **Dezibel** *nt (dB)* AKUSTIK, AUFNAHME, ELEKTRONIK *logarithmisches Dämpfungsmaß*, PHYS *Einheit der Dämpfung*, RADIO, STRAHLPHYS, UMWELTSCHMUTZ decibel *(dB)*; **Dezibel über Isotropstrahler** *nt pl (dBi)* STRAHLPHYS decibels over isotropic *(dBi)*; **Dezibelskale** *f* AUFNAHME decibel scale; **Dezigramm** *nt* METROL decigram; **Deziliter** *m (dl)* METROL deciliter (AmE), decilitre (BrE) *(dl)*

dezimal *adj* COMP & DV decimal

Dezimal- *pref* COMP & DV, ELEKTRONIK, LABOR, MATH decimal; **Dezimal-Binär-Umsetzer** *m* ELEKTRONIK, GERÄT decimal-to-binary converter; **Dezimal-Binär-Umsetzung** *f* ELEKTRONIK, LABOR decimal-to-binary conversion; **Dezimalbruch** *m* MATH decimal fraction; **Dezimalbruchentwicklung** *f* MATH decimal series; **Dezimal-Dual-Umsetzer** *m* ELEKTRONIK, GERÄT decimal-to-binary converter; **Dezimalkomma** *nt* COMP & DV, MATH decimal point; **Dezimalschreibweise** *f* COMP & DV, MATH decimal notation; **Dezimalskale** *f* GERÄT decimal scale; **Dezimalstelle** *f* COMP & DV decimal point, MATH decimal place; **Dezimalsystem** *nt* MATH decimal system; **Dezimalteiler** *m* ELEKTRONIK decade scaler; **Dezimalwaage** *f* GERÄT decimal balance; **Dezimalzahl** *f* MATH decimal

Dezimeter *m* METROL decimeter (AmE), decimetre (BrE); **Dezimeterwelle** *f* ELEKTRONIK, FERNSEH, RADIO, TELEKOM ultrahigh frequency, WELLPHYS decimetric wave, ultrahigh frequency wave

Dezineper *nt* AKUSTIK decineper

Dezi-: **Dezitonne** *f* METROL quintal (AmE); **Dezi-Verstärker** *m* ELEKTRONIK microwave amplifier; **Dezi-Verstärkerröhre** *f* ELEKTRONIK microwave amplifier tube; **Dezi-Verstärkung** *f* ELEKTRONIK microwave amplification

DFT *abbr (diskrete Fourier-Transformation)* ELEKTRONIK DFT *(discrete Fourier transform)*

DFV *abbr (Datenfernverarbeitung)* COMP & DV TP *(teleprocessing)*

DFV-Verbindung *f* COMP & DV TP connection, communication link

D-Glied *nt* REGELUNG derivative element

D-Glucosamin *nt* CHEMIE D-glucosamine

DGPS *abbr (Differential-GPS)* WASSERTRANS *Satellitennavigation* DGPS *(differential global positioning system)*

Di *abbr (Richtwirkungsindex)* AKUSTIK Di *(directivity index)*

Dia *nt* FOTO slide, transparency (AmE)

Diac *abbr (bidirektionale Triggerdiode)* ELEKTRONIK *Wechselstromdiodenschalter*, RADIO diac *(diode alternating-current switch)*

Diacetyl *nt* CHEMIE diacetyl

Diacetylen *nt* CHEMIE diacetylene

Diagenese *f* ERDÖL *Geologie*, NICHTFOSS ENERG diagenesis

diagenetisch *adj* ERDÖL *Geologie*, NICHTFOSS ENERG diagenetic

Diagnose *f* COMP & DV diagnosis; **Diagnosecode** *m* COMP & DV flag code; **Diagnoseexpertensystem** *nt* KÜNSTL INT diagnostic expert system; **Diagnosehilfe** *f* TELEKOM diagnostic aid; **Diagnoseprogramm** *nt* COMP & DV

diagnostic program; **Diagnosetest** *m* COMP & DV diagnostic test

Diagnostik *f* COMP & DV diagnostics

Diagonal- *pref* KERNTECH, KFZTECH, KONSTZEICH diagonal

diagonal[1] *adj* GEOM, KERNTECH, MATH diagonal

diagonal[2] *adv* GEOM diagonally

diagonal:[3] **~e Strebe** *f* KERNTECH diagonal member rod

Diagonale *f* MATH diagonal, WASSERTRANS diagonal line

Diagonal-: **Diagonalkreuz** *nt* KONSTZEICH diagonal cross; **Diagonalreifen** *m* KFZTECH bias ply tire (AmE), bias ply tyre (BrE), fabric-laminated thread tire (AmE), fabric-laminated thread tyre (BrE), KUNSTSTOFF cross ply tire (AmE), cross ply tyre (BrE), diagonal ply tire (AmE), diagonal ply tyre (BrE); **Diagonalschneidemaschine** *f* MECHAN angle cutter; **Diagonalstab** *m* BAU brace; **Diagonalstrebe** *f* HYDRAUL diagonal stay, KERNTECH diagonal, KFZTECH antiroll bar; **Diagonalstütze** *f* HYDRAUL *Kessel* diagonal stay; **Diagonalverband** *m* BAU diagonal bracing; **Diagonalverstrebung** *f* WASSERVERSORG *eines Schleusentors* diagonal brace

Diagramm[1] *nt* COMP & DV, MASCHINEN, TELEKOM diagram

Diagramm:[2] **~ aufnehmen** *vi* MASCHINEN take a diagram

Diagramm: **Diagrammabreißstab** *m* GERÄT chart paper tear-off bar; **Diagrammantriebsmotor** *m* GERÄT chart motor; **Diagrammstreifen** *m* GERÄT chart, continuous diagram, recording chart, strip chart; **Diagrammtransport** *m* GERÄT chart transport; **Diagrammtrommel** *f* GERÄT chart drum

Dia: **Diakasten** *m* FOTO slide box

Diakaustik *f* OPTIK diacaustic

diakaustisch *adj* OPTIK diacaustic

Dia: **Diakopieraufsatz** *m* FOTO slide copying attachment; **Diakopieren** *nt* FOTO slide copying, slide duplication; **Diakopiergerät** *nt* FOTO slide copying device

diakritisch[1] *adj* COMP & DV, DRUCK, KONSTZEICH diacritical

diakritisch:[2] **~es Zeichen** *nt* KONSTZEICH diacritical sign; **~e Zeichen** *nt pl* DRUCK diacritical marks

Dialin *nt* CHEMIE dialin, dihydronaphthalene

Diallylphthalat- *pref* KUNSTSTOFF diallylphthalate; **Diallylphthalat-Formmasse** *f* KUNSTSTOFF diallylphthalate molding compound (AmE), diallylphthalate moulding compound (BrE); **Diallylphthalat-Preßmasse** *f* KUNSTSTOFF *PDAP* diallylphthalate molding compound (AmE), diallylphthalate moulding compound (BrE)

Dialog *m* COMP & DV dialog (AmE), dialogue (BrE)

Dialogbetrieb:[1] **im ~ arbeitend** *adj* COMP & DV interactive

Dialogbetrieb[2] *m* COMP & DV conversational mode, interactive mode; **Dialogbetriebmodus** *m* COMP & DV interactive mode

Dialog: **Dialogentzerrer** *m* AUFNAHME dialog equalizer (AmE), dialogue equalizer (BrE)

dialogfähig: **~e Datenstation** *f* COMP & DV interactive terminal; **~e Grafikverarbeitung** *f* COMP & DV interactive graphics

Dialog: **Dialogfenster** *nt* COMP & DV pop-down, pop-up window; **Dialogfenstermenü** *nt* COMP & DV pop-up menu; **Dialoggerät** *nt* TELEKOM interactive terminal; **Dialogkommunikation** *f* COMP & DV conversational communication; **Dialognetz** *nt* TELEKOM interactive network

dialogorientiert *adj* KÜNSTL INT dialog-oriented (AmE), dialogue-oriented (BrE)

Dialog: Dialogspur *f* FERNSEH dialog track (AmE), dialogue track (BrE); **Dialogsystem** *nt* TELEKOM interactive system

Dialursäure *f* CHEMIE dialuric acid, hydroxybarbituric acid, tartronylurea

Dialysat *nt* CHEMIE dialyzate

Dialyse[1] *f* CHEMIE dialysis

Dialyse:[2] **durch ~ trennen** *vt* CHEMIE dialyze

dialysieren *vt* CHEMIE dialyze

dialytisch *adj* CHEMIE dialytic, dialytical

diamagnetisch[1] *adj* ELEKTRIZ, PHYS, STRAHLPHYS diamagnetic

diamagnetisch:[2] **~e Abschirmung des Atomkerns** *f* STRAHLPHYS diamagnetic shielding of the nucleus; **~e Anisotropie** *f* STRAHLPHYS diamagnetic anisotropy; **~er Stoff** *m* ELEKTRIZ diamagnetic material

Diamagnetismus *m* CHEMIE, ELEKTRIZ, ELEKTROTECH, PHYS diamagnetism, STRAHLPHYS diamagnetics, diamagnetism

Diamant:[1] **durch ~ gerissen** *adj* FERTIG *Meßoptik* diamond-scribed

Diamant[2] *m* MASCHINEN diamond, MECHAN diamond (AmE)

diamantbesetzt *adj* MECHAN jeweled (AmE), jewelled (BrE)

Diamant: **Diamantbohrmeißel** *m* ERDÖL *Bohrtechnik* diamond bit; **Diamantgitter** *nt* METALL diamond lattice; **Diamantglanz** *m* FERTIG adamantine luster (AmE), adamantine lustre (BrE)

diamanthart *adj* FERTIG adamantine

Diamant: **Diamanthohlbohrmeißel** *m* ERDÖL *Bohrtechnik* diamond core drill; **Diamantkegel** *m* FERTIG brale

Diamantkronen: **mit ~ bohren** *vt* ERDÖL *Bohrtechnik* diamond drilling

Diamant: **Diamantmarkierungsstift** *m* LABOR diamond-tipped pen; **Diamantmeißel** *m* MASCHINEN diamond nose chisel, diamond point chisel; **Diamantmörser** *m* LABOR *Schleifen* percussion mortar; **Diamantnadel** *f* AUFNAHME diamond stylus; **Diamantpaste** *f* MASCHINEN, METALL diamond paste; **Diamantpunktierung** *f* KER & GLAS diamond point engraving; **Diamantsäge** *f* MASCHINEN diamond saw; **Diamantschleifscheibe** *f* MASCHINEN diamond-grinding wheel; **Diamantschneidrad** *nt* KER & GLAS diamond-slitting wheel; **Diamantspitze** *f* BAU, MASCHINEN diamond point; **Diamantstahl** *m* MECHAN carbon steel; **Diamantwerkzeug** *nt* MECHAN diamond tool

diametral *adj* GEOM diametric, diametrical; **~ entgegengesetzt** *adj* GEOM diametrically opposed

Diametral-Pitch *m (DP)* MASCHINEN diametral pitch *(DP)*

diametrisch: **~e Projektion** *f* KONSTZEICH diametric projection

Diamid *nt* CHEMIE diamide, diazane, hydrazine

Diamin *nt* CHEMIE diamine, diazane, hydrazine

Diaminodiphenylmethan *nt* KUNSTSTOFF diaminodiphenylmethane

Diamontriffelung *f* WASSERVERSORG diamond riffle

Diaper *m* TEXTIL diaper

Diaphon *nt* WASSERTRANS *Navigation* diaphone

Diaphragmapumpe *f* WASSERVERSORG diaphragm pump

Diapir *m* ERDÖL *Geologie* diapir

Dia: **Diapositiv** *nt* FOTO slide, transparency (AmE); **Diapositivabtaster** *m* FERNSEH slide scanner; **Diapositivaufnahme** *f* FERNSEH slide pick-up; **Diapro-**

jektor *m* FOTO slide projector; **Diarähmchen** *nt* FOTO slide holder; **Diarahmung** *f* FOTO slide mounting

Diarsenat *nt* CHEMIE diarsenate, pyroarsenate;

Diastase *f* LEBENSMITTEL diastase

Diastereomer *nt* CHEMIE diastereomer, epimer

Diät *f* LEBENSMITTEL diet

diathermisch *adj* THERMOD diathermanous, diathermic

diatonisch: **~er Halbton** *m* AKUSTIK diatonic semitone; **~e Tonleiter** *f* AKUSTIK diatonic scale, gamut; **~er Vierklang** *m* AKUSTIK diatonic tetrachord

Diät: **Diätsalz** *nt* LEBENSMITTEL salt substitute; **Diätzucker** *m* LEBENSMITTEL dietary sugar

Dia: **Diavorlage** *f* KONSTZEICH original for slides; **Diawechsler** *m* FOTO slide changer

Diazan *nt* CHEMIE diazane, hydrazine

Diazo- *pref* CHEMIE *Diazoverbindung* diazo; **Diazobenzol** *nt* CHEMIE diazobenzene

Diazoessig- *pref* CHEMIE diazoacetic

Diazo-: **Diazoimid** *nt* CHEMIE diazoimide, hydrogen azide

Diazol *nt* CHEMIE diazole

Diazonium- *pref* CHEMIE diazonium

Diazo-: **Diazoschicht** *f* DRUCK diazo coating

diazotieren *vt* CHEMIE diazotize

Dibenzanthracen *nt* CHEMIE dibenzanthracene, naphthophenanthrene

Dibenzoparadiazin *nt* CHEMIE dibenzopyrazine, phenazine

Dibenzopyran *nt* CHEMIE xanthene

Dibenzopyrazin *nt* CHEMIE dibenzopyrazine, phenazine

Dibenzopyron *nt* CHEMIE xanthone

Dibenzopyrrol *nt* CHEMIE carbazole

Dibenzoyl- *pref* CHEMIE dibenzoyl

Dibenzylamin *nt* CHEMIE dibenzylamine

Dibrom- *pref* CHEMIE dibromo; **Dibrombenzol** *nt* CHEMIE dibromobenzene; **Dibromhydrin** *nt* CHEMIE dibromohydrin

Dibutylphthalat *nt* KUNSTSTOFF dibutylphthalate

Dichlor- *pref* CHEMIE dichloro; **Dichloraceton** *nt* CHEMIE dichloroacetone; **Dichlorbenzol** *nt* CHEMIE dichlorobenzene; **Dichlordiphenyltrichlorproäthan** *nt (DDT)* CHEMIE dichlordiphenyltrichlorproethane *(DDT)*

Dichloressig- *pref* CHEMIE dichloroacetic

Dichlorid *nt* CHEMIE bichloride, dichloride

Dichroismus *m* CHEMIE dicroism, PHYS dichroism

dichroitisch[1] *adj* FOTO, PHYS, TELEKOM dichroic

dichroitisch:[2] **~er Schleier** *m* FOTO dichroic fog; **~er Spiegel** *m* OPTIK dichroic mirror

Dichromat *nt* CHEMIE bichromate, dichromate

Dicht- *pref* FERTIG sealing, MASCHINEN packing, sealing

dicht[1] *adj* ERDÖL *Geologie* impervious; **~ angeholt** *adj* WASSERTRANS *Segeln* close-hauled; **~ gepackt** *adj* ANSTRICH closely-packed

dicht:[2] **~ am Wind** *adv* WASSERTRANS *Segeln* close-hauled

dicht:[3] **~es Bohrloch** *nt* ERDÖL tight hole; **~es Erz** *nt* KOHLEN compact ore

Dichte *f* AKUSTIK optical density, BAU, CHEMIE, COMP & DV, ERDÖL, KOHLEN, KUNSTSTOFF, MECHAN, PHYS density, STRAHLPHYS, TEXTIL density, specific gravity; **~ der freien Elektronen** *f* STRAHLPHYS free-electron density; **~ der kinetischen Energie** *f* AKUSTIK kinetic energy density; **Dichteänderung** *f* STRÖMPHYS density variation; **Dichtefühler** *m* GERÄT density probe; **Dichtelog** *nt* ERDÖL *Bohrlochmessung* density log; **Dichtemesser** *m* LABOR, METROL densimeter, PHYS densimeter, viscosimeter; **Dichtemeßfühler** *m* GERÄT density probe; **Dichtemeßgerät** *nt* METROL densime-ter, PHYS densimeter, gravimeter; **Dichtemessung** *f* GERÄT densimetry, density measurement, LABOR density measurement, LEBENSMITTEL, METROL densimetry, PHYS densimetry, density measurement; **Dichtemodifikator** *m* LEBENSMITTEL density modifier; **Dichtemodulation** *f* ELEKTRONIK *Mikrowellen* density modulation

Dichten *nt* BAU stopping

dichten *vt* BAU stop

Dichte: **Dichtepegel** *m* AKUSTIK density level; **Dichte-verhältnis** *nt* ERDÖL specific gravity, KOHLEN relative density; **Dichtewaage** *f* GERÄT density balance

Dichtfilz *m* MASCHINEN packing felt

Dichtfläche *f* FERTIG *Kunststoffinstallationen*, KER & GLAS, MASCHINEN sealing surface

Dichtgas *nt* KERNTECH seal gas

dichtgelagert: **~er Kies** *m* BAU tight gravel

dichtgepackt: **~es Gitter** *nt* METALL close-packed lattice

Dichtheit *f* FERTIG *Kunststoffinstallationen* leakproof closure, KERNTECH leak tightness; **Dichtheitsprüfung** *f* KERNTECH leak test

dichtholen *vt* WASSERTRANS *Tauwerk* set taut

Dichtigkeit *f* KOHLEN density, MASCHINEN tightness, NICHTFOSS ENERG solidity, SICHERHEIT tightness; **Dichtigkeitsprüfung** *f* KERNTECH leak test; **Dichtig-keitstest** *m (DT)* ERDÖL *Bohrtechnik, Flüssigkeiten, Gase* leak-off test *(LOT)*

Dicht-: **Dichtkante** *f* KER & GLAS sealing edge; **Dichtlippe** *f* MASCHINEN sealing lip; **Dichtmanschette** *f* MASCHI-NEN cup; **Dichtmasse** *f* CHEMIE, KUNSTSTOFF sealant; **Dichtmaterial** *nt* MASCHINEN packing material; **Dicht-mittel** *nt* ANSTRICH, KER & GLAS, KFZTECH *Karosserie* sealant; **Dichtnut** *f* MASCHINEN sealing groove; **Dicht-prüfung** *f* BAU density test; **Dichtring** *m* KFZTECH sealing ring, MASCHINEN packing ring, sealing ring, MECHAN gasket, PAPIER sealing ring; **Dichtscheibe** *f* MASCHINEN gasket; **Dichtschweißen** *nt* FERTIG, caul-king; **Dichtstoff** *m* HEIZ & KÄLTE sealant; **Dichtstreifen** *m* VERPACK band sealer

Dichtung *f* BAU *zwischen beweglichen Teilen* packing, ELEKTRIZ seal, ERDÖL sealing, seal, FERTIG gasket, *Kunststoffinstallationen* gasket, seal, KER & GLAS sea-ling, seal, KERNTECH packing seal, KFZTECH gasket, LABOR seal, MASCHINEN gasket, jointing, seal, ME-CHAN gasket, packing, VERPACK, WASSERTRANS *Schiffbau* seal; **~ durch luftleeren Raum** *f* VERPACK chamber-type vacuum sealing; **Dichtungsbahn** *f* AB-FALL liner sheet; **Dichtungseinheit** *f* KERNTECH seal unit; **Dichtungsgraben** *m* BAU cutoff ditch; **Dich-tungsgummiring** *m* BAU washer; **Dichtungsmanschette** *f* MASCHINEN cup, MECHAN gasket; **Dichtungsmasse** *f* BAU sealing compound; **Dichtungsmaterial** *nt* KERNTECH sealing material; **Dichtungsmittel** *nt* BAU *zur Nachbehandlung* curing compound; **Dichtungsmontage** *f* KERNTECH seal as-sembly; **Dichtungsring** *m* FERTIG toroidal ring, washer, KERNTECH joint ring, MASCHINEN packing ring; **Dichtungsscheibe** *f* FERTIG packing washer, ME-CHAN gasket; **Dichtungsschleier** *m* WASSERVERSORG *eines Wehres* cutoff wall; **Dichtungsschweißnaht** *f* KERNTECH sealing weld; **Dichtungsstutzen** *m* WASSER-TRANS gland; **Dichtungswand** *f* ABFALL slurry wall; **Dichtungszange** *f* MASCHINEN sealing pliers

Dicht-: **Dichtwerkstoff** *m* FERTIG *Kunststoffinstallatio-nen* sealing material

Dick- *pref* FERTIG thick

dick[1] *adj* KER & GLAS *Schulter, Boden, Ecke eines Behäl-ters* heavy; **sehr ~ umhüllt** *adj* FERTIG *Elektrode* shielded

dick:[2] **~e Blase** *f* KER & GLAS heavy seed; **~e Platte** *f* KER & GLAS heavy panel

Dick-: **Dickdruckpapier** *nt* PAPIER bulking paper

Dicke *f* ANSTRICH thickness, DRUCK set, set width, width, KUNSTSTOFF thickness, MASCHINEN gage (AmE), gauge (BrE), MECHAN thickness, PAPIER thickness, *des Papiers* caliper (AmE), calliper (BrE); **~ des Luftschraubenblattes** *f* LUFTTRANS *Hubschrauber* blade depth; **~ des Ziehbalkens** *f* KER & GLAS depth of the drawbar; **Dickenabnahme** *f* FERTIG *Walzen* reduc-tion; **Dickenlehre** *f* GERÄT thickness gage (AmE), thickness gauge (BrE); **Dickenmeßeinrichtung** *f* GE-RÄT thickness gage (AmE), thickness gauge (BrE); **Dickenmesser** *m* KUNSTSTOFF, PAPIER thickness gage (AmE), thickness gauge (BrE); **Dickenmeßgerät mit Gammastrahlen** *nt* GERÄT gamma thickness meter; **Dickenmeßlehre** *f* METROL caliper (AmE), calliper (BrE); **Dickensensor** *m* GERÄT thickness gage (AmE), thickness gauge (BrE); **Dickenverhältnis** *nt* LUFT-TRANS thickness ratio; **Dickenverlust** *m* AUFNAHME, FERNSEH thickness loss

Dick-: **Dickfilmschaltung** *f* PHYS printed circuit

dickflüssig *adj* FERTIG viscid

Dickflüssigkeit *f* FERTIG viscidity, LEBENSMITTEL ropi-ness

Dickoxid *nt* ELEKTRONIK thick oxide; **Dickoxid-Metall-gate-MOS-Schaltung** *f* ELEKTRONIK thick oxide metal-gate MOS circuit

Dickschicht *f* ELEKTRONIK, RAUMFAHRT thick film; **Dickschichtbauelement** *nt* ELEKTRONIK thick film de-vice; **Dickschichthybridschaltung** *f* ELEKTRONIK thick film hybrid circuit; **Dickschichtkondensator** *m* ELEK-TRONIK thick film capacitor; **Dickschichtleiter** *m* ELEKTRONIK thick film conductor; **Dickschichtmate-rial** *nt* ELEKTRONIK thick film material; **Dickschichttechnik** *f* ELEKTRONIK, RAUMFAHRT *Raumschiff* thick film technology; **Dickschichtwider-stand** *m* ELEKTRONIK thick film resistor

Dickspiegelglas *nt* KER & GLAS thick polished plate glass

Dicktafelglas *nt* KER & GLAS crystal sheet glass (AmE), thick sheet glass (BrE)

Dickten- *pref* DRUCK width, MASCHINEN thickness, METROL feeler; **Dickenhobelmaschine** *f* MASCHINEN planing and thicknessing machine, thicknessing ma-chine; **Dicktenhobeln** *nt* MASCHINEN thicknessing; **Dicktenlehre** *f* METROL feeler gage (AmE), feeler gauge (BrE); **Dicktenschablone** *f* METROL feeler gage (AmE), feeler gauge (BrE); **Dicktentabelle** *f* DRUCK width table

Dicyan *nt* CHEMIE cyanogen

Didotsystem *nt* DRUCK Didot system

Didymium *nt* CHEMIE didymium

Diebstahl *m* SICHERHEIT theft; **Diebstahlalarmanlage** *f* SICHERHEIT theft alarm installation

diebstahlsicher *adj* VERPACK pilfer-proof

Diebstahl: **Diebstahlssicherung** *f* COMP & DV lock; **Diebstahlsicherung mit Trickschaltung** *f* KFZTECH an-titheft ignition lock, lock; **Diebstahlverhütung** *f* SICHERHEIT theft prevention device

Dieldrin *nt* CHEMIE, LEBENSMITTEL *Insektizid* dieldrin

Diele *f* BAU plank

Dielektrikum *nt* ELEKTRIZ, ELEKTROTECH, PHYS, RADIO,

TELEKOM dielectric; ~ mit Verlust *nt* ELEKTRIZ lossy dielectric

dielektrisch[1] *adj* CHEMIE, ELEKTRIZ, ELEKTROTECH, MASCHINEN, PHYS, RADIO, RAUMFAHRT, TELEKOM dielectric

dielektrisch:[2] ~e Absorption *f* ELEKTROTECH dielectric absorption; ~es Anschwellen *nt* KERNTECH dielectric swelling; ~e Antenne *f* RAUMFAHRT *Weltraumfunk*, TELEKOM dielectric antenna; ~er Durchbruch *m* ELEKTRIZ dielectric breakdown; ~e Eigenschaften *f pl* ELEKTRIZ dielectric properties; ~e Erwärmung *f* ELEKTRIZ, ELEKTROTECH, HEIZ & KÄLTE, KUNSTSTOFF dielectric heating; ~e Hysterese *f* ELEKTRIZ, ELEKTROTECH dielectric hysteresis; ~e Isolierung *f* ELEKTROTECH dielectric isolation; ~e Ladung *f* TELEKOM dielectric charge; ~e Leitfähigkeit *f* RAUMFAHRT permittivity; ~es Medium *nt* ELEKTROTECH dielectric medium; ~e Polarisation *f* ELEKTROTECH dielectric polarization; ~e Prüfung *f* ELEKTROTECH dielectric test; ~es Resonanzfilter *nt* RAUMFAHRT *Weltraumfunk* dielectric resonator filter; ~er Resonator *m* RAUMFAHRT, TELEKOM dielectric resonator; ~e Stärke *f* ELEKTRIZ, ELEKTROTECH dielectric strength; ~er Stoff *m* ELEKTROTECH dielectric material; ~e Suszeptibilität *f* ELEKTRIZ dielectric susceptibility; ~er Verlust *m* ELEKTRIZ, ELEKTROTECH, PHYS dielectric loss; ~er Verlustwinkel *m* ELEKTRIZ dielectric loss angle

Dielektrizität *f* ELEKTROTECH dielectricity; **Dielektrizitätskonstante** *f* ELEKTRIZ permittivity, relative permittivity, ELEKTROTECH dielectric constant, permittivity, FERNSEH specific inductive capacity, KUNSTSTOFF dielectric constant, permittivity, PHYS, RADIO, TELEKOM permittivity; **Dielektrizitätskonstante des Vakuums** *f* ELEKTROTECH, PHYS permittivity of free space; **Dielektrizitätskonstante der Luft** *f* ELEKTROTECH permittivity of air; **Dielektrizitätszahl** *f* ELEKTROTECH, PHYS relative permittivity

Dielektronen-Spektrometer: ~ mit hoher Akzeptanz *nt (HADES)* TEILPHYS high acceptance di-electron spectrometer *(HADES)*

dielen *vt* BAU floor

Dielung *f* BAU flooring, planking

Dien *nt* CHEMIE diene

Dienst:[1] außer ~ gestellt *adj* WASSERTRANS *Schiff* decommissioned; in ~ befindlich *adj* WASSERTRANS *Schiff* in commission

Dienst[2] *m* TELEKOM service; ~ zum Grundtarif *m* TELEKOM basic rate service; ~ unterer Ebene *m* TELEKOM lower level service

Dienst:[3] in ~ stellen *vt* WASSERTRANS *Schiff* commission

Dienst: **Dienstanbieter** *m* TELEKOM service provider; **Dienstanforderung** *f* TELEKOM request for service

diensteintegrierend: ~es digitales Breitbandnetz *nt* TELEKOM wideband integrated services digital network; ~e Selbstwählnebenstelle *f* TELEKOM integrated services PABX; ~e Vermittlungsstelle *f* TELEKOM integrated services exchange

Dienst: **Diensterbringer** *m* TELEKOM service provider; **Dienstewechsel** *m* TELEKOM swap; **Dienstgipfelhöhe** *f* LUFTTRANS service ceiling; **Dienstgüte** *f* TELEKOM grade of service

diensthabend: ~er Operator *m* KERNTECH on shift operator

dienstintegrierend: ~es Digitalnetz *nt* TELEKOM integrated service digital network

Dienst: **Dienstleistungsmarke** *f* PATENT service mark;

Dienstleitung *f* TELEKOM order wire, traffic circuit; **Dienstmerkmal** *nt* TELEKOM *ISDN* facility; **Dienstpersonal** *nt* KERNTECH service staff; **Dienstprogramm** *nt* COMP & DV service program, utility program; **Dienstschicht** *f* TELEKOM service layer; **Dienstunterbrechung** *f* TELEKOM service disruption; **Dienstzeit** *f* TELEKOM service time

Diesel[1] *m* ERDÖL diesel fuel

Diesel:[2] auf ~ umstellen *vt* KFZTECH convert to diesel

Diesel: **Dieselaggregat** *nt* ELEKTROTECH diesel-driven generating set

dieselbetrieben: ~es Notstromaggregat *nt* KERNTECH diesel generator standby power plant

dieselelektrisch: ~es Kraftwerk *nt* ELEKTROTECH diesel electric power station; ~e Lokomotive *f* EISENBAHN diesel electric locomotive; ~er Motor *m* KFZTECH diesel electric engine; ~e Rangierkleinlokomotive *f* EISENBAHN diesel-electric shunting motor tractor; ~er Triebwagen *m* EISENBAHN diesel electric railcar

Diesel: **Dieselelektroantrieb** *m* KFZTECH diesel electric drive; **Dieselhammer** *m* KOHLEN diesel hammer; **Dieselhorst-Martin-Kabel** *nt* ELEKTROTECH multiple-twin quad

dieselhydraulisch: ~e Lokomotive *f* EISENBAHN diesel hydraulic locomotive; ~er Motor *m* MASCHINEN diesel hydraulic engine

Diesel: **Dieselkraftstoff** *m* ERDÖL diesel fuel, KFZTECH diesel fuel, fuel; **Dieselkraftwerk** *nt* ELEKTROTECH diesel electric power station; **Diesellokomotive** *f* EISENBAHN diesel locomotive; **Dieselmannschaftswagen** *m* EISENBAHN diesel generator unit crew car; **Dieselmotor** *m* KFZTECH, MASCHINEN compression-ignition engine, diesel engine, WASSERTRANS diesel engine

Dieselmotor: mit ~ *adj* MASCHINEN diesel-powered

Diesel: **Dieselmotor mit indirekter Einspritzung** *m* KFZTECH indirect injection diesel engine; **Dieselmotor in Kreuzkopfbauart** *m* WASSERTRANS crosshead engine; **Dieselöl** *nt* EISENBAHN diesel oil, KFZTECH diesel fuel, diesel oil; **Dieseltriebwagenzug** *m* EISENBAHN diesel motorcoach

diesig *adj* WASSERTRANS *Wetter* hazy

Diesigkeit *f* WASSERTRANS haze

Diethen *nt* CHEMIE bivinyl

Diethylen *nt* CHEMIE bivinyl, diethene

Diethylendiamin *nt* CHEMIE diethylenediamine, piperazine

Differential *nt* AUFNAHME, ELEKTRIZ, ELEKTRONIK, ELEKTROTECH, FERNSEH, KFZTECH, KUNSTSTOFF, LUFTTRANS, MASCHINEN differential, MATH differential derivative, differential coefficient, differential, MECHAN, THERMOD differential; ~ mit regelbarem Schlupf *nt* MECHAN controlled slip differential

differential: ~es Magnetometer *nt* ELEKTRIZ differential magnetometer

Differential: **Differential-Amperemeter** *nt* ELEKTRIZ differential ammeter; **Differentialbetrieb** *m* ELEKTRONIK differential mode; **Differentialbremsung** *f* LUFTTRANS differential braking

differentialerregt: ~er Doppelschlußgenerator *m* ELEKTRIZ differentially excited compound generator

Differential: **Differentialflaschenzug** *m* KERNTECH differential chain block, MECHAN differential pulley, differential chain block; **Differential-Galvanometer** *nt* ELEKTROTECH differential galvanometer; **Differentialgehäuse** *nt* KFZTECH differential case;

Differentialgetriebe *nt* KFZTECH differential, MASCHINEN differential gear; **Differentialgewinn** *m* FERNSEH differential gain; **Differentialgleichung** *f* MATH differential equation; **Differential-GPS** *f* *(DGPS)* WASSERTRANS differential global positioning system *(DGPS)*; **Differential-Kalorimeter** *nt* THERMOD differential scanning calorimeter; **Differential-Kalorimetrie** *f* THERMOD differential scanning calorimetry; **Differentialkondensator** *m* ELEKTROTECH differential capacitor; **Differentialmikrofon** *nt* AUFNAHME differential microphone; **Differentialphase** *f* FERNSEH differential phase; **Differentialquotient** *m* MATH differential coefficient; **Differentialrechnung** *f* MATH differential calculus; **Differentialrelais** *nt* ELEKTRIZ, ELEKTROTECH differential relay; **Differential-Scanningkalorimeter** *nt* THERMOD differential scanning calorimeter; **Differential-Scanningkalorimetrie** *f* KUNSTSTOFF, THERMOD differential scanning calorimetry; **Differentialschraube** *f* MASCHINEN compound screw, differential screw; **Differentialschutzrelais** *nt* ELEKTRIZ differential protection relay; **Differentialspannung** *f* ELEKTROTECH differential voltage; **Differentialsperre** *f* KFZTECH *Triebstrang* differential lock; **Differentialspule** *f* ELEKTRIZ differential coil; **Differentialsteuerung** *f* *(PID-Steuerung)* ELEKTRIZ derivative control; **Differentialteilen** *nt* MASCHINEN differential indexing; **Differentialthermoanalyse** *f* *(DTA)* KUNSTSTOFF, THERMOD, UMWELTSCHMUTZ differential thermal analysis *(DTA)*; **Differentialtransducer** *m* ELEKTROTECH differential transducer; **Differentialtransformator** *m* ELEKTRIZ, REGELUNG differential transformer; **Differentialverhältnis** *nt* KFZTECH differential ratio; **Differentialverstärker** *m* ELEKTRONIK, MECHAN differential amplifier; **Differentialverzögerung** *f* ELEKTRONIK differential delay; **Differentialwandler** *m* ELEKTROTECH differential transducer; **Differentialwelle** *f* KFZTECH differential shaft; **Differentialwicklung** *f* ELEKTROTECH differential winding; **Differentialwirkung** *f* LUFTTRANS differential effect; **Differentialzeit** *f* ELEKTRONIK differential time; **Differentialzwischenrad** *nt* KFZTECH differential pinion

differentiell: **~e Modendämpfung** *f* OPTIK, TELEKOM differential mode attenuation; **~e Modenverzögerung** *f* OPTIK differential mode delay; **~e Phase** *f* ELEKTRONIK *Fernsehen, Radio* differential phase; **~e Quantenausbeute** *f* TELEKOM differential quantum efficiency; **~er Quantenwirkungsgrad** *m* OPTIK, TELEKOM differential quantum efficiency

Differenz *f* MATH difference

Differenzdruck *m* ERDÖL *Meßtechnik* differential pressure, HEIZ & KÄLTE differential pressure, pressure differential, LABOR, MECHAN, NICHTFOSS ENERG differential pressure; **Differenzdruck-Durchflußmesser** *m* GERÄT differential pressure flowmeter; **Differenzdruckhöhe** *f* NICHTFOSS ENERG differential head; **Differenzdruckmesser** *m* MECHAN differential pressure gage (AmE), differential pressure gauge (BrE); **Differenzdruck-Meßumformer** *m* GERÄT differential pressure transducer, differential head pressure transducer; **Differenzdruck-Meßwandler** *m* GERÄT differential pressure transducer; **Differenzdruck-Meßzelle** *f* GERÄT differential pressure cell; **Differenzdruckwandler** *m* GERÄT differential pressure transducer

Differenz: **Differenzeingang** *m* ELEKTRONIK *am Verstär-*

ker differential input; **Differenzierbeiwert** *m* REGELUNG derivative action coefficient; **Differenzieren** *nt* MATH differentiation

differenzieren *vt* MATH differentiate

differenzierend: **~es Glied** *nt* REGELUNG derivative element; **~e Regelung** *f* REGELUNG derivative control; **~es Verhalten** *nt* REGELUNG derivative action

Differenz: **Differenzierer** *m* REGELUNG derivative unit; **Differenzierschaltung** *f* ELEKTRONIK differentiating circuit

differenziert: **~es Signal** *nt* ELEKTRONIK differentiated signal

Differenzierung: **~ einer impliziten Funktion** *f* MATH implicit differentiation

Differenz: **Differenzierzeit** *f* REGELUNG derivative action time; **Differenzkanal** *m* AUFNAHME difference channel; **Differenzkomparator** *m* ELEKTRONIK differential comparator; **Differenzmodulation** *f* ELEKTRONIK differential modulation; **Differenznote** *f* AUFNAHME difference note; **Differenz-Pulscodemodulation** *f* *(DPCM)* ELEKTRONIK differential pulse code modulation *(DPCM)*; **Differenzsignal** *nt* ELEKTRONIK difference signal, differential signal, differential mode signal; **Differenzsignalquelle** *f* ELEKTRONIK differential signal source; **Differenzspannungsmeßgerät** *nt* ELEKTRIZ differential voltmeter; **Differenztemperatur** *f* ERDÖL *Meßtechnik* differential temperature; **Differenzthermoanalyse** *f* UMWELTSCHMUTZ differential thermal analysis; **Differenzthermoelement** *nt* THERMOD differential thermocouple; **Differenzton** *m* AKUSTIK difference tone, RADIO difference frequency; **Differenzverstärker** *m* ELEKTRONIK differential amplifier, instrumentation amplifier, RADIO, TELEKOM differential amplifier; **Differenzverstärkung** *f* ELEKTRONIK differential gain

Diffraktion *f* ELEKTROTECH, TELEKOM diffraction; **Diffraktionstechnik** *f* ERDÖL, PHYS *Lichtwellen* diffractometry

diffundiert: **~er Emitter-Kollektor-Transistor** *m* ELEKTRONIK diffused emitter-collector transistor; **~e Schicht** *f* ELEKTRONIK diffused layer; **~er Übergang** *m* ELEKTRONIK *Halbleiter* diffused junction

diffus: **~er Nebel** *m* RAUMFAHRT diffuse nebula; **~e Reflexion** *f* STRAHLPHYS diffuse reflection; **~er Schallpegel** *m* AKUSTIK diffuse sound level; **~e Strahlung** *f* NICHTFOSS ENERG, RAUMFAHRT diffuse radiation

Diffusion *f* BAU, CHEMIE *von Flüssigkeiten*, CHEMTECH, ELEKTRIZ, ELEKTRONIK, KERNTECH, KOHLEN, MASCHINEN, PHYS, RADIO, UMWELTSCHMUTZ diffusion; **~ im Magnetfeld** *f* KERNTECH diffusion across the magnetic field; **Diffusionsapparat** *m* CHEMTECH diffusion apparatus, diffusion cell, *Lebensmittel* diffuser; **Diffusionsdotierung** *f* ELEKTRONIK diffusion doping; **Diffusionsfehlerstelle** *f* ELEKTRONIK diffusion defect; **Diffusionsfläche** *f* HEIZ & KÄLTE diffusion area; **Diffusionsfotodiode** *f* ELEKTRONIK diffused photodiode; **Diffusionsgalvanisierung** *f* ANSTRICH diffused plating; **Diffusionsglühen** *nt* CHEMTECH diffusion annealing; **Diffusionskern** *m* KERNTECH diffusion kernel; **Diffusionskoeffizient** *m* *(D)* ELEKTRONIK, PHYS, RADIO diffusion coefficient *(D)*; **Diffusionslänge** *f* ELEKTRONIK diffusion length, KERNTECH diffusion length

diffusionslegiert: **~er Transistor** *m* ELEKTRONIK *Legierung kombiniert mit Diffusion* diffused alloy transistor

diffusionslos: **~e Rückwirkung** *f* METALL diffusionless reaction

Diffusion: **Diffusionsmethode** *f* KERNTECH diffuse scattering method; **Diffusionsofen** *m* ELEKTRONIK diffusion oven; **Diffusionspumpe** *f* MASCHINEN, PHYS diffusion pump; **Diffusionsstrom** *m* ELEKTRIZ diffusion current; **Diffusionswiderstand** *m* LUFTTRANS *Luftfahrzeug* spray drag; **Diffusionszelle** *f* CHEMTECH diffusion cell

Diffusor *m* NICHTFOSS ENERG, RAUMFAHRT *für gasförmigen Sauerstoff*, TELEKOM diffuser, WASSERVERSORG volute chamber; *~* **für Auflichtmessung** *m* FOTO diffuser for incident measurement

Diffusverstärker *m* FERNSEH matting amplifier

Digital- *pref* AUFNAHME, COMP & DV, ELEKTRONIK, FERNSEH, LABOR, TELEKOM digital

digital[1] *adj* AUFNAHME, COMP & DV, ELEKTRIZ, ELEKTRONIK, FERNSEH, LABOR, PHYS, RADIO, RAUMFAHRT, TELEKOM digital

digital:[2] **~er Addierer** *m* ELEKTRONIK digital adder; **~es angepaßtes Filter** *nt* ELEKTRONIK digital-matched filter; **~e Anzeige** *f* ELEKTRIZ, GERÄT digital readout; **~e Audiocassette** *f* AUFNAHME digital audio tape cassette; **~e Auffüllung** *f* TELEKOM digital filling; **~e Aufzeichnung** *f* AUFNAHME, FERNSEH, TELEKOM digital recording; **~es Aufzeichnungsgerät** *nt* KERNTECH digital recorder; **~es Ausgabesignal** *nt* ELEKTRONIK digital output signal; **~es Befehlszeichen** *nt* TELEKOM DCS, digital command signal; **~e Bildverarbeitung** *f* ELEKTRONIK digital image processing; **~e CD** *f* OPTIK digital optical disc (BrE), digital optical disk (AmE); **~ codierte Videoplatte** *f* OPTIK digitally-encoded videodisc (BrE), digitally-encoded videodisk (AmE); **~e Codierung** *f* TELEKOM digital coding; **~er Computer** *m* COMP & DV digital computer; **~es Computersystem** *nt* KERNTECH digital process computer system; **~es Dämpfungsglied** *nt* ELEKTRONIK digital attenuator; **~e Darstellung** *f* COMP & DV, ELEKTRONIK digital representation; **~e Datenfernverarbeitung** *f* COMP & DV digital communications; **~es Drehzahlmeßgerät** *nt* GERÄT counter; **~es Eingangssignal** *nt* ELEKTRONIK, REGELUNG digital input signal; **~er Fernseher** *m* FERNSEH digital TV receiver; **~es Filtern** *nt* COMP & DV, ELEKTRONIK digital filtering; **~e Filterung** *f* TELEKOM digital filtering; **~er Flugdatenschreiber** *m* LUFTTRANS digital flight data recorder; **~er Frequenzzähler** *m* GERÄT counter; **~es Gerät** *nt* ELEKTRONIK digital device; **~er Halbbilderzeuger** *m* FERNSEH digital framer; **~e Hauptvermittlungstelle** *f* TELEKOM DMNSC, digital main network switching center (AmE), digital main network switching centre (BrE); **~e Hierarchie** *f* TELEKOM digital hierarchy; **~e Impulsfolge** *f* TELEKOM digital pulse stream; **~es Instrument** *nt* ELEKTRIZ digital instrument; **~e Integration** *f* ELEKTRONIK digital integration; **~es Integrierglied** *nt* ELEKTRONIK digital integrator; **~e integrierte Schaltung** *f* ELEKTRONIK digital-integrated circuit; **~er Kennungsrahmen** *m* TELEKOM digital identification frame; **~es Koppelelement** *nt* TELEKOM digital switching element; **~e Koppelmatrix** *f* TELEKOM digital switching matrix; **~es Koppelvielfach** *nt* TELEKOM digital switching matrix; **~e Leitung** *f* TELEKOM digital circuit; **~e Logik** *f* ELEKTRONIK *Schaltalgebra* digital logic; **~es Meßgerät** *nt* GERÄT digital measuring instrument; **~es Meßinstrument** *nt* GERÄT digital measuring instrument, METROL digital readout measuring instrument; **~er Meßschritt** *m* REGELUNG digital measuring step; **~er Meßwert** *m* GERÄT digital reading; **~e Modulation** *f* ELEKTRONIK, PHYS, TELEKOM digital modulation; **~e Momentanfrequenzmessung** *f* ELEKTRONIK digital instantaneous frequency measurement; **~es Multimeter** *nt* ELEKTROTECH digital multimeter; **~es Multiplexverfahren** *nt* ELEKTRONIK digital multiplexing; **~e Multiplikation** *f* ELEKTRONIK digital multiplication; **~er Multiplizierer** *m* ELEKTRONIK digital multiplier; **~e optische Platte** *f* COMP & DV digital optical disk; **~e Phasenmodulation** *f* COMP & DV, TELEKOM digital phase modulation; **~e Phasenverschiebung** *f* ELEKTRONIK digital phase shifting; **~er Plotter** *m* COMP & DV digital plotter; **~e Pseudorauschfolge** *f* TELEKOM digital pseudo noise sequence; **~er Rahmenaufbau** *m* TELEKOM digital frame structure; **~e Rahmenstruktur** *f* TELEKOM digital frame structure; **~er Regenerator** *m* ELEKTRONIK digital regenerator; **~e Regenerierung** *f* ELEKTRONIK digital regeneration; **~e Rückkopplung** *f* TELEKOM digital feedback; **~er Satz** *m* DRUCK digital typesetting; **~e Schaltung** *f* COMP & DV digital circuit; **~e Schnittstelle** *f* TELEKOM digital interface; **~e Schrift** *f* DRUCK digital font; **~er Selektivruf** *m* TELEKOM DSC, digital selective calling; **~e Sichtanzeige** *f* COMP & DV digital readout; **~es Signal** *nt* COMP & DV, ELEKTRONIK, PHYS, TELEKOM digital signal; **~e Signalverarbeitung** *f* COMP & DV, ELEKTRONIK digital signal processing; **~e Sprachinterpolation** *f* *(DSI)* RAUMFAHRT, TELEKOM digital speech interpolation *(DSI)*; **~e Sprachsynthese** *f* ELEKTRONIK digital speech synthesis; **~es Stellglied** *nt* ELEKTROTECH digital actuator; **~es Steuergerät** *nt* KFZTECH digital control box; **~e Steuerung** *f* FERNSEH, TELEKOM digital control; **~e Störung** *f* TELEKOM digital interference; **~er Stromkreis** *m* COMP & DV digital circuit; **~e Teilnehmeranschlußeinheit** *f* TELEKOM digital subscriber access unit; **~es Tonband** *nt* COMP & DV digital audio tape; **~er Trägerbaustein** *m* TELEKOM digital carrier module; **~e Transitsteuerung** *f* TELEKOM digital transit command; **~e Übertragung** *f* TELEKOM digital transmission; **~er Übertragungsweg** *m* TELEKOM digital circuit; **~ umgesetztes Signal** *nt* ELEKTRONIK digitized signal; **~e Verarbeitung** *f* TELEKOM digital processing; **~es Vermitteln** *nt* TELEKOM digital switching; **~e Vermittlungsanlage** *f* ELEKTROTECH digital switching equipment; **~es Vermittlungsnetz** *nt* TELEKOM digital switching network; **~e Vermittlungsstelle** *f* TELEKOM digital exchange, digital switch, digital switching center (AmE), digital switching centre (BrE); **~es Vermittlungssystem** *nt* TELEKOM digital switch, digital switching system; **~e Videoeffekte** *m pl* FERNSEH DVE, digital video effects; **~e Videoplatte** *f* OPTIK digital videodisc (BrE), digital videodisk (AmE); **~er Videorecorder** *m* FERNSEH DVTR, digital videotape recorder; **~es Voltmeter** *nt* ELEKTROTECH digital voltmeter; **~er Zähler** *m* GERÄT digital counter

digital:[3] **~ darstellen** *vt* ELEKTRONIK *Signale* digitize

Digital-: **Digitalabstimmung** *f* ELEKTRONIK digital tuning

Digital-Analog- *pref* *(D/A)* AUFNAHME, COMP & DV, ELEKTRONIK, FERNSEH, LABOR, TELEKOM digital-analog *(D/A)*; **Digital-Analog-Umsetzer** *m* *(DAU, Digital-Analog-Wandler)* COMP & DV digital-analog converter *(DAC)*, ELEKTRONIK, FERNSEH, TELEKOM digital-analog converter *(DAC)*; **Digital-Analog-Umsetzung** *f* AUFNAHME digital-analog conversion, COMP & DV digital-analog conversion, ELEKTRONIK, GERÄT, TELEKOM digital-analog conversion; **Digital-**

Analog-Wandler *m* COMP & DV digital-analog converter, ELEKTRONIK, FERNSEH, TELEKOM digital-analog converter; **Digital-Analog-Wandlung** *f* AUFNAHME digital-analog conversion, COMP & DV digital-analog conversion, ELEKTRONIK, GERÄT, TELEKOM digital-analog conversion

Digital-: **Digitalanzeige** *f* ELEKTRONIK digital display, GERÄT digital display, digital readout, TELEKOM digital readout; **Digital-Audio-Tape** *nt (DAT)* AUFNAHME digital audio tape *(DAT)*; **Digitalaufzeichnung** *f* AUFNAHME, FERNSEH, TELEKOM digital recording; **Digitalausgabe** *f* COMP & DV digital output; **Digitalausgang** *m* ELEKTRONIK digital output; **Digitalbereich** *m* ELEKTRONIK digital domain; **Digitalchip** *m* ELEKTRONIK *Speicherbaustein* digital chip; **Digitalcode** *m* ELEKTRONIK digital code; **Digitalcodierung** *f* ELEKTRONIK digital coding; **Digitaldaten** *nt pl* ELEKTRONIK digital data; **Digital-Digital-Umsetzung** *f* GERÄT digital-digital conversion

Digital: **in ~ e Darstellung umsetzen** *vt* GERÄT digitalize

Digitalein *nt* CHEMIE digitalein

Digital-: **Digitaleingabe** *f* ELEKTRONIK digital input; **Digitalfehler** *m* TELEKOM digital error; **Digitalfernsehen** *nt* FERNSEH digital television; **Digitalfilter** *m* ELEKTRONIK, TELEKOM digital filter; **Digitalfüllzeichen** *nt* TELEKOM digital pad; **Digitalhierarchie** *f* TELEKOM digital hierarchy

Digitalin *nt* CHEMIE, LEBENSMITTEL digitalin

digitalisieren[1] *vt* AUFNAHME, COMP & DV, ELEKTRIZ, FERNSEH digitize

digitalisieren[2] *vi* MASCHINEN *Modell*, PHYS digitize

Digitalisierer *m* COMP & DV, ELEKTRONIK digitizer

Digitalisiergerät *nt* COMP & DV, RADIO digitizer

digitalisiert[1] *adj* DRUCK digitized, RAUMFAHRT *Weltraumfunk* digitalized

digitalisiert:[2] **~es Bild** *nt* ELEKTRONIK digital image, digitized image; **~e Daten** *nt pl* ELEKTRONIK, TELEKOM digitized data; **~e Sprache** *f* TELEKOM digitized speech

Digitalisiertablett *nt* COMP & DV, ELEKTRONIK digitizing tablet

Digitalisierung *f* COMP & DV digitization, ELEKTRONIK *Umsetzung von Grafiken in digitale Daten* digitizing, KERNTECH, PHYS digitization, TELEKOM digitalization, digitization; **~ von Signalen** *f* ELEKTRONIK signal digitization; **Digitalisierungstablett** *nt* COMP & DV, ELEKTRONIK digitizing tablet

Digital-: **Digitalkamera** *f* FERNSEH digital camera; **Digitalkassette** *f* COMP & DV digital cassette; **Digitalkonverter** *m* GERÄT digital converter; **Digitalmeßgerät** *nt* GERÄT digital measuring instrument; **Digitalmikrometer** *nt* METROL digital readout micrometer; **Digital-Multiplexeinrichtung** *f* ELEKTRONIK digital multiplex; **Digitalrechner** *m* COMP & DV digital computer; **Digitalschaltung** *f* ELEKTRONIK digital circuit

Digitalschaltung: **als ~ ausgelegte Konzeption** *f* ELEKTRONIK digital-circuit design

Digital-: **Digitalsignal** *nt* COMP & DV digital signal, ELEKTRONIK digital signal, discrete signal, PHYS, TELEKOM digital signal; **Digitalsignalanalysator** *m* ELEKTRONIK digital signal analyser (BrE), digital signal analyzer (AmE); **Digitalsignalanalyse** *f* ELEKTRONIK digital signal analysis; **Digitalsignalverbindung** *f (DSV)* TELEKOM digital connection; **Digitalsignalverteiler** *m* TELEKOM digital distribution frame; **Digitalsprache** *f* ELEKTRONIK digital speech; **Digitalstrommeßgerät** *nt*

ELEKTRIZ digital ammeter; **Digitalsubtrahierer** *m* ELEKTRONIK digital subtractor; **Digitalübertragung** *f* TELEKOM digital transmission; **Digitaluhr** *f* COMP & DV digital clock; **Digitalumsetzer** *m* ELEKTRONIK, GERÄT digital converter; **Digitalverarbeitung** *f* ELEKTRONIK digital processing; **Digitalvermittlung** *f* TELEKOM digital switching; **Digitalvideorecorder** *m* FERNSEH DVTR, digital videotape recorder; **Digitalvoltmeter** *nt* ELEKTRIZ digital voltmeter; **Digitalzähler** *m* GERÄT digital counter

Diglycidether *m* CHEMIE diglycidyl ether

Diglycidylether *m* CHEMIE diglycidyl ether

Diglykololeat *nt* LEBENSMITTEL diglycol oleate

Digraph *m* KÜNSTL INT digraph, directed graph, oriented graph

Dihydro- *pref* CHEMIE dihydro-; **Dihydrobenzol** *nt* CHEMIE cyclohexadiene, dihydrobenzene; **Dihydrodioxonaphthalin** *nt* CHEMIE dihydrodiketonaphthalene, naphthoquinone; **Dihydroergotamin** *nt* CHEMIE dihydroergotamine; **Dihydronaphthalin** *nt* CHEMIE dialin, dihydronaphthalene; **Dihydrostreptomycin** *nt* CHEMIE dihydrostreptomycin; **Dihydrotachysterin** *nt* CHEMIE dihydrotachysterol; **Dihydrothiazol** *nt* CHEMIE dihydrothiazole, thiazoline

Dihydroxyaceton *nt (DHA)* CHEMIE dihydroxyacetone

Dihydroxypropanon *nt (DHA)* CHEMIE dihydroxyacetone

Dihydroxy-α-Carotin *nt* CHEMIE dihydroxy-α-carotene, lutein

Diiodmethan *nt* CHEMIE diiodomethane, methylene iodide

Diisopropylidenaceton *nt* CHEMIE diisopropylidene acetone, phorone

Diktiergerät *nt* AUFNAHME dictation machine

Dilatanz *f* KUNSTSTOFF dilatancy

DIL-Gehäuse *nt (Doppelreihenanschlußgehäuse)* ELEKTRONIK, ELEKTROTECH, RADIO DIP *(dual-in-line package)*

Dimension *f* COMP & DV, DRUCK, MASCHINEN, MATH dimension; **~ einer Größe** *f* PHYS dimension of a quantity; **Dimensionalität** *f* ERGON dimensional characteristic

dimensionieren *vt* BAU size

Dimensionierung *f* COMP & DV dimensioning, MASCHINEN dimensioning, sizing; **Dimensionierungsstabilität** *f* VERPACK dimensional stability

Dimension: **Dimensionsgleichung** *f* PHYS dimensional equation

dimensionslos: **~e Darstellung** *f* KONSTZEICH dimensionless representation

Dimension: **Dimensionsstabilität** *f* KUNSTSTOFF dimensional stability

Dimer *nt* CHEMIE dimer

dimer *adj* CHEMIE dimeric

Dimeres *nt* CHEMIE dimer

Dimethoxyphthalid *nt* CHEMIE dimethoxyphthalide, meconin, opianyl

Dimethyl- *pref* CHEMIE dimethyl-; **Dimethylamin** *nt* CHEMIE dimethylamine; **Dimethylanilin** *nt* CHEMIE dimethylaniline, xylidine; **Dimethylarsan** *nt* CHEMIE dimethylarsane; **Dimethylarsin** *nt* CHEMIE dimethylarsane; **Dimethylbenzol** *nt* CHEMIE dimethylbenzene, xylol; **Dimethylbutanon** *nt* CHEMIE dimethylbutanone

Dimethylessig- *pref* CHEMIE dimethylacetic

Dimethyl-: **Dimethylhydroxybenzol** *nt* CHEMIE hydroxydimethylbenzene, xylenol; **Dimethylketon** *nt* CHEMIE acetone, propanone; **Dimethylmorphin** *nt* CHEMIE dimethylmorphine, paramorphine, thebaine; **Dimethyloctadienol** *nt* CHEMIE dimethyloctadienol, nerol; **Dimethyloctenal** *nt* CHEMIE citronellal, dimethyloctenal; **Dimethylpyridin** *nt* CHEMIE lutidine; **Dimethylxanthin** *nt* CHEMIE dimethylxanthine, theobromine

dimetrisch[1] *adj* GEOM dimetric

dimetrisch:[2] **~e Projektion** *f* GEOM, KONSTZEICH dimetric projection

Dimmer *m* ELEKTRIZ, ELEKTROTECH, LUFTTRANS *Beleuchtung* dimmer; **Dimmerabdeckung** *f* LUFTTRANS dimmer cap; **Dimmerschalter** *m* ELEKTRIZ, ELEKTROTECH dimmer switch

dimolekular *adj* CHEMIE bimolecular

DIN *abbr (Deutsches Institut für Normung)* MASCHINEN DIN, German Standards Institution

Dinasstein *m* KER & GLAS dinas brick

Dinatriumtetraborat-Dekahydrat *nt* CHEMIE borax, disodium tetraborate decahydrate

DIN-Format *nt* DRUCK DIN size

Dingi *nt* WASSERTRANS *Boot* dinghy

DIN-Größe *f* DRUCK DIN size

Dinitro- *pref* CHEMIE dinitro-; **Dinitrobenzol** *nt* CHEMIE dinitrobenzene; **Dinitrogenoxid** *nt* CHEMIE dinitrogen oxide; **Dinitronaphthalin** *nt* CHEMIE dinitronaphthalene; **Dinitrophenol** *nt* CHEMIE dinitrophenol; **Dinitrotoluol** *nt* CHEMIE binitrotoluene, dinitrotoluene

Dioctylphthalat *nt (DOP)* KUNSTSTOFF dioctylphthalate *(DOP)*

Diode *f* COMP & DV, ELEKTRIZ, ELEKTRONIK *zweipoliges Halbleiterbauelement mit nichtlinearer Strom-Spannungskennlinie,* KERNTECH, KFZTECH *Elektrikzündung,* PHYS, RADIO, TELEKOM diode; **~ mit einfachem pn-Übergang** *f* ELEKTRONIK p-n homojunction diode; **als ~ geschaltete Röhre** *f* ELEKTRONIK diode-connected tube; **als ~ geschalteter Transistor** *m* ELEKTRONIK diode-connected transistor; **~ mit hoher Trägerbeweglichkeit** *f* ELEKTRONIK hot carrier diode; **~ mit niedriger Verlustleistung** *f* ELEKTRONIK low-power diode; **~ mit pn-Übergang** *f* ELEKTRONIK p-n junction diode

Dioden: aufeinander abgestimmte ~ *f pl* ELEKTRONIK matched diodes

Diode: **Diodenbegrenzer** *m* ELEKTRONIK diode limiter; **Dioden-Entstörbaugruppe** *f* ELEKTRONIK diode suppressor; **Diodenentstörung** *f* ELEKTRONIK diode suppression; **Diodenfolge** *f* ELEKTRONIK diode string; **Diodenfrequenzvervielfacher** *m* ELEKTRONIK diode frequency multiplier; **Diodengatter** *nt* ELEKTRONIK diode gate; **Diodengleichrichter** *m* ELEKTRONIK diode rectifier; **Diodenkennlinie** *f* ELEKTRONIK diode characteristic; **Diodenkoppelpunkt** *m* TELEKOM diode crosspoint; **Diodenlaser** *m* ELEKTRONIK diode laser; **Diodenlogik** *f* ELEKTRONIK diode logic; **Diodenmatrix** *f* TELEKOM diode array; **Diodenmischer** *m* ELEKTRONIK diode mixer; **Diodenmodulation** *f* ELEKTRONIK diode modulation; **Diodenmodulator** *m* ELEKTRONIK diode modulator; **Diodenphasenschieber** *m* ELEKTRONIK diode phase shifter; **Diodenprüfgerät** *nt* ELEKTRONIK diode tester; **Diodenschalter** *m* FERNSEH diode switch; **Diodenspannung** *f* ELEKTRONIK diode voltage; **Dioden-Transistor-Logik** *f (DTL)* ELEKTRONIK diode transistor logic *(DTL)*; **Diodenumsetzer** *m* ELEKTRONIK diode modulator; **Diodenverstärker** *m* ELEKTRONIK diode amplifier; **Diode-Triode** *f* ELEK-

TRONIK diode triode

Diolefin *nt* CHEMIE dialkene, diene, diolefin, ERDÖL *Petrochemie* diolefin

Diopter *nt* BAU *Vermessung* vane, PHYS *optisches Instrument,* RAUMFAHRT *Raumschiff* diopter

Dioptrie *f (dpt)* OPTIK diopter (AmE), dioptre (BrE) *(dpt)*

Dioptrik *f* OPTIK dioptrics

Dioxid *nt* CHEMIE dioxide

Dioxobor- *pref* CHEMIE metaboric; **Dioxoborat** *nt* CHEMIE dioxoborate, metaborate

Dipalmitin *nt* CHEMIE dipalmitin

Diphenyl- *pref* CHEMIE diphenyl; **Diphenylenimid** *nt* CHEMIE carbazole; **Diphenylether** *m* CHEMIE diphenyl ether, phenoxybenzene; **Diphenylglyoxal** *nt* CHEMIE benzil, bibenzoyl; **Diphenylharnstoff** *m* CHEMIE carbanilide; **Diphenylimid** *nt* CHEMIE carbazole; **Diphenylketon** *nt* CHEMIE benzophenone, diphenyl ketone; **Diphenylmethandiisocyanat** *nt (MDI)* KUNSTSTOFF diphenylmethane diisocyanate *(MDI)*; **Diphenylsulfoharnstoff** *m* CHEMIE *Pharmazie* thiambutosine

Diphosphat *nt* CHEMIE pyrophosphate

diphosphorig *adj* CHEMIE pyrophosphorous

Dipikrylamin *nt* CHEMIE dipicrylamin, hexanitrodiphenylamine

Diplexer *m* TELEKOM diplexer

Dipol *m* ELEKTRIZ, ELEKTROTECH, METALL, TELEKOM dipole; **Dipolantenne** *f* FERNSEH dipole aerial, RADIO, TELEKOM dipole, WASSERTRANS *Funk* dipole aerial (BrE); **Dipol-Dipol-Wechselwirkung** *f* STRAHLPHYS dipole-dipole interaction; **Dipolmoment** *nt* ELEKTROTECH, PHYS dipole moment; **Dipolreihe** *f* ELEKTRONIK linear array

dippen *vt* WASSERTRANS *Flagge* dip

DIP-Relais *nt* ELEKTROTECH DIP relay; **DIP-Schalter** *m* ELEKTRIZ, ELEKTROTECH DIP switch

Dirac-Konstante *f* PHYS h-quer Dirac constant

Direkt- *pref* AUFNAHME, COMP & DV, ELEKTRONIK, FERTIG, FOTO, TELEKOM, TRANS, UMWELTSCHMUTZ, direct

direkt[1] *adj* AUFNAHME, COMP & DV, ELEKTRONIK, FERTIG, FOTO, TELEKOM, TRANS, UMWELTSCHMUTZ, direct; **~ geerdet** *adj* ELEKTROTECH directly-earthed

direkt:[2] **~er Abbruch** *m* COMP & DV immediate cancel; **~er AC-Umformer** *m* ELEKTRIZ direct AC converter; **~e Adresse** *f* COMP & DV immediate address, ELEKTRONIK *Angabe im Befehlsadreßteil der Speicheradresse* direct address; **~e Adressierung** *f* COMP & DV direct addressing; **~ angetriebene Pumpe** *f* WASSERVERSORG direct-acting pump, direct-action pump; **~ angetriebener Propeller** *m* LUFTTRANS direct drive propeller; **~es Auffangen** *nt* UMWELTSCHMUTZ direct interception; **~e Brennstoffzelle** *f* KFZTECH direct cell; **~e Datei** *f* COMP & DV direct file; **~e Dateneingabe** *f (DDE)* COMP & DV direct data entry *(DDE)*; **~er Dateneintrag** *m (DDE)* COMP & DV direct data entry *(DDE)*; **~e Destillatfraktion** *f* ERDÖL straight run product; **~e Digitalsteuerung** *f* COMP & DV direct digital control; **~er Durchbruch** *m* KERNTECH direct breakthrough; **~e Einwahl** *f* TELEKOM DDI (BrE), direct dialing-in (AmE), direct dialling-in (BrE); **~e Elektronenstrahl-Belichtung** *f* ELEKTRONIK direct electron beam writing; **~e Energieumwandlung** *f* ELEKTROTECH direct energy conversion; **~er Gang** *m* KFZTECH *Getriebe* direct drive; **~e Kaltwasserstoffbrennstoffzelle** *f* KFZTECH direct cold hydrogen cell; **~er Kernfotoeffekt**

m KERNTECH direct photonuclear effect; ~e Komponente *f* ELEKTRIZ direct component; ~e Kupplung *f* NICHTFOSS ENERG direct coupling; ~es Licht *nt* FOTO direct light; ~er Lichtbogenofen *m* FERTIG direct arc furnace; ~es Methylalkohol-Luftsauerstoffelement *nt* TRANS direct methanol air cell; ~er Mustervergleich *m* COMP & DV template matching, templet matching; ~ netzbetriebener Motor *m* ELEKTRIZ across the line motor; ~er Piezoeffekt *m* ELEKTROTECH direct piezoelectric effect; ~e Rundfunkübertragung über Satellit *f* TELEKOM direct broadcasting by satellite; ~er Schallpegel *m* AUFNAHME direct sound level; ~er Speicherzugriff *m* COMP & DV direct memory access; ~es Spinnen von Glasseidensträngen *nt* KER & GLAS direct roving; ~e Strahlung *f* NICHTFOSS ENERG direct radiation; ~e Überstromauslösung *f* ELEKTRIZ direct overcurrent release; ~e Umlaufbahn *f* RAUMFAHRT direct orbit; ~e Verarbeitung *f* COMP & DV random processing; ~e Verdrahtung *f* ELEKTRIZ point-to-point wiring; ~e Verseuchung *f* UMWELTSCHMUTZ direct poisoning; ~er Vielfachzugriff *m* TELEKOM random multiple access; ~e Wasserstoff-Sauerstoff-Brennstoffzelle *f* TRANS direct hydrogen-oxygen cell; ~ wirkender Propeller *m* LUFTTRANS direct drive propeller; ~er Zugriff *m* COMP & DV random access, COMP & DV *(DA)* direct access *(DA)*; ~e zyklische Verstellung *f* LUFTTRANS *Hubschrauber* primary cyclic variation

Direkt-: **Direktablesung** *f* MASCHINEN direct reading; **Direktanlassen** *nt* ELEKTRIZ *Elektromotor* direct starting; **Direktantrieb** *m* KFZTECH *Getriebe*, MASCHINEN direct drive

direktanzeigend: ~es Instrument *nt* GERÄT direct-reading instrument; ~es **Meßgerät** *nt* GERÄT direct-reading instrument; ~es **Meßinstrument** *nt* ELEKTRIZ, GERÄT direct-reading instrument

Direkt-: **Direktausgabe** *f* ELEKTRONIK direct output; **Direktbefehl** *m* COMP & DV immediate instruction; **Direktbelichtung** *f* ELEKTRONIK direct writing; **Direktdampf** *m* HYDRAUL live steam; **Direktdampfinjektor** *m* HYDRAUL live steam injector; **Direktdaten** *nt pl* COMP & DV immediate data; **Direktdestillat** *nt* ERDÖL straight run product; **Direkt-Duplikatfilm** *m* FOTO direct duplicating film; **Direkteingabe** *f* ELEKTRONIK direct input; **Direkteinspritzung** *f* KFZTECH, MASCHINEN direct injection; **Direktfarbstoff** *m* TEXTIL direct dyestuff; **Direktflug** *m* LUFTTRANS direct flight; **Direktfrequenzgenerator** *m* ELEKTRONIK direct frequency synthesizer; **Direktfrequenzmodulation** *f* ELEKTRONIK direct frequency modulation; **Direktfrequenzsynthese** *f* ELEKTRONIK direct frequency synthesis

direktgeheizt: ~e Kathode *f* ELEKTROTECH directly-heated cathode

direktgekoppelt[1] *adj* COMP & DV close-coupled, ELEKTRIZ direct-coupled

direktgekoppelt:[2] ~e Transistorlogik *f (DCTL)* ELEKTRONIK direct-coupled transistor logic *(DCTL)*

direktgekuppelt *adj* COMP & DV close-coupled, direct-coupled, ELEKTRIZ direct-coupled

Direkt-: **Direktkopplung** *f* COMP & DV close coupling, ELEKTRIZ direct coupling; **Direktleitung** *f* TELEKOM direct line; **Direktmodulation** *f* ELEKTRONIK direct modulation; **Direktmodus** *m* COMP & DV immediate mode; **Direktmustererzeugung** *f* ELEKTRONIK direct pattern generation

Direktor *m* RAUMFAHRT *Antennenteil* director

Direkt-: **Direktregler** *m* GERÄT primary controller; **Di-**rektrundfunksatellit *m* FERNSEH direct broadcast satellite; **Direktsatellitenrundfunk** *m* FERNSEH direct satellite broadcasting; **Direktschreiben** *nt* ELEKTRONIK *IC-Herstellung durch Direktbelichtung* direct writing; **Direktsichtbildröhre** *f* ELEKTRONIK direct view storage tube; **Direkt-Speicherzugriff** *m (DMA)* COMP & DV direct memory access *(DMA)*; **Direktsteuerung** *f* MASCHINEN DC, direct control; **Direktstrom** *m* KER & GLAS *der Glasströmung im Ofen* direct current

direktübertragen: ~e Musik *f* AUFNAHME *nicht im Studio* live music; ~er Ton *m* AUFNAHME live sound

Direkt-: **Direktumwandlung** *f* NICHTFOSS ENERG direct conversion

direktwirkend: ~e obenliegende Nockenwelle *f* KFZTECH direct-acting overhead camshaft; ~er Temperaturregler *m* HEIZ & KÄLTE thermostatic valve

Direktzugriff *m* COMP & DV, ELEKTROTECH direct access, random access; **Direktzugriffsdatei** *f* COMP & DV random access file; **Direktzugriffsspeicher** *m* COMP & DV random access storage, COMP & DV *(DMA)* direct access storage, memory random access, COMP & DV *(RAM)*, ELEKTRONIK *(RAM)* random access memory *(RAM)*, ELEKTROTECH direct access memory

Disassemblierer *m* COMP & DV disassembler

Disazofarbstoff *m* CHEMIE bis-azo dye

Dischwefel- *pref* CHEMIE pyrosulfuric (AmE), pyrosulphuric (BrE); **Dischwefelsäure** *f* CHEMIE hydrosulfurous acid (AmE), hydrosulphurous acid (BrE)

Disilan *nt* CHEMIE disilane

Disilicoethan *nt* CHEMIE disilane

Disilikat *nt* CHEMIE disilicate

disjunkt: ~e Mengen *f pl* MATH disjoint sets

Disjunktion *f* COMP & DV disjunction

Disk *f (Diskette)* COMP & DV disk

Diskette *f* COMP & DV *fl* floppy disk, disk, diskette, DRUCK diskette, floppy disk, TELEKOM floppy disk; **Diskettenlaufwerk** *nt* COMP & DV disk drive, diskette drive, floppy disk drive; **Diskettenlesegerät** *nt* TELEKOM floppy disk reader

diskontinuierlich: ~e Arbeitsweise *f* CHEMTECH batch processing; ~e Belastung *f* ELEKTRIZ intermittent load; ~er Betrieb *m* ELEKTRIZ intermittent duty; ~er Fehler *m* ELEKTRIZ intermittent fault; ~er Kocher *m* PAPIER batch digester; ~er Mischer *m* CHEMTECH batch mixer; ~er Pulper *m* PAPIER batch pulper; ~er Speiseeisbereiter *m* LEBENSMITTEL batch freezer

Diskordanz *f* ERDÖL *Geologie* unconformity; **Diskordanzfalle** *f* ERDÖL *Geologie* unconformity trap

diskret[1] *adj* COMP & DV, ELEKTRONIK discrete, FERNSEH quantized, QUAL, TELEKOM discrete

diskret:[2] ~es Bauelement *nt* TELEKOM discrete component; ~er Bipolar-Transistor *m* ELEKTRONIK discrete bipolar transistor; ~es Filter *m* ELEKTRONIK discrete filter; ~e Fourier-Transformation *f (DFT)* ELEKTRONIK discrete Fourier transform *(DFT)*; ~e Fourier-Transform-Technik *f* ELEKTRONIK discrete Fourier transform; ~es Gitter *nt* FERNSEH quantized gate; ~es Halbleiterbauelement *nt* ELEKTRONIK discrete semiconductor device; ~er Kanal *m* TELEKOM discrete channel; ~es Merkmal *nt* QUAL discrete characteristic; ~er N-Kanal-Feldeffekttransistor *m* ELEKTRONIK n-channel discrete FET; ~es Signal *nt* ELEKTRONIK discrete signal; ~er Verstärker *m* ELEKTRONIK discrete amplifier; ~e Verzögerungsleitung *f*

FERNSEH quantized delay line
Diskretisierung *f* MATH truncation
Diskrimination *f* ERGON discrimination
Diskriminator *m* ELEKTRONIK *Entscheider*, FERNSEH, RADIO *Schaltung, Schaltkreis*, TELEKOM discriminator
Diskriminierungsvermögen *nt* ERGON sensory discrimination
Dispatcher *m* COMP & DV, KFZTECH *Schmieranlage, Öl* dispatcher
Dispergator *m* KUNSTSTOFF deflocculating agent, MEERSCHMUTZ dispersant, dispersing agent
Dispergens *nt* CHEMIE deflocculant, CHEMTECH dispersive medium, ERDÖL dispersant, MEERSCHMUTZ, UMWELTSCHMUTZ dispersant, dispersing agent
dispergieren *vt* CHEMIE deflocculate
dispergierend: **~e Laufzeitkette** *f* ELEKTRONIK, RADIO dispersive delay line
Dispergiermittel *nt* CHEMIE deflocculant, CHEMTECH dispersive medium, KUNSTSTOFF deflocculating agent, dispersant, dispersing agent, LEBENSMITTEL dispersing agent
dispergiert: **~er Brennstoff** *m* KERNTECH dispersion fuel
Dispergierung *f* CHEMIE deflocculation; **Dispergierungsmittel** *nt* KOHLEN dispersing agent
dispers: **~e Phase** *f* UMWELTSCHMUTZ disperse phase
Dispersant *nt* FERTIG dispersant, MEERSCHMUTZ, UMWELTSCHMUTZ dispersant, dispersing agent; **Dispersantbehälter** *m* MEERSCHMUTZ *unter einem Helikopter befestigter Behälter zum Ausbringen von Dispersionsmitteln* bucket
Dispersion *f* ANSTRICH dispersion, CHEMTECH dispersion, dispersivity, COMP & DV, ELEKTRIZ, KOHLEN, KUNSTSTOFF, PHYS, TELEKOM, WELLPHYS dispersion; **~ von Farben** *f* PHYS *aufgrund von Brechung*, WELLPHYS *aufgrund von Brechung* dispersion of colors (AmE), dispersion of colours (BrE); **Dispersionseinrichtung** *f* MEERSCHMUTZ *zur Bekämpfung von Ölverschmutzungen* dispersing equipment; **Dispersionsfarbe** *f* BAU water-based paint; **Dispersionsfarbstoff** *m* TEXTIL disperse dyestuff
dispersionsgekühlt: **~er Reaktor** *m* KERNTECH dispersion-cooled reactor
Dispersion: **Dispersionsgleichung** *f* PHYS, WELLPHYS dispersion equation; **Dispersionshärten** *nt* METALL precipitation hardening; **Dispersionshärtung** *f* METALL dispersion hardening; **Dispersionskneter** *m* CHEMTECH dispersion kneader; **Dispersionsmedium** *nt* PHYS dispersion medium; **Dispersionsmittel** *nt* KERNTECH dispersion agent, KUNSTSTOFF, MEERSCHMUTZ dispersant, dispersing agent; **Dispersionsrelation** *f* WELLPHYS dispersion relation; **Dispersionsteilchen** *nt* CHEMTECH *Schmutzteilchen* particulate
Dispersoid *nt* CHEMTECH dispersoid
Display *nt* DRUCK, VERPACK display; **Displayschachtel** *f* VERPACK presentation box
Dispositionsgleis *nt* EISENBAHN relief track
dissipativ: **~es Medium** *nt* PHYS dissipative medium
Dissonanz *f* AKUSTIK, RADIO discordance, dissonance
Dissousgasflasche *f* FERTIG acetylene cylinder
Dissoziation *f* KOHLEN dissociation; **Dissoziationswärme** *f* THERMOD heat of dissociation
dissoziierbar *adj* CHEMIE dissociable
dissoziieren *vt* CHEMIE dissociate
Dissoziierung *f* CHEMIE dissociation
Dissymmetrie *f* CHEMIE, GEOM dissymmetry

dissymmetrisch *adj* GEOM dissymmetric, dissymmetrical
distal *adj* ERGON distal
Distanz *f* FERTIG distance, MASCHINEN spacer; **Distanzadresse** *f* COMP & DV displacement address; **Distanzblech** *nt* ERDÖL stabilizer; **Distanzblock** *m* MASCHINEN spacer block; **Distanzbuchse** *f* FERTIG *Kunststoffinstallationen* distance bush, distance piece; **Distanzscheibe** *f* MASCHINEN shim
Distickoxid *nt* CHEMIE nitrous oxide
Distickstoffmonoxid *nt* CHEMIE dinitrogen monoxide
Distickstoffoxid *nt* UMWELTSCHMUTZ nitrous oxide
Distributivgesetz *nt* MATH distributive law
Disulfat *nt* CHEMIE disulfate (AmE), disulphate (BrE), pyrosulfate (AmE), pyrosulphate (BrE)
Disulfid *nt* CHEMIE disulfide (AmE), disulphide (BrE)
Disulfit *nt* CHEMIE pyrosulfite (AmE), pyrosulphite (BrE)
Disulfuryl- *pref* CHEMIE pyrosulfuryl (AmE), pyrosulphuryl (BrE)
Dithion- *pref* CHEMIE dithionic; **Dithionat** *nt* CHEMIE dithionate
dithionig: **~e Säure** *f* CHEMIE dithionous acid, tetraoxodisulfuric acid (AmE), tetraoxodisulphuric acid (BrE)
Dithionit *nt* CHEMIE dithionite, hyposulfite (AmE), hyposulphite (BrE)
ditonisch: **~es Komma** *nt* AKUSTIK Didyme comma
diurnal *adj* ERGON diurnal
divergent[1] *adj* GEOM, OPTIK divergent
divergent:[2] **~e Düse** *f* PHYS *im Windkanal* divergent nozzle; **~e Reihe** *f* MATH divergent series
Divergenz *f* PHYS *eines Vektorfeldes* divergence
divergierend: **~e Reihe** *f* MATH divergent series
Diversity *f* TELEKOM diversity
Dividend *m* COMP & DV dividend, recognition, MATH dividend
dividieren[1] *vt* MATH divide
dividieren[2] *vi* GEOM divide
Divinyl *nt* CHEMIE bivinyl, divinyl
Division *f* COMP & DV, MATH *Grundrechenart* division
Divisor *m* COMP & DV, MATH divisor
D-Kanal *m* TELEKOM D-channel
dl *abbr* (*Deziliter*) LABOR dl (*deciliter*)
DM *abbr* (*Deltamodulation*) ELEKTRONIK, RAUMFAHRT, TELEKOM DM (*delta modulation*)
DMA *abbr* (*Direkt-Speicherzugriff, Direktzugriffsspeicher*) COMP & DV DMA (*direct memory access*)
DMC *abbr* (*kittartige Formmasse*) KUNSTSTOFF DMC (*dough-moulding compound*)
DM-Vierer *m* ELEKTROTECH multiple-twin quad
D$_2$O *abbr* (*Deuteriumoxid*) CHEMIE D$_2$O (*deuterium oxide*)
Dock *nt* WASSERTRANS dock; **Dockadaptor** *m* RAUMFAHRT docking adaptor
Docke *f* TEXTIL *Warendocke* batch
Dock: **Dockgeld** *nt* WASSERTRANS dockage
Docking *nt* RAUMFAHRT docking; **Docking-Fenster** *nt* RAUMFAHRT docking port; **Docking-Stutzen** *m* RAUMFAHRT docking probe; **Docking-Tunnel** *m* RAUMFAHRT docking tunnel
Dock: **Dockmöglichkeiten** *f pl* WASSERTRANS dockage; **Dockstück** *nt* RAUMFAHRT docking piece
Dodecan *nt* CHEMIE bihexyl, dihexyl, dodecane
Dodecanoyl- *pref* CHEMIE lauryl
Dodecawolframatophosphat *nt* CHEMIE phosphatodo-

decatungstate, phosphotungstate

Dodecyl- *pref* CHEMIE dodecyl

Dodeka- *pref* MATH dodeca-; **Dodekaeder** *nt* GEOM dodecahedron; **Dodekagon** *nt* GEOM dodecagon

DOHC-Motor *m* (*Querstromkopfmotor*) KFZTECH DOHC engine (*direct-acting overhead camshaft engine*)

doktornegativ *adj* CHEMIE *Erdöl* sweet

Dokument *nt* COMP & DV document

Dokumentation *f* COMP & DV documentation

Dokument: **Dokumentenabruf** *m* COMP & DV document retrieval; **Dokumenten-Archivierungssystem mit CD** *nt* COMP & DV, OPTIK optical data disk document filing system; **Dokumentenfilm** *m* FOTO document film; **Dokumentenglas** *nt* KER & GLAS document glass

Doline *f* WASSERVERSORG doline

Dollbord *nt* WASSERTRANS *Schiffbau* gunnel, gunwale

Dolle *f* WASSERTRANS rowlock (BrE), *Bootszubehör* oarlock (AmE)

Dolomit *m* ERDÖL *Geologie*, KER & GLAS dolomite; **Dolomitstein** *m* BAU dolomite brick

Domäne *f* KÜNSTL INT *des Wissens* domain; **Domänenstruktur** *f* PHYS domain structure; **Domänenwissen** *nt* KÜNSTL INT domain knowledge

dominant: **~es Anion** *nt* UMWELTSCHMUTZ dominant anion; **~es Kation** *nt* UMWELTSCHMUTZ dominant cation

Dominante *f* AKUSTIK dominant

Donator *m* COMP & DV donor, ELEKTRONIK *elektronenabgebendes Atom oder Störstelle* donator, donor; **Donatoratom** *nt* ELEKTRONIK, PHYS donor atom; **Donatorniveau** *nt* ELEKTRONIK donor level; **Donatorverschmutzung** *f* ELEKTRONIK donor impurity; **Donatorverunreinigung** *f* ELEKTRONIK donor impurity

DOP *abbr* (*Dioctylphthalat*) KUNSTSTOFF DOP (*dioctylphthalate*)

Dopamin *nt* CHEMIE dopamine

Dopans *nt* OPTIK dopant

Doppel- *pref* AKUSTIK, DRUCK double, ELEKTROTECH twin, KFZTECH tandem, LUFTTRANS, VERPACK twin; **Doppelabsacksystem** *nt* VERPACK twin bagging system; **Doppelachse** *f* KFZTECH *LKW* tandem axle, MASCHINEN double axle

doppeladrig[1] *adj* RADIO bifilar

doppeladrig:[2] **~es Kabel** *nt* ELEKTRIZ double-core cable

Doppel-: **Doppelankerrelais** *nt* ELEKTRIZ double-armature relay

doppelatomig *adj* CHEMIE biatomic, diatomic

Doppel-: **Doppel-b** *nt* AKUSTIK double flat; **Doppelbakkenbremse** *f* EISENBAHN clasp brake (AmE); **Doppelbandpolieren** *nt* KER & GLAS twin polishing; **Doppelbandpoliermaschine** *f* KER & GLAS twin polisher; **Doppelbandschleifmaschine** *f* KER & GLAS twin grinder

doppelbasisch *adj* CHEMIE bibasic, dibasic

Doppel-: **Doppelbasisdiode** *f* ELEKTRONIK double base diode; **Doppelbelegung** *f* TELEKOM double seizure; **Doppelbelichtung** *f* FOTO double exposure; **Doppelbeschichtung** *f* TELEKOM double layer coating; **Doppelboden** *m* BAU double floor, HEIZ & KÄLTE raised floor, WASSERTRANS *Schiffbau* double bottom; **Doppelbohrung** *f* MASCHINEN twin bore

doppelbrechend[1] *adj* OPTIK birefringent

doppelbrechend:[2] **~es Medium** *nt* OPTIK birefringent medium

Doppel-: **Doppelbrechung** *f* OPTIK, STRAHLPHYS birefringence; **Doppelbruch** *m* MATH complex fraction; **Doppelbuchstabe** *m* DRUCK double letter; **Doppelchlorid** *nt* CHEMIE bichloride, dichloride; **Doppeldeckpalette** *f* TRANS reversible pallet, VERPACK double-decked pallet; **Doppeldeltaflügel** *m* LUFTTRANS double delta wing; **Doppeldiodenpentode** *f* (*DDP*) ELEKTRONIK double diode pentode (*DDP*); **Doppeldrahtschaltung** *f* ELEKTRIZ two-wire circuit; **Doppeldruckregler** *m* HEIZ & KÄLTE dual pressure controller; **Doppelelementrelais** *nt* ELEKTRIZ two-element relay; **Doppelfadenaufhängung** *f* ELEKTRIZ, PHYS bifilar suspension

doppelfädig[1] *adj* ELEKTRIZ, PHYS bifilar

doppelfädig:[2] **~es Elektrometer** *nt* ELEKTRIZ bifilar electrometer

Doppel-: **Doppelfarbigkeit** *f* CHEMIE dicroism; **Doppelfensterfaser** *f* OPTIK double-window fiber (AmE), double-window fibre (BrE); **Doppelflugzeug** *nt* LUFTTRANS composite aircraft; **Doppelflüssigtreibstoffantrieb** *m* RAUMFAHRT *Raumschiff* liquid bipropellant propulsion; **Doppelformatkamera** *f* FOTO dual-format camera; **Doppelfußboden** *m* BAU framed floor

doppelgängig: **~es Gewinde** *nt* MASCHINEN two-start thread

Doppel-: **Doppelgarn** *nt* TEXTIL two-ply yarn; **Doppelgegensprechedieren** *nt* FERNSEH physical quadruplex editing; **Doppelgehäuse** *nt* MASCHINEN double casing; **Doppelgelenk** *nt* KFZTECH *Antriebswelle, Kardanwelle* constant-velocity universal joint, MASCHINEN double joint

doppelgewickelt: **~er Generator** *m* ELEKTRIZ double-wound generator

Doppel-: **Doppelgewindeschraube** *f* BAU double-threaded screw; **Doppelhaken** *m* MASCHINEN clip hooks; **Doppelhebel** *m* FERTIG *Kunststoffinstallationen* double lever handle; **Doppelherzstück** *nt* EISENBAHN diamond crossing, double diamond crossing; **Doppelhiebfeile** *f* FERTIG double-cut file

doppelhiebig: **~e Feile** *f* MASCHINEN double-cut file

doppelhörig *adj* AKUSTIK binaural

Doppel-: **Doppelhub** *m* FERTIG cycle, reciprocation, MASCHINEN double stroke; **Doppelhülle** *f* WASSERTRANS *Schiffbau, U-Boote* double hull; **Doppelisolator** *m* ELEKTROTECH double insulator; **Doppelisolierung** *f* ELEKTROTECH double insulation; **Doppeljersey** *m* TEXTIL double jersey; **Doppelkabel** *nt* ELEKTRIZ duplex cable, foto double cable; **Doppelkabelauslöser** *m* FOTO double cable release; **Doppelkäfigmotor** *m* ELEKTRIZ double-squirrel cage motor; **Doppelkäfigwicklung** *f* ELEKTROTECH double-squirrel cage winding; **Doppelkamm-Magnetron** *nt* ELEKTRONIK, PHYS interdigital magnetron; **Doppelkapselmikrofon** *nt* AKUSTIK differential microphone; **Doppelkassette** *f* FOTO twin magazine; **Doppelkegelhälfte** *f* GEOM nappe; **Doppelkeilriemen** *m* MASCHINEN double-V belt; **Doppelkettfäden** *m pl* TEXTIL twin ends; **Doppelklikken** *nt* COMP & DV *mit Maus* double click; **Doppelklinke** *f* MASCHINEN double ratchet; **Doppelkolben** *m* KFZTECH, MASCHINEN double piston, twin piston; **Doppelkolbenkompressor** *m* HYDRAUL duplex compressor; **Doppelkolbenmotor** *m* KFZTECH twin-piston engine, MASCHINEN double-piston engine; **Doppelkolbenpumpe** *f* HYDRAUL duplex pump; **Doppelkondensator-Motor** *m* ELEKTRIZ dual capacitor motor; **Doppelkontaktrelais** *nt* ELEKTRIZ two-element relay; **Doppelkonusantenne** *f* RADIO discone, TELEKOM biconical antenna; **Doppelkonuslautsprecher** *m* AUFNAHME dual-cone loudspeaker; **Doppelkopfniete** *f* BAU bullhead rivet; **Doppelkopfschiene** *f* EISENBAHN bull-headed rail, double-headed rail; **Doppelkörpervergaser** *m* KFZTECH twin-barreled carburetor (AmE), twin-barrelled carburettor (BrE); **Doppelkreuz** *nt* AKUSTIK double sharp, OPTIK double crucible; **Doppelkreuzmethode** *f* OPTIK double crucible method; **Doppelkreuzverfahren** *nt* OPTIK double crucible technique; **Doppelkristall** *m* METALL twin; **Doppelkurbel** *f* MASCHINEN double crank, duplex crank; **Doppelkurbelpresse** *f* MASCHINEN double-crank press; **Doppellaschennietung** *f* MASCHINEN double-strap butt joint; **Doppellattenkiste** *f* VERPACK double-battened case; **Doppelleinen** *nt* DRUCK buckram; **Doppelleitwerk** *nt* LUFTTRANS twin-tail unit; **Doppellinie** *f* DRUCK double rule, OPTIK *Spektralanalyse* doublet; **Doppellinse** *f* KER & GLAS twins; **Doppelmast** *m* WASSERTRANS derrick mast

doppelmäulig *adj* FERTIG double-end

Doppel-: **Doppelmesserschalter** *m* ELEKTRIZ double-throw knife switch; **Doppelmesserschneider** *m* PAPIER dual knife cutter; **Doppelmesserumschalter** *m* ELEKTRIZ double-pole double-throw knife switch; **Doppelmikrofon** *nt* AUFNAHME double-button microphone; **Doppelmodulation** *f* ELEKTRONIK compound modulation, double modulation; **Doppelmotor** *m* KONTROLL tandem motor; **Doppelmuffe** *f* LABOR Feststellvorrichtung bosshead

doppeln *vt* WASSERTRANS double

Doppel-: **Doppelnetzspannung** *f* ELEKTROTECH dual supply voltage; **Doppelnormmonitor** *m* FERNSEH dual standard monitor; **Doppelobjektiv** *nt* FOTO doubled lens, doublet lens; **Doppel-Öffner-Kontakt** *m* ELEKTRIZ break-break contact; **Doppelöffnerschalter** *m* ELEKTRIZ double break switch; **Doppelpackung** *f* VERPACK twin pack; **Doppelpeilung** *f* WASSERTRANS *Navigation* running fix

doppelphasig *adj* ELEKTRIZ biphase

Doppel-: **Doppelplattformpalette** *f* VERPACK double-platform pallet

doppelpolig: **~e Elektrode** *f* ELEKTRIZ bipolar electrode; **~e Leitung** *f* ELEKTRIZ bipolar line

Doppel-: **Doppelpoller** *m* WASSERTRANS bitts; **Doppelpolwicklung** *f* ELEKTRIZ bipolar winding; **Doppelprisma** *nt* OPTIK biprism; **Doppelprofilglas** *nt* KER & GLAS double-bended glass; **Doppelquerlenkeraufhängung** *f* KFZTECH double-wishbone suspension; **Doppelräder** *f pl* LUFTTRANS dual wheel; **Doppelrampe** *f* LUFTTRANS dual platform; **Doppelreflektorantenne** *f* TELEKOM double reflector antenna; **Doppelregistervergaser** *m* KFZTECH four-barrel carburetor (AmE), four-barrel carburettor (BrE), quad carburetor (AmE), quad carburettor (BrE); **Doppelreihenanschlußgehäuse** *nt* *(DIL-Gehäuse)* ELEKTRONIK, ELEKTROTECH, RADIO dual-in-line package *(DIP)*; **Doppelringschlüssel** *m* MASCHINEN double open-ended spanner (BrE), double open-ended wrench, double-ended box spanner (BrE), double-ended box wrench, double-ended open-jaw spanner (BrE), double-ended open-jaw wrench, double-ended ring spanner (BrE), double-ended ring wrench, double-ended spanner (BrE),

double-ended wrench; **Doppelrumpfboot** *nt* WASSERTRANS *Boottyp* catamaran; **Doppelschaufelabscheider** *m* UMWELTSCHMUTZ double bucket collector

doppelschichtig: **~e Wellfaserplatte** *f* VERPACK double-wall corrugated fiberboard (AmE), double-wall corrugated fibreboard (BrE)

Doppel-: **Doppelschichtwicklung** *f* ELEKTRIZ double layer winding; **Doppelschlichtfeile** *f* FERTIG dead smooth cut file; **Doppelschlußmotor** *m* ELEKTROTECH compound motor; **Doppelschlußwicklung** *f* ELEKTROTECH compound winding; **Doppelschneckenextruder** *m* ABFALL, KUNSTSTOFF twin-screw extruder; **Doppelschrauben** *f pl* WASSERTRANS *Schiffantrieb* twin propellers; **Doppelschraubendampfer** *m* WASSERTRANS twin-screw steamer; **Doppelschwinge** *f* MASCHINEN double rocker; **Doppelseitenband** *nt* *(DSB)* ELEKTRONIK, RADIO double sideband *(DSB)*; **Doppelseitenbandsendung** *f* FERNSEH double-sideband transmission

doppelseitig [1] *adj* BAU double-faced, DRUCK back-to-back, ELEKTRONIK double-sided, OPTIK two-sided, TELEKOM double-sided, VERPACK double-faced, double-sided; **~ platiert** *adj* FERTIG duo-clad

doppelseitig [2]: **~er Amplitudenbegrenzer** *m* ELEKTRONIK amplitude gate; **~es Bedrucken** *nt* DRUCK back-to-back printing; **~ klebendes Band** *nt* VERPACK double-sided tape; **~es Kreppapier** *nt* PAPIER, VERPACK double-faced crepe paper; **~e Scheibe** *f* OPTIK two-sided disc (BrE), two-sided disk (AmE); **~es Trägermaterial** *nt* ELEKTRONIK *für Leiterplatten* double-sided substrate; **~er Verteiler** *m* TELEKOM double-sided distribution frame; **~es Wachspapier** *nt* PAPIER, VERPACK double-faced wax paper; **~e Wellpappe** *f* VERPACK double-faced corrugated board

Doppel-: **Doppelsilicat** *nt* CHEMIE bisilicate; **Doppelspalt-Löschkopf** *m* AUFNAHME double-gap erase head; **Doppelspielband** *nt* AUFNAHME double-play tape; **Doppelspinsatellit** *m* RAUMFAHRT *Raumschiff* dual spin satellite; **Doppelspinstabilisierung** *f* RAUMFAHRT *Raumschiff* dual spin stabilization; **Doppelspitzhacke** *f* KOHLEN coal pick; **Doppelspur** *f* AKUSTIK dual track, AUFNAHME twin track; **Doppelspur-Aufnahmegerät** *nt* AUFNAHME twin-track recorder; **Doppelstatordrehkondensator** *m* ELEKTROTECH split stator variable capacitor; **Doppelstecker** *m* FERTIG biplug; **Doppelsteghohlleiter** *m* ELEKTROTECH double ridge waveguide; **Doppelsteuerschulung** *f* LUFTTRANS dual instruction; **Doppelsteuerstange** *f* LUFTTRANS dual rod; **Doppelstichprobenentnahme** *f* QUAL double sampling; **Doppelstichprobenprüfplan** *m* QUAL double-sampling plan; **Doppelstift-Steckverbindung** *f* ELEKTRIZ two-contact connector; **Doppelstrahl-Kathodenstrahlröhre** *f* ELEKTRONIK dual-beam cathode-ray tube; **Doppelstrangpolymer** *nt* KUNSTSTOFF double-strand polymer, ladder polymer; **Doppelstrich** *m* DRUCK double rule; **Doppelstrombetrieb** *m* TELEKOM double current operation; **Doppelstromtor-Strahlsteuerungsröhre** *f* FERNSEH gated beam tube; **Doppelstromversorgung** *f* ELEKTROTECH dual power supply; **Doppelsupereffekt** *m* FERNSEH double super effect

doppelt [1]: **~ mit Baumwolle umhüllt** *adj* ELEKTRIZ double-cotton-covered, DCC; **~ kautschukbedeckt** *adj* ELEKTRIZ double-pure-rubber-covered

doppelt [2]: **~er Anschnitt** *m* KER & GLAS double bevel; **~e**

bituminöse Oberflächenbehandlung *f* BAU double bituminous surface treatment; **~e D-Schaltung** *f* ELEKTRIZ double delta connection; **~er Erdfehler** *m* ELEKTRIZ double-earth fault (BrE), double-ground fault (AmE); **~er Erdschluß** *m* ELEKTRIZ double-earth fault (BrE), double-ground fault (AmE); **~e Flachspule** *f* ELEKTRIZ double disc winding (BrE), double disk winding (AmE); **~e Gleisverbindung** *f* EISENBAHN double crossover; **~er Kameraauszug** *m* FOTO double camera extension; **~e Kreuzungsweiche** *f* BAU double crossover; **~e Linie** *f* DRUCK double rule; **~er Netzanschluß** *m* ELEKTRIZ duplicate supply; **~e obenliegende Nockenwelle** *f* KFZTECH *Motor* double overhead camshaft; **~e Pufferung** *f* COMP & DV double buffering; **~er Scheitelwert** *m* AKUSTIK, PHYS peak-to-peak value; **~e Schreibdichte** *f* COMP & DV DD, double density; **~e Speicherkapazität** *f* COMP & DV double density; **~es Tandemradfahrgestell** *nt* LUFTTRANS dual tandem wheel undercarriage

doppeltabgestimmt: ~er Mischer *m* ELEKTRONIK *Hochfrequenztechnik* double-balanced mixer

Doppel-T-Anker *m* ELEKTRIZ shuttle armature; **Doppel-T-Eisen** *nt* BAU H-iron

Doppel-: Doppeltetrode *f* RADIO *Röhre* double tetrode

doppeltgerichtet: ~es Bündel *nt* TELEKOM both-way group; **~e Leitung** *f* TELEKOM both-way circuit, both-way line

doppeltgespeist: ~er Motor *m* ELEKTRIZ double-fed motor

Doppel-: Doppeltiegelverfahren *nt* TELEKOM double crucible technique; **Doppeltischmaschine** *f* KER & GLAS two-table machine; **Doppel-T-Netz** *nt* ELEKTROTECH twin-T network; **Doppeltreibstoffdruckmesser** *m* LUFTTRANS dual-fuel pressure gage (AmE), dual-fuel pressure gauge (BrE); **Doppeltrommelkessel** *m* HEIZ & KÄLTE bi-drum boiler; **Doppel-T-Träger** *m* BAU H-beam, H-girder, I-beam, FERTIG I-beam, METALL I beam

doppeltwirkend[1] *adj* FERTIG *Kunststoffinstallationen*, MASCHINEN double-acting

doppeltwirkend:[2] **~er Kompressor** *m* HEIZ & KÄLTE double-acting compressor; **~e Presse** *f* MASCHINEN double-acting press; **~e Pumpe** *f* MASCHINEN double-acting pump; **~er Servomotor** *m* NICHTFOSS ENERG double-acting servomotor; **~er Stoßdämpfer** *m* KFZTECH double-acting shock absorber; **~er Verdichter** *m* HEIZ & KÄLTE double-acting compressor; **~er Zylinder** *m* MASCHINEN double-acting cylinder

Doppel-: Doppelüberlagerung *f* ELEKTRONIK, RADIO double conversion; **Doppelumschalter** *m* PHYS double-throw switch; **Doppelunterbrecher** *m* KFZTECH dual point breaker; **Doppelvergaser** *m* KFZTECH dual carburetor (AmE), dual carburettor (BrE), twin carburetor (AmE), twin carburettor (BrE), twin-choke carburetor (AmE), twin-choke carburettor (BrE), MECHAN dual carburetor (AmE), dual carburettor (BrE); **Doppelverglasung** *f* BAU, HEIZ & KÄLTE double glazing; **Doppelverglasungseinheit** *f* KER & GLAS double glazing unit

doppelwandig *adj* HEIZ & KÄLTE *Rolle*, WASSERTRANS *Schiffkonstruktion* double-skin

Doppel-: Doppelweggleichrichten *nt* ELEKTRIZ bridge rectification, ELEKTROTECH full-wave rectification; **Doppelweggleichrichter** *m* ELEKTRIZ bridge rectifier, ELEKTROTECH full-wave rectifier; **Doppelwegspeisung** *f* ELEKTRIZ two-way feed; **Doppelwendel** *f*

ELEKTRIZ coiled coil, MASCHINEN double helix; **Doppelwendelfaden** *m* ELEKTRIZ coiled coil filament; **Doppelwendelglühfaden** *m* ELEKTRIZ coiled coil filament; **Doppelwendellampe** *f* ELEKTRIZ coiled coil lamp; **Doppelwicklungsanker** *m* ELEKTRIZ double-wound armature; **Doppelwicklungstransformator** *m* ELEKTRIZ double-wound transformer; **Doppel-Windom-Antenne** *f* RADIO double Windom; **Doppelzeilensprungabtastung** *f* FERNSEH twin-interlaced scanning; **Doppelzellenkondensator** *m* ELEKTRIZ two-cell capacitor; **Doppelzirkel** *m* BAU double calipers (AmE), double callipers (BrE)

Döpper *m* BAU rivet set, rivet snap, riveting set, FERTIG holding-up snap, snap, MASCHINEN header (AmE), snap die

Doppler *m* ELEKTRONIK Doppler; **Doppler-Bandbreite** *f* ELEKTRONIK Doppler bandwidth; **Doppler-Breite** *f* STRAHLPHYS *im optischen Frequenzbereich* Doppler width; **Doppler-Effekt** *m* AKUSTIK, ELEKTRONIK, RADIO, WELLPHYS Doppler effect; **Doppler-Filter** *nt* ELEKTRONIK Doppler filter; **Doppler-Filterung** *f* ELEKTRONIK Doppler filtering; **~sche Frequenz** *f* ELEKTRONIK Doppler frequency; **Doppler-Modulation** *f* ELEKTRONIK Doppler modulation; **Doppler-Navigation** *f* RAUMFAHRT *Raumschiff* Doppler navigation; **Doppler-Trägheitsnavigation** *f* RAUMFAHRT *Raumschiff* Doppler inertial navigation; **Doppler-Verbreiterung** *f* STRAHLPHYS Doppler broadening; **Doppler-Verschiebung** *f* AUFNAHME, RAUMFAHRT Doppler shift

Dorn *m* BAU bolt, pin drift, spur, *eines Schlosses* broach, FERTIG core bar, pritchel, tongue, KER & GLAS spike, KUNSTSTOFF mandrel, mandril, MASCHINEN arbor (AmE), arbour (BrE), gudgeon, mandrel, mandril; **Dorndurchmesser** *m* FERTIG arbor diameter; **Dornpresse** *f* MASCHINEN arbor press, mandrel press, mandril press; **Dornschaft** *m* FERTIG arbor shank; **Dornschraubzwinge** *f* FERTIG arbor clamp; **Dornstange** *f* FERTIG *Bending* mandrel supporting rod, mandril supporting rod, *Stopfenzug* bar; **Dorntraglager** *nt* FERTIG arbor bracket

dorsal *adj* ERGON dorsal

DOS®-Betriebssystem *nt* COMP & DV DOS®, disk operating system

Dose *f* VERPACK can (AmE), tin (BrE)

Dosen: in ~ konserviert *adj* LEBENSMITTEL canned (AmE), tinned (BrE)

Dose: Dosenabfüllautomat *m* VERPACK can filling machine (AmE), tin filling machine (BrE); **Dosenabfüllinie** *f* VERPACK can filling line (AmE), tin filling line (BrE); **Dosenbarometer** *nt* LABOR, LUFTTRANS aneroid barometer; **Dosendichtungsmasse** *f* VERPACK can sealing compound (AmE), tin sealing compound (BrE); **Dosenhüllenentfernung** *f* VERPACK can delabeling (AmE), tin delabelling (BrE); **Dosenkontakt** *m* ELEKTROTECH female contact; **Dosenneuetikettierung** *f* VERPACK can relabeling (AmE), tin relabelling (BrE); **Dosenring** *m* VERPACK pull ring; **Dosenverpackungsmaschine** *f* VERPACK can packing machine (AmE), tin packing machine (BrE); **Dosenverschließmaschine** *f* VERPACK can closing machine (AmE), tin closing machine (BrE)

Dosier- *pref* GERÄT metering, proportioning, VERPACK dosing; **Dosieranlage** *f* BAU batch plant; **Dosierautomat** *m* GERÄT automatic proportioner;

Dosierbandwaage _f_ GERÄT metering conveyor balance; **Dosiereinrichtung** _f_ GERÄT proportioning device

dosieren _vt_ BAU batch, METROL measure out

Dosierer _m_ VERPACK dosing feeder

Dosier-: **Dosiergerät** _nt_ GERÄT proportioning device; **Dosierkugelhahn** _m_ FERTIG _Kunststoffinstallationen_ metering ball valve; **Dosiermaschine** _f_ VERPACK dosing machine; **Dosierpumpe** _f_ GERÄT, LABOR _Weiterleitung von Flüssigkeiten_, MASCHINEN metering pump, VERPACK dosing pump; **Dosiertank** _m_ KERN-TECH batching tank

Dosierung _f_ KOHLEN dosage, MASCHINEN metering; **Dosierungsöffnung** _f_ MASCHINEN metering hole

Dosier-: **Dosierventil** _nt_ KFZTECH metering valve, proportioning valve, MASCHINEN metering valve; **Dosiervorrichtung** _f_ FERTIG batcher, VERPACK dosing apparatus, metering equipment; **Dosierwaage** _f_ GERÄT gravimetric meter, metering balance; **Dosierzähler** _m_ GERÄT batching counter

Dosimeter _nt_ ERGON dosimeter, GERÄT radiation dosimeter, STRAHLPHYS dosimeter; **Dosimeterglas** _nt_ KER & GLAS dosimeter glass

Dosimetrie _f_ PHYS, STRAHLPHYS dosimetry; ~ **bei hohem Strahlungspegel** _f_ STRAHLPHYS high-level dosimetry

Dosis _f_ KERNTECH dose rate, STRAHLPHYS dose; **Dosisgrenzwert für berufliche Bestrahlung** _m_ UMWELTSCHMUTZ occupational dose limit; **Dosisleistung** _f_ STRAHLPHYS R, dose rate; **Dosisleistungseffekt** _m_ STRAHLPHYS dose rate effect; **Dosismesser** _m_ GERÄT radiation dosimeter; **Dosismeßgerät** _nt_ GERÄT, PHYS dosemeter; **Dosisrate** _f_ STRAHLPHYS R, dose rate; **Dosiswirkung** _f_ UMWELT-SCHMUTZ dose response; **Dosis-Wirkungsbeziehung** _f_ UMWELTSCHMUTZ dose response relationship

Dotier- _pref_ ELEKTRONIK implant, PHYS dope; **Dotierdosis** _f_ ELEKTRONIK implant dose; **Dotierelement** _nt_ PHYS dopant

dotieren _vt_ ELEKTRONIK implant, OPTIK, PHYS, TELEKOM dope

Dotier-: **Dotierstoff** _m_ PHYS dopant

dotiert[1] _adj_ COMP & DV, ELEKTRONIK, OPTIK, PHYS doped

dotiert:[2] ~**er Halbleiter** _m_ ELEKTRONIK, PHYS doped semiconductor; ~**e Silicafaser** _f_ OPTIK doped silica fiber (AmE), doped silica fibre (BrE)

Dotierung _f_ ELEKTRONIK implantation, _Verunreinigung zur Veränderung von Halbleitereigenschaften_ doping, PHYS _von Halbleitern mit Fremdelementen_, TELEKOM doping; **Dotierungsausgleich** _m_ ELEKTRONIK doping compensation; **Dotierungsmaterial** _nt_ ELEKTRONIK dopant, doping agent; **Dotierungsniveau** _nt_ ELEKTRONIK doping level; **Dotierungsprofil** _nt_ ELEKTRONIK doping profile, impurity concentration profile; **Dotierungsstoff** _m_ COMP & DV dopant; **Dotierungssubstanz** _f_ TELEKOM dopant

Doublet _nt_ FOTO doubled lens, doublet

Dove: ~**sches Umkehrprisma** _nt_ OPTIK Dove prism

Dozer: ~ **mit neigbarem Schild** _m_ TRANS tilting dozer

DP _abbr_ (_Diametral-Pitch_) MASCHINEN DP (_diametral pitch_)

DPCM _abbr_ (_Differenz-Pulscodemodulation_) ELEKTRONIK DPCM (_differential pulse code modulation_)

DPDT _abbr_ (_zweipoliger Umschalter, zweipoliger Wechselschalter_) ELEKTROTECH DPDT (_double-pole double-throw_)

DPP-Film _m_ VERPACK orientated polypropylene film

DPSK _abbr_ (_Phasendifferenzmodulation, Phasendifferenzumtastung_) ELEKTRONIK DPSK (_differential phase shift keying_)

DPST _abbr_ (_zweipoliger Einl Aus-Schalter_) ELEKTRO-TECH DPST (_double-pole single-throw_)

dpt _abbr_ (_Dioptrie_) OPTIK dpt (_dioptre_)

Drachenviereck _nt_ GEOM kite

Dragganker _m_ WASSERTRANS _Festmachen_ grapnel

Draggen _m_ WASSERTRANS _Festmachen_ grapnel

dragiert _adj_ LEBENSMITTEL _Süßwaren_ panned

Draht _m_ ELEKTROTECH wire, FERTIG _Schweißen_ rod (AmE); ~ **mit Flußmittelkern** _m_ BAU _Schweißen_ flux-cored wire; **Drahtantenne** _f_ TELEKOM wire aerial; **Drahtauslöser** _m_ FOTO cable release; **Drahtauslösernippel** _m_ FOTO cable release socket; **Drahtbonden** _nt_ ELEKTROTECH wire bonding; **Drahtbündel** _nt_ ELEK-TROTECH wire bundle; **Drahtbürste** _f_ BAU scratch brush, FERTIG wire brush; **Drahtdicke** _f_ MASCHINEN wire gage (AmE), wire gauge (BrE); **Drahtelektrode** _f_ ELEKTRIZ wire electrode; **Drahtende** _nt_ ELEKTROTECH wire end; **Drahtgeflecht** _nt_ BAU wire netting; **Drahtgewebe** _nt_ FERTIG wire cloth, KUNSTSTOFF wire mesh

drahtgewickelt: ~**er Anker** _m_ ELEKTRIZ wire-wound armature; ~**e Spule** _f_ ELEKTRIZ wire-wound coil; ~**er Widerstand** _m_ ELEKTROTECH wire-wound resistor; **nicht** ~**er Widerstand** _m_ ELEKTROTECH nonwirewound resistor

Draht: **Drahtgitter** _nt_ KER & GLAS wire mesh; **Drahtgittercontainer** _m_ TRANS lattice-sided container, skeleton container; **Drahtgitterverstärkung** _f_ KER & GLAS wire mesh reinforcement; **Drahtglas** _nt_ BAU armored glass (AmE), armoured glass (BrE), KER & GLAS armored glass (AmE), armoured glass (BrE), wire glass, wired glass; **Drahtgußglas** _nt_ KER & GLAS wired cast glass; **Drahtheftklammer** _f_ BAU wire staple, VERPACK wire staple; **Drahtheftmaschine** _f_ VERPACK stapling machine; **Drahtkammer** _f_ TEILPHYS wire chamber; **Drahtkern** _m_ ELEKTROTECH wire core; **Drahtkontaktieren** _nt_ ELEK-TROTECH wire bonding; **Drahtkugellager** _nt_ MASCHINEN wire race ball bearing; **Drahtlehre** _f_ MA-SCHINEN SWG, standard wire gage (AmE), standard wire gauge (BrE), wire gage (AmE), wire gauge (BrE); **Drahtlitze** _f_ MASCHINEN strand wire; **Drahtlitzenleiter** _m_ ELEKTRIZ tinsel conductor

drahtlos:[1] ~ **ausgesandt** _adj_ PHYS radio

drahtlos:[2] ~**er Infrarot-Kopfhörer** _m_ AUFNAHME wireless infrared headphones; ~**e Kopfgarnitur** _f_ AUFNAHME _Kopfhörer und Mikrofon_ wireless headset; ~**es Schwerhörigengerät** _nt_ TELEKOM wireless hearing aid receiver; ~**e Steuerungsautomatik** _f_ LUFTTRANS, TRANS, WASSERTRANS radio telecontrol

Draht: **Drahtmodelldarstellung** _f_ COMP & DV wire frame representation; **Drahtnachlaufschweißen** _nt_ FERTIG backward welding; **Drahtnachricht** _f_ ELEKTROTECH cablegram; **Drahtnagel** _m_ BAU brad, MASCHINEN wire nail; **Drahtnetz** _nt_ LABOR wire gauze; **Drahtpaar** _nt_ ELEKTROTECH wire pair; **Drahtpotentiometer** _nt_ ELEK-TRIZ wire-wound potentiometer; **Drahtquerschnitt** _m_ METROL wire gage (AmE), wire gauge (BrE); **Drahtrolle** _f_ BAU wire reel; **Drahtrollenlager** _nt_ MASCHINEN wire race roller bearing; **Drahtseil** _nt_ FERTIG, MASCHINEN, SICHERHEIT wire rope; **Drahtseilbahn** _f_ TRANS cable railroad (AmE), cable railway (BrE), cable road, ropeway; **Drahtseilschlaufe** _f_ SICHERHEIT wire rope sling; **Drahtspeichenrad** _nt_ KFZTECH wire wheel; **Drahtspeichergerät** _nt_ AUFNAHME wire recorder; **Drahtstärke** _f_

MASCHINEN wire gage (AmE), wire gauge (BrE); **Drahtsteigung** *f* ELEKTRIZ pitch; **Drahtstöpselverschluß** *m* KER & GLAS wired stopper finish (AmE); **Drahtstraße** *f* MASCHINEN wire mill; **Drahttarget** *nt* STRAHLPHYS wire mesh target; **Drahtübertragungsweg** *m* ELEKTROTECH metallic circuit; **Drahtumschnürungsapparat** *m* VERPACK wire strapping equipment; **Drahtverschnürung für Beutel** *f* VERPACK wire bag tie

drahtverstärkt: ~es Brandschutzglas *nt* KER & GLAS Georgian-wired glass; ~er Schlauch *m* KUNSTSTOFF, MASCHINEN wire-reinforced hose

Draht: **Drahtwalzwerk** *nt* KOHLEN rod mill; **Drahtwiderstand** *m* ELEKTRIZ, PHYS wire-wound resistor; **Drahtzange** *f* MASCHINEN tongs; **Drahtzange mit flachem Maul** *f* MECHAN flat-nosed pliers; **Drahtzaun** *m* BAU wire fence; **Drahtziehbank** *f* FERTIG wire-drawing bench; **Drahtzieheisen** *nt* MASCHINEN wire-drawing die; **Drahtziehen** *nt* MASCHINEN wire drawing; **Drahtzuführung** *f* KER & GLAS wire guide; **Drahtzug** *m* FERTIG wire drawing; **Drahtzusammenstapelmaschine** *f* VERPACK wire stacking machine

Drain *m* ELEKTRONIK, ELEKTROTECH, PHYS, RADIO *Drainanschluß des FET* drain; **Drainanschluß** *m* ELEKTROTECH drain terminal; **Drainelektrode** *f* PHYS *beim Feldeffekttransistor* drain; **Drainschalter** *m* ELEKTROTECH drain contact; **Drainschaltung** *f* ELEKTROTECH drain connection; **Drainstrom** *m* ELEKTROTECH drain current; **Drainverstärker** *m* ELEKTRONIK drain amplifier; **Drainvorspannung** *f* ELEKTROTECH drain bias

Drall *m* ELEKTRIZ lay, FERTIG helix, moment of impulse, spiral, MASCHINEN twist, RAUMFAHRT spin, TEXTIL twist; **Dralllänge** *f* ELEKTRIZ *Kabelherstellung* length of lay, ELEKTROTECH lay

drallfrei: ~es Tau *nt* WASSERTRANS nonkinking rope

Drall: **Drallnut** *f* FERTIG helical broaching; **Drallnutenräumen** *nt* FERTIG helical broaching; **Drallrichtung** *f* ELEKTRIZ direction of lay, FERTIG hand of helix, hand of spiral, TEXTIL direction of twist; **Drallverhältnis** *nt* ELEKTRIZ lay ratio; **Drallwinkel** *m* FERTIG angle of the tooth helix, MECHAN *Drahtseiltechnik* angle of twist

DRAM *abbr (dynamischer RAM)* COMP & DV DRAM *(dynamic random access memory)*

Dränage *f* ERDÖL *Geologie*, WASSERVERSORG drainage

drapieren *vt* TEXTIL drape

Drapierung *f* TEXTIL draping

Drechselbank *f* MASCHINEN lathe

Drechseln *nt* MASCHINEN turning

drechseln *vt* MASCHINEN turn

Drechsler *m* MASCHINEN turner, wood turner; **Drechslerbank** *f* BAU wood-turning lathe; **Drechslerwerkzeug** *nt* BAU wood-turning tools

D-Regeleinrichtung *f* REGELUNG derivative control system

dreggen *vt* WASSERTRANS drag

Dreggnetz *nt* WASSERTRANS *Fischerei* dredge net

Dreh- *pref* MECHAN torsional; **Drehachse** *f* FERTIG fulcrum, hinge, MASCHINEN axis of rotation, swivel axis, MECHAN axis of revolution, hinge, PHYS axis of revolution; **Drehanker** *m* ELEKTRIZ rotary armature, rotating armature, ELEKTROTECH pivoted armature, revolving armature; **Dreharbeit** *f* FERTIG, MASCHINEN lathe work; **Dreharm** *m* KFZTECH torque arm, MECHAN swivel, MEERSCHMUTZ rotatable arm; **Drehautomat** *m* MASCHINEN automatic lathe

Drehbank *f* BAU, FERTIG, MASCHINEN, MECHAN lathe;

Drehbankarbeit *f* MASCHINEN lathe work; **Drehbankbett** *nt* MASCHINEN, MECHAN lathe bed; **Drehbankfutter** *nt* MASCHINEN, MECHAN lathe chuck; **Drehbankschlitten** *m* MASCHINEN, MECHAN lathe slide; **Drehbankspindel** *f* MASCHINEN lathe spindle; **Drehbankspindelstock** *m* MASCHINEN lathe headstock; **Drehbankspitze** *f* MASCHINEN lathe center (AmE), lathe centre (BrE); **Drehbankwerkzeughalter** *m* MASCHINEN lathe toolpost

drehbar[1] *adj* FERTIG hinged, LABOR revolving, rotary, MECHAN pivoted, RADIO revolving, RAUMFAHRT, TELEKOM rotatable

drehbar:[2] ~e Antenne *f* TELEKOM rotatable antenna; ~e Düse *f* RAUMFAHRT *Raumschiff* rotatable nozzle; ~er Pfeifenkopf *m* LABOR *Mikroskop* revolving nose piece; ~e Reflektorantenne *f* RADIO revolving radar reflector; ~e Stellung *f* LABOR *Mikroskop* revolving stage; ~er Tisch *m* METROL rotary table; ~er Zeichenkopf *m* METROL protractor

Dreh-: **Drehbeanspruchung** *f* METALL twisting strain; **Drehbewegung** *f* FERTIG *Kunststoffinstallationen*, MASCHINEN, PHYS rotation; **Drehbohren** *nt* BAU, KOHLEN rotary drilling; **Drehbohrer** *m* BAU rotary drill, twist gimlet, FERTIG rotary tool; **Drehbohrmaschine** *f* KOHLEN rotary machine; **Drehbolzen** *m* FERTIG pivot; **Drehbrett** *nt* FERTIG loam board; **Drehbrücke** *f* BAU pivot bridge, swing bridge, turn bridge, turning bridge, MASCHINEN turn bridge, WASSERTRANS swing bridge; **Drehdiamanten** *m pl* MASCHINEN turning diamonds; **Drehdurchmesser** *m* MASCHINEN swing; **Dreheiseninstrument** *nt* ELEKTROTECH moving-iron instrument, GERÄT moving-iron instrument, soft iron instrument; **Dreheiseninstrument mit Magnet** *nt* GERÄT permanent magnet moving-iron instrument; **Dreheisenmeßgerät** *nt* ELEKTROTECH moving-iron instrument; **Dreheisenmeßwerk** *nt* GERÄT moving-iron instrument

drehelastisch *adj* MASCHINEN torsionally elastic

Dreh : **Drehelastizität** *f* MASCHINEN torsional elasticity

Drehen *nt* BAU slewing (BrE), sluing (AmE), *eines Krans* turning, MASCHINEN turning; ~ **von der Stange** *nt* MASCHINEN bar turning

drehen[1] *vt* COMP & DV rotate, KER & GLAS throw, MASCHINEN rotate, turn, WASSERTRANS *Schiff* turn

drehen[2] *vi* COMP & DV, MASCHINEN rotate, WASSERTRANS *Schiff* turn

drehen:[3] **sich ~** *v refl* WASSERTRANS *Wind* veer

drehend[1] *adj* PHYS *Molekül* rotatory

drehend:[2] ~er Videokopf *m* FERNSEH rotary video head

Dreher *m* KER & GLAS thrower, MASCHINEN turner, MECHAN lathe operator

Dreh-: **Drehfeld** *nt* ELEKTRIZ rotating field, ELEKTROTECH, LABOR rotary field, TELEKOM rotating field; **Drehfeldinstrument** *nt* GERÄT rotating field instrument; **Drehfeldumformer** *m* ELEKTRIZ rotary field converter; **Drehfenster** *nt* BAU pivot-hung window; **Drehfensterflügel** *m* BAU pivot-hung sash; **Drehfeuer** *nt* LUFTTRANS rotating beacon; **Drehfilter** *nt* KOHLEN, WASSERVERSORG rotary filter; **Drehflügelfenster** *nt* BAU side-hung window; **Drehflügelflugzeug** *nt* LUFTTRANS gyroplane, rotary wing aircraft, rotating wing aircraft, rotor aircraft, TRANS gyroplane; **Drehflügelzähler** *m* GERÄT rotating blade meter; **Drehformblasverfahren** *nt* KER & GLAS paste mould blowing; **Drehform-Press-Blasverfahren** *nt* KER & GLAS paste mould press-and-blow process; **Drehfunk-**

feuer *nt* LUFTTRANS omnirange indicator
drehgelagert: **~er Anker** *m* ELEKTROTECH pivoted armature
Drehgelenk: **über ~ verbunden** *adj* FERTIG pin-connected
Dreh-: **Drehgelenk** *nt* LUFTTRANS *Hubschrauber* blade pitch change hinge, MASCHINEN hinge, hinge joint
drehgelenkig[1] *adj* FERTIG pivoting; **~ angeordnet** *adj* FERTIG pivoted
drehgelenkig:[2] **~e Anordnung** *f* FERTIG pivoting
drehgelenkig:[3] **~ anordnen** *vt* FERTIG pivot
Dreh-: **Drehgelenkverbindung** *f* MASCHINEN swivel joint; **Drehgeschwindigkeit** *f* LUFTTRANS rate of turn, MASCHINEN rotating speed; **Drehgestell** *nt* FERTIG dolly; **Drehgestellgüterwagen** *m* KFZTECH *mit Schwenkdach* bogie wagon; **Drehgestellrahmen** *m* EISENBAHN bogie frame; **Drehgestellwagen** *m* MASCHINEN bogie car; **Drehgriff** *m* KFZTECH *Motorrad* twist grip; **Drehhaken** *m* WASSERTRANS *Takelage, Beschläge* swivel hook; **Drehherz** *nt* FERTIG, MASCHINEN driver, driving dog, lathe carrier, lathe dog; **Drehimpuls** *m* PHYS, TEILPHYS angular momentum; **Drehimpulsquantenzahl** *f* TEILPHYS spin; **Drehkippfenster** *nt* BAU *horizontal oder vertikal* center-hung window (AmE), centre-hung window (BrE); **Drehknopf** *m* ELEKTROTECH knob, rotary knob, MASCHINEN knob; **Drehkolben** *m* MASCHINEN rotary piston; **Drehkolbengasmeßgerät** *nt* GERÄT lobed-impeller gas meter; **Drehkolbenmotor** *m* KFZTECH rotating piston engine, MASCHINEN rotary engine; **Drehkolbenpumpe** *f* KONTROLL, MASCHINEN, WASSERVERSORG rotary pump; **Drehkolbenverdichter** *m* MASCHINEN rotary compressor; **Drehkondensator** *m* ELEKTRIZ rotary capacitor, variable capacitor, ELEKTROTECH variable capacitor; **Drehkondensatorbereich** *m* ELEKTROTECH variable capacitor sector; **Drehkopf** *m* MECHAN turret; **Drehkörper** *m* KONTROLL rotor; **Drehkraft** *f* PHYS rotatory power; **Drehkran** *m* BAU all-round swing crane (BrE), rotary crane, slewing crane (BrE), sluing crane (AmE), KERNTECH slewing crane (BrE), sluing crane (AmE); **Drehkranz** *m* KONTROLL turntable; **Drehkreis** *m* WASSERTRANS *Schiff* turning circle; **Drehkreuz** *nt* FERTIG capstan, turnstile, LUFTTRANS *Hubschrauber* spider unit, MASCHINEN capstan wheel, spider wheel; **Drehkristallmethode** *f* STRAHLPHYS *Röntgenbeugung* rotating crystal method; **Drehkuppel** *f* FERTIG turret; **Drehlager** *nt* EISENBAHN pivot bearing, FERTIG *Kunststoffinstallationen* rotary bearing, KERNTECH pivot bearing; **Drehling** *m* FERTIG tool holder bit; **Drehmagnetcassette** *f* AUFNAHME moving-magnet cartridge; **Drehmagnet-Galvanometer** *nt* ELEKTROTECH, GERÄT moving-magnet galvanometer; **Drehmagnetmedium** *nt* ELEKTROTECH moving-magnet medium; **Drehmagnetmeßwerk** *nt* GERÄT moving-magnet movement; **Drehmantel** *m* FERTIG outer sleeve; **Drehmaschine** *f* FERTIG duplex lathe, gear lathe, MASCHINEN turning lathe; **Drehmaschine mit Brücke** *f* MASCHINEN break lathe, gap lathe; **Drehmaschine mit Sechskantrevolverkopf** *f* MASCHINEN hexagon turret lathe; **Drehmeißel** *m* FERTIG lathe tool, MASCHINEN lathe tool, turning tool; **Drehmelder für Drehmomente** *m* GERÄT synchro torque transmitter
Drehmoment *nt* ELEKTRIZ, ELEKTROTECH, ERDÖL torque, FERTIG radial force, FERTIG torque, *Kunststoffinstallationen* torque, KFZTECH *Motor* torque, MASCHINEN turning moment, MASCHINEN torque, MECHAN angular momentum, MECHAN torque, PHYS rotational moment; **~ eines blockierten Läufers** *nt* ELEKTRIZ locked rotor torque; **~ eines blockierten Rotors** *nt* ELEKTRIZ locked rotor torque; **~ des Motors** *nt* KFZTECH, LUFTTRANS engine torque; **~ des Triebwerks** *nt* KFZTECH, LUFTTRANS engine torque; **Drehmomentanzeiger** *m* GERÄT torque indicator; **Drehmomentausgleichsluftschraube** *f* LUFTTRANS antitorque rotor; **Drehmomentausgleichspropeller** *m* LUFTTRANS antitorque propeller; **Drehmomentausgleichsvorrichtung** *f* LUFTTRANS antitorque device; **Drehmomentenstückegabel** *f* LUFTTRANS *Fahrwerk* torque link; **Drehmomentmesser** *m* FERTIG dynamometer, MASCHINEN torquemeter, torsiometer; **Drehmomentminderer** *m* FERTIG automatic torque limiting device; **Drehmomentschlüssel** *m* KERNTECH torque spanner, KFZTECH *Werkzeug*, MASCHINEN torque wrench; **Drehmomentskoeffizient** *m* NICHTFOSS ENERG coefficient of torque; **Drehmomentwandler** *m* KFZTECH *Automatikgetriebe* converter, *Getriebe* torque converter, MASCHINEN torque converter; **Drehmomentwandlergehäuse** *nt* KFZTECH torque converter housing
Dreh-: **Drehofen** *m* KOHLEN rotary kiln; **Drehpfanne** *f* KFZTECH *Anhänger* bogie pivot (BrE), truck pivot (AmE); **Drehplatte** *f* KONTROLL turntable; **Drehpol** *m* MASCHINEN center of revolution (AmE), centre of revolution (BrE); **Drehpositionsbestimmung** *f* COMP & DV rotation position sensing, rotational position sensing; **Drehpotentiometer** *nt* ELEKTRIZ, ELEKTROTECH rotary potentiometer; **Drehprisma** *nt* OPTIK rotating prism; **Drehpunkt** *m* FERTIG fulcrum, MASCHINEN pivot, pivot point, MECHAN center of motion (AmE), centre of motion (BrE), pivot, PHYS center of motion (AmE), centre of motion (BrE), fulcrum; **Drehrahmen** *m* FOTO *Kamera* revolving back; **Drehregelventil** *nt* BAU plug cock, plug tap; **Drehregler** *m* ELEKTRIZ induction regulator; **Drehrichtung** *f* FERTIG hand of rotation, MASCHINEN sense of rotation; **Drehrichtungsanzeiger** *m* GERÄT rotation indicator
drehrichtungsunabhängig: **~er Lüfter** *m* HEIZ & KÄLTE bidirectional fan
Dreh-: **Drehring** *m* MECHAN swivel; **Drehrohrofen** *m* ABFALL rotary furnace, rotary kiln, KER & GLAS rotary kiln; **Drehsäule** *f* WASSERVERSORG *einer Schleuse* quoin post; **Drehschalter** *m* ELEKTRIZ rotary-type switch, ELEKTROTECH rotary switch, KONTROLL rotary wafer switch; **Drehscheibe** *f* EISENBAHN turntable, FERTIG swivel, KER & GLAS throwing wheel, MASCHINEN rotating disc (BrE), rotating disk (AmE); **Drehscheibenfluglehrapparat** *m* LUFTTRANS link trainer; **Drehscheibenschalter** *m* ELEKTROTECH rotary wafer switch; **Drehscheibenventil** *nt* KFZTECH *Zweitaktmotor* rotary disc valve (BrE), rotary disk valve (AmE); **Drehschieber** *m* KFZTECH *Zweitaktmotor* rotary disc valve (BrE), rotary disk valve (AmE), MASCHINEN, NICHTFOSS ENERG rotary valve; **Drehschlauch** *m* ERDÖL *Bohrtechnik* rotary hose; **Drehschraubstock** *m* MASCHINEN swivel vice (BrE), swivel vise (AmE); **Drehschüssel** *f* KER & GLAS rotating bowl; **Drehschwingung** *f* MASCHINEN rotary oscillation; **Drehseil** *nt* ERDÖL *Bohrtechnik* spinning line; **Drehspäne** *m pl* MASCHINEN turnings; **Drehspiegel** *m* PHYS rotating mirror; **Drehspindel** *f* MASCHINEN lathe spindle

Dreh-: **Drehspul-Amperemeter** *nt* ELEKTRIZ moving-coil ammeter; **Drehspule** *f* ELEKTROTECH *Galvanometer* moving coil; **Drehspulgalvanometer** *nt* ELEKTRIZ, ELEKTROTECH, PHYS moving-coil galvanometer; **Drehspulinstrument** *nt* GERÄT moving-coil instrument, permanent magnet moving-coil instrument; **Drehspulmeßgerät** *nt* ELEKTRIZ, ELEKTROTECH moving-coil meter, GERÄT moving-coil instrument; **Drehspulrelais** *nt* ELEKTRIZ moving-coil relay; **Drehspulspannungsmeßgerät** *nt* ELEKTRIZ moving-coil voltmeter; **Drehspulstrommeßgerät** *nt* ELEKTRIZ moving-coil ammeter; **Drehspultonabnehmer** *m* AUFNAHME moving-coil pickup; **Drehstab** *m* KFZTECH torsion bar, *Federung, Aufhängung* stabilizer bar; **Drehstabstabilisator** *m* KFZTECH torque stabilizer, *Federung* antiroll bar; **Drehstahl** *m* MASCHINEN lathe tool; **Drehstift** *m* BAU hinge pin, turn pin

Drehstrom *m* ELEKTRIZ, ELEKTROTECH three-phase current; **Drehstromalternator** *m* ELEKTRIZ three-phase alternator; **Drehstromanker** *m* ELEKTRIZ three-phase current armature; **Drehstromgenerator** *m* ELEKTRIZ alternator, three-phase generator, ELEKTROTECH, PHYS alternator; **Drehstromgleichrichterbrücke** *f* ELEKTRIZ three-phase rectifier; **Drehstrominduktionsmotor** *m* KFZTECH three-phase induction motor; **Drehstromlichtmaschine** *f* KFZTECH, NICHTFOSS ENERG alternator; **Drehstrommotor** *m* ELEKTRIZ three-phase motor; **Drehstromnetz** *nt* ELEKTRIZ three-phase supply network; **Drehstromschaltung** *f* ELEKTRIZ polyphase circuit; **Drehstromschrittmotor** *m* ELEKTROTECH three-phase stepper motor; **Drehstromschutzleiterdrossel** *f* ELEKTRIZ three-phase neutral reactor; **Drehstromsynchronmotor** *m* ELEKTROTECH three-phase synchronous motor; **Drehstromtransformator** *m* ELEKTROTECH three-phase transformer; **Drehstromversorgung** *f* ELEKTROTECH three-phase supply

Dreh-: **Drehsupport** *m* MASCHINEN swivel head, swivel slide rest; **Drehteil** *nt* FERTIG lathe work, *Waagerechtstoßmaschine* harp, *Wälzfräsen* hob swivel head, MASCHINEN turned part; **Drehteller** *m* AKUSTIK turntable; **Drehtisch** *m* ERDÖL *Bohrtechnik* rotary table, KONTROLL turntable, MASCHINEN revolving table, rotary table, rotating table, MECHAN turntable; **Drehtischzuführung** *f* VERPACK turntable feed; **Drehtor** *nt* BAU swing gate; **Drehtransformator** *m* ELEKTROTECH rotary transformer; **Drehtrommel** *f* ABFALL revolving drum; **Drehtrommelzuführung** *f* MASCHINEN rotary drum feeder; **Drehtür** *f* BAU swing door, swinging door; **Drehumformer** *m* ELEKTRIZ inverted rotary converter, rotary converter

Drehung[1] *f* ELEKTROTECH *Rotation* turn, GEOM revolution, rotation, *Koordinatenachsen* rotation, MASCHINEN rotation, PHYS turn; **~ entgegen dem Uhrzeigersinn** *f* MASCHINEN rotation anticlockwise; **~ im Uhrzeigersinn** *f* MASCHINEN rotation clockwise

Drehung:[2] **in ~ versetzen** *vt* MASCHINEN *Welle* impart a rotary motion

Drehungen: **~ pro Meter** *f pl* TEXTIL turns per meter (AmE), turns per metre (BrE); **~ pro Zoll** *f pl* TEXTIL turns per inch

Drehung: **Drehungsbeiwert** *m* TEXTIL twist factor **drehungsfrei** *adj* PHYS irrotational, nonkinking

Drehung: **Drehungsgeschwindigkeit** *f* LUFTTRANS rotation speed

Dreh-: **Drehventil** *nt* HYDRAUL rotary valve; **Drehverbin-**dung *f* ELEKTROTECH rotary joint; **Drehversuch** *m* METALL torsion test; **Drehvorrichtung** *f* KERNTECH, WASSERTRANS *Motor* turning gear; **Drehwähler** *m* ELEKTROTECH *Fernmeldewesen* uniselector; **Drehwählersystem** *nt* TELEKOM rotary system; **Drehwählervermittlungsstelle** *f* TELEKOM rotary exchange; **Drehwechselfestigkeit** *f* FERTIG alternate torsional strength; **Drehwerkzeug** *nt* MASCHINEN lathe tool; **Drehwinkel** *m* FERTIG *Kunststoffinstallationen*, GERÄT angle of rotation, MASCHINEN angle of twist; **Drehwinkelbegrenzung** *f* FERTIG *Kunststoffinstallationen* limitation of rotation angle; **Drehwinkelrate** *f* LUFTTRANS angular roll rate

Drehzahl *f* ELEKTRIZ RPM, revolutions per minute, GERÄT rotational speed, KFZTECH *Motor* revs, MASCHINEN rotational speed, speed, PHYS speed; **~ des Rotors** *f* LUFTTRANS *Hubschrauber* rotor speed; **~ der Schleifscheibe** *f* FERTIG grinding wheel RPM; **Drehzahlanzeige** *f* MASCHINEN revolution indication; **Drehzahlanzeigegerät** *nt* GERÄT speed indicator; **Drehzahlanzeiger** *m* MASCHINEN revolution indicator; **Drehzahlbegrenzer** *m* KFZTECH speed limiter, MASCHINEN overspeed protection; **Drehzahlbereich** *m* MASCHINEN range of speeds, speed range; **Drehzahldrehmomentkennlinie** *f* HEIZ & KÄLTE speed torque characteristic

Dreh-: **Drehzähler** *m* FERTIG counter

Drehzahl: **Drehzahlmesser** *m* KFZTECH *Motor, Zubehör* revolution counter, MASCHINEN revolution counter, speed counter; **Drehzahlminderer** *m* MASCHINEN speed reducer; **Drehzahlregelung** *f* ELEKTRIZ, TEXTIL speed control; **Drehzahlregler** *m* ELEKTROTECH, KFZTECH actuator, *Motordrehzahlbegrenzer* governor, MASCHINEN speed controller, speed governor, MECHAN governor, NICHTFOSS ENERG speed control device, OPTIK *für CD-Spieler* controller, TRANS *KFZ* actuator; **Drehzahlreihe** *f* FERTIG group of speeds; **Drehzahlsichtanzeigesystem** *nt* TRANS displayed speed system; **Drehzahlüberschreitungsprüfung** *f* ELEKTRIZ overspeed test; **Drehzahlverhältnis** *nt* MASCHINEN speed ratio

Dreh-: **Drehzahn** *m* FERTIG tool bit; **Drehzapfen** *m* FERTIG gudgeon, KERNTECH king journal, trunnion, KFZTECH *Anhänger* bogie pin (BrE), truck pin (AmE), pivot pin, *Universalgelenk* trunnion, KOHLEN trunnion, MASCHINEN fulcrum pin, gudgeon pin, hinge pin, piston pin, pivot pin, swivel pin, MECHAN journal, pivot; **Drehzapfenlager** *nt* EISENBAHN center plate (AmE), centre plate (BrE)

Drei- *pref* BAU three; **Dreiadern-Kabel** *nt* ELEKTRIZ triple core cable; **Dreiadreßbefehl** *m* COMP & DV three-address instruction

Dreiachs- *pref* RAUMFAHRT three-axis; **Dreiachsenanzeige** *f* RAUMFAHRT *Raumschiff* three-axis indicator; **Dreiachsenkreisel** *m* RAUMFAHRT *Raumschiff* three-axis gyro unit; **Dreiachsen-Pinchversuch** *m* KERNTECH triaxial pinch experiment; **Dreiachsenstabilisierung** *f* RAUMFAHRT *Raumschiff* three-axis stabilization

dreiachsig: **~e Spannung** *f* METALL triaxial stress

Dreiachs-: **Dreiachs-Winkeldrehsensor** *m* LUFTTRANS angular three-axis rate sensor

dreiadrig: **~es Kabel** *nt* ELEKTROTECH three-conductor cable

Drei-: **Dreiaxialprüfung** *f* BAU triaxial test, MASCHINEN three-jaw chuck; **Dreibackensetzstock** *m* MASCHINEN three-jaw steady, three-jaw steadyrest

dreibasig: ~e Säure *f* CHEMIE triacid

Dreibein *nt* BAU gin; **Dreibeinbohrbühne** *f* ERDÖL *Bohrtechnik* shear leg; **Dreibeinfahrwerk** *nt* LUFTTRANS *Fahrwerk* tricycle landing gear; **Dreibeinkran** *m* BAU shear leg

3-D *abbr (dreidimensional)* MASCHINEN, PHYS 3-D *(three-dimensional)*

Drei-: **Dreidecker** *m* LUFTTRANS triplane

dreidimensional[1] *adj (3-D)* MASCHINEN three-dimensional, PHYS three-dimensional *(3-D)*

dreidimensional:[2] ~es Bild *nt* TELEKOM three-dimensional image; ~e Geometrie *f* GEOM geometry of three dimensions; ~e Grafik *f* COMP & DV three-dimensional graphics; ~er IC *m* ELEKTRONIK three-dimensional integrated circuit; ~e Integration *f* ELEKTRONIK three-dimensional integration; ~e Koordinaten *f pl* GEOM x-y-z coordinates; ~es Nachformfräsen *nt* FERTIG kellering

dreidimensional:[3] ~ fräsen *vt* FERTIG *Gesenke* pocket

Drei-: **Dreidimensionalität** *f* GEOM three dimensionality; **Dreidrahtgenerator** *m* ELEKTRIZ three-wire generator; **Dreidrahtsystem** *nt* ELEKTRIZ three-wire system

Dreieck *nt* ELEKTROTECH delta, GEOM triangle; **Dreieckbogen** *m* BAU triangular arch

dreieckig[1] *adj* GEOM triangular

dreieckig:[2] ~er Nocken *m* MASCHINEN triangular cam

Dreieck: **Dreieckigkeit** *f* KER & GLAS triangularity; **Dreieckschaltung** *f* ELEKTRIZ delta connection, ELEKTROTECH delta connection, *Speicherröhrenanschlüsse* mesh connection; **Dreiecksmatrix** *f* COMP & DV triangular matrix; **Dreiecksschaltung** *f* PHYS delta connection; **Dreieck-Sternschaltung** *f* ELEKTRIZ delta star connection; **Dreieck-Sternumformung** *f* ELEKTRIZ delta-to-star conversion; **Dreieckstest** *m* LEBENSMITTEL triangle test, triangle testing; **Dreiecksvermessung** *f* BAU triangulation; **Dreieckszahn** *m* MASCHINEN fleam tooth

Drei-: **Dreielektrodenröhre** *f* CHEMIE *Elektrizität* three-electrode valve, triode, ELEKTRONIK three-electrode tube; **Dreierpackung** *f* VERPACK triple pack; **Dreierverbindung** *f* TELEKOM three-way call

Dreifach- *pref* CHEMIE triple

dreifach[1] *adj* CHEMIE ternary, triple

dreifach:[2] ~er Alphaprozeß *m* KERNTECH triple alpha process; ~ beschichtetes Teilchen *nt* KERNTECH triplex-coated particle; ~ gekröpfte Kurbel *f* MASCHINEN three-throw crank; ~ gekröpfte Kurbelwelle *f* MASCHINEN three-throw crankshaft; ~ gewickelter Transformator *m* ELEKTRIZ triple-wound transformer

Dreifach-: **Dreifachform** *f* KER & GLAS triple cavity mould; **Dreifachkabel** *nt* ELEKTROTECH three-conductor cable; **Dreifachnorm** *f* FERNSEH triple standard

Dreifarben- *pref* ELEKTRONIK three-beam, FOTO three-color (AmE), three-colour (BrE); **Dreifarben-Bildröhre** *f* ELEKTRONIK three-beam color picture tube (AmE), three-beam colour picture tube (BrE); **Dreifarbenfotografie** *f* FOTO three-color photography (AmE), three-colour photography (BrE); **Dreifarbenplatte** *f* FOTO three-color plate (AmE), three-colour plate (BrE)

Drei-: **Dreifingerregel** *f* ELEKTRIZ left-hand rule

dreiflächig *adj* GEOM trihedral

Drei-: **Dreifuß** *m* LABOR tripod

dreigängig[1] *adj* FERTIG, MASCHINEN three-start

dreigängig:[2] ~es Gewinde *nt* MASCHINEN three-start thread

Drei-: **Dreigelenkbogen** *m* BAU three-hinged arch

dreigestaltig *adj* CHEMIE trimorphic, trimorphous

Drei-: **Dreigestaltigkeit** *f* CHEMIE trimorphism; **Dreigitterröhre** *f* ELEKTRONIK three-grid tube

dreigliedrig *adj* MATH trinomial

Drei-: **Dreihalskolben** *m* LABOR three-necked flask; **Dreikanalzweitaktmotor** *m* KFZTECH three-port two-stroke engine

Dreikant- *pref* BAU triangular, MASCHINEN three-square; **Dreikantfeile** *f* MASCHINEN three-square file, tri square file, triangular file; **Dreikantleiste** *f* BAU triangular fillet; **Dreikantprisma** *nt* PHYS roof prism

Drei-: **Dreiklauenfutter** *nt* MASCHINEN three-pronged chuck; **Dreikomponentenlegierung** *f* METALL three component alloy; **Dreikreis-Kernkraftwerk** *nt* KERNTECH three-circuit nuclear power plant; **Dreilagenholz** *nt* BAU three-ply wood; **Dreileiterkabel** *nt* ELEKTROTECH three-conductor cable; **Dreileiternetz** *nt* ELEKTROTECH three-wire mains; **Dreilochbrenner** *m* HEIZ & KÄLTE treble jet burner; **Dreimastmarssegelschoner** *m* TRANS barque schooner (BrE); **Dreimessermaschine** *f* DRUCK three-sided cutting machine; **Dreiniveaulaser** *m* ELEKTRONIK three-level laser; **Dreiniveaumaser** *m* ELEKTRONIK three-level maser; **Dreinullen-Antialiasing-Filter** *nt* ELEKTRONIK *zur Verhinderung von Faltungsfrequenzen* three-zeros antialiasing filter

Dreiphasen- *pref* ELEKTRIZ, ELEKTROTECH three-phase; **Dreiphasen-Erdungstransformator** *m* ELEKTRIZ three-phase earthing transformer (BrE), three-phase grounding transformer (AmE); **Dreiphasen-Induktionsmotor** *m* ELEKTROTECH three-phase induction motor; **Dreiphasenläufer** *m* ELEKTROTECH three-phase rotor; **Dreiphasenmaschine** *f* ELEKTRIZ, ELEKTROTECH three-phase machine; **Dreiphasenmotor** *m* ELEKTROTECH three-phase motor; **Dreiphasennetz** *nt* ELEKTROTECH three-wire mains; **Dreiphasenrotor** *m* ELEKTROTECH three-phase rotor; **Dreiphasenrotorwicklung** *f* ELEKTROTECH three-phase rotor winding; **Dreiphasenschaltung** *f* TELEKOM three-phase circuit; **Dreiphasenstator** *m* ELEKTROTECH three-phase stator; **Dreiphasen-Statorwicklung** *f* ELEKTROTECH three-phase stator winding; **Dreiphasenstrom** *m* ELEKTROTECH three-phase current; **Dreiphasen-Stromversorgung** *f* ELEKTROTECH three-phase supply; **Dreiphasen-Synchronmotor** *m* ELEKTROTECH three-phase synchronous motor; **Dreiphasensystem** *nt* ELEKTROTECH three-phase system, three-wire system; **Dreiphasenwechselstrommotor** *m* KFZTECH three-phase alternomotor

dreiphasig *adj* CHEMIE, ELEKTRIZ, ELEKTROTECH, PHYS three-phase

dreipolig: ~es Filter *nt* ELEKTRONIK three-pole filter; ~er Schalter *m* ELEKTROTECH three-pole switch

dreiprotonig: ~e Säure *f* CHEMIE triacid

Dreipunkt- *pref* LUFTTRANS, MASCHINEN three-point, REGELUNG three-step; **Dreipunktbiegen** *nt* METALL three-point bending; **Dreipunktbiegeprobe** *f* KERNTECH three-point bending specimen; **Dreipunktgurt** *m* KFZTECH *Sicherheitszubehör* safety belt; **Dreipunktlagenwinkel** *m* LUFTTRANS ground angle; **Dreipunktlager** *nt* MASCHINEN three-point support; **Dreipunktlandung** *f* LUFTTRANS three-point landing; **Dreipunktregelung** *f* REGELUNG three-step control; **Dreipunktsicherheitsgurt** *m* KFZTECH three-point seat belt; **Dreipunktsignal** *nt* ELEKTRONIK three-level signal, REGELUNG three-step signal

dreirädrig *adj* MASCHINEN three-wheeled

Drei-: **Dreirad-Zweikreisbremsanlage** *f* KFZTECH L-split system

dreiringig *adj* CHEMIE tricyclic

Drei-: **Dreiröhrenkamera** *f* FERNSEH three-tube camera; **Dreirollenbohrmeißel** *m* ERDÖL three-cone bit, *Bohrtechnik* tricone bit; **Dreisatz** *m* MATH rule of three

dreischäftig *adj* WASSERTRANS *Tauwerk* three-stranded

Drei-: **Dreischichtenfilm** *m* FOTO tripack film

dreischichtig: **~e Wellpappe** *f* VERPACK triple wall corrugated board

Drei-: **Dreischritt-Relais** *nt* ELEKTRIZ three-step relay

dreiseitig[1] *adj* GEOM three-sided

dreiseitig:[2] **~e Matrix** *f* COMP & DV triangular matrix

Drei-: **Dreiseitenbeschneidemaschine** *f* DRUCK three-sided cutting machine; **Dreispur-Stereo** *nt* AUFNAHME three-track stereo; **Dreistellungsschalter** *m* ELEKTRIZ three-position switch, three-way switch; **Dreistift-Steckbüchse** *f* ELEKTRIZ three-pin socket

Dreistrahl- *pref* ELEKTRONIK three-gun, KERNTECH triple beam; **Dreistrahl-Farbfernsehröhre** *f* ELEKTRONIK three-gun color picture tube (AmE), three-gun colour picture tube (BrE); **Dreistrahl-Koinzidenzspektrometer** *nt* KERNTECH triple beam coincidence spectrometer

dreistufig: **~er Verstärker** *m* ELEKTRONIK three-stage amplifier

Drei-: **Dreitastenmaus** *f* COMP & DV three-button mouse

dreiteilig: **~er Ölabstreifring** *m* KFZTECH three-piece oil control ring

Drei-: **Drei-Teilnehmer-Gespräch** *nt* TELEKOM three-way call; **Dreiteilung** *f* GEOM trisection; **Dreiviertelwind** *m* WASSERTRANS quarter wind

Dreiwege- *pref* AUFNAHME, BAU three-way, ELEKTRIZ, KUNSTSTOFF, MASCHINEN trifurcate, MECHAN three-way; **Dreiwegehahn** *m* BAU, MASCHINEN three-way cock; **Dreiwegekugelhahn** *m* FERTIG *Kunststoffinstallationen* three-way ball valve; **Dreiwegesystem** *nt* AUFNAHME three-way system; **Dreiwegeventil** *nt* HYDRAUL, MASCHINEN three-way valve; **Dreiwegexpander** *m* ELEKTRIZ trifurcator; **Dreiwegexpansionskasten** *m* ELEKTRIZ trifurcating box; **Dreiwegexpansionsspleiß** *m* ELEKTRIZ trifurcating joint; **Dreiwegezapfluftventil** *nt* LUFTTRANS air cross bleed valve

dreiwertig[1] *adj* CHEMIE tribasic, trivalent

dreiwertig:[2] **~er Alkohol** *m* CHEMIE trihydric acid, triol; **~e Logik** *f* ELEKTRONIK tristate logic

Drei-: **Dreiwertigkeit** *f* CHEMIE tervalence, trivalence, trivalency; **Dreiwicklungstransformator** *m* ELEKTROTECH three-winding transformer

Dreizustand- *pref* ELEKTRONIK three-state; **Dreizustandsausgang** *m* ELEKTRONIK three-state output; **Dreizustandsgatter** *nt* ELEKTRONIK three-state gate; **Dreizustandslogik** *f* ELEKTRONIK three-state logic

Drei-: **Dreizylindermotor** *m* MASCHINEN three-cylinder engine

Drempel *m* BAU miter sill (AmE), mitre sill (BrE), WASSERVERSORG clap sill

dressieren *vt* FERTIG *Blech* kill

dressiert *adj* FERTIG *Blech* killed, nonkinking, pinch-passed

Drexon-Karte *f* OPTIK Drexon card

Drift *f* AKUSTIK, ELEKTRIZ drift, ELEKTRONIK droop,

RAUMFAHRT *Raumschiff*, TELEKOM drift, WASSERTRANS drift current, drift; **Driftanzeige** *f* LUFTTRANS drift indicator

driftarm: **~er Oszillator** *m* ELEKTRONIK low-drift oscillator

Drift: **Driftausgleich** *m* GERÄT drift compensation

Driften *nt* BAU drifting

driften *vi* METROL drift

Drift: **Driftfehler** *m* LUFTTRANS *Höhenmesser* drift error; **Driftgeschwindigkeit** *f* METALL drift velocity; **Driftkammer** *f* TEILPHYS drift chamber; **Driftkompensation** *f* GERÄT drift compensation; **Driftstabilisierung** *f* FERNSEH driftlock; **Driftströmung** *f* WASSERTRANS drift current

Drillbohrer *m* MASCHINEN Archimedean drill

Drillen *nt* KER & GLAS lacing

Drillings- *pref* METALL triple; **Drillingspreßpumpe** *f* WASSERVERSORG three-throw pump; **Drillingsverbindung** *f* METALL triple junction

Drillschraubendreher *m* MASCHINEN spiral ratchet screwdriver

Drillstem-Test *m* NICHTFOSS ENERG drill stem test

Dringlichkeit *f* COMP & DV precedence

dritt:[1] **~e** *adj* MATH third

dritt-[2] *pref* MATH three; **~er Brand** *m* KER & GLAS third firing; **~er Hauptsatz der Thermodynamik** *m* PHYS third law of thermodynamics **~e Harmonische** *f* ELEKTRONIK third harmonic; **~e Oberwelle** *f* ELEKTRONIK third harmonic; **~e Potenz** *f* FERTIG, MATH cube; **~e Reinigungsstufe** *f* ABFALL tertiary sewage treatment; **~e Schiene** *f* EISENBAHN live rail, third rail; **~e Wurzel** *f* MATH cube root

dritt: **in ~e Potenz erheben** *vt* MATH cube

dritten Grades *phr* MATH cubic

Dritte-Partei *f* PATENT third party

Drittel *nt* MATH third; **Drittelgeviert** *nt* DRUCK three-to-em space; **Drittelspatium** *nt* DRUCK thick space

Droop-Snoot-Blatt *nt* LUFTTRANS *Concorde* droop snoot

Drop-Frame *nt* FERNSEH drop-frame; **Drop-Frame-Anzeige** *f* FERNSEH drop-frame indicator; **Drop-Frame-Betrieb** *m* FERNSEH drop-frame mode

Drossel *f* ELEKTRIZ, ELEKTROTECH choke, reactor, ERDÖL *Bohrtechnik* jet, *um Rohrströmung zu verhindern* choke, FERTIG damper, restrictor, LUFTTRANS *Luftfahrzeug* throttle, RADIO, TELEKOM choke; **Drosselanschlagschraube** *f* KFZTECH *Vergaser* throttle stop screw; **Drosselblende** *f* ERDÖL, HEIZ & KÄLTE orifice plate, MASCHINEN orifice meter; **Drosselklappe** *f* BAU damper, FERTIG choke, *Kunststoffinstallationen* throttle valve, HEIZ & KÄLTE butterfly damper, damper flap, KFZTECH throttle plate, throttle valve, *Vergaser* throttle, MASCHINEN butterfly valve, throttle valve; **Drosselklappendämpfer** *m* KFZTECH *Vergaser* throttle dashpot; **Drosselklappenhebel** *m* KFZTECH throttle control lever; **Drosselklappenschalter** *m* KFZTECH throttle valve switch; **Drosselklappenventil** *nt* HYDRAUL butterfly throttle-valve, LUFTTRANS *Luftfahrzeug* throttle; **Drosselkolben** *m* ELEKTROTECH choke plunger; **Drosselladedruckventil** *nt* KFZTECH throttle boost pressure valve; **Drosselluftklappe des Vergasers** *f* MECHAN choke; **Drosseln** *nt* EISENBAHN, MASCHINEN throttling, LUFTTRANS choking

drosseln *vt* FERTIG *Kunststoffinstallationen* throttle, KFZTECH choke, LUFTTRANS throttle back, MASCHINEN throttle

Drossel: **Drosselschaltung** f ELEKTRIZ choke circuit; **Drosselschieber** m HEIZ & KÄLTE damper slide, KFZTECH *Vergaser* throttle slide; **Drosselspeisung** f ELEKTRIZ choke feed; **Drosselspule** f ELEKTRIZ choke coil, ELEKTROTECH choke, choke coil, inductor, reactance coil, reactor, TELEKOM choke; **Drosselstoß der Schienen** m EISENBAHN impedance bond, reactance bond

Drosselung f AKUSTIK partial masking, EISENBAHN throttling, LUFTTRANS choking, MASCHINEN throttling

Drossel: **Drosselventil** nt FERTIG throttle valve, HEIZ & KÄLTE restrictor valve, throttle valve, HYDRAUL butterfly valve, throttle valve, KFZTECH throttle valve, KOHLEN choker valve, MASCHINEN butterfly valve; **Drosselventilhebel** m HYDRAUL throttle lever; **Drosselventilstange** f HYDRAUL throttle rod, throttle stem; **Drosselwirkung** f RAUMFAHRT *Raumschiff* throttle control; **Drosselzapfendüse** f KFZTECH throttle pintle nozzle

Druck[1] m BAU thrust, COMP & DV print, printout, ELEKTROTECH pressure, HYDRAUL head, pressure delivery, pressure head, *Dampf* pressure, *zum Gegenpumpen* head, MECHAN pressure, push, MEERSCHMUTZ thrust, PAPIER pressure, PHYS sound pressure, RAUMFAHRT *Raumschiff*, TEXTIL, THERMOD pressure; **Druck-** *pref* FERTIG compressed; **äußerer ~** f DRUCK outer form; **~ auf volle Bogen** m COMP & DV, DRUCK even working

Druck:[2] **mit ~ beaufschlagen** vt HEIZ & KÄLTE pressurize

Druck: **Druckabbau** m RAUMFAHRT *Raumschiff* depressurization; **Druckabdichtung** f HYDRAUL pressure seal; **Druckabfall** m FERTIG friction pressure drop, pressure drop, *Hydraulik* head loss, HEIZ & KÄLTE, HYDRAUL, NICHTFOSS ENERG, PAPIER pressure drop

druckabhängig adj FERTIG pressure-dependent

Druck: **Druckabhängigkeit** f FERTIG pressure dependence; **Druckablaßventil** nt KFZTECH *Schmierung* relief valve; **Druckamplitude** f AKUSTIK pressure amplitude; **Druckänderung** f WELLPHYS pressure variation; **Druckänderungs-Geschwindigkeitsregulierung** f LUFTTRANS pressure rate-of-change regulating; **Druckänderungs-Geschwindigkeitsschalter** m LUFTTRANS pressure rate-of-change switch; **Druckangleichsunfall** m KERNTECH blowdown accident; **Druckanschluß** m ELEKTROTECH pressurized connection; **Druckanstieg** m HEIZ & KÄLTE pressure rise, MASCHINEN pressure build-up; **Druckanzeiger** m GERÄT pressure indicator, HEIZ & KÄLTE indicating pressure gage (AmE), indicating pressure gauge (BrE); **Druckanzug** m RAUMFAHRT *Raumschiff* G-suit, pressure suit; **Druckaufbau** m LUFTTRANS pressure build-up; **Druckaufbauventil** nt LUFTTRANS pressurizing valve; **Druckauflage** f COMP & DV print run; **Druckauftrag** m DRUCK print job; **Druckausbreitung** f PHYS pressure broadening; **Druckausgabe** f COMP & DV hard copy, DRUCK printer output, TELEKOM printout; **Druckausgabepuffer** m DRUCK print buffer; **Druckausgabeverkleinerung** f (COR) COMP & DV character output reduction (COR); **Druckausgleich** m FERTIG pressure balance, pressure compensation, HEIZ & KÄLTE expansion; **Druckausgleichbehälter** m NICHTFOSS ENERG surge tank; **Druckausgleichdose** f MECHAN expansion bellows; **Druckausgleichkolben** m HYDRAUL balancing piston; **Druckausgleichventil** nt HYDRAUL balanced valve; **Druckausrichtung** f COMP & DV print position; **Druckausrüstung** f ERDÖL *Tief-*

tauchtechnik pressure equipment; **Druckautomat** m DRUCK flat-bed cylinder press; **Druckbalg** m GERÄT pressure bellows

Drückbank f FERTIG *Metalldrücken* lathe, MASCHINEN spinning lathe

Druck: **Druckbeanspruchung** f MASCHINEN, MECHAN, METALL compression stress, VERPACK compression load, WERKPRÜF compressive strength; **Druckbefehl** m COMP & DV print command; **Druckbegrenzungsventil** nt MASCHINEN pressure relief valve; **Druckbehälter** m FERTIG, KERNTECH, MASCHINEN pressure vessel

druckbelüftet: **~er Motor** m ELEKTRIZ forced-ventilation motor

Druck: **Druckbelüftung** f LUFTTRANS pressurization

druckbeständig adj WERKPRÜF compression-proof

Druck: **Druckbogen** m DRUCK sheet, signature; **Druckbolzen** m KFZTECH nozzle holder spindle; **Druckbuchstabe** m DRUCK printing letter; **Druckbügelregler** m GERÄT chopper bar controller; **Druckcharakteristik** f WASSERTRANS *Wetterkunde* pressure characteristic; **Druckdateien** f pl DRUCK print files; **Druckdecke** f TEXTIL blanket

druckdicht[1] adj FERTIG pressure-sealed, pressure-tight, *Kunststoffinstallationen* leakproof under pressure

druckdicht:[2] **~er Boden** m LUFTTRANS pressurized floor; **~er Druckluftverteiler** m LUFTTRANS pressurized manifold; **~er Wagen** m EISENBAHN pressure-sealed wagon

Druck: **Druckdichtung** f EISENBAHN pressure sealing; **Druckdifferenz** f HYDRAUL pressure difference, KFZTECH pressure differential; **Druckdifferenzmelder** m REGELUNG pneumatic limit operator; **Druckdifferenzregelventil** nt KFZTECH pressure differential warning valve; **Druckdose** f MECHAN crusher gage (AmE), crusher gauge (BrE); **Druckecho** nt AUFNAHME printing echo

Drucken nt COMP & DV printing, DRUCK printing, printing process, KER & GLAS, PAPIER, TEXTIL printing; **~ von Hand** nt DRUCK hand printing

Drücken nt COMP & DV push, FERTIG *Spanung* dragging, KUNSTSTOFF pressure forming, MASCHINEN spinning

drucken vt COMP & DV, DRUCK, PAPIER, TEXTIL print

drücken vt COMP & DV push, *Taste* push, FERTIG *Schneidenrücken* drag, KUNSTSTOFF pressure-form, MASCHINEN spin, MECHAN push

druckentlastet: **~es Ventil** nt HYDRAUL balanced valve

Druck: **Druckentnahmebohrung** f FERTIG pressure tap; **Druckentspannungsventil** nt HYDRAUL pressure relief valve

Drucker m COMP & DV printer, DRUCK *Maschine* printer, *Person* printer, TELEKOM printer; **~ mit fliegendem Abdruck** m COMP & DV hit-on-the-fly printer; **~ und Setzer** m DRUCK printer and typesetter; **~ mit Typenradwalze** m COMP & DV barrel printer (BrE), drum printer (AmE)

Drücker m FERTIG spinner

Drucker: **Druckerauftrag** m COMP & DV *in Druckerwarteschlange* print job; **Druckerausgabe** f DRUCK printer output

Drückerauslöser m FOTO *Kameraverschluß* trigger release

Drucker: **Druckerbefehle** m pl DRUCK printer commands

Druckerei f DRUCK print shop, printing trade, printing works; **Druckereiarbeiter** m DRUCK printing trade worker; **Druckereibedarf** m DRUCK printer's supply;

Druckereigeräte nt pl DRUCK printing equipment; **Druckereizubehör** nt DRUCK printing accessories

Drucker: **Druckerfarbe** f DRUCK printer's ink, printing ink; **Druckergewerbe** nt DRUCK printing trade; **Druckerhöhungspumpe** f ERDÖL booster pump, RAUMFAHRT boost pump; **Druckerkunst** f DRUCK art of printing

Druckerlaubnis: ~ erteilen vi DRUCK pass for press

Drucker: **Druckerlehrling** m DRUCK printer's devil; **Druckerpapier** nt DRUCK printing paper; **Druckerpresse** f DRUCK press; **Druckerpuffer** m DRUCK print buffer; **Druckerschnittstelle** f COMP & DV hard copy interface; **Druckerschwärze** f DRUCK printer's ink, printing ink; **Druckerserver** m COMP & DV print server; **Druckertreiber** m COMP & DV printer driver; **Druckerzeichen** nt DRUCK printer's mark

Druck: **Druckerzeuger** m FERTIG pressure generator; **Druckerzeugung** f TRANS pressurization; **Druckfarbe** f KUNSTSTOFF printing ink, PAPIER ink, printing ink

druckfärben vt TEXTIL dye under pressure

Druck: **Druckfeder** f MASCHINEN compression spring; **Druckfehler** m DRUCK misprint, typo

druckfest adj WERKPRÜF compression-proof

Druckfestigkeit f BAU, KUNSTSTOFF compressive strength, MASCHINEN, VERPACK compression strength; **Druckfestigkeitsversuch** m BAU crushing test

Drückfett nt FERTIG spinning lubricate

Druck: **Druckfilter** nt ABFALL, CHEMTECH, KOHLEN, WASSERVERSORG pressure filter; **Druckfirnis** m DRUCK printing varnish; **Druckfläche** f DRUCK printing area

Druckfläche: über die ~ hinausgehen vi DRUCK bleed

Druck: **Druckflasche für Helium** f RAUMFAHRT Raumschiff compressed-helium bottle; **Druckflüssigkeit** f FERTIG pressure liquid; **Druckform** f COMP & DV form, DRUCK forme (BrE), printing form (AmE), printing forme (BrE), type form (AmE), type forme (BrE); **Druckformat** nt COMP & DV print format; **Druckformträger** m DRUCK carriage; **Druckfreistrahlgebläse zum Gußputzen** nt FERTIG air blast cleaning unit; **Druckfüllung** f VERPACK für Sprühdosen press filling

Drückfutter nt MASCHINEN spinning mandrel

Druckgas nt RAUMFAHRT Raumschiff pressurizing gas; **Druckgasflasche** f FERTIG Schweißen pressure cylinder

druckgasisoliert: ~es Kabel nt ELEKTRIZ external gas pressure cable, internal gas pressure cable

Druckgas: **Druckgastank** m RAUMFAHRT Raumschiff pressurizing gas tank

Druck: **Druckgefälle** nt ERDÖL, FERTIG pressure gradient, HEIZ & KÄLTE pressure drop; **Druckgefäß** nt BAU, HEIZ & KÄLTE pressure vessel, LABOR autoclave, MECHAN pressure vessel, PHYS reactor pressure vessel

druckgegossen adj FERTIG Metall die-cast

druckgekühlt: ~er Motor m ELEKTRIZ forced-ventilation motor

Druck: **Druckgeschwindigkeit** f COMP & DV print speed

druckgießen vt MASCHINEN die-cast

Druck: **Druckgießform** f FERTIG die-casting die; **Druckglied** nt BAU strut; **Druckgradient** m ERDÖL, STRÖMPHYS pressure gradient; **Druckgradient null** m STRÖMPHYS Untersuchung von Grenzschichten zero pressure gradient; **Druckgradientendiagramm** nt ERDÖL Geologie: Darstellung von Druck in Abhängigkeit zur Tiefe pressure vs depth plot; **Druckgradientenmikrofon** nt AKUSTIK velocity microphone; **Druckgrenze**

f HYDRAUL head limit; **Druckguß** m FERTIG Metall, MASCHINEN die casting; **Druckgußautomat** m FERTIG automatic die-casting machine; **Druckgußform** f MASCHINEN die-casting die, pressure die-casting die; **Druckgußlegierung** f FERTIG die-casting alloy; **Druckgußmaschine** f MASCHINEN die-casting machine; **Druckhammer** m DRUCK printing hammer; **Druckhebewinde** f FERTIG hydraulic jack; **Druckhöhe** f HEIZ & KÄLTE head, pump head, HYDRAUL static head, KERNTECH einer Pumpe elevation head, KOHLEN pressure head, LUFTTRANS pressure altitude, pressure height, MASCHINEN elevation head, NICHTFOSS ENERG effective head; **Druckhöhenmeßgerät** nt GERÄT head meter; **Druckimpuls** m AKUSTIK pressure impulse; **Druckindustrie** f DRUCK printing industry; **Druckkabel** nt ELEKTRIZ pressure cable; **Druckkabine** f RAUMFAHRT Raumschiff cabin; **Druckkammer** f FERTIG casting chamber, pressure chamber; **Druckkammerlautsprecher** m AKUSTIK pneumatic loudspeaker; **Druckkappe** f KFZTECH pressure cap; **Druckkessel** m MECHAN pressure vessel; **Druckkissen** nt VERPACK zur Unterlage pressure pad; **Druckknopf** m COMP & DV, ELEKTRIZ push button, ELEKTROTECH button, KONTROLL button, push button, LUFTTRANS für das Wiederanstellen des Triebwerks im Flug, MASCHINEN, MECHAN push button, TELEKOM button, press button, push button; **Druckknopfanlasser** m ELEKTRIZ push-button starter; **Druckknopfschalter** m TRANS pedestrian push button; **Druckknopfsteuerung** f MECHAN push-button control; **Druckknoten** m FERTIG pressure node; **Druckkochtopf** m MASCHINEN pressure cooker; **Druckkoeffizient** m MASCHINEN, NICHTFOSS ENERG pressure coefficient; **Druckkolben** m BAU ram; **Druckkopf** m COMP & DV print head, DRUCK, PAPIER printing head; **Druckkraft** f FERTIG tonnage, MASCHINEN compressive force; **Druckkraftfestigkeit** f MECHAN compression strength; **Druckkufe** f AUFNAHME pressure pad; **Druckkühlung** f MASCHINEN compression refrigeration; **Druckkurve** f HYDRAUL pressure curve; **Drucklager** nt MASCHINEN thrust bearing, WASSERTRANS Motor thrust bearing, thrust block; **Drucklegung** f DRUCK going to press; **Druckleiste** f FERTIG thrust strip; **Druckleitung** f HYDRAUL head pipe, KFZTECH delivery pipe, NICHTFOSS ENERG penstock, WASSERVERSORG delivery pipe, penstock; **Druckleitungsanschluß** m FERTIG outlet; **Drucklinie** f KOHLEN compression curve

drucklos:[1] ~ geöffnet adj FERTIG Kunststoffinstallationen fail-safe to open; ~ geschlossen adj FERTIG Kunststoffinstallationen fail-safe to close

drucklos:[2] ~er Abschnitt des Flugzeugrumpfes m LUFTTRANS fuselage non-pressurized section; ~e Leitung f KERNTECH unpressurized line; ~er Refiner m PAPIER atmospheric refiner

Druckluft f ANSTRICH, MASCHINEN compressed air; **Druckluftakkumulator** m FERTIG hydropneumatic accumulator; **Druckluftanhebung** f FERTIG airlift; **Druckluftatemgerät** nt SICHERHEIT für industrielle Einsätze breathing apparatus

druckluftbetätigt: ~e Spanneinrichtung f FERTIG air clamp; ~es Ventil nt MASCHINEN pneumatically operated valve

Druckluft: **Druckluftbohren** nt ERDÖL Bohrtechnik air flooding; **Druckluftbohrer** m BAU pneumatic drill, MASCHINEN air drill, compressed air drill, MECHAN, PHYS air drill; **Druckluftbohrmaschine** f FERTIG pneumatic drill; **Druckluftbremse** *f* KFZTECH air brake, air pressure brake, pneumatic brake, MASCHINEN air brake, compressed air brake, pneumatic brake, MECHAN, PHYS air brake; **Druckluftbremsschlauch** *m* KUNSTSTOFF air brake hose; **Druckluftbremssystem** *nt* MASCHINEN compressed air braking system; **Druckluft-Differentialkolbenakkumulator** *m* FERTIG differential accumulator; **Drucklufteinbringung** *f* ERDÖL *Öllagerstätte* air repressuring

Drucklüfter *m* HEIZ & KÄLTE forced-draft fan (AmE), forced-draught fan (BrE)

Druckluft: **Druckluftflasche** *f* FERTIG, HEIZ & KÄLTE air bottle, MECHAN, PHYS air cylinder; **Druckluftförderer** *m* FERTIG pneumatic conveyor; **Druckluftförderung** *f* KOHLEN pneumatic handling; **Druckluftfutter** *nt* FERTIG air-actuated chuck, MASCHINEN air chuck, air-operated chuck; **Druckluftgebläse** *nt* FERTIG air lance

druckluftgekühlt: **~er Transformator** *m* ELEKTRIZ air blast transformer

Druckluft: **Druckluftgeräte** *nt pl* MASCHINEN compressed air equipment

druckluftgesteuert: **~e Vakuumbremse** *f* EISENBAHN air-pressure-controlled vacuum brake

Druckluft: **Druckluftgußputzen** *nt* FERTIG air blasting; **Drucklufthammer** *m* MASCHINEN pneumatic hammer; **Drucklufttheber** *m* CHEMTECH airlift pump, MASCHINEN air hoist, pneumatic hoist; **Druckluft-Kolbenakkumulator** *m* FERTIG air-loaded accumulator with piston; **Druckluftkreisel** *m* LUFTTRANS *Navigation* aerogyro; **Druckluftleistungsschalter** *m* ELEKTROTECH air blast circuit breaker; **Druckluftleitung** *f* MASCHINEN compressed air line; **Druckluftmeißel** *m* FERTIG pneumatic chipping hammer; **Druckluftmotor** *m* MASCHINEN air engine, air motor, compressed air engine; **Druckluft-Niethammer** *m* MASCHINEN pneumatic riveter; **Druckluft-Preßformmaschine** *f* FERTIG air-operated squeezer; **Druckluft-Putzstrahlen** *nt* FERTIG air blast cleaning, compressed air blast-cleaning; **Druckluftschalter** *m* ELEKTRIZ air blast breaker, air blast switch, air breaker; **Druckluftschlagbohrer** *m* BAU pneumatic hammer drill; **Druckluftschlauch** *m* BAU, FERTIG, MASCHINEN, MECHAN, PHYS compressed air hose; **Druckluftschleuse** *f* WASSERVERSORG lock; **Druckluftschrauber** *m* FERTIG pneumatic screw driver; **Druckluftspanndorn** *m* FERTIG pneumatic expanding mandrel; **Druckluftspannung** *f* FERTIG air chucking; **Druckluftspeicher** *m* FERTIG air accumulator, air hydraulic accumulator; **Druckluftstampfer** *m* FERTIG *Gießen* pneumatic rammer; **Druckluftstrom** *m* FERTIG air blast; **Druckluftstutzen** *m* MASCHINEN compressed air socket; **Druckluftsystem** *nt* LUFTTRANS air pressure system, MASCHINEN compressed air system; **Drucklufttechnik** *f* KFZTECH pneumatics; **Druckluftturbine** *f* MASCHINEN air turbine

Drucklüftungssystem *nt* HEIZ & KÄLTE plenum system

Druckluft: **Druckluftventil** *nt* MASCHINEN pneumatic valve; **Druckluftwerkzeug** *nt* MASCHINEN air tool, pneumatic tool; **Druckluftzange** *f* FERTIG pneumatic collet; **Druckluftziehkissen** *nt* FERTIG pneumatic die cushion; **Druckluftzylinder** *m* LUFTTRANS *Hubschrauber* pneumatic cylinder, MASCHINEN compressed air cylinder, pneumatic cylinder, MECHAN, PHYS air cylinder

Druck: **Druckmaschine** *f* DRUCK press printing machine,

printing press, TEXTIL printing machine

Drückmaschine *f* MASCHINEN spinning lathe

Druck: **Druckmeßdose** *f* GERÄT load cell, KOHLEN pressure cell; **Druckmeßeinrichtung** *f* GERÄT pressure-measuring equipment; **Druckmesser** *m* BAU pressure gage (AmE), pressure gauge (BrE), FERTIG manometer, pressure gage (AmE), pressure gauge (BrE), HEIZ & KÄLTE, HYDRAUL pressure gage (AmE), pressure gauge (BrE), KOHLEN compressometer, KONTROLL pressure gage (AmE), pressure gauge (BrE), LABOR manometer, PAPIER pressure gage (AmE), pressure gauge (BrE), PHYS manometer; **Druckmeßgerät** *nt* ERDÖL manometer, pressure gage (AmE), pressure gauge (BrE), GERÄT head meter, HYDRAUL, KOHLEN, LABOR, PHYS pressure gage (AmE), pressure gauge (BrE); **Druckmessung** *f* RAUMFAHRT *Raumschiff* pressure measurement; **Druckmikrofon** *nt* AKUSTIK pressure microphone; **Druckminderer** *m* LUFTTRANS pressure reducer; **Druckminderung** *f* MASCHINEN depressurization; **Druckminderungsventil** *nt* HEIZ & KÄLTE pressure-reducing valve, MASCHINEN reducing valve; **Druckminderventil** *nt* BAU pressure-reducing valve, FERTIG pressure relief valve, pressure-reducing valve, MASCHINEN depressurization valve, pressure-reducing valve; **Druckmittelpunkt** *m* LUFTTRANS *Aerodynamik*, PHYS center of pressure (AmE), centre of pressure (BrE); **Druckmittelpunkt des Blattes der Luftschraube** *m* LUFTTRANS *Hubschrauber* blade center of pressure (AmE), blade centre of pressure (BrE); **Druckmodul** *m* KUNSTSTOFF compressive modulus

druckölbetätigt *adj* FERTIG oil-actuated

Druck: **Druckölbetätigung** *f* FERTIG oil actuation; **Druckölbrenner** *m* HEIZ & KÄLTE pressure jet oil burner; **Druckölschmierung** *f* MASCHINEN forced-oil cooling; **Druckpapier** *nt* FOTO printing paper, VERPACK printings

Druckplatte *f* DRUCK plate, printing plate, FERTIG *Kunststoffinstallationen* pressure plate, KFZTECH pressure plate, *Kupplung* driven plate, MASCHINEN thrust plate; **Druckplattenantriebsriemen** *m* KFZTECH pressure plate drive strap; **Druckplattenausrückgabel** *f* KFZTECH *Kupplung* pressure plate release lever; **Druckplattenausrückhebel** *m* KFZTECH pressure plate release lever; **Druckplattenfeder** *f* KFZTECH pressure plate spring; **Druckplattenherstellung** *f* DRUCK platemaking

Druck: **Druckposition** *f* COMP & DV print position; **Druckpresse** *f* DRUCK press, press printing machine, printing press; **Druckpresse für einzelne Bogen** *f* DRUCK sheet-fed machine; **Druckprobe** *f* MASCHINEN pressure test, MECHAN compression test; **Druckpropeller** *m* LUFTTRANS pusher propeller; **Druckprüfmaschine** *f* VERPACK compression test machine; **Druckprüfung** *f* KOHLEN, VERPACK, WERKPRÜF compression test; **Druckpuffer** *m* DRUCK print buffer; **Druckpumpe** *f* HYDRAUL, KOHLEN pressure pump, MASCHINEN double-acting pump, WASSERVERSORG force pump, pressure pump, ram pump; **Druckpunkt** *m* COMP & DV key force; **Druckraumabschluß** *m* FERTIG pressure seal; **Druckreduzierer** *m* RAUMFAHRT *Raumschiff* pressure reducer; **Druckreduzierung** *f* PHYS pressure reduction; **Druckreduzierventil** *nt* HEIZ & KÄLTE, HYDRAUL pressure-reducing valve; **Druckreflexionsfaktor** *m* AKUSTIK pressure reflection coefficient; **Druckregelung** *f* HEIZ & KÄLTE pressure control; **Druckregelventil** *nt* FERTIG pressure control valve, pressure-regulating valve; **Druckregler** m BAU, ELEKTROTECH pressure regulator, HEIZ & KÄLTE pressure controller, HYDRAUL pressure regulator, LUFTTRANS barostat, PAPIER pressure controller

druckreif: ~**e Vorlage** f DRUCK CRC, camera ready copy

Druck: **Druckring** m FERTIG reaction ring, KFZTECH, MASCHINEN thrust collar; **Druckriß** m KER & GLAS pressure check; **Druckrohr** nt FERTIG gun, KFZTECH pressure tube, MASCHINEN pressure pipe; **Druckröhrenreaktor** m KERNTECH pressure tube reactor; **Druckrohrleitung** f NICHTFOSS ENERG penstock, WASSERVERSORG penstock, pentrough; **Druckrohrtemperatur** f PHYS, THERMOD discharge temperature; **Druckrolle** f MASCHINEN pressure roller; **Drucksache** f DRUCK printed matter; **Drucksammler** m PAPIER pressure accumulator; **Druckschacht** m WASSERVERSORG pressure well; **Druckschalter** m ELEKTROTECH, FERTIG, HYDRAUL pressure switch; **Druckschaltungsverbinder** m ELEKTROTECH printed circuit connector; **Druckscheibe** f FERTIG thrust washer, *Kunststoffinstallationen* washer; **Druckschmieden** nt MASCHINEN press forging; **Druckschmierung** f FERTIG force-feed lubrication, pressure-feed lubrication, HEIZ & KÄLTE forced lubrication, KFZTECH pressure lubrication, MASCHINEN pressure-feed lubrication; **Druckschott** nt LUFTTRANS pressure bulkhead; **Druckschraube** f FERTIG clamping nut, MASCHINEN pressure screw; **Druckschreiber** m GERÄT pressure recorder, recording manometer; **Druckschwankung** f FERTIG pressure fluctuation; **Druckschwankungs-Ausgleichsakkumulator** m FERTIG alleviator; **Druckschweißen** nt THERMOD pressure welding; **Druckschweißung** f FERTIG upset welding, THERMOD pressure welding; **Druckseite** f DRUCK page, printed sheet, FERTIG discharge side, HYDRAUL pressure side; **Drucksensordetektor** m EISENBAHN pressure-sensitive detector; **Druckserver** m COMP & DV print server; **Drucksintern** nt CHEMTECH sintering under pressure; **Druckspalte** f DRUCK column; **Druckspant** m RAUMFAHRT *Raumschiff* pressure bulkhead; **Druckspeicher** m HEIZ & KÄLTE pressurized hot water tank, KUNSTSTOFF, MASCHINEN hydraulic accumulator; **Druckstab** m BAU strut, FERTIG compression member, MECHAN strut; **Druckstelle** f COMP & DV print position; **Druckstempel** m FERTIG thrust die; **Drucksterilisator** m LEBENSMITTEL autoclave; **Drucksteuerung** f HEIZ & KÄLTE pressure control; **Drucksteuerzeichen** nt COMP & DV print control character; **Druckstift** m MASCHINEN pressure pin; **Druckstock** m DRUCK block, printing block; **Druckstockherstellung** f DRUCK blockmaking; **Druckstockhöhenprüfer** m DRUCK type height gage (AmE), type height gauge (BrE); **Druckstoß** m ERDÖL surge, *Rohrleitungen* water hammer; **Druckstoßdrossel** f LUFTTRANS antisurge baffle; **Druckstoßventil** nt LUFTTRANS antisurge valve; **Druckstück** nt FERTIG *Kunststoffinstallationen* compressor; **Druckstufe** f FERTIG, HYDRAUL pressure stage; **Drucksturz** m THERMOD explosive decompression; **Drucksystem** nt LUFTTRANS pressure system; **Drucktaste** f COMP & DV push button, ELEKTROTECH key, FERTIG punchbutton key, MASCHINEN push button, TELEKOM press button, push button

drucktastengeschaltet adj FERTIG punchbutton-operated

Druck: **Drucktastenschalttafel** f FERTIG punchbutton panel; **Drucktastensteuerung** f FERTIG punchbutton control; **Drucktastentafel** f FERTIG punchbutton panel

Drückteil m FERTIG spun part

Druck: **Druck-Temperatur-Schreiber** m PHYS barothermograph; **Drucktendenz** f WASSERTRANS *Wetterkunde* pressure tendency; **Drucktest** m HYDRAUL pressure test; **Drucktisch** m DRUCK printing table; **Drucktransmitter** m HYDRAUL pressure transmitter; **Drucktuch** nt TEXTIL blanket; **Druckturbine** f HYDRAUL pressure turbine; **Drucktype** f DRUCK movable type, printing type; **Druckübertragung** f FERTIG pressure transmission; **Druckübertragungsgerät** nt HYDRAUL pressure transmitter; **Druckumformmaschine** f VERPACK pressure-forming machine; **Druckumlaufschmierung** f FERTIG pressure circulation lubrication, pressure lubrication, HEIZ & KÄLTE forced lubrication, KFZTECH forced-feed lubrication, MASCHINEN force-feed lubrication; **Druckunterlegscheibe** f KFZTECH thrust washer; **Druckunterschied** m HEIZ & KÄLTE pressure differential; **Druckventil** nt HEIZ & KÄLTE discharge valve, MASCHINEN delivery valve, head valve; **Druckverbindung** f ELEKTROTECH pressurized connection; **Druckverbreiterung** f STRAHLPHYS *von Spektrallinien* pressure broadening; **Druckverformung** f VERPACK compression damage; **Druckverformungsrest** m KUNSTSTOFF compression set, residual set; **Druckverhältnis im Triebwerk** nt LUFTTRANS engine pressure ratio; **Druckverlust** m ERDÖL, HEIZ & KÄLTE pressure drop, HYDRAUL loss of pressure, KFZTECH *Reifen* deflation, MASCHINEN pressure loss, NICHTFOSS ENERG pressure drop; **Druckvermerk** m KONSTZEICH notation; **Druckverringerung** f MASCHINEN depressurization; **Druckverstärker** m HYDRAUL intensifier; **Druckverstärkerpumpe** f MECHAN booster pump; **Druckversuch** m FERTIG, KOHLEN, MASCHINEN, METALL, VERPACK compression test; **Druckversuch an Rohren** m FERTIG collapse test; **Druckverteilung** f FERTIG pressure distribution; **Druck-Volumen-Diagramm** nt *(P/V-Diagramm)* THERMOD pressure volume diagram; **Druckvorgang** m DRUCK printing process; **Druckvorlage** f KONSTZEICH photomaster; **Druckvorlagenhersteller** m DRUCK process engraver; **Druckvorrichtung** f DRUCK printing apparatus; **Druckwaage** f FERTIG pressure-maintaining valve; **Druckwächter** m HEIZ & KÄLTE pressure switch; **Druckwalze** f COMP & DV print drum, DRUCK printing roller, roller; **Druckwalzenmasse** f DRUCK printing roller composition; **Druckwandler** m GERÄT pressure transducer; **Druckware** f TEXTIL printed fabric; **Druckwasser** nt WASSERVERSORG pressurized water, water under pressure; **Druckwasserkolben** m BAU hydraulic piston; **Druckwasserkühlung** f HEIZ & KÄLTE pressurized water cooling; **Druckwasserreaktor** m KERNTECH, PHYS pressurized water reactor; **Druckwasserspeicher** m FERTIG, PAPIER hydraulic accumulator; **Druckwassersystem** nt HYDRAUL hydraulic system; **Druckwelle** f AKUSTIK, AUFNAHME compressional wave, HYDRAUL pressure surge, TELEKOM pressure wave

Drückwerkzeug nt MASCHINEN spinning tool

Druck: **Druckwiderstand** m LUFTTRANS pressure drag; **Druckzentrum** nt MASCHINEN center of pressure (AmE), centre of pressure (BrE); **Druckzone** f COMP & DV print position; **Druckzuführung** f KFZTECH pressure feed; **Druckzug** m HEIZ & KÄLTE forced draft (AmE), forced draught (BrE); **Druckzylinder** m

DRUCK cylinder, printing cylinder, KUNSTSTOFF impression cylinder, LUFTTRANS *Bremse* master cylinder, PAPIER printing cylinder

Drüse *f* LEBENSMITTEL gland

drusenreich *adj* ERDÖL vuggy, vugular

drusig *adj* ERDÖL *Geologie* vuggy, vugular

DSB *abbr (Doppelseitenband)* ELEKTRONIK, RADIO DSB *(double sideband)*

D-Schicht *f* PHYS D-layer, RADIO D-region

DSI *abbr (digitale Sprachinterpolation)* RAUMFAHRT, TELEKOM DSI *(digital speech interpolation)*

D-Steuerung *f* ELEKTRIZ derivative control

DSV *abbr (Digitalsignalverbindung)* TELEKOM digital connection

DT *abbr (Dichtigkeitstest)* ERDÖL LOT *(leak-off test)*

DTA *abbr (Differentialthermoanalyse)* KUNSTSTOFF, THERMOD, UMWELTSCHMUTZ DTA *(differential thermal analysis)*

DTL *abbr (Dioden-Transistor-Logik)* ELEKTRONIK DTL *(diode transistor logic)*

DTP *abbr (Desktop-Publishing)* COMP & DV, DRUCK DTP *(desktop publishing)*

Dual- *pref* COMP & DV dual, ELEKTRONIK, TELEKOM binary

dual: **~es Kartenbild** *nt* TELEKOM binary image; **~e Schaltung** *f* PHYS dual network

Dual-: **Dualdividierer** *m* ELEKTRONIK binary divider; **Dualinput** *m* FERNSEH dual input; **Dualmultiplizierer** *m* ELEKTRONIK, TELEKOM binary multiplier; **Dual-Port-Speicher** *m* COMP & DV dual port memory; **Dualprozessor-Lastteilungssystem** *nt* TELEKOM dual-processor load-sharing system; **Dualprozessorsystem** *nt* TELEKOM dual-processor system; **Dualsubtrahierer** *m* ELEKTRONIK binary subtractor; **Dualzähler** *m* GERÄT binary counter, dual counter

Dübel *m* BAU dowel, dowel pin, joggle, plug, tenon, trenail, *Holzbau* key, FERTIG dowel pin, dowel slip, MECHAN key, peg; **Dübelbohrer** *m* BAU bradawl, MASCHINEN pin drill; **Dübelloch** *nt* BAU dowel hole

dübeln *vt* BAU joggle, plug, FERTIG dowel pin

Dübel: **Dübelstein** *m* BAU anchorage block

Dublett *nt* NICHTFOSS ENERG *elektronisch*, PHYS *Spektroskopie* doublet

Dublette *f* DRUCK doublet

Dublett: **Dublettstruktur** *f* STRAHLPHYS *von Spektrallinien* doublet structure

Dückdalbe *f* WASSERTRANS *Festmachen* mooring pile

Dückdalben *m* WASSERTRANS *Festmachen* mooring post

DÜE *abbr (Datenübertragungseinrichtung)* COMP & DV DCE *(data communication terminating equipment)*, TELEKOM DCE *(data circuit terminating equipment)*

Düker *m* BAU culvert

Dukt *m* RADIO duct

duktil *adj* METALL ductile

Dulcin *nt* CHEMIE dulcin, dulcine

Dulcit *nt* CHEMIE ducite, ducitol, melampyrit

Dulcitol *nt* CHEMIE ducite, ducitol, melampyrit

duldbar: **~e tägliche Aufnahmemenge** *f (ADI)* LEBENSMITTEL acceptable daily intake *(ADI)*

Du-Long-Petit: **~sches Gesetz** *nt* PHYS DuLong and Petit's law

Dunkel- *pref* ELEKTRONIK, ELEKTROTECH, ERGON, FERTIG, PHYS dark

dunkel: **dunkle Interferenzringe** *m pl* PHYS dark fringe; **dunkler Interferenzstreifen** *m* PHYS dark fringe; **~ste Rotglühhitze** *f* METALL dark red heat; **dunkle Rothitze**

f METALL blood red heat;

Dunkel-: **Dunkeladaptation** *f* ERGON dark adaptation; **Dunkelfeldbeleuchtung** *f* FERTIG dark field illumination, PHYS dark field illumination, dark ground illumination; **Dunkelkammer** *f* FOTO darkroom; **Dunkelkammerbeleuchtung** *f* FOTO safelight; **Dunkelkorrektur** *f* FERNSEH shading corrector; **Dunkelleitung** *f* ELEKTROTECH dark conduction; **Dunkellinienspektrum** *nt* RAUMFAHRT dark line spectrum; **Dunkelschriftschirm** *m* ELEKTRONIK dark trace screen; **Dunkelsignal** *nt* FERNSEH shading signal; **Dunkelsteuerung** *f* ELEKTRONIK *End- und Peripherigeräte* blanking, FERNSEH shading; **Dunkelsteuerungssignal** *nt* ELEKTRONIK blanking signal; **Dunkelstrom** *m* ELEKTROTECH, OPTIK, PHYS, TELEKOM dark current; **Dunkelwiderstand** *m* ELEKTROTECH, KERNTECH dark resistance

Dünn- *pref* DRUCK, ELEKTRONIK thin, FERTIG light gage (AmE), light gauge (BrE), PAPIER lightweight, TELEKOM thin

dünn: **~es Blech** *nt* METALL thin plate; **~e Linse** *f* PHYS thin lens; **~e Magnetschicht** *f* ELEKTRONIK magnetic thin film; **~es Präparat** *nt* KERNTECH *radioaktive Quelle* thin source; **~e Schicht** *f* CHEMIE film, lamina; **~es Spatium** *nt* DRUCK thin space; **~e transparente Goldschicht** *f* KER & GLAS starved gold; **~e Verblendung** *f* BAU veneer

Dünn-: **Dünnblech** *nt* FERTIG light gage sheet metal (AmE), light gauge sheet metal (BrE); **Dünndruckpapier** *nt* DRUCK thin paper

Dünne *f* CHEMIE tenuity

dünnflüssig: **~er Schlamm** *m* KERNTECH liquid slurry

Dünn-: **Dünnpapier** *nt* PAPIER lightweight paper; **Dünnschaftschraube** *f* MASCHINEN reduced shaft bolt

Dünnschicht: *f* ELEKTRONIK, TELEKOM thin film, thin layer; **Dünnschichtbauelement** *nt* ELEKTRONIK thin film device; **Dünnschicht-Chromatographie** *f* ELEKTRONIK thin layer chromatography; **Dünnschicht-Elektrolumineszenz** *f (TFEL)* ELEKTRONIK thin film electroluminescence *(TFEL)*; **Dünnschichthybridschaltung** *f* ELEKTRONIK thin film hybrid circuit; **Dünnschichtkondensator** *m* ELEKTRONIK thin film capacitor, TELEKOM thin layer capacitor; **Dünnschichtleiter** *m* ELEKTRONIK thin film conductor; **Dünnschichtmaterial** *nt* ELEKTRONIK thin film material; **Dünnschichtspeicher** *m* COMP & DV thin film memory; **Dünnschichttechnik** *f* ELEKTRONIK thin film technology; **Dünnschichttransistor** *m* ELEKTRONIK thin film transistor; **Dünnschicht-Wärmeaustauscher** *m* HEIZ & KÄLTE scraped-surface heat exchanger; **Dünnschichtwellenleiter** *m* TELEKOM thin film waveguide; **Dünnschichtwiderstand** *m* ELEKTRONIK thin film resistor

Dünntafelglas *nt* KER & GLAS thin sheet glass

dünnwandig[1] *adj* MASCHINEN thin-walled

dünnwandig:[2] **~e Lagerschale** *f* MASCHINEN thin-walled half-bearing; **~er Zylinder** *m* MASCHINEN thin-walled cylinder

Dünn-: **Dünnware** *f* KER & GLAS thin ware

Dunst *m* ELEKTROTECH damp, FOTO *Atmosphäre* atmospheric haze, UMWELTSCHMUTZ haze, WASSERTRANS *leichter Nebel* mist

dünsten *vt* LEBENSMITTEL steam

Dunst: **Dunstkoeffizient** *m* UMWELTSCHMUTZ coefficient of haze; **Dunstventil** *nt* LUFTTRANS exhalation valve

Dünung *f* WASSERTRANS *Seezustand* swell

Duodezbogen *m* DRUCK duodecimo

Duodezimalsystem *nt* MATH duodecimal system

Duotriode *f* ELEKTRONIK double triode

Duowalzwerk *nt* FERTIG two-high mill

Duplex *nt* COMP & DV duplex, full duplex, ELEKTROTECH duplex; Duplexbetrieb *m* COMP & DV duplex operation, duplexing, RADIO *Sprechfunk* full duplex; Duplexbrenner *m* LUFTTRANS duplex burner; Duplexkabel *nt* ELEKTRIZ duplex cable, foto double cable; Duplexkarton *m* VERPACK duplex board; Duplexkette *f* KFZTECH double roller chain; Duplexkompressor *m* HYDRAUL duplex compressor; Duplexpappe *f* VERPACK duplex board; Duplexpumpe *f* HYDRAUL duplex pump; Duplexschmelzverfahren *nt* FERTIG duplex process, duplexing; Duplex-Sprechweg *m* TELEKOM two-frequency channel; Duplexübertragung *f* COMP & DV duplex; Duplexverfahren *nt* FERTIG duplex process, duplexing; Duplexverkehr *m* RADIO duplex

Duplikat *nt* FOTO duplicate; Duplikatfilm *m* FOTO duplicating film

duplizieren *vt* ANSTRICH forge

Dur-Akkord *m* AKUSTIK major chord

Duralumin *nt* METALL duralumin

Duraluminium *nt* MECHAN duralumin

Durchbiegen *nt* BAU bending, FERTIG forming

durchbiegen *vt* FERTIG form

Durchbiegung *f* BAU bending, camber, deflection, flexion, EISENBAHN sagging, KERNTECH sag, MASCHINEN deflection, PAPIER bending, WASSERTRANS *Schiffbau* sagging; ~ unter Last *f* MASCHINEN deflection under load

Durchblättern *nt* COMP & DV *einer Datenbank, eines Textes* browsing

durchbohren *vt* BAU hole, pierce

Durchbrechen: mit ~ *adj* FERTIG holed

durchbrechen *vt* BAU break through, hole, pierce, FERTIG hole

Durchbrennen *nt* ELEKTRIZ *einer Sicherung* blowing, blowing out

durchbrennen[1] *vt* RADIO fuse

durchbrennen[2] *vi* ELEKTRIZ *Sicherung* blow

durchbrochen: ~es Mauerwerk *nt* BAU trellis work; ~e weiße Linie *f* BAU *Straßenmarkierung* broken white line

Durchbruch *m* BAU breakpoint, breakthrough, *für Fenster, Tür* opening, ELEKTRIZ breakdown, HYDRAUL *in Trennwand, Platte* opening, TEXTIL breakthrough; Durchbruchfeldstärke *f* ELEKTROTECH disruptive strength; Durchbruchspannung *f* ELEKTRIZ, PHYS, TELEKOM *Halbleiter* breakdown voltage; Durchbruchstelle *f* KOHLEN breakthrough point; Durchbruchszeichnung *f* KONSTZEICH penetration drawing

Durchdrehen *nt* LUFTTRANS belting-in; ~ des Rades *nt* KFZTECH spinning of the wheel

durchdringbar *adj* CHEMIE permeable

Durchdringbarkeit *f* NICHTFOSS ENERG permeability

durchdringen *vt* ANSTRICH penetrate, BAU intersect, penetrate

durchdringend *adj* ANSTRICH penetrant, FERTIG *Strahl* hard

Durchdringung *f* ELEKTRONIK, ERDÖL penetration, GEOM, KERNTECH interpenetration, MECHAN penetration; Durchdringungsgrad *m* ERDÖL *Tiefbohrtechnik* penetration rate; Durchdringungspotential *nt* KERNTECH penetration potential; Durchdringungs-

wahrscheinlichkeit *f* KERNTECH penetration factor

Durchdrückpackung *f* VERPACK push-through pill pack; Durchdrückpackungsfolie *f* VERPACK push-through packaging sheet; Durchdrückverpackung *f* VERPACK blister pack

Durchfahrt *f* WASSERTRANS *Navigation* pass; Durchfahrtstraße *f* TRANS thoroughfare (BrE), thruway (AmE)

Durchfeuchten *nt* BAU soaking

Durchfluß *m* BAU flow, FERTIG *Kunststoffinstallationen* throughput (BrE), thruput (AmE), HYDRAUL, KER & GLAS flow, KFZTECH passage, KOHLEN, WASSERVERSORG flow; Durchflußanzeiger *m* MASCHINEN flow indicator; Durchflußdichtemeßgerät *nt* GERÄT continuous flow density analyser (BrE), continuous flow density analyzer (AmE); Durchflußgeschwindigkeit *f* FERTIG *Kunststoffinstallationen* speed of flow, HEIZ & KÄLTE, KOHLEN, PHYS rate of flow; Durchflußkalorimeter *nt* THERMOD continuous flow calorimeter; Durchflußkennlinie *f* MASCHINEN flow characteristic; Durchflußkoeffizient *m* HYDRAUL discharge coefficient, NICHTFOSS ENERG flow coefficient; Durchflußkorrekturrechner *m* GERÄT correcting flow calculator; Durchflußmenge *f* ERDÖL flow rate, HEIZ & KÄLTE, KUNSTSTOFF flow rate, rate of flow; Durchflußmengenmesser *m* METROL rate-of-flow meter; Durchflußmengenmessung *f* GERÄT flow measurement; Durchflußmengenregler *m* MASCHINEN flow rate controller; Durchflußmeßblende *f* GERÄT orifice plate; Durchflußmesser *m* BAU, KOHLEN, LABOR, MASCHINEN, PAPIER, PHYS, THERMOD flowmeter, WASSERVERSORG flowmeter, *für Wasser* instant flowmeter; Durchflußmesser mit Permanentmagnet *m* KERNTECH permanent-magnet flowmeter; Durchflußmesser mit Tauchglockenwirkdruckgeber *m* GERÄT bell flowmeter; Durchflußmeßgerät *nt* ELEKTROTECH flowmeter, GERÄT aneroid flowmeter, *für Rohre* pipe flowmeter; Durchflußmeßgerät mit Balgfeder als Wirkdruckgeber *nt* GERÄT bellows flowmeter; Durchflußmeßzelle *f* GERÄT continuous flow cell, flow-through cell, flow-through-type cell; Durchflußquerschnitt *m* RAUMFAHRT *Raumschiff* bore; Durchflußrate *f* HEIZ & KÄLTE flow rate, rate of flow, WASSERVERSORG discharge, rate of flow; Durchflußrechner für den Volumenstrom *m* GERÄT volumetric flow calculator; Durchflußrefraktometer *nt* GERÄT continuous flow refractometer; Durchflußregelung *f* HEIZ & KÄLTE flow control; Durchflußregelventil *nt* MASCHINEN flow control valve; Durchflußrichtung *f* FERTIG *Kunststoffinstallationen* flow direction; Durchflußrohr *nt* MASCHINEN flow pipe; Durchflußschalter *m* ELEKTRIZ flow switch; Durchflußvolumen *nt* PHYS volume rate; Durchflußzähler *m* GERÄT flow-counting device, volumetric flow meter, HEIZ & KÄLTE liquid flow counter, THERMOD flowmeter; Durchflußzählung *f* GERÄT flow counting; Durchflußzelle *f* GERÄT flow-through cell, flow-through-type cell

Durchführbarkeit *f* BAU, COMP & DV feasibility; Durchführbarkeitsbericht *m* COMP & DV feasibility report; Durchführbarkeitsstudie *f* BAU feasibility study

durchführen *vt* COMP & DV implement, PATENT carry out, TELEKOM *Kabel* pass through

Durchführung *f* COMP & DV execution, implementation, ELEKTROTECH grommet, FERTIG *Kunststoffinstallationen* duct, KONTROLL execution, MECHAN duct, feedthrough, PATENT carrying out, PHYS, RAUMFAHRT feedthrough, TELEKOM inlet; **Durchführungseingang** *m* ELEKTROTECH feedthrough input; **Durchführungshülse** *f* ELEKTROTECH grommet; **Durchführungsisolator** *m* ELEKTROTECH feedthrough insulator; **Durchführungskondensator** *m* ELEKTROTECH, PHYS feedthrough capacitor; **Durchführungsstelle** *f* WASSERTRANS *Behörde* regulatory agency

Durchgang:[1] in einem ~ hergestellt *adj* FERTIG one-holed

Durchgang[2] *m* COMP & DV walkthrough, FERTIG throat, *Riemen* sag, KERNTECH *eines geladenen Teilchens* transit, MASCHINEN undersize; **Durchgangsamt** *nt* TELEKOM tandem exchange; **Durchgangsbahnhof** *m* TRANS through station; **Durchgangsbohrung** *f* FERTIG through hole, MASCHINEN clearance hole, through hole; **Durchgangsdämpfung** *f* AKUSTIK, TELEKOM *Vierpol* transmission loss; **Durchgangsdämpfung im Gebäude** *f* TELEKOM building penetration loss; **Durchgangsdrehzahl** *f* NICHTFOSS ENERG runaway speed; **Durchgangsdurchmesser** *m* FERTIG *Spanung* diametral capacity; **Durchgangseilgüterzug** *m* EISENBAHN through freight train (AmE), through goods train (BrE); **Durchgangsfernamt** *nt* TELEKOM transit switching center (AmE), transit switching centre (BrE); **Durchgangshafen** *m* WASSERTRANS port of transit; **Durchgangsknotenamt** *nt* TELEKOM junction tandem exchange (BrE); **Durchgangskontrolle** *f* GERÄT conduction test; **Durchgangsleitung** *f* TELEKOM through line; **Durchgangsprüfer** *m* ELEKTRIZ continuity tester, GERÄT continuity tester, *für elektrische Leitungen* circuit continuity tester; **Durchgangsprüfung** *f* GERÄT conduction test; **Durchgangsrichtung** *f* ELEKTRIZ forward-conducting direction; **Durchgangsschalter** *m* ELEKTRIZ continuity switch; **Durchgangsschraube** *f* MASCHINEN through bolt; **Durchgangsunterbrechung** *f* TELEKOM continuity fault; **Durchgangsventil** *nt* HEIZ & KÄLTE two-way valve, MASCHINEN full-way valve, straight-way valve, NICHTFOSS ENERG straight flow valve; **Durchgangsverkehr** *m* TELEKOM transit traffic, TRANS bypassable traffic, external-external traffic, through traffic, transient currents; **Durchgangsvermittlungsstelle** *f* TELEKOM tandem exchange, transit exchange; **Durchgangszeit** *f* ELEKTROTECH, KERNTECH *von geladenen Teilchen* transit time

durchgebrannt: ~er Kontakt *m* KFZTECH *Ventil* burnt contact; ~e Sicherung *f* ELEKTRIZ open fuse, ELEKTROTECH blown fuse

durchgehend: ~e bewehrte Fundamentplatte *f* FERTIG raft foundation; ~e digitale Verbindungsmöglichkeit *f* TELEKOM end-to-end digital connectivity; ~ geschweißte Schienen *f pl* EISENBAHN continuous-welded rail; ~es Gleis *nt* EISENBAHN main track; ~es Loch *nt* MASCHINEN through hole; ~es Mauerwerk *nt* BAU blank wall, blind wall; ~e Neigung *f* EISENBAHN continuous gradient; ~es Protokoll *nt* COMP & DV end-to-end protocol; ~e weiße Linie *f* TRANS *Straßenmarkierung* continuous white line; ~es Zeitband *nt* TRANS through band; ~er Zug *m* EISENBAHN nonstop train

durchgelassen: ~er Strahl *m* PHYS transmitted beam; ~e Welle *f* PHYS transmitted wave

durchgestrichen: ~e Null *f* DRUCK slashed zero

durchgezogen: ~e Maßlinie *f* KONSTZEICH continuous dimension line

durchgießen *vt* FERTIG strain

Durchgreifspannung *f* ELEKTRONIK punch-through

Durchgriff *m* ELEKTRONIK punch-through

Durchhang *m* BAU *von Leitungen* dip, sag, WASSERTRANS *Tauwerk* slack; ~ einer Schwärzungskurve *m* FOTO toe region of characteristic curve

durchhängen *vi* BAU sag

durchkohlen *vt* KOHLEN, THERMOD carbonize

durchkontaktiert: ~es Loch *nt* ELEKTRIZ metalized hole (AmE), metallized hole (BrE)

Durchkontaktierung *f* KONTROLL, TELEKOM through connection

Durchlaß *m* FERTIG *Werkstück* passage, KER & GLAS throat, KFZTECH passage, MECHAN feedthrough, port; **Durchlaßabdeckstein** *m* KER & GLAS throat cover; **Durchlaßband** *nt* COMP & DV, RADIO, TELEKOM passband; **Durchlaßbereich** *m* AUFNAHME, COMP & DV passband, ELEKTRONIK filter pass band, passband, ELEKTROTECH conducting zone, PHYS, RADIO passband; **Durchlaßcharakteristik** *f* TELEKOM *Filter* transmission characteristic; **Durchlaßdämpfung** *f* ELEKTRONIK passband attenuation; **Durchlaßfunktion** *f* KERNTECH transmission function; **Durchlaßgrad** *m* TELEKOM transmittance

durchlässig[1] *adj* AKUSTIK, ANSTRICH porous, CHEMIE, KOHLEN, KUNSTSTOFF permeable, METALL, NICHTFOSS ENERG porous, TELEKOM transparent, TEXTIL, WERKPRÜF permeable

durchlässig:[2] ~e Scheibe *f* OPTIK transmissive disc (BrE), transmissive disk (AmE)

Durchlässigkeit *f* AKUSTIK porosity, transmission, ANSTRICH porosity, CHEMIE, ERDÖL, KOHLEN, KUNSTSTOFF permeability, METALL porosity, NICHTFOSS ENERG perviousness, porosity, OPTIK transmission, PHYS transmission power, transmittance, TELEKOM transmission, transparency, TEXTIL permeability, WELLPHYS transmittance, WERKPRÜF permeability; **Durchlässigkeitsbeiwert** *m* NICHTFOSS ENERG hydraulic conductivity; **Durchlässigkeitsbereich** *m* MASCHINEN passband; **Durchlässigkeitsfaktor** *m* AKUSTIK diffuse density, PHYS *Schall* transmission coefficient; **Durchlässigkeitsgrad** *m* OPTIK transmittance; **Durchlässigkeitskoeffizient** *m* ABFALL coefficient of permeability; **Durchlässigkeitsspektrum** *nt* KERNTECH transmission spectrum; **Durchlässigkeitswert** *m* ABFALL coefficient of permeability

Durchlaß: **Durchlaßintervall** *nt* FERNSEH forward-stroke interval; **Durchlaßöffnung** *f* KERNTECH *an Handschuhkasten* transfer port; **Durchlaßseitenstein** *m* KER & GLAS throat cheek; **Durchlaßspannung** *f* PHYS forward voltage; **Durchlaßstrom** *m* ELEKTROTECH forward current, on-state current; **Durchlaßtransistor** *m* ELEKTRONIK pass transistor; **Durchlaßverhalten** *nt* ELEKTRONIK passband response; **Durchlaßvorspannung** *f* ELEKTROTECH forward bias; **Durchlaßzeit** *f* ELEKTROTECH *bei Thyristor* conduction angle; **Durchlaßzustand** *m* ELEKTRONIK *Halbleiter* conducting state, ELEKTROTECH *Thyristor* on-state

Durchlauf *m* COMP & DV pass, run, run-through; **Durchlaufanzeiger** *m* MASCHINEN flow indicator; **Durchlaufbalkenträger** *m* BAU continuous beam; **Durchlaufbelichter** *m* VERPACK continuous printer; **Durchlaufdampfgenerator** *m* KERNTECH OTSG, once-through steam generator; **Durchlaufdosenreiniger** *m* LEBENSMITTEL straight-through can washer (AmE), straight-through tin washer (BrE)

Durchlaufen *nt* CHEMIE percolation

durchlaufen *vt* TELEKOM pass through

durchlaufend: **~er Träger** *m* ELEKTRONIK *Hochbau* continuous beam

Durchlauf: **Durchlauf-Entwicklungsmaschine** *f* FOTO continuous processing machine

Durchläufer *m* QUAL passed component

Durchlauf: **Durchlauferhitzer** *m* HEIZ & KÄLTE flow-type heater, hot-water heater, instantaneous water heater; **Durchlaufglühen** *nt* FERTIG continuous annealing; **Durchlaufkochanlage** *f* LEBENSMITTEL continuous cooker; **Durchlaufofen** *m* HEIZ & KÄLTE continuous kiln; **Durchlaufplatte** *f* BAU continuous slab; **Durchlaufschleifen** *nt* FERTIG through-feed grinding; **Durchlaufschmierung** *f* MASCHINEN once-through lubrication; **Durchlaufträger** *m* FERTIG continuous beam; **Durchlaufvernetzung** *f* KUNSTSTOFF continuous vulcanization; **Durchlaufzeit** *f* COMP & DV, KONTROLL, TELEKOM turnaround time (AmE), turnround time (BrE)

Durchleuchtung *f* ELEKTROTECH *Röntgen* fluoroscopy

Durchlicht *nt* FOTO, LABOR, STRAHLPHYS transmitted light

Durchlichtmikroskop *nt* METROL microscope for transmitted light

Durchlüfter *m* LUFTTRANS aerator

Durchmesser *m (D)* FERTIG, GEOM, MASCHINEN diameter *(D)*; **~ der Blattsteigungsachse** *m* LUFTTRANS pitch center diameter (AmE), pitch centre diameter (BrE); **Durchmessermaß** *nt* KONSTZEICH diametral dimension; **Durchmesserreduktion** *f* FERTIG *Walzen* breaking down; **Durchmesserteilung** *f* MASCHINEN diametral pitch; **Durchmessertoleranz** *f* MASCHINEN tolerance on the diameter; **Durchmesserverjüngung** *f* FERTIG *Bohrer* longitudinal clearance; **Durchmesserwicklung** *f* ELEKTROTECH full-pitch diametrical winding; **Durchmesserzeichen** *nt* KONSTZEICH diameter symbol

durchperlen *vi* PHYS bubble through

durchplattiert: **~es Loch** *nt* ELEKTRONIK *in Leiterplatten* plated-through hole

durchpoltern *vt* FERTIG dish

Durchprüfung *f* COMP & DV *eines Programms auf Fehler* program checkout

Durchreiben *nt* KERNTECH chafing

durchreißen *vt* FERTIG *Blechbearbeitung* louver (AmE), louvre (BrE)

Durchrutschen *nt* KFZTECH clutch slip; **~ des Bandes** *nt* AUFNAHME tape slippage

Durchsacken *nt* FERTIG sag, LUFTTRANS *Strömungsabriß eines Flugzeugs* stall

durchsacken *vi* WASSERTRANS *Schiff* sag

Durchsackwarngerät *nt* LUFTTRANS stall warning device

Durchsageanlage *f* LUFTTRANS PA system, public address system

Durchsatz *m* ERDÖL flow rate, throughput (BrE), thruput (AmE), HEIZ & KÄLTE rate of flow, KONTROLL, MASCHINEN throughput (BrE), thruput (AmE), MECHAN flow rate; **Durchsatzgeschwindigkeit** *f* KONTROLL throughput rate; **Durchsatzrate** *f* KONTROLL throughput rate; **Durchsatzzeit** *f* KONTROLL throughput time

Durchschalte- *pref* TELEKOM switching; **Durchschalteeinheit** *f* TELEKOM switching unit; **Durchschaltesystem** *nt* TELEKOM circuit switching system; **Durchschalte-**

vermittlung *f* COMP & DV *(CS)* circuit switching *(CS)*, TELEKOM circuit switch, TELEKOM *(CS)* circuit switching *(CS)*; **Durchschalte-Vermittlungseinrichtung** *f* TELEKOM circuit switching unit; **Durchschalte-Vermittlungsnetz** *nt (CSN)* COMP & DV, TELEKOM circuit-switched network *(CSN)*; **Durchschaltnetzwerk** *nt* ELEKTROTECH *Fernmeldewesen* switching network

Durchschaltung *f* TELEKOM through connection

Durchscheinen *nt* STRAHLPHYS translucence

durchscheinend[1] *adj* TEXTIL sheer

durchscheinend:[2] **~e Materialien** *nt pl* STRAHLPHYS translucent substances; **~es Medium** *nt* PHYS translucent medium

Durchscheuern *nt* WASSERTRANS *Segeln, Tauwerk* chafing

Durchschießen *nt* COMP & DV interleaving

durchschießen *vt* DRUCK lead out, TEXTIL *Druck* interline

Durchschlag *m* ELEKTRIZ breakdown, ELEKTRONIK *im Kondensatorwickel* puncture, *von Gasröhren* breakdown, ELEKTROTECH disruptive discharge, insulation breakdown, *bei p-n Anschlußisolator* breakdown, KUNSTSTOFF breakdown, MASCHINEN drift, drift punch, piercer, PAPIER puncture

durchschlagen[1] *vt* BAU hole, MECHAN overshoot

durchschlagen[2] *vi* KUNSTSTOFF bleed

durchschlagend *adj* ELEKTROTECH disruptive

Durchschläger *m* MASCHINEN drift, solid punch

Durchschlag: **Durchschlagfestigkeit** *f* PHYS dielectric strength; **Durchschlagprüfung** *f* ELEKTRIZ puncture test; **Durchschlagpunkt** *m* PAPIER puncture point; **Durchschlagspannung** *f* ELEKTRIZ breakdown voltage, disruptive voltage, ELEKTROTECH disruptive voltage, *Gas* breakdown voltage, *bei p-n Anschlußisolator* breakdown voltage, *Ölleitung* breakdown voltage, MASCHINEN, TELEKOM breakdown voltage; **Durchschlagsprüfer** *m* PAPIER puncture tester

Durchschlämmung *f* CHEMIE *Boden* percolation

durchschleifen *vt* FERNSEH pipe

Durchschleusen *nt* WASSERVERSORG sluicing, *eines Schiffs* lockage

Durchschlupf *m* QUAL average outgoing quality

Durchschnitt *m* MATH intersection

durchschnittlich[1] *adj* COMP & DV mean, KERNTECH, MASCHINEN, NICHTFOSS ENERG, PHYS, QUAL, TRANS average

durchschnittlich:[2] **~e Anhaltezeit** *f* TRANS average stopped time; **~e Anzahl der geprüften Einheiten je Los** *f* QUAL average total inspection; **~e Energie** *f (W)* KERNTECH *pro Ionenpaar* average energy *(W)*; **~e Fahrzeuglänge** *f* TRANS average vehicle length; **~e Fertigproduktqualität** *f (AOQ)* QUAL average outgoing quality *(AOQ)*; **~er Fertigproduktqualitätsgrenzwert** *m (AOQL)* QUAL average outgoing quality limit *(AOQL)*; **~er Gesamtprüfumfang** *m* QUAL average total inspection; **~er Gleitwegfehler** *m* LUFTTRANS mean glide path error; **~e kinetische Molekularenergie** *f (ε)* PHYS average molecular kinetic energy (ε); **~e mittlere Temperatur** *f* HEIZ & KÄLTE average mean temperature; **~e Momentgeschwindigkeit** *f* TRANS average spot speed; **~e Reisegeschwindigkeit** *f* TRANS average overall travel speed; **~e Reisezeit** *f* TRANS average journey time; **~e Stichprobengröße** *f* QUAL average sample number; **~er Stichprobenumfang** *m* QUAL average sample number; **~e Tagesleistung** *f*

NICHTFOSS ENERG average daily output; **~es Tagesverkehrsaufkommen** *nt* TRANS ADT, average daily traffic; **~es Tagesverkehrsaufkommen pro Jahr** *nt (AADT)* TRANS annual average daily traffic *(AADT)*; **~er Wasserspiegel** *m* WASSERVERSORG intermediate water level; **~e Windgeschwindigkeit** *f* NICHTFOSS ENERG average wind speed

Durchschnitt: **Durchschnittsdichte** *f* TRANS average density; **Durchschnittsgeschwindigkeit** *f* EISENBAHN, KFZTECH, LUFTTRANS mean speed, TRANS average running speed, WASSERTRANS mean speed; **Durchschnittsleistung** *f* PHYS average output; **Durchschnittsprobe** *f* QUAL average sample; **Durchschnittswert** *m* COMP & DV mean, mean value; **Durchschnittszeitintervall** *nt* TRANS average time interval

durchschossen *adj* COMP & DV interleaved

Durchschreibmöglichkeit *f* ELEKTRONIK write-through capability

Durchschuß *m* COMP & DV, DRUCK leading, ELEKTRONIK *Druckwesen* lead, TEXTIL pick

durchsetzend: ~e Stelle *f* QUAL enforcement authority

Durchsicht *f* PAPIER lookthrough

durchsichtig[1] *adj* ANSTRICH glassy, COMP & DV transparent, KER & GLAS seethrough, PHYS, STRAHLPHYS transparent

durchsichtig:[2] **~er Fleck** *m* KER & GLAS clear spot; **~es Material** *nt* PHYS transparent medium; **~e Materialien** *nt pl* STRAHLPHYS translucent substances, transparent substances; **~es Medium** *nt* PHYS transparent medium; **~er Vorhangstoff** *m* TEXTIL casement cloth

Durchsichtigkeit *f* WELLPHYS transmittance

Durchsichtprisma *nt* PHYS Amici prism

Durchsickern *nt* MEERSCHMUTZ seepage

durchsickern[1] *vt* BAU leak, pass through

durchsickern[2] *vi* BAU seep

Durchsieben *nt* CHEMTECH sieving, MEERSCHMUTZ screening

durchsieben *vt* BAU *Erde*, KOHLEN screen, MEERSCHMUTZ sift

durchspülen *vt* BAU, MASCHINEN, WASSERVERSORG flush

Durchspülung *f* MECHAN scavenging

Durchsteckschraube *f* BAU bolt and nut, FERTIG bolt

durchstellen *vt* TELEKOM put through

Durchstoß *m* ABFALL puncture, GEOM penetration; **Durchstoßfestigkeit** *f* ABFALL puncturability, puncture resistance; **Durchstoßpunkt** *m* GEOM penetration point; **Durchstoßungspunkt** *m* GEOM penetration point; **Durchstoßwicklung** *f* ELEKTRIZ push-through winding

Durchstrahlung *f* ELEKTRONIK, KERNTECH, LABOR, PHYS transmission; **Durchstrahlungselektronenmikroskop** *nt* ELEKTRONIK, KERNTECH, LABOR, PHYS transmission electron microscope; **Durchstrahlungs-Kathodenstrahlröhre** *f* ELEKTRONIK penetration CRT

Durchstrahlverfahren *nt* KERNTECH transmission technique

durchströmen *vt* BAU pass

Durchströmungskanal *m* PHYS port

durchsuchen *vt* COMP & DV browse, scan

durchtränken *vt* LEBENSMITTEL soak, steep

durchtreiben *vt* FERTIG drift

Durchtreiber *m* BAU pin punch, MASCHINEN drift punch

Durchtrittsfrequenz *f* ELEKTRONIK , RADIO, TELEKOM gain crossover frequency

durchverbinden *vt* RADIO interconnect, TELEKOM put

through

Durchwahl *f* TELEKOM *Nebenstelle* direct inward dialing (AmE), direct inward dialling (BrE)

Durchwärmdauer *f* THERMOD heat penetration time

durchwärmen *vt* KER & GLAS, METALL soak

durchweicht *adj* PAPIER soggy

Durchziehvorrichtung *f* ELEKTRIZ pull box

Durchzugspule *f* ELEKTRIZ pull-through winding

Dur-Dreiklang *m* AKUSTIK major common chord

Duren *nt* CHEMIE durene

Durometer *nt* KUNSTSTOFF durometer

Duroplast *m* FERTIG *Kunststoffinstallationen* thermosetting plastic, KUNSTSTOFF thermoset, thermosetting plastic

duroplastisch: ~e Kunststoffmasse *f* KUNSTSTOFF thermosetting compound

Dur-Tonart *f* AKUSTIK major key

Dur-Tonleiter *f* AKUSTIK major scale

Düse[1] *f* BAU nozzle, DRUCK air vent, FERTIG nozzle, orifice, tue iron, tuyere, *Matrize* aperture, *Schneidbrenner* tip, HYDRAUL *Unterwasser* orifice, KFZTECH jet, nozzle, KOHLEN, KUNSTSTOFF, LABOR, LUFTTRANS nozzle, MASCHINEN mouth, nozzle, opening, orifice, port, porthole, MECHAN, NICHTFOSS ENERG, PAPIER nozzle, PHYS, RAUMFAHRT *Raumschiff* jet, nozzle; **~ an der Spitze des Luftschraubenblattes** *f* LUFTTRANS *Hubschrauber* blade tip nozzle; **~ des Strahltriebwerks** *f* LUFTTRANS jet nozzle; **~ mit Strahlumlenkung** *f* LUFTTRANS thrust vectoring nozzle

Düse:[2] **~ am Rohrende anbringen** *vi* MASCHINEN fit nozzle on end of pipe

Düsen *f pl* MASCHINEN dies

Düse: **Düsenansatz** *m* MASCHINEN nozzle adaptor; **Düsenantrieb** *m* LUFTTRANS, RAUMFAHRT *Raumschiff* jet propulsion; **Düsendorn** *m* FERTIG *Extruder* core; **Düsendurchmesser** *m* NICHTFOSS ENERG jet diameter; **Düsenfächer** *m* LUFTTRANS ducted fan; **Düsenfläche** *f* RAUMFAHRT *Raumschiff* nozzle area; **Düsenflugzeug** *nt* LUFTTRANS jet, jet plane; **Düsengeschwindigkeit** *f* RAUMFAHRT *Raumschiff* jet velocity; **Düsengeschwindigkeitskoeffizient** *m* NICHTFOSS ENERG nozzle velocity coefficient; **Düsenhals** *m* MASCHINEN nozzle throat; **Düsenhalsquerschnitt** *m* RAUMFAHRT *Raumschiff* nozzle throat, throat of nozzle; **Düsenhalter** *m* KFZTECH nozzle holder; **Düsenhaubenverkleidung** *f* LUFTTRANS *Flugwesen* nozzle cowl; **Düsenlastflugzeug** *nt* TRANS heavy jet; **Düsenlippen** *f pl* KER & GLAS slot lips; **Düsenmund** *m* PHYS nozzle exit; **Düsenpropeller** *m* EISENBAHN ducted propeller, TRANS carinated propeller, shrouded propeller; **Düsenschwefelbrenner** *m* PAPIER jet sulfur burner (AmE), jet sulphur burner (BrE); **Düsenstein** *m* KER & GLAS burner block; **Düsenstock** *m* FERTIG penstock; **Düsenstrahl** *m* LUFTTRANS jet wash, *eines Vergasers* jet; **Düsenstrahlschutzwand** *f* LUFTTRANS *Fangeinrichtung für Flugzeuge* blast fence; **Düsenstrahltriebwerk** *nt* LUFTTRANS jet engine; **Düsentemperaturanzeige** *f* LUFTTRANS *Flugwesen* nozzle temperature indicator; **Düsentragflächenboot** *nt* WASSERTRANS *Schifftyp* jetfoil; **Düsentriebwerk** *nt* LUFTTRANS, RAUMFAHRT *Raumschiff*, THERMOD jet engine; **Düsenverkehrsflugzeug** *nt* LUFTTRANS jet aeroplane (BrE), jet airplane (AmE); **Düsenwirkungsgrad** *m* RAUMFAHRT *Raumschiff* nozzle efficiency

Dutch-Roll *f* LUFTTRANS *Flugzeug mit gepfeiltem Flügel* Dutch roll; **Dutch-Tropfen** *m* KER & GLAS Dutch drop

Dutzend *nt* MATH dozen

DV *abbr (Datenverarbeitung)* COMP & DV, ELEKTRONIK, KONTROLL, TELEKOM DP *(data processing)*

D-Ventil *nt* HYDRAUL D-valve

Dwars- *pref* WASSERTRANS beam, breast

dwars *adv* WASSERTRANS abeam

Dwars-: Dwarsbalken *m* WASSERTRANS *Schiffbau* crossbeam, crosspiece; **Dwarsfeste** *f* WASSERTRANS breast line

dwarsschiffs *adv* WASSERTRANS athwartships

Dwarssee *f* WASSERTRANS beam sea

Dy *(Dysprosium)* CHEMIE Dy *(dysprosium)*

Dyn *nt* METROL dyn, dyne

Dynamik *f* AUFNAHME, FERNSEH, MASCHINEN, MECHAN, PHYS, RADIO dynamics; **Dynamikbereich** *m* AUFNAHME volume range, FERNSEH, RADIO dynamic range; **Dynamikdehner** *m* AUFNAHME expander; **Dynamikdehnung** *f* RADIO expansion; **Dynamikkompression** *f* ELEKTRONIK volume compression; **Dynamikkonvergenz** *f* FERNSEH dynamic convergence; **Dynamikpresser** *m* AUFNAHME volume compressor; **Dynamikpresser und-dehner** *m* AUFNAHME compander; **Dynamikpressung** *f* AUFNAHME compression; **Dynamikregelung** *f* TELEKOM companding; **Dynamikumfang** *m* AKUSTIK volume range

dynamisch[1] *adj* AKUSTIK, AUFNAHME, BAU, COMP & DV, ELEKTROTECH, FERNSEH, KOHLEN, KUNSTSTOFF, MASCHINEN, RADIO, RAUMFAHRT, TELEKOM, dynamic

dynamisch:[2] ~**es Abschöpfgerät** *nt* MEERSCHMUTZ dynamic skimmer; ~**e Adreßumsetzung** *f* COMP & DV dynamic address translation; ~**e Ähnlichkeit** *f* STRÖMPHYS *von zwei Strömungen* dynamic similarity; ~**e Arbeit** *f* ERGON dynamic effort; ~**e Auftriebskraft** *f* PHYS lifting force; ~**er Ausgleich** *m* LUFTTRANS dynamic balancing; ~**es Auswuchten** *nt* LUFTTRANS dynamic balancing; ~**e Auswuchtung** *f* FERTIG dynamic balancing; ~**e Bedingungen** *f pl* ELEKTROTECH dynamic conditions; ~**e Belastung** *f* BAU dynamic loading, LUFTTRANS impact load, METALL dynamic loading, WERKPRÜF dynamic load; ~**er Belegungsdetektor** *m* LUFTTRANS dynamic presence detector; ~**er Bereich** *m* STRAHLPHYS dynamic range; ~**er Bewegungsdetektor** *m* LUFTTRANS dynamic movement detector; ~**er Dauerspeicher** *m* COMP & DV permanent dynamic memory; ~**e Dichtung** *f* MASCHINEN dynamic seal; ~**er Druck** *m* FERTIG dynamic head, LUFTTRANS dynamic pressure; ~**e Druckhöhe** *f* HEIZ & KÄLTE velocity head; ~**e Eigenschaften** *f pl* KUNSTSTOFF dynamic properties; ~**er Eluationstest** *m* ABFALL dynamic leaching test; ~**e Entkopplung** *f* RAUMFAHRT *Raumschiff* dynamic decoupling; ~**e Erholung** *f* METALL dynamical recovery; ~**e Erwärmung** *f* THERMOD dyna-

mic heating; ~**e Fokussierung** *f* FERNSEH dynamic focusing; ~**es Gleichgewicht** *nt* MASCHINEN dynamic balance; ~**er Haltestrom** *m* ELEKTROTECH latching current; ~**e Komponente** *f* LUFTTRANS dynamic component; ~**e Last** *f* BAU dynamic loading; ~**er Lautsprecher** *m* AKUSTIK, AUFNAHME dynamic loudspeaker; ~**e Leistungsaufnahme** *f* ELEKTROTECH dynamic power consumption; ~**es Loten** *nt* KOHLEN dynamic sounding; ~**e Lotung** *f* KOHLEN dynamic sounding; ~**es Modell** *nt* RAUMFAHRT *Raumschiff* dynamic model; ~**e Muskelarbeit** *f* ERGON dynamic effort; ~**er Parameter** *m* COMP & DV dynamic parameter; ~**e Positionierung** *f* ERDÖL *Nautik* dynamic positioning; ~**er Programmaustausch** *m* COMP & DV swapping; ~**e Programmierung** *f* COMP & DV dynamic programming; ~**e Prüfung** *f* WERKPRÜF dynamic test; ~**er RAM** *m (DRAM)* COMP & DV dynamic random access memory *(DRAM)*; ~**e Rauschunterdrückung** *f* AUFNAHME dynamic noise suppressor; ~**e Reibung** *f* PHYS dynamic friction; ~**er Speicher** *m* COMP & DV dynamic memory, KERNTECH delay line storage; ~**er Speicherauszug** *m* COMP & DV dynamic dump, snapshot dump; ~**er Speicherbereich** *m* COMP & DV dynamic storage area; ~**er Spurwinkel** *m* KFZTECH *Lenkung* dynamic toe angle; ~**e Stabilität** *f* LUFTTRANS dynamic stability; ~**es Trimmen** *nt* ELEKTROTECH dynamic trimming; ~**e Überspannung** *f* ELEKTROTECH dynamic overvoltage; ~**e Verzerrung** *f* AKUSTIK dynamic distortion; ~**e Viskosität** *f* FERTIG absolute viscosity, KUNSTSTOFF, MASCHINEN, NICHTFOSS ENERG, PHYS, STRÖMPHYS dynamic viscosity; ~**e Wechselwirkung** *f* METALL dynamic interaction; ~**er Widerstand** *m* ELEKTRIZ *Resonanzzustand eines Schwingkreises*, RADIO dynamic resistance; ~**e Zuordnung** *f* COMP & DV dynamic allocation; ~**e Zuweisung** *f* COMP & DV dynamic allocation

Dynamo *m* ELEKTRIZ, ELEKTROTECH, KFZTECH, RADIO, WASSERTRANS *Elektrik* dynamo; ~ **mit englischer Rahmenmontierung** *m* ELEKTRIZ cradle dynamo; ~ **mit konstanter Spannung** *m* ELEKTRIZ constant-voltage dynamo; **Dynamoeffekt** *m* RAUMFAHRT dynamo effect

dynamoelektrisch *adj* ELEKTROTECH dynamo-electric

Dynamo: Dynamograph *m* MECHAN dynamograph; **Dynamometamorphose** *f* NICHTFOSS ENERG dynamic metamorphism; **Dynamometer** *nt* ELEKTRIZ, ERGON, LABOR *Energie*, MASCHINEN, MECHAN dynamometer; **Dynamometer-Leistungsmesser** *m* ELEKTRIZ dynamometer wattmeter

Dynamotor *m* ELEKTROTECH dynamotor

Dynode *f* PHYS dynode

Dysakusis *f* ERGON dysacusis

Dysodil *nt* KOHLEN paper coal

Dysprosium *nt (Dy)* CHEMIE dysprosium *(Dy)*

D-Zug *m* EISENBAHN express train, fast train

E

E[1] *abbr* DRUCK *(Evaporation, Verdampfung)* E *(evaporation)*, ELEKTRIZ *(elektrische Feldstärke)* E *(electric field strength)*, ELEKTRIZ *(Energie)* E *(energy)*, ELEKTROTECH *(elektrischer Feldvektor)* E *(electric field vector)*, ELEKTROTECH *(elektrische Feldstärke)* E *(electric field strength)*, ELEKTROTECH *(Energie)* E *(energy)*, ERDÖL *(Evaporation, Verdampfung)* E *(evaporation)*, ERDÖL *(Youngscher Modul) Elastizität* E *(Young's modulus)*, HEIZ & KÄLTE *(Evaporation, Verdampfung)*, HYDRAUL *(Evaporation, Verdampfung)* E *(evaporation)*, HYDRAUL *(Youngscher Modul) Elastizität* E *(Young's modulus)*, KERNTECH *(Energie)* E *(energy)*, KOHLEN *(Youngscher Modul) Elastizität*, KUNSTSTOFF *(Youngscher Modul) Elastizität* E *(Young's modulus)*, MASCHINEN *(Evaporation, Verdampfung)* E *(evaporation)*, MECHAN *(Energie)* E *(energy)*, METALL *(Youngscher Modul) Elastizität* E *(Young's modulus)*, METROL *(Energie)* E *(energy)*, NICHTFOSS ENERG *(Evaporation, Verdampfung)* E *(evaporation)*, OPTIK *(Energie)* power, PHYS *(elektrische Feldstärke)* E *(electric field strength)*, PHYS *(Energie)* E *(energy)*, PHYS *(Evaporation, Verdampfung)* E *(evaporation)*, PHYS *(Youngscher Modul) Elastizität* E *(Young's modulus)*, THERMOD *(Energie)* E *(energy)*, THERMOD *(Evaporation, Verdampfung)* E *(evaporation)*

E:[2] **E-Modul** *m* BAU, KOHLEN, KUNSTSTOFF, LUFTTRANS, MASCHINEN, METALL, PHYS, WERKPRÜF modulus of elasticity; **E-Modus** *m* ELEKTROTECH E mode, TM mode, OPTIK E Mode, TM mode, TELEKOM E mode, TM mode

e *abbr (Elektron)* ELEKTRIZ, ELEKTROTECH, PHYS, RADIO, TEILPHYS e *(electron)*

E/A[1] *abbr* COMP & DV *(Eingabel Ausgabe)*, ELEKTRIZ *(Eingabel Ausgabe, Eingangl Ausgang)* I/O *(input/output)*

E/A:[2] **E/A-Prozessor** *m* COMP & DV input/output processor; **E/A-System** *nt* COMP & DV input/output system

Early-Effekt *m* ELEKTRONIK *Transistoren* Early effect

Earnshaw: **~sches Theorem** *nt* PHYS Earnshaw's theorem

EAS *abbr (äquivalente Fluggeschwindigkeit)* LUFTTRANS EAS *(equivalent airspeed)*

Easy-Gleitbereich *m* METALL easy-glide region

Ebbe *f* NICHTFOSS ENERG falling tide, low tide, WASSERTRANS ebb, ebb tide, low tide; **Ebbekrafterzeugung** *f* NICHTFOSS ENERG ebb generation

ebben *vi* WASSERTRANS *Gezeiten* ebb

Ebbe: **Ebbeströmung** *f* NICHTFOSS ENERG ebb tide; **Ebbetor** *nt* WASSERVERSORG aft gate, tail gate

Ebbstrom *m* WASSERTRANS ebb stream

EBCDIC-Code *m (erweiterter Binärcode für Dezimalziffern)* COMP & DV, ELEKTRONIK EBCDIC *(extended binary-coded decimal interchange code)*

EBCS-System *nt (europäisches Leichterträgersystem)* WASSERTRANS EBCS *(European barge carrier system)*

eben[1] *adj* BAU flush, level, FERTIG *Kräfte* coplanar, GEOM planar; **~ mit der Oberfläche eingebaut** *adj* FERTIG flush-mounted; **ebenerdig** *adj* BAU at grade, even with the ground; **ebenflächig** *adj* FERTIG planar

eben:[2] **auf ~em Kiel** *adv* WASSERTRANS even keel

eben:[3] **~es Dreieck** *nt* GEOM plane triangle; **~e Figuren** *f pl* GEOM plane figures; **~e Fläche** *f* MASCHINEN plain surface; **~e Geometrie** *f* GEOM plane geometry; **~er Kiel** *m* WASSERTRANS *Schiffkonstruktion* even keel; **~e parallele Wellen** *f pl* WELLPHYS *von weit entfernter Quelle* plane parallel waves; **~ polarisierte Welle** *f* WELLPHYS plane-polarized wave; **~es Polygon** *nt* GEOM plane polygon; **~es Schallfeld** *nt* AKUSTIK free sound field; **~er Spiegel** *m* PHYS plane mirror; **~e Welle** *f* AKUSTIK, ELEKTROTECH, OPTIK, PHYS, TELEKOM plane wave; **~er Winkel** *m* GEOM plane angle

Ebene:[1] **nicht in einer ~ liegend** *adj* FERTIG noncoplanar

Ebene[2] *f* COMP & DV, ELEKTRONIK *Fläche* level, GEOM plane, MECHAN flat

ebenerdig: **~e Führungsschiene** *f* EISENBAHN guideway at grade

Ebenheit *f* PAPIER flatness; **~ der Straßendecke** *f* BAU pavement surface evenness (BrE), sidewalk surface evenness (AmE); **Ebenheitstoleranz** *f* MASCHINEN flatness tolerance

ebnen *vt* BAU *Straßenbau* level, MASCHINEN flatten, MECHAN plane

E-Bogen *m* ELEKTROTECH *Hohlleiter* E-plane bend, *Wellenleiter* E bend, E plane

Ebonit *nt* KUNSTSTOFF ebonite, vulcanite

EC *abbr (Ethylcellulose)* KUNSTSTOFF EC *(ethyl cellulose)*

Ecdyson *nt* CHEMIE ecdysone

Ecgonin *nt* CHEMIE ecgonine

Echelette-Gitter *nt* PHYS echelette grating

Echinochrom *nt* CHEMIE echinochrome

Echinus *m* BAU ovolo

Echo *nt* AKUSTIK, AUFNAHME, COMP & DV, ELEKTRONIK *mit deutlichem Verzug wahrgenommene Schallreflexion*, PHYS, RADIO, WELLPHYS *reflektierter Schall* echo; **Echoanzeige** *f* WASSERTRANS radar blip, radar pip; **Echoimpuls** *m* FERTIG reflected pulse, TELEKOM blip; **Echoimpulsgerät** *nt* FERTIG reflectorscope; **Echokompensation** *f* ELEKTRONIK echo cancellation; **Echokompensator** *m* ELEKTRONIK *zur Einspeisung des kompensierenden Gegensignals* echo canceler (AmE), echo canceller (BrE); **Echokompensator-Chip** *m* ELEKTRONIK echo-canceling chip (AmE), echo-cancelling chip (BrE); **Echokontrolle** *f* COMP & DV read back check; **Echolot** *nt* STRAHLPHYS sonar, supersonic radar, WASSERTRANS echo sounder, echo sounding, sonar, *Navigation* echo depth finder, WELLPHYS echo sounder

echometrisch: **~e Messung** *f* ERDÖL *Bohrlochmessung* acoustic well logging

Echo: **Echoortung** *f* AKUSTIK echolocation; **Echoplex** *nt* COMP & DV echoplex; **Echoprüfung** *f* COMP & DV echo check; **Echoschreiber** *m* PHYS echograph; **Echosignal** *nt* ELEKTRONIK echo signal; **Echosperre** *f* COMP & DV, ELEKTRONIK *Telefon* echo suppressor; **Echostrom** *m*

ELEKTROTECH return current; **Echounterdrückung** *f* ELEKTRONIK *Telefon* echo suppression; **Echounterdrückungsschaltung** *f* RAUMFAHRT *Weltraumfunk* echo suppressor; **Echoverzerrung** *f* ELEKTRONIK echo distortion; **Echozeichen** *nt* TELEKOM pip

echt[1] *adj* COMP & DV real, TEXTIL actual

echt:[2] **~e Adresse** *f* COMP & DV real address; **~er Bruch** *m* MATH proper fraction; **~e Farbe** *f* TEXTIL fast color (AmE), fast colour (BrE); **~e Halbwertsbreite** *f* STRAHLPHYS true half-width; **~e Klassengrenzen** *f pl* QUAL true class limits; **~es Labkraut** *nt* LEBENSMITTEL lady's bedstraw; **~es Lösemittel** *nt* KUNSTSTOFF true solvent; **~er Mehltau** *m* LEBENSMITTEL *Pflanzenkrankheitslehre* powdery mildew; **~e Untermenge** *f* COMP & DV proper subset

Echtheit *f* TEXTIL fastness

Echtzeit:[1] **in ~** *adj* TELEKOM real-time

Echtzeit[2] *f* COMP & DV, ELEKTRONIK, KONTROLL, TELEKOM real time; **Echtzeitanalysator** *m* AKUSTIK real-time analyser (BrE), real-time analyzer (AmE); **Echtzeitanalyse** *f* ELEKTRONIK real-time analysis; **Echtzeitausgabe** *f* COMP & DV real-time output; **Echtzeitbetrieb** *m* COMP & DV real-time operation; **Echtzeiteingabe** *f* COMP & DV real-time input; **Echtzeit-Signalverarbeitung** *f* ELEKTRONIK real-time signal processing; **Echtzeitsimulation** *f* ELEKTRONIK real-time simulation; **Echtzeitsimulator** *m* ELEKTRONIK real-time simulator; **Echtzeit-Spektralanalysator** *m* ELEKTRONIK real-time spectral analyser (BrE), real-time spectral analyzer (AmE); **Echtzeit-Spektralanalyse** *f* ELEKTRONIK real-time spectral analysis; **Echtzeitsprache** *f* COMP & DV real-time language; **Echtzeitsteuerung** *f* TRANS real-time control; **Echtzeitsystem** *nt* COMP & DV real-time system; **Echtzeituhr** *f* COMP & DV real-time clock; **Echtzeitumsetzer** *m* TELEKOM real-time conversion facility; **Echtzeitverarbeitung** *f* COMP & DV real-time processing

Eckband *nt* BAU corner band

Eckblech *nt* FERTIG gusset plate

Ecke *f* BAU corner, GEOM corner, vertex, MASCHINEN nose, PHYS edge; **Eckenheftmaschine** *f* VERPACK corner stapling machine; **Eckenheftung** *f* VERPACK corner stapling; **Eckenmaß** *nt* MASCHINEN width across corners; **Eckenversteifung** *f* VERPACK corner reinforcement

Eckhahn *m* MASCHINEN right-angle stop cock

eckig: ~e Klammer *f* COMP & DV bracket, MATH square bracket

Ecklautsprecher *m* AUFNAHME corner loudspeaker

Ecknaht *f* FERTIG *Schweißen* corner weld

Eckpfeiler *m* BAU corner pillar, jamb stone

Eckpfosten *m* BAU corner post

Eckrohrzange *f* MASCHINEN multiple pliers

Eckschiene *f* FERTIG angle bar

Eckstab *m* KERNTECH *in Brennelementkonfiguration* corner rod; **~ eines Brennelementbündels** *m* KERNTECH bundle corner rod; **~ in Bündelelement** *m* KERNTECH fuel assembly corner rod

Eckstein *m* BAU pillar stone, quoin, KER & GLAS corner block

Ecksteuerelement *nt* KERNTECH edge control assembly, edge control element

Eckventil *nt* FERTIG *Kunststoffinstallationen* right angle valve, MASCHINEN angle valve

ECL *abbr* (*emittergekoppelte Logik*) COMP & DV, ELEKTRONIK ECL (*emitter-coupled logic*)

ECL-Gatteranordnung *f* ELEKTRONIK ECL gate array

Edelgas *nt* KERNTECH inert gas; **Edelgasröhre** *f* ELEKTRONIK rare gas tube; **Edelgasschutzmantel** *m* FERTIG inert gas shield

Edelgasschutzmantel- *pref* FERTIG inert gas-shielded

Edelgasschutzmantel: mit ~ *adj* FERTIG inert gas-shielded

Edelkohle *f* KOHLEN pure coal

Edelmetall *nt* METALL, UMWELTSCHMUTZ noble metal; **Edelmetallthermoelement** *nt* GERÄT noble metal thermocouple

Edelpassung *f* MASCHINEN force fit

Edelrost[1] *m* FERTIG patina

Edelrost:[2] **mit ~ überziehen** *vt* FERTIG patinate

Edelstahl *m* FERTIG *Kunststoffinstallationen* high-alloyed steel, KFZTECH stainless steel, METALL refined steel, special steel; **Edelstahlbecher** *m* LABOR stainless steel beaker

Edestin *nt* CHEMIE edestin

Edieren: ~ von Hand *nt* FERNSEH manual editing

Edison: Edison-Batterie *f* ELEKTRIZ Edison cell; **Edison-Sockel** *m* ELEKTROTECH *Glühbirnen* screw cap; **Edison-Zelle** *f* ELEKTRIZ Edison cell

Editbetrieb *m* FERNSEH edit mode

editgesteuert: ~e Synchronisierung *f* FERNSEH edit sync

editieren *vt* COMP & DV edit

Editimpuls *m* FERNSEH edit pulse

Editor *m* COMP & DV, FERNSEH editor

edles: ~ Metall *nt* METALL, UMWELTSCHMUTZ noble metal; **~ Thermoelement** *nt* GERÄT noble metal thermocouple

EDTV *abbr* (*hochauflösendes Fernsehen*) FERNSEH EDTV (*extended definition television*)

EDV *abbr* (*elektronische Datenverarbeitung*) COMP & DV, ELEKTRIZ, ELEKTRONIK, KONTROLL EDP (*electronic data processing*)

EEB *abbr* (*elektroerosive Bearbeitung*) MASCHINEN EDM (*electro-discharge machining*)

E-Ebene *f* RADIO E-plane

EEPROM *abbr* (*elektrisch löschbarer programmierbarer Lesespeicher*) ELEKTRONIK EEPROM (*electrically-erasable programmable read-only memory*)

EEROM *abbr* (*elektronisch löschbarer Festwertspeicher, elektronisch löschbarer Lesespeicher*) COMP & DV EEROM (*electronically erasable read-only memory*)

Effekt *m* ELEKTRIZ effect; **äußerer fotoelektrischer ~** *m* OPTIK external photoelectric effect, TELEKOM external photoelectric effect, photoemissive effect; **Effektbogen** *m* ELEKTROTECH flame mode; **Effektbus** *m* FERNSEH effects bus; **Effekte** *m pl* FERNSEH effects; **Effektgarn** *nt* TEXTIL fancy yarn; **Effektgenerator** *m* FERNSEH effects generator

effektiv[1] *adj* AKUSTIK effective

effektiv:[2] **~e Adresse** *f* COMP & DV effective address; **~er Dampfdruck** *m* HYDRAUL, KERNTECH effective steam pressure; **~e Datenübertragungsgeschwindigkeit** *f* COMP & DV effective data transfer rate; **~e Druckhöhe** *f* HYDRAUL effective head; **~e Evaporation** *f* WASSERVERSORG effective evaporation; **~e Fallhöhe** *f* KOHLEN effective drop height; **~e Korngröße** *f* KOHLEN effective grain size; **~e Leistung** *f* MECHAN actual power; **~e Lückenlänge** *f* FERNSEH effective gap length; **~e Masse** *f* AKUSTIK effective mass; **~e Modenamplitude** *f* OPTIK effective mode volume; **~e Neutronenlebensdauer** *f* (*l*) KERNTECH effective neutron lifetime (*l*); **~e Neutronen-Multiplikationskonstante** *f* (*keff*)

KERNTECH effective neutron multiplication constant; **~e Pferdestärke-Stunde** *f (effektive PS-Stunde)* MECHAN actual horsepower hour; **~e PS-Stunde** *f (effektive Pferdestärke-Stunde)* MECHAN actual horsepower hour; **~er Schalldruck** *m* AKUSTIK, UMWELTSCHMUTZ effective sound pressure; **~e Schlitzbreite** *f* FERNSEH effective slit width; **~e Spaltbreite** *f* AKUSTIK, AUFNAHME effective gap length; **~e Teilchendichte** *f* KERNTECH effective particle density; **~er Temperaturbereich** *m* THERMOD effective temperature range; **~e Verdunstung** *f* WASSERVERSORG effective evaporation; **~er Widerstand** *m* PHYS effective resistance

Effektiv-EMK *f* ELEKTRIZ effective electromotive force

Effektivleistung: ~ in Pferdestärke *f (Effektivleistung in PS)* MECHAN actual horsepower; **~ in PS** *f (Effektivleistung in Pferdestärke)* MECHAN actual horsepower

Effektivspannung *f* ELEKTRIZ root mean square voltage

Effektivstrom *m* ELEKTROTECH rms current

Effektivwert *m* AUFNAHME, ELEKTRONIK, OPTIK, PHYS root mean square value; **~ des Stromes** *m* ELEKTROTECH rms current

Effekt: Effektlautsprecher *m* AUFNAHME effects loudspeaker; **Effektmikrofon** *nt* AUFNAHME effects microphone

effektorisch: ~es Handeln *nt* ERGON effector process

Effekt: Effektspeicher *m* FERNSEH effects bank

efferent: ~er Nerv *m* ERGON efferent nerve

effloreszierend *adj* CHEMIE efflorescent

Effusion *f* KERNTECH effusion; **Effusionsofen** *m* ELEKTRONIK *Lava-Ausflußofen* effusion oven

EFS *abbr (essentielle Fettsäure)* LEBENSMITTEL EFA *(essential fatty acid)*

EFuRD *abbr (Europäischer Funkrufdienst)* TELEKOM European radio-paging system

Egalisierer *m* TEXTIL leveling agent (AmE), levelling agent (BrE)

Egalisiermittel *nt* TEXTIL leveling agent (AmE), levelling agent (BrE)

Egalisierwalze *f* PAPIER evener roll

Egoutteur *m* PAPIER, VERPACK dandy roll; **Egoutteurwalze** *f* PAPIER forming roll

EHF *abbr (Millimeterwellen)* RADIO EHF *(extremely high frequency)*

Ehrenfest-Gleichung *f* PHYS Ehrenfest's equation

E.h.t. *abbr (Hochspannung, Höchstspannung)* FERNSEH EHT *(extremely high tension)*

Eichamt *nt* METROL calibration service

Eichanordnung *f* GERÄT calibration set-up

Eicheinrichtung *f* GERÄT calibration equipment

Eichelzucker *m* CHEMIE quercite, quercitol

Eichen *nt* ERDÖL gaging (AmE), gauging (BrE)

eichen *vt* BAU gage (AmE), gauge (BrE), ELEKTRIZ, LABOR, PHYS, STRAHLPHYS calibrate

Eichengerb- *pref* CHEMIE quercitannic

Eichfehlergrenze *f* GERÄT calibration limit

Eichflug *m* LUFTTRANS calibration flight

Eichfrequenz *f* AKUSTIK SF, standard frequency

Eichgenauigkeit *f* GERÄT accuracy of calibration

Eichgerät *nt* GERÄT calibration instrument, RADIO calibrator

Eichgewicht *nt* LABOR calibration weight

Eichimpuls *m* ELEKTRONIK *zur Entfernungseichung eines Radargeräts* calibration pip

Eichinstrument *nt* GERÄT, MECHAN calibration instrument

Eichinvarianz *f* MECHAN gage invariance (AmE), gauge invariance (BrE)

Eichmaß *nt* FERTIG, KFZTECH gage (AmE), gauge (BrE), METROL, PHYS, TELEKOM standard

Eichmikrofon *nt* AKUSTIK standard microphone

Eichsignal *nt* ELEKTRONIK *Datenkommunikation* calibration signal

Eichtank *m* ERDÖL gaging tank (AmE), gauging tank (BrE)

Eichton *m* AKUSTIK reference tone

Eichtrafo *m* KERNTECH calibrating transformer

Eichtransformator *m* KERNTECH calibrating transformer

Eichung *f* AUFNAHME, COMP & DV, ELEKTRIZ, ELEKTRONIK calibration, ERDÖL gaging (AmE), gauging (BrE), LABOR, METROL, PHYS calibration

Eichversuch *m* MASCHINEN calibration test

Eichverzerrer *m* ELEKTRONIK harmonic generator

Eichwert *m* GERÄT calibration value

eiförmig *adj* METALL oval

Eigen- *pref* ANSTRICH, CHEMIE, GERÄT, STRAHLPHYS self-; **Eigenabgleich** *m* GERÄT self-balance; **Eigenabsorption** *f* CHEMIE self-absorption; **Eigenabsorption von Strahlung** *f* STRAHLPHYS *durch angeregte Atome* self-absorption of radiation

eigen *adj* ANSTRICH inherent

Eigenantrieb: mit ~ *adj* KFZTECH automotive, WASSERTRANS self-propelled

eigenbetrieben *adj* ELEKTROTECH self-powered

Eigen-: Eigendämpfung *f* LUFTTRANS internal damping; **Eigenempfindlichkeit** *f* AKUSTIK characteristic sensitivity; **Eigenerwärmung** *f* ELEKTROTECH self-heating; **Eigenerweichungstemperatur** *f* KER & GLAS self-sagging temperature; **Eigenfeedback** *nt* KERNTECH inherent feedback; **Eigenfluß** *m* PHYS self-flux; **Eigenfrequenz** *f* AKUSTIK natural frequency, ELEKTRONIK characteristic frequency, natural frequency, FERNSEH characteristic frequency, PHYS natural frequency, RADIO characteristic frequency, RAUMFAHRT *Raumschiff*, STRAHLPHYS eigenfrequency; **Eigenfrequenzen** *f pl* WELLPHYS natural harmonics; **Eigenfrequenzschwingung** *f* AKUSTIK, ELEKTRONIK, PHYS natural frequency oscillation; **Eigenfunktion** *f* PHYS, STRAHLPHYS eigenfunction; **Eigengeschwindigkeit** *f* LUFTTRANS airspeed; **Eigengeschwindigkeitsanzeiger** *m (ASI)* LUFTTRANS airspeed indicator *(ASI)*; **Eigengewicht** *nt* FERTIG *Kunststoffinstallationen* dead weight; **Eigenhalbleiter** *m* COMP & DV intrinsic semiconductor, ELEKTRONIK i-type semiconductor, intrinsic semiconductor, PHYS intrinsic semiconductor; **Eigenidentifizierung** *f* TELEKOM self-identification; **Eigenionisierung** *f* PHYS, STRAHLPHYS autoionization; **Eigenjustierung** *f* GERÄT automatic adjustment; **Eigenkapazität** *f* ELEKTRIZ self-capacitance, ELEKTROTECH distributed capacitance, PHYS self-capacitance; **Eigenkapital** *nt* ERDÖL *Finanzen* equity capital; **Eigenkonvektion** *f* HEIZ & KÄLTE natural convection; **Eigenkopie** *f* TELEKOM local copy; **Eigenkorrelation** *f* ELEKTRONIK autocorrelation; **Eigenkühlung** *f* HEIZ & KÄLTE self-cooling; **Eigenlast** *f* BAU dead load, permanent weight; **Eigenleiterschichtdiode** *f* ELEKTRONIK intrinsic-barrier diode; **Eigenleitfähigkeit** *f* ELEKTROTECH intrinsic conductivity; **Eigenmasse** *f* BAU permanent weight; **Eigenmodulation** *f* TELEKOM automodulation; **Eigenmodus** *m* COMP & DV native mode; **Eigennachführung** *f*

TELEKOM autotracking; **Eigenperiode** f ELEKTRONIK natural period; **Eigenpotentiallog** nt ERDÖL self-potential log, *Meßtechnik* spontaneous potential log; **Eigenrauschen** nt AKUSTIK *Mikrofon* inherent noise pressure, AUFNAHME inherent noise, ELEKTRONIK ground noise; **Eigenregelung** f ELEKTRONIK *bei gleichbleibender Drehzahl* inherent regulation; **Eigenreibung** f KER & GLAS internal friction

eigenrelativ: ~e **Adressierung** f COMP & DV self-relative addressing

Eigen-: **Eigenrückkopplung** f ELEKTRONIK inherent feedback

Eigenschaft f KÜNSTL INT feature; ~ **der Quarks** f PHYS, TEILPHYS charm; **Eigenschaften** f pl TELEKOM characteristics; **Eigenschaften von Winkeln** f pl GEOM properties of angles

Eigen-: **Eigenschatten** m RAUMFAHRT *Raumschiff* eigenshadow; **Eigenscherben** f pl KER & GLAS factory cullet; **Eigenschwingung** f MASCHINEN self-oscillation; **Eigenschwingungen** f pl FERTIG self-exited vibrations, self-induced vibrations; **Eigenschwingungszustand** m AKUSTIK natural mode of vibration

eigensicher adj ELEKTROTECH intrinsically safe

Eigen-: **Eigenspannung** f MASCHINEN, METALL internal stress

eigenständig[1] adj COMP & DV stand-alone

eigenständig:[2] ~e **Substanz** f UMWELTSCHMUTZ autochthonous matter; ~e **Zeichnung** f KONSTZEICH independent drawing

Eigen-: **Eigensynchronisierung** f TELEKOM autosynchronization; **Eigentemperatur** f ELEKTRONIK intrinsic temperature; **Eigentemperaturbereich** m ELEKTRONIK intrinsic temperature range; **Eigentümer** m COMP & DV owner; **Eigenvektor** m COMP & DV, ELEKTRONIK, PHYS eigenvector; **Eigenverbrauch** m ELEKTROTECH power consumption; **Eigenverlust an der Verbindungsstelle** m OPTIK intrinsic joint loss; **Eigenverstärkung** f ELEKTRONIK internal gain; **Eigenverzerrung** f TELEKOM inherent distortion; **Eigenvolumen** nt PHYS specific volume; **Eigenwärme** f HEIZ & KÄLTE specific heat; **Eigenwert** m COMP & DV, ELEKTRONIK, PHYS, STRAHLPHYS eigenvalue; **Eigenzeit** f PHYS proper time, REGELUNG inherent delay; **Eigenzündung** f KFZTECH *Zündanlage bei Dieselmotor* compression ignition

Eightball-Mikrofon nt AUFNAHME eightball mike

Eigner m COMP & DV owner

Eignung f ERGON aptitude; **Eignungsprüfung** f KERNTECH qualification test, QUAL performance test; **Eignungstest** m ERGON ability test, aptitude test, normal arm's reach

Eikosylalkohol m CHEMIE eicosyl alcohol

Eilauftrag m DRUCK rush order

Eilgang m MASCHINEN fast traverse; **Eilgangwelle** f MASCHINEN quick-motion shaft

Eilgutbahnhof m EISENBAHN parcels depot

Eilgüterzug m EISENBAHN express parcels train

Eilrücklauf m MASCHINEN quick return

Eilvorschub m MASCHINEN quick feed

Eilwartung f COMP & DV emergency maintenance

Eimer m BAU, LABOR, MECHAN, WASSERTRANS bucket; **Eimerbagger** m WASSERTRANS bucket dredge, bucket dredger; **Eimerkette** f WASSERTRANS *Baggern* bucket chain; **Eimerkettenaufzug** m BAU bucket elevator; **Eimerkettenbagger** m BAU bucket excavator, WASSERTRANS ladder dredge, ladder dredger; **Eimer-**

kettenschaltung f (*BBD*) TELEKOM bucket brigade device (*BBD*); **Eimerkettenspeicher** m (*BBD*) ELEKTROTECH bucket brigade device (*BBD*); **Eimerleiter** f WASSERTRANS *Baggern* ladder

Ein- und Ausstiegsluke f RAUMFAHRT manhole

ein- und mehrschichtiges Glas nt SICHERHEIT single and multi-layer glass

Einadreßbefehl m COMP & DV one-address instruction, single address instruction; **Einadreßcode** m COMP & DV single address code; **Einadreßrechner** m COMP & DV one-address computer

einadrig: ~er **Hohlleiter** m ELEKTROTECH uniconductor waveguide; ~es **Kabel** nt ELEKTRIZ single conductor cable, single-core cable, ELEKTROTECH single conductor cable

einander: ~ **durchdringende Ebenen** f pl GEOM intersecting planes

Einanker-Frequenzumformer m ELEKTRIZ rotary frequency converter; **Einankerumformer** m ELEKTROTECH rotary converter, synchronous converter, synchronous inverter

Einanodengleichrichter m ELEKTROTECH single anode rectifier; **Einanodenröhre** f ELEKTRONIK single anode tube

Einarbeiten nt FERTIG sinking

einarbeiten vt KUNSTSTOFF incorporate

Einarbeitung f QUAL indoctrination, TEXTIL contraction

Einarmhebel m FERTIG *Kunststoffinstallationen* single-armed lever handle

einarmig: ~e **Spindelpresse** f MASCHINEN swan neck fly press, swan neck screw press

Einarmzapfverbindung f BAU *Holzbau* housed joint

einatomig[1] adj CHEMIE monoatomic

einatomig:[2] ~es **Gas** nt PHYS monatomic gas

einäugig: ~e **Spiegelreflexkamera** f (*SLR*) FOTO single lens reflex camera (*SLR*)

Ein-/Aus- pref COMP & DV, ELEKTRIZ, HYDRAUL on/off; **Ein-/Ausgabe parallel zu Rechenprogramm** nt (*Spool-Programm*) COMP & DV simultaneous peripheral operations on-line (*SPOOL*); **Ein-/Ausgabewerk** nt TELEKOM interface processor; **Ein-/Aushebelschalter** m ELEKTRIZ lever on-off switch; **Ein-/Auslagerungsrate** f COMP & DV swap rate; **Ein-/Auslaßöffnung** f HYDRAUL port opening, *Dampfturbine* gate; **Ein-/Auslaßöffnungsfläche** f HYDRAUL port face; **Ein-/Auslaßschieber** m HYDRAUL gate valve; **Ein-/Auslaßschiebersteuerung** f HYDRAUL gate gear; **Ein-/Auslaßschiebestange** f HYDRAUL gate stem; **Ein-/Auslaßsteuerung** f HYDRAUL gate gear; **Ein-/Ausschalter** m ELEKTRIZ, ELEKTROTECH, FOTO, MASCHINEN, PHYS on-off switch; **Ein-/Ausspeicherung** f COMP & DV roll in/roll out; **Ein-/Aussteuerung** f ELEKTRIZ on-off control

ein/aus adv MASCHINEN on/off

Einbadentwickler m FOTO single bath developer

Einband m DRUCK cover

einbasisch adj CHEMIE monobasic

Einbau m ELEKTRONIK mounting, MASCHINEN installation, mounting; **Einbauanleitung** f MASCHINEN fitting instructions; **Einbaubrenner** m HEIZ & KÄLTE built-in burner

einbauen vt BAU build in, embed, fit in, house, mount, ELEKTRONIK mount, WASSERTRANS install

Einbau: **Einbauhöhe** f FERTIG *Kunststoffinstallationen* overall height; **Einbauinstrument** nt GERÄT flush instrument; **Einbaulage** f FERTIG assembling position,

Kunststoffinstallationen positioning, HEIZ & KÄLTE mounting position; **Einbaulautsprecher** *m* AUFNAHME cabinet loudspeaker; **Einbaumaß** *nt* FERTIG tool fitting dimension, MASCHINEN fitting dimension, mounting dimension; **Einbaumaße** *nt pl* FERTIG *Kunststoffinstallationen* overall dimensions; **Einbaumikrofon** *nt* AUFNAHME built-in microphone; **Einbaumodem** *nt* COMP & DV built-in modem, integrated modem, line adaptor; **Einbaumotor** *m* ELEKTROTECH built-in motor; **Einbaureibahle** *f* FERTIG block-type reamer; **Einbausatz** *m* MASCHINEN installation kit; **Einbaustück** *nt* FERTIG *Walzen* chuck; **Einbautank** *m* MASCHINEN built-in tank; **Einbautechnik** *f* ABFALL refuse deposition technique; **Einbauten** *m pl* BAU fixed equipment; **Einbauvorrichtung** *f* KERNTECH fitting stand

Einbechern *nt* KUNSTSTOFF potting
Einbereichinstrument *nt* GERÄT single range instrument
einbetonieren *vt* BAU set in concrete
Einbetten *nt* KUNSTSTOFF embedding, encapsulation
einbetten *vt* BAU bed in, embed
Einbettmasse *f* KUNSTSTOFF encapsulant
Einbettung *f* ELEKTRIZ bedding, GEOM immersion, MASCHINEN embedding; **Einbettungsvermögen** *nt* FERTIG embeddability
einbeulen *vt* MECHAN dent
Einbeulung *f* FERTIG dome, MASCHINEN buckle
einbinden *vt* BAU fix, fix in, tail in
Einbindung *f* ABFALL *Sondermüll* grain encapsulation, BAU *einer Stütze* embedment
einblatten *vt* FERTIG adze
Einblenden *nt* FERNSEH inlay
einblenden *vt* AUFNAHME fade in
Einblicklinse *f* OPTIK ocular
Einblicksöffnung *f* FOTO eyepiece
einbrechen *vt* ANSTRICH disrupt
einbrennbar: **~es Abziehbild** *nt* KER & GLAS ceramic transfer
Einbrenne *f* LEBENSMITTEL roux
Einbrennen *nt* DRUCK burning-in, ELEKTRONIK *Dickschicht-Leiterplatten*, ELEKTROTECH *Reaktoren* firing, KUNSTSTOFF baking
einbrennen *vt* BAU bake, FERNSEH burn in, FERTIG bake
Einbrennetikett *nt* VERPACK hot-transfer label
Einbrennlack *m* BAU baking varnish, KUNSTSTOFF stoving enamel, stoving finish, stoving varnish, VERPACK enameling (AmE), enamelling (BrE)
Einbrennmuffel *f* KER & GLAS decorating lehr
Einbrennofen *m* KER & GLAS decorating kiln, TEXTIL baking stove
Einbringen: **~ der ersten Rohrtour** *nt* ERDÖL *Bohrtechnik* spudding in
Einbruch *m* ERDÖL *Bohrtechnik* caving, MECHAN breaking in, WASSERVERSORG irruption; **~ von Wasser** *m* WASSERVERSORG irruption of water; **Einbruchsalarm** *m* SICHERHEIT alarm
einbruchssicher *adj* SICHERHEIT burglar-proof
Einbuchen: **~ des Teilnehmer-Aufenthaltsortes** *nt* TELEKOM mobile location registration
Einbuchung *f* TELEKOM log in
Eindampfen: **~ einer Säure** *nt* UMWELTSCHMUTZ acid concentration
eindampfen *vt* CHEMIE *bis zur Trocken* evaporate
Eindampfkessel *m* CHEMTECH vaporizer
Eindampfung *f* CHEMIE inspissation
eindecken *vt* BAU roof

Eindeck: **Eindeck-Flachpalette** *f* TRANS single-faced pallet; **Eindeckpalette** *f* TRANS single-decked pallet; **Eindeckschiff** *nt* WASSERTRANS single-decked ship
eindeutig: **~es Wort** *nt* RAUMFAHRT *Weltraumfunk* UW, unique word; **~e Worterkennung** *f* RAUMFAHRT *Weltraumfunk* unique word detection
Eindickapparat *m* CHEMTECH *Gerät* thickener
eindicken[1] *vt* CHEMTECH condense, FERTIG body, body up, inspissate, LEBENSMITTEL boil down
eindicken[2] *vi* CHEMTECH condense
Eindicker *m* KUNSTSTOFF, LEBENSMITTEL thickener
Eindickkegel *m* KOHLEN thickening cone
Eindickung *f* CHEMIE inspissation, FERTIG inspissation, *Öl* bodying
Eindickzylinder *m* PAPIER concentrator
eindimensional *adj* PHYS one-dimensional
eindocken *vt* WASSERTRANS dock, drydock
Eindockung *f* WASSERTRANS *Schiff* docking
Eindosen *nt* LEBENSMITTEL canning
Eindraht: **Eindrahtspeisung** *f* ELEKTRIZ single supply; **Eindrahtsystem** *nt* ELEKTRIZ single wire system
eindrehen *vt* FERTIG *kreisförmige Nut* neck
Eindrehung *f* MASCHINEN groove, recess
Eindringen: **~ von Wasser in ein Brennelement** *nt* KERNTECH water logging
eindringen *vt* ANSTRICH, BAU penetrate
Eindringkörper *m* MASCHINEN indenter
Eindringkraft *f* STRAHLPHYS penetrating power
Eindringtiefe *f* BAU penetration depth, COMP & DV penetration, ELEKTRONIK, KERNTECH, MASCHINEN, WERKPRÜF penetration depth; **Eindringtiefenmesser** *m* BAU penetrometer
Eindringung *f* MECHAN penetration; **Eindringungsversuch** *m* KOHLEN penetration test
Eindringverfahren *nt* KERNTECH *bei Werkstoffprüfung* penetration method
Eindruck *m* MASCHINEN, METALL indentation
Eindrückdeckel *m* VERPACK lever lid
Eindruck: **Eindruckhärte** *f* KUNSTSTOFF indentation hardness, MASCHINEN indentation hardness, penetration hardness; **Eindruckkalotte** *f* FERTIG ball impression
Einebnen *nt* BAU leveling (AmE), levelling (BrE), MECHAN equalization, leveling (AmE), levelling (BrE)
einebnen *vt* FERTIG flush
Einerkomplement *nt* COMP & DV one's complement
Einfach- *pref* COMP & DV single
einfach[1] *adj* COMP & DV single, KONTROLL straightforward, TEXTIL plain; **~ mit Baumwolle isoliert** *adj* ELEKTRIZ SCC; **~ mit Gummi isoliert** *adj* ELEKTRIZ single-rubber-covered; **~ mit Papier isoliert** *adj* ELEKTRIZ single-paper-covered
einfach:[2] **~e Baumwolleisolierung** *f* ELEKTRIZ SCC; **~e bituminöse Oberflächenbehandlung** *f* BAU single bituminous surface treatment; **~er Bootskörper** *m* WASSERTRANS single hull; **~e Einspeisung** *f* ELEKTRIZ single feeder; **~e Erde** *f* ELEKTRIZ single earth (BrE), single ground (AmE); **~er Flammofen** *m* METALL air furnace; **~e Gegentaktmischstufe** *f* ELEKTRONIK single-balanced mixer; **~e Genauigkeit** *f* COMP & DV single precision; **~e Gleiskreuzung** *f* EISENBAHN common crossing; **~e harmonische Bewegung** *f* PHYS, WELLPHYS simple harmonic motion; **~e Hybridschaltung** *f* ELEKTRONIK simple hybrid circuit; **~er Kameraauszug** *m* FOTO single camera extension; **~es Kreuz** *nt* TEXTIL end-and-end lease, one-and-one lea-

se; ~es **Objektiv** *nt* FOTO single lens; ~er **Öffnungskontakt** *m* ELEKTROTECH single break contact; ~es **Pendel** *nt* PHYS simple pendulum; ~er **Polykristallinprozeß** *m* ELEKTRONIK single level polysilicon process; ~e **Scherspannung** *f* METALL simple shear stress; ~es **schritthaltendes Paket** *nt (SIP-Paket)* COMP & DV, ELEKTRONIK single in-line package *(SIP)*; ~es **schritthaltendes Speichermodul** *nt (SIMM)* COMP & DV single in-line memory module *(SIMM)*; ~e **Speiseleitung** *f* ELEKTRIZ single feeder; ~er **Strebebogen** *m* BAU flying buttress; ~er **Taljereepsknoten** *m* WASSERTRANS *Knoten* single Matthew Walker; ~er **Zeilenabstand** *m* COMP & DV monospacing; ~er **Zwirn** *m* TEXTIL *Spinnen* twine

Einfach-: **Einfachabdeckstruktur** *f* ELEKTRONIK single level masking structure; **Einfachbettdrehmaschine** *f* MASCHINEN plain-bed lathe; **Einfachdrehbank** *f* MASCHINEN plain lathe; **Einfachdrehmaschine** *f* MASCHINEN plain lathe; **Einfachexpansionsmaschine** *f* MASCHINEN simple expansion engine, single expansion engine; **Einfachfahrschein** *m* TRANS one-way ticket (AmE), single ticket (BrE); **Einfachfilter** *nt* ELEKTRONIK single section filter; **Einfachform** *f* MASCHINEN single impression mold (AmE), single impression mould (BrE); **Einfachfräsmaschine** *f* MASCHINEN plain-milling machine

einfachgerichtet[1] *adj* TELEKOM one-way

einfachgerichtet:[2] ~er **Verstärker** *m* ELEKTRONIK, TELEKOM one-way repeater

Einfach-: **Einfachimpuls** *m* ELEKTRONIK single pulse; **Einfachimpulssignal** *nt* ELEKTRONIK single pulse signal; **Einfachraketentreibstoff** *m* CHEMIE, RAUMFAHRT monopropellant; **Einfachschlüssel** *m* MASCHINEN single-ended spanner; **Einfachschraubenschlüssel** *m* MASCHINEN single-ended spanner; **Einfachstapelfasergarn** *nt* KER & GLAS single staple-fiber yarn (AmE), single staple-fibre yarn (BrE); **Einfachstichprobe** *f* QUAL single sample; **Einfachstichprobenentnahme** *f* QUAL single sampling; **Einfachstichprobenprüfplan** *m* QUAL single sampling plan; **Einfachstichprobenprüfung** *f* QUAL single sampling inspection; **Einfachtafelglas** *nt* KER & GLAS single thickness sheet glass; **Einfachteilen** *nt* MASCHINEN single indexing; **Einfachüberlappung** *f* MASCHINEN single overlap; **Einfachverstärker** *m* ELEKTRONIK monolithic amplifier

einfachwirkend[1] *adj* HEIZ & KÄLTE single-acting

einfachwirkend:[2] ~e **Maschine** *f* MASCHINEN single action engine, single-acting engine; ~e **Pumpe** *f* HYDRAUL single-acting pump; ~er **Servomotor** *m* NICHTFOSS ENERG single-acting servomotor; ~er **Verdichter** *m* HEIZ & KÄLTE single-acting compressor

Einfädelband *nt* FERNSEH line-up tape

Einfädeln: ~ **von Papier** *nt* PAPIER threading of paper

Einfädelung *f* KFZTECH weaving maneuver (AmE), weaving manoeuvre (BrE), TRANS joining a traffic system; **Einfädelungsaufkommen** *nt* TRANS *Verkehrsströme* merge volume

Einfadenaufhängung *f* ELEKTRIZ unifilar suspension

Einfahren *nt* ERDÖL *Bohrtechnik* going-in hole, *Zapfer in Muffengewinde, Gestänge* stabbing, MASCHINEN running-in

einfahren *vt* KFZTECH *Motor* run in

einfahrend: ~er **Verkehr** *m* TRANS entering traffic

Einfahrt *f* WASSERTRANS *Geographie, Hafen* mouth, *Hafen* inlet; **äußeres Einfahrtsignal** *nt* EISENBAHN outer home signal

Einfahrvorsignal *nt* EISENBAHN entry warning signal

Einfall *m* KERNTECH fall-back, OPTIK *Strahl*, PHYS incidence

Einfallen *nt* ERDÖL dip, *Geologie* dipping, NICHTFOSS ENERG *Geologie* dip

einfallend[1] *adj* OPTIK *Strahl* incident, TELEKOM *Welle* incoming

einfallend:[2] ~es **Licht** *nt* FOTO, PHYS, WELLPHYS incident light; ~er **Strahl** *m* PHYS, WELLPHYS incident beam, incident ray; ~e **Welle** *f* PHYS, WELLPHYS incident wave

Einfall: **Einfallsebene** *f* PHYS plane of incidence; **Einfallstelle** *f* FERTIG *Gießen* shrink mark; **Einfallstellentropfen** *nt* KER & GLAS crater drip (BrE), top tin (AmE); **Einfallswinkel** *m* ELEKTROTECH acceptance angle, FERTIG, LUFTTRANS, OPTIK, PHYS angle of incidence, TELEKOM angle of arrival, WELLPHYS angle of incidence; **Einfallwinkelsonde** *f* LUFTTRANS incidence probe

einfalzen *vt* BAU join, FERTIG rabbet

Einfang *m* KERNTECH capture

Einfangen *nt* FERTIG aligning, *Meßgerät* alignment, RAUMFAHRT *eines Satelliten* capture

einfangen *vt* RAUMFAHRT *Raumschiff* capture

Einfang: **Einfangstrahlung** *f* KERNTECH capture radiation

einfärben *vt* BAU color (AmE), colour (BrE)

Einfarbenpunktschreiber *m* GERÄT single color point recorder (AmE), single colour point recorder (BrE)

einfarbig *adj* COMP & DV, DRUCK, FOTO monochrome, TEXTIL plain

Einfärbung *f* PAPIER inking

Einfaserkabel *nt* ELEKTROTECH single fiber cable (AmE), single fibre cable (BrE)

Einfaserleitung *f* ELEKTROTECH single fiber line (AmE), single fibre line (BrE)

Einfaßborte *f* TEXTIL braid

einfassen *vt* BAU border, TEXTIL face

Einfassung *f* BAU skirting, KFZTECH *Scheinwerfer* rim, MEERSCHMUTZ skirt

Einfeldträger *m* BAU simple beam

Einfettmittel *nt* LEBENSMITTEL *Trennmittel für Backbleche* greasing agent

Einfingerwahl *f* TELEKOM single digit dialing (AmE), single digit dialling (BrE)

Einfliegen *nt* LUFTTRANS flight test

Einfluchten *nt* BAU running, KER & GLAS marking out

einfluchten *vt* FERTIG flush

Einflugsteuerkurs *m* LUFTTRANS inbound heading; **äußeres Einflugzeichennt** LUFTTRANS *Startbahn* outer marker

Einflußfunktion *f* KERNTECH importance function

Einflußgebiet *nt* WASSERVERSORG area of influence

Einflußlinie *f* BAU *Brückenbau* influence line

einförmig *adj* CHEMIE monotonic, uniform

Einfressung *f* KERNTECH corrosion

Einfriedung *f* BAU boundary fence, enclosure

Einfrieren *nt* HEIZ & KÄLTE freezing, VERPACK deep-freezing

einfrieren[1] *vt* LEBENSMITTEL, PAPIER freeze

einfrieren[2] *vi* HEIZ & KÄLTE freeze

einfrieren:[3] **sich ~ lassen** *v refl* HEIZ & KÄLTE freeze

Einfriertemperatur *f* KUNSTSTOFF glass transition temperature

Einfügedämpfungsmeßmethode *f* TELEKOM *Lichtleitfaser* reference test method

Einfügen *nt* FERNSEH edit-in, insert edit, insert editing

einfügen *vt* BAU join, COMP & DV paste, patch, FERTIG rabbet

Einfügung *f* COMP & DV insert; **Einfügungsdämpfung** *f* PHYS insertion loss, TELEKOM extrinsic joint loss, insertion loss; **Einfügungsverlust** *m* OPTIK insertion loss; **Einfügungsverstärkung** *f* PHYS insertion gain

einführen *vt* ELEKTROTECH plug in

Einführkabel *nt* ELEKTRIZ lead-in cable

Einfuhrlizenz *f* WASSERTRANS *Dokument* import licence (BrE), import license (AmE)

Einführungsdraht *m* ELEKTROTECH lead-in wire

Einführungsrille *f* AUFNAHME lead-in groove

Einfülladapter *m* KFZTECH filler adaptor

Einfülldeckel *m* MECHAN filler cap

Einfüllöffnung *f* RAUMFAHRT *Raumschiff* filling hole

Einfüllstutzen *m* KFZTECH filler neck; **~ für Reaktorkühlmittel** *m* KERNTECH reactor coolant inlet nozzle

Einfülltrichter *m* TEXTIL hopper

Einfüllventil *nt* KFZTECH filler valve, filling valve, RAUMFAHRT *Raumschiff* filling valve

Einfüllverlust *m* RAUMFAHRT spillover loss

Einfüllverschluß *m* KFZTECH radiator cap

Eingabe *f* COMP & DV entry, input IP, ELEKTRIZ IP, input, ELEKTRONIK IP, input FERNSEH, HYDRAUL, KONTROLL, PHYS, RADIO IP, input; **~ am Steuerpult** *f* KONTROLL console input; **~ von Hand** *f* COMP & DV manual input; **~ über Tastatur** *f* COMP & DV keyboard entry; **Eingabeanschluß** *m* COMP & DV input port; **Eingabeanweisung** *f* COMP & DV input statement; **Eingabearbeitswarteschlange** *f* COMP & DV input work queue; **Eingabeaufforderung** *f* COMP & DV prompt

Eingabe/Ausgabe *f* (*E/A*) COMP & DV, ELEKTRIZ input/output (*I/O*); **Eingabe/Ausgabeanforderung** *f* COMP & DV input/output request; **Eingabe/Ausgabeanschluß** *m* COMP & DV input/output port; **Eingabe/Ausgabebefehl** *m* COMP & DV input/output instruction

eingabe-/ausgabebegrenzt *adj* COMP & DV input/output limited

Eingabe/Ausgabe: **Eingabe/Ausgabebus** *m* COMP & DV input/output bus; **Eingabe/Ausgabedatei** *f* COMP & DV input/output file; **Eingabe/Ausgabeeinheit** *f* COMP & DV input/output device; **Eingabe/Ausgabegerät** *nt* COMP & DV input/output device; **Eingabe/Ausgabeinstruktion** *m* COMP & DV input/output instruction; **Eingabe/Ausgabeinterrupt** *m* COMP & DV input/output interrupt; **Eingabe/Ausgabekanal** *m* COMP & DV input/output channel; **Eingabe/Ausgabeprozessor** *m* COMP & DV IOP, input/output processor; **Eingabe/Ausgabepuffer** *m* COMP & DV input/output buffer; **Eingabe/Ausgaberegister** *nt* COMP & DV input/output register; **Eingabe/Ausgabesteuerung** *f* COMP & DV input/output control; **Eingabe/Ausgabesystem** *nt* COMP & DV IOS, input/output system; **Eingabe/Ausgabeunterbrechung** *f* COMP & DV input/output interrupt

Eingabe: **Eingabebedingung** *f* COMP & DV entry condition; **Eingabebefehl** *m* COMP & DV entry instruction

eingabebegrenzt *adj* COMP & DV input-limited

Eingabe: **Eingabebereich** *m* COMP & DV input area; **Eingabeblock** *m* COMP & DV input block; **Eingabedatei** *f* COMP & DV input file; **Eingabedaten** *nt pl* COMP & DV input data; **Eingabedatensatz** *m* COMP & DV input record; **Eingabeeinheit** *f* COMP & DV input device, input unit; **Eingabefehler** *m* TELEKOM keying error; **Eingabefolge** *f* COMP & DV input sequence; **Eingabegerät** *nt* COMP & DV input device, input unit, ELEKTROTECH

input device; **Eingabeglied** *nt* REGELUNG input element; **Eingabekanal** *m* KONTROLL input port; **Eingabeleitung** *f* COMP & DV input lead; **Eingabemodus** *m* COMP & DV input mode; **Eingabemultiplexer** *m* TELEKOM *Datenverarbeitung* scanner; **Eingabeprogramm** *nt* COMP & DV input routine, reader; **Eingabepuffer** *m* COMP & DV input buffer; **Eingabepufferverstärker** *m* ELEKTRONIK input buffer amplifier; **Eingaberegister** *nt* COMP & DV input register; **Eingaberoutine** *f* COMP & DV input routine; **Eingaberückstellung** *f* RAUMFAHRT *Wanderwellenröhre* input back-off; **Eingabesatz** *m* COMP & DV input record; **Eingabespeicherbereich** *m* COMP & DV input storage; **Eingabesteuerung** *f* ELEKTRONIK input control; **Eingabetablett** *nt* COMP & DV data tablet; **Eingabetaste** *f* COMP & DV return, return key; **Eingabevorgang** *m* COMP & DV transaction; **Eingabewarteschlange** *f* COMP & DV entry queue, input queue, input work queue; **Eingabezeile** *f* COMP & DV entry line

Eingang *m* ELEKTRIZ, ELEKTRONIK, FERNSEH, IP, input, FERTIG *Kunststoffinstallationen* mouth, KONTROLL, RADIO IP, input; **Eingang/Ausgang** *m* (*E/A*) ELEKTRIZ input/output (*I/O*)

eingängig[1] *adj* MASCHINEN single-start, single-thread

eingängig:[2] **~es Gewinde** *nt* MASCHINEN single thread

Eingang: **Eingangsabgriff** *m* ELEKTROTECH input tapping; **Eingangsablauf** *m* TELEKOM incoming procedure; **Eingangsadmittanz** *f* ELEKTROTECH input admittance; **Eingangsbestand** *m* VERPACK accepted stock; **Eingangsdämpfungsglied** *nt* ELEKTRONIK input attenuator; **Eingangsdruck** *m* KOHLEN inlet pressure; **Eingangselektrode** *f* ELEKTROTECH input electrode; **Eingangselement** *nt* REGELUNG receiver element; **Eingangsfächerung** *f* ELEKTROTECH fan-in; **Eingangsfehler** *m* COMP & DV inherited error; **Eingangsfilter** *nt* ELEKTRONIK, RADIO, RAUMFAHRT *Weltraumfunk* input filter; **Eingangsfilter mit Drossel** *nt* RADIO choke-input filter; **Eingangsfilterung** *f* ELEKTRONIK input filtering; **Eingangsflughafen** *m* LUFTTRANS airport of entry; **Eingangsfolgeliste** *f* COMP & DV push-up list; **Eingangsfolgestapel** *f* COMP & DV push-up stack; **Eingangsfunkvermittlungsstelle** *f* TELEKOM gateway mobile switching center (AmE), gateway mobile switching centre (BrE); **Eingangsgatter** *nt* ELEKTRONIK input gate; **Eingangsgleichstrom** *m* ELEKTROTECH DC input; **Eingangsglied** *nt* GERÄT *einer Meßeinrichtung* receiving element; **Eingangshohlraum** *m* ELEKTRONIK input cavity; **Eingangsimpedanz** *f* AKUSTIK *bei Nennbelastung* loaded impedance, ELEKTROTECH, FERNSEH, TELEKOM input impedance; **Eingangsimpuls** *m* ELEKTRONIK input pulse; **Eingangskanal** *m* KONTROLL input port; **Eingangskapazität** *f* ELEKTROTECH input capacitance; **Eingangskegelritzelwelle** *f* LUFTTRANS *Hubschrauber* input bevel pinion shaft; **Eingangsklemme** *f* ELEKTRIZ, ELEKTROTECH input terminal; **Eingangskondensatorfilter** *nt* RADIO capacitor input filter; **Eingangskontrolle** *f* ABFALL *einer Deponie* weigh office, QUAL incoming inspection; **Eingangskreis** *m* ELEKTROTECH input circuit; **Eingangsleistung** *f* ELEKTROTECH, FERNSEH, MASCHINEN, TELEKOM input power; **Eingangsleitung** *f* AUFNAHME, FERNSEH line in; **Eingangsmeßwandler** *m* ELEKTROTECH input transductor; **Eingangs-MSC** *f* TELEKOM gateway MSC; **Eingangspegel** *m* FERNSEH, TELEKOM input level; **Eingangspegel für Tonfrequenzsignal** *m* AUF-

NAHME audio signal input level; **Eingangsprüfung** *f* QUAL incoming inspection, on-receipt inspection, receiving inspection; **Eingangspunkt** *m* COMP & DV entry point; **Eingangsregister** *nt* TELEKOM incoming register; **Eingangsresonator** *m* ELEKTRONIK *Klystron* input resonator, *verursacht Geschwindigkeitsmodulation* buncher resonator; **Eingangsschaltung** *f* ELEKTRIZ input circuit; **Eingangsscheinleitwert** *m* ELEKTROTECH input admittance; **Eingangsscheinwiderstand** *m* ELEKTROTECH input impedance; **Eingangssignal** *nt* ELEKTRONIK, FERNSEH input signal, TELEKOM incoming signal; **Eingangssignalleistung** *f* ELEKTRONIK input signal power; **Eingangssignalquantelung** *f* ELEKTRONIK input signal quantization; **Eingangssignal-Rausch-Verhältnis** *nt* ELEKTRONIK input signal-to-noise ratio; **Eingangsspannung** *f* ELEKTRIZ, ELEKTROTECH input voltage; **Eingangsstelle** *f* PATENT receiving section; **Eingangssteuerung** *f* ELEKTRONIK input control; **Eingangsstrom** *m* ELEKTRIZ input current; **Eingangsstufe** *f* ELEKTRONIK input stage, RADIO premixer; **Eingangstransformator** *m* ELEKTROTECH, PHYS input transformer; **Eingangsverhalten** *nt* ELEKTRONIK input response; **Eingangsverstärker** *m* ELEKTRONIK input amplifier; **Eingangswelle** *f* KFZTECH *Kupplung, Getriebe,* MASCHINEN input shaft; **Eingangswiderstand** *m* ELEKTROTECH input resistance, PHYS input impedance; **Eingangszuleitung** *f* ELEKTROTECH input lead

eingebaut[1] *adj* BAU encastré, ELEKTROTECH, MASCHINEN, MECHAN built-in

eingebaut:[2] ~e **Alterung** *f* ABFALL built-in obsolescence; ~e **Barriere** *f* KERNTECH *zur Sicherheit in Atomkraftwerken* engineered barrier; ~e **Batterie** *f* ELEKTROTECH internal battery; ~er **Belichtungsmesser** *m* FOTO built-in exposure meter; ~es **Ladegerät** *nt* TRANS built-in charger; ~er **Motor** *m* ELEKTROTECH built-in motor; ~er **Oszillator** *m* PHYS local oscillator; ~e **Prüfeinrichtung** *f* GERÄT built-in test equipment; ~e **Standardfunktion** *f* COMP & DV built-in function

Eingeben *nt* ELEKTRONIK inputting

eingeben *vt* COMP & DV type, *Daten, Befehl* enter, key in, ELEKTRONIK input

eingebettet[1] *adj* COMP & DV, MASCHINEN embedded

eingebettet:[2] ~er **Befehl** *m* COMP & DV embedded command; ~er **Code** *m* COMP & DV embedded code; ~es **System** *nt* COMP & DV embedded computer, embedded system

eingebrannt: ~es **Ventil** *nt* KFZTECH *Motor* burnt valve; ~er **Zeitcode** *m* FERNSEH burnt-in time code

eingebunden: ~es **Post-Script** *nt* COMP & DV encapsulated PostScript; ~es **Programm** *nt* COMP & DV encapsulated program

eingedämmt *adj* THERMOD banked-up

eingedampft: ~er **Latex** *nt* KUNSTSTOFF evaporated latex

eingedickt: ~er **Schlamm** *m* KOHLEN thickened slime

eingedost *adj* CHEMIE canned (AmE), tinned (BrE)

eingedrückt: ~er **Mantel** *m* OPTIK depressed cladding

eingeebnet *adj* BAU leveled (AmE), levelled (BrE)

eingeengt: ~er **Sattelpunkt** *m* METALL constricted node

eingefahren: ~er **Notabschaltstab** *m* KERNTECH inserted scram rod; ~er **Schnellabschaltstab** *m* KERNTECH scrammed rod

eingefroren *adj* WASSERTRANS *Schiff* icebound

eingegangen: ~er **Bestand** *m* VERPACK accepted stock

Eingehen *nt* TEXTIL shrinkage

eingehen *vi* TEXTIL contract, shrink

eingehend: ~e **Meldung** *f* COMP & DV incoming message; ~e **Nachricht** *f* COMP & DV incoming message

eingekapselt: ~e **Strahlungsquelle** *f* KERNTECH encapsulated source

eingekehlt *adj* FERTIG *Schmieden* necked-down

eingekerbt: ~e **Düse** *f* LUFTTRANS notched nozzle

eingeklebt *adj* DRUCK tipped-in

eingelagert[1] *adj* MASCHINEN embedded

eingelagert:[2] ~er **Abfall** *m* ABFALL emplaced waste

eingelassen[1] *adj* ELEKTRIZ flush-mounting

eingelassen:[2] ~er **Heißring** *m* WASSERTRANS *Deckbeschläge* flush lifting ring; ~er **Schalter** *m* ELEKTRIZ flush switch; ~e **Schleife** *f* TRANS embedded loop

eingelegt: ~e **Drähte** *m pl* ELEKTRIZ flush wiring

eingeleitet *adj* PHYS induced

eingenäht: ~es **Etikett** *nt* TEXTIL sewn-in label

eingeprägt: ~e **Kraft** *f* FERTIG *auf einen Körper wirkend* active force

eingerastet *adj* FERTIG engaged

eingereicht: ~er **Flugplan** *m* LUFTTRANS air-filed flight plan

eingerissen *adj* FERTIG ragged

eingeschalt *adj* BAU timbered

eingeschaltet[1] *adj* ELEKTROTECH on active, *Schaltung* on

eingeschaltet:[2] ~er **Stromkreis** *m* ELEKTROTECH closed circuit; ~er **Zustand** *m* ELEKTROTECH on-state; nicht ~er **Zustand** *m* ELEKTROTECH off-state

eingeschliffen[1] *adj* MASCHINEN ground-in

eingeschliffen:[2] ~er **Glasstopfen** *m* LABOR ground stopper

eingeschlossen: ~e **Luft** *f* KUNSTSTOFF, VERPACK entrapped air; ~es **Teilchen** *nt* KERNTECH trapped particle

eingeschnitten: ~es **Walmdach** *nt* BAU hip and valley roof

eingeschränkt: ~er **Belegungsdetektor** *m* TRANS limited presence detector; ~er **Dienst mit 64 kbit/s** *m* TELEKOM ISDN sixty-four kbps restricted service; ~es **Progressivsystem** *nt* TRANS limited progressive system

eingeschrieben: ~er **Kreis** *m* GEOM inscribed circle; ~e **Kugel** *f* FERTIG insphere; ~es **Quadrat** *nt* GEOM inscribed square; ~er **Winkel** *m* GEOM inscribed angle

eingeschwungen: ~er **Zustand** *m* COMP & DV, TELEKOM *Oszillation* steady state

eingesenkt: ~er **Faden** *m* KER & GLAS depressed thread

eingesetzt[1] *adj* MASCHINEN inserted

eingesetzt:[2] ~er **Stahl** *m* METALL case-hardened steel; ~er **Zahn** *m* FERTIG cog

eingespannt[1] *adj* BAU encastré

eingespannt:[2] ~er **Träger** *m* BAU encastré beam

eingestellt *adj* PAPIER adjusted

eingestochen *adj* FERTIG recessed

eingetaucht *adj* PHYS immersed

eingetragen: ~er **Benutzer** *m* PATENT registered user; ~e **Marke** *f* PATENT registered trade mark; nicht ~e **Marke** *f* PATENT unregistered mark; ~es **Warenzeichen** *nt* PATENT registered trade mark

Eingeweide *nt pl* LEBENSMITTEL gut

Eingewöhnung *f* HEIZ & KÄLTE acclimatization

eingezapft: ~er **Mauerstein** *m* BAU tusk

eingezäunt: nicht ~ *adj* BAU unfenced

Eingießen *nt* KUNSTSTOFF potting

Eingitterröhre *f* ELEKTRONIK single grid tube

Einglasen *nt* KER & GLAS *Einbauen von Fenstern* glazing

eingleisig: ~e **Gleisabzweigung** *f* EISENBAHN single line

turnout; **~e Strecke** *f* EISENBAHN single track line
Eingreifen *nt* MASCHINEN meshing, MECHAN mating
eingreifen *vi* MASCHINEN engage, mesh
Eingreifswinkel *m* FERTIG *Getriebelehre* angle of obliquity of action
eingrenzen *vt* COMP & DV localize, MEERSCHMUTZ *Ölverschmutzung* corral
Eingrenzung *f* COMP & DV *einer Fehlerquelle* isolation, TELEKOM locating; **allgemeine ~** *f* TELEKOM general localization
Eingriff:[1] **im ~** *adj* FERTIG engaged, MASCHINEN engaged, meshed
Eingriff:[2] **nicht im ~** *adv* MASCHINEN out of gear
Eingriff[3] *m* COMP & DV intervention, FERTIG mesh, *Getriebelehre* contact, MASCHINEN contact, engagement, gearing, intermeshing, meshing
Eingriff:[4] **außer ~ bringen** *vt* FERTIG *Zahnräder* disengage; **in ~ bringen** *vt* MASCHINEN mesh; **in ~ kommen** *vi* MASCHINEN come into gear; **wieder in ~ bringen** *vt* MASCHINEN re-engage
Eingriff: **Eingriffsbogen** *m* LUFTTRANS *des Gurtes, Riemens* arc of contact; **Eingriffsbogen vor dem Wälzpunkt** *m* FERTIG *Getriebelehre* arc of action; **Eingriffsfeld** *nt* FERTIG zone of action; **Eingriffsgrenze** *f* QUAL action limit; **Eingriffslinie** *f* MASCHINEN line of action, line of engagement; **Eingriffsstörung** *f* FERTIG tooth interference; **Eingriffssteuerung** *f* LUFTTRANS override control; **Eingriffstiefe** *f* MASCHINEN depth, working depth of teeth; **Eingriffswinkel** *m* FERTIG *Getriebelehre* angle of approach, MASCHINEN angle of obliquity, angle of pressure, pressure angle
Einguß *m* MASCHINEN sprue; **Eingußabschneider** *m* FERTIG sprue cutter; **Eingußbolzen** *m* MASCHINEN sprue pin
Einhakdeckel *m* VERPACK hooked lid
Einhaken *nt* FERTIG *Spanung* binding
einhaken *vt* FERTIG *Bohren* bind
Einhaltung *f* FERTIG *Toleranz* maintenance
einhängbar: **~er Sack** *m* VERPACK insertable sack
Einhängefeld *nt* BAU *Brücke* suspended span
Einhängemaschine *f* DRUCK casing-in machine
einhängen *vt* BAU hinge, DRUCK case in
Einheftkante *f* DRUCK binding edge
Einheit *f* COMP & DV device, unit, ELEKTRIZ, KFZTECH, MASCHINEN, OPTIK, PHYS, TELEKOM unit; **~ der absorbierten Strahlungsdosis** *f* STRAHLPHYS unit of absorbed dose; **~ der Bestrahlung** *f* STRAHLPHYS unit of exposure; **~ des Dosisäquivalents** *f* STRAHLPHYS *als Maß für biologische Wirkung* unit of dose equivalent; **~ der Entropie** *f* THERMOD unit of entropy; **~ mit einem oder mehreren Hauptfehlern** *f* QUAL major defective; **~ mit einem oder mehreren Nebenfehlern** *f* QUAL minor defective; **~ im Raumwinkelmaß** *f* GEOM steradian; **Einheitencode** *m* COMP & DV device code; **Einheitenfolge** *f* COMP & DV unit string; **Einheitensteuerung** *f* COMP & DV device control; **Einheitensteuerzeichen** *nt* COMP & DV device control character; **Einheitensystem** *nt* ELEKTRIZ, MASCHINEN system of units
einheitlich: **~er Aufbau** *m* COMP & DV unified architecture; **~es Feld** *nt* PHYS uniform field; **~es Kabel** *nt* OPTIK unit-type cable; **~e Leitung** *f* ELEKTROTECH uniform line; **~e Rufnummer** *f* TELEKOM universal number
Einheitlichkeit: **~ der Erfindung** *f* PATENT unity of invention
Einheit: **Einheitsbohrung** *f* FERTIG, MASCHINEN basic

bore; **Einheitselement** *nt* MATH identity element; **Einheitsignal** *nt* REGELUNG standard signal; **Einheitsmatrix** *f* MATH identity matrix; **Einheitsmeßumformer für Mischungsabweichungen** *m* REGELUNG composition deviation transmitter; **Einheitssatz** *m* PATENT flat-rate fee; **Einheitsschritt** *m* COMP & DV unit element; **Einheitsschub** *m* RAUMFAHRT *Raumschiff* unit thrust; **Einheitsvektor** *m* MATH identity vector, unit vector, PHYS unit vector; **Einheitswelle** *f* MASCHINEN basic shaft
Einhiebfeile *f* MASCHINEN single-cut file
einhiebig[1] *adj* FERTIG *Feile* float-cut
einhiebig:[2] **~e Feile** *f* FERTIG float, MASCHINEN float, float-cut file, single-cut file
einhieven *vt* WASSERTRANS *Tauwerk* heave in
Einholen: **~ auf der Umlaufbahn** *nt* RAUMFAHRT orbital catchup
einholen *vt* WASSERTRANS *Schiff* hoist, *Tauwerk* haul in
Einholtau *nt* WASSERTRANS *Deckausrüstung* dead man
Einhüllung *f* PHYS enclosure
Einimpfen *nt* KERNTECH seeding
Einkanalprotokoll *nt* COMP & DV single channel protocol
Ein-Kanal-Träger *m* *(SCPC)* RAUMFAHRT *Weltraumfunk*, TELEKOM single channel per carrier *(SCPC)*
Einkanalträger *m* RAUMFAHRT *Weltraumfunk* single channel carrier
Einkanalverstärker *m* ELEKTRONIK single channel amplifier
Einkapselung *f* ABFALL *Deponie* sealing, KERNTECH encapsulation
Einkaufsbedingungen *f pl* RAUMFAHRT *Raumschiff* procurement specifications
Einkerben *nt* FERTIG brinelling
einkerben *vt* BAU score, FERTIG incise, nick, serrate
Einkerbung *f* BAU indentation, FERTIG incision, indentation, MASCHINEN dent, indentation
einklammern *vt* DRUCK bracket
Einklang *m* AKUSTIK concord, consonance
einkleben *vt* DRUCK tip in
Einklinken *nt* ELEKTROTECH latching
einklinken *vt* ERDÖL *Bohrtechnik* latch on
einkochen *vt* CHEMTECH thicken by boiling, LEBENSMITTEL boil down, *Früchte oder Gemüse* bottle
Einkoppelstrecke *f* ELEKTRONIK *Klystron* buncher space, *Wellenleiter* input gap
Einkoppelungsfaser *f* OPTIK launching fiber (AmE), launching fibre (BrE)
Einkopplung *f* TELEKOM launching; **Einkopplungsbedingung bei stationärer Modenverteilung** *f* TELEKOM steady state launching condition
Einkörperschiff *nt* WASSERTRANS single hull ship
Einkörperverdampfer *m* LEBENSMITTEL single effect evaporator
Einkreisreaktor *m* KERNTECH one-cycle reactor
Einkreisschaltung *f* ELEKTRONIK one-shot circuit
Einkristall *m* ELEKTRONIK *Monokristall* single crystal; **Einkristallfaden** *m* KUNSTSTOFF whisker; **Einkristallhalbleiter** *m* ELEKTRONIK single crystal semiconductor; **Einkristallzüchtung** *f* ELEKTRONIK single crystal growth
Einkuppeln *nt* MASCHINEN meshing
einkuppeln *vt* KFZTECH engage
einladen *vt* COMP & DV roll in
Einlage *f* BAU core, FERTIG *Kunststoffinstallationen* insert, KERNTECH, KOHLEN liner, KUNSTSTOFF insert,

VERPACK inlay, insert, liner; **Einlagern** *nt* COMP & DV swap-in

einlagern *vt* COMP & DV roll in

Einlagerung *f* WERKPRÜF inclusion

Einlagestoff *m* TEXTIL interlining

einlagig *adj* BAU single-layer, FERTIG *Riemen* single-ply

Einlaß *m* HYDRAUL gating, KER & GLAS inlet port, KFZTECH induction, inlet, MASCHINEN admission, inlet, intake, MECHAN, TELEKOM inlet

einlassen *vt* HYDRAUL gate

Einlaß: **Einlaßgeschwindigkeit** *f* HYDRAUL inlet velocity; **Einlaßhub** *m* KFZTECH induction stroke; **Einlaßkanal** *m* HYDRAUL *Dampfzylinder* induction port, KFZTECH inlet port; **Einlaßkrümmer** *m* KFZTECH *Motor* induction manifold; **Einlaßlufttrichter** *m* LUFTTRANS inlet throat; **Einlaßöffnung** *f* HYDRAUL *Dampfzylinder* induction port, KFZTECH inlet port, MASCHINEN inlet, intake; **Einlaßring am Flugzeugrumpf** *m* LUFTTRANS nacelle intake ring; **Einlaßrohr** *nt* HYDRAUL induction pipe; **Einlaßseite** *f* MASCHINEN inlet side, intake side; **Einlaßsonde** *f* KERNTECH injection well; **Einlaßspinne** *f* KFZTECH *Motor* induction manifold, inlet manifold; **Einlaßstutzen** *m* FERTIG inlet connection; **Einlaßsystem** *nt* MASCHINEN intake system; **Einlaßüberdeckung** *f* HYDRAUL *Steuerschieber* outside lap; **Einlaßventil** *nt* HYDRAUL induction valve, inlet valve, *Dampf* intake valve, KFZTECH induction valve, suction valve, *Motor* inlet valve, MASCHINEN admission valve; **Einlaßverbindungskabel** *nt* KERNTECH inlet jumper

Einlauf *m* BAU *Regenrohr* hopper head, FERTIG *Gießen* gate, MECHAN intake, WASSERVERSORG inlet, intake; **Einlaufanschluß** *m* PAPIER inlet

Einlaufen *nt* MASCHINEN running-in, TEXTIL shrinkage

einlaufen *vt* MASCHINEN run in

einlaufend[1] *adj* WASSERTRANS inward-bound

einlaufend:[2] **~er Verkehr** *m* TRANS inbound traffic, incoming traffic (AmE), inward traffic (BrE)

Einlauf: **Einlaufrille** *f* AKUSTIK lead-in groove; **Einlaufschacht** *m* UMWELTSCHMUTZ sink; **Einlaufzeit** *f* THERMOD warm-up time

einlegbar: **~er Schalter** *m* ELEKTRIZ recessed switch

Einlegeende *nt* KER & GLAS charging end; **Einlegekeil** *m* MASCHINEN sunk key

Einlegen *nt* KER & GLAS charging; **~ von nur einem Glasposten** *nt* KER & GLAS single gob feeding

einlegen *vt* AUFNAHME *eines Bandes in Gerät* thread, BAU insert, *Holz* inlay, FERTIG *Spanung* inject, *Werkstück* insert

Einleger *m* FERTIG *Gießen* feeder

Einlegering *m* FERTIG *Kunststoffinstallationen* spacing ring; **Einlegestreifen** *m* TEXTIL paper collar; **Einlegeteil** *nt* FERTIG *Kunststoffinstallationen* valve end; **Einlegevorbau** *m* KER & GLAS dog house, filling end

Einleiten *nt* MEERSCHMUTZ, WASSERVERSORG discharge

einleiten *vt* COMP & DV initialize, PHYS induce

Einleiterkabel *nt* ELEKTROTECH single conductor cable

Einleitung *f* ABFALL discharge, *von Abwässern* discharge, MEERSCHMUTZ *von Abwässern*, UMWELTSCHMUTZ *von Abwässern*, WASSERVERSORG *von Abwässern* discharge; **Einleitungsanlage** *f* ABFALL discharge system; **Einleitungsbremse** *f* EISENBAHN single pipe brake; **Einleitungskanal** *m* WASSERVERSORG effluent channel

einlesen *vt* GERÄT *Programm* read

Einlocheinspritzdüse *f* KFZTECH single jet injection nozzle

einloten *vt* BAU plumb

Einmachglas *nt* KER & GLAS canning jar (AmE), preserving jar (BrE), VERPACK glass jar

Einmaischen *nt* LEBENSMITTEL mashing

einmal: **~ beschreibbare Platte** *f* COMP & DV write-once disk, write-once read many times disk; **~ gestrichenes Papier** *nt* PAPIER single-coated paper

Einmalartikel: **~ aus gepreßtem Zellstoff** *m* VERPACK *in Krankenhaus* molded pulp article (AmE), moulded pulp article (BrE)

Einmalbeschreibung-Mehrfachlesen *nt* (*WORM*) OPTIK write once read many times (*WORM*)

einmalig: **~e Beladung** *f* KERNTECH once-through charge; **~er Impuls** *m* ELEKTRONIK nonrecurrent pulse, nonrecursive pulse; **~e Kosten** *f pl* RAUMFAHRT nonrecurrent cost

Einmalkarbon-Farbband *nt* KONSTZEICH once-only ribbon

einmanteln *vt* BAU box

einmauern *vt* BAU brick in

einmäulig *adj* FERTIG *Lehre* single-end

Einmessen *nt* METROL calibration

Einmoden- *pref* ELEKTRONIK, ELEKTROTECH, FERNSEH, OPTIK, PHYS, TELEKOM single mode; **Einmodenfaser** *f* OPTIK single mode fiber (AmE), single mode fibre (BrE), TELEKOM monomode fiber (AmE), monomode fibre (BrE), single mode fiber (AmE), single mode fibre (BrE); **Einmodenglasfaser** *f* ELEKTROTECH single mode optical fiber (AmE), single mode optical fibre (BrE); **Einmodenkabel** *nt* ELEKTROTECH single mode cable; **Einmodenlaser** *m* ELEKTRONIK, FERNSEH, RADIO, TELEKOM single frequency laser; **Einmoden-Lichtleiter** *m* PHYS monomode fiber (AmE), monomode fibre (BrE); **Einmoden-Lichtwellenleiter** *m* TELEKOM monomode fiber (AmE), monomode fibre (BrE)

einmolekular *adj* CHEMIE monomolecular, unimolecular

einohrig *adj* AKUSTIK, AUFNAHME monaural

einordnen *vt* LEBENSMITTEL grade

einparametrisch: **~es digitales Signal** *nt* REGELUNG single parameter digital signal

Einpassen *nt* COMP & DV sizing, MASCHINEN, MECHAN fitting

einpassen *vt* BAU fit in, fit, seat, MASCHINEN fit in, fit into, MECHAN fit

Einpegelungston *m* AUFNAHME line-up tone

einpeilen *vt* BAU locate

Einpendeln *nt* ELEKTROTECH *Regler*regler hunting

Einphasen *nt* ELEKTRONIK phasing, KONTROLL singlephase; **Einphasenmotor mit Anlaufkondensator** *m* ELEKTROTECH capacitor-start motor; **Einphasenreaktion** *f* METALL monophase reaction; **Einphasensteuergerät** *nt* TRANS one-phase controller; **Einphasenstrom** *m* BAU single phase electric current, ELEKTROTECH single phase current

einphasig[1] *adj* ELEKTRIZ monophase, single-phase, uniphase, ELEKTROTECH one phase, single-phase, uniphase, KONTROLL single-phase

einphasig:[2] **~er Brückengleichrichter** *m* ELEKTRIZ single phase bridge rectifier; **~er Gleichrichter** *m* ELEKTRIZ single wave rectifier; **~er Induktionsmotor** *m* ELEKTROTECH single phase induction motor; **~e Leitung** *f* ELEKTRIZ monopolar line; **~e Maschine** *f* ELEKTROTECH single phase machine; **~er Motor** *m* ELEKTRIZ, ELEKTROTECH single phase motor; **~er Strom** *m* ELEK-

TROTECH single phase current; ~e **Stromversorgung** f ELEKTRIZ, ELEKTROTECH single phase supply; ~er **Transformator** m ELEKTROTECH single phase transformer; ~e **Wicklung** f ELEKTROTECH single phase winding

Einplatinenrechner m COMP & DV single board computer

Einplattenruder nt WASSERTRANS single plate rudder

einpolar adj ELEKTROTECH unipolar

einpolig[1] adj COMP & DV unipolar, ELEKTRIZ monopolar, single-pole, unipolar, ELEKTRONIK one-pole, FERNSEH single-pole, unipolar

einpolig:[2] ~er **Ein-/Ausschalter** m (SPST-Schalter) ELEKTRIZ single pole single-throw switch, single toggle switch (SPST switch), ELEKTROTECH, KONTROLL single pole single-throw switch (SPST switch), single toggle switch; ~es **Einschaltrelais** nt ELEKTROTECH SPST relay; ~er **Schalter** m ELEKTRIZ, ELEKTROTECH single pole switch; ~er **Umschalter** m (SPDT-Schalter) ELEKTROTECH single pole double-throw switch (SPDT switch); ~es **Umschaltrelais** nt ELEKTROTECH SPDT relay; ~er **Wechselschalter** m (SPDT-Schalter) ELEKTRIZ mit mittlerer Ruhelage single pole double-throw switch (SPDT switch)

Einprägen nt DRUCK stamping

einprägsam: ~e **Darstellung** f KONSTZEICH expressive representation

Einpreßbohrung f ERDÖL Tiefbohrtechnik injection well

Einpressen nt BAU Spannbeton, KOHLEN grouting

einpressen vt BAU Zementmörtel grout

Einpreßmutter f MASCHINEN press nut

Einpreßpumpe f BAU injection pump

einprofilig adj FERTIG Schleifscheibe single-edge

Einprogrammsystem nt COMP & DV monoprogramming system

einprotonig adj CHEMIE Säure monobasic

Einpunktverbindung f ELEKTRIZ single point bonding

Einrahmung f BAU eines Fensters, einer Tür casing

Einrammen nt BAU Pfähle ramming, FERTIG driving

einrammen vt BAU Nägel drive in

Einrasten nt FERTIG insertion

einrasten vt FERTIG pawl, Stift insert, MASCHINEN Klinke engage, MECHAN lock

einrastend: ~er **Elektromagnet** m ELEKTRIZ latching electromagnet

Einrastknopf m BAU lock knob

Einrastung f MASCHINEN stop

Einreichung f PATENT filing

einreihig[1] adj MASCHINEN single-row

einreihig:[2] ~e **Nietüberlappung** f BAU single-riveted lap joint; ~e **Nietverbindung** f BAU single-riveted joint

Einreißen nt KER & GLAS rip-in, KUNSTSTOFF tear

einreißen vt ANSTRICH crack

Einreißfestigkeit f KUNSTSTOFF tear resistance, tear strength

Einrichten nt LUFTTRANS eines Instrumentes setting, MASCHINEN setting, setup

einrichten vt BAU set, COMP & DV initialize, ein System set-up, MASCHINEN set, set-up

Einrichtprozedur f COMP & DV initial set-up procedure

Einrichtung f FERTIG Kunststoffinstallationen facility, MASCHINEN installation, MEERSCHMUTZ device, TELEKOM device, facility, Ausrüstung unit; ~ zur Erzeugung von Mehrfachbelastungen f ERGON multistress facility; ~ zur Hochfrequenzschweißung f VERPACK high-frequency welding equipment; ~ für Probebetrieb f MASCHINEN try-out facility; ~ zur

Verfahrensüberwachung f ELEKTROTECH process controller

Einriegelschloß nt BAU deadlock

einringen vt BAU Beton place

einrollen vt FERTIG crush, TEXTIL curl

einrotorig adj LUFTTRANS Hubschrauber single rotor

Einrücken nt MASCHINEN engagement, engaging, gearing

einrücken vt MASCHINEN mesh, throw into action, throw into gears

Einrüsten nt BAU scaffolding

Eins f MATH one

Einsabstoff m ERDÖL Raffinerie, Vergasung feedstock

Einsackapparat m VERPACK bagging machine

Einsacken nt PAPIER bagging

einsacken vt LEBENSMITTEL, VERPACK bag

einsalzen vt LEBENSMITTEL cure

Einsammeln nt ABFALL collection; ~ von Altöl nt ABFALL collection of waste oil; ~ von Müllsäcken nt ABFALL refuse sack collection

Einsatz m AKUSTIK attack, FERTIG Kunststoffinstallationen application, Stahl case, KFZTECH, KUNSTSTOFF insert, MASCHINEN insert, socket, MECHAN insert, lining, TEXTIL batch, VERPACK insert; ~ in Fertigungsreihe m FERTIG in-line operation; **Einsatzbereich** m GERÄT range; **Einsatzbereich eines Geräts** m GERÄT instrument range

einsatzbereit: ~er **Wartebetrieb** m RAUMFAHRT Raumschiff hot standby

Einsatz: **Einsatzbohrer** m ERDÖL Bohrtechnik insert bit; **Einsatzbrücke** f MASCHINEN gap bridge, gap piece; **Einsatzdaten** nt pl QUAL failure risks; **Einsatzentfernung** f LUFTTRANS Flugwesen operating range; **Einsatzergebnisse** nt pl QUAL failure risks; **Einsatzfilter** nt HEIZ & KÄLTE cartridge-type filter

einsatzgehärtet: ~er **Stahl** m MECHAN case-hardened steel

Einsatz: **Einsatzgeschwindigkeit** f LUFTTRANS operating speed; **Einsatzhärten** nt FERTIG carbon case hardening, pack hardening, MASCHINEN case hardening

einsatzhärten vt FERTIG carburize, Stahl case-harden, cement

Einsatz: **Einsatzhärteofen** m MASCHINEN carburizing furnace; **Einsatzhärtung** f FERTIG carburization, METALL case hardening; **Einsatzlaufbüchse** f MECHAN liner; **Einsatzlebensdauer** f RAUMFAHRT Raumschiff service life; **Einsatzmeißel** m FERTIG bit insert; **Einsatzmittel** nt COMP & DV resource; **Einsatzofen** m CHEMTECH batch furnace; **Einsatzpause** f LUFTTRANS rest period; **Einsatzprüfung** f RAUMFAHRT field trial; **Einsatzreichweite** f LUFTTRANS Flugwesen operating range; **Einsatzspirale** f FOTO tank reel; **Einsatztiefe** f MASCHINEN case depth; **Einsatzversuch** m RAUMFAHRT field trial; **Einsatzzentrale** f SICHERHEIT emergency center (AmE), emergency centre (BrE)

Einsaugen nt HEIZ & KÄLTE, MECHAN suction

einsaugen vt FERTIG inspire, HEIZ & KÄLTE aspirate

Einsaugung f FERTIG inspiration

einsäurig adj CHEMIE monoacidic

Einschalt- pref COMP & DV, ELEKTROTECH, FERNSEH, FERTIG turn-on; **Einschaltantwort** f ELEKTROTECH transient response; **Einschaltdauer** f FERTIG Kunststoffinstallationen duty cycle

Einschalten nt ELEKTROTECH Lampe turn-on, eines elektrischen Stromkreises closure, STRAHLPHYS eines

Magnetfeldes onset

einschalten *vt* COMP & DV connect, *Rechner* enable, ELEKTRIZ switch on, ELEKTROTECH make, power up, *Lampe* turn on, FERNSEH, KONTROLL switch on, PHYS *elektrischer Stromkreis* energize

einschaltend: ~e Windgeschwindigkeit *f* NICHTFOSS ENERG cut-in wind speed

Einschalter *m* ELEKTROTECH circuit closer

Einschalt-: Einschaltimpuls *m* ELEKTRONIK turn-on pulse, ELEKTROTECH make pulse; **Einschaltlaststrom** *m* ELEKTROTECH on-load current; **Einschaltprellen** *nt* ELEKTRIZ pull-in bouncing; **Einschaltstellung** *f* ELEKTROTECH on position; **Einschaltstoß** *m* ELEKTROTECH, PHYS transient; **Einschaltstoßstrom** *m* ELEKTROTECH inrush current; **Einschaltstoßstrom-Begrenzer** *m* ELEKTROTECH inrush current limiter; **Einschaltstrom** *m* ELEKTRIZ inrush current, ELEKTROTECH make current, HEIZ & KÄLTE starting current; **Einschalttor** *nt* REGELUNG normally open gate; **Einschaltung** *f* ELEKTROTECH power up

einschaltverzögert: ~es Relais *nt* ELEKTROTECH on-delay relay

Einschalt-: Einschaltverzögerung *f* KONTROLL turn-on delay; **Einschaltwiderstand** *m* ELEKTROTECH on resistance; **Einschaltzeit** *f* ELEKTRONIK turn-on time, ELEKTROTECH on period, turn-on time, *Schaltung* on period, KONTROLL turn-on time; **Einschaltzustand** *m* ELEKTROTECH on-state

Einscheiben- *pref* MASCHINEN single pulley; **Einscheibenantrieb** *m* MASCHINEN single pulley drive; **Einscheibenfensterglas** *nt* KER & GLAS single thickness window glass; **Einscheibentrockenkupplung** *f* KFZTECH single dry plate clutch, MASCHINEN dry single-disc clutch (BrE), dry single-disk clutch (AmE)

einscheren *vt* WASSERTRANS *Tauwerk* reeve

einschichtig *adj* BAU single-layer; **~ mit Baumwolle bedeckt** *adj* ELEKTRIZ single cotton covered

Einschicht-Keramikkondensator *m* ELEKTROTECH single layer ceramic capacitor

Einschiebeinheit *f* ELEKTRIZ plug-in unit

Einschieben *nt* KER & GLAS setting in; **~ der Scherben** *nt* KER & GLAS pushing down the cullet

einschieben *vt* COMP & DV *Zeichen, Absatz* insert

Einschiebtreppe *f* BAU folding staircase

Einschienen- *pref* EISENBAHN monorail; **Einschienenbahn** *f* BAU, EISENBAHN *System* monorail; **Einschienenbahn mit asymmetrischer Aufhängung** *f* EISENBAHN monorail with asymmetric suspension; **Einschienenbahn mit Pendelfahrzeugaufhängung** *f* EISENBAHN monorail with pendulum vehicle suspension; **Einschienenbahn mit pneumatischer Aufhängung** *f* EISENBAHN monorail with pneumatic suspension; **Einschienengreiferlaufkatze** *f* EISENBAHN monorail grab trolley; **Einschienenhängebahn** *f* EISENBAHN monorail conveyor, monorail with hanging cars, suspended monorail; **Einschienenhochbahn** *f* EISENBAHN elevated monorail; **Einschienensattelbahn** *f* EISENBAHN supported monorail

einschiffen: sich ~ *v refl* WASSERTRANS *Passagiere* ship; **sich wieder ~** *v refl* WASSERTRANS *Passagiere* re-embark

Einschiffung *f* WASSERTRANS *Passagiere* boarding

einschlafen *vi* WASSERTRANS *Wind* drop

einschlagen *vt* BAU *Nagel* drive in, FERTIG *Ventilsitz* pocket, MASCHINEN drive, drive in

Einschlagfaden *m* TEXTIL pick

Einschlagmaschine *f* VERPACK envelope machine, wrapping machine

Einschlagszentrum *nt* MECHAN, PHYS center of impact (AmE), centre of impact (BrE)

Einschleifen *nt* KER & GLAS truing, *eines Stopfens* grinding, MASCHINEN grinding-in

einschleifen: neu ~ *vt* FERTIG *Ventil*, KFZTECH *Ventil* reseat

Einschleifpaste *f* FERTIG grinding paste

Einschließen *nt* KERNTECH *von radioaktiven Stoffen* containment, *von Aktivabfall* encapsulation; **~ in Beton** *nt* KERNTECH embedding in concrete

einschließen *vt* ANSTRICH encapsule, BAU enclose, include, CHEMIE occlude, MEERSCHMUTZ *einen Ölteppich* entrap

Einschließung *f* BAU housing, KERNTECH *von radioaktiven Stoffen* containment

Einschluß *m* ABFALL *von Sondermüll* grain encapsulation, CHEMIE occlusion, KERNTECH *von radioaktivem Material* enclosure, *von Verunreinigungen* inclusion, METALL inclusion, PHYS confinement, containment, RAUMFAHRT envelope, TEILPHYS confinement, WERKPRÜF inclusion; **~ in Beton** *m* KERNTECH embedding in concrete; **~ von Medien** *m* ANSTRICH media entrapment

Einschmelzen *nt* TEXTIL oiling

einschmelzen *vt* TEXTIL melt

Einschmelztiefe *f* FERTIG *Schweißen* depth of fusion

Einschnappverschluß *m* VERPACK snap-on closure

einschneiden *vt* BAU notch

einschneidig[1] *adj* FERTIG *Werkzeug* single-edge, MASCHINEN single-point

einschneidig:[2] **~es Werkzeug** *nt* MASCHINEN single point cutting tool

Einschnitt *m* BAU indentation, WASSERVERSORG notch

einschnittig *adj* MASCHINEN single-shear

Einschnüreffekt *m* ELEKTRONIK pinch-off effect, PHYS pinch effect

Einschnürung *f* FERTIG formation of neck, *Plaste* choking, MASCHINEN, METALL, PHYS necking

Einschnurvermittlungsschrank *m* TELEKOM single cord switchboard

einschränkend *adj* ELEKTRONIK limiting

Einschränkung *f* KÜNSTL INT constraint

einschrauben *vt* BAU drive

Einschraubenschiff *nt* WASSERTRANS single screw ship

Einschraubteil *m* FERTIG *Kunststoffinstallationen* union bush

einschreiben *vt* GEOM inscribe

Einschritt- *pref* COMP & DV single step; **Einschrittbetrieb** *m* COMP & DV single step operation; **Einschrittoperation** *f* COMP & DV single step operation

Einschrumpfen *nt* VERPACK shrink wrapping

Einschub *m* VERPACK compartmented tray, insert; **Einschubmodul** *nt* ELEKTRONIK card module

Einschuß *m* TEXTIL pick, *Weben* weft; **Einschußfaden** *m* TEXTIL weft

einschwalben *vt* BAU dovetail

Einschweißfolie *f* DRUCK blister pack

einschwenkbar: ~er Filter *nt* FOTO swing-in filter

Einschwing- *pref* ELEKTRIZ, FERNSEH transient; **Einschwingbedingungen** *f pl* ELEKTROTECH transient conditions

Einschwingen *nt* PHYS transient oscillation

Einschwing-: Einschwingspannung *f* ELEKTRIZ transient voltage; **Einschwingverhalten** *nt* ELEKTROTECH,

FERNSEH transient response, GERÄT transient behavior (AmE), transient behaviour (BrE); **Einschwingverzögerung** f TELEKOM *Stufenfunktion* delay; **Einschwingvorgang** m AKUSTIK, KONTROLL, PHYS transient; **Einschwingzeit** f GERÄT damping period, settling time, transient time, WERKPRÜF response time; **Einschwingzustand** m ELEKTRIZ transient state

Einschwungprellen nt ELEKTRIZ pull-in bouncing

Einseitenband nt *(SSB)* ELEKTRONIK, FERNSEH, RADIO, TELEKOM, WASSERTRANS single sideband *(SSB)*; ~ **mit kompandierter Amplitude** nt *(ACSR)* RADIO amplitude-compandered single sideband *(ACSS)*; **Einseitenbandfilter** nt ELEKTRONIK single sideband filter; **Einseitenbandmodulation** f ELEKTRONIK single sideband modulation; **Einseitenbandmodulator** m ELEKTRONIK single sideband modulator; **Einseitenbandsendung** f FERNSEH single sideband transmission; **Einseitenbandübertragung** f PHYS single sideband transmission

einseitig:[1] ~ **beschreibbare Diskette** f COMP & DV single-sided disk, single-sided diskette; ~**e Diskette** f OPTIK single-sided disc (BrE), single-sided disk (AmE); ~ **geglättete Pappe** f DRUCK, PAPIER MG board, machine-glazed board; ~ **geglättetes Papier** nt DRUCK, PAPIER MG paper, machine-glazed paper; ~ **gelagerte Kurbel** f MASCHINEN outside crank; ~ **gerichteter Strom** m ELEKTRIZ unidirectional current; ~ **gerichteter Transducer** m ELEKTROTECH unidirectional transducer; ~ **gestrichene Pappe** f VERPACK one-sided coated board; ~**e Leiterplatte** f ELEKTRONIK single-sided printed circuit; ~**e Palette** f KFZTECH single platform pallet; ~**er Strom** m ELEKTRIZ unidirectional current; ~**es Verteilergestell** nt TELEKOM single-sided distribution frame

einseitig:[2] ~ **gerichtet** adj TELEKOM unidirectional

Eins: **Eins-Element** nt MATH identity element; **Einsenken** nt MASCHINEN recessing; **Einsenkpresse** f MASCHINEN hobbing press; **Einsenkung** f EISENBAHN subsidence, MASCHINEN counterbore; **Einsenkung des Index** f OPTIK index dip

einsetzbar: ~**es Fach** nt VERPACK compartmented insert

Einsetzen nt BAU sealing, MATH substitution, STRAHLPHYS *eines Magnetfeldes* onset

einsetzen[1] vt BAU insert, set, COMP & DV insert, paste, *Variable* set, MATH *Wert in Formel, Lösung in Gleichung* substitute, METALL case-harden

einsetzen[2] vi WASSERTRANS *von Gezeiten* set in

Einsetzkamera f FERNSEH insert camera

Einsickern nt KOHLEN infiltration

einsickern vt BAU penetrate

Einsickerung f WASSERVERSORG infiltration

Einsinken nt UMWELTSCHMUTZ subsidence

Einsinkpunkt m KER & GLAS sinking point

einsitzig: ~**es Ventil** nt HYDRAUL single-seated valve

Einspannen nt BAU stretching, MASCHINEN mounting, MECHAN chucking

einspannen vt BAU clamp, *Balken, Träger* fix, COMP & DV *Papier* load, FERTIG *Spannung* chuck, MASCHINEN chuck, clamp, mount, MECHAN hitch

Einspannfutter nt MECHAN chuck

Einspannkopf m FERTIG *Zerreißstab* gripping head

Einspannmoment nt BAU fixed-end moment

Einspannstelle f MASCHINEN bearing point

Einspannung f FERTIG *Balken* constraint, MASCHINEN fixing, MECHAN clamping

Einspannvorrichtung f BAU shackle, MASCHINEN chucking device, clamping device, clamping fixture, gripping device, MECHAN jig

einspeichern vt COMP & DV roll in

Einspeicherung f COMP & DV roll in; **Einspeicherungsimpuls** m COMP & DV write pulse; **Einspeicherungszeit** f COMP & DV write time

Einspeisarmatur f ERDÖL feed tank

einspeisen vt BAU supply, FERNSEH, MECHAN feed

Einspeisepegel m ELEKTRONIK injection level **Einspeiseschlauchverbindung** f ERDÖL feed hose union; **Einspeiseschleuse** f PAPIER airlock feeder; **Einspeiseventil** nt ERDÖL feed valve; **Einspeisung** f ELEKTRONIK *eines Signals in Schaltung* injection, FERNSEH feed, incoming feed, HYDRAUL, KFZTECH, MECHAN feed

einspeisungsstabilisierter Oszillator m RAUMFAHRT *Weltraumfunk* injection-locked oscillator

einspielen vt FERNSEH play in

Einspielzeit f WERKPRÜF response time

Einspindelautomat m MASCHINEN single spindle automatic

Einspindelbohrmaschine f MASCHINEN single spindle boring machine

Einspindeldrehmaschine f MASCHINEN single spindle lathe

Eins-plus-Eins-Adreßbefehl m COMP & DV one-plus-one address instruction

Eins-plus-Eins-Trägersystem nt TELEKOM one-plus-one carrier system

einspringend adj GEOM reentrant

Einspritz: ~**- und Zündungsrechner** m KFZTECH digital control box

Einspritzaggregat nt MASCHINEN fuel injector

Einspritzbohrung f KERNTECH injection borehole

Einspritzdruck m MASCHINEN injection pressure

Einspritzdüse f CHEMTECH, KFZTECH *Kraftstoff* injection nozzle, MECHAN injector; **Einspritzdüse mit Halter** f KFZTECH *Kraftstoff* injector; **Einspritzdüsenhalter** m KFZTECH injection nozzle holder

Einspritzen: ~ **von Anlaßkraftstoff** nt LUFTTRANS priming

einspritzen vt RAUMFAHRT inject

Einspritzhahn m HYDRAUL injection cock

Einspritzkniehebel m LUFTTRANS *Hubschrauber* mixer bellcrank

Einspritzkompressor m HYDRAUL injection compressor

Einspritzkondensator m HYDRAUL injection condenser, jet condenser

Einspritzleitung f KFZTECH delivery pipe

Einspritzmenge f RAUMFAHRT *Raumschiff* priming charge

Einspritzpumpe f KFZTECH, MASCHINEN, WASSERTRANS *Motor* injection pump

Einspritzrohr nt HYDRAUL injection pipe

Einspritzung f KFZTECH *Kraftstoff* injection, RAUMFAHRT *Raumschiff* primer

Einspritzventil nt LABOR *Gaschromatographie* injection valve

Einspritzzapfendüse f KFZTECH pintle injection nozzle

Einspruch m PATENT opposition; **Einspruchsgründe** m pl PATENT grounds for opposition; **Einspruchsschrift** f PATENT notice of opposition; **Einspruchsverfahren** nt PATENT opposition proceedings

einspulig: ~**es Stromstoßrelais** nt ELEKTROTECH single coil latching relay; ~**es Stützrelais** nt ELEKTROTECH single coil latching relay

Einspülschiff *nt* ERDÖL *Schiff zum Einspülen von Seeleitungen* bury barge

Einspuraufnahme *f* AUFNAHME single track recording

Einspuraufzeichnung *f* AKUSTIK one-track recording

Einstahlschneidwerkzeug *nt* MASCHINEN single point cutting tool

einstampfbar: ~er Klebstoff *m* ABFALL repulpable adhesive

Einstampfgerät *nt* VERPACK repulping equipment

Einständerblechkanten-Hobelmaschine *f* FERTIG open-side plate planing machine

Einständerhobelmaschine *f* MASCHINEN open-side planing machine

Einstandspreis *m* KUNSTSTOFF *Lagerwert* cost price

Einstaubewässerung *f* WASSERVERSORG subsurface irrigation

Einstechdrehen *nt* MASCHINEN recessing

Einstechdrehmaschine *f* MASCHINEN grooving machine

einstechen *vt* MASCHINEN recess

Einstechgewindeschleifen *nt* MASCHINEN plunge-cut thread grinding

Einstechmeißel *m* MASCHINEN recessing tool

Einstechschleifen *nt* MASCHINEN plunge grinding, plunge-cut grinding

Einstechwerkzeug *nt* MASCHINEN plunging tool

Einsteck- *pref* BAU, ELEKTROTECH plug-in; Einsteckbaugruppe *f* ELEKTROTECH plug-in unit; Einsteckeinheit *f* ELEKTRIZ plug-in unit

einstecken *vt* ELEKTRIZ plug in, ELEKTROTECH plug, plug in, FERTIG *Niet*, RADIO plug, TELEKOM plug in

Einsteck-: Einsteckende *nt* BAU *einer Muffenrohrverbindung* spigot; Einsteckfeder *f* BAU *Holzbau* loose tongue; Einsteckgruppe *f* ELEKTROTECH plug-in unit; Einsteckmeißel *m* FERTIG boring-bar cutter, inserted tool, tool holder bit; Einsteckmodul *m* ELEKTROTECH plug-in module; Einsteckrelais *nt* ELEKTROTECH plug-in relay; Einsteckschloß *nt* BAU mortise dead lock, mortise lock; Einsteckspule *f* ELEKTROTECH plug-in coil; Einsteckteil *nt* ELEKTROTECH plug-in component

Einsteigeplattform *f* EISENBAHN boarding platform

Einsteigöffnung *f* MASCHINEN access hole

Einstein: ~sche Koeffizienten *m pl* PHYS, STRAHLPHYS Einstein coefficients; ~sche Temperatur *f* PHYS Einstein temperature, THERMOD *(θK)* Einstein temperature *(θK)*

Einstein-de Haas: ~ scher Effekt *m* PHYS, THERMOD Einstein-de Haas effect

Einsteinium *nt (Es)* CHEMIE, STRAHLPHYS einsteinium *(Es)*

Einstell- *pref* MASCHINEN adjusting; Einstellanschlag *m* MECHAN adjustable stop

einstellbar[1] *adj* ELEKTRIZ variable, KONTROLL, MASCHINEN adjustable

einstellbar:[2] ~er Generator *m* RAUMFAHRT *Raumschiff* pointable generator; ~es Kontaktthermometer *nt* GERÄT adjustable contact thermometer; ~e Kurzschlußbrücke *f* PHYS adjustable short-circuit bridge; ~es Relais *nt* TELEKOM variable relay; ~es Schneidmesser *nt* BAU *für Furniere* cutting gage (AmE), cutting gauge (BrE); ~er Schraubenschlüssel *m* MECHAN adjustable spanner (BrE), adjustable wrench (AmE); ~er Spannungserzeuger *m* ELEKTRIZ variable voltage generator; ~er Spannungsteiler *m* ELEKTRIZ adjustable voltage divider; ~er Thermoschalter *m* HEIZ & KÄLTE adjustable thermostatic switch; ~er Wellenleiter *m* RADIO adjustable wave-guide; ~er Widerstand *m* ELEKTRIZ adjustable resistor

Einstell-: Einstellbrett *nt* FOTO *des Vergrößerungsapparates* enlarger baseboard; Einstelldruck *m* HEIZ & KÄLTE setting pressure; Einstellehre *f* MASCHINEN setting gage (AmE), setting gauge (BrE); Einstellelement *nt* GERÄT setting device

Einstellen *nt* BAU, LUFTTRANS *von Instrumenten* setting, REGELUNG positioning; ~ des Luftschraubenblattes *nt* LUFTTRANS *Hubschrauber* blade setting

einstellen *vt* BAU adjust, set, COMP & DV, KONTROLL set, METROL *Mikroskop* adjust, PAPIER adjust, set up; neu ~ *vt* MECHAN reset

Einstell-: Einstellfilter *nt* FOTO red swing filter; Einstellgenauigkeit *f* GERÄT accuracy of adjustment; Einstellglied *nt* GERÄT adjusting element; Einstellhülse *f* KFZTECH adjusting sleeve

einstellig[1] *adj* COMP & DV unary

einstellig:[2] ~e Operation *f* COMP & DV unary operation

Einstell-: Einstellknopf *m* ELEKTRIZ control knob, MECHAN adjusting knob; Einstellmaß *nt* KONSTZEICH setting dimension; Einstellmutter *f* MASCHINEN regulating nut, set nut; Einstellscheibe *f* FERTIG *Kunststoffinstallationen* adjustment dial; Einstellschraube *f* ELEKTRIZ tuning screw, MASCHINEN adjusting screw, regulating screw, set screw, temper screw, MECHAN adjusting screw, PHYS tuning screw, TRANS adjustable pitch propeller; Einstellskala am Meßgerät *f* GERÄT meter dial; Einstellspannung *f* ELEKTRIZ *Abgleichspannung* adjusting voltage; Einstellstift *m* MASCHINEN set pin, MECHAN alignment pin

Einstellung *f* BAU *Vermessung* sight, COMP & DV computer setting, ELEKTRONIK adjustment, ERGON attitude, set, KUNSTSTOFF formulation, MASCHINEN adjustment, regulation, setting, setup, METROL adjustment, PAPIER adjusting, adjustment, RADIO adjustment, TRANS *auf konstant Grün* synchronization; ~ auf Null *f* MASCHINEN zeroizing; Einstellungsänderung *f* ERGON attitude change; Einstellungsgesundheitsuntersuchung *f* SICHERHEIT pre-employment health screening; Einstellungsskalen *f pl* ERGON attitude scales

Einstell-: Einstellvorrichtung *f* PAPIER adjuster; Einstellwert *m* GERÄT setting value, KERNTECH index value, MASCHINEN setting; Einstellwiderstand *m* ELEKTROTECH adjustable resistor; Einstellwinkel *m* MASCHINEN entering angle; Einstellwinkel des Blattes *m* LUFTTRANS *Hubschrauber* blade angle; Einstellwinkel der Luftschraube *m* LUFTTRANS *Hubschrauber* blade angle; Einstellwinkel des Luftschraubenblattes *m* LUFTTRANS *Hubschrauber* blade-setting angle; Einstellwinkelschwankung *f* LUFTTRANS incidence oscillation; Einstellzeit *f* COMP & DV response time, GERÄT settling time, *Brücke* balance time; Einstellzeit einer Frequenzdekade *f* TELEKOM synthesizer setting time

Einstemmen *nt* BAU morticing (BrE), mortising (AmE), FERTIG, MECHAN caulking

einstemmen *vt* FERTIG mortice, mortise

Einstich *m* FERTIG *Spiralbohrer* neck, MASCHINEN plunge cut, recess; Einstichboden *m* KER & GLAS push-up, pushed punt

Einstieg *m* ERDÖL manway; Einstiegloch *nt* MASCHINEN access hole; Einstiegsluke *f* LUFTTRANS hatch; Einstiegsöffnung *f* BAU, KERNTECH manhole; Einstiegsstelle *f* FERNSEH in point einstöpseln *vt* FERNSEH *Stecker* plug in

Einstrahl-Kathodenstrahlröhre *f* ELEKTRONIK single beam cathode ray tube

Einstrahloszilloskop *nt* GERÄT single beam oscilloscope

Einstrahlröhre *f* ELEKTRONIK single beam tube

Einstrahlspektrometer *nt* STRAHLPHYS single beam spectrophotometer

Einstrahlung *f* RAUMFAHRT *Weltraumfunk* irradiation

Einstreichen: ~ mit Flußmittel *nt* BAU fluxing

einstrippen *vt* DRUCK strip in

Einströmen *nt* MASCHINEN inlet

Einströmkanal *m* FERTIG sprue hole

Einströmöffnung *f* MASCHINEN inlet

Einströmrate *f* LUFTTRANS inflow ratio

Einströmung *f* LUFTTRANS inflow; **Einströmungsöffnung** *f* KERNTECH *einer Turbine* inlet end

Einströmwinkel *m* LUFTTRANS inflow angle

Einstufen- *pref* FERTIG *Stauchautomat* one-blow; **Einstufenkompressor** *m* MASCHINEN single stage compressor; **Einstufenrückführung** *f* KERNTECH rabbit; **Einstufenverdampfer** *m* LEBENSMITTEL single effect evaporator; **Einstufenverstärker** *m* ELEKTRONIK, KERNTECH, LEBENSMITTEL, MASCHINEN single stage amplifier

einstufig[1] *adj* COMP & DV single-level

einstufig:[2] **~er Kompressor** *m* HYDRAUL single stage compressor; **~e Turbine** *f* HYDRAUL single stage turbine; **~er Verdichter** *m* HEIZ & KÄLTE, MASCHINEN single stage compressor; **~er Verstärker** *m* ELEKTRIZ single stage amplifier

Einstufung *f* ERGON rating, score

Einsturz *m* BAU collapse, ERDÖL caving

einstürzen *vi* BAU fail, fall in

einstweilig: ~er Schutz *m* PATENT provisional protection; **~e Verfügung** *f* PATENT interim injunction

Einsumpfen *nt* BAU *Kalk* soaking

Einsumpfzeit *f* BAU soaking period

Eins: Eins-Verstärker *m* ELEKTRONIK *Verstärker mit Verstärkungsfaktor Eins* unity gain amplifier; **Eins-Verstärkung** *f* ELEKTRONIK unity gain; **Eins-Zustand** *m* ELEKTRONIK one state

Eintagstide *f* WASSERTRANS diurnal tide

Eintaktröhre *f* ELEKTRONIK single-ended tube

Eintaktverstärker *m* ELEKTRONIK single-ended amplifier

Eintasten *nt* TELEKOM keying

eintasten *vt* DRUCK key in, keyboard, TELEKOM *Nummer* key in

Eintauchen *nt* BAU plunging, CHEMIE immersion, KER & GLAS *des Fangeisens bei der Herstellung von Tafelglas* dip, PAPIER immersion, RAUMFAHRT dive

eintauchen[1] *vt* METALL dip, PAPIER immerse, TEXTIL steep, VERPACK dip

eintauchen[2] *vi* RAUMFAHRT *Raumschiff* dive

Eintauchmeßzelle *f* GERÄT immersion cell

eintauchmetallisieren *vt* FERTIG whiten

Eintauchobjektiv *nt* PHYS *Mikroskop* immersion objective

Eintauch-Thermostat *m* HEIZ & KÄLTE immersion-type thermostat

Eintauchtiefe *f* WASSERTRANS depth of immersion

einteilen *vt* MECHAN index

einteilig[1] *adj* FERTIG solid

einteilig:[2] **~e Bifokallinsen** *f pl* KER & GLAS solid bifocals; **~es Lager** *nt* MASCHINEN solid bearing; **~er Schieber** *m* HEIZ & KÄLTE single leaf damper; **~e Schneidkluppe**

f MASCHINEN one-part screw plate

Einteilung *f* COMP & DV partitioning; **~ in Gruppen** *f* ELEKTROTECH grouping

Einthoven: ~sches Galvanometer *nt* ELEKTRIZ Einthoven galvanometer

Eintonnenvertäuung *f* ERDÖL single buoy mooring

Eintrag *m* COMP & DV entry, *in Liste* item

eintragen *vt* COMP & DV enter, register

Einträgersystem *nt* TRANS monobeam system

Eintrag: Eintraggabel *f* KER & GLAS carrying-in fork

Eintragung *f* LUFTTRANS, PATENT, TRANS, WASSERTRANS registration

eintreiben *vt* BAU *von Pfählen* pile

Eintreten: ~ in Umlaufbahn *nt* RAUMFAHRT *Raumschiff* entry into orbit

Eintritt *m* LUFTTRANS *Motor, Triebwerk* intake, MASCHINEN inlet, intake; **Eintrittskanal** *m* FERTIG inlet port; **Eintrittsleitschaufel** *f* LUFTTRANS intake guide vane; **Eintrittsleitschaufel-Staudruck** *m* LUFTTRANS intake guide vane ram; **Eintrittsöffnung** *f* BAU throat, MASCHINEN inlet, intake; **Eintrittsorbit** *m* RAUMFAHRT injection orbit; **Eintrittspupille** *f* PHYS entrance pupil; **Eintrittsschalldämpfer** *m* MECHAN inlet muffler (AmE), inlet silencer (BrE); **Eintrittstemperatur** *f* UMWELTSCHMUTZ inlet temperature; **Eintrittswahrscheinlichkeit** *f* COMP & DV probability; **Eintrittswinkel** *m* ELEKTRONIK acceptance angle, PHYS angle of contact

eintrommeln *vt* MEERSCHMUTZ *eine Sperre* reel in

Einwahl: ~ ins Netz *f* TELEKOM direct outward dialing (AmE), direct outward dialling (BrE)

Einwählvorgang *m* TELEKOM access via switched lines

Einwalzen *nt* BAU rolling

einwandern *vt* FERTIG diffuse

Einwanderung *f* FERTIG diffusion

einwandfrei *adj* BAU sound

Einwärtsfluß *m* PHYS inward flux

einwässern *vt* FERTIG macerate

einwecken *vt* LEBENSMITTEL *Früchte oder Gemüse* bottle

Einweg- *pref* ABFALL half-wave, ELEKTRIZ half wave, HEIZ & KÄLTE, KER & GLAS, KFZTECH, LEBENSMITTEL, PHYS, SICHERHEIT, TRANS, VERPACK half-wave; **Einwegbehälter** *m* VERPACK one-way container; **Einwegfilter** *nt* HEIZ & KÄLTE disposable filter; **Einwegflasche** *f* ABFALL disposable bottle, nonreturnable bottle, one-way bottle, KER & GLAS single trip bottle, VERPACK disposable bottle, nonreturnable bottle, one-way bottle; **Einweggleichrichter** *m* ELEKTRIZ, PHYS half-wave rectifier; **Einwegkupplung** *f* KFZTECH free engine clutch; **Einwegölfilter** *nt* KFZTECH throw-away oil filter; **Einwegpackung** *f* VERPACK one-way pack; **Einwegpalette** *f* TRANS expendable pallet, nonreusable pallet, one-way pallet, VERPACK expandable pallet, nonreturnable pallet, one-way pallet; **Einwegpolythenverpackung** *f* VERPACK expanded polythene packaging; **Einwegprodukt** *nt* ABFALL throw-away product; **Einwegschutzkleidung** *f* SICHERHEIT disposable protective clothing; **Einwegspiegel** *m* KER & GLAS seethrough mirror; **Einwegverpackung** *f* ABFALL disposable container, nonreturnable container, one-way pack, throw-away pack, LEBENSMITTEL, VERPACK nonreturnable packaging

Einweichen *nt* PAPIER, TEXTIL soaking

einweichen *vt* CHEMIE macerate, LEBENSMITTEL macerate, soak, steep, PAPIER batch, soak, TEXTIL soak through, soak, steep

einwellig[1] *adj* MASCHINEN single-shaft

einwellig:[2] **~e integrierte Optikschaltung** *f* ELEKTRONIK single mode optical integrated circuit; **~es Licht** *nt* METALL monochromatic light

einwertig[1] *adj* CHEMIE monobasic, monovalent, univalent

einwertig:[2] **~e Säure** *f* CHEMIE primary acid

Einwertigkeit *f* CHEMIE monovalence, univalence, monovalency, univalency

Einwicklungstransformator *m* ELEKTRIZ one-coil transformer

einwirken: ~ auf *vt* PHYS act upon

Einwohnergleichwert *m* ABFALL, WASSERVERSORG inhabitant equivalent, population equivalent

Einzahnschlagfräser *m* FERTIG single point cutter

einzapfen *vt* FERTIG mortice, mortise

einzäunen *vt* BAU fence in

Einzeilenfenster *nt* COMP & DV strip window

Einzel- *pref* COMP & DV, FERNSEH, FERTIG, KONTROLL, TELEKOM, TEXTIL, VERPACK single; **Einzeladreßcode** *m* COMP & DV single address code, single address instruction; **Einzeladreßnachricht** *f* COMP & DV single address message; **Einzelalarm** *m* TELEKOM minor alarm; **Einzelantrieb** *m* FERTIG individual drive, self-contained drive, MASCHINEN individual drive; **Einzelbauelement** *nt* ELEKTROTECH discrete component; **Einzelbenutzersystem** *nt* COMP & DV single user system; **Einzelbenutzerzugriff** *m* COMP & DV single user access; **Einzelberechnung** *f* TELEKOM detailed billing; **Einzelbild** *nt* COMP & DV frame, FERNSEH frame by frame; **Einzelbitfehler** *m* COMP & DV single bit error; **Einzelblattzuführung** *f* COMP & DV sheet feeding; **Einzelbuchstabensetz- und -gießmaschine** *f* DRUCK single-type composing and casting machine; **Einzeldiffusionsvorgang** *m* ELEKTRONIK single diffusion process; **Einzeldruck** *m* KONSTZEICH one-off print; **Einzelfaden-Schlichten** *nt* TEXTIL single end sizing; **Einzelfahrzeug ohne Fahrer** *nt* KFZTECH driverless single car; **Einzelfederung** *f* MASCHINEN individual suspension; **Einzelfertigung** *f* FERTIG jobbing; **Einzelflotation** *f* KOHLEN single flotation; **Einzelfundament** *nt* BAU footing, foundation block, single footing; **Einzelgerät** *nt* KONTROLL stand-alone device; **Einzelgußteil** *nt* FERTIG jobbing casting; **Einzelhandelpackung** *f* VERPACK retail package; **Einzelhub** *m* MASCHINEN single stroke

einzelhüllig *adj* WASSERTRANS single-hull

Einzel-: **Einzelkläranlage** *f* WASSERVERSORG separate sewerage system; **Einzelkondensator** *m* ELEKTROTECH discrete capacitor; **Einzelkontrolle** *f* TRANS individual control; **Einzelkristalldiodenmischer** *m* ELEKTRONIK single-ended crystal mixer; **Einzelleitung** *f* ELEKTRIZ independent feeder; **Einzellinearinduktionsmotor** *m* TRANS SLIM, single linear inductor motor; **Einzellinse** *f* KERNTECH Einzel lens; **Einzelmeßwert** *m* GERÄT individual measuring value, measurement value

einzeln[1] *adj* COMP & DV single

einzeln:[2] **~es Anführungszeichen** *nt* DRUCK turned comma; **~er Escape-Peak** *m* STRAHLPHYS single escape peak

Einzel-: **Einzelnetzgerät** *nt* ELEKTROTECH single supply; **Einzeloperation** *f* COMP & DV single operation; **Einzelpackung** *f* VERPACK unit pack; **Einzelplatzsystem** *nt* COMP & DV single user system; **Einzelplatzzugriff** *m* COMP & DV single user access; **Einzelpreis** *m* MASCHI-

NEN break-up price; **Einzelprobe** *f* QUAL increment; **Einzelresonanz** *f* KERNTECH single level resonance; **Einzelschicht-Wellfaserplatte** *f* VERPACK single wall-corrugated fiberboard (AmE), single wall-corrugated fibreboard (BrE); **Einzelschrittbetrieb** *m* KONTROLL step-by-step operation; **Einzelschrittsignal** *nt* ELEKTRONIK one-shot signal; **Einzelspeicher** *m* TELEKOM individual store; **Einzelstaubabscheider** *m* SICHERHEIT individual dust removal apparatus; **Einzelsteuerung** *f* TRANS individual control; **Einzelsteuerung des Durchflusses in Kühlkanälen** *f* KERNTECH individual channel flow control; **Einzelstrahlbrechung** *f* OPTIK monorefringence; **Einzelstromelement** *nt* ELEKTROTECH discrete power component; **Einzelstromversorgung** *f* ELEKTROTECH single supply; **Einzelstromversorgungsspannung** *f* ELEKTROTECH single supply voltage; **Einzelteil** *nt* ELEKTRONIK component, FERTIG *Kunststoffinstallationen* component part, KFZTECH part, KONSTZEICH component, MASCHINEN component, *der Drehmaschine* separate parts; **Einzelteilzeichnung** *f* KONSTZEICH component drawing; **Einzeltonaudiogramm** *nt* AKUSTIK pure tone audiogram; **Einzeltonnenfestmachen** *nt* ERDÖL single buoy mooring, *Schiffahrt* single buoy mooring; **Einzeltreibstoffschubtriebwerk** *nt* RAUMFAHRT *Raumschiff* monopropellant thruster; **Einzeltype** *f* DRUCK movable type; **Einzelverfahren** *nt* QUAL detailed procedure; **Einzelwasserversorgung** *f* WASSERVERSORG individual water supply; **Einzelwiderstand** *m* ELEKTROTECH discrete resistor; **Einzelworterkennung** *f* KÜNSTL INT isolated words recognition

einziehbar[1] *adj* MECHAN retractable

einziehbar:[2] **~e Antenne** *f* FERNSEH retractable antenna; **~es Filter** *nt* FOTO retractable filter; **~e Räder** *nt pl* KFZTECH retractable wheels

Einziehen *nt* PAPIER draw, TELEKOM *Kabel* pulling-in

einziehen *vt* WASSERTRANS *Tauende in Block* reeve

Einzifferaddierglied *nt* ELEKTRONIK one-digit adder

Einziffersubtrahierglied *nt* ELEKTRONIK one-digit subtractor

Einzonenreaktor *m* KERNTECH one-zone reactor

einzufügend: ~er Text *m* DRUCK inside forme

Einzug *m* TEXTIL *Weben* draft; **Einzugsbereich** *m* RADIO capture area, RAUMFAHRT range; **Einzugsbereich eines Knotenamts** *m* TELEKOM group-switching center catchment area (AmE), group-switching centre catchment area (BrE); **Einzugsgebiet** *nt* BAU, NICHTFOSS ENERG catchment area, WASSERVERSORG catchment area, drainage area, drainage basin; **Einzugsgebiet mit Binnenentwässerung** *nt* WASSERVERSORG blind drainage area; **Einzugsrolle** *f* FERTIG *Draht* feed roll

Einzweckmaschine *f* MASCHINEN single purpose machine

Einzylindermotor *m* KFZTECH one-cylinder engine, MASCHINEN one-cylinder engine, single cylinder engine

Einzylindertrockner *m* PAPIER yankee dryer

EIRP *abbr* (*äquivalente Isotropenstrahlungsleistung*) RADIO, RAUMFAHRT EIRP (*effective isotropically-radiated power*)

Eis *nt* THERMOD ice

eisbehindert *adj* WASSERTRANS *Schiff, Hafen* icebound

Eis: **Eisblumenglas** *nt* KER & GLAS ice-patterned glass; **Eisbrecher** *m* LUFTTRANS ice guard, WASSERTRANS ice guard, icebreaker; **Eisbrecherfrachtschiff** *nt* TRANS icebreaking cargo ship; **Eisbrechertanker** *m* TRANS icebreaking oil tanker

Eisen *nt* CHEMIE *(Fe)* iron *(Fe)*, METALL iron

Eisen- *pref* CHEMIE ferric

Eisenbahn *f* EISENBAHN railroad (AmE), railway (BrE); **Eisenbahnanschnitt** *m* EISENBAHN rail cutting; **Eisenbahnbediensteter** *m* EISENBAHN railroadman (AmE), railwayman (BrE); **Eisenbahnbetrieb** *m* EISENBAHN railroad operation (AmE), railway operation (BrE); **Eisenbahnbrücke** *f* EISENBAHN railroad bridge (AmE), railway bridge (BrE); **Eisenbahndamm** *m* EISENBAHN embankment; **Eisenbahneinschnitt** *m* EISENBAHN railroad cutting (AmE), railway cutting (BrE); **Eisenbahnfährdock** *nt* TRANS train ferry dock; **Eisenbahnfähre** *f* WASSERTRANS ferry; **Eisenbahnfahrplan** *m* EISENBAHN railroad schedule (AmE), railway schedule (BrE), railroad timetable (AmE), railway timetable (BrE); **Eisenbahnfahrzeuge** *nt pl* EISENBAHN railroad vehicles (AmE), railway vehicles (BrE); **Eisenbahnforschungs- und Versuchsamt** *nt* EISENBAHN ORE, Office for Research and Experiments; **Eisenbahnfrachtterminal** *m* EISENBAHN railroad freight terminal (AmE), railway freight terminal (BrE); **Eisenbahnkarte** *f* EISENBAHN railroad map (AmE), railway map (BrE); **Eisenbahnknotenpunkt** *m* EISENBAHN railroad center (AmE), railway centre (BrE), railroad junction (AmE), railway junction (BrE); **Eisenbahnmaterial** *nt* EISENBAHN railroad material (AmE), railway material (BrE), railroad stock (AmE), railway stock (BrE); **Eisenbahnschiene** *f* EISENBAHN railroad track (AmE), railway track (BrE); **Eisenbahnschwelle** *f* EISENBAHN cross tie (AmE), sleeper (BrE), tie (AmE); **Eisenbahnsicherheit** *f* SICHERHEIT rail safety; **Eisenbahnstrecke** *f* EISENBAHN railroad line (AmE), railway line (BrE); **Eisenbahntransport** *m* EISENBAHN railroad transport (AmE), railway transport (BrE); **Eisenbahnüberführung** *f* EISENBAHN *für Straßen* railroad overbridge (AmE), railway overbridge (BrE); **Eisenbahnunterführung** *f* EISENBAHN *für Straßen* railroad underbridge (AmE), railway underbridge (BrE); **Eisenbahnverkehr** *m* EISENBAHN railroad traffic (AmE), railway traffic (BrE); **Eisenbahnverkehrsordnung** *f* EISENBAHN railroad regulations (BrE), railway regulations (AmE); **Eisenbahnwagen** *m* EISENBAHN freight car (AmE), wagon (BrE); **Eisenbahnwaggon** *m* EISENBAHN railroad car (AmE), railway carriage (BrE)

Eisen: **Eisenband** *nt* MECHAN ferrule; **Eisenbandcutter** *m* VERPACK iron band cutter; **Eisenbeschläge** *m pl* BAU ironwork; **Eisenblech** *nt* FERTIG, METALL sheet iron; **Eisenbrücke** *f* BAU iron bridge; **Eisenfeilspäne** *m pl* PHYS iron filings

eisengeschirmt: **~es Meßwerk** *nt* GERÄT iron-screened movement

Eisen: **Eisengießerei** *f* FERTIG iron foundry; **Eisenglimmer** *m* KUNSTSTOFF micaceous iron oxide; **Eisenglut** *f* METALL red-hot iron; **Eisengraupe** *f* METALL granular iron; **Eisenguß** *m* METALL iron casting; **Eisenhüttenkunde** *f* METALL metallurgy; **Eisenkarbid** *nt* METALL cementite

Eisenkern *m* ELEKTROTECH iron core; **Eisenkernspannungsmeßgerät** *nt* ELEKTRIZ iron core voltmeter; **Eisenkernstrommeßgerät** *nt* ELEKTRIZ iron core ammeter; **Eisenkerntransformator** *m* ELEKTROTECH iron core transformer

Eisen: **Eisenlegierung** *f* ANSTRICH ferrous alloy

eisenlos *adj* ELEKTROTECH *Spule* air core

Eisen: **Eisenmetalle** *nt pl* METALL ferrous metals; **Eisennadelinstrument** *nt* GERÄT permanent magnet moving-iron instrument; **Eisen-Nickel-Akkumulator** *m* ELEKTRIZ Edison cell, RAUMFAHRT *Raumschiff* Ni-Fe battery; **Eisennippel** *m* MECHAN ferrule; **Eisenoxid** *nt* AUFNAHME ferric oxide, KER & GLAS ferrous oxide, CHEMIE *Schiff* iron-oxide; METALL black iron oxide; **Eisenrohr** *nt* BAU iron pipe; **Eisensalzlicht-Pausverfahren** *nt* KONSTZEICH ferrosalt method of reproduction; **Eisensättigung** *f* ELEKTROTECH magnetic saturation; **Eisenschlacke** *f* METALL iron slag; **Eisenschlechten** *f pl* KER & GLAS iron slips; **Eisenschrott** *m* ABFALL ferrous scrap, junk iron, scrap iron; **Eisenschrottpresse** *f* ABFALL junk press, scrap-baling press; **Eisenstab** *m* METALL iron bar; **Eisensulfat-Heptahydrat** *nt* CHEMIE iron sulfate (AmE), iron sulphate (BrE); **Eisenträger** *m* BAU iron girder; **Eisenverlust** *m* ELEKTRIZ, PHYS iron loss; **Eisenverluste** *m pl* ELEKTRIZ, PHYS core losses; **Eisenvitriol** *nt* CHEMIE copperas, iron vitriol; **Eisenwaren** *f pl* MASCHINEN hardware; **Eisenwasserstoffröhre** *f* ELEKTROTECH barretter; **Eisenwasserstoffwiderstand** *m* ELEKTROTECH barretter

eisern: **~er Vorhang** *m* THERMOD *zum Feuerschutz im Theater* fire curtain

Eis: **Eisessig** *m* CHEMIE, LEBENSMITTEL glacial acetic acid; **Eisfabrik** *f* THERMOD ice-making plant; **Eisfach** *nt* MASCHINEN ice-making compartment

eisig *adj* THERMOD icy

eiskalt *adj* THERMOD ice-cold

Eis: **Eiskondensator** *m* HEIZ & KÄLTE, KERNTECH ice condenser; **Eislinse** *f* KOHLEN ice lens; **Eismaschine** *f* THERMOD ice-making machine; **Eismeßfühler** *m* LUFTTRANS, WASSERTRANS ice probe; **Eispack** *nt* LUFTTRANS, WASSERTRANS ice pack; **Eispunkt** *m* HEIZ & KÄLTE, PHYS ice point; **Eisscholle** *f* WASSERTRANS ice floe; **Eisstücke** *nt pl* HEIZ & KÄLTE broken ice; **Eistarget** *nt* KERNTECH ice target; **Eiswarnzeichen** *nt* LUFTTRANS, WASSERTRANS ice-warning sign; **Eiswürfel** *m* THERMOD ice cube

Eiweiß *nt* LEBENSMITTEL albumen; **Eiweißfasern** *f pl* TEXTIL protein fibers (AmE), protein fibres (BrE)

eiweißreich *adj* LEBENSMITTEL high-protein

Eiweißschlichte *f* TEXTIL protein size

Ejektor *m* LABOR syphon, MECHAN ejector

ejektorartig: **~es Schneidabfallausstoßsystem** *nt* VERPACK ejector-type trim exhaust system

Ejektor: **Ejektorpumpe** *f* MASCHINEN ejector pump

Ekliptik *f* RAUMFAHRT *scheinbare Sonnenbahn* ecliptic

E-Krümmer *m* ELEKTROTECH *Wellenleiter* E bend, E plane

EL *abbr (Elektrolumineszenz-Anzeige)* ELEKTRONIK EL *(electroluminescent display)*

Elaidin *nt* CHEMIE elaidin; **Elaidin-** *pref* CHEMIE elaidic

Elain *nt* CHEMIE olein

Elast *nt* CHEMIE elastomer

elastisch[1] *adj* FERTIG resilient, *Hysterese* mechanical, KUNSTSTOFF, MECHAN elastic, TEXTIL flexible

elastisch:[2] **~er Aufprall** *m* KERNTECH elastic impact; **~e Ausdehnung** *f* VERPACK elastic elongation; **~er Bereich** *m* MECHAN elastic range; **~e Dehnung** *f* KUNSTSTOFF stretch; **~e Durchbiegung** *f* VERPACK elastic deformation; **~e Eigenschaften** *f pl* STRÖMPHYS *Flüssigkeiten* elastic properties; **~es Gelenk** *nt* MASCHINEN flexible joint; **~e Konstante** *f* STRÖMPHYS elastic constant; **~e Kupplung** *f* HEIZ & KÄLTE flexible coupling; ~e **Masse** *f* CHEMIE elastomer; ~er **Modus** *m* RAUMFAHRT elastic mode; ~e **Nachwirkung** *f* KUNST-STOFF retarded elasticity; ~e **Nachwirkungen** *f pl* STRÖMPHYS *Turbulenz* elastic aftereffects; ~es **Rad** *nt* TRANS elastic wheel; ~e **Schiene** *f* EISENBAHN resilient rail; ~er **Schlupf** *m* FERTIG stretch; ~es **Seil** *nt* WASSER-TRANS sandow; ~e **Spannung** *f* PHYS stress; ~er **Stoß** *m* KERNTECH, PHYS, STRAHLPHYS elastic collision; ~e **Streuung** *f* PHYS, STRAHLPHYS, TEILPHYS elastic scattering; nicht ~e **Verformung** *f* KUNSTSTOFF plastic yield; ~es **Vorspannen** *nt* FERTIG prespringing; ~e **Wellen** *f pl* PHYS elastic waves

elastisch:[3] ~ **zurückfedern** *vi* FERTIG resile

Elastizität *f* KUNSTSTOFF elasticity, MASCHINEN elasticity, resilience, resiliency, MECHAN, METALL elasticity, PAPIER resiliency, PHYS elasticity, TEXTIL flexibility, resilience, VERPACK, WASSERTRANS *Holz, Metall* elasticity; **Elastizitätsbereich** *m* MECHAN elastic range; **Elastizitätsgebiet** *nt* MECHAN elastic range; **Elastizitätsgrenze** *f* BAU elastic limit, KERNTECH yield point, KUNSTSTOFF, MECHAN, PHYS, VERPACK elastic limit; **Elastizitätskoeffizient** *m* KUNSTSTOFF, METALL coefficient of elasticity; **Elastizitätskonstante** *f* MASCHINEN, METALL elastic constant; **Elastizitätsmodul** *m* BAU modulus of elasticity, HYDRAUL *(K)* bulk modulus of elasticity *(K)*, KOHLEN, KUNSTSTOFF, LUFTTRANS, MASCHINEN, METALL modulus of elasticity, PHYS bulk modulus, modulus of elasticity, WERKPRÜF modulus of elasticity; **Elastizitätsmodus** *m* RAUMFAHRT elastic mode

Elastomer *nt* CHEMIE, ERDÖL *Kunststoff*, FERTIG *Kunststoffinstallationen*, KUNSTSTOFF elastomer

Elastomeres *nt* CHEMIE elastomer

Elastomer: **Elastomerverschnitt** *m* KUNSTSTOFF elastomer blend

elastoplastisch *adj* KUNSTSTOFF elastoplastic

Electronic-Publishing *nt* COMP & DV, DRUCK, ELEKTRO-NIK *Erstellen von Druckerzeugnissen auf Großrechnern* electronic publishing

ELED *abbr (Kantenemitter-Lumineszenzdiode, kantenstrahlende Lumineszenzdiode)* TELEKOM ELED (edge-emitting light-emitting diode)

Elefantenhaut *f* KUNSTSTOFF alligatoring, crazing

Elektret *nt* ELEKTRIZ, PHYS electret; **Elektretfolienmikrofon** *nt* AKUSTIK, AUFNAHME electret-foil microphone

elektrifizieren *vt* ELEKTROTECH electrify

Elektrifizierung *f* ELEKTRIZ, PHYS electrification

elektrisch[1] *adj* ELEKTRIZ, ELEKTRONIK electric, electrical; ~ **angetrieben** *adj* FOTO, MECHAN electrically-driven; mit ~em **Antrieb** *adj* FOTO electrically-driven; ~ **betrieben** *adj* FERTIG electric-powered; ~ **neutral** *adj* CHEMIE *Punkt* uncharged

elektrisch:[2] ~ **abgestimmter Oszillator** *m* ELEKTRONIK electrically-tuned oscillator; ~e **Abstimmung** *f* ELEK-TRONIK electric tuning; ~e **Anlage** *f* ELEKTRIZ electrical plant, ELEKTROTECH, WASSERTRANS electrical installation; ~er **Anlasser** *m* ELEKTRIZ electric starter; ~er **Anschluß** *m* ELEKTROTECH electrical connection, electrical connector; ~e **Ausgabe** *f* ELEKTRONIK electrical output; ~er **Ausgang** *m* ELEK-TROTECH electrical output; ~es **Bauteil** *nt* ELEKTROTECH electrical component; ~e **Beleuchtung** *f* ELEKTRIZ electric lighting; ~e **Beschaltung** *f* ELEKTRO-TECH electrical wiring; ~e **Bewegungsimpedanz** *f* AKUSTIK electrical motional impedance; ~er **Bewegungsscheinwiderstand** *m* AKUSTIK electrical

motional impedance; ~es **Bild** *f* ELEKTROTECH electric image; ~er **Blindleitwert** *m (BE)* ELEKTRIZ electric susceptance *(BE)*; ~e **Bogenentladung** *f* PHYS electric arc; ~er **Bohrer** *m* ELEKTRIZ electric drill; ~e **Bohrmaschine** *f* BAU power drill, MASCHINEN electric drill; ~e **Bremsung** *f* EISENBAHN electric braking; ~er **Brennofen** *m* ELEKTRIZ electric furnace; ~er **Bus** *m* TRANS battery bus; ~er **CO2-Entladungslaser** *m* ELEKTRONIK electric-discharge CO_2 laser; ~er **Dipol** *m* PHYS electric dipole; ~es **Dipolmoment** *nt* PHYS electric dipole moment; ~e **Durchgangsprüfung** *f* ELEKTRIZ continuity test; ~e **Eigenschaft** *f* ELEKTRONIK electrical characteristic; ~e **Eindringtiefe** *f* KERNTECH electric penetration; ~er **Eingang** *m* ELEKTROTECH electrical input; ~e **Eingangsimpedanz** *f* AKUSTIK *bei unbelastetem Ausgang* free electrical impedance; ~e **Einrichtung** *f* ELEKTRIZ electrical installation; ~e **Energie** *f* ELEK-TRIZ electric power, electrical power, ELEKTRIZ electrical energy, ELEKTROTECH electrical energy, PHYS electric energy; ~er **Entladungslaser** *m* ELEKTRONIK electric discharge laser; ~e **Entstaubung** *f* SICHERHEIT electrical dust removal installation; ~e **Erhitzung** *f* KERNTECH joule heating; ~er **Fehler** *m* ELEKTROTECH electrical breakdown; ~es **Feld** *nt* AUFNAHME, ELEK-TRIZ, ELEKTROTECH, FERNSEH, PHYS electric field; ~e **Feldkonstante** *f* PHYS permittivity of free space; ~e **Feldstärke** *f (E)* ELEKTRIZ, ELEKTROTECH, PHYS electric field strength *(E)*; ~er **Feldvektor** *m (E)* ELEKTROTECH electric field vector *(E)*; ~e **Feuerung** *f* ELEKTRIZ electric lighting; ~es **Filter** *nt* ELEKTRONIK electric filter, electrical filter; ~er **Fluß** *m* ELEKTRIZ flow, PHYS electric flux; ~er **Funke** *m* ELEKTRIZ electric spark; ~e **Gefahr** *f* SICHERHEIT electrical hazard; ~ **gehaltener Koppelpunkt** *m* TELEKOM electrically-held crosspoint; ~e **Größe** *f* ELEKTRIZ electric variable; ~es **Haushaltgerät** *nt* ELEKTRIZ electrical household appliance; ~es **Haushaltsgerät** *nt* ELEKTRIZ domestic appliance; ~er **Hauteffekt** *m* AKUSTIK electrodermal effect; ~er **Heizapparat** *m* ELEKTRIZ electric heater; ~es **Heizelement** *nt* ELEKTRIZ electric heater; ~es **Heizgerät** *nt* MASCHINEN electric heater; ~es **Heizkissen** *nt* THERMOD electric heating pad; ~e **Heizung** *f* ELEK-TRIZ, HEIZ & KÄLTE electric heating; ~e **Impedanz** *f* AUFNAHME electrical impedance; ~er **Impuls** *m* ELEK-TROTECH electric pulse; ~er **Induktionsofen** *m* ELEKTROTECH electric induction furnace; ~e **Installation** *f* WASSERTRANS electrical installation; ~e **Installationsarbeit** *f* ELEKTRIZ electrical installation work; ~e **Isolierplatte** *f* ELEKTRIZ electrical-insulating board; ~e **Isolierung** *f* ELEKTROTECH electrical insulation; ~e **Kapazität** *f (CE)* AKUSTIK electric capacitance *(CE)*; ~e **Kennlinie** *f* ELEKTROTECH electrical characteristic; ~er **Kleinmotor** *m* ELEKTROTECH fractional horsepower motor; ~e **Komponente** *f* ELEK-TROTECH electrical component; ~e **Konstante** *f* PHYS electric constant; ~er **Kontakt** *m* ELEKTRIZ, ELEKTRO-TECH electrical contact; ~e **Kontinuität** *f* ELEKTROTECH electrical continuity; ~er **Konvektionsofen** *m* THER-MOD electric convector; ~e **Kraftstoffpumpe** *f* KFZTECH *Kraftstoffzufuhr* electric fuel pump; ~es **Kraftwerk** *nt* ELEKTRIZ, ELEKTROTECH electric power station; ~e **Ladung** *f* ELEKTRIZ, PHYS, TEILPHYS electric charge; ~e **Laufzeitkette** *f* ELEKTRONIK electric delay line; ~e **Leistung** *f* ELEKTRIZ electric power, electrical power, KERNTECH, TELEKOM electrical power; ~ **leitende Versiegelung** *f* KERNTECH electrical conductor seal; **~er Leiter** *m* ELEKTROTECH electrical conductor, PHYS electric conductor; **~e Leitfähigkeit** *f* ELEKTROTECH electrical conduction, electrical conductivity; **~er Leitungsbruchalarm** *m* ELEKTRIZ electric wire-break alarm; **~es Leuchten** *nt* RAUMFAHRT electroglow; **~er Lichtbogen** *m* ELEKTRIZ electric arc; **~er Lichtbogenschmelzofen** *m* ELEKTRIZ EAF, electric-arc furnace; **~e Lieferfahrzeug** *nt* KFZTECH electrovan; **~e Lokomotive** *f* ELEKTRIZ electric locomotive; **~ löschbarer programmierbarer Lesespeicher** *m (EEPROM)* ELEKTRONIK electrically-erasable programmable read-only memory *(EEPROM)*; **~e Maschine** *f* ELEKTROTECH electrical machine; **~es Meßgerät** *nt* SICHERHEIT electric-measuring apparatus; **~es Meßgerät für nichtelektrische Größen** *nt* GERÄT electrically-measuring instrument; **~e Messung** *f* ELEKTROTECH electrical test; **~e Mittelführerstandlok mit langen und flachen Aufbauten** *f* EISENBAHN crocodile; **~es Mixgerät** *nt* LEBENSMITTEL electric mixer; **~es Netzwerk** *nt* PHYS electric network; **~er Nullpunkt** *m* ELEKTRIZ electrical zero; **~er Nullsteller** *m* ELEKTRIZ electrical zero adjuster; **~er Ofen** *m* ELEKTRIZ, THERMOD electric oven; **~e Pferdestärke** *f* ELEKTRIZ electric horsepower; **~e Pferdestärkestunde** *f* ELEKTRIZ electric horsepower hour; **~er Pol** *m* ELEKTROTECH electric pole; **~e Polarisation** *f* ELEKTRIZ, PHYS electric polarization; **~es Potential** *nt* ELEKTRIZ, ELEKTROTECH, PHYS electric potential, electrical potential; **~e Prüfung** *f* ELEKTROTECH, WERKPRÜF electrical test; **~es Quadrupolmoment** *nt* PHYS quadrupole electrical moment; **~es Relais** *nt* ELEKTRIZ, ELEKTROTECH electric relay, electrical relay; **~er Resonator** *m* ELEKTRONIK electrical resonator; **~e Säge** *f* ELEKTRIZ electric saw; **~e Schaltdifferenz** *f* AUFNAHME electric hysteresis; **~e Schaltuhr** *f* GERÄT automatic electric timer; **~e Schaltung** *f* ELEKTRIZ, ELEKTRONIK electric circuit, ELEKTROTECH electric wiring, electrical wiring; **~er Schienenwagen** *m* ELEKTRIZ electric railcar; **~es Schneiden** *nt* THERMOD electric-arc cutting; **~er Schock** *m* ELEKTRIZ electric shock; **~es Schutzgerät** *nt* SICHERHEIT electrical protection equipment; **~e Schwingung** *f* ELEKTRONIK electric oscillation; **~e Schwingungen** *f pl* WELLPHYS electrical oscillations; **~er Schwingungserzeuger** *m* ELEKTRONIK electrical oscillator; **~es Signal** *nt* ELEKTRONIK electrical signal, ELEKTROTECH electric signal; **~er Signalwandler** *m* ELEKTROTECH electric transducer; **~e Spannung** *f* ELEKTRIZ electric potential, PHYS voltage; **~er Stecker** *m* LABOR electric plug; **~er Steckverbinder** *m* ELEKTROTECH electrical connector; **~es Stellglied** *nt* RAUMFAHRT *Raumschiff* electric actuator; **~er Strom** *m* ELEKTRIZ conduction current, ELEKTRIZ electric current, ELEKTROTECH electric power, electrical power, PHYS electric current; **~e Stromdichte** *f* ELEKTRIZ electric current density; **~e Suszeptanz** *f* ELEKTRIZ electric susceptance; **~e Suszeptibilität** *f* ELEKTROTECH, PHYS electric susceptibility; **~e Technologie** *f* ELEKTRIZ electrotechnology; **~er Transducer** *m* ELEKTROTECH electric transducer; **~es Triebfahrzeug** *nt* ELEKTRIZ electric locomotive; **~er Trockner** *m* ELEKTRIZ electric dryer; **~e Übertragungsleitung** *f* ELEKTROTECH electrical transmission line; **~e Übertragungsschaltung** *f* ELEKTROTECH electric transducer; **~e Variable** *f* ELEKTRIZ electric variable; **~e Verbindung** *f* ELEKTRIZ electric linkage, ELEKTROTECH electrical connection; **~e Verdrahtung** *f*

ELEKTROTECH electric wiring, electrical wiring; **~er Verdrahtungsplan** *m* WASSERTRANS electrical-wiring diagram; **~e Verlustleistung** *f* ELEKTRIZ electric losses; **~es Verriegelungssystem** *nt* ELEKTRIZ electric-interlocking system; **~e Verschiebung** *f* ELEKTROTECH electric flux, PHYS electric displacement; **~es Versorgungsunternehmen** *nt* ELEKTROTECH electric utility; **~er Vierpol** *m* ELEKTROTECH electric quadrupole; **~e Vierpolübergänge** *m pl* STRAHLPHYS electric quadrupole transitions; **~ vorgespanntes Relais** *nt* ELEKTRIZ biased relay; **~er Wandler** *m* ELEKTROTECH electric transducer; **~es Wärmeäquivalent** *nt* ELEKTRIZ Joule's equivalent; **~es Wechselfeld** *nt* ELEKTROTECH alternating electric field; **~e Welle** *f* ELEKTROTECH electric wave; **~er Widerstand** *m* PHYS *physikalische Größe* electric resistance; **~er Wirkungsgrad** *m* ELEKTROTECH electrical efficiency; **~es Zählgerät** *nt* GERÄT counting instrument; **~er Zünder** *m* ELEKTRIZ electric lighter; **~e Zündung** *f* ELEKTRIZ electric lighting

elektrisieren *vt* ELEKTROTECH electrify

Elektrisiermaschine *f* ELEKTROTECH electric machine, static electrical machine

Elektrizität *f* ELEKTRIZ, ELEKTROTECH, PHYS, RADIO electricity; **Elektrizitätsausgangsleistung** *f* KERNTECH *eines Reaktors* electrical output; **Elektrizitätserzeugung** *f* ELEKTRIZ generation of electricity; **Elektrizitätskontrolltafel** *f* KERNTECH electrical control board; **Elektrizitätskraftwerk** *nt (E-Werk)* ELEKTRONIK electric power station; **Elektrizitätsmeßgerät** *nt* ELEKTRIZ electricity meter; **Elektrizitätsnetz** *nt* ELEKTRIZ *großes oder flächendeckendes Versorgungsnetz*, ELEKTROTECH *Verteilung der E-Energie* grid; **Elektrizitätsschalttafel** *f* KERNTECH electrical control board; **Elektrizitätsschaltwarte** *f* KERNTECH electrical control room; **Elektrizitätssystem mit ungeerdetem Mittelleiter** *nt* ELEKTRIZ isolated neutral system; **Elektrizitätstransformierung** *f* ELEKTRIZ transformation of electricity; **Elektrizitätsübertragung** *f* ELEKTRIZ transmission of electricity; **Elektrizitätsunterwerk** *nt* ELEKTRIZ electric power substation; **Elektrizitätsversorgung** *f* ELEKTRIZ electricity supply; **Elektrizitätsversorgungsunternehmen** *nt (EVU)* ELEKTRIZ electricity supply company; **Elektrizitätswerk** *nt* BAU, ELEKTROTECH electricity generation station, generating plant; **Elektrizitätswirtschaft** *f* ELEKTRIZ electricity sector economics; **Elektrizitätszähler** *m* ELEKTRIZ electricity meter

Elektro- *pref* AKUSTIK, ELEKTRONIK, ELEKTROTECH, MASCHINEN, MECHAN, PHYS electrical; **Elektroakustik** *f* ELEKTROTECH electroacoustics

elektroakustisch[1] *adj* AUFNAHME electroacoustic

elektroakustisch:[2] **~er Frequenzgang** *m* AUFNAHME electroacoustical frequency response; **~e Kette** *f* AKUSTIK electroacoustic chain; **~er Reziprozitätskoeffizient** *m* AKUSTIK electroacoustical reciprocity coefficient; **~er Wandler** *m* AKUSTIK, ELEKTROTECH electroacoustic transducer

Elektro-: **Elektroanalyse** *f* ELEKTRIZ electroanalysis; **Elektroantrieb** *m* FOTO electric drive, KERNTECH electrical drive; **Elektroblech** *nt* METALL silicone steel sheet; **Elektrobohrer** *m* MASCHINEN, MECHAN electric drill; **Elektrobus** *m* KFZTECH electric bus, electrobus; **Elektrochemie** *f* ELEKTRIZ electrochemistry

elektrochemisch:[1] **~e Energie** *f* ELEKTROTECH electrochemical energy; **~er Sekundärgenerator** *m* KFZTECH secondary electrochemical generator

elektrochemisch:[2] ~ **überziehen** *vt* ANSTRICH galvanize
Elektro-: **Elektrocochleographie** *f* AKUSTIK electro-cochleography; **Elektrocureverfahren** *nt* KERNTECH electron beam curing; **Elektrodampfkessel** *m* MASCHINEN electric steam boiler
Elektrode *f* ELEKTRIZ electrode, plate, ELEKTROTECH, FERNSEH, LABOR, MECHAN, METALL, PHYS electrode; **Elektrodenabstand** *m* HEIZ & KÄLTE electrode gap, spark gap, KFZTECH spark plug gap; **Elektrodenanordnung** *f* TELEKOM electrode configuration; **Elektrodenhalter** *m* BAU, ELEKTROTECH electrode holder; **Elektrodenkapazität** *f* ELEKTROTECH inter-electrode capacitance; **Elektrodenkennlinie** *f* ELEKTROTECH electrode characteristic; **Elektrodenkessel** *m* HEIZ & KÄLTE electrode boiler; **Elektrodenkohle** *f* ELEKTROTECH electrode carbon; **Elektrodenleitwert** *m* ELEKTRIZ electrode admittance; **Elektrodenmantel** *m* FERTIG *Schweißen* electrode coating; **Elektrodenpotential** *nt* ELEKTRIZ, MECHAN, PHYS electrode potential; **Elektrodenschweißen** *nt* BAU electrode welding; **Elektrodenspannung** *f* ELEKTRIZ electrode potential; **Elektrodenspitze** *f* ELEKTRIZ electrode tip; **Elektrodenstrahloszilloskop** *nt* ELEKTRONIK *zur Bildschirmdarstellung von schnell schwankenden, periodischen Spannungswerten* cathode-ray oscilloscope; **Elektrodenvorspannung** *f* ELEKTROTECH electrode bias, electrode bias voltage
Elektro-: **Elektrodialyse** *f* CHEMIE electrodialysis; **Elektrodynamik** *f* ELEKTRIZ, PHYS, TEILPHYS electrodynamics
elektrodynamisch: ~**e Gleisbremse** *f* EISENBAHN eddy current rail brake; ~**es Instrument** *nt* ELEKTRIZ electrodynamic instrument; ~**er Lautsprecher** *m* AKUSTIK electrodynamic loudspeaker; ~**es Meßinstrument** *nt* ELEKTRIZ electrodynamic instrument; ~**es Meßwerk** *nt* GERÄT electrodynamic movement; ~**es Mikrofon** *nt* AKUSTIK, AUFNAHME electrodynamic microphone; ~**es Relais** *nt* ELEKTRIZ electrodynamic relay; ~**es Schwebesystem** *nt* EISENBAHN electrodynamic levitation; ~**er Schwingungsaufnehmer** *m* GERÄT electrodynamic vibration pick-up
Elektro-: **Elektrodynamometer** *nt* ELEKTRIZ *Messung mechanischer Leistung*, PHYS electrodynamometer
elektrodynamometrisch *adj* ELEKTRIZ electrodynamometric
Elektro-: **Elektroeingang** *m* ELEKTRONIK electrical input; **Elektroenergieübertragung** *f* ELEKTROTECH electric power transmission
elektroerosiv: ~**e Bearbeitung** *f (EEB)* MASCHINEN electro-discharge machining *(EDM)*
Elektro-: **Elektrofahrzeug** *nt* ELEKTROTECH battery vehicle; **Elektrofahrzeug für den Stadtverkehr** *nt* TRANS urban electric vehicle; **Elektrofilter** *nt* ELEKTRONIK, HEIZ & KÄLTE electrostatic filter; **Elektroformen** *nt* MASCHINEN electroforming
elektrofotografisch: ~**er Drucker** *m* COMP & DV electro-photographic printer
Elektro-: **Elektrogerät** *nt* LEBENSMITTEL electrical appliance
elektrographisch: ~**er Drucker** *m* COMP & DV electrographic printer
Elektro-: **Elektrohebezeug** *nt* MECHAN electric hoist; **Elektroheizung** *f* HEIZ & KÄLTE electric heating
elektrohydraulisch: ~**es Bohren** *nt* KOHLEN electrodrilling
Elektro-: **Elektroingenieur** *m* FERNSEH electrical engineer; **Elektroinstallation** *f* ELEKTROTECH electrical installation; **Elektrokinetik** *f* ELEKTROTECH, PHYS electrokinetics
elektrokinetisch: ~**e Energie** *f* ELEKTRIZ electrokinetic energy
Elektro-: **Elektrokochplatte** *f* THERMOD electric hot plate; **Elektroleitung** *f* THERMOD electric power line; **Elektrolieferfahrzeug** *nt* KFZTECH electric pickup; **Elektrolieferwagen** *m* KFZTECH electric delivery truck; **Elektrolog** *nt* ERDÖL *Bohrlochmeßtechnik* electric log
Elektrolumineszenz *f* ELEKTRONIK *durch elektrische Felder induziert* electroluminescence, KERNTECH electrofluorescence, electroluminescence, OPTIK, PHYS, TELEKOM electroluminescence; **Elektrolumineszenz-Anzeige** *f (EL)* ELEKTRONIK electroluminescent display *(EL)*
Elektrolyse *f* DRUCK, ELEKTRIZ, ELEKTROTECH, PHYS electrolysis; ~ **von Wasser** *f* KERNTECH water electrolysis; **Elektrolyseapparat** *m* ELEKTROTECH electrolytic unit; **Elektrolysebad** *nt* ELEKTRIZ, ELEKTROTECH electrolytic bath, PHYS electrolytic cell
Elektrolyseur *m* CHEMIE electrolyzer
Elektrolyse: **Elektrolysezelle** *f* ELEKTROTECH electrolytic cell, FERTIG pot, PHYS electrolytic unit, electrolytic cell
elektrolysieren *vt* CHEMIE, PHYS electrolyze
Elektrolysierung *f* ELEKTRIZ electrolyzation
Elektrolyt *m* CHEMIE, ELEKTRIZ, ELEKTROTECH, KUNSTSTOFF, PHYS, TELEKOM electrolyte
Elektrolyt- *pref* CHEMIE electrolytic
Elektrolyt: **Elektrolytätzen** *nt* KERNTECH electrolytic etching; **Elektrolytglas** *nt* KER & GLAS copper light; **Elektrolytgleichrichter** *m* ELEKTROTECH electrolytic rectifier
elektrolytisch[1] *adj* CHEMIE, ELEKTRIZ, METALL, PHYS electrolytic
elektrolytisch:[2] ~**e Abscheidung** *f* ELEKTROTECH, FERTIG electrodeposition; ~**er Gleichrichter** *m* ELEKTROTECH electrolytic rectifier; ~**e Korrosion** *f* METALL electrolytic corrosion; ~**e Leitfähigkeit** *f* ELEKTRIZ electrolytic conductivity; ~**e Reinigung** *f* METALL electrolytic cleaning; ~**es Ventil** *nt* ELEKTROTECH electrolytic rectifier; ~**e Zelle** *f* CHEMIE electrolyzer
elektrolytisch:[3] ~ **behandeln** *vt* WASSERTRANS *Metall* anodize; ~ **plattieren** *vt* ELEKTROTECH electroplate; ~ **zerlegen** *vt* CHEMIE electrolyze
Elektrolyt: **Elektrolytkondensator** *m* ELEKTROTECH *(Elkom)*, PHYS, RADIO electrolytic capacitor, TELEKOM electrochemical capacitor; **Elektrolytstand** *m* KFZTECH acid level
Elektro-: **Elektromagnet** *m* CHEMIE, ELEKTRIZ, ELEKTROTECH, FERNSEH, PHYS electromagnet
elektromagnetisch[1] *adj* ELEKTRIZ electromagnetic, FERTIG solenoid, PHYS, RADIO electromagnetic; ~ **betrieben** *adj* ELEKTROTECH electromagnetically-operated
elektromagnetisch:[2] ~**e Ablenkung** *f* ELEKTROTECH electromagnetic deflection; ~**e Abschirmung** *f* PHYS, TEILPHYS, WELLPHYS electromagnetic screen; ~**e Abstimmung** *f* ELEKTRONIK electromagnetic tuning; ~**er Auslöser** *m* FOTO electromagnetic shutter release; ~**e Dämpfung** *f* ELEKTRIZ *Schwingungen* electromagnetic damping; ~**es Drehmoment** *nt* ELEKTRIZ electromagnetic moment; ~**e Einheit** *f* ELEKTRIZ electromagnetic unit; ~**e Energie** *f* ELEKTROTECH, PHYS, WELLPHYS electromagnetic energy; ~**er Energieimpuls**

m ELEKTROTECH electromagnetic energy pulse; ~es **Feld** *nt* ELEKTRIZ, ELEKTROTECH, PHYS, TELEKOM, WELLPHYS electromagnetic field; ~e **Fokussierung** *f* ELEKTROTECH electromagnetic focusing; ~es **Futter** *nt* MASCHINEN electromagnetic chuck; ~er **Impuls** *m* ELEKTROTECH, TELEKOM electromagnetic pulse; ~e **Induktion** *f* ELEKTROTECH, PHYS, TEILPHYS, WELLPHYS electromagnetic induction; ~e **Interferenz** *f* ELEKTROTECH EMI, electromagnetic interference; ~e **Isolierung** *f* ELEKTROTECH electromagnetic isolation; ~es **Kalorimeter** *nt* STRAHLPHYS, TEILPHYS electromagnetic calorimeter; ~e **Kompatibilität** *f* ELEKTROTECH electromagnetic compatibility; ~e **Kopplung** *f* ELEKTRIZ coupling, ELEKTROTECH electromagnetic coupling; ~e **Kraft** *f* ELEKTRIZ, ELEKTROTECH, PHYS, TEILPHYS, WELLPHYS electromagnetic force; ~e **Kupplung** *f* EISENBAHN, KFZTECH electromagnetic clutch, electromagnetic coupling, MECHAN electromagnetic clutch; ~er **Lautsprecher** *m* AKUSTIK, AUFNAHME electromagnetic loudspeaker; ~e **Linse** *f* ELEKTROTECH, FERNSEH electromagnetic lens; ~es **Mikrofon** *nt* AKUSTIK, AUFNAHME electromagnetic microphone; ~es **Moment** *nt* ELEKTRIZ, PHYS, TEILPHYS, WELLPHYS electromagnetic moment; ~e **Pumpe** *f* KERNTECH electromagnetic pump; ~es **Querführungssystem** *nt* EISENBAHN, KFZTECH electromagnetic lateral guidance system; ~e **Querwelle** *f* ELEKTROTECH, TELEKOM transverse electromagnetic wave; ~es **Relais** *nt* ELEKTRIZ, ELEKTROTECH electromagnetic relay; ~er **Resonator** *m* ELEKTRONIK electromagnetic resonator; ~e **Schirmung** *f* ELEKTRIZ electromagnetic shielding; ~er **Schrittmotor** *m* ELEKTROTECH variable reluctance stepper motor; ~e **Schwebeführung** *f* EISENBAHN, KFZTECH electromagnetic levitation; ~es **Spektrum** *nt* ELEKTRONIK, ELEKTROTECH, PHYS, TEILPHYS, WELLPHYS electromagnetic spectrum; ~e **Störung** *f* COMP & DV, ELEKTROTECH, RAUMFAHRT EMI, electromagnetic interference; ~e **Strahlen** *m pl* ELEKTRIZ, ELEKTROTECH, OPTIK, PHYS, TEILPHYS, TELEKOM, WELLPHYS electromagnetic radiation; ~e **Strahlung** *f* ELEKTRIZ, ELEKTROTECH, OPTIK, PHYS, TEILPHYS, TELEKOM, WELLPHYS electromagnetic radiation; ~es **Umfeld** *nt* RAUMFAHRT electromagnetic environment; ~es **Ventil** *nt* HYDRAUL solenoid valve; ~e **Verträglichkeit** *f* (EMV) ELEKTRIZ, RADIO, RAUMFAHRT electromagnetic compatibility (EMC); ~e **Wechselwirkung** *f* PHYS, TEILPHYS, WELLPHYS electromagnetic interaction; ~e **Welle** *f* ELEKTRIZ, ELEKTROTECH, PHYS, TEILPHYS, TELEKOM, WELLPHYS electromagnetic wave; ~e **Wellengleichungen** *f pl* PHYS, TEILPHYS, WELLPHYS electromagnetic-wave equations; ~e **Zündung** *f* EISENBAHN, KFZTECH electromagnetic ignition

Elektro-: **Elektromagnetismus** *m* ELEKTRIZ, PHYS electromagnetism; **Elektromagnetlautsprecher** *m* AKUSTIK electromagnet loudspeaker; **Elektromaschine** *f* ELEKTROTECH electric machine; **Elektromechanik** *f* ELEKTRIZ electromechanics

elektromechanisch: ~es **Filter** *nt* ELEKTRONIK electromechanical filter; ~es **Gerät** *nt* ELEKTROTECH electromechanical device; ~er **Kopplungsfaktor** *m* AKUSTIK electromechanical coupling factor; ~es **Relais** *nt* ELEKTROTECH electromechanical relay; ~e **Tonaufzeichnung** *f* AUFNAHME electromechanical recording; ~er **Transducer** *m* ELEKTROTECH electromechanical transducer; ~e **Vermittlung** *f* TELEKOM electromechanical switching; ~e **Vermittlungseinrichtung** *f* TELEKOM electromechanical switching unit; ~e **Vermittlungsstelle** *f* TELEKOM electromechanical exchange; ~es **Vermittlungssystem** *nt* TELEKOM electromechanical switching system; ~er **Wandler** *m* AKUSTIK, ELEKTROTECH electromechanical transducer

elektromer: ~er **Effekt** *m* CHEMIE mesomeric effect

Elektro-: **Elektrometallurgie** *f* ELEKTRIZ electrometallurgy

Elektrometer *nt* ELEKTRIZ, ELEKTROTECH, LABOR *elektrisches Laden*, PHYS electrometer; **Elektrometerröhre** *f* ELEKTRONIK, ELEKTROTECH electrometer tube; **Elektrometerverstärker** *m* ELEKTRONIK electrometer amplifier

Elektro-: **Elektrometrie** *f* ELEKTROTECH electrometry

elektrometrisch: ~e **Titration** *f* CHEMIE electrometric titration

Elektromotor *m* ELEKTROTECH electric motor, electromotor, KFZTECH electric motor

elektromotorisch: ~e **Gegenkraft** *f* EISENBAHN back electromotive force; ~e **Kraft** *f* (EMK) BAU, EISENBAHN, ELEKTRIZ, ELEKTROTECH, FERNSEH, PHYS, RADIO electromotive force (EMF)

Elektron *nt* (*e*) ELEKTRIZ, ELEKTROTECH, PHYS *Elementarteilchen*, RADIO, TEILPHYS electron (*e*); **äußeres ~** *nt* METALL valence electron

Elektronen: **durch ~ induzierte Aktivierung** *f* STRAHLPHYS electron-induced activation; **Elektronenabbildung** *f* ELEKTRONIK electron imaging

elektronenabgebend: ~es **Atom** *nt* PHYS donor atom

Elektron: **Elektronenabspaltung durch Fotoeffekt** *f* KERNTECH photodetachment; **Elektronenabtaststrahl** *m* FERNSEH electron scanning beam; **Elektronenabtastung** *f* KERNTECH electron scanning; **Elektronenanlagerung** *f* KERNTECH electron attachment

elektronenanziehend *adj* CHEMIE electrophilic

Elektron: **Elektronenapparatur** *f* ELEKTROTECH electron device; **Elektronenbahn** *f* KERNTECH electron path; **Elektronenbeschleuniger** *m* TEILPHYS electron accelerator; **Elektronenbeschuß** *m* ELEKTRONIK, TEILPHYS electron bombardment; **Elektronenbeschußtriebwerk** *nt* RAUMFAHRT *Raumschiff* electron bombardment thruster; **Elektronenbeugung** *f* STRAHLPHYS electron diffraction, electron spectroscopic diffraction; **Elektronenbild** *nt* ELEKTRONIK electron image; **Elektronenbildwandler** *m* ELEKTRONIK *Bildwandlerröhre* electron image tube; **Elektronendichte** *f* PHYS electron density, RAUMFAHRT *Raumschiff* electron population; **Elektroneneinfang** *m* PHYS *Kernphysik*, STRAHLPHYS electron capture; **Elektroneneinfangdetektor** *m* UMWELTSCHMUTZ electron capture detector; **Elektroneneinstrahlung** *f* RAUMFAHRT electron irradiation; **Elektronenemission** *f* ELEKTRONIK, TEILPHYS electron emission; **Elektronenfahrplan** *m* ELEKTRONIK *Klystron* Applegate diagram; **Elektronenfelderzeugung** *f* FERNSEH electronic field production; **Elektronenfluß** *m* FERNSEH electron stream; **Elektronenflutlithographie** *f* ELEKTRONIK electron flood lithography; **Elektronengas** *nt* PHYS electron gas; **Elektronengerät** *nt* ELEKTROTECH electron device; **Elektronenhülle** *f* KERNTECH electron shell; **Elektronenkanone** *f* ELEKTRONIK, FERNSEH, PHYS, STRAHLPHYS electron gun; **Elektronenkanonenstrom** *m* FERNSEH electron gun current; **Elektronenkaskade** *f*

KERNTECH electron cascade; **Elektronenkonfiguration** *f* PHYS, STRAHLPHYS, TEILPHYS electronic configuration; **Elektronenkontinuum** *nt* KERNTECH electron continuum

elektronenkoppelnd: ~er Oszillator *m* ELEKTRONIK electron-coupling oscillator

Elektron: **Elektronenkopplung** *f* ELEKTRONIK, ELEKTROTECH electron coupling; **Elektronenkühlung** *f* TEILPHYS electron cooling; **Elektronenlaufzeit** *f* ELEKTROTECH *von Kathode zu Anode* transit time

elektronenleitend[1] *adj* ELEKTRONIK n-type

elektronenleitend:[2] ~e Epitaxialschicht *f* ELEKTRONIK n-type epitaxial layer; ~es Silizium *nt* ELEKTRONIK n-type silicon; ~e Störstelle *m* ELEKTRONIK n-type impurity; ~es Trägermaterial *nt* ELEKTRONIK n-type substrate

Elektron: **Elektronenleitfähigkeit** *f* STRAHLPHYS electron conductivity; **Elektronenleitvermögen** *nt* STRAHLPHYS electron conductivity; **Elektronenlinearbeschleuniger** *m* TEILPHYS electron linear accelerator; **Elektronenlinse** *f* ELEKTRONIK, FERNSEH, PHYS electron lens; **Elektronenlochrekombination** *f* KERNTECH electron hole recombination; **Elektronenmasse** *f (me)* CHEMIE, KERNTECH, TEILPHYS electron mass *(me)*; **Elektronenmikrofon** *nt* AUFNAHME electronic microphone; **Elektronenmikroskop** *nt* ELEKTRONIK, LABOR, METALL, PHYS, STRAHLPHYS, TELEKOM electron microscope; **Elektronenmikroskopbild** *nt* STRAHLPHYS electron micrograph; **Elektronenmikroskopie** *f* ELEKTRONIK electron microscopy; **Elektronenniederschlag** *m* BAU electrodeposition; **Elektronenoptik** *f* PHYS electron optics; **Elektronenpaar** *nt* TEILPHYS electron pair; **Elektronenpolarisation** *f* PHYS, STRAHLPHYS, TEILPHYS electronic polarization; **Elektronenpolarisierung** *f* PHYS, STRAHLPHYS, TEILPHYS electronic polarization; **Elektronenpopulation** *f* RAUMFAHRT *Raumschiff* electron population; **Elektronen-Positronen-Kollideranlage** *f (LEP)* TEILPHYS large electron-positron collider *(LEP)*; **Elektronenquelle** *f* ELEKTRONIK electron source, *Physik* electron gun, STRAHLPHYS electron source; **Elektronenradiographie** *f* KERNTECH electron radiography; **Elektronenradius** *m (re)* KERNTECH electron radius *(re)*

Elektronenröhre *f* ELEKTRONIK electron tube, electronic tube, electronic valve, RADIO thermionic tube, thermionic valve, RAUMFAHRT *Weltraumfunk* electron tube; **Elektronenröhrenansatz** *m* ELEKTRONIK electron tube neck; **Elektronenröhrengitter** *nt* ELEKTRONIK electron tube grid; **Elektronenröhrenhalter** *m* ELEKTRONIK electron tube holder; **Elektronenröhrenheizung** *f* ELEKTRONIK electron tube heater; **Elektronenröhrenkolben** *m* ELEKTRONIK electron tube envelope; **Elektronenröhrenoszillator** *m* ELEKTRONIK electron tube oscillator; **Elektronenröhrensockel** *m* ELEKTRONIK electron tube base

Elektron: **Elektronenschale** *f* PHYS, STRAHLPHYS, TEILPHYS electron shell, electronic subshell

Elektronenschalen: äußere ~ *f pl* STRAHLPHYS outer orbital complex

Elektron: **Elektronenschauer** *m* KERNTECH electron shower; **Elektronensenke** *f* KERNTECH electron sink; **Elektronensonde** *f* KERNTECH electron probe; **Elektronenspeicher** *m* ELEKTROTECH electronic memory; **Elektronenspeicherring** *m* TEILPHYS electron storage ring; **Elektronenspektroskopie** *f* PHYS electron spectroscopy, STRAHLPHYS electron energy loss spectroscopy, electron spectroscopic imaging

elektronenspendend *adj* CHEMIE *Valenz* nucleophilic

Elektron: **Elektronenspiegel** *m* ELEKTRONIK electron mirror; **Elektronenspinresonanz** *f (ESR)* PHYS, STRAHLPHYS, TEILPHYS electron spin resonance *(ESR)*; **Elektronenspinresonanz-Magnetometer** *nt* KERNTECH electron spin resonance magnetometer; **Elektronenstoßionentriebwerk** *nt* RAUMFAHRT *Raumschiff* electron impact ion engine

Elektronenstrahl *m (ES)* COMP & DV, ELEKTRIZ, ELEKTRONIK, FERNSEH, KERNTECH, STRAHLPHYS, TELEKOM, WELLPHYS electron beam, electronic beam *(EB)*; ~ für Direktbelichtung *m* ELEKTRONIK direct-write electron beam; **Elektronenstrahlabdecklack** *m* ELEKTRONIK electron beam resist; **Elektronenstrahlabtastung** *f* ELEKTRONIK electron beam scanning; **Elektronenstrahlaufzeichnung** *f* GERÄT electron beam recording, electronic beam recording; **Elektronenstrahlausrichtmethode** *f* ELEKTRONIK electron beam alignment method; **Elektronenstrahlbearbeitung** *f* ELEKTRONIK electron beam machining; **Elektronenstrahlbildung** *f* ELEKTRONIK electronic beam forming; **Elektronenstrahlbündelung** *f* ELEKTRONIK electron beam focusing; **Elektronenstrahldirektbelichtung** *f* ELEKTRONIK electron beam direct writing; **Elektronenstrahlkolonne** *f* ELEKTRONIK electron beam column; **Elektronenstrahllaser** *m* ELEKTRONIK electron beam laser; **Elektronenstrahllithographie** *f* ELEKTRONIK electron beam lithography; **Elektronenstrahl-Lithographiebearbeitungsmaschine** *f* ELEKTRONIK electron beam lithography machine; **Elektronenstrahlmaske** *f* ELEKTRONIK electron beam mask; **Elektronenstrahlnachbeschleunigung** *f* ELEKTRONIK electron beam acceleration; **Elektronenstrahl-Projektionslithografie** *f* ELEKTRONIK projection electron-beam lithography; **Elektronenstrahl-Projektionsschreiber** *m* ELEKTRONIK electron beam projection printer; **Elektronenstrahlresist** *m* ELEKTRONIK electron beam resist; **Elektronenstrahlröhre** *f* ELEKTRONIK electron beam tube; **Elektronenstrahlschmelzen** *nt* KERNTECH electron beam melting; **Elektronenstrahlschneiden** *nt* ELEKTRONIK electron beam cutting; **Elektronenstrahlschweißen** *nt* BAU, ELEKTRIZ, KERNTECH electron beam welding; **Elektronenstrahlspannung** *f* FERNSEH electron beam voltage; **Elektronenstrahlsystem** *nt* ELEKTRONIK color gun (AmE), colour gun (BrE); **Elektronenstrahlung** *f* METALL electron beam; **Elektronenstrahlverarbeitung** *f* ELEKTRONIK electron beam processing; **Elektronenstrahlvergütung** *f* ELEKTRONIK electron beam annealing

Elektron: **Elektronenstreuung** *f* KERNTECH electron scattering; **Elektronenstrom** *m* ELEKTROTECH electron current; **Elektronenstruktur** *f* KERNTECH electronic structure; **Elektronensynchrotron** *nt* TEILPHYS electron synchrotron; **Elektronentheorie der Metalle** *f* STRAHLPHYS electron theory of metals; **Elektronentrajektorie** *f* KERNTECH electron trajectory; **Elektronentransportdiode** *f* ELEKTRONIK transferred-electron diode; **Elektronenüberlauf** *m* FERNSEH spillover; **Elektronenverbindung** *f* METALL electron compound; **Elektronenverdampfung** *f* PHYS thermionic emission; **Elektronenvervielfacher** *m* ELEKTRONIK, STRAHLPHYS electron multiplier; **Elektronenvervielfacherröhre** *f* ELEKTRONIK electron multiplier tube; **Elektronenvolt** *nt (eV)* ELEKTRIZ, ELEKTROTECH,

PHYS, STRAHLPHYS, TEILPHYS electronvolt *(eV)*; **Elektronenwanderung** *f* KERNTECH electron drift; **Elektronenweg** *m* FERNSEH electron path; **Elektronenwellenmagnetron** *nt* ELEKTRONIK electron wave magnetron; **Elektronenwellenröhre** *f* ELEKTRONIK electron wave tube; **Elektronenwolke** *f* FERNSEH, KERNTECH, STRAHLPHYS electron cloud; **Elektronenzusammenstoß** *m* TELEKOM electron collision; **Elektronenzyklotron** *nt* TEILPHYS microtron

Elektronik *f* COMP & DV, EISENBAHN, ELEKTRONIK, KFZTECH, LUFTTRANS, WASSERTRANS *Steuereinrichtungen* electronics; **Elektronikbremse** *f* KFZTECH electronic-braking control; **Elektronikmeßgerät** *nt* METROL electronic gage (AmE), electronic gauge (BrE); **Elektronikmodum** *nt* ELEKTRONIK electronic module; **Elektronikschablone** *f* ELEKTRONIK electronic stencil

elektronisch[1] *adj* ELEKTRIZ, ELEKTRONIK electronic; ~ **gesteuert** *adj* ELEKTRONIK electronically-controlled

elektronisch:[2] ~ **abgestimmter Oszillator** *m* ELEKTRONIK electronically-controlled oscillator; ~ **abgestimmtes Filter** *nt* ELEKTRONIK electronically-tuned filter; ~**es Ablagesystem** *nt* COMP & DV electronic filing; ~**er Abstimmbereich** *m* ELEKTRONIK *Klystron* electronic-tuning range; ~**e Abstimmung** *f* ELEKTRONIK *Klystron*, TELEKOM electronic tuning; ~**e Abtastung** *f* ELEKTRONIK, RADIO, TELEKOM frequency scanning; ~**es Antiblockiersystem** *nt* KFZTECH electronic antiskid system, electronic antilocking device; ~**es Arbeitsblatt** *nt* COMP & DV spreadsheet; ~**e Aufklärung** *f* ELEKTRONIK electronic intelligence; ~**es Bauelement** *nt* ELEKTRONIK electronic component, electronic device, KERNTECH electronic instrument module, MECHAN chip, TELEKOM electronic component; ~**es Bauteil** *nt* COMP & DV electronic component; ~**e Benzineinspritzung** *f* KFZTECH electronic metering of fuel injection; ~**e Berichterstattung** *f* COMP & DV electronic news reporting; ~**e Bilderzeugung** *f* ELEKTRONIK electronic imaging; ~**er Bleistift** *m* ELEKTRONIK electronic pencil; ~**e Bremsschlupfregelung** *f* KFZTECH antiblocking system, antiskid braking system; ~**e Bremssteuerung** *f* KFZTECH electronic-braking control; ~**er Briefkasten** *m* COMP & DV electronic mailbox, TELEKOM electronic mailbox, user agent; ~**es Büro** *nt* COMP & DV electronic office; ~**e Datenverarbeitung** *f (EDV)* COMP & DV, ELEKTRIZ, ELEKTRONIK, KONTROLL electronic data processing *(EDP)*; ~**er Drehzahlregler** *m* KFZTECH electronic speed controller; ~**es Editieren** *nt* COMP & DV electronic editing; ~**er Fahrtrichtungsschalter** *m* KFZTECH electronic direction reverser; ~**es Fahrzeug** *nt* KFZTECH electronic car; ~**e Frequenzsteuerung** *f* ELEKTRONIK electronic frequency control; ~**e Gegenmaßnahmen** *f pl* RAUMFAHRT *Weltraumfunk* electronic countermeasures; ~**e Geldanweisung** *f* TELEKOM EFT, electronic funds transfer; ~**e Geldüberweisung an Verkaufsort** *f* TELEKOM EFT-POS, electronic funds transfer at point of sale; ~**es Gerät** *nt* ELEKTRONIK electronic equipment; ~**es Gerät für die Industrie** *nt* ELEKTROTECH industrial electronic equipment; ~**e Geschwindigkeitskontrolle** *f* KFZTECH electronic speed control; ~ **gesteuerte Einspritzung** *f* KFZTECH electronic injection; ~ **gesteuertes Ventil** *nt* BAU electronically-controlled valve; ~**es Gravieren** *nt* DRUCK electronic engraving; ~**er Halbleiter** *m* KERNTECH electronic semiconductor; ~**e integrierte Schaltung** *f* ELEKTRONIK electronic integrated circuit;

~**e Kampfführung** *f* ELEKTRONIK electronic warfare; ~**e Karte** *f* WASSERTRANS *Navigation* electronic chart, electronic map; ~**e Kassenanzeige** *f (POS-Anzeige)* VERPACK point of sale display *(POS display)*; ~**es Kassenterminal** *nt* COMP & DV EPS, electronic point-of-sale; ~**er Kommutator** *m* KFZTECH electronic commutation; ~**er Koppelpunkt** *m* TELEKOM electronic crosspoint; ~**e Kriegsführung** *f* ELEKTRONIK *militärische Nachrichtentechnik* electronic warfare; ~**er Lichtsatz** *m* DRUCK electronic photocomposition; ~ **löschbarer Festwertspeicher** *m (EEROM)* COMP & DV electronically erasable read-only memory *(EEROM)*; ~ **löschbarer Lesespeicher** *m (EEROM)* COMP & DV electronically erasable read-only memory *(EEROM)*; ~ **löschbarer ROM** *m* COMP & DV electronically erasable ROM; ~**e Mailbox** *f* COMP & DV electronic mailbox; ~**es Mattieren** *nt* FERNSEH electronic matting; ~**es Meßgerät** *nt* ELEKTRONIK, GERÄT electronic instrument, METROL electronic gage (AmE), electronic gauge (BrE); ~**es Mitteilungssystem** *nt* TELEKOM electronic message system; ~**er Modum** *m* KERNTECH electronic instrument module; ~**e Morsetaste** *f* RADIO El bug; ~**e Musik** *f* ELEKTRONIK electronic music; ~**er Nachrichtendienst** *m* FERNSEH electronic news gathering; ~**e Nachrichtenspeichervermittlung** *f* TELEKOM electronic message switch; ~**e Nachrichtenübermittlung** *f* COMP & DV, ELEKTRONIK electronic messaging; ~**e Post** *f (E-Mail)* COMP & DV, ELEKTRONIK, TELEKOM electronic mail *(e-mail)*; ~**er Postdienst** *m* COMP & DV electronic mail service; ~**es Postfach** *nt* TELEKOM electronic mailbox; ~**e Prüfmuster** *nt pl* ELEKTRONIK electronic test patterns; ~**es Publizieren** *nt* COMP & DV, DRUCK, ELEKTRONIK electronic publishing; ~**er Rauschgenerator** *m (RG)* FERNSEH electronic noise generator *(ENG)*; ~**er Rechner** *m* COMP & DV electronic calculator; ~**e Regelung** *f* KFZTECH electronic control; ~**er Regler** *m* KFZTECH transistorized regulator; ~**es Relais** *nt* ELEKTRIZ *elektronisch gesteuerter Schalter* electronic relay; ~**es Scannen** *nt* DRUCK electronic scanning; ~**er Schaltkreis** *m* ELEKTRONIK electronic circuit; ~**e Schaltuhr** *f* FOTO electronic timer; ~**e Schaltung** *f* PHYS electronic network, TELEKOM electronic circuit; ~**es Schlüsselsystem** *nt* TELEKOM electronic key system; ~**e Signalverarbeitung** *f* ELEKTRONIK electronic signal processing; ~**er Speicher** *m* ELEKTROTECH electronic memory; ~**e Sperre** *f* COMP & DV electronic lock; ~**e Sprachsynthese** *f* ELEKTRONIK electronic speech synthesis; ~**es Steuergerät** *nt* KFZTECH electronic control unit; ~**e Steuerung** *f* WASSERTRANS electronic control; ~**es Steuerungssystem** *nt* ELEKTRONIK electronic control system; ~**e Stromversorgung** *f* ELEKTROTECH electronic power supply; ~**er Taktgeber** *m* ELEKTRONIK electronic clock; ~**e Technik** *f* ELEKTRONIK electronic engineering; ~**es Telefonbuch** *nt* TELEKOM electronic directory; ~**er Theodolit mit Digitalanzeige** *m* BAU *Vermessung* electronic digital theodolite; ~**e Überwachung** *f* TELEKOM electronic surveillance; ~**e Uhr** *f* TELEKOM electronic clock; ~**es Umbruchterminal** *m* DRUCK electronic makeup terminal; ~**er Vergaser** *m* KFZTECH electronic carburetor (AmE), electronic carburettor (BrE); ~**e Verkehrshilfen** *f pl* TRANS electronic traffic aids; ~**e Vermittlung** *f* TELEKOM electronic switching; ~**e Vermittlung mit Reed-Relais** *f* TELEKOM reed relay electronic exchange; ~**e Vermittlungsstelle** *f* TELEKOM electronic exchange; ~**es**

Vermittlungssystem *nt* TELEKOM electronic switching system; ~er Verstimmbereich *m* ELEKTRONIK - *Oszillator* electronic-tuning range; ~e Verstimmempfindlichkeit *f* ELEKTRONIK electronic-tuning sensitivity; ~e Verstimmung *f* ELEKTRONIK *Oszillator* electronic tuning; ~e Verteilungsfunktion *f* KERNTECH electronic partition function; ~e Waage *f* LABOR electronic balance, VERPACK electronic-weighing scales; ~e Wärmekapazität *f* PHYS, STRAHLPHYS, TEILPHYS electronic heat capacity; ~e Wärmeleitfähigkeit *f* KERNTECH electronic heat conductivity; ~es Zählen *nt* ELEKTRONIK electronic counting; ~er Zähler *m* ELEKTRONIK *mit elektronischen Schaltungen aufgebaut* electronic counter; ~er Zahlungsverkehr *m* COMP & DV EFT, electronic funds transfer; ~er Zeitschalter *m* ELEKTRONIK electronic timer; ~e Zündung *f* KFZTECH electronic ignition

Elektron: Elektronlochpaar *nt* PHYS electron hole pair; Elektronneutrino *nt* PHYS electron neutrino; Elektronstrahlpumpen *nt* ELEKTRONIK electron beam pumping

Elektro-: Elektronutzfahrzeug *nt* KFZTECH commercial electric vehicle; Elektroofen *m* ELEKTRIZ electric oven, FERTIG, KOHLEN electric furnace, THERMOD electric oven

elektrooptisch[1] *adj* ELEKTRONIK electrically-tuned oscillator, electro-optical, TELEKOM electro-optic

elektrooptisch:[2] ~er Effekt *m* OPTIK electro-optic effect; ~er Modulator *m* ELEKTRONIK electro-optical modulator; ~er Schalter *m* TELEKOM electro-optic switch; ~e Signalverarbeitung *f* ELEKTRONIK electro-optical signal processing; ~er Tonabnehmer *m* AUFNAHME light beam pickup

Elektro-: Elektroosmose *f* CHEMIE electro-osmosis

elektroosmotisch *adj* CHEMIE electro-osmotic

elektrophil *adj* CHEMIE electrophilic

Elektro-: Elektrophor *m* ELEKTROTECH electrophorus

Elektrophorese *f* ELEKTRIZ, LABOR electrophoresis; Elektrophoresekammer *f* LABOR electrophoresis cell; Elektrophoresezelle *f* LABOR electrophoresis cell

elektrophoretisch: ~e Wanderung *f* KERNTECH electrophoretic migration

Elektro-: Elektroplattieren *nt* ELEKTROTECH, FERTIG electroplating

elektroplattieren *vt* ELEKTROTECH electroplate

Elektro-: Elektroplattierung *f* ELEKTROTECH electroplating, plating

elektropneumatisch: ~e Bremse *f* EISENBAHN, KFZTECH electropneumatic brake

elektropositiv: ~e Elemente *nt pl* PHYS, STRAHLPHYS, TEILPHYS electropositive elements

Elektro-: Elektroproduktion *f* PHYS, STRAHLPHYS, TEILPHYS electroproduction; Elektrorauschen *nt* ELEKTRONIK electric noise, electrical noise; Elektrorund *m* FERTIG manufactured corundum; Elektrosägen *nt* KERNTECH electrical sawing; Elektroschlackeschweißen *nt* BAU, KERNTECH electroslag welding; Elektroschlepper *m* KFZTECH electric truck

elektroschwach: ~e Theorie *f* TEILPHYS electroweak theory; ~e Wechselwirkung *f* TEILPHYS electroweak interaction

Elektro-: Elektroschweißen *nt* ELEKTRIZ electric welding, MECHAN arc welding, THERMOD electric-arc welding; Elektroschweißer *m* MECHAN arc welder; Elektroschweißmaschine *f* MECHAN arc-welding machine

elektrosensitiv: ~er Drucker *m* COMP & DV electrosensitive printer; ~es Papier *nt* COMP & DV electrosensitive paper

Elektro-: Elektrosicherheitssystem *nt* SICHERHEIT electrosensitive safety system; Elektroskop *nt* ELEKTRIZ *Instrument zur Messung elektrostatischer Ladungen*, PHYS, STRAHLPHYS, TEILPHYS electroscope; Elektrosprayen *nt* KERNTECH electrospraying; Elektrostatik *f* ELEKTRIZ, ELEKTROTECH, PHYS electrostatics; Elektrostatikladungsmeßgerät *nt* ELEKTRIZ static meter

elektrostatisch[1] *adj* ELEKTRIZ, TELEKOM electrostatic

elektrostatisch:[2] ~e Abschirmung *f* ELEKTRIZ static screen, PHYS electrostatic screen; ~e Anziehung *f* ELEKTROTECH electrostatic attraction; ~e Anziehungskraft *f* ELEKTRIZ electrostatic attraction; ~er Drucker *m* COMP & DV electrographic printer, electrostatic printer; ~e Elektronenbündelung *f* ELEKTROTECH electrostatic focusing; ~er Fehler *m* FERNSEH static error; ~es Feld *nt* ELEKTRIZ, PHYS electrostatic field; ~es Filter *nt* ELEKTRONIK *Kohlekraftwerk*, HEIZ & KÄLTE electrostatic filter; ~er Fluß *m* ELEKTRIZ electrostatic flux; ~e Flußdichte *f* ELEKTRIZ electrostatic flux density; ~er Generator *m* ELEKTROTECH electrostatic generator; ~e Induktion *f* ELEKTRIZ, PHYS electrostatic induction; ~es Instrument *nt* ELEKTRIZ, ELEKTROTECH, LABOR, PHYS electrometer; ~e Ionenoszillation *f* KERNTECH electrostatic ion oscillation; ~er Kollektor *m* KERNTECH electrostatic collector; ~e Kraft *f* ELEKTROTECH electrostatic force; ~e Ladung *f* ELEKTRIZ electrostatic charge; ~er Lautsprecher *m* AKUSTIK, AUFNAHME electrostatic loudspeaker; ~e Linse *f* ELEKTRONIK *Kathodenstrahlröhren* electrostatic CRT, ELEKTROTECH electrostatic lens, focusing electrode, PHYS electrostatic lens; ~es Luftfilter *nt* SICHERHEIT electrostatic air filter; ~es Mikrofon *nt* AKUSTIK, AUFNAHME condenser microphone, electrostatic microphone; ~er Plotter *m* COMP & DV electrostatic plotter; ~es Pulverbeschichten *nt* KUNSTSTOFF electrostatic powder coating; ~es Relais *nt* ELEKTRIZ electrostatic relay; ~er Schirm *m* ELEKTRONIK electrostatic screen; ~er Staubabscheider *m* (ESA) UMWELTSCHMUTZ electrostatic precipitator (ESP)

Elektro-: Elektrostauchen *nt* FERTIG metal gathering; Elektrostraßenfahrzeug *nt* KFZTECH electric road vehicle; Elektrostriktion *f* ELEKTRIZ, PHYS electrostriction; Elektrosynthese *f* CHEMIE electrosynthesis

elektrothermal *adj* ELEKTRIZ electrothermal

elektrothermisch *adj* ELEKTRIZ electrothermal, electrothermic

Elektro-: Elektrowärmegerät *nt* HEIZ & KÄLTE electric-heating appliance; Elektrowelle *f* (*E-Welle*) ELEKTROTECH, PHYS, TELEKOM electric wave (*E wave*)

Element *nt* BAU member, COMP & DV element, item, ELEKTRIZ element, ELEKTROTECH cell, FERTIG *Kraftmaschine* detail, HYDRAUL element, KÜNSTL INT *eines Schemas* slot, MASCHINEN element, link, MATH, OPTIK, RADIO element, TELEKOM chip; ~ der Actinidenreihe *nt* STRAHLPHYS actinide element

Elemente *nt pl* MATH *einer Menge* members

elementar[1] *adj* MATH elementary

elementar:[2] ~er Anreicherungsfaktor *m* KERNTECH elementary enrichment factor; ~e Rechenzeit *f* COMP & DV basic machine time; ~er Trenneffekt *m* KERNTECH elementary separation effect; ~es Trennvermögen *nt* KERNTECH elementary separative power

Element: **Elementarfaden** *m* KUNSTSTOFF monofilament; **Elementarladung** *f* PHYS, TEILPHYS elementary charge; **Elementarlautsprecher** *m* AKUSTIK elementary loudspeaker; **Elementarteilchen** *nt* PHYS, TEILPHYS charm, charmed quark, elementary particle; **Elementarteilchenphysik** *f* PHYS particle physics; **Elementarwelle** *f* FERTIG wavelet; **Elementarzelle** *f* KERNTECH unit cell; **Elementenfamilie** *f* STRAHLPHYS family of elements; **Elementenreihe** *f* STRAHLPHYS family of elements

elementfremd: ~e **Mengen** *f pl* MATH disjoint sets

Element: **Elementtriade** *f* CHEMIE triad; **Elementzeichen** *nt* MATH inclusion symbols

Eleostearin- *pref* CHEMIE elaeostearic

Elevation *f* WASSERTRANS *Navigation* elevation; **Elevationswinkel** *m* RAUMFAHRT elevation angle

Elite *f* DRUCK *Schrift* elite

Elkom *m* *(Elektrolytkondensator)* ELEKTROTECH electrolytic capacitor

Ellag- *pref* CHEMIE ellagic

Ellagengerbstoff *m* CHEMIE ellagitannin

Ellbogen *m* WASSERTRANS bend; **Ellbogengelenk** *nt* KERNTECH *eines Manipulators* elbow; **Ellbogenschutz** *m* SICHERHEIT elbow pad

Ellipse *f* GEOM ellipse; **Ellipsenbogen** *m* BAU elliptical arch; **Ellipsenzirkel** *m* FERTIG trammel point, KER & GLAS trammel, MASCHINEN egg calipers (AmE), egg callipers (BrE), trammel

Ellipsoid *nt* GEOM, PHYS ellipsoid

ellipsoid *adj* GEOM ellipsoidal

Ellipsometer *nt* PHYS ellipsometer

Elliptikfeder *f* MASCHINEN elliptic spring

elliptisch[1] *adj* GEOM elliptic, elliptical

elliptisch:[2] ~e **Bahn** *f* PHYS elliptical orbit; ~e **Frequenzgangkurve** *f* ELEKTRONIK elliptic response curve; ~e **Geometrie** *f* GEOM *nicht-euklidische Geometrie zweiter Art* elliptical geometry; ~es **Gewölbe** *nt* BAU three-centered arch (AmE), three-centred arch (BrE); ~e **Polarisation** *f* PHYS, RAUMFAHRT *Weltraumfunk* elliptical polarization; ~ **polarisierte Welle** *f* AKUSTIK, PHYS elliptical-polarized wave; ~er **Raum** *m* GEOM elliptical space; ~er **Spiegel** *m* PHYS elliptical mirror; ~es **Zahnrad** *nt* MASCHINEN elliptical gear

Elliptizität *f* RAUMFAHRT *Weltraumfunk* ellipticity

Ellipton *nt* CHEMIE elliptone

Ellsworthit *m* KERNTECH ellsworthite

Elmsfeuer *nt* WASSERTRANS *Wetterkunde* St Elmo's fire, corposant

Elongation *f* FERTIG *Schwingung* displacement

Eloxalaluminium *nt* HEIZ & KÄLTE anodized aluminium (BrE), anodized aluminum (AmE)

Eloxalqualität *f* METALL anodizing quality

Eloxalverfahren *nt* FERTIG aluminite process (AmE), METALL anodizing

eloxieren *vt* CHEMIE, FERTIG, WASSERTRANS *Metall* anodize

Eloxierung *f* FERTIG anodization

ELSBM *abbr* *(ungeschützte Einzeltonnenvertäuung)* ERDÖL ELSBM *(exposed location single buoy mooring)*

Eluat *nt* CHEMIE eluate

Eluationsversuch *m* ABFALL leaching test

Eluent *m* CHEMIE eluant, elution agent

Eluieren *nt* CHEMIE, CHEMTECH elution

eluieren *vt* CHEMIE elute

Elution *f* CHEMIE elution; **Elutionsmittel** *nt* CHEMIE eluant, elution agent; **Elutionsversuch** *m* ABFALL leachability test

E-Mail *f* *(elektronische Post)* COMP & DV, ELEKTRONIK, TELEKOM e-mail *(electronic mail)*

Emaille *f* BAU, KER & GLAS enamel; **Emailledraht** *m* ELEKTRIZ, ELEKTROTECH enameled wire (AmE), enamelled wire (BrE); **Emaillefarbe** *f* KER & GLAS enamel color (AmE), enamel colour (BrE); **Emaillelack** *m* BAU baking varnish; **Emaillemischung** *f* FERTIG slip

Emaillierung *f* VERPACK enameling (AmE), enamelling (BrE)

E-Mail: **E-Mail-Mitteilung** *f* COMP & DV mail message

Emanation *f* KERNTECH, STRAHLPHYS emanation

Embelin *nt* CHEMIE embelin

EMC-Kollaboration *f* TEILPHYS European collaboration for muon physics

Emetin *nt* CHEMIE emetin, emetine

EMI-Filterung *f* *(Filterung gegen elektromagnetische Beeinflussung)* ELEKTRONIK EMI filtering

Emission *f* COMP & DV, KFZTECH, LUFTTRANS, PHYS, STRAHLPHYS *spontane, induzierte Emission*, TEILPHYS, UMWELTSCHMUTZ emission; ~ **in die Luft** *f* PHYS, STRAHLPHYS emission-into-the-air; **Emissionsbande** *f* PHYS, STRAHLPHYS emission band; **Emissionsbegrenzer** *m* KERNTECH gag; **Emissionsdaten** *nt pl* UMWELTSCHMUTZ emission data; **Emissionselektrode** *f* ELEKTROTECH emitter; **Emissionsfotoschicht** *f* ELEKTRONIK photoemissive layer; **Emissionslinie** *f* PHYS, STRAHLPHYS emission line; **Emissionsmikroskop** *nt* METALL emission microscope; **Emissionsort** *m* UMWELTSCHMUTZ emission point; **Emissionsquelle** *f* UMWELTSCHMUTZ emission source, pollution emitter; **Emissionsquelle in einem Gebiet** *f* UMWELTSCHMUTZ area emission source; **Emissionsspektralanalyse** *f* PHYS, STRAHLPHYS emission spectral analysis; **Emissionsspektrum** *nt* PHYS, STRAHLPHYS emission spectrum; **Emissionsstandard** *m* UMWELTSCHMUTZ emission standard, level of emission; **Emissionsstärke** *f* OPTIK, PHYS, STRAHLPHYS emissivity; **Emissionsverhinderung** *f* PHYS blocking effect; **Emissionsvermeidung** *f* UMWELTSCHMUTZ avoidance of emissions; **Emissionsvermögen** *nt* HEIZ & KÄLTE, PHYS, STRAHLPHYS, TELEKOM emissivity; **Emissionsverzeichnis** *nt* UMWELTSCHMUTZ emission inventory

Emittanz *f* NICHTFOSS ENERG emittance

Emitter *m* COMP & DV, ELEKTROTECH, PHYS *elektronenliefernde Transistorelektrode*, RADIO, TELEKOM emitter; ~ **des Transistors** *m* TELEKOM transistor emitter; **Emitterbasisanschluß** *m* ELEKTROTECH earthed-emitter connection (BrE), grounded-emitter connection (AmE); **Emitterbasisdurchschlag** *m* ELEKTRONIK emitter-base breakdown; **Emitterbasissperrschicht** *f* ELEKTRONIK emitter-base junction; **Emitterelektrode** *f* ELEKTROTECH emitter electrode; **Emitterfolger** *m* ELEKTROTECH, PHYS emitter follower; **Emittergebiet** *nt* ELEKTROTECH emitter region

emittergekoppelt: ~e **Logik** *f* *(ECL)* COMP & DV, ELEKTRONIK emitter-coupled logic *(ECL)*

Emitter: **Emitterkontakt** *m* ELEKTROTECH emitter contact; **Emitterschaltung** *f* ELEKTROTECH common-emitter connection; **Emitterverstärker** *m* ELEKTRONIK common-emitter amplifier; **Emitterzone** *f* ELEKTROTECH emitter region

emittierend: ~e **Diode** *f* ELEKTRONIK emissive diode

emittiert: ~e **Strahlung** *f* STRAHLPHYS emitted radiation

EMK *abbr* *(elektromotorische Kraft)* BAU, EISENBAHN,

ELEKTRIZ, ELEKTROTECH, FERNSEH, PHYS, RADIO **EMF** *(electromotive force)*

Emodin *nt* CHEMIE emodin

Emodin- *pref* CHEMIE emodic

Emodol *nt* CHEMIE emodin

Empfang *m* COMP & DV receipt, reception, RADIO reception; ~ **mit faseroptischem Endgerät** *m* OPTIK receive fiberoptic terminal device (AmE), receive fibreoptic terminal device (BrE)

empfangen:[1] **-es Signal** *nt* ELEKTRONIK received signal

empfangen[2] *vt* COMP & DV *Daten* receive

Empfänger *m* COMP & DV addressee, ELEKTRONIK, FERNSEH, RADIO, RAUMFAHRT *Weltraumfunk,* TELEKOM receiver, TRANS consignee, UMWELTSCHMUTZ receptor, WASSERTRANS *Satellitenfunk* receiver; ~ **für Lichtwellenleiterübertragung** *m* TELEKOM fiberoptic receiver (AmE), fibreoptic receiver (BrE); ~ **mit Stummabstimmung** *m* RADIO muting receiver; **Empfängerbandpaß** *m* FERNSEH receiver bandpass; **Empfängerbereich** *m* UMWELTSCHMUTZ receptor region; **Empfängerdiode** *f* ELEKTRONIK receiver diode; **Empfängerfeinabstimmung** *f (RIT)* RADIO receiver incremental tuning *(RIT);* **Empfängerkarte** *f* ELEKTRONIK receiver board; **Empfängerröhre** *f* ELEKTRONIK receiving tube; **Empfängersperrröhre** *f* ELEKTRONIK TR tube; **Empfängerverstärkung** *f* ELEKTRONIK receiver gain

empfänglich *adj* ANSTRICH prone

Empfang: **Empfangsanlage** *f* COMP & DV receive-only equipment; **Empfangsantenne** *f* FERNSEH, PHYS, RADIO receiving aerial, receiving antenna, TELEKOM receive antenna; **Empfangsbereich** *m* FERNSEH receiving range, RADIO range; **Empfangsbescheinigung** *f* PATENT *für Unterlagen* receipt; **Empfangsbestätigungszeichen** *nt* COMP & DV acknowledgement character; **Empfangsfilter** *nt* ELEKTRONIK receive filter; **Empfangsfrequenz** *f* ELEKTRONIK, FERNSEH, RADIO, TELEKOM reception frequency; - **Empfangsgerät** *nt* TELEKOM receive machine; **Empfangsgleichrichtung** *f* PHYS *Funkwellen* demodulation; **Empfangskarte** *f* ELEKTRONIK receiver board; **Empfangsloch** *nt* FERNSEH shadow; **Empfangslücke** *f* GERÄT dead spot

Empfangsoszillator *m* ELEKTRONIK, RADIO, TELEKOM local oscillator; ~ **mit Frequenzaufbereitung** *m* ELEKTRONIK synthesized local oscillator; **Empfangsoszillatorfrequenz** *f* ELEKTRONIK, RADIO, TELEKOM local oscillator frequency; **Empfangsoszillatorröhre** *f* ELEKTRONIK local oscillator tube; **Empfangsoszillatorsignal** *nt* ELEKTRONIK local oscillator signal

Empfang: **Empfangspegel** *m* ELEKTRONIK reception level; **Empfangsquarz** *m* ELEKTRONIK receive crystal; **Empfangsquittung** *f* COMP & DV receipt; **Empfangsschüsselantenne** *f* FERNSEH receiving dish antenna; **Empfangssignal** *nt* TELEKOM *Empfänger* incoming signal; **Empfangssucher** *m* ELEKTRONIK ranger finder

Empfehlung *f* TRANS advisory message; **Empfehlungen für die Nährstoffzufuhr** *f pl* LEBENSMITTEL RDA, recommended dietary allowances

empfindlich:[1] ~ **für alle Farben** *adj* CHEMIE *Photographie,* DRUCK, FOTO panchromatic

empfindlich:[2] **-e Emulsion** *f* FOTO orthochromatic emulsion; **-es Papier** *nt* FOTO sensitive paper

empfindlich[3] ~ **machen** *vt* FOTO sensitize

Empfindlichkeit *f* AKUSTIK response, COMP & DV, ELEKTRIZ, ELEKTROTECH, GERÄT, KOHLEN, KONTROLL,

OPTIK sensitivity, PHYS sensitivity, susceptibility, RADIO, RAUMFAHRT *Weltraumfunk,* TELEKOM sensitivity; ~ **nach DIN** *f* FOTO DIN speed; ~ **am Skalenanfangswert** *f* GERÄT minimum scale sensitivity; **Empfindlichkeitsindex** *m* FOTO exposure index; **Empfindlichkeitsschwelle** *f* GERÄT threshold of sensitivity

Empfindung *f* AKUSTIK sensation; **Empfindungsfunktion** *f* AKUSTIK stimulus-sensation relation; **Empfindungsgrößen** *f pl* AKUSTIK values of sensation; **Empfindungsniveau** *nt* ERGON sensitivity level; **Empfindungsschwelle** *f* ERGON threshold of feeling; **Empfindungsstufen** *f pl* AKUSTIK sensation steps

EMS[1] *abbr (Expansionsspeicher-Spezifikation)* COMP & DV EMS *(expanded memory specification)*

EMS:[2] **EMS-Speicherverwalter** *m* COMP & DV expanded memory manager

Emulation *f* COMP & DV, ELEKTRONIK *Simulation eines anderen Computersystems mit Hardware- oder Softwaremitteln* emulation

Emulator *m* COMP & DV emulator, ELEKTRONIK *Hardware-Zusatz* emulator, *Programm* emulator, TELEKOM emulator

Emulgator *m* CHEMTECH, KERNTECH, KUNSTSTOFF, LEBENSMITTEL, PAPIER, VERPACK emulsifier, emulsifying agent; **Emulgatorflüssigkeit** *f* SICHERHEIT emulsifying liquid

Emulgier- *pref* CHEMTECH emulsifying

emulgierbar *adj* CHEMTECH emulsifiable

Emulgierbarkeit *f* CHEMTECH emulsifiability

Emulgieren *nt* CHEMTECH emulsification

emulgieren *vt* CHEMTECH, FOTO, KUNSTSTOFF, PAPIER, UMWELTSCHMUTZ emulsify

Emulgier-: **Emulgiermaschine** *f* CHEMTECH, KERNTECH emulsifying machine; **Emulgiermittel** *nt* CHEMTECH, KERNTECH emulsifier, KUNSTSTOFF emulsifier, emulsifying agent, LEBENSMITTEL, PAPIER emulsifier, VERPACK emulsifying agent

Emulgierung *f* CHEMIE emulsification

Emulgierungs- *pref* CHEMTECH emulsifying

emulieren *vt* COMP & DV, ELEKTRONIK *Verhalten eines anderen Programms simulieren* emulate

Emulsin *nt* CHEMTECH emulsin

Emulsion *f* BAU, CHEMTECH *Binder,* ERDÖL, FOTO, KERNTECH, KUNSTSTOFF, LEBENSMITTEL, MEERSCHMUTZ, PHYS emulsion

emulsionbeschichtet *adj* VERPACK emulsion-coated

Emulsionieren *nt* CHEMIE emulsification

Emulsion: **Emulsionsanlage** *f* KERNTECH emulsifying machine; **Emulsionsbeständigkeit** *f* CHEMTECH emulsion persistence; **Emulsionschargennummer** *f* FOTO emulsion batch number; **Emulsionsfarbe** *f* BAU, KUNSTSTOFF emulsion paint; **Emulsionsflüssigkeit** *f* CHEMTECH, SICHERHEIT emulsifying liquid; **Emulsionspolymerisation** *f* KUNSTSTOFF emulsion polymerization; **Emulsionsspalter** *m* LEBENSMITTEL de-emulsifying agent, MEERSCHMUTZ demulsifier, emulsion breaker, UMWELTSCHMUTZ emulsion breaker; **Emulsionstest** *m* CHEMTECH emulsion test

EMV *abbr (elektromagnetische Verträglichkeit)* ELEKTRIZ, RADIO, RAUMFAHRT *Raumfahrt* EMC *(electromagnetic compatibility)*

EMV-gerecht *adj* ELEKTRIZ EMC-compatible

EN *abbr (Europäische Norm)* ELEKTRIZ European Standard

Enantiomer *nt* CHEMIE enantiomer, optical isomer

enantiomorph *adj* CHEMIE enantiomorphic, enantiomorphous

Enantiomorphie *f* CHEMIE enantiomorphism

enantiotrop *adj* CHEMIE enantiotropic

End- *pref* ABFALL, FERTIG, GERÄT, KERNTECH, LUFT-TRANS, TELEKOM final, ultimate; **Endabbrand** *m* KERNTECH ultimate burn up, *von Brennelementen* final fuel burnup; **Endabdeckung** *f* ABFALL *einer Deponie* final covering, final cover; **Endablesung** *f* GERÄT final reading; **Endabnahme** *f* QUAL final acceptance; **Endabschaltung** *f* FERTIG *Kunststoffinstallationen* end switch; **Endabschnitt** *m* KERNTECH *eines Brennelementes* end section; **Endamt** *nt* TELE-KOM terminating exchange; **Endanflug** *m* LUFTTRANS final approach; **Endanflugsbahn** *f* LUFTTRANS final approach path; **Endanflugspunkt** *m* LUFTTRANS final approach fix, final approach point; **Endanode** *f* FERN-SEH final anode; **Endanschlag** *m* FERTIG end stop; **Endanwendung** *f* TEXTIL end use; **Endauflager** *nt* BAU *Architektur* abutment; **Endauslösevorrichtung** *f* KERNTECH final trip assembly; **Endaustastung** *f* FERN-SEH final blanking; **Endbahnhof** *m* EISENBAHN terminal station; **Endbearbeitung** *f* KER & GLAS finishing; **Endbedingung** *f* COMP & DV end condition; **Endbegrenzungsleuchte** *f* KFZTECH end outline marker lamp; **Endbenutzer** *m* TELEKOM end user; **Endbogenstück** *nt* LUFTTRANS edge box member; **Endcode** *m* COMP & DV tail; **Enddeckel** *m* PAPIER end deckle; **Enddruck** *m* MASCHINEN final pressure

Ende: [1] **am ~ herausgezogen** *adj* KER & GLAS drawn out at end

Ende [2] *nt* COMP & DV, PAPIER end; **~ der Blankschmelze** *nt* KER & GLAS seed-free time; **~ ohne Kuppe** *nt* MASCHI-NEN as-rolled end; **~ des Übertragungsblocks** *nt* COMP & DV end-of-transmission block

Ende: [3] **~ werfen** *vi* WASSERTRANS *Tauwerk* throw a line

End-: **Endeinheit** *f* COMP & DV terminal device; **Endeinrichtung** *f* COMP & DV, TELEKOM terminal, terminal equipment

Ende: **Endemarke** *f* FERTIG *Datenverarbeitung* block-mark

End-: **Endflansch** *m* MASCHINEN end flange; **Endformat** *nt* PAPIER trimmed size; **Endgehalt** *m* KERNTECH *von Natururan* tail assay; **Endgerät** *nt* COMP & DV terminal, terminal device, TELEKOM terminal; **Endgeräteanpassung** *f* TELEKOM terminal adaptor; **Endgerätesubadressierung** *f* TELEKOM terminal sub-addressing; **Endgeschwindigkeit** *f* RAUMFAHRT *Raumschiff* all-burnt velocity; **Endglied** *nt* MASCHI-NEN end link

endgültig: **~er Befehl** *m* COMP & DV effective instruction; **~e Tonmischung** *f* AUFNAHME final mix

End-: **Endinstallation** *f* KERNTECH ultimate installation; **Endkeil** *m* KOHLEN end cleat; **Endknoten** *m* KÜNSTL INT *eines Baumes* end node, terminal node, TELEKOM terminating junction; **Endkontrolle** *f* QUAL final inspection; **Endlage** *f* FERTIG *Kunststoffinstallationen* end position, GERÄT *Zeiger* end-point position, KERN-TECH *eines Regel- oder Moderatorstabes* limit of travel; **Endlageneinstellung** *f* KERNTECH final position setting; **Endlager** *nt* ABFALL disposal zone, vitrification process, MASCHINEN end bearing; **Endlagerstätte** *f* UMWELTSCHMUTZ *für radioaktiven Abfall* repository

Endlagerung *f* ABFALL *von Atommüll oder radioaktivem Abfall* final dumping, *von Müll* final storage, ultimate storage, KERNTECH *von Atommüll* ultimate waste disposal; **~ von Abfällen** *f* ABFALL permanent waste

storage; **Endlagerungsstätte** *f* ABFALL disposal zone, vitrification process

End-: **Endleistungsverstärker** *m* FERNSEH output amplifier

endlich [1] *adj* MATH finite

endlich: [2] **~e Reihe** *f* MATH finite series

Endlos- *pref* PAPIER, TEXTIL endless

endlos [1] *adj* PAPIER, TEXTIL endless

endlos: [2] **~er Breitkeilriemen** *m* MASCHINEN endless wide V-belt

Endlos-: **Endlosantrieb** *m* AUFNAHME closed-loop drive; **Endlosfaden** *m* TEXTIL filament; **Endlosfaser** *f* KUNST-STOFF filament, METALL continuous fiber (AmE), continuous fibre (BrE); **Endlosfasermatte** *f* KUNST-STOFF continuous strand mat; **Endloskabel** *nt* KFZTECH endless cable; **Endloskette** *f* KFZTECH, PA-PIER endless chain; **Endlosmagnetbandkassette** *f* AKUSTIK endless magnetic loop cartridge; **Endlos-matte** *f* KUNSTSTOFF continuous strand mat; **Endlospapier** *nt* COMP & DV continuous forms (AmE), continuous stationery (BrE), continuous-feed paper (AmE), fanfold stationery, DRUCK continuous forms (AmE), continuous stationery (BrE), continuous-feed paper (AmE); **Endlospapiereinzug** *m* COMP & DV continuous feed; **Endlosriemen** *m* KFZTECH endless belt; **Endlosschleife** *f* COMP & DV infinite loop; **Endlos-spinnfaden** *m* KER & GLAS continuous filament; **Endlosverfahren** *nt* KER & GLAS continuous-drawing process

End-: **Endmarke** *f* COMP & DV terminator; **Endmaß** *nt* MASCHINEN· end gage (AmE), end gauge (BrE), METROL end measure, gage block (AmE), gauge block (BrE), length bar; **Endmaßvergleichsmesser** *m* METROL gage block comparator (AmE), gauge block comparator (BrE); **Endmast** *m* ELEKTRIZ terminal tower; **Endmontage** *f* KERNTECH final assembly, ultimate installation

Endoenzym *nt* CHEMIE endo-enzyme

Endoskop *nt* PHYS endoscope

Endoskopie *f* KERNTECH endoscopy

Endosperm *nt* LEBENSMITTEL *Nährgewebe im Samen* endosperm

endotherm [1] *adj* KER & GLAS, RAUMFAHRT *Raumschiff* endothermic, THERMOD endothermal, endothermic

endotherm: [2] **~er Prozeß** *m* THERM endothermic process; **~e Reaktion** *f* NICHTFOSS ENERG endothermic reaction

endothermisch [1] *adj* KER & GLAS, RAUMFAHRT *Raumschiff* endothermic, THERMOD endothermal, endothermic

endothermisch: [2] **~er Prozeß** *m* THERM endothermic process; **~e Reaktion** *f* NICHTFOSS ENERG endothermic reaction

End-: **Endpflock** *m* KOHLEN end cleat; **Endplatte** *f* MA-SCHINEN end plate; **Endprodukt** *nt* KOHLEN *Kohle* commercial coal; **Endprüfung** *f* QUAL final inspection; **Endpunkt** *m* COMP & DV exit point, FERNSEH out point; **Endpunktkoordinaten** *f pl* GEOM end-point coordinates; **Endrahmenstück** *nt* VERPACK end frame member; **Endreinigungsvorgang** *m* KERNTECH tail end process; **Endrille** *f* AKUSTIK finishing groove; **Endrippe** *f* LUFT-TRANS end rib; **Endrohr** *nt* KFZTECH tail pipe; **Endrohrverlängerung** *f* KFZTECH tail pipe extension; **Endschalter** *m* ELEKTRIZ limit switch, proximity switch, ELEKTROTECH limit switch, FERTIG depth-control limit switch, KONTROLL end position switch, limit switch, MECHAN limit switch; **Endserienverpackung** *f*

VERPACK end-of-line packaging; **Endspalte** *f* COMP &
DV end column; **Endspeisung** *f* RADIO *Antenne* end
feeding; **Endspiel** *nt* MASCHINEN, MECHAN end play
endspiralig: ~**er Bohrer** *m* FERTIG high-helix drill
End-: **Endstelle** *f* COMP & DV station (BrE); **Endstellung** *f*
GERÄT *Zeiger* end-point position, ultimate position;
Endstück *nt* FERTIG butt, KERNTECH end fitting; **Endstufe** *f* ELEKTROTECH *(PA)*, RADIO *(PA)* power
amplifier *(PA)*, TELEKOM terminating stage; **End-
symbol** *nt* COMP & DV terminal symbol; **Endsystemteil**
nt TELEKOM user agent; **Endtetrode mit Elektronenbündelung** *f* ELEKTRONIK beam power tube;
Endumsetzer *m* ELEKTRONIK *Trägerfrequenz* final
modulator; **Endvakuum** *nt* THERMOD ultimate vacuum; **Endverbraucher** *m* COMP & DV end user;
Endverkehr *m* TELEKOM terminating traffic; **Endvermittlungsstelle** *f (EVS)* TELEKOM terminating
exchange; **Endverstärker** *m* ELEKTRONIK final amplifier, ELEKTROTECH power amplifier; **Endverstärkung** *f*
ELEKTRONIK *Radio* final amplification; **Endverzwei-
ger** *m* TELEKOM block terminal; **Endwert** *m* QUAL
target; **Endzusammenbau** *m* KERNTECH final assembly
energetisch: ~**e Verwertung** *f* ABFALL energy recovery;
~**er Wirkungsgrad** *m* THERMOD energy efficiency
Energie[1] *f (E)* ELEKTRIZ energy, power *(P)*, ELEKTRO-
TECH, KERNTECH, LABOR, MECHAN energy *(E)*, OPTIK
power, PHYS, THERMOD energy *(E)*
Energie:[2] ~ **abschalten** *vi* ELEKTROTECH de-energize
Energie: ~ **aus Abfall** *f* ABFALL residue derived energy; ~
der elektroschwachen Vereinigung *f* TEILPHYS electroweak unification energy; ~ **der großen Vereinigung** *f*
TEILPHYS grand unification energy; **Energieabbau** *m*
KERNTECH energy degradation; **Energieabsorption** *f*
TELEKOM energy absorption; **Energieanschluß** *m*
ELEKTROTECH power supply
energiearm: ~**er Laser** *m* ELEKTRONIK low-energy laser;
~**er Strahl** *m* ELEKTRONIK low-energy beam
Energie: **Energieaustauschreaktion** *f* KERNTECH energy
exchange reaction; **Energiebedarf** *m* THERMOD energy
demand; **Energiebereich** *m* STRAHLPHYS energy
range; **Energiebilanz** *f* WASSERVERSORG energy balance; **Energiedichte** *f* TELEKOM power density;
Energiedichte einer Strahlung *f* STRAHLPHYS energy
density of radiation; **Energiedosis** *f* PHYS, STRAHL-
PHYS absorbed dose of ionizing radiation;
Energieeinheit *f* THERMOD unit of energy; **Energieer-
haltung** *f* PHYS conservation of energy, THERMOD
energy conservation; **Energieersparnis** *f* THERMOD
energy saving; **Energieerzeugung** *f* ELEKTROTECH power generation; **Energieerzeugungsanlage** *f*
ELEKTROTECH power plant; **Energiefluß** *m* PHYS energy fluence; **Energieflußbild** *nt* THERMOD energy flow
chart; **Energieflußdiagramm** *nt* THERMOD energy flow
chart; **Energieflußdichte** *f* KERNTECH *(I)* energy flux
density *(I)*, OPTIK power flux density; **Energieflußrate**
f PHYS energy fluence rate; **Energiegehalt** *m* THERMOD
energy content; **Energiegewinnung** *f* NICHTFOSS
ENERG energy extraction; **Energiegleichgewicht** *nt*
STRÖMPHYS *bei turbulenter Bewegung*, THERMOD
energy balance; **Energiehaushalt** *m* UMWELTSCHMUTZ
energy budget; **Energieinhalt** *m* THERMOD energy content
energie-intensiv *adj* THERMOD *Verfahren, Industrie*
energy-intensive
Energie: **Energiekaskade** *f* STRÖMPHYS energy cascade;

Energiekonverter *m* ELEKTROTECH energy converter;
Energiekrise *f* THERMOD energy crisis; **Energieleitung**
f ELEKTROTECH transmission line; **Energieleitungs-
netz** *nt* ELEKTRIZ transmission line network
energielos *adj* ELEKTRIZ wattless
Energie: **Energielücke** *f* PHYS *Halbleiter* energy gap;
Energiemusterfaktor *m* NICHTFOSS ENERG energy pattern factor; **Energieniveau** *nt* PHYS energy level;
Energiequelle *f* ELEKTRIZ energy source, ELEKTRO-
TECH power source, power supply, source;
Energiereflexionskoeffizient *m* OPTIK power reflection
coefficient
energiereich: ~**es Elektron** *nt* ELEKTRONIK high-energy
electron; ~**es Ion** *nt* ELEKTRONIK high-energy ion; ~**er
Strahl** *m* ELEKTRONIK high-energy beam; ~**es Teilchen**
nt ELEKTRONIK high-energy particle
Energie: **Energieressourcen** *f pl* ABFALL energy resources; **Energierückgewinnung** *f* ABFALL energy recovery,
THERMOD energy recovery, energy regeneration; **Ener-
gierückgewinnungsfaktor** *m* NICHTFOSS ENERG energy
recovery factor; **Energiesparen** *nt* THERMOD energy
saving
energiesparend[1] *adj* THERMOD energy-saving
energiesparend:[2] ~**e Technologie** *f* ABFALL energy-
saving technology
Energie: **Energiespeicher** *m* RAUMFAHRT *Raumschiff*
energy storage device; **Energiespeicherung** *f* ELEK-
TROTECH, THERMOD energy storage;
Energiespeicherung in der Schwachlastzeit *f* KERN-
TECH off-peak energy storage; **Energiespektrum** *nt*
RAUMFAHRT energy spectrum; **Energiestreuung** *f*
RAUMFAHRT *Weltraumfunk* energy dispersal; **Energie-
tal** *nt* KERNTECH energy valley; **Energietechnik** *f*
UMWELTSCHMUTZ energy technology; **Energieträger**
m ELEKTRIZ energy source; **Energietransportkoeffi-
zient** *m* PHYS energy transfer coefficient;
Energieübertragung *f* ELEKTROTECH energy transmission, power transmission, THERMOD energy transfer,
energy transmission; **Energieübertragung durch mechanische Schwingung** *f* WELLPHYS *Körperschall*
energy transfer by vibration; **Energieumformung** *f*
ELEKTRIZ energy transformation; **Energieumsatz** *m*
ERGON energy expenditure, metabolic rate; **Energie-
umwandler** *m* ELEKTROTECH, THERMOD energy
converter; **Energieumwandlung** *f* ELEKTROTECH,
THERMOD energy conversion; **Energieumwandlungs-
koeffizient** *m* KERNTECH mass energy transfer
coefficient
energieunabhängig: ~**er Speicher** *m* COMP & DV nonvolatile memory, permanent memory, permanent
storage
Energie: **Energieverbrauch** *m* ELEKTRIZ power consumption, PHYS, THERMOD energy consumption;
Energieverengung *f* METALL constriction energy;
Energieverlust *m* ELEKTRIZ energy loss, ELEKTROTECH
power loss, PHYS degradation of energy, THERMOD
energy loss; **Energieverlust von Elektronen** *m* STRAHL-
PHYS electron energy loss; **Energieverschwendung** *f*
THERMOD, UMWELTSCHMUTZ waste of energy; **Energieversorgung** *f* EISENBAHN, ELEKTROTECH power
supply, NICHTFOSS ENERG, THERMOD energy supply;
Energieversorgungswagen *m* EISENBAHN power
source car; **Energiewandler** *m* ELEKTROTECH, -
TELEKOM, THERMOD energy converter;
Energiewiedergewinnung *f* THERMOD energy recupe-
ration; **Energiezustand eines Atoms** *m* KERNTECH,

PHYS, STRAHLPHYS atomic state

ENF *abbr (extrem niedrige Frequenz)* RADIO ELF *(extremely low frequency)*

eng:[1] **~e Bohrung** *f* ERDÖL *Bohrtechnik* slim hole; **~e Kopplung** *f* ELEKTROTECH, PHYS tight coupling; **~e Passung** *f* MASCHINEN close fit; **~e Toleranz** *f* MASCHINEN close tolerance

eng:[2] **~er ausschließen** *vt* DRUCK close up, keep in

Engel *m pl* ELEKTRONIK *Radartechnik* clutter filter

Enghalsflasche *f* LABOR narrow-necked bottle

Enghalspackung *f* KER & GLAS narrow neck container

Engländer *m* MASCHINEN coach wrench, shifting spanner (BrE)

Englergrad *m* FERTIG, MASCHINEN Engler degree

englisch: ~e Schreibschrift *f* DRUCK script type

Engpaß *m* MECHAN, TRANS bottleneck

Engschrift *f* KONSTZEICH close-spaced characters, close-spaced lettering

Engspaltschweißen *nt* MECHAN narrow-gap welding

engtoleriert *adj* MASCHINEN close-tolerance

enharmonisch: ~e Noten *f pl* AKUSTIK enharmonic notes

Enol *nt* CHEMIE enol

Enol- *pref* CHEMIE enolic

Enolase *f* CHEMIE enolase

enolisch *adj* CHEMIE enolic

Enolisierung *f* CHEMIE enolization

entartet[1] *adj* ELEKTRONIK, METALL, PHYS degenerate

entartet:[2] **~es Elektronengas** *nt* STRAHLPHYS degenerate electron gas; **~er Halbleiter** *m* ELEKTRONIK degenerate semiconductor

Entartung *f* ELEKTRONIK degeneracy, degeneration, KERNTECH *von Teilchen, Energieniveaus* degradation, PHYS degeneracy, STRAHLPHYS *von Energieniveaus* degeneration

Entbastungsmittel *nt* CHEMIE *Textil, Seide* scouring agent

Entbasung *f* KOHLEN desorption

entbehrlich *adj* RAUMFAHRT *Raumschiff* expendable

Entbituminieren *nt* KOHLEN debituminization

Entblätterungsmittel *nt* CHEMIE defoliant

Entblocken *nt* COMP & DV deblocking

entblocken *vt* COMP & DV deblock

Entblößung *f* METALL denudation

Entbrummspule *f* AUFNAHME, ELEKTROTECH, FERNSEH humbucking coil

Entbündeln *nt* ELEKTRONIK debunching

enteisen *vt* HEIZ & KÄLTE, RAUMFAHRT *Raumschiff* de-ice

Enteisenung *f* ABFALL deferrization, KER & GLAS de-ironing

Enteiser *m* KFZTECH, LUFTTRANS, RAUMFAHRT *Raumschiff* de-icer; **Enteiserhaube** *f* LUFTTRANS de-icer boot, de-icer trunk; **Enteiserleitung** *f* LUFTTRANS de-icing duct; **Enteiserluftauslaß** *m* LUFTTRANS de-icing air outlet; **Enteiserpumpe** *f* LUFTTRANS de-icing pump

Enteisung *f* HEIZ & KÄLTE de-icing, RAUMFAHRT anti-icing, de-icing; **~ des Motors** *f* LUFTTRANS *des Triebwerks* engine de-icing; **Enteisungsflüssigkeit** *f* ANSTRICH de-icing fluid; **Enteisungsluft** *f* LUFTTRANS de-icing air; **Enteisungsstiefel** *m* RAUMFAHRT de-icer boot; **Enteisungssystem** *nt* RAUMFAHRT anti-icing system

Entemulgator *m* LEBENSMITTEL demulsifier

Entenflugzeug *nt* LUFTTRANS canard wing aircraft, tail first configuration aircraft

Enterhaken *m* WASSERTRANS grapple

Entermannschaft *f* WASSERTRANS *Seeräuberei* boarding party

entern *vt* WASSERTRANS board

Entfälschung *f* FERNSEH antialiasing

entfaltbar: ~e Antenne *f* RAUMFAHRT *Weltraumfunk* unfurlable antenna

Entfaltung *f* TELEKOM deconvolution

entfärben *vt* TEXTIL bleach

Entfärber *m* KER & GLAS decolorizer (AmE), decolourizer (BrE)

Entfärbungspulver *nt* TEXTIL bleaching powder

entfeint: ~er Beton *m* BAU no-fines concrete

entfernbar[1] *adj* OPTIK removable

entfernbar:[2] **~es Teil** *nt* ELEKTRIZ removable part

Entfernen[1] *nt* BAU removing, MEERSCHMUTZ removal; **~ von Randbeschnitt** *nt* PAPIER trim removal

Entfernen:[2] **~ von Glastafeln von den Tischen nach dem Schleifen** *phr* KER & GLAS stripping

entfernt[1] *adj* COMP & DV remote

entfernt:[2] **~ aufgestelltes Netzgerät** *nt* ELEKTROTECH remote power supply; **~e Quelle** *f* UMWELTSCHMUTZ distant source

Entfernung *f* EISENBAHN *der Stangenkupplung* removal, ELEKTRONIK, GERÄT range, RADIO distance, TELEKOM, WASSERTRANS *Navigation, Radar, Funk* range; **~ bewegungsunfähiger Lutfahrzeuge** *f* LUFTTRANS *Flughafen* disabled aircraft removal; **~ von der Schallquelle** *f (r)* AKUSTIK distance from source *(r)*; **Entfernungseinstellring** *m* FOTO focusing ring; **Entfernungsmeßeinrichtung** *f* GERÄT, LUFTTRANS DME, distance-measuring equipment; **Entfernungsmessen mit einer Kette** *nt* BAU chaining; **Entfernungsmesser** *m* BAU odometer, FOTO rangefinder, WASSERTRANS RF, range finder, *Navigation* distance finder; **Entfernungsmeßgerät** *nt* GERÄT RF, range finder; **Entfernungsmessung** *f* ELEKTRONIK range finding, RAUMFAHRT ranging; **Entfernungsring** *m* FOTO focusing ring, WASSERTRANS *Radar* calibration ring; **Entfernungsskale** *f* FOTO distance scale; **Entfernungstaste** *f (Taste Entf)* COMP & DV delete key *(DEL key)*

Entfetten *nt* MASCHINEN, MECHAN degreasing, TEXTIL scouring

entfetten *vt* BAU, ELEKTRIZ, MASCHINEN, MECHAN degrease, TEXTIL *Wolle* scour

Entfetter *m* ANSTRICH degreaser

Entfettung *f* BAU, KER & GLAS degreasing; **Entfettungsbehälter** *m* LEBENSMITTEL degreasing tank; **Entfettungseinrichtung** *f* ELEKTRIZ degreaser; **Entfettungsmittel** *nt* MECHAN degreasing agent, VERPACK degreasing compound

entfeuchten *vt* HEIZ & KÄLTE dehumidify

Entfeuchter *m* CHEMIE, CHEMTECH desiccator, HEIZ & KÄLTE dehydrator, KERNTECH dehumidifier

Entfeuchtung *f* HEIZ & KÄLTE dehumidification; **Entfeuchtungsgerät** *nt* HEIZ & KÄLTE dehumidifier; **Entfeuchtungsmittel** *nt* LEBENSMITTEL desiccant

entflammbar[1] *adj* KUNSTSTOFF, SICHERHEIT flammable; **nicht ~** *adj* CHEMIE nonflammable, VERPACK flameproof, noninflammable, WERKPRÜF nonflammable

entflammbar:[2] **~er Dampf** *m* SICHERHEIT flammable vapor (AmE), flammable vapour (BrE); **~e Flüssigkeit** *f* SICHERHEIT flammable liquid; **nicht ~e Kleidung** *f* SICHERHEIT flameproof clothing; **~er Werkstoff** *m* SICHERHEIT flammable material

Entflammbarkeit *f* CHEMIE ignitability, SICHERHEIT

flammability
entflammen vt THERMOD fire up
Entflammungspunkt m HEIZ & KÄLTE flash point, THERMOD kindling point
Entflechtung f ELEKTRIZ *Leiterplatte* layout
Entflocken nt CHEMIE deflocculation
Entformen nt KER & GLAS *Herausnehmen des Gegenstands aus Form* take-out, KUNSTSTOFF demolding (AmE), demoulding (BrE); **~ mit Einstechen** nt KER & GLAS take-out with push-up
Entformer m KER & GLAS *Vorrichtung zum Entformen* take-out
Entformungsmittel nt KUNSTSTOFF mold release agent (AmE), mould release agent (BrE), release agent
Entformungsvorrichtung f KUNSTSTOFF extractor
entfrieren vi BAU freeze
Entfrittung f METALL decohesion
Entfrosten nt HEIZ & KÄLTE, MASCHINEN defrosting
entfrosten vt HEIZ & KÄLTE de-ice, defrost
Entfroster m KFZTECH demister, *Zubehör* defroster
Entfrostung f HEIZ & KÄLTE de-icing
entführen vt LUFTTRANS *Flugzeug* hijack, skyjack
Entgasen nt CHEMTECH, ELEKTRONIK *Elektronenröhre*, KUNSTSTOFF degassing
entgasen vt ABFALL degasify, CHEMTECH, ELEKTRONIK *Elektronenröhre* degas, THERMOD free from gas
Entgaser m ERDÖL deaerator, HEIZ & KÄLTE degasser
entgast[1] adj THERMOD free from gas
entgast:[2] **~es Brennelement** nt KERNTECH vented fuel assembly; **~er Brennstab** m KERNTECH vented fuel rod; **~es Öl** nt ERDÖL dead oil
Entgasung f ABFALL degassing, *Deponie* gas drainage, *einer Deponie* degasification; **Entgasungsindex** m KER & GLAS outgassing index
entgegengerichtet: ~er Gradient m STRÖMPHYS adverse gradient
entgegengesetzt adj MATH inverse
entgegennehmen vt TELEKOM *Anruf* answer
entgegenwirkend: ~es Feld nt ELEKTRIZ opposing field
Entgiftung f KERNTECH decontamination, depoisoning, STRAHLPHYS *Kernspaltprodukte* decontamination
entglasen vt KER & GLAS devitrify
Entglasung f KER & GLAS devitrification; **Entglasungssteinchen** nt KER & GLAS devitrification stone
entgleisen vt EISENBAHN derail
Entgleisung f EISENBAHN derailment; **Entgleisungsweichen** f pl EISENBAHN catch points, derailing points (BrE), derailing switch (AmE)
Entgrat- und Abfasmaschine f FERTIG deburring and chamfering machine
Entgraten nt KER & GLAS, MASCHINEN deburring
entgraten vt FERTIG deburr, *Kunststoffinstallationen* deburr, *Plaste* deflash, KUNSTSTOFF deflash, MASCHINEN, MECHAN deburr
Entgratwerkzeug nt MASCHINEN burr remover
Enthacken nt RAUMFAHRT *Weltraumfunk* descrambling
Enthacker m RAUMFAHRT descrambler
Enthalpie f *(H)* HEIZ & KÄLTE, KOHLEN, MECHAN, NICHTFOSS ENERG, PHYS, RAUMFAHRT, THERMOD enthalpy *(H)*
enthalten vt BAU include
Enthärten nt METALL softening
Enthärter m TEXTIL *Wasser* softener
enthärtet: ~es Wasser nt WASSERVERSORG soft water
Enthärtung: Enthärtungsanlage f FERTIG *Kunststoffinstallationen* water-softening plant; **Enthärtungsmittel**

nt TEXTIL *Wasser* softening agent
entharzen vt FERTIG deresinify
Enthitzer m HEIZ & KÄLTE desuperheater
Enthülsen nt KERNTECH *von Brennelementen* decanning, decladding
enthülsen vt LEBENSMITTEL husk
enthülst: ~es Brennelement nt KERNTECH uncanned fuel element
entionisiert: ~es Wasser nt ELEKTRIZ de-ionized water
Entionisierungsgitter nt ELEKTRONIK de-ionizing grid
Entionisierungsmittel nt LABOR *Wasser* de-ionizer
Entität f KÜNSTL INT entity
entkalken vt CHEMIE decalcify
Entkarbonisieren nt CHEMIE decarbonization
entkarbonisieren vt CHEMIE, KOHLEN decarbonate
entkeimt adj LEBENSMITTEL sterilized
entkernen vt LEBENSMITTEL *Früchte* pit (AmE), stone (BrE)
Entkerner m ERDÖL *Bohrtechnik* corer
entkoffeiniert adj LEBENSMITTEL decaffeinated
entkohlen vt FERTIG decarburize, THERMOD decarbonize
entkohlt[1] adj FERTIG *Randzone* soft
entkohlt:[2] **~e Schicht** f FERTIG bark
Entkohlung f FERTIG decarburization, THERMOD decarbonization
entkomprimieren vt COMP & DV *data* unpack
entkoppelt[1] adj COMP & DV decoupled
entkoppelt:[2] **~e Mehrgrößenregelung** f REGELUNG noninteracting control
Entkoppelungskreis m LUFTTRANS antiresonant circuit
Entkopplung f ELEKTROTECH, RADIO, RAUMFAHRT *Weltraumfunk*, TELEKOM decoupling; **Entkopplungsfilter** nt ELEKTRONIK decoupling filter; **Entkopplungskondensator** m ELEKTRIZ, ELEKTROTECH decoupling capacitor, decoupling condensor
Entkorkmaschine f VERPACK uncorking machine
entkrusten vt MECHAN descale
Entkupplungsstange f EISENBAHN shunter's pole
Entlade- pref LUFTTRANS, RAUMFAHRT discharge; **Entladebunker** m ABFALL unloading hopper; **Entladehaken** m LUFTTRANS cargo release hook; **Entladekondensator** m ELEKTROTECH discharge capacitor; **Entladekreis** m ELEKTROTECH discharge circuit
Entladen nt COMP & DV unloading, TRANS unstuffing
entladen vt BAU dump, COMP & DV unload, MASCHINEN discharge, TRANS unstuff
Entladeregler m RAUMFAHRT *Raumschiff* discharge regulator; **Entladeschaltung** f ELEKTROTECH discharge circuit; **Entladestab** m KERNTECH unloading rod; **Entladestation** f LUFTTRANS discharging station; **Entladestrom** m ELEKTROTECH discharge current
Entladung f ELEKTRIZ, ELEKTROTECH discharge, METALL unloading, PHYS unloading, *elektrische* discharge, TELEKOM discharge, TRANS unloading; **Entladungskanal** m KERNTECH transfer canal; **Entladungskreis** m ELEKTROTECH discharge circuit; **Entladungslampe** f ELEKTROTECH discharge lamp; **Entladungsmikrofon** nt AUFNAHME discharge microphone; **Entladungsröhre** f ELEKTRONIK *Glimmlampe*, PHYS discharge tube; **Entladungsspitzenspannung** f ELEKTRIZ peak arc voltage; **Entladungsstrom** m ELEKTRIZ discharge current; **Entladungswiderstand** m ELEKTRIZ *Bauelement* discharge resistor, *physikalische Größe* discharge resistance, RADIO bleeder resistance

entlanggleiten *vi* BAU ride

Entlassungsbrunnen *m* WASSERVERSORG relief well

Entlasten *nt* BAU removing

entlasten *vt* BAU ease

entlastend: ~es Wasser *nt* UMWELTSCHMUTZ deballasting water

entlastet[1] *adj* FERTIG *Dichtung* pressure-balanced

entlastet:[2] **~es Querruder** *nt* LUFTTRANS balanced aileron; **~er Schieber** *m* MASCHINEN balanced slide valve

Entlastung *f* MASCHINEN relief, PHYS unloading; **Entlastungsanlage** *f* BAU spillway; **Entlastungsbogen** *m* BAU safety arch, *Mauerwerk* discharging arch; **Entlastungsgerinne** *nt* WASSERVERSORG discharge flume; **Entlastungskanal** *m* HYDRAUL *Hydraulik* spillway canal; **Entlastungsöffnung** *f* MECHAN lightening hole; **Entlastungsschleuse** *f* WASSERVERSORG discharge sluice; **Entlastungsstrecke** *f* EISENBAHN bypass line; **Entlastungsventil** *nt* HEIZ & KÄLTE relief valve, MASCHINEN unloading valve, MECHAN, NICHTFOSS ENERG relief valve; **Entlastungswehr** *nt* WASSERVERSORG spillway, waste weir; **Entlastungszug** *m* EISENBAHN relief train

Entlaufen *nt* EISENBAHN *von Wagen* runaway

Entlaugen *nt* FERTIG washing

entlaugen *vt* FERTIG wash

Entleeren *nt* FERTIG *Kunststoffinstallationen* drainage

entleeren *vt* BAU drain, ELEKTRONIK *Röhren*, WASSERTRANS *Schiff* evacuate, WASSERVERSORG blow off

Entleerung *f* ERDÖL drain, WASSERVERSORG depletion; **Entleerungshahn** *m* ERDÖL drain tap

Entleerventil *nt* NICHTFOSS ENERG purging valve

entlieschen *vt* LEBENSMITTEL *Mais* husk

Entlöten *nt* MASCHINEN unsoldering

entlöten *vt* MASCHINEN unsolder

Entlüften *nt* ERDÖL bleeding, HEIZ & KÄLTE, KERNTECH venting

entlüften *vt* BAU vent, FERTIG *Luft* bleed, HEIZ & KÄLTE vent, MASCHINEN *Luft* bleed, vent

Entlüfter *m* ERDÖL air exhaust, HEIZ & KÄLTE air bleeder, vent, KFZTECH breather, *Kurbelgehäuse des Motors* breather, MECHAN exhaust pump; **Entlüfterstutzen** *m* BAU vent plug

Entlüftung *f* BAU airing, ERDÖL air vent, FERTIG air drain, air escape, HEIZ & KÄLTE ventilation, KER & GLAS vent, KERNTECH air drain, vent, KFZTECH bleeding, ventilation, KUNSTSTOFF, LABOR vent, MASCHINEN bleeding, vent, venting, ventilation, MECHAN vent, THERMOD, WASSERTRANS ventilation; **Entlüftungsanlage** *f* LEBENSMITTEL exhauster; **Entlüftungsarmatur** *f* ERDÖL bleed valve; **Entlüftungsbehälter** *m* LEBENSMITTEL exhaustion box; **Entlüftungsbohrung** *f* FERTIG *Ziehwerkzeug* air vent; **Entlüftungshahn** *m* FERTIG air drain petcock; **Entlüftungshaubenventil** *nt* LUFTTRANS air vent valve; **Entlüftungsklappe** *f* BAU vent cap, KERNTECH air vent; **Entlüftungsleitung** *f* MECHAN exhaust line; **Entlüftungsöffnung** *f* BAU vent, FERTIG *Formen* whistler, HEIZ & KÄLTE vent, vent port, KERNTECH, KUNSTSTOFF, LABOR vent, MASCHINEN vent, vent hole; **Entlüftungsrohr** *nt* BAU, HEIZ & KÄLTE, KER & GLAS, KERNTECH vent pipe, KFZTECH breather, KUNSTSTOFF, LABOR, MASCHINEN, MECHAN vent pipe, RAUMFAHRT standpipe; **Entlüftungsschraube** *f* KFZTECH, MASCHINEN bleeder screw; **Entlüftungsstopfen** *m* MASCHINEN bleed plug; **Entlüftungsventil** *nt* FERTIG air drain valve, air relief valve, breather, KERNTECH air drain valve,

KFZTECH bleed valve, LEBENSMITTEL air bleed valve, LUFTTRANS air bleed valve, *für luftführende Leitungen* vent valve, MASCHINEN air vent valve, bleed valve

Entmagnetisieren *nt* COMP & DV, FERNSEH, MASCHINEN degaussing

entmagnetisieren *vti* AUFNAHME, COMP & DV degauss, FERNSEH degauss, demagnetize, KOHLEN demagnetize, MASCHINEN degauss, demagnetize, PHYS, TELEKOM demagnetize

Entmagnetisierer *m* AUFNAHME degausser

Entmagnetisiergerät *nt* FERNSEH degausser, MASCHINEN demagnetizer

Entmagnetisierspule *f* FERNSEH degaussing coil

Entmagnetisierung *f* AUFNAHME demagnetization, COMP & DV degaussing, ELEKTRIZ demagnetization, FERNSEH degaussing, demagnetization, MASCHINEN degaussing, MECHAN, PHYS demagnetization; **Entmagnetisierungsfeld** *nt* ELEKTRIZ, PHYS demagnetizing field; **Entmagnetisierungsgerät** *nt* COMP & DV degausser; **Entmagnetisierungsverlust** *m* AUFNAHME demagnetization loss

entmasten *vt* WASSERTRANS *Schiff* dismast

entmineralisieren *vt* CHEMTECH demineralize

Entmineralisierung *f* CHEMTECH demineralization; **Entmineralisierungsanlage** *f* KERNTECH demineralizing plant

Entmischen *nt* BAU *Frischbeton* settlement, KERNTECH *von Legierungen*, KUNSTSTOFF segregation

Entmischungseffekt *m* CHEMTECH *Phasen oder Gemische* separation effect

Entmischungsvorgang *m* CHEMTECH separation process

Entnahme *f* MASCHINEN discharge, WASSERVERSORG intake; **~ von Wasser** *f* WASSERVERSORG tapping; **Entnahmegerät** *nt* ABFALL extractor; **Entnahmematerial** *nt* BAU borrow; **Entnahmestelle** *f* BAU borrow pit; **Entnahmeversuch** *m* WASSERVERSORG pumping test

Entnebeler *m* LUFTTRANS demister

Entnebelungsventilator *m* LUFTTRANS defogging fan

entnehmen *vt* ELEKTRIZ abstract, PAPIER pick

Entnickelung *f* FERTIG denickelfication

Entölen *nt* ABFALL oil removal, oil separation

entölen *vt* BAU, ELEKTRIZ, MASCHINEN, MECHAN degrease

Entölung *f* BAU degreasing

entpacken *vt* COMP & DV *Daten* unpack

entpaketieren *vt* COMP & DV unpack

Entpalettisiermaschine *f* VERPACK depalletizer

Entphosphoren *nt* CHEMIE dephosphorization

Entphosphorungsverfahren *nt* METALL dephosphorizing process

Entpolymerisation *f* VERPACK depolymerization

Entrahmungszentrifuge *f* LEBENSMITTEL cream separator

entregen *vi* PHYS de-energize

Entriegeln *nt* COMP & DV unlocking

Entriegelung *f* KERNTECH unlatching; **~ der Ladung** *f* LUFTTRANS *Flugwesen* load release

Entriegelungs- *pref* COMP & DV, KONTROLL nonlocking; **Entriegelungstaste** *f* KONTROLL unlock key

Entrinden *nt* PAPIER barking

Entrindungstrommel *f* PAPIER barking drum

Entropie *f* COMP & DV, FERTIG, MECHAN, NICHTFOSS ENERG, PHYS, TELEKOM, THERMOD entropy; **Entropiecode** *m* TELEKOM variable-length code; **Entropiefluß** *m* THERMOD entropic flux

Entrosten *nt* MASCHINEN derusting

Entsalzen *nt* CHEMTECH desalination, desalinization, desalting

entsalzen *vt* CHEMTECH desalinate, desalinize, desalt, WASSERVERSORG desalinate, desalinize

Entsalzung *f* CHEMTECH desalination, desalinization, *Hydrochemie* demineralizing, FERTIG desalinization, *Kunststoffinstallationen* desalination, MASCHINEN desalting, WASSERVERSORG desalination, desalinization; **Entsalzungsanlage** *f* BAU, CHEMTECH desalination plant, desalinization plant, WASSERVERSORG desalination plant, salt water plant; **Entsalzungsreaktor** *m* KERNTECH desalination reactor; **Entsalzungsverfahren** *nt* ABFALL *Abfälle werden so behandelt, daß sie wie Kies oder Sand abgelagert werden* mineralization technique

Entsander *m* ERDÖL *Bohrtechnik* desander

entsättigen *vt* FERNSEH desaturate

entsättigt: ~e Farben *f pl* FERNSEH desaturated colors (AmE), desaturated colours (BrE)

Entsäuerung *f* CHEMIE *Ölraffination* neutralization

entschädigen *vt* SICHERHEIT compensate, *für erlittene Verletzungen* compensate

Entschädigung *f* SICHERHEIT compensation; **~ für Industrieverletzungen** *f* SICHERHEIT industrial injury benefit

entschalen *vt* BAU dismantle

Entschärfung: **~ von Hand** *f* RAUMFAHRT *Raumschiff* manual disarming

Entschäumen *nt* FERTIG scumming, skimming

entschäumen *vt* FERTIG scum, skim

Entschäumer *m* LEBENSMITTEL defoaming agent, PAPIER defoamer

Entscheidung *f* COMP & DV decision; **Entscheidungsbaum** *m* COMP & DV decision tree; **Entscheidungsgehalt** *m* COMP & DV decision content; **Entscheidungsgeschwindigkeit** *f* LUFTTRANS decision speed; **Entscheidungsgraph** *m* KÜNSTL INT decision graph; **Entscheidungshilfesystem** *nt* KÜNSTL INT decision-support system; **Entscheidungshöhe** *f* LUFTTRANS decision height; **Entscheidungssymbol** *nt* COMP & DV decision box; **Entscheidungstabelle** *f* COMP & DV, KÜNSTL INT decision table

entscheidungsunterstützend: **~es System** *nt* KÜNSTL INT decision-support system

Entschieferung *f* ERDÖL deslating

entschlammen *vt* KOHLEN deslurry, WASSERVERSORG scour

Entschlammer *m* ERDÖL desilter

Entschlämmsieb *nt* KOHLEN depulping screen, desliming screen

Entschlämmung *f* KOHLEN deslurrying

Entschleimung *f* LEBENSMITTEL degumming

Entschlichten *nt* TEXTIL desizing

entschlichten *vt* TEXTIL desize

Entschlichtung *f* KER & GLAS, TEXTIL desizing

entschlüsseln *vt* COMP & DV decode, ELEKTRONIK decipher, decrypt, FERNSEH unscramble

Entschlüsselung *f* COMP & DV decoding, decryption, ELEKTRONIK deciphering, FERNSEH unscrambler, RAUMFAHRT *Weltraumfunk* decoding; **Entschlüsselungsvorlage** *f* RAUMFAHRT *Weltraumfunk* filter mask

Entschrottung *f* ABFALL scrap metal separation

Entschwärzen: **~ von Schlamm** *nt* ABFALL de-inking

Entschwefelung *f* KOHLEN, UMWELTSCHMUTZ desulfurization (AmE), desulphurization (BrE)

Entschweißen *nt* TEXTIL *Wolle* scouring

entseuchen *vt* KERNTECH decontaminate, SICHERHEIT decontaminate, disinfest

Entseuchung *f* KERNTECH, SICHERHEIT decontamination; **Entseuchungsgrad** *m* KERNTECH degree of decontamination

entsilbern *vt* METALL desilver

Entsilberung *f* METALL desilverization

Entsorgung *f* ABFALL, WASSERVERSORG disposal; **~ von Kernreaktoren** *f* KERNTECH nuclear reactor poison removal; **Entsorgungsanlage an Land** *f* MEERSCHMUTZ shore reception facility; **Entsorgungslogistik** *f* UMWELTSCHMUTZ logistics of disposal; **Entsorgungstank** *m* RAUMFAHRT *Raumschiff* disposal tank; **Entsorgungsweg** *m* ABFALL disposal route

entspannen[1] *vt* TEXTIL relax

entspannen[2] *vi* HYDRAUL *Dampf* expand, THERMOD relieve stress

entspannt: **~e Faser** *f* TEXTIL relaxed fiber (AmE), relaxed fibre (BrE); **~e Luft** *f* HEIZ & KÄLTE expanded air

Entspannung *f* HYDRAUL *Dampf* expansion, KER & GLAS stress relaxation, METALL relaxation, WERKPRÜF *mechanisch* stress relief; **Entspannungsglühen** *nt* THERMOD stress-relieving anneal; **Entspannungsmittel** *nt* ANSTRICH *Wasser* surfactant; **Entspannungsunterkühlung** *f* KERNTECH flash subcooling, flash undercooling; **Entspannungsventil** *nt* HEIZ & KÄLTE, HYDRAUL expansion valve; **Entspannungsverdampfung** *f* KERNTECH flash evaporation, THERMOD, WASSERVERSORG flash distillation; **Entspannungszeit** *f* METALL relaxation time; **Entspannungszentrum** *nt* METALL relaxation center (AmE), relaxation centre (BrE)

entspelzen *vt* LEBENSMITTEL *Reis* husk

Entsperren *nt* COMP & DV unlocking

entspiegelt[1] *adj* KER & GLAS bloomed

entspiegelt:[2] **~es Glas** *nt* KER & GLAS coated glass, nonreflecting glass

Entspiegelung *f* FOTO blooming

entsprechend: **~e Lufttüchtigkeitsanforderung** *f* LUFTTRANS appropriate airworthiness requirement

entstanden: **~e Helligkeit** *f* STRAHLPHYS developed luminosity

entstauben *vt* KOHLEN dedust

Entstauber *m* ABFALL dust separator, CHEMTECH, KOHLEN dust collector

Entstaubung: **Entstaubungsanlage** *f* KUNSTSTOFF dust collector; **Entstaubungsgerät** *nt* BAU dedusting unit; **Entstaubungssystem** *nt* VERPACK dust removal system

entstearinisieren *vt* CHEMIE winterize

Entstehung *f* PAPIER formation

Entstipper *m* PAPIER deflaker

Entstördrossel *f* ELEKTRIZ suppressor choke

entstörend *adj* ELEKTRIZ anti-interference

Entstörer *m* ELEKTRIZ, ELEKTRONIK, ELEKTROTECH, TELEKOM suppressor

Entstörkondensator *m* ELEKTRIZ decoupling capacitor, decoupling condenser, suppressor capacitor, ELEKTROTECH *BrE* decoupling capacitor, decoupling condenser

Entstörung *f* ELEKTRONIK interference rejection, RADIO interference elimination, TELEKOM fault clearance

Entstörvorrichtung *f* ELEKTRIZ, ELEKTRONIK, ELEKTROTECH, TELEKOM suppressor

Enttonung *f* ERDÖL *Bohrtechnik* deslating

Enttrichtern *nt* FERTIG spruing

enttrichtern vt FERTIG *Gießen* sprue

Enttrübung f WASSERTRANS *Radar* anticlutter control

Entwässerer m KERNTECH dephlegmator

Entwässern nt TEXTIL dewatering

entwässern vt BAU drain, FERTIG, HEIZ & KÄLTE dehydrate, HYDRAUL *Pumpe* dewater, PAPIER drain, TEXTIL dewater, WASSERVERSORG drain

entwässert[1] adj CHEMIE anhydrous, dehydrated, ERDÖL anhydrous

entwässert:[2] **~er Abfall** m ABFALL, KERNTECH dewatered waste; **~er Schlamm** m ABFALL dewatered sludge

Entwässerung f BAU dewatering, CHEMIE dehydration, ERDÖL *Gasförderung* water knock-out, KOHLEN drain, MASCHINEN, PAPIER drainage, WASSERVERSORG drainage, draining; **Entwässerungsbauwerk** nt BAU drainage structure; **Entwässerungsgefällestufe** f LUFTTRANS drainage terrace; **Entwässerungsgerinne** nt BAU drainage channel; **Entwässerungsgraben** m BAU drain, drainage channel, WASSERVERSORG drainage ditch; **Entwässerungsgraben mit Böschung** m WASSERVERSORG berm ditch; **Entwässerungshahn** m BAU drip cock; **Entwässerungskanal** m NICHTFOSS ENERG dike (AmE), dyke (BrE), WASSERVERSORG drainage channel, sewer; **Entwässerungsloch** nt BAU weephole; **Entwässerungsmittel** nt CHEMTECH, HEIZ & KÄLTE dehydrator; **Entwässerungspresse** f PAPIER dewatering press; **Entwässerungspumpe** f WASSERVERSORG drainage pump, draining engine, draining pump; **Entwässerungsrohr** nt BAU drain; **Entwässerungsschicht** f ABFALL *einer Deponie* drainage layer; **Entwässerungssieb** nt KOHLEN draining screen; **Entwässerungsstollen** m WASSERVERSORG water adit; **Entwässerungsventil** nt EISENBAHN, MASCHINEN, WASSERTRANS drain valve; **Entwässerungsvorrichtung** f WASSERTRANS drain; **Entwässerungswalze** f PAPIER dewatering roll

Entweichen nt ELEKTROTECH leakage; **~ durch Leck** nt SICHERHEIT leakage

Entweichgeschwindigkeit f PHYS escape velocity

Entwerfen nt TEXTIL styling

entwerfen vt MECHAN design, TEXTIL style

entwickeln vt ANSTRICH, BAU, MASCHINEN develop

entwickelt: ~es Bild nt FOTO developed picture

Entwickler m ANSTRICH developer, FERTIG *Schweißen* generator, FOTO developer; **Entwicklerflüssigkeit** f FOTO developer; **Entwicklerrahmen** m FOTO tray; **Entwicklerschale** f FOTO tray; **Entwicklerzange** f FOTO print tongs

Entwicklung f BAU development, FOTO processing MASCHINEN development, PHYS evolution; **Entwicklungsbad** nt FOTO developing bath; **Entwicklungsbohrung** f ERDÖL development well, extension well; **Entwicklungsklammer** f FOTO developing clip; **Entwicklungsmaschine** f FOTO processing machine; **Entwicklungsrahmen** m FOTO developing frame; **Entwicklungsspirale** f FOTO developing spiral; **Entwicklungstank** m FOTO developing tank; **Entwicklungstankthermometer** nt FOTO developing tank thermometer; **Entwicklungstrommel** f FOTO processing drum; **Entwicklungswerkzeug** nt KÜNSTL INT development tool; **Entwicklungszange** f FOTO developing tongs

Entwurf m COMP & DV design, layout, HEIZ & KÄLTE design; **Entwurfbüro** nt BAU design office

Entwürfeln nt TELEKOM descrambling

entwürfeln vt TELEKOM descramble

Entwürfler m TELEKOM descrambler

Entwurf: Entwurfsautomatisierung f COMP & DV design automation; **Entwurfshandbuch** nt TELEKOM designer handbook; **Entwurfsprogramm** nt COMP & DV design aid; **Entwurfsprüfung** f QUAL design review; **Entwurfszeichnung** f HEIZ & KÄLTE draft drawing, KONSTZEICH preliminary drawing

Entzerrer m AUFNAHME equalizer, COMP & DV equalizer, repeater, ELEKTRONIK equalizer, ELEKTROTECH balancer, compensator, TELEKOM equalizer; **~ mit Vorabfühlung** m AUFNAHME presence equalizer; **Entzerrerschaltung** f TELEKOM equalizer circuit

Entzerrung f AKUSTIK de-emphasis, equalization, AUFNAHME, COMP & DV, ELEKTRONIK equalization, FERTIG *Meßgerät* correction, TELEKOM equalization; **Entzerrungskreis** m LUFTTRANS antiresonant circuit; **Entzerrungsschaltung** f ELEKTROTECH balancing network

entzinken vt CHEMIE dezincify

Entzinkung f FERTIG dezincification

Entzinnen nt FERTIG, METALL detinning

Entzinnung f ABFALL detinning

entzündbar adj CHEMIE, FERTIG, THERMOD combustible

Entzünden nt KUNSTSTOFF ignition

entzünden vt UMWELTSCHMUTZ ignite

Entzunderer m METALL descaler

Entzundern nt FERTIG descaling, scouring

entzundern vt FERTIG descale, scour, MECHAN descale

Entzündlichkeit f CHEMIE ignitability, THERMOD combustibility

Entzündungsexperiment nt KERNTECH ignition experiment

Entzündungspunkt m THERMOD flash point

Entzündungstemperatur f THERMOD inflammation point, inflammation temperature

Enveloppe f MECHAN envelope curve

Enzianblau nt STRÖMPHYS *Strömungsvisualisierung* gentian violet

Enzym nt LEBENSMITTEL enzyme; **Enzyminhibitor** m LEBENSMITTEL anti-enzyme

EOB abbr (*Blockende*) COMP & DV EOB (*end of block*)

EOD abbr (*Datenende*) COMP & DV EOD (*end of data*)

EOF abbr (*Dateiende*) COMP & DV EOF (*end of file*)

E-Ofen m FERTIG electric furnace

EOM abbr (*Nachrichtenende*) COMP & DV EOM (*end of message*)

Eosin nt CHEMIE eosin, tetrabromofluorosceine

EOT abbr (*Bandende*) COMP & DV EOT (*end of tape*)

Eötvös-Gravitationswaage f PHYS Eotvos balance

EP abbr (*Höchstdruck*) MASCHINEN EP (*extreme pressure*)

Ephedrin nt CHEMIE ephedrine

Ephemeriden f pl RAUMFAHRT ephemerides

Epichlorhydrin nt CHEMIE epichlorhydrin

Epidiaskop nt FOTO epidiascope

Epikoprostanol nt CHEMIE epicoprostanol

Epimer nt CHEMIE epimer

Epimerisierung f CHEMIE epimerization

EPIRB abbr (*Satellitennetzwerk zur Ortung von Schiffen in Seenot*) WASSERTRANS *Funk* EPIRB (*emergency position-indicating radio beacon*)

epitaktisch[1] adj ELEKTRONIK epitactic

epitaktisch:[2] **~e Ablagerung** f ELEKTRONIK epitaxial diffusion-junction transistor; **~es Abscheiden aus Dampfphase** nt CHEMTECH vapor phase epitaxy (AmE), vapour phase epitaxy (BrE)

Epitaxial- *pref* ELEKTRONIK, METALL, TELEKOM epitaxial

epitaxial: ~**er Siliziumplanartransistor** *m* ELEKTRONIK silicon epitaxial planar transistor

Epitaxial-: **Epitaxialplanartransistor** *m* ELEKTRONIK epitaxial diffusion-junction transistor; **Epitaxialreaktor** *m* ELEKTRONIK epitaxy reactor; **Epitaxialschicht** *f* ELEKTRONIK, TELEKOM epitaxial layer; **Epitaxialtransistor** *m* ELEKTRONIK epitaxial transistor; **Epitaxialversetzung** *f* METALL epitaxial dislocation; **Epitaxialwafer** *m* ELEKTRONIK epitaxial wafer

Epitaxie *f* ELEKTRONIK *Aufwachstechnik*, METALL, STRAHLPHYS epitaxy

epitaxisch *adj* ELEKTRONIK epitactic

Epitrochoide *f* GEOM epitrochoid

Epizentrum *nt* PHYS epicenter (AmE), epicentre (BrE)

epizyklisch *adj* FERTIG epicycloidal

epizykloid *adj* GEOM epicycloidal; **epizykloidal** *adj* MECHAN epicycloidal

Epizykloide *f* FERTIG, GEOM epicycloid

epizykloidisch *adj* MASCHINEN epicycloidal

EPM *abbr* *(Äquivalent je Million)* UMWELTSCHMUTZ EPM *(equivalent per million)*

EPNS *abbr* *(versilberte Gegenstände)* METALL EPNS *(electroplated nickel silver)*

Epoxidharz *nt* BAU, CHEMIE, ELEKTRIZ, FERTIG *Kunststoffinstallationen*, KUNSTSTOFF, VERPACK epoxy resin

epoxidieren *vt* CHEMIE peroxidize

epoxidiert: ~**es Öl** *nt* KUNSTSTOFF epoxidized oil

Epoxidmatrix *f* RAUMFAHRT *Raumschiff* epoxy matrix

Epoxy- *pref* BAU, CHEMIE, ELEKTRIZ, FERTIG, KUNSTSTOFF, TELEKOM, VERPACK epoxy; **Epoxydharz** *nt* BAU, ELEKTRIZ, FERTIG *Kunststoffinstallationen*, KUNSTSTOFF, VERPACK epoxy resin; **Epoxydpolster** *nt* TELEKOM epoxy buffer

EPROM *abbr* *(löschbarer programmierbarer Lesespeicher)* COMP & DV, RADIO EPROM *(erasable programmable read-only memory)*

EP-Schmierstoff *m* MASCHINEN EP lubricant

ε *abbr* HYDRAUL *(kinematische Wirbelzähigkeit)* ε *(kinematic eddy viscosity)*, PHYS *(durchschnittliche kinetische Molekularenergie)* ε *(average molecular kinetic energy)*

Equalizer *m* ELEKTRONIK, FERNSEH equalizer; **Equalizerverstärker** *m* FERNSEH equalizing amplifier

Equilenin *nt* CHEMIE equilenin

Er *(Erbium)* CHEMIE Er *(erbium)*

Erbeulen *nt* MECHAN buckling

Erbium *nt* *(Er)* CHEMIE erbium *(Er)*

erblindet *adj* KER & GLAS struck

Erbsenkette *f* MASCHINEN beaded chain

Erbskohle *f* KOHLEN pea coal, smalls

Erdanschluß *m* ELEKTRIZ earth (BrE), ground (AmE), earth connection (BrE), ground connection (AmE), ELEKTROTECH earth terminal (BrE), ground terminal (AmE)

Erdanziehungskraft *f* PHYS gravitation

Erdanziehungspotential *nt* PHYS gravitational potential

Erdarbeit *f* BAU digging

Erdaufschüttung *f* BAU earth fill

Erdbau *m* BAU earthwork; **Erdbauarbeiten** *f pl* BAU earthwork; **Erdbaumaschinen** *f pl* BAU earthworking machinery

Erdbeben *nt* BAU earthquake; **Erdbebenkunde** *f* PHYS seismology; **Erdbebenmesser** *m* BAU seismograph; **Erdbebenregistriergerät** *m* PHYS seismograph

erdbebensicher: ~**e Bemessung** *f* BAU seismic design

Erdbeben: **Erdbebensicherheitsuntersuchung** *f* WERKPRÜF earthquake safety study; **Erdbebensimulator** *m* WERKPRÜF earthquake simulator; **Erdbebenwelle** *f* AKUSTIK Rayleigh wave, WELLPHYS seismic wave

Erdbehälter *m* WASSERVERSORG earth reservoir

Erdbeobachtungssatellit *m* RAUMFAHRT earth observation satellite

Erdbeschleunigung *f* MECHAN, PHYS acceleration, RAUMFAHRT *(g)* gravitational acceleration *(g)*

Erdbewegungsmaschinen *f pl* MASCHINEN earth-moving machinery

Erdbohrer *m* BAU auger

Erddamm *m* BAU bank; **Erddammpfahl** *m* KOHLEN embankment pile; **Erddammpfahltreiben** *nt* KOHLEN embankment piling

Erddruck *m* ERDÖL *Geologie* geopressure, KOHLEN earth pressure, soil pressure; **Erddruckbeiwert** *m* KOHLEN earth pressure coefficient

Erde:[1] **an** ~ **gelegt** *adj* ELEKTROTECH connected to earth (BrE), connected to ground (AmE), earthed (BrE), grounded (AmE); **mit** ~ **verbunden** *adj* ELEKTROTECH connected to earth (BrE), connected to ground (AmE), earthed (BrE), grounded (AmE)

Erde:[2] **an** ~ **legen** *vt* ELEKTRIZ earth (BrE), ground (AmE), TELEKOM ground (AmE)

Erdeinsturz *m* BAU fall of earth

Erdelektrode *f* ELEKTRIZ earth rod (BrE), ground rod (AmE)

Erdempfänger *m* RAUMFAHRT *Weltraumfunk* earth receiver

erden *vt* ELEKTRIZ, ELEKTROTECH earth (BrE), ground (AmE), TELEKOM ground (AmE)

Erdfehler *m* ELEKTRIZ *an elektrischer Leitung* earth fault (BrE), ground fault (AmE); **Erdfehlerschutz** *m* ELEKTRIZ earth fault protection (BrE), ground fault protection (AmE); **Erdfehlerschutzeinrichtung** *f* ELEKTRIZ earth fault protection (BrE), ground fault protection (AmE)

Erdfixpunktumlaufbahn *f* RAUMFAHRT earth-parking orbit

Erdfluchtgeschwindigkeit *f* RAUMFAHRT *zweite kosmische Geschwindigkeit* earth escape velocity

Erdfluchtstufe *f* RAUMFAHRT *Raketenstufe mit zweiter kosmischer Geschwindigkeit* earth escape stage

erdfrei *adj* ELEKTROTECH floating

Erdfunkenstrecke *f* ELEKTRIZ earth terminal arrester

Erdfunkstelle *f* RAUMFAHRT CES, coast earth station, *Weltraumfunk* earth station, land station; ~ **auf einem Schiff** *f* RAUMFAHRT *Weltraumfunk* shipborne earth station

Erdgas *nt* ERDÖL, HEIZ & KÄLTE, THERMOD, UMWELTSCHMUTZ natural gas; **Erdgasaustauschgas** *nt* *(SNG)* ERDÖL synthetic natural gas *(SNG)*; **Erdgasfeld** *nt* THERMOD gas field; **Erdgaskondensat** *nt* ERDÖL NGL, natural gas liquid; **Erdgastanker** *m* TRANS liquid natural gas carrier, WASSERTRANS methane carrier; **Erdgastanker mit integriertem Behälter** *m* WASSERTRANS methane carrier with integrated tank; **Erdgastanker mit selbsttragendem Behälter** *m* WASSERTRANS methane carrier with self-supporting tank

Erdgleiche *f* KERNTECH ground level

Erdhobel *m* BAU scraper

Erdinduktionskompaß *m* LUFTTRANS gyrosyn compass; **Erdinduktionskompaßanzeige** *f* LUFTTRANS gyrosyn compass indicator

Erdkabel *nt* ELEKTRIZ, ELEKTROTECH earth lead (BrE),

ground lead (AmE), underground cable

Erdkern *m* NICHTFOSS ENERG earth's core

Erdklemme *f* ELEKTRIZ earth clamp (BrE), ground clamp (AmE), earth clip (BrE), ground clip (AmE), earth terminal (BrE), ground terminal (AmE)

Erdklumpen *m* BAU clod

Erdkommandostation *f* RAUMFAHRT command earth station

Erdkriechstrom *m* ELEKTRIZ earth leakage current (BrE), ground leakage current (AmE)

Erdkrümmung *f* RAUMFAHRT earth curvature

Erdkruste *f* NICHTFOSS ENERG earth's crust

Erdlader *m* BAU scraper

Erdlast *f* FERTIG *Kunststoffinstallationen* backfill material

Erdleiter *m* ELEKTRIZ earth conductor (BrE), ground conductor (AmE), ELEKTROTECH earth line (BrE), ground line (AmE), earth wire (BrE), ground wire (AmE)

Erdleitung *f* ELEKTROTECH earth line (BrE), ground line (AmE), underground line

Erdmagnetfeld *nt* PHYS, RAUMFAHRT earth's magnetic field

erdmagnetisch: **~es Feld** *nt* ELEKTRIZ earth's magnetic field

Erdmagnetismus *m* PHYS geomagnetism, terrestrial magnetism

Erdnähe *f* PHYS perigee

Erdnetz *nt* TELEKOM earth network (BrE), ground network (AmE)

Erdoberfläche *f* RAUMFAHRT terrestrial surface

Erdöl *nt* ERDÖL crude, crude oil; **Erdölanalyse** *f* ERDÖL crude assay, crude oil analysis; **Erdölbegleitgas** *nt* ERDÖL *Ölförderung* associated gas (AmE), associated petrol (BrE); **Erdölbetrieb** *m* ERDÖL petroleum workings; **Erdölbohrlocheinrichtung** *f* ERDÖL oil well appliance; **Erdölbohrturm** *m* ERDÖL oil well derrick; **Erdölbohrung** *f* ERDÖL *Ölförderung* oil well; **Erdölerzeugnis** *nt* UMWELTSCHMUTZ petroleum product; **Erdölexploration** *f* ERDÖL *Erdölsuche* oil exploration; **Erdölfalle** *f* ERDÖL *Erdölgeologie* oil trap; **Erdölförderpumpe** *f* ERDÖL *Ölförderung* oil well pump; **Erdölförderung** *f* ERDÖL drawing petroleum

erdölführend *adj* ERDÖL oil-bearing

Erdöl: **Erdölgas** *nt* ERDÖL associated gas (AmE), associated petrol (BrE); **Erdölgeologie** *f* ERDÖL petroleum geology

erdölhaltig *adj* ERDÖL *Erdölgeologie* oil-bearing

Erdöl: **Erdölingenieur** *m* ERDÖL *Person* petroleum engineer; **Erdöllagerstätte** *f* ERDÖL oilfield, pool of petroleum, *Erdölexploration* oil reservoir, petroleum reservoir; **Erdölraffinerie** *f* ERDÖL refinery, *Ölindustrie* oil refinery, petroleum refinery; **Erdölverarbeitung** *f* ERDÖL *Ölindustrie, Raffinerie* oil refining

Erdorbit: **im ~** *adj* RAUMFAHRT earth-orbiting

Erdparkorbit *m* RAUMFAHRT earth-parking orbit

Erdpech *nt* BAU mineral pitch

Erdplanum *nt* BAU grade

Erdrückleitung *f* ELEKTROTECH ground return

Erdruhedruck *m* KOHLEN earth pressure at rest

Erdrutsch *m* TRANS landslide, landslip

Erdsatellit *m* RAUMFAHRT *Erforschung von Bodenschätzen* earth satellite; **~ zur Ferndatenaufnahme** *m* RAUMFAHRT earth remote-sensing satellite

Erdschalter *m* ELEKTRIZ earth switch

Erdschein *m* RAUMFAHRT earthshine

Erdschelle *f* ELEKTRIZ earth clamp (BrE), ground clamp (AmE)

Erdschiene *f* ELEKTRIZ earth bus (BrE), ground bus (AmE), earthing bus (BrE), grounding bus (AmE)

Erdschluß *m* ELEKTRIZ earth leakage (BrE), ground fault (AmE), ground leakage (AmE), *Fehler an elektrischer Leitung* earth fault (BrE); **Erdschlußanzeiger** *m* ELEKTRIZ earth leakage detector (BrE), ground leakage detector (AmE), ELEKTROTECH earth indicator (BrE), ground indicator (AmE); **Erdschlußlöschspule** *f* ELEKTROTECH arc suppression coil; **Erdschlußmeßgerät** *nt* ELEKTRIZ earth leakage meter (BrE), ground leakage meter (AmE); **Erdschlußprüfer** *m* ELEKTROTECH earth detector (BrE), ground detector (AmE), earth leakage indicator (BrE), ground leakage indicator (BrE); **Erdschlußreaktanz** *f* ELEKTROTECH neutral compensator; **Erdschlußschutz** *m* ELEKTRIZ earth fault protection (BrE), ground fault protection (AmE); **Erdschlußstrom** *m* ELEKTRIZ earth leakage current (BrE), ground leakage current (AmE); **Erdschlußstromunterbrecher** *m* ELEKTRIZ earth leakage circuit breaker (BrE), ground leakage circuit breaker (AmE)

Erdschüttdamm *m* WASSERVERSORG earth dam

Erdsieb *nt* KOHLEN screen

Erdspannung *f* ELEKTRIZ earth potential

Erdspiralbohrer *m* KOHLEN earth drill

Erdstab *m* ELEKTRIZ earth rod (BrE), ground rod (AmE)

Erdstampfer *m* BAU earth rammer

Erdstaudamm *m* WASSERVERSORG earth dam

Erdstoffstruktur *f* KOHLEN soil structure

Erdstrom *m* ELEKTRIZ earth current (BrE), ground current (AmE)

erdsymmetrisch *adj* ELEKTROTECH balanced to earth

erdsynchron: **~er Satellit** *m* RAUMFAHRT earth synchronous satellite; **~e Umlaufbahn** *f* RAUMFAHRT earth synchronous orbit

Erdteer *m* BAU mineral tar

Erdumlaufbahn *f* RAUMFAHRT earth orbit; **Erdumlaufbahntreffen** *nt* RAUMFAHRT earth orbit rendezvous

Erdumsegelung *f* WASSERTRANS circumnavigation

Erdung *f* BAU, EISENBAHN, ELEKTRIZ, ELEKTROTECH, KFZTECH, KOHLEN, RADIO earth (BrE), earthing (BrE), ground (AmE), grounding (AmE), SICHERHEIT earthing installation, WASSERTRANS earth (BrE), earthing (BrE), ground (AmE), grounding (AmE); **~ des Flugzeugrumpfes** *f* LUFTTRANS fuselage ground connection; **~ des Flugzeugs** *f* LUFTTRANS grounding of aircraft; **Erdungsabschnitt** *m* RAUMFAHRT *Weltraumfunk* earth segment; **Erdungsanschluß** *m* EISENBAHN, KFZTECH, WASSERTRANS earth connector (BrE), ground connector (AmE); **Erdungsdraht** *m* FERNSEH earth wire (BrE), ground wire (AmE); **Erdungseinstellung** *f* ELEKTRIZ *Schalterstellung zur Erdung* earthing position (BrE), grounding position (AmE); **Erdungselektrode** *f* ELEKTRIZ earth electrode (BrE), ground electrode (AmE), earth rod (BrE), ground rod (AmE), earthing rod (BrE), grounding rod (AmE); **Erdungskabel** *nt* EISENBAHN earth cable (BrE), ground cable (AmE), ELEKTROTECH earth cable (BrE), earth lead (BrE), ground cable (AmE), ground lead (AmE), KFZTECH, WASSERTRANS earth cable (BrE), ground cable (AmE); **Erdungsklemme** *f* ELEKTRIZ earthing clip (BrE), grounding clip (AmE); **Erdungsleiter** *m* ELEKTROTECH earth wire (BrE), ground wire (AmE); **Erdungsleitung** f ELEKTROTECH earth line (BrE), ground line (AmE); **Erdungsplatte** f PHYS earth plate (BrE), ground plate (AmE); **Erdungsschalter** m ELEKTRIZ earthing switch (BrE), grounding switch (AmE); **Erdungsschelle** f ELEKTRIZ earthing clip (BrE), grounding clip (AmE); **Erdungsschiene** f ELEKTRIZ earth bar (BrE), ground bar (AmE), earth bus (BrE), ground bus (AmE); **Erdungsstab** m ELEKTRIZ earth electrode (BrE), ground electrode (AmE), earthing rod (BrE), grounding rod (AmE); **Erdungsstange** f LUFTTRANS earthing bar (BrE), grounding bar (AmE)

Erdverkabelung f BAU underground cabling
erdverlegt: ~e Schleife f TRANS buried loop
Erdverlegung f ERDÖL *Rohrleitung* burial
Erdvermessungskunde f GEOM geodesy
Erdwärme f ERDÖL geothermics
Erdwiderstand m ELEKTRIZ earth leakage meter (BrE), ground leakage meter (AmE), earth resistance (BrE), ground resistance (AmE); **Erdwiderstandsmeßgerät** nt ELEKTRIZ earth resistance meter (BrE), ground resistance meter (AmE)
Ereignis nt COMP & DV, PHYS *in der Relativitätstheorie,* TEILPHYS event; **Ereignisbehandlung** f COMP & DV event handling
ereignisbezogen: ~e Potentiale nt pl ERGON event-related potentials
Ereignis: **Ereignisbit** nt COMP & DV event bit
ereignisgesteuert adj KÜNSTL INT event-driven
Ereignis: **Ereignisschreiber** m ELEKTRIZ event recorder, GERÄT event recorder, time recorder; **Ereignisverfolgung** f COMP & DV event trapping; **Ereigniszähler** m ELEKTRIZ operation counter, GERÄT event counter; **Ereigniszeit** f PHYS time of event
Erfahrungswissen nt KÜNSTL INT experiential knowledge
Erfassungsbereich m GERÄT coverage
Erfassungssystem nt KFZTECH detection system
erfinden vt PATENT invent
Erfinder m PATENT inventor; **alleiniger ~** m PATENT sole inventor
erfinderisch:[1] ~e Tätigkeit f PATENT inventive step
erfinderisch:[2] auf ~er Tätigkeit beruhen phr PATENT involve an inventive step
Erfindernennung f PATENT designation of the inventor
Erfindung f PATENT invention
erfolglos: ~er Anruf m TELEKOM ineffective call
erfolgreich: ~ abgewickelter Anruf m TELEKOM successful call
Erfolgsrate f COMP & DV yield
erforderlich: ~e Frequenz f NICHTFOSS ENERG required frequency; ~e Zulaufhöhe f KERNTECH *einer Pumpe* net positive suction head
Erfüllung: ~ der Zielvorstellung f KÜNSTL INT goal satisfaction
Erg nt METROL erg
ergänzend adj PATENT supplementary
Ergänzung f COMP & DV *Programmiersprache* attribute; **Ergänzungswinkel** m MATH conjugate angle; **Ergänzungszeichnung** f KONSTZEICH supplementary drawing
Ergebnis nt KERNTECH issue, MASCHINEN output, QUAL result; **Ergebnisabweichung** f QUAL error of result
ergebnislos: ~er Versuch m PHYS inconclusive test
Ergol nt RAUMFAHRT, THERMOD ergol
Ergometer nt METROL ergometer

Ergonomie f COMP & DV, ERGON, MASCHINEN, RAUMFAHRT, SICHERHEIT ergonomics
ergonomisch adj ERGON ergonomic, MASCHINEN ergonomical, VERPACK ergonomic
Ergot-Alkaloid nt CHEMIE ergot alkaloid
Ergotinin nt CHEMIE ergotinine
Erguß m PHYS effusion; **Ergußgestein** nt NICHTFOSS ENERG extrusive rocks, igneous rocks
erhaben: ~e Fuge f KER & GLAS prominent joint
Erhalten nt RAUMFAHRT acquisition
erhalten vt MASCHINEN *Werkzeug, Geräte,* MECHAN *Werkzeuge, Geräte* maintain, SICHERHEIT *Geldbetrag* receive
Erhaltung f ELEKTROTECH *bei Thyristoren* holding, ERDÖL, PHYS, STRÖMPHYS, THERMOD conservation; ~ der rotationsfreien Bewegung f STRÖMPHYS permanence of irrotational motion; ~ der Strahlungsdichte f TELEKOM conservation of radiance; **Erhaltungsstützen** f pl THERMOD conservation laws
Erhärten nt BAU hardening
erhärten vt BAU harden, *Beton* freeze
Erhärtung f BAU *Beton* seasoning
erheben vt BAU rise, MATH *einer Zahl in die x-te Potenz* raise
Erhebungswinkel m MECHAN quadrant angle, NICHTFOSS ENERG angle of incidence; ~ der Sonne m NICHTFOSS ENERG solar altitude angle
Erhitzen nt TEXTIL heating
erhitzen vt TEXTIL, THERMOD heat
Erhitzer m MECHAN heater
Erhitzung f CHEMIE calefaction; ~ durch Luftreibung f RAUMFAHRT *Raumschiff* air friction heating; **Erhitzungsgeschwindigkeit** f THERMOD rate of heating; **Erhitzungskurve** f THERMOD heating curve
Erhöhen nt BAU heightening, *Angebot* keying-up
erhöhen vt BAU raise, FERNSEH *Zuschauerrate* bump up
erhöht: ~er Durchlaß m KER & GLAS lifted throat; ~er Fußweg m WASSERTRANS causeway; ~e Straße f TRANS flyover (BrE), skyway (AmE); ~e Temperatur f THERMOD excess temperature
Erhöhung f TELEKOM enhancement; **Erhöhungswinkel** m NICHTFOSS ENERG angle of incidence; **Erhöhungszeichen** nt AKUSTIK sharp
Erholpause f ERGON fatigue allowance, relaxation allowance, rest pause
Erholspannung f ELEKTRIZ recovery voltage
Erholung f ELEKTROTECH *von dynamischen Lasten,* METALL, TEXTIL recovery; **Erholungsgrad** m METALL recovery rate; **Erholungszuschlag** m ERGON relaxation allowance
Erichsen: ~scher Tiefziehversuch m FERTIG Erichsentype ductility test
Erinnerungsalarmdienst m TELEKOM reminder alarm service
Erinnerungsanruf m TELEKOM reminder call
erkannt: ~es Signal nt ELEKTRONIK detected signal
Erkennen nt ERGON cognition, recognition, RAUMFAHRT detection; ~ einzelner Wörter nt KÜNSTL INT isolated words recognition; ~ kontinuierlicher Sprechsprache nt KÜNSTL INT connected speech recognition, continuous speech recognition
erkennen vt ELEKTRONIK detect, KONTROLL identify
Erkennung f AKUSTIK identification, recognition, COMP & DV recognition, ELEKTRONIK detection, KONTROLL identification, KÜNSTL INT recognition; ~ kontinuierlicher Sprechsprache f KÜNSTL INT isolated words

recognition; **Erkennungssystem** *nt* KÜNSTL INT recognition system; **Erkennungsteil** *nt* COMP & DV identification division; **Erkennungsvorrichtung für fehlende Kappen** *f* VERPACK missing cap detector
Erkerfenster *nt* BAU bay window
erklärend: ~**e Anweisung** *f* COMP & DV narrative statement
Erklärung *f* COMP & DV narrative; **Erklärungskomponente** *f* KÜNSTL INT *eines Expertensystems* explanation subsystem, explanation component; **Erklärungsteil** *nt* KÜNSTL INT *eines Expertensystems* explanation subsystem, explanation component
Erl *abbr (Erlang)* TELEKOM Erl *(Erlang)*
Erlang *nt (Erl)* TELEKOM *Einheit des Verkehrswertes* Erlang *(Erl)*
erlaubt: ~**er Elektrondipolübergang** *m* STRAHLPHYS allowed electron dipole transition; ~**es Energieband** *nt* STRAHLPHYS allowed energy band; ~**er Übergang** *m* STRAHLPHYS allowed transition
erleichtern *vt* BAU ease
Erleichterung: ~ **der Arbeit** *f* RAUMFAHRT ergonomics; **Erleichterungsloch** *nt* LUFTTRANS lightening hole
Erlenmeyer-Kolben *m* LABOR Erlenmeyer flask, conical flask
erlöschen *vt* ELEKTROTECH *Licht* go out
Ermächtigungsbescheinigung *f* QUAL certificate of authorization
Ermangelungsschließen *nt* KÜNSTL INT default reasoning
ermäßigt: ~**e Gesprächsgebühr** *f* TELEKOM cheap call rate; ~**er Tarif** *m* TELEKOM reduced rate
Ermitteln: ~ **böswilliger Anrufe** *nt* TELEKOM malicious call tracing
Ermittlung *f* COMP & DV identification; ~ **der Wortzahl** *f* COMP & DV word count
Ermittlungsergebnis *nt* QUAL result of determination
ermüden *vi* ANSTRICH fatigue
Ermüdung *f* ANSTRICH, BAU, KUNSTSTOFF, MASCHINEN, MECHAN, WERKPRÜF fatigue; ~ **bei niedriger Lastspielzahl** *f* METALL low-cycle fatigue; **Ermüdungsanriß** *m* METALL fatigue crack; **Ermüdungsausfall** *m* KONTROLL wearout failure; **Ermüdungsbruch** *m* METALL fatigue failure; **Ermüdungseigenschaften** *f pl* MECHAN fatigue properties; **Ermüdungsfestigkeit** *f* WERKPRÜF fatigue resistance, fatigue strength; **Ermüdungshärten** *nt* METALL fatigue hardening; **Ermüdungsprüfung** *f* WERKPRÜF fatigue test; **Ermüdungsriß** *m* WERKPRÜF fatigue crack; **Ermüdungsverhalten** *nt* MASCHINEN fatigue behavior (AmE), fatigue behaviour (BrE); **Ermüdungsverschleiß** *m* MASCHINEN fatigue wear; **Ermüdungsversuch** *m* METALL fatigue test, WERKPRÜF endurance test; **Ermüdungsvorriß** *m* KERNTECH fatigue precrack; **Ermüdungsweichmachen** *nt* METALL fatigue softening
Ernährung *f* LEBENSMITTEL nutrition; **Ernährungsergänzungsstoff** *m* LEBENSMITTEL nutritional supplement; **Ernährungsstörung** *f* LEBENSMITTEL nutritional disorder; **Ernährungsumstellung** *f* LEBENSMITTEL dietary change
erneuerbar: ~**e Energiequelle** *f* ELEKTRIZ renewable energy source
Erneuerung: ~ **der Qualifikationen** *f* QUAL requalification
erneut:[1] ~**e Qualifizierung** *f* QUAL requalification; ~**er Schreibvorgang** *m* COMP & DV rewrite

erneut:[2] ~ **anzeigen** *vt* COMP & DV refresh; ~ **speichern** *vt* COMP & DV resave
Erniedrigungszeichen *nt* AKUSTIK *Musik* flat
Ernteabfall *m* ABFALL crop waste
erodieren *vt* ANSTRICH, BAU, ELEKTRIZ erode
Erosion *f* BAU, KOHLEN, NICHTFOSS ENERG erosion; **Erosionsabbrand** *m* RAUMFAHRT erosive burning; **Erosionsrate** *f* RAUMFAHRT *Raumschiff* erosion rate
erproben *vt* QUAL try out test
Erprobung *f* GERÄT, KERNTECH trial; **Erprobungsflug** *m* LUFTTRANS proving flight, test flight
errechnet: ~**e Adresse** *f* COMP & DV generated address; ~**e Flügelfläche** *f* LUFTTRANS design wing area; ~**e Fluggeschwindigkeit** *f* LUFTTRANS design airspeed; ~**es Fluggewicht** *nt* LUFTTRANS design flight weight; ~**e Geschwindigkeit bei größter Böenintensität** *f* LUFTTRANS *Lufttüchtigkeit* design speed for maximum gust intensity; ~**es Gewicht** *nt* LUFTTRANS design weight; ~**e Landegeschwindigkeit** *f* LUFTTRANS design-landing speed; ~**es Landegewicht** *nt* LUFTTRANS design-landing weight; ~**e Landeklappengeschwindigkeit** *f* LUFTTRANS *Lufttüchtigkeit* design flap speed; ~**e Last** *f* LUFTTRANS design load; ~**e Radbelastung** *f* LUFTTRANS design wheel load; ~**er Raddruck** *m* LUFTTRANS design wheel load; ~**e Reisefluggeschwindigkeit** *f* LUFTTRANS design-cruising speed; ~**es Rollgewicht** *nt* LUFTTRANS design taxi weight; ~**e Startmasse** *f* LUFTTRANS design takeoff mass; ~**e Sturzfluggeschwindigkeit** *f* LUFTTRANS design-diving speed; ~**e Tragflügelfläche** *f* LUFTTRANS design wing area
erregen *vt* ELEKTROTECH energize
Erreger *m* ELEKTRIZ, ELEKTROTECH, NICHTFOSS ENERG exciter; **Erregeranode** *f* ELEKTROTECH excitation anode, keep-alive electrode; **Erregerdynamo** *m* ELEKTRIZ exciting dynamo; **Erregerfeld** *nt* ELEKTROTECH exciting field; **Erregerfrequenz** *f* WERKPRÜF excitation frequency; **Erregerkreis** *m* ELEKTRIZ field circuit, ELEKTROTECH energizing circuit; **Erregerspule** *f* ELEKTRIZ field coil; **Erregerstrom** *m* ELEKTRIZ excitation current, field current, ELEKTROTECH energizing current, induction current; **Erregerstufe** *f* RADIO *Sender* exciter; **Erregerwicklung** *f* ELEKTRIZ excitation winding, field coil; **Erregerwiderstand** *m* ELEKTROTECH field rheostat
erregt *adj* ELEKTROTECH energized
Erregung *f* AKUSTIK, ELEKTRIZ excitation, ELEKTROTECH energization, excitation, ERGON arousal, TELEKOM excitation; ~ **durch Strahlungskopplung** *f* RADIO parasitic excitation; **Erregungspegel** *m* AKUSTIK excitation level
Erreichen *nt* RAUMFAHRT acquisition; ~ **der Fluglage** *nt* RAUMFAHRT *Raumschiff* acquisition of attitude; ~ **des Normalmodus** *nt* RAUMFAHRT *Raumschiff* acquisition of normal mode; ~ **der Umlaufbahn** *nt* RAUMFAHRT *Raumschiff* acquisition of orbit
erreichen *vt* TELEKOM *Teilnehmer* reach
erreicht: ~**er Meßwert** *m* GERÄT achieved-measuring value; ~**er Wert** *m* GERÄT achieved-measuring value
errichten *vt* BAU construct, put up
Errichtung *f* BAU erection
Ersatz *m* LUFTTRANS reserves; **Ersatzboot** *nt* ERDÖL *Schiffahrt* stand-by boat; **Ersatzglied** *nt* MASCHINEN repair link; **Ersatzkreis** *m* ELEKTROTECH analog circuit (AmE), analogue circuit (BrE); **Ersatzlampe** *f* FOTO spare bulb; **Ersatzleitweg** *m* TELEKOM alterna-

tive route; **Ersatzmittel** *nt* LEBENSMITTEL surrogate;
Ersatzrad *nt* KFZTECH spare wheel; **Ersatzrädersatz** *m*
MASCHINEN set of change wheels; **Ersatzschaltung** *f*
ELEKTRIZ, ELEKTRONIK equivalent circuit, ELEKTRO-
TECH analog circuit, equivalent circuit, PHYS
equivalent circuit; **Ersatzstromkreis** *m* ELEKTROTECH
equivalent circuit; **Ersatzteil** *nt* EISENBAHN, FERTIG
Kunststoffinstallationen, KFZTECH, LUFTTRANS, MA-
SCHINEN, WASSERTRANS spare part; **Ersatzteile** *nt pl*
MASCHINEN spares; **Ersatzteileölfilter** *nt* KFZTECH re-
placeable element oil filter; **Ersatzweg** *m* TELEKOM
alternative route; **Ersatzwerkzeug** *nt* MASCHINEN
spare tool; **Ersatzwiderstand** *m* ELEKTRIZ equivalent
resistance; **Ersatzzeichen** *nt* COMP & DV substitute
character
Erscheinungsbild *nt* WERKPRÜF aesthetics
erschließen *vt* BAU *von Bauland* develop
Erschließung *f* BAU *Bauland*, ERDÖL *Lagerstätte* development; **Erschließungsphase** *f* ERDÖL *Lagerstätte*
development phase; **Erschließungsvorhaben** *nt* ERD-
ÖL *Lagerstätte* development project
erschöpft: ~**e Batteriekapazität** *f* COMP & DV low battery
charge; ~**er Kernbrennstoff** *m* KERNTECH depleted
nuclear fuel
Erschöpfung *f* WASSERVERSORG depletion
Erschütterung *f* PHYS vibration, RAUMFAHRT *Raumschiff* judder, shock; **Erschütterungsdämpfer** *m*
LUFTTRANS vibration damper; **Erschütterungsfestig-
keit** *f* KUNSTSTOFF shock resistance;
Erschütterungsprobe *f* VERPACK jarring test
erschwert: ~**e Prüfung** *f* QUAL tightened inspection
ersetzbar: nicht ~**e Sicherung** *f* ELEKTRIZ nonrenewable
fuse
ersetzen *vt* MATH substitute
ersoffen: ~**e Turbine** *f* HYDRAUL drowned turbine
Erspinnen *nt* TEXTIL spinning
Erst- *pref* RAUMFAHRT initial
erst: ~**es Anfahren** *nt* KERNTECH beginning of life; ~**er
Detektor** *m* ELEKTRONIK *in Überlagerungsempfängern*
first detector, first mixer; ~**e Generation** *f* COMP & DV
first generation; ~**e Harmonische** *f* ELEKTRONIK first
harmonic; ~**er Hauptsatz der Wärmelehre** *m* PHYS first
law of thermodynamics; ~**er Ingenieur** *m* WASSER-
TRANS *Besatzung* chief engineer; ~**e Injektion** *f*
ELEKTRONIK *Transistoren* first injection; ~**e Ionisationsstufe** *f* PHYS first ionization potential; ~**er
kritischer Test** *m* KERNTECH first critical experiment;
~**es kritisches Experiment** *nt* KERNTECH first critical
experiment; ~**es Kritischwerden** *nt* KERNTECH first
criticality, first divergence; ~**e Lage der Y-Schweiß-
naht** *f* MECHAN root pass; ~**er Naßfilz** *m* PAPIER first
dryer; ~**er Offizier** *m* WASSERTRANS *Handelsmarine,
Besatzung* chief mate; ~**er Oxidationsbrand** *m* KER &
GLAS first oxidizing firing; ~**e Projektionsebene** *f*
GEOM ground plane; ~**er Summand** *m* COMP & DV
augend; ~**es Transmissionsfenster** *nt* OPTIK *Lichtleitfaser* first fiber window (AmE), first fibre window
(BrE); ~**er Überlagerungsoszillator** *m* ELEKTRONIK
first local oscillator; ~**er Vergaserlufttrichter** *m*
KFZTECH primary barrel; ~**es Walzenpaar** *nt* KER &
GLAS first pair of rollers; ~**er ZF-Verstärker** *m (erster
Zwischenfrequenzverstärker)* ELEKTRONIK first IF
amplifier *(first intermediate frequency amplifier)*; ~**e
Zwischenfrequenz** *f* ELEKTRONIK first intermediate
frequency; ~**er Zwischenfrequenzverstärker** *m (erster
ZF-Verstärker)* ELEKTRONIK first intermediate fre-

quency amplifier *(first IF amplifier)*
erstarren[1] *vt* FERTIG *Metall* freeze
erstarren[2] *vi* ABFALL, BAU set, FERTIG congeal
Erstarrung *f* ABFALL, BAU setting, CHEMTECH coagulation, gelation; **Erstarrungsbad** *nt* CHEMTECH
coagulating bath; **Erstarrungsflüssigkeit** *f* CHEMTECH
coagulation liquid; **Erstarrungsgeschwindigkeit** *f* BAU
rate of curing, KER & GLAS setting rate; **Erstarrungs-
punkt** *m* STRÖMPHYS congealing point, THERMOD
solidification point; **Erstarrungszeit** *f* KUNSTSTOFF
setting time
Erstattung *f* PATENT reimbursement
Erst-: Erstausbau *m* TELEKOM *Amt* initially-installed
capacity; **Erstausrüstung** *f* MASCHINEN original
equipment; **Erstbelegung** *f* COMP & DV *Programm* initialization; **Erstbündel** *nt* TELEKOM first-choice group
Erste-Hilfe *f* SICHERHEIT first aid; **Erste-Hilfe-Kasten** *m*
SICHERHEIT first-aid box; **Erste-Hilfe-Kurs** *m* SICHER-
HEIT first-aid class; **Erste-Hilfe-Raum** *m* SICHERHEIT
first-aid treatment room; **Erste-Hilfe-Schrank** *m* SI-
CHERHEIT first-aid cupboard; **Erste-Hilfe-Verfahren** *nt*
SICHERHEIT first-aid procedure, *Notfälle* first-aid pro-
cedure
erstellen *vt* COMP & DV create, load
Ersteller *m* KONSTZEICH draftsman (AmE), draughts-
man (BrE)
Erstellung *f* COMP & DV creation, preparation; ~ **von
Modellen** *f* COMP & DV, ELEKTRONIK, GEOM modeling
(AmE), modelling (BrE); **Erstellungsnummer** *f* COMP
& DV generation number
Erst-: Ersthelfer *m* SICHERHEIT first-aid personnel, first-
aider
ersticken[1] *vt* SICHERHEIT suffocate, THERMOD *Feuer*
smother
ersticken[2] *vi* SICHERHEIT suffocate
Erstickung *f* SICHERHEIT *Dämpfe* suffocation; **Erstik-
kungsgefahr** *f* SICHERHEIT risk of suffocation
Erst-: Erstmahlen *nt* KOHLEN primary grinding; **Erst-
neutron** *nt* KERNTECH first-flight neutron; **Erstprobe** *f*
KOHLEN primary sample; **Erstprüfung** *f* QUAL original
inspection
erstrecken: sich ~ **von** *v refl* TELEKOM range from
Erst-: Erstsetzung *f* KOHLEN primary settlement; **Erst-
ziehen** *nt* MASCHINEN first drawing
erteilen *vt* WASSERTRANS *Praktika* admit
Erteilung *f* PATENT grant
Ertrag *m* CHEMIE, ELEKTRONIK, NICHTFOSS ENERG, TEX-
TIL yield
Eruca- *pref* CHEMIE erucic
Eruption *f* ERDÖL breakout, *Bohrtechnik* blowout
Erwärmen *nt* TEXTIL heating
erwärmen *vt* TEXTIL, THERMOD heat
Erwärmung *f* THERMOD temperature rise
erwartet: ~**e Betriebsbedingungen** *f pl* LUFTTRANS an-
ticipated-operating conditions; ~**es Potential** *nt* PHYS
advanced potential
Erwartung *f* ERGON set; **Erwartungsbohrung** *f* ERDÖL
Lagerstättenerkundung appraisal well; **Erwartungs-
wert** *m* QUAL expected value
erweichen *vt* FERTIG plasticize
Erweichung *f* FERTIG plasticization, KER & GLAS *Keramik* sagging; **Erweichungsintervall** *nt* KER & GLAS
softening range; **Erweichungsofen** *m* KER & GLAS softening furnace; **Erweichungspunkt** *m* HEIZ & KÄLTE
softening point, KER & GLAS deformation point,
KUNSTSTOFF, TEXTIL softening point; **Erweichungs-**

temperatur *f* KUNSTSTOFF softing point, WERKPRÜF *Kunststoffe* heat distortion temperature

erweiterbar: ~**e Adressierung** *f* COMP & DV extensible addressing; ~**es Etikettiersystem** *nt* VERPACK modular labeling system (AmE), modular labelling system (BrE); ~**e Sprache** *f* COMP & DV extensible language

Erweiterbarkeit *f* COMP & DV extensibility

erweitern *vt* BAU expand, COMP & DV extend, upgrade, MATH *von Brüchen* extend, MECHAN ream

erweitert[1] *adj* MECHAN flared

erweitert:[2] **nicht mit ~em ausgeprägtem Pol** *m* ELEKTRIZ nonsalient pole; ~**e Adressierung** *f* COMP & DV extended addressing; ~**er Binärcode für Dezimalziffern** *m* *(EBCDIC-Code)* COMP & DV, ELEKTRONIK extended binary-coded decimal interchange code *(EBCDIC)*; ~**e Bohrung** *f* ERDÖL development well; ~**er Dienst** *m* TELEKOM enhanced service; ~**e indizierte Zugriffsmöglichkeit für sequentielle Dateien** *f* *(QUISAM)* COMP & DV *(QUISAM)* Queued Unique Index Sequential Access Method; ~**e Zugriffsmethode** *f* COMP & DV queued access method; ~**e Zugriffsmöglichkeit für sequentielle Dateien** *f* *(QSAM)* COMP & DV queued sequential access method *(QSAM)*

Erweiterung *f* BAU development, COMP & DV *Hardware* upgrade, DRUCK expansion, TEXTIL flare; ~ **eines Ausdrucks** *f* MATH expansion of an expression; **Erweiterungsanweisung** *f* COMP & DV option instruction; **Erweiterungsbohren** *nt* ERDÖL *Lagerstättenerkundung* appraisal drilling; **Erweiterungsbohrer** *m* ERDÖL *Bohrtechnik* reaming bit, shell; **Erweiterungsbohrmeißel** *m* ERDÖL eccentric bit, *Bohrtechnik* expansion bit; **Erweiterungsbohrung** *f* ERDÖL *Bohrtechnik* extension well, outpost well, *Lagerstättenabbau* outpost well; **Erweiterungsfeld** *nt* KONSTZEICH extension block; **Erweiterungskarte** *f* COMP & DV expansion card, feature expansion card, ELEKTRONIK extension card; **Erweiterungsnetz** *nt* TELEKOM expansion network; **Erweiterungsplatine** *f* COMP & DV expansion board, expansion card; **Erweiterungsposition** *f* COMP & DV expansion slot; **Erweiterungsring** *m* ERDÖL *Bohrtechnik* expansion ring; **Erweiterungsspeicher** *m* *(XMS)* COMP & DV extended memory specification *(XMS)*; **Erweiterungsspeicherröhre** *f* ELEKTRONIK expansion storage tube; **Erweiterungssteckkarte** *f* COMP & DV plug-in board; **Erweiterungssteckplatz** *m* COMP & DV expansion slot

Erwerb *m* KÜNSTL INT *des Wissens* acquisition

Erythrin *nt* CHEMIE erythrine, tetraiodofluorescein

Erythrit *nt* CHEMIE erythritol; **Erythrittetranitrat** *nt* CHEMIE tetranitrol

Erythrose *f* CHEMIE erythrose

Erythrosin *nt* CHEMIE erythrosine

Erythrulose *f* CHEMIE erythrulose

Erz *nt* FERTIG, KOHLEN ore; **Erzanalyse** *f* KERNTECH ore assaying, ore testing; **Erzanreicherungsanlage** *f* KERNTECH ore enrichment plant; **Erzaufbereitung** *f* KOHLEN mineral processing; **Erz-Bulk-Öl-Frachter** *m* WASSERTRANS combination bulk carrier

Erzen *nt* FERTIG oreing down

erzen *vt* FERTIG ore down

erzeugen *vt* BAU prepare, GEOM generate, HEIZ & KÄLTE *Druck* develop

Erzeuger *m* RADIO generator

Erzeugnis *nt* COMP & DV product, PAPIER make

erzeugt: ~**e Elektrizität** *f* KERNTECH generated electricity

Erzeugungskopie *f* FERNSEH generation copy

Erz: **Erzfrachter** *m* WASSERTRANS *Schifftyp* ore carrier

erzielt: ~**e Qualität** *f* QUAL quality achievement

Erz-Kohle-Öl *m* *(OCO)* TRANS ore-coal-oil *(OCO)*; **Erz-Kohle-Öl-Frachtschiff** *nt* TRANS ore-coal-oil carrier

Erz: **Erzlager** *nt* KERNTECH ore deposit; **Erzniere** *f* KOHLEN nodule; **Erz-Öl-Schiff** *nt* WASSERTRANS *Schifftyp* ore-oil carrier; **Erz-Öl-Tanker** *m* WASSERTRANS *Schiff* ore-oil carrier; **Erz-Schlamm-Öl** *m* *(OSO)* WASSERTRANS ore-slurry-oil *(OSO)*; **Erz-Schlamm-Öl-Tanker** *m* WASSERTRANS ore-slurry-oil tanker; **Erz-Schüttgut-Öl** *nt* *(OBO)* WASSERTRANS ore-bulk oil *(OBO)*; **Erz-Schüttgut-Öl-Frachter** *m* WASSERTRANS *Schiff* ore-bulk-oil carrier; **Erzvorkommen** *nt* KERNTECH ore deposit

erzwungen: ~**e Emission** *f* ELEKTRONIK, PHYS, TELEKOM stimulated emission; ~**e Konvektion** *f* PHYS forced convection; ~**e Schwingung** *f* AKUSTIK forced vibration, ELEKTRONIK forced oscillation, PHYS *meist elektrisch* forced oscillation, *meist mechanisch* forced vibration

ES *abbr* ELEKTRONIK *(Elektronenstrahl)* EB *(electronic beam)*, KERNTECH *(Elektronenstrahl)* EB *(electronic beam)*, KÜNSTL INT *(Expertensystem)* ES *(expert system)*,

Es *abbr* *(Einsteinium)* CHEMIE, STRAHLPHYS Es *(einsteinium)*

ESA *abbr* RAUMFAHRT *(Europäische Raumfahrtbehörde)* ESA *(European Space Agency)*, UMWELTSCHMUTZ *(elektrostatischer Staubabscheider)* ESP *(electrostatic precipitator)*

Esaki-Diode *f* ELEKTRONIK Esaki diode, PHYS Esaki diode, tunnel diode

ESCA *abbr* *(Fotoelektronenspektroskopie)* PHYS ESCA *(electron spectroscopy for chemical analysis)*

Escape: **Escape-Peak** *m* STRAHLPHYS *bei Gamma-Strahlung* escape peak; **Escape-Sequenz** *f* COMP & DV escape sequence; **Escape-Zeichen** *nt* COMP & DV escape character; **Escape-Zeichenfolge** *f* COMP & DV escape sequence

E-Schicht *f* PHYS, RADIO E layer

E-Schmelzung *f* ELEKTROTECH electric smelting

Eserin *nt* CHEMIE eserine, physostigmine

ESPRIT *abbr* ELEKTRIZ ESPRIT, European Semiconductor Production Research Initiative

ESR *abbr* *(Elektronenspinresonanz)* PHYS, STRAHLPHYS, TEILPHYS ESR *(electron spin resonance)*

essentiell: ~**e Fettsäure** *f* *(EFS)* LEBENSMITTEL essential fatty acid *(EFA)*

essigartig *adj* CHEMIE acetic, acetous

Essigerzeuger *m* LEBENSMITTEL vinegar generator

Essigester *m* LEBENSMITTEL ethyl acetate

essigsauer *adj* CHEMIE acetous

Essigsäure *f* FERTIG *Kunststoffinstallationen*, KUNSTSTOFF, LEBENSMITTEL acetic acid; **Essigsäureanhydrid** *nt* LEBENSMITTEL acetic anhydride; **Essigsäurebacterium** *nt* LEBENSMITTEL acetobacter; **Essigsäurebakterien** *f pl* LEBENSMITTEL acetic bacteria; **Essigsäurebildung** *f* CHEMIE acetification; **Essigsäureester** *m* CHEMIE acetate; **Essigsäureethylester** *m* LEBENSMITTEL acetic ether; **Essigsäuregärung** *f* LEBENSMITTEL acetic fermentation; **Essigsäuremethylester** *m* CHEMIE methyl acetate

Ester *m* CHEMIE ester; ~ **der Arsensäure** *m* CHEMIE arsenate; **Estergummi** *m* KUNSTSTOFF ester gum;

Esterharz *nt* KUNSTSTOFF ester gum

Estrichstärke *f* BAU screed height

Estron *nt* CHEMIE oestrone, theelin

ETA *abbr (voraussichtliche Ankunftszeit)* LUFTTRANS, WASSERTRANS ETA *(estimated time of arrival)*

Eta-Faktor *m* PHYS *Neutronenausbeute bei Absorption* eta-factor

Etage *f* BAU floor; **Etagenbogen** *m* ERDÖL *Rohrleitung* dogleg; **Etagenhöhe** *f* KUNSTSTOFF daylight; **Etagenofen** *m* ABFALL multiple-hearth incinerator; **Etagenpresse** *f* KUNSTSTOFF daylight press, multiple-daylight press; **Etagenschalter** *m* ELEKTRIZ floor switch, landing switch; **Etagentrockenpartie** *f* PAPIER stacked dryer section; **Etagenwagen** *m* LUFTTRANS *Werkstatt* service trolley

Etalon *nt* PHYS etalon, primary standard, standard

Eta-Mason *f* PHYS eta mason

ETD *abbr (voraussichtliche Abflugzeit)* LUFTTRANS, WASSERTRANS ETD *(estimated time of departure)*

Ethal *nt* CHEMIE ethal

Ethan *nt* CHEMIE ethane, hexadecanol, ERDÖL *Petrochemie* ethane; **Ethanal** *nt* CHEMIE ethanal, LEBENSMITTEL acetaldehyde; **Ethandiamid** *nt* CHEMIE oxamide; **Ethandinitril** *nt* CHEMIE cyanogen

Ethandioyl- *pref* CHEMIE oxalyl

Ethandisäuremonoureid *nt* CHEMIE oxaluric acid

Ethannitril *nt* CHEMIE acetonitrile, ethanenitrile

Ethanol *nt* CHEMIE, ERDÖL *Petrochemie* ethanol, LEBENSMITTEL ethanol, ethyl alcohol; **Ethanolat** *nt* CHEMIE ethanolate; **Ethanolyse** *f* CHEMIE ethanolysis

Ethan: **Ethansäure** *f* LEBENSMITTEL acetic acid; **Ethanthiol** *nt* CHEMIE ethanethiol

Ethen *nt* CHEMIE ethene, ethylene

Ethenyl- *pref* CHEMIE vinyl

Ethenyliden- *pref* CHEMIE vinylidene

Ether *m* CHEMIE ether

etherartig *adj* CHEMIE ethereal

etherisch *adj* CHEMIE ethereal

Ethin *nt* CHEMIE acetylene, ethine, ethyne

Ethion- *pref* CHEMIE ethionic

Ethlen *nt* ERDÖL ethene

Ethoxyacetanilid *nt* CHEMIE ethoxyacetanilide, phenacetin

Ethoxyanilin *nt* CHEMIE ethoxyaniline, phenetidine

Ethoxybenzol *nt* CHEMIE ethoxybenzene, phenetole

Ethyl *nt* ERDÖL *Petrochemie* ethyl; **Ethylacetat** *nt* KUNSTSTOFF, LEBENSMITTEL ethyl acetate; **Ethylaldehyd** *m* LEBENSMITTEL acetaldehyde; **Ethylalkohol** *m* ERDÖL *Petrochemie*, FOTO ethyl alcohol, LEBENSMITTEL ethanol, ethyl alcohol; **Ethylamin** *nt* CHEMIE aminoethane, ethylamine; **Ethylanilin** *nt* CHEMIE ethylaniline; **Ethylat** *nt* CHEMIE ethylate; **Ethylcellulose** *f (EC)* KUNSTSTOFF ethyl cellulose *(EC)*; **Ethyldimethylmethan** *nt* CHEMIE isopentane

Ethylen *nt* CHEMIE, ERDÖL *Petrochemie* ethene, ethylene, KUNSTSTOFF, LEBENSMITTEL ethylene

Ethylen- *pref* CHEMIE ethylenic

Ethylen: **Ethylenkohlenwasserstoff** *m* CHEMIE alkene, olefin, olefine; **Ethylen-Propylen-Kautschuk** *m* KUNSTSTOFF ethylene propylene rubber; **Ethylenvinylacetat** *nt (EVA)* KUNSTSTOFF ethylene vinyl acetate *(EVA)*

Ethyl: **Ethylhydrosulfid** *nt* CHEMIE ethanethiol

Ethyliden *nt* CHEMIE ethylidene; **Ethylidenradikal** *nt* CHEMIE ethylidene

ethylieren *vt* CHEMIE ethylate

Ethyl: **Ethylierung** *f* CHEMIE ethylation; **Ethylmercaptan** *nt* CHEMIE ethanethiol; **Ethylmorphin** *nt* CHEMIE ethylmorphine; **Ethylphenylether** *m* CHEMIE ethoxybenzene, phenetole; **Ethylschwefel-** *pref* CHEMIE ethylsulfuric (AmE), ethylsulphuric (BrE), *Säure* vinic; **Ethylthioethanol** *nt* ERDÖL *Petrochemie* ethylthioethanol; **Ethylurethan** *nt* CHEMIE ethyl urethane; **Ethylvanillin** *nt* LEBENSMITTEL *Aromastoff* ethyl-vanillin

Etikett *nt* COMP & DV external label, label, TEXTIL label, tag, VERPACK label; **Etikettausgabe** *f* VERPACK label dispenser; **Etikettenaufdruckmaschine** *f* VERPACK label-overprinting machine; **Etikettenauszeichnungsmaschine** *nt* VERPACK label-coding machine; **Etikettenfolie** *f* VERPACK label film

Etikettieren *nt* TEXTIL labeling (AmE), labelling (BrE), tagging; **~ mit Druckluft** *nt* VERPACK air-blast labeling (AmE), air-blast labelling (BrE); **~ mit Luftdruck** *nt* VERPACK air-jet labeling (AmE), air-jet labelling (BrE)

etikettieren *vt* TEXTIL label, tag

Etikett: **Etikettierer** *m* VERPACK labeler (AmE), labeller (BrE); **Etikettiermaschine** *f* VERPACK labeling machine (AmE), labelling machine (BrE); **Etikettiermaschine für Packungsoberseiten** *f* VERPACK front of pack labeler (AmE), front of pack labeller (BrE); **Etikettierung** *f* VERPACK labeling (AmE), labelling (BrE); **Etikettrückseite** *f* VERPACK back

Eu *(Europium)* CHEMIE Eu *(europium)*

Eucalyptol *nt* CHEMIE eucalyptol

Eudiometer *nt* CHEMIE eudiometer

Eudiometrie *f* CHEMIE eudiometry

Eugenol *nt* CHEMIE eugenol

euklidisch: **~e Geometrie** *f* GEOM Euclidean geometry; **nicht ~e Geometrie** *f* GEOM non-Euclidean geometry; **nicht ~e Geometrie der 1 Art** *f* GEOM hyperbolic geometry **~er Raum** *m* GEOM, PHYS Euclidean space

Eule: **eine ~ fangen** *vt* WASSERTRANS *Segeln* broach to

Euler: **~sche Bewegungsgleichungen** *f pl* STRÖMPHYS Eulerian equations; **~sche Formel** *f* GEOM Euler's formula; **~sche Kurve** *f* MATH Euler circles; **~sche Winkel** *m pl* PHYS Euler angles

EURATOM *abbr (Europäische Atomgemeinschaft)* TEILPHYS EURATOM *(European Organization for Nuclear Research)*

Euroflasche *f* KER & GLAS Euro bottle

Europäisch: **~er Alkohol-, Branntwein- und Spirituosenverband** *m* LEBENSMITTEL European Alcohol, Brandy and Spirit Union; **~e Atomgemeinschaft** *f (EURATOM)* TEILPHYS European Organization for Nuclear Research *(EURATOM)*; **~er Funkrufdienst** *m (EFuRD)* TELEKOM European radio-paging system; **~es Kernforschungszentrum** *nt (CERN)* TEILPHYS European Organization for Nuclear Research *(CERN)*; **~e Norm** *f (EN)* ELEKTRIZ European Standard; **~e Raumfahrtbehörde** *f (ESA)* RAUMFAHRT European Space Agency *(ESA)*

europäisch: **~es Leichterträgersystem** *nt (EBCS-System)* WASSERTRANS European barge carrier system *(EBCS)*; **~es Patent** *nt* PATENT European patent; **~e Patentanmeldung** *f* PATENT European patent application

europaweit: **~e GSM-Standards** *m pl* TELEKOM pan-European GSM standards

Europiep *m* TELEKOM European radio-paging system

Europium *nt (Eu)* CHEMIE europium *(Eu)*

Euroschlitz *m* VERPACK euroslot

eustatisch *adj* NICHTFOSS ENERG eustatic

Eutektikum *nt* CHEMIE, KER & GLAS eutectic

eutektisch[1] *adj* CHEMIE eutectic

eutektisch:[2] **~e Legierung** *f* METALL eutectic alloy; **~e Reaktion** *f* METALL eutetic reaction; **~er Stahl** *m* METALL eutectoid steel; **~e Transformation** *f* METALL eutetic transformation

Eutektoid *nt* METALL eutectoid

Eutrophierung *f* UMWELTSCHMUTZ eutrophication

eV *abbr (Elektronenvolt)* ELEKTRIZ, ELEKTROTECH, PHYS, STRAHLPHYS, TEILPHYS eV *(electronvolt)*

EVA *abbr (Ethylenvinylacetat)* KUNSTSTOFF EVA *(ethylene vinyl acetate)*

evakuieren *vt* ELEKTRONIK *Röhren*, WASSERTRANS *Schiff* evacuate

evakuiert *adv* PHYS, THERMOD under vacuum

Evakuierung: ~ und Fluchtmöglichkeit *f* SICHERHEIT evacuation and means of escape

Evaluierung *f* KÜNSTL INT evaluation

Evaporation *f (E)* DRUCK, ERDÖL, HEIZ & KÄLTE, HYDRAUL, MASCHINEN, NICHTFOSS ENERG, PHYS, THERMOD evaporation *(E)*; **Evaporationskühlung** *f* HEIZ & KÄLTE, THERMOD evaporative cooling

Evaporator *m* CHEMTECH evaporator

Evaporimeter *nt* CHEMTECH evaporimeter

Evaporit *nt* ERDÖL *Geologie* evaporite

E-Verhüttung *f* ELEKTROTECH electric smelting

Evolute *f* GEOM evolute

Evolvente *f* FERTIG involute curve, GEOM involute; **Evolventenkerbverzahnung** *f* MASCHINEN involute serrations, involute spline; **Evolventenrad** *nt* MASCHINEN involute gear; **Evolventenverzahnung** *f* MASCHINEN involute gearing

evolventisch *adj* FERTIG involute

evozieren *vt* ERGON evoke

evoziert: ~es Potential *nt* ERGON evoked potential; **~e Reaktion** *f* ERGON evoked response

EVS *abbr (Endvermittlungsstelle)* TELEKOM terminating exchange

EVU *abbr (Elektrizitätsversorgungsunternehmen)* ELEKTRIZ electricity supply company

E-Welle *f (Elektrowelle)* ELEKTROTECH E wave, TM wave, PHYS, TELEKOM E wave, TM wave *(electric wave)*

E-Werk *nt* ELEKTROTECH *Kraftwerk* station, ELEKTROTECH electric power station

exakt *adj* MECHAN, PHYS accurate

Exemplar *nt* DRUCK copy

Exhaustor *m* CHEMTECH dust catcher, MASCHINEN exhauster, MECHAN exhaust pump

Exiton *nt* PHYS exciton

exklusiv: ~e ODER-Verknüpfung *f* COMP & DV nonequivalence operation; **~es-ODER-Glied** *nt* ELEKTRONIK exclusive OR circuit, exclusive OR gate

Ex-Motor *m (explosionsgeschützter Motor)* ELEKTROTECH, THERMOD flameproof motor

exorheisch *adj* WASSERVERSORG exorheic

exotherm[1] *adj* THERMOD exothermal, exothermic; **exothermisch** *adj* RAUMFAHRT *Raumschiff* exothermic

exotherm:[2] **~er Prozeß** *m* THERM exothermic process

exotisch: ~er Chip *m* ELEKTRONIK exotic chip; **~es Signal** *nt* ELEKTRONIK exotic signal

expandieren *vi* HYDRAUL *Dampf* expand

expandiert[1] *adj* RAUMFAHRT *Raumschiff* expanded

expandiert:[2] **~er Graph** *m* KÜNSTL INT expanded graph

Expansion *f* HYDRAUL *Dampf*, MASCHINEN, RAUMFAHRT *Raumschiff*, THERMOD expansion; **Expansionsbeanspruchung** *f* HYDRAUL expansion stress; **Expansionsbohrmeißel** *m* ERDÖL expansion bit; **Expansionsdüse** *f* LUFTTRANS *Strahltriebwerk* expansion nozzle; **Expansionsfalle** *f* HYDRAUL expansion trap; **Expansionshub** *m* MASCHINEN, MECHAN, THERMOD expansion stroke; **Expansionskammer** *f* MASCHINEN expansion chamber; **Expansionskasten** *m* HYDRAUL expansion box; **Expansionskoeffizient** *m* MASCHINEN expansion coefficient; **Expansionskupplung** *f* MASCHINEN slip joint; **Expansionsmaschine** *f* MASCHINEN expansion engine; **Expansionsperiode** *f* HYDRAUL expansion period; **Expansionsplatte** *f* HYDRAUL expansion plate; **Expansionspunkt** *m* HYDRAUL expansion point; **Expansionsraum** *m* KER & GLAS expansion space; **Expansionsring** *m* ERDÖL expansion ring; **Expansionsrohr** *nt* LABOR expansion tube; **Expansionsschalter** *m* ELEKTRIZ air breaker; **Expansionsschaltkulisse** *f* HYDRAUL *Quadrant* expansion notch; **Expansionsschaltnocke** *f* HYDRAUL *Quadrant* expansion notch; **Expansionsschieber** *m* HYDRAUL expansion slide; **Expansionsspannung** *f* HYDRAUL expansion stress; **Expansionsspeicher** *m* COMP & DV expanded memory; **Expansionsspeicher-Spezifikation** *m (EMS)* COMP & DV expanded memory specification *(EMS)*; **Expansionssteuernocke** *f* HYDRAUL *Dampfmaschine* expansion cam; **Expansionsstufe** *f* TELEKOM expansion stage; **Expansionsturbine** *f* HEIZ & KÄLTE expansion turbine; **Expansionsventil** *nt* HEIZ & KÄLTE, HYDRAUL, MASCHINEN expansion valve; **Expansionswelle** *f* LUFTTRANS *Überschallknall* expansion wave; **Expansionszeitraum** *m* HYDRAUL expansion period

Experiment *nt* KOHLEN trial, PHYS experiment; **~ innerhalb des Reaktors** *nt* KERNTECH in-reactor experiment; **Experimentalphysiker** *m* TEILPHYS experimental physicist; **Experimentalsicherheitsauto** *nt* KFZTECH ESV, experimental safety vehicle; **~e mit hochenergetischem Teilchenstrahl** *nt pl* STRAHLPHYS fast beam experiments

experimentell[1] *adj* PHYS experimental

experimentell:[2] **~es Fernsehen** *nt* FERNSEH experimental television

Experiment: Experimentenpaket *nt* RAUMFAHRT experiment package; **Experimentiermodul** *nt* RAUMFAHRT experiment module

Expertensystem *nt* COMP & DV *(XPS)*, KÜNSTL INT *(ES, XPS)* expert system *(XPS)*; **Expertensystem-Shell** *f* KÜNSTL INT expert system shell

explodieren *vt* THERMOD detonate

Exploration *f* ERDÖL *Lagerstätten* exploration; **Explorationsbohranlage** *f* ERDÖL *Lagerstätten* exploration rig; **Explorationsbohren** *nt* ERDÖL *Lagerstätten* exploration drilling, exploratory drilling; **Explorationsphase** *f* ERDÖL *Lagerstätten* exploration phase

Explosion *f* ERDÖL *Petrochemie, Physik*, SICHERHEIT explosion, THERMOD detonation

explosionsartig: ~es Feuer *nt* THERMOD flash fire

Explosion: Explosionsbürette *f* CHEMIE eudiometer; **Explosionsformgebung** *f* MECHAN explosive forming; **Explosionsformung** *f* THERMOD explosive forming

explosionsgefährdet: ~er Bereich *m* ELEKTRIZ explosive

gas atmosphere

Explosion: **Explosionsgemisch** *nt* KFZTECH explosive mixture

explosionsgeschützt[1] *adj* ELEKTRIZ, LUFTTRANS, MECHAN explosion-proof, THERMOD flameproof, VERPACK explosion-proof

explosionsgeschützt:[2] ~**er Motor** *m* *(Ex-Motor)* ELEKTROTECH, THERMOD flameproof motor

Explosion: **Explosionsmesser** *m* LABOR *brennbare Gase* explosimeter; **Explosionsmotor** *m* MECHAN internal combustion machine

explosionssicher[1] *adj* ELEKTRIZ, LUFTTRANS, MECHAN, VERPACK explosion-proof

explosionssicher:[2] ~**e Verglasung** *f* KER & GLAS explosion-proof glazing

Explosion: **Explosionszeichnung** *f* MASCHINEN exploded view

explosiv[1] *adj* KFZTECH explosive, THERMOD detonatable, explosive

explosiv:[2] ~**er Abfall** *m* ABFALL explosive waste; ~**e Luft** *f* SICHERHEIT explosive atmosphere

Explosivstoffe *m pl* THERMOD explosives

Explosivumformung *f* MASCHINEN explosive forming

Exponent *m* COMP & DV exponent, MATH exponent, index

Exponential- *pref* AKUSTIK, ELEKTRIZ, ELEKTRONIK, MATH exponential; **Exponentialfunktion** *f* MATH exponential function; **Exponentialkurve** *f* ELEKTRIZ exponential curve; **Exponentialröhre** *f* ELEKTRONIK exponential tube; **Exponentialtrichter** *m* AKUSTIK exponential horn; **Exponentialverstärker** *m* ELEKTRONIK exponential amplifier; **Exponentialverteilung** *f* COMP & DV exponential distribution

exponentiell[1] *adj* MATH exponential

exponentiell:[2] ~**es Brechzahlprofil** *nt* TELEKOM power law index profile; ~**e Glättung** *f* GEOM exponential smoothing; ~**er Zerfall** *m* ELEKTRONIK *Kerntechnik* exponential decay

Exportgüterverpackung *f* VERPACK export packaging

Exportlizenz *f* WASSERTRANS *Dokumente* export licence (BrE), export license (AmE)

Expositionszeit *f* ERGON exposure time

Exsikkator *m* CHEMIE, CHEMTECH, LABOR *Trocknen*, LEBENSMITTEL desiccator

Extender *m* KUNSTSTOFF extender

Extensionsgröße *f* PHYS extensive quantity

extern: ~**e Blockierung** *f* TELEKOM external blocking; ~**e Datei** *f* COMP & DV external data file; ~**es Drehmoment** *nt* MASCHINEN external torque; ~**e Eingabe** *f* COMP & DV external input; ~**e Einspritzung** *f* KFZTECH external injection; ~ **erregter Motor** *m* ELEKTRIZ separately-excited motor; ~**es Gerät** *nt* COMP & DV external device; ~**es Interface** *nt* RAUMFAHRT *Raumschiff* external interface; ~**es Magnetfeld** *nt* ELEKTRIZ external magnetic field; ~**e Modulation** *f* ELEKTRONIK external modulation; ~**e Quelle** *f* ELEKTRONIK external source; ~**er Radioaktivitätspegel** *m* STRAHLPHYS level of external radioactivity; ~**er Schnittstellenadapter** *m* COMP & DV peripheral interface adaptor; ~**es Signal** *nt* ELEKTRONIK external signal; ~**e Sortierung** *f* COMP & DV external sort; ~**er Speicher** *m* COMP & DV external memory, external storage, external store, external memory, ELEKTROTECH external memory; ~**e Steuereinheit** *f* *(PCU)* COMP & DV peripheral control unit *(PCU)*; ~**er Taktgeber** *m* COMP & DV external clock; ~**e Unterbrechung** *f* COMP & DV, ELEKTRONIK external

interrupt; ~**er Ursprung** *m* ELEKTRONIK external source; ~**er Verstärker** *m* ELEKTRONIK remote amplifier; ~**es Vorspannen** *nt* BAU *Beton* external prestressing; ~**er Widerstand** *m* ELEKTRIZ external resistance

Externumschaltung *f* TELEKOM intercell hand-off, interhandoff

Extinktionsmeßgerät *nt* GERÄT haze meter

extradünn: ~**es Tafelglas** *nt* KER & GLAS extra-thin sheet glass

extragalaktisch *adj* RAUMFAHRT extra-galactic

extrahart: ~**es Papier** *nt* FOTO extra-hard paper

extrahierbar: ~**er Schwefel** *m* KUNSTSTOFF extractable sulfur (AmE), extractable sulphur (BrE)

extrahieren *vt* CHEMIE abstract, extract, leach, PAPIER extract

Extrahochspannungskabel *nt* ELEKTRIZ extra-high voltage cable

Extrakt *nt* PAPIER extract

Extrakteur *m* CHEMTECH extractor

Extraktion *f* CHEMTECH, LABOR, extraction; **Extraktionsapparat** *m* CHEMTECH extractor; **Extraktionshaube** *f* LABOR extraction hood; **Extraktionshülse** *f* LABOR *Soxhlet-Apparat*, LEBENSMITTEL extraction thimble; **Extraktionsmittel** *nt* CHEMIE *für Drogenauszüge* menstruum, KERNTECH eluant, eluting agent, LEBENSMITTEL extraction solvent; **Extraktionssäule** *f* PAPIER extractor; **Extraktionsventilator** *m* LABOR extraction fan

extraktiv: ~**e Destillation** *f* LEBENSMITTEL extractive distillation

Extrapolation *f* MATH extrapolation

extrapolieren *vti* MATH extrapolate

extraterrestrisch: ~**es Rauschen** *nt* RADIO external noise

extraweich: ~**es Papier** *nt* FOTO extra-soft paper

extrem: ~ **niedrige Frequenz** *f* *(ENF)* RADIO extremely low frequency *(ELF)*

Extrempunkt *m* GEOM turning point

Extremum *nt* MATH extreme

Extremwert *m* QUAL extreme value; **Extremwertauswahleinheit** *f* REGELUNG high-low signal selector

Extrinsic-Halbleiter *m* PHYS extrinsic semiconductor

Extruder *m* KUNSTSTOFF extruder; **Extruderdüse** *f* KUNSTSTOFF extrusion die; **Extruderfolie** *f* KUNSTSTOFF extruded film

Extrudierbarkeit *f* KUNSTSTOFF extrudability

Extrudieren *nt* KUNSTSTOFF extrusion

extrudieren *vt* KUNSTSTOFF extrude

extrudiert[1] *adj* FERTIG extrusion molded (AmE), extrusion moulded (BrE)

extrudiert:[2] ~**e Folie** *f* KUNSTSTOFF extruded film

Extrusion *f* FERTIG extrusion molding (AmE), extrusion moulding (BrE), KUNSTSTOFF, PAPIER extrusion; **Extrusionsblasen** *nt* VERPACK extrusion blow molding (AmE), extrusion blow moulding (BrE); **Extrusionsmaschine** *f* KUNSTSTOFF extrusion machine; **Extrusionswerkzeug** *nt* KUNSTSTOFF extrusion die

Exzenter *m* MASCHINEN, TEXTIL eccentric; **Exzenterbohrmeißel** *m* ERDÖL *Bohrtechnik* eccentric bit; **Exzenterbolzen** *m* MASCHINEN eccentric bolt; **Exzenterbuchse** *f* MASCHINEN eccentric bush; **Exzenterbügel** *m* MASCHINEN eccentric strap; **Exzenterdrehen** *nt* FERTIG eccentric turning; **Exzenternocken** *m* MASCHINEN eccentric cam; **Exzenterpresse** *f* FERTIG, MASCHINEN eccentric press; **Exzenterscheibe** *f* MASCHINEN eccentric disc (BrE),

eccentric disk (AmE), eccentric sheave; **Exzenterstange** f MECHAN eccentric rod; **Exzenterstift** m FERTIG calm pin; **Exzenterwelle** f FERTIG, MASCHINEN eccentric shaft; **Exzenterzapfen** m MASCHINEN eccentric pin
exzentrisch[1] *adj* MECHAN eccentric
exzentrisch:[2] **~e Anomalie** f RAUMFAHRT eccentric anomaly; **~e Belastung** f BAU eccentric loading; **~es Futter** nt MASCHINEN eccentric chuck

Exzentrizität f AKUSTIK eccentricity, MASCHINEN eccentricity, throw, MECHAN eccentricity, OPTIK *Lichtleiter, von Kern zu Mantel* core-cladding concentricity error, RAUMFAHRT eccentricity; **Exzentrizitätsmaß** nt MASCHINEN throw
Exzitron nt ELEKTROTECH excitron

F

F [1] *abbr* AKUSTIK *(Frequenz)*, AUFNAHME *(Frequenz)*, COMP & DV *(Frequenz)* f *(frequency)*, ELEKTRIZ *(Farad)* F *(farad)*, ELEKTRONIK *(Rauschzahl)* F *(noise figure)*, ELEKTRONIK *(Frequenz)* f *(frequency)*, ELEKTROTECH *(Farad)* F *(farad)*, HYDRAUL *(Froudensche Zahl)* F *(Froude number)*, KERNTECH *(hyperfeine Quantenzahl)* F *(hyperfine quantum number)*, METALL *(Kraft)* F *(force)*, METALL *(freie Energie)* F *(free energy)*, METROL *(Fahrenheit)* F *(Fahrenheit)*, METROL *(Farad)* F *(farad)*, METROL *(Femto-)* f *(femto-)*, PHYS *(Froudensche Zahl)* F *(Froude number)*, PHYS *(Farad)* F *(farad)*, PHYS *(Kraft)* F *(force)*, PHYS *(freie Energie)* F *(free energy)*, PHYS *(Frequenz)* f *(frequency)*, RADIO *(Rauschzahl)* F *(noise figure)*, RADIO *(Frequenz)* f *(frequency)*

F [2] *(Fluor)* CHEMIE F *(fluorine)*

F&E-Ingenieur m *(Forschungs- und Entwicklungsingenieur)* MASCHINEN research-development engineer

fA *abbr (Antiresonanzfrequenz)* AKUSTIK, ELEKTRONIK fA *(antiresonant frequency)*

Fabrik f MECHAN factory, VERPACK board mill; **Fabrikabnehmer** m MASCHINEN OEM, original equipment manufacturer; **Fabrikanlage** f MASCHINEN mill; **Fabrikanschlußgleis** nt EISENBAHN factory siding

Fabrikationsnummer f MASCHINEN serial number

Fabrik: Fabrikdämpfe m pl SICHERHEIT factory fumes

fabrikfertig [1] *adj* HEIZ & KÄLTE factory-assembled

fabrikfertig: [2] **~e Anlage** f HEIZ & KÄLTE factory-assembled system; **~e Verpackung** f VERPACK prefabricated package

Fabrik: Fabrikhalle f MECHAN fabricating shop; **Fabrikprüfung** f QUAL shop test; **Fabrikschiff** nt WASSERTRANS factory ship

Fabry-Pérot: ~sches Interferometer nt PHYS, RAUMFAHRT Fabry-Pérot interferometer

Faceplatte f WASSERTRANS *Schiffbau* face plate

Facette f KER & GLAS arrissed edge

facettiert [1] *adj* KER & GLAS facetted

facettiert: [2] **~es Bläschen** nt KERNTECH facetted bubble; **~er Ring** m KERNTECH facetted ring

Fach nt MASCHINEN compartment, MECHAN, TELEKOM bay; **Fachbereichswissen** nt KÜNSTL INT domain knowledge

Fächer m HEIZ & KÄLTE fan, ventilator

fächerförmig: ~es Lichtbündel nt ELEKTRONIK *Beleuchtungstechnik* fan beam

Fächer: Fächerfunkfeuer nt WASSERTRANS *Seezeichen* fan marker beacon; **Fächerkasten** m VERPACK compartment case; **Fächerkeule** f ELEKTRONIK *Antennentechnik* fan beam; **Fächermaschine** f PAPIER harper machine; **Fächermethode** f ABFALL cell method; **Fächerplatte** f WASSERTRANS *Schiffbau* gusset plate; **Fächerscheibe** f MASCHINEN serrated lock washer; **Fächerwand** f VERPACK partition wall

Fachwerk nt BAU framework, lattice, truss, trussing; **Fachwerkbinder** m BAU open-web girder; **Fachwerkbinderdach** nt BAU trussed roof; **Fachwerkbrücke** f BAU frame bridge, truss bridge; **Fachwerkhaus** nt BAU frame house, half-timbered house; **Fachwerkholzträger** m BAU trussed wooden beam; **Fachwerkträger** m BAU lattice girder, trussed beam, trussed girder; **Fachwerkwand** f BAU stud wall

Fackel f ERDÖL *Raffinerie, Bohrfeld* flare, MECHAN torch

fackeln vt TEXTIL blaze

Fackelrohr nt ERDÖL *Raffinerie, Bohrfeld* flare stack

fade *adj* LEBENSMITTEL unflavored (AmE), unflavoured (BrE)

Faden [1] m BAU filament, KER & GLAS string, thread, METROL fathom, PAPIER thread, TEXTIL thread, yarn, WASSERTRANS *Maßeinheit* fathom

Faden: [2] **mit ~ heften** vt DRUCK thread

Faden: Fadenanzahl f TEXTIL *Garn* ply; **Fadenauflage** f KER & GLAS applied thread; **Fadenbruch** m TEXTIL broken end; **Fadenende** nt TEXTIL yarn end

fadenförmig: ~er Knoten m KER & GLAS stringy knot

Faden: Fadenführer m TEXTIL feeder, yarn carrier, *Spinnen* carrier; **Fadenkreuz** nt COMP & DV crosshair, ELEKTRONIK reticle, FERTIG hair cross, OPTIK spider lines; **Fadenkreuzlinie** f OPTIK webspider line; **Fadenkreuzokular** nt OPTIK eyepiece with cross-wires; **Fadenlieferer** m TEXTIL guide; **Fadennetz** nt FERTIG reticle; **Fadenscheinigkeit** f TEXTIL scratching; **Fadenschluß** m TEXTIL cover; **Fadenverdickung** f TEXTIL slub; **Fadenwächter am Gatter** m TEXTIL stop motion on creel; **Fadenzähler** m DRUCK line, PAPIER thread counter; **Fadenziehen** nt LEBENSMITTEL *Brot* ropiness; **Fadenzufuhrregelung** f TEXTIL yarn feed control

Fading nt AKUSTIK, RADIO, TELEKOM fade, fading; **Fadingregelung** f ELEKTROTECH automatic volume control

Fähigkeit f ERGON ability, PHYS power; **~ zur Korrektur von Fehlerbursts** f TELEKOM burst error-correcting capability; **~ zu Was-wäre-wenn-Folgerungen** f KÜNSTL INT *eines Expertensystems* what-if capability

Fähigkeiten f pl COMP & DV *eines Programms, Computers, Benutzers* capabilities

Fahne f TEXTIL *Wolle* ply, WASSERTRANS *Flagge* flag; **Fahnenabzug** m DRUCK galley, galley proof, slip proof

Fahr- *pref* TRANS driving; **Fahrabschaltventil** nt HYDRAUL riding cutoff valve; **Fahrbahn** f BAU *eines Krans* runway, TRANS roadway; **Fahrbahn für allgemeinen Verkehr** f TRANS nonreserved space; **Fahrbahnmarkierung** f BAU road painting; **Fahrbahnunstetigkeit** f EISENBAHN unevenness of trackway; **Fahrbalken** m TRANS track girder

fahrbar: ~e Hubbühne f BAU portable hoisting platform; **~er Portalkran** m WASSERTRANS *Hafen* traveling gantry crane (AmE), travelling gantry crane (BrE); **~er Schraubstock** m BAU portable vice; **~er Verdichter** m ABFALL compactor vehicle, compression vehicle, packer body; **~er Wagenheber** m TRANS mobile jack

Fährbetrieb m WASSERTRANS ferrying

Fährdienst m WASSERTRANS ferry service

Fähre *f* RAUMFAHRT *Raumschiff* shuttle, WASSERTRANS ferry

fahren[1] *vt* TRANS carry

fahren[2] *vi* WASSERTRANS sail, *Schiff* run

Fahrenheit *nt (F)* METROL Fahrenheit *(F)*; **Fahrenheit-Temperaturskale** *f* PHYS Fahrenheit scale

Fahrer *m* TRANS driver; **Fahrerbereich** *m* KFZTECH cockpit; **Fahrerhaus** *nt* EISENBAHN, KFZTECH *Karosserie* cab;

Fahr-: **Fahrerlaubnis** *f* KFZTECH *Rechtsvorschriften* driver's licence (BrE), driver's license (AmE)

fahrerlos: **~er Zug** *m* EISENBAHN unmanned train

Fahrer: **Fahrerseite** *f* KFZTECH offside

Fahr-: **Fahrfläche** *f* LUFTTRANS *Fahrwerk* tread

Fahrgast *m* TRANS passenger; **Fahrgastflug** *m* TRANS passenger flight; **Fahrgastraum** *m* EISENBAHN passenger compartment; **Fahrgastsitz** *m* TRANS passenger seat

Fahr-: **Fahrgemeinschaft** *f* TRANS car pool; **Fahrgeschwindigkeit** *f* TRANS progression speed, running speed

Fahrgestell *nt* FERTIG bogie, KFZTECH undercarriage, *Anhänger* bogie (BrE), *Karosserie* chassis, MASCHINEN bogie, MECHAN carriage, TRANS carriage, *Kran* bogie (BrE), bogie truck (AmE), trailer (AmE); **Fahrgestell-A mit Motor** *nt* KFZTECH carriage A containing the motor; **Fahrgestell mit Kabine** *nt* KFZTECH *LKW* chassis-cab; **Fahrgestellachswelle** *f* LUFTTRANS landing-gear shaft; **Fahrgestellauskreuzungseinrichtung** *f* LUFTTRANS landing-gear bracing installation; **Fahrgestelleinfahrverriegelungskasten** *m* LUFTTRANS landing-gear up-lock box; **Fahrgestellhaubenhalterung** *f* LUFTTRANS landing-gear boot retainer (BrE), landing-gear trunk retainer (AmE); **Fahrgestellkompensierungsstange** *f* LUFTTRANS landing-gear compensation rod; **Fahrgestellquerbock** *m* LUFTTRANS landing-gear diagonal truss; **Fahrgestellquerstrebe** *f* LUFTTRANS landing-gear diagonal truss; **Fahrgestellspur** *f* LUFTTRANS landing-gear track; **Fahrgestellstoßdämpfer** *m* LUFTTRANS landing-gear bumper; **Fahrgestellstütze** *f* LUFTTRANS landing leg support; **Fahrgestellverschlußhalterung** *f* LUFTTRANS landing-gear boot retainer (BrE), landing-gear trunk retainer (AmE)

Fahr-: **Fahrkarte** *f* EISENBAHN railroad ticket (AmE), railway ticket (BrE); **Fahrkorb** *m* TRANS *eines Aufzugs* car; **Fahrkran** *m* BAU portable crane, MECHAN traveling crane (AmE), travelling crane (BrE)

Fährlandungsbrücke *f* WASSERTRANS ferry-landing stage

Fahrleitung *f* MECHAN, PHYS catenary; **Fahrleitungsmast** *m* EISENBAHN catenary support

Fahr-: **Fahrmanipulator** *m* KERNTECH traveling manipulator (AmE), travelling manipulator (BrE); **Fahrpedal** *nt* KFZTECH accelerator (BrE), gas pedal (AmE)

Fahrplan *m* EISENBAHN schedule (AmE), timetable (BrE); **Fahrplankonstruktion** *f* EISENBAHN schedule compilation (AmE); timetable compilation (BrE); **Fahrplantrasse** *f* EISENBAHN train path; **nicht nach ~ verkehrender Zug** *m* EISENBAHN out-of-course running

Fahrrad *nt* MASCHINEN bicycle; **Fahrradergometer** *nt* ERGON bicycle ergometer; **Fahrradpumpe** *f* MASCHINEN bicycle pump; **Fahrradventil** *nt* MASCHINEN bicycle valve; **Fahrradwerkzeuge** *nt pl* MASCHINEN bicycle tools

Fahr-: **Fahrrinne** *f* WASSERTRANS ship canal, *Navigation* channel

Fährseil *nt* WASSERTRANS ferry cable

Fahrspur *f* TRANS lane; **Fahrspurrichtungssignal** *nt* TRANS lane direction control signal; **Fahrspurwechsel** *m* TRANS lane switching

Fahr-: **Fahrsteig** *m* TRANS moving pavement (BrE), moving sidewalk (AmE); **Fahrstrahl** *m* PHYS position vector

Fahrstraße *f* TRANS road; **Fahrstraßeneinstellung durch Rechner** *f* EISENBAHN computer route setting; **Fahrstraßenfestlegung** *f* EISENBAHN holding of a route; **Fahrstraßenmatrix** *f* EISENBAHN routing diagram; **Fahrstraßensperre** *f* EISENBAHN route locking

Fahr-: **Fahrstrecke** *f* LUFTTRANS, TRANS *Auto, Bahn* distance covered; **Fahrstuhl** *m* ELEKTRIZ, MECHAN, TRANS elevator (AmE), lift (BrE)

Fahrt: **in ~** *adj* WASSERTRANS under way; **~ voraus** *adj* WASSERTRANS headway

Fahrt *f* TRANS running, WASSERTRANS way of ship; **~ zur Arbeit gegen den hauptsächlichen Verkehrsstrom** *f* TRANS reverse commute; **Fahrtbericht** *m* TRANS trip report analysis; **Fahrtdauer** *f* TRANS journey time; **Fahrtenbuch** *nt* LUFTTRANS, TRANS, WASSERTRANS logbook; **Fahrtenschreiber** *m* KFZTECH tachograph, trip recorder; **Fahrtgeschwindigkeit** *f* WASSERTRANS rate of sailing; **Fahrtmeßanlage** *f* WASSERTRANS speedometer; **Fahrtmesser** *m* LUFTTRANS, WASSERTRANS log; **Fahrtregler** *m* KFZTECH cruise control; **Fahrtrichtungsanzeiger** *m* KFZTECH direction indicator, indicator, TRANS trafficator; **Fahrtsignal** *nt* EISENBAHN, WASSERTRANS clear signal; **Fahrtstörungslaterne** *f* WASSERTRANS *Signal* not-under-command light; **Fahrtrimm** *f* WASSERTRANS squat

fahrtüchtig *adj* WASSERTRANS navigable

Fahr-: **Fahrtüchtigkeit** *f* WASSERTRANS navigability

Fahrt: **Fahrtwender** *m* EISENBAHN braking switchgroup, reversing switchgroup; **Fahrtwind** *m* WASSERTRANS headwind; **Fahrtzweck** *m* TRANS trip purpose

Fahr-: **Fahrvorrichtung** *f* KERNTECH *an Dickenmeßgerät* traversing mechanism

Fahrwasser *nt* WASSERTRANS *Navigation* channel, fairway

Fahrwasser: **in ~ einlaufen** *vi* WASSERTRANS *Navigation* enter a channel

Fahrwasser: **Fahrwassermarkierungen** *f pl* WASSERTRANS channel markings, *Seezeichen* fairway markings; **Fahrwasserzeichen** *nt* WASSERTRANS fairway mark

Fahrwerk *nt* LUFTTRANS landing gear, undercarriage, MASCHINEN bogie assembly, running gear; **Fahrwerkabwerftest** *m* LUFTTRANS landing-gear drop test; **Fahrwerkanzeige** *f* LUFTTRANS landing-gear position indicator; **Fahrwerkausfahren** *nt* LUFTTRANS landing-gear extension; **Fahrwerkbein** *nt* LUFTTRANS landing-gear leg; **Fahrwerkeinfahrverriegelung** *f* LUFTTRANS landing-gear up-lock, landing-gear retraction lock; **Fahrwerkentriegelung** *f* LUFTTRANS landing-gear unlocking; **Fahrwerkgabelstange** *f* LUFTTRANS landing-gear fork rod; **Fahrwerkgelenkträger** *m* LUFTTRANS landing-gear hinge beam; **Fahrwerkgelenkträgeranschluß** *m* LUFTTRANS landing-gear hinge beam fitting; **Fahrwerkgrube** *f* LUFTTRANS landing-gear well; **Fahrwerkhauptbremszylinder** *m* LUFTTRANS landing-gear master brake cylinder; **Fahrwerkhauptfederbein** *nt* LUFTTRANS landing-gear main shock strut; **Fahrwerkklappenentriegelung** *f* LUFTTRANS landing-gear door unlatching; **Fahrwerkklappenverschluß** *m* LUFTTRANS landing-gear door latch; **Fahrwerkklappenverschlußkasten** *m* LUFTTRANS landing-gear door latching box; **Fahrwerkschieberventil** *nt* LUFTTRANS landing-gear sliding valve; **Fahrwerksicherheitssteuerung** *f* LUFTTRANS landing-gear safety override; **Fahrwerksicherheitsverschluß** *m* LUFTTRANS landing-gear safety lock; **Fahrwerksperre** *f* LUFTTRANS landing-gear down latch; **Fahrwerksteuergerät** *nt* LUFTTRANS landing-gear control unit; **Fahrwerksteuerung** *f* LUFTTRANS landing-gear control unit; **Fahrwerkverriegelung** *f* LUFTTRANS landing-gear down latch; **Fahrwerkverriegelungsbolzen** *m* LUFTTRANS landing-gear lock pin

Fahr-: **Fahrwiderstand** *m* KFZTECH *Reifen* road resistance; **Fahrzeit** *f* TRANS running time

Fahrzeug *nt* KFZTECH car, MECHAN vehicle, MEERSCHMUTZ *in das geleichtert wird* lightening vessel, WASSERTRANS craft; **~ mit Allradantrieb** *nt* KFZTECH four-wheel drive vehicle; **~ innerhalb der Erdgravitation** *nt* RAUMFAHRT *Raumschiff* earth capture vehicle; **~ mit Unterdruckaufhängung** *f* KFZTECH suction-suspended vehicle; **~ mit Vergasermotor** *nt* UMWELTSCHMUTZ gasoline engine vehicle (AmE), petrol engine vehicle (BrE); **Fahrzeugabstand** *m* TRANS vehicular gap; **Fahrzeugantriebsdifferential** *nt* KFZTECH traction differential; **Fahrzeugausstattung** *f* KFZTECH car accessories; **Fahrzeugbremsweg** *m* KFZTECH braking distance; **Fahrzeugbrief** *m* KFZTECH *KFZ* engine logbook; **Fahrzeugerfassung** *f* TRANS vehicle intercept survey; **Fahrzeugfähre** *f* WASSERTRANS vehicle ferry; **Fahrzeugfluß zur Hauptverkehrszeit** *m* TRANS vehicular flow at the peak hour; **Fahrzeugfolgeabstand** *m* TRANS *Verkehr* headway; **Fahrzeugfolgezeit** *f* TRANS gap, time headway, vehicle extension period; **Fahrzeugfolgezeitanalyse** *f* TRANS headways distribution analysis; **Fahrzeugfolgezeitdetektor** *m* TRANS gap detector; **Fahrzeuginnenraum** *m* KFZTECH interior of car; **Fahrzeugmarkierung** *f* TRANS vehicle tagging

fahrzeugmontiert: **~er kurzer Primärlinearmotor** *m* KFZTECH vehicle-mounted short primary linear motor

Fahrzeug: **Fahrzeugortungssubsystem** *nt* TELEKOM vehicle location subsystem; **Fahrzeugpark** *m* KFZTECH rolling stock; **Fahrzeugschein** *m* KFZTECH engine logbook; **Fahrzeugschlange** *f* TRANS line (AmE), queue (BrE); **Fahrzeugschlangendetektor** *m* TRANS line detector (AmE), queue detector (BrE); **Fahrzeugschwebesystem** *nt* EISENBAHN SVS, suspended vehicle system; **Fahrzeugtanker** *m* WASSERTRANS vehicle tanker; **Fahrzeugverkehr** *m* LUFTTRANS aerodrome vehicle operations (BrE), airdrome vehicle operations (AmE); **Fahrzeugzufahrt** *f* TRANS vehicle ramp

Failsafe-Design *f* KERNTECH fail-safe design

Faksimile *nt (Fax)* COMP & DV, RADIO, TELEKOM facsimile *(fax)*; **Faksimile-Mitteilung** *f* COMP & DV, TELEKOM facsimile message; **Faksimile-Telegraphie** *f* COMP & DV, TELEKOM facsimile telegraphy

Faktenwissen *nt* KÜNSTL INT factual knowledge

Faktor *m* COMP & DV, MATH factor; **~ der schnellen Spaltung** *f* PHYS *Kernphysik* fast fission factor

Faktoren-[1] *pref* MATH factorial

Faktoren:[2] **in ~ zerlegen** *vt* MATH factorize

Faktorenanalyse *f* ERGON factor analysis

faktoriell[1] *adj* MATH factorial

faktoriell:[2] **~e Gestaltung** *f* ERGON factorial design

Faktorisierung *f* MATH factorization

Fakultät *f* MATH factorial

fakultativ: **~er Aerobier** *m* LEBENSMITTEL facultative aerobe

Fall *m* COMP & DV instance, METROL case, TEXTIL draping properties, WASSERTRANS rake, *Tauwerk* halyard; **Fallbär** *m* MECHAN ram; **Fallbetankung** *f* LUFTTRANS gravity refueling (AmE), gravity refuelling (BrE); **Fallbetankungshahn** *m* LUFTTRANS gravity filler plug; **Fallbirne** *f* BAU breaker ball; **Fallbügelpunktschreiber** *m* GERÄT chopper bar dot recorder; **Fallbügelregler** *m* GERÄT chopper bar controller; **Fallbügelschreiber** *m* GERÄT hoop drop recorder

Falle *f* ERDÖL *Geologie* trap

Falleitung *f* KERNTECH penstock

Fallen *nt* ERDÖL *Geologie* dip, THERMOD fall

fallend: **~es Gießen** *nt* FERTIG direct casting; **~er Guß** *m* FERTIG top pouring; **~e Tide** *f* WASSERTRANS *Gezeiten* falling tide; **~e Widerstandscharakteristik** *f* ELEKTROTECH negative resistance characteristic

fallenlassen *vt* PATENT *Anmeldung* abandon

Fall: **Fallfüllung** *f* RAUMFAHRT *Raumschiff* gravity filling; **Fallgesetz** *nt* MASCHINEN law of gravitation; **Fallgewicht** *nt* MASCHINEN drop weight; **Fallgewichtsprüfung** *f* MASCHINEN hammer test; **Fallhammer** *m* BAU monkey, FERTIG drop stamp, tup, KOHLEN, MASCHINEN drop hammer; **Fallhärteprüfung** *f* METALL ball test; **Fallhöhe** *f* BAU head, HYDRAUL head, head of water, KOHLEN drop height, VERPACK drop height, height of fall; **Fallkabel** *nt* FERNSEH drop cable; **Fallkasten** *m* WASSERVERSORG drip pump, drop box; **Fallklappentafel** *f* ELEKTROTECH annunciator; **Fallmauer** *f* WASSERVERSORG *Kanalschleuse* lift wall

Fällmittel *nt* ABFALL coagulant

Fallout *m* KERNTECH, UMWELTSCHMUTZ fallout

Fall: **Fallprobe** *f* MASCHINEN drop test, falling-weight test; **Fallreepstreppe** *f* WASSERTRANS accommodation ladder; **Fallrichtung** *f* ERDÖL *Geologie* down dip; **Fallrinne** *f* MECHAN chute; **Fallrohr** *nt* BAU downspout, leader, *Dachrinne* rainwater pipe, *Kaminschacht* band, ERDÖL *Destillationstechnik*, KERNTECH downcomer, PAPIER drop leg, WASSERVERSORG soil pipe; **Fallrohrauslauf** *m* BAU shoe; **Fallrohreindicker** *m* PAPIER gravity thickener; **Fallschacht** *m* WASSERVERSORG pressure well

Fallschirm: mit ~ abwerfen *vt* LUFTTRANS airdrop

Fall: **Fallschirmaufziehleine** *f* LUFTTRANS parachute release handle; **Fallschirmbremsung** *f* RAUMFAHRT *Raumschiff* parabrake; **Fallschirmlicht** *nt* WASSERTRANS *Signal* parachute flare; **Fallschloß** *nt* BAU spring lock; **Fallschmierung** *f* MASCHINEN gravity lubrication; **Fallschnecke** *f* FERTIG drop worm; **Fallstrom** *m* MASCHINEN downdraft (AmE), downdraught (BrE); **Fallstromkühler** *m* KFZTECH upright radiator; **Fallstromvergaser** *m* KFZTECH downdraft carburetor (AmE), downdraught carburettor (BrE); **Fallstudie** *f* ERGON, KÜNSTL INT case study; **Falltür** *f* BAU trap door; **Fallüberlaufdamm** *m* LUFTTRANS gravity spillway dam

Fällungsanalyse *f* CHEMTECH precipitation analysis; **Fällungsmittel** *nt* CHEMTECH precipitating agent

Fall: **Fallverschluß** *m* FOTO guillotine shutter; **Fallversuch** *m* MASCHINEN drop test, falling-weight test, VERPACK drop test; **Fallwind** *m* LUFTTRANS down gust, downwash, downwind

falsch[1] *adj* COMP & DV false; **~ verbunden** *adj* TELEKOM wrongly-connected

falsch:[2] **~e akustische Wahrnehmung** *f* AKUSTIK paracusis; **~es Heben** *nt* SICHERHEIT *Unfallursachen* incorrect manual lifting; **~es Körpergehalt** *m* KER & GLAS false body; **~e Nummer** *f* TELEKOM wrong number; **~er Rücken** *m* DRUCK false back; **~es Wiederauffinden** *nt* COMP & DV false retrieval

falsch:[3] **~ beschneiden** *vt* FERTIG mistrim

Falschfahrt *f* EISENBAHN running on wrong line

Falschluft *f* KFZTECH air leak

Falschsignal *nt* ELEKTRONIK false signal

Falt- *pref* KONSTZEICH, RADIO, RAUMFAHRT, VERPACK folding; **Falt- und Aufrichtmaschine** *f* VERPACK large case erector; **Faltantenne** *f* RAUMFAHRT *Weltraumfunk* collapsible antenna; **Faltart** *f* KONSTZEICH folding mode

faltbar[1] *adj* MASCHINEN collapsible

faltbar:[2] **~es und wiederzuverwertendes Verpackungssystem** *nt* VERPACK collapsible and reusable packaging system

Falt-: **Faltbett** *nt* SICHERHEIT *Erste-Hilfe* folding bed; **Faltboot** *nt* WASSERTRANS collapsible boat; **Faltdipol** *m* RADIO, TELEKOM folded dipole

Falte *f* ANSTRICH lap, FERTIG pucker, *Blech* flopper, KER & GLAS crimp, lap, PAPIER wrinkle, TEXTIL crease, pleat

Falten *nt* PAPIER folding, TEXTIL pleating; **Faltenbalg** *m* MASCHINEN, MECHAN bellows; **Faltenbildung** *f* FERTIG puckering

falten *vt* FERTIG crease, PAPIER fold, TEXTIL pleat

faltenfrei *adj* ANSTRICH unlapped

Falte: **Faltenhalter** *m* FERTIG blank holder; **Faltenhalterkraft** *f* FERTIG blank-holder force; **Faltenrohr** *nt* MASCHINEN quill tube

Falt-: **Faltflügelflugzeug** *nt* LUFTTRANS folding-wing aircraft; **Faltgut** *nt* KONSTZEICH folded material; **Faltkante** *f* KONSTZEICH folding edge; **Faltkarton** *m* VERPACK collapsible case, folding carton; **Faltprospekt** *m* DRUCK folder; **Falt-Quad-Antenne** *f* RADIO *Antenne* folded quad; **Faltschachtel** *f* PAPIER folding box, VERPACK folding cardboard box; **Falttür** *f* BAU flexible door, folding door

Faltung *f* ELEKTRONIK folding; **Faltungscode** *m* TELEKOM convolution code, convolutional code, convolutive code; **Faltungscodierung mit halber Geschwindigkeit** *f* TELEKOM rate one-half convolutional coding; **Faltungsfrequenz** *f* COMP & DV aliasing; **Faltungsoperation** *f* ELEKTRONIK *Nachrichtenverarbeitung* convolution; **Faltungsprodukt** *nt* ELEKTRONIK *Nachrichtenverarbeitung* convolution product

Falt-: **Faltverschluß** *m* VERPACK tuck-in closure; **Faltversuch** *m* MASCHINEN folding test, METALL cold bend test, doubling-over test, *Platten, Stäben* bend test, VERPACK folding test

Falz *m* BAU joggle, lap, mortise, plough (BrE), plow (AmE), rabbet, seam, FERTIG rabbet, PAPIER fold; **Falz- und Anleimmaschine** *f* VERPACK crease and glueing machine; **Falz- und Verschließmaschine** *f* VERPACK folding and seaming machine; **Falzbarkeit** *f* FERTIG foldability; **Falzbodenkarton** *m* VERPACK folded-bottom box

Falzen *nt* BAU bending, FERTIG bending, folding, seaming

falzen *vt* BAU bead, bend, rabbet, FERTIG bend, welt, *Blech* seam, MECHAN crimp, VERPACK crease

Falz: **Falzfestigkeit** *f* VERPACK folding strength; **Falzfuge** *f* BAU rebated joint; **Falzhobel** *m* BAU fillister, rabbet plane, rebate plane; **Falzmarken** *f pl* DRUCK folding marks; **Falzmaschine** *f* DRUCK folder unit, MASCHINEN folding machine, seaming machine; **Falzmeißel** *m* FERTIG groover; **Falztrichter** *m* PAPIER former

Falzung *f* BAU feather edge

Falz: **Falzwalzen** *f pl* DRUCK folding rollers; **Falzzudrükken** *nt* FERTIG grooving

Familienpackung *f* VERPACK economy-size pack, family packet

Fan *m* LUFTTRANS fan

Fang- *pref* ELEKTRONIK capture; **Fangarbeit** *f* ERDÖL fishing; **Fangbereich** *m* ELEKTRONIK lock-in range, *AFC* capture range, RADIO locking range; **Fangdamm** *m* BAU batardeau, cofferdam, WASSERVERSORG cofferdam, *einer Schleuse* coffer; **Fangeisen** *nt* KER & GLAS bait

Fangen *nt* TELEKOM call interception, call trace

Fang-: **Fanggerät** *nt* ERDÖL fishing tool; **Fanggitter** *nt* ELEKTROTECH suppression grid; **Fangglocke** *f* ERDÖL overshot; **Fanghilfeverstärker** *m* ELEKTRONIK lock-in amplifier; **Fangleine** *f* WASSERTRANS *Festmachen* painter; **Fangort** *m* ELEKTROTECH trapping site; **Fangstelle** *f* COMP & DV trap, ELEKTROTECH trapping site; **Fangstoff** *m* ELEKTROTECH getter; **Fangwerkzeug** *nt* ERDÖL fishing tool

Fantfracht *f* ERDÖL dead freight

Fan-Triebwerk *nt* LUFTTRANS fan jet engine

Farad *nt* ELEKTRIZ *(F)*, ELEKTROTECH *(F)*, METROL *(F)*, PHYS *(F)* farad *(F)*, RADIO *Einheit der Kapazität* farad

Faraday: **~sche Drehung** *f* RAUMFAHRT Faraday rotation; **~scher Dunkelraum** *m* ELEKTRONIK, PHYS Faraday dark space; **~scher Effekt** *m* ELEKTROTECH, PHYS Faraday effect; **~sches Gefäß** *nt* ELEKTRIZ Faraday ice pail; **~sche Gesetze** *nt pl* ELEKTRIZ, PHYS Faraday's laws; **~sches Induktionsgesetz** *nt* ELEKTRIZ, PHYS Faraday's law; **~scher Käfig** *m* ELEKTRIZ Faraday cage, ELEKTROTECH Faraday cage, Faraday screen, KERNTECH Faraday cage, Faraday shield, PHYS Faraday cage, RADIO Faraday screen; **~sche Konstante** *f* PHYS Faraday constant, faraday; **~sche Scheibe** *f* ELEKTROTECH Faraday disc (BrE), Faraday disk (AmE); **~sche Schlitzscheibe** *f* PHYS Faraday disc (BrE), Faraday disk (AmE); **~scher Zylinder** *m* PHYS Faraday cylinder

Farb- *pref* ANSTRICH, FERNSEH color (AmE), colour (BrE); **Farbabbrennlampe** *f* BAU paint-burning lamp; **Farbabgleich** *m* DRUCK color matching (AmE), colour matching (BrE); **Farbabgleichung** *f* ERGON color matching (AmE), colour matching (BrE); **Farbabmusterung** *f* DRUCK color matching (AmE), colour matching (BrE); **Farbabstimmung** *f* COMP & DV color balance (AmE), colour balance (BrE); **Farbabweichung** *f* FERNSEH chromaticity aberration; **Farbabzug** *m* FOTO color print (AmE), colour print (BrE); **Farbadapter** *m* COMP & DV color adaptor (AmE), colour adaptor (BrE); **Farbaffinität** *f* TEXTIL dyeing affinity; **Farbanalysator** *m* FOTO color analyzer (AmE), colour analyser (BrE); **Farbanteile** *m pl* FERNSEH chrominance components; **Farbanzeige** *f* COMP & DV color display (AmE), colour display (BrE); **Farbanzeige für Strahlungsdosis** *f* STRAHLPHYS dose color indicators (AmE), dose colour indicators (BrE); **Farbauflösungsvermögen** *nt* PHYS chromatic resolving power; **Farbaufnahme** *f* FOTO color picture (AmE), colour picture (BrE); **Farbaufrollen** *nt* BAU roller painting; **Farbaufsatz** *m* FOTO color head (AmE), colour head (BrE); **Farbauszugsfilter** *nt* FOTO color separation filter (AmE), colour separation filter (BrE); **Farbauszugsnegativ** *nt* FOTO color separation negative (AmE), colour separation negative (BrE); **Farbauszugsüberlagerung** *f* FERNSEH chromakey (AmE), color separation overlay (AmE), colour separation overlay (BrE); **Farbauszugverfahren** *nt* DRUCK color separation (AmE), colour separation (BrE); **Farbbalken** *m pl* FERNSEH color bars (AmE), colour bars (BrE); **Farbbalkengenerator** *m* FERNSEH color bar generator, colour bar generator (BrE); **Farbband** *nt* COMP & DV inked ribbon, ribbon; **Farbbandführung** *f* AUFNAHME, GERÄT *Registriergerät* ribbon guide; **Farbbeizen** *nt* KER & GLAS staining; **Farbbeständigkeit** *f* KUNSTSTOFF color fastness (AmE), colour fastness (BrE); **Farbbezugssignal** *nt* FERNSEH color reference signal (AmE), colour reference signal (BrE); **Farbbildschirm** *m* COMP & DV color display (AmE), color monitor (AmE), colour display (BrE), colour monitor (BrE); **Farbburst** *m* FERNSEH color burst (AmE), colour burst (BrE); **Farbcode für Feuerlöscher** *m* SICHERHEIT fire extinguisher color code (AmE), fire extinguisher colour code; **Farbdecoder** *m* FERNSEH color decoder (AmE), colour decoder (BrE); **Farbdecodierer** *m* COMP & DV color decoder (AmE), colour decoder (BrE); **Farbdichtemesser** *m* PAPIER colour densitometer (BrE); **Farbdifferenz** *f* FERNSEH color difference (AmE), colour difference (BrE); **Farbdifferenzsignal** *nt* FERNSEH color difference signal (AmE), colour difference signal (BrE); **Farbdreieck** *nt* PHYS color triangle (AmE), colour triangle (BrE); **Farbdruck** *m* DRUCK color printing (AmE), colour printing (BrE), colorwork (AmE), colourwork (BrE)

Farbe[1] *f* ANSTRICH paint, DRUCK color (AmE), colour (BrE), FERNSEH chroma, LEBENSMITTEL, PAPIER, TEILPHYS, TELEKOM color (AmE), colour (BrE), TEXTIL color (AmE), colour (BrE), dye

Farbe:[2] **die ~ abstimmen** *vi* TEXTIL match the shade

Färbebad *nt* TEXTIL bath

Färbebaum *m* TEXTIL beam

Färbebeschleuniger *m* TEXTIL carrier

farbecht *adj* VERPACK colorfast (AmE), colourfast (BrE)

Farb-: **Farbechtheit** *f* KUNSTSTOFF color fastness (AmE), colour fastness (BrE)

Färbeflotte *f* FERTIG *Kunststoffinstallationen* dyeing solution

Färbehülse *f* TEXTIL cone tube

Farb-: **Farbeindringprüfung** *f* MECHAN dye penetrant test

färben *vt* FOTO, TEXTIL dye

Farbe: **Farbenanalyse** *f* FERNSEH color analysis (AmE), colour analysis (BrE)

färbend: **nicht ~** *adj* KUNSTSTOFF nonstaining

Farbe: **Farbendruck** *m* DRUCK color printing (AmE), colour printing (BrE), colorwork (AmE), colourwork (BrE); **Farbendruckmaschine** *f* DRUCK color printing

machine (AmE), colour printing machine (BrE); **Farbenform** *f* DRUCK colorform (AmE), colour form (BrE); **Farbenlichtdruck** *m* DRUCK color collotype (AmE), colour collotype (BrE); **Farbenmesser** *m* PHYS colorimeter; **Farbenmessung** *f* PHYS, STRAHLPHYS colorimetry; **Farbenphase** *f* FERNSEH color phase (AmE), colour phase (BrE); **Farbensehen** *nt* ERGON color vision (AmE), colour vision (BrE); **Farbensinn** *m* ERGON color vision (AmE), colour vision (BrE); **Farbenspektrum** *nt* FOTO chromatic spectrum; **Farbentrennung** *f* FERNSEH color separation (AmE), colour separation (BrE); **Farbentwickler** *m* FOTO color developer (AmE), colour developer (BrE); **Farbentwicklung** *f* FOTO color development (AmE), colour development (BrE); **Farbenzerlegung** *f* FERNSEH color break-up (AmE), colour break-up (BrE)

Färberei *f* TEXTIL dyeing

Färbewickel *m* TEXTIL mock cake

Farb-: **Farbfehler** *m* ELEKTRONIK *Nachrichtentechnik* color artefact (AmE), colour artefact (BrE), FERNSEH chromatic aberration, color error (AmE), colour error (BrE), OPTIK chromatic distortion, *Linsenfehler* chromatic aberration, STRAHLPHYS chromatic aberration; **Farbfeld** *nt* FERNSEH color field (AmE), colour field (BrE); **Farbfeldkorrektur** *f* FERNSEH color field corrector (AmE), colour field corrector (BrE); **Farbflimmern** *nt* FERNSEH chromatic flicker; **Farbfotografie** *f* FOTO color photography (AmE), colour photography (BrE); **Farbfotoverfahren** *nt* FOTO color printing process (AmE), colour printing process (BrE); **Farbgarn** *nt* TEXTIL dyed yarn; **Farbgebung** *f* COMP & DV painting; **Farbglas** *nt* KER & GLAS colored glass (AmE), coloured glass (BrE); **Farbgleichgewicht** *nt* FERNSEH chromatic balance, FOTO color balance (AmE), colour balance (BrE); **Farbgrafik** *f* COMP & DV color graphics (AmE), colour graphics (BrE); **Farbgrafikadapter** *m (CGA)* COMP & DV color graphics adaptor (AmE), colour graphics adaptor (BrE) *(CGA)*; **Farbhilfsträgerbezug** *m* FERNSEH chrominance subcarrier reference; **Farbhintergrundgenerator** *m* FERNSEH color background generator (AmE), colour background generator (BrE)

farbig[1] *adj* TELEKOM colored (AmE), coloured (BrE)

farbig:[2] **~es Paketband** *nt* VERPACK colored strapping (AmE), coloured strapping (BrE); **~e Ränder** *m pl* DRUCK colored edges (AmE), coloured edges (BrE); **~es Rauschen** *nt* PHYS pink noise; **~es Umführungsband** *nt* VERPACK colored strapping (AmE), coloured strapping (BrE)

farbig:[3] **~ verzieren** *vt* KER & GLAS put down in color work (AmE), put down in colour work (BrE)

Farb-: **Farbkasten** *m* FERNSEH paintbox; **Farbkomponente** *f* FERNSEH chromatic component; **Farbkoordinaten** *f pl* PHYS chromaticity coordinates, *Farbdreieck* chromatic coordinates, STRAHLPHYS color coordinates (AmE), colour coordinates (BrE); **Farbkörper** *m* KUNSTSTOFF, TEXTIL pigment; **Farbkorrektur** *f* FERNSEH color correction (AmE), colour correction (BrE); **Farbkorrekturfilter** *nt* ELEKTRONIK color correction filter (AmE), colour correction filter (BrE)

farbkorrigiert: **~es Objektiv** *nt* FOTO color-corrected lens (AmE), colour-corrected lens (BrE)

farbkundlich *adj* ANSTRICH chromate

farblos[1] *adj* LEBENSMITTEL colorless (AmE), colourless (BrE)

farblos:[2] **~es Glas** *nt* KER & GLAS colorless glass, colourless glass (BrE); **~e Masse** *f* KER & GLAS colorless flux, colourless flux (BrE); **~es Produkt** *nt* MEERSCHMUTZ white product

Farb-: Farbmaßzahl *f* FERNSEH chromaticity; **Farbmessung** *f* WASSERVERSORG colorimetry; **Farbmetallographie** *f* METALL color metallography (AmE), colour metallography (BrE); **Farbmischung** *f* COMP & DV dithering, KER & GLAS color mix (AmE), colour mix (BrE); **Farbmodulator** *m* FERNSEH color modulator (AmE), colour modulator (BrE); **Farbmonitor** *m* COMP & DV color monitor (AmE), colour monitor (BrE); **Farbmühle** *f* KER & GLAS paint mill; **Farbnachlauf** *m* FERNSEH chroma delay; **Farboszillator** *m* ELEKTRONIK chrominance subcarrier oscillator; **Farbpalette** *f* COMP & DV color palette (AmE), colour palette (BrE); **Farbphase** *f* FERNSEH chrominance phase; **Farbphasendiagramm** *nt* FERNSEH color phase diagram (AmE), colour phase diagram (BrE); **Farbpigment** *nt* ANSTRICH pigment; **Farbpyrometer** *nt* STRAHLPHYS color pyrometer (AmE), colour pyrometer (BrE), THERMOD colorimetric pyrometer; **Farbrad** *nt* OPTIK color wheel (AmE), colour wheel (BrE); **Farbrahmen** *m* FERNSEH color framing (AmE), colour framing (BrE); **Farbraster** *nt* DRUCK, FOTO color screen (AmE), colour screen (BrE); **Farbrauschen** *nt* FERNSEH color noise (AmE), colour noise (BrE), cross-colour noise (AmE), cross-colour noise (BrE); **Farbsättigung** *f* TV color saturation (AmE), colour saturation (BrE); **Farbschaltung** *f* AUFNAHME color sampling (AmE), colour sampling (BrE); **Farbschaltungsabfolge** *f* FERNSEH color sampling sequence (AmE), colour sampling sequence (BrE); **Farbschaltungsgeschwindigkeit** *f* FERNSEH color sampling rate (AmE), colour sampling rate (BrE); **Farbschattierungstreifenbildung** *f* FERNSEH banding on hue; **Farbschlieren** *f pl* KER & GLAS color streaks (AmE), colour streaks (BrE); **Farbschlüssel** *m* FERNSEH chromakey (AmE), color separation overlay (AmE), colour separation overlay (BrE); **Farbschwankung** *f* FERNSEH chroma flutter; **Farbschwellwert** *m* FERNSEH color threshold (AmE), colour threshold (BrE); **Farbsignal** *nt* FERNSEH color signal (AmE), colour signal (BrE); **Farbsplitten** *nt* FERNSEH chromatic splitting; **Farbsplitter** *m* ANSTRICH paint chip; **Farbspritzen** *nt* ANSTRICH spray painting; **Farbspritzgerät** *nt* ANSTRICH paint-spraying apparatus; **Farbsprühen** *nt* ANSTRICH spray painting; **Farbstärke** *f* KUNSTSTOFF color strength (AmE), colour strength (BrE); **Farbsteuergitter** *nt* FERNSEH color grid (AmE), colour grid (BrE); **Farbsteuerung** *f* FERNSEH chroma control, chroma pilot; **Farbstich** *m* FOTO color cast (AmE), colour cast (BrE)

Farbstoff *m* DRUCK coloring matter (AmE), colouring matter (BrE), KER & GLAS coloring agent (AmE), colouring agent (BrE), PAPIER stain, TEXTIL dye, dyestuff; **~ zur Flächenrißprüfung** *m* FERTIG dye penetrant; **Farbstoffaufnahme** *f* TEXTIL dye uptake; **Farbstoffherstellung** *f* KER & GLAS color striking (AmE), colour striking (BrE); **Farbstofflaser** *m* PHYS dye laser

Farb-: Farbsynchrongatter *nt* FERNSEH burst gate; **Farbsynchronisierung** *f* FERNSEH color lock (AmE), colour lock (BrE); **Farbsynchronisierungssignal** *nt* FERNSEH color sync signal (AmE), colour sync signal (BrE); **Farbsynchronphase** *f* FERNSEH burst phase; **Farbsynchronsignal** *nt* TV burst; **Farbsynchrontrennung** *f* FERNSEH burst separator; **Farbsynthesizer** *m* FERNSEH color synthesiser (AmE), colour synthesizer (BrE); **Farbtafel** *f* FERNSEH chromaticity diagram,- color chart (AmE), colour chart (BrE); **Farbtemperaturmeßgerät** *nt* FOTO color temperature meter (AmE), colour temperature meter (BrE); **Farbtestbild mit Balken** *nt* FERNSEH color bar test pattern (AmE), colour bar test pattern (BrE); **Farbtiefe** *f* TEXTIL depth of shade; **Farbton** *m* DRUCK hue, tint, FERNSEH chromaticity, FOTO hue, tint, KER & GLAS tint, KUNSTSTOFF color tone (AmE), colour tone (BrE), TEXTIL shade; **Farbtonregelung** *f* FERNSEH hue control; **Farbtönung** *f* KUNSTSTOFF color tone (AmE), colour tone (BrE)

Farbträger *m* FERNSEH color subcarrier (AmE), colour subcarrier (BrE), TV chrominance subcarrier; **Farbträger-Demodulation** *f* ELEKTRONIK chrominance subcarrier demodulation; **Farbträger-Demodulator** *m* ELEKTRONIK chrominance subcarrier demodulator; **Farbträger-Modulation** *f* ELEKTRONIK chrominance subcarrier modulation; **Farbträger-Modulator** *m* ELEKTRONIK chrominance subcarrier modulator; **Farbträger-Unterdrückung** *f* FERNSEH color kill (AmE), colour kill (BrE)

Farb-: Farbtrennverfahren *nt* DRUCK color separation (AmE), colour separation (BrE); **Farbtüchtigkeit** *f* ERGON acuity of color perception (AmE), acuity of colour perception (BrE); **Farbumkehrentwicklung** *f* FOTO color reversal process (AmE), colour reversal process (BrE); **Farbumkehrfilm** *m* FOTO color reversal film (AmE), colour reversal film (BrE), reversal-type color film (AmE), reversal-type colour film; **Farbumrandung** *f* FERNSEH color fringing (AmE), colour fringing (BrE)

Färbung *f* LEBENSMITTEL coloring (AmE), colouring (BrE)

Farbunterscheidung *f* ERGON color discrimination (AmE), colour discrimination (BrE); **Farbunterscheidungsvermögen** *nt* ERGON color discrimination (AmE), colour discrimination (BrE)

Farb-: Farbveränderung *f* KER & GLAS color change (AmE), colour change (BrE); **Farbverbrauch** *m* PAPIER ink coverage; **Farbverfahrenchemikalien** *f pl* FOTO color processing chemicals (AmE), colour processing chemicals (BrE); **Farbverschiebung** *f* COMP & DV color shift (AmE), colour shift (BrE); **Farbwert** *m* ELEKTRONIK chrominance, PHYS tristimulus value; **Farbzerlegung** *f* OPTIK Licht chromatic dispersion; **Farbzuordnungstabelle** *f* COMP & DV color map (AmE), colour map (BrE)

Farinograph *m* LEBENSMITTEL farinograph

Farmer: ~scher Abschwächer *m* FOTO Farmer's reducer

fas *abbr (frei Längsseite Schiff)* WASSERTRANS fas *(free alongside ship)*

Fase:[1] **mit ~** *adj* FERTIG landed

Fase[2] *f* BAU chamfer, *Holz* scarf, FERTIG bevel, heel, MASCHINEN land

fasen *vt* FERTIG chamfer

fasenartig: ~er Anschliff *m* FERTIG ridge; **~er Anschliff an der Schneide** *m* FERTIG primary land

Fase: Fasenfreiwinkel *m* FERTIG secondary clearance angle; **Fasenhöhe** *f* FERTIG *Spiralbohrer* depth of body clearance; **Fasenring** *m* MASCHINEN bevel ring

fasenringartig: ~ nach außen erweiterte Stummelwelle *f* LUFTTRANS bevel ring-flared stub shaft
Fasenwinkel *m* MASCHINEN angle of bevel
Faser *f* OPTIK, PAPIER, TELEKOM, TEXTIL fiber (AmE), fibre (BrE); ~ mit einheitlichem Brechungsindex *f* OPTIK uniform-index fiber (AmE), uniform-index fibre (BrE); ~ mit quadratischem Index *f* OPTIK parabolic-index fiber (AmE), parabolic-index fibre (BrE); ~ mit zweitem Transmissionsfenster *f* OPTIK second window fiber (AmE), second window fibre (BrE); **Faserabschluß** *m* OPTIK fiber buffer (AmE), fibre buffer (BrE); **Faserachse** *f* OPTIK fiber axis (AmE), fibre axis (BrE); **Faserband** *nt* TEXTIL sliver; **Faserbart** *m* TEXTIL *Spinnen* tuft; **Faserbündel** *nt* KER & GLAS, OPTIK, TELEKOM fiber bundle (AmE), fibre bundle (BrE); **Faserdämpfung** *f* TELEKOM fiber loss (AmE), fibre loss (BrE); **Faserflor** *m* TEXTIL pile; **Fasergehalt** *m* TEXTIL fiber content (AmE), fibre content (BrE); **Faserholz** *nt* ABFALL, PAPIER pulpwood; **Faserhülle** *f* TELEKOM fiber buffer (AmE), fibre buffer (BrE), fiber jacket (AmE), fibre jacket (BrE); **Faserhülse** *f* TELEKOM *Lichtleitfaser* ferrule
faserig[1] *adj* PAPIER fibrous
faserig:[2] ~e Mikrostruktur *f* METALL fibrous microstructure
Faser: **Faserisolierung** *f* HEIZ & KÄLTE fibrous insulation; **Faserkalk** *m* PAPIER *Asbest* agalite; **Faserkern** *m* FERNSEH fiber core (AmE), fibre core (BrE); **Faserlänge** *f* TEXTIL staple length; **Fasermantel** *m* OPTIK fiber cladding (AmE), fiber coating (AmE), fibre coating (BrE), fiber jacket (AmE), fibre cladding (BrE), fibre jacket (BrE)
Faseroptik *f* COMP & DV, ELEKTROTECH, KER & GLAS, PHYS fiber optics (AmE), fibre optics (BrE); ~ zur Lichtübertragung *f* OPTIK transit fiberoptic (AmE), transit fibreoptic (BrE); **Faseroptik-Ausrüstung** *f* LABOR fiber optics equipment (AmE), fibre optics equipment (BrE)
faseroptisch: ~er Empfänger *m* ELEKTROTECH fiberoptic receiver (AmE), fibreoptic receiver (BrE); ~es Endgerät *nt* OPTIK fiberoptic terminal device (AmE), fibreoptic terminal device (BrE); ~es Kabel *nt* OPTIK fiberoptic cable (AmE), fibreoptic cable (BrE); ~es Kabelnetz *nt* ELEKTROTECH fiberoptic network (AmE), fibreoptic network (BrE); ~er Meßwandler *m* ELEKTROTECH fiberoptic transducer (AmE), fibreoptic transducer (BrE); ~er Sender *m* ELEKTROTECH fiberoptic transmitter (AmE), fibreoptic transmitter (BrE); ~er Steckverbinder *m* ELEKTROTECH fiberoptic connector (AmE), fibreoptic connector (BrE); ~e Technologie *f* ELEKTROTECH fiberoptic technology (AmE), fibreoptic technology (BrE); ~es Terminal *nt* OPTIK fiberoptic terminal device (AmE), fibreoptic terminal device (BrE); ~er Transducer *m* ELEKTROTECH fiberoptic transducer (AmE), fibreoptic transducer (BrE); ~e Übertragung *f* OPTIK fiberoptic transmission (AmE), fibreoptic transmission (BrE); ~es Übertragungssystem *nt* ELEKTROTECH fiberoptic transmission system (AmE), fibreoptic transmission system (BrE)
Faser: **Faserquetschung** *f* FERTIG ruptured fiber structure (AmE), ruptured fibre structure (BrE); **Faserschichtglas** *nt* KER & GLAS *Flachglas* ply glass; **Faserschlaufe** *f* SICHERHEIT fiber-type sling (AmE), fibre-type sling (BrE); **Faserschnittmatte** *f* KUNSTSTOFF chopped-strand mat; **Faserspeiser** *m* KER &

GLAS fiber feeder (AmE), fibre feeder (BrE); **Faserspleiß** *m* TELEKOM optical fiber splice (AmE), optical fibre splice (BrE); **Faserstippe** *f* PAPIER flake; **Faserstoff** *m* PAPIER pulp; **Faserstoffdichtung** *f* MECHAN fiber gasket (AmE), fibre gasket (BrE); **Faserstoffriemen** *m* MASCHINEN fiber belt (AmE), fibre belt (BrE); **Faserstoffschicht** *f* PAPIER furnish layer; **Faserstoffzusammensetzung** *f* PAPIER, VERPACK fiber composition (AmE), fibre composition (BrE); **Faserstreuung** *f* OPTIK fiber scattering (AmE), fibre scattering (BrE); **Faserstruktur** *f* METALL fiber texture (AmE), fibre texture (BrE); **Fasertaper** *m* TELEKOM tapered fiber (AmE), tapered fibre (BrE); **Fasertorf** *m* KOHLEN fibrous peat; **Faserüberlänge** *f* OPTIK fiber excess length (AmE), fibre excess length (BrE); **Faserverstärkung** *f* BAU fiber reinforcement (AmE), fibre reinforcement (BrE); **Faserwendel** *f* OPTIK fiber helix (AmE), fibre helix (BrE); **Faserziehen** *nt* TELEKOM fiber drawing (AmE), fibre drawing (BrE)
Faß *nt* BAU, KOHLEN barrel, KUNSTSTOFF drum, LEBENSMITTEL barrel, vat, MECHAN, PHYS, TRANS barrel; ~ für Atommüll *nt* KERNTECH waste drum; **Faßbinden** *nt* VERPACK hooping
Fassade *f* BAU *Gebäude* façade; **Fassadenfarbe** *f* KUNSTSTOFF house paint
fassen *vt* FERTIG *Flüssigkeit* hold, *Werkzeug* bite, WASSERTRANS grip
Fassonschmieden *nt* FERTIG swaging
Faß: **Faßreifen** *m* FERTIG, VERPACK hoop; **Faßtonne** *f* WASSERTRANS *Navigation* barrel buoy
Fassung *f* ELEKTROTECH *Glühlampe* holder, *Sicherung* fuse base, *elektrische Lampen* snubber resistor, socket, FERTIG receptacle, FOTO *Kamera, Licht* mounting, MASCHINEN mount, setting; ~ der Frontlinse *f* FOTO mount of front element; **Fassungsvermögen** *nt* BAU, ELEKTRIZ *Behälter* capacitance, capacity, HEIZ & KÄLTE *Tiefkühlgerät* freezer capacity, MASCHINEN capacity, WASSERTRANS *Maßeinheit* volume
Fastsenkrechtstarter *m* (*STOL-Flugzeug*) LUFTTRANS short takeoff and landing aircraft (*STOL aircraft*)
Fastzusammenstoß *m* LUFTTRANS near collision, near miss
Faszie *f* BAU fascia
Faul- *pref* ABFALL digesting; **Faulbaumbitter** *nt* CHEMIE frangulin; **Faulbecken** *nt* WASSERVERSORG septic tank; **Faulbehälter** *m* ABFALL digester, digestion tank, digestion sump
Fäule *f* WASSERTRANS *Holz* rot
faulfähig: ~er Schlamm *m* ABFALL putrescible sludge
Faul-: **Faulfähigkeit** *f* ABFALL putrescibility; **Faulgas** *nt* ABFALL biogas, digester gas, fermentation gas, THERMOD digester gas; **Faulgrube** *f* WASSERVERSORG septic tank
Fäulnisalkaloid *nt* CHEMIE ptomaine
fäulnisfähig: ~er Stoff *m* ABFALL putrescible matter
fäulnissicher *adj* PAPIER rotproof
Faul-: **Faulraum** *m* ABFALL digestion tank, digestion sump, THERMOD digestion tank; **Faulschlamm** *m* ABFALL, BAU, CHEMIE digested sludge; **Faulteich** *m* ABFALL anaerobic lagoon; **Faulung** *f* ABFALL fouling
Faustachse *f* KFZTECH *Rad* stub axle
Fäustel *m* FERTIG hammer, MASCHINEN club hammer
Fax *nt* COMP & DV (*Faksimile, Faxgerät, Fernkopieren, Fernkopierer*), RADIO (*Faksimile, Fernkopieren, Telefax*), TELEKOM (*Faksimile, Faxgerät, Fernkopieren, Fernkopierer, Telefax*) fax (*facsimile*)

faxen *vt* TELEKOM fax

Faxgerät *nt (Fax)* COMP & DV, TELEKOM facsimile machine

FB *abbr (Flughafenbake)* LUFTTRANS, RAUMFAHRT *(aerodrome beacon BrE, airdrome beacon AmE)*

FCKW *abbr (Fluorchlorokohlenwasserstoff)* UMWELTSCHMUTZ, VERPACK CFC *(chlorofluorocarbon)*

FCNE *abbr (Flugüberwachungs- und Navigationsausrüstung)* LUFTTRANS FCNE *(flight control and navigational equipment)*

Fe *(Eisen)* CHEMIE Fe *(iron)*

Feder[1] *f* BAU feather, spring, tongue, KFZTECH spring, MASCHINEN key, spring, MECHAN, PHYS spring

Feder:[2] ~ **kalibrieren** *vt* MASCHINEN scale

Feder: ~ **mit geschlossener Wicklung** *f* MASCHINEN close-coil spring; ~ **mit gleichbleibender Federkraft** *f* FERTIG constant-force spring; ~ **und Nut** *f* FERTIG key and slot, MASCHINEN key and feather; **Federauflage** *f* KFZTECH spring seat; **Federbandkupplung** *f* MASCHINEN coil clutch, spring band clutch; **Federbein** *nt* KFZTECH *Fahrwerk* strut

federbelastet: ~**es Ventil** *nt* HYDRAUL spring-loaded valve

Feder: **Federbogen** *m* FERTIG *Kunststoffinstallationen* swing arm; **Federbolzen** *m* BAU spring bolt, spring hanger pin; **Federbuchse** *f* ELEKTROTECH spring jack; **Federbügel** *m* MASCHINEN spring band, spring buckle, spring shackle, strap; **Federcharakteristik** *f* MASCHINEN spring characteristic; **Federdruckkörper** *m* FERTIG automatic center punch (AmE), automatic centre punch (BrE); **Federdynamometer** *nt* METROL spring balance; **Federfalle** *f* BAU latch bolt; **Federfassung** *f* ELEKTROTECH snap-in socket

federgespannt: ~**er Spannhebel** *m* FOTO spring-tensioned pressure lever

Feder: **Federhaken** *m* MASCHINEN spring hook; **Federhaltebügel** *m* KFZTECH spring retainer; **Federkeil** *m* BAU *Holz* feather, feather tongue, MASCHINEN feather, feather key; **Federkennlinie** *f* MASCHINEN spring characteristic; **Federklammer** *f* KFZTECH rebound clip; **Federklemme am Ende des Hefteisens** *f* KER & GLAS gadget; **Federkommutator** *m* ELEKTRIZ spring commutator; **Federkonstante** *f* MASCHINEN spring constant; **Federkorbpresse** *f* KER & GLAS spring cage press; **Federkraft** *f* MASCHINEN spring force, MECHAN spring; **Federkraftregler** *m* MASCHINEN spring governor; **Federleiste für die gedruckte Schaltung** *f* ELEKTROTECH printed circuit connector; **Federlösemechanismus** *m* RAUMFAHRT *Raumschiff* spring release device; **Federmanometer** *nt* PHYS spring manometer

federn *vi* MASCHINEN be resilient

federnd[1] *adj* KUNSTSTOFF resilient

federnd:[2] ~**er Anschlag** *m* MASCHINEN spring stop; ~**e Dichtung** *f* MASCHINEN resilient seal; ~**e Windung** *f* FERTIG active coil

Feder: **Federopazität** *f* KER & GLAS plume opacity; **Federpaket** *nt* FERTIG *Kunststoffinstallationen* spring unit; **Federpuffer** *m* EISENBAHN spring buffer; **Federrate** *f* MASCHINEN spring rate; **Federring** *m* FERTIG lock washer, MASCHINEN lock washer, split washer, spring clip, MECHAN lock washer; **Federringdichtung** *f* MASCHINEN spring lock washer; **Federrollenlager** *nt* MASCHINEN flexible roller bearing; **Federrückstellschalter** *m* ELEKTRIZ spring return switch; **Federrückstellung** *f* FERTIG *Kunststoffinstallationen*

spring return mechanism; **Federsatz** *m* MASCHINEN nest of springs; **Federschalter** *m* ELEKTRIZ spring switch, ELEKTROTECH snap-action switch; **Federscheibe** *f* MASCHINEN spring washer; **Federschloß** *nt* BAU spring lock; **Federsitz** *m* KFZTECH spring seat; **Federspannmotor** *m* MECHAN clockwork; **Federstahl** *m* METALL spring steel; **Federteilzirkel** *m pl* MASCHINEN spring dividers; **Federteller** *m* MASCHINEN spring plate

Federung *f* FERTIG cushioning, MASCHINEN spring suspension

Feder: **Federventil** *nt* HYDRAUL spring valve; **Federverbindung** *f* BAU ploughed-and-feathered joint (BrE), plowed-and-feathered joint (AmE), slip tongue joint, tongue-and-groove joint; **Federvorsteckstift** *m* MASCHINEN spring cotter; **Federwaage** *f* MASCHINEN spring balance, METROL spiral balance, spring balance, PHYS spring balance

Feedback *nt* KERNTECH, PHYS feedback

FEF-Ruß *m (schnell spritzbarer Furnace-Ruß)* KUNSTSTOFF FEF carbon black *(fast extruding furnace carbon black)*

Fehlalarm *m* TELEKOM false alarm; **Fehlalarmwahrscheinlichkeit** *f* TELEKOM false alarm probability

Fehlanflugsverfahren *nt* LUFTTRANS missed approach procedure

fehlangepaßt *adj* FERNSEH, PHYS mismatched

Fehlanruf *m* TELEKOM false call; **Fehlanrufhäufigkeit** *f* TELEKOM false calling rate

Fehlauslösung *f* ELEKTRIZ false trip

Fehlaustrag *m* KOHLEN outsize

Fehlbohrung *f* ERDÖL *Tiefbohrtechnik* dry hole

fehleingestellt[1] *adj* LUFTTRANS *Hubschrauber* out-of-pitch

fehleingestellt:[2] ~**es Blatt** *nt* LUFTTRANS *Hubschrauber* out-of-pitch blade

Fehler *m* COMP & DV failure, fault, ELEKTRIZ fault, ELEKTRONIK error, ELEKTROTECH defect, failure, fault, KER & GLAS, KERNTECH *Material* defect, LEBENSMITTEL blemish, MASCHINEN fault, MATH error, MECHAN fault, flaw, METALL defect, flaw, PHYS error, QUAL defect, error, nonconformance, nonconformity, TEXTIL flaw; ~ **bei der Ausführung** *m* COMP & DV run-time error; ~ **durch Synchronisationsverlust** *m* TELEKOM out-of-synchronization error; ~ **im Flankendurchmesser** *m* METROL pitch diameter error; ~ **im Teilkreisdurchmesser** *m* METROL pitch diameter error; **Fehlerabschätzung** *f* MATH error estimation; **Fehleranalyse** *f* COMP & DV, MATH error analysis, STRAHLPHYS failure analysis; **Fehleranteil** *m* QUAL fraction defective; **Fehleranzahl pro Einheit** *f* QUAL defects per unit; **Fehleranzeige** *f* TELEKOM fault display; **Fehleranzeiger** *m* ELEKTRIZ fault detector; **Fehlerbedingung** *f* COMP & DV error condition, fault

fehlerbehaftet: ~**e Sekunde** *f* TELEKOM errored second

Fehler: **Fehlerbehandlungsprogramm** *nt* COMP & DV failure routine; **Fehlerbehebung** *f* COMP & DV error handling, error management, error recovery, error trapping, TELEKOM fault maintenance; **Fehlerbericht** *m* COMP & DV error report, QUAL defect note; **Fehlerberichterstattung** *f* QUAL nonconformance reporting; **Fehlerbeseitigung** *f* COMP & DV debugging; **Fehlercode** *m* COMP & DV error code; **Fehlerdiagnose** *f* COMP & DV error diagnosis, fault diagnosis, ELEKTRIZ fault diagnosis, TELEKOM error diagnosis; **Fehlerdiagnostik** *f* COMP & DV error diagnostics; **Fehlerdichte** *f*

ELEKTRONIK defect density; **Fehlerempfindlichkeit** *f* TELEKOM error susceptibility; **Fehlerentdeckung** *f* COMP & DV fault detection

fehlererkennend: ~e **Codierung** *f* TELEKOM error detection coding

Fehler: **Fehlererkennung** *f* COMP & DV error detection, problem diagnosis, ELEKTRONIK error detection, - TELEKOM error detection, fault detection; **Fehlererkennungscode** *m* COMP & DV, ELEKTRONIK error-detecting code, TELEKOM error detection code; **Fehlererkennungseinrichtung** *f* TELEKOM error detector; **Fehlererkennungsprogramm** *nt* COMP & DV fault location program; **Fehlerfeststellung** *f* FERNSEH error detection; **Fehlerfortpflanzung** *f* COMP & DV error propagation

fehlerfrei[1] *adj* TEXTIL faultless

fehlerfrei:[2] ~e **Einheit** *f* QUAL conforming item

Fehler: **Fehlergrenze** *f* METROL limit of error

fehlerhaft[1] *adj* COMP & DV *Daten* corrupt, ELEKTRIZ faulty, out of operation, MECHAN faulty, QUAL nonconforming, *Werkstoff* defective, TEXTIL faulty

fehlerhaft:[2] ~er **Block** *m* TELEKOM erroneous block; ~e **Datei** *f* COMP & DV corrupt file; ~e **Eingabe** *f* COMP & DV garbage; ~e **Einheit** *f* QUAL nonconforming item; ~e **Funktion des Lesekopfes** *f* COMP & DV head crash; ~e **Funktion des Leseschreibkopfes** *f* COMP & DV head crash; ~e **Funktion des Schreibkopfes** *f* COMP & DV head crash; ~er **Zeitabschnitt** *m* TELEKOM erroneous period

Fehler: **Fehlerhäufigkeit** *f* COMP & DV error rate, MATH frequency of errors, TELEKOM error rate; **Fehlerhäufung** *f* COMP & DV burst, error burst, TELEKOM error density; **Fehlerklasse** *f* GERÄT *Meßgerät* class; **Fehlerklassifizierung** *f* QUAL classification of nonconformance, classification of nonconformities; **Fehlerkontrolle** *f* TELEKOM error check; **Fehlerkontrollzeichen** *nt* TELEKOM error check character, error check signal; **Fehlerkorrektur** *f* COMP & DV error correction, ELEKTRONIK defect annealing, error correction, TELEKOM error correction; **Fehlerkorrekturcode** *m* COMP & DV error-correcting code, self-checking code, ELEKTRONIK, RAUMFAHRT *Weltraumfunk* error-correcting code; **Fehlerkorrekturschlüssel** *m* RAUMFAHRT *Weltraumfunk* error-correcting code

fehlerkorrigierend: ~er **Code** *m* TELEKOM error correction code; ~e **Codierung** *f* TELEKOM error correction coding

Fehler: **Fehlerliste** *f* COMP & DV error list; **Fehlerlokalisierung** *f* ELEKTRIZ fault location

fehlerlos: ~es **Programm** *nt* COMP & DV star program

Fehler: **Fehlermeldung** *f* COMP & DV error message, QUAL defect note, TELEKOM error message; **Fehlermuster** *nt* TELEKOM error pattern; **Fehlernachricht** *f* COMP & DV error message

Fehlernährung *f* LEBENSMITTEL malnutrition

Fehler: **Fehlerortung** *f* ELEKTRIZ fault location, KONTROLL troubleshooting; **Fehlerortungsgerät** *nt* GERÄT fault location instrument; **Fehlerprogramm** *nt* COMP & DV error program; **Fehlerprotokollierung** *f* COMP & DV error logging, failure logging; **Fehlerprüfcode** *m* COMP & DV error-checking code; **Fehlerprüfung** *f* COMP & DV error checking; **Fehlerquote** *f* COMP & DV, TELEKOM error rate; **Fehlerquotenmessung** *f* TELEKOM error rate measurement; **Fehlerrate** *f* COMP & DV error rate, failure rate, ELEKTRONIK error rate, QUAL failure rate,

outage rate, TELEKOM error rate; **Fehlerroutine** *f* COMP & DV error routine; **Fehlerschutz** *m* TELEKOM error protection; **Fehlerschutzcode** *m* TELEKOM error protection code; **Fehlersicherung** *f* TELEKOM error protection; **Fehlersicherungsgerät** *nt* TELEKOM ECD, error control device; **Fehlersignal** *nt* ELEKTRONIK error signal; **Fehlerspanne** *f* COMP & DV margin of error; **Fehlerspannungs-Stromunterbrecher** *m* ELEKTRIZ fault voltage circuit breaker; **Fehlerstrom** *m* ELEKTROTECH leakage current; **Fehlersuche** *f* ELEKTROTECH fault finding, KONTROLL troubleshooting; **Fehlersuchprogramm** *nt* COMP & DV debugger; **Fehlersuchtabelle** *f* MASCHINEN fault-finding table

fehlertolerant[1] *adj* COMP & DV, ELEKTROTECH fault-tolerant

fehlertolerant:[2] ~es **System** *nt* COMP & DV fault-tolerant system

Fehler: **Fehlertoleranz** *f* COMP & DV, ELEKTROTECH fault tolerance; **Fehlerüberwachung** *f* COMP & DV error control; **Fehlerwahrscheinlichkeit** *f* KÜNSTL INT, TELEKOM error probability; **Fehlerwiderstand** *m* ELEKTROTECH fault resistance; **Fehlerwiederherstellung** *f* TELEKOM error recovery

Fehlfarbe *f* COMP & DV false colour

Fehlfunktion *f* ELEKTRIZ, METROL, RAUMFAHRT *Raumschiff* malfunction

fehlgeleitet: ~er **Anruf** *m* TELEKOM misdirected call

fehlgeordnet *adj* FERTIG *Kristall* disordered

Fehlguß *m* KER & GLAS waste

Fehlinhalt *m* KER & GLAS off-content

Fehlkontakt *m* ELEKTROTECH bad contact

Fehlmenge *f* LEBENSMITTEL *Flüssigkeit* ullage

Fehlmessung *f* GERÄT faulty measurement

Fehlprodukt *nt* QUAL nonconforming product

Fehlregistrierung *f* FERNSEH misregistration

Fehlschalten *nt* ELEKTRIZ false switching

fehlschlagen *vi* BAU fail

Fehlschließung *f* ELEKTROTECH false closure

Fehlsignal *nt* ELEKTRONIK false signal

Fehlstelle *f* CHEMIE void, FERTIG *Lösen von Plastschichten* let-go, METALL void; **Fehlstellenleitfähigkeit** *f* ELEKTROTECH p-type conductivity; **Fehlstellenstreuung** *f* KERNTECH defect scattering

fehlsynchronisiert *adj* FERNSEH out of sync

Fehlweisung *f* LUFTTRANS, WASSERTRANS *Navigation* compass error

Fehlzündung *f* ELEKTRONIK *Magnetron* mode jump, KFZTECH backfire, misfire, misfiring

Feile *f* KFZTECH *Werkzeug*, MASCHINEN, MECHAN file

Feilen *nt* MASCHINEN filing; **Feilenbürste** *f* MASCHINEN file card; **Feilenhärte** *f* MASCHINEN file hardness; **Feilenhärteprüfung** *f* MASCHINEN file test; **Feilenhauerei** *f* MASCHINEN file cutting; **Feilenhieb** *m* MASCHINEN cut, file cut

feilen *vi* MASCHINEN file

Feilkolben *m* BAU pin vice (BrE), pin vise (AmE), MASCHINEN filing vice (BrE), filing vise (AmE), tail vice (BrE), tail vise (AmE), hand vice (BrE), hand vise (AmE)

Feilmaschine *f* MASCHINEN filing machine

Feilscheibe *f* MASCHINEN circular-cut file

Feilspan *m* FERTIG filing

Fein- *pref* ELEKTRONIK, GERÄT, TELEKOM fine; **Feinabstimmung** *f* ELEKTRONIK, GERÄT, TELEKOM fine tuning; **Feinanalyse** *f* ERGON fine analysis; **Feinbearbeitung** *f* FERTIG finishing, MASCHINEN fine machining, precision machining; **Feinblech** *nt* MET-ALL sheet, thin sheet; **Feinblechwalzen** *nt* FERTIG roller sheet, sheet rolling; **Feinblechwalzwerk** *nt* FER-TIG sheet mill; **Feinbohren** *nt* FERTIG borizing (AmE), fine boring, MASCHINEN fine boring, precision boring; **Feinbrechen** *nt* KOHLEN fine crushing; **Feinbrecher** *m* CHEMTECH fine-crushing mill; **Feindosierventil** *nt* GERÄT fine-metering valve; **Feindrehmaschine** *f* MASCHINEN precision lathe; **Feindruckmeßgerät** *nt* GERÄT micromanometer

fein: ~**er Furnace-Ruß** *m (FF-Ruß)* KUNSTSTOFF fine furnace carbon black *(FF carbon black)*; ~**es Garn** *nt* TEXTIL fine-count yarn; ~**e Garnnummer** *f* TEXTIL fine count; ~**e Skalenmarke** *f* GERÄT hairline; ~**er Skalenstrich** *m* GERÄT hairline; ~**er Strich** *m* DRUCK fine line

Feine *f* METALL fineness

Fein-: **Feineinstellschraube** *f* OPTIK fine adjustment screw; **Feineinstellskale** *f* GERÄT vernier scale; **Feineinstellung** *f* ELEKTRONIK, FERNSEH fine adjustment, FERTIG fine adjustment, vernier adjustment, GERÄT fine setting, vernier adjustment, KERNTECH, OPTIK *mittels Mikrometerschraube* fine adjustment

Feinen *nt* FERTIG refining

Fein-: **Feinerde** *f* KOHLEN fine soil; **Feinfilter** *nt* MASCHINEN fine-mesh filter, WASSERVERSORG microfilter; **Feinfiltration** *f* CHEMIE clarification; **Feinfolie** *f* KUNSTSTOFF film; **Feinfräsen** *nt* MASCHINEN fine milling, precision milling; **Feingehalt** *m* METALL fineness; **Feingemisch** *nt* LUFTTRANS lean mixture; **Feingewindeschraube** *f* BAU fine-pitch screw; **Feingleiten** *nt* METALL fine slip; **Feingold** *nt* METALL fine gold, gold of standard fineness; **Feingut** *nt pl* MASCHINEN fine sizes

Feinheit *f* BAU, PAPIER fineness; **Feinheitanalyse** *f* CHEM-TECH particle size analysis; **Feinheitsfestigkeit** *f* TEXTIL breaking length; **Feinheitsgrad** *m* MASCHINEN fineness ratio

Fein-: **Feinhöhenmesser** *m* LUFTTRANS sensitive altimeter; **Feinjustierung** *f* KERNTECH fine adjustment; **Feinkeramikmaschine** *f* KER & GLAS machine for fine ceramics; **Feinkies** *m* BAU fine gravel; **Feinkohle** *f* KOHLEN culm; **Feinkorn** *nt* METALL close grain, fine grain; **Feinkornbild** *nt* FOTO fine-grain image; **Feinkornentwickler** *m* FOTO fine-grain developer

feinkörnig[1] *adj* FERTIG sappy, *Bruchfläche* even, METALL close-grained, fine-grained

feinkörnig:[2] ~**er Kies** *m* BAU fine gravel; ~**er Sand** *m* BAU fine sand; ~**er Stahl** *m* KERNTECH fine-grained steel

Fein-: **Feinkornstahl** *m* KERNTECH fine-grained steel

feinkristallin *adj* CHEMIE microcrystalline

Fein-: **Feinlinie** *f* ELEKTRONIK fine line; **Feinlinienleiterplatte** *f* ELEKTRONIK fine-line printed circuit; **Feinlunker** *m* OPTIK pinhole; **Feinmahlen** *nt* KOHLEN fine grinding

feinmahlen *vt* CHEMTECH pulverize

Fein-: **Feinmahlung** *f* KOHLEN pulverization; **Feinmeßmanometer** *nt* GERÄT precision gage (AmE), precision gauge (BrE); **Feinmühle** *f* BAU pulverizer; **Feinraster** *m* DRUCK fine screen; **Feinrechen** *m* AB-FALL fine screen

feinregeln *vt* HEIZ & KÄLTE control finely

Fein-: **Feinsand** *m* KOHLEN fine sand; **Feinschicht** *f* KUNSTSTOFF, WASSERTRANS *Schiffbau* gel coat; **Feinschlämme** *f* BAU laitance; **Feinschliff** *m* ANSTRICH microsection; **Feinschnitt** *m* ANSTRICH microsection; **Feinschraubengewinde nach britischem Standard** *nt*

MASCHINEN British standard fine screw thread; **Feinsieb** *nt* MASCHINEN fine screen; **Feinsilber** *nt* METALL fine silver; **Feinstbohren** *nt* MASCHINEN precision boring; **Feinstdreharbeit** *f* FERTIG superfinish turning; **Feinstdrehmaschine** *f* FERTIG superfinisher

Feinsteinstellung *f* FERTIG metal adjustment

Feinsteinstellung: **mit** ~ *adj* FERTIG micrometer-adjustable

Fein-: **Feinstellskale** *f* GERÄT micrometric scale; **Feinsteuerstab** *m* KERNTECH fine control member; **Feinsteuerung** *f* KERNTECH *Reaktor* fine control; **Feinstoff** *m* BAU, PAPIER fines; **Feinstruktur** *f* PHYS *Atomphysik*, STRAHLPHYS fine structure; **Feinstrukturaufspaltung** *f* KERNTECH fine-structure splitting; **Feinstrukturkonstante** *f* PHYS fine-structure constant

feinstufig *adj* FERTIG sensitive

Feinstvermahlung *f* KERNTECH comminution

feinstzerteilt *adj* KUNSTSTOFF micronized

Fein-: **Feintaster** *m* FERTIG precision dial gage (AmE), precision dial gauge (BrE); **Feinungsschlacke** *f* FER-TIG finishing slag; **Feinverteilen** *nt* CHEMTECH dispersion; **Feinwaage** *f* METROL special accuracy weighing machine; **Feinwerktechnik** *f* MASCHINEN precision engineering; **Feinzuschlagstoff** *m* BAU fine aggregate

Feld *nt* AKUSTIK field, BAU bay, *Trägern* span, COMP & DV, ELEKTRIZ, ELEKTROTECH *Leiter* field, ERDÖL block, field, KONSTZEICH block, panel, RADIO field, TELEKOM array, section; ~ **mit abklingender Stärke** *nt* OPTIK, TELEKOM evanescent field; ~ **für Maßstabsangaben** *nt* KONSTZEICH panel provided for scale particulars; **Feldbahnlokomotive** *f* EISENBAHN pug; **Feldbegrenzung** *f* KFZTECH field frame; **Feldbuch** *nt* BAU *Vermessung* field book; **Felddesorptions-Massenspektrometer** *nt* KERNTECH field desorption mass spectrometer

Feldeffekt *m* ELEKTRONIK, TELEKOM field effect; **Feldeffekttransistor** *m (FET)* COMP & DV, ELEKTRONIK, OPTIK, PHYS, RADIO, RAUMFAHRT field effect transistor *(FET)*; **Feldeffekttransistor mit bipolarisoliertem Gatter** *m (BIGFET)* ELEKTRONIK bipolar-insulated gate field-effect transistor *(BIG-FET)*; **Feldeffekttransistor mit Verarmungsschicht** *m* ELEKTRONIK depletion mode FET; **Feldeffektverstärker** *m* ELEKTRONIK field effect amplifier

Feld: **Feldeinteilung** *f* KONSTZEICH block subdivision; **Feldemission** *f* ELEKTRONIK *Elektronenröhre* field emission, ELEKTROTECH cold emission, PHYS field emission; **Feldemissionsmikroskop** *nt* PHYS field emission microscope; **Feldendezeichen** *nt* COMP & DV field delimiter; **Felderprobung** *f* TELEKOM field trial; **Felderregung** *f* ELEKTRIZ field excitation; **Feldflakkern** *nt* KERNTECH field flutter

feldfrei: ~**er Emissionsstrom** *m* KERNTECH field-free emission current

Feld: **Feldgehäuse** *nt* KFZTECH field frame; **Feldgenerator** *m* FERNSEH safe area generator; **Feldgradient** *m* ELEKTROTECH electric field gradient; **Feldgruppe** *f* COMP & DV array; **Feldgruppenelement** *nt* COMP & DV array element; **Feldionenemissionsmikroskop** *nt* PHYS field ion microscope; **Feldkabel** *nt* ELEKTRO-TECH field wire; **Feldkrümmung** *f* PHYS curvature of the field; **Feldleitung** *f* ERDÖL *Leitung von Bohrung zu Sammelstation* flow line; **Feldleitungstemperatur** *f* ERDÖL flow line temperature; **Feldlinie** *f* ELEKTRO-TECH, PHYS field line; **Feldlinse** *f* FOTO *Objektiv* front element, *Okular* field lens; **Feldmagnet** *m* AUFNAHME, ELEKTROTECH field magnet; **Feldmeßkette** *f* BAU land measuring chain; **Feldmessung** *f* BAU land measuring; **Feldmikrofon** *nt* AUFNAHME field microphone; **Feldoxid** *nt* ELEKTRONIK field oxide; **Feldpol** *m* ELEKTROTECH field pole; **Feldregler** *m* ELEKTRIZ field regulator, ELEKTROTECH field regulator, field rheostat, KERNTECH field regulator; **Feldreglerrheostat** *nt* ELEKTRIZ field rheostat

Feld: **Feldrichtung** *f* ELEKTROTECH field direction; **Feldschaltung** *f* ELEKTRIZ field circuit; **Feldspannung** *f* ELEKTRIZ field voltage; **Feldspat** *m* KER & GLAS feldspar; **Feldspule** *f* AUFNAHME, ELEKTRIZ, ELEKTROTECH field coil

Feldstärke *f* ELEKTRIZ field intensity, field strength, magnetizing force, ELEKTROTECH field strength, RADIO field strength, signal strength; **Feldstärkelinie** *f* ELEKTROTECH line of force; **Feldstärkemesser** *m* RADIO field strength meter; **Feldstärkemeßgerät** *nt* ELEKTRIZ field strength meter; **Feldstärkepegel** *m* TELEKOM signal level

Feld: **Feldstrom** *m* ELEKTRIZ, ELEKTROTECH field current; **Feldübertragungsfaktor** *m* AKUSTIK free-field tension sensitivity; **Feldunterbrecher** *m* KERNTECH field discharge switch, field-breaking switch; **Feldunterdrücker** *m* ELEKTRIZ field suppressor; **Felduntersuchung** *f* KOHLEN field investigation; **Feldvektor** *m* ELEKTROTECH field vector; **Feldvermesser** *m* BAU Ordnance Surveyor; **Feldversuch** *m* MASCHINEN field test, MEERSCHMUTZ, TELEKOM field trial; **Feldwicklung** *f* ELEKTRIZ field coil, field winding, ELEKTROTECH field winding

Felge *f* FERTIG felloe, KFZTECH *Rad* rim; **Felgenflansch** *m* KFZTECH *Rad* rim flange; **Felgenschulter** *f* KFZTECH *Autofelge* flange

Fels *m* KOHLEN rock; **Felsband** *nt* KOHLEN rock ledge; **Felsbohrmeißel** *m* ERDÖL *Bohrtechnik* rock bit; **Felsdruck** *m* KOHLEN rock pressure

Felsen *m* WASSERTRANS *Geographie* rock

Fels: **Felsgründung** *f* KOHLEN rock foundation; **Felshöhle** *f* KOHLEN rock cut; **Felsmechanik** *f* KOHLEN rock mechanics

FEM *abbr* *(Finite-Elemente-Methode)* MASCHINEN FEM *(finite elements method)*

Femto- *pref (F)* METROL femto- *(f)*; **Femtometer** *nt* LABOR femtometer

Fenchen *nt* CHEMIE fenchene

Fenchon *nt* CHEMIE fenchone

Fenchyl- *pref* CHEMIE fenchyl

Fender[1] *m* MEERSCHMUTZ fender, WASSERTRANS bumper (BrE), *Deckausrüstung* fender

Fender:[2] **~ ausbringen** *vt* WASSERTRANS *Festmachen* put out

Fenske-Ringe *m pl* LABOR *Destillation* Fenske helices

Fenster *nt* COMP & DV, KFZTECH, MASCHINEN, WASSERTRANS *Schiffbau* window; **~ der Atmosphäre** *nt* PHYS, STRAHLPHYS atmospheric window; **Fensterblende gegen Seeschlag** *f* WASSERTRANS *Schiffbau* deadlight; **Fensterblendrahmen** *m* BAU window frame; **Fensterbrüstung** *f* BAU spandrel; **Fensterdichtung** *f* KFZTECH window seal; **Fensterfilter** *nt* ELEKTRONIK window filter; **Fensterflügel** *m* BAU, KER & GLAS casement; **Fensterflügelrahmen** *m* BAU sash; **Fenstergitter** *nt* BAU window bars; **Fensterglas** *nt* BAU window glass; **Fensterglasflügel** *m* BAU glazed sash; **Fenstergummi** *nt* KFZTECH window seal, *Windschutzscheibe* pane rab-

bet; **Fensterheber** *m* KFZTECH window regulator; **Fensterkitt** *m* BAU bedding putty; **Fensterladen** *m* BAU folding shutter, shutter; **Fensteröffnung** *f* BAU window opening; **Fensterrahmen** *m* KFZTECH window frame; **Fensterriegel** *m* BAU sash rail, window catch; **Fensterschließer** *m* BAU window fastener; **Fenstersprosse** *f* BAU sash bar, window bar; **Fensterstab** *m* BAU sash bar; **Fenstersturz** *m* BAU *Fenster* lintel; **Fenstertechnik** *f* COMP & DV *Bildschirmunterteilung* window clipping, windowing; **Fenstertransformation** *f* COMP & DV window transformation; **Fenstertür** *f* BAU French casement, glazed door

Fermat: **~sche Primzahl** *f* MATH Fermat number; **~sches Prinzip** *nt* PHYS Fermat's principle

Fermate *f* AKUSTIK rest

Fermentation *f* CHEMIE fermentation, zymosis

Fermi: **~sche Energie** *f* PHYS Fermi energy; **~sche Grenze** *f* PHYS Fermi limit; **~sche Kugel** *f* PHYS Fermi sphere; **~sches Niveau** *nt* PHYS Fermi level; **~sche Oberfläche** *f* PHYS Fermi surface; **~scher Wellenvektor** *m* PHYS Fermi wave vector

Fermi-Dirac: **~sche Statistik** *f* PHYS Fermi-Dirac statistics; **~sche Verteilung** *f* PHYS *Quantenstatistik* Fermi-Dirac distribution

Fermion *nt* PHYS, TEILPHYS fermion

Fermium *nt (Fm)* CHEMIE fermium *(Fm)*

Fern- *pref* COMP & DV, KONTROLL remote

fern:[1] **~ am ~ en Leitungsende** *adj* TELEKOM at the far end

fern:[2] **~e Datenstation** *f* COMP & DV remote terminal; **~es Infrarot** *nt* STRAHLPHYS far infrared; **~e Infrarotstrahlung** *f* STRAHLPHYS far infrared; **~es Laden** *nt* COMP & DV remote loading; **~e Stapeldatenstation** *f* COMP & DV remote batch terminal; **~er Test** *m* COMP & DV remote test; **~es Ultraviolett** *nt* PHYS, STRAHLPHYS far ultraviolet; **~e UV-Strahlung** *f* STRAHLPHYS far ultraviolet

Fern-: **Fernabtastung** *f* COMP & DV remote sensing; **Fernamt** *nt* TELEKOM toll exchange (AmE), toll switch, trunk exchange (BrE); **Fernanzeige** *f* GERÄT remote indication; **Fernanzeigegerät** *nt* GERÄT remote indicating instrument; **Fernaufnahmepunkt** *m* FERNSEH remote pickup point

fernbedient: **~e Weiche** *f* EISENBAHN automatic switch

Fernbedienung *f* FOTO, RADIO remote control, SICHERHEIT remote-handling device, TELEKOM remote control; **Fernbedienungsgerät** *nt* AUFNAHME remote control device; **Fernbedienungsinstrument** *nt* KERNTECH remote handling tool; **Fernbedienungsvorrichtung** *f* KERNTECH remote handling tool

Fern-: **Fernbeförderung** *f* TRANS long-haul carriage

fernbetätigt: **~es Zeichen** *nt* TRANS remote control sign

Fern-: **Fernbetrieb** *m* TELEKOM remote operation; **Ferndrucken** *nt* COMP & DV remote printing; **Fernerfassung** *f* TELEKOM remote detection; **Fernerkundung** *f* MEERSCHMUTZ remote sensing; **Fernfahrer** *m* KFZTECH long-haul lorry driver (BrE), long-haul truck driver (AmE)

Fernfeld *nt* TELEKOM distant field; **Fernfeldanalyse** *f* TELEKOM far-field analysis; **Fernfeldbereich** *m* OPTIK, TELEKOM far-field region; **Fernfeldbrechungsmuster** *nt* OPTIK far-field diffraction pattern; **Fernfeldmuster** *nt* OPTIK far-field pattern; **Fernfeldstrahlungsdiagramm** *nt* TELEKOM far-field pattern; **Fernfeldstrahlungsmuster** *nt* OPTIK far-field radiation pattern

Fern-: **Fernflug** *m* LUFTTRANS long-distance flight;

Fernfühler *m* BAU remote sensor

Ferngas *nt* HEIZ & KÄLTE grid gas; **Ferngasleitung** *f* THERMOD gas pipeline; **Ferngasnetz** *nt* THERMOD gas grid; **Ferngastransport** *m* TRANS long-distance gas transport

Fern-: **Ferngeber** *m* GERÄT retransmitting slide wire; **Ferngespräch** *nt* TELEKOM toll call (AmE), trunk call (BrE); **Ferngespräch zu Ortsgebühr** *nt* TELEKOM local-charge-rate trunk call

ferngesteuert[1] *adj* FERNSEH, MASCHINEN remote-controlled

ferngesteuert:[2] **~es Entsicherungs- und Sicherungsgerät** *nt* RAUMFAHRT *Raumschiff* remote arming and safety unit; **~e Fokussierung** *f* FERNSEH remote control focusing; **~e Kamera** *f* FERNSEH remote-controlled camera; **~er Oszillator** *m* ELEKTRONIK labile oscillator; **~e Sendung** *f* FERNSEH remote broadcast

Fern-: **Fernglas** *nt* KER & GLAS field glass magnifier, PHYS, WASSERTRANS binoculars; **Fernheizung** *f* BAU, HEIZ & KÄLTE district heating; **Fernheizwerk** *nt* THERMOD district-heating station; **Fernhörer** *m* TELEKOM *Telefon* receiver; **Ferninstandhaltung** *f* TELEKOM remote maintenance; **Fernkabel** *nt* ELEKTROTECH long-distance cable, TELEKOM trunk cable; **Fernkontrolle** *f* ELEKTRIZ remote control; **Fernkopieren** *nt* *(Fax)* COMP & DV, RADIO, TELEKOM facsimile *(fax)*
fernkopieren *vt* TELEKOM facsimile, fax

Fern-: **Fernkopierer** *m* *(Fax)* COMP & DV, TELEKOM facsimile machine; **Fernladen** *nt* COMP & DV, TELEKOM remote loading; **Fernlastzug** *m* KFZTECH long-distance road train; **Fernleitung** *f* ELEKTROTECH, TELEKOM long-distance line; **Fernleitungsbetrieb** *m* ELEKTROTECH trunking; **Fernleitungshauptverteiler** *m* *(FHV)* TELEKOM trunk distribution frame *(TDF)*; **Fernleitungsnetz** *nt* TELEKOM trunk network; **Fernmanagement** *nt* TELEKOM remote management; **Fernmanipulation** *f* SICHERHEIT remote-handling device; **Fernmeldegeheimnis** *nt* TELEKOM secrecy of telecommunications; **Fernmeldegesellschaft** *f* TELEKOM telecommunication operator; **Fernmeldekabel** *nt* TELEKOM telecommunication cable; **Fernmeldeleitung** *f* TELEKOM telecommunications line; **Fernmeldelinie** *f* TELEKOM trunk; **Fernmeldenetz** *nt* TELEKOM telecommunication network; **Fernmeldesatellit** *m* *(ComSat)* TELEKOM communication satellite *(comsat)*; **Fernmeldeschaltung** *f* TELEKOM communications circuit; **Fernmeldetechnik** *f* TELEKOM telecommunications; **Fernmeldeverbindung** *f* TELEKOM telecommunications line; **Fernmeldewesen** *nt* TELEKOM telecommunications; **Fernmeßgerät** *nt* MASCHINEN telemeter; **Fernmeßsystem** *nt* GERÄT telemetering system; **Fernmeßtechnik** *f* COMP & DV telemetry; **Fernmessung** *f* ELEKTRIZ telemetry, GERÄT remote sensing, KERNTECH remote metering, telemetry, MEERSCHMUTZ remote sensing, RADIO, TELEKOM telemetry; **Fernnebensprechen** *nt* TELEKOM far-end crosstalk; **Fernnetz** *nt* TELEKOM trunk network, trunking network; **Fernnetzgerät** *nt* ELEKTROTECH remote power supply; **Fernordnungsstoß** *m* KERNTECH distant collision; **Fernreisebus** *m* KFZTECH long-distance bus; **Fernrohr** *nt* PHYS refracting telescope, refractor, RAUMFAHRT, WASSERTRANS telescope; **Fernrohrlinse** *f* FOTO telescopic lens; **Fernsatz** *m* DRUCK teletypesetting; **Fernschaltanlage** *f* TELEKOM remote-switching system; **Fernschaltung** *f* FERNSEH remote switching; **Fernschnellzug** *m* EISENBAHN express train; **Fernschreiben** *nt* TELEKOM telex message; **Fernschreib-Entzerrer** *m* ELEKTRONIK *Telegrafie* regenerative repeater; **Fernschreiber** *m* *(FS)* COMP & DV Teletype®, teleprinter (BrE), teletypewriter (AmE) *(TTY)*, TELEKOM Teletype®, teleprinter (BrE), teletypewriter (AmE)

Fernseh- *pref* FERNSEH television; **Fernsehaufzeichnung** *f* FERNSEH telerecording; **Fernseh-Bildröhre** *f* FERNSEH television picture tube; **Fernsehempfänger** *m* FERNSEH television receiver; **Fernsehempfangsstörung** *f* *(TVI)* FERNSEH television interference *(TVI)*

Fernsehen[1] *nt* *(TV)* FERNSEH television *(TV)*; **~ mit langsamer Abtastung** *nt* *(SSTV)* FERNSEH slow scan television *(SSTV)*; **~ über Gemeinschaftsantenne** *nt* *(CATV)* FERNSEH community antenna television system *(CATV)*; **~ über Projektoren** *nt* FERNSEH projection television

Fernsehen:[2] **im ~ senden** *vt* FERNSEH telecast

Fernseh-: **Fernsehfunk** *m* FERNSEH television broadcasting; **Fernsehgerät** *nt* FERNSEH television set; **Fernsehkabel** *nt* FERNSEH television cable; **Fernsehkamera** *f* FERNSEH television camera; **Fernseh-Kamerafernsteuerung** *f* FERNSEH, TRANS remote control by television camera; **Fernsehkamera-Röhre** *f* FERNSEH television camera tube; **Fernsehkanal** *m* ELEKTROTECH channel; **Fernsehnorm** *f* FERNSEH television standard; **Fernsehrelais** *nt* FERNSEH television relay; **Fernsehröhre** *f* FERNSEH, KER & GLAS television tube; **Fernsehrundfunk** *m* FERNSEH television broadcasting; **Fernsehsender** *m* FERNSEH television transmitter

Fernsehsendung: als ~ ausstrahlen *vt* FERNSEH televise
Fernseh-: **Fernsehstörung** *f* *(TVI)* FERNSEH television interference *(TVI)*; **Fernsehübertragungsrechte** *nt pl* FERNSEH television rights; **Fernsehzuschauer** *m* FERNSEH television viewer

Fernsprech- *pref* TELEKOM telephone; **Fernsprechamt** *nt* TELEKOM telephone exchange; **Fernsprechansagedienst** *m* TELEKOM recorded public information service; **Fernsprechapparat** *m* TELEKOM telephone instrument; **Fernsprechauftragsdienst** *m* TELEKOM absent subscriber service; **Fernsprechauskunft** *f* TELEKOM directory enquiries; **Fernsprechen** *nt* TELEKOM telephony; **Fernsprechendgerät** *nt* TELEKOM telephone terminal

Fernsprecher *m* TELEKOM telephone

Fernsprech-: **Fernsprechgebühr** *f* TELEKOM call charge; **Fernsprechkabel** *nt* ELEKTROTECH telephone line; **Fernsprechleitung** *f* ELEKTROTECH telephone line; **Fernsprechnebenstelle** *f* TELEKOM telephone extension; **Fernsprechnetz** *nt* TELEKOM telephone network, voice network; **Fernsprechschrank** *m* TELEKOM telephone switchboard; **Fernsprechschrank mit Stöpselschnüren** *m* TELEKOM plug and cord switchboard; **Fernsprechübertrager** *m* ELEKTROTECH repeating coil; **Fernsprechverbindung** *f* PHYS telecommunication; **Fernsprechvermittlung mit ZB-Betrieb** *f* TELEKOM central battery switchboard; **Fernsprechvermittlungsstelle** *f* TELEKOM telephone exchange; **Fernsprechverzeichnis** *nt* TELEKOM telephone directory; **Fernsprechwesen** *nt* TELEKOM telephony; **Fernsprechzelle** *f* TELEKOM telephone box

Fern-: **Fernsteuern** *nt* RADIO telecommand
fernsteuern *vt* RADIO, TRANS radioguide

Fern-: **Fernsteuerung** *f* ELEKTRIZ, KONTROLL, MECHAN, TELEKOM remote control; **Fernstoß** *m* KERNTECH distant collision; **Fernstrecke** *f* EISENBAHN trunk line; **Fernstromversorgung** *f* ELEKTROTECH remote power supply; **Ferntest** *m* COMP & DV remote test; **Fernthermometer** *nt* HEIZ & KÄLTE remote thermometer, THERMOD remote temperature gage (AmE), remote temperature gauge (BrE); **Fernüberwachung** *f* FERNSEH, TELEKOM remote monitoring; **Fernverarbeitung** *f* COMP & DV *von Daten* teleprocessing; **Fernverbindungskabel** *nt* ELEKTROTECH, TELEKOM trunk cable; **Fernverkehrsdienst zu Ortsgebühren** *m* TELEKOM extended-area service

Fernvermittlung *f* TELEKOM toll exchange (AmE), trunk exchange (BrE), trunk switching; **Fernvermittlungsstelle** *f (FVSt)* TELEKOM toll exchange (AmE), trunk exchange (BrE), trunk switching center (AmE), trunk switching centre (BrE) *(toll exchange)*

Fernwahl *f* TELEKOM STD, subscriber trunk-dialing (AmE), subscriber trunk-dialling (BrE); **Fernwahlzugangskennzahl** *f* TELEKOM direct distance-dialing access code (AmE), subscriber trunk-dialling access code (BrE)

Fernwärme *f* HEIZ & KÄLTE, THERMOD district heating; **Fernwärmekraftwerk** *nt* THERMOD district-heating station

Fern-: **Fernwasserversorgung** *f* WASSERVERSORG distant water supply; **Fernwirkungsfeldstärke** *f* RAUMFAHRT far-field intensity; **Fernzähler** *m* GERÄT telecounter; **Fernzeichnen** *nt* TELEKOM telewriting; **Fernzugriff** *m* COMP & DV remote access

Ferrat *nt* CHEMIE ferrate

Ferredoxin *nt* CHEMIE ferredoxin

Ferricyan *nt* CHEMIE ferricyanogen

ferrimagnetisch *adj* PHYS ferrimagnetic

Ferrimagnetismus *m* PHYS ferrimagnetism

Ferrit *nt* CHEMIE, ELEKTRIZ, ELEKTROTECH, PHYS ferrite; **~ mit rechteckiger Magnetisierungsschleife** *nt* ELEKTROTECH square loop ferrite; **Ferritbegrenzer** *m* ELEKTROTECH ferrite limiter; **Ferritdreher** *m* ELEKTROTECH ferrite rotator

Ferritin *nt* CHEMIE ferritin

ferritisch[1] *adj* METALL, PHYS ferritic

ferritisch:[2] **~er rostfreier Stahl** *m* PHYS ferritic stainless steel

Ferrit: **Ferritisolator** *m* ELEKTROTECH ferrite isolator; **Ferritkern** *m* COMP & DV ferrite core, magnetic core, ELEKTRIZ, ELEKTROTECH ferrite core; **Ferritkopf** *m* AUFNAHME, FERNSEH ferrite head; **Ferritmodulator** *m* ELEKTRONIK microwave amplitude modulator; **Ferritperle** *f* RADIO ferrite bead; **Ferritphasenregler** *m* ELEKTROTECH ferrite phase shifter; **Ferritphasenschieber** *m* ELEKTROTECH ferrite phase shifter; **Ferritringleiter** *m* ELEKTROTECH ferrite circulator; **Ferritspulenkern** *m* RADIO ferrite slug; **Ferritstab** *m* ELEKTROTECH, PHYS, RADIO ferrite rod; **Ferritstabantenne** *f* WASSERTRANS *Funk* ferrite rod antenna

Ferrocyan *nt* CHEMIE ferrocyanogen

ferrodynamisch: **~er Leistungsmesser** *m* ELEKTRIZ ferrodynamic wattmeter; **~es Wattmeter** *nt* ELEKTRIZ ferrodynamic wattmeter

Ferroelektrikum *nt* ELEKTROTECH ferroelectricity

ferroelektrisch[1] *adj* PHYS ferroelectric

ferroelektrisch:[2] **~er Kristall** *m* ELEKTROTECH ferroelectric crystal

Ferroelektrizität *f* PHYS ferroelectricity

Ferromagnetikum *nt* ELEKTROTECH ferromagnetic material

ferromagnetisch[1] *adj* AUFNAHME, PHYS ferromagnetic

ferromagnetisch:[2] **~es Material** *nt* ELEKTRIZ ferromagnetic material; **~er Verstärker** *m* ELEKTRONIK ferromagnetic amplifier

Ferromagnetismus *m* AUFNAHME, ELEKTRIZ, PHYS ferromagnetism

Ferroresonanz *f* ELEKTROTECH ferroresonance; **Ferroresonanzkreis** *m* ELEKTROTECH ferroresonance circuit

Ferse *f* KER & GLAS heel

fertig:[1] **~ montiert** *adj* HEIZ & KÄLTE factory-assembled

fertig:[2] **~ bearbeitetes Teil** *nt* MASCHINEN finished part; **~er Quarzkristall** *m* ELEKTRONIK finished quartz

Fertigbeton *m* BAU ready-mixed concrete

Fertigblasen *nt* KER & GLAS final blow, settle blow

Fertigbohren *nt* MASCHINEN finish boring; **~ mit Diamanten** *nt* FERTIG diamond boring

Fertigbohrkopf *m* FERTIG boring head

Fertigdrehen *nt* MASCHINEN final turning

fertigen *vt* MECHAN fabricate

Fertiger *m* BAU *Tiefbau* finisher

Fertiggesenk *nt* MASCHINEN finishing die

fertiggesenkschmieden *vi* FERTIG finish-stamp

Fertigkaliber *nt* FERTIG finishing groove

Fertigkeit *f* ERGON skill; **Fertigkeitsanalyse** *f* ERGON skills analysis

Fertigläppen *nt* FERTIG finish lap

Fertigmachen *nt* DRUCK finishing

Fertigmaß *nt* MASCHINEN actual size

Fertigmehl *nt* LEBENSMITTEL self-raising flour (BrE)

Fertigpackung *f* ABFALL prepackaging

Fertigproduktelager *nt* VERPACK finished goods store

fertigputzen *vt* FERTIG rumble

Fertigreibahle *f* MASCHINEN finishing reamer

fertigschmieden *vi* FERTIG finish-stamp

Fertigschneideeisen *nt* FERTIG bottoming die

Fertigschneider *m* FERTIG *Gewinde* final tap, finishing tap, MASCHINEN third tap

Fertigschnitt *m* MASCHINEN finishing cut

fertigstellen *vt* BAU finish

Fertigstellung *f* BAU completion; **Fertigstellungsdatum** *nt* BAU completion date

Fertigteil *nt* BAU precast unit; **Fertigteilbau** *m* BAU system building construction; **Fertigteilbeton** *m* BAU precast concrete

Fertigung *f* FERTIG manufacturing; **Fertigungsautomation** *f* ELEKTRIZ manufacturing automation; **Fertigungsfehler** *m* FERTIG *Getriebelehre* error of gear cutting

fertigungsgerecht: **~e Maßeinteilung** *f* KONSTZEICH production-oriented dimensioning

Fertigung: **Fertigungsmittelzeichnung** *f* KONSTZEICH production facility drawing; **Fertigungsplan** *m* COMP & DV production schedule; **Fertigungsprüfer** *m* QUAL in-process inspector; **Fertigungsprüfplan** *m* QUAL in-process inspection plan; **Fertigungsprüfung** *f* QUAL in-process inspection, manufacturing inspection, process inspection; **Fertigungsregel** *f* COMP & DV production rule; **Fertigungsroboter** *m* MECHAN assembly robot; **Fertigungssteuerung** *f* COMP & DV production control, KONTROLL, MASCHINEN manufacturing control; **Fertigungsstraße** *f* MASCHINEN, VERPACK, WASSERTRANS *Schiffbau* production line; **Fertigungsstückliste** *f* KONSTZEICH production parts list; **Fertigungstechnik** *f* COMP & DV production engin-

eering, ELEKTRONIK manufacturing technique, MA-
SCHINEN production engineering
fertigungstechnisch: ~er **Arbeitsvorgang** *m* FERTIG
machining operation
Fertigung: **Fertigungsüberwachung** *f* QUAL process
control, production surveillance; **Fertigungsüber-
wachungsunterlagen** *f pl* QUAL process-controlling
documents; **Fertigungsverfahren** *nt* FERTIG operating
procedure; **Fertigungszeichnung** *f* HEIZ & KÄLTE,
KONSTZEICH production drawing, MASCHINEN working drawing; **Fertigungszyklus** *m* KUNSTSTOFF
molding cycle (AmE), moulding cycle (BrE)
Fertigwalzen *nt* FERTIG finish roll-forming
Fertigware *f* TEXTIL finished goods
Fertigzeichnung *f* MASCHINEN final drawing
Fertigziehen *nt* MASCHINEN final drawing, finish
drawing
Ferula- *pref* CHEMIE ferulic
Fessel *f* RAUMFAHRT *Raumschiff* tether; **Fesselflug** *m*
RAUMFAHRT captive flight
fest[1] *adj* ANSTRICH, BAU *Untergrund* solid, COMP & DV
static, MASCHINEN fixed, permanent, MECHAN fixed,
TEXTIL firm, VERPACK moisture-proof; ~ **angeschlos-
sen** *adj* ELEKTROTECH hard-wired; **mit ~er Anordnung
der Spindeln** *adj* FERTIG fixed center (AmE), fixed
centre (BrE); ~ **gekoppelt** *adj* ELEKTRIZ close-
coupled; ~ **verlegt** *adj* BAU permanent; **mit ~en
Zähnen** *adj* FERTIG solid
fest:[2] ~er **Abfall** *m* ABFALL solid waste; ~er **Abfallstoff** *m*
ABFALL solid waste; ~e **Ablaufsteuerung** *f* COMP & DV,
TELEKOM fixed sequencer; ~er **Aggregatzustand** *m*
ELEKTRONIK, TEILPHYS solid state; ~er **Anschlag** *m*
MASCHINEN fixed stop, hard stop; ~es **Aufspulen** *nt*
FOTO tight spooling; ~er **Block** *m* WASSERTRANS *Be-
schläge* standing block; ~er **Brennstoff** *m* HEIZ &
KÄLTE, MASCHINEN solid fuel; ~es **Bullauge** *nt* WAS-
SERTRANS *Schiffbau* deadlight; ~es **Dämpfungsglied**
nt ELEKTRONIK fixed attenuator, TELEKOM pad; ~es
Dielektrikum *nt* ELEKTROTECH solid dielectric; ~er
Einband *m* DRUCK hardback; ~e **Entfernungsbefeue-
rung** *f* LUFTTRANS *Flughafen* fixed distance lights; ~er
Fehler *m* LUFTTRANS *Funkhöhenmesser* fixed error;
~es **Feld** *nt* COMP & DV fixed field; ~e **Feuerlöschanlage** *f* SICHERHEIT stationary fire-fighting installation;
~er **Flugfunkdienst** *m (AFS)* LUFTTRANS *Bodenfunk-
stationen* aeronautical-fixed network (AmE),
aeronautical-fixed service (BrE), aeronautical-fixed
system (AmE) *(aeronautical-fixed service)*; ~es **Flugfunknetz** *nt (AFTN)* LUFTTRANS aeronautical-fixed
telecommunication network *(AFTN)*; ~e **Flugfunk-
stelle** *f* LUFTTRANS aeronautical-fixed station; ~e
Flugmeldeverbindung *f* LUFTTRANS aeronautical-
fixed circuit; ~es **Gehrungsdreieck** *nt* BAU miter
square (AmE), mitre square (BrE); ~ **gewordenes
Fett** *nt* LEBENSMITTEL solidified fat; ~er **Griff** *m* TEXTIL
firm handle; **mit ~em Griff gehaltener Diamant** *m* KER
& GLAS diamond held with firm grip; ~er **Kernbrennstoff** *m* KERNTECH solid nuclear fuel; ~er **Kohlenstoff**
m CHEMIE fixed carbon; ~e **Kopplung** *f* ELEKTRIZ
close coupling, ELEKTROTECH tight coupling; ~e
Kupplung *f* MASCHINEN permanent coupling, solid
coupling; ~e **Länge** *f* COMP & DV fixed length; ~es
Material *nt* PHYS solid; ~e **Phase** *f* THERMOD solid
phase; ~es **Rad** *nt* MASCHINEN fixed wheel; ~e **Riemenscheibe** *f* MASCHINEN fixed pulley; ~e **Rolle** *f*
MASCHINEN fixed pulley; ~er **Rost** *m* HEIZ & KÄLTE

fixed grate; ~er **Schenkel** *m* FERTIG *Winkelmesser*
blade, stock; ~e **Schürze** *f* WASSERTRANS rigid skirt;
~er **Setzstock** *m* MASCHINEN fixed steadyrest; ~er
Siedlungsabfall *m* ABFALL MSW, municipal solid
waste; ~e **Sperre** *f* SICHERHEIT fixed guard; ~e **Spitze** *f*
FERTIG dead center (AmE), dead centre (BrE), MA-
SCHINEN dead center (AmE), dead centre (BrE), fixed
center (AmE), fixed centre (BrE); ~e **Versetzung** *f*
METALL immobile dislocation; ~e **virtuelle Verbindung** *f* COMP & DV, TELEKOM PVC, permanent virtual
circuit; ~er **virtueller Schaltkreis** *m* COMP & DV PVC,
permanent virtual circuit; ~e **Wortlänge** *f* COMP & DV
fixed word length; ~er **Zahnkranz** *m* LUFTTRANS fixed
ring gear; ~ **zugeordnete Frequenz** *f* TELEKOM dedicated frequency; ~er **Zustand** *m* TEILPHYS solid state
festabgestimmt: ~er **Hohlraumresonator** *m* ELEKTRO-
NIK fixed-tuned cavity resonator
Festabstimmung *f* ELEKTRONIK fixed tuning
Festaderkabel *nt* TELEKOM tight-jacketed cable
Festamplitude *f* ELEKTRONIK fixed amplitude
Festanschlag *m* FERTIG positive stop
festbacken *vt* CHEMTECH cake
festbinden *vt* WASSERTRANS lash
festbrennen *vt* TEXTIL *Verschmutzung* bake
Festdaten *nt pl* COMP & DV fixed data
Festdielektrikum *nt* ELEKTROTECH solid dielectric
festeingebaut: ~e **Wohnungsgegenstände** *m pl* BAU fix-
tures and fittings
festfahren *vi* NICHTFOSS ENERG stall
Festfeuer *nt* WASSERTRANS *Seezeichen* fixed light
Festformat *nt* COMP & DV fixed format
Festfrequenzgenerator *m* ELEKTRONIK fixed-frequency
synthesizer
Festfrequenzmagnetron *nt* ELEKTRONIK fixed-frequency magnetron
Festfrequenzoszillator *m* ELEKTRONIK fixed-frequency
oscillator, RAUMFAHRT local oscillator
Festfressen *nt* FERTIG galling, KFZTECH *Kolbenringe*
jamming, *Lager, Kolben* seizing
festfressen[1] *vt* FERTIG *Werkzeug* bind
festfressen:[2] **sich** ~ *v refl* KERNTECH seize
festgefressen *adj* KFZTECH jammed
festgelegt: ~er **Fahrweg** *m* WASSERTRANS lane; ~es **Verfahren** *nt* QUAL routine
Festgenerator *m* RAUMFAHRT fixed generator
festgeschaltet: ~er **Anschluß** *m* TELEKOM dedicated
port; ~er **Kanal** *m* TELEKOM dedicated channel; ~e
Leitung *f* COMP & DV, TELEKOM dedicated line; ~er
Zeichengabekanal *m* TELEKOM dedicated signaling
channel (AmE), dedicated signalling channel (BrE);
nicht ~er Zeichengabekanal *m* TELEKOM nondedicated signaling channel (AmE), nondedicated
signalling channel (BrE)
festgezurrt: ~ **und aufgehängt** *adj* RAUMFAHRT *Raumschiff* strapdown-mounted
festhaken[1] *vt* MASCHINEN clasp, hook, MECHAN hitch
festhaken:[2] **sich** ~ *v refl* FERTIG *Säge* clog, WASSERTRANS
Festmachen grip
Festhalten: ~ **der Darstellung** *nt* ELEKTRONIK display
retention
Festhöhe *f* FERTIG fixed height
Festigkeit *f* KERNTECH toughness, KOHLEN strength,
LEBENSMITTEL consistency, MASCHINEN strength, ME-
CHAN stress, METALL strength, NICHTFOSS ENERG
solidity, PAPIER, PHYS strength, TELEKOM stability,
TEXTIL strength, tenacity; **Festigkeitsberechnung** *f*

MASCHINEN stability calculation; **Festigkeitseigen-schaften** *f pl* WERKPRÜF physical properties; **Festigkeitsgrenze** *f* MECHAN breaking point; **Festigkeitsprüfung** *f* RAUMFAHRT *Raumschiff* stress analysis

festkleben *vi* BAU stick

Festklemmen *nt* FERTIG *Bohrer* sticking

festklemmen[1] *vt* BAU clamp, FERTIG choke, MASCHINEN lock, MECHAN, WASSERTRANS jam

festklemmen:[2] **sich ~** *v refl* MECHAN jam

Festklopfen *nt* BAU ramming

Festkomma *nt* COMP & DV fixed point, MATH fixed decimal point, TELEKOM fixed point; **Festkommabetrieb** *m* COMP & DV fixed-point operation; **Festkommarechnung** *f* COMP & DV fixed-point arithmetic; **Festkommaschreibweise** *f* COMP & DV fixed-point notation

festkommen *vi* WASSERTRANS *Schiff* run aground

Festkondensator *m* ELEKTROTECH, PHYS fixed capacitor

Festkontakt *m* ELEKTRIZ, ELEKTROTECH fixed contact

Festkörper *m* COMP & DV, PHYS, STRAHLPHYS, TEILPHYS solid; **Festkörperbauelement** *nt* ELEKTRIZ, PHYS, TE-LEKOM solid state device; **Festkörpereffekt** *m* KERNTECH solid state effect; **Festkörpergeometrie** *f* GEOM CSG, constructive solid geometry; **Festkörperphysik** *f* PHYS, TEILPHYS solid state physics; **Festkörperrelais** *nt* ELEKTROTECH solid state relay; **Festkörperspannungsableiter** *m* ELEKTROTECH solid state surge arrester; **Festkörperspeicher** *m* COMP & DV, ELEKTROTECH solid state memory device; **Festkörperverstärker** *m* TELEKOM solid state amplifier; **Festkörperzähler** *m* STRAHLPHYS solid state detector

Festlandsockel *m* ERDÖL, WASSERTRANS *Geologie* continental shelf

Festlast *f* ELEKTROTECH fixed load

festlegen *vt* COMP & DV declare, set

Festlegung *f* FERTIG convention *n*; **~ der Prioritätsfolge** *f* COMP & DV priority sequencing; **~ der Werkzeugwinkel** *f* FERTIG tool angle convention; **~ der Wirkwinkel** *f* FERTIG working angle convention

Festluftkissen *nt* WASSERTRANS static air cushion

Festmachen *nt* WASSERTRANS mooring

festmachen[1] *vt* MEERSCHMUTZ *Schiff* moor, WASSER-TRANS make fast, moor, secure, *Segeln* furl

festmachen[2] *vi* WASSERTRANS moor

Festmachleine *f* WASSERTRANS *Tauwerk* mooring line

Festoxidbrennstoffzelle *f* ELEKTRIZ solid oxide fuel cell

Festplatte *f* COMP & DV Winchester disk, fixed disk, disk (AmE), COMP & DV *(HD)* hard disk, hard disk *(HD)*, TELEKOM *(HD)* hard disk *(HD)*; **Festplattencontroller** *m* COMP & DV disk controller; **Festplattenlaufwerk** *nt* COMP & DV disk drive

Festpol *m* ELEKTRIZ fixed pole

Festpunkt *m* BAU datum, fixed point, *Vermessung* benchmark, EISENBAHN *Fahrleitung* midpoint anchor, KERNTECH fixed point; **Festpunkteinstellung** *f* REGEL-UNG terminal-based conformity; **Festpunktnetz** *nt* BAU *Vermessung* observation grid

Festrad *nt* MASCHINEN fixed wheel

Festsattel *m* KFZTECH fixed caliper (AmE), fixed calliper (BrE); **Festsattelscheibenbremse** *f* KFZTECH fixed caliper disk brake (AmE), fixed calliper disc brake (BrE)

Festscheibe *f* FERTIG fast pulley

Festschelle *f* FERTIG *Kunststoffinstallationen* fixed-point bracket

Festschrauben *nt* MASCHINEN screwing

festschrauben *vt* BAU bolt, MASCHINEN screw

Festsetzen *nt* FERTIG *Kunststoffinstallationen* seizing

festsetzen: sich ~ *v refl* CHEMTECH settle on

Festsitz *m (FS)* MASCHINEN driving fit, force fit

Festspannen *nt* BAU stretching, MASCHINEN mounting

festspannen *vt* MASCHINEN clamp, mount

Festspeicherinstruktion *f* COMP & DV read-only instruction

feststampfen *vt* BAU, EISENBAHN tamp

feststehend[1] *adj* MECHAN fixed

feststehend:[2] **~e Achse** *f* MASCHINEN dead axle; **~er Flügel** *m* LUFTTRANS fixed wing; **~er Querbalken** *m* FERTIG fixed rail; **~e Richtungsschaufel** *f* LUFTTRANS fixed stator vane; **~e Spule** *f* ELEKTRIZ fixed coil; **~es Teil** *nt* PHYS stator; **~er Tisch** *m* KER & GLAS *Spiegelherstellung* fixed table

Feststellbremse *f* KFZTECH, MECHAN parking brake

Feststelleinrichtung *f* FERTIG retainer

Feststellen: ~ des Bildschirms *nt* COMP & DV *Gegensatz zu Blättern* screen locking; **~ des Luftschraubenblattes** *nt* LUFTTRANS *Hubschrauber* blade setting

feststellen *vt* BAU lock, FERNSEH park

Feststeller *m* FERTIG *Kunststoffinstallationen* locking pin, RAUMFAHRT *Raumschiff* fastener

Feststellring *m* MASCHINEN lock ring

Feststellvorrichtung *f* MASCHINEN blocking device

Feststoff *m* ANSTRICH, MASCHINEN solid; **Feststoffabfall** *m* UMWELTSCHMUTZ solid waste; **Feststoffaustauscher** *m* KOHLEN solid exchanger; **Feststoffextraktion** *f* CHEMIE leaching; **Feststoffgehalt** *m* ABFALL solids content; **Feststoffrakete** *f* MASCHINEN solid propellant rocket engine, RAUMFAHRT dry-fuelled rocket; **Feststoffschmierung** *f* MASCHINEN solid lubrication; **Feststoffschubtriebwerk** *nt* RAUMFAHRT solid fuel booster; **Feststoffsystem** *nt* RAUMFAHRT solid propellant system; **Feststoffteilchen** *nt* CHEMTECH, UMWELTSCHMUTZ solid particle

Festtantalkondensator *m* ELEKTROTECH solid tantalum capacitor

Festtreibstoff *m* RAUMFAHRT *Raumschiff* solid propellant

festverdrahtet[1] *adj* COMP & DV, ELEKTROTECH hardwired

festverdrahtet:[2] **~e Logik** *f* COMP & DV hard-wired logic; **~es Programm** *nt* COMP & DV hard-wired program; **~es programmierbares Vermittlungssystem** *nt* TELE-KOM hard-wired programmable switching system; **~e Verbindung** *f* COMP & DV hard-wired connection

Festwertregelung *f* ELEKTROTECH regulation, REGEL-UNG fixed command control

Festwertspeicher *m (ROM)* COMP & DV nonerasable storage, read-only memory, ELEKTRIZ, ELEKTROTECH, RADIO read-only memory *(ROM)*

Festwiderstand *m* ELEKTRIZ, ELEKTROTECH, PHYS fixed resistor

festzeitgesteuert: ~es Signal *nt* TRANS pretimed signal

Festzeitrelais *nt* ELEKTRIZ definitive-time relay

Festziehen *nt* MASCHINEN tightening

festziehen *vt* MASCHINEN fasten, tighten

festzuzurrend: ~e Gerätschaft *f* RAUMFAHRT *Raumschiff* strapdown equipment; **~e Trägheitsplattform** *f* RAUM-FAHRT *Raumschiff* strapdown inertial platform

FET[1] *abbr (Feldeffekttransistor)* COMP & DV, ELEKTRO-NIK, OPTIK, PHYS, RADIO, RAUMFAHRT FET *(field effect transistor)*

FET:[2] **FET-Eingang** *m* ELEKTRONIK FET front end, FET

input; **FET-Frequenzmesser** *m* RADIO gate dip meter
Fett[1] *nt* DRUCK, KFZTECH grease, LEBENSMITTEL fat,
MASCHINEN, MECHAN grease, PAPIER fat, grease
Fett:[2] **mit ~ abdichten** *vt* MASCHINEN pack with grease
fett[1] *adj* DRUCK bold
fett:[2] **~er Beton** *m* BAU fat concrete; **~er Druck** *m* DRUCK
bold face; **~es Gemisch** *nt* KFZTECH rich mixture; **~es
Öl** *nt* CHEMIE fixed oil; **~e Schrift** *f* DRUCK heavy type;
~er Ton *m* ERDÖL *Mineral* fat clay, KER & GLAS rich
clay
Fett: **Fettabscheider** *m* ABFALL grease separator, grease
trap, MEERSCHMUTZ skimming tank
fettabweisend: **~es Papier** *nt* VERPACK grease-resistant
paper
fettaffin *adj* CHEMIE lipophile, lipophilic
fettähnlich *adj* CHEMIE lipoid
fettarm *adj* LEBENSMITTEL low-fat
fettartig *adj* CHEMIE lipoid
Fett: **Fettbeständigkeit** *f* KUNSTSTOFF grease resistance;
Fettbüchse *f* FERTIG grease cup, greaser, MASCHINEN
grease cup
fettdicht[1] *adj* PAPIER, VERPACK greaseproof
fettdicht:[2] **~es Papier** *nt* LEBENSMITTEL greaseproof paper, PAPIER grease-resistant paper
Fett: **Fettdichtigkeitsprobe** *f* PAPIER greaseproof proof
Fettdruck *m* COMP & DV bold face, bold print, DRUCK
bold face; **Fettdrucken** *nt* DRUCK emboldening
Fett: **Fettdurchlässigkeit** *f* VERPACK permeability to
grease; **Fettfänger** *m* MEERSCHMUTZ skimming tank
fettfrei *adj* LEBENSMITTEL nonfat
fettgeschmiert *adj* FERTIG grease-lubricated
Fett: **Fettharz** *nt* CHEMIE oleoresin
fettig: **~es Alkyd** *nt* KUNSTSTOFF long oil alkyd
Fett: **Fettkalk** *m* PAPIER fat lime; **Fettkante** *f* KUNST-
STOFF fat edge; **Fettkappe** *f* KFZTECH grease cap;
Fettkennzahl *f* LEBENSMITTEL lipid value; **Fettkohle** *f*
KOHLEN fat coal, rich coal
fettlöslich *adj* CHEMIE liposoluble
Fetton *m* CHEMIE smectite
Fett: **Fettpackung** *f* MASCHINEN grease packing; **Fettpi-
stole** *f* KFZTECH *Werkzeug* grease gun; **Fettpresse** *f*
BAU, MASCHINEN grease gun; **Fettreif** *m* LEBENSMIT-
TEL *Schokolade* bloom; **Fettsäure** *f* CHEMIE,
LEBENSMITTEL, PAPIER fatty acid; **Fettsäureglycerid**
nt LEBENSMITTEL fatty acid glyceride
fettundurchlässig: **~es Papier** *nt* LEBENSMITTEL grease-
proof paper
FET-Verstärker *m* ELEKTRONIK FET amplifier; **~ in
Gateschaltung** *m* RADIO common gate FET amplifier
feucht *adj* BAU damp, PAPIER damp, moist, PHYS hygroscopic, TEXTIL wet, THERMOD humid, moist
Feuchte *f* BAU, PHYS, TEXTIL, VERPACK, WERKPRÜF
moisture; **Feuchteanzeiger** *m* PHYS hygroscope;
Feuchtegehalt *m* BAU, PHYS, TEXTIL, VERPACK, WERK-
PRÜF moisture content
feuchtehaltig *adj* PHYS hygroscopic
Feuchte: **Feuchtemesser** *m* HEIZ & KÄLTE moisture
meter, PHYS moisture meter, psychrometer; **Feuchte-
meßfühler** *m* GERÄT moisture head; **Feuchtemeßgerät**
nt GERÄT moisture content meter; **Feuchtemessung** *f*
PHYS psychrometry
Feuchter *m* PAPIER dampener
feuchtgeglättet: **~es Papier** *nt* DRUCK water-finished
paper
Feuchtglättwerk *nt* PAPIER breaker stack
Feuchtigkeit[1] *f* ANSTRICH humidity, ELEKTROTECH

damp, FERTIG *Kunststoffinstallationen*, HEIZ & KÄLTE
humidity, PAPIER moisture, PHYS, THERMOD humidity
Feuchtigkeit- und Temperaturfühler *m* TRANS moisture and temperature detector
Feuchtigkeit:[2] **~ entziehen** *vi* HEIZ & KÄLTE dehumidify
feuchtigkeitsabweisend *adj* VERPACK moisture-
repellent
Feuchtigkeit: **Feuchtigkeitsanzeige** *f* VERPACK humidity
indicator; **Feuchtigkeitsaufnahme** *f* PAPIER moisture
regain, VERPACK humidity absorber, WERKPRÜF
moisture regain; **Feuchtigkeitsaufnahme im Normal-
klima** *f* WERKPRÜF moisture regain in the standard
atmosphere
feuchtigkeitsbeständig *adj* VERPACK moisture-proof
Feuchtigkeit: **Feuchtigkeitsbestimmung** *f* VERPACK
moisture determination; **Feuchtigkeitsdämmschicht**
f BAU damp-proof course, dpc
feuchtigkeitsfest *adj* BAU, VERPACK damp-proof
Feuchtigkeit: **Feuchtigkeitsgehalt** *m* HEIZ & KÄLTE, KOH-
LEN, LEBENSMITTEL, PAPIER, TEXTIL,
WASSERVERSORG, WERKPRÜF moisture content;
Feuchtigkeitsmesser *m* HEIZ & KÄLTE, PHYS moisture
meter; **Feuchtigkeitsmessung** *f* WASSERTRANS humi-
dity measurement; **Feuchtigkeitsprobe** *f* VERPACK
moisture test; **Feuchtigkeitsregler** *m* HEIZ & KÄLTE
humidistat
Feuchtkugelthermometer *nt* THERMOD wet bulb ther-
mometer
Feuchtraum *m* HEIZ & KÄLTE damp location; **Feucht-
raumisolator** *m* ELEKTROTECH mushroom insulator
Feuchtstaubabsaugung *f* SICHERHEIT wet dust removal
installation
Feuchtverfahren *nt* KONSTZEICH semidry-method
Feuchtwalze *f* VERPACK damping roll
Feuer[1] *nt* SICHERHEIT, THERMOD fire, WASSERTRANS *unter der Kimm* loom; **Feuer- und Hitzeschutzkleidung** *f*
SICHERHEIT protective clothing against heat and fire
Feuer:[2] **ein ~ löschen** *vi* SICHERHEIT put out a fire
Feuer: **Feueralarm** *m* SICHERHEIT, THERMOD fire alarm;
Feueranzünder *m* HEIZ & KÄLTE fire lighter
feuerbeständig[1] *adj* HEIZ & KÄLTE, SICHERHEIT fire-
resistant, THERMOD fire-resisting
feuerbeständig:[2] **~e Beschichtung** *f* THERMOD fire-
resisting coating; **~e Farbe** *f* THERMOD fire-resisting
paint; **~e Trennwand** *f* THERMOD fire-resisting bulkhead; **~e Tür** *f* SICHERHEIT fire-resistant door
Feuer: **Feuerbeständigkeit** *f* FERTIG refractoriness,
KUNSTSTOFF fire resistance; **Feuerbrücke** *f* THERMOD
fire stop; **Feuerbüchse** *f* EISENBAHN firebox; **Feuer-
falle** *f* SICHERHEIT firetrap, flame trap
feuerfest[1] *adj* HEIZ & KÄLTE refractory, MECHAN, SICHER-
HEIT fireproof, THERMOD fire-resisting, fireproofed,
fireproof, refractory, VERPACK fireproof
feuerfest:[2] **~e Auskleidung** *f* HEIZ & KÄLTE refractory
lining; **~e Ausmauerung** *f* HEIZ & KÄLTE refractory
lining; **~e Beschichtung** *f* THERMOD fire-resisting
coating; **~e Farbe** *f* THERMOD fire-resisting paint; **~es
Geschirr** *nt* KER & GLAS oven-to-table ware; **~es Glas**
nt THERMOD oven proof glass; **~er Handschuh** *m*
LABOR heat-resistant glove; **~es Material** *nt* THERMOD
refractory; **~es Metall** *nt* METALL refractory metal;
~es Papier *nt* PAPIER flameproof paper; **~er Sandstein**
m KER & GLAS fire resisting sandstone; **~es Schott** *nt*
RAUMFAHRT *Raumschiff* fireproof bulkhead; **~er Stoff**
m FERTIG refractory; **~er Ton** *m* KER & GLAS chamotte,
THERMOD fireclay; **~e Töpferwaren** *f pl* KER & GLAS

fireproof pottery; **~e Trennwand** *f* LUFTTRANS fire wall; **~er Ziegel** *m* BAU fire brick

feuerfest:[3] **~ machen** *vt* SICHERHEIT, THERMOD fireproof

Feuer: **Feuerfestbetonerzeugnis** *nt* KER & GLAS castable; **Feuerfesterzeugnis** *nt* KER & GLAS refractory; **Feuerfestglas** *nt* KER & GLAS flameproof glass; **Feuerfestigkeit** *f* OPTIK *Materialwissenschaft* refractoriness; **Feuerfestmaterial** *m* KOHLEN refractory material; **Feuerflecken** *m pl* KER & GLAS fire marks; **Feuergefahr** *f* THERMOD fire hazard; **Feuergefährlichkeit** *f* THERMOD flammability

feuerhemmend[1] *adj* HEIZ & KÄLTE, SICHERHEIT fire-retardant, THERMOD fire-retarding

feuerhemmend:[2] **~e Beschichtung** *f* KERNTECH fire-retardant coat

Feuer: **Feuerholz** *nt* THERMOD firewood; **Feuerklappe** *f* HEIZ & KÄLTE fire damper; **Feuerleiter** *f* BAU fire escape, SICHERHEIT fire ladder, THERMOD fire escape; **Feuerleitung** *f* WASSERTRANS *Marine* fire control; **Feuerlöschanlage mit Sprinkler und Wassersprühanlage** *f* SICHERHEIT sprinkler and water spray fire-extinguishing installation; **Feuerlöschboot** *nt* WASSERTRANS fire boat; **Feuerlöschdecke** *f* SICHERHEIT fire blanket; **Feuerlöscheimer** *m* SICHERHEIT fire bucket; **Feuerlöscheinrichtung** *f* LUFTTRANS firefighting equipment, SICHERHEIT fixed fire extinguisher, WASSERTRANS firefighting equipment; **Feuerlöscher** *m* KFZTECH, LUFTTRANS, SICHERHEIT, THERMOD, WASSERTRANS fire extinguisher; **Feuerlöscherladung** *f* SICHERHEIT fire extinguisher filling; **Feuerlöscherschlagbolzen** *m* LUFTTRANS extinguisher striker; **Feuerlöscherzuschläger** *m* LUFTTRANS extinguisher striker; **Feuerlöschfahrzeug** *nt* THERMOD fire engine; **Feuerlöschhydrant** *m* THERMOD, WASSERTRANS fire hydrant; **Feuerlöschmittel** *nt* SICHERHEIT fire-extinguishing agent; **Feuerlöschmonitor** *m* MEERSCHMUTZ fire monitor; **Feuerlöschpumpe** *f* THERMOD fire pump; **Feuerlöschsteigleitung** *f* THERMOD fire riser, fire-rising main; **Feuermeldeanlage** *f* LUFTTRANS, WASSERTRANS *Notfall* fire detection system; **Feuermelder** *m* ELEKTRIZ fire alarm, SICHERHEIT fire detector; **Feuermelderdraht** *m* LUFTTRANS, WASSERTRANS fire-detecting wire; **Feuermelderkabelbaum** *m* LUFTTRANS, WASSERTRANS fire detection harness; **Feuermeldersystem** *nt* SICHERHEIT fire detection and alarm system; **Feuermeldeschleife** *f* RAUMFAHRT *Raumschiff* fire detection loop

feuern[1] *vt* THERMOD fuel

feuern[2] *vi* KÜNSTL INT *Regel* fire

Feuer: **Feuerplatte** *f* KER & GLAS deadplate; **Feuerpolierer** *m* KER & GLAS fire finisher

feuerpoliert[1] *adj* KER & GLAS fire-polished

feuerpoliert:[2] **~e Kante** *f* KER & GLAS fire-polished edge

Feuer: **Feuerpolitur** *f* KER & GLAS fire finish, fire polishing; **Feuerraum** *m* HEIZ & KÄLTE combustion chamber, HYDRAUL *Dampfkessel* combustion chamber, fire chamber; **Feuerrisiko durch elektrische Ursache** *f* SICHERHEIT electric fire risk; **Feuerrohr** *nt* HEIZ & KÄLTE smoke tube

Feuerschaden[1] *m* SICHERHEIT fire damage

Feuerschaden:[2] **den ~ ermitteln** *vi* SICHERHEIT evaluate the loss occasioned by a fire

Feuer: **Feuerschein** *m* THERMOD firelight; **Feuerschiff** *nt* THERMOD fireship, WASSERTRANS lightship, lightvessel; **Feuerschneise** *f* THERMOD firebreak;

Feuerschott *nt* WASSERTRANS *Schiffkonstruktion* fire bulkhead

Feuerschutz *m* SICHERHEIT *Personen* fire guard, THERMOD fire guard, protection against fire; **Feuerschutzgitter** *nt* SICHERHEIT fire screen; **Feuerschutzisolierglas** *nt* SICHERHEIT insulating glass for fire protection; **Feuerschutzschott** *nt* RAUMFAHRT *Raumschiff* fire bulkhead; **Feuerschutztür** *f* THERMOD fire door; **Feuerschutzwand** *f* RAUMFAHRT *Raumschiff* fire wall

Feuer: **Feuerschweißen** *nt* FERTIG forge welding; **Feuersektor** *m* WASSERTRANS *Seezeichen* sector of a light

feuersicher[1] *adj* ELEKTRIZ, MECHAN fireproof

feuersicher:[2] **~e Telefonanlage** *f* BAU fireproof elephone system

Feuer: **Feuersicherheit** *f* SICHERHEIT *in Gebäuden* fire safety; **Feuersirene** *f* SICHERHEIT fire siren; **Feuerspritze** *f* THERMOD fire hose; **Feuerton** *m* KER & GLAS pipe clay; **Feuertür** *f* EISENBAHN firebox door, THERMOD fire door; **Feuerübung** *f* THERMOD fire drill

Feuerung *f* ELEKTROTECH firing, FERTIG furnace, MASCHINEN firing system, MECHAN heating; **Feuerungsanlage** *f* MASCHINEN firing plant; **Feuerungsdecke** *f* FERTIG *Ofen* crown; **Feuerungsstoß** *m* RAUMFAHRT *Raumschiff* pyrotechnical shock; **Feuerungssystem** *nt* MASCHINEN firing system; **Feuerungstechnik** *f* RAUMFAHRT pyrotechnics; **Feuerungsventil** *nt* RAUMFAHRT *Raumschiff* pyrotechnic valve; **Feuerungswandung** *f* MASCHINEN furnace wall

Feuer: **Feuerverhinderung** *f* THERMOD fire prevention; **Feuerverhütung** *f* SICHERHEIT fire prevention

feuerverzinken *vt* ANSTRICH galvanize

feuerverzinkt *adj* HEIZ & KÄLTE hot-dip galvanized

Feuer: **Feuerverzinkung** *f* FERTIG pot galvanizing; **Feuervorhang** *m* THERMOD fire curtain; **Feuerwache** *f* THERMOD fire station

Feuerwehr *f* SICHERHEIT, THERMOD fire brigade; **Feuerwehrauto** *nt* THERMOD fire engine; **Feuerwehraxt** *f* SICHERHEIT firefighting axe; **Feuerwehrfahrzeug** *nt* SICHERHEIT firefighting vehicle; **Feuerwehrgerät** *nt* SICHERHEIT firefighting equipment; **Feuerwehrhelm** *m* SICHERHEIT fireman's helmet; **Feuerwehrpersonal** *nt* SICHERHEIT firefighting personnel; **Feuerwehrschlauch** *m* SICHERHEIT, THERMOD fire hose; **Feuerwehrwagen** *m* SICHERHEIT fire engine

Feuerwerk *nt* THERMOD firework display; **Feuerwerkskörper** *m* THERMOD firework

Feuer: **Feuerwiderstandsdauer** *f* HEIZ & KÄLTE fire-resistance time; **Feuerwiderstandsfähigkeit** *f* KUNSTSTOFF fire resistance; **Feuerwiderstandsklasse** *f* HEIZ & KÄLTE fire rating; **Feuerzelle** *f* KERNTECH fire cell; **Feuerzone** *f* KERNTECH *durch Feuersperren abgetrennt* fire area

Feynman: **~sches Diagramm** *nt* PHYS Feynman diagram

FF-Ruß *m* (*feiner Furnace-Ruß*) KUNSTSTOFF FF carbon black (*fine furnace carbon black*)

FFS *abbr* (*flexibles Fertigungssystem*) KÜNSTL INT FMS (*flexible manufacturing system*)

FFT *abbr* (*schnelle Fourier-Transformation*) ELEKTRONIK FFT (*fast Fourier transform*)

FHV *abbr* (*Fernleitungshauptverteiler*) TELEKOM TDF (*trunk distribution frame*)

Fiberdichtung *f* MECHAN fiber gasket (AmE), fibre gasket (BrE)

Fiberglas *nt* BAU glass fiber (AmE), glass fibre (BrE),

WASSERTRANS *Schiffbau* fiberglass (AmE), fibreglass (BrE)

Fibonacci-Verfahren *nt* COMP & DV Fibonacci search

Fibonacci-Zahlen *f pl* MATH Fibonacci numbers

Fibrillierung *f* PAPIER fibrillating

Fibroin *nt* CHEMIE fibroin

Ficim *nt* CHEMIE ficin

Fick: **~sches Gesetz** *nt* PHYS Fick's law

Fiedelbohrer *m* MASCHINEN bow drill

fieren[1] *vt* WASSERTRANS *Kette* pay out, *Segeln* lower, *Tauwerk* slacken

fieren[2] *vi* WASSERTRANS *Tauwerk* veer

FIFA *abbr* *(Spaltstoffabbrand, Spaltstoffverbrauch)* KERNTECH FIFA *(fissions per initial fissile atom)*

FIFA-Wert *m* KERNTECH FIFA value

FIFO-Prinzip *nt* *(zuerst Abgelegtes wird als erstes bearbeitet)* COMP & DV FIFO *(first-in-first-out)*

Figur *f* DRUCK, PATENT *Zeichen* figure

figurativ: **~es Element** *nt* PATENT *Zeichen* figurative element; **~e Konstante** *f* COMP & DV figurative constant

fiktiv: **~e Bindungsenergie** *f* KERNTECH fictitious binding energy

Filament *nt* KUNSTSTOFF, TEXTIL filament; **Filamentdenier** *nt* TEXTIL filament denier

Filicin- *pref* CHEMIE filicic

Film *m* FOTO, HYDRAUL *Wasser*, KUNSTSTOFF, MECHAN film; **Filmabtaster** *m* FERNSEH film scanner; **Filmabtastung** *f* FERNSEH telecine scan; **Filmandruckplatte** *f* FOTO *Kamera* pressure pad; **Filmanzeiger** *m* FOTO film type indicator; **Filmaufnahme** *f* FERNSEH film pick-up

filmbildend *adj* KUNSTSTOFF film-forming

Film: **Film-Coating** *nt* VERPACK film coating; **Filmdicke** *f* KUNSTSTOFF film thickness; **Filmdosimeter** *nt* KERNTECH, STRAHLPHYS film badge, film dosimeter; **Filmdosimetrie** *f* KERNTECH film dosimetry; **Filmdruck** *m* DRUCK serigraphy; **Filmführung** *f* FOTO film advance leader; **Filmgelenk** *nt* KUNSTSTOFF integral hinge, living hinge; **Filmgestell** *nt* FOTO film rack; **Filmhaltevorrichtung** *f* FOTO film holder; **Filmkartonierung** *f* VERPACK film cartoning; **Filmkassette** *f* FOTO cassette; **Filmklammer** *f* FOTO film clip; **Filmladegerät** *nt* FOTO bulk film loader; **Filmmontage** *f* DRUCK film mounting; **Filmpatrone** *f* FOTO *Kleinbildkamera* cartridge; **Filmplakette** *f* KERNTECH film badge; **Filmprojektor** *m* ELEKTRIZ movie projector; **Filmrißbildung** *f* KUNSTSTOFF mud cracking; **Filmrolle** *f* FOTO spool of films; **Filmrückschicht** *f* FOTO film backing; **Filmrückspulgabel** *f* FOTO film rewind handle; **Filmscharnier** *nt* KUNSTSTOFF integral hinge, living hinge; **Filmschlüsselschalter** *m* ELEKTROTECH membrane keyswitch; **Filmschrumpfung** *f* FOTO film shrinkage; **Filmsender** *m* FERNSEH film transmitter; **Filmsieden** *nt* HEIZ & KÄLTE, KERNTECH film boiling; **Filmspeicher** *m* COMP & DV thin film memory; **Filmspule** *f* FOTO *Kleinbildfilm* film spool; **Filmtastatur** *f* ELEKTROTECH membrane keyboard; **Filmtransport** *m* FOTO film transport; **Filmtransporthebel** *m* FOTO film transport lever; **Filmtransportkurbel** *f* FOTO film advance crank, film transport crank; **Filmtransportzahntrommel** *f* FOTO film transport sprocket; **Filmtrockengerät** *nt* FOTO film dryer; **Filmvorspann** *m* FOTO *Projektor* film leader

Filter *nt* CHEMIE, COMP & DV, ELEKTRIK, ELEKTRONIK filter, ERDÖL filter, strainer, FERTIG strainer, FOTO, KFZTECH *Vergaser, Öl*, KOHLEN, LABOR, MECHAN, PAPIER, PHYS, RADIO, TELEKOM filter; **~ mit drei Nullstellen** *nt* ELEKTRONIK three-zeros filter; **~ dritter Ordnung** *nt* ELEKTRONIK third-order filter; **~ für elliptisch polarisiertes Licht** *nt* ELEKTRONIK elliptic filter; **~ erster Ordnung** *nt* ELEKTRONIK first-order filter; **~ mit fester Verstärkung** *nt* ELEKTRONIK fixed-gain filter; **~ gegen elektromagnetische Beeinflußung** *nt* ELEKTRONIK electromagnetic-interference filter; **~ geradzahliger Ordnung** *nt* ELEKTRONIK even-order filter; **~ mit geringer Durchlaßbreite** *nt* ELEKTRONIK narrow-band filter; **~ höherer Ordnung** *nt* ELEKTRONIK high-order filter; **~ mit induktivem Eingang** *nt* ELEKTROTECH choke-input filter; **~ niedriger Ordnung** *nt* ELEKTRONIK low-order filter; **~ für relativ konstante Bandbreite** *nt* ELEKTRONIK constant-percentage bandwidth filter; **~ mit unbegrenztem Impulsansprechverhalten** *nt* ELEKTRONIK infinite impulse response filter; **~ ungerader Ordnung** *nt* ELEKTRONIK odd-order filter; **~ für unteres Seitenband** *nt* FERNSEH lower sideband filter; **~ zweiter Ordnung** *nt* ELEKTRONIK second-order filter; **Filter-Abtast-Detektor** *m* TELEKOM filter-and-sample detector; **Filteramplitudenfrequenzgang** *m* ELEKTRONIK filter amplitude response; **Filteranlage** *f* SICHERHEIT *gegen Staub, Fasern* filter plant, UMWELTSCHMUTZ filtering unit, WASSERVERSORG filter plant; **Filteraufnahme** *f* FERNSEH filter holder; **Filterbanksystem** *nt* TELEKOM filterbank system; **Filterbelag** *m* CHEMTECH filter cake; **Filterbett** *nt* CHEMTECH, KERNTECH, WASSERVERSORG filter bed; **Filterbeutel** *m* CHEMTECH filter bag; **Filterbohrung** *f* CHEMTECH filtering well; **Filterbrunnen** *m* CHEMTECH, WASSERVERSORG filtering well; **Filterdämpfung** *f* ELEKTRONIK filter attenuation; **Filterdeckel** *m* KFZTECH filter plug; **Filterdrossel** *f* ELEKTRIZ, ELEKTROTECH filter choke, KFZTECH filter choke unit, filter choke; **Filterdurchlauf** *m* KERNTECH filter run; **Filtereigenfunktion** *f* ELEKTRONIK filter characteristic function; **Filtereinsatz** *m* FERTIG strainer, HEIZ & KÄLTE, KFZTECH, MECHAN filter cartridge; **Filterelement** *nt* KFZTECH filter cartridge, filter element; **Filterfaktor** *m* FOTO filter factor; **Filterflanke** *f* ELEKTRONIK filter slope; **Filterflasche** *f* CHEMTECH filter flask, filtering flask; **Filterfrequenz** *f* ELEKTRONIK filter frequency; **Filterfrequenzgang** *m* ELEKTRONIK filter frequency response; **Filtergehäuse** *nt* KFZTECH filter housing, *Vergaser* filter bowl; **Filtergestaltung** *f* ELEKTRONIK filter shaping; **Filtergewebe** *nt* CHEMTECH filter cloth; **Filtergrenzfrequenz** *f* ELEKTRONIK filter cut-off frequency; **Filtergruppe** *f* ELEKTRONIK bank of filters; **Filterhalter** *m* LABOR filter support; **Filterhalterung** *f* FERNSEH filter holder; **Filterhaus** *nt* KERNTECH filter house; **Filterhilfe** *f* CHEMTECH filter aid; **Filterhilfsmittel** *nt* CHEMTECH filter aid; **Filterkammer** *f* WASSERVERSORG filter gallery; **Filterkartusche** *f* CHEMTECH filter cartridge; **Filterkerze** *f* KERNTECH filtering candle, MECHAN filter cartridge; **Filterkies** *m* CHEMTECH, KERNTECH, WASSERVERSORG filter gravel; **Filterkohle** *f* KOHLEN filtering charcoal; **Filterkondensator** *m* ELEKTROTECH filter capacitor; **Filterkuchen** *m* KOHLEN, PAPIER filter cake; **Filtermanschette** *f* LABOR filter funnel; **Filtermasse** *f* CHEMTECH filter pulp, filter stuff; **Filtermembrane** *f* LABOR filter membrane

Filtern *nt* CHEMIE, CHEMTECH, COMP & DV, TELEKOM filtering; **~ mit fester Verstärkung** *nt* ELEKTRONIK fixed-gain filtering

filtern *vt* CHEMTECH *Gasfeststoff*, COMP & DV, ELEKTRO-

NIK, FOTO filter

Filter: **Filternullpunkt** *m* ELEKTRONIK filter zero; **Filternutsche nach Büchner** *f* LABOR *Filtrieren* Büchner funnel; **Filterordnung** *f* ELEKTRONIK filter order; **Filterpapier** *nt* LABOR filter paper; **Filterpaßbereich** *m* ELEKTRONIK filter pass band; **Filterpatrone** *f* KFZTECH filter cartridge, MASCHINEN cartridge filter; **Filterphasenverhalten** *nt* ELEKTRONIK filter phase response; **Filterplattenhahn** *m* FERTIG *Kunststoffinstallationen* filter plate valve; **Filterpol** *m* ELEKTRONIK filter pole; **Filterpresse** *f* ABFALL, CHEMTECH filter press, KER & GLAS clay press, filter press, KOHLEN, LABOR, LEBENSMITTEL, PAPIER filter press; **Filterpressenstoff** *m* CHEMTECH filter-press cloth; **Filterpumpe** *f* KFZTECH, LABOR filter pump; **Filterquarz** *m* ELEKTRONIK filter crystal; **Filterrahmen** *m* CHEMTECH filter frame; **Filterreihe** *f* ELEKTRONIK filter bank; **Filterrest** *m* ANSTRICH residue; **Filterrückstand** *m* CHEMTECH filter cake; **Filtersatz** *m* FOTO filter set; **Filterschicht** *f* CHEMTECH filter bed, filtering layer, WASSERVERSORG filter bed; **Filtersieb** *nt* KUNSTSTOFF filter screen; **Filterstoff** *m* KER & GLAS, WASSERVERSORG filter cloth; **Filtersynthese** *f* ELEKTRONIK filter synthesis; **Filtertrennschärfe** *f* ELEKTRONIK filter discrimination; **Filtertrichter** *m* CHEMTECH filtering cone, LABOR filter funnel; **Filtertrog** *m* KOHLEN filter feed trough; **Filtertrommel** *f* CHEMTECH filter drum; **Filtertuch** *nt* TEXTIL bolting fabric, WASSERVERSORG filter cloth

Filterung *f* ELEKTRONIK, TELEKOM filtering; **~ auf der negativen Zuleitung** *f* RADIO negative lead filtering; **~ gegen elektromagnetische Beeinflussung** *f* *(EMI-Filterung)* ELEKTRONIK electromagnetic-interference filtering

Filter: **Filterverdickungsmittel** *nt* KOHLEN filter thickener; **Filterverhalten** *nt* ELEKTRONIK filter response; **Filterverschmutzung** *f* HEIZ & KÄLTE filter fouling; **Filterverstärker** *m* ELEKTRONIK filter amplifier

Filtrat *nt* CHEMTECH, KOHLEN filtrate

Filtration *f* ABFALL, ERDÖL, PAPIER filtration; **Filtrationsanlage** *f* KOHLEN filtration plant; **Filtrationsprüfer** *m* PAPIER filtration tester; **Filtrationsverhältnis** *nt* ANSTRICH strain rate

Filtrierapparat *m* CHEMTECH filter

Filtrierbarkeit *f* KOHLEN filterability

filtrieren *vt* CHEMTECH filter

Filtrierkolben *m* LABOR filtration flask

Filtriermasse *f* PAPIER filter mass

Filtrierpapier *nt* CHEMTECH filter paper

Filtriersieb *nt* CHEMTECH filtering screen

Filtrierstativ *nt* LABOR funnel stand

Filtriertuch *nt* CHEMTECH filter cloth

Filtrierung *f* ABFALL, ERDÖL filtration

Filz *m* DRUCK blanket, FERTIG, PAPIER, TEXTIL felt; **Filzdichtung** *f* MASCHINEN felt packing; **Filzfilter** *nt* MASCHINEN felt filter; **Filzkonditionierer** *m* PAPIER felt conditioner; **Filzleitwalze** *f* PAPIER felt-carrying roll; **Filzmarke** *f* PAPIER felt mark; **Filzpolierer** *m* KER & GLAS felt polisher; **Filzreinigungsvorrichtung** *f* PAPIER felt whipper; **Filzscheibe** *f* MASCHINEN felt washer; **Filzseite** *f* DRUCK felt side; **Filzspannvorrichtung** *f* PAPIER felt stretcher; **Filztrockner** *m* PAPIER felt dryer

finanziell: **~er Gewinn eines Raumfluges** *m* RAUMFAHRT payoff

FINGAL-Verfahren *nt* KERNTECH FINGAL process

Fingerhut *m* KER & GLAS thimble

Fingerhutrohr *nt* KERNTECH thimble

Fingerling *m* WASSERTRANS pintle

Fingerschutz *m* SICHERHEIT finger stall

Finish-Presse *f* TEXTIL press finishing machine

finit: **~es Element** *nt* MASCHINEN finite element

Finite-Elemente-Methode *f* *(FEM)* MASCHINEN finite elements method *(FEM)*

Finne *f* FERTIG, MASCHINEN pane, peen

Finsternisdauer *f* RAUMFAHRT eclipse period

FIR *abbr* *(begrenztes Ansprechen auf einen Impuls)* ELEKTRONIK FIR *(finite impulse response)*

FIR-Filter *nt* ELEKTRONIK finite impulse response filter, TELEKOM FIR filter

Firmenkapazität *f* KERNTECH firm capacity

Firmenname *m* PATENT trade name

Firmware *f* COMP & DV firmware

Firnis *m* FERTIG boiled oil, MECHAN lacquer

First[1] *m* BAU *Dach* ridge

First[2] **mit ~ versehen** *vt* BAU ridge

First: **Firstabdeckung** *f* BAU ridge capping; **Firstbalken** *m* BAU ridge beam; **Firstbrett** *nt* BAU ridge piece; **Firstlinie** *f* BAU ridge line; **Firstpfosten** *m* BAU crown post, *Dachstuhl* king post; **Firststein** *m* BAU crown tile, ridge tile; **Firststück** *nt* BAU ridge piece; **Firstziegel** *m* BAU crest tile, head, ridge tile, KER & GLAS ridge tile

FIR-System *nt* ELEKTRONIK finite impulse response

Fisch *m* WASSERTRANS fish; **Fischauge** *nt* KUNSTSTOFF fish eye; **Fischaugenobjektiv** *nt* FOTO fish-eye lens; **Fischerboot** *nt* WASSERTRANS fishing boat, fishing smack

Fischerei *f* WASSERTRANS fishery; **Fischereifahrzeug** *nt* WASSERTRANS fishing boat, fishing vessel; **Fischereiflotte** *f* WASSERTRANS fishing fleet; **Fischereihafen** *m* WASSERTRANS fishing port; **Fischereirechte** *nt pl* WASSERTRANS fishing rights; **Fischereischutzboot** *nt* WASSERTRANS fishery protection vessel

Fisch: **Fischernetz** *nt* WASSERTRANS fishing net; **Fischfanggebiet** *nt* WASSERTRANS fishery; **Fischgerinne** *nt* NICHTFOSS ENERG fish pass; **Fischgraben** *m* NICHTFOSS ENERG fish pass; **Fischgrätenantenne** *f* RADIO fishbone antenna; **Fischgrätenbildung** *f* FERNSEH herringboning; **Fischgrätenmuster** *nt* BAU *Parkettbodenbelag* herringbone pattern; **Fischgrätenstoff** *m* TEXTIL herringbone; **Fischgrätenverkrümmung** *f* KER & GLAS herringbone distortion; **Fischgrätkühlrippen** *f pl* KERNTECH herringbone fins; **Fischgrund** *m* WASSERTRANS fishing ground; **Fischleim** *m* DRUCK fish glue, LEBENSMITTEL isinglass; **Fischplanke** *f* WASSERTRANS *Schiffbau* king plank; **Fischschwanzbohrer** *m* ERDÖL *Bohrtechnik* fishtail bit; **Fischschwanzbohrmeißel** *m* ERDÖL fishtail bit; **Fischzucht** *f* LEBENSMITTEL fish breeding

Fisetin *nt* CHEMIE fisetin

Fissium *nt* KERNTECH fissium

Fitting *nt* MASCHINEN fitting, screwed fitting

Fix *m* WASSERTRANS *Navigation* fix

fix: **~er Kohlenstoff** *m* CHEMIE fixed carbon

Fixationspunkt *m* ERGON point of fixation

Fixationsreflex *m* ERGON fixation reflex

Fixfocus-Kamera *f* FOTO fixed-focus camera

Fixfocus-Objektiv *nt* FOTO fixed-focus lens

Fixierbolzen *m* MASCHINEN locating stud

Fixieren *nt* FOTO fixing, TEXTIL boarding

Fixierfaden *m* FOTO fixing thread

Fixiermittel *nt* FOTO fixing agent, TEXTIL fastener

Fixierschraube *f* MASCHINEN locating screw

Fixierstift *m* MASCHINEN alignment pin, locating pin

fixiert: ~es Walzenwehr *nt* NICHTFOSS ENERG fixed roller sluice gate

Fixierung *f* KONSTZEICH fixing, TEXTIL curing

Fixpunkt *m* MECHAN benchmark; Fixpunkte *m pl* THERMOD *Temperaturskale* fixed reference points

Fizeau: ~sche Ringe *m pl* PHYS Fizeau fringes

Fjord *m* WASSERTRANS fjord

FKO *abbr (Fließkommaoperation)* COMP & DV FLOP *(floating-point operation)*

FKP *abbr (Fließkommaprozessor)* COMP & DV FPP *(floating-point processor)*

Flach- *pref* ELEKTRONIK, RADIO, TELEKOM flat

flach[1] *adj* BAU level, KER & GLAS, KOHLEN, WASSERTRANS *Wasser* shallow; ~ geneigt *adj* BAU low-gradient

flach:[2] ~er Auswerferstift *m* MASCHINEN flat ejector pin; ~e Beleuchtung *f* FOTO flat lighting; ~er Bildschirm *m* COMP & DV flat screen, ELEKTRONIK flat panel display, TELEKOM flat screen; ~er Bipolartransistor *m* ELEKTRONIK planar bipolar transistor; ~es Gehäuse *nt* ELEKTRONIK flatpack; ~e integrierte Schaltung *f* ELEKTRONIK planar integrated circuit; ~e Kante *f* KER & GLAS flat edge; ~e Kante und Schräge *f* KER & GLAS flat edge and bevel; ~e Kehre *f* LUFTTRANS flat turn; ~e Kümpelvertiefung *f* KERNTECH *Brennstoffpellets* dishing shallow depression; ~e Kurve *f* GEOM flat curve; ~es Optikwerkzeug *nt* KER & GLAS flat optical tool; ~er Plattenkollektor *m* NICHTFOSS ENERG flat plate collector; ~e ringförmige Kammer *f* KERNTECH pancake-shaped annular chamber; ~er Schlauchbeutel *m* VERPACK lay flat film bag; ~er Sinkflug *m* LUFTTRANS shallow descent; ~er Stab *m* METALL flat bar; ~er Treibriemen *m* MASCHINEN flat transmission belt; ~es Überlaufwehr *nt* HYDRAUL flat-crested weir; ~e Wiedergabe *f* AUFNAHME, ELEKTRONIK flat response

Flach-: Flachantenne *f* TELEKOM flat antenna; Flachbandfilter *nt* ELEKTRONIK flat band-pass filter; Flachbandkabel *nt* RADIO flat line; Flachbatterie *f* TELEKOM flat battery; Flachbauelement *nt (SMD)* ELEKTRIZ surface mounting device *(SMD)*; Flachbettdruck *m* DRUCK flat-bed printing; Flachbettgerät *nt* COMP & DV flat bed; Flachbettplotter *m* COMP & DV flat bed plotter; Flachbett-Scanner *m* COMP & DV flat bed scanner; Flachbildschirm *m* COMP & DV flat screen, ELEKTRONIK flat panel display, FERNSEH flat screen; Flachboden *m* BAU flat top; Flachbodenätzgrübchen *nt* METALL flat-bottomed etch pit

flachbödig *adj* WASSERTRANS *Schiff* flat-bottomed

Flach-: Flachbogen *m* BAU flat arch, scheme arch, segmental arch; Flachbohrer *m* MASCHINEN flat drill; Flachdach *nt* BAU decking; Flachdeck *nt* WASSERTRANS flat top; Flachdichtung *f* FERTIG *Kunststoffinstallationen* flat gasket, KERNTECH flat gasket, flat-packing gasket, KFZTECH gasket, MASCHINEN flat packing, gasket, WASSERTRANS gasket; Flachdraht *m* ELEKTROTECH flat wire; Flachdruck *m* DRUCK flat printing, planography

Fläche *f* ANSTRICH area, GEOM area, face, surface, MATH *unter einer Kurve,* PAPIER, PHYS area; ~ eines Kreises *f* GEOM area of a circle; ~ zweiter Ordnung *f* GEOM quadric surface

Flach-: Flacheisen *nt* MASCHINEN flat bar

Flächen[1] *nt* FERTIG slabbing

Flächen:[2] ~ bearbeiten *vi* FERTIG slab; ~ fräsen *vi* FERTIG face

Fläche: Flächenabtaster *m* GERÄT area scanner; Flä-

chenbearbeitung *f* KER & GLAS surface working; Flächenberechnung *f* FERTIG mensuration; Flächendeckung *f* TELEKOM coverage; Flächendiode *f* ELEKTRONIK junction diode; Flächendruckkraft *f* EISENBAHN surface pressure; Flächeneinheit *f* METROL unit of area; Flächenemitter-Lumineszenzdiode *f* TELEKOM surface-emitting light-emitting diode; Flächenfräsen *nt* MASCHINEN surface milling; Flächenfräsmaschine *f* MASCHINEN surface-milling machine; Flächengewicht *nt* PAPIER basis weight, substance; Flächengitter *nt* METALL plane lattice; Flächengründung *f* KOHLEN pad foundation; Flächenheizkörper *m* HEIZ & KÄLTE panel heater, LABOR heating mantle; Flächenheizung *f* HEIZ & KÄLTE radiant panel heating, radiant-heating system; Flächenhelle *f* ELEKTROTECH luminance; Flächenhelligkeit *f* OPTIK brightness; Flächenhelligkeitsmesser *m* GERÄT brightness meter; Flächeninhalt *m* BAU, GEOM area; Flächeninhaltsbestimmung *f* NICHTFOSS ENERG quadrature; Flächenkontaktdiode *f* ELEKTRONIK junction diode; Flächenkrümmung *f* GEOM curvature of surfaces; Flächenladungsdichte *f* ELEKTROTECH surface density; Flächenlast *f* MASCHINEN surface load; Flächenmaße *nt pl* METROL square measures; Flächenmassenmessung *f* GERÄT area mass measurement; Flächennutzungsplan *m* WASSERVERSORG zoning plan; Flächenpressung *f* FERTIG pressure intensity, MASCHINEN surface pressure; Flächenprofil *nt* MASCHINEN surface profile; Flächenregel *f* LUFTTRANS area rule; Flächenschleifmaschine *f* FERTIG surface-grinding machine; Flächenschwerpunkt *m* PHYS centroid; Flächenträgheitsmoment *nt* MASCHINEN geometrical moment of inertia; Flächentransistor *m* ELEKTRONIK junction transistor; Flächenverlust *m* KER & GLAS loss of sheet; Flächenversetzung *f* KERNTECH face gap; Flächenwiderstand *m* ELEKTROTECH sheet resistance

Flach-: Flachfacette *f* KER & GLAS flat facet; Flachfeile *f* MASCHINEN flat file; Flachformzylinderpresse *f* DRUCK flat-bed cylinder press; Flachführung *f* FERTIG square guide

flachgängig *adj* FERTIG *Gewinde* square

Flach-: Flachgehäuse *nt* ELEKTRONIK flatpack

flachgehend: ~es Schiff *nt* WASSERTRANS shallow-draught vessel

Flach-: Flachgewinde *nt* MASCHINEN flat thread, square thread; Flachgewindemeißel *m* FERTIG square thread tool; Flachgewölbe *nt* KER & GLAS jack arch; Flachglas *nt* BAU plate glass, KER & GLAS flat glass; Flachgurt *m* MASCHINEN flat belt; Flachheizkörper *m* HEIZ & KÄLTE flat radiator; Flachinstrument *nt* GERÄT flat-face instrument; Flachkabel *nt* ELEKTRIZ flat cable, ribbon cable, ELEKTROTECH flat cable, TELEKOM ribbon cable; Flachkämmmaschine *f* TEXTIL rectilinear-combing machine; Flachkarton *m* VERPACK flat pack; Flachkeil *m* FERTIG flat key, parallel key, MASCHINEN flat key, key on flat, rectangular key

Flachkopf *m* MASCHINEN pan head; Flachkopfniet *m* MASCHINEN pan head rivet; Flachkopfschraube *f* MASCHINEN pan head screw

flachliegend: ~e Hülsen *f pl* VERPACK lay flat tubing

Flach-: Flachlitzenseil *nt* FERTIG flattened strand rope; Flachmaterial *nt* KER & GLAS, MASCHINEN flats; Flachmeißel *m* FERTIG square-nosed tool, MASCHINEN flat chisel; Flachpackung *f* VERPACK flat pack; Flachpalette *f* VERPACK flat pallet; **Flachprofilgerät** *nt* GERÄT flat edgewise pattern instrument; **Flachrelais** *nt* ELEKTRO-TECH flat relay; **Flachriemen** *m* MASCHINEN flat belt; **Flachriementrieb** *m* MASCHINEN flat-belt drive; **Flachringdynamo** *m* ELEKTRIZ flat ring dynamo; **Flachrücken** *m* DRUCK flat back

Flachrundkopf *m* FERTIG truss head, MASCHINEN mushroom head; **Flachrundkopfniet** *m* BAU cup head rivet; **Flachrundkopfschraube** *f* MASCHINEN mushroom-head bolt

Flach-: **Flachrundschraube** *f* MASCHINEN saucer head screw; **Flachsauger** *m* PAPIER flat box; **Flachschieber** *m* HYDRAUL plain slide valve, MASCHINEN flat slide valve; **Flachschiene** *f* EISENBAHN strap rail; **Flachschleifen** *nt* MASCHINEN surface grinding; **Flachschleifmaschine** *f* KER & GLAS flat-grinding machine, MASCHINEN surface grinder, surface-grinding machine; **Flachseil** *nt* MASCHINEN flat rope; **Flachsenken** *nt* MASCHINEN end facing, spot facing; **Flachspan** *m* FERTIG flake; **Flachspitzenimpuls** *m* FERNSEH tach pulse; **Flachspritzen** *nt* FERTIG *Plaste* quenching

flachspritzen *vt* FERTIG *Plaste* quench

Flach-: **Flachspule** *f* ELEKTRIZ loop coil, pancake coil, ELEKTROTECH pancake coil; **Flachspulinstrument** *nt* GERÄT flat-coil instrument; **Flachstahl** *m* METALL flat bar, flats; **Flachstampfer** *m* FERTIG *Formen* flat rammer; **Flachstößel** *m* FERTIG *Getriebelehre* flat follower; **Flachstrickerei** *f* TEXTIL flat knitting; **Flachstrickmaschine** *f* TEXTIL flat-knitting machine; **Flachstromvergaser** *m* KFZTECH horizontal carburetor (AmE), horizontal carburettor (BrE), *veraltetes Prinzip* sidedraft carburetor (AmE), sidedraft carburettor (BrE); **Flachtrudeln** *nt* LUFTTRANS flat spin; **Flachwagen** *m* EISENBAHN, KFZTECH flat wagon

flachwalzen *vt* FERTIG slab

Flach-: **Flachwasser** *nt* WASSERTRANS shallows; **Flachwicklung** *f* ELEKTRIZ disc winding (BrE), disk winding (AmE); **Flachzange** *f* FERTIG flat-nosed pliers; **Flachziegel** *m* BAU plain tile, KER & GLAS flat tile

Flackerfrequenz *f* FERNSEH flicker frequency

Flackern *nt* COMP & DV, FERNSEH flicker, TELEKOM flickering

flackern *vi* ELEKTRONIK flicker, FERTIG flare

Flagge[1] *f* WASSERTRANS colors (AmE), colours (BrE), flag

Flagge:[2] **eine ~ führen** *vi* WASSERTRANS fly a flag; **eine ~ hissen** *vi* WASSERTRANS fly a flag, hoist the colours (BrE), hoist the colors (AmE); **die ~ streichen** *vi* WASSERTRANS strike colors (AmE), strike colours (BrE)

Flagge: **Flaggenkasten** *m* WASSERTRANS flag locker, signal locker; **Flaggenknopf** *m* WASSERTRANS truck; **Flaggenmast** *m* WASSERTRANS signal mast; **Flaggensignal** *nt* WASSERTRANS *Kommunikation* flag signal; **Flaggenspind** *m* WASSERTRANS flag locker, signal locker; **Flaggenstock** *m* WASSERTRANS flagstaff; **Flaggenzeichen** *nt* WASSERTRANS *Kommunikation* flag signal; **Flagge-Q** *f* WASSERTRANS Q flag

Flaggleine *f* LUFTTRANS halyard

Flaggschiff *nt* WASSERTRANS *Marine* flagship

Flamm- *pref* TEXTIL blazing

flammbar *adj* THERMOD flammable

Flammbarkeit *f* THERMOD flammability, VERPACK combustibility, flammability

flammbeständig *adj* SICHERHEIT flame-resistant

Flamme *f* SICHERHEIT, THERMOD fire, flame

Flämmen *nt* FERTIG scarfing

flämmen *vt* FERTIG scarf

Flamme: **Flammenabsorptionsfotometrie** *f* GERÄT absorption flame photometry; **Flammenausbreitungsgeschwindigkeit** *f* THERMOD rate of spread of flame; **Flammenaussetzer** *m* THERMOD flame failure

flammenbeständig[1] *adj* ELEKTRIZ flameproof

flammenbeständig:[2] **~e Beleuchtungseinrichtung** *f* ELEKTRIZ flameproof lighting installation; **~er Schalter** *m* ELEKTRIZ flameproof switch

flammend *adj* TEXTIL blazing, THERMOD blazing, flaming

Flamme: **Flammendämpfung** *f* KER & GLAS flame attenuation; **Flammenemissionsspektroskopie** *f* PHYS flame emission spectroscopy

flammenfest *adj* VERPACK flameproof

Flamme: **Flammenfotometer** *nt* LABOR flame photometer

flammenfotometrisch: **~er Detektor** *m* UMWELT-SCHMUTZ flame photometric detector

flammengehärtet *adj* FERTIG flame-hardened

Flamme: **Flammenhärtemaschine** *f* FERTIG flame-hardening machine; **Flammenhärtung** *f* FERTIG flame hardening; **Flammenhemmstoff** *m* LUFTTRANS flame retardant; **Flammenhemmung** *f* WERKPRÜF *Kunststoffe* flame retardancy; **Flammenhydrolyse** *f* OPTIK flame hydrolysis; **Flammenlöscher** *m* RAUMFAHRT flame arrester; **Flammenlötung** *f* FERTIG torch brazing; **Flammenmelder** *m* HEIZ & KÄLTE flame detector; **Flammenplatieren** *nt* FERTIG flame plating; **Flammenrückschlag** *m* BAU flashback, *Schweißen* backfire, KFZTECH backfire, THERMOD flashback; **Flammenrückschlagsicherung** *f* KFZTECH *Motor* flame trap

flammensicher[1] *adj* FERTIG, LUFTTRANS, VERPACK flameproof

flammensicher:[2] **~es Gehäuse für elektrische Einrichtungen** *nt* SICHERHEIT flameproof enclosure of electrical apparatus; **~er Schalter** *m* ELEKTRIZ flameproof switch

Flamme: **Flammenspektroskopie** *f* THERMOD flame spectroscopy; **Flammenspektrum** *nt* PHYS, THERMOD flame spectrum; **Flammensperre** *f* ERDÖL *Sicherheitstechnik* flame arrester, LUFTTRANS, THERMOD flame trap; **Flammenstabilisator** *m* LUFTTRANS flame holder; **Flammenstrahlbohren** *nt* KOHLEN jet drilling; **Flammenwächter** *m* HEIZ & KÄLTE flame detector; **Flammenwerfer** *m* THERMOD flame thrower

flammfest *adj* WERKPRÜF nonflammable

Flamm-: **Flammfugenhobeln** *nt* BAU flame gouging; **Flammhärten** *nt* METALL flame hardening

flammhemmend[1] *adj* KUNSTSTOFF flame-retardant; **~ eingestellt** *adj* KUNSTSTOFF fire-retardant

flammhemmend:[2] **~es Zusatzmittel** *nt* KUNSTSTOFF flame-retardant

Flamm-: **Flammkohle** *f* KOHLEN flaming coal; **Flammofen** *m* FERTIG air furnace, reverberatory furnace, HEIZ & KÄLTE air furnace, METALL reverberatory furnace; **Flammofenfrischen** *nt* FERTIG puddling

flammofenfrischen *vt* FERTIG puddle

Flamm-: **Flammpunkt** *m* ERDÖL *Destillation*, HEIZ & KÄLTE, KFZTECH, KUNSTSTOFF, LEBENSMITTEL, MASCHINEN, THERMOD, WASSERTRANS *Material* flash point; **Flammpunktprüfer** *m* MASCHINEN flash tester; **Flammpunktprüfgerät** *nt* LABOR flash point apparatus

Flammrohr *nt* FERTIG, HEIZ & KÄLTE flue, KERNTECH *Gasturbine* flame tube; **Flammrohrkessel** *m* HEIZ &

KÄLTE flue boiler

Flamm-: **Flammrückschlagsicherung** *f* LUFTTRANS flame trap; **Flammschutz** *m* SICHERHEIT flame protection; **Flammschutzmittel** *nt* KUNSTSTOFF flame-retardant; **Flammschweißen** *nt* KUNSTSTOFF flame welding

flammsicher[1] *adj* SICHERHEIT flameproof

flammsicher:[2] **~er Rührer** *m* LABOR flameproof stirrer

Flamm-: **Flammsperre** *f* BAU flame arrester; **Flammspritzen** *nt* FERTIG, KERNTECH flame spraying; **Flammstrahlen** *nt* FERTIG flame blasting, KER & GLAS scarfing; **Flammstrahlen zum Entzundern** *nt* FERTIG flame cleaning; **Flammstrahlreinigen** *nt* BAU flame cleaning

flammwidrig *adj* HEIZ & KÄLTE flame-retardant, KUNSTSTOFF fire-retardant

Flanke *f* BAU flank, FERTIG *Getriebelehre* side, *Gewinde* flank, MASCHINEN flank, side, MECHAN flank; **Flankendurchmesser** *m* MASCHINEN effective diameter, minor diameter, pitch diameter; **Flankenformfehler** *m* MASCHINEN flank form error

flankengesteuert: **~er Multivibrator** *m* ELEKTRONIK edge-triggered flip-flop

Flanke: **Flankenkorrektur** *f* FERNSEH edge correction; **Flankenlinie** *f* MASCHINEN flank line; **Flankenrate** *f* ELEKTRONIK edge rate; **Flankenspiel** *nt* FERTIG *Getriebelehre* backlash, MASCHINEN flank clearance, MECHAN backlash; **Flankensteilheit** *f* ELEKTRONIK edge steepness; **Flankenverriegelung** *f* ELEKTRONIK edge latching; **Flankenverstärkung** *f* FERNSEH edge enhancement; **Flankenwinkel** *m* FERTIG thread angle, *Gewinde* profile angle, MASCHINEN thread angle

Flansch *m* AKUSTIK flange, BAU boom, ELEKTRIZ flange, ELEKTROTECH coupling, flange, ERDÖL *Rohrleitungen*, FERTIG flange, KFZTECH flange, *Kurbelwelle* web, LABOR, MASCHINEN, MECHAN, MEERSCHMUTZ, RAUMFAHRT flange, TELEKOM *Wellenleiter* connector, coupling; **Flanscharmaturen** *f pl* MASCHINEN flanged fittings; **Flanschbefestigung** *f* MASCHINEN, RAUMFAHRT flange mounting

Flanschen *nt* FERTIG, MASCHINEN flanging

flanschen *vt* ERDÖL flange up, MASCHINEN flange

Flansch: **Flanschengußrohr** *nt* BAU flanged cast-iron pipe; **Flanschhälfte** *f* MASCHINEN half-flange; **Flanschkupplung** *f* MASCHINEN flange coupling, half-coupling

flanschlos: **~e Bremssohle** *f* EISENBAHN flangeless brake shoe

Flansch: **Flanschmotor** *m* ELEKTRIZ, MECHAN flange motor; **Flanschpressenbearbeitung** *f* KER & GLAS flange press finish; **Flanschrohr** *nt* BAU flange pipe, MASCHINEN flanged pipe; **Flanschstahl** *m* METALL flange steel; **Flanschverbindung** *f* MASCHINEN flange connection, flange coupling, flange joint, flange union, flanged connection, flanged coupling, flanged joint, flanged union; **Flanschwelle** *f* MASCHINEN flange shaft, flanged shaft

Fläschchen *nt* LABOR phial (BrE), vial (AmE)

Flasche *f* FERTIG, KER & GLAS flask, MASCHINEN pulley; **~ mit formgepreßtem Hals** *f* LABOR bottle with molded neck (AmE), bottle with moulded neck (BrE); **~ ohne Pfand** *f* VERPACK nonreturnable bottle; **~ mit Schraubverschluß** *f* VERPACK screw cap bottle; **~ mit unebenem Boden** *f* KER & GLAS rocker

Flaschen:[1] **in ~ abgefüllt** *adj* LEBENSMITTEL bottled

Flaschen:[2] **auf ~ abfüllen** *vt* LEBENSMITTEL bottle

Flasche: **Flaschenabfüllmaschine** *f* LEBENSMITTEL bottling machine; **Flaschenabpackungsanlage** *f* VERPACK bottle-packing machine; **Flaschenausrichter** *m* VERPACK bottle unscrambler; **Flaschenbrennofen** *m* KER & GLAS *Keramik* bottle kiln; **Flaschenetikettaufdruck** *m* VERPACK graphics coordinated with bottle labels; **Flaschenfüllapparat** *m* LEBENSMITTEL bottle filler; **Flaschengas** *nt* THERMOD bottled gas; **Flaschenglas** *nt* KER & GLAS bottle glass; **Flaschenhals** *m* KER & GLAS neck of a bottle, LEBENSMITTEL, MECHAN bottleneck; **Flaschenhülle** *f* VERPACK bottle jacket; **Flaschenhülse** *f* VERPACK bottle sleeve; **Flaschenindustrie** *f* KER & GLAS bottle industry; **Flaschenkappenaufsetzer** *m* VERPACK bottle-capping machine; **Flaschenkapsel** *f* VERPACK bottle capsule; **Flaschenkasten** *m* VERPACK bottle crate, crate; **Flaschenkorkmaschine** *f* VERPACK bottle-corking machine; **Flaschenlecksensor** *m* VERPACK bottle leak detector; **Flaschenpfand** *nt* VERPACK bottle deposit, deposit; **Flaschenspülmaschine** *f* LEBENSMITTEL bottle washer; **Flaschenstopfen** *m* VERPACK bottle stopper; **Flaschenträger** *m* VERPACK bottle carrier; **Flaschenummantellungsmaschine** *f* KER & GLAS bottle-casing machine; **Flaschenverschließmaschine** *f* VERPACK bottle-closing machine, bottle-sealing machine; **Flaschenverschluß** *m* KER & GLAS closure for bottles, VERPACK bottle closure; **Flaschenverschlußkappe** *f* VERPACK bottle cap; **Flaschenwagen** *m* FERTIG *Schweißen* trolley; **Flaschenwaschmaschine** *f* VERPACK bottle-rinsing machine, bottle-washing machine; **Flaschenwinde** *f* MASCHINEN bottle jack; **Flaschenzähler** *m* GERÄT bottle counter; **Flaschenzählgerät** *nt* GERÄT bottle counter; **Flaschenzug** *m* BAU tackle, FERTIG block and tackle, pulley, tackle, MASCHINEN block and pulley, block and tackle, lifting block, lifting tackle, pulley block, MECHAN chain block, tackle, PHYS pulley, SICHERHEIT hoist, WASSERTRANS *Deckausrüstung* pulley block; **Flaschenzuggehäuse** *nt* MASCHINEN pulley shell; **Flaschenzughaken** *m* MASCHINEN pulley block hook

Flashdestillation *f* THERMOD flash distillation

Flatter- *pref* LUFTTRANS flutter; **Flatterdämpfer** *m* LUFTTRANS *Luftfahrzeug* shimmy damper; **Flatterecho** *nt* AKUSTIK flutter echo; **Flattereffekt** *m* FERNSEH flutter effect; **Flatterfaktor** *m* AUFNAHME flutter factor

Flattern *nt* AUFNAHME *schnelle Tonhöhenschwankungen* flutter, COMP & DV jitter, FERNSEH flutter, LUFTTRANS buffeting, *Aerodynamik* flutter MASCHINEN knocking, RADIO flutter

flattern *vi* MASCHINEN chatter, knock

Flatter-: **Flattersatz rechts** *m* DRUCK ragged right setting; **Flatterschwingung** *f* LUFTTRANS *Aerodynamik* flutter; **Flattersitz** *m* HYDRAUL fluttering seat

flau: **~e Kühle** *f* WASSERTRANS light airs

Flaute *f* WASSERTRANS *Wind* calm

Flavan *nt* CHEMIE flavan

Flavanon *nt* CHEMIE flavanone

Flavin *nt* CHEMIE flavin

Flavon *nt* CHEMIE flavone, phenylchromone, LEBENSMITTEL *Pflanzenfarbstoff* flavone

Flavonoid *nt* LEBENSMITTEL flavonoid

Flavonol *nt* CHEMIE flavonol

Flavoprotein *nt* LEBENSMITTEL flavoprotein

Flavopurpurin *nt* CHEMIE flavopurpurin

Flechtdraht *m* ELEKTROTECH braided wire

Flechte *f* TEXTIL braid

Flechten *nt* TEXTIL braiding
flechten *vt* BAU *Bewehrungsstahl* bend
***Flechte*: Flechtenrot** *nt* CHEMIE *Farbstoff* orcein
Flechttechnik *f* TEXTIL braiding technique
Flechtwerk *nt* BAU trellis, trellis work
Fleck *m* DRUCK speckle, KER & GLAS freak, TEXTIL blotch, speckle; **~ unter Oberfläche** *m* KER & GLAS pip under finish; **Fleckempfindlichkeitsklasse** *f* KER & GLAS *zur Charakterisierung von optischem Glas* staining class; **Fleckenbildung** *f* KER & GLAS specking, *atmosphärischer Angriff* staining
fleckenfrei *adj* PAPIER stainless
Fleisch *nt* DRUCK beard, LEBENSMITTEL meat; **Fleischbeschaugesetz** *nt* ABFALL Meat Inspection Act; **Fleischmilch** *f* CHEMIE *Säure* sarcolactic; **Fleischseite** *f* FERTIG *Riemen* flesh side; **Fleischwolf** *m* LEBENSMITTEL meat grinder, mincer, mincing machine
Fleißspannung *f* PHYS yield stress
FLEI-Verkehr *m* *(Flugzeug-Eisenbahn-Verkehr)* TRANS rail-air-rail service
Fleming: ~sche Dreifingerregel *f* ELEKTRIZ Fleming's rules; **~sche rechtshändige Dreifingerregel** *f* ELEKTRIZ right-hand rule
flexibel[1] *adj* ELEKTRIZ flexible
flexibel:[2] **flexibler Datenträger** *m* COMP & DV flexible disk; **flexibler Einband** *m* DRUCK soft cover; **flexible Feldgruppe** *f* COMP & DV flexible array; **flexibles Fertigungssystem** *nt* *(FFS)* KÜNSTL INT flexible manufacturing system *(FMS)*; **flexible Flachbaugruppe** *f* ELEKTRONIK flexible printed circuit; **flexible gedruckte Schaltung** *f* ELEKTRONIK flexible printed circuit; **flexibler Hohlleiter** *m* ELEKTROTECH *Weltraumfunk* flexible waveguide; **flexible Isolierplatte** *f* FERTIG blanket insulator; **flexibles Kabel** *nt* ELEKTRIZ flexible cable; **flexible Kupplung** *f* MASCHINEN flexible coupling; **flexibler Leiter** *m* ELEKTRIZ flexible conductor; **flexible Leiterplatte** *f* ELEKTRONIK flexible printed circuit; **flexibles Produktionssteuerungssystem** *nt* KÜNSTL INT flexible manufacturing system; **flexibler Reflektor** *m* RAUMFAHRT *Raumschiff* flexible reflector; **flexibler Schlauch** *m* MEERSCHMUTZ flexible hose; **flexibler Schwimmtank** *m* MEERSCHMUTZ *zur Aufnahme von Öl* floating flexible tank; **flexible Stahlschlauchleitung** *f* MASCHINEN flexible steel piping; **flexibler Umschlag** *m* DRUCK limp binding; **flexible Verbindung** *f* EISENBAHN flexible connection; **flexibler Widerstand** *m* ELEKTROTECH flexible resistor
Flexibilität *f* KUNSTSTOFF flexibility
Flexion *f* ERGON flexion
Flexodruck *m* DRUCK aniline print, flexographic printing, flexography, KUNSTSTOFF flexographic printing
Flexofaltschachtel-Klebmaschine *f* VERPACK flexo-folder gluer
Flicken *nt* TEXTIL mending; **~ des Ofenfutters** *nt* KER & GLAS patching
flicken *vti* TEXTIL mend
Flickstein *m* KER & GLAS patch block
fliegen *vt* LUFTTRANS pilot
fliegend: ~er Akzent *m* DRUCK floating accent, piece accent; **~ aufgespannter Dorn** *m* FERTIG stub arbor (AmE), stub arbour (BrE); **~e Brücke** *f* BAU, WASSERTRANS flying bridge; **~e Fertigungsprüfung** *f* QUAL patrol inspection; **~e Lagerung** *f* FERTIG *Walze* cantilever support; **~e Verbindung** *f* TELEKOM jumper
Fliehgewicht *nt* MASCHINEN centrifugal weight, flyweight

Fliehkraft *f* CHEMTECH, MASCHINEN, PHYS, RAUMFAHRT, STRÖMPHYS, UMWELTSCHMUTZ centrifugal force; **Fliehkraft- und Vakuumregler** *m* LUFTTRANS centrifugal and vacuum governor; **Fliehkraftabsauggebläse** *nt* KERNTECH centrifugal extractor; **Fliehkraftabscheider** *m* CHEMTECH centrifugal separator, UMWELTSCHMUTZ cyclone-recovery skimmer; **Fliehkraftabschneider** *m* ERDÖL cyclone; **Fliehkraftbeschleunigung** *f* LUFTTRANS centrifugal acceleration; **Fliehkraftgebläse** *nt* KFZTECH centrifugal supercharger; **Fliehkraftkupplung** *f* KFZTECH, MASCHINEN centrifugal clutch; **Fliehkraftlüfter** *m* HEIZ & KÄLTE centrifugal fan; **Fliehkraftregelung** *f* LUFTTRANS governor control link; **Fliehkraftregler** *m* KFZTECH *Motordrehzahlbegrenzer*, NICHTFOSS ENERG governor; **Fliehkraftreiniger** *m* CHEMTECH centrifugal cleaner; **Fliehkraftschalter** *m* GERÄT tachometric relay, MASCHINEN centrifugal switch; **Fliehkraftschmierung** *f* MASCHINEN centrifugal lubrication; **Fliehkraftversteller** *m* KFZTECH *Zündung* centrifugal advance mechanism; **Fliehkraftzündversteller** *m* KFZTECH centrifugal advance mechanism
Fliehpendeltachometer *nt* GERÄT flyweight tachometer
Fliese *f* BAU slab, tile
fliesen *vt* BAU tile
***Fliese*: Fliesenboden** *m* KER & GLAS tiling; **Fliesenfußboden** *m* BAU tile floor, tile flooring
Fließ- *pref* COMP & DV, ELEKTROTECH, ERDÖL flow
Fließband *nt* KONTROLL line, MASCHINEN conveyor line, MECHAN assembly line; **Fließbandarchitektur** *f* KONTROLL pipelined architecture; **Fließbandstraße** *f* MASCHINEN assembly line
Fließbett *nt* CHEMTECH, UMWELTSCHMUTZ fluidized bed; **Fließbetttrockner** *nt* CHEMTECH fluidized-bed dryer; **Fließbettverfahren** *nt* CHEMTECH fluid-catalyst process
Fließ-: Fließbild *nt* COMP & DV flowchart; **Fließdiagramm** *nt* ERDÖL flow sheet
Fließdruck: allgemeiner ~ *m* METALL general yield load
Fließen *nt* BAU creep, ELEKTROTECH, KUNSTSTOFF, MASCHINEN, TEXTIL flow
fließen *vi* COMP & DV, PHYS, STRÖMPHYS, TEXTIL, WASSERTRANS *Fluß*, *Gezeiten* flow
fließend[1] *adj* PHYS floating
fließend:[2] **~er Erdstoff** *m* KOHLEN running soil; **~es Gewässer** *nt* WASSERVERSORG running water; **~er Verkehr** *m* BAU, TRANS moving traffic; **~es Wasser** *nt* WASSERVERSORG running water
fließfähig: ~es Produkt *nt* VERPACK free-flow product
Fließ-: Fließfertigung *f* VERPACK continuous production line; **Fließfigur** *f* FERTIG worm
fließgepreßt *adj* MASCHINEN extruded
Fließ-: Fließgeschwindigkeit *f* HEIZ & KÄLTE flow velocity, KUNSTSTOFF flow rate; **Fließgrenze** *f* ANSTRICH yield strength, BAU liquid limit, KERNTECH yield point, KOHLEN liquid limit, MECHAN yield point, PHYS yield point, WERKPRÜF yield strength; **Fließgrenzgerät** *nt* KOHLEN liquid limit device; **Fließkommamodus** *m* COMP & DV noisy mode; **Fließkommaoperation** *f* *(FKO)* COMP & DV floating-point operation *(FLOP)*; **Fließkommaprozessor** *m* *(FKP)* COMP & DV floating-point processor *(FPP)*; **Fließlehre** *f* KOHLEN rheology; **Fließlinien-Schrumpfverpackungen** *f pl* VERPACK shrink flow line wrappers; **Fließlöten** *nt* ELEKTROTECH reflow soldering; **Fließpresse** *f* MASCHINEN extruder, METALL

extrusion press; **Fließpressen** *nt* MASCHINEN, METALL extrusion

fließpressen *vt* MASCHINEN, METALL extrude

Fließ-: Fließpreßteil *nt* MASCHINEN extruded part; **Fließpunkt** *m* ERDÖL flow point, HEIZ & KÄLTE pour point, KER & GLAS flow point, KFZTECH *Öl* pour point, STRÖMPHYS flow point; **Fließsand** *m* KOHLEN quicksand; **Fließsatz** *m* DRUCK body matter, solid matter; **Fließschaumverpackung** *f* VERPACK flow foam wrap; **Fließschema** *nt* ERDÖL, KOHLEN flow sheet; **Fließschweißen** *nt* FERTIG *Plaste* flow welding; **Fließspan** *m* MASCHINEN continuous chip; **Fließton** *m* KOHLEN quick clay; **Fließverhalten** *nt* KUNSTSTOFF flow characteristics; **Fließvermögen** *nt* MASCHINEN, MECHAN fluidity, METALL plasticity, PHYS, STRÖMPHYS fluidity; **Fließvermögen bei Kälte** *nt* MECHAN cold flow; **Fließwasser** *nt* WASSERVERSORG running water; **Fließwiderstand** *m* PHYS flow stress; **Fließzeit** *f* KUNSTSTOFF *Kautschukmischung* scorch time; **Fließzonenbildung** *f* KUNSTSTOFF crazing

Flimmerfotometer *nt* PHYS flicker photometer

flimmerfrei *adj* COMP & DV flicker-free, ELEKTRONIK *Leuchtdioden* jitter-free

Flimmern *nt* COMP & DV flicker, RAUMFAHRT *Weltraumfunk* scintillation, TELEKOM scintillation, *Video* flickering

flimmern *vi* ELEKTRONIK flicker

Flimmerrauschen *nt* RAUMFAHRT *Weltraumfunk* scintillation noise

flink: ~e Sicherung *f* ELEKTROTECH fast-acting fuse

Flip-Chip *m* ELEKTRONIK flip chip

Flip-Flop *m* COMP & DV toggle; **Flip-Flop-Schaltung** *f* COMP & DV, PHYS flip-flop; **Flip-Flop-Vorgang** *m* KERNTECH flop-over process

Floatglas *nt* KER & GLAS float glass

Flocke *f* FERTIG shatter crack, thermal burst, KUNSTSTOFF flock

flockenförmig *adj* CHEMTECH flocculent

flockengefärbt *adj* TEXTIL stock-dyed

Flockenriß *m* FERTIG *Stahl* fish eye

Flockigkeit *f* CHEMTECH flocculence

Flockpunkt *m* CHEMTECH flocculation point

Flockspritzen *nt* VERPACK flock spraying

Flocktest *m* CHEMTECH flocculation test

Flockung *f* ABFALL, CHEMIE, CHEMTECH, ERDÖL *Aufbereitungstechnik*, KOHLEN, KUNSTSTOFF, LEBENSMITTEL flocculation; **Flockungschemikalie** *f* CHEMTECH flocculent; **Flockungseinrichtung** *f* CHEMTECH flocculator; **Flockungshilfsmittel** *nt* KUNSTSTOFF flocculant, flocculating agent; **Flockungsmittel** *nt* ABFALL coagulant, flocculant, CHEMTECH flocculent, KOHLEN flocculant, KUNSTSTOFF flocculant, flocculating agent; **Flockungsreaktor** *m* CHEMTECH flocculator

Floppy *f* COMP & DV FD, floppy disk, DRUCK FD, diskette, floppy disk

Flor *m* TEXTIL pile; **Flordichte** *f* TEXTIL density of pile; **Florgewicht** *nt* TEXTIL pile weight; **Florhöhe** *f* TEXTIL pile height; **Florteiler** *m* TEXTIL tape condenser

Floß *nt* WASSERTRANS raft; **Floßbrücke** *f* WASSERTRANS floating bridge

Flosse *f* WASSERTRANS *Schiffbau* fin; **Flossenkiel** *m* WASSERTRANS *Schiffbau* fin keel

Flotation *f* KOHLEN flotation; **Flotationsanlage** *f* CHEMTECH flotation plant; **Flotationsflüssigkeit** *f* CHEMTECH flotation liquid; **Flotationskammer** *f*

MEERSCHMUTZ *Ölsperre* flotation chamber; **Flotationsschaum** *m* CHEMTECH flotation froth; **Flotationsverfahren** *nt* KOHLEN flotation process; **Flotationszelle mit Lufterührung** *f* KOHLEN pneumatic flotation cell

Flotille *f* WASSERTRANS flotilla

flott *adj* WASSERTRANS *Schiff* afloat

Flotte *f* TEXTIL bath, WASSERTRANS fleet, navy; **Flottenbasis** *f* WASSERTRANS naval base

flottmachen: wieder ~ *vt* WASSERTRANS *Schiff* refloat

Flowmeter *m* WASSERVERSORG flowmeter

Flöz *nt* KOHLEN seam; **Flözarbeit** *f* KOHLEN seam work

Flucht *f* FERTIG alignment; **Fluchten** *nt* FERTIG aligning; MASCHINEN alignment, lining-in

fluchten *vt* BAU align

fluchtend *adj* FERTIG lining-up, MASCHINEN in-line; **nicht ~** *adj* FERTIG misaligned

Fluchtendmachen *nt* MASCHINEN lining-up

Flucht: Fluchtgeschwindigkeitsstartmotor *m* RAUMFAHRT launch escape motor

flüchtig[1] *adj* CHEMIE, COMP & DV volatile, DRUCK fugitive, ELEKTROTECH transient, KUNSTSTOFF volatile, PHYS transient, TEXTIL volatile; **nicht ~** *adj* COMP & DV nonvolatile

flüchtig:[2] **nicht ~e Bestandteile** *m pl* KUNSTSTOFF nonvolatile content; **~e Emissionen** *f pl* UMWELTSCHMUTZ fugitive emissions; **~e Masse** *f* KOHLEN volatile body; **~er Netzvorgang** *m* ELEKTRIZ line transient; **~er Speicher** *m* COMP & DV, ELEKTROTECH volatile memory; **nicht ~er Speicher** *m* COMP & DV, ELEKTROTECH nonvolatile memory

Flüchtigkeit *f* CHEMIE, KUNSTSTOFF, TEXTIL volatility; **~ von Gasen** *f* THERMOD fugacity of gases

Flucht: Fluchtkapsel *f* ERDÖL *Offshore* escape capsule; **Fluchtlinie** *f* MECHAN alignment; **Fluchtmöglichkeit** *f* SICHERHEIT *aus brennenden Gebäuden* means of escape

Fluchtpunkt *m* GEOM, KONSTZEICH vanishing point; **Fluchtpunktperspektive** *f* GEOM true perspective; **Fluchtpunktprojektion** *f* KONSTZEICH vanishing point projection

Flucht: Fluchtstab *m* BAU *Vermessung* range pole, range rod; **Fluchtstange** *f* BAU *Vermessung* rod, target

Fluchtungsfehler *m* FERTIG malalignment, misalignment, MASCHINEN alignment error, misalignment

Fluchtungsfernrohr *nt* FERTIG optical alignment-testing telescope

Flucht: Fluchtweg *m* SICHERHEIT fire rescue path

Fluenz *f* PHYS fluence

Flug *m* LUFTTRANS *mit Reisegeschwindigkeit* flight; **~ mit doppelter Besatzung** *m* LUFTTRANS double-crew operation; **Flugasche** *f* PAPIER, UMWELTSCHMUTZ fly ash

Flugbahn *f* LUFTTRANS flight path, path; **Flugbahnabfangen** *nt* LUFTTRANS flight path levelling; **Flugbahnkurskreisel** *m* LUFTTRANS directional gyro

Flug: Flugbegleitpersonal *nt* LUFTTRANS flight crew; **Flugbenzin** *nt* ERDÖL *Destillationsprodukt* aviation gasoline (AmE), aviation petrol (BrE), LUFTTRANS aviation fuel (BrE); **Flugbereich** *m* LUFTTRANS flight envelope; **Flugbesatzung** *f* LUFTTRANS flight crew; **Flugbetrieb** *m* RAUMFAHRT *Raumschiff* in-flight operation; **Flugbetriebsmeldung** *f* LUFTTRANS dismantling, flight regularity message; **Flugbetriebs-**

plannung *f* LUFTTRANS in-flight operational planning; **Flugbewegung** *f* LUFTTRANS aircraft movement; **Flugbewegungsleitung** *f* LUFTTRANS flight controls; **Flugblatt** *nt* PAPIER fly sheet; **Flugboot** *nt* TRANS flying boat; **Flugcomputer** *m* LUFTTRANS flight computer; **Flugdaten** *nt pl* LUFTTRANS flight data; **Flugdatenschreiber** *m* LUFTTRANS flight data recorder; **Flugdeck** *nt* LUFTTRANS flight deck

Flügel *m* FERTIG lobe, vane, *Rührwerk* blade, HEIZ & KÄLTE blade, vane, MASCHINEN blade, impeller, vane, wing, PHYS wing; ~ **in Mitteldeckeranordnung** *m* LUFTTRANS midwing; **Flügelanode** *f* ELEKTROTECH vane-type anode; **Flügelausrundung** *f* LUFTTRANS wing fillet; **Flügelbohrmeißel** *m* ERDÖL *Bohrtechnik* blade bit; **Flügelbremse** *f* MASCHINEN fan brake; **Flügelfenster** *nt* BAU French window, casement window; **Flügelgeschwindigkeit** *f* NICHTFOSS ENERG vane velocity; **Flügelhahn** *m* NICHTFOSS ENERG butterfly cock, butterfly valve; **Flügelhinterkante** *f* LUFTTRANS trailing edge; **Flügelholm** *m* FERTIG spar; **Flügelklappe** *f* LUFTTRANS wing flap; **Flügelmauer** *f* BAU wing wall, *Brücken* head wall; **Flügelmutter** *f* BAU butterfly nut, fly nut, thumb nut, wing nut, KFZTECH butterfly nut, finger nut, fly nut, thumb nut, wing nut, MASCHINEN butterfly nut, fly nut, thumb nut, wing nut; **Flügeloberseite** *f* PHYS upper surface of wing; **Flügelpumpe** *f* WASSERVERSORG semirotary pump, vane pump; **Flügelrad** *nt* HEIZ & KÄLTE vane wheel, KFZTECH *Pumpe* impeller, LUFTTRANS impeller, *Turbomotor* impeller, MASCHINEN, MECHAN impeller; **Flügelradanemometer** *nt* GERÄT rotating cup anemometer, rotating vane anemometer, HEIZ & KÄLTE windmill-type anemometer; **Flügelradwattmeßgerät** *nt* ELEKTRIZ vane wattmeter; **Flügelradzähler** *m* GERÄT vane meter; **Flügelrelais** *nt* ELEKTRIZ vane-type relay; **Flügelschiene** *f* EISENBAHN wing rail; **Flügelschraube** *f* BAU, FERTIG, MASCHINEN butterfly screw, thumb bolt, thumb screw, wing bolt, wing screw; **Flügelspalt** *m* LUFTTRANS wing slot; **Flügelspitze** *f* LUFTTRANS wing tip; **Flügelspitzenwirbel** *m* LUFTTRANS wing tip vortex; **Flügelstreckung** *f* LUFTTRANS *Tragfläche* aspect ratio; **Flügelstützschwimmer** *m* LUFTTRANS wing tank; **Flügeltiefe** *f* LUFTTRANS chord, NICHTFOSS ENERG *Aerodynamik* chord length; **Flügeltür** *f* BAU folding door; **Flügelübergang** *m* LUFTTRANS wing fillet; **Flügelvorderklappenkante** *f* LUFTTRANS slat of the leading edge; **Flügelwand** *f* BAU return wall; **Flügelzellenpumpe** *f* MASCHINEN vane pump

Flugerlaubnis: ~ **entziehen** *vi* LUFTTRANS earth (BrE), ground (AmE)

Flug: **Flugerprobungszentrum** *nt* LUFTTRANS flight test center (AmE), flight test centre (BrE); **Flugfeld** *nt* LUFTTRANS airfield; **Flugfreigabe** *f* LUFTTRANS flight clearance; **Flugfreigabeüberprüfung** *f* RAUMFAHRT FRR, flight readiness review; **Flugfunke** *m* SICHERHEIT flying spark

Fluggast *m* TRANS passenger; **Fluggastbetreuung** *f* LUFTTRANS passenger service; **Fluggastbrücke** *f* LUFTTRANS aerobridge, air bridge, boarding bridge, jetway, passenger bridge; **Fluggastraum** *m* LUFTTRANS passenger cabin

Flug: **Fluggeschwindigkeit** *f* LUFTTRANS airspeed; **Fluggesellschaft** *f* LUFTTRANS airline; **Flughafen** *m* LUFTTRANS aerodrome (BrE), airdrome (AmE), airport; **Flughafenabfertigungsgebäude** *nt* TRANS air terminal; **Flughafenbake** *f* LUFTTRANS aerodrome

beacon (BrE), airdrome beacon (AmE), RAUMFAHRT *(FB)* aerodrome beacon (BrE), airdrome beacon (AmE), airport beacon; **Flughafengebühr** *f* LUFTTRANS airport fee; **Flughafenleuchtfeuer** *nt* LUFTTRANS airport beacon; **Flughafen-Überwachungsradar** *nt* *(ASR)* LUFTTRANS airport surveillance radar *(ASR)*; **Flughalle** *f* LUFTTRANS air terminal; **Flughalle einer Luftverkehrsgesellschaft** *f* LUFTTRANS airways terminal; **Flughandbuch** *nt* LUFTTRANS flight manual; **Flughöhe** *f* LUFTTRANS flight altitude, flight level, RAUMFAHRT altitude; **Fluginformationsdienst** *m* LUFTTRANS flight information service; **Fluginformationszentrale** *f* LUFTTRANS flight information center (AmE), flight information centre (BrE); **Flugkabine** *f* LUFTTRANS flight compartment; **Flugkabinenbeleuchtung** *f* LUFTTRANS flight compartment lights; **Flugkabinenzugangstreppe** *f* LUFTTRANS flight compartment access stairway; **Flugkommandoanlage** *f* LUFTTRANS flight director; **Fluglage** *f* RAUMFAHRT attitude, pitch attitude; **Fluglage- und Umlaufbahnkontrollsystem** *nt* *(AOCS)* RAUMFAHRT attitude and orbit control system *(AOCS)*; **Fluglagebezugssystem** *nt* RAUMFAHRT attitude reference unit; **Fluglagekontrollsystem** *nt* RAUMFAHRT attitude control unit; **Flugleistungsstörung** *f* LUFTTRANS flight technical error; **Flugleiter** *m* LUFTTRANS flight controller; **Fluglogbuch** *nt* LUFTTRANS flight log; **Fluglotse** *m* LUFTTRANS air traffic controller; **Flugmasse** *f* LUFTTRANS gross weight; **Flugnachbesprechung** *f* LUFTTRANS postflying check; **Flugnavigationsfunkdienst** *m* LUFTTRANS aeronautical radio navigation service; **Flugnormengruppe** *f* *(ASG)* RAUMFAHRT aeronautical standards group *(ASG)*; **Flugnormwirkungsgrad** *m* *(ase)* RAUMFAHRT air standard efficiency *(ase)*; **Flugparameter** *nt pl* LUFTTRANS flight data; **Flugplan** *m* LUFTTRANS aerial timetable; **Flugplandaten** *nt pl* LUFTTRANS flight plan data; **Flugplatz** *m* LUFTTRANS aerodrome (BrE), airdrome (AmE); **Flugradar** *nt* ELEKTRONIK airborne radar; **Flugrechnersystem** *nt* RAUMFAHRT flight data system; **Flugrettung** *f* LUFTTRANS air emergency; **Flugsand** *m* BAU flying sand; **Flugschneise** *f* LUFTTRANS lane; **Flugschrauber** *m* LUFTTRANS gyrodyne; **Flugschreiber** *m* LUFTTRANS black box, flight recorder; **Flugschubvektorierung** *f* RAUMFAHRT *Raumschiff* in-flight thrust vectoring; **Flugsequenz** *f* RAUMFAHRT *Raumschiff* in-flight sequence; **Flugsicherung** *f* *(FS)* LUFTTRANS air traffic control *(ATC)*; **Flugsicherungszentrale** *f* LUFTTRANS air traffic control center (AmE), air traffic control centre (BrE); **Flugsicht** *f* LUFTTRANS flight visibility; **Flugsimulator** *m* COMP & DV flight simulator; **Flugspektrum** *nt* LUFTTRANS flight spectrum; **Flugstaub** *m* KOHLEN flue dust; **Flugsteig** *m* LUFTTRANS gate, ramp; **Flugsteuerungen** *f pl* LUFTTRANS flight controls; **Flugstrecke** *f* LUFTTRANS, TRANS *Flugzeug* distance covered; **Flugstreckeneinrichtungen** *f pl* LUFTTRANS air route facilities; **Flugstützpunkt** *m* TRANS air base

flugtechnisch: ~ **bedingter Ausfall** *m* LUFTTRANS flight technical error

Flug: **Flugtestanlage** *f* LUFTTRANS flying test bench; **Flugturbinenkerosin** *nt* ERDÖL *Destillationsprodukt* ATK, aviation turbine kerosene; **Flugüberwachungs- und Navigationsausrüstung** *f* *(FCNE)* LUFTTRANS flight control and navigational equipment *(FCNE)*; **Flugüberwachungsinstrumente** *nt pl* LUFTTRANS

flight instruments; **Flugüberwachungsradar** *nt* *(ARSR)* RAUMFAHRT air route surveillance radar *(ARSR)*; **Flugverkehr** *m* LUFTTRANS air traffic; **Flugverlaufsplan** *m* LUFTTRANS flight progress board; **Flugvorbereitung** *f* LUFTTRANS preflight planning; **Flugvorbereitungsinformationen** *f pl* LUFTTRANS preflight information; **Flugweg** *m* LUFTTRANS flight path; **Flugwegzeichnen** *nt* LUFTTRANS radar plotting; **Flugwerk** *nt* LUFTTRANS *ohne Motor* airframe; **Flugwerksleitebene** *f* LUFTTRANS airframe reference plane; **Flugwerterechner** *m* LUFTTRANS air data computer; **Flugwetterwarte** *f* LUFTTRANS aeronautical meteorological station; **Flugzeitdatenanalyse** *f* STRAHLPHYS time-of-flight data analysis; **Flugzeitmethode** *f* STRAHLPHYS time-of-flight method
Flugzeug *nt* LUFTTRANS aeroplane (BrE), airplane (AmE), aircraft, plane; ~ **mit absenkbarer Rumpfspitze** *nt* LUFTTRANS droop-nose aircraft; ~ **mit nur einem Mittelgang** *nt* LUFTTRANS single aisle aircraft; ~ **für Raketenstarts** *nt* RAUMFAHRT launching aircraft; ~ **mit variabler Geometrie** *nt* LUFTTRANS variable-geometry aircraft; ~ **mit vier Strahltriebwerken** *nt* LUFTTRANS four-engine jet aircraft; **Flugzeugabgas** *nt* UMWELTSCHMUTZ aircraft waste gas; **Flugzeugabstellplatz** *m* LUFTTRANS *Flughafen* aircraft-parking position; **Flugzeugachse** *f* LUFTTRANS aircraft axis; **Flugzeugaufzug** *m* LUFTTRANS aircraft lift; **Flugzeugausrüstung** *f* LUFTTRANS aircraft equipment; **Flugzeugbeleuchtung** *f* LUFTTRANS aircraft light; **Flugzeug-Eisenbahn-Verkehr** *m* *(FLEI-Verkehr)* TRANS rail-air-rail service; **Flugzeugentführung** *f* LUFTTRANS hijack, skyjack; **Flugzeuggleichgewicht** *nt* LUFTTRANS aircraft balance; **Flugzeughalle** *f* LUFTTRANS hangar; **Flugzeugkategorie** *f* LUFTTRANS aircraft category; **Flugzeugkennung** *f* LUFTTRANS aircraft identification; **Flugzeuglängsfeld** *nt* LUFTTRANS *Magnetfeld* aircraft longitudinal field; **Flugzeugnutzleistung** *f* LUFTTRANS aircraft effectivity; **Flugzeugquerfeld** *nt* LUFTTRANS *Magnetfeld* aircraft lateral field; **Flugzeugradar** *nt* TELEKOM airborne radar; **Flugzeugrumpf** *m* LUFTTRANS fuselage, nacelle; **Flugzeugrumpfbasis** *f* LUFTTRANS fuselage datum line; **Flugzeugrumpfkasten** *m* LUFTTRANS fuselage box; **Flugzeugrumpfmittelkasten** *m* LUFTTRANS fuselage center box (AmE), fuselage centre box (BrE); **Flugzeugschlepper** *m* LUFTTRANS aircraft tug, TRANS aircraft tractor; **Flugzeugschleppstart** *m* LUFTTRANS aeroplane tow launch (BrE), airplane tow launch (AmE); **Flugzeugschwerpunkt** *m* LUFTTRANS aircraft balance; **Flugzeugträger** *m* LUFTTRANS carrier, WASSERTRANS *Marine* aircraft carrier; **Flugzeugtreppe** *f* LUFTTRANS air stairs; **Flugzeugtriebwerksemissionen** *f pl* LUFTTRANS aircraft engine emissions; **Flugzeugüberholungsdaten** *nt pl* LUFTTRANS aircraft overhaul rating; **Flugzeugvereisungsanzeiger** *m* LUFTTRANS aircraft icing indicator; **Flugzeugwartungsdaten** *nt pl* LUFTTRANS aircraft maintenance rating
Flug: **Flugzustand** *m* LUFTTRANS flight status
Fluid *nt* CHEMIE fluid
fluid *adj* MASCHINEN fluidal
Fluid: **Fluidantrieb** *m* MECHAN fluid drive; **Fluidelement** *nt* MASCHINEN fluidic device; **Fluidgetriebe** *nt* MASCHINEN fluidic transmission; **Fluidics** *f* STRÖMPHYS fluidics; **Fluidität** *f* MASCHINEN, MECHAN, PHYS, STRÖMPHYS fluidity; **Fluidkompaß** *m* WASSERTRANS liquid compass

Fluktuation *f* ERGON labor turnover (AmE), labour turnover (BrE)
fluktuierend: ~**es Rauschen** *nt* AKUSTIK fluctuating noise
Fluor *nt* *(F)* CHEMIE fluorine *(F)*
Fluoranthen *nt* CHEMIE fluoranthene
Fluor: **Fluorchlorokohlenwasserstoff** *m* *(FCKW)* UMWELTSCHMUTZ, VERPACK chlorofluorocarbon *(CFC)*
Fluoren *nt* CHEMIE fluorene
Fluorenon *nt* CHEMIE fluorenone
Fluor: **Fluorescein** *nt* CHEMIE fluorescein
Fluoreszenz *f* CHEMIE, PHYS fluorescence; **Fluoreszenzpref** CHEMIE fluorescent; **Fluoreszenzanalyse** *f* PHYS, STRAHLPHYS, WELLPHYS fluorescence analysis; **Fluoreszenzanregungsspektrum** *nt* PHYS, STRAHLPHYS, WELLPHYS fluorescence excitation spectrum; **Fluoreszenzlampe** *f* STRAHLPHYS fluorescent lamp; **Fluoreszenzschirm** *m* STRAHLPHYS fluorescent screen
fluoreszierend *adj* CHEMIE, DRUCK fluorescent
Fluorid *nt* CHEMIE fluoride
Fluoridierung *f* CHEMIE fluoridation
Fluorid: **Fluorid-Opalglas** *nt* KER & GLAS fluoride opal glass; **Fluoridzusatz** *m* CHEMIE *Trinkwasser* fluoridation
Fluor: **Fluorkältemittel** *nt* HEIZ & KÄLTE fluorocarbon refrigerant
Fluorkiesel- *pref* CHEMIE fluosilicic
Fluor: **Fluorkohlenstoff** *m* KUNSTSTOFF fluorocarbon resin; **Fluoroaluminat** *nt* CHEMIE fluoaluminate; **Fluorobor-** *pref* CHEMIE fluoboric; **Fluoroborat** *nt* CHEMIE borofluoride
fluoroborsauer: ~**es Salz** *nt* CHEMIE fluoborate
Fluor: **Fluoroform** *nt* CHEMIE fluoroform; **Fluorophosphat** *nt* CHEMIE fluophosphate; **Fluorosilicat** *nt* CHEMIE hexafluorosilite; **Fluorozirconat** *nt* CHEMIE zirconifluoride; **Fluorpolymer** *nt* KUNSTSTOFF fluorocarbon resin; **Fluorsiliciumverbindung** *f* CHEMIE hexafluorosilite
Fluorsulfon- *pref* CHEMIE fluosulfonic (AmE), fluosulphonic (BrE)
fluorwasserstoffsauer *adj* CHEMIE hydrofluoric
Flurplatte *f* WASSERTRANS *Schiffbau* floor plate
Fluß *m* COMP & DV flow, ELEKTRIZ flux, ELEKTROTECH current, flow, KONTROLL, MASCHINEN flow, MECHAN flux, METALL, NICHTFOSS ENERG flow, PHYS flow, flux, WASSERTRANS river; **Flußablagerung** *f* WASSERVERSORG aggradational deposit
flußabwärts *adv* BAU downstream
Fluß: **Flußaufsichtsbehörde** *f* WASSERVERSORG river authority; **Flußbau** *m* WASSERVERSORG river works; **Flußbett** *nt* WASSERVERSORG river bed; **Flußboot** *nt* WASSERTRANS river boat
Flüßchen *nt* WASSERTRANS creek (AmE)
Fluß: **Flußdampfer** *m* WASSERTRANS water bus; **Flußdelta** *nt* ERDÖL delta; **Flußdiagramm** *nt* COMP & DV, PHYS flowchart; **Flußdiagrammbeschriftung** *f* COMP & DV flowchart text; **Flußdiagrammsymbol** *nt* COMP & DV flowchart symbol; **Flußdichte** *f* ELEKTRIZ, PHYS flux density; **Flußdichtemeßgerät** *nt* GERÄT flux meter; **Flußdichtewölbung** *f* KERNTECH Bg^2, geometric buckling; **Flußeinzugsgebiet** *nt* WASSERTRANS, WASSERVERSORG river basin; **Flußeisen** *nt* BAU structural iron; **Flußfähre** *f* WASSERTRANS river ferry; **Flußgebiet** *nt* WASSERVERSORG river basin; **Flußgeschwindigkeit des Reaktorkernkühlmittels** *f* KERNTECH core coolant flow rate; **Flußhafen** *m* WAS-

SERTRANS river port

Flüssig- *pref* UMWELTSCHMUTZ fluid

flüssig[1] *adj* STRÖMPHYS fluid, THERMOD liquid

flüssig:[2] **~er Abfall** *m* ABFALL liquid waste; **~er Ammoniak** *m* THERMOD liquid ammonia; **~er Anlaßwiderstand** *m* ELEKTRIZ liquid starter resistance; **~es Begleitprodukt** *nt* ERDÖL *Erdgasförderung* associated liquids; **~e Brennstoffe** *m pl* HEIZ & KÄLTE liquid fuels; **~es Chlor** *nt* THERMOD liquid chlorine; **~es Helium** *nt* THERMOD liquid helium; **~e Kathode** *f* ELEKTROTECH pool cathode; **~er Kautschuk** *m* KUNSTSTOFF liquid rubber; **~e Luft** *f* THERMOD liquid air; **~es Monergol** *nt* THERMOD liquid monopropellant; **~es Paraffin** *nt* THERMOD liquid paraffin; **~er Stickstoff** *m* THERMOD liquid air; **~es Triergol** *nt* THERMOD liquid tripropellant; **~er Wasserstoff** *m* THERMOD liquid hydrogen

Flüssig-: **Flüssigantriebsystem** *nt* RAUMFAHRT *Raumschiff* liquid propellant system; **Flüssigbett** *nt* UMWELTSCHMUTZ fluidized bed; **Flüssigchromatographie** *f* UMWELTSCHMUTZ liquid chromatography; **Flüssigerdgas** *nt (LNG)* ERDÖL, THERMOD liquefied natural gas *(LNG)*; **Flüssigerdgasbus** *m* KFZTECH liquid natural gas bus; **Flüssigerdgastanker** *m* WASSERTRANS liquefied natural gas tanker; **Flüssigerdgastransporter** *m* THERMOD liquid natural gas carrier

Flüssiggas *nt (LPG)* ERDÖL, HEIZ & KÄLTE, KFZTECH, THERMOD, WASSERTRANS liquefied petroleum gas *(LPG)*; **Flüssiggasbus** *m* KFZTECH liquefied petroleum gas bus; **Flüssiggasmotor** *m* KFZTECH liquefied petroleum gas engine; **Flüssiggastanker** *m* WASSERTRANS liquefied petroleum gas tanker; **Flüssiggastransporter** *m* THERMOD liquefied petroleum gas carrier

flüssiggekühlt: **~er Motor** *m* KFZTECH liquid-cooled engine

Flüssigkeit[1] *f* HEIZ & KÄLTE liquid, PHYS, STRÖMPHYS fluid, THERMOD liquid

Flüssigkeit:[2] **~ rückführen** *vi* FERTIG *Hydraulik* vent

Flüssigkeiten: **~ in rotierenden Systemen** *f pl* STRÖMPHYS fluids in rotating systems

Flüssigkeit: **Flüssigkeitsanlasser** *m* ELEKTROTECH liquid starter; **Flüssigkeitsbremse** *f* MASCHINEN hydraulic brake; **Flüssigkeitsdichtemeßgerät** *nt* GERÄT areometer; **Flüssigkeitsdruck** *m* HEIZ & KÄLTE hydrostatic pressure, STRÖMPHYS fluid pressure

Flüssigkeitsdruck: durch ~ angepreßte Dichtung *f* FERTIG automatic packing

Flüssigkeit: **Flüssigkeitsdruckmeßdose** *f* GERÄT hydraulic capsule; **Flüssigkeitseinlaß** *m* MASCHINEN fluid inlet

flüssigkeitsfest[1] *adj* VERPACK liquidproof

flüssigkeitsfest:[2] **~er Karton** *m* VERPACK liquidproof carton

flüssigkeitsgekühlt *adj* THERMOD liquid-cooled

Flüssigkeit: **Flüssigkeitsgetriebe** *nt* MASCHINEN hydraulic transmission, MECHAN fluid drive; **Flüssigkeitsguß** *m* RAUMFAHRT *Raumschiff* liquid slosh; **Flüssigkeitshonen** *nt* MASCHINEN liquid honing; **Flüssigkeitsindex** *m* KOHLEN liquidity index; **Flüssigkeitskathode** *f* ELEKTROTECH pool cathode; **Flüssigkeitskühler** *m* HEIZ & KÄLTE liquid chiller; **Flüssigkeitskühlung** *f* THERMOD liquid cooling; **Flüssigkeitskupplung** *f* HYDRAUL hydraulic clutch, KFZTECH *Kraftübertragung*, MASCHINEN fluid coupling; **Flüssigkeitslaser** *m* ELEKTRONIK liquid laser; **Flüssigkeitslasermedium** *nt* ELEKTRONIK liquid laser medium; **Flüssigkeitsleitung** *f* MASCHINEN fluid pipeline; **Flüssigkeitslöscher** *m* SICHERHEIT nonflammable liquid extinguisher; **Flüssigkeitsmaß** *nt* METROL liquid measure; **Flüssigkeitsmassengut** *nt (OBO)* WASSERTRANS ore-bulk oil *(OBO)*; **Flüssigkeitsmassengutfrachter** *m* WASSERTRANS ore-bulk oil carrier; **Flüssigkeitsmotor** *m* KFZTECH organic fluid engine; **Flüssigkeitsregler** *m* ELEKTROTECH liquid controller; **Flüssigkeitsreibung** *f* HEIZ & KÄLTE fluid friction, LEBENSMITTEL, MASCHINEN, PHYS viscous friction; **Flüssigkeitssäule** *f* MASCHINEN liquid column; **Flüssigkeitsschwund** *m* RAUMFAHRT *Raumschiff* ullage

Flüssigkeitsspiegel: durch ~ betätigt *adj* FERTIG float-operated

Flüssigkeitsstand *m* VERPACK liquid level; **Flüssigkeitsstandanzeiger** *m* ERDÖL *Meßtechnik* gage glass (AmE), gauge glass (BrE), GERÄT liquid level indicator, MASCHINEN level indicator, VERPACK liquid level indicator; **Flüssigkeitsstandglas** *nt* HEIZ & KÄLTE gage glass (AmE), gauge glass (BrE); **Flüssigkeitsstandregler** *m* VERPACK liquid level control

Flüssigkeit: **Flüssigkeitsstrahl** *m* FERTIG jet of liquid; **Flüssigkeitsstrahlbohren** *nt* FERTIG abrasive jet drilling; **Flüssigkeitsstrom** *m* KERNTECH liquid flow; **Flüssigkeitsströmung** *f* STRÖMPHYS fluid flow, liquid flow; **Flüssigkeitsteilchen** *nt* STRÖMPHYS fluid particle; **Flüssigkeitsthermometer** *nt* THERMOD liquid expansion thermometer, liquid thermometer; **Flüssigkeitstropfenmodell** *nt* PHYS *Kernphysik* liquid drop model; **Flüssigkeitsverlust** *m* CHEMIE ullage; **Flüssigkeitsverschluß** *m* MASCHINEN liquid seal; **Flüssigkeitswaage** *f* LEBENSMITTEL hydrometer; **Flüssigkeitswiderstand** *m* ELEKTRIZ liquid rheostat; **Flüssigkeitszerstäuber** *m* WASSERVERSORG pulverizer

Flüssigkristall *m* COMP & DV *(LC)* liquid crystal, ELEKTRIZ *(LC)* liquid crystal *(LC)*, ELEKTRONIK, KERNTECH, TELEKOM liquid crystal; **Flüssigkristallanzeige** *f (LCD)* COMP & DV, ELEKTRIZ, ELEKTRONIK, FERNSEH, GERÄT, TELEKOM, THERMOD liquid crystal display *(LCD)*

Flüssigmetall *nt* KOHLEN liquid metal; **Flüssigmetallionenquelle** *f* STRAHLPHYS liquid metal ion source

Flüssigmetallkühlung: mit ~ *adj* THERMOD liquid metal cooled

Flüssigmetall: **Flüssigmetallreaktor** *m (FMR)* KERNTECH flowable solids reactor *(FSR)*; **Flüssigmetall-Wärmeaustauscher** *m* THERMOD liquid metal heat exchanger

Flüssig-: **Flüssigmist** *m* ABFALL slurry; **Flüssigphase** *f* THERMOD liquid phase; **Flüssigphasenepitaxie** *f* ELEKTRONIK liquid phase epitaxy; **Flüssigrakete** *f* THERMOD liquid fuel rocket, liquid propellant rocket; **Flüssigsauerstoff** *m (LOX)* RAUMFAHRT, THERMOD liquid oxygen *(lox)*; **Flüssigschlamm** *m* ABFALL liquid sludge, slurry; **Flüssigschmiere** *f* RAUMFAHRT *Raumschiff* liquid slosh; **Flüssigstickstoff** *m* RAUMFAHRT liquid nitrogen; **Flüssigtreibstoff** *m* RAUMFAHRT liquid propellant, THERMOD liquid fuel, liquid propellant; **Flüssigwasserstoff** *m* RAUMFAHRT liquid hydrogen

Fluß: **Flußkanalisierung** *f* WASSERVERSORG river training; **Flußlauf von Oberwasser** *m* WASSERVERSORG headwater reach; **Flußlinie** *f* ELEKTROTECH flux line,

line of flux; **Flußmeßgerät** *nt* GERÄT flux meter, PHYS
fluxmeter; **Flußmeter** *nt* GERÄT flux meter
Flußmittel[1] *nt* ELEKTROTECH flux, soldering flux, KER &
GLAS flux, KOHLEN flux powder, MASCHINEN flux ad-
ditive, METALL, RADIO *Löthilfe* flux; ~ **zum
Lichtbogenschweißen** *nt* FERTIG arc flux
Flußmittel:[2] **in ~ tauchen** *vt* METALL flux
Flußmittel:[3] ~ **zusetzen** *vi* FERTIG flux
flußmittelgefüllt: ~**es Lot** *nt* ELEKTRIZ cored solder
Fluß: **Flußmündung** *f* NICHTFOSS ENERG estuary, WAS-
SERVERSORG river mouth; **Flußprojektierung** *f*
NICHTFOSS ENERG run-of-river scheme; **Flußquantum**
nt PHYS flux quantum; **Flußrate** *f* PHYS flow rate;
Flußregulierung *f* WASSERVERSORG river training;
Flußrichtung *f* COMP & DV flow direction; **Flußröhre** *f*
PHYS tube
flußsauer: flußsaures Salz *nt* CHEMIE fluoride
Fluß: **Flußschiff** *nt* WASSERTRANS river boat; **Flußschiff-
fahrt** *f* WASSERTRANS river navigation, river traffic;
Flußschlepper *m* WASSERTRANS river tug; **Flußspat** *m*
KER & GLAS fluorspar; **Flußstahl** *m* METALL mild steel;
Flußsteuerung *f* COMP & DV, TELEKOM flow control;
Flußstrom *m* ELEKTROTECH forward current
Flußufer:[1] **am ~ lebend** *adj* WASSERVERSORG riparian
Flußufer[2] *nt* WASSERTRANS river bank; **Flußufermauer** *f*
WASSERVERSORG river wall
Fluß: **Flußventil** *nt* LUFTTRANS flux valve; **Flußwechsel-
dichte** *f* COMP & DV packing density; **Flußwölbung** *f*
KERNTECH buckling, geometric buckling; **Flußzeit** *f*
ELEKTROTECH on period
Flut *f* NICHTFOSS ENERG high tide, rising tide, WASSER-
TRANS flood tide, flood, high tide, high water, tide;
Flutbecken *nt* NICHTFOSS ENERG tidal basin; **Flutbe-
leuchtung** *f* ELEKTRIZ floodlighting
fluten[1] *vt* KFZTECH *Motor* flood
fluten[2] *vi* WASSERTRANS *Schleusen* flood
Flut: **Fluthafen** *m* WASSERTRANS tidal harbor (AmE),
tidal harbour (BrE), tidal port; **Flutkraftwerk** *nt*
NICHTFOSS ENERG tidal power station; **Flutlicht** *nt*
ELEKTROTECH floodlight; **Flutöffnung** *f* WASSERVER-
SORG flood arch; **Flutstrom** *m* WASSERTRANS
Navigation, Gezeiten flood stream; **Flutströmung** *f*
NICHTFOSS ENERG flowing tide; **Flutstunde** *f* NICHT-
FOSS ENERG lagging of the tide; **Fluttor** *nt*
WASSERTRANS *Schleuse* floodgate
Flutung *f* KER & GLAS flooding
Flut: **Flutventil** *nt* WASSERTRANS *Schiffbau* seacock, WAS-
SERVERSORG flooding cock; **Flutverlust** *m* NICHTFOSS
ENERG flood loss; **Flutwechsel** *m* WASSERTRANS turn
of the tide; **Flutwelle** *f* WASSERTRANS tidal wave
fluvial: ~**es Schwemmland** *nt* WASSERVERSORG fluvial
alluvium
Fluxmeter *nt* ELEKTROTECH fluxmeter
Fly-By-Punkt *m* RAUMFAHRT *Raumschiff* fly-by point
Flyer *m* TEXTIL flyer spinning frame, roving frame;
Flyergarn *nt* TEXTIL rove
FM *abbr* (*Frequenzmodulation*) COMP & DV, ELEKTRO-
NIK, PHYS, RADIO, TELEKOM FM (*frequency
modulation*)
Fm (*Fermium*) CHEMIE Fm (*fermium*)
FM: **FM-Aufzeichnung** *f* AUFNAHME FM recording; **FM-
Modem** *m* ELEKTRONIK FM modem
FMR *abbr* (*Flüssigmetallreaktor*) KERNTECH FSR
(*flowable solids reactor*)
FM: **FM-Signal** *nt* ELEKTRONIK FM signal; **FM-Stereo-
phonie** *f* AUFNAHME FM stereo; **FM-Träger** *m*

ELEKTRONIK FM carrier
fob *abbr* (*frei an Bord*) ERDÖL, WASSERTRANS fob
(*free on board*)
Fockmast *m* WASSERTRANS *Segeln* foremast
Fockstag *nt* WASSERTRANS forestay
Fogging *nt* KUNSTSTOFF fogging
Fokalebene *f* FOTO focal plane
Fokalfläche *f* PHYS *Optik* caustic surface
Fokallinie *f* OPT caustic curve
Fokus *m* FOTO focal point, GEOM focus; **Fokuseinstel-
lung** *f* FOTO focus setting; **Fokuslampe** *f* ELEKTRIZ
focusing lamp; **Fokus-Servo** *m* OPTIK focus servo
Fokussieraufsatz *m* FOTO focusing stage
fokussieren[1] *vt* ELEKTRONIK, FOTO, GERÄT *Elektronen-
strahl*, PHYS focusing
fokussieren[2] *vi* FOTO, LABOR *Elektronenstrahl* focus
Fokussierhilfe *f* FOTO focusing aid
Fokussierknopf *m* FOTO focusing knob
Fokussiermagnet *m* ELEKTROTECH focusing magnet
Fokussierpunkt *m* FERNSEH crossover
Fokussierspule *f* ELEKTROTECH focusing coil
fokussiert[1] *adj* FOTO in focus, PHYS focused
fokussiert:[2] ~**er Ionenstrahl** *m* PHYS focused ion beam;
~**er Strahl** *m* PHYS focused beam
Fokussierung *f* ELEKTRONIK *Kathodenstrahlröhre* focusing, *Teilchenstrahl* focusing; **Fokussierungsanlage
für Ionenstrahlen** *f* STRAHLPHYS ion beam-focusing
column; **Fokussierungsanode** *f* ELEKTROTECH focusing anode; **Fokussierungselektrode** *f* ELEKTROTECH
focusing electrode; **Fokussierungsmagnet** *m* RAUM-
FAHRT *Weltraumfunk* focusing magnet
Foley-Spur *f* AUFNAHME Foleysche track
Folge *f* COMP & DV series, suite, KONTROLL routine,
sequence, MATH *Zahlen* sequence; **Folgeausfall** *m*
QUAL subsequent failure; **Folgebereich** *m* COMP & DV
overflow area, ELEKTRONIK follow range; **Folgeblatt**
nt KONSTZEICH continuation sheet; **Folgedrosselung** *f*
AKUSTIK temporal partial masking; **Folgefeld** *nt* PHYS
wake field
folgegedrosselt: ~**e Lautheit** *f* AKUSTIK temporally
partial-masked loudness
Folgegerät *nt* KONTROLL *führungsabhängig* slave
folgegesteuert[1] *adj* COMP & DV sequence-controlled
folgegesteuert:[2] ~**er Ablauf** *m* COMP & DV sequencing
Folge: **Folgenummer** *f* COMP & DV sequence number;
Folgenutzung *f* ABFALL after use; **Folgeprüfung** *f*
COMP & DV sequence control, QUAL sequential test;
Folgeregelung *f* ELEKTROTECH servomechanism,
KONTROLL servo control, REGELUNG sequence control; **Folgeregelungssystem** *nt* ELEKTROTECH
servomechanism, KONTROLL servo control system,
servo system; **Folgerelais** *nt* ELEKTROTECH sequence
relay; **Folgesatz** *m* MATH corollary; **Folgeschäden** *m
pl* KERNTECH consequential damage; **Folgesteuerung**
f COMP & DV, ELEKTROTECH sequencing; **Folgesteue-
rungseinheit** *f* TELEKOM sequencer;
Folgesteuerungsmechanismus *m* COMP & DV servomechanism; **Folgestichprobenentnahme** *f* QUAL
sequential sampling; **Folgestichprobenplan** *m* QUAL
sequential-sampling plan; **Folgewerkzeug** *nt* MASCHI-
NEN follow-on tool, progressive tool
Folie *f* CHEMIE hauchdünn film, FERTIG leaf, KOHLEN foil,
KUNSTSTOFF film, sheet, PAPIER foil; **Folienabpreßma-
schine** *f* VERPACK foil-backing machine; **Folienblasen**
nt KUNSTSTOFF film blowing; **Folieneinschweißung** *f*
LEBENSMITTEL *in Folie* shrink-wrap; **Folienextrudier-**

anlage *f* VERPACK film extrusion equipment; **Folienextrusion** *f* KUNSTSTOFF film extrusion; **Foliengießen** *nt* KUNSTSTOFF film casting; **Folienkondensator** *m* ELEKTRIZ capacitor film; **Folienpapier** *nt* PAPIER foil paper; **Folienversiegelung** *f* VERPACK foil sealing

Folin- *pref* CHEMIE folinic

Folio *m* DRUCK folio; **Folioformat** *nt* DRUCK folio

Folsäure *f* LEBENSMITTEL folic acid

Fond *m* TEXTIL *Naßverfahren* blotch

Foolscap *nt* DRUCK foolscap

Footcandle *f* METROL footcandle

Förde *f* WASSERTRANS firth

Förder- *pref* ERDÖL, FERTIG production; **Förderabgabe** *f* ERDÖL royalty; **Förderanlage** *f* BAU conveyor system, KERNTECH conveyor, MASCHINEN transporter, TRANS conveying plant; **Förderapparat** *m* TRANS conveyor

Förderband *nt* ABFALL, MASCHINEN, MECHAN, TRANS, VERPACK band conveyor, belt conveyor, conveying belt; **~ zur Ölaufnahme** *nt* MEERSCHMUTZ *Verschmutzung*, UMWELTSCHMUTZ belt skimmer; **Förderbandfilter** *nt* KERNTECH TBF, traveling belt filter (AmE), travelling belt filter (BrE); **Förderbandskimmer** *m* UMWELTSCHMUTZ conveyor belt skimmer; **Förderbandtrockner** *m* CHEMTECH belt drier, belt dryer; **Förderbandwaage** *f* GERÄT belt balance; **Förderbandwerkstoff** *m* TEXTIL conveyor belting

Förder-: **Förderbohrung** *f* ERDÖL production well; **Förderdruck** *m* HEIZ & KÄLTE delivery pressure, HYDRAUL head, WASSERVERSORG delivery pressure

Forderer *m* BAU, VERPACK conveyor; **~ mit veränderlicher Geschwindigkeit** *m* TRANS variable-speed conveyor belt

Forder-: **Fördererz** *nt* KOHLEN crude ore; **Fördergerät** *nt* BAU conveyor; **Förderguß** *m* KOHLEN dross

Förde: **Förderhöhe** *f* BAU *Pumpe*, ERDÖL head, FERTIG discharge head, HEIZ & KÄLTE delivery head, pump head, HYDRAUL head, static head, KERNTECH *Pumpe* delivery head, MASCHINEN discharge head, lift, WASSERVERSORG delivery head, delivery lift, discharge head; **Förderhöhengrenze** *f* HYDRAUL head limit

Förder-: **Förderhorizont** *m* ERDÖL *Fördertechnik* pay zone, production horizon; **Förderkasten** *m* FERTIG tote box; **Förderkette** *f* MASCHINEN conveyor chain; **Förderkohle** *f* KOHLEN pit coal, rough coal, run of mine coal, unscreened coal; **Förderkohlesieb** *nt* KOHLEN raw coal screen; **Förderkolonne** *f* ERDÖL production string; **Förderkopf** *m* ERDÖL wellhead; **Förderkorb** *m* TRANS skip; **Förderleistung** *f* BAU capacity, HEIZ & KÄLTE delivery rate, discharge capacity, MASCHINEN carrying capacity, delivery rate, discharge, VERPACK *Transportband* carrying capacity, WASSERVERSORG *Pumpe* delivery; **Fördermenge** *f* FERTIG discharge, MASCHINEN delivery, discharge, output, WASSERVERSORG capacity

Fördern *nt* MASCHINEN delivery

fördern *vt* BAU haul

Förder-: **Förderphase** *f* ERDÖL production phase; **Förderplattform** *f* ERDÖL production platform; **Förderpumpe** *f* FERTIG, HEIZ & KÄLTE, MASCHINEN feed pump; **Förderrichtung** *f* HEIZ & KÄLTE discharge direction; **Förderrohr** *nt* BAU screw elevator; **Förderrutsche** *f* MASCHINEN chute, slide; **Förderschnecke** *f* HYDRAUL Archimedean screw, MASCHINEN, VERPACK screw, screw conveyor, worm, worm conveyor; **Förderseil** *nt* EISENBAHN traction cable, MASCHINEN hoisting rope; **Förderseite** *f* FERTIG discharge side,

HYDRAUL pressure side, MASCHINEN discharge side; **Förderstrom** *m* FERTIG delivery, oil flow, HEIZ & KÄLTE flow of discharge; **Fördertechnik** *f* FERTIG handling engineering, hoisting and conveying

Förderung *f* MASCHINEN delivery, discharge, WASSERVERSORG offtake; **die ~ aufnehmen** *vt* ERDÖL *Öl-und Erdgasförderung* bring into production

Förder-: **Fördervolumen** *nt* MASCHINEN delivery, displacement; **Fördervorrichtung** *f* PAPIER conveyor; **Förderwagen** *m* EISENBAHN *Bergbau* trolley (BrE), KOHLEN, LABOR trolley, TRANS cart (AmE), truck (BrE); **Förderzins** *m* ERDÖL *Recht* royalty

Form *f* BAU form, DRUCK forme (BrE), printing form (AmE), FERTIG chase, die, KUNSTSTOFF, MASCHINEN mold (AmE), mould (BrE), METALL mold (AmE), mould (BrE), shape, PATENT *Zusammenfassung* form, TEXTIL shape; **äußere ~** *f* WERKPRÜF geometry; **~ für thermoplastischen Guß** *f* MASCHINEN thermoplastic mold (AmE), thermoplastic mould (BrE); **~ für Wachsausschmelzverfahren** *f* MASCHINEN lost wax mold (AmE), lost wax mould (BrE)

Formabweichung *f* METROL form errors

formal: **~e Logik** *f* COMP & DV formal logic; **~es Parameter** *nt* COMP & DV formal parameter; **~e Sprache** *f* COMP & DV formal language

Formaldehyd *m* CHEMIE formaldehyde, methanal, KUNSTSTOFF, TEXTIL formaldehyde; **Formaldehydsulfoxylat** *nt* LEBENSMITTEL formaldehyde sulfoxylate (AmE), formaldehyde sulphoxylate (BrE)

Formalin *nt* CHEMIE formalin

Formamid *nt* CHEMIE formamide, methanamide

Formänderung *f* AKUSTIK warp, KUNSTSTOFF strain, MASCHINEN deformation, yield, METALL shape change; **Formänderungsarbeit** *f* MASCHINEN deformation work; **Formänderungsfestigkeit** *f* MASCHINEN yield strength; **Formänderungswiderstand** *m* FERTIG consistency

Formant *m* AKUSTIK formant; **Formant-Vocoder** *m* TELEKOM formant vocoder

Format *nt* COMP & DV, DRUCK, FERNSEH format; **Formatbreite** *f* DRUCK measure

formatieren *vt* COMP & DV *Diskette, Text*, DRUCK format

Formatierung *f* TELEKOM formatting; **Formatierungsanweisung** *f* COMP & DV tag; **Formatierungsprogramm** *nt* COMP & DV formatter; **Formatierungssequenz** *f* COMP & DV tag

Formation *f* ERDÖL, KOHLEN, LUFTTRANS formation; **Formationsbewertung** *f* ERDÖL *Geologie* formation evaluation; **Formationsdruck** *m* ERDÖL *Geologie* formation pressure; **Formationsdruckgradient** *m* ERDÖL *Geologie* formation pressure gradient; **Formationsflug** *m* LUFTTRANS formation flight; **Formationskunde** *f* KOHLEN stratigraphy; **Formationstest** *m* ERDÖL *Geologie* formation test; **Formationstester** *m* PAPIER formation tester; **Formationswasser** *nt* ERDÖL *Geologie* formation water

Format: **Formatleiste** *f* PAPIER deckle board

Formazyl *nt* CHEMIE formazyl

Form: **Formbarkeit** *f* METALL plasticity; **Formbeständigkeit** *f* KERNTECH *Brennelement* dimensional stability; **Formbetätigungseinrichtung** *f* FERTIG die-actuating mechanism; **Formblasen** *nt* KER & GLAS mold-blowing (AmE), mould-blowing (BrE); **Formdeckel** *m* PAPIER deckle strap; **Formdrehen** *nt* MASCHINEN contouring; **Formdrehmaschine** *f* MASCHINEN forming lathe; **Formeinsatz** *m* KUNSTSTOFF mold insert (AmE), mould insert (BrE)

Formel *f* COMP & DV rule, MATH formula

Formen *nt* KER & GLAS *mit Tafeln*, MASCHINEN, MECHAN forming; ~ **mit Tonplatten** *nt* KER & GLAS molding with clay sheets (AmE), moulding with clay sheets (BrE)

formen *vt* ANSTRICH forge, BAU, KER & GLAS *Ton* mold (AmE), mould (BrE)

Form: **Formenbauer** *m* KER & GLAS mold maker (AmE), mould maker (BrE); **Formenbrecher** *m* KOHLEN breaker; **Formentleerer** *m* KER & GLAS mold emptier (AmE), mould emptier (BrE); **Formentrocknen** *nt* FERTIG mold drying (AmE), mould drying (BrE)

Former *m* FERTIG molder (AmE), moulder (BrE)

Formerei *f* FERTIG, METALL molding shop (AmE), moulding shop (BrE)

Form: **Formfaktor** *m* TEILPHYS form factor; **Formfräsen** *nt* MASCHINEN form milling, profile milling; **Formfräser** *m* FERTIG formed circular cutter, multiple-tooth gear cutter, MASCHINEN form cutter, form-milling cutter, formed cutter, formed-milling cutter; **Formfräsmaschine** *f* FERTIG form-milling machine, KER & GLAS shape-cutting machine; **Formgebung** *f* MASCHINEN design, METALL forming

formgeschäumt: ~**es Polystyrol und PET** *nt* VERPACK form-molded polystyrene and PET (AmE), form-moulded polystyrene and PET (BrE)

formgewickelt: ~**e Spule** *f* ELEKTRIZ form-wound coil

Form: **Formgleichheit** *f* CHEMIE isomorphism; **Formgravieren** *nt* MASCHINEN mold engraving (AmE), mould engraving (BrE); **Formgrube** *f* FERTIG molding hole (AmE), moulding hole (BrE), KER & GLAS pit; **Formgrubentür** *f* KER & GLAS pit door; **Formhalter** *m* KER & GLAS mold holder (AmE), mould holder (BrE); **Formholz** *nt* FERTIG wood die, *Streckziehen* former

Formiat *nt* CHEMIE formate

Form: **Formkachel** *f* BAU trimmer; **Formkasten** *m* FERTIG molding box (AmE), moulding box (BrE), molding flask (AmE), moulding flask (BrE), METALL molding box (AmE), moulding box (BrE); **Formkonduktor** *m* ELEKTRIZ sector-shaped conductor, shaped conductor; **Formkurven** *f pl* WASSERTRANS *Schiffkonstruktion* hydrostatic curves; **Formlehre** *f* METROL receiving gage (AmE), receiving gauge (BrE); **Formleiter** *m* ELEKTRIZ sector-shaped conductor

Formling *m* KER & GLAS briquette

formlos *adj* ANSTRICH amorphous

Form: **Formmarkierung** *f* KER & GLAS mold mark (AmE), mould mark (BrE); **Formmaschine** *f* FERTIG *Gießen* molding machine (AmE), moulding machine (BrE); **Formmaske** *f* FERTIG molding shell (AmE), moulding shell (BrE); **Formmaskenverfahren** *nt* FERTIG C-process, *Gießen* shell-molding process (AmE), shell-moulding process (BrE); **Formmassepulver** *nt* KUNSTSTOFF molding powder (AmE), moulding powder (BrE); **Formmeißel** *m* MASCHINEN forming cutter, forming tool; **Formmodell** *nt* FERTIG mold pattern (AmE), mould pattern (BrE); **Formpappe** *f* PAPIER, VERPACK molded board (AmE), moulded board (BrE); **Formpresse** *f* KUNSTSTOFF compression-molding machine (AmE), compression-moulding machine (BrE); **Formpressen** *nt* FERTIG, KER & GLAS compression molding (AmE), compression moulding (BrE), KUNSTSTOFF compression molding (AmE), compression moulding (BrE), molding (AmE), moulding (BrE), VERPACK compression molding (AmE), compression moulding (BrE);

Formrippe *f* LUFTTRANS false rib; **Formsand** *m* FERTIG molding sand (AmE), moulding sand (BrE); **Formsatz** *m* DRUCK runaround; **Formscheibe** *f* KER & GLAS former, MASCHINEN form shim; **Formschleifen** *nt* MASCHINEN form grinding, profile grinding, profiling; **Formschlichte** *f* ANSTRICH mold coating (AmE), mould coating (BrE), FERTIG dressing, KER & GLAS mold coating (AmE), mould coating (BrE); **Formschließen** *nt* DRUCK lock-up

formschlüssig[1] *adj* FERTIG positive

formschlüssig:[2] ~**es Kuppeln** *nt* KFZTECH jaw clutching; ~**e Kupplung** *f* MASCHINEN positive clutch; ~**e Ventildrehvorrichtung** *f* KFZTECH positive-type valve rotator

Form: **Formschräge** *f* KER & GLAS shaped bevel; **Formschuh** *m* PAPIER forming shoe; **Formsignal** *nt* EISENBAHN semaphore signal; **Formstahl** *m* MASCHINEN forming tool; **Formstahlhalter** *m* MASCHINEN forming tool holder; **Formstanzen** *nt* KUNSTSTOFF pressure forming; **Formsteifigkeit** *f* KERNTECH inherent stability; **Formstempel** *m* PAPIER mold stamp (AmE), mould stamp (BrE); **Formstich** *m* FERTIG *Walzen* former; **Formstück** *nt* MASCHINEN plain fitting; **Formteil** *nt* ELEKTROTECH molding (AmE), moulding (BrE), FERTIG compact; **Formteilgrat** *m* KUNSTSTOFF flash; **Formteilherstellung** *f* KUNSTSTOFF molding (AmE), moulding (BrE); **Formtoleranz** *f* MASCHINEN form tolerance; **Formtrennfuge** *f* FERTIG *Plaste* cutoff; **Formtrennmittel** *nt* KUNSTSTOFF mold release agent (AmE), mould release agent (BrE), release agent; **Formtrocknen** *nt* FERTIG mold drying (AmE), mould drying (BrE)

Formular *nt* COMP & DV form, DRUCK printed form, PATENT form; **Formularmaske** *f* COMP & DV form overlay; **Formularmodus** *m* COMP & DV form mode; **Formulartransport** *m* DRUCK form feed; **Formularvorschub** *m* COMP & DV form feed; **Formularzufuhr** *f* DRUCK form feed

Formulierung *f* KUNSTSTOFF formulation

Formung *f* TEXTIL boarding; **Formungs-, Abfüll- und Siegelanlage** *f* VERPACK form, fill and seal machine; **Formungs-, Abfüll- und Siegelmaschine** *f* VERPACK *waagerecht und senkrecht arbeitend* form, fill and seal machine; **Formungstemperatur** *f* VERPACK *Wärmeformung* forming temperature; **Formungsverstärker** *m* ELEKTRONIK shaping amplifier

Form: **Formwalze** *f* KER & GLAS former roller; **Formwerkzeug** *nt* KUNSTSTOFF mold (AmE), mould (BrE); **Formwiderstand** *m* FERTIG form drag, *Strömung* body drag, LUFTTRANS form drag, WASSERTRANS *Schiffkonstruktion* hull resistance

Formyl *nt* CHEMIE formyl; **Formylgruppe** *f* CHEMIE formyl

Form: **Formzyklus** *m* KUNSTSTOFF molding cycle (AmE), moulding cycle (BrE)

Forschungs: -- **und Entwicklungsingenieur** *m (F&E-Ingenieur)* MASCHINEN research-development engineer

Forschungsreaktor *m* KERNTECH laboratory reactor, research reactor

Forschungszentrum *nt* TELEKOM research center (AmE), research centre (BrE)

Forstwirtschaftsforschung *f* UMWELTSCHUTZ forestry research

fortgeschritten: ~**er Gas-Graphit-Reaktor** *m (AGR)* KERNTECH advanced gas-cooled reactor *(AGR)*

Fortin: ~sches Barometer *nt* PHYS Fortin barometer

fortlaufend[1] *adj* KONTROLL successive

fortlaufend:[2] ~e Nummer *f* PATENT serial number; ~e **Qualifikationsprüfung** *f* KERNTECH on-going qualification test; ~er **Text** *m* DRUCK running text

fortlaufend:[3] ~ **numerieren** *vt* PATENT number consecutively

Fortluft *f* HEIZ & KÄLTE exhaust air, outgoing air; **Fortluftstrom** *m* HEIZ & KÄLTE exhaust airstream

Fortpflanzung *f* COMP & DV, KÜNSTL INT propagation; ~ **von Schallwellen** *f* ELEKTROTECH acoustic-wave propagation; **Fortpflanzungsgleichung** *f* PHYS propagation equation; **Fortpflanzungskonstante** *f* AKUSTIK propagation coefficient, TELEKOM propagation coefficient, propagation constant

Fortschaltrelais *nt* ELEKTRIZ multiposition relay, stepping relay, stepping switch

Fortschaltung *f* ELEKTRONIK increment; **Fortschaltungsadressierung** *f* COMP & DV implied addressing

fortschreiben *vt* COMP & DV update

Fortschreibung *f* COMP & DV file maintenance, file updating

fortschreitend: ~e **Welle** *f* AKUSTIK traveling wave (AmE), travelling wave (BrE), TELEKOM outward-propagating wave, traveling wave (AmE), travelling wave (BrE), WELLPHYS traveling wave (AmE), travelling wave (BrE); ~e **Wellen** *f pl* WELLPHYS progressive waves

fortschrittlich: ~e **Festkörperlogik** *f (ASLT)* ELEKTRONIK advanced solid logic technology *(ASLT)*; ~e **Luftunterstützung** *f* LUFTTRANS *Militär* advanced airborne fire support system; ~e **Technologie** *f (AT)* COMP & DV advanced technology *(AT)*

Fortsetzungsblatt *nt* DRUCK continuation sheet

fossil: ~er **Brennstoff** *m* THERMOD, UMWELTSCHMUTZ fossil fuel; ~e **Brennstoffe** *m pl* UMWELTSCHMUTZ combustible fossil fuels, combustible fossils; ~e **Strahlung** *f* RAUMFAHRT fossil radiation

Fotikon *nt* ELEKTRONIK photicon

Foto *nt* FOTO picture; **Fotoabzug** *m* DRUCK photographic print, photoprint

fotoaktiv: ~er **Transducer** *m* ELEKTROTECH photoactive transducer; ~er **Wandler** *m* ELEKTROTECH photoactive transducer

Foto: **Fotoapparat** *m* FOTO camera; **Fotoätzung** *f* DRUCK photoetching; **Fotobox** *f* FOTO box camera; **Fotochemie** *f* FOTO photochemistry; **Fotochemigrafie** *f* DRUCK photoengraving

fotochemisch[1] *adj* UMWELTSCHMUTZ photochemical

fotochemisch:[2] ~er **Smog** *m* UMWELTSCHMUTZ photochemical smog; ~e **Strahlung** *f* STRAHLPHYS actinic light; ~ **wirksame Strahlen** *m pl* FOTO actinic rays; ~e **Wirkung** *f* NICHTFOSS ENERG photochemical effect

Foto: **Fotodetektion** *f* ELEKTRONIK photodetection; **Fotodetektor** *m* ELEKTRIZ photocell, ELEKTRONIK, OPTIK photodetector, TELEKOM light detector; **Fotodiode** *f* ELEKTRONIK photodetector diode, photodiode, FOTO photodiode, OPTIK photodetector diode, photodiode, PHYS photodiode, TELEKOM photodetector diode, photodiode; **Fotodiodengruppe** *f* ELEKTRONIK photodiode array; **Fotoecken** *f pl* FOTO corner mounts

Fotoeffekt *m* ELEKTRONIK photoelectric effect, RAUMFAHRT *Raumschiff* photovoltaic effect, STRAHLPHYS photoelectric effect, photoemissive effect; **äußerer** ~ *m* ELEKTRONIK photoelectric emission, OPTIK photo-emissive effect

fotoelektrisch[1] *adj* ELEKTRIZ photoelectric

fotoelektrisch:[2] ~ **betriebenes Relais** *nt* ELEKTROTECH photoelectrically-operated relay; ~er **Detektor** *m* TRANS photoelectric detector; ~er **Effekt** *m* OPTIK, PHYS, STRAHLPHYS, TELEKOM photoelectric effect; ~e **Einsatzschwelle** *f* PHYS photoelectric threshold; ~e **Lichtschranken und Scanner** *f pl* VERPACK photoelectric light barriers and scanner; ~es **Relais** *nt* ELEKTRIZ, ELEKTROTECH photoelectric relay; ~er **Strom** *m* ELEKTRIZ photoelectric current; ~er **Tonabnehmer** *m* AUFNAHME photoelectric pick-up; ~er **Transducer** *m* ELEKTROTECH photoelectric transducer

Fotoelektron *nt* ELEKTRONIK photoelectron; **Fotoelektronen-Spektroskopie** *f* PHYS photoelectron spectroscopy, PHYS *(ESCA)* electron spectroscopy for chemical analysis *(ESCA)*; **Fotoelektronen-Vervielfacher** *m* ELEKTRONIK photomultiplier

fotoelektronisch: ~e **Röhre** *f* ELEKTRONIK photosensitive tube

Foto: **Fotoelement** *nt* ELEKTROTECH, NICHTFOSS ENERG photovoltaic cell; **Fotoemission** *f* FERNSEH photoemission

fotoemissiv *adj* FOTO photoemissive

fotoempfindlich *adj* ELEKTRONIK light-sensitive

fotogalvanisch: ~e **Zelle** *f* NICHTFOSS ENERG photogalvanic cell

Foto: **Fotogenerator** *m* ELEKTROTECH photogenerator; **Fotogerät** *nt* FOTO photographic apparatus; **Fotograf** *m* FOTO, PHYS photographer; **Fotografie** *f* FOTO photograph

fotografieren *vt* FOTO photograph

fotografisch: ~er **Abzug** *m* DRUCK photographic print, photoprint; ~e **Belichtung** *f* AKUSTIK photographic exposure; ~e **Platte** *f* DRUCK photographic plate

Foto: **Fotogrammetrie** *f* BAU, RAUMFAHRT *Raumschiff* photogrammetry; **Fotogravierverfahren** *nt* ELEKTRONIK photoengraving; **Fotohalogenid** *nt* FOTO photohalide; **Fotoinitiator** *m* KUNSTSTOFF photoinitiator; **Fotoionisation** *f* PHYS photoionization; **Fotokathode** *f* ELEKTROTECH, FERNSEH, PHYS photocathode; **Fotolabor** *nt* FOTO photographic laboratory

Fotolack *m* ELEKTRONIK photoresist, resist; **mit** ~ **überzogene Halbleiterscheibe** *f* ELEKTRONIK resist-coated wafer; **Fotolacküberzug** *m* ELEKTRONIK photoresist coating

fotoleitend: ~e **Schicht** *f* OPTIK photoconducting layer; ~e **Trommel** *f* OPTIK photoconducting drum

fotoleitfähig *adj* FOTO photoconductive

Foto: **Fotoleitfähigkeit** *f* ELEKTRONIK, OPTIK, PHYS, TELEKOM photoconductivity; **Fotolithographie** *f* DRUCK, ELEKTRONIK photolithography; **Fotolumineszenz** *f* STRAHLPHYS photoluminescence; **Fotolyse** *f* NICHTFOSS ENERG photolysis; **Fotomaske** *f* ELEKTRONIK photomask

fotomechanisch *adj* DRUCK photomechanical

Foto: **Fotometer** *nt* FOTO, KUNSTSTOFF, PHYS photometer; **Fotometrie** *f* PHYS photometry; **Fotomultiplier** *m* STRAHLPHYS photomultiplier

fotonuklear: ~er **Effekt** *m* KERNTECH direct photonuclear effect

Foto: **Fotopapier** *nt* DRUCK bromide paper, photopaper, FOTO photographic paper; **Fotoplotter** *m* COMP & DV photoplotter; **Fotopolymerisation** *f* CHEMIE photopolymerization; **Fotoprobeabzüge** *m pl* DRUCK photographic proofs; **Fotoproduktion** *f* TEILPHYS photoproduction; **Fotoresist** *nt* ELEKTRONIK photoresist; **Fotoröhre** *f* ELEKTRONIK phototube

Fotosatz *m* DRUCK photocomposition, phototypesetting; **Fotosatzanlage** *f* DRUCK filmsetter, phototypesetter; **Fotosatzmaschine** *f* DRUCK filmsetter, phototypesetter

Foto: **Fotoseite** *f* DRUCK photopage

fotosensibel: fotosensibles Glas *nt* KER & GLAS photosensitive glass

Foto: **Fotosensor** *m* ELEKTRIZ photocell, ELEKTRONIK photosensor; **Fotosetzer** *m* DRUCK photocomposer; **Fotospaltung** *f* PHYS *Kernphysik* photodisintegration; **Fotosphäre** *f* RADIO, RAUMFAHRT photosphere

fotosphärisch: ~e Absorption *f* STRAHLPHYS photospheric absorption

Foto: **Fotostrom** *m* ELEKTRIZ photoelectric current, OPTIK, TELEKOM photocurrent; **Fotosynthese** *f* NICHTFOSS ENERG photosynthesis; **Fotothek** *f* FOTO picture library; **Fototransistor** *m* COMP & DV, ELEKTRONIK, STRAHLPHYS phototransistor; **Fotovaristor** *m* ELEKTROTECH photovaristor; **Fotovernetzung** *f* CHEMIE photopolymerization; **Fotovervielfacher** *m* ELEKTRONIK, PHYS, STRAHLPHYS photomultiplier

fotovoltaisch: ~er Effekt *m* ELEKTRIZ photovoltaic effect; **~e Solarstromanlage** *f* ELEKTROTECH photovoltaic solar power plant; **~e Zelle** *f* ELEKTRIZ *PV-Zelle* solar cell

Foto: **Fotovoltgenerator** *m* ELEKTROTECH photovoltaic generator; **Fotovoltstrom** *m* ELEKTROTECH photovoltaic current; **Fotowiderstand** *m* ELEKTRONIK, RADIO photoconductive cell, STRAHLPHYS photoresistor

Fotozelle *f* COMP & DV photocell, phototransistor, DRUCK *(PEC)* photocell, photoelectric cell *(PEC)*, ELEKTRIZ photocell, ELEKTRIZ *(PEC)* photoelectric cell *(PEC)*, ELEKTRONIK *(PEC)* photocell, photoelectric cell, photoelectric tube, phototube, ELEKTROTECH phototube, photovoltaic cell, FERNSEH *(PEC)* photoelectric cell *(PEC)*, FOTO *(PEC)* photocell, photoelectric cell, PHYS *(PEC)* photocell, photoelectric cell *(PEC)*, RAUMFAHRT *Raumschiff* photovoltaic cell, STRAHLPHYS *(PEC)* photocell, photoelectric cell *(PEC)*; **Fotozellen-Registersteuerung** *f* VERPACK photoelectric register control; **Fotozellenrelais** *nt* ELEKTROTECH phototube relay; **Fotozellenverstärker** *m* ELEKTRONIK electron multiplier phototube; **Fotozellenzerhacker** *m* ELEKTRONIK electronic chopper

Foucault-Pendel *nt* PHYS Foucault pendulum

Foucault-Strom *m* ELEKTRIZ eddy current

Foulard *m* TEXTIL pad mangle, *Färben* pad; **Foulardfärbung** *f* TEXTIL pad dyeing

Foulardieren *nt* TEXTIL padding

foulardieren *vt* TEXTIL pad

Fourier: **Fourier-Analyse** *f* ELEKTRONIK, ERGON, MATH, PHYS, TELEKOM Fourier analysis, harmonic analysis; **Fourier-Entwicklung** *f* MATH Fourier series; **Fourier-Integral** *nt* PHYS Fourier integral; **Fourier-Reihe** *f* PHYS Fourier series; **Fourier-Transformation** *f* ELEKTRONIK Fourier transformation, Fourier transform, PHYS Fourier transform, Fourier transformation; **Fourier-Transformationsspektroskopie** *f* PHYS Fourier transform spectroscopy; **Fourier-Transformierte** *f* ELEKTRONIK Fourier transform

FPS *abbr (schnelle Paketvermittlung)* TELEKOM FPS *(fast packet server)*

Fr *(Francium)* CHEMIE Fr *(francium)*

fR *abbr (Resonanzfrequenz)* AKUSTIK, ELEKTRONIK, TELEKOM, WELLPHYS fR *(resonant frequency)*

Frac-Behandlung *f* ERDÖL *Förderung* fracturing

Fracht *f* ERDÖL *Handel, Schiffahrt* freight, TRANS carriage, WASSERTRANS load, *Ladung* cargo; **Fracht- und Passagierschiff** *nt* WASSERTRANS cargo and passenger ship; **Frachtabfertigung** *f* LUFTTRANS cargo handling; **Frachtabfertigungsterminal** *nt* LUFTTRANS cargo terminal; **Frachtaufseher** *m* WASSERTRANS *Handelsmarine* supercargo; **Frachtbehälter** *m* MEERSCHMUTZ scoop

Fracht: **Frachtbrief** *m* LUFTTRANS, TRANS, WASSERTRANS waybill

Frachter *m* WASSERTRANS freighter

Fracht: **Frachtflugzeug** *nt* LUFTTRANS cargo plane, freighter; **Frachtgeld** *nt* TRANS carriage

Frachtgut *nt* EISENBAHN ordinary freight; **Frachtgutwagenladung** *f* TRANS carload (AmE), wagonload (BrE)

Fracht: **Frachthubschrauber** *m* LUFTTRANS cargo helicopter; **Frachtkabine** *f* LUFTTRANS *Flugwesen* cargo compartment; **Frachtkabineneinrichtung** *f* LUFTTRANS *Flugwesen* cargo compartment equipment; **Frachtkabinentür** *f* LUFTTRANS *Flugwesen* cargo compartment door; **Frachtkahn** *m* WASSERTRANS cargo barge; **Frachtkosten** *pl* VERPACK freight rate; **Frachtraum** *m* LUFTTRANS *Flugzeug* hold, RAUMFAHRT *Raumschiff* cargo hold; **Frachtsatzanzeiger** *m* EISENBAHN, WASSERTRANS scale rates

Frachtschiff *nt* TRANS cargo ship, WASSERTRANS cargo ship, dry-cargo ship, freight barge, freighter; **~ mit Fahrgastbeförderung** *nt* TRANS passenger cargo ship

Fracht: **Frachtschlinge** *f* LUFTTRANS *Hubschrauber* cargo sling; **Frachttarif** *m* VERPACK freight rate; **Frachtterminal** *nt* LUFTTRANS cargo terminal; **Frachttonne** *f* METROL freight ton; **Frachtumschlagplatz** *m* LUFTTRANS, WASSERTRANS cargo-handling berth; **Frachtzahlung** *f* EISENBAHN freight payment

Frage/Antwort-Gerät *nt* TELEKOM interrogator-transponder

Fragebogen *m* ERGON questionnaire

Fragmentierung *f* COMP & DV fragmentation

Fraktal *nt* COMP & DV fractal

fraktal: ~e Geometrie *f* GEOM fractal geometry

Fraktil *nt* QUAL fractile

Fraktion *f* ERDÖL *Destillation* fraction

Fraktionierapparat *m* CHEMTECH fractionating apparatus

Fraktionieren *nt* CHEMIE fractionation, CHEMTECH fractional distillation

fraktionierend: ~e Destillation *f* CHEMIE fractionation, CHEMTECH fractional distillation

Fraktionierkolben *m* CHEMTECH distillation flask

Fraktionierkolonne *f* CHEMTECH fractionating column

Fraktioniersäule *f* LABOR *Destillation* fractionation column

fraktioniert: ~e Destillation *f* ERDÖL fractional distillation; **~e Trennung** *f* CHEMIE fractionation

Frame *m* KÜNSTL INT frame

Francis-Turbine *f* NICHTFOSS ENERG Francis turbine

Francium *nt (Fr)* CHEMIE francium *(Fr)*

Franck-Condon: ~sches Prinzip *nt* PHYS Franck-Condon principle

Franck-Hertz: ~scher Versuch *m* PHYS Franck-Hertz experiment

Frangulin *nt* CHEMIE frangulin

Französisch: ~e Norm *f* MASCHINEN French standard;

~e Prägung *f* KER & GLAS French embossing

Franzstandort *m* LUFTTRANS pinpoint

Fräsdorn *m* MASCHINEN cutter arbor, milling cutting arbor; **Fräsdornmutter** *f* FERTIG arbor nut; **Fräsdornstützlager** *nt* FERTIG arbor support; **Fräsdorntraglager** *nt* FERTIG arbor yoke, arbor-supporting bracket, MASCHINEN arbor support

Fräsen *nt* FERTIG, MASCHINEN, TEXTIL *Maschine* milling; ~ **schräger Flächen** *nt* FERTIG angle milling

fräsen *vt* BAU, MASCHINEN mill

Fräser *m* BAU cutter, FERTIG mill, milling cutter, rotary multipoint cutter, MASCHINEN milling cutter, milling worker; ~ **mit eingesetzten Zähnen** *m* MASCHINEN inserted tooth-milling cutter; ~ **mit geraden Zähnen** *m* MASCHINEN milling cutter with straight teeth; ~ **mit grober Zahnteilung** *m* FERTIG coarse-pitch cutter; ~ **mit hinterdrehten Zähnen** *m* MASCHINEN relieved-milling cutter; ~ **mit sägeförmigen Zähnen** *m* MASCHINEN sawtooth cutter; ~ **für Scheibenfedern** *m* MASCHINEN Woodruff key cutter; ~ **mit Spiralzähnen** *m* MASCHINEN milling cutter with spiral teeth; **Fräserabhebung** *f* FERTIG cutter lift, cutter relief; **Fräserdorn** *m* MASCHINEN milling machine arbor; **Fräsermesser** *nt* KER & GLAS cutter blade; **Fräsersatz** *m* FERTIG set of cutters; **Fräserschaft** *f* FERTIG cutter shank; **Fräserschleifmaschine** *f* MASCHINEN cutter grinder; **Fräserstandzeit** *f* FERTIG cutter life; **Fräserwiege** *f* FERTIG cutter cradle

Fräskopf *m* MASCHINEN cutter head, milling head

Fräsmaschine *f* FERTIG milling machine, offset-milling machine, MASCHINEN, MECHAN milling machine; ~ **mit Handvorschub** *f* FERTIG router; **Fräsmaschinendorn** *m* FERTIG milling machine arbor; **Fräsmaschinenständer** *m* FERTIG milling machine column; **Fräsmaschinentisch** *m* MASCHINEN milling machine table, milling table

Frässchnitt *m* FERTIG milling cut

Frässpan *m* FERTIG milling

Frässpindel *f* FERTIG cutter spindle, milling spindle, MASCHINEN cutter mandrel, cutter spindle, milling spindle; **Frässpindelstock** *m* FERTIG cutter head

Frästisch *m* MASCHINEN milling machine table, milling table

Fräsvorrichtung *f* MASCHINEN milling attachment, milling jig

Fräsvorschub *m* FERTIG milling feed

Fräswerkzeug *nt* FERTIG milling tool, MASCHINEN cutter, milling cutter

Fraunhofer: ~**scher Bereich** *m* RAUMFAHRT *Weltraumfunk* Fraunhofer region; ~**sche Beugungserscheinung** *f* PHYS Fraunhofer diffraction; ~**sches Beugungsmuster** *nt* OPTIK Fraunhofer diffraction pattern; ~**sche Linien** *f pl* PHYS Fraunhofer lines

Freeware *f* COMP & DV *Programm* freeware package

Fregatte *f* WASSERTRANS *Marine* frigate

frei[1] *adj* TELEKOM idle; ~ **an Bord** *adj (fob)* ERDÖL *Handel, Schiffahrt,* WASSERTRANS *Seehandel* free on board *(fob)*; ~ **aufliegend** *adj* BAU simply-supported; ~ **geblasen** *adj* KER & GLAS free-blown; ~ **von Geruchsbeeinflussung** *adj* VERPACK odor proof (AmE), odour proof (BrE); ~ **Kai** *adj* WASSERTRANS *Seehandel* free on quay; ~ **Längsseite Schiff** *adj (fas)* WASSERTRANS *Seehandel* free alongside ship *(fas)*; **in** ~**er Strömung** *adj* STRÖMPHYS in free stream; ~ **verstellbar** *adj* MASCHINEN adjustable at will

frei:[2] ~**e Baustelle** *f* BAU delivered site; ~ **belegbare Funktionstaste** *f* COMP & DV soft key; ~ **belegbare Tastatur** *f* COMP & DV soft keyboard; ~**er Betriebskanal** *m* TELEKOM idle-working channel; ~**e elektrische Bewegungsimpedanz** *f* AKUSTIK free electrical motional impedance; ~**es Elektron** *nt* ELEKTRIZ, PHYS, TEILPHYS free electron; ~**e Elektronendichte** *f* STRAHLPHYS free-electron density; ~**e Energie** *f (F)* METALL, PHYS free energy *(F)*; ~**e Energie nach Helmholtz** *f* PHYS Helmholtz free energy, Helmholtz function; ~**e Flüssigkeitsoberfläche** *f* PHYS free surface of liquid; ~**es Format** *nt* COMP & DV free format; ~**es Grundwasser** *nt* WASSERVERSORG free groundwater; ~**er Kanal** *m* TELEKOM clear channel; ~**e Konvektionsströmung** *f* STRÖMPHYS free convection flow; ~**e Ladung** *f* PHYS free charge; ~**e Liste** *f* COMP & DV free list; ~**e Mode** *f* OPTIK unbound mode; ~**e Oberfläche** *f* WASSERTRANS *Schiffkonstruktion* free surface; ~**er Platz** *m* COMP & DV empty slot; ~**es Radikal** *nt* LEBENSMITTEL free radical; ~**er Raum für den Kuppler** *m* EISENBAHN Berne rectangle; ~**er Rotor** *m* LUFTTRANS *Hubschrauber* free rotor; ~**es Schweben** *nt* PHYS levitation; ~**er Schwefel** *m* KUNSTSTOFF free sulfur (AmE), free sulphur (BrE); ~**e Schwingung** *f* AKUSTIK free vibration, ELEKTRIZ, ELEKTRONIK, FERTIG free oscillation, PHYS free oscillation, *mechanisch* free vibration; ~**e Strahlenquelle** *f* KERNTECH free source; ~**er Träger** *m* BAU free beam; ~ **umlaufende vom Fahrtwind getriebene Luftschraube** *f* LUFTTRANS windmilling propeller; ~**e Variable** *f (cf gebundene Variable)* KÜNSTL INT free variable; ~**es Walzenwehr** *nt* NICHTFOSS ENERG free roller sluice gate; ~**e Wärme** *f* THERMOD free heat; ~**er Zugriff** *m* RAUMFAHRT *Weltraumfunk* random access

frei:[3] ~**e Fahrt geben** *vi* EISENBAHN, WASSERTRANS clear the line

Freibiegeversuch *m* FERTIG *Schweißen* free bend test

Freibord *m* ERDÖL ullage, WASSERTRANS *Schiffbau* freeboard; **Freibordhöhe** *f* WASSERTRANS *Schiffkonstruktion* depth for freeboard; **Freibordmarke** *f* WASSERTRANS plimsoll line; **Freibordzuschlag** *m* WASSERTRANS *Schiffkonstruktion* freeboard allowances

freifahrend: ~**e Turbine** *f* LUFTTRANS free turbine

Freifall *m* VERPACK free fall; **Freifallbohrung** *f* BAU free-fall boring, free-fall drilling; **Freifallstanze** *f* BAU free-falling stamp

Freifeld *nt* COMP & DV free field; **Freifeld-Bedingungen** *f pl* AUFNAHME free-field conditions; **Freifeld-Übertragungsfaktor** *m* AUFNAHME free-field response

Freifläche *f* BAU open area, FERTIG tool flank, *Spanung* flank, relief face, LUFTTRANS *Flughafen* clearway, MASCHINEN flank; ~ **am Umfang** *f* FERTIG *Spiralbohrer* body clearance, diametral clearance; ~ **an Fase** *f* FERTIG land clearance; **Freiflächenfase** *f* FERTIG tool flank chamfer; **Freiflächen-Orthogonalebene** *f* FERTIG tool flank orthogonal plane

freiformgeschmiedet *adj* FERTIG hammer-forged, hand-forged

Freiformkurve *f* GEOM free-form curve

Freiformschmieden *nt* FERTIG hammer forging, hammering, MASCHINEN open die forging

freiformschmieden *vt* FERTIG hammer-forge, hand-hammer

Freifräsung: ~ **am Umfang** *f* FERTIG *Spiralbohrer* land clearance

Freigabe *f* COMP & DV release, ELEKTRONIK enabling, LUFTTRANS *Genehmigung* clearance, TELEKOM release, WASSERTRANS *Genehmigung* clearance; ~ **zur Ausführung von Arbeiten** *f* QUAL permit to work; ~ **durch die Flugsicherung** *f* LUFTTRANS air traffic control clearance; **Freigabeauflage** *f* ERDÖL *Recht* relinquishment requirement; **Freigabedauer** *f* LUFTTRANS, WASSERTRANS clearance period; **Freigabeimpuls** *m* COMP & DV, ELEKTRONIK enable pulse; **Freigabeknopf** *m* FERNSEH release button; **Freigabesignal** *nt* COMP & DV enabling signal, ELEKTRONIK enable signal; **Freigabezeit** *f* TRANS green period

freigeben *vt* ELEKTRONIK, KONTROLL enable, MECHAN release, SICHERHEIT approve, TELEKOM enable

freigegeben: **~es Gatter** *nt* ELEKTRONIK enabled gate

freigelegt[1] *adj* ANSTRICH exposed

freigelegt:[2] **~er Schußfaden** *m* TEXTIL loose pick

freigeschaltet: **~er Kanal** *m* TELEKOM blanked channel

freigesetzt: **~e Energie** *f* PHYS released energy; **~e kinetische Energie geladener Teilchen in Materie** *f (K)* PHYS *Kerma* kerma *(K)* kinetic energy released mass; **~e Wärme** *f* HEIZ & KÄLTE released heat

freigestellt: **~e Prüfung** *f* QUAL optional test

Freihafen *m* WASSERTRANS free port

freihalten: sich ~ von *vt* WASSERTRANS *Navigation* steer clear

Freihandel *m* WASSERTRANS *Seehandel* free trade

freihändig: ~ erstellte Zeichnung *f* KONSTZEICH freehand drawing

Freihandlinie *f* KONSTZEICH continuous irregular line, freehand line

Freihandschleifen *nt* MASCHINEN freehand grinding

freihandschmieden *vt* FERTIG hammer

Freiheit: ~ von Einbrandkerben *f* FERTIG *Schweißen* absence of undercutting

Freiheitsgrad *m* ERGON, MASCHINEN, PHYS, QUAL, THERMOD degree of freedom; **Freiheitsgradzahl** *f* PHYS variance

Freikolbengasturbine *f* MASCHINEN free-piston gas turbine

Freikolbenmaschine *f* MASCHINEN free-piston engine

freikreuzen: sich ~ *v refl* WASSERTRANS *absegeln vom Legerwall* claw off

Freilager *nt* WASSERTRANS *Zoll* bonded warehouse

Freilauf *m* MASCHINEN freewheel, MECHAN freewheel mechanism; **Freilauf- und Kuppelungseinheit** *f* LUFTTRANS freewheel and clutch unit; **Freilaufdiode** *f* ELEKTRONIK freewheeling diode

freilaufend: ~er Rotor *m* LUFTTRANS *Hubschrauber* free rotor; **~es Signal** *nt* ELEKTRONIK free-running signal

Freilauf: Freilaufkupplung *f* KFZTECH free engine clutch, overrunning clutch, roller clutch, MASCHINEN freewheel clutch, MECHAN roller clutch; **Freilaufvorrichtung** *f* MASCHINEN freewheel mechanism

freilegen *vt* ANSTRICH expose

Freileitung *f* EISENBAHN overhead line, ELEKTRIZ aerial line, ELEKTROTECH open-wire line, overhead line, TELEKOM overhead line; **Freileitungskabel** *nt* ELEKTROTECH overhead cable, TELEKOM aerial cable; **Freileitungsnetz** *nt* TELEKOM overhead network; **Freileitungssystem** *nt* ELEKTROTECH overhead system; **Freileitungsübertragung** *f* ELEKTROTECH open-wire transmission line

Freiluft *f* BAU open air; **Freiluftkabel** *nt* ELEKTRIZ outdoor cable, overhead cable; **Freiluftkegelresonanz** *f* AUFNAHME free-air cone resonance; **Freiluftleitung** *f* ELEKTRIZ overhead line; **Freiluftquarzoszillator** *m* ELEKTRONIK free-air crystal oscillator; **Freiluftschaltanlage** *f* ELEKTRIZ outdoor switchgear

Freimachung: ~ der Baustelle *f* BAU clearing and grubbing

Freipfeiler *m* BAU pillar

freiprogrammierbar: ~es logisches Feld *nt* COMP & DV field programmable device, field programmable logic array

Freiraumausbreitung *f* RADIO free space propagation

Freiraumgrunddämpfung *f* TELEKOM free space basic loss

freischwebend *adj* MECHAN cantilevered

freischwimmend *adj* WASSERTRANS hull borne

freischwingend: ~er Oszillator *m* ELEKTRONIK free-running oscillator

Freischwingfrequenz *f* ELEKTRONIK free-running frequency

Freisetzung *f* ABFALL discharge, release

Freispeicher *m* COMP & DV heap

freistehend[1] *adj* BAU self-supporting, VERPACK free-standing

freistehend:[2] **~es Gerät** *nt* KONTROLL stand-alone device; **~er Kran** *m* BAU independent crane; **~e Zwischenwand** *f* BAU self-supporting partition

freisteuern: ~ von *vi* WASSERTRANS *Navigation* steer clear

Freistich *m* MASCHINEN undercut

Freistrahlturbine *f* MECHAN impulse turbine

Freistrahlwindkanal *m* PHYS open-jet wind tunnel

freitragend[1] *adj* BAU overhanging

freitragend:[2] **~es Pultdach** *nt* BAU single pitch roof; **~e Treppe** *f* BAU fliers; **~e Wand** *f* BAU cantilevered wall; **~e Windung** *f* RAUMFAHRT *Raumschiff* air core winding

Freiträger *m* FERTIG cantilever beam; **Freiträgertreppe** *f* BAU hanging stairs

Freiwahl *f* TELEKOM hunting

Freiwange *f* BAU face string, outside string

Freiwasser *nt* WASSERVERSORG surplus water

freiwerden *vi* TELEKOM to be released

freiwerdend: ~es Neutron *nt* KERNTECH nascent neutron; **~e Wärme** *f* HEIZ & KÄLTE released heat

Freiwinkel *m* FERTIG back-off clearance, clearance angle, relief angle, MASCHINEN clearance angle, orthogonal clearance, relief angle

Freiziehen *nt* TRANS *Schlamm* debogging

Freizustand *m* COMP & DV idle condition, TELEKOM idle state

Fremdantrieb *m* LUFTTRANS belting-in run

Fremdatom *nt* ELEKTRONIK impurity

fremdbewegt: ~es Kühlmittel *nt* HEIZ & KÄLTE forced-circulated coolant

Fremdemissionen *f pl* UMWELTSCHMUTZ foreign emissions

fremderregt: ~er Dynamo *m* ELEKTROTECH separate excitation, separate-excited dynamo; **~er Generator** *m* ELEKTROTECH separate-excited generator; **~er Magnet** *m* CHEMIE electromagnet

Fremdgeräusch *nt* AUFNAHME extraneous noise

Fremdgeschmack *m* LEBENSMITTEL off-flavour

Fremdkapazität *f* ELEKTROTECH parasitic capacitance

Fremdkomponente *f* ELEKTROTECH parasitic component

Fremdkörper *m* FERTIG fish, LEBENSMITTEL foreign body

Fremdkraftbremse *f* KFZTECH power brake

Fremdkühlung *f* HEIZ & KÄLTE separate cooling; **~ mit Luft** *f* HEIZ & KÄLTE air blast cooling

Fremdorganisation *f* QUAL outside agency

Fremdquelle *f* FERTIG outside source, UMWELTSCHMUTZ foreign source

Fremdscherben *f pl* KER & GLAS foreign cullet

Fremdspannung *f* ELEKTROTECH external voltage; **Fremdspannungsquelle** *f* ELEKTROTECH external voltage source

Fremdstelle *f* QUAL outside agency

Fremdstoff *m* ANSTRICH contaminant, LEBENSMITTEL foreign matter; **Fremdstoffniederschlag** *m* UMWELTSCHMUTZ contamination fallout

Fremdstrom *m* ELEKTROTECH parasitic current

Fremdsynchronisierung *f* ELEKTRONIK external synchronization; **Fremdsynchronisierungseinrichtung** *f* FERNSEH slaving unit

Fremdteil *nt* ELEKTROTECH parasitic component; **Fremdteilzeichnung** *f* KONSTZEICH foreign part drawing

Fremdzufuhr *f* UMWELTSCHMUTZ external input

Frequenz *f (F)* AKUSTIK, AUFNAHME, COMP & DV, ELEKTRONIK, PHYS, RADIO frequency *(f)*; **~ des Grundzustandes** *f* ELEKTRONIK, FERNSEH, RADIO basic state frequency; **~ des übernächsten Kanals** *f* ELEKTRONIK, FERNSEH, RADIO, TELEKOM second channel frequency; **Frequenzabfall** *m* ELEKTRONIK, RADIO, TELEKOM frequency fall-off; **Frequenzabgleich** *m* ELEKTRONIK, FERNSEH, RADIO, TELEKOM frequency adjustment, frequency alignment; **Frequenzabstand** *m* ELEKTRONIK frequency separation, mode separation, RADIO, TELEKOM frequency separation; **Frequenzabstimmung** *f* ELEKTRONIK, RADIO, TELEKOM frequency tuning; **Frequenzabtastung** *f* ELEKTRONIK, RADIO, TELEKOM frequency scanning; **Frequenzabweichung** *f* COMP & DV frequency deviation; **Frequenzagilität** *f* ELEKTRONIK, FERNSEH, RADIO, TELEKOM frequency agility; **Frequenzanalysator** *m* ELEKTRONIK wave analyser (BrE), wave analyzer (AmE); **Frequenzauflösung** *f* ELEKTRONIK, RADIO, TELEKOM frequency resolution; **Frequenzaufnahme** *f* ELEKTRONIK, RADIO, TELEKOM frequency record; **Frequenzauswanderung** *f* ELEKTRONIK *bei Belastung*, RADIO frequency pulling, TELEKOM frequency pulling, frequency drift; **Frequenzband** *nt* ELEKTRONIK, FERNSEH frequency band, RADIO frequency band, waveband, TELEKOM frequency band; **Frequenzbandentstörungsfilter** *nt* COMP & DV band-rejection filter; **Frequenzbandsperrfilter** *nt* COMP & DV band-stop filter; **Frequenzbereich** *m* AKUSTIK, AUFNAHME *von Mikrofonen*, COMP & DV, ELEKTRONIK, RADIO, TELEKOM frequency band, frequency domain, frequency range, WELLPHYS waveband; **Frequenzcharakteristik** *f* TELEKOM frequency characteristic; **Frequenzdekade** *f* TELEKOM synthesizer; **Frequenzdemodulation** *f* ELEKTRONIK, RADIO, TELEKOM frequency demodulation; **Frequenzdemodulator** *m* ELEKTRONIK, RADIO, TELEKOM frequency demodulator, frequency detector; **Frequenzdemodulator mit Rückkoppelung** *m* RADIO frequency compressive feedback demodulator; **Frequenzdiversität** *f* ELEKTRONIK, RADIO, TELEKOM frequency diversity; **Frequenzdrift** *f* ELEKTRONIK, TELEKOM frequency drift; **Frequenzeicher** *m* ELEKTRONIK, FERNSEH frequency calibrator; **Frequenzeinstellung** *f* ELEKTRONIK, FERNSEH, RADIO, TELEKOM frequency adjustment, frequency setting; **Frequenzentkoppelung** *f* ELEKTRONIK, RADIO, TELEKOM frequency decoupling; **Frequenzfenster in Erdatmosphäre** *nt* PHYS, STRAHLPHYS atmospheric window; **Frequenzgang** *m* AKUSTIK response, COMP & DV, ELEKTRONIK, RADIO, TELEKOM, WELLPHYS frequency response; **Frequenzgangkurve** *f* ELEKTRONIK, RADIO, TELEKOM frequency response curve

frequenzgesteuert: ~e Antenne *f* ELEKTRONIK, RADIO, TELEKOM frequency scanner

frequenzgeteilt: ~es Vermittlungssystem *nt* ELEKTRONIK, RADIO, TELEKOM frequency division switching system

Frequenz: **Frequenzgrenze** *f* ELEKTRONIK, RADIO, TELEKOM frequency cut-off; **Frequenzgruppe** *f* AKUSTIK critical band; **Frequenzgruppenbreite** *f* AKUSTIK critical band width; **Frequenzgruppenintensität** *f* AKUSTIK critical band intensity; **Frequenzgruppenpegel** *m* AKUSTIK critical band level; **Frequenzhalbierschaltung** *f* ELEKTRONIK *Schaltkreistechnik* binary counter; **Frequenzhub** *m* ELEKTRONIK, RADIO frequency deviation, frequency sweep, RAUMFAHRT *Weltraumfunk* deviation, TELEKOM frequency sweep, *Frequenzmodulation* frequency deviation; **Frequenzkanal** *m* ELEKTROTECH channel; **Frequenzkennlinie** *f* ELEKTRONIK, RADIO, TELEKOM gain-frequency characteristic; **Frequenzkompensation** *f* AUFNAHME, ELEKTRONIK frequency compensation; **Frequenzkomponente** *f* AUFNAHME, ELEKTRONIK frequency component; **Frequenzkontrollgerät** *nt* PHYS wavemeter; **Frequenzlücke** *f* ELEKTRONIK, RADIO, TELEKOM frequency gap; **Frequenzmeßbrücke** *f* GERÄT frequency-measuring bridge; **Frequenzmesser** *m* ELEKTRONIK frequency meter, PHYS wavemeter, RADIO, TELEKOM frequency meter, WASSERTRANS *Funk* wavemeter; **Frequenzmodulation** *f (FM)* COMP & DV, ELEKTRONIK, PHYS, RADIO, TELEKOM frequency modulation *(FM)*; **Frequenzmodulationsrauschen** *nt* ELEKTRONIK, RADIO, TELEKOM frequency modulation noise; **Frequenzmodulator** *m* ELEKTRONIK, RADIO, TELEKOM frequency modulator

frequenzmoduliert *adj* ELEKTRONIK frequency-modulated

Frequenz: **Frequenzmultiplexverfahren** *nt* ELEKTRONIK, RADIO, TELEKOM FDM, frequency division multiplexing; **Frequenznachführung** *f* ELEKTRONIK, RADIO, TELEKOM frequency tracking; **Frequenznormal** *nt* ELEKTRONIK, RADIO, TELEKOM frequency standard; **Frequenzökonomie** *f* TELEKOM spectrum efficiency; **Frequenzquelle** *f* ELEKTRONIK, RADIO, TELEKOM frequency source; **Frequenzrauschen** *nt* ELEKTRONIK, RADIO, TELEKOM frequency noise; **Frequenzregelung** *f* ELEKTRONIK, RADIO, TELEKOM frequency control, frequency regulation, frequency stabilization; **Frequenzrelais** *nt* ELEKTRONIK, RADIO, TELEKOM frequency relay; **Frequenzrücklauf** *m* ELEKTRONIK, RADIO, TELEKOM frequency retrace; **Frequenzschieben** *nt* ELEKTRONIK, RADIO, TELEKOM frequency pushing; **Frequenzschwankungen** *f pl* AKUSTIK wow

frequenzselektiv: ~es Filter *nt* ELEKTRONIK, RADIO, TELEKOM frequency-selective filter; **~e Flüssigkristallanzeige** *f* ELEKTRONIK dichroic LCD; **~er Verstärker** *m* ELEKTRONIK, RADIO, TELEKOM frequency-selective amplifier

Frequenz: **Frequenzskala** *f* ELEKTRONIK, RADIO, TELEKOM frequency scale; **Frequenzspektrum** *nt*

AUFNAHME, COMP & DV, ELEKTRONIK, RADIO, TELE-KOM frequency spectrum; **Frequenzsprungverfahren** *nt* ELEKTRONIK, RADIO, TELEKOM frequency hopping; **Frequenzstabilisierung** *f* ELEKTRONIK, RADIO, TELE-KOM frequency stabilization; **Frequenzstromwandler** *m* ELEKTRONIK, RADIO, TELEKOM frequency-current converter; **Frequenzstufe** *f* AKUSTIK step difference limen, ELEKTRONIK, RADIO, TELEKOM frequency difference limen; **Frequenzsynthese** *f* ELEKTRONIK, RADIO, TELEKOM frequency synthesis; **Frequenzteil-bereich** *m* ELEKTRONIK, RADIO, TELEKOM frequency subband; **Frequenzteiler** *m* ELEKTRIZ, RADIO, TELE-KOM frequency divider; **Frequenztonhöhe** *f* ELEKTRONIK, RADIO, TELEKOM frequency pitch; **Fre-quenzüberdeckung** *f* ELEKTRONIK, RADIO, TELEKOM frequency coverage; **Frequenzüberschneidung** *f* ELEKTRONIK, RADIO, TELEKOM frequency overlap; **Frequenzübertragungsverhalten** *nt* ELEKTRONIK, RA-DIO, TELEKOM, WELLPHYS frequency response; **Frequenzüberwachung** *f* ELEKTRONIK, RADIO, TELE-KOM frequency monitoring; **Frequenzumformer** *m* COMP & DV frequency changer, ELEKTRONIK, RADIO, TELEKOM frequency transformer; **Frequenzumformer-Unterwerk** *nt* ELEKTRIZ substation for frequency conversion; **Frequenzumkehrung** *f* ELEKTRONIK, RA-DIO, TELEKOM frequency inversion; **Frequenzumsetzer** *m* ELEKTRONIK, RADIO, TELEKOM frequency converter; **Frequenzumsetzung** *f* ELEKTRO-NIK, RADIO, TELEKOM frequency conversion, frequency translation, frequency transposition; **Fre-quenzumtastung** *f (FSK)* COMP & DV, ELEKTRONIK, RADIO, TELEKOM frequency shift keying *(FSK)*; **Fre-quenzunsicherheitsband** *nt* ELEKTRONIK, RADIO, TELEKOM frequency uncertainty band; **Frequenzun-terdrückung** *f* ELEKTRONIK, RADIO, TELEKOM frequency rejection; **Frequenzverdoppler** *m* ELEKTRO-NIK, RADIO, TELEKOM frequency doubler; **Frequenzverluste** *m pl* ELEKTRONIK, RADIO, TELEKOM frequency losses; **Frequenzversatz** *m* COMP & DV fre-quency shift, ELEKTRONIK, RADIO, TELEKOM frequency departure, frequency offset; **Frequenzver-schachtelung** *f* ELEKTRONIK, RADIO, TELEKOM frequency interlace; **Frequenzverschiebung** *f* COMP & DV frequency drift, ELEKTRONIK, RADIO, TELEKOM frequency displacement, frequency shift; **Frequenz-verschiebung durch Dopplereffekt** *f* RADIO Doppler shift; **Frequenzverteilung** *f* COMP & DV, ELEKTRONIK, TELEKOM frequency distribution; **Frequenzvervielfa-cher** *m* ELEKTRONIK frequency multiplier, harmonic generator, RADIO, TELEKOM frequency multiplier; **Frequenzvervielfachung** *f* ELEKTRONIK frequency multiplication, harmonic generation, RADIO, TELEKOM frequency multiplication; **Frequenzverviel-fachungsklystron** *nt* ELEKTRONIK, RADIO, TELEKOM frequency multiplier klystron; **Frequenzvervielfa-chungs-Reaktanzdiode** *f* ELEKTRONIK harmonic generator varactor; **Frequenzverzerrung** *f* ELEKTRO-NIK, RADIO, TELEKOM frequency distortion; **Frequenzvielfach-Zugriffsverfahren** *nt* ELEKTRONIK, RADIO, TELEKOM FDMA, frequency division multi-ple access; **Frequenzwahlschalter** *m* ELEKTRONIK, RADIO, TELEKOM frequency selector; **Frequenzwande-rung eines Oszillators** *f* ELEKTRONIK oscillator drift; **Frequenzwandler** *m* ELEKTRONIK, RADIO, TELEKOM frequency converter; **Frequenzwandlung** *f* ELEKTRO-NIK, RADIO, TELEKOM frequency conversion;

Frequenzwechsel *m* ELEKTRONIK frequency change; **Frequenzwechsler** *m* ELEKTRONIK frequency chan-ger; **Frequenzweiche** *f* AUFNAHME crossover network, ELEKTRONIK, RADIO frequency-separating filter, TELE-KOM diplexer, frequency-separating filter; **Frequenzwiederbenutzung** *f* ELEKTRONIK, RADIO, TE-LEKOM frequency reuse; **Frequenzwiederverwendung** *f* ELEKTRONIK, RADIO, TELEKOM frequency reuse; **Fre-quenzwobbelung** *f* ELEKTRONIK frequency sweep, wobbling, RADIO, TELEKOM frequency sweep; **Fre-quenzzähler** *m* ELEKTRONIK frequency counter, GERÄT counter, RADIO, TELEKOM frequency counter; **Frequenzzuteilung** *f* RADIO *Frequenzplan*, TELEKOM frequency allocation; **Frequenzzuweisung** *f* ELEKTRO-NIK, FERNSEH frequency allocation

Fresnel: **~sche Beugung** *f* PHYS Fresnel diffraction; **~sches Beugungsdiagramm** *nt* TELEKOM Fresnel dif-fraction pattern; **~sches Beugungsmuster** *nt* OPTIK Fresnel diffraction pattern; **~sche Beugungszone** *f* RADIO, TELEKOM Fresnel zone; **~sches Biprisma** *nt* PHYS Fresnel biprism; **~sches Gebiet** *nt* TELEKOM Fresnel region; **~sche Gleichungen** *f pl* PHYS Fresnel's formulae; **~sche Linse** *f* FOTO, PHYS Fresnel lens; **~sche Reflexion** *f* OPTIK, TELEKOM Fresnel reflection; **~sche Reflexionsmethode** *f* TELEKOM Fresnel reflec-tion method; **~scher Spiegel** *m* PHYS Fresnel mirrors; **~sche Zone** *f* RADIO, TELEKOM Fresnel zone

Fressen:[1] **das ~ verhindernd** *adj* MECHAN antiseize

Fressen[2] *nt* MASCHINEN seizing, seizure

fressen[1] *vt* ANSTRICH *Korrosion, Reiben* fret, FERTIG scuff

fressen[2] *vi* MASCHINEN seize

Frettbohrer *m* BAU auger gimlet

Freunde: **~ der Erde** *m pl* UMWELTSCHMUTZ Friends Of The Earth

friemeln *vt* MASCHINEN cross-roll

Friemelwalzwerk *nt* FERTIG reeler

frierend *adj* THERMOD freezing

Fries *m* BAU molding (AmE), moulding (BrE), *Tür, Fenster* style

Friktion *f* MASCHINEN, PAPIER friction

friktioniert *adj* PAPIER friction-glazed

Friktion: **Friktionsfeder** *f* MASCHINEN friction spring; **Friktionskalander** *m* PAPIER friction-glazing calender; **Friktionsrolle** *f* PAPIER friction reel

Frisch- *pref* LEBENSMITTEL fresh

frisch:[1] **~ vom Faß gezapft** *adj* LEBENSMITTEL drawn from the wood

frisch:[2] **~er Brennstoff** *m* KERNTECH fresh fuel; **~er Uran-Brennstoff** *m* KERNTECH fresh uranium

Frisch-: **Frischbeton** *m* BAU green concrete; **Frisch-dampf** *m* HYDRAUL, KERNTECH, MASCHINEN, THERMOD live steam; **Frischdampfinjektor** *m* HY-DRAUL live steam injector

Frischen *nt* FERTIG *Stahl* oxidation of impurities

frischen *vt* FERTIG decarburize, METALL refine

Frisch: **Frischhaltefolie** *f* VERPACK cling film; **Frischhal-temittel** *nt* LEBENSMITTEL *Brot* antistaling agent; **Frischluft** *f* HEIZ & KÄLTE fresh air; **Frischlüfter** *m* HEIZ & KÄLTE forced-draft fan (AmE), forced-draught fan (BrE); **Frischluftkühlung** *f* HEIZ & KÄLTE fresh-air cooling; **Frischölschmierung** *f* MASCHINEN total loss lubrication; **Frischschlamm** *m* ABFALL fresh sludge

Frischwasser *nt* ABFALL, WASSERTRANS, WASSER-VERSORG freshwater; **Frischwassererzeuger** *m* WASSERTRANS freshwater condenser; **Frischwasser-**

freibord *m* WASSERTRANS *Schiffkonstruktion* freshwater freeboard

Frist *f* PATENT time limit

Fritte *f* KER & GLAS frit

Fritten *nt* KER & GLAS *der Charge* fritting; **Frittenglasur** *f* KER & GLAS fritted glaze

Frittezone *f* KER & GLAS fritting zone

Frittung *f* CHEMIE *Geologie* vitrification

Front *f* COMP & DV, KONSTZEICH front; **Frontabschnitt** *m* KONSTZEICH frontal section

Frontalbereich *m* MASCHINEN frontal area

Frontalzusammenstoß *m* KFZTECH, RAUMFAHRT *Raumschiff*, SICHERHEIT head-on collision

Front: **Frontantrieb** *m* MECHAN front wheel drive; **Front-End-Computer** *m* COMP & DV front-end computer; **Front-End-System** *nt* COMP & DV front-end system

Front: **Frontlader-Tieflöffelkombination** *f* BAU *Straßenbau* loader backhoe; **Frontlenker** *m* KFZTECH *Karosserie* cab over engine; **Frontlinse** *f* FOTO *Objektiv* front element; **Frontmotor** *m* KFZTECH front engine, front-mounted engine; **Frontplatte** *f* FERNSEH face plate, FOTO lens panel, GERÄT front panel, MASCHINEN breast plate, front panel, panel; **Frontschaufellader** *m* MEERSCHMUTZ front-end loader; **Frontscheibe** *f* KFZTECH, RAUMFAHRT *Raumschiff* windscreen (BrE), windshield (AmE); **Frontschott** *nt* TRANS break-bulkhead; **Frontseite** *f* MASCHINEN face; **Frontspalt** *m* AKUSTIK front gap; **Fronttafel** *f* GERÄT *Gerät* front panel; **Frontwalze** *f* PAPIER face roll; **Frontwand** *f* BAU face wall

Froschbeinwicklung *f* ELEKTROTECH frog-leg winding

Frost *m* KOHLEN frost

frostanfällig: **nicht ~er Boden** *m* KOHLEN nonfrost susceptible soil

Frostanfälligkeit *f* KOHLEN frost susceptibility; **Frostaufbruch** *m* KOHLEN frost heave

frostbeständig: **~er Boden** *m* KOHLEN frost-resistant soil

Frost: **Frosteindringtiefe** *f* KOHLEN frost penetration depth

frostfrei: **~e Tiefe** *f* KOHLEN frost-free level

Frost: **Frostgrenze** *f* KOHLEN frost limit; **Frostpunkt** *m* HEIZ & KÄLTE ice point; **Frostschadstelle** *f* KOHLEN frost boil

Frostschutz *m* BAU, KFZTECH *Kühlsystem* antifreeze

Frostschutz- *pref* HEIZE & KÄLTE anti-freeze; **Frostschutzmittel** *nt* HEIZ & KÄLTE antifreeze agent, KFZTECH antifreeze, VERPACK frost-preventive agent; **Frostschutzpapier** *nt* PAPIER antifreeze paper; **Frostschutzschicht** *f* BAU *Tiefbau* subbase; **Frostschutzwächter** *m* HEIZ & KÄLTE antifreeze detector

froststabilisiert: **~er Latex** *m* KUNSTSTOFF freeze-thaw resistant latex

Frost: **Frost-Tau-Beständigkeit** *f* HEIZ & KÄLTE freeze-thaw resistance

Frouden: **~sche Zahl** *f (F)* HYDRAUL, PHYS *Strömungslehre* Froude number *(F)*

Fruchtfleisch *nt* LEBENSMITTEL pulp

Fruchtzucker *m* LEBENSMITTEL fructose, laevulose (BrE), levulose (AmE)

Fructosan *nt* CHEMIE fructosan, inulin

Fructose *f* CHEMIE, LEBENSMITTEL fructose

früh: **~e Veröffentlichung** *f* PATENT early publication; **~ere Anmeldung** *f* PATENT earlier application; **~ere Priorität** *f* PATENT earlier priority

Frühausfall *m* ELEKTROTECH early failure, KONTROLL wear-in failure

frühhochfest: **~er Zement** *m* BAU rapid-hardening cement

Frühjahrs-Tagundnachtgleiche *f* RAUMFAHRT vernal equinox

Frühlingsmaximum *nt* UMWELTSCHMUTZ spring maximum of fallout

Frühlingssäureschock *m* UMWELTSCHMUTZ spring acid shock

Frühstart *m* FERNSEH early start; **Frühstartbild** *nt* FERNSEH early-start video; **Frühstartton** *m* FERNSEH early-start audio

Frühwarnradar *nt* WASSERTRANS early-warning radar

Frühzündung *f* KFZTECH advance, advanced ignition, premature ignition, LUFTTRANS ignition advance, spark advance

FS *abbr* COMP & DV *(Fernschreiber)* TTY *(teletypewriter)*, LUFTTRANS *(Flugsicherung)* ATC *(air traffic control)*, MASCHINEN *(Festsitz)* force fit, TELEKOM *(Fernschreiber)* TTY *(teletypewriter)*

F-Schicht *f* PHYS Appleton layer, F layer, RADIO F layer

FSK *abbr* *(Frequenzumtastung)* COMP & DV, ELEKTRONIK, RADIO, TELEKOM FSK *(frequency shift keying)*

FSK-Modem *m* ELEKTRONIK FSK modem

FS: **FS-Nachrichtenblatt** *nt* LUFTTRANS aeronautical information circular; **FS-Nachrichtendienst** *m* LUFTTRANS aeronautical information service

FSTV *abbr* *(Breitbandfernsehen)* FERNSEH FSTV *(fast-scan television)*

Fuchs *m* KER & GLAS flue

Fuchson *nt* CHEMIE fuchsone

Fuchs: **Fuchsschwanz** *m* BAU handsaw, tenon saw, MASCHINEN handsaw

Fucose *f* CHEMIE fucose

Fucosterin *nt* CHEMIE fucosterol

Fucoxanthin *nt* CHEMIE fucoxanthin

Fuge *f* BAU joint, meeting, mortise, seam, FERTIG interstice, KERNTECH *Schweißen* joint, MASCHINEN, MECHAN gap; **~ auf Fuge** *f* BAU *Mauerwerk* straight joint

Fugeisen *nt* BAU jointer

Fuge: **Fugenflanke** *f* FERTIG joint face; **Fugenhobel** *m* BAU gouging plane; **Fugenhobeln** *nt* FERTIG gas gouging, gouging, groove cutting

fugenhobeln *vt* FERTIG torch-gouge

Fuge: **Fugenmasse** *f* BAU joint sealer; **Fugenmörtelbrett** *nt* BAU hawk; **Fugennaht** *f* FERTIG groove weld; **Fugenschneidegerät** *nt* BAU joint cutter; **Fugenvergußmasse** *f* BAU sealing compound; **Fugenvorbereitung** *f* FERTIG *Schweißen* edge preparation, plate-edge preparation

Fügung *f* FERTIG mating

fühlbar: **~e Kühlwirkung** *f* HEIZ & KÄLTE sensible-cooling effect; **~e Wärme** *f* HEIZ & KÄLTE sensible heat; **~e Wärmelast** *f* HEIZ & KÄLTE sensible heat load

Fühler *m* ELEKTRIZ pick-up, probe, GERÄT, KOHLEN probe, MASCHINEN feeler, probe, tracer pin, OPTIK *Meßglied* detector, RAUMFAHRT *Weltraumfunk*, WASSERTRANS *Meßinstrumente* sensor; **~ und Geber** *m* TELEKOM scanner distributor; **Fühlerlehre** *f* KERNTECH feeler gage (AmE), feeler gauge (BrE), MASCHINEN feeler gage (AmE), feeler gauge (BrE), thickness gage (AmE), thickness gauge (BrE)

Fühlglied *nt* RAUMFAHRT *Weltraumfunk* sensor

Fühllehre *f* KFZTECH *Werkzeug*, METROL feeler gage

(AmE), feeler gauge (BrE)

Fühlschiene *f* EISENBAHN locking bar

Fühlsensor *m* GERÄT tactile sensor

Fühluhr *f* METROL dial indicating gage (AmE), dial indicating gauge (BrE)

führen[1] *vt* HYDRAUL gate, LUFTTRANS pilot, steer, TRANS steer, WASSERTRANS steer, *Schiff* con, handle, navigate

führen[2] *vi* LUFTTRANS, TRANS steer, WASSERTRANS steer, *Schiff* navigate

Führerschein *m* KFZTECH *Rechtsvorschriften* driver's licence (BrE), driver's license (AmE)

Führerstand *m* EISENBAHN cab, driver's cab, KFZTECH *Karosserie* cab; **Führerstandssignal** *nt* EISENBAHN cab signaling (AmE), cab signalling (BrE)

Fuhrlohn *m* TRANS cartage

Fuhrpark *m* BAU rolling stock

Führschraube *f* MECHAN lead screw

Führung *f* BAU *Schloss* forcing, ELEKTRIZ *Kabelrohr, Schutzrohr* conduit, HYDRAUL *Turbine*, KONTROLL guide, MASCHINEN guide, guiding, slide bar, PAPIER guide; **~ für Luftschraubenblatt** *f* LUFTTRANS *Hubschrauber* blade sleeve

Führungen *f pl* KER & GLAS guides, MASCHINEN ways

Führung: **Führungsantenne** *f* RAUMFAHRT *Raumschiff* guidance antenna; **Führungsbahn** *f* FERTIG bearing, MASCHINEN guideway, ways; **Führungsbereich** *m* REGELUNG range of command; **Führungsblock** *m* MASCHINEN guide block; **Führungsbuchse** *f* FERNSEH female guide, FERTIG adaptor bushing, KERNTECH guide bushing, KFZTECH pilot bushing, MASCHINEN guide bush; **Führungsempfänger** *m* RAUMFAHRT *Raumschiff* guidance receiver; **Führungsfase** *f* FERTIG *Spiralbohrer* land; **Führungsfehler** *m* FERNSEH guide errors; **Führungsgestell** *nt* MASCHINEN die set; **Führungsgröße** *f* REGELUNG reference variable; **Führungslager** *nt* KFZTECH pilot bearing, MASCHINEN guide bearing; **Führungsleiste** *f* FERTIG *Spitzenlosschleife* plate, MASCHINEN guide rail, work rest blade; **Führungslenker** *m* KFZTECH *Aufhängung* radius arm; **Führungslicht** *nt* FOTO key light; **Führungslineal** *nt* FERTIG fence, MASCHINEN gib; **Führungsloch** *nt* COMP & DV feed hole, sprocket hole; **Führungsmagnet** *m* TRANS guidance magnet; **Führungsmeißel** *m* ERDÖL *Bohrtechnik* pilot bit; **Führungsnase** *f* MECHAN locating key; **Führungsnavigationssystem** *nt* RAUMFAHRT *Raumschiff* guidance navigation system; **Führungsplatte** *f* MASCHINEN guide plate; **Führungspolster** *nt* TRANS guidance cushion; **Führungsprismen** *nt pl* FERTIG vees; **Führungspunkte** *m pl* DRUCK dot leaders; **Führungsräder** *nt pl* TRANS guide wheels; **Führungsring** *m* HYDRAUL guide ring; **Führungsrohr** *nt* MASCHINEN guide tube; **Führungsrolle** *f* FERTIG *Bandsäge* guide roller, MASCHINEN jockey, jockey pulley, jockey roller, jockey wheel, MECHAN jockey pulley, TEXTIL guide roller, WASSERTRANS *Decksausrüstung* fairlead; **Führungssäule** *f* MASCHINEN guide pillar; **Führungsschaft** *m* FERTIG rear pilot, *Reibahle* back pilot; **Führungsscheibe** *f* MASCHINEN guide, guide pulley; **Führungsschiene** *f* EISENBAHN guide rail, FERTIG *Meßschieber* beam, MASCHINEN guide bar, work rest blade; **Führungsschiff** *nt* WASSERTRANS *Marine* command ship; **Führungsschlitten** *m* MASCHINEN pilot carriage; **Führungsschnitt** *m* FERTIG subpress die; **Führungsstange** *f* BAU *Ramme* guide pole, MASCHINEN guide bar, slide bar, TEXTIL guide bar; **Führungsstein** *m* MASCHINEN slide block; **Führungs-**

stift *m* MASCHINEN box pin, guide pin, MECHAN alignment pin, guide pin; **Führungsverhalten** *nt* REGELUNG command action; **Führungswalze** *f* TEXTIL guide roller; **Führungswelle** *f* MECHAN idler; **Führungszapfen** *m* ELEKTROTECH *Röhre* aligning plug, FERTIG teat (AmE), *Reibahle* pilot, MASCHINEN guide pin, pilot, pilot pin; **Führungszentrum** *nt* TELEKOM management center (AmE), management centre (BrE)

Fuhrunternehmen *nt* TRANS forwarding agent

Fuhrunternehmer *m* TRANS road haulier

Fuhrwerk *nt* KFZTECH carriage

Füll- *pref* ELEKTROTECH, KOHLEN, VERPACK filling; **Füllapparat** *m* VERPACK feeder; **Füllart der Deponie** *f* ABFALL tip-filling method; **Fülldichte** *f* KOHLEN bulk density; **Fülldüse** *f* RAUMFAHRT *Raumschiff* nozzle; **Fülleinrichtung** *f* VERPACK feeding device, filling device; **Füllelement** *nt* ELEKTROTECH wet cell; **Füllelemente** *nt pl* HEIZ & KÄLTE infill panels

Füllen: **~ des Ofens** *nt* KER & GLAS *vor Beginn des Schmelzvorgangs* filling the furnace

füllen *vt* KER & GLAS, TRANS fill

Fuller-Bonnot-Luftstromkegelmühle *f* KOHLEN Fuller-Bonnot mill

Fullererde *f* BAU Fuller's earth; **Fullerkreide** *f* BAU Fuller's chalk

Füll-: **Füllfaktor** *m* TELEKOM filling coefficient; **Füllgrad der Schallplatte** *m* AUFNAHME *Rillenabstand* groove spacing; **Füllhahn** *m* FERTIG feed cock; **Füllhöhe** *f* MASCHINEN filling level; **Füllholz** *nt* KER & GLAS packing piece

füllig: **~er Griff** *m* TEXTIL full handle

Füll-: **Fülligkeit** *f* TEXTIL *Garn* bulk; **Füllkit** *m* FERTIG beaumontage; **Füllkoksäule** *f* KOHLEN coke bed

Füllkörperabscheider: *m* UMWELTSCHMUTZ packed-bed scrubber; **Füllkörperkolonne** *f* CHEMTECH *Destillation, Absorption* packed column, packed tower, ERDÖL *Raffinerie* packed column; **Füllkörpersäule** *f* CHEMTECH packed column, packed tower

Füll-: **Füllmaschine** *f* MASCHINEN filler, filling machine; **Füllmaschine bis zur Dichtheitsgrenze** *f* VERPACK density-filling machine; **Füllmaterial** *nt* KERNTECH filling, filling material, TEXTIL filling; **Fülloch** *nt* VERPACK filling hole; **Füllöffnung** *f* MECHAN, VERPACK filling hole; **Füllpunkt** *m* KER & GLAS filling point

Füllraum *m* FERTIG *Plaste* pot; **Füllraum-Abquetschwerkzeug** *nt* KUNSTSTOFF semipositive mold (AmE), semipositive mould (BrE); **Füllraumwerkzeug** *nt* KUNSTSTOFF positive mold (AmE), positive mould (BrE)

Füll-: **Füllrohr** *nt* WASSERTRANS filling pipe; **Füllschlauchverbindung** *f* ERDÖL feed hose union; **Füllsender** *m* FERNSEH booster station; **Füllspant** *m* WASSERTRANS filling frame

Füllstand *m* BAU level, ERDÖL *Behälter, Tanks* liquid level, GERÄT level, VERPACK fill level, level of filling; **Füllstandanzeige** *f* KERNTECH level meter; **Füllstandsanzeigegerät** *nt* GERÄT indicating level meter; **Füllstandsanzeiger** *m* BAU level indicator, GERÄT filling level indicator, level indicator, liquid level indicator; **Füllstandsmeßgerät** *nt* GERÄT level gage (AmE), level gauge (BrE); **Füllstandsmessung** *f* GERÄT level measurement; **Füllstandswächter** *m* GERÄT level indicator; **Füllstandüberwachung** *f* VERPACK liquid level control

Füll-: **Füllstoff** *m* ELEKTROTECH, KER & GLAS, KUNST-

STOFF filler; **Füllstück** *nt* ELEKTRIZ filler; **Füllstutzen** *m* VERPACK filling nozzle; **Fülltrichter** *m* MECHAN hopper; **Füllung** *f* ELEKTROTECH charge, KER & GLAS fill, LEBENSMITTEL *Fleisch* stuffing, MASCHINEN admission, MECHAN batch; **Füllzeichen** *nt* COMP & DV filler, filler character, gap character, pad, DRUCK filler; **Füllziffer** *f* COMP & DV gap digit; **Füllzylinder** *m* FERTIG hopper

Fulminat *nt* CHEMIE fulminate

Fulven *nt* CHEMIE fulvene

Fumar- *pref* CHEMIE fumaric

Fundament *nt* BAU base, base plate, foundation, DRUCK bed, forme bed, KOHLEN foundation, PAPIER basement

fundamental: **~e Kraft** *f* TEILPHYS *Wechselwirkung* fundamental force

Fundamentalmode *f* OPTIK fundamental mode

Fundament: **Fundamentanker** *m* BAU anchor bolt; **Fundamentblock** *m* BAU footing block, foundation block; **Fundamentgewölbe** *nt* BAU inverted arch; **Fundamentkonstruktion** *f* BAU substructure; **Fundamentplatte** *f* BAU bottom plate, foundation plate, KOHLEN raft, MASCHINEN bed plate; **Fundamentschraube** *f* BAU foundation bolt, lag screw; **Fundamentzeichnung** *f* KONSTZEICH foundation drawing

Fünf *f* MATH five

fünfatomig *adj* CHEMIE pentatomic

Fünf: **Fünfeck** *nt* GEOM pentagon

fünfeckig *adj* GEOM pentagonal

Fünf: **Fünfermarkierung** *f* QUAL tally

fünfflächig *adj* GEOM pentahedral

Fünf: **Fünfgittermischröhre** *f* ELEKTROTECH pentagrid converter; **Fünfgitterröhre** *f* ELEKTRONIK pentode

fünfkantig: **~es Räumwerkzeug** *nt* MASCHINEN five-sided broach

Fünf: **Fünfkantmutter** *f* MASCHINEN pentagon nut

fünfschichtig: **~e Sperrfolie** *f* VERPACK five-layer barrier film

fünfstufig: **~e Ganztonleiter** *f* AKUSTIK pentatonic scale

fünfte *adj* MATH fifth

Fünf: **Fünftel** *nt* MATH fifth

fünfwertig[1] *adj* CHEMIE pentavalent, quinquevalent

fünfwertig:[2] **~es Element** *nt* CHEMIE pentad

Fünf: **Fünfwertigkeit** *f* CHEMIE pentavalence, quinquevalence

50%-Punkt: **~ der Annahmekennlinie** *m* QUAL point of control; **~ der OC-Kurve** *m* QUAL point of control

Fungistatikum *nt* LEBENSMITTEL fungistat

Fungizid *nt* CHEMIE, KUNSTSTOFF fungicide

Funk *m* RADIO radio; **Funkamateur** *m* RADIO ham, TELEKOM radio amateur; **Funkanflughilfen** *f pl* LUFTTRANS radio approach aids; **Funkantenne** *f* KFZTECH *Zubehör*, RADIO, TRANS radio aerial (BrE), radio antenna (AmE); **Funkbake** *f* LUFTTRANS, WASSERTRANS *Seezeichen* radio beacon; **Funkbereich** *m* LUFTTRANS, RADIO, TRANS radio range; **Funkbereichskennzahl** *f* TELEKOM area code; **Funkbetrieb** *m* RAUMFAHRT *Weltraumfunk* operation; **Funkbrücke** *f* LUFTTRANS, TRANS, WASSERTRANS radio link; **Funkdienst** *m* RAUMFAHRT *Weltraumfunk* service

Funke *m* ELEKTRIZ, ELEKTROTECH, KER & GLAS, PHYS spark

Funk: **Funkeinrichtung** *f* LUFTTRANS, RADIO, TRANS, WASSERTRANS radio facility; **Funkeleffekt** *m* ELEKTRONIK Schottky effect; **Funkelfeuer** *nt* WASSERTRANS *Seezeichen* quick-flashing light

Funkeln *nt* TEXTIL scintillation

Funkelrauschen *nt* ELEKTRONIK *Halbleiterrauschen*, RAD flicker noise

Funk: **Funkempfänger** *m* PHYS radio receiver, TELEKOM *Radio* receiver

Funken *m* ELEKTRIZ spark

funkenbildend: **nicht ~** *adj* ELEKTROTECH nonarcing

Funken: **Funkenbildung** *f* ELEKTROTECH, FERNSEH, FERTIG sparking; **Funkenentladung** *f* PHYS spark discharge

funkenerodieren *vt* ELEKTRIZ spark-erode

Funken: **Funkenerosion** *f* MASCHINEN spark erosion; **Funkenerosionsbearbeitung** *f* MASCHINEN electro-spark machining, spark machining

funkenfrei *adj* ELEKTROTECH nonarcing

Funken: **Funkeninduktor** *m* ELEKTROTECH spark coil; **Funkenkammer** *f* PHYS, TEILPHYS spark chamber; **Funkenkondensator** *m* ELEKTROTECH spark capacitor; **Funkenlänge** *f* ELEKTROTECH sparking distance; **Funkenlöscher** *m* ELEKTRIZ spark arrester, spark blow out, spark extinguisher, spark quencher, ELEKTROTECH spark suppressor; **Funkenlöschspule** *f* ELEKTROTECH blowout coil; **Funkenlöschung** *f* ELEKTROTECH spark quenching, spark suppression; **Funkenregen** *m* BAU shower of sparks; **Funkensieb** *nt* EISENBAHN chimney netting; **Funkenspektrum** *nt* STRAHLPHYS spark spectrum; **Funkenstrecke** *f* ELEKTRIZ spark absorber, spark gap, ELEKTROTECH spark gap, KFZTECH spark plug gap, PHYS spark gap

Funk: **Funkentfernungsmeßausrüstung** *f* LUFTTRANS distance-measuring radio equipment; **Funkentstörung** *f* AUFNAHME, ELEKTROTECH noise suppression

Funken: **Funkenüberschlag** *m* ELEKTROTECH arc-over, THERMOD flashover; **Funkenunterdrückung** *f* ELEKTROTECH spark suppression; **Funkenzähler** *m* STRAHLPHYS spark counter; **Funkenzündung** *f* KFZTECH spark ignition

Funker *m* WASSERTRANS radio operator

Funk: **Funkfehlweisung** *f* LUFTTRANS quadrantal error; **Funkfelddämpfung** *f* TELEKOM transmission loss; **Funkfeldlänge** *f* TELEKOM hop length; **Funkfernschreiben** *nt* (*RTTY*) RADIO radioteletype (*RTTY*); **Funkfernsprechen** *nt* TELEKOM radiotelephony, wireless telephony; **Funkfernsteuerung** *f* LUFTTRANS, RADIO, TRANS, WASSERTRANS radio remote control, radio steering; **Funkfeststation** *f* TELEKOM base station; **Funkfeuer** *nt* LUFTTRANS beacon, radio beacon, radio range, RADIO radio range, STRAHLPHYS radio beacon, TRANS radio range, WASSERTRANS radio range, *Seezeichen* radio beacon; **Funkfrequenz** *f* (*HF*) AUFNAHME, ELEKTRONIK, FERNSEH, RADIO, TELEKOM radio frequency (*RF*); **Funkfrequenzbereich** *m* LUFTTRANS, RADIO, TRANS radio range; **Funkfrequenzspektrum** *nt* ELEKTRONIK radio spectrum; **Funkgerät** *nt* LUFTTRANS, RADIO, TRANS, WASSERTRANS radio equipment; **Funkgeräusch** *nt* ELEKTRONIK radio noise

funkgesteuert *adj* RADIO, TRANS radio-controlled

Funk: **Funkkanal** *m* LUFTTRANS radio channel; **Funkkompaß** *m* LUFTTRANS radio compass, PHYS, STRAHLPHYS radiogoniometer, WASSERTRANS radio compass; **Funkkontakt** *m* WASSERTRANS radio contact; **Funkkonzentrator** *m* TELEKOM base station; **Funkleitstrahl** *m* LUFTTRANS glide path beam, radio beacon, *Flugwesen* localizer beam, STRAHLPHYS radio beam,

WASSERTRANS radio beacon; **Funkleitung** *f* LUFTTRANS radio guidance; **Funkmeßverfahren** *nt* RADIO radio detecting and ranging; **Funknavigation** *f* LUFTTRANS, RADIO, TRANS, WASSERTRANS radio navigation; **Funknavigationssystem** *nt* WASSERTRANS long-range navigation system; **Funknetz** *nt* TELEKOM radio network; **Funknetz mit Pulsamplitudenmodulation** *nt* TELEKOM pulse amplitude modulation network; **Funknotrufsystem** *nt* TELEKOM distress radio call system; **Funkortung** *f* LUFTTRANS radar control, STRAHLPHYS radiolocation, TRANS radar control; **Funkpeilantenne** *f* RADIO, TRANS, WASSERTRANS RDF antenna, radio direction finding antenna; **Funkpeiler** *m* PHYS, RADIO, TRANS radio direction finder, WASSERTRANS direction finder, radio direction finder; **Funkpeilgerät** *nt* *(ADF)* LUFTTRANS *Funknavigation*, RADIO, TELEKOM automatic direction finder *(ADF)*; **Funkpeilgerätantenne** *f* LUFTTRANS, TRANS, WASSERTRANS radio direction finder antenna; **Funkpeilkompaß** *m* LUFTTRANS, WASSERTRANS radio compass; **Funkpeilrahmen** *m* RADIO radio direction finder frame; **Funkpeilstelle** *f* LUFTTRANS, TRANS, WASSERTRANS radio direction finding station; **Funkpeiltechnik** *f* PHYS, STRAHLPHYS radiogoniometry; **Funkpeilung** *f* LUFTTRANS radio bearing, radio position fixing, RADIO RDF, radio direction finding, radio bearing, TRANS, WASSERTRANS RDF, radio direction finding, radio position fixing; **Funkraum** *m* WASSERTRANS radio room; **Funkreichweite** *f* LUFTTRANS, RADIO, TRANS radio range; **Funkruf** *m* TELEKOM paging, radiopaging; **Funkrufempfänger mit alphanumerischer Anzeige** *m* TELEKOM alphanumeric pager; **Funkrufsystem mit Tonfolgecodierung** *nt* TELEKOM sequential tone-coded radiopaging system; **Funkseitenpeilung** *f* LUFTTRANS curved azimuth approach path, relative bearing; **Funksender** *m* PHYS radio transmitter; **Funksignal** *nt* ELEKTRONIK radio signal, RAUMFAHRT *Weltraumfunk* signaling (AmE), signalling (BrE); **Funksonde** *f* TELEKOM radiosonde; **Funkspektrum** *nt* ELEKTRONIK radio spectrum; **Funksprechanlage** *f* LUFTTRANS, RADIO, TRANS, WASSERTRANS radio link; **Funksprechgerät** *nt* RADIO, WASSERTRANS radiotelephone; **Funkstandort** *m* LUFTTRANS, TRANS, WASSERTRANS *Navigation* radio fix; **Funkstation** *f* RAUMFAHRT *Weltraumfunk* station; **Funksteuerung** *f* LUFTTRANS radio guidance; **Funkstrecke** *f* RADIO radio path; **Funkstreckendämpfung** *f* FERNSEH path attenuation; **Funkstreckenprofil** *nt* RADIO path profile; **Funkstreifenwagen** *m* TRANS radio patrol car; **Funktagebuch** *nt* RAD log; **Funktaxi** *nt* KFZTECH radio taxicab; **Funktechnik** *f* LUFTTRANS, RADIO, TRANS, WASSERTRANS radio engineering; **Funkteilnehmer** *m* TELEKOM radio subscriber

Funkteilnehmer: vom ~ abgehend *adj* TELEKOM mobile-originated

Funk: **Funkteilsystem** *nt* TELEKOM radio -subsystem; **Funktelefon** *nt* RADIO, TRANS radiophone

funktelefonisch: ~ anrufen *vi* RADIO, TRANS radiophone

Funktion *f* COMP & DV function, *Programm* feature, ELEKTRONIK function, MASCHINEN action, MATH function; **~ auf zwei Ebenen** *f* ELEKTROTECH bilevel operation; **~ dritten Grades** *f* MATH cubic

funktional: ~ aufgeteiltes System *nt* TELEKOM functionally divided system; **~e Sprache** *f* COMP & DV functional language

Funktionalanalyse *f* MATH functional analysis

funktionell: ~es Design *nt* COMP & DV functional design; **~er Entwurf** *m* COMP & DV functional design; **~er Hörverlust** *m* ERGON functional hearing loss

funktionieren *vi* MASCHINEN operate, work

Funktion: **Funktionsablauf** *m* FERTIG operational sequence

funktionsbedingt: ~es Maß *nt* KONSTZEICH functionally significant dimension

Funktion: **Funktionsbereich** *m* COMP & DV functional area

funktionsbezogen: ~e Bezugsebene *f* KONSTZEICH functionally important datum plane; **~e Maßeintragung** *f* KONSTZEICH function-related dimensioning

Funktion: **Funktionsblock** *m* COMP & DV functional block; **Funktionscode** *m* COMP & DV function code, function digit; **Funktionsdiagramm** *nt* COMP & DV functional diagram; **Funktionseinheit** *f* COMP & DV functional unit; **Funktionsempfänger** *m* ELEKTROTECH synchro transformer

funktionsfähig: ~e Windgeschwindigkeit *f* NICHTFOSS ENERG survival wind speed

Funktion: **Funktionsgeber** *m* ELEKTRONIK function generator; **Funktionsgleichung einer Kurve** *f* MATH equation of a curve; **Funktionsgraph** *m* KÜNSTL INT function graph; **Funktionskontrolle** *f* TELEKOM functional test; **Funktionskurve** *f* MATH curve; **Funktionsminderung des Gehörs** *f* ERGON hearing disability; **Funktionsplan** *m* KONSTZEICH function plan, MASCHINEN functional diagram; **Funktionsprüfung** *f* COMP & DV, QUAL functional test; **Funktionsschema** *nt* KONSTZEICH function diagram, MASCHINEN functional diagram

funktionssicher *adj* FERTIG *Kunststoffinstallationen* reliable

Funktion: **Funktionstabelle** *f* COMP & DV truth table; **Funktionstaste** *f* COMP & DV dead key, function key; **Funktionstüchtigkeit** *f* KERNTECH *eines Brennstabs* serviceability; **Funktionsverlauf** *m* REGELUNG course of the function; **Funktionswähler** *m* ELEKTRIZ function selector; **Funktionszeichen** *nt* COMP & DV functional character

Funk: **Funkverbindung** *f* FERNSEH, LUFTTRANS radio link, TELEKOM radiocommunication, TRANS radio link, WASSERTRANS radio contact, radio link; **Funkverbindung von Erdstationen mit Mondreflexion** *f* *(EME)* RADIO earth-moon-earth communications; **Funkverbindung über Meteorschwarmreflektion** *f* RAUMFAHRT *Weltraumfunk* meteor burst communication, meteor scatter communication; **Funkverkehr** *m* RADIO radio communication, TELEKOM radiocommunication, TRANS, WASSERTRANS radio communication; **Funkverkehrsleitung** *f* LUFTTRANS, TRANS, WASSERTRANS radio link; **Funkvermittlungsstelle** *f* *(MSC)* TELEKOM home exchange, mobile switching center (AmE), mobile switching centre (BrE); **Funkversorgung** *f* TELEKOM *Radio* coverage; **Funkwelle** *f* ELEKTRONIK radio-wave, PHYS, RADIO, TELEKOM radio wave

funkwellenundurchlässig *adj* STRAHLPHYS radio-opaque

Funk: **Funkzielflug** *m* LUFTTRANS radio homing; **Funkzonengrenze** *f* TELEKOM cell boundary; **Funkzonengruppe** *f* TELEKOM cluster; **Funkzonenwechsel** *m* TELEKOM cell change

Furaldehyd *m* KUNSTSTOFF furfuraldehyde

Furan *nt* CHEMIE furan

Furche *f* MASCHINEN ridge, MECHAN, OPTIK *Beugungs-gitter* groove

furchen *vt* BAU, FERTIG, MASCHINEN ridge

Furfural *nt* KUNSTSTOFF furfural

Furfuran *nt* CHEMIE furan

Furfuryl- *pref* CHEMIE furfuryl

Furil *nt* CHEMIE furil; **Furil-** *pref* CHEMIE furilic

Furling-Geschwindigkeit *f* NICHTFOSS ENERG Furling speed

Furnier *nt* BAU veneer

Furnieren *nt* BAU veneering

Furnier: **Furnierholz** *nt* BAU veneer; **Furnierplatte** *f* FERTIG ply; **Furnierpresse** *f* MASCHINEN veneering press; **Furniersäge** *f* FERTIG veneer saw

Fusarc-Verfahren *nt* FERTIG fusarc process

Fuselöl *nt* LEBENSMITTEL fusel oil

Fusion *f* ERGON, PHYS fusion; **Fusionsprozesse** *m pl* KERNTECH nuclear fusions, TEILPHYS nuclear fusion; **Fusionsreaktion** *f* KERNTECH thermonuclear reaction; **Fusionsreaktor mit Linearbeschleuniger** *m* KERNTECH LADR, linear accelerator-driven reactor; **Fusionswelle** *f* KERNTECH thermonuclear combustion wave

Fuß *m* BAU *Maßeinheit* foot, *eines Hügels* bottom, DRUCK base, FERTIG *Säule, Schiene* patten, KER & GLAS root, MASCHINEN base, leg, root, METROL, WASSERTRANS *Maßeinheit* foot; **~ pro Sekunde** *m* METROL foot per second; **~ pro Sekunde-Quadrat** *m* METROL foot per second squared; **Fußausrundung** *f* MASCHINEN fillet; **Fußbalken** *m* BAU sole plate; **Fußbedienung** *f* MASCHINEN foot-operated control; **Fußbetätigung** *f* MASCHINEN foot-operated control

fußbetrieben: **~er Rollenschneider** *m* KER & GLAS foot-operated score

Fußboden *m* BAU floor; **Fußbodenbelag** *m* BAU flooring; **Fußbodenfliese** *f* BAU flooring tile; **Fußbodenheizung** *f* BAU screed heating, HEIZ & KÄLTE floor heating, underfloor heating, THERMOD underfloor heating; **Fußbodennagel** *m* BAU flooring nail; **Fußbodenplatte** *f* BAU flooring tile, KER & GLAS floor tile; **Fußbodenquerträger** *m* EISENBAHN floor beam; **Fußbodenspeicherheizung** *f* HEIZ & KÄLTE thermal storage floor heating

Fuß: **Fußbremse** *f* KFZTECH brake pedal, foot brake; **Fußbrett** *nt* BAU toeboard

fusselfrei: **~e Kleidung** *f* MECHAN lint-free cloth

Fuß: **Fußfläche** *f* MASCHINEN root surface; **Fußgänger** *m* TRANS pedestrian

Fußgänger: **durch ~ gelenkt** *adj* TRANS pedestrian-controlled

Fußgänger *pref* TRANS pedestrian

fußgängerbetätigt: **~es Signal** *nt* TRANS pedestrian-actuated signal

Fußgänger-: **Fußgängerbrücke** *f* TRANS pedestrian bridge; **Fußgängerphase** *f* TRANS pedestrian phase; **Fußgängerschutzinsel** *f* BAU refuge; **Fußgängertunnel** *m* TRANS pedestrian underpass; **Fußgängerüberführung** *f* EISENBAHN footbridge; **Fußgängerverkehr** *m* TRANS pedestrian traffic

Fuß: **Fußgangschaltung** *f* KFZTECH foot change; **Fußhebel** *m* KER & GLAS foot boards, MASCHINEN treadle; **Fußhebeldämpfungsgestänge** *nt* LUFTTRANS *Flugzeug* pedal damper assembly; **Fußhöhe** *f* FERTIG *Getriebelehre*, MASCHINEN dedendum; **Fußholz** *nt* BAU bottom rail, ground plate, groundsill, sole piece, *Dachkonstruktion* pole plate; **Fußkreis** *m* MASCHINEN root line; **Fußkreisdurchmesser** *m* MASCHINEN dedendum circle, root diameter; **Fußkreislinie** *f* MASCHINEN dedendum line; **Fußlager** *nt* MASCHINEN footstep bearing; **Fußleiste** *f* BAU base, base board, baseboard (AmE), mopboard (AmE), skirting board (BrE), skirting; **Fußpfette** *f* BAU wall plate; **Fußplatte** *f* BAU sole plate, WASSERTRANS *Schiffbau* heel plate; **Fußpumpe** *f* MASCHINEN foot pump; **Fußpunkt** *m* METROL foot, TELEKOM *Antenne* base; **Fußraste** *f* KFZTECH *Motorrad* foot rest; **Fußrohr** *nt* WASSERVERSORG tail pipe; **Fußschalterkontakt** *m* ELEKTRIZ floor contact switch; **Fußschalthebel** *m* KFZTECH foot change lever; **Fußschicht** *f* KER & GLAS eaves course; **Fußschraube** *f* MASCHINEN foot screw; **Fußträger** *m* KER & GLAS foot carrier; **Fußventil** *nt* MASCHINEN foot valve

Futter *nt* BAU lining, KERNTECH liner, MASCHINEN chuck, MECHAN lining; **~ mit einzeln verstellbaren Backen** *nt* MASCHINEN independent chuck; **~ mit vier Einzelverstellbacken** *nt* MASCHINEN four-jaw independent chuck; **Futterautomat** *m* MASCHINEN automatic chucking lathe, chucker, chucking automatic lathe; **Futterholz** *nt* BAU furring, furring piece; **Futterplatte** *f* MASCHINEN back plate, chuck plate; **Futterrohr** *nt* ERDÖL casing

Futterrohre: **~abhängen** *vt* ERDÖL *Bohrtechnik* set

Futter: **Futterscheibe** *f* FERTIG *Spannfutter* back plate; **Futterschutz** *m* MASCHINEN chuck guard; **Futterspannung** *f* FERTIG *Metallspanung* chucking; **Futterstoff** *m* TEXTIL lining fabric

Fuzzy-Logik *f* COMP & DV, KÜNSTL INT fuzzy logic

FVSt *abbr* (*Fernvermittlungsstelle*) TELEKOM toll exchange (AmE), trunk exchange (BrE), trunk switching center (AmE), trunk switching centre (BrE) (*toll exchange*)

f-Zahl *f* PHYS f-number

F2-Schicht *f* RADIO F2 layer

G

G *abbr* AUFNAHME (*Gau*β), ELEKTRIZ (*Gau*β) G (*gauss*), ELEKTRONIK (*Gewinn*), ERGON (*Gewinn*), FERNSEH (*Gewinn*) G (*gain*), MASCHINEN (*Schermodul*) G (*shear modulus*), METROL (*Giga-*) G (*giga*), PHYS (*Gibbssche Funktion*) G (*Gibbs function*), PHYS (*Schermodul*) G (*shear modulus*), RADIO (*Gewinn*), RAUMFAHRT (*Gewinn*), TELEKOM (*Gewinn*) G (*gain*), THERMOD (*Gibbssche Funktion*) G (*Gibbs function*)

g *abbr* CHEMIE (*Gramm*) g (*gram*), KERNTECH (*gyromagnetisches Verhältnis*) g (*gyromagnetic ratio*), LABOR (*Gramm*), PHYS (*Gramm*) g (*gram*), PHYS (*gyromagnetisches Verhältnis*) g (*gyromagnetic ratio*), PHYS (*statistisches Gewicht*) g (*statistical weight*), RAUMFAHRT (*Erdbeschleunigung*) g (*gravitational acceleration*)

Ga (*Gallium*) CHEMIE Ga (*gallium*)

GaAs *abbr* (*Galliumarsenid*) ELEKTRONIK, OPTIK, PHYS, RADIO GaAs (*gallium arsenide*)

GaAs-Laser *m* PHYS GaAs laser

Gabel *f* HYDRAUL gab, KER & GLAS fork, KFZTECH *Motorradgetriebe* fork, *Universalgelenk* yoke, MASCHINEN fork, MECHAN bracket; **~ mit Bremsnickausgleich** *f* KFZTECH *Motorrad* antidive fork; **Gabelbein** *nt* KFZTECH *Motorrad* fork leg; **Gabelgelenk** *nt* MASCHINEN knuckle joint

gabelgesteuert: ~e Ventilbewegung *f* HYDRAUL hook gear valve motion

Gabel: **Gabelhebel** *m* MASCHINEN fork lever, forked lever; **Gabelkopf** *m* MASCHINEN fork head, yoke, MECHAN clevis, yoke; **Gabellehre** *f* METROL caliper gage (AmE), calliper gauge (BrE)

gabeln *vt* FERTIG bisect

Gabel: **Gabelpfanne** *f* FERTIG *Gießen* shank ladle; **Gabelpleuel** *nt* MASCHINEN fork-end connecting rod; **Gabelpleuelstange** *f* MASCHINEN connecting rod with fork end; **Gabelpunkt** *m* TELEKOM two-to-four wire transition point; **Gabelrohr** *nt* BAU forked pipe, MECHAN Y-tube; **Gabelrückholfeder** *f* KFZTECH *Kupplung* fork return spring; **Gabelschaltung** *f* TELEKOM hybrid circuit; **Gabelschlüssel** *m* FERTIG *Kunststoffinstallationen* spanner (BrE), wrench, MASCHINEN engineer's wrench, face spanner (BrE), face wrench, fork wrench, open spanner (BrE), open wrench, open-end spanner (BrE), open-end wrench; **Gabelschraubenschlüssel** *m* MECHAN open-end spanner (BrE), open-end wrench; **Gabelschweißung** *f* FERTIG cleft weld; **Gabelspanneisen** *nt* FERTIG U-clamp

Gabelstapler *m* BAU, KFZTECH, VERPACK forklift, forklift truck; **~ an Gabelstapler Umschlag** *m* TRANS truck-to-truck handling (AmE), truck-to-truck operation (AmE)

Gabelstaplerbetrieb: auf ~ umstellen *vt* TRANS palletize

Gabel: **Gabelstößel** *m* KFZTECH *Kupplung* fork push rod; **Gabelstück** *nt* BAU Y branch; **Gabelumschalter** *m* TELEKOM cradle switch; **Gabelverbindung** *f* ELEKTRIZ forked connection; **Gabelzinke** *f* MASCHINEN fork arm

Gablonzer-Ware *f* KER & GLAS Gablonz glassware

Gadolinium *nt* (*Gd*) CHEMIE gadolinum (*Gd*)

Gaffel *f* WASSERTRANS *Segeln* gaff; **Gaffelklaue** *f* WASSERTRANS *Segeln* crutch

Galactan *nt* CHEMIE galactan, gelose

Galacton- *pref* CHEMIE galactonic

Galactosamin *nt* CHEMIE aminodeoxy-D-galactose, galactosamine

Galactosan *nt* CHEMIE galactan, gelose

galaktisch: ~e Wolke *f* RAUMFAHRT galactic cloud

Galaktose *f* LEBENSMITTEL *Milchsaccharid* galactose

Galaxienhaufen *m* RAUMFAHRT galaxy cluster

Galilei: **~sches Bezugssystem** *nt* PHYS Galilean frame; **~sches Fernrohr** *nt* PHYS Galilean telescope; **~sches Teleskop** *nt* PHYS Galilean telescope; **~sche Transformation** *f* PHYS, STRÖMPHYS Galilean transformation

Gallat *nt* CHEMIE gallate

Galle *f* KER & GLAS gall

Gallein *nt* CHEMIE gallein

Gallert *f* VERPACK gelatine

gallertartig: ~er Bohrschlamm *m* ERDÖL colloidal mud

Gallertbildung *f* CHEMTECH gelation, jellification

Gallium *nt* (*Ga*) CHEMIE gallium (*Ga*)

Galliumarsenid *nt* (*GaAs*) ELEKTRONIK, OPTIK, PHYS, RADIO gallium arsenide (*GaAs*); **Galliumarsenid-Chip** *m* ELEKTRONIK gallium arsenide chip; **Galliumarsenid-Diode** *f* ELEKTRONIK gallium arsenide diode; **Galliumarsenid-Laser** *m* STRAHLPHYS gallium arsenide laser; **Galliumarsenid-Logik** *f* ELEKTRONIK gallium arsenide logic; **Galliumarsenid-MOS-Transistor** *m* ELEKTRONIK gallium arsenide MOS transistor; **Galliumarsenid-Solarzelle** *f* ELEKTRONIK gallium arsenide solar cell; **Galliumarsenid-Trägermaterial** *nt* ELEKTRONIK gallium arsenide substrate

Gall-Kette *f* MASCHINEN plate link chain

Gallone *f* METROL gallon; **Gallonenflasche** *f* KER & GLAS gallon jug

Gallotannin *nt* CHEMIE gallotannin

Gallusgerbsäure *f* CHEMIE gallotannic acid

Gallussäure *f* CHEMIE gallic acid

Galvanisation *f* CHEMIE voltaization, ELEKTROTECH electroplating

galvanisch[1] *adj* CHEMIE, ELEKTRIZ *Elektrochemie* galvanic; **~ aktiv** *adj* ANSTRICH galvanically sacrificial, sacrificial; **~ getrennt** *adj* ELEKTRIZ DC-isolated

galvanisch[2] **~e Anode** *f* ERDÖL sacrificial anode; **~es Element** *nt* CHEMIE, ELEKTRIZ, ELEKTROTECH galvanic cell, voltaic cell; **~ gekoppelter Verstärker** *m* ELEKTRONIK DC-coupled amplifier, direct-coupled amplifier; **~ isolierte Stromversorgung** *f* ELEKTRIZ floating supply; **~e Isolierung** *f* ELEKTROTECH galvanic isolation; **~e Kette** *f* CHEMIE galvanic cell; **~e Kopplung** *f* ELEKTRONIK direct coupling, ELEKTROTECH direct coupling, galvanic couple; **~ leitende Verbindung** *f* NICHTFOSS ENERG ohmic contact; **~er Strom** *m* ELEKTROTECH galvanic current; **~er Überzug** *m* FERTIG electroplate; **~es Verbleien** *nt* FERTIG lead plating, terne plating; **~es Vernickeln** *nt* FERTIG nickel plating; **~e Versilberung** *f* ELEKTROTECH electrosilvering; **~es Verzinken** *nt* FERTIG electrogalvanizing; **~er Vorgang**

m ANSTRICH galvanic action; **~e Zelle** *f* ELEKTROTECH galvanic cell

galvanisch:[3] **mit ~em Überzug versehen** *vt* METALL plate; **~ versilbern** *vt* ELEKTROTECH electrosilver; **~ verzinken** *vt* FERTIG electrogalvanize

Galvanisieren *nt* ANSTRICH plating, ELEKTROTECH electroplating, plating, FERTIG electroplating

galvanisieren *vt* ELEKTROTECH electroplate

galvanisiert *adj* ANSTRICH, ELEKTRIZ electroplated, FERTIG plated, MECHAN galvanized; **im ~en Zustand** *adj* FERTIG as-deposited

Galvanisierung *f* BAU electrodeposition, ELEKTRIZ electroplating

Galvano *nt* DRUCK electro, electrotype

Galvanometer *nt* ELEKTRIZ, ELEKTROTECH, LABOR, PHYS galvanometer; **Galvanometermeßwerk** *nt* GERÄT galvanometer movement; **Galvanometer-Nebenschlußwiderstand** *m* ELEKTRIZ galvanometer shunt; **Galvanometer-Shunt** *m* ELEKTROTECH galvanometer shunt

Galvano: **Galvanoplastik** *f* ELEKTROTECH electroforming, FERTIG electroform

galvanoplastisch *adj* FERTIG galvanoplastic

Galvano: **Galvanotechnik** *f* FERTIG *Kunststoffinstallationen* electroplating industry

Gamaschen *f pl* SICHERHEIT gaiters; **~ und Schuhschutz** *f pl* SICHERHEIT *gegen Verbrennungen* gaiters and footwear protection

Gambir *m* CHEMIE gambier

Gamma *nt* FERNSEH gamma; **Gamma-Abschirmung** *f* KERNTECH gamma shield; **Gamma-Anpassung** *f* RADIO *Antenne* gamma match; **Gamma-Aufheizung** *f* KERNTECH gamma heating; **Gamma-Eigenschaft** *f* ELEKTRONIK *Bildaufnahmeröhre* gamma characteristic; **Gamma-Eisen** *nt* METALL gamma iron; **Gamma-Erzbreikonzentrationsmeßgerät** *nt* KERNTECH gamma ore pulp content meter; **Gamma-Escape-Peak** *nt* STRAHLPHYS, TEILPHYS, WELLPHYS gamma ray escape peak; **Gamma-Fehler** *m* FERNSEH gamma error; **Gamma-Gamma Log** *nt* ERDÖL *Bohrlochmessung* gamma-gamma log; **Gamma-Korrektur** *f* FERNSEH gamma corrector; **Gamma-Kurve** *f* ELEKTRONIK *Bildaufnahmeröhre* gamma characteristic; **Gamma-Log** *nt* ERDÖL gamma-gamma log, *Bohrlochmessung* gamma ray log

gammametrisch: **~e Qualitätsbestimmung des Erzes** *f* KERNTECH gammametric ore assaying

Gamma: **Gammaquant** *nt* STRAHLPHYS, TEILPHYS, WELLPHYS gamma particle, gamma quantum; **Gammaradiographie** *f* STRAHLPHYS, TEILPHYS, WELLPHYS gamma radiation; **Gamma-Rückstreumethode** *f* KERNTECH gamma backscatter method; **Gamma-Spektrometer** *nt* STRAHLPHYS, TEILPHYS, WELLPHYS gamma ray spectrometer; **Gammaspektrum** *nt* STRAHLPHYS, TEILPHYS, WELLPHYS gamma ray spectrum

Gammastrahl *m* ELEKTRONIK gamma ray, STRAHLPHYS, TEILPHYS, WELLPHYS gamma beam, gamma ray; **Gammastrahlen** *m pl* STRAHLPHYS, TEILPHYS, WELLPHYS gamma radiation; **Gammastrahlenabsorptionsanalyse** *f* STRAHLPHYS, TEILPHYS, WELLPHYS gamma ray absorption analysis; **Gammastrahlenaktivierungsanalyse** *f* STRAHLPHYS photoactivation analysis; **Gammastrahlenaufheizung** *f* STRAHLPHYS, TEILPHYS, WELLPHYS gamma ray heating; **Gammastrahlenaufzeichnung** *f* NICHTFOSS ENERG gamma ray log;

Gammastrahlenbohrlochmessung *f* ERDÖL *Meßtechnik* gamma ray well logging; **Gammastrahlendetektor** *m* GERÄT gamma radiation detector; **Gammastrahlendickenmeßgerät** *nt* GERÄT gamma thickness meter; **Gammastrahlenfilm** *m* STRAHLPHYS *im Strahlenschutz*, TEILPHYS *im Strahlenschutz*, WELLPHYS *im Strahlenschutz* gamma film; **Gammastrahlenkonstante** *f* STRAHLPHYS, TEILPHYS, WELLPHYS gamma constant; **Gammastrahlenspektrometer** *nt* STRAHLPHYS, TEILPHYS, WELLPHYS gamma ray spectrometer; **Gammastrahlung** *f* ELEKTRIZ gamma radiation, ELEKTRONIK gamma ray, STRAHLPHYS gamma emission, gamma radiation, TEILPHYS, WELLPHYS gamma emission, gamma radiation, gamma ray; **Gammastrahlungsüberwachung** *f* KERNTECH gamma ray survey; **Gammastrahlverfahren** *nt* STRAHLPHYS, TEILPHYS, WELLPHYS gamma radiation

Gammaübergang *m* STRAHLPHYS, TEILPHYS, WELLPHYS gamma ray transformation

Gammaumwandlung *f* CHEMIE *Gummiherstellung* vitrification

Gammexan *nt* CHEMIE gammexane

Gang[1] *m* COMP & DV running, FERTIG *Extruderschnecke* channel, *Schnecke* start, *Schraubenlinie* flight, MASCHINEN action, operation, run, running, work, working, MECHAN gear

Gang:[2] **~ einlegen** *vi* KFZTECH put into gear

Gang: **Gangerz** *nt* KOHLEN gangue mineral; **Ganghöhe** *f* ELEKTRIZ, ELEKTROTECH pitch, FERTIG screw pitch, MASCHINEN lead, pitch, MECHAN pitch; **Ganglinie** *f* WASSERVERSORG hydrograph; **Gangschalthebel** *m* KFZTECH *Getriebe* gear lever (BrE), gear shift (AmE); **Gangschaltung** *f* KFZTECH *Getriebe* gear lever (BrE), gear shift (AmE), MASCHINEN speed-changing device, speed-changing mechanism, MECHAN gear lever (BrE), gear shift (AmE); **Gangwechsel** *m* KFZTECH *Getriebe* gear change; **Gangwerk** *nt* MASCHINEN motion; **Gangzahl** *f* MASCHINEN number of starts

Gänseaugenstoff *m* TEXTIL *Jacquardgewebe* diaper

ganz:[1] **~ langsam voraus** *adv* WASSERTRANS dead slow ahead; **~ langsam zurück** *adv* WASSERTRANS dead slow astern

ganz:[2] **~er Ton** *m* AKUSTIK whole tone; **~e Zahl** *f* COMP & DV, MATH integer

Ganzglasfaser *f* TELEKOM all-glass fiber (AmE), all-glass fibre (BrE)

Ganzjahresöl *nt* KFZTECH multigrade oil

ganzjährig: **~e Klimatisierung** *f* HEIZ & KÄLTE all-year air conditioning

Ganzkörper- *pref* KERNTECH whole-body; **Ganzkörperbestrahlung** *f* KERNTECH whole-body irradiation; **Ganzkörperspektrometer** *nt* KERNTECH whole-body counter; **Ganzkörperzähler** *m* KERNTECH HBC, human-body counter, whole-body counter

Ganzpolteilwicklung *f* ELEKTRIZ full-pitch winding

Ganzseitenmontagesystem *nt* DRUCK page composition system

Ganzstoffkasten *m* PAPIER stuff chest

Ganzzahl *f* COMP & DV integer

ganzzahlig: **~er Bruch** *m* MATH common fraction; **~er Datentyp** *m* COMP & DV integer type; **~er Spin** *m* PHYS integral spin

Ganzzeichen *nt* DRUCK solid letter

Garage *f* TRANS garage; **Garagenlüftung** *f* SICHERHEIT garage ventilation apparatus

Garantie *f* QUAL guarantee; **Garantiegewicht** *nt* LUFT-

TRANS guaranteed weight; **Garantiekappe** f VERPACK guarantee cap

garantiert:[1] ~ **farbecht** adj TEXTIL guaranteed not to fade

garantiert:[2] ~e **Entnahme** f NICHTFOSS ENERG guaranteed draw-off; ~e **Flugbahn** f LUFTTRANS guaranteed flight path; ~er **Schub** m LUFTTRANS guaranteed thrust

Garantie: **Garantieverschluß** m VERPACK guarantee closure; **Garantiezeitraum** m RAUMFAHRT guarantee period

Garbe f FERTIG sheaf

Gärbehälter m LEBENSMITTEL fermenter

Gardine f TEXTIL curtain; **Gardinenbildung** f KUNSTSTOFF sagging

gären vi CHEMIE Flüssigkeit ferment

Garn[1] nt KER & GLAS, KUNSTSTOFF, PAPIER, TEXTIL yarn

Garn:[2] **im ~ färben** vt TEXTIL yarn-dye

Garn: **Garnapplikator** m KER & GLAS yarn applicator; **Garnfärben** nt TEXTIL yarn dyeing

Garnitur f BAU set, DRUCK series, FERTIG Kunststoffinstallationen fittings, TEXTIL set

Garn: **Garnkörper** m TEXTIL package; **Garnnummer** f TEXTIL size; **Garnspule** f KER & GLAS, TEXTIL pirn; **Garnsträhne** f TEXTIL hank; **Garnstrang** m TEXTIL hank; **Garnträger** m TEXTIL bobbin

Gartenblankglas nt KER & GLAS horticultural glass

Gartenklarglas nt KER & GLAS horticultural cast glass

Gärung f CHEMIE Vorgang, LEBENSMITTEL fermentation; **Gärungsgase** nt pl ABFALL fermentation gases

Gas[1] nt HEIZ & KÄLTE, PHYS gas, THERMOD gas (AmE), gasoline (AmE)

Gas:[2] ~ **geben** vi LUFTTRANS advance throttle; ~ **wegnehmen** vi LUFTTRANS throttle back

Gas: **Gasabsaugbohrung** f KOHLEN methane-draining boring; **Gasabscheider** m KERNTECH für Kühlwasser gas stripper; **Gasabsorption** f ERDÖL absorption of gases; **Gasabzug** m KERNTECH gas vent; **Gasanalyse** f ERDÖL Meßtechnik gas analysis; **Gasanalysegerät** nt ERDÖL Meßtechnik gas analyser (BrE), gas analyzer (AmE); **Gasanalysengerät mit Wärmeleitfähigkeitszelle** nt GERÄT conduction-of-heat gas analyser (BrE), conduction-of-heat gas analyzer (AmE); **Gasanreicherung** f THERMOD gas enrichment; **Gasanzeichen** nt ERDÖL Exploration gas show; **Gasanzünder** m HEIZ & KÄLTE gas lighter

gasarm[1] adj KFZTECH lean

gasarm:[2] ~es **Gemisch** nt KFZTECH poor mixture

Gas: **Gasaufkohlen** nt THERMOD gas carburizing; **Gasaufkohlung** f FERTIG gas carburization; **Gasausgang** m KFZTECH gas outlet; **Gasausscheidung** f METALL gas precipitate; **Gasaustritt** m ERDÖL Bohrtechnik trip gas; **Gasaustrittsöffnung** f KFZTECH gas outlet; **Gasaustrittstemperatur** f KERNTECH gas outlet temperature; **Gasbadeofen** m HEIZ & KÄLTE gas geyser; **Gasbehälter** m THERMOD gas holder

gasbeheizt[1] adj HEIZ & KÄLTE gas-fired

gasbeheizt:[2] ~er **Ofen** m HEIZ & KÄLTE, THERMOD gas-fired furnace

gasbenzinelektrisch: ~es **Fahrzeug** nt KFZTECH gas electric vehicle (AmE)

gasbeständig adj THERMOD gasproof

gasbetrieben: ~es **Auto** nt KFZTECH gas-fueled car (AmE), petrol-fuelled car (BrE); ~er **Bus** m KFZTECH gas-fueled bus (AmE), petrol-fuelled bus (BrE); ~er **Motor** m MASCHINEN gas engine

Gas: **Gasbildungsvermögen** nt LEBENSMITTEL beim Teig gassing power; **Gasblase** f FERTIG blister, gas cavity, KER & GLAS air bell, bubble; **Gasblasendurchflußmesser** m LABOR bubble flow meter; **Gasblasenströmungsmesser** m CHEMTECH bubble gage (AmE), bubble gauge (BrE); **Gasboiler** m THERMOD gas boiler; **Gasbrenner** m HEIZ & KÄLTE gas burner, THERMOD gas burner, gas ring; **Gasbrenner ohne Gebläse** m THERMOD atmospheric burner

gasbrenngeschnitten adj FERTIG flame cut

Gas: **Gasbrennschnitt** m FERTIG flame-cut; **Gasbürette** f LABOR gas burette; **Gaschromatograph** m LABOR gas chromatograph; **Gaschromatographie** f LEBENSMITTEL, THERMOD gas chromatography; **Gasdetektor** m THERMOD gas leak detector

gasdicht adj FERTIG gastight, Kunststoffinstallationen gastight, MASCHINEN gasproof, MECHAN gastight, THERMOD gasproof, gastight

Gas: **Gasdichteschreiber** m GERÄT gas density recorder; **Gasdichtewaage** f GERÄT buoyancy gas balance; **Gasdrossel** f KFZTECH Vergaser accelerator (BrE), gas pedal (AmE), MECHAN gooseneck; **Gasdrosselung** f KERNTECH gas baffle; **Gasdruck** m PHYS, THERMOD gas pressure; **Gasdruckminderungsventil** nt THERMOD gas pressure-reducing valve; **Gasdruckregler** m HEIZ & KÄLTE, MASCHINEN gas pressure regulator; **Gasdurchlässigkeit** f KUNSTSTOFF, THERMOD gas permeability; **Gasdurchsatz** m RAUMFAHRT Raumschiff gas flow; **Gasdynamik** f MASCHINEN gas dynamics; **Gaseinpressung** f ERDÖL gas injection; **Gaseinschluß** m KERNTECH gas cavity

Gasen nt TEXTIL singeing

gasen vt TEXTIL gas

Gasentladung f ELEKTRONIK gas discharge; **Gasentladungslampe** f ELEKTRIZ gas discharge lamp; **Gasentladungsrelais** nt ELEKTRONIK, ELEKTROTECH gas-filled relay; **Gasentladungsröhre** f ELEKTRONIK gas discharge tube, gas tube; **Gasentladungsspalt** m KERNTECH gas discharge gap; **Gasentladungsstrecke** f KERNTECH gas discharge gap; **Gasentladungsventil** nt ELEKTROTECH gas-filled rectifier

Gas: **Gasentölungstrieb** m ERDÖL Fördertechnik solution gas drive; **Gasentschwefelung** f UMWELTSCHMUTZ gas desulfurization (AmE), gas desulphurization (BrE); **Gasentwickler nach Kipp** m LABOR Generator Kipp's apparatus; **Gaserzeuger** m THERMOD gas generator; **Gasexplosion** f KOHLEN gas explosion; **Gasfackel** f THERMOD zum Abfackeln gas flare; **Gasfeder** f MASCHINEN gas spring; **Gasfeld** nt ERDÖL, THERMOD gas field; **Gas-Fest-Chromatographie** f UMWELTSCHMUTZ gas-solid chromatography; **Gasfeuerung** f HEIZ & KÄLTE gas-heating system; **Gasfeuerungsautomat** m HEIZ & KÄLTE automatic gas-firing unit

Gasflamme: mit ~ getrocknet adj FERTIG Form skindried

Gasflasche f KERNTECH gas bottle, MASCHINEN gas cylinder, SICHERHEIT transportable gas container, THERMOD gas bottle, gas cylinder; **Gasflaschenlager** nt SICHERHEIT storage of gas cylinders; **Gas-Flüssigkeit-Chromatographie** f THERMOD, UMWELTSCHMUTZ gas-liquid chromatography; **Gasfokussierung** f ELEKTRONIK Strahlkonzentrierung durch Gasfüllung gas focusing

gasförmig[1] adj PHYS, THERMOD gaseous

gasförmig:[2] ~er **Abfall** m UMWELTSCHMUTZ gaseous

waste; ~**es aktives Medium** *nt* ELEKTRONIK gaseous active medium; ~**er Brennstoff** *m* ERDÖL, HEIZ & KÄLTE gaseous fuel; ~**es Medium** *nt* UMWELTSCHUTZ gaseous medium; ~**e Phase** *f* THERMOD gaseous phase; ~**es Verbrennungsprodukt** *nt* UMWELTSCHUTZ gaseous combustion product; ~**er Zustand** *m* THERMOD gaseous phase

Gas: **Gasfotozelle** *f* ELEKTRONIK gas phototube

gasfrei *adj* THERMOD free from gas

gasgefeuert *adj* HEIZ & KÄLTE gas-fired

gasgefüllt[1] *adj* THERMOD gas-filled

gasgefüllt:[2] ~**e Diode** *f* ELEKTRONIK gas diode; ~**e Fotozelle** *f* ELEKTRONIK gas phototube; ~**e Gleichrichterröhre** *f* ELEKTRIZ gas-filled rectifier, ELEKTRONIK gas-filled detector tube; ~**e Röhre** *f* ELEKTRONIK soft tube; ~**e Schaltröhre** *f* ELEKTRONIK gas-filled switching tube; ~**e Stabilisierungsröhre** *f* RADIO gaseous regulator tube

Gasgehalt *m* THERMOD gas content; ~ **im Bohrschlamm** *m* ERDÖL *Tiefbohrtechnik* gas-cut mud

gasgekohlt *adj* FERTIG gas-carburized

gasgekühlt[1] *adj* THERMOD gas-cooled

gasgekühlt:[2] ~**er Brutreaktor** *m* KERNTECH GCBR, gas-cooled breeder reactor; ~**er Reaktor** *m* KERNTECH gas-cooled nuclear power plant

Gas: **Gasgenerator** *m* TRANS gas generator

gasgeschmiert: ~**es Lager** *nt* KERNTECH gas-lubricated bearing

Gas: **Gasgestänge** *nt* KFZTECH throttle control rod, *Vergaser* accelerator linkage, throttle linkage; **Gasgewinde** *nt* MASCHINEN gas threads; **Gasgewinnung aus Mülldeponien** *f* UMWELTSCHUTZ landfill gas extraction; **Gasgleichrichterröhre** *f* ELEKTROTECH gas-filled rectifier; **Gasgleichung** *f* THERMOD gas equation

gashaltig[1] *adj* THERMOD gassy

gashaltig:[2] ~**es Öl** *nt* THERMOD live oil

Gas: **Gashebel** *m* RAUMFAHRT *Raumschiff* throttle control; **Gasheizung** *f* HEIZ & KÄLTE gas-heating system, THERMOD *Gerät* gas fire, *Heizen mit Gas* gas heating; **Gashinweis** *m* ERDÖL gas show; **Gashydrat** *nt* CHEMIE *Erdgasaufbereitung* gas hydrate

gasiert: ~**es Garn** *nt* TEXTIL gassed yarn

Gas: **Gasinjektion** *f* ERDÖL *Ölgewinnung* gas injection

gasisoliert: ~**es Kabel** *nt* ELEKTRIZ gas-filled cable, gas-insulated line

Gas: **Gaskältemaschine** *f* HEIZ & KÄLTE gas-refrigerating machine; **Gaskanal** *m* FERTIG vent hole; **Gaskappe** *f* ERDÖL *Lagerstättenkunde* gas cap; **Gaskappenantrieb** *m* ERDÖL *Ölförderung* gas cap drive; **Gaskissen** *nt* KERNTECH gas cushion; **Gaskohle** *f* KOHLEN gas coal; **Gaskoks** *m* KOHLEN gas-coke; **Gaskonstante** *f* (*R*) PHYS, THERMOD gas constant (*R*); **Gaskreislauf** *m* HEIZ & KÄLTE gas circuit, KERNTECH gas circulation loop; **Gaskühler** *m* HEIZ & KÄLTE gas cooler; **Gaskühlschrank** *m* THERMOD gas refrigerator; **Gaslagerstätte** *f* ERDÖL gas field; **Gaslagerung** *f* LEBENSMITTEL gas storage; **Gaslaser** *m* ELEKTRONIK gas dynamic laser, gas laser, STRAHLPHYS gas laser; **Gasleitung** *f* BAU, ERDÖL *Erdgastransport* gas pipeline, THERMOD gas pipe; **Gasleitungsleck** *nt* THERMOD gas leak; **Gasleitungsnetz** *nt* ERDÖL gas grid; **Gaslift** *m* ERDÖL *Erdölgewinnung* gaslift; **Gaslöten** *nt* BAU torch brazing; **Gasluftgemisch** *nt* PHYS, THERMOD gas-air mixture; **Gas-Maser** *m* ELEKTRONIK gas maser; **Gasmessung** *f* THERMOD gasometry; **Gasmotor** *m* MASCHINEN gas engine, THERMOD gas engine (AmE),

gasoline engine (AmE), petrol engine (BrE); **Gasmultiplikationsfaktor** *m* ELEKTRONIK gas multiplication factor; **Gasnitrieren** *nt* THERMOD gas nitriding; **Gasofen** *m* THERMOD gas fire

Gasöl *nt* ERDÖL *Raffinerie, Destillationsprodukt*, THERMOD gas oil

Gas: **Gas-Öl-Verhältnis** *nt* (*GÖV*) ERDÖL *Erdölgewinnung* gas-to-oil ratio (*GOR*); **Gasometrie** *f* THERMOD gasometry; **Gaspatrone** *f* THERMOD gas bottle; **Gaspedal** *nt* KFZTECH *Vergaser* accelerator (BrE), accelerator pedal, gas pedal (AmE); **Gasphasenabscheidung** *f* (*CVD*) ELEKTRONIK *nach chemischen Verfahren*, TELEKOM chemical vapor deposition (AmE), chemical vapour deposition (BrE) (*CVD*); **Gasphasennitrierung** *f* CHEMTECH vapor phase nitration (AmE), vapour phase nitration (BrE); **Gasphasenpropfen** *m* KERNTECH gas phase grafting; **Gaspore** *f* OPTIK pinhole; **Gasprüfer** *m* CHEMIE eudiometer; **Gasrauschen** *nt* ELEKTRONIK gas noise

gasreich *adj* THERMOD gassy

Gas: **Gasreiniger** *m* SICHERHEIT gas-cleaning equipment; **Gasreinigung** *f* SICHERHEIT gas cleaning; **Gasreinigungsanlage** *f* KERNTECH gas purifiers; **Gasrelais** *nt* ELEKTRONIK, ELEKTROTECH gas-filled relay; **Gasrohr** *nt* BAU, KFZTECH, THERMOD gas pipe; **Gasröhre** *f* ELEKTRONIK gas tube; **Gasrohr-Innengewinde** *nt* FERTIG *Kunststoffinstallationen* BSP parallel female thread; **Gasrohrzange** *f* BAU gas pliers; **Gasrückgewinnung** *f* UMWELTSCHUTZ gas recovery; **Gasrückstand** *m* ELEKTRONIK, UMWELTSCHUTZ residual gas; **Gasruß** *m* KUNSTSTOFF channel black; **Gassammler** *m* FERTIG *Schweißen* gas holder; **Gasschieber** *m* MASCHINEN gas valve; **Gasschleuse** *f* HEIZ & KÄLTE, KERNTECH gas lock; **Gasschweißen** *nt* MASCHINEN gas welding, THERMOD oxyacetylene welding; **Gasschweißung** *f* MASCHINEN gas welding

Gasse *f* TRANS gap; **Gassen** *f pl* DRUCK rivers of white; **Gassenbesetztzustand** *m* TELEKOM *Telefonverkehr* congestion

Gas: **Gasspürgerät** *nt* LABOR gas detector, leak detector; **Gasstrahl** *m* MASCHINEN gas jet; **Gasstrom** *m* THERMOD gas flow; **Gasströmung** *f* THERMOD gas flow; **Gastanker** *m* WASSERTRANS gas tanker; **Gasteer** *m* KOHLEN gas tar; **Gastetrode** *f* ELEKTRONIK *Elektronenröhre* gas tetrode; **Gasthermometer** *nt* GERÄT gas-filled thermometer, HEIZ & KÄLTE, PHYS, THERMOD gas thermometer

Gastlandflagge *f* WASSERTRANS courtesy ensign, courtesy flag

Gas: **Gastriode** *f* ELEKTRONIK gas triode

Gasturbine *f* FERTIG, MASCHINEN, MECHAN, THERMOD, WASSERTRANS *Motor* gas turbine; ~ **mit geschlossenem Kreislauf** *f* TRANS closed cycle gas turbine; ~ **mit offenem Kreislauf** *f* TRANS open-cycle gas turbine; **Gasturbinenbus** *m* KFZTECH gas turbine bus; **Gasturbinen-Elektrizitätswerk** *nt* ELEKTRIZ gas turbine power station; **Gasturbinen-Kraftwerk** *nt* ELEKTRIZ gas turbine power station; **Gasturbinen-Reisebus** *m* KFZTECH gas turbine motor coach; **Gasturbinen-Triebwagen** *m* EISENBAHN gas turbine railcar; **Gasturbinen-Triebwerk** *nt* LUFTTRANS gas turbine engine; **Gasturbinen-Zug** *m* EISENBAHN gas turbine train

Gas: **Gasverflüssigung** *f* MASCHINEN, THERMOD liquefaction of gases

gasverpackt *adj* LEBENSMITTEL gas-packed

Gas: **Gaswaschanlage** *f* KERNTECH gas washer, THER-

MOD gas-scrubbing plant; **Gaswäsche** f THERMOD gas scrubbing; **Gaswaschen** nt CHEMTECH scrubbing; **Gaswaschflasche** f LABOR wash bottle; **Gaswaschflasche nach Dreschel** f LABOR Dreschel gas-washing bottle; **Gaswaschturm** m CHEMTECH scrubber; **Gaswegnahme** f LUFTTRANS engine shut-off stop; **Gaszähler** m LABOR, THERMOD gas meter; **Gaszug** m KFZTECH carburetor control cable (AmE), carburettor control cable (BrE); **Gaszylinder** m KERNTECH gas cylinder

Gate nt COMP & DV gate, ELEKTROTECH *Thyristorelektrode* gate, *Transistorelektrode* gate, PHYS *Elektrode beim Feldeffekttransistor*, RADIO *FET* gate; **Gate-Array** nt ELEKTRONIK *anwendungsspezifisch verdrahtbare Standard-Anordnung von Gattern*, TELEKOM gate array; **Gate-Array-Chip** m ELEKTRONIK gate-array chip; **Gate-Dielektrikum** nt ELEKTROTECH gate dielectric; **Gate-Drain-Sperrkapazität** f ELEKTROTECH gate-to-drain capacitance; **Gate-Fehlerstrom** m ELEKTROTECH gate leakage current; **Gate-Kathoden-Widerstand** m ELEKTROTECH gate-to-cathode resistor; **Gate-Kontakt** m ELEKTROTECH gate contact; **Gate-Schaltung** f ELEKTROTECH common-gate connection; **Gate-Senke-Sperrkapazität** f ELEKTROTECH gate-to-drain capacitance; **Gate-Source-Spannung** f ELEKTROTECH gate-to-source voltage; **Gate-Source-Sperrkapazität** f ELEKTROTECH gate-to-source capacitance; **Gate-Spannung** f ELEKTROTECH gate voltage; **Gate-Substrat-Sperrkapazität** f ELEKTROTECH gate-to-substrate capacitance; **Gateverstärker** m ELEKTRONIK common-gate amplifier; **Gateway** m COMP & DV gateway, TELEKOM gateway, *zwischen ungleichen Netzen* network gateway

Gattchen nt WASSERTRANS *Segeln* grommet

Gatter nt COMP & DV, ELEKTRONIK, FERTIG *Säge*, PHYS gate; **Gatteranordnung** f ELEKTRONIK gate array, logic array, PHYS gate array; **Gatteransteuerungssignal** nt ELEKTRONIK gate-drive signal; **Gatterdichte** f ELEKTRONIK gate density; **Gatterfeld** nt TELEKOM gate array; **Gatterführung** f MASCHINEN saw guide; **Gattermatrix** f COMP & DV gate array; **Gatterschaltung** f ELEKTRONIK logic gate; **Gatterverzögerung** f ELEKTRONIK gate delay

Gattierung f FERTIG composition

Gattungsname m COMP & DV generic name

GAU abbr (*größter anzunehmender Unfall*) KERNTECH MCA (*maximum credible accident*)

Gaufrage f PAPIER embossing

gaufrieren vt PAPIER emboss

Gaufrierkalander m PAPIER embossing calender

Gaufrierwalze f PAPIER embossing roll

Gauge nt TEXTIL gage (AmE), gauge (BrE)

Gault-Ton m BAU *Geologie* Gault Clay

Gauß nt (G) AUFNAHME *Einheit der magnetischen Induktion*, ELEKTRIZ gauss (G); **~sche Fehlerverteilung** f AUFNAHME Gaussian distribution; **~-Filter-Minimalphasenumtastung** f TELEKOM GMSK, Gaussian filtered minimum shift keying; **~sche Glockenkurve** f MATH bell-shaped curve; **~scher Impuls** m TELEKOM Gaussian pulse; **~sche Krümmung** f GEOM Gaussian curvature; **~sche Kurve** f GEOM Gaussian curve; **~scher Lehrsatz** m ELEKTRIZ Gauss's theorem; **~sche Quadratur** f COMP & DV Gaussian quadrature; **~sches Rauschen** nt ELEKTRONIK, TELEKOM Gaussian noise; **~scher Satz** m PHYS *Elektrostatik* Gauss's law, *Vektoranalysis* Gauss's theorem; **~scher Strahl** m TE-LEKOM Gaussian beam; **~sche Verteilung** f COMP & DV, ELEKTRIZ PHYS Gaussian distribution

gautschen vt PAPIER couch

Gautschpresse f PAPIER couch press

Gautschwalze f PAPIER couch roll; **Gautschwalzenbezug** m PAPIER couch roll jacket; **Gautschwalzenfilzbürste** f PAPIER jacket brush

Gay-Lussac: **~sches Gesetz** nt MASCHINEN, PHYS Charles's law, Gay-Lussac's law

Gazepapier nt VERPACK reinforced paper

GB abbr (*Gigabyte*) COMP & DV, OPTIK GB (*gigabyte*)

GCA-System nt LUFTTRANS *Landesystem* GCA system, ground-controlled approach system

Gd (*Gadolinium*) CHEMIE Gd (*gadolinum*)

gealtert adj THERMOD aged

Gebäckfehler m LEBENSMITTEL baking fault

Gebälk nt BAU beams

Gebäude nt EISENBAHN, KONTROLL structure; **Gebäudeanschlußleitung** f BAU branch line; **Gebäudebrand** m SICHERHEIT structural fire; **Gebäudeflügel** m BAU wing; **Gebäudeleitung** f BAU building line; **Gebäuderäumung** f SICHERHEIT evacuation of buildings; **Gebäudeschutz** m SICHERHEIT safeguarding of buildings

Geber m TELEKOM *Telegrafie* sender

gebeugt: **~e Welle** f PHYS diffracted wave

Gebiet nt AKUSTIK field, BAU area, KOHLEN zone, KÜNSTL INT *des Wissens* domain, METALL zone; **~ mit schlechtem Empfang** nt FERNSEH poor reception area; **Gebietsauslaß** m WASSERVERSORG outfall; **Gebietsrückhalt** m WASSERVERSORG retention; **Gebietsspeicherung** f WASSERVERSORG retention; **Gebietsüberdeckung** f TELEKOM area coverage

Gebilde nt BAU form

Gebirgsbahn f EISENBAHN mountain railroad (AmE), mountain railway (BrE)

Gebirgsdruck m ERDÖL *Geologie* overburden pressure

Gebirgsmasse f KOHLEN mountain mass

Gebläse nt BAU fan, ventilating fan, ELEKTRIZ fan, FERTIG fanner, KFZTECH fan, *Kühlanlage* blower, LEBENSMITTEL blower, LUFTTRANS defogging fan, fan, MASCHINEN blast engine, blower, MECHAN, PAPIER blower; **Gebläsebrenner** m BAU blowlamp (BrE); **Gebläsebürste** f FOTO blower brush; **Gebläseflügel** m HEIZ & KÄLTE, MECHAN, THERMOD fan blade; **Gebläseflügelrad** nt MASCHINEN fan wheel

gebläsekühlen vt HEIZ & KÄLTE, MECHAN, THERMOD fan-cool

Gebläse: **Gebläsekühlung** f HEIZ & KÄLTE, MECHAN, THERMOD fan cooling; **Gebläsekupolofen** m FERTIG blast cupola; **Gebläselaufrad** nt MASCHINEN blower wheel; **Gebläsemaschine** f MASCHINEN blast engine

geblasen: **~es Glasrohr** nt LABOR blown-glass tube; **~e Glasröhre** f LABOR blown-glass tube; **~es Tafelglas** nt KER & GLAS blown sheet (AmE), cylinder glass (BrE)

Gebläse: **Gebläseofen** m HEIZ & KÄLTE, THERMOD blast furnace; **Gebläserad** nt KERNTECH, KOHLEN impeller

geblaut adj METALL blued

gebläut: **~es Blech** nt METALL blued sheet

gebleicht: **~es Mehl** nt LEBENSMITTEL bleached flour; **~er Papierbrei** m VERPACK bleached pulp; **~er Zellstoff** m VERPACK bleached pulp

gebogen[1] adj BAU arched, KER & GLAS bent, MATH *Verlauf eines Graphen* curved, METALL bent

gebogen:[2] **~er Abschnitt** m METALL bent section; **~e Linie** f GEOM curved line; **~er Meißel** m MASCHINEN cranked tool; **~er Schraubenschlüssel** *m* MASCHINEN S-shaped spanner (BrE), S-shaped wrench, curved spanner (BrE), curved wrench

gebördelt: ~er Boden *m* KER & GLAS flanged bottom; **~e Kappe** *f* VERPACK flanged cap; **~er Papierbecher** *m* VERPACK crimp paper cup; **~er Rand** *m* MASCHINEN flanged edge

gebrannt: ~es Eisen *nt* METALL burnt iron; **~e Form** *f* KER & GLAS burnt mold (AmE), burnt mould (BrE); **~er Kalk** *m* BAU quicklime; **~es Steingut** *nt* KER & GLAS burnt earthenware; **~er Ton** *m* KER & GLAS burnt clay; **~er Ziegel** *m* BAU burnt brick

Gebrauch *m* COMP & DV use; **Gebrauchs- und Installationsanweisungen** *f pl* VERPACK handling and installation instructions; **Gebrauchsanweisungen** *f pl* VERPACK directions for use, instructions for use; **Gebrauchsdauer** *f* FERTIG *Kunststoffinstallationen* operational life, KUNSTSTOFF pot life, MASCHINEN working life

gebrauchsfertig *adj* FOTO *Lösung* ready-made

gebrauchsgetestet *adj* MECHAN field-tested

Gebrauch: Gebrauchsgrafik *f* DRUCK commercial art; **Gebrauchsmuster** *nt* PATENT utility model; **Gebrauchsnormal** *nt* QUAL service standard, working standard; **Gebrauchsschrift** *f* DRUCK body type; **Gebrauchstauglichkeit** *f* QUAL fitness for use; **Gebrauchszertifikat** *nt* PATENT utility certificate

gebrochen[1] *adj* FERTIG *Härtung* stepped

gebrochen:[2] **~es Dach** *nt* BAU gambrel roof (BrE), mansard roof (AmE); **~er Exponent** *m* MATH fractional exponent; **~es Licht** *nt* OPTIK refracted light; **~e Linie** *f* GEOM broken line; **~er Strahl** *m* OPTIK *Lichtleiter* refracted rayoptical fiber (AmE), refracted rayoptical fibre (BrE), PHYS, TELEKOM refracted ray; **~e Zahl** *f* MATH fractional

gebucht: ~er Zusteigeverkehr *m* TRANS pick-up traffic

Gebühr[1] *f* TELEKOM call charge, charge

Gebühr:[2] **~ entrichten** *vi* PATENT pay a fee

Gebühr: Gebührenabrechnungssystem *nt* TELEKOM call-accounting system; **Gebührenangabe** *f* TELEKOM charging information; **Gebührenanzeiger beim Teilnehmer** *m* TELEKOM subscriber's private meter; **Gebührenerfassung** *f* TELEKOM call metering, metering; **Gebührenfernsehnetz** *nt* TELEKOM paytelevision network

gebührenfrei[1] *adj* TELEKOM free of charge

gebührenfrei:[2] **~er Anruf** *m* TELEKOM Freephone call (BrE), toll-free call (AmE), no-charge call; **~e Nummer** *f* TELEKOM freephone number; **~e Rufnummer** *f* TELEKOM Freefone number (BrE), toll-free number (AmE); **~e Schnellstraße** *f* TRANS freeway (AmE)

gebührengünstig: ~e Zeit *f* TELEKOM low-charge period

Gebühreninformation: ~ im laufenden Gespräch *f* TELEKOM call-in-progress cost information

gebührenpflichtig: ~e Ansprüche *m pl* PATENT claims incurring fees; **~e Autobahn** *f* TRANS toll road, turnpike (AmE); **~e Fernsehen** *nt* FERNSEH pay television; **~es Kabel** *nt* FERNSEH pay cable; **~e Straße** *f* TRANS turnpike (AmE)

Gebühr: Gebührenstelle *f* TELEKOM billing center (AmE), billing centre (BrE); **Gebührenübernahme** *f* COMP & DV reverse charge; **Gebührenverrechnung** *f* TELEKOM billing; **Gebührenzähler** *m* TELEKOM call-charging equipment, subscriber's meter; **Gebührenzone** *f* TELEKOM charging area

gebündelt: ~er Strahl *m* ELEKTRONIK collimated beam

gebunden[1] *adj* KER & GLAS bonded

gebunden:[2] **~es Buch** *nt* DRUCK bound book; **~es Elektron** *nt* TEILPHYS bound electron; **~es Glasfaservlies** *nt* KER & GLAS bonded mat; **~e Schleifmittel** *f pl* MASCHINEN bonded abrasive products; **~er Schwefel** *m* KUNSTSTOFF combined sulfur (AmE), combined sulphur (BrE); **~e Variable** *f* KÜNSTL INT bound variable; **~e Wärme** *f* BAU, ERDÖL, HEIZ & KÄLTE, THERMOD latent heat; **~es Wasser** *nt* LEBENSMITTEL bound water

gebürstet *adj* ELEKTROTECH, KER & GLAS, KFZTECH, MECHAN brushed

Gedächtnis: ins ~ zurückrufen *vi* ERGON recall

Gedächtnisspanne *f* ERGON memory span

gedämmt *adj* BAU insulated

gedämpft[1] *adj* PHYS damped, THERMOD banked-up

gedämpft:[2] **~er Schallmessraum** *m* RAUMFAHRT reverberation chamber; **~ schwingendes Instrument** *nt* GERÄT damped periodic instrument; **~e Schwingung** *f* AUFNAHME, ELEKTRONIK damped oscillation; **~e Schwingungen** *f pl* WELLPHYS damped vibrations; **~e Sinusgröße** *f* ELEKTROTECH damped sinusoidal quantity; **~es System** *nt* GERÄT attenuated system

Gedankenflußanalyse *f* ERGON thought-stream analysis

gedeckt[1] *adj* WASSERTRANS *Schiffbau* decked

gedeckt:[2] **~er Güterwagen** *m* EISENBAHN boxcar (AmE), freight car (AmE), wagon (BrE); **~er Hafen** *m* KER & GLAS closed port; **~er Wagen** *m* EISENBAHN covered car (AmE), covered wagon (BrE), freight van (AmE), goods van (BrE)

gedehnt[1] *adj* DRUCK elongated

gedehnt:[2] **~e x-Ablenkung** *f* ELEKTRONIK *Radar* expanded sweep

gedornt *adj* FERTIG indented

gedreht: ~er Rand *m* KER & GLAS turned rim; **~e Scheibe** *f* MASCHINEN turned washer; **~es Teil** *nt* MASCHINEN turned part

gedrosselt: ~e Lautheit *f* AKUSTIK partially-masked loudness

gedruckt[1] *adj* PATENT printed

gedruckt:[2] **~es Buch** *nt* DRUCK printed book; **~e Mikrowellenschaltung** *f* ELEKTRONIK microwave-printed circuit; **~e Schaltkarte** *f* ELEKTRONIK logic card; **~e Schaltung** *f* COMP & DV printed circuit, ELEKTRONIK *(PCB)* printed circuit board *(PCB)*, PHYS, TELEKOM printed circuit; **~e Verdrahtung** *f* ELEKTRONIK printed wiring

gedrückt[1] *adj* FERTIG *Metall, Blech* spun

gedrückt:[2] **~er Spitzbogen** *m* BAU four-centered arch (AmE), four-centred arch (BrE)

geeicht: ~er Eimer *m* BAU stamped bucket; **~e Unterlegscheibe** *f* MASCHINEN calibrated spacer; **~es Wasserrückhaltebecken** *nt* UMWELTSCHMUTZ *Landwirtschaft* calibrated watershed

geerdet[1] *adj* ELEKTRIZ, ELEKTROTECH earthed (BrE), grounded (AmE); **nicht ~** *adj* ELEKTRIZ earth-free

geerdet:[2] **~er Schalter** *m* ELEKTRIZ earthed switch (BrE), grounded switch (AmE)

Gefahr *f* SICHERHEIT hazard; **~ durch Hochfrequenzwellen** *f* SICHERHEIT radio-wave hazard; **~ durch Laserstrahlung** *f* SICHERHEIT laser radiation hazard; **~ durch Ultraschall** *f* SICHERHEIT ultrasonic hazard; **Gefahrbereichklassifizierung** *f* SICHERHEIT *für elektrische Geräte* hazardous zones classification

gefährden *vt* SICHERHEIT be a danger to

Gefahren: ~ beim Quersägen *f pl* SICHERHEIT crosscut

saw hazards; ~ **beim Querschnittssägen** *f pl* SICHERHEIT crosscut saw hazards; **Gefahrenbake** *f* LUFTTRANS hazard beacon; **Gefahrenbereich** *m* SICHERHEIT danger area, danger zone, high-risk area; **Gefahrenfeuer** *nt* LUFTTRANS hazard beacon; **Gefahrenkennzeichnung** *f* SICHERHEIT identification of hazards; **Gefahrenpunkt** *m* SICHERHEIT danger point; **Gefahrensignal** *nt* SICHERHEIT danger signal; **Gefahrensituation** *f* UMWELTSCHMUTZ episode; **Gefahrenverhütung** *f* SICHERHEIT *in Gebäuden* hazard prevention

Gefahr: **Gefahrgutbeauftragter** *m* UMWELTSCHMUTZ authorized person for hazardous goods; **Gefahrgüter** *nt pl* VERPACK dangerous goods; **Gefahrgutumschlag** *m* UMWELTSCHMUTZ transshipment of hazardous goods

gefährlich: ~**er Abfall** *m* ABFALL hazardous waste; ~**e Frachtgüter** *nt pl* LUFTTRANS dangerous goods; ~**e Ladungen** *f pl* VERPACK dangerous loads; ~**e Maschine** *f* SICHERHEIT dangerous machine; ~**er Stoff** *m* SICHERHEIT dangerous material

gefahrlos: ~**e Konzentration** *f* KERNTECH *von Kernbrennstoff* safe concentration

Gefahr: **Gefahrmeldeeinrichtung** *f* REGELUNG alarm unit; **Gefahrstoff** *m* SICHERHEIT dangerous substance, hazardous substance; **Gefahrstoffkataster** *nt* UMWELTSCHMUTZ register of hazardous substances; **Gefahrstofflager** *nt* SICHERHEIT storage of dangerous materials

Gefälle *nt* BAU downward gradient, falling gradient, gradient, incline, pitch, slant, slope, *Gelände* grade, GEOM grade, slope, HYDRAUL head, head of water, *(S)* slope *(S)*; ~ **des Wasserspiegels** *nt* WASSERVERSORG fall; ~ **einer Geraden** *nt* GEOM gradient of a straight line; **Gefällewinkelmesser** *m* METROL clinometer

gefaltet *adj* TEXTIL pleated

gefalzt: ~**e Verbindung** *f* BAU rabbeted joint

gefärbt[1] *adj* TELEKOM colored (AmE), coloured (BrE)

gefärbt:[2] ~**es Verbundglas** *nt* KER & GLAS tinted-laminated glass

Gefäß *nt* LABOR vessel; **Gefäßdurchdringen** *nt* KERNTECH vessel penetration; **Gefäßförderanlage** *f* KOHLEN skip extraction; **Gefäßreinigungsanlage** *f* BAU tank-cleaning plant

Gefechtskopf *m* RAUMFAHRT *Raumschiff* warhead

gefedert[1] *adj* MASCHINEN spring-loaded

gefedert:[2] ~**e Andruckplatte** *f* FOTO spring-mounted pressure plate; ~**r Dielenfußboden** *m* BAU tongued flooring; ~**es Gewicht** *nt* KFZTECH *Karosserie* sprung weight; ~**es Rad** *nt* KFZTECH *Getriebe* sprung gear; ~**e Verbindung** *f* BAU *Holzbau* feather joint

gefertigt: ~**e Fläche** *f* FERTIG machined surface

gefesselt *adj* MECHAN captive

gefiltert: ~**e Quadraturphasenumtastung** *f* TELEKOM filtered QPSK; ~**r Schlamm** *m* ABFALL filtration sludge

geflanscht[1] *adj* ELEKTRIZ flanged

geflanscht:[2] ~**es Rohr** *nt* MASCHINEN flanged pipe

Geflecht *nt* BAU netting, ELEKTROTECH *Isolierung von elektrischer Leitung* braid, *Kupferdraht-Abschirmung* braid

geflutet *adj* WASSERTRANS *Schleuse* flooded

gefordert: ~**e Verfügbarkeitszeit** *f* QUAL required time

gefördert: ~**e Luftmenge** *f* HEIZ & KÄLTE rate of air delivered

geformt[1] *adj* MASCHINEN shaped, PAPIER molded

(AmE), moulded (BrE)

geformt:[2] ~**er Impuls** *m* ELEKTRONIK shaped pulse; ~**er Reflektor** *m* RAUMFAHRT *Weltraumfunk* shaped reflector

gefräst *adj* MECHAN milled

Gefrier- *pref* HEIZ & KÄLTE, LEBENSMITTEL, THERMOD freezing, frozen; **Gefrieranlage** *f* HEIZ & KÄLTE freezing plant, refrigerating plant; **Gefrierbrand** *m* LEBENSMITTEL freezerburn, THERMOD humidity loss by sublimation; **Gefriercontainer** *m* HEIZ & KÄLTE refrigerated container; **Gefriereffekt** *m* THERMOD *von Helium* mechanothermal effect

Gefrieren *nt* HEIZ & KÄLTE, LEBENSMITTEL, METALL, PAPIER freezing

gefrieren[1] *vt* HEIZ & KÄLTE *von Wasser* freeze

gefrieren[2] *vi* BAU freeze

Gefrier-: **Gefrierfach** *nt* HEIZ & KÄLTE *eines Kühlschranks* freezer compartment, MASCHINEN household freezer compartment

gefrierfest *adj* HEIZ & KÄLTE, LUFTTRANS antifreezing

Gefrier-: **Gefriergerät** *nt* HEIZ & KÄLTE, MASCHINEN freezer; **Gefriergerät für Lebensmittel** *nt* MASCHINEN food freezer

gefriergetrocknet[1] *adj* CHEMTECH, HEIZ & KÄLTE, LEBENSMITTEL, THERMOD freeze-dried

gefriergetrocknet:[2] ~**es Produkt** *nt* VERPACK freeze-dried product

Gefrier-: **Gefrierkette** *f* LEBENSMITTEL *Weg vom Hersteller zum Endverbraucher* freezer chain; **Gefrierkonzentration** *f* CHEMTECH freeze concentration, HEIZ & KÄLTE freeze-concentration; **Gefrierkost** *f* VERPACK deep-frozen food; **Gefrierkurve** *f* METALL freezing curve; **Gefriermaschine** *f* HEIZ & KÄLTE freezer; **Gefriermischung** *f* HEIZ & KÄLTE freezing mixture; **Gefriermittel** *nt* HEIZ & KÄLTE freezing medium; **Gefriermöbel** *nt* HEIZ & KÄLTE display case; **Gefrierpunkt** *m* HEIZ & KÄLTE, THERMOD, VERPACK, WASSERTRANS freezing point; **Gefrierpunktserniedrigung** *f* THERMOD depression of freezing point; **Gefrierraum** *m* HEIZ & KÄLTE chill room, freezing room; **Gefrierschachtverfahren** *nt* THERMOD low-temperature sinking; **Gefrierschrank** *m* LEBENSMITTEL *Verpackung* deep freeze; **Gefrierschutzmittel** *nt* HEIZ & KÄLTE antifreeze agent; **Gefriertheke** *f* HEIZ & KÄLTE display case; **Gefriertrocknen** *nt* CHEMTECH, THERMOD, VERPACK freeze-drying

gefriertrocknen *vt* LEBENSMITTEL, THERMOD freeze-dry

Gefrier-: **Gefriertrockner** *m* CHEMTECH, HEIZ & KÄLTE freeze-drier; **Gefriertrocknung** *f* CHEMTECH, HEIZ & KÄLTE freeze-drying, lyophilization, LEBENSMITTEL dehydrofreezing, freeze-drying, VERPACK freeze-drying; **Gefriertrocknungskolben** *m* KER & GLAS lyophilization flask; **Gefriertruhe** *f* HEIZ & KÄLTE chest freezer, LEBENSMITTEL freezer chest, THERMOD freezer; **Gefriertunnel** *m* HEIZ & KÄLTE freezing tunnel, lyophilization tunnel; **Gefrierverpackung** *f* VERPACK deep freeze packaging

gefroren: ~**er Boden** *m* KOHLEN frozen ground

Gefüge *nt* FERTIG *Schleifscheibe* spacing; **Gefügeausbildung** *f* KOHLEN crystal structure; **Gefügebeständigkeit** *f* WERKPRÜF *Kunststoffe* structural stability; **Gefügeumwandlung** *f* FERTIG *Stahl* structural change

Gefühlssimulator *m* RAUMFAHRT feel simulator

geführt: ~**er Modus** *m* TELEKOM bound mode; **nicht ~er Modus** *m* TELEKOM unbound mode

gefüllt[1] *adj* BAU filled

gefüllt:[2] ~es PTFE *nt* FERTIG *Kunststoffinstallationen* PTFE and graphite

gefunkt *adj* PHYS radio

gefurcht *adj* FERTIG grooved

gegeben: ~e Größe *f* COMP & DV datum

gegen:[1] ~ Luftverschmutzung *adj* MECHAN antipollution

gegen:[2] ~ den Strom *adv* WASSERTRANS upstream; ~ den Uhrzeigersinn *adv* GERÄT ccw, counterclockwise; ~ den Wind *adv* WASSERTRANS upwind

gegen:[3] ~ Basen resistente Bespannung für Industriezwecke *f* SICHERHEIT alkaline-resistant lining for industrial plants

gegen:[4] ~ Eingriff sichern *vt* VERPACK tamper-proof; ~ die Faser arbeiten *vt* BAU work against the grain

Gegenbegrenzer *m* ELEKTRONIK inverse limiter

Gegenbogen *m* BAU inflected arch, reversed arch

Gegendruck *m* HYDRAUL *Zylinder*, MASCHINEN, PAPIER back pressure; Gegendruckturbine *f* MASCHINEN back-pressure turbine, MECHAN impulse turbine; Gegendruckventil *nt* HYDRAUL back-pressure valve; Gegendruckzylinder *m* KUNSTSTOFF impression cylinder

gegeneinandergeschaltet[1] *adj* ELEKTRIZ back-to-back connected

gegeneinandergeschaltet:[2] ~e Anordnung *f* ELEKTROTECH *Dioden* back-to-back arrangement

gegenelektromotorisch: ~e Kraft *f* (*Gegen-EMK*) EISENBAHN, ELEKTRIZ, ELEKTROTECH, LUFTTRANS back electromotive force *(bemf)*, counter electromotive force *(cemf)*

Gegen-EMK *f* (*gegenelektromotorische Kraft*) EISENBAHN, ELEKTRIZ, ELEKTROTECH, LUFTTRANS bemf, *(back electromotive force)*, cemf *(counter electromotive force)*

Gegenfeder *f* FERTIG return spring

Gegenflansch *m* KERNTECH counter flange, mating flange, MASCHINEN counter flange

Gegenflutung *f* WASSERTRANS counterflooding

Gegengewicht *nt* AUFNAHME *des Plattenspielerarms*, BAU counterweight, FERTIG dolly, LUFTTRANS balance weight, counterbalance, MASCHINEN, MECHAN balance weight, counterbalance, counterweight, RADIO *Viertelwellenantenne* counterpoise, radial; ~ des Luftschraubenblattes *nt* LUFTTRANS blade balance weight

Gegengewölbe *nt* BAU inverted arch

Gegengift *nt* CHEMIE antidote

Gegengrünphase *f* TRANS opposing green

Gegenhalten *nt* MASCHINEN holding-up

gegenhalten *vt* FERTIG *Nieten* dolly, MASCHINEN hold up

Gegenhalter *m* BAU rivet dolly, FERTIG *Fräsmaschine* overarm, overhanging arm, MASCHINEN holder-up, holding-up hammer, overarm, overhanging arm; Gegenhalterschere *f* FERTIG arbor brace, *Fräsmaschine* brace

Gegeninduktion *f* ELEKTRIZ mutual inductance, mutual induction, mutual induction, PHYS mutual induction; Gegeninduktionskoeffizient *m* ELEKTRIZ, ELEKTROTECH coefficient of mutual inductance

Gegeninduktivität *f* ELEKTROTECH mutual inductance, PHYS mutual inductance; Gegeninduktivitätskopplung *f* ELEKTROTECH mutual inductance coupling

Gegeninduktoren *m pl* ELEKTRIZ mutual inductors

gegeninduziert: ~er Anker *m* ELEKTRIZ inverse-induced armature

Gegenkolbenmotor *m* MASCHINEN opposed piston engine

Gegenkopplung *f* AUFNAHME negative feedback, ELEKTRONIK inverse feedback, negative feedback, ELEKTROTECH inverse feedback, WELLPHYS negative feedback; Gegenkopplungsfilter *nt* ELEKTRONIK inverse feedback filter

Gegenkraft *f* MASCHINEN counteracting force

Gegenkurs *m* WASSERTRANS *Navigation* reciprocal course, reciprocal track

Gegenlauf *m* FERNSEH reverse action, FERTIG reverse rotation

gegenlaufend: ~e Welle *f* ELEKTROTECH reverse traveling-wave (AmE), reverse travelling-wave (BrE)

Gegenlauf: Gegenlauffräsen *nt* FERTIG conventional milling, out-cut milling, up-milling, upcut milling, MASCHINEN conventional milling, standard milling, upcut milling; Gegenlauffrässchnitt *m* FERTIG conventional cut

gegenläufig: ~er Axiallüfter *m* LUFTTRANS counter-revolving axial fan; ~e Propeller *m pl* LUFTTRANS counter-rotating propellers; ~e Treppe *f* BAU dogleg stairs; ~e Walzenstreichmaschine *f* PAPIER reverse roll coater

Gegenlauf: Gegenlaufschleifen *nt* FERTIG up-grinding; Gegenlaufwirbeln *nt* FERTIG opposed whirling

Gegenlicht:[1] im ~ *adj* FOTO backlit

Gegenlicht:[2] im ~ *adv* FOTO backlight

Gegenlichtaufnahme *f* FOTO backlighted photo

Gegenlichtblende *f* FOTO hood, lens hood

Gegenmodulation *f* ELEKTRONIK inverse modulation

Gegenmutter *f* MASCHINEN jam nut, locknut, MECHAN locknut

Gegenpassat *m* WASSERTRANS *Windart* antitrades

gegenphasig[1] *adj* ELEKTRIZ opposite phase, ELEKTRONIK in-phase opposition

gegenphasig[2] *adv* FERNSEH antiphase

gegenphasig:[3] ~e Antenne *f* RAUMFAHRT *Weltraumfunk* endfire antenna

Gegenprobe *f* KOHLEN check sample, MASCHINEN countertest

Gegenprofil *nt* MASCHINEN mating profile

Gegenrad *nt* MASCHINEN mating gear

Gegenschaltung *f* ELEKTRIZ bucking circuit

Gegenschiene *f* EISENBAHN safety rail

Gegenschlaghammer *m* FERTIG impacter

Gegensee *f* WASSERTRANS head sea

gegenseitig:[1] ~e Abhängigkeit *f* KONTROLL interplay; ~e Blockierung *f* KONTROLL deadlock; ~e Induktivität *f* ELEKTROTECH mutual inductance; ~e Peilung *f* LUFTTRANS *Navigation* reciprocal bearing; ~es Sperren *nt* COMP & DV deadlock, deadly embrace; ~e Störung der Kanäle *f* ELEKTROTECH interchannel interference; ~e Synchronisierung *f* TELEKOM mutual synchronization

gegenseitig:[2] ~ anziehen *vi* PHYS attract each other

gegenseitig:[3] ~ versetzen *vt* COMP & DV interleave

Gegenspannung *f* ELEKTROTECH reverse voltage; Gegenspannungsschutz *m* ELEKTROTECH reverse-voltage protection

Gegensprechanlage *f* AUFNAHME talkback

Gegensprechen *nt* AUFNAHME talkback

Gegensprechmikrofon *nt* AUFNAHME talkback microphone

Gegenstand *m* PATENT subject matter

Gegenständer *m* MASCHINEN back rest

Gegenstelle *f* TELEKOM distant end

Gegenstempel *m* MASCHINEN counterpunch

Gegenstößel *m* MECHAN plunger

Gegenstrom *m* ELEKTROTECH countercurrent, KOHLEN, MASCHINEN counterflow; **Gegenstrombremsung** *f* ELEKTROTECH plugging; **Gegenstromdestillation** *f* CHEMIE rectification; **Gegenstromdiffusionsanlage** *f* KERNTECH countercurrent diffusion plant; **Gegenstromfilter** *nt* ABFALL reverse flow filter; **Gegenstromklassierer** *m* KOHLEN countercurrent classifier; **Gegenstromkondensation** *f* HEIZ & KÄLTE counterflow condensation; **Gegenstromkühlturm** *m* HEIZ & KÄLTE counterflow-cooling tower; **Gegenstromkühlung** *f* HEIZ & KÄLTE counterflow cooling; **Gegenstromlinie** *f* HYDRAUL counter streamline; **Gegenstromwärmeaustauscher** *m* HEIZ & KÄLTE, LEBENSMITTEL counterflow heat exchanger

Gegentakt *m* MECHAN push-pull; **Gegentaktbetrieb** *m* RADIO push-pull operation; **Gegentaktmischer** *m* ELEKTRONIK balanced mixer; **Gegentaktmodulator** *m* ELEKTRONIK balanced modulator; **Gegentaktschalter** *m* ELEKTRIZ push-pull switch; **Gegentaktschaltung** *f* AUFNAHME push-pull circuit; **Gegentaktumsetzer** *m* ELEKTRONIK push-pull modulator; **Gegentaktverstärker** *m* AUFNAHME balanced amplifier, ELEKTRONIK balanced amplifier, paraphrase amplifier, push-pull amplifier

gegenüberliegend[1] *adj* GEOM opposite

gegenüberliegend:[2] ~e Seiten *f pl* GEOM *eines Quadrats* opposite sides; ~e Zylinder *m pl* KFZTECH opposed cylinders

Gegenüberwicklung *f* ELEKTRIZ diametrical winding

Gegenvakuumventil *nt* NICHTFOSS ENERG antivacuum valve

Gegenverkehr *m* TRANS opposing traffic

Gegenwelle *f* MASCHINEN second motion shaft

Gegenwind *m* LUFTTRANS, WASSERTRANS headwind

Gegenwinkel *m pl* GEOM corresponding angles

gegenwirkend[1] *adj* MASCHINEN reactive

gegenwirkend:[2] ~e Drehkraft *f* LUFTTRANS antagonistic torque

Gegenwirkleitwert *m* ELEKTROTECH transconductance

gegißt: ~es Besteck *nt* WASSERTRANS *Navigation* dead-reckoning position, estimated position

geglättet: ~e Kante *f* KER & GLAS smoothed edge; ~er Verkehr *m* TRANS smooth traffic

gegliedert *adj* BAU jointed

geglüht *adj* METALL, THERMOD *Stahl* annealed

gegoren: ~er Malztrank *m* LEBENSMITTEL malt extract

gegossen: ~es Loch *nt* MASCHINEN cast hole; ~e Type *f* DRUCK metal type; ~e Zeile *f* DRUCK slug; in ~em Zustand *adj* FERTIG *ohne weitere Bearbeitung* as-cast

Gehalt *m* ANSTRICH, KOHLEN, KUNSTSTOFF content, MASCHINEN tenor, METALL, PAPIER content, TEXTIL analysis, content

gehalten: ~e Verbindung *f* TELEKOM call held

gehämmert *adj* KER & GLAS hammered

Gehänge *nt* FERTIG *Gießen, Gießkran* ball, KFZTECH *Blattfeder* shackle, MASCHINEN hanger

gehärtet *adj* CHEMIE *Fett, Öl*, LEBENSMITTEL hydrogenated, METALL *Stahl* hardened, THERMOD heat-treated

Gehäuse *nt* BAU casing, frame, housing, ELEKTRIZ casing, ELEKTROTECH *eines elektronischen Geräts* frame, FERTIG *Kunststoffinstallationen* body, housing, HEIZ & KÄLTE enclosure, HYDRAUL *Dampfzylinder, Gebläse,*

Zentrifugalpumpe, Turbine, KFZTECH *Motor, Getriebe* casing, KOHLEN *Maschine* shell, KONTROLL enclosure, LUFTTRANS *Flugwesen* case, MASCHINEN box, cage, case, casing, housing, shell, MECHAN case, casing, NICHTFOSS ENERG housing, RAUMFAHRT *Raumschiff* pod, TELEKOM cabinet, WASSERTRANS casing; **Gehäuseabstrahlung** *f* TELEKOM cabinet radiation; **Gehäusedeckel** *m* FOTO body cap, MASCHINEN casing cover; **Gehäusedichtung** *f* FERTIG *Kunststoffinstallationen* body seal

geheftet[1] *adj* DRUCK stitched

geheftet:[2] ~e Schachtel *f* VERPACK stitched box

Geheimtür *f* BAU jib door

gehemmt *adj* FERTIG *Getriebelehre* held back

gehen *vi* MASCHINEN work

gehend[1] *adj* TELEKOM outgoing

gehend:[2] ~er Ablauf *m* TELEKOM outgoing procedure

Gehlinie *f* BAU *Treppe* walking line

gehoben: ~e Last *f* LUFTTRANS lifted load

Gehör *nt* AKUSTIK audio, auditory, ERGON audition; **Gehörempfindlichkeit** *f* AKUSTIK aural sensitivity; **Gehörempfindlichkeitsmeßgerät** *nt* AKUSTIK audiometer; **Gehörempfindlichkeitsmessung** *f* AKUSTIK audiometry; **Gehörempfindlichkeitsskale** *f* AKUSTIK aural sensation scale; **Gehörempfindung** *f* AKUSTIK auditory sensation; **Gehörermüdung** *f* AKUSTIK hearing fatigue

gehörevoziert: ~e Spannung *f* AKUSTIK hearing-evoked voltage

Gehör: **Gehörgang** *m* AKUSTIK auditory canal; **Gehörmesser** *m* AUFNAHME audiometer; **Gehörmeßgerät** *nt* WELLPHYS sonometer; **Gehörprüfkabine** *f* AUFNAHME audiometric booth; **Gehörschärfemessung** *f* AKUSTIK audiometry; **Gehörschutz** *m* AKUSTIK ear protection, ERGON ear protector, SICHERHEIT hearing conservation; **Gehörschwankungen** *f pl* AKUSTIK *in der Tonhöhe* aural flutter; **Gehörtestraum** *m* AKUSTIK audiometric test room; **Gehörverlust** *m* ERGON hearing loss

gehren *vt* FERTIG miter (AmE), mitre (BrE)

Gehrstoß *m* BAU miter joint (AmE), mitre joint (BrE)

Gehrung *f* BAU bevel, miter (AmE), mitre (BrE), DRUCK, FERTIG, KER & GLAS miter (AmE), mitre (BrE); **Gehrungsfuge** *f* BAU miter joint (AmE), mitre joint (BrE); **Gehrungskrümmung** *f* KER & GLAS miter return (AmE), mitre return (BrE); **Gehrungsschere** *f* FERTIG beveling shear (AmE), bevelling shear (BrE); **Gehrungsschleifmaschine** *f* KER & GLAS miter-grinding machine (AmE), mitre-grinding machine (BrE); **Gehrungsschnitt** *m* FERTIG miter cut (AmE), mitre cut (BrE); **Gehrungsschnittlehre** *f* BAU miter board (AmE), miter box (AmE), mitre board (BrE), mitre box (BrE); **Gehrungsstanzmaschine** *f* BAU miter-cutting machine (AmE), mitre-cutting machine (BrE); **Gehrungswinkel** *m* BAU miter square (AmE), mitre square (BrE), FERTIG bevel, KER & GLAS miter bevel (AmE), mitre bevel (BrE), METROL bevel

Gehweg *m* BAU banquette, pavement (BrE), sidewalk (AmE); **Gehwegplatte** *f* BAU flag, paving stone; **Gehwegplattenbelag** *m* BAU flagstone pavement (BrE), flagstone sidewalk (AmE)

Gei *f* WASSERTRANS *Tauwerk* guy

Geigenharz *nt* CHEMIE rosin

Geiger: **Geiger-Müller-Zählrohr** *nt* PHYS, STRAHLPHYS, TEILPHYS Geiger-Muller tube; **Geigerzähler** *m* FERTIG, PHYS, STRAHLPHYS, TEILPHYS, UMWELTSCHMUTZ Geiger counter, contamination meter; **Geiger-Zählrohr** *nt* PHYS, STRAHLPHYS, TEILPHYS Geiger tube

Geiser *m* NICHTFOSS ENERG geyser

Geißler-Röhre *f* ELEKTRONIK Geissler tube

Geisterbild *nt* FERNSEH ghost image, multipath signals, FOTO ghost

Geisterecho *nt* WASSERTRANS *Radar* ghost echo

geistig: ~es Eigentum *nt* PATENT intellectual property

Geitau *nt* WASSERTRANS *Tauwerk* guy

gekämmt *adj* TEXTIL combed

gekapselt[1] *adj* MASCHINEN enclosed

gekapselt:[2] ~e Induktanz *f* ELEKTRIZ sealed reactor; ~e Kontakte *m pl* ELEKTROTECH sealed contacts; ~er Motor *m* ELEKTRIZ closed motor, enclosed motor, sealed motor, ELEKTROTECH, MASCHINEN enclosed motor, MECHAN canned motor; ~e Sicherung *f* ELEKTRIZ, ELEKTROTECH enclosed fuse; ~er Transformator *m* ELEKTRIZ sealed transformer

gekehlt *adj* MECHAN keyed

gekennzeichnet: ~er Name *m* COMP & DV qualified name

gekerbt[1] *adj* FERTIG notched, scalloped, serrated, MASCHINEN notched

gekerbt:[2] ~e Mutter *f* MASCHINEN notched nut

gekettet: ~e Baumstruktur *f* COMP & DV threaded tree; ~e Datei *f* COMP & DV chained file, threaded file, TELEKOM threaded file; ~e Liste *f* COMP & DV chained list; ~es Programm *nt* COMP & DV thread; ~e Programmiersprache *f* COMP & DV threaded language

geklebt[1] *adj* DRUCK pasted, ELEKTRIZ laminated

geklebt:[2] ~e Bindung *f* DRUCK perfect binding; ~es Glasleinen *nt* KER & GLAS bonded glass cloth

geknickt: ~e Freifläche *f* FERTIG offset tool flank; ~er Linienzug *m* KONSTZEICH zigzag line; ~e Spanfläche *f* FERTIG offset tool face

gekniffen: ~e Fadenauflage *f* KER & GLAS pinched thread

gekocht: ~e Stärke *f* LEBENSMITTEL boiled starch

gekohlt: ~er Stahl *m* MASCHINEN carbon steel

gekoppelt[1] *adj* ELEKTRIZ ganged, ELEKTROTECH coupled, MASCHINEN connected

gekoppelt:[2] ~er Entfernungsmesser *m* FOTO coupled rangefinder; ~e Gleichungen *f pl* MATH simultaneous equations; ~e Kondensatoren *m pl* ELEKTRIZ ganged capacitors; ~e Kontakte *f* ELEKTROTECH mated contacts; ~er Kreis *m* FERNSEH ganged circuit; ~e Moden *f pl* OPTIK, TELEKOM coupled modes; ~e Oszillatoren *m pl* PHYS coupled oscillators; ~es Potentiometerpaar *nt* ELEKTRIZ dual-ganged potentiometer; ~e Stromkreise *m pl* ELEKTRIZ coupled circuits; ~e Systeme *nt pl* PHYS coupled systems; ~e Verschluß- und Blendeneinstellung *f* FOTO coupled speed and F-stop setting

gekräuselt *adj* TEXTIL crimped

gekreppt *adj* PAPIER creped

gekreuzt[1] *adj* MASCHINEN crossed

gekreuzt:[2] ~e Nicol-Prismen *nt pl* PHYS crossed Nicols

gekröpft[1] *adj* MASCHINEN cranked, swan-necked

gekröpft:[2] ~e Achse *f* KFZTECH *Triebstrang*, MASCHINEN dropped axle; ~es Drehherz *nt* MASCHINEN bent-tail lathe dog; ~er Gewindemeißel *m* FERTIG offset single-point threading tool; ~er Meißel *m* MASCHINEN goosenecked tool; ~er Schraubenschlüssel *m* MASCHINEN bent spanner (BrE), gooseneck wrench, offset wrench; ~es Werkzeug *nt* MASCHINEN bent tool

gekrümmt: ~er Flaschenhals *m* KER & GLAS bent neck; ~e Linie *f* GEOM curved line; ~es Schaufelblatt *nt* HYDRAUL *Turbine, Kreiselpumpe* curved vane; ~e Wand *f* BAU bulged wall

gekühlt[1] *adj* HEIZ & KÄLTE refrigerated, LEBENSMITTEL chilled, THERMOD chilled, cooled

gekühlt:[2] ~e Abstellfläche *f* HEIZ & KÄLTE refrigerated shelf area

gekümpelt[1] *adj* FERTIG dished

gekümpelt:[2] ~er Boden *m* KERNTECH *eines Reaktordruckgefäßes* dished bottom

gekuppelt[1] *adj* FERTIG engaged, interlocked, MASCHINEN coupled

gekuppelt:[2] ~er verstellbarer Nutenfräser *m* FERTIG interlocking mill

gekürzt:[1] ~er Bruch *m* MATH basic fraction; ~e Fassung *f* DRUCK abridged edition

gekürzt:[2] ~ zeichnen *vt* KONSTZEICH draw in shortened form

Gel *nt* ERDÖL, KUNSTSTOFF gel

geladen: ~e Kapazität *f* KOHLEN loaded capacity; ~es Teilchen *nt* ELEKTRONIK, ELEKTROTECH, KERNTECH, STRAHLPHYS, TEILPHYS charged particle

Gelände *nt* BAU field; ~ für Schleudertraining *nt* KFZTECH *Straßenfahrt* skidpad; **Geländefahrzeug** *nt* KFZTECH all-terrain vehicle

geländegängig: ~er LKW *m* KFZTECH cross-country lorry (BrE), cross-country truck (AmE)

Gelände: **Geländehöhe** *f* BAU level, EISENBAHN ground level; **Geländemotorrad** *nt* KFZTECH cross-country motorcycle, scrambling motor cycle; **Geländeneigung** *f* BAU fall of ground

Geländer *nt* BAU balustrade, guard rail, handrail, railing, MECHAN handrail, SICHERHEIT guard rail; **Geländerausfachung** *f* BAU paling; **Geländerpfosten** *m* BAU baluster

Gelände: **Geländespiegel** *m* PHYS periscope

Gelatine *f* DRUCK, VERPACK gelatine; **Gelatinekapsel** *f* VERPACK gelatine capsule

Gelatinierung *f* KUNSTSTOFF gelation

Gelatinierung *f* KUNSTSTOFF gelation; **Gelatinierungsmittel** *nt* KUNSTSTOFF gelling agent

Gelb *nt* FOTO yellow; **Gelbbrennsäure** *f* CHEMIE aqua fortis

gelb: ~es Katechu *nt* CHEMIE gambier

Gelb: **Gelbfiltereinstellung** *f* FOTO minus blue filter adjustment, yellow filter adjustment; **Gelbguß** *m* FERTIG high brass; **Gelbkörperhormon** *nt* CHEMIE progesterone

gelblich *adj* TEXTIL yellowish

Gelb: **Gelbsignaldauer** *f* TRANS hour of yellow signal indication; **Gelbstich** *m* TEXTIL yellowness

gelbstichig *adj* TEXTIL yellowish

Gelb: **Gelbstrohpapier** *nt* PAPIER yellow straw paper; **Gelbstrohstoff** *m* PAPIER yellow straw pulp

Gel: **Gelchromatographie** *f* LABOR gel permeation chromatography; **Gelcoat** *m* KUNSTSTOFF, WASSERTRANS *Schiffbau* gel coat

Geldausgabeautomat *m* COMP & DV ATM, automatic teller machine

Geldkartentelefon *nt* TELEKOM card-operated payphone

geleiten *vt* WASSERTRANS *Schiff* convoy

geleitet: ~e Welle *f* OPTIK guided wave

Geleitfahrzeug *nt* WASSERTRANS *Marine* escort ship

Geleitzug *m* WASSERTRANS *Marine* convoy

Gelenk:[1] mit ~ verbunden *adj* MECHAN articulated

Gelenk[2] *nt* BAU joint, COMP & DV link, ERGON joint, KFZTECH knuckle, LUFTTRANS cardan, MASCHINEN joint, MECHAN knuckle, TRANS articulated; **Gelenkarm** *m* FERTIG articulated arm; **Gelenkbolzen** *m* BAU joint bolt, MASCHINEN hinged bolt, pintle; **Gelenkbus** *m* TRANS articulated bus; **Gelenkfahrsteig** *m* TRANS articulated-type moving pavement (BrE), articulated-type moving sidewalk (AmE); **Gelenkfahrzeug** *nt* KFZTECH articulated vehicle, twister; **Gelenkflügel der Luftschraube** *m* LUFTTRANS *Hubschrauber* articulated blade

gelenkig *adj* BAU jointed; **~ verbunden** *adj* MECHAN linked

Gelenk: **Gelenkkette** *f* MECHAN sprocket chain; **Gelenkketteneinstellung** *f* KFZTECH sprocket and chain timing; **Gelenkkreuz** *nt* KFZTECH *Universalgelenk* spider; **Gelenkkupplung** *f* MASCHINEN universal joint coupling, TRANS articulated coupling; **Gelenklager** *nt* MASCHINEN swing support, MECHAN ball-and-socket joint; **Gelenkoberleitungsbus** *m* KFZTECH articulated trolleybus; **Gelenkpunkt** *m* PHYS fulcrum; **Gelenkrotor** *m* LUFTTRANS *Hubschrauber* articulated rotor; **Gelenkschienenfahrzeug** *nt* EISENBAHN articulated railcar; **Gelenkstellung** *f* ERGON joint posture; **Gelenkstraßenbahn** *f* KFZTECH articulated tramway

gelenkt: **~es Rad** *nt* KFZTECH *Lenkung* steered wheel; **~er unbemannter Hubschrauber** *m* LUFTTRANS drone helicopter

Gelenk: **Gelenktriebwagen** *m* KFZTECH articulated streetcar (AmE), articulated tramcar (BrE); **Gelenkverbindung** *f* BAU hinge joint, ERGON articulation, MASCHINEN articulation, link joint; **Gelenkwagen** *m* KFZTECH articulated car, articulated lorry (BrE), articulated truck (AmE); **Gelenkwelle** *f* FERTIG universal shaft, KFZTECH propeller shaft, MECHAN cardan shaft

Gelierdauer *f* VERPACK gel time

Gelieren *nt* CHEMTECH jellification

gelieren *vi* CHEMTECH coagulate

Geliermittel *nt* KUNSTSTOFF, LEBENSMITTEL, MEERSCHMUTZ gelling agent

Gelierung *f* CHEMTECH jellification

Gelierzeit *f* VERPACK gel time

gelind:[1] **~e Hitze** *f* THERMOD gentle heat; **~e Wärme** *f* THERMOD gentle heat

gelind:[2] **~e kochen** *vi* THERMOD boil slowly

gelitzt: **~er Draht** *m* ELEKTRIZ stranded cable, ELEKTROTECH stranded conductor; **~er Leiter** *m* ELEKTRIZ stranded conductor

gelocht[1] *adj* COMP & DV perforated

gelocht:[2] **~e Dämmplatte** *f* AUFNAHME perforated absorbent tile; **~e Platte** *f* METALL perforated plate

geloggt: **~e Entfernung** *f* WASSERTRANS *Navigation* distance logged

gelöscht: **~er Kalk** *m* LEBENSMITTEL slaked lime

gelöst[1] *adj* CHEMTECH dissolved

gelöst:[2] **~er anorganischer Kohlenstoff** *m* UMWELTSCHMUTZ dissolved inorganic carbon; **~er organischer Kohlenstoff** *m* UMWELTSCHMUTZ dissolved organic carbon; **~e organische Substanz** *f* UMWELTSCHMUTZ dissolved organic matter; **~er Sauerstoff** *m* UMWELTSCHMUTZ dissolved oxygen

gelotet *adj* FERTIG cast

gelötet: **~e Blechverbindung** *f* BAU plumb joint

Gel-Permeations-Chromatographie *f* *(GPC)* KUNSTSTOFF, LABOR gel permeation chromatography *(GPC)*

Gelsemin *nt* CHEMIE gelsemine

Geltungsbereich *m* MASCHINEN scope

Geltungsdauer *f* BAU validity period

gelüftet *adj* HEIZ & KÄLTE, THERMOD ventilated

Gel-Zeit *f* KUNSTSTOFF gel time

Gel-Zelle *f* ELEKTROTECH gel cell

gemahlen *adj* PAPIER beaten

gemallt: **~e Breite** *f* WASSERTRANS *Schiffkonstruktion* molded breadth (AmE), moulded breadth (BrE); **~e Seitenhöhe** *f* WASSERTRANS *Schiffbau* molded depth (AmE), moulded depth (BrE)

gemein: **~er Bruch** *m* MATH common fraction, vulgar fraction

gemeinsam:[1] **~e Abfrage** *f* COMP & DV partitioning sensing; **~e Anmelder** *m pl* PATENT joint applicants; **~er Anodenanschluß** *m* ELEKTROTECH common anode connection; **~e Benennung** *f* PATENT joint designation; **~ benutzbarer virtueller Bereich** *m (SVA)* COMP & DV shared virtual area *(SVA)*; **~ benutzte Datei** *f* COMP & DV shared file; **~ benutzter Speicher** *m* COMP & DV shared memory; **~ benutztes Speichersystem** *nt* COMP & DV shared memory system; **~er Bereich** *m* COMP & DV common area; **~e Busleitung** *f* TELEKOM common highway; **~er Dateizugriff** *m* COMP & DV file sharing; **~e Eigenschaften** *f pl* STRAHLPHYS *elektromagnetischer Wellen* common properties; **~er Highway** *m* TELEKOM common highway; **~e Kathode** *f* ELEKTROTECH common cathode; **~e Luftschnittstelle** *f* TELEKOM common air interface; **~er Nenner** *m* MATH common denominator; **~e Nutzung** *f* COMP & DV sharing; **~e Nutzung der Betriebsmittel** *f* COMP & DV resource sharing; **~es Phänomen** *nt* PHYS cooperative phenomenon; **~e Rückleitung** *f* EISENBAHN common return; **~er Speicher** *m* TELEKOM common store; **~er Teiler** *m* MATH common factor, common ratio; **~er Träger** *m* FERNSEH common carrier; **~e Zahnhöhe** *f* FERTIG *Getriebelehre* depth of engagement; **~er Zugriff** *m* COMP & DV shared access; **~er Zweig** *m* ELEKTROTECH *bei Strompfad* common branch; **~e Zweigleitung** *f* ELEKTRIZ *elektrisches Versorgungsnetz* common branch

gemeinsam:[2] **~ benutzen** *vt* COMP & DV share; **~ nutzen** *vt* COMP & DV share

Gemeinschaft *f* TELEKOM community

gemeinschaftlich: **~es Fahrzeug** *nt* TRANS public automobile; **~ stranggepreßte Folie** *f* VERPACK coextruded film

Gemeinschaft: **Gemeinschaftsantenne** *f* FERNSEH community antenna, TELEKOM collective aerial, collective antenna, common aerial, community aerial; **Gemeinschaftseinrichtung** *f* TELEKOM common equipment; **Gemeinschaftskläranlage** *f* WASSERVERSORG community sewage works, public water supply; **Gemeinschaftsleitung** *f* TELEKOM party line, shared service line; **Gemeinschaftssystem** *nt* COMP & DV multiuser system

Gemenge *nt* KER & GLAS *Glasherstellung* batch; **Gemengecharge ohne Scherben** *f* KER & GLAS batch charge without cullet

gemengefrei *adj* KER & GLAS batch-free

Gemenge: **Gemengehaus** *nt* KER & GLAS batch house; **Gemengehaut** *f* KER & GLAS batch crust; **Gemengemischung** *f* KER & GLAS batch mixing; **Gemengesatz** *m* KER & GLAS batch pile; **Gemengeschmelzgrenze** *f* KER & GLAS batch-melting line (AmE), silica scum line (BrE); **Gemengespeiser** *m* KER & GLAS batch charger; **Gemengestaub** *m* KER & GLAS batch dust; **Gemengestein** *m* KER & GLAS batch stone; **Gemengeturm** *m* KER & GLAS batch tower

gemessen: **~e Schwelle** *f* KERNTECH *einer Kernreaktion* observed threshold; **~e Spannung** *f* ELEKTRIZ measured voltage; ~er **Stromwert** *m* ELEKTRIZ measured current; ~er **Überdruck** *m* HEIZ & KÄLTE *Überdruck über atmosphärischem Druck* gage pressure (AmE), gauge pressure (BrE); ~er **Wert** *m* GERÄT measured value

Gemisch *nt* KUNSTSTOFF blend, LEBENSMITTEL, MASCHINEN mixture; **Gemischregler** *m* KFZTECH mixture control unit; **Gemischregulierung** *f* LUFTTRANS *Motor und Triebwerk* mixture control; **Gemischschmierung** *f* MASCHINEN oil-in-gasoline lubrication

gemischt: ~e **Ablagerung** *f* ABFALL codeposition, codisposal; ~ **algebraische Ausdrücke** *m pl* MATH mixed algebraic expressions; ~ **betriebene Leitung** *f* TELEKOM both-way circuit; ~e **Datenaufzeichnung** *f* COMP & DV MDR, miscellaneous data recording; ~e **Energieversorgung** *f* TRANS mixed power supply; ~es **Produkt** *nt* MATH *von Vektoren* triple scalar product; ~er **Prozeß** *m* ELEKTRONIK mixed process; ~er **Satz** *m* DRUCK mixed styles; ~e **Strahlung** *f* STRAHLPHYS mixed radiation; ~e **Versetzung** *f* METALL mixed dislocation; ~e **Zahl** *f* MATH mixed number, mixed numeral

gemischtadrig: ~es **Kabel** *nt* ELEKTROTECH composite cable

Gemischtbasisschreibweise *f* COMP & DV mixed-base notation, mixed-radix notation

Gemischtbremsventil *nt* EISENBAHN brake-blending valve

gemischtpaarig: ~es **Kabel** *nt* ELEKTROTECH composite cable

genähert *adj* MATH approximate

genau[1] *adj* MECHAN, METROL, PHYS accurate

genau:[2] ~ **achteraus** *adv* WASSERTRANS dead astern; ~ **voraus** *adv* WASSERTRANS dead ahead

genau:[3] ~e **Druckmarkierung** *f* VERPACK accurate print registration; ~e **Karte** *f* METROL accurate map; ~e **Mitte** *f* MECHAN dead center (AmE), dead centre (BrE); ~e **Registrierung** *f* VERPACK accurate print registration; ~e **Überprüfung** *f* BAU meticulous inspection; ~e **Wiedergabe** *f* FOTO accurate reproduction

Genaubohren *nt* MASCHINEN precision drilling

Genauigkeit *f* COMP & DV, MASCHINEN, MECHAN, METROL, PHYS accuracy, precision, QUAL, WASSERTRANS *des Schiffsstandortes* accuracy; ~ **des Sollwertes** *f* KERNTECH set point accuracy; **Genauigkeitsgießform** *f* FERTIG, MASCHINEN investment mold (AmE), investment mould (BrE); **Genauigkeitsklasse** *f* GERÄT *Meßgerät* class; **Genauigkeitsprüfung** *f* MASCHINEN accuracy test; **Genauigkeitsspiralbohrer** *m* FERTIG cylinder bit

genehmigen *vt* QUAL, SICHERHEIT approve

genehmigt *adj* SICHERHEIT approved

Genehmigung *f* ELEKTRIZ, QUAL approval, RADIO *Funkverwaltung* licence (BrE), license (AmE), TRANS approval; **Genehmigungszeichnung** *f* HEIZ & KÄLTE approval drawing

geneigt:[1] ~ **um einen Winkel von** *adv* GEOM inclined at an angle of

geneigt:[2] ~er **Dipol** *m* RADIO drooping dipole; ~e **Ebene** *f* PHYS inclined plane; ~e **Fläche** *f* GEOM inclined plane, MASCHINEN cant; ~e **Linie** *f* KONSTZEICH sloping line

General- *pref* ELEKTROTECH, TELEKOM, WASSERTRANS master; **Generalplan** *m* WASSERTRANS *Schiffbau* general arrangement plan; **Generalruf** *m* TELEKOM global call; **Generalschalter** *m* ELEKTROTECH master switch; **Generalschlüssel** *m* BAU master key; **Generalüberholung** *f* TRANS overhaulage; **Generalunternehmer** *m* BAU general contractor; **Generalverkehrsplan** *m* TRANS traffic master plan

Generator *m* BAU, COMP & DV, ELEKTRIZ generator, ELEKTROTECH electric generator, generator, HYDRAUL generator, KERNTECH generation time, MASCHINEN producer, PHYS generator, voltage generator, RADIO dynamo, generator, TELEKOM, WASSERTRANS *Elektrik* generator; ~ **mit ausgeprägten Polkanten** *m* ELEKTRIZ salient pole generator; ~ **mit Doppelwicklung** *m* ELEKTRIZ double-wound generator; ~ **mit erweitertem Luftspalt** *m* ELEKTRIZ salient pole generator; ~ **für die Gittervorspannung** *m* ELEKTROTECH bias generator; **Generatoranlage** *f* ELEKTROTECH generating plant; **Generatorbürste** *f* KFZTECH *KFZ-Elektrik* generator brush; **Generatorgeschwindigkeit** *f* NICHTFOSS ENERG generator speed; **Generatorgruppe** *f* ELEKTROTECH generating set

generatorisch: ~es **Bremsen** *nt* EISENBAHN dynamic braking

Generator: **Generatorkohle** *f* KOHLEN generator coal, producer coal; **Generatorleistung** *f* ELEKTROTECH generator output power; **Generatorsatz** *m* ELEKTROTECH generating set; **Generator-Signalgabe** *f* ELEKTROTECH generator signaling (AmE), generator signalling (BrE)

generell: ~es **Problemlösen** *nt* KÜNSTL INT GPS, general problem solving

generieren *vt* GEOM generate

generiert: ~er **Fehler** *m* COMP & DV generated error

Generierung *f* COMP & DV generation; **Generierungsprogramm** *nt* COMP & DV generating program, generator

generisch[1] *adj* COMP & DV generic

generisch:[2] ~e **Kaskade** *f* KERNTECH generic cascade; ~er **Name** *m* COMP & DV generic name

genetisch: ~ **wichtige Dosis** *f* UMWELTSCHUTZ genetically significant dose

genietet: ~e **Überlappung** *f* MASCHINEN riveted lap joint

Genistein *nt* CHEMIE genistein, prunetol

genormt: ~e **Bemessungswerte** *m pl* HEIZ & KÄLTE standard ratings; ~e **Schnittstelle** *f* TELEKOM standard interface

Gentex *nt* (*Telegrammwähldienst*) TELEKOM gentex (*general telegraph exchange*)

Gentianin *nt* CHEMIE gentianin

Gentiobiose *f* CHEMIE gentiobiose

Gentiopikrin *nt* CHEMIE gentiopicrin

Gentiopikrosid *nt* CHEMIE gentiopicrin

Gentisin *nt* CHEMIE gentisin; **Gentisin-** *pref* CHEMIE gentisic

Genußsäure *f* LEBENSMITTEL edible acid

genutet[1] *adj* FERTIG grooved, slotted

genutet:[2] ~er **Anker** *m* ELEKTROTECH slotted armature; ~es **Kabel** *nt* OPTIK grooved cable

Geodäsie *f* GEOM geodesy

Geodäte *f* GEOM geodesic

geodätisch[1] *adj* WASSERTRANS geodesic, geodetic

geodätisch:[2] ~e **Linie** *f* GEOM geodesic

Geodimeter *nt* BAU geodimeter

geoelektrisch: ~es **Log** *nt* ERDÖL electric log

geöffnet[1] *adj* PHYS *Stromkreis* open

geöffnet:[2] ~er **Kontakt** *m* ELEKTRIZ open contact; ~e **Schaltung** *f* ELEKTROTECH broken circuit

geographisch: ~e **Abweichung** *f* UMWELTSCHUTZ geographic variation; ~e **Breite** *f* WASSERTRANS *Navigation* latitude; ~e **Flugbahn** *f* LUFTTRANS required flightpath; ~e **Länge** *f* WASSERTRANS *Navigation* longitude; ~e **Sichtweite** *f* WASSERTRANS *Navigation* geographical range

Geologie *f* ERDÖL, KOHLEN geology

geologisch: ~e **Vermessung** *f* ERDÖL, KOHLEN geological survey

geölt: ~e **Lager** *nt pl* MASCHINEN oiled bearings

geomagnetisch[1] *adj* RAUMFAHRT geomagnetic

geomagnetisch:[2] ~e **Abrißenergie** *f* RAUMFAHRT geomagnetic cut-off energy; ~e **Albedo** *f* RAUMFAHRT *Raumschiff* geomagnetic albedo

Geomagnetismus *m* PHYS, RAUMFAHRT geomagnetism

Geometer *nt* GEOM geometer, geometrician

Geometrie *f* ELEKTROTECH, FERNSEH, KERNTECH, RADIO geometry; **Geometrie-Eichung** *f* FERNSEH geometric calibration; **Geometriefaktor** *m* KERNTECH geometry factor; **Geometriefehler** *m* FERNSEH geometric error; **Geometrieverhältnis** *nt* ELEKTROTECH *MOS-FET* aspect ratio

geometrisch[1] *adj* GEOM geometric, geometrical

geometrisch:[2] ~e **Auflösungslänge** *f* KERNTECH geometrical resolution length; ~es **Buckling** *nt* *(Bg)* KERNTECH geometric buckling *(Bg);* ~e **Eigenschaften** *f pl* GEOM geometric properties; ~e **Fläche** *f* GEOM geometric surface; **nicht** ~e **Größe** *f* KONSTZEICH nongeometrical quantity; ~er **Körper** *m* GEOM geometric solid; ~es **Mittel** *nt* COMP & DV, GEOM, MATH, QUAL geometric mean; ~er **Mittelwert** *m* MATH, QUAL geometric mean; ~e **Optik** *f* OPTIK geometric optics, PHYS geometrical optics, TELEKOM geometric optics; ~er **Ort** *m* GEOM geometric locus, locus; ~e **Reihe** *f* GEOM geometric progression, MATH geometric series; ~e **Steigung** *f* LUFTTRANS *Propeller* geometrical pitch; ~e **Strahlauflösung** *f* KERNTECH geometric beam resolution; ~e **Trennung** *f* KERNTECH separation by geometry; ~er **Werkzeugspanwinkel** *m* FERTIG tool geometrical rake; ~e **Werte** *m pl* BAU geometrical data

Geophon *nt* ERDÖL, KOHLEN geophone

Geophysik *f* ERDÖL, KOHLEN, PHYS geophysics

geophysikalisch: ~e **Aufnahme** *f* BAU geophysical survey; ~es **Log** *nt* ERDÖL *Meßtechnik* geophysical log; ~e **Untersuchung** *f* ERDÖL *Geologie* geophysical survey

geordnet: ~es **Ablagern** *nt* ABFALL, MEERSCHMUTZ landfilling; ~e **Ablagerung** *f* ABFALL proper disposal, sanitary landfilling, sound disposal; ~er **Baum** *m* COMP & DV ordered tree; ~e **Beseitigung** *f* ABFALL safe disposal; ~e **Datenmenge** *f* COMP & DV data set document; ~e **Deponie** *f* ABFALL controlled dumping, controlled tipping, sanitary landfill; ~e **Festlösung** *f* METALL ordered solid solution; ~e **Legierung** *f* METALL ordered alloy; ~e **Liste** *f* COMP & DV ordered list; ~e **Menge** *f* MATH, METALL ordered set; ~es **Paar** *nt* MATH ordered pair; ~e **Suche** *f* KÜNSTL INT ordered search

Georgi: ~sches **Einheitssystem** *nt* METROL Giorgi system of units

geostationär[1] *adj* RADIO geostationary

geostationär:[2] ~e **Bahn** *f* PHYS geostationary orbit; ~er **Satellit** *m* FERNSEH, PHYS, RAUMFAHRT, TELEKOM, WASSERTRANS *Navigation, Satellitenfunk* geostationary satellite; ~e **Satellitenumlaufbahn** *f* RAUMFAHRT geostationary satellite orbit

geostatisch: ~er **Druck** *m* ERDÖL *Geologie* geostatic pressure

geosynchron *adj* RADIO, RAUMFAHRT geosynchronous

Geosynklinale *f* ERDÖL *Geologie* geosyncline

geothermal: ~e **Energie** *f* UMWELTSCHMUTZ geothermal energy

Geothermik *f* ERDÖL *Erdformationswärme* geothermics

geothermisch[1] *adj* NICHTFOSS ENERG geothermal

geothermisch:[2] ~e **Anlage** *f* NICHTFOSS ENERG geothermal plant; ~e **Bohrausrüstung** *f* NICHTFOSS ENERG geothermal drilling equipment; ~e **Energie** *f* NICHTFOSS ENERG geothermal power, PHYS geothermal energy; ~es **Feld** *nt* NICHTFOSS ENERG geothermal field; ~er **Gradient** *m* ERDÖL *Geophysik* geothermal gradient; ~es **Kraftwerk** *nt* ELEKTRIZ, ELEKTROTECH geothermal power station; ~er **Kreislauf** *m* NICHTFOSS ENERG geothermal circuit; ~es **Log** *nt* ERDÖL *Meßtechnik* geothermal log; ~e **Quellen** *f pl* NICHTFOSS ENERG geothermal resources; ~e **Tiefenstufe** *f* NICHTFOSS ENERG geothermal gradient

gepaart: ~es **Kabel** *nt* ELEKTROTECH paired cable

Gepäck *nt* EISENBAHN baggage, luggage; **Gepäckabteil** *nt* EISENBAHN baggage compartment, baggage room (AmE), luggage compartment (BrE); **Gepäckannahmestelle** *f* TRANS parcels office; **Gepäckausgabeband** *nt* LUFTTRANS baggage claim belt; **Gepäckfördereinrichtung** *f* TRANS bag conveyor; **Gepäckkarren** *m* TRANS barrow; **Gepäcklader** *m* LUFTTRANS baggage loader; **Gepäcknetz** *nt* EISENBAHN rack; **Gepäckraum** *m* EISENBAHN vestibule; **Gepäckschlepper** *m* EISENBAHN luggage trolley

gepackt: ~e **Dezimalzahl** *f* COMP & DV packed decimal; ~es **Format** *nt* COMP & DV packed format

Gepäck: **Gepäckterminal** *nt* TRANS baggage terminal; **Gepäckwagen** *m* EISENBAHN baggage car (AmE), luggage van (BrE)

gepanzert[1] *adj* ELEKTROTECH armored clad (AmE), armoured clad (BrE)

gepanzert:[2] ~es **Kabel** *nt* ELEKTROTECH shielded cable; ~er **Transformator** *m* ELEKTROTECH shielded transformer; ~es **Transportfahrzeug** *nt* TRANS AT vehicle, armored transport vehicle (AmE), armoured transport vehicle (BrE)

geparkt[1] *adj* TELEKOM parked

geparkt:[2] ~e **Leitung** *f* TELEKOM parked line

gepastet: ~e **Form** *f* KER & GLAS paste mold (AmE), paste mould (BrE)

gepfeilt: ~er **Flügel** *m* LUFTTRANS back-swept wing

geplant: ~e **Nichtverfügbarkeit** *f* QUAL scheduled outage

geplatzt: ~es **Brennelement** *nt* KERNTECH burst can, burst slug

gepolstert[1] *adj* MECHAN padded

gepolstert:[2] ~e **Kleidung** *f* SICHERHEIT padded clothing; ~er **Kopfhörerbügel** *m* AUFNAHME padded headband

gepolt: ~er **Elektrolytkondensator** *m* ELEKTROTECH polarized electrolytic capacitor; ~er **Kondensator** *m* ELEKTROTECH polarized capacitor; ~es **Relais** *nt* ELEKTRIZ, ELEKTROTECH polarized relay; **nicht** ~es **Relais** *nt* ELEKTRIZ nonpolarized relay; ~es **Relais ohne Vorspannung** *nt* ELEKTRIZ unbiased-polarized relay; ~er **Stecker** *m* ELEKTROTECH polarized plug; ~er **Verbinder** *m* ELEKTROTECH polarized connector

geprägt *adj* MASCHINEN embossed

geprüft[1] *adj* QUAL tested

geprüft:[2] ~er **Sicherheitsbereich** *m* SICHERHEIT approved safety area

gepulst: ~e **Elektronenkanone** *f* STRAHLPHYS pulsed electron gun; ~e **Elektronenquelle** *f* STRAHLPHYS pulsed electron gun; ~er **Laser** *m* ELEKTRONIK pulsed laser; ~e **Strömung** *f* STRÖMPHYS pulsating flow

Geraddrehen *nt* FERTIG straight turning

gerade[1] *adj* BAU *Türöffnung* square-headed, COMP & DV even, DRUCK regular, MATH *Zahl, Funktion* even; **mit ~n Zähnen** *adj* MASCHINEN straight-tooth

gerade:[2] **~s Band** *nt* BAU T-hinge, cross-garnet hinge; **~ Destillation** *f* THERMOD distillation by ascent; **~r Durchlaß** *m* KER & GLAS straight throat; **~einfaches Herzstück** *nt* EISENBAHN straight common crossing; **~r Flußlauf zwischen zwei Biegungen** *m* WASSERVERSORG reach of a river; **~ Frequenz** *f* ELEKTROTECH straight line frequency; **~r Frequenzgang** *m* AUFNAHME flat frequency response; **~ Kante** *f* KER & GLAS straight edge; **~r Kreiskegel** *m* GEOM right circular cone; **~r Kreiszylinder** *m* GEOM right circular cylinder; **~ Linie** *f* PHYS straight line; **~ Packung** *f* KER & GLAS straight packing; **~ Parität** *f* COMP & DV *Prüfung auf gerade Bitzahl* even parity; **~r Rücken** *m* DRUCK square back; **~ Schleifscheibe** *f* MASCHINEN straight wheel, straight-grinding wheel; **~ Seite** *f* DRUCK verso; **~r Spleiß** *m* ELEKTRIZ straight joint; **~ Stirn** *f* FERTIG *Schaftfräser* square end; **~r Strang** *m* EISENBAHN straight track; **~r Treppenlauf** *m* BAU flyers; **~r Vorsteven** *m* WASSERTRANS *Bootbau* straight stem; **~ Zahl** *f* MATH even number

Gerade *f* GEOM line, straight line; **Geradeausanflug** *m* LUFTTRANS straight-in approach; **Geradeaustest** *m* TELEKOM quick test; **Geradeausverkehr** *m* TRANS straight-through traffic

geradegedreht: ~e Riemenscheibe *f* MASCHINEN straight-faced pulley

geradestehend *adj* DRUCK regular

geradestoßen *vt* DRUCK jog

Geradführung *f* MASCHINEN slide bar, straight guide

Geradheitstoleranz *f* MASCHINEN straightness tolerance

geradlinig[1] *adj* MECHAN rectilineal

geradlinig:[2] **~e Antenne** *f* TELEKOM rectilinear antenna; **~er Asynchronmotor** *m* ELEKTRIZ linear induction motor; **~e Ausbreitung** *f* FERNSEH, WELLPHYS *von Lichtwellen* rectilinear propagation; **~e Bewegung** *f* MECHAN, PHYS rectilinear motion

Geradlinigkeitsprüfinstrument *nt* METROL straightness-measuring instrument

Geradsichtprisma *nt* PHYS Amici prism, direct-vision prism

Geradstirnrad *nt* MASCHINEN spur gear, spur wheel

geradverzahnt[1] *adj* MASCHINEN straight

geradverzahnt:[2] **~es Rad** *nt* MASCHINEN straight tooth wheel

Geradverzahnung *f* FERTIG straight gear cutting, MASCHINEN spur teeth

geradzahlig: ~e harmonische Schwingungen *f pl* PHYS even harmonic vibrations; **~e Oberwelle** *f* ELEKTRONIK even harmonic; **~e Parität** *f* PHYS even parity

geradzahlig-geradzahlig: ~er Kern *m* PHYS even-even nucleus

geradzahlig-ungeradzahlig: ~er Kern *m* PHYS even-odd nucleus

geradzahnig *adj* MASCHINEN straight-tooth

Geradzahnrad *nt* MASCHINEN spur wheel

gerafft *adj* TEXTIL gathered

gerahmt: ~es Fenster *nt* COMP & DV tiled window

gerammt: ~er Bereich *m* KERNTECH *als Lager* rammed area

gerändelt *adj* MECHAN knurled

Geraniol *nt* CHEMIE geraniol

Geraniumaldehyd *nt* CHEMIE citral, geranialaldehyde

Geranyl- *pref* CHEMIE geranyl; **Geranylalkohol** *m* CHEMIE geraniol

Gerät *nt* BAU equipment, utensil, COMP & DV device, instrument, KONTROLL device, LEBENSMITTEL appliance, MASCHINEN appliance, device, tackle, MEERSCHMUTZ device, TELEKOM device, unit, TEXTIL appliance; **~ zur automatischen Aufzeichnung von Verkehrsverstößen** *nt* TRANS automatic infringement recorder; **~ zu Fernsprechgebühr** *nt* TELEKOM telephony-rated device; **~ zur Geräuschisolierung** *nt* SICHERHEIT noise-insulating equipment; **~ der Konsumelektronik** *nt* RADIO consumer electronic device; **~ zur radiologischen Bohrlochvermessung** *nt* KERNTECH well-logging equipment; **~ mit seriellem Zugriff** *nt* COMP & DV serial access device; **~ zur Signaleingabe** *nt* REGELUNG device for signal input; **~e der Unterhaltungselektronik** *nt pl* ELEKTROTECH consumer electronic equipment; **~ mit wahlfreiem Zugriff** *nt* COMP & DV random access device; **~ für die Zufallsabtastung** *nt* COMP & DV random-scan device

Geräte *nt pl* MASCHINEN equipment

Gerät: Geräteanordnung *f* COMP & DV hardware configuration; **Geräteausfall** *m* GERÄT instrument malfunction; **Geräteausrüstung** *f* FERTIG instrumentation; **Geräteausstattung** *f* GERÄT instrumentation; **Gerätefehler** *m* GERÄT instrumental error; **Gerätegehäuse** *nt* GERÄT instrument cabinet; **Gerätegruppe** *f* COMP & DV cluster; **Gerätekennung** *f* COMP & DV device code, device flag; **Gerätekonfiguration** *f* COMP & DV hardware configuration; **Gerätelebenserwartung** *f* RAUMFAHRT commercial life; **Gerätemotor** *m* KONTROLL system motor; **Geräteprüfung** *f* COMP & DV hardware check; **Gerätesatz** *m* ELEKTROTECH set; **Geräteschicht** *f* TELEKOM equipment layer; **Geräteschnittstelle** *f* COMP & DV terminal interface; **Geräteschuppen** *m* BAU tool shed; **Gerätestecker** *m* ELEKTROTECH connector; **Gerätesteckvorrichtung** *f* ELEKTROTECH coupler; **Gerätesteuerprogramm** *nt* COMP & DV peripheral software driver; **Gerätesteuerung** *f* COMP & DV, TELEKOM DC, device controller

gerätetechnisch[1] *adj* REGELUNG device-related

gerätetechnisch:[2] **~e Ausrüstung** *f* GERÄT instrumentation

Gerät: Geräteträger *m* GERÄT instrument rack; **Gerätetreiber** *m* COMP & DV device driver; **Geräteverbundgruppe** *f* KONTROLL cluster

gerauht *adj* FERTIG raised

Geräusch *nt* AKUSTIK, ELEKTRONIK, PHYS, TELEKOM noise; **Geräuschabstand** *m* TELEKOM signal-to-noise ratio

geräuscharm: ~es Aufnahmesystem *nt* AUFNAHME noiseless-recording system; **~e Hupe** *f* KFZTECH low-tone horn; **~es Kurzstart-und Landeflugzeug** *nt* LUFTTRANS QSTOL aircraft, quiet short takeoff and landing aircraft; **~er Modus** *m* DRUCK quiet mode; **~ startendes und landendes Flugzeug** *nt* LUFTTRANS QTOL aircraft, quiet takeoff and landing aircraft

geräuschdämpfend *adj* AKUSTIK antinoise

Geräusch: Geräuschdämpfer *m* HEIZ & KÄLTE muffler (AmE), silencer (BrE); **Geräuscheffekte** *m pl* FERNSEH sound effects; **Geräuschfilter** *nt* AUFNAHME scratch filter; **Geräusch-Instrumentarium** *nt* AUFNAHME sound equipment; **Geräuschkulisse** *f* AUFNAHME sound effects

geräuschlos[1] *adj* SICHERHEIT noiseless

geräuschlos:[2] **~er Lauf** *m* SICHERHEIT noiseless running; **~er Motor** *m* SICHERHEIT noiseless motor; **~e Steuerkette** *f* KFZTECH noiseless-timing chain

Geräusch: **Geräuschmeßgerät** *nt* GERÄT interference
level meter, sound level meter; **Geräuschmodulation** *f*
AUFNAHME noise modulation; **Geräuschpegel** *m* TE-
LEKOM noise level; **Geräuschpegelanzeiger** *m*
UMWELTSCHMUTZ weighted noise level indicator; **Ge-
räuschsperre** *f* TELEKOM squelch; **Geräuschspur** *f*
AUFNAHME *auf Band* buzz track

gerbstoffartig *adj* CHEMIE tannic

gereckt: **~es Polypropylen-Etikett** *nt* VERPACK orientated polypropylene label; **~e Polypropylenfolie** *f*
VERPACK orientated polypropylene film; **~e Salzbla-
sen** *f pl* KER & GLAS gray blibes (AmE), grey blibes
(BrE)

geregelt[1] *adj* KONTROLL regulated, stabilized

geregelt:[2] **~e Ablagerung** *f* UMWELTSCHMUTZ regulated
deposition; **~es Bussystem** *nt* RAUMFAHRT *Raumschiff* regulated bus system; **~er Druck** *m* MASCHINEN
controlled pressure; **~es Netzgerät** *nt* ELEKTROTECH
regulated power supply; **~e Temperatur** *f* HEIZ & KÄLTE
controlled temperature; **~es Verbrennungssystem** *nt*
LUFTTRANS controlled combustion system

gereinigt: **~es Wasser** *nt* UMWELTSCHMUTZ depolluted
water

gerichtet: **~e Bohrung** *f* ERDÖL *Bohrtechnik* directional
well; **~es Glied** *nt* REGELUNG directional element; **~er
Graph** *m* KÜNSTL INT digraph, directed graph, oriented graph; **~er Lautsprecher** *m* AKUSTIK directional
loudspeaker; **nicht ~er Graph** *m* KÜNSTL INT nondirected graph, nonoriented graph, undirected graph;
nicht ~es Mikrofon *nt* AUFNAHME astatic microphone;
nicht ~e Schallquelle *f* AKUSTIK simple acoustic
source; **~er Strahl** *m* ELEKTRONIK shaped beam

gerieft *adj* FERTIG serrated, striated

geriffelt *adj* FERTIG corrugated, MECHAN fluted, knurled

gering: **~e Konzentration** *f* ELEKTRONIK low concentration; **~e Steigung** *f* LUFTTRANS *Luftschraube* fine
pitch; **~er Verlust** *m* TELEKOM low loss

geringfügig: **~es Gleiten** *nt* METALL banal slip

geringpermeable: **~r Grundwasserleiter** *m* WASSERVER-
SORG aquiclude, aquitard

geringwertig: **~e Kohle** *f* KOHLEN inferior coal

Gerinne *nt* BAU flume, gutter, launder, NICHTFOSS ENERG
flume, WASSERVERSORG raceway, race, sluice box

Gerinnen *nt* CHEMIE clotting

gerinnen:[1] **~ lassen** *vt* CHEMTECH coagulate

gerinnen[2] *vi* CHEMTECH coagulate, FERTIG congeal

Gerinnung *f* LEBENSMITTEL coagulating; **Gerinnungs-
mittel** *nt* CHEMTECH coagulator

Gerippe *nt* BAU *Fachwerk* stud, LUFTTRANS hull

gerippt[1] *adj* HEIZ & KÄLTE finned, MECHAN, TEXTIL ribbed

gerippt:[2] **~e Fläche** *f* HEIZ & KÄLTE finned surface; **~es
Glas** *nt* KER & GLAS reeded glass

gerissen[1] *adj* MECHAN cracked

gerissen:[2] **~e Blase** *f* KER & GLAS broken seed; **~er Faden**
m TEXTIL broken end; **~e Oberfläche** *f* KER & GLAS
checked finish, crizzled finish; **~e Schwelle** *f* EISEN-
BAHN split sleeper (BrE), split tie (AmE)

Germanatglas *nt* KER & GLAS germanide glass

Germanium-Avalanche-Photodiode *f* ELEKTRONIK germanium avalanche photodiode

Germaniumdiode *f* ELEKTRIZ germanium diode

Germaniumgleichrichter *m* ELEKTRIZ, ELEKTROTECH
germanium rectifier

Geröllblock *m* BAU *Geologie* boulder

geronnen[1] *adj* CHEMTECH coagulated

geronnen:[2] **~e Milch** *f* LEBENSMITTEL curd

Geruch *m* ABFALL, CHEMTECH odor (AmE), odour
(BrE)

geruchlos *adj* VERPACK nonodorous

Geruch: **Geruchsbekämpfung** *f* ABFALL, CHEMTECH,
UMWELTSCHMUTZ odor control (AmE), odour control (BrE); **Geruchsbelästigung** *f* ABFALL odor
nuisance (AmE), odour nuisance (BrE); **Geruchs-
emission** *f* UMWELTSCHMUTZ odor emissions (AmE),
odour emissions (BrE)

geruchsverbessernd: **~er Stoff** *m* KUNSTSTOFF deodorant

Geruchsverschluß *m* BAU drain trap, stench trap, stink
trap, trap, CHEMTECH trap

gerufen: **~er Fernsprecher** *m* TELEKOM called telephone;
~er Teilnehmer *m* TELEKOM called party; **~es Telefon** *nt*
TELEKOM called telephone

Gerümpel *nt* ABFALL litter

gerundet: **~e Zahlen** *f pl* MATH round figures

Gerüst[1] *nt* BAU gantry, scaffolding, scaffold, MASCHINEN
skeleton, MECHAN frame

Gerüst:[2] **~ abbauen** *vi* BAU take down scaffolding

Gerüst: **Gerüstbau** *m* BAU staging; **Gerüstbock** *m* BAU
trestle; **Gerüstboden** *m* BAU stage; **Gerüstbohle** *f* BAU
scaffold board; **Gerüsteiweiß** *nt* LEBENSMITTEL sclero-
protein; **Gerüsteiweißstoff** *m* LEBENSMITTEL
albuminoid; **Gerüstfangnetz** *nt* SICHERHEIT scaffolding protective net; **Gerüstpfosten** *m* BAU standard;
Gerüststange *f* BAU putlog, scaffold pole

Gesamt- *pref* MASCHINEN total, TRANS overall

gesamt[1] *adj* MASCHINEN overall

gesamt:[2] **~es atomares Bremsvermögen** *nt* PHYS total-
atomic stopping power; **~es lineares Bremsvermögen**
nt PHYS total-linear stopping power; **~e mittlere freie
Weglänge** *f* KERNTECH total mean free path

Gesamt-: **Gesamtabfallaufkommen** *nt* UMWELT-
SCHMUTZ total appearance of waste;
Gesamtablagerung *f* UMWELTSCHMUTZ total deposition; **Gesamtabmessungen** *f pl* MASCHINEN overall
dimensions; **Gesamtabnahme** *f* BAU *eines Projektes*
general acceptance; **Gesamtachsstand** *m* EISENBAHN
total wheelbase; **Gesamtauftrieb** *m* LUFTTRANS total
lift; **Gesamtbearbeitungszeit** *f* COMP & DV processing
time; **Gesamtbeladung** *f* KERNTECH total charge; **Ge-
samtbetrag** *m* COMP & DV sum; **Gesamtbild-
schirmeditor** *m* COMP & DV full screen editor; **Gesamt-
breite** *f* MASCHINEN overall width; **Gesamtdämp-
fungsverlauf** *m* AKUSTIK overall response curve; **Ge-
samtdrehimpuls** *m* PHYS total angular momentum;
Gesamtdrehimpulsquantenzahl *f* PHYS total angular
momentum quantum number; **Gesamtdruck** *m* MA-
SCHINEN overall pressure; **Gesamtenergie** *f*
MASCHINEN total energy; **Gesamtenergiedichte** *f* AKU-
STIK total energy per unit volume; **Gesamtfahrstraße** *f*
EISENBAHN *einer Kurve* negotiation; **Gesamtfahrzeit** *f*
TRANS overall travel time; **Gesamtfehler** *m* GERÄT
total error; **Gesamtfläche** *f* BAU total area, NICHTFOSS
ENERG *eines Kollektors* gross area, PAPIER overall face;
Gesamtfluggewicht *nt* LUFTTRANS AUW, all-up
weight; **Gesamtflugmasse** *f* LUFTTRANS AUW, all-up
weight; **Gesamtfluß** *m* KERNTECH gross flow

Gesamtgewicht: **~ des Fahrzeugs** *nt* KFZTECH gross
vehicle weight

Gesamt-: **Gesamtgröße** *f* METROL total size

Gesamtheit: **~ aller Geräte** *f* MECHAN hardware; **Ge-
samtheitsumkehr** *f* ELEKTRONIK *Statistik* population

inversion

Gesamt-: **Gesamtheizfläche** *f* HEIZ & KÄLTE aggregate heating surface; **Gesamthöhe** *f* KERNTECH total height, MASCHINEN overall height; **Gesamtkonfiguration** *f* TELEKOM total configuration; **Gesamtlänge** *f* MASCHINEN length overall, overall length, METROL, TEXTIL overall length, WASSERTRANS *Schiff* length overall; **Gesamtlautheit** *f* AKUSTIK total loudness; **Gesamtmassenbremsvermögen** *nt* PHYS total mass stopping power; **Gesamtölvolumen** *nt* ERDÖL *Erdölgeologie* oil in place; **Gesamtreisegeschwindigkeit** *f* TRANS overall travel speed; **Gesamtsäurezahl** *f (GSZ)* CHEMIE total acid number *(TAN)*; **Gesamtschattierung** *f* TEXTIL overall shade; **Gesamtschub** *m* LUFTTRANS gross thrust; **Gesamtschwefelgehalt** *m* KUNSTSTOFF total sulfur (AmE), total sulphur (BrE); **Gesamtstrahlungs-Pyrometer** *nt* GERÄT, THERMOD total radiation pyrometer; **Gesamtsumme** *f* MATH amount; **Gesamtteilung** *f* MASCHINEN total pitch; **Gesamttiter** *m* TEXTIL total denier; **Gesamtüberdeckungsgrad** *m* FERTIG *Getriebelehre* total contact ratio; **Gesamtverluste** *m pl* ELEKTRIZ total losses; **Gesamtvolumenstrom** *m* HEIZ & KÄLTE total volumetric flow; **Gesamtwiderstand** *m* ELEKTRIZ all-in resistance, LUFTTRANS total drag; **Gesamtwirkungsgrad** *m* HEIZ & KÄLTE, NICHTFOSS ENERG overall efficiency; **Gesamtzeitintervall** *nt* TRANS overall time interval

gesättigt[1] *adj* HEIZ & KÄLTE saturated; **~ alicyclisch** *adj* CHEMIE naphthenic

gesättigt:[2] **~er Dampf** *m* PHYS saturated vapor (AmE), saturated vapour (BrE), THERMOD saturated steam; **~e Erde** *f* KOHLEN saturated soil; **~er Kern** *m* ELEKTROTECH saturated core; **~er Kohlenwasserstoff** *m* ERDÖL alkane, *Geologie* saturated hydrocarbon; **~e Logik** *f* ELEKTRONIK saturated logic; **~er Ringkerntransformator** *m* ELEKTROTECH saturated toroidal transformer; **~er Transformator** *m* ELEKTROTECH saturated transformer

geschachtelt: **~e Intervalle** *nt pl* MATH nest of intervals

Geschäft *nt* DRUCK, LUFTTRANS, PAPIER business; **Geschäftsdrucksachen** *f pl* DRUCK business stationery; **Geschäftsflugzeug** *nt* LUFTTRANS business aircraft, executive aircraft; **Geschäftshubschrauber** *m* LUFTTRANS executive helicopter; **Geschäftskommunikationssystem** *nt* TELEKOM business communication system; **Geschäftsnetz** *nt* TELEKOM business system

geschält: **~er Reis** *m* LEBENSMITTEL hulled rice

geschaltet[1] *adj* TELEKOM switched

geschaltet:[2] **~er Strom** *m* ELEKTRIZ switched current

geschätzt: **~e verstrichene Zeit** *f* LUFTTRANS estimated elapsed time

geschäumt: **~es Polysterol** *nt (Schaum-PS)* VERPACK expanded polystyrene *(ep)*

geschichtet[1] *adj* KOHLEN stratified, STRÖMPHYS laminar

geschichtet:[2] **~er Kunststoff** *m* ELEKTRIZ laminated plastic; **~e Probe** *f* SICHERHEIT stratified sampling; **~e Probenahme** *f* KOHLEN stratified sampling; **~e Stichprobe** *f* QUAL stratified sample; **~e Strömung** *f* STRÖMPHYS stratified flow; **~e Unterlegscheibe** *f* MASCHINEN peel shim; **~e Zufallsstichprobe** *f* QUAL stratified random sample

Geschicklichkeit *f* ERGON design parameter

Geschiebe *nt* KOHLEN boulder; **Geschiebeboden** *m* KOHLEN boulder soil; **Geschiebefracht** *f* WASSERVERSORG sediment discharge; **Geschiebelehm** *m* KOHLEN boulder clay, glacial clay, till; **Geschiebemergel** *m* KOHLEN glacial clay

Geschirr *nt* FERTIG tackle, RAUMFAHRT safety harness; **Geschirreinschiebevorrichtung** *f* KER & GLAS ware pusher; **Geschirrkeramik- und Haushaltsglasindustrie** *f* KER & GLAS tableware and domestic glass industry

geschleppt: **~es Wasserfahrzeug** *nt* WASSERTRANS tow

geschlichtet: **~e Kette** *f* TEXTIL sized warp

geschliffen: **~es Drahtglas** *nt* KER & GLAS polished-wired glass; **~es Glas** *nt* KER & GLAS cut glass; **~e Kante** *f* KER & GLAS polished edge

geschlitzt[1] *adj* FERTIG notched

geschlitzt:[2] **~er Wellenleiter** *m* ELEKTROTECH slotted waveguide

geschlossen[1] *adj* FERTIG compact, MEERSCHMUTZ sealed; **in sich ~** *adj* BAU, PHYS self-contained; **im ~en Raum bestimmter Flammpunkt** *m* KUNSTSTOFF closed-cup flash point

geschlossen:[2] **~e Benutzergruppe** *f (CUG)* COMP & DV, TELEKOM closed user group *(CUG)*; **~er Benutzerkreis** *m (CUG)* COMP & DV, TELEKOM closed user group *(CUG)*; **~er Betrieb** *m* COMP & DV closed shop operation; **~ Brennstoffkreislauf** *m* KERNTECH closed fuel cycle; **~er Container** *m* TRANS closed container, covered container; **~es Druckgaskabel** *nt* ELEKTRIZ self-contained pressure cable; **~e Ecke** *f* BAU tight corner; **~es Gefäß** *nt* LABOR closed vessel; **~es Gesenk** *nt* MASCHINEN closed die; **~er Getriebekasten** *m* MASCHINEN enclosed gears; **~er Gleichrichter** *m* ELEKTROTECH sealed rectifier; **~es Hafenbecken** *nt* WASSERTRANS wet dock; **~e Heizungsanlage** *f* HEIZ & KÄLTE closed-type heating system; **~er Hohlkastenträger** *m* TRANS closed box girder; **~es Kaliber** *nt* FERTIG *Walzen* close pass; **~e Kompostierung** *f* ABFALL mechanical composting, rapid fermentation; **~er Kreislauf** *m* LUFTTRANS closed loop, MASCHINEN closed circuit, closed loop; **~er Kühlkreislauf** *m* KERNTECH closed cycle cooling system; **~es Kühlsystem** *nt* KFZTECH closed and sealed cooling system; **~e Kurve** *f* GEOM, MATH closed curve; **~e Maßkette** *f* KONSTZEICH closed chain dimensioning, closed chain dimension; **~e Membran** *f* AKUSTIK closed diaphragm; **~es Meßgerät** *nt* GERÄT self-contained instrument; **~es Polygon** *nt* GEOM closed polygon; **~er Regelkreis** *m* ELEKTRIZ, ELEKTRONIK *Regeltechnik* closed loop; **~es Regelsystem** *nt* LUFTTRANS closed loop; **~er Scheibendrehschalter** *m* ELEKTROTECH sealed wafer rotary switch; **~e Schleife** *f* KONTROLL closed loop; **in sich ~es Servolenksystem** *nt* KFZTECH self-contained power steering system; **~er Spind** *m* WASSERTRANS closed locker; **~e Stellung** *f* ELEKTRIZ closed position; **~er Stromkreis** *m* ELEKTRIZ, ELEKTROTECH closed circuit; **~es System** *nt* THERMOD closed system; **~er Überdruck-Windkanal** *m* NICHTFOSS ENERG pressure tunnel; **~er Wirkungskreis** *m* FERTIG feedback loop; **~e Zelle** *f* KUNSTSTOFF closed cell; **~er Zug** *m* EISENBAHN block train; **~e Zugeinheit** *f* EISENBAHN unsplittable train

geschlossenzellig: **~er Schaumkunststoff** *m* KUNSTSTOFF closed-cell cellular plastic; **~er Schaumstoff** *m* HEIZ & KÄLTE closed-cell foamed plastic, VERPACK closed-cell foam

Geschmack *m* LEBENSMITTEL, TEILPHYS flavor (AmE), flavour (BrE); **Geschmacksstoff** *m* LEBENSMITTEL flavoring (AmE), flavouring (BrE); **Geschmacksverstärker** *m* LEBENSMITTEL flavor enhancer (AmE), flavour enhancer (BrE), flavor potentiator (AmE), flavour potentiator (BrE)

geschmiedet[1] *adj* MASCHINEN forged, MECHAN forged, wrought

geschmiedet:[2] **~er Stahl** *m* METALL forge steel

geschmiert: ~es Band *nt* AUFNAHME lubricated tape

geschmolzen[1] *adj* THERMOD fused, melted, molten

geschmolzen:[2] **~er Kern** *m* RAUMFAHRT molten core; **~es Metall** *nt* METALL, SICHERHEIT molten metal; **~er Quarz** *m* OPTIK fused quartz; **~es Silica** *nt* OPTIK fused silica; **~es Silikatglas** *nt* TELEKOM fused silica

geschnitten[1] *adj* KOHLEN cutoff

geschnitten:[2] **~e Viskose-Filamentfasern** *f pl* TEXTIL cut staple

geschoben: ~er Zug *m* EISENBAHN backup train

Geschoß *nt* BAU floor; **Geschoßdecke** *f* BAU floor; **Geschoßquerbalken** *m* BAU summer, summer tree

geschraubt: ~e Verbindung *f* KERNTECH screwed joint

geschrumpft: ~er Abschnitt *m* HYDRAUL contracted section

Geschützbronze *f* FERTIG gunmetal

Geschützmetall *nt* MECHAN gunmetal

geschützt[1] *adj* BAU screened, SICHERHEIT guarded

geschützt:[2] **~e Anlage im Freien** *f* HEIZ & KÄLTE sheltered installation; **~es Feld** *nt* COMP & DV protected field; **~es Getriebe** *nt* SICHERHEIT guarded gears; **~er Speicher** *m* COMP & DV protected storage; **~er Speicherplatz** *m* COMP & DV protected location; **~e Zahnräder** *nt pl* MASCHINEN guarded gears

geschwärzt[1] *adj* THERMOD blackened

geschwärzt:[2] **~ darstellen** *vt* KONSTZEICH show in black

geschweift: ~e Klammern *f pl* MATH *Notierung in der Mengenlehre* braces

geschweißt[1] *adj* MASCHINEN, THERMOD welded

geschweißt:[2] **~e Hülse** *f* KERNTECH *eines Brennelementes* weld-deposited cladding

Geschwindigkeit[1] *f* AKUSTIK velocity, COMP & DV rate, ELEKTRONIK velocity, MASCHINEN speed, velocity, MECHAN velocity, METROL rate, PAPIER speed, PHYS speed, velocity, STRÖMPHYS velocity, TEXTIL, TRANS speed; **~ des Anwachsens der Viskosität** *f* LEBENSMITTEL bodying speed; **~ der Außenströmung** *f* STRÖMPHYS *außerhalb der Grenzschicht* free-stream velocity; **~ über Grund** *f* LUFTTRANS ground speed, TRANS group speed, WASSERTRANS ground speed; **~ von Längswellen** *f (cl)* AKUSTIK velocity of longitudinal waves *(cl)*; **~ von Transversalwellen** *f (ct)* LABOR velocity of transversal waves *(ct)*

Geschwindigkeit:[2] **~ verringern** *vi* MASCHINEN reduce speed, TRANS slow down

geschwindigkeitsabhängig: ~e Frequenz *f* AKUSTIK speed variation frequency

Geschwindigkeit: Geschwindigkeitsabnahme *f* KFZTECH *bei einem Motor* deceleration; **Geschwindigkeitsanzeige** *f* MASCHINEN speed indicator; **Geschwindigkeitsanzeiger** *m* MASCHINEN speedometer, PAPIER speed indicator, RAUMFAHRT *(ASI)* airspeed indicator *(ASI)*; **Geschwindigkeitsbegrenzer** *m* KFZTECH speed limiter; **Geschwindigkeitsdetektor** *m* TRANS speed detector; **Geschwindigkeitsdiagramm** *nt* MASCHINEN, NICHTFOSS ENERG velocity diagram; **Geschwindigkeitsdruckhöhe** *f* HYDRAUL velocity head; **Geschwindigkeitseinheit** *f* RAUMFAHRT velocity increment; **Geschwindigkeitsempfänger** *m* AUFNAHME velocity microphone; **Geschwindigkeitsfeld** *nt* LUFTTRANS wing velocity field;

Geschwindigkeitsgefälle *nt* KUNSTSTOFF shear rate; **Geschwindigkeitskoeffizient** *m* NICHTFOSS ENERG velocity coefficient; **Geschwindigkeitskonstante** *f* METALL rate constant; **Geschwindigkeitsmesser** *m* KFZTECH tachometer, *Zubehör* speedometer, LUFTTRANS *(ASI)* airspeed indicator *(ASI)*, PHYS tachometer; **Geschwindigkeitsmesserantrieb** *m* KFZTECH speedometer drive gear; **Geschwindigkeitsmeßgerät** *nt* GERÄT rate-measuring instrument, speed indicator, PHYS velocimeter; **Geschwindigkeitsmessung** *f* PHYS velocimetry; **Geschwindigkeitsmodulation** *f* ELEKTRONIK, FERNSEH, PHYS velocity modulation; **Geschwindigkeitspotential** *nt (φ)* AKUSTIK velocity potential *(φ)*; **Geschwindigkeitsprofil** *nt* PHYS velocity profile; **Geschwindigkeitsregelung** *f* EISENBAHN, ELEKTRIZ, KONTROLL, TRANS speed control; **Geschwindigkeitsregler** *m* FERNSEH velocity control servo; **Geschwindigkeitsschreiber** *m* EISENBAHN, KFZTECH speed recorder; **Geschwindigkeitsschwankung** *f* FERNSEH wow; **Geschwindigkeitsschwankungen** *f pl* STRÖMPHYS velocity fluctuations; **Geschwindigkeitssteuerung** *f* KONTROLL speed control, PHYS velocity modulation; **Geschwindigkeitsstufenturbine** *f* HYDRAUL velocity stage turbine; **Geschwindigkeitstiefenkurve** *f* ERDÖL *Seismik* velocity depth curve; **Geschwindigkeitsüberwachung** *f* EISENBAHN speed supervision; **Geschwindigkeitsverlust** *m* KERNTECH velocity loss; **Geschwindigkeitswähler nach Flugzeitmessung** *m* KERNTECH time-of-flight velocity selector; **Geschwindigkeitswählschalter** *m* EISENBAHN speed selector; **Geschwindigkeitszunahme** *f* RAUMFAHRT velocity increment; **Geschwindigkeit-Verkehrsaufkommen-Kurve** *f* TRANS speed volume curve

geschwungen: ~er Deckel *m* KER & GLAS swung baffle

Gesellschaft: ~ für Schwerionenforschung *f* TEILPHYS Research Institute for Nuclear and Particle Physics

Gesenk:[1] **im ~ geschmiedet** *adj* MASCHINEN drop-forged

Gesenk[2] *nt* FERTIG swage, *Schmieden* die, MASCHINEN die, forging die, swage, MECHAN die, swage; **Gesenkformen** *nt* MECHAN die-stamping; **Gesenkfräsen** *nt* FERTIG, MASCHINEN die-sinking; **Gesenkfräser** *m* FERTIG cherry; **Gesenkfräsmaschine** *f* MASCHINEN die-sinking machine

gesenkgeschmieden: ~er Stahl *m* METALL drop-forged steel

gesenkgeschmiedet *adj* FERTIG drop-forged

Gesenk: Gesenkhalter *m* FERTIG holding shoe; **Gesenkoberteil** *nt* MASCHINEN top swage; **Gesenkplatte** *f* MASCHINEN swage block; **Gesenkpresse** *f* FERTIG stamping press

gesenkpreßschmieden *vt* FERTIG *Gießen* iron

Gesenkschmiedeanteil *nt* FERTIG stamping plant

Gesenkschmiedehammer *m* FERTIG drop stamp, stamp

Gesenkschmieden *nt* FERTIG die-forging, drop-forging, impact die forging, *Schmieden* die-stamping, MASCHINEN, MECHAN drop-forging

Gesenkschmiederohling *m* FERTIG dummy

Gesenkschmiedeteil *nt* FERTIG drop-forging, stamping

Gesetz *nt* SICHERHEIT act; **~ von der Erhaltung der Teilchenzahl** *nt* KERNTECH particle number conservation law; **~ über Fabriken** *nt* SICHERHEIT Factory Act (BrE); **~ der korrespondierenden Zustände** *nt* PHYS law of corresponding states; **~ von der Paritätserhaltung** *nt* STRAHLPHYS parity conservation law; **~ zur Reinhaltung der Luft** *nt* UMWELTSCHMUTZ Clean Air

Act; ~ **zur Wasserreinhaltung** *nt* MEERSCHMUTZ *CWA* Clean Water Act

gesetzlich: ~**e Längeneinheiten** *f pl* METROL legal units of length; ~**e Vorschrift** *f* SICHERHEIT statutory regulation

Gesetztes *nt* DRUCK matter

gesichert *adj* MECHAN fused

Gesichtsfeld *nt* ERGON visual field

Gesichtsmaske *f* SICHERHEIT *Schutzkleidung* mask

Gesichtsschlagschutz *m* SICHERHEIT *mit Schutzglas* filtering facepiece

Gesichtsschutz *m* FERTIG face shield, SICHERHEIT face shield, face visor, visor

Gesiebe *nt* CHEMTECH sieve cloth

gesiebt[1] *adj* BAU screened

gesiebt:[2] ~**er Poliersand** *m* ANSTRICH mesh abrasive grit

Gesims *nt* BAU cornice, molding (AmE), moulding (BrE); **Gesimsband** *nt* BAU string

gesintert *adj* CHEMTECH, MASCHINEN, MECHAN sintered

gespalten: ~**er Kern** *m* ELEKTROTECH gapped core; **nicht ~er Kernbrennstoff** *m* KERNTECH unfissioned nuclear fuel

Gespannguß *m* FERTIG group casting, group teeming

Gespannplatte *f* FERTIG *Getriebelehre* bottom plate, bottom-pouring plate

gespannt: ~**es Grundwasser** *nt* KOHLEN, WASSERVERSORG confined ground water; ~**er Grundwasserleiter** *m* WASSERVERSORG confined aquifer

gespeichert: ~**e Ansage** *f* TELEKOM prerecorded message; ~**e Energie** *f* METALL, PHYS, STRAHLPHYS stored energy; ~**es Programm** *nt* COMP & DV stored program

Gesperre *nt* MASCHINEN locking mechanism

gesperrt[1] *adj* ELEKTROTECH off, KONTROLL disabled, TELEKOM *Teilnehmerstation* barred, *aus- und eingehende Telefongespräche* barred

gesperrt:[2] ~**er Eingabebereich** *m* COMP & DV dead zone; ~**e Flächen** *f pl* LUFTTRANS *Flughafen* unserviceable areas; ~**e Kapazität** *f* AUFNAHME clamped capacitance

gespleißt: ~**es Kabel** *nt* TELEKOM spliced cable; ~**es Tau** *nt* WASSERTRANS spliced rope

Gespräch[1] *nt* TELEKOM call; ~ **mit ermäßigter Gebühr** *nt* TELEKOM cheap call; ~ **zu Ortsgebühr** *nt* TELEKOM local-charge-rate call; ~ **mit Voranmeldung** *nt* TELEKOM booked call; ~ **in Wartestellung** *nt* TELEKOM camp-on call

Gespräch:[2] **ein ~ anmelden** *vi* TELEKOM book a call

Gespräch: **Gesprächsabwicklung** *f* TELEKOM *Telefon* call handling; **Gesprächsdatenerfassung** *f* TELEKOM call logging; **Gesprächsdauer** *f* TELEKOM *Telefon* call duration; **Gesprächsendezeichen** *nt* TELEKOM end-of-communication signal; **Gesprächsgebühr** *f* TELEKOM *Telefon* call charge; **Gesprächsgebührenzähler** *m* TELEKOM *Telefon* call-charging equipment; **Gesprächsgeheimhaltung** *f* TELEKOM voice privacy; **Gesprächsmodus** *m* COMP & DV conversational mode; **Gesprächsverbindung** *f* TELEKOM *Telefon* call; **Gesprächsweiterleitung** *f* TELEKOM *Funkzellenwechsel* automatic handoff; **Gesprächsweiterverbindung** *f* TELEKOM call transfer; **Gesprächszähler** *m* TELEKOM message register, subscriber's meter

gesprengt: ~**es Gestein** *nt* KOHLEN blasted stone

gesprenkelt *adj* VERPACK mottled

gesprungen *adj* MECHAN cracked

gespundet *adj* BAU tongued-and-grooved

gestaffelt: ~ **abgestimmter Verstärker** *m* ELEKTRONIK stagger-tuned amplifier

Gestaltänderungsenergie *f* FERTIG distortion energy

gestalten *vt* BAU develop

Gestaltfestigkeit *f* MASCHINEN fatigue strength

Gestaltung *f* DRUCK, ERGON, MASCHINEN design, TELEKOM configuration

Gestänge *nt* KFZTECH linkage, MASCHINEN bar linkage, rod, rod linkage, MECHAN linkage, rod system; **Gestängeanheber** *m* ERDÖL elevator

gestanzt: ~**es Blech** *nt* ELEKTROTECH stamping; ~**er Stahl** *m* METALL stamped steel; ~**es Trafoblech** *nt* ELEKTROTECH core lamination

Gestein *nt* KOHLEN rock; **Gesteinsabbau** *m* KOHLEN stoneworking; **Gesteinsanker** *m* BAU rockbolt; **Gesteinsbohrer** *m* BAU rock borer, rock drill, tapped valve drill, KOHLEN rock drill; **Gesteinsbohrmaschine** *f* KOHLEN rock drill; **Gesteinsdruck** *m* KOHLEN rock pressure; **Gesteinsmehl** *nt* KOHLEN stone dust; **Gesteinsprallmühle** *f* KOHLEN impact breaker; **Gesteinsschotter** *m* HYDRAUL rock rubble; **Gesteinsstaub** *m* KOHLEN stone dust; **Gesteinsstrecke** *f* KOHLEN stone drift; **Gesteinsverwitterung** *f* KOHLEN rock decay

Gestell *nt* BAU trestle, KER & GLAS horse, MASCHINEN column, cradle, frame, support, MECHAN cradle, rack, PAPIER rack, TELEKOM bay, rack, TEXTIL, VERPACK frame

gestellbefestigt *adj* VERPACK *auf Gestell* rack-mount

Gestell: **Gestellrahmen** *m* TELEKOM rack; **Gestellsäge** *f* MASCHINEN frame saw

gesteuert: ~**es Fräsen** *nt* SICHERHEIT jig routing; ~**e Leitwegumlenkung** *f* TELEKOM controlled routing; ~**er Oszillator** *m* ELEKTRONIK controlled oscillator; ~**er Thermonuklearreaktor** *m* (*TNR*) KERNTECH controlled thermonuclear reactor (*CTR*); ~**e Verzögerungsschaltung** *f* FERNSEH controlled delay lock

gestockt: ~**e Antennengruppen** *f pl* RADIO baying aerials; ~**e Köpfe** *m pl* FERNSEH stacked heads

gestopft *adj* FERTIG *Windform* blind

gestört[1] *adj* MASCHINEN, TELEKOM out of order

gestört:[2] ~**er Betrieb** *m* MASCHINEN faulty operation; ~**e Bodenprobe** *f* KOHLEN remolded sample (AmE), remoulded sample (BrE); ~**e Frequenz** *f* STRAHLPHYS perturbed frequency; ~**es Gespräch** *nt* TELEKOM faulty call; ~**er Kompaß** *m* WASSERTRANS *Navigation* disturbed compass; ~**e Leitung** *f* TELEKOM faulty line; ~**e Verbindung** *f* TELEKOM faulty connection; ~**e Verdichterförderung** *f* LUFTTRANS *Turbomotor* surge; ~**e Welle** *f* PHYS distorted wave

gestoßen: ~**e Verbindung** *f* BAU *Holzbau* abutting joint

gestrandet[1] *adj* WASSERTRANS stranded, *Schiff* shipwrecked

gestrandet:[2] ~**es Schiff** *nt* WASSERTRANS shipwreck

gestreckt[1] *adj* BAU square-headed, GEOM prolate, MECHAN elongated

gestreckt:[2] ~**e kleine Blase** *f* KER & GLAS blibe; ~**e Länge** *f* KONSTZEICH developed view; ~**es Rotationsellipsoid** *nt* GEOM prolate spheroid, PHYS prolate ellipsoid; ~**e Spule** *f* PHYS solenoid; ~**er Winkel** *m* GEOM flat angle

gestreut:[1] ~**es Laden** *nt* COMP & DV scatter load, scattered load; ~**es Lesen** *nt* COMP & DV scatter read, scattered read; ~**es Licht** *nt* OPTIK scattered light; ~**e Speicherungsform** *f* COMP & DV random organization

gestreut:[2] ~ **laden** *vt* COMP & DV scatter-load; ~ **lesen** *vt* COMP & DV scatter-read

gestrichen: ~**es Papier** *nt* PAPIER, VERPACK coated

paper; **~e Pappe** *f* VERPACK enamel board

Gestrick *nt* TEXTIL knitted fabric

Gestübbe *nt* METALL brasque

gestuft *adj* MASCHINEN stepped

gestülpt *adj* FERTIG *Ziehen* inside-out redrawn

gestutzt: ~e Tragfläche *f* LUFTTRANS clipped wing

gesundheitlich: ~ abträglich *adj* CHEMIE noxious

Gesundheits: ~ und Sicherheitsbedingungen *f pl* SI-CHERHEIT health and safety requirements; **~ und Sicherheitsvorschriften** *f pl* SICHERHEIT *Arbeitsplatz* health, safety and welfare requirements

Gesundheitspaß *m* WASSERTRANS *Dokumente* bill of health

Gesundheitsrisiken *nt pl* SICHERHEIT health hazards

gesundheitsschädlich *adj* SICHERHEIT harmful to health

Gesundheitsüberwachung *f* SICHERHEIT health surveillance

gesüßt *adj* LEBENSMITTEL sweetened

getaktet: ~e Arbeit *f* ERGON paced work; **~e Schaltung** *f* ELEKTRONIK clocked circuit; **~es System** *nt* KONTROLL clocked system

geteert: ~es Tau *nt* WASSERTRANS *Tauwerk* tarred rope

geteilt: ~e Anflugbahn *f* LUFTTRANS segmented approach path; **~er Balken** *m* METROL *Waage* divided beam; **~er Bildschirm** *m* COMP & DV split screen; **~e Felge** *f* MASCHINEN split rim; **~es Gehäuse** *nt* KFZTECH *Hinterachsgruppe* split housing; **~es Lager** *nt* MASCHINEN split bearing; **~e Muffe** *f* MASCHINEN split collar, split sleeve; **~e Reibscheibe** *f* EISENBAHN split friction disc (BrE), split friction disk (AmE); **~e Riemenscheibe** *f* MASCHINEN split pulley; **~e Skala** *f* MASCHINEN divided dial; **~e Stromschiene** *f* ELEKTRIZ sectionalized busbar

getempert *adj* MECHAN tempered

getestet *adj* QUAL tested

getönt: ~es Normalglas *nt* KER & GLAS neutral-tinted glass; **~e Schweißschutzbrille** *f* SICHERHEIT sunglasses for welding protection

Getränkeverpackung *f* ABFALL beverage container

getränkt: ~es Papier *nt* KONSTZEICH impregnated paper

Getreidebrand *m* LEBENSMITTEL smut

Getreidekäfer *m* LEBENSMITTEL weevil

Getreidemotte *f* LEBENSMITTEL *Pflanzenkrankheitslehre* grain moth

getrennt: ~e Abfallagerung *f* ABFALL waste segregation; **~e Aufbewahrung** *f* QUAL quarantining; **~e Empfängerfeinabstimmung** *f* RADIO receiver incremental tuning; **~ erstellte Zeichnung** *f* KONSTZEICH separately-elaborated drawing; **~e Klärung von Abwässern** *f* WASSERVERSORG separate sewerage system; **~e Müllabfuhr** *f* ABFALL selective collection, separate collection; **~e Müllsammlung** *f* ABFALL selective collection, separate collection; **~er Perlit** *m* METALL divorced pearlite; **~e Schaltung** *f* ELEKTROTECH broken circuit; **~er Stromkreis** *m* ELEKTROTECH broken circuit

getreu: ~e Wiedergabe *f* AUFNAHME faithful reproduction

Getriebe:[1] **mit ~** *adj* MECHAN geared

Getriebe[2] *nt* FERTIG gear, KFZTECH transmission, MASCHINEN driving gear, gear, gearbox, gearing, mechanism, transmission gear, MECHAN, PAPIER, WASSERTRANS *Motor* gear; **~ für Hilfseinrichtungen** *nt* LUFTTRANS accessory gearbox; **~ für die Schaltung des Vorschubs** *nt* MASCHINEN change-feed box; **Getriebeaggregat** *nt* MASCHINEN gear assembly;

Getriebeantriebswelle *f* KFZTECH gearbox drive shaft, primary shaft; **Getriebeautomatik** *f* MASCHINEN automatic transmission; **Getriebebremse** *f* MASCHINEN transmission brake; **Getriebedeckel** *m* MASCHINEN gear cover; **Getriebeeingangswelle** *f* MASCHINEN gearbox input shaft; **Getriebegehäuse** *nt* KFZTECH gearbox, gearbox housing; **Getriebehauptwelle** *f* KFZTECH mainshaft, third motion shaft; **Getriebekasten** *m* FERTIG gearbox, MASCHINEN gear case, gear casing, gearbox, MECHAN gearbox; **Getriebekopf** *m* MASCHINEN gear head; **Getriebelehre** *f* FERTIG kinematics

getriebelos *adj* MECHAN gearless

Getriebe: Getriebemotor *m* MECHAN geared motor

getrieben: ~e Scheibe *f* MASCHINEN driven disc (BrE), driven disk (AmE)

Getriebe: Getrieberad *nt* MASCHINEN gear, gearwheel; **Getrieberäder** *nt pl* MASCHINEN gearing; **Getrieberadsatz** *m* KFZTECH set of gears; **Getriebeturbine** *f* MECHAN geared turbine; **Getriebeuntersetzung** *f* KFZTECH transmission reduction; **Getriebewelle** *f* MASCHINEN gear shaft; **Getriebezahnrad** *nt* MASCHINEN gear

getrocknet *adj* LEBENSMITTEL, THERMOD desiccated, dried

Getter *nt* ELEKTRIZ, ELEKTROTECH, TELEKOM getter; **Getterstoff** *m* ELEKTROTECH getter

getunt: ~er Motor *m* KFZTECH hotted-up engine

Geübtheit *f* ERGON proficiency

Geviert *nt* DRUCK em, mutton

gewachsen: ~er Boden *m* UMWELTSCHMUTZ unspoilt land; **~er Übergang** *m* ELEKTRONIK *Halbleiter* grown junction

gewählt: ~e virtuelle Verbindung *f* TELEKOM switched virtual circuit

gewährleistet: ~e Flugbahn *f* LUFTTRANS guaranteed flight path; **~es Gewicht** *nt* LUFTTRANS guaranteed weight

Gewährleistungsmarke *f* PATENT certification mark

gewalzt *adj* ELEKTRIZ laminated, METALL rolled; **mit ~em Gewinde** *adj* FERTIG roll-threaded

Gewände *nt* BAU jamb

gewartet *adj* MASCHINEN serviced

gewaschen: ~e und ausgepreßte Pappartikel *m pl* VER-PACK *aus dem Handel zur Entsorgung* washed and squashed consumer waste cartons; **~e Kohle** *f* KOHLEN cleaned coal

Gewässer *nt pl* WASSERTRANS waters; **Gewässerbelastung** *f* UMWELTSCHMUTZ impact of waters; **Gewässergüte** *f* WASSERVERSORG quality of water; **Gewässerkunde** *f* NICHTFOSS ENERG, WASSERTRANS hydrography, WASSERVERSORG hydrology

gewässerkundlich *adj* WASSERTRANS hydrographic

Gewässer: Gewässerreinigungsschiff *nt* UMWELT-SCHMUTZ depolluting ship; **Gewässerschutz** *m* UMWELTSCHMUTZ river and lake protection, water protection; **Gewässerverschmutzung** *f* WASSERVER-SORG water pollution; **Gewässerverunreinigung** *f* WASSERVERSORG water pollution; **Gewässerwissenschaft** *f* WASSERVERSORG hydroscience

Gewebe *nt* PAPIER fabric, TEXTIL cloth, fabric, web, woven fabric, *in Strangform* fabric; **~ mit Lichtpausschicht** *nt* KONSTZEICH cloth with diazo coating; **Gewebebandpresse** *f* PAPIER fabric press; **Gewebebindung** *f* TEXTIL weave of a fabric; **Gewebefilter** *nt* ABFALL fabric filter; **Gewebekonstruktion** *f* TEXTIL fabric construction; **Geweberiemen** *m* MASCHINEN fabric belt; **Gewebestrang** *m* TEXTIL rope

gewebt: nicht ~es Glasgarngelege *nt* KER & GLAS nonwoven scrim; nicht ~e Matte *nt* KER & GLAS nonwoven scrim; nicht ~er Teppich *m* TEXTIL nonwoven carpet

gewellt[1] *adj* FERTIG corrugated, KER & GLAS wavy, MASCHINEN corrugated, PAPIER corrugated, fluted

gewellt:[2] ~e Ausdehnungsverbindung *f* KERNTECH corrugated expansion joint; ~e Federscheibe *f* MASCHINEN corrugated spring washer, crinkle washer; ~e Kante *f* KER & GLAS curled edge; ~er Rohrausgleicher *m* KERNTECH corrugated tube compensator; ~e Scheibe *f* MASCHINEN corrugated washer

Gewerbe *nt* ABFALL, ERGON business; **Gewerbeabfall** *m* ABFALL industrial waste; **Gewerbehygiene** *f* ERGON industrial hygiene; **Gewerbekühlschrank** *m* HEIZ & KÄLTE commercial refrigerator

gewerblich:[1] ~er Abfall *m* ABFALL commercial waste, industrial waste, process waste, trade waste; ~es Abwasser *nt* ABFALL industrial effluent; ~e Anwendbarkeit *f* PATENT industrial application; ~e Anwendung *f* PATENT exploitation in industry; ~es Eigentum *nt* PATENT industrial property; ~e Funkdienste *m pl* RAUMFAHRT business services; ~er Müll *m* ABFALL industrial waste; ~er Verkehr *m* TRANS commercial traffic

gewerblich:[2] ~ anwendbar sein *vi* PATENT to be susceptible of industrial application

Gewerk *nt* BAU trade

gewetzt: ~e Freifläche *f* FERTIG *Reibahle* primary clearance

Gewicht *nt* DRUCK weight, MATH place value, *Statistik* weight, METROL, PHYS weight; ~ des Seils *nt* LUFTTRANS cable weight; ~ pro Quadratmeter *nt* DRUCK grams per square meter (AmE), grams per square metre (BrE)

Gewichte: ~ und Maße *nt pl* METROL weights and measures

gewichten *vti* ERGON weight

gewichtet: ~er Durchschnitt *m* QUAL weighted average; ~er Graph *m* KÜNSTL INT weighted graph; ~es Mittel *nt* MATH, PHYS weighted mean; ~er Mittelwert *m* QUAL weighted average

Gewicht: **Gewichtsanteil** *m* KERNTECH weight fraction; **Gewichtsausgleich des Luftschraubenblattes** *m* LUFTTRANS *Hubschrauber* blade balance weight

gewichtsbelastet: ~es Manometer *nt* GERÄT deadweight gage (AmE), dead-weight gauge (BrE)

Gewichtsdifferenz: der ~ Rechnung tragen *vi* METROL make allowance for difference in weight

Gewicht: **Gewichtseinheit** *f* METROL weight unit; **Gewichtskraft** *f* METROL, PHYS weight; **Gewichtslosigkeit** *f* PHYS weightlessness

gewichtsmolar *adj* CHEMIE molal

Gewicht: **Gewichtsoptimierung** *f* RAUMFAHRT *Raumschiff* weight optimization; **Gewichtsplattform** *f* ERDÖL *Offshore-Technik* gravity platform; **Gewichtsschwerpunkt** *m* WASSERTRANS *Schiffkonstruktion* center of gravity (AmE), centre of gravity (BrE); **Gewichtsskale** *f* METROL weighing scale; **Gewichtsversuch** *m* KOHLEN weight penetration test

Gewichtung *f* COMP & DV weighting, LABOR, MATH weight; **Gewichtungsfaktor** *m* RAUMFAHRT *Weltraumfunk* weighting factor

gewickelt: ~er Stator *m* ELEKTROTECH wound stator

Gewinde:[1] mit ~ *adj* FERTIG, MASCHINEN threaded

Gewinde[2] *nt* FERTIG thread, MASCHINEN thread, *einer Mutter* thread, MECHAN coil; ~ nach britischem Standard *nt* MASCHINEN *(BSF-Gewinde)* British standard fine screw thread *(BSF)*, MASCHINEN *(BSP-Gewinde)* British standard pipe thread *(BSP)*

Gewinde:[3] mit ~ versehen *vt* MASCHINEN screw

Gewinde:[4] ~ bohren *vi* BAU tap; ~ fertigen *vi* MASCHINEN thread; ~ herstellen *vi* FERTIG, MASCHINEN thread

Gewinde: **Gewindeachse** *f* FERTIG thread axis; **Gewindeanschluß** *m* FERTIG *Kunststoffinstallationen* threaded joint; **Gewindebearbeitungsmaschine** *f* MASCHINEN screwing machine; **Gewindebemaßung** *f* KONSTZEICH thread dimensioning; **Gewindebohreinheit** *f* MASCHINEN tapping unit; **Gewindebohreinrichtung** *f* MASCHINEN tapping attachment; **Gewindebohren** *nt* MASCHINEN tapping; **Gewindebohrer** *m* BAU screw tap, tap (BrE), FERTIG tap, *für Acme-Trapezgewinde* acme thread tap, MASCHINEN screw tap, tap; **Gewindebohrer Nr. 3** *m* FERTIG, MASCHINEN tap No 3, third tap; **Gewindebohrer Nr. 1** *m* FERTIG, MASCHINEN first-cut tap, tap No1; **Gewindebohrer Nr. 2** *m* FERTIG, MASCHINEN intermediate tap, second tap, tap No 2; **Gewindebohrerhalter** *m* MASCHINEN tap holder; **Gewindebohrmaschine** *f* MASCHINEN tapping machine; **Gewindebohr-und-schneidmaschine** *f* MASCHINEN screwing and tapping machine; **Gewindebohrung** *f* FERTIG taphole, *Innengewinde* tapped hole; **Gewindebolzen** *m* KFZTECH threaded bolt, MASCHINEN stud, stud bolt, threaded fastener; **Gewindebolzenabschneider** *m* FERTIG bolt clipper; **Gewindebuchse** *f* FERTIG screwed bush, *Kunststoffinstallationen* threaded bush; **Gewindedarstellung** *f* KONSTZEICH representation of a thread; **Gewindedrehen** *nt* MASCHINEN screw cutting, thread turning; **Gewindedreher** *m* BAU pipe threader; **Gewindedrehmaschine** *f* MASCHINEN threading lathe; **Gewindedrücken** *nt* MASCHINEN thread bulging; **Gewindedurchmesser** *m* MASCHINEN thread diameter; **Gewindeeinsatz** *m* MASCHINEN thread insert; **Gewindeflanke** *f* MASCHINEN thread flank; **Gewindeform** *f* MASCHINEN thread form

gewindeformend: ~e Schraube *f* MASCHINEN thread-forming screw

Gewinde: **Gewindefräsen** *nt* FERTIG, MASCHINEN thread milling; **Gewindefräser** *m* FERTIG, MASCHINEN thread-milling cutter; **Gewindefräsmaschine** *f* FERTIG thread-milling machine; **Gewindefreistich** *m* MASCHINEN thread undercut; **Gewindefurchen** *nt* MECHAN thread ridging; **Gewindeganganzeiger** *m* MASCHINEN thread dial indicator; **Gewindeherstellung** *f* FERTIG threading; **Gewindeinstallation** *f* MASCHINEN screwing; **Gewindelänge** *f* MASCHINEN thread length; **Gewindelehrdorn** *m* METROL plug thread gage (AmE), plug thread gauge (BrE); **Gewindelehre** *f* MASCHINEN screw pitch gage (AmE), screw pitch gauge (BrE), screw thread gage (AmE), screw thread gauge (BrE), thread gage (BrE), thread gauge (BrE), METROL center gage (AmE), centre gauge (BrE), screw thread gage (AmE), screw thread gauge (BrE); **Gewindeloch** *nt* FERTIG taphole, *Kunststoffinstallationen* threaded hole, MASCHINEN taphole, tapped hole; **Gewindemeißel** *m* FERTIG, MASCHINEN threading tool; **Gewindemeßschraube** *f* FERTIG thread micrometer; **Gewindemeßzylinder** *m* METROL screw-thread measuring cylinder; **Gewindemuffe** *f* FERTIG *Kunststoffinstallationen* threaded socket end, MASCHINEN threaded sleeve; **Gewindemutter** *f* MASCHINEN threaded nut; **Gewindenachbohrer** *m* BAU, MASCHINEN plug tap; **Gewindenachschneiden** *nt* MASCHINEN rethreading; **Gewindenippel** *m* MASCHINEN threaded nipple; **Gewindeprofil** *nt* FERTIG, MASCHINEN thread profile; **Gewinderille** *f* FERTIG thread groove; **Gewindering** *m* MASCHINEN ring nut; **Gewinderohr** *nt* MASCHINEN threaded pipe; **Gewinderollen** *nt* MASCHINEN thread rolling; **Gewindeschablone** *f* MASCHINEN screw pitch gage (AmE), screw pitch gauge (BrE); **Gewindeschälen** *nt* FERTIG thread peeling, MASCHINEN thread whirling; **Gewindeschleifen** *nt* FERTIG, MASCHINEN, MECHAN thread grinding; **Gewindeschleifmaschine** *f* FERTIG thread-grinding wheel; **Gewindeschneidbacke** *f* FERTIG chaser, threading die; **Gewindeschneidbohrer** *m* FERTIG tap; **Gewindeschneideinrichtung** *f* FERTIG thread-cutting attachment, MASCHINEN screw-cutting attachment, thread-cutting attachment; **Gewindeschneideisen** *nt* MASCHINEN screwing die; **Gewindeschneiden** *nt* FERTIG thread cutting, threading, MASCHINEN screw cutting, thread cutting

gewindeschneidend: ~**er Bohrer** *m* MASCHINEN tapping drill; ~**e Schraube** *f* MASCHINEN thread-cutting screw

Gewinde: **Gewindeschneider** *m* MASCHINEN threader; **Gewindeschneidkluppe** *f* MASCHINEN screw plate, tap plate; **Gewindeschneidkluppe mit Ratsche** *f* MASCHINEN ratchet-screwing stock; **Gewindeschneidkopf** *m* FERTIG die head, MASCHINEN die head, die stock, screw stock, screwing chuck, screwing head; **Gewindeschneidkopf für Außengewinde** *m* FERTIG bolt die head; **Gewindeschneidmaschine** *f* MASCHINEN machine tapper, threading machine; **Gewindeschneidschraube** *f* MASCHINEN self-cutting screw; **Gewindespitzenabrundung** *f* FERTIG crest truncation; **Gewindesteigung** *f* KFZTECH thread pitch; **Gewindesteigungswinkel** *m* MASCHINEN thread lead angle; **Gewindestift** *m* BAU stud bolt, FERTIG *Kunststoffinstallationen* grub screw, MASCHINEN grub screw, headless pin, MECHAN headless screw; **Gewindestopfen** *m* BAU screw plug; **Gewindestrehlen** *nt* FERTIG thread chasing, MASCHINEN screw chasing, thread chasing

gewindestrehlen *vt* FERTIG chase

Gewinde: **Gewindestrehler** *m* FERTIG, MASCHINEN screw chaser, thread chaser; **Gewindeteilung** *f* MASCHINEN screw pitch, thread pitch; **Gewindetiefe** *f* BAU, FERTIG, MASCHINEN thread depth; **Gewindetiefenmesser** *m* METROL height gage (AmE), height gauge (BrE); **Gewindewalzautomat mit Backen** *m* FERTIG automatic flat-die thread-rolling machine; **Gewindewalzen** *nt* MASCHINEN thread rolling; **Gewindewälzen** *nt* FERTIG thread hobbing; **Gewindewälzfräser** *m* FERTIG thread-milling hob; **Gewindewirbeln** *nt* MASCHINEN thread whirling; **Gewindezahn** *m* FERTIG thread ridge

Gewindezapfen: mit ~ *adj* FERTIG *Spindel*, MASCHINEN threaded

Gewinn *m* ELEKTRONIK *(G)*, ERGON *(G)*, FERNSEH *(G)* gain *(G)*, NICHTFOSS ENERG yield, RADIO *Antenne* RADIO *(G)*, RAUMFAHRT *(G)* *Weltraumfunk*, TELEKOM *(G)* *Antenne* gain *(G)*

gewinnbar: ~**e Reserven** *f pl* ERDÖL recoverable reserves

gewinnen *vt* KOHLEN get

gewinnend: ~**er Strom** *m* WASSERVERSORG gaining stream

gewinngeführt *adj* ELEKTRONIK *Laser* gain-controlled

Gewinnung *f* ERDÖL *Bohrtechnik*, FERTIG *Kunststoffinstallationen*, KOHLEN extraction; **Gewinnungserlaubnis** *f* ERDÖL *Recht* production licence (BrE), production license (AmE)

Gewinn: **Gewinnveränderung** *f* ELEKTRONIK gain change

Gewirk *nt* TEXTIL knitted fabric

Gewißheitsfaktor *m* KÜNSTL INT certainty factor, confidence factor

gewogen: ~**es Mittel** *nt* MATH weighted mean

gewöhnlich: ~**er Portlandzement** *m* BAU ordinary Portland cement; ~**e Sechskantmutter** *f* MASCHINEN ordinary hexagonal nut; ~**e wechselseitig betriebene Leitung** *f* TELEKOM ordinary bothway line

Gewöhnung *f* ERGON habituation

Gewölbe *nt* BAU vault, KER & GLAS *des Glashafens* arch; **Gewölbefläche** *f* BAU intrados; **Gewölberücken** *m* BAU extrados; **Gewölberückenfläche** *f* BAU back; **Gewölbesperrmauer** *f* BAU arch dam; **Gewölbestein** *m* BAU arch stone

gewölbt[1] *adj* BAU arched, bonneted, MASCHINEN dished

gewölbt:[2] ~**er Boden** *m* MECHAN dished head; ~**es Deck** *nt* WASSERTRANS cambered deck; ~**e Federscheibe** *f* MASCHINEN curved spring washer; ~**er Luftsaugekanal** *m* LUFTTRANS variable geometry inlet; ~**e Oberfläche** *f* KER & GLAS warped finish; ~**es Tafelglas** *nt* KER & GLAS bow and warp (AmE), warped sheet (BrE); ~**er Verschluß** *m* KER & GLAS bulged finish

gewunden *adj* BAU meandering

gewürfelt *adj* MATH aleatoric

Geysir *m* NICHTFOSS ENERG geyser

gezackt[1] *adj* FERTIG scalloped, MECHAN, SICHERHEIT jagged

gezackt:[2] ~**e Kante** *f* MASCHINEN pinked edge; ~**er Riß** *m* KER & GLAS hackle; ~**e Schaufel** *f* BAU pronged shovel; ~**e Schneide** *f* SICHERHEIT *einer Klinge* jagged edge

gezählt: ~**er Impuls** *m* GERÄT count

gezähmt: ~**e Frequenzmodulation** *f* ELEKTRONIK, FERNSEH, RADIO, TELEKOM tamed frequency modulation

gezahnt[1] *adj* MASCHINEN geared, toothed, MECHAN cogged

gezahnt:[2] ~**er Keilriemen** *m* MASCHINEN cogged V belt; ~**er Synchronisationsimpuls** *m* FERNSEH serrated pulse; ~**er Treibriemen** *m* MASCHINEN toothed drive belt

Gezeit *f* NICHTFOSS ENERG, WASSERTRANS tide

Gezeiten *f pl* WASSERTRANS tides; **Gezeitenaufzeichnung** *f* NICHTFOSS ENERG marigram; **Gezeitenbereich** *m* NICHTFOSS ENERG tidal range; **Gezeitenbewegung** *f* NICHTFOSS ENERG tidal movement; **Gezeitenenergie** *f* NICHTFOSS ENERG tidal power, PHYS tidal energy; **Gezeitenhub** *m* WASSERTRANS range of tide; **Gezeitenkraft** *f* NICHTFOSS ENERG tidal power; **Gezeitenkraftwerk** *nt* ELEKTROTECH tidal power plant, NICHTFOSS ENERG tidal power station; **Gezeitenmesser** *m* NICHTFOSS ENERG tide gage (AmE), tide gauge (BrE); **Gezeitenmühle** *f* NICHTFOSS ENERG tide mill; **Gezeitenprisma** *nt* NICHTFOSS ENERG tidal prism; **Gezeitensignale** *nt pl* WASSERTRANS tidal signals, tide signals; **Gezeitenstrom** *m* NICHTFOSS ENERG tidal current, WASSERTRANS, WASSERVERSORG tidal current, tidal flow, tidal stream; **Gezeitenstromatlas** *m* WASSERTRANS tidal stream atlas; **Gezeitenstromschnelle** *f* WASSERTRANS tide race; **Gezeitentabelle** *f* WASSERTRANS tide chart, *Navigation* tidal chart; **Gezeitentafel** *f* WASSERTRANS tide chart, *Navigation* tidal chart; **Gezeitentafeln** *f pl* WASSERTRANS tide tables; **Gezeitenwechsel** *m* WASSERTRANS turn of the tide; **Gezeitenzone** *f* WASSERTRANS littoral

gezielt: **~e Sendung** *f* FERNSEH narrowcasting

gezogen: **~er Draht** *m* MASCHINEN drawn wire; **~er Stiel** *m* KER & GLAS drawn stem; **~er Zonenübergang** *m* ELEKTRONIK *Halbleiter* drawn junction; **~er Zucker** *m* LEBENSMITTEL *Süßwaren* pulled sugar

gezündet: **~e Röhre** *f* ELEKTRONIK fired tube; **nicht ~e Röhre** *f* ELEKTRONIK unfired tube

g-Faktor *m* PHYS g-factor

GFK *abbr* KUNSTSTOFF *(Glasfaserkunststoff, glasfaserverstärkter Kunststoff)*, VERPACK *(glasfaserverstärkter Kunststoff)*, WASSERTRANS *(glasfaserverstärkter Kunststoff) Schiffbau* GRP *(glass fibre-reinforced plastic)*

ggT *abbr (größter gemeinsamer Teiler)* MATH HCF *(highest common factor)*

Gibbs: **~sche freie Energie** *f* PHYS Gibbs free energy; **~sche Funktion** *f (G)* PHYS, THERMOD Gibbs function *(G)*; **~sche Phasenregel** *f* KERNTECH, THERMOD Gibbs phase rule

Gicht *f* FERTIG batch, top; **Gichtbühne** *f* FERTIG charging platform; **Gichtgas** *nt* FERTIG blast furnace gas, KERNTECH stack gas; **Gichtglocke** *f* FERTIG bell; **Gichtverschluß** *m* FERTIG bell and hopper

Giebel *m* BAU gable; **Giebelbogen** *m* BAU triangular arch; **Giebeldach** *nt* BAU gable roof; **Giebelfußstein** *m* BAU skew; **Giebelmauer** *f* KER & GLAS gable wall; **Giebelwand** *f* BAU flank wall

Gientalje *f* WASSERTRANS *Deckausrüstung* winding tackle

Gier- *pref* LUFTTRANS, MASCHINEN, NICHTFOSS ENERG, RAUMFAHRT yaw; **Gierachse** *f* LUFTTRANS yaw axis; **Gierbewegung** *f* LUFTTRANS yaw

Gieren *nt* LUFTTRANS, NICHTFOSS ENERG, RAUMFAHRT *Raumschiff* yaw

gieren *vi* NICHTFOSS ENERG, RAUMFAHRT *Raumschiff*, WASSERTRANS *Navigation* yaw

Gier-: **Gierjustierung** *f* NICHTFOSS ENERG yaw adjustment; **Gierkontrolle** *f* NICHTFOSS ENERG yaw control; **Giermoment** *nt* LUFTTRANS, MASCHINEN, NICHTFOSS ENERG yawing moment; **Gierschwingung** *f* LUFTTRANS *Aerodynamik* snaking

Gierung *f* RAUMFAHRT *Quantität* yaw rate; **Gierungsachse** *f* RAUMFAHRT *Raumschiff* yaw axis; **Gierungswinkel** *m* RAUMFAHRT *Raumschiff* yaw angle

Gier-: **Gierwinkelgeschwindigkeit** *f* LUFTTRANS angular yaw rate

Gieß- *pref* DRUCK, KER & GLAS, MASCHINEN casting; **Gießakt** *m* FERTIG *Gießen* shot; **Gießansatz** *m* KER & GLAS casting scar; **Gießaufsatz** *m* FERTIG *Gießen* feeder; **Gießbäche** *m pl* DRUCK rivers of white

Gießen *nt* FERTIG casting, founding, KER & GLAS *von Feuerfesterzeugnissen* casting, *von Spiegelglas* casting, KUNSTSTOFF, MASCHINEN, MECHAN, METALL casting, SICHERHEIT pouring; **~ in Mehrfachform** *nt* FERTIG gating

gießen *vt* BAU *Beton* pour, DRUCK cast, LEBENSMITTEL pour, MASCHINEN, PAPIER cast

Gießer *m* DRUCK composition caster, FERTIG founder, KER & GLAS ladler

Gießerei *f* FERTIG, KOHLEN foundry; **Gießereiformschwärze** *f* FERTIG *Gießen* blackening; **Gießereikran** *m* KER & GLAS casting crane; **Gießereisand** *m* BAU foundry sand

Gieß-: **Gießfolie** *f* KUNSTSTOFF cast film; **Gießform** *f*

DRUCK casting mold (AmE), casting mould (BrE), mold (AmE), mould (BrE), MASCHINEN casting mold (AmE), casting mould (BrE), mold for casting (AmE), mould for casting (BrE), MECHAN ingot mold (AmE), ingot mould (BrE), METALL mold (AmE), mould (BrE); **Gießkasten** *m* PAPIER casting box; **Gießlippe** *f* KER & GLAS casting lip; **Gießloch** *nt* KER & GLAS orifice; **Gießlochring** *m* KER & GLAS orifice ring; **Gießlöffel** *m* BAU *Maurerwerkzeug* ladle, FERTIG handladle, ladle, MASCHINEN pouring spoon; **Gießmaschine** *f* DRUCK caster, casting machine, type caster, KER & GLAS casting unit, PAPIER casting machine; **Gießpfanne** *f* FERTIG foundry ladle; **Gießpfannenkran** *m* FERTIG ladle crane

Gießrinne *f* FERTIG spout, KER & GLAS *bei der Herstellung von Walzglas* trough; **Gießrinnenlippe** *f* KER & GLAS trough lip

Gieß-: **Gießschlicker** *m* KER & GLAS casting slip; **Gießspirale** *f* FERTIG fluidity mold (AmE), fluidity mould (BrE); **Gießteil** *nt* KUNSTSTOFF casting; **Gießtisch** *m* KER & GLAS casting table

Gießtrichter *m* FERTIG cast gate, ingate, pouring gate, skim gate, METALL sprue; **Gießtrichteransatz** *m* FERTIG sprue; **Gießtrichtermodell** *nt* FERTIG gate pin, gate stick

Gieß-: **Gießtümpel** *m* FERTIG runner basin; **Gießverfahren** *nt* KUNSTSTOFF casting; **Gießwalzen** *f pl* KER & GLAS casting rollers; **Gießwanne** *f* FERTIG tundish

giftig *adj* ANSTRICH, ERDÖL, KOHLEN toxic

Giftigkeit *f* CHEMIE, ERDÖL, KUNSTSTOFF, SICHERHEIT toxicity

Giftmüll *m* ABFALL poisonous waste, toxic waste; **Giftmüllentsorgungsanlage** *f* UMWELTSCHMUTZ toxic waste disposal plant

Giftschrank *m* LABOR poisons cupboard

Giftstoff *m* CHEMIE, UMWELTSCHMUTZ toxic agent, toxicant; **Giftstoffentfernung aus Kernreaktoren** *f* KERNTECH nuclear reactor poison removal

Giga- *pref (G)* METROL giga *(G)*; **Gigabyte** *nt (GB)* COMP & DV, OPTIK *Informationseinheit* gigabyte *(GB)*; **Gigahertz** *nt* RADIO gigahertz; **Gigaplatte** *f* COMP & DV, OPTIK gigadisk

GIGO *abbr (Müll rein, Müll raus)* COMP & DV GIGO *(garbage in, garbage out)*

GII *abbr (globale Informations-Infrastruktur)* COMP & DV GII *(Global Information Infrastructure)*

Gilbert *nt* ELEKTROTECH *CGS-Einheit* gilbert

Gill *nt* METROL gill

Gillung *f* WASSERTRANS *Schiffbau* counter; **Gillungsheck** *nt* WASSERTRANS *Schiffbau* counter stern

Gimpe *f* TEXTIL gimp

Ginn: **~sche Gleichung** *f* KERNTECH Ginn equation

Gipfelstation *f* TRANS top station

Gips *m* ERDÖL *Mineral* gypsum; **Gips-** *pref* CHEMIE *Kalk* selenitic; **Gipsgestein** *nt* BAU plaster rock, plaster stone; **Gipskartonplatte** *f* BAU plasterboard; **Gipsmörtel** *m* BAU plaster; **Gipsputzunterlage** *f* BAU *aus Streckmetall* furring

Girlande *f* PAPIER festoon

Gischt *f* WASSERTRANS *Meer* foam, spray

Gispe *f* KER & GLAS *Blase* seed

Gitter *nt* BAU lattice, screen, trellis, ELEKTRIZ grid, ELEKTRONIK lattice, *Elektronenröhre* grid, ELEKTROTECH, FERNSEH grating, FERTIG grid, lattice, KERNTECH *Elektrode*, KOHLEN grid, MATH lattice, PHYS, RADIO grid, RAUMFAHRT *Raumschiff* lattice; **Gitterableitwi-**

derstand *m* PHYS grid-leak resistor; **Gitterabstand** *m* METALL lattice spacing; **Gitterbalken** *m* BAU lattice truss; **Gitterboxpalette** *f* TRANS crate pallet, VERPACK box pallet with sidewalls; **Gitterbrücke** *f* BAU lattice bridge; **Gittereigenschaft** *f* ELEKTRONIK grid characteristic; **Gitterfehler** *m* ELEKTRONIK *Halbleiter*, METALL lattice defect

gitterförmig *adj* FERTIG latticed

Gitter: **Gitterfurche** *f* OPTIK *Beugungsgitter* groove

gittergesteuert: **~er Quecksilberbogen-Gleichrichter** *m* ELEKTROTECH grid-controlled mercury arc rectifier; **~e Röhre** *f* ELEKTRONIK grid-controlled tube

Gitter: **Gitterkammer** *f* KER & GLAS checker chamber; **Gitterkathodenkondensator** *m* ELEKTROTECH grid-cathode capacitance; **Gitterkisteneinlage** *f* PAPIER crate liners; **Gitterkondensator** *m* ELEKTROTECH grid capacitor; **Gitterkonstante** *f* METALL lattice constant; **Gitterlast** *f* RADIO grid loading; **Gitterlücke** *f* METALL *Kristalle* vacancy; **Gitterluftschraubenblätter** *nt pl* LUFTTRANS cascade blades, cascade vanes; **Gittermast** *m* BAU pylon, tower, RADIO lattice mast; **Gittermauer** *f* BAU screen wall; **Gittermauerwerk** *nt* KER & GLAS checkers; **Gittermodulation** *f* ELEKTRONIK, FERNSEH grid modulation; **Gitternetz** *nt* RAUMFAHRT *Sieb* mesh; **Gitterpfosten** *m* BAU trellis post; **Gitterplatte** *f* ELEKTRIZ battery electrode, battery plate; **Gitterpunkt** *m* METALL lattice point; **Gitterrippe** *f* LUFTTRANS lattice rib; **Gitterrost** *nt* BAU grate, HEIZ & KÄLTE grating, grille; **Gitterschaufeln** *f pl* LUFTTRANS *Turbine* cascade vanes; **Gittersonde** *f* KERNTECH grid probe; **Gitterspektrograph** *m* KERNTECH diffraction spectrograph, grating spectrograph; **Gitterspiegel** *m* RAUMFAHRT *Raumschiff* reticulated mirror; **Gitterstab** *m* BAU screen bar; **Gitterstein** *m* FERTIG, KER & GLAS checker brick; **Gittersteuerleistung** *f* ELEKTROTECH grid-driving power; **Gitterstrich** *m* OPTIK *Beugungsgitter* groove; **Gitterstrom** *m* ELEKTROTECH grid current; **Gitterträger** *m* BAU lattice beam, lattice girder, MECHAN, RAUMFAHRT *Raumschiff* lattice girder; **Gitterträgerbogen** *m* BAU lattice girder arch; **Gitterträgerplatte** *f* KERNTECH grid support plate; **Gitterturbulenz** *f* STRÖMPHYS grid turbulence; **Gitterumformer** *m* ELEKTROTECH grating converter; **Gitterverformung** *f* METALL lattice deformation; **Gitterverlustleistung** *f (Pg)* RADIO grid dissipation power *(Pg)*; **Gittervorspannung** *f* ELEKTROTECH bias, grid bias, *Thyristoren* gate bias, RADIO grid bias; **Gittervorspannung durch Kathodenwiderstand** *f* ELEKTROTECH self-bias; **Gittervorwiderstand** *m* PHYS *Elektronenröhre* bias resistor; **Gitterwandler** *m* ELEKTROTECH grating converter; **Gitterwerk** *nt* BAU latticework; **Gitterwerkmast** *m* ELEKTRIZ lattice tower; **Gitterwiderstand** *m* RADIO grid-leak resistor; **Gitterzerkleinerer** *m* ABFALL grid crusher; **Gitterziegel** *m* BAU perforated brick; **Gitterzuordnung** *f* METALL lattice correspondence -

Glanz *m* DRUCK, KUNSTSTOFF gloss, METALL brightness, brilliance, burnish, PAPIER gloss, TEXTIL glaze, luster (AmE), lustre (BrE), radiance, sheen, VERPACK gloss; **Glanzappretur** *f* TEXTIL glazing

glänzen *vt* TEXTIL glaze

glänzend *adj* KUNSTSTOFF glossy, TEXTIL bright, glossy, lustrous, VERPACK glossy

Glanz: **Glanzfarbe** *f* BAU gloss paint; **Glanzgarn** *nt* TEXTIL glazed yarn; **Glanzgold** *nt* KER & GLAS bright gold, burnishing gold; **Glanzkarton** *m* VERPACK glazed board; **Glanzkohle** *f* KOHLEN glance coal; **Glanzlack für Anstrich** *m* VERPACK gloss

glanzlos *adj* BAU *Farbe* dull, flat, TEXTIL lusterless (AmE), lustreless (BrE)

Glanz: **Glanzmaschine** *f* VERPACK glazing machine; **Glanzmesser** *m* KUNSTSTOFF gloss meter; **Glanzpapier** *nt* DRUCK glossy paper, PAPIER glazed paper, VERPACK glazed paper, glossy paper; **Glanzpappe** *f* VERPACK glazed board; **Glanzschleifen** *nt* PAPIER rubbing; **Glanzsilber** *nt* KER & GLAS bright silver, burnishing silver; **Glanzwinkelgitter** *nt* PHYS blazed grating

Glas *nt* ANSTRICH, CHEMIE glass, VERPACK glass container, glass jar; **~ mit hohem Brechungsindex** *nt* KER & GLAS flint glass; **nur aus Gemenge erschmolzenes ~** *nt* KER & GLAS glass melted from batch only; **Glasanalyse** *f* KER & GLAS glass analysis; **Glasandruckplatte** *f* FOTO glass pressure plate

glasartig *adj* ANSTRICH glassy, CHEMIE, FERTIG vitreous, KER & GLAS glassy

Glas: **Glasausbeute** *f* KER & GLAS glass yield; **Glasauskleidung** *f* ELEKTROTECH glass cladding; **Glasballon** *m* KER & GLAS, LABOR carboy; **Glasbaustein** *m* KER & GLAS glass block; **Glasbehälter** *m* ABFALL bottle bank, VERPACK glass container; **Glasbetonplatte** *f* KER & GLAS glass concrete panel; **Glasbildner** *m* KER & GLAS glass former; **Glasblasen** *nt* KER & GLAS blowing, glassblowing; **Glasbläser** *m* KER & GLAS blower, glassblower; **Glasblock** *m* KERNTECH glass block; **Glasbruch** *m* ABFALL cullet; **Glascontainer** *m* ABFALL bottle bank; **Glasdach** *nt* KER & GLAS glass roof; **Glasdachziegel** *m* KER & GLAS glass roof tile; **Glaselektrode** *f* LABOR glass electrode; **Glasemail** *nt* KER & GLAS vitreous enamel; **Glasemailschild** *nt* KER & GLAS vitreous enamel label; **Glasendmaß** *nt* METROL optical flat; **Glas-Epoxid-Laminat** *nt* ELEKTRONIK glass-epoxy laminate; **Glas-Epoxid-Leiterplatte** *f* ELEKTRONIK glass-epoxy printed circuit board

Glaser *m* BAU glazier; **Glaserdiamant** *m* BAU diamond pencil, glass cutter, glazier's diamond, KER & GLAS diamond pencil; **Glaserkitt** *m* BAU putty, sash putty, KER & GLAS putty; **Glaserzange** *f* KER & GLAS glazier's pliers

Gläser: **in ~ einmachen** *vt* LEBENSMITTEL *Früchte, Gemüse* bottle

Glas: **Glasfarbe** *f* KER & GLAS glass color (AmE), glass colour (BrE)

Glasfaser *f* BAU glass fiber (AmE), glass fibre (BrE), COMP & DV optical fiber (AmE), optical fibre (BrE), ELEKTROTECH glass fiber (AmE), glass fibre (BrE), optical fiber (AmE), optical fibre (BrE), KUNSTSTOFF glass fiber (AmE), glass fibre (BrE), RAUMFAHRT *zur Signalübertragung* optical fiber (AmE), optical fibre (BrE), WASSERTRANS *Schiffbaumaterial* glass fiber (AmE), glass fibre (BrE); **Glasfaseranschluß** *nt* ELEKTROTECH fiberoptic connection (AmE), fibreoptic connection (BrE); **Glasfaserkabel** *nt* COMP & DV, ELEKTROTECH, TELEKOM fiberoptic cable (AmE), fibreoptic cable (BrE); **Glasfaserkabel mit großem Durchmesser** *nt* ELEKTROTECH large-core glass fiber (AmE), large-core glass fibre (BrE); **Glasfaserkabel für mehrere Einsatzarten** *nt* ELEKTROTECH multimode optical fiber (AmE), multimode optical fibre (BrE); **Glasfaserkabel-Steckverbinder** *m* ELEKTROTECH fiberoptic connector (AmE), fibreoptic connector (BrE); **Glasfaserkreisel** *m* RAUMFAHRT *Raumschiff* fiberoptic gyrometer (AmE), fibreoptic gyrometer

(BrE); **Glasfaserkunststoff** *m (GFK)* KUNSTSTOFF
glass fiber-reinforced plastic (AmE), glass fibre-reinforced plastic (BrE) *(GRP)*; **Glasfaserlaminat** *nt*
VERPACK glass fiber laminate (AmE), glass fibre laminate (BrE); **Glasfaserschichtkunststoff** *m* VERPACK
glass fiber laminate (AmE), glass fibre laminate
(BrE); **Glasfaserstoff** *m* TEXTIL fiberglass (AmE), fibreglass (BrE); **Glasfaserstrang** *m* KER & GLAS strand;
Glasfasertechnik *f* COMP & DV fiber optics (AmE),
fibre optics (BrE); **Glasfasertechnologie** *f* ELEKTRO-
TECH fiberoptic technology (AmE), fibreoptic
technology (BrE)

glasfaserverstärkt[1] *adj* VERPACK glass fiber-reinforced
(AmE), glass fibre-reinforced (BrE)

glasfaserverstärkt:[2] ~**er Kunststoff** *m (GFK)* KUNST-
STOFF, VERPACK, WASSERTRANS glass fiber-reinforced
plastic (AmE), glass fibre-reinforced plastic (BrE)
(GRP)

Glasfaser: **Glasfaserverstärkung** *f* KER & GLAS glass
fiber reinforcement (AmE), glass fibre reinforcement
(BrE); **Glasfaservlies** *nt* KER & GLAS chopped-strand
mat, glass fiber mat (AmE), glass fibre mat (BrE)

Glas: **Glasfilament** *nt* KER & GLAS glass filament; **Glas-
film** *m* KER & GLAS glass film; **Glasfläschchen** *nt* KER &
GLAS phial (BrE), vial (AmE); **Glasformzange** *f* KER &
GLAS pucella; **Glasfritte** *f* KER & GLAS glass frit; **Glas-
füllungstür** *f* BAU sash door; **Glasgefäß** *nt* VERPACK
glass jar; **Glasgestrick** *nt* KER & GLAS knitted glass
fabric; **Glasgewebe** *nt* VERPACK glass fabric; **Glasglok-
ke** *f* KER & GLAS *Uhr*, LABOR bell jar; **Glashafenton** *m*
KER & GLAS pot clay; **Glashafenträger mit Schwanenhals** *m* KER & GLAS goosenecked pot carriage;
Glashalbleiter *m* ELEKTRONIK amorphous semiconductor; **Glashalter** *m* ELEKTROTECH glass holder;
Glashärte *f* METALL glass hardness; **Glashartgewebe**
nt KERNTECH glass-reinforced laminate; **Glasheizkör-
per** *m* KER & GLAS glass heating panel

glasieren *vt* FERTIG, FOTO, KER & GLAS *Substrat*, LEBENS-
MITTEL glaze

Glasiermaschine *f* KER & GLAS glazing machine

glasiert[1] *adj* KER & GLAS *Töpferwaren* glazed

glasiert:[2] ~**e Ofenkachel** *f* KER & GLAS Dutch tile; ~**es
Steingut** *nt* KER & GLAS glazed earthenware; ~**e Töpferwaren** *f pl* KER & GLAS glazed pottery

glasig[1] *adj* ANSTRICH glassy

glasig:[2] ~**er Feldspat** *m* KER & GLAS glassy feldspar

Glas: **Glasisolator** *m* ELEKTRIZ, KER & GLAS glass insulator; **Glaskamee** *f* KER & GLAS glass cameo; **Glaskappe** *f*
KER & GLAS blank seam; **Glaskeramik** *f* KER & GLAS,
KERNTECH glass ceramic; **Glaskolben** *m* KER & GLAS
bulb, LEBENSMITTEL *Laborgerät* flask; **Glaskondensa-
tor** *m* ELEKTROTECH glass capacitor; **Glaskrug** *m* KER &
GLAS glass jug; **Glaskugel** *f* KER & GLAS bead; **Glasla-
ser** *m* ELEKTRONIK glass laser; **Glasleiste** *f* BAU
window bar; **Glaslot** *nt* KER & GLAS solder glass; **Glas-
lüftungsstein** *m* KER & GLAS glass ventilating brick;
Glasmacherlehrling *m* KER & GLAS taker-in; **Glasma-
cherstuhl** *m* KER & GLAS chair; **Glasmacherwerkzeug**
nt KER & GLAS glassmaker's tool; **Glasmalerei** *f* KER &
GLAS painting on glass; **Glasmarmor** *m* KER & GLAS *zur
Herstellung von Glasfasern* glass marble; **Glasmi-
krosphäre** *f* KER & GLAS glass microsphere;
Glasoberfläche *f* KER & GLAS overlay, overlaying; **Glas-
ofenreise** *f* KER & GLAS campaign; **Glaspassivierung** *f*
ELEKTRONIK glass passivation, *Halbleiter* glassiva-
tion; **Glaspegelregler** *m* KER & GLAS glass level

controller; **Glasperle** *f* ANSTRICH glass bead, KER &
GLAS bead, glass bead; **Glaspflasterplatte** *f* KER & GLAS
glass-paving slab; **Glasplatte** *f* LABOR glass plate

Glasposten *m* KER & GLAS gob; **Glaspostenende** *nt* KER
& GLAS gob tail; **Glaspostentemperatur** *f* KER & GLAS
gob temperature; **Glaspostenverarbeitung** *f* KER &
GLAS gobbing; **Glaspostenverteiler** *m* KER & GLAS gob
distributor

Glas: **Glaspressen** *nt* KER & GLAS pressing; **Glaspunkt** *m*
KUNSTSTOFF glass transition temperature; **Glasrecy-
cling** *nt* ABFALL glass recycling; **Glasrohr** *nt*
ELEKTRONIK, KER & GLAS glass tube; **Glasröhre** *f* ELEK-
TRONIK glass tube; **Glasroving** *nt* TEXTIL roving;
Glasrührstab *m* LABOR glass-stirring rod; **Glassatz** *m*
KER & GLAS batch formula; **Glasschale** *f* KER & GLAS
glass dish; **Glasscheibe** *f* BAU pane; **Glasscherben** *f pl*
ABFALL, KER & GLAS cullet; **Glasschleifer** *m* KER &
GLAS *Person* glass cutter; **Glasschmuckperle** *f* KER &
GLAS prunt; **Glasschneidediamant** *m* KER & GLAS diamond for glass cutting; **Glasschneider** *m* BAU glass
cutter, KER & GLAS vitrea cutter, *Werkzeug* glass cutter; **Glasschneiderdiamant** *m* KER & GLAS cutting
diamond; **Glasschneidertisch** *m* KER & GLAS cutter's
table; **Glasschneidertischlineal** *nt* KER & GLAS cutter's
table ruler; **Glasschneidezange** *f* KER & GLAS cutter's
pliers; **Glasseidenmatte** *f* WASSERTRANS *Schiffbau*
chopped-strand mat; **Glasseidenvlies** *nt* KER & GLAS
continuous strand mat; **Glasseidenzwirn** *m* KER &
GLAS spun roving; **Glassinterfiltertiegel** *m* LABOR sintered glass filter crucible; **Glassinterfiltertrichter** *m*
LABOR sintered glass filter funnel; **Glasspinnfaden-
garn** *nt* KER & GLAS glass continuous filament yarn;
Glaspulver *nt* KER & GLAS powdered glass; **Glasstab**
m LABOR glass rod; **Glasstahlbeton** *m* KER & GLAS
glass-reinforced concrete; **Glasstapelfasergarn** *nt* KER
& GLAS glass staple-fiber yarn (AmE), glass staple-fibre yarn (BrE); **Glasstaub** *m* KER & GLAS glass dust;
Glas-Substrat *nt* ELEKTRONIK glass substrate; **Glasta-
sche** *f* KER & GLAS glass pocket; **Glastuch** *nt*
WASSERTRANS *Schiffbaumaterial* glass cloth; **Glas-
übergangstemperatur** *f* KUNSTSTOFF glass transition
temperature; **Glasumwandlungstemperatur** *f* KUNST-
STOFF glass transition temperature

Glasur *f* BAU enamel, KER & GLAS glaze, glossing, LE-
BENSMITTEL frosting, icing, TEXTIL glazing; **Glasurerz**
nt KER & GLAS potter's ore; **Glasurofen** *m* KER & GLAS
glaze kiln; **Glasurqualität** *f* KER & GLAS glazing quality;
Glasurschleifer *m* KER & GLAS glaze grinder; **Glasur-
stein** *m* BAU glazed brick; **Glasurziegel** *m* BAU glazed
brick

Glas: **Glaswalzendämpfer** *m* KER & GLAS glass roll dam-
pener; **Glaswaren** *f pl* KER & GLAS glassware;
Glaswaschapparat *m* LABOR glass washer; **Glaswatte** *f*
VERPACK glass wadding; **Glaswolle** *f* KER & GLAS spun
glass, KUNSTSTOFF glass wool, WASSERTRANS -
Schiffbau fiberglass (AmE), fibreglass (BrE);
Glaswollefilter *m* KER & GLAS glass wool filter; **Glas-
zange** *f* KER & GLAS chipping tool; **Glasziegel** *m* KER &
GLAS glass brick; **Glaszustand** *m* KER & GLAS vitreous
state

Glatt- *pref* KER & GLAS, PAPIER, WASSERTRANS flush,
straight

glatt[1] *adj* ANSTRICH smooth, FERTIG slick, KER & GLAS
ohne Dekor plain, PAPIER even, smooth

glatt:[2] ~**es Gewebe** *nt* TEXTIL plain fabric; ~**er Satz** *m*
DRUCK straight text matter

Glatt-: **Glattbeplattung** *f* WASSERTRANS *Schiffbau* flush plating; **Glattbrand** *m* KER & GLAS sharp fire; **Glattdeck** *nt* WASSERTRANS *Schiffbau* flush deck

Glätte *f* PAPIER smoothness, TRANS slipperiness

Glätten *nt* BAU planing, COMP & DV *von Rundungen*, KER & GLAS *von Hohlglas* smoothing, MASCHINEN, METALL burnishing

glätten *vt* BAU even, flush, skim, smooth, trowel, *Mauern* level, FERTIG *Gießform* slick, MASCHINEN flat, MECHAN polish, METALL burnish, TEXTIL glaze, iron out, surface

Glätteprüfer *m* PAPIER smoothness tester

Glatt-: **Glattgarn** *nt* TEXTIL flat yarn

glatthobeln *vt* BAU surface, *Holzkanten* shoot

Glatt-: **Glattmantelwalze** *f* BAU smooth roller; **Glattnegativ** *nt* FOTO straight negative; **Glattpresse** *f* PAPIER plain press

Glättpresse *f* PAPIER smoothing press

Glatt-: **Glattpressenwalze** *f* PAPIER plain press roll; **Glattsandstrahlen** *nt* KER & GLAS plain sandblast; **Glattschachtpackung** *f* KER & GLAS smooth plain packing; **Glattstoßmaschine** *f* DRUCK jogging machine; **Glattstreichen** *nt* FERTIG *Gießen* sleeking

glattstreichen *vt* BAU *Fugen* strike, FERTIG *Gießen* sleek

Glättung *f* ELEKTRONIK, GERÄT smoothing, MECHAN burnishing, PAPIER glaze, polish, smooth finish; **Glättungsdrossel** *f* ELEKTRIZ, ELEKTROTECH smoothing choke; **Glättungskondensator** *m* ELEKTRIZ, ELEKTROTECH smoothing capacitor; **Glättungskreis** *m* ELEKTRIZ, ELEKTROTECH smoothing circuit; **Glättungsschaltung** *f* ELEKTRIZ, ELEKTRONIK smoothing filter; **Glättungswiderstand** *m* ELEKTRIZ, ELEKTROTECH smoothing resistor

Glättwalze *f* PAPIER smoothing roll

Glatt-: **Glattwalzenstuhl** *m* FERTIG smooth roller mill

Glättwerk *nt* PAPIER thickness calender; **Glättwerkzeug** *nt* MASCHINEN burnishing tool

Glättzahn *m* FERTIG *Räumwerkzeug* button, MASCHINEN burnishing tooth

Glättzylinder *m* PAPIER MG cylinder, machine-glazing cylinder, glazing cylinder

Glaubensmaß *nt* KÜNSTL INT MB, measure of belief

Glaukonitmergel *m* BAU glauconite marl

Gleason-Verzahnung *f* MASCHINEN Gleason gear teeth

gleich[1] *adj* MATH equal; **auf ~er Höhe mit** *adj* BAU level with; **gleichförmig** *adj* METALL homogeneous

gleich:[2] **auf ~er Höhe** *adv* WASSERTRANS abreast

gleich:[3] **~e Mengen** *f pl* MATH *Mengenlehre* equal sets

gleich:[4] **auf ~e Höhe bringen** *vt* DRUCK level

gleichachsig: ~er gegenläufiger Propeller *m* LUFTTRANS coaxial propeller; **~es Korn** *nt* METALL equiaxed grain

gleicharmig: ~e Brücke *f* ELEKTRIZ equal arm bridge

Gleichbarkanalstörung *f* FERNSEH cochannel interference

gleichberechtigt: ~er Spontanbetrieb *m* TELEKOM balanced mode

gleichbleibend: ~er Differenzialdruck *m* LUFTTRANS constant differential pressure; **mit ~er Fördermenge** *adj* FERTIG constant-flow; **~e Peilung** *f* WASSERTRANS *Navigation* steady bearing; **~er Schaltschritt** *m* COMP & DV monospacing

Gleichdruck *m* HEIZ & KÄLTE balanced pressure; **Gleichdruckturbine** *f* HYDRAUL action turbine, NICHTFOSS ENERG impulse turbine; **Gleichdruckvergaser** *m* KFZTECH suction carburetor (AmE), suction carburettor (BrE)

gleichen *vt* GEOM equal

gleichförmig: ~ angeregte Gassäule *f* STRAHLPHYS uniformly-excited column of gas; **~e Bewegung** *f* PHYS uniform motion

gleichgerichtet: ~er Ausgang *m* ELEKTROTECH rectified output; **~er Strom** *m* ELEKTROTECH rectified current, unidirectional current; **~er Wechselstrom** *m* ELEKTRIZ rectified alternating current; **nicht ~er Wechselstrom** *m* ELEKTRIZ unrectified ac

Gleichgewicht:[1] **aus dem ~** *adj* METROL out of balance

Gleichgewicht:[2] **nicht im ~** *adv* PHYS not in equilibrium

Gleichgewicht[3] *nt* FERTIG poise, LUFTTRANS aerodynamic balance, MECHAN equilibrium, METROL, PAPIER balance, PHYS balance, equilibrium; **~ des Luftschraubenblattes** *nt* LUFTTRANS *Hubschrauber* blade balance

Gleichgewicht:[4] **aus dem ~ bringen** *vt* SICHERHEIT overbalance

Gleichgewicht: Gleichgewichtsanflug *m* LUFTTRANS steady approach; **Gleichgewichtsbedingung** *f* MECHAN equation of equilibrium, OPTIK steady state condition; **Gleichgewichtsdichte** *f* ERDÖL *Bohrtechnik* equilibrium density; **Gleichgewichtsfehler** *m* MECHAN unbalance; **Gleichgewichtskonstante** *f (K)* THERMOD equilibrium constant *(K)*; **Gleichgewichtskraft** *f* LUFTTRANS equalizing; **Gleichgewichtskurve** *f* METALL equilibrium curve; **Gleichgewichtslänge** *f* TELEKOM equilibrium-mode distribution length, equilibrium length; **Gleichgewichtsmodenverteilung** *f* TELEKOM equilibrium mode distribution; **Gleichgewichtspunkt** *m* BAU center of gravity (AmE), centre of gravity (BrE), GERÄT *Brücke* balance point; **Gleichgewichtsstrahlungsdiagramm** *nt* TELEKOM equilibrium radiation pattern; **Gleichgewichtsthermodynamik** *f* THERMOD thermostatics; **Gleichgewichtsventil** *nt* HYDRAUL equilibrium valve; **Gleichgewichtszustand** *m* PHYS steady state, THERMOD state of equilibrium; **Gleichgewichtszustand des Gezeitenwechsels** *m* NICHTFOSS ENERG equilibrium tide

Gleichheit *f* COMP & DV, MATH equality; **Gleichheitsprüfer** *m* PHYS comparator

Gleichkanal- *pref* TELEKOM cochannel; **Gleichkanalschutzabstand** *m* TELEKOM cochannel protection ratio; **Gleichkanalstörung** *f* AUFNAHME, TELEKOM cochannel interference; **Gleichkanalwiederholabstand** *m* TELEKOM cochannel reuse distance

Gleichklang *m* AKUSTIK consonance, unison

gleichkörnig: ~e Erde *f* KOHLEN even-grained soil; **~er Kieszuschlagstoff** *m* BAU single size gravel aggregate

gleichlastig *adj* WASSERTRANS on-even-keel

Gleichlauf[1] *m* ELEKTRONIK synchronism, FERNSEH tracking, KFZTECH synchronization, KONTROLL, MASCHINEN synchronism

Gleichlauf:[2] **~ wiederherstellen** *vi* TELEKOM resynchronize

gleichlaufend[1] *adj* ELEKTROTECH in step; **~ existent** *adj* KONTROLL concurrent

gleichlaufend:[2] **~e Kondensatoren** *m pl* ELEKTRIZ ganged capacitors

Gleichlauf: **Gleichlauffehler** *m* ELEKTRONIK clocking error; **Gleichlauffräsen** *nt* FERTIG, MASCHINEN down-cut milling; **Gleichlaufgelenk** *nt* KFZTECH *Antriebswelle, Kardanwelle* constant-velocity universal joint; **Gleichlaufgenerator** *m* FERNSEH tracking generator; **Gleichlaufgetriebe** *nt* MASCHINEN synchromesh gear; **Gleichlaufimpuls** *m* ELEKTRONIK clocking pulse;

Gleichlaufregler *m* FERNSEH tracking control; **Gleich-laufschleifen** *nt* FERTIG down grinding; **Gleichlaufschwankung** *f* AKUSTIK, TELEKOM *Aufzeichnung* flutter; **Gleichlaufschwankungen** *f pl* FERNSEH *Tonbandgerät* wow and flutter; **Gleichlaufsteuerung** *f* KONTROLL synchronization

Gleichlichtfotometer *nt* GERÄT continuous-light photometer

Gleichmaß *nt* AKUSTIK time

gleichmäßig[1] *adj* FERTIG *Druck* even, MATH monotone; ~ **verteilt** *adj* ANSTRICH smooth

gleichmäßig:[2] ~**er Anflug** *m* LUFTTRANS steady approach; ~ **anregendes Rauschen** *nt* AKUSTIK uniform-exciting noise; ~**e Beschleunigung** *f* PAPIER uniform acceleration; ~**e Korrosion** *f* METALL uniform corrosion; ~**e Lagenwicklung** *f* ELEKTRIZ uniform-layer winding; ~**er Lauf** *m* MASCHINEN smooth running; ~**es Rauschen** *nt* AKUSTIK steady noise; ~ **verdeckendes Rauschen** *nt* AKUSTIK uniform-masking noise

Gleichmäßigkeitskoeffizient *m* KOHLEN uniformity coefficient

Gleichmäßigkeitsprüfung *f* METALL homogeneity test

gleichmolar *adj* CHEMIE equimolecular

gleichnamig: ~**e Pole** *m pl* PHYS like poles

gleichphasig[1] *adj* ELEKTRIZ, ELEKTRONIK in-phase

gleichphasig:[2] ~**e Fläche** *f* ELEKTROTECH equiphase surface; ~**e Komponente** *f* ELEKTRONIK in-phase component; ~**es Signal** *nt* ELEKTRONIK in-phase signal; ~**er Strom** *m* ELEKTRIZ in-phase current

Gleichpolgenerator *m* ELEKTROTECH homopolar generator

Gleichpotential-Linse *f* KERNTECH unipotential lens

gleichrichten *vt* ELEKTRIZ, ELEKTROTECH, RADIO rectify

Gleichrichter *m* AUFNAHME *elektrisches Ventil*, ELEKTRIZ rectifier, ELEKTRONIK detector, ELEKTROTECH, KFZTECH *KFZ-Elektrik* rectifier, PHYS detector, rectifier, RADIO, TELEKOM rectifier; ~ **zur Batterieladung** *m* ELEKTRIZ charging rectifier; ~ **als Brücke geschaltet** *m* ELEKTROTECH bridge rectifier; **Gleichrichteranode** *f* ELEKTROTECH rectifier anode; **Gleichrichteranschluß** *m* ELEKTROTECH rectifying junction; **Gleichrichterbrücke** *f* ELEKTROTECH bridge rectifier, rectifier bridge; **Gleichrichterdiode** *f* ELEKTRONIK rectifier diode; **Gleichrichterfilter** *nt* AUFNAHME rectifier filter; **Gleichrichtergerät** *nt* TELEKOM rectifier unit; **Gleichrichterinstrument** *nt* GERÄT rectifier instrument; **Gleichrichterkreis** *m* ELEKTROTECH rectifying circuit; **Gleichrichterlokomotive** *f* EISENBAHN rectifier locomotive; **Gleichrichtermeßgerät** *nt* GERÄT rectifier instrument; **Gleichrichterrauschen** *nt* ELEKTRONIK detector noise; **Gleichrichterröhre** *f* ELEKTROTECH rectifier tube; **Gleichrichterschaltung** *f* ELEKTROTECH rectifying circuit; **Gleichrichterstation** *f* ELEKTROTECH rectifier substation; **Gleichrichtertrafo** *m* ELEKTROTECH rectifier transformer; **Gleichrichtertransformator** *m* ELEKTROTECH rectifier transformer; **Gleichrichterwandler** *m* ELEKTROTECH rectifier transformer; **Gleichrichterzelle** *f* ELEKTROTECH rectifier cell

Gleichrichtung *f* AKUSTIK detection, ELEKTRIZ, ELEKTROTECH, RADIO rectification, RAUMFAHRT *Weltraumfunk* detection

gleichschenklig[1] *adj* GEOM isosceles

gleichschenklig:[2] ~**es Dreieck** *nt* GEOM isosceles triangle; ~**es Winkeleisen** *nt* BAU equal-sided angles

Gleichschlagseil *nt* MASCHINEN long-lay rope

gleichschwebend: ~**e Temperatur** *f* AKUSTIK equal temperament

gleichschwer: ~**e Kerne** *m pl* KERNTECH isobar

gleichseitig[1] *adj* GEOM equilateral

gleichseitig:[2] ~**es Giebeldach** *nt* BAU span roof

Gleichspannung *f* ELEKTROTECH DC voltage; **Gleichspannungsmesser** *m* ELEKTROTECH DC voltmeter; **Gleichspannungsquelle** *f* ELEKTROTECH DC voltage source; **Gleichspannungteiler** *m* ELEKTRIZ DC potentiometer; **Gleichspannungswandler** *m* ELEKTROTECH DC-DC converter, TELEKOM direct-current converter; **Gleichspannungswandlung** *f* ELEKTROTECH DC-DC conversion

Gleichspulenwicklung *f* ELEKTROTECH diamond winding

Gleichstrom *m* *(GS)* AUFNAHME, COMP & DV, EISENBAHN, ELEKTRIZ, ELEKTROTECH, FERNSEH, FERTIG, PHYS, RADIO, TELEKOM direct current *(DC)*; **Gleichstromamperemeter** *nt* ELEKTROTECH DC ammeter; **Gleichstrombrücke** *f* ELEKTROTECH DC bridge; **Gleichstromdatenübertragungseinrichtung** *f* COMP & DV baseband modem; **Gleichstromdirektumformer** *m* ELEKTRIZ direct d-c converter; **Gleichstromdynamo** *m* ELEKTRIZ direct-current generator; **Gleichstromelektronenbeschleuniger** *m* *(CEBAF)* TEILPHYS continuous electron beam facility *(CEBAF)*; **Gleichstromerzeuger** *m* ELEKTROTECH DC generator; **Gleichstromerzeugung** *f* ELEKTROTECH DC generation

gleichstromgekoppelt *adj* ELEKTRIZ direct-coupled

Gleichstrom: **Gleichstromgenerator** *m* ELEKTRIZ DC generator, direct-current generator, dynamo, ELEKTROTECH, PHYS DC generator; **Gleichstromisolation** *f* ELEKTROTECH DC isolation; **Gleichstrom-Josephson-Effekt** *m* PHYS DC Josephson effect; **Gleichstromkompensator** *m* ELEKTRIZ DC potentiometer, direct-current potentiometer; **Gleichstromkomponente** *f* ELEKTRIZ, TELEKOM DC component, direct-current component; **Gleichstromkonverter** *m* TELEKOM direct-current converter; **Gleichstromkoppler** *m* TELEKOM DCC, direct-current coupler; **Gleichstromkopplung** *f* ELEKTRIZ direct coupling; **Gleichstromkreis** *m* EISENBAHN track circuit, ELEKTROTECH DC circuit; **Gleichstromlichtbogenschweißen** *nt* FERTIG DC welding; **Gleichstromlöschkopf** *m* AUFNAHME DC erase head; **Gleichstrommaschine** *f* ELEKTROTECH DC machine; **Gleichstrommesser** *m* ELEKTRIZ DC meter; **Gleichstrommittenabgleich** *m* FERNSEH DC centering (AmE), DC centring (BrE); **Gleichstrommotor** *m* ELEKTRIZ, ELEKTROTECH, FERTIG, PHYS DC motor, direct-current motor; **Gleichstrommotor in Bürstenbauweise** *m* ELEKTROTECH brush-type DC motor; **Gleichstromnetz** *nt* ELEKTRIZ, ELEKTROTECH DC network, direct-current network; **Gleichstromnetzwerk** *nt* ELEKTROTECH DC network, direct-current network; **Gleichstrompegel** *m* FERNSEH DC level; **Gleichstrompotentiometer** *nt* ELEKTRIZ DC potentiometer, direct-current potentiometer; **Gleichstromprüfzeile** *f* FERNSEH dc insertion; **Gleichstromquelle** *f* ELEKTROTECH DC supply, direct-current supply; **Gleichstromrauschen** *nt* AUFNAHME DC noise; **Gleichstromregelung** *f* ELEKTRIZ DC regulation, direct-voltage regulation; **Gleichstromrelais** *nt* ELEKTRIZ, ELEKTROTECH DC relay, direct-current relay; **Gleichstromschaltvorrichtung** *f* ELEKTROTECH DC switching; **Gleichstromschweißen** *nt* FERTIG DC welding; **Gleichstromservometer** *nt* ELEKTROTECH DC servometer; **Gleichstromsignalisierung** *f* ELEKTRONIK DC signaling (AmE), DC signalling (BrE); **Gleichstromtrafo** *m* ELEKTROTECH DC transformer; **Gleichstromtransformator** *m* ELEKTROTECH DC transformer; **Gleichstromturbine** *f* HYDRAUL parallel flow turbine; **Gleichstromumformer** *m* ELEKTRIZ DC converter; **Gleichstromumrichter** *m* COMP & DV inverter; **Gleichstromverdichter** *m* HEIZ & KÄLTE uniflow compressor; **Gleichstromversorgung** *f* ELEKTRIZ, ELEKTROTECH DC supply, direct-current supply; **Gleichstromverstärker** *m* ELEKTRONIK DC amplifier; **Gleichstromverstärkung** *f* ELEKTRONIK DC amplification, DC current gain; **Gleichstromverzerrung** *f* KERNTECH direct-current distortion; **Gleichstromvoltmeter** *nt* ELEKTROTECH DC voltmeter; **Gleichstromvorspannung** *f* FERNSEH DC biasing; **Gleichstromvorwärmer** *m* HEIZ & KÄLTE uniflow preheater; **Gleichstromwandler** *m* ELEKTRIZ direct-current transformer, ELEKTROTECH DC transducer, RAUMFAHRT *Raumschiff* DC-AC converter; **Gleichstromwärmeaustauscher** *m* HEIZ & KÄLTE, KERNTECH parallel-flow heat exchanger; **Gleichstrom-Wechselstrom-Konverter** *m* ELEKTROTECH inverter; **Gleichstromwiderstand** *m* ELEKTROTECH DC resistance, ohmic resistance; **Gleichstrom Zugförderungsmotor** *m* TRANS direct-current traction motor

Gleichtakt *m* ELEKTRONIK *Differentialverstärker* common mode; **Gleichtaktbetrieb** *m* RADIO push-push operation; **Gleichtaktsignal** *nt* ELEKTRONIK common-mode signal; **Gleichtaktspannung** *f* ELEKTROTECH common-mode voltage; **Gleichtaktunterdrückung** *f* ELEKTRONIK, TELEKOM common-mode rejection; **Gleichtaktunterdrückungsverhältnis** *nt* ELEKTRONIK common-mode rejection ratio; **Gleichtaktverstärkung** *f* ELEKTRONIK common-mode gain

gleichtemperiert *adj* MECHAN, PHYS, THERMOD isothermal

Gleichung *f* CHEMIE, MATH, RADIO, STRÖMPHYS equation; **~ dritten Grades** *f* FERTIG, MATH cubic equation; **~ ersten Grades** *f* MATH equation of first degree, simple equation; **Gleichungen für reibungsbehaftete Strömungen** *f pl* PHYS viscous flow equations; **Gleichungsseiten** *f pl* MATH equation members

Gleichverteilung: **~ der Energie** *f* PHYS equipartition of energy

gleichweit: **~ entfernt** *adj* BAU, GEOM equidistant

Gleichwellensignal *nt* ELEKTROTECH CW signal, continuous-wave signal

Gleichwertigkeit *f* COMP & DV equivalence

gleichwinklig[1] *adj* GEOM equiangular, isogonal

gleichwinklig:[2] **~es Dreieck** *nt* GEOM equiangular triangle

gleichzeitig[1] *adj* COMP & DV, KONTROLL simultaneous; **~ ablaufend** *adj* COMP & DV concurrent

gleichzeitig:[2] **~er Ablauf mehrerer Programme** *m* COMP & DV multitasking; **~e Ausführung** *f* COMP & DV concurrent execution; **~e Ausführung mehrerer Jobs** *f* COMP & DV multitasking; **~e Führung** *f* RAUMFAHRT iterative guidance; **nicht ~er Mehrfachzugriff** *m* *(TDMA)* COMP & DV, ELEKTRONIK, RAUMFAHRT *Weltraumfunk*, TELEKOM time division multiple access *(TDMA)*; **~e Verarbeitung** *f* COMP & DV concurrent processing; **~e Verarbeitung von zwei Kübeln** *f* KER & GLAS double gobbing

Gleichzeitigkeit *f* PHYS simultaneity

Gleis:[1] **~ frei** *adj* EISENBAHN line-clear

Gleis[2] *nt* EISENBAHN line, rail track, track; **~ außer Betrieb** *nt* EISENBAHN track out of service; **~ in Betrieb** *nt* EISENBAHN track in service; **~ mit dritter Schiene** *nt* EISENBAHN mixed-gage track (AmE), mixed-gauge track (BrE); **Gleisabschnitt** *m* EISENBAHN track section; **Gleisanschluß** *m* BAU siding; **Gleisarbeiten** *nt* EISENBAHN track laying; **Gleisarbeiter** *m* EISENBAHN track layer; **Gleisbild** *nt* EISENBAHN track diagram; **Gleisbremse** *f* EISENBAHN rail brake; **Gleisdrossel** *f* EISENBAHN impedance bond

Gleise *nt pl* EISENBAHN metals

Gleis: **Gleisinstabilität** *f* EISENBAHN instability of track; **Gleisjochlegemaschine** *f* EISENBAHN track-panel laying machine; **Gleiskette** *f* MECHAN track; **Gleiskettenschrappwagen** *m* TRANS caterpillar-hauling scraper; **Gleislage** *f* EISENBAHN track bed; **Gleislagerung** *f* EISENBAHN track bed; **Gleismontage** *f* EISENBAHN track assembly; **Gleisrelais** *nt* EISENBAHN track relay; **Gleisschotter** *m* EISENBAHN track ballast; **Gleissenkung** *f* EISENBAHN depression of track; **Gleisstrang aus endlos zusammengeschweißten Schienen** *m* EISENBAHN long-welded rail; **Gleistafel** *f* EISENBAHN track diagram; **Gleisüberführung** *f* EISENBAHN flyover (BrE), skyway (AmE); **Gleisverbindung** *f* EISENBAHN crossover; **Gleisverformung** *f* EISENBAHN distortion of the track; **Gleisverlegung** *f* BAU track laying; **Gleisverschlingungen** *f pl* EISENBAHN crossover; **Gleisverwerfung** *f* EISENBAHN distortion of the track, warping of track; **Gleisvorarbeiter** *m* EISENBAHN *Person* track-laying foreman; **Gleiszwischenraum** *m* EISENBAHN space between rails

Gleit- *pref* MECHAN antifriction; **~ und Widerstandsbeiwert** *m* *(LD-Beiwert)* LUFTTRANS *Nutzeffekt des Luftfahrzeugs* lift and drag ratio *(LD ratio)*; **Gleitaxiallager** *nt* MASCHINEN plain thrust bearing; **Gleitbacke** *f* FERTIG flat die; **Gleitbahn** *f* LUFTTRANS glide path, MASCHINEN slideway, track; **Gleitbahnkurs-Funkfeuer** *nt* LUFTTRANS glide path localizer; **Gleitband** *nt* METALL glide band; **Gleitbereich** *m* COMP & DV floating area; **Gleitbewegung** *f* ELEKTROTECH slip; **Gleitboot** *nt* WASSERTRANS gliding boat, hydroplane; **Gleitbruch** *m* KERNTECH gliding fracture, sliding fracture; **Gleitbügel** *m* EISENBAHN pantograph; **Gleitebene** *f* KERNTECH glide plane; **Gleiten** *nt* ELEKTROTECH slip, MASCHINEN slide, sliding

gleiten *vi* MASCHINEN, MECHAN slide

gleitend: **~e Last** *f* ELEKTROTECH sliding load; **~er Löschkopf** *m* FERNSEH flying erase head

Gleiter *m* TRANS skidder

Gleit-: **Gleitfeder** *f* MASCHINEN sliding key; **Gleitfestigkeit** *f* MASCHINEN resistance to sliding; **Gleitfläche** *f* FERTIG rubbing surface, KOHLEN slip surface, METALL gliding plane; **Gleitflächendichtung** *f* MASCHINEN floating seal; **Gleitflosse** *f* LUFTTRANS *Wasserflugzeug* chine

Gleitflug *m* LUFTTRANS gliding flight; **Gleitflugentfernung** *f* LUFTTRANS gliding distance; **Gleitflugwinkel** *m* LUFTTRANS gliding angle

Gleit-: **Gleitfrequenz** *f* ELEKTRONIK, FERNSEH, RADIO, TELEKOM sliding frequency; **Gleitfrequenzgenerator** *m* ELEKTRONIK, FERNSEH, RADIO, TELEKOM sliding frequency generator; **Gleitgelenk** *nt* MASCHINEN slip joint; **Gleitgeometrie** *f* METALL geometry of glide; **Gleitgeschwindigkeit** *f* EISENBAHN *Rad* sliding speed; **Gleithemmung** *f* AKUSTIK antiskating

Gleitkomma *nt* COMP & DV floating point, MATH floating decimal point; **Gleitkomma-Arithmetik** *f* COMP & DV floating-point arithmetic; **Gleitkommabetrieb** *m* COMP & DV FLOP, floating-point operation; **Gleitkommaoperation** *f* COMP & DV FLOP, floating-point operation; **Gleitkommaschreibweise** *f* COMP & DV floating-point notation; **Gleitkommazahl** *f* COMP & DV floating-point number

Gleit-: **Gleitkontakt** *m* ELEKTROTECH sliding contact; **Gleitkreis** *m* BAU *Bodenmechanik* slip circle; **Gleitkufe** *f* FERTIG skid; **Gleitlager** *nt* KFZTECH plain bearing, MASCHINEN bearing, friction-type bearing, plain bearing; **Gleitmarkierung** *f* METALL slip marking; **Gleitmittel** *nt* KER & GLAS, KUNSTSTOFF lubricant; **Gleitmodul** *m* KOHLEN rigidity modulus, MASCHINEN modulus of transverse elasticity; **Gleitpfad** *m* LUFT-TRANS glide path, glide slope; **Gleitpfadantenne** *f* LUFTTRANS glide aerial; **Gleitpotentiometer** *nt* ELEKTROTECH slide potentiometer; **Gleitreibung** *f* ERGON, MASCHINEN, PHYS sliding friction; **Gleitreibungszahl** *f* MECHAN, PHYS coefficient of sliding friction; **Gleitring** *m* ELEKTROTECH slip ring; **Gleitringdichtung** *f* FERTIG face seal, *Kunststoffinstallationen* mechanical seal; **Gleitschaftkolben** *m* KFZTECH full slipper piston; **Gleitschalung** *f* BAU sliding formwork, sliding shuttering; **Gleitschicht** *f* MASCHINEN antifriction layer; **Gleitschiene** *f* EISENBAHN slide rail, FERTIG skid, KOHLEN slide, MASCHINEN crosshead guide, slide bar, slide rail; **Gleitschienenträger** *m* MASCHINEN slide bar carrier; **Gleitschirm** *m* RAUMFAHRT *Raumschiff* parafoil; **Gleitschuh** *m* FERTIG shoe, slipper, MASCHINEN crosshead shoe, sliding block; **Gleitschuhkolben** *m* KFZTECH full slipper piston; **Gleitschutz-Deckfarbe** *f* WASSERTRANS *Schiff und Bootsbau* nonslip deck paint; **Gleitsitz** *m* MASCHINEN sliding fit, MECHAN close-sliding fit, sliding fit; **Gleitstange** *f* FERTIG tiller; **Gleitstein** *m* EISENBAHN link-block guide; **Gleitstrahl** *m* LUFTTRANS glide path beam; **Gleitstück** *nt* MASCHI-NEN slide, slide block, slipper; **Gleitstufenhöhe** *f* METALL slip step height

Gleitung *f* ELEKTROTECH slip, FERTIG slipping

Gleit-: **Gleitverhältnis** *nt* LUFTTRANS glide ratio; **Gleitwagen** *m* KFZTECH glide car; **Gleitwegfunkfeuer** *nt* LUFTTRANS glide path beacon; **Gleitweggleitstrahler** *m* LUFTTRANS glide path beam; **Gleitzahl** *f* LUFTTRANS lift-to-drag ratio, MASCHINEN skid number, WASSER-TRANS *Bootbau* lift-drag ratio; **Gleitzeiger** *m* MATH cursor; **Gleitzylinder** *m* METALL slip cylinder

Glied *nt* COMP & DV member, *Reihe* term, ELEKTRIZ *eines Systems* link, MASCHINEN link, member, *Filter* section, WASSERTRANS link; **~ mit Zweipunktverhalten** *nt* REGELUNG element with two-step action; **Gliederbandförderer** *m* TRANS apron conveyor; **Gliederkessel** *m* HEIZ & KÄLTE sectional boiler; **Gliederkette** *f* MASCHINEN link chain; **Gliederriemen** *m* KUNSTSTOFF link belting, MASCHINEN link belt; **Gliederschiff** *nt* WASSERTRANS articulated ship

Gliederung *f* BAU division

Gliederzug *m* EISENBAHN articulated train

glimmen *vi* THERMOD *Glut, schwelendes Feuer* smolder (AmE), smoulder (BrE)

Glimmentladung *f* ELEKTRIZ glow discharge, ELEKTRIZ corona discharge, ELEKTRONIK, ELEKTROTECH, PHYS, STRAHLPHYS glow discharge; **Glimmentladungslampe** *f* ELEKTRIZ glow discharge lamp; **Glimmentladungsröhre** *f* ELEKTRONIK glow discharge tube;

Glimmentladungsventil *nt* ELEKTROTECH glow discharge rectifier

Glimmer *m* ELEKTRIZ, FERTIG, KER & GLAS, KUNSTSTOFF mica; **Glimmerkondensator** *m* ELEKTRIZ mica dielectric capacitor, ELEKTROTECH mica capacitor

Glimmkathode *f* ELEKTROTECH glow discharge cathode

Glimmlampe *f* ELEKTROTECH glow lamp; **~ mit Neonfüllung** *f* ELEKTROTECH neon lamp

Glimmlichtgleichrichter *m* ELEKTROTECH glow discharge rectifier

Glimmschalter *m* ELEKTROTECH glow switch

global[1] *adj* COMP & DV global

global:[2] **~es Ersetzen** *nt* COMP & DV *Funktion bei Textprogrammen* global change; **~e Informations-Infrastruktur** *f (GII)* COMP & DV Global Information Infrastructure *(GII)*; **~es Positionsbestimmungssystem** *nt (GPS)* WASSERTRANS *Satellitennavigation* global-positioning system *(GPS)*; **~es Suchen und Ersetzen** *nt* COMP & DV global search and replace; **~es Umweltüberwachungssystem** *nt* UMWELTSCHMUTZ Global Environment Monitoring System; **~e Variable** *f* COMP & DV global variable

Globalstrahl *m* RAUMFAHRT *Weltraumfunk* global beam

Globoid *nt* MASCHINEN globoid; **Globoidgetriebe** *nt* MA-SCHINEN enveloping worm drive, globoid gear, globoidal gear, globoidal worm gear; **Globoidschnecke** *f* MASCHINEN double-enveloping worm, enveloping tooth wheel

Glocke *f* BAU *eines Dachfirstes* cap, CHEMTECH bubble, ELEKTRIZ bell, ERDÖL *Destillationstechnik* bubble cap, *Raffinerie, Fraktioniertechnik* bubble cap; **Glockenbatterie** *f* ELEKTRIZ bell battery; **Glockenboden** *m* CHEMTECH, ERDÖL *Fraktioniertechnik* bubble tray, KERNTECH bubble cap; **Glockenbodenkolonne** *f* CHEMTECH bubble-cap tray column, ERDÖL *Fraktioniertechnik* bubble-cap tower

glockenförmig: **~er Aufnahmestutzen** *m* RAUMFAHRT bell mouth; **~e Kurve** *f* GEOM bell-shaped curve

Glocke: **Glockengut** *nt* METALL bell metal; **Glockenhaube** *f* KERNTECH bubble hood; **Glockenisolator** *m* ELEKTROTECH bell-shaped insulator, petticoat insulator; **Glockenkappe** *f* ERDÖL *Raffinerie* bell cap; **Glockenkegel** *m* KER & GLAS bell cone; **Glockenkreis** *m* FERNSEH Gaussian filter circuit; **Glockenkurve** *f* GEOM, MATH bell-shaped curve; **Glockenmanometer** *nt* GERÄT bell-type manometer; **Glockenmetall** *nt* MET-ALL bell metal; **Glockenrock** *m* TEXTIL flared skirt; **Glockenspinnmaschine** *f* TEXTIL cap-spinning frame; **Glockentonne** *f* WASSERTRANS *Seezeichen* bell buoy; **Glockentransformator** *m* ELEKTRIZ bell transformer; **Glockentrichter** *m* LABOR thistle funnel; **Glockenventil** *nt* HYDRAUL bell valve, MASCHINEN bell-shaped valve, bellows valve; **Glockenzentriervorrichtung** *f* MASCHI-NEN bell-centering punch (AmE), bell-centring punch (BrE)

Glosskalander *m* PAPIER gloss calender

Glove-Box *f* KERNTECH glove box (AmE), glove compartment (BrE)

Glucagon *nt* CHEMIE glucagon

Glucamin *nt* CHEMIE glucamine

Glucar- *pref* CHEMIE glucaric

Glucin *nt* CHEMIE glucin

Glucon- *pref* CHEMIE gluconic

Glucopyranose *f* CHEMIE glucopyranose

Glucosamin *nt* CHEMIE glucosamine

Glucosan *nt* CHEMIE glucosan

Glucose *f* LEBENSMITTEL grape sugar

Glucosid *nt* CHEMIE glucoside

Glüh- *pref* FERTIG, THERMOD annealing; **Glühanlage** *f* METALL annealing plant; **Glühbad** *nt* FERTIG, THERMOD annealing bath; **Glühbehandlung** *f* FERTIG heat exchange; **Glühbirne** *f* ELEKTRIZ bulb, incandescent lamp, ELEKTROTECH *Lampe* bulb; **Glühdraht** *m* ELEKTRIZ filament; **Glühdrahthalterung** *f* ELEKTRIZ *Lampenkolben* anchor

glühelektrisch: ~e Elektronenemission *f* PHYS thermionic emission

Glüh-: **Glühemission** *f* ELEKTROTECH thermionic emission; **Glühemissionskonverter** *m* ELEKTROTECH thermionic converter; **Glühemissionswandlung** *f* ELEKTROTECH thermionic conversion

glühen[1] *vt* THERMOD *Stahl* bake

glühen[2] *vi* THERMOD glow

glühend[1] *adj* METALL red-hot, THERMOD glowing

glühend[2]: ~e Kohle *f* KOHLEN live coal

Glüh-: **Glühentladung** *f* ELEKTRIZ, ELEKTRONIK, PHYS, STRAHLPHYS glow discharge; **Glühfaden** *m* ELEKTROTECH filament; **Glühfadenpyrometer** *nt* PHYS disappearing filament pyrometer; **Glühfrischen** *nt* FERTIG malleablizing

glühfrischen *vt* FERTIG malleablize

Glüh-: **Glühhaube** *f* FERTIG annealing bell; **Glühhitze** *f* THERMOD glowing heat

Glühkathode *f* ELEKTROTECH hot cathode, thermionic cathode; **Glühkathodenentladung** *f* ELEKTROTECH glow discharge; **Glühkathodenröhre** *f* ELEKTRONIK hot-cathode tube, thermionic tube; **Glühkathodentriode** *f* ELEKTRONIK thermionic triode

Glüh-: **Glühkerze** *f* KFZTECH glow plug, THERMOD heat plug, *im Motor* glow plug; **Glühkopfmotor** *m* KFZTECH hot-bulb engine, semidiesel engine; **Glühlampe** *f* ELEKTROTECH incandescent lamp, lamp; **Glühofen** *m* FERTIG, KERNTECH, METALL annealing furnace; **Glühpunkt** *m* *(GP)* METALL annealing point *(AP)*; **Glühschiffchen** *nt* LABOR combustion boat; **Glühschmelzer** *m* BAU *Tiefbau* heating melter; **Glühspan** *m* MECHAN scale; **Glühstrumpf** *m* THERMOD gas mantle; **Glühverlust** *m* KOHLEN, UMWELTSCHMUTZ ignition loss; **Glühzyklus** *m* THERMOD heat cycle

Gluon *nt* PHYS *Elementarteilchen*, TEILPHYS gluon

Glut *f* THERMOD burning heat

Glutamin *nt* CHEMIE glutamine; **Glutamin-** *pref* CHEMIE glutamic

Glutaminat *nt* CHEMIE glutamate

Glutaraldehyd *m* CHEMIE glutaraldehyde

Glutardialdehyd *nt* CHEMIE glutaraldehyde

Glutathion *nt* CHEMIE glutathione

glutenfrei *adj* LEBENSMITTEL gluten-free

Gluthitze *f* THERMOD glowing heat

Glyceraldehyd *m* CHEMIE glyceraldehyde

Glycerid *nt* CHEMIE, LEBENSMITTEL glyceride

Glycerin *nt* CHEMIE glyceric, CHEMIE glycerine, glycerol; **Glycerinacetat** *nt* LEBENSMITTEL acetin; **Glycerinaldehyd** *m* CHEMIE glyceraldehyde; **Glycerindibutyrat** *nt* CHEMIE dibutyrin; **Glycerinmonoacetat** *nt* CHEMIE monoacetin, LEBENSMITTEL glycerol monoacetate; **Glycerintriacetat** *nt* CHEMIE triacetin; **Glycerintributyrat** *nt* CHEMIE tributyrin; **Glycerintrimyristat** *nt* CHEMIE myristin; **Glycerintrinitrat** *nt* CHEMIE nitroglycerin; **Glycerintrioleat** *nt* CHEMIE triolein; **Glycerintripalmitin** *nt* CHEMIE tripalmitin; **Glycerintripalmitinsäureester** *m* CHEMIE tripalmitin

Glycerol *nt* CHEMIE glycerine, glycerol; **Glycerolmonoacetat** *nt* CHEMIE monoacetin; **Glycerolmonostearat** *nt* CHEMIE monostearin; **Glyceroltrinitrat** *nt* CHEMIE nitroglycerin; **Glyceroltrioleat** *nt* CHEMIE olein

Glycerophosphat *nt* CHEMIE glycerophosphate

Glycerophosphor- *pref* CHEMIE glycerophosphoric

Glyceryl- *pref* CHEMIE glyceryl; **Glycerylmonostearat** *nt* CHEMIE monostearin; **Glyceryltetradecanoat** *nt* CHEMIE myristin; **Glyceryltripalmitat** *nt* CHEMIE palmitin; **Glyceryltristearat** *nt* CHEMIE glyceryl tristeate, tristearin

Glycid- *pref* CHEMIE glycidic

Glycogen *nt* CHEMIE glycogen

Glycol *nt* CHEMIE glycol; **Glycol-** *pref* CHEMIE glycolic

Glycolylharnstoff *m* CHEMIE hydantoin

Glycosidase *f* CHEMIE carbohydrase

Glycyl- *pref* CHEMIE glycyl

Glycyrrhizinsäure *f* CHEMIE glycyrrhizine

Glykogen *nt* LEBENSMITTEL animal starch, glycogen

Glykokoll *nt* LEBENSMITTEL glycine

Glykol- *pref* CHEMIE glycollic; **Glykolid** *nt* CHEMIE glycolide; **Glykolipid** *nt* CHEMIE glycolipid; **Glykolyse** *f* LEBENSMITTEL glycolysis

Glykoprotein *nt* CHEMIE glucoprotein

Glykosid *nt* LEBENSMITTEL glycoside

Glykuron- *pref* CHEMIE glycuronic

Glyoxal *nt* CHEMIE glyoxal; **Glyoxalin** *nt* CHEMIE glyoxaline

Glyoxim *nt* CHEMIE glyoxime

Glyoxyl- *pref* CHEMIE glyoxylic; **Glyoxyldiureid** *nt* CHEMIE allantoin, glyoxydiureide

Glyptalharz *nt* KUNSTSTOFF glyptal resin

g/m^2 *abbr* *(Gramm pro Quadratmeter)* DRUCK gsm *(grams per square metre)*

GMDSS *abbr* *(System zur Rettung von Menschenleben bei Seenotfällen)* WASSERTRANS GMDSS *(global marine distress and safety system)*

Gneis *m* BAU, ERDÖL *Mineralogie* gneiss

gnomonisch: ~e Projektion *f* RADIO, WASSERTRANS *Navigation* gnomonic projection

Golay-Zelle *f* PHYS Golay cell

Gold *nt* METALL gold; **Goldamalgam** *nt* METALL gold amalgam; **Goldbeschichtung** *f* RAUMFAHRT *Raumschiff* gold plating; **Goldblatt-Elektroskop** *nt* ELEKTRIZ, ELEKTROTECH, PHYS gold leaf electroscope; **Goldchlorid** *nt* CHEMIE gold chloride, gold trichloride; **Goldcyanid** *nt* CHEMIE gold cyanide

golddotiert: ~e Diode *f* ELEKTRONIK gold-doped diode

Gold: **Golddotierung** *f* ELEKTRONIK gold doping

golden: ~er Schnitt *m* GEOM golden section

Gold: **Goldepoxid** *nt* ELEKTRONIK gold epoxy; **Goldfolie** *f* DRUCK gold foil; **Goldgehalt** *m* METALL gold content

goldplattieren *vt* METALL plate

Gold: **Goldpulver** *nt* KER & GLAS powdered gold; **Goldschnitt** *m* DRUCK gilt edges; **Goldsondenmethode** *f* KERNTECH *der Eichung* gold probe method; **Goldtonbad** *nt* FOTO gold toning; **Goldwaschen** *nt* CHEMIE panning

Golf *m* WASSERTRANS gulf

Gondel *f* EISENBAHN gondola

Gongtonne *f* WASSERTRANS *Seezeichen* gong buoy

Goniometer *nt* GEOM goniometer METROL angulometer, RADIO goniometer

Gooch-Tiegel *m* LABOR *Filtrieren* Gooch crucible

Göpel *m* BAU *Bohrarbeiten* gin

Görtlerzahl *f* STRÖMPHYS *Grenzschichttheorie* Görtler

number

Gösch *f* WASSERTRANS *Flagge* jack flag

Gotisch *nt* DRUCK gothic

GÖV *abbr* *(Gas-Öl-Verhältnis)* ERDÖL *Lagerstätten-technik* GOR *(gas-to-oil ratio)*

GP *abbr* *(Glühpunkt)* METALL AP *(annealing point)*

GPC *abbr* *(Gel-Permeations-Chromatographie)* KUNST-STOFF, LABOR GPC *(gel permeation chromatography)*

GPF-Ruß *m* KUNSTSTOFF GPF carbon black, general-purpose furnace carbon black

GPG *abbr* *(Grundprimärgruppe)* TELEKOM basic group

GPS *abbr* *(globales Positionsbestimmungssystem)* WASSERTRANS *Satellitennavigation* GPS *(global-positioning system)*

Graben *m* BAU digging, trench, *Entwässerung* ditch, ERDÖL *Leitungsbau* trench, KOHLEN ditch, trench, MEERSCHMUTZ trench, NICHTFOSS ENERG dike (AmE), dyke (BrE), WASSERVERSORG ditch line, ditch, race; **Grabenarbeiten** *f pl* BAU trenchwork; **Grabenaushub** *m* BAU trenching; **Grabenbagger** *m* BAU trench excavator; **Grabenbewässerung** *f* WASSERVERSORG ditch irrigation; **Grabenherstellung** *f* BAU trenching; **Grabenmethode** *f* ABFALL trench method; **Grabenverbau** *m* BAU trench sheeting; **Grabenverfüllgerät** *nt* TRANS back filler

Grabzähne *m pl* BAU cutting teeth

Grad:[1] in ~ **Celsius geteilt** *adj* MECHAN centigrade

Grad[2] *m* FERTIG order, GEOM degree, METROL rate, PHYS, THERMOD degree; ~ **Celsius** *m* METROL degree Celsius; ~ **Kelvin** *m* THERMOD degree Kelvin; **Gradbogen** *m* MASCHINEN protractor, MECHAN quadrant scale; **Gradeinteilung** *f* COMP & DV calibration, KONSTZEICH angular spacing, LABOR graduation

Gradient *m* ELEKTROTECH graded index, gradient, GEOM *einer Kurve*, KÜNSTL INT, MATH *Vektorrechnung*, STRÖMPHYS *Temperatur- und Druckgradient* gradient; ~ **des elektrischen Feldes** *m* ELEKTROTECH electric field gradient; ~ **einer Geraden** *m* GEOM gradient of a straight line; **Gradientenfaser** *f* TELEKOM gradient index fiber (AmE), gradient index fibre (BrE); **Gradientenindexprofil** *nt* TELEKOM graded index profile; **Gradientenkern** *m* ELEKTROTECH graded index core; **Gradientenlichtleiter** *m* OPTIK power law index fiber (AmE), power law index fibre (BrE); **Gradientenlichtleitfaser** *f* ELEKTROTECH *mit mehreren Arbeitsweisen* graded index multimode optical fiber (AmE), graded index multimode optical fibre (BrE); **Gradientenlichtwellenleiter** *m* TELEKOM gradient index fiber (AmE), gradient index fibre (BrE); **Gradientenzug** *m* BAU line of levels; **Gradientmikrofon** *nt* AKUSTIK gradient microphone

Gradteiler *m* MECHAN vernier

Grafik *f* COMP & DV graphics, DRUCK art work, graphic arts; **Grafikadapter** *m* COMP & DV graphic display adaptor; **Grafikarbeitsplatz** *m* COMP & DV graphics workstation; **Grafikbildschirmadapter** *m* COMP & DV graphic display adaptor; **Grafikblock** *m* COMP & DV Rand tablet, graphics pad, graphics tablet; **Grafikdrucker** *m* COMP & DV graphics printer; **Grafikkarte** *f* COMP & DV graphic display adaptor; **Grafikkurvenschreiber** *m* COMP & DV graphics plotter; **Grafikmodus** *m* COMP & DV graphics mode, plotting mode; **Grafikplotter** *m* COMP & DV graphics plotter; **Grafikprozessor** *m* COMP & DV graphics processor; **Grafiksoftwarepaket** *nt* COMP & DV graphic software package; **Grafiktablett** *nt* COMP & DV graphics tablet; **Grafikvorlage** *f* DRUCK

art work; **Grafikzeichen** *nt* COMP & DV graphic character, graphics character

grafisch[1] *adj* DRUCK graphic, graphical

grafisch:[2] ~er **Arbeitsplatz** *m* COMP & DV graphics workstation; ~e **Benutzeroberfläche** *f* COMP & DV graphical interface; ~e **Darstellung** *f* COMP & DV graphical representation; ~es **Editieren** *nt* COMP & DV graphical editing; ~e **Methoden** *f pl* MATH graphical methods; ~e **Symbole** *nt pl* SICHERHEIT *für Brandschutzpläne* graphical symbols

grafisch:[3] ~ **darstellen** *vt* COMP & DV plot

Graham: ~**sches Diffusionsgesetz** *nt* PHYS Graham's law of diffusion

Gramm *nt* (g) CHEMIE, METROL, PHYS gram (g); ~ **pro Quadratmeter** *nt* (g/m²) DRUCK grams per square meter (AmE), grams per square metre (BrE) (gsm)

grammatisch: ~e **Markierung** *f* COMP & DV grammatical tagger

Gramme-Ring *m* ELEKTRIZ Gramme winding

Grammion *nt* METROL gram-ion

Grammkalorie *f* METROL gram calorie, gram centimeter heat-unit (AmE), gram centimetre heat-unit (BrE)

Grammophon *nt* AUFNAHME gramophone (BrE), phonograph (AmE)

Gran *nt* METROL grain

Granalie *f* METALL shot

Granit *m* BAU granite

Granulat *nt* CHEMTECH granulate

Granulation *f* CHEMTECH granulation; **Granulationsrauschen** *nt* TELEKOM speckle noise

Granulator *m* CHEMTECH *Zucker* granulating machine, granulator, VERPACK granulating machine

Granulierapparat *m* CHEMTECH granulator

Granulieren *nt* KUNSTSTOFF pelletizing

granulieren *vt* CHEMTECH granulate, FERTIG grain, VER-PACK granulate

Granulierextruder *m* KUNSTSTOFF *Kautschuk* pelletizer

Granuliermühle *f* CHEMTECH granulating crusher

Granulit *nt* ERDÖL *Mineralogie* granulite

Graph[1] *m* COMP & DV, KÜNSTL INT graph

Graph:[2] **als** ~ **zeichnen** *vt* MATH graph

Graph[3] **einen** ~ **zeichnen** *vi* MATH plot a graph

Graph: **Graphensuche** *f* KÜNSTL INT graph search; **Graphensuchverfahren** *nt* KÜNSTL INT graph search; **Graphentheorie** *f* KÜNSTL INT, MATH graph theory

graphisch:[1] ~e **Darstellung** *f* LUFTTRANS *Navigation* plot, MATH graph; ~es **Gerät** *nt* GERÄT display device; ~es **Gewerbe** *nt* DRUCK printing industry; ~e **Massenberechnung** *f* NICHTFOSS ENERG mass diagram

graphisch:[2] ~ **darstellen** *vt* MATH graph

Graphit *m* CHEMIE, FERTIG plumbago; **Graphitabschirmung** *f* KERNTECH graphite shielding

graphitbeschichtet: ~es **Brennelement** *nt* KERNTECH graphite-clad fuel element

Graphit: **Graphitbeschichtung** *f* KERNTECH graphite coating; **Graphitblock** *m* BAU graphite block; **Graphitbürste** *f* ELEKTRIZ graphite brush; **Graphitformschwärzung** *f* FERTIG *Gießen* graphite blacking; **Graphitführungsrohr** *nt* KERNTECH graphite guide tube

Graphitisation *f* METALL graphitization

Graphitkugel *f* KERNTECH graphite pebble

graphitmoderiert[1] *adj* KERNTECH graphite-moderated

graphitmoderiert:[2] ~er **gasgekühlter Reaktor** *m* KERN-TECH graphite-moderated gas-cooled reactor

Graphit: **Graphitpackung** *f* MASCHINEN graphite packing; **Graphitschmierung** f MECHAN graphite grease; **Graphitschwund** m KERNTECH graphite shrinkage; **Graphitstaub** m CHEMIE *Gießerei* plumbago; **Graphitstruktur** f KERNTECH graphite structure; **Graphittiegel** m FERTIG graphite crucible, plumbago crucible

graphitumhüllt: ~es Brennelement nt KERNTECH graphite-clad fuel element

Gras nt KERNTECH *Störung auf Oszilloskop* grass

Grat:[1] **mit ~** adj FERTIG, MASCHINEN, MECHAN burred

Grat[2] m BAU *Architektur* Architektur groin, FERTIG rag, KOHLEN rib, MASCHINEN burr, wire edge, MECHAN burr, PHYS *Werkstück* fin line

Grat:[3] **~ abscheren** vi FERTIG trim

Gratbildung f FERTIG formation of burrs, *Walzen* finning

Gräting f WASSERTRANS *Schiffbau* grating

Gratsparren m BAU angle rafter, hip rafter; **Gratsparrendach** nt BAU hip and ridge roof

Grätzgleichrichter m ELEKTRIZ bridge rectifier

Grat: Gratziegel m BAU hip tile

Grau nt DRUCK, FERNSEH, FOTO gray (AmE), grey (BrE)

grau: ~er Körper m FERNSEH gray body (AmE), grey body (BrE); **~er Star bei Glasmachern** m KER & GLAS glassworker's cataract

Grau: Grauglasscheibe f FERNSEH black screen; **Grauguß** m FERTIG *Kunststoffinstallationen* cast iron, MECHAN gray-cast iron (AmE), grey-cast iron (BrE); **Graugußimpfungszusatz** m FERTIG inoculant; **Graugußrohr** nt MASCHINEN gray iron pipe (AmE), grey iron pipe (BrE); **Graugußzusatz** m FERTIG inoculant; **Graukeil** m FERNSEH staircase; **Graukeilsignal** nt FERNSEH staircase signal; **Graupappe** f DRUCK, VERPACK millboard; **Grauschatten** m FERNSEH black shading; **Grauskala** f FERNSEH gray scale (AmE), grey scale (BrE); **Grauskalenwert** m FERNSEH gray scale value (AmE), grey scale value (BrE); **Graustufe** f COMP & DV gray scale (AmE), grey scale (BrE); **Graustufung** f FOTO gray scale (AmE), grey scale (BrE); **Grautönung** f KONSTZEICH gray shading (AmE), grey shading (BrE), gray toning (AmE), grey toning (BrE); **Grauwertstauchung** f FERNSEH black crush

Graveur m KER & GLAS engraver

Gravieren nt DRUCK, ELEKTRONIK engraving

gravieren vt DRUCK engrave

Gravierfräsen nt MASCHINEN engraving

Gravimetrie f PHYS gravimetry

gravimetrisch[1] adj KOHLEN gravimetric

gravimetrisch:[2] **~e Messung** f ERDÖL *Prospektion* gravimetric analysis

Gravitation f UMWELTSCHMUTZ gravity; **Gravitationskonstante** f PHYS, RAUMFAHRT gravitation constant; **Gravitationskraft** f PHYS force of inertia, gravitation; **Gravitationswellen** f pl PHYS, STRAHLPHYS, WELLPHYS *theoretische Ausbreitung der Gravitationskraft* gravity waves

Graviton nt PHYS, TEILPHYS graviton

Gravur[1] f DRUCK, KER & GLAS engraving

Gravur:[2] **~en einsenken** vi FERTIG type

Gravur: Gravurmaschine f KER & GLAS engraving lathe

Gray nt *(gy)* PHYS *Einheit der Energiedosis*, TEILPHYS gray (AmE) *(gy)*

Gregorianisch: ~es Teleskop nt PHYS *Spiegelteleskop* Gregorian telescope

Gregory-Antenne f TELEKOM Gregorian reflector antenna

Greifanker m WASSERTRANS *Festmachen* grappling hook

Greifbagger m BAU grab crane, WASSERTRANS grab dredge, grab dredger

Greifen nt MASCHINEN biting; **~ der Walzen** nt MASCHINEN biting of the rolls

greifen[1] vt BAU *Schrauben* bite, ERGON grab

greifen[2] vi MASCHINEN *Feile*, WASSERTRANS bite

Greifer m BAU grab, DRUCK gripper, ERGON gripper, pantograph, KERNTECH gripper, *eines Manipulators* finger action tool, MASCHINEN clutch, gripper, METALL, WASSERTRANS *Baggern* grab; **~ und Garnträger** m pl TEXTIL gripper and yarn carriers; **Greiferauflage** f DRUCK gripper pad; **Greiferkorb** m BAU grab bucket; **Greiferkübel** m MASCHINEN grab bucket; **Greiferscheibe** f TRANS clip pulley; **Greiferseilscheibe** f TRANS clip pulley

Greifhaken m KERNTECH grip hook

Greifvermögen nt FERTIG *Walzen* bite

Greifvorrichtung f MASCHINEN gripping device; **~ eines Roboters** f MASCHINEN robot gripping device

Greifwerkzeug nt ERGON gripper, KERNTECH gripper tool

Greifwinkel m FERTIG *Walzen* angle of contact, angle of nip

Greifzange f KERNTECH grapple

Greifzirkel m METROL caliper (AmE), calliper (BrE)

Grellweiß nt METALL dazzling white

Grenz- pref MATH, QUAL limiting; **Grenzabmessungen** f pl MASCHINEN limit dimensions; **Grenzabweichung** f QUAL limiting deviation; **Grenzanteil** m QUAL limiting proportion; **Grenzbedingung** f MATH *eines Gleichungssystems* boundary condition; **Grenzbrennstoffkassette** f KERNTECH limiting fuel assembly; **Grenzdauer** f AKUSTIK critical duration

Grenze f BAU boundary, MASCHINEN limit, METALL boundary

Grenzempfindlichkeit f GERÄT threshold of sensitivity, PHYS tangential signal sensitivity

Grenzfläche f FERTIG interface, HEIZ & KÄLTE, LUFTTRANS boundary layer, METALL interface boundary, *zwischen Medien* interface, OPTIK *Lichtleiter, zwischen Kern und Mantel* core-cladding interface, PHYS surface, TELEKOM interface

grenzflächenaktiv[1] adj CHEMIE surface-active

grenzflächenaktiv:[2] **~es Mittel** nt CHEMIE surfactant; **~er Stoff** m UMWELTSCHMUTZ surfactant

Grenzfläche: Grenzflächenenergie f METALL interface energy; **Grenzflächenspannung** f KOHLEN surface tension, MEERSCHMUTZ interfacial tension

Grenz-: Grenzfrequenz f ELEKTRONIK cutoff frequency, threshold frequency, FERNSEH, RADIO cutoff frequency; **Grenzgatter** nt ELEKTRONIK threshold gate; **Grenzkonzentration** f KUNSTSTOFF critical concentration, UMWELTSCHMUTZ limiting concentration; **Grenzkorn** nt KOHLEN near-mesh material

Grenzkosten: zu ~ abbaubare Lagerstätte f ERDÖL *Grenze der wirtschaftlichen Förderwürdigkeit* marginal field

Grenz-: Grenzlast f ELEKTRIZ limit load, KOHLEN failure load, LUFTTRANS *eines Luftschraubenblattes*, MASCHINEN limit load; **Grenzlastfaktor** m LUFTTRANS limit load factor; **Grenzlehrdorn** m MASCHINEN internal limit gage (AmE), internal limit gauge (BrE); **Grenzlehre** f MASCHINEN go and no-go limit gage (AmE), go and no-go limit gauge (BrE), limit gage (AmE), limit gauge (BrE), METROL limit gage (AmE), limit gauge (BrE); **Grenzleistung bei Schnellabschaltung** f KERN-

TECH emergency shutdown power; **Grenzlinie** *f* TRANS cordon line; **Grenzlinienübersicht** *f* TRANS cordon line survey; **Grenzmarkierung** *f* BAU boundary mark; **Grenzmaß** *nt* MASCHINEN boundary dimensions, limit size, size limit, MECHAN limit size; **Grenzpfosten** *m* BAU boundary post; **Grenzpunkt** *m* HYDRAUL cutoff point; **Grenzqualität** *f* QUAL limiting quality; **Grenzrachenlehre** *f* MASCHINEN external caliper gage (AmE), external caliper gauge (BrE); **Grenzreibung** *f* MASCHINEN boundary friction; **Grenzrelais** *nt* ELEKTRIZ limit value relay; **Grenzschalter** *m* ELEKTRIZ check switch, limit switch, ELEKTROTECH, KONTROLL, MECHAN limit switch; **Grenzschaufelturbine** *f* HYDRAUL limit turbine

Grenzschicht *f* FERTIG *Strömung*, HEIZ & KÄLTE, MASCHINEN, MECHAN, NICHTFOSS ENERG boundary layer, OPTIK barrier layer, PHYS interface, *in Wandnähe eines Flüssigkeitscontainers oder Kanals* boundary layer, STRÖMPHYS boundary layer; **Grenzschichtablösung** *f* STRÖMPHYS boundary layer separation; **Grenzschichtbeeinflussung** *f* STRÖMPHYS, TRANS boundary layer control; **Grenzschichtdicke** *f* HYDRAUL boundary layer momentum thickness, STRÖMPHYS boundary layer thickness; **Grenzschichteinfluß** *m* STRÖMPHYS boundary layer effect; **Grenzschichtgleichung** *f* STRÖMPHYS boundary layer equation; **Grenzschichtkapazität** *f* ELEKTROTECH junction capacitance; **Grenzschichtschmierung** *f* LUFTTRANS boundary lubrication

Grenz-: **Grenzschmierung** *f* MASCHINEN boundary lubrication; **Grenzspannung** *f* ELEKTROTECH critical voltage; **Grenzstein** *m* BAU boundary stone, landmark; **Grenzsteinmarkierung** *f* BAU *Vermessung* monument; **Grenzstrom** *m* ELEKTRIZ limiting current; **Grenztaster** *m* ELEKTRIZ microswitch

grenzübergreifend: **~e Systeme** *nt pl* TELEKOM cross-border systems

grenzüberschreitend: **~e Abfallverbringung** *f* ABFALL transboundary movement of waste

Grenz-: **Grenzviskosität** *f* STRÖMPHYS limiting viscosity number; **Grenzwellenlänge** *f* ELEKTRONIK threshold wavelength, OPTIK *einer Einzelmode* cutoff wavelength, *einer Schwingungsmode* cutoff wavelength, PHYS *Hohlleiter*, TELEKOM cutoff wavelength

Grenzwert *m* AKUSTIK threshold value, ERGON limen, threshold, MATH limit, QUAL limiting value, tolerance limit, SICHERHEIT *für Aussetzung von gefährlichen Substanzen* exposure limit, TELEKOM limiting value; **Grenzwertanzeiger** *m* GERÄT limit indicator; **Grenzwertdesign** *nt* RAUMFAHRT *konstruiert bis zur Bruchlast* design to breaking strength; **Grenzwerteinstellung** *f* KERNTECH limit setting; **Grenzwertmelder** *m* GERÄT limit indicator; **Grenzwertprüfung** *f* COMP & DV MC, marginal check, marginal test; **Grenzwertsensor** *m* GERÄT threshold detector; **Grenzwertüberwachung** *f* COMP & DV marginal check; **Grenzwertvergleich** *m* GERÄT limit comparison

Grenz-: **Grenzwinkel** *m* FERTIG, OPTIK, PHYS, TELEKOM critical angle; **Grenzwinkel der Totalreflexion** *m* OPTIK angle of total reflection

Griddipper *m* RADIO *Resonanzmeßgerät* grid dip oscillator

Grieß *m* KERNTECH *Störung auf Oszilloskop* grass, LEBENSMITTEL middlings; **Grießkleie** *f* LEBENSMITTEL middlings bran; **Grießkohle** *f* KOHLEN smalls; **Grießkohle ohne Feinkohle** *f* KOHLEN small coal without fines

Griff *m* ERGON grip, FERTIG hilt, FOTO handgrip, KER & GLAS grip, KFZTECH handle, KOHLEN grip, MASCHINEN grip, handle, MECHAN handle, knob, PAPIER, RAUMFAHRT *Raumschiff*, TEXTIL *Stoff*, VERPACK handle

griffig[1] *adj* FERTIG *Schleifscheibe* open

griffig:[2] **~ machen** *vt* FERTIG sharpen

Griffith: **~sche Risse** *m pl* KER & GLAS Griffith flaw

Griff: **Griffkraft** *f* ERGON grip strength; **Griffkreuz** *nt* MASCHINEN star handle; **Griffrippe** *f* FERTIG *Kunststoffinstallationen* reinforcing rib; **Griffschalter** *m* ELEKTROTECH lever switch

Grignard- *pref* CHEMIE organomagnesium; **Grignard-Verbindung** *f* CHEMIE organomagnesium compound

Grob- *pref* TEXTIL coarse-count

grob[1] *adj* MASCHINEN coarse, unfinished; **mit ~er Zahnteilung** *adj* FERTIG coarse-pitch

grob:[2] **~es Filter** *nt* WASSERVERSORG coarse filter; **~eres Gewebe** *nt* TEXTIL coarser woven fabric; **~es Sieb** *nt* KOHLEN riddle; **~e Teilung** *f* MASCHINEN coarse-pitch; **~e Übereinstimmung** *f* COMP & DV fuzzy match; **~e Unterlegscheibe** *f* MASCHINEN coarse washer

grob:[3] **~ entwerfen** *vt* BAU sketch

Grob-: **Grobabgleich** *m* GERÄT *Brücke* coarse balance; **Grobabtastung** *f* FERNSEH coarse scanning; **Grobblech** *nt* METALL heavy plates, plate, WASSERTRANS *Schiffbau* plate; **Grobbrechen** *nt* FERTIG coarse crushing; **Grobbrecher** *m* KOHLEN primary crusher

grobdendritisch: **~es Gefüge** *nt* FERTIG ingotism

Grobeinstellung *f* ELEKTRIZ, FERTIG coarse adjustment; **~ mittels Gestell und Zahnrad** *f* OPTIK *Mikroskop* coarse adjustment by rack and pinion

Grob-: **Grobfeile** *f* MASCHINEN coarse file, rough file, rough-cut file; **Grob-Fein-Einstellung** *f* GERÄT coarse-fine adjustment; **Grobfilter** *nt* MASCHINEN coarse filter; **Grobflyer** *m* TEXTIL slubbing frame

grobgängig: **~e Schraube** *f* BAU coarse-pitch screw

Grob-: **Grobgarn** *nt* TEXTIL coarse yarn; **Grobgewinde** *nt* MASCHINEN coarse thread; **Grobhieb** *m* FERTIG *Feile* coarse cut, MASCHINEN rough cut; **Grobholz** *nt* BAU rough wood; **Grobkeramik** *f* KER & GLAS ordinary ceramic; **Grobkies** *m* BAU rubble

grobkiesig: **~er Sand** *m* BAU coarse gravelly sand

Grob-: **Grobklärbecken** *nt* WASSERVERSORG roughing tank; **Grobkohle** *f* KOHLEN lump coal

grobkonzentrieren *vt* FERTIG rag

Grobkorn *nt* FERTIG, METALL coarse grain; **Grobkorngefüge** *nt* FERTIG pebbles; **Grobkornglühen** *nt* FERTIG coarse-grain annealing

grobkörnig[1] *adj* BAU rough-grained, METALL coarse-grained

grobkörnig:[2] **~es Bild** *nt* FOTO coarse-grain image; **~e Erde** *f* KOHLEN coarse soil

grobporig: **~e Schleifscheibe** *f* FERTIG open-structure wheel

Grob-: **Grobraster** *nt* DRUCK coarse screen; **Grobrechen** *m* ABFALL coarse screen; **Grobsand** *m* ANSTRICH, BAU, MECHAN grit; **Grobschleifen** *nt* MASCHINEN rough grinding; **Grobschleifscheibe** *f* MASCHINEN rough-grinding wheel; **Grobschmieden** *nt* FERTIG preliminary drawing, rough forging

grobschmieden *vt* FERTIG rough-forge

Grob-: **Grobsieb** *nt* KOHLEN scalping screen; **Grobsieben** *nt* KOHLEN scalping

Grobstoff *m* CHEMIE *Papier* screenings; **Grobstoffänger** *m* WASSERVERSORG roughing tank; **Grobstoffentferner** *m* PAPIER junk remover

Grob-: Grobstraße *f* FERTIG blooming train; **Grobstruktur** *f* CHEMIE macrostructure; **Grobvakuum** *nt* PHYS coarse vacuum; **Grobverstellung** *f* MASCHINEN coarse feed; **Grobvorschub** *m* FERTIG coarse feed; **Grobvorschubreihe** *f* FERTIG coarse-feed series; **Grobwalze** *f* MASCHINEN breaking-down roll; **Grobwalzen** *nt* FERTIG roughing, METALL blooming; **Grobwalzwerk** *nt* MASCHINEN blooming mill; **Grobzerkleiner** *m* KOHLEN coarse crusher; **Grobzerkleinerung** *f* KOHLEN coarse crushing, coarse grinding, PAPIER breaking; **Grobzerkleinerungsmaschine** *f* CHEMTECH coarse-crushing mill; **Grobzug** *m* FERTIG *Draht* roughing block; **Grobzuschlagstoff** *m* BAU coarse aggregate; **Grobzuschlagstoffe** *m pl* BAU ballasting material

Gros *nt* MATH *Dutzend*, METROL gross

Groß- *pref* COMP & DV, FOTO, TRANS large, main

groß:[1] von ~er Dicke *adj* FERTIG heavy-gage (AmE), heavy-gauge (BrE)

groß:[2] ~e Bahnhalbachse *f* RAUMFAHRT *eines Orbits* semimajor axis; ~es Bohrloch *nt* ERDÖL *Bohrtechnik* big hole; ~er Ganzton *m* AKUSTIK major whole tone; ~er Kondensator *m* ELEKTROTECH large-value capacitor; ~e Menge *f* BAU bulk; ~e Mutter *f* MASCHINEN heavy nut; ~es Pleuelauge *nt* KFZTECH connecting rod big end; ~e Reynoldszahl *f* STRÖMPHYS high Reynolds number; ~e Sekunde *f* AKUSTIK major second; ~e Septime *f* AKUSTIK major seventh; ~e Sext *f* AKUSTIK major sixth; ~e Spantiefe *f* MASCHINEN heavy cut; ~e Steigung *f* LUFTTRANS *Hubschrauber* high pitch, *am Propeller* coarse pitch; ~er Streuwinkel *m* KERNTECH large-angle scattering; ~e Sturzwelle *f* WASSERTRANS *Seezustand* roller; ~e Terz *f* AKUSTIK major third; ~e Tonne *f* METROL long ton; ~e Vereinigung *f* TEILPHYS grand unification; zu ~e Vorspannung *f* AUFNAHME overbias; ~er Wasserfall *m* WASSERVERSORG cataract; ~er Widerstand *m* ELEKTROTECH large-value resistor

Groß-: Großaufnahme *f* FOTO close-up; **Großbaum** *m* WASSERTRANS *Segeln* main boom; **Großbehälterumschlag** *m* TRANS containerization; **Großbildschirm** *m* COMP & DV LSD, large-screen display; **Großbohrloch** *nt* KOHLEN well drill hole; **Großboot** *nt* WASSERTRANS *Beiboot* longboat; **Großbrasse** *f* WASSERTRANS *Tauwerk* main brace; **Großbuchstabe** *m* DRUCK upper case

Großbuchstaben: alles in ~ *phr* DRUCK all caps; **in ~** *adj* COMP & DV in upper case

Groß-: Großcontainer *m* VERPACK large-size container

Größe *f* DRUCK weight, ELEKTRONIK quantity, FERTIG quantity, value, METROL gage (AmE), gauge (BrE), TEXTIL size; ~ des Spanraums *f* FERTIG amount of chip space; **Größendarstellung** *f* COMP & DV signed magnitude representation; **Größenklasse** *f* PHYS *Stern* magnitude; **Größenordnung** *f* COMP & DV, PHYS order of magnitude, STRAHLPHYS *des Hintergrundrauschens* order; **Größenordnung einer physikalischen Größe** *f* PHYS magnitude of quantity; **Größenschwelle** *f* ERGON size threshold; **Größenwandler** *m* COMP & DV quantizer; **Größenzusammenhang** *m* REGELUNG relationship between variables, relationship between quantities

größer: ~ als *adj* MATH greater than

Größergleichzeichen *nt* MATH chevron

Größerzeichen *nt* MATH chevron

Groß-: Großflächenwärmetauscher *m* MASCHINEN extended-surface heat exchanger

großflächig: ~e Bestrahlungsnorm *f* KERNTECH large-area radiation standard; ~es **System** *nt* TELEKOM wide-area system

Groß-: Großflughafen *m* LUFTTRANS air terminal; **Großformatklappkamera** *f* FOTO large-format folding camera; **Großintegration** *f (LSI)* COMP & DV, ELEKTRONIK, PHYS, TELEKOM large-scale integration *(LSI)*

Großkreis *m* PHYS, RADIO great circle, RAUMFAHRT meridian

großkreisabhängig *adj* RAUMFAHRT meridional

Großkreis: Großkreisfunkstrecke *f* RADIO great circle radio path; **Großkreiskarte** *f* WASSERTRANS *Navigation* great circle chart; **Großkreiskurs** *m* WASSERTRANS great circle route, *Navigation* great circle course; **Großkreisroute** *f* RAUMFAHRT great circle path

Groß-: Großlochbohrung *f* KOHLEN large-hole boring; **Großmast** *m* WASSERTRANS *Segeln* mainmast; **Großmotorrad** *nt* KFZTECH large-capacity motorcycle; **Großoberflächenfehler** *m* FERTIG rat; **Großplatten** *f pl* METALL large plates

Großraum- *pref* LUFTTRANS wide-bodied; **Großraumcontainer** *m (HC)* TRANS High Cube *(HC)*; **Großraumdüsenflugzeug** *nt* LUFTTRANS jumbo jet; **Großraumfrachter** *m* WASSERTRANS bulk carrier; **Großraumjet** *m* LUFTTRANS wide-bodied aircraft; **Großraum-LKW** *m* KFZTECH large-capacity truck; **Großraumwagen** *m* EISENBAHN *für Personen* saloon coach

Groß-: Großrechner *m* COMP & DV large-scale computer, mainframe computer, supercomputer; **Großring-** *pref* CHEMIE macrocyclic; **Großsack** *m* VERPACK multiply sack; **Großschot** *f* WASSERTRANS *Segeln* mainsheet; **Großschreibung** *f* DRUCK capitalization; **Großsegel** *nt* WASSERTRANS *Segeln* mainsail; **Großserienfertigung** *f* FERTIG large-batch production, quantity production

Großsignal *nt* ELEKTRONIK large signal; **Großsignal-Bandbreite** *f* ELEKTRONIK large-signal bandwidth; **Großsignal-Bedingungen** *f pl* ELEKTRONIK large-signal conditions; **Großsignal-Betrieb** *m* ELEKTRONIK large-signal operation

Großspeicher *m* COMP & DV mass storage; **Großspeicher-Chip** *m* ELEKTRONIK random logic chip; **Großspeicherschaltung** *f* ELEKTRONIK random logic circuit

Groß-: Großstag *nt* WASSERTRANS *Takelage* mainstay

größt: ~e Abmessungen *f pl* WASSERTRANS *Schiffbau* extreme dimensions; ~er **anzunehmender Unfall** *m (GAU)* KERNTECH maximum credible accident *(MCA)*; ~e **Breite** *f* WASSERTRANS *Schiffkonstruktion* extreme breadth; ~er **Durchschlupf** *m* QUAL average outgoing quality limit; ~er **gemeinsamer Teiler** *m (ggT)* MATH highest common factor *(HCF)*; ~er **Leistungseingang** *m* ELEKTROTECH maximum power input; ~e **Schiffsbreite** *f* WASSERTRANS *Schiff und Bootsbau* maximum beam; ~er **Tiefgang** *m* WASSERTRANS *Schiffkonstruktion* extreme draught; ~er **Wassergehalt** *m* KOHLEN liquid limit; ~e **zulässige Nutzleistung** *f* ELEKTROTECH overload level; ~er **zulässiger Fehler** *m* METROL maximum permissible error

Größtmaß *nt* MASCHINEN maximum size

größtmöglich: ~e Schlepptiefe *f* WASSERVERSORG full-dredging depth; ~e **Signalempfindlichkeit** *f* ELEKTRONIK minimum detectable signal

Größtspiel *nt* MASCHINEN maximum clearance

Größtübermaß *nt* MASCHINEN maximum allowance

Groß-: Großvaterdatei *f* COMP & DV grandfather file; **Großwant** *f* WASSERTRANS *Tauwerk* main shroud

Groteskschrift *f* DRUCK, KONSTZEICH sans serif
Grübchen *nt* METALL dimple; **Grübchenbildung** *f* KER &
GLAS pitting, RAUMFAHRT *Raumschiff* potting
Grube *f* ABFALL trench landfill, ERDÖL, KOHLEN, WAS-
SERVERSORG pit; **Grubenarbeiter** *m* KOHLEN collier,
miner; **Grubenbahn** *f* EISENBAHN, KOHLEN mine rail-
road (AmE), mine railway (BrE); **Grubengas** *nt*
KOHLEN, THERMOD firedamp; **Grubengasprüfgerät** *nt*
KOHLEN firedamp-proof machine; **Grubenholz** *nt*
KOHLEN timber; **Grubenlampe** *f* KOHLEN Davy lamp;
Grubenlokomotive *f* EISENBAHN hauling engine; **Gru-
benwagen** *m* EISENBAHN tram; **Grubenwand** *f* ABFALL
einer Deponie embankment; **Grubenzimmerung** *f*
KOHLEN timbering
Grün *nt* FERNSEH, TRANS green
grün: ~es Elektronenstrahlsystem *nt* ELEKTRONIK green
gun; ~er Sand *m* FERTIG *naß* green sand; ~e Welle *f*
TRANS progressive signal system, *Ampelschaltung*
phased traffic lights (BrE), synchronized lights
(AmE), *KFZ-Verkehr* linked lights
Grund:[1] auf ~ *adv* WASSERTRANS aground
Grund[2] *m* MASCHINEN root
Grund:[3] auf ~ setzen *vt* WASSERTRANS *Schiff* ground, run
aground
Grund:[4] den ~ berühren *vi* WASSERTRANS *Schiff* touch
bottom; auf ~ laufen *vi* WASSERTRANS go aground, run
ashore, *Schiff* ground, run aground
Grund: **Grundablaß** *m* WASSERVERSORG bottom outlet;
Grundarmierung *f* BAU main reinforcement; **Grund-
backe** *f* FERTIG actual chuck jaw; **Grundbaustein** *m*
ELEKTRIZ basic module; **Grundbefehl** *m* COMP & DV
basic instruction; **Grundbindung** *f* TEXTIL plain weave;
Grundbitrate *f* TELEKOM basic bit rate; **Grundbogen** *m*
BAU reversed arch; **Grundbohrung** *f* FERTIG blind bore,
blind hole; **Grundbruch** *m* BAU base failure; **Grund-
büchse** *f* FERTIG *Bohren* liner bushing, MASCHINEN
bottom brass; **Grundcodierung** *f* COMP & DV basic
coding; **Grunddesign** *nt* KERNTECH base design;
Grundebene *f* FERTIG basal plane, GEOM ground plane; **Grundeinheit** *f* ELEKTRIZ, MASCHINEN
fundamental unit
gründen *vt* BAU *Gebäudefundament* lay
Grund: **Grundfalte** *f* KONSTZEICH basic fold; **Grundfarbe**
f COMP & DV, DRUCK primary color (AmE), primary
colour (BrE), KER & GLAS ground color (AmE),
ground colour, OPTIK, PHYS primary color (AmE),
primary colour (BrE); **Grundfarben** *f pl* DRUCK fundamental colors (AmE), fundamental colours (BrE),
STRAHLPHYS prime colors (AmE), prime colours
(BrE); **Grundfarbstoff** *m* PAPIER basic dye; **Grundfehler**
m METROL *Meßinstrument* intrinsic error; **Grundfern-
sprechgebühr** *f* TELEKOM basic call charge;
Grundfläche *f* BAU area, floor space, METALL basal
plane; **Grundflächengleiten** *nt* METALL basal slip;
Grundformen *f pl* GEOM basic shapes; **Grundfrequenz** *f*
ELEKTRONIK, FERNSEH, RADIO, TELEKOM BF, base
frequency, fundamental frequency; **Grundgebühr** *f* TE-
LEKOM basic call charge; **Grundgefüge** *nt* FERTIG
matrix; **Grundgerät** *nt* GERÄT basic instrument;
Grundgeräusch *nt* AKUSTIK ground noise, ELEKTRO-
NIK *Telefontechnik* basic noise, WERKPRÜF
background noise; **Grundgesamtheit** *f* QUAL popula-
tion; **Grundgeschwindigkeit** *f* KONTROLL basic speed;
Grundgestein *nt* WASSERVERSORG bedrock; **Grundge-
webe** *nt* TEXTIL ground cloth, ground fabric,
Frottierware backing fabric, *Teppich* backing; **Grund-**

gruppe *f* ELEKTROTECH, TELEKOM basic group; **Grund-
hieb** *m* FERTIG *Feile* undercut
grundieren *vt* BAU prime, *Farbe* precoat, PAPIER stain
Grundierfarbe *f* KER & GLAS flat color (AmE), flat colour
(BrE)
Grundiermasse *f* FERTIG size
Grundiermittel *nt* KUNSTSTOFF primer
grundiert: ~e Rohkarosserie *f* KFZTECH body in white
Grundierung *f* ANSTRICH base coat, BAU prime coat,
Farbe undercoat, FERTIG priming, KUNSTSTOFF,
RAUMFAHRT *Raumschiff* primer
Grund: **Grundkegel** *m* MASCHINEN base cone; **Grundket-
tenfilter** *nt* RADIO constant-k filter;
Grundkomponente *f* PHYS *Schwingung* fundamental
component; **Grundkonzentration** *f* UMWELTSCHMUTZ
background concentration, instantaneous concentra-
tion; **Grundkörper** *m* FERTIG main casting, stock;
Grundkreis *m* MASCHINEN base circle, root circle;
Grundladung *f* RAUMFAHRT *Raumschiff* priming
charge; **Grundlagen eines Axiomensystems** *f pl* GEOM
bases of an axiomatic system; **Grundlagenwissen** *nt*
COMP & DV knowledge base
Grundlänge: ~ der Start- und Landebahn *f* LUFTTRANS
runway basic length
Grundlast *f* TRANS basic load; **Grundlastbündel** *nt* TELE-
KOM *Schaltung* first-choice group; **Grundlastkessel** *m*
KERNTECH base load boiler
grundlegend: ~e Leistungsfähigkeit *f* TRANS basic capa-
city; ~e Verschmutzung *f* UMWELTSCHMUTZ back-
ground pollution
Grund: **Grundleistung** *f* KERNTECH base power
gründlich: ~e Überholung *f* KERNTECH major overhaul
Grundlinie *f* BAU *Vermessung* base, baseline, DRUCK ba-
seline, GEOM *einer geometrischen Figur* base;
Grundlinienkontrolle *f* MECHAN baseline inspection
Grundloch *nt* MASCHINEN blind hole, bottom hole;
Grundlochgewindebohrer *m* MASCHINEN bottoming
tap, plug tap; **Grundlochreibahle** *f* MASCHINEN
bottoming reamer
Grund: **Grundmasse** *f* BAU matrix; **Grundmaterial** *nt*
ANSTRICH substrate; **Grundmauer** *f* BAU base wall;
Grundmetall *nt* MASCHINEN base metal, parent metal,
METALL base metal, basis metal; **Grundmode** *f* OPTIK
fundamental mode; **Grundmodus** *m* PHYS *Hohlleiter*
dominant mode; **Grundnahrungsmittel** *nt* LEBENSMIT-
TEL staple food; **Grundnetz** *nt* MEERSCHMUTZ trawl
net; **Grundpetrochemikalien** *f pl* ERDÖL basic petro-
chemicals; **Grundplatine** *f* COMP & DV motherboard;
Grundplatte *f* BAU *Hoch und Tiefbau*, EISENBAHN, ERD-
ÖL *Offshore* bed plate, FERTIG die bed, die shoe,
Schnitt shoe, KFZTECH *Bremsanlage* backing plate,
MASCHINEN base plate, bed plate, MECHAN base plate,
WASSERTRANS *Maschine* bed plate; **Grundprimärgruppe** *f (GPG)* TELEKOM basic group; **Grundrahmen** *m*
KERNTECH base frame; **Grundrauschen** *nt* GERÄT ba-
sic noise, TELEKOM background noise; **Grundriß** *m* BAU
sketch, MASCHINEN plan view
grundsätzlich: ~e Sicherheitsvorschriften *f pl* SICHER-
HEIT basic safety rules
Grund: **Grundschaltbild** *nt* KERNTECH basic circuit diagram; **Grundschicht** *f* ANSTRICH base coat, FERTIG
primer; **Grundschleier** *m* FOTO base fog; **Grund-
schleppnetz** *nt* MEERSCHMUTZ trawl net;
Grundschriftfeld *nt* KONSTZEICH basic title block;
Grundschwelle *f* BAU ground plate, groundsill, sill, sill
plate, WASSERTRANS *Hafen*, WASSERVERSORG sill;

Grundschwingung f ELEKTRONIK first harmonic, fundamental frequency, funnel, ELEKTROTECH *Wellenleiter* dominant mode, PHYS fundamental mode, RADIO, TELEKOM fundamental frequency; **Grundschwingungsmode** f AKUSTIK fundamental vibration mode, OPTIK fundamental mode; **Grundsee** f WASSERTRANS *Seezustand* ground swell

grundsohlig adj ERDÖL *Bohrtechnik* bottom-hole

Grund: **Grundstellung** f COMP & DV initial state, reset; **Grundstruktur** f COMP & DV framework

Grundstück nt BAU plot; **Grundstücksbegrenzungsmauer** f BAU party wall; **Grundstücksleitung** f BAU supply pipe; **Grundstücksmakler** m BAU estate agent

Grund: **Grundtaktgenerator** m COMP & DV master clock; **Grundton** m AKUSTIK fundamental tone, keynote, WELLPHYS fundamental tone; **Grundtyp** m ELEKTROTECH *Wellenleiter* dominant mode, *einer Welle* fundamental mode, PHYS dominant mode

grundüberholen vt WASSERTRANS refit

Grund: **Grundüberholung** f KERNTECH major overhaul, WASSERTRANS refit

Gründung f BAU *Gebäude* footing; **Gründungspfahl** m BAU pier; **Gründungssohle** f BAU foundation; **Gründungswanne** f BAU *Grundbau* tank

Grund: **Grundverbindung** f COMP & DV basic linkage

Grundwasser nt KOHLEN ground water, UMWELTSCHMUTZ underground water, WASSERVERSORG ground water, subsoil water, subterranean water; **Grundwasserangebot** nt WASSERVERSORG ground water resources; **Grundwasserbelastung** f UMWELTSCHMUTZ impact on ground water; **Grundwassereinzugsgebiet** nt WASSERVERSORG ground water basin; **Grundwassererneuerung** f WASSERVERSORG natural ground water recharge

grundwasserführend adj: **~e Schicht** f WASSERVERSORG water-bearing stratum

Grundwasser: **Grundwasserkunde** f KOHLEN geohydrology; **Grundwasserleiter** m WASSERVERSORG aquifer; **Grundwasserschließung** f WASSERVERSORG capture of ground water; **Grundwasserschutz** m ABFALL ground water protection; **Grundwasserspiegel** m BAU ground water level, ERDÖL water table, KOHLEN ground water table, WASSERVERSORG ground water level, phreatic water level; **Grundwasserstand** m WASSERVERSORG ground water level, ground water table; **Grundwasserstauer** m WASSERVERSORG aquifuge; **Grundwasserstrom** m UMWELTSCHMUTZ underground water flow; **Grundwassertiefe** f WASSERVERSORG ground water depth; **Grundwasserversorgung** f KOHLEN ground water supply

Grund: **Grundwehr** nt HYDRAUL, WASSERVERSORG drowned weir, submerged weir; **Grundwelle** f AKUSTIK fundamental wave, ELEKTROTECH fundamental mode, PHYS carrier, WASSERTRANS *Seezustand* ground wave, WELLPHYS carrier

Grundwerk nt PAPIER bed plate; **Grundwerkkasten** m PAPIER bed plate box; **Grundwerkstoff** m BAU base material; **Grundwerkwalze** f PAPIER bed roll

Grund: **Grundzahl** f MATH radix; **Grundzahlen** f pl MATH radices; **Grundzeit** f COMP & DV productive time; **Grundzustand** m COMP & DV stable state, PHYS ground state, STRAHLPHYS basic state, TEILPHYS ground state; **Grundzyklus** m COMP & DV basic machine time

Grün: **Grüne-Welle-Verkehrssignalsteuerung** f TRANS linked traffic signal control; **Grüngitter** nt FERNSEH green screen-grid; **Grünkanone** f FERNSEH green gun;

Grünlaser m ELEKTRONIK green beam laser

Grünling m BAU sun-dried brick, KERNTECH green compact

Grün: **Grünmischer** m FERNSEH green adder; **Grünpellet** nt KERNTECH green pellet; **Grünphase** f TRANS green phase; **Grün-Schwarz-Pegel** m FERNSEH green-black level; **Grünsignaldauer** f TRANS hour of green signal indication; **Grünspan** m CHEMIE, FERTIG verdigris; **Grünspitzenwert** m FERNSEH green peak level; **Grünstein** m BAU green stone

Grünstrahl m FERNSEH green beam; **Grünstrahllaser** m ELEKTRONIK green beam laser; **Grünstrahlsystem** nt ELEKTRONIK *Fernsehen* green gun

Grünzeit f TRANS green period, green time; **Grünzeitverschiebung** f TRANS offset

Gruppe f AKUSTIK field, CHEMIE residue, COMP & DV cluster, group, set, ELEKTROTECH group, *Tasten, Kontakte* bank, *von Kondensatoren* bank, MASCHINEN battery, cluster, MATH group, RADIO *Antennen* array, TELEKOM array, group; **Gruppenanrufkennung** f TELEKOM group call identity; **Gruppenantenne** f TELEKOM array antenna; **Gruppenauslese** f ERGON group selection; **Gruppenauswahl** f QUAL stratified sampling; **Gruppenbrechungsindex** m OPTIK group index; **Gruppenbrechzahl** f TELEKOM group index

gruppencodiert: **~es Aufzeichnen** nt COMP & DV GCR, group code recording

Gruppe: **Gruppenfahrkarte** f EISENBAHN group ticket; **Gruppengeschwindigkeit** f AKUSTIK, OPTIK *Wellenausbreitung*, PHYS group velocity, TELEKOM envelope velocity, group velocity

gruppenkollektiv: **~e Dosis** f UMWELTSCHMUTZ group collective dose

Gruppe: **Gruppenlaufzeit** f COMP & DV, ELEKTROTECH group delay, TELEKOM group transmission delay; **Gruppenlaufzeitdifferenz durch Modendispersion** f TELEKOM differential mode delay, multimode group delay; **Gruppenmarke** f COMP & DV group mark, group marker; **Gruppenschalter** m ELEKTROTECH gang switch; **Gruppensteuereinheit** f COMP & DV cluster controller; **Gruppentheorie** f MATH group theory; **Gruppenvermittlungsstelle** f (*GrVST*) TELEKOM group-switching center (AmE), group-switching centre (BrE) (*GSC*); **Gruppenverschlüsselung** f COMP & DV GCR, group code recording; **Gruppenverzögerung** f ELEKTROTECH group delay; **Gruppenzeichnung** f KONSTZEICH group drawing

gruppiert adj COMP & DV ganged

Gruppierung f ELEKTRIZ layout, ELEKTROTECH grouping, TRANS consolidation; **~ im Rechteck** f RAD rectangular wiring; **Gruppierungsschalter** m ELEKTROTECH grouping switch

Grus m KOHLEN slack coal; **Gruskohle** f KOHLEN slack coal

GrVST abbr (*Gruppenvermittlungsstelle*) TELEKOM GSC (*group-switching centre*)

GS[1] abbr (*Gleichstrom*) AUFNAHME, COMP & DV, EISENBAHN, ELEKTRIZ, ELEKTROTECH, FERNSEH, FERTIG, PHYS, RADIO, TELEKOM DC (*direct current*)

GS:[2] **GS-Löschkopf** m AUFNAHME DC erase head; **GS-Motor mit Bürsten** m ELEKTROTECH brush-type DC motor; **GS-Vormagnetisierung** f AUFNAHME DC bias; **GS-WS-Wandler** m PHYS DC-AC converter; **GS-WS-Wandlung** f PHYS DC-AC conversion

GSZ abbr (*Gesamtsäurezahl*) CHEMIE TAN (*total acid number*)

Guajacol nt CHEMIE guaiacol
Guajacon- pref CHEMIE guaiaconic
Guajakharz nt LEBENSMITTEL guaiac resin, gum guaiacum
Guajakholz nt MECHAN lignum vitae
Guajaret- pref CHEMIE guaiaretic
Guanidin nt CHEMIE guanidine; Guanidinabspaltung f CHEMIE depurination
Guanin nt CHEMIE guanine
Guano m CHEMIE guano; Guanosin nt CHEMIE guanosine, vernine
Guanyl- pref CHEMIE guanyl; Guanylguanidin nt CHEMIE biguanide
Guckloch nt MASCHINEN spyhole, RAUMFAHRT Raumschiff peep hole
Gülle f ABFALL slurry
Gully m UMWELTSCHMUTZ sink
Gulon- pref CHEMIE gulonic
Gulose f CHEMIE gulose
gültig: für ~ erklären vt COMP & DV validate
Gültigkeit f TELEKOM validity; Gültigkeitsbereich m COMP & DV scope; Gültigkeitsprüfung f COMP & DV, TELEKOM validation, validity check
Gumbo nt ERDÖL Geologie gumbo
Gummi nt ELEKTRIZ rubber, KUNSTSTOFF india rubber, rubber; Gummiabfall m ABFALL rubber waste, waste rubber; Gummiabfallverwertung f KUNSTSTOFF rubber scrap recycling, scrap recycling; Gummiarabikum nt LEBENSMITTEL Klebstoff gum arabic; Gummiarbeitshandschuhe m pl SICHERHEIT working gloves; Gummiboot nt WASSERTRANS rubber boat, rubber dinghy; Gummibuchse f FERTIG Kunststoffinstallationen rubber bush; Gummidichtring m ELEKTROTECH grommet; Gummidichtung f ELEKTROTECH grommet, FERTIG, MASCHINEN rubber gasket; Gummidichtungsring m MASCHINEN grommet; Gummidruckschlauch m WASSERVERSORG rubber delivery hose
gummielastisch adj FERTIG rubber-like
gummieren vt DRUCK gum
Gummiermaschine f VERPACK glue-gumming machine, gumming machine
gummiert[1] adj KUNSTSTOFF rubberized
gummiert:[2] ~es Etikett nt VERPACK gummed label; ~es Gewebe nt KUNSTSTOFF coated fabric; ~es Papier nt VERPACK gummed paper; ~er Rand m VERPACK gummed edge
Gummi: Gummifeder f MASCHINEN rubber spring; Gummiförderschlauch m WASSERVERSORG rubber delivery hose; Gummiform f MASCHINEN rubber mould; Gummigurt m MASCHINEN rubber belt; Gummihandschuh m KUNSTSTOFF india rubber glove, SICHERHEIT, für elektrische Einsätze rubber glove
gummiisoliert: ~es Kabel nt ELEKTROTECH rubber-insulated cable
Gummi: Gummikabel nt ELEKTROTECH rubber cable, rubber-insulated cable; Gummikissen nt KFZTECH rubber pad; Gummiklotz m KFZTECH rubber pad; Gummikolben m LABOR Pipette rubber bulb; Gummilager nt KFZTECH Motor, MASCHINEN rubber mounting; Gummimembran f MASCHINEN rubber diaphragm; Gummimotoraufhängung f KFZTECH rubber engine mounting; Gummipuffer m FOTO rubber tip, MASCHINEN rubber buffer; Gummiquetschwalze f FOTO squeegee; Gummiradwalze f BAU rubber-tired roller (AmE), rubber-tyred roller (BrE), Straßenbau pneumatic-tired roller (AmE), pneumatic-tyred roller

(BrE); Gummiriemen m MASCHINEN rubber belting; Gummisaugschlauch m WASSERVERSORG rubber suction-hose; Gummischlauch m KUNSTSTOFF india rubber hose, rubber hose, LABOR rubber tubing, MASCHINEN rubber hose; Gummistoff m ELEKTRIZ rubberized material; Gummistopfen m LABOR rubber stopper; Gummituch nt DRUCK rubber blanket; Gummiwalze f FERTIG, KER & GLAS für optisches Glas squeegee; Gummiwendelantenne f RADIO rubber ducky antenna; Gummizylinder m DRUCK blanket cylinder
Gundiode f ELEKTRONIK gun diode
Gunn: Gunn-Diode f PHYS electron transfer diode, Halbeiterphysik Gunn diode, RADIO Gunn-effect diode; Gunn-Effekt m ELEKTRONIK Gunn effect
günstig: ~ste Geschwindigkeit f TRANS optimum speed
Gunverstärker m ELEKTRONIK gun amplifier
Gurt m BAU boom, fascia, KOHLEN wale, waling, LUFTTRANS brace, MASCHINEN band, strap, NICHTFOSS ENERG chord; Gurtband nt TEXTIL webbing; Gurtbandförderer m MASCHINEN band conveyor, belt conveyor; Gurtblech nt BAU boom plate
Gurte m pl RAUMFAHRT safety harness
Gürtel m KFZTECH Gürtelreifen belt, Reifen ply; Gürtelreifen m KFZTECH Reifen radial tire (AmE), radial tyre (BrE), KUNSTSTOFF radial ply tire (AmE), radial ply tyre (BrE)
Gurt: Gurtholz nt BAU waling; Gurtplatte f BAU eines Trägers flange plate; Gurtsims m BAU fascia; Gurttrommel f FERTIG belt fastener; Gurtwerkstoff m KUNSTSTOFF belting; Gurtzuführer m CHEMTECH belt feed
Guß m METALL, PAPIER casting; Guß- pref METALL castiron; Gußblase f FERTIG blister; Gußbronze f MECHAN cast bronze; Gußeisen nt FERTIG, MASCHINEN, MECHAN, METALL, PAPIER cast iron; Gußeisengelenk nt BAU cast-iron joint; Gußeisenrohr nt BAU cast-iron pipe
gußeisern[1] adj METALL cast-iron
gußeisern:[2] ~er Krümmer m BAU cast-iron elbow
Guß: Gußfehler m FERTIG shift; Gußform f MASCHINEN mold for casting (AmE), mould for casting (BrE), WASSERTRANS mold (AmE), mould (BrE); Gußglas nt KER & GLAS cast glass; Gußhaut f FERTIG scale; Gußmessing nt METALL cast brass; Gußmodell nt MECHAN casting pattern; Gußnaht f FERTIG, MASCHINEN burr; Gußnarbe f MECHAN flaw; Gußputzen nt FERTIG tumbling; Gußputztrommel f FERTIG rumble, shaker barrel, tumbler; Gußrohrleitung f MASCHINEN castiron pipeline; Gußschablone f PAPIER casting template; Gußspiegelglas nt KER & GLAS cast plate glass; Gußstahl m MECHAN cast steel, METALL casting steel; Gußstück nt METALL casting; Gußteil nt FERTIG casting; Gußzinnbronze f METALL cannon metal, gunmetal
Gut nt QUAL commodity, WASSERTRANS Tauwerk rigging
gut:[1] ~ erreichbar adj MASCHINEN Hebel conveniently-placed; ~ funktionierend adj COMP & DV Programm well-behaving; ~ verbunden adj ANSTRICH well-bonded
gut:[2] ~ leitende Diode f ELEKTRONIK high-conductance diode; ~ sichtbare Kleidung f SICHERHEIT highly visible clothing
gut:[3] ~ freihalten von vt WASSERTRANS Schiffsführung give a wide berth; nicht ~ passen vt METALL misfit
Gutachten nt QUAL expert's report

Güte *f* AKUSTIK quality, METALL grade, QUAL quality; ~ der Oberfläche *f* ANSTRICH surface finish; ~ des Zuschlagstoffs *f* BAU quality of aggregate; **Güteanforderung** *f* TEXTIL spec, specification; **Gütebestätigungsstufe** *f* QUAL assessment level; **Gütebestätigungssystem** *nt* QUAL system of quality assessment; **Gütebewertung** *f* QUAL quality appraisal; **Gütefaktor** *m* ELEKTRONIK figure of merit, MECHAN *(Q-Faktor)*, PHYS *(Q-Faktor)*, QUAL *(Q-Faktor)*, RADIO *(Q-Faktor)*, UMWELTSCHMUTZ *(Q-Faktor)* quality factor *(Q factor)*; **Gütefaktor einer Spule** *m* ELEKTRIZ coil Q-factor; **Gütefaktormesser** *m (Q-Meter)* PHYS Q meter; **Gütefunktion** *f* QUAL power function

gütegeschaltet: ~er Laser *m* KERNTECH Q-switched laser

Güte: Gütegrad *m* MECHAN rating; **Güteklasse** *f* GERÄT *Meßgerät* class, MECHAN, QUAL quality class; **Gütekontrolle** *f* FERTIG inspection and quality control; **Gütekriterium** *nt* CHEMIE performance index; **Gütemerkmal** *nt* QUAL quality criterion; **Güteminderung** *f* QUAL deterioration

Gutenberg: ~sche Diskontinuität *f* NICHTFOSS ENERG Gutenberg discontinuity

Güte: Güteprüfung durch den öffentlichen Auftraggeber *m* QUAL government quality assurance

Güter *nt pl* RAIL goods; **Güterannahme** *f* EISENBAHN freight inwards (AmE), goods inwards (BrE); **Güterbahnhof** *m* EISENBAHN freight station (AmE), goods station (BrE), freight yard (AmE), goods yard (BrE), TRANS freight depot (AmE), goods depot (BrE); **Güterboden** *m* EISENBAHN freight shed (AmE), goods shed (BrE); **Güterfernverkehr** *m* TRANS long-distance goods traffic, road haulage, road transport; **Güterlastkraftwagen** *m (Güter-LKW)* KFZTECH freight truck (AmE), goods lorry (BrE) *(freight truck)*; **Güter-LKW** *m (Güterlastkraftwagen)* KFZTECH freight truck (AmE), goods lorry (BrE) *(goods lorry)*; **Güterlokomotive** *f* EISENBAHN freight locomotive; **Güterrutsche** *f* EISENBAHN freight chute (AmE), goods chute (BrE); **Güterschuppen** *m* EISENBAHN freight shed (AmE), goods shed (BrE), TRANS freight depot (AmE), goods depot (BrE); **Güterträger** *m* EISENBAHN freight porter (AmE), goods porter (BrE);

Güterwagen *m* EISENBAHN railroad freight car (AmE), railway freight car (BrE), van; **Güterwagendrehgestell** *nt* EISENBAHN freight truck (AmE), goods lorry (BrE); **Güterwaren** *f pl* VERPACK goods; **Güterzug** *m* EISENBAHN freight train (AmE), goods train (BrE)

Güte: Güteschaltbetrieb *m* ELEKTRONIK *Laser-Sperrung* Q switching; **Gütezahl** *f* MECHAN quality index; **Gütezeichen** *nt* MECHAN quality sign, PATENT certification mark, QUAL mark of conformity, VERPACK quality mark

Gutlehrdorn *m* FERTIG go-screw plug

Gutlehre *f* FERTIG go gage (AmE), go gauge (BrE), MASCHINEN go gage (AmE), go gauge (BrE), pass gage (AmE), pass gauge (BrE)

gutmoderiert: ~er Reaktorkern *m* KERNTECH well-moderated core

Gutrachenlehre *f* FERTIG go snap-gage (AmE), go snap-gauge (BrE)

Gut-/Schlecht-Entscheidung *f* QUAL go/no-go decision, pass/fail decision

Gutseite *f* FERTIG *Lehre*, MASCHINEN go end

Gutseitelehrung *f* FERTIG go end gaging (AmE), go end gauging (BrE)

Gutstoff *m* PAPIER accepted stock

Guttapercha *f* CHEMIE, KUNSTSTOFF gutta-percha

Gut- und Ausschußlehre *f* MASCHINEN go and no-go gage (AmE), go and no-go gauge (BrE)

Gx *abbr (Systemkonstante)* AKUSTIK Gx *(system-rating constant)*

gy *abbr (Gray)* PHYS *Einheit der Energiedosis*, TEILPHYS *Einheit der Strahlendosis* gy *(gray)*

Gynocard- *pref* CHEMIE gynocardic

Gyrator *m* PHYS gyrator

Gyrobus *m* KFZTECH gyrobus

Gyrograph *m* RAUMFAHRT gyrograph

gyromagnetisch: ~er Effekt *m* PHYS gyromagnetic effect; ~es Verhältnis *nt (g)* KERNTECH, PHYS gyromagnetic ratio *(g)*

Gyroskop *nt* PHYS gyroscope

Gyrostat *m* CHEMIE gyrostat

gyrostatisch *adj* CHEMIE gyrostatic

Gyrotron *nt* TELEKOM gyrotron

H

H¹ *abbr* ELEKTRIZ *(Henry)* H *(henry)*, ELEKTRIZ *(magnetische Feldstärke)* H *(magnetic field strength)*, ELEKTROTECH *(Henry)* H *(henry)*, ELEKTROTECH *(magnetische Feldstärke)* H *(magnetic field strength)*, HEIZ & KÄLTE *(Enthalpie)* H *(enthalpy)*, HYDRAUL *(Hamiltonsche Funktion)* H *(Hamiltonian function)*, KOHLEN *(Enthalpie)*, MECHAN *(Enthalpie)* H *(enthalpy)*, METROL *(Henry)* H *(henry)*, NICHT-FOSS ENERG *(Enthalpie)* H *(enthalpy)*, OPTIK *(Bestrahlungsstärke)* H *(irradiance)*, PHYS *(Enthalpie)* H *(enthalpy)*, PHYS *(Henry)* H *(henry)*, PHYS *(Magnetfeldstärke)* H *(magnetic field strength)*, RADIO *(Henry)* H *(henry)*, RAUMFAHRT *(Enthalpie)*, THERMOD *(Enthalpie)* H *(enthalpy)*

H² *(Wasserstoff)* CHEMIE H *(hydrogen)*

h ¹ *abbr* COMP & DV *(Höhe)*, GEOM *(Höhe)* h *(height)*, METROL *(Hekto-)* h *(hecto-)*, METROL *(Stunde)* h *(hour)*, PHYS *(Plancksche Konstante, Plancksches Wirkungsquantum)* h *(Planck's constant)*, RADIO *(Höhe)* h *(height)*, STRAHLPHYS *(Plancksche Konstante, Plancksches Wirkungsquantum)*, TEILPHYS *(Plancksche Konstante, Plancksches Wirkungsquantum)* h *(Planck's constant)*

h :² ~ **quer** *adj* PHYS *Dirac-Konstante* h-bar

ha *abbr (Hektar)* LABOR ha *(hectare)*

Haar *nt* TEXTIL hair; **Haarfeuchtigkeitsmesser** *m* HEIZ & KÄLTE hair hygrometer; **Haargarnteppich** *m* TEXTIL haircord carpet; **Haarhygrometer** *nt* HEIZ & KÄLTE, LABOR, PHYS *Feuchtigkeitsmesser* hair hygrometer; **Haarkristall** *m* ELEKTRONIK, KUNSTSTOFF, METALL whisker; **Haarlineal** *nt* MASCHINEN knife edge straight edge, straight edge; **Haarlinie** *f* DRUCK hairline; **Haarnadelfeder** *f* MASCHINEN hairpin spring; **Haarnadeltrockner** *m* KER & GLAS hairpin cooler; **Haarriß** *m* FERTIG shatter crack, KERNTECH capillary crack, hairline crack, MECHAN hairline crack, TEXTIL craze; **Haarrißbildung** *f* FERTIG *Gießen*, KER & GLAS *auf Ziegeln, Glas* crazing; **Haar-Roving** *nt* KER & GLAS hairy roving; **Haarseite** *f* FERTIG *Riemen* grain side; **Haarspatium** *nt* DRUCK hairline space; **Haarstrich** *m* GERÄT *auf Skale* hairline

Habitus *m* METALL *Kristalle* habit; **Habitusfläche** *f* METALL habit plane

Hacker *m* TEXTIL *Spinnen* comb; **Hackerkamm** *m* TEXTIL doffer comb

Hackmaschine *f* PAPIER chipper

Hackmesser *nt* PAPIER chipper knife

Hackschnitzel *m* PAPIER chip

Häcksler *m* PAPIER chopper

Ha-Dec-Befestigung *f* RAUMFAHRT Ha-Dec mount

Hadernpapier *nt* DRUCK, PAPIER rag paper

Hadernsortierer *m* PAPIER rag sorter

HADES *abbr (Dielektronen-Spektrometer mit hoher Akzeptanz)* TEILPHYS HADES *(high acceptance di-electron spectrometer)*

Hadron *nt* PHYS, TEILPHYS hadron; **Hadron-Elektron-Ring-Anlage** *f* *(HERA)* TEILPHYS hadron-electron ring collider *(HERA)*

hadronisch¹ *adj* TEILPHYS hadronic

hadronisch:² ~**es Kalorimeter** *nt* STRAHLPHYS, TEILPHYS hadronic calorimeter

Hadron: **Hadronkollideranlage** *f* *(LHC)* PHYS large hadron collider *(LHC)*

Hafen *m* PHYS port, WASSERTRANS harbor (AmE), harbour (BrE), port; ~ **der Inbetriebnahme** *m* WASSERTRANS port of commissioning; **Hafenabstich** *m* KER & GLAS pot mouth; **Hafenamt** *nt* WASSERTRANS harbor master's office (AmE), harbour master's office (BrE); **Hafenarbeiter** *m* WASSERTRANS docker; **Hafenbahnhof** *m* EISENBAHN maritime terminal; **Hafenbecken** *nt* WASSERTRANS basin; **Hafenbehörde** *f* WASSERTRANS port authorities

Hafenbehörde: **sich bei der ~ melden** *v refl* WASSERTRANS report to the port authorities

Hafen: **Hafendamm** *m* BAU breakwater, WASSERTRANS mole; **Hafeneinrichtungen** *f pl* WASSERTRANS port facilities; **Hafeneinsatz** *m* KER & GLAS pot setting; **Hafenfähre** *f* WASSERTRANS harbor ferry (AmE), harbour ferry (BrE); **Hafengebühren** *f pl* WASSERTRANS harbor dues (AmE), harbour dues (BrE), port charges; **Hafengeld** *nt* WASSERTRANS harbor dues (AmE), harbour dues (BrE); **Hafengewölbe** *nt* KER & GLAS pot arch; **Hafenkapitän** *m* WASSERTRANS harbor master (AmE), harbour master (BrE); **Hafenkran** *m* WASSERTRANS quay crane; **Hafenkühlung** *f* KER & GLAS pot cooling; **Hafenmeister** *m* WASSERTRANS harbor master (AmE), harbour master (BrE)

Hafenofen: **im ~ erschmolzenes Opalglas** *nt* KER & GLAS pot opal; **im ~ erschmolzenen Rubinglas** *nt* KER & GLAS pot ruby

Hafen: **Hafenschlitten** *m* KER & GLAS pot carriage; **Hafenspeicher** *m* WASSERTRANS dock warehouse; **Hafenspeiserkopf** *m* KER & GLAS pot spout; **Hafensperre** *f* WASSERTRANS boom; **Hafenstadt** *f* WASSERTRANS port, seaport; **Hafenverwaltungsbüro** *nt* WASSERTRANS port administration office; **Hafenwache** *f* WASSERTRANS port watch; **Hafenzollamt** *nt* WASSERTRANS port custom house

Hafnium *nt* *(Hf)* CHEMIE hafnium *(Hf)*

HAF-Ruß *m* *(hochabriebfester Furnace-Ruß)* KUNSTSTOFF HAF carbon black *(high abrasion furnace carbon black)*

Haftband *nt* VERPACK pressure-sensitive tape

Haftbedingung *f* STRÖMPHYS no-slip condition

Haftbestückung *f* ELEKTRONIK surface mounting

Haften *nt* ELEKTROTECH sticking, FERTIG holding, KER & GLAS sticking

haften *vi* BAU stick, KUNSTSTOFF, PAPIER, VERPACK adhere

haftend *adj* PAPIER adherent

Haftenergie *f* METALL bond energy

Haftfähigkeit *f* PAPIER adhesiveness

haftfest *adj* ANSTRICH well-bonded

Haftfestigkeit *f* ANSTRICH bond strength, KERNTECH bonding strength, KUNSTSTOFF adhesive strength, bond strength, VERPACK adherence; **Haftfestigkeits-**

prüfung *f* KUNSTSTOFF adhesion test; **Haftfestigkeits-versuch** *m* MASCHINEN adhesion strength test

Haftgrund *m* KUNSTSTOFF primer, wash primer

Haftklebepapier *nt* VERPACK pressure-adhesive paper, pressure-sensitive paper

Haftmarkierung *f* KER & GLAS sticking mark

Haftmittel *nt* KUNSTSTOFF bonding agent

Haftprüfung *f* VERPACK bonding test

Haftpulver *nt* FERTIG *Fluoreszenzverfahren* blotter powder

Haftreibung *f* ERGON static friction, MASCHINEN static friction, stiction

haftreibungsfrei: **~er Oszillator** *m* ELEKTRONIK antistiction oscillator

Haftscheibe *f* VERPACK adhesive disc (BrE), adhesive disk (AmE)

Haftschicht *f* ANSTRICH bonding layer

Haftschweißen *nt* MECHAN tack welding

Haftstoff *m* RAUMFAHRT *Raumschiff* bonding agent

Haftung *f* ANSTRICH bond, BAU adhesion, bond, bonding, FERTIG stick, KOHLEN, KUNSTSTOFF adhesion, MEERSCHMUTZ liability

Haftverbindung *f* FERTIG joint

Haftvermittler *m* KUNSTSTOFF coupling agent, primer

Haftvermögen *nt* BAU adhesion, FERTIG *Riemen* grip, PAPIER adherence, tackiness, WERKPRÜF peel strength

Haftverstärker *m* KUNSTSTOFF adhesion promoter

Haftwasser *nt* ERDÖL *Geologie* interstitial water, KOHLEN pellicular water

Haftwert *m* KFZTECH adhesion coefficient

Hagen-Poisseuille: **~sches Gesetz** *nt* PHYS Hagen-Poisseuille law

Hager-Schleuderscheibe *f* KER & GLAS Hager disc (BrE), Hager disk (AmE)

Hahn *m* BAU cock, FERTIG *Kunststoffinstallationen* plug valve, valve, KERNTECH valve, LABOR *Bedienung* faucet (AmE), tap (BrE), MASCHINEN cock, faucet (AmE), spigot, tap (BrE), MECHAN cock, faucet (AmE), tap (BrE), valve, WASSERTRANS cock

Hahnepot *f* WASSERTRANS *Tauwerk* bridle

Hahn: **Hahnhülse** *f* LABOR *Spritzgerät* barrel; **Hahnkegel** *m* BAU plug; **Hahnküken** *nt* FERTIG taper plug, HYDRAUL plug; **Hahnventil** *nt* LABOR cock, MASCHINEN cock valve, MECHAN cock

Haidinger: **~sche Ringe** *m pl* PHYS Haidinger fringes

Haken[1] *m* BAU hook, FERTIG crochet, holdfast, HYDRAUL gab, KER & GLAS hook, pick, snap, MASCHINEN hook, MECHAN hitch, hook, TEXTIL hook; **~ zum Lösen der Fracht** *m* LUFTTRANS *Hubschrauber* cargo release hook

Haken:[2] **an ~ befestigen** *vt* MASCHINEN hook

Haken: **Hakenbügel** *m* BAU U-bolt; **Hakeneisen** *nt* KER & GLAS trying iron; **Hakenkeil** *m* FERTIG dog key; **Hakenlast** *f* ERDÖL *Bohrtechnik* hook load; **Hakenmarkierung** *f* KER & GLAS hook mark; **Hakennagel** *m* BAU spike; **Hakenschalter** *m* ELEKTROTECH gravity switch; **Hakenschlag** *m* WASSERTRANS blackwall hitch; **Hakenschlüssel** *m* MASCHINEN hook spanner; **Hakenschraube** *f* BAU screw hook, MASCHINEN hook bolt; **Hakenstift** *m* BAU sprig bolt; **Hakenverschluß** *m* VERPACK hooked lock; **Hakenzahn** *m* MASCHINEN peg tooth

halb:[1] **~e Fahrt voraus** *adv* WASSERTRANS half ahead; **~e Fahrt zurück** *adv* WASSERTRANS half astern

halb:[2] **~er Balken** *m* WASSERTRANS *Schiffbau* half beam; **~er Hub** *m* MASCHINEN midtravel; **~e Hubhöhe** *f* MA-

SCHINEN half-travel; **~er Schritt** *m* COMP & DV half-space

Halbacetal *nt* CHEMIE hemiacetal

Halbachse *f* GEOM semiaxis

Halbaddierer *m* COMP & DV, ELEKTRONIK *vernachlässigte Überträge* half-adder

halbaktiv: **~es Fahrwerk** *nt* LUFTTRANS semiactive landing gear; **~e Zielsuchlenkung** *f* LUFTTRANS homing semi-active guidance

Halbanthrazit *m* KOHLEN semianthracite

Halbautomatik *f* KFZTECH *Triebstrang, Getriebe* semiautomatic transmission

halbautomatisch[1] *adj* KER & GLAS, MASCHINEN, TELEKOM, VERPACK semiautomatic

halbautomatisch:[2] **~e Etikettiermaschine** *f* VERPACK semiautomatic labeling machine (AmE), semiautomatic labelling machine (BrE); **~er Fernbetrieb** *m* TELEKOM semiautomatic trunk working; **~e Paketiermaschine** *f* VERPACK semiautomatic strapping machine; **~es Pressen** *nt* KER & GLAS semiautomatic pressing; **~es System** *nt* TELEKOM semiautomatic system; **~er Vermittlungsschrank** *m* TELEKOM automanual switchboard

Halbband *m* DRUCK quarter binding

Halbbaum *m* TEXTIL *für Kettenwirkerei* half beam

halbberuhigt *adj* FERTIG *Stahl* balanced

halbbeweglich *adj* MASCHINEN semiportable

Halbbild *nt* FERNSEH field; **Halbbildabschluß** *m* FERNSEH interfield cut

Halbbinder *m* BAU half-truss

Halbbogen *m* BAU haunch

Halbbyte *nt* COMP & DV nibble, nybble

Halbcellulose *f* CHEMIE hemicellulose

Halbdach *nt* BAU pent roof

Halbdieselmotor *m* MASCHINEN semidiesel engine

Halbdunkelaufnahme *f* FOTO twilight shot

Halbduplex *m* COMP & DV half duplex

halbduplex *adj* *(HD)* COMP & DV half-duplex *(HDX)*

Halbduplex: **Halbduplexbetrieb** *m* COMP & DV half-duplex operation; **Halbduplexmodus** *m* COMP & DV half-duplex mode; **Halbduplex-Operation** *f* COMP & DV half-duplex operation

halbdurchlässig: **~e Farbe** *f* KER & GLAS semitransparent color (AmE), semitransparent colour (BrE); **~Fotokathode** *f* ELEKTROTECH semitransparent photocathode; **~e Membran** *f* PHYS semipermeable membrane; **~e Platte** *f* PHYS semireflecting plate; **~e Scheibe** *f* PHYS semireflecting plate

halbellipsenförmig: **~er Boden** *m* KERNTECH hemiellipsoidal bottom; **~er Deckel** *m* KERNTECH hemiellipsoidal head

Halbelliptikfeder *f* MASCHINEN half-elliptic spring, semielliptic spring

halbem: **mit ~ Wind segeln** *vi* WASSERTRANS *Segeln* sail on a beam reach

halbfest: **~er brennbarer Abfall** *m* UMWELTSCHMUTZ semisolid combustible waste

Halbfett *nt* DRUCK medium face

halbfett: **~e Kohle** *f* KOHLEN semibituminous coal; **~e Schrift** *f* DRUCK medium face

Halbfeuchttrennung *f* ABFALL semiwet sorting

halbfliegend: **~e Achse** *f* KFZTECH semifloating axle

halbformatig: **~e Leiterplatte** *f* ELEKTRONIK half-sized board

Halbfranzband *nt* DRUCK half-bound

halbgebleicht: **~er Zellstoff** *m* PAPIER semibleached pulp halbgedreht: ~e Treppe *f* BAU half-turn stairs

halbgekapselt: ~er Motor *m* ELEKTRIZ semienclosed motor

halbgerichtet: ~es Mikrofon *nt* AUFNAHME semidirectional microphone

halbgetaucht: ~es Tragflächenboot *nt* WASSERTRANS surface piercing craft

Halbgeviert *nt* DRUCK en; Halbgeviert-Zwischenraum *m* DRUCK en space

halbieren *vt* BAU halve, GEOM bisect

halbierend *adj* GEOM bisecting

Halbierung *f* GEOM bisection; Halbierungslinie *f* GEOM bisector; Halbierungspunkt *m* GEOM midpoint; Halbierungssuchverfahren *nt* COMP & DV dichotomizing search, TELEKOM binary search procedure

Halbimpuls *m* ELEKTRONIK *Daten* half-pulse

Halbinsel *f* WASSERTRANS peninsula

halbisolierend: ~es Trägermaterial *nt* ELEKTRONIK semi-insulating substrate

halbjährlich *adj* MATH biannual

halbkalibriert: ~e Walze *f* FERTIG half-roll

Halbkanten *f pl* GEOM half edges

Halbkartonaufrichter *m* VERPACK tray erector

Halbkettenfahrzeug *nt* TRANS half-track vehicle

halbklassisch: ~e Näherung *f* KERNTECH semiclassical approximation

halbkompiliert *adj* COMP & DV semicompiled

halbkontinuierlich: ~es Gießen *nt* KER & GLAS semicontinuous casting

Halbkreis *m* BAU, GEOM semicircle; Halbkreisbogen *m* BAU round arch, semicircular arch

halbkreisförmig *adj* GEOM, KERNTECH semicircular

halbkreisförmig: ~es Betaspektrometer *nt* KERNTECH semicircular beta spectrograph

Halbkugel *f* GEOM hemisphere; Halbkugelendspant *m* RAUMFAHRT *Raumschiff* hemispherical end rib

halbkugelförmig: ~er Brennraum *m* KFZTECH hemispherical combustion chamber

halbleitend *adj* ANSTRICH semiconductive

Halbleiter *m* COMP & DV semiconductor, solid, ELEKTRIZ, ELEKTRONIK, PHYS semiconductor, RADIO solid; ~ unter Elektronenbeschuß *m* ELEKTRONIK electron-bombarded semiconductor; ~ vom Typ n⁻ *m* ELEKTRONIK n⁻ type semiconductor; ~ vom Typ n⁺ *m* ELEKTRONIK n⁺-type semiconductor; Halbleiterband-Elementekonstruktion *f* ELEKTRONIK VMOS, vertical metal oxide semiconductor; Halbleiterbauelement *nt* COMP & DV semiconductor device, ELEKTRONIK semiconductor device, solid state device, TELEKOM solid state device; Halbleiterbauteil *nt* COMP & DV solid state device, ELEKTRONIK semiconductor component; Halbleiterchip *m* ELEKTRONIK semiconductor chip; Halbleiterdehnungsmeßstreifen *m* GERÄT semiconductor strain gage (AmE), semiconductor strain gauge (BrE); Halbleiterdiode *f* COMP & DV, ELEKTRONIK semiconductor diode; Halbleiterdotierung *f* ELEKTRONIK semiconductor doping; Halbleitereinkristall *m* ELEKTRONIK semiconductor single crystal; Halbleiter-Feldeffekttransistor mit Rückgatter *m* (*BMOSFET*) ELEKTRONIK back-gate metal-oxide semiconductor field-effect transistor (*BMOSFET*); Halbleiterfotodetektor *m* ELEKTRONIK semiconductor photodetector; Halbleitergleichrichter *m* ELEKTRIZ, ELEKTROTECH semiconductor rectifier; Halbleiterherstellung *f* ELEKTRONIK semiconductor fabrication; Halbleiterkamera *f* ELEKTRONIK solid state camera;

Halbleiterkomponente *f* ELEKTRONIK semiconductor component; Halbleiterkoppelpunkt *m* TELEKOM semiconductor crosspoint; Halbleiterkristall *m* ELEKTRONIK semiconductor crystal; Halbleiterkristallscheibe *f* ELEKTROTECH wafer; Halbleiterlaser *m* ELEKTRONIK semiconductor laser, solid state laser, OPTIK, STRAHLPHYS, TELEKOM semiconductor laser; Halbleitermaser *m* ELEKTRONIK solid state maser; Halbleitermaterial *nt* ELEKTRONIK semiconductor material; Halbleitermikrofon *nt* AUFNAHME semiconductor microphone; Halbleiterpapier *nt* PHOTO semiconductor layer paper; Halbleiterrelais *nt* ELEKTRIZ static relay, ELEKTROTECH semiconductor relay; Halbleiterschaltelement *nt* ELEKTRIZ semiconductor switching device; Halbleiterschalter *m* ELEKTROTECH semiconductor switch; Halbleiterscheibe *f* COMP & DV, ELEKTRONIK semiconductor wafer; Halbleiterschicht *f* ELEKTRONIK semiconductor layer; Halbleiterspeicher *m* COMP & DV, ELEKTROTECH semiconductor memory; Halbleitertechnik *f* ELEKTRONIK semiconductor technology; Halbleiterthermoelement *nt* GERÄT semiconductor thermocouple; Halbleiterträgermaterial *nt* ELEKTRONIK semiconductor substrate; Halbleiterverstärker *m* TELEKOM semiconductor amplifier; Halbleiterwerkstoff *m* ELEKTRONIK semiconductor material; Halbleiterwiderstand *m* ELEKTROTECH semiconductor resistor; Halbleiterzähler *m* STRAHLPHYS semiconductor counter

Halbmaske *f* SICHERHEIT half-mask

halbmast *adv* WASSERTRANS *Flagge* half-mast

halbmatt *adj* TEXTIL semimatt

Halbmesserlehre *f* FERTIG radius gage (AmE), radius gauge (BrE)

halbmondförmig *adj* GEOM crescent-shaped

Halbparabelbrücke *f* BAU hogbacked bridge

Halbportalkran *m* BAU semigantry crane

Halbradiallüfter *m* HEIZ & KÄLTE mixed-flow fan

Halbring *m* MASCHINEN half-ring

Halbbrücke *f* ELEKTROTECH half-bridge; Halbbrücken-Anordnung *f* ELEKTROTECH half-bridge arrangement

Halbrund *nt* ELEKTROTECH half round

halbrund: ~e Kante *f* KER & GLAS half-round edge

Halbrund: Halbrundfeile *f* MASCHINEN half-round file; Halbrundkopf *m* ELEKTRIZ button, MASCHINEN cup head, round head; Halbrundkopfschraube *f* MASCHINEN button-headed screw (AmE), cup head bolt, half-round screw; Halbrundniet *m* FERTIG button-headed rivet, round-head rivet; Halbrundschraube *f* FERTIG *Kunststoffinstallationen* securing screw, MASCHINEN button-headed screw (AmE), cup head bolt, half-round screw; Halbrundzange *f* MASCHINEN half-round pliers

Halbschale *f* MASCHINEN half-liner

Halbschatten:¹ im ~ *adj* OPTIK penumbral; ~ erzeugend *adj* OPTIK penumbrous

Halbschatten² *m* OPTIK, PHYS penumbra

Halbscheibe *f* MASCHINEN half-washer

Halbschnitt *m* FERTIG, KONSTZEICH half-section; Halbschnittzeichnung *f* KONSTZEICH half-section drawing

Halbschwingachse *f* KFZTECH de Dion axle

halbseitig: ~e Spur *f* AKUSTIK unilateral track

halbspröd: ~er Bruch *m* METALL semibrittle fracture

Halbstahl *m* METALL half-steel

halbstarr: ~e automatische Kupplung *f* KFZTECH semirigid automatic coupling

halbsteif: ~er Löschschlauch *m* SICHERHEIT *Feuerwehr-*

gerät semirigid delivery hose

halbstocks: ~ **setzen** *vt* WASSERTRANS *Flagge* half-mast

Halbstrahl *m* GEOM half-line

Halbsubtrahierer *m* COMP & DV, ELEKTRONIK half subtractor

Halbsubtrahierglied *nt* COMP & DV half subtractor

Halbsubtrahiersignal *nt* COMP & DV half subtractor

Halbtagstide *f* WASSERTRANS *Gezeiten* semidiurnal tide

Halbtaucher *m* ERDÖL *Offshore-Technik* semisubmersible rig

Halbtide *f* WASSERTRANS *Gezeiten* half-tide

Halbton *m* AKUSTIK semitone, DRUCK continuous tone, halftone, PHYS semitone

halbweiß: **~es Glas** *nt* KER & GLAS half-white glass

Halbwelle *f* ELEKTRIZ half wave, KFZTECH *Triebstrang* half shaft, PHYS, STRAHLPHYS half-wave; **Halbwellendipol** *m* PHYS half-wave dipole; **Halbwellendipolantenne** *f* STRAHLPHYS half-wave dipole aerial, half-wave dipole antenna; **Halbwellengleichrichter** *m* ELEKTROTECH half-wave rectifier; **Halbwellengleichrichtung** *f* ELEKTROTECH half-wave rectification; **Halbwellenleitung** *f* PHYS half-wave line

Halbwertdicke *f* PHYS half-thickness, half-value thickness

Halbwertsbreite *f* ELEKTRONIK half-power width, OPTIK FWHM, full width at half maximum, full duration at half maximum, PHYS, STRAHLPHYS half-width

Halbwertszeit *f* KERNTECH *(HWZ, $T^{1}/_2$)* half-life, operating lifetime, PHYS *(HWZ, $T^{1}/_2$)*, STRAHLPHYS *(HWZ, $T^{1}/_2$)*, TEILPHYS *(HWZ, $T^{1}/_2$)* half-life *($T^{1}/_2$)*, TELEKOM *(HWZ)* full duration half maximum *(FDHM)*; **Halbwertszeitbereich** *m* STRAHLPHYS range of half-life

Halbwort *nt* COMP & DV half-word

halbzählig[1] *adj* FERTIG *Spin* half-integer

halbzählig:[2] **~er Spin** *m* PHYS half-integral spin

Halbzellstoff *m* PAPIER semichemical pulp

Halbzeug *nt* ELEKTRIZ, KUNSTSTOFF semifinished product; **Halbzeugholländer** *m* PAPIER breaker

Halbzyklus *m* ELEKTROTECH half-cycle

Halde[1] *f* BAU spoil heap, stockpile, KOHLEN dump, tip

Halde:[2] **auf ~ lagern** *vt* BAU stockpile

Halde: **Haldenabfall** *m* KOHLEN tails; **Haldenabfallbeseitigung** *f* KOHLEN tail disposal; **Haldenkohle** *f* KOHLEN stock coal

Half-Plate-Kamera *f* FOTO half-plate camera

Hall: **~sche Beweglichkeit** *f* PHYS Hall mobility; **~scher Effekt** *m* ELEKTRIZ *durch querliegenden Strom und Magnetfeld erzeugte Spannung in Halbleitern*, PHYS, RAUMFAHRT, STRAHLPHYS Hall effect; **~sches Feld** *nt* PHYS Hall field; **~scher Geber** *m* KFZTECH Hall generator; **~scher Generator** *m* KFZTECH Hall generator; **~scher IC** *m* KFZTECH Hall IC; **~sches Ionentriebwerk** *nt* RAUMFAHRT *Raumschiff* Hall-ion thruster; **~scher Koeffizient** *m (RH)*, RADIO Hall coefficient *(RH)*; **~sches Magnetometer** *nt* PHYS Hall magnetometer; **~sche Mobilität** *f (µH)* RADIO Hall mobility *(µH)*; **~sche Sonde** *f* PHYS, STRAHLPHYS Hall probe; **~sche Spannung** *f* PHYS Hall voltage **~scher Widerstand** *m* PHYS Hall resistance

Halle *f* BAU shed; **Hallenschiff** *nt* BAU span

hallig: **~es Studio** *nt* AUFNAHME live studio

Halligkeit *f* AKUSTIK liveness

Hallraum *m* AKUSTIK echo chamber, reverberation room, AUFNAHME reverberant room, reverberation chamber, reverb

Hallwachs-Effekt *m* OPTIK photoemissive effect

Halo *m* RAUMFAHRT halo; **Haloantenne** *f* RADIO, RAUMFAHRT halo

Halogen *nt* CHEMIE halogen

halogenartig *adj* CHEMIE haloid

Halogenation *f* CHEMIE halogenation

Halogenid *nt* CHEMIE halide, halogenide

Halogenisierung *f* CHEMIE halogenation

Halogen: **Halogenkohlenwasserstoff** *nt* RAUMFAHRT *Raumschiff* halon; **Halogenkohlenwasserstoff-Kältemittel** *nt* HEIZ & KÄLTE halocarbon refrigerant; **Halogenlampe** *f* ELEKTRIZ halogen lamp; **Halogensilberemulsion** *f* FOTO silver halide emulsion; **Halogensilberpapier** *nt* FOTO silver halide paper

Halographie *f* CHEMIE halography

Halokinese *f* ERDÖL *Salztektonik* halokinesis

Halon *nt* RAUMFAHRT *Raumschiff* halon; **Halonfeuerlöscher** *m* SICHERHEIT halon fire extinguisher

Haloumlaufbahn *f* RAUMFAHRT halo orbit

Hals *m* ELEKTRONIK *einer Kathodenstrahlröhre*, KER & GLAS, KFZTECH, LABOR neck, MASCHINEN collar, neck, throat, WASSERTRANS *Segeln* tack

halsen[1] *vt* WASSERTRANS *Segeln* wear

halsen[2] *vi* WASSERTRANS *Segeln* jibe

Hals: **Halslager** *nt* MASCHINEN collar bearing, neck bearing; **Halsring** *m* KER & GLAS neck ring, *der Owens-Maschine* spout; **Halsringhalter** *m* KER & GLAS neck ring holder; **Halsstück** *nt* BAU throat; **Halszapfen** *m* MECHAN gudgeon pin (BrE)

Halt[1] *m* COMP & DV halt, KFZTECH, MASCHINEN, MECHAN stop

haltbar[1] *adj* KUNSTSTOFF lasting, TEXTIL fast; **~ bis zum** *adj* VERPACK best before

haltbar:[2] **~ machen** *vt* LEBENSMITTEL preserve, *Räuchern, Salzen, Pökeln* cure

Haltbarkeit *f* BAU service life, KUNSTSTOFF durability, shelf life, LEBENSMITTEL keeping quality, MASCHINEN, TEXTIL durability, VERPACK shelf impact; **Haltbarkeitsdatum** *nt* VERPACK sell-by date; **Haltbarkeitsdauer** *f* LEBENSMITTEL shelf life; **Haltbarkeitsprüfung** *f* VERPACK shelf life test; **Haltbarkeitstest** *m* VERPACK durability test

Halt: **Halteanode** *f* ELEKTROTECH holding anode, keepalive electrode; **Haltearm** *m* LUFTTRANS *Luftfahrzeug* hold; **Haltebedingung** *f* COMP & DV halt condition, stop condition; **Haltebefehl** *m* COMP & DV halt instruction, stop instruction; **Haltebremse** *f* EISENBAHN holding brake; **Haltebucht** *f* TRANS bus bay; **Haltecode** *m* COMP & DV stop code; **Haltefahrstreifen für Busse** *m* TRANS bus stopping lane; **Haltegestell für Reagenzgläser** *nt* LABOR rack for test tubes; **Halteimpuls** *m* COMP & DV hold; **Halteklemme für Mikroskopstellung** *f* LABOR clip of microscope stage; **Haltekraft** *f* BAU cohesion

Halten *nt* ELEKTROTECH *Quecksilberdampfröhren* holding, **~ einer Verbindung** *nt* TELEKOM call hold

halten *vt* TELEKOM put on hold

Halt: **Haltenetz** *nt* LUFTTRANS mooring harness; **Halteplatte** *f* MASCHINEN retaining plate; **Halteplattform** *f* KERNTECH holding pedestal; **Haltepodest** *nt* KERNTECH holding pedestal

Haltepunkt *m* KONTROLL breakpoint, MECHAN stop, PHYS recalescence, QUAL hold point; **~ bei Abkühlung** *m* FERTIG APT, Ar point, aspiration point temperature; **~ bei Erwärmung** *m* FERTIG decalescence point

Halter *m* FERTIG *Reibahle* arbor (AmE), arbour (BrE), *Schneidbacke* cap, KFZTECH handle, MASCHINEN holder, MECHAN clamp, fastener, handle

Haltering *m* LUFTTRANS mooring ring, MASCHINEN holding ring, retaining ring, MECHAN retaining ring

Halterung *f* FERTIG fastening, *Kunststoffinstallationen* bracket, holder, KER & GLAS mechanical boy, KFZTECH *für Karosserieblech* panel mounting, KOHLEN attachment, LUFTTRANS fairlead, MASCHINEN attachment, holder, holding fixture, support; **Halterungsklammer** *f* RAUMFAHRT *für Rakete beim Start* launcher release gear

Halt: **Halteschelle am Luftschraubenblatt** *f* LUFTTRANS *Hubschrauber* blade retention strap; **Halteseil** *nt* MASCHINEN holding rope; **Haltespeicher** *m* TELEKOM control memory, hold latch; **Haltestelle** *f* TEXTIL stopping mark, TRANS *Station* halt, stop; **Haltestift** *m* FERTIG retaining pin; **Haltestock** *m* BAU *Zimmermannsarbeiten* bench stop; **Haltestrahl** *m* COMP & DV, ELEKTRONIK *Computer*, STRAHLPHYS holding beam; **Haltestrom** *m* ELEKTRIZ, ELEKTROTECH holding current; **Halteturm mit Fluchtmöglichkeit** *m* RAUMFAHRT *Raumschiff* emergency escape tower; **Haltewicklung** *f* ELEKTRIZ *eines Relais* holding winding; **Haltezeit** *f* COMP & DV hold time, RADIO lock-up time, TRANS halt

Haltezustand: **im ~** *adj* TELEKOM on-hold

Halt: **Haltgliedsteuerung** *f* REGELUNG holding element control; **Haltscheibe** *f* EISENBAHN *für Rangierfahrten* stop signal; **Haltsignal** *nt* EISENBAHN stop board, stop signal

Haltung *f* ERGON attitude, posture

Hämatein *nt* CHEMIE haematein (BrE), hematein (AmE)

Hämatin *nt* CHEMIE haematin (BrE), hematin (AmE); **Hämatin-** *pref* CHEMIE haematic (BrE), hematic (AmE)

Hämatit *m* FERTIG haematite (BrE), hematite (AmE)

Hämatoporphyrin *nt* CHEMIE haematoporphyrin (BrE), hematoporphyrin (AmE)

Hämatoxylin *nt* CHEMIE haematoxylin (BrE), hematoxylin (AmE)

Hamilton- *pref* TEILPHYS Hamiltonian; **~scher Operator** *m* PHYS Hamiltonian operator; **~sche Funktion** *f (H)* HYDRAUL Hamiltonian function *(H)*; **~sche Gleichungen** *f pl* PHYS Hamilton's equations

Hamilton-Jacobi: **~sche Gleichung** *f* PHYS Hamilton-Jacobi equation

Hammer *m* KER & GLAS, KOHLEN, MASCHINEN hammer, MECHAN hammer, mallet; **~ mit gerader Finne** *m* BAU straight-pane hammer, straight-peen hammer; **~ mit Kugelfinne** *m* MASCHINEN ball-pane hammer, ball-peen hammer; **Hammerbacken** *m* FERTIG rotary swaging die; **Hammerbär** *m* FERTIG hammer tup

hämmerbar *adj* MECHAN malleable

Hämmerbarkeit *f* METALL ductility

Hammer: **Hammerbrecher** *m* KOHLEN, MASCHINEN hammer crusher; **Hammerfinne** *f* FERTIG hammer peen

hammergeschmiedet: **~es Teil** *nt* FERTIG hammered forging

Hammer: **Hammerhärten** *nt* METALL hammer hardening; **Hammerkopf** *m* MASCHINEN hammer head; **Hammerkopfschraube** *f* MASCHINEN T-head bolt, hammer-head bolt, hammer-head screw; **Hammermühle** *f* ABFALL hammer mill, hammer-mill crusher, LEBENSMITTEL hammer mill

Hämmern *nt* BAU hammering, FERTIG forging, swaging,

KERNTECH hammering, MASCHINEN hammering, peening

hämmern[1] *vt* BAU sledge, FERTIG chase, forge, peen, rotary-swage, MASCHINEN hammer

hämmern[2] *vi* BAU beat, MASCHINEN hammer

Hammer: **Hammernieten** *nt* FERTIG hammer riveting

hammernieten *vt* FERTIG hammer-rivet

Hammer: **Hammeröhr** *nt* FERTIG hammer eye

Hammerschlag *m* FERTIG forge scale, hammer scale, MASCHINEN hammer blow, MECHAN scale; **Hammerschlaganstrich** *m* KUNSTSTOFF hammer finish; **Hammerschlaglack** *m* KUNSTSTOFF hammer finish paint; **Hammerschraube** *f* MASCHINEN T-head bolt, hammer-head bolt, hammer-head screw; **Hammerschweißen** *nt* BAU forge welding; **Hammerunterbrecher** *m* ELEKTROTECH trembler; **Hammerzerkleinerer** *m* ABFALL hammer mill, hammer-mill crusher

Hamming-Abstand *m* TELEKOM Hamming distance

Hämoglobin *nt* CHEMIE haemoglobin (BrE), hemoglobin (AmE)

Hämolyse *f* CHEMIE haemolysis (BrE), hemolysis (AmE)

Hämolysin *nt* CHEMIE haemolysin (BrE), hemolysin (AmE)

Hämopyrrol *nt* CHEMIE haemopyrrole (BrE), hemopyrrole (AmE)

Hämosiderin *nt* CHEMIE haemosiderin (BrE), hemosiderin (AmE)

Hämotoxin *nt* CHEMIE haemotoxin (BrE), hemotoxin (AmE)

Hand:[1] **von ~** *adj* MECHAN manual; **von ~ zusammengestellt** *adj* VERPACK hand-assembled

Hand:[2] **von ~ bediente Maschine** *f* VERPACK hand-operated machine; **über die ~ übertragene Vibration** *f* SICHERHEIT hand-transmitted vibration

Hand:[3] **von ~ mischen** *vt* BAU *Beton* spade; **von ~ stampfen** *vt* FERTIG hand-ram

Hand-: *pref* DRUCK, FERTIG, KERNTECH, TELEKOM manual; **Handabschaltung** *f* KERNTECH manual shutdown; **Handapparat** *m* TELEKOM hand-held receiver; **Handapparateschnur** *f* TELEKOM handset cord; **Handarbeit** *f* DRUCK handwork, KER & GLAS offhand working; **Handarmatur** *f* FERTIG *Kunststoffinstallationen* hand-operated valve; **Hand-Arm-System** *nt* ERGON hand-arm system; **Handauflage** *f* MASCHINEN handrest, turning rest; **Handauflegeverfahren** *nt* KUNSTSTOFF hand lay-up; **Handauslösesignal** *nt* REGELUNG manually-operated releasing signal; **Handauslösung** *f* ELEKTRIZ manual reset; **Handautomatikschalter** *m* KERNTECH hand-automatic switch

handbedient[1] *adj* MECHAN hand-operated, manually-operated

handbedient:[2] **~er Drehzahlmesser** *m* VERPACK hand tachometer; **~es Fernsprechsystem** *nt* TELEKOM manual system; **~er Zug** *m* KERNTECH hand-operated pull

Hand-: **Handbedienung** *f* COMP & DV manual operation, MECHAN manual control, TELEKOM manual working

handbetätigt[1] *adj* KONTROLL, MASCHINEN hand-operated, manually-operated

handbetätigt:[2] **~er Schalter** *m* ELEKTRIZ hand-operated switch; **~es Werkzeug** *nt* MECHAN handtool

Hand-: **Handbetätigung** *f* COMP & DV manual operation, FERTIG *Kunststoffinstallationen* manual override; **Handbetrieb** *m* COMP & DV manual operation

handbetrieben *adj* KONTROLL, MECHAN, RAUMFAHRT hand-operated, manually-operated

Hand-: **Handbetriebsanzeiger** *m* FOTO manual control indicator; **Handblasebalg** *m* KER & GLAS hand bellow; **Handblechschere** *f* FERTIG handshears; **Handbohrer** *m* BAU gimlet, MASCHINEN hand brace, handdrill; **Handbohrmaschine** *f* MASCHINEN crank brace, MECHAN handdrill; **Handbremse** *f* KFZTECH handbrake, parking brake, MASCHINEN handbrake, MECHAN parking brake; **Handbuch** *nt* COMP & DV documentation, manual, KONTROLL manual, MASCHINEN handbook, RADIO manual; **Handdrahtzug** *m* KERNTECH hand wire pull

Handdruck *m* TEXTIL hand-block printing; **Handdruckmaschine** *f* DRUCK hand-printing machine

Hand-: **Handdurchschläger** *m* BAU nail set, set

Handels- *pref* WASSERTRANS merchant; **Handelsflotte** *f* WASSERTRANS *Handelsmarine* merchant fleet; **Handelsgüter** *nt pl* VERPACK goods; **Handelshafen** *m* WASSERTRANS trading port, *Hafen* commercial port; **Handelsmarine** *f* WASSERTRANS mercantile marine, merchant marine, merchant navy; **Handelsschiff** *nt* WASSERTRANS *Handelsmarine* merchant ship; **Handelsschiffsmatrose** *m* WASSERTRANS *Handelsmarine* merchant seaman; **Handelstoluol** *nt* CHEMIE toluol

handelsüblich: **~er Verstärker** *m* ELEKTRONIK commercial amplifier

Hand-: **Handendgerät** *nt* TELEKOM hand-held terminal; **Handetikettiermaschine** *f* VERPACK hand labeller; **Handfackel** *f* WASSERTRANS *Signal* handflare; **Handfeuerlöscher** *m* SICHERHEIT portable fire extinguisher; **Handform** *f* KUNSTSTOFF portable mold (AmE), portable mould (BrE); **Handfunksprechgerät** *nt* TELEKOM hand-carried transceiver; **Handgaszugsteuerung** *f* KFZTECH hand throttle control

handgeführt *adj* FERTIG *Läppwerkzeug* hand-held

Hand-: **Handgelenkschutz** *m* SICHERHEIT wrist protector

handgemischt: **~er Beton** *m* BAU hand-mixed concrete

Hand-: **Handgepäck** *nt* EISENBAHN hand luggage

handgeregelt *adj* ELEKTROTECH manually-controlled

Hand-: **Handgeschicklichkeit** *f* ERGON manual dexterity

handgeschöpft: **~es Papier** *nt* DRUCK handmade paper

Hand-: **Handgetriebe** *nt* FERTIG *Kunststoffinstallationen* manual drive unit, reduction gear; **Handgewindebohrer** *m* FERTIG handtap; **Handgießpfanne** *f* FERTIG handladle; **Handgriff** *m* BAU handle, MASCHINEN grip, handgrip

handhaben *vt* BAU handle, ERGON manipulate, MECHAN, WASSERTRANS *Schiff* handle

Handhabung *f* ERGON manipulation, TELEKOM, TEXTIL, VERPACK handling; **~ von Gütern** *f* VERPACK handling of goods; **~ von Mehrwegflaschen** *f* VERPACK handling of returnables; **Handhabungsgerät** *nt* ERGON manipulator

Handhebel *m* MASCHINEN hand lever; **Handhebelbohrer** *m* MASCHINEN sensitive drill; **Handhebelpresse** *f* KER & GLAS side lever press; **Handhebel-Reihenbohrmaschine** *f* MASCHINEN sensitive gang drill; **Handhebelschere** *f* FERTIG handshears, MASCHINEN crocodile shears; **Handhebelvorschub** *m* FERTIG sensitive feed, MASCHINEN hand lever feed

Handhebelvorschub: **mit ~** *adj* FERTIG sensitive

Hand-: **Handhubwagen** *m* VERPACK manual lift truck

Händigkeit *f* ERGON handedness

Hand-: **Handkette** *f* BAU handchain; **Handklassierung** *f*

KOHLEN hand screening; **Handkontrolle** *f* ELEKTRIZ manual control; **Handkreuz** *nt* FERTIG, MASCHINEN pilot wheel; **Handkurbel** *f* FERTIG ball handle crank, MASCHINEN manual crank, MECHAN crank; **Handlaminat** *nt* KUNSTSTOFF hand lay-up laminate; **Handlaminieren** *nt* KUNSTSTOFF hand lay-up; **Handlampe** *f* ELEKTRIZ portable lamp, ELEKTROTECH inspection lamp; **Handlauf** *m* BAU, KERNTECH, WASSERTRANS handrail; **Handlaufkrümmling** *m* BAU *Treppe* wreath; **Handleuchte** *f* BAU portable light

handlich *adj* MECHAN handy

Handling *nt* RAUMFAHRT *des Raumschiffs*, VERPACK handling

Hand-: **Handlocher** *m* COMP & DV keypunch; **Handluftschieber** *m* HEIZ & KÄLTE main valve, manual damper

Handlung *f* ERGON action; **Handlungsanalyse** *f* ERGON activity analysis; **Handlungsfolge** *f* ERGON serial behavior (AmE), serial behaviour (BrE); **Handlungsträger** *m* KÜNSTL INT actor

Hand-: **Handmaschinenvibration** *f* SICHERHEIT vibration emitted by portable hand-held machines; **Handmatrizen** *f pl* DRUCK sorts; **Handmikrofon** *nt* AUFNAHME hand microphone; **Handnachbildung** *f* ERGON artificial hand; **Handpeilkompaß** *m* WASSERTRANS hand-bearing compass; **Handpfanne** *f* FERTIG *Gießen* handladle; **Handpresse** *f* DRUCK handpress; **Handpressenrähmchen** *nt* DRUCK frisket; **Handpumpe** *f* FERTIG, SICHERHEIT *Feuerlöschgerät* handpump; **Handrad** *nt* FERTIG *Kunststoffinstallationen*, MASCHINEN, MECHAN handwheel; **Handregelung** *f* MASCHINEN manual setting, REGELUNG manual control; **Handreglerschalter** *m* REGELUNG manual control switch; **Handreibahle** *f* KFZTECH *Werkzeug*, MASCHINEN handreamer, reamer; **Handrückstellung** *f* ELEKTRIZ manual reset; **Handsäge** *f* BAU, MASCHINEN handsaw; **Handsatz** *m* DRUCK hand composition, hand setting, manual typesetting; **Handsauger** *m* KER & GLAS handsucker; **Handschachten** *nt* BAU shovel work; **Handschalten** *nt* ELEKTROTECH manual switching; **Handschalter** *m* REGELUNG manual control switch; **Handschere** *f* FERTIG handshears; **Handschleifen** *nt* MASCHINEN hand grinding; **Handschliff** *m* FERTIG offhand grinding; **Handschmierung** *f* MASCHINEN hand lubrication, manual lubrication; **Handschmiervorrichtung** *f* MASCHINEN manual-lubricating device; **Handschneidbrenner** *m* FERTIG hand flame-cutting torch; **Handschraube** *f* MASCHINEN handscrew; **Handschraubspindel** *f* MASCHINEN handscrew; **Handschraubstock** *m* MASCHINEN hand vice (BrE), hand vise (AmE); **Handschrifterkennung** *f* KÜNSTL INT handwriting recognition

Handschuh *m* FERTIG *Schweißen* gauntlet; **Handschuheingriff** *m* KERNTECH glove port; **Handschuhfach** *nt* KFZTECH *Innenausstattung* glove box (AmE), glove compartment (BrE); **Handschuhkasten** *m* KERNTECH glove box (AmE), glove compartment (BrE); **Handschuhöffnung** *f* KERNTECH glove port

Handschutz *m* SICHERHEIT handshield; **Handschutzschild** *m* BAU welding handshield

Hand-: **Handshake** *m* COMP & DV, KONTROLL handshake; **Handsiebdruck** *m* TEXTIL hand screen printing; **Handsignal** *nt* TRANS handsignal; **Handsortierung** *f* ABFALL *von Müll* hand sorting, manual sorting; **Handspindelbremse** *f* EISENBAHN screw brake with crank handle; **Handstellteil** *nt* ERGON hand control; **Handsteuerung** *f* BAU, ELEKTRIZ manual control, KERNTECH manual handling, LUFTTRANS manual control; **Handstichprobe** f KOHLEN hand sampling; **Handtalje** f WASSERTRANS *Deckausrüstung* handy billy, *Tauwerk* jigger; **Handtuchstoff** m TEXTIL towelling

Handvermittlung f TELEKOM manual board; **Handvermittlungsschrank** m TELEKOM cord switchbord; **Handvermittlungsstelle** f TELEKOM manual exchange

Hand-: **Handverpacken** nt VERPACK hand packing

Handvorschub: **mit ~ ausfräsen** vt FERTIG *Blech* rout

Hand-: **Handwagen** m TRANS trolley; **Handwasserspritze** f SICHERHEIT stirrup pump for water; **Handwerkszeug** nt BAU set of tools; **Handzeichen** nt SICHERHEIT hand signal; **Handzentrifuge** f LABOR *Trennen* hand centrifuge; **Handzufuhr** f VERPACK hand feed

Handzuführung:[1] **mit ~** adj DRUCK hand-fed

Handzuführung[2] f MASCHINEN hand feed; **Handzuführungslocher** m COMP & DV hand-feed punch

Handzustellung f MASCHINEN hand feed

Hanf m FERTIG, WASSERTRANS *Tauwerk* hemp; **Hanfdichtung** f FERTIG hemp packing; **Hanfseil** nt MASCHINEN, VERPACK hemp rope

Hang m KOHLEN slope

Hangar m LUFTTRANS hangar

Hängebahn f EISENBAHN suspended railroad (AmE), suspended railway (BrE)

Hängebaugerüst nt BAU boat scaffold

Hängebrücke f BAU cable-stayed bridge, suspension bridge

Hängebügel m MASCHINEN stirrup hanger

Hängebühne f BAU cradle, hanging scaffold

Hängedecke f KER & GLAS flying arch

Hängeeisen nt BAU hanger

Hängegerüst nt BAU flying scaffold, hanging scaffold, hanging stage, suspended scaffold, traveling cradle (AmE), travelling cradle (BrE)

Hängehaken m MASCHINEN suspension hook

Hangeinschnitt m BAU sidehill cut

Hängeisolator m ELEKTROTECH suspension insulator

Hängekran m MASCHINEN overhead crane, suspension crane, MECHAN overhead crane

Hängelager nt BAU hanger, MASCHINEN hanging bearing

Hängelampe f ELEKTRIZ luminaire, ELEKTROTECH hanging lamp

Hängelaufkran m MASCHINEN overhead traveling crane (AmE), overhead travelling crane (BrE)

Hängematte f WASSERTRANS hammock

hängend: **~er Einzug** m COMP & DV reverse indention; **~er Torpfosten** m BAU hanging post, hinge post; **~es Ventil** nt HYDRAUL *Dampfmaschine* drop valve, KFZTECH OHV, overhead valve

Hanger m WASSERTRANS *Tauwerk* topping lift

Hängeruder nt WASSERTRANS underhung rudder

Hängesäule f MASCHINEN joggle piece, joggle post, WASSERVERSORG *einer Schleuse* heelpost

Hängetrockner m PAPIER festoon dryer

Hängeventil nt HYDRAUL *Dampfmaschine* drop valve; **Hängeventilsteuerung** f HYDRAUL drop valvegear

Hängevorlagespeicher m HYDRAUL inverted pattern accumulator

Hangkanal m NICHTFOSS ENERG headrace canal, WASSERVERSORG headrace

Hank nt TEXTIL hank

Hantel f METALL dumbbell

haptisch adj ERGON *Tastsinn* haptic

Hardcopy f COMP & DV hard copy

Hardenit m METALL hardenite

Hardware f COMP & DV, TELEKOM hardware; **Hardware-Aufrüstung** f COMP & DV hardware upgrade; **Hardware-Ausrüstung** f COMP & DV hardware resources; **Hardware-Betriebsmittel** nt pl COMP & DV hardware resources; **Hardware-Fehler** m COMP & DV machine error; **Hardwarefehler** m COMP & DV hard failure; **Hardware-Kompatibilität** f COMP & DV hardware compatibility; **Hardware-Konfiguration** f COMP & DV hardware configuration

hardwarenah adj COMP & DV machine-intimate

Hardware: **Hardware-Service** m COMP & DV hardware maintenance; **Hardware-Sicherheit** f COMP & DV hardware security; **Hardware-Stack** m COMP & DV hardware stack; **Hardware-Unterbrechung** f COMP & DV hardware interrupt; **Hardware-Upgrade** nt COMP & DV hardware upgrade

Hardy-Scheibe f MASCHINEN Hardy disc (BrE), Hardy disk (AmE)

Harmalin nt CHEMIE harmaline

Harmin nt CHEMIE harmine, yageine

Harmonie f AKUSTIK harmony

Harmonik f AKUSTIK harmonics

Harmonika: **Harmonikatrennwand** f BAU slip partition

harmonisch[1] adj AKUSTIK harmonic

harmonisch:[2] **~er Analysator** m PHYS harmonic analyser (BrE), harmonic analyzer (AmE); **~e Analyse** f MATH, MECHAN, PHYS harmonic analysis; **~er Mischer** m ELEKTRONIK harmonic mixer; **~es Mittel** nt MATH harmonic mean; **~er Mittelwert** m MATH harmonic mean; **~e Molltonleiter** f AKUSTIK harmonic minor scale; **~e Ordnung** f ELEKTRONIK harmonic order; **~er Oszillator** m PHYS harmonic oscillator; **~e Reihe** f AKUSTIK harmonic series; **~e Schwingung** f ELEKTRONIK harmonic oscillation, PHYS harmonic vibration, *Oberschwingungen* harmonic oscillation; **~e Verzerrung** f AUFNAHME, ELEKTRONIK harmonic distortion; **~e Wellen** f pl WELLPHYS harmonic waves

Harmonische f AKUSTIK, MECHAN, RADIO harmonic; **~ höherer Ordnung** f ELEKTRONIK high-order harmonic; **~ niedriger Ordnung** f ELEKTRONIK low-order harmonic

Harn-: pref CHEMIE *Säure* uric

Harnstoff m CHEMIE carbamide, urea; **Harnstoffadditionsverbindung** f LEBENSMITTEL urea adduct; **Harnstoffaddukt** nt LEBENSMITTEL urea adduct

harnstoffausscheidend adj CHEMIE ureotelic

Harnstoff: **Harnstoff-Formaldehydharz** nt (*UFH*) ELEKTRIZ, FERTIG, KUNSTSTOFF urea formaldehyde resin (*UFR*); **Harnstoffharz** nt ELEKTRIZ, FERTIG, KUNSTSTOFF urea resin

Hart-: pref VERPACK rigid

hart:[1] **~ eingelötet** adj FERTIG sandwich-brazed; **mit ~em Kern** adj FERTIG hard-centered (AmE), hard-centred (BrE)

hart:[2] **~ aufgelötetes Plättchen** nt FERTIG brazed-on tip; **~er Begrenzer** m ELEKTRONIK hard limiter; **~e Begrenzung** f ELEKTRONIK hard limiting; **~es Bromsilberpapier** nt FOTO hard bromide paper; **~er Griff** m TEXTIL hard handle; **~er Kunststoff** m KUNSTSTOFF rigid plastic; **~e Landung** f LUFTTRANS hard landing, rough landing, RAUMFAHRT hard landing; **~e Röntgenstrahlen** m pl PHYS, STRAHLPHYS hard X-rays

härtbar adj MASCHINEN hardenable, THERMOD heat-treatable

Härtbarkeit f ANSTRICH, MASCHINEN, METALL hardenability

Hart-: **Hartblei** *nt* FERTIG antimonial lead

Härte *f* KUNSTSTOFF, MASCHINEN, MECHAN, METALL, PAPIER hardness; ~ **einer Prüfung** *f* QUAL test item; **Härtebad** *nt* FOTO hardener, METALL hardening bath, quenching bath; **Härtegeschwindigkeit** *f* KUNSTSTOFF cure rate; **Härtegrad** *m* KER & GLAS temper, MASCHINEN grade, hardness, METALL temper

Hart-: **Harteisen** *nt* METALL hard iron

Härte: **Härtekomponente** *f* KUNSTSTOFF hardener

Härtemesser *m* KUNSTSTOFF, LABOR durometer

Härten *nt* KOHLEN, KUNSTSTOFF, MASCHINEN, METALL hardening, TEXTIL baking

härten *vt* ANSTRICH *Legierungen* temper, BAU condition, CHEMIE *Fett, Öl* hydrogenate, KUNSTSTOFF cure, LEBENSMITTEL *Fett, Öl* hydrogenate, MASCHINEN, METALL harden

härtend: **~es Säurebad** *nt* FOTO acid-hardening bath

Härte: **Härteofen** *m* FERTIG quench furnace, METALL hardening furnace; **Härteöl** *nt* CHEMIE tallow oil; **Härteprüfer** *m* LABOR durometer, hardness tester, MASCHINEN, PAPIER hardness tester; **Härteprüfgerät** *nt* KUNSTSTOFF durometer

Härter *m* KER & GLAS *auf der Glasur* hardening, KUNSTSTOFF hardener

Härte: **Härterei** *f* METALL hardening shop; **Härteriß** *m* THERMOD heat treatment crack; **Härteskala** *f* MECHAN hardness scale; **Härtetest** *m* MECHAN, PHYS hardness test; **Härtetester** *m* METROL hardness tester; **Härtezeit** *f* KUNSTSTOFF curing time, setting time

Hart-: **Hartfaserplatte** *f* BAU hardboard; **Hartfett** *nt* LEBENSMITTEL hydrogenated fat

hartformatiert[1] *adj* COMP & DV hard-sectored

hartformatiert:[2] **~e Platte** *f* COMP & DV hard-sectored disk

Hart-: **Hartformatierung** *f* COMP & DV hard-sectoring

hartgelötet *adj* FERTIG brazed, hard-soldered, THERMOD brazed

Hart-: **Hartgesteinbohrmeißel** *m* ERDÖL *Bohrtechnik* hard formation bit

hartgezogen *adj* THERMOD cold-drawn

Hart-: **Hartglas** *nt* BAU toughened glass, KER & GLAS fused silica, hard glass, tempered glass, METALL silica glass; **Hartgummi** *nt* ELEKTRIZ vulcanite, KUNSTSTOFF ebonite, vulcanite; **Hartgußeisen** *nt* METALL hard cast iron; **Hartgußstrahlmittel** *nt* METALL chill cast shot; **Hartholz** *nt* BAU hardwood; **Hartimpuls** *m* ELEKTRONIK hard pulse; **Hartkautschuk** *m* KUNSTSTOFF ebonite, vulcanite; **Hartlandung** *f* LUFTTRANS hard landing, rough landing, RAUMFAHRT hard landing

Hartlegierung *f* FERTIG hard alloy; **Hartlegierungsauflage** *f* FERTIG alloy facing

Hartlegierungsauflage: **mit ~** *adj* FERTIG alloy-faced

Hartley-Oszillator *m* ELEKTRONIK Hartley oscillator

Härtling *m* FERTIG hard head

Hart-: **Hartlot** *nt* MASCHINEN brazing solder; **Hartlötbrenner** *m* BAU brazing blowpipe

Hartlöten *nt* ELEKTRIZ, FERTIG hard-soldering, THERMOD brazing

hartlöten *vt* FERTIG braze, hard-solder, MASCHINEN, MECHAN, THERMOD braze

Hartlötflußmittel *nt* BAU brazing flux

Hartlötung *f* FERTIG hard solder, *Lötmittel* brazing, *Verfahren* braze, MASCHINEN brazing, METALL *Lötmittel* hard solder, hard-brazing solder, SICHERHEIT *Verfahren* brazing

hartmagnetisch: **~er Werkstoff** *m* MECHAN, PHYS hard magnetic material

Hart-: **Hartmessinglot** *nt* METALL hard brass solder

Hartmetall *nt* FERTIG carbide, cemented carbide, MASCHINEN tungsten carbide; **Hartmetallauflage** *f* MECHAN hard-facing

hartmetallbestückt[1] *adj* MASCHINEN carbide-tipped

hartmetallbestückt:[2] **~er Drehstahl** *m* MASCHINEN turning tool with carbide tip; **~er Meißel** *m* MASCHINEN carbide-tipped tool

Hartmetall: **Hartmetallgesenk** *nt* FERTIG carbide die; **Hartmetallmeißel** *m* FERTIG, MASCHINEN carbide tool; **Hartmetallscheibe** *f* FERTIG *Bohrer* carbide tip; **Hartmetallschneidplättchen** *nt* MASCHINEN carbide tip; **Hartmetallspitze** *f* MASCHINEN tungsten carbide tip; **Hartmetall-Wendeschneidplatte** *f* MASCHINEN indexable hard metal insert; **Hartmetallwerkzeug** *nt* MASCHINEN tungsten carbide tool

Hart-: **Hartpappe** *f* VERPACK hardboard, millboard; **Hartperlit** *m* METALL troostite; **Hartporzellan** *nt* KER & GLAS hard porcelain; **Hart-PVC** *nt* VERPACK rigid PVC; **Hartroheisen** *nt* METALL hard pig iron; **Hartrudersignal** *nt* ELEKTRONIK *Luftfahrt* hard-over signal; **Hartschmiedeeisen** *nt* METALL hard iron; **Hartschweißen** *nt* BAU hard-facing; **Hartsektorieren** *nt* COMP & DV hard-sectoring

hartsektoriert[1] *adj* COMP & DV hard-sectored

hartsektoriert:[2] **~e Platte** *f* COMP & DV hard-sectored disk

Hart-: **Hartstrahlung** *f* STRAHLPHYS hard radiation; **Hartumpolung** *f* TELEKOM line reversal

Härtung *f* KUNSTSTOFF curing, LEBENSMITTEL *Fett, Öl* hydrogenation, METALL hardening; **~ durch Diffusion** *f* KERNTECH *des Neutronenspektrums* diffusion hardening

Hart-: **Hartverchromung** *f* FERTIG industrial chromium plating, MASCHINEN hard chromium plating; **Hartweizen** *m* LEBENSMITTEL durum wheat; **Hartzinn** *nt* FERTIG pewter

Harz *nt* FERTIG gum, KUNSTSTOFF, TEXTIL resin; **~ im A-Zustand** *nt* KUNSTSTOFF A-stage resin, resol; **~ im B-Zustand** *nt* KUNSTSTOFF B-stage resin; **~ im C-Zustand** *nt* KUNSTSTOFF C-stage resin, resite; **~ für Formmaskenverfahren** *nt* KUNSTSTOFF shell-molding resin (AmE), shell-moulding resin (BrE); **~ im Resolzustand** *nt* KUNSTSTOFF A-stage resin, resol

harzartig *adj* FERTIG gummy

harzfrei *adj* FERTIG nonresinous

harzgebunden: **~es Sperrholz** *nt* KUNSTSTOFF resin-bonded plywood

Harz: **Harzmittel** *nt* FERTIG binder; **Harzrückstand** *m* FERTIG *Öl* gum; **Harzträger** *m* FERTIG filler

Hash *m* COMP & DV hash; **Hash-Code** *m* COMP & DV hash code; **Hash-Funktion** *f* COMP & DV hash function

Hashing *nt* COMP & DV *Abbildung mit Hilfe der Streuspeichertechnik* hashing

Hash: **Hash-Tabelle** *f* COMP & DV hash table; **Hash-Verfahren** *nt* COMP & DV *Abbildung mit Hilfe der Streuspeichertechnik* hashing; **Hash-Zeichen** *nt* COMP & DV hashmark

Haspe *f* BAU *Fenster, Tür* knuckle, *Schloß* hasp, staple

Haspel *f* AUFNAHME reel, BAU winder, FERTIG reel, roll, spool, KER & GLAS winder, PAPIER reel, TEXTIL winch

Haspeln *nt* BAU winding

haspeln *vt* TEXTIL wind

Haspeltrommel *f* TEXTIL swift

Haspen *m* FERTIG catch

Hatchettin *m* KERNTECH hatchettite, PHYS *Mineralogie* adipocerite

Haube *f* BAU coping, COMP & DV hood, ELEKTROTECH cap, FERTIG *Wärmebehandlung* bell, LABOR *eines Destillationsapparats* head, MASCHINEN bonnet (BrE), hood (AmE), shroud, MECHAN cap, PAPIER hood, SICHERHEIT cover; **Haubenschloß** *nt* KFZTECH bonnet catch (BrE), hood catch (AmE); **Haubenverkleidung** *f* MECHAN cowl

Haueisen *nt* BAU mattock

Hauen *nt* MASCHINEN cutting

hauen *vt* KOHLEN hew

Hauer *m* BAU *von Stein, Holz* hewer

Haufen *m* BAU heap; **Haufenwolke** *f* LUFTTRANS, WASSERTRANS cumulus

Häufigkeit *f* PHYS abundance; ~ **der Elemente** *f* STRAHLPHYS nuclear abundance; **Häufigkeitsdichte** *f* ELEKTRONIK, RADIO, TELEKOM frequency density; **Häufigkeitskoeffizient** *m* WASSERVERSORG coefficient of abundance; **Häufigkeitsverteilung** *f* RADIO frequency distribution

haufwerksporig: ~**er Beton** *m* BAU no-fines concrete

Haupt *nt* MASCHINEN head; **Haupt-** *pref* COMP & DV, RADIO master; **Haupt- und Nebenkanäle** *m pl* HEIZ & KÄLTE main and branch ductwork; **Hauptabrechnungsstelle** *f* TELEKOM major account holder; **Hauptachse** *f* GEOM major axis, MASCHINEN main axle, OPTIK *eines gewölbten Spiegels oder einer Linse*, PHYS *eines Festkörperkristalls* principal axis; **Hauptalarm** *m* TELEKOM major alarm; **Hauptamt** *nt* TELEKOM central exchange, host exchange, main exchange; **Hauptanode** *f* ELEKTROTECH main anode; **Hauptanschlußbereich eines Fernamtes** *m* TELEKOM main trunk exchange area; **Hauptanschlußbereich einer Fernvermittlungsstelle** *m* TELEKOM main trunk-switching center area (AmE), main trunk-switching centre area (BrE); **Hauptanschlußklemme** *f* KFZTECH main terminal; **Hauptanschlußleitung** *f* TELEKOM main line; **Hauptansicht** *f* KONSTZEICH principal view; **Hauptantrieb** *m* MASCHINEN main drive, master drive; **Hauptantriebswelle** *f* KFZTECH *Getriebe* mainshaft, LUFTTRANS *Hubschrauber* main drive shaft; **Hauptantriebszahnrad** *nt* KFZTECH main drive gear; **Hauptanzapfstelle** *f* ELEKTRIZ principal tapping; **Hauptauftragnehmer** *m* BAU general contractor; **Hauptausfall** *m* LUFTTRANS *einer technischen Anlage* basic failure; **Hauptbalken** *m* BAU main beam; **Hauptband** *nt* COMP & DV master tape; **Hauptbatterie** *f* LUFTTRANS *eines Luftfahrzeugs* main battery; **Hauptbehälterdruck** *m* EISENBAHN *Bremse* main air reservoir pressure; **Hauptbewehrung** *f* BAU main reinforcement; **Hauptblatt** *nt* KFZTECH *der Blattfeder* main leaf, top leaf; **Hauptbremsleitung** *f* EISENBAHN main brake pipe; **Hauptbremsschlauch** *m* EISENBAHN main brake hose; **Hauptbremszylinder** *m* KFZTECH brake master cylinder, master cylinder; **Hauptbrenner** *m* HEIZ & KÄLTE main burner; **Hauptdampf** *m* KERNTECH mainsteam; **Hauptdampfleitung** *f* HYDRAUL mainsteam pipe; **Hauptdatei** *f* COMP & DV master file; **Hauptdatenstation** *f* COMP & DV master terminal; **Hauptdeck** *nt* WASSERTRANS main deck; **Hauptdüse** *f* KFZTECH *Vergaser* main jet; **Hauptebene** *f* FOTO nodal plane, principal plane, OPTIK principal plane; **Haupteinflugzeichen** *nt* LUFTTRANS *ILS* middle marker; **Haupteintrag** *m* COMP & DV primary entry; **Hauptentladungsstrecke** *f* ELEKTROTECH main gap;

Hauptentwässerungsleitung *f* BAU main sewer; **Haupterzeugnis** *nt* LEBENSMITTEL staple

Hauptfahrwerk *nt* LUFTTRANS *Hubschrauber* main-landing gear; **Hauptfahrwerkachsenträger** *m* LUFTTRANS main gear axle beam; **Hauptfahrwerkschiebeklappe** *f* LUFTTRANS main gear-sliding door; **Hauptfahrwerksklappe** *f* LUFTTRANS main landing gear door; **Hauptfahrwerksstützstrebe** *f* LUFTTRANS main landing gear brace strut

Haupt: **Hauptfaktor** *m* TEXTIL chief factor; **Hauptfeder** *f* MASCHINEN mainspring; **Hauptfehler** *m* QUAL major defect, major failure; **Hauptförderstrecke** *f* KOHLEN gangway; **Hauptfreifläche** *f* FERTIG major flank; **Hauptgasleitung** *f* THERMOD gas main; **Hauptgebälk** *nt* BAU principal; **Hauptgleis** *nt* EISENBAHN main track; **Haupthahn** *m* MASCHINEN main tap; **Hauptintensität** *f* OPTIK principal maxima; **Hauptkabel** *nt* ELEKTROTECH main; **Hauptkarte** *f* COMP & DV master card; **Hauptknotenpunkt** *m* EISENBAHN major railroad junction (AmE), major railway junction (BrE); **Hauptkonsole** *f* COMP & DV master console; **Hauptkontakte** *m pl* ELEKTRIZ main contacts; **Hauptkrümmung** *f* KER & GLAS principal curvature; **Hauptlager** *nt* BAU, KFZTECH, MASCHINEN, WASSERTRANS main bearing; **Hauptlagerbuchse** *f* KFZTECH main-bearing bushing; **Hauptlagerhülse** *f* KFZTECH main-bearing bushing; **Hauptlandevorrichtung** *f* LUFTTRANS *Hubschrauber* main-landing gear; **Hauptlast** *f* BAU main load; **Hauptleitung** *f* BAU main line, *Wasser, Strom* main, COMP & DV ethyne, ELEKTROTECH bus, main, HEIZ & KÄLTE main, WASSERVERSORG head pipe; **Hauptluftbehälter** *m* EISENBAHN *Bremse* main air reservoir; **Hauptmaske** *f* ELEKTRONIK master mask; **Hauptmaßstab** *m* KONSTZEICH principal scale; **Hauptmast** *m* WASSERTRANS *Segeln* mainmast; **Hauptmaximum** *nt* PHYS principal maxima; **Hauptmenge** *f* PHYS bulk; **Hauptmischregler** *m* FERNSEH master control fader; **Hauptmodus** *m* RAUMFAHRT *Raumschiff* fundamental mode; **Hauptmonitor** *m* FERNSEH master monitor; **Hauptmotor** *m* LUFTTRANS master engine; **Hauptnetzleitung** *f* ELEKTRIZ trunk main; **Hauptnormal** *nt* QUAL master standard, primary standard; **Hauptplatine** *f* COMP & DV motherboard, wraparound, ELEKTRONIK motherboard; **Hauptplatte** *f* COMP & DV master disk; **Hauptpleuel** *nt* MASCHINEN main rod; **Hauptpleuelstange** *f* MASCHINEN main rod; **Hauptpol** *m* ELEKTRIZ main pole, ELEKTROTECH field pole; **Hauptpresse** *f* PAPIER main press; **Hauptprogramm** *nt* TRANS master program (AmE), master programme (BrE); **Hauptprozessor** *m* TELEKOM master processor, regional processor; **Hauptpunkte** *m pl* OPTIK cardinal points, PHYS principal points; **Hauptquantenzahl** *f* LUFTTRANS main quantum number, PHYS principal quantum number; **Hauptquelle** *f* UMWELTSCHMUTZ major source; **Hauptrechner** *m* COMP & DV host computer, master computer; **Hauptregelventil** *nt* KFZTECH main regulator valve; **Hauptregieraum** *m* FERNSEH central control room; **Hauptregler** *m* FERNSEH master control; **Hauptrichtantenne** *f* RAUMFAHRT *Weltraumfunk* main beam; **Hauptrippe** *f* LUFTTRANS main rib; **Hauptriß** *m* METALL main crack; **Hauptrohrleitung** *f* UMWELTSCHMUTZ pipeline

Hauptrotor *m* LUFTTRANS *Hubschrauber* main rotor; **Hauptrotorblatt** *nt* LUFTTRANS main rotor blade; **Hauptrotorkopf** *m* LUFTTRANS main rotor head; **Hauptrotornabe** *f* LUFTTRANS main rotor hub; **Haupt-**

rotorwelle *f* LUFTTRANS main rotor shaft

Haupt: **Hauptroutine** *f* COMP & DV main routine, master routine; **Hauptrücksetzsignal** *nt* KONTROLL master reset signal; **Hauptsammelkanal** *m* ABFALL interceptor sewer, BAU main sewer; **Hauptsammelschiene** *f* ELEKTROTECH main bar, TELEKOM main busbar; **Hauptsammler** *m* ABFALL interceptor sewer, main collector, main sewer, BAU *Abwasser* main drain; **Hauptsatz** *m* COMP & DV master record; **Hauptsatz der Thermodynamik** *m* THERMOD law of thermodynamics; **Hauptschalter** *m* ELEKTRIZ, ELEKTROTECH main switch, master switch, FERNSEH master switch

Hauptschaltgetriebe *nt* LUFTTRANS *Hubschrauber* main gearbox; **Hauptschaltgetriebeaufnahme** *f* LUFTTRANS main gearbox support; **Hauptschaltgetriebegehäusearm** *m* LUFTTRANS main gearbox support; **Hauptschaltgetriebehalterung** *f* LUFTTRANS main gearbox support

Haupt: **Hauptschaltkontakte** *m pl* ELEKTRIZ main-switching contacts; **Hauptschenkel** *m* KERNTECH *eines Transformatorkernes* main leg; **Hauptschiene** *f* ELEKTROTECH main bar; **Hauptschiffahrtsroute** *f* WASSERTRANS *Seehandel* main-trading route; **Hauptschlüssel** *m* BAU master key; **Hauptschlußmaschine** *f* ELEKTRIZ series-excited machine; **Hauptschlußmotor** *m* ELEKTRIZ series motor; **Hauptschneide** *f* FERTIG active-cutting edge, lip, major-cutting edge, working cutting edge, MASCHINEN major-cutting edge; **Hauptschnittdruck** *m* FERTIG main tool thrust; **Hauptschnittfläche** *f* FERTIG work surface; **Hauptschnittkraft** *f* FERTIG main-cutting force

Hauptsignal *nt* EISENBAHN home signal; **Hauptsignalsteuergerät** *nt* RAIL *Verkehrsregelung* master controller

Haupt: **Hauptskalenteilung** *f* GERÄT major graduation; **Hauptsolargenerator** *m* RAUMFAHRT *Raumschiff* main solar generator; **Hauptspant** *nt* WASSERTRANS *Schiffbau* midship frame, midship section; **Hauptsparren** *m* BAU principal rafter

Hauptspeicher *m* COMP & DV central memory, main memory, main store, primary memory, primary storage, primary store; **Hauptspeicherabbild** *nt* COMP & DV memory map; **Hauptspeicherauszug** *m* COMP & DV memory dump; **Hauptspeichererweiterung** *f* COMP & DV memory expansion; **Hauptspeicherkapazität** *f* COMP & DV memory capacity; **Hauptspeicherstruktur** *f* COMP & DV memory map; **Hauptspeicherzugriff** *m* COMP & DV memory access

Haupt: **Hauptspindel** *f* MASCHINEN main spindle; **Hauptspindelgetriebe** *nt* LUFTTRANS headgear; **Hauptstart- und Landebahn** *f* LUFTTRANS main runway, primary runway; **Hauptstation** *f* COMP & DV master station; **Hauptstellenimpuls** *m* ELEKTRONIK master pulse; **Hauptsteuerpult** *nt* FERNSEH master control panel; **Hauptstrahl** *m* OPTIK, PHYS principal ray, RAUMFAHRT *Weltraumfunk* main beam; **Hauptstrecke** *f* EISENBAHN arterial railroad (AmE), arterial railway (BrE), main line, main-line railroad (AmE), main-line railway (BrE), ELEKTROTECH main gap

Hauptstrom *m* ELEKTRIZ main current, ELEKTROTECH series

hauptstromgeregelt: **~es Netzgerät** *nt* ELEKTROTECH series-regulated power supply

Hauptstrom: **Hauptstromkreis** *m* ELEKTRIZ main circuit; **Hauptstromölfilter** *nt* KFZTECH *Schmierung* full-flow oil filter; **Hauptstromregelung** *f* ELEKTROTECH series

regulation; **Hauptstromregler** *m* ELEKTROTECH series regulator

Haupttakt *m* TELEKOM master clock; **Haupttaktgeber** *m* COMP & DV master clock

Haupt: **Hauptteilstrich** *m* GERÄT major graduation; **Hauptterminal** *nt* COMP & DV central terminal; **Hauptträger** *m* BAU main girder; **Hauptträgheitsachse** *f* MASCHINEN main axis of inertia; **Haupttrennventil** *nt* KERNTECH main-isolating valve; **Haupttriebwerk** *nt* LUFTTRANS master engine; **Haupttyp** *m* ELEKTROTECH *Wellenleiter* dominant mode; **Hauptuhr** *f* COMP & DV master clock; **Hauptverbindung** *f* COMP & DV busbar, EISENBAHN main line; **Hauptverbindungsstraße** *f* TRANS main road

Hauptverkehr *m* EISENBAHN peak hour traffic; **Hauptverkehrsader** *f* TRANS thoroughfare (BrE), thruway (AmE); **Hauptverkehrsstraße** *f* TRANS arterial highway (AmE), arterial motorway (BrE), arterial road, main road; **Hauptverkehrsstunde** *f* *(HVStd)* TELEKOM busy hour; **Hauptverkehrszeit** *f* EISENBAHN peak hours, TELEKOM busy period, TRANS peak hour

Haupt: **Hauptvermittlungsstelle** *f* *(HVSt)* TELEKOM main exchange; **Hauptverstärker** *m* *(PA)* PHYS power amplifier *(PA)*; **Hauptverstärkerröhre** *f* ELEKTRONIK power amplifier tube; **Hauptverstärkertransistor** *m* ELEKTRONIK power amplifier transistor; **Hauptverstärkungsregler** *m* AUFNAHME, ELEKTRONIK master gain control; **Hauptverteiler** *m* *(HVt)* TELEKOM main distribution frame *(MDF)*; **Hauptverteiler für Verstärkerämter** *m* TELEKOM main repeater distribution frame; **Hauptverteilung** *f* TELEKOM *Starkstromtechnik* distribution center (AmE), distribution centre (BrE); **Hauptvorschubbewegung** *f* MASCHINEN main feed motion; **Hauptwärmeaustauscher** *m* LUFTTRANS primary heat exchanger; **Hauptwasserleitung** *f* WASSERVERSORG delivery main, mains (BrE), supply network (AmE), water main; **Hauptwasserrohr** *nt* WASSERVERSORG water main; **Hauptwechsel** *m* TRANS master change; **Hauptwelle** *f* KFZTECH, LUFTTRANS, MASCHINEN, MECHAN mainshaft; **Hauptwellenlager** *nt* WASSERTRANS *Schiffbau* mainshaft bearing; **Hauptwert** *m* MATH median; **Hauptzeichnung** *f* KONSTZEICH general arrangement drawing; **Hauptzeit beim Schleifen** *f* FERTIG actual-grinding time; **Hauptzylinder** *m* KFZTECH, LUFTTRANS *Bremse* master cylinder

Haus *nt* BAU domestic; **Hausanschlußkasten** *m* BAU *Elektroversorgung* branch box; **Hausbrandkohle** *f* KOHLEN domestic coal

Hausenblase *f* LEBENSMITTEL *Klärmittel* isinglass

Haushalt *m* WASSERVERSORG household; **Haushaltabfall** *m* WASSERVERSORG domestic waste; **Haushaltabwasser** *nt* WASSERVERSORG domestic waste water; **Haushaltabwässer** *nt pl* ABFALL household wastewater; **Haushaltboiler** *m* HEIZ & KÄLTE, MASCHINEN domestic boiler; **Haushaltbrennstoff** *m* KOHLEN household fuel; **Haushaltelektronik** *f* ELEKTROTECH domestic electronic equipment

Haushalten *nt* SICHERHEIT good housekeeping

Haushalt: **Haushaltgasgerät** *nt* HEIZ & KÄLTE domestic gas appliance; **Haushaltkeramik** *f* KER & GLAS crockery ware; **Haushaltkühlschrank** *m* MASCHINEN domestic refrigerator, household refrigerator; **Haushaltnetzinstallation** *f* ELEKTROTECH domestic electric installation; **Haushaltporzellan** *nt* KER & GLAS household porcelain; **Haushaltroboter** *m* KÜNSTL INT domestic robot; **Haushalttextilien** *f pl* TEXTIL household textiles

Haushaltung f RAUMFAHRT housekeeping

Haushalt: **Haushaltverbraucher** m ELEKTRIZ domestic consumer; **Haushaltwasser** nt WASSERVERSORG domestic water; **Haushaltwasserversorgung** f WASSERVERSORG domestic water supply

Hausinstallation f ELEKTRIZ indoor installation; **Hausinstallationskabel** nt ELEKTRIZ indoor cable; **Hausinstallationsschalter** m ELEKTRIZ house-wiring switch

Haus: **Hausisolierung** f ELEKTRIZ indoor insulation; **Hauskorrektur** f DRUCK house corrections; **Hausleiterkabel** nt ELEKTRIZ indoor cable; **Hausmüll** m ABFALL consumer waste, domestic waste, UMWELTSCHMUTZ consumer waste, domestic waste, municipal waste, WASSERVERSORG municipal waste; **Hausmülldeponie** f ABFALL municipal waste landfill; **Hausmüllzusammensetzung** f ABFALL waste composition; **Hausnebenstelle mit Wählbetrieb** f TELEKOM private automatic exchange; **Haussprechanlage** f AUFNAHME intercom; **Hausvermittlungssystem** nt TELEKOM house exchange system; **Hausvorschriften** f pl DRUCK house style; **Hauswirtschaftslehre** f LEBENSMITTEL home economics; **Hauszeitschrift** f DRUCK house organ; **Haus-zu-Hauslieferung** f KFZTECH door-to-door delivery

Haut f KOHLEN, KUNSTSTOFF, LEBENSMITTEL skin; **Hautblase** f KER & GLAS skin blister; **Hauteffekt** m ELEKTRIZ, ELEKTROTECH, PHYS, WERKPRÜF skin effect; **Hautsalbe** f SICHERHEIT skin cream; **Hauttiefe** f PHYS skin depth

Häutungshormon nt CHEMIE ecdyson

Haut: **Hautverhütungsmittel** nt KUNSTSTOFF antiskinning agent; **Hautwiderstand** m KOHLEN skin resistance; **Hautwiderstandsänderung** f ERGON galvanic skin response

Havarie f KERNTECH average, WASSERTRANS average, *Schiff* damage by sea

havariebedingt: **~er Ausfluß** m UMWELTSCHMUTZ *Öl, Chemikalien* accidental discharge

Havarie: **Havariekommissar** m WASSERTRANS *Versicherung* average adjuster; **Havarieschutz** m KERNTECH RPS, reactor protection system

H-Bahn f *(hochgeständerte Einschienenhängebahn)* EISENBAHN overhead monorail

H-Band nt BAU H hinge

H-Bogen m ELEKTROTECH H-plane bend

HC abbr *(Großraumcontainer)* TRANS HC *(High Cube)*

HD abbr COMP & DV *(Festplatte)* HD *(hard disk)*, COMP & DV *(halbduplex)* HDX *(half-duplex)*, MASCHINEN *(Hochleistung)* HD *(heavy duty)*, TELEKOM *(Festplatte)* HD *(hard disk)*

HDLC-Prozedur f COMP & DV, TELEKOM HDLC, high-level data link control

HDLC-Verfahren nt COMP & DV HDLC, high-level data link control

HD-Öl nt *(Heavy-Duty-Öl, Hochleistungsöl)* MASCHINEN HD oil *(heavy-duty oil)*

HDTV abbr *(hochauflösendes Fernsehen, hochzeiliges Fernsehverfahren)* FERNSEH HDTV *(high-definition television)*

He *(Helium)* CHEMIE He *(helium)*

Head-Down-Display nt RAUMFAHRT *Instrumentenbrettdarstellung* head-down display

Head-Up- pref WASSERTRANS head-up

Head-Up-Display nt RAUMFAHRT *Frontscheibensichtan-* *zeige, Blickfelddarstellung* head-up display

Heavy-Duty-Öl nt *(HD-Öl)* MASCHINEN heavy-duty oil *(HD oil)*

Hebdrehwählersystem nt TELEKOM Strowger system

Hebearm m LUFTTRANS *Hubschrauber* hoist arm

Hebeauge nt LUFTTRANS hoisting eye

Hebeausleger m LUFTTRANS hoist boom

Hebebaum m MECHAN handspike

Hebebock m MASCHINEN jack

Hebebremsklotz m LUFTTRANS hoisting block

Hebebrücke f BAU lift bridge

Hebebühne f EISENBAHN, LUFTTRANS lifting platform, MASCHINEN elevating platform, MECHAN hydraulic jack, WASSERTRANS lifting platform

Hebedaumen m FERTIG wiper, MASCHINEN lifter

Hebegerät nt MASCHINEN lifting apparatus, lifting device, lifting equipment, SICHERHEIT lifting appliance

Hebehaken m MASCHINEN lifting hook

Hebekette f SICHERHEIT lifting chain

Hebekranführer m LUFTTRANS hoist operator

Hebel m FERTIG, MASCHINEN lever; **Hebelarm** m BAU lever arm, MASCHINEN lever arm, moment arm; **Hebelausschalter** m ELEKTROTECH single throw switch; **Hebelbremse** f MASCHINEN lever brake; **Hebeldrehpunkt** m FERTIG leveling fulcrum (AmE), levelling fulcrum (BrE); **Hebelgestänge** nt MASCHINEN leverage; **Hebelgriff** m BAU lever handle; **Hebelhammer** m FERTIG tilt hammer; **Hebelkraft** f ERGON, FERTIG, MASCHINEN leverage

hebeln vt MASCHINEN lever

Hebel: **Hebelpresse** f MASCHINEN lever press; **Hebelpunkt** m PHYS fulcrum; **Hebelrelais** nt ELEKTROTECH single throw relay; **Hebelschalter** m ELEKTRIZ toggle switch, ELEKTROTECH lever switch; **Hebelschere** f MASCHINEN lever shears; **Hebelstrecker** m WASSERTRANS forestay release lever; **Hebelsystem** nt MASCHINEN lever system; **Hebelübersetzung** f MASCHINEN leverage; **Hebelventil** nt HYDRAUL lever valve; **Hebelvorschub** m MASCHINEN lever feed; **Hebelwechslerschalter** m ELEKTRIZ double-throw switch; **Hebelwerk** nt MASCHINEN compound lever; **Hebelwirkung** f ERGON leverage

Hebemagnet m ELEKTRIZ lifting magnet

Hebemaschine f MASCHINEN hoisting machine

Heben nt BAU raising, MASCHINEN hoisting, lifting, SICHERHEIT lifting

heben¹ vt MASCHINEN hoist, jack up, lift, WASSERTRANS heave in

heben:² **sich ~ und senken** v refl WASSERTRANS heave

hebend: **~es Kissen** nt TRANS height-on cushion

H-Ebene f ELEKTROTECH, RADIO H-plane

Hebeponton m WASSERTRANS camel

Hebepumpe f LUFTTRANS hoist pump

Heber m BAU lifter, LABOR siphon, syphon, MASCHINEN jack, PHYS siphon, syphon

hebern vt LABOR siphon, syphon, NICHTFOSS ENERG syphon, PHYS siphon, syphon

Hebeschaft m MASCHINEN lifting shaft

Hebeseilschlaufe f LUFTTRANS hoisting sling

Hebeseiltrenner m LUFTTRANS *Hubschrauber* hoist cable cutter

Hebetisch m MECHAN elevating table

Hebevorrichtung f EISENBAHN lifting gear, lifting tackle, LABOR jack, LUFTTRANS lifting gear, lifting tackle, MASCHINEN lifting apparatus, WASSERTRANS lifting gear, lifting tackle

Hebewerk nt BAU lift, ERDÖL Bohrtechnik draw works, MASCHINEN elevator

Hebewinde f BAU windlass

Hebezeug nt BAU elevator (AmE), lift (BrE), lifting table, gin, tackle, ELEKTRIZ, FERTIG elevator (AmE), lift (BrE), gin, lifting table, tackle, LUFTTRANS gin, lift, lifting table, tackle, MASCHINEN elevator (AmE), lift (BrE), gin, lifting table, tackle, purchase, MECHAN gin, lift (BrE), tackle, lifting table, WASSERTRANS elevator (AmE), lift (BrE), gin, lifting table, tackle

Hebezug m SICHERHEIT hoist

Hebung f WASSERVERSORG des Wasserspiegels lift

Hecheln nt TEXTIL hackling

hecheln vt TEXTIL hackle

Heck nt KFZTECH Karosserie rear end, tail, RAUMFAHRT Raumschiff afterbody, WASSERTRANS Schiffbau stern; **Heckaufreißer** m TRANS rear-mounted ripper; **Heckfenster** nt KFZTECH Karosserie rear window; **Heckflagge** f WASSERTRANS stern flag; **Heckkanzel** f WASSERTRANS Decksausrüstung stern pulpit; **Heckklappe** f KFZTECH, MECHAN, TRANS tailgate; **Heckkorb** m WASSERTRANS Deckausrüstung pushpit; **Hecklaterne** f WASSERTRANS Navigation stern light; **Heckleine** f WASSERTRANS Festmachen stern line; **Heckleuchte** f KFZTECH Beleuchtung rear lamp, tail light, tail lamp; **Heckluftschraube** f LUFTTRANS tail propeller; **Heckmotor** m KFZTECH rear engine, rear-mounted engine; **Heckreling** f WASSERTRANS Schiffbau taffrail; **Heckrotor** m LUFTTRANS Hubschrauber tail rotor; **Heckscheibe** f KFZTECH Karosserie back window, rear window; **Heckschraube** f LUFTTRANS Hubschrauber tail rotor; **Heckspiegel** m WASSERTRANS Schiffbau transom; **Hecksporn** m LUFTTRANS tail skid; **Heckstoßwelle** f LUFTTRANS tail shock wave; **Heckstrahlpropeller** m WASSERTRANS Schiffantrieb stern thruster; **Hecktür** f KFZTECH hatchback, tailgate, TRANS tailgate; **Hecküberhang** m WASSERTRANS Schiffkonstruktion aft rake, Schiffbau fantail

Hede f TEXTIL tow

hedonisch: ~er Maßstab m LEBENSMITTEL hedonic scale

Heft nt FERTIG handle, hilt; **Heftahle** f MASCHINEN elevating machinery, hoist, hoisting gear, jack, lift; **Heftapparat** m VERPACK stapling equipment; **Heftbolzen** m MECHAN locating pin; **Heftdraht** m VERPACK stapling wire, stitching wire; **Hefteisen** nt KER & GLAS punty, sticking up iron

Hefteisen: mit ~ aufnehmen vt KER & GLAS put on the punty

heften vt BAU tack

Heften nt DRUCK sewing

Heftfaden m DRUCK binding thread

Heftfalte f KONSTZEICH filling fold

heftig: ~es Sieden nt TEXTIL violent boiling

Heft: **Heftklammer** f VERPACK staple; **Heftmaschine** f DRUCK sewing machine; **Heftniet** m FERTIG dummy rivet; **Heftrand** m KONSTZEICH binding margin, einer Zeichnung filling margin

heilen vt ANSTRICH cure

Heimarbeit: ~ am Computer f COMP & DV telecommuting

Heimat-Bahnbetriebswerk nt EISENBAHN home depot

Heimatbahnhof m EISENBAHN home station

Heimatdatei f TELEKOM home location register

Heimathafen m WASSERTRANS port of documentation, port of registry, port of registration, Hafen home port

Heimcomputer m COMP & DV home computer

heimkehrend adj WASSERTRANS Boot, Schiff inward-bound

Heimreise f WASSERTRANS homeward passage

Heimroboter m KÜNSTL INT domestic robot

Heimtextilien nt pl TEXTIL home textiles

Heimvideo-Aufzeichnungssystem nt (VHS-C) FERNSEH video home system-compact (VHS-C)

Heimvideosystem nt (VHS) FERNSEH video home system (VHS)

heimwärts adv WASSERTRANS homeward

Heisenberg: ~sche Unbestimmtheitsrelation f TEILPHYS Heisenberg uncertainty principle

heiß[1] adj KERNTECH hot

heiß:[2] ~e Chemie f KERNTECH hot chemistry; ~es Labor nt KERNTECH hot laboratory; ~es Triebwerksteil nt LUFTTRANS eines Triebwerkes hot section; ~es Wasser nt THERMOD hot strength, hot water; ~e Zelle f KERNTECH hot cell

Heiß- pref HEIZ & KÄLTE, KERNTECH, MASCHINEN, PHYS, THERMOD, VERPACK hot; **Heißabfüllung** f VERPACK hot-filling; **Heißaufladung** f KERNTECH hot-refueling (AmE), hot-refuelling (BrE); **Heißauge** nt WASSERTRANS Schiffbau, Deckbeschläge lifting eye; **Heißbeschickung** f KERNTECH hot-refueling (AmE), hot-refuelling (BrE); **Heißdampf** m HEIZ & KÄLTE, MASCHINEN, PHYS, THERMOD superheated steam; **Heißdampfkühler** m HEIZ & KÄLTE desuperheater; **Heißendvergütung** f KER & GLAS hot end coating

heißfixierbar adj THERMOD heat-setting

Heiß-: **Heißfolien-Kartoncodierer** m VERPACK hot foil carton coder; **Heißform** f KER & GLAS hot mold (AmE), hot mould (BrE); **Heißgas-Entlastungsventil** nt HEIZ & KÄLTE hot-gas by-pass valve

heißgelaufen: ~es Lager nt FERTIG overheating bearing

Heiß-: **Heißgemisch** nt BAU Bitumen hot mix

heißgesiegelt adj THERMOD heat-sealed

Heiß-: **Heißglasdraht** m KER & GLAS hot glass wire; **Heißglasdrahtschneiden** nt KER & GLAS hot glass wire cutting; **Heißkalandrieren** nt PAPIER hot calendering; **Heißkanalfaktor** m KERNTECH hot channel factor; **Heißkanalwerkzeug** nt KUNSTSTOFF hot runner mold (AmE), hot runner mould (BrE); **Heißkaschieren** nt VERPACK heat lamination; **Heißklebeband** nt VERPACK heat-fix tape; **Heißklebeetikett** nt VERPACK heat seal label, heat-activated label; **Heißklebefolie** f VERPACK heat-sealing tape; **Heißkleben** nt VERPACK thermal sealing; **Heißlabor** nt KERNTECH hot laboratory; **Heißlaufen** nt KFZTECH overheating

heißlaufen vi KFZTECH overheat, MASCHINEN run hot

Heißläufer m EISENBAHN hot box; **Heißläufersuchgerät** nt EISENBAHN hot-box detector

Heiß-: **Heißleim** m VERPACK hot-setting glue; **Heißleiter** m PHYS, TELEKOM thermistor; **Heißlötstelle** f ELEKTRIZ hot junction

Heißluft f KFZTECH, LABOR, MASCHINEN, SICHERHEIT hot-air; **Heißluft- und Flammenausstoß des Ofens** m KER & GLAS sting-out; **Heißluftgebläse** nt LABOR hot-air blower; **Heißluftheizung** f SICHERHEIT hot-air radiation heating system; **Heißluftmaschine** f MASCHINEN caloric engine; **Heißluftmotor** m KFZTECH, MASCHINEN hot-air engine; **Heißluftofen** m KUNSTSTOFF air oven; **Heißluftschlichtmaschine** f TEXTIL hot-air sizing machine; **Heißluftstrom** m TEXTIL hot-air stream; **Heißlufttrockner** m TEXTIL hot-air dryer; **Heißluftturbine mit geschlossenem Kreislauf** f TRANS closed cycle hot-air turbine; **Heißluftventil** *nt* LUFT-TRANS hot-air valve; **Heißluftventilator** *m* HEIZ & KÄLTE hot-air fan

Heiß-: **Heißprägen** *nt* VERPACK *von Folien* hot-stamping; **Heißpresse** *f* MASCHINEN hot press; **Heißpressen** *nt* VERPACK hot-pressing; **Heißräucherung** *f* LEBENSMIT-TEL hot-smoking; **Heißring** *m* WASSERTRANS *Deckbeschläge* lifting ring; **Heißschmelzbeschichter** *m* PAPIER hot-melt coating; **Heißschmelzkleber** *m* KUNSTSTOFF hot-melt adhesive; **Heißschrumpfsitz** *m* MASCHINEN hot-shrink fit; **Heißsiegel- und Ver-schweißmaschine** *f* VERPACK *für Schrumpfpackungen* heat-sealing and welding machine; **Heißsiegelanlage** *f* VERPACK heat-sealing equipment; **Heißsiegelbe-schichtung** *f* VERPACK heat seal coating

heißsiegelfähig *adj* FERTIG hot-sealing, PAPIER heat-sea-ling, THERMOD heat-sealable

Heiß-: **Heißsiegeln** *nt* KUNSTSTOFF, THERMOD heat-sea-ling, VERPACK hot-blade sealing

heißsiegeln *vt* FERTIG hot-seal, *Plaste* heat-seal, THER-MOD heat-seal

Heiß-: **Heißsiegelpapier** *nt* VERPACK heat-sealable pa-per; **Heißsiegelverpackungen** *f pl* THERMOD heat-sealed wrappings; **Heißspülung** *f* ANSTRICH hot rinse; **Heißstrahltriebwerk** *nt* LUFTTRANS thermal jet engine; **Heißverkleben** *nt* THERMOD heat-sealing

heißverklebt *adj* THERMOD heat-sealed

Heiß-: **Heißverschweißgerät** *nt* LABOR *Polyäthylenbeu-tel* heat seal apparatus

heißversiegelt *adj* FERTIG hot-sealed

heißverstreckt: **~e Faser** *f* TEXTIL heat-stretched fiber (AmE), heat-stretched fibre (BrE)

Heiß-: **Heißvulkanisation** *f* THERMOD hot creep, hot-cu-ring; **Heißwäsche** *f* ANSTRICH hot wash

Heißwasser *nt* THERMOD hot water; **Heißwasserboiler** *m* THERMOD hot-water boiler; **Heißwassererzeuger** *m* HEIZ & KÄLTE high-temperature water heating appli-ance; **Heißwassergerät** *nt* THERMOD hot-water boiler; **Heißwasserheizungsanlage** *f* HEIZ & KÄLTE high-tem-perature water heating system; **Heißwasserspeicher** *m* HEIZ & KÄLTE thermal storage water heater; **Heiß-wassertrichter** *m* LABOR funnel heater; **Heißwasservulkanisation** *f* KUNSTSTOFF hot-water vulcanization; **Heißwasserwaschen** *nt* MEER-SCHMUTZ hot-water washing

Heiz- *pref* HEIZ & KÄLTE, KFZTECH heating; **Heizanlage** *f* KFZTECH *Zubehör* heating system; **Heizbalg** *m* KUNST-STOFF bladder; **Heizband** *nt* LABOR heating tape; **Heizdraht** *m* ELEKTROTECH filament, HEIZ & KÄLTE fire bar, MECHAN filament, METALL resistance wire; **Heiz-einsatz** *m* HEIZ & KÄLTE heating element; **Heizelement** *nt* ELEKTRIZ heating element, ELEKTROTECH heater, FOTO element heater, HEIZ & KÄLTE fire bar, heater, heating element; **Heizen** *nt* THERMOD heating; **Heizer** *m* HEIZ & KÄLTE heater; **Heizergebläse** *nt* HEIZ & KÄLTE heater fan; **Heizfaden** *m* ELEKTROTECH, RADIO *Elek-tronenröhre* heater; **Heizfadenspannung** *f* ELEKTROTECH heater voltage; **Heizfadentemperatur** *f* ELEKTRIZ filament temperature; **Heizfadenwider-stand** *m* ELEKTRIZ filament resistance, filament resistor; **Heizfähigkeit** *f* HEIZ & KÄLTE, THERMOD hea-ting capacity; **Heizfläche** *f* HEIZ & KÄLTE flat radiator, heating surface, KERNTECH heating surface, THERMOD effective heating surface, heating surface; **Heizflä-chenrohr** *nt* KERNTECH heating surface tube; **Heizgebläse** *nt* HEIZ & KÄLTE fan-assisted air heater,

KFZTECH *Zubehör* heater; **Heizgerät** *nt* HEIZ & KÄLTE heater, heating appliance, MASCHINEN heating device, THERMOD heater; **Heizgürtel** *m* HEIZ & KÄLTE heating belt; **Heizkabel** *nt* ELEKTRIZ heating cable; **Heizkam-mer** *f* THERMOD heating chamber; **Heizkanal** *m* VERPACK heating channel; **Heizkathode** *f* ELEKTRO-TECH hot cathode; **Heizkessel** *m* HEIZ & KÄLTE heating and hot water boiler; **Heizkörper** *m* ELEKTROTECH heater, HEIZ & KÄLTE heater, radiator, THERMOD radia-tor; **Heizkraft** *f* MECHAN heating, THERMOD heating power; **Heizkraftwerk** *nt* THERMOD CHPS, combined heat and power station; **Heizkreis** *m* HEIZ & KÄLTE heating circuit; **Heizleistung** *f* HEIZ & KÄLTE heat out-put, heating capacity, PHYS, THERMOD calorific output, calorific power; **Heizleiter** *m* ELEKTROTECH heater; **Heizlüfter** *m* HEIZ & KÄLTE fan heater, LUFT-TRANS heater blower, MASCHINEN, MECHAN fan heater, SICHERHEIT fan-assisted air heater, THERMOD fan heater; **Heizmantel** *m* LABOR heating mantle, THERMOD heating jacket; **Heizofen** *m* MECHAN heater, THERMOD heating furnace, VERPACK heating tunnel; **Heizöl** *nt* BAU, ERDÖL *Destillationsprodukt*, HEIZ & KÄLTE fuel oil, THERMOD heating oil, oil fuel; **Heiz-platte** *f* KUNSTSTOFF heated plate, LABOR hotplate; **Heizraum** *m* HEIZ & KÄLTE boiler room, combustion chamber

Heizrohr *nt* KERNTECH fire tube, WASSERTRANS heat pipe; **Heizrohrkessel** *m* HEIZ & KÄLTE multitubular boiler; **Heizrohrschlange** *f* BAU coil

Heiz-: **Heizschlange** *f* HEIZ & KÄLTE calorifier, coil, hea-ting coil; **Heizspule** *f* THERMOD heating coil; **Heizstab** *m* HEIZ & KÄLTE heating element, immersion heater, KERNTECH heater rod; **Heizstift** *m* KERNTECH heating pin; **Heizstrahler** *m* HEIZ & KÄLTE, MASCHINEN, STRAHLPHYS, THERMOD radiant heater; **Heizstrom** *m* ELEKTRIZ *Glühkathodenröhre*, ELEKTROTECH filament current, THERMOD heating current; **Heiztechniker** *m* MASCHINEN heating technician; **Heiztransformator** *m* ELEKTROTECH filament transformer; **Heizung** *f* ELEK-TROTECH heater, HEIZ & KÄLTE heating, KFZTECH *Zubehör* heater, THERMOD heating; **Heizungs-, Lüf-tungs- und Klimatechnik** *f* HEIZ & KÄLTE heating, ventilation and air conditioning; **Heizungsanlage** *f* THERMOD heating installation, heating plant; **Hei-zungsbau** *m* HEIZ & KÄLTE heating installation; **Hei-zungskanal** *m* HEIZ & KÄLTE heating duct; **Hei-zungsnetzteil** *nt* ELEKTROTECH heater power supply; **Heizungssystem** *nt* THERMOD heating system; **Hei-zungstechnik** *f* RAUMFAHRT heat transfer engineer; **Heizvorrichtung** *f* ELEKTROTECH heater; **Heizwert** *m* ABFALL, FERTIG, HEIZ & KÄLTE, PHYS calorific value, THERMOD calorific value, thermal power; **Heizwert-messer** *m* MASCHINEN calorimeter; **Heizwicklung** *f* THERMOD heating coil; **Heizzug** *m* THERMOD flue

Hektar *m (ha)* METROL hectare *(ha)*; **Hektarzähler** *m* METROL acremeter

Hekto- *pref (h)* METROL hecto- *(h)*; **Hektogramm** *nt* METROL hectogram; **Hektographie** *f* DRUCK hectogra-phy; **Hektoliter** *m (hl)* LABOR hectoliter (AmE), hectolitre (BrE) *(hl)*; **Hektowatt** *nt* ELEKTROTECH hectowatt

Helianthin *nt* CHEMIE helianthin, helianthine

Helicin *nt* CHEMIE helicin

Helikoid *nt* GEOM helicoid

helikoid *adj* GEOM helicoid

Heliostat *m* NICHTFOSS ENERG heliostat

Heliotropin *nt* CHEMIE heliotropin, piperonal
heliotropisch *adj* NICHTFOSS ENERG heliotropic
Helipot *nt* ELEKTRIZ *Mehrdrehungspotentiometer* helical potentiometer
Helium *nt (He)* CHEMIE helium *(He)*; **Helium-Entwässerungsanlage** *f* KERNTECH helium dehydrator unit; **Helium-Gasflasche** *f* RAUMFAHRT *Raumschiff* compressed-helium bottle; **Helium-Lecksortung** *f* KERNTECH helium leak detection; **Helium-Lecktest** *m* KERNTECH helium leak test; **Helium-Lösungskältemaschine** *f* PHYS helium dilution refrigerator; **Helium-Neonlaser** *m* STRAHLPHYS helium neon laser; **Heliumschutz-Gasschweißen** *nt* FERTIG heliarc welding
Helix *f* GEOM helix; **Helixantenne** *f* RAUMFAHRT *Weltraumfunk* helix antenna
hell[1] *adj* OPTIK light, TEXTIL bright
hell:[2] **~e Flamme** *f* THERMOD blaze; **~e Hinterlegung** *f* COMP & DV *auf dem Bildschirm* highlighting; **~e Kante** *f* PHYS bright edge; **~er Lichtschein** *m* THERMOD blaze; **~es Weizenmehl** *nt* LEBENSMITTEL patent flour
Hellegatt *nt* WASSERTRANS *Ladung* storeroom
heller: ~ es Zentrum *nt* FOTO *des Lichtkegels einer Atelierlampe* hot spot
Hellfeld *nt* METALL bright field; **Hellfeldbeleuchtung** *f* PHYS bright field illumination
Helligkeit *f* ELEKTRONIK *Fernsehtechnik*, ERGON brightness, FERNSEH brightness, luminance, OPTIK brightness, PHYS luminosity, *nicht allgemein definierbare Größe* brightness, STRAHLPHYS brightness; **Helligkeitskurve** *f* FERNSEH brightness curve; **Helligkeitsmeßgerät** *nt* GERÄT brightness meter; **Helligkeitsmodulation** *f* ELEKTRONIK intensity modulation; **Helligkeitspegel** *m* FERNSEH bright level; **Helligkeitsregler** *m* ELEKTROTECH dimmer switch, FERNSEH brightness control; **Helligkeitsschwankung** *f* FERNSEH fluttering of brightness level; **Helligkeitsschwellwert** *m* FERNSEH luminescence threshold; **Helligkeitssignal** *nt* FERNSEH luminance signal; **Helligkeitssteuerung** *f* ELEKTRONIK brightness modulation; **Helligkeitsumfang** *m* FOTO brightness range; **Helligkeitsverhältnis** *nt* FERNSEH, PHYS, STRAHLPHYS brightness ratio; **Helligkeitsverzögerung** *f* FERNSEH luminance delay; **Helligkeitsverzögerungssignal** *nt* FERNSEH luminance difference signal; **Helligkeitswert** *m* FERNSEH brightness value
Helling *f* WASSERTRANS building berth, building slip, *Schiffbau* slip, *Schiffbau* slipway
Hellmarke *f* ELEKTRONIK *Kathodenstrahlröhre* intensify pip
Hellrotglühhitze *f* METALL bright red heat
Hellsteuerimpuls *m* ELEKTRONIK indicator gate
Hellsteuerung *f* ELEKTRONIK *Kathodenstrahlröhre* unblanking
Helmholtz: ~sches Galvanometer *nt* ELEKTRIZ Helmholtz galvanometer; **~scher Resonator** *m* AKUSTIK, PHYS Helmholtz resonator; **~sche Spulen** *f pl* PHYS Helmholtz coils
Helvetica *f* DRUCK *Schrift* Helvetica
Hemdenstoff *m* TEXTIL shirting
Hemiacetal *nt* CHEMIE hemiacetal
Hemicellulose *f* CHEMIE hemicellulose
Hemipin- *pref* CHEMIE hemipinic
Hemisphäre *f* GEOM hemisphere
hemmen *vt* MASCHINEN inhibit, MECHAN jam
Hemmnis *nt* BAU obstruction

Hemmschiene *f* BAU skid track
Hemmschuh *m* MASCHINEN scotch, MECHAN shoe, skid; **Hemmschuh-Auswurfvorrichtung** *f* EISENBAHN rail slipper
Hemmstoff *m* ANSTRICH, LEBENSMITTEL inhibitor
Hemmung *f* FERTIG escapement, MASCHINEN escapement mechanism
Hemmwerk *nt* FERTIG escapement
Hennegatt *nt* WASSERTRANS rudder port
Henry *nt (H)* ELEKTRIZ, ELEKTROTECH, METROL, PHYS, RADIO *Einheit der Induktivität* henry *(H)*
Hentriacontanon *nt* CHEMIE hentriacontanone, palmitone
Heparin *nt* CHEMIE heparin
Heptaeder *nt* GEOM heptahedron
Heptagon *nt* GEOM heptagon
heptagonal *adj* GEOM heptagonal
Heptan *nt* CHEMIE, ERDÖL *Kohlenwasserstoff* heptane; **Heptan-1-al** *nt* CHEMIE oenanthal
heptavalent *adj* CHEMIE heptavalent
Hept-1-in *nt* CHEMIE heptyne
Hepten *nt* CHEMIE heptene, heptylene
Heptode *f* ELEKTRONIK *Elektronenröhre* heptode
Heptose *f* CHEMIE heptose
Heptyl- *pref* CHEMIE heptyl, heptylic
Heptylen *nt* CHEMIE heptene, heptylene
HERA *abbr (Hadron-Elektron-Ring-Anlage)* TEILPHYS HERA *(hadron-electron ring collider)*
herablassen *vt* SICHERHEIT lower
herabsetzen *vt* ELEKTROTECH *Spannung* drop
herabsetzend: ~e Äußerungen *f pl* PATENT disparaging statements
Herabsetzung: ~ des pH-Wertes *f* UMWELTSCHMUTZ pH depression
heranführen *vt* TELEKOM *eine Leitung* link up
herausgequetscht: ~er Rand *m* FERTIG spew
Herausheber *m* BAU extractor
herauslösen *vt* CHEMIE *adsorbierte Stoffe aus festen Adsorptionsmitteln* elute, CHEMTECH dissolve away, dissolve out
herausquetschen *vt* FERTIG spew
Herausschmelzen *nt* FERTIG eliquation
herausschmelzen *vt* FERTIG eliquate
Herausschneiden *nt* FERNSEH edit-out
herausspringen *vi* FERTIG *Kette* jump
herausspritzen *vt* FERTIG squirt
Herauszeichnen: ~ von Einzelheiten *nt* KONSTZEICH separate drawing of details
herauszeichnen *vt* KONSTZEICH draw separately
Herausziehen *nt* BAU *eines Nagels* extraction, *von Nägeln* drawing, FERTIG *Bohrer* retraction
herausziehen *vt* BAU *Nagel* pull out
Herd *m* FERTIG hearth; **Herdformerei** *f* FERTIG open-sand molding (AmE), open-sand moulding (BrE); **Herdfrischverfahren** *nt* METALL Siemens-Martin process; **Herdglas** *nt* KER & GLAS slag glass; **Herdofen** *m* KOHLEN open hearth furnace; **Herdraum** *m* BAU hearth; **Herdraum des Hafenofens** *m* KER & GLAS pot room; **Herdwanderung** *f* FERTIG bottom bank
hereinkommend: ~er Fluß *m* PHYS inward flux
hergestellt *adj* LEBENSMITTEL prepared
herkömmlich: ~es Telefonnetz *nt* TELEKOM traditional telephone network
Herkunft *f* COMP & DV, ELEKTROTECH source; **Herkunftsangabe** *f* PATENT indication of source
hermetisch:[1] **~ abgeschlossen** *adj* ELEKTROTECH her-

metically-sealed, HEIZ & KÄLTE, MECHAN airtight, hermetically-sealed, PHYS airtight

hermetisch:[2] ~ **abgeschlossene Baugruppe** *f* ELEKTRO-TECH hermetically-sealed unit; ~ **abgeschlossener Verdichtersatz** *m* HEIZ & KÄLTE hermetically-sealed compressor unit; ~ **abgeschlossenes Gerät** *nt* ELEK-TROTECH hermetically-sealed unit; ~**er Luftabschluß** *m* KERNTECH hermetic sealing; ~**er Verdichter** *m* MA-SCHINEN hermetic refrigerant compressor; ~**er Verschluß** *m* TELEKOM hermetic sealing, VERPACK hermetic closure; ~**e Versiegelung** *f* KERNTECH hermetic sealing, VERPACK hermetic seal

Herstellen: ~ **einer Intersatellitenfunkverbindung** *nt* RAUMFAHRT *Weltraumfunk* intersatellite link acquisition; ~ **der Mater** *nt* OPTIK mastering; ~ **U-förmiger Biegeteile** *nt* FERTIG channel bending

herstellen *vt* BAU, MECHAN fabricate, TELEKOM *Verbindung* set up

Hersteller: beim ~ vorgenommene Einstellung *f* GERÄT factory setting

Herstellgrenzqualität *f* QUAL manufacturing quality limit

Herstellung *f* COMP & DV production, KER & GLAS manufacture, LEBENSMITTEL preparation; ~ **auf einem Glasposten** *f* KER & GLAS making on a post; ~ **balligtragender Flächen** *f* FERTIG *Spanung* crowning; ~ **mit Glasmacherpfeife** *f* KER & GLAS making on blowpipe; ~ **des Gleichgewichtes** *f* KERNTECH balancing; ~ **integrierter Schaltung** *f* ELEKTRONIK integrated-circuit fabrication; ~ **im Wälzverfahren** *f* FERTIG generating

herstellungsbedingt: ~**er Brennelementdefekt** *m* KERN-TECH fabrication-related fuel defect

Herstellung: **Herstellungsdatum** *nt* VERPACK date of manufacture; **Herstellungswert** *m* QUAL objective value

Hertz *nt (Hz)* ELEKTRIZ, ELEKTROTECH, FERNSEH, METROL, PHYS, RADIO hertz *(Hz)*; **Hertz-** *pref* ELEK-TRIZ Hertzian; ~**scher Bruch** *m* KER & GLAS Hertzian fracture; ~**scher Dipol** *m* RAUMFAHRT *Weltraumfunk* Hertzian dipole; ~**-Oszillator** *m* ELEKTRIZ Hertzian oscillator; ~**sche Pressung** *f* FERTIG Hertz-calculated stresses, hertz equation; ~**scher Strahl** *m* FERNSEH Hertzian beam

herumhantieren: ~ **an** *vt* SICHERHEIT tamper with

herunterdrücken *vt* VERPACK press down

Heruntergehen *nt* LUFTTRANS letdown

herunterwalzen *vt* FERTIG *Walzen* cog

Herunterziehen: ~ **von Glasfasern** *nt* KER & GLAS picking down

hervorholen *vt* KONTROLL retrieve

Hervorströmen *nt* BAU outpouring

Herz *nt* MASCHINEN dog

Herzblatt-Polierschaufel *f* BAU heart trowel

Herzkurve *f* AUFNAHME cardioid diagram, MASCHINEN cardioid

Hesperidin *nt* LEBENSMITTEL hesperidin

Hesse: ~sche Normalform *f* COMP & DV normal form

Hessian *m* TEXTIL hessian

heteroatomig *adj* CHEMIE heteroatomic

Heteroauxin *nt* CHEMIE heteroauxin

heterocyclisch *adj* CHEMIE heterocyclic

Heterodynempfang *m* TELEKOM heterodyne reception

heterogen[1] *adj* METALL heterogeneous

heterogen:[2] ~**er Reaktor** *m* WASSERTRANS heterogeneous reactor; ~**e Strahlung** *f* KERNTECH heteroradiation

Heterojunktion *f* OPTIK heterojunction

heteropolar *adj* ELEKTRIZ, ELEKTROTECH heteropolar

Heterosid *nt* CHEMIE heteroside

Heteroübergang *m* ELEKTRONIK *Halbleiter*, OPTIK, TELEKOM heterojunction; **Heteroübergangs-Feldeffekttransistor** *m* ELEKTRONIK heterojunction FET

Heteroxanthin *nt* CHEMIE heteroxanthine

Heuerbüro *nt* WASSERTRANS shipping office

Heuler *m* TELEKOM howler

Heultonne *f* WASSERTRANS *Seezeichen* whistle buoy

Heuristik *f* KÜNSTL INT heuristics

heuristisch[1] *adj* COMP & DV, KÜNSTL INT heuristic

heuristisch:[2] ~**es Wissen** *nt* KÜNSTL INT heuristic knowledge

Heusler: ~sche Legierung *f* FERTIG magnet alloy

HEX *abbr* COMP & DV *(hexadezimal)*, GEOM *(hexadezimal)*, GEOM *(hexadecimal)*, GEOM *(Hexagon)* hex *(hexagon)*

Hexacontan *nt* CHEMIE hexacontane

Hexacosan *nt* CHEMIE cerane, hexacosane

Hexacyanoferrat *nt* CHEMIE prussiate

Hexadecan *nt* CHEMIE hexadecane

Hexadecanoat *nt* CHEMIE hexadecanoate, palmitate

Hexadecanol *nt* CHEMIE ethal, hexadecanol

Hexadecyl *nt* CHEMIE cetyl, hexadecyl; **Hexadecylalkohol** *m* CHEMIE hexadecanol

Hexadecylen *nt* CHEMIE cetene, hexadecylene

hexadezimal[1] *adj (HEX)* COMP & DV hexadecimal, sexadecimal, GEOM hexadecimal *(hex)*

hexadezimal:[2] ~**e Zahlendarstellung** *f* COMP & DV hexadecimal notation

Hexadezimal-Darstellung *f* COMP & DV hexadecimal notation

Hexaeder *nt* GEOM hexahedron

hexaedrisch *adj* GEOM, KERNTECH hexahedral

Hexafluorsilicat *nt* CHEMIE hexafluorosilicate

Hexagon *nt (HEX)* GEOM hexagon *(hex)*

hexagonal *adj* GEOM, KERNTECH hexagonal

Hexahydropyrazin *nt* CHEMIE diethylenediamine, hexahydropyrazine, piperazine

Hexahydropyridin *nt* CHEMIE hexahydropyridine, piperidine

Hexamethylendiisocyanat *nt* KUNSTSTOFF hexamethylene diisocyanate

Hexamethylentetramin *nt* CHEMIE methenamine, urotropine

Hexamin *nt* CHEMIE methenamine, urotropine

Hexamincobalt *nt* CHEMIE luteocobaltic

Hexan *nt* CHEMIE, ERDÖL *Kohlenwasserstoff* hexane; **Hexan-** *pref* CHEMIE caproic

Hexanitrodiphenylamin *nt* CHEMIE dipicrylamin, hexanitrodiphenylamine

Hexanol *nt* CHEMIE hexyl alcohol

hexavalent *adj* CHEMIE hexavalent

Hexen *nt* CHEMIE hexene, hexylene; **Hexenspiegel** *m* KER & GLAS witch mirror

Hexin *nt* CHEMIE hexyne

Hexode *f* ELEKTRONIK hexode

Hexogen *nt* CHEMIE cyclonite, hexogen

Hexosan *nt* CHEMIE hemicellulose

Hexose *f* CHEMIE hexose

Hexyl- *pref* CHEMIE capryl, hexylic; **Hexylalkohol** *m* CHE-MIE hexyl alcohol

Hexylen *nt* CHEMIE hexene, hexylene

HF[1] *abbr* AUFNAHME *(Funkfrequenz, Hochfrequenz)* HF *(high frequency)*, RF *(radio frequency)*, ELEKTRIZ

(Hochfrequenz) HF *(high frequency)*, ELEKTRONIK *(Funkfrequenz, Hochfrequenz)*, FERNSEH *(Funkfrequenz, Hochfrequenz)* HF *(high frequency)*, RF *(radio frequency)*, RADIO *(Funkfrequenz, Hochfrequenz)* HF *(high frequency)*, RF *(radio frequency)*, TELEKOM *(Funkfrequenz, Hochfrequenz)* HF *(high frequency)*, RF *(radio frequency)*, WASSERTRANS *(Hochfrequenz)* HF *(high frequency)*, RF *(radio frequency)*

HF:[2] **HF-Abschirmung** *f* AUFNAHME, FERNSEH RF shielding; **HF-Abschnitt** *m* ELEKTRONIK RF section; **HF-Abschnittsgenerator** *m* ELEKTRONIK RF section generator; **HF-Generator** *m* ELEKTROTECH RF alternator, RF generator; **HF-Linearität** *f* RADIO RF linearity; **HF-Löschkopf** *m* AUFNAHME HF erase head; **HF-Mikrofon** *nt* AUFNAHME RF microphone; **HF-Nachsynchronisierung** *f* FERNSEH RF dub; **HF-Oszillator** *m* ELEKTRONIK RF oscillator; **HF-Puls** *m* FERNSEH RF pulse; **HF-Signal** *nt* ELEKTRONIK HF signal; **HF-Signalgenerator** *m* ELEKTRONIK HF signal generator; **HF-Sonde** *f* RAUMFAHRT *Weltraumfunk* RF sensor; **HF-Spektrum** *nt* ELEKTRONIK HF spectrum; **HF-Spule** *f* ELEKTROTECH RF coil; **HF-Störung** *f* ELEKTRONIK radio interference, FERNSEH RF interference; **HF-Strecke** *f* ELEKTRONIK RF section; **HF-Streckengenerator** *m* ELEKTRONIK RF section generator; **HF-Strom** *m* ELEKTROTECH RF current; **HF-Stromquelle** *f* ELEKTROTECH RF current source; **HF-Stufe** *f* ELEKTRONIK RF stage; **HF-Träger** *m* ELEKTRONIK RF carrier; **HF-Transformator** *m* ELEKTROTECH RF transformer; **HF-Transistor** *m* ELEKTRONIK RF transistor; **HF-Verstärker** *m* ELEKTRONIK, TELEKOM RF amplifier; **HF-Verstärkung** *f* ELEKTRONIK RF amplification; **HF-Vorstufe** *f* ELEKTRONIK *des Empfängers* RF stage

Hf *(Hafnium)* CHEMIE Hf *(hafnium)*

Hg *(Quecksilber)* CHEMIE Hg *(mercury)*

H-Glied *nt* ELEKTROTECH H-network

Hieb *m* MASCHINEN cut; **Hiebteilung** *f* FERTIG *Feile* coarseness

Hierarchie *f* COMP & DV hierarchy; **~ einer Regelung** *f* REGELUNG control hierarchy; **~ einer Steuerung** *f* REGELUNG control hierarchy

hierarchisch: ~es Modell *nt* COMP & DV hierarchical model; **~er objektorientierter Entwurf** *m* COMP & DV hierarchical object-oriented design; **~es Programmieren** *nt* KÜNSTL INT hierarchical programming; **~es System** *nt* TELEKOM hierarchical system; **nicht ~es System** *nt* TELEKOM nonhierarchical system

hieven *vt* WASSERTRANS haul up

Hifiklang *m* FERNSEH hi-fi sound

Higgs-Boson *nt* TEILPHYS Higgs boson

Higgs-Teilchen *nt* TEILPHYS Higgs particle

Highway *m* TELEKOM highway

Hilfe[1] *f* COMP & DV help

Hilfe:[2] **nach ~ rufen** *vi* SICHERHEIT call for help

Hilfe: **Hilfeanzeige** *f* COMP & DV help display; **Hilfebereich** *m* COMP & DV help area; **Hilfebildschirm** *m* COMP & DV help screen; **Hilfedatei** *f* COMP & DV help file; **Hilfefunktion** *f* COMP & DV help function; **Hilfemeldung** *f* COMP & DV help message; **Hilfemenü** *nt* COMP & DV help menu; **Hilfenachricht** *f* COMP & DV help message; **Hilfeprogramm** *nt* COMP & DV help program; **Hilferuf** *m* SICHERHEIT call for help

Hilfs- *pref* MASCHINEN auxiliary; **Hilfsanlage** *f* TELEKOM emergency installation; **Hilfsansteuerungsfunkfeuer** *nt* LUFTTRANS, WASSERTRANS compass locator; **Hilfs-**

antrieb *m* LUFTTRANS accessory drive; **Hilfsausrüstung** *f* FERTIG ancillary equipment; **Hilfsbit** *nt* COMP & DV service bit; **Hilfsbremsanlage** *f* KFZTECH emergency brake system; **Hilfsdienstplatz** *m* TELEKOM auxiliary service position; **Hilfsdynamo** *m* ELEKTRIZ booster dynamo; **Hilfseinrichtung** *f* MECHAN ancillary equipment; **Hilfselektrode** *f* KER & GLAS auxiliary electrode; **Hilfsfahrstraße** *f* TRANS auxiliary route; **Hilfsfahrzeug** *nt* WASSERTRANS auxiliary vessel; **Hilfsflügel** *m* LUFTTRANS *Flugzeug* flap; **Hilfsflügelrollenlager** *nt* LUFTTRANS flap roller carriage; **Hilfsflügelspurrippe** *f* LUFTTRANS flap track rib; **Hilfsgerät** *nt* GERÄT autoranging, auxiliary device; **Hilfsgitter** *nt* ELEKTRONIK *zur zusätzlichen Steuerung des Elektronenstroms* injection grid; **Hilfshammer** *m* FERTIG anvil top tool; **Hilfskanal** *m* AUFNAHME return channel; **Hilfskessel** *m* HEIZ & KÄLTE auxiliary boiler; **Hilfskompaß** *m* LUFTTRANS stand-by compass; **Hilfskontakt** *m* ELEKTRIZ, ELEKTROTECH auxiliary contact; **Hilfskoordinatensystem** *nt* GEOM auxiliary coordinate system; **Hilfskoppelgruppe** *f* TELEKOM auxiliary switching unit; **Hilfskoppelstelle** *f* TELEKOM auxiliary switching point; **Hilfskraftbremse** *f* KFZTECH servo brake; **Hilfskraftlenkung** *f* KFZTECH power steering, power-assisted steering; **Hilfskraftmodulatorventil** *nt* KFZTECH servo modulator valve; **Hilfskran** *m* EISENBAHN wrecking crane; **Hilfskreisbogen** *m* KONSTZEICH auxiliary arc; **Hilfslinien** *f pl* DRUCK feint rules; **Hilfsmaschine** *f* WASSERTRANS *Schiffantrieb* auxiliary engine; **Hilfsmaschinen** *f pl* WASSERTRANS auxiliary machinery; **Hilfsmaß** *nt* KONSTZEICH auxiliary dimension; **Hilfsmaßstab** *m* GERÄT auxiliary scale; **Hilfsmittel** *nt* FERTIG resource, KOHLEN adjuvant, TEXTIL appliance; **Hilfsmotor** *m* ELEKTRIZ auxiliary motor, ELEKTROTECH servomotor, MASCHINEN, WASSERTRANS *Schiffantrieb* auxiliary engine; **Hilfsmühle** *f* NICHTFOSS ENERG booster mill; **Hilfsoperation** *f* COMP & DV auxiliary operation; **Hilfsoszillator** *m* ELEKTRONIK keep-alive oscillator, local oscillator; **Hilfsprogramm** *nt* COMP & DV tool, utility; **Hilfsprozessor** *m* COMP & DV auxiliary processor; **Hilfspumpe** *f* MECHAN booster pump; **Hilfsrelais** *nt* COMP & DV slave relay, ELEKTRIZ secondary relay, ELEKTROTECH all-or-nothing relay; **Hilfsrippe** *f* LUFTTRANS false frame; **Hilfsrotor** *m* LUFTTRANS *Hubschrauber* auxiliary rotor; **Hilfsschalter** *m* ELEKTRIZ auxiliary switch, FERTIG *Kunststoffinstallationen* auxiliary control, TELEKOM auxiliary switch; **Hilfsschiff** *nt* WASSERTRANS *Schifftyp* support vessel; **Hilfsschnitt** *m* KER & GLAS auxiliary cut; **Hilfsseil** *nt* TRANS emergency cable; **Hilfsservosteuerung** *f* MASCHINEN auxiliary servo control; **Hilfsskale** *f* GERÄT auxiliary scale; **Hilfsspeicher** *m* COMP & DV secondary memory, secondary storage; **Hilfsständer** *m* FERTIG *Einständerhobelmaschine* auxiliary housing; **Hilfssteuerungsventil** *nt* MASCHINEN pilot valve; **Hilfsstromversorgung** *f* ELEKTRIZ stand-by supply; **Hilfsstütze** *f* BAU flying shore; **Hilfsträgerfrequenz** *f* ELEKTRONIK, FERNSEH, RADIO, TELEKOM subcarrier frequency; **Hilfsträgergeräuschsperre** *f* *(CTCSS)* RADIO continuous tone-coded squelch system *(CTCSS)*; **Hilfstransformator** *m* ELEKTRIZ auxiliary transformer; **Hilfstriebwerk** *nt* LUFTTRANS auxiliary power unit; **Hilfsventil** *nt* MASCHINEN auxiliary valve; **Hilfszug** *m* EISENBAHN breakdown train, breakdown car (AmE), breakdown wagon (BrE); **Hilfszugriffsspeicher** *m* COMP & DV intermediate access memory

Himmelskörper *m* RAUMFAHRT heavenly body

Himmelsrauschen *nt* RADIO external noise

hin:[1] **~ und her** *adv* MASCHINEN to and fro

hin:[2] **~ und hergehend** *adj* MASCHINEN reciprocating; **~ und herlaufend** *adj* MECHAN reciprocating

hin:[3] **~ und herschalten** *vi* COMP & DV toggle

Hin: ~ und Herbewegung *f* MASCHINEN alternating motion, reciprocating motion

hinausfahren: ~ über *vt* EISENBAHN *ein Haltesignal* overshoot

Hinausschießen *nt* LUFTTRANS *Flugwesen*, METALL overshooting

hinausschießen: ~ über *vt* LUFTTRANS overshoot

hindern *vt* RAUMFAHRT *Raumschiff* retard

Hindernis *nt* BAU barricade, obstruction, METALL obstacle; **~ in geschichteter Flüssigkeit** *nt* STRÖMPHYS *Turbulenzuntersuchung* obstacle in stratified fluid; **~ in rotierendem Fluid** *nt* STRÖMPHYS *Turbulenzuntersuchung* obstacle in rotating fluid; **Hindernisbegrenzungsfläche** *f* LUFTTRANS obstacle limitation surface; **Hindernisbeseitigung** *f* LUFTTRANS *Flughafen* clearing; **Hindernisgewinn** *m* ELEKTRONIK, RADIO obstacle gain

hindurchfließen *vi* TELEKOM *Strom* pass through

hindurchgehen *vi* TELEKOM pass through

Hineinfegen *nt* KER & GLAS insweep

hineinpassen *vt* MASCHINEN fit into

Hineinschneiden *nt* FERNSEH in-edit

hinlaufend: ~e Welle *f* ELEKTROTECH forward wave

Hinreise *f* WASSERTRANS outward passage

hinten: hintere Brennebene *f* FOTO rear focal plane; **hinteres Drehmoment** *nt* KFZTECH rear end torque; **hintere Einzelradaufhängung** *f* KFZTECH independent rear suspension; **hinteres Ende** *nt* ELEKTRONIK tail; **hintere Flanke** *des Impulses* ELEKTRONIK tail; **hintere Führung** *f* FERTIG *Reibahle* rear pilot; **hintere Kantenplatte** *f* KER & GLAS rear lip tile; **hinterer Kolben** *m* KFZTECH secondary piston; **hinterer Kontakt** *m* ELEKTRIZ back contact; **hinteres Lot** *nt* WASSERTRANS *Schiffkonstruktion* aft perpendicular; **hintere Scheibe** *f* MASCHINEN tail pulley; **hintere Schwarzschulter** *f* FERNSEH back porch; **hinterer Spalt** *m* AKUSTIK, AUFNAHME back gap; **hintere Spannung** *f* AUFNAHME *Tonband* back tension; **hinterer Verkleidungskonus** *m* RAUMFAHRT *Raumschiff* aft skirt; **hinterer Verschlußstein** *m* KER & GLAS back tweel; **hinterer Zellenring** *m* RAUMFAHRT *Raumschiff* aft frame section

Hinterachsantriebswelle *f* KFZTECH *Triebstrang* rear axle drive shaft

Hinterachsbrücke *f* KFZTECH differential casing

Hinterachse *f* KFZTECH *Triebstrang* back axle, rear axle; **~ mit doppelter Untersetzung** *f* KFZTECH double-reduction rear axle

Hinterachsgehäuse *nt* KFZTECH *Triebstrang* rear axle housing; **Hinterachsgehäusekörper** *m* KFZTECH rear axle housing assembly

Hinterachskörper *m* KFZTECH rear axle assembly

Hinterachstrichter *m* KFZTECH rear axle flared tube

Hinterachswelle *f* KFZTECH rear axle shaft; **Hinterachswellenrad** *nt* KFZTECH differential side gear

Hinterarbeiten *nt* FERTIG backing-off, relief, relieving, MASCHINEN backing-off, relief

hinterarbeiten *vt* FERTIG machine-relieve, *Spanung* clear, MASCHINEN *Maschine* back off, relieve

Hinterbohren *nt* MASCHINEN backing-off boring

Hinterdrehen *nt* MASCHINEN backing-off, relief, relieving

hinterdrehen *vt* FERTIG relieve by turning, MASCHINEN back off, relieve by turning

Hinterdrehmaschine *f* FERTIG relieving lathe, MASCHINEN backing-off lathe, relieving lathe

hinterdreht: ~er Fräser *m* MASCHINEN relieved-milling cutter; **~e Zähne** *m pl* MASCHINEN backed-off teeth, relieved teeth

hintereinandergeschaltet[1] *adj* ELEKTRIZ, ELEKTROTECH series, series-connected, GERÄT series-connected, KONTROLL serial

hintereinandergeschaltet:[2] **~er Transformator** *m* ELEKTRIZ series transformer; **~er Widerstand** *m* ELEKTRIZ series-connected resistance

Hintereinanderschaltung *f* ELEKTRIZ series connection, tandem connection, ELEKTROTECH series arrangement, series connection

Hinterflanke *f* ELEKTRONIK, FERNSEH, PHYS trailing edge

Hinterfräsen *nt* MASCHINEN relief milling

hinterfüllen *vt* BAU backfill

Hinterfüllung *f* BAU, KOHLEN backfill

Hintergrund *m* COMP & DV, DRUCK, FOTO background; **Hintergrundabsorption** *f* PHYS, STRAHLPHYS, TEILPHYS background absorption; **Hintergrundbeleuchtung** *f* ELEKTROTECH backlighting; **Hintergrundgeräusch** *nt* AKUSTIK, AUFNAHME, WERKPRÜF background noise; **Hintergrundmusik** *f* AUFNAHME background music; **Hintergrundprogramm** *nt* COMP & DV background program; **Hintergrundrauschen** *nt* AKUSTIK background noise, ELEKTRONIK background noise, grass, RAUMFAHRT background noise; **Hintergrundsrauschtemperatur** *f* RAUMFAHRT *Weltraumfunk* sky noise temperature; **Hintergrundstrahlung** *f* PHYS, STRAHLPHYS, TEILPHYS background radiation; **Hintergrundverarbeitung** *f* COMP & DV background processing

Hinterkante: ~ des Luftschraubenblattes *f* LUFTTRANS *Hubschrauber* blade trailing edge; **Hinterkantenwirbel** *m pl* STRÖMPHYS trailing vortices

Hinterkipperanhänger *m* TRANS rear tipping trailer

Hinterkippung *f* BAU *Kfz* end dump

Hinterlagedichtung *f* FERTIG *Kunststoffinstallationen* backing seal

Hinterlegung *f* PATENT deposit

hintermauern *vt* BAU back up

Hintermauerungsmaterial *nt* BAU backing

Hinterrad *nt* KFZTECH rear wheel; **Hinterradachse** *f* MECHAN rear axle; **Hinterradantrieb** *m* KFZTECH rear wheel drive; **Hinterradantrieb beim Heckmotor** *m* KFZTECH rear engine rear wheel drive; **Hinterradaufhängung** *f* KFZTECH rear suspension

Hinterschleifen *nt* MASCHINEN backing-off, relieving

hinterschleifen *vt* FERTIG relief-grind

Hinterschleifwinkel *m* FERTIG relief angle

Hinterschliff *m* FERTIG back-off clearance, relief, MASCHINEN relief; **~ der Fase** *m* FERTIG *Spanung* primary clearance

Hinterschlifffläche *f* FERTIG *Bohrer* flank

hinterschneiden *vt* MASCHINEN undercut

Hinterschneidung *f* KUNSTSTOFF, MASCHINEN undercut

Hinterschraube *f* LUFTTRANS rear propeller

Hintersetzwinkel *m* FERTIG *Reibahle* radial relief

Hintersteven *m* WASSERTRANS *Schiffbau* stern frame, sternpost

Hinterwand *f* MASCHINEN back-end plate
hinübernehmen *vt* DRUCK overrun
Hinweis *m* EISENBAHN notice; **~ auf Spezifikationsände-rungen** *m (SCN)* TRANS specification change notice *(SCN);* **Hinweisansagegerät** *nt* TELEKOM intercep-tion equipment
hinweisend *adj* PHYS point
Hinweis: **Hinweislinie** *f* KONSTZEICH leader line; **Hin-weissymbol** *nt* COMP & DV sentinel; **Hinweistafel für Hydranten und Wasseranschlüsse** *f* SICHERHEIT *Brandbekämpfung* indicator plate for hydrants and water supply points; **Hinweiston** *m* TELEKOM alerting tone; **Hinweiszeichen** *nt* COMP & DV reference mark
hinzufügen *vt* COMP & DV add
hissen *vt* WASSERTRANS *Segeln, Flagge* hoist
Histogramm *nt* COMP & DV, ERGON, MATH, PHYS, QUAL, TELEKOM histogram
histologisch: ~es Bad *nt* LABOR *Schnitt aufziehen*
Histon *nt* CHEMIE histone
Hittorf: ~scher Dunkelraum *m* ELEKTRONIK Hittorf dark space, PHYS Crookes dark space
Hitzdraht *m* GERÄT hot wire; **Hitzdrahtdurchfluß-meßgerät** *nt* GERÄT hot-wire flowmeter; **Hitzdraht-instrument** *nt* GERÄT thermal expansion instrument, PHYS hot-wire anemometer; **Hitzdrahtleistungs-messer** *m* ELEKTRIZ hot-wire wattmeter; **Hitzdrahtmeßwerk** *nt* GERÄT expansion movement; **Hitzdrahtmikrofon** *nt* AKUSTIK hot-wire microphone; **Hitzdrahtrelais** *nt* ELEKTRIZ hot-wire relay; **Hitzdraht-strommeßgerät** *nt* ELEKTRIZ hot-wire ammeter, thermal ammeter
Hitze *f* HEIZ & KÄLTE, KOHLEN, PHYS, TEXTIL heat, THERMOD burning heat, heat; **Hitze- und UV-Bestrahlungstest** *m* KER & GLAS bake and UV-irradiation test
hitzeabweisend *adj* SICHERHEIT heat-resistant, heat-proof
Hitze: **Hitzeausgleich** *m* RAUMFAHRT heat transfer engi-neer; **Hitzebarriere** *f* ANSTRICH thermal barrier; **Hitzebehandlung** *f* ANSTRICH, METALL heat treatment, TEXTIL baking
hitzebeständig [1] *adj* ERDÖL thermostable, HEIZ & KÄLTE, PHYS, RAUMFAHRT *Raumschiff*, VERPACK heat-resi-stant
hitzebeständig: [2] **~es Glas** *nt* KER & GLAS heat-resisting glass; **~er Stahl** *m* METALL heat-resisting steel
Hitzebeständigkeit *f* THERMOD resistance to heat, tem-perature resistance
Hitze: **Hitzeerschöpfung** *f* ERGON heat exhaustion; **Hitzefarbe** *f* METALL heat tint; **Hitzefärben** *nt* METALL heat-tinting; **Hitzefluß** *m* RAUMFAHRT heat flux; **Hitzekachel** *f* RAUMFAHRT tile; **Hitzekollaps** *m* ERGON heat syncope; **Hitzemantel** *m* RAUMFAHRT heat shroud; **Hitzemauer** *f* ANSTRICH, LUFTTRANS thermal barrier; **Hitzeriß** *m* MECHAN hot tear; **Hitzeschild** *m* LUFTTRANS heat shield, heating shield, RAUMFAHRT *Raumschiff* heat shield, thermal protection shield, THERMOD heat shield; **Hitzeschutzhandschuh** *m* SICHERHEIT heat-resistant glove; **Hitzeschutzkleidung** *f* SICHERHEIT heat-protective clothing, heatproof clothing; **Hitzeschutzmaterial** *nt* SICHERHEIT heat-protective material; **Hitzeschutzwand** *f* LUFTTRANS heat-insulating wall; **Hitzestrahlung** *f* RAUMFAHRT *Raumschiff* radiative heat transfer; **Hitzestrahlungs-messer** *m* THERMOD pyrometer
hitzesuchend *adj* RAUMFAHRT *Raumschiff* heat-seeking

hitzetrocknen *vt* THERMOD dry by heat
Hitze: **Hitzeverschweißen** *nt* VERPACK heat welding; **Hitze-versiegelmaschine** *f* VERPACK heat-sealing machine; **Hitzeversiegelung** *f* VERPACK heat induction seal, heat sealing; **Hitzeversiegler** *m* VERPACK heat-sealing device; **Hitzewelle** *f* THERMOD heat wave; **Hitzewiderstand** *m* LUFTTRANS heating resistor
H-Krümmer *m* ELEKTROTECH H-plane bend
hl *abbr (Hektoliter)* LABOR hl *(hectoliter)*
HMF-Ruß *m* KUNSTSTOFF HMF carbon black
H-Modus *m* ELEKTROTECH, TELEKOM H-mode, TE mode
HNF *abbr (höchste nutzbare Frequenz)* RADIO MUF *(maximum usable frequency)*
Ho *(Holmium)* CHEMIE Ho *(holmium)*
Hobel *m* BAU *Werkzeug*, FERTIG *Werkzeug* plane; **Hobel-bank** *f* BAU carpenter's bench, joiner's bench; **Hobeleisen** *nt* BAU, MASCHINEN plane iron; **Hobelka-sten** *m* BAU plane stock; **Hobelmaschine** *f* BAU, FERTIG, MASCHINEN, MECHAN planer, planing machi-ne; **Hobelmeißel** *m* BAU paring chisel, MASCHINEN planer tool; **Hobelmesser** *nt* BAU plane iron
Hobeln *nt* BAU, MASCHINEN planing
hobeln *vt* FERTIG, MASCHINEN, MECHAN plane
Hobel: **Hobelspan** *m* BAU shaving, FERTIG planing chip; **Hobelspäne** *m pl* BAU wood shavings; **Hobeltisch** *m* MASCHINEN planer table; **Hobelwerkzeug** *nt* BAU pla-ning tools
hoch [1] *adj* MASCHINEN, PAPIER, PHYS *Temperatur*, UM-WELTSCHUTZ *Konzentration* high **für hohe Geschwindigkeit** *adj* MECHAN high-speed; **~ radioaktiv** *adj* KERNTECH highly-radioactive; **mit hoher Wieder-gabetreue** *adj* AUFNAHME high fidelity
hoch [2] *adv* MATH to the power of
hoch [3]: **hoher Anstellwinkel** *m* LUFTTRANS *Hubschrauber* high pitch; **hoher Anzeigewert** *m* GERÄT high reading; **hohe Auflösung** *f* COMP & DV high resolution; **hoher Bahnsteig** *m* EISENBAHN elevated platform; **hoher Bildpegel** *m* FERNSEH high picture level; **hohe Dämp-fung** *f* TELEKOM *Transmission* high loss; **hohe Drehzahl** *f* MASCHINEN high speed; **hohes Einheits-drehzahlrad** *nt* NICHTFOSS ENERG high specific speed wheel; **hohe Geschwindigkeit** *f* MASCHINEN high speed; **hoher Integrationsgrad** *m (LSI)* COMP & DV, ELEKTRONIK, PHYS *mehr als etwa 1000 Bauelemente*, TELEKOM large-scale integration *(LSI);* **hohe Losgröße** *f* FERTIG high-quantity lot; **hoher Schwe-felgehalt** *nt* ERDÖL *Erdöl, Erdgas, Raffinerieprodukte* high sulfur content (AmE), high sulphur content (BrE); **hohe See** *f* WASSERTRANS open sea; **hoher Verlust** *m* TELEKOM high loss; **hohe Wassersäule** *f* NICHTFOSS ENERG high head; **hohe Welle** *f* WASSER-TRANS *Seezustand* billow; **hoher Widerstand** *m* PHYS, TELEKOM high resistance
hoch [4]: **zu ~ ansteuern** *vt* RAUMFAHRT *Weltraumfunk* overdrive; **~ drei nehmen** *vt* MATH cube; **mit hoher Geschwindigkeit laufen lassen** *vt* FERTIG overspeed; **~ zwei nehmen** *vt* MATH square
Hoch *nt* WASSERTRANS high
hochabriebfest: ~er Furnace-Ruß *m (HAF-Ruß)* KUNSTSTOFF high abrasion furnace carbon black *(HAF carbon black)*
Hochachse *f* LUFTTRANS normal axis; **Hochachsewind-turbine** *f* NICHTFOSS ENERG vertical-axis wind turbine
hochaktiv: ~er Abfall *m* KERNTECH HAW, highly-active waste

hochangereichert: ~es Uran *nt* KERNTECH highly-enriched uranium

hochauflösend[1] *adj* COMP & DV high-resolution

hochauflösend:[2] ~e Abtastung *f* STRAHLPHYS high-resolution scan; ~es Fernsehen *nt* FERNSEH *(EDTV)* extended definition television *(EDTV)*, FERNSEH *(HDTV)* high-definition television *(HDTV)*; ~er Scan *m* STRAHLPHYS high-resolution scan; ~e Untersuchung *f* STRAHLPHYS *Linienprofile* high-resolution study

Hoch: **Hochausbeute-Faserstoff** *m* PAPIER high-yield pulp; **Hochbahn** *f* EISENBAHN elevated railroad (AmE), elevated railway (BrE), overhead railroad (AmE), overhead railway (BrE), TRANS overhead track; **Hochbau** *m* BAU building construction; **Hochbauschgarn** *nt* TEXTIL high-bulk spun yarn; **Hochbehälter** *m* BAU tower tank; **Hochdach-Kastenwagen** *m* KFZTECH raised roof van; **Hochdach-Transporter** *m* KFZTECH raised roof van

hochdotiert *adj* ELEKTRONIK high-dose

Hochdruck *m* DRUCK letterpress, letterpress printing, PHYS high performance, high pressure; **Hochdruckadditiv** *nt* ERDÖL *Bohrtechnik* extreme-pressure additive; **Hochdruckaufnehmer** *m* HEIZ & KÄLTE high-pressure pickup; **Hochdruckflüssigchromatographie** *f* *(HPLC)* LABOR, LEBENSMITTEL high-pressure liquid chromatography *(HPLC)*; **Hochdruckgebiet** *nt* WASSERTRANS *Wetterkunde* high-pressure area; **Hochdruckheizung** *f* HEIZ & KÄLTE high-pressure heating system; **Hochdruckkeil** *m* WASSERTRANS *barometrischer Druck* ridge; **Hochdruckkessel** *m* HEIZ & KÄLTE high-pressure boiler; **Hochdruckkolbenverdichter** *m* MASCHINEN high-pressure piston compressor; **Hochdruckkompressor** *m* MASCHINEN high-pressure compressor; **Hochdruckkraftstoffpumpe** *f* KFZTECH high-pressure fuel pump; **Hochdruckmanometer** *nt* GERÄT high-range gauge (BrE), high-range gage (AmE); **Hochdruckmesser** *m* HEIZ & KÄLTE high-pressure gage (AmE), high-pressure gauge (BrE); **Hochdruckquecksilberdampflampe** *f* ELEKTRIZ high-pressure mercury lamp; **Hochdruckregler** *m* HEIZ & KÄLTE high-pressure controller; **Hochdruckreifen** *m* KFZTECH high-pressure tire (AmE), high-pressure tyre (BrE); **Hochdruckreinigung** *f* MEERSCHMUTZ high-pressure water blasting; **Hochdruckrotationsmaschine** *f* DRUCK letterpress rotary; **Hochdruckschmierstoff** *m* MASCHINEN extreme-pressure lubricant, high-pressure lubricant; **Hochdruckschwimmerventil** *nt* HEIZ & KÄLTE high-pressure float valve; **Hochdruckspülen** *nt* MEERSCHMUTZ high-pressure flushing; **Hochdrucktank** *m* RAUMFAHRT *Raumschiff* high-pressure tank; **Hochdruckumgebung** *f* SICHERHEIT high-pressure atmosphere; **Hochdruckvakuumpumpe** *f* MASCHINEN high-pressure vacuum pump; **Hochdruckventil** *nt* MASCHINEN high-pressure valve; **Hochdruckzylinder** *m* MASCHINEN high-pressure cylinder

Hoch: **Hochebene** *f* ERDÖL plateau

hochenergetisch: ~e Strahlung *f* STRAHLPHYS high-level radiation

Hoch: **Hochenergieband** *nt* FERNSEH high-energy tape; **Hochenergiefusion** *f* KERNTECH high-energy fusion; **Hochenergiemetallumformung** *f* MASCHINEN high-energy metal forming; **Hochenergiephysik** *f* PHYS high-energy physics; **Hochenergieproton** *nt* RAUMFAHRT high-energy proton; **Hochenergiestrahlung** *f* STRAHLPHYS high-energy radiation; **Hochfahrbahn** *f* EISENBAHN overhead trackway

hochfahren *vt* AUFNAHME bring up

Hoch: **Hochfahrzeit** *f* AUFNAHME run-up time

hochfest: ~er Bohrschlamm *m* ERDÖL *Bohrtechnik* high-solid mud; ~e Faser *f* TEXTIL high-tenacity fiber (AmE), high-tenacity fibre (BrE); ~er Stahl *m* METALL high-tensile steel

Hoch: **Hochflußreaktor** *m* KERNTECH high flux reactor; **Hochformat** *nt* COMP & DV portrait format, portrait representation, DRUCK portrait format

hochfrequent[1] *adj* ELEKTRIZ, ELEKTRONIK, RADIO high-frequency, radio-frequency

hochfrequent:[2] ~e Erwärmung *f* ELEKTROTECH electronic heating

Hochfrequenz *f* *(HF)* AUFNAHME, ELEKTRIZ, ELEKTRONIK, FERNSEH, RADIO, TELEKOM, WASSERTRANS high frequency *(HF)*, radio frequency *(RF)*; **Hochfrequenzausgleich** *m* AUFNAHME, ELEKTRONIK high-frequency compensation; **Hochfrequenzeisenkern** *m* ELEKTROTECH powdered iron core; **Hochfrequenzerwärmung** *f* KUNSTSTOFF dielectric heating, radio-frequency heating; **Hochfrequenzfilter** *nt* AUFNAHME, ELEKTRONIK high-frequency filter; **Hochfrequenzgenerator** *m* ELEKTRIZ high-frequency generator, ELEKTROTECH radio-frequency alternator; **Hochfrequenzheizung** *f* ELEKTROTECH electronic heating, high-frequency heating; **Hochfrequenzinduktionserwärmung** *f* ELEKTRIZ dielectric heating, eddy current heating, high-frequency heating; **Hochfrequenzinduktionslöten** *nt* BAU high-frequency induction brazing; **Hochfrequenzkabel** *nt* ELEKTRIZ high-frequency cable; **Hochfrequenzkomponente** *f* ELEKTRONIK high-frequency component; **Hochfrequenzleiterplatte** *f* ELEKTRONIK high-frequency printed circuit, high frequency printed-circuit board; **Hochfrequenzleitung** *f* RADIO high-frequency line; **Hochfrequenzlitze** *f* ELEKTROTECH stranded conductor; **Hochfrequenznetzanalyse** *f* ELEKTROTECH high-frequency network analysis; **Hochfrequenzofen** *m* ELEKTROTECH high-frequency furnace; **Hochfrequenzschalten** *nt* ELEKTROTECH high-frequency switching; **Hochfrequenzschweißung** *f* VERPACK *von Folien* high-frequency welding; **Hochfrequenzsignal** *nt* ELEKTRONIK high-frequency signal, radio signal; **Hochfrequenzspektrum** *nt* ELEKTRONIK high-frequency spectrum; **Hochfrequenzstörung** *f* AUFNAHME radio-frequency interference, ELEKTRONIK radio interference, radio noise, radio-frequency interference, RADIO, TELEKOM radio-frequency interference; **Hochfrequenzstrom** *m* ELEKTRIZ high-frequency current, ELEKTROTECH radio-frequency current; **Hochfrequenzträger** *m* ELEKTRONIK radio-frequency carrier; **Hochfrequenztransformator** *m* ELEKTROTECH high-frequency transformer; **Hochfrequenztransistor** *m* ELEKTRONIK high-frequency transistor; **Hochfrequenztrichterlautsprecher** *m* AUFNAHME high-frequency horn loudspeaker; **Hochfrequenzverstärkung** *f* ELEKTRONIK high-frequency amplification

Hoch: **Hochgebirgsbahn** *f* EISENBAHN mountain railroad (AmE), mountain railway (BrE)

hochgeleimt: ~es Papier *nt* DRUCK hard-sized paper

hochgemahlen: ~er Zellstoff *m* PAPIER wet-beaten pulp

hochgenau: ~e Abwiegung *f* VERPACK ultrahigh accuracy weighing

Hochgeschwindigkeit *f* MASCHINEN high speed,

WASSERVERSORG high velocity; **Hochgeschwindigkeitsabtastung** *f* FERNSEH high-velocity scanning; **Hochgeschwindigkeitsfahrzeug** *nt* KFZTECH HHSV, high hypothetical speed vehicle; **Hochgeschwindigkeitsgasturbinenreisebus** *m* KFZTECH high-speed gas turbine motor coach; **Hochgeschwindigkeitsgasturbinentriebwagen** *m* EISENBAHN high-speed gas turbine railcar; **Hochgeschwindigkeitskopie** *f* FERNSEH high-speed duplication; **Hochgeschwindigkeitsschienenfahrzeug** *nt* EISENBAHN super high-speed rail vehicle; **Hochgeschwindigkeitsschleifmaschine** *f* MASCHINEN high-speed grinding machine; **Hochgeschwindigkeitsschütteln** *nt* LUFTTRANS high-speed buffeting; **Hochgeschwindigkeitsteilchen** *nt* KERNTECH high-speed particle; **Hochgeschwindigkeitsverkehr** *m* TRANS super high-speed traffic; **Hochgeschwindigkeitszug** *m* EISENBAHN APT, advanced passenger train (BrE), high-speed train

hochgeständert: ~e Einschienenhängebahn *f (H-Bahn)* EISENBAHN overhead monorail

hochgestellt: ~es Zeichen *nt* COMP & DV, DRUCK superscript

Hochglanz[1] *m* KUNSTSTOFF high gloss

Hochglanz:[2] auf ~ bringen *vt* ANSTRICH polish

Hochglanz: **Hochglanzfolie** *f* VERPACK high-gloss foil; **Hochglanzfoto** *nt* FOTO glossy print; **Hochglanzmaschine** *f* FOTO glazing machine; **Hochglanzpapier** *nt* FOTO glossy paper, VERPACK high-gloss paper; **Hochglanzplatte** *f* FOTO glazing sheet

hochglanzpolieren *vt* ANSTRICH burnish

Hochglanz: **Hochglanzpolitur** *f* MASCHINEN mirror finish; **Hochglanztrockenpresse** *f* FOTO dryer-glazer

Hoch: **Hochgleis** *nt* EISENBAHN elevated track; **Hochglühen** *nt* METALL full annealing

hochgradig: ~e Hitze *f* KERNTECH high-grade heat

hochhebeln *vt* MASCHINEN lever up

Hochheben *nt* BAU raising

hochheben *vt* MASCHINEN hoist

hochintegriert: ~er logischer Schaltkreis *m* ELEKTRONIK high-density logic; ~er Schaltkreis *m (LSI-Kreis)* ELEKTRONIK, PHYS, TELEKOM large-scale integrated circuit *(LSI circuit)*; ~e Schaltung *f* ELEKTRONIK high-density integrated circuit

Hoch: **Hochintensitätslichtbogen** *m* ELEKTRIZ high-intensity electric arc

hochkantbiegen *vt* BAU bend on edge

hochkanten *vt* BAU raise on edge

hochkantig: ~es Wachstum *nt* METALL edgewise growth

Hoch: **Hochkomma** *nt* DRUCK turned comma; **Hochkurzzeiterhitzung** *f* LEBENSMITTEL HTST, high-temperature short time pasteurization; **Hochladen** *nt* COMP & DV uploading

hochladen *vt* COMP & DV upload

Hoch: **Hochlastwiderstand** *m* ELEKTROTECH power resistor; **Hochlaufen** *nt* LUFTTRANS *Leistung des Motors* engine run-up, *Motor und Triebwerk* run-up

hochlaufen *vi* LUFTTRANS *Motor und Triebwerk* run-up

Hochleistung *f* FERTIG, MASCHINEN heavy duty, MASCHINEN *(HD)* heavy duty *(HD)*, MECHAN heavy duty, PHYS high performance; **Hochleistungsband** *nt* AUFNAHME high-output tape; **Hochleistungsbatterie** *f* TRANS high-performance battery; **Hochleistungsbipolartransistor** *m* ELEKTRONIK high-power bipolar transistor; **Hochleistungsbrenner** *m* BAU high-pressure blowpipe; **Hochleistungsdrehmaschine** *f*

MASCHINEN heavy-duty lathe; **Hochleistungsdüse** *f* KFZTECH high-speed auxiliary jet; **Hochleistungsfilterung** *f* ABFALL high-rate filtration; **Hochleistungs-Flüssigkeitschromatographie** *f* UMWELTSCHMUTZ high-performance liquid chromatography; **Hochleistungsgleichrichter** *m* ELEKTROTECH high-power rectifier; **Hochleistungskontakt** *m* ELEKTROTECH heavy-duty contact; **Hochleistungslaser** *m* ELEKTRONIK high-energy laser, KERNTECH high-power laser; **Hochleistungslift** *m* BAU heavy duty lift; **Hochleistungslüfter** *m* HEIZ & KÄLTE high-performance fan; **Hochleistungsmanipulator im Reaktorkern** *m* KERNTECH in-core power manipulator; **Hochleistungsöl** *nt (HD-Öl)* MASCHINEN heavy-duty oil *(HD oil)*; **Hochleistungsröhre** *f* ELEKTRONIK highpower tube; **Hochleistungsthyristor** *m* ELEKTROTECH high-power SCR; **Hochleistungstransformator** *m* ELEKTRIZ high-power transformer; **Hochleistungsverbraucher** *m* ELEKTROTECH high-power load; **Hochleistungsverstärker** *m* RAUMFAHRT *Weltraumfunk* high-power amplifier

Hoch: **Hochlicht** *nt* DRUCK highlight; **Hochlinie** *f* EISENBAHN elevated line; **Hochmodul-Furnace-Ruß** *m* KUNSTSTOFF high-modulus furnace carbon black

hochmolekular *adj* CHEMIE macromolecular

Hochofen *m* FERTIG, KER & GLAS, KOHLEN, MASCHINEN, THERMOD blast furnace; **Hochofenausmauerung** *f* FERTIG blast furnace lining, shirt (AmE); **Hochofengas** *nt* FERTIG blast furnace gas; **Hochofenzement** *m* BAU blast furnace cement

hochohmig[1] *adj* RADIO high-impedance, TELEKOM high-resistance

hochohmig:[2] ~er Zustand *m* ELEKTROTECH high-impedance state

Hoch: **Hochohmigkeit** *f* RADIO high impedance; **Hochohmwiderstand** *m* TELEKOM high resistance

Hochpaß *m* TELEKOM high-pass; **Hochpaßfilter** *nt* AUFNAHME, COMP & DV, ELEKTRIZ, ELEKTRONIK, FERNSEH, PHYS, TELEKOM high-pass filter; **Hochpaßfilter zweiter Ordnung** *nt* ELEKTRONIK second order high-pass filter; **Hochpaßfilterung** *f* ELEKTRONIK high-pass filtering

Hochprägung *f* DRUCK embossing, relief printing

hochratig: ~es Faksimile *nt* TELEKOM high-speed facsimile

hochrein: ~es Pigment *nt* KUNSTSTOFF high-purity pigment

hochrot *adj* METALL bright red

Hoch: **Hochschulterlager** *nt* MASCHINEN rigid deep-groove ball bearing

Hochsee *f* WASSERTRANS high seas; **Hochsee-** *pref* WASSERTRANS deep-sea; **Hochseebagger** *m* MEERSCHMUTZ marine dredge; **Hochseebergungsschlepper** *m* TRANS seagoing salvage tug; **Hochseefischerei** *f* WASSERTRANS *Fischerei* deep-sea fishing; **Hochseeflotte** *f* WASSERTRANS sea fleet; **Hochseekreuzer** *m* WASSERTRANS ocean-going cruiser; **Hochseeschiff** *nt* MEERSCHMUTZ seagoing vessel, WASSERTRANS seagoing vessel, *Schifftyp* ocean-going ship; **Hochseeschiffahrt** *f* WASSERTRANS deep-sea navigation; **Hochseeschlepper** *m* WASSERTRANS seagoing tug; **Hochseevermessungsschiff** *nt* WASSERTRANS ocean survey vessel

Hochsicherheitsverglasung *f* KFZTECH high-safety glazing

Hochsiedendes *nt* THERMOD distillation tail

Hochspannung *f* ELEKTRIZ HT, high tension, high voltage, FERNSEH EHT, extra-high tension; **Hochspannungsanschlußklemme** *f* KFZTECH high-tension terminal; **Hochspannungsblitzschutz** *m* SICHERHEIT lightning arrester for high voltage; **Hochspannungseinrichtung** *f* ELEKTRIZ high-voltage equipment; **Hochspannungsgleichrichter** *m* ELEKTRIZ high-voltage rectifier, FERNSEH EHT rectifier; **Hochspannungsgleichstromkraftübertragung** *f* ELEKTROTECH DC high-tension power transmission; **Hochspannungsimpulsgenerator** *m* ELEKTRIZ high-voltage impulse generator; **Hochspannungsisolierung** *f* ELEKTRIZ high-voltage insulation; **Hochspannungskabel** *nt* ELEKTRIZ high-voltage cable; **Hochspannungsleitung** *f* BAU transmission line, ELEKTRIZ high-voltage transmission line; **Hochspannungsmotor** *m* ELEKTRIZ high-voltage motor; **Hochspannungsnetz** *nt* ELEKTROTECH high-tension power supply, high-voltage power supply; **Hochspannungspol** *m* KFZTECH high-tension terminal; **Hochspannungsporzellanisolator** *m* ELEKTRIZ high-voltage porcelain insulator; **Hochspannungsprüfgerät** *nt* ELEKTRIZ high-voltage tester; **Hochspannungsschaltanlage** *f* ELEKTRIZ high-voltage switchgear; **Hochspannungsseekabel** *nt* ELEKTRIZ high-voltage undersea cable; **Hochspannungssteckdose** *f* KERNTECH high-potential socket; **Hochspannungsstoßgenerator** *m* ELEKTRIZ high-voltage impulse generator; **Hochspannungsstromunterbrecher** *m* ELEKTRIZ high-voltage circuit breaker; **Hochspannungsstromversorgung** *f* ELEKTRIZ HT power supply; **Hochspannungsstromversorgungsnetz** *nt* ELEKTRIZ high-voltage grid; **Hochspannungstransformator** *m* ELEKTRIZ high-voltage transformer; **Hochspannungsversorgung** *f* FERNSEH EHT supply; **Hochspannungswicklung** *f* ELEKTRIZ high-voltage winding

höchst:[1] ~ **eben** *adj* ANSTRICH ultrasmooth; ~ **glatt** *adj* ANSTRICH ultrasmooth

höchst:[2] ~**e Amplitude** *f* ELEKTRONIK peak amplitude; ~**er Außenluftüberdruck** *m* LUFTTRANS *Überschallknall* free-air peak overpressure; ~**e brauchbare Übertragungsfrequenz** *f* ELEKTROTECH maximum usable frequency; ~**e Dauerleistung** *f* LUFTTRANS maximum continuous power; ~**e für längere Zeit entnehmbare Leistung** *f* LUFTTRANS METO power, maximum except takeoff power; ~**e nutzbare Frequenz** *f* (*HNF*) RADIO maximum usable frequency (MUF); ~**er Punkt vor Sinkflug** *m* LUFTTRANS *künstlicher Flugsimulator* top of descent; ~**e Rotordrehzahl** *f* LUFTTRANS maximum rotor speed; ~**e Schlagbelastung** *f* LUFTTRANS *Hubschrauber* flapping stress peak

hochstabil: ~**er Bohrschlamm** *m* ERDÖL high-solid mud; ~**er Oszillator** *m* ELEKTRONIK highly stable oscillator

Höchst- *pref* ELEKTRONIK, KFZTECH, LUFTTRANS, MASCHINEN maximum; **Höchstanteil** *m* QUAL upper limiting proportion

hochstapeln *vt* VERPACK stack up

Höchst-: **Höchstauftrieb** *m* LUFTTRANS maximum lift; **Höchstbelastung** *f* ELEKTROTECH peak load, LUFTTRANS maximum load; **Höchstbelastungsgrenze** *f* SICHERHEIT maximum exposure limit; **Höchstbetriebshöhe** *f* LUFTTRANS maximum operating altitude; **Höchstdrehzahl** *f* KFZTECH *Motor* peak revs, MASCHINEN maximum speed; **Höchstdrehzahl des**

Motors *f* KFZTECH peak engine speed; **Höchstdruck** *m* (*EP*) MASCHINEN extreme pressure (*EP*)

hochstegig *adj* FERTIG high-webbed

Hoch: **Hochstellen** *nt* KERNTECH *Regeln* setup; **Hochstellung** *f* COMP & DV superscript

Höchst-: **Höchstflugdauer** *f* LUFTTRANS endurance, maximum flying time

Höchstfrequenz *f* ELEKTRONIK microwave, superhigh frequency; **Höchstfrequenzgenerator** *m* ELEKTRONIK microwave generator, microwave synthesizer; **Höchstfrequenzoszillator** *m* ELEKTRONIK microwave oscillator; **Höchstfrequenzsignal** *nt* ELEKTRONIK microwave signal; **Höchstfrequenzsignalgenerator** *m* ELEKTRONIK microwave signal generator; **Höchstfrequenzsignalquelle** *f* ELEKTRONIK microwave signal source

Höchstgeschwindigkeit:[1] **mit** ~ *adj* TRANS at full speed

Höchstgeschwindigkeit[2] *f* EISENBAHN, KFZTECH, LUFTTRANS, MASCHINEN maximum speed, TRANS *Geschwindigkeitsbegrenzung* speed limit, WASSERTRANS maximum speed; ~ **in Normalfluglage mit Nennleistung** *f* LUFTTRANS maximum speed in level flight with rated power

Höchst-: **Höchstgewicht** *nt* VERPACK maximum weight; **Höchstintegration** *f* (*VLSI*) COMP & DV, ELEKTRONIK, TELEKOM very large-scale integration (*VLSI*); **Höchstintegrationsschaltkreis** *m* PHYS very large-scale integrated circuit; **Höchstlast** *f* ELEKTROTECH, PAPIER peak load, WASSERTRANS maximum load; **Höchstlautstärke-Geschwindigkeit** *f* AUFNAHME peak volume velocity

Höchstleistung *f* ELEKTRIZ maximum output, maximum power, ELEKTROTECH peak power; ~ **bei Nennwindgeschwindigkeit** *f* NICHTFOSS ENERG maximum power at rated wind speed; **Höchstleistungsmischungsverhältnis** *nt* KFZTECH maximum output mixture ratio; **Höchstleistungsrechner** *m* COMP & DV number cruncher, supercomputer

Höchst-: **Höchstnennstrom** *m* ELEKTROTECH maximum current rating; **Höchstnutzlast** *f* LUFTTRANS maximum payload; **Höchstquantil** *nt* QUAL upper limiting quantile

Hoch: **Hochstraße** *f* BAU elevated highway, elevated motorway, TRANS flyover (BrE), skyway (AmE); **Hochstromdiode** *f* ELEKTRONIK high-current diode; **Hochstromtransistor** *m* ELEKTRONIK high-current transistor

höchstschmelzend: ~**es Metall** *nt* ANSTRICH refractory metal

Höchst-: **Höchstschweißstrom** *m* BAU maximum welding current; **Höchstspannung** *f* ELEKTRIZ maximum voltage, ELEKTROTECH peak voltage, FERNSEH extremely high tension; **Höchstspannungsrelais** *nt* ELEKTRIZ maximum voltage relay; **Höchststromstärke** *f* ELEKTROTECH peak current; **Höchsttemperatur in der Brennelementhülse** *f* KERNTECH PCT, peak cladding temperature; **Höchstverbrauch** *m* ELEKTRIZ maximum demand; **Höchstverbrauchszähler** *m* ELEKTROTECH demand meter; **Höchstvergrößerung** *f* METALL ultimate magnification; **Höchstwert** *m* ELEKTRIZ maximum value, ELEKTRONIK peak value, KERNTECH maximum, PAPIER peak, QUAL upper limiting value; **Höchstwertanzeiger** *m* ELEKTRONIK peak indicator

höchstwertig: ~**e Binärstelle** *f* COMP & DV MSB, most significant bit; ~**es Bit** *nt* COMP & DV MSB, most

significant bit; **~es Zeichen** *nt* COMP & DV most significant character; **~e Ziffer** *f* COMP & DV most significant
digit

höchstzulässig: ~e Betriebsgeschwindigkeit *f* LUFT-
TRANS maximum permissible operating speed; **~e
Dosis** *f* STRAHLPHYS *ionisierende Strahlung* maximum
permissible dose; **~e Fahrwerkbetriebsgeschwindig-
keit** *f* LUFTTRANS maximum landing-gear operating
speed; **~es Gesamtgewicht** *nt* KFZTECH, LUFTTRANS,
WASSERTRANS maximum total weight; **~e Geschwindigkeit** *f* KFZTECH maximum design speed **~e
Geschwindigkeit bei ausgefahrenem Fahrwerk** *nt*
LUFTTRANS maximum landing-gear extended speed;
~e Geschwindigkeit bei ausgefahrenen Klappen *f*
LUFTTRANS maximum flap extended speed; **~e Konzentration** *f* *(HZK)* UMWELTSCHMUTZ maximum
allowable concentration *(MAC),* threshold limit
value *(TLV);* **~e Konzentration in der Umwelt** *f* UM-
WELTSCHMUTZ threshold limit value in the free
environment; **~e Machzahl** *f* LUFTTRANS maximum
permissible Mach number; **~e Riemenspannung** *f* MA-
SCHINEN maximum allowable belt tension; **~e
Überdrehzahl des Motors** *f* LUFTTRANS maximum engine overspeed

Hoch: **Hochtank** *m* TRANS, WASSERTRANS deep tank
Hochtemperatur *f* METALL, KERNTECH, PHYS high temperature

hochtemperaturbeständig: ~e Isolierung *f* ELEKTRIZ
high-temperature insulation;

Hochtemperatur : **Hochtemperatur-Festigkeitsprüfung**
f WERKPRÜF high-temperature strength test; **Hoch-
temperaturfett** *nt* MECHAN high-temperature grease;
Hochtemperaturkriechen *nt* METALL high-temperature creep; **Hochtemperaturreaktor** *m* *(HTR)*
KERNTECH high-temperature reactor *(HTR);* **Hochtemperaturreaktor mit Bündelelementen** *m*
KERNTECH block-type element-fueled high temperature reactor (AmE), block-type element-fuelled high
temperature reactor (BrE); **Hochtemperatur-Salz-
schmelztreibstoffzelle** *f* KFZ-TECH high-temperature
molten salts fuel battery; **Hochtemperatursupraleit-
fähigkeit** *f* PHYS high-temperature superconductivity;
Hochtemperaturtreibstoffzelle *f* KFZTECH high-temperature fuel cell; **Hochtemperaturwindkanal** *m*
LUFTTRANS hot shot wind tunnel

Hoch: **Hoch-Tief-Verhalten** *nt* REGELUNG high-low action; **Hochtonausgleich** *m* AUFNAHME treble
compensation

hochtonig *adj* AUFNAHME treble

Hoch: **Hochtonlautsprecher** *m* AUFNAHME tweeter

**Hochvakuum: ** *nt* ELEKTRONIK hard vacuum, MECHAN,
PHYS high vacuum; **Hochvakuumbildröhre** *f* FERNSEH
high-vacuum cathode ray tube; **Hochvakuumfotozelle**
f ELEKTRONIK vacuum phototube; **Hochvakuumofen**
m MASCHINEN high-vacuum furnace; **Hochvakuum-
röhre** *f* ELEKTRONIK hard-vacuum tube, high-vacuum
tube, FERNSEH vacuum tube

hochverfügbar *adj* COMP & DV fault-tolerant

Hochwasser *nt* WASSERTRANS high tide, high water;
Hochwasserentlastungsanlage *f* WASSERVERSORG
flood spillway, spillway; **Hochwassermarke** *f* WASSER-
TRANS high-water mark; **Hochwasserschutz** *m*
NICHTFOSS ENERG flood control, WASSERVERSORG
flood abatement, flood control, flood prevention;
Hochwasserspiegel *m* BAU high-water level; **Hoch-
wasserüberlauf** *m* WASSERVERSORG high-water

overflow; **Hochwasserüberschwemmungsgebiet** *nt*
WASSERVERSORG flood plain; **Hochwasserüberwa-
chung** *f* WASSERVERSORG flood control

hochwertig[1] *adj* KOHLEN high-grade, MECHAN high-tensile

hochwertig:[2] **~es Benzin** *nt* KFZTECH high-test gasoline
(AmE), high-test petrol (BrE); **~es Erz** *nt* KOHLEN
high-grade ore; **~er Stahl** *m* MECHAN high-tensile steel

hochwinden *vt* BAU hoist, FERTIG hoist, jack, WASSER-
TRANS winch up

Hoch: **Hochzahl** *f* MATH exponent

hochzeilig: ~es Fernsehverfahren *nt* *(HDTV)* FERNSEH
high-definition television *(HDTV)*

Hoch: **Hochziehen** *nt* LUFTTRANS pitch-up

hochziehen *vt* MECHAN hoist

höffig: ~es Gebiet *nt* ERDÖL zone of petroleum accumulation

Hoffman-Elektrometer *nt* ELEKTRIZ Hoffman electrometer

hoch: sehr hohe Dichtigkeit *f* *(VHD)* OPTIK very high
density *(VHD)*

Höhe *f* BAU elevation, grade, COMP & DV height, GEOM
altitude, GEOM height, HYDRAUL *zum Gegenpumpen*
head, PHYS altitude, RADIO height, WASSERTRANS *Navigation* elevation, *astronomische Navigation* altitude;
~ der Dünung *f* WASSERTRANS height of the swell; **~ der
Gezeiten** *f* WASSERTRANS height of the tide; **~ über
alles** *f* MASCHINEN overall height; **~ über dem durch-
schnittlichen Geländeniveau** *f* RADIO height above
average terrain; **~ über dem Meeresspiegel** *f* BAU
height above sea level, WASSERTRANS *Navigation* elevation above sea level

Hoheitsgewässer *nt pl* WASSERTRANS territorial waters

Höhe: **Höhen- und Breitenverhältnis** *nt* DRUCK aspect
ratio; **Höhenanhebung** *f* AUFNAHME treble boost; **Hö-
henaufnahme** *f* BAU leveling (AmE), levelling (BrE);
Höhendämpfung *f* AUFNAHME treble roll-off; **Höhen-
einstellung** *f* KERNTECH *eines Kontrollstabs* height
position; **Höhenfehler** *m* LUFTTRANS height-keeping
error; **Höhenflosse** *f* LUFTTRANS horizontal stabilizer,
tailplane; **Höhenförderer** *m* FERTIG elevator; **Höhen-
fries** *m* BAU *einer Tür* stile

höhengleich: ~er Bahnübergang *m* BAU, EISENBAHN
grade crossing (AmE), level crossing (BrE)

Höhe: **Höhenkammeraufstieg** *m* LUFTTRANS chamber
ascent; **Höhenkorrektureinrichtung** *f* KFZTECH ride
height corrector; **Höhenleitwerk** *nt* LUFTTRANS horizontal stabilizer, tailplane; **Höhenlinie** *f* BAU contour,
contour line; **Höhenmarke** *f* MECHAN benchmark; **Höh-
enmaßstab** *m* METROL height gage (AmE), height
gauge (BrE); **Höhenmesser** *m* PHYS, TRANS altimeter;
Höhenmessereinstellung *f* LUFTTRANS altimeter setting; **Höhenmesserkontrollorte** *m pl* LUFTTRANS
preflight altimeter check locations; **Höhenmeßgerät**
nt GERÄT altimeter; **Höhenplan** *m* BAU longitudinal
section, *Landvermessung* contour map; **Höhenquer-
ruder** *nt* LUFTTRANS elevon; **Höhenregler** *m*
AUFNAHME treble control; **Höhenreißer** *m* MASCHINEN
scribing block, METROL height gage (AmE), height
gauge (BrE), vernier height gage (AmE), vernier
height gauge (BrE), surface gage (AmE), surface gauge (BrE), surface geometry meter; **Höhenrichtwerk** *nt*
LUFTTRANS elevator

Höhenruder *nt* LUFTTRANS elevator; **Höhenruderaus-
schlag** *m* LUFTTRANS elevator deflection;
Höhenruderservosteuerung *f* LUFTTRANS elevator fol-

low-up; **Höhenrudersteuerung** *f* LUFTTRANS elevator control; **Höhenrudertrimmklappe** *f* LUFTTRANS elevator trim

Höhe: **Höhenschnitt** *m* KONSTZEICH vertical section; **Höhenschnittpunkt** *m* GEOM orthocenter (AmE), orthocentre (BrE); **Höhenschreiber** *m* PHYS barograph; **Höhensteuer** *nt* LUFTTRANS elevator; **Höhensteuerung** *f* LUFTTRANS altitude controller; **Höhenstrahlung** *f* PHYS cosmic rays, STRAHLPHYS cosmic ray background

höhenverstellbar[1] *adj* FERTIG *Radialbohrer* elevating

höhenverstellbar:[2] **~er Tisch** *m* MASCHINEN height-adjustable table

Höhe: **Höhenwinkel** *m* BAU elevation angle, NICHTFOSS ENERG angle of incidence, RAUMFAHRT, TELEKOM elevation angle

höher: **~e Ableitungen** *f pl* MATH higher derivatives; **~e Dienste** *m pl* TELEKOM higher-level services; **~es Elementenpaar** *nt* FERTIG *Getriebelehre* higher pair; **~e Energieleistung** *f* ABFALL UCV, upper calorific value; **~e Gewalt** *f* TRANS *Versicherung* act of God; **~er Grad** *m* GEOM higher degree; **~e Logik** *f* ELEKTRONIK high-level logic; **~e Mathematik** *f* MATH higher mathematics; **~e Programmiersprache** *f (HPS)* COMP & DV high-order language, high-level language, *(HLL)*, KÜNSTL INT advanced language, high-level language *(HLL)*, TELEKOM high-level language *(HLL)*, high-order language; **~e zyklische Steigung** *f* LUFTTRANS *Hubschrauber* high-order cyclic pitch

höher: **auf ~en Meßbereich umschalten** *vt* GERÄT *Mehrbereichsinstrument* uprange

höherwertig *adj* COMP & DV high-order

hohes: **für ~ Drehmoment geeignet** *adj* MECHAN high-torque

hohl[1] *adj* BAU hollow

hohl:[2] **~er Flaschenboden** *m* KER & GLAS punt; **~es Gegenstück** *nt* FERTIG female part; **~e See** *f* WASSERTRANS *Seezustand* heavy swell

Hohladerkabel *nt* TELEKOM loose cable structure

Hohladerstruktur *f* TELEKOM loose tube structure

Hohlanode *f* ELEKTRIZ hollow anode

Hohlbohrer *m* MASCHINEN hollow drill

Hohleisen *nt* BAU gouge

Hohlfahrbalken *m* TRANS hollow-type track girder

Hohlfeder *f* MASCHINEN hollow spring

hohlflächig *adj* FERTIG dished

Hohlfräser *m* MASCHINEN running-down cutter

hohlgeschliffen *adj* MECHAN dished

Hohlglasblock *m* KER & GLAS hollow glass block

Hohlhals *m* KER & GLAS hollow neck

Hohlheit *f* BAU hollowness

Hohlkammerplatte *f* KUNSTSTOFF cellular sheet

Hohlkathoden-Ionenquelle *f* KERNTECH hollow cathode ion source

Hohlkehle *f* BAU fillet, gorge, quirk, EISENBAHN tire groove (AmE), tyre groove (BrE), FERTIG fillet

hohlkehlen *vt* FERTIG rebate

Hohlkeil *m* MASCHINEN saddle key

Hohlkörper *m* BAU hollow

Hohlkugel *f* FERTIG hollow sphere

Hohlleiter *m* ELEKTRIZ hollow conductor, ELEKTROTECH wave duct, waveguide, RADIO, TELEKOM waveguide; **~ mit nur einem Leiter** *m* ELEKTROTECH uniconductor waveguide; **Hohlleiterantenne** *f* TELEKOM waveguide antenna; **Hohlleiterbereich** *m* ELEKTROTECH waveguide section; **Hohlleiterbereich mit Schlitz** *m*

ELEKTROTECH waveguide slotted section; **Hohlleiterfestlast** *f* ELEKTROTECH waveguide fixed load; **Hohlleitergleitlast** *f* ELEKTROTECH waveguide sliding load; **Hohlleiterisolator** *m* ELEKTROTECH waveguide isolator; **Hohlleiterkolben** *m* ELEKTROTECH waveguide plunger; **Hohlleiterkomponente** *f* ELEKTROTECH waveguide component; **Hohlleiterkopplung** *f* ELEKTROTECH waveguide coupling; **Hohlleiterlast** *f* ELEKTROTECH waveguide load; **Hohlleiterphasenregler** *m* ELEKTROTECH waveguide phase shifter; **Hohlleitertransformator** *m* ELEKTROTECH waveguide transformer; **Hohlleiterübergang** *m* ELEKTROTECH waveguide transition

Hohlmaß *nt* FERTIG, METROL liquid measure

Hohlmeißel *m* BAU *Holzbearbeitung* gouge

Hohlniet *m* MASCHINEN hollow rivet

Hohlpfanne *f* KER & GLAS gutter tile

Hohlprägen *nt* FERTIG, MASCHINEN embossing

Hohlprofil *nt* HEIZ & KÄLTE hollow section

Hohlrad *nt* KFZTECH annulus

Hohlraum *m* BAU cavity, *eines Ziegels* core, ELEKTRONIK cavity, FERTIG cavity, hollow, KERNTECH *eines Druckgefäßes* cavity, KOHLEN cavity, cell, void, MECHAN cavity, METALL cavity, void, PHYS, RADIO, STRÖMPHYS cavity; **Hohlraumbildung** *f* BAU, MECHAN, METALL, NICHTFOSS ENERG, PHYS cavitation, RAUMFAHRT *Weltraumfunk* cavity, STRÖMPHYS cavitation; **Hohlraumgehalt** *m* BAU porosity; **Hohlraumgitter** *nt* ELEKTRONIK resonator grid; **Hohlraummagnetron** *nt* ELEKTRONIK cavity magnetron; **Hohlraumresonanz** *f* ELEKTRONIK cavity resonance; **Hohlraumresonanzeffekt** *m* AUFNAHME cavity resonance effect; **Hohlraumresonator** *m* ELEKTRONIK cavity oscillator, cavity resonator, PHYS, TEILPHYS, TELEKOM cavity resonator; **Hohlraumvolumen** *nt* TEXTIL void volume

hohlschleifen *vt* FERTIG dish

Hohlschlüssel *m* MECHAN box spanner (BrE), box wrench

Hohlschraube *f* MASCHINEN banjo bolt, hollow bolt; **Hohlschraubenverbindung** *f* FERTIG banjo fitting, MASCHINEN banjo union

Hohlspiegel *m* PHYS concave mirror

Hohlsteindecke *f* BAU hollow pot flooring

Hohlstelle *f* FERTIG rag

Hohlstift *m* MASCHINEN hollow pin

Hohltarget *nt* KERNTECH hollow target

Hohlträger *m* BAU box girder; **Hohlträgerbrücke** *f* BAU box girder bridge

Höhlung *f* BAU hole, MASCHINEN cavity

Hohlwelle *f* FERTIG, MASCHINEN hollow shaft

Hohlzeug *nt* KER & GLAS hollow ware; **Hohlzeugpressmaschine** *f* KER & GLAS hollow-ware presser

Holden: **~scher Effekt** *m* KERNTECH Holden effect

Holländermesser *nt* PAPIER beater bar, rag knife; **Holländertropfen** *m* KER & GLAS Dutch drop; **Holländerwalze** *f* PAPIER beater roll

Hollerith: **Hollerith-Code** *m* COMP & DV Hollerith code; **Hollerith-Karte** *f* COMP & DV Hollerith card

Holm *m* LUFTTRANS *Luftfahrzeug* spar, MECHAN boom, RAUMFAHRT *Raumschiff* spar; **Holmbeschlag des Luftschraubenblattes** *m* LUFTTRANS *Hubschrauber* blade attachment fitting; **Holmenkasten des Leitwerks** *m* LUFTTRANS fin spar box; **Holmenwand des Flugzeugrumpfkastens** *f* LUFTTRANS fuselage box beam wall

Holmium *nt (Ho)* CHEMIE holmium *(Ho)*

holoedrisch *adj* FERTIG holohedral

Hologramm *nt* COMP & DV holographic image, PHYS, WELLPHYS hologram

Holographie *f* COMP & DV, PHYS, RAUMFAHRT *Raumschiff*, STRAHLPHYS, WELLPHYS holography

holographisch: **~er Scanner** *m* COMP & DV holographic scanner; **~er Speicher** *m* COMP & DV holographic memory, holographic storage, TELEKOM holographic memory

Holz[1] *nt* KER & GLAS, PAPIER wood

Holz:[2] **mit ~ verkleiden** *vt* BAU timber

Holz: **Holzabfall** *m* ABFALL wood waste; **Holzarbeiten** *f* BAU woodwork; **Holzbalkenzug-Ankerverbindung** *f* BAU haunched mortise and tenon joint; **Holzbau** *m* BAU building in wood, woodwork; **Holzbock** *m* BAU timber jack; **Holzbolzen** *m* BAU needle; **Holzbrücke** *f* BAU timber bridge; **Holzbuchstaben** *m pl* DRUCK woodtypes; **Holzdrehbank** *f* BAU wood-turning lathe

hölzern: **~e Typen** *f pl* DRUCK woodtypes

Holz: **Holzfachwerk** *nt* BAU timber framing; **Holzfachwerkträger** *m* BAU timber truss; **Holzfaserbruch** *m* FERTIG woody fracture, KERNTECH fibrous fracture; **Holzfloß** *nt* BAU timber raft

holzfrei[1] *adj* VERPACK woodfree

holzfrei:[2] **~es Papier** *nt* DRUCK, PAPIER woodfree paper

Holz: **Holzgurtgesims** *nt* BAU stringer

holzhaltig[1] *adj* PAPIER woody

holzhaltig:[2] **~es Papier** *nt* DRUCK, PAPIER wood-containing paper

Holz: **Holzhammer** *m* BAU *Plasterarbeiten* beetle, FERTIG wood mallet, KER & GLAS, MASCHINEN, MECHAN mallet; **Holzklammer** *f* BAU timber dog; **Holzkohle** *f* FERTIG, KOHLEN charcoal, wood charcoal; **Holzkohlefilter** *nt* LABOR charcoal filter; **Holzkohlenstaub** *m* KOHLEN pulverized charcoal; **Holzleiste** *f* BAU cleat; **Holzmehl** *nt* KUNSTSTOFF wood flour; **Holznagel** *m* BAU trenail; **Holzpfahl** *m* BAU pale, spile, KOHLEN wooden pile; **Holzpflock** *m* BAU spile, FERTIG runner stick; **Holzplatte** *f* KER & GLAS nog plate; **Holzplatte für Anwärmgefäß der Pfeife** *f* KER & GLAS shoe nog plate; **Holzplatz** *m* BAU timber yard; **Holzrahmen** *m* BAU timber frame; **Holzriegel** *m* BAU nogging piece; **Holzrost** *m* BAU pontoon; **Holzsäge** *f* BAU wood saw; **Holzschlaghammer** *m* BAU bossing mallet; **Holzschleifen** *nt* FERTIG glasspapering, sanding; **Holzschleifer** *m* PAPIER grinder; **Holzschleifmaschine** *f* FERTIG sander, sandpapering machine; **Holzschliff** *m* PAPIER groundwood pulp, mechanical wood pulp, VERPACK mechanical wood pulp; **Holzschliffkarton** *m* VERPACK mechanical pulp board; **Holzschliffpappe** *f* PAPIER mechanical pulp board; **Holzschraube** *f* BAU woodscrew; **Holzschutzmittel** *nt* BAU wood preservative; **Holzschwelle** *f* BAU abutment, wooden sleeper; **Holzspaltkeil** *m* BAU timber splitting wedge; **Holzspanplatte** *f* VERPACK chipboard; **Holzsparren** *m* BAU timber rafter; **Holzspiritus** *m* THERMOD wood alcohol; **Holzstoff** *m* VERPACK molded pulp article (AmE), moulded pulp article (BrE); **Holzstopfen** *m* WASSERTRANS *Schiffbau* wooden plug; **Holzverkleidung** *f* BAU timbering, HYDRAUL wood lagging; **Holzverlattung** *f* BAU battening, lathing; **Holzverschalung** *f* HYDRAUL wood lagging; **Holzverstärkung** *f* WASSERTRANS *Schiffbau* wood reinforcement; **Holzwolle** *f* VERPACK wood wool; **Holzzellstoff** *m* DRUCK chemical wood pulp, PAPIER wood pulp; **Holzziegel** *m* BAU wood brick

Homobrenzcatechin *nt* CHEMIE homopyrocatechol

homocyclisch *adj* CHEMIE carbocyclic, homocyclic, isocyclic

Homodynoszillator *m* ELEKTRONIK homodyne oscillator

homogen[1] *adj* MATH homogeneous

homogen:[2] **~e Anregung** *f* STRAHLPHYS homogeneous stimulus; **~e isotrope Turbulenz** *f* STRÖMPHYS homogeneous isotropic turbulence; **~er Mantel** *m* OPTIK *Lichtleiter*, TELEKOM homogeneous cladding; **~es Medium** *nt* PHYS homogeneous medium; **~er Reaktor** *m* KERNTECH, TRANS homogeneous reactor; **~er Stimulus** *m* STRAHLPHYS homogeneous stimulus; **~e Strahlung** *f* PHYS homogeneous radiation; **~es System** *nt* THERMOD heating zone, homogeneous system

Homogenisator *m* LABOR *Präparation* homogenizer

Homogenisieren *nt* KUNSTSTOFF homogenization, homogenizing

Homogenisierung *f* METALL homogenization, homogenizing

Homojunktion *f* OPTIK homojunction

homolog: **~e Temperatur** *f* METALL homologous temperature

homologe: **~ Reihe** *f* ERDÖL *Petrochemie* homologous series

Homöostase *f* ERGON homeostasis

homopolar *adj* ELEKTRIZ homopolar, unipolar

Homopolymer *nt* KUNSTSTOFF homopolymer; **Homopolymerisat** *nt* KUNSTSTOFF homopolymer; **Homopolymerisation** *f* KUNSTSTOFF homopolymerization

Homoterephtal- *pref* CHEMIE homoterephthalic

Homoübergang *m* ELEKTRONIK *einfacher Übergang*, OPTIK, TELEKOM homojunction

homozyklisch *adj* CHEMIE carbocyclic, homocyclic, isocyclic

Honahle *f* FERTIG, MASCHINEN hone, honing tool

Honen *nt* FERTIG, MASCHINEN honing

honen *vt* FERTIG, MASCHINEN, MECHAN hone

Honmaschine *f* FERTIG, MASCHINEN honing machine

Honstein *m* MASCHINEN honestone, honing stone

Hooke: **~sches Gesetz** *nt* BAU, PHYS Hooke's law

Hopcalit *nt* CHEMIE hopcalite

hopfenähnlich *adj* CHEMIE lupuline

Hopperbagger *m* WASSERTRANS hopper dredge, hopper dredger

Hopperschute *f* WASSERTRANS hopper barge

Hopping-Verbindung *f* FERNSEH hopping patch

Hör- *pref* AKUSTIK aural, COMP & DV audio

hörbar[1] *adj* ERGON audible

hörbar:[2] **~er Frequenzbereich** *m* AKUSTIK audible frequency range; **~es Signal** *nt* AUFNAHME audible signal

Hörbarkeitsgrenze *f* AKUSTIK hearing threshold level

Hörbarkeitsmesser *m* AUFNAHME audibility meter

Hörbarkeitsschwelle *f* UMWELTSCHMUTZ threshold of audibility

Hör-: **Hörbehinderung** *f* ERGON hearing handicap; **Hörbereich** *m* AUFNAHME, ERGON audible range

Horchgerät *nt* AKUSTIK sound locator

Horchortung *f* WELLPHYS sound ranging

Hordein *nt* CHEMIE hordein

Höreindruck *m* ERGON hearing experience

Hörer *m* TELEKOM handset, receiver; **~ aufgelegt** *m* TELEKOM on-hook condition; **~ mit Verstärker** *m* TELEKOM amplified handset; **Hörerschnur** *f* TELEKOM handset cord

Hör-: **Hörfeld** *f* AKUSTIK auditory sensation area; **Hörfläche** *f* AKUSTIK auditory sensation area
hörfrequent *adj* AUFNAHME audio-frequency
Hör-: **Hörfrequenz** *f* AKUSTIK acoustic frequency, audio frequency, AUFNAHME, ELEKTRONIK acoustic frequency; **Hörfrequenzmesser** *m* STRAHLPHYS audiometer; **Hörfunk** *m* RADIO sound broadcasting; **Hörgerät** *nt* AKUSTIK hearing aid, ERGON artificial ear; **Hörgrenzen** *f pl* ERGON audible limits; **Hörhilfe** *f* AKUSTIK hearing aid, ERGON artificial ear
horizontal[1] *adj* GEOM horizontal
horizontal:[2] **~e Ablenkung** *f* ELEKTRONIK horizontal deflection; **~e Achse** *f (X-Achse)* MATH horizontal axis *(x-axis)*; **~er Bilddurchlauf** *m* COMP & DV scrolling; **~e Bildzentrierung** *f* FERNSEH horizontal-centering control (AmE), horizontal-centring control (BrE); **~e Ebene** *f* GEOM horizontal plane; **~e eingebauter Motor** *m* KFZTECH horizontal engine; **~e Einwicklung** *f* VERPACK horizontal wrapping; **~e Kartonfüllmaschine** *f* VERPACK horizontal case loader; **~e Komponente** *f* PHYS horizontal component; **~e Luftströmung** *f* PHYS, STRÖMPHYS advection; **~e Polarisation** *f* ELEKTROTECH, PHYS, TELEKOM horizontal polarization; **~er Reiseflug** *m* LUFTTRANS level cruise; **~e Schichten** *f pl* STRÖMPHYS horizontal layers; **~ und topladende Kartoniereinrichtung** *f* VERPACK horizontal and top loader cartoner; **~e und vertikale Linien** *f pl* LUFTTRANS *flugrichtungsanzeigend* horizontal and vertical bars; **~er Windgradient** *m* LUFTTRANS horizontal wind shear
Horizontal- *pref* ELEKTRONIK, FERNSEH, VERPACK horizontal; **Horizontal- und Vertikaleinschlagmaschine** *f* VERPACK horizontal and vertical wrapping machine; **Horizontalablenkplatte** *f* ELEKTRONIK horizontal deflection plate, FERNSEH X-plate; **Horizontalablenkplatten** *f pl* PHYS horizontal-deflecting plates; **Horizontalablenkspule** *f* ELEKTROTECH horizontal deflection coil; **Horizontalablenkungssteuerung** *f* FERNSEH horizontal deflection control; **Horizontalablenkverstärker** *m* GERÄT *Oszilloskop* sweep deflection amplifier; **Horizontalabtastfrequenz** *f* ELEKTRONIK, RADIO, TELEKOM horizontal-scanning frequency; **Horizontalabtastung** *f* FERNSEH horizontal scanning; **Horizontalachse** *f* BAU horizontal axis; **Horizontalauflösung** *f* FERNSEH horizontal resolution; **Horizontalaufzug** *m* TRANS horizontal elevator; **Horizontalaustastintervall** *nt* FERNSEH horizontal-blanking interval; **Horizontalaustastung** *f* FERNSEH horizontal blanking; **Horizontalbalken** *m* FERNSEH horizontal bar; **Horizontaldynamikkonvergenz** *f* FERNSEH horizontal dynamic convergence
Horizontale *f* GEOM horizontal, MECHAN datum line
Horizontal-: **Horizontaleinfangen** *nt* FERNSEH horizontal lock, horizontal hold; **Horizontalflug** *m* LUFTTRANS level flight; **Horizontalformat** *nt* DRUCK landscape format; **Horizontalkartoniermaschine** *f* VERPACK horizontal-cartoning machine; **Horizontalkraft** *f* BAU horizontal thrust; **Horizontallauf** *m* FERNSEH horizontal sweep; **Horizontalmühle** *f* SICHERHEIT horizontal-milling machine; **Horizontalregler** *nt* FERNSEH horizontal hold control; **Horizontalschnitt** *m* KONSTZEICH horizontal section; **Horizontalsynchronisierimpuls** *m* FERNSEH breezeway; **Horizontalsynchronisierung** *f* FERNSEH horizontal synchronization; **Horizontaltabulator** *m* COMP & DV HT, horizontal tabulator; **Horizontalvergaser** *m*

KFZTECH horizontal carburetor (AmE), horizontal carburettor (BrE); **Horizontalverstärker** *m* ELEKTRONIK horizontal amplifier
horizontieren *vt* LUFTTRANS level out
Horizontierungseinheit *f* LUFTTRANS leveling unit (AmE), levelling unit (BrE)
Horizontmelder *m* RAUMFAHRT *Raumschiff* horizon sensor
Hör-: **Hörkapsel** *f* TELEKOM receiver inset; **Hörmelder** *m* GERÄT acoustic alarm device, audible alarm device
Horn *nt* FERTIG *Schmieden,* MASCHINEN beak; **Hornantenne** *f* RADIO horn, RAUMFAHRT horn, horn antenna; **Hornausgleich** *m* LUFTTRANS balance horn; **Hornklausel** *f* KÜNSTL INT Horn clause; **Hornschiene** *f* EISENBAHN wing rail; **Hornstein** *nt* ERDÖL *Geologie* chert; **Hornstrahler** *m* LUFTTRANS *Funkwesen* horn
Hör-: **Hörpegel** *m* ERGON hearing level; **Hörprothese** *f* ERGON auditory prosthesis; **Hörrundfunk** *m* RADIO sound broadcasting; **Hörrundfunksender** *m* RADIO sound broadcast transmitter; **Hörsaal** *m* AUFNAHME auditorium; **Hörschädigung** *f* ERGON hearing impairment; **Hörschärfe** *f* AKUSTIK auditory acuity, ERGON hearing acuity; **Hörschwelle** *f* AKUSTIK aural threshold, hearing threshold, threshold of audibility, ERGON hearing threshold, hearing threshold level, PHYS hearing threshold; **Hörschwellendifferenz** *f* AKUSTIK hearing threshold difference; **Hörschwellenmeßgerät** *nt* AKUSTIK, GERÄT audiometer; **Hörschwellenpegel** *m* AKUSTIK hearing threshold level; **Hör-Sprech-Schalter** *m* AUFNAHME talk-listen switch; **Hörstörungen** *f pl* ERGON hearing defects; **Hörtest** *m* AKUSTIK hearing test; **Hörverlustfaktor** *m* AKUSTIK hearing loss factor; **Hörvermögen** *nt* ERGON audition, hearing; **Hörverständigung im Fahrzeug** *f* KFZTECH in-vehicle aural communication
Hosenboje *f* WASSERTRANS breeches buoy
Hosenrohr *nt* FERTIG Y-pipe, MASCHINEN, MECHAN breeches pipe
Host *m* COMP & DV host; **Hostcomputer** *m* COMP & DV host computer; **Hostsystem** *nt* COMP & DV host system
Hot-Carrier-Diode *f* ELEKTRONIK, RADIO hot carrier diode
Hot-Spot *m* KERNTECH hot spot
Hovercraft *nt* WASSERTRANS *Schifftyp* hovercraft (BrE)
h-Parameter *m (Hybrid-Parameter)* ELEKTRONIK hybrid parameter
HPC-Ruß *m (schwer verarbeitbarer Kanalruß)* KUNSTSTOFF HPC carbon black *(hard-processing channel carbon black)*
HPLC *abbr (Hochdruckflüssigchromatographie)* LABOR, LEBENSMITTEL HPLC *(high-pressure liquid chromatography)*
H-Profil *m* FERTIG H-section
HPS *abbr (höhere Programmiersprache)* COMP & DV, TELEKOM HLL *(high-level language)*
HTR *abbr (Hochtemperaturreaktor)* KERNTECH HTR *(high-temperature reactor)*
Hub *m* BAU lift, ERDÖL *Seegang* heave, FERTIG stroke, *Kunststoffinstallationen* stroke, *Presse, Schere* blow, HYDRAUL elevator (AmE), lift (BrE), *Steuerkolben* stroke, KERNTECH lift, KFZTECH stroke, LUFTTRANS lift, MASCHINEN daylight, displacement, stroke, throw, travel, PHYS stroke, TEXTIL traverse; **Hubanzeigestift** *m* FERTIG *Kunststoffinstallationen* position indicator; **Hubbegrenzer** *m* FERTIG stop; **Hubbegren-**

zung *f* FERTIG *Kunststoffinstallationen* lift limiter, stroke limiter; **Hubbereich** *m* KERNTECH *eines Steuerstabes* range of movement; **Hubbrücke** *f* BAU lifting bridge, TRANS lift bridge, WASSERTRANS lifting bridge; **Hubdruck** *m* TRANS lifting pressure; **Hubel** *m* KER & GLAS blank; **Hubende** *nt* FERTIG bottom stroke, MASCHINEN end of stroke, end of travel; **Hubfenster** *nt* BAU sash window; **Hubgebläse** *nt* LUFTTRANS lift fan; **Hubgerät** *nt* NICHTFOSS ENERG lift-type device; **Hubgeschwindigkeit** *f* KERNTECH *eines Steuerstabes* rate of travel, MASCHINEN hoisting speed; **Hubglied** *nt* FERTIG *Kurve* follower; **Hubgriff** *m* BAU lift; **Hubhöhe** *f* KERNTECH *eines Elementes* stroke, MASCHINEN lift; **Hubkarren** *m* VERPACK lifting vehicle; **Hubkette** *f* BAU lifting chain; **Hubklinke** *f* BAU lift latch; **Hubkolbenmotor** *m* KFZTECH, LUFTTRANS, MASCHINEN, WASSERTRANS piston engine, reciprocating engine; **Hubkolbenverbrennungsmaschine** *f* KFZTECH reciprocating internal combustion engine; **Hubkolbenverdichter** *m* MASCHINEN reciprocating compressor, reciprocating piston compressor; **Hubkolbenzähler** *m* GERÄT reciprocating piston-type meter, REGELUNG ball prover flow measuring device; **Hubkraft** *f* MASCHINEN, TRANS lifting power; **Hublader** *m* BAU *Tiefbau* loading shovel; **Hublänge** *f* MASCHINEN length of stroke; **Hublänge des Kolbens** *f* MASCHINEN piston stroke; **Hubmagnet** *m* MASCHINEN lifting magnet; **Hubmessung** *f* TELEKOM deviation measurement; **Hubmitte** *f* FERTIG midstroke; **Hubmotor** *m* MASCHINEN hoisting motor, lift motor; **Hubplattform** *f* ERDÖL jack-up rig, MASCHINEN lift platform, MECHAN elevating table; **Hubrad** *nt* MASCHINEN elevating wheel, lifting wheel; **Hubraum** *m* KFZTECH displacement, *Motor* capacity, MASCHINEN displacement, MECHAN, PHYS cubic capacity; **Hubrohr** *nt* BAU lift pipe; **Hubscheibe** *f* FERTIG *Getriebelehre* main driving gear

Hubschrauber[1] *m* LUFTTRANS helicopter; ~ **mit Doppelfunktion** *m* LUFTTRANS dual-role helicopter

Hubschrauber:[2] **mit ~ befördern** *vt* LUFTTRANS helicopter

Hubschrauber: **Hubschrauberavionikausrüstung** *f* LUFTTRANS helicopter avionics package; **Hubschrauberflughafen** *m* TRANS heliport; **Hubschrauberlandedeck** *nt* LUFTTRANS helicopter landing deck; **Hubschrauberlandefläche** *f* LUFTTRANS helicopter landing surface, heliport deck; **Hubschrauberlandeplattform** *f* LUFTTRANS helicopter landing platform, WASSERTRANS helicopter landing pad; **Hubschrauberlandeplatz** *m* ERDÖL heliport, *auf Plattform* helipad, LUFTTRANS helipad, helistop, *auf Schiffen* spot, TRANS heliport; **Hubschrauberstation** *f* LUFTTRANS helicopter station; **Hubschrauberverhalten** *nt* LUFTTRANS helicopter behavior (AmE), helicopter behaviour (BrE); **Hubschrauberzubringerdienst** *m* LUFTTRANS helicopter shuttle service

Hub: **Hubseil** *nt* EISENBAHN fall rope, MASCHINEN hoisting rope; **Hubspiegel** *m* FOTO swing-up mirror; **Hubspindel** *f* FERTIG raising screw, MASCHINEN elevating screw; **Hubstange** *f* HYDRAUL lifting rod; **Hubstapler** *m* FERTIG stacker truck, MECHAN lifting truck; **Hubtor** *nt* BAU lift gate; **Hubtragschrauber** *m* TRANS heligyro; **Hubventil** *nt* HYDRAUL lifting valve, MASCHINEN lift valve; **Hubverhältnis** *nt* ELEKTRONIK *Modulation* deviation ratio; **Hubverlagerung** *f* FERTIG ram positioning; **Hubvermögen mit Haken** *nt* KERNTECH lifting capacity with hook; **Hubvolumen** *nt* FERTIG piston displacement; **Hubwagen** *m* MECHAN lifting truck, VERPACK lift truck; **Hubweg** *m* MASCHINEN stroke; **Hubwelle** *f* LUFTTRANS lift shaft; **Hubwerk** *nt* ERDÖL elevator, FERTIG hoisting gear

Hubwinde *f* LUFTTRANS hoist; **Hubwindeanschlußstück** *nt* LUFTTRANS *Hubschrauber* hoist fitting; **Hubwindehebel** *m* LUFTTRANS hoist lever; **Hubwindenfahrgestell** *nt* LUFTTRANS hoisting carriage

Hub: **Hubzähler** *m* GERÄT stroke counter; **Hubzählgerät** *nt* GERÄT stroke counter; **Hubzapfen** *m* FERTIG crankpin; **Hubzeit** *f* ELEKTRIZ traveling time (AmE), travelling time (BrE)

Huckepackbahn *f* EISENBAHN piggyback rail

Huckepackreaktor *m* KERNTECH package reactor, transportable reactor

Huckepackverkehr *m* EISENBAHN piggyback traffic, piggyback transport, rail transport of road trailers, LUFTTRANS piggyback traffic, piggyback transport, TRANS TOFC, trailers on flat cars

Huf *m* ELEKTRIZ, PHYS horse shoe; **Hufeisengewölbe** *nt* BAU horseshoe arch; **Hufeisenmagnet** *m* ELEKTRIZ, PHYS horseshoe magnet; **Hufeisenofen** *m* KER & GLAS horseshoe-fired furnace; **Hufeisenprofile** *nt pl* MASCHINEN horseshoe sections; **Hufeisenrettungsboje** *f* WASSERTRANS horseshoe lifebuoy; **Hufeisenwirbel** *m* STRÖMPHYS horseshoe vortex

Hula-Hoop-Antenne *f* RADIO hula hoop aerial, hula hoop antenna

Hülle *f* COMP & DV hood, ELEKTROTECH envelope, FERTIG, LABOR *Glasartikel* jacket, LEBENSMITTEL skin, MECHAN cover, RAUMFAHRT *Raumschiff* case, jacket, shell; **Hüllengewebe** *nt* FERTIG *Keilriemen* casing

Hüllkurve *f* FERNSEH, MATH envelope, MECHAN envelope curve, RAUMFAHRT *Weltraumfunk*, TELEKOM envelope; **Hüllkurvenmonitor** *m* FERNSEH waveform monitor; **Hüllkurvenverzögerung** *f* RAUMFAHRT *Weltraumfunk* envelope delay

Hüllmaterial *nt* KERNTECH cladding material

Hüllschnitt *m* MASCHINEN profiling cut

Hülltemperaturgrenze *f* KERNTECH cladding temperature limit

Hülse *f* BAU tube, *eines Schlosses* barrel, FERTIG quill, sleeve, thimble, *Kunststoffinstallationen* shell, KERNTECH cladding, MASCHINEN bush, bushing, collar, collet, runner, sleeve, MECHAN collar, sheath, PAPIER *der Papierrolle* core, TELEKOM ferrule, TEXTIL bobbin, VERPACK sleeve; ~ **mit Außengewinde** *f* MASCHINEN threaded bush; **Hülsenfrucht** *f* LEBENSMITTEL legume, pulse; **Hülsenkette** *f* MASCHINEN bushed roller chain; **Hülsenlehre** *f* KER & GLAS, METROL ring gage (AmE), ring gauge (BrE)

hülsenlos: ~**es Brennelement** *nt* KERNTECH canal-ray discharge

Hülse: **Hülsenrohr** *nt* BAU socket pipe; **Hülsenschiebermotor** *m* KFZTECH sleeve valve engine; **Hülsenüberwachung** *f* KERNTECH cladding monitoring

Human-Engineering *nt* ERGON human engineering

Humulen *nt* CHEMIE humulene

Humus *m* KOHLEN humus; **Humusbehälter** *m* WASSERVERSORG humus tank

Hund: ~**sche Regeln** *f pl* PHYS Hund's rules

Hundekoje *f* WASSERTRANS quarter berth

Hundert: **Hundert-Jahr-Sturm** *m* ERDÖL *Offshore* hundred year storm; **Hundert-Jahr-Welle** *f* ERDÖL

Offshore hundred year wave; **Hundertprozentprüfung** *f* QUAL one-hundred-percent inspection

Hundertstel: in ~ unterteilt *adj* MECHAN centigrade

Hutmutter *f* FERTIG acorn nut, *Kunststoffinstallationen* handwheel nut, LUFTTRANS acorn nut, MASCHINEN cap nut, dome nut, MECHAN cap nut

Hutschraube *f* MASCHINEN cap bolt

Hütte *f* METALL smeltery; **Hütteneis** *nt* KER & GLAS granulated glass; **Hüttenkunde** *f* FERTIG metallurgy, process metallurgy

hüttenmännisch *adj* FERTIG metallurgical

Hütte: **Hüttenofen** *m* MASCHINEN metallurgical furnace; **Hüttenwerk** *nt* METALL smeltery; **Hüttenzement** *m* METALL slag cement; **Hüttenzink** *nt* METALL spelter

Huygens: ~sches Okular *nt* PHYS Huygens' eyepiece; **~sches Prinzip** *nt* PHYS Huygens' principle

HV-Naht *f* FERTIG *Schweißen* single bevel groove weld

HVSt *abbr (Hauptvermittlungsstelle)* TELEKOM main exchange

HVStd *abbr (Hauptverkehrsstunde)* TELEKOM busy hour

HVt *abbr (Hauptverteiler)* TELEKOM MDF *(main distribution frame)*

H-Welle *f* ELEKTROTECH, TELEKOM H-wave, TE wave

HWZ *abbr (Halbwertszeit)* KERNTECH, PHYS, STRAHLPHYS, TEILPHYS $T^1/2$ *(half-life)*, TELEKOM FDHM *(full duration half maximum)*

Hyacinthenaldehyd *m* CHEMIE hyacinthin, phenylacetaldehyde

Hyacinthin *nt* CHEMIE hyacinthin, phenylacetaldehyde

Hybrid- *pref* KFZTECH, TELEKOM, THERMOD hybrid

hybrid: ~er Treibstoff *m* THERMOD lithergol; **~er Vermittlungsprozessor** *m* TELEKOM hybrid call processor

Hybrid-: Hybridantrieb *m* KFZTECH hybrid propulsion; **Hybridbus** *m* KFZTECH hybrid bus

Hybride *f* ELEKTRONIK *Mikrowellen* hybrid junction

Hybrid-: **Hybridfahrzeug** *nt* KFZTECH hybrid vehicle; **Hybridlager** *nt* MASCHINEN hybrid bearing; **Hybrid-Mikroschaltung** *f* ELEKTRONIK hybrid microcircuit; **Hybridmode** *f* OPTIK *Wellenausbreitung* hybrid mode; **Hybridmodus** *m* TELEKOM hybrid mode; **Hybridmotor** *m* KFZTECH hybrid engine; **Hybrid-Parameter** *m* *(h-Parameter)* ELEKTRONIK hybrid parameter; **Hybridplattform** *f* ERDÖL *Offshore-Betrieb* hybrid platform; **Hybridrechner** *m* COMP & DV hybrid computer; **Hybridringmischer** *m* RADIO hybrid ring mixer; **Hybridschaltkreis** *m* PHYS hybrid circuit, TELEKOM hybrid integrated circuit; **Hybridschaltung** *f* COMP & DV hybrid circuit, ELEKTRONIK hybrid circuit, hybrid integrated circuit; **Hybridschnittstelle** *f* COMP & DV hybrid interface; **Hybridsystem** *nt* KFZTECH, TELEKOM hybrid system; **Hybridtragflächenboot** *nt* WASSERTRANS hybrid foil craft; **Hybridwerkzeug** *nt* KÜNSTL INT *Expertensysteme* hybrid tool

Hydantoin *nt* CHEMIE hydantoin; **Hydantoinsäure** *f* CHEMIE hydantoic acid

Hydracryl- *pref* CHEMIE hydracrylic

Hydrant *m* SICHERHEIT fire hydrant, WASSERVERSORG hydrant, plug (AmE), water hydrant, water plug (AmE)

Hydrast- *pref* CHEMIE hydrastic; **Hydrastin** *nt* CHEMIE hydrastine

Hydrat[1] *nt* CHEMIE hydrate

Hydrat:[2] **~ bilden** *vi* CHEMIE hydrate

Hydratation *f* BAU *Zement*, CHEMIE hydration; **Hydratationswärme** *f* BAU *Zement*, THERMOD heat of hydration

Hydratbildung *f* CHEMIE hydration

hydratisch *adj* CHEMIE hydrous

hydratisieren *vt* CHEMIE hydrate

hydratisiert[1] *adj* CHEMIE hydrous

hydratisiert:[2] **~es Proton** *nt* CHEMIE oxonium

Hydratropa- *pref* CHEMIE hydratropic

Hydraulik *f* ERDÖL, HYDRAUL, MASCHINEN hydraulics; **Hydraulikaggregat** *nt* FERTIG power pack; **Hydraulikanlage** *f* WASSERTRANS hydraulic system; **Hydraulikantrieb** *m* MASCHINEN hydraulic drive; **Hydraulikarmaturen** *f pl* HYDRAUL hydraulic fittings; **Hydraulikbehälter** *m* HYDRAUL hydraulic reservoir; **Hydraulikdetektor** *m* KFZTECH hydraulic detector

Hydraulikflüssigkeit *f* ANSTRICH, HYDRAUL, MASCHINEN hydraulic fluid; **Hydraulikflüssigkeitsbehälter** *m* MASCHINEN hydraulic fluid reservoir

Hydraulik: **Hydraulikgenerator** *m* HYDRAUL hydraulic generator; **Hydraulikgetriebe** *nt* MASCHINEN hydraulic transmission; **Hydraulikheber** *m* MASCHINEN hydraulic jack; **Hydraulikkolben** *m* FERTIG hydraulic jack, MASCHINEN hydraulic ram; **Hydraulikkraft** *f* HYDRAUL hydraulic power; **Hydraulikkupplung** *f* HYDRAUL hydraulic clutch; **Hydrauliköl** *nt* HYDRAUL hydraulic fluid; **Hydraulikpresse** *f* BAU, HYDRAUL hydraulic jack, LABOR hydraulic press; **Hydraulikpumpe** *f* MASCHINEN, MEERSCHMUTZ hydraulic pump; **Hydraulikschaltbild** *nt* KONTROLL hydraulic diagram; **Hydraulikschlauch** *m* KUNSTSTOFF hydraulic hose; **Hydraulikspeicher** *m* KUNSTSTOFF hydraulic accumulator; **Hydrauliksystem** *nt* HYDRAUL, MASCHINEN hydraulic system; **Hydraulikverriegelung** *f* HYDRAUL hydraulic locking; **Hydraulikverschluß** *m* HYDRAUL hydraulic locking; **Hydraulikwinde** *nt* HYDRAUL hydraulic jack; **Hydraulikzylinder** *m* MASCHINEN hydraulic cylinder

hydraulisch[1] *adj* MECHAN, WASSERTRANS hydraulic; **~ vorgesteuert** *adj* FERTIG pilot-operated

hydraulisch:[2] **~ angetriebener Zylinder** *m* HYDRAUL hydraulic actuating cylinder; **~er Antrieb** *m* MASCHINEN hydraulic drive; **~ betätigter Zylinder** *m* HYDRAUL hydraulic actuating cylinder; **~ betätigtes Ventil** *nt* HEIZ & KÄLTE hydraulically-operated valve; **~ betriebenes Gerät** *nt* MASCHINEN hydraulically-operated device; **~e Bremse** *f* MASCHINEN hydraulic brake; **~er Bremskraftverstärker** *m* KFZTECH hydraulic brake servo; **~es Bremssystem** *nt* MASCHINEN hydraulic brake system; **~e Druckquelle** *f* HYDRAUL hydraulic pressure source; **~e Druckversorgung** *f* HYDRAUL hydraulic pressure supply; **~e Förderhöhe** *f* ERDÖL hydraulic head; **~e Geräte** *nt pl* MASCHINEN hydraulic equipment; **~es Gestänge** *nt* KFZTECH hydraulic linkage; **~es Getriebe** *nt* MASCHINEN hydraulic transmission; **~er Heber** *m* MASCHINEN, MECHAN hydraulic jack; **~er Kompensator** *m* ERDÖL *Plattform* hydraulic compensator; **~e Kopierfräsmaschine** *f* MASCHINEN hydraulic copy mill; **~e Kupplung** *f* KFZTECH *Kraftübertragung* hydraulic clutch, MASCHINEN hydraulic coupling; **~e Maschinen** *f pl* MASCHINEN hydraulic machinery; **~e Presse** *f* KUNSTSTOFF hydraulic press; **~e Pumpe** *f* MASCHINEN hydraulic pump; **~er Regler** *m* KFZTECH hydraulic control system; **~e Rißbildung** *f* NICHTFOSS ENERG hydraulic fracturing; **~e Setzmaschine** *f* KOHLEN plunger-type jig; **~er Sohlenauftrieb** *m* KOHLEN hydraulic bottom heave; **~er Stoßdämpfer** *m* KFZTECH *Vergaser* dashpot; **~er Strahlantrieb** *m* KFZTECH hydraulic jet propulsion; **~e Strangpresse** *f* MASCHINEN hydraulic extruder; ~er **Ventilfederheber** *m* KFZTECH hydraulic tappet, hydraulic valve lifter; ~er **Ventilstößel** *m* KFZTECH hydraulic tappet, hydraulic valve lifter; ~er **Verlust** *m* KERNTECH hydraulic loss; ~e **Wasserkraft** *f* HYDRAUL hydraulic power; ~er **Widder** *m* NICHTFOSS ENERG hydraulic ram; ~er **Wirkungsgrad** *m* NICHTFOSS ENERG hydraulic efficiency; ~es **Zirkulationssystem** *nt* ERDÖL *Bohrtechnik* hydraulic circulation system

Hydrazid *nt* CHEMIE hydrazide

Hydrazin *nt* CHEMIE diamide, diazane, hydrazine, RAUMFAHRT hydrazine; **Hydrazinantrieb** *m* RAUMFAHRT *Raumschiff* hydrazine propulsion; **Hydrazinantriebssystem** *nt* RAUMFAHRT *Raumschiff* hydrazine propulsion system

Hydrazobenzol *nt* CHEMIE phenylhydrazine

Hydrid *nt* CHEMIE, METALL hydride

Hydrierapparat *m* LEBENSMITTEL hydrogenator

Hydrieren *nt* CHEMIE hydrogenation

hydrieren *vt* CHEMIE, LEBENSMITTEL hydrogenate

hydrierend: ~e **Spaltung** *f* ERDÖL *Raffinerie* hydroracking

hydriert[1] *adj* CHEMIE hydrous, LEBENSMITTEL hydrogenated

hydriert:[2] ~es **Fett** *nt* LEBENSMITTEL hydrogenated fat; ~e **Schicht** *f* KER & GLAS hydrated layer

Hydrierung *f* CHEMIE, ERDÖL *Raffinerie*, LEBENSMITTEL hydrogenation

Hydrinden *nt* CHEMIE hydrindene, indan

Hydro- *pref* CHEMIE hydro-

hydroaromatisch *adj* CHEMIE hydroaromatic

Hydro-: **Hydrobilirubin** *nt* CHEMIE hydrobilirubin, urobilin; **Hydrobrom-** *pref* CHEMIE hydrobromic; **Hydrobromid** *nt* CHEMIE hydrobromide; **Hydrocellulose** *f* CHEMIE hydrocellulose; **Hydrochinon** *nt* CHEMIE hydroquinone; **Hydrochlorid** *nt* CHEMIE hydrochloride; **Hydrocortison** *nt* CHEMIE hydrocortisone; **Hydrocotarnin** *nt* CHEMIE hydrocotarnine; **Hydrodynamik** *f* ERDÖL, MASCHINEN, PHYS, STRÖMPHYS, WASSERTRANS *Schiffkonstruktion* hydrodynamics

hydrodynamisch[1] *adj* CHEMIE, ERDÖL *Hydraulik*, PHYS hydrodynamic

hydrodynamisch:[2] ~er **Auftrieb** *m* WASSERTRANS hydrodynamic lift; ~er **Dämpfungsfaktor** *m* NICHTFOSS ENERG hydrodynamic damping factor; ~e **Faserverwirbelung** *f* KUNSTSTOFF hydraulic entanglement process, hydroentanglement process; ~e **Kupplung** *f* KFZTECH *Kraftübertragung* fluid coupling, MASCHINEN hydrodynamic clutch; ~es **Modell** *nt* NICHTFOSS ENERG hydrodynamic model; ~e **Peilung** *f* RAUMFAHRT *Raumschiff* hydrodynamic bearing; ~e **Schmierung** *f* MASCHINEN hydrodynamic lubrication; ~er **Strömungswiderstand** *m* WASSERTRANS hydrodynamic drag

hydroelastisch: ~e **Radaufhängung** *f* KFZTECH Hydrolastic suspension

hydroelektrisch: ~er **Generator** *m* ELEKTROTECH hydroelectric generator; ~es **Umformen** *nt* MASCHINEN electrohydraulic forming; ~e **Umformung** *f* MASCHINEN hydroelectric forming

Hydro-: **Hydroelektrizität** *f* ELEKTRIZ hydroelectricity; **Hydrofluorid** *nt* CHEMIE hydrofluoride

Hydrogen- *pref* CHEMIE hydrogen, monohydric; **Hydrogenazid** *nt* CHEMIE diazoimide; **Hydrogencarbonat** *nt* CHEMIE hydrocarbonate; **Hydrogenperoxid** *nt* CHEMIE hydrogen peroxide; **Hydrogensalz** *nt* LEBENSMITTEL

acid salt; **Hydrogensulfat** *nt* CHEMIE hydrosulfate (AmE), hydrosulphate (BrE); **Hydrogensulfid** *nt* CHEMIE hydrogen sulfide (AmE), hydrogen sulphide (BrE), hydrosulfide (AmE), hydrosulphide (BrE), sulfhydrate (AmE), sulphydrate (BrE); **Hydrogensulfit** *nt* CHEMIE hydrogen sulfite (AmE), hydrogen sulphite (BrE), hydrosulfite (AmE), hydrosulphite (BrE)

Hydro-: **Hydrogeologie** *f* WASSERVERSORG hydrogeology; **Hydrographie** *f* NICHTFOSS ENERG, WASSERTRANS hydrography

hydrographisch *adj* WASSERTRANS hydrographic

Hydro-: **Hydrolastikfederung** *f* KFZTECH Hydrolastic suspension; **Hydrologie** *f* WASSERVERSORG hydrology

hydrologisch: ~e **Bilanz** *f* WASSERVERSORG hydrological balance; ~e **Untersuchung** *f* BAU hydrological study; ~er **Zyklus** *m* WASSERVERSORG hydrologic cycle

Hydro-: **Hydrolyse** *f* KUNSTSTOFF, LEBENSMITTEL hydrolysis; **Hydromechanik** *f* STRÖMPHYS hydromechanics

hydromechanisch: ~e **Diessellokomotive** *f* EISENBAHN diesel-hydromechanical locomotive; ~er **Fliehkraftregler** *m* NICHTFOSS ENERG hydromechanical governor; ~e **Kupplung** *f* MASCHINEN hydromechanical clutch; ~er **Zentrifugalregler** *m* NICHTFOSS ENERG hydromechanical governor

Hydro-: **Hydrometallurgie** *f* KOHLEN, METALL hydrometallurgy; **Hydrometer** *nt* ELEKTRIZ, ERDÖL *Meßtechnik*, KOHLEN, QUAL *Batterie* hydrometer; **Hydrometrie** *f* CHEMIE, WASSERVERSORG hydrometry; **Hydromotor** *m* MASCHINEN hydraulic motor; **Hydroniumion** *nt* CHEMIE hydroxonium ion

hydrophil *adj* KOHLEN hydrophilic

hydrophob *adj* CHEMIE, KOHLEN hydrophobic

Hydro-: **Hydrophobiermittel** *nt* TEXTIL water repellent; **Hydrophon** *nt* ERDÖL *Offshore-Seismik*, TELEKOM hydrophone

hydropneumatisch: ~e **Aufhängung** *f* KFZTECH hydropneumatic suspension; ~e **Bremse** *f* KFZTECH hydropneumatic brake; ~er **Speicher** *m* MASCHINEN hydropneumatic accumulator; ~er **Stoßdämpfer** *m* KFZTECH oleopneumatic shock absorber

Hydro-: **Hydropulsor** *m* NICHTFOSS ENERG hydraulic ram; **Hydropumpe** *f* MEERSCHMUTZ hydraulic pump; **Hydrosilicat** *nt* CHEMIE hydrosilicate; **Hydrosol** *nt* CHEMIE hydrosol; **Hydrosphäre** *f* UMWELTSCHMUTZ hydrosphere; **Hydrostatik** *f* BAU, MASCHINEN, MECHAN, PHYS, STRÖMPHYS, WASSERVERSORG hydrostatics

hydrostatisch[1] *adj* MASCHINEN, PHYS hydrostatic

hydrostatisch:[2] ~er **Druck** *m* ERDÖL *Geologie*, HEIZ & KÄLTE, KOHLEN hydrostatic pressure, NICHTFOSS ENERG hydraulic thrust, STRÖMPHYS hydrostatic pressure; ~es **Gleichgewicht** *nt* STRÖMPHYS hydrostatic balance, THERMOD hydrostatic equilibrium; ~e **Höhe** *f* ERDÖL hydrostatic head; ~es **Lager** *nt* MASCHINEN hydrostatic bearing; ~e **Lagerung** *f* MECHAN hydrostatic bearing; ~e **Schmierung** *f* MASCHINEN hydrostatic lubrication; ~e **Spannung** *f* METALL hydrostatic stress; ~e **Übertragung** *f* MECHAN hydrostatic transmission

Hydro-: **Hydrosulfid** *nt* CHEMIE hydrogen sulfide (AmE), hydrogen sulphide (BrE), sulfhydrate (AmE), sulphydrate (BrE), hydrosulfide (AmE), hydrosulphide (BrE); **Hydrosystem** *nt* MASCHINEN fluid-power system

hydrothermal: ~e **Prozesse** *m pl* NICHTFOSS ENERG hydrothermal processes

Hydro-: **Hydroventil** *nt* MASCHINEN hydraulically-operated valve

Hydroxozinkat *nt* CHEMIE zincate

Hydroxybarbitursäure *f* CHEMIE dialuric acid, hydroxybarbituric acid, tartronylurea

Hydroxycarbonsäure *f* CHEMIE hydroxycarboxylic acid

Hydroxycholin *nt* CHEMIE muscarine

Hydroxydinitrobenzol *nt* CHEMIE dinitrophenol

Hydroxyethylzellulose *f* ERDÖL *Petrochemie* hydroxyethylcellulose

Hydroxyindol *nt* CHEMIE hydroxyindole, indolol, indoxyl

Hydroxyketon *nt* CHEMIE ketol

hydroxyliert *adj* LEBENSMITTEL hydroxylated

Hydroxynaphthalin *nt* CHEMIE naphthol

Hydroxynaphthochinon *nt* CHEMIE hydroxynaphthoquinone, juglone

Hydroxyphenanthren *nt* CHEMIE phenanthrol

Hydroxytryptamin *nt* CHEMIE serotonin

Hydrozimt- *pref* CHEMIE hydrocinnamic

Hydro-: **Hydrozyklon** *m* ABFALL, CHEMTECH, ERDÖL *Bohrtechnik*, KOHLEN hydrocyclone; **Hydrozylinder** *m* MASCHINEN fluid-power cylinder

Hygrometer *nt* ERDÖL *Meßtechnik*, GERÄT, HEIZ & KÄLTE, MASCHINEN, PHYS, THERMOD hygrometer

Hygrometrie *f* WASSERVERSORG hygrometry

hygroskopisch *adj* BAU, MECHAN, WASSERVERSORG hygroscopic

Hyochol- *pref* CHEMIE hyocholic

Hyoscin *nt* CHEMIE hyoscine

hyperabrupt: ~er **Übergang** *m* ELEKTRONIK hyperabrupt junction

hyperballistisch *adj* RAUMFAHRT hyperballistic

Hyperbel *f* GEOM hyperbola; **Hyperbelnavigation** *f* WASSERTRANS hyperbolic navigation; **Hyperbelorbit** *m* RAUMFAHRT hyperbolic orbit; **Hyperbelräder** *nt pl* MASCHINEN hyperbolical wheels; **Hyperbelverfahren zur Positionsbestimmung** *nt* WASSERTRANS *Navigation* hyperbolic position-fixing system

hyperbolisch[1] *adj* GEOM hyperbolic

hyperbolisch:[2] ~e **Geometrie** *f* GEOM hyperbolic geometry; ~er **Raum** *m* GEOM hyperbolic space; ~e **Spirale** *f* GEOM hyperbolic spiral

Hyperboloid *nt* GEOM hyperboloid; **Hyperboloidgetriebe** *nt* MASCHINEN hyperbolical gear

Hyperebene *f* GEOM hyperplane

hypereutektisch *adj* METALL hypereutectic

hypereutektoidisch: ~er **Stahl** *adj* METALL hypereutectoid steel

hyperfein: ~e **Quantenzahl** *f (F)* KERNTECH hyperfine quantum number *(F)*

Hyperfeinstruktur *f* PHYS, STRAHLPHYS hyperfine structure

Hyperfläche *f* GEOM hypersurface

Hypergol- *pref* RAUMFAHRT *Raumschiff* hypergol

hypergolisch[1] *adj* RAUMFAHRT *Raumschiff* hypergolic

hypergolisch:[2] ~e **Eigenschaft** *f* RAUMFAHRT hypergolic property

Hyperkardioid-Mikrofon *nt* AKUSTIK hypercardioid microphone

Hyperladung *f* PHYS hypercharge

Hyperon *nt* PHYS, TEILPHYS hyperon

Hyperoxid *nt* CHEMIE hyperoxide

Hyperschallströmung *f* STRÖMPHYS hypersonic flow

Hypertext *m* COMP & DV hypertext

hyperthermisch: ~e **Felder** *nt pl* NICHTFOSS ENERG hyperthermal fields

Hypochlorid *nt* CHEMIE oxychloride

hypochlorig: ~e **Säure** *f* CHEMIE hypochlorous acid

Hypochlorit *nt* CHEMIE hypochlorite

Hypochlorsäure *f* CHEMIE hypochlorous acid

Hypodiphosphor- *pref* CHEMIE hypophosphoric

hypoeutektisch *adj* METALL hypoeutectic

Hypoid- *pref* MATH hypoid; **Hypoidgetriebe** *nt* KFZTECH hypoid gearing, MASCHINEN hypoid bevel gears; **Hypoidkegelgetriebe** *nt* KFZTECH hypoid bevel gearing; **Hypoidkegelrad** *nt* MASCHINEN, MECHAN hypoid bevel gear; **Hypoidkegelschraubgetriebe** *nt* MASCHINEN hypoid bevel gears; **Hypoidrad** *nt* MASCHINEN hypoid gear; **Hypoidwälzfräsautomat** *m* FERTIG automatic hypoid generator

Hyponitrit *nt* CHEMIE hyponitrite

Hypophosphat *nt* CHEMIE hypophosphate

hypophosphorisch *adj* CHEMIE hypophosphorous

Hypotenuse *f* GEOM hypotenuse

Hypothermie *f* WASSERTRANS hypothermia

Hypothese *f* KÜNSTL INT hypothesis; ~ **des elastischen Grenzzustandes** *f* FERTIG Mohr's strength theory

Hypothesenbildung *f* KÜNSTL INT hypothesis generation

Hypothesengenerierung *f* KÜNSTL INT hypothesis generation

hypothesengesteuert *adj* KÜNSTL INT hypothesis-driven

hypothesengetrieben *adj* KÜNSTL INT hypothesis-driven

hypotonisch *adj* CHEMIE hypotonic

Hypotrochoide *f* GEOM hypotrochoid

Hypoxanthin *nt* CHEMIE hypoxanthine, sarkine

Hypozykloide *f* GEOM hypocycloid

Hystazarin *nt* CHEMIE hystazarin

Hysterese *f* AUFNAHME, ELEKTRIZ, ELEKTROTECH, FERNSEH, KUNSTSTOFF, MASCHINEN, METALL, PHYS hysteresis; **Hysteresefehler** *m* LUFTTRANS *Höhenmesser* hysteresis error; **Hysteresekurve** *f* RADIO hysteresis; **Hystereseschleife** *f* ELEKTRIZ B/H loop, hysteresis loop, ELEKTROTECH, KUNSTSTOFF, MASCHINEN, METALL, PHYS hysteresis loop; **Hystereseverlust** *m* ELEKTROTECH, KUNSTSTOFF hysteresis loss; **Hystereseverlustzahl** *f* ELEKTRIZ hysteresis coefficient

Hysteresis *f* MASCHINEN hysteresis; **Hysteresismotor** *m* ELEKTROTECH hysteresis motor

Hz *abbr (Hertz)* ELEKTRIZ, ELEKTROTECH, FERNSEH, METROL, PHYS, RADIO Hz *(hertz)*

HZK[1] *abbr (höchstzulässige Konzentration)* UMWELTSCHMUTZ MAC *(maximum allowable concentration)*, TLV *(threshold limit value)*

HZK:[2] ~ **am Arbeitsplatz** *f* UMWELTSCHMUTZ MAC in the workplace, TLV in the workplace; ~ **in Umwelt** *f* UMWELTSCHMUTZ MAC in the free environment, TLV in the free environment

I

I [1] *abbr* AKUSTIK *(Intensität, Stärke)* I *(intensity)*, ELEKTRIZ *(elektrischer Strom)* I *(electric current)*, ELEKTRIZ *(Intensität)* I *(intensity)*, KERNTECH *(Energieflußdichte)* I *(energy flux density)*, KERNTECH *(nukleare Spinquantenzahl)* I *(nuclear spin quantum number)*, OPTIK *(Intensität)* I *(intensity)*, PHYS *(elektrischer Strom)*, TELEKOM *(elektrischer Strom)* I *(electric current)*

I [2] *(Iod, Jod)* CHEMIE I *(iodine)*

I-Achse *f* FERNSEH I axis

I-Anker *m* ELEKTRIZ shuttle armature

I-Beiwert *m* REGELUNG integral action coefficient

ICAS *abbr (Kommerzieller und Amateurfunkdienst)* RADIO ICAS *(Intermittent Commercial and Amateur Services)*

IC-Maske *f* ELEKTRONIK IS mask

Icosan *nt* CHEMIE icosane

ICRP *abbr (Internationale Strahlenschutzkommission)* STRAHLPHYS ICRP *(International Commission on Radiological Protection)*

IC-Verfahren *nt (Spritzprägeverfahren)* KUNSTSTOFF injection compression process

ID *abbr (Identifikation, Kennung)* COMP & DV identification

ideal: ~**es Filter** *nt* ELEKTRONIK ideal filter; ~**e Flüssigkeit** *f* PHYS perfect fluid; ~**es Gas** *nt* PHYS, THERMOD ideal gas, perfect gas; ~**e Phasenfokussierung** *f* ELEKTRONIK ideal bunching

Ideal- *pref* ELEKTROTECH, TRANS ideal; **Idealbedingungen** *f pl* TRANS ideal conditions; **Idealgeschwindigkeit** *f* NICHTFOSS ENERG ideal velocity; **Idealgleichrichter** *m* ELEKTROTECH ideal rectifier; **Idealtransformator** *m* ELEKTROTECH ideal transformer

I-Demodulator *m* FERNSEH I demodulator

Identifikation *f* COMP & DV identity, COMP & DV, MASCHINEN identification; **Identifikationscode** *m* COMP & DV authentication code, identification code; **Identifikationskennzeichen** *nt* COMP & DV tag, identification character

identifizieren *vt* COMP & DV identify

Identifizierer *m* COMP & DV identifier

identifiziert: **nicht** ~**es Flugobjekt** *nt (UFO)* RAUMFAHRT unidentified flying object *(UFO)*; ~**e Quellen** *f pl* NICHTFOSS ENERG identified resources

Identifizierung *f* COMP & DV identity; ~ **des rufenden Anschlusses** *f* TELEKOM CLI, calling line identification

identisch: ~**e Gleichheit** *f* MATH identity

Identität *f* MATH identity

Identkarte *f* QUAL identity card

Identnummer *f* QUAL identity number

Ideogramm *nt* COMP & DV ideogram

idiomorph: ~**er Kristall** *m* METALL idiomorphic crystal

Idit *nt* CHEMIE idite, iditol

Iditol *nt* CHEMIE idite, iditol

Idler-Frequenz *f* ELEKTRONIK, RADIO, TELEKOM idler frequency

Idon- *pref* CHEMIE idonic

Idose *f* CHEMIE idose

Idozucker- *pref* CHEMIE idosaccharic

IFR *abbr (Instrumentenflugregeln)* LUFTTRANS IFR *(instrument flight rules)*

IFRB *abbr (Internationale Frequenz-Zuweisungsbehörde)* RAUMFAHRT IFRB *(International Frequency Registration Board)*

IGFET *abbr (Isolierschicht-Feldeffekttransistor)* ELEKTRONIK, RADIO IGFET *(insulated gate field-effect transistor)*

I-Glied *nt (Integralelement)* REGELUNG integral element

Iglu-Container *m* LUFTTRANS igloo container

Ignitron *nt* ELEKTRIZ ignitron; **Ignitronlokomotive** *f* EISENBAHN ignitron locomotive; **Ignitronröhre** *f* ELEKTROTECH ignitron

I-Halbleiter *m* COMP & DV intrinsic semiconductor

IIR *abbr (unbegrenztes Ansprechen auf Impuls)* ELEKTRONIK IIR *(infinite impulse response)*

IIR-Digitalfilter *nt* TELEKOM IIR digital filter; **IIR-Filter** *nt* TELEKOM IIR filter

Ikonoskop *nt* ELEKTRONIK iconoscope

Ikosaeder *nt* GEOM icosahedron

ikosaedrisch *adj* GEOM icosahedral

illegal: ~**e Dünnsäureverklappung** *f* UMWELTSCHMUTZ illegal barging of spent acid

Illit *m* ERDÖL, KOHLEN illite

I²L-Logik *f (integrierte Injektionslogik)* ELEKTRONIK I²L *(integrated injection logic)*

Illumination *f* ELEKTRIZ illumination

Illustration *f* DRUCK illustration; **Illustrationsfarbe** *f* DRUCK halftone ink

illustrieren *vt* DRUCK illustrate

ILS *abbr (Blindfluglandesystem durch Eigenpeilung, Instrumentenlandesystem)* LUFTTRANS, RAUMFAHRT ILS *(instrument landing system)*

IM *abbr* FERTIG *(Injection-Moulding, Spritzgießen)*, KUNSTSTOFF *(Injection-Moulding, Spritzgießen, Spritzgießmasse)*, KUNSTSTOFF *(Spritzgießmaschine)*, VERPACK *(Injection-Moulding, Spritzgießen)* IM *(injection molding, injection moulding)*

imaginär: ~**e Einheit i** *f* MATH imaginary unit i; ~**e Zahl** *f* MATH imaginary number

Imband-Zeichengabe *f* TELEKOM in-band signaling (AmE), in-band signalling (BrE)

IMD *abbr* AUFNAHME *(Intermodulationsverzerrung)*, ELEKTRONIK *(Zwischenmodulationsverzerrung)*, RADIO *(Intermodulationsverzerrung)* IMD *(intermodulation distortion)*

Imhoffbrunnen *m* ABFALL Imhoff tank

Imid *nt* CHEMIE imide

Imidazo- Pyrimidin *nt* CHEMIE purine

Imido- *pref* CHEMIE imido; **Imidogruppe** *f* CHEMIE imido group; **Imidoxanthin** *nt* CHEMIE aminohypoxanthine, guanine, imidoxanthine

Iminoharnstoff *m* CHEMIE guanidine

Immediatanalyse *f* CHEMIE proximate analysis

Immersion *f* CHEMIE immersion; **Immersionslinse** *f*

FERNSEH immersion electron lens, LABOR *Mikroskop* immersion lens; **Immersionsobjektiv** *nt* METALL immersion objective; **Immersionsöl-Linse** *f* LABOR *Mikroskop* oil immersion lens

Immissionsgrenzwert: ~ **der Luft** *m* UMWELTSCHMUTZ ambient air emission standard, ambient air quality standard

IMO *abbr (Internationale Schifffahrtorganisation)* WASSERTRANS *Behörde* IMO *(International Maritime Organization)*

Impaktion *f* UMWELTSCHMUTZ impaction

Impatt-Diode *f (Lawinenlaufzeitdiode)* ELEKTRONIK, PHYS, RADIO impatt diode *(impact ionization avalanche transit-time diode)*

Impatt-Oszillator *m* ELEKTRONIK impatt oscillator

Impedanz *f* AUFNAHME impedance, ELEKTRIZ *(Z)* impedance *(Z)*, ELEKTROTECH impedance, *als Bauelement* impedor, PHYS, RADIO, TELEKOM impedance; **durch ~ abgeschlossene Leitung** *f* PHYS line terminated by an impedance; **Impedanzanpassung** *f* ELEKTROTECH, PHYS impedance matching; **Impedanzanpassungsnetz** *nt* ELEKTROTECH impedance matching network; **Impedanzausgleicher** *m* ELEKTRIZ impedance corrector; **Impedanzbrücke** *f* GERÄT impedance measuring bridge; **Impedanzfehlanpassung** *f* ELEKTROTECH impedance mismatch; **Impedanzkupplung** *f* ELEKTROTECH impedance coupling; **Impedanzkurve** *f* ELEKTROTECH impedance characteristic; **Impedanzkurve eines blockierten Läufers** *f* ELEKTRIZ locked rotor impedance characteristic; **Impedanzmeßbrücke** *f* ELEKTROTECH impedance bridge, GERÄT impedance measuring bridge; **Impedanzrelais** *nt* ELEKTRIZ impedance relay; **Impedanzspannung** *f* ELEKTROTECH impedance voltage; **Impedanzspannungsabfall** *m* ELEKTRIZ impedance drop; **Impedanzspule** *f* ELEKTROTECH impedance coil; **Impedanzwandler** *m* PHYS impedance transformer; **Impedanzwandlung** *f* ELEKTROTECH impedance conversion

Impfen *nt* KERNTECH inoculation

Impfkompostrückführung *f* ABFALL recycling of inoculated compost

Impfkristall *m* FERTIG, THERMOD seed crystal

Impfung *f* KERNTECH inoculation

Implantation: ~ **radioaktiver Ionen** *f* TEILPHYS radioactive ion implantation

implantiert: ~**e Basis** *f* ELEKTRONIK implanted base; ~**e Diode** *f* ELEKTRONIK implanted diode; ~**er Transistor** *m* ELEKTRONIK implanted transistor

implementieren *vt* MASCHINEN implement

Implementierung *f* COMP & DV implementation

impliziert: ~**e Adressierung** *f* COMP & DV implied addressing

implizit[1] *adj* MATH implicit

implizit:[2] ~**e Adressierung** *f* COMP & DV inherent addressing

implodieren *vt* ELEKTRONIK implode

Implosion *f* ELEKTRONIK implosion; ~ **der schwarzen Strahlung** *f* KERNTECH implosion of black body radiation

Importlizenz *f* WASSERTRANS *Dokument* import licence (BrE), import license (AmE)

Imprägnieren *nt* BAU soaking, KUNSTSTOFF impregnation

imprägnieren *vt* BAU proof, temper, TEXTIL dip, impregnate

Imprägnierlack *m* ELEKTRIZ *Tränklack* impregnating varnish

Imprägniermaschine *f* VERPACK impregnating machine

Imprägniermasse *f* VERPACK impregnating agent

Imprägniermittel *nt* CHEMIE impregnant, saturant, VERPACK impregnating agent

imprägniert[1] *adj* PAPIER impregnated

imprägniert:[2] ~**es Gewebe** *nt* VERPACK impregnated fabric; **nicht ~es Gewebe** *nt* TEXTIL undipped fabric; ~**es Kabel** *nt* ELEKTRIZ impregnated cable; ~**e Kathode** *f* ELEKTROTECH impregnated cathode; ~**es Papier** *nt* DRUCK, VERPACK impregnated paper; ~**es papierisoliertes Kabel** *nt* ELEKTRIZ impregnated paper insulation; ~**e Spule** *f* ELEKTROTECH impregnated coil

Imprägnierung *f* BAU, PAPIER, TEXTIL impregnation

Imprägnierwachs *nt* VERPACK impregnating wax

imprimaturbereit *adj* DRUCK passed for press

Improved-Ruß *m* KUNSTSTOFF improved carbon black

Impuls *m* AUFNAHME pulse, COMP & DV pulse, signal, ELEKTRIZ, ELEKTRONIK pulse, ELEKTROTECH momentary action, FERNSEH spike, KONTROLL pulse, MASCHINEN impetus, impulse, impulsion, momentum, MECHAN impulse, momentum, OPTIK pulse, PAPIER impulse, PHYS momentum, *Zeitintegral der Kraft* impulse, RADIO pulse, TELEKOM impulse, WASSERTRANS *Radar* pulse; ~ **mit hoher Amplitude** *m* ELEKTRONIK high-amplitude pulse; ~ **mit kurzer Anstiegszeit** *m* ELEKTRONIK fast-rise pulse; ~ **eines Schaltkennzeichens** *m* ELEKTRONIK signal pulse; **Impulsabfall** *m* ELEKTRONIK pulse tilt; **Impulsabfallzeit** *f* AUFNAHME, TELEKOM pulse decay time; **Impulsamplitude** *f* AUFNAHME, ELEKTRONIK pulse amplitude; **Impulsantwort** *f* TELEKOM impulse response

impulsartig: ~ **rauschen** *vi* COMP & DV burst

Impuls: Impulsbeschleuniger *m* STRAHLPHYS impulse accelerator; **Impulsbetrieb** *m* ELEKTRONIK pulsed operation; **Impulsbildung** *f* ELEKTRONIK *in Laufzeitröhren* bunching; **Impulsbreite** *f* COMP & DV pulse width, ELEKTRONIK pulse duration, pulse width, FERNSEH, PHYS, TELEKOM pulse width; **Impulsbreitemodulation** *f* ELEKTRONIK pulse width modulation; **Impulscharakteristik** *f* FERNSEH surge characteristic; **Impulsdauer** *f* COMP & DV, ELEKTRONIK, FERNSEH pulse width, KONTROLL impulse length, PHYS pulse width, TELEKOM pulse length, pulse width; **Impulsdiskriminator** *m* RADIO pulse count discriminator; **Impulsdispersion** *f* OPTIK, TELEKOM pulse dispersion

Impulse: ~ **je Sekunde** *m pl* TELEKOM pulses per second

Impuls: Impulsentzerrung *f* FERNSEH pulse restoration; **Impulserhaltung** *f* PHYS conservation of momentum; **Impulserzeuger** *m* FERTIG pulser; **Impulsfolge** *f* COMP & DV pulse train, ELEKTRONIK pulse sequence, pulse train; **Impulsfolgefrequenz** *f* COMP & DV, ELEKTRONIK, PHYS, TELEKOM PRF, pulse repetition frequency; **Impulsfolgeperiode** *f* ELEKTRONIK pulse repetition period; **Impulsform** *f* ELEKTRONIK pulse shape; **Impulsformung** *f* COMP & DV pulse shaping; **Impulsfrequenz** *f* ELEKTRONIK impulse frequency; **Impulsfunktion** *f* ELEKTRONIK impulse function; **Impulsgang** *m* OPTIK impulse response; **Impulsgeber** *m* ELEKTRONIK pulser, KERNTECH surge generator; **Impulsgeberrad** *nt* KFZTECH trigger wheel; **Impulsgenerator** *m* COMP & DV PG, pulse generator, ELEKTRIZ PG, pulse generator, impulse generator, ELEKTRONIK pulse synthesizer, ELEKTROTECH impulse generator, TELEKOM PG, pulse generator

impulshaltig: ~es Rauschen *nt* AKUSTIK impulsive noise

Impuls: **Impulshitzesiegler** *m* VERPACK impulse heat sealer; **Impulshöhe** *f* COMP & DV pulse height, ELEKTRONIK pulse amplitude; **Impulskennlinien** *f pl* ELEKTRONIK pulse characteristics; **Impulskette** *f* COMP & DV pulse train; **Impulskompression** *f* TELEKOM pulse compression; **Impulskondensator** *m* ELEKTRIZ pulse capacitor; **Impulskorrektor** *m* ELEKTRONIK pulse regenerator; **Impulslänge** *f* TELEKOM, WASSERTRANS *Radar* pulse length; **Impulslaser** *m* ELEKTRONIK, STRAHLPHYS pulsed laser; **Impulsmagnetron** *nt* ELEKTRONIK pulsed magnetron; **Impulsmaser** *m* ELEKTRONIK pulsed maser; **Impulsmodulierung** *f* ELEKTRIZ pulse modulation; **Impulsmoment** *nt* LUFTTRANS angular momentum; **Impulsoszillator** *m* ELEKTRONIK pulsed oscillator; **Impulspause** *f* ELEKTRONIK pulse separation; **Impulspegel** *m* AKUSTIK burst level; **Impulsperiodendauer** *f* ELEKTRONIK pulse spacing; **Impulsprofil** *nt* TELEKOM pulse profile; **Impulsrauschen** *nt* RAUMFAHRT *Weltraumfunk* pulse noise; **Impulsregenerierung** *f* FERNSEH pulse regeneration; **Impulsrelais** *nt* ELEKTRIZ pulse relay, surge relay, ELEKTROTECH impulse relay; **Impulsrückflanke** *f* TELEKOM pulse trailing edge; **Impulsschalter** *m* ELEKTROTECH momentary action switch; **Impulsschaltung** *f* ELEKTRONIK pulse circuit; **Impulssignal** *nt* ELEKTRONIK pulse signal; **Impulsspannung** *f* ELEKTRIZ impulse voltage; **Impulsspitze** *f* ELEKTRIZ pulse spike; **Impulsspitzenfrequenz** *f* ELEKTRONIK, FERNSEH, RADIO, TELEKOM sync tip frequency; **Impulsstopfen** *nt* TELEKOM justification; **Impulsstörung** *f* AKUSTIK, COMP & DV, TELEKOM impulse noise; **Impulsstörungsbegrenzer** *m* RADIO noise pulse limiter; **Impulsstrom** *m* ELEKTRIZ impulse current, pulsed current; **Impulstastverhältnis** *nt* PHYS mark space ratio; **Impulstechnik** *f* WERKPRÜF pulse technique; **Impulstriggern** *nt* FERNSEH pulse triggering; **Impulsübertrager** *m* TELEKOM PT, pulse transformer; **Impulsübertragungsgang** *m* OPTIK impulse response; **Impulsultraschalldetektor** *m* TRANS pulsed ultrasonic detector; **Impulsverbesserung** *f* ELEKTRONIK pulse regeneration; **Impulsverbreiterung** *f* OPTIK pulse broadening, pulse spreading, TELEKOM pulse broadening, pulse widening; **Impulsverkehrsradar** *nt* TRANS pulsed radar detector; **Impulsverschlüssler** *m* STRAHLPHYS pulse coder; **Impulsverstärker** *m* AUFNAHME, ELEKTRONIK pulse amplifier; **Impulsverstärkung** *f* ELEKTRONIK pulse amplification; **Impulsversteilerungsschaltung** *f* ELEKTRONIK peaking circuit; **Impulsvorderflanke** *f* TELEKOM pulse leading edge; **Impulswiederholer** *m* ELEKTRONIK regenerator; **Impulszähler** *m* ELEKTRIZ impulse counter, ELEKTRONIK pulse counter; **Impulszähltechnik** *f* TELEKOM pulse-counting technique; **Impulszeichengabe** *f* TELEKOM impulse signaling (AmE), impulse signalling (BrE); **Impulszentrale** *f* TELEKOM central pulse distributor

In *(Indium)* CHEMIE In *(indium)*

inaktinisch: ~es Glas *nt* KER & GLAS inactinic glass

inaktiv[1] *adj* CHEMIE, COMP & DV inactive

inaktiv:[2] ~er Reaktor *m* KERNTECH cold reactor

inaktivieren *vt* COMP & DV disable

Inaktivierung *f* COMP & DV disarmed state

inakzeptabel: **inakzeptable Qualität** *f* TELEKOM unacceptable quality

Inanspruchnahme *f* PATENT claiming

Inbetriebnahme[1] *f* COMP & DV installation, KONTROLL initial operation phase, MECHAN commissioning; **Inbetriebnahmeprüfung** *f* TELEKOM commissioning test; **Inbetriebnahmeventil** *nt* HYDRAUL equilibrium valve; **Inbetriebnahmevorbereitung** *f* HYDRAUL priming

Inbetriebnahme:[2] **für die ~ vorbereiten** *vt* HYDRAUL *Dampfkessel* prime

inbetriebsetzen *vt* KERNTECH set into operation

Inbusschlüssel *m* MASCHINEN Allen key (BrE), Allen wrench (AmE)

Inbusschraube *f* MASCHINEN Allen screw, socket head screw

Inch *m* FERTIG *Kunststoffinstallationen* in, inch; **Inchgewinde** *nt* MASCHINEN inch thread; **Inchscrap-Verfahren** *nt* ABFALL cryogrinding, freeze-grinding

In-Circuit-Tester *m* ELEKTRIZ in-circuit tester

Incore- *pref* KERNTECH in-core; **Incore-Brennstoffkreislauf** *m* KERNTECH in-core fuel cycle; **Incore-Lebensdauer des Brennstoffes** *f* KERNTECH in-core fuel life

Indan *nt* CHEMIE hydrindene, indan; **Indanon** *nt* CHEMIE indanone; **Indanthron** *nt* CHEMIE indanthrene

Indazin *nt* CHEMIE indazine

Indazol *nt* CHEMIE indazole

Inden *nt* CHEMIE indene

Index *m* COMP & DV, MASCHINEN, MATH index; **~ der Wärmebelastung** *f* ERGON heat stress index

Indexieren *nt* COMP & DV, MASCHINEN indexing

indexieren *vt* COMP & DV index

indexiert: **~er Befehl** *m* COMP & DV indexed instruction; **~e Datei** *f* COMP & DV indexed file; **~e Variable** *f* COMP & DV subscripted variable

Index: **Indexliste** *f* COMP & DV *FORTRAN* subscript; **Indexloch** *nt* COMP & DV index hole; **Indexprofil** *nt* OPTIK, TELEKOM index profile; **Indexregister** *nt* COMP & DV index register; **Indexröhre** *f* FERNSEH index tube

indexsequentiell: **~e Datei** *f* COMP & DV indexed sequential file; **~er Zugriff** *m* COMP & DV indexed sequential access

Index: **Indexsequenz** *f* COMP & DV IS, indexed sequence

indexsequenziert: **~e Datei** *f* COMP & DV indexed sequential file; **~er Zugriff** *m* COMP & DV indexed sequential access

Indican *nt* CHEMIE indicane

Indienststellung *f* MECHAN, WASSERTRANS *Schiff* commissioning

indifferent: **~es Lösemittel** *nt* CHEMIE aprotic solvent

Indikator *m* HYDRAUL indicator, KER & GLAS tracer, MASCHINEN, WASSERVERSORG indicator; **Indikatoratom** *nt* KERNTECH labeled atom (AmE), labelled atom (BrE); **Indikatordiagramm** *nt* MASCHINEN indicator diagram; **Indikatorpapier** *nt* FOTO, VERPACK indicator paper

indirekt: **~e Adressierung** *f* COMP & DV deferred addressing, indirect addressing; **~ beeinflußte Regelstrecke** *f* REGELUNG indirectly controlled system; **~ beeinflußte Steuerstrecke** *f* REGELUNG indirectly controlled system; **~e Beleuchtung** *f* ELEKTROTECH indirect illumination; **~ geheizte Kathode** *f* ELEKTROTECH heater-type cathode, indirectly heated cathode; **~ gesteuertes System** *nt* TELEKOM indirect-control system; **~e Photoleitfähigkeit** *f* ELEKTRONIK indirect photoconductivity; **~e Regelung** *f* ELEKTROTECH indirect control; **~e Überstromabschaltung** *f* ELEKTRIZ indirect over-current release; **~ wirkende obenliegende Nockenwelle** *f* KFZTECH indirect overhead camshaft

Indium *nt (In)* CHEMIE indium *(In)*

Individual-Section-Flaschenblasmaschine *f (IS-Maschine)* KER & GLAS individual section machine *(IS machine)*; **Individualverkehr** *m* TRANS private vehicle traffic

individuell: ~e **Unterschiede** *m pl* ERGON individual differences

indizieren *vt* COMP & DV index

indiziert: ~e **Adresse** *f* COMP & DV indexed address; ~e **Adressierung** *f* COMP & DV indexed addressing; ~e **Datei** *f* COMP & DV indexed file; ~e **Instruktion** *f* COMP & DV indexed instruction

Indol *nt* CHEMIE indole; **Indolol** *nt* CHEMIE hydroxyindole, indolol, indoxyl

Indolylessig- *pref* CHEMIE indolylacetic

Indonaphthen *nt* CHEMIE indene

Indophenin *nt* CHEMIE indophenine, induline

Indophenol *nt* CHEMIE indophenol

Indoxyl *nt* CHEMIE hydroxyindole, indolol, indoxyl; **Indoxyl-** *pref* CHEMIE indoxylic; **Indoxylschwefel-** *pref* CHEMIE indoxylsulfuric (AmE), indoxylsulphuric (BrE)

Induktanz *f* ELEKTRIZ reactor, self-induction, self-inductance, ELEKTROTECH inductive reactance; **äußere** ~ *f* ELEKTRIZ external inductance; **Induktanzbrücke** *f* ELEKTRIZ *Meßbrücke* inductance bridge; **Induktanzmeßgerät** *nt* ELEKTRIZ inductance meter

Induktion *f* ELEKTRIZ, ELEKTROTECH, MASCHINEN, TELEKOM induction; **Induktionsfeld** *nt* ELEKTROTECH, FERNSEH induction field; **Induktionsfluß** *m* ELEKTROTECH induction flux, magnetic flux

induktionsfrei[1] *adj* ELEKTRIZ noninductive

induktionsfrei:[2] ~e **Last** *f* ELEKTRIZ noninductive load; ~er **Stromkreis** *m* ELEKTRIZ noninductive circuit; ~er **Widerstand** *m* ELEKTRIZ noninductive resistor

Induktion: **Induktionsfrequenzumformer** *m* ELEKTRIZ induction frequency converter; **Induktionsgenerator** *m* ELEKTRIZ, ELEKTROTECH induction generator; **Induktionshartlöten** *nt* FERTIG induction brazing

induktionshartlöten *vt* FERTIG induction-braze

Induktion: **Induktionshärtung** *f* ELEKTROTECH induction hardening; **Induktionsheizgerät** *nt* ELEKTROTECH induction heater; **Induktionsheizung** *f* ELEKTROTECH, MECHAN, THERMOD *Verfahren* induction heating; **Induktionsinstrument** *nt* ELEKTROTECH induction instrument; **Induktionskoeffizient** *m* PHYS coefficient of induction; **Induktionskopplung** *f* ELEKTRIZ coupling; **Induktionslöten** *nt* FERTIG induction brazing

induktionslöten *vi* FERTIG induction-braze

Induktion: **Induktionsmotor** *m* ELEKTRIZ, ELEKTROTECH, FERTIG, KFZTECH, PHYS induction motor; **Induktionsmotor mit Schleifringläufer** *m* ELEKTROTECH wound-rotor induction motor; **Induktionsofen** *m* ELEKTROTECH, PHYS induction furnace; **Induktionspumpe** *f* ELEKTROTECH induction pump; **Induktionsregler** *m* ELEKTROTECH induction voltage regulator; **Induktionsrelais** *nt* ELEKTRIZ, ELEKTROTECH induction relay; **Induktionsrinnenofen** *m* HEIZ & KÄLTE channel induction furnace; **Induktionsschleifendetektor** *m* KFZTECH induction loop detector; **Induktionsschweißen** *nt* ELEKTRIZ, FERTIG induction welding; **Induktionssiegler** *m* VERPACK induction sealer; **Induktionsspannung** *f* ELEKTROTECH induced electromotive force, induction voltage, TELEKOM induced voltage; **Induktionsspannungsregler** *m* ELEKTROTECH induction voltage regulator; **Induk-**

tionsspule *f* ELEKTRIZ, ELEKTROTECH, KFZTECH induction coil; **Induktionsspule mit Luftspaltkern** *f* ELEKTRIZ air gap induction coil; **Induktionsstrom** *m* TELEKOM induced current; **Induktionssystem** *nt* PHYS inducing system; **Induktionswiderstand** *m* PHYS inductive reactance; **Induktionszeit** *f* METALL induction period

induktiv:[1] **nicht** ~ *adj* ELEKTRIZ noninductive

induktiv:[2] ~e **Abstimmung** *f* ELEKTROTECH inductive tuning; ~es **AC-Potentiometer** *nt* ELEKTRIZ inductive potential divider; ~e **Belastung** *f* TELEKOM inductive load; ~er **Blindwiderstand** *m (XL)* ELEKTRIZ inductive reactance *(XL)*; ~er **Drahtwicklungswiderstand** *m* ELEKTROTECH inductive wirewound resistor; ~es **Durchflußmengenmeßgerät** *nt* GERÄT inductive flowmeter; ~er **Durchflußmesser** *m* ELEKTROTECH electromagnetic flowmeter; ~e **Erwärmung** *f* KUNSTSTOFF induction heating; ~er **Kondensator** *m* ELEKTROTECH inductive capacitor; ~e **Kopplung** *f* ELEKTRIZ inductive coupling, magnetic coupling, ELEKTROTECH flux linkage, inductive coupling; ~e **Last** *f* ELEKTRIZ, ELEKTROTECH inductive load; **nicht** ~e **Last** *f* ELEKTRIZ noninductive load; ~er **Näherungsschalter** *m* ELEKTROTECH inductive proximity switch; ~e **Pi-Schaltung** *f* RADIO pi-L network; ~e **Reaktanz** *f* ELEKTRIZ, ELEKTROTECH inductive reactance; ~e **Rückkopplung** *f* ELEKTROTECH inductive feedback; ~e **Schaltung** *f* ELEKTRIZ inductive circuit; **nicht** ~e **Schaltung** *f* ELEKTRIZ noninductive circuit; ~er **Spannungsteiler** *m* ELEKTRIZ inductive potential divider; **nicht** ~e **Wicklung** *f* ELEKTRIZ noninductive winding; ~er **Widerstand** *m* ELEKTROTECH inductive reactance

Induktivität *f (L)* AUFNAHME *Spule*, ELEKTRIZ, ELEKTROTECH, LABOR, PHYS, RADIO, TELEKOM inductance *(L)*

induktivitätbehaftet: ~er **Widerstand** *m* ELEKTROTECH inductive resistor

Induktivität: **Induktivitätskasten** *m* ELEKTROTECH inductance box; **Induktivitätsmeßbrücke** *f* ELEKTROTECH inductance bridge; **Induktivitätsmeßgerät** *nt* GERÄT inductance measuring instrument; **Induktivitätsspule** *f* ELEKTROTECH inductance coil

Induktometer *nt* ELEKTRIZ, ELEKTROTECH inductometer

Induktor *m* ELEKTROTECH inductor; **Induktoralternator** *m* ELEKTRIZ inductor alternator; **Induktorgenerator** *m* ELEKTROTECH inductor generator

Indulin *nt* CHEMIE induline

Industrie *f* ABFALL, ELEKTRONIK industry; **Industrieabfall** *m* WASSERVERSORG industrial waste; **Industrieabwasser** *nt* ABFALL industrial waste water, WASSERVERSORG industrial effluent; **Industriealkohol** *m* LEBENSMITTEL *Lösungsmittel* industrial alcohol; **Industriearbeitskleidung** *f* SICHERHEIT industrial clothing; **Industrieautomation** *f* MASCHINEN industrial automation; **Industriedichtung** *f* VERPACK industrial packing; **Industrieelektronik** *f* ELEKTROTECH industrial electronics; **Industrieelektronikröhre** *f* ELEKTRONIK industrial electronic tube; **Industriefernbedienung** *f* SICHERHEIT remote control system for industrial applications; **Industriefotografie** *f* FOTO commercial photography; **Industriehygiene** *f* SICHERHEIT industrial hygiene; **Industrie-LKW** *m* SICHERHEIT *Sicherheitsvorschriften* industrial truck

industriell: ~e **Bestrahlungsanlage** *f* KERNTECH industrial irradiator; ~e **Einleitung** *f* WASSERVERSORG industrial discharge; **~e Kernenergie** *f* KERNTECH industrial nuclear power; **~er Klärschlamm** *m* ABFALL industrial sewage sludge; **~es Nutzwasser** *nt*-WASSERVERSORG industrial water; **~es Schüttgutcontainersystem** *nt* VERPACK industrial bulk container system

Industrie: **Industriemagnetron** *nt* ELEKTRONIK industrial magnetron; **Industriemüll** *m* ABFALL industrial waste; **Industriemülldeponie** *f* ABFALL industrial landfill; **Industrienorm** *f* COMP & DV, QUAL industrial standard; **Industrieofen** *m* FERTIG furnace, MASCHINEN furnace, industrial furnace, industrial oven; **Industrie-Overall** *m* SICHERHEIT industrial overall; **Industrieroboter** *m* KÜNSTL INT, SICHERHEIT *Sicherheitsvorkehrungen* IR, industrial robot; **Industrieschornstein** *m* BAU stack; **Industrieschutzhelm** *m* SICHERHEIT industrial safety helmet; **Industriestandard** *m* COMP & DV, QUAL industrial standard; **Industrieunfall** *m* SICHERHEIT industrial accident; **Industrieverfrachter** *m* WASSERTRANS industrial carrier; **Industrieverpackung** *f* KERNTECH industrial packaging; **Industrieversicherung** *f* SICHERHEIT industrial insurance

induzieren *vt* ELEKTRIZ, PHYS induce

induzierend: ~er Durchfluß *m* BAU *Brunnen* inducing flow

induziert[1] *adj* ELEKTRIZ *Spannung*, PHYS induced

induziert:[2] **~er Anstellwinkel** *m* LUFTTRANS induced attack angle; **~e elektromotorische Kraft** *f* ELEKTRIZ, ELEKTROTECH induced electromotive force; **~e Emission** *f* ELEKTRONIK stimulated emission, STRAHLPHYS induced emission; **~e EMK** *f* PHYS induced EMF; **~er Fehler** *m* COMP & DV induced failure; **~es Feld** *nt* ELEKTRIZ induced field; **~es Gitterrauschen** *nt* RADIO induced grid noise; **~e Kernreaktion** *f* KERNTECH artificial nuclear reaction, induced nuclear reaction; **~e Ladung** *f* ELEKTRIZ, ELEKTROTECH induced charge; **~er Luftwiderstand** *m* LUFTTRANS induced drag; **~e Radioaktivität** *f* KERNTECH induced radioactivity; **~e Spannung** *f* ELEKTRIZ induced voltage; **~e Störung** *f* COMP & DV induced interference; **~er Strom** *m* ELEKTRIZ induced current

ineinanderfließen *vi* CHEMIE coalesce

Ineinandergreifen *nt* MASCHINEN mating, MECHAN meshing; **~ der Phasen** *nt* TRANS phase skipping

ineinandergreifen *vi* COMP & DV interlace, MASCHINEN engage, interlock, mate, mesh

ineinandergreifend *adj* FERTIG mating, *Getriebelehre* interengaging

ineinanderzeichnen *vt* KONSTZEICH draw in the mated condition

inelastisch: ~e Neutronenstreuung *f* STRAHLPHYS, TEILPHYS inelastic neutron scattering; **~er Stoß** *m* STRAHLPHYS, TEILPHYS inelastic collision; **~e Streuung** *f* KERNTECH, STRAHLPHYS, TEILPHYS inelastic scattering

inert[1] *adj* ERDÖL *Petrochemie* inert

inert:[2] **~er Abfall** *m* ABFALL inert waste; **~es Material** *nt* ABFALL inert material

Inertgas *nt* FERTIG, KERNTECH *Schweißen*, MASCHINEN inert gas; **Inertgasschutzmantel** *m* FERTIG inert gas shield; **Inertgasschweißen** *nt* FERTIG sigma welding; **Inertgasschweißen mit abschmelzender Elektrode** *nt* FERTIG inert arc welding with a consumable electrode; **Inertgasschweißen mit nicht abschmelzender Elektrode** *nt* FERTIG inert arc welding with

non-consumable electrode

Inertialnavigationssystem *nt* LUFTTRANS, RAUMFAHRT, WASSERTRANS INS, inertial navigation system

Inertialsystem *nt* PHYS inertial frame

inertial: ~es Bezugssystem *nt* PHYS inertial frame

Inertisieren *nt* ERDÖL *Sicherheit* inerting

inertisiert: ~er Rückstand *m* ABFALL noncombustible residue

Inertisierung *f* ERDÖL *Sicherheit* blanketing

infektiös: ~er Abfall *m* ABFALL anatomical waste, infectious waste, pathological waste

Inferenz *f* COMP & DV, KÜNSTL INT inference; **Inferenzeinheit** *f* COMP & DV inference engine; **Inferenzkomponente** *f* KÜNSTL INT *eines Expertensystems* inference engine; **Inferenzmaschine** *f* KÜNSTL INT *eines Expertensystems* inference engine; **Inferenzregel** *f* KÜNSTL INT inference rule; **Inferenzstrategie** *f* KÜNSTL INT inference strategy, reasoning strategy

Inferieren *nt* KÜNSTL INT inference, reasoning

Infiltration *f* ABFALL *Schadstoffe*, WASSERVERSORG infiltration

infinitesimal *adj* GEOM infinitesimal

Infinitesimalrechnung *f* MATH calculus

Infinitum *nt* MATH infinity

Infixschreibweise *f* COMP & DV infix notation

Influenzmaschine *f* ELEKTROTECH electrostatic generator

Infobahn *f* COMP & DV information super-highway

Informatik *f* COMP & DV computer science, informatics

Information *f* COMP & DV, ELEKTRONIK information; **Informationsabruf** *m* COMP & DV information retrieval; **Informationsausgabe** *f* COMP & DV information output; **Informationsbit** *nt* COMP & DV information bit; **Informationseingabe** *f* COMP & DV information input; **Informationsempfangsstelle** *f* TELEKOM information receiver station; **Informationsentropie** *f* COMP & DV information entropy; **Informationsfluß** *m* COMP & DV information flow; **Informationsgehalt** *m* COMP & DV information content; **Informationsquelle** *f* COMP & DV information source; **Informationsschutz** *m* COMP & DV privacy of information; **Informationssendestelle** *f* - TELEKOM information sending station; **Informationsspeicher** *m* COMP & DV data storage, information storage; **Informationsspeicherung** *f* COMP & DV information storage; **Informationsspeicherung und-abfrage** *f* COMP & DV ISR, information storage and retrieval; **Informationsspeicherung und- wiederauffindung** *f* COMP & DV ISR, information storage and retrieval; **Informationsstand** *m* FERTIG *Messe* information booth; **Informationssystem** *nt* COMP & DV, TELEKOM IS, information system; **Informationstechnik** *f* COMP & DV information technology; **Informationstheorie** *f* COMP & DV, ELEKTRONIK information theory; **Informationstrennzeichen** *nt* COMP & DV information separator; **Informationsverarbeitung** *f* COMP & DV, ELEKTRONIK information processing; **Informationsverwaltungssystem** *nt* COMP & DV information management system

Infraprotein *nt* CHEMIE infraprotein

Infrarot *nt* (*IR*) KUNSTSTOFF, OPTIK, PHYS, STRAHLPHYS infrared (*IR*); **Infrarotabgasprüfgerät** *nt* KFZTECH infrared exhaust gas analyser (BrE), infrared exhaust gas analyzer (AmE); **Infrarotabtaster** *m* GERÄT infrared scanner; **Infrarotbehandlung** *f* STRAHLPHYS infrared therapy; **Infrarotbewegungsmelder** *m* SICHERHEIT infrared motion alarm;

Infrarotbildkonverter m FERNSEH infrared image converter; **Infrarotdetektor** m TRANS infrared detector
infrarotempfindlich[1] adj STRAHLPHYS infrared-sensitive
infrarotempfindlich:[2] ~e Emulsion f FOTO infrared emulsion, infrared-sensitive emulsion
Infrarot: **Infraroterdmelder** m RAUMFAHRT infrared earth sensor; **Infrarotfernbedienung** f MASCHINEN infrared remote control; **Infrarotfilm** m FOTO infrared film; **Infrarotfilter** nt STRAHLPHYS infrared filter; **Infrarotfotografie** f FOTO infrared photography; **Infrarotheizung** f HEIZ & KÄLTE, STRAHLPHYS infrared heating; **Infrarot-Laser** m ELEKTRONIK infrared laser; **Infrarot-LED** f ELEKTRONIK infrared LED, infrared light-emitting diode; **Infrarotlicht** nt STRAHLPHYS infrared light; **Infrarot-Lumineszenzdiode** f ELEKTRONIK infrared LED, infrared light-emitting diode; **Infrarotraumheizung** f HEIZ & KÄLTE infrared panel heating; **Infrarotspektralfotometer** nt LABOR infrared spectrophotometer; **Infrarot-Spektrometer** nt NICHTFOSS ENERG spectroradiometer, STRAHLPHYS infrared spectrometer; **Infrarotspektroskopie** f STRAHLPHYS infrared spectroscopy; **Infrarotspektrum** nt STRAHLPHYS infrared spectrum; **Infrarotstrahlen** m pl OPTIK, STRAHLPHYS infrared radiation, infrared rays; **Infrarotverbindung** f FERNSEH infrared link
Infraschall m AKUSTIK, PHYS infrasound; **Infraschallbereich** m AKUSTIK, PHYS infrasonic frequency range; **Infraschallfrequenz** f AKUSTIK, PHYS infrasonic frequency
Infrastruktur f COMP & DV infrastructure
Infusion f LEBENSMITTEL infusion; **Infusionsflasche** f KER & GLAS infusion bottle
Ingangsetzen nt LUFTTRANS actuation
ingangsetzen vt KERNTECH set into operation
Ingenieur m MECHAN engineer; **Ingenieurbüro** nt MECHAN engineering office; **Ingenieurhochbau** m BAU structural engineering; **Ingenieurwissenschaft** f MECHAN engineering
Inhaber: ~ eines Patents m PATENT proprietor of a patent
Inhalt m ANSTRICH, COMP & DV content, GEOM volume, KOHLEN, PATENT content, WASSERTRANS volume; ~ der Kanalhaltung m NICHTFOSS ENERG pondage
inhaltsadressierbar: ~er Speicher m (CAM) COMP & DV, KÜNSTL INT associative memory, content-addressable memory (CAM)
Inhalt: **Inhaltsangabe** f VERPACK contents declaration; **Inhaltskennzeichnung** f SICHERHEIT identification of contents; **Inhaltsstoff** m KUNSTSTOFF ingredient; **Inhaltsverzeichnis** nt COMP & DV contents directory
inhärent: ~e Adressierung f COMP & DV inherent addressing; ~ stabiler Reaktor m KERNTECH inherently stable reactor; ~e Verfügbarkeit f LUFTTRANS inherent availability
Inhibitor m KUNSTSTOFF, WASSERVERSORG inhibitor
inhomogen: ~e Strahlungsquelle f STRAHLPHYS nonuniform source of radiation; ~es System nt THERMOD inhomogeneous system
Inhomogenität f KER & GLAS inhomogeneity
Initialbestätigung f METROL initial verification
Initialdruck m MASCHINEN initial pressure
initialisieren vt COMP & DV initialize
Initialisierung f COMP & DV initialization; **Initialisierungsabsicht** f COMP & DV scheduling intent
Initialprogrammlader m (IPL) COMP & DV initial program loader (IPL)

Initialzündung f LUFTTRANS priming
Initiator m GERÄT approximating pick-up, LEBENSMITTEL initiator
Injection-Moulding nt (IM) FERTIG Kunststoffinstallationen, KUNSTSTOFF, VERPACK injection molding (AmE), injection moulding (BrE)
Injektion f CHEMTECH, ELEKTRONIK injection; **Injektionsdüse** f CHEMTECH injection nozzle; **Injektionsgerät** nt BAU grouting equipment; **Injektionslaser** m ELEKTRONIK injection laser; **Injektionslaserdiode** f OPTIK, TELEKOM ILD, injection laser diode; **Injektionslogik** f ELEKTRONIK Mikroelektronik injection logic; **Injektionsmörtel** m BAU grout; **Injektionsschürze** f BAU grout curtain
injektionsstabilisiert: ~er Laser m TELEKOM injection-locked laser
injektionssynchronisiert: ~er Oszillator m ELEKTRONIK injection-locked oscillator
Injektionsverfahren nt WASSERTRANS Bootsbau injection procedure
injektionsverriegelt: ~er Laser m OPTIK injection-locked laser
Injektionswinkel m KERNTECH angle of injection
Injektor m ELEKTRONIK, HYDRAUL injector; **Injektordrossel** f HYDRAUL injector throttle
Injizieren nt ELEKTRONIK Transistor injection
Inklination f RAUMFAHRT inclination; **Inklinationsmesser** m KOHLEN clinometer, inclinometer; **Inklinationsmeßgerät** nt PHYS inclinometer; **Inklinationswinkel** m PHYS angle of dip
inklusiv: ~es ODER-Gate nt COMP & DV inclusive OR gate; ~es ODER-Glied nt COMP & DV inclusive OR circuit; ~e ODER-Operation f COMP & DV inclusive OR operation; ~es UND-Glied nt COMP & DV inclusive AND circuit, inclusive AND gate; ~e UND-Operation f COMP & DV inclusive AND operation
inkohärent[1] adj METALL, OPTIK incoherent
inkohärent:[2] ~es Licht nt PHYS, TELEKOM incoherent light; ~er Schall m AKUSTIK incoherent sound; ~e Strahlung f PHYS, TELEKOM incoherent radiation; ~er Zwilling m METALL incoherent twin
Inkohärenz f OPTIK, TELEKOM incoherence
inkohlen vt KOHLEN carbonize, coke
inkommensurabel adj MATH incommensurable
inkompressibel adj CHEMIE incompressible
Inkompressibilität f STRÖMPHYS incompressibility; ~ von Flüssigkeiten f THERMOD incompressibility of liquids
inkompressibel: inkompressible Flüssigkeit f PHYS incompressible flow; inkompressible Strömung f STRÖMPHYS incompressible flow
Inkrafttreten nt PATENT entry into force
Inkreis m GEOM incircle, inscribed circle; **Inkreisradius** m GEOM apothem, short radius
Inkrement nt ELEKTRONIK, MATH increment; **Inkrementalkompilierer** m COMP & DV incremental compiler; **Inkrementalrechner** m COMP & DV incremental computer
inkrementell: ~e Bemaßung f GERÄT incremental measure system
inkrementieren vt ELEKTRONIK increment
Inland nt TELEKOM, TRANS inland; **Inlands- oder Binnenemissionen** f pl UMWELTSCHMUTZ domestic emissions; **Inlandsanruf** m TELEKOM inland call; **Inlandsflug** m LUFTTRANS domestic flight; **Inlandsflugverkehr** m LUFTTRANS domestic service;

Inlandshafen *m* WASSERTRANS home port; **Inlandsquelle** *f* UMWELTSCHMUTZ internal source; **Inlandsverkehr** *m* TELEKOM national traffic
Inline-Kopf *m* AUFNAHME in-line head
Inline-Stereophonieband *nt* AUFNAHME in-line stereophonic tape
Innen- *pref* FERTIG female, UMWELTSCHMUTZ internal; **Innen- und Außentaster** *m* MASCHINEN inside and outside calipers (AmE), inside and outside callipers (BrE)
innen: innere Abdeckklappe der Landeklappenschlitze *f* LUFTTRANS inner shroud; **innere Beschichtung** *f* VERPACK interior coating; **innere Blockierung** *f* TELEKOM internal blocking; **innere Dämpfung** *f* LUFTTRANS internal damping; **inneres Einflugzeichen** *nt* LUFTTRANS inner marker; **innere Elektronen** *nt pl* STRAHLPHYS inner electrons; **innere Elektronenschalen** *f pl* STRAHLPHYS inner orbital complex; **innere Energie** *f* PHYS internal energy, THERMOD internal energy, intrinsic energy; **innere Form** *f* DRUCK inside forme; **innerer Fotoeffekt** *m* ELEKTRONIK, OPTIK internal photoelectric effect; **innerer fotoelektrischer Effekt** *m* OPTIK, TELEKOM internal photoelectric effect; **innere Induktionsdichtung** *f* VERPACK induction inner seal; **innere Konversion** *f* KERNTECH, STRAHLPHYS internal conversion; **innerer Laufring** *m* MASCHINEN ball inner race; **innere Leitfähigkeit** *f* ELEKTRIZ intrinsic conductivity; **innere molare Energie** *f* PHYS molar internal energy; **innere Oxydation** *f* METALL internal oxidation; **innere Permeabilität** *f* ELEKTRIZ intrinsic permeability; **innerer Planet** *m* RAUMFAHRT inner planet; **inneres Radgehäuse** *nt* LUFTTRANS internal wheel case; **innere Reibung** *f* METALL internal friction; **innere Rückkopplung** *f* ELEKTRONIK *in Trioden* inherent feedback; **innerste Schale mit zwei Elektronen** *f* KERNTECH two-electron innermost shell; **innere Schirmung** *f* ELEKTRONIK *bei Elektronenröhren* internal shield; **innere Spannung** *f* METALL internal stress; **innere Störgröße** *f* FERTIG *Maschine* failure; **innere Totalreflexion** *f* OPTIK, WELLPHYS total internal reflection; **innerer Türstein** *m* KER & GLAS inside jamb block; **innere Überlappung** *f* HYDRAUL *Steuerschieber, Steuerkolben* inside lap slide valve; **innere Umwandlung** *f* KERNTECH, STRAHLPHYS internal conversion; **innere Umwicklung** *f* VERPACK interior wrapping; **innere Verpackung** *f* VERPACK interior packaging; **innere Viskosität** *f* STRÖMPHYS intrinsic viscosity; **innere Wechselwinkel** *m pl* GEOM alternate interior angles; **innerer Weichmacher** *m* KUNSTSTOFF internal plasticizer
Innen-: Innenabdeckung *f* HYDRAUL inside cover; **Innenabscheidungsverfahren** *nt* TELEKOM inside vapor phase oxidation (AmE), inside vapour phase oxidation (BrE); **Innenantenne** *f* ELEKTROTECH indoor antenna; **Innenarchitektur** *f* BAU interior design; **Innenausbau** *m* BAU interior work; **Innenauskleidung** *f* VERPACK interior lining; **Innenbackenbremse** *f* MASCHINEN internal expanding brake; **Innenbeleuchtung** *f* ELEKTROTECH indoor lighting; **Innenbeschichtungsprozeß** *m* TELEKOM inside vapor phase oxidation (AmE), inside vapour phase oxidation (BrE); **Innenbeutel** *m* VERPACK bag-in-a-can; **Innenboden** *m* WASSERTRANS *Schiffbau* inner bottom; **Innenbodenbeplattung** *f* WASSERTRANS inner bottom plating; **Innenbodenlängsverband** *m* WASSERTRANS inner bottom longitudinal; **Innenbrenner** *m* KER & GLAS

internal burner; **Innendeckel** *m* HYDRAUL inside cover; **Innendrehen** *nt* MASCHINEN internal turning
innendrehen *vt* FERTIG bore
Innen-: Innendrehmeißel *m* MASCHINEN boring tool; **Innendruckfestigkeit** *f* WERKPRÜF *Glas* inside surface strength, internal pressure strength; **Innendruckversuch** *m* FERTIG destructive hydrostatic test; **Innendurchmesser** *m* FERTIG, MASCHINEN, MECHAN ID, inner diameter, inside diameter; **Inneneckmeißel** *m* MASCHINEN internal facing tool; **Inneneckrand** *m* VERPACK inside corner edge; **Inneneinrichtung** *f* BAU interior fittings
innengekühlt *adj* KERNTECH internally cooled
innengetrieben *adj* FERTIG *Malteserkreuz* internal
Innengewinde[1] *nt* FERTIG *Kunststoffinstallationen* female thread, KER & GLAS internal screw, MASCHINEN female thread, inside thread, internal screw thread, internal thread
Innengewinde:[2] **~ schneiden** *vi* FERTIG, MASCHINEN tap
Innengewinde:**Innengewindebohrer** *m* BAU tapped valve drill; **Innengewinderäumen** *nt* MASCHINEN internal thread broaching; **Innengewindeschneiden** *nt* FERTIG internal threading, tapping; **Innengewindeschneider** *m* MASCHINEN inside threading tool
Innen-: Innenhaut *f* WASSERTRANS *Schiffbau* inner skin; **Inneninstallation** *f* ELEKTROTECH internal installation; **Innenisolierung** *f* ELEKTRIZ indoor insulation
innenkern- *pref* KERNTECH in-core
Innen-: Innenlackierung *f* VERPACK internal lacquering
innenlastig *adj* FERTIG *Flurförderer* inboard
Innen-: Innenleiter *m* TELEKOM inner conductor; **Innenlenker** *m* KFZTECH saloon (BrE), sedan (AmE); **Innenlunker** *m* FERTIG internal shrinkage; **Innenmantel** *m* TELEKOM inner cladding; **Innenmantelung** *f* ELEKTRIZ inner covering; **Innenmeßgerät** *nt* METROL bore gage (AmE), bore gauge (BrE); **Innenmikrometer** *nt* MASCHINEN inside micrometer calipers (AmE), inside micrometer callipers (BrE), internal micrometer; **Innenpoldynamo** *m* ELEKTRIZ internal pole dynamo, internal pole generator; **Innenpolgenerator** *m* ELEKTRIZ internal pole dynamo, internal pole generator; **Innenputz** *m* BAU interior plaster; **Innenrad** *nt* MASCHINEN inside gear; **Innenraster** *m* ELEKTRONIK *CRT* internal graticule; **Innenraum** *m* KERNTECH *Reaktordruckgefäß* cavity; **Innenräumen** *nt* MASCHINEN internal broaching; **Innenräummaschine** *f* MASCHINEN internal-broaching machine; **Innenräumwerkzeug** *nt* FERTIG, MASCHINEN internal broach; **Innenreibung** *f* MASCHINEN internal friction; **Innenring** *m* MASCHINEN inner ring; **Innenriß** *m* FERTIG *Schmiedestück* shatter crack, METALL internal crack; **Innenrückspiegel** *m* KFZTECH *Zubehör* rear-view mirror; **Innenrundschleifen** *nt* MASCHINEN internal cylindrical grinding; **Innenrüttler** *m* BAU poker vibrator; **Innensäule** *f* FERTIG *Radialbohrmaschine* column; **Innenschicht** *f* VERPACK interior coating, internal lacquering; **Innenschleifen** *nt* MASCHINEN internal grinding; **Innenschleifer** *m* MASCHINEN internal grinder; **Innenschleifmaschine** *f* FERTIG internal-grinding machine; **Innenschneidestahl** *m* MECHAN inside tool; **Innenschraube** *f* MASCHINEN inside screw; **Innenschweißung** *f* MECHAN inside welding; **Innensechskant** *m* MASCHINEN hex socket, hexagon socket; **Innensechskantschlüssel** *m* FERTIG *Kunststoffinstallationen* hexagonal recess wrench, MASCHINEN Allen key (BrE), Allen wrench (AmE); **Innensechskant-**

schraube *f* MASCHINEN Allen screw, hexagon socket head screw; **Innenspannung** *f* FERTIG internal gripping; **Innenspiegel** *m* KFZTECH driving mirror; **Innenspielsteuerschieber** *m* HYDRAUL inside clearance slide valve; **Innenspülung** *f* KOHLEN internal scour

innenstehend: ~**er Pfeil** *m* KONSTZEICH inward-positioned arrowhead

Innen-: **Innentaster** *m* MASCHINEN inside calipers (AmE), inside callipers (BrE), internal caliper gage (AmE), internal calliper gauge (BrE); **Innenteil** *nt* FERTIG *Passung* insert, MASCHINEN insert, internal member; **Innentemperatur** *f* VERPACK internal temperature; **Innenthermostat** *m* HEIZ & KÄLTE room thermostat; **Innenüberdeckungs-Steuerschieber** *m* HYDRAUL inside lap slide valve; **Innenverdrahtung** *f* ELEKTROTECH indoor wiring, TELEKOM internal wiring; **Innenverkleidung** *f* WASSERTRANS inner lining; **Innenverstärkung** *f* VERPACK interior strengthening bar

innenverzahnt: ~**es Getriebe** *nt* KFZTECH, MASCHINEN internal gear

Innen-: **Innenverzahnung** *f* MASCHINEN internal toothing; **Innenvolumen** *nt* GEOM space inside; **Innenvoreinström-Steuerschieber** *m* HYDRAUL inside lead slide valve; **Innenwiderstand** *m* ELEKTRIZ internal resistance; **Innenwinkel** *m* GEOM interior angle

innerhalb: ~ **eines Moleküls** *adj* CHEMIE intramolecular

innerörtliche: ~**e Verkehrsbedienung** *f* TRANS local traffic information

innewohnend *adj* ANSTRICH inherent

Inosin *nt* CHEMIE, LEBENSMITTEL inosine

Inosit *m* CHEMIE inositol

Inositol *m* CHEMIE, LEBENSMITTEL inositol

In-Pile-Kreislauf *m* KERNTECH in-pile loop

Input *m* HYDRAUL, PHYS IP, input; **Input-Filter** *nt* RAUMFAHRT *Weltraumfunk* input filter

Inquadrat *nt* GEOM inscribed square, insquare

insektenfest *adj* VERPACK insect-proof

Insel *f* WASSERTRANS *Geographie* island; **Inselbahnhof** *m* EISENBAHN island depot; **Inselgruppe** *f* WASSERTRANS *Geographie* archipelago

Inserat *nt* DRUCK advertisement; **Inseratenabteilung** *f* DRUCK advertising department; **Inseratensetzerei** *f* DRUCK advertisement composing room

Insert-Technik *f* KUNSTSTOFF insert molding (AmE), insert moulding (BrE)

insgesamt: ~ **digital** *adj* ELEKTRONIK all-digital

Insolation *f* NICHTFOSS ENERG insolation

Inspektion *f* MASCHINEN, MECHAN inspection, WASSERTRANS *Schiff* surveying; **Inspektionsöffnung** *f* RAUMFAHRT *Raumschiff* inspection door; **Inspektionszyklus** *m* LUFTTRANS inspection cycle

Inspektor *m* MEERSCHMUTZ supervisor, SICHERHEIT factory inspector

Inspirationskapazität *f* ERGON inspiratory capacity

instabil[1] *adj* ELEKTRIZ unstable, ELEKTROTECH transient

instabil:[2] ~**er Abbrand** *m* RAUMFAHRT chuffing; ~**es Ausbuchten** *nt* KERNTECH ballooning instability; ~**es Isotop** *nt* CHEMIE radioisotope; ~**er Kern** *m* TEILPHYS unstable nucleus; ~**e Strömungen** *f pl* STRÖMPHYS unstable flows; ~**e Zerspanung** *f* FERTIG unstable metal cutting

Instabilität *f* ELEKTROTECH, VERPACK instability; ~ **aufgrund der Oberflächenspannung** *f* STRÖMPHYS surface tension instabilities; ~ **der rotierenden Couetteströ**mung *f* STRÖMPHYS instability of rotating Couette flow; **Instabilitätserscheinungen** *f pl* STRÖMPHYS instability phenomena

Installateur *m* BAU plumber

Installation *f* BAU plumbing, COMP & DV installation, *eines Rechners* setup, FERTIG utility, MASCHINEN, TELEKOM installation; **Installationsobjekte** *nt pl* BAU fixtures and fittings, METROL fixtures; **Installationsoption** *f* COMP & DV set-up option; **Installationsplan** *m* ELEKTRIZ wiring diagram; **Installationsplanung** *f* COMP & DV physical planning; **Installationsrohr** *nt* BAU conduit; **Installationszeit** *f* COMP & DV set-up time

installieren *vt* BAU plumb, COMP & DV install, mount, set up, DRUCK install, ELEKTRONIK mount, FERTIG provide, VERPACK erect, WASSERTRANS *Technik* install

installiert: ~**er Hubraum** *m* KFZTECH installed capacity; ~**e Leistung** *f* ELEKTRIZ installed capacity

instandhalten *vt* COMP & DV service, MASCHINEN maintain, service, MECHAN *Geräte* maintain, *Werkzeuge* service

Instandhaltung *f* COMP & DV maintenance, upkeep, EISENBAHN, MASCHINEN, MECHAN maintenance; **Instandhaltungsdauer** *f* QUAL active maintenance time; **Instandhaltungskonzept** *nt* QUAL maintenance concept; **Instandhaltungsprozessor** *m* TELEKOM maintenance processor

instandsetzen *vt* BAU make good, WASSERTRANS repair

Instandsetzung *f* KFZTECH *Motor* overhaul, QUAL corrective maintenance, WASSERTRANS *eines Schiffes* repair; **Instandsetzungsarbeiten** *f pl* BAU repairs; **Instandsetzungsdauer** *f* COMP & DV repair time; **Instandsetzungshandbuch** *nt* KFZTECH overhaul manual

instantiieren *vt* KÜNSTL INT instantiate

Instant-Replay *nt* FERNSEH instant replay

Instanz *f* KÜNSTL INT instance; ~ **des Systemmanagements** *f* TELEKOM system management application entity

instationär: ~**e Strömungen** *f pl* STRÖMPHYS unsteady flows

Instruktion *f* COMP & DV instruction; **Instruktionsabruf** *m* COMP & DV instruction fetching; **Instruktionscode** *m* COMP & DV instruction code; **Instruktionsregister** *nt* COMP & DV instruction register; **Instruktionsstrom** *m* COMP & DV instruction stream; **Instruktionszyklus** *m* COMP & DV instruction cycle

Instrument *nt* COMP & DV, EISENBAHN, ELEKTRIZ, ELEKTROTECH, KFZTECH, LUFTTRANS instrument, MASCHINEN apparatus, implement, instrument, WASSERTRANS instrument; ~ **für Einzelmessungen** *nt* GERÄT single shot instrument; ~ **zur Messung von Leuchtdichte und Beleuchtungsstärke** *nt* OPTIK nitometer-luxmeter; ~ **mit Nebenwiderstand** *nt* GERÄT shunted instrument; ~ **mit Nullpunkt in der Skalenmitte** *nt* GERÄT center-reading instrument (AmE), centre-reading instrument (BrE); ~ **mit Shunt** *nt* GERÄT shunted instrument

Instrumentenanflug *m* LUFTTRANS instrument approach; **Instrumentenanflugkarte** *f* LUFTTRANS instrument approach chart; **Instrumentenanflugpiste** *f* LUFTTRANS instrument approach runway; **Instrumentenanflugverfahren** *nt* LUFTTRANS instrument approach procedure

Instrument: **Instrumentenaufbau im Reaktorkern** *m* KERNTECH in-core instrument assembly; **Instrumentenausrüstung** *f* COMP & DV instrumentation;

Instrumentenbeleuchtung *f* WASSERTRANS scale illumination; **Instrumentenbrett** *nt* LUFTTRANS console, instrument panel; **Instrumentenfehler** *m* GERÄT instrumental error, MASCHINEN instrument error, WASSERTRANS *Navigation* index error

Instrumentenflug *m* LUFTTRANS instrument flying, instrument flight; **Instrumentenflugberechtigung** *f* LUFTTRANS instrument rating; **Instrumentenflugberechtigung für Piloten** *f* LUFTTRANS single pilot instrument rating; **Instrumentenflugregeln** *f pl (IFR)* LUFTTRANS instrument flight rules *(IFR)*; **Instrumentenflugsimulator für die Grundschulung** *m* LUFTTRANS basic instrument flight trainer

Instrument: **Instrumentenhöhe** *f* BAU *Vermessung* height of instrument; **Instrumentenlandesystem** *nt (ILS)* LUFTTRANS, RAUMFAHRT instrument landing system *(ILS)*; **Instrumentenlandung** *f* LUFTTRANS instrument landing; **Instrumentenschalter** *m* ELEKTROTECH instrument switch; **Instrumententafel** *f* KFZTECH dash, dashboard, *Zubehör* instrument panel, LUFTTRANS, WASSERTRANS instrument panel; **Instrumentenverluste** *m pl* ELEKTRIZ meter losses

instrumentieren *vt* WASSERTRANS instrument

Instrumentierung *f* COMP & DV instrumentation

instrumentlos: **~es Brennelement** *nt* KERNTECH uninstrumented fuel assembly

intakt *adj* ANSTRICH intact

Intaktstabilität *f* WASSERTRANS *Schiffkonstruktion* intact stability

Integral *nt* MATH integral; **~ einer Funktion** *nt* MATH integral of a function

integral: **~e Abtastung** *f* TELEKOM integral sampling; **~es Laufrad** *nt* NICHTFOSS ENERG *Wasserturbine* integral runner; **~ versteifte Leichtmetallbeplankung** *f* RAUMFAHRT *Raumschiff* integrally-stiffened light alloy skin

Integral: **Integralelement** *nt* LABOR integral element; **Integralrechnung** *f* MATH integral calculus; **Integralregler** *m* LABOR integral action controller; **Integralschaumstoff** *m* KUNSTSTOFF integral foam, integral skin foam

Integration *f* ELEKTRONIK, TELEKOM integration; **~ einer Elektronikschaltung** *f* ELEKTRONIK electronic circuit integration; **Integrationsbereich** *m* MATH integral domain; **Integrationsdichte** *f* ELEKTRONIK integration density; **Integrationsschaltung** *f* ELEKTROTECH integrating circuit; **Integrationsverstärkung** *f* ELEKTRONIK integration gain; **Integrationszeit** *f* ELEKTRONIK, ELEKTROTECH integration period, integration time

Integrator *m* ELEKTRONIK, ELEKTROTECH, LUFTTRANS integrator

Integrierbeiwert *m* REGELUNG integral action coefficient

Integrieren *nt* MATH integration

integrieren[1] *vt* COMP & DV integrate

integrieren[2] *vi* COMP & DV integrate

integrierend: **~es Bauelment** *nt* ELEKTRONIK integrator; **~er Fehler** *m* GERÄT cumulative error; **~es Glied** *nt* REGELUNG integral element; **~es Meßgerät** *nt* ELEKTROTECH integrating meter; **~es Netz** *nt* LUFTTRANS integrating network; **~es Verhalten** *nt* REGELUNG integral action; **~er Zähler** *m* GERÄT totalizing counter

Integrierkondensator *m* ELEKTROTECH integrating capacitor

Integrierschaltung *f (IS)* COMP & DV, ELEKTRIZ, ELEK-TRONIK, KONTROLL, PHYS, RADIO, TELEKOM integrated circuit *(IC)*

integriert[1] *adj* ELEKTRONIK integrated, FERNSEH solid state

integriert:[2] **~er Bipolartransistor** *m* ELEKTRONIK integrated bipolar transistor; **~es Bürokommunikationssystem** *nt* TELEKOM integrated office system; **~e Datenbank** *f* COMP & DV integrated database; **~e Datenverarbeitung** *f* COMP & DV integrated data processing; **~e Dickschichtschaltung** *f* TELEKOM thick layer integrated circuit; **~e digitale Vermittlung** *f* TELEKOM integrated digital exchange; **~es digitales Fernmeldenetz** *nt (ISDN)* TELEKOM integrated service digital network *(ISDN)*; **~es Digitalnetz** *nt* TELEKOM integrated digital network; **~er Digitalzugriff** *m* COMP & DV IDA, integrated digital access; **~e Einheit** *f* COMP & DV integrated device; **~e Einspritzung** *f* KFZTECH integral injection; **~es Filter** *nt* ELEKTRONIK integrated filter; **~e Funktion** *f* ELEKTRONIK integrated function; **~es Gerät** *nt* COMP & DV integrated device; **~e Halbleiterschaltung** *f* ELEKTRONIK semiconductor integrated circuit; **~e Hybridkomponente** *f* ELEKTRONIK integrated hybrid component; **~e Hybridschaltung** *f* TELEKOM hybrid integrated circuit; **~er Hybridwiderstand** *m* ELEKTROTECH integrated hybrid resistor; **~e Injektionslogik** *f* (I^2L-*Logik*) ELEKTRONIK integrated injection logic (I^2L); **~er Kondensator** *m* ELEKTRO-TECH integrated capacitor, on-chip capacitor; **~e Ladung** *f* ELEKTROTECH integrated charge; **~e Laufzeit** *f* ERDÖL *Seismik* ITT, integrated transit time; **~e Logikschaltung** *f* ELEKTRONIK integrated logic circuit; **~er Mikrowellenschaltkreis** *m (MIC)* ELEKTRONIK, WELLPHYS microwave integrated circuit *(MIC)*; **~er MOS-Transistor** *m* ELEKTRONIK integrated MOS transistor; **~er N-Kanal-MOS-Transistor** *m* ELEKTRONIK n-channel integrated MOS transistor; **~e optische Koppelmatrix** *f* TELEKOM integrated optical switching matrix; **~e optische Schaltung** *f (IOS)* TELEKOM integrated optical circuit *(IOC)*; **~er optischer Schalter** *m* TELEKOM integrated optical switch; **~er optischer Schaltkreis** *m (IOS)* ELEKTRONIK, OPTIK integrated optical circuit, optical integrated circuit; **~e optoelektronische Schaltung** *f* TELEKOM integrated optoelectronic circuit; **~er PIN-FET-Empfänger** *m* OP-TIK, TELEKOM PIN-FET integrated receiver; **~er P-Kanal-FET** *m* ELEKTRONIK P-channel integrated FET; **~e Quellenfindung** *f* COMP & DV IHS, integrated home system; **~er Schaltkreis** *m (IS)* COMP & DV, ELEKTRIZ, ELEKTRONIK, KONTROLL, PHYS, RADIO, TE-LEKOM integrated circuit *(IC)*; **~e Schaltkreise für bestimmte Funktionen** *f pl* COMP & DV application-specific integrated circuits; **~e Schaltkreismaske** *f* ELEKTRONIK integrated circuit mask; **~e Schaltung** *f* *(IS)* COMP & DV, ELEKTRIZ, ELEKTRONIK, KONTROLL, PHYS, RADIO, TELEKOM integrated circuit *(IC)*; **~e Schaltung in Metall-Gate-CMOS-Technologie** *f* ELEK-TRONIK metal gate CMOS integrated circuit; **~er Schottky-Bipolarschaltkreis** *m* ELEKTRONIK Schottky bipolar-integrated circuit; **~e Siliziumschaltung** *f* ELEKTRONIK silicon integrated circuit; **~es System** *nt* TELEKOM integrated system; **~es Text- und Datennetz** *nt* TELEKOM integrated digital network; **~e Transistorlogik** *f (MTL-Logik)* ELEKTRONIK merged transistor logic *(MTL)*; **~es Verknüpfungsglied** *nt* ELEKTRONIK integrated logic gate; **~er verstärkter Griff** *m* VERPACK integral reinforced handle; **~er Zugang** *m* TELEKOM integrated access

Integrierung *f* MATH integration

Integrität *f* COMP & DV integrity

intelligent: ~**e Datenstation** *f* COMP & DV intelligent terminal, smart terminal; ~**e frei programmierbare Datenstation** *f* COMP & DV intelligent terminal; ~**es Lernprogramm** *nt* *(KI-Lernprogramm)* KÜNSTL INT intelligent tutoring system *(ITS)*

Intelligenzquotient *m* ERGON intelligence quotient; **Intelligenztest** *m* ERGON intelligence test

Intensionsgröße *f* PHYS intensive quantity

Intensität *f* *(I)* AKUSTIK, ELEKTRIZ, OPTIK *proportional zur Strahlung* intensity *(I)*; **Intensitätspegel** *m* ELEKTROTECH intensity level; **Intensitätsschrift** *f* AKUSTIK variable density recording; **Intensitätsstufe** *f* AUFNAHME intensity spectrum level; **Intensitätstonspur** *f* AUFNAHME variable density sound track; **Intensitätsverteilung** *f* STRAHLPHYS intensity distribution; **Intensitätswert** *m* STRAHLPHYS level of intensity

Interaktion *f* COMP & DV dialog (AmE), dialogue (BrE), interaction, MASCHINEN interaction

interaktiv[1] *adj* COMP & DV, KONTROLL interactive, OPTIK compact disc-interactive (BrE), compact disk-interactive (AmE)

interaktiv:[2] ~**e Bildplatte** *f* OPTIK interactive videodisc (BrE), interactive videodisk (AmE); ~**es Fernsehen** *nt* FERNSEH interactive television; ~**e Grafikverarbeitung** *f* COMP & DV interactive graphics; ~**e Routine** *f* COMP & DV interactive routine; ~**es Terminal** *nt* TELEKOM interactive terminal; ~**e Verarbeitung** *f* COMP & DV interactive processing; ~**e Videographie** *f* TELEKOM interactive videography

interatomar: ~**e Kraft** *f* STRAHLPHYS interatomic force; ~**er Stoß** *m* KERNTECH atom-atom collision

Interchip-Signalverzögerung *f* ELEKTRONIK interchip signal delay

Intercircuit-Signalverzögerung *f* ELEKTRONIK intercircuit signal delay

Intercity-Flugdienst *m* EISENBAHN intercity air service

Intercity-Flugverbindungen *f pl* EISENBAHN intercity air service

Intercity-Zug *m* EISENBAHN intercity train (BrE)

interdigital *adj* RADIO interdigital

Interdigital- *pref* RADIO, TELEKOM interdigital; **Interdigitalfilter** *nt* RADIO interdigital bandpass; **Interdigitalleitung** *f* PHYS *Akusto-Elektronik* interdigital line; **Interdigitalwandler** *m* TELEKOM interdigital transducer

Interface *nt* COMP & DV, TELEKOM interface

Interferenz *f* COMP & DV, FERNSEH *Wellen* interference, OPTIK fringe, interference, PHYS, RADIO, TELEKOM, WELLPHYS interference; ~ **mit Datenverlust** *f* ELEKTROTECH destructive interference; ~ **mit Informationsverlust** *f* ELEKTROTECH destructive interference; **Interferenzbänder** *nt pl* WELLPHYS interference bands; **Interferenzbild** *nt* OPTIK interference figure; **Interferenzfarben** *f pl* FOTO Newton's rings; **Interferenzfilter** *nt* AUFNAHME, ELEKTRONIK, FERNSEH, OPTIK, PHYS, TELEKOM interference filter; **Interferenzkomparator** *m* METROL *Optik* gage block interferometer (AmE), gauge block interferometer (BrE); **Interferenzmaschine** *f* COMP & DV inference machine; **Interferenzmikroskop** *nt* METALL, PHYS interference microscope; **Interferenzmuster** *nt* OPTIK interference fringe, WELLPHYS interference pattern; **Interferenzrefraktometer** *nt* OPTIK interference refrac-

tometer; **Interferenzringe** *f pl* PHYS interference fringes; **Interferenzstreifen** *m pl* FERNSEH fringes, PHYS interference fringes, *gleicher Dichte* fringes, WELLPHYS interference fringes

interferieren *vt* PHYS interfere

Interferometer *nt* METROL, OPTIK, PHYS, TELEKOM interferometer

intergranular *adj* FERTIG intercrystalline, METALL intergranular

interindividuell: ~**e Unterschiede** *m pl* ERGON interindividual differences

Interkanalstörung *f* ELEKTROTECH interchannel interference

interkristallin[1] *adj* FERTIG intercrystalline

interkristallin:[2] ~**e Korrosion** *f* CHEMIE intercrystalline corrosion, intergranular corrosion; ~**e Spannungsriß- korrosion** *f* FERTIG caustic embrittlement

interlaminar: ~**e Festigkeit** *f* KUNSTSTOFF interlaminar strength; ~**e Scherfestigkeit** *f* KUNSTSTOFF interlaminar shear strength

intermediär: ~**e Bodenart** *f* KOHLEN intermediate type of soil; ~**es Boson** *nt* PHYS intermediate boson

intermetallisch: ~**e Verbindung** *f* METALL intermetallic compound

intermittierend: ~**es Luftstrahltriebwerk** *nt* LUFTTRANS pulsojet; ~**e Quelle** *f* WASSERVERSORG intermittent spring; ~**es Rauschen** *nt* AKUSTIK intermittent noise

Intermodulation *f* FERNSEH, RADIO, RAUMFAHRT *Weltraumfunk*, TELEKOM intermodulation; **Intermodulationsprodukt** *nt* RAUMFAHRT *Weltraumfunk*, TELEKOM intermodulation product; **Intermodulationsrauschen** *nt* RAUMFAHRT *Weltraumfunk* intermodulation noise; **Intermodulationsstörung** *f* RADIO intermodulation interference; **Intermodulationsverzerrung** *f* *(IMD)* AUFNAHME, RADIO intermodulation distortion *(IMD)*

intermolekular *adj* CHEMIE intermolecular

intern: ~**es Eingangssignal** *nt* TELEKOM internal input signal; ~**e Nebenstelle** *f* TELEKOM internal extension; ~**e Sortierung** *f* COMP & DV internal sort; ~**er Speicher** *m* COMP & DV internal memory, internal storage (AmE), internal store (BrE), ELEKTROTECH internal memory; ~**er Takt** *m* TELEKOM internal clock; ~**es Target** *nt* TEILPHYS internal target; ~**e Uhr** *f* COMP & DV clock device; ~**er Wartestatus** *m* COMP & DV quiesced state, quiescent state; ~**er Widerstand** *m* ELEKTRIZ internal resistance

International: ~**er Amateurfunkdachverband** *m* RADIO International Amateur Radio Union; ~**er Eisenbahnverband** *m* *(UIC)* EISENBAHN International Railway Union *(UIC)*; ~**er Fernmeldeberatungsausschuß** *m* *(CCITT)* TELEKOM International Telegraph and Telephone Consultative Committee *(CCITT)*; ~**e Fernmeldeunion** *f* *(ITU)* RADIO, WASSERTRANS *Behörde* International Telecommunications Union *(ITU)*; ~**e Frequenz-Zuweisungsbehörde** *f* *(IFRB)* RAUMFAHRT International Frequency Registration Board *(IFRB)*; ~**er Lichtnormausschuß** *m* PHYS International Commission on Illumination; ~**e Normungsorganisation** *f* *(ISO)* ELEKTRIZ, MASCHINEN International Standards Organization *(ISO)*; ~**es Referenzsystem** *nt* *(IRS)* UMWELTSCHUTZ International Referral System *(IRS)*; ~**e Schifffahrtorganisation** *f* *(IMO)* WASSERTRANS International Maritime Organization *(IMO)*; ~**e Strahlenschutzkommission** *f* *(ICRP)* STRAHLPHYS International

Commission on Radiological Protection *(ICRP)*; ~es **Transit-Zentrum** *nt* RAUMFAHRT *Weltraumfunk* International Transit Centre; ~es **Verzeichnis für potentiell toxische Chemikalien** *nt (IRPTC)* UMWELT-SCHMUTZ International Register of Potentially Toxic Chemicals *(IRPTC)*

international: ~e **Anmeldung** *f* PATENT international application; ~er **Betriebsdienst** *m* TELEKOM international operations service; ~e **Datumsgrenze** *f* LUFTTRANS international date line; ~e **Einheit** *f* ELEKTRIZ international unit; ~es **Einheitensystem** *nt (SI-Einheit)* ELEKTRIZ, METROL, PHYS international system of units *(SI unit)*; ~es **Fernamt** *nt* TELEKOM international-switching center (AmE), international-switching centre (BrE); ~er **Flughafen** *m* LUFTTRANS international airport; ~e **Flugroute** *f* LUFTTRANS international air route; ~e **Gerätekennung** *f* TELEKOM IMEI, international mobile station equipment identity; ~e **Gewässer** *nt pl* WASSERTRANS international waters; ~es **Hauptamt** *nt* TELEKOM main international-switching center (AmE), main international-switching centre (BrE); ~e **Hauptvermittlungsstelle** *f* TELEKOM *im Fernwahlnetz* main international trunk-switching center (AmE), main international trunk-switching centre (BrE); ~es **Kopfamt** *nt* TELEKOM international gateway exchange; ~es **Normal** *nt* QUAL international standard; ~es **Normgewinde** *nt* MASCHINEN international standard thread; ~es **paketvermitteltes Datennetz** *nt* TELEKOM international packet-switching data network; ~es **paketvermitteltes Kopfamt** *nt* TELEKOM international packet-switching gateway exchange; ~e **Recherchenbehörde** *f* PATENT international searching authority; ~e **Registrierung** *f* PATENT international registration; ~e **Selbstwahl** *f (ISW)* TELEKOM international direct dialing (AmE), international direct dialling (BrE), international direct distance dialing (AmE), international direct distance dialling (BrE) *(IDDD)*; ~er **Selbstwählferndienst** *m* TELEKOM ISD, international subscriber dialing (AmE), international subscriber dialling (BrE); ~er **Standard** *m* BAU international standard; ~er **Standardruß** *m (IRB-Ruß)* KUNSTSTOFF industry reference black *(IRB)*; ~e **Teilnehmerselbstwahl** *f* TELEKOM ISD, international subscriber dialing (AmE), international subscriber dialling (BrE); ~es **Telegrafenalphabet** *nt (ITA)* LUFTTRANS, WASSERTRANS international telegraph alphabet *(ITA)*; ~e **Vermittlungsstelle** *f* TELEKOM international-switching center (AmE), international-switching centre (BrE)

Internverbindungsleitungssatz *m* TELEKOM intra-office junctor circuit

Internverkehr *m* TELEKOM internal traffic

Interplanetar- *pref* RAUMFAHRT interplanetary; **Interplanetarflug** *m* RAUMFAHRT interplanetary flight; **Interplanetarsonde** *f* RAUMFAHRT interplanetary probe

Interpolation *f* COMP & DV, MATH, TELEKOM interpolation; **Interpolationsfilter** *nt* ELEKTRONIK interpolating filter

Interpolator *m* TELEKOM interpolator

Interpolieren *nt* MATH interpolation

interpolieren *vt* DRUCK interpolate

interpretierend: *f* DRUCK punctuation; ~es **Programm** *nt* COMP & DV interpreter

Interpunktion *f* DRUCK punctuation; **Interpunktionspunkt** *m* DRUCK full point; **Interpunktionszeichen** *nt pl* DRUCK punctuation marks

Interrogator-Responsor *m* TELEKOM interrogator-transponder

Interrupt *m* COMP & DV interrupt

interruptgesteuert: ~es **System** *nt* KONTROLL interrupt-driven system

Intersatellitenfunk *m* RAUMFAHRT *Weltraumfunk* intersatellite link; **Intersatellitenfunkdienst** *m* RAUMFAHRT intersatellite service

Intersektion *f* COMP & DV intersection

intersensorisch: ~e **Wahrnehmung** *f* ERGON intersensory perception

interstellar: ~e **Materie** *f* RAUMFAHRT interstellar matter; ~er **Raum** *m* RAUMFAHRT interstellar space

Intersymbol *nt* ELEKTRONIK intersymbol; **Intersymbolrauschen** *nt* ELEKTRONIK intersymbol noise; **Intersymbolstörung** *f* ELEKTRONIK *ISI*, TELEKOM intersymbol interference

Intervall *nt* AKUSTIK, MATH interval; **Intervallgeschwindigkeit** *f* ERDÖL *Seismik* interval velocity; **Intervall-Länge** *f* METROL interval length; **Intervallschmierung** *f* MASCHINEN intermittent lubrication; **Intervallzeitgeber** *m* COMP & DV interval timer

Interworking *nt* TELEKOM interworking

Intonation *f* AKUSTIK intonation

intra-individuell: ~e **Unterschiede** *m pl* ERGON intra-individual differences

intramolekular *adj* CHEMIE, METALL intramolecular

Intrinsic-Halbleiter nt PHYS intrinsic semiconductor

Intrinsic-I-Halbleiter *m* ELEKTRONIK i-type semiconductor

intrinsisch:[1] ~ **sicher** *adj* SICHERHEIT intrinsically safe

intrinsisch:[2] ~er **Koppelverlust** *m* TELEKOM intrinsic joint loss

Intrittfallen *nt* FERNSEH pulling

Intrittkommen *nt* ELEKTROTECH *bei Wechselstrommaschinen, mit der Grundfrequenz* paralleling

Introskopie *f* KERNTECH introscopy

intrusiv *adj* NICHTFOSS ENERG intrusive

Inulin *nt* CHEMIE alantin, dahlin, inulin, LEBENSMITTEL inulin

Invar *nt* FERTIG *Nickelstahl*, METALL invar

invariant *adj* GEOM invariant

Invariante *f* GEOM invariant

Inventar *nt* ERDÖL, VERPACK inventory

invers[1] *adj* MATH inverse

invers:[2] ~er **Compton-Effekt** *m* PHYS inverse Compton effect; ~er **fotoelektrischer Effekt** *m* ELEKTRONIK inverse photoelectric effect; ~e **Funktion** *f* MATH inverse function; ~er **piezoelektrischer Effekt** *m* ELEKTROTECH, PHYS inverse piezoelectric effect; ~es **Verhalten** *nt* REGELUNG reverse action

Inverse *nt* MATH inverse

Inversionskappe *f* UMWELTSCHMUTZ lid; **Inversionsschicht** *f* ELEKTRONIK *Halbleiter*, TELEKOM inversion layer, UMWELTSCHMUTZ atmospheric inversion, inversion layer; **Inversionstemperatur** *f* ELEKTRIZ, PHYS inversion temperature

Inversprimärkriechen *nt* METALL inverse primary creep

Invertase *f* LEBENSMITTEL invertase, saccharase, sucrase

Inverter *m* COMP & DV inverter, negator, ELEKTROTECH, TELEKOM inverter

Invertglas *nt* KER & GLAS invert glass

invertieren *vt* MATH *Matrix*, RADIO invert

invertierend:[1] **nicht** ~ *adj* ELEKTROTECH noninverting

invertierend:[2] **nicht** ~er **Puffer** *m* RADIO noninverting buffer

Invertierschaltung *f* TELEKOM inverter

invertiert: ~**er Chip** *m* ELEKTRONIK inverted chip; ~**e Darstellung** *f* COMP & DV reverse video; ~**e Datei** *f* COMP & DV inverted file; ~**es Videobild** *nt* COMP & DV inverse video

Invertose *f* LEBENSMITTEL invert sugar

Invertzeitrelais *nt* ELEKTRIZ inverse time relay

Invertzucker *m* LEBENSMITTEL invert sugar

involut *adj* GEOM involute

Involute *f* GEOM involute

Iod *nt* (*I*) CHEMIE iodine (*I*); **Iod-** *pref* CHEMIE iodous; **Iodat** *nt* CHEMIE iodate; **Iodbenzol** *nt* CHEMIE iodobenzene, phenyl iodide; **Iodeosin** *nt* CHEMIE iodeosin, tetraiodofluorescein; **Iodhydrin** *nt* CHEMIE iodohydrin

iodieren *vt* CHEMIE iodize

iodig *adj* CHEMIE iodous

Iod: **Iodimetrie** *f* CHEMIE iodometry; **Iodlaser** *m* ELEKTRONIK iodine laser; **Iodoaurat** *nt* CHEMIE iodoaurate, tetraiodoaurate; **Iodoform** *nt* CHEMIE iodoform, triiodomethane; **Iodometrie** *f* CHEMIE iodometry

iodometrisch[1] *adj* CHEMIE iodometric

iodometrisch:[2] ~**e Titration** *f* CHEMIE iodometry

Iod: **Iodonium** *nt* CHEMIE iodonium; **Iodopsin** *nt* CHEMIE iodopsin

Iodoso- *pref* CHEMIE iodoso-; **Iodosobenzol** *nt* CHEMIE iodosobenzene; **Iodosolbenzyl** *nt* CHEMIE iodosobenzene

Iod-: **Iodwasserstoff-** *pref* CHEMIE hydriodic; **Iodzahl** *f* LEBENSMITTEL iodine number, iodine value

Ion *nt* ELEKTRIZ, ELEKTRONIK, ERDÖL *Petrochemie*, PHYS, RADIO, TEILPHYS ion

Ionen- *pref* STRAHLPHYS ionic; **Ionenabstand** *m* CHEMIE interionic distance; **Ionenantrieb** *m* RAUMFAHRT *Raumschiff* ion propulsion; **Ionenausbeute** *f* STRAHLPHYS ion yield; **Ionenaustauscherharz** *nt* FERTIG *Kunststoffinstallationen* ion exchange resin; **Ionenaustauschglas** *nt* KER & GLAS ion exchange glass; **Ionenaustauschisotherme** *f* STRAHLPHYS ion exchange isotherm; **Ionenaustauschverfahren** *nt* OPTIK, TELEKOM ion exchange technique; **Ionenaustausch-Wasserreiniger** *m* LABOR ion exchange water purifier; **Ionenbeschleuniger** *m* TEILPHYS ion accelerator; **Ionenbeschuß** *m* ELEKTRONIK, METALL, TEILPHYS ion bombardment; **Ionenbeweglichkeit** *f* STRAHLPHYS ion mobility; **Ionenbindung** *f* STRAHLPHYS ionic bond; **Ionenbrennfleck** *m* ELEKTRONIK ion burn; **Ionencluster** *m* STRAHLPHYS ion cluster; **Ionenfalle** *f* ELEKTRONIK, FERNSEH ion trap; **Ionenfleck** *m* FERNSEH ion spot; **Ionengetterpumpe** *f* PHYS ion pump; **Ionenimplantation** *f* ELEKTRONIK *Halbleiter*, TEILPHYS ion implantation; **Ionenlaser** *m* ELEKTRONIK, MASCHINEN ion laser; **Ionenlautsprecher** *m* AKUSTIK, AUFNAHME ionic loudspeaker; **Ionenleitung** *f* STRAHLPHYS ionic conductance; **Ionenöffnungswinkel** *m* KERNTECH angle of acceptance of ions; **Ionenpaar** *nt* STRAHLPHYS ion pair; **Ionenpolarisation** *f* STRAHLPHYS ionic polarization; **Ionenpumpe** *f* MASCHINEN ion pump; **Ionenquelle** *f* PHYS, STRAHLPHYS ion source; **Ionenradius** *m* STRAHLPHYS ionic radius; **Ionenrakete** *f* RAUMFAHRT ion rocket; **Ionenröhre** *f* ELEKTRONIK gas tube; **Ionenschalter** *m* ELEKTRONIK, ELEKTROTECH gas-filled relay; **Ionenschubtriebwerk** *nt* RAUMFAHRT ion thruster; **Ionenspaltung** *f* ELEKTRIZ ionization; **Ionenspektrum** *nt* STRAHLPHYS ion spectrum; **Ionenstärke** *f* STRAHLPHYS ionic strength;

Ionenstrahl *m* ELEKTRONIK, STRAHLPHYS ion beam; **Ionenstrahl mit hoher Intensität** *m* STRAHLPHYS high-intensity ion beam; **Ionenstrahl-Lithographie** *f* ELEKTRONIK ion beam lithography; **Ionentriebwerk** *nt* RAUMFAHRT *Raumschiff* ion engine; **Ionenverdampferpumpe** *f* CHEMTECH evaporating-ion pump, evaporation-ion pump; **Ionenwanderung** *f* ELEKTRONIK ion migration

Ion: **Ionhaushalt** *m* UMWELTSCHMUTZ ion budget

Ionisation *f* ELEKTROTECH, STRAHLPHYS, TEILPHYS ionization; **Ionisationsargonlaser** *m* ELEKTRONIK ionized argon laser; **Ionisationsenergie** *f* TEILPHYS ionization energy; **Ionisationskammer** *f* STRAHLPHYS, TEILPHYS ionization chamber; **Ionisationsmanometer** *nt* GERÄT ion gage (AmE), ion gauge (BrE); **Ionisationsmeßgerät nach Bayard-Alpert** *nt* KERNTECH Bayard-Alpert ionization gage (AmE), Bayard-Alpert ionization gauge (BrE); **Ionisationspotential** *nt* STRAHLPHYS, TEILPHYS ionization potential; **Ionisationsrate** *f* STRAHLPHYS, TEILPHYS ionization rate; **Ionisationsstrom** *m* ELEKTRONIK ionization current; **Ionisationsvakuummeter** *nt* GERÄT ion gage (AmE), ion gauge (BrE), ionization vacuum gage (AmE), ionization vacuum gauge (BrE), thermionic vacuum gauge (BrE), thermionic vacuum gage (AmE), HEIZ & KÄLTE ionization vacuum gage (AmE), ionization vacuum gauge (BrE), STRAHLPHYS, TEILPHYS ionization gage (AmE), ionization gauge (BrE); **Ionisationsverlust** *m* STRAHLPHYS, TEILPHYS ionization loss

ionisch: ~**er Antrieb** *m* RAUMFAHRT *Raumschiff* ionic propulsion

ionisierend: ~**e Strahlung** *f* ELEKTRIZ, STRAHLPHYS, TEILPHYS, UMWELTSCHMUTZ ionizing radiation; **nicht** ~**e Strahlung** *f* STRAHLPHYS nonionizing radiation; ~**es Teilchen** *nt* STRAHLPHYS, TEILPHYS ionizing particle

ionisiert: ~**er Zustand** *m* STRAHLPHYS, TEILPHYS ionized state

Ionisierung *f* ELEKTRIZ, ELEKTROTECH, RADIO ionization; **Ionisierungsdetektor** *m* STRAHLPHYS, TEILPHYS ionization detector; **Ionisierungsenergie** *f* STRAHLPHYS ionization energy; **Ionisierungskammer im Reaktorkern** *f* KERNTECH in-core ionization chamber; **Ionisierungspotential** *nt* STRAHLPHYS, TEILPHYS ionization potential; **Ionisierungsschicht** *f* ELEKTRIZ ionizing layer; **Ionisierungsstrom** *m* ELEKTRONIK ionization current; **Ionisierungsverlust** *m* STRAHLPHYS, TEILPHYS ionization loss

Ionogramm *nt* RADIO ionogram

Ionon *nt* CHEMIE ionone

Ionophorese *f* ELEKTRIZ electrophoresis

Ionosphäre *f* RADIO ionosphere, STRAHLPHYS ionic atmosphere, ionosphere, TEILPHYS ionosphere

ionosphärisch: ~**e Ausbreitung** *f* RADIO ionospheric propagation; ~**e Streuung** *f* RADIO ionospheric scatter

Ionotropie *f* CHEMIE ionotropy

IOS *abbr* ELEKTRONIK (*integrierter optischer Schaltkreis*), OPTIK (*integrierter optischer Schaltkreis*), TELEKOM (*integrierte optische Schaltung*) IOC (*integrated optical circuit*)

IP *abbr* (*Eingabe*) COMP & DV IP (*input*)

Ipecin *nt* CHEMIE emetin, emetine

Ipekakuanha *f* LEBENSMITTEL *Pharmakologie* ipecac, ipecacuanha

IPL *abbr* (*Initialprogrammlader*) COMP & DV IPL (*initial*

program loader)

IR *abbr* COMP & DV *(Wiederauffinden von Informationen)* IR *(information retrieval)*, KUNSTSTOFF *(Infrarot)*, OPTIK *(Infrarot)*, PHYS *(Infrarot)*, STRAHLPHYS *(Infrarot)* IR *(infrared)*

Iraser *m* ELEKTRONIK iraser

IRB-Ruß *m (internationaler Standardruß)* KUNSTSTOFF IRB *(industry reference black)*

I-Regler *m (Integralregler)* REGELUNG integral action controller

Iridium- *pref* CHEMIE iridic

Irisblende *f* PHYS iris

Irisch: ~es Moos *nt* LEBENSMITTEL carrageen

Irisieren *nt* MEERSCHMUTZ, OPTIK iridescence; **~ von Farben** *nt* OPTIK irisplay of colours

irisierend: ~es Glas *nt* KER & GLAS iridescent glass

Iron *nt* CHEMIE irone

IRPTC *abbr (Internationales Verzeichnis für potentiell toxische Chemikalien)* UMWELTSCHUTZ IRPTC *(International Register of Potentially Toxic Chemicals)*

irrational[1] *adj* MATH irrational

irrational:[2] **~e Zahl** *f* COMP & DV irrational number, MATH irrational number, surd

irreduzibel: irreduzibles Polynom *nt* COMP & DV irreducible polynomial

irreführend *adj* PATENT misleading

irrelevant *adj* PATENT irrelevant

irreversibel[1] *adj* PHYS, THERMOD irreversible

irreversibel:[2] **irreversible Abschaltung** *f* KERNTECH irreversible shutdown; **irreversibles Kolloid** *nt* CHEMIE irreversible colloid

Irrfahrt *f* COMP & DV *Statistik* random walk

IRS *abbr (Internationales Referenzsystem)* UMWELTSCHUTZ IRS *(International Referral System)*

IR-Spannungsabfall *m* ELEKTRIZ IR-drop

IS *abbr* COMP & DV *(Integrierschaltung, integrierte Schaltung, integrierter Schaltkreis)*, ELEKTRIZ *(Integrierschaltung, integrierte Schaltung, integrierter Schaltkreis)*, ELEKTRONIK *(Integrierschaltung, integrierte Schaltung, integrierter Schaltkreis)* IC *(integrated circuit)*, ELEKTRONIK *(Sättigungsstrom)* IS *(saturation current)*, KONTROLL *(Integrierschaltung, integrierte Schaltung, integrierter Schaltkreis)*, PHYS *(Integrierschaltung, integrierte Schaltung, integrierter Schaltkreis)* IC *(integrated circuit)*, PHYS *(Sättigungsstrom)* IS *(saturation current)*, RADIO *(Integrierschaltung, integrierte Schaltung, integrierter Schaltkreis)* IC *(integrated circuit)*, RADIO *(Sättigungsstrom)* IS *(saturation current)*, TELEKOM *(Integrierschaltung, integrierte Schaltung, integrierter Schaltkreis)* IC *(integrated circuit)*

Isatin *nt* CHEMIE isatin; **Isatin-** *pref* CHEMIE isatic

Isatogen- *pref* CHEMIE isatogenic

Isatropa- *pref* CHEMIE isatropic

ISB *abbr (unabhängiges Seitenband)* RADIO ISB *(independent sideband)*

ISB-Modulation *f* ELEKTRONIK ISB modulation

ISDN *abbr (integriertes digitales Fernmeldenetz)* TELEKOM ISDN *(integrated service digital network)*

ISDN-Anschluß *m* TELEKOM ISDN access; **ISDN-Breitbanddienst** *m* TELEKOM BISDN service, Broadband Integrated Services Digital Network; **ISDN-Primärratenanschluß** *m* TELEKOM ISDN primary rate access; **ISDN-Vermittlung** *f* TELEKOM ISDN exchange

.isentropisch *adj* PHYS, THERMOD isentropic

Isethion- *pref* CHEMIE isethionic; **Isethionat** *nt* CHEMIE isethionate

IS-Gehäuse *nt* ELEKTRONIK integrated-circuit package

ISM *abbr (Betriebsüberwachung)* TELEKOM ISM *(in-service monitoring)*

IS-Maschine *f (Individual-Section-Flaschenblasmaschine)* KER & GLAS IS machine *(individual section machine)*

ISO *abbr (Internationale Normungsorganisation)* ELEKTRIZ, MASCHINEN ISO *(International Standards Organization)*

Isoalloxazin *nt* CHEMIE isoalloxazine

Isoamyl- *pref* CHEMIE isoamyl, isopentyl

isobar *adj* THERMOD isobaric

Isobare *f* KERNTECH, PHYS, THERMOD, WASSERTRANS isobar

Isobarenspin *m* PHYS isobaric spin

Isobathe *f* WASSERTRANS isobath

Isobelastung *f* LUFTTRANS isostress

Isoborneol *nt* CHEMIE isoborneol

Isobutan *nt* CHEMIE isobutane, methylpropane, ERDÖL *Kohlenwasserstoff* isobutane

Isobuten *nt* CHEMIE isobutene, isobutylene, methylpropene

Isobutter- *pref* CHEMIE isobutyric

Isobutyl- *pref* CHEMIE isobutyl; **Isobutylalkohol** *m* CHEMIE isopropanol, isopropylcarbinol, methylpropanol

Isochinolin *nt* CHEMIE isoquinoline, leucoline

isochor *adj* THERMOD isochore

Isochore *f* PHYS isochor

Isochromatenbild *nt* FERTIG stress pattern

isochron[1] *adj* COMP & DV isochronous

isochron:[2] **~es Glühen** *nt* METALL isochronal annealing; **~e Übertragung** *f* COMP & DV isochronous transmission

Isocinchomeron- *pref* CHEMIE isocinchomeronic

Isocroton- *pref* CHEMIE isocrotonic

Isocyan- *pref* CHEMIE isocyanic

Isocyanat *nt* CHEMIE, KUNSTSTOFF isocyanate

Isocyanid *nt* CHEMIE carbylamine, isocyanide

isocyclisch *adj* CHEMIE homocyclic, isocyclic

Isodipren *nt* CHEMIE carene

Isodulcit *nt* CHEMIE isodulcite

isoelektrisch[1] *adj* ELEKTRIZ equipotential

isoelektrisch[2] *m* CHEMIE isoelectric; **~es Fahrzeug** *nt* KFZTECH isoelectric vehicle

isoelektronisch *adj* CHEMIE isosteric

Isofenchol *nt* CHEMIE isofenchol

Isoflavon *nt* CHEMIE isoflavone

Isogewichtskurve *f* LUFTTRANS iso-weight curve

isogonal *adj* GEOM isogonal

Isokline *f* PHYS isocline

Isolation *f* COMP & DV, ELEKTROTECH *Isolationsstrom*, HEIZ & KÄLTE *Eigenschaft, Zustand*, PHYS, TELEKOM insulation, isolation; **Isolationsdurchschlag** *m* ELEKTRIZ insulation breakdown; **Isolationsfehler** *m* ELEKTROTECH insulation defect; **Isolationsgrad** *m* ELEKTRIZ insulation class; **Isolationsklasse** *f* ELEKTRIZ, HEIZ & KÄLTE insulation class; **Isolationsmaterial** *nt* CHEMIE insulator; **Isolationsmeßgerät** *nt* ELEKTROTECH Megger®; **Isolationspapier** *nt* ELEKTROTECH fish paper; **Isolationsprüfer** *m* ELEKTROTECH earth leakage indicator (BrE), ground leakage indicator (BrE); **Isolationsprüfgerät** *nt* ELEKTRIZ, GERÄT insulation tester; **Isolationsstrecke** *f* ELEKTROTECH insulation distance; **Isolationswiderstand** *m* ELEKTROTECH, PHYS insulation resistance

Isolator *m* ELEKTRIZ, ELEKTROTECH *elektrisch oder thermisch*, FERTIG, HEIZ & KÄLTE, PHYS, RADIO insulator, TELEKOM insulator, isolator; ~ **mit Vergußkammer** *m* ELEKTRIZ pot insulator; **Isolatorklemme** *f* ELEKTROTECH insulator clamp

Isoleucin *nt* CHEMIE aminomethylpentanoic acid, isoleucine

Isolier- *pref* CHEMIE, ELEKTROTECH, FERTIG, KER & GLAS, PHYS, SICHERHEIT, TELEKOM insulating; **Isolierband** *nt* ELEKTRIZ, ELEKTROTECH insulating tape

isolierbar *adj* CHEMIE isolable

Isolier-: **Isolierbehälter** *m* THERMOD heat-insulated container, insulated container; **Isolierblech** *nt* HYDRAUL clothing plate; **Isolierdecke** *f* VERPACK insulating sheet; **Isolierei** *nt* KER & GLAS porcelain insulator

Isolieren *nt* FERTIG, TELEKOM insulation

isolieren *vt* BAU insulate, CHEMIE isolate, ELEKTRIZ, FERTIG, HEIZ & KÄLTE, PHYS insulate, SICHERHEIT insulate, isolate

isolierend[1] *adj* ELEKTROTECH, FERTIG insulating

isolierend:[2] ~**e Umhüllung** *f* ELEKTROTECH insulating covering

Isolier-: **Isolierfähigkeit** *f* VERPACK insulating property; **Isolierhandschuhe** *m pl* SICHERHEIT insulating gloves; **Isolierhülle** *f* ELEKTROTECH insulating covering; **Isolierhülse** *f* ELEKTROTECH insulating sheath; **Isolierkörper** *m* ELEKTROTECH, TELEKOM insulator; **Isolierlack** *m* ELEKTRIZ insulating varnish; **Isoliermantel** *m* ELEKTROTECH insulating sheath; **Isoliermasse** *f* ELEKTROTECH, VERPACK insulating compound; **Isoliermaterial** *nt* ELEKTROTECH insulating material, HEIZ & KÄLTE insulant, MECHAN insulating material, THERMOD lagging; **Isoliermatte** *f* ELEKTRIZ insulating mat; **Isoliermittel** *nt* BAU insulator; **Isoliermuffe** *f* ELEKTROTECH insulating joint; **Isolieröl** *nt* ELEKTRIZ, ELEKTROTECH, ERDÖL *Hochspannungstransformatoren* insulating oil; **Isolierpapier** *nt* ELEKTRIZ, PAPIER insulating paper; **Isolierplatte** *f* ELEKTROTECH insulating plate, HEIZ & KÄLTE insulating board; **Isolierporzellan** *nt* ELEKTROTECH electrotechnical porcelain; **Isolierrohr** *nt* ELEKTROTECH conduit, insulating sleeve, MASCHINEN insulation pipe, NICHTFOSS ENERG *elektrisch* conduit; **Isolierscheibe** *f* ELEKTRIZ, ELEKTROTECH insulating washer

Isolierschicht *f* ELEKTROTECH, VERPACK insulating layer; **Isolierschicht-Feldeffekttransistor** *m (IGFET)* ELEKTRONIK, RADIO insulated gate field-effect transistor *(IGFET)*

Isolier-: **Isolierschienenlasche** *f* EISENBAHN insulating fishplate; **Isolierschlauch** *m* ELEKTROTECH insulating sleeve, KUNSTSTOFF electrical sleeving

Isolierstoff *m* BAU insulating material, FERTIG insulant, HEIZ & KÄLTE insulant, insulator, TELEKOM insulation, VERPACK insulating material; **Isolierstoffklasse** *f* HEIZ & KÄLTE insulation class

Isolier-: **Isolierstoß** *m* EISENBAHN insulated rail joint; **Isoliersubstrat** *nt* ELEKTROTECH insulating substrate

isoliert[1] *adj* BAU, ELEKTROTECH, HEIZ & KÄLTE insulated

isoliert:[2] ~**e Abschirmung** *f* ELEKTRIZ insulation screen; ~**e Antennenleitung** *f* ELEKTRIZ insulated antenna cable; ~**er Draht** *m* ELEKTRIZ insulated conductor, ELEKTROTECH insulated wire; ~**e Durchführung** *f* ELEKTROTECH grommet; ~**es Kabel** *nt* ELEKTRIZ, ELEKTROTECH insulated cable; ~**es Kabelrohr** *nt* ELEKTRIZ insulated conduit; ~**e Kabelseele** *f* ELEKTRIZ insulated core; ~**er Leiter** *m* ELEKTROTECH, TELEKOM

insulated conductor; **nicht ~er Leiter** *m* ELEKTRIZ bare conductor; ~**er Stromleiter** *m* ELEKTRIZ insulated conductor; ~**es System** *nt* PHYS isolated system; ~**e Werkzeuge** *nt pl* SICHERHEIT insulated tools

Isolierung *f* BAU, ELEKTRIZ, ELEKTROTECH *eines Leiters* insulation, FERTIG *Rohre* lagging, HEIZ & KÄLTE *Werkstoff* insulation, HYDRAUL cladding, clothing, *Dampfmaschine* lagging, KER & GLAS, KUNSTSTOFF, MASCHINEN, MECHAN, NICHTFOSS ENERG, SICHERHEIT, TELEKOM, WASSERTRANS *Elektrik* insulation; **äußere** ~ *f* ELEKTRIZ external insulation, outer insulation; ~ **zwischen Wicklungen** *f* ELEKTRIZ coil-to-coil insulation, interturn insulation; **Isolierungsträger** *m* RAUMFAHRT *Raumschiff* insulating substrate

Isolier-: **Isolierventil** *nt* LABOR isolating valve; **Isolierverkleidung des Nutzlastraums** *f* RAUMFAHRT payload bay insulation; **Isoliervermögen** *nt* VERPACK insulating property; **Isolierwachs** *nt* ELEKTROTECH insulating wax

Isolog *nt* CHEMIE isolog (AmE), isologue (BrE)

isolog *adj* CHEMIE isologous

Isomaltose *f* CHEMIE isomaltose

Isomer *nt* CHEMIE, ERDÖL, KERNTECH, STRAHLPHYS isomer

isomer: ~**er Übergang** *m* STRAHLPHYS isomeric transition; ~**e Umwandlung** *f* CHEMIE isomerization

Isomerie *f* CHEMIE, PHYS isomerism

Isomerisation *f* CHEMIE, ERDÖL isomerization

Isomerisierung *f* CHEMIE isomerization, ERDÖL *Petrochemie* isomerization, *Umlagerung chemischer Verbindungen in Isomere* isomerization

Isomerismus *f* FERTIG allotropy

Isometrie *f* GEOM isometry

isometrisch[1] *adj* GEOM isometric

isometrisch:[2] ~**e Darstellung** *f* KONSTZEICH isometric projection; ~**e Kraft** *f* ERGON isometric force; ~**e Muskelkontraktion** *f* ERGON isometric contraction; ~**e Projektion** *f* GEOM, KONSTZEICH isometric projection

Isomorphie *f* CHEMIE isomorphism

Isonicotin- *pref* CHEMIE isonicotinic

Isonitril *nt* CHEMIE isocyanide, isonitrile

Isooctan *nt* CHEMIE isooctane

Isopachenkarte *f* ERDÖL *Geologie* isopach map

Isoparaffin *nt* CHEMIE isoparaffin

Isopelletierin *nt* CHEMIE isopelletierin

Isopentan *nt* CHEMIE isopentane, methylbutane

Isopentyl- *pref* CHEMIE isoamyl, isopentyl

Isophorondiamin *nt* KUNSTSTOFF isophorone diamine

Isoplethe *f* CHEMIE isopleth

Isopolysäure *f* CHEMIE isopoly acid

Isopren *nt* CHEMIE isoprene, methylbutadiene

Isoprenoid *nt* CHEMIE isoprenoid

Isopropanol *nt* CHEMIE propanol, LEBENSMITTEL isopropyl alcohol

Isopropenyl- *pref* CHEMIE isoallyl, isopropenyl

Isopropyl- *pref* CHEMIE isopropyl; **Isopropylalkohol** *m* CHEMIE isopropanol, propanol; **Isopropylbenzol** *nt* CHEMIE cumene, isopropylbenzene

Isospin *m* STRAHLPHYS, TEILPHYS isospin; **Isospin-Multiplett** *nt* PHYS, STRAHLPHYS, TEILPHYS charge multiplet

Isostasie *f* NICHTFOSS ENERG isostasy

isoster *adj* CHEMIE isosteric

Isosterie *f* CHEMIE isosterism

isosterisch *adj* CHEMIE *Enzym* isosteric

isotherm[1] *adj* MECHAN, PHYS, THERMOD isothermal

isotherm:[2] **~e Ausdehnung** *f* PHYS isothermal expansion; **~e Kompressibilität** *f* PHYS isothermal compressibility

Isothermbehälter *m* KFZTECH insulated container

Isotherme *f* LUFTTRANS isotherm, PHYS isotherm, isothermal curve, isothermal line, THERMOD isothermal curve, isothermal line, WASSERTRANS isotherm

isothermisch: **~es Abschrecken** *nt* METALL isothermal quenching; **~e Prüfung** *f* METALL isothermal test; **~e Reaktion** *f* METALL isothermal reaction

Isotone *f* PHYS isotone

isotonisch: **~e Muskelkontraktion** *f* ERGON isotonic contraction

Isotop *nt* KERNTECH, PHYS, STRAHLPHYS, TEILPHYS isotope; **~ zur industriellen Bestrahlung** *nt* KERNTECH industrial isotope; **Isotopenanalyse** *f* PHYS isotopic analysis; **Isotopengenerator** *m* RAUMFAHRT *Raumschiff* isotopic generator; **Isotopenhäufigkeit** *f* PHYS isotopic abundance; **Isotopenhäufigkeitsverhältnis** *nt* KERNTECH abundance ratio

isotopenmarkiert: **~es Material** *nt* KERNTECH isotopically-tagged compound

Isotop: **Isotopenmasse** *f* PHYS nucleon number, PHYS mass number; **Isotopenmessung** *f* KOHLEN isotope measurement; **Isotopenspin** *m* PHYS isotopic spin; **Isotopentrennung** *f* PHYS, STRAHLPHYS, TEILPHYS isotope separation

Isotopie *f* CHEMIE isotopy

isotrop[1] *adj* OPTIK *elektromagnetische Wellen*, RADIO isotropic

isotrop:[2] **~e Abbildung** *f* GEOM isotropic mapping; **~e Turbulenz** *f* STRÖMPHYS isotropic turbulence

Isotropantenne *f* RAUMFAHRT *Kugelstrahler* isotropic antenna

isotropisch[1] *adj* RAUMFAHRT *Weltraumfunk*, TELEKOM isotropic

isotropisch:[2] **~er Gewinn** *m* RAUMFAHRT *Weltraumfunk* isotropic gain; **~e Verstärkung** *f* RAUMFAHRT isotropic gain

Isovanillin *nt* CHEMIE isovanilline

Isoxazol *nt* CHEMIE isoxazole

IS: **IS-Scheibe** *f* ELEKTRONIK integrated-circuit wafer

Ist- *pref* TEXTIL actual; **Istabmaß** *nt* FERTIG actual deviation; **Istabweichung** *f* GERÄT actual deviation; **Istdurchmesser** *m* FERTIG *Bohrung* actual size

Isthmus *m* WASSERTRANS isthmus

Ist-: **Istmaß** *nt* MASCHINEN actual size

IS: **IS-Trägermaterial** *nt* ELEKTRONIK integrated-circuit substrate

Ist-: **Iststrom** *m* GERÄT actual current; **Istvorschub** *m* FERTIG actual feed rate; **Istwert** *m* GERÄT instantaneous value, MASCHINEN actual value; **Istwert der Teilkreisteilung** *m* FERTIG actual tooth spacing on pitch circle; **Istwertanzeige** *f* GERÄT actual indication; **Istwertferntasten** *nt* COMP & DV remote sensing

ISW *abbr (internationale Selbstwahl)* TELEKOM IDD *(international direct dialling)*, IDDD *(international direct distance dialling)*

ITA *abbr (internationales Telegraphenalphabet)* LUFTTRANS, WASSERTRANS ITA *(international telegraph alphabet)*

Itacon- *pref* CHEMIE itaconic

Iteration *f* COMP & DV, MATH, UMWELTSCHMUTZ iteration; **Iterationsmethode** *f* COMP & DV iterative method; **Iterationsschleife** *f* COMP & DV iterative routine

iterativ[1] *adj* COMP & DV iterative

iterativ:[2] **~e Operation** *f* COMP & DV iterative process; **~er Prozeß** *m* COMP & DV iterative process; **~es Rechnen** *nt* COMP & DV iterative operation; **~e Suche** *f* KÜNSTL INT iterative search

I-Träger *m* BAU *gewalzt* I-beam, METALL I beam

ITU *abbr (Internationale Fernmeldeunion)* RADIO, WASSERTRANS ITU *(International Telecommunications Union)*

IUC *abbr (Meß- und Regeltechnik)* ELEKTRONIK IUC *(instrumentation and control)*

I-Wagen *m* EISENBAHN refrigerated car, refrigerated wagon

J

J *abbr* AKUSTIK *(Schallenergiefluß)* J *(sound-energy flux)*, ELEKTRIZ *(Joule)* J *(joule)*, KERNTECH *(Winkelmomentquantenzahl)* J *(total angular momentum quantum number)*, LEBENSMITTEL *(Joule)*, MECHAN *(Joule)* J *(joule)*, MECHAN *(mechanisches Wärmeäquivalent)* J *(mechanical equivalent of heat)*, METROL *(Joule)*, PHYS *(Joule)* J *(joule)*, PHYS *(Schallenergiefluß)* J *(sound-energy flux)*, THERMOD *(Joule)* J *(joule)*, THERMOD *(mechanisches Wärmeäquivalent)* J *(mechanical equivalent of heat)*

j *abbr (Sprunghöhe)* HYDRAUL j *(height of hydraulic jump)*

Jacht *f* WASSERTRANS yacht; **Jachthafen** *m* WASSERTRANS marina; **Jachtheck** *nt* WASSERTRANS *Schiffbau* counter stern

Jackson: **~sches Modell** *nt* KERNTECH Jackson model

Jacquard- *pref* TEXTIL jacquard; **Jacquardgewebe** *nt* TEXTIL jacquard fabric; **Jacquardpapier** *nt* VERPACK jacquard paper; **Jacquardpappe** *f* VERPACK jacquard board; **Jacquardwebstuhl** *m* TEXTIL jacquard loom

Jahres- *pref* WASSERVERSORG annual, yearly; **Jahresabfluß** *m* WASSERVERSORG annual runoff; **Jahresdurchfluß** *m* WASSERVERSORG annual flow; **Jahresgebühr** *f* PATENT renewal fee; **Jahreshochwasser** *nt* WASSERVERSORG annual flood

jährlich: **~e Entwässerung** *f* WASSERVERSORG annual drainage; **~e Evaporation** *f* WASSERVERSORG annual evaporation; **~er Kapazitätsfaktor** *m* NICHTFOSS ENERG annual capacity factor; **~e Last** *f* WASSERVERSORG annual load; **~er Mittelwasserstand** *m* WASSERVERSORG annual mean water level; **~e natürliche Hintergrundstrahlung** *f* STRAHLPHYS natural annual background radiation

Jalapin *nt* CHEMIE jalapin, orizabin

Jalousie *f* KER & GLAS, KFZTECH *Verglasung* louver (AmE), louvre (BrE); **Jalousieeffekt** *m* FERNSEH venetian-blind effect; **Jalousieplattenkassette** *f* FOTO roller-blind dark slide

Jaspégarn *nt* TEXTIL jaspe yarn

Jauche *f* ABFALL slurry

Jaulen *nt* AKUSTIK wow, RADIO yoop; **~ des Plattentellers** *nt* AUFNAHME turntable wow

Javellauge *f* FERTIG *Kunststoffinstallationen* javel water

Jedermann-Funk *m* TELEKOM citizens' band radio

Jena: **~er Glas** ® *nt* THERMOD oven-proof glass

Jerobeam *f* KER & GLAS jeroboam

Jersey *m* TEXTIL jersey

Jervin *nt* CHEMIE jervine

JET *abbr* STRAHLPHYS JET, Joint European Torus

Jetstream *m* LUFTTRANS jet stream

JET-Tokamak *m* KERNTECH, STRAHLPHYS JET Tokamac

Jigger *m* ABFALL, TEXTIL jigger

J-Integral-Methode *f* KERNTECH J-integral method

Jitter *m* TELEKOM jitter

jitterfrei: **~es Signal** *nt* TELEKOM jitter-free signal

Jitterreduktion *f* TELEKOM jitter reduction

j-j-Kopplung *f* KERNTECH, PHYS j-j coupling

Job *m* COMP & DV job; **Jobabrechnung** *f* COMP & DV job accounting; **Jobabschnitt** *m* COMP & DV job step; **Jobanfang** *m* COMP & DV job begin; **Jobanforderung** *f* COMP & DV job request; **Jobanfrage** *f* COMP & DV job request; **Jobbefehl** *m* COMP & DV job command; **Jobbeschreibung** *f* COMP & DV job description; **Jobdatum** *nt* COMP & DV job date; **Jobdefinition** *f* COMP & DV job definition; **Jobende** *nt* COMP & DV EOJ, end of job; **Jobferneingabe** *f* COMP & DV RJE, remote job entry; **Jobfernverarbeitung** *f* COMP & DV RJE, remote job entry; **Jobfolge** *f* COMP & DV job step; **Jobkatalog** *m* COMP & DV job catalog (AmE), job catalogue (BrE); **Jobklasse** *f* COMP & DV job class

joborientiert: **~e Datenstation** *f* COMP & DV job-oriented terminal; **~e Programmiersprache** *f* COMP & DV job-oriented language

Job: **Jobplanung** *f* COMP & DV job scheduling; **Jobschritt** *m* COMP & DV job step; **Jobstapel** *m* COMP & DV job batch, job stack; **Jobsteuerdatei** *f* COMP & DV job control file; **Jobsteuerprogramm** *nt* COMP & DV job control program, job scheduler; **Jobsteuersprache** *f* COMP & DV JCL, job control language; **Jobsteuerung** *f* COMP & DV job control; **Jobstrom** *m* COMP & DV job stream; **Jobverarbeitungssystem** *nt* COMP & DV job-processing system; **Jobwarteschlange** *f* COMP & DV job queue, job stream

Joch *nt* BAU *Brücke* frame, ELEKTRIZ, KERNTECH *Magnet*, KFZTECH *Universalgelenk*, MASCHINEN, MECHAN yoke; **Jochbalken** *m* BAU straining piece; **Jochspule** *f* ELEKTROTECH yoke coil

Jod *nt (I)* CHEMIE iodine *(I)*

Jodeldetektor *m* KERNTECH Jodel detector

Jod: **Jodkolben** *m* LABOR iodine flask; **Jodsilber** *nt* FOTO silver iodide; **Jodzahl** *f* KUNSTSTOFF iodine value

Johannit *m* KERNTECH johannite

Johnson: **~sches Rauschen** *nt* PHYS Johnson noise

Jojo-Entspinnen *nt* RAUMFAHRT *Raumschiff* yoyo despin

Jokerzeichen *nt* COMP & DV wildcard character

Jolle *f* WASSERTRANS dinghy

Josephson: **~scher Effekt** *m* KERNTECH, PHYS Josephson effect; **~scher Übergang** *m* ELEKTRONIK, KERNTECH Josephson junction; **~sche Verbindung** *f* PHYS Josephson junction

Jost-Funktion *f* KERNTECH Jost function

Joule *nt (J)* ELEKTRIZ, LEBENSMITTEL, MECHAN, METROL, PHYS, THERMOD joule *(J)*; **~scher Effekt** *m* ELEKTRIZ, ELEKTROTECH, PHYS *Wärmelehre, Magnetismus*, THERMOD Joule effect; **~sches Gesetz** *nt* PHYS *Elektrizitätslehre*, THERMOD Joule's law; **~scher Wärmeverlust** *m* ELEKTRIZ Joule's heat loss

Joule-Thomson: **~scher Effekt** *m* PHYS, THERMOD Joule-Kelvin expansion, Joule-Thomson effect, Joule-Thomson expansion, joule expansion; **~scher Koeffizient** *m* PHYS, THERMOD Joule-Thomson coefficient

Joule: **Joule-Verlust** *m* ELEKTRIZ copper loss

Joy: **~sche Ventilsteuerung** *f* HYDRAUL Joy's valve-gear

Joystick *m* COMP & DV, FERNSEH joystick; **Joystick-Schalter** *m* ELEKTRIZ joystick selector

J-Teilchen *nt* PHYS J particle

Juglon *nt* CHEMIE hydroxynaphthoquinone, juglone

Jukebox-Archivierungssystem *nt* OPTIK jukebox filing system

Jumper *m* ELEKTROTECH jumper

Jumpstagspreize *f* WASSERTRANS jumper strut

Junctiondiode *f* ELEKTRIZ junction diode

Jungfernfahrt *f* WASSERTRANS maiden voyage

Jungfernflug *m* LUFTTRANS maiden flight

jungfräulich[1] *adj* COMP & DV virgin

jungfräulich:[2] **~e Faser** *f* KER & GLAS pristine fiber (AmE), pristine fibre (BrE); **~es Glas** *nt* KER & GLAS pristine glass; **~es Neutron** *nt* KERNTECH uncollided neutron, virgin neutron

Junkers-Kalorimeter *nt* THERMOD continuous flow calorimeter

Jura *m* ERDÖL *Geologie* Jurassic period

juristisch: ~e Person *f* PATENT legal person

Justier- *pref* MASCHINEN adjusting

justierbar: ~e Blende *f* PHYS adjustable aperture; **~er Keramikkondensator** *m* ELEKTROTECH adjustable ceramic capacitor; **~er Kern** *m* ELEKTROTECH adjustable core

Justier-: Justiereinrichtung *f* GERÄT calibration equipment; **Justierelement** *nt* GERÄT trimming element

Justieren *nt* CHEMIE rectification, LUFTTRANS *von Instrumenten* setting, METROL adjustment

justieren *vt* MASCHINEN set

Justier-: Justierfehler *m* TELEKOM alignment fault; **Justierglied** *nt* GERÄT adjusting element; **Justierknopf** *m* GERÄT, MECHAN adjusting knob; **Justiermutter** *f* FERTIG leveling nut (AmE), levelling nut (BrE); **Justierpotentiometer** *nt* ELEKTROTECH trimming potentiometer; **Justierring** *m* GERÄT adjustment ring; **Justierschraube** *f* GERÄT adjustable screw, trimming screw, MASCHINEN adjusting screw, set screw, MECHAN adjusting screw; **Justierspannung** *f* ELEKTRIZ adjusting voltage

Justierung *f* DRUCK adjustment, ELEKTRONIK adjustment, fine adjustment, *von Feldgeräten* calibration, MASCHINEN, RADIO adjustment

Justier-: Justierwiderstand *m* GERÄT trimming resistor

Just-in-Time-Lieferung *f* VERPACK just in time delivery

Jute *f* TEXTIL jute; **Jutedrell** *m* VERPACK jute sacking; **Jutegarn** *nt* TEXTIL jute yarn; **Juteseil** *nt* MASCHINEN jute rope; **Jutespinnerei** *f* TEXTIL jute spinning; **Juteumhüllung** *f* ELEKTROTECH jute covering

juvenil: ~es Grundwasser *nt* WASSERVERSORG juvenile water

K

K[1] *abbr* AKUSTIK *(Magnetostriktionskonstante)* K *(magnetostriction constant)*, ELEKTRIZ *(Kelvin)* K *(kelvin)*, HYDRAUL *(Kompressionsmodul)* K *(bulk modulus of compression)*, HYDRAUL *(Elastizitätsmodul)* K *(bulk modulus of elasticity)*, KERNTECH *(Kerma)* K *(kerma)*, METROL *(Kelvin)*, PHYS *(Kelvin)* K *(kelvin)*, PHYS *(freigesetzte kinetische Energie geladener Teilchen in Materie)* K *(kerma)*, THERMOD *(Gleichgewichtskonstante)* K *(equilibrium constant)*, THERMOD *(Kelvin)* K *(kelvin)*

K[2] *(Kalium)* CHEMIE K *(potassium)*

k *abbr* AKUSTIK *(Wellenkonstante)* k *(wave constant)*, ELEKTRIZ *(Kopplungskoeffizient)* k *(coupling coefficient)*, KERNTECH *(Multiplikationskonstante für infinite Systeme)* k *(multiplication constant for an infinite system)*, KERNTECH *(Neutronenmultiplikationskonstante)* k *(neutron multiplication constant)*, LABOR *(Kilo, Kilogramm)* k *(kilo)*, PHYS *(Boltzmannsche Konstante, Boltzmannsche Zahl)* k *(Boltzmann constant)*, PHYS *(Kopplungskoeffizient)* k *(coupling coefficient)*, THERMOD *(Boltzmannsche Konstante, Boltzmannsche Zahl)* k *(Boltzmann constant)*

kabbelig: ~**e See** *f* WASSERTRANS *Seezustand* choppy sea

Kabel[1] *nt* AUFNAHME, COMP & DV, ELEKTRIZ cable, ELEKTROTECH cable, lead, FERNSEH, FERTIG, KFZTECH, KUNSTSTOFF, MASCHINEN, MECHAN cable, OPTIK cable assembly, RADIO, TELEKOM, TRANS, VERPACK, WASSERTRANS cable; ~ **mit abgestufter Koppeldämpfung** *nt* TELEKOM grading coupling loss cable; ~ **zwischen Eingabegerät und Computer** *nt* COMP & DV input lead; ~ **mit losem Aufbau** *nt* OPTIK loose construction cable; ~ **mit metallischen Leitern** *nt* TELEKOM metal conductor cable; ~ **mit Nutenstruktur** *nt* TELEKOM grooved cable; ~ **mit separater Bleiumhüllung** *nt* ELEKTRIZ separately lead-sheathed cable; ~ **mit separater Bleiummantelung** *nt* ELEKTRIZ separately lead-sheathed cable; ~ **mit symmetrischen Adernpaaren** *nt* TELEKOM symmetrical pair cable

Kabel:[2] ~ **verlegen** *vi* AUFNAHME lay tracks

Kabel: **Kabelabschluß** *m* ELEKTRIZ cable termination, ELEKTROTECH cable head; **Kabelabschnitt** *m* ELEKTROTECH cable section; **Kabelabzweigdose** *f* ELEKTRIZ cable junction box; **Kabelabzweigkasten** *m* ELEKTRIZ cable junction box; **Kabelader** *f* ELEKTROTECH cable core; **Kabeladernpaar** *nt* ELEKTROTECH cable pair; **Kabelarmatur** *f* ELEKTROTECH cable fitting; **Kabelaufhängung** *f* ELEKTROTECH, KFZTECH cable support; **Kabelaufhängungsdraht** *m* ELEKTROTECH cable suspension wire; **Kabelausziehvorrichtung** *f* ELEKTRIZ pull box; **Kabelbahn** *f* TRANS cable railroad (AmE), cable railway (BrE); **Kabelbaum** *m* ELEKTROTECH cable harness, RAUMFAHRT *Raumschiff* safety harness, wiring harness; **Kabelbewehrung** *f* FERTIG cable armoring (AmE), cable armouring (BrE); **Kabelbinder** *m* FERNSEH binder, RADIO lace; **Kabelbündel** *nt* ELEKTRIZ, ELEKTROTECH bunched cable (BrE), bundled cable (AmE), cable bundle; **Kabeldämpfung** *f* ELEKTROTECH cable loss; **Kabeldefekt** *m* ELEKTRO-TECH cable defect; **Kabeldose** *f* ELEKTRIZ cable box; **Kabeleinführung** *f* HEIZ & KÄLTE cable entry; **Kabeleinstieg** *m* ELEKTRIZ cable manhole; **Kabeleinziehvorrichtung** *f* ELEKTRIZ cable pull box; **Kabelendgestell** *nt* ELEKTRIZ, TELEKOM cable support rack; **Kabelendstück** *nt* ELEKTRIZ cable end piece; **Kabelendverschluß** *m* ELEKTRIZ cable box; **Kabelfehlernachweisgerät** *nt* ELEKTRIZ cable fault detector; **Kabelfernsehanlage** *f* TELEKOM cable television system; **Kabelfernsehen** *nt* FERNSEH cable TV, cable television, wired television; **Kabelfernsehen zu Überwachungszwecken** *nt (CCTV)* FERNSEH closed-circuit television *(CCTV)*; **Kabelfernsehnetz** *nt* FERNSEH, TELEKOM cable television network; **Kabelfernsehstörung** *f (CATVI)* RADIO cable television interference *(CATVI)*; **Kabelfett** *nt* ELEKTROTECH cable grease; **Kabelführung** *f* ELEKTROTECH cable conduit, cable duct, KFZTECH *Elektrik* cable guide; **Kabelfunk** *m* FERNSEH cablecast; **Kabelgarnitur für Deckdurchführung** *f* WASSERTRANS *Tauwerk* through deck cable fitting

kabelgefärbt *adj* TEXTIL tow-dyed

Kabel: **Kabelgeschirr** *nt* MECHAN harness

kabelgeschlagen *adj* WASSERTRANS *Tauwerk* cable-laid

Kabel: **Kabelgestell** *nt* ELEKTROTECH cable rack; **Kabelgraben** *m* ELEKTRIZ, ELEKTROTECH cable trench, cable trough; **Kabelhalterung** *f* KFZTECH cable support; **Kabelisolator** *m* ELEKTROTECH cable insulator, cable isolator; **Kabelisolierer** *m* ELEKTROTECH cable insulator, cable isolator; **Kabelisolierung** *f* ELEKTRIZ, ELEKTROTECH cable covering, cable insulation; **Kabeljacke** *f* ELEKTRIZ jacket; **Kabel-Kammzug-Konverter** *m* TEXTIL tow-to-top converter; **Kabelkanal** *m* ELEKTROTECH cable conduit, cable duct, KERNTECH raceway; **Kabelkanal des Luftschraubenblattes** *m* LUFTTRANS *Hubschrauber* blade duct; **Kabelkasten** *m* ELEKTROTECH cable box; **Kabelkeller** *m* TELEKOM underground chamber; **Kabelkette** *f* MASCHINEN chain cable, WASSERTRANS *Festmachen* cable chain; **Kabelklemme** *f* ELEKTRIZ armor clamp (AmE), armour clamp (BrE), cable clip, clamp, ELEKTROTECH cable clamp, cable lug, KFZTECH *KFZ-Elektrik* cable clip, MECHAN cable clamp; **Kabelkompaktierung** *f* OPTIK tight buffering; **Kabelkopf** *m* ELEKTROTECH cable head, FERTIG *Kunststoffinstallationen* cable plug; **Kabelkran** *m* TRANS cableway; **Kabellänge** *f* WASSERTRANS *Marinemaßeinheit* cable, cable length; **Kabellauf** *m* ELEKTRIZ cable run; **Kabelleger** *m* KFZTECH cable ship; **Kabellegeschiff** *nt* TELEKOM cable ship; **Kabellegung** *f* ELEKTROTECH cabling; **Kabellehre** *f* ELEKTROTECH cable gage (AmE), cable gauge (BrE); **Kabelleitungsdurchführung** *f* ELEKTROTECH grommet; **Kabellogcomputerprogramm** *nt* COMP & DV, ERDÖL *Meßtechnik*, LABOR program for computer processing of wireline logs; **Kabellöter** *m* TELEKOM cable jointer; **Kabelmantel** *m* ELEKTROTECH cable sheath; **Kabelmeßbrücke** *f* GERÄT post office bridge box; **Kabelmesser** *nt* BAU hacking knife, RAUMFAHRT

Raumschiff cable cutter; **Kabelmontage** *f* TELEKOM cable assembly; **Kabelmuffe** *f* BAU, ELEKTRIZ cable joint box, ELEKTROTECH cable fitting, cable joint box; **Kabelnachricht** *f* ELEKTROTECH cablegram; **Kabelnetz** *nt* ELEKTROTECH, FERNSEH cable network, cabled network; **Kabelortungsgerät** *nt* ELEKTRIZ cable detector, cable locator; **Kabelöse** *f* ELEKTROTECH cable lug; **Kabelpaar** *nt* COMP & DV cable pair; **Kabelprüfdraht** *m* ELEKTROTECH pilot wire; **Kabelrepeater** *m* ELEKTROTECH cable repeater; **Kabelrohr** *nt* ELEKTROTECH conduit; **Kabelrost** *m* ELEKTROTECH cable rack; **Kabelrundfunk** *m* FERNSEH wired broadcasting; **Kabelschacht** *m* ELEKTROTECH cable shaft, TELEKOM cable manhole; **Kabelschelle** *f* ELEKTRIZ, ELEKTROTECH cable clamp, cable clip; **Kabelschirm** *m* ELEKTRIZ cable screen; **Kabelschuh** *m* ELEKTROTECH cable lug, terminal; **Kabelschutz** *m* ELEKTRIZ armor (AmE), armour (BrE); **Kabelschutzrohr** *nt* ELEKTROTECH cable conduit; **Kabelseele** *f* ELEKTROTECH, KUNSTSTOFF cable core; **Kabelsendung** *f* FERNSEH cable transmission; **Kabelspanner** *m* ELEKTROTECH cable tensioner; **Kabelspleißung** *f* ELEKTRIZ cable joint, cable splicing, cable splicing, TELEKOM cable joint; **Kabelstück** *nt* ELEKTROTECH cable section; **Kabelstumpf** *m* ELEKTROTECH cable end; **Kabelsuchgerät** *nt* ELEKTRIZ cable detector; **Kabeltrommel** *f* BAU, ELEKTRIZ, ELEKTROTECH, VERPACK cable drum; **Kabelummantelung** *f* KUNSTSTOFF cable covering, cable sheathing; **Kabelverbinder** *m* ELEKTRIZ, ELEKTROTECH cable connector, cable fitting; **Kabelverbindung** *f* ELEKTROTECH cable coupling, FERNSEH cable link, TELEKOM cable communication, cable joint; **Kabelverlegung** *f* ELEKTRIZ, ELEKTROTECH, TELEKOM cable laying; **Kabelverschraubung** *f* FERTIG *Kunststoffinstallationen* cable connection; **Kabelverstärker** *m* ELEKTROTECH cable repeater; **Kabelverteiler** *m* ELEKTROTECH cable junction; **Kabelverteilpunkt** *m* ELEKTROTECH cable junction; **Kabelverzweiger** *m* ELEKTROTECH cable distributor, distribution cabinet, terminal box; **Kabelverzweigerkasten** *m* TELEKOM cross-connect cabinet; **Kabelverzweigung** *f* ELEKTROTECH cable distribution point; **Kabelverzweigungspunkt** *m* ELEKTROTECH cable distribution point; **Kabelweg** *m* ELEKTRIZ cable run; **Kabelwinde** *f* ELEKTROTECH cable winch; **Kabelzuschlag** *m* TELEKOM slack

Kabine *f* TRANS *eines Aufzugs* car, WASSERTRANS cabin, stateroom; **Kabinenbandrollsteig** *m* LUFTTRANS cabin-type moving pavement (BrE), cabin-type moving sidewalk (AmE); **Kabinendruck** *m* LUFTTRANS, RAUMFAHRT *Raumschiff* cabin pressure; **Kabinenförderband** *nt* LUFTTRANS cabin conveyer; **Kabinenhöhe** *f* LUFTTRANS cabin altitude; **Kabinenhöhenmesser** *m* LUFTTRANS cabin altimeter; **Kabinenkreuzer** *m* WASSERTRANS *Schifftyp* cabin cruiser; **Kabinenschwebekorb** *m* TRANS *Bauwesen* cabin pulley cradle; **Kabinenstehhöhe** *f* WASSERTRANS *Schiffbau* cabin headroom

Kabinettprojektion *f* KONSTZEICH cabinet projection
K-Absorptionskante *f* KERNTECH K-absorption edge
Kachel *f* BAU tile
kacheln *vt* BAU tile
Kadmieren *nt* METALL cadmium plating
Kadmium *nt* (*Cd*) CHEMIE cadmium (*Cd*); **Kadmiumamalgam-Kryptomat** *nt* KERNTECH kryptonate of cadmium amalgam; **Kadmiumbatterie** *f* ELEKTRIZ

cadmium cell
kadmium-beschichtet *adj* MECHAN cadmium-plated
Kadmium: **Kadmiumblende** *f* FERTIG greenockite; **Kadmiumelement** *nt* FERTIG cadmium cell; **Kadmiumsulfidzelle** *f* ELEKTRIZ cadmium sulfide cell (AmE), cadmium sulphide cell (BrE); **Kadmiumzelle** *f* ELEKTRIZ cadmium cell

Käfig *m* ELEKTRIZ, ELEKTROTECH cage, squirrel cage, FERTIG *Lager* retainer, MASCHINEN cage; **Käfiganker** *m* ELEKTROTECH (*Käfigläufer*) cage rotor, ELEKTROTECH squirrel cage rotor; **Käfigläufer** *m* ELEKTRIZ cage armature, ELEKTROTECH cage rotor, ELEKTROTECH squirrel cage rotor; **Käfigläufermotor** *m* ELEKTRIZ, ELEKTROTECH squirrel cage motor; **Käfigrelais** *nt* ELEKTROTECH cage relay; **Käfigwicklung** *f* ELEKTROTECH squirrel cage winding
Kahlerit *m* KERNTECH kahlerite
Kahn *m* LABOR *Analyse* boat
Kai *m* WASSERTRANS dock, quay, wharf; **Kaibahn** *f* EISENBAHN quayside railroad (AmE), quayside railway (BrE); **Kaibandförderer** *m* TRANS quayside conveyor
Kainit *m* FERTIG kainite
Kaistraße *f* TRANS quayside roadway
Kajüte *f* WASSERTRANS cabin; **Kajütenaufbau** *m* WASSERTRANS *Schiffbau* cabin roof
Kajütsboden *m* WASSERTRANS *Schiffbau* cabin sole
Kalander *m* KUNSTSTOFF, PAPIER, TEXTIL calender; **Kalanderfolie** *f* KUNSTSTOFF calendered film; **Kalanderwalze** *f* PAPIER bowl, calender roll; **Kalanderwalzensatz** *m* PAPIER calender stack; **Kalanderwasserkasten** *m* PAPIER calender water box
Kalandria *f* KERNTECH calandria; **Kalandriagefäß** *nt* KERNTECH calandria
Kalandrieren *nt* KUNSTSTOFF, PAPIER calendering
kalandrieren *vt* KUNSTSTOFF calender, VERPACK *Papier* glaze
Kalfaterer *m* WASSERTRANS caulker
kalfatern *vt* WASSERTRANS *Schiffbau* caulk
Kalfaterung *f* WASSERTRANS *Schiffbau* caulked joint
Kalialaun *m* CHEMIE potash alum
Kaliapparat *m* LABOR potash bulb
Kaliatron-Oszillator *m* RADIO *VFO-Typ* Kaliatron oscillator
Kaliber *nt* ERDÖL caliber (AmE), calibre (BrE), FERTIG groove, *Walzen* pass, MASCHINEN bore, caliber (AmE), calibre (BrE), MECHAN gage (AmE), gauge (BrE), PAPIER groove; **Kaliberfolge** *f* FERTIG *Walzen* passes and reductions; **Kaliberlehre** *f* METROL ring gage (AmE), ring gauge (BrE); **Kaliberlog** *nt* ERDÖL *Bohrlochmeßtechnik* caliber log (AmE), calibre log (BrE); **Kaliberwalze** *f* FERTIG, PAPIER grooved roll
Kalibrator *m* HEIZ & KÄLTE calibrator
Kalibrierdruck *m* LUFTTRANS calibration pressure
Kalibriereinrichtung *f* ELEKTRONIK, GERÄT calibration equipment, calibrator
Kalibrieren *nt* ERDÖL *Meßtechnik* calibration, FERTIG end sizing, LABOR, METROL *bei Glasmeßgeräten*, PAPIER calibration
kalibrieren *vt* BAU size, ELEKTRIZ calibrate, FERTIG size, LABOR, MASCHINEN, PAPIER calibrate
Kalibriermeßeinheit *f* LUFTTRANS calibration module
Kalibriermodul *nt* LUFTTRANS calibration module
Kalibriernachweis *m* QUAL documented verification of calibration
Kalibriernormal *nt* QUAL calibration standard
Kalibrierplakette *f* QUAL calibration tag

kalibriert[1] *adj* ERDÖL gaged (AmE), gauged (BrE), FERTIG scaled, MASCHINEN calibrated, PAPIER grooved

kalibriert:[2] **~e Bohrung** *f* ERDÖL *Meßtechnik* gaged orifice (AmE), gauged orifice (BrE); **~e Drossel** *f* ERDÖL *Meßtechnik* gaged restriction (AmE), gauged restriction (BrE)

Kalibrierung *f* COMP & DV, ELEKTRIZ, ELEKTRONIK *von Meßgeräten* calibration, FERTIG *Walzen* grooving, matrix, KERNTECH, LUFTTRANS, MASCHINEN *einer Feder*, PHYS, STRAHLPHYS, WELLPHYS calibration; **~ eines Radars** *f* WELLPHYS radar calibration; **~ des Signalgebers** *f* ELEKTRONIK signal generator calibration

Kaliglas *nt* KER & GLAS potash glass

Kalisalpeter *m* CHEMIE *Kaliumnitrat* potash niter (AmE), potash nitre (BrE), saltpeter (AmE), saltpetre (BrE); **Kalisalpeterverfahren** *nt* KERNTECH saltpeter process (AmE), saltpetre process (BrE)

Kalisalz *nt* CHEMIE potash

Kalium *nt (K)* CHEMIE potassium *(K)*; **Kaliumalaun** *m* CHEMIE potash alum; **Kaliumaluminiumsulfat** *nt* CHEMIE potash alum, potassium aluminium; **Kaliumcarbonat** *nt* CHEMIE potash; **Kaliumchlorat** *nt* CHEMIE potassium chlorate; **Kaliumchlorid** *nt* CHEMIE potassium chloride; **Kaliumchromalaun** *m* CHEMIE chrome alum; **Kaliumchromsulfat** *nt* CHEMIE chrome alum; **Kaliumcyanid** *nt* CHEMIE potassium cyanide; **Kaliumhydrogentartrat** *nt* CHEMIE tartar; **Kaliumhydroxid** *nt* CHEMIE potash, potassium hydroxide; **Kaliummanganat** *nt* CHEMIE potassium manganate, potassium permanganate; **Kaliumnitrat** *nt* CHEMIE *Kalisalpeter* niter (AmE), nitre (BrE), potassium nitrate, LEBENSMITTEL potassium nitrate; **Kaliumoxid** *nt* CHEMIE potash, potassium oxide; **Kaliumpermanganat** *nt* CHEMIE potassium manganate, potassium permanganate

Kalk *m* BAU, ERDÖL, FERTIG, KER & GLAS, KOHLEN, LEBENSMITTEL *Mineral* lime; **Kalkablagerung** *f* LEBENSMITTEL lime scale; **Kalkanreicherung von Seen** *f* UMWELTSCHMUTZ lake liming

kalkbehandelt: ~er Bohrschlamm *m* ERDÖL *Bohrtechnik* lime-treated mud

Kalk: Kalkbohrschlamm *m* ERDÖL *Bohrtechnik* lime mud

Kalken *nt* BAU limewashing, liming, whitewashing

kalkhaltig: ~er Ton *m* WASSERVERSORG chalky clay; **~es Wasser** *nt* WASSERVERSORG hard water

Kalk: Kalkhydrat *nt* BAU hydrated lime; **Kalkkaseinfarbe** *f* KUNSTSTOFF distemper; **Kalkmilch** *f* BAU, FERTIG whitewash; **Kalkscheidepfanne** *f* LEBENSMITTEL *Zuckerfabrikation* liming tank; **Kalkscheidung** *f* LEBENSMITTEL *Zuckerfabrikation* lime defecation; **Kalkschlamm** *m* KER & GLAS lime slurry; **Kalkstein** *m* BAU, FERTIG, KER & GLAS limestone, LEBENSMITTEL calcium carbonate; **Kalktuff** *m* BAU tufa; **Kalktünche** *f* BAU limewash

Kalkulation *f* GEOM calculation

Kalkung *f* CHEMTECH Zucker, LEBENSMITTEL *zur Gewinnung des Scheidesaftes in der Zuckerherstellung* defecation

Kalk: Kalkverfestigung *f* BAU lime stabilization; **Kalkzuschlag** *m* METALL limestone flux

Kalman-Filter *nt* ELEKTRONIK Kalman filter; **Kalman-Filterung** *f* ELEKTRONIK Kalman filtering

Kalmen *f pl* WASSERTRANS *Tiefdruckgürtel um Äquator* doldrums

Kalomel *nt* CHEMIE, ELEKTRIZ calomel; **Kalomelelektrode** *f* ELEKTRIZ calomel electrode

Kalorie *f* ERGON, LABOR cal, calorie, LEBENSMITTEL cal, calorie, energy

kalorienarm *adj* LEBENSMITTEL low-calorie, low-energy

Kalorie: Kalorienverbrauch *m* LEBENSMITTEL caloric expenditure; **Kalorienzufuhr** *f* ERGON caloric intake

Kalorimeter *nt* GERÄT, LABOR, MASCHINEN, PHYS, THERMOD calorimeter; **~ zum Hadronnachweis** *nt* STRAHLPHYS, TEILPHYS hadronic calorimeter; **Kalorimeterbombe** *f* LABOR *Hitzemessung* calorimetric bomb

Kalorimetrie *f* PHYS, THERMOD calorimetry

kalorimetrisch[1] *adj* CHEMIE calorimetric

kalorimetrisch:[2] **~e Bombe** *f* GERÄT bomb calorimeter; **~es Thermometer** *nt* THERMOD calorimetric thermometer

kalorisch *adj* PHYS, THERMOD calorific

Kalorisieren *nt* FERTIG aluminium impregnation (BrE), aluminum impregnation (AmE)

kalorisieren *vt* FERTIG aluminium-impregnate (BrE), aluminum-impregnate (AmE)

Kalotte *f* FERTIG spherical surface; **Kalottenfläche** *f* FERTIG impression

Kalt- *pref* ANSTRICH, MASCHINEN, MECHAN cold

kalt[1] *adj* ANSTRICH cold, cool, ELEKTROTECH cold, HEIZ & KÄLTE cold, dry, KERNTECH, KOHLEN, KUNSTSTOFF, METALL, THERMOD cold; **~ eingesenkt** *adj* FERTIG hobbed; **~ gewalzt und ausgeglüht** *adj (CRCA)* METALL cold-rolled and annealed *(CRCA)*; **~ gezogen** *adj* THERMOD cold-drawn; **~ verformt** *adj* THERMOD cold-forged

kalt:[2] **~er Bereich** *m* LUFTTRANS *eines Strahltriebwerkes* cold section; **~er Biegeversuch** *m* METALL cold bend test; **~es Fließen** *nt* KUNSTSTOFF cold flow; **~er Fluß** *m* THERMOD cold creep; **~er Gehalt** *m* KOHLEN cold content; **~e Kathode** *f* ELEKTROTECH cold cathode; **~es Leuchten** *nt* ELEKTROTECH, FERNSEH luminescence; **~e Lötstelle** *f* ELEKTRIZ dry joint, MASCHINEN dry joint, dry solder joint; **~e Quelle** *f* KERNTECH cold source; **~er Reaktor** *m* KERNTECH cold reactor; **~e Verbindungsstelle** *f* ELEKTRIZ, GERÄT *beim Thermoelement* cold junction

kalt:[3] **~ abtrennen** *vt* MASCHINEN cold-shear; **~ härten** *vt* THERMOD cold-harden; **~ nieten** *vt* FERTIG clinch; **~ verformen** *vt* THERMOD cold-forge

kaltabbindend: ~er Klebstoff *m* KUNSTSTOFF cold setting adhesive

kaltaushärten *vt* FERTIG age at room temperature

Kalt-: Kaltbearbeitung *f* ANSTRICH cold work; **Kaltbiegen** *nt* MECHAN cold bending; **Kaltbiegeprobe** *f* MASCHINEN cold-bending test

kaltbrüchig: ~es Eisen *nt* METALL cold-short iron

Kalt-: Kaltbrüchigkeit *f* THERMOD cold brittleness

Kälte *f* HEIZ & KÄLTE cold, low temperature, refrigerating, THERMOD cold strength, coldness, cold, low temperature, refrigerating, VERPACK refrigerating; **Kälteanlage** *f* HEIZ & KÄLTE, THERMOD refrigerating plant, VERPACK refrigeration machine; **Kältebad** *nt* HEIZ & KÄLTE cryogenic bath

kältebeständig *adj* HEIZ & KÄLTE antifreezing, nonfreezing, LUFTTRANS antifreezing

Kälte: Kältebeständigkeit *f* THERMOD temperature resistance; **Kältechemie** *f* HEIZ & KÄLTE cryochemistry; **Kältedämmung** *f* THERMOD low-temperature insulation; **Kältefach** *nt* HEIZ & KÄLTE low-temperature compartment; **Kältefestigkeit** *f* KUNSTSTOFF low-temperature resistance, WERKPRÜF low temperature toughness

kalteinsenken *vt* FERTIG broach

Kälte: **Kälteisolierung** *f* THERMOD low-temperature insulation; **Kältekompressor** *m* HEIZ & KÄLTE chiller, refrigerating compressor; **Kältekreislauf** *m* HEIZ & KÄLTE refrigeration cycle; **Kältelagerraum** *m* HEIZ & KÄLTE chill room; **Kältemaschine** *f* HEIZ & KÄLTE, THERMOD refrigerating machine; **Kältemischung** *f* HEIZ & KÄLTE, THERMOD freezing mixture, frigorific mixture; **Kältemittel** *nt* HEIZ & KÄLTE cryogen, cryogenic fluid, refrigerant, refrigerating medium, KFZTECH, MASCHINEN, THERMOD, UMWELTSCHMUTZ refrigerant; **Kältemittelkreislauf** *m* HEIZ & KÄLTE refrigerant circuit; **Kältemittelverdichter** *m* MASCHINEN refrigerant compressor

Kalt-: **Kaltendvergütung** *f* KER & GLAS cold-end coating

Kälte: **Kälteofen** *m* LABOR refrigerated oven; **Kälteraum** *m* HEIZ & KÄLTE cold chamber, cold room; **Kälteschrank** *m* HEIZ & KÄLTE cold chamber, refrigeration cabinet; **Kälteschrumpfung** *f* THERMOD contraction due to cold; **Kältetechnik** *f* COMP & DV cryogenics, HEIZ & KÄLTE cryogenics, refrigeration, refrigeration engineering, LEBENSMITTEL refrigeration engineering, PHYS, RAUMFAHRT *Raumschiff*, THERMOD cryogenics; **Kältetechniker** *m* HEIZ & KÄLTE refrigeration engineer, THERMOD refrigerating engineer

kältetechnisch *adj* PHYS cryogenic

Kälte: **Kälteturbine** *f* HEIZ & KÄLTE, LUFTTRANS expansion turbine; **Kälteverhalten** *nt* HEIZ & KÄLTE low-temperature characteristics, KUNSTSTOFF low-temperature performance, MASCHINEN low-temperature behavior (AmE), low-temperature behaviour (BrE); **Kältezentrale** *f* HEIZ & KÄLTE refrigeration control center (AmE), refrigeration control centre (BrE)

Kalt-: **Kaltfließen** *nt* KUNSTSTOFF cold flow, creep; **Kaltfließvermögen** *nt* MECHAN cold flow; **Kaltfluß** *m* MECHAN cold flow; **Kaltform** *f* KER & GLAS cold mold (AmE), cold mould (BrE); **Kaltformen** *nt* FERTIG cold working, KUNSTSTOFF cold molding (AmE), cold moulding (BrE); **Kaltfront** *f* WASSERTRANS *Wetter* cold front; **Kaltgasblasen** *nt* FERTIG gas quenching; **Kaltgasschubsystem** *nt* RAUMFAHRT *Raumschiff* cold gas thrust system

kaltgeformt: **~es Holz** *nt* WASSERTRANS *Schiffbau* cold-molded wood (AmE), cold-moulded wood (BrE)

Kalt-: **Kaltgesenk** *nt* MASCHINEN cold die

kaltgewalzt[1] *adj* THERMOD cold-rolled

kaltgewalzt:[2] **~er Träger** *m* THERMOD cold-rolled joist

kaltgezogen: **~er Stahldraht** *m* METALL cold-draw steel wire

Kalt-: **Kaltgießen** *nt* THERMOD cold casting; **Kalthämmern** *nt* METALL cold hammering; **Kalthärtbarkeit** *f* FERTIG strain-hardening ability; **Kalthärten** *nt* KUNSTSTOFF cold setting

kalthärtend: **~er Klebstoff** *m* KUNSTSTOFF cold setting adhesive

Kalt-: **Kalthärtung** *f* METALL strain hardening; **Kaltkanalwerkzeug** *nt* KUNSTSTOFF cold runner mold (AmE), cold runner mould (BrE); **Kaltkathodenröhre** *f* ELEKTRONIK cold cathode tube; **Kaltkautschuk** *m* KUNSTSTOFF cold rubber; **Kaltkleben** *nt* THERMOD cold bonding

kaltkleben *vt* THERMOD cold-bond

Kalt-: **Kaltklebestelle** *f* THERMOD cold bond; **Kaltlagerung** *f* LEBENSMITTEL cold storage; **Kaltlagerungsschaden** *m* LEBENSMITTEL cold storage injury; **Kaltleimsystem** *nt* VERPACK cold glueing system; **Kaltlötstelle** *f* ELEKTROTECH cold junction; **Kaltluftgefrieren** *nt* LEBENSMITTEL blast freezing

kaltlufttrocknen *vt* THERMOD dry by cold air

Kalt-: **Kaltluftturbulenzen** *f pl (CAT)* LUFTTRANS cold air turbulence *(CAT)*; **Kaltluftvorhang** *m* HEIZ & KÄLTE air curtain; **Kaltmeißel** *m* MASCHINEN cold chisel

kaltprägen *vt* METALL cold-stamp

Kalt-: **Kaltpressen** *nt* KUNSTSTOFF cold molding (AmE), cold moulding (BrE), MASCHINEN cold forging; **Kaltpreßschweißen** *nt* BAU, MASCHINEN, MECHAN cold pressure welding; **Kaltrauch** *m* LEBENSMITTEL cold smoke; **Kaltrecken** *nt* MECHAN cold drawing, cold working

kaltrecken *vt* METALL cold-hammer

Kalt-: **Kaltriß** *m* KER & GLAS crizzle, WERKPRÜF cold crack; **Kaltrißanfälligkeit** *f* WERKPRÜF cold cracking risk; **Kaltsäge** *f* MASCHINEN cold saw; **Kaltsatz** *m* DRUCK cold type; **Kaltschere** *f* MASCHINEN cold shears; **Kaltschweißstelle** *f* FERTIG shut; **Kaltsprödigkeit** *f* THERMOD cold brittleness

Kaltstart *m* COMP & DV, ELEKTRIZ, KFZTECH, MASCHINEN, THERMOD cold start; **Kaltstartlampe** *f* ELEKTRIZ cold-start lamp; **Kaltstartvorrichtung** *f* KFZTECH *Motor, Vergaser* cold-start device; **Kaltstartzug** *m* KFZTECH choke

Kalt-: **Kaltverfestigung** *f* FERTIG strain hardening, work hardening, MECHAN cold working, METALL strain hardening; **Kaltverfestigungskoeffizient** *m* METALL work-hardening coefficient; **Kaltvulkanisation** *f* FERTIG acid cure; **Kaltvulkanisieren** *nt* THERMOD cold curing

kaltvulkanisieren *vt* THERMOD cold-cure

kaltvulkanisiert *adj* THERMOD cold-cured

Kalt-: **Kaltwalzen** *nt* METALL, THERMOD cold rolling

kaltwalzen *vt* METALL, THERMOD cold-roll

Kalt-: **Kaltwassereinbruch** *m* KERNTECH intrusion of cold water; **Kaltwiderstand** *m* ELEKTROTECH cold resistance

kaltzäh: **~er Stahl** *m* METALL tough-at-subzero steel

Kalt-: **Kaltziehen** *nt* MASCHINEN, MECHAN, METALL, THERMOD cold drawing

kaltziehen *vt* METALL, THERMOD cold-draw

Kalzinieren *nt* METALL calcination

kalzinieren *vt* FERTIG calcinate, KOHLEN calcine

Kalzinierofen *m* KOHLEN calcining kiln

kalziniert *adj* METALL calcined

Kalzinierung *f* ABFALL calcination

Kalziumkarbid *nt* FERTIG carbide

Kamee *f* KER & GLAS cameo

Kamera *f* ELEKTRONIK, FERNSEH, FOTO, RADIO camera; **~ mit abnehmbaren Mattscheibensucher** *f* FOTO camera with detachable reflex viewfinder; **~ mit auswechselbarem Objektiv** *f* FOTO camera with interchangeable lens; **~ mit Blendenverschluß** *f* FOTO camera with diaphragm shutter; **~ mit eckigen Balgen** *f* FOTO square bellows camera; **~ mit gekoppeltem Belichtungsmesser** *f* FOTO camera with coupled exposure meter; **~ mit gekoppeltem Entfernungsmesser** *f* FOTO camera with coupled rangefinder; **~ mit großem Balgenauszug** *f* FOTO camera with large bellows extension; **~ mit kurzem Balgenauszug** *f* FOTO camera with short bellows extension; **~ mit Spiegelreflex-Fo-**

kussierung *f* FOTO camera with mirror reflex focusing; ~ **mit versenkbarer Objektivfassung** *f* FOTO camera with collapsible mount; ~ **mit verstellbarer und schwenkbarer Standarte** *f* FOTO camera with rising and swinging front; ~ **mit Zeitautomatik** *f* FOTO aperture priority camera; **Kameraanpassung** *f* FERNSEH camera matching; **Kameraaufstellung** *f* FERNSEH camera line up; **Kameraauszug** *m* FOTO camera extension; **Kamerafassung** *f* FOTO camera mount; **Kameragehäuse** *nt* FOTO camera body, camera housing; **Kamerahülle** *f* FOTO covering; **Kamerakanal** *m* FERNSEH camera channel; **Kamerakette** *f* FERNSEH camera chain; **Kamerakommandosystem** *nt* FERNSEH camera prompting system; **Kameramann** *m* FERNSEH cameraman; **Kameramonitor** *m* FERNSEH camera monitor; **Kameraneiger** *m* FOTO tilt head; **Kameraröhre** *f* FERNSEH camera tube; **Kameraröhre mit hochwertiger Gradation** *f* ELEKTRONIK high-gamma camera tube; **Kameraschwenk-Potentiometer** *nt* AUFNAHME pan pot; **Kamerasignal** *nt* FERNSEH camera signal; **Kamerastativ** *nt* FOTO camera stand; **Kamerasteuerung** *f* FERNSEH camera control unit; **Kameraumschaltung** *f* FERNSEH camera switching; **Kamerawagen** *m* FERNSEH dolly

Kamin *m* BAU stack, HEIZ & KÄLTE chimney flue, THERMOD flue; **Kamineinsatzrohr** *nt* HEIZ & KÄLTE flue lining; **Kaminschacht** *m* BAU shaft; **Kaminwirkung** *f* HEIZ & KÄLTE chimney effect; **Kaminzug** *m* BAU draft (AmE), draught (BrE)

Kamm *m* BAU ridge, NICHTFOSS ENERG *Wellenkamm* crest, TEXTIL comb, reed

Kämmaschine *f* TEXTIL combing machine

Kamm: **Kammelektrode** *f* RAUMFAHRT *Raumschiff* comb-shaped electrode

Kämmen *nt* FERTIG, MASCHINEN intermeshing, mating, TEXTIL combing

kämmen[1] *vt* FERTIG *Zahnräder* intermesh, TEXTIL comb

kämmen[2] *vi* MASCHINEN mate, mesh, pitch

kämmend *adj* FERTIG *Zahnräder* intermeshing

Kammer *f* ABFALL chamber, BAU cavity, CHEMTECH chamber, KUNSTSTOFF cabinet, LABOR cell, MASCHINEN, MECHAN chamber, WASSERVERSORG coffer; **Kammerfilterpresse** *f* ABFALL chamber filter press; **Kammermauer** *f* WASSERVERSORG side wall; **Kammerofen** *m* HEIZ & KÄLTE box furnace, THERMOD batch furnace; **Kammersäure** *f* CHEMTECH chamber acid; **Kammerschleuse** *f* WASSERVERSORG lift lock; **Kammerton** *m* AUFNAHME standard pitch; **Kammertongenerator** *m* AUFNAHME standard tone generator; **Kammerwand** *f* WASSERVERSORG side wall

Kamm: **Kammfilter** *nt* ELEKTRONIK *Mikrowellentechnik* comb filter; **Kammfilterung** *f* ELEKTRONIK comb filtering

Kammgarn *nt* TEXTIL combed yarn, worsted yarn; **Kammgarnanzugstoff** *m* TEXTIL worsted suiting, worsted yarn; **Kammgarnnumerierung** *f* TEXTIL worsted count, worsted yarn

Kamm: **Kammhöhe** *f* NICHTFOSS ENERG *Wellenkamm* crest height; **Kammlager** *nt* MASCHINEN multicollar thrust bearing; **Kammwalze** *f* FERTIG *Walzen* pinion, TEXTIL porcupine; **Kammzug** *m* TEXTIL *Spinnen* top; **Kammzugfärben** *nt* TEXTIL top dyeing

kammzuggefärbt *adj* TEXTIL top-dyed

Kämpfer *m* BAU impost, transom, traverse, *eines Bogens* springer; **Kämpferholz** *nt* BAU *Fenster* impost; **Kämpferlinie** *f* BAU springing line; **Kämpferschicht** *f* BAU

springing course; **Kämpferstein** *m* BAU springer stone

Kampfhubschrauber *m* LUFTTRANS combat helicopter

Kampfverband *m* WASSERTRANS *Marine* task force

Kanal *m* AUFNAHME, BAU, COMP & DV, ELEKTRONIK, ELEKTROTECH, FERNSEH channel, FERTIG duct, flue, HEIZ & KÄLTE duct, HYDRAUL port, KER & GLAS *des Tafelglas-Wannenofens* canal, KOHLEN, KONTROLL channel, MASCHINEN channel, duct, passage, MECHAN channel, NICHTFOSS ENERG channel, conduit, RADIO, STRÖMPHYS channel, TELEKOM duct, WASSERTRANS canal, channel; **Kanalabgleich** *m* AUFNAHME channel phasing; **Kanalabschnitt** *m* WASSERVERSORG reach; **Kanalabstand** *m* COMP & DV, FERNSEH channel spacing, TELEKOM interchannel spacing; **Kanaladapter** *m* COMP & DV channel adaptor; **Kanaladreßwort** *nt* *(KAW)* COMP & DV channel address word *(CAW)*; **Kanalaufteilung** *f* TELEKOM channeling (AmE), channelling (BrE); **Kanalausnutzung** *f* TELEKOM channel efficiency; **Kanalbandbreite** *f* FERNSEH channel bandwidth; **Kanalbau** *m* WASSERVERSORG canalization; **Kanalbefehlswort** *nt* COMP & DV channel command word; **Kanalbelastung** *f* TELEKOM channel loading; **Kanalbelegung** *f* TELEKOM channel occupancy; **Kanalbildung** *f* NICHTFOSS ENERG chaneling (AmE), channelling (BrE); **Kanalboot** *nt* WASSERTRANS *Schifftyp* canal boat; **Kanalbündelung** *f* TELEKOM trunking; **Kanaldotierung** *f* ELEKTRONIK channel doping

Kanäle[1] *m pl* HEIZ & KÄLTE ducting

Kanäle:[2] **mit Kanälen** *adj* FERTIG ported

Kanäle:[3] **in Kanälen fortleiten** *vt* HEIZ & KÄLTE duct away

Kanal: **Kanaleinfahrt** *f* WASSERTRANS canal entrance; **Kanaleinrichtung** *f* TELEKOM channel equipment; **Kanalfilter** *nt* ELEKTRONIK channel filter; **Kanalhaltung** *f* WASSERVERSORG reach

Kanalisation *f* ABFALL drain system, sewer system, sewerage system, WASSERVERSORG canalization, sewerage; **Kanalisationsnetz** *nt* WASSERVERSORG canalization, sewerage, sewerage system; **Kanalisationssystem** *nt* WASSERVERSORG canalization

kanalisieren *vt* WASSERVERSORG canalize

Kanal: **Kanalkapazität** *f* COMP & DV, TELEKOM channel capacity; **Kanalkohle** *f* KOHLEN channel coal; **Kanalkompensation** *f* AUFNAHME channel balancing; **Kanallandmarken** *f pl* WASSERTRANS channel marks; **Kanallänge** *f* NICHTFOSS ENERG length of channel; **Kanalrauschen** *nt* ELEKTRONIK channel noise; **Kanalroute** *f* WASSERTRANS channel track; **Kanalruß** *m* KUNSTSTOFF channel black; **Kanalschiffahrt** *f* WASSERTRANS canal transport; **Kanalschleuse** *f* WASSERVERSORG canal lock; **Kanalschleusentor** *nt* WASSERVERSORG canal lock gate; **Kanalsohle** *f* WASSERVERSORG canal bottom, channel bed, channel bottom, *künstlicher Kanal* canal bottom; **Kanalstatustabelle** *f* COMP & DV channel status table; **Kanalstatuswort** *nt* COMP & DV channel status word; **Kanalsteuerung** *f* TELEKOM channel control; **Kanalstopper** *m* ELEKTROTECH channel stopper; **Kanalstrahl** *m* KERNTECH PHYS canal ray; **Kanalstrahlenanalyse** *f* KERNTECH canal-ray analysis; **Kanalstrahlentladung** *f* KERNTECH canal-ray discharge; **Kanalströmung** *f* *(cf Rohrströmung)* STRÖMPHYS *Strömung im offenen Gerinne* channel flow, flow in channels; **Kanalsystem** *nt* HEIZ & KÄLTE duct system, ducting; **Kanaltrennfilter** *nt* ELEKTRONIK channel filter; **Kanaltrennung** *f* AUFNAHME channel separation; **Kanalumsetzung** *f* ELEKTRONIK *Trägerfrequenztech-*

nik channel modulation; **Kanalverstärker** *m* FERNSEH channel amplifier; **Kanalvocoder** *m* TELEKOM channel vocoder; **Kanalvorwahl** *f* FERNSEH presetting of channels; **Kanalwähler** *m* FERNSEH channel selector, TELEKOM channel selector, *Kanalselektion* tuner; **Kanalwählschalter** *m* AUFNAHME channel selector switch; **Kanalweiche** *f* TELEKOM channel branching filter; **Kanalzuweisung** *f* FERNSEH channel allocation; **Kanalzuweisungszeit** *f* TELEKOM channel allocation time; **Kanalzwischenraum** *m* COMP & DV channel spacing

Känguruh-Frachter *m* WASSERTRANS barge-carrying ship

Kanne: ~**sche Kammer** *f* KERNTECH *zur Überwachung radioaktiven Gases* Kanne chamber

Kannelkohle *f* KOHLEN cannel coal

Kännelkohle *f* KOHLEN kennel coal

Kanneneintauchkühler *m* LEBENSMITTEL in-can immersion cooler

Kannette *f* TEXTIL pirn

Kanone *f* MECHAN, PHYS barrel; **Kanonenbohrer** *m* - FERTIG cylinder bit, half-round bit; **Kanonenwirkungsgrad** *m* FERNSEH gun efficiency

kanonisch: ~**e Gesamtheit** *f* PHYS canonical ensemble; ~**e Gleichung** *f* PHYS canonical equation; ~**e Variable** *f* PHYS canonical variable

Kante:[1] **von ~ zu Kante** *adj* MASCHINEN edge-to-edge

Kante[2] *f* BAU corner, skirt, COMP & DV, GEOM edge, KÜNSTL INT *Graph* arc, *zwischen Knoten in Graph* edge, link, MASCHINEN edge, outline, PAPIER, PHYS, TEXTIL, VERPACK edge

Kanten: ~ **abschlagen** *vi* BAU spall

kanten *vt* BAU tip

Kante: **Kantenabschälen** *nt* KER & GLAS edge peeling; **Kantenbeschneiden mit Schneidstift** *nt* KER & GLAS pencil edging; **Kanteneffekt** *m* FOTO Eberhard effect, edge effect; **Kantenfeinschleifen** *nt* KER & GLAS edge fine-grinding; **Kantenfeuchter** *m* PAPIER edge spray, edging spray; **Kantenfließen** *nt* KER & GLAS edge creep; **Kantengummiermaschine** *f* VERPACK edge-gumming machine; **Kanteninterpretation** *f* KÜNSTL INT *im Bildverstehen* edge interpretation; **Kantenkorrosion** *f* WERKPRÜF edge corrosion; **Kantenplatte** *f* LUFTTRANS edging panel; **Kantenpressung** *f* MASCHINEN edge pressure; **Kantenriß** *m* KER & GLAS edge crack, edge fracture; **Kantenschliff** *m* KER & GLAS edging; **Kantenschloß** *nt* BAU flush lock; **Kantenschmelzen** *nt* KER & GLAS edge melting; **Kantenschneider** *m* PAPIER edge cutters; **Kantenschneidevorgang** *m* TEXTIL selvedge cutting process; **Kantenschutz** *m* VERPACK edge cushion, edge protection; **Kantenschutzschiene** *f* BAU nosing; **Kantenstein** *m* KER & GLAS edger block; **Kantenversetzung** *f* METALL edge dislocation; **Kantenvorbereitung** *f* MECHAN edge preparation; **Kantenwalze** *f* KER & GLAS edge bowl; **Kantenwalzen** *f pl* KER & GLAS edge rolls; **Kantenwirkung** *f* LUFTTRANS fringe effect

Kantholz *nt* BAU scantling, square timber

Kanvas *m* TEXTIL canvas

Kanzel *f* LUFTTRANS canopy, cockpit, WASSERTRANS *Deckausrüstung* pulpit

Kaolin *nt* DRUCK kaolin, KER & GLAS china clay, KUNSTSTOFF china clay, kaolin; **Kaolinerde** *f* DRUCK kaolin

Kaolinit *m* ERDÖL, KOHLEN, NICHTFOSS ENERG kaolinite

Kaolin: **Kaolinschlämmen** *nt* KER & GLAS china clay washing; **Kaolinsteinbruch** *m* KER & GLAS china clay

quarry

Kaon *nt* PHYS *Elementarteilchen*, TEILPHYS kaon

Kap[1] *nt* WASSERTRANS *Geographie* cape

Kap:[2] **von einem ~ freikommen** *vi* WASSERTRANS *Segeln, Sturm* weather a cape

Kapazitanz *f* ELEKTROTECH, HEIZ & KÄLTE capacitance

Kapazität *f* BAU *(C)*, ELEKTRIZ *(C)* capacitance, capacity *(C)*, ELEKTROTECH *(C)* capacitance, capacity, ERDÖL *(C)* capacitance, capacity *(C)*, FOTO *Batterie* ampere-hour capacity, HEIZ & KÄLTE *(C)* capacity *(C)*, PHYS *(C)*, RADIO *(C)*, TELEKOM *(C)* capacitance, capacity *(C)*; ~ **zwischen Elektroden** *f* RADIO interelectrode capacitance; ~ **einer Straße** *f* TRANS capacity of a road; ~ **unter vorherrschenden Bedingungen** *f* TRANS capacity under prevailing conditions; ~ **zwischen Wicklungen** *f* ELEKTRIZ interturn capacitance

kapazitätsarm *adj* GERÄT anticapacitance

Kapazität: **Kapazitätsbelastung** *f* VERPACK *des Förderbands* carrying capacity; **Kapazitätsbrücke** *f* ELEKTRIZ, GERÄT capacitance bridge; **Kapazitätsdiode** *f* PHYS capacitance diode, varactor diode

kapazitätsfrei[1] *adj* ELEKTRIZ, ELEKTROTECH noncapacitive

kapazitätsfrei:[2] ~ **Last** *f* ELEKTROTECH noncapacitive load

Kapazität: **Kapazitätskasten** *m* ELEKTROTECH capacitance box; **Kapazitätsklausel** *f* LUFTTRANS capacity clause; **Kapazitätskoeffizient** *m* PHYS capacitance coefficient; **Kapazitätskontrolle** *f* LUFTTRANS capacity control; **Kapazitätsmeßbrücke** *f* ELEKTRIZ capacity bridge, GERÄT capacitance bridge; **Kapazitätsmeßgerät** *nt* ELEKTROTECH capacitance meter, GERÄT capacitance measuring instrument; **Kapazitätsmessung** *f* OPTIK capacitance sensing; **Kapazitätsrelais** *nt* ELEKTRIZ capacitance relay; **Kapazitätsscheibe** *f* OPTIK *Scheibenkondensator* capacitance disc (BrE), capacitance disk (AmE); **Kapazitätsüberschreitung** *f* COMP & DV overflow

kapazitiv[1] *adj* ELEKTRIZ capacitive, ELEKTROTECH capacitance, capacitive, LABOR, PHYS, RADIO, TELEKOM capacitance; **nicht ~** *adj* ELEKTRIZ noncapacitive

kapazitiv:[2] ~**er Abschluß** *m* ELEKTROTECH capacitive load; ~**e Antennenanpassung** *f (ATC)* RADIO aerial-tuning capacitor, antenna-tuning capacitor *(ATC)*; ~**e Belastung** *f* ELEKTROTECH, TELEKOM capacitive load; ~**er Blindwiderstand** *m* ELEKTRIZ *(XC)* capacitive reactance *(XC)*, ELEKTROTECH capacitive reactance, negative reactance, PHYS capacitive reactance; ~**er Dehnungsmeßstreifen** *m* GERÄT capacitive strain gage (AmE), capacitive strain gauge (BrE); ~**es Dickenmeßgerät** *nt* GERÄT capacitive thickness gage (AmE), capacitive thickness gauge (BrE); ~**er Druckwandler** *m* PHYS CPT, capacitive pressure transducer; ~**es Feedback** *nt* ELEKTROTECH capacitive feedback; ~**e Komponente** *f* ELEKTRIZ capacitive component; ~**e Kopplung** *f* ELEKTRIZ capacitive coupling, ELEKTROTECH capacitance coupling, TELEKOM capacitive coupling; ~**er Kurzschlußkolben** *m* ELEKTROTECH choke plunger; ~**e Last** *f* ELEKTRIZ, ELEKTROTECH capacitive load; ~**e Reaktanz** *f* ELEKTRIZ capacitive reactance, ELEKTROTECH capacitive reactance, negative reactance, PHYS capacitive reactance; ~**e Rückkopplung** *f* ELEKTROTECH capacitive feedback; ~**er Spannungsteiler** *m* ELEKTROTECH capacitive voltage divider; ~**er Widerstand** *m* ELEKTROTECH capacitive resistance

Kapellenofen *m* HEIZ & KÄLTE assay furnace

Kapillar- *pref* FERTIG, KOHLEN, STRÖMPHYS capillary

kapillar[1] *adj* FERTIG, MASCHINEN capillary

kapillar:[2] **~es Wasser** *nt* KOHLEN capillary water

kapillaraktiv *adj* CHEMIE surface-active

kapillarbrechend: ~e Schicht *f* BAU *Straßenbau* anticapillary course

Kapillar-: **Kapillardruck** *m* STRÖMPHYS capillary pressure; **Kapillare** *f* ERDÖL, PHYS capillary tube, STRÖMPHYS capillary; **Kapillareffekt** *m* ERDÖL, PHYS capillary action; **Kapillarfusion** *f* KERNTECH capillary fusion; **Kapillarimeter** *nt* KOHLEN capillarimeter

Kapillarität *f* FERTIG, KOHLEN, PHYS, STRÖMPHYS capillarity; **Kapillaritätsbruchschicht** *f* KOHLEN capillarity breaking layer; **Kapillaritätszahl** *f* STRÖMPHYS capillary number

Kapillar-: **Kapillarkraft** *f* STRÖMPHYS capillary force; **Kapillar-Mengenstrommesser** *m* LABOR capillary flowmeter; **Kapillar-Rheometer** *nt* GERÄT capillary rheometer; **Kapillarrohr** *nt* HEIZ & KÄLTE capillary tube; **Kapillarröhrchen** *nt* LABOR, STRÖMPHYS capillary tube; **Kapillarsäule** *f* GERÄT *Gaschromatographie* capillary column; **Kapillar-Viskosimeter** *nt* CHEMTECH capillary viscometer, GERÄT capillary viscosimeter, LABOR *Flüssigkeitsdurchfluß* capillary viscometer; **Kapillarwellen** *f pl* STRÖMPHYS capillary waves; **Kapillarwirkung** *f* BAU, MASCHINEN, STRÖMPHYS capillarity, capillary action

Kapitälchen *nt pl* DRUCK small caps

Kapitalrückfluß *m* ERDÖL *Finanzen* return of assets

Kapitän *m* WASSERTRANS *Besatzung* captain; **Kapitänspatent** *nt* WASSERTRANS *Dokuments* master's certificate; **Kapitänsrang** *m* WASSERTRANS captaincy; **Kapitänsruf** *m* LUFTTRANS captain call

Kaplanschaufel *f* FERTIG kaplan blade

Kappdiode *f* ELEKTRONIK limiter diode

Kappe *f* ELEKTROTECH, HYDRAUL, MASCHINEN, MECHAN cap, WASSERVERSORG *eines Schleusentors* cap sill

Kappen *nt* COMP & DV scissoring, KÜNSTL INT *eines Baumes* pruning

Kappe: **Kappenaufsetzer** *m* VERPACK capper; **Kappendichtmasse** *f* VERPACK cap-sealing compound; **Kappenisolator** *m* ELEKTROTECH cap-and-pin insulator, cap-and-rod insulator; **Kappenmutter** *f* MECHAN cap nut; **Kappenpresse** *f* VERPACK capping press; **Kappensensor** *m* VERPACK missing cap detector; **Kappensiegelung** *f* VERPACK cap sealing; **Kappenversiegelungsmaschine** *f* VERPACK cap-sealing equipment

Kapplage *f* FERTIG backing bead

Kapsel *f* AKUSTIK enclosure, ELEKTROTECH cap, FERTIG case, LABOR capsule, MECHAN cap, PHYS enclosure, TELEKOM *Mikrofon* button; **Kapselfederdruckmeßglied** *nt* GERÄT diaphragm pressure element; **Kapselfeder-Manometer** *nt* GERÄT, METROL pneumatic capsule gage (AmE), pneumatic capsule gauge (BrE); **Kapselfederwirkdrucksensor** *m* GERÄT aneroid flowmeter; **Kapselgehäuse** *nt* HYDRAUL *Turbine* enclosed casing; **Kapselhöhenmesser** *m* LUFTTRANS aneroid altimeter; **Kapselmutter** *f* MECHAN cap nut

kapseln *vt* FERTIG case, seal

Kapselton *m* KER & GLAS sagger clay

Kapselung *f* ABFALL encapsulation, FERTIG containment

Karabinerhaken *m* MASCHINEN snap hook

Karat *nt* METALL carat (BrE), karat (AmE), METROL *Edelmetalle* carat (BrE), carat fine, karat (AmE), *Edelsteine* carat; **Karatgewicht** *nt* METROL caratage

Karayagummi *nt* LEBENSMITTEL crystal gum, karaya gum

Karbid *nt* FERTIG, MECHAN, METALL carbide

karbidbildend: ~er Zusatz *m* FERTIG carbide former

Karbid: **Karbidentstehung** *f* METALL carbide formation; **Karbidrißbildung** *f* METALL carbide cracking; **Karbidzelle** *f* FERTIG carbide band

Karbolinium *nt* FERTIG carbolinium

Karbon *nt* ERDÖL *Geologie* carboniferous

Karbonatation *f* CHEMIE carbonatation

Karbonisation *f* KOHLEN carbonization

karbonisieren *vt* KOHLEN, METALL carbonize, carburize

Karbonisierung *f* METALL carburization

Karbonitrieren *nt* FERTIG carbonitriting; **~ in Gas** *nt* FERTIG gas cyaniding

Karbonstahl *m* METALL high-carbon steel

Karborund *nt* FERTIG, MASCHINEN carborundum; **Karborundschleifscheibe** *f* FERTIG carborundum wheel

Karborundum *nt* FERTIG carborundum

karburieren *vt* CHEMIE, METALL carburet

karburierend *adj* METALL carbureting (AmE), carburetting (BrE)

karburiert *adj* METALL carbureted (AmE), carburetted (BrE)

Karburierung *f* METALL carburation, carbureting (AmE), carburetting (BrE)

Kardamomöl *nt* LEBENSMITTEL cardamom oil

Kardan- *pref* FERTIG cardan; **Kardanantrieb** *m* FERTIG cardan drive, universal drive; **Kardandrehzapfen** *m* MECHAN knuckle; **Kardangelenk** *nt* FERTIG cardan joint, KFZTECH *Triebstrang* universal joint, MASCHINEN cardan joint, gimbal joint, universal joint, MECHAN cardan joint

kardanisch:[1] **~ gelagert** *adj* RAUMFAHRT *Raumfahrttechnik* gimbal-mounted

kardanisch:[2] **~e Aufhängung** *f* MASCHINEN cardanic suspension, gimbal suspension, WASSERTRANS gimbal

Kardan-: **Kardanring** *m* FERTIG, MECHAN, WASSERTRANS gimbal; **Kardantunnel** *m* KFZTECH *Getriebe* propeller shaft tunnel; **Kardanwelle** *f* FERTIG cardan shaft, KFZTECH cardan shaft, propeller shaft

Karde *f* TEXTIL card; **Kardeel** *nt* WASSERTRANS *Tauwerk* strand

karden *vt* TEXTIL card

Karde: **Kardenbeschlag** *m* TEXTIL card clothing; **Kardengarnitur** *f* TEXTIL card clothing; **Kardensaal** *m* TEXTIL card room; **Karderie** *f* TEXTIL card room

Kardieren *nt* TEXTIL carding

kardieren *vt* TEXTIL card

kardiert: ~e Display-Verpackung *f* VERPACK visual-carded packaging; **~e Produkte** *nt pl* VERPACK carded packaging

Kardinal- *pref* FERTIG, MATH, WASSERTRANS cardinal; **Kardinalpunkt** *m* FERTIG Gaussian point; **Kardinalpunkte** *m pl* WASSERTRANS *Kompaß* cardinal points; **Kardinalstriche** *m pl* WASSERTRANS *Kompaß* cardinal points; **Kardinalsystem** *nt* WASSERTRANS *Navigation* cardinal system; **Kardinalzahl** *f* MATH cardinal number

Kardiograph *m* ERGON cardiograph

Kardioidmikrofon *nt* AKUSTIK cardioid microphone

Kardiotachometer *nt* ERGON cardiotachometer

karieren *vt* FERTIG checker (AmE), chequer (BrE)

kariert: ~**e Waren** *f pl* TEXTIL checks
Karkasse *f* TEXTIL carcass
Karnaubawachs *nt* LEBENSMITTEL *Pflanzenwachs* carnauba wax
Karnaugh-Diagramm *nt* COMP & DV Veitch diagram
Karnaugh-Tabelle *f* COMP & DV Karnaugh map
Karnieshobel *m* BAU ogee plane
Karnotit *m* KERNTECH carnotite
Karosserie *f* FERTIG body, KFZTECH body, coach, *Fahrzeug* car body, MECHAN car body; ~ **nach dem Baukastenprinzip** *f* KFZTECH unitized body; **Karosseriehersteller** *m* FERTIG body maker; **Karosseriewerkzeuge** *nt pl* MASCHINEN car body tooling; **Karosserieziehpresse** *f* FERTIG body drag press
Karrageen *nt* LEBENSMITTEL carrageen
Karren *m* DRUCK carriage
KARS *abbr (kohärente Antistokes-Raman-Streuung)* STRAHLPHYS, WELLPHYS CARS *(coherent anti-Stokes Raman scattering)*
Karsthydrologie *f* WASSERVERSORG karst hydrology
Karstquelle *f* WASSERVERSORG intermittent spring, karstic spring
Karte[1] *f* COMP & DV card, PHYS chart, TEXTIL *Weben* card, TRANS map, WASSERTRANS *Navigation* chart; ~ **mit großem Maßstab** *f* TRANS large-scale map
Karte:[2] **auf** ~ **eintragen** *vt* WASSERTRANS *Navigation* chart
Karte: **Kartenabtastung** *f* COMP & DV card sensing; **Kartenbahn** *f* COMP & DV card channel; **Kartenberichtigung** *f* WASSERTRANS *Navigation* chart correction; **Kartenbildschirm** *m* WASSERTRANS *Navigation* chart display; **Kartencode** *m* COMP & DV card code; **Kartenführung** *f* COMP & DV card bed; **Kartenkäfig** *m* COMP & DV card cage; **Kartenleser** *m* COMP & DV, TELEKOM card reader; **Kartenlochen** *nt* TEXTIL card cutting; **Kartenlocher** *m* COMP & DV card punch, keypunch; **Kartenmagazin** *nt* COMP & DV card hopper; **Kartenmaßstab** *m* METROL scale, WASSERTRANS *Navigation* chart scale, map scale; **Kartenmischer** *m* COMP & DV collator; **Kartennull** *f* WASSERTRANS *Navigation, Gezeiten* chart datum, map datum; **Kartensatz** *m* COMP & DV card deck, card record; **Kartenschlagen** *nt* TEXTIL card cutting; **Kartenstanzen** *nt* TEXTIL card cutting; **Kartenstau** *m* COMP & DV card jam; **Kartentelefon** *nt* TELEKOM card phone; **Kartentisch** *m* WASSERTRANS *Navigation* chart table, map table; **Kartenwassertiefe** *f* WASSERTRANS *Navigation* charted depth, mapped depth; **Kartenwender** *m* ELEKTRONIK *Computer-Peripheriegeräte* card reverser; **Kartenzuführung** *f* COMP & DV card feed
kartesisch: ~**e Geometrie** *f* GEOM Cartesian geometry; ~**e Koordinaten** *f pl* BAU, GEOM, KONSTZEICH, MATH, PHYS Cartesian coordinates; ~**es Koordinatensystem** *nt* ELEKTRONIK Cartesian coordinate system; ~**es Produkt** *nt* COMP & DV, MATH Cartesian product
Kartierer *m* BAU *Vermessung* mapper
Kartierung *f* BAU *Vermessung* mapping
Kartoffelfäule *f* LEBENSMITTEL *Pflanzenkrankheitslehre* potato blight
Kartoffelkäfer *m* LEBENSMITTEL *Zoologie, Pflanzenschädlinge* Colorado beetle, potato beetle (BrE), potato bug (AmE)
Karton *m* DRUCK cardboard, paste board, pulp board, PAPIER board, SICHERHEIT box, VERPACK box, cardboard, paper board, carton; ~ **aus Kistenpappe** *m* VERPACK container board box; **Kartonabfüllanlage** *f* VERPACK carton filler; **Kartonabfüllmaschine** *f* VERPACK carton-filling machine
Kartonage *f* VERPACK cardboard packaging; **Kartonagen-Aufrichtmaschine** *f* VERPACK folding cardboard box erecting machine; **Kartonagen-Einrichtmaschine** *f* VERPACK folding cardboard box setting machine; **Kartonagenmaschine** *f* VERPACK cardboard machine
Karton: **Kartonaufricht- und verschließmaschine** *f* VERPACK carton erector and closer; **Kartonaufrichtmaschine** *f* VERPACK carton-erecting machine; **Kartonautomat** *m* VERPACK carton-making machine; **Kartondosiermaschine** *f* VERPACK carton-dosing machine; **Kartondrucker mit Einzelblatteinzug** *m* VERPACK sheet-fed carton printer; **Kartoneinlage** *f* VERPACK cardboard backing
Kartoniereinrichtung *f* VERPACK cartoner, cartoning equipment
Kartoniermaschine *f* VERPACK boxing machine, cartoning machine
Karton: **Kartonmaschine** *f* PAPIER board machine; **Kartonrecycling** *nt* VERPACK paper carton recycling; **Kartonröhre** *f* VERPACK cardboard tube; **Kartons** *m pl* SICHERHEIT boxes
kartonstark: ~**es Papier** *nt* FOTO double-weight paper
Karton: **Kartonverpackung** *f* VERPACK cardboard packaging; **Kartonversteifung** *f* VERPACK cardboard backing; **Kartonwiederverwertung** *f* VERPACK paper carton recycling
Kartusche *f* DRUCK, KFZTECH, VERPACK cartridge; **Kartuschenfilter** *nt* KFZTECH *Schmierung* cartridge filter; **Kartuschenpapier** *nt* VERPACK cartridge paper
Karusseldrehmaschine *f* FERTIG vertical turret lathe, MASCHINEN vertical boring and turning mill
karweelgebaut *adj* WASSERTRANS *Schiffbau* carvel-built
Karyokinese *f* KERNTECH karyokinesis
Karyolyse *f* KERNTECH karyolisis
Karzinogen *nt* LEBENSMITTEL carcinogen, SICHERHEIT carcinogenic substance
Karzinotron *nt* ELEKTRONIK carcinotron, *Mikrowellentechnik* backward-wave oscillator, PHYS backward-wave oscillator, carcinotron, TELEKOM carcinotron
Kaschieren *nt* KUNSTSTOFF, VERPACK *von Papier, Pappe* coating
kaschieren *vt* KUNSTSTOFF coat, PAPIER paste, VERPACK coat
Kaschiermaschine *f* PAPIER pasting machine, VERPACK laminating machine
Kaschierpapier *nt* PAPIER liner paper, VERPACK liner paper, lining paper
kaschiert: ~**es Gewebe** *nt* KUNSTSTOFF coated fabric; ~**e Graupappe** *f* VERPACK lined chipboard; ~**er Kunststoff** *m* ELEKTRIZ laminated plastic; ~**es Papier** *nt* PAPIER pasted paper
Kaschierung *f* PAPIER pasting
Kascode *f* RADIO cascode
Käsebruch *m* LEBENSMITTEL cheese curd, curd
Kasein *nt* CHEMIE, LEBENSMITTEL casein
Kaseinat *nt* LEBENSMITTEL caseinate; **Kaseinatgummi** *nt* LEBENSMITTEL caseinate gum
Kasein: **Kaseinhydrolysat** *nt* LEBENSMITTEL casein hydrolysate; **Kaseinleim** *m* LEBENSMITTEL casein glue
Kaserne *f* BAU barracks
Kaskade[1] *f* ELEKTROTECH cascade set, *Reihenschaltung* cascade
Kaskade:[2] **in** ~ **schalten** *vt* ELEKTROTECH cascade

Kaskadenanordnung *f* ELEKTROTECH cascade arrangement, tandem arrangement

Kaskade: **Kaskadenfolge schweißen** *vi* FERTIG cascade

Kaskade: **Kaskadenmühle** *f* KOHLEN cascade mill; **Kaskadenofen** *m* HEIZ & KÄLTE cascade furnace; **Kaskadenprozeß** *f* STRAHLPHYS cascade process; **Kaskadenschaltung** *f* ELEKTRIZ tandem connection, ELEKTROTECH tandem connection, *Reihenschaltung* cascade connection, KERNTECH tandem connection; **Kaskadenteilchen** *nt* PHYS *Elementarteilchen* Xi particle; **Kaskadenübertrag** *m* ELEKTRONIK *Computertechnik* cascaded carry; **Kaskadenumformer** *m* ELEKTROTECH motor converter; **Kaskadenverbindung** *f* KERNTECH cascade connection; **Kaskadenverstärker** *m* ELEKTRONIK *mehrstufig* cascade amplifier; **Kaskadenwandler** *m* KERNTECH cascade transformer; **Kaskadenwässerung** *f* FOTO cascade washing

Kaskadieren *nt* KOHLEN cascading

Kaskoversicherung *f* TRANS *Versicherung* hull insurance

Kasse *f* COMP & DV point of sale, VERPACK counter top machine

Kassette *f* ABFALL landfill cell, refuse cell, *Verfüllung von Deponien* subcell, BAU caisson; **Kassettendecke** *f* BAU pan ceiling

Kassiaöl *nt* LEBENSMITTEL cassia oil

Kassierer *m* TRANS collector

Kasten *m* BAU box, caisson, DRUCK, FERTIG, MASCHINEN box, VERPACK carton, case; **~ mit Metallbeschlägen** *m* VERPACK metal edging case

Kastenaufricht: ~, -abfüll- und - verschließmaschine *f* VERPACK case erecting, filling and closing machine

Kasten: **Kastendurchlaß** *m* BAU box culvert; **Kastenformerei** *f* FERTIG flask moulding

kastenförmig: ~er Fahrbalken *m* TRANS box-section track girder; **~e Stabilisierung** *f* LUFTTRANS box-type stiffener; **~e Struktur** *f* LUFTTRANS box-type structure; **~e Versteifung** *f* LUFTTRANS box-type stiffener

Kasten: **Kastenguß** *m* MASCHINEN box casting; **Kastenkaliber** *nt* FERTIG *Walzen* box groove; **Kastenkalibrierung** *f* FERTIG box pass; **Kastenkipper** *m* KOHLEN tip box car; **Kastenkopierrahmen** *m* DRUCK printing frame; **Kastenleiter** *m* ELEKTROTECH rectangular waveguide; **Kastenmetall** *nt* METALL boxmetal; **Kastenofen** *m* HEIZ & KÄLTE box kiln; **Kastenrahmen** *m* KFZTECH *Motor* box-type chassis, box-type frame, MASCHINEN box frame, box-form frame, box-section frame; **Kastenrinne** *f* BAU *Dachrinne* box gutter, *Dach* trough gutter, *Gebäude* parallel gutter; **Kastenschloß** *nt* BAU box lock; **Kastenständer** *m* FERTIG box column; **Kastenständerbohrmaschine** *f* FERTIG box-column drilling machine; **Kastentisch** *m* MASCHINEN box table; **Kastenträger** *m* BAU box girder; **Kastenvorkalibrierung** *f* FERTIG box pass; **Kastenzange** *f* FERTIG square tongs, KER & GLAS pinchers

katadioptrisch *adj* PHYS catadioptric

Katalase *f* CHEMIE, LEBENSMITTEL catalase

Katalog *m* COMP & DV catalog (AmE), catalogue (BrE)

katalogisieren *vt* COMP & DV catalog (AmE), catalogue (BrE)

Katalysator *m* ERDÖL *Reaktionsbeschleuniger beim Crack-Prozeß* catalyst, KFZTECH catalytic converter (BrE), catalytic muffler (AmE), catalytic silencer (BrE), *Abgassystem, Auspuffanlage* catalyst, KUNSTSTOFF, TEXTIL catalyst, UMWELTSCHMUTZ catalytic converter (BrE), catalytic muffler (AmE), catalytic silencer (BrE), WASSERVERSORG catalyst; **Katalysatorauspuff** *m* KFZTECH exhaust catalytic converter system; **Katalysatorbett** *nt* KERNTECH catalyst bed; **Katalysatorgift** *nt* CHEMTECH catalytic poison

katalysatorinduziert: ~e Deuteriumreaktion *f* KERNTECH catalysed deuterium reaction

Katalyse *f* CHEMIE, LEBENSMITTEL catalysis

katalysieren *vt* KUNSTSTOFF catalyze

katalysiert: ~e Deuteriumreaktion *f* KERNTECH catalysed deuterium reaction

katalytisch: ~er Inhibitor *m* CHEMTECH catalytic poison; **~e Krackanlage** *f* ERDÖL *Raffinerietechnik* catalytic cracking plant; **~es Kracken** *nt* ERDÖL *Raffinerie* catalytic cracking; **~er Reaktor** *m* CHEMTECH catalytic reactor; **~es Reduktionsverfahren** *nt* UMWELTSCHMUTZ catalytic process; **~es Reformieren** *nt* ERDÖL *Raffinerie* catalytic reforming; **~e Reformierung** *f* CHEMIE *Erdöl* catalytic reforming, catforming, ERDÖL *Raffinerie* catalytic reforming; **~e Spaltung** *f* ERDÖL catalytic cracking; **~er Umformer** *m* UMWELTSCHMUTZ catalytic converter (BrE), catalytic muffler (AmE), catalytic silencer (BrE)

Katamaran *m* WASSERTRANS catamaran ship, twin-hull ship, *Boottyp* catamaran, WASSERVERSORG catamaran dredge; **Katamaran-Trägerschiff** *nt* TRANS bacat ship, barge-aboard catamaran-ship

Katarakt *m* KOHLEN, WASSERVERSORG cataract

Kataster *nt* BAU land register; **Katasteramt** *nt* BAU land registry; **Katasteraufnahme** *f* BAU cadastral survey

Katathermometer *nt* HEIZ & KÄLTE katathermometer

Kategorie *f* PATENT category

Katenoid *nt* GEOM catenoid

Katergol *nt* RAUMFAHRT *Raumschiff* katergol

Kathedralglas *nt* KER & GLAS cathedral glass

Kathepsin *nt* CHEMIE cathepsin

Kathete *f* GEOM leg

Kathetometer *nt* LABOR *Längenmessung*, PHYS cathetometer

Kathode *f* ELEKTRIZ, ELEKTRONIK, ELEKTROTECH, FERNSEH, METALL., PHYS, RADIO cathode; **Kathodendunkelraum** *m* ELEKTROTECH cathode dark space; **Kathodenfleck** *m* ELEKTROTECH cathode spot; **Kathodenfolger** *m* PHYS cathode follower

kathodengekoppelt: ~e Gegentaktstufe *f* ELEKTRONIK long-tail pair

Kathode: **Kathodengitter** *nt* FERNSEH cathode screen; **Kathodenglimmlicht** *nt* PHYS cathode glow; **Kathodenmodulation** *f* ELEKTRONIK cathode modulation; **Kathodenschaltung** *f* ELEKTROTECH cathode circuit

Kathodenstrahl *m* COMP & DV, DRUCK, ELEKTRIZ, ELEKTRONIK cathode ray, electron ray, FERNSEH, RADIO, STRAHLPHYS cathode ray, TELEKOM cathode ray, electron ray; **Kathodenstrahlanzeigegerät** *nt* KONTROLL cathode-ray display; **Kathodenstrahlbildschirm** *m* TELEKOM cathode-ray screen; **Kathodenstrahlbündel** *nt* ELEKTRIZ cathode-ray pencil; **Kathodenstrahldisplay** *nt* KONTROLL cathode-ray display; **Kathodenstrahlen** *m pl* ELEKTRONIK, FERNSEH, PHYS, STRAHLPHYS cathode rays; **Kathodenstrahloszillograph** *m* ELEKTRONIK *registriert schnelle Größen* cathode-ray oscillograph; **Kathodenstrahloszilloskop** *nt* PHYS, STRAHLPHYS cathode-ray oscilloscope; **Kathodenstrahlröhre** *f* *(KSR)* COMP & DV, DRUCK, ELEKTRIZ, ELEKTRONIK, FERNSEH, KER & GLAS, RADIO cathode-ray tube *(CRT)*

Kathode: **Kathodensumpfröhre** *f* ELEKTRONIK mercury

pool tube; **Kathodenverstärker** m ELEKTROTECH cathode follower; **Kathodenzerstäubung** f ELEKTROTECH, METALL cathode sputtering

kathodisch: ~er **Schutz** m KOHLEN cathodic protection

Kathodolumineszenz f ELEKTROTECH, PHYS cathodoluminescence

Kation nt ELEKTRIZ, ELEKTROTECH, ERDÖL, KOHLEN, LEBENSMITTEL, PHYS, STRAHLPHYS cation; **Kationenaustauscher** m KOHLEN, UMWELTSCHMUTZ cation exchanger; **Kationenaustauschkapazität** f ERDÖL *Petrochemie, Elektrolyse,* UMWELTSCHMUTZ *Boden* cation exchange capacity; **Kationendenudationsrate** f UMWELTSCHMUTZ cation denudation rate

kationisch[1] adj KOHLEN cationic

kationisch:[2] ~er **Farbstoff** m TEXTIL basic dye

kationoid adj CHEMIE electrophilic

Katkracker m ERDÖL cat cracker

Katzenauge nt BAU cats' eyes, KFZTECH *Sicherheitszubehör, Fahrrad* reflector

Katzenkopf m MASCHINEN cat head, spider

Kauri-Butanolwert m CHEMIE kauri butanol number

kausal: ~es **Wissen** nt KÜNSTL INT causal knowledge

Kausalgraph m KÜNSTL INT causal graph

Kausch f WASSERTRANS *Beschläge* thimble

kaustifizieren vt CHEMIE causticize

Kaustik f CHEMIE, PHYS caustic

kaustisch adj CHEMIE caustic

Kaustizität f CHEMIE causticity

Kautschuk m CHEMIE, DRUCK caoutchouc, ELEKTRIZ rubber, KUNSTSTOFF raw rubber, rubber

Kavalier-Projektion f KONSTZEICH cavalier projection

Kavitation f BAU, ERDÖL *an Laufrädern von Wasserturbinen, Schiffsschrauben,* MECHAN, METALL, NICHTFOSS ENERG, PHYS cavitation, RAUMFAHRT *Weltraumfunk* cavity, STRÖMPHYS cavitation; **Kavitationsversagen** nt METALL cavitation failure; **Kavitationszahl** f PHYS, STRÖMPHYS cavitation number

kavitierend adj MECHAN cavitating

KAW abbr (*Kanaladreßwort*) COMP & DV CAW (*channel address word*)

KB abbr (*Kilobyte*) COMP & DV, TELEKOM KB (*kilobyte*)

kcal abbr (*Kilokalorie*) LEBENSMITTEL kcal (*kilocalorie*)

keff abbr (*effektive Neutronen-Multiplikationskonstante*) KERNTECH keff

Kegel m DRUCK body, FERNSEH cone, FERTIG taper, *Kunststoffinstallationen* cotter, GEOM cone, KER & GLAS taper, KOHLEN, MASCHINEN cone; **Kegel-** pref GEOM conical; **Kegelanschlagschräge** f KER & GLAS tapered stop bevel; **Kegelanschnitt** m KER & GLAS taper bevel; **Kegelaufschläger** m PAPIER banger; **Kegelband** nt BAU T-hinge; **Kegelbohren** nt FERTIG taper boring; **Kegelbrecher** m KOHLEN cone crusher; **Kegelbremse** f MASCHINEN cone brake; **Kegelfeder** f FERTIG volute spring, MASCHINEN conical spring

kegelförmig: ~er **Abschnitt** m ELEKTROTECH tapered section; ~er **Bestandteil** m ELEKTROTECH tapered section; ~er **Kompressionsring** m KFZTECH tapered compression ring; ~es **Sieb** nt LEBENSMITTEL conical sieve; ~er **Trichter** m AKUSTIK conical horn

Kegel: **Kegelfräsen** nt FERTIG taper milling; **Kegelgewinde** nt MASCHINEN taper thread; **Kegelgriff** m FERTIG ball handle, MASCHINEN ball handle, clamping lever; **Kegelhülse** f MASCHINEN taper sleeve

kegelig:[1] ~ **verjüngt** adj MASCHINEN tapered; **mit kegeligem Anschnitt** adj FERTIG tapered-ended; **mit**

kegeligem Gewinde adj MASCHINEN taper-threaded

kegelig:[2] ~es **Rohrgewinde** nt MASCHINEN taper pipe thread

Kegeligdrehen nt MASCHINEN taper turning

Kegeligdrehvorrichtung f MASCHINEN taper-turning attachment

Kegeligsenken nt MASCHINEN countersinking

Kegelkopf m MASCHINEN cone head, pan head; **Kegelkopfniet** m BAU cone head rivet, MASCHINEN pan head rivet; **Kegelkopfschraube** f MASCHINEN pan head screw

Kegel: **Kegelkuppe** f MASCHINEN blunt start, flat point; **Kegelkupplung** f KFZTECH, MASCHINEN cone clutch; **Kegellager** nt MASCHINEN cone bearing; **Kegelleuchte** f ELEKTRIZ cone light; **Kegelnabe** f KFZTECH *Rad* tapered hub; **Kegelniet** m FERTIG cone head rivet; **Kegelpolster** nt KER & GLAS tapered pad; **Kegelprober** m KOHLEN cone sampler; **Kegelprojektion** f GEOM conic projection

Kegelrad nt FERTIG, KFZTECH, LUFTTRANS bevel gear, MASCHINEN bevel gear, bevel wheel, conical gear, miter wheel (AmE), mitre wheel (BrE), MECHAN bevel gear; ~ **mit Oktoidverzahnung** nt MASCHINEN octoid bevel gear; ~ **für den Radantrieb** nt KFZTECH *beim Ausgleichsgetriebe* side gear; ~ **und Tellerrad** nt KFZTECH *Triebstrang, Differential* crown and pinion; **Kegelradantrieb** m EISENBAHN, FERTIG, MASCHINEN bevel gear drive; **Kegelradformfräser** m FERTIG bevel-gear-formed cutter; **Kegelradfräsmaschine** f FERTIG bevel gear cutting machine; **Kegelradgetriebe** nt FERTIG obtuse-angle bevel gear, KFZTECH *Hinterachse* bevel gear set, MASCHINEN bevel gears; **Kegelradgetriebegehäuse** nt LUFTTRANS *Hubschrauber* bevel gear housing; **Kegelradhobelmaschine** f FERTIG bevel gear planing machine; **Kegelradpaar** nt FERTIG miter gearing (AmE), mitre gearing (BrE); **Kegelradumlaufgetriebe** nt FERTIG bevel epicyclic train; **Kegelradverzahnung** f KFZTECH, MASCHINEN bevel gearing; **Kegelradwälzfräsmaschine** f FERTIG bevel gear generating machine

Kegel: **Kegelreibahle** f MASCHINEN taper reamer; **Kegelreibungskupplung** f FERTIG cone friction clutch; **Kegelritzel** nt FERTIG bevel gear pinion; **Kegelrollenlager** nt KFZTECH taper roller bearing, tapered roller bearing, MASCHINEN taper rolling bearing, tapered roller bearing, timken bearing (AmE); **Kegelschaft** m MASCHINEN taper shank; **Kegelschale** f FERTIG conical shell; **Kegelscheibenantrieb** m MASCHINEN cone drive, cone gear; **Kegelschleifen** nt FERTIG taper grinding; **Kegelschliff-Verbindungsstück** nt LABOR cone-and-socket joint; **Kegelschnecke** f MASCHINEN conical worm, tapered worm; **Kegelschnitt** m GEOM conic section; **Kegelsenker** m MASCHINEN cone countersink, countersink, rose countersink, rose-head countersink bit; **Kegelseparator** m KOHLEN cone separator; **Kegelsieb** nt KOHLEN cone classifier; **Kegelsitz** m MASCHINEN conical seat; **Kegelspitze** f MASCHINEN truncated cone point; **Kegelstift** m MASCHINEN taper dowel, taper pin, tapered pin, MECHAN taper pin; **Kegelstumpf** m FERTIG truncated cone; **Kegeltoleranz** f MASCHINEN cone tolerance; **Kegelventil** nt FERTIG, HYDRAUL, MASCHINEN cone valve; **Kegelverhältnis** nt MECHAN taper; **Kegelverjüngung** f FERTIG amount of taper; **Kegelwinkel** m GEOM cone angle, MASCHINEN angle of taper; **Kegelzahnrad** nt FERTIG, MECHAN bevel gear

Kehlbalken *m* BAU collar beam, span piece; **Kehlbalkenbinder** *m* BAU collar beam truss; **Kehlbalkendach** *nt* BAU collar roof; **Kehlbalkenstütze** *f* BAU side post

Kehle *f* AKUSTIK throat, BAU groove, plough (BrE), plow (AmE), valley, FERTIG throat

Kehleisen *nt* FERTIG vee sett, *Schmieden* necking tool

kehlen *vt* FERTIG recess

Kehlhammer *m* FERTIG top fuller

Kehlhobel *m* BAU plough (BrE), plow (AmE)

Kehlkopf *m* AKUSTIK throat; **Kehlkopfmikrofon** *nt* AKUSTIK, AUFNAHME throat microphone

Kehlmaschine *f* FERTIG molding machine (AmE), moulding machine (BrE)

Kehlnaht *f* BAU *Holzbau* fillet joint, FERTIG *Schweißen* fillet, MASCHINEN, MECHAN fillet weld

kehlschneiden *vt* WASSERTRANS *Schiffbau* mold (AmE), mould (BrE)

Kehrbild *nt* FOTO inverted image

kehren *vt* BAU *Kamin* sweep

Kehrfahrzeug *nt* ABFALL road-sweeping lorry, street cleaner, street-cleaning lorry (BrE), street-cleaning truck (AmE), KFZTECH street cleaner, street-cleaning lorry (BrE), street-cleaning truck (AmE)

Kehrlage *f* TELEKOM reverse frequency position

Kehrmaschine *f* ABFALL sweeper

Kehrwalze *f* ABFALL *Kehrfahrzeug* cylinder broom

Kehrwert *m* ELEKTRONIK complement, GEOM reciprocal, MATH conjugate, inverse proportion, inverse ratio, multiplicative inverse

Keil *m* BAU key, wedge, ELEKTROTECH key, FERTIG chock, key, male spline, wedge, *Einsatzmesser* calm, MASCHINEN cotter, machine key, quoin, taper key, wedge, MECHAN cotter pin, key, spline, wedge, VERPACK arrowhead; **Keilbruch** *m* METALL wedge-type fracture; **Keildensitometer** *nt* FOTO wedge densitometer; **Keilfänger** *m* ERDÖL *Fangwerkzeug* fishing socket; **Keilflankenschleifen** *nt* FERTIG grinding of splines

keilförmig[1] *adj* FERTIG sphenoid

keilförmig[2] **-er Brennraum** *m* KFZTECH wedge-type combustion chamber

Keil: **Keillängsnut** *f* FERTIG keyway; **Keillehre** *f* KER & GLAS V-gage (AmE), V-gauge (BrE), METROL spline gage (AmE), spline gauge (BrE); **Keilloch** *nt* MASCHINEN cotter slot, MECHAN key slot; **Keillochhammer** *m* KOHLEN stone-splitting hammer; **Keilmeßebene** *f* FERTIG wedge measurement plane; **Keilnabe** *f* FERTIG splined hub; **Keilnabenprofil** *nt* MASCHINEN internal splines

Keilnut[1] *f* BAU key, FERTIG key slot, spine, KERNTECH key bed, keygroove, keyway, MASCHINEN V-groove, key seating, keyway, spline, MECHAN keyway

Keilnut:[2] **Keilnuten ziehen** *vi* FERTIG keygroove

Keilnut: **Keilnutenfräsen** *nt* MASCHINEN keyway milling, keywaying; **Keilnutenfräser** *m* FERTIG keyway cutter; **Keilnutenfräserspannfutter** *nt* FERTIG keyway cutter chuck; **Keilnutenfräsmaschine** *f* MASCHINEN keyway-milling machine; **Keilnutenräumnadel** *f* MASCHINEN keyway broach; **Keilnutenstoßen** *nt* MASCHINEN keyway slotting; **Keilnutenstoßmaschine** *f* MASCHINEN keyseater; **Keilnutenziehen** *nt* FERTIG keygrooving; **Keilnutfräser** *m* MASCHINEN splining tool; **Keilnutmaschine** *f* MASCHINEN keywaying machine

Keilprofil:[1] **mit ~** *adj* FERTIG splined

Keilprofil[2] *nt* FERTIG spline

keilprofilfräsen *vi* FERTIG spline

Keilprofilräumnadel *f* FERTIG spline broach

Keilriemen *m* FERTIG, HEIZ & KÄLTE V-belt, vee belt, KFZTECH *Kühlsystem*, KUNSTSTOFF V-belt, MASCHINEN vee belt, MECHAN V-belt; **Keilriemenantrieb** *m* MASCHINEN V-belt drive; **Keilriemenscheibe** *f* MASCHINEN V-belt pulley; **Keilriemenspannung** *f* MASCHINEN V-belt tension; **Keilriementrieb** *m* MASCHINEN V-belt drive

Keil: **Keilrille** *f* MASCHINEN V-groove, MECHAN keyway; **Keilriß** *m* METALL wedge crack; **Keilschieber** *m* MASCHINEN wedge-type valve, WASSERVERSORG sluice valve; **Keilschloß** *nt* MASCHINEN gib and cotter, gib and key; **Keilschweißung** *f* FERTIG cleft weld; **Keilstein** *m* BAU arch stone, voussoir, FERTIG skewback; **Keilstift** *m* MECHAN taper pin; **Keilstück** *nt* FERTIG taper parallel; **Keilverzahnung** *f* FERTIG splining; **Keilverzahnungsfräsmaschine** *f* FERTIG spline milling machine

Keilwelle *f* FERTIG, MASCHINEN spline shaft, splined shaft; **Keilwellenprofil** *nt* FERTIG spine, MASCHINEN external splines, spline profile; **Keilwellenprofil mit Evolventenflanken** *nt* MASCHINEN involute spline; **Keilwellenverbindung** *f* MASCHINEN spline

Keil: **Keilwinkel** *m* FERTIG wedge angle, *Spiralbohrer* lip angle (AmE), MASCHINEN wedge angle; **Keilzapfenverbindung** *f* BAU wedged mortice and tenon joint; **Keilziegel** *m* BAU feather-edged brick, gage brick (AmE), gauge brick (BrE); **Keilzugprobe** *f* METALL wedge draw test

Keim *m* FERTIG *Kristall*, KER & GLAS nucleus

keimfrei *adj* LEBENSMITTEL aseptic

Keimfreitechnologie *f* SICHERHEIT aseptic engineering

kein:[1] **~e Operation** *f (NO-OP)* COMP & DV no-operation *(NO-OP)*

kein:[2] **~ Anschluß unter dieser Nummer** *phr (NU-Ton)* TELEKOM number-unobtainable tone *(NUT)*

K-Einfang *m* PHYS *Kernphysik* K-capture

Kelle[1] *f* BAU trowel

Kelle:[2] **mit ~ abreiben** *vt* BAU trowel off

Kellenrückstand *m* KER & GLAS scull

Kellerbasis *f* COMP & DV stack base

Kellergeschoßwand *f* BAU basement wall

Keller-Kopiereinrichtung *f* FERTIG Keller attachment

Kellerspeicher *m* COMP & DV push-down stack

Kelly *f* ERDÖL kelly

Kelp *nt* LEBENSMITTEL kelp

Keltapapier *nt* CHEMIE, FOTO gelatino-chloride paper

Kelvin *nt (K)* ELEKTRIZ, METROL, PHYS, THERMOD kelvin *(K)*; **~sche Skale** *f* BAU Kelvin scale; **~sche Stromwaage** *f* ELEKTRIZ Kelvin balance; **Kelvinbrücke** *f* ELEKTRIZ Kelvin bridge; **Kelvinbrückenschaltung** *f* PHYS Kelvin bridge; **Kelvindoppelbrücke** *f* ELEKTRIZ double Kelvin bridge; **Kelvineffekt** *m* ELEKTRIZ Kelvin effect; **Kelvinsformulierung** *f* PHYS *zweiter Hauptsatz der Thermodynamik* Kelvin statement; **Kelvintemperatur** *f* LEBENSMITTEL absolute temperature, PHYS, RAUMFAHRT, THERMOD Kelvin temperature; **Kelvintemperaturskale** *f* RAUMFAHRT Kelvin scale

K-Emitter *m* KERNTECH K-emitter

Kennbuchstabe *m* COMP & DV code letter

Kenndämpfungswiderstand *m* PHYS iterative impedance

Kenndaten *nt pl* TELEKOM *Datenblatt* characteristics

Kennelly-Heaviside-Schicht *f* PHYS Kennelly-Heaviside layer

Kennfeuer *nt* LUFTTRANS identification beacon

Kenngleichung *f* RAUMFAHRT characteristic equation

Kennkurve *f* RADIO characteristic, RAUMFAHRT characteristic curve

Kennlicht *nt* LUFTTRANS identification light, navigation light

Kennlinie *f* AKUSTIK characteristic curve, ELEKTRIZ characteristic, ELEKTRONIK, GERÄT, PHYS characteristic curve

Kennsatz *m* COMP & DV header, label, label record; **Kennsatzanfang** *m* COMP & DV SOH, start of header

Kennung *f* COMP & DV identifier, tag, COMP & DV identification, FERNSEH identification signal, KONTROLL identification, TELEKOM answer-back; ~ **der Küstenfunkstelle** *f* TELEKOM coastal station identity; ~ **der Schiffsfunkstelle** *f* TELEKOM ship station identity

Kennwert *m* GEOM, TELEKOM characteristic, parameter, value

Kennwiderstand *m* ELEKTROTECH image impedance

Kennwort *nt* COMP & DV identifier word, keyword, password, TELEKOM password; **Kennwortdateischutz** *m* COMP & DV password protection; **Kennwortschutz** *m* COMP & DV password protection, password security

Kennzeichen *nt* COMP & DV identifier, snowflake topology, token, KER & GLAS badge, KFZTECH license plate (AmE), numberplate (BrE), QUAL identification; **Kennzeichengabe** *f* TELEKOM *Telefon* signaling (AmE), signalling (BrE); **Kennzeichenregister** *nt* COMP & DV flag register

Kennzeichnen *nt* KER & GLAS badging, TEXTIL marking

kennzeichnen *vt* COMP & DV identify, tag, TEXTIL label

Kennzeichnung *f* COMP & DV certification, QUAL identifying marking, WERKPRÜF marking

Kennziffer *f* TELEKOM prefix

Kentern: **zum** ~ **bringen** *vt* WASSERTRANS *Schiff* capsize

kentern *vi* WASSERTRANS *Schiff* capsize

Kepler: ~**sches Flächengesetz** *nt* RAUMFAHRT Kepler's law of areas; ~**sche Gesetze** *nt pl* PHYS Kepler's laws; ~**scher Umlauf** *m* RAUMFAHRT Keplerian orbit

Kerabitumen *nt* ERDÖL *Geologie* kerogen

Kerametall *nt* ANSTRICH, KER & GLAS ceramal, cermet; **Kerametall-Beschichtung** *f* ANSTRICH cermet coating

Keramik *f* BAU, KER & GLAS, KERNTECH, MECHAN ceramic; **Keramikbrennofen** *m* KER & GLAS ceramic kiln; **Keramikfaser** *f* HEIZ & KÄLTE ceramic fiber (AmE), ceramic fibre (BrE); **Keramikfliese** *f* BAU glazed tile; **Keramikglasur** *f* KER & GLAS ceramic glaze; **Keramikindustrie** *f* KER & GLAS ceramic industry; **Keramikkondensator** *m* ELEKTRIZ, ELEKTROTECH, TELEKOM ceramic capacitor; **Keramikkondensator mit Glasbeschichtung** *m* ELEKTROTECH glass-coated ceramic capacitor; **Keramikkunst** *f* KER & GLAS ceramic art; **Keramikmaschine** *f* KER & GLAS ceramic machine; **Keramikpflasterstein** *m* KER & GLAS ceramic pavement slab (BrE), ceramic sidewalk slab (AmE); **Keramiktrimmer** *m* ELEKTROTECH adjustable ceramic capacitor; **Keramikwandfliese** *f* KER & GLAS ceramic wall tile

keramisch[1] *adj* ANSTRICH, ELEKTRIZ, ELEKTROTECH ceramic, FERTIG *Bindung* vitrified

keramisch:[2] ~**er Brennstoff** *m* KERNTECH ceramic fuel; ~**er Isolator** *m* ELEKTRIZ ceramic insulator; ~**es Isoliermaterial** *nt* ELEKTROTECH ceramic insulating material; ~**er Kondensator** *m* ELEKTROTECH, PHYS ceramic capacitor; ~**er Plättchenkondensator** *m* ELEKTROTECH ceramic chip capacitor; ~**er Rohrkondensator** *m* ELEKTROTECH tubular ceramic capacitor

Kerb *m* FERTIG rag, KOHLEN cut

Kerbbiegeversuch *m* MASCHINEN notch bending test

Kerbe *f* BAU notch, FERTIG groove, jag, nick, notch, undercut, KERNTECH groove, MASCHINEN dent, nick, notch, MECHAN, METALL notch

kerbempfindlich *adj* FERTIG notch-sensitive

Kerbempfindlichkeit *f* MASCHINEN notch sensitivity; **Kerbempfindlichkeitszahl** *f* FERTIG fatigue notch sensitivity

Kerb: **Kerbfilter** *nt* ELEKTRONIK *Radio*, RADIO *schmalbandige Bandsperre*, TELEKOM notch filter; **Kerbmessung** *f* HYDRAUL notch gaging (AmE), notch gauging (BrE); **Kerbnagel** *m* MASCHINEN grooved pin, splined pin; **Kerbschlagprobe** *f* KERNTECH notch impact test, MECHAN notched bar impact test; **Kerbschlagversuch** *m* ANSTRICH impact test, FERTIG notched bar impact test, METROL impact test; **Kerbschlagzähigkeitswert** *m* METALL impact test; **Kerbstab** *m* FERTIG notched bar; **Kerbstift** *m* *(KS)* FERTIG, MASCHINEN grooved pin, splined pin

Kerbung *f* FERTIG nicking, KER & GLAS scoring

Kerbverbindung *f* BAU notch joint

kerbverzahnt *adj* FERTIG splined, MASCHINEN serrate

Kerbverzahnung *f* FERTIG serration, spline, MASCHINEN serration; **Kerbverzahnungswälzfräser** *m* FERTIG serration hob

Kerb: **Kerbwinkel** *m* METALL notch angle; **Kerbwirkung** *f* MASCHINEN notch effect; **Kerbzähigkeit** *f* FERTIG impact value, KERNTECH notch toughness

Kerma *nt* *(K)* KERNTECH kerma *(K)*

Kermarate *f* PHYS kerma rate

Kern *m* BAU, COMP & DV, ELEKTRIZ core, ELEKTROTECH core, *Hohlleiter, Wicklung* slug, ERDÖL *Bohrtechnik* core, FERTIG pit, *Magnet* limb, *Spiralbohrer* web, KERNTECH, MECHAN, OPTIK *Lichtleiter*, PAPIER core, PHYS nucleus, RADIO, RAUMFAHRT core, TEILPHYS nucleus, TELEKOM *elektrisch*, TEXTIL core; **Kern- und Hülsenschliff** *m* KER & GLAS graded seal; **Kernabschirmung** *f* ELEKTRIZ screened core; **Kernanalyse** *f* ERDÖL core analysis; **Kernansatz** *m* FERTIG half dog; **Kernbaustein** *m* PHYS nucleon; **Kernbeton** *m* BAU mass concrete; **Kernbildung** *f* METALL nucleation; **Kernbildungsgeschwindigkeit** *f* METALL nucleation rate; **Kernbindungsenergie** *f* *(B)* STRAHLPHYS, TEILPHYS binding energy *(B)*; **Kernblasmaschine** *f* MASCHINEN core-blowing machine; **Kernblech** *nt* ELEKTROTECH core plate, stamping; **Kernbock** *m* WASSERVERSORG chaplet; **Kernbohren** *nt* FERTIG trepanning, MASCHINEN core drilling, trepanning (BrE)

kernbohren *vt* FERTIG trepan

Kern: **Kernbohrer** *m* ERDÖL *Bohrtechnik* core bit, core drill; **Kernbohrmaschine** *f* MASCHINEN core drill; **Kernbohrmeißel** *m* ERDÖL core bit, *Bohrtechnik* annular bit

Kernbohrung *f* BAU core drilling

Kern: **Kernbohrwerkzeug** *nt* ERDÖL *Bohrtechnik* coring tool; **Kernbrennstoff** *m* KERNTECH fuel; **Kernbrett** *nt* FERTIG *Gießen* core board; **Kerndeformation** *f* KERNTECH nuclear deformation; **Kerndrehbank** *f* FERTIG core bar; **Kerndurchmesser** *m* FERTIG *Getriebelehre, Gewinde* core diameter, MASCHINEN core diameter, inside diameter, OPTIK *Lichtleiter* core diameter; **Kerndurchmessertoleranz** *f* TELEKOM core diameter tolerance; **Kerneisen** *nt* FERTIG *Gießen* core iron

Kernel *m* COMP & DV kernel

Kern: **Kernelement** *nt* ELEKTROTECH nuclear cell

Kernenergie f ELEKTRIZ, KERNTECH, TEILPHYS nuclear energy; **Kernenergieanlage** f ELEKTROTECH, KERNTECH nuclear power plant

Kern: **Kernerbohrung** f ERDÖL coring; **Kernerregung** f AKUSTIK main excitation; **Kernfänger** m KERNTECH *Öltechnologie* core catcher; **Kernflutsystem** nt KERNTECH core-flooding train; **Kernformen** nt FERTIG *Gießen* coring; **Kernformung** f FERTIG coremaking; **Kernforschung** f KERNTECH, STRAHLPHYS atomic research, nuclear research; **Kernfusion** f KERNTECH, TEILPHYS nuclear fusion; **Kerngewinnung** f ERDÖL *Bohrtechnik* coring; **Kernguß** m FERTIG core casting

kernig[1] *adj* TEXTIL crisp

kernig:[2] **~er Griff** m TEXTIL crisp handle

kerninnen- *pref* KERNTECH in-core

Kern: **Kernisomerie** f STRAHLPHYS nuclear isomerism; **Kernkasten** m FERTIG *Gießen* core box; **Kernkopfverankerungseinheit** f KERNTECH core head plug unit; **Kernkraft** f KERNTECH nuclear power; **Kernkraftanteil** m ELEKTRIZ, KERNTECH nuclear tranche; **Kernkraftwerk** nt ELEKTRIZ, ELEKTROTECH, KERNTECH nuclear power station; **Kernkraftwerk mit Spitzenlast** nt KERNTECH peak load nuclear power plant; **Kernkraftwerk mit zwei Kühlkreisen** nt KERNTECH two-circuit nuclear power plant; **Kernladung** f TEILPHYS nuclear charge; **Kernladungszahl** f KERNTECH, PHYS, STRAHLPHYS atomic number, TEILPHYS proton number; **Kernlautheit** f AKUSTIK main loudness; **Kernleitwert** m TELEKOM transfer impedance; **Kernlochdurchmesser** m MASCHINEN core hole

kernlos: **~er Anker** m ELEKTRIZ coreless armature; **~er Induktionsofen** m HEIZ & KÄLTE coreless induction furnace

Kern: **Kernmagneton** nt TEILPHYS nuclear magneton; **Kern-Mantel-Exzentrizität** f TELEKOM core-cladding concentricity error; **Kernmarke** f FERTIG *Gießen* core print, print; **Kernmasse** f *(MN)* KERNTECH nuclear mass *(MN)*; **Kernmitte** f OPTIK *Lichtleiter* core center (AmE), core centre (BrE); **Kernmittelpunkt** m TELEKOM core center (AmE), core centre (BrE); **Kernmodell** nt TEILPHYS nuclear model; **Kernmodell mit variablem Kernträgheitsmoment** nt KERNTECH variable moment of inertia model; **Kernmodus** m TELEKOM guided mode; **Kernnagel** m BAU core nail, FERTIG *Getriebelehre* chaplet, *Gießen* sprig; **Kernobst** nt LEBENSMITTEL pomaceous fruit; **Kernphysik** f KERNTECH nuclear physics, PHYS atomic physics; **Kernphysik im mittleren Energiebereich** f KERNTECH medium-energy nuclear physics; **Kernpotential** nt STRAHLPHYS, TEILPHYS nuclear potential; **Kernprobe** f BAU core sample; **Kernprüfung** f ELEKTRIZ core test; **Kernquadrupolmoment** nt PHYS nuclear quadrupole moment; **Kernquerschnitt** m OPTIK core area; **Kernradius** m *(r)* KERNTECH nuclear radius *(r)*; **Kernreaktion** f TEILPHYS nuclear reaction; **Kernreaktionsmechanismus** m TEILPHYS nuclear reaction channel; **Kernreaktor** m ELEKTRIZ, ELEKTROTECH nuclear reactor, KERNTECH atomic pile, nuclear reactor, pile, PHYS atomic pile, reactor pressure vessel, STRAHLPHYS atomic pile; **Kernrohr** nt ERDÖL core barrel; **Kernsand** m FERTIG *Gießen* core sand; **Kernschablone** f FERTIG *Gießen* core board; **Kernschatten** m PHYS umbra; **Kernspaltung** f KERNTECH, TEILPHYS fission, nuclear fission; **Kernspaltungswirkungsquerschnitt** m PHYS fission cross section; **Kernspeicher** m COMP & DV core storage (AmE), core store (BrE); **Kernspektrum**

nt STRAHLPHYS nuclear radiation spectrum; **Kernspin** m STRAHLPHYS nuclear spin; **Kernspinresonanzlog** nt KERNTECH NMR log; **Kernspur** f KERNTECH nuclear track; **Kernstahlgerippe** nt FERTIG *Gießen* core grid; **Kernstrahlung** f KERNTECH, STRAHLPHYS nuclear radiation; **Kernstück** nt FERTIG *Riemen* center (AmE), centre (BrE); **Kernsymmetrie-Energie** f STRAHLPHYS nuclear symmetry energy; **Kerntechnik** f KERNTECH, PHYS nucleonics

kerntechnisch: **~e Prüfaufsicht** f KERNTECH ANIS, QUAL authorized nuclear inspector supervisor; **~er Prüfsachverständiger** m QUAL ANI, authorized nuclear inspector

Kern: **Kerntoleranzbereich** m TELEKOM core tolerance field; **Kerntoleranzfeld** nt OPTIK *Lichtleiter* core tolerance field; **Kerntransformator** m ELEKTRIZ, ELEKTROTECH core transformer, core-type transformer; **Kerntrockenkammer** f FERTIG *Gießen* core stove; **Kernverformung** f KERNTECH nuclear deformation; **Kernverlust** m ELEKTRIZ iron loss; **Kernverluste** m pl ELEKTRIZ, PHYS core losses; **Kernverschmelzung** f KERNTECH karyogamy; **Kernwiderstand** m TELEKOM mutual impedance; **Kernzerschmiedung** f FERTIG hammer pipe; **Kernzone** f TELEKOM core area; **Kernzustandsgleichung** f STRAHLPHYS nuclear equation of state

Kerogen nt ERDÖL kerogen

Kerosin nt ERDÖL *(RP-1)* *Destillationsprodukt* kerosene (AmE) *(RP-1)*, RAUMFAHRT *(RP-1)* kerosene *(RP-1)*, THERMOD kerosene (AmE), paraffin (BrE), TRANS *(RP-1)* kerosene (AmE), paraffin (BrE) *(RP-1)*

Kerr-Effekt m PHYS *elektro-optisch* Kerr electro-optical effect, *magneto-optisch* Kerr magneto-optical effect

Kerr-Zelle f PHYS Kerr cell

Kerze f KFZTECH *Zündung* plug, spark plug; **neue ~** f OPTIK new candle; **Kerzenfuß** m KFZTECH *Zündung* plug socket, spark plug socket

Kessel m EISENBAHN, KOHLEN, LEBENSMITTEL, MASCHINEN, MECHAN boiler, METROL *Zentrifuge* bowl, THERMOD, WASSERTRANS *Schiffantrieb* boiler; **~ mit Klöpperböden** m HYDRAUL disc-ended boiler (BrE), disk-ended boiler (AmE); **Kesselalarm** m HYDRAUL boiler alarm; **Kesselalarmschwimmer** m HYDRAUL *Sicherheitseinrichtung* boiler emergency float; **Kesselanlage** f HEIZ & KÄLTE boiler plant; **Kesselarmaturen** f pl HYDRAUL boiler fittings; **Kesselausrüstung** f HYDRAUL boiler fittings; **Kesselbau** m HEIZ & KÄLTE boiler engineering; **Kesselbauer** m HYDRAUL boilermaker; **Kesselbeschickung** f HYDRAUL boiler feeding; **Kesselblech** nt HYDRAUL boiler plate; **Kesseldruck** m MASCHINEN boiler pressure; **Kesselersatzspeisepumpe** f HYDRAUL *Kesselhilfsspeisepumpe* auxiliary boiler feeder; **Kesselexplosion** f HYDRAUL, SICHERHEIT boiler explosion; **Kesselfeuerraum** m HEIZ & KÄLTE, HYDRAUL boiler furnace; **Kesselfeuerung** f HYDRAUL boiler furnace; **Kesselflammrohr** nt HYDRAUL boiler flue; **Kesselfront** f HYDRAUL boiler front; **Kesselfuchs** m HYDRAUL boiler flue; **Kesselführung** f HEIZ & KÄLTE boiler operation; **Kesselhammer** m HYDRAUL boiler-scaling hammer; **Kesselhaus** nt HEIZ & KÄLTE, HYDRAUL boiler house; **Kesselhersteller** m HYDRAUL boilermaker; **Kesselherstellung** f HEIZ & KÄLTE, HYDRAUL boilermaking; **Kesselhilfsspeisepumpe** f HYDRAUL *Kesselersatzspeisepumpe* auxiliary boiler feeder; **Kesselkohle** f KOHLEN boiler coal; **Kes-**

selkohle *f* KOHLEN boiler coal; **Kessellagerung** *f* FERTIG boiler bedding; **Kesselleistung** *f* HEIZ & KÄLTE boiler capacity, boiler output; **Kesselmanometer** *nt* GERÄT boiler gage (AmE), boiler gauge (BrE); **Kesselmantel** *m* FERTIG boiler barrel, HYDRAUL boiler jacket, boiler jacketing, boiler shell; **Kesselnaht** *f* FERTIG boiler weld; **Kesselniet** *nt* HYDRAUL boiler rivet; **Kesselofen** *m* FERTIG rotary furnace; **Kesselprüfblech** *nt* HYDRAUL boiler test plate; **Kesselrauchgaskanal** *m* HYDRAUL boiler flue; **Kesselraum** *m* HYDRAUL boiler room; **Kesselrohr** *nt* MASCHINEN boiler tube; **Kesselrohrwalze** *f* HYDRAUL boiler tube expander; **Kesselrost** *m* HEIZ & KÄLTE boiler grate; **Kesselschlacke** *f* BAU clinker, MECHAN boiler slag; **Kesselschmied** *m* HYDRAUL boiler smith; **Kesselschweißen** *nt* FERTIG boiler welding; **Kesselschweißer** *m* FERTIG boiler welder; **Kesselschwimmer** *m* HYDRAUL *Niveauregelung* boiler float; **Kesselspeisepumpe** *f* HEIZ & KÄLTE boiler feed pump, boiler feeder; **Kesselspeisewasser** *nt* ERDÖL *Dampferzeugung* boiler feed water; **Kesselspeisung** *f* HYDRAUL boiler feeding

Kesselstein[1] *m* EISENBAHN boiler scale, FERTIG boiler scale, fur, scale, HEIZ & KÄLTE scale, HYDRAUL boiler scale

Kesselstein:[2] ~ **ansetzen** *vi* FERTIG fur; ~ **entfernen** *vi* FERTIG descale

Kesselstein: **Kesselsteinablagerung** *f* LEBENSMITTEL, WASSERVERSORG boiler scale formation; **Kesselsteinbildung** *f* WASSERVERSORG boiler scale formation; **Kesselsteinhammer** *m* MASCHINEN scaling hammer; **Kesselsteinlösemittel** *nt* HEIZ & KÄLTE boiler-cleaning compound; **Kesselsteinmittel** *nt* CHEMIE anti-incrustant

kesselsteinverhütend *adj* FERTIG anti-ager scale

Kesselsteinverhütungsmittel *nt* HEIZ & KÄLTE scale inhibitor

Kessel: **Kesseltemperaturmeßgerät** *nt* GERÄT boiler temperature meter; **Kesselüberprüfung** *f* SICHERHEIT boiler inspection; **Kesselummantelung** *f* HEIZ & KÄLTE jacket, HYDRAUL boiler jacketing; **Kesselverkleidung** *f* HEIZ & KÄLTE jacket, HYDRAUL boiler jacket, boiler lagging; **Kesselwagen** *m* EISENBAHN, KFZTECH tank car (AmE), tank wagon (BrE); **Kesselwasserbehandlung** *f* HEIZ & KÄLTE boiler water purification, boiler water treatment; **Kesselwasserreinigung** *f* HEIZ & KÄLTE boiler water purification, boiler water treatment; **Kesselwerk** *nt* HYDRAUL boiler works; **Kesselwirkungsgrad** *m* HEIZ & KÄLTE boiler efficiency; **Kesselzug** *m* HYDRAUL boiler flue

Ketazin *nt* CHEMIE ketazine

Keten *nt* CHEMIE ketene

Ketimin *nt* CHEMIE ketimine

Ketobernstein- *pref* CHEMIE oxalacetic

Ketocarbonsäure *f* CHEMIE keto acid, oxo acid

Ketoform *f* CHEMIE keto form

Ketol *nt* CHEMIE ketol

Keton *nt* CHEMIE, KUNSTSTOFF, LEBENSMITTEL ketone; **Keton-** *pref* CHEMIE ketonic

ketonartig *adj* CHEMIE ketonic

ketonisch *adj* CHEMIE ketonic

Ketosäure *f* CHEMIE keto acid, oxo acid

Ketsch *f* WASSERTRANS *Segeln* ketch

Kettbaum:[1] **auf den ~ gewickelt** *adj* TEXTIL wound onto the beam

Kettbaum[2] *m* TEXTIL beam, warp beam, weaver's beam, yarn roller; **Kettbaumfärbeapparat** *m* TEXTIL beam-dyeing machine; **Kettbaumfärben** *nt* TEXTIL beam dyeing; **Kettbaumfärbung** *f* TEXTIL beam dyeing

Kette *f* BAU, COMP & DV chain, FERTIG *Drahtweben* warp, *Fertigung* line, KFZTECH, KONSTZEICH, MASCHINEN, MECHAN chain, PAPIER, TEXTIL chain, warp, WASSERTRANS chain; **Ketten** *nt* COMP & DV chaining; **Kettenanschärer** *m* TEXTIL beamer; **Kettenantrieb** *m* KFZTECH *Kraftübertragung, Motorrad* chain drive, MASCHINEN chain drive, chain transmission, MECHAN chain drive; **Kettenantriebsritzel** *nt* KFZTECH drive sprocket; **Kettenbecherwerk** *nt* MASCHINEN chain elevator (AmE), chain lift (BrE); **Kettenbefehl** *m* COMP & DV chain; **Kettenbemaßung** *f* KONSTZEICH chain dimensioning; **Kettenblock** *m* MECHAN chain block; **Kettenbruchentwicklung** *f* MATH arithmetic progression; **Kettenbrücke** *f* BAU chain bridge; **Kettendrucker** *m* COMP & DV chain printer (AmE), train printer (BrE); **Kettenfähre** *f* WASSERTRANS chain ferry; **Kettenfahrleitung** *f* EISENBAHN catenary; **Kettenfahrzeug** *nt* KFZTECH tracked vehicle; **Kettenfläche** *f* GEOM catenoid; **Kettenflaschenzug** *m* MASCHINEN chain block, chain hoist, chain pulley block; **Kettenförderer** *m* MASCHINEN chain conveyor; **Kettenförderung** *f* KOHLEN chain haulage; **Kettenführung** *f* KFZTECH *Motor*, MASCHINEN chain guide; **Kettengehäuse** *nt* KFZTECH *Kraftübertragung, Motorrad* chain case; **Kettengetriebe** *nt* MASCHINEN chain gear, chain gearing, MECHAN sprocket wheel

kettengetrieben *adj* MASCHINEN chain-driven

Kette: **Kettenglied** *nt* KFZTECH *Kraftübertragung, Motorrad*, MASCHINEN chain link, MECHAN link, shackle; **Kettengreifer** *m* WASSERTRANS chain grab; **Kettenhebel** *m* MASCHINEN chain lever; **Kettenimpedanz** *f* AKUSTIK, ELEKTROTECH iterative impedance; **Kettenkasten** *m* SICHERHEIT chain case, WASSERTRANS chain locker, *Festmachen* cable locker; **Kettenkranz** *m* MASCHINEN sprocket wheel; **Kettenkupplung** *f* MASCHINEN chain coupling; **Kettenlänge** *f* KUNSTSTOFF chain length; **Kettenlaufwerk** *nt* MECHAN crawler; **Kettenleiter** *m* ELEKTROTECH interactive network, lattice network; **Kettenleiternetzwerk** *nt* ELEKTROTECH, PHYS ladder network; **Kettenlinie** *f* GEOM, MASCHINEN, MECHAN, PHYS, WASSERTRANS catenary; **Kettenmaßsystem** *nt* FERTIG, GERÄT incremental system; **Kettenmolekül** *nt* CHEMIE chain molecule, macromolecule; **Kettennuß** *f* MASCHINEN chain sprocket, sprocket wheel; **Kettenpumpe** *f* MASCHINEN chain pump, WASSERVERSORG chain pump, paternoster pump; **Kettenrad** *nt* FERTIG chain wheel, sprocket, KFZTECH *Motorradgetriebe* sprocket, MASCHINEN chain sheave, chain wheel, sprocket, MECHAN sprocket wheel; **Kettenradwalzfräser** *m* FERTIG sprocket hob

Kettenreaktion *f* KERNTECH, MASCHINEN, PHYS chain reaction, STRAHLPHYS chain explosion; ~ **von Neutronen bei der Kernspaltung** *f* KERNTECH, STRAHLPHYS chain reaction of neutrons in nuclear fission; **Kettenreaktionsausmaß** *nt* KERNTECH chain-reacting amount

Kette: **Kettenregel** *f* MATH *zur Differenzierung von impliziten Funktionen* chain rule; **Kettenrelais** *nt* ELEKTROTECH link relay; **Kettenrohrzange** *f* MASCHINEN chain wrench; **Kettenrolle** *f* MASCHINEN chain sprocket; **Kettenrost** *m* MASCHINEN chain grate; **Kettensäge** *f* FERTIG, MASCHINEN chain saw; **Kettenschaltung** *f* ELEKTROTECH, PHYS ladder network;

Kettenschärmaschine *f* TEXTIL warper; **Kettenschlaufe** *f* SICHERHEIT chain sling; **Kettenschleifer** *m* PAPIER chain grinder; **Kettenschlinge** *f* MASCHINEN chain sling; **Kettenschlüssel** *m* MASCHINEN chain pipe wrench; **Kettenschutz** *m* KFZTECH *Kraftübertragung, Motorrad* chainguard, MASCHINEN chain guard; **Kettenspanner** *m* KFZTECH *Kraftübertragung, Motorrad* chain tensioner, PAPIER chain tightener; **Kettenspannungsteiler** *m* ELEKTRONIK ladder attenuator; **Kettenstruktur** *f* REGELUNG chain structure; **Kettenteiler** *m* ELEKTRONIK ladder attenuator; **Kettenteilung** *f* FERTIG, MASCHINEN chain pitch; **Kettentrieb** *m* KFZTECH, MASCHINEN chain and sprocket wheel drive; **Kettentrommel** *f* MASCHINEN chain drum; **Kettenwicklung** *f* ELEKTROTECH basket winding; **Kettenwiderstand** *m* ELEKTRIZ, PHYS iterative impedance; **Kettenwirken** *nt* TEXTIL warp knitting; **Kettenwirkerei** *f* TEXTIL warp knitting; **Kettenwirkmaschine** *f* TEXTIL warp knitting machine; **Kettenzugmaschine** *f* BAU tracked tractor

Kettfaden *m* TEXTIL end; **Kettfadenablaßvorrichtung** *f* TEXTIL let-off motion; **Kettfadenbruch** *m* TEXTIL breakage, warp break; **Kettfadenwächter** *m* TEXTIL warp stop motion; **Kettfadenwächterlamelle** *f* TEXTIL drop wire

Kettgarn *nt* PAPIER warp yarn

Kettschären *nt* TEXTIL warping

Kettschlichten *nt* TEXTIL slasher sizing

kettschlichtgefärbt *adj* TEXTIL slasher dyed

Kettstreifen *m pl* TEXTIL warp streaks

Kettstuhlwirkerei *f* TEXTIL warp knitting

Kettung *f* KÜNSTL INT chaining

Keulenbreite *f* ELEKTRONIK *Antennentechnik* beamwidth

Keulengriff *m* MASCHINEN club handle

keV *abbr (Kilo-Elektronenvolt)* TEILPHYS keV *(kilo electronvolt)*

Kevlar *nt* WASSERTRANS *Schiffbau* kevlar

Keyboard *nt* COMP & DV keyboard

Keyes-Verfahren *nt* LEBENSMITTEL *Destillation* Keyes process

KF *abbr (Konfidenzfaktor)* KÜNSTL INT CF *(confidence factor)*

kfG *abbr (kontextfreie Grammatik)* KÜNSTL INT CFG *(context-free grammar)*

K-förmig: ~**er Zahn** *m* MASCHINEN hook tooth, hooked tooth

Kf-Wert *m* ABFALL coefficient of permeability

Kfz[1] *abbr (Kraftfahrzeug)* KFZTECH MC *(motorcar)*

Kfz:[2] **Kfz-Sicherheitseinrichtung** *f* SICHERHEIT road safety device; **Kfz-Teile** *nt pl* KFZTECH motorcar parts

kg *abbr* LABOR *(Kilo, Kilogramm)* kg *(kilogram)*, PHYS *(Kilogramm)* kg *(kilogramme)*

kgN *abbr (kleinster gemeinsamer Nenner)* MATH LCD *(least common denominator)*

kgT *abbr (kleinster gemeinsamer Teiler)* GEOM LCD *(least common denominator)*

kgV *abbr (kleinstes gemeinsames Vielfaches)* COMP & DV LCM *(least common multiple)*, GEOM LCM *(lowest common multiple)*

kHz *abbr (Kilohertz)* ELEKTRIZ, RADIO kHz *(kilohertz)*

Kick *m* ERDÖL *Bohrtechnik* kick; **Kickdown** *m* KFZTECH *Automatikgetriebe* kickdown; **Kickdown-Schalter** *m* KFZTECH kickdown switch; **Kickstarter** *m* KFZTECH *Motorradmotor* kick starter

Kiel *m* WASSERTRANS keel; ~ **zum Auflaufen auf Land** *m* WASSERTRANS *Schiffbau* beaching keel

Kielbank *f* WASSERTRANS *Instandhaltung* careening grid

kielbrüchig *adj* WASSERTRANS *Schiff* broken-backed

Kiel: Kielbucht *f* WASSERTRANS *Schiffbau* sagging; **Kielgang** *m* WASSERTRANS keel strake, *Schiffbau* garboard strake

kielholen *vt* WASSERTRANS *Instandhaltung* careen

Kiel: Kiellegung *f* WASSERTRANS keel laying; **Kielplanke** *f* WASSERTRANS garboard plank; **Kielplatte** *f* WASSERTRANS keel plate; **Kielschwein** *nt* WASSERTRANS keelson; **Kielstapelung** *f* WASSERTRANS *Schiffbau* cribbing; **Kielträger** *m* RAUMFAHRT keel; **Kielwasser** *nt* MEERSCHMUTZ, STRÖMPHYS, WASSERTRANS *Schiff* wake

Kies *m* BAU, KOHLEN gravel

Kiese *m pl* BAU pebbles

Kiesel- *pref* CHEMIE siliceous; **Kieselerde** *f* ELEKTRONIK, PHYS, SICHERHEIT silica; **Kieselerdestaub** *m* SICHERHEIT silica dust; **Kieselfilterschicht** *f* ABFALL *Deponie* gravel filter layer; **Kieselgel** *nt* LEBENSMITTEL *Trokkenmittel*, VERPACK silica gel; **Kieselgur** *f* LEBENSMITTEL diatomaceous earth; **Kieselhydrogel** *nt* KUNSTSTOFF precipitated silica; **Kieselsäure** *f* CHEMIE silicic acid; **Kieselstein** *m* BAU pebble; **Kieselwolfram-** *pref* CHEMIE *Säure* silicotungstic

Kies: Kiesgrube *f* BAU, WASSERVERSORG gravel pit; **Kiespreßdach** *nt* BAU felt and gravel roof; **Kiessand** *m* BAU grit; **Kiesschotter** *m* BAU ballast; **Kiesstrand** *m* WASSERTRANS *Meer* shingle

Kikuchi-Linie *f* KERNTECH Kikuchi line

KI-Lernprogramm *nt (intelligentes Lernprogramm)* KÜNSTL INT ITS *(intelligent tutoring system)*

Kiln *m* KOHLEN kiln

Kilo *nt (Kilogramm)* LABOR kilo *(k)*; **Kilobyte** *nt (KB)* COMP & DV, TELEKOM kilobyte *(KB)*; **Kilo-Elektronenvolt** *m (keV)* TEILPHYS kilo electronvolt *(keV)*; **Kilogramm** *nt* LABOR *(Kilo, k, kg)*, PHYS *(kg)* SI-Einheit der Masse kilogram, kilogramme *(kg)*; **Kilohertz** *nt (kHz)* ELEKTRIZ, RADIO kilohertz *(kHz)*; **Kilokalorie** *f (kcal)* LEBENSMITTEL kilocalorie, kilogram calorie, kilogramme calorie *(kcal)*

Kilometer *m (km)* METROL kilometer (AmE), kilometre (BrE) *(km)*; **Kilometerpunkt** *m* EISENBAHN mileage point; **Kilometerstein** *m* TRANS milestone

Kilo: Kilonem *nt* CHEMIE kilonem; **Kilopondmeter** *m* METROL kilogram force meter; **Kilostream** *m* TELEKOM *Punkt-zu-Punkt Analog-Datenverbindung* kilostream circuit; **Kilovolt** *nt (kV)* ELEKTROTECH kilovolt *(kV)*; **Kilowatt** *nt (kW)* ELEKTRIZ kilowatt *(kW)*; **Kilowattstunde** *f (kWh)* ELEKTRIZ kilowatt-hour *(kWh)*, ELEKTROTECH, PHYS *Energieeinheit* kilowatt hour *(kWh)*

Kimm *f* WASSERTRANS *astronomische Navigation* visible horizon; **Kimmbeplattung** *f* WASSERTRANS bilge plating

Kimme *f* LUFTTRANS *Wasserflugzeug* chine

kimmerisch: ~**e Gebirgsbildung** *f* ERDÖL Cimmerian orogeny; ~**e Orogenese** *f* ERDÖL *Geologie* Cimmerian orogeny; ~**e Schichtenkontinuitätsstörung** *f* ERDÖL *Geologie* Cimmerian unconformity

Kimm: Kimmgang *m* WASSERTRANS bilge strake; **Kimmlinie** *f* WASSERTRANS sea line; **Kimmplatte** *f* WASSERTRANS bilge plate; **Kimmstringer** *m* WASSERTRANS bilge stringer; **Kimmstütze** *f* WASSERTRANS bilge shore; **Kimmtiefe** *f* WASSERTRANS *Navigation* dip of horizon

kindersicher: ~e Verpackung *f* VERPACK child-resistant packaging; ~er Verschluß *m* KER & GLAS childproof finish

Kindersicherungsverschluß *m* VERPACK CRC, child-resistant closure

K-Index *m* RADIO K-index

Kinematik *f* FERTIG, MASCHINEN, MECHAN kinematics

kinematisch[1] *adj* EISENBAHN, ERGON, FERTIG, MASCHINEN, MECHAN, NICHTFOSS ENERG, PHYS kinematic

kinematisch:[2] ~e Begrenzungslinie *f* EISENBAHN kinematic gage (AmE), kinematic gauge (BrE); ~e Fahrzeugbegrenzungslinie *f* EISENBAHN kinematic vehicle gage (AmE), kinematic vehicle gauge (BrE); ~e Kette *f* MASCHINEN kinematic chain; ~e Viskosität *f* HEIZ & KÄLTE, MASCHINEN, MECHAN, NICHTFOSS ENERG, PHYS kinematic viscosity; ~e Wirbelzähigkeit *f* (ε) HYDRAUL kinematic eddy viscosity (ε); ~e Zähigkeit *f* MECHAN, NICHTFOSS ENERG, PHYS kinematic viscosity; ~er Zwang *m* FERTIG constraint, *Getriebelehre* geometrical constraint

Kinesiologie *f* ERGON kinesiology

Kineskop *nt* ELEKTRONIK *Fernsehen* cinescope

Kinetik *f* MASCHINEN, MECHAN, METALL, PHYS, THERMOD kinetics; ~ der Gase *f* THERMOD gas kinetics

kinetisch[1] *adj* ERGON, FERTIG, KERNTECH, MASCHINEN, MECHAN, PHYS, RAUMFAHRT, STRAHLPHYS kinetic

kinetisch:[2] ~e Aufheizung *f* RAUMFAHRT *Raumschiff* kinetic heating; ~e Energie *f* ERGON, MASCHINEN, MECHAN, PHYS, RAUMFAHRT kinetic energy; ~ erzeugter Auftrieb *m* UMWELTSCHMUTZ kinetically-induced buoyancy; ~e Gastheorie *f* PHYS, THERMOD kinetic theory of gases; ~er Isotopeneffekt *m* KERNTECH kinetic isotope effect; ~e Spektrofotometrie *f* STRAHLPHYS kinetic spectrophotometry; ~e Trennung *f* KERNTECH kinetic separation; ~e Wärme *f* MECHAN, PHYS kinetic heat

Kingston-Ventil *nt* WASSERTRANS *Schiff* Kingston valve

Kink *f* WASSERTRANS kink

Kipp-[1] *pref* BAU, KFZTECH tilting

Kipp:[2] ~scher Apparat *m* LABOR *Generator* Kipp's apparatus

Kipp-: Kippachse *f* BAU horizontal axis

kippbar: ~er Turm *m* NICHTFOSS ENERG tiltable tower

Kipp-: Kippbecherwerk *nt* TRANS tipping bucket conveyor; **Kippbehälter** *m* KERNTECH tilting basket; **Kippbühne** *f* TRANS tipping platform

Kippe *f* KOHLEN tip

Kippen *nt* BAU tipping, FERNSEH tilt, FERTIG tilting, LUFTTRANS pitching

kippen *vt* BAU tilt, tip, KOHLEN dump

Kipper *m* ABFALL skip, tipper truck, BAU tipper, KFZTECH dump car, dump truck, dump wagon, KOHLEN tipper; **Kipperaufbau** *m* KFZTECH tilting body

kippfähig: ~er Wagen *m* EISENBAHN tip-up car, tip-up wagon

Kipp-: Kippfahrzeug *nt* BAU tipper; **Kippfenster** *nt* BAU pivot-hung window; **Kippfensterflügel** *m* BAU pivot-hung sash; **Kippflügelflugzeug** *nt* LUFTTRANS gyroplane, tilt wing plane; **Kippform** *f* KER & GLAS tilting mould; **Kippfrequenz** *f* ELEKTRONIK, FERNSEH, LABOR, TELEKOM sweep frequency; **Kippglied** *nt* ELEKTRONIK bistable

Kipphebel *m* ELEKTROTECH tumbler, FERTIG *Kunststoffinstallationen* tilting lever, KFZTECH rocker, rocker arm, MASCHINEN rocking arm, tumbler lever, MECHAN rocker; **Kipphebelabdeckung** *f* KFZTECH rocker cover; **Kipphebelbock** *m* KFZTECH rocker arm support; **Kipphebeleinheit** *f* KFZTECH rocker arm assembly; **Kipphebelgehäuse** *nt* KFZTECH rocker box; **Kipphebelschalter** *m* ELEKTROTECH tumbler switch; **Kipphebelwelle** *f* KFZTECH rocker arm shaft

Kipp-: Kippkreis *m* FERNSEH sweep circuit; **Kippkübel** *m* BAU dumping bucket, tipping bucket, MEERSCHMUTZ skip, TRANS dumping bucket, tilting skip; **Kipplager** *nt* MASCHINEN rocker bearing; **Kipp-LKW** *m* KFZTECH dump truck; **Kipplore** *f* TRANS tilting wagon; **Kippmischer** *m* FERNSEH tilt mixer; **Kippmoment** *nt* BAU overturning moment, MASCHINEN tilting moment, NICHTFOSS ENERG pitching moment; **Kippregel** *f* BAU *Vermessung* leveling alidade (AmE), levelling alidade (BrE); **Kippschalter** *m* ELEKTRIZ rocker switch, ELEKTROTECH toggle switch, tumbler switch, KONTROLL toggle switch; **Kippschaltung** *f* ELEKTRONIK flip-flop, multivibrator

Kipp-: Kippschwingung *f* ELEKTRIZ, ELEKTRONIK, PHYS relaxation oscillation; **Kippstromgatter** *nt* FERNSEH scanning gate; **Kippstufe** *f* FERNSEH dumping circuit; **Kippstufenrost** *m* ABFALL rocking grate; **Kippstuhl** *m* KERNTECH upender; **Kipptisch** *m* FERTIG, MASCHINEN tilting table; **Kippverstärker** *m* ELEKTRONIK bistable amplifier, GERÄT sweep deflection amplifier; **Kippvorrichtung** *f* BAU tipping device, KERNTECH tilting device, KFZTECH dump; **Kippwagen** *m* KFZTECH dump wagon, tipper

KI-Programmiersprache *f* KÜNSTL INT AI programing language (AmE), AI programming language (BrE)

Kirchhoff: ~sche Gesetze *nt pl* ELEKTRIZ, ELEKTROTECH *bei Stromnetzen* Kirchhoff's laws; ~sches Strahlungsgesetz *nt* STRAHLPHYS Kirchhoff's law of emission of radiation

Kirnen *nt* LEBENSMITTEL *Margarineherstellung* churning

Kirschrotglut *f* METALL cherry-red heat

kissenförmig: ~e Verzeichnung *f* FOTO, OPTIK, PHYS negative distortion (AmE), pincushion distortion (BrE)

Kiste *f* FERTIG *Wärmebehandlung*, TRANS box, VERPACK carton; **Kistenabfüllung** *f* VERPACK case packing; **Kistenglühen** *nt* FERTIG box annealing; **Kistenheber** *m* MASCHINEN box hook; **Kistenofen** *m* THERMOD pot furnace; **Kistenöffner** *m* VERPACK nail puller; **Kistenpalette** *f* TRANS box pallet; **Kistenpalette mit Gittergeflecht** *f* TRANS box pallet with mesh

KI-System *nt* KÜNSTL INT AI system

Kitt *m* BAU putty

kittartig: ~e Formmasse *f* (DMC) KUNSTSTOFF dough-molding compound (AmE), dough-moulding compound (BrE) (DMC)

kitten *vt* FERTIG putty, KER & GLAS cement

Kitt: Kittentfernungsmesser *nt* BAU hacking knife; **Kittfalz** *m* BAU *Fenster* fillister; **Kittmesser** *nt* BAU putty knife, stopping knife

Kjeldahl: Kjeldahl-Apparat *m* LABOR *Stickstoffbestimmung* Kjeldahl digestion apparatus; **Kjeldahlmethode** *f* KERNTECH *Stickstoffbestimmung* Kjeldahl method

K-Jetronic-Einspritzanlage *f* KFZTECH K-Jetronic fuel injection, continuous injection system

K-Kanten-Gamma-Densitometrie *f* KERNTECH K-edge gamma densitometry

Klammer[1] *f* BAU staple, DRUCK parenthesis, FERTIG staple, MASCHINEN clamp, clamping band, clasp, cramp, MECHAN clip, RAUMFAHRT *Raumschiff* brace

Klammer:[2] in ~ setzen *vt* MATH bracket together
Klammer: Klammerflansch *m* MASCHINEN clamped tube flange
klammerfrei: ~er Ausdruck *m* COMP & DV prefix notation; **~e Schreibweise** *f* COMP & DV Polish notation, parenthesis-free notation
Klammer: Klammerhaken *m* MASCHINEN dog hook; **Klammerimpulse** *m pl* FERNSEH clamping pulses
Klammern *f pl* DRUCK *eckige* brackets, FERNSEH cramping, MATH brackets
Klammerpulsgenerator *m* FERNSEH clamp pulse generator
Klammerung *f* FERNSEH clamping; **Klammerungsschaltung** *f* FERNSEH clamping circuit
Klammer: Klammerverbindungen für Rohre *f pl* MASCHINEN clamped pipe connections; **Klammerzeichen** *nt* MATH *Logik* quantifier
Klang *m* AKUSTIK, AUFNAHME combination sound, tone; **Klanganalysator** *m* AKUSTIK sound analyser (BrE), sound analyzer (AmE); **Klangcode** *m* AKUSTIK, AUFNAHME sound code; **Klangdiffusor** *m* AUFNAHME sound diffuser; **Klangfarbe** *f* AKUSTIK timbre, timbre of sound; **Klangfarbenregler** *m* AUFNAHME tone control; **Klangspektrograph** *m* AKUSTIK sound spectrograph; **Klangverzerrung** *f* AUFNAHME sound distortion
Klapp- *pref* FERTIG, FOTO, LUFTTRANS folding; **Klappachse** *f* LUFTTRANS *Hubschrauber* folding axis
klappbar[1] *adj* LUFTTRANS folding, MECHAN, VERPACK hinged
klappbar:[2] **~er Außenlastträger** *m* LUFTTRANS *Hubschrauber* folding pylon; **~es Luftschraubenblatt** *nt* LUFTTRANS *Hubschrauber* folding blade; **~er Steckverschluß** *m* VERPACK hinged plug orifice closure
Klapp-: Klappbrücke *f* BAU balance bridge, bascule bridge, counterpoise bridge; **Klappdeckel** *m* FERTIG hinged cover, VERPACK hinged lid
Klappe *f* AKUSTIK key, BAU valve, FERTIG leaf, *Kunststoffinstallationen* hinged cover, valve, HEIZ & KÄLTE damper, trap, HYDRAUL shutter, *Absperrorgan von Rohrleitungen* valve, KERNTECH valve, LABOR lid, MASCHINEN bascule, cap, clack, flap, MECHAN flap, valve, PAPIER, RAUMFAHRT *Raumschiff*, TEXTIL, VERPACK flap; **äußere ~** *f* VERPACK outer flap; **~ mit Schnappverschluß** *f* VERPACK flap snap; **Klappendurchflußmesser** *m* GERÄT airfoil flow meter, flap flow meter; **Klappenflügel** *m* HEIZ & KÄLTE damper blade; **Klappenführungsrippe** *f* LUFTTRANS flap track rib; **Klappenheber** *m* LUFTTRANS flap jack; **Klappenkolben** *m* HYDRAUL bucket; **Klappenkolbenpumpe** *f* HYDRAUL bucket pump; **Klappenscharnier** *nt* BAU flap hinge; **Klappenschrank** *m* TELEKOM switchboard; **Klappenschrank für Induktoranruf** *m* TELEKOM magneto switchboard; **Klappenströmungsmesser** *m* GERÄT airfoil flow meter; **Klappenteller** *m* FERTIG *Kunststoffinstallationen* valve disc (BrE), valve disk (AmE); **Klappentext** *m* DRUCK blurb; **Klappenträger** *m* FERTIG clapper box; **Klappenträgerklemmschraube** *f* FERTIG apron-clamping bolt; **Klappenventil** *nt* HYDRAUL butterfly valve, clapper valve, flap valve, leaf valve; **Klappenwehr** *nt* WASSERVERSORG lever weir
Klapp-: Klappfahrrad *nt* KFZTECH folding bicycle; **Klappflügelflugzeug** *nt* LUFTTRANS folding-wing aircraft; **Klappflügelpropeller** *m* WASSERTRANS *Schiffbau* folding propeller; **Klappgabel** *f* LUFTTRANS hinge fork; **Klappgelenk des Luftschraubenblattes** *nt* LUFTTRANS

Hubschrauber blade-folding hinge; **Klappkamera** *f* FOTO folding camera; **Klappladen** *m* BAU folding shutter; **Klappschütz** *nt* NICHTFOSS ENERG tilting gate; **Klappsitz** *m* KFZTECH tip-up seat; **Klappsucher** *m* FOTO collapsible viewfinder; **Klappsucher mit Gegenlichtblende** *m* FOTO folding viewfinder with hood; **Klapptisch** *m* MASCHINEN folding table; **Klapptor** *nt* NICHTFOSS ENERG flap gate; **Klapptür** *f* BAU flap door
klar[1] *adj* EISENBAHN, OPTIK clear, TEXTIL bright, WASSERTRANS clear
klar:[2] **~e Abbildung** *f* OPTIK clear image; **~e Konfiguration** *f* LUFTTRANS clean configuration
klar:[3] **~ passieren** *vt* EISENBAHN, WASSERTRANS clear
Kläranlage *f* ABFALL clarification plant, purification plant, sewage treatment plant, sewage works, wastewater purification plant, wastewater treatment plant; **Kläranlagebehälter** *m* WASSERVERSORG filtration vat; **Kläranlagenabfluß** *m* WASSERVERSORG sewage effluent
Klärapparat *m* CHEMIE clarifier
Klärbecken *nt* ABFALL clarification basin, clarification tank, CHEMTECH sedimentation basin, settling basin, ERDÖL *Bohrtechnik* clarifier basin, KOHLEN settling basin, WASSERVERSORG clarification basin, clarification tank
Klärbehälter *m* CHEMTECH sedimentation tank, WASSERVERSORG filtering basin, filtering tank
Klardauer *f* QUAL uptime
Klären *nt* CHEMTECH defecation
klären *vt* BAU, CHEMTECH, LEBENSMITTEL clarify
Klarfritte *f* KER & GLAS clear frit
Klärgas *nt* THERMOD digester gas
Klarglas *nt* KER & GLAS clear glass
Klärgrube *f* BAU dry well, settling pit, ERDÖL *Abscheidetechnik* decanting pit, WASSERVERSORG cess pit, cess pool
Klarheit *f* OPTIK *einer Abbildung*, WASSERVERSORG *des Wassers* clearness
klarieren *vt* EISENBAHN, WASSERTRANS clear
Klarifikator *m* CHEMIE clarifier
Klarlack *m* KUNSTSTOFF varnish
Klärleitung *f* ERDÖL *Abscheidetechnik* decanting trunk
klarmachen: ~ zum *vt* WASSERTRANS make ready, rig for
Klärmittel *nt* LEBENSMITTEL clarifier, fining agent
Klärschlamm *m* ABFALL sewage sludge, wastewater sludge, BAU digested sludge, WASSERVERSORG sewage sludge
Klarschriftleser *m* COMP & DV character reader
Klarsichtfolie *f* VERPACK cellophane, cling film, film wrap, transparent film; **Klarsichtfolienverpackung** *f* VERPACK seethrough packaging
Klarsichtkartonage *f* VERPACK skin pack
Klarsichtscheibe *f* WASSERTRANS clear-view screen
Klärspitze *f* KOHLEN settling cone
Klärsumpf *m* CHEMTECH settling sump, WASSERVERSORG settling tank
Klärteich *m* KOHLEN clear pond, settling pond
Klartext *m* COMP & DV plain text
Klärung *f* CHEMTECH purification, *durch Abgießen* decantation, ERDÖL *Abscheidetechnik* decantation, LEBENSMITTEL decantation, fining, *von Lösungen* defecation
Klärvorrichtung *f* LEBENSMITTEL clarifier
Klarwasser *nt* WASSERVERSORG clear water
Klärwerk *nt* ABFALL clarification plant, purification plant, sewage treatment plant, sewage works, wastewater treatment plant, wastewater treatment works,

WASSERVERSORG clarification plant

Klasse f COMP & DV, GERÄT *Meßgerät*, MASCHINEN class; **Klasse-AB-Verstärker** m ELEKTRONIK class AB-amplifier; **Klassenbreite** f QUAL class interval; **Klassengrenze** f QUAL class boundary, class limit; **Klassenmitte** f QUAL midpoint of class, midvalue of class interval

Klassierapparat m CHEMTECH classifier

Klassieren nt FERTIG *Erz* separation, KOHLEN grading

klassieren vt CHEMTECH classify, PAPIER screen

Klassierer m CHEMTECH, KOHLEN classifier

Klassierfachmann m KOHLEN classifier

Klassiermaschine f MASCHINEN grading machine

klassiert: ~**e Kohle** f KOHLEN graded coal

Klassiertrichter m KOHLEN cone classifier

Klassierung f BAU screening, *nach Korngrößen* grading; **Klassierungsdetektor** m TRANS selective vehicle detector

Klassifikation f WASSERTRANS *Handelsmarine* classification

Klassifizierung f VERPACK grading

klassisch: ~**er Elektronenradius** m PHYS classical radius of the electron; ~**es Pressen** nt KER & GLAS straight pressing; ~**e Thermodynamik** f THERMOD classic thermodynamics

Klaubarbeit f KOHLEN sorting by hand

klauben vt KOHLEN cob

Klaue f FERTIG dog, MASCHINEN, MECHAN claw, dog, jaw, PAPIER jaw; **Klauenfutter** nt MASCHINEN prong chuck; **Klauenkupplung** f FERTIG dog clutch, KFZTECH jaw clutch, *Getriebe* dog clutch, MASCHINEN claw clutch, dog clutch, dog coupling, jaw clutch, PAPIER jaw clutch; **Klauenpolmaschine** f ELEKTROTECH inductor machine

Klausel f KÜNSTL INT clause

Klaviersaitendraht m MASCHINEN piano string, piano wire

Klebeband nt ELEKTROTECH, KUNSTSTOFF, MECHAN adhesive tape, VERPACK adhesive tape, self-adhesive tape

Klebebindung f DRUCK perfect binding, unsewn binding, VERPACK parallel glueing

Klebeblock m DRUCK perfect-bound block

Klebeemulsion f VERPACK emulsion adhesive

Klebefläche f PAPIER adherend

Klebefolie f VERPACK adhesive film

Klebeheftung f DRUCK perfect binding, unsewn binding

Klebemaschine f DRUCK gluer, VERPACK adhesive machine, binding machine

Klebemittel nt CHEMIE, FERTIG agglutinant

Kleben nt DRUCK gluing up, ELEKTROTECH sticking, FERTIG *Metalle* bonding, VERPACK gluing

kleben[1] vt BAU glue, stick, DRUCK paste up, FERTIG *Metall* bond

kleben[2] vi KUNSTSTOFF, PAPIER, VERPACK adhere

klebend[1] adj CHEMIE, CHEMTECH agglutinant, PAPIER adhesive

klebend:[2] ~**er Kontakt** m ELEKTRIZ sticking contact

Klebepaste f DRUCK adhesive paste

Kleber m BAU cementing material, KUNSTSTOFF adhesive, glue, LEBENSMITTEL gluten, RADIO, SICHERHEIT adhesive; **Kleberdehnbarkeit** f LEBENSMITTEL gluten extensibility

Klebesandform f FERTIG *Thermitschweißen* sand and clay mold (AmE), sand and clay mould (BrE)

Klebeseite f VERPACK adhesive side

Klebesiegel nt SICHERHEIT tamper-proof seal

Klebestelle f FERNSEH *Band* splice; **Klebestellengeräusch** nt AUFNAHME bloop, blooping; **Klebestellenvertiefung** f AUFNAHME bloop punch

Klebestreifen m KUNSTSTOFF adhesive tape, self-adhesive tape

Klebeumbruch m DRUCK paste-up

Klebeverbindung f FERTIG adhesive-bonded joint, glued joint

Klebevorrichtung f VERPACK gluing device

Klebfestigkeit f KUNSTSTOFF bond strength

Klebfilm m VERPACK adhesive film

Klebfläche f KUNSTSTOFF adherend

Klebfuge f KUNSTSTOFF glue line, VERPACK glued joint

Klebfügeteil nt KUNSTSTOFF adherend

Klebkarton m VERPACK glued box

Klebmuffe f FERTIG *Kunststoffinstallationen* solvent cement socket

klebrig adj KUNSTSTOFF sticky, tacky, LEBENSMITTEL sticky, VERPACK tacky

Klebrigkeit f LEBENSMITTEL ropiness; **Klebrigkeitsniveau** nt VERPACK tack level

Klebrigmacher m CHEMIE tackiness agent, KUNSTSTOFF tackifier, tackifying agent

Klebstoff m KUNSTSTOFF, MECHAN, RADIO adhesive, TEXTIL glue, VERPACK adhesive glue, bonding agent, glue

klebstoffbeständig adj PAPIER adhesive-resistant

Klebstoffschicht f VERPACK adhesive film

Klebstutzen m FERTIG *Kunststoffinstallationen* spigot

Klebung f FERTIG *Kunststoffinstallationen* cementing

Klebverbindung f KUNSTSTOFF bond, VERPACK glued joint

Klebverschluß m VERPACK binding closure

Klebzement m KUNSTSTOFF cement

Kleeblatt nt RADIO *Antennentyp* cloverleaf; **Kleeblattzapfen** m FERTIG *Walze* wobbler

Kleesäure f FOTO oxalic acid

Kleiderstoffe m pl TEXTIL dress materials

Kleidung f SICHERHEIT *Schutzmaßnahmen* clothing, TEXTIL apparel; ~ **für die keimfreie Zelle** f SICHERHEIT asceptic room clothing; ~ **für die staubfreie Zelle** f SICHERHEIT asceptic room clothing

Kleidungsstück nt TEXTIL garment

Kleie f LEBENSMITTEL tailings, *Müllerei* break tailings; **Kleiebürste** f LEBENSMITTEL bran finisher

Klein:[1] ~**sche Flasche** f GEOM Klein bottle

klein:[1] ~**er gleich** adj MATH equal to or less than; **auf zu** ~**es Maß bearbeitet** adj FERTIG overmachined

klein:[2] ~**es Beiboot** nt WASSERTRANS cock; ~**erer Durchmesser** m MASCHINEN minor diameter; ~**e Fahrt** f KFZTECH *Schiff* slow speed; ~**er Fermatscher Satz** m MATH Fermat's little theory of prime numbers; ~**er Ganzton** m *(cf großer Ganzton)* AKUSTIK minor whole tone; ~**e Gasblase** f FERTIG pepper blister, pinhead; ~**ster gemeinsamer Nenner** m *(kgN)* MATH lowest common denominator *(LCD)*; ~**ster gemeinsamer Teiler** m *(kgT)* MATH least common denominator *(LCD)*; ~**stes gemeinsames Vielfaches** nt *(kgV)* COMP & DV, MATH least common multiple, lowest common multiple *(LCM)*; ~**es Gewicht** nt METROL net weight, short weight; ~**e und große Wartungsarbeiten** f pl LUFTTRANS minor and major servicing operation; ~**er Halbton** m AKUSTIK minor semitone; ~**er Holzpfropfen** m BAU spile; ~**e Kohlensorte** f KER & GLAS burgee; ~**er Kupolofen** m FERTIG cupolette; ~**e Leistung** f ELEKTROTECH low power; ~**ste nachweis-**

bare Spur f CHEMIE *Analyse* ultratrace; ~es Pleuelauge nt KFZTECH connecting rod small end, small end; ~e Sekunde f AKUSTIK minor second; ~e Septime f AKUSTIK minor seventh; ~e Sext f AKUSTIK minor sixth; ~e Stückzahl f FERTIG batch; ~e Terz f AKUSTIK minor third; ~e Tonne f METROL short ton; ~ste Umtastung f (MSK) ELEKTRONIK minimum-shift keying (MSK); ~es unbemanntes Wählamt nt TELEKOM CDO, community dial office; ~er vernachlässigbarer Durchmesserfehler m METROL minor diameter error; ~e Vorwölbung auf Glas f KER & GLAS tit; ~ster wahrnehmbarer Unterschied m ERGON just noticeable difference; ~er Wasserlauf m WASSERTRANS *Geographie* creek (AmE); ~er Widerstand m PHYS low resistance

Klein-² *pref* FOTO, VERPACK small; **Kleinauflage** f VERPACK short run; **Kleinbildfilm** m FOTO *35mm* miniature film; **Kleinbildkamera** f FOTO *35mm* miniature camera; **Kleinbuchstaben** m pl DRUCK lc, lower case; Kleinbus m KFZTECH microbus, minibus; **Kleindarstellung** f KONSTZEICH small-scale representation; **Kleindruck** m DRUCK fine print, LABOR low pressure; **Kleindruck-Manometer** nt GERÄT low-pressure gauge (BrE), low-pressure gage (AmE)

klein: auf ~eren Meßbereich umschalten *vt* GERÄT downrange

Kleinergleichzeichen nt MATH chevron

Kleinerzeichen nt MATH chevron

Klein-Gordon-Gleichung f PHYS Klein-Gordon equation

Klein-: Kleinhebezeug nt MASCHINEN small hoists; **Kleinintegration** f (SSI-Schaltung) COMP & DV small-scale integration (SSI), ELEKTRONIK single scale integration (SSI); **Kleinkamera** f FERNSEH minicam; **Kleinkonverter** m FERTIG baby Bessemer converter; **Kleinlader** m ELEKTROTECH trickle charger; **Kleinladung** f ELEKTROTECH trickle charge; **Kleinlaster** m KFZTECH light lorry (BrE), light truck (AmE); **Kleinlastwagen** m KFZTECH pick-up, pick-up truck; **Kleinlieferwagen** m KFZTECH minivan; **Kleinlokomotive** f EISENBAHN light rail motor tractor; **Kleinmagnetron** nt ELEKTRONIK miniature magnetron; **Kleinmotor** m ELEKTRIZ fractional horsepower motor; **Kleinoffset** nt DRUCK small offset print; **Kleinoffsetdruck** m DRUCK small offset print; **Kleinpflaster** nt BAU pebble pavement (BrE), pebble sidewalk (AmE)

kleinporig *adj* FERTIG *Gefüge* close

Klein-: Kleinpresse f FERTIG subpress; **Kleinschalter** m ELEKTRIZ installation switch

Kleinserien mit Laschen versehen *vi* VERPACK batch tabbing

Klein-: Kleinserienproduktion f MASCHINEN short run

Kleinsignal nt ELEKTRONIK low-level signal, small signal; **Kleinsignal-Parameter** m ELEKTRONIK small signal parameter; **Kleinsignal-Transistor** m ELEKTRONIK small signal transistor; **Kleinsignal-Verstärker** m ELEKTRONIK small signal amplifier; **Kleinsignal-Verstärkung** f ELEKTRONIK small signal amplification

Kleinst- *pref* MASCHINEN minimum; **Kleinstbildkamera** f FOTO subminiature camera; **Kleinsthörgerät** nt AKUSTIK *mit Ohranpassung* insert earphone; **Kleist-integration** f (SSI-Schaltung) ELEKTRONIK small-scale integration (SSI); **Kleinstluftfahrzeugindex** m LUFTTRANS miniature aircraft index; **Kleinstmaß** nt MASCHINEN minimum size; **Kleinstrelais** nt ELEKTRO-

TECH subminiature relay; **Kleinströhre** f ELEKTRONIK acorn tube; **Kleinstsignal** nt ELEKTRONIK minimum signal; **Kleinstspiel** nt MASCHINEN minimum clearance; **Kleinstübermaß** nt MASCHINEN minimum interference; **Kleinstzone** f TELEKOM microcell

Klein-: Kleinwählerzentrale f TELEKOM UAX, unit automatic exchange; **Kleinware auf Kartonunterlagen** f pl VERPACK carded packaging; **Kleinwerkzeuge** nt pl MASCHINEN small tools; **Kleinwinkelprisma** nt PHYS small-angle prism; **Kleinzelle** f TELEKOM minicell; **Kleinzellenfangdamm** m BAU gabion

Kleister m FERTIG slipping, KUNSTSTOFF glue

Klemm- *pref* MASCHINEN gripping; **Klemmbacke** f FERTIG *Stauchmaschine* gripping die, KERNTECH jaw, MASCHINEN gripping jaw; **Klemmblock** m KER & GLAS chuck block; **Klemmbügel** m MASCHINEN clamp; **Klemmdiode** f ELEKTRONIK, PHYS clamping diode; **Klemmdose** f ELEKTROTECH connection box

Klemme f ELEKTRIZ terminal, FERTIG connector, terminal, FOTO, KFZTECH, MASCHINEN clamp, MECHAN clamp, clip, TELEKOM *Leitung* hub

Klemm-: Klemmechanismus m MASCHINEN clamping mechanism; **Klemmeffekt** m AKUSTIK pinch effect; **Klemmen** nt KFZTECH *Bremsen*, MASCHINEN jamming

klemmen *vt* MASCHINEN jam, MECHAN clamp

Klemme: Klemmenblock m ELEKTRIZ, ELEKTROTECH, KONTROLL terminal block; **Klemmenbrett** nt ELEKTROTECH terminal strip; **Klemmenimpedanz** f KONTROLL terminal impedance; **Klemmenkasten** m ELEKTRIZ terminal box; **Klemmenleiste** f ELEKTRIZ, ELEKTROTECH terminal block, terminal strip, FERTIG *Kunststoffinstallationen*, KONTROLL terminal strip, TELEKOM connection strip, terminal strip; **Klemmenstreifen** m ELEKTROTECH terminal strip

Klemm-: Klemmgesperre nt MASCHINEN silent ratchet; **Klemmgriff** m FERTIG clamping lever; **Klemmhebel** m FERTIG binder lever, clamping lever, lock lever; **Klemmhülse** f FERTIG collet, MASCHINEN clamping sleeve; **Klemmkasten** m ELEKTROTECH conduit box; **Klemmklampe** f WASSERTRANS *Deckbeschläge* jam cleat; **Klemmkopf** m MASCHINEN clamping handle; **Klemmnabe** f FERTIG *Kunststoffinstallationen* clamping collar; **Klemmplatte** f EISENBAHN rail clip; **Klemmreflektor** m FOTO clamping reflector; **Klemmring** m FERTIG adjusting collar, MASCHINEN clamp ring, clamping ring, lock ring; **Klemmschaltung** f ELEKTRONIK *Schaltkreistechnik* clamping circuit; **Klemmschraube** f ELEKTROTECH binding post, terminal, FERTIG clamp, clamping bolt, set screw, *Kunststoffinstallationen* clamping screw, MASCHINEN binding screw, clamping screw, lock screw, locking screw, set bolt; **Klemmsitz** m MECHAN force fit; **Klemmstück** nt FERTIG *Stößel* block

Klemmung f BAU *Nivellierinstrument* clamp, ELEKTRONIK *Fernsehtechnik* clamping

Klemm-: Klemmutter f FERTIG locking nut; **Klemmvorrichtung** f LABOR clamp

Klempner m BAU plumber; **Klempnerarbeiten** f pl BAU plumbing

Kletterfilmverdampfer m LEBENSMITTEL climbing film evaporator

Klickspur f AUFNAHME click track

Klima:¹ mit Klimaanlage *adj* FERTIG air-conditioned

Klima² nt BAU, HEIZ & KÄLTE, SICHERHEIT climate; **Klimaaggregat** nt HEIZ & KÄLTE air conditioner; **Klimaanlage** f FERTIG air-conditioning plant, HEIZ &

KÄLTE air-conditioning plant, air-conditioning system, KFZTECH *Innenraum* air conditioner, SICHERHEIT air-conditioning plant; **Klimadecke** *f* HEIZ & KÄLTE air-handling ceiling, ventilated ceiling; **Klimadetektor** *m* TRANS climatic detector; **Klimafestigkeit** *f* BAU, MASCHINEN weathering resistance; **Klimagefahr** *f* SICHERHEIT climatic hazard; **Klimagerät** *nt* HEIZ & KÄLTE, MASCHINEN air conditioner; **Klimakammer** *f* ERGON, HEIZ & KÄLTE, VERPACK, WERKPRÜF climatic chamber, environmental chamber; **Klimaleuchte** *f* HEIZ & KÄLTE air-handling luminaire; **Klimaprüfung** *f* WERKPRÜF climatic test; **Klimaraum** *m* VERPACK climatic chamber; **Klimaregelung** *f* HEIZ & KÄLTE air conditioning; **Klimaschutz** *m* SICHERHEIT climatic protection; **Klimatechnik** *f* HEIZ & KÄLTE air conditioning

klimatisch: ~**e Bedingungen** *f pl* VERPACK climatic conditions

klimatisieren *vt* BAU, HEIZ & KÄLTE air-condition

klimatisiert: ~**er Inspektionsraum** *m* MASCHINEN temperature-controlled inspection room; ~**e Raumluft** *f* HEIZ & KÄLTE conditioned air

Klimatisierung *f* HEIZ & KÄLTE air conditioning, climatization, PAPIER air conditioning

Klima: **Klimaversuch** *m* VERPACK climatic test

Klinge *f* FERTIG *Schraubenzieher*, MASCHINEN blade

Klingel *f* COMP & DV bell character, ELEKTROTECH bell, TELEKOM ringer; **Klingeldraht** *m* ELEKTROTECH bell wire

Klingeln *nt* ELEKTROTECH *Telefonglocke* ringing, ERDÖL knock, KFZTECH pinking, *Motor* pinging, MECHAN, TELEKOM ringing; ~ **des Motors** *nt* MASCHINEN ringing engine

klingeln *vi* TELEKOM ring

Klingel: **Klingeltrafo** *m* ELEKTROTECH bell transformer; **Klingeltransformator** *m* ELEKTROTECH bell transformer

Klingen *nt* AUFNAHME ringing

Klinke *f* ELEKTRIZ jack, FERTIG pawl, *Kunststoffinstallationen* ratchet, MASCHINEN, MECHAN catch, dog, pawl, ratchet, TELEKOM *Schalttafel* jack, *Telefon* jack; **Klinkenfeder** *f* FERTIG pawl spring; **Klinkenhülse** *f* ELEKTROTECH jack bush; **Klinkenkupplung** *f* MASCHINEN pawl coupling; **Klinkenrad** *nt* FERTIG ratchet, MASCHINEN dog wheel, ratchet, ratchet wheel; **Klinkenradvorschub** *m* MASCHINEN ratchet feed; **Klinkenschaltwerk** *nt* MASCHINEN ratchet mechanism

Klinkenstecker: [1] **mit** ~ **angeschlossen** *adj* ELEKTROTECH jacked

Klinkenstecker [2] *m* ELEKTRIZ jack, ELEKTROTECH *Schalttafel* jack plug, TELEKOM switchboard plug

Klinke: **Klinkenstreifen** *m* ELEKTROTECH jack strip; **Klinkenumschalter** *m* ELEKTRIZ jack switchboard; **Klinkenumschaltertafel** *f* ELEKTRIZ jack switchboard

Klinker *m* BAU, KER & GLAS clinker, clinker brick; **Klinkerkitt** *m* BAU, KER & GLAS clinker cement

Klinsch *m* WASSERTRANS *Knoten* clinch

Klippe *f* WASSERTRANS *Geographie* cliff, rock

Klippegel *m* FERNSEH clipping level

Klipper *m* FERNSEH clipper; **Klipperverstärker** *m* FERNSEH clipper amplifier

Klirrdämpfung *f* AKUSTIK harmonic distortion

Klirren *nt* ELEKTRONIK harmonic distortion

Klirrfaktor *m* AKUSTIK distortion, harmonic distortion, AUFNAHME distortion, ELEKTRONIK relative harmonic content, TELEKOM harmonic distortion;

Klirrfaktor-Meßbrücke *f* AUFNAHME distortion-measuring bridge; **Klirrfaktormesser** *m* AUFNAHME distortion meter

Klischee *nt* DRUCK block, printing block; **Klischeehersteller** *m* DRUCK process engraver; **Klischeeherstellung** *f* DRUCK blockmaking; **Klischeeprüfer** *m* DRUCK type height gage (AmE), type height gauge (BrE)

Klon *m* COMP & DV clone

Klopfbrett *nt* DRUCK planer

Klopfen *nt* ERDÖL *Ottomotor: Kraftstoffselbstzündung mit Verbrennung* knock, KFZTECH beat, pinking, *Vorzündung des Motors* knocking, MASCHINEN knocking, PHYS tapping

klopfen [1] *vt* KOHLEN tap, MASCHINEN hammer, PHYS tap

klopfen [2] *vi* BAU beat, MASCHINEN hammer, knock

klopffest: ~**e Mischung** *f* KFZTECH antiknock mixture

Klopffestigkeit *f* ERDÖL *Kraftstoff* knock rating, KFZTECH antiknock resistance

Klopfung *f* UMWELTSCHMUTZ rapping

Klöppel *m* FERTIG clapper; **Klöppelverbindung** *f* KERNTECH ball coupling

Klotz *m* KOHLEN block; **Klotzbremse** *f* EISENBAHN, MASCHINEN block brake, shoe brake; **Klotzdruck** *m* TEXTIL block printing

Klotzen *nt* TEXTIL *Färben* padding

Klotz: **Klotzfärbung** *f* TEXTIL pad dyeing; **Klotzmaschine** *f* TEXTIL pad mangle

Klumpen [1] *m* KER & GLAS chunk, stick, LEBENSMITTEL caking, PAPIER lump

Klumpen: [2] ~ **bilden** *vi* PAPIER clot

klumpen *vi* LEBENSMITTEL cake

Klumpenglas *nt* KER & GLAS chunk glass

Kluppe *f* MASCHINEN screw plate; **Kluppenrahmen** *m* TEXTIL clip frame; **Kluppenspannrahmen** *m* TEXTIL clip stenter

Klüse *f* WASSERTRANS *Tauwerk* hawse

Klüver *m* WASSERTRANS *Segeln* jib

Klystron *nt* ELEKTRONIK, PHYS, RADIO, RAUMFAHRT, STRAHLPHYS, TELEKOM klystron; ~ **mit drei Resonanzkammern** *nt* ELEKTRONIK three-cavity klystron; **Klystronoszillator** *m* ELEKTRONIK klystron oscillator; **Klystronverstärker** *m* ELEKTRONIK klystron amplifier, klystron repeater

km *m (Kilometer)* LABOR km *(kilometer)*

Knack *m* AKUSTIK click

Knacken *nt* AKUSTIK crackle

Knackfilter *nt* TELEKOM click filter

Knackgeräusch *nt* AKUSTIK click

Knagge *f* BAU toe

Knall *m* SICHERHEIT noise; **Knall-** *pref* CHEMIE fulminic; **Knallgas** *nt* CHEMIE oxyhydrogen; **Knallsignal** *nt* EISENBAHN torpedo; **Knalltrauma** *nt* AKUSTIK acoustic trauma; **Knallvorrichtung** *f* EISENBAHN detonator; **Knallvorrichtungsexplosion** *f* EISENBAHN exploding of detonator

Knarre *f* MASCHINEN ratchet, ratchet lever

Knauf *m* MECHAN knob

Knautschzone *f* KFZTECH crumple zone, deformable zone

Knebel *m* KOHLEN, WASSERTRANS toggle; **Knebelgriff** *m* BAU, FERTIG, MECHAN T-handle, locking handle; **Knebelkerbstift** *m* FERTIG *Kunststoffinstallationen* grooved pin; **Knebelschraube** *f* BAU capstan-headed screw, MASCHINEN T-screw, tommy screw

Kneifzange *f* BAU nipper pliers, pincers, nippers, FERTIG,

MASCHINEN nipper pliers, nippers, pincers
Kneten *nt* LEBENSMITTEL kneading
kneten *vt* FERTIG *Kunststoffe* masticate, *Ton* temper
Kneter *m* CHEMTECH mixer, KUNSTSTOFF internal mixer,
kneader, PAPIER kneader; **~ mit gegenläufigen Schaufeln** *m* KUNSTSTOFF dough mixer
Knetlegierung *f* FERTIG plastic alloy
Knetmaschine *f* FERTIG *Kunststoffe* masticator
Knick: **~ einer Kurve** *m* MASCHINEN knee of a curve;
Knickband *nt* METALL kink band; **Knickbelastung** *f*
TRANS buckling load
Knicken *nt* MASCHINEN buckling
knicken *vt* MASCHINEN buckle
Knick: **Knickfestigkeit** *f* MASCHINEN buckling resistance; **Knickinstabilität** *f* KERNTECH kink instability;
Knickkraft *f* FERTIG critical compressive force; **Knicklast** *f* MASCHINEN buckling load; **Knickpunkt** *m* BAU
knee; **Knickspannung** *f* MECHAN breaking stress;
Knickstab *m* FERTIG column; **Knickstelle** *f* METALL
kink; **Knickung** *f* MASCHINEN buckling; **Knickversuch**
m MECHAN breaking test
Knie *nt* WASSERTRANS *Schiffbau* knee; **Knieblech** *nt* WASSERTRANS *Schiffbau* bracket; **Kniegelenkbolzen** *m*
MASCHINEN fulcrum pin; **Kniehebel** *m* KER & GLAS,
KUNSTSTOFF toggle, LUFTTRANS *Hubschrauber* bell
crank, MASCHINEN knee joint, knuckle joint, toggle,
toggle joint; **Kniehebelpresse** *f* KER & GLAS, MASCHINEN toggle press; **Knierohr** *nt* BAU, MECHAN bend,
knee bend, pipe bend; **Knieschoner** *m* SICHERHEIT
knee pad; **Kniestück** *nt* BAU knee, LABOR elbow, MASCHINEN knee, WASSERTRANS *Schiffbau* angle
Kniff *m* PAPIER crease
Knight: **~sche Verschiebung** *f* KERNTECH Knight shift
Knistern *nt* AKUSTIK, AUFNAHME crackle
Knitter *m* PAPIER crumpling, TEXTIL crease; **Knittererholung** *f* TEXTIL crease recovery; **Knitterfestausrüstung** *f*
TEXTIL crease-resist finish; **Knitterfestigkeit** *f* TEXTIL
crease resistance, crush resistance
Knittern *nt* TEXTIL crushing
knittern *vt* TEXTIL crease, crush
KNN *abbr (künstliches neuronales Netzwerk)* KÜNSTL
INT ANN *(artificial neural network)*
Knochen *m* AKUSTIK, CHEMIE, KER & GLAS, KOHLEN,
TEXTIL bone; **Knochenasche** *f* KER & GLAS bone ash;
Knochengallerte *f* CHEMIE ossein; **Knochenkohle** *f*
KOHLEN animal charcoal, bone coal; **Knochenleim** *m*
TEXTIL bone glue; **Knochenleitung** *f* AKUSTIK bone
conduction; **Knochenporzellan** *nt* KER & GLAS bone
china; **Knochenvibrator** *m* AKUSTIK bone vibrator
knollenförmig *adj* METALL nodular
Knopf *m* ELEKTROTECH button
knopfförmig *adj* ELEKTRIZ, ELEKTROTECH, KONTROLL,
TELEKOM button-shaped
Knopflochmikrofon *nt* AKUSTIK, AUFNAHME lapel
microphone
Knötchen *nt* FERTIG *Kunstoffe* fish eye; **Knötchenbildung** *f* TEXTIL pilling
Knoten *m* COMP & DV, ELEKTRIZ, FERTIG node, KER &
GLAS knot, *Blaswolle* nodule, KÜNSTL INT *Graph* node,
NICHTFOSS ENERG, PAPIER knot, TELECOM node, TEXTIL knot, WASSERTRANS *Knoten* knot, *Maßeinheit*
knot, WELLPHYS *einer stehenden Welle* node; **Knotenbahnhof** *m* EISENBAHN railroad center (AmE), railway
centre (BrE); **Knotenblech** *nt* FERTIG junction plate,
MASCHINEN gusset plate; **Knotendehnbarkeit** *f* TEXTIL
knot extensibility; **Knotenebene** *f* PHYS nodal plane;

Knotenfänger *m* PAPIER knotter; **Knotenfängerstoff** *m*
PAPIER knotter pulp; **Knotenfestigkeit** *f* TEXTIL knot
tenacity; **Knotenlinie** *f* AKUSTIK, AUFNAHME nodal
line
knoten *vt* TEXTIL knot
knotenlos[1] *adj* TEXTIL knotless
knotenlos:[2] **~e Garnlänge** *f* TEXTIL knotless yarn length
Knoten: **Knotenprozessor** *m* COMP & DV node processor
Knotenpunkt *m* AKUSTIK *einer Schwingung*, ELEKTRIZ
node, FERTIG *Schwingung*, PHYS nodal point, TELEKOM *Netzwerk* junction; **Knotenpunktentwicklungsmethode** *f* KERNTECH *Theorie* nodal expansion
method; **Knotenpunktverbindung** *f* BAU knee bracket
plate
Knoten: **Knotenseil** *nt* TRANS *Kabelbahn* button rope;
Knotenstrom *m* ELEKTRIZ nodal current; **Knotenverteiler** *m* TELEKOM JDF, junction distribution frame
(BrE); **Knotenvorbrecher** *m* PAPIER knot prebreaker
knotig *adj* TEXTIL knotty
Knowledge-Engineering *nt* KÜNSTL INT KE, knowledge
engineering
Knudsen-Effekt *m* KERNTECH *Molekularströmung*
Knudsen effect
Knüppel *m* FERTIG *Walzen*, MECHAN, METALL billet,
SICHERHEIT push stick; **Knüppelausstoßer** *m* FERTIG
billet pusher; **Knüppelbohrmaschine** *f* FERTIG billet-drilling machine; **Knüppelfertigwalzen** *nt* FERTIG
billet finishing; **Knüppelschaltung** *f* KFZTECH *Getriebe*
floor shift; **Knüppelschere** *f* MASCHINEN billet shears;
Knüppelschlepper *m* FERTIG billet buggy; **Knüppeltasche** *f* FERTIG *Walzen* billet cradle; **Knüppelwalze** *f*
FERTIG billet roll, MASCHINEN billeting roll, blooming
roll; **Knüppelwalzwerk** *nt* FERTIG billet mill
Koagulans *nt* KUNSTSTOFF coagulating agent
Koagulation *f* CHEMIE clotting, coagulation, CHEMTECH, KUNSTSTOFF coagulation; **Koagulationsbad** *nt*
CHEMTECH coagulating bath; **Koagulationsmittel** *nt*
KUNSTSTOFF coagulating agent
Koagulieren *nt* CHEMIE clotting, LEBENSMITTEL coagulating
koagulieren *vt* CHEMIE clot
Koaguliermittel *nt* CHEMTECH coagulator
koaguliert *adj* CHEMTECH coagulated
Koagulierungsflüssigkeit *f* CHEMTECH coagulation
liquid
Koagulum *nt* KUNSTSTOFF coagulum
koaleszieren *vi* CHEMIE coalesce
koalisieren *vi* CHEMIE coalesce
Koaxial- *pref* ELEKTRONIK, ELEKTROTECH, TELEKOM
coaxial
koaxial[1] *adj* AUFNAHME, ELEKTRONIK, ELEKTROTECH,
LUFTTRANS coaxial, RADIO coaxial
koaxial:[2] **~es Dämpfungsglied** *nt* ELEKTRONIK coaxial
attenuator; **~e Doppelleitung** *f* ELEKTROTECH coaxial
pair, coaxial-pair cable; **~e Festlast** *f* ELEKTROTECH
coaxial-fixed load; **~er Hubschraubertyp** *m* LUFTTRANS coaxial-type helicopter; **~e Leitung** *f*
AUFNAHME coaxial line; **~er Phasenregler** *m* ELEKTROTECH coaxial phase shifter; **~er Phasenschieber** *m*
ELEKTROTECH coaxial phase shifter; **~er Phasensteller**
m ELEKTROTECH coaxial phase shifter
Koaxial-: **Koaxialantenne** *f* TELEKOM coaxial antenna;
Koaxialbalun *m* RADIO sleeve balun; **Koaxialdiode** *f*
ELEKTRONIK coaxial diode; **Koaxialfilter** *nt* TELECOM
coaxial filter; **Koaxialkabel** *nt* AUFNAHME, COMP & DV,
ELEKTRIZ, ELEKTROTECH, FERNSEH, PHYS, TELEKOM

coaxial cable; **Koaxiallast** *f* ELEKTROTECH coaxial load; **Koaxiallautsprecher** *m* AKUSTIK, AUFNAHME coaxial loudspeaker; **Koaxialleitung** *f* ELEKTROTECH, PHYS, TELEKOM coaxial line; **Koaxialleitungssystem** *nt* TELEKOM coaxial-line system; **Koaxialmagnetron** *nt* ELEKTRONIK coaxial magnetron; **Koaxialstecker** *m* ELEKTROTECH coaxial connector; **Koaxialtopfkreis** *m* ELEKTRONIK coaxial cavity

Koaxkabel *nt* ELEKTROTECH coaxial cable

Koazervat *nt* CHEMIE coacervate; **Koazervation** *f* CHEMIE coacervation

Koazervierung *f* CHEMIE coacervation

Kobalt *nt* (*Co*) CHEMIE cobalt (*Co*); **Kobalt-Arsen-Kies** *m* HYDRAUL danaide; **Kobaltblüte** *f* CHEMIE erythrine, erythrite; **Kobaltbombe** *f* KERNTECH cobalt bomb; **Kobaltchlorid** *nt* KER & GLAS cobalt chloride; **Kobaltglasflasche** *f* KER & GLAS cobalt bottle; **Kobaltlegierung** *f* ANSTRICH cobalt alloy; **~ 60** *nt* KERNTECH cobalt 60, radiocobalt; **~ 60 Bestrahlungsanlage** *f* KERNTECH cobalt 60 irradiation plant

Kobold *m* COMP & DV sprite

Koch- *pref* CHEMTECH, PAPIER boiling; **Kochbecher** *m* PAPIER beaker

köcheln *vi* LEBENSMITTEL simmer

Kochen *nt* LEBENSMITTEL boiling, PAPIER digestion, THERMOD boiling

kochen *vti* THERMOD boil

kochend[1] *adj* CHEMTECH, KERNTECH, LEBENSMITTEL, THERMOD boiling

kochend:[2] **~es Fließbett** *nt* KERNTECH boiling bed; **~e Gärung** *f* CHEMTECH, LEBENSMITTEL boiling fermentation

Koch-: **Kochflasche** *f* CHEMTECH boiling flask; **Kochkessel** *m* LEBENSMITTEL kettle; **Kochkolben** *m* CHEMTECH boiling flask; **Kochplatte** *f* CHEMTECH boiling plate; **Kochpunkt** *m* LEBENSMITTEL boiling point; **Kochsalzersatz** *nt* LEBENSMITTEL salt substitute; **Kochsäureanlage** *f* PAPIER acid plant

Kodachrome-Verfahren® *nt* FOTO dye-transfer process, kodachrome process®

Koeffizient *m* ELEKTRIZ coefficient, HYDRAUL *Kontraktion* coefficient, *Leistung, Beaufschlagung* coefficient, MATH, MECHAN, PHYS coefficient; **~ der linearen Ausdehnung** *m* PHYS coefficient of linear expansion; **~ der linearen Wärmedehnzahl** *m* PHYS coefficient of linear expansion; **~ der Thermospaltung** *m* PHYS thermal fission factor

Koerzitivfeldstärke *f* ELEKTRIZ coercive force, coercive field strength, ELEKTROTECH coercive force, FERNSEH coercivity

Koerzitivkraft *f* AUFNAHME coercivity, ELEKTRIZ, ELEKTROTECH coercive force, FERNSEH coercivity, METALL coercive force, PHYS coercive force, coercivity

Kofferdamm *m* WASSERVERSORG cofferdam

Kofferraum *m* KFZTECH boot (BrE), rear boot (BrE), rear trunk (AmE), trunk (AmE), receiving boot (BrE), receiving trunk (AmE)

kognitiv[1] *adj* ERGON cognitive

kognitiv:[2] **~es Abbild** *nt* ERGON cognitive map

kohärent[1] *adj* AUFNAHME, ELEKTRIZ, ELEKTRONIK, METALL, OPTIK, STRAHLPHYS, TELEKOM, WELLPHYS coherent

kohärent:[2] **~e Ableitung** *f* ELEKTRONIK coherent deduction; **~e Antistokes-Raman-Streuung** *f* (*KARS*) STRAHLPHYS, WELLPHYS coherent anti-Stokes Raman scattering (*CARS*); **~er Bereich** *m* TELEKOM coherent area; **~e Grenze** *f* METALL coherent boundary; **~e Grenzfläche** *f* METALL coherent interface; **~er Impulsradar** *m* ELEKTRONIK coherent pulse radar; **~er Impulsradarstrahl** *m* STRAHLPHYS coherent pulse radar; **~es Licht** *nt* ELEKTRONIK *aus dem Laser*, STRAHLPHYS, TELEKOM, WELLPHYS coherent light; **~er monochromatischer Lichtstrahl** *m* STRAHLPHYS *laser-erzeugt* coherent monochromatic beam; **~e Morsetastung** *f* RADIO coherent cw; **~e Phasenumtastung** *f* TELEKOM CPSK, coherent phase shift keying; **~es Rauschen** *nt* AUFNAHME coherent noise; **~er Schall** *m* AKUSTIK coherent sound; **~e Signalverarbeitung** *f* ELEKTRONIK coherent signal processing; **~er Strahl** *m* ELEKTRONIK coherent beam; **~e Strahlung** *f* OPTIK, TELEKOM coherent radiation; **~es Teilchen** *nt* METALL coherent particle; **~e Übertragung** *f* TELEKOM coherent transmission; **~e Wellen** *f pl* STRAHLPHYS, WELLPHYS coherent waves; **nicht ~e Wobbeltonmodulation** *f* TELEKOM noncoherent swept tone modulation

Kohärenz *f* ELEKTRONIK *Nachrichtentechnik* coherence, *systematischer logischer Zusammenhang* coherence, OPTIK, PHYS, TELEKOM coherence, WELLPHYS coherency; **~ eines Laserstrahls** *f* WELLPHYS *über große Entfernungen hinweg* coherency of a laser beam; **Kohärenzbandbreite** *f* TELEKOM coherence bandwidth; **Kohärenzbereich** *m* OPTIK coherence area; **Kohärenzgrad** *m* OPTIK, TELEKOM degree of coherence; **Kohärenzlänge** *f* OPTIK, PHYS, TELEKOM coherence length; **Kohärenzoszillator** *m* ELEKTRONIK *Radartechnik* coherent oscillator; **Kohärenzzeit** *f* OPTIK, PHYS, TELEKOM coherence time

Kohäsion *f* BAU, METALL, PHYS cohesion; **Kohäsionsenergie** *f* METALL cohesive energy; **Kohäsionsfestigkeit** *f* KUNSTSTOFF adhesive shear strength; **Kohäsionskraft** *f* PHYS cohesive force

Kohle *f* KOHLEN coal

kohleartig *adj* CHEMIE carbonaceous

Kohle: **Kohleaufdampfverfahren** *nt* KERNTECH carbon replica method; **Kohlebecken** *nt* KOHLEN coal basin

kohlebefeuert *adj* KOHLEN coal-fired

Kohle: **Kohlebürste** *f* ELEKTRIZ carbon brush, graphite brush, ELEKTROTECH, KFZTECH, MASCHINEN carbon brush; **Kohleelektrode** *f* CHEMIE, ELEKTROTECH carbon electrode; **Kohlefadenlampe** *f* ELEKTROTECH carbon filament lamp; **Kohlefaser** *f* KUNSTSTOFF carbon fiber (AmE), carbon fibre (BrE); **Kohleförderung** *f* KOHLEN coal extraction

kohlegeheizt: **~er Kessel** *m* HEIZ & KÄLTE coal-fired boiler

Kohle: **Kohlehalterlampe** *f* ELEKTROTECH carbon holder lamp

kohlehaltig *adj* KOHLEN coal-bearing

Kohle: **Kohlehydrat** *nt* LEBENSMITTEL carbohydrate; **Kohlekontakt** *m* ELEKTROTECH carbon contact; **Kohlekraftwerk** *nt* THERMOD fossil fuel power station

Kohlelichtbogen *m* ELEKTRIZ, ELEKTROTECH, FERTIG, MASCHINEN carbon arc; **Kohlelichtbogenlampe** *f* ELEKTRIZ carbon arc lamp; **Kohlelichtbogenschneiden** *nt* FERTIG, MASCHINEN carbon arc cutting; **Kohlelichtbogenschweißen** *nt* FERTIG carbon arc welding

Kohle: **Kohlemassewiderstand** *m* ELEKTROTECH carbon composition resistor; **Kohlemikrofon** *nt* AKUSTIK carbon microphone; **Kohlenabbau** *m* KOHLEN coal mining; **Kohlenachbrechen** *nt* KOHLEN breaking down coal; **Kohlenauffüllung** *f* KOHLEN coal backing;

Kohlenbecken nt KOHLEN coalfield; **Kohlenbergbau** m KOHLEN coal mining; **Kohlenbergwerk** nt KOHLEN coal mine, coal pit, coal works; **Kohlenbergwerksprengstoff** m KOHLEN coal-mining explosive; **Kohlenbohrer** m KOHLEN coal drill; **Kohlenbunker** m KOHLEN coal bunker

Kohlendioxid nt CHEMIE, ELEKTRONIK, KOHLEN, MASCHINEN, UMWELTSCHMUTZ carbon dioxide; **Kohlendioxidlaser** m (CO₂-Laser) ELEKTRONIK carbon dioxide laser (CO₂ laser); **Kohlendioxidtreibhauseffekt** m UMWELTSCHMUTZ carbon dioxide greenhouse effect

Kohle: **Kohlendisulfid** nt CHEMIE carbon disulfide (AmE), carbon disulphide (BrE); **Kohlenelektrode** f ELEKTRIZ carbon electrode; **Kohlenfaserfilz** m RAUMFAHRT *Raumschiff* carbon fiber felt (AmE), carbon fibre felt (BrE); **Kohlenfaserverbundstoff** m RAUMFAHRT *Raumschiff* carbon fiber (AmE), carbon fibre (BrE); **Kohlenfeld** nt KOHLEN coalfield; **Kohlenfließband** nt KOHLEN coal belt; **Kohlenflöz** nt KOHLEN coal seam; **Kohlenflözsohle** f KOHLEN coal-seam floor; **Kohlenförderband** nt KOHLEN coal belt; **Kohlenformation** f KOHLEN coal formation; **Kohlengrieß** m KOHLEN small coal; **Kohlengrube** f KOHLEN coal mine, coal pit; **Kohlengrus** m KER & GLAS culm, KOHLEN coal beans, duff, slack coal; **Kohlenhacke** f KOHLEN coal pick; **Kohlenhalde** f KOHLEN coal yard; **Kohlenhauer** m KOHLEN coal breaker; **Kohlenhydrat** nt CHEMIE, LEBENSMITTEL carbohydrate; **Kohlenklein** nt KOHLEN breeze, charcoal duff, small coal; **Kohlenkorb** m KOHLEN coal basket; **Kohlenkübel** m KOHLEN coal basket; **Kohlenladeplatz** m EISENBAHN, WASSERTRANS coal wharf; **Kohlenlagerplatz** m KOHLEN coal yard

Kohlenmonoxid nt CHEMIE, ELEKTRONIK, KFZTECH *Abgase*, KOHLEN, MASCHINEN, SICHERHEIT, UMWELTSCHMUTZ carbon monoxide; **Kohlenmonoxidfilter** nt SICHERHEIT carbon monoxide filter; **Kohlenmonoxidlaser** m ELEKTRONIK carbon monoxide laser

Kohlenoxid nt CHEMIE carbon monoxide; **Kohlenoxidchlorid** nt CHEMIE phosgene

Kohle: **Kohlenpulver** nt KOHLEN coal powder; **Kohlenrutsche** f KOHLEN coal chute; **Kohlensack** m FERTIG *Gießen* belly

Kohlensäure[1] f FERTIG *Kunststoffinstallationen* carbon dioxide, carbonic acid

Kohlensäure:[2] **mit ~ versetzen** vt FERTIG aerate

Kohlensäure:[3] **~ entziehen** vi KOHLEN decarbonate

Kohlensäure: **Kohlensäurediamid** nt CHEMIE carbamide, urea; **Kohlensäuredichlorid** nt CHEMIE phosgene; **Kohlensäurefeuerlöscher** m SICHERHEIT carbon dioxide fire extinguisher

kohlensäurehaltig adj LEBENSMITTEL carbonated

Kohlensäure: **Kohlensäurelöscher** m SICHERHEIT carbon dioxide fire extinguisher

kohlensaures: **~ Calcium** nt LEBENSMITTEL calcium carbonate

Kohlensäure: **Kohlensäuresättigung** f CHEMIE carbonatation

Kohle: **Kohlenschacht** m KOHLEN coal mine; **Kohlenschicht** f KOHLEN coal seam; **Kohlenschichtboden** m KOHLEN bottom of a coal seam; **Kohlenschiff** nt KOHLEN coal ship, WASSERTRANS coal ship, collier; **Kohlenschlacke** f KOHLEN slag; **Kohlenschlamm** m KOHLEN coal sludge; **Kohlenschrämmaschine** f KOHLEN coal cracker, coal cutter; **Kohlenschurre** f KOHLEN

coal chute; **Kohlensilo** m KOHLEN coal bunker

Kohlenstaub m KOHLEN coal powder, coaldust, MASCHINEN pulverized coal, UMWELTSCHMUTZ coal dust; **Kohlenstaubbrenner** m HEIZ & KÄLTE pulverized coal burner; **Kohlenstaubfeuerung** f HEIZ & KÄLTE pulverized coal firing; **Kohlenstaubmikrofon** nt AUFNAHME carbon microphone

Kohlenstoff:[1] **auf ~ basiert** adj ANSTRICH organic

Kohlenstoff[2] m (C) CHEMIE carbon (C)

kohlenstoffarm[1] adj FERTIG *Stahl* mild

kohlenstoffarm:[2] **~er Stahl** m METALL low-carbon steel

Kohlenstoff: **Kohlenstoffaser** f KUNSTSTOFF carbon fiber (AmE), carbon fibre (BrE); **Kohlenstoffdioxid** nt CHEMIE carbon dioxide; **Kohlenstoffdisulfid** nt CHEMIE carbon disulfide (AmE), carbon disulphide (BrE); **Kohlenstoffentziehung** f KOHLEN decarbonization; **Kohlenstoffeuerlöscher** m SICHERHEIT carbon dioxide fire extinguisher

kohlenstoffhaltig adj CHEMIE carbonaceous

Kohlenstoff: **Kohlenstoffkreislauf** m LEBENSMITTEL carbon cycle; **Kohlenstoffmassentransport** m KERNTECH carbon mass transfer

kohlenstofffrei adj METALL carbon-free

kohlenstoffreich: **~er Stahl** m METALL high-carbon steel

Kohlenstoff: **Kohlenstoffstahl** m ANSTRICH carbon steel, FERTIG ordinary steel, KERNTECH, KOHLEN, MECHAN carbon steel, METALL carbon steel, ordinary steel; **Kohlenstoffstahlstaub** m KOHLEN carbon steel dust; **Kohlenstofftetrachlorid** nt CHEMIE carbon tetrachloride, tetrachloromethane

Kohle: **Kohlenstoß** m KOHLEN coalface; **Kohlenstoßpflock** m KOHLEN coalface cleat; **Kohlenstraße** f KOHLEN coal road; **Kohlenwagen** m EISENBAHN tender, KFZTECH, KOHLEN mine car; **Kohlenwand** f KOHLEN coal wall; **Kohlenwaschanlage** f KOHLEN coal washer

Kohlenwasserstoff m CHEMIE (KW-Stoff), ERDÖL, MEERSCHMUTZ, UMWELTSCHMUTZ hydrocarbon; **Kohlenwasserstoff-Aerosoltreibgas** nt ERDÖL hydrocarbon aerosol propellant; **Kohlenwasserstoffalle** f ERDÖL *Geologie* hydrocarbon trap; **Kohlenwasserstoff-Einsatzprodukt** nt ERDÖL *Raffinerie* hydrocarbon feedstocks; **Kohlenwasserstoffteppich** m UMWELTSCHMUTZ hydrocarbon slick

Kohle: **Kohlenzeche** f KOHLEN coal mine, coal pit; **Kohleschicht** f ELEKTROTECH carbon film; **Kohleschichtwiderstand** m ELEKTROTECH carbon film resistor; **Kohleverbrennung** f KERNTECH carbon burning; **Kohleverflüssigung** f ERDÖL *Kohlehydrierung* coal liquefaction; **Kohlevergasung** f ERDÖL *Gaserzeugung*, THERMOD coal gasification; **Kohlevorkommen** nt KOHLEN coal deposit; **Kohlewiderstand** m ELEKTRIZ, ELEKTROTECH, PHYS carbon resistor; **Kohle-Zink-Zelle** f LABOR Leclanché cell

kohobieren vt CHEMIE *Destillation* cohobate

Koinzidenz f AUFNAHME, ELEKTRONIK, PHYS, STRAHLPHYS coincidence; **Koinzidenzeffekt** m AUFNAHME coincidence effect; **Koinzidenzschaltung** f ELEKTRONIK *Datenverarbeitung*, PHYS, STRAHLPHYS coincidence circuit

Koje f WASSERTRANS berth

Kokille f FERTIG metallic die, permanent mold (AmE), permanent mould (BrE), *Gießen* chill, MECHAN ingot mold (AmE), ingot mould (BrE)

Kokillen: **in ~ gießen** vt FERTIG chill

Kokille: **Kokillenausbruch** m FERTIG dressing; **Kokillenguß** m FERTIG chill casting, chilling, die casting, permanent-mold casting (AmE), permanent-mould casting (BrE), MASCHINEN gravity die-casting, METALL chill casting, gravity die-casting; **Kokillenkleber** *m* VERPACK chill permanent adhesive

Kokosbast *m* WASSERTRANS *Tauwerk* coir

Koks *m* KER & GLAS, KOHLEN, MASCHINEN, METALL coke; **Koksbrechanlage** *f* KOHLEN coke breaker; **Koksbrechen** *nt* KOHLEN coking cracking; **Koksgabel** *f* KOHLEN coke fork; **Koksgrus** *m* KOHLEN coking duff; **Kokskohle** *f* KOHLEN coking coal; **Kokskorb** *m* KOHLEN coke basket; **Koksmühle** *f* KOHLEN coke mill; **Koksofen** *m* HEIZ & KÄLTE, KER & GLAS coke oven; **Koksroheisen** *nt* METALL coke iron, coke pig; **Kokssäule** *f* KOHLEN coke column; **Koksschmiedeeisen** *nt* METALL coke iron; **Koksstaub** *m* KOHLEN coke dust

Kolben *m* ELEKTRIZ bulb, *Thermometer* bulb, ELEKTRONIK *einer Kathodenstrahlröhre* cone, ELEKTROTECH bulb, envelope, FERTIG flask, HYDRAUL, KFZTECH *Motor* piston, KUNSTSTOFF ram, LABOR flask, MASCHINEN bulb, MECHAN, WASSERTRANS *Motor* piston; **Kolbenabschwächer** *m* ELEKTRONIK *Mikrowellen* piston attenuator; **Kolbenachsendichtung** *f* RAUMFAHRT *Raumschiff* gland; **Kolbenblitz** *m* FOTO flash bulb; **Kolbenboden** *m* KFZTECH piston head, piston top, *Motor* piston crown, MASCHINEN piston head; **Kolbenbohrung** *f* FERTIG *Kolbenpumpe* cylinder

Kolbenbolzen *m* KFZTECH wrist pin (AmE), *Motor, Kolben* gudgeon pin (BrE), MASCHINEN, MECHAN gudgeon pin (BrE), wrist pin (AmE); **Kolbenbolzenauge** *nt* KFZTECH piston pin boss; **Kolbenbolzenbuchse** *f* KFZTECH piston-pin bushing, small end bushing; **Kolbenbolzennabe** *f* KFZTECH piston pin boss

kolbenbolzenseitig: **~es Ende** *nt* MASCHINEN small end; **~er Pleuelkopf** *m* MASCHINEN connecting rod small end

Kolbenbolzen: **Kolbenbolzensicherung** *f* KFZTECH gudgeon pin lock (BrE), piston-pin lock (AmE), wrist pin lock (AmE)

Kolben: **Kolbenbuchse** *f* KFZTECH piston boss bushing; **Kolbendichtung** *f* MASCHINEN piston packing; **Kolbendosierpumpe** *f* GERÄT piston-type metering pump; **Kolbenentlastungskanal** *m* BAU piston relief duct; **Kolbenfläche** *f* MASCHINEN piston area; **Kolbenfresser** *m* KFZTECH piston seizing; **Kolbengebläse** *nt* MASCHINEN piston blower; **Kolbengeschwindigkeit** *f* MASCHINEN piston speed; **Kolbenhub** *m* BAU, MASCHINEN piston stroke; **Kolbenhublänge** *f* BAU length of piston stroke; **Kolbenklopfen** *nt* KFZTECH piston knock; **Kolbenkompressor** *m* MASCHINEN piston compressor, positive-displacement compressor; **Kolbenkopf** *m* KFZTECH piston top; **Kolbenmanometer** *nt* GERÄT piston-type pressure gage (AmE), piston-type pressure gauge (BrE); **Kolbenmantel** *m* KFZTECH piston body, piston skirt, MASCHINEN piston surface; **Kolbenmaschine** *f* KFZTECH, LUFTTRANS, MASCHINEN, WASSERTRANS reciprocating engine; **Kolbenmotor** *m* KFZTECH, LUFTTRANS, WASSERTRANS piston engine, reciprocating engine; **Kolbenplatte** *f* MECHAN butt plate; **Kolbenpleuelstange** *f* KFZTECH piston connecting rod; **Kolbenpumpe** *f* MASCHINEN, WASSERVERSORG piston pump, reciprocating pump

Kolbenring *m* KFZTECH, MASCHINEN, MECHAN piston ring; **Kolbenringfressen** *nt* MASCHINEN piston ring sticking; **Kolbenringnut** *f* KFZTECH piston ring groove; **Kolbenringnute** *f* KFZTECH piston ring groove; **Kol-**

benringspanner *m* KFZTECH *Werkzeug* piston ring clamp; **Kolbenringstoßfuge** *f* KFZTECH piston ring gap; **Kolbenringteilfuge** *f* KFZTECH piston ring joint

Kolben: **Kolbenschaft** *m* KFZTECH piston body, piston skirt, MASCHINEN piston body; **Kolbenschieber** *m* MASCHINEN piston valve; **Kolbenschlag** *m* KFZTECH *Motor* piston slap

kolbenseitig: **~es Pleuelstangenende** *nt* KFZTECH small end; **~er Pleuelstangenkopf** *m* KFZTECH connecting rod small end

Kolben: **Kolbenspiel** *nt* KFZTECH, MASCHINEN piston clearance; **Kolbenstange** *f* EISENBAHN piston rod, FERTIG piston rod, stem, KFZTECH, MASCHINEN, WASSERTRANS piston rod; **Kolbenstange der Pumpe** *f* WASSERVERSORG pump rod; **Kolbensteg** *m* KFZTECH *Motor* piston land; **Kolbensteuerventil** *nt* FERTIG *Kunststoffinstallationen* plunger valve; **Kolbenverdichter** *m* HEIZ & KÄLTE reciprocating compressor, MASCHINEN piston compressor, positive-displacement compressor, reciprocating compressor, reciprocating piston compressor; **Kolbenverklemmung** *f* FERTIG mug lock; **Kolbenweg** *m* MASCHINEN piston travel; **Kolbenzähler** *m* GERÄT piston-type flowmeter

Kolk *m* FERTIG, MASCHINEN crater; **Kolkbildung** *f* FERTIG *Spanung* cratering, *Spanfläche* erosion

Kolkung *f* FERTIG *Spanfläche* crater

Kolk: **Kolkverschleiß** *m* MASCHINEN crater wear

Kollagen *nt* LEBENSMITTEL collagen

Kollargol *nt* CHEMIE collargol

kollationieren *vt* DRUCK collate

Kollationiermarken *f pl* DRUCK collating marks

Kollationiermaschine *f* DRUCK collating machine

Kollationiertisch *m* DRUCK collating table

kollektiv: **~e Anregung bei Teilchenwechselwirkung** *f* STRAHLPHYS collective excitation in particle interaction

Kollektivkniehebelsystem *nt* LUFTTRANS *Hubschrauber* collective bellcrank

Kollektivmarke *f* PATENT collective mark

Kollektivmodell *nt* KERNTECH collective model

Kollektivsteigung *f* LUFTTRANS *Hubschrauber* collective pitch; **Kollektivsteigungsanzeiger** *m* LUFTTRANS collective pitch indicator; **Kollektivsteigungssteuerung** *f* LUFTTRANS *Hubschrauber* collective pitch control; **Kollektivsteigungssynchronisierung** *f* LUFTTRANS *Hubschrauber* collective pitch synchronizer

Kollektor *m* ELEKTRIZ commutator, ELEKTRONIK collector, ELEKTROTECH commutator, drain, *bei dynamoelektrischer Maschine* collector, LUFTTRANS manifold, NICHTFOSS ENERG, PHYS *elektrisch*, TELEKOM collector; **~ des Transistors** *m* TELEKOM transistor collector; **Kollektorabdeckplatte** *f* NICHTFOSS ENERG collector cover plate; **Kollektoranreicherung** *f* ELEKTRONIK collector doping; **Kollektoranschluß** *m* ELEKTROTECH common collector connection; **Kollektorbasisstufe** *f* ELEKTROTECH emitter follower; **Kollektorbürste** *f* ELEKTRIZ commutator brush; **Kollektorelektrode** *f* ELEKTROTECH collector electrode; **Kollektorgebiet** *nt* ELEKTROTECH collector region; **Kollektorkontakt** *m* ELEKTROTECH collector contact; **Kollektorleistungsvermögen** *nt* NICHTFOSS ENERG collector efficiency; **Kollektormotor** *m* ELEKTROTECH collector motor; **Kollektorring** *m* ELEKTROTECH collector ring, PHYS slip ring; **Kollektorschaltung** *f* ELEKTROTECH earthed collector connection (BrE), grounded collector connection (AmE); **Kollektorstab** m ELEKTROTECH commutator bar; **Kollektortiltwinkel** m NICHTFOSS ENERG collector tilt angle; **Kollektorverstärker** m ELEKTROTECH emitter follower; **Kollektorzone** f ELEKTROTECH collector region

Kollergang m FERTIG pug mill, sand mill, HYDRAUL pug mill, PAPIER edge runner

Kollermühle f KER & GLAS edge runner mill, KUNSTSTOFF edge mill

kollidieren[1] vt WASSERTRANS mit Schiff collide; ~ **mit** vt TRANS collide with

kollidieren[2] vi TRANS collide

kolligativ adj CHEMIE colligative

Kolliko nt TRANS collico

Kollimation f ELEKTRONIK Antennentechnik, FERTIG, NICHTFOSS ENERG, OPTIK collimation; **Kollimationslicht** nt NICHTFOSS ENERG collimated light

Kollimator m FERTIG, FOTO, PHYS, TELEKOM collimator; **Kollimatorfehler** m FOTO collimating fault; **Kollimatorlinse** f FOTO collimated lens

kollimiert: ~**e Punktquelle** f KERNTECH collimated point source

kollinear[1] adj GEOM collinear

kollinear[2]: ~**e Laserspektroskopie** f STRAHLPHYS collinear laser spectroscopy

Kollision f COMP & DV, EISENBAHN, RAUMFAHRT Raumschiff, TEILPHYS, TELEKOM, WASSERTRANS collision; **Kollisionsenergie** f TEILPHYS collision energy; **Kollisionserkennung** f (CD) COMP & DV, TELEKOM collision detection (CD); **Kollisionskurs** m RAUMFAHRT Raumschiff, WASSERTRANS Navigation collision course; **Kollisionsverhütungshilfen** f WASSERTRANS Radar collision avoidance aids; **Kollisionswarner** m WASSERTRANS anticollision marker; **Kollisionswarnsystem** nt RAUMFAHRT Raumschiff collision warning system

Kollodium nt DRUCK, FOTO collodion; **Kollodiumplatte** f FOTO collodion plate

Kolloid nt KER & GLAS, KOHLEN, KUNSTSTOFF, LEBENSMITTEL gallertartiger Stoff colloid; **Kolloid-** pref CHEMIE colloidal

kolloidal[1] adj CHEMIE colloidal

kolloidal[2]: ~**er Bohrschlamm** m ERDÖL Bohrtechnik colloidal mud

Kolloidantrieb m RAUMFAHRT Raumschiff colloid propulsion

kolloiddispers: ~**es System** nt UMWELTSCHMUTZ colloide disperse system

Kolloidmühle f LEBENSMITTEL colloid mill

Kolonne f CHEMIE, DRUCK column, TRANS platoon; **Kolonnenauflösung** f TRANS platoon dispersion

Kolophonium nt FERTIG, KUNSTSTOFF rosin

kolorieren vt DRUCK color (AmE), colour (BrE)

Kolorimeter nt ERGON, KUNSTSTOFF, LABOR, PAPIER, PHYS, STRAHLPHYS colorimeter

Kolorimetrie f ERGON, PHYS, STRAHLPHYS , WASSERVERSORG colorimetry

Kolormetrie f WASSERVERSORG colorimetry

Kolumne f DRUCK column

Koma nt ELEKTRONIK kometenschweifartiger Abbildungsfehler, OPTIK Asymmetriefehler coma

Kombi m KFZTECH combined; **Kombiflugschrauber** m LUFTTRANS gyrodyne; **Kombimassengutfrachter** m WASSERTRANS combination bulk carrier

Kombination f AKUSTIK, AUFNAHME, BAU, COMP & DV, LUFTTRANS Hubschrauber, MASCHINEN combination; **Kombinationsfutter** nt MASCHINEN combination chuck; **Kombinationsmikrofon** nt AUFNAHME combination microphone; **Kombinationsschloß** nt BAU combination lock, puzzle lock; **Kombinationston** m AKUSTIK combination tone, complex tone

Kombinator m TELEKOM combiner

kombinatorisch[1] adj ELEKTRONIK, GEOM, KÜNSTL INT combinatorial

kombinatorisch[2]: ~**e Analyse** f MATH combinatorial analysis; ~**e Explosion** f KÜNSTL INT combinatorial explosion; ~**e Logik** f ELEKTRONIK, KÜNSTL INT combinatorial logic; ~**e Mathematik** f MATH combinational mathematics

kombinieren vt COMP & DV combine

kombiniert: ~**e Abfrage** f COMP & DV relational query; ~**er Anzeiger für Gleitweg und Landkurs** m LUFTTRANS glide path localizer; ~**e Axial-Radialturbine** f HYDRAUL combined flow turbine; ~**er Deckel-Böden-Flaschenkarton** m VERPACK coupled lid-base bottle tray; ~**es Förder- und Tragseil** nt WASSERTRANS combined hauling and carrying rope; ~**es Höhen- und Querruder** nt LUFTTRANS elevon; ~**es Kabel** nt ELEKTROTECH composite cable; ~**er Querneigungs- und Steigungsanzeiger** m LUFTTRANS bank-and-pitch indicator (BrE), turn-and-bank indicator (AmE); ~**er Repulsions-Induktionsmotor** m ELEKTROTECH repulsion-induction motor; ~**es Straßen-See-Transportsystem** nt TRANS road-sea combined transport system; ~**er Verkehr** m EISENBAHN intermodal traffic; ~**e Verpackung** f VERPACK combined packaging; ~**er Verteiler** m (KV) TELEKOM combined distribution frame (CDF)

Kombi: **Kombischaltung** f COMP & DV combinational circuit (AmE), combinatorial circuit (BrE); **Kombischiff** nt WASSERTRANS combined vessel; **Kombiwagen** m KFZTECH estate car (BrE), shooting brake (BrE), shooting break (AmE), station wagon (AmE); **Kombiwerk** nt ELEKTRIZ combined heat and power station; **Kombiwerkzeug** nt MASCHINEN combination tool; **Kombizange** f MASCHINEN all-purpose wrench, combination pliers

Kombüse f WASSERTRANS Schiff galley; **Kombüsenausstattung** f LUFTTRANS, WASSERTRANS galley furnishings

Kometenkern m RAUMFAHRT Raumschiff comet core

Komfortklimaanlage f HEIZ & KÄLTE comfort air-conditioning plant

Komforttelefon nt TELEKOM added feature telephone

Komma nt AKUSTIK, DRUCK comma, MATH point

Kommandant m RAUMFAHRT, WASSERTRANS Marine commander

Kommando nt RAUMFAHRT command; **Kommando- und Servicemodul** nt (CSM) RAUMFAHRT Raumschiff command and service module (CSM); **Kommandobrücke** f WASSERTRANS Handelsmarine navigation bridge; **Kommandoempfänger** m RAUMFAHRT command receiver; **Kommandokanal** m RAUMFAHRT command channel; **Kommandokapsel** f RAUMFAHRT command module; **Kommandokreis** m FERNSEH talkback circuit; **Kommandomodul** nt RAUMFAHRT command module; **Kommandoverbindung** f RAUMFAHRT command link; **Kommandozentrale** f WASSERTRANS Schiff command-and-control center (AmE), command-and-control centre (BrE)

kommensurabel adj MATH commensurable

Kommentar¹ *m* COMP & DV comment
Kommentar:² **auf ~ setzen** *vt* COMP & DV comment
Kommentarspur *f* AUFNAHME commentary track
kommentieren *vt* COMP & DV comment
kommerziell: ~e Datenverarbeitung *f* COMP & DV commercial computing; **~er Verkehr** *m* TRANS revenue-earning traffic
Kommerzieller: ~ und Amateurfunkdienst *m* (*ICAS*) RADIO Intermittent Commercial and Amateur Services (*ICAS*)
Kommodore *m* WASSERTRANS *Marine* commodore
kommunal: ~er Abfall *m* ABFALL municipal waste, urban solid waste, urban waste; **~es Abwasser** *nt* ABFALL municipal sewage; **~er Güterverkehr** *m* TRANS public hauling; **~e Kläranlage** *f* ABFALL municipal sewage works; **~es Wasser** *nt* WASSERVERSORG town water
Kommunikation *f* COMP & DV, KONTROLL, TELEKOM communication; **~ offener Systeme** *f* (*OSI*) COMP & DV, TELEKOM open systems interconnection (*OSI*); **~ vor Ort** *f* TELEKOM on-scene communications; **Kommunikationsfilter** *nt* ELEKTRONIK communications filter; **Kommunikationskanal** *m* COMP & DV pipe; **Kommunikationsmedium** *nt* COMP & DV communication medium; **Kommunikationsnetz** *nt* KONTROLL communication network; **Kommunikationsprotokoll** *nt* TELEKOM communication protocol; **Kommunikationsschnittstelle** *f* KÜNSTL INT communication interface; **Kommunikationssoftware** *f* COMP & DV communication software; **Kommunikationssteuerungsschicht** *f* COMP & DV session layer; **Kommunikationssystem** *nt* COMP & DV communication system; **Kommunikationstheorie** *f* COMP & DV communication theory; **Kommunikationsverbindung** *f* COMP & DV data link
Kommutation *f* ELEKTRIZ, ELEKTROTECH, MATH commutation
kommutativ *adj* MATH commutative
Kommutativgesetz *nt* MATH commutative law
Kommutator *m* ELEKTRIZ, ELEKTROTECH, KFZTECH commutator; **Kommutatorbürste** *f* KFZTECH *KFZ-Elektrik, Kollektorbürste* commutator brush; **Kommutatorgleichstrommotor** *m* ELEKTROTECH commutator dc motor; **Kommutatorhebelschalter** *m* ELEKTRIZ lever commutator switch; **Kommutatorlamelle** *f* ELEKTRIZ commutator segment, ELEKTROTECH commutator bar, commutator segment; **Kommutatormotor** *m* ELEKTRIZ, ELEKTROTECH commutator motor; **Kommutatorrichtungsschalter** *m* ELEKTRIZ commutator switch; **Kommutatorring** *m* ELEKTRIZ commutator ring; **Kommutatorsprühen** *nt* ELEKTRIZ commutator sparking; **Kommutatorstab** *m* ELEKTRIZ commutator bar; **Kommutatorsteg** *m* ELEKTROTECH commutator segment
Kommutierpol *m* ELEKTRIZ commutating pole
Kommutierwicklung *f* ELEKTRIZ commutating winding
kompakt¹ *adj* ANSTRICH, AUFNAHME, ELEKTRIZ, KFZTECH compact, solid, MASCHINEN compact, OPTIK tight
kompakt:² **~e Hochtemperatur-Elektrolysezelle** *f* KFZTECH high-temperature solid electrolyte cell; **~es Mantelkabel** *nt* OPTIK tight-jacketed cable
Kompaktader *f* OPTIK *Lichtwellenleiter* tight buffer
Kompaktierung *f* ABFALL compaction
Kompaktkabel *nt* OPTIK tight construction cable
Kompaktkassette *f* AUFNAHME compact cassette
Kompaktleiter *m* ELEKTRIZ compacted conductor

Kompaktor *m* ABFALL landfill compactor, packer unit
Kompakt-Quarzoszillator *m* ELEKTRONIK simple-packaged crystal oscillator
Kompander *m* COMP & DV, ELEKTRONIK *Kompressor und Expander*, RAUMFAHRT compander, TELEKOM compressor-expander; **Kompandersignal** *nt* ELEKTRONIK companded signal
Kompandierer *m* TELEKOM compressor-expander
kompandiert: ~e Deltamodulation *f* (*CDM*) TELEKOM companded delta modulation (*CDM*)
Kompandierung *f* ELEKTRONIK, RADIO, TELEKOM companding
Komparator *m* COMP & DV, ELEKTRONIK, KONTROLL, METROL, TELEKOM comparator; **Komparatorschaltung** *f* ELEKTRONIK comparator circuit
Kompaß *m* BAU leveling compass (AmE), levelling compass (BrE), LUFTTRANS compass; **Kompaßberichtigung** *f* LUFTTRANS, WASSERTRANS compass compensating; **Kompaßbüchse** *f* PHYS compass bowl; **Kompaßdiopter** *m* BAU sight vane; **Kompaßeingang** *m* LUFTTRANS, WASSERTRANS *Radar* compass input; **Kompaßgefäß** *nt* PHYS compass bowl; **Kompaßgehäuse** *nt* WASSERTRANS binnacle; **Kompaßhaube** *f* WASSERTRANS binnacle cover; **Kompaßhausdeckel** *m* WASSERTRANS binnacle cover; **Kompaßkompensierscheibe** *f* LUFTTRANS, WASSERTRANS compass compensation base; **Kompaßkurs** *m* LUFTTRANS, WASSERTRANS *Navigation* compass heading; **Kompaßmißweisung** *f* LUFTTRANS, WASSERTRANS compass variation; **Kompaßnadel** *f* PHYS compass needle; **Kompaßpeilung** *f* LUFTTRANS, WASSERTRANS *Navigation* compass bearing; **Kompaßrose** *f* LUFTTRANS, WASSERTRANS compass card, compass dial; **Kompaßstrich** *m* WASSERTRANS *Kompaß* rhumb
kompatibel *adj* COMP & DV compatible
Kompatibilität *f* COMP & DV, ERGON, FERNSEH, MASCHINEN compatibility
Kompendium *nt* FOTO *Linse* matte box
Kompensation *f* ELEKTRIZ compensating, ELEKTRONIK, ELEKTROTECH compensation, KERNTECH compensating, PHYS, TELEKOM compensation; **Kompensationsbandschreiber** *m* GERÄT compensating strip chart recorder, strip chart potentiometric recorder; **Kompensationsentwickler** *m* FOTO compensating developer; **Kompensationsfilter** *nt* FOTO compensating filter; **Kompensationshalbleiter** *m* ELEKTROTECH compensated semiconductor; **Kompensationsinstrument** *nt* GERÄT potentiometer instrument; **Kompensationskreis** *m* FERNSEH bucking circuit, GERÄT potentiometer circuit; **Kompensationsmagnet** *m* WASSERTRANS *Kompaß* compensating magnet; **Kompensationsmeßgerät** *nt* GERÄT compensating instrument, potentiometer instrument, potentiometric meter; **Kompensationsmethode** *f* AKUSTIK cancellation method; **Kompensationspendel** *nt* PHYS compensated pendulum; **Kompensationsschaltung** *f* ELEKTRIZ compensating circuit, GERÄT compensating circuit, potentiometer circuit, TELEKOM compensation circuit; **Kompensationsschreiber** *m* GERÄT compensating recorder, null balance recorder, potentiometer recorder, self-balancing recorder; **Kompensationsspannung** *f* ELEKTRIZ compensating voltage; **Kompensationsspule** *f* AUFNAHME, ELEKTROTECH bucking coil; **Kompensationsstab** *m* KERNTECH compensating rod; **Kompensationsstrom** *m* ELEKTRIZ

compensating current; **Kompensationstheorem** *nt* ELEKTRIZ compensation theorem; **Kompensationsverstärker** *m* ELEKTRONIK compensated amplifier; **Kompensations-Voltmeter** *nt* GERÄT compensated voltmeter; **Kompensationswicklung** *f* ELEKTROTECH compensation winding

Kompensator *m* ELEKTRONIK, ELEKTROTECH, GERÄT compensator, HYDRAUL expansion joint, PHYS compensator; **Kompensatormaschine** *f* ELEKTRIZ compensator; **Kompensatorschaltung** *f* GERÄT potentiometer circuit

kompensieren *vt* KOHLEN, PHYS, WASSERTRANS *Kompaß* compensate

kompensierend: **~es Registriergerät** *nt* GERÄT compensating recorder

kompensiert: nicht ~er Motor *m* ELEKTROTECH noncompensated motor

Kompetenz *f* ERGON proficiency

Kompilierbefehl *m* COMP & DV compiler directive

kompilieren *vt* COMP & DV compile

kompilierend: **~es Programm** *nt* COMP & DV compiler generator

Kompilierer *m* COMP & DV, TELEKOM compiler

Kompilierfehler *m* COMP & DV compilation error

Kompilierung *f* COMP & DV compilation

Kompilierzeit *f* COMP & DV compilation time

komplan *adj* FERTIG coplanar

Komplement *nt* COMP & DV, ELEKTRONIK *zur Darstellung von Negativwerten* complement

Komplementär- *pref* FOTO, PHYS complementary; **Komplementärausgaben** *f pl* ELEKTRONIK complementary outputs; **Komplementärfarbe** *f* FOTO, PHYS complementary color (AmE), complementary colour (BrE)

komplementär: **~es Paar** *nt* ELEKTRONIK *Transistoren* complementary pair

Komplementarität *f* PHYS, TEILPHYS complementarity; **Komplementaritätsprinzip** *nt* PHYS principle of complementarity

Komplementär-: **Komplementär-Metalloxid-Halbleiter** *m (CMOS)* COMP & DV, ELEKTRONIK complementary metal oxide semiconductor *(CMOS)*; **Komplementär-Symmetrischer Metalloxid-Halbleiter** *m (COSMOS)* ELEKTRONIK complementary-symmetrical metal oxide semiconductor *(COSMOS)*; **Komplementärtransistoren** *m pl* ELEKTRONIK complementary transistors; **Komplementärwinkel** *m* GEOM complementary angles

Komplementmenge *f* MATH complementary set

komplett: ~e Bremse *f* KFZTECH brake assembly

Komplettierung *f* ERDÖL *Bohrtechnik* completion

Komplettschnitt *m* MASCHINEN combination die, compound die

komplex[1] *adj* COMP & DV, ELEKTRIZ, ELEKTROTECH, GEOM, KONTROLL, PHYS complex

komplex:[2] **~e Admittanz** *f* ELEKTRIZ complex admittance; **~er Brechungsindex** *m* PHYS complex refractive index; **~e Impedanz** *f* ELEKTRIZ complex impedance; **~e Kreisverstärkung** *f* REGELUNG complex loop chain; **~e Leistung** *f* ELEKTRIZ *AC-Leistungsberechnung* complex power; **~e Permeabilität** *f* ELEKTRIZ complex permeability; **~er Regelfaktor** *m* REGELUNG complex control factor; **~er Scheinwiderstand** *m* ELEKTROTECH complex impedance; **~es Signal** *nt* ELEKTRONIK complex signal; **~e Variable** *f* COMP & DV complex variable; **~e Wellenform** *f* ELEKTRIZ complex waveform; **~er Widerstand** *m* PHYS complex impedance; **~er Wirkleit-**

wert *m* PHYS complex admittance; **~e Zahl** *f* COMP & DV, MATH complex number

Komplexbildner *m* CHEMIE chelating agent, complexing agent, KERNTECH complexing agent

Komplexbildung *f* CHEMIE chelation, complexing

Komplexerz *nt* KOHLEN complex ore

Komplexität *f* CHEMIE, COMP & DV complexity

Komponente *f* ELEKTRIZ, ELEKTRONIK *Funktionselement*, KERNTECH, KOHLEN, MASCHINEN, MATH *eines Vektors*, MECHAN, TELEKOM *physikalisch* component

Kompost *m* ABFALL compost; **Kompostaufbereitungsanlage** *f* ABFALL composting plant; **Kompostaufbetrieb** *m* ABFALL composting plant; **Kompostbelüftung** *f* ABFALL compost aeration; **Kompostbereitung** *f* ABFALL composting

kompostierbar: ~er Abfall *m* ABFALL compostable waste; **nicht ~er Abfall** *m* ABFALL noncompostable waste

Kompostierung *f* ABFALL *von Hausmüll* composting; **Kompostierungsanlage** *f* ABFALL composting plant; **Kompostierungsrückstand** *m* ABFALL composting residue; **Kompostierungstechnik** *f* ABFALL composting technique

Kompost: **Kompostreifung** *f* ABFALL compost maturing, compost ripening; **Kompostwerk** *nt* ABFALL composting plant

Kompoundierung *f* ELEKTROTECH compounding

Kompoundmotor *m* ELEKTRIZ, ELEKTROTECH compound motor

Kompressibilität *f* LUFTTRANS, METALL, PAPIER, PHYS, STRÖMPHYS, THERMOD *Gas* compressibility; **Kompressibilitätseffekte** *m pl* LUFTTRANS compressibility effects; **Kompressibilitätsfaktor** *m (z)* THERMOD compressibility factor *(z)*; **Kompressibilitätswiderstand** *m* LUFTTRANS compressibility drag

kompressible: **~ Strömung** *f* STRÖMPHYS compressible flow

Kompression *f* ABFALL compaction, AUFNAHME compression, COMP & DV *von Daten* compaction, ELEKTRONIK, ERDÖL, HYDRAUL, KFZTECH, KUNSTSTOFF, PAPIER, PHYS, THERMOD, WELLPHYS compression; **Kompressionsarbeit** *f* MASCHINEN compression work; **Kompressionsbeiwert** *m* KOHLEN compression index; **Kompressionsfeder** *f* HYDRAUL compression spring; **Kompressionsfilter** *nt* ELEKTRONIK compression filter; **Kompressionshahn** *m* HYDRAUL compression cock; **Kompressionshub** *m* KFZTECH *Motor* compression stroke; **Kompressionskältemaschine** *f* THERMOD compression plant, compression refrigerator; **Kompressionskammer** *f* ERDÖL *Tieftauchtechnik*, HYDRAUL, KOHLEN compression chamber; **Kompressionskoeffizient** *m* PHYS coefficient of compressibility; **Kompressionskühlung** *f* HEIZ & KÄLTE compression refrigeration; **Kompressionsmesser** *m* PAPIER compressometer; **Kompressionsmodul** *nt (K)* HYDRAUL bulk modulus of compression *(K)*; **Kompressionsperiode** *f* HYDRAUL compression period; **Kompressionspumpe** *f* HYDRAUL compression pump; **Kompressionspunkt** *m* HYDRAUL compression point; **Kompressionsraum** *m* KFZTECH compression chamber; **Kompressionsring** *m* KFZTECH *Motor* compression ring; **Kompressionsstufe** *f* MASCHINEN compression stage; **Kompressionstreiber** *m* AUFNAHME compression driver; **Kompressionsverhältnis** *nt* AUFNAHME, ELEKTRONIK *Mikrowellen*, HEIZ & KÄLTE, KFZTECH *Motor*, MASCHINEN, THERMOD compression ratio;

Kompressionswärme *f* THERMOD heat of compression; **Kompressionszeitraum** *m* HYDRAUL compression period

Kompressor *m* ERDÖL *Maschine*, FERTIG, KFZTECH *Motor*, LABOR, MASCHINEN, MECHAN, PAPIER, TELEKOM compressor; **Kompressoranlage** *f* MASCHINEN compressor plant; **Kompressorenschalldämpfer** *m* SICHERHEIT noise protection for compressors

Kompreßschrift *f* DRUCK condensed face

komprimierbar: **~er Abfall** *m* ABFALL compressible waste

komprimieren *vt* COMP & DV *Daten* compress, pack

komprimiert[1] *adj* ELEKTRONIK, FERNSEH, KERNTECH, TELEKOM, VERPACK compressed

komprimiert:[2] **~e Digitalübertragung** *f* TELEKOM compressed digital transmission; **~es Kernmaterial** *nt* KERNTECH compressed nuclear matter; **~e Klebstoffzufuhr** *f* VERPACK pressurized glue feed; **~es Signal** *nt* ELEKTRONIK compressed signal; **~e Sprachinformationen** *f pl* ELEKTRONIK compressed speech; **~er Videopegel** *m* FERNSEH compressed video level

Komprimierung *f* COMP & DV, ELEKTRONIK *Hochfrequenztechnik* compression

Kondensat *nt* CHEMTECH *Produkt*, ERDÖL, HEIZ & KÄLTE, MASCHINEN, THERMOD condensate; **Kondensatablaßventil** *nt* HYDRAUL pet valve; **Kondensatabscheider** *m* CHEMIE condenser, CHEMTECH condenser cooler, ERDÖL steam trap; **Kondensatdurchdringung** *f* FERTIG *Kunststoffinstallationen* condensate permeation

Kondensation *f* CHEMTECH *durch Oberflächenkülung*, FERTIG *Kunststoffinstallationen*, HEIZ & KÄLTE, KER & GLAS *von Doppelverglasung*, LABOR, MASCHINEN, PHYS, THERMOD, UMWELTSCHMUTZ, VERPACK condensation; **Kondensationsanlage** *f* CHEMTECH condensing plant; **Kondensationsauffanggefäß** *nt* LABOR condensing trap; **Kondensationskern** *m* THERMOD, UMWELTSCHMUTZ condensation nucleus; **Kondensationskernzähler** *m* UMWELTSCHMUTZ condensation nucleus counter; **Kondensationspolymer** *nt* KUNSTSTOFF condensation polymer; **Kondensationspolymerisation** *f* KUNSTSTOFF condensation polymerization; **Kondensationsprodukt** *nt* CHEMTECH condensate; **Kondensationssatz** *m* HEIZ & KÄLTE condensing set; **Kondensationssatz mit Zwischenüberhitzung** *m* HEIZ & KÄLTE condensing set with reheat; **Kondensationssäule** *f* CHEMTECH condensation column; **Kondensationsturbine** *f* HEIZ & KÄLTE condensing turbine; **Kondensationsturm** *m* CHEMTECH cooling tower; **Kondensationswärme** *f* THERMOD condensation heat

Kondensator *m* AKUSTIK, AUFNAHME, CHEMTECH condenser, COMP & DV capacitor, ELEKTRIZ, ELEKTROTECH capacitor, condenser, ERDÖL *Kühltechnik* condenser, FERNSEH capacitor, KFZTECH condenser, *Zündung* capacitor, KOHLEN condenser, LABOR, MASCHINEN, PAPIER capacitor, condenser, PHYS, RADIO, TELEKOM capacitor, WASSERTRANS condenser; **~ mit Festelektrolyt** *m* ELEKTROTECH solid electrolyte capacitor; **~ für punktförmig verteilte Kapazität** *m* ELEKTROTECH lumped capacitor; **Kondensatorblindwiderstand** *m* ELEKTROTECH reactance capacitance, resistance capacitance; **Kondensatorenblock** *m* ELEKTROTECH capacitor bank; **Kondensatorenreihe** *f* ELEKTROTECH capacitor bank; **Kondensatorentladung** *f* ELEKTROTECH capacitor discharge; **Kondensatorgruppe** *f* ELEKTROTECH bank of capacitors; **Kondensatorküh-**

ler *m* CHEMTECH condenser cooler; **Kondensatorkühlwasserpumpe** *f* HEIZ & KÄLTE condenser circulating pump; **Kondensatorlautsprecher** *m* AUFNAHME electrostatic loudspeaker; **Kondensatormikrofon** *nt* AKUSTIK condenser microphone, AUFNAHME capacitor microphone, condenser microphone, electrostatic microphone, RADIO condenser microphone; **Kondensatormotor** *m* ELEKTRIZ capacitive starting motor, ELEKTROTECH permanent split capacitor motor, *mit Betriebskondensator* capacitor motor; **Kondensatorplatte** *f* ELEKTRIZ, PHYS capacitor plate; **Kondensatorreihe** *f* ELEKTROTECH bank of capacitors; **Kondensatorreststrom** *m* ELEKTROTECH capacitor leakage current; **Kondensatorrohr** *nt* MASCHINEN condenser tube; **Kondensatorspeicher** *m* COMP & DV capacitor store; **Kondensatorzündung** *f* KFZTECH capacitor ignition

Kondensat: **Kondensatpumpe** *f* CHEMTECH condensate pump; **Kondensatsammelgefäß** *nt* CHEMTECH condensation trap; **Kondensattopf** *m* HYDRAUL steam trap

Kondenser *m* CHEMIE condenser

Kondensfahne *f* LUFTTRANS condensation trail

kondensierbar *adj* PHYS condensable

kondensieren[1] *vt* CHEMTECH *Lebensmittel*, THERMOD *Flüssigkeit*, VERPACK condense

kondensieren[2] *vi* CHEMTECH, THERMOD condense

kondensiert[1] *adj* CHEMTECH, THERMOD condensed

kondensiert:[2] **~es System** *nt* CHEMTECH condensed system

Kondensierung *f* MASCHINEN, VERPACK condensation; **Kondensierungswärme** *f* THERMOD condensation heat

Kondensmilch *f* LEBENSMITTEL *gezuckert* condensed milk

Kondensor *m* FOTO, LABOR *Linsen-System*, OPTIK condenser; **Kondensorlampe** *f* FOTO condenser lamp; **Kondensorlinse** *f* FOTO condensing lens; **Kondensorsystem** *nt* FOTO *Vergrößerer* condenser system

Kondensstreifen *m* LUFTTRANS condensation trail

Kondenstopf *m* HEIZ & KÄLTE, PAPIER steam trap

Kondenswasser *nt* CHEMTECH, HEIZ & KÄLTE condensate; **Kondenswasserablauf** *m* HEIZ & KÄLTE condensate drain; **Kondenswasserabscheider** *m* HEIZ & KÄLTE steam trap; **Kondenswasserheizung** *f* HEIZ & KÄLTE anticondensation heater; **Kondenswasserpumpe** *f* CHEMTECH condensate pump

Konditionieren *nt* KUNSTSTOFF, PAPIER conditioning

konditioniert *adj* TEXTIL conditioned

Konditionierung *f* ERGON, KUNSTSTOFF conditioning

Konduktanz *f* ELEKTRIZ, ELEKTROTECH, PHYS, TELEKOM conductance; **Konduktanzbrücke** *f* ELEKTRIZ conductance bridge

Konduktionsstrom *m* ELEKTRIZ conduction current

Konfektion *f* TEXTIL making-up; **Konfektionsklebrigkeit** *f* KUNSTSTOFF green tack, tack

Konferenz *f* FERNSEH, TELEKOM conference; **Konferenzbridge** *f* TELEKOM conference bridge; **Konferenzschaltung** *f* FERNSEH conference network; **Konferenzverbindung** *f* TELEKOM conference call

Konfidenzfaktor *m* (*KF*) KÜNSTL INT certainty factor, confidence factor (*CF*)

Konfiguration *f* COMP & DV, ELEKTRONIK, METALL, PHYS, TELEKOM configuration; **Konfigurationseinstellung** *f* COMP & DV configuration setting; **Konfigurationsentropie** *f* METALL configurational entropy;

Konfigurationsmanagement *nt* COMP & DV configuration management; **Konfigurationsraum** *m* PHYS configuration space
konfigurieren *vt* COMP & DV, KONTROLL configure
konfiguriert *adj* COMP & DV configured-in; **nicht ~** *adj* COMP & DV configured-out
Konfigurierung: ~ für reduzierte Last *f* RAUMFAHRT *Raumschiff* reduced load configuration
Konflikt *m* TELEKOM contention; **Konfliktauflösung** *f* KÜNSTL INT conflict resolution, TELEKOM contention control
konfliktfrei: ~e Verkehrsströme *f pl* TRANS nonconflicting traffic flows
Konflikt: Konfliktlösung *f* KÜNSTL INT conflict resolution; **Konfliktstelle** *f* TRANS conflict point; **Konfliktverkehrsströme** *m pl* TRANS conflicting traffic flows
Konformität *f* QUAL compliance, conformity; **Konformitätsbescheinigung** *f* MASCHINEN certificate, QUAL COC, certificate of compliance, certificate of conformance, conformity certificate; **Konformitätszeichen** *nt* QUAL mark of conformity; **Konformitätszertifikat** *nt* QUAL certificate of conformity
Konglomerat *nt* NICHTFOSS ENERG conglomerate
kongruent[1] *adj* GEOM, MATH *Dreiecke, Zahlen* congruent
kongruent:[2] **~e Dreiecke** *nt pl* GEOM congruent triangles; **~e Zahlen** *f pl* MATH *kongruent bezüglich eines Modulus* congruent numbers
Kongruenz *f* GEOM congruence
Koniferosid *nt* CHEMIE coniferin
Königlich: ~ Britische Marine *f* WASSERTRANS Royal Navy
Königswelle *f* MECHAN mainshaft
Königszapfen *m* MASCHINEN, MECHAN kingbolt (AmE), kingpin (BrE)
Koniin *nt* CHEMIE conicine, coniine, propylpiperidine
konisch[1] *adj* AKUSTIK conical, FERTIG taper, GEOM, KER & GLAS, LABOR conical, MASCHINEN tapered, TEXTIL conic
konisch:[2] **~er Becher** *m* LABOR conical beaker; **~e Hohlform** *f* FERTIG cup; **~es Horn** *nt* AKUSTIK conical horn; **~e Hülle** *f* RAUMFAHRT *Raumschiff* conical shell; **~e Klemmverbindung** *f* MASCHINEN conical clamping connection; **~e Kreuzspule** *f* TEXTIL cone; **~e Nadel** *f* MASCHINEN tapered needle; **~es Rohrstück** *nt* MASCHINEN taper pipe; **~e Schliffverbindung** *f* LABOR conical ground glass point; **~e Unterlegscheibe** *f* MASCHINEN taper washer; **~er verstärkter Rand** *m* KER & GLAS conical reinforced rim; **~e Verzahnung** *f* MASCHINEN tapered teeth; **~es Wellenende** *nt* MASCHINEN conical shaft end
konisch:[3] **~ zulaufen** *vi* FERTIG taper
Konischdrehen *nt* MASCHINEN conical turning, taper turning
Konischdrehvorrichtung *f* MASCHINEN taper-turning attachment
Konizität *f* FERTIG amount of taper, MECHAN taper
konjugiert[1] *adj* GEOM, METALL, PHYS conjugate
konjugiert:[2] **~er Durchmesser** *m* METALL conjugate diameter; **~e Ebene** *f* METALL conjugate plane; **~es Gleiten** *nt* METALL conjugate slip; **~e Halbmesser** *m pl* GEOM conjugate radii; **~e Punkte** *m pl* PHYS conjugate points; **~e Zweige** *f pl* ELEKTROTECH conjugate branches

konjugiert-komplex[1] *adj* MATH conjugate, conjugate-complex
konjugiert-komplex:[2] **~e Scheinwiderstände** *f pl* AKUSTIK conjugate impedances
Konkatenation *f* ELEKTROTECH concatenation
konkav[1] *adj* GEOM, KER & GLAS, OPTIK concave
konkav:[2] **~e Fläche** *f* GEOM concave surface; **~e Krümmung** *f* KER & GLAS concave bow; **~es Optikwerkzeug** *nt* KER & GLAS concave optical tool
Konkavgitter: ~ von Rowland *nt* PHYS concave grating of Rowland
Konkavität *f* OPTIK concavity
konkavkonvex *adj* OPTIK concavo-convex
Konkav: Konkavlinse *f* FOTO concave lens; **Konkavspiegel** *m* PHYS concave mirror
Konkordanz *f* ERDÖL *Geologie* conformity
konkretisieren *vt* KÜNSTL INT instantiate
Konkurrenz *f* COMP & DV, METALL competition; **Konkurrenzbetrieb** *m* COMP & DV contention mode; **Konkurrenzsituation** *f* COMP & DV contention; **Konkurrenzwachstum** *nt* METALL competition growth
Konnektivität *f* COMP & DV connectivity
Konnektor *m* ELEKTROTECH connector
Konnossement *nt* ERDÖL *Schiffahrt, Handel,* WASSERTRANS *Dokumente* bill of lading; **Konnossementsbedingung** *f* WASSERTRANS *Dokumente* clause of bill of lading; **Konnossementsvorbehalt** *m* WASSERTRANS *Dokumente* clause of bill of lading
Konode *f* FERTIG conode
kononisch: ~e Verteilung *f* PHYS canonical distribution
Konservation *f* STRÖMPHYS conservation
konservativ: ~e Kraft *f* PHYS conservative force
Konserven *f pl* VERPACK canned food (AmE), tinned food (BrE); **Konservenbüchse** *f* ABFALL can (AmE), tin (BrE); **Konservenglas** *nt* KER & GLAS canning jar (AmE), preserving jar (BrE); **Konservenherstellung** *f* LEBENSMITTEL canning
konservieren *vt* LEBENSMITTEL preserve
konserviert: ~er Latex *m* KUNSTSTOFF preserved latex
Konservierung *f* ERDÖL, LEBENSMITTEL, PHYS, THERMOD, VERPACK conservation; **Konservierungsmittel** *nt* VERPACK preservative; **Konservierungsstoff** *m* LEBENSMITTEL preservative
Konsignant *m* TRANS *Überseehandel* consignor
Konsistenz *f* COMP & DV, KOHLEN, KÜNSTL INT, LEBENSMITTEL consistency; **Konsistenzgrenze** *f* KOHLEN limit of consistency; **Konsistenzprüfung** *f* KÜNSTL INT consistency check; **Konsistenzzahl** *f* KOHLEN consistency index
Konsole *f* BAU bracket, corbel, support, COMP & DV console, panel, FERTIG knee, GERÄT *Ein-Ausgabe-Einheit*, KONTROLL console, MASCHINEN bracket, MECHAN pad, WASSERTRANS *Schiffelektronik* console
Konsolfräsmaschine *f* FERTIG knee-and-column milling machine, MASCHINEN knee-and-column milling machine, knee-type milling machine
Konsolführung *f* FERTIG key slide
Konsolidierung *f* KOHLEN consolidation; **Konsolidierungsprüfung** *f* KOHLEN consolidation test
Konsoltisch *m* FERTIG knee table
Konsonant *m* AKUSTIK consonant
konsonant: ~er Akkord *m* AKUSTIK concord; **~er Grundakkord** *m* AKUSTIK fundamental concord
Konstant- *pref* ELEKTRIZ, ELEKTRONIK, MASCHINEN, TELEKOM constant
konstant[1] *adj* DRUCK, ELEKTRIZ, FOTO, LUFTTRANS,

MATH, PHYS, RADIO, TELEKOM, TRANS constant

konstant:[2] **~e Brennweite** *f* FOTO fixed focus; **~e Differenz** *f* MATH *zwischen Termen einer arithmetischen Folge* common difference; **~e Drehzahl** *f* OPTIK constant angular velocity; **~e Erreichbarkeit** *f* TELEKOM constant availability; **~er Faktor** *m* MATH common ratio; **~es Feld** *nt* ELEKTRIZ constant field; **~ geringe Batterieentladung** *f* RAUMFAHRT *Raumschiff* battery drain; **~ Lineargeschwindigkeit** *f* COMP & DV, OPTIK constant linear velocity; **~e Spationierung** *f* DRUCK monospace; **~er Steigungswinkel** *m* LUFTTRANS collective pitch angle; **~er Verkehrsfluß** *m* TRANS stable flow; **~e Verzögerung** *f* ELEKTRIZ fixed delay; **~e Winkelgeschwindigkeit** *f* COMP & DV, GERÄT, OPTIK constant angular velocity

Konstantan *nt* ELEKTRIZ constantan

Konstant-: **Konstantausgangsspannung** *f* ELEKTROTECH regulated output voltage; **Konstantausgangsstrom** *m* ELEKTROTECH regulated output current

Konstante *f* COMP & DV, GERÄT, MATH, PHYS, RADIO constant

Konstant-: **Konstantfett** *nt* MASCHINEN set grease; **Konstanthalter** *m* TELEKOM regulator; **Konstantlast** *f* ELEKTRIZ constant load; **Konstantlithografie** *f* ELEKTRONIK constant lithography; **Konstantspannung** *f* ELEKTRIZ, ELEKTROTECH, LABOR constant voltage, regulated voltage; **Konstantspannungsquelle** *f* ELEKTRIZ, ELEKTROTECH, GERÄT constant-voltage source

Konstantstrom *m* ELEKTRIZ, ELEKTROTECH, LABOR constant current; **Konstantstromdynamo** *m* ELEKTRIZ constant-current dynamo; **Konstantstrom-Modulation** *f* ELEKTRONIK constant-current modulation; **Konstantstromoszillator** *m* ELEKTRONIK constant-current oscillator; **Konstantstromquelle** *f* GERÄT constant-current source; **Konstantstromtransformator** *m* ELEKTROTECH constant-current transformer; **Konstantstromversorgung** *f* ELEKTROTECH regulated power supply

Konstant-: **Konstantzeilenbetrieb** *m* FERNSEH constant line number operation; **Konstantzugwinde** *f* WASSERTRANS *Deckbeschläge* self-tensioning winch

Konstanz *f* TELEKOM stability

Konstitutionstyp *m* ERGON body type

Konstitutionswasser *nt* WASSERVERSORG combined water

Konstringenz *f* PHYS constringence

konstruieren *vt* BAU construct, design, GEOM construct

Konstrukteur *m* BAU, ERGON, MASCHINEN design engineer, designer

Konstruktion *f* BAU structure, COMP & DV design, GEOM construction, MASCHINEN design; **Konstruktionsabteilung** *f* MECHAN engineering department

konstruktionsbedingt: **~er Defekt** *m* KERNTECH design-related defect

Konstruktion: **Konstruktionsbüro** *nt* WASSERTRANS design department, *Schiffbau drawing office;* **Konstruktionsendprüfung** *f* RAUMFAHRT FDR, final design review; **Konstruktionsmerkmal** *nt* MASCHINEN, WASSERTRANS *Schiffbau* constructional feature, design feature; **Konstruktionsplan** *m* WASSERTRANS *Schiffbau* construction plan; **Konstruktionsprogramm** *nt* COMP & DV design aid; **Konstruktionsriß** *m* WASSERTRANS *Schiffbau* construction plan; **Konstruktionsstückliste** *f* KONSTZEICH design parts list;

Konstruktionssystem *nt* COMP & DV design system; **Konstruktionsüberprüfung** *f* QUAL design review; **Konstruktionsvorgaben** *f pl* QUAL design input; **Konstruktionswasserlinie** *f* WASSERTRANS *Schiffkonstruktion* design waterline, *Schiffbau* load waterline; **Konstruktionswasser-Linienebene** *f* WASSERTRANS *Schiffskonstruktion* design waterplane; **Konstruktionszeichner** *m* MECHAN designer draftsman (AmE), designer draughtsman (BrE), WASSERTRANS *Schiffkonstruktion* draftsman (AmE), draughtsman (BrE); **Konstruktionszeichnung** *f* KONSTZEICH design drawing

konstruktiv[1] *adj* BAU structural

konstruktiv:[2] **~e Interferenz** *f* PHYS, WELLPHYS constructive interference

Konsumgüter *nt pl* VERPACK consumer goods

Kontakt[1] *m* COMP & DV, ELEKTRIZ, ELEKTROTECH, FERTIG *Kunststoffinstallationen*, FOTO, KFZTECH, MASCHINEN, TRANS, VERPACK contact

Kontakt:[2] **~ herstellen** *vi* ELEKTRONIK contact making

Kontakt: **Kontaktabstand** *m* ELEKTRIZ contact gap, ELEKTROTECH break distance, KFZTECH contact gap; **Kontaktabtasten** *nt* COMP & DV contact scanning; **Kontaktabzug** *m* FOTO contact print; **Kontaktanordnung** *f* ELEKTROTECH contact arrangement; **Kontaktarm** *m* ELEKTRIZ contact blade; **Kontaktarmträger** *m* ELEKTROTECH brush rod; **Kontaktbahn** *f* TELEKOM bank contact; **Kontaktbemessung** *f* ELEKTROTECH contact rating; **Kontaktbildschirm** *m* COMP & DV touch-sensitive screen; **Kontaktbombe** *f* CHEMTECH catalytic bomb; **Kontaktbuchse** *f* ELEKTROTECH female contact; **Kontaktcodierung im seriellen Betrieb** *f* VERPACK in-line contact coding; **Kontaktdetektor** *m* TRANS contact detector; **Kontaktelement** *nt* ELEKTROTECH contact; **Kontakt-EMK** *m* ELEKTROTECH, PHYS contact emf; **Kontaktfeder** *f* ELEKTRIZ contact blade, contact spring, MASCHINEN, WASSERVERSORG contact spring; **Kontaktfehler** *m* ELEKTROTECH contact fault; **Kontaktfenster** *nt* ELEKTROTECH *bei Halbleitern* contact window; **Kontaktfläche** *f* MASCHINEN contact surface; **Kontaktflattern** *nt* KFZTECH contact chatter; **Kontaktfroster** *m* HEIZ & KÄLTE contact freezer; **Kontaktgefrieren** *nt* HEIZ & KÄLTE contact freezing; **Kontaktgift** *nt* UMWELTSCHMUTZ catalyst poison; **Kontakthaftmittel** *nt* VERPACK contact adhesive; **Kontakthammer** *m* ELEKTROTECH trembler; **Kontaktkleber** *m* KUNSTSTOFF, VERPACK contact adhesive; **Kontaktklebstoff** *m* KUNSTSTOFF contact adhesive; **Kontaktkopie** *f* DRUCK, FOTO contact print; **Kontaktkopieren** *nt* FOTO contact printing; **Kontaktkopiergerät** *nt* FOTO contact printer; **Kontaktkopierrahmen** *m* FOTO contact-printing frame; **Kontaktlinse** *f* KER & GLAS contact lens; **Kontaktlog** *nt* ERDÖL *Bohrlochmeßtechnik* contact log

kontaktlos: **~e Aufhängung** *f* KFZTECH noncontact suspension; **~es Relais** *nt* ELEKTROTECH solid state relay; **~e Steuerung** *f* KFZTECH breakerless triggering; **~e Transistorzündung** *f* KFZTECH contactless-transistorized ignition

Kontakt: **Kontaktmaske** *f* ELEKTRONIK *Grafik* contact mask; **Kontaktmaskierung** *f* ELEKTRONIK contact masking; **Kontaktmeßinstrument** *nt* GERÄT contact-measuring instrument; **Kontaktmikrofon** *nt* AKUSTIK, AUFNAHME contact microphone; **Kontaktnegativ** *nt* FOTO contact negative; **Kontaktprellen** *nt* ELEKTRIZ contact bounce, KFZTECH contact chatter; **Kontakt-**

pressen *nt* KER & GLAS contact molding (AmE), contact moulding (BrE); **Kontaktpunkt** *m* LUFTTRANS contact point; **Kontaktsatz** *m* ELEKTRIZ, KFZTECH *Zündung* contact set, TELEKOM bank contact; **Kontaktschalter** *m* ELEKTROTECH touch switch; **Kontaktschlammverfahren** *nt* ABFALL sludge contact process; **Kontaktschuh** *m* EISENBAHN collector shoe; **Kontaktspalt** *m* ELEKTRIZ contact gap; **Kontaktspannung** *f* ELEKTRIZ contact potential; **Kontaktstift** *m* ELEKTROTECH contact pin, pin; **Kontaktstück** *nt* ELEKTROTECH contact; **Kontakt-Thermometer** *nt* GERÄT contact thermometer; **Kontaktunterbrecher** *m* KFZTECH breaker; **Kontaktverschleiß** *m* ELEKTRIZ contact wear; **Kontaktwiderstand** *m* ELEKTRIZ, ELEKTROTECH contact resistance; **Kontaktwinkel** *m* KOHLEN contact angle; **Kontaktzunge** *f* TELEKOM reed
Kontamination *f* CHEMIE, KOHLEN, LABOR contamination; **Kontaminationsüberwachung** *f* GERÄT contamination monitoring
kontaminieren *vt* KERNTECH contaminate
kontaminiert: ~**er Standort** *m* ABFALL contaminated site, problem site
Kontaminierung *f* KERNTECH contamination
Kontermutter *f* FERTIG locking nut, MASCHINEN jam nut, locknut, MECHAN locknut
Kontern *nt* DRUCK retransfer
Kontext *m* COMP & DV context
kontextabhängig *adj* COMP & DV context-sensitive, contextual
kontextfrei[1] *adj* COMP & DV context-free
kontextfrei:[2] ~**e Grammatik** *f (kfG)* KÜNSTL INT CF grammar, context-free grammar
kontextsensitiv: ~**e Grammatik** *f (ksG)* KÜNSTL INT context-sensitive grammar *(CSG)*
Kontinentalabfall *m* ERDÖL continental slope
Kontinentalböschung *f* ERDÖL *Geomorphologie* continental slope
Kontinentalschelf *nt* ERDÖL *Geomorphologie* continental shelf
Kontinue-Garn *nt* TEXTIL continuous spun yarn, continuous yarn
kontinuierlich[1] *adj* AKUSTIK, COMP & DV, ELEKTRONIK, KFZTECH, KONTROLL, METALL, PHYS, STRAHLPHYS, TRANS continuous
kontinuierlich:[2] ~ **abstimmbares Filter** *nt* AUFNAHME continuously tunable filter; ~**e Abstimmung** *f* ELEKTRONIK continuous tuning; ~ **arbeitende Gewichtsdosierung** *f* VERPACK continuous motion weight filling; ~**e Aushärtung** *f* METALL continuous precipitation; ~ **gesteuerte Geräuschsperre** *f* TELEKOM continuous-controlled squelch system; ~**er Kocher** *m* PAPIER continuous digester; ~**e Kraftstoffeinspritzung** *f* KFZTECH K-Jetronic fuel injection; ~**er Laser** *m* ELEKTRONIK continuous laser; ~**es Lasern** *nt* ELEKTRONIK continuous laser action; ~**er Laserstrahl** *m* ELEKTRONIK continuous laser beam; ~**e mechanische Zwillingsnachbildung** *f* METALL continual mechanical twinning; ~**es Spektrum** *nt* AKUSTIK, ELEKTRONIK, PHYS, STRAHLPHYS continuous spectrum; ~**e Strahlmodulation** *f* FERNSEH continuous beam modulation; ~**er Transport** *m* TRANS continuous transport; ~**er Umlaufkühlofen** *m* KER & GLAS continuous recirculation lehr; ~**es Walzen von Gußglas** *nt* KER & GLAS continuous casting
Kontinuität *f* FERNSEH, PHYS, STRÖMPHYS, WERKPRÜF continuity; **Kontinuitätdiskontinuität** *f* WERKPRÜF

continuity-discontinuity; **Kontinuitätsgleichung** *f* PHYS, STRÖMPHYS continuity equation; **Kontinuitätsschleife** *f* FERNSEH continuity log; **Kontinuitätssteuerung** *f* FERNSEH continuity control
Kontinuum *nt* MATH continuum
Kontourenmeßgerät *nt* METROL contour-measuring equipment
Kontourringe *m pl* PHYS contour fringes
kontrahiert: ~**er Abschnitt** *m* HYDRAUL contracted section
Kontraktion *f* MASCHINEN contraction, METALL constriction; **Kontraktionskoeffizient** *m* HYDRAUL contraction coefficient; **Kontraktionsziffer** *f* HYDRAUL coefficient of contraction
Kontrast *m* PHYS contrast; **Kontrastabschwächung** *f* FOTO contrast reduction; **Kontrasteffekt** *m* FERNSEH contrast effect; **Kontrast-Filterscheibe** *f* FOTO filter screen; **Kontrastregler** *m* FERNSEH contrast control
kontrastreich: ~**e Wiedergabe** *f* KONSTZEICH high-contrast reproduction
Kontrast: **Kontrastschwelle** *f* ERGON contrast threshold; **Kontraststeigerung** *f* FOTO increase in contrast; **Kontrastverhältnis** *nt* FERNSEH, PAPIER contrast ratio
Kontroll- *pref* AUFNAHME, EISENBAHN, LUFTTRANS, MASCHINEN, SICHERHEIT control; **Kontrollämpchen** *nt* ELEKTROTECH pilot light; **Kontrollampe** *f* EISENBAHN telltale lamp, ELEKTROTECH pilot lamp, pilot light; **Kontrollanzeige** *f* LUFTTRANS *Lichtsignal* indicator; **Kontrollart** *f* UMWELTSCHMUTZ indicator species; **Kontrollautsprecher** *m* AUFNAHME monitoring loudspeaker; **Kontrollbericht** *m* QUAL check report; **Kontrollbildschirm** *m* TELEKOM *Video* monitor; **Kontrollbit** *nt* RADIO control bit; **Kontrollbrunnen** *m* ABFALL monitoring well, observation well
Kontrolle *f* COMP & DV check, control, KFZTECH, LUFTTRANS control, MECHAN inspection, TELEKOM control, TEXTIL monitoring, VERPACK check; ~ **des Luftkorridors** *f* LUFTTRANS corridor control; ~ **der Zeitüberwachung** *f* TELEKOM time-out supervision
Kontroll-: **Kontrolleuchte** *f* KFZTECH *Zubehör* indicator; **Kontrolleur** *m* SICHERHEIT factory inspector; **Kontrollfeld** *nt* COMP & DV control field; **Kontrollgerät** *nt* TELEKOM monitor, monitor unit; **Kontrollgrenze** *f* QUAL control limit
Kontrollicht *nt* LUFTTRANS indicator light
kontrollieren[1] *vt* KONTROLL inspect, MEERSCHMUTZ monitor, TELEKOM control, TEXTIL, UMWELTSCHMUTZ monitor
kontrollieren[2] *vti* VERPACK check
kontrolliert: ~**er Abflußkanal** *m* WASSERVERSORG controlled spillway; ~**es Abladen von Schutt** *nt* UMWELTSCHMUTZ controlled dumping; ~**e Atmosphäre** *f* HEIZ & KÄLTE controlled atmosphere, VERPACK CA, controlled atmosphere; ~**er Flug** *m* LUFTTRANS controlled flight; ~**e Gärung** *f* ABFALL controlled fermentation; ~**er Leistungsrückgang** *m* COMP & DV graceful degradation; ~**er Luftraum** *m* LUFTTRANS *auf Instrumentenflug beschränkt* controlled airspace; ~**e Müllablagerung** *f* ABFALL controlled dumping, controlled tipping, sanitary landfill; ~**es Trudeln** *nt* LUFTTRANS controlled spin
Kontroll-: **Kontrollkarte für kumulierte Werte** *f* QUAL consum chart; **Kontrollmeßgerät** *nt* GERÄT checking instrument; **Kontrollmonitor** *m* FERNSEH image and waveform monitor, off-air monitor; **Kontrolloch** *nt* MASCHINEN inspection hole; **Kontrollprobe** *f* KOHLEN

control assay; **Kontrollprüfung** *f* QUAL check test; **Kontrollpunkte** *m pl* GEOM control points; **Kontrollschranke** *f* BAU control barrier; **Kontrollschuß** *m* ERDÖL *Seismik* checkshot; **Kontrollspur** *f* AUFNAHME guide track; **Kontrollsumme** *f* COMP & DV checksum; **Kontrollsystem** *nt* AUFNAHME pilot system, STRAHLPHYS monitoring system, TELEKOM control system; **Kontrollton** *m* AUFNAHME pilot tone; **Kontrollturm** *m* LUFTTRANS control tower; **Kontrolluhr** *f* MECHAN punch clock; **Kontrollventil** *nt* HYDRAUL control valve; **Kontrollverstärker** *m* AUFNAHME bridging amplifier, monitoring amplifier; **Kontrollvorrichtung** *f* VERPACK checking apparatus, inspection equipment; **Kontrollwaage** *f* VERPACK checkweigher

kontrollwiegen *vt* VERPACK check weigh

Kontroll-: **Kontrollzettel zum Aufkleben** *m* VERPACK control tag; **Kontrollzone** *f* LUFTTRANS control sector

Kontur *f* ANSTRICH profile, DRUCK, MASCHINEN outline; **Konturätzen** *nt* FERTIG chemical milling; **Kontureffekt** *m* AKUSTIK contour effect; **Konturenausgleich** *m* COMP & DV anti-aliasing; **Konturensatz** *m* DRUCK runaround; **Konturenschärfe** *f* FOTO acutance

konturenscharf: **~es Zeichnen** *nt* KONSTZEICH sharp-contoured impression

konturgetreu: **~er Überzug** *m* KUNSTSTOFF conformal coating

Konus *m* AKUSTIK, AUFNAHME, DRUCK bevel, cone, ERDÖL, GEOM, KER & GLAS, KFZTECH, MASCHINEN cone; **Konusbohrer** *m* ERDÖL *Bohrtechnik* cone bit; **Konusbohrmeißel** *m* ERDÖL cone bit; **Konusbremse** *f* MASCHINEN wedge brake; **Konuskupplung** *f* FERTIG, KFZTECH, MASCHINEN cone clutch, conical clutch; **Konuslager** *nt* MASCHINEN cone-type bearing; **Konuslautsprecher** *m* AUFNAHME cone loudspeaker; **Konusmembran** *f* AKUSTIK conical diaphragm; **Konusnabe** *f* KFZTECH *Rad* tapered hub; **Konusresonanz** *f* AUFNAHME cone resonance; **Konustreiber** *m* FERTIG drift; **Konustrichter** *m* AKUSTIK conical horn; **Konuswinkel** *m* LUFTTRANS flapping angle

Konvektion *f* ELEKTROTECH, ERDÖL, HEIZ & KÄLTE, KER & GLAS, PHYS, RAUMFAHRT, STRÖMPHYS, THERMOD convection; **~ im rotierenden Ringspalt** *f* STRÖMPHYS rotating annulus convection; **Konvektionsabriß** *m* RAUMFAHRT *Raumschiff* absence of convection; **Konvektionskühler** *m* HEIZ & KÄLTE, PHYS, THERMOD convection cooler; **Konvektionskühlung** *f* HEIZ & KÄLTE convection cooling, jet cooling, PHYS, THERMOD convection cooling; **Konvektionsmangel** *m* RAUMFAHRT *Raumschiff* absence of convection; **Konvektionsofen** *m* HEIZ & KÄLTE, PHYS, THERMOD convection oven; **Konvektionsstrom** *m* ELEKTROTECH, KER & GLAS, PHYS convection current; **Konvektionsströmung** *f* HEIZ & KÄLTE, THERMOD convection current; **Konvektionstrocknen** *nt* HEIZ & KÄLTE, PHYS, THERMOD convection drying; **Konvektionstrockner** *m* HEIZ & KÄLTE, PHYS, THERMOD convection dryer; **Konvektionsüberhitzer** *m* HEIZ & KÄLTE, PHYS, THERMOD convection superheater; **Konvektionswärme** *f* HEIZ & KÄLTE, PHYS, THERMOD convection heat; **Konvektionszahl** *f* HEIZ & KÄLTE, PHYS, THERMOD convection coefficient

konvektiv[1] *adj* HEIZ & KÄLTE, LUFTTRANS, PHYS, STRAHLPHYS, THERMOD convective

konvektiv:[2] **~e Strömungen** *f pl* STRÖMPHYS convective flows; **~e Turbulenz** *f* LUFTTRANS convective turbulence; **~e Verwirbelung** *f* LUFTTRANS convective

turbulence

Konvektor *m* THERMOD convector, convector heater

konventionell: **~e Leitung** *f* OPTIK conventional cable; **~er Rechner** *m (CISC)* COMP & DV complex instruction set computer *(CISC)*; **~er Satz** *m* DRUCK hot-metal typesetting; **~ startendes und landendes Flugzeug** *nt (CTOL-Flugzeug)* LUFTTRANS conventional takeoff and landing aircraft *(CTOL aircraft)*; **~e Transportpalette** *f* VERPACK conventional transportable pallet

konvergent[1] *adj* GEOM, OPTIK convergent

konvergent:[2] **~e Geraden** *f pl* GEOM convergent lines; **~e Reihe** *f* MATH convergent series; **~er Strahl** *m* OPTIK convergent beam

Konvergenz *f* FERNSEH, GEOM, MATH convergence; **Konvergenzbaugruppe** *f* FERNSEH convergence assembly; **Konvergenzfehler** *m* FERNSEH convergence errors; **Konvergenzkreise** *m pl* FERNSEH convergence circuits

konvergieren *vi* MATH converge

Konversion *f* ELEKTRONIK, ELEKTROTECH, ERDÖL, KERNTECH, TRANS conversion; **Konversionsanlage** *f* KERNTECH conversion plant; **Konversionselektronen** *nt pl* STRAHLPHYS conversion electrons; **Konversionsfaktor** *m* KERNTECH conversion factor; **Konversionsfrequenz** *f* ELEKTRONIK, FERNSEH, RADIO conversion frequency; **Konversionsgewinn** *m* ELEKTRONIK *Atomphysik* conversion gain; **Konversionsgrad** *m* TRANS conversion degree; **Konversionsöl** *nt* ERDÖL conversion oil; **Konversionsspannungsverstärkung** *f* ELEKTROTECH conversion voltage gain; **Konversionswandler** *m* ELEKTROTECH conversion transducer

Konverter *m* ELEKTRONIK, ELEKTROTECH, FERTIG, HEIZ & KÄLTE converter, KERNTECH converter reactor, MASCHINEN, METALL, PAPIER, RADIO, TELEKOM converter; **Konvertereinsatz** *m* FERTIG converter charge; **Konverterfutter** *nt* FERTIG converter lining; **Konverterkammzug** *m* TEXTIL converted top; **Konverterkippung** *f* FERTIG converter tilting; **Konverterreaktor** *m* KERNTECH thermal converter reactor; **Konvertersatz** *m* ELEKTROTECH converter set; **Konverterstahl** *m* FERTIG converter steel

konvertieren *vt* COMP & DV convert

Konvertierung *f* COMP & DV conversion; **Konvertierungsprogramm** *nt* COMP & DV conversion program

Konvertkupfer *nt* CHEMIE black copper

konvex[1] *adj* BAU, GEOM, KER & GLAS, OPTIK, PHYS convex

konvex:[2] **~e Fläche** *f* GEOM, KER & GLAS *der Plankonvexlinse* convex surface; **~e Krümmung** *f* KER & GLAS convex bow; **~es Optikwerkzeug** *nt* KER & GLAS convex optical tool; **~er Spiegel** *m* PHYS convex mirror; **~er Stab** *m* BAU ovolo

Konvexität *f* OPTIK convexity

konvexkonkav[1] *adj* OPTIK convexo-concave

konvexkonkav:[2] **~e Linse** *f* BAU meniscus

Konvexlinse *f* FOTO convex lens

Konvoi *m* WASSERTRANS *Marine* convoy

konvolutionell: **~es Filter** *nt* ELEKTRONIK convolutional filter; **~es Filtern** *nt* ELEKTRONIK convolutional filtering

Konvolutionscode *m* TELEKOM convolution code, convolutional code, convolutive code

Konzentrat *nt* KOHLEN, LEBENSMITTEL concentrate

Konzentration *f* ELEKTRIZ *(c)*, ELEKTRONIK *(c)*, KOHLEN *(c)*, KUNSTSTOFF *(c)*, TELEKOM *(c)* concentration *(c)*, TEXTIL strength, UMWELT-

SCHMUTZ *(c)* concentration *(c)*; ~ in der Atmosphäre *f* UMWELTSCHMUTZ atmospheric concentration; ~ auf Bodenhöhe *f* UMWELTSCHMUTZ *von Schadstoffen* GLC, ground level concentration; ~ der Umweltschadstoffe *f* UMWELTSCHMUTZ ambient pollutant concentration; Konzentrationselektrode *f* ELEKTROTECH focusing electrode; Konzentrationskoppelfeld *nt* TELEKOM concentration network; Konzentrationsstufe *f* TELEKOM concentration stage; Konzentrationstabelle *f* KOHLEN concentrating table; Konzentrationsüberspannung *f* RAUMFAHRT *Raumschiff* concentration overvoltage; Konzentrationsverhältnis *nt* KOHLEN, NICHTFOSS ENERG concentration ratio; Konzentrationszelle *f* ELEKTRIZ concentration cell

Konzentrator *m* ELEKTRONIK, HEIZ & KÄLTE, NICHTFOSS ENERG, TELEKOM concentrator; Konzentratorzentrale *f* TELEKOM RSU, remote switching unit, remote switching stage

konzentrieren *vt* KOHLEN concentrate

konzentriert[1] *adj* LEBENSMITTEL concentrated

konzentriert:[2] ~e Salpetersäure *f* CHEMIE aqua fortis; ~es Schaltelement *nt* ELEKTROTECH, PHYS lumped circuit element

Konzentrierung *f* KOHLEN concentration

konzentrisch[1] *adj* ELEKTRIZ, GEOM, MASCHINEN, MECHAN, OPTIK concentric

konzentrisch:[2] ~es Dreibackenfutter *nt* MASCHINEN triple jaw concentric chuck, triple jaw concentric gripping chuck; ~e Kreise *m pl* GEOM concentric circles; ~er Leiter *m* ELEKTRIZ concentric conductor; ~er Mantellichtleiter *m* OPTIK concentric optical cable; ~ verdrillter Leiter *m* ELEKTRIZ concentrically-stranded circular conductor; ~e Wicklungen *f pl* ELEKTRIZ concentric windings

Konzentrizität *f* MECHAN concentricity; Konzentrizitätsfehler zwischen Kern und Mantel *m* TELEKOM core-cladding concentricity error; Konzentrizitätsfehler Kern-Bezugsfläche *f* OPTIK, TELEKOM core-reference surface concentricity error

Konzeptbildung *f* ERGON concept formation

konzeptionell *adj* COMP & DV conceptual

Konzeptqualität *f* DRUCK draft quality

konzeptuell: ~e Dependenz *f* KÜNSTL INT CD, conceptual dependency, CD

Konzession *f* ERDÖL *Handel, Recht* concession, *Recht* licence (BrE), license (AmE)

kooperativ: ~e Emission *f* METALL cooperative emission

Koordinate *f* BAU, COMP & DV, GEOM, KONSTZEICH, KONTROLL, LABOR, MASCHINEN, MATH, PHYS coordinate

Koordinaten *f pl* BAU coordinates; Koordinatenachsen *f pl* GEOM coordinate axes; Koordinatenbemaßung *f* KONSTZEICH coordinate dimensioning; Koordinatenbohrmaschine *f* MASCHINEN coordinate boring and drilling machine; Koordinatendrucker *m* RAUMFAHRT X-Y recorder; Koordinatenfräsen *nt* MASCHINEN jig milling; Koordinatenfräsmaschine *f* MASCHINEN coordinate-milling machine; Koordinatengeometrie *f* GEOM coordinate geometry; Koordinatenmeßgerät *nt* METROL coordinate-measuring machine; Koordinatenpaar *nt* GEOM pair of coordinates; Koordinatenplotter *m* RAUMFAHRT X-Y plotter; Koordinatenschaltersystem *nt* TELEKOM crossbar system; Koordinatenschaltervermittlungsstelle *f* TELEKOM crossbar exchange; Koordinatenschleifen *nt* MASCHINEN jig grinding; Koordinatenschreiber *m* GERÄT graph plotter, two-axis plotter; Koordinatensystem *nt* GEOM, MATH, PHYS coordinate system; Koordinatentransformation *f* KONTROLL coordinate transformation; Koordinatenverschiebung *f* KONTROLL coordinate displacement; Koordinatenwähler *m* ELEKTROTECH cross coupling, crossbar selector; Koordinatenwandlung *f* ELEKTRONIK coordinate transformation; Koordinatenzeichentisch *m* GERÄT X-Y plotting table

Koordination *f* ERGON, KUNSTSTOFF, METALL coordination; Koordinationsblatt *nt* FERTIG *Kunststoffinstallationen* coordination sheet; Koordinationszahl *f* METALL coordination number

koordinieren *vt* BAU coordinate

koordiniert: ~e Verbindung *f* METALL coordinate linkage

Köper *m* TEXTIL *Weben* twill

Kopf:[1] über ~ *adv* MASCHINEN overhead

Kopf[2] *m* COMP & DV head, header, MASCHINEN head, MECHAN crown, TELEKOM head, header; Kopf- und Gesichtschutz *m* SICHERHEIT full face mask; ~ eines Hammers *m* MASCHINEN hammer head; ~ einer Schraube *m* MASCHINEN screw head; Kopfabnutzung *f* FERNSEH head wear; Kopfanfangszeichen *nt* COMP & DV SOH, start of header; Kopfanschlußkappe *f* ELEKTRONIK *Elektronenröhre* top cap; Kopfanstauchwerkzeug *nt* LUFTTRANS heading tool; Kopfausrichtung *f* AUFNAHME, COMP & DV, FERNSEH head alignment; Kopfbahn *f* MASCHINEN crest track; Kopfbahnhof *m* EISENBAHN dead-end station, rail head, railroad terminus (AmE), railway terminus (BrE)

Kopfband *nt* BAU angle brace, angle tie, raker, *Holzbau* knee brace, strut; Kopfbandberührung *f* FERNSEH head-to-tape contact; Kopfbandgeschwindigkeit *f* FERNSEH head-to-tape velocity

Kopf: Kopfbaugruppe *f* AUFNAHME, FERNSEH head assembly; Kopfbrett *nt* WASSERTRANS *Segeln* headboard; Kopfdrehmaschine *f* MASCHINEN face lathe; Kopfempfindlichkeit *f* FERNSEH head response; Kopfentmagnetisierer *m* AUFNAHME head demagnetizer; Kopfflanke *f* FERTIG *Zahnrad* face; Kopfgeschirr *nt* AUFNAHME *Mikrofon, Kopfhörer* headset

kopfgesteuert: ~es Flugzeug *nt* LUFTTRANS canard wing aircraft; ~er Motor *m* KFZTECH overhead valve engine

Kopf: Kopfhaube *f* SICHERHEIT hair protector; Kopfhöhe *f* BAU headroom, FERTIG, MASCHINEN, MECHAN addendum; Kopfhöhe des Großrades *f* FERTIG gear addendum (AmE)

Kopfhörer *m* AKUSTIK circumaural earphone, earphone, AUFNAHME headphone, headset, headphones, RADIO headphone, TELEKOM headphone, headphones, headset; Kopfhörer-Anschlußbuchse *f* AUFNAHME headphone jack; Kopfhörerentzerrer *m* AKUSTIK equalizer for earphone

Kopf: Kopfjustierung *f* FERNSEH head adjustment; Kopfkanal *m* FERNSEH head channel

Kopfkreis *m* FERTIG, MASCHINEN addendum circle, addendum line; Kopfkreisdurchmesser *m* MASCHINEN addendum circle; Kopfkreiszylinder *m* FERTIG addendum cylinder

Kopf: Kopfkürzung *f* FERTIG addendum reduction

kopflastig: ~ untergehen *vi* WASSERTRANS go down by the bows

Kopflastigkeit *f* LUFTTRANS nose heaviness

Kopf: Kopflebensdauer *f* FERNSEH head life; Kopfleine *f* WASSERTRANS *Festmachen* head line; Kopfleiste *f* DRUCK headband, KONSTZEICH column heading

panel; **Kopfleitwerk** *nt* NICHTFOSS ENERG headworks
kopflos: **~e Schraube** *f* MASCHINEN headless screw
Kopf: **Kopfnachführung** *f* FERNSEH head tracking; **Kopf-platte** *f* BAU cap, MASCHINEN top plate; **Kopfplattform** *f* EISENBAHN bay platform; **Kopfpositionierungimpuls** *m* FERNSEH head position pulse; **Kopfrad** *nt* FERNSEH head wheel, HYDRAUL breast wheel; **Kopfraum** *m* LE-BENSMITTEL head space; **Kopfrechnen** *nt* MATH mental arithmetic; **Kopfregelung** *f* FERNSEH head banding; **Kopfrohr** *nt* HYDRAUL head pipe; **Kopf-schraube** *f* MASCHINEN screw with head; **Kopfservoeinstellung** *f* FERNSEH head servo lock; **Kopfspiel** *nt* FERTIG *Zahnrad* bottom clearance, clear-ance, crest clearance, MASCHINEN clearance; **Kopfsteg** *m* DRUCK head; **Kopfstein** *m* BAU *Mauerwerk* header; **Kopfsteinschicht** *f* BAU header course; **Kopfstelle** *f* COMP & DV head end; **Kopfstück** *nt* KERNTECH head piece, MASCHINEN head end; **Kopfstütze** *f* KFZTECH headrest; **Kopfteil** *m* KERNTECH head piece; **Kopftrom-mel** *f* FERNSEH head drum; **Kopfverband** *m* BAU header bond; **Kopfverschmutzung** *f* FERNSEH head clogging; **Kopfverstärker** *m* RAUMFAHRT *Weltraumfunk* head amplifier; **Kopfwelle** *f* KERNTECH head wave; **Kopf-windung** *f* FERNSEH head winding; **Kopfzeile** *f* COMP & DV header
Kopie *f* AKUSTIK rerecording, COMP & DV, DRUCK, FERN-SEH copy
Kopier- *pref* AUFNAHME, FERTIG, FOTO, MASCHINEN co-pying; **Kopierbezugsstück** *nt* FERTIG copying master; **Kopierdauer** *f* FOTO printing time; **Kopierdrehen** *nt* MASCHINEN copy turning; **Kopierdrehmaschine** *f* MA-SCHINEN copying lathe; **Kopierdrehmeißel** *m* MASCHINEN copying lathe tool; **Kopierecho** *nt* FERN-SEH printing echo; **Kopiereffekt** *m* AUFNAHME print-through
Kopieren *nt* AUFNAHME dubbing, FERNSEH print-through, FERTIG forming, FOTO printing, MASCHINEN copying; **~ mit Fotopapier** *nt* FOTO printing through photo paper
kopieren *vt* COMP & DV copy, duplicate, DRUCK copy, FERNSEH duplicate, FERTIG form, FOTO duplicate, MA-SCHINEN copy
kopierfähig: **~e Zeichnung** *f* KONSTZEICH copyable drawing
Kopier-: **Kopierfräsen** *nt* FERTIG copy milling, MASCHI-NEN copy milling, copy turning, tracer milling; **Kopierfräsmaschine** *f* MASCHINEN copy-milling ma-chine; **Kopiergenehmigung** *f* COMP & DV ATC, authorization to copy; **Kopiermaschine** *f* FOTO prin-ter, MASCHINEN copying machine, duplicator; **Kopiermaske** *f* FOTO printing mask; **Kopierpegel** *m* FERNSEH print-through level; **Kopierschablone** *f* FER-TIG template, templet; **Kopierschutz** *m* COMP & DV copy protection; **Kopierstift** *m* MASCHINEN follower; **Kopiertechnik** *f* FOTO printing technique; **Kopiertisch** *m* FOTO printing stage; **Kopiervorlage** *f* ELEKTRONIK *Werkzeugmaschinen* master pattern; **Kopiervorrich-tung** *f* FERTIG, MASCHINEN copying attachment
koplanar[1] *adj* GEOM, PHYS coplanar
koplanar:[2] **~er Lichtleiter** *m* PHYS coplanar waveguide; **~er Wellenleiter** *m* PHYS coplanar waveguide
kopolar: **~e Dämpfung** *f* RAUMFAHRT *Weltraumfunk* co-polar attenuation
Koppel *f* MASCHINEN coupler
koppelbar *adj* EISENBAHN coupleable
Koppel: **Koppeldämpfung** *f* TELEKOM coupling loss;

Koppelebene *f* FERTIG *Getriebelehre* coupler plane; **Koppelelement** *nt* OPTIK *Lichtleiter* coupler; **Koppel-feld** *nt* TELEKOM switching network, switching network complex, switching stage; **Koppelkondensa-tor** *m* ELEKTROTECH, PHYS *für Wechselspannungen* blocking capacitor; **Koppelkurve** *f* FERTIG *Getriebe-lehre* coupler curve; **Koppelleitung** *f* PHYS *eines Magnetrons* strapping; **Koppellenkerachse** *f* KFZTECH dead beam axle; **Koppelmatrix** *f* TELEKOM switching matrix; **Koppelmittellinie** *f* FERTIG *Getriebelehre* coup-ler link
Koppeln *nt* LUFTTRANS *Navigation*, WASSERTRANS *Navi-gation* dead reckoning
Koppel: **Koppelnetz** *nt* TELEKOM switching network; **Koppelnetzwerk** *nt* GERÄT coupling network; **Kop-pelort** *m* WASSERTRANS *Navigation* dead-reckoning position; **Koppelproduktverwertung** *f* ABFALL by-pro-duct recovery; **Koppelpunkt** *m* TELEKOM switching point; **Koppelschaltung** *f* GERÄT coupling network; **Koppelspule** *f* ELEKTROTECH coupling transformer; **Koppelstelle** *f* TELEKOM switching point
Koppelung: **~ des Funkempfängers und- senders mit Telefonnetzen** *f* RADIO *Sprechfunk* autopatch; **Koppe-lungsverfahren** *nt* LUFTTRANS docking procedure
Koppel: **Koppelverlust** *m* OPTIK, TELEKOM coupling loss; **Koppelvielfach** *nt* TELEKOM switching matrix; **Koppel-wirkungsgrad** *m* OPTIK, TELEKOM coupling efficiency; **Koppelzuordnung** *f* FERTIG *Getriebelehre* coupler coordination
Koppler *m* AKUSTIK, COMP & DV, ELEKTROTECH, OPTIK, RADIO, TELEKOM coupler; **~ für Lichtleitfasern** *m* OP-TIK optical fiber coupler (AmE), optical fibre coupler (BrE); **Kopplerverlust** *m* OPTIK coupler loss
Kopplung *f* COMP & DV coupling, ELEKTRIZ coupling, interconnection, ELEKTROTECH coupler, coupling, in-terconnection, FERTIG, KFZTECH, LABOR, LUFTTRANS coupling, MASCHINEN linkage, linking, MECHAN, PHYS, TELEKOM coupling; **~ mit nächstem Nachbar-atom** *f* KERNTECH *in Kristallen* nearest neighbor coupling (AmE), nearest neighbour coupling (BrE); **~ zwischen Stufen** *f* ELEKTRONIK, RADIO interstage coupling; **Kopplungsfaktor** *m* ELEKTRIZ coefficient of coupling; **Kopplungsimpedanz** *f* ELEKTRIZ coupling impedance; **Kopplungskoeffizient** *m* (k) ELEKTRIZ, PHYS coupling coefficient (k); **Kopplungskondensa-tor** *m* ELEKTRIZ, PHYS coupling capacitor; **Kopplungskonstante** *f* KERNTECH, MECHAN, PHYS coupling constant; **Kopplungsnetz** *nt* GERÄT coupling network; **Kopplungsschleife** *f* ELEKTROTECH coupling loop; **Kopplungsspule** *f* AKUSTIK coupler, ELEKTRIZ coupling coil, ELEKTROTECH coupler; **Kopplungstrafo** *m* ELEKTROTECH coupling transformer; **Kopplungs-transformator** *m* ELEKTRIZ, ELEKTROTECH coupling transformer; **Kopplungsübertrager** *m* ELEKTROTECH coupling transformer; **Kopplungswiderstand** *m* ELEK-TRIZ coupling resistance
Kopräzipitation *f* KERNTECH coprecipitation
Kops *m* KER & GLAS cop
Korb *m* BAU, ELEKTROTECH, LEBENSMITTEL basket; **Korbbodenspule** *f* ELEKTROTECH basket coil; **Korbbo-denwicklung** *f* ELEKTROTECH basket winding; **Korbbogen** *m* BAU basket handle arch, three-centered arch (AmE), three-centred arch (BrE); **Korbgeflecht-packung** *f* KER & GLAS basketweave packing; **Korbspule** *f* ELEKTROTECH basket coil
Kordel *f* TEXTIL cord

Kordeln *nt* FERTIG diamond knurling, MASCHINEN cross knurling, diamond knurling

Kork *m* BAU, KER & GLAS, LABOR, MASCHINEN cork; **Korkbohrer** *m* LABOR cork borer; **Korkenzieherregel** *f* ELEKTRIZ, ELEKTROTECH, PHYS corkscrew rule; **Korkradpolitur** *f* KER & GLAS cork polishing; **Korkscheibe** *f* MASCHINEN cork washer; **Korkstoff** *m* CHEMIE suberin; **Korkstopfen** *m* VERPACK corking plug; **Korkverschluß** *m* KER & GLAS cork finish, LABOR cork

Korn *nt* CHEMTECH particle, KOHLEN grain, TEXTIL particle; **Kornabstumpfung** *f* FERTIG *Schleifscheibe* glazing; **Kornanalyse** *f* BAU grading analysis; **Kornbranntwein** *m* LEBENSMITTEL grain alcohol

Körnchen *nt* CHEMTECH, VERPACK granule

Korndurchmesser *m* CHEMTECH particle size

körnen *vt* FERTIG grain, MASCHINEN, MECHAN centerpunch (AmE), centre-punch (BrE), VERPACK granulate

Körner *m* FERTIG puncher, punch, MASCHINEN center punch (AmE), centre punch (BrE), prick punch, punch, MECHAN center punch (AmE), centre punch (BrE); **Körnermarke** *f* FERTIG center punch mark (AmE), centre punch mark (BrE), MASCHINEN center mark (AmE), centre mark (BrE); **Körnerspitze** *f* MASCHINEN center (AmE), centre (BrE)

Kornett *nt* METALL cornet

Korn: **Kornform** *f* KOHLEN grain shape; **Kornfraktion** *f* KOHLEN grain fraction; **Korngefüge** *nt* METALL grain structure

Korngrenze *f* KERNTECH, METALL grain boundary; **Korngrenzendiffusion** *f* METALL grain boundary diffusion; **Korngrenzenkorrosion** *f* CHEMIE intergranular corrosion; **Korngrenzenverschiebung** *f* METALL grain boundary migration

Korngröße[1] *f* CHEMTECH particle size, KOHLEN grain size, KUNSTSTOFF particle size, MASCHINEN, METALL grain size

Korngröße:[2] **nach Korngrößen trennen** *vt* BAU size

Korngröße: **Korngrößenabstufung** *f* KOHLEN granulometry; **Korngrößenanalyse** *f* CHEMTECH particle size analyser (BrE), particle size analysis, particle size analyzer (AmE); **Korngrößenanteil** *m* KOHLEN size fraction; **Korngrößenbestimmung** *f* KOHLEN size grading, KUNSTSTOFF particle size measurement; **Korngrößenkurve** *f* KER & GLAS particle size curve; **Korngrößenverteilung** *f* BAU particle size distribution

körnig[1] *adj* BAU, KER & GLAS, METALL granular

körnig:[2] **~er Bruch** *m* KERNTECH, METALL granular fracture; **~er Korund** *m* KER & GLAS emery; **~es Material** *nt* BAU granular material; **~er Schliff** *m* KER & GLAS sugary cut

Körnigkeit *f* FOTO granularity

Kornklassierung *f* KOHLEN size grading

kornlos *adj* FOTO grainless

Korn: **Kornoberflächenentwicklung** *f* FOTO grain surface development; **Kornstruktur** *f* KOHLEN grain structure

Körnung *f* AKUSTIK graininess, BAU grading, COMP & DV granularity, DRUCK graining, FERTIG grit, KOHLEN granulation, METALL grain size, PAPIER grain; **~ des Gemenges** *f* KER & GLAS granulation of the batch; **Körnungsprüfung** *f* KER & GLAS grain test; **Körnungspunkt** *m* MASCHINEN punch mark

kornverfeinernd: **~es Glühen** *nt* THERMOD grain-refining anneal

Kornverfeinung *f* METALL grain refinement

Korn: **Kornzerfall** *m* FERTIG weld decay; **Kornzerkleinerung** *f* KOHLEN particle size reduction

Korollar *nt* MATH corollary

Korona *f* ELEKTRIZ, ELEKTROTECH, KUNSTSTOFF, PHYS, RADIO *Strahlenkranz*, STRAHLPHYS corona; **Koronaeffekt** *m* ELEKTRIZ corona effect; **Koronaentladung** *f* ELEKTRIZ corona discharge, ELEKTROTECH corona discharge, corona effect, KUNSTSTOFF, PHYS, RAUMFAHRT corona discharge; **Koronafestigkeit** *f* KUNSTSTOFF corona resistance; **Koronallinien** *f pl* STRAHLPHYS *Sonne* coronal emission lines

Körper *m* GEOM body, solid, MASCHINEN, MECHAN, WASSERVERSORG body; **~ in Bewegung** *m* MECHAN body in motion; **~ in Ruhe** *m* MECHAN body at rest; **vom ~ übertragene Vibrationsgefahr** *f* SICHERHEIT body-transmitted vibration hazard; **Körperabstützung** *f* ERGON body support; **Körperbautyp** *m* ERGON somatotype

körperfest: **~er Drehkegel** *m* FERTIG polhode cone

Körper: **Körperhaltung** *f* ERGON posture; **Körperkante** *f* FERTIG, KONSTZEICH edge; **Körperlage** *f* ERGON posture; **Körpermaße** *f pl* ERGON body dimensions; **Körperschall** *m* AKUSTIK structure-borne noise, structure-borne sound

Korpuskel *f* ELEKTRONIK, TEILPHYS particle; **Korpuskelstrahl** *m* ELEKTRONIK particle beam

Korpuskularstrahlung *f* STRAHLPHYS corpuscular radiation

Korrektionsfilter *nt* FOTO correction filter

Korrektur *f* COMP & DV patch, LABOR, MASCHINEN correction; **Korrekturabzug** *m* DRUCK proof; **Korrekturbefehl** *m* ELEKTROTECH *bei Rechnern, Programmen* patch; **Korrekturfaktor** *m* METROL correction factor; **Korrekturlesen** *nt* DRUCK proofreading; **Korrekturlinse** *f* FOTO correcting lens, correction lens, OPTIK correcting optics; **Korrekturmanöver** *nt* RAUMFAHRT correction maneuver (AmE), correction manoeuvre (BrE); **Korrekturmaßnahmen** *f pl* QUAL corrective measures; **Korrekturschaltung** *f* FERNSEH corrector circuit; **Korrekturseiten** *f pl* DRUCK page proofs; **Korrekturzeichen** *nt pl* DRUCK editing marks, proof correction marks, proofreader's marks

Korrelation *f* COMP & DV, ELEKTRONIK, LABOR, MATH, PHYS, STRÖMPHYS, TELEKOM correlation; **Korrelationsdauer** *f* GERÄT correlation interval; **Korrelationsfunktion** *f* ELEKTRONIK correlation function; **Korrelationsintervall** *nt* GERÄT correlation interval; **Korrelationskoeffizient** *m* COMP & DV, PHYS, STRÖMPHYS correlation coefficient; **Korrelationsmeßverfahren** *nt* GERÄT correlation-measuring procedure; **Korrelationsphasenumtastung** *f* TELEKOM correlative phase shift keying

Korrelator *m* ELEKTRONIK, TELEKOM correlator

korreliert *adj* MATH correlated

korrespondenzfähig: **~es Schriftbild** *nt* COMP & DV, DRUCK NLQ, near-letter quality

Korrespondenzprinzip *nt* PHYS correspondence principle

Korrespondenzqualität *f (LQ)* COMP & DV letter-quality *(LQ)*, DRUCK letter quality *(LQ)*

korrespondierend: **~e Winkel** *m pl* GEOM corresponding angles

korrigieren *vt* COMP & DV debug, patch, DRUCK patch

korrigierend: **~e Schutzeigenschaften** *f pl* SICHERHEIT corrective protective properties

korrigiert: **~er Abzug** *m* DRUCK clean proof; **~es Ergeb-**

nis *nt* METROL corrected result; ~e **Stelle** *f* DRUCK patch

korrodierbar *adj* CHEMIE corrodible

korrodierend: ~er Stoff *m* SICHERHEIT corrosive substance

Korrosion *f* ANSTRICH, BAU, CHEMIE, ERDÖL, KER & GLAS, KERNTECH, KFZTECH, KOHLEN, KUNSTSTOFF, MASCHINEN, MECHAN, METALL, RADIO, VERPACK corrosion; **~ verursachender Stoff** *m* ANSTRICH corrodent

korrosionsanfällig *adj* CHEMIE corrodible

Korrosion: **Korrosionsanfälligkeit** *f* KERNTECH corrodibility; **Korrosionsbeizen** *nt* KERNTECH corrosion pickling

korrosionsbeständig[1] *adj* CHEMIE, MASCHINEN corrosion-resistant

korrosionsbeständig:[2] **~er Edelstahl** *m* MASCHINEN corrosion-resistant stainless steel

Korrosion: **Korrosionsbeständigkeit** *f* BAU, KUNSTSTOFF corrosion resistance; **Korrosionselement** *nt* FERTIG corrosion cell; **Korrosionsermüdung** *f* METALL corrosion fatigue

korrosionsgeschützt *adj* MECHAN anticorrosive

Korrosion: **Korrosionshemmer** *m* KFZTECH, RAUMFAHRT corrosion inhibitor; **Korrosionshemmstoff** *m* VERPACK corrosion preventive; **Korrosionsinhibitor** *m* ERDÖL anticorrosion additive; **Korrosionsknoten** *m* KERNTECH corrosion nodule; **Korrosionsmedium** *nt* CHEMIE corrodent

korrosionsresistent *adj* ANSTRICH corrosion-resistant

Korrosion: **Korrosionsriß** *m* KERNTECH corrosion fatigue crack

Korrosionsschutz *m* ELEKTRIZ, VERPACK corrosion prevention; **Korrosionsschutzanstrich** *m* KUNSTSTOFF anticorrosive coating; **Korrosionsschutzbeschichtung** *f* KERNTECH anticorrosion coating; **Korrosionsschutzmittel** *nt* KFZTECH corrosion inhibitor; PAPIER anticorrosive agent; **Korrosionsschutzpapier** *nt* PAPIER antitarnish paper, VERPACK corrosion preventative paper

korrosionssicher *adj* FERTIG *Kunststoffinstallationen* corrosion-resistant

Korrosionsverschleiß *m* MASCHINEN corrosive wear

korrosiv: ~er Abnutzungsverschleiß *m* MECHAN abrasion-fretting corrosion; **~es Wasser** *nt* WASSERVERSORG corrosive water

Korund *m* KER & GLAS corundum, emery, MECHAN emery; **Korundschlämmung** *f* KER & GLAS emery washing

Kosekans *m* GEOM cosecant

Kosekante *f* GEOM cosecant

Kosinus *m* BAU, COMP & DV, FERNSEH, GEOM, TELEKOM cosine; **Kosinusequalizer** *m* FERNSEH cosine equalizer; **Kosinusquadrat-Impuls** *m* TELEKOM raised-cosine pulse; **Kosinussatz** *m* GEOM cosine rule

Kosmetikfläschchen *nt* KER & GLAS cosmetic jar

kosmisch[1] *adj* RAUMFAHRT cosmic

kosmisch:[2] **~e Astronomie** *f* RAUMFAHRT space astronomy; **~e Geschwindigkeit** *f* RAUMFAHRT cosmic velocity; **~e Hintergrundstrahlung** *f* PHYS cosmic background radiation; **~er Schauer** *m* RAUMFAHRT cosmic shower; **~e Strahlung** *f* RAUMFAHRT cosmic radiation

Kosmodrom *m* RAUMFAHRT cosmodrome

Kosmogonie *f* RAUMFAHRT cosmogony

Kosmographie *f* RAUMFAHRT cosmography

Kosmologie *f* RAUMFAHRT cosmology

Kosmonaut *m* RAUMFAHRT cosmonaut

Kosmos *m* RAUMFAHRT cosmic space

Kossel-Linie *f* KERNTECH *in Röntgenspektren* Kossel line

Kosten *f pl* PATENT costs, TELEKOM call charges, charge; **~ durch Ausfallzeit** *f pl* VERPACK downtime cost; **Kostenanschlag** *m* BAU tender; **Kostenfestsetzung** *f* PATENT awarding of costs; **Kostenfunktion** *f* QUAL cost function; **Kostenplaner** *m* BAU quantity surveyor; **Kostenstelle** *f* FERTIG *Kunststoffinstallationen* cost center (AmE), cost centre (BrE); **Kostenträger** *m* FERTIG *Kunststoffinstallationen* cost bearer

Kotangens *m* *(cot)* GEOM cotangent *(cot)*

kotangential: ~e Umlaufbahn *f* RAUMFAHRT cotangential orbit

Kotflügel *m* KFZTECH *Karosserie* fender (AmE), mudguard (BrE), wing (BrE), MECHAN fender

kovalent: ~e Bindung *f* KERNTECH covalency, METALL covalent bond

Kovalenz *f* KERNTECH *Bindung* covalency, *Wertigkeit* covalence

Kovarianz *f* COMP & DV covariance

KPK *abbr* *(kritische Pigmentvolumenkonzentration)* KUNSTSTOFF cpvc *(critical pigment volume concentration)*

krachen *vi* SICHERHEIT crash into

Kracken *nt* ERDÖL *Raffinerie* cracking

Kraft[1] *f* ELEKTROTECH energy, power, KFZTECH, MASCHINEN power, METALL *(F)* force *(F)*, PAPIER power, PHYS *(F)* force *(F)*; **äußere ~** *f* METALL external force; **~ der Masse** *f* METALL body force

Kraft:[2] **außer ~ setzen** *vt* ELEKTROTECH override; **in ~ setzen** *vt* KONTROLL activate, enable

Kraft:[3] **außer ~ gesezt** *adj* KONTROLL disabled

Kraft: **Kraftanlage** *f* NICHTFOSS ENERG powerhouse; **Kraftarm** *m* FERTIG, MASCHINEN moment arm; **Kraftauslegepapier** *nt* VERPACK kraft liner; **Kraftdroschke** *f* KFZTECH cab

Kräfte: ~ in einer Ebene *f pl* PHYS coplanar forces; **Kräftediagramm** *nt* MASCHINEN force diagram; **Kräftedreieck** *nt* BAU triangle of forces, PHYS TWT, traveling wave tube (AmE), travelling wave tube (BrE), triangle of forces

kräftefrei: ~er Kreisel *m* LUFTTRANS, RAUMFAHRT free gyroscope

Kräfte: **Kräfteparallelogramm** *nt* GEOM, MASCHINEN parallelogram of forces; **Kräfteplan** *m* KONSTZEICH force diagram; **Kräftepolygon** *nt* MASCHINEN polygon of forces; **Kräftevieleck** *nt* PHYS polygon of forces

Kraft: **Kraftfahrzeug** *nt* KFZTECH automobile, KFZTECH *(Kfz)* motorcar *(MC)*; **Kraftfeld** *nt* FERTIG, KERNTECH field of force; **Kraftflußlinie** *f* ELEKTROTECH line of flux; **Kraftgewebe** *nt* PAPIER power fabric

kräftig: ~er Farbton *m* KUNSTSTOFF deep color tone (AmE), deep colour tone (BrE)

Kraft: **Kraftlinie** *f* ELEKTRIZ, ELEKTROTECH, MASCHINEN, PHYS line of force; **Kraftlinienfeld** *nt* ELEKTROTECH field of force; **Kraftmaschine** *f* KFZTECH motor, MASCHINEN engine; **Kraftmaschine mit äußerer Verbrennung** *f* KFZTECH, MASCHINEN external combustion engine; **Kraftmeßdose** *f* GERÄT load cell; **Kraftmesser** *m* MECHAN dynamometer; **Kraftmeßfühler** *m* GERÄT force sensor; **Kraftmeßplatte** *f* ERGON force platform; **Kraftpapier** *nt* VERPACK *braunes Hartpapier* kraft paper; **Kraftpappe** *f* VERPACK kraft board; **Kraftsackpapier** *nt* VERPACK kraft sack paper; **Kraft-**

schalter *m* LUFTTRANS, MECHAN actuator; **Kraft-schlepper** *m* KFZTECH traction engine; **Kraftschluß** *m* BAU traction; **Kraftschlußbeiwert** *m* KFZTECH adhesion coefficient

kraftschlüssig[1] *adj* FERTIG, MASCHINEN nonpositive

kraftschlüssig:[2] ~er Schnappverschluß *m* VERPACK friction snap-on cap

Kraft: **Kraftschrauber** *m* MASCHINEN power wrench; **Kraftschreiber** *m* MECHAN dynamograph; **Kraftsensor** *m* GERÄT force sensor; **Kraftspannfutter** *nt* MASCHINEN power-operated lathe chuck

Kraftstoff *m* KFZTECH, WASSERTRANS fuel; **Kraftstoffanlage** *f* MASCHINEN engine fuel system, WASSERTRANS *Schiffantrieb* fuel system; **Kraftstoffanzeiger** *m* KFZTECH fuel gage (AmE), fuel gauge (BrE), fuel indicator; **Kraftstoffassungsvermögen** *nt* LUFTTRANS fuel load; **Kraftstoffaufnahme** *f* MEERSCHMUTZ refueling (AmE), refuelling (BrE); **Kraftstoffbehälterdeckel** *m* KFZTECH gas tank cap (AmE), gasoline tank cap (AmE), petrol tank cap (BrE); **Kraftstoffdoppelfilter** *nt* KFZTECH two-stage fuel filter; **Kraftstoffdosierung** *f* GERÄT fuel metering; **Kraftstoffdüse** *f* MASCHINEN fuel nozzle; **Kraftstoffdüsenhalterungabdeckung** *f* LUFTTRANS fuel jet support cover; **Kraftstoffeinlaßventil** *nt* KFZTECH fuel inlet valve; **Kraftstoffeinspritzdüse** *f* KFZTECH fuel nozzle; **Kraftstoffeinspritzpumpe** *f* KFZTECH fuel injection pump; **Kraftstoffeinspritzung** *f* KFZTECH, THERMOD fuel injection; **Kraftstofffilter** *nt* KFZTECH fuel filter, gas filter (AmE), gasoline filter (AmE), petrol filter (BrE), MASCHINEN fuel filter; **Kraftstoffkolbenpumpe** *f* KFZTECH plunger fuel pump; **Kraftstoffleitung** *f* KFZTECH fuel line, *Kraftstoff* gas hose (AmE), gasoline hose (AmE), petrol hose (BrE); **Kraftstoffluftgemisch** *nt* THERMOD fuel-air mixture; **Kraftstoff-Luft-Verhältnis** *nt* KFZTECH mixture ratio; **Kraftstoffmeßanzeiger** *m* LUFTTRANS fuel gage indicator (AmE), fuel gauge indicator (BrE); **Kraftstoffmeßgeber** *m* LUFTTRANS fuel gage transmitter (AmE), fuel gauge transmitter (BrE); **Kraftstofförderpumpe** *f* RAUMFAHRT boost pump; **Kraftstoffpumpe** *f* KFZTECH fuel pump, gas pump (AmE), gasoline pump (AmE), petrol pump (BrE), MASCHINEN, WASSERTRANS fuel pump

kraftstoffreich: ~es Gemisch *nt* KFZTECH rich mixture

Kraftstoff: **Kraftstoffschlauch** *m* KUNSTSTOFF fuel hose; **Kraftstoffsorte nach Oktanzahl** *f* KFZTECH fuel grade; **Kraftstoffstandsprogrammsteuerung** *f* LUFTTRANS fuel level pre-setting controls; **Kraftstofftank** *m* KFZTECH gas tank (AmE), gasoline tank (AmE), petrol tank (BrE), tank; **Kraftstoffverbrauch** *m* KFZTECH consumption, gas consumption (AmE), gasoline consumption (AmE), petrol consumption (BrE); **Kraftstoffverbrauch pro Meile** *m* KFZTECH, WASSERTRANS mileage; **Kraftstoffvorratsübermittler** *m* LUFTTRANS fuel level transmitter; **Kraftstoffzufuhr** *f* KFZTECH, WASSERTRANS engine fuel supply; **Kraftstoffzusatz gegen Klopfen** *m* KFZTECH antiknock agent

Kraftstrom *m* ELEKTRIZ, ELEKTROTECH, LUFTTRANS electric power; **Kraftstromeinrichtungen** *f pl* ELEKTRIZ power plant; **Kraftstromkabel** *nt* ELEKTRIZ power cable; **Kraftstromkreis** *m* ELEKTRIZ power circuit

Kraft: **Kraftsystem mit durch resonanten Schwingungskreis geerdetem Mittel** *nt* ELEKTRIZ resonant-earthed neutral system (BrE), resonant-grounded neutral sy-

stem (AmE); **Kraftturm** *m* NICHTFOSS ENERG power tower

Kraftübertragung *f* ELEKTROTECH power transmission, KFZTECH drive line, transmission, MASCHINEN transmission of forces; ~ **durch Riementrieb** *f* MASCHINEN power transmission by belt drive; **Kraftübertragungsritzel** *nt* KFZTECH transmission pinion; **Kraftübertragungssystem** *nt* MASCHINEN power transmission system; **Kraftübertragungsweg** *m* KFZTECH, LUFTTRANS power train

Kraft: **Kraftventilator** *m* KFZTECH power fan; **Kraftverbindung** *f* LUFTTRANS force link; **Kraftvergleichsglied** *nt* GERÄT force-balance element; **Kraftvergleichsmeßwandler** *m* ELEKTROTECH force-balance transducer; **Kraftvergleichstransducer** *m* ELEKTROTECH force-balance transducer; **Kraftverstärker** *m* (*PA*) AUFNAHME power amplifier (*PA*)

Kraftwagen *m* MECHAN car; **Kraftwagenkupplung** *f* MASCHINEN automotive clutch

Kraft: **Kraft-Wärme-Kopplung** *f* ELEKTRIZ cogeneration; **Kraftwerk** *nt* ELEKTROTECH generating plant, power plant, MASCHINEN, NICHTFOSS ENERG, PHYS, TELEKOM power station; **Kraftwerksteilanlage** *f* KERNTECH unit; **Kraftzellstoff** *m* PAPIER kraft pulp; **Kraftzentrale** *f* ELEKTROTECH central power plant

Krag-: *pref* BAU cantilever; **Kragarm** *m* BAU cantilever, jib, FERTIG cantilever; **Kragelement** *nt* BAU jetty; **Kragendichtung** *f* MASCHINEN collar joint; **Kraglast** *f* BAU cantilever load; **Kragträger** *m* BAU cantilever beam; **Kragtreppe** *f* BAU hanging stairs

Krählarm *m* ABFALL rabble arm

Kralle *f* BAU, MASCHINEN claw

Krampe *f* BAU staple, MASCHINEN cramp

Kran *m* MASCHINEN, MECHAN, WASSERTRANS crane; **Kranauslegearm** *m* MECHAN crane jib; **Kranausleger** *m* MECHAN crane jib; **Kranbein** *nt* BAU crane leg; **Krandreharm** *m* MECHAN crane jib; **Kranführer** *m* BAU, WASSERTRANS crane operator; **Kranführerhaus** *nt* BAU cabin, house

krängen *vi* WASSERTRANS *vorübergehende Seitenneigung eines Schiffes* heel

Kran: **Krangerüst** *nt* BAU framework

Krängung *f* WASSERTRANS heel; **Krängungsmoment** *nt* WASSERTRANS *Schiffkonstruktion* heeling moment; **Krängungsversuch** *m* WASSERTRANS *Schiffbau* inclining test; **Krängungswinkel** *m* WASSERTRANS *Schiffkonstruktion* angle of heel

Krankenbahre *f* SICHERHEIT stretcher

Krankenhausabfall *m* ABFALL hospital waste

Kran: **Kranlasthaken** *m* BAU crane hook; **Kranlaufbahn** *f* BAU craneway; **Kranpfanne** *f* FERTIG *Getriebelehre* crane ladle; **Kranportal** *nt* BAU gantry; **Kransäule** *f* MASCHINEN crane post; **Kranschiene** *f* BAU crane rail; **Kranschiff** *nt* ERDÖL *Schiffahrt* crane barge

Kranz *m* BAU wreath, MASCHINEN rim; **Kranzleiste** *f* BAU platband

Krarupisierung *f* ELEKTROTECH continuous loading, krarup loading

Krarupkabel *nt* ELEKTROTECH krarup cable

Krarupleitung *f* ELEKTROTECH *Telefonleitung* continuously-loaded cable

Krater[1] *m* FERTIG *Lichtbogenschweißen* cup, KER & GLAS dimple, KUNSTSTOFF crater, pinhole

Krater:[2] ~ **bilden** *vi* FERTIG *Schweißen* crater

Kraterbildung *f* FERTIG *Schweißen* cratering, KUNSTSTOFF crawling

Kratzbandförderer *m* MASCHINEN scraper
Kratze *f* FERTIG skimmer, TEXTIL *Wolle* card
Krätze *f* FERTIG dross
Kratzeisen *nt* BAU, MASCHINEN raker, scraper
Kratzen *nt* TEXTIL carding
kratzen[1] *vt* ANSTRICH, TEXTIL scratch
kratzen[2] *vi* ANSTRICH scratch
Kratzenbeschlag *m* TEXTIL card clothing
Kratzer *m* ANSTRICH, KUNSTSTOFF, PAPIER scratch; ~ auf dem Schichtträger *m* FOTO base scratch
Kratzfestigkeit *f* KUNSTSTOFF, WERKPRÜF scratch resistance
Kratzhobel *m* BAU scraper
Krause *f* TEXTIL ruffle
Kräusel- *pref* TEXTIL curling; **Kräuselfaser** *f* TEXTIL crimped fiber (AmE), crimped fibre (BrE); **Kräuselgarn** *nt* TEXTIL crimped yarn; **Kräusellack** *m* KUNSTSTOFF wrinkle paint
kräuseln[1] *vt* TEXTIL crimp, curl, gather, VERPACK falten
kräuseln:[2] sich ~ *v refl* PAPIER curl
Kräuselung *f* PAPIER curling, TEXTIL crimp, curl; **Kräuselungsgrad** *m* TEXTIL degree of crimp
Krebserreger *m* LEBENSMITTEL carcinogen
krebserzeugend: ~er Stoff *m* SICHERHEIT carcinogenic substance
Kreditkartenanruf *m* TELEKOM credit card call
Kreide *f* ERDÖL *Geologie* cretaceous period, KER & GLAS chalk; **Kreideformation** *f* WASSERVERSORG chalk formation; **Kreidemergel** *m* BAU chalk marl
Kreiden *nt* KUNSTSTOFF chalking
Kreide: **Kreideschicht** *f* BAU chalk stratum
Kreis[1] *m* ELEKTROTECH circuit, cycle, GEOM circle, RADIO circuit; ~ mit konzentriertem Schaltelement *m* ELEKTROTECH lumped-element circuit; ~ mit verteilten Elementen *m* ELEKTROTECH distributed-element circuit
Kreis:[2] ~ schließen *vi* FERTIG *Stromkreis* make a circuit
Kreis: **Kreisbahn** *f* RAUMFAHRT circular route; **Kreisbekken** *nt* ABFALL clarification basin; **Kreisbeschleuniger** *m* TEILPHYS cyclic accelerator; **Kreisbewegung** *f* FERTIG gyration, MASCHINEN, PHYS circular motion; **Kreisblattdiagramm** *nt* GERÄT circular chart diagram; **Kreisblattschreiber** *m* GERÄT circular chart recorder; **Kreisblende** *f* PHYS circular aperture; **Kreisbogen** *m* GEOM arc of a circle, circular arc; **Kreisbüschel** *nt* FERTIG family of circles; **Kreisdiagramm** *nt* COMP & DV, MATH pie chart
Kreisel *m* MASCHINEN, MECHAN gyroscope; **Kreiselaufzeichnungsgerät** *nt* RAUMFAHRT gyrograph; **Kreiselbrecher** *m* LEBENSMITTEL gyratory crusher; **Kreiselgehäuse** *nt* LUFTTRANS gyrocaging
kreiselgesteuert: ~e Datenvermittlung *f* LUFTTRANS gyro data-switching control
kreiselgestützt *adj* MECHAN gyroscopic
Kreisel: **Kreiselhorizont** *m* LUFTTRANS, TRANS artificial horizon, gyro horizon; **Kreiselinstrumente** *nt pl* LUFTTRANS gyro instruments; **Kreiselkompaß** *m* LUFTTRANS gyrocompass, gyroscopic compass, MASCHINEN gyrostat, WASSERTRANS *Navigation* gyrocompass; **Kreiselkompaßkoppelung** *f* WASSERTRANS *Radar* azimuth stabilization; **Kreiselkraft** *f* NICHTFOSS ENERG gyroscopic force; **Kreisellader** *m* KFZTECH centrifugal supercharger; **Kreiselmoment** *nt* LUFTTRANS gyroscopic torque; **Kreiselnullstellung** *f* LUFTTRANS gyro resetting; **Kreiselplattform** *f* LUFTTRANS gyroscopic platform; **Kreiselpumpe** *f*

CHEMTECH centrifugal pump, FERTIG centrifugal pump, *Kunststoffinstallationen* centrifugal pump, HEIZ & KÄLTE, MASCHINEN, MEERSCHMUTZ centrifugal pump; **Kreiselradius** *m* PHYS radius of gyration; **Kreiselstabilisierung** *f* TRANS gyro stabilization; **Kreiselsteuergerät** *nt* LUFTTRANS autogyro, autopilot; **Kreiselströmungsdurchflußmesser** *m* GERÄT gyroscopic flow meter; **Kreiselunwucht** *f* LUFTTRANS gyro unbalance; **Kreiselverstärkerstufe** *f* LUFTTRANS gyro amplifier; **Kreiselwendeanzeiger** *m* RAUMFAHRT *Raumschiff* gyro turn indicator; **Kreiselzurückstellung** *f* LUFTTRANS gyro resetting
kreisen *vi* RAUMFAHRT orbit
Kreis: **Kreisevolvente** *f* GEOM involute of a circle; **Kreisfläche** *f* GEOM area of a circle; **Kreisformel** *f* GEOM circle formula
kreisförmig[1] *adj* ELEKTRONIK, GEOM circular
kreisförmig:[2] ~e Abtastung *f* ELEKTRONIK circular scan; ~er Riß *m* METALL penny-shaped crack
Kreis: **Kreisfrequenz** *f* AKUSTIK, ELEKTRONIK angular frequency, ELEKTROTECH angular velocity, FERTIG pulsatance, NICHTFOSS ENERG angular velocity, PHYS angular frequency, pulsatance; **Kreisgeschwindigkeit** *f* ELEKTROTECH angular velocity
Kreis: **Kreisgleichung**: allgemeine ~ *f* GEOM general equation of the circle; **Kreisgrad** *m* ELEKTRIZ radian; **Kreiskolbenmotor** *m* KFZTECH rotary engine, rotary piston engine
Kreislauf:[1] ~ zur Wiederaufbereitung des Schutzgases *m* KERNTECH blanket-reprocessing circuit
Kreislauf:[2] im ~ umpumpen *vt* KOHLEN recirculate
Kreislauf: **Kreislaufschmierung** *f* MASCHINEN recirculating lubrication, recirculation lubrication; **Kreislaufwasserführung** *f* WASSERVERSORG recirculating water economy; **Kreislaufwirtschaft** *f* ABFALL recycling economy
Kreis: **Kreisneigung** *f* MECHAN circular pitch; **Kreispolarisation** *f* TELEKOM circular polarization; **Kreisring** *m* FERTIG, GEOM, LUFTTRANS annulus, MASCHINEN torus
kreisrund: ~er Schleifkörper *m* FERTIG grinding wheel
Kreis: **Kreissäge** *f* MASCHINEN annular saw, circular saw; **Kreissägeblatt** *nt* MASCHINEN circular saw blade; **Kreisschnitt** *m* ELEKTROTECH pie section; **Kreisschwingsieb** *nt* KOHLEN circular-vibrating screen; **Kreissektor** *m* BAU sector, GEOM sector of a circle; **Kreisskale** *f* GERÄT dial scale; **Kreisskalenanzeigegerät** *nt* GERÄT round scale indicator; **Kreissperre** *f* ELEKTRONIK loop lock
kreisstabilisiert: ~e Plattform *f* LUFTTRANS gyroscopic platform
Kreis: **Kreisstellung** *f* MECHAN circular pitch; **Kreisstruktur** *f* REGELUNG closed-loop structure; **Kreistangente** *f* GEOM tangent to the circle; **Kreisumlaufbahn** *f* RAUMFAHRT circular orbit; **Kreisverkehr** *m* TRANS traffic rotary (AmE), traffic roundabout (BrE); **Kreisverkehrsdokument** *nt* COMP & DV turn-around document (AmE), turnround document (BrE); **Kreisverkehrsplatz** *m* TRANS rotary intersection (AmE), roundabout intersection (BrE); **Kreisverschiebung** *f* ELEKTRONIK *Datenverarbeitung* circular shift; **Kreisverstärkung** *f* ELEKTRONIK loop gain
Krempe *f* BAU *Dachziegel* flap
Krempel *f* TEXTIL *Spinnen* card; **Krempelbeschlag** *m* TEXTIL card clothing; **Krempelei** *f* TEXTIL card room

Krempeln nt TEXTIL carding
krempeln vt TEXTIL card
Krempelsaal m TEXTIL card room
Kreosot nt CHEMIE creosote
Kreppapier nt PAPIER, VERPACK crepe paper
Kreppen nt PAPIER creping
Kreppverband m TEXTIL crepe bandage
Kreuz nt AKUSTIK sharp, COMP & DV, KER & GLAS, PHYS, STRAHLPHYS, TEILPHYS cross; **Kreuzanschnitt** m KER & GLAS cross bevel; **Kreuzassemblierer** m COMP & DV cross assembler; **Kreuzbeschuß** m PHYS, STRAHLPHYS, TEILPHYS cross bombardment; **Kreuzbett** nt MASCHINEN crossbed; **Kreuzbettfräsmaschine** f MASCHINEN crossbed-milling machine; **Kreuzblume** f BAU finial; **Kreuzbohrmeißel** m ERDÖL star bit, Bohrtechnik cross bit, FERTIG star bit
Kreuzen: ~ vor dem Wind nt WASSERTRANS Segeln downwind tacking
kreuzen[1] vt BAU, WASSERTRANS cross
kreuzen[2] vi WASSERTRANS Marine cruise
Kreuzer m WASSERTRANS Kriegsschiff cruiser; **Kreuzerheck** nt WASSERTRANS Schiffbau cruiser stern; **Kreuzerjacht** f WASSERTRANS Hochseejacht cruiser
Kreuzfahrt f WASSERTRANS cruise; **Kreuzfahrtschiff** nt WASSERTRANS cruise liner, cruise ship, passenger cruiser
Kreuzfeld nt ELEKTRONIK, TELEKOM crossed field; **Kreuzfeldmikrowellenröhre** f ELEKTRONIK M-type microwave tube; **Kreuzfeldröhre** f ELEKTRONIK crossed field tube; **Kreuzfeldröhren** f pl PHYS Mikrowellenröhren crossed field tube; **Kreuzfeldverstärker** m ELEKTRONIK, TELEKOM crossed field amplifier
Kreuzgelenk nt KFZTECH Triebstrang universal joint, MASCHINEN cardan joint, universal joint; **Kreuzgelenkgabel** f FERTIG universal joint yoke
kreuzgewickelt: ~e Spule f ELEKTROTECH lattice-wound coil
Kreuz: **Kreuzgewölbe** nt BAU groined vault; **Kreuzgriff** m MASCHINEN cross handle, spider, star handle; **Kreuzhiebfeile** f FERTIG, MASCHINEN crosscut file; **Kreuzknoten** m WASSERTRANS Knoten carrick bend; **Kreuzkompilierer** m COMP & DV cross compiler; **Kreuzkompilierung** f COMP & DV cross compilation
Kreuzkopf m MASCHINEN, PHYS, WASSERTRANS crosshead; **Kreuzkopfbolzen** m HYDRAUL pin of cross head; **Kreuzkopfdieselmotor** m WASSERTRANS Motor crosshead engine; **Kreuzkopfverschiebungsgeschwindigkeit** f PHYS crosshead displacement rate; **Kreuzkopfzapfen** m MASCHINEN crosshead pin
Kreuz: **Kreuzkopplung** f ELEKTROTECH von Wellen cross coupling
Kreuzkorrelation f TELEKOM cross correlation; ~ der Geschwindigkeit f STRÖMPHYS Turbulenz double velocity correlations; **Kreuzkorrelationsfunktion** f ELEKTRONIK cross-correlation function
Kreuz: **Kreuzkorrelator** m ELEKTRONIK cross correlator; **Kreuzlatte** f BAU brace; **Kreuzleistungsspektrum** nt GERÄT cross power spectrum; **Kreuzloch** nt MASCHINEN cross hole; **Kreuzlochmutter** f MASCHINEN capstan nut; **Kreuzlochschraube** f BAU capstan screw; **Kreuzmaß** nt BAU cross; **Kreuzmeißel** m FERTIG crosscut chisel; **Kreuzmodulation** f ELEKTRONIK, FERNSEH, RADIO cross modulation; **Kreuzprodukt** nt MATH von Vektoren cross product; **Kreuzrändeln** nt MASCHINEN cross knurling, diamond knurling; **Kreuzriet** nt TEXTIL leasing reed; **Kreuzrohrstück** nt BAU cross; **Kreuz-**

scheibe f BAU cross-staff head; **Kreuzschieber** m FERTIG Fräsmaschine saddle; **Kreuzschienenverteiler** m TELEKOM crossbar distributor; **Kreuzschienenwähler** m ELEKTROTECH cross coupling, crossbar selector; **Kreuzschlaghammer** m BAU cross-peen sledge hammer; **Kreuzschlagseil** nt MASCHINEN regular-lay rope; **Kreuzschliff** m FERTIG cross hatch; **Kreuzschlitten** m MASCHINEN compound rest, compound slide rest; **Kreuzschlitz** m MASCHINEN cross recess; **Kreuzschlitzschraube** f MASCHINEN Phillips screw; **Kreuzschlitzschraubendreher** m MASCHINEN Phillips screwdriver; **Kreuzschlitzschraubenzieher** m MASCHINEN Phillips screwdriver; **Kreuzschlüssel** m MASCHINEN spider spanner (BrE), spider wrench (AmE); **Kreuzschnur** f TEXTIL lease band; **Kreuzspring** f WASSERTRANS Festmachen cross spring; **Kreuzspule** f TEXTIL cheese; **Kreuzspulinstrument** nt GERÄT crossed coil instrument; **Kreuzspulmeßwerk** nt GERÄT crossed coil movement; **Kreuzstab** m TEXTIL lease rod; **Kreuzstoß** m FERTIG double-tee joint; **Kreuzstück** nt BAU crosspiece, MASCHINEN cross fitting, double junction, double tee, pipe cross; **Kreuztisch** m FOTO mechanical stage, MASCHINEN compound table; **Kreuztischeinrichtung** f FOTO mechanical stage; **Kreuzumwandlung** f COMP & DV cross assembly
Kreuzung f BAU junction; **Kreuzungsbahnhof** m EISENBAHN crossing station; **Kreuzungsmast** m ELEKTRIZ transposition tower; **Kreuzungspunkt** m COMP & DV intersection, TELEKOM crosspoint; **Kreuzungsweiche** f EISENBAHN slip; **Kreuzungswinkel** m TRANS drift angle
Kreuz: **Kreuzverband** m EISENBAHN crossbond; **Kreuzverschraubung** f MASCHINEN cross union
kreuzverzahnt: ~er Fräser m FERTIG alternate helical tooth cutter; ~er Walzenfräser m FERTIG alternate gash plain mill
Kreuzwickel m TEXTIL cheese; **Kreuzwickelhülse** f TEXTIL cheese tube
Kreuz: **Kreuz-Yagi-Antenne** f ELEKTRONIK crossed Yagi array; **Kreuzzahnscheibenfräser** m FERTIG alternate angle side and face cutter
Kriech- pref PHYS creeping in; **Kriechbeanspruchung** f WERKPRÜF creep loading; **Kriechbewegung** f STRÖMPHYS in Verbindung mit zähen Strömungen creeping motion; **Kriechboden** m HEIZ & KÄLTE false floor, raised floor; **Kriechbruchdehnung** f METALL creep rupture elongation; **Kriechdehnung** f MASCHINEN creep strain; **Kriecheigenschaften** f pl MECHAN creep properties; **Kriechen** nt BAU, ERDÖL, KOHLEN creep, KUNSTSTOFF cissing, creep, MASCHINEN creeping, MECHAN, METALL creep; **Kriecherholung** f METALL recovery creep; **Kriechfestigkeit** f KUNSTSTOFF creep resistance; **Kriechöl** nt KFZTECH penetrating oil; **Kriechspur** f BAU Straße climbing lane; **Kriechstrom** m ELEKTROTECH leakage current, FERNSEH crawling current, RADIO leak current, TELEKOM leakage current; ~ zur Erde m ELEKTRIZ earth leakage (BrE), ground leakage (AmE); **Kriechstromverlust** m ELEKTRIZ leakage loss; **Kriechverhalten** nt MECHAN creep properties; **Kriechversuch** m WERKPRÜF creep test; **Kriechweg** m ELEKTROTECH leakage path; **Kriechwegbildung** f ELEKTRIZ tracking
Krimpen nt WASSERTRANS des Windes backing
Krimpwerkzeug nt ELEKTRIZ Quetschverbinden crimping tool

Kristall *m* CHEMIE, ELEKTRONIK crystal, FERTIG grain, KER & GLAS, STRAHLPHYS crystal; **Kristalldiode** *f* ELEKTRONIK crystal diode; **Kristallfilter** *nt* STRAHLPHYS crystal filter; **Kristallflächenwachstum** *nt* METALL facetted growth; **Kristallfrequenz** *f* ELEKTRONIK, FERNSEH, RADIO crystal frequency; **Kristallfrequenzwanderung** *f* ELEKTRONIK crystal frequency drift; **Kristallgitter** *nt* CHEMIE crystal lattice; **Kristallgitter-Filter** *nt* ELEKTRONIK crystal lattice filter; **Kristallglas** *nt* KER & GLAS crystal glass; **Kristallhalter** *m* ELEKTRONIK crystal holder

kristallin: ~er **Kieselerdestaub** *m* SICHERHEIT crystalline silica dust

Kristalline *f* KER & GLAS celluloid varnish

kristallinisch: ~er **Bruch** *m* METALL crystalline fracture

Kristallisation *f* CHEMIE crystallization; **Kristallisationsbeginn** *m* CHEMTECH crystallization point; **Kristallisationsgefäß** *nt* CHEMTECH crystallizer; **Kristallisationskeim** *m* FERTIG initial nucleus, seed crystal, THERMOD initial nucleus; **Kristallisationspunkt** *m* STRÖMPHYS pour point

Kristallisierbecken *nt* CHEMTECH crystallizing pond

Kristallisierschale *f* LABOR crystallizing dish

kristallisiert: ~e **Essigsäure** *f* CHEMIE glacial acetic acid

Kristall: **Kristallkeim** *m* FERTIG seed crystal; **Kristallkettenfilter** *nt* ELEKTRONIK crystal ladder filter; **Kristall-Laser** *m* ELEKTRONIK crystal laser; **Kristallmikrofon** *nt* AUFNAHME crystal microphone

Kristallographie *f* METALL crystallography

kristallographisch: ~es **Gleiten** *nt* METALL crystallographic slip

Kristall: **Kristalloszillator** *m* STRAHLPHYS crystal oscillator; **Kristallperlwand** *f* FOTO beaded screen; **Kristallplastizität** *f* METALL crystal plasticity; **Kristallresonator** *m* ELEKTROTECH piezoelectric resonator; **Kristallscheibe** *f* ELEKTRONIK silicon wafer; **Kristallseigerung** *f* FERTIG coring; **Kristallskelett** *nt* FERTIG *Gefüge* dendrite; **Kristallspektrometer** *nt* STRAHLPHYS crystal spectrometer; **Kristallspiegelglas** *nt* BAU polished plate glass; **Kristallstruktur** *f* METALL crystal structure; **Kristalltafelglas** *nt* KER & GLAS crystal sheet glass (AmE), thick sheet glass (BrE); **Kristallwachstum** *nt* METALL crystal growth

kristallwasserfrei *adj* CHEMIE anhydrous

Kristall: **Kristallzüchtung** *f* FERTIG growing of crystals

Kriterium *nt* COMP & DV criterion

Kritikalitätsabweichung *f* KERNTECH *eines Reaktors* deviation from criticality

Kritikalitätsdurchlauf *m* KERNTECH passage of criticality

kritisch[1] *adj* KONTROLL critical

kritisch:[2] ~er **Abschnitt** *m* COMP & DV critical section; ~e **Anordnung** *f* KERNTECH critical assembly; ~er **Anstellwinkel** *m* LUFTTRANS angle of stall; ~er **Aufbau** *m* KERNTECH critical assembly; ~e **Betriebsmittel** *nt pl* COMP & DV critical resource; ~e **Bruchspannung** *f* METALL critical fracture stress; ~e **Dämpfung** *f* ELEKTROTECH, PHYS critical damping; ~e **Dichte** *f* TRANS critical density; ~er **Druck** *m* HEIZ & KÄLTE, PHYS, THERMOD critical pressure; ~es **Ereignis** *nt* ERGON critical incident; ~er **Fehler** *m* QUAL critical defect, critical non-conformance; ~es **Feld** *nt* ELEKTROTECH *bei Magnetron* critical field; ~e **Flackerfrequenz** *f* ELEKTRONIK, FERNSEH, RADIO critical flicker frequency; ~e **Frequenz** *f* ELEKTRONIK, FERNSEH, RADIO critical frequency, TELEKOM *Mikrowellenmodus* criti-

cal frequency, *Wellenleitermodus* cutoff frequency; ~es **Frequenzband** *nt* AUFNAHME critical band; ~ **gedämpftes Galvanometer** *nt* ELEKTRIZ dead beat galvanometer; ~e **Geschwindigkeit** *f* MECHAN, PHYS critical speed; ~e **Höhe** *f* LUFTTRANS critical altitude; ~er **Kraftverstärker** *m* LUFTTRANS *Lufttüchtigkeit* critical power unit; ~e **Last** *f* MASCHINEN critical load; ~er **Lastpunkt** *m* KERNTECH hot spot; ~e **Masse** *f* KERNTECH critical amount, PHYS critical mass; ~e **Menge** *f* KERNTECH *von Brennmaterial* critical amount; ~er **Pfad** *m* COMP & DV critical path; ~e **Pigmentvolumenkonzentration** *f* (*KPK*) KUNSTSTOFF critical pigment volume concentration (*cpvc*); ~er **Punkt** *m* MASCHINEN, PHYS, THERMOD critical point; ~e **Reaktion** *f* PHYS, THERMOD critical reaction; ~er **Reaktor** *m* KERNTECH critical reactor; ~e **Rißlänge** *f* METALL critical crack length; ~e **Schubspannung** *f* METALL critical shear strain; ~e **Spannung** *f* ELEKTRIZ, ELEKTROTECH critical voltage, METALL critical stress; ~e **Temperatur** *f* ERDÖL, HEIZ & KÄLTE, PHYS, THERMOD critical temperature; ~er **Temperaturbereich** *m* PHYS, THERMOD critical temperature range; ~e **Temperaturkurve** *f* PHYS, THERMOD critical temperature curve; ~e **Tragfläche** *f* LUFTTRANS *Lufttüchtigkeit* critical wing; ~es **Triebwerk** *nt* LUFTTRANS *Lufttüchtigkeit* critical engine; ~e **Überhitzung** *f* KERNTECH departure from nuclear boiling; ~e **Vergleichsdifferenz** *f* QUAL reproducibility critical difference; ~e **Wärmestromdichte** *f* KERNTECH burnout, critical heat flow; ~e **Wasserlinie** *f* WASSERVERSORG critical water level; ~er **Wasserstand** *m* WASSERVERSORG critical water level; ~er **Weg** *m* BAU critical path; ~e **Wellenlänge** *f* PHYS critical wavelength, TELEKOM *Wellenleitermodus* cutoff wavelength; ~er **Widerstand** *m* ELEKTRIZ critical resistance; ~e **Wiederholdifferenz** *f* QUAL repeatability critical difference; ~er **Winkel** *m* FERTIG, OPTIK, PHYS, TELEKOM critical angle

kritisch:[3] ~ **werden** *vi* KERNTECH *Reaktor* go critical

Kritischwerden *nt* KERNTECH divergence

Krokodilklemme *f* ELEKTRIZ, ELEKTROTECH, MASCHINEN alligator clip, crocodile clip

Krokon- *pref* CHEMIE croconic

Kronen *m* VERPACK crown; **Kronenbecher** *m* VERPACK crown cup

Kronenbohrmeißel *m* ERDÖL *Bohrtechnik* crown bit

Kronenkapsel *f* VERPACK crown closure

Kronenkorken *m* VERPACK crown cork

Kronenmutter *f* BAU, FERTIG, MASCHINEN castellated nut, castle nut

Kronglas *nt* KER & GLAS crown glass; **Kronglaslinse** *f* KER & GLAS crown glass lens; **Kronglastropfen** *m* KER & GLAS crown glass drop

Krook: ~scher **Kollisionsoperator** *m* KERNTECH Krook collision operator

Kropf *m* PAPIER backfall

Kröpfen *nt* MASCHINEN cranking

kröpfen *vt* BAU joggle, FERTIG, MASCHINEN crank

Kröpfmaschine *f* MASCHINEN joggling machine, MECHAN crimping tool

Kröpfung *f* MASCHINEN, MECHAN offset

Kröseleisen *nt* BAU grooving iron, rabbet iron

Krume *f* LEBENSMITTEL crumb; **Krumenbeschaffenheit** *f* LEBENSMITTEL bread texture, crumb texture; **Krumenbildung** *f* LEBENSMITTEL crumb formation; **Krumenelastizität** *f* LEBENSMITTEL crumb elasticity;

Krumenfestigkeit *f* LEBENSMITTEL crumb firmness
Krümmen *nt* EISENBAHN flexion, MECHAN bending
krümmen *vt* BAU bend, camber, inflect
Krümmer *m* BAU bend, elbow, LUFTTRANS *Flugzeugtriebwerk* manifold, MASCHINEN bend, elbow, knee, manifold, MECHAN bend, knee, manifold, elbow; **Krümmerüberwurf** *m* BAU elbow union
krummlinig[1] *adj* FERTIG, GEOM, PHYS curvilinear
krummlinig:[2] **~e Koordinate** *f* GEOM, PHYS curvilinear coordinate
Krümmung *f* AKUSTIK *an Bauteilen* camber, BAU curve, ELEKTROTECH *Wellenleiter* bend, GEOM curvature, KER & GLAS *von optischem Glas* warp, LUFTTRANS *Start- und Landebahn* camber, MECHAN bend, PHYS curvature; **~ von Flächen** *f* GEOM curvature of surfaces; **~ der Interferenzstreifen** *f* FERTIG band deflection; **Krümmungs- und Torsionsprüfung** *f* WERKPRÜF curvature-and-twisting test; **~ und Verdrehung** *f* KER & GLAS bow and warp (AmE), warped sheet (BrE); **Krümmungskreis** *m* GEOM circle of curvature; **Krümmungsmittelpunkt** *m* GEOM, PHYS, STRAHLPHYS center of curvature (AmE), centre of curvature (BrE); **Krümmungsmittelpunktskurve** *f* GEOM evolute; **Krümmungsradius** *m* GEOM radius of curvature; **Krümmungsverlust** *m* ELEKTROTECH bending loss; **Krümmungsversuch** *m* METALL *Rohren* bend test; **Krümmungszentrum** *nt* PHYS, STRAHLPHYS center of curvature (AmE), centre of curvature (BrE)
krumpfecht *adj* TEXTIL shrink-proof
Krumpfen *nt* TEXTIL shrinkage
krumpfen *vi* TEXTIL shrink
Kruskalgrenze *f* KERNTECH Kruskal limit
Kruskalgrenzwert *m* KERNTECH Kruskal limit
Kryo- *pref* THERMOD cryogenic; **Kryochemie** *f* HEIZ & KÄLTE cryochemistry; **Kryoflüssigkeit** *f* HEIZ & KÄLTE cryogen, cryogenic fluid
kryogen[1] *adj* RAUMFAHRT *Raumschiff* cryogenic
kryogen:[2] **~er Brennstoff** *m* RAUMFAHRT *Raumschiff* cryogenic fuel; **~e Stufe** *f* RAUMFAHRT *Raumschiff* cryogenic stage; **~er Tank** *m* RAUMFAHRT *Raumschiff* cryogenic tank; **~er Treibstoff** *m* RAUMFAHRT *Raumschiff* cryogenic propellant
Kryolit *m* KER & GLAS cryolite
Kryo-: **Kryophysik** *f* HEIZ & KÄLTE cryophysics; **Kryopumpe** *f* RAUMFAHRT *Raumschiff* cryopump; **Kryoskopie** *f* THERMOD cryoscopy, freezing point method; **Kryostat** *m* LABOR, PHYS, RAUMFAHRT cryostat; **Kryotechnik** *f* HEIZ & KÄLTE cryoengineering; **Kryotron** *nt* ELEKTROTECH cryotron
Kryptographie *f* COMP & DV, RAUMFAHRT *Weltraumfunk* cryptography
Kryptonabsorbtion: **~ im flüssigen Kohlendioxid** *f* KERNTECH KALC process, krypton absorption in liquid carbon dioxide
Kryptosterin *nt* CHEMIE lanosterol
KS *abbr (Kerbstift)* FERTIG, MASCHINEN grooved pin, splined pin
K-Schale *f* KERNTECH, PHYS *Atomphysik* K-shell
ksG *abbr (kontextsensitive Grammatik)* KÜNSTL INT CSG *(context-sensitive grammar)*
KSR *abbr (Kathodenstrahlröhre)* COMP & DV, DRUCK, ELEKTRIZ, ELEKTRONIK, FERNSEH, RADIO CRT *(cathode-ray tube)*
K-Strahler *m* KERNTECH K-emitter
Kübel *m* BAU bucket, pail, FERTIG skip, tub; **Kübelfördergerät** *nt* BAU bucket conveyor; **Kübelsitz** *m*

KFZTECH bucket seat
Kubik- *pref* MATH cubic; **Kubikberechnung im Erdbau** *f* BAU earthworks cubature; **Kubikdezimeter** *m* METROL cubic decimeter (AmE), cubic decimetre (BrE); **Kubikmaß** *nt* KOHLEN cubage, METROL cubic measure; **Kubikmeter** *m* METROL cu.m., cubic meter (AmE), cubic metre (BrE); **Kubikwindgeschwindigkeit** *f* NICHTFOSS ENERG wind velocity cubed; **Kubikwurzel** *f* MATH cube root; **Kubik-Yard** *nt* METROL cubic yard; **Kubikzentimeter** *m* METROL cc, cubic centimeter (AmE), cubic centimetre (BrE); **Kubikzoll** *m* METROL cubic inch; **Kubikzoll pro Minute** *m (cim)* METROL cubic inches per minute *(cim)*
kubisch[1] *adj* GEOM, MATH, MECHAN, METALL, PHYS cubic
kubisch:[2] **~er Ausdehnungskoeffizient** *m* MECHAN, PHYS coefficient of cubic expansion; **~e Dilation** *f* METALL cubic dilatation; **~e Gleichung** *f* MATH cubic equation; **~es System** *nt* METALL cubic system; **~e Verzerrung** *f* METALL cubic distortion
kubischflächenzentriert: **~es Gitter** *nt* KERNTECH face-centered cubic lattice (AmE), face-centred cubic lattice (BrE)
Kubooktaeder *nt* GEOM cubic octahedron
Kubus *m* GEOM cube
Kuchendiagramm *nt* COMP & DV pie chart
Kufe *f* TEXTIL vat; **Kufenfahrgestell** *nt* LUFTTRANS landing skid
Kugel *f* BAU ball, FERTIG ball, pellet, sphere, *Kunststoffinstallationen* ball, GEOM sphere, KOHLEN, MASCHINEN ball, PHYS sphere
Kugel: **Kugelabsperrhahn** *m* MASCHINEN ball valve; **Kugelarretierung** *f* MASCHINEN ball stop; **Kugelbehälter** *m* FERTIG spherical vessel; **Kugelbemaßung** *f* KONSTZEICH dimensioning of a sphere; **Kugeldichtung** *f* FERTIG *Kunststoffinstallationen* ball retainer; **Kugeldrehen** *nt* MASCHINEN spherical turning; **Kugeldrehmaschine** *f* FERTIG ball-turning lathe; **Kugeldrehsupport** *m* FERTIG ball-turning rest; **Kugeldreieck** *nt* FERTIG spherical triangle
Kugeldruck: **~ prüfen** *vi* METALL ball-test
Kugel: **Kugeldruckhärte** *f* FERTIG ball impression hardness; **Kugeldrucklager** *nt* MASCHINEN, MECHAN ball thrust bearing; **Kugeldruckprüfung** *f* METALL ball test; **Kugeleindruckhärte** *f* WERKPRÜF *Kunststoffe* ball indentation hardness; **Kugelfall-Viscosimeter** *nt* LABOR *Viskosität von Flüssigkeiten* falling sphere viscometer; **Kugelfinne** *f* MASCHINEN ball pane, ball peen; **Kugelform** *f* FERTIG spheroidal form
kugelförmig[1] *adj* FERTIG, MASCHINEN spherical, METALL globular
kugelförmig:[2] **~es Achsende** *nt* KFZTECH tapered axle end
Kugel: **Kugelfräseeinrichtung** *f* MASCHINEN cherrying attachment; **Kugelfräsen** *nt* FERTIG cherrying; **Kugelfräser** *m* FERTIG cherry; **Kugelfunkenstrecke** *f* ELEKTROTECH measuring spark gap, sphere gap; **Kugelfunkenwelle** *f* ELEKTROTECH sphere wave; **Kugelgefüge** *nt* LABOR spheroidized structure
kugelgelagert *adj* FERTIG ball-bearing
Kugelgelenk *nt* FERTIG ball joint, ball-and-socket joint, spherical joint, FOTO ball-and-socket joint, KFZTECH ball joint, MASCHINEN ball joint, ball-and-socket joint, globe joint, socket joint, MECHAN ball-and-socket joint; **Kugelgelenkgehäuse** *nt* MASCHINEN ball joint cage; **Kugelgelenkkopf** *m* FOTO, MASCHINEN

ball-and-socket head; **Kugelgelenklager** *nt* FERTIG ball-and-socket bearing

Kugel: **Kugelgestalt** *f* FERTIG sphericity

kugelgestrahlt *adj* ANSTRICH shot-peened

Kugel: **Kugelglühen** *nt* LABOR spheroidizing

Kugelgraphit[1] *m* FERTIG *Gefüge* spheroidal graphite

Kugelgraphit:[2] **~ bilden** *vi* FERTIG nodularize, spheroidize

Kugelgraphitguß *m* FERTIG spheroidal graphite cast iron

Kugel: **Kugelhahn** *m* BAU ball cock, FERTIG *Kunststoffinstallationen*, MASCHINEN ball valve; **Kugelhaufen** *m* KERNTECH pebble bed; **Kugelhaufenreaktor** *m* KERNTECH pebble bed reactor

kugelig[1] *adj* FERTIG nodular, spheroidal; **~ gelagert** *adj* FERTIG spherically-seated

kugelig:[2] **~es Gelenklager** *nt* MASCHINEN spherical plain bearing

Kugel: **Kugelkäfig** *m* MASCHINEN ball cage; **Kugelkalotte** *f* FERTIG calotte, spherical indentation; **Kugelkeil** *m* FERTIG spherical wedge; **Kugelkoks** *m* KOHLEN globular coke; **Kugelkoordinaten** *f pl* GEOM, PHYS spherical coordinates; **Kugelkopfverbindung** *f* MASCHINEN ball-ended linkage; **Kugelkuppe** *f* FERTIG ball point

Kugellager *nt* KFZTECH, MASCHINEN, MECHAN ball-bearing; **Kugellageraußenring** *m* FERTIG ball-bearing outer race; **Kugellagerfett** *nt* MASCHINEN ball-bearing grease; **Kugellagerführung** *f* MASCHINEN ball-bearing guideway; **Kugellagerinnenring** *m* FERTIG ball-bearing inner race; **Kugellagerkäfig** *m* MASCHINEN ball-bearing cage; **Kugellagerlaufbahn** *f* FERTIG ball track; **Kugellagerring** *m* KFZTECH ball-bearing race

Kugel: **Kugelläppmaschine** *f* FERTIG ball-lapping machine; **Kugellaufbahn** *f* MASCHINEN ball track; **Kugellaufrille** *f* FERTIG ball groove; **Kugellehre** *f* FERTIG, METROL ball gage (AmE), ball gauge (BrE); **Kugellinse** *f* PHYS spherical lens; **Kugelmahlen** *nt* KOHLEN ball milling; **Kugelmanipulator** *m* KERNTECH ball manipulator; **Kugelmühle** *f* CHEMTECH ball mill, FERTIG ball crusher, KER & GLAS, KOHLEN, KUNSTSTOFF, LABOR, LEBENSMITTEL, MASCHINEN, PAPIER ball mill; **Kugelmutter** *f* KERNTECH ball nut

Kugeln: **~ bilden** *vi* FERTIG coalesce

Kugel: **Kugeloberwelle** *f* RAUMFAHRT spherical harmonic; **Kugelpfanne** *f* FERTIG ball cup; **Kugelrückschlagventil** *nt* FERTIG ball check valve, *Kunststoffinstallationen* ball check valve, MASCHINEN ball check valve; **Kugelsacktest** *m* KER & GLAS shot bag test; **Kugelschale** *f* FERTIG spherical shell, MASCHINEN ball cup, race; **Kugelschalensitz** *m* MASCHINEN ball socket seat; **Kugelschaltung** *f* KFZTECH *Getriebe* floor shift; **Kugelschlaghärteprüfung** *f* FERTIG ball-impact hardness testing; **Kugelschlagprüfung** *f* METALL ball test; **Kugelschraubtrieb** *m* FERTIG recirculating ball screw and nut; **Kugelschußgerät** *nt* ERDÖL *Bohrtechnik* perforating gun; **Kugelsektor** *m* GEOM spherical sector; **Kugelsperre** *f* MASCHINEN ball lock; **Kugelspiegel** *m* LABOR, TELEKOM spherical mirror; **Kugelstrahlen** *nt* FERTIG, KER & GLAS peening, shot peening

kugelstrahlen *vt* FERTIG peen

Kugelstrahler *m* RADIO isotropic radiator, TELEKOM spherical antenna

Kugeltank *m* RAUMFAHRT *Raumschiff*, WASSERTRANS spherical tank; **Kugeltank-Flüssiggastransportschiff** *nt* WASSERTRANS methane carrier with spherical tanks

Kugel: **Kugeltraglager** *nt* MECHAN angular ball bearing; **Kugeltrommel** *f* KOHLEN balling drum; **Kugelumlaufbuchse** *f* FERTIG recirculating ball bushing; **Kugelumlauflenkgetriebe** *nt* KFZTECH recirculating ball steering gear; **Kugelumlaufmutter** *f* FERTIG recirculating ball nut; **Kugelumlaufspindel** *f* FERTIG recirculating ball screw, MASCHINEN ball screw, circulating ball spindle; **Kugelventil** *nt* BAU ball valve, HYDRAUL globe valve, KERNTECH ball check valve, MASCHINEN ball check valve, ball valve, spherical valve, MECHAN, PAPIER ball valve; **Kugelverschluß** *m* MASCHINEN ball lock; **Kugelweiten** *nt* FERTIG ballizing; **Kugelwelle** *f* AKUSTIK, PHYS, WELLPHYS spherical wave; **Kugelzapfen** *m* FERTIG ball journal, MASCHINEN ball and socket; **Kugelzweieck** *nt* FERTIG lune

Kuhfuß *m* MECHAN crowbar

kühl[1] *adj* HEIZ & KÄLTE, THERMOD cool

kühl:[2] **~ aufbewahren** *vt* VERPACK keep cool; **~ lagern** *vt* VERPACK keep cool

Kühl- *pref* MASCHINEN refrigerating; **Kühlaggregat** *nt* THERMOD refrigerator; **Kühlanlage** *f* BAU cooling system, HEIZ & KÄLTE cooling plant, cooling system, refrigerating plant, KERNTECH cooler, MASCHINEN cooling equipment, refrigerating plant, THERMOD refrigerating plant; **Kühlart** *f* HEIZ & KÄLTE method of ventilation; **Kühlbandeindrücke** *m pl* KER & GLAS belt marks; **Kühlbecken** *nt* WASSERVERSORG cooling pond; **Kühlbereich** *m* KER & GLAS annealing range; **Kühlblech** *nt* PHYS, RAUMFAHRT heat sink; **Kühlcontainer** *m* EISENBAHN, HEIZ & KÄLTE, WASSERTRANS refrigerated container

Kühle *f* THERMOD coolness

Kühl-: **Kühleinrichtung** *f* HEIZ & KÄLTE cooler, cooling system, TEXTIL cooling equipment

Kühlen *nt* KER & GLAS annealing, KUNSTSTOFF, THERMOD *von Substanzen* chilling

kühlen *vt* ANSTRICH cool, HEIZ & KÄLTE chill, cool, refrigerate, KER & GLAS anneal, MECHAN chill, PAPIER cool, THERMOD chill, cool, refrigerate

Kühler *m* ERDÖL cooler, HEIZ & KÄLTE chiller, cooler, heat exchanger, radiator, KFZTECH, MECHAN, RAUMFAHRT *Raumschiff*, THERMOD cooler; **Kühlerablaßhahn** *m* KFZTECH radiator drain cock, radiator drain tap; **Kühlerblock** *m* KFZTECH radiator core; **Kühlerdeckel** *m* KFZTECH radiator cap; **Kühlerdruckverschluß** *m* KFZTECH radiator pressure cap; **Kühlereinfüllstutzen** *m* KFZTECH radiator filler neck; **Kühlereinfüllverschluß** *m* KFZTECH radiator filler cap; **Kühlerelement** *nt* HEIZ & KÄLTE cooler element; **Kühlerentlüftungsschlauch** *m* KFZTECH radiator vent hose; **Kühlerflansch** *m* KFZTECH radiator flange; **Kühlerfuß** *m* KFZTECH radiator support; **Kühlergehäuse** *nt* KFZTECH radiator frame; **Kühlergrädigkeit** *f* HEIZ & KÄLTE temperature difference rating; **Kühlergrill** *m* KFZTECH radiator grill; **Kühlerjalousie** *f* KFZTECH radiator blind; **Kühlerkern** *m* KFZTECH radiator core; **Kühlerrippe** *f* KFZTECH radiator fin; **Kühlerschlauch** *m* KFZTECH radiator hose; **Kühlerstütze** *f* KFZTECH radiator support; **Kühlerteilblock** *m* KFZTECH radiator element; **Kühlerverschluß** *m* KFZTECH radiator cap; **Kühlerwasserkasten** *m* KFZTECH radiator header

Kühl-: **Kühlfahrzeug** *nt* HEIZ & KÄLTE refrigerated vehicle, KFZTECH insulated lorry (BrE), insulated truck (AmE), MASCHINEN refrigerated vehicle, THERMOD heat-insulated lorry (BrE), heat-insulated truck

(AmE), insulated lorry (BrE), insulated truck (AmE); **Kühlfalle** *f* CHEMTECH, HEIZ & KÄLTE cold trap, condensation trap, cryotrap; **Kühlfalte** *f* KER & GLAS chill mark (BrE), chill wrinkle (AmE); **Kühlfiltersystem** *nt* KERNTECH component cooling filter; **Kühlflüssigkeit** *f* MASCHINEN, THERMOD coolant, cooling liquid; **Kühlgebläse** *nt* KFZTECH cooling fan; **Kühlgerät** *nt* HEIZ & KÄLTE refrigerator; **Kühlhalle** *f* HEIZ & KÄLTE cold store; **Kühlhaus** *nt* HEIZ & KÄLTE cold store, refrigerated warehouse; **Kühlhochhaus** *nt* HEIZ & KÄLTE high-rise cold store; **Kühlkanal** *m* KERNTECH cooling channel; **Kühlkasten** *m* METALL monkey; **Kühlkette** *f* HEIZ & KÄLTE cold chain; **Kühlkörper** *m* ELEKTRIZ, ELEKTROTECH, RADIO, RAUMFAHRT heat sink; **Kühlkreis** *m* HEIZ & KÄLTE cooling circuit; **Kühlkreislauf** *m* HEIZ & KÄLTE cooling circuit, ventilation circuit, KERNTECH heat-removal loop; **Kühllast** *f* HEIZ & KÄLTE cooling load, heat gain; **Kühlleistung** *f* HEIZ & KÄLTE cooling capacity, refrigerating capacity; **Kühlleitung** *f* MASCHINEN cooling duct, RAUMFAHRT *Raumschiff* coolant feed line

Kühlluft *f* HEIZ & KÄLTE air coolant, cooling air; **Kühlluftbedarf** *m* HEIZ & KÄLTE rate of coolant air required; **Kühlluftdurchflußmenge** *f* HEIZ & KÄLTE rate of coolant air flow; **Kühlluftgebläse** *nt* HEIZ & KÄLTE cooling air fan; **Kühlluftkanal** *m* HEIZ & KÄLTE cooling air duct; **Kühlluftklappe** *f* LUFTTRANS cooling flap; **Kühlluftmenge** *f* HEIZ & KÄLTE rate of coolant air flow; **Kühlluftregulierklappe** *f* LUFTTRANS *Motor, Triebwerk* cowl flap; **Kühlluftstrom** *m* HEIZ & KÄLTE rate of coolant air flow; **Kühlluftweg** *m* HEIZ & KÄLTE cooling air passage, ventilating passage

Kühl-: **Kühlmantel** *m* HEIZ & KÄLTE, KFZTECH cooling jacket; **Kühlmaschine** *f* HEIZ & KÄLTE refrigerating machine; **Kühlmedium** *nt* HEIZ & KÄLTE coolant, cooling agent, cooling medium

Kühlmittel *nt* HEIZ & KÄLTE coolant, cooling agent, refrigerant, KFZTECH refrigerant, *Motor* coolant, MASCHINEN refrigerant, PHYS coolant, THERMOD refrigerant, UMWELTSCHMUTZ cooling medium, refrigerant; **Kühlmittelbewegung** *f* HEIZ & KÄLTE circulation, coolant circulation; **Kühlmitteldurchflußmenge** *f* HEIZ & KÄLTE rate of coolant flow; **Kühlmittelstrom** *m* HEIZ & KÄLTE rate of coolant flow; **Kühlmitteltemperatur** *f* THERMOD coolant temperature, temperature of cooling medium; **Kühlmittelumlauf** *m* HEIZ & KÄLTE coolant circulation; **Kühlmittelumwälzung** *f* HEIZ & KÄLTE coolant circulation; **Kühlmittelzufuhr** *f* MASCHINEN coolant supply

Kühl-: **Kühlnagel** *m* FERTIG *Gießen* chill; **Kühlnebel** *m* HEIZ & KÄLTE coolant mist

Kühlofen *m* KER & GLAS annealing lehr, annealing furnace, annealing kiln, leer, lehr, THERMOD annealing furnace; **Kühlofenband** *nt* KER & GLAS leer belt, lehr belt; **Kühlofenbediener** *m* KER & GLAS leer attendant, lehr attendant; **Kühlofenhelfer** *m* KER & GLAS leer assistant, lehr assistant

Kühl-: **Kühlöl** *nt* ABFALL cutting oil, MASCHINEN cooling oil; **Kühlplan** *m* KER & GLAS annealing schedule

Kühlraum *m* HEIZ & KÄLTE chill room, cold storage room, KERNTECH cooling cavity, THERMOD chill room, WASSERTRANS refrigerating hold; **Kühlraumladung** *f* HEIZ & KÄLTE, WASSERTRANS refrigerated cargo; **Kühlraumlagerung** *f* LEBENSMITTEL cold storage

Kühl-: **Kühlrippe** *f* HEIZ & KÄLTE fin, *außen* cooling fin, *innen* cooling rib, KERNTECH cooling fin, fin, rib,

LUFTTRANS fin, MASCHINEN cooling fin, gill

Kühlrippen:[1] **mit ~ versehen** *adj* HEIZ & KÄLTE finned
Kühlrippen:[2] **mit ~ versehene Fläche** *f* HEIZ & KÄLTE finned surface

Kühl-: **Kühlrohr** *nt* MASCHINEN cooling tube; **Kühlschiff** *nt* WASSERTRANS refrigeration ship, refrigerated cargo ship, *Schifftyp* cold storage ship, reefer ship; **Kühlschlange** *f* HEIZ & KÄLTE coil, condensing coil, cooling coil, KERNTECH cooling coil; **Kühlschlitz** *m* HEIZ & KÄLTE cooling air duct; **Kühlschmierstoffe** *m pl* ABFALL cutting oil; **Kühlschrank** *m* HEIZ & KÄLTE domestic refrigerator, MASCHINEN, THERMOD refrigerator; **Kühlsole** *f* FERTIG *Kunststoffinstallationen* cooling liquid; **Kühlspirale** *f* MASCHINEN cooling spiral; **Kühlstation** *f* BAU fan station; **Kühlsystem** *nt* ELEKTRIZ, HEIZ & KÄLTE, KFZTECH cooling system, MASCHINEN refrigerating system, TEXTIL, UMWELTSCHMUTZ cooling system; **Kühlsystem für die Abschirmung** *nt* KERNTECH shield cooling system; **Kühlteich** *m* WASSERVERSORG cooling pond; **Kühltransport** *m* EISENBAHN, LEBENSMITTEL refrigerated transport; **Kühltunnel** *m* LEBENSMITTEL cooling tunnel; **Kühlturm** *m* CHEMTECH, HEIZ & KÄLTE, MASCHINEN, TEXTIL, THERMOD cooling tower

Kühlung *f* HEIZ & KÄLTE chilling, KER & GLAS, MASCHINEN, RADIO cooling, THERMOD refrigeration, VERPACK cooling; **~ durch Kälteerzeugung** *f* HEIZ & KÄLTE refrigeration; **~ durch natürlichen Luftzug** *f* THERMOD natural draft cooling (AmE), natural draught cooling (BrE); **~ mit Naturumlauf** *f* KERNTECH natural circulation cooling; **~ durch Verdampfung** *f* CHEMTECH evaporation cooling

Kühl-: **Kühlvorrichtung** *f* PAPIER cooler; **Kühlwagen** *m* EISENBAHN refrigerated car, refrigerated truck, refrigerated wagon, HEIZ & KÄLTE cold storage car, freezer, refrigerated truck; **Kühlwalze** *f* HEIZ & KÄLTE, KUNSTSTOFF chill roll, PAPIER cooling cylinder; **Kühlwaren** *f pl* VERPACK chilled goods

Kühlwasser *nt* HEIZ & KÄLTE chilled water, cooling water; **Kühlwasserablaß** *m* KFZTECH radiator draining; **Kühlwasser-Durchflußmenge** *f* HEIZ & KÄLTE flow rate of cooling water; **Kühlwassermantel** *m* FERTIG water jacket, KFZTECH *doppelwandig* water galleries; **Kühlwasserrohr** *nt* MASCHINEN cooling-water pipe; **Kühlwasserstrom** *m* HEIZ & KÄLTE flow rate of cooling water

Kühl-: **Kühlzahl** *f* HEIZ & KÄLTE cooling coefficient; **Kühlzone** *f* KER & GLAS cooling zone, LEBENSMITTEL cooling section; **Kühlzonenbreite** *f* HEIZ & KÄLTE cooling range; **Kühlzylinder** *m* PAPIER sweat roll

Kuhn-Thomas-Reich: **~sche-Summenformel** *f* KERNTECH Kuhn-Thomas-Reich sum rule

Küken *nt* BAU plug

Külbel *m* KER & GLAS parison, *Glas* blank; **Külbelaufnehmer** *m* KER & GLAS parison gatherer; **Külbelriß** *m* KER & GLAS parison check; **Külbelübertragung aus der Vorform in die Fertigform** *f* KER & GLAS blank transfer

Kulierware *f* TEXTIL weft-knitted fabric

Kulisse *f* FERTIG crank, rocker, *Getriebelehre* rocker arm; **Kulissenrad** *nt* FERTIG *Getriebelehre* main driving gear, MASCHINEN bull gear; **Kulissenstein** *m* MASCHINEN slide block; **Kulissensteuerung** *f* MASCHINEN link motion

Kulmination *f* WASSERTRANS *astronomische Navigation* transit

Kulturplatte *f* LABOR *Bakteriologie* culture plate

Kümpeln *nt* FERTIG cupping, MASCHINEN dishing
kümpeln *vt* FERTIG dish
kumulativ: ~**er Ausfluß** *m* NICHTFOSS ENERG cumulative discharge; ~**er Fehler** *m* GERÄT cumulative error; ~**e Wahrscheinlichkeit** *f* QUAL cumulative probability
kumulierend: ~**er Zähler** *m* GERÄT accumulating counter
kumuliert: ~**er Index** *m* DRUCK bulk index
Kumulus *m* LUFTTRANS, WASSERTRANS *Wolkenart* cumulus
Kundenangaben: nach ~ **angefertigt** *adj* VERPACK custom-made; **nach** ~ **entworfen** *adj* VERPACK purpose-designed
Kundenanpassungsentwicklung *f* ELEKTRONIK customization
Kundendienst *m* BAU after-sales service
Kundenspezifikation: nach ~ **hergestellt** *adj* COMP & DV custom-made
kundenspezifisch[1] *adj* COMP & DV custom-built, ELEKTRONIK custom-designed; ~ **ausgeführt** *adj* ELEKTRONIK custom-designed, customized
kundenspezifisch:[2] ~**e Anpassung** *f* ELEKTRONIK customization; ~**er Chip** *m* COMP & DV, ELEKTRONIK custom chip; ~**e Großintegration** *f* ELEKTRONIK custom LSI
Kundt: ~**sche Röhre** *f* PHYS Kundt's tube
Kunst- *pref* DRUCK, FERTIG, FOTO, PAPIER, VERPACK artificial; **Kunstchromopapier** *nt* VERPACK imitation chromoboard; **Kunstdruckkarton** *m* DRUCK artboard; **Kunstdruckpapier** *nt* DRUCK, PAPIER art paper, coated paper; **Kunstfaser** *f* VERPACK man-made fiber (AmE), man-made fibre (BrE)
Kunstharz *nt* BAU, ELEKTRIZ epoxy resin, ERDÖL *Petrochemie* synthetic resin, FERTIG synthetic resin, *Kunststoffinstallationen* epoxy resin, KUNSTSTOFF epoxy resin, synthetic resin, VERPACK epoxy resin; **Kunstharzbeton** *m* KUNSTSTOFF polymer concrete; **Kunstharzlack** *m* KUNSTSTOFF enamel
kunstharzverleimt: ~**es Sperrholz** *nt* KUNSTSTOFF resin-bonded plywood
Kunstleder *nt* KUNSTSTOFF artificial leather, mutation leather, leatherette
künstlich[1] *adj* KÜNSTL INT, PAPIER artificial; ~ **gealtert** *adj* THERMOD artificially-aged
künstlich:[2] ~**e Abdichtung** *f* ABFALL synthetic lining; ~**e Alterung** *f* ABFALL, THERMOD artificial ageing (BrE), artificial aging (AmE); ~**e Antenne** *f* RADIO dummy load; ~**es Aufrauhen** *nt* KERNTECH artificial roughening; ~**e Belüftung** *f* SICHERHEIT artificial ventilation; ~**e Bewitterung** *f* KUNSTSTOFF artificial weathering; ~ **erzeugte Radioaktivität** *f* STRAHLPHYS artificial radioactivity; ~ **erzeugte Sprache** *f* KÜNSTL INT synthetic speech; ~**er Flugsimulator** *m* LUFTTRANS synthetic flight trainer; ~**es Geräusch** *nt* TELEKOM artificial noise; ~**er Hafen** *m* WASSERTRANS artificial harbour, artificial port; ~**er Horizont** *m* LUFTTRANS artificial horizon, RAUMFAHRT *Fluglageanzeiger* artificial horizon, gyrohorizon, TRANS artificial horizon; ~**e Intelligenz** *f* COMP & DV artificial intelligence, machine intelligence; ~**er Kehlkopf** *m* AKUSTIK artificial larynx; ~**e Kohle** *f* CHEMIE charcoal; ~**er Luftzug** *m* MASCHINEN forced draft (AmE), forced draught (BrE); ~**er Mondsatellit** *m* RAUMFAHRT lunar artificial satellite; ~**er Mund** *m* AKUSTIK artificial mouth; ~**es neuronales Netzwerk** *nt* *(KNN)* KÜNSTL INT artificial neural net, artificial neural network *(ANN)*; ~**es Ohr** *nt* AKUSTIK, ERGON artificial ear; ~**e Radioaktivität** *f* STRAHLPHYS artificial radioactivity; ~**er Satellit** *m* TELEKOM artificial satellite; ~**es Sehen** *nt* KÜNSTL INT artificial vision, computer vision; ~**e Sprache** *f* TELEKOM simulated speech; ~**e Stimme** *f* AKUSTIK, ERGON artificial voice; ~**e Störung** *f* TELEKOM man-made noise; ~**e Übersäuerung** *f* UMWELTSCHMUTZ artificial acidification; ~**er Zug** *m* HEIZ & KÄLTE forced draft (AmE), forced draught (BrE)
künstlich:[3] ~ **altern** *vi* THERMOD age artificially
Kunst-: Kunstlichtfarbfilm *m* FOTO artificial light color film (AmE), artificial light colour film (BrE); **Kunstlichtfotografie** *f* FOTO artificial light photography; **Kunstmilchprodukt** *nt* LEBENSMITTEL nondairy product; **Kunstporzellan** *nt* KER & GLAS artistic porcelain; **Kunstseide** *f* KUNSTSTOFF rayon; **Kunstspeisefett** *nt* LEBENSMITTEL *gehärtet* manufactured edible fat
Kunststoff *m* ABFALL, ELEKTROTECH, ERDÖL plastic, FERTIG plastomer, *Kunststoffinstallationen* plastic, FOTO, KUNSTSTOFF, TELEKOM, VERPACK plastic; **Kunststoffabfall** *m* ABFALL plastic waste; **Kunststoffaser** *f* ELEKTROTECH plastic fiber (AmE), plastic fibre (BrE), TELEKOM all-plastic fiber (AmE), all-plastic fibre (BrE); **Kunststoffaserkabel** *nt* ELEKTROTECH plastic fiber cable (AmE), plastic fibre cable (BrE); **Kunststoffassung** *f* FOTO plastic mounting; **Kunststoffauskleidung** *f* VERPACK plastic liner; **Kunststoffbehälter** *m* FERTIG plastainer, MEERSCHMUTZ dracone; **Kunststoffbeschichtung** *f* TELEKOM plastic coating; **Kunststoffeinfassung** *f* ELEKTROTECH plastic cladding; **Kunststoffentwicklungstank** *m* FOTO plastic developing tank; **Kunststoffgebinde** *nt* ABFALL plastic container; **Kunststoffilm** *m* VERPACK plastic sheeting
kunststoffisoliert: ~**es Kabel** *nt* ELEKTROTECH, TELEKOM plastic-insulated cable
Kunststoff-: Kunststoff-Kabelführung *f* ELEKTRIZ insulated conduit; **Kunststoffkondensator** *m* ELEKTROTECH plastic capacitor; **Kunststoffmembran** *f* BAU synthetic membrane; **Kunststoffolie** *f* VERPACK plastic sheeting; **Kunststoffpreßform** *f* MASCHINEN mold for plastics (AmE), mould for plastics (BrE); **Kunststoffpreßmatrize** *f* MASCHINEN extrusion die for plastics; **Kunststoffrecycling** *nt* ABFALL plastics recycling; **Kunststoffriemen** *m* MASCHINEN plastic belt; **Kunststoffschale** *f* FOTO plastic dish; **Kunststoffschichtkondensator** *m* ELEKTROTECH plastic film capacitor; **Kunststoffstöpsel** *m* VERPACK plastic plug
kunststoffummantelt: ~**e Flüssigkristallanzeige** *f* ELEKTRONIK plastic-sealing liquid crystal display
Kunststoff: Kunststoffummantelung *f* TELEKOM plastic coating; **Kunststoffverkleidung** *f* ELEKTROTECH plastic cladding; **Kunststoffverpackung** *f* ABFALL plastic container, plastic packing material; **Kunststoffverwertung** *f* ABFALL plastics recycling
Kunst-: Kunsttischlerei *f* BAU cabinet-making; **Kunsttöpferwaren** *f pl* KER & GLAS art pottery
Küpe *f* TEXTIL *Färben* vat
Kupelle *f* CHEMIE cupel
Kupellieren *nt* METALL cupellation
Kupellierofen *m* METALL cupellation furnace
Küpenfarbstoff *m* TEXTIL vat dye
Kupfer *nt (Cu)* CHEMIE, METALL copper *(Cu)*; **Kupferacetat** *nt* FERTIG cupric acetate
kupferartig *adj* CHEMIE cupreous
Kupfer: Kupferasbestdichtung *f* KFZTECH, MASCHINEN

copper asbestos gasket

kupferbedeckt *adj* ELEKTRIZ copper-clad

Kupfer: **Kupferbeizen** *nt* KER & GLAS copper staining; **Kupferblech** *nt* BAU copper sheet, METALL sheet copper; **Kupferblock** *m* METALL copper ingot; **Kupferdraht** *m* BAU, ELEKTRIZ copper wire

Kupferdruck *m* DRUCK copperplate printing; **Kupferdruckpapier** *nt* DRUCK copperplate-printing paper; **Kupferdruckpresse** *f* DRUCK copperplate-printing press

Kupfer: **Kupfergarherd** *m* METALL copper-refining furnace

kupferhaltig *adj* CHEMIE cupreous

Kupfer: **Kupferkabel** *nt* TELEKOM copper cable

kupferkaschiert *adj* ELEKTRIZ copper-clad

Kupfer: **Kupferknetlegierung** *f* MASCHINEN wrought copper alloy; **Kupferlackdraht** *m* ELEKTRIZ, ELEKTRO-TECH enameled copper wire (AmE), enamelled copper wire (BrE); **Kupferlegierung** *f* MASCHINEN copper alloy; **Kupferleiter** *m* ELEKTRIZ copper conductor; **Kupferlitze** *f* FERTIG copper braid; **Kupferlitzenabschirmung** *f* ELEKTRIZ copper-braid shielding; **Kupferniet** *m* BAU copper rivet; **Kupferoxidammoniak** *m* TEXTIL cuprammonium; **Kupferoxydul-Gleichrichter** *m* ELEKTROTECH copper oxide rectifier; **Kupferplatte** *f* DRUCK copperplate; **Kupferrohstein** *m* METALL copper matte; **Kupferschwärze** *f* CHEMIE black copper; **Kupfersulfat** *nt* CHEMIE blue vitriol, copper tetraoxosulfate (AmE), copper tetraoxosulphate (BrE), FOTO copper sulfate (AmE), copper sulphate (BrE); **Kupfertiefdruck** *m* DRUCK copperplate printing; **Kupferuranit** *nt* KERN-TECH copper uranite; **Kupferverlust** *m* ELEKTROTECH, PHYS copper loss; **Kupfervitriol** *nt* CHEMIE blue vitriol, bluestone; **Kupferzylinder** *m* DRUCK copper-plated cylinder

Kupolofen *m* EISENBAHN cupola, FERTIG cupola furnace, cupola, KER & GLAS, KOHLEN cupola, cupola furnace

Kuppe *f* BAU crest, knoll, meniscus, MASCHINEN point

Kuppel *f* BAU cupola, dome, EISENBAHN, FERTIG cupola, KER & GLAS dome, KOHLEN cupola; **Kuppeldach** *nt* BAU dome roof

kuppeln *vt* FERTIG, MASCHINEN *zweier Wellen* couple

Kuppel: **Kuppelschlauch** *m* EISENBAHN coupling hose; **Kuppelstange** *f* EISENBAHN coupling rod, drawbar; **Kuppeltisch** *m* FERTIG tandem table; **Kuppelvorrichtung** *f* MASCHINEN coupling

Kuppenkreis *m* FERTIG *Kurve* nose circle

Kuppler *m* EISENBAHN *Person* shunter

Kupplung[1] *f* EISENBAHN coupling, FERTIG jigger, *Getriebelehre* coupler, KFZTECH clutch, LUFTTRANS coupling, MASCHINEN attachment, clutch, MECHAN clutch, coupling, PHYS, WASSERTRANS *Motor* coupling

Kupplung:[2] ~ **ausrücken** *vi* KFZTECH declutch

Kupplung: **Kupplungsaufnahme** *f* KFZTECH clutch pick-off; **Kupplungsausrückgabel** *f* KFZTECH clutch fork; **Kupplungsausrückgabelstrebe** *f* KFZTECH throw-out fork strut; **Kupplungsausrückgabelzapfen** *m* KFZTECH throw-out fork pivot; **Kupplungsausrückhebelbolzen** *m* KFZTECH release lever pin; **Kupplungsausrückhebelfeder** *f* KFZTECH release lever spring; **Kupplungsausrücklager** *nt* KFZTECH clutch release stop, release bearing; **Kupplungsausrücklagerbuchse** *f* KFZTECH release-bearing sleeve, throw-out bearing sleeve;

Kupplungsausrücklagernabe *f* KFZTECH release-bearing hub; **Kupplungsausrückstange** *f* KFZTECH release rod; **Kupplungsbelag** *m* KFZTECH, MASCHINEN, ME-CHAN clutch lining; **Kupplungsbolzen** *m* MASCHINEN coupling pin; **Kupplungsbügel** *m* EISENBAHN D-link; **Kupplungsdämpfer** *m* LUFTTRANS coupling buffer; **Kupplungsdrucklager** *nt* KFZTECH release bearing; **Kupplungsdruckplatte** *f* MASCHINEN clutch pressure plate; **Kupplungsfeder** *f* KFZTECH clutch spring; **Kupplungsflansch** *m* MASCHINEN coupling flange; **Kupplungsgehäuse** *nt* KFZTECH bell housing, clutch casing, clutch drum, clutch housing, LUFTTRANS *Hubschrauber* coupling cover, MASCHINEN clutch housing; **Kupplungsgelenk** *nt* MASCHINEN clutch coupling, coupling joint; **Kupplungsgestänge** *nt* KFZTECH clutch linkage, *Kupplung* clutch pedal push-rod; **Kupplungshaken** *m* EISENBAHN coupling hook, draw-hook bar, MASCHINEN coupling hook; **Kupplungshauptzylinder** *m* KFZTECH *Hauptzylinder für die Kupplungsbetätigung* master cylinder; **Kupplungshülse** *f* KFZTECH clutch sleeve, MECHAN, PHYS coupling sleeve; **Kupplungsmuffe** *f* KFZTECH clutch sleeve, MA-SCHINEN clutch collar, coupling box, coupling sleeve; **Kupplungsnehmerzylinder** *m* KFZTECH clutch output cylinder; **Kupplungspedal** *nt* KFZTECH, MASCHINEN clutch pedal; **Kupplungspedalausrückhebel** *m* KFZTECH clutch pedal release lever; **Kupplungspedalspiel** *nt* KFZTECH clutch pedal clearance; **Kupplungspuffer** *m* LUFTTRANS coupling buffer; **Kupplungsring** *m* KFZTECH clutch plate; **Kupplungsscheibe** *f* KFZTECH clutch disk (AmE), clutch disc (BrE), clutch plate, driven plate, MASCHINEN driven plate, friction disc (BrE), friction disk (AmE); **Kupplungsschlupf** *m* KFZTECH clutch slip; **Kupplungsseil** *nt* KFZTECH clutch cable; **Kupplungsseilzug** *m* KFZTECH clutch cable; **Kupplungsspiel** *nt* KFZTECH clutch clearance; **Kupplungsstange** *f* KFZTECH clutch rod; **Kupplungsstück** *nt* ELEKTROTECH, MASCHINEN coupling; **Kupplungstreibscheibe** *f* KFZTECH clutch drive plate; **Kupplungswelle** *f* KFZTECH clutch shaft; **Kupplungszapfen** *m* FERTIG wobbler, *Walze* palm end

Kuproxgleichrichter *m* ELEKTROTECH copper oxide rectifier

Kurbel *f* BAU winch, FERTIG crank, winch, KFZTECH handle, *Motor* crank, MASCHINEN crank, crank handle; **Kurbelbohrer** *m* MASCHINEN bit stock drill

Kurbelgehäuse *nt* FERTIG, KFZTECH, MECHAN crank-case; **Kurbelgehäusebelüftung** *f* KFZTECH crankcase ventilation; **Kurbelgehäuseentlüfter** *m* KFZTECH crankcase breather, crankcase ventilator; **Kurbelgehäuseoberteil** *nt* KFZTECH crankcase top half; **Kurbelgehäuseunterteil** *nt* KFZTECH crankcase bottom half; **Kurbelgehäusezwangsentlüftung** *f* (*PCV-Ventilation*) KFZTECH positive crankcase ventilation (*PCV*)

Kurbel: **Kurbelgetriebe** *nt* MASCHINEN crank mechanism; **Kurbelgriff** *m* MASCHINEN crank handle, MECHAN cránkpin; **Kurbelinduktor** *m* ELEKTROTECH Megger (TM), magneto; **Kurbellager** *nt* MASCHINEN crank bearing; **Kurbelpresse** *f* MASCHINEN crank press; **Kurbelrad** *nt* MASCHINEN crank wheel; **Kurbelschwinge** *f* FERTIG *Getriebelehre* oscillating lever; **Kurbelstange** *f* KFZTECH, MECHAN connecting rod; **Kurbeltrieb** *m* KFZTECH crankshaft drive, MASCHINEN crank drive, crank mechanism; **Kurbelwange** *f* KFZTECH crank web, MASCHINEN crank arm, crank cheek, crank web; **Kurbelwanne** *f* FERTIG crankcase; **Kurbelwannensumpf** *m* KFZTECH crankcase bottom half

Kurbelwelle *f* FERTIG, KFZTECH, MASCHINEN, WASSER-TRANS crankshaft; **Kurbelwellenbohrer** *m* MASCHINEN crankshaft drill; **Kurbelwellendrehmaschine** *f* MA-SCHINEN crankshaft lathe; **Kurbelwellendrehzahl** *f* KFZTECH engine speed; **Kurbelwellenlager** *nt* KFZTECH main bearing, *Motor* crankshaft bearing, MASCHINEN crankshaft bearing

kurbelwellenseitig: **~es Pleuelende** *nt* KFZTECH big end, connecting rod big end; **~er Pleuelkopf** *m* MASCHINEN big end, connecting rod big end; **~er Pleuelstangenkopf** *m* MASCHINEN connecting rod big end; **~er Totpunkt** *m* MASCHINEN crank-end dead-center (AmE), crank-end dead-centre (BrE)

Kurbelwelle: **Kurbelwellenzapfen** *m* KFZTECH crankpin

Kurbel: **Kurbelzapfen** *m* FERTIG, KFZTECH, MASCHINEN, MECHAN crankpin

Kurs:[1] **auf ~** *adj* WASSERTRANS *Navigation* on course; **vom ~ abgewichen** *adj* RAUMFAHRT off-course

Kurs[2] *m* METROL bearings, RAUMFAHRT heading, WAS-SERTRANS track, *Navigation* course; **~ über Grund** *m* WASSERTRANS *Navigation* course made good; **~ durch Wasser** *m* WASSERTRANS course to steer

Kurs:[3] **~ haben auf** *vt* WASSERTRANS *Navigation* stand for; **~ halten auf** *vt* WASSERTRANS head for; **~ nehmen auf** *vt* WASSERTRANS head for, *Navigation* steer for

Kurs:[4] **vom ~ abdrehen** *vi* WASSERTRANS *Schiff* veer off course; **~ und Fahrt halten** *vi* WASSERTRANS *Navigation* maintain course and speed; **~ halten** *vi* WASSERTRANS *Navigation* keep course

Kurs: **Kurs- und Vertikalbezugssystem** *nt* RAUMFAHRT *Raumschiff* heading and vertical reference system; **Kursabweichung** *f* PHYS yaw; **Kursanalyse** *f* ERGON course analysis; **Kursänderung** *f* RAUMFAHRT alteration of course, WASSERTRANS alteration of course, *Navigation* change of course; **Kursanzeige** *f* RAUM-FAHRT *Raumschiff* heading indicator

kursanzeigend: **~er Kurswähler** *m* LUFTTRANS course indicator selector

Kurs: **Kursanzeiger** *m* LUFTTRANS, WASSERTRANS *Navigation* course indicator; **Kurs-Blip-Impuls** *m* TELEKOM course-blip pulse; **Kursbuch** *nt* EISENBAHN railroad guide (AmE), railway guide (BrE), schedule (AmE), timetable (BrE); **Kursdatengeber** *m* LUFTTRANS heading data generator; **Kursdreieck** *nt* WASSERTRANS protractor; **Kurseinstellung** *f* LUFTTRANS *Instrumentenlandesystem* course alignment; **Kursfehlerintegrator** *m* LUFTTRANS heading error integrator; **Kursfehler-Sychronismus-Anzeigerverstärker** *m* LUFTTRANS heading error sychronizer amplifier; **Kursfunksteuerkurs** *m* LUFTTRANS localizer beam heading; **Kursgeber** *m* LUFTTRANS course selector; **Kursindikator** *m* LUFTTRANS course tracer

kursiv[1] *adj* DRUCK italic

kursiv:[2] **~ setzen** *vt* DRUCK italicize

Kursivschrift *f* DRUCK italic type

Kurs: **Kurskarte** *f* WASSERTRANS track chart; **Kurslineal** *nt* WASSERTRANS parallel ruler; **Kurslinie** *f* LUFTTRANS *Instrumentenlandesystem* course line; **Kursmaterial** *nt* COMP & DV courseware; **Kursstabilität** *f* LUFTTRANS directional stability; **Kursstrich** *m* WASSERTRANS *Kompaß* lubber's line; **Kurswagen** *m* EISENBAHN through wagon; **Kurswähler** *m* LUFTTRANS *Flugwesen* omnibearing selector; **Kurswechsel** *m* WASSERTRANS

Navigation change of course; **Kurswinkel** *m* LUFT-TRANS course angle

Kurtosis *f* QUAL kurtosis

Kurve[1] *f* BAU bend, curve, FERTIG calm, GEOM, MATH curve, TRANS turning; **~ gleicher Lautstärke** *f* AKUSTIK equal-loudness contours; **~ gleicher Temperatur** *f* PHYS isotherm; **~ für den mittleren Stichprobenumfang** *f* QUAL average sample number curve

Kurve:[2] **in ~ legen** *vt* RAUMFAHRT bank; **als ~ zeichnen** *vt* GEOM graph

Kurve:[3] **eine ~ zeichnen** *vi* MATH plot a curve

Kurve: **Kurvenanflug** *m* LUFTTRANS curved approach; **Kurvenfaktor** *m* NICHTFOSS ENERG curve factor; **Kurvenform** *f* LUFTTRANS cam contour; **Kurvenfräseinrichtung** *f* FERTIG cam-milling attachment; **Kurvenfräsmaschine** *f* FERTIG cam-milling machine, MASCHINEN cam copy miller, cam-milling machine; **Kurvengetriebe** *nt* MASCHINEN cam mechanism; **Kurvengleichung** *f* MATH equation of a curve; **Kurvenhub** *m* FERTIG *Getriebelehre* calm throw; **Kurvenlage** *f* TRANS *Flugzeug* banking; **Kurvenlineal** *nt* FERTIG curve; **Kurvenmechanismus** *m* FERTIG *Getriebelehre* calm mechanism; **Kurvenmeßgerät** *nt* METROL cam-measuring equipment; **Kurvenparameter** *m* REGELUNG curve parameter; **Kurvenpunkt** *m* KONSTZEICH plotpoint on curves; **Kurvenrolle** *f* MASCHINEN cam roller, follower

Kurvenscheibe *f* FERTIG *Getriebelehre* disc cam (BrE), disk cam (AmE), MASCHINEN cam plate, cam wheel, disc cam (BrE), disk cam (AmE); **Kurvenscheibengetriebe** *nt* FERTIG disc cam mechanism (BrE), disk cam mechanism (AmE)

Kurvenscheibe: **mit Kurvenscheibensteuerung** *adj* FER-TIG *Getriebelehre* disc-cam-operated (BrE), disk-cam-operated (AmE)

Kurve: **Kurvenschreiber** *m* COMP & DV graph plotter, plotter, FERTIG plotter, GERÄT curve plotter, graph plotter; **Kurvensteuerung** *f* FERTIG cam control; **Kurvenstößel** *m* FERTIG *Getriebelehre* cam follower; **Kurventrommel** *f* FERTIG barrel cam, cylinder cam; **Kurvenverbreiterung** *f* BAU curve widening; **Kurvenverzerrungsanalysator** *m* GERÄT distortion analyser (BrE), distortion analyzer (AmE); **Kurvenwelle** *f* FER-TIG undulation

kurz[1] *adj* ELEKTRIZ, ELEKTRONIK short

kurz:[2] **~es Glas** *nt* KER & GLAS short glass; **~er Impuls** *m* WASSERTRANS short pulse; **mit ~ en Impulsen gepulster Laser** *m* WELLPHYS short-pulsed laser; **~er Spiralbohrer** *m* MASCHINEN stub drill; **~er Ton** *m* WAS-SERTRANS short blast; **~e Trompete** *f* WASSERTRANS *Knoten* cat's paw; **~es Verbindungsstück** *nt* BAU *von Rohren* faucet joint; **~er Zapfen** *m* BAU stub tenon; **~es Zapfenloch** *nt* BAU stub mortise

Kurzbaulänge *f* FERTIG *Kunststoffinstallationen* minimum overall length

Kurzbewitterungsversuch *m* KUNSTSTOFF accelerated weathering test

Kurzbezeichnung *f* KONSTZEICH abbreviated designation

kurzbrennweitig: **~es Objektiv** *nt* FOTO short-focus lens

Kurzdarstellung *f* COMP & DV abstract

Kürzen: **~ von Fasern** *nt* PAPIER shortening of fibers (AmE), shortening of fibres (BrE)

kürzen *vt* MATH *Brüche vollständig* reduce, PAPIER shorten

Kürzester-Weg-Programm *nt* TRANS shortest path program (AmE), shortest path programme (BrE)

Kurzfaservlies *nt* KUNSTSTOFF chopped-strand mat

Kurzfassung *f* DRUCK abridged edition

kurzgeschlossen[1] *adj* ELEKTRIZ, ELEKTROTECH, PHYS short-circuited

kurzgeschlossen:[2] ~**er Anker** *m* ELEKTRIZ short circuit armature, ELEKTROTECH short-circuited armature; ~**er Rotor** *m* ELEKTRIZ short-circuited rotor; ~**er Schleifringanker** *m* ELEKTRIZ short-circuited slip-ring rotor; ~**e Windung** *f* ELEKTROTECH shorted turn

kurzgliedrig: ~**e Kette** *f* MASCHINEN short link chain

Kurzhals-Projektionsröhre *f* ELEKTRONIK short neck projection tube

Kurzhubhonen *nt* MASCHINEN superfinishing

Kurzhubhonstein *nt* MASCHINEN superfinishing honing stone, superfinishing stone

kurzhubig *adj* MASCHINEN short-stroke

Kurzhubmotor *m* KFZTECH oversquare engine, short stroke engine

Kurzimpuls *m* ELEKTRONIK short pulse

Kurzkanal *m* ELEKTRONIK short channel; **Kurzkanaltransistor** *m* ELEKTRONIK short channel transistor

Kurznummer *f* TELEKOM abbreviated number

kurzölig: ~**es Alkydharz** *nt* KUNSTSTOFF short oil alkyd

Kurzprüfung *f* METALL short time test

Kurzrohr *nt* HYDRAUL short pipe

Kurzrufnummer *f* TELEKOM abbreviated number

Kurzschließen *nt* ELEKTROTECH shorting

kurzschließen *vt* TELEKOM short-circuit

Kurzschließer *m* ELEKTRIZ short-circuiting device

Kurzschluß *m* COMP & DV, ELEKTRIZ short circuit, ELEKTROTECH short, short circuit, PHYS closed circuit, short circuit, TELEKOM short circuit; ~ **zwischen Phasen** *m* ELEKTRIZ interphase short circuit; **Kurzschlußanker** *m* ELEKTRIZ closed-coil armature, ELEKTROTECH short-circuited armature, squirrel cage rotor; **Kurzschlußbrücke** *f* ELEKTROTECH bonding jumper, jumper; **Kurzschlußdrossel** *f* ELEKTROTECH current-limiting reactor; **Kurzschlußfluß** *m* AKUSTIK short circuit flux

kurzschlußfrei: ~**e Kontakte** *m pl* ELEKTROTECH nonbridging contacts

Kurzschluß: **Kurzschlußimpedanz** *f* ELEKTRIZ, ELEKTROTECH short circuit impedance; **Kurzschlußkäfig** *m* ELEKTROTECH squirrel cage; **Kurzschlußkontakt** *m* ELEKTROTECH shorting contact; **Kurzschlußkontaktschalter** *m* ELEKTROTECH shorting contact switch; **Kurzschlußläufer** *m* ELEKTROTECH squirrel cage rotor; **Kurzschlußläufermotor** *m* ELEKTROTECH squirrel cage motor; **Kurzschlußleitung** *f* ELEKTROTECH adjustable short; **Kurzschlußlos-Schalter** *m* ELEKTROTECH nonshorting switch; **Kurzschlußschalter** *m* ELEKTROTECH shorting switch; **Kurzschlußschutz** *m* ELEKTROTECH short circuit protection; **Kurzschlußstrom** *m* FERNSEH short circuit flux; **Kurzschlußwiderstand** *m* ELEKTROTECH short circuit impedance

Kurzspan *m* FERTIG finely broken chip, short chip

Kurzstart: **Kurzstart- und Landung** *f* LUFTTRANS short takeoff and landing; **Kurzstartflugzeug** *nt* (*STOL-Flugzeug*) LUFTTRANS short takeoff and landing aircraft (*STOL aircraft*); **Kurzstart-Kurzlande-Flugzeug** *nt* (*STOL-Flugzeug*) LUFTTRANS short takeoff and landing aircraft (*STOL aircraft*)

Kurzstrecke: **Kurzstreckengleiter** *m* TRANS short haul skidder; **Kurzstreckentransport** *m* TRANS short distance transport; **Kurzstreckenverkehrsflugzeug** *nt*

TRANS short haul airliner; **Kurzstreckenzähler** *m* KFZTECH trip mileage indicator

Kurzversuch *m* QUAL accelerated test

Kurzwahl *f* TELEKOM short code dialing (AmE), short code dialling (BrE)

Kurzwelle *f* ELEKTRIZ, RADIO short wave

Kurzwort *nt* COMP & DV acronym

Kurzzange *f* MASCHINEN short-nosed pliers

Kurzzapfverbindung *f* BAU spur tenon joint

Kurzzeit- *pref* KUNSTSTOFF, KÜNSTL INT short-term; **Kurzzeitalterungsversuch** *m* KUNSTSTOFF accelerated ageing test (BrE), accelerated aging test (AmE); **Kurzzeitermüdungsversuch** *m* METALL rapid fatigue test; **Kurzzeit-Erträglichkeitsgrenze** *f* ERGON just tolerable limit; **Kurzzeitgedächtnis** *nt* (*KZG*) ERGON, KÜNSTL INT short-term memory (*STM*)

kurzzeitig[1] *adj* ELEKTRONIK short term, FERTIG transient

kurzzeitig:[2] ~**e Drift** *f* ELEKTRONIK short-term drift; ~**er Fehler** *m* COMP & DV transient error; ~**e Frequenzstabilität** *f* ELEKTRONIK, FERNSEH, RADIO, TELEKOM short-term frequency stability

Kurzzeit-: **Kurzzeitleistung** *f* ELEKTRIZ short time rating; **Kurzzeitmeßgerät** *nt* GERÄT time interval measuring instrument; **Kurzzeitnachleuchten** *nt* ELEKTRONIK CRT-lag; **Kurzzeitprüfung** *f* ELEKTRIZ short time test; **Kurzzeitregistriergerät** *nt* GERÄT time interval recorder; **Kurzzeitschankungsrate** *f* FERNSEH flutter rate; **Kurzzeitschutz** *m* ELEKTROTECH short-term protection; **Kurzzeitspannung** *f* KER & GLAS temporary stress; **Kurzzeit-Stromnennwert** *m* ELEKTRIZ rated short-time current; **Kurzzeitversuch** *m* QUAL accelerated test

Küste[1] *f* WASSERTRANS *Geographie* coast

Küste:[2] **die ~ anlaufen** *vt* WASSERTRANS *Navigation* stand inshore

Küste:[3] **an der ~ entlanglaufen** *vi* WASSERTRANS follow the coast; **die ~ entlangsegeln** *vi* WASSERTRANS *Seehandel* coast; **auf die ~ zusteuern** *vi* WASSERTRANS *Navigation* stand inshore

Küsten- *pref* WASSERTRANS coastal, *Geographie* littoral

küsteneinwärts *adv* WASSERTRANS inshore

Küste: **Küstenendkabel** *nt* ELEKTROTECH shore end cable; **Küstenfahrt** *f* WASSERTRANS coasting trade, coastwise trade, *Seehandel* coastal trade; **Küstenfahrzeug** *nt* WASSERTRANS coaster, coasting vessel

küstenfern *adj* WASSERTRANS offshore

Küste: **Küstenfluß** *m* WASSERVERSORG coastal river; **Küstenfunkstelle** *f* RADIO, TELEKOM coastal station; **Küstengewässer** *nt pl* WASSERTRANS coastal waters; **Küstenkarte** *f* WASSERTRANS *Navigation* coastal chart, plan; **Küstenkreuzer** *m* WASSERTRANS coastal cruiser; **Küstenlinie** *f* MEERSCHMUTZ shoreline, WASSERTRANS shoreline, *Geographie* coastline; **Küstenlotse** *m* WASSERTRANS inshore pilot; **Küstenlotsenwesen** *nt* WASSERTRANS inshore pilotage

küstennah[1] *adj* WASSERTRANS inshore, offshore

küstennah:[2] ~**e Ölbohrung** *f* UMWELTSCHMUTZ offshore well

Küste: **Küstennavigation** *f* WASSERTRANS *Navigation* coastal navigation; **Küstenringstraße** *f* BAU coastal ring road; **Küstenschiff** *nt* WASSERTRANS coastal vessel, coasting vessel; **Küstenschiffahrt** *f* WASSERTRANS cabotage, *Handelsmarine* coastal navigation, *Seehandel* coastal trade; **Küstenschlamm** *m* WASSERVERSORG coastal deposit; **Küstenschlick** *m* WASSERVERSORG coastal deposit; **Küstenschutz** *m* WASSERVERSORG shore protection; **Küstensockel** *m* WASSERTRANS shelf; **Küstenstation** *f* TELEKOM coastal station; **Küstenstreifen** *m* WASSERTRANS shoreline; **Küstenverteidigung** *f* WASSERTRANS *Marine* coastal defence (BrE), coastal defense (AmE); **Küstenwache** *f* WASSERTRANS coastguard; **Küstenwachkutter** *m* WASSERTRANS coastguard cutter

küstenwärts *adv* WASSERTRANS shoreward

Kutter *m* WASSERTRANS *Schifftyp* cutter

Kuverwasser *nt* MEERSCHMUTZ seepage

Küvette *f* LABOR vessel

KV *abbr (kombinierter Verteiler)* TELEKOM CDF *(combined distribution frame)*

kV *abbr (Kilovolt)* ELEKTROTECH kV *(kilovolt)*

kW *abbr (Kilowatt)* ELEKTRIZ kW *(kilowatt)*

K-Wert *m* HEIZ & KÄLTE K-factor

kWh *abbr (Kilowattstunde)* ELEKTRIZ kWh *(kilowatt-hour)*, ELEKTROTECH, PHYS kWh *(kilowatt hour)*

KWIC *m* COMP & DV KWIC, keyword in context

KWOC-Index *m (Stichwortanalyse mit Text)* COMP & DV KWOC, keyword out of context *(keyword out of context)*

KW-Stoff *m (Kohlenwasserstoff)* CHEMIE hydrocarbon

Kybernetik *f* COMP & DV, FERTIG, RAUMFAHRT cybernetics

Kynch: **~sche Trennungstheorie** *f* KERNTECH Kynch separation theory

kyrillisch: **~es Zeichen** *nt* KONSTZEICH cyrillic letter

KZG *abbr (Kurzzeitgedächtnis)* ERGON, KÜNSTL INT STM *(short-term memory)*

K-Zustand *m* KERNTECH K-state

L

L *abbr* AKUSTIK *(Lautstärke)* L *(loudness)*, AUFNAHME *(Induktivität)*, ELEKTRIZ *(Induktivität)*, ELEKTRO-TECH *(Induktivität)* L *(inductance)*, KERNTECH *(Diffusionslänge)* L *(diffusion length)*, KERNTECH *(lineare Energieübertragung)* L *(linear energy transfer)*, KERNTECH *(Orbitalwinkelmomentzahl)* L *(total orbital angular momentum number)*, MECHAN *(Lagrangesche Funktion)* L *(Lagrangian function)*, METROL *(Induktivität)* L *(inductance)*, OPTIK *(Luminanz)* L *(luminance)*, PHYS *(Induktivität)*, RADIO *(Induktivität)* L *(inductance)*, STRAHLPHYS *(lineare Energieübertragung)* L *(linear energy transfer)*, TELEKOM *(Induktivität)* L *(inductance)*, THERMOD *(Lorenzsche Einheit)* L *(Lorenz unit)*

l *abbr* COMP & DV *(Länge)*, GEOM *(Länge)* l *(length)*, KERNTECH l, KERNTECH *(effektive Neutronenlebensdauer)* l *(effective neutron lifetime)*, PHYS *(Länge)*, TELEKOM *(Länge)* l *(length)*

La *(Lanthan)* CHEMIE La *(lanthanium)*

Lab *nt* LEBENSMITTEL rennet; **Labferment** *nt* LEBENSMITTEL rennin

labil: **~es Gleichgewicht** *nt* PHYS unstable equilibrium

Lab: **Labkasein** *nt* LEBENSMITTEL rennet casein

Laboratorium: *nt* KOHLEN assay office

Labor *nt* ELEKTRIZ, PHYS laboratory; **Laborbedingungen** *f pl* ELEKTRIZ laboratory conditions; **Laborkittel** *m* LABOR laboratory coat, SICHERHEIT laboratory clothing; **Laborkugelhahn** *m* FERTIG *Kunststoffinstallationen* laboratory ball cock; **Labormeßgerät** *nt* GERÄT laboratory instrument; **Labormühle** *f* MASCHINEN triturator; **Laborschemel** *m* LABOR laboratory stool; **Laborstandard** *m* KERNTECH laboratory standard; **Laborstruktur** *f* PHYS laboratory frame; **Laborstuhl** *m* LABOR laboratory stool; **Laborversuch** *m* BAU, LEBENSMITTEL bench test

Laburnin *nt* CHEMIE cytisine, laburnine, ulexine

Labyrinthdichtung *f* FERTIG labyrinth packing, KERNTECH, MASCHINEN labyrinth seal

Labyrinthpackung *f* MASCHINEN labyrinth packing

Laccain- *pref* CHEMIE laccaic

Laccol *nt* CHEMIE laccol

Lachgas *nt* CHEMIE laughing gas

Lack *m* BAU lacquer, DRUCK, ELEKTRIZ varnish, KFZTECH *Karosserie* paint, KUNSTSTOFF varnish, MECHAN lacquer; **Lackabfall** *m* ABFALL varnish waste; **Lackdraht** *m* ELEKTRIZ, ELEKTROTECH enameled wire (AmE), enamelled wire (BrE); **Lackfarbe** *f* BAU enamel, lacquer, varnish; **Lackfirnis** *m* BAU shellac; **Lackfolienaufnahme** *f* AUFNAHME lacquer recording

Lackieren *nt* BAU varnishing

lackieren *vt* ANSTRICH paint, FERTIG japan, lacquer

Lackierkabine *f* ANSTRICH spray booth

Lackiermaschine *f* VERPACK coating machine, lacquering machine

lackiert *adj* MECHAN lacquered

Lackierung *f* BAU varnishing

Lackmuspapier *nt* FERTIG litmus paper

Lack: **Lackrest** *m* ABFALL varnish waste; **Lackschlamm**

m ABFALL paint sludge; **Lacksplitter** *m* ANSTRICH paint chip; **Lackversiegelung** *f* VERPACK lacquer sealing

Lactam *nt* CHEMIE lactam; **Lactamid** *nt* CHEMIE hydropropanamide, lactamide

Lactat *nt* CHEMIE lactate

Lactid *nt* CHEMIE lactide

Lacto-Butyrometer *nt* LEBENSMITTEL lactobutyrometer

Lactometer *nt* LEBENSMITTEL lactometer

Lacton *nt* CHEMIE lactone; **Lacton-** *pref* CHEMIE lactonic; **Lactonbildung** *f* CHEMIE lactonization

Lactonisierung *f* CHEMIE lactonization

Lactonitril *nt* CHEMIE hydropropanenitrile, lactonitrile

Lactose *f* CHEMIE lactose

Laddertron *nt* ELEKTRONIK *Mikrowellen-Klystron* laddertron

Lade- *pref* BAU, COMP & DV, TRANS, WASSERTRANS loading; **Lade- und Löschbord** *m* TRANS skids; **Ladeadresse** *f* COMP & DV load point; **Ladeanzeige** *f* WASSERTRANS *Elektrik* charge indicator; **Ladeband** *nt* BAU conveyor

Ladebaum *m* MECHAN boom, derrick, hoist, WASSERTRANS *Ladung* cargo boom, cargo derrick, derrick, derrick boom; **Ladebaumpfosten** *m* WASSERTRANS *Schiffbau* Samson post

Lade-: **Ladebereich** *m* LUFTTRANS *Flughafen* loading area; **Ladebrücke** *f* BAU deck, EISENBAHN loading bridge; **Ladebucht** *f* RAUMFAHRT *Raumschiff* cargo bay; **Ladedruck** *m* KFZTECH boost pressure, LUFTTRANS manifold pressure, *Überdruck* boost pressure; **Ladedruckventil** *nt* KFZTECH pressure boost valve; **Lade-Entladezyklus** *m* WASSERTRANS charge-discharge cycle; **Ladefähigkeit** *f* LUFTTRANS load capacity, WASSERTRANS *Schiffkonstruktion* cargo capacity; **Ladefaktor** *m* MECHAN load factor, RAUMFAHRT *Weltraumfunk* loading factor; **Ladefläche** *f* MASCHINEN platform; **Ladegerät** *nt* FOTO, RADIO charger, TRANS *an Stromversorgungsnetz angeschlossen* loader; **Ladegerät für langsames Aufladen** *nt* ELEKTROTECH trickle charger; **Ladegeschirr** *nt* WASSERTRANS *Ladung* cargo gear; **Ladegestell** *nt* MECHAN skid; **Ladegleis** *nt* TRANS loading siding; **Ladehaken** *m* WASSERTRANS *Ladung* cargo hook; **Ladekai** *m* WASSERTRANS loading dock; **Ladeklappe** *f* LUFTTRANS *Flugzeug* loading door; **Ladekondensator** *m* ELEKTROTECH input capacitor; **Ladekran** *m* EISENBAHN loading crane, WASSERTRANS *Ladung* cargo crane; **Ladeleitung** *f* LUFTTRANS manifold; **Ladelinie** *f* WASSERTRANS loadline; **Ladeliste** *f* WASSERTRANS *Dokumente* cargo manifest; **Ladeluke** *f* LUFTTRANS *Flugzeug* loading door, RAUMFAHRT *Raumschiff* cargo hatch, WASSERTRANS cargo hatchway, *Ladung* cargo hatch; **Lademarke** *f* LUFTTRANS load line; **Lademaß** *nt* EISENBAHN loading gage (AmE), loading gauge (BrE)

Laden *nt* COMP & DV loading, ELEKTROTECH charging

laden *vt* COMP & DV boot, load, ELEKTRONIK *Programm* input, RADIO charge, load; **neu~** *vt* COMP & DV reload; **wieder~** *vt* BAU recharge

Laden: **Ladenanschlag** m TEXTIL beat-up
Lade-: **Ladenetz** nt WASSERTRANS *Ladung* net sling; **Ladepfosten** m WASSERTRANS *Deckbeschläge* king post, *Ladung* cargo post; **Ladeplan** m WASSERTRANS *Ladung* capacity plan, cargo plan; **Ladeprogramm** nt COMP & DV loader, loading routine; **Ladepumpe** f MEERSCHMUTZ, WASSERTRANS cargo pump; **Ladepunkt** m COMP & DV load point
Lader m COMP & DV loader, KFZTECH supercharger
Lade-: **Laderampe** f BAU, EISENBAHN loading platform, LUFTTRANS *Flugzeug* loading ramp, TRANS loading platform; **Laderaum** m KFZTECH *Lkw* cargo hold, RAUMFAHRT *Raumschiff* payload bay, TRANS *Lkw* cargo space, WASSERTRANS *Ladung* hold, *Schiff* cargo hold, hold; **Laderegler** m RAUMFAHRT charging regulator; **Laderelais-Ausschalter** m ELEKTRIZ, KFZTECH regulator cutout; **Ladeschaltung** f ELEKTRIZ charging circuit; **Ladeschaufel** f BAU loading shovel; **Ladeschlitz** m FERNSEH loading slot; **Ladespannung** f ELEKTRIZ charging voltage; **Ladestation** f ELEKTROTECH *für Akkumulatoren/Batterien* charging station
Ladestrom m ELEKTRIZ charging current; **Ladestrommeßgerät** nt GERÄT charge rate meter
Lade-: **Ladetank** m UMWELTSCHMUTZ cargo tank; **Ladeverdrängung** f WASSERTRANS loaded displacement, *Schiffskonstruktion* heavy displacement, *Schiffkonstruktion* load displacement; **Ladevorrichtung** f TELEKOM charging equipment; **Ladewert** m TRANS load value; **Ladewinde** f WASSERTRANS *Ladung* cargo winch; **Ladezeit** f FOTO recharge time
Ladung f ELEKTRIZ, ELEKTROTECH charge, ERDÖL freight, KOHLEN load, LEBENSMITTEL batch, LUFTTRANS cargo, PHYS, RADIO charge, RAUMFAHRT *Raumschiff* batch, cargo, STRAHLPHYS, TEILPHYS, TELEKOM *elektrisch* charge, TRANS batch, loading, WASSERTRANS cargo, load; **Ladungs- und Abfüllgeräte** nt pl VERPACK handling and filling equipment; **Ladungsaufbau** m ELEKTROTECH charge buildup; **Ladungsdichte** f ELEKTRIZ, PHYS, STRAHLPHYS, TEILPHYS charge density; **Ladungsdichte eines Teilchens** f PHYS, STRAHLPHYS, TEILPHYS charge density of particle; **Ladungserhaltung** f PHYS connection, conservation of charge
ladungsgekoppelt: **~es Bauelement** nt ELEKTRONIK *(CCD)* charge-coupled device *(CCD)*, PHYS *(CTD)* charge transfer device *(CTD)*; **~e Kamera** f VERPACK CCD camera, charge-coupled device camera
Ladung: **Ladungskompensierung** f ELEKTRIZ charge neutralization; **Ladungsleckstrom** m ELEKTRIZ charge leakage; **Ladungsmanifest** nt LUFTTRANS, WASSERTRANS *Dokumente* cargo manifest; **Ladungsmassenverhältnis** nt PHYS, STRAHLPHYS, TEILPHYS charge-mass ratio; **Ladungsmengenmesser** m ELEKTROTECH coulometer, voltameter; **Ladungsmeßgerät** nt ELEKTRIZ coulombmeter, coulometer; **Ladungsmultiplett** nt PHYS, STRAHLPHYS, TEILPHYS charge multiplet; **Ladungsparitätssymmetrie** f PHYS, STRAHLPHYS, TEILPHYS charge-parity symmetry; **Ladungspumpe** f ELEKTROTECH charge pump; **Ladungsspeicher** m ELEKTROTECH charge storage; **Ladungsspeicherdiode** f ELEKTRONIK CCD diode, charge-storage diode; **Ladungsspeicherröhre** f ELEKTRONIK charge-storage tube; **Ladungssumme** f ELEKTROTECH net charge
Ladungsträger m ELEKTRIZ carrier, ELEKTROTECH charge carrier, PHYS carrier, RAUMFAHRT charge carrier; **Ladungsträgerbeweglichkeit** f ELEKTRIZ, PHYS carrier mobility; **Ladungsträgerstrahl** m ELEKTRONIK charged-particle beam; **Ladungsträgervervielfachung** f ELEKTRONIK *Mikroelektronik* carrier multiplication
Ladung: **Ladungstransferelement** nt *(CTD)* TELEKOM charge transfer device *(CTD)*; **Ladungsübertragung** f KERNTECH, STRAHLPHYS, TEILPHYS charge transfer; **Ladungsübertragungsgerät** nt *(CTD)* RAUMFAHRT charge transfer device *(CTD)*; **Ladungsumschlag** m WASSERTRANS *Ladung* cargo handling; **Ladungsverluststrom** m ELEKTRIZ charge leakage; **Ladungsverschiebeband** nt KERNTECH, STRAHLPHYS, TEILPHYS charge transfer band; **Ladungsverschiebeelement** nt *(CCD)* ELEKTRONIK, PHYS, TELEKOM charge-coupled device *(CCD)*; **Ladungsverschiebeschaltung** f *(CTD)* ELEKTROTECH *Halbleiter* charge transfer device *(CTD)*; **Ladungsverstärker** m ELEKTRONIK charge amplifier; **Ladungswolke** f PHYS, STRAHLPHYS, TEILPHYS charge cloud
LAGA abbr *(Länderarbeitsgemeinschaft Abfall)* ABFALL *in Deutschland* Federal States Working Group on Waste
Lage[1] f BAU lie, site, *Geographie* lay, ELEKTROTECH *eines Kabels* lay, FERTIG *der Schneide* orientation, KER & GLAS course, KOHLEN layer, MASCHINEN, RAUMFAHRT *Raumschiff* ply, WASSERVERSORG layer; **~ Papier** f DRUCK quire; **~ eines Pegels** f WASSERVERSORG gaging station (AmE), gauging station (BrE)
Lage[2] in **~ bringen** vt BAU locate
Lage: **Lagefehler** m MASCHINEN error of position, position error; **Lagegenauigkeit der Bohrung** f FERTIG accuracy in hole positioning; **Lageindex** m ERGON position index; **Lagemeßgerät** nt GERÄT position measuring instrument; **Lagenenergie** f MASCHINEN potential energy; **Lagenhaftung** f KUNSTSTOFF ply bond strength; **Lagenisolierung** f ELEKTRIZ interturn insulation; **Lagenlösung** f KUNSTSTOFF ply separation; **Lagentrennung** f KUNSTSTOFF ply separation; **Lagenwicklung** f ELEKTROTECH *bei Bürsten* layer winding
Lager nt BAU bearing, stockpile, ELEKTRIZ bearing, KOHLEN deposit, MASCHINEN, MECHAN, TRANS bearing; **~ mit Weißmetallausguß** nt MASCHINEN babbitted bearing; **Lagerausguß** m MASCHINEN lining, MECHAN bearing lining; **Lagerbehälter** m HEIZ & KÄLTE storage tank; **Lagerbestand** m ERDÖL inventory, stock; **Lagerbeständigkeit** f VERPACK shelf impact, storage durability, WERKPRÜF *Kunststoffe* shelf life; **Lagerbestandsaufnahme** f VERPACK inventory; **Lagerbock** m MASCHINEN bearing block, pedestal, MECHAN bracket, pedestal; **Lagerbuchse** f MASCHINEN brass, MECHAN bushing; **Lagerbüchse** f MASCHINEN bearing bush, bearing bushing, bushing; **Lagerbunker** m ABFALL receiving bin, refuse bunker; **Lagerdauer** f FOTO storage period; **Lagerdeckel** m FERTIG top bearing, KFZTECH, MASCHINEN bearing cap; **Lagerregelungsrakete** f RAUMFAHRT attitude control rocket; **Lagerfähigkeit** f LEBENSMITTEL keeping quality; **Lagerfaß für neue Brennelemente** nt KERNTECH new element storage drum; **Lagerfestigkeit** f VERPACK shelf stability; **Lagerfläche** f BAU bed, VERPACK floor space; **Lagergehäuse** nt MASCHINEN, PAPIER bearing housing; **Lagergestell** nt KER & GLAS storage rack; **Lagergut** nt ABFALL fill mass, waste mass; **Lagerhaus** nt EISENBAHN freight house (AmE), warehouse (BrE); **Lagerhülse** f MASCHINEN bearing

bush, bearing bushing

lagerichtig[1] *adj* KONSTZEICH in correct positional arrangement

lagerichtig:[2] ~e Darstellung *f* KONSTZEICH topographical representation

Lager: **Lagerkäfig** *m* MASCHINEN bearing cage; **Lagerkammer** *f* ABFALL *für radioaktive Abfälle* storage chamber; **Lagerkonfiguration** *f* RAUMFAHRT *Raumschiff* storage configuration; **Lagerkontrolle** *f* EISENBAHN stock control; **Lagerluft** *f* MASCHINEN bearing clearance; **Lagermetall** *nt* MASCHINEN bearing alloy, bearing metal, METALL babbitt metal, bearing metal; **Lagermöglichkeit** *f* UMWELTSCHMUTZ storage facility

Lagern *nt* COMP & DV store;

lagern *vt* BAU keep, stock; ~ **lassen** *vt* KOHLEN store

Lager: **Lagerplatz** *m* BAU stockyard, yard; **Lagerraum** *m* VERPACK storage space, WASSERTRANS *Ladung* storeroom; **Lagerraum für Tiefkühlkost** *m* HEIZ & KÄLTE frozen-food storage room; **Lagerraumkosten** *f pl* VERPACK cost of space; **Lagerregal** *nt* VERPACK bin, storing shelf; **Lagerreibung** *f* MASCHINEN bearing friction; **Lagerring** *m* FERTIG roller race; **Lagerrolle** *f* FERTIG *Schleudergießmaschine* bottom roller; **Lagerschale** *f* FERTIG pillow, MASCHINEN bearing bush, bearing shell, liner, pillow; **Lagerschale mit Bund** *f* MASCHINEN flanged liner; **Lagerschalenhälfte** *f* MASCHINEN half-bushing; **Lagerschild** *nt* MASCHINEN bearing plate; **Lagerschmierung** *f* FERTIG bearing lubrication; **Lagerseite** *f* MASCHINEN bearing end; **Lagerspiel** *nt* FERTIG diametral clearance, MASCHINEN bearing clearance

Lagerstätte *f* ABFALL repository, storage facility, ERDÖL field, reservoir; **Lagerstättendruck** *m* ERDÖL formation pressure, reservoir pressure; **Lagerstättenmedium** *nt* ERDÖL formation fluid; **Lagerstättenvergasung** *f* THERMOD underground gasification; **Lagerstättenwasser** *nt* ERDÖL formation water

Lager: **Lagerstuhl** *m* MECHAN cradle; **Lagersystem in geregelter Umgebung** *nt* VERPACK controlled environment storage system; **Lagertank** *m* ERDÖL, RAUMFAHRT *Raumschiff* storage tank

Lagerung *f* COMP & DV storage, ELEKTROTECH *in Meßwerken* suspension, FOTO *Fotomaterialien* storage, KOHLEN stratification, MASCHINEN bearing, MEERSCHMUTZ storage; **Lagerungsbeständigkeit** *f* KUNSTSTOFF shelf life; **Lagerungsdichte** *f* BAU *Geologie* compactness; **Lagerungszapfen** *m* MASCHINEN locating spigot

Lager: **Lagerweißmetall** *nt* FERTIG babbitt; **Lagerwerkstoffe** *m pl* MASCHINEN bearing materials; **Lagerzapfen** *m* KERNTECH journal, KFZTECH journal, *Universalgelenk* trunnion, MASCHINEN bearing journal, MECHAN journal, trunnion

Lage: **Lagestabilisierung** *f* TELEKOM orientation control; **Lagetoleranz** *f* MASCHINEN positional tolerance, tolerance of position; **Lagewinkel** *m* FERTIG orientation angle; **Lagewinkel der Freiflächen-Orthogonalebene** *m* FERTIG tool flank orthogonal plane orientation angle; **Lagezuordnung** *f* FERTIG position co-ordination

Lagrange: ~**sche Betrachtungsweise** *f* STRÖMPHYS Lagrangian viewpoint; ~**sche Funktion** *f (L)* MECHAN Lagrangian function, angular momentum *(L)*; ~**sche Gleichung** *f* PHYS Lagrange's equation; ~**scher**

Multiplikator *m* PHYS Lagrangian multiplier; ~**scher Operator** *m* PHYS Lagrangian operator

Lagune *f* WASSERVERSORG lagoon

Laktam *nt* CHEMIE lactam

Laktat *nt* CHEMIE lactate

Lambda *nt* KFZTECH, PHYS lambda; **Lambdapunkt** *m* PHYS *Kryotechnik* lambda point; **Lambdasonde** *f* KFZTECH lambda probe; **Lambdateilchen** *nt* PHYS lambda particle; **Lambda/4-Blättchen** *nt* PHYS quarter-wave plate; **Lambda/2-Blättchen** *nt* PHYS half-wave plate

Lambert *nt* OPTIK lambert; ~**sches Cosinusgesetz** *nt* OPTIK Lambert's cosine law; ~**sches Gesetz** *nt* PHYS Lambert's law; ~**scher Strahler** *m* OPTIK, TELEKOM lambertian source, lambertian radiator; **Lambertreflektor** *m* OPTIK lambertian reflector

Lambverschiebung *f* PHYS Lamb shift

Lamellargraphitgußeisen *nt* MECHAN lamellar graphite cast iron

Lamelle *f* FERTIG lamination, MASCHINEN, MECHAN fin, METALL lamella; **Lamellenanker** *m* ELEKTRIZ laminated armature; **Lamellenblech** *nt* ELEKTROTECH stamping; **Lamellenfeder** *f* MASCHINEN blade spring; **Lamellenheizgerät** *nt* THERMOD finned heater; **Lamellenheizung** *f* HEIZ & KÄLTE strip heating; **Lamellenkern** *m* ELEKTRIZ laminated core; **Lamellenkühler** *m* KFZTECH finned radiator, ribbon cellular radiator, THERMOD finned cooler; **Lamellenkupplung** *f* KFZTECH multiple-disc clutch (BrE), multiple-disk clutch (AmE), MASCHINEN multidisc clutch (BrE), multidisk clutch (AmE), multiple-disc clutch (BrE), multiple-disk clutch (AmE), multiple-plate clutch; **Lamellenmagnet** *m* PHYS compound magnet; **Lamellenschleifscheibe** *f* MASCHINEN abrasive flap wheel; **Lamellenstruktur** *f* METALL lamellar structure; **Lamellenverschluß** *m* FOTO leaf shutter

lamelliert: ~**e Bürste** *f* ELEKTRIZ laminated brush; ~**er Magnet** *m* ELEKTRIZ laminated magnet

Laminar- *pref* CHEMIE laminar

laminar[1] *adj* CHEMIE, STRÖMPHYS laminar

laminar:[2] ~**e Ablösung** *f* STRÖMPHYS laminar separation; ~ **fluidisierter Brennstoff** *m* KERNTECH paste fuel; ~**e Rohrströmung** *f* STRÖMPHYS laminar pipe flow; ~**e Strömung** *f* HEIZ & KÄLTE, LUFTTRANS, STRÖMPHYS laminar flow

Laminarin *nt* CHEMIE laminarin

Laminartransistor *m* ELEKTRONIK laminar transistor

Laminat *nt* ELEKTRONIK laminate, KUNSTSTOFF laminate, laminated plastic; **Laminatprofil** *nt* KUNSTSTOFF laminated section

Laminieren *nt* KUNSTSTOFF lamination, PAPIER laminating, RADIO *Transformatorkern* lamination

laminieren *vt* BAU, DRUCK, FERTIG laminate

laminiert[1] *adj* ELEKTRIZ, FERTIG, KUNSTSTOFF, WASSERTRANS laminated

laminiert:[2] ~**e Drehstabfeder** *f* LUFTTRANS laminated torsion bar; ~**es Plastik** *nt* WASSERTRANS laminated plastic

Laminierung: ~ **aus Siliziumstahl** *f* ELEKTROTECH silicon steel lamination

Lampard-Thomson-Kondensator *m* PHYS Lampard and Thomson capacitor

Lampe *f* KFZTECH *Zubehör* lamp; **Lampenbrett** *nt* FOTO bank of lights; **Lampenfassung** *f* ELEKTROTECH lamp cap, lamp holder, FOTO lamp socket; **Lampengehäuse** *nt* FOTO *Projektor* lamphouse; **Lampenkolben** *m* ELEK-

TRIZ bulb, KER & GLAS lamp bulb; **Lampenschirm** *m*
ELEKTROTECH hood, lampshade; **Lampenwechsel** *m*
FOTO lamp replacement; **Lampenzylinder** *m* KER &
GLAS lamp chimney

LAN *abbr (lokales Netz)* COMP & DV, TELEKOM LAN
(local area network)

Land:[1] **auf ~** *adj* ERDÖL onshore

Land:[2] **an ~** *adv* WASSERTRANS ashore, on shore

Land[3] *nt* WASSERTRANS shore

Land:[4] **an ~ absetzen** *vt* WASSERTRANS *Ladung, Passagie-*
re land; **an ~ setzen** *vt* WASSERTRANS *Passagiere* land

Land: Landaufnahme *f* BAU geodetic survey; **Land-Bord-**
Alarmierung *f* TELEKOM shore-to-ship alerting;
Landbrise *f* WASSERTRANS land breeze; **Landcontainer**
m TRANS land container

Lande- *pref* LUFTTRANS, WASSERTRANS landing

Landeanflug *m* RAUMFAHRT *Raumschiff* descent,
descent path; **Landeanflugsgeschwindigkeit** *f* LUFT-
TRANS landing approach speed

Lande-: Landeauslaufstrecke *f* LUFTTRANS landing run

Landebahn *f* LUFTTRANS landing strip; **Landebahnmar-**
kierung *f* LUFTTRANS landing strip marker,
Vorfeldmarkierung, -befeuerung hold-short line
(AmE), lead-in line (BrE); **Landebahnmittellinienver-**
längerung *f* LUFTTRANS extended runway centerline
(AmE), extended runway centreline (BrE); **Lande-**
bahnscheinwerfer *m* ELEKTRIZ apron floodlight;
Landebahnsichtweite *f* LUFTTRANS runway visual
range

Lande-: Landedeck *nt* WASSERTRANS landing deck; **Lan-**
defahrgestell *nt* LUFTTRANS landing-gear leg;
Landefahrzeug *nt* RAUMFAHRT *Raumschiff* lander,
landing vehicle

Landé-Faktor *m* PHYS Landé factor

Lande-: Landefolge *f* LUFTTRANS landing sequence;
Landeführungsgerät *nt* TRANS localizer; **Landegebiet**
nt RAUMFAHRT *Raumschiff* landing area; **Landege-**
schwindigkeit *f* LUFTTRANS landing speed;
Landegestell *nt* LUFTTRANS landing gear; **Landege-**
wicht *nt* LUFTTRANS landing weight; **Landekapsel** *f*
RAUMFAHRT *Raumschiff* landing capsule; **Landekarte**
f LUFTTRANS landing chart; **Landeklappe** *f* LUFT-
TRANS landing flap, *Flugzeug* flap; **Landekufe** *f*
LUFTTRANS landing skid, landing-gear leg; **Landelän-**
ge *f* LUFTTRANS landing distance; **Landeleitlinie** *f*
LUFTTRANS glide slope; **Landelicht** *nt* LUFTTRANS
landing light

Landen *nt* TRANS *einer Ladung* landing

landen *vi* RAUMFAHRT *Raumschiff* touch down, WASSER-
TRANS land

Land: Landenge *f* WASSERTRANS isthmus

Lande-: Landepfad *m* LUFTTRANS landing path; **Lande-**
piste *f* LUFTTRANS landing strip; **Landepunkt** *m*
RAUMFAHRT *Raumschiff* touchdown point

Länderarbeitsgemeinschaft: ~ Abfall *f (LAGA)* ABFALL
in Deutschland Federal States Working Group on
Waste

Lande-: Landerichtungsanzeiger *m* LUFTTRANS landing
direction indicator

Land: Landerschließung *f* UMWELTSCHMUTZ reclamation of land

Lande-: Landeschleife *f* LUFTTRANS landing pattern
turn

Land: Landeskenner *m* RADIO *Amateurfunk* prefix; **Lan-**
deskennzahl *f* TELEKOM country code; **Landesmarine**
f WASSERTRANS national navy; **Landesstraße** *f* TRANS

in Deutschland state road

Lande-: Landestrecke *f* LUFTTRANS landing distance;
Landestufe *f* RAUMFAHRT *Raumschiff* descent stage,
lander stage; **Landesystem** *nt* LUFTTRANS, WASSER-
TRANS landing system; **Landeumlaufbahn** *f*
RAUMFAHRT descent orbit; **Landeverfahren** *nt* LUFT-
TRANS landing procedure; **Landezone** *f* LUFTTRANS
landing area

Land: Landfahrzeug *nt* RAUMFAHRT *Raumschiff* land
vehicle; **Landflugzeug** *nt* LUFTTRANS terraplane;
Landgang *m* WASSERTRANS gangway

landgebunden: ~es Luftkissenfahrzeug *nt* TRANS land
air cushion vehicle

Land: Landgewinnung *f* UMWELTSCHMUTZ reclamation
of land, WASSERVERSORG land reclamation; **Landka-**
bel *nt* TELEKOM land cable

ländlich: ~er Bezirk *m* ELEKTROTECH rural district

Land: Landluftwegtransport *m* TRANS road-air combined transport; **Landmarke** *f* WASSERTRANS
Seezeichen landmark; **Landmesser** *m* BAU surveyor;
Landnetz *nt* TELEKOM rural network; **Landnutzungs-**
plan *m* BAU land use plan; **Landschaftsfotograf** *m*
FOTO landscape photographer; **Landschaftsgestal-**
tung *f* BAU landscaping

landseitig: ~e Basis *f* ERDÖL

Land: Landspitze *f* WASSERTRANS *Geographie* point;
Landstraße *f* TRANS secondary road

Landung *f* LUFTTRANS, RAUMFAHRT *Raumschiff*, WAS-
SERTRANS landing; **~ mit anschließendem**
Durchstarten *f* LUFTTRANS touch-and-go landing; **~**
mit ausgefallenem Triebwerk *f* LUFTTRANS dead stick
landing; **~ mit eingefahrenem Fahrwerk** *f* LUFTTRANS
wheels-up landing; **~ bei geringer Sicht** *f* LUFTTRANS
low visibility landing; **Landungsboot** *nt* WASSERTRANS
landing craft; **Landungsbrücke** *f* BAU pier, TRANS
landing stage, WASSERTRANS jetty; **Landungsgebühr** *f*
LUFTTRANS, WASSERTRANS landing charge (BrE),
landing fee (AmE); **Landungskosten** *f pl* LUFTTRANS
landing charge (BrE), landing fee (AmE); **Landungs-**
ponton *m* WASSERTRANS landing pontoon

Land: Landurlaub *m* WASSERTRANS shore leave; **Landver-**
messung *f* BAU land survey, land surveying;
Landvermittlungsstelle *f* TELEKOM rural switch; **Land-**
wind *m* WASSERTRANS land wind, offshore wind

landwirtschaftlich: ~er Abfall *m* ABFALL agricultural
waste, farm waste

Land: Landzentrale *f* TELEKOM rural exchange; **Land-**
zunge *f* WASSERTRANS *Geographie* headland;
Landzuwachs *m* WASSERVERSORG land accretion

Lang- *pref* MASCHINEN, RADIO long

lang: ~er Impuls *m* WASSERTRANS *Radar* long pulse; **~**
nachleuchtender Bildschirm *m* FERNSEH long-persist-
ence screen; **~e Ringleitung** *f* TRANS long loop; **~er**
Sturzbalken *m* BAU breastsummer; **~er Ton** *m* WASSER-
TRANS long blast; **~e Unterlängen** *f pl* DRUCK long
descenders

lang: mit ~ er Standzeit *adj* FERTIG long-life

langbrennweitig: ~es Objektiv *nt* FOTO long-focus lens

Lang-: Langdrahtantenne *f* RADIO long-wire antenna;
Langdrehautomat *m* MASCHINEN Swiss-type automatic; **Langdrehen** *nt* MASCHINEN plain turning,
straight turning; **Langdrehmaschine** *f* MASCHINEN
plain-turning lathe, sliding lathe

Länge *f* COMP & DV *(l)*, GEOM *(l)* length *(l)*, METROL
yardage, PHYS *(l)*, TELEKOM *(l)* length *(l)*; **~ über**
alles *f* MASCHINEN overall length, WASSERTRANS *Maß-*

einheit ram; ~ **der Erzeugenden** *f* GEOM slant height; ~ **der Fahrzeugschlange** *f* TRANS queue length; ~ **zwischen den Loten** *f* WASSERTRANS *Schiffkonstruktion* length between perpendiculars; **Längen- und Seitenverhältnis** *nt* COMP & DV aspect ratio; ~ **im stationären Zustand** *f* OPTIK equilibrium length; ~ **der Zeichenfolge** *f* COMP & DV string length; **Längen** *nt* MASCHINEN elongation **Längenänderung** *f* FERTIG *Kunststoffinstallationen* displacement; **Längenausdehnungskoeffizient** *m* KUNSTSTOFF coefficient of linear expansion; **Längeneinheit** *f* FERTIG, METROL unit of length; **Längengrad** *m* WASSERTRANS *Geographie, Navigation* longitude; **Längenkontraktion** *f* PHYS length contraction; **Längenmaß** *nt* MATH linear measurement, METROL long measure; **Längenmeßgeräte** *nt pl* METROL dimensional measuring instruments; **Längenmeßinstrument** *nt* MASCHINEN length measuring instrument; **Längenmeßmaschine** *f* GERÄT length measuring machine; **Längenmetazentrum** *nt* WASSERTRANS *Schiffbau* longitudinal metacenter (AmE), longitudinal metacentre (BrE)

längenspezifisch: ~**e Strömungsresistanz** *f* AKUSTIK flow resistivity

längentreu: ~**e Azimutalprojektion** *f* RADIO *Kartographie* azimuthal equidistant projection

Länge: **Längenverhältnis** *nt* MECHAN aspect ratio; **Längenverhältnis des Luftschraubenblattes** *nt* LUFTTRANS blade aspect ratio; **Längenverkürzung** *f* PHYS length contraction

Lang-: **Langfaser** *f* TEXTIL long line; **Langflachs** *m* TEXTIL line flax; **Langfräsmaschine** *f* MASCHINEN planomiller, planomilling machine; **Langgewinde** *nt* MASCHINEN longscrew; **Langhalsflasche** *f* LABOR long-necked flask; **Langhalskolben** *m* LABOR long-necked flask; **Langhobel** *m* BAU trying plane; **Langhobelfräsen** *nt* MASCHINEN planer milling; **Langholzwagen** *m* EISENBAHN timber wagon

langhubig *adj* MASCHINEN long-stroke

Lang-: **Langkorn** *nt* METALL elongated grain

langlebig[1] *adj* LEBENSMITTEL long-life

langlebig:[2] ~**es Isotop** *nt* STRAHLPHYS long-lived isotope

Lang-: **Langlebigkeit** *f* ANSTRICH longevity, KUNSTSTOFF durability; **Langleitungseffekt** *m* ELEKTRONIK *Mikrowellen* long-line effect

länglich *adj* GEOM oblong

Lang-: **Langlichtbogen** *m* FERTIG long arc

Langloch *nt* MASCHINEN, MECHAN elongated hole; **Langlochfräsen** *nt* FERTIG slotting; **Langlochfräser** *m* FERTIG router, MASCHINEN slot drill, slot mill; **Langlochfräsmaschine** *f* FERTIG slot milling machine, MASCHINEN slot drilling machine

Lang-: **Langölalkydharz** *nt* KUNSTSTOFF long oil alkyd

Längs- *pref* ELEKTRONIK, WASSERTRANS longitudinal

längs *adv* MASCHINEN lengthways, lengthwise; ~ **der Küste** *adv* WASSERTRANS alongshore

Längs-: **Längsabweichung** *f* LUFTTRANS longitudinal divergence; **Längsachse** *f* LUFTTRANS, MASCHINEN longitudinal axis

langsam:[1] ~ **voraus** *adv* WASSERTRANS *Motor* slow ahead; ~ **zurück** *adv* WASSERTRANS *Motor* slow astern

langsam:[2] ~**es Abschrecken** *nt* METALL slow quenching; ~ **drehender Elektromotor** *m* ELEKTROTECH low-speed electric motor; ~ **erstarrendes Glas** *nt* KER & GLAS slow-setting glass; ~**e Gärung** *f* ABFALL slow fermentation; ~**es Gefrieren** *nt* LEBENSMITTEL slow freezing; ~**e Kompostierung** *f* ABFALL slow composting; ~ **laufen-**

der Dieselmotor *m* TRANS, WASSERTRANS slow-running diesel engine; ~**es Modem** *nt* ELEKTRONIK low-speed modem; ~**es Neutron** *nt* PHYS slow neutron; ~**e Nullpunktsveränderung** *f* METALL zero creep; ~ **variierende Spannung** *f* ELEKTROTECH slowly varying voltage; ~**e Welle** *f* ELEKTROTECH slow wave

Langsamfahrsignal *nt* EISENBAHN speed restriction board, speed-restricting signal

Langsamfilter *nt* WASSERVERSORG slow sand filter

Langsamkeit *f* TRANS slowness

Langsamladung *f* ELEKTROTECH trickle charge

langsamlaufend: ~**er Kompressor** *m* HYDRAUL slow speed compressor

Langsamläufer *m* WASSERTRANS low-speed engine, *Dieselmotor* low-speed diesel engine

Langsamsandfiltration *f* WASSERVERSORG slow sand filtration

Langsamwellenstruktur *f* ELEKTROTECH slow wave structure

Längs-: **Längsanker** *m* ELEKTRIZ axial armature; **Längsanschlag** *m* FERTIG length stop; **Längsbalken** *m* BAU stringer; **Längsband** *nt* WASSERTRANS *Schiffbau* tie plate; **Längsbeanspruchung** *f* METALL longitudinal stress; **Längsbespannung** *f* WASSERTRANS *Schiffbau* longitudinal framing; **Längsbewehrung** *f* BAU longitudinal reinforcement

Lang-: **Langschienen** *f pl* EISENBAHN continuous-welded rail, ribbon rails; **Langschwelle** *f* EISENBAHN stringer

Längs-: **Längsdrehen** *nt* FERTIG straight turning, MASCHINEN plain turning; **Längsdruck** *m* MASCHINEN thrust; **Längsfaltung** *f* KONSTZEICH Leporello folding, longitudinal folding; **Längsfehler** *m* RAUMFAHRT along-track error; **Längsfilter** *nt* ELEKTRONIK longitudinal filter; **Längsglied** *nt* LUFTTRANS longitudinal member

Langsieb *nt* PAPIER fourdrinier; **Langsiebpapiermaschine** *f* PAPIER fourdrinier paper machine

Längs-: **Längskeil** *m* FERTIG machine key; **Längskomponente** *f* PHYS longitudinal component; **Längskugellager** *nt* MASCHINEN thrust ball-bearing; **Längslager** *nt* FERTIG thrust bearing, MASCHINEN thrust bearing, thrust block; **Längslagestabilisierung** *f* LUFTTRANS pitch attitude; **Längsleistungstransistor** *m* ELEKTRONIK series pass power transistor; **Längslenker** *m* KFZTECH *Radaufhängung* trailing arm; **Längsmagnetisierung** *f* AKUSTIK longitudinal magnetization; **Längsneigungsmesser des Luftschraubenblattes** *m* LUFTTRANS *Hubschrauber* blade pitch indicator; **Längsneigungswinkel** *m* LUFTTRANS pitch angle

längsnuten *vt* FERTIG spline

Längs-: **Längsparität** *f* COMP & DV horizontal parity

Lang-: **Langspielband** *nt* AUFNAHME long-play tape; **Langspielplatte** *f* (*LP*) AUFNAHME extended-play record, long-playing record (*EP*); **Langspleiß** *m* WASSERTRANS *Tauwerk* long splice

Längs-: **Längsreibemaschine** *f* LEBENSMITTEL conche; **Längsrichtung** *f* DRUCK grain, grain direction; **Längsriß** *m* FERTIG shear draft, WASSERTRANS *Schiffkonstruktion* sheer drawing, sheer plan

längsschiffs *adv* WASSERTRANS fore and aft

Längs-: **Längsschiffsplan** *m* WASSERTRANS *Schiffkonstruktion* profile; **Längsschleifen** *nt* MASCHINEN traverse grinding, PAPIER longitudinal grinding; **Längsschlitten** *m* MASCHINEN longitudinal slide;

Längsschlitz *m* TELEKOM longitudinal slot; **Längsschneidemaschine** *f* DRUCK slitter; **Längsschnitt** *m* BAU, EISENBAHN longitudinal section; **Längsschnittlinie** *f* WASSERTRANS *Schiffbau* buttock; **Längsschruppen** *nt* FERTIG straight rough turning; **Längsschwingung** *f* MASCHINEN longitudinal oscillation

längsseits[1] *adj* WASSERTRANS alongside
längsseits[2] *adv* WASSERTRANS *Festmachen* alongside
längsseits:[3] ~ **gehen** *vi* WASSERTRANS draw alongside, *Schiff* go alongside; ~ **verholen** *vi* WASSERTRANS haul alongside

Längs-: **Längsspannung** *f* METALL line tension; **Längsspant** *m* RAUMFAHRT *Raumschiff* stringer, WASSERTRANS *Schiffkonstruktion* longitudinal; **Längsspiel** *nt* KERNTECH end float; **Längsspuraufzeichnung** *f* AUFNAHME, FERNSEH longitudinal recording; **Längsstabilität** *f* AIR TRANS longitudinal stability; **Längsstrahler** *m* RADIO *längsstrahlende Dipolanordnung* endfire array, TELEKOM endfire antenna, endfire array; **Längsströmung** *f* KER & GLAS longitudinal current; **Längssummenkontrolle** *f* COMP & DV LRC, longitudinal redundancy check

langstielig: ~**e Zange** *f* KERNTECH long-handed tongs
Längs-: **Längsträger** *m* KFZTECH *Chassis, Fahrgestell* side member; **Längsträgerkoppelung** *f* LUFTTRANS longitudinal beam coupler; **Längstransistor** *m* ELEKTRONIK series pass transistor

Lang-: **Langstreckenlinienflugzeug** *nt* LUFTTRANS longhaul airliner; **Langstreckennavigationskeite** *f* (*LORAN*) LUFTTRANS, WASSERTRANS long-range navigation (*loran*); **Langstreckenverkehr** *m* LUFTTRANS long-haul service

Längs-: **Längstrimmung** *f* LUFTTRANS pitch trim; **Längsversteifung** *f* RAUMFAHRT *Raumschiff* stringer

langwegig: ~**es Signal** *nt* ELEKTRONIK long-way signal
Lang-: **Langwelle** *f* (*LW*) RADIO long wave (*LW*)
langwellig: ~**es fernes Infrarot** *nt* PHYS *Strahlung* far infrared

Langzeit- *pref* LEBENSMITTEL long-life; **Langzeitbatterie** *f* ELEKTROTECH long-life battery; **Langzeitgedächtnis** *nt* (*LZG*) ERGON, KÜNSTL INT long-term memory (*LTM*); **Langzeitkonstante** *f* ELEKTRONIK long-time constant; **Langzeitmessung** *f* GERÄT long-term measurement; **Langzeitmission** *f* RAUMFAHRT *Raumschiff* long mission; **Langzeitprüfung** *f* ELEKTRIZ long-term test; **Langzeitquotient** *m* KERNTECH endurance ratio; **Langzeitrelais** *nt* ELEKTROTECH slow operate relay; **Langzeitstabilität** *f* ELEKTRONIK long-term stability; **Langzeittauchen** *nt* ERDÖL saturation diving; **Langzeittaucher** *m* ERDÖL saturation diver; **Langzeitverhalten** *nt* KERNTECH long-term behavior (AmE), long-term behaviour (BrE)

Lanosterin *nt* CHEMIE lanosterol
Lanthan *nt* (*La*) CHEMIE lanthanium (*La*)
Lanthanoid *nt* CHEMIE lanthanoide
Lanze *f* MASCHINEN lance
Lanzette *f* FERTIG *Formen* slick, slicker
Laplace: ~**sche Gleichung** *f* PHYS Laplace's equation; ~**scher Operator** *m* KERNTECH, PHYS Laplacian operator; ~**sche Transformation** *f* ELEKTRONIK, MATH, PHYS Laplace transformation

Lappaconitin *nt* CHEMIE lappaconitine
Läppaste *f* FERTIG lapping compound
Läppblasen *f pl* KER & GLAS lap blisters
Läppdorn *m* FERTIG cylindrical lap

Läppeinrichtung *f* MASCHINEN lapping fixture
Lappen *m* FERTIG lobe, *Schaft* tang, MECHAN flap
Läppen *nt* FERTIG lapping, HYDRAUL *Feinstschleifen* lap, MASCHINEN lapping
lappen *vt* FERTIG tongue
läppen *vt* FERTIG, MECHAN lap
lappenförmig:[1] ~ **abgesetzt** *adj* FERTIG tanged
lappenförmig:[2] ~ **absetzen** *vt* FERTIG tang
Läppkäfig *m* FERTIG *Werkstückträger* cage
Läppmarkierung *f* KER & GLAS lap mark
Läppmaschine *f* FERTIG, MASCHINEN, MECHAN lapping machine
Läpprippen *f pl* KER & GLAS lapping ribs
Läppwerkzeug *nt* FERTIG lap, MASCHINEN lapping tool
Laptop *m* COMP & DV laptop, laptop computer
L-Arabinose *f* CHEMIE pectinose
Larizin *nt* CHEMIE coniferin
Lärm *m* AKUSTIK, ERGON, SICHERHEIT *Fabrik, Verkehr*, WELLPHYS noise; **durch ~ verursachter Hörschaden** *m* SICHERHEIT noise-induced hearing impairment; ~ **mit Vibration** *m* SICHERHEIT noise with vibration; **Lärmbekämpfung** *f* BAU noise control; **Lärmbelästigung** *f* AKUSTIK noise nuisance, SICHERHEIT noise pollution, UMWELTSCHMUTZ noise pollution, sound pollution; **Lärmbelastungsmesser für Personen** *m* SICHERHEIT personal sound exposure meter; **Lärmbeurteilungskurven** *f pl* ERGON noise rating curves; **Lärmemission** *f* KERNTECH acoustic emission; **Lärmexposition** *f* ERGON noise exposure
Larmor: ~**sche Frequenz** *f* PHYS Larmor frequency; ~**sche Präzession** *f* PHYS Larmor precession
Lärm: **Lärmquelle** *f* UMWELTSCHMUTZ noise source; **Lärmreduzierung** *f* SICHERHEIT noise control; **Lärmschutz** *m* ELEKTRIZ soundproofing; **Lärmschutzvorrichtung** *f* MASCHINEN noise absorption device; **Lärmschutzwand** *f* BAU noise barrier; **Lärmschutzzaun** *m* BAU acoustic fencing; **Lärmschwerhörigkeit** *f* ERGON noise-induced hearing loss
Lasche *f* BAU shackle, tongue, EISENBAHN rail splice, FERTIG cover plate, fish plate, shin, *Kette* link plate, sideplate, MASCHINEN clip, link plate, plate, strap, MECHAN lug, shackle, tab, VERPACK tab; **Laschenkette** *f* MASCHINEN pitch chain, pitched chain, plate link chain, sprocket chain; **Laschennietung** *f* MASCHINEN butt-strap riveting; **Laschenschraube** *f* FERTIG fish bolt; **Laschenverband** *m* EISENBAHN fishplating; **Laschenverbindung** *f* BAU scarf, splice joint, FERTIG *Nieten* butt joint
Laschung *f* BAU *von zwei Holzstücken* scarf
Laser *m* (*Lichtverstärkung durch stimulierte Strahlungsemission*) COMP & DV, DRUCK, ELEKTRONIK, PHYS, STRAHLPHYS laser (*light amplification by stimulated emission of radiation*); ~ **mit Elektropumpe** *m* ELEKTRONIK electrically-pumped laser; ~ **mit kurzer Wellenlänge** *m* ELEKTRONIK short wavelength laser; **Laserabgleich** *m* ELEKTRONIK laser trimming; **Laserabstrahlung** *f* ELEKTRONIK laser emission; **Laseralarmempfänger** *m* ELEKTRONIK laser warning receiver; **Laseranemometer** *nt* GERÄT laser anemometer; **Laseranregung** *f* PHYS, STRAHLPHYS laser excitation; **Laserantrieb** *m* RAUMFAHRT *Raumschiff* laser propulsion; **Laseraufnahmekopf** *m* OPTIK laser pick-up head; **Laseraufzeichnung** *f* OPTIK laser optic recording; **Laserband** *nt* OPTIK laser optic tape; **Laserbandbreite** *f* ELEKTRONIK laser bandwidth; **Laserbearbeitung** *f* MECHAN laser machining; **Laser-**

beleuchtung *f* ELEKTRONIK laser illumination; **Laserbezeichnung** *f* ELEKTRONIK laser designation; **Laserbildplatte** *f* OPTIK laservision disc (BrE), laservision disk (AmE), laservision videodisc (BrE), laservision videodisk (AmE); **Laserbohrer** *m* ELEKTRONIK laser drill; **Laserbündel** *nt* ELEKTRONIK laser burst; **Laser-CD** *f* OPTIK laser videodisc (BrE), laser videodisk (AmE); **Lasercode** *m* ELEKTRONIK laser code; **Laserdiode** *f* ELEKTRONIK, OPTIK, PHYS, STRAHLPHYS, TELEKOM LD, laser diode; **Laserdiode mit Einfach-Heteroübergang** *f* ELEKTRONIK single heterojunction laser diode; **Laserdiode kleiner Leistung** *f* TELEKOM low-power laser diode; **Laserdruck** *m* OPTIK laser printing; **Laserdrucker** *m* COMP & DV, DRUCK, OPTIK laser printer; **Laserdrucker/Kopierer** *m* OPTIK laser printer-copier; **Laserdüse** *f* OPTIK laserjet (TM); **Laserentfernungsmesser** *m* ELEKTRONIK laser range-finder; **Laserentfernungsmessung** *f* TELEKOM laser telemetry; **Laserführung** *f* ELEKTRONIK laser guidance; **Laserfusion** *f* KERNTECH laser fusion; **Laserfusionshohlraum** *m* ELEKTRONIK laser cavity

lasergeführt *adj* ELEKTRONIK laser-guided

lasergesteuert: ~e **Maschine** *f* BAU laser-controlled machine

Laser: **Laserglas** *nt* KER & GLAS laser glass; **Laserglühen** *nt* ELEKTRONIK laser annealing; **Laserhohlraum** *m* ELEKTRONIK laser cavity; **Laserimpuls** *m* ELEKTRONIK laser pulse

laserinduziert: ~e **Fusion** *f* KERNTECH laser-driven fusion

Laser: **Laserinterferometer** *nt* ELEKTRONIK laser interferometer; **Laserjet®** *m* OPTIK Laserjet®; **Laserkalibrierung** *f* ELEKTRONIK laser trimming; **Laserkarte** *f* OPTIK lasercard; **Laserkommunikation** *f* ELEKTRONIK laser communications; **Laserkopf** *m* OPTIK laser head; **Laserkreisel** *m* RAUMFAHRT *Raumschiff* laser gyro; **Lasermechanismus** *m* OPTIK laser mechanism; **Lasermedium** *nt* ELEKTRONIK laser medium, OPTIK laser medium, laser optic medium, TELEKOM laser medium; **Lasermeßgerät** *nt* METROL laser measuring instrument

Lasern *nt* ELEKTRONIK laser action, lasing

Laser: **Lasernachführer** *m* ELEKTRONIK laser tracker, laser tracking; **Laseroptikdiskette** *f* OPTIK laser optic disc (BrE), laser optic disk (AmE)

laseroptisch: ~e **Karte** *f* OPTIK laser optic card

Laser: **Laserplatte** *f* COMP & DV optical disk; **Laserscheibe** *f* OPTIK laser disc (BrE), laser disk (AmE); **Laserschmelzen** *nt* ELEKTRONIK laser melting; **Laserschneiden** *nt* BAU, ELEKTRONIK laser cutting, MASCHINEN laser beam cutting, laser cutting; **Laserschreiben** *nt* ELEKTRONIK laser scribing; **Laserschreibstift** *m* ELEKTRONIK laser scriber; **Laserschweißen** *nt* BAU, ELEKTRONIK laser welding; **Laserschwelle** *f* OPTIK, TELEKOM lasing threshold; **Lasersensor** *m* ELEKTRONIK laser sensor; **Lasersondemassenspektrographie** *f* KERNTECH laser probe mass spectrography; **Laserspeicher** *m* COMP & DV photodigital memory; **Laserspektroskopie** *f* PHYS, STRAHLPHYS laser spectroscopy

Laserstrahl *m* ELEKTRONIK, KERNTECH laser beam, PHYS, STRAHLPHYS laser beam, laser light beam, TELEKOM laser beam; **Laserstrahlaufzeichnung** *f* COMP & DV, FERNSEH laser beam recording; **Laserstrahl-Energie** *f* ELEKTRONIK laser beam energy; **Laserstrahlmodulation** *f* ELEKTRONIK laser beam modulation; **Laserstrahlschweißen** *nt* BAU laser beam welding

Laser: **Laserstrahlung** *f* ELEKTRONIK, PHYS, STRAHLPHYS laser radiation; **Lasertätigkeit** *f* ELEKTRONIK lasing; **Lasertrennen** *nt* BAU laser cutting; **Laserübergang** *m* PHYS, STRAHLPHYS laser transition; **Laserüberwachungssystem** *nt* PHYS, STRAHLPHYS laser monitoring system; **Laserwaffe** *f* ELEKTRONIK laser weapon; **Laserwendeanzeiger** *m* PHYS, STRAHLPHYS laser gyro

LASH-Schiff *nt* *(Leichtertransporter, Leichterträgerschiff)* WASSERTRANS LASH carrier *(lighter aboard ship carrier)*.

Last *f* ELEKTRIZ, HYDRAUL *Ventil,* MASCHINEN, MECHAN, METALL, TELEKOM load

lastabhängig: ~e **Bremsung** *f* TRANS load-sensitive braking

Last: **Lastabschaltung** *f* ELEKTRIZ load shedding; **Lastabwurf** *m* ELEKTRIZ load loss, load shedding, ELEKTROTECH load shedding; **Lastannahme** *f* FERTIG design load; **Lastannahmen** *f pl* QUAL design loadings; **Lastbegrenzung** *f* ELEKTROTECH load limiting; **Lastcharakteristik** *f* ELEKTROTECH load characteristic; **Lastdauerkurve** *f* ELEKTRIZ load duration curve; **Lastenaufzug** *m* TRANS elevator (AmE), lift (BrE), hoist; **Lastenbeförderung außerhalb des Hubschraubers** *f* LUFTTRANS external load carrying; **Lastenhebemagnet** *nt* TRANS lift magnet; **Lastenmaßstab** *m* WASSERTRANS *Schiffkonstruktion* dead-weight scale; **Lastfaktor** *m* HEIZ & KÄLTE, TRANS load factor

lastfrei: ~er **Betrieb** *m* ELEKTROTECH no-load operation, KFZTECH *Motor* off-load operation; ~e **Prüfung** *f* ELEKTRIZ no-load test

Last: **Lastfrequenzregelung** *f* ELEKTRIZ load frequency control; **Lastfuhrwerk** *nt* TRANS cart (AmE), truck (BrE); **Lasthaken** *m* BAU lifting hook, LUFTTRANS *Hubschrauber* load hook up, MASCHINEN lifting hook; **Lasthebegerät** *nt* MASCHINEN lifting device

Lastigkeit *f* WASSERTRANS *Schiff* trim

Last: **Lastimpedanz** *f* ELEKTROTECH, PHYS, TELEKOM load impedance; **Lastinduktanz** *f* ELEKTROTECH load inductance

Last-in First-out *adj* *(LIFO)* COMP & DV last-in-first-out *(LIFO)*

Last: **Lastkahncontainer** *m* TRANS barge container; **Lastkapazität** *f* ELEKTROTECH load capacitance, *bei Meßsonden* input capacitance; **Lastkennlinie** *f* ELEKTROTECH load characteristic; **Lastkette** *f* MASCHINEN lifting chain, load chain, SICHERHEIT *Hebevorrichtung* load chain

Lastkraftwagen *m* *(Lkw)* KFZTECH heavy goods vehicle, lorry (BrE), trailer (AmE), truck (AmE) *(HGV)*; **Lastkraftwagen-Pooling** *nt* KFZTECH lorry pooling (BrE), truck pooling (AmE)

Last: **Lastkurve** *f* ELEKTRIZ load curve; **Last-Leer-Verhältnis** *nt* KFZTECH load no-load ratio; **Lastminderung** *f* ELEKTRIZ load derating; **Lastöse** *f* MASCHINEN clevis; **Lastösenbolzen** *m* MASCHINEN clevis pin; **Lastprüfung** *f* ELEKTRIZ load test; **Lastschalter** *m* ELEKTRIZ load switch; **Lastschwankung** *f* ELEKTRIZ load fluctuation; **Lastseil** *nt* EISENBAHN fall rope, FERTIG hoisting rope; **Lastspannung** *f* ELEKTRIZ on-load voltage; **Lastspiel** *nt* FERTIG stress cycle; **Lastspielzeit** *f* FERTIG endurance; **Lastspitze** *f* ELEKTRIZ load peak, ELEKTROTECH peak load; **Lastspule** *f* ELEKTRIZ, ELEKTROTECH loading coil; **Laststromkreis** *m* ELEKTRIZ load circuit;

Lastteilungssystem *nt* TELEKOM load-sharing system; **Lasttransfer** *m* TELEKOM load transfer; **Lastübergabe** *f* ELEKTRIZ load transfer; **Lastumschaltung** *f* ELEKTRIZ load transfer; **Lastverlauf** *m* ELEKTRIZ load variation; **Lastverlaufkurve** *f* ELEKTRIZ load duration curve

Lastverteilung *f* BAU, LUFTTRANS, MASCHINEN load distribution; **Lastverteilungsliste** *f* LUFTTRANS load distribution manifest; **Lastverteilungsmanifest** *nt* LUFTTRANS load distribution manifest; **Lastverteilungsplatte** *f* BAU base plate

Last: **Lastvielfaches** *nt* TRANS load factor; **Lastwagentransport** *m* TRANS trucking (AmE); **Lastwechsel** *m* FERTIG alternation of stress, stress cycle; **Lastwechselprüfung** *f* METROL endurance test; **Lastwiderstand** *m* ELEKTRIZ, ELEKTROTECH *Bauteil* load resistor, PHYS load resistance; **Lastwinkel** *m* ELEKTRIZ load angle; **Lastzug** *m* EISENBAHN trailer train, KFZTECH articulated lorry (BrE), articulated truck (AmE)

Lasur *f* KUNSTSTOFF scumble

Latensifikation *f* FOTO latensification

latent: **~e Ausdehnungswärme** *f* PHYS, THERMOD latent heat of expansion; **~es Bild** *nt* FOTO, OPTIK, PHYS latent image; **~e Kristallisationswärme** *f* PHYS, THERMOD latent heat of solidification; **~e Schmelzwärme** *f* PHYS latent heat of fusion, THERMOD effective latent heat of fusion, latent heat of fusion; **~e Umwandlungswärme** *f* PHYS, THERMOD latent heat of transformation; **~e Verdampfungswärme** *f* PHYS latent heat of evaporation, latent heat of vaporization, THERMOD latent heat of vaporization, latent heat of evaporation; **~e Verdichtungswärme** *f* PHYS, THERMOD latent heat of compression; **~e Wärme** *f* BAU, ERDÖL, HEIZ & KÄLTE, PHYS, THERMOD latent heat; **~e Wärmelast** *f* HEIZ & KÄLTE latent heat load

Latentmodul *nt* METALL latent modulus

Latenzzeit *f* COMP & DV latency, ERGON latency, latency period, OPTIK latency

lateral[1] *adj* ERGON lateral

lateral:[2] **~e Dominanz** *f* ERGON lateral dominance; **~e Hemmung** *f* ERGON lateral inhibition; **~e Plasmaabscheidung** *f* TELEKOM lateral plasma deposition

Lateralität *f* ERGON handedness

Lateralschwerpunkt *m* WASSERTRANS *Schiffkonstruktion* center of lateral resistance (AmE), centre of lateral resistance (BrE)

Lateralsystem *nt* WASSERTRANS lateral system

Lateraltransistor *m* ELEKTRONIK lateral transistor

Laterit *m* BAU *Geologie* laterite

Laterne *f* EISENBAHN lamp

Latex *m* KUNSTSTOFF, TEXTIL latex; **Latexschaum** *m* KUNSTSTOFF latex foam; **Latexuntergrund** *m* TEXTIL latex backing

Latte *f* BAU *Holzbau* lath, MASCHINEN batten; **Lattenholz** *nt* BAU lathwood; **Lattenstift** *m* BAU lath nail; **Lattentasche** *f* WASSERTRANS *Segeln* batten pocket; **Lattenzaun** *m* BAU paling

Laubbaum *m* BAU hardwood

Laubholz *nt* PAPIER hardwood

Laubsäge *f* MASCHINEN scroll saw

Laudanidin *nt* CHEMIE laudanine

Laudaninmethylether *nt* CHEMIE laudanosine

Laudanosin *nt* CHEMIE laudanosine

Laue: **~sches Diagramm** *nt* STRAHLPHYS Laue pattern

Lauf *m* COMP & DV running, MASCHINEN action, operation, running, working, TEXTIL running; **Laufbahn** *f* MASCHINEN runway; **Laufbandflachsauger** *m* PAPIER moving-belt flat box; **Laufboden** *m* FOTO baseboard; **Laufbohrung** *f* FERTIG *Gewehr* barrel bore; **Laufbrett** *nt* BAU duck board, *Gerüst* toeboard; **Laufbrücke** *f* WASSERTRANS flying bridge; **Laufbuchse** *f* EISENBAHN bushing; **Laufbüchse** *f* MASCHINEN bushing; **Laufdecke** *f* KFZTECH *amerikanischer Reifentyp* cover; **Laufeigenschaften** *f pl* FERTIG eccentricity

Laufen *nt* KUNSTSTOFF, PAPIER running

laufen:[1] **~ lassen** *vt* COMP & DV *Programm* run

laufen[2] *vi* COMP & DV *Programm*, MASCHINEN run

laufend: **~er Block** *m* MASCHINEN running block; **~es Gespräch in Vermittlung** *nt* TELEKOM switching call-in-progress; **~es Gut** *nt* WASSERTRANS *Tauwerk* running gear, running rigging; **~e Nummer** *f* FOTO serial number; **~er Text** *m* DRUCK running text; **~e Wartung** *f* HEIZ & KÄLTE routine maintenance

Läufer *m* ELEKTRIZ, ELEKTROTECH, KFZTECH *umlaufender Teil eines Generators* rotor, MASCHINEN traveler (AmE), MATH cursor, MECHAN runner; **~ mit erhöhtem Widerstand** *m* ELEKTRIZ increased resistance rotor; **~ ohne Schleifring** *m* ELEKTROTECH nonwound rotor; **Läuferanlasser** *m* ELEKTRIZ rotor starter; **Läuferbalken** *m* KER & GLAS runner bar; **Läuferbildung** *f* KUNSTSTOFF curtaining, sagging; **Läuferfeld** *nt* ELEKTRIZ rotor field; **Läuferschicht** *f* BAU stretching course; **Läuferstein** *m* BAU stretcher; **Läuferverband** *m* BAU stretching bond, *Mauerwerk* running bond; **Läuferwelle** *f* ELEKTRIZ rotor shaft; **Läuferwicklung** *f* ELEKTROTECH rotor winding

Lauf: **Lauffähigkeit von Papier** *f* PAPIER runnability of paper; **Lauffläche** *f* EISENBAHN running surface, *von Rädern* tread, MASCHINEN face; **Laufgang** *m* EISENBAHN gangway, KERNTECH gallery, gangway, MECHAN catwalk, WASSERTRANS *Schiffbau* alleyway; **Laufgestell** *nt* TRANS bogie (BrE), bogie truck (AmE), trailer (AmE); **Laufgewicht** *nt* MASCHINEN jockey weight, movable weight, slider, sliding weight; **Laufgewichtswaage** *f* METROL Roman steelyard, PHYS steelyard; **Laufkarte** *f* QUAL routing card, traveler (AmE), traveller (BrE); **Laufkatze** *f* BAU traveling winch (AmE), travelling winch (BrE), *eines Krans* crab, FERTIG, KERNTECH, WASSERTRANS traveling crab (AmE), travelling crab (BrE); **Laufkraftwerk** *nt* NICHTFOSS ENERG run-of-river station; **Laufkran** *m* BAU overhead crane, traveling crane (AmE), travelling crane (BrE), MASCHINEN, MECHAN traveling crane (AmE), travelling crane (BrE)

Laufkranz *m* EISENBAHN, LUFTTRANS *Fahrwerk* tread; **Laufkranztrommel** *f* KOHLEN trommel

Lauf: **Lauflänge** *f* TEXTIL yardage; **Laufplanke** *f* WASSERTRANS gangplank

Laufrad *nt* FERTIG *Kunststoffinstallationen*, HEIZ & KÄLTE impeller, KFZTECH *Pumpe* impeller, *einer Turbine* rotor, KOHLEN impeller, MASCHINEN impeller, rotor, runner, running wheel, NICHTFOSS ENERG *Wasserturbine* runner; **Laufradblatt** *nt* HYDRAUL *Kreiselpumpe, Turbine, Wasserrad* runner blade; **Laufradmantel** *m* LUFTTRANS *Motor* chine tire (AmE), chine tyre (BrE); **Laufradschaufel** *f* HYDRAUL runner vane, *Kreiselpumpe, Turbine, Wasserrad* runner blade, MASCHINEN rotor blade

Laufraum *m* ELEKTRONIK *in Laufzeitröhren* drift space; **Laufraumelektrode** *f* ELEKTRONIK drift tunnel

Lauf: **Laufrichtung** *f* DRUCK grain, PAPIER machine direction, making direction; **Laufrille** *f* MASCHINEN ball race, ball ring, groove, MECHAN race; **Laufring** m FERTIG *Lager* raceway; **Laufrinne** f FERTIG *flüssiges Metall* launder; **Laufrolle** f FERTIG guiding roller, MASCHINEN ball race, ball ring, bearing race, runner, WASSERTRANS *Tauwerk* runner; **Laufschaufel** f NICHTFOSS ENERG runner blade; **Laufschicht** f MASCHINEN antifriction layer; **Laufschiene** f EISENBAHN running rail, slide rail, *der Einschienenbahn* monorail, MASCHINEN runner, running rail; **Laufsetzstock** m MASCHINEN traveling steadyrest (AmE), travelling steadyrest (BrE); **Laufsitz** m *(LS)* MASCHINEN running fit; **Laufstatus** m COMP & DV running state; **Laufsteg** m BAU catwalk, MECHAN catwalk, walkway; **Lauftest** m MASCHINEN running test; **Lauftisch** m MASCHINEN traveling table (AmE), travelling table (BrE); **Laufwagenzeichenmaschine** f KONSTZEICH carriage-type drafting machine; **Laufweg** m MECHAN walkway; **Laufwerk** nt AKUSTIK tape deck, COMP & DV disk drive, drive, MASCHINEN carriage; **Laufwerk für beschreibbare CD** nt OPTIK writable optical drive; **Laufwerk für beschreibbare Scheiben** nt OPTIK writable optical disk drive; **Laufwerk für löschbare CD** nt OPTIK erasable optical drive; **Laufwerk für löschbare Scheiben** nt OPTIK erasable disk drive; **Laufwerksschalter** m ELEKTROTECH deck switch; **Laufzapfen** m FERTIG *Walze* journal, MECHAN neck

Laufzeit f COMP & DV propagation, run duration, run time, running duration, running time, ELEKTRONIK *eines Signals* time delay, KER & GLAS running time, TELEKOM *Laufzeitkette* delay, *Signal* time delay; **Laufzeit eines Patents** f PATENT term of patent; **Laufzeitdiode** f ELEKTRONIK transit time diode; **Laufzeitentzerrer** m ELEKTRONIK delay equalizer; **Laufzeiterzeugung** f ELEKTRONIK time delay generation; **Laufzeitfehler** m FERNSEH velocity error; **Laufzeitfilter** nt ELEKTRONIK transit time filter; **Laufzeitfiltern** nt ELEKTRONIK transit time filtering; **Laufzeitgenerator** m ELEKTRONIK delay generator; **Laufzeitgerät** nt ELEKTROTECH transit time device; **Laufzeitkette** f GERÄT delay network, TELEKOM delay circuit; **Laufzeitleistung** f COMP & DV run-time output; **Laufzeitleitung** f ELEKTRONIK delay line; **Laufzeitoszillator** m ELEKTRONIK velocity-modulated oscillator; **Laufzeitröhre** f ELEKTRONIK drift tube, velocity-modulated tube; **Laufzeitschaltung** f ELEKTRONIK time delay circuit; **Laufzeitspeicher** m KERNTECH delay line storage; **Laufzeitstrahl** m ELEKTRONIK velocity-modulated beam; **Laufzeitsystem** nt COMP & DV run-time system; **Laufzeitverzerrung** f AUFNAHME delay distortion, ELEKTRONIK delay distortion, time delay distortion, KONTROLL delay distortion; **Laufzeitverzögerung** f COMP & DV propagation delay

Lauge f CHEMIE alkali, FERTIG lye

laugen vt BAU, CHEMIE, MEERSCHMUTZ leach

Lauge: **Laugenbeständigkeit** f WERKPRÜF *Glas* caustic solution resistance; **Laugenfestigkeit** f KUNSTSTOFF alkali resistance; **Laugenlösung** f CHEMTECH leach liquor; **Laugenmesser** m LEBENSMITTEL alkalimeter; **Laugenmessung** f CHEMIE alkalimetry; **Laugenprüfer** m GERÄT alkaline tester; **Laugensalz** nt CHEMIE alkali; **Laugensprödigkeit** f FERTIG caustic embrittlement

Laugerei f KOHLEN leaching plant

Laugfähigkeit f KOHLEN leachability

Laugflüssigkeit f KOHLEN barren solution

Laugung f KER & GLAS leaching

Laugzeit f KOHLEN leaching time

Laurin- pref CHEMIE lauric

Lauryl- pref CHEMIE lauryl

Laut m AKUSTIK tone; **Lautbildung** f AKUSTIK phonation

läuten vi TELEKOM ring

läutern vt FERTIG wash

Läuterung f CHEMTECH *Flüssigkeiten* purification, KER & GLAS refining; **Läuterungsmittel** nt CHEMTECH purifying agent; **Läuterungszone** f KER & GLAS refining zone

Lautheit f PHYS *Stärke der Lautempfindung* loudness; **Lautheitsdrosselung** f AKUSTIK partial masked loudness

Lauthören nt TELEKOM open listening

Läutprobe f ELEKTRIZ ringing test

Lautsprecher m AKUSTIK loudspeaker, AUFNAHME loudspeaker, *mit unendlicher Resonanzwand* infinite-baffle loudspeaker, ELEKTRIZ, PHYS loudspeaker, RADIO loudspeaker, speaker, TELEKOM loudspeaker; **~ mit Richtwirkung** m AKUSTIK directional loudspeaker; **Lautsprecherdämpfung** f AUFNAHME loudspeaker damping; **Lautsprechergehäuse** nt AUFNAHME loudspeaker enclosure, loudspeaker housing; **Lautsprecherkombination** f AUFNAHME composite loudspeaker; **Lautsprechersäule** f AUFNAHME column loudspeaker; **Lautsprechersystem** nt AKUSTIK, AUFNAHME loudspeaker system; **Lautsprechertrichter** m AUFNAHME loudspeaker cone, loudspeaker horn; **Lautsprecherwand** f AKUSTIK loudspeaker baffle

Lautstärke f AKUSTIK loudness level, volume, AKUSTIK *(L)* loudness *(L)*, AUFNAHME loudness level, loudness, volume, COMP & DV volume, ERGON loudness, sound intensity, PHYS loudness level; **~ der Sprache** f AKUSTIK volume speech; **Lautstärkeanzeige** f AUFNAHME volume indicator; **Lautstärkebereich** m AUFNAHME dynamic range; **Lautstärkeempfindung** f AKUSTIK loudness; **Lautstärkeentzerrer** m AUFNAHME volume equalizer; **Lautstärkefunktion** f AUFNAHME loudness function; **Lautstärkekurve** f AKUSTIK loudness function; **Lautstärkemesser** m AKUSTIK loudness meter, sound level meter; **Lautstärkemeßgerät** nt GERÄT volume meter; **Lautstärkemuster** nt AUFNAHME loudness pattern; **Lautstärkenbereich** m AKUSTIK volume range; **Lautstärkepegel** m AKUSTIK, ERGON loudness level; **Lautstärkeregler** m AUFNAHME volume control; **Lautstärkeumfang** m AKUSTIK dynamic range; **Lautstärkeunterschiedsschwelle** f AKUSTIK differential threshold of sound pressure level

lauwarm adj THERMOD tepid

Lavagestein nt NICHTFOSS ENERG extrusive rocks

Lavalier-Mikrofon nt AUFNAHME Lavalier microphone

Lävan nt CHEMIE levan

Lavendelkopie f FOTO lavender print

Lävulin nt CHEMIE levulin, synanthrose; **Lävulin-** pref CHEMIE levulinic

Lävulosan nt CHEMIE fructosan, levulosan

Lävulose f CHEMIE fructose, levulose, LEBENSMITTEL laevulose (BrE), levulose (AmE)

Lawine f ELEKTROTECH avalanche; **Lawinendiode** f ELEKTRONIK, PHYS avalanche diode; **Lawinendurchbruch** m ELEKTRIZ, ELEKTRONIK *Mikroelektronik* avalanche breakdown; **Lawinendurchbruchspannung** f ELEKTRIZ avalanche voltage; **Lawinenfotodiode** f ELEKTRONIK, OPTIK avalanche photodiode; **Lawinenlaufzeitdiode** f *(Impatt-Diode)* ELEKTRONIK, PHYS, RADIO impact ionization avalanche transit-time diode *(impatt diode)*; **Lawinenverstärkung** f ELEKTRONIK avalanche gain

Lawson nt CHEMIE lawsone

Layout nt COMP & DV zweidimensionale Darstellung eines Teils, DRUCK, VERPACK layout

Lazarettschiff nt WASSERTRANS Marine hospital ship

LB abbr COMP & DV (Ortsbatterie), ELEKTROTECH (lokale Batterie) LB (local battery)

L-Band nt ELEKTRONIK 390-1550 MHz, RAUMFAHRT Weltraumfunk, WASSERTRANS Satellitenfunk L-band

LC abbr (Flüssigkristall) COMP & DV, ELEKTRIZ LC (liquid crystal)

LCD[1] abbr (Flüssigkristallanzeige) COMP & DV, ELEKTRIZ, ELEKTRONIK, FERNSEH, LABOR, TELEKOM, THERMOD LCD (liquid crystal display)

LCD:[2] **LCD-Anzeigetafel** f ELEKTRONIK LCD panel; **LCD-Modul** nt ELEKTRONIK LCD module

LC-Filter nt ELEKTRONIK, RADIO LC filter

LD-Beiwert m (Gleit und Widerstandsbeiwert) LUFTTRANS Nutzeffekt des Luftfahrzeugs LD ratio (lift and drag ratio)

LD$_{50}$ abbr (mittlere letale Dosis) STRAHLPHYS LD$_{50}$ (median lethal dose)

L-Dock nt TRANS offshore dock

Leak: ~ **in der Rohrleitung** nt WASSERVERSORG piping seepage

LEAR abbr (Antiprotonenring mit geringer Energie) TEILPHYS LEAR (Low-Energy Antiproton Ring)

lebend: ~**er Kolumnentitel** m DRUCK running head, running title; ~**es Werk** nt WASSERTRANS Schiffkonstruktion quickwork

Lebendmasse f NICHTFOSS ENERG biomass

Lebensdauer f ANSTRICH Mehrkomponentenlacken pot life, ELEKTROTECH lifetime, FERTIG fatigue life, Kunststoffinstallationen service life, KERNTECH eines Nutzgerätes service life, KOHLEN service life, MASCHINEN life cycle, working life, TELEKOM lifetime; ~ **der Atmosphäre** f UMWELTSCHMUTZ atmospheric lifetime; ~ **der Batterie-Schwebespannung** f ELEKTROTECH Akkumulatoren float life; ~ **des Brennstoffes im Reaktorkern** f KERNTECH in-core fuel life; ~ **bei Gebrauch** f FOTO Lösung working life; ~ **des Minoritätsträgers** f ELEKTRONIK versenkter Kanal, Transistortechnik bulk lifetime; **Lebensdauererwartung** f TELEKOM lifetime expectancy; **Lebensdauerprüfmenge** f QUAL life test quantity; **Lebensdauerprüfung** f ELEKTROTECH life test, METROL endurance test, QUAL life test; **Lebensdauerschmierung** f MASCHINEN for-life lubrication, lifetime lubrication; **Lebensdauerschmierung: mit ~** f HEIZ & KÄLTE sealed for life; **Lebensdauerschnelltest** m WERKPRÜF accelerated life test

Lebenserhaltungsgerät nt RAUMFAHRT Raumschiff environmental control system

Lebenserwartung f BAU, TELEKOM life expectancy

lebensfähig: ~**e Bakterien** nt pl WASSERVERSORG viable bacteria

Lebensgemeinschaft f UMWELTSCHMUTZ living community

Lebensmittel: nicht für ~ geeignete Verpackung f VERPACK nonfood packaging; **Lebensmittelbedarf** m LEBENSMITTEL food requirements; **Lebensmittelbestrahlung** f VERPACK irradiation of food; **Lebensmittelchemie** f LEBENSMITTEL food chemistry; **Lebensmittelfarbstoff** m LEBENSMITTEL food color (AmE), food colour (BrE)

lebensmittelgerecht: ~**e Frischhaltefolienverpackung** f VERPACK food-grade packaging film

Lebensmittel: Lebensmittelknappheit f LEBENSMITTEL food shortage; **Lebensmittelüberschuß** m LEBENSMITTEL food surplus; **Lebensmittelüberwachung** f LEBENSMITTEL food inspection; **Lebensmittelverarbeitungsanlage** f LEBENSMITTEL food-processing plant; **Lebensmittelvergiftung** f LEBENSMITTEL food poisoning; **Lebensmittelverpackung** f VERPACK food packaging; **Lebensmittelverpackungsmaschinen** f pl VERPACK food-wrapping machinery; **Lebensmittelwissenschaft** f LEBENSMITTEL food science; **Lebensmittelzusatzstoff** m LEBENSMITTEL food additive

Lebensraum: ~ **im Wasser** m WASSERVERSORG aquatic system

Lebensrettungsgerät nt SICHERHEIT life-saving apparatus

Lebensrettungskurs m SICHERHEIT course of training for rescue work

Leberstärke f LEBENSMITTEL animal starch, glycogen

lebhaft adj TEXTIL Farbe bright

Leblanc: ~**sche Schaltung** f ELEKTRIZ Leblanc connection

Lecherleitung f RADIO Lecher line

Lecithin nt LEBENSMITTEL lecithin

Leck[1] nt ELEKTRIZ, KER & GLAS leak, NICHTFOSS ENERG leak, leakage, PHYS, SICHERHEIT, WASSERTRANS leak

Leck:[2] **ein ~ stopfen** vi WASSERTRANS plug a leak, WASSERVERSORG stop a leak

leck[1] adj WASSERTRANS leaky

leck:[2] ~ **werden** vi WASSERTRANS Schiff make water

Leckage f CHEMIE, LEBENSMITTEL bei Behältern ullage, MEERSCHMUTZ, NICHTFOSS ENERG, WASSERVERSORG leakage

Leck: Leckalarm m SICHERHEIT leakage warning; **Leckauffanggefäß** nt KERNTECH leakage interception vessel; **Leckbestimmung** f ABFALL leak detection

leckdicht adj MECHAN leak-tight

Leckdichtheit f KERNTECH des Druckgefäßes leak tightness

Leckdruck m ERDÖL Bohrtechnik leak-off pressure

lecken vi BAU, SICHERHEIT, WASSERTRANS leak

Leck: Leckfeld nt ELEKTRIZ stray field; **Leckgeschwindigkeit** f KERNTECH leak rate; **Leckluftlüfter** m HEIZ & KÄLTE make-up fan; **Leckmesser** m ELEKTRIZ leakage meter; **Leckmeßgerät** nt ELEKTRIZ leakage meter; **Leckmodus** m TELEKOM leaky mode, tunneling mode (AmE), tunnelling mode (BrE); **Leckortungsgerät** nt HEIZ & KÄLTE leak detector; **Leckrate** f KERNTECH leak rate; **Lecksicherung** f WASSERTRANS damage control; **Leckspürgerät** nt GERÄT leak detector; **Leckstrahl** m TELEKOM leaky ray, tunnelling ray (BrE); **Leckstrom** m ELEKTRIZ leakage current, leakage, ELEKTROTECH, TELEKOM leakage current; **Leckstromkorrosion** f ELEKTROTECH stray current corrosion; **Lecksucher** m GERÄT, VERPACK leak detector; **Lecksuchgerät** nt HEIZ & KÄLTE leak detector; **Leckverlust** m ELEKTRIZ leakage loss; **Leckwarnsystem** nt SICHERHEIT leakage indicator system; **Leckwasserpumpe** f KERNTECH leakage water pump; **Leckweg** m ELEKTRIZ leakage path; **Leckwiderstand** m PHYS leakage resistance

Leclanché-Element nt ELEKTRIZ, ELEKTROTECH, LABOR Leclanché cell

LED abbr (Leuchtdiode, Lumineszenzdiode, lichtmittierende Diode) COMP & DV, ELEKTRIZ, ELEKTRONIK, FERNSEH, OPTIK, PHYS, TELEKOM LED (light-emitting *diode)*

Ledeburit *m* METALL ledeburite

Leder *nt* FOTO, TEXTIL leather; **Lederbalgen** *m* FOTO leather bellows; **Lederdichtungsscheibe** *f* FERTIG leather gasket; **Lederetui** *nt* FOTO leather case; **Lederfutteral** *nt* FOTO leather case; **Lederhobel** *m* BAU spokeshave; **Ledermanschette** *f* FERTIG leather packing; **Ledermanschettendichtung** *f* FERTIG leather cup; **Lederschürze** *f* SICHERHEIT leather apron; **Lederstulpenhandschuh** *m* SICHERHEIT leather gauntlet glove; **Ledertreibriemen** *m* FERTIG, MASCHINEN leather belt

Lee *f* WASSERTRANS lee

Leeküste *f* WASSERTRANS lee shore

leer[1] *adj* COMP & DV blank

leer:[2] **~e Anweisung** *f* COMP & DV dummy instruction, null instruction; **~es Band** *nt* PHYS *Festkörperphysik* empty band; **~er Bereich** *m* COMP & DV sparse array; **~er Datenträger** *m* COMP & DV blank medium, empty medium; **~es Magnetband** *nt* FERNSEH blank magnetic tape; **~e Menge** *f* MATH empty set; **~es Schriftelement** *nt* COMP & DV empty font; **~e Zeichenfolge** *f* COMP & DV null string

leer:[3] **~e Kamera bedienen** *vi* FOTO *Auslöser-Test* operate empty camera

Leerbefehl *m* COMP & DV do-nothing instruction

Leeren *nt* METALL exhaustion

leeren *vt* TRANS dump

Leerfahrt: auf ~ *f* EISENBAHN, WASSERTRANS running light

Leerfracht *f* ERDÖL *Schiffahrt* dead freight

Leergewicht *nt* KFZTECH unladen weight, MECHAN dead weight

Leergut *nt* VERPACK empties

Leerhub *m* MASCHINEN idle stroke

Leerkarte *f* WASSERTRANS *Navigation* plotting chart, plotting sheet

Leerlauf:[1] **im ~** *adj* MASCHINEN on no load

Leerlauf[2] *m* FERTIG free motion, loafing, KFZTECH *Motor* idling, MASCHINEN idle speed, no-load operation, MECHAN idler; **Leerlauf-** *pref* FERTIG no-load

Leerlauf:[3] **im ~ fahren** *vi* KFZTECH coast; **im ~ laufen** *vi* KFZTECH *Motor* idle

Leerlaufbetrieb *m* ELEKTRIZ open circuit operation, KONTROLL idle mode, LUFTTRANS no-load operation; **Leerlaufbetriebszustand beim Anflug** *m* LUFTTRANS approach idling conditions

Leerlauf: Leerlaufcharakteristik *f* LUFTTRANS no-load characteristic; **Leerlaufdrehzahl** *f* MECHAN idling speed; **Leerlaufdrosselanschlag** *m* LUFTTRANS idle throttle stop; **Leerlaufdüse** *f* KFZTECH *Vergaser* idle jet; **Leerlaufeigenschaften** *f pl* ELEKTRIZ open circuit characteristics

leerlaufen[1] *vt* FERTIG loaf

leerlaufen[2] *vi* FERTIG idle, MASCHINEN run light, run on no load, MECHAN idle, WASSERVERSORG drain

Leerlaufen *nt* MASCHINEN running light, running on no load

leerlaufend *adj* ELEKTRIZ idling, MASCHINEN light-running

Leerlauf: Leerlaufenergie *f* THERMOD waste energy; **Leerlaufgleichspannung** *f* ELEKTROTECH floating potential; **Leerlaufimpedanz** *f* AKUSTIK blocked electrical impedance, ELEKTRIZ open circuit impedance, ELEKTROTECH blocked impedance, open circuit impedance; **Leerlaufkomponente** *f* ELEKTRIZ idle component; **Leerlaufladung** *f* ELEKTROTECH floating charge; **Leerlaufleistung** *f* MASCHINEN idle power, idling power; **Leerlaufmodus** *m* KONTROLL idle mode; **Leerlaufprüfung** *f* ELEKTRIZ open circuit test; **Leerlaufrolle** *f* FERTIG idler; **Leerlaufschaltung** *f* KOHLEN open circuit; **Leerlaufscheinwiderstand** *m* ELEKTROTECH open circuit impedance; **Leerlaufspannung** *f* ELEKTRIZ, ELEKTROTECH, NICHTFOSS ENERG open circuit voltage; **Leerlaufstellschraube** *f* KFZTECH *Vergaser* idle adjustment screw; **Leerlaufstellung** *f* KFZTECH neutral position, *Getriebe* neutral; **Leerlaufstrom** *m* COMP & DV *Datenverarbeitung* idle current, ELEKTRIZ idle current, open circuit current; **Leerlaufwiderstand** *m* ELEKTROTECH open circuit impedance; **Leerlaufzeit** *f* COMP & DV idle time; **Leerlaufzustand** *m* COMP & DV idle condition, ELEKTROTECH open circuit

Leerliste *f* COMP & DV empty list

Leerlokomotive *f* EISENBAHN light engine, light locomotive

leerpumpen *vt* WASSERVERSORG pump out

Leerraumkoeffizient *m* KERNTECH *der Reaktivität* void coefficient

Leerrückfahrt *f* TRANS deadhead

Leerschein *m* VERPACK blank ticket

Leerschritt *m* COMP & DV blank

Leerstelle *f* COMP & DV blank, space, PHYS vacancy; **Leerstellendiffusion** *f* METALL vacancy diffusion; **Leerstellenwanderung** *f* METALL vacancy migration

Leerstring *m* COMP & DV empty string

Leertaste *f* COMP & DV blank key, space bar

Leertrum *nt* FERTIG *Kette* nondriving free length

Leeruder *nt* WASSERTRANS lee helm

Leerwagensammelgleis *nt* EISENBAHN empties siding

Leerzeichen *nt* COMP & DV idle character, space, space character; **Leerzeicheneinfügung** *f* COMP & DV idle insertion

Leerzeile *f* COMP & DV null line

leewärtig *adj* WASSERTRANS leeward

leewärts *adv* WASSERTRANS alee, leeward

Legel *m* WASSERTRANS *Segeln* cringle

legen[1] *vt* TELEKOM lay

legen:[2] **sich ~** *v refl* WASSERTRANS *Wind* drop

Legende *f* FERTIG *Kunststoffinstallationen* key

Legendre-Polynom *nt* PHYS Legendre polynomial

Legerwall *m* WASSERTRANS lee shore

legierbar *adj* FERTIG *Metall* alloyable

Legierbarkeit *f* FERTIG *Metall* alloyability

Legieren *nt* METALL alloyage, alloying

legieren *vt* FERTIG *Stahl*, METALL alloy

legiert: ~e Diode *f* ELEKTRONIK *Mikroelektronik* alloy diode; **~er Grauguß** *m* FERTIG alloy cast iron; **~es Karbid** *nt* METALL alloy carbide; **~er Stahl** *m* FERTIG alloy steel, KOHLEN alloyed steel, METALL alloy steel; **~er Übergang** *m* ELEKTRONIK *Halbleiter* alloy junction; **~er Zonenübergang** *m* ELEKTRONIK *Halbleiter* alloyed junction

Legierung *f* ANSTRICH alloy, METALL alloyage, alloying, alloy, PAPIER alloy; **~ für das Weichlöten** *f* MASCHINEN soft solder alloy; **Legierungsbestandteil** *m* FERTIG alloy component; **Legierungsgehalt** *m* FERTIG alloy content; **Legierungsgrundgefüge** *nt* FERTIG alloy matrix; **Legierungsmetall** *nt* KOHLEN steel alloy; **Legierungsmethode** *f* ELEKTRONIK alloying method; **Legierungsplattierschicht** *f* FERTIG alloy cladding; **Legierungstransistor** *m* ELEKTRONIK *Mikroelektronik* alloyed junction transistor; **Legierungszusatz** *m* FERTIG alloy addition

Leguminose *f* LEBENSMITTEL legume
Lehm *m* BAU, FERTIG loam, HYDRAUL pug, KOHLEN clay, WASSERVERSORG loam; **Lehmbaustein** *m* BAU sundried brick; **Lehmform** *f* FERTIG loam mold (AmE), loam mould (BrE); **Lehmgehalt** *m* KOHLEN clay content; **Lehmmörtel** *m* KER & GLAS clay mortar; **Lehmwall** *m* ABFALL clay barrier
Lehrdorn *m* MASCHINEN, METROL plug gage (AmE), plug gauge (BrE)
Lehre[1] *f* ELEKTRIZ gage (AmE), gauge (BrE), ERDÖL template, templet, FERTIG, GERÄT, KFZTECH *Werkzeug* gage (AmE), gauge (BrE); **~ von den Kegelschnitten** *f* GEOM conics; **~ der Weltentstehung** *f* RAUMFAHRT cosmology
Lehre:[2] **mit ~ messen** *vt* MASCHINEN gage (AmE), gauge (BrE)
Lehrenbohren *nt* FERTIG, MASCHINEN jig boring
lehrenbohren *vt* FERTIG jig-bore
Lehrenbohrgerät *nt* MASCHINEN jig boring tool
Lehrenbohrmaschine *f* MASCHINEN jig borer, jig boring machine, MECHAN jig borer
Lehrenbohrwerk *nt* FERTIG jig borer
Lehrenform *f* FERTIG template, templet
Lehrenschleifen *nt* MASCHINEN jig grinding
Lehrenschleifmaschine *f* MASCHINEN jig grinder
Lehrgerüst *nt* BAU *eines Mauerwerksbogens* center (AmE), centre (BrE)
Lehrrad *nt* FERTIG gear master
Lehrring *m* MASCHINEN female gage (AmE), female gauge (BrE), ring gage (AmE), ring gauge (BrE), METROL ring gage (AmE), ring gauge (BrE)
Lehrsatz *m* MATH, PHYS theorem; **~ von Pythagoras** *m* GEOM, MATH Pythagorean theorem
Leibung *f* BAU *Fenster, Tür* jamb, reveal
Leiche *f* DRUCK *jargon* out; **Leichengift** *nt* CHEMIE ptomaine
leicht[1] *adj* MECHAN lightweight; **~ entflammbar** *adj* THERMOD flammable, inflammable; **~ salzig** *adj* LEBENSMITTEL brackish; **~ schmelzbar** *adj* THERMOD fusible
leicht:[2] **~ angereicherter Halbleiter** *m* ELEKTRONIK lightly-doped semiconductor; **~e Bearbeitbarkeit** *f* MECHAN ease of machining; **~e Behandelbarkeit** *f* MECHAN ease of machining; **~er Beobachtungshubschrauber** *m* LUFTTRANS light observation helicopter; **~e Bespulung** *f* ELEKTROTECH *Pupinisierung des Kabels* light loading; **~ entflammbare Flüssigkeit** *f* SICHERHEIT highly inflammable liquid; **~es Erdöl** *nt* ERDÖL light crude oil; **~e Fraktionen** *f* ERDÖL light fractions; **~es Gewebe** *nt* TEXTIL lightweight fabric; **~es Heizöl** *nt* ERDÖL *Destillationsprodukt* domestic fuel oil; **~e Kohlenwasserstofffraktionen** *f pl* ERDÖL light hydrocarbon fractions; **~er Mehrzweckhubschrauber** *m* LUFTTRANS light multirole helicopter; **~er Nebel** *m* UMWELTSCHMUTZ mist; **~es Rohöl** *nt* ERDÖL light crude oil; **~e Schnitte** *m pl* ERDÖL light fractions; **~e Schweißnaht** *f* KERNTECH concave weld, light weld; **~es spurgeführtes Transportsystem** *nt* EISENBAHN light guideway transit system; **~e Strahlung** *f* KERNTECH light radiation; **~e Wartung** *f* MECHAN ease of maintenance; **~es Wasser** *nt* KERNTECH ordinary water; **~er Wind** *m* WASSERTRANS light airs
Leichtanschlußsteckverbinder *m* ELEKTROTECH low-insertion-force connector
Leichtbauschnelltriebzug *m* EISENBAHN LRC, light-rapid-comfortable

Leichtbenzin *nt* ERDÖL *Destillationsprodukt* light distillates, KFZTECH light gasoline (AmE), light petrol (BrE)
Leichtbeton *m* BAU lightweight concrete
Leichter *m* MEERSCHMUTZ lighter, WASSERTRANS *Schifftyp* barge, *Schiff* lighter; **~ ohne Eigenantrieb** *m* WASSERTRANS dumb barge; **Leichterführer** *m* WASSERTRANS bargee (BrE), bargeman (AmE), lighterman; **Leichtergeld** *nt* WASSERTRANS *Handel* lighterage, lighterage charges
Leichtern *nt* MEERSCHMUTZ *Ölabgabe von Schiff zu Schiff* lightening
Leichter: **Leichterschiff** *nt* TRANS lighter carrier; **Leichterträgerschiff** *nt* *(LASH-Schiff)* WASSERTRANS *Schiff mit Schlepper an Bord* lighter aboard ship carrier *(LASH carrier)*; **Leichtertransport** *m* WASSERTRANS *Handel* lighterage; **Leichtertransporter** *m* *(LASH-Schiff)* WASSERTRANS *Schiff* lighter aboard ship carrier *(LASH carrier)*
Leichtfaß *nt* KERNTECH *aus faserverstärktem Kunststoff* fiber drum (AmE), fibre drum (BrE), VERPACK fiber drum (AmE), fibre drum (BrE), plywood drum
Leichtflintglas *nt* KER & GLAS light flint
Leichtgewichtwabenkonstruktion *f* VERPACK lightweight honeycomb structure
Leichtkolben *m* KFZTECH full slipper piston
Leichtkraftrad *nt* KFZTECH *mit Tretanlasser* light motorcycle
Leichtkronglas *nt* KER & GLAS light crown
Leichtmatrose *m* WASSERTRANS *Besatzung* ordinary seaman
Leichtmesonenspektrum *nt* STRAHLPHYS light meson spectrum
Leichtmetall *nt* METALL light alloy; **Leichtmetallegierung** *f* MECHAN light alloy; **Leichtmetallguß** *m* FERTIG *Kunststoffinstallationen* light metal casting
Leichtplatten *f pl* KER & GLAS light panels
leichtwassergekühlt: **~er Hybridreaktor** *m* KERNTECH LWHR, light water hybrid reactor; **~er Reaktor** *m* KERNTECH light water-cooled reactor
Leichtwasserlinie *f* WASSERTRANS light waterline
Leim *m* CHEMIE *Papier* sizing agent, DRUCK glue, size, FERTIG size, KUNSTSTOFF glue, PAPIER glue, size, TEXTIL, VERPACK glue; **Leimauftragmaschine** *f* VERPACK glue spreading machine, glue-gumming machine, gluing machine
Leimen *nt* DRUCK gluing up
leimen *vt* BAU, PAPIER glue
Leim: **Leimfarbe** *f* BAU, KUNSTSTOFF distemper; **Leimfuge** *f* KUNSTSTOFF glue line; **Leimgewebe** *nt* LEBENSMITTEL collagen; **Leimmattierung** *f* KER & GLAS glue-etching; **Leimpresse** *f* PAPIER size press
Leimung *f* PAPIER gluing, sizing; **Leimungsprüfer** *m* PAPIER *Gerät zur Überprüfung des Leimungsgrades von Papier* sizing tester
Leim: **Leimwalze** *f* PAPIER size roll; **Leimzwinge** *f* VERPACK glue press
Leine[1] *f* WASSERTRANS *Tauwerk* line
Leine:[2] **~ werfen** *vi* WASSERTRANS *Tauwerk* throw a line
Leinen *nt* DRUCK, TEXTIL linen; **Leinenkanevas** *m* TEXTIL canvas; **Leinenkleidung** *f* TEXTIL linen clothing; **Leinenschießgerät** *nt* WASSERTRANS line thrower
Leinöl *nt* BAU, WASSERTRANS linseed oil; **Leinölfirnis** *m* CHEMIE boiled linseed oil
Leinsaatöl *nt* CHEMIE linseed oil
Leinwandbindung *f* PAPIER, TEXTIL plain weave

L-Eisen *nt* BAU angle bar, METALL L-iron
Leiste *f* BAU batten, *Holz* strip, DRUCK border, FERTIG tongue, MASCHINEN ledge; **Leistenhobelmaschine** *f* BAU *Holzbau* molding machine (AmE), moulding machine (BrE)
Leistung *f* COMP & DV performance, ELEKTRIZ *Maschine* capacitance, capacity, ELEKTRIZ *(P)* power *(P)*, ELEKTROTECH power, ERDÖL *Kapazität einer Bohrung* capacity, FERTIG *Kunststoffinstallationen* performance, HEIZ & KÄLTE capacitance, capacity, KERNTECH output, KFZTECH power, KONTROLL performance, MASCHINEN performance, power, throughput (BrE), thruput (AmE), MECHAN effect, power, OPTIK, RADIO, TELEKOM *elektrisch* power; ~ **ohne Last** *f* KERNTECH no-load force; ~ **pro Flächeneinheit** *f* RAUMFAHRT *Raumschiff* power per unit area; ~ **in Schwachlastzeit** *f* KERNTECH off-peak power; ~ **des Turbogenerators** *f* KERNTECH thermal steam generator output; ~ **bei Wasserkühlung** *f* HEIZ & KÄLTE water-cooled rating; **Leistungsabfall** *m* TELEKOM attenuation; **Leistungsabgabe** *f* ELEKTROTECH power output, MASCHINEN output, power output, NICHTFOSS ENERG power output; **Leistungsaggregat** *nt* ELEKTROTECH power pack; **Leistungsanforderungen** *f pl* MASCHINEN performance specification; **Leistungsangabe** *f* ELEKTROTECH power rating; **Leistungsangabe eines radioaktiven Präparats** *f* KERNTECH nameplate source strength; **Leistungsaufnahme** *f* AUFNAHME power-handling capacity, ELEKTROTECH power consumption, power input, HEIZ & KÄLTE power input; **Leistungsbandbreite** *f* ELEKTRONIK power bandwidth; **Leistungsbegrenzer** *m* MASCHINEN power limiter; **Leistungsbelastung** *f* METROL power loading; **Leistungsbereich** *m* MASCHINEN performance range, power range; **Leistungsbilanz** *f* ELEKTRIZ energy balance; **Leistungsbilanz einer Übertragungsstrecke** *f* TELEKOM link power budget; **Leistungsdaten** *nt pl* TELEKOM performance data; **Leistungsdiagramm** *nt* PHYS indicator diagram; **Leistungsdichte** *f* KERNTECH, NICHTFOSS ENERG, TELEKOM *Antenne* power density; **Leistungsdiode** *f* ELEKTRONIK power diode; **Leistungsdrahtwiderstand** *m* ELEKTROTECH power wirewound resistor; **Leistungseinbruch** *m* KERNTECH trip; **Leistungselektronik** *f* ELEKTRIZ power electronics; **Leistungserhöhung** *f* ELEKTRONIK power amplification
leistungsfähig *adj* PHYS efficient
Leistungsfähigkeit *f* BAU capacitance, capacity, ELEKTROTECH, ERGON capacity, KERNTECH *eines Kraftwerkes* canyon
Leistung: **Leistungsfaktor** *m* ELEKTRIZ, ELEKTROTECH, KUNSTSTOFF, PHYS power factor; **Leistungsfernmeßgerät** *nt* GERÄT telewattmeter; **Leistungsflußdichte** *f* RAUMFAHRT *Raumschiff* power flux density; **Leistungsflußrichtungsrelais** *nt* ELEKTRIZ power directional relay; **Leistungsganglinie** *f* ELEKTRIZ load characteristic; **Leistungsgenerator** *m* ELEKTRONIK power oscillator; **Leistungsgrad** *m* AUFNAHME *Verstärker* power efficiency; **Leistungsgröße** *f* ERGON performance variable; **Leistungskabel** *nt* ELEKTRIZ power cable; **Leistungskennlinien** *f pl* HEIZ & KÄLTE performance characteristics, performance curves; **Leistungskoeffizient** *m* NICHTFOSS ENERG power coefficient; **Leistungskoeffizient der Reaktivität** *m* KERNTECH reactivity power coefficient; **Leistungskomponente** *f* ELEKTRIZ active component;

Leistungskondensator *m* ELEKTRIZ, ELEKTROTECH power capacitor; **Leistungskoppler** *m* RADIO power combiner; **Leistungskurve** *f* MASCHINEN performance curve, NICHTFOSS ENERG power curve; **Leistungsleitungen** *f pl* ELEKTROTECH load leads; **Leistungsmerkmal** *nt* FERNSEH rating, TELEKOM facility; **Leistungsmesser** *m* ELEKTROTECH demand meter; **Leistungsmeßgerät** *nt* ELEKTRIZ active energy meter, GERÄT power-measuring instrument, PHYS wattmeter; **Leistungsminderung** *f* ERGON disability; **Leistungsprüfung** *f* ELEKTRIZ, MASCHINEN performance test; **Leistungsquelle** *f* ELEKTROTECH power source; **Leistungsrate** *f* COMP & DV yield; **Leistungsreaktor** *m* KERNTECH power reactor; **Leistungsregler** *m* ELEKTROTECH gov-ernor, RAUMFAHRT *Raumschiff* power conditioning unit; **Leistungsrelais** *nt* ELEKTROTECH power relay; **Leistungsröhre** *f* ELEKTRONIK power tube; **Leistungsschalter** *m* ELEKTROTECH circuit breaker, switch; **Leistungsschalter mit Minimalauslösung** *m* ELEKTROTECH minimum circuit breaker; **Leistungsschreiber** *m* GERÄT power recorder; **Leistungsspektrum** *nt* ELEKTROTECH, ERGON power spectrum; **Leistungsspektrumsdichte** *f* RAUMFAHRT *Weltraumfunk* power spectral density; **Leistungsspitze** *f* ELEKTROTECH power surge; **Leistungsstufe** *f* MASCHINEN power stage; **Leistungsteiler** *m* ELEKTRIZ, ELEKTROTECH, TELEKOM power divider; **Leistungsthyristor** *m* TELEKOM power thyristor; **Leistungstransformator** *m* ELEKTROTECH power transformer; **Leistungstransistor** *m* ELEKTRONIK power transistor; **Leistungsübertragung** *f* ELEKTROTECH power transmission; **Leistungsübertragungsfaktor** *m* AKUSTIK response to power; **Leistungsumschalttransistor** *m* ELEKTRONIK power-switching transistor; **Leistungsumsetzer** *m* ELEKTROTECH power converter; **Leistungsverbrauch** *m* ELEKTRIZ, ELEKTROTECH power consumption; **Leistungsverhalten** *nt* MASCHINEN performance properties; **Leistungsverlust** *m* ELEKTROTECH power loss, MASCHINEN loss of power, TELEKOM attenuation; **Leistungsvermögen** *nt* COMP & DV capacity, KERNTECH *eines Kraftwerkes* canyon, *einer Anlage* unit capacity; **Leistungsversorgung** *f* ELEKTROTECH power supply; **Leistungsversorgunseinrichtung** *f* MASCHINEN engine lathe; **Leistungsverstärker** *m* AUFNAHME *(PA)*, ELEKTRONIK *(PA)*, ELEKTROTECH *(PA)* power amplifier *(PA)*, KFZTECH power booster, PHYS *(PA)*, RADIO *(PA)*, RAUMFAHRT *(PA) Weltraumfunk*, TELEKOM *(PA)* power amplifier *(PA)*; **Leistungsverstärker mit hohem Verstärkungsgrad** *m* ELEKTRONIK high-gain power amplifier; **Leistungsverstärkerröhre** *f* ELEKTRONIK power amplifier tube; **Leistungsverstärkertransistor** *m* ELEKTRONIK power amplifier transistor; **Leistungsverstärkung** *f* AUFNAHME power gain, ELEKTRONIK power amplification, power gain, PHYS power gain; **Leistungsverzeichnis** *nt* BAU specifications; **Leistungswandler** *m* ELEKTROTECH power converter
Leit- *pref* COMP & DV master; **Leit- und Zugspindeldrehmaschine** *f* MASCHINEN engine lathe; **Leitartikel** *m* DRUCK lead; **Leitbefehl** *m* COMP & DV routing directive; **Leitblatt** *nt* HYDRAUL guide blade, *Turbine, Kreiselpumpe* stationary blade
Leitblech[1] *nt* BAU baffle, CHEMTECH baffle plate, FERTIG baffle plate, deflector, HEIZ & KÄLTE baffle plate, MASCHINEN baffle, deflector plate; **Leitblechring** *m* ERDÖL baffle ring

Leitblech:[2] **mit ~ versehen** *vt* FERTIG baffle
Leit-: Leitblock *m* WASSERTRANS *Beschläge* lead block,
leading block; **Leitdaten** *nt pl* COMP & DV master data;
Leiteinrichtung *f* MASCHINEN guide
leiten *vt* BAU carry
leitend[1] *adj* ANSTRICH conducting, conductive, ELEK-
TRIZ conductible, conducting, conductive; **nicht ~** *adj*
CHEMIE dielectric, ELEKTROTECH nonconductive
leitend:[2] **~e Abschirmung** *f* ELEKTRIZ conducting screen,
conductor screen; **~er Auditor** *m* QUAL lead auditor;
~er Offizier *m* WASSERTRANS *Handelsmarine, Besatzung* chief mate; **nicht ~er Zustand** *m* ELEKTROTECH
nonconducting state
Leiter[1] *m* ELEKTRIZ conductor, ELEKTROTECH conductor, wire, *bei Glasfaserkabel* core, *eines elektrischen
Kabels* core, ERDÖL *für Wärme, Kälte, Elektrizität,*
PHYS conductor, SICHERHEIT safety ladder, TELEKOM
conductor; **~ für hohe Stromstärken** *m* ELEKTRIZ ampere conductor; **Leiteraddierer** *m* ELEKTRONIK ladder
adder; **Leiterbagger** *m* WASSERTRANS *Baggern* ladder
dredge, ladder dredger; **Leiterbündel** *nt* ELEKTRIZ
bunched conductor (BrE), bundled conductor
(AmE); **Leiter-Leiter-Spannung** *f* ELEKTRIZ line-to-
line voltage
Leiterplatte[1] **auf der ~** *adj* ELEKTRONIK on board
Leiterplatte:[2] **nicht auf der ~** *adv* ELEKTRONIK off-board
Leiterplatte[3] *f* COMP & DV, ELEKTRIZ printed circuit
board, ELEKTRONIK printed wiring board, ELEKTRO-
NIK, FERNSEH, RADIO, TELEKOM printed circuit board;
Leiterplatten-Laminat *nt* ELEKTRONIK printed circuit
laminate; **Leiterplattenstecker** *m* ELEKTRONIK printed
circuit connector; **Leiterplattenträgermaterial** *nt*
ELEKTRONIK printed circuit substrate
leitfähig[1] *adj* ELEKTRIZ conductible, conducting, conductive
leitfähig:[2] **~es Fett** *nt* RAUMFAHRT *Raumschiff* conductive grease; **~er Gummi** *m* KUNSTSTOFF conductive
rubber
Leitfähigkeit *f* ANSTRICH, AUFNAHME conductivity,
ELEKTRIZ conductance, conductibility, conductivity,
ELEKTROTECH conductance, conductivity, KUNST-
STOFF conductivity, PHYS, TELEKOM conductance,
conductivity, WASSERVERSORG conductivity; **~ im Einschaltzustand** *f* ELEKTROTECH on-state conductivity;
Leitfähigkeitsmesser *m* LABOR conductivity meter;
Leitfähigkeitsmeßgerät *nt* GERÄT conductivity measuring instrument, conductometric instrument;
Leitfähigkeitsmeßzelle *f* GERÄT conductivity cell; **Leit-
fähigkeitsmodulation** *f* ELEKTRONIK conductivity
modulation; **Leitfähigkeitsschreiber** *m* GERÄT conductivity recorder; **Leitfähigkeitszelle** *f* GERÄT
conductivity cell, LABOR conductance cell
Leit-: Leitfeuer *nt* WASSERTRANS leading light; **Leitflügel**
m NICHTFOSS ENERG *Aerodynamik* guide vane; **Leitflü-
gel-Servomotor** *m* NICHTFOSS ENERG guide vane
servomotor; **Leitflügelvibration** *f* NICHTFOSS ENERG
guide vane vibration; **Leitgummi** *m* KUNSTSTOFF conductive rubber; **Leitintensität** *f* AUFNAHME standard
reference intensity; **Leitkabel** *nt* KERNTECH leader;
Leitkarte *f* COMP & DV master card; **Leitkegel** *m* BAU
Verkehr traffic cone; **Leitklampe** *f* WASSERTRANS
Deckausrüstung fairlead; **Leitlinie** *f* WASSERTRANS
leading line; **Leitmarke** *f* WASSERTRANS leading mark;
Leitoszillator *m* PHYS master oscillator; **Leitpfad** *m*
COMP & DV routing path; **Leitpfosten** *m* BAU guide post;
Leitplanke *f* BAU guard rail, side rail, SICHERHEIT

crash barrier, TRANS crash barrier (BrE); **Leitplatte** *f*
MASCHINEN deflector plate; **Leitprozessor** *m* TELE-
KOM administrative processor; **Leitpunkte** *m pl* GEOM
control points; **Leitrad** *nt* KFZTECH stator, *Teil des
Drehmomentwandlers* reactor; **Leitrechner** *m* COMP &
DV host, host computer, master; **Leitrechnersystem** *nt*
COMP & DV master computer system; **Leitring** *m* HY-
DRAUL guide ring; **Leitrolle** *f* FERTIG belt idler, idle
pulley, KFZTECH belt idler, MASCHINEN guide pulley,
idler, PAPIER jockey pulley; **Leitschaufel** *f* HEIZ & KÄLTE
guide vane, HYDRAUL guide blade, guide vane, *Turbine, Pumpe* stationary vane, LUFTTRANS compressor
blade, *Kompressor* stator vane, MASCHINEN, MECHAN,
NICHTFOSS ENERG *Turbine* guide vane; **Leitscheibe** *f*
MASCHINEN guide pulley; **Leitschicht** *f* ELEK-
TROTECH wave duct; **Leitschiene** *f* BAU check rail,
MASCHINEN guide, guide bar; **Leitseitenstrahlkoppler**
m LUFTTRANS lateral beam coupler; **Leitspindel** *f* FER-
TIG *Drehmaschine* leadscrew, MASCHINEN guide screw,
lead screw, leading screw, MECHAN lead screw; **Leit-
spindelmutter** *f* MASCHINEN half-nut; **Leitstand** *m*
RAUMFAHRT operation center (AmE), operation
centre (BrE); **Leitstange** *f* MASCHINEN slide bar; **Leit-
station** *f* COMP & DV control terminal, RAUMFAHRT *in
Funknetzwerken* network coordination station; **Leit-
stelle** *f* KONTROLL master
Leitstrahl[1]**: einen ~ erfassen** *vi* LUFTTRANS *flugwesen*
capture a beam
Leitstrahl[2] *m* RAUMFAHRT beacon, WASSERTRANS guide
beam; **Leitstrahlerzeuger** *m* RAUMFAHRT *Raumschiff*
beacon generator
leitstrahlgeführt *adj* RAUMFAHRT abeam
Leitstrahl: Leitstrahllenkung *f* LUFTTRANS beam following
Leit-: Leitton *m* AKUSTIK leading note, AUFNAHME neo-
pilot tone; **Leittuch** *nt* TEXTIL leader cloth
Leitung[1] *f* AUFNAHME line, COMP & DV line, link, pipeline,
transmission line, ELEKTRIZ cable, line, ELEKTROTECH
transmission line, *Stromdrahtversorgung* lead, *elektrisch* cable, *von Strom* conduction, ERDÖL *zum
Transport von flüssigen oder gasförmigen Medien* pipeline, FERNSEH line, FERTIG main, HEIZ & KÄLTE
conduction, HYDRAUL *Turbine* guide, KERNTECH line,
KFZTECH cable, MASCHINEN, MECHAN duct, PHYS conduction, TELEKOM *Telefon* line; **für abgehende Anrufe
gesperrte ~** *f* TELEKOM outgoing calls barred line; **für
ankommende Anrufe gesperrte ~** *f* TELEKOM incoming calls barred line; **~ elektrischer Länge** *f*
ELEKTRIZ *gleich einer halben Wellenlänge* half-wave
transmission line; **~ mit Verstärker** *f* TELEKOM amplified circuit; **~ ohne Verstärker** *f* TELEKOM unamplified
circuit; **~ der Vorfelddienstleistungen** *f* LUFTTRANS
apron management service
Leitung:[2] **in ~ gehen** *vi* TELEKOM go into circuit; **über die
~ gehen** *vi* TELEKOM go via the circuit
Leitungen: alle ~ belegt *phr* TELEKOM ATB all trunks
busy
Leitung: Leitung-Nulleiter-Spannung *f* ELEKTRIZ line-
to-neutral voltage; **Leitungsabfertiger** *m* ELEKTRIZ
load dispatcher; **Leitungsabschluß** *m* COMP & DV line
termination; **Leitungsabschnitt** *m* TELEKOM link; **Lei-
tungsanschluß** *m* COMP & DV line adaptor;
Leitungsanschlußeinrichtung *f* TELEKOM line connection unit; **Leitungsanschlußfeld** *nt* ELEKTROTECH line
pad; **Leitungsband** *nt* PHYS, STRAHLPHYS conduction
band; **Leitungsbelegungstaste** *f* TELEKOM line seizure

button; **Leitungsbetrieb** *m* ELEKTROTECH line operation

leitungsbetrieben *adj* ELEKTROTECH line-operated

Leitung: **Leitungsbündel** *nt* TELEKOM group, line group; **Leitungscode** *m* TELEKOM line code; **Leitungsdraht** *m* ELEKTROTECH conductor wire, *Zuleitungsdraht* lead; **Leitungsdurchgangsprüfer** *m* GERÄT circuit continuity tester; **Leitungsendeinrichtung** *f* TELEKOM line-terminating equipment; **Leitungsendgerät** *nt* TELEKOM line terminal; **Leitungs-Erde-Spannung** *f* ELEKTRIZ line-to-earth voltage (BrE), line-to-ground voltage (AmE); **Leitungsfehler** *m* ELEKTROTECH line fault

leitungsgebunden: **~e Störstrahlung** *f* TELEKOM conducted spurious emission; **~e Störung** *f* TELEKOM conducted interference

Leitung: **Leitungsgerüst** *nt* ELEKTROTECH lead frame; **Leitungsgraben** *m* BAU utility trench; **Leitungshalterung** *f* LUFTTRANS fairlead; **Leitungsimpedanz** *f* ELEKTROTECH line impedance; **Leitungsisolator** *m* ELEKTROTECH line insulator; **Leitungskommutator** *m* ELEKTRIZ line commutator; **Leitungskompensation** *f* FERNSEH cable compensation circuits; **Leitungskonfiguration** *f* ELEKTROTECH line configuration; **Leitungskonzentrator** *m* TELEKOM line concentrator, remote concentrator; **Leitungskopplung** *f* ELEKTROTECH line coupling; **Leitungskopplungstrafo** *m* ELEKTROTECH line-coupling transformer; **Leitungskreis** *m* HEIZ & KÄLTE circuit; **Leitungskreuzung** *f* ELEKTRIZ transposition of insulated cables

leitungslos: **~er Chip-Träger** *m* ELEKTROTECH leadless chip carrier

Leitung: **Leitungsmast** *m* ELEKTRIZ transmission tower; **Leitungsmietgebühr** *f* TELEKOM line rental; **Leitungsmodul** *nt* TELEKOM line module; **Leitungsnummer** *f* COMP & DV *Datenfernverarbeitung* line number; **Leitungspegel** *m* AUFNAHME line level; **Leitungsprüfer** *m* GERÄT circuit continuity tester, *elektrische Leitung auf Stromdurchgang* continuity tester; **Leitungspumpe** *f* ELEKTROTECH conduction pump; **Leitung-srahmen** *m* ELEKTROTECH lead frame; **Leitungsrauschen** *nt* ELEKTRONIK circuit noise, line noise, ELEKTROTECH line noise; **Leitungsregelung** *f* ELEKTROTECH line regulation; **Leitungsrohr** *nt* BAU conduit pipe, NICHTFOSS ENERG conduit; **Leitungssatz** *m* TELEKOM junctor, *Kreislauf* line terminal; **Leitungsschleife** *f* TELEKOM loop; **Leitungsschnittstelle** *f* ELEKTROTECH line interface; **Leitungsschnittstellenmodul** *nt* TELEKOM line interface module; **Leitungsschnur** *f* TELEKOM *elektrisch* cord; **Leitungsschutz** *m* ELEKTRIZ line protection, line relay; **Leitungsschutzdrossel** *f* ELEKTROTECH line-choking coil; **Leitungsspannung** *f* ELEKTROTECH line voltage

leitungsstabilisiert: **~er Oszillator** *m* ELEKTRONIK line-stabilized oscillator

Leitung: **Leitungssteuerung** *f* ELEKTROTECH line controller; **Leitungsstörung** *f* ELEKTROTECH, TELEKOM line fault; **Leitungsstrecke** *f* WASSERVERSORG section; **Leitungsstrom** *m* ELEKTROTECH line current, PHYS conduction current; **Leitungssystem** *nt* TELEKOM line system; **Leitungstreiber** *m* COMP & DV line driver; **Leitungstrennschalter** *m* ELEKTRIZ line breaker; **Leitungsübertrager** *m* ELEKTROTECH repeating coil, RADIO line transformer; **Leitungsübertragung** *f* COMP & DV line communication; **Leitungsüberwachung** *f* FERNSEH line monitor; **Leitungsunterbrechung** *f*

ELEKTRIZ line break; **Leitungsverbinder** *m* ELEKTROTECH cable connector, connector; **Leitungsverbindung über Schnittstellen** *f* ELEKTROTECH line interfacing; **Leitungsverlegung** *f* BAU cut and cover

leitungsvermittelnd: **~es Amt** *nt* TELEKOM circuit switching center (AmE), circuit switching centre (BrE)

leitungsvermittelt: **~er Dienst** *m* TELEKOM switched service; **~es Netz** *nt* COMP & DV, TELEKOM circuit-switched network; **~er Trägerdienst** *m* TELEKOM circuit-mode bearer service

Leitung: **Leitungsvermittlung** *f* COMP & DV circuit switching, line switching, TELEKOM circuit switching, circuit switching system; **Leitungsversetzung** *f* ELEKTRIZ transposition of insulated cables; **Leitungsverstärker** *m* AUFNAHME line amplifier, COMP & DV line driver, ELEKTRONIK, RADIO line amplifier, TELEKOM line repeater; **Leitungswähler** *m* TELEKOM *Schaltung* connector; **Leitungswasser** *nt* BAU tap water; **Leitungszeichen** *nt* ELEKTRONIK line signal; **Leitungszeichengabegerät** *nt* TELEKOM line-signaling equipment (AmE), line-signalling equipment (BrE)

Leit-: **Leitvermögen** *nt* ELEKTROTECH conductivity; **Leitwalze** *f* PAPIER guide roll, leading roll

Leitweg *m* COMP & DV route, TELEKOM route, routing; **Leitweganzeiger** *m* COMP & DV routing indicator; **Leitwegbefehl** *m* COMP & DV routing directive; **Leitwegcode** *m* COMP & DV routing code; **Leitweginformationen** *f pl* COMP & DV routing information; **Leitweglenkung** *f* TELEKOM automatic routing; **Leitwegprogramm** *nt* COMP & DV router; **Leitwegwahl** *f* COMP & DV routing

Leitwerk *nt* LUFTTRANS horizontal stabilizer, tail unit, TELEKOM control unit; **Leitwerksansatzfläche** *f* LUFTTRANS fin stub frame

Leitwert *m* ELEKTRIZ conductance, susceptance, ELEKTROTECH, PHYS admittance, conductance, TELEKOM conductance; **Leitwertbrücke** *f* GERÄT conductance bridge; **Leitwertschreiber** *m* GERÄT conductivity recorder

Leit-: **Leitzahl** *f* FOTO guide number

LEM *abbr* (*Mondlandefahrzeug, Mondlandefähre*) RAUMFAHRT LEM (*lunar excursion module*)

Lemma *nt* MATH lemma

Lemniskate *f* GEOM lemniscate

Lemniskoide *f* FERTIG *Wattkurve* lemniscoid

Lemonal *nt* CHEMIE citral

Lenkachse *f* EISENBAHN leading axle, KFZTECH *Lenkung, Räder* steering axle

Lenkanschlag *m* KFZTECH *Lenkung* steering lock

Lenkbarkeit *f* KERNTECH *des Kraftniveaus* maneuverability (AmE), manoeuvrability (BrE)

Lenkeinschlag *m* KFZTECH *Lenkung* steer angle

lenken[1] *vt* LUFTTRANS pilot, steer, NICHTFOSS ENERG channel, TELEKOM direct, TRANS, WASSERTRANS steer

lenken[2] *vi* LUFTTRANS, TRANS, WASSERTRANS steer

Lenker *m* LUFTTRANS connecting rod

Lenkgehäuse *nt* KFZTECH steering gearbox

Lenkgeometrie *f* KFZTECH steering geometry

Lenkgestänge *nt* KFZTECH steering linkage

Lenkgetriebe *nt* KFZTECH steering gear, *Lenkung* steering gearbox

Lenkhebel *m* KFZTECH steering arm, LUFTTRANS drop arm

Lenkknüppelfuß: **~ des Bugradfahrwerks** *m* LUFTTRANS nose gear steering base post

Lenkkopf *m* KFZTECH *Motorradlenkung* steering head

Lenkkreis *m* KFZTECH *Lenkung* steering circle
Lenkrad *nt* KFZTECH wheel, *Lenkung* steering wheel; **Lenkradschloß** *nt* KFZTECH *Lenkung* steering column lock; **Lenkradseite** *f* KFZTECH offside
Lenkrolle *f* MASCHINEN caster, castor, guide pulley
Lenkrollradius *m* KFZTECH offset radius
Lenksäule *f* KFZTECH steering column
Lenkschubstange *f* KFZTECH *Lenkung* drag rod
Lenkspurstange *f* KFZTECH *Lenkung* drag rod
Lenkstockhebel *m* KFZTECH pitman arm, *Lenkung* drop arm
Lenkung *f* KFZTECH steering system, steering; **Lenkungsspiel** *nt* KFZTECH *Lenkung* steering play
Lenkwelle *f* KFZTECH steering shaft
Lenkzapfen *m* KFZTECH steering knuckle pin; **Lenkzapfensturz** *m* KFZTECH kingbolt inclination (AmE), kingpin inclination (BrE), steering axis inclination
Lenkzwischenhebel *m* KFZTECH idler arm, relay arm
Lenkzwischenstange *f* KFZTECH *Lenkung* center link (AmE), centre link (BrE)
Lenzanlage *f* WASSERTRANS drainage system
lenzen *vt* WASSERTRANS pump
Lenzpumpe *f* WASSERTRANS bilge pump
Lenz: **~sches Gesetz** *nt* ELEKTRIZ, PHYS Lenz's law; **~sche Regel** *f* ELEKTRIZ, PHYS Lenz's law
Lenzvorrichtung: **~ der Plicht** *f* WASSERTRANS cockpit drainage
Leonhardtit *m* KERNTECH leonhardite
LEP *abbr* (*Elektronen-Positronen-Kollideranlage*) TEILPHYS LEP (*large electron-positron collider*)
Leporellofalzung *f* DRUCK concertina fold, PAPIER accordion fold
Lepton *nt* PHYS, TEILPHYS lepton; **Leptonenzahl** *f* PHYS lepton number
leptonisch *adj* TEILPHYS leptonic
Lernautomat *m* ELEKTRONIK *lernender Automat* learning machine
Lerneinstellung *f* ERGON learning set
Lernen: **~ durch Wahrnehmung** *f* ERGON perceptual learning
lernend: **~e Banderol-Klebmaschine** *f* VERPACK intelligent labeling machine (AmE), intelligent labelling machine (BrE); **~e Etikettiermaschine** *f* VERPACK intelligent labeling machine (AmE), intelligent labelling machine (BrE)
lernfähig *adj* COMP & DV adaptive
Lernkurve *f* ELEKTRIZ, ERGON learning curve
Lernphase *f* ELEKTRONIK learning phase
Lernprogramm *nt* COMP & DV tutorial
Lernregel *f* KÜNSTL INT learning rule
lesbar:[1] **~e und dauerhafte Kennzeichnung** *f* QUAL legible and durable marking
lesbar:[2] **nur einmal beschreibbar mehrfach ~** *adj* COMP & DV, OPTIK write-once read many times
Lesbarkeit *f* ERGON legibility
Lesefehler *m* COMP & DV read error
Lesegerät *nt* ELEKTRONIK reading gun
Lesegeschwindigkeit *f* COMP & DV read rate, reading rate
Leseglas *nt* OPTIK reading glass
Lesekopf *m* COMP & DV head, magnetic head, read head, OPTIK read head
Leselaser *m* OPTIK read laser
Leselupe *f* OPTIK reading lens
Lesen *nt* COMP & DV read; **~ von Markierungen** *nt* COMP & DV mark reading; **~ beim Schreiben** *nt* COMP & DV read while write **~ nach dem Schreiben** *nt* COMP & DV read after write
lesen *vt* COMP & DV read, retrieve, GERÄT *Speicherdaten* read
Leser *m* COMP & DV, DRUCK reader
Lese-/Schreib *pref* COMP & DV read/write; **Lese-/Schreibkanal** *m* COMP & DV read/write channel; **Lese-/Schreibkopf** *m* COMP & DV read/write head; **Lese-/Schreibspeicher** *m* (*RAM*) COMP & DV random access memory (*RAM*)
Lesesperre *f* COMP & DV fetch protection
Lesestift *m* COMP & DV wand
Lesestiftscanner *m* COMP & DV wand scanner
Lesestrahl *m* ELEKTRONIK reading beam, OPTIK read beam
Lesetransistor *m* ELEKTRONIK read transistor
Lese-und-Schreibkopf *m* OPTIK read-write head
Leseverstärker *m* COMP & DV read amplifier, ELEKTRONIK read amplifier, sense amplifier
Lesezeichen *nt* DRUCK bookmark
Lesezeit *f* COMP & DV read time
Lesezugriffszeit *f* COMP & DV read access time
Letaldosis *f* UMWELTSCHMUTZ lethal dose
Lethargie *f* KERNTECH, PHYS lethargy
Letten *m* BAU clay; **Lettenbohrer** *m* ERDÖL claying bar
Letter *f* DRUCK metal type; **Letternmetall** *nt* DRUCK type metal
letzt:[1] **~e Bildschirmmaske** *f* ELEKTRONIK *eines Programms* end screen; **~e Notfallmaßnahme** *f* LUFTTRANS last emergency action; **~e Schicht** *f* ANSTRICH finish
letzt:[2] **mit ~er Schicht versehen** *vt* ANSTRICH finish
Letztweg *m* TELEKOM last choice route; **Letztwegbündel** *nt* TELEKOM last choice circuit group
Leuchtanzeige *f* COMP & DV electroluminescent display
Leuchtbalkenanzeige *f* GERÄT bar graph display
Leuchtboje *f* WASSERTRANS *Seezeichen* light buoy
Leuchtdichte *f* ELEKTROTECH, FERNSEH luminance, OPTIK brightness, PHYS, TELEKOM luminance; **Leuchtdichtefaktor** *m* STRAHLPHYS luminosity coefficient; **Leuchtdichtemessung** *f* GERÄT luminance measurement; **Leuchtdichtendifferenzschwelle** *f* ERGON luminance difference threshold; **Leuchtdichtenfaktor** *m* ERGON luminance factor; **Leuchtdichtenkontrast** *m* ERGON luminance contrast; **Leuchtdichtenunterschied** *m* ERGON luminance difference; **Leuchtdichtesignal** *nt* FERNSEH luminance signal; **Leuchtdichtetheorem** *nt* OPTIK brightness theorem
Leuchtdiode *f* (*LED*) COMP & DV, ELEKTRIZ light-emitting diode (*LED*), ELEKTRONIK light-emitting diode, luminance, luminescent diode (*LED*), FERNSEH, OPTIK, PHYS, TELEKOM light-emitting diode (*LED*)
Leuchte *f* KFZTECH light, *zur Warnung* lamp
leuchtend[1] *adj* ELEKTROTECH luminescent, TELEKOM illuminated, TEXTIL bright
leuchtend:[2] **~ farbige Schutzkleidung** *f* SICHERHEIT luminous and colored protective clothing (AmE), luminous and coloured protective clothing (BrE)
Leuchtfaden *m* ELEKTRIZ filament
Leuchtfeuer *nt* LUFTTRANS beacon, WASSERTRANS light; **Leuchtfeuertonne** *f* WASSERTRANS *Seezeichen* light buoy; **Leuchtfeuerverzeichnis** *nt* WASSERTRANS *Navigation* list of lights
Leuchtgerät *nt* LABOR *Mikroskop* illuminating apparatus
Leuchtglas *nt* KER & GLAS luminescent glass

Leuchthorizont *m* LUFTTRANS *Anflugsbefeuerungssystem* crossbar
Leuchtkasten *m* FOTO lightbox
Leuchtkörper *m* ELEKTRIZ luminaire, OPTIK illuminated body
Leuchtkraft *f* LUFTTRANS lighting efficiency
Leuchtkugel *f* WASSERTRANS Very light, flare; **Leuchtkugelpistole** *f* WASSERTRANS Very pistol
Leuchtlupe *f* FERTIG illuminated magnifier
Leuchtpetroleum *nt* ERDÖL *Erdölfraktion* lamp oil
Leuchtpunkt *m* FERNSEH beam impact point
Leuchtschirm *m* ELEKTRIZ, ELEKTRONIK fluorescent screen
Leuchtsignal *nt* LUFTTRANS indicator light
Leuchtskale *f* GERÄT luminous dial
Leuchtstärke *f* STRAHLPHYS luminous intensity
Leuchtstoff *m* ELEKTROTECH, FERNSEH, STRAHLPHYS fluorescent substance; **Leuchtstofflampe** *f* ELEKTROTECH fluorescent lamp; **Leuchtstoffpunkt** *m* FERNSEH phosphor dot; **Leuchtstoffröhre** *f* ELEKTRIZ fluorescent tube, tubular incandescent lamp, STRAHLPHYS fluorescent discharge tube
Leuchtstreifen *m* FERNSEH phosphor strip
Leuchttisch *m* DRUCK light table
Leuchtturm *m* WASSERTRANS lighthouse; **Leuchtturmwärter** *m* lighthouse keeper
Leuchtwirksamkeit *f* PHYS luminous efficiency
Leuchtzeit *f* STRAHLPHYS luminosity life-time
Levothyroxin *nt* CHEMIE thyroiodine
lexikalisch: ~e **Analyse** *f* COMP & DV lexical analysis
lexikographisch: ~e **Anordnung** *f* COMP & DV lexicographic order
LHC *abbr* (*Hadronkollideranlage*) PHYS LHC (*large hadron collider*)
Li (*Lithium*) CHEMIE Li (*lithium*)
Liapunovexponenten *m pl* STRÖMPHYS Liapunov exponents
Libelle *f* MECHAN bubble level, level, METROL level; **Libellenblase** *f* FERTIG air bubble
Librationspunkt *m* RADIO libration point
Licht *nt* FOTO, KFZTECH, PHYS light
licht: ~e **Höhe** *f* BAU headroom, ELEKTROTECH clearance, FERTIG maximum daylight, MASCHINEN clearance height, daylight, overall internal height, WASSERTRANS *zwischen den Decks* headroom under beams; ~e **Weite** *f* ELEKTROTECH clearance, FERTIG internal diameter, *Rohr* bore size, MASCHINEN inside diameter
Licht: **Lichtabdeckschirm** *m* FERNSEH flag; **Lichtablenkung** *f* OPTIK deflection; **Lichtabsorption** *f* STRAHLPHYS absorption of light
lichtaktiviert: ~er **silikongesteuerter Gleichrichter** *m* ELEKTROTECH light-activated silicon-controlled rectifier
Licht: **Lichtaufnehmer** *m* ELEKTRONIK light sensor; **Lichtausbeute** *f* ERGON luminous efficiency, LUFTTRANS *Hubschrauber* lighting efficiency, PHYS efficiency, luminous efficacy, STRAHLPHYS light yield
lichtbeständig *adj* VERPACK stable to light
Licht: **Lichtbeständigkeit** *f* KUNSTSTOFF light resistance; **Lichtbeugung** *f* PHYS diffraction of light; **Lichtbildkompaß** *m* WASSERTRANS *Kompaß* projector compass
Lichtbogen *m* ELEKTRIZ arc; **Lichtbogenableiter** *m* ELEKTRIZ arc arrester
lichtbogenbeständig *adj* FERTIG arc-resistant
Lichtbogen: **Lichtbogenbildung** *f* ELEKTROTECH arcing; **Lichtbogenbrennschneiden** *nt* FERTIG arc cutting;

Lichtbogenbrennschneider *m* MASCHINEN arc cutter; **Lichtbogendauer** *f* ELEKTRIZ arc duration; **Lichtbogenentladung** *f* ELEKTROTECH arc discharge; **Lichtbogengleichrichter** *m* ELEKTRIZ, ELEKTROTECH arc rectifier; **Lichtbogenhandschweißen** *nt* BAU manual arc welding; **Lichtbogenheizgerät** *nt* MASCHINEN arc heater; **Lichtbogenkennlinie** *f* FERTIG arc characteristic; **Lichtbogenkontakte** *m pl* ELEKTRIZ arcing contacts; **Lichtbogenlampe** *f* ELEKTRIZ arc lamp; **Lichtbogenleistungsschalter** *m* ELEKTROTECH arc breaker; **Lichtbogenleuchte** *f* ELEKTRIZ arc light; **Lichtbogenlöschkammer** *f* ELEKTROTECH arc quench chamber; **Lichtbogenlöschung** *f* ELEKTRIZ arc extinction, ELEKTROTECH arc quenching; **Lichtbogenofen** *m* FERTIG, HEIZ & KÄLTE arc furnace, KOHLEN EAF, electric-arc furnace, MASCHINEN arc furnace, THERMOD electric-arc furnace; **Lichtbogenregler** *m* ELEKTRIZ arc regulator; **Lichtbogensauerstoffschweißen** *nt* BAU oxygen arc welding; **Lichtbogenschneiden** *nt* BAU arc cutting, THERMOD electric-arc cutting; **Lichtbogenschutzarmatur** *f* FERTIG arcing shield; **Lichtbogenschutzring** *m* FERTIG arcing ring; **Lichtbogenschweißautomat** *m* MASCHINEN automatic arc-welding machine; **Lichtbogenschweißelektrode** *f* ELEKTRIZ arc-welding electrode; **Lichtbogenschweißen** *nt* BAU arc welding, arc weld, ELEKTRIZ arc welding, FERTIG arc welding, electric-arc welding, THERMOD electric-arc welding; **Lichtbogenschweißen mit Fülldrahtelektroden** *nt* BAU flux-cored arc welding; **Lichtbogenschweißen mit der Hand** *nt* MECHAN manual arc welding; **Lichtbogenschweißrauch** *m* FERTIG arc fume; **Lichtbogenschweißstab** *m* ELEKTRIZ arc-welding electrode; **Lichtbogenstrom** *m* ELEKTRIZ arc current; **Lichtbogenstromrichter** *m* ELEKTROTECH arc rectifier; **Lichtbogentrennschalter** *m* ELEKTRIZ arc breaker; **Lichtbogenüberschlag** *m* ELEKTRIZ arc over, arc striking; **Lichtbogenunterdrückung** *f* ELEKTROTECH arc suppression; **Lichtbogenunterdrückungsspule** *f* ELEKTRIZ *Lichtbogenlöschspule* arc suppression coil; **Lichtbogenzündung** *f* ELEKTRIZ, ELEKTROTECH arc ignition
Lichtbrechung *f* OPTIK refringency; **Lichtbrechungsvermögen** *nt* FOTO refractive power
Licht: **Lichtbündel** *nt* OPTIK pencil of light; **Lichtbüschel** *nt* OPTIK pencil of light
lichtchemisch *adj* PHYS actinic
Licht: **Lichtdämpfungssystem** *nt* LUFTTRANS *Beleuchtung* dimmer
lichtdicht *adj* VERPACK lightproof
Licht: **Lichtdiffuser** *m* OPTIK diffuser; **Lichtdruckplatte** *f* DRUCK collotype plate
lichtdurchlässig: ~e **Scheibe** *f* OPTIK transparent disc (BrE), transparent disk (AmE)
Licht: **Lichtdurchlässigkeit** *f* OPTIK transmittance
Lichtechtheit *f* TEXTIL fastness to light
lichtelektrisch:[1] ~ **leitend** *adj* ELEKTRONIK photoconductive
lichtelektrisch:[2] ~er **Effekt** *m* ELEKTRONIK photoelectric emission; ~e **Emission** *f* ELEKTRONIK photoemission; ~es **Gerät** *nt* ELEKTRONIK photoelectric device; ~er **Strom** *m* TELEKOM light current; ~er **Verstärker** *m* ELEKTRONIK photoelectric amplifier; ~e **Verstärkung** *f* ELEKTRONIK photoconductive gain; ~e **Wirkung** *f* ELEKTRONIK photoelectric effect; ~e **Zelle** *f* PHYS pho-

toconductive cell, photoelectric cell; ~er **Zerhacker** *m* ELEKTRONIK electronic chopper

lichtelektrisch:[3] ~ **gravieren** *vt* ELEKTRONIK photoengrave

lichtemittierend: ~e **Diode** *f (LED)* COMP & DV, ELEKTRIZ, ELEKTRONIK, FERNSEH, OPTIK, PHYS, TELEKOM light-emitting diode *(LED)*

lichtempfindlich[1] *adj* ELEKTRONIK light-sensitive, FOTO light-sensitive, photosensitive, PHYS photosensitive

lichtempfindlich:[2] ~e **Platte** *f* DRUCK light-sensitive plate

Lichtempfindlichkeit *f* ELEKTRONIK photosensitivity, FOTO film speed, PHYS actinism, photosensitivity, STRAHLPHYS sensitivity to light; **Lichtempfindlichkeitskurve** *f* ELEKTRONIK response curve

Lichten *nt* TRANS lifting

Lichtenberg: ~sche **Figur** *f* PHYS Lichtenberg figure

Lichtenergie *f* STRAHLPHYS light energy

lichtfest *adj* VERPACK stable to light

Licht: **Lichtfilter** *nt* DRUCK light filter; **Lichtfleck** *m* ELEKTRONIK light spot; **Lichtgeschwindigkeit** *f* LABOR *(c)* velocity of light *(c)*, OPTIK *(c) im Vakuum* speed of light in empty space *(c)*, PHYS, WELLPHYS speed of light; **Lichtgriffel** *m* COMP & DV, FERNSEH light pen

Lichthof *m* ELEKTRONIK halo; **Lichthofbildung** *f* ELEKTRONIK *Kathodenstrahlröhre*, FOTO halation; **Lichthofschutzschicht** *f* FOTO antihalo layer

Licht: **Lichthupe** *f* KFZTECH *Beleuchtung* headlamp flasher; **Lichtimpuls** *m* ELEKTRONIK light pulse

lichtinduziert: ~e **Polymerisation** *f* CHEMIE photopolymerization

Licht: **Lichtintensität** *f* STRAHLPHYS intensity of light; **Lichtjahr** *nt* PHYS light year; **Lichtkabel** *nt* ELEKTROTECH light cable; **Lichtkante** *f* KONSTZEICH imaginary intersection; **Lichtkegel** *m* OPTIK cone of rays; **Lichtleistung** *f* FOTO light output; **Lichtleitbündeltechnik** *f* COMP & DV fiber optics (AmE), fibre optics (BrE); **Lichtleiter** *m* PHYS light guide; **Lichtleiter mit sich parabolisch änderndem Brechungsindex** *m* OPTIK parabolic-index fiber (AmE), parabolic-index fibre (BrE); **Lichtleitfaser** *f* ELEKTROTECH, KER & GLAS optical fiber (AmE), optical fibre (BrE), OPTIK optical fibre (BrE), optical fiber (AmE); **Lichtleitfaser mit abgestuftem Brechungsindex** *f* PHYS step index fiber (AmE), step index fibre (BrE); **Lichtleitfaser mit kontinuierlich veränderlichem Brechungsindex** *f* PHYS graded index fiber (AmE), graded index fibre (BrE); **Lichtleitkabel** *nt* OPTIK fiberoptic cable (AmE), fibreoptic cable (BrE), optical fiber cable (AmE), optical fibre cable (BrE); **Lichtleitstein** *m* KER & GLAS light-directing block; **Lichtleitung** *f* ELEKTROTECH light pipe

Lichtmarke *f* ELEKTRONIK light spot; **Lichtmarken-Galvanometer** *nt* GERÄT luminous pointer galvanometer, STRAHLPHYS light beam galvanometer; **Lichtmarkeninstrument** *nt* GERÄT optical pointer instrument; **Lichtmarkenleistungsmeßgerät** *nt* GERÄT luminous pointer power meter

Licht: **Lichtmaschine** *f* KFZTECH *KFZ-Elektrik* generator; **Lichtmenge** *f* OPTIK *(Q)* quantity of light *(Q)*, PHYS quantity of light; **Lichtmesser** *m* FOTO photometer; **Lichtmikroskopie** *f* METALL light microscopy; **Lichtmodulation** *f* ELEKTRONIK, FERNSEH light modulation; **Lichtmodulator** *m* AKUSTIK light modulator; **Lichtmülle** *f* PHYS radiometer; **Lichtnetz** *nt* ELEKTROTECH mains (BrE), supply network (AmE); **Lichtpause** *f* FERTIG print; **Lichtpausfilm** *m* KONSTZEICH diazotype film; **Lichtpausmaterial** *nt*

KONSTZEICH diazotype material; **Lichtpauspapier auf Gewebe** *nt* KONSTZEICH mount diazo paper; **Lichtpausschicht** *f* KONSTZEICH diazo coating; **Lichtpult** *nt* DRUCK light table

Lichtpunkt *m* FERNSEH scanning spot; **Lichtpunktabtaster** *m* FERNSEH, RADIO flying-spot scanner; **Lichtpunktkorrektur** *f* FERNSEH spot shape corrector; **Lichtpunktröhrenabtaster** *m* FERNSEH flying spot tube scanner

Licht: **Lichtquelle** *f* ELEKTRONIK light source, ELEKTROTECH source, FOTO, LABOR, OPTIK, PHYS light source, STRAHLPHYS luminous source; **Lichtreflexion** *f* STRAHLPHYS luminous reflectance; **Lichtregelsystem** *nt* LUFTTRANS *Beleuchtung* dimmer; **Lichtsatz** *m* DRUCK photocomposition, phototypesetting; **Lichtschacht** *m* BAU funnel; **Lichtschein** *m* WASSERTRANS loom; **Lichtschirm** *m* OPTIK screen; **Lichtschnittmikroskop** *nt* FERTIG light-slit microscope; **Lichtschnittverfahren** *nt* FERTIG light-slit method; **Lichtschreiber** *m* PHYS light pen; **Lichtschutzfilter** *nt* FOTO safelight filter; **Lichtsensor** *m* ELEKTRONIK optical sensor; **Lichtsensorsignal** *nt* ELEKTRONIK optical sensor signal; **Lichtsignal** *nt* EISENBAHN colour light signal (BrE), light signal, ELEKTRONIK light signal; **Lichtsignal an Fußgängerüberwegen** *nt* TRANS *fußgängerbetätigt* pedestrian crossing light; **Lichtskalenschalter** *m* FOTO light scale switch; **Lichtsonde** *f* STRAHLPHYS light detector; **Lichtspalt** *m* ANSTRICH graticule; **Lichtspektrum** *nt* WELLPHYS light spectrum; **Lichtstärke** *f* ELEKTROTECH, ERGON luminous intensity, FOTO candle power, *einer Linse* f-number, PHYS luminous intensity, STRAHLPHYS intensity of light; **Lichtstärkeeinheit** *f* OPTIK light unit; **Lichtstärkemessung** *f* GERÄT luminous intensity measurement; **Lichtstift** *m* COMP & DV light pen; **Lichtstifterkennung** *f* COMP & DV light-pen detection; **Lichtstrahl** *m* FERNSEH light beam, FOTO light beam, PHYS beam, light beam, light ray, TEILPHYS beam, TELEKOM light beam, WASSERTRANS *Signal* beam; **Lichtstrahlschweißen** *nt* ELEKTRONIK laser welding

lichtstreuend: ~er **Körper** *m* OPTIK diffuser

Licht: **Lichtstreuung** *f* ELEKTRONIK scattering; **Lichtstrom** *m* ELEKTROTECH luminous flux, OPTIK light current, optical flux, PHYS luminous flux; **Lichtstrommeßgerät** *nt* PHYS lumenmeter; **Lichttonspalt** *m* AUFNAHME recording slit

lichtundurchlässig *adj* VERPACK lightproof

Licht: **Lichtundurchlässigkeit** *f* WELLPHYS opacity; **Lichtverstärker** *m* ELEKTRONIK light amplifier; **Lichtverstärkung durch stimulierte Strahlungsemission** *f (Laser)* COMP & DV, DRUCK, ELEKTRONIK, PHYS, STRAHLPHYS light amplification by stimulated emission of radiation *(laser)*; **Lichtweg** *m* TELEKOM optical path

Lichtwelle *f* ELEKTRONIK light wave, ELEKTROTECH optical guided wave, OPTIK, WELLPHYS light wave

Lichtwellenleiter *m* OPTIK, TELEKOM optical waveguide; **Lichtwellenleiterachse** *f* TELEKOM fiber axis (AmE), fibre axis (BrE); **Lichtwellenleiteranschluß** *m* TELEKOM optical fiber pigtail (AmE), optical fibre pigtail (BrE); **Lichtwellenleiterdämpfung** *f* TELEKOM fiber loss (AmE), fibre loss (BrE); **Lichtwellenleiterendeinrichtung** *f* TELEKOM fiberoptic terminal device (AmE), fibreoptic terminal device (BrE); **Lichtwellenleiterkabel** *nt* COMP & DV fiberoptic cable (AmE), fiberoptic connection (AmE), fibreoptic cable (BrE), fibreoptic connection (BrE), TELEKOM fiberoptic cable (AmE), fibreoptic cable (BrE); **Lichtwellenleiterkoppler** *m* TELEKOM optical fiber coupler (AmE), optical fibre coupler (BrE); **Lichtwellenleitermantel** *m* TELEKOM fiberoptic cladding (AmE), fibreoptic cladding (BrE); **Lichtwellenleitermehrfachverbindung** *f* TELEKOM multifiber joint (AmE), multifibre joint (BrE); **Lichtwellenleitermodem** *nt* ELEKTRONIK *faseroptisches Modem* fiberoptic modem (AmE), fibreoptic modem (BrE); **Lichtwellenleiterspleiß** *m* TELEKOM fiberoptic splice (AmE), fibreoptic splice (BrE), optical fiber splice (AmE), optical fibre splice (BrE); **Lichtwellenleitersteckverbinder** *m* TELEKOM optical fiber connector (AmE), optical fibre connector (BrE); **Lichtwellenleitertaper** *m* TELEKOM tapered fiber (AmE), tapered fibre (BrE); **Lichtwellenleitertechnik** *f* COMP & DV fiber optics (AmE), fibre optics (BrE); **Lichtwellenleiterübertragung** *f* TELEKOM fiberoptic transmission (AmE), fibreoptic transmission (BrE), optical fiber transmission (AmE), optical fibre transmission (BrE); **Lichtwellenleiterverbindung** *f* TELEKOM optical fiber link (AmE), optical fibre link (BrE)

Licht: **Lichtwert** *m* FOTO light value; **Lichtwerteinstellring** *m* FOTO light value setting ring; **Lichtwirkungsgrad** *m* LUFTTRANS *Hubschrauber* lighting efficiency; **Lichtzeichenmaschine** *f* COMP & DV photoplotter; **Lichtzeiger** *m* COMP & DV light pen; **Lichtzerhacker** *m* ELEKTRONIK light chopper; **Lichtzuleitung** *f* ELEKTROTECH light cable

Lieberkühn-Reflektor *m* FOTO Lieberkühn reflector

Lieferangebot *nt* BAU tender

Lieferant *m* VERPACK deliverer; **Lieferantenbeurteilung** *f* QUAL vendor appraisal, vendor assessment, vendor inspection, vendor rating; **Lieferantenrisiko** *nt* QUAL producer's risk

lieferbar *adj* FERTIG *Kunststoffinstallationen* available

Lieferdatum *nt* VERPACK delivery date

Lieferer *m* VERPACK deliverer

Lieferfirma *f* QUAL vendor

Lieferinformation *f* VERPACK off the shelf information

liefern *vt* ELEKTRIZ supply, MASCHINEN deliver, discharge

Lieferposten *m* TRANS consignment

Lieferpreis *m* FERTIG *Kunststoffinstallationen* delivery price

Lieferqualität *f* QUAL delivery quality

Liefertermin *m* VERPACK delivery date

Lieferung *f* KERNTECH, LEBENSMITTEL delivery, QUAL consignment; **Lieferungsbeurteilung** *f* QUAL consignment appraisal

Lieferverzögerung *f* VERPACK delivery delay

Lieferwagen *m* EISENBAHN van, KFZTECH delivery truck, van; ~ **mit offener Pritsche** *m* KFZTECH pick-up, pick-up truck

Lieferzeichnung *f* QUAL as-delivered condition

liegen: ~ **in** *vi* COMP & DV reside

liegend[1]: *adj* MASCHINEN horizontal

liegend:[2] ~**er Motor** *m* KFZTECH horizontal engine; ~**e Welle** *f* MASCHINEN lying shaft

Liegeplatz *m* WASSERTRANS berth, shelter, *Festmachen* mooring

Liegepresse *f* PAPIER straight-through press

Liegesitz *m* KFZTECH *Sitz* reclining seat

Liegetage *m pl* ERDÖL *Schiffahrt* lay days

Liek *nt* WASSERTRANS leech; **Liektau** *nt* WASSERTRANS

Tauwerk bolt rope

LIFO *abbr (Last-in First-out)* COMP & DV LIFO *(last-in-first-out)*

LIFO-Prinzip *nt* COMP & DV LIFO principle

Lift *m* HYDRAUL, MASCHINEN, TRANS elevator (AmE), lift (BrE)

Liftfan *m* LUFTTRANS lift fan

Lift-On-Lift-Off-Schiff *nt* WASSERTRANS lift-on lift-off vessel, *Vertikalumschlag* lift-on lift-off ship

Lift-On-Lift-Off-System *nt* WASSERTRANS lift-on lift-off system

Ligand *m* CHEMIE, METALL ligand

Ligatur *f* DRUCK double letter

Lignan *nt* CHEMIE lignan

Lignin *nt* KUNSTSTOFF lignin

Lignit *m* KOHLEN lignite

Ligroin *nt* CHEMIE ligarine, naphtha, ligroin

Li-Li ~ Schiff *nt* WASSERTRANS *Vertikalumschlag* lift-on lift-off ship, lift-on lift-off vessel

Limit *nt* MASCHINEN limit

Limma *nt* AKUSTIK limma

Limone *f* LEBENSMITTEL *Art kleine Zitrone* lime

Limonit *m* CHEMIE brown haematite (BrE), brown hematite (AmE), limonite, brown iron ore

LIM-Verfahren *nt* KUNSTSTOFF LIM, liquid injection moulding

Linalool *nt* CHEMIE linalool

Lindan *nt* CHEMIE gammexane

Lindenholz *nt* FERTIG lime

Linderung *f* MEERSCHMUTZ mitigation

LINEAC *abbr (Linearbeschleuniger)* ELEKTROTECH, PHYS LINAC *(linear accelerator)*, TEILPHYS LINEAC *(linear accelerator)*

Lineal *nt* METROL straight edge

Linear- *pref* TEILPHYS linear

linear[1] *adj* GEOM, MATH, PAPIER, PHYS, RADIO linear; **nicht ~** *adj* ELEKTRIZ, PHYS, RADIO, TELEKOM nonlinear

linear:[2] ~**e Abmessung** *f* MATH linear measurement; ~**er Abschwächungskoeffizient** *m* KERNTECH, TELEKOM linear attenuation coefficient; ~**er Absorptionskoeffizient** *m* PHYS linear absorption coefficient; ~**e Aktivität** *f* KERNTECH *einer linienförmigen Quelle* linear activity; ~**e Algebra** *f* COMP & DV, MATH linear algebra; ~**e Amplitudenverzerrung** *f* ELEKTRONIK, TELEKOM amplitude-frequency distortion; **nicht ~e Amplitudenverzerrung** *f* AUFNAHME amplitude distortion; ~**er Asynchronmotor** *m* ELEKTRIZ linear induction motor; ~**er Ausdehnungskoeffizient** *m* PHYS linear expansion coefficient; **nicht ~e Bedingungen** *f* ELEKTROTECH nonlinear conditions; ~**er Bereich** *m* *(R)* KERNTECH linear range *(R)*; ~**er Dämpfungskoeffizient** *m* PHYS attenuation coefficient; ~**er Defekt** *m* METALL linear defect; ~**er digitaler Sprachverwürfler** *m* TELEKOM linear digital voice scrambler; **nicht ~es digitales Sprachsignal** *nt* TELEKOM nonlinear digital speech; ~**e Dipolgruppe** *f* RADIO collinear array; ~**e Dispersion** *f* STRAHLPHYS linear dispersion; ~**er Elektromotor** *m* ELEKTROTECH linear electric motor; ~**e Energieübertragung** *f (L)* KERNTECH, STRAHLPHYS linear energy transfer *(L)*; ~**es Feedback-Steuersystem** *nt* ELEKTROTECH linear feedback control system; ~**es Filter** *nt* TELEKOM linear filter; ~**es Filtern** *nt* TELEKOM linear filtering; **nicht ~es Filtern** *nt* TELEKOM nonlinear filtering; ~**e Geschwindigkeit** *f* FERTIG velocity; ~**er Gleichrichter** *m* ELEKTRONIK linear detector; ~e Gleichrichtung f ELEKTRONIK linear detection; ~e Gleichung f MATH linear equation, simple equation; nicht ~es Glied nt ELEKTROTECH nonlinear element; ~er Hochleistungsmotor m KFZTECH high-power linear motor; ~er Induktionsmotor m ELEKTRIZ linear induction motor; ~e integrierte Schaltung f ELEKTRONIK linear-integrated circuit; ~e Interpolation f TELEKOM linear interpolation; nicht ~e Interpolation f TELEKOM nonlinear interpolation; ~e Ionisation f PHYS linear ionization; ~e Kalthärtung f METALL linear work hardening; ~er Kanal m TELEKOM linear channel; ~e Kennlinie f ELEKTRONIK linear characteristic; ~e kinetische Energie f MASCHINEN linear kinetic energy; ~er Konzentrator m NICHTFOSS ENERG linear concentrator; ~e Ladungsdichte f PHYS linear charge density; ~er Leistungsverstärker m ELEKTRONIK, RADIO, TELEKOM linear power amplifier; ~e Liste f COMP & DV linear list; ~er Meßwandler m ELEKTROTECH linear transducer; ~e Modulation f ELEKTRONIK linear modulation; ~e Näherung f TELEKOM linear approximation; nicht ~es Netzwerk nt ELEKTROTECH nonlinear network; ~e OEM-Stromversorgung f ELEKTROTECH linear OEM power supply; ~e Optimierung f COMP & DV linear optimization, linear programming, MATH linear optimization; nicht ~e Phasenverzerrung f RAUMFAHRT phase nonlinear distortion; ~e Platte f OPTIK linear disc (BrE), linear disk (AmE); ~e Polarisation f ELEKTROTECH linear polarization; ~ polarisierte Mode f (LP-Mode) OPTIK, TELEKOM linearly-polarized mode (LP mode); ~ polarisierte Welle f AKUSTIK, ELEKTROTECH linearly-polarized wave, PHYS linearly-polarized wave, plane-polarized wave; ~ polarisierter Wellentyp m (LP-Mode) OPTIK, TELEKOM linearly-polarized mode (LP mode); ~es Polymer nt KUNSTSTOFF linear polymer; nicht ~es Potentiometer nt ELEKTROTECH nonlinear potentiometer; ~er Prädiktionscodierer mit Codebuch-Erregung m TELEKOM CELP, codebook-excited linear predictive coder; ~e Prädiktionscodierung f (LPC) ELEKTRONIK, TELEKOM linear predictive coding (LPC); nicht ~es Programmieren nt COMP & DV nonlinear programming; ~e Programmierung f COMP & DV linear optimization, linear programming, ELEKTRONIK linear programing (AmE), linear programming (BrE); nicht ~e Programmierung f COMP & DV nonlinear programming; ~e Regelung f ELEKTROTECH linear regulation; ~e Schaltung f PHYS linear network, TELEKOM linear circuit; nicht ~e Schaltung f TELEKOM nonlinear circuit; ~er Schwächungskoeffizient m KERNTECH linear attenuation coefficient, PHYS linear absorption coefficient; ~e Schwingung f TELEKOM linear oscillation; nicht ~e Schwingung f TELEKOM nonlinear oscillation; ~e Skale f ELEKTRIZ linear scale; nicht ~e Skale f ELEKTROTECH, METROL nonlinear scale; ~e Skalierungsberechnung f TELEKOM linear-scaling calculation; ~er Spannungsanstieg m ELEKTROTECH ramp voltage; ~er Stark-Effekt m PHYS linear Stark effect; nicht ~er Stark-Effekt m PHYS nonlinear Stark effect; ~e Steuerung f ELEKTRIZ linear control; nicht ~e Streuung f OPTIK, TELEKOM nonlinear scattering; ~e Stromdichte f (A) ELEKTRIZ linear current density (A); ~er Stromkreis m ELEKTRIZ linear circuit; ~es Stromkreiselement nt ELEKTRONIK linear circuit element; ~es Stromnetz nt ELEKTRIZ linear current network; ~e Stromversorgung f ELEKTROTECH linear power supply; ~e Thermodynamik f THERMOD linear thermodynamics; ~er Transducer m ELEKTROTECH linear transducer; ~e Unabhängigkeit f MATH linear independence; ~ variabler Differentialtransformator m ELEKTROTECH linear variable differential transformer; ~e Vergrößerung f PHYS linear magnification; ~er Verstärker m ELEKTRONIK, TELEKOM linear amplifier; nicht ~er Verstärker m ELEKTRONIK nonlinear amplifier; ~e Verstärkung f ELEKTRONIK linear amplification; nicht ~e Verstärkung f TELEKOM nonlinear amplification; ~e Verzerrung f AUFNAHME, TELEKOM linear distortion; nicht ~e Verzerrung f AUFNAHME, ELEKTRONIK, TELEKOM nonlinear distortion; ~er Vierpolstromkreis m ELEKTRIZ linear four-terminal network; ~er Wandler m AKUSTIK linear transducer; nicht ~er Widerstand m ELEKTRIZ nonlinear resistor, TELEKOM nonlinear resistance

Linear-: **Linearabtastung** f ELEKTRONIK linear scan; **Linearbedingungen** f pl ELEKTROTECH linear conditions; **Linearbeschleuniger** m (LINEAC) ELEKTROTECH, PHYS linear accelerator (LINAC), TEILPHYS linear accelerator (LINEAC); **Linearbetrieb** m ELEKTROTECH linear operation; **Linearcode** m TELEKOM linear code; **Linear-Collider** m TEILPHYS linear collider; **Lineardruck** m PAPIER linear pressure; **Linearimpulsverstärker** m ELEKTRONIK linear pulse amplifier

linearisieren vt CHEMIE linearize

Linearisierungsglied nt RAUMFAHRT *Weltraumfunk* linearizer

Linearität f AUFNAHME, ELEKTRIZ, ELEKTRONIK, RADIO, TELEKOM linearity; ~ bei Festpunkteinstellung f REGELUNG terminal-based linearity; ~ bei Nullpunkteinstellung f REGELUNG zero-based linearity; **Linearitätsfehler** m FERNSEH linearity error; **Linearitätssteuerung** f FERNSEH linearity control

Linear-: **Linearkreis** m ELEKTRONIK linear circuit; **Linearmaßstab** m ELEKTRONIK linear scale; **Linearmatrix** f FERNSEH linear matrix; **Linearmodulator** m ELEKTRONIK linear modulator; **Linearmotor** m KFZTECH linear motor; **Linearnetz** nt ELEKTROTECH linear network; **Linear-Potentiometer** nt ELEKTROTECH linear potentiometer; **Linearschaltung** f ELEKTRONIK *für integrierte Schaltung* linear circuit; **Linearschwingung** f MASCHINEN linear oscillation; **Linearskale** f METROL linear scale; **Linearspannung** f ELEKTROTECH linear voltage; **Linearstrahlröhre** f ELEKTRONIK linear beam tube, linear tube; **Linearstrahl-Rückwärtswellen-Oszillator** m ELEKTRONIK linear beam backward wave oscillator; **Linearstrahlverstärker** m ELEKTRONIK linear beam amplifier; **Linearturbine** f WASSERTRANS linear turbine; **Linearverhalten** nt ELEKTRONIK linear behavior (AmE), linear behaviour (BrE); **Linearverzerrung durch Gruppenverzögerung** f RAUMFAHRT *Weltraumfunk* group delay linear distortion; **Linearwiderstand** m ELEKTRIZ, ELEKTROTECH, PHYS linear resistor

Liner m ERDÖL, VERPACK liner

Linie[1] f DRUCK line, rule, EISENBAHN line, ELEKTRONIK *der Schutzschicht* line, *des Spektrums* line, GEOM, KER & GLAS line, KERNTECH *in einem Spektrum* peak, MATH, STRAHLPHYS line; ~ gleicher Inklination f PHYS isoclinal line; ~ haltende Ziffern f pl DRUCK lining figures, modern figures

Linie:[2] eine ~ durchziehen vt KONSTZEICH draw a continuous line

Linie:[3] **~ in Betrieb** *phr* EISENBAHN line in service
Linien:[1] **~ der Paschenserie** *f pl* STRAHLPHYS Paschen series lines
Linien:[2] **die ~ abschnüren** *vi* WASSERTRANS *Schiffkonstruktion* lay down the lines
Linie: **Linienabstand** *m* KONSTZEICH line spacing; **Linienangriff** *m* FERTIG line application; **Linienbe-schickungsgeräte** *nt pl* VERPACK line-feeding equipment; **Linienbreite** *f* KONSTZEICH line thickness, STRAHLPHYS line width; **Liniendicke** *f* METROL thickness of lines; **Liniendienst** *m* LUFTTRANS scheduled service; **Linienflug** *m* LUFTTRANS scheduled flight; **Linienflugzeug** *nt* LUFTTRANS airliner, liner; **Liniengeometrie** *f* GEOM line geometry; **Liniengeschwindigkeit** *f* VERPACK line speed; **Liniengrafik** *f* COMP & DV line graphics; **Liniengruppe** *f* KONSTZEICH line group; **Linienintegral** *nt* PHYS line integral; **Linienprofil** *nt* STRAHLPHYS line profile; **Linienprofil von Spektrallinien** *nt pl* STRAHLPHYS profiles of spectral lines; **Linienquelle** *f* UMWELTSCHMUTZ line source; **Linienriß** *m* WASSERTRANS *Schiffkonstruktion* lines drawing, lines plan; **Linienschreiber** *m* GERÄT strip chart line recorder; **Linienspannung** *f* METALL line tension; **Linienspektrum** *nt* AKUSTIK, OPTIK, PHYS line spectrum, RAUMFAHRT bright-line spectrum, STRAHLPHYS discontinuous spectrum, line spectrum, TELEKOM line spectrum; **Linienzugbeeinflussung** *f* EISENBAHN continuous automatic train control
Linierung *f* PAPIER *auf Schreibpapier* lining
liniieren *vt* DRUCK line, rule
Linkage-Editor *m* COMP & DV linkage editor
Linke-Hand-Regel *f* PHYS left-hand rule
Link-Kopplung *f* ELEKTROTECH link coupling
Link-Relais *nt* ELEKTROTECH link relay
Links- *pref* COMP & DV, TRANS left
links:[1] **~ flatternd** *adj* DRUCK ragged left
links:[2] **linker Rand** *m* DRUCK left margin; **linke Seite** *f* DRUCK verso, PHYS *einer Gleichung* left-hand side; **linker Stereo-Kanal** *m* AUFNAHME left stereo channel
linksabbiegend: ~er Verkehr *m* TRANS left-turning traffic
Links-: **Linksabbiegephase** *f* TRANS left turn phase; **Linksausrichtung** *f* COMP & DV left justification
linksbündig: ~ ausrichten *vt* COMP & DV left justify
Links-: **Linksbündigkeit** *f* COMP & DV left justification; **Linksdraht** *m* TEXTIL S-twist
Linksdrall: mit ~ *adj* FERTIG left-helix
Linksdrall *m* FERTIG left-hand helix
linksdrehend[1] *adj* FERTIG laevorotatory, GERÄT ccw, counterclockwise
linksdrehend:[2] **~e Zirkularpolarisation** *f* RADIO, RAUMFAHRT *Weltraumfunk* LHCP, left-hand circular polarization
Links-: **Linksdrehung** *f* TEXTIL S-twist; **Linksflanke** *f* MASCHINEN left-hand tooth flank
linksgängig *adj* MASCHINEN left-hand, left-handed
Links-: **Linksgewindeschraube** *f* MASCHINEN left-handed screw; **Linkshändigkeit** *f* ERGON left handedness
Link-Sicherung *f* ELEKTROTECH link fuse
Links-: **Linkslauf** *m* MASCHINEN reverse action
linksläufig *adj* FERTIG left-hand helix
linksschief *adj* GEOM positively skewed
linksschneidend *adj* MASCHINEN left-handed
linkssteigend *adj* FERTIG left-hand helical
Links-: **Linksverschiebung** *f* COMP & DV left shift
Linol- *pref* CHEMIE linoleic

Linoleat *nt* CHEMIE linoleate
Linolein *nt* CHEMIE linoleine
Linolen- *pref* CHEMIE linolenic
Linol-: **Linolsäure** *f* KUNSTSTOFF, LEBENSMITTEL *essentielle Fettsäure* linoleic acid; **Linolschnitt** *m* DRUCK linocut
Linotype® *f* DRUCK Linotype®
Linse *f* LABOR, OPTIK, PHYS lens; **~ mit Begrenzungsblende** *f* PHYS stopped lens; **Linsenantenne** *f* RAUMFAHRT *Weltraumfunk*, TELEKOM lens antenna; **Linseneffekte** *m pl* FOTO lens flares; **Linsenfassung** *f* FOTO lens mount; **Linsenfehler** *m* OPTIK aberration
linsenförmig *adj* FOTO lens-shaped
Linse: **Linsenhalter** *m* KER & GLAS lens holder; **Linsenkopf** *m* MASCHINEN raised head; **Linsenkopfschraube** *f* BAU cheese-head screw, MASCHINEN fillister-head screw, raised head screw; **Linsenkuppe** *f* MASCHINEN blunt start, oval point; **Linsenlichtflecke** *m pl* FOTO lens flares; **Linsenscheitel** *m* FOTO lens vertex; **Linsenschirm** *m* FERNSEH flag; **Linsenschraube** *f* BAU slotted fillister head screw, MASCHINEN oval-head screw; **Linsensenkkopf** *m* MASCHINEN raised countersunk head; **Linsensenkniet** *m* MASCHINEN oval countersunk rivet; **Linsensenkschraube** *f* MASCHINEN raised countersunk head screw; **Linsenvergütung** *f* FOTO lens coating; **Linsenzwilling** *m* METALL lenticular twin
Lipase *f* CHEMIE lipase
Lipid *nt* CHEMIE lipid
lipoid *adj* CHEMIE lipoid
lipophil *adj* CHEMIE lipophile, lipophilic
Lipopolysaccharid *nt* CHEMIE lipopolysaccharide
Lippe *f* FERTIG *Dichtung*, MASCHINEN lip; **Lippendichtung** *f* MASCHINEN lip seal, lip-type seal, MECHAN lip seal; **Lippenlesen** *nt* AKUSTIK lip reading; **Lippenmikrofon** *nt* AKUSTIK lip microphone; **Lippensynchronisation** *f* AUFNAHME lip-sync
Liquiduslinie *f* METALL liquidus line
LISP *abbr (Listenprogrammiersprache)* COMP & DV LISP *(list-programming language)*
Lissajous: ~sche Figur *f* PHYS, RADIO Lissajous figure
Liste *f* COMP & DV list; **~ freier Speicherplätze** *f* COMP & DV available list; **~ qualifizierter Lieferanten** *f* QUAL approved vendors list; **~ zugelassener Erzeugnisse** *f* QUAL qualified products list; **Listenerstellung** *f* COMP & DV report generation; **Listenpreis** *m* FERTIG *Kunststoffinstallationen* list price; **Listenprogrammgenerator** *m* COMP & DV RPG, report program generator; **Listenprogrammiersprache** *f (LISP)* COMP & DV list-programming language *(LISP)*; **Listenstruktur** *f* COMP & DV list structure; **Listenverarbeitung** *f* COMP & DV list processing
Listing *nt* COMP & DV program listing, *eines Programms* listing
Liter *m* METROL, PHYS *Einheit des Volumens* liter (AmE), litre (BrE)
Literal *nt* COMP & DV literal
Litermolarität *f* CHEMIE molarity
Lithargit *m* KUNSTSTOFF lead oxide, litharge
Lithergol *nt* RAUMFAHRT lithergol
Lithium *nt (Li)* CHEMIE lithium *(Li)*; **Lithiumbatterie** *f* ELEKTROTECH lithium battery; **Lithiumchloridakkumulator** *m* KFZTECH lithium-chlorine storage battery
Lithografie *f* DRUCK lithograph, lithographic print, lithography; **Lithografieglas** *nt* KER & GLAS glass for lithography

lithografiert: ~e **Packung** *f* VERPACK lithographed package
lithografisch: ~e **Platte** *f* DRUCK lithoplate; ~er **Vorgang** *m* ELEKTRONIK lithographic process
Lithomaske *f* ELEKTRONIK lithographic mask
Lithosphäre *f* NICHTFOSS ENERG earth's crust, lithosphere
Litoral *nt* WASSERTRANS littoral
litoral *adj* WASSERTRANS *Geographie* littoral
Litosphäre *f* UMWELTSCHMUTZ litosphere
Littletontemperatur *f* KER & GLAS Littleton softening point
Litze *f* FERTIG, MASCHINEN, PHYS strand, TEXTIL braid, braiding, heald; **Litzenbesatz** *m* TEXTIL braiding; **Litzendraht** *m* ELEKTRIZ braided wire, ELEKTROTECH stranded conductor, TEXTIL heald wire; **Litzenkabel** *nt* ELEKTROTECH flexible cable; **Litzenseil** *nt* MASCHINEN stranded rope
live *adj* FERNSEH live
Live-Kamera *f* FERNSEH live camera
Live-Sendung *f* FERNSEH live broadcast
Live-Übertragung *f* FERNSEH live coverage
Lizenz[1] *f* PATENT licence (BrE), license (AmE)
Lizenz:[2] ~ **erteilen** *vi* PATENT grant a licence
Lizenz: **Lizenzgeber** *m* PATENT licensor; **Lizenzgebühren** *f pl* PATENT royalties
LKF *abbr (Luftkissenfahrzeug)* KFZTECH SEV *(surface effect vehicle)*, TRANS ACV, *(air cushion vehicle)*, WASSERTRANS hovercraft (BrE), hydroskimmer (AmE), surface effect ship
LKT *abbr (luftgekühlte Triode)* ELEKTRONIK ACT *(air-cooled triode)*
Lkw[1] *abbr (Lastkraftwagen)* KFZTECH HGV *(heavy goods vehicle)*
Lkw:[2] ~ **mit Hubladeklappe** *m* KFZTECH tail lift truck; ~ **mit offener Ladefläche** *m* KFZTECH rack body truck; **Lkw-Dienst** *m* TRANS cartage service; **Lkw-Fahrer** *m* TRANS trucker (AmE); **Lkw-Faktor** *m* TRANS truck factor; **Lkw-Transportunternehmen** *nt* TRANS cartage contractor; **Lkw-Zug** *m* KFZTECH road train
Lloyd: ~scher **Spiegel** *m* PHYS Lloyd's mirror
LM[1] *abbr (Lunar-Modul)* RAUMFAHRT *Raumschiff* LM *(lunar module)*
LM:[2] **LM-Hangar** *m* RAUMFAHRT *Raumschiff* LM hangar
lm *abbr (Lumen)* FERNSEH, METROL, PHYS lm *(lumen)*
L-Netz *nt* ELEKTROTECH L-network
LNG[1] *abbr (Flüssigerdgas)* ERDÖL, THERMOD LNG *(liquefied natural gas)*
LNG:[2] **LNG-Bus** *m* KFZTECH LNG bus; **LNG-Tanker** *m* WASSERTRANS LNG tanker; **LNG-Transporter** *m* THERMOD, TRANS LNG carrier
Load-on-Top *f* UMWELTSCHMUTZ load on top
Lobeliaalkaloid *nt* CHEMIE lobelia alkaloid
Lobelin *nt* CHEMIE lobeline
Loch[1] *nt* BAU opening, ELEKTROTECH *Elektronloch*, ERDÖL *Bohrtechnik*, KERNTECH, MASCHINEN, PHYS *fehlender Ladungsträger im Halbleiter* hole
Loch:[2] ~ **graben** *vi* BAU hole
Loch: **Lochabstand** *m* FOTO *beim Film* pitch; **Lochband** *nt* MEERSCHMUTZ sifting belt; **Lochbild** *nt* KONSTZEICH hole pattern; **Lochblech** *nt* BAU punched plate, KERNTECH perforated plate; **Lochblende** *f* FERNSEH scanning aperture; **Lochbohrung** *f* BAU boreholing; **Lochdorn** *m* FERTIG drift, tapered punch, MASCHINEN piercer; **Lochdurchmesser** *m* FERTIG *Kunststoffinstallationen* perforation; **Locheisen** *nt* BAU punch, MASCHINEN hollow punch, MECHAN broaching, punch
Lochen *nt* BAU boring, COMP & DV punching
lochen *vt* MECHAN punch
Locher *m* COMP & DV perforator, punch
Löcherhalbleiter *m* ELEKTRONIK p-type semiconductor
Löcherleitung *f* ELEKTROTECH hole conduction
Loch: **Lochfeile** *f* MASCHINEN riffler; **Lochfotografie** *f* FOTO pinhole photography; **Lochfräser** *m* MASCHINEN arbor-type cutter; **Lochfraß** *m* ANSTRICH, KER & GLAS *Korrosion*, MASCHINEN pitting; **Lochkamera** *f* FOTO pinhole camera; **Lochkameraobjektiv** *nt* OPTIK pinpoint lens
Lochkarte *f* COMP & DV punch card, punched card; **Lochkartendoppler** *m* COMP & DV punched-card reproducer; **Lochkartenleser** *m* COMP & DV punched-card reader; **Lochkartenmischer** *m* COMP & DV collator; **Lochkartenstanzer** *m* COMP & DV card punch
Loch: **Lochkreis** *m* FERTIG *Bohren* scribed circle; **Lochlehre** *f* BAU *Meßtechnik* plug gage (AmE), plug gauge (BrE); **Lochmaschine** *f* DRUCK perforating machine; **Lochmaske** *f* ELEKTRONIK *Video* shadow mask, FERNSEH aperture mask; **Lochmutter** *f* MASCHINEN ring nut; **Lochplatte** *f* FERTIG boss, *Schmieden* swage block, MECHAN swage block; **Lochpresse** *f* MASCHINEN perforating press, piercing press; **Lochring** *m* FERTIG *Schmieden* bolster; **Lochsäge** *f* BAU lock saw, MASCHINEN keyhole saw; **Lochscheibe** *f* KER & GLAS bushing; **Lochspalte** *f* COMP & DV card column; **Lochstanze** *f* BAU, MECHAN drift, PAPIER punching press; **Lochstempel** *m* MASCHINEN piercing die
Lochstreifen *m* AUFNAHME perforated tape, COMP & DV perforated tape, punch tape, punched tape, TELEKOM perforated tape, punched tape; **Lochstreifendoppler** *m* COMP & DV punched-tape reproducer; **Lochstreifenleser** *m* COMP & DV punched-tape reader, tape reader; **Lochstreifenstanzer** *m* COMP & DV tape punch; **Lochstreifensteuerung** *f* FERTIG taping·
Lochung *f* BAU *Ziegel* core
Loch: **Lochwalze** *f* PAPIER holy roll; **Lochzeile** *f* COMP & DV row; **Lochziegel** *m* BAU perforated brick
locker: ~es **Bandkabel** *nt* OPTIK loose flat cable; ~ **gehaltener Diamant** *m* KER & GLAS diamond held trailing; ~es **Schlauchkabel** *nt* OPTIK loose tube cable; ~e **Schwelle** *f* EISENBAHN pumping sleeper (BrE), pumping tie (AmE)
lockerbar *adj* FERTIG strippable
Lockern *nt* MASCHINEN slackening, slacking
lockern[1] *vt* BAU ease, FERTIG *Schraube* strip, LEBENSMITTEL *Teig* aerate, MASCHINEN slacken, MECHAN loosen
lockern:[2] **sich** ~ *v refl* MASCHINEN work loose
lodernd *adj* THERMOD blazing
Löffel *m* MEERSCHMUTZ *Löffelbagger* shovel; **Löffelbagger** *m* BAU *Tiefbau* power shovel, WASSERTRANS *Baggern* dipper dredge, dipper dredger, WASSERVERSORG spoon dredge, spoon dredger; **Löffelbohrer** *m* BAU *Tiefbau* shell auger, spoon auger; **Löffelbug** *m* WASSERTRANS *Schiffbau* spoon bow; **Löffelschaber** *m* FERTIG half-round scraper; **Löffeltiefbagger** *m* MEERSCHMUTZ backhoe
Log *nt* ERDÖL *Bohrtechnik*, LUFTTRANS log, MATH - *Zehnerlogarithmus* log, WASSERTRANS *Schiffgeschwindigkeitsmesser* log
Logarithmenpapier *nt* MATH logarithmic paper
logarithmisch[1] *adj* MATH logarithmic
logarithmisch:[2] ~e **Darstellung** *f* COMP & DV logarithmic

graph; ~es **Dekrement** *nt* ELEKTRONIK, PHYS logarithmic decrement; ~e **Kennlinie** *f* ELEKTRONIK logarithmic characteristic; ~es **Kriechen** *nt* METALL logarithmic creep; ~er **Maßstab** *m* ELEKTRONIK logarithmic scale; **logarithmisch-normale Abschattung** *f* TELEKOM log-normal shadowing; **logarithmisch-periodische Antenne** *f* RADIO log periodic antenna; ~es **Potentiometer** *nt* ELEKTROTECH logarithmic potentiometer; ~e **Skale** *f* ELEKTRIZ, ELEKTRONIK *Meßtechnik* logarithmic scale; ~e **Spirale** *f* GEOM logarithmic spiral; ~er **Verstärker** *m* ELEKTRONIK logarithmic amplifier; ~er **Videoverstärker** *m* ELEKTRONIK logarithmic video amplifier; ~es **Wobbeln** *nt* ELEKTRONIK *Meßtechnik* logarithmic sweep

Logarithmus *m* COMP & DV log, logarithm, MATH *(Log)* logarithm *(log)*

Logatom *nt* AKUSTIK logatom

Logbuch *nt* LUFTTRANS, TRANS logbook, WASSERTRANS ship's log, *Dokumente* logbook; **Logbucheintrag** *m* LUFTTRANS, WASSERTRANS log

Logger *m* WASSERTRANS *Boottyp* drifter

Logik *f* COMP & DV logic, logic device, ELEKTRONIK, MATH logic; **Logik- und Taktanalysator** *m* ELEKTRONIK logic state and timing analyser (BrE), logic state and timing analyzer (AmE); **Logikanalysator** *m* COMP & DV, ELEKTRONIK logic analyser (BrE), logic analyzer (AmE); **Logikanalyse** *f* COMP & DV, ELEKTRONIK logic analysis; **Logikaufbau** *m* COMP & DV logic design, ELEKTRONIK logic pattern; **Logikbaustein** *m* COMP & DV, ELEKTRONIK logic device; **Logikeinheit** *f* COMP & DV logic unit; **Logikelement** *nt* COMP & DV logic element; **Logikentwurf** *m* COMP & DV logic design; **Logikfamilie** *f* COMP & DV, ELEKTRONIK *Schaltkreisfamilie* logic family; **Logikgatter** *nt* PHYS logic gate; **Logikkonzeption** *f* ELEKTRONIK logic design; **Logikoperation** *f* COMP & DV logic operation; **Logikoperator** *m* COMP & DV, ELEKTRONIK logic operator; **Logikpegel** *m* COMP & DV logic level; **Logikraster** *nt* COMP & DV logic grid; **Logikschaltbild** *nt* ELEKTRONIK logic diagram; **Logikschaltkarte** *f* COMP & DV logic card; **Logikschaltung** *f* COMP & DV logic circuit, PHYS logic gate, TELEKOM logic circuit; **Logiksignal** *nt* ELEKTRONIK logic signal; **Logiksimulation** *f* ELEKTRONIK logic simulation; **Logiksimulator** *m* ELEKTRONIK logic simulator; **Logiksymbol** *nt* COMP & DV logic symbol; **Logiktaktanalyse** *f* ELEKTRONIK logic timing analysis; **Logiktaktsteuerung** *f* ELEKTRONIK logic timing; **Logiktest** *m* ELEKTRONIK logic test; **Logiktester** *m* ELEKTRONIK logic tester; **Logikverknüpfung** *f* ELEKTRONIK logic operation; **Logikzeichen** *nt* COMP & DV logic symbol; **Logikzeitmessung** *f* ELEKTRONIK logic timing; **Logikzustand** *m* ELEKTRONIK logic state; **Logikzustandsanalyse** *f* ELEKTRONIK logic state analysis

logisch[1] *adj* COMP & DV logical; ~ **eins** *adj* ELEKTRONIK logic high; ~ **null** *adj* ELEKTRONIK logic low

logisch:[2] ~e **Adressierung** *f* COMP & DV logical addressing; ~es **Ausgangssignal** *nt* ELEKTRONIK logic output signal; ~er **Befehl** *m* COMP & DV logic instruction; ~er **Block** *m* COMP & DV logical block; ~e **Datei** *f* COMP & DV logical file; ~es **Diagramm** *nt* COMP & DV logical chart; ~es **Eingangssignal** *nt* ELEKTRONIK logic input signal; ~e **Entscheidung** *f* COMP & DV decision instruction; ~e **Fortschreibung** *f* COMP & DV indexed sequence; ~ **integrierte Schaltung** *f* ELEKTRONIK logic-integrated circuit; ~er **Kanal** *m* COMP & DV logical channel; ~e **Mikroschaltung** *f* ELEKTRONIK logic microcircuit; ~e

Operation *f* COMP & DV, MATH logical operation; ~er **Operator** *m* COMP & DV logical operator; ~er **Satz** *m* COMP & DV logical record; ~es **Schließen** *nt* COMP & DV inference; ~er **Schluß** *m* COMP & DV inference; ~e **Schlüsse pro Sekunde** *m pl* KÜNSTL INT LIPS, *Maß für Leistung von KI-Systemen* logical inferences per second; ~e **Seitenlänge** *f* DRUCK logical page length; ~e **Variable** *f* COMP & DV logical variable; ~es **Verknüpfungsglied** *nt* ELEKTRONIK logic operator; ~es **Verschieben** *nt* COMP & DV logical shift

Logistik *f* COMP & DV logistics

logistisch: ~e **Unterstützung** *f* TRANS logistic support

Logleine *f* WASSERTRANS *Tauwerk* log line

lohgar *adj* FERTIG *Gerberei* tanned

LOI *abbr* (*Sauerstoffindex*) KUNSTSTOFF LOI (*limiting oxygen index*)

Lok *f* (*Lokomotive*) EISENBAHN locomotive

Lokal- *pref* COMP & DV local

lokal[1] *adj* COMP & DV local

lokal:[2] ~e **Batterie** *f* (*LB*) ELEKTROTECH local battery (*LB*); ~e **Erklärung** *f* COMP & DV local declaration; ~ **gemessene Geschwindigkeit** *f* TRANS spot speed; ~e **Korrosion** *f* MASCHINEN local corrosion; ~es **Kreuzungssteuergerät** *nt* TRANS local intersection controller; ~es **Netz** *nt* (*LAN*) COMP & DV, TELEKOM local area network (*LAN*); ~er **Oszillator** *m* ELEKTRONIK phase local oscillator; ~ **oxidierter Übergang** *m* ELEKTRONIK locally-oxided junction; ~er **Rundfunk** *m* FERNSEH community broadcasting; ~es **Steuergerät** *f* TRANS local controller; ~e **Variable** *f* COMP & DV local variable

Lokal-: **Lokalbetrieb** *m* COMP & DV local mode

lokalisieren *vt* COMP & DV localize

lokalisiert: ~e **Interferenzen** *f pl* PHYS *in einer Schicht* localized fringes; **nicht** ~e **Interferenzlinien** *f pl* PHYS nonlocalized fringes

Lokalisierung *f* TELEKOM *Satellit* tracking

Lokal-: **Lokalmodus** *m* COMP & DV local mode; **Lokaloszillator** *m* RADIO local oscillator; **Lokalspeicher** *m* COMP & DV local memory

Lokomotivbetriebswerk *nt* EISENBAHN locomotive depot

Lokomotive *f* (*Lok*) EISENBAHN locomotive; ~ **mit Reibungs- und Zahnradantrieb** *f* EISENBAHN rack rail locomotive

Lokomotivführer *m* EISENBAHN train engineer

Lokomotivschuppen *nt* EISENBAHN engine shed

Lok: **Lokschuppen** *nt* EISENBAHN locomotive shed

Loktalsockel *m* ELEKTRONIK *Elektronenröhren* loctal base

Lok: **Lokwartegleis** *nt* EISENBAHN locomotive holding track

Longifolen *nt* CHEMIE longifolene

Longitudinal: **Longitudinalprüfung** *f* COMP & DV LRC, longitudinal redundancy check; **Longitudinalwelle** *f* PHYS, WELLPHYS *Schallwellen* longitudinal wave

longitudinal: ~er **zyklischer Steuerknüppel** *m* LUFTTRANS *Hubschrauber* fore-and-aft cyclic stick; ~e **zyklische Steuerungshilfe** *f* LUFTTRANS *Hubschrauber* fore-and-aft cyclic control support

Long-Line-Effekt *m* TELEKOM long-line effect

LOOP-Anweisung *f* COMP & DV *EDV-Programm* LOOP statement

Lophin *nt* CHEMIE lophine

LORAN *abbr* (*Langstreckennavigationskette*) LUFTTRANS, WASSERTRANS loran (*long-range navigation*)

Lore *f* EISENBAHN small tip wagon (BrE), spoil car (AmE), trolley (BrE), KOHLEN trolley

Lorentz: ~**sche Bedingung** *f* PHYS Lorentz gage (AmE), Lorentz gauge (BrE); ~**sche Kraft** *f* ELEKTROTECH, PHYS Lorentz force; ~**sche Transformation** *f* PHYS Lorentz transformation

Lorentz-Fitzgerald: ~**sche Kontraktion** *f* PHYS Lorentz-Fitzgerald contraction

Lorentz-Lorenz: ~**sche Gleichung** *f* PHYS Lorentz-Lorenz formula

Lorenz: ~**sche Einheit** *f (L)* THERMOD Lorenz unit *(L)*; ~**sche Konstante** *f* PHYS *Wärmeleitung* Lorenz constant

Lorinmaschine *f* LUFTTRANS athodyd

Los *nt* FERTIG run, *Kunststoffinstallationen* batch, QUAL lot

lösbar[1] *adj* FERTIG *Verbindungen* removable, MASCHINEN detachable, separable; **nicht** ~ *adj* MASCHINEN permanent

lösbar:[2] ~**e Verbindung** *f* FERTIG fastening, MASCHINEN detachable union

Losbrechmoment *nt* MASCHINEN breakaway torque

löschbar: ~**e CD** *f* OPTIK erasable optical disk; ~**e Datenträgerscheibe** *f* OPTIK erasable data disk; ~**es optisches Datenträgermedium** *nt* OPTIK erasable optical medium; ~**er optischer Speicher** *m* OPTIK erasable optical storage; ~**er programmierbarer Lesespeicher** *m (EPROM)* COMP & DV, RADIO erasable programmable read-only memory *(EPROM)*; ~**er Speicher** *m* COMP & DV erasable memory, erasable storage; **nicht** ~**er Speicher** *m* COMP & DV nonerasable storage

Löschbereich *m* COMP & DV purge area

löschbereit *adj* COMP & DV clear-to-zero

Löschdämpfung *f* AKUSTIK, FERNSEH erasure

Löschdrossel *f* FERNSEH bulk eraser

Löschen *nt* AKUSTIK erasure, COMP & DV deletion, purging, ELEKTRIZ blowing out, FERNSEH erasure, TELEKOM deletion, TRANS *einer Ladung*, WASSERTRANS landing

löschen *vt* AUFNAHME erase, BAU *Kalk* quench, COMP & DV clear, erase, zeroize, erase, *Zeichen* delete, DRUCK kill, FERTIG *Kalk* slake, MECHAN quench, MEERSCHMUTZ *bei Schiffen* unload, RADIO cancel, THERMOD *Feuer* quench, TRANS dump, WASSERTRANS *Ladung* discharge, unload, unship

löschend: ~**er Cursor** *m* COMP & DV destructive cursor; ~**es Lesen** *nt* COMP & DV destructive read; **nicht** ~**es Lesen** *nt* COMP & DV nondestructive read

Löscher *m* MASCHINEN extinguisher

Löschfrequenz *f* AUFNAHME erase frequency

Löschgerät *nt* FERNSEH eraser

Löschkalk *m* BAU hydrated lime, CHEMIE quicklime, slaked lime

Löschkopf *m* AUFNAHME, COMP & DV, FERNSEH erase head

Loschmidt: ~**sche Zahl** *f (n0)* PHYS Loschmidt number *(n0)*

Löschpapierzwischenlage *f* FERTIG blotting-paper washer

Löschrohrblitzableiter *m* ELEKTROTECH expulsion-type lightning arrester

Löschrohrsicherung *f* ELEKTROTECH expulsion fuse

Löschsatz *m* COMP & DV deletion record

Löschschaum *m* THERMOD foam

Löschschlauch *m* SICHERHEIT fire hose

Löschschlauchanschluß *m* SICHERHEIT fire hose coupling

Löschschlauchhaspel *f* SICHERHEIT fire hose reel

Löschspannung *f* ELEKTROTECH extinction potential

Löschspule *f* AUFNAHME bulk eraser, ELEKTROTECH blowout coil

Löschstrom *m* AUFNAHME, FERNSEH erasing current

Löschtransformator *m* ELEKTROTECH neutral compensator

Löschtrog *m* FERTIG *Schmieden* bosh, water bosh

Löschung *f* AKUSTIK, FERNSEH erasure, KONTROLL clearing, PATENT *der Eintragung* cancelation (AmE), cancellation (BrE), TELEKOM deletion; **Löschungsvollzug** *m* TELEKOM cancellation completed

Löschwasserpumpe *f* SICHERHEIT fire pump

Löschzeichen *nt* COMP & DV delete character

Lose *f* MASCHINEN backlash, play, slack

lose[1] *adj* MASCHINEN, PAPIER loose

lose:[2] ~ **Ablagerung** *f* UMWELTSCHMUTZ bulk deposition; ~**r Flansch** *m* FERTIG *Kunststoffinstallationen* backing flange; ~**s Formwerkzeug** *nt* KUNSTSTOFF portable mold (AmE), portable mould (BrE); ~ **gewickelte Windungen** *f pl* ELEKTROTECH loosely-wound turns; ~**s Glas** *nt* KER & GLAS loose glass; ~**r Kabelaufbau** *m* OPTIK loose cable structure; ~ **Klemme** *f* ELEKTRIZ loose terminal; ~ **Kupplung** *f* COMP & DV, ELEKTROTECH, MASCHINEN, PHYS loose coupling; ~ **Querschwelle** *f* EISENBAHN dancing sleeper (BrE), dancing tie (AmE); ~ **Riemenscheibe** *f* MASCHINEN dead pulley, loose pulley; ~ **Rolle** *f* MASCHINEN idle pulley; ~ **Schüttung** *f* EISENBAHN loose ballasting; ~**s Stoßen** *nt* OPTIK loose buffering; ~ **Stoßstelle** *f* OPTIK loose buffer; ~**r Transport** *m* VERPACK bulk transport; ~**r Umschlag** *m* VERPACK wraparound; ~ **Wolle** *f* KER & GLAS loose wool; ~**r Zement** *m* BAU bulk cement

Lose: Loseblatt *nt* DRUCK, PAPIER loose-leaf; **Losefehler** *m* LUFTTRANS *Höhenmesser* backlash error

Losekeil *m* MASCHINEN loosening wedge

Lösemittel *nt* CHEMIE dissolvent, menstruum, CHEMTECH dissolvent

lösemittelabstoßend *adj* CHEMIE lyophobic

lösemittelanziehend *adj* CHEMIE lyophilic

Lösen *nt* EISENBAHN *einer Kupplung* loosening, FERTIG release

lösen *vt* BAU ease, KFZTECH *die Bremse* release, MASCHINEN disengage, PAPIER dissolve, WASSERTRANS *Tauwerk* loosen

Los: Losgröße *f* FERTIG, QUAL lot size; **Loslager** *nt* MASCHINEN movable bearing

löslich *adj* ERDÖL, MASCHINEN soluble

Löslichkeit *f* CHEMIE dissolubility, solubility, KOHLEN, KUNSTSTOFF solubility; **Löslichkeitsverbesserer** *m* CHEMIE solutizer

loslösen *vt* MECHAN loosen

Los: Losmachen *nt* WASSERTRANS unmooring

losmachen *vti* WASSERTRANS unmoor

Los: Losrad *nt* MASCHINEN loose wheel; **Losscheibe** *f* MASCHINEN loose pulley, loose wheel; **Losschlagen** *nt* FERTIG *Modell* rapping

losschlagen *vt* FERTIG *Modell* rap

Los: Losschrauben *nt* MASCHINEN unbolting, unscrewing

losschrauben *vt* MASCHINEN unscrew

lossegeln *vi* WASSERTRANS sail away

Los: Lossitz *m* HYDRAUL *Ventil* loose seat; **Losumfang** *m* QUAL lot size

Lösung[1] *f* CHEMIE dissolution, *verdünnt* dilution, MATH root, THERMOD solution; **~ einer Aufgabe** *f* PATENT solution of a problem

Lösung:[2] **in ~ schwimmen** *vi* ANSTRICH suspend

Lösung: **Lösungs- und- Verdünnungs-Kältemaschine** *f* PHYS dilution refrigerator; **Lösungsbenzin** *nt* ERDÖL *Destillationsprodukt* petroleum spirit; **Lösungsglühen** *nt* METALL solution annealing; **Lösungsgraph** *m* KÜNSTL INT solution graph

Lösungsmittel *nt* ANSTRICH, KOHLEN, KUNSTSTOFF, LEBENSMITTEL, METALL solvent, PAPIER dissolver, TEXTIL, UMWELTSCHMUTZ solvent; **Lösungsmitteldampf** *m* KOHLEN solvent vapour; **Lösungsmittelextraktion** *f* LEBENSMITTEL solvent extraction; **Lösungsmittelresistenz** *f* ANSTRICH solvent resistance; **Lösungsmittelretention** *f* KUNSTSTOFF solvent retention; **Lösungsmittelrückgewinnung** *f* DRUCK, LEBENSMITTEL solvent recovery; **Lösungsmittelrückgewinnungsanlage** *f* ABFALL solvent recovery plant, solvent recovery unit

Lösung: **Lösungspolymerisation** *f* KUNSTSTOFF solution polymerization; **Lösungsschweißen** *nt* KUNSTSTOFF solvent welding; **Lösungsvermittler** *m* CHEMIE solutizer; **Lösungswärme** *f* THERMOD heat of solution

losweise: ~ Prüfung *f* QUAL lot-by-lot inspection

loswerfen *vt* WASSERTRANS cast off

Lot:[1] **im ~** *adv* BAU plumb

Lot[2] *nt* BAU bob, plummet, solder, ELEKTRONIK *vertikales Referenzmaß* lead, ELEKTROTECH solder, FERTIG bob, plumb, solder, GEOM perpendicular, MASCHINEN, RADIO solder

Lot:[3] **ins ~ bringen** *vt* BAU plumb

Lot:[4] **~ einführen** *vi* ELEKTRIZ run solder

Lötanschluß *m* MASCHINEN soldered fitting

Lötbad *nt* FERTIG molten solder, solder bath, MASCHINEN soldering bath

Lot: **Lotband** *nt* MASCHINEN strip solder

lotbar: ~er Grund *m* WASSERTRANS *Meer* soundings

lötbar *adj* ELEKTRIZ, FERTIG solderable

Lötbarkeit *f* ELEKTRIZ solderability

Lot: **Lotblei** *nt* WASSERTRANS sounding lead

Lötbrüchigkeit *f* FERTIG solder embrittlement

Lötdraht *m* FERTIG solder wire, MASCHINEN filler wire

Loten *nt* BAU plumbing

Löten *nt* ELEKTRIZ, FERTIG, MASCHINEN soldering

loten *vt* RADIO *Navigation* sound

löten[1] *vt* FERTIG solder, sweat, MASCHINEN, RADIO solder

löten[2] *vti* MASCHINEN solder

Lötfahne *f* FERTIG soldering ear, soldering tag

Lötfluß *m* ELEKTRIZ soldering flux; **Lötflußmittel** *nt* FERTIG flux, solder flux

lötfrei *adj* RADIO solderless

Lötfuge *f* FERTIG joint clearance, soldering joint gap

lotgerecht: nicht ~ *adv* BAU off plumb, out of plumb

Lötkolben *m* BAU soldering iron, FERTIG bit, copper bit, iron, soldering bit, soldering iron, soldering copper, MASCHINEN, RADIO soldering iron

Lot: **Lotkreisel** *m* RAUMFAHRT gyroscopic verticant

Lötlampe *f* BAU blowlamp (BrE), blowtorch (AmE), FERTIG blowlamp (BrE), MASCHINEN blowlamp, blowtorch

Lot: **Lotleine** *f* WASSERTRANS lead line, sounding line

Lötmittel *nt* ELEKTROTECH flux, soldering flux, solder, FERTIG flux

Lötnaht *f* FERTIG solder, LEBENSMITTEL *Konservendosen* soldered seam

Lötofen *m* FERTIG brazier

Lötöse *f* FERTIG lug, soldering ear, RADIO solder lug

Lötpistole *f* ELEKTRIZ soldering gun

lotrecht[1] *adj* FERTIG perpendicular; **~ einfallend** *adj* FERTIG incident normally

lotrecht[2] *adv* BAU plumb

Lötrohr *nt* BAU soldering blowpipe

Lot: **Lotschnur** *f* BAU plumb line

Lötschweißung *f* BAU braze welding

Lotse *m* WASSERTRANS pilot

Lötseite *f* TELEKOM soldered side

lotsen *vt* LUFTTRANS, WASSERTRANS pilot

Lotse: **Lotsenboot** *nt* WASSERTRANS pilot boat; **Lotsenflagge** *f* WASSERTRANS pilot flag; **Lotsengebühr** *f* WASSERTRANS pilotage; **Lotsenkutter** *m* WASSERTRANS pilot cutter; **Lotsenrevier** *nt* WASSERTRANS pilot waters; **Lotsenstrecke** *f* WASSERTRANS pilot waters; **Lotsenwesen** *nt* WASSERTRANS pilotage

Lötstelle *f* BAU wiped joint, MASCHINEN soldering joint, RADIO junction

Lot: **Lotung** *f* WASSERTRANS sounding

Lötung *f* MASCHINEN soldering

Lötverbindung *f* MASCHINEN soldered joint

Lötzinn *nt* BAU plumber's solder, MASCHINEN tin-lead solder, RADIO solder

Low-Level-Injektion *f* ELEKTRONIK low-level injection

LOX *abbr* (*Flüssigsauerstoff*) RAUMFAHRT, THERMOD lox (*liquid oxygen*)

Loxodrome *f* RAUMFAHRT loxodromic line, WASSERTRANS *Navigation* rhumb line

loxodromisch: ~e Navigation *f* WASSERTRANS *Navigation* rhumb line navigation

LP *abbr* (*Langspielplatte*) AUFNAHME EP, (*extended-play record*) LP (*long-playing record*)

LPC[1] *abbr* (*lineare Prädiktionscodierung*) ELEKTRONIK, TELEKOM LPC (*linear predictive coding*)

LPC:[2] **LPC-Kodierung** *f* ELEKTRONIK LPC-coding; **LPC-Vocoder** *m* TELEKOM linear predictive coding vocoder

LPG[1] *abbr* (*Flüssiggas*) ERDÖL, HEIZ & KÄLTE, KFZTECH, THERMOD, WASSERTRANS LPG (*liquefied petroleum gas*)

LPG:[2] **LPG-Bus** *m* KFZTECH LPG bus; **LPG-Motor** *m* KFZTECH LPG engine; **LPG-Tanker** *m* WASSERTRANS LPG tanker; **LPG-Transporter** *m* THERMOD LPG carrier

LPM *abbr* (*Zeilen pro Minute*) COMP & DV LPM (*lines per minute*)

LP-Mode *f* (*linear polarisierte Mode, linear polarisierter Wellentyp*) OPTIK, TELEKOM LP mode (*linearly-polarized mode*)

L-Profil *nt* METALL L-section

LQ *abbr* (*Korrespondenzqualität*) COMP & DV, DRUCK LQ (*letter quality*)

LS *abbr* (*Laufsitz*) MASCHINEN running fit

LSB *abbr* COMP & DV (*niederwertigstes Bit*) LSB (*least significant bit*), ELEKTRONIK (*unteres Seitenband*), RADIO (*unteres Seitenband*), TELEKOM (*unteres Seiteband*) LSB (*lower sideband*)

L-Schale *f* PHYS *Atomphysik* L-shell

LSI *abbr* (*Großintegration, hoher Integrationsgrad*) COMP & DV, ELEKTRONIK, PHYS, TELEKOM LSI (*large-scale integration*)

L-Signal *nt* ELEKTRONIK L-signal, low-level signal

LSI-Kreis *f* (*hochintegrierter Schaltkreis*) ELEKTRONIK, PHYS, TELEKOM LSI circuit (*large-scale integrated circuit*)

L-S-Kopplung *f* *(Russell-Saunders-Kopplung)* KERN-
TECH l-s coupling *(Russell-Saunders coupling)*
L-Stein *m* KER & GLAS L-block
L-Träger *m* BAU L-beam
Lu *(Lutetium)* CHEMIE Lu *(lutetium)*
Lucit *nt* KUNSTSTOFF Lucite
Lücke *f* BAU interstice, COMP & DV, ELEKTROTECH *Ma-
gnetkreis*, MASCHINEN gap; **Lückenbildung** *f* METALL
void formation; **Lückeneffekt** *m* FERNSEH gap effect;
Lückenfräser *m* MASCHINEN gap cutter, MECHAN an-
gular milling cutter; **Lückengrad** *m* METALL voids
fraction; **Lückengrund** *m* FERTIG *Zahnrad* space bot-
tom; **Lückenschalter** *m* FERNSEH gapping switch;
Lückenwachstum *nt* METALL void growth
Lüder: ~sche Linie *f* FERTIG line of yielding
Luft:[1] **mit ~ als Dielektrikum ausgestattet** *adj* ELEKTRIZ
air-dielectric
Luft[2] *f* ELEKTROTECH clearance, MASCHINEN backlash,
bearing slackness, clearance, play, TELEKOM clearance; **~ und Raumfahrt** *f* RAUMFAHRT aerospace;
Luft-und Raumfahrtelektronik *f* LUFTTRANS avionics;
Luft- und Raumfahrtmedizin *f* RAUMFAHRT aerospace
medicine; **Luft- und Seestreitkräfte** *f pl* WASSERTRANS
Marine air and sea forces; **durch die ~ verbreiteter
akustischer Lärm** *m* SICHERHEIT airborne acoustical
noise; **durch die ~ verbreiteter Lärm** *m* SICHERHEIT
airborne noise emitted
Luft:[3] **mit ~ kühlen** *vt* THERMOD air-cool
Luft: **Luftabfluß** *m* MECHAN, PHYS air discharge; **Luftab-
gleichkondensator** *m* ELEKTROTECH air trimmer
capacitor; **Luftabscheider** *m* ABFALL air separator,
LUFTTRANS deaerator, MASCHINEN air separator; **Luft-
abscheidung** *f* CHEMTECH air separation
Luftabzug *m* FERTIG air exhaust, WASSERTRANS air vent;
Luftabzugsöffnung *f* HEIZ & KÄLTE vent port; **Luftab-
zugssystem** *nt* SICHERHEIT extraction fan system;
Luftabzugventil *nt* FERTIG air escape valve
Luft: **Luftagens** *nt* ERDÖL atmospheric agent; **Luftanlas-
ser** *m* MASCHINEN air starter; **Luftansaugstutzen** *m*
LUFTTRANS inducer; **Luftansaugung** *f* FERTIG air inta-
ke, MASCHINEN indraught of air
luftartig *adj* CHEMIE aeriform
Luftaufklärung *f* MEERSCHMUTZ aerial reconnaissance;
Luftaufklärungsflugzeug *nt* MEERSCHMUTZ *für Ölverschmutzungen* spotter plane
Luft: **Luftauftanksystem** *nt* LUFTTRANS refueling in-
flight system (AmE), refuelling in-flight system
(BrE); **Luftausfällung** *f* UMWELTSCHMUTZ air shed;
Luftauslaß *m* ERDÖL air exhaust, HEIZ & KÄLTE air
discharge, air outlet, MASCHINEN air outlet, MECHAN,
PHYS air discharge, WASSERTRANS air vent; **Luftauslaß-
düse** *f* MECHAN, PHYS air discharge nozzle; **Luftaustritt**
m HEIZ & KÄLTE air discharge, air outlet; **Luftaustritts-
gitter** *nt* HEIZ & KÄLTE air discharge grille; **Luftbedarf**
m MASCHINEN air consumption; **Luftbefeuchter** *m*
HEIZ & KÄLTE, LUFTTRANS, PAPIER humidifier, SICHER-
HEIT air humidifier, THERMOD humidifier;
Luftbehälter *m* ERDÖL air tank, MASCHINEN air box,
air receiver; **Luftbetankungssonde** *f* LUFTTRANS flight
refueling probe (AmE), flight refuelling probe (BrE),
in-flight refueling probe (AmE), in-flight refuelling
probe (BrE)
luftbetrieben: ~es Meßgerät *nt* METROL air-operated
gage (AmE), air-operated gauge (BrE)
Luft: **Luftbewegung** *f* HEIZ & KÄLTE air movement, LUFT-
TRANS blast; **Luftbildauswertung** *f* KOHLEN air photo

interpretation; **Luftbildfernerkundung** *f* MEER-
SCHMUTZ airborne remote sensing; **Luftbildkamera** *f*
FOTO aerial mapping camera; **Luftbildmeßkamera** *f*
FOTO aerial mapping camera; **Luftbildvermessung** *f*
LUFTTRANS aerial survey; **Luftbildwesen** *nt* LUFT-
TRANS aerial survey; **Luftblase** *f* FERTIG *Guß* cavity,
MECHAN, PHYS air bubble; **Luftblasenflotation** *f* UM-
WELTSCHMUTZ air flotation; **Luftbohren** *nt* ERDÖL
Bohrtechnik air drilling; **Luftbremse** *f* LUFTTRANS air
brake, speed brake
luftbremsen *vt* RAUMFAHRT *Raumschiff* aerobrake
Luft: **Luft-Brennstoff-Verhältnis** *nt* TRANS air-fuel ratio;
Luftbrücke *f* LUFTTRANS airlift; **Luftbürste** *f* FERTIG air
knife, KUNSTSTOFF, PAPIER air brush; **Luftbürsten-
streichmaschine** *f* PAPIER airbrush coater; **Luftchemie**
f UMWELTSCHMUTZ atmospheric chemistry; **Luft-
dämpfung** *f* GERÄT *am Meßwerk* air damping
luftdicht[1] *adj* ERDÖL, LEBENSMITTEL, MASCHINEN, ME-
CHAN airtight, PAPIER air-proof, airtight, PHYS,
VERPACK, WASSERTRANS airtight; **~ abgeschlossen** *adj*
ELEKTROTECH, HEIZ & KÄLTE, MECHAN hermetically-
sealed
luftdicht:[2] **~er Verschluß** *m* TELEKOM hermetic sealing,
VERPACK hermetic closure; **~e Versiegelung** *f* VERPACK
hermetic seal
Luft: **Luftdichte** *f* HEIZ & KÄLTE air density; **Luftdichte-
meßgerät** *nt* METROL, PAPIER, PHYS aerometer;
Luftdiffusor *m* HEIZ & KÄLTE air diffuser; **Luftdrehkon-
densator** *m* ELEKTROTECH air variable capacitor;
Luftdruck *m* FERTIG air pressure, LUFTTRANS baromc-
tric pressure, MASCHINEN air pressure, PHYS,
WASSERTRANS atmospheric pressure
luftdruckbedingt: ~e Spektrallinie *f* PHYS atmospheric
line
Luft: **Luftdruckmeißel** *m* FERTIG air chipper; **Luftdruck-
messer** *m* LABOR barometer, METROL air gage (AmE),
air gauge (BrE); **Luftdruckmeßgerät** *nt* ERDÖL *Meßtechnik* air pressure gage (AmE), air pressure gauge
(BrE); **Luftdruckmotor** *m* LUFTTRANS air motor; **Luft-
druckschalter** *m* LUFTTRANS barometric switch;
Luftdruckschreiber *m* GERÄT, LABOR, WASSERTRANS
barograph; **Luftdruckwirkung** *f* LUFTTRANS blast;
Luftdurchflußmenge *f* HEIZ & KÄLTE airflow rate, rate
of air flow; **Luftdurchflußzähler** *m* MASCHINEN air
meter; **Luftdurchgang** *m* MASCHINEN air passage
luftdurchlässig *adj* VERPACK impermeable
Luft: **Luftdurchlässigkeit** *f* HEIZ & KÄLTE air permeability; **Luftdurchsatz** *m* HEIZ & KÄLTE rate of air
flow; **Luftdusche** *f* PAPIER air shower; **Luftdüse** *f*
MASCHINEN air nozzle, MECHAN choke; **Luftdüsen-
streichmaschine** *f* PAPIER air jet coater; **Lufteinblasen**
nt MASCHINEN air blowing
Lufteinlaß *m* FERTIG air admission, air intake, HEIZ &
KÄLTE air inlet, air intake, KER & GLAS air inlet, MA-
SCHINEN air inlet, air intake, WASSERTRANS air intake;
~ am Triebwerk *m* LUFTTRANS engine air intake; **~ mit
variabler Geometrie** *m* LUFTTRANS variable-geometry
intake; **Lufteinlaßdüse** *f* MASCHINEN air inlet nozzle;
Lufteinlaßhahn *m* FERTIG, MASCHINEN air inlet cock,
WASSERVERSORG bleeding cock; **Lufteinlaßventil** *nt*
LUFTTRANS air-charging valve, WASSERVERSORG
bleeding valve
Luft: **Lufteinpreßbohrung** *f* ERDÖL *Förderung* air input
well; **Lufteinschluß** *m* FERTIG air cavity, KUNSTSTOFF
entrapped air, STRÖMPHYS *Röhren* airlock, VERPACK
entrapped air

Lufteintritt *m* HEIZ & KÄLTE air inlet, air intake; **Lufteintrittsdruck** *m* LUFTTRANS air intake pressure; **Lufteintrittsöffnung** *f* LUFTTRANS inducer; **Lufteintrittsventil** *nt* LUFTTRANS air intake valve

luftelektrisch: **~e Störung** *f* ELEKTROTECH atmospherics, static

lüften[1] *vt* BAU vent, ventilate, HEIZ & KÄLTE ventilate, MASCHINEN vent, THERMOD ventilate, TRANS air

lüften[2] *vi* HEIZ & KÄLTE vent

Luft: **Luftentfeuchter** *m* HEIZ & KÄLTE dehydrating breather, SICHERHEIT air dehumidifier

Lüfter *m* EISENBAHN, ELEKTRIZ fan, HEIZ & KÄLTE blower, fan, ventilator, KFZTECH cooling fan, fan, ventilator, LEBENSMITTEL blower, MASCHINEN ventilating fan, MECHAN exhauster, fan, RADIO blower, SICHERHEIT ventilator, THERMOD fan, WASSERTRANS ventilator; **~ mit verschiebbarer Schlitzplatte** *m* HEIZ & KÄLTE hit-and-miss damper; **~ für zwei Richtungen** *m* HEIZ & KÄLTE bidirectional fan; **Lüfterabdeckhaube** *f* HEIZ & KÄLTE fan cowl, fan shroud; **Lüfteraggregat** *nt* HEIZ & KÄLTE fan set, fan unit; **Lüfterbaugruppe** *f* HEIZ & KÄLTE fan unit; **Lüfterdrehzahl** *f* HEIZ & KÄLTE fan speed; **Lüftergehäuse** *nt* HEIZ & KÄLTE fan casing, fan enclosure, fan housing; **Lüfterhaube** *f* HEIZ & KÄLTE cowl, fan cowl, fan guard, shroud, KFZTECH, WASSERTRANS *Deckbeschläge* ventilator cowl

Luft: **Lufterhitzer** *m* FERTIG, HEIZ & KÄLTE, MASCHINEN air heater

Lüfter: **Lüfterkeilriemen** *m* KFZTECH fan belt; **Lüfterkennlinie** *f* HEIZ & KÄLTE fan characteristic; **Lüfterkragen** *m* HEIZ & KÄLTE cowl, fan cowl, fan shroud; **Lüfterkranz** *m* HEIZ & KÄLTE fan impeller; **Lüfterleistung** *f* HEIZ & KÄLTE fan performance; **Lüfterleistungskennlinie** *f* HEIZ & KÄLTE fan performance curve

Luft: **Luftermessung** *f* LUFTTRANS *Filmaufnahmen* aerial motion picture survey

Lüfter: **Lüftermotor** *m* HEIZ & KÄLTE fan motor; **Lüfterpumpe** *f* MECHAN exhaust pump; **Lüfterrad** *nt* HEIZ & KÄLTE fan impeller, impeller; **Lüfterriemenscheibe** *f* KFZTECH *Kühlsystem* fan pulley; **Lüfterschaufel** *f* HEIZ & KÄLTE, KFZTECH, MASCHINEN, THERMOD fan blade; **Lüfterstation** *f* BAU fan station; **Lüfterstufe** *f* HEIZ & KÄLTE fan stage; **Lüfterstutzen** *m* HEIZ & KÄLTE fan cowl; **Lüfterumfangsgeschwindigkeit** *f* HEIZ & KÄLTE tip speed; **Lüfterwirkung** *f* HEIZ & KÄLTE fanning action

Luftfahrt *f* LUFTTRANS aeronautics; **Luftfahrtfunkdienst** *m (AACS)* RAUMFAHRT airways and air communications service *(AACS)*; **Luftfahrtindustrie** *f* TRANS aeronautical industry; **Luftfahrt-Navigationsausschuß** *m (ANC)* LUFTTRANS International Civil Aviation Organization *(ICAO)*; **Luftfahrtregeln** *f pl* LUFTTRANS rules of the air; **Luftfahrtregister** *nt* LUFTTRANS aeronautical register; **Luftfahrttechnik** *f* LUFTTRANS aerotechnics (AmE)

Luftfahrzeug *nt* LUFTTRANS aircraft; **vom ~ zurückgelegter Kilometer** *m* LUFTTRANS aircraft kilometre performed; **Luftfahrzeugklasse** *f* LUFTTRANS aircraft classification; **Luftfahrzeugleitwerk** *nt* LUFTTRANS aircraft tail unit; **Luftfahrzeugradar** *nt* TELEKOM airborne radar; **Luftfahrzeugrufzeichen** *nt* LUFTTRANS aircraft call signal; **Luftfahrzeugstromversorgung** *f* LUFTTRANS aircraft mains; **Luftfahrzeugzulassungsbescheinigung** *f* LUFTTRANS certificate of airworthiness; **Luftfahrzeugverteilernetz** *nt* LUFTTRANS aircraft mains

Luft: **Luftfernsehen** *nt* FERNSEH airborne television; **Luftfeuchtemeßgerät** *nt* GERÄT air humidity meter; **Luftfeuchteschreiber** *m* GERÄT air humidity recorder

Luftfeuchtigkeit *f* ANSTRICH, FERTIG *Kunststoffinstallationen*, HEIZ & KÄLTE humidity, KOHLEN air moisture, PHYS, THERMOD humidity, VERPACK air humidity; **Luftfeuchtigkeitsanzeige** *f* VERPACK humidity indicator; **Luftfeuchtigkeitsmesser** *m* ERDÖL, GERÄT hygrometer, HEIZ & KÄLTE, LABOR *Feuchtigkeit* hygrometer, psychrometer, MASCHINEN, PHYS, THERMOD hygrometer; **Luftfeuchtigkeitsmessung** *f* HEIZ & KÄLTE hygrometry, WASSERTRANS humidity measurement

Luft: **Luftfilmsystem** *nt* WASSERTRANS air film system; **Luftfilter** *nt* CHEMTECH, HEIZ & KÄLTE air filter, KFZTECH *Vergaser* air cleaner, air filter, KOHLEN air filter, MASCHINEN air cleaner, MECHAN, PHYS air filter; **Luftfilter für Submikronstaub** *nt* SICHERHEIT submicron particulate airfilter; **Luftfilterung** *f* FERTIG air cleaning

luftförmig *adj* CHEMIE aeriform

Luft: **Luftfotografie** *f* FOTO aerial photography; **Luftfracht** *f* LUFTTRANS air freight, VERPACK air cargo, air freight; **Luftfrachtbrief** *m* LUFTTRANS air waybill; **Luftführungsbahn** *f* TRANS aerial guideway; **Luftführungsblech** *nt* HEIZ & KÄLTE air baffle plate; **Luftgang** *m* WASSERTRANS *Schiffbau* air course; **Luftgardine** *f* KFZTECH air curtain; **Luftgefrierapparat** *m* HEIZ & KÄLTE air blast freezer; **Luftgefrieren** *nt* HEIZ & KÄLTE air blast freezing

luftgekühlt[1] *adj* ELEKTRIZ air-cooled, FERTIG air-cooled, air-dried, HEIZ & KÄLTE, MASCHINEN, PAPIER, THERMOD air-cooled

luftgekühlt:[2] **~er Kondensator** *m* HEIZ & KÄLTE air-cooled condenser; **~er Motor** *m* KFZTECH, MASCHINEN air-cooled engine; **~e Röhre** *f* ELEKTRONIK air-cooled tube; **~es System** *nt* MASCHINEN air-cooled system; **~er Transformator** *m* ELEKTRIZ air-cooled transformer; **~e Triode** *f (LKT)* ELEKTRONIK air-cooled triode *(ACT)*

luftgelagert *adj* FERTIG air-bearinged

luftgelöscht: **~er Kalk** *m* CHEMIE air-slaked lime

Luft: **Luftgeräusch** *nt* HEIZ & KÄLTE aerodynamic noise

luftgeschmiert *adj* FERTIG air-lubricated

Luft: **Luftgeschwindigkeit** *f* HEIZ & KÄLTE air velocity

luftgesteuert: **~e Setzmaschine** *f* KOHLEN Baum box, Baum jig

luftgestützt: **~er Abstandswarnanzeiger** *m* LUFTTRANS airborne proximity warning indicator; **~es Kollisionswarnsystem** *nt* LUFTTRANS airborne collision avoidance system

luftgetrocknet *adj* LEBENSMITTEL air-dried, PAPIER *auf Trockenboden* loft-dried, VERPACK air-dried

Luft: **Lufthahn** *m* FERTIG air cock; **Lufthärtestahl** *m* FERTIG air hardening steel, METALL air-hardening steel; **Lufthärtungsstahl** *m* FERTIG air hardening steel, METALL air-hardening steel; **Luftheizgerät mit Gebläse** *nt* THERMOD unit heater; **Luftheizung** *f* HEIZ & KÄLTE hot-air heater; **Luftherd** *m* KOHLEN pneumatic table

lufthydraulisch *adj* FERTIG air-hydraulic

Luft: **Lufthygiene** *f* UMWELTSCHUTZ air pollution control; **Luftinjektor** *m* MASCHINEN air injector; **Luftisolation** *f* ELEKTROTECH air insulation

luftisoliert: **~er Kondensator** *m* ELEKTRIZ air capacitor

Luft: **Luftisolierung** *f* ELEKTRIZ, ELEKTROTECH air insulation, HEIZ & KÄLTE airspace insulation; **Luftkabel** *nt*

ELEKTROTECH overhead cable, TELEKOM aerial cable; **Luftkanal** *m* FERTIG air conduit, HEIZ & KÄLTE air duct, duct, KOHLEN air duct, LUFTTRANS airway, MASCHINEN air conduit; **Luftkasten** *m* ERDÖL *Raffinerie* air box, WASSERTRANS *Bootbau* air tank; **Luftkern** *m* ELEKTROTECH *Spule* air core; **Luftkernspule** *f* ELEKTRIZ air core coil; **Luftkerntransformator** *m* ELEKTRIZ air core transformer, air transformer, air-cored transformer

Luftkissen *nt* KFZTECH air bag, LUFTTRANS air dashpot, MASCHINEN, TRANS air cushion; **~ mit eingegangenen Lufblasen** *nt* LUFTTRANS sidewall air cushion; **~ mit Ringstrahl** *nt* TRANS peripheral jet air cushion; **~ mit starren Schürzen** *nt* LUFTTRANS rigid sidewall air cushion

luftkissenbefördert *adj* TRANS cushion-borne

Luftkissen: **Luftkissenboot** *nt* WASSERTRANS hydroskimmer (AmE), marine air cushion vehicle, marine hovercraft

Luftkissenfahrzeug *nt (LKF)* KFZTECH surface effect vehicle *(SEV)*, TRANS aeromobile- (AmE), air cushion vehicle, WASSERTRANS *Schifftyp* hovercraft (BrE), hydroskimmer (AmE), surface effect ship; **~ mit festen Schürzen** *nt* WASSERTRANS rigid sidewall hovercraft; **~ mit Luftschraubenantrieb** *nt* TRANS air propelled hovercraft; **~ mit starren Schürzen** *nt* - WASSERTRANS rigid skirt hovercraft; **~ mit Wasserschrauben** *nt* WASSERTRANS water-propelled hovercraft; **Luftkissenfahrzeughafen** *m* WASSERTRANS hoverport

Luftkissen: **Luftkissenhaltesystem** *nt* TRANS air cushion restraint system; **Luftkissenplattform** *f* WASSERTRANS hover pallet; **Luftkissenschwebesystem** *nt* TRANS air cushion levitation; **Luftkissenschwebezug** *m* WASSERTRANS hovertrain; **Luftkissentransportrinne** *f* TRANS aeroglide; **Luftkissenzug** *m* EISENBAHN aerotrain

Luft: **Luftklappe** *f* FERTIG air choke, air valve, HEIZ & KÄLTE air damper, KFZTECH *Vergaser* choke, MASCHINEN air valve; **Luftklappensystem** *nt* TRANS blown-flap system; **Luftklassierer** *m* ABFALL air classifier, air separation plant; **Luftkompressor** *m* HYDRAUL, KFZTECH, LABOR, MASCHINEN air compressor; **Luftkondensator** *m* MECHAN, PHYS air capacitor; **Luftkorrekturdüse** *f* KFZTECH air correction jet; **Luftkorridor** *m* LUFTTRANS air corridor; **Luftkreislauf** *m* HEIZ & KÄLTE ventilation circuit; **Luftkühlapparat** *m* HEIZ & KÄLTE air cooler

luftkühlen *vt* HEIZ & KÄLTE, MECHAN, THERMOD fan-cool

Luft: **Luftkühler** *m* HEIZ & KÄLTE, KERNTECH air cooler; **Luftkühlkreislauf** *m* HEIZ & KÄLTE air refrigeration cycle; **Luftkühlmittel** *nt* KERNTECH air coolant

Luftkühlung *f* ELEKTROTECH air cooling, HEIZ & KÄLTE fan cooling, KFZTECH, MASCHINEN air cooling, MECHAN, THERMOD fan cooling; **Luftkühlungssystem** *nt* MASCHINEN air-cooling installation

Luft: **Luftkursbuch** *nt* LUFTTRANS aerial timetable; **Luftlager** *nt* FERTIG air bearing, MECHAN gas bearing; **Luftleistung** *f* HEIZ & KÄLTE airflow rate, flow rate, rate of air flow; **Luftleitblech** *nt* HEIZ & KÄLTE air baffle plate, shroud, KFZTECH *Karosserie* louver (AmE), louvre (BrE), spoiler; **Luftleitung** *f* AKUSTIK air conduction, KER & GLAS airline, MASCHINEN air main, air pipeline, airline, PAPIER airline; **Luftleitungen** *f pl* MASCHINEN air ducting; **Luftloch** *nt* WASSERTRANS *Schiffbau* air course

luftlos: **~e Einspritzung** *f* MASCHINEN solid injection; **~er**

Reifen *m* KFZTECH flat tire (AmE), flat tyre (BrE)

Luft: **Luft-Luft-Wärmetauscher** *m* HEIZ & KÄLTE, MASCHINEN air-to-air heat exchanger; **Luftmenge** *f* HEIZ & KÄLTE air volume; **Luftmengenmesser** *m* LUFTTRANS airflow sensor; **Luftmesser** *nt* FERTIG, KUNSTSTOFF air knife, PAPIER air blade, air knife; **Luftmesserstreichmaschine** *f* PAPIER air knife coater; **Luftnavigationskarte** *f* LUFTTRANS aeronautical chart (BrE), sectional chart (AmE)

Luftpatentieren *nt* FERTIG air patenting

luftpatentiert *adj* FERTIG air-patented

Luft: **Luftpinsel** *m* DRUCK aerograph; **Luftporenbeton** *m* BAU air-entrained concrete; **Luftporenbildner** *m* BAU *Beton* air-entraining admixture; **Luftpostpapier** *nt* DRUCK, PAPIER airmail paper; **Luftprobenahmetechnik** *f* SICHERHEIT air-sampling technique; **Luftpuffer** *m* FERTIG air buffer, LUFTTRANS air dashpot; **Luftpumpe** *f* MASCHINEN, MECHAN, PHYS air pump; **Luftqualität** *f* SICHERHEIT air quality; **Luftqualitätsdaten** *nt pl* UMWELTSCHMUTZ air quality data; **Luftrakel** *f* KUNSTSTOFF air knife, PAPIER air doctor; **Luftrakelfeuchtsystem** *nt* DRUCK air doctor dampening system; **Luftraumbeschränkung** *f* LUFTTRANS airspace restriction; **Luftraumüberwachungsradar** *nt* WASSERTRANS *Marine* air search radar; **Luftregulierung** *f* MASCHINEN air regulator; **Luftreibung** *f* RAUMFAHRT *Raumschiff* air friction; **Luftreibungsverluste** *m pl* ELEKTRIZ windage losses; **Luftreifen** *m* KFZTECH, TRANS pneumatic tire (AmE), pneumatic tyre (BrE); **Luftreifenstadtbahn** *f* EISENBAHN pneumatic-tired metropolitan railroad (AmE), pneumatic-tyred metropolitan railway (BrE); **Luftreinheit** *f* UMWELTSCHMUTZ air purity; **Luftreiniger** *m* KOHLEN air cleaner, SICHERHEIT gas-cleaning equipment, VERPACK air purger

Luftreinigung *f* KOHLEN air cleaning, SICHERHEIT *Umweltschutz* clean air device; **Luftreinigungs- und Deodorisierungsgerät** *nt* SICHERHEIT air purification and deodorization equipment

Luft: **Luftrohr** *nt* MASCHINEN air pipe; **Luftröhrenkühler** *m* KFZTECH honeycomb radiator; **Luftsauerstoffbatterie** *f* ELEKTROTECH air depolarized battery; **Luftsauerstoffelement** *nt* ELEKTROTECH air cell; **Luftsauerstoffzelle** *f* ELEKTROTECH air cell; **Luftsaugrohr** *nt* FERTIG air intake; **Luftsäulenlautsprecher** *m* AUFNAHME air column loudspeaker; **Luftschacht** *m* HEIZ & KÄLTE air duct; **Luftschadstoff** *m* UMWELTSCHMUTZ air pollutant; **Luftschall** *m* HEIZ & KÄLTE air noise; **Luftschallemission** *f* MASCHINEN airborne noise emitted; **Luftschalter** *m* ELEKTROTECH air break switch; **Luftschlauch** *m* BAU *Druckluft* air hose, ERDÖL air hoist, KFZTECH inner tube, MASCHINEN, MECHAN, PHYS air hose; **Luftschleiertür** *f* SICHERHEIT air curtain installation for open doors

Luftschleuse *f* HEIZ & KÄLTE, LUFTTRANS, RAUMFAHRT *Raumschiff*, SICHERHEIT, WASSERVERSORG airlock; **Luftschleusensystem** *nt* KERNTECH airlock system

Luft: **Luftschlitz** *m* HEIZ & KÄLTE air duct, duct, MECHAN louver (AmE), louvre (BrE); **Luftschmierung** *f* FERTIG air lubrication

Luftschraube *f* LUFTTRANS airscrew, TRANS air propeller; **Luftschraubenansatz** *m* LUFTTRANS *Hubschrauber* blade root; **Luftschraubenblatt- und Spaltflügelantrieb** *m* LUFTTRANS blade and slot drive; **Luftschraubenblattachse** *f* LUFTTRANS *Hubschrauber* blade pocket; **Luftschraubenblattbelastung** *f* LUFT-

TRANS *Hubschrauber* blade loading; **Luftschrauben-blattbreitenverhältnis** nt LUFTTRANS *Hubschrauber* blade width ratio; **Luftschraubenblattfuß** m LUFT-TRANS blade shank; **Luftschraubenblatthülle** f LUFTTRANS *Hubschrauber* blade sleeve; **Luftschrau-benblattmanschette** f LUFTTRANS *Hubschrauber* blade cuff; **Luftschraubenblattoberseite** f LUFTTRANS *Hubschrauber* blade upper surface; **Luftschrauben-blattpfeilung** f LUFTTRANS *Hubschrauber* blade sweep; **Luftschraubenblattprofil** nt LUFTTRANS *Hubschrauber* blade profile; **Luftschraubenblattradius** m LUFTTRANS *Hubschrauber* blade radius; **Luftschraubenblattschaft** m LUFTTRANS *Hubschrauber* blade shank; **Luftschrau-benblattschlagwinkel** m LUFTTRANS *Hubschrauber* bladder flapping angle; **Luftschraubenblattsehne** f LUFTTRANS *Hubschrauber* blade chord; **Luftschrau-benblattspitze** f LUFTTRANS *Hubschrauber* blade tip; **Luftschraubenblattspitzenhütchen** nt LUFTTRANS *Hubschrauber* blade tip cap; **Luftschraubenblattstei-gungskoeffizient** m LUFTTRANS *Hubschrauber* blade lift coefficient; **Luftschraubenblattsteuersystem** nt LUFTTRANS *Hubschrauber* blade control system; **Luft-schraubenblattzeilung** f LUFTTRANS *Hubschrauber* blade spacing system; **Luftschraubendrehmoment** nt LUFTTRANS propeller torque; **Luftschraubeneinstell-winkel** m LUFTTRANS *Propeller* effective pitch; **Luftschraubenhaube** f LUFTTRANS *Propeller* spinner; **Luftschraubennabe** f LUFTTRANS propeller hub; **Luft-schraubenschlupf** m LUFTTRANS slip of a propeller; **Luftschraubensteigung** f LUFTTRANS propeller pitch; **Luftschraubensteigungseinstellung** f LUFTTRANS *Hubschrauber* blade pitch setting; **Luftschraubenstei-gungsregler** m LUFTTRANS propeller governor; **Luftschraubenstrahl** m LUFTTRANS slipstream; **Luft-schraubenturbine** f NICHTFOSS ENERG propeller turbine; **Luftschraubenwelle** f LUFTTRANS propeller shaft

Luft: **Luftselbstkühlung** f HEIZ & KÄLTE natural air cool-ing; **Luftsetzmaschine** f KOHLEN air jig, pneumatic jig; **Luftsortierer** m ABFALL air classifier, air separator, air separation plant; **Luftspalt** m COMP & DV *eines Ma-gnetkopfes* gap, ELEKTRIZ, ELEKTROTECH *Magnet-Stromkreis*, ERDÖL *Motor* air gap, PHYS *Elek-tromagnet* air gap, *Magnet* gap, TRANS air gap; **Luftspalt zwischen Elektrode und Werkstück** m FER-TIG arc gap; **Luftspalt-Magnetometer** nt ELEKTROTECH flux-gate magnetometer; **Luftspeicher-dieselmotor** m KFZTECH air cell diesel engine; **Luftsperre** f MEERSCHMUTZ air bubble boom; **Luft-spieß** m FERTIG *Gießen* pricker
luftspießen vt FERTIG *Gießen* vent
Luft: **Luftspule** f ELEKTRIZ air reactor; **Luftstartanlaß-schalter** m LUFTTRANS air start ignition switch; **Luftstift** m DRUCK air piston; **Luftstoß** m KOHLEN air blast; **Luftstrahl** m FERTIG air jet; **Luftstrahltriebwerk** nt LUFTTRANS air breathing engine; **Luftstrecke** f ELEKTRIZ air gap
Luftstrom m BAU air flow, LUFTTRANS airflow; **Luft-stromschalter** m ELEKTROTECH air blast circuit breaker; **Luftstromscheider** m LUFTTRANS airstream separation
Luftströmung f HEIZ & KÄLTE air flow, LUFTTRANS, STRÖMPHYS airflow; **Luftströmungsmelder** m HEIZ & KÄLTE airflow indicator; **Luftströmungsmesser** m PHYS anemometer; **Luftströmungspuffer** m LUFT-TRANS friction damper; **Luftströmungswächter** m

HEIZ & KÄLTE airflow monitor, airflow proving switch; **Luftströmungswiderstand** m LUFTTRANS friction drag
Luft: **Lufttank** m ERDÖL air tank; **Lufttankflugzeug** nt LUFTTRANS refueling craft (AmE), refuelling craft (BrE); **Lufttauglichkeitsprüfung** f LUFTTRANS certifi-cation test; **Lufttemperaturanzeige des Enteisers** f LUFTTRANS de-icing air temperature indicator; **Luft-trafo** m ELEKTROTECH air core transformer; **Lufttransformator** m ELEKTRIZ air transformer, air-cored transformer, ELEKTROTECH air core transformer; **Lufttransport** m LUFTTRANS air trans-port, airlift; **Lufttrennschalter** m ELEKTRIZ air break switch; **Lufttrichter** m KFZTECH *Vergaser* venturi
lufttrocken[1] adj PAPIER air-dry
lufttrocken:[2] **~es Papier** nt DRUCK air-dried paper, air-dry paper
Luft: **Lufttrocknen** nt DRUCK air drying
lufttüchtig adj LUFTTRANS airworthy
Luft: **Lufttüchtigkeit** f LUFTTRANS airworthiness; **Luft-tüchtigkeit bescheinigen** vi LUFTTRANS certify as airworthy; **Lufttüchtigkeitszeugnis** nt LUFTTRANS cer-tificate of airworthiness; **Luftturbulenzen** f pl LUFTTRANS atmospheric turbulence; **Luftüberschuß** m MASCHINEN excess air
luftübertragen adj FERTIG airborne
Luft: **Luftüberwachung** f MEERSCHMUTZ aerial surveil-lance; **Luftumlauftrockner** m PAPIER air float dryer; **Luftumwälzofen** m FERTIG air-circulating furnace; **Luftumwälzung** f FERTIG, HEIZ & KÄLTE air circulation
Lüftung f HEIZ & KÄLTE venting, LUFTTRANS air renewal, MASCHINEN airing, venting, SICHERHEIT ventilation system; **Lüftungsanlage** f HEIZ & KÄLTE air-handling system, KFZTECH, WASSERTRANS ventilation system; **Lüftungseinheit** nt HEIZ & KÄLTE AH unit, air-hand-ling unit; **Lüftungsflügelfenster** nt BAU projected window; **Lüftungskanal** m BAU ventiduct, ventilation duct; **Lüftungsleitung** f HEIZ & KÄLTE ventilation duct; **Lüftungsöffnung** f MASCHINEN air vent; **Lüftungs-schacht** m BAU funnel; **Lüftungsschlitz** m HEIZ & KÄLTE venting slot; **Lüftungsstutzen** m KERNTECH vent nozzle, KFZTECH, WASSERTRANS ventilator socket; **Lüftungstür** f BAU ventilating door; **Lüftungszentrale** f HEIZ & KÄLTE ventilation control center (AmE), venti-lation control centre (BrE)
Luft: **Luftventil** nt FERTIG air choke, NICHTFOSS ENERG air valve; **Luftverbrauch** m MASCHINEN air consump-tion; **Luftverdichter** m HYDRAUL air compressor; **Luftverdichtung** f FERTIG air compression; **Luftvergif-tung** f UMWELTSCHMUTZ air poisoning; **Luftverhältnis** nt KFZTECH air ratio
Luftverkehr m LUFTTRANS air traffic; **Luftverkehrsge-sellschaft** f LUFTTRANS airline; **Luftverkehrskontrolle** f LUFTTRANS air traffic control service; **Luftverkehrsre-geln** f pl LUFTTRANS rules of the air; **Luftverkehrsschema** nt LUFTTRANS air traffic pattern; **Luftverkehrszentrale** f LUFTTRANS air traffic control center (AmE), air traffic control centre (BrE)
Luftverschmutzung f UMWELTSCHMUTZ air pollution, atmospheric pollution; **Luftverschmutzungsvorher-sage** f UMWELTSCHMUTZ air pollution forecast
Luft: **Luftversorgung** f LUFTTRANS air supply; **Luftver-teiler** m HEIZ & KÄLTE air diffuser, diffuser; **Luftverteilergehäuse** nt KFZTECH plenum chamber
luftverunreinigend: **~er Stoff** m UMWELTSCHMUTZ air-polluting substance
Luftverunreinigung f UMWELTSCHMUTZ air pollution;

Luftverunreinigungsemission *f* UMWELTSCHUTZ air pollution emission; **Luftverunreinigungsereignis** *nt* UMWELTSCHUTZ air pollution incident; **Luftverunreinigungsgefahrensituation** *f* UMWELTSCHUTZ air pollution episode; **Luftverunreinigungsstandard** *m* UMWELTSCHUTZ level of pollution

Luft: **Luftvorwärmer** *m* MASCHINEN air preheater, PAPIER air heater; **Luftvulkanisation** *f* KUNSTSTOFF air cure; **Luftwalze** *f* PAPIER air roll; **Luft-Wasser-Wärmetauscher** *m* HEIZ & KÄLTE air-to-water heat exchanger; **Luftwechsel** *m pl* HEIZ & KÄLTE air changes, LUFTTRANS air renewal; **Luftwechselgeschwindigkeit** *f* HEIZ & KÄLTE rate of air change; **Luftwechsler** *m* PAPIER air exchanger; **Luftweg** *m* LUFTTRANS airway, *Flugsicherung* advisory route

Luftweg: auf dem ~ *adj* LUFTTRANS airborne

Luft: **Luftwegnavigationskarte** *f* LUFTTRANS aeronautical route chart

Luftwiderstand *m* HEIZ & KÄLTE drag, LUFTTRANS drag, ohmic resistance, RAUMFAHRT drag, TRANS aerodynamic drag; **Luftwiderstandsbeiwert** *m* KFZTECH drag coefficient, NICHTFOSS ENERG *(DD)* coefficient of drag *(DD)*, TRANS aerodynamic drag factor; **Luftwiderstandsdämpfer** *m* LUFTTRANS compensating developer, drag damper; **Luftwiderstandsmoment** *nt* LUFTTRANS drag moment; **Luftwiderstandsstützstrebe** *f* LUFTTRANS drag brace; **Luftwiderstandsverspannung** *f* LUFTTRANS drag brace; **Luftwiderstandswinkel** *m* LUFTTRANS drag angle

Luft: **Luftzahl** *f* KFZTECH air ratio; **Luftzerlegung** *f* CHEMTECH, LEBENSMITTEL air separation; **Luftziegel** *m* KER & GLAS adobe; **Luftzufuhr** *f* BAU aeration, LUFTTRANS air supply, MASCHINEN air intake, air supply; **Luftzuführung** *f* MASCHINEN air inlet; **Luftzuführungsrohr** *nt* MASCHINEN air inlet pipe; **Luftzug** *m* BAU, MASCHINEN draft (AmE), draught (BrE); **Luftzutritt** *m* FERTIG air admission; **Luftzwischenraum** *m* TRANS air gap

Lugger *m* WASSERTRANS *Segeln* lugger; **Luggersegel** *nt* WASSERTRANS *Segeln* lug

Luke *f* LUFTTRANS hatch, RAUMFAHRT *Raumschiff* access, hatch, WASSERTRANS *Schiff* hatch; **Lukendeckel** *m* WASSERTRANS *Schiffteil* hatch cover; **Lukenöffnung** *f* WASSERTRANS hatchway; **Lukensüll** *nt* WASSERTRANS hatch coaming

Lumen *nt (lm)* FERNSEH, METROL, PHYS *Einheit des Lichtstromes* lumen *(lm)*

Luminanz *f* ELEKTRONIK, ELEKTROTECH, FERNSEH luminance, OPTIK luminance, STRAHLPHYS luminance; **Luminanzträgerleistung** *f* FERNSEH luminance carrier output; **Luminanzverstärker** *m* ELEKTRONIK luminance amplifier

lumineszent *adj* ELEKTROTECH luminescent

Lumineszenz *f* ELEKTROTECH, PHYS, STRAHLPHYS luminescence; **Lumineszenzdiode** *f (LED)* COMP & DV, ELEKTRIZ, ELEKTRONIK, FERNSEH, OPTIK, PHYS, TELEKOM light-emitting diode *(LED)*

Luminophor *m* CHEMIE luminophore

Luminosität *f* TEILPHYS luminosity

Lümmel *m* WASSERTRANS *Beschläge* gooseneck

Lummer-Brodhun-Würfel *m* PHYS *Fotometer* Lummer-Brodhun photometer

Lumpen *m* PAPIER rag; **Lumpenbrecher** *m* PAPIER rag breaker; **Lumpenentstaubungstrommel** *f* PAPIER rag duster; **Lumpensammler** *m* ABFALL scavenger; **Lumpensammlung** *f* ABFALL collection by tatters; **Lumpenshredder** *m* PAPIER rag shredder

Lunar-Modul *nt (LM)* RAUMFAHRT lunar module *(LM)*

Lünette *f* FERTIG back rest, boring-bar steady bracket, lathe steady, steady rest, MASCHINEN back rest, back stay, center rest (AmE), centre rest (BrE); **Lünettenständer** *m* FERTIG boring stay, end-support column, outer stay

lunisolar: ~es Potential *nt* RAUMFAHRT luni-solar potential

Lunker *m* BAU pipe, FERTIG pipe cavity, pocket, shrink hole, KER & GLAS, KUNSTSTOFF void, METALL blow hole, pipe

lunker-: von ~ und fehlerfreiem Gefüge *adj* FERTIG metallurgically sound

lunkerfrei *adj* FERTIG pipeless

Lunkern *nt* FERTIG shrinking

Lunte: als ~ gefärbt *adj* TEXTIL slubbing dyed

Lupe *f* KER & GLAS glass, LABOR, MECHAN magnifying glass, OPTIK *Vergrößerungsglas* lens; **Lupenhalter** *m* OPTIK lens holder

Lupinidin *nt* CHEMIE lupinidine, sparteine

Luppe *f* FERTIG ball, bloom, puddle ball, puddled ball, METALL balled iron, loop, puddle ball; **Luppeneisen** *nt* FERTIG ball iron; **Luppenstab** *m* FERTIG puddle bar

Lüster *m* KER & GLAS luster (AmE), lustre (BrE)

LUT *abbr (Bodenstation)* WASSERTRANS *Satellitennavigation* LUT *(local user terminal)*

Lutein *nt* CHEMIE lutein, xanthophyll

Luteol *nt* CHEMIE luteol

Luteolin *nt* CHEMIE lutcolin

Lutetium *nt (Lu)* CHEMIE lutetium *(Lu)*

Lutidin *nt* CHEMIE lutidine; **Lutidin-** *pref* CHEMIE lutidinic

Lutidon *nt* CHEMIE lutidone

luven *vt* WASSERTRANS luff

luvgierig[1] *adj* WASSERTRANS weatherly

luvgierig:[2] **~ sein** *vi* WASSERTRANS *Segeln* carry weather helm

Luvliek *nt* WASSERTRANS *Segeln* luff

Luvruder *nt* WASSERTRANS *Pinnestellung* weather helm

Luvseite *f* WASSERTRANS weather side

luvwärtig *adj* WASSERTRANS windward

luvwärts *adv* WASSERTRANS windward

Lux *nt (lx)* FOTO, METROL *Beleuchtungsstärke*, OPTIK, PHYS lux *(lx)*; **Luxmeter** *nt* GERÄT luxmeter; **Luxwert** *m* FOTO lux value

LW *abbr (Langwelle)* RADIO LW *(long wave)*

LWL-Kabel *nt* TELEKOM fiberoptic cable (AmE), fibreoptic cable (BrE)

lx *abbr (Lux)* FOTO, LABOR, OPTIK, PHYS lx *(lux)*

Lyman-Serie *f* PHYS Lyman series

Lyogel *nt* CHEMIE lyogel

lyophil *adj* CHEMIE lyophilic

Lyophilisation *f* CHEMTECH lyophilization, LEBENSMITTEL freeze-drying

Lyophilisierung *f* CHEMTECH lyophilization

lyophob *adj* CHEMIE lyophobic

Lyosol *nt* CHEMIE lyosol

lyraförmig: ~er Flugsteuerungswinkelhebel *m* LUFTTRANS flight controls lyre-shaped bellcrank

Lysin *nt* CHEMIE lysine

Lysolecithin *nt* CHEMIE lysolecithin

Lyxon- *pref* CHEMIE lyxonic

Lyxose *f* CHEMIE lyxose

LZG *abbr (Langzeitgedächtnis)* ERGON, KÜNSTL INT LTM *(long-term memory)*

M

M *abbr* ERDÖL *(Molendkulargewicht)* M *(molecular weight)*, M *(Mach number)*, KERNTECH *(Reaktormultiplikation)* M *(multiplication of a reactor)*, LUFTTRANS *(Machzahl)* M *(Mach number)*, METROL *(Mega-)* M *(mega-)*, PHYS *(Machzahl)* M *(Mach number)*, PHYS *(Molekulargewicht)*, THERMOD *(Molekulargewicht)* M *(molecular weight)*

m *abbr* AKUSTIK *(Streukoeffizient, Öffnungskoeffizient)* m *(flare coefficient of horn)*, AKUSTIK *(Scherelastizität)* m *(shear elasticity)*, MASCHINEN *(Masse)* m *(mass)*, METROL *(Meter)* m *(meter)*, METROL *(Milli-)* m *(milli-)*, PHYS *(Masse)* m *(mass)*, PHYS *(Molekularmasse)* m *(molecular mass)*, PHYS *(Gegenindukctivität)* m *(mutual inductance)*, THERMOD *(Masse)* m *(mass)*

m-Höhe *f* DRUCK x-height, z-height

m_0 *abbr (Restmasse)* KERNTECH m_0 *(rest mass)*

MA *abbr (Mittabstand)* FERTIG, KFZTECH, MASCHINEN CD *(centre distance)*

Ma *abbr (Atommasse)* KERNTECH Ma *(atomic mass)*

Mäanderbildung *f* MASCHINEN meandering

Maat *m* WASSERTRANS *Besatzung* leading seaman, *Marine* petty officer

M-Ablauf *m* FERNSEH M-wrap

MAC *abbr (magnetisches Kalorimeter)* TEILPHYS MAC *(magnetic calorimeter)*

Mach: **~sches Prinzip** *nt* PHYS Mach's principle

machbar: **~er Abbrand** *m* KERNTECH achievable burn-up

Machbarkeitsstudie *f* COMP & DV feasibility study

Machkompensator *m* LUFTTRANS Mach compensator

Machmeter *nt* GERÄT *Geschwindigkeitsmeßgerät für strömende Gase, meist mit Pitot-Rohr* machmeter, LUFTTRANS Mach meter

Macht *f* QUAL power; **Machtfunktion** *f* QUAL power function

Machzahl *f (M)* HYDRAUL, LUFTTRANS, PHYS Mach number *(M)*

Mach-Zehender-Interferometrie *f* OPTIK axial slab interferometry

Maclurin *nt* CHEMIE maclurin

Mac-Pherson: **~ Federbein** *nt* KFZTECH *Federung* MacPherson strut

MAG-Schweißen *nt* *(Metall-Aktivgas-Schweißen)* THERMOD MAG welding *(metal active gas welding)*

Magazin *nt* DRUCK, MASCHINEN magazine, RAUMFAHRT *Raumschiff* pod; **Magazinautomat** *m* FERTIG magazine automatic; **Magazinrückwand** *f* FOTO magazine back

Magenta *nt* DRUCK magenta; **Magentaeinstellung** *f* FOTO magenta filter adjustment

Mager- *pref* BAU, KFZTECH, KOHLEN, LUFTTRANS lean

mager: **~es Alkydharz** *nt* KUNSTSTOFF short oil alkyd; **~es Gemisch** *nt* KFZTECH poor mixture; **~e Schrift** *f* DRUCK light face; **~e Steinkohle** *f* KOHLEN close-burning coal; **~er Ton** *m* BAU sandy clay

Mager-: **Magerbeton** *m* BAU lean concrete; **Magergemisch** *nt* KFZTECH, LUFTTRANS lean mixture; **Magerkohle** *f* KOHLEN lean coal, nonbituminous coal;

Magermilchpulver *nt* LEBENSMITTEL skimmed-milk powder; **Magerton** *m* KER & GLAS meager clay

Magerungszusatz *m* KER & GLAS leaner

magisch: **~es Auge** *nt* ELEKTRONIK magic eye, ELEKTROTECH electric eye; **~es Quadrat** *nt* MATH magic square; **~e Zahlen** *f pl* PHYS *Kernphysik*, STRAHLPHYS *bei Kernen mit speziell hoher Bindungsenergie* magic numbers

Magnesia *f* CHEMIE bitter earth, magnesia; **Magnesia-** *pref* CHEMIE magnesian

Magnesit *m* KUNSTSTOFF magnesite; **Magnesit-Chrom-Feuerfesterzeugnis** *nt* KER & GLAS magnesite chrome refractory; **Magnesitstein** *m* BAU magnesite brick; **Magnesitziegel** *m* BAU magnesite brick

Magnesium *nt (Mg)* CHEMIE magnesium *(Mg)*; **Magnesiumblitzlicht** *nt* FOTO flashlight

magnesiumhaltig *adj* CHEMIE magnesian

Magnesium: **Magnesiumoxid** *nt* CHEMIE bitter earth, magnesium oxide, KUNSTSTOFF calcined magnesia; **Magnesiumsilberchloridelement** *nt* ELEKTROTECH magnesium-silver chloride cell

Magneson *nt* CHEMIE magneson

Magnet *m* AUFNAHME, ELEKTRIZ, ELEKTROTECH, -LABOR, PHYS, TEILPHYS, TELEKOM magnet; **Magnetablenkung** *f* KERNTECH magnetic deflection; **Magnetabscheider** *m* ABFALL, KERNTECH, KOHLEN magnetic separator; **Magnetabscheidung** *f* ABFALL magnetic separation; **Magnetabschirmung** *f* ELEKTROTECH magnetic shielding, PHYS magnetic shield; **Magnetabstoßung** *f* ELEKTROTECH magnetic repulsion; **Magnetabstreifung** *f* AUFNAHME magnetic stripping; **Magnetachse** *f* RAUMFAHRT magnetic axis; **Magnetanker** *m* ELEKTRIZ *(cf Magnetzunge)*, PHYS keeper; **Magnetankerlautsprecher** *m* AUFNAHME magnetic armature loudspeaker; **Magnetanlasser** *m* ELEKTRIZ magnetic starter; **Magnetaufnahme** *f* COMP & DV magnetic recording; **Magnetaufnahmestandard** *m* AUFNAHME magnetic-recording standard; **Magnetaufzeichnung** *f* COMP & DV, FERNSEH, TELEKOM magnetic recording; **Magnetaufzeichnungsmedium** *nt* FERNSEH magnetic-recording medium

Magnetband *nt* AUFNAHME, COMP & DV magnetic tape, tape, DRUCK, ELEKTRIZ, FERNSEH, TELEKOM magnetic tape; **Magnetbandeinheit** *f* COMP & DV magnetic tape unit, streamer; **Magnetbandgerät** *nt* COMP & DV magnetic tape recorder, magnetic tape unit, tape deck

magnetbandgesteuert: **~e Werkzeugmaschine** *f* FERTIG magnetic-tape-controlled machine tool

Magnetband: **Magnetbandkassette** *f* COMP & DV magnetic tape cartridge, tape cartridge; **Magnetbandkassettenlaufwerk** *nt* COMP & DV cartridge drive; **Magnetbandrauschen** *nt* AUFNAHME magnetic tape noise; **Magnetband-Streamer** *m* COMP & DV streaming tape drive, stringy floppy

Magnet: **Magnetbeschichtung** *f* FERNSEH magnetic coating; **Magnetblasenspeicher** *m* COMP & DV magnetic bubble memory; **Magnetbremse** *f* EISENBAHN, KFZTECH electromagnetic brake; **Magnetdetektor** *m* TRANS magnetic detector; **Magnetdickenmesser** *m*

LABOR *bei Magnetrelais* magnetic thickness gage (AmE), magnetic thickness gauge (BrE); **Magnetdiode** *f* ELEKTRONIK magnetodiode; **Magnetdoppelschicht** *f* PHYS magnetic shell; **Magnetdraht** *m* AKUSTIK magnetic wire; **Magnetdynamo** *m* ELEKTRIZ, KFZTECH magnetodynamo; **Magneteisen** *nt* METALL magnetic iron; **Magneteisenstein** *m* METALL magnetic ore

magnetelektrisch: ~e **Maschine** *f* WASSERTRANS magneto

Magnet: **Magnetfangwerkzeug** *nt* ERDÖL *Bohrtechnik* magnetic fishing tool; **Magnetfarbe** *f* COMP & DV magnetic ink

Magnetfeld *nt* ELEKTRIZ, ELEKTROTECH, FERNSEH, TELEKOM magnetic field; **durch** ~ **variierbares Potentiometer** *nt* ELEKTRIZ magnetoresistor potentiometer; ~ **wechselnder Richtung** *nt* ELEKTROTECH alternating magnetic field; **Magnetfeldkonfiguration** *f* KERNTECH, STRAHLPHYS magnetic field configuration; **Magnetfeldlinie** *f* STRAHLPHYS magnetic field line; **Magnetfeldmesser** *m* LUFTTRANS magnetometer; **Magnetfeldmeßgerät** *nt* ELEKTRIZ gaussmeter; **Magnetfeldregler** *m* ELEKTROTECH field regulator; **Magnetfeldröhre** *f* ELEKTRONIK magnetron; **Magnetfeldstärke** *f* ELEKTRIZ magnetic flux density, PHYS magnetic field strength, STRAHLPHYS magnetic intensity

Magnet: **Magnetfilter** *nt* MASCHINEN magnetic filter; **Magnetfluß** *m* ELEKTRIZ, ELEKTROTECH, FERNSEH, STRAHLPHYS magnetic flux; **Magnetflußdichte** *f* ELEKTRIZ, PHYS magnetic flux density; **Magnetflüssigkeitsbad** *nt* FERTIG wet bath; **Magnetfutteraufspannung** *f* FERTIG magnetic chucking; **Magnethörkopf** *m* AKUSTIK reproducing magnetic head; **Magnetinduktion** *f* (*B*) ELEKTRIZ, ELEKTROTECH, PHYS, TELEKOM magnetic induction (*B*); **Magnetinduktionsdichte** *f* ELEKTRIZ magnetic induction density; **Magnetinduktionsschleife** *f* TELEKOM magnetic induction current loop

magnetisch[1] *adj* AUFNAHME, ELEKTRIZ, PHYS magnetic; **nicht** ~ *adj* CHEMIE, ELEKTRIZ nonmagnetic

magnetisch:[2] ~**er Ablaßstopfen** *m* MASCHINEN magnetic drain plug; ~e **Anordnung** *f* METALL magnetic order; ~**er Anzeiger** *m* MASCHINEN magnetic indicator; ~e **Anziehung** *f* ELEKTRIZ magnetic attraction; ~**er Äquator** *m* PHYS magnetic equator; ~**es Aufzeichnungsmaterial** *nt* AKUSTIK magnetic medium; ~e **Ausrichtung** *f* AUFNAHME magnetic alignment; ~e **Beblasung** *f* ELEKTRIZ magnetic blowout; ~e **Beschichtung** *f* AUFNAHME magnetic coating; ~**er Bezirk** *m* ELEKTROTECH magnetic domain; ~**er Blasenspeicher** *m* ELEKTROTECH magnetic bubble memory; ~e **Breite** *f* PHYS magnetic latitude; ~e **Dämpfung** *f* ELEKTROTECH magnetic damping; ~e **Datenträger** *m pl* COMP & DV magnetic media; ~e **Deklination** *f* PHYS magnetic declination; ~e **Depolarisation** *f* STRAHLPHYS *von Resonanzstrahlung* magnetic depolarization; ~**er Dipol** *m* PHYS magnetic dipole; ~**es Dipolmoment** *nt* PHYS magnetic dipole moment; ~**er Dipolübergang** *m* STRAHLPHYS magnetic dipole transition; ~e **Durchdringbarkeit** *f* ELEKTROTECH magnetic permeability; ~**er Durchflußmeßumformer** *m* REGELUNG magnetic flow transducer; ~e **Durchlässigkeit** *f* ELEKTROTECH magnetic permeability; ~**es Echo** *nt* AUFNAHME magnetic echo; ~**er Einschluß** *m* PHYS *Plasmaphysik* magnetic confinement; ~e **Energie** *f*

ELEKTRIZ, ELEKTROTECH, PHYS magnetic energy; ~**es Feld** *nt* AUFNAHME, ELEKTRIZ, PHYS, TELEKOM magnetic field; ~**er Feldgradient** *m* ELEKTROTECH magnetic field gradient; ~e **Feldintensität** *f* ELEKTRIZ magnetic field intensity; ~e **Feldkonstante** *f* ELEKTROTECH, PHYS permeability of free space; ~e **Feldlinie** *f* KERNTECH magnetic flux line; ~e **Feldstärke** *f* (*H*) ELEKTRIZ, ELEKTROTECH magnetic field strength (*H*); ~e **Flasche** *f* PHYS magnetic bottle; ~**er Fluß** *m* ELEKTROTECH flux, magnetic flux, STRAHLPHYS magnetic flux; ~**er Flußmesser** *m* ELEKTRIZ *Meßinstrument* fluxmeter; ~e **Flußverkettung** *f* ELEKTROTECH flux linkage, NICHTFOSS ENERG magnetic flux linkage; ~e **Fokussierung** *f* ELEKTROTECH magnetic focusing; ~ **gehaltener Koppelpunkt** *m* TELEKOM magnetically-latched crosspoint; ~**es Halterelais** *nt* ELEKTROTECH magnetic latching relay; ~e **Halterung** *f* MASCHINEN magnetic holding; ~e **Hysterese** *f* ELEKTRIZ, ELEKTROTECH magnetic hysteresis; ~e **Hystereseschleife** *f* ELEKTRIZ magnetic hysteresis loop; ~**er Induktionsfluß** *m* AUFNAHME magnetic flux; ~e **Isotopentrennung** *f* KERNTECH magnetic isotope separation; ~**es Kalorimeter** *nt* (*MAC*) TEILPHYS magnetic calorimeter (*MAC*); ~e **Karte** *f* COMP & DV magnetic card; ~e **Kernresonanz** *f* (*NMR*) ERDÖL, TEILPHYS nuclear magnetic resonance (*NMR*); ~e **Konstante** *f* PHYS magnetic constant; ~e **Kopplung** *f* ELEKTRIZ magnetic coupling, ELEKTROTECH inductive coupling; ~**er Kopplungsfaktor** *m* ELEKTRIZ magnetic-coupling coefficient; ~**er Kopplungskoeffizient** *m* ELEKTRIZ magnetic-coupling coefficient; ~e **Kraft** *f* ELEKTRIZ magnetic force; ~e **Kraftlinie** *f* ELEKTROTECH flux line, magnetic line of force; ~e **Kraftlinienstreuung** *f* ELEKTROTECH flux leakage; ~e **Kupplung** *f* ELEKTRIZ magnetic clutch; ~**er Kurs** *m* WASSERTRANS magnetic course; ~e **Leitfähigkeit** *f* ELEKTRIZ, ELEKTROTECH permeance, TELEKOM magnetoconductivity; ~**er Leitwert** *m* ELEKTRIZ (*P*) permeance (*P*), ELEKTROTECH, PHYS permeance; ~**er Löschkopf** *m* AKUSTIK erasing magnetic head; ~**es Medium** *nt* COMP & DV, ELEKTROTECH magnetic medium; ~**er Meridian** *m* PHYS magnetic meridian; ~**es Moment eines Müons** *nt* STRAHLPHYS muon magnetic moment; ~**er Nord-Süd-Pol** *m* PHYS magnetic north/south pole; ~e **Nord-Süd-Richtung** *f* PHYS magnetic meridian; ~e **Peilung** *f* RAUMFAHRT *Raumschiff* magnetic bearing; ~e **Permeabilität** *f* ELEKTRIZ, ELEKTROTECH magnetic permeability; ~e **Permeabilität des Vakuums** *f* ELEKTROTECH permeability of free space; ~e **Polarisation** *f* AKUSTIK, ELEKTROTECH magnetic polarization; ~**er Rißdetektor** *m* MASCHINEN magnetic crack detector; ~**er Scheinwiderstand** *m* (*B*) AUFNAHME magnetic induction (*B*); ~**es Schwungrad** *nt* ELEKTROTECH magnetic flywheel; ~**es skalares Potential** *nt* PHYS magnetic scalar potential; ~e **Spiralstruktur** *f* PHYS helimagnetism; **nicht** ~**er Stahl** *m* ELEKTRIZ nonmagnetic steel; ~e **Stoffe** *m pl* ELEKTROTECH magnetic material; ~**er Streufaktor** *m* ELEKTRIZ coefficient of magnetic dispersion; ~e **Streuung** *f* ELEKTROTECH magnetic leakage; ~e **Streuzahl** *f* ELEKTRIZ coefficient of magnetic dispersion; ~**er Strom** *m* ELEKTROTECH flux; ~**es Teilchen** *nt* FERNSEH magnetic particle; ~**er Tonabnehmer** *m* AUFNAHME magnetic pickup; ~**es Überlastrelais** *nt* ELEKTRIZ magnetic overload relay; ~**er Verstärker** *m* ELEKTROTECH, PHYS, RAUMFAHRT *Raumschiff* magamp, magnetic amplifier; ~e Verzögerung ƒ LUFTTRANS magnetic drag; ~e Vorspannung ƒ AUFNAHME, FERNSEH magnetic bias; ~es Wechselfeld nt ELEKTROTECH alternating magnetic field; ~e Wechselvorspannung ƒ FERNSEH AC magnetic biasing; ~er Widerstand m ELEKTROTECH reluctance, PHYS magnetoresistance, reluctance, reluctivity; ~e Zelle ƒ COMP & DV magnetic cell; ~er Zentrierring m RAUMFAHRT Raumschiff magnetic-centering ring (AmE), magnetic-centring ring (BrE)

magnetisch-epitaxial: ~e Schicht ƒ ELEKTRONIK magnetic epitaxial layer

magnetisieren vt ELEKTROTECH, PHYS magnetize

magnetisiert[1] adj AUFNAHME, ELEKTRIZ, KERNTECH magnetized

magnetisiert:[2] ~er Kopf m AUFNAHME magnetized head; ~es Plasma nt KERNTECH magnetized plasma

Magnetisierung ƒ AUFNAHME, ELEKTRIZ, ELEKTROTECH, FERNSEH, PHYS, TELEKOM magnetization; **Magnetisierungsfeld** nt ELEKTROTECH magnetizing field; **Magnetisierungs-Koeffizient** m ELEKTRIZ susceptibility; **Magnetisierungskraft** ƒ ELEKTRIZ magnetizing force; **Magnetisierungskurve** ƒ ELEKTROTECH magnetization curve; **Magnetisierungsmoment** nt ELEKTROTECH magnetizing moment; **Magnetisierungsschleife** ƒ ELEKTRIZ B/H loop; **Magnetisierungsspule** ƒ ELEKTRIZ, ELEKTROTECH magnetizing coil

Magnet: **Magnetismus** m ELEKTRIZ, PHYS, RADIO magnetism

Magnetit m KERNTECH schwerer Betonzuschlagstoff magnetite, METALL magnetic ore, magnetite

Magnet: **Magnetjoch** nt PHYS yoke of magnet

Magnetkarte ƒ COMP & DV magnetic card, ELEKTRONIK Datenkommunikation card; **Magnetkartenlesegerät** nt COMP & DV magnetic card reader; **Magnetkartenleser** m COMP & DV magnetic card reader; **Magnetkartenspeicher** m COMP & DV magnetic card memory

Magnet: **Magnetkern** m COMP & DV ferrite core, magnetic core, ELEKTROTECH Teil eines Magnetkreises, bei Magnetspeicher magnetic core, PHYS core; **Magnetkernspeicher** m ELEKTROTECH magnetic core memory

Magnetkissen nt TRANS magnetic cushion; **Magnetkissenaufhängung** ƒ TRANS magnetic suspension; **Magnetkissenzug** m TRANS magnetic cushion train

Magnet: **Magnetkompaß** m LUFTTRANS magnetic compass

Magnetkopf m AKUSTIK, AUFNAHME, COMP & DV, FERNSEH magnetic head; **Magnetkopfkern** m FERNSEH magnetic head core; **Magnetkopfspalt** m COMP & DV head gap, FERNSEH head gap, magnetic head gap; **Magnetkopfspaltbreite** ƒ FERNSEH gap

Magnet: **Magnetkopierer** m FERNSEH magnetic reproducer; **Magnetkraftschweißen** nt KERNTECH magnetic force welding; **Magnetkreis** m ELEKTRIZ, ELEKTROTECH, PHYS, RAUMFAHRT Raumschiff magnetic circuit; **Magnetkupplung** ƒ ELEKTROTECH, MASCHINEN magnetic clutch; **Magnetkurs** m LUFTTRANS magnetic heading; **Magnetlager** nt pl ELEKTRIZ magnetic bearing, MASCHINEN magneto bearings, MECHAN magnetic bearing; **Magnetlinse** ƒ ELEKTROTECH, STRAHLPHYS magnetic lens; **Magnetlöschkopf** m FERNSEH magnetic-erasing head; **Magnetmaterial** nt ELEKTROTECH magnetic material; **Magnetmoment** nt ELEKTRIZ, PHYS, TEILPHYS magnetic moment; **Magnetmonopol** nt PHYS magnetic monopole; **Magnetnadel** ƒ MASCHINEN magnetic needle

Magneto- pref magneto; **Magnetoelektrizität** ƒ ELEKTROTECH magnetoelectricity; **Magnetogasdynamik** ƒ (MGD) KERNTECH magnetogasdynamics (MGD); **Magnetogramm** nt RADIO magnetogram; **Magnetograph** m COMP & DV magnetographic printer; **Magnetohydrodynamik** ƒ KERNTECH, MASCHINEN, PHYS, STRÖMPHYS magnetohydrodynamics

magnetohydrodynamisch[1] adj ELEKTROTECH, KERNTECH, MASCHINEN, PHYS, RAUMFAHRT magnetohydrodynamic

magnetohydrodynamisch:[2] ~er Generator m ELEKTROTECH magnetohydrodynamic generator; ~er Konverter m (MHD-Konverter) RAUMFAHRT magnetohydrodynamic converter (MHD converter); ~es Lager nt MASCHINEN magnetohydrodynamic bearing; ~e Pumpe ƒ ELEKTROTECH magnetohydrodynamic pump; ~e Stromerzeugung ƒ ELEKTROTECH magnetohydrodynamic generation; ~er Wandler m (MHD-Wandler) ELEKTROTECH, KERNTECH magnetohydrodynamic converter (MHD converter); ~e Wandlung ƒ ELEKTROTECH magnetohydrodynamic conversion

Magnetometer nt ELEKTRIZ, ERDÖL, LUFTTRANS, PHYS, RADIO, RAUMFAHRT, STRÖMPHYS magnetometer; **Magnetometer-Ausleger** m RAUMFAHRT Raumschiff magnetometer boom; **Magnetometer-Meßtechnik** ƒ ELEKTRIZ, ERDÖL Erdmagnetfeld, PHYS magnetometry; **Magnetometer-Vermessung** ƒ ERDÖL Erdmagnetfeld magnetometer survey

magnetomotorisch: ~e Kraft ƒ (MMK) ELEKTRIZ, PHYS, STRÖMPHYS magnetomotive force (mmf)

Magneton nt TEILPHYS magneton

magneto-optisch[1] adj OPTIK m-o, magneto-optic, magneto-optical

magneto-optisch:[2] ~e Drehung ƒ ELEKTROTECH Faraday effect; ~er Effekt m OPTIK magneto-optical effect; ~es Medium nt OPTIK magneto-optical medium; ~e Platte ƒ COMP & DV magneto-optical disk, OPTIK m-o disc (BrE), m-o disk (AmE), magneto-optical disc (BrE), magneto-optical disk (AmE)

Magneto-: **Magnetoplasma** nt KERNTECH magnetoplasma; **Magnetoskop** nt TELEKOM magnetoscope; **Magnetosphäre** ƒ RADIO magnetosphere

magnetostatisch: ~es Feld nt KERNTECH, PHYS magnetostatic field

Magnetostriktion ƒ AKUSTIK, ELEKTROTECH, PHYS magnetostriction; **Magnetostriktionskonstante** ƒ (K) AKUSTIK magnetostriction constant (K); **Magnetostriktionslautsprecher** m AKUSTIK magnetostriction loudspeaker; **Magnetostriktionsmikrofon** nt AKUSTIK magnetostriction microphone

magnetostriktiv: ~es Material nt ELEKTROTECH magnetostrictive material; ~er Wandler m ELEKTROTECH magnetostrictive transductor, GERÄT magnetostrictive transducer

Magnetothek ƒ COMP & DV tape library

Magnet: **Magnetpeilung** ƒ LUFTTRANS magnetic bearing; **Magnetplatte** ƒ AUFNAHME, COMP & DV, ELEKTRIZ, ELEKTROTECH magnetic disc (BrE), magnetic disk (AmE); **Magnetpol** m ELEKTRIZ, PHYS magnetic pole; **Magnetpotential** nt ELEKTROTECH magnetic potential; **Magnetpulveraufschwämmung** ƒ FERTIG magnetic paste; **Magnetpulverkupplung** ƒ MASCHINEN magnetic particle clutch, magnetic powder clutch, powder clutch; **Magnetpulverprüfung** ƒ FERTIG magnaflux testing, MASCHINEN magnetic particle inspection, MECHAN magnetic particle examination;

Magnetquantenzahl *f* KERNTECH total magnetic quantum number, PHYS magnetic quantum number; **Magnetresonanz** *f* ELEKTROTECH, PHYS magnetic resonance; **Magnetresonanzspektroskopie** *f* STRAHLPHYS magnetic resonance spectroscopy

Magnetron *nt* ELEKTRONIK, RADIO magnetron; **Magnetrongenerator** *m* ELEKTRONIK magnetron oscillator; **Magnetronlichtbogenbildung** *f* ELEKTROTECH magnetron arcing; **Magnetronverstärker** *m* ELEKTRONIK magnetron amplifier

Magnet: **Magnetrührer** *m* LABOR magnetic stirrer;- **Magnetsättigung** *f* ELEKTRIZ, ELEKTROTECH magnetic saturation; **Magnetscheibe** *f* ELEKTROTECH magnetic disc (BrE), magnetic disk (AmE); **Magnetschirmung** *f* ELEKTRIZ magnetic screening; **Magnetschleifendetektor** *m* TRANS magnetic loop detector

Magnetschrift *f* COMP & DV magnetic ink; **Magnetschrifterkennung** *f* (*MICR*) COMP & DV magnetic ink character recognition (*MICR*); **Magnetschriftlesegerät** *nt* COMP & DV magnetic ink character reader; **Magnetschriftleser** *m* COMP & DV magnetic ink character reader; **Magnetschriftzeichenerkennung** *f* (*MICR*) COMP & DV magnetic ink character recognition (*MICR*)

Magnet: **Magnetschwebetechnik** *f* PHYS, TRANS magnetic levitation; **Magnetschweif** *m* RAUMFAHRT magnetotail; **Magnetsonde** *f* KERNTECH magnetic probe; **Magnetsortierung** *f* ABFALL *von Müll* magnetic separation; **Magnetspeicher** *m* COMP & DV magnetic memory; **Magnetspeichermedium** *nt* ELEKTROTECH magnetic storage medium; **Magnetspiegel** *m* PHYS magnetic mirror; **Magnetspule** *f* ELEKTRIZ electromagnet, solenoid, ELEKTROTECH magnet coil, HEIZ & KÄLTE solenoid coil, KFZTECH *Anlasser* solenoid; **Magnetspule mit Luftspaltkern** *f* ELEKTRIZ air gap coil; **Magnetspur** *f* COMP & DV track; **Magnetstreifen** *m* AUFNAHME magnetic stripe; **Magnetstreifen-Streamer** *m* COMP & DV streamer; **Magnetstrom** *m* PHYS magnetron; **Magnetsturm** *m* RAUMFAHRT magnetic storm; **Magnetsuszeptibilität** *f* ELEKTRIZ, PHYS magnetic susceptibility; **Magnettinte** *f* COMP & DV magnetic ink

Magnetton *m* AKUSTIK, AUFNAHME magnetic sound; **Magnettonaufzeichnung** *f* AKUSTIK, AUFNAHME magnetic recording; **Magnettonband** *nt* AKUSTIK magnetic tape; **Magnettonfilm** *m* AUFNAHME magnetic-recording film; **Magnettongerät** *nt* AKUSTIK magnetic recorder; **Magnettonspur** *f* AUFNAHME magnetic sound track

Magnet: **Magnetträger** *m* COMP & DV magnetic material, magnetic medium; **Magnettrommel** *f* COMP & DV, ELEKTROTECH magnetic drum; **Magnettrommelspeicher** *m* COMP & DV, ELEKTROTECH magnetic drum memory; **Magnetübergang** *m* METALL magnetic transition; **Magnetvektorpotential** *nt* PHYS magnetic vector potential; **Magnetventil** *nt* ELEKTRIZ, FERTIG *Kunststoffinstallationen*, HEIZ & KÄLTE, HYDRAUL solenoid valve, MASCHINEN magnetic valve; **Magnetverstärker** *m* ELEKTROTECH magamp, magnetic amplifier; **Magnetwelle** *f* ELEKTROTECH magnetic wave; **Magnetwerkstoff** *m* COMP & DV magnetic material; **Magnetwiderstand** *m* ELEKTROTECH magnetic resistance; **Magnetzähler** *m* GERÄT magnetic counter; **Magnetzelle** *f* COMP & DV magnetic cell; **Magnetzünder** *m* ELEKTROTECH magneto; **Magnetzündung** *f* ELEKTRIZ magneto, KFZTECH magneto ignition; **Magnetzunge** *m* (*cf Magnetanker*) ELEKTRIZ keeper

Magnon *nt* PHYS magnon
Magnox-Reaktor *m* KERNTECH magnox reactor
Magnum *nt* KER & GLAS magnum
Magnus-Effekt *m* PHYS Magnus effect
Mahlanlage *f* CHEMTECH grinding plant, pulverizing equipment, PAPIER refining plant
Mahlbarkeit *f* CHEMTECH grindability, PAPIER beatability
Mahlen *nt* CHEMTECH milling, KOHLEN, KUNSTSTOFF grinding, LEBENSMITTEL milling, METALL grinding, PAPIER beating, milling, TEXTIL grinding, milling; **~ im geschlossenen Kreislauf** *nt* KOHLEN closed-circuit grinding
mahlen *vt* CHEMTECH grind, KOHLEN mill, LEBENSMITTEL grind, MECHAN mill, PAPIER beat
Mahl-: **~ und Extrahierprozeß** *m* KERNTECH grind and leach process
Mahlfeinheitsmeßgerät *nt* LABOR fineness-of-grind gage (AmE), fineness-of-grind gauge (BrE)
Mahlgerät *nt* CHEMTECH grinding device
Mahlgrad *m* PAPIER freeness, freeness value; **Mahlgradmeßgerät nach Hegman** *nt* KUNSTSTOFF Hegman fineness of grind gage (AmE), Hegman fineness of grind gauge (BrE); **Mahlgradprüfer** *m* PAPIER freeness tester
Mahlholländer *m* PAPIER beater
Mahlkammer *f* CHEMTECH pulverizing chamber
Mahlkörper *m* KOHLEN grinding medium
Mahlraum *m* CHEMTECH pulverizing chamber
Mahlring *m* CHEMTECH grinding ring
Mahlschüssel *f* FERTIG *Kollergang* pan
Mahlstein *m* LEBENSMITTEL millstone
Mahltrommel *f* CHEMTECH grinding drum
Mahlverfahren *nt* LEBENSMITTEL milling process
Mail *f* COMP & DV mail message
Mailing *nt* COMP & DV mailing
Mail-Server *m* TELEKOM mail server
Maisbrei *m* LEBENSMITTEL hominy
Maischbottich *m* LEBENSMITTEL mash tub
Maische *f* LEBENSMITTEL pulp, *Bierbrauen und Keltern* pomace, *Brauerei* mash; **Maischeapparat** *m* LEBENSMITTEL masher; **Maischebereiter** *m* LEBENSMITTEL masher
Maischwasser *nt* LEBENSMITTEL mash liquor
Maisgrieß *m* LEBENSMITTEL hominy grits
Maiskleber *m* CHEMIE maize gluten
Majolika *f* KER & GLAS majolica; **Majolikafarben** *f pl* KER & GLAS majolica colors (AmE), majolica colours (BrE); **Majolikafliese** *f* KER & GLAS majolica tile; **Majolikamaler** *m* KER & GLAS majolica painter; **Majolikawaren** *f pl* KER & GLAS majolica ware
Majorana-Kraft *f* KERNTECH Majorana force
Majorität *f* ELEKTRONIK, PHYS majority; **Majoritätsgatter** *nt* ELEKTRONIK majority gate; **Majoritätsladungsträger** *m* PHYS majority carrier; **Majoritätslogik** *f* ELEKTRONIK majority logic; **Majoritätsschaltung** *f* ELEKTRONIK majority gate; **Majoritätsträger** *m* ELEKTRONIK majority carrier; **Majoritätsträgerdiode** *f* ELEKTRONIK majority carrier diode; **Majoritätsträger-Transistor** *m* ELEKTRONIK majority carrier transistor
MAK *m* (*maximale Arbeitsplatzkonzentration*) KERNTECH MAC (*maximum allowable concentration*), TLV (*threshold limit value*)
Makadam *m* BAU, TRANS macadam
Makeln *nt* TELEKOM broker's call; **~ zwischen Abfrageor-**

ganen *nt* TELEKOM alternating between call keys

Makro *nt* COMP & DV *(Makrocode)* macro *(macrocode)*, COMP & DV *(Makrobefehl, Makroinstruktion)* macro *(macroinstruction)*; **Makroabfall** *m* UMWELTSCHMUTZ macrowaste; **Makroassembler** *m* COMP & DV macroassembler; **Makroätzprüfverfahren** *nt* FERTIG macroetch test; **Makroätzung** *f* FERTIG macroetching; **Makroaufruf** *m* COMP & DV macrocall; **Makrobefehl** *m* *(Makro)* COMP & DV macrocommand, macroinstruction *(macro)*; **Makrobiegeverlust** *m* OPTIK macrobend loss; **Makrobiegung** *f* OPTIK, TELEKOM macrobending; **Makrobogen** *m* ELEKTROTECH macrobend; **Makrocode** *m* *(Makro)* COMP & DV macrocode *(macro)*

makrocyclisch *adj* CHEMIE macrocyclic

Makro: **Makroerweiterung** *f* COMP & DV macroexpansion; **Makrogefüge** *nt* CHEMIE macrostructure; **Makrogenerierung** *f* COMP & DV macrogeneration

makrogeometrisch: **~e Oberflächengestalt** *f* FERTIG macrogeometrical surface pattern

Makro: **Makrohärte** *f* MASCHINEN macrohardness; **Makroinstruktion** *f* *(Makro)* COMP & DV macrocommand, macroinstruction *(macro)*

makromodular: **~er Dampfgenerator** *m* KERNTECH macromodular steam generator

Makro: **Makromolekül** *nt* CHEMIE, KUNSTSTOFF macromolecule

makromolekular[1] *adj* CHEMIE macromolecular

makromolekular:[2] **~e Dispersion** *f* LEBENSMITTEL macromolecular dispersion

makromolisch: **~e Kohlenstoffverbindung** *f* ANSTRICH organic polymer

Makro: **Makroprogramm** *nt* TRANS macroprogram; **Makroprozessor** *m* COMP & DV macroprocessor; **Makroradiographie** *f* KERNTECH macroradiography

makroskopisch: **~e Flußschwankung** *f* KERNTECH macroscopic flux variation; **~er Querschnitt** *m* KERNTECH cross-section density, macroscopic cross section; **~e Veränderliche** *f* PHYS macroscopic variable

Makro: **Makrostativ** *nt* FOTO macrophoto stand; **Makrosteuerung** *f* TRANS macrocontrol; **Makro-Umwandler** *m* COMP & DV macroprocessor

makrozyklisch *adj* CHEMIE macrocyclic

Makulaturbogen *m* DRUCK waste sheet

Malakon *nt* KERNTECH malacon

Malat *nt* CHEMIE malate; **Malat-** *pref* CHEMIE malic

Maleinimid *nt* CHEMIE maleinimide

Maleinsäure *f* CHEMIE maleic acid

Malerarbeiten *f pl* ANSTRICH paintwork

Mall *nt* WASSERTRANS *Schiffbau* mold (AmE), mould (BrE); **Mallbreite** *f* WASSERTRANS *Schiffbau* molding (AmE), moulding (BrE); **Mallbrett** *nt* WASSERTRANS *Schiffbau* template, templet

Mallungen *f pl* WASSERTRANS *Tiefdruckgürtel um Äquator* doldrums

Malnehmen *nt* MATH multiplication

malnehmen *vt* COMP & DV multiply

Malon- *pref* CHEMIE malonic

Malonamid *nt* CHEMIE malonamide, propanediamide

Malonat *nt* CHEMIE malonate

Malonester *m* CHEMIE malonate

Malonsäuredinitril *nt* CHEMIE malononitrile

Maltase *f* LEBENSMITTEL maltase

Malteserkreuzgetriebe *nt* FERTIG Geneva stop, MASCHINEN Geneva mechanism

Malteserkreuzscheibe *f* FERTIG Geneva wheel

Malteserkreuztrieb *m* FERTIG Geneva drive

Malus: **~sches Gesetz** *nt* PHYS Malus's law

Malz *nt* LEBENSMITTEL malt; **Malzbereitung** *f* LEBENSMITTEL malting

malzen *vt* LEBENSMITTEL malt

Mälzerei *f* LEBENSMITTEL malt house, malting

Malz: **Malzextrakt** *m* LEBENSMITTEL malt extract; **Malzfabrik** *f* LEBENSMITTEL malt house

Management-Informationsbasis *f* TELEKOM management information base

Management-Informationssystem *nt* *(MIS)* COMP & DV management information system *(MIS)*

Mangan *nt* *(Mn)* CHEMIE manganese *(Mn)*; **Mangan-** *pref* CHEMIE manganic, manganous

Manganat *nt* CHEMIE manganate, manganite, manganate, permanganate

Mangan: **Manganbronze** *f* CHEMIE manganese bronze; **Manganbronzelegierung** *f* MECHAN manganese bronze; **Mangandioxid** *nt* ELEKTROTECH manganese dioxide; **Manganite** *nt* CHEMIE manganite; **Mangankupfer** *nt* CHEMIE cupromanganese; **Manganmassel** *f* METALL manganese pig

Mangano- *pref* CHEMIE manganous

Mangan: **Manganstahl** *m* MECHAN, METALL manganese steel; **Mangansulfatbadverfahren** *nt* KERNTECH manganous sulfate bath method (AmE), manganous sulphate bath method (BrE)

Mangel *m* KERNTECH *in Material* flaw, TEXTIL calender

Mängel *m pl* QUAL defect, deficiency; **Mängelbericht** *m* QUAL nonconformance report, nonconformity report

Mangel: **Mangelhalbleiter** *m* ELEKTRONIK p-type semiconductor; **Mangelleitfähigkeit** *f* ELEKTROTECH p-type conductivity

Mängel: **Mängelliste** *f* BAU completion list; **Mängelrüge** *f* QUAL notification of defects, notification of nonconformance

Manipulator *m* KERNTECH manipulator

Mannid *nt* CHEMIE mannide

mannigfaltig *adj* GEOM manifold

Mannigfaltigkeit *f* GEOM manifold

Mannit *m* CHEMIE mannite, mannitol

Mannitan *nt* CHEMIE mannitan

Mannithexanitrat *nt* CHEMIE nitromannite

Mannitol *nt* CHEMIE mannite, mannitol

Mannloch *nt* ERDÖL *Behälter, Tank* manway, RAUMFAHRT manhole; **Mannlochdeckel** *m* MECHAN manhole cover; **Mannlochdichtung** *f* MECHAN manhole gasket; **Mannlochverschluß** *m* MECHAN manhole cover

Mannonsäure *f* CHEMIE mannonic acid

Mannose *f* CHEMIE mannose

Mannschaft[1] *f* ERDÖL *auf Bohrturm, Bohrinsel, Schiff*, WASSERTRANS *Besatzung* crew

Mannschaft:[2] **~ anheuern** *vi* WASSERTRANS *Besatzung* take on hands

Mannschaft: **Mannschaftsdeck** *nt* WASSERTRANS *Schiff* mess deck; **Mannschaftsliste** *f* WASSERTRANS crew list; **Mannschaftsräume** *m pl* WASSERTRANS crew's quarters; **Mannschaftsschleuse** *f* RAUMFAHRT crew entry tunnel

Manometer *nt* BAU gage (AmE), gauge (BrE), pressure gage (AmE), pressure gauge (BrE), ERDÖL *Meßtechnik* manometer, FERTIG manometer, pressure gage (AmE), pressure gauge (BrE), GERÄT gage (AmE), gauge (BrE), HEIZ & KÄLTE, KONTROLL pressure gage (AmE), pressure gauge (BrE), LABOR manometer, MASCHINEN gage (AmE), gauge (BrE), pressure gage

(AmE), pressure gauge (BrE), PHYS manometer, pressure gage (AmE), pressure gauge (BrE); ~ **mit Druckkompensation** nt GERÄT dead-weight gage (AmE), dead-weight gauge (BrE), PHYS dead-weight pressure gage (AmE), dead-weight pressure gauge (BrE); ~ **für Kessel** nt GERÄT boiler gage (AmE), boiler gauge (BrE); ~ **mit Kraftvergleich** nt GERÄT dead-weight gage (AmE), dead-weight gauge (BrE), PHYS dead-weight pressure gage (AmE), dead-weight pressure gauge (BrE); **Manometerschalter** m ELEKTRIZ manometric switch

Manöver nt WASSERTRANS maneuver (AmE), manoeuvre (BrE)

Manövrierbarkeit f MASCHINEN, TRANS maneuverability (AmE), manoeuvrability (BrE)

manövrieren vi WASSERTRANS maneuver (AmE), manoeuvre (BrE)

manövrierfähig adj WASSERTRANS maneuverable (AmE), manoeuvrable (BrE)

Manövrierfähigkeit f LUFTTRANS maneuverability (AmE), manoeuvrability (BrE), WASSERTRANS maneuverability (AmE), Schiff manoeuvrability (BrE)

Manövriergeschwindigkeit f LUFTTRANS design-maneuvering speed (AmE), design-manoeuvring speed (BrE)

Manövrierlast f LUFTTRANS maneuvering load (AmE), manoeuvring load (BrE)

manövrierunfähig adj WASSERTRANS Schiff NUC, not under command

Mansardendach nt BAU French roof

Mansardenwalmdach nt BAU curb roof, double pitch roof

Manschette f BAU collar, FERTIG Kunststoffinstallationen sleeve, MASCHINEN, MECHAN collar

Mantel m ELEKTROTECH jacket, HYDRAUL cladding, KERNTECH shell casing, Umhüllung shell, zum Kühlen, Erwärmen jacket, KFZTECH amerikanischer Reifentyp cover, LABOR Glasartikel jacket, MASCHINEN jacket, skirt, MECHAN jacket, OPTIK Lichtleiter cladding, RAUMFAHRT Kabel shielding, TELEKOM cladding; **Manteldraht** m ELEKTROTECH bimetallic wire; **Manteldurchmesser** m OPTIK Lichtleiter cladding diameter; **Mantelelektrode** f BAU covered electrode; **Manteletikett** nt VERPACK wraparound label; **Mantelfaser** f OPTIK Lichtleiter compound glass fiber (AmE), compound glass fibre (BrE); **Mantelfläche** f GEOM lateral area; **Mantelgebläse** nt LUFTTRANS, MASCHINEN ducted fan; **Mantelglas** nt KER & GLAS encapsulating glass; **Mantelkabel** nt ELEKTROTECH sheathed cable; **Mantelkühlung** f HEIZ & KÄLTE, KERNTECH jacket cooling; **Mantelkurve** f FERTIG barrel cam, cylinder cam, drum cam, MASCHINEN barrel cam; **Mantelmaterial** nt TEXTIL jacketing; **Mantelmitte** f OPTIK Lichtleiter cladding center (AmE), cladding centre (BrE); **Mantelmittelpunkt** m TELEKOM cladding center (AmE), cladding centre (BrE); **Mantelmode** f OPTIK Schwingungsmode im Lichtleitermantel cladding mode; **Mantelmodenstripper** m OPTIK cladding mode stripper; **Mantelmodus** m TELEKOM cladding mode; **Mantelofen** m HEIZ & KÄLTE jacket furnace; **Mantelpropeller** m LUFTTRANS ducted propeller; **Mantelrohr** nt BAU casing, FERTIG outer sleeve, KOHLEN pipe casing, MASCHINEN jacket pipe; **Mantelstein** m KER & GLAS mantle block; **Mantelstromstrahltriebwerk** nt LUFTTRANS bypass engine; **Mantelstromtriebwerk** nt LUFTTRANS fan engine; **Manteltoleranzfeld** nt OPTIK,

TELEKOM cladding tolerance field; **Manteltrafo** m ELEKTROTECH shell-type transformer; **Manteltransformator** m ELEKTRIZ, ELEKTROTECH shell-type transformer

Mantisse f COMP & DV, MATH mantissa

manuell[1] adj KONTROLL, MECHAN, RADIO manual; ~ **betrieben** adj KONTROLL manually-operated

manuell:[2] ~ **bediente Maschine** f VERPACK hand-operated machine; ~**e Betätigung des Fahrwerks** f LUFTTRANS landing-gear manual release; ~**er Betrieb** m TELEKOM manual working; ~**e Datenverarbeitung** f COMP & DV manual data processing; ~**e Eingabe** f COMP & DV manual entry, manual input; ~**e Fernbedienung** f LUFTTRANS manual remote control; ~**e Geschicklichkeit** f ERGON manual dexterity; ~**es Heben** nt SICHERHEIT manual lifting technique; ~**e Kühlofenbeschickung** f KER & GLAS carry-in; ~**e Steuerung der Starterklappe** f KFZTECH manual choke control; ~**e Verstärkungseinstellung** f ELEKTRONIK manual gain control; ~**e Zufuhr** f VERPACK hand feed

Manufacturing: ~ **Automation Protocol** nt (MAP) KONTROLL Standard für Fabriksautomatisierungsgeräte manufacturing automation protocol (MAP)

Manuskript nt DRUCK copy, manuscript

MAP abbr (Manufacturing Automation Protocol) KONTROLL Standard für Fabrikautomatisierungsgeräte MAP (manufacturing automation protocol)

Map f COMP & DV map

Marantastärke f LEBENSMITTEL arrowroot

Marbelmarkierung f KER & GLAS marver mark

Marbeln nt KER & GLAS marvering

Marbeltisch m KER & GLAS marver

Marginalie f DRUCK formal side note

Marienglas nt CHEMIE selenite

marin: ~**e Verschmutzung** f WASSERVERSORG aquatic pollutant

Marina f WASSERTRANS Hafen marina

Marine f WASSERTRANS marine (BrE), navy (AmE); **Marineingenieur** m WASSERTRANS naval engineer; **Marineingenieurwesen** nt WASSERTRANS naval architecture; **Marineluftwaffe** f WASSERTRANS naval air force, Streitkräfte Fleet Air Arm (BrE), Naval Air Service (AmE); **Marineradar** nt WASSERTRANS marine radar; **Marinestützpunkt** m WASSERTRANS naval base; **Marinewerft** f WASSERTRANS dockyard, naval dockyard

maritim[1] adj WASSERTRANS maritime

maritim:[2] ~**er Satellit** m RAUMFAHRT Weltraumfunk maritime satellite

Marke f BAU datum level, COMP & DV mark, marker, PATENT Gemeinschaftsmarke trademark; ~ **auf der Abschlußseite** f COMP & DV trailer label; **Markenname** m PATENT trade name; **Marketerie** f KER & GLAS marquetry

Markierbit nt COMP & DV marker, TELEKOM marker bit

Markieren nt COMP & DV flagging, KERNTECH durch chemischen Austausch labeling (AmE), labelling (BrE)

markieren vt BAU beacon, COMP & DV flag, tag, KONTROLL strobe

Markierer m KER & GLAS, RADIO, TELEKOM marker

Markierfilz m PAPIER marking felt, ribbing felt

Markierfolge f TELEKOM marking sequence

Markierimpuls m COMP & DV, ELEKTRONIK marker pulse, TELEKOM Radar strobe pulse

Markiernadel f BAU scratch awl

markiert: ~**er freier Kanal** m TELEKOM marked idle channel; **~e Verbindung** *f* KERNTECH *radioaktiv* labeled compound (AmE), labelled compound (BrE)

Markierung *f* COMP & DV flag, marker, tab, tag, *auf dem Bildschirm* highlighting, MASCHINEN marker, PAPIER marking, QUAL tally, TELEKOM, TEXTIL marking, WASSERTRANS mark; **~ eines sicheren Gewässers** *f* WASSERTRANS safe water mark; **~ mit typisierender Information** *f* KÜNSTL INT tagging; **Markierungsabtasten** *nt* COMP & DV mark scanning; **Markierungsatom** *nt* KERNTECH tracer atom; **Markierungsbit** *nt* COMP & DV flag bit; **Markierungsboje** *f* WASSERTRANS marker buoy; **Markierungseisen** *nt* BAU scribing iron; - **Markierungsende** *nt* COMP & DV end mark; **Markierungsfunkfeuer** *nt* LUFTTRANS fan marker beacon; **Markierungsimpuls** *m* ELEKTRONIK marker pulse; **Markierungsintensität** *f* COMP & DV mark density; **Markierungslesen** *nt* COMP & DV mark reading, mark sensing, mark scanning; **Markierungsleser** *m* COMP & DV mark reader, mark sense device; **Markierungspunkt** *m* BAU *Vermessung* monument; **Markierungsschild** *nt* VERPACK marking label; **Markierungssprache** *f* DRUCK markup language; **Markierungsstab** *m* BAU *Vermessung* arrow; **Markierungssystem** *nt* TELEKOM marker system; **Markierungstechnik** *f* KERNTECH labeling technique (AmE), labelling technique (BrE); **Markierungsverfahren** *nt* KERNTECH labeling technique (AmE), labelling technique (BrE)

Markisenstoff *m* TEXTIL canvas

Markröhre *f* CHEMIE pith

Marksensing *nt* COMP & DV mark sensing

Marlspieker *m* WASSERTRANS *Tauwerk* marline spike

Marmorieren *nt* DRUCK marbling

marmorieren *vt* BAU mottle, PAPIER marble

marmoriert *adj* BAU mottled, PAPIER marbled

Marmorierung *f* PAPIER marbling

Marmorofen *m* KER & GLAS marble furnace

Marmorziehscheibe *f* KER & GLAS marble bushing

maron *adj* KUNSTSTOFF maroon

Marsch *f* WASSERVERSORG marsh; **Marschflugkörper** *m* RAUMFAHRT *Raumschiff*, WASSERTRANS *Militär* cruise missile; **Marschgeschwindigkeit** *f* WASSERTRANS cruising speed

Marshall-Probe *f* BAU Marshall test

Marshall-Prüfung *f* BAU Marshall test

Martens-Prüfung *f* KUNSTSTOFF Martens test

Martens-Spiegelgerät *nt* FERTIG Martens strain gage (AmE), Martens strain gauge (BrE)

martensiaushärtbar: ~er Stahl *m* METALL maraging steel

Martensit *m* METALL martensite

martensitisch: ~es Härten *nt* FERTIG maraging

Martensit: Martensitstahl *m* METALL martensitic steel

Marxgenerator *m* KERNTECH Marx generator

Masche *f* ELEKTRIZ, ELEKTRONIK mesh, ELEKTROTECH delta network, mesh, KOHLEN, LEBENSMITTEL *eines Siebes*, RAUMFAHRT *Sieb* mesh, TEXTIL mesh, stitch, WASSERVERSORG mesh; **Maschendraht** *m* BAU wire netting; **Maschennetz** *nt* COMP & DV meshed network; **Maschenschaltung** *f* ELEKTROTECH mesh, *Speicherröhrenanschlüsse* mesh connection; **Maschenspeicherröhre** *f* ELEKTRONIK mesh storage tube; **Maschenstrom** *m* ELEKTROTECH mesh current; **Maschenware** *f* TEXTIL knitted fabric; **Maschenweite** *f* ELEKTRIZ, KOHLEN mesh size, MASCHINEN aperture; **Maschenzahl** *f* TEXTIL mesh

Maschine[1] *f* COMP & DV, ELEKTROTECH, KER & GLAS, MASCHINEN machine, MECHAN engine, PAPIER machine, WASSERTRANS engine; **~ zum Auseinanderschachteln** *f* VERPACK denesting machine; **~ zum Einsetzen von Fächern und Unterteilungen** *f* VERPACK division-inserting equipment; **~ mit Gegenhalter** *f* MASCHINEN overarm machine; **~ zum Herausheben, Packen und Abdecken von Trays** *f* VERPACK tray denesting, filling and lidding machine; **~ für weich-elastische Verpackung** *f* VERPACK flexible packaging machine; **~ zum Zahnkanten-Abrunden und -Entgraten** *f* FERTIG gear-tooth rounding and deburring machine; **~ zum Zahnrad-Abrunden und -Abdachen** *f* FERTIG gear-tooth rounding-off and pointing machine

maschinell:[1] **~e Ausrüstung** *f* MASCHINEN machinery; **~es Bügeln** *nt* TEXTIL pressing; **~er Entwickler** *m* FOTO machine processor; **~es Fertigbearbeiten** *nt* MASCHINEN machine finishing; **~ hergestellte Muttern** *f pl* MASCHINEN machine-made nuts; **~er Kohlenabbau** *m* KOHLEN machine coalmining; **~es Lernen** *nt* KÜNSTL INT machine learning; **~es Nieten** *nt* MASCHINEN machine riveting; **~es Polieren** *nt* METALL mechanical polishing; **~e Qualitätskontrolle** *f* VERPACK machine version verification of production quality; **~es Sehen** *nt* KÜNSTL INT machine vision

maschinell:[2] **~ bearbeiten** *vt* FERTIG machine

Maschinen: ~ anhalten *vi* WASSERTRANS *Schiffantrieb* stop engines; **~ stoppen** *vi* WASSERTRANS *Schiffantrieb* stop engines

maschinenabhängig *adj* COMP & DV machine-dependent

maschinenabschalten *vi* KER & GLAS stop machines

Maschine: Maschinenabteilung *f* WASSERTRANS *Schiff* engine compartment; **Maschinenachse** *f* FERTIG *geometrische Zerlegung* machine axis; **Maschinenadresse** *f* COMP & DV machine address; **Maschinenanfahren** *nt* KER & GLAS machine start-up; **Maschinenanlage** *f* WASSERTRANS power plant; **Maschinenarbeit** *f* MASCHINEN machine work; **Maschinenausfall** *m* COMP & DV machine failure; **Maschinenausfallzeit** *f* ERGON machine downtime; **Maschinenausrüstung** *f* COMP & DV hardware, MASCHINEN machinery

Maschinenbau *m* FERTIG, MASCHINEN mechanical engineering; **Maschinenbaufabriken** *f pl* MECHAN engineering facilities; **Maschinenbauingenieur** *m* FERTIG, MASCHINEN mechanical engineer

Maschine: Maschinenbedienung *f* COMP & DV machine operation; **Maschinenbefehl** *m* COMP & DV machine instruction; **Maschinenbefehlscode** *m* COMP & DV machine instruction code; **Maschinenbefüllung** *f* PAPIER machine fill; **Maschinenbelastung** *f* KONTROLL machine load; **Maschinenbelüftungsanlage** *f* KFZTECH, WASSERTRANS engine ventilation system

maschinenbestimmt: ~e Arbeitsgeschwindigkeit *f* ERGON machine-paced work

Maschine: Maschinenbetrieb *m* COMP & DV machine operation, WASSERTRANS *Motor* engine operation; **Maschinenbetriebsstundenanzeiger** *m* WASSERTRANS *Motor* engine hours indicator; **Maschinenbezugsachse** *f* FERTIG machine reference axis; **Maschinenbreite** *f* DRUCK machine width; **Maschinenbügelsäge** *f* MASCHINEN power hacksaw; **Maschinenbütte** *f* DRUCK, PAPIER machine chest; **Maschinencode** *m* COMP & DV machine code, machine language; **Maschinendeckel** *m* PAPIER machine deckle; **Maschinendefekt** *m* KFZTECH, WASSERTRANS engine failure; **Maschinendrehzahl** *f* KER & GLAS machine speed;

Maschinendruck *m* DRUCK printing by machine
maschineneigen: **~er Zeichensatz** *m* COMP & DV native character set
Maschine: **Maschinenelement** *nt* MASCHINEN machine part; **Maschinenfehler** *m* COMP & DV machine error; **Maschinenfertigungsanlagen** *f pl* MECHAN engineering facilities; **Maschinenfundament** *nt* MASCHINEN engine bed, WASSERTRANS *Motor* engine seating; **Maschinengefahr** *f* SICHERHEIT machinery hazard; **Maschinengestell** *nt* KFZTECH, WASSERTRANS engine frame
maschinengestrichen *adj* VERPACK *Papier* machine-coated
maschinengestützt: **~es Lernen** *nt* COMP & DV machine learning
Maschine: **Maschinengewindebohrer** *m* MASCHINEN machine tap, power tap
maschinengezogen: **~es Antikglas** *nt* KER & GLAS antique drawn glass
maschinenglatt: **~es Papier** *nt* DRUCK mill-finished paper, VERPACK MG paper, machine-glazed paper
Maschine: **Maschinengrundreibahle** *f* FERTIG rose reamer; **Maschinenhammer** *m* FERTIG, MASCHINEN power hammer; **Maschinenhaus** *nt* EISENBAHN engine shed; **Maschineninstruktion** *f* COMP & DV machine instruction; **Maschineninstruktionscode** *m* COMP & DV machine instruction code; **Maschinenklarschriftleser** *m* METROL optical reader for machine tools; **Maschinenlauf** *m* MASCHINEN machine run; **Maschinenlauf unter Last** *m* MASCHINEN machine running under load; **Maschinenleistung** *f* FERTIG machine capacity, machine efficiency; **Maschinenlernen** *nt* KÜNSTL INT machine learning
maschinenlesbar[1] *adj* COMP & DV machine-readable
maschinenlesbar:[2] **~e Daten** *nt pl* COMP & DV machine-readable data
Maschine: **Maschinennietung** *f* MASCHINEN machine riveting; **Maschinenöl** *nt* MASCHINEN machine oil, machinery oil; **Maschinenoperation** *f* COMP & DV machine operation
maschinenorientiert[1] *adj* COMP & DV machine-oriented
maschinenorientiert:[2] **~e Programmiersprache** *f* COMP & DV LLL, low-level language
Maschine: **Maschinenpappe** *f* VERPACK machine-made board; **Maschinenprogramm** *nt* COMP & DV machine program, object program; **Maschinenprüfbedingung** *f* COMP & DV *Datenverarbeitung* machine check; **Maschinenprüfung** *f* COMP & DV *Basissystem* machine check; **Maschinenraum** *m* WASSERTRANS *Motor* engine room; **Maschinenreibahle** *f* MASCHINEN chucking reamer, machine reamer; **Maschinenrichtung** *f* DRUCK grain, grain direction; **Maschinenrüstzeit** *f* KONTROLL machine set-up time; **Maschinensäge** *f* MASCHINEN power saw; **Maschinensatz** *m* DRUCK mechanical typesetting, ELEKTROTECH cascade set
Maschinensatz: **im ~ gesetzt** *adj* DRUCK mechanically-set
Maschine: **Maschinenschere** *f* MASCHINEN machine shears, shearing machine; **Maschinenschleifen** *nt* MASCHINEN machine grinding; **Maschinenschlosser** *m* MASCHINEN fitter, locksmith, MECHAN fitter; **Maschinenschnitt** *m* MASCHINEN machine cutting; **Maschinenschraube** *f* MASCHINEN machine bolt, machine screw; **Maschinenschutz** *m* SICHERHEIT machine guard; **Maschinenschutzkäfig** *m* SICHERHEIT machine cage; **Maschinensendung** *f* TELEKOM automatic transmission; **Maschinensetzer** *m* DRUCK machine compositor; **Maschinenspannstock** *m* MASCHINEN machine vice (BrE), machine vise (AmE); **Maschinensprache** *f* COMP & DV machine code, machine language, object code, object language; **Maschinenstörung** *f* COMP & DV machine malfunction, KFZTECH, WASSERTRANS engine malfunction; **Maschinenstreichen** *nt* PAPIER on-machine coating; **Maschinenstundenkosten** *f pl* FERTIG overheads (BrE); **Maschinentagebuch** *nt* WASSERTRANS engine room log; **Maschinenteil** *nt* COMP & DV environment division, machine element, MASCHINEN machine part; **Maschinentelegraf** *m* WASSERTRANS *Motor* engine room telegraph; **Maschinentisch** *m* FERTIG, MASCHINEN machine table; **Maschinentrog** *m* KER & GLAS machine tray; **Maschinenüberholung** *f* WASSERTRANS *Motor* engine overhaul; **Maschinenübersetzung** *f (MÜ)* KÜNSTL INT machine translation *(MT)*; **Maschinenumzäunung** *f* SICHERHEIT machine fence
maschinenunabhängig *adj* COMP & DV machine-independent
Maschine: **Maschinenunterbau** *m* MECHAN engine pedestal; **Maschinenwartung** *f* KFZTECH, WASSERTRANS engine maintenance; **Maschinenwort** *nt* COMP & DV computer word; **Maschinenzeit** *f* COMP & DV machine time, FERTIG time per cut; **Maschinenzentrale** *f* ELEKTROTECH central power plant; **Maschin enzuverlässigkeit** *f* COMP & DV hardware reliability; **Maschinenzyklus** *m* COMP & DV machine cycle
Maser *m (Mikrowellenverstärkung durch stimulierte Strahlungsabgabe)* ELEKTRONIK, PHYS, RAUMFAHRT *Weltraumfunk*, TELEKOM maser *(microwave amplification by stimulated emission of radiation)*
masern *vt* FERTIG grain
Maserpapier *nt* PAPIER grained paper
Maserung *f* BAU *Holz* grain, *Holz, Stein* vein, FERTIG grain, streak, PAPIER *von Holz* streak
Maske *f* COMP & DV mask, FERTIG *Formmaskenverfahren* shell, FOTO mask; **Maskenauslauf** *m* ELEKTRONIK mask runout; **Maskenausrichtung** *f* ELEKTRONIK mask alignment; **Maskenausrichtungsschablone** *f* ELEKTRONIK *Halbleiter* mask alignment jig; **Maskenbit** *nt* COMP & DV mask bit; **Maskengenerierung** *f* ELEKTRONIK mask generation
maskenlos: **~e Lithografie** *f* ELEKTRONIK maskless lithography
Maske: **Maskenmikrofon** *nt* AKUSTIK mask microphone; **Maskenöffnung** *f* ELEKTRONIK aperture mask
maskenprogrammierbar[1] *adj* COMP & DV, ELEKTRONIK mask-programmable
maskenprogrammierbar:[2] **~es Feld** *nt* ELEKTRONIK mask-programmable array; **~es Filter** *nt* ELEKTRONIK mask-programmable filter
maskenprogrammiert: **~e Lithografie** *f* ELEKTRONIK masked lithography
Maske: **Maskenprogrammierung** *f* COMP & DV mask programming; **Maskenregister** *nt* COMP & DV mask register; **Maskenröhre** *f* ELEKTRONIK *Video* shadow mask tube; **Maskensatz** *m* ELEKTRONIK mask set; **Maskenträger** *m* ELEKTRONIK mask carrier
maskierbar: **~e Unterbrechung** *f* COMP & DV maskable interrupt; **nicht ~e Unterbrechung** *f* COMP & DV NMI, nonmaskable interrupt
maskieren *vt* CHEMIE sequester
Maskierfolie *f* DRUCK masking film
Maskierung *f* COMP & DV, ELEKTRONIK masking; **Mas-**

kierungsmittel *nt* CHEMIE sequestering agent

Maß *nt* COMP & DV measure, measurement, metric, MASCHINEN dimension, measure, METROL measure, measurement; **~ der Glaubwürdigkeit** *nt* KÜNSTL INT MB, measure of belief; **Maßabweichung** *f* BAU margin, MASCHINEN error of size, offsize; **Maßanalyse** *f* GERÄT titrimetry; **Maßband** *nt* METROL measure, measuring tape, tape measure; **Maßbeständigkeit** *f* KUNSTSTOFF, WERKPRÜF dimensional stability; **Maßbild** *nt* KONSTZEICH dimension illustration; **Maßblatt** *nt* KONSTZEICH dimension sheet; **Maßbuchstabe** *m* KONSTZEICH dimension letter

Masse:[1] **an ~ gelegt** *adj* ELEKTROTECH connected to earth (BrE), connected to ground (AmE)

Masse[2] *f* EISENBAHN, ELEKTRIZ *elektrisch* , ELEKTROTECH, KFZTECH earth (BrE), ground (AmE), MASCHINEN mass, MECHAN batch, METROL weight, PHYS bulk, PHYS mass, TEXTIL bulk, THERMOD mass, WASSERTRANS earth (BrE), ground (AmE); **Masseanschluß** *m* ELEKTRIZ earth connection (BrE), ground connection (AmE), ELEKTROTECH connection to earth (BrE), connection to ground (AmE), earth terminal (BrE), ground terminal (AmE), KFZTECH earth connection (BrE), ground connection (AmE); **Massedraht** *m* ELEKTROTECH earth wire (BrE), ground wire (AmE); **Masseelektrode** *f* KFZTECH earth electrode (BrE), ground electrode (AmE); **Masse-Energie-Äquivalenz** *f* PHYS mass energy equivalence

Masse:[3] **an ~ legen** *vt* ELEKTROTECH earth (BrE), ground (AmE)

Maß: **Maßeinheit** *f* ERDÖL unit of measurement, KONSTZEICH dimension unit

Masse: **Massekabel** *nt* EISENBAHN earth cable (BrE), ground cable (AmE), ELEKTROTECH earth cable (BrE), earth lead (BrE), ground cable (AmE), ground lead (AmE), KFZTECH, WASSERTRANS earth cable (BrE), ground cable (AmE); **Massekern** *m* ELEKTROTECH powdered iron core

Massel *f* FERTIG blind riser, iron pig, pig; **Masselbett** *nt* FERTIG pig bed

Masse: **Masseleiter** *m* ELEKTROTECH earth wire (BrE), ground wire (AmE); **Masseleitung** *f* ELEKTROTECH earth line (BrE), ground line (AmE)

Massel: **Masselform** *f* FERTIG pig mold (AmE), pig mould (BrE)

Masse: **Massenabsorptionskoeffizient** *m* KERNTECH mass absorption coefficient; **Massenauffahrunfall** *m* TRANS multiple-pile-up; **Massenausgleich** *m* MASCHINEN mass balancing, MECHAN counterbalance; **Massenausgleich am Luftschraubenblatt** *m* LUFTTRANS *Hubschrauber* blade balance weight; **Massenbelegung** *f* PHYS mass; **Massenbeton** *m* BAU mass concrete; **Massenbezugslinie** *f* KERNTECH *in Massenspektrum* parent mass peak, parent peak; **Massenbruchteil** *m* KERNTECH mass fraction; **Massendefekt** *m* KERNTECH mass defect, packing effect, STRAHLPHYS mass deficit; **Massendichte** *f* PHYS mass; **Massendurchsatz** *m* LUFTTRANS mass flow; **Masseneffekt** *m* KERNTECH mass effect; **Massenentnahme** *f* BAU borrow; **Massenerhaltung** *f* PHYS, STRÖMPHYS conservation of mass; **Massenfertigung** *f* FERTIG, KFZTECH, WASSERTRANS mass production; **Massenfluß** *m* STRÖMPHYS *durch Rohr, Masse pro Zeiteinheit* mass flux; **Massenform** *f* METALL bed pig; **Massenfraktion** *f* KERNTECH mass fraction; **Massengleichgewicht** *nt* KERNTECH mass balance; **Massen-**

gramm *nt* METROL gram in mass (AmE), gram in mass; **Massengut** *nt* BAU bulk material, WASSERTRANS *Ladung* bulk cargo; **Massengutfrachter** *m* WASSERTRANS bulk carrier

massenimprägniert: **~e Papierisolierung** *f* ELEKTRIZ mass-impregnated paper insulation

Masse: **Massenkraft** *f* FERTIG inertia force; **Massenluftdurchsatz** *m* LUFTTRANS mass airflow; **Massenmittelpunkt** *m* MECHAN, PHYS center of mass (AmE), centre of mass (BrE); **Massenmittelpunktskoordinaten** *f pl* MECHAN, PHYS center of mass coordinates (AmE), centre of mass coordinates (BrE); **Massenparallelverarbeitung** *f* KÜNSTL INT MPP, massively parallel processing; **Massenspeicher** *m* COMP & DV bulk memory, mass storage, mass memory; **Massenspeichereinheit** *f* COMP & DV mass storage device; **Massenspeichersystem** *nt* COMP & DV mass storage system; **Massenspektrograph** *m* PHYS mass spectrograph; **Massenspektrometer** *nt* LABOR, MASCHINEN, PHYS mass spectrometer, STRAHLPHYS mass spectrograph; **Massenspektrometrie** *f* PHYS mass spectrometry; **Massenspektroskopanalyse** *f* STRAHLPHYS mass spectral analysis; **Massenspektrum** *nt* PHYS, STRAHLPHYS mass spectrum; **Massenstrom** *m* LUFTTRANS mass flow; **Massenstrommeßgerät** *nt* GERÄT mass flow meter; **Massenträgheitsmoment** *nt* LUFTTRANS angular momentum, MASCHINEN mass moment of inertia; **Massenüberschuß** *m* PHYS *Kernphysik* mass excess; **Massenverlustberechnung** *f* RAUMFAHRT *Weltraumfunk* mass budget; **Massenwiderstand** *m* FERTIG inertness; **Massenwirkungsgesetz** *nt* MASCHINEN, PHYS law of mass action; **Massenzahl** *f* KERNTECH mass number, PHYS isotope number, nucleon number, PHYS mass number, STRAHLPHYS, TEILPHYS isotope number, TEILPHYS mass number; **Massenzuordnung** *f* KERNTECH mass assignment; **Massepotential** *nt* RAUMFAHRT *Erdung* earth potential (BrE), ground potential (AmE); **Masseschlinge** *f* ELEKTRIZ earth loop (BrE), ground loop (AmE); **Massezylinder** *m* FERTIG *Plaste* heating cylinder

maßgenau *adj* MASCHINEN true-to-size

maßgeschneidert *adj* ELEKTRONIK *werbetechnisch* custom-designed

maßhaltig[1] *adj* MASCHINEN true-to-size; **nicht ~** *adj* MASCHINEN out of tolerance

maßhaltig:[2] **nicht ~e Meß- und Prüfmittel** *nt pl* QUAL out-of-calibration devices

Maß: **Maßhaltigkeit** *f* FERTIG *Kunststoffinstallationen* accuracy to gage (AmE), accuracy to gauge (BrE), KUNSTSTOFF, WERKPRÜF dimensional stability; **Maßhilfslinie** *f* KONSTZEICH projection line, MASCHINEN extension line

massiv[1] *adj* BAU *Holz, Stein* solid, MECHAN heavy

massiv:[2] **~er Guß** *m* FERTIG solid casting; **~er Leiter** *m* ELEKTROTECH solid conductor; **~e Parallelität** *f* KÜNSTL INT MPP, massivelyparallel processing; **~e Reaktion** *f* METALL massive reaction; **~e Treppenspindel** *f* BAU newel post

Massivanode *f* ELEKTROTECH heavy anode

Massivbeton *m* BAU mass concrete

Massivschale *f* MASCHINEN solid liner

Massivumformung *f* MASCHINEN massive forming

Maß: **Maßkennzeichen** *nt* KONSTZEICH identification marking of dimensions; **Maßkette** *f* KONSTZEICH chain dimensioning; **Maßkolben** *m* LABOR volumetric flask; **Maßlehre** *f* METROL limit gage (AmE), limit gauge (BrE)

maßlich: ~**es Prüfen** *nt* METROL measuring; ~**e Überbestimmung** *f* KONSTZEICH redundant dimensioning

Maß: **Maßlinie** *f* KONSTZEICH, MASCHINEN dimension line; **Maßlinienbegrenzung** *f* KONSTZEICH dimension line termination; **Maßlücke** *f* KONSTZEICH dimension gap; **Maßnahme** *f* COMP & DV measure, QUAL action; **Maßpfeil** *m* BAU *Vermessung* arrowhead; **Maßprüfung** *f* QUAL dimensional check; **Maßskizze** *f* FERTIG dimensional sketch

Maßstab *m* BAU gage (AmE), gauge (BrE), scale, COMP & DV, DRUCK, GEOM, GERÄT, MASCHINEN scale, METROL measuring rod, scale

maßstabgetreu: ~**e Darstellung** *f* KONSTZEICH true-to-scale representation; ~**es Modell** *nt* GEOM, WASSERTRANS scale model; ~**e Zeichnung** *f* GEOM scale drawing

maßstäblich:[1] ~**e Darstellung** *f* KONSTZEICH representation to scale; ~**es Modell** *nt* WASSERTRANS scale model

maßstäblich:[2] ~ **verändern** *vt* GERÄT *normieren* scale

Maßstab: **Maßstabpapier** *nt* PAPIER scale paper; **Maßstabsangaben** *f pl* KONSTZEICH scale particulars; **Maßstabsanpassung einer Feder** *f* METROL scaling a spring; **Maßstabsfaktor** *m* COMP & DV scale factor

Maßstabsfaktor: ~**festlegen** *vt* COMP & DV scale; **mit** ~ **multiplizieren** *vt* GERÄT *normieren* scale

maßstabsgerecht[1] *adj* FERTIG *Modell* scale

maßstabsgerecht:[2] ~**e Zeichnung** *f* KONSTZEICH scaled drawing

Maß: **Maßstelle** *f* KONSTZEICH dimension joint; **Maßtoleranz** *f* FERTIG tolerance in size, MASCHINEN dimensional tolerance, size margin, size tolerance

Mast[1] *m* BAU pole, ELEKTRIZ pylon, tower, RADIO mast, pedestal, WASSERTRANS mast; **am** ~ **montierter Transformator** *m* ELEKTRIZ pole-mounted transformer

Mast:[2] **den** ~ **einsetzen** *vi* WASSERTRANS *Schiffbau* step the mast; ~ **herausnehmen** *vi* WASSERTRANS unstep the mast

Mast: **Mastantenne** *f* TELEKOM mast antenna; **Mastausleger** *m* BAU, TRANS derrick boom; **Mastbacken** *f pl* WASSERTRANS hounds; **Mastenkran** *m* BAU derrick

Master *f* OPTIK master; **Masterband** *nt* FERNSEH master tape; **Masterbatch** *m* KUNSTSTOFF master batch; **Mastern von Platten** *nt* OPTIK disc mastering (BrE), disk mastering (AmE); **Masterplatte** *f* OPTIK master disc (BrE)

Master-Slave: **Master-Slave-Flipflop** *nt* ELEKTRONIK master-slave flip-flop; **Master-Slave-Manipulator** *m* KERNTECH master-slave manipulator; **Master-Slave-Rechnersystem** *nt* COMP & DV master-slave system

Mast: **Mastfall** *m* WASSERTRANS mast rake; **Mastfuß** *m* WASSERTRANS mast foot; **Mastfußschiene** *f* WASSERTRANS *Bootbau, Deckbeschlag* mast foot rail

Mastikation *f* KUNSTSTOFF mastication

Mastix *m* WASSERTRANS *Schiffbau* mastic

mastizieren *vt* FERTIG *Plaste* masticate

Mastiziermittel *nt* KUNSTSTOFF peptizer

Mast: **Mastkran** *m* WASSERTRANS *Ladung* mast crane; **Mastschulter** *f* WASSERTRANS hounds; **Mastspitze** *f* WASSERTRANS masthead; **Mastspur** *f* WASSERTRANS mast step; **Maststrecke** *f* TELEKOM pole route; **Maststuhl** *m* WASSERTRANS mast tabernacle; **Masttransformator** *m* ELEKTRIZ pole-type transformer

Maß: **Maßverkörperung** *f* FERTIG standard, QUAL material measure

Mater *f* DRUCK flong, matrix, OPTIK master

Material *nt* RAUMFAHRT fabric; ~ **mit angepaßter Brechzahl** *nt* TELEKOM index-matching material; ~ **zur Anpassung des Index** *nt* OPTIK index-matching material; **Materialabnahme** *f* MASCHINEN stock removal; **Materialabtragung** *f* MASCHINEN material removal; **Materialdispersion** *f* OPTIK, TELEKOM material dispersion; **Materialdispersionskoeffizient** *m* TELEKOM material dispersion parameter; **Materialermüdungsriß** *m* RAUMFAHRT *Raumschiff* fatigue crack; **Materialermüdungswiderstand** *m* RAUMFAHRT *Raumschiff* fatigue strength; **Materialfehler** *m* KERNTECH flaw, MASCHINEN material defect, QUAL defect of material, TEXTIL flaw, WERKPRÜF material flaw; **Materialfluß** *m* VERPACK material flow; **Materialgröße** *f* KER & GLAS stock size; **Materialgrube** *f* KOHLEN borrow pit; **Materialhandhabung** *f* KERNTECH materials handling; **Materialplaner** *m* KER & GLAS estimator; **Materialplatte** *f* KER & GLAS stock sheet; **Materialprüfanstalt** *f* QUAL material-testing institute; **Materialprüfreaktor** *m* (*MTR*) KERNTECH materials-testing reactor (*MTR*); **Materialprüfung** *f* MASCHINEN material testing, MASCHINEN materials inspection, testing of materials; **Materialrückgewinnung** *f* ABFALL material recovery; **Materialstärke** *f* WASSERTRANS *Schiffbau* scantling; **Materialstreuung** *f* OPTIK, TELEKOM material scattering; **Materialtrichter** *m* FERTIG *Extrudieren* feed hopper; **Materialzuführungstrommel** *f* VERPACK vibratory hopper

materiell: ~**e Flußdichtewölbung** *f* KERNTECH material buckling

Materiewelle *f* ELEKTROTECH, PHYS, STRAHLPHYS de Broglie wave

Maternpappe *f* DRUCK flong

Materplatte *f* OPTIK master disk (AmE)

Mathematik *f* COMP & DV, MATH mathematics

mathematisch[1] *adj* MATH mathematical

mathematisch:[2] ~**e Analyse** *f* MATH mathematical analysis; ~**er Ausdruck** *m* MATH mathematical expression; ~**e Berechnungen** *f pl* MATH mathematical calculations; ~**e Grundlagen** *f pl* COMP & DV, MATH mathematics; ~**e Hoffnung** *f* COMP & DV expectation; ~**e Induktion** *f* COMP & DV, MATH mathematical induction; ~**e Logik** *f* COMP & DV symbolic logic, MATH mathematical logic; ~**es Modell** *nt* COMP & DV, ELEKTRONIK mathematical model; ~**e Operationen** *f pl* MATH mathematical operations; ~**es Pendel** *nt* PHYS simple pendulum; ~**e Physik** *f* PHYS mathematical physics; ~**es Programmieren** *nt* COMP & DV mathematical programming; ~**e Programmierung** *f* COMP & DV mathematical programming; ~**es Teilchen** *nt* KERNTECH mathematical particle; ~**e Wahrscheinlichkeit** *f* MATH mathematical probability

Matrix *f* BAU *Tiefbau*, COMP & DV, DRUCK, FERNSEH matrix, MATH array, matrix, METALL matrix; ~ **mit reellen Zahlen** *f* MATH matrix of real numbers; **Matrixalgebra** *f* MATH matrix algebra; **Matrixanzeige** *f* TELEKOM matrix display; **Matrixdisplay** *nt* TELEKOM matrix display; **Matrixdrucker** *m* COMP & DV dot matrix printer, matrix printer, DRUCK matrix printer; **Matrixschaltung** *f* FERNSEH matrixing; **Matrixsignalisation** *f* TRANS matrix signalization

Matrize *f* COMP & DV matrix, DRUCK matrix, stencil, FERTIG female die, swage, OPTIK master; **Matrizenalgebra** *f* MATH matrix algebra; **Matrizenform** *f* TELEKOM matrix configuration; **Matrizenhalter** *m* FERTIG *Loch-*

en die holder; **Matrizenmagazin** *nt* DRUCK matrix magazine; **Matrizenmechanik** *f* MECHAN, PHYS matrix mechanics; **Matrizenpappe** *f* DRUCK stereotype drymat; **Matrizenschaltung** *f* TELEKOM matrix circuit; **Matrizenstahl** *m* FERTIG die steel

matt[1] *adj* BAU dull, flat, DRUCK matt, METALL dull, matt, TEXTIL lusterless (AmE), lustreless (BrE), matt

matt:[2] ~**es Papier** *nt* DRUCK matt surface paper, FOTO matt paper; ~**e Satinierung** *f* DRUCK English finish

matt:[3] ~ **werden** *vi* BAU *Glas* blind

Mattappretur *f* TEXTIL dull finish

Mattätzpaste *f* KER & GLAS matt-etching paste

Mattätzsalz *nt* KER & GLAS matt-etching salt

Mattblech *nt* FERTIG terne plate

Mattenbewehrung *f* BAU wire mesh reinforcement

mattgeschliffen: ~**er Fuß** *m* KER & GLAS ground base; ~**es Glas** *nt* KER & GLAS satin finish glass

Mattglas *nt* KER & GLAS frosted glass

Mattglasur *f* KER & GLAS matt glaze

Mattheit *f* FERTIG flatness

Mattieren *nt* BAU deadening

mattieren *vt* TEXTIL delustre

mattiert: ~**e Buchstaben** *m pl* KER & GLAS dim letters

Mattierung *f* KER & GLAS frosting, KUNSTSTOFF matting; **Mattierungsbad** *nt* KER & GLAS frosting bath; **Mattierungsmittel** *nt* KUNSTSTOFF flatting agent

Mattkohle *f* KOHLEN dull coal, kennel coal

Mattscheibe *f* FERNSEH screen, FOTO focusing screen, groundglass screen; ~ **mit Fadenkreuz** *f* FOTO groundglass screen with reticule; ~ **mit Fresnellinse** *f* FOTO groundglass with Fresnel lens; ~ **mit Mikroprismenring** *f* FOTO groundglass screen with microprism collar; **Mattscheibenrahmen** *m* FOTO focusing screen frame; **Mattscheibenring** *m* FOTO matt collar

Mattschliff *m* KER & GLAS matt cutting

Mattschmelzfarbe *f* KER & GLAS matt vitrifiable color (AmE), matt vitrifiable colour (BrE)

Matzen *m* LEBENSMITTEL matzoth

Mauer *f* BAU wall; **Mauerabdeckung** *f* BAU, WASSERVERSORG *einer Schleuse* coping; **Mauerband** *nt* BAU string; **Mauerbohrer** *m* FERTIG, MASCHINEN masonry drill; **Mauerecke** *f* BAU quoin; **Mauerfuß** *m* KER & GLAS curb; **Mauerhaken** *m* BAU spike; **Mauerkappe** *f* BAU hood; **Mauerkrone** *f* BAU crown; **Mauermantel** *m* KOHLEN mantle

mauern *vt* BAU brick, lay, mason

Mauerschale: **äußere** ~ *f* KOHLEN mantle

Mauer: **Mauerspalt** *m* KOHLEN crevice; **Mauerung** *f* BAU walling; **Mauervorsprung** *m* BAU spur; **Mauerwerk** *nt* BAU masonry, walling, KER & GLAS brickwork; **Mauerwerksanker** *m* BAU anchor; **Mauerwerksarbeiten** *f pl* BAU masonry work; **Mauerziegel** *m* BAU brick

Maul *nt* FERTIG *Zange* mouth, MASCHINEN chaps; **Maulhöhe** *f* FERTIG *Nietmaschine* gap; **Maulpresse** *f* KUNSTSTOFF C-frame press; **Maulschlüssel** *m* KER & GLAS mouth tools, MASCHINEN face spanner (BrE), face wrench, open spanner (BrE), open wrench, open-end spanner (BrE), open-end wrench, MECHAN open-end spanner (BrE), open-end wrench; **Maulweite** *f* MASCHINEN spanner opening (BrE), wrench opening; **Maulwurf** *m* WASSERVERSORG mole

Maurer *m* BAU bricklayer, mason; **Maurerkelle** *f* BAU brick trowel

Maus *f* COMP & DV mouse, WASSERTRANS noseband; ~ **mit zwei Tasten** *f* COMP & DV two-button mouse; **Mauseloch** *nt* ERDÖL *Bohrturm* mousehole; **Mausprogramm**

nt COMP & DV mouse software; **Maussoftware** *f* COMP & DV mouse software; **Mauszeiger** *m* COMP & DV pointer

Mautbrücke *f* BAU toll bridge

Mautentrichtung *f* TRANS toll payment

Mautstraße *f* TRANS toll road

Maximal- *pref* AKUSTIK, ELEKTRIZ, ELEKTROTECH, KERNTECH, METROL maximum

maximal: ~**e Arbeitsplatzkonzentration** *f* *(MAK)* KERNTECH maximum allowable concentration *(MAC)*, threshold limit value *(TLV)*; ~**er Axialdruck** *m* NICHTFOSS ENERG maximum axial thrust; ~**e Bahnbreite** *f* PAPIER maximum deckle; ~**e beschnittene Bahnbreite** *f* PAPIER maximum-trimmed machine width; ~**e beschnittene Maschinenbreite** *f* VERPACK maximum-trimmed machine width; ~**e Bewicklungsbreite** *f* TEXTIL maximum dressed width of warp; ~**es Biegemoment** *nt* RAUMFAHRT maximum bending moment; ~**es bis mittleres Leistungsverhältnis** *nt* KERNTECH peak heat flux; ~**er Durchsatz** *m* ERDÖL operational capacity; ~**er Durchschlupf** *m* QUAL average outgoing quality limit; ~**e Emissionskonzentration** *f* *(MEK)* UMWELTSCHMUTZ maximum emission concentration; ~**e Fördermenge** *f* ERDÖL capacity; ~**er Frequenzhub** *m* RAUMFAHRT, TELEKOM peak frequency deviation; ~**e Gesamtbelastung** *f* BAU maximum total load; ~ **glaubhafter Unfall** *m* KERNTECH maximum credible accident; ~**e Höhe** *f* RAUMFAHRT ceiling; ~**e Kapazität** *f* PAPIER maximum capacity; ~**e Last** *f* LUFTTRANS maximum load; ~**er Laststrom** *m* ELEKTRIZ limiting overload current; ~**e Leistungsübertragung** *f* ELEKTROTECH maximum power transmission; ~**e Momentleistung** *f* RAUMFAHRT maximum instantaneous power; ~**e Motordrehzahl** *f* KFZTECH peak engine speed; ~**e Rückfederungsbelastung** *f* LUFTTRANS maximum spring-back load; ~**er Schalldruck** *m* AKUSTIK peak sound pressure; ~**e Schmelzrate** *f* KER & GLAS maximum melting rate; ~**e Sprechleistung** *f* AKUSTIK peak speech power; ~**e Stromübertragung** *f* ELEKTROTECH maximum power transmission; ~**er vertikaler Raddruck** *m* LUFTTRANS maximum wheel vertical load; ~**er Wärmefluß** *m* KERNTECH maximum flux heat, peak heat flux; ~**e Wellengeschwindigkeit** *f* NICHTFOSS ENERG maximum shaft speed; ~**er Wert** *m* GERÄT crest value; ~**e Zugspannung** *f* KERNTECH ultimate tensile stress; ~ **zulässige Abweichung** *f* MASCHINEN maximum permissible deviation; ~ **zulässige Arbeitsplatzkonzentration** *f* UMWELTSCHMUTZ occupational MAC, threshold limit value in the workplace; ~ **zulässige Dosis** *f* KERNTECH maximum admissible dose; ~ **zulässige Leistung** *f* TELEKOM maximum admissible power

Maximal-: **Maximalausgabe** *f* ELEKTRIZ maximum output; **Maximalausschalter** *m* ELEKTROTECH maximum cutout; **Maximalbelastung** *f* ELEKTROTECH maximum demand; **Maximal-Eichungskennzeichen** *nt* METROL approval sign; **Maximalleistung** *f* ELEKTRIZ maximum output, maximum power, KERNTECH maximum capacity; **Maximalschalldruck** *m* AKUSTIK maximum sound pressure; **Maximalsignal** *nt* ELEKTRONIK maximum signal; **Maximalsignalamplitude** *f* ELEKTRONIK maximum signal amplitude; **Maximalspannung** *f* ELEKTRIZ maximum voltage, *eines Gerätes* highest voltage, PHYS peak voltage; **Maximalstrom** *m* ELEKTRIZ maximum current, ELEKTROTECH peak current; **Maximaltemperatur im Brennelementinneren** *f* KERN-

TECH maximum fuel central temperature; **Maximal-tiefgang** *m* WASSERTRANS *Schiffkonstruktion* deepest draught; **Maximalwert** *m* GERÄT crest value, PHYS peak value

Maximierung *f* TELEKOM maximization

Maximum *nt* KERNTECH, MATH maximum; **Maximum-Minimum-Thermometer** *nt* HEIZ & KÄLTE, LABOR maximum and minimum thermometer; **Maximumver-kehrsaufkommen pro Stunde** *nt* TRANS maximum hourly volume; **Maximumzähler** *m* ELEKTROTECH demand meter

Maxwell *nt (Mx)* ELEKTRIZ, ELEKTROTECH maxwell *(Mx)*; **~sche Gleichungen** *f pl* PHYS Maxwell's equations; **Maxwell-Verteilung** *f* PHYS Maxwell distribution

Mayday *m* LUFTTRANS, WASSERTRANS *Notfall* mayday

Mazerieren *nt* CHEMIE maceration

mazerieren *vt* CHEMIE, FERTIG macerate

Mazeriergefäß *nt* CHEMIE macerator

Mazza *f* LEBENSMITTEL matzoth

MB *abbr (Mbyte, Megabyte)* COMP & DV MB *(megabyte)*

MBE *abbr (Molekularstrahlepitaxie)* ELEKTRONIK, STRAHLPHYS MBE *(molecular-beam epitaxy)*

M-box *abbr* COMP & DV *bei E-Mail* bb

Mbyte *nt (MB)* COMP & DV megabyte *(MB)*

McPherson-Federbein *nt* KFZTECH McPherson strut; **McPherson-Federbein-Vorderachse** *f* KFZTECH McPherson strut front suspension

Md *(Mendelevium)* CHEMIE Md *(mendelevium)*

MDI *abbr (Diphenylmethandiisocyanat)* KUNSTSTOFF MDI *(diphenylmethane diisocyanate)*

MDR *abbr (Speicherdatenregister)* COMP & DV MDR *(memory data register)*

me *abbr (Elektronenmasse)* CHEMIE, KERNTECH, TEILPHYS me *(electron mass)*

MEA *abbr (Means-End-Analyse, Mittel-Zweck-Analyse)* KÜNSTL INT MEA *(means-end analysis)*

Means-End-Analyse *f (MEA)* KÜNSTL INT *Methode der Problemlösung* means-end analysis *(MEA)*

Mechanik *f* MASCHINEN mechanical system, mechanics

Mechanikerdrehmaschine *f* MASCHINEN bench lathe

mechanisch[1] *adj* MASCHINEN mechanical

mechanisch:[2] **nicht ~e Gefahr** *f* SICHERHEIT nonmechanical hazard; **~ abgestimmtes Magnetron** *nt* ELEKTRONIK mechanically-tuned magnetron; **~ abgestimmter Oszillator** *m* ELEKTRONIK mechanically-tuned oscillator; **~es Abluftsystem** *nt* SICHERHEIT mechanical exhaust air installation; **~e Abnutzung** *f* BAU mechanical wear; **~er Abscheider** *m* UMWELTSCHMUTZ mechanical collector; **~e Abwasser-behandlung** *f* WASSERVERSORG *der ersten Stufe* primary clarification; **~e Abwasserreinigung** *f* ABFALL primary sewage treatment; **~e Admittanz** *f* AKUSTIK mechanical admittance; **~er Antrieb** *m* MASCHINEN mechanical drive; **~e Aufnahme** *f* AKUSTIK mechanical recording; **~es Aufnahmegerät** *nt* AKUSTIK mechanical recorder; **~e Auslenkung** *f (CM)* AKUSTIK mechanical compliance *(CM)*; **~es Auslesen mit konstanter Amplitude** *nt* AKUSTIK constant-amplitude mechanical reading; **~es Auslesen mit konstanter Geschwindigkeit** *nt* AKUSTIK constant-velocity mechanical reading; **~er Auslöser** *m* ELEKTRIZ mechanical tripping device; **~e Benzinpumpe** *f* KFZTECH mechanical fuel pump; **~ betriebener Greifer** *m* BAU mechanical grab; **~ betriebenes Schütz** *nt* ELEKTRIZ

mechanical contactor; **~er Blindleitwert** *m* AKUSTIK mechanical susceptance; **~er Drucker** *m* COMP & DV impact printer; **nicht ~er Drucker** *m* COMP & DV nonimpact printer; **~es Edieren** *nt* FERNSEH mechanical editing; **~e Eigenschaften** *f pl* BAU, KUNSTSTOFF, MASCHINEN, METALL *von Nickelstahl*, STRÖMPHYS mechanical properties; **~e Eingangsimpedanz** *f* AKUSTIK *bei unbelastetem Ausgang* free mechanical impedance; **~er Einschluß** *m* ABFALL *von Schadstoffen* physical stabilization; **~er Endanschlag** *m* ELEKTRIZ mechanical end stop; **~e Energie** *f* MASCHINEN mechanical energy; **~es Enthülsen** *nt* KERNTECH mechanical decanning, mechanical decladding; **~e Feder** *f* MASCHINEN mechanical spring; **~e Fehler** *m pl* FERNSEH mechanical errors; **~es Filter** *nt* ELEKTRONIK mechanical filter; **~es Filter mit Scheibendraht** *nt* AUFNAHME disc-wire-type mechanical filter (BrE), disk-wire-type mechanical filter (AmE); **~e Förder-einrichtung** *f* MASCHINEN mechanical handling equipment; **~e Gefahr** *f* SICHERHEIT mechanical hazard; **~es Getriebe** *nt* MASCHINEN mechanical transmission system; **~er Gleichlauf** *m* ELEKTROTECH ganging; **~er Holzstoff** *m* VERPACK mechanical wood pulp; **~e Impedanz** *f* AKUSTIK, ELEKTROTECH mechanical impedance; **~e Kabelverbindung** *f* FERNSEH mechanical splice; **~e Kernimpedanz** *f* AKUSTIK transfer mechanical impedance; **~e Klärung** *f* ABFALL sedimentation; **~er Klassierer** *m* KOHLEN mechanical classifier; **~e Kraftübertragung** *f* NICHTFOSS ENERG mechanical transmission; **~e Kupplung** *f* ELEKTROTECH ganging; **~es Luftfilter** *nt* HEIZ & KÄLTE mechanical air filter; **~e Modulation** *f* ELEKTRONIK mechanical modulation; **~e Nullstellung** *f* ELEKTRIZ mechanical zero adjustment; **~er optischer Schalter** *m* TELEKOM mechanical optical switch; **~e Presse** *f* MASCHINEN power press; **~er Prober** *m* KOHLEN mechanical sampler; **~e Reaktanz** *f* AKUSTIK mechanical reactance; **~e Resistanz** *f* AKUSTIK, MECHAN mechanical resistance; **~e Resonanz** *f* AKUSTIK, MECHAN mechanical resonance; **~e Schläge** *m pl* SICHERHEIT mechanical shock; **~e Schwingung** *f* AKUSTIK mechanical oscillation; **~e Sortierung** *f* ABFALL mechanical separation; **~e Spannung** *f* MEERSCHMUTZ stress; **~er Spleiß** *m* TELEKOM mechanical splice; **~e Spleißstelle** *f* OPTIK mechanical splice; **~e Stabilität** *f* KUNSTSTOFF mechanical stability; **~e Stoßprüfung** *f* METROL mechanical shock test; **~es System** *nt* AKUSTIK mechanical system; **~e Teile** *nt pl* MASCHINEN mechanical components; **~er Teilkopf** *m* MASCHINEN mechanical-dividing head; **~es Testen** *nt* MASCHINEN, WERKPRÜF mechanical testing; **~e Tonaufzeichnung** *f* AUFNAHME mechanical recording; **~e Trennung** *f* ABFALL automatic sorting, mechanical separation; **~e Unstabilität** *f* METALL mechanical instability; **~e Verbindung** *f* KERNTECH mechanical bond; **~es Verhalten von Werkstoffen** *nt* WERKPRÜF mechanical behavior of materials (AmE), mechanical behaviour of materials (BrE); **~e Vibration** *f* SICHERHEIT mechanical vibration; **~e Vibrationsdämpfung** *f* SICHERHEIT mechanical isolation against vibration; **~e Vibrationsisolierung** *f* SICHERHEIT mechanical isolation against vibration; **~es Wärmeäquivalent** *nt* MECHAN *(J)* mechanical equivalent of heat *(J)*, PHYS Joule's equivalent, THERMOD Joule's equivalent, thermal equivalent, THERMOD *(J)* mechanical equivalent of heat *(J)*; **~e Wasseraufbereitung** *f* WASSERVERSORG physical water treatment; ~e **Welle** *f* ELEKTROTECH mechanical wave; ~e **Werte** *m pl* KUNSTSTOFF mechanical properties; ~er **Wirkungsgrad** *m* ERGON *der Muskelarbeit*, MASCHINEN, NICHTFOSS ENERG mechanical efficiency; ~er **Zerhacker** *m* KERNTECH mechanical chopper; ~e **Zurichtung** *f* DRUCK mechanical overlay

Mechanismus *m* MASCHINEN mechanism; ~ **zur Besetzungsumkehr** *m* STRAHLPHYS population inversion mechanism; ~ **zur Populationsumkehr** *m* PHYS *bei Lasern*, STRAHLPHYS laser population mechanism

Mechanorezeptor *m* ERGON mechanoreceptor

Meconin *nt* CHEMIE dimethoxyphthalide, meconin, opianyl

medial *adj* ERGON medial

Median *m* QUAL median; **Medianebene** *f* ERGON median plane

Mediante *f* AKUSTIK mediant

Medianwert *m* COMP & DV median

Mediävalschrift *f* DRUCK old style

Mediävalziffern *f pl* DRUCK nonlining figures

Medien *nt pl* FERNSEH media

Medium *nt* CHEMIE agent, COMP & DV, DRUCK medium, FERTIG *Kunststoffinstallationen* agent, PHYS medium

medizinisch: ~es **Expertensystem** *nt* KÜNSTL INT medical expert system

Meer:[1] **im** ~ *adj* ERDÖL offshore

Meer[2] *nt* WASSERTRANS sea; **Meerbusen** *m* WASSERTRANS *Geographie* gulf; **Meerenge** *f* WASSERTRANS sound, *Geographie* narrows, strait

Meere: die ~ **befahren** *vi* WASSERTRANS sail over the seas

Meerenge: in ~ **einlaufen** *vi* WASSERTRANS *Navigation* enter straits

Meeres- *pref* WASSERTRANS maritime; **Meeresarm** *m* WASSERTRANS *Geographie* inlet; **Meeresboden** *m* NICHTFOSS ENERG, WASSERTRANS seabed; **Meeresbodenreinigung** *f* ERDÖL *Offshore-Technik* sea floor housekeeping

meeresbürtig: ~e **Verschmutzung** *f* MEERSCHMUTZ seabased pollution

Meeres-: **Meeresforschungsschiff** *nt* WASSERTRANS oceanographic research ship; **Meeresgebiet** *nt* WASSERTRANS sea area; **Meeresgrund** *m* BAU, NICHTFOSS ENERG, WASSERTRANS seabed; **Meereshöhe** *f* WASSERTRANS sea level; **Meereskunde** *f* WASSERTRANS oceanography; **Meeresspiegel** *m* BAU, NICHTFOSS ENERG, WASSERTRANS, WASSERVERSORG sea; **Meeresströmung** *f* WASSERTRANS ocean current

meerestechnisch: ~e **Industrie** *f* WASSERTRANS maritime industry

Meeres-: **Meerestiefen** *f pl* WASSERTRANS ocean deeps, ocean depths; **Meeresumwelt** *f* MEERSCHMUTZ marine environment

Meer: **Meersalz** *nt* LEBENSMITTEL sea salt; **Meerwasser** *nt* WASSERTRANS seawater; **Meerwassereinbruch** *m* WASSERVERSORG seawater intrusion

meerwassergekühlt *adj* THERMOD sea water cooled

Mega- *pref (M)* METROL mega- *(M)*; **Megabyte** *nt (MB)* COMP & DV megabyte *(MB)*; **Megachip** *m* ELEKTRONIK megachip; **Megadoc®** *nt* OPTIK Megadoc®; **Megadyn** *nt* METROL megadyne; **Megahertz** *nt (MHz)* ELEKTRIZ, ELEKTROTECH, FERNSEH, RADIO megahertz *(MHz)*; **Megastream** *nt* TELEKOM *Punkt-zu-Punkt-Digitalverbindung* megastream circuit; **Megawatt** *nt* ELEKTRIZ megawatt

Megger® *m* ELEKTROTECH Megger

Megohm *nt* ELEKTRIZ, ELEKTROTECH megohm

mehlig *adj* LEBENSMITTEL farinaceous

Mehlschwitze *f* LEBENSMITTEL roux

Mehltau *m* LEBENSMITTEL mildew

Mehr- *pref* COMP & DV, ELEKTRONIK, ELEKTROTECH, RADIO, TELEKOM, VERPACK multi-

mehrachsig: ~es **Schwerlastfahrzeug** *nt* KFZTECH multiaxle heavy goods vehicle; ~e **Spannung** *f* KUNSTSTOFF multiaxial stress

Mehr-: **Mehradreßbefehl** *m* COMP & DV multiaddress instruction; **Mehradreßinstruktion** *f* COMP & DV multiaddress instruction

mehradrig[1] *adj* MASCHINEN multiwire

mehradrig:[2] ~es **Kabel** *nt* ELEKTRIZ multiconductor cable, multicore cable, ELEKTROTECH, FERNSEH multicore cable

Mehr-: **Mehramplitudenmodulation** *f* ELEKTRONIK multilevel modulation; **Mehranodengleichrichter** *m* ELEKTROTECH multianode rectifier

mehratomig *adj* CHEMIE polyatomic

Mehr-: **Mehrbahnenetikettiersystem** *nt* VERPACK multilane labeling system (AmE), multilane labelling system (BrE); **Mehrbahnmaschine** *f* VERPACK multilane machine; **Mehrband-** *pref* RADIO multiband; **Mehrbandfilter** *nt* TELEKOM multiband filter; **Mehrbenutzer-** *pref* RAUMFAHRT *Weltraumfunk* multiple-access; **Mehrbenutzersystem** *nt* COMP & DV multiuser system; **Mehrbereichsboden** *m* KOHLEN multigraded soil; **Mehrbereichsmeßgerät** *nt* ELEKTRIZ multirange meter; **Mehrbereichsöl** *nt* KFZTECH, MASCHINEN multigrade oil; **Mehrblattfeder** *f* MASCHINEN multiple-blade spring; **Mehrdecksystem** *nt* TRANS multidecking system; **Mehrdienstevermittlungssystem** *nt* TELEKOM multiservice switching system

mehrdimensional: ~e **Filterung** *f* TELEKOM multidimensional filtering

Mehr-: **Mehreinheitcontainer** *m* VERPACK multiunit container; **Mehrelektronenröhre** *f* ELEKTRONIK multigrid tube; **Mehremittertransistor** *m* ELEKTRONIK multiemitter transistor

mehrere: für ~ **Fernsehnormen ausgelegt** *adj* FERNSEH multistandard

Mehrfach- *pref* AKUSTIK, AUFNAHME multi-, multiple, COMP & DV multi-, multiple, multiport, ELEKTRIZ, FERNSEH, FERTIG, FOTO, MECHAN, TELEKOM multi-, multiple

mehrfach[1] *adj* ELEKTRIZ multiple; ~ **ungesättigt** *adj* CHEMIE, LEBENSMITTEL *Fettsäure* polyunsaturated

mehrfach:[2] ~ **gelitzter Leiter** *m* ELEKTRIZ multiple-stranded conductor; ~e **Schutzerde** *f* ELEKTRIZ protective multiple earthing (BrE), protective multiple grounding (AmE)

mehrfach:[3] ~ **ausnützen** *vt* TELEKOM multiplex; ~ **nutzen** *vt* COMP & DV multiplex

Mehrfach-: **Mehrfachabstimmung** *f* ELEKTROTECH ganged tuning; **Mehrfachabstimmungskreis** *m* ELEKTROTECH ganged circuit; **Mehrfachabtastung** *f* TELEKOM multiple sampling; **Mehrfachanweisungszeile** *f* COMP & DV multistatement line; **Mehrfachausgangsstecker** *m* FERNSEH multiple-outlet plug; **Mehrfachbandpaßfilter** *nt* AUFNAHME multiple-band-pass filter; **Mehrfachbefehlsstrom-Einfachdatenstrom-Rechner** *m (MISD-Rechner)* COMP & DV multiple-instruction single-data machine *(MISD machine)*; **Mehrfachbefehlsstrom-Mehrfach-**

datenstrom-Rechner *m (MIMD-Rechner)* COMP & DV multiple-instruction multiple-data machine *(MIMD machine)*; **Mehrfachbelegung** *f* TELEKOM multiple seizure; **Mehrfachbelichtung** *f* FOTO multiple exposure; **Mehrfachbespielung** *f* AUFNAHME sound on sound; **Mehrfachbetrieb** *m* COMP & DV multiprocessing; **Mehrfachbeugung** *f* TELEKOM multiple diffraction; **Mehrfachbildschirm** *m* FERNSEH multiscreen; **Mehrfachbohren** *nt* FERTIG multidrilling; **Mehrfachbohrmaschine** *f* MECHAN multiple-drilling machine; **Mehrfachbruch** *m* MATH complex fraction; **Mehrfachburst** *m* FERNSEH multiburst; **Mehrfachdrahtsystem** *nt* ELEKTRIZ multiple-wire system; **Mehrfachdrehkondensator** *m* ELEKTROTECH gang capacitor; **Mehrfachecho** *nt* AKUSTIK flutter echo, multiple echo; **Mehrfacheinsatzorbiter** *m* RAUMFAHRT recoverable orbiter; **Mehrfacheinsatztreibsatz** *m* RAUMFAHRT recoverable thruster; **Mehrfachexpansionsmaschine** *f* MASCHINEN compound expansion engine, multiple-expansion engine; **Mehrfachfallschirm** *m* LUFTTRANS cluster; **Mehrfachfestkondensator** *m* ELEKTROTECH capacitor bank; **Mehrfachform** *f* MASCHINEN multi-impression mold (AmE), multi-impression mould (BrE); **Mehrfachfrequenz** *f (MF)* ELEKTRONIK, RADIO, TELEKOM multiple frequency *(MF)*; **Mehrfachgarn** *nt* TEXTIL plied yarn; **Mehrfachgesenk** *nt* MASCHINEN multiple die; **Mehrfachglasiermaschine** *f* KER & GLAS multiple-glazing unit; **Mehrfachkeilriemenantrieb** *m* MASCHINEN multiple-V-belt drive; **Mehrfachkeilwelle** *f* MASCHINEN multispline shaft; **Mehrfachkeule** *f* TELEKOM multiple beam; **Mehrfachkeulenanntenne** *f* TELEKOM multiple-beam aerial, multiple-beam antenna; **Mehrfachkoppler** *m* COMP & DV multiplexer; **Mehrfachleitungskabel** *nt* ELEKTRIZ multiple feeder; **Mehrfachmikrofon** *nt* AUFNAHME multiple micro-phone; **Mehrfachmikrofonanordnung** *f* AKUSTIK multiple microphone; **Mehrfachnutzung** *f* ELEKTRONIK multiplex; **Mehrfachprogrammierung** *f* COMP & DV multiprogramming; **Mehrfachpumpe** *f* FERTIG double pump; **Mehrfachräumen** *nt* MASCHINEN multiple broaching; **Mehrfachreflektorantenne** *f* TELEKOM multiple-reflector aerial, multiple-reflector antenna; **Mehrfachröhrendüse** *f* LUFTTRANS multitube nozzle; **Mehrfachrufnummer** *f* TELEKOM multiple-subscriber number; **Mehrfachschalter** *m.* ELEKTROTECH gang switch; **Mehrfachschnitt** *m* FERTIG multiple blanking; **Mehrfach-Server** *m* TELEKOM multiple-server queue; **Mehrfachstahl** *nt* MASCHINEN gang tool; **Mehrfachstichprobenentnahme** *f* QUAL multiple sampling; **Mehrfachstichprobenprüfplan** *m* QUAL multiple-sampling plan; **Mehrfachstichprobenprüfung** *f* QUAL multiple-sampling inspection; **Mehrfachtonspur** *f* AUFNAHME multiple soundtrack; **Mehrfachverbindung** *f* COMP & DV multipoint link; **Mehrfachverstärker** *m* ELEKTRONIK multistage amplifier; **Mehrfachwahlmethode** *f* ERGON multiple-choice method; **Mehrfachwegsignale** *nt pl* FERNSEH multipath signals; **Mehrfachwerkzeug** *nt* KUNSTSTOFF multi-impression mold (AmE), multi-impression mould (BrE); **Mehrfachwicklung** *f* ELEKTRIZ, ELEKTROTECH multiple winding; **Mehrfachzugriff** *m* RAUMFAHRT *Weltraumfunk*, TELEKOM multiple access; **Mehrfachzugriff durch Trägerprüfung** *m (CSMA)* COMP & DV carrier sense multiple access *(CSMA)*; **Mehrfachzugriff im Zeitmultiplex** *m (TDMA)* COMP & DV, ELEKTRONIK, RAUMFAHRT, TELEKOM time division multiple access *(TDMA)*; **Mehrfachzugriffscode** *m* COMP & DV multiple-address code; **Mehrfachzugriffssystem** *nt* COMP & DV multiaccess system

mehrfädig: **~es Garn** *nt* TEXTIL plied yarn

Mehr-: **Mehrfarbendruck** *m* DRUCK, VERPACK multicolor printing (AmE), multicolour printing (BrE); **Mehrfarbenlichtpauspapier** *nt* KONSTZEICH multicolor diazotype paper (AmE), multicolour diazotype paper (BrE); **Mehrfarbenrotationspresse** *f* DRUCK multi-color rotary printing machine (AmE), multicolour rotary printing machine (BrE)

mehrfarbig *adj* DRUCK polychrome

Mehr-: **Mehrfaserkabel** *nt* ELEKTROTECH, TELEKOM multifiber cable (AmE), multifibre cable (BrE); **Mehrfaserverbindung** *f* OPTIK *Verbindung mehrerer Glasfasern*, TELEKOM multifiber joint (AmE), multifibre joint (BrE); **Mehrfeldplatte** *f* BAU continuous slab

Mehrfrequenz- *pref* ELEKTRONIK, RADIO, TELEKOM multifrequency; **Mehrfrequenzantenne** *f* ELEKTRONIK, RADIO, TELEKOM multifrequency aerial, multifrequency antenna; **Mehrfrequenzempfänger** *m* ELEKTRONIK, RADIO, TELEKOM multifrequency receiver; **Mehrfrequenz-Geber-Empfänger** *m* ELEKTRONIK, RADIO, TELEKOM multifrequency sender-receiver; **Mehrfrequenzgenerator** *m* ELEKTRONIK, RADIO, TELEKOM multifrequency generator; **Mehrfrequenz-Sender-Empfänger** *m* ELEKTRONIK, RADIO, TELEKOM multifrequency sender-receiver; **Mehrfrequenzwahl** *f (MFW)* RADIO dual-tone multifrequency *(DTMF)*, TELEKOM multifrequency dialing (AmE), multifrequency dialling (BrE) *(MFD)*

mehrgängig[1] *adj* FERTIG *Gewinde* multiple-screw, *Schnecke* multistart, MASCHINEN *Schnecke* multistart

mehrgängig:[2] **~es Gewinde** *nt* MASCHINEN multiple thread, multistart thread; **~es Potentiometer** *nt* ELEKTROTECH multiturn potentiometer; **~e Schnecke** *f* MASCHINEN multistart worm; **~e Schraube** *f* MASCHINEN multiple-threaded screw

Mehr-: **Mehrgewicht** *nt* VERPACK excess weight; **Mehrgitterröhre** *f* ELEKTRONIK multielectrode tube, multigrid tube, RADIO multigrid valve

mehrgliedrig *adj* MASCHINEN multilink

Mehr-: **Mehrkammerklystron** *nt* ELEKTRONIK, PHYS multicavity klystron; **Mehrkammerverbundrohrmühle** *f* KOHLEN compartment pebble mill; **Mehrkanal-** *pref* AUFNAHME multichannel, COMP & DV multiport, ELEKTRONIK, RADIO multichannel; **Mehrkanalelementarlautsprecher** *m* AKUSTIK multichannel elementary loudspeaker; **Mehrkanalfilter** *nt* TELEKOM multichannel filter; **Mehrkanallautsprecher** *m* AUFNAHME multichannel loudspeaker; **Mehrkanalprotokoll** *nt* COMP & DV multichannel protocol; **Mehrkanalregister** *nt* COMP & DV multiport register; **Mehrkanalträger** *m* RAUMFAHRT *Weltraumfunk* multichannel carrier; **Mehrkanalübertragung** *f* COMP & DV multiplexing; **Mehrkanalüberwachung** *f* RADIO, WASSERTRANS *Funk* multichannel monitoring; **Mehrkanalverstärker** *m* ELEKTRONIK multichannel amplifier; **Mehrkanalwähler** *m* FERNSEH multichannel selector; **Mehrkolbenmotor** *m* MASCHINEN multipiston engine; **Mehrkollektortransistor** *m* ELEKTRONIK multicollector transistor; **Mehrkomponentenkleber** *m* VERPACK mixed adhesive; **Mehrkopf-** *pref* TEXTIL multihead; **Mehrkörperproblem** *nt* RAUMFAHRT many-body problem; **Mehrkörperschiff** *nt*

WASSERTRANS multihull ship, multihulled ship; **Mehrkreisfilter** *nt* ELEKTRONIK multisection filter; **Mehrkristallhalbleiter** *m* ELEKTRONIK polycrystalline semiconductor; **Mehrlagen-** *pref* MASCHINEN multilayer; **Mehrlagenabdeckung** *f* ELEKTRONIK *Leiterplatten* multilayer resist; **Mehrlagendickfilme** *m pl* ELEKTRONIK multilayer thick films; **Mehrlagendünnfilme** *m pl* ELEKTRONIK multilayer thin films; **Mehrlagenkarton** *m* PAPIER multilayer board, VERPACK multiple board; **Mehrlagenleiterplatte** *f* ELEKTRONIK multilayer printed circuit; **Mehrlagensack** *m* VERPACK multiply sack, multiwall sack

mehrlagig[1] *adj* VERPACK multiply

mehrlagig:[2] **~e gedruckte Schaltung** *f* TELEKOM multilayer printed circuit; **~er Plattenheizkörper** *m* HEIZ & KÄLTE multilevel panel-type radiator; **~e Spule** *f* ELEKTRIZ multilayer coil; **~e Wicklung** *f* ELEKTRIZ multilayer coil

Mehr-: **Mehrleiterkabel** *nt* ELEKTROTECH multiconductor cable, multicore cable

mehrlinsig: **~es Objektiv** *nt* FOTO composite lens

Mehr-: **Mehrlippenbohrer** *m* FERTIG subland drill

mehrlösig: **~e Bremse** *f* EISENBAHN graduated brake

Mehr-: **Mehrmeißeldrehmaschine** *f* MASCHINEN multiple-tool lathe, multitool lathe; **Mehrmeißelhalter** *m* MASCHINEN turret; **Mehrmodenfaser** *f* OPTIK *Lichtleitfaser* multimode fiber (AmE), multimode fibre (BrE); **Mehrmodengruppenlaufzeit** *f* OPTIK *Lichtleitfaser* multimode group decay; **Mehrmodenlaser** *m* OPTIK multimode laser; **Mehrmodenverzerrung** *f* OPTIK *Lichtleitfaser* multimode distortion

mehrmotorig: **~er Hubschrauber** *m* LUFTTRANS multiengine helicopter

Mehr-: **Mehrordnungsfilter** *nt* ELEKTRONIK multiple-order filter

mehrpaarig: **~es Kabel** *nt* ELEKTRIZ multipair cable

Mehr-: **Mehrpfadbetrieb** *m* COMP & DV multithreading; **Mehrpfadprogramm** *nt* COMP & DV multithread program

Mehrphasen- *pref* ELEKTROTECH polyphase; **Mehrphasenauflösung** *f* RAUMFAHRT *Weltraumfunk* phase ambiguity resolution; **Mehrphasengenerator** *m* ELEKTROTECH polyphase generator; **Mehrphaseninduktionsmotor** *m* ELEKTROTECH polyphase induction motor; **Mehrphasenmotor** *m* ELEKTROTECH polyphase motor; **Mehrphasensteuergerät** *nt* KFZTECH multiphase controller; **Mehrphasenstufenbohrer** *m* MASCHINEN subland twist drill; **Mehrphasensynchronmotor** *m* ELEKTROTECH polyphase synchronous motor; **Mehrphasentransformator** *m* ELEKTROTECH poly-phase transformer

mehrphasig[1] *adj* ELEKTRIZ multiphase, polyphase, ELEKTRONIK multiphase, ELEKTROTECH polyphase

mehrphasig:[2] **~er Motor** *m* ELEKTRIZ polyphase motor; **~es Netz** *nt* ELEKTRIZ polyphase network; **~e Schaltung** *f* ELEKTRIZ polyphase circuit; **~er Strom** *m* ELEKTRIZ polyphase current; **~er Transformator** *m* ELEKTRIZ polyphase transformer

Mehr-: **Mehrplatinencomputer** *m* COMP & DV multiboard computer

mehrplattig: **~er Kondensator** *m* ELEKTRIZ multiple-plate capacitor

Mehr-: **Mehrplatzsystem** *nt* COMP & DV multiuser system

mehrpolig[1] *adj* ELEKTRIZ multipolar, ELEKTROTECH multipin

mehrpolig:[2] **~er Anker** *m* ELEKTRIZ multipolar arma-

ture; **~e Buchse** *f* ELEKTRIZ multiple socket; **~es Filter** *nt* ELEKTRONIK multipole filter; **~er Stecker** *m* ELEKTRIZ multiple plug; **~er Stecker mit Verriegelung** *m* ELEKTRIZ multiconductor locking plug

Mehr-: **Mehrpolschalter** *m* ELEKTRIZ multiple switch; **Mehrprogrammbetrieb** *m* COMP & DV multiprogramming; **Mehrprogrammsystem** *nt* COMP & DV multiprogramming system

Mehrprozessor *m* COMP & DV multiprocessor; **Mehrprozessorbetrieb** *m* COMP & DV multiprocessing; **Mehrprozessorsystem** *nt* COMP & DV multiprocessing system; **Mehrprozessorverschachtelung** *f* COMP & DV multiprocessor interleaving

Mehrpunkt- *pref* COMP & DV multidrop, multipoint; **Mehrpunktglied** *nt* REGELUNG multiposition element; **Mehrpunkt-Klebemaschine** *f* VERPACK multipoint glueing machine; **Mehrpunkt-Regeleinrichtung** *f* REGELUNG multiposition controller; **Mehrpunktschalter** *m* ELEKTROTECH multiposition switch; **Mehrpunktverbindung** *f* COMP & DV multidrop line, multidrop link, multipoint connection, multipoint link; **Mehrpunktverhalten** *nt* REGELUNG *von Gliedern* multiposition action

mehrreihig: **~er Plattenheizkörper** *m* HEIZ & KÄLTE multibank panel-type radiator

Mehr-: **Mehrrundsiebmaschine** *f* PAPIER multivat board machine

mehrschäftig: **~es Tau** *nt* WASSERTRANS *Tauwerk* multistrand rope

Mehr-: **Mehrscheibenkupplung** *f* KFZTECH multiple-disc clutch (BrE), multiple-disk clutch (AmE), MASCHINEN multiple-disc clutch (BrE), multiple-disk clutch (AmE), multiple-plate clutch

Mehrschicht- *pref* ANSTRICH, MASCHINEN, RAUMFAHRT multilayer; **Mehrschichten-CRT** *f* ELEKTRONIK penetration CRT; **Mehrschichtenglas** *nt* KER & GLAS laminated glass; **Mehrschichtenglasfrontscheibe** *f* KFZTECH *Karosserie* laminated windscreen (BrE), laminated windshield (AmE); **Mehrschichtenglasherstellung** *f* KER & GLAS laminating; **Mehrschichtenkarton** *m* VERPACK multiply board; **Mehrschichtenphosphorschirm** *m* ELEKTRONIK, FERNSEH penetration screen; **Mehrschichtensicherheitsglas** *nt* KER & GLAS laminated safety glass

mehrschichtig[1] *adj* FERTIG, KUNSTSTOFF laminated, KÜNSTL INT *neurales Netz*, VERPACK multilayered

mehrschichtig:[2] **~e Filtration** *f* WASSERVERSORG multilayer filtration

Mehrschicht-: **Mehrschichtleiterplatte** *f* TELEKOM multilayer printed circuit; **Mehrschichtprinzip** *nt* ABFALL *Deponie* multibarrier principle

mehrschneidig *adj* MASCHINEN multiblade

Mehr-: **Mehrschürzensystem** *nt* WASSERTRANS multipleskirt system, multiskirt system

mehrskalig[1] *adj* ELEKTRIZ multirange

mehrskalig:[2] **~es Meßinstrument** *nt* ELEKTRIZ multirange meter .

Mehr-: **Mehrspaltensatz** *m* DRUCK multicolumn setting; **Mehrspannungsmotor** *m* ELEKTRIZ universal motor; **Mehrspindelanordnung** *f* FERTIG multispindle arrangement; **Mehrspindelautomat** *m* FERTIG multispindle automatic; **Mehrspindelbauart** *f* FERTIG multispindle design; **Mehrspindelbohrmaschine** *f* FERTIG multispindle drilling machine, MASCHINEN multiple drill, multiple-spindle drilling machine; **Mehrspindelbohrwerk** *nt* MASCHINEN multiple-boring machine; **Mehrspindeldrehautomat** *m* FERTIG multispindle chucking automatic, multispindle automatic, MASCHINEN multispindle automatic machine; **Mehrspindelfutterautomat** *m* FERTIG multispindle chucking automatic; **Mehrspindelstangenautomat** *m* FERTIG multispindle bar automatic, MECHAN automatic lathe; **Mehrspiralenabtastscheibe** *f* FERNSEH multispiral scanning disc (BrE), multispiral scanning disk (AmE); **Mehrspur-Aufnahmesystem** *nt* AUFNAHME multitrack recording system; **Mehrspuraufzeichnung** *f* AKUSTIK multitrack recording

mehrspurig: ~e **Strecke** *f* EISENBAHN mixed-gage track (AmE), mixed-gauge track (BrE)

Mehr-: **Mehrstationenverbindung** *f* COMP & DV multidrop link; **Mehrstoffauflauf** *m* PAPIER multistock headbox; **Mehrstoffheizanlage** *f* MASCHINEN multifuel heater; **Mehrstofflager** *nt* MASCHINEN compound bearing; **Mehrstoffmotor** *m* KFZTECH,THERMOD multifuel engine; **Mehrstrahlantenne** *f* PHYS, TELEKOM multiple-beam aerial, multiple-beam antenna

mehrstrahlig *adj* RAUMFAHRT *Weltraumfunk* multibeam

Mehr-: **Mehrstrahlinterferenz** *f* PHYS multiple-beam interference; **Mehrstrahlröhre** *f* ELEKTRONIK multigun tube; **Mehrstromgenerator** *m* ELEKTROTECH multiple-current generator; **Mehrstückpackung** *f* VERPACK multipack; **Mehrstufen-** *pref* FERTIG multiple-shot; **Mehrstufengesenk** *nt* MASCHINEN progression dies, progressive dies; **Mehrstufenkompressor** *m* HEIZ & KÄLTE, MASCHINEN multistage compressor; **Mehrstufenrakete** *f* RAUMFAHRT multistage rocket; **Mehrstufenturbine** *f* MASCHINEN multistage turbine; **Mehrstufenverstärker** *m* ELEKTRONIK multistage amplifier

mehrstufig[1] *adj* FERTIG, MASCHINEN, TELEKOM multistage

mehrstufig:[2] ~e **Behandlungsanlage** *f* WASSERVERSORG comprehensive water treatment plant; ~es **Folgewerkzeug** *nt* MASCHINEN multistage progression tooling; ~es **Netz** *nt* TELEKOM multistage network; ~e **Schaltung** *f* TELEKOM multistage circuit; ~e **Stichprobenentnahme** *f* QUAL multistage sampling; ~es **System** *nt* TELEKOM multilevel system; ~e **Turbine** *f* MASCHINEN multistage turbine

mehrteilig[1] *adj* KER & GLAS split

mehrteilig:[2] ~er **Brennstoffstab** *m* KERNTECH segmented fuel rod; ~er **Entwicklungsbehälter** *m* FOTO multiunit developing tank; ~er **Fernschnelltriebwagen** *m* EISENBAHN multiple-unit train; ~e **Form** *f* KER & GLAS split mold (AmE), split mould (BrE); ~e **Walzen** *f pl* KER & GLAS split rollers; ~es **Werkzeug** *nt* KUNSTSTOFF split mold (AmE), split mould (BrE); ~e **Zugeinheit** *f* EISENBAHN multiple-train unit

Mehr-: **Mehrträgerdienst** *m* TELEKOM multibearer service; **Mehrtrichter-Lautsprecher** *m* AUFNAHME multiple-cone loudspeaker; **Mehrwegbetrieb** *m* COMP & DV multithreading; **Mehrwegefading** *nt* TELEKOM multipath fading; **Mehrwegeführung** *f* TELEKOM redundant routing; **Mehrwegereflexionen** *f pl* TELEKOM multipath reflections; **Mehrwegflasche** *f* ABFALL deposit bottle, returnable bottle, VERPACK recycled bottle; **Mehrweggebinde** *nt* ABFALL returnable pack, returnable container; **Mehrwegkarton** *m* VERPACK reusable box; **Mehrwegschieber** *m* MASCHINEN multiple-way slide valve; **Mehrwegventil** *nt* FERTIG *Kunststoffinstallationen* L-port valve, multiport

valve, MASCHINEN multiple-way valve; **Mehrwegverpackung** *f* VERPACK returnable packaging

Mehrwert- *pref* COMP & DV value-added; **Mehrwertdienste** *m pl* TELEKOM value-added services; **Mehrwertdienstnetz** *nt* (*VAN*) COMP & DV, TELEKOM value-added network (*VAN*)

mehrwertig[1] *adj* CHEMIE polyvalent

mehrwertig:[2] ~e **Menge** *f* COMP & DV, KÜNSTL INT fuzzy set

Mehr-: **Mehrwertigkeit** *f* CHEMIE polyvalence, polyvalency; **Mehrwertnetz** *nt* (*VAN*) COMP & DV, TELEKOM value-added network (*VAN*); **Mehrwicklungs-Transformator** *m* ELEKTRIZ multiwinding transformer

mehrzählig *adj* CHEMIE *Komplexchemie* polydentate

mehrzähnig *adj* CHEMIE polydentate

Mehrzweck- *pref* CHEMIE multifunctional, polyfunctional, KFZTECH utility, MECHAN GP, general-purpose; **Mehrzweckanhänger** *m* KFZTECH all-purpose trailer; **Mehrzweckbehälter** *m* ERDÖL, WASSERTRANS multiservice vessel; **Mehrzweckdrehmaschine** *f* FERTIG universal lathe; **Mehrzweckelektrofahrzeug** *nt* KFZTECH electric vehicle for general-purpose use; **Mehrzweckfrachter** *m* WASSERTRANS multipurpose carrier; **Mehrzweckgerät** *nt* GERÄT general-purpose instrument; **Mehrzweckhubschrauber** *m* LUFTTRANS multipurpose helicopter; **Mehrzweckkühlraum** *m* HEIZ & KÄLTE multiple-purpose cold store; **Mehrzweckmeßgerät** *nt* GERÄT general-purpose instrument; **Mehrzweckreaktor** *m* KERNTECH multipurpose reactor; **Mehrzweckrohrleitung** *f* TRANS multipurpose material pipeline; **Mehrzweckschiff** *nt* ERDÖL *Schiffahrt* multiservice vessel, WASSERTRANS *Handelsmarine* multipurpose ship, multiservice vessel; **Mehrzwecktank** *m* ERDÖL *Lagertechnik*, WASSERTRANS *Lagertechnik* multiservice vessel; **Mehrzwecktanker** *m* WASSERTRANS multipurpose tanker

Mehr-: **Mehrzylindermaschine** *f* KFZTECH, MASCHINEN multicylinder engine; **Mehrzylindertrockenpartie** *f* PAPIER multicylinder dryer section

Meile *f* METROL, TRANS mile; **Meilen je Gallone** *f pl* TRANS miles per gallon; **Meilenfahrt** *f* WASSERTRANS *Navigation* distance run

Meißel *m* BAU bit, chisel, sett, FERTIG gad, *Spanung* chisel, MASCHINEN tool; ~ **mit abgeschrägter Kante** *m* MASCHINEN beveled-edge chisel (AmE), bevelled-edge chisel (BrE); ~ **mit gerader Schneidkante** *m* FERTIG square-nosed tool; ~ **mit hochgekröpftem Schneidkopf** *m* FERTIG raised-face tool; **Meißelbohren** *nt* BAU boring with the bit; **Meißelbohrer** *m* ERDÖL *Tiefbohrtechnik* chisel bit; **Meißelhalter** *m* MASCHINEN tool head; **Meißelhalter mit Klappe und Klappenträger** *m* FERTIG *Hobelmaschine, Waagrechtstoßmaschine* apron; **Meißelhalterschlitten** *m* MASCHINEN tool carrier slide; **Meißelhammer** *m* BAU chipper; **Meißelklappe** *f* FERTIG, MASCHINEN clapper; **Meißelklappenträger** *m* FERTIG box

Meißeln *nt* FERTIG, MASCHINEN chiseling (AmE), chiselling (BrE)

meißeln *vt* BAU chip, chisel, FERTIG chip

Meißel-: **Meißelschaft** *m* MASCHINEN tool shank; **Meißelschlitten** *m* FERTIG downfeed slide, *Waagerechtstoßmaschine* head slide; **Meißelvorschub** *m* FERTIG tool feed

Meißner-: ~**scher Effekt** *m* PHYS Meissner effect; ~**scher Oszillator** *m* ELEKTRONIK Meissner oscillator; ~**sche Schaltung** *f* ELEKTRONIK Meissner oscillator

Meistermodus m KONTROLL master mode
Meisterrücksetzsignal nt KONTROLL master reset signal
Meisterstelle f KONTROLL master
MEK abbr KUNSTSTOFF (Methylethylketon) MEK (methyl ethyl ketone), UMWELTSCHMUTZ (maximale Emissionskonzentration) maximum emission concentration
Meker-Brenner m LABOR Meker burner
Mel nt AKUSTIK, AUFNAHME mel
Melamin nt CHEMIE, TEXTIL melamine; **Melamin-Formaldehydharz** nt (MF) ELEKTRIZ melamine resin (MF), KUNSTSTOFF melamine formaldehyde resin (MF); **Melaminharz** nt (MF) ELEKTRIZ melamine resin (MF), KUNSTSTOFF melamine formaldehyde resin (MF)
Melange f TEXTIL blend
Melanin nt CHEMIE melanin
Melanterit m CHEMIE copperas
Melde: ~scher Versuch m PHYS Melde's experiment
Meldeleitung f TELEKOM Telefon control circuit
melden vt COMP & DV return
meldepflichtig[1] adj QUAL notifiable
meldepflichtig:[2] ~e Abweichung f QUAL reportable nonconformance; ~er Unfall m SICHERHEIT notifiable accident
Melder m ELEKTRONIK Signal- und Sicherungstechnik detector, ELEKTROTECH, GERÄT annunciator; **Melderelais** nt ELEKTRIZ pilot relay
Meldesignal nt TELEKOM answer signal
Meldeverzug m TELEKOM answering delay
Meldung f COMP & DV message, EISENBAHN notice, MEERSCHMUTZ notification, RADIO, TELEKOM message; **Meldungskopf** m COMP & DV message header; **Meldungsquelle** f COMP & DV message source; **Meldungstext** m COMP & DV message text; **Meldungsvermittlungssystem** nt TELEKOM message switching system
Meletin nt CHEMIE meletin
Melezitose f CHEMIE melicitose, raffinose
Melibiose f CHEMIE melibiose
melieren vt TEXTIL blend
meliert: ~es Gußeisen nt FERTIG mottled iron
Mellith- pref CHEMIE mellitic
Mellon nt CHEMIE mellon
Member nt COMP & DV Teildatei member
Membran f AUFNAHME diaphragm, MASCHINEN diaphragm, membrane, MECHAN diaphragm, RAUMFAHRT Raumschiff membrane; **Membrandichtung** f RAUMFAHRT bellows seal; **Membrandruckdose** f RAUMFAHRT bellows; **Membranfeder** f MASCHINEN diaphragm spring; **Membranfederkupplung** f KFZTECH diaphragm clutch; **Membranfilter** nt CHEMTECH, LABOR membrane filter; **Membranklappe** f FERTIG Kunststoffinstallationen diaphragm disc valve (BrE), diaphragm disk valve (AmE); **Membrankraftstoffpumpe** f KFZTECH diaphragm fuel pump; **Membranlautsprecher** m AKUSTIK membrane loudspeaker; **Membranmeßwerk** nt GERÄT diaphragm movement; **Membranpumpe** f MASCHINEN, MEERSCHMUTZ, WASSERVERSORG diaphragm pump; **Membranregler** m KFZTECH suction-type governor; **Membranscheibe** f MASCHINEN diaphragm disc (BrE), diaphragm disk (AmE); **Membranschlüsselschalter** m ELEKTROTECH membrane keyswitch; **Membransetzkasten** m KOHLEN diaphragm-type washbox; **Membransiegelung** f VERPACK foil sealing;

Membrantastatur f ELEKTROTECH membrane keyboard; **Membranventil** nt FERTIG Kunststoffinstallationen, MASCHINEN diaphragm valve; **Membranverdichter** m MASCHINEN diaphragm compressor; **Membranverschließ- und Heißsiegelmaschine** f VERPACK film-applying lid and heat-sealing machine; **Membranversiegelung** f VERPACK diaphragm sealing
Memory-Funktion f COMP & DV memory function
Mendelevium nt (Md) CHEMIE mendelevium (Md)
Menge f BAU aggregate, ELEKTRONIK, KONTROLL quantity, MATH set, Quantität amount, METROL rate, QUAL batch; **Mengenbestimmung** f BAU measurement of quantities; **Mengendosierung** f GERÄT volume dosage; **Mengendurchfluß** m HEIZ & KÄLTE mass flow rate, PHYS mass rate of flow; **Mengendurchflußmeßgerät** nt GERÄT mass flow meter; **Mengendurchsatz** m HEIZ & KÄLTE mass flow rate; **Mengenfluß** m KERNTECH mass flow; **Mengenlehre** f MATH set theory; **Mengenmeßgerät** nt ERDÖL Meßtechnik flowmeter; **Mengenregelklappe** f HEIZ & KÄLTE volume control damper; **Mengenregelungsventil** nt FERTIG flow control valve, flow controller; **Mengenstrommesser von Gasblasen** m LABOR bubble flow meter; **Mengenverpackungsanlage** f VERPACK flow wrapping machine; **Mengenzählung** f GERÄT volume counting
Mengfutter nt LEBENSMITTEL Landwirtschaft mash
Meniskus m PHYS Flüssigkeitsspiegel meniscus; **Meniskuslinse** f FOTO Linse, PHYS meniscus lens
Mennige f CHEMIE minium, red lead
menschlich: ~ bedingte Übersäuerung f UMWELTSCHMUTZ anthropogenic acidification
Mensch-Maschine-Dialog m COMP & DV man-machine interaction
Mensch-Maschine-Interaktion f COMP & DV man-machine interaction
Mensch-Maschine-Interface nt (MMI) COMP & DV, KONTROLL, KÜNSTL INT, RAUMFAHRT man-machine interface (MMI)
Mensch-Maschine-Schnittstelle f (MMI) COMP & DV, KONTROLL, KÜNSTL INT, RAUMFAHRT man-machine interface (MMI)
Mensch-Maschine-System nt ERGON man-machine system
Mensur f LABOR measuring cylinder
mental: ~e Belastung f ERGON mental load
Menthan nt CHEMIE menthane; **Menthandiamin** nt CHEMIE menthanediamine
Menthanol nt CHEMIE menthanol
Menthanon nt CHEMIE menthanone
Menthen nt CHEMIE menthene; **Menthenol** nt CHEMIE menthenol; **Menthenon** nt CHEMIE menthenone
Menthofuran nt CHEMIE menthofuran
Menü nt COMP & DV, KONTROLL menu; **Menüanzeige** f COMP & DV menu screen; **Menüauswahl** f COMP & DV menu selection; **Menübildschirm** m COMP & DV menu screen
menügeführt[1] adj COMP & DV menu-driven
menügeführt:[2] ~e Anwendung f COMP & DV menu-driven application
menügesteuert[1] adj COMP & DV menu-driven
menügesteuert:[2] ~e Anwendung f COMP & DV menu-driven application
menügestützt: ~e Benutzeroberfläche f KÜNSTL INT menu-based user interface
MEP abbr (mittlerer Nutzdruck) LUFTTRANS, MASCHINEN mep (mean effective pressure)

Mepacrin *nt* CHEMIE atebrin, mepacrine, quinacrine

Meprobamat *nt* CHEMIE meprobamate

Mercaptal *nt* CHEMIE mercaptal

Mercaptan *nt* CHEMIE mercaptan, thiol

Mercapto- *pref* CHEMIE sulfhydryl (AmE), sulphhydryl (BrE); **Mercaptoessig-** *pref* CHEMIE *Säure* mercapto-acetic, thioglycolic

Mercaptol *nt* CHEMIE mercaptol, thioacetol

Mercaptomerin *nt* CHEMIE mercaptomerin

Mercatorkarte *f* WASSERTRANS *Navigation* Mercator chart

Mercatorprojektion *f* RAUMFAHRT, WASSERTRANS *Navigation* Mercator projection

Mercurochrom® *nt* CHEMIE merbromin, Mercuro-chrome®

Mergel *m* WASSERVERSORG marl; **Mergelton** *m* WASSERVERSORG marly clay

Meridian *m* RAUMFAHRT meridian; **Meridiandurchgang** *m* RAUMFAHRT meridian transit; **Meridiankreisel** *m* RAUMFAHRT *Raumschiff* meridian gyro

meridional *adj* RAUMFAHRT meridional

Meridionalschnitt *m* PHYS tangential focal line

Meridionalstrahl *m* OPTIK, TELEKOM meridional ray

Merkaptan *nt* ERDÖL *Petrochemie*, KUNSTSTOFF mercaptan

Merkmal *nt* COMP & DV attribute, characteristic, feature, ELEKTRONIK characteristic, KÜNSTL INT, PATENT feature, QUAL characteristic; **Merkmalausblendung** *f* COMP & DV feature extraction

Merkmarke *f* AUFNAHME cue mark

Merkpunkt *m* AUFNAHME cue dot

Mesacon- *pref* CHEMIE mesaconic

Mesadiode *f* ELEKTRONIK mesa diode

Mesaprozeß *m* ELEKTRONIK mesa process

Mesatransistor *m* RADIO mesa transistor

MESFET *abbr* (*Metallhalbleiter-Feldeffekttransistor*) ELEKTRONIK MESFET (*metal semiconductor field effect transistor*)

Mesidin *nt* CHEMIE mesidine

Mesitylen *nt* CHEMIE mesitylene; **Mesitylen-** *pref* CHEMIE mesitylenic

Mesomerie-Effekt *m* CHEMIE mesomeric effect

Meson *nt* CHEMIE, PHYS, TEILPHYS meson

Mesopause *f* RADIO mesopause

Mesorcin *nt* CHEMIE mesorcin

Mesosphäre *f* RADIO mesosphere

Mesothorium *nt* CHEMIE mesothorium

Mesotron *nt* CHEMIE meson

Mesoweinsäure *f* CHEMIE mesotartaric acid

Mesoxal- *pref* CHEMIE mesoxalic

Mesozoikum *nt* ERDÖL *Geologie* Mesozoic

Meß- *pref* BAU, GERÄT, KER & GLAS, QUAL measuring; **Meß- und Prüfeinrichtungen** *f pl* QUAL measuring and test equipment; **Meß- und Regeltechnik** *f* (*IUC*) ELEKTRONIK *Leittechnik* instrumentation and control (*IUC*); **Meßabweichung** *f* QUAL error of measurement; **Meßader** *f* ELEKTROTECH *bei Kabel* pilot wire, TELEKOM *Kabel* pilot; **Meßanlage** *f* GERÄT measuring equipment, measuring system; **Meßanordnung** *f* GERÄT measuring arrangement; **Meßanzeige** *f* MASCHINEN dial indicator; **Meßapparat** *m* BAU measuring apparatus; **Meßapparatur** *f* GERÄT measuring equipment; **Meßaufgabe** *f* GERÄT measuring task; **Meßaufnehmer** *m* HEIZ & KÄLTE sensor; **Meßband** *nt* BAU surveyor's tape

meßbar: **~e Menge** *f* METROL measurable quantity

Meß-: **Meßbarkeit** *f* GERÄT measurability; **Meßbarkeitsgrenze** *f* GERÄT limit of measurability

Meßbereich *m* GERÄT instrument range, measurement range, measuring range, range of measurement: **Meßbereichsänderung** *f* GERÄT change in range; **Meßbereichschalter** *m* ELEKTRIZ range switch; **Meßbereichsendewert** *m* GERÄT full-scale point; **Meßbereichserweiterung** *f* GERÄT extension of the measuring range; **Meßbereichsüberschreitung** *f* GERÄT overrange; **Meßbereichsunterdrückung** *f* GERÄT suppression of range; **Meßbereichswahl** *f* GERÄT automatic ranging

Meß-: **Meßbildverfahren** *nt* BAU photogrammetry; **Meßblättchen** *nt* METROL gap gage (AmE), gap gauge (BrE); **Meßblende** *f* ERDÖL orifice plate, FERTIG calibrated orifice, GERÄT orifice plate, *Pneumatik* measuring orifice, HEIZ & KÄLTE orifice plate, MASCHINEN orifice meter, OPTIK measuring orifice; **Meßbolzen** *m* FERTIG spindle; **Meßbrücke** *f* ELEKTRIZ, ELEKTROTECH bridge, GERÄT bridge, measuring bridge, test bridge, MASCHINEN measuring bridge; **Meßbuchse** *f* ELEKTROTECH test jack

Meßdaten *nt pl* METROL measuring data; **Meßdatenabtastung** *f* GERÄT data sampling, measuring data sampling, measuring data scanning; **Meßdatenerfassung** *f* GERÄT acquisition of measured data, data logging, measurement data acquisition; **Meßdatengewinnung** *f* GERÄT measurement data acquisition; **Meßdatenregistrierung** *f* GERÄT data logging; **Meßdatensichtgerät** *nt* GERÄT data display unit; **Meßdatenübertragungssystem** *nt* GERÄT data transmission system; **Meßdatenumformung** *f* GERÄT data conversion; **Meßdatenumsetzer** *m* GERÄT data converter; **Meßdatenumsetzung** *f* GERÄT data conversion; **Meßdatenverarbeitung** *f* GERÄT measurement data processing, processing of measured data; **Meßdatenverdichtung** *f* GERÄT measuring data reduction; **Meßdatenverstärker** *m* GERÄT data amplifier

Meß-: **Meßdorn** *m* FERTIG feeler; **Meßdruck** *m* GERÄT measuring pressure; **Meßdüse** *f* FERTIG gaging jet cutlet (AmE), gauging jet cutlet (BrE), MASCHINEN metering jet

Messe *f* WASSERTRANS mess

Meß-: **Meßeinheit** *f* METROL unit of measurement; **Meßeinrichtung** *f* GERÄT measuring equipment, measuring set; **Meßelektrode** *f* ELEKTROTECH sensing electrode

Messen *nt* ERDÖL gaging (AmE), gauging (BrE), LABOR measuring, METROL gaging (AmE), gauging (BrE); **~ der Beschichtungsdicke** *nt* METROL coating-thickness measurement

messen *vt* BAU gage (AmE), gauge (BrE), COMP & DV measure, ELEKTRIZ, KONTROLL gage (AmE), gauge (BrE), MASCHINEN, METROL measure, RADIO meter

messend: **~e Maschine** *f* METROL measuring machine; **~es Relais** *nt* GERÄT detecting relay

Messer *nt* ELEKTRIZ gage (AmE), gauge (BrE), MASCHINEN knife, meter, MECHAN blade, PAPIER blade, knife; **Messerfeile** *f* MASCHINEN cant file, knife edge file, knife file

Meß-: **Meßergebnis** *nt* GERÄT measuring result, result of measurement

Messer: **Messerhalter** *m* MASCHINEN blade holder, PAPIER knife holder; **Messerkopf** *m* FERTIG face-milling cutter with inserted blades, MASCHINEN cutter head, inserted blade cutter, inserted blade milling cutter, inserted tooth cutter; **Messerschalter** m ELEKTRIZ knife switch, KERNTECH knife edge switch; **Messerschneide** f MASCHINEN knife edge; **Messerwalze** f MASCHINEN cutter wheel, knife drum; **Messerzylinder** m PAPIER knife cylinder

Meß-: Meßfehler m METROL measuring error; **Meßflasche** f LABOR graduated flask, volumetric flask; **Meßfolgegeschwindigkeit** f ELEKTRONIK von AD-Wandler conversion rate; **Meßfühler** m COMP & DV sensor, GERÄT gage (AmE), gauge (BrE), KFZTECH sensor, MEERSCHMUTZ sensing device, METROL sensor, OPTIK detector, PHYS, RAUMFAHRT Weltraumfunk, TELEKOM sensor; **Meßfunkenstrecke** f ELEKTROTECH measuring spark gap; **Meßgegenstand** m GERÄT measurand, object of measurement; **Meßgenauigkeit** f METROL accuracy of measurement

Meßgerät nt EISENBAHN instrument, ELEKTRIZ measuring instrument, ERDÖL instrument, GERÄT gage (AmE), gauge (BrE), measuring equipment, measuring set, measuring instrument, KFZTECH, KONTROLL, LABOR gage (AmE), gauge (BrE), LUFTTRANS instrument, MEERSCHMUTZ sensing device, METROL gage (AmE), gauge (BrE), measuring device, measuring instrument, PAPIER gage (AmE), gauge (BrE), RADIO meter, WASSERTRANS instrument; **~ mit Analogausgang** nt GERÄT analog output instrument; **~ zur Analyse** nt SICHERHEIT measuring and analysis apparatus; **~ zur Bestimmung des Berylliumgehaltes** nt KERNTECH beryllium content meter, beryllium prospecting meter; **~ für elektrische Größen** nt GERÄT electric measuring instrument, electrical measuring instrument; **~ mit gedehnter Skale** nt GERÄT expanded scale meter; **~ mit interner Meßdatenverarbeitung** nt GERÄT processing measuring instrument; **~ mit lebendigem Nullpunkt** nt GERÄT live-zero instrument; **~ mit Nullpunkt in der Skalenmitte** nt GERÄT central-zero instrument; **~ mit Projektionsskale** nt GERÄT projected-scale instrument; **~ mit unterdrücktem Nullpunkt** nt GERÄT set-up scale instrument; **~ mit Zeigeranzeige** nt METROL dial indicating gage (AmE), dial indicating gauge (BrE); **Meßgerätefehler** m GERÄT instrumental error; **Meßgeräteklemme** f GERÄT meter terminal; **Meßgeräteschutzschaltung** f GERÄT meter protecting circuit; **Meßgeräteskale** f GERÄT meter dial; **Meßgeräteverstärker** m GERÄT meter amplifier; **Meßgerätständer** m METROL gage stand (AmE), gauge stand (BrE)

Meß-: Meßglas nt KER & GLAS gage glass (AmE), gauge glass (BrE); **Meßglied** nt GERÄT Meßeinrichtung receiving element; **Meßgröße** f ELEKTRONIK feedback signal, measurand, measured quantity, GERÄT, METROL measurand; **Meßgrößenwandler** m GERÄT converter

Messing[1] nt ELEKTRIZ, FERTIG, MASCHINEN, METALL brass

Messing:[2] **mit ~ löten** vt MECHAN, THERMOD braze

Messing: Messingarbeiten f pl BAU brass works; **Messingdraht** m BAU brass wire; **Messinggießerei** f BAU brass foundry; **Messingguß** m METALL cast brass; **Messinglot** nt BAU, MASCHINEN brass solder; **Messingrevolverdrehmaschine** f FERTIG monitor lathe; **Messingrundkopfschraube** f BAU brass round-head wood screw; **Messingschmied** m BAU brass smith; **Messingschraube** f MASCHINEN brass screw; **Messingstab** m NICHTFOSS ENERG brass rod; **Messingtype** f DRUCK brass type

Meßinstrument nt EISENBAHN instrument, ELEKTRIZ measuring instrument, ERDÖL instrument, GERÄT measuring instrument, KFZTECH, KONTROLL gage (AmE), gauge (BrE), LABOR gage (AmE), gauge (BrE), measuring equipment, measuring set, LUFTTRANS instrument, MEERSCHMUTZ sensing device, METROL measuring device, measuring instrument, PAPIER gage (AmE), gauge (BrE), PHYS electrodynamometer, RADIO meter, WASSERTRANS instrument; **~ mit Nebenwiderstand** nt GERÄT shunted instrument; **~ mit Shunt** nt GERÄT shunted instrument; **Meßinstrumentfehler** m GERÄT instrumental error

Meß-: Meßkabel nt ELEKTROTECH test lead; **Meßkette** f BAU chain, engineer's chain, measuring chain, Vermessung band chain, METROL chain; **Meßklemme** f ELEKTROTECH test terminal; **Meßkolben** m LABOR graduated flask, volumetric flask; **Meßkopf** m GERÄT measuring head, probe, sensing head, PHYS probe; **Meßkraft** f GERÄT measuring force; **Meßkrümmer** m REGELUNG flow elbow; **Meßkunde** f BAU surveying; **Meßkurslinie** f LUFTTRANS slant course line; **Meßlatte** f BAU rod, Vermessung staff, mit Ablesemarkierungen speaking rod, FERTIG staff, METROL rod; **Meßlattenträger** m BAU staff holder; **Meßlehre** f MECHAN gage (AmE), gauge (BrE), METROL caliper (AmE), calliper (BrE); **Meßleitung** f ELEKTROTECH sensing lead, slotted line, test lead; **Meßleitungssonde** f ELEKTROTECH slotted line probe; **Meßmarke** f FERTIG pop mark; **Meßmaschine** f GERÄT zur numerisch gesteuerten Fertigung check station, METROL measuring machine; **Meßmikrofon** nt AKUSTIK standard microphone; **Meßnorm** f METROL measurement standard; **Meßobjekt** nt GERÄT object of measurement, QUAL device under test; **Meßort** m GERÄT measuring position, sensing point, sensor location; **Meßoszilloskop** nt ELEKTRIZ measuring oscilloscope; **Meßpfad** m GERÄT measuring path; **Meßpipette** f LABOR graduated pipette; **Meßplatte** f AUFNAHME test record; **Meßplatz** m KERNTECH measuring desk; **Meß-projektor** m METROL optical comparator

Meßpunkt m TELEKOM test point; **~ für Überfluglärm** m LUFTTRANS flyover noise measurement point; **Meßpunktabtaster** m KONTROLL scanner

Meß-: Meßrahmen m EISENBAHN loading gage (AmE), loading gauge (BrE); **Meßreaktor** m KERNTECH measurements reactor, source reactor; **Meßrelais** nt ELEKTROTECH instrument-type relay, measuring relay, meter-type relay, sensing relay, GERÄT detecting relay, measuring relay; **Meßreproduzierbarkeit** f METROL reproducibility of measurements; **Meßschalter** m ELEKTROTECH instrument switch, sensing switch; **Meßschieber** m MASCHINEN caliper square (AmE), calliper square (BrE), METROL caliper (AmE), calliper (BrE), vernier caliper (AmE), vernier calliper (BrE); **Meßschrank** m GERÄT test board; **Meßschraube** f METROL micrometer; **Meßschreiber** m ELEKTRIZ, LABOR pen recorder; **Meßsender** m RADIO, TELEKOM signal generator; **Meßshunt** nt ELEKTROTECH instrument shunt; **Meßsignal** nt GERÄT measurement signal; **Meßskale** f GERÄT meter dial, MASCHINEN measuring scale; **Meßskalenantrieb** m RAUMFAHRT vernier motor; **Meßsonde** f RAUMFAHRT Raumschiff measuring probe; **Meßspannenfehler** m REGELUNG span error; **Meßspannenverschiebung** f REGELUNG span shift; **Meßspion** m METROL feeler gage (AmE), feeler gauge (BrE); **Meßspitze** f GERÄT test prod; **Meßspule** f ELEK-

TROTECH search coil; **Meßstab** *m* KFZTECH *Schmierung* dipstick; **Meßstange** *f* BAU gage bar (AmE), gauge bar (BrE)

Meßstelle *f* GERÄT measuring position, sensing point; ~ **mit analoger Meßdatenerfassung** *f* GERÄT analog point; ~ **mit digitaler Meßdatenerfassung** *f* GERÄT digital point; **Meßstellenabtaster** *m* GERÄT scanner; **Meßstellentemperatur** *f* GERÄT measuring junction temperature; **Meßstellenumschalter** *m* GERÄT scanner

Meß-: **Meßstellung** *f* GERÄT *Bedienungselement* measuring position; **Meßsteuerung** *f* FERTIG in-process gaging (AmE), in-process gauging (BrE), sizing; **Meßstift** *m* KER & GLAS roller gage (AmE), roller gauge (BrE), METROL *Meßuhr* feeler pin; **Meßstrahl** *m* METROL beam; **Meßstrecke** *f* FERTIG *Windkanal* conduit, PHYS working section; **Meßstrom** *m* GERÄT measuring current; **Meßsystem** *nt* ELEKTRIZ, GERÄT measuring system; **Meßtank** *m* ERDÖL *Meßtechnik* gaging tank (AmE), gauging tank (BrE)

meßtechnisch: ~**e Ausrüstung** *f* GERÄT instrumentation

Meß-: **Meßtemperatur** *f* GERÄT measured temperature; **Meßtisch** *m* BAU *Vermessung* plane table; **Meßüberträger** *m* TELEKOM test transformer; **Meßuhr** *f* MASCHINEN dial gage (AmE), dial gauge (BrE), dial indicator, METROL dial indicating gage (AmE), dial indicating gauge (BrE); **Meßumformer** *m* COMP & DV transducer, ELEKTRIZ current transformer (AmE), mains transformer (BrE), instrument transformer, ELEKTROTECH transducer, GERÄT measuring transducer, transducer, METROL measuring transducer; **Meßumsetzer** *m* GERÄT measuring converter

Messung *f* ELEKTRONIK measurement, GEOM mensuration, LABOR measuring, METROL measurement, TELEKOM metering; ~ **durch Bewegungsgitter** *f* OPTIK measurement by diffraction grating; ~ **des Linienprofils** *f* STRAHLPHYS *von Spektrallinien* line profile measurement; ~ **der Luftqualität** *f* UMWELTSCHMUTZ air quality measurement; ~ **der Luftverschmutzung** *f* GERÄT atmospheric pollution measurement, SICHERHEIT measurement of air pollution; ~ **der Vibration** *f* SICHERHEIT *von tragbaren Geräten und Maschinen* measurement of vibration

Meß-: **Meßungenauigkeit** *f* METROL inaccuracy of measurement; **Meßunsicherheit** *f* GERÄT measurement uncertainty, uncertainty of measurement; **Meßventil** *nt* GERÄT measuring valve; **Meßverfahren** *nt* BAU method of measurement, METROL measurement process; **Meßverkörperung** *f* QUAL material measure; **Meßverstärker** *m* ELEKTRONIK measuring amplifier, GERÄT instrumentation amplifier; **Meßwagen** *m* FERTIG *Steigerungsmeßmaschine* carriage; **Meßwandler** *m* ELEKTRIZ instrument transformer, ELEKTROTECH instrument transformer, transducer, FERTIG resolver, GERÄT instrument transformer, measuring transducer, transducer, MASCHINEN transducer; **Meßwandler ohne Hilfsenergie** *m* ELEKTROTECH self-generating transducer; **Meßwehr** *nt* WASSERVERSORG *mit Einschnitt* measuring weir; **Meßwendekreisel** *m* PHYS rate gyro

Meßwerk *nt* ELEKTROTECH meter movement, GERÄT instrument movement, measuring system, measuring movement, meter movement; **Meßwerkaufhängung** *f* GERÄT movement suspension; **Meßwerkdämpfung** *f* GERÄT meter damping; **Meßwerkregler** *m* GERÄT control meter, movement controller, primary controller; **Meßwerkzeug** *nt* MASCHINEN measuring instrument

Meßwert *m* ELEKTRONIK measurement, GERÄT measurand, measured value, measurement value, measuring value, observed value, test value; ~ **vor Auftreten eines Fehlers** *m* GERÄT prefault measuring value; ~ **nach Auftreten eines Fehlers** *m* GERÄT postfault measuring value; **Meßwertabtastung** *f* GERÄT data sampling, measuring data sampling, measuring data scanning, measuring data sampling; **Meßwerterfassung** *f* GERÄT data logging; **Meßwertgeber** *m* COMP & DV sensor, transducer, LUFTTRANS *Kreisfrequenzen, Winkelgeschwindigkeit* angular velocity rate sensor; **Meßwertglättung** *f* GERÄT *von Meßkurven durch Mittelwertbildung* smoothing; **Meßwertprüfung** *f* GERÄT data checking; **Meßwertregistrierung** *f* GERÄT data logging; **Meßwertübertragungssystem** *nt* GERÄT data transmission system; **Meßwertumformer** *m* COMP & DV, ELEKTROTECH transducer; **Meßwertumformung** *f* GERÄT data conversion; **Meßwertumsetzer** *m* GERÄT data converter, measuring converter; **Meßwertverarbeitung** *f* GERÄT processing of measured data; **Meßwertverdichtung** *f* GERÄT measuring data reduction; **Meßwertverstärker** *m* GERÄT data amplifier; **Meßwertwandler** *m* PHYS transducer

Meß-: **Meßwesen** *nt* METROL metrology; **Meßwiderstand** *m* ELEKTROTECH instrument shunt, sensing resistor; **Meßzange** *f* ELEKTRIZ clip-on instrument; **Meßzeit** *f* GERÄT detection time; **Meßzelle** *f* GERÄT detector cell, measuring cell; **Meßzylinder** *m* FOTO *Entwicklungschemikalien,* LABOR measuring cylinder

Metabisulfit *nt* CHEMIE metabisulfite (AmE), metabisulphite (BrE)

metabolisch: ~**es Indican** *nt* CHEMIE indicane; ~**e Wärmeproduktion** *f* ERGON metabolic heat production

Metabolismus *m* ERGON metabolism

Metabor- *pref* CHEMIE metaboric

Metaborat *nt* CHEMIE dioxoborate, metaborate

Metadyne *f* ELEKTRONIK *Elektromaschinen* metadyne

Metakiesel- *pref* CHEMIE metasilicic

Metaldehyd *nt* CHEMIE metaldehyde

Metall *nt* KER & GLAS, METALL metal; ~ **im Nachsaugesteiger** *nt* FERTIG *Gießen* head metal; **Metallabfall** *m* ABFALL metal waste; **Metallabnahme** *f* MASCHINEN metal removal; **Metall-Aktivgas-Schweißen** *nt* (*MAG-Schweißen*) THERMOD metal active gas welding (*MAG welding*); **Metallbanddrucker** *m* COMP & DV band printer, belt printer; **Metallbandsägeblatt** *nt* MASCHINEN metal-cutting bandsaw blade; **Metallbandverschluß** *m* VERPACK metal strip closure; **Metallbarometer** *nt* BAU *Vermessung* surveying aneroid barometer; **Metallbauwerk** *nt* BAU metallic structure; **Metallbearbeitung** *f* FERTIG machining of metals; **Metallbedampfung** *f* ELEKTRONIK *im Vakuum* vacuum metalization (AmE), vacuum metallization (BrE); **Metallbelag** *m* BAU metalization (AmE), metallization (BrE); **Metallbeschichtung** *f* ANSTRICH metallic coating, FERNSEH metal coating, MASCHINEN metallic coating; **Metallbindung** *f* METALL metallic bond; **Metallbolzen** *m* BAU gate hook, FERTIG gudgeon; **Metalldampf-Laser** *m* ELEKTRONIK metal vapor laser (AmE), metal vapour laser (BrE); **Metalldetektor** *m* VERPACK metal detector; **Metalldicke** *f* KER & GLAS metal depth; **Metalldraht** *m* ELEKTROTECH metal filament; **Metalldrückbank** *f* FERTIG spinning lathe; **Metalldrücken** *nt* FERTIG metal spinning; **Metalleffektlack** *m* KUNSTSTOFF metallic paint; **Metallfaden** *m* ELEKTROTECH metal filament; **Metallfließpreßmatrize**

f MASCHINEN extrusion die for metal; **Metallfolie** *f* FERTIG spangle, VERPACK metal foil, metalized film (AmE), metallized film (BrE)

metallgekapselt *adj* MECHAN metal-clad

metallgeschützt *adj* ELEKTRIZ metal-clad

Metall: **Metallgesteinsstrecke** *f* KOHLEN metal drift; **Metallglasur** *f* ELEKTRONIK metal glaze; **Metallgleichrichter** *m* ELEKTRIZ metal rectifier; **Metallgummifeder** *f* MASCHINEN rubber-metal spring; **Metallguß** *m* FERTIG nonferrous castings; **Metallhalbleiter-Feldeffekttransistor** *m (MESFET)* ELEKTRONIK metal semiconductor field effect transistor *(MESFET)*; **Metallhalbleiter-Übergang** *m* ELEKTRONIK metal semiconductor junction; **Metallinertgasschweißen** *nt (MIG-Schweißen)* BAU, FERTIG, THERMOD metal inert gas welding *(MIG welding)*; **Metall-Lichtbogenschweißen** *nt* THERMOD metal arc welding

metallisch[1] *adj* ANSTRICH metallic

metallisch:[2] **nicht ~er Einschluß** *m* FERTIG sonim, METALL nonmetallic inclusion; **~er Gleichrichter** *m* ELEKTROTECH metallic rectifier; **~er Koppelpunkt** *m* TELEKOM metallic crosspoint; **~e Kupplung** *f* MASCHINEN metal-to-metal clutch; **~er Leiter** *m* ELEKTROTECH metallic conductor; **~e Leitung** *f* ELEKTROTECH metallic circuit; **~es Natururan** *nt* KERNTECH metallic natural uranium; **~e Sperrfolie** *f* AUFNAHME metallic stop foil; **~er Überzug** *m* MECHAN cladding, VERPACK metallic coating

Metallisieren *nt* FERTIG metal coating, MASCHINEN metalization (AmE), metalizing (AmE), metallization (BrE), metallizing (BrE)

metallisiert: **~er Bildschirm** *m* ELEKTRONIK metalized screen (AmE), metallized screen (BrE); **~er Farbstoff** *m* TEXTIL premetalized dye (AmE), premetallized dye (BrE); **~er Glimmerkondensator** *m* ELEKTROTECH metalized mica capacitor (AmE), metallized mica capacitor (BrE); **~er Kondensator** *m* ELEKTROTECH metalized capacitor (AmE), metallized capacitor (BrE); **~er Papierkondensator** *m* ELEKTRIZ metalized paper capacitor (AmE), metallized paper capacitor (BrE)

Metallisierung *f* ELEKTRONIK *Plattierung, Galvanisierung* metalization (AmE), metallization (BrE), KER & GLAS metalizing (AmE), metallizing (BrE), PHYS, RAUMFAHRT *Raumschiff* metalization (AmE), metallization (BrE), VERPACK metal coating; **Metallisierungsmaske** *f* ELEKTRONIK metalization mask (AmE), metallization mask (BrE); **Metallisierungsschicht** *f* ELEKTRONIK metalization layer (AmE), metallization layer (BrE)

Metall: **Metallisolator-Feldeffekttransistor** *m (MISFET)* ELEKTRONIK metal insulator semiconductor field effect transistor *(MISFET)*; **Metallisolator-Halbleiter** *m (MIS)* ELEKTRONIK metal insulator semiconductor *(MIS)*

metallkaschiert *adj* ELEKTRIZ metal-clad

Metall: **Metallkassette** *f* FOTO metal dark slide, VERPACK metal box; **Metallkeramikbeschichtung** *f* ANSTRICH metallic-ceramic coating; **Metallkeramikwiderstand** *m* ELEKTROTECH metal glaze resistor

metallkiesgestrahlt *adj* ANSTRICH shot-peened

Metall: **Metallkiesstrahlen** *nt* FERTIG shot-peening

metallkiesstrahlen *vt* FERTIG shot-peen

Metall: **Metallkonusröhre** *f* ELEKTRONIK metal-cone tube; **Metallkunde** *f* METALL metallography; **Metall-Luftbatterie** *f* KFZTECH metal air battery; **Metallmantel**

m ELEKTROTECH metal sheath; **Metallograph** *m* METALL metallographer

metallographisch: **~es Mikroskop** *nt* LABOR metallographic microscope

Metalloid *nt* METALL metalloid

metallorganisch *adj* CHEMIE organometallic

Metalloxid-Halbleiter *m (MOS)* COMP & DV, ELEKTRONIK metal oxide semiconductor *(MOS)*

Metalloxid-Silizium-Feldeffekttransistor *m (MOSFET)* RADIO metal oxide silicon field effect transistor *(MOSFET)*

Metalloxid-Transistor *m (MOS)* ELEKTRONIK metal oxide semiconductor *(MOS)*

Metall: **Metallpackung** *f* MASCHINEN metallic packing; **Metallpapier** *nt (MP)* VERPACK metalized paper (AmE), metallic paper, metallized paper (BrE) *(MP)*; **Metallpigmentfarbe** *f* KUNSTSTOFF metallic paint

metallplattiert: **~es Loch** *nt* ELEKTRIZ metalized hole (AmE), metallized hole (BrE)

Metall: **Metallpulver** *nt* METALL metal powder; **Metallrohr** *nt* MASCHINEN metal tube; **Metallröhre** *f* ELEKTRONIK metal tube; **Metallsägeblatt** *nt* MASCHINEN hacksaw blade, metal-cutting saw blade; **Metallsägebogen** *m* MASCHINEN hacksaw frame; **Metallschicht** *f* ELEKTRONIK metal film, metalization (AmE), metallization (BrE); **Metallschichtwiderstand** *m* ELEKTROTECH metal film resistor; **Metallschlauch** *m* MASCHINEN flexible metal tube, flexible metallic hose; **Metallschleifvorschriften** *f pl* SICHERHEIT grinding of metal regulations; **Metallschlitzsäge** *f* MASCHINEN metal slitting saw; **Metallschrott** *m* ABFALL metal waste; **Metallsortieranlage** *f* ABFALL *magnetische Abtrennung* metal separator; **Metallspritzen** *nt* FERTIG metal spraying, MASCHINEN metal powder spraying; **Metallspritzer** *m* SICHERHEIT *Schutzkleidung* molten metal splash; **Metallspritzverfahren** *nt* MASCHINEN metal spraying process; **Metallsteuerelektrode** *f* ELEKTRONIK metal gate; **Metallsucher** *m* MASCHINEN metal detector; **Metallsuchgerät** *nt* VERPACK metal detector; **Metallthermometer** *nt* THERMOD differential thermometer; **Metalltröpfchen** *nt* FERTIG *Schweißen* droplet of metal

metallüberzogen *adj* FERTIG plated

Metall: **Metallüberzug** *m* FERTIG, MASCHINEN metal coating, TELEKOM metallic coating, VERPACK metal coating

Metallüberzug: **mit ~** *adj* FERTIG metal-coated

Metall: **Metallummantelung** *f* ELEKTRIZ metallic sheath; **Metallurg** *m* METALL metallurgist

Metallurgie *f* FERTIG metallurgy

metallurgisch *adj* ANSTRICH, FERTIG, KOHLEN *Abfall* metallurgical

metallverkleidet *adj* ELEKTRIZ metal-coated

Metall: **Metallwaren** *f pl* MASCHINEN hardware; **Metallwerkzeug** *nt* FERTIG metal die; **Metallwiderstand** *m* ELEKTRIZ metallic resistor; **Metallwiedergewinnung** *f* KOHLEN metal recovery; **Metallzierarbeiten** *f pl* BAU *Geländer, Tore* art metal work

metamorph: **~es Gestein** *nt* NICHTFOSS ENERG metamorphic rocks

Metamorphit *m* NICHTFOSS ENERG metamorphic rocks

Metaphosphat *nt* CHEMIE metaphosphate

Metaphosphor- *pref* CHEMIE metaphosphoric

Metaregel *f* KÜNSTL INT metarule

Metasilicat *nt* CHEMIE metasilicate

Metasprache *f* COMP & DV metalanguage

metastabil¹ *adj* STRAHLPHYS metastable
metastabil:² ~es Atom *nt* STRAHLPHYS metastable atom; ~es Gleichgewicht *nt* PHYS metastable equilibrium; ~er Zustand *m* METALL metastable state
Metathese *f* CHEMIE metathesis
Metathesis *f* CHEMIE metathesis
Metazentrum *nt* PHYS, WASSERTRANS *Schiffbau* metacenter (AmE), metacentre (BrE)
Metazinn- *pref* CHEMIE metastannic
Meteor *m* RAUMFAHRT meteor; Meteorenecho *nt* RAUMFAHRT meteor echo; Meteoriteneinsturm *m* RAUMFAHRT meteorite influx; Meteoritenstaub *m* RAUMFAHRT meteor dust; Meteorschwarmfunkverbindung *f* RAUMFAHRT *Weltraumfunk* meteor burst link
Meter *m* METROL *Meßgerät* meter, METROL *Meßeinheit* meter (AmE), metre (BrE)
Meterküvette *f* FOTO, OPTIK meter cell
Meterspurweite *f* EISENBAHN meter gage (AmE), metre gauge (BrE)
Meterware *f* FOTO *Film* bulk film
Meterwellen-Hochfrequenz *f* ELEKTRONIK very high frequency, RADIO very high frequency
Methacryl- *pref* CHEMIE methacrylic; Methacrylat *nt* KUNSTSTOFF methacrylate; Methacrylatklebstoff *m* KUNSTSTOFF methacrylic adhesive
Methan *nt* CHEMIE, ERDÖL methane; Methan- *pref* CHEMIE methanoic
Methanal *nt* CHEMIE formaldehyde, methanal
Methanamid *nt* CHEMIE formamide, methanamide
Methangärung *f* ABFALL alkaline fermentation, methane digestion, methane digestion, methane fermentation
Methangastanker *m* WASSERTRANS methane carrier
Methanol *nt* CHEMIE methane alcohol, methanol; Methanolbrennstoffzelle *f* KFZTECH methanol cell
methanolisch *adj* CHEMIE methanolic
Methenamin *nt* CHEMIE methenamine, urotropine
Methion- *pref* CHEMIE methionic
Methode: ~ mit gebrochenem Strahl *f* OPTIK refracted ray method; ~ der gewichteten Rückstände *f* KERNTECH Gelerkin method; ~ der kleinsten Quadrate *f* ERGON, MATH, PHYS least squares method; ~ des kritischen Weges *f* (CPM) COMP & DV critical path method (CPM); Methodenstudie *f* ERGON method study
Methoxybenzaldehyd *nt* CHEMIE anisaldehyde, methoxybenzaldehyde
Methoxybenzen *nt* CHEMIE anisole, methoxybenzene
Methoxyl- *pref* CHEMIE methoxyl
Methusalem *m* KER & GLAS methuselah
Methyl *nt* CHEMIE methyl; Methylacetat *nt* CHEMIE methyl acetate; Methylacrolein *nt* CHEMIE crotonaldehyde, methylacrolein; Methylalkohol *m* CHEMIE methane alcohol, methanol, KUNSTSTOFF methyl alcohol; Methylamin *nt* CHEMIE aminomethane, methylamine; Methylaminoessigsäure *f* CHEMIE N-methylaminoacetic acid, sarcosine; Methylanilin *nt* CHEMIE methylaniline; Methylat *nt* CHEMIE methylate; Methylbenzol *nt* CHEMIE methylbenzene, toluene; Methylcyanid *nt* CHEMIE acetonitrile, ethanenitrile; Methylenblautest *m* ABFALL *Verfahren zum Feststellen der Fäulnisfähigkeit von Wasser* methylene blue test; Methylendioxybenzaldehyd *m* CHEMIE heliotropin, methylenedioxybenzaldehyde, piperonal; Methyleniodid *nt* CHEMIE diiodomethane, methylene iodide;

Methylethin *nt* CHEMIE allylene, methylacetylene, propyne; Methylethylketon *nt* (MEK) KUNSTSTOFF methyl ethyl ketone (MEK); Methylgruppe *f* CHEMIE methyl group
methylieren *vt* CHEMIE methylate
Methylierung *f* CHEMIE *organische Chemie* methylation
Methyl: Methylindol *nt* CHEMIE methylindole, skatole; Methylkautschuk *m* KUNSTSTOFF methyl rubber; Methylmorphin *nt* CHEMIE codeine, methylmorphine; Methylnaphthalen *nt* CHEMIE methylnaphthalene; Methylorange *nt* CHEMIE helianthine; Methylphenyl- *pref* CHEMIE tolyl; Methylphenylether *m* CHEMIE anisole, methoxybenzene, LEBENSMITTEL anisole; Methylphenylketon *nt* CHEMIE acetophenone; Methylpiperidin *nt* CHEMIE methylpiperidine, pipecoline; Methylpyridin *nt* CHEMIE methylpyridine, pikoline; Methylquercetin *nt* CHEMIE methylquercitin, rhamnetin; Methylradikal *nt* CHEMIE methyl radical; Methyltertiärbutylether *m* ERDÖL *Petrochemie* methyl tertiary-butyl ether
Metol *nt* CHEMIE metol
Metrik *f* COMP & DV metric
metrisch¹ *adj* COMP & DV metric, FERTIG French, METROL metric, metrical, RADIO metric
metrisch:² ~e Geometrie *f* GEOM metrical geometry; ~es Gewinde *nt* MASCHINEN metric thread; ~es ISO-Gewinde *nt* MASCHINEN ISO metric thread; ~es Karat *nt* METROL metric carat; ~e Pferdestärke *f* METROL metric horsepower; ~er Punkt *m* DRUCK metric point; ~er Schlüssel *m* KERNTECH metric key; ~es System *nt* METROL metric system; ~e Tonne *f* METROL metric ton; ~es Trapezgewinde *nt* MASCHINEN metric trapezoidal screw thread
Metteurtisch *m* DRUCK imposing table
MeV *abbr* (*Million Elektronenvolt*) TEILPHYS MeV (*million electron volts*)
MF *abbr* ELEKTRIZ (*Melamin-Formaldehydharz, Melaminharz*) MF (*melamine resin*), ELEKTRONIK (*Mittelfrequenz*) MF (*medium frequency*), ELEKTRONIK (*Mehrfachfrequenz*) MF (*multiple frequency*), KUNSTSTOFF (*Melamin-Formaldehydharz, Melaminharz*) MF (*melamine formaldehyde resin*), RADIO (*Mittelfrequenz*) MF (*medium frequency*), RADIO (*Mehrfachfrequenz*) MF (*multiple frequency*), TELEKOM (*Mittelfrequenz*) MF (*medium frequency*), TELEKOM (*Mehrfachfrequenz*) MF (*multiple frequency*)
MF-Band *nt* RADIO MF band
MFC *abbr* (*Multifrequenzcode*) TELEKOM MFC (*multifrequency code*)
MFC-Telefon *nt* TELEKOM MFC telephone
MF-Generator *m* TELEKOM MF generator
MFM *abbr* (*modifizierte Frequenzmodulation*) ELEKTRONIK, RADIO, TELEKOM MFM (*modified frequency modulation*)
MFW *abbr* (*Mehrfrequenzwahl*) RADIO DTMF (*dual-tone multifrequency*), TELEKOM MFD (*multifrequency dialling*)
Mg (*Magnesium*) CHEMIE Mg (*magnesium*)
MGD *abbr* (*Magnetogasdynamik*) KERNTECH MGD (*magnetogasdynamics*)
MHD-Konverter *m* (*magnetohydrodynamischer Konverter*) RAUMFAHRT MHD converter (*magnetohydrodynamic converter*)
MHD-Wandler *m* (*magnetohydrodynamischer Wandler*) ELEKTROTECH, KERNTECH MHD converter (*magne-*

tohydrodynamic converter)

MHz *abbr (Megahertz)* ELEKTRIZ, ELEKTROTECH, FERN-SEH, RADIO MHz *(megahertz)*

MIC *abbr (integrierter Mikrowellenschaltkreis)* ELEK-TRONIK, WELLPHYS MIC *(microwave integrated circuit)*

Michelson-Interferometer *nt* PHYS Michelson interferometer

Michelson-Morley-Experiment *nt* PHYS Michelson-Morley experiment

MICR *abbr (Magnetschrifterkennung, Magnetschriftzeichenerkennung)* COMP & DV MICR *(magnetic ink character recognition)*

Micro: ~ **Channel** *m* COMP & DV *Warenzeichen* microchannel

micronisiert *adj* KUNSTSTOFF micronized

mieten *vt* WASSERTRANS *Schiff* charter

Mietleitung *f* COMP & DV leased circuit, leased line, TELE-KOM leased line, private wire; ~ **mit Fernsprechqualität** *f* TELEKOM speech-grade private wire

Mietleitungsnetz *nt* COMP & DV leased line network

MIG-MAG-Schweißbrenner *m* BAU torch for MIG-MAG welding

Migration *f* ERDÖL *Erdölgeologie,* KUNSTSTOFF migration

migrierend: nicht ~er Weichmacher *m* KUNSTSTOFF non-migratory plasticizer

MIG-Schweißen *nt (Metallinertgasschweißen)* BAU, FERTIG, THERMOD MIG welding *(metal inert gas welding)*

Mikro *nt (Mikrofon)* AKUSTIK, AUFNAHME, ELEKTRIZ, RADIO mike *(microphone)*

Mikro- *pref* COMP & DV, METROL micro-; **Mikroampere** *nt* ELEKTRIZ microampere; **Mikro-Amperemeter** *nt* ELEK-TROTECH microammeter; **Mikrobaustein** *m* COMP & DV microassembly; **Mikrobefehl** *m* COMP & DV microinstruction; **Mikrobefehlscode** *m* COMP & DV microcode; **Mikrobiegeverlust** *m* OPTIK microbend loss; **Mikrobiegung** *f* OPTIK microbending

mikrobielle: ~ Laugung *f* CHEMIE leaching

Mikro-: Mikrobild *nt* METALL photomicrograph

mikrobiologisch: ~e Gefahr *f* SICHERHEIT microbiological hazard

Mikro-: Mikrochip *m* ELEKTRONIK microchip; **Mikrocode** *m* COMP & DV microcode; **Mikrocomputer** *m* COMP & DV microcomputer; **Mikrocontroller** *m* COMP & DV microcontroller; **Mikrodevitrifikation** *f* OPTIK microdevitrification; **Mikrodiskette** *f* COMP & DV microfloppy disk; **Mikroeinkapselung** *f* ABFALL *von Sondermüll* grain encapsulation; **Mikroelektronik** *f* COMP & DV microelectronics; **Mikroentglasung** *f* OPTIK microdevitrification; **Mikrofarad** *nt* ELEKTRIZ, ELEK-TROTECH microfarad; **Mikrofiche** *f* COMP & DV fiche, microfiche, DRUCK microfiche; **Mikrofichelesegerät** *nt* COMP & DV, DRUCK microfiche reader

Mikrofilm[1] *m* COMP & DV, DRUCK, FOTO microfilm

Mikrofilm:[2] **auf ~ aufnehmen** *vt* COMP & DV microfilm

Mikrofilm: Mikrofilmaufnahmegerät *nt* COMP & DV microfilm recorder; **Mikrofilmaufzeichnungsgerät** *nt* COMP & DV microfilm recorder; **Mikrofilmlesegerät** *nt* COMP & DV microfilm reader; **Mikrofilmleser** *m* COMP & DV microfilm reader; **Mikrofilmlochkarte** *f* COMP & DV aperture card; **Mikrofilmrecorder** *m* COMP & DV microfilm recorder; **Mikrofilmtechnik** *f* KONSTZEICH microcopying technique, microfilming technique

Mikrofon *nt (Mikro)* AKUSTIK, AUFNAHME, ELEKTRIZ,

RADIO microphone *(mike)*; ~ **mit herzförmiger Charakteristik** *nt* AKUSTIK, AUFNAHME cardioid microphone; ~ **mit Parabolreflektor** *nt* AUFNAHME parabolic reflector microphone; **Mikrofonabschirmung** *f* AUFNAHME microphone shield; **Mikrofongalgen** *m* AUFNAHME microphone boom; **Mikrofonie-Effekt in der Cochlear** *m* AKUSTIK cochlear microphonic effect

mikrofonisch *adj* AUFNAHME microphonic

Mikrofon: Mikrofonkabel *nt* AUFNAHME microphone cable; **Mikrofonkappe** *f* AUFNAHME microphone blanket; **Mikrofonmembran** *f* AUFNAHME microphone diaphragm; **Mikrofonnetzteil** *nt* AUFNAHME microphone power supply; **Mikrofonstativ** *nt* AUFNAHME microphone stand; **Mikrofonstummschaltung** *f* RADIO microphone cancellation; **Mikrofontrafo** *m* AUFNAH-ME microphone transformer

mikrofonunabhängig *adj* AUFNAHME off-mike

Mikrofon: Mikrofonverstärker *m* AUFNAHME microphone amplifier

Mikro-: Mikrofotoansatz *m* FOTO microattachment; **Mikrofotogramm** *nt* METALL photomicrogram; **Mikrofotometer** *nt* STRAHLPHYS microphotometer; **Mikrohärte** *f* KUNSTSTOFF, METALL microhardness; **Mikrohenry** *nt* ELEKTRIZ microhenry; **Mikrohöhlung** *f* OPTIK micropit; **Mikroinstruktion** *f* COMP & DV microinstruction; **Mikrokanal** *m* ELEKTRONIK microchannel; **Mikrokanal-Bildverstärker** *m* ELEKTRONIK microchannel image intensifier; **Mikrokanalplatte** *f* ELEKTRONIK microchannel plate; **Mikrokopie** *f* COMP & DV microcopy; **Mikrokopieaufzeichnungsgerät** *nt* COMP & DV microfilm recorder

mikrokristallin *adj* CHEMIE microcrystalline

Mikro-: Mikrokrümmung *f* ELEKTROTECH microbend, TELEKOM microbending; **Mikromanometer** *nt* GERÄT micromanometer

Mikrometer *nt* GERÄT, LABOR *Dickenmessung,* MASCHI-NEN, MECHAN micrometer, METROL micrometer, micromil, PAPIER, PHYS micrometer; ~ **mit elektronischer Anzeige** *nt* METROL electronic display micrometric head; ~ **mit Okular** *nt* MASCHINEN eyepiece micrometer; **Mikrometermeßuhr** *f* METROL dial indicating micrometer; **Mikrometerschraube** *f* LABOR calipers (AmE), callipers (BrE), MASCHINEN, PHYS micrometer screw; **Mikrometerschraube mit Feingewinde** *f* MASCHINEN finely threaded micrometer screw; **Mikrometer-Schraubenkopf** *m* METROL micrometric head; **Mikrometertaster** *m* MASCHINEN micrometer calipers (AmE), micrometer callipers (BrE)

Mikrometrie *f* MASCHINEN micrometry

Mikro-: Mikromillimeter *m* LABOR micromillimeter (AmE), micromillimetre (BrE)

mikrominiaturisiert: ~e Schaltung *f* COMP & DV microcircuit

Mikro-: Mikrominiaturisierung *f* ELEKTRONIK microminiaturization

Mikron: *nt* METROL micron; **Mikronfilter** *nt* MASCHINEN micronic filter

mikronisieren *vt* CHEMIE micronize

Mikron: Mikronschaltung *f* ELEKTRONIK micron circuit; **Mikronschranke** *f* ELEKTRONIK micron barrier

Mikro-: Mikroohm *nt* ELEKTROTECH microhm; **Mikroorganismus** *m* UMWELTSCHUTZ microorganism; **Mikropipette** *f* LABOR micropipette; **Mikroplanfilm** *m* COMP & DV microfiche; **Mikroprogramm** *nt* COMP & DV microprogram, microroutine; **Mikroprogrammieren**

nt COMP & DV microprogramming

Mikroprozessor *m (MP)* COMP & DV, ELEKTRIZ, MA-SCHINEN microprocessor *(MP)*; **Mikroprozessor-Chip** *m* ELEKTRONIK microprocessor chip; **Mikroprozessoreinheit** *f* COMP & DV MPU, microprocessor unit; **Mikroprozessorsteuerung** *f* COMP & DV microcontroller, TELEKOM microprocessor control

Mikro-: **Mikropulsieren** *nt* RADIO micropulsation; **Mikropumpe** *f* MASCHINEN micropump; **Mikrorakete** *f* RAUMFAHRT *Raumschiff* microrocket; **Mikrorechner** *m* COMP & DV microcomputer; **Mikrorheologie** *f* METALL microrheology; **Mikrorille** *f* AKUSTIK microgroove; **Mikrorillenaufnahme** *f* AUFNAHME microgroove recording; **Mikrorillenplatte** *f* AUFNAHME microgroove record; **Mikroriß** *m* OPTIK microcrack; **Mikroschalter** *m* ELEKTRIZ, ELEKTROTECH, FERTIG *Kunststoffinstallationen*, KONTROLL *Grenzschalter* microswitch; **Mikroschaltkreis** *m* FERTIG microcircuit

Mikroschaltung *f* COMP & DV, ELEKTRONIK microcircuit; **Mikroschaltungsaufbau** *m* COMP & DV, ELEKTRONIK microcircuitry

Mikroschlitz- *pref* TELEKOM microslot

Mikro-: **Mikroschraube** *f* KONTROLL microscrew; **Mikroschubtriebwerk** *nt* RAUMFAHRT microthruster; **Mikroschwerkraft** *f* RAUMFAHRT microgravity; **Mikroseigerung** *f* METALL microsegregation; **Mikrosekunde** *f* COMP & DV microsecond; **Mikrosieb** *nt* WASSERVERSORG microstrainer; **Mikrosiebfilter** *nt* WASSERVERSORG microstrainer

Mikroskop *nt* LABOR, METROL microscope; **Mikroskop-Adapter** *m* FOTO microscope adaptor

mikroskopisch: **~es Kriechen** *nt* METALL microcreep; **~er Staub** *m* SICHERHEIT microscopic dust; **~er Zustand** *m* STRAHLPHYS microscopic state

Mikroskop: **Mikroskop-Kondensator** *m* LABOR microscope condenser; **Mikroskop-Objektträger** *m* LABOR microscope slide; **Mikroskop-Objektträgerabdeckung** *f* LABOR microscope slide cover slip

Mikro-: **Mikrosonde** *f* STRAHLPHYS microprobe; **Mikrospritze** *f* LABOR *Gaschromatografie* microsyringe; **Mikrosteuerung** *f* KFZTECH microcontrol; **Mikrostreifen** *m* ELEKTRONIK, PHYS, RADIO microstrip; **Mikrostreifenleitung** *f* RADIO microstripline; **Mikrostrip** *m* ELEKTRONIK, PHYS, RADIO microstrip, TELEKOM microribbon; **Mikrostripantenne** *f* ELEKTRONIK microstrip aerial, microstrip antenna; **Mikrostruktur** *f* KOHLEN microstructure; **Mikrotechnik** *f* COMP & DV, ELEKTRONIK microcircuitry; **Mikrotom** *nt* LABOR *Mikroskopie* microtome; **Mikrotriebwerk** *nt* RAUMFAHRT microrocket; **Mikrotron** *nt* TEILPHYS microtron

mikroverfilmen *vt* COMP & DV, FOTO microfilm, KONSTZEICH microcopy, microfilm

Mikro-: **Mikroverformung** *f* METALL microstrain; **Mikrovolt** *nt* (μV) ELEKTRIZ, ELEKTROTECH microvolt (μV)

Mikrowelle *f* ELEKTRIZ, ELEKTRONIK, RADIO, WELLPHYS microwave; **Mikrowellenabsorption** *f* TELEKOM microwave absorption

mikrowellenabstimmbar: **~es Filter** *nt* ELEKTRONIK microwave tunable filter

Mikrowelle: **Mikrowellenantenne** *f* TELEKOM microwave aerial, microwave antenna; **Mikrowellen-Bandpaßfilter** *nt* ELEKTRONIK microwave band-pass filter; **Mikrowellenbegrenzer** *m* ELEKTRONIK microwave limiter; **Mikrowellendämpfung** *f* ELEKTRONIK microwave attenuation; **Mikrowellen-Dämpfungsglied**

nt ELEKTRONIK, TELEKOM microwave attenuator; **Mikrowellendiode** *f* ELEKTRONIK microwave diode; **Mikrowellen-Elektronenröhre** *f* ELEKTRONIK microwave tube

mikrowellenfest: **~e Verpackung** *f* VERPACK microwaveable packaging

Mikrowelle: **Mikrowellenfilter** *nt* ELEKTRONIK microwave filter; **Mikrowellenfrequenz** *f* ELEKTRONIK, WELLPHYS microwave frequency; **Mikrowellengenerator** *m* ELEKTRONIK microwave generator; **Mikrowellenherd** *m* ELEKTROTECH, LEBENSMITTEL microwave oven; **Mikrowellenhintergrundstrahlung** *f* WELLPHYS microwave background radiation; **Mikrowellenhohlraum** *m* ELEKTRONIK microwave cavity; **Mikrowellenleistung** *f* ELEKTROTECH microwave power; **Mikrowellenleistungstransistor** *m* ELEKTRONIK microwave power transistor; **Mikrowellenleistungsverstärker** *m* ELEKTRONIK microwave power amplifier; **Mikrowellenleistungsverstärkung** *f* ELEKTRONIK microwave power amplification; **Mikrowellenmischer** *m* ELEKTRONIK microwave mixer; **Mikrowellenmodul** *nt* ELEKTRONIK microwave module; **Mikrowellenmodulator** *m* TELEKOM microwave modulator; **Mikrowellenofen** *m* ELEKTROTECH, LEBENSMITTEL microwave oven; **Mikrowellenoszillator** *m* ELEKTRONIK microwave oscillator; **Mikrowellenoszillatorröhre** *f* ELEKTRONIK microwave oscillator tube; **Mikrowellen-Phasenschieber** *m* TELEKOM microwave phase changer; **Mikrowellenresonator** *m* ELEKTRONIK, TELEKOM microwave resonator; **Mikrowellenröhre** *f* MASCHINEN microwave tube; **Mikrowellenröhre vom Typ M** *f* ELEKTRONIK M-type microwave tube; **Mikrowellenschaltkreis** *m* ELEKTRONIK microwave circuit; **Mikrowellensignal** *nt* ELEKTRONIK microwave signal; **Mikrowellensignalgenerator** *m* ELEKTRONIK microwave signal generator; **Mikrowellensignalquelle** *f* ELEKTRONIK microwave signal source; **Mikrowellenspektroskopie** *f* WELLPHYS microwave spectroscopy; **Mikrowellenspektrum** *nt* WELLPHYS microwave spectrum; **Mikrowellen-Sperrfilter** *nt* ELEKTRONIK microwave band-stop filter; **Mikrowellenstrahl** *m* TELEKOM microwave beam; **Mikrowellensubstrat** *nt* ELEKTRONIK microwave substrate; **Mikrowellentechnik** *f* RAUMFAHRT microwave technology; **Mikrowellen-Tiefpaßfilter** *nt* ELEKTRONIK microwave low-pass filter; **Mikrowellen-Trägermaterial** *nt* ELEKTRONIK microwave substrate; **Mikrowellentransistor** *m* ELEKTRONIK microwave transistor; **Mikrowellentransistorverstärker** *m* ELEKTRONIK microwave transistor amplifier; **Mikrowellenübertragung** *f* ELEKTROTECH microwave transmission; **Mikrowellenverbindung** *f* FERNSEH, WELLPHYS microwave link; **Mikrowellenverstärker** *m* TELEKOM, WELLPHYS microwave amplifier; **Mikrowellenverstärkung durch stimulierte Strahlungsabgabe** *f* (*Maser*) ELEKTRONIK, PHYS, RAUMFAHRT *Weltraumfunk*, TELEKOM microwave amplification by stimulated emission of radiation *(maser)*; **Mikrowellenverzögerungsleitung** *f* ELEKTRONIK microwave delay line; **Mikrowellenzirkulator** *m* TELEKOM microwave circulator

Mikro-: **Mikrozwilling** *m* METALL microtwin; **Mikrozwischenstück** *nt* FOTO *Kamera* microscope adaptor

Milch- *pref* CHEMIE, LEBENSMITTEL lactic; **Milch-Butyrometer** *nt* LEBENSMITTEL lactobutyrometer; **Milcheiweiß** *nt* LEBENSMITTEL milk protein; **Milchfett**

nt LEBENSMITTEL milk fat; **Milchglas** *nt* KER & GLAS milk glass, translucent glass

milchig: ~e Trübung *f* KER & GLAS milkiness

Milch-: Milchimitat *nt* LEBENSMITTEL nondairy product; **Milchpulver** *nt* LEBENSMITTEL milk powder

milchsauer: ~es Salz *nt* CHEMIE lactate

Milch-: Milchsäure *f* LEBENSMITTEL lactic acid; **Milchsäurenitril** *nt* CHEMIE hydropropanenitrile, lactonitrile; **Milchschleuder** *f* LEBENSMITTEL cream separator; **Milchtanker** *m* KFZTECH milk tanker; **Milchzucker** *m* CHEMIE lactose

Millefiori *nt* KER & GLAS glass mosaic

Miller: ~sche Indizes *nt pl* METALL Miller indices; **Millersche-Brücke** *f* ELEKTRIZ Miller bridge

Milli- *pref (m)* METROL milli- *(m)*; **Milliampere** *nt* ELEKTRIZ, ELEKTROTECH milliampere; **Milli-Amperemeter** *nt* ELEKTROTECH milliammeter

Milliarde *f* MATH billion (AmE), milliard (BrE *dated*), a thousand million (BrE)

Milli-: Milligramm *nt* METROL milligram

Millikan-Leiter *m* ELEKTRIZ Millikan conductor; **Millikan-Versuch** *m* PHYS Millikan's experiment

Millimeter *m* METROL millimeter (AmE), millimetre (BrE); **Millimeterpapier** *nt* BAU plotting paper, MATH graph paper; **Millimeter-Wanderwellenröhre** *f* ELEKTRONIK millimeter-wave traveling-wave tube (AmE), millimetre-wave travelling-wave tube (BrE); **Millimeterwelle** *f* ELEKTRONIK millimetric wave, PHYS millimeter wave (AmE), millimetre wave (BrE)

Millimeterwellen *f pl (EHF)* RADIO extremely high frequency *(EHF)*; **Millimeterwellen-Elektronenröhre** *f* ELEKTRONIK millimeter-wave tube (AmE), millimetre-wave tube (BrE); **Millimeterwellen-Magnetron** *nt* ELEKTRONIK millimeter-wave magnetron (AmE), millimetre-wave magnetron (BrE); **Millimeterwellen-Quelle** *f* ELEKTRONIK millimeter-wave source (AmE), millimetre-wave source (BrE); **Millimeterwellenröhre** *f* ELEKTRONIK millimeter-wave tube (AmE), millimetre-wave tube (BrE); **Millimeterwellen-Ursprung** *m* ELEKTRONIK millimeter-wave source (AmE), millimetre-wave source (BrE); **Millimeterwellenverstärker** *m* ELEKTRONIK millimeter-wave amplifier (AmE), millimetre-wave amplifier (BrE); **Millimeterwellenverstärkung** *f* ELEKTRONIK millimeter-wave amplification (AmE), millimetre-wave amplification (BrE)

Million *f* MATH million; **~ Elektronenvolt** *nt (MeV)* TEILPHYS million electron volts *(MeV)*

Millionen: ~ Befehle pro Sekunde *f pl (MIPS)* COMP & DV millions of instructions per second *(MIPS)*; **~ logischer Inferenzen pro Sekunde** *f pl (MLIPS)* KÜNSTL INT millions of logical inferences per second *(MLIPS)*

Millionstel *nt* MATH millionth

Milli-: Millisekunde *f* COMP & DV millisecond

Millivolt *nt* ELEKTRIZ, ELEKTROTECH millivolt; **Millivoltbandschreiber** *m* GERÄT millivolt stripchart recorder; **Millivoltmeter** *nt* ELEKTRIZ millivoltmeter

Milliwatt *nt* ELEKTRIZ milliwatt; **Milliwattmeter** *nt* ELEKTRIZ milliwattmeter

MIMD-Rechner *m (Mehrfachbefehlsstrom-Mehrfachdatenstrom-Rechner)* COMP & DV MIMD machine *(multiple-instruction multiple-data machine)*

Mindergewicht *nt* VERPACK short weight

Minderung *f* MEERSCHMUTZ mitigation

minderwertig: ~es Benzin *nt* KFZTECH low-test gasoline

(AmE), low-test petrol (BrE)

Mindest- *pref* LUFTTRANS, MASCHINEN, QUAL, STRAHLPHYS, TELEKOM, TRANS minimum; **Mindestabhebegeschwindigkeit** *f* LUFTTRANS minimum unstick speed; **Mindestabstandskontrolle** *f* TRANS control of minimum headway; **Mindestannahmewahrscheinlichkeit** *f* QUAL minimum probability of acceptance; **Mindestbestrahlungsdauer einer Probe** *f* STRAHLPHYS minimum specimen irradiation; **Mindestbetrag** *m* TELEKOM minimum amount; **Mindestdrehzahl** *f* MASCHINEN minimum speed; **Mindestfreibord** *nt* WASSERTRANS minimum required freeboard; **Mindestgebühr** *f* TELEKOM initial period charge; **Mindestgeschwindigkeit** *f* MASCHINEN minimum speed; **Mindestgewicht** *nt* VERPACK m i n i m u m weight; **Mindesthaltbarkeitsdatum** *nt* LEBENSMITTEL best before date; **Mindestleistungsanforderungen** *f pl* QUAL minimum grade requirements; **Mindestschweißstrom** *m* BAU minimum welding current; **Mindestsinkhöhe** *f* LUFTTRANS minimum descent altitude, minimum descent height; **Mindestwert** *m* QUAL lower limiting value; **Mindestwetterbedingungen** *f pl* LUFTTRANS minimum weather conditions

Mine *f* KOHLEN, WASSERTRANS mine; **Minenlegen** *nt* WASSERTRANS *Marine* minelaying; **Minenleger** *m* WASSERTRANS *Marine* minelayer, minelaying ship; **Minenräumen** *nt* WASSERTRANS *Marine* minesweeping; **Minenräumer** *m* WASSERTRANS *Marine* minesweeper; **Minensuchboot** *nt* WASSERTRANS *Marine* minesweeper; **Minensuchen** *nt* WASSERTRANS *Marine* minesweeping

Mineral *nt* KOHLEN mineral; **Mineralboden** *m* KOHLEN mineral soil; **Mineralisator** *m* CHEMIE mineralizer

mineralisch[1] *adj* KOHLEN mineral

mineralisch:[2] **~e Substanzen entfernen** *vt* CHEMTECH demineralize

mineralisoliert: ~es Kabel *nt* ELEKTRIZ, ELEKTROTECH mineral-insulated cable

Mineral: Mineralisolierung *f* ELEKTRIZ mineral insulation; **Mineralmörser** *m* LABOR *Schleifen* percussion mortar; **Mineralogie** *f* ERDÖL, KOHLEN mineralogy; **Mineralöl** *nt* KFZTECH, KUNSTSTOFF, MASCHINEN mineral oil; **Mineralölwirtschaft** *f* ERDÖL oil industry, petroleum industry; **Mineralquelle** *f* WASSERVERSORG mineral spring

mineralstofffrei *adj* UMWELTSCHMUTZ mineral-matter-free

Minette *f* ERDÖL *Geologie* minette

Mini- *pref* AUFNAHME, COMP & DV, ELEKTROTECH, OPTIK mini-; **Minimum** *nt* MATH minimum

Miniatur *f* COMP & DV, ELEKTRONIK, ELEKTROTECH, KER & GLAS, MASCHINEN miniature; **Miniaturelektronik** *f* ELEKTRONIK microelectronics; **Miniaturflasche** *f* KER & GLAS miniature bottle; **Miniaturisierung** *f* COMP & DV miniaturization; **Miniaturkugellager** *nt* MASCHINEN miniature ball bearing; **Miniaturleistungsschalter** *m* ELEKTROTECH miniature circuit breaker; **Miniaturrelais** *nt* ELEKTROTECH miniature relay; **Miniaturstromschütz** *nt* ELEKTRIZ miniature circuit breaker; **Miniatur-Wanderwellenröhre** *f* ELEKTRONIK miniature traveling-wave tube (AmE), miniature travelling-wave tube (BrE)

Mini-: Minibündelkabel *nt* OPTIK minibundle cable; **Minicomputer** *m* COMP & DV minicomputer; **Minikassette** *f* AUFNAHME minicassette; **Minileistungsschalter** *m* ELEKTROTECH miniature circuit breaker

Minimal- *pref* COMP & DV, ELEKTRIZ, ELEKTROTECH, LUFTTRANS, MATH, RADIO, TELEKOM minimal

minimal: **~e Abweichung** *f* PHYS minimum deviation; **~e Bewicklungsbreite** *f* TEXTIL minimum dressed width of warp; **~e fehlerfreie Paketierung/Depaketierung** *f* TELEKOM MEFP, minimum error-free PAD

Minimal-: **Minimalflächen** *f pl* GEOM minimal surfaces; **Minimalgebühr** *f* TELEKOM minimum charge; **Minimalgleitweg** *m* LUFTTRANS minimum glide path; **Minimalleistungsrelais** *nt* ELEKTRIZ minimum power relay; **Minimalphasenumtastung** *f (MSK)* COMP & DV, RADIO, TELEKOM minimum-shift keying *(MSK)*; **Minimalschalter** *m* ELEKTROTECH minimum circuit breaker; **Minimalspannung** *f* ELEKTRIZ minimum voltage

Mini-: **Minimax-Thermometer** *nt* STRAHLPHYS minimum and maximum thermometer

Minimum-Maximum-Thermometer *nt* STRAHLPHYS minimum and maximum thermometer; **Minimumstromrelais** *nt* ELEKTRIZ minimum current relay

Mini-: **Minirail** *f* EISENBAHN minirail; **Minirechner** *m* COMP & DV minicomputer; **Minirillenaufnahme** *f* AUFNAHME minigroove recording; **Minischubboot** *nt* WASSERTRANS minipusher tug

Minkowski-Raum *m* PHYS Minkowski space

Minorität *f* ELEKTRONIK, PHYS minority; **Minoritätsladungsträger** *m* PHYS minority carrier; **Minoritätsträger** *m* ELEKTRONIK minority carrier; **Minoritätsträgerkanal** *m* ELEKTRONIK *Transistortechnik* bulk channel

Minus *nt* MATH minus

minus *adj* MATH minus

Minus: **Minusanschlußklemme** *f* KFZTECH minus terminal; **Minusleiter** *m* ELEKTROTECH negative conductor; **Minusplatte** *f* KFZTECH negative plate; **Minuspol** *m* ELEKTRIZ negative pole, negative terminal, ELEKTROTECH cathode, negative pole, negative terminal, KFZTECH minus terminal, negative terminal; **Minuszeichen** *nt* MATH minus sign

Minute *f* METROL, PHYS *Einheit des ebenen Winkels* minute; **~ mit verminderter Dienstgüte** *f* TELEKOM degraded minute; **Minutenzeiger** *m* METROL minute hand

MIPS *abbr (Millionen Befehle pro Sekunde)* COMP & DV MIPS *(millions of instructions per second)*

Mirban- *pref* CHEMIE mirbane

MIS *abbr* COMP & DV *(Management-Informationssystem)* MIS *(management information system)*, ELEKTRONIK *(Metallisolator-Halbleiter)* MIS *(metal insulator semiconductor)*

Misch- *pref* CHEMIE, ERDÖL, FERTIG, PAPIER mixing; **Misch-und Ausgabe-Vorratsautomat** *m* VERPACK mix and dispense storage system **Mischanlage** *f* PAPIER proportioner; **Mischapparat** *m* CHEMTECH mixer

mischbar[1] *adj* CHEMIE, ERDÖL miscible, FERTIG *synthetische Harze* alloyable; **nicht ~** *adj* CHEMIE, ERDÖL, FERTIG immiscible

mischbar[2]: **nicht ~e Flüssigkeiten** *f pl* STRÖMPHYS immiscible fluids; **~e Substanz** *f* UMWELTSCHMUTZ miscible substance

Misch-: **Mischbarkeit** *f* FERTIG *synthetische Harze* alloyability; **Mischbehälter** *m* CHEMTECH mixing tank, mixing vessel; **Mischbohrschlamm** *m* ERDÖL *Bohrtechnik* mixing mud; **Mischbütte** *f* PAPIER blending chest, mixing chest; **Mischchargenlager** *nt* KER & GLAS

mixed batch store; **Mischdauer** *f* BAU mixing time; **Mischdeponie** *f* ABFALL co-disposal landfill; **Mischdiode** *f* ELEKTRONIK mixer diode; **Mischdüse** *f* MASCHINEN inspirator, METALL *Schweißarbeiten* mixer

Mischen *nt* BAU mixing, COMP & DV merge, merging, LEBENSMITTEL blending

mischen *vt* ANSTRICH, AUFNAHME mix, BAU prepare, *Beton* mix, COMP & DV merge, FERNSEH dub up, mix, KUNSTSTOFF, MASCHINEN blend, METALL *synthetische Harze* alloy, PAPIER blend, mix, TEXTIL *Fasern* blend; **~ in Stereo** *vt* AUFNAHME mix down

mischend: **nicht ~e Kaskade** *f* KERNTECH no-mixing cascade; **~es Sortieren** *nt* COMP & DV merge sort

Misch-: **Mischentwässerung** *f* WASSERVERSORG combined sewer system

Mischer *m* AUFNAHME, DRUCK, ELEKTRONIK *Mikrowellen* mixer, FERNSEH adder, mixer, KER & GLAS blender, *Bediener der Mischanlage* mixer, KUNSTSTOFF blender, mixer, MASCHINEN mixer, PAPIER blender, RADIO mixer; **Mischer-Vorverstärker** *m* ELEKTRONIK mixer preamplifier

Misch-: **Mischgarn** *nt* TEXTIL *Garn* blend; **Mischgerät** *nt* LUFTTRANS *Hubschrauber* mixing unit; **Mischgestänge** *nt* LUFTTRANS *Hubschrauber* mixer rod; **Mischgewebe** *nt* TEXTIL union cloth; **Mischgewebefärben** *nt* TEXTIL union dyeing; **Mischgitter** *nt* LUFTTRANS injection grid; **Mischglied** *nt* GERÄT comparing element; **Mischheptode** *f* ELEKTROTECH *Mischröhre mit fünf Gittern* pentagrid converter; **Mischkammer** *f* KFZTECH *Vergaser* mixing chamber; **Mischkanalisation** *f* ABFALL combined sewerage system, WASSERVERSORG combined sewer system; **Mischkarbid** *nt* METALL composite carbide; **Mischkasten** *m* KER & GLAS, PAPIER mixing box; **Mischkniehebel** *m* LUFTTRANS *Hubschrauber* mixer bellcrank; **Mischkonzentrat-Flotation** *f* KOHLEN bulk flotation; **Mischlicht** *nt* FOTO mixed light; **Mischlogikboard** *nt* ELEKTRONIK mixed-logic board; **Mischlogikkarte** *f* ELEKTRONIK mixed-logic board; **Mischmaschine** *f* BAU, MASCHINEN mixer; **Mischmühle** *f* CHEMTECH mixing mill; **Mischpolymerisat** *nt* CHEMIE, ERDÖL, KUNSTSTOFF, TEXTIL copolymer; **Mischpolymerisation** *f* KUNSTSTOFF copolymerization; **Mischprobe** *f* KOHLEN composite sample; **Mischpult** *nt* AUFNAHME mixing desk, *im Studio* mixer, FERNSEH mixing desk; **Mischraum** *m* AUFNAHME mixing booth, mixing room, KER & GLAS port neck; **Mischrohr** *nt* MASCHINEN combining cone, combining nozzle, combining tube; **Mischröhre** *f* ELEKTRONIK mixer tube; **Mischrührwerk** *nt* CHEMTECH agitating mixer; **Mischsatz** *m* DRUCK mixed styles; **Mischschwebesystem** *nt* TRANS mixed levitation; **Mischsortieren** *nt* COMP & DV merge sort; **Mischsteilheit** *f* ELEKTROTECH conversion conductance; **Mischströmung** *f* RAUMFAHRT mixed flow; **Mischstufe** *f* ELEKTRONIK mixing stage, ELEKTROTECH converter, FERNSEH, RADIO, RAUMFAHRT *Weltraumfunk* mixer; **Mischtafel** *f* AUFNAHME mixing sheet; **Mischtechnik** *f* CHEMTECH mixing technique; **Mischtechnologie** *f* ELEKTRONIK mixed technology; **Mischtransistor** *m* ELEKTRONIK mixing transistor; **Mischtrommel** *f* FERTIG, HYDRAUL pug mill, MECHAN batch

Mischung *f* AKUSTIK mixing, ANSTRICH mix, KUNSTSTOFF blend, mix, *Kautschuk* compound, LEBENSMITTEL mix, MASCHINEN mixture, PAPIER blend, mixing, TELEKOM grading, TEXTIL blend; ~ aus Lehm und Sand *f* KER & GLAS hogging; **Mischungsauflösung** *f* FERNSEH mix dissolve; **Mischungsentwurf** *m* BAU mix design; **Mischungslücke** *f* METALL miscibility gap; **Mischungsverhältnis** *nt* BAU mix proportions, KFZTECH mixture ratio, TEXTIL blend ratio; **Mischungswärme** *f* THERMOD heat of mixing

Misch-: **Mischventil** *nt* MASCHINEN mixing valve, WASSERVERSORG combined sewer system; **Mischverstärker** *m* FERNSEH mixer amplifier; **Mischverstärkung** *f* ELEKTRONIK *Elektronenröhren* conversion gain; **Mischvorgang** *m* AKUSTIK mixing; **Mischware** *f* KER & GLAS mixed ware; **Mischwerk** *nt* CHEMTECH agitator; **Mischzeit** *f* BAU mixing time

MISD-Rechner *m* (*Mehrfachbefehlsstrom-Einfachdatenstrom-Rechner*) COMP & DV MISD machine (*multiple-instruction single-data machine*)

MISFET *abbr* (*Metallisolator-Feldeffekttransistor*) ELEKTRONIK MISFET (*metal insulator semiconductor field effect transistor*)

Mißbrauch *m* PATENT abuse

Mißfärbung *f* KER & GLAS discoloration (AmE), discolouration (BrE)

Mission: ~ **in Erdumlaufbahn** *f* RAUMFAHRT earth-orbiting mission; ~ **in den tiefen Weltraum** *f* RAUMFAHRT deep-space mission

Mißklang *m* AKUSTIK discordance, dissonance

mißlingen *vi* BAU fail

mißweisend: **~er Kurs** *m* LUFTTRANS magnetic heading, WASSERTRANS magnetic course; **~e Peilung** *f* LUFTTRANS magnetic bearing

Mißweisung *f* METROL angle error, WASSERTRANS magnetic declination, magnetic variation; **Mißweisungsgeber** *m* LUFTTRANS deviation detector; **Mißweisungswinkel** *m* PHYS angle of magnetic declination

Mitbenutzer *m* TELEKOM joint user

Mitfällung *f* KERNTECH coprecipitation

mitgehend: **~e Lünette** *f* FERTIG follow rest; **~er Setzstock** *m* MASCHINEN follow rest

mitgeltend: **~e Unterlagen** *f pl* QUAL referenced documents

Mithören *nt* RADIO monitoring, TELEKOM listening in, *Telefon* monitoring

mithören *vt* TELEKOM monitor

Mithörschwelle *f* AKUSTIK masked threshold

Mithörtelefon *nt* TELEKOM observation telephone

Mitkoppeln *nt* WASSERTRANS *Radar* plotting

Mitkopplung *f* AUFNAHME positive feedback, ELEKTRONIK *Radio* regenerative feedback

mitlaufen *vi* MASCHINEN follow

mitlaufend[1] *adj* FERTIG *Setzstock* moving, *Spitze* live, MASCHINEN live, revolving, traveling (AmE), travelling (BrE)

mitlaufend:[2] **~er Fehler** *m* COMP & DV propagated error; **~er Setzstock** *m* MASCHINEN traveling stay (AmE), traveling steadyrest (AmE), travelling stay (BrE), travelling steadyrest (BrE); **~e Spitze** *f* MASCHINEN live center (AmE), live centre (BrE), revolving center (AmE), revolving centre (BrE)

Mitläufer *m* TEXTIL wrapper

Mitlaufgenerator *m* ELEKTRONIK tracking generator

Mitlaut *m* AKUSTIK consonant

Mitnahme *f* RADIO, TELEKOM pulling-in; **Mitnahmeeffekt** *m* TELEKOM capture effect; **Mitnahmegenerator** *m* ELEKTRONIK locked oscillator

Mitnehmer *m* BAU *eines Türriegels* nosing, ELEKTRONIK *Oszillator* lock, FERTIG catch, striker, MASCHINEN carrier, catch, dog, tappet, TRANS carrier; **Mitnehmerbolzen** *m* FERTIG drive, driver; **Mitnehmerkeil** *m* FERTIG driving key; **Mitnehmernut** *f* FERTIG drive slot; **Mitnehmerscheibe** *f* FERTIG driver plate, KFZTECH driven plate, MASCHINEN catch plate, driver chuck, driver plate, driving plate; **Mitnehmerscheibeneinheit** *f* KFZTECH driven plate assembly; **Mitnehmerspindel** *f* MASCHINEN live spindle; **Mitnehmerstange** *f* ERDÖL *Bohrtechnik* kelly; **Mitnehmerstangenlager** *nt* ERDÖL *Bohrtechnik* kelly bushing; **Mitnehmerstift** *m* MASCHINEN follower pin

Mitreeder *m* WASSERTRANS *Schiff* part owner

Mitreißen *nt* STRÖMPHYS entrainment

Mitschwingen *nt* ELEKTRONIK resonance

mitschwingen *vt* FERTIG covibrate

mitsprechen *vt* COMP & DV monitor

Mittabstand *m* (*MA*) FERTIG, KFZTECH, MASCHINEN center distance (AmE), centre distance (BrE) (*CD*)

Mittagsbesteck *nt* WASSERTRANS *astronomische Navigation* noon sight

Mitte:[1] **von ~ zu Mitte** *adv* MASCHINEN from center to center (AmE), from centre to centre (BrE)

Mitte[2] *f* MASCHINEN center (AmE), centre (BrE); **~ des Schiffes** *f* WASSERTRANS midship; **~ Schrifthöhe** *f* KONSTZEICH midheight of the character

Mitteilung *f* PATENT *der Prüfungsabteilung* communication, RADIO, TELEKOM *Datentransfer* message; **Mitteilungsspeicherung** *f* (*MS*) TELEKOM message storing (*MS*); **Mitteilungstransfersystem** *nt* TELEKOM message transfer system; **Mitteilungs-Übermittlungsdienst** *m* TELEKOM MHS, message handling system

mittel: **mittlere Abweichung** *f* ELEKTRIZ mean deviation, ELEKTRONIK, METALL standard deviation, QUAL mean deviation; **mittlerer Abweichungsbetrag** *m* QUAL mean deviation; **mittlere aerodynamische Flügeltiefe** *f* LUFTTRANS *Tragflügel* mean aerodynamic chord; **mittlere aerodynamische Sehne** *f* LUFTTRANS *Tragflügel* mean aerodynamic chord; **mittlere alkalische radioaktive Abfälle** *m pl* KERNTECH alkaline medium-level radioactive waste; **mittlere Anomalität** *f* RAUMFAHRT mean anomaly; **mittlerer Anstellwinkel** *m* LUFTTRANS mean pitch angle; **mittlere Aufenthaltszeit** *f* QUAL mean abode time; **mittlerer Ausfallabstand** *m* COMP & DV, ELEKTROTECH, TELEKOM MTBF, mean time between failures; **mittlere Belastung** *f* ELEKTRIZ average load; **mittlere Belegungsdauer** *f* TELEKOM mean holding time; **mittlere Bindungsenergie** *f* KERNTECH mean bond energy; **mittlere Bremsleistung** *f* LUFTTRANS brake mean effective pressure; **mittlerer Druck** *m* MASCHINEN mean pressure; **mittlere Durchgangsrate** *f* TELEKOM average crossing rate; **mittlerer Durchmesser für Bezugsoberfläche** *m* OPTIK average reference surface diameter; **mittlerer Fehler** *m* ELEKTRIZ mean error, GERÄT average error; **mittlerer Fehleranteil der Fertigung** *m* QUAL process-average defective; **mittlere fehlerfreie Betriebszeit** *f* COMP & DV MTBF, mean time between failures; **mittlere Flügeltiefe der Steuerfläche** *f* LUFTTRANS mean chord of the control surface; **mittlere freie Diffusionsweglänge** *f* KERNTECH diffusion mean free path; **mittleres Fehlerquadrat** *nt* ELEKTRIZ mean square value; **mittlere freie Weglänge** *f* AKUSTIK, METALL, PHYS, THERMOD mean free path; **mittlere Gebühr** *f* TELEKOM medium rate; **mittlerer Gesamtfehler** *m* COMP & DV mean square error; **mittlerer Gleitwegfehler** *m* LUFTTRANS mean glide path error; **mittlere Hauptverkehrsstunde** *f* TELEKOM mean busy hour; **mittleres Infrarot** *nt* STRAHLPHYS middle infrared; **mittlere Instandsetzungszeit** *f (MTTR)* MECHAN mean time to repair *(MTTR)*; **mittlerer Integrationsgrad** *m (MSI)* COMP & DV, ELEKTRONIK, TELEKOM medium-scale integration *(MSI)*; **mittlere Integrationsdichte** *f (MSI)* COMP & DV medium-scale integration *(MSI)*; **mittlere Integrationstechnik** *f (MSI)* COMP & DV, ELEKTRONIK medium-scale integration *(MSI)*; **mittlere jährliche Änderung** *f* WASSERTRANS *Gezeiten* mean annual variation; **mittlerer Kernabbrand** *m* KERNTECH core average burn-up; **mittlerer Kerndurchmesser** *m* OPTIK, TELEKOM average core diameter; **mittlere Lasche der Höhenflosse** *f* LUFTTRANS horizontal stabilizer center fishplate (AmE), horizontal stabilizer centre fishplate (BrE); **mittlere Lebensdauer** *f* COMP & DV MTTF, mean time to failure, median life, ELEKTROTECH MTBF, mean time between failures, KERNTECH mean life, PHYS average life, mean life; **mittlere Leistung** *f* TELEKOM average power; **mittlere letale Dosis** *f* STRAHLPHYS MLD, mean lethal dose, STRAHLPHYS median lethal dose; **mittlere Letalkonzentration** *f* UMWELTSCHMUTZ median lethal concentration; **mittlere Letalzeit** *f* UMWELTSCHMUTZ median lethal time; **mittlerer Manteldurchmesser** *m* OPTIK *Lichtleitfaser,* TELEKOM average cladding diameter; **mittlere Monatsdosis** *f* UMWELTSCHMUTZ average monthly dose; **mittlerer Nutzdruck** *m (MEP)* LUFTTRANS *Triebwerk,* MASCHINEN mean effective pressure *(mep)*; **mittlere Ortszeit** *f* TRANS local mean time; **mittlerer Prüfumfang** *m* QUAL average amount of inspection; **mittlerer quadratischer Fehler** *m* COMP & DV mean square error; **mittlere Qualitätslage** *f* QUAL process average; **mittlere Rauhtiefe** *f* MASCHINEN average depth; **mittlere Reparaturdauer** *f (MTTR)* COMP & DV, QUAL, RAUMFAHRT mean time to repair *(MTTR)*; **mittlere Schallausstrahlung** *f* AKUSTIK *Sprache* average speech power; **mittlere Schallintensität** *f* AKUSTIK sound power; **mittlere Seehöhe** *f* WASSERTRANS mean sea level; **mittlere Sonnenzeit** *f* RAUMFAHRT mean solar time; **mittlere Spannweite** *f* QUAL mean range; **mittlere Sprachleistung** *f* AKUSTIK average speech power; **mittlerer Steigungswinkel** *m* LUFTTRANS mean pitch angle; **mittlere Steinkohle** *f* KOHLEN cob coal; **mittlere Tageswassermenge** *f* WASSERVERSORG mean daily flow; **mittlerer Temperaturunterschied** *m* HEIZ & KÄLTE mean temperature difference; **mittlerer Tidehub** *m* NICHTFOSS ENERG mean tidal range; **mittlerer Tiefgang** *m* WASSERTRANS *Schiffkonstruktion* mean draft (AmE), mean draught (BrE); **mittlere veranschlagte Zeit zwischen zwei Ausfällen** *f* QUAL assessed mean time between failures; **mittlere Verfügbarkeit** *f* REGELUNG average availability; **mittlere Wartezeit** *f* TRANS average delay; **mittlere Wassersäule** *f* NICHTFOSS ENERG medium head; **mittlere Windgeschwindigkeit** *f* NICHTFOSS ENERG mean wind speed; **mittlere Zeit zwischen Ausfällen** *f* MECHAN MTBF, mean time between failures; **mittlere Zeit bis zum ersten Ausfall** *f* QUAL mean time to first failure; **mittlere Zeit bis zur Reparatur** *f (MTTR)* ELEKTROTECH mean time to repair *(MTTR)*; **mittlere Zeit zwischen Wartungsarbeiten** *f* QUAL mean time between maintenance; **mittlere Zeit zur Wiederherstellung des betriebsfähigen Zustands** *f* QUAL mean time to restore; **mittlere**

Zeitdauer zwischen Ausfällen *f* RAUMFAHRT MTBF, mean time between failures; **mittlere Zeitdauer zwischen Entnahmen** *f* RAUMFAHRT *Ausbau* MTBR, mean time between removals

Mittel *nt* COMP & DV medium, KOHLEN agent, MATH mean, MEERSCHMUTZ *zur Modifizierung der Oberflächenspannung* surface tension modifier, QUAL mean; **Mittel-** *pref* BAU center (AmE), centre (BrE), COMP & DV medium, EISENBAHN, ELEKTRIZ, FERTIG, FOTO, KOHLEN, LEBENSMITTEL, MASCHINEN, METALL center (AmE), centre (BrE)

mittel *adj* COMP & DV mean

Mittel: **Mittelachsensatz** *m* DRUCK ragged center setting (AmE), ragged centre setting (BrE); **Mittelanzapfung** *f* ELEKTRIZ center tap (AmE), centre tap (BrE); **Mittelbalken** *m* WASSERTRANS *Schiffbau* midship beam

mittelbituminös *adj* KOHLEN semibituminous

Mittel: **Mittelblech** *nt* METALL medium plate; **Mitteldeck** *nt* WASSERTRANS *Schiffkonstruktion* orlop deck; **Mitteldecker** *m* LUFTTRANS midwing plane; **Mitteldestillate** *nt pl* ERDÖL *Destillationsprodukt* medium distillates; **Mitteldruck-Dampfmaschine** *f* HYDRAUL *Dampfmaschine* intermediate cylinder steam engine; **Mitteldruckzylinder** *m* HYDRAUL *Dampfmaschine* intermediate pressure cylinder; **Mitteleisen** *nt* METALL medium iron; **Mittelfalzhülse** *f* VERPACK center folding tubing (AmE), centre folding tubing (BrE); **Mittelfeld** *nt* LUFTTRANS center panel (AmE), centre panel (BrE); **Mittelflyer** *m* TEXTIL intermediate frame

Mittelfrequenz *f (MF)* ELEKTRONIK, RADIO, TELEKOM medium frequency *(MF)*; **Mittelfrequenzband** *nt* ELEKTRONIK, RADIO, TELEKOM medium-frequency band; **Mittelfrequenzerwärmung** *f* ELEKTROTECH medium-frequency heating; **Mittelfrequenzheizung** *f* ELEKTROTECH medium-frequency heating; **Mittelfrequenzofen** *m* ELEKTROTECH medium-frequency furnace

Mittel: **Mittelgang** *m* EISENBAHN central gangway; **Mittelgerüst** *nt* FERTIG *Walzen* intermediate roll stand; **Mittelgrund** *m* WASSERTRANS *Geographie* middle ground; **Mittelgut** *nt* KOHLEN finished middlings; **Mittelhieb** *m* MASCHINEN bastard cut; **Mittelkasten** *m* FERTIG *Formen* cheek, intermediate box; **Mittelkiel** *m* WASSERTRANS *Schiffbau* center girder (AmE), centre girder (BrE); **Mittellager** *nt* KFZTECH center bearing (AmE), centre bearing (BrE); **Mittellänge** *f* DRUCK x-height, z-height; **Mittellängsschott** *nt* WASSERTRANS *Schiffkonstruktion* center line bulkhead (AmE), centre-line bulkhead (BrE); **Mittellast** *f* TRANS average load; **Mittel-Leistungsverstärker** *m* ELEKTRONIK medium-power amplifier; **Mittel-Leiter** *m* ELEKTROTECH *Verteilung* neutral conductor; **Mittellinie** *f* COMP & DV, GEOM median, MASCHINEN, MECHAN, RAUMFAHRT center line (AmE), centre line (BrE); **Mittellinienkreuz** *nt* KONSTZEICH center line cross (AmE), centre line cross (BrE); **Mittellot** *nt* WASSERTRANS *Schiffkonstruktion* perpendicular amidships

mittelmäßig: **~ verarbeiteter Kanalruß** *m (MPC-Ruß)* KUNSTSTOFF medium-processing channel carbon black *(MPC carbon black)*

Mittel: **Mittelmehl** *nt* LEBENSMITTEL middlings; **Mittelmotor** *m* KFZTECH center engine (AmE), centre engine (BrE), midengine

Mitteln: **~ von Signalen** *nt* ELEKTRONIK signal averaging

mitteln *vt* GERÄT average

Mittel: **Mittelöl** *nt* KOHLEN middle oil; **Mittelpfosten** *m* KER & GLAS mullion; **Mittelpufferkupplung** *f* EISEN-BAHN central buffer coupling

Mittelpunkt *m* GEOM midpoint, MASCHINEN, TELEKOM center (AmE), centre (BrE); **Mittelpunkterdung** *f* ELEKTRIZ midpoint earthing (BrE), midpoint grounding (AmE); **Mittelpunkttransformator** *m* ELEK-TROTECH static balancer

Mittel: **Mittelrippe** *f* METALL midrib; **Mittelrumpflängsträger** *m* RAUMFAHRT *Raumschiff* waist longeron

mittels: ~ **Lichtleitfaser übertragen** *vt* OPTIK fiber (AmE), fibre (BrE);

Mittel: **Mittelsäule eines Stativs** *f* FOTO central column of a tripod; **Mittelschaltung** *f* KFZTECH *Getriebe* floor shift; **Mittelschiene** *f* EISENBAHN center rail (AmE), centre rail (BrE), middle rail; **Mittelschiff** *nt* WASSER-TRANS *Schiffbau* midbody

mittelschlächtig: ~**es Wasserrad** *nt* HYDRAUL breast wheel

Mittel: **Mittelschneider** *m* FERTIG, MASCHINEN *Gewinde* intermediate tap, second tap, tap No2; **Mittelschneidkante** *f* NICHTFOSS ENERG central splitter edge; **Mittelschnelläufer** *m* WASSERTRANS *Dieselmotor* medium-speed engine; **Mittelsenkrechte** *f* GEOM midperpendicular; **Mittelspannung** *f* ELEKTROTECH medium voltage, METALL mean stress; **Mittelspannungssystem** *nt* ELEKTROTECH medium-voltage system; **Mittelspur** *f* AUFNAHME center track (AmE), centre track (BrE); **Mittelstreckenflugzeug** *nt* LUFTTRANS medium-range aircraft; **Mittelstreckenlinienflugzeug** *nt* LUFTTRANS medium-range airliner; **Mittelstreckenverkehrsflugzeug** *nt* LUFTTRANS medium-range airliner; **Mittelteer** *m* KOHLEN middle tar; **Mitteltonlautsprecher** *m* AUFNAHME midrange loudspeaker

Mittelung *f* STRÖMPHYS *in turbulenter Strömung* averaging

Mittel: **Mittelwalze** *f* METALL middle roll; **Mittelwelle** *f* (*MW*) FERNSEH medium wave, RADIO medium wave (*MW*); **Mittelwellenbereich** *m* RADIO medium-wave band; **Mittelwert** *m* COMP & DV mean, mean value, median, ELEKTRIZ average value, MATH average, mean, PHYS average, average value, mean value

Mittelwert bilden *vi* GERÄT average

Mittel: **Mittelwertbildung** *f* GERÄT *bei Signalen* signal averaging

mittelwertig: ~**er Boden** *m* KOHLEN medium-graded soil

Mittel: **Mittelzapfen** *m* BAU king rod; **Mittelzeitverhalten** *nt* KERNTECH medium-term behavior (AmE), medium-term behaviour (BrE); **Mittel-Zweck-Analyse** *f* (*MEA*) KÜNSTL INT *Methode der Problemlösung* means-end analysis (*MEA*)

Mitte: **Mittenabgleich** *m* FERNSEH centering control (AmE), centring control (BrE); **Mittenabstand** *m* MA-SCHINEN distance between centers (AmE), distance between centres (BrE); **Mittenbereich** *m* QUAL mean range; **Mittenfrequenz** *f* ELEKTRONIK, FERNSEH, RA-DIO center frequency (AmE), centre frequency (BrE)

mittengespeist: ~**er Horizontaldraht** *m* RADIO center-fed horizontal wire (AmE), centre-fed horizontal wire (BrE)

Mitte: **Mittenkontakt** *m* FOTO hot-shoe flash contact; **Mittenlinie** *f* MASCHINEN line of centers (AmE), line of centres (BrE); **Mittenloch** *nt* MASCHINEN center hole (AmE), centre hole (BrE); **Mittenrichtigkeit** *f* MECHAN concentricity

mittig:[1] **nicht** ~ *adj* RAUMFAHRT off-center (AmE), off-centre (BrE)

mittig:[2] ~**e Last** *f* BAU *Statik* concentric load

mittschiffs[1] *adj* WASSERTRANS midship

mittschiffs[2] *adv* WASSERTRANS amidships

Mittschiffsebene *f* WASSERTRANS *Schiffbau* center plane (AmE), centre plane (BrE)

Mittschiffslinie *f* WASSERTRANS *Schiffbau* center line (AmE), centre line (BrE), *Schiffkonstruktion* fore-and-aft line

Mix- und Püriergerät *nt* VERPACK mixing and blending equipment

Mizelle *f* KUNSTSTOFF micelle

MKSA-System *nt* METROL MKSA system, meter-kilo-gram-second-ampere system (AmE), metre-kilogram-second-ampere system (BrE)

MLIPS *abbr* (*Millionen logischer Inferenzen pro Sekunde*) KÜNSTL INT MLIPS (*millions of logical inferences per second*)

MMI *abbr* (*Mensch-Maschine-Interface, Mensch-Maschine-Schnittstelle*) COMP & DV, KONTROLL, KÜNSTL INT, RAUMFAHRT MMI (*man-machine interface*)

MMK *abbr* (*magnetomotorische Kraft*) ELEKTRIZ, PHYS, STRÖMPHYS mmf (*magnetomotive force*)

MN *abbr* (*Kernmasse*) KERNTECH MN (*nuclear mass*)

Mn (*Mangan*) CHEMIE Mn (*manganese*)

mn *abbr* (*Neutronenmasse*) KERNTECH, STRAHLPHYS, TEILPHYS mn (*neutron mass*)

Mnemonik *f* COMP & DV, KÜNSTL INT mnemonics

mnemonisch[1] *adj* COMP & DV, KÜNSTL INT mnemonic

mnemonisch:[2] ~**er Code** *m* COMP & DV mnemonic code; ~**er Name** *m* COMP & DV mnemonic name; ~**es Symbol** *nt* COMP & DV mnemonic symbol

mnemotechnisch *adj* COMP & DV, KÜNSTL INT mnemonic

Mo (*Molybdän*) CHEMIE Mo (*molybdenum*)

Möbelschreiner *m* BAU cabinet-maker

Möbeltischlerei *f* BAU cabinet-making

Möbelwagen *m* TRANS removal truck (AmE), removal van (BrE)

mobil[1] *adj* TELEKOM mobile

mobil:[2] ~**er Feuerlöscher** *m* SICHERHEIT mobile fire extinguisher; ~**e Kamera** *f* FERNSEH mobile camera; ~**er Satellitenfunk** *m* RAUMFAHRT *Kommunikation* mobile satellite communications

Mobilfunkkanal *m* RADIO, TELEKOM mobile radio channel

Mobilfunkstelle *f* RADIO, TELEKOM mobile radio station

Mobilstation *f* (*MS*) TELEKOM mobile station (*MS*)

Mobiltelefondienst *m* TELEKOM mobile telephone service

Möbiusband *nt* GEOM Möbius strip

möblieren *vt* BAU furnish

Modacryl *nt* TEXTIL modacrylic

Modalität *f* ERGON *Art der Sinneswahrnehmung* modality

Modalnoten *f pl* AKUSTIK modal notes

Modalwert *m* GEOM mode

Mode *f* OPTIK *Schwingung* mode

Modell *nt* COMP & DV model, ELEKTRONIK pattern, FER-TIG *Formguß* pattern, *Metalldrücken* chuck, MASCHINEN copy, pattern, TELEKOM, WASSERTRANS *Schiffbau* model; **Modell-** *pref* COMP & DV model; ~ **unabhängiger Teilchen** *nt* PHYS *Kernphysik* independent particle model; **Modellarm** *m* LUFTTRANS *Luftfahrzeug* hold; **Modellaufspanntisch** *m* MASCHI-NEN pattern table; **Modellausschmelzgießen** *nt*

FERTIG investment casting; **Modelldruck** *m* TEXTIL block printing; **Modelldruckmaschine** *f* DRUCK block printing machine; **Modelleichung** *f* UMWELTSCHMUTZ model calibration; **Modellformstoff** *m* FERTIG *Modellausschmelzverfahren* investment compound; **Modellholz** *nt* FERTIG *Gießen* pattern lumber

Modellieren *nt* COMP & DV, ELEKTRONIK, MATH modeling (AmE), modelling (BrE)

Modell: **Modellplatte** *f* FERTIG *Formen* match plate, *Gießen* pattern plate; **Modellsand** *m* FERTIG *Gießen* facing sand; **Modellschraube** *f* FERTIG *Gießen* lifting screw; **Modellspitze** *f* FERTIG *Formen* draw spike; **Modelltisch** *m* MASCHINEN copyholder; **Modelltischlerei** *f* FERTIG pattern shop; **Modellversuch** *m* WASSERTRANS *Schiffbau* model test

Modem:[1] **~ betriebsbereit** *adj* COMP & DV modem-ready

Modem[2] *nt* *(Modulator-Demodulator)* COMP & DV, ELEKTRONIK, RADIO, TELEKOM modem *(modulator-demodulator)*; **~ auf Leiterplattenebene** *nt* ELEKTRONIK board-level modem; **Modem-Anschluß** *m* COMP & DV, ELEKTRONIK modem interface; **Modembuchse** *f* COMP & DV data jack; **Modem-Empfänger** *m* COMP & DV, ELEKTRONIK modem receiver; **Modem-Interface** *nt* COMP & DV, ELEKTRONIK modem interface; **Modem-Schnittstelle** *f* COMP & DV, ELEKTRONIK modem interface; **Modem-Sender** *m* COMP & DV, ELEKTRONIK modem transmitter; **Modem-Wechsel** *m* COMP & DV, ELEKTRONIK modem interchange

Mode: **Modenabstreifer** *m* OPTIK mode stripper, TELEKOM cladding mode stripper, mode stripper; **Modendispersion** *f* OPTIK modal dispersion, TELEKOM intermodal distortion, intramodal distortion, modal distortion, mode distortion, multimode distortion; **Modenfelddetektor** *m* TELEKOM mode field detector; **Modenfelddurchmesser** *m* OPTIK mode field diameter; **Modenfilter** *m* OPTIK, TELEKOM mode filter; **Modenkopplung** *f* OPTIK, TELEKOM mode coupling; **Modenmischer** *m* OPTIK, TELEKOM mode mixer, mode scrambler; **Modenrauschen** *nt* OPTIK, TELEKOM modal noise; **Modenscrambler** *m* OPTIK, TELEKOM mode mixer, mode scrambler; **Modenspringen** *nt* OPTIK, TELEKOM mode hopping, mode jumping; **Modensprung** *m* OPTIK, TELEKOM mode hopping, mode jumping; **Modenstripper** *m* OPTIK mode stripper, TELEKOM cladding mode stripper, mode stripper; **Modenumfang** *m* OPTIK mode volume

Modenverteilung: **~ im stationären Zustand** *f* OPTIK equilibrium mode distribution; **~ bei Ungleichgewicht** *f* OPTIK nonequilibrium mode distribution; **Modenverteilungslänge im stationären Zustand** *f* OPTIK equilibrium mode distribution length

Mode: **Modenvolumen** *nt* TELEKOM mode volume

Moderator *m* KERNTECH, PHYS STRAHLPHYS moderator; **Moderator-Brennstoff-Verhältnis** *nt* KERNTECH moderator-fuel ratio; **Moderator-Spaltstoff-Verhältnis** *nt* KERNTECH moderator-fuel ratio; **Moderatortrimmung** *f* KERNTECH moderator control

moderieren *vt* KERNTECH moderate

moderiert: **nicht ~es Spaltneutron** *nt* KERNTECH unmoderated fission neutron

modern: **~es Bauelement** *nt* GERÄT advanced component; **~e Schrift** *f* DRUCK modern face; **~e Signalverarbeitung** *f* ELEKTRONIK advanced signal processing

Modifikation *f* FERTIG *Stoff* allotrope

modifizieren *vt* COMP & DV, GEOM modify

Modifizierer *m* KOHLEN modifier

modifiziert: **~e FM** *f* ELEKTRONIK, RADIO, TELEKOM modified FM; **~e Frequenzmodulation** *f* *(MFM)* ELEKTRONIK, RADIO, TELEKOM modified frequency modulation *(MFM)*; **~e Stärke** *f* LEBENSMITTEL modified starch; **~es System** *nt* TEXTIL modified system; **~e Wechseltaktschrift** *f* ELEKTRONIK, RADIO, TELEKOM modified frequency modulation

Modul *nt* COMP & DV module

modular[1] *adj* COMP & DV, FERTIG modular

modular:[2] **~e Arithmetik** *f* COMP & DV modular arithmetic; **~e Einheit** *f* MASCHINEN modular unit; **~es Meßsystem** *nt* METROL modular gaging system (AmE), modular gauging system (BrE); **~es Oberflächenreinigungsmittel** *nt* VERPACK modular surface cleaner; **~es Programmieren** *nt* COMP & DV modular programming; **~es Rechnen** *nt* COMP & DV modular arithmetic; **~es Werkzeugsystem** *nt* FERTIG modular tool system

Modularität *f* COMP & DV modularity

Modulation *f* AKUSTIK, AUFNAHME, COMP & DV, ELEKTRIZ, ELEKTRONIK, PHYS, RAUMFAHRT *Weltraumfunk*, TELEKOM, WELLPHYS *einer Welle* modulation; **~ mit freiem Träger** *f* ELEKTRONIK floating-carrier modulation; **~ mit konstanter Amplitude** *f* ELEKTRONIK constant-amplitude modulation; **~ ohne Rückkehr zu Null** *f* *(NRZ-Modulation)* TELEKOM nonreturn-to-zero modulation *(NRZ modulation)*; **~ mit unabhängigen Seitenbändern** *f* ELEKTRONIK independent sideband modulation; **Modulationsband** *nt* ELEKTRONIK modulation band; **Modulationselektrode** *f* FERNSEH modulation electrode; **Modulationsfaktor** *m* PHYS modulation factor; **Modulationsfrequenz** *f* ELEKTRONIK, RADIO, TELEKOM modulation frequency; **Modulationsgitter** *nt* FERNSEH modulation grid; **Modulationsgrad** *m* ELEKTRONIK modulation depth, modulation factor, PHYS modulation depth; **Modulationshüllkurve** *f* AUFNAHME modulation envelope; **Modulationsindex** *m* ELEKTRONIK, RADIO modulation index; **Modulationskarte** *f* COMP & DV, ELEKTRONIK modem board; **Modulationsrauschen** *nt* AKUSTIK, AUFNAHME, ELEKTRONIK, FERNSEH, TELEKOM modulation noise; **Modulationssignal** *nt* AUFNAHME, ELEKTRONIK modulating signal; **Modulationstiefe** *f* ELEKTRONIK modulation depth, modulation factor; **Modulationsübertragung** *f* ELEKTRONIK *von einem Träger auf einen anderen* remodulation; **Modulations-Übertragungsfunktion** *f* ELEKTRONIK modulation transfer function; **Modulationsverstärker** *m* ELEKTRONIK modulation amplifier; **Modulationswelle** *f* ELEKTRONIK, FERNSEH modulating wave; **Modulationswinkel** *m* AKUSTIK modulation angle

Modulator *m* COMP & DV, ELEKTRONIK *A/D-Wandler für Datensignale*, FERNSEH, TELEKOM modulator; **~ mit Null-Vorspannung** *m* RADIO zero-bias modulator; **Modulator-Demodulator** *m* *(Modem)* COMP & DV, ELEKTRONIK, RADIO, TELEKOM modulator-demodulator *(modem)*; **Modulatordiode** *f* ELEKTRONIK modulator diode; **Modulatortreiberstufe** *f* ELEKTRONIK modulator driver

Modul: **Modulfräser** *m* MASCHINEN module milling cutter

modulieren *vt* AUFNAHME, ELEKTRONIK, FERNSEH, PHYS, RADIO, TELEKOM modulate

moduliert: **~er Dauerträger** *m* FERNSEH MCW, modulated continuous wave; ~er **Oszillator** m ELEKTRONIK modulated oscillator; ~e **Rille** f AKUSTIK modulated groove; ~e **Schwingung** f ELEKTRONIK modulated oscillation; ~es **Signal** nt TELEKOM modulated signal; ~er **Strahl** m ELEKTRONIK modulated beam; ~e **Struktur** f METALL modulated structure; ~er **Träger** m ELEKTRONIK, FERNSEH modulated carrier; ~e **Welle** f AUFNAHME, ELEKTRONIK modulated wave

Modul: **Modulkehrwert** m FERTIG diametral pitch; **Modulon-Kontrolle** f COMP & DV residue check; **Modulsatz** m ELEKTRONIK module set; **Modulus** m MATH *einer komplexen Zahl* modulus; **Modulwälzfräser** m FERTIG module hob

Modum m COMP & DV, ELEKTRIZ, ELEKTRONIK, ERDÖL *Teil einer Offshore-Plattform* module, FERTIG module, *Kunststoffinstallationen* module, KONTROLL module, MASCHINEN module, modulus, RADIO module, TELEKOM board

Modus m COMP & DV, DRUCK, ELEKTRONIK mode; **Modusanzeiger** m COMP & DV mode indicator; **Modusauswahl** f COMP & DV mode selection; **Modusbeschreibung** f COMP & DV mode description; **Modusverteilung** f COMP & DV mode distribution; **Moduswechsel** m COMP & DV mode change, mode switching

Mofette f NICHTFOSS ENERG mofette

möglich[1] adj ANSTRICH potential

möglich:[2] ~e **Leistungsfähigkeit** f TRANS possible capacity; ~e **Reserven** f pl ERDÖL *Lagerstätteninhalt* possible reserves

Mohr: ~scher **Quetschhahn** m LABOR *Gummischlauch* Mohr's clip; ~scher **Spannungs-und Trägheitskreis** m FERTIG Mohr's circles

Mohs: ~sche **Härteskale** f FERTIG Mohs' scale

Moiré nt FERNSEH moiré; **Moiré-Muster** nt AKUSTIK moiré pattern, PHYS moiré fringe

Mol nt METROL gram molecule

mol abbr *(Mole)* CHEMIE, LABOR, PHYS mol *(mole)*

molal adj CHEMIE molal

molar: ~es **Brechungsvermögen** nt THERMOD molecular refractivity; ~e **Gaskonstante** f PHYS molar gas constant; ~e **Wärmekapazität** f PHYS molar heat capacity

Molarität f CHEMIE molarity

Molbruchzahl f METALL mole fraction

Molch m ERDÖL go-devil, pig, scraper, *Gerät zum Reinigen von Rohrleitungen* scraper, FERTIG *Kunststoffinstallationen* scraper

Mole f BAU breakwater, pier, CHEMIE *(mol)*, METROL *(mol)*, PHYS *(mol)* *Einheit der Stoffmenge* mole *(mol)*, WASSERTRANS *Hafen* jetty, mole, pier

Molekül nt CHEMIE, ERDÖL *Petrochemie*, PHYS molecule

molekular: ~es **Brechungsvermögen** nt PHYS molecular refractivity; ~e **Depression** f PHYS, THERMOD molecular depression of freezing point; ~es **Feld** nt PHYS, THERMOD molecular field; ~e **Gefrierpunkterniedrigung** f PHYS, THERMOD molecular depression of freezing point; ~e **Leitfähigkeit** f PHYS, THERMOD molecular conductivity; ~es **Schwingungsniveau** nt STRAHLPHYS molecular vibrational energy level; ~e **Siedepunkterhöhung** f PHYS, THERMOD molecular elevation of boiling point; ~e **Spektralanalyse** f STRAHLPHYS molecular spectroanalysis; ~e **Umlaufbahn** f PHYS molecular orbital

Molekular- pref ELEKTRONIK, KERNTECH, PHYS, THERMOD molecular; **Molekulardichte** f *(n)* PHYS, THERMOD molecular density *(n)*; **Molekularelektronik** f ELEKTRONIK molecular electronics; **Molekulargewicht** nt *(M)* ERDÖL *Petrochemie*, PHYS, THERMOD molecular weight *(M)*; **Molekularkräfte** f pl METALL intermolecular forces; **Molekularmasse** f *(m)* PHYS molecular mass *(m)*; **Molekularpumpe** f MECHAN, PHYS kinetic vacuum pump; **Molekularstrahlepitaxie** f *(MBE)* ELEKTRONIK, STRAHLPHYS molecular-beam epitaxy *(MBE)*

Molekül: **Moleküldurchmesser** m PHYS diameter of molecule; **Molekülgaslaser** m ELEKTRONIK molecular gas laser; **Moleküllaser** m ELEKTRONIK molecular laser; **Molekülspektrum** nt PHYS, THERMOD molecular spectrum; **Molekülstrahl** m TELEKOM molecule beam; **Molekülzahl** f *(N)* PHYS number of molecules *(N)*

Molenkopf m WASSERTRANS *Hafen* pierhead

Möller m FERTIG ore and flux, METALL burden

Molvolumen nt PHYS molar volume

Molwärme f PHYS, THERMOD molecular heat

Molybdän nt *(Mo)* CHEMIE molybdenum *(Mo)*; **Molybdändisulfid** nt MASCHINEN molybdenum disulfide (AmE), molybdenum disulphide (BrE); **Molybdänkarbid** nt FERTIG molybdenum carbide; **Molybdänstahl** m METALL molybdenum steel

Molybdat nt CHEMIE molybdate, tetraoxomolybdate

Moment nt MASCHINEN, MECHAN *Kräftepaar* moment

Momentan- pref MASCHINEN instantaneous: **Momentanachse** f MASCHINEN instantaneous axis; **Momentananzeige** f GERÄT instantaneous display, PHYS live display

momentan: ~e **Dichte der kinetischen Energie** f AKUSTIK instantaneous kinetic energy; ~e **Dichte der potentiellen Energie** f AKUSTIK instantaneous potential energy; ~e **Dichte der Schallenergie** f AKUSTIK instantaneous acoustic energy; ~er **Druckanstieg** m FERTIG surge; ~er **Nachführungsfehler** m RAUMFAHRT *Weltraumfunk* instantaneous tracking error; ~er **Schalldruck** m AKUSTIK instantaneous sound pressure; ~e **Schalleistung** f AKUSTIK instantaneous sound power, PHYS sound-energy flux; ~e **Schallintensität** f AKUSTIK instantaneous sound power; ~e **Sprachleistung** f AKUSTIK instantaneous speech power; ~e **Sprechleistung** f ERGON instantaneous speech power

Momentan-: **Momentangeschwindigkeit** f FERTIG instantaneous velocity; **Momentanpol** m FERTIG *Getriebelehre* instant center (AmE), instant centre (BrE); **Momentanspannung** f ELEKTRIZ instantaneous voltage; **Momentanstrom** m ELEKTRIZ, ELEKTROTECH instantaneous current; **Momentanwert** m ELEKTRIZ, FERTIG, GERÄT, PHYS instantaneous value

Moment: **Momentaufnahme** f COMP & DV snapshot; **Momentenausgleich** m MASCHINEN balancing of moments; **Momentenbeiwert** m MASCHINEN moment coefficient; **Momentenkurve** f MASCHINEN moment curve; **Momentenlinie** f MASCHINEN moment line; **Momentgleichrichter** m KFZTECH *Getriebe* torque rectifier; **Momentrelais** nt ELEKTROTECH instantaneous relay

monadisch[1] adj COMP & DV monadic, unary

monadisch:[2] ~e **Operation** f COMP & DV monadic operation

Mond m RAUMFAHRT moon

Möndchen nt GEOM meniscus

Mond: **Mondflutintervall** nt NICHTFOSS ENERG lagging of the tide; **Mondlandeeinheit** f RAUMFAHRT lunar module; **Mondlandefähre** f *(LEM)* RAUMFAHRT *Apollo-Raumschiff* lunar excursion module *(LEM)*; **Mond-**

landefahrzeug nt (LEM) RAUMFAHRT Apollo-Raum-schiff lunar excursion module (LEM); **Mondlandung** f RAUMFAHRT lunar landing; **Mondsonde** f RAUM-FAHRT lunar probe; **Mondtag** m RAUMFAHRT lunar day; **Mondumlaufbahn** f RAUMFAHRT lunar orbit; **Mondversorgungsfahrzeug** nt RAUMFAHRT LLV, lunar logistics vehicle

Monitor m AUFNAHME, COMP & DV, ELEKTRIZ monitor, FERNSEH monitor, video display unit, KON-TROLL VDU, monitor, PHYS VDU, STRAHLPHYS, TELEKOM monitor; **Monitoraufruf** m COMP & DV moni-tor call; **Monitorcode** m COMP & DV monitor code; **Monitorklasse** f COMP & DV monitor class; **Monitormo-dus** m COMP & DV monitor mode

Mono- pref EISENBAHN, ELEKTRONIK mono-
Monoacetin nt CHEMIE monoacetin
Monoamid nt CHEMIE monoamide
Monoamin nt CHEMIE monoamine
Monoamino- pref CHEMIE monoamino
monoatomar adj CHEMIE monoatomic
Mono-: **Mono-Beschleunigungsanode** f ELEKTRONIK monoaccelerator CRT; **Monoblock-Betonschwelle** f EISENBAHN monobloc concrete sleeper (BrE), mono-bloc concrete tie (AmE); **Monoblockrad** nt EISENBAHN solid wheel; **Monobrombenzol** nt CHEMIE mono-bromobenzene; **Monochord** nt AKUSTIK monochord
monochrom adj COMP & DV, DRUCK, FOTO monochrome; **monochromatisch** adj OPTIK, PHYS monochromatic
monochromatisch: **~es Licht** nt WELLPHYS monochro-matic light; **~e Strahlung** f OPTIK, STRAHLPHYS, TELEKOM monochromatic radiation
Mono-: **Monochromator** m OPTIK, PHYS, TELEKOM monochromator; **Monochromsignal** nt RAUMFAHRT Weltraumfunk monochrome signal
monoenergetisch adj PHYS monoenergetic
Mono-: **Monoethylamin** nt CHEMIE aminoethane, ethyla-mine; **Monofil** nt KUNSTSTOFF monofilament; **Monofilament** nt KUNSTSTOFF monofilament; **Monofi-lamentgarn** nt TEXTIL monofilament yarn; **Monofilgarn** nt TEXTIL monofilament yarn; **Monohy-drat** nt CHEMIE monohydrate; **Monohydrogen-** pref CHEMIE monohydric; **Monohydroxyketon** nt CHEMIE ketol; **Monoklinsystem** nt METALL monoclinic system
monokrystallin: **~es Silizium** nt RAUMFAHRT Raumschiff monocrystalline silicon
monolithisch: **~es Feld** nt ELEKTRONIK monolithic ar-ray; **~es Filter** nt ELEKTRONIK, TELEKOM monolithic filter; **~ integrierte Schaltung** f ELEKTRONIK, TELEKOM monolithic integrated circuit; **~er Mikrowellenschalt-kreis** m PHYS monolithic microwave integrated circuit; **~er Verstärker** m ELEKTRONIK monolithic amplifier
Monom nt MATH monomial
Monomer nt CHEMIE, ERDÖL Petrochemie, KUNSTSTOFF monomer
monomer[1] adj KUNSTSTOFF monomeric
monomer:[2] **~e Substanz** f CHEMIE monomer
Monomethylamin nt CHEMIE aminomethane, methyla-mine
Monomethyl-Aminophenolsulfat nt CHEMIE methylami-nophenol sulfate (AmE), methylaminophenol sulphate (BrE), metol
Mono-: **Monomodefaser** f OPTIK monomode fiber (AmE), monomode fibre (BrE), TELEKOM single mode fiber (AmE), single mode fibre (BrE)
monomolekular[1] adj CHEMIE monomolecular, unimole-cular

monomolekular:[2] **~e Reaktion** f CHEMIE monomolecular reaction
Mono-: **Monomolekularfilm** m CHEMIE monolayer, monomolecular layer; **Mononatriumglutamat** nt LE-BENSMITTEL Geschmacksstoff MSG, monosodium glutamate
monophon: **~er Abtaster** m AKUSTIK monophonic pick-up; **~e Aufzeichnung** f AKUSTIK monophonic recording
monophonisch: **~e Aufnahme** f AUFNAHME mono-pho-nic recording
Monopol nt RADIO, TEILPHYS monopole; **Monopolan-tenne** f TELEKOM monopole aerial, monopole antenna, unipole aerial, unipole antenna
Mono-: **Monoschicht** f CHEMIE monolayer, monomole-cular layer; **Monosilan** nt CHEMIE monosilane, silicomethane
monostabil[1] adj COMP & DV, ELEKTRONIK monostable.
monostabil:[2] **~e Kippschaltung** f ELEKTRONIK gated flip-flop, one-shot multivibrator, PHYS monostable; **~er Multivibrator** m ELEKTRONIK monostable multivibrat-or
Mono-: **Monostearat** nt CHEMIE monostearin; **Monota-ste** f FERNSEH monkey
monoton[1] adj MATH Folgen, Reihen monotone
monoton:[2] **~es Schließen** nt KÜNSTL INT monotonic reasoning; **nicht ~es Schließen** nt KÜNSTL INT non-monotonic reasoning
Mono-: **Mono-Tonsystem** nt AUFNAHME monophonic sound system; **Monotreibstoff** m CHEMIE, RAUMFAHRT monopropellant; **Monotron** nt ELEKTRONIK Bildröhre für Prüfzwecke monotron
monotrop: **~e Reaktion** f METALL monotropic reaction
Monotype ® f DRUCK Monotype ®; **Monotypegießma-schine** f DRUCK Monotype casting machine
monovalent adj CHEMIE monovalent, univalent
Mono-: **Monoverstärker** m AUFNAHME monoamplifier; **Monovinylacetylen** nt CHEMIE vinylacetylene; **Mon-oxid** nt CHEMIE monoxide
Monsun m WASSERTRANS monsoon
Montage f AUFNAHME editing, BAU assembly, ELEKTRO-NIK mounting, FERNSEH editing, FERTIG erection, mounting, MASCHINEN assembly, mounting, MECHAN assembly, PAPIER assembly, TRANS assembly; **~ oberhalb des Reaktorbodens** f KERNTECH upper shell assembly; **~ eines optischen Kabels** f TELEKOM optical cable assembly; **Montageautomat** m MASCHINEN automatic assembly machine; **Montageband** nt COMP & DV, FERTIG flow line; **Montagebauweise** f BAU dry construction; **Montagebetrieb** m MASCHINEN assem-bly plant; **Montageblock** m AUFNAHME editing block; **Montagebock** m MASCHINEN assembly jig; **Montage-fehler** m FERTIG installation error; **Montagefolie** f DRUCK mounting foil; **Montagegerät** nt MASCHINEN assembly machine, fitting device; **Montagehalle** f ME-CHAN assembly shop, erecting shop, WASSERTRANS Schiffbau assembly hall, erecting shop; **Montagekle-ber** m DRUCK mounting glue; **Montageloch** nt MASCHINEN mounting hole; **Montagemaße** nt pl FER-TIG Kunststoffinstallationen assembly dimensions; **Montageniet** m MASCHINEN field rivet, site rivet; **Mon-tageplatte** f FERTIG Kunststoffinstallationen mounting plate, MASCHINEN mounting base, RADIO mounting plate; **Montagepunkt** m TRANS assembly point; **Mon-tageroboter** m MECHAN assembly robot; **Montageroller** m MASCHINEN dolly; **Montageschrau-**

be *f* MASCHINEN assembling bolt, fitting bolt, mounting bolt; **Montageschweißen** *nt* KERNTECH field weld; **Montagesteg** *m* KERNTECH catwalk; **Montagestraße** *f* MECHAN assembly line; **Montagewerkstatt** *f* MECHAN assembly shop; **Montagewerkzeuge** *nt pl* MASCHINEN assembly tools; **Montagezeichnung** *f* MECHAN assembly drawing

Monte-Carlo-Methode *f* COMP & DV Monte-Carlo-method, random walk method

Monte-Carlo-Verfahren *nt* COMP & DV Monte-Carlo-method

Montejus *m* CHEMTECH acid elevator

Monteur *m* FERTIG erector, MASCHINEN assembler, fitter, MECHAN erector, fitter, WASSERTRANS erector

montieren *vt* BAU assemble, fit, set up, COMP & DV, FERTIG mount, MECHAN erect, PAPIER assemble, RADIO mount, WASSERTRANS *Schiffteile* fit

montiert: **~e Zeichnung** *f* KONSTZEICH assembled drawing

Montierung *f* FERTIG mount

Montmorillonit *m* ERDÖL *Mineral*, KOHLEN montmorillonite

Mooney-Anvulkanisationsdauer *f* KUNSTSTOFF Mooney scorch time

Mooney-Viskosität *f* KUNSTSTOFF Mooney viscosity

Moor *nt* WASSERVERSORG swamp

Mooring *nt* MEERSCHMUTZ mooring

Moosgummi *nt* KUNSTSTOFF microcellular rubber

Moräne *f* KOHLEN moraine; **Moränenfilterschicht** *f* ABFALL *Deponie* morainic filter layer

Morast *m* WASSERVERSORG swamp

Morin *nt* CHEMIE morin

Morindin *nt* CHEMIE morindin

Morpholin *nt* CHEMIE morpholine, tetrahydrooxazine

Morphotropie *f* CHEMIE morphotropism

Morsecode *m* RADIO Morse code

Morsekegel *m* MASCHINEN Morse taper; **Morsekegelstift** *m* MASCHINEN Morse taper pin

Mörser *m* CHEMTECH, FERTIG, LABOR mortar; **Mörserkeule** *f* CHEMTECH pestle

Morsetaste *f* RADIO key

Mörtel *m* BAU plaster, FERTIG mortar; **Mörtelbett** *nt* BAU mortar; **Mörtelmischmaschine** *f* BAU mortar mixer

MOS *abbr* COMP & DV *(Metalloxid-Halbleiter)*, ELEKTRONIK *(Metalloxid-Halbleiter, Metalloxid-Transistor)* MOS *(metal oxide semiconductor)*

Mosaik *nt* ELEKTRONIK mosaic; **Mosaikdrucker** *m* COMP & DV matrix printer; **Mosaikkrankheit** *f* LEBENSMITTEL *Pflanzenkrankheitslehre* mosaic; **Mosaikstein** *m* KER & GLAS tessera

Moseley: **~sches Gesetz** *nt* PHYS Moseley's law

MOSFET *abbr* *(Metalloxid-Silizium-Feldeffekttransistor)* RADIO MOSFET *(metal oxide silicon field effect transistor)*

MOS: **MOS-Gatter** *nt* ELEKTRONIK MOS gate; **MOS-Kondensator** *m* ELEKTROTECH MOS capacitor; **MOS-Laufzeitkette** *f* ELEKTRONIK MOS delay line; **MOS-Leistungstransistor** *m* ELEKTRONIK MOS power transistor; **MOS-Logikschaltkreis** *m* ELEKTRONIK MOS logic circuit

Mößbauer: **~scher Effekt** *m* PHYS Mossbauer effect

Most *m* LEBENSMITTEL stum}

MOS: **MOS-Transistor** *m* ELEKTRONIK MOS transistor; **MOS-Treiber** *m* ELEKTRONIK MOS driver

Motor[1] *m* ELEKTRIZ, ELEKTROTECH motor, KFZTECH engine, MASCHINEN engine, motor, MECHAN, WASSERTRANS engine; **~ mit Doppelschlußwicklung** *m* ELEKTROTECH compound-winding motor; **~ mit Eigenkühlung** *m* KFZTECH ventilated motor; **~ mit einstellbarer Drehzahl** *m* ELEKTRIZ adjustable varying speed motor; **~ für Flüssigtreibstoff** *m* THERMOD liquid fuel engine; **~ mit Gangschaltung** *m* MECHAN geared motor; **~ mit gewickeltem Stator** *m* ELEKTROTECH wound-stator motor; **~ mit gleichbleibendem Schluckvolumen** *m* FERTIG constant-capacity motor; **~ mit hängenden Ventilen** *m* KFZTECH overhead valve engine; **~ mit hohem Anzugsmoment** *m* MECHAN high-torque motor; **~ mit Kompensationswicklung** *m* ELEKTRIZ compensated motor, compound motor, compound-wound motor; **~ mit Kondensator für Anlauf und Betrieb** *m* ELEKTROTECH capacitor start-run motor; **~ mit phasengewickeltem Läufer** *m* ELEKTRIZ phase-wound rotor motor; **~ mit Querstromspülung** *m* KFZTECH three-port two-stroke engine; **~ mit Schleifringläufer** *m* ELEKTROTECH wound-rotor motor; **~ mit Selbstzündung** *m* KFZTECH compression-ignition engine; **~ mit stehenden Ventilen** *m* KFZTECH L-head engine; **~ mit stehenden Zylindern** *m* KFZTECH vertical engine; **~ mit stellbarer Geschwindigkeit** *m* ELEKTRIZ adjustable speed motor; **~ mit T-förmigem Verbrennungsraum** *m* KFZTECH T-head engine; **~ mit Turboaufladung** *m* KFZTECH, WASSERTRANS turbocharged engine; **~ mit übereinander angeordneten Ventilen** *m* KFZTECH F-Head engine; **~ mit Ventilen zu beiden Seiten** *m* KFZTECH T-head engine; **~ mit veränderlicher Drehzahl** *m* ELEKTROTECH variable speed motor; **~ mit zwei Drehzahlen** *m* ELEKTRIZ double-speed motor; **~ mit Zylindern in V-Anordnung** *m* MASCHINEN V-cylinder engine

Motor:[2] **den ~ absaufen lassen** *vi* KFZTECH flood the carburetor (AmE), flood the carburettor (BrE); **den ~ voll ausfahren** *vi* MASCHINEN run an engine to its full capacity, work an engine to its full capacity

motorangetrieben *adj* ELEKTROTECH motor-driven

Motor: **Motoranker** *m* ELEKTRIZ motor armature; **Motoranlasser** *m* ELEKTROTECH motor starter, KFZTECH, LUFTTRANS, WASSERTRANS engine starter; **Motorantrieb** *m* ELEKTROTECH, FOTO motor drive; **Motorantriebmechanismus** *m* ELEKTRIZ motor drive mechanism; **Motoraufhängung** *f* KFZTECH engine support, engine support lug; **Motoraufzug** *m* TRANS powered lift; **Motorauspuffsystem** *nt* MASCHINEN engine exhaust system

motorbetrieben: **~es Abschöpfgerät** *nt* MEERSCHMUTZ *für Öl* self-propelled skimmer

Motor: **Motorblock** *m* KFZTECH, MASCHINEN, MECHAN, WASSERTRANS engine block; **Motorboot** *nt* WASSERTRANS motorboat; **Motorbremse** *f* KFZTECH engine brake, *Bremsanlage* exhaust brake; **Motorbrennkammer** *f* MASCHINEN engine combustion chamber; **Motordrehmoment** *nt* KFZTECH, LUFTTRANS engine torque; **Motordrehzahl** *f* KFZTECH engine speed; **Motordrehzahlaufnehmer** *m* KFZTECH engine speed pick-up; **Motoreinstellung** *f* KFZTECH tuning; **Motorenabgasanlage** *f* KFZTECH, WASSERTRANS engine exhaust system; **Motorenauslaufzeit** *f* LUFTTRANS engine coasting-down time; **Motorenbauer** *m* MASCHINEN engine builder; **Motorenbenzin** *nt* ERDÖL motor spirit, KFZTECH gas (AmE), gasoline (AmE), petrol (BrE); **Motorenfundament** *nt* MECHAN engine pedestal; **Motorengehäusebogen** *m* LUFTTRANS engine support arch; **Motorenhalterungsbogen** *m*

LUFTTRANS engine support arch; **Motorenhersteller** *m* KFZTECH engine manufacturer; **Motorenkühlanlage** *f* WASSERTRANS engine cooling system; **Motorenöl** *nt* ERDÖL motor oil; **Motorenprüfstand** *m* LUFTTRANS engine test stand; **Motorensteuerzentrale** *f* KONTROLL motor control center (AmE), motor control centre (BrE); **Motorfähre** *f* WASSERTRANS motor ferry; **Motorfahrzeug** *nt* WASSERTRANS motor vessel; **Motorgebläse** *nt* KFZTECH engine fan; **Motorgehäuse** *nt* KFZTECH crankcase; **Motorgenerator** *m* ELEKTROTECH motor generator; **Motorgetriebeeinheit** *f* KFZTECH power unit

motorgetrieben: ~**e Pumpe** *f* LUFTTRANS engine-driven pump

Motor: **Motorhaube** *f* KFZTECH engine bonnet (BrE), engine hood (AmE), *Karosserie* bonnet (BrE), hood (AmE); **Motorhaubenverriegelung** *f* KFZTECH bonnet catch (BrE), hood catch (AmE); **Motorhubraum** *m* KFZTECH engine capacity, MASCHINEN capacity of an engine

motorisch: ~**e Aktivität** *f* ERGON motor activity

motorisiert: ~**er Förderwagen** *m* KFZTECH powered barrow; ~**er Handkarren** *m* KFZTECH powered barrow

Motor: **Motorkurbel** *f* MASCHINEN engine crank; **Motorlager** *nt* MASCHINEN, WASSERTRANS engine bearing; **Motorleistung** *f* HEIZ & KÄLTE motor rating; **Motorluftanlage** *f* KFZTECH, WASSERTRANS engine ventilation system; **Motornachlauf** *m* KFZTECH engine second rating; **Motoröl** *nt* ERDÖL motor oil, KFZTECH, MASCHINEN, WASSERTRANS engine oil; **Motorpumpe** *f* MEERSCHMUTZ motor pump; **Motorradvergaser** *m* KFZTECH carburetors for motorcycles (AmE), carburettors for motorcycles (BrE); **Motorrahmen** *m* MASCHINEN engine frame; **Motorraum** *m* KFZTECH engine compartment; **Motorrüstung** *f* LUFTTRANS engine instruments; **Motorschaden** *m* KFZTECH engine failure, engine malfunction, *Motor* engine breakdown, WASSERTRANS engine failure, engine malfunction; **Motorschalldämpfer** *m* MASCHINEN engine muffler (AmE), engine silencer (BrE); **Motorschiff** *nt* WASSERTRANS motor ship; **Motorschwungrad** *nt* MASCHINEN engine flywheel; **Motorsegler** *m* WASSERTRANS auxiliary engine sailing ship, motor sailer; **Motorspritze** *f* MEERSCHMUTZ motor pump; **Motorsteuerung** *f* FERNSEH motor control, KFZTECH timing gear; **Motorstraßenhobel** *m* BAU *Straßenbau* motor grader; **Motorträger** *m* LUFTTRANS engine mount; **Motorträgerschraube** *f* KFZTECH engine support plug; **Motortriebwagen** *m* EISENBAHN rail coach; **Motorüberholung** *f* WASSERTRANS engine overhaul; **Motorventil** *nt* MASCHINEN engine valve; **Motorventilator** *m* KFZTECH engine fan; **Motorverkleidung** *f* LUFTTRANS cowling; **Motorwagen** *m* EISENBAHN rail motor car; **Motorwartung** *f* KFZTECH, WASSERTRANS engine maintenance; **Motorwelle** *f* MASCHINEN engine shaft

moussierend *adj* LEBENSMITTEL effervescent

MP *abbr* COMP & DV *(Mikroprozessor)*, ELEKTRIZ *(Mikroprozessor)*, MASCHINEN *(Mikroprozessor)* MP *(microprocessor)*, VERPACK *(Metallpapier)* MP *(metallic paper)*

mp *abbr* *(Protonenmasse)* KERNTECH mp *(proton mass)*

MPC-Ruß *m* *(mittelmäßig verarbeiteter Kanalruß)* KUNSTSTOFF MPC carbon black *(medium-processing channel carbon black)*

MS *abbr* *(Mitteilungsspeicherung, Mobilstation)* TELEKOM MS *(message storing)*

MSC *abbr* *(Funkvermittlungsstelle)* TELEKOM MSC *(mobile switching centre)*

M-Schale *f* PHYS *Atomphysik* M-shell

MSI *abbr* COMP & DV *(mittlere Integrationsdichte, mittlere Integrationstechnik, mittlerer Integrationsgrad)*, ELEKTRONIK *(mittlere Integrationstechnik, mittlerer Integrationsgrad, mittlerere Integrationsdichte)*, TELEKOM *(mittlerer Integrationsgrad, mittlerere Integrationsdichte)* MSI *(medium-scale integration)*

MSI-Schaltkreis *m* TELEKOM MSI circuit

MSK *abbr* COMP & DV *(Minimalphasenumtastung)*, ELEKTRONIK *(kleinste Umtastung)*, RADIO *(Minimalphasenumtastung)*, TELEKOM *(Minimalphasenumtastung)* MSK *(minimum-shift keying)*

MTL-Logik *f* *(integrierte Transistorlogik)* ELEKTRONIK MTL *(merged transistor logic)*

MTR *abbr* *(Materialprüfreaktor)* KERNTECH MTR *(materials-testing reactor)*

MT-Ruß *m* KUNSTSTOFF *mittlerer Thermalruß* MT carbon black, medium thermal carbon black

MTTR *abbr* COMP & DV *(mittlere Reparaturdauer)*, ELEKTROTECH *(mittlere Zeit bis zur Reparatur)*, MECHAN *(mittlere Instandsetzungszeit)*, QUAL *(mittlere Reparaturdauer)*, RAUMFAHRT *(mittlere Reparaturdauer)* MTTR *(mean time to repair)*

MÜ *abbr* *(Maschinenübersetzung)* KÜNSTL INT MT *(machine translation)*

mu *abbr* *(Atommassenkonstante)* KERNTECH mu *(unified atomic mass constant)*

µ *abbr* ELEKTRIZ *(Permeabilität)* µ *(permeability)*, - RADIO *(Verstärkung)* µ *(amplification factor)*, THERMOD µ

µH *abbr* *(Hallsche Mobilität)* RADIO µH *(Hall mobility)*

Mucin *nt* CHEMIE mucin

Mucoitinschwefel *m* CHEMIE mucoitinsulfur (AmE), mucoitinsulphur (BrE)

Mucon- *pref* CHEMIE muconic

Mucoproteid *nt* CHEMIE mucoprotein

Mucoprotein *nt* CHEMIE mucoprotein

Muffe *f* BAU socket, FERTIG bell, hose, MASCHINEN collar, coupling sleeve, muff, sleeve, socket, MECHAN clamp, sleeve, RAUMFAHRT *Raumschiff* gland

Muffel *f* FERTIG, KER & GLAS, METALL muffle; **Muffelkühlofen** *m* KER & GLAS muffle lehr; **Muffelofen** *m* FERTIG, LABOR muffle furnace; **Muffelstütze** *f* KER & GLAS muffle support

Muffe: **Muffengrund** *m* FERTIG *Kunststoffinstallationen* root; **Muffenkupplung** *f* MASCHINEN box coupling, butt coupling, muff coupling, sleeve coupling; **Muffenrohr** *nt* BAU, FERTIG socket pipe; **Muffenrohrverbindung** *f* BAU spigot joint; **Muffenschweißen** *nt* FERTIG *Kunststoffinstallationen* socket fusion jointing; **Muffenstück** *nt* FERTIG flange; **Muffenverbindung** *f* BAU spigot and socket joint, tailpiece, MASCHINEN sleeve joint, socket joint; **Muffenverbindungsrohre** *nt pl* BAU spigot and socket joint pipes

Mühle *f* KUNSTSTOFF, PAPIER *Schleifvorrichtung* mill; **Mühlenindustrie** *f* LEBENSMITTEL milling industry; **Mühlenstaub** *m* LEBENSMITTEL mill dust

Mühlgerinne *nt* WASSERVERSORG mill course, millrace

Mühlgraben *m* WASSERVERSORG mill course, millrace

Mühlrad *nt* MASCHINEN millwheel

Mühlstein *m* LEBENSMITTEL millstone

Mulde f ERDÖL syncline, FERTIG basin, spherical depression, LABOR, MASCHINEN trough; **Muldenkipper** m BAU dumper, EISENBAHN skip wagon, KFZTECH dump truck, skip lorry (BrE), skip truck (AmE); **Muldenkippwagen** m MEERSCHMUTZ skip lorry (BrE), skip truck (AmE); **Muldenofen** m THERMOD crucible furnace

Müll m COMP & DV, VERPACK garbage (AmE), rubbish (BrE), WASSERVERSORG refuse; **~ rein, Müll raus** phr *(GIGO)* COMP & DV garbage in, garbage out *(GIGO)*; **Müllabfuhr** f ABFALL collection service, garbage collection (AmE), refuse collection (BrE), garbage disposal (AmE), refuse disposal (BrE), refuse collection service, waste collection; **Müllabfuhrunternehmen** nt ABFALL collector; **Müllabfuhrwagen** m ABFALL, KFZTECH dust cart (BrE), garbage truck (AmE); **Müllabladen** nt UMWELTSCHMUTZ dumping; **Müllabladeplatz** m UMWELTSCHMUTZ dump ground; **Müllablagerung** f WASSERVERSORG refuse tipping; **Müllabwurfschacht** m ABFALL refuse chute; **Müllanfall** m ABFALL waste formation, waste production, waste stream; **Müllaufbereitung** f UMWELTSCHMUTZ conditioning of waste; **Müllaufgabetrichter** m ABFALL hopper-furnace feed chute; **Müllballen** m ABFALL waste bale; **Müllbehälter** m ABFALL garbage can (AmE), rubbish bin (BrE), waste container; **Müllbeseitigung** f UMWELTSCHMUTZ waste disposal; **Müllbeutel** m ABFALL garbage bag (AmE), rubbish bag (BrE), VERPACK refuse sack; **Müllbrennstoff** m ABFALL RDF, refuse-derived fuel; **Müllbunker** m ABFALL receiving bunker; **Müllcontainer** m ABFALL roll-out container, MEERSCHMUTZ skip; **Mülldeponie** f ABFALL landfill, UMWELTSCHMUTZ landfill, sanitary landfill; **Mülleimer** m ABFALL garbage can (AmE), rubbish bin (BrE); **Mülleinfülltrichter** m ABFALL loading hopper

Müllerei f LEBENSMITTEL milling

Müll: **Müllfahrzeug** nt ABFALL collection body, collection vehicle, dust cart (BrE), garbage truck (AmE), refuse body, refuse collection vehicle, KFZTECH dust cart (BrE), garbage truck (AmE)

Mullins-Effekt m KUNSTSTOFF Mullins effect

Müll: **Müllkippe** f ABFALL illegal dump site, waste dump, waste tip, BAU disposal site, UMWELTSCHMUTZ refuse disposal site; **Müllsack** m ABFALL garbage bag (AmE), rubbish bag (BrE), refuse sack; **Müllsammelfahrzeug** nt ABFALL collection vehicle; **Müllsammlung** f ABFALL garbage collection (AmE), refuse collection (BrE); **Müllschacht** m BAU waste chute; **Müllschlacke** f ABFALL clinker, slag; **Müllschlucker** m ABFALL refuse chute; **Müllsortieranlage** f ABFALL refuse separation plant, sorting plant; **Mülltonne** f ABFALL garbage can (AmE), rubbish bin (BrE), waste container; **Mülltourismus** m ABFALL waste tourism; **Müllumladeanlage** f ABFALL transfer station; **Müllumschlagstation** f ABFALL transfer station; **Müllverbrennung** f ABFALL refuse incineration, trash burning; **Müllverbrennungsanlage** f *(MVA)* ABFALL garbage incineration plant (AmE), refuse incineration plant (BrE), waste incineration plant, waste incinerator, VERPACK garbage incinerator (AmE), refuse incinerator (BrE); **Müllverbrennungsofen** m THERMOD destructor; **Müllverdichter** m ABFALL landfill compactor, packer unit; **Müllverdichtung** f ABFALL compaction, waste compaction; **Müllwagen** m ABFALL collection body, collection vehicle, dust cart (BrE), garbage truck (AmE), refuse body, refuse collection vehicle, KFZTECH dust cart (BrE), garbage truck (AmE), refuse collection lorry; **Müllwagen mit Förderschnecke** m ABFALL screw conveyor; **Müllzerkleinerer** m ABFALL garbage grinder (AmE), refuse grinder (BrE)

Multi- pref COMP & DV, ELEKTROTECH, KÜNSTL INT, OPTIK, TELEKOM, TEXTIL multi-; **Multibussystem** nt COMP & DV multibus system

multidimensional: **~e Stellelemente** nt pl ERGON multidimensional controls

Multi-: **Multifaserkabel** nt OPTIK multifiber cable (AmE), multifibre cable (BrE); **Multifilamentgarn** nt TEXTIL multifilament yarn; **Multifilamentmaschine** f TEXTIL multifilament machine; **Multifilgarn** nt TEXTIL multifilament yarn; **Multifrequenzcode** m *(MFC)* TELEKOM multifrequency code *(MFC)*; **Multikomponentenfaser** f OPTIK *Glasfaser aus mehreren Komponenten* multicomponent glass fiber (AmE), multicomponent glass fibre (BrE); **Multimeter** nt ELEKTROTECH, FERNSEH multimeter; **Multimode-Laser** m TELEKOM multimode laser

multioktav: **~ abstimmbares Filter** nt ELEKTRONIK multioctave-tunable filter; **~ abstimmbarer Oszillator** m ELEKTRONIK multioctave-tunable oscillator

Multi-: **Multioktavabstimmung** f ELEKTRONIK multioctave tuning; **Multiplaybacktechnik** f AKUSTIK multiplayback

Multiplett nt PHYS *Spektrallinien*, TEILPHYS multiplet; **Multiplettaufspaltung** f KERNTECH multiplet splitting

Multiplex nt RAUMFAHRT *Weltraumfunk*, TELEKOM multiplex; **Multiplexbetrieb** m COMP & DV, ELEKTRONIK multiplex operation; **Multiplexen** nt COMP & DV, TELEKOM multiplexing

multiplexen vt ELEKTRONIK, TELEKOM multiplex

Multiplex: **Multiplexen von Signalen** nt ELEKTRONIK signal multiplexing; **Multiplexen mit Zeitteilung** nt *(TDM)* COMP & DV, ELEKTRONIK, TELEKOM time division multiplex *(TDM)*; **Multiplexer** m *(MUX)* COMP & DV, ELEKTRONIK, FERNSEH, TELEKOM multiplexer *(MUX)*; **Multiplexfrequenz** f ELEKTRONIK, RADIO, TELEKOM multiplexing frequency; **Multiplexieren** nt TELEKOM multiplexing

multiplexieren vt ELEKTRONIK, TELEKOM multiplex

Multiplex: **Multiplexkanal** m COMP & DV multiplexer channel, multiplexor channel, ELEKTRONIK multiplex channel; **Multiplexkarton** m PAPIER multilayer board; **Multiplexleitung** f COMP & DV bus (BrE), highway, trunk (AmE); **Multiplexmodus** m COMP & DV multiplex mode; **Multiplexsendung** f FERNSEH multiplex transmission; **Multiplexverfahren** nt COMP & DV multiplex, multiplexing, ELEKTRONIK multiplex

Multiplikand m COMP & DV multiplicand

Multiplikation f COMP & DV, MATH multiplication; **Multiplikationskonstante für infinite Systeme** f *(k)* KERNTECH multiplication constant for an infinite system *(k)*; **Multiplikationstabelle** f MATH multiplication table; **Multiplikationszeichen** nt MATH multiplication sign

multiplikativ adj MATH multiplicative

Multiplikator m COMP & DV multiplier, MATH multiplicand, TELEKOM multiplicator

multiplizieren vt COMP & DV multiply; **~ mit** vt MATH multiply by

Multipliziergerät nt COMP & DV multiplier

Multiplizität f PHYS multiplicity

Multipol m PHYS multipole

Multi-: **Multiprocessing** nt COMP & DV multiprocessing; **Multiprozessor** m COMP & DV multiprocessor; **Multiprozessorsystem** nt COMP & DV, TELEKOM multiprocessor system; **Multiscan-Monitor** m COMP & DV multiscan monitor, multisync monitor; **Multi-Tasking** nt COMP & DV multitasking

multivariat adj ERGON multivariate

Multi-: **Multivibrator** m PHYS, RADIO, TELEKOM multivibrator; **Multizellularlautsprecher** m AKUSTIK multicellular loudspeaker

Mumetall nt PHYS mumetal

Mundblasen nt KER & GLAS mouth blowing

mundgeblasen: **~es Glas** nt KER & GLAS hand-blown glass

mündlich: **~e Verhandlung** f PATENT oral proceedings

Mundloch nt KER & GLAS port; **Mundlochschürze** f KER & GLAS port apron

Mundstück nt BAU nozzle, KER & GLAS die, TELEKOM mouthpiece

Mündung f HYDRAUL Unterwasser, KER & GLAS orifice, WASSERTRANS Geographie mouth; **Mündungsgebiet** nt WASSERTRANS Geographie estuary

Munitionskasten m WASSERTRANS Marine caisson

Münzer m TELEKOM payphone

Münzfernsprecher m TELEKOM coin-operated payphone, payphone

Münzgold nt METALL gold bullion

Münzrelais nt ELEKTRIZ bei Telefonsystem coin box relay

Münzsilber nt METALL silver bullion

Münzzähler m GERÄT prepayment meter

Müon nt PHYS Elementarteilchen muon; **Müonenzerfallsspuren** f pl STRAHLPHYS muon decay tracks; **Müonneutrino** nt PHYS Elementarteilchen muon neutrino

Murexid nt CHEMIE murexide

Muring f WASSERTRANS Festmachen mooring; **Muringgeschirr** nt WASSERTRANS Festmachen mooring gear

Muscarin nt CHEMIE muscarine

muschelförmig: **~e Blisterpackung** f VERPACK clamshell blister

muschelig: **~er Bruch** m KER & GLAS conchoidal fracture

Muschelschale f VERPACK clamshell

musikalisch: **~es Intervall** nt WELLPHYS zwischen zwei Noten musical interval

Musikautomat m OPTIK jukebox

Musikbelastbarkeit f AUFNAHME music-power-handling capacity

Musik-CD f OPTIK CD audio disc (BrE), CD audio disk (AmE), compact audio disc (BrE); **Musik-CD-Spieler** m OPTIK CD audio player

Muskatblütenöl nt LEBENSMITTEL mace oil

Muskeleiweiß nt CHEMIE myosin

Muskelfibrin nt CHEMIE syntonin

Muskelstärke f ERGON muscular strength

muskulär: **~e Ausdauer** f ERGON muscular endurance

Muster nt COMP & DV model, pattern, template, templet, ELEKTRONIK pattern, KOHLEN sample, specimen, KUNSTSTOFF, LABOR specimen, MASCHINEN copy, specimen, MECHAN specimen, PATENT gewerbliches Muster, Geschmackmuster design, QUAL specimen, TELEKOM model, TEXTIL pattern; **~ der Bruchfläche** nt MECHAN breaking pattern; **Musterbuch** nt DRUCK swatchbook; **Mustererfassung** f ELEKTRONIK pattern registration; **Mustererkennung** f COMP & DV pattern recognition, ELEKTRONIK pattern recognition, Litho-

grafie patterning, KÜNSTL INT pattern recognition; **Mustererzeugung** f ELEKTRONIK pattern generation; **Mustergenerator** m FERNSEH pattern generator; **Musterklassifizierung** f KÜNSTL INT pattern classification; **Musterlänge** f TEXTIL pattern length; **Musterlos** nt QUAL pilot lot; **Musterprüfung** f WERKPRÜF sampling; **Mustersortierpumpe** f LABOR sampling pump

Musterung f FERNSEH, TEXTIL patterning

Muster: **Mustervergleich** m COMP & DV, KÜNSTL INT pattern matching; **Musterzeichnung** f TEXTIL pattern

Mutter f AKUSTIK mother, FERTIG, KFZTECH, MASCHINEN, MECHAN nut

Mutterboden m BAU, KOHLEN topsoil; **Mutterbodenabtrag** m BAU topsoil stripping

Mutter: **Muttererde** f KOHLEN top soil; **Mutterfrequenz** f ELEKTRONIK master frequency; **Muttergestein** nt ERDÖL Geologie bedrock, source rock; **Mutterkorn** nt LEBENSMITTEL Getreidekrankheit ergot; **Mutterkornalkaloid** nt CHEMIE ergot alkaloid; **Mutterkristall** m ELEKTRONIK mother crystal; **Mutterlauge** f LEBENSMITTEL mother liquor; **Muttermodell** nt ELEKTRONIK master pattern; **Mutteranziehmaschine** f MASCHINEN nut tightener; **Mutterngewindebohrer** m MASCHINEN nut tap; **Mutterngewindeschneidmaschine** f MASCHINEN nut-threading machine; **Mutternsicherung** f MASCHINEN nut lock; **Mutternuklid** nt KERNTECH, STRAHLPHYS parent nuclide; **Mutternzange** f MASCHINEN nut pliers; **Mutterpause** f KONSTZEICH master print, master tracing; **Mutterplatte** f AKUSTIK mother; **Mutterraumschiff** nt RAUMFAHRT mother ship; **Mutterschiff** nt WASSERTRANS mother ship; **Mutterschloß** nt MASCHINEN half-nut; **Mutterschraube** f BAU bolt and nut; **Muttersteckverbinder** m ELEKTROTECH female connector; **Muttersubstanz** f FERTIG parent

µV abbr (Mikrovolt) ELEKTRIZ, ELEKTROTECH µV (microvolt)

MUX abbr (Multiplexer) COMP & DV, ELEKTRONIK, FERNSEH, TELEKOM MUX (multiplexer)

MVA abbr (Müllverbrennungsanlage) ABFALL garbage incineration plant (AmE), refuse incineration plant (BrE), waste incineration plant, waste incinerator (garbage incineration plant), VERPACK garbage incinerator (AmE), refuse incinerator (BrE)

MW abbr (Mittelwelle) FERNSEH, RADIO MW (medium wave)

MW-Bereich m RADIO MW band

Mx abbr (Maxwell) ELEKTRIZ, ELEKTROTECH Mx (maxwell)

Mycoprotein nt LEBENSMITTEL mycoprotein

Mycotoxin nt LEBENSMITTEL Pflanzenkrankheitslehre mycotoxin

Mylarsockel m FERNSEH mylar base

Myon nt TEILPHYS muon; **Myonneutrino** nt TEILPHYS muon neutrino

Myosin nt CHEMIE myosin

Myrcen nt CHEMIE myrcene

Myria- pref METROL myria; **Myriagramm** nt METROL myriagram

Myristin- pref CHEMIE myristic

Myristyl- pref CHEMIE myristyl

Myron- pref CHEMIE myronic

Myrosin nt CHEMIE myrosin

Mytilotoxin nt CHEMIE mytilotoxin

N

N[1] *abbr* ELEKTRIZ *(Newton)* N *(newton)*, ELEKTRIZ *(Windungszahl)* N *(number of turns in a winding)*, ELEKTRONIK *(Rauschleistung)* N *(noise power)*, HYDRAUL *(Newton)* N *(newton)*, KERNTECH *(Rauschleistung)* N *(noise power)*, LABOR *(Newton)* N *(newton)*, METROL *(Strahlung)*, OPTIK *(Strahlung)* N *(radiance)*, PHYS *(Molekülzahl)* N *(number of molecules)*, STRÖMPHYS *(Newton)* N *(newton)*

N[2] *(Nitrogenium)* CHEMIE N *(nitrogen)*

N$_A$ *abbr (Avogadrosche Zahl, Loschmidtsche Zahl)* PHYS, THERMOD N$_A$ *(Avogadro's number, Loschmidt number)*

n *abbr* ELEKTRIZ *(Neutron)* n *(neutron)*, ELEKTRIZ *(Windungszahl pro Längeneinheit)* n *(turns per unit length)*, KERNTECH *(Neutron)* n *(neutron)*, KERNTECH *(Quantenzahl)*, METROL *(Quantenzahl)* n *(principal quantum number)*, PHYS *(Molekulardichte)* n *(molecular density)*, STRAHLPHYS *(Neutron)*, - TEILPHYS *(Neutron)* n *(neutron)*, THERMOD *(Molekulardichte)* n *(molecular density)*

Na *(Natrium)* CHEMIE Na *(sodium)*

Nabe *f* COMP & DV hub, FERTIG boss, LUFTTRANS *Hubschrauber* hub, MASCHINEN boss, hub

Nabel *m* KER & GLAS, RAUMFAHRT nose; **~ der Glasmacherpfeife** *m* KER & GLAS nose of blowpipe; **Nabelschnur** *f* RAUMFAHRT umbilical cable; **Nabelschnuranschluß** *m* RAUMFAHRT umbilical connector

Nabe: **Nabenabdeckplatte** *f* LUFTTRANS hub cover plate; **Nabenabzieher** *m* MASCHINEN hub extractor, hub puller, MECHAN hub puller; **Nabendeckel** *m* FERTIG *Kunststoffinstallationen* collar cover, KFZTECH *Rad* hubcap; **Nabendeckplatte** *f* LUFTTRANS *Hubschrauber* hub cover plate; **Nabenkappe** *f* KFZTECH *Rad* hubcap; **Nabenkippanschlag** *m* LUFTTRANS *Sperre* hub tilt stop; **Nabenunterlegring** *m* LUFTTRANS *Hubschrauber* hub spacer; **Nabenwulst am Steuerknüppel** *m* LUFTTRANS control column boss

nachabgleichen *vt* GERÄT rebalance

Nachahmung *f* COMP & DV simulation

Nacharbeiten *nt* FERTIG *Spannung* remachining, KER & GLAS touching-up, MASCHINEN remachining

nacharbeiten[1] *vt* FERTIG *Spannung* remachine, QUAL refinish

nacharbeiten[2] *vti* QUAL rework

Nachaudit *nt* QUAL reaudit

Nachbar- *pref* CHEMIE vicinal, FERNSEH, TELEKOM adjacent; **Nachbarkanal** *m* FERNSEH adjacent channel; **Nachbarkanalselektion** *f* TELEKOM adjacent channel selectivity; **Nachbarkanalunterdrückung** *f* TELEKOM adjacent channel rejection; **Nachbarschaft** *f* CHEMIE vicinity, METALL neighbourhood; **Nachbarzeichenstörung** *f* TELEKOM intersymbol interference; **Nachbarzone** *f* THERMOD heat-affected zone

Nachbearbeiten *nt* MASCHINEN remachining

Nachbearbeitung *f* ELEKTRONIK postprocessing; **~ von Daten** *f* COMP & DV postediting

Nachbedienung *f* MECHAN local control

nachbehandeln *vt* BAU *Beton* cure, FERTIG retreat

Nachbehandlung *f* BAU retreatment, MECHAN curing; **Nachbehandlungsfilm** *m* BAU curing membrane; **Nachbehandlungstunnel** *m* BAU curing tunnel; **Nachbehandlungszeit** *f* BAU cure period

Nachbelichtung *f* FOTO postexposure

Nachbeschleunigungs-CRT *f* ELEKTRONIK postaccelerator CRT

Nachbesprechung *f* RAUMFAHRT debriefing

nachbessern *vt* FOTO retouch

Nachbild *nt* ERGON, FERNSEH afterimage

Nachbildung *f* TELEKOM balancing

Nachbildwirkung *f* OPTIK persistence of vision

Nachblasen *nt* FERTIG *Thomasverfahren* Bessemer afterblow

Nachbohren *nt* MASCHINEN reboring

nachbohren *vt* KFZTECH *Motor, Zylinder*, MASCHINEN rebore

Nachbohrung *f* KFZTECH reboring

Nachbrecher *m* KOHLEN secondary crusher

Nachbrennen *nt* METALL, STRAHLPHYS, THERMOD afterglow

Nachbrenner *m* KFZTECH *Motor*, LUFTTRANS, MASCHINEN, THERMOD afterburner

Nachbrennkammer *f* *(SCC)* ABFALL, MASCHINEN afterburner chamber, secondary combustion chamber

nachdecken *vt* TEXTIL cross-dye

Nachdieseln *nt* KFZTECH dieseling

nachdrehen *vt* FERTIG *Spanung*, MASCHINEN re-turn

Nachdrehmaschine *f* MASCHINEN finishing lathe

nachdrucken *vt* DRUCK reprint

nachdunkelnd: ~es Sonnenschutzglas *nt* KER & GLAS solar control glass

nacheichen *vt* FERTIG, QUAL recalibrate

Nacheichung *f* FERTIG, KERNTECH recalibration

Nacheilen *nt* LUFTTRANS *Hubschrauber*, MECHAN lagging

nacheilen *vi* FERTIG *Phase* lag

nacheilend[1] *adj* ELEKTROTECH lagging

nacheilend:[2] **~e Phasenverschiebung** *f* PHYS lag in phase

Nacheilung *f* ELEKTRONIK lag

Nacheilwinkel *m* ELEKTRIZ, MASCHINEN angle of lag

Nachempfindung *f* ERGON aftersensation

nachempfunden: ~es Muster *nt* ELEKTRONIK replicated pattern

Nachentzerrung *f* AUFNAHME de-emphasis, postequalization, FERNSEH de-emphasis

nachfedernd *adj* MECHAN elastic

Nachfließen *nt* KUNSTSTOFF cold flow

Nachflügel *m* LUFTTRANS *Flugzeug* flap

Nachfolger *m* COMP & DV descendant

Nachfolgesatz *m* COMP & DV trailer record

Nachformdrehen *nt* MASCHINEN copy turning

Nachformdrehmaschine *f* MASCHINEN contour lathe, copying lathe

Nachformen *nt* KUNSTSTOFF postforming, MASCHINEN copying

nachformen *vt* MASCHINEN copy

Nachformfräsen *nt* FERTIG copy milling, MASCHINEN

copy milling, profile milling, tracer milling

Nachformfräsmaschine *f* MASCHINEN profile-milling machine, profiler

Nachformfrässchablone *f* FERTIG milling template

Nachformhobeln *nt* FERTIG copy planing

Nachformmaschine *f* MASCHINEN copier, copying machine

Nachformrolle *f* MASCHINEN contour follower, profiling roller

Nachformschleifen *nt* MASCHINEN form grinding

Nachfräsen *nt* FERTIG recutting

nachfräsen *vt* FERTIG recut

Nachfrist *f* PATENT period of grace

Nachführstation *f* RAUMFAHRT tracking station

Nachführung *f* RAUMFAHRT *Raumschiff*, TELEKOM *Antenne* tracking; **Nachführungsantenne** *f* RAUMFAHRT tracking antenna; **Nachführungsfehler** *m* METROL, TELEKOM tracking error; **Nachführungsgenauigkeit** *f* RAUMFAHRT *Weltraumfunk* tracking accuracy

Nachfüllen *nt* EISENBAHN *von Bremsluft* refilling

Nachfülllösung *f* FOTO replenisher

Nachfüllung *f* LEBENSMITTEL, PAPIER refill

Nachgeben *nt* KERNTECH *von Metallen unter Druck* yielding

nachgeben *vi* BAU give way, MASCHINEN yield

nachgeordnet[1] *adj* HEIZ & KÄLTE down-stream

nachgeordnet[2] *adv* BAU downstream

nachgeschaltet[1] *adj* HEIZ & KÄLTE, MASCHINEN downstream

nachgeschaltet:[2] **-es Bauglied** *nt* REGELUNG *des Meßumformers* structural element next in line

Nachgeschmack *m* LEBENSMITTEL aftertaste

nachgewiesen: ~e Lagerstätte *f* ERDÖL proven field; **~e Reserven** *f pl* ERDÖL proven reserves

Nachgiebigkeit *f* METALL yielding

Nachglimmen *nt* STRAHLPHYS, THERMOD afterglow

Nachglühen *nt* RAUMFAHRT *Raumschiff* afterglow

Nachhall *m* AKUSTIK reverberation; **Nachhallmeßgerät** *nt* AUFNAHME reverberation unit; **Nachhallplatte** *f* AUFNAHME reverberation plate; **Nachhallraum** *m* AKUSTIK reverberation room; **Nachhallspirale** *f* AUFNAHME spring reverberation unit; **Nachhallzeit** *f* (*T*) AKUSTIK, AUFNAHME reverberation time (*T*)

Nachhärten *nt* FERTIG afterbake, KUNSTSTOFF age hardening

nachhärten *vt* ANSTRICH *Metall* retemper, FERTIG *Legierungen* age

Nachhauen *nt* FERTIG *Feile* recutting

nachhauen *vt* FERTIG *Feile* recut

nachkalibrieren *vt* QUAL recalibrate

Nachkalibrierung *f* KERNTECH, QUAL recalibration; **Nachkalibrierungsbereich** *m* QUAL recalibration range

Nachklärbecken *nt* ABFALL final settling tank, secondary sedimentation basin, secondary settling tank

Nachklassierung *f* KOHLEN sizing

Nachkommaziffern: ~ des Logarithmus *f pl* COMP & DV mantissa

Nachkühler *m* HEIZ & KÄLTE after cooler

nachlassen *vi* WASSERTRANS *Wind* abate

Nachlauf *m* AUFNAHME tracking, KFZTECH caster action, LUFTTRANS *Hubschrauber* lagging, STRÖMPHYS *eine Zylinder* wake; **Nachlaufachse** *f* KFZTECH trailing axle; **Nachlaufdelle** *f* STRÖMPHYS wake depression; **Nachlauf-Empfangsoszillator** *m* ELEKTRONIK tracking local oscillator

Nachlaufen *nt* FERNSEH lag, trailing, KFZTECH dieseling

nachlaufend: ~e Chrominanz *f* FERNSEH lagging chrominance

Nachlauf: **Nachlauffilter** *nt* ELEKTRONIK tracking filter; **Nachlaufintensität** *f* STRÖMPHYS wake intensity; **Nachlauf-Konfiguration** *f* AUFNAHME tracking configuration; **Nachlaufoszillator** *m* ELEKTRONIK tracking oscillator; **Nachlaufregelung** *f* ELEKTROTECH servomechanism; **Nachlaufwinkel** *m* KFZTECH castor angle

Nachleuchtcharakteristik *f* ELEKTRONIK persistence characteristic, ELEKTROTECH decay characteristic

Nachleuchtdauer *f* COMP & DV afterglow, ELEKTRIZ, ELEKTRONIK, RADIO persistence

Nachleuchten *nt* ELEKTRONIK phosphorescence, *Bildschirm* afterglow, FERNSEH afterglow, KERNTECH hangover, STRAHLPHYS, THERMOD, WASSERTRANS *Radar* afterglow

nachleuchtend: ~e Substanz *f* PHYS phosphor

Nachleuchtung *f* ELEKTRIZ persistence

Nachleuchtzeit *f* ELEKTRONIK *eines Elektronenstrahlröhrenbildschirms* decay time

Nachmahlen *nt* KOHLEN secondary grinding

nachmessen *vti* METROL check the measurements made

Nachmittagsspitze *f* TRANS pm peak

Nachprüfung *f* QUAL check test, repeat test, retest

nachrangig: ~e Verarbeitung *f* COMP & DV *Betriebsart* background processing

Nachricht *f* COMP & DV message, EISENBAHN notice, RADIO, TELEKOM message; **Nachrichten** *f pl* FERNSEH news; **Nachrichtenauslauf** *m* COMP & DV quiescing; **Nachrichtenbehandlung** *f* COMP & DV message handling; **Nachrichteneinheit** *f* COMP & DV message unit; **Nachrichtenempfänger** *m* COMP & DV message sink; **Nachrichtenende** *nt* (*EOM*) COMP & DV end of message (*EOM*); **Nachrichtenkanal** *m* ELEKTROTECH channel; **Nachrichtenkopf** *m* COMP & DV message header, TELEKOM header; **Nachrichtenleitung** *f* ELEKTROTECH communications line; **Nachrichtennetz** *nt* COMP & DV communication network, TELEKOM telecommunication network; **Nachrichtenquelle** *f* COMP & DV information source, message source; **Nachrichtenredaktion** *f* FERNSEH editorial newsroom; **Nachrichtensatellit** *m* (*ComSat*) RAUMFAHRT communication satellite (comsat); **Nachrichtensatz** *m* COMP & DV message set; **Nachrichtensenderkette** *f* FERNSEH news network; **Nachrichtensendung** *f* FERNSEH newscast; **Nachrichtensenke** *f* COMP & DV message sink; **Nachrichtensprecher** *m* FERNSEH newscaster; **Nachrichtenstruktur** *m* COMP & DV message structure; **Nachrichtenstudio** *nt* FERNSEH newsroom; **Nachrichtentechnik** *f* ELEKTRIZ telecommunications engineering; **Nachrichtentext** *m* COMP & DV message text; **Nachrichtenübermittlung** *f* COMP & DV message routing; **Nachrichtenübertragung** *f* COMP & DV message transfer; **Nachrichtenverarbeitung** *f* COMP & DV message processing; **Nachrichtenverarbeitungsgeräte** *nt pl* WASSERTRANS *Kommunikation* message processing equipment; **Nachrichtenvermittlung** *f* COMP & DV message routing, message switching, messaging, TELEKOM message switch; **Nachrichtenvermittlungsnetz** *nt* COMP & DV message-switched network, TELEKOM MSN, message switching network; **Nachrichtenvermittlungsprozessor** *m* TELEKOM message switching processor; **Nachrichtenverteilung** *f* COMP & DV message switching; **Nachrichtenverteilungsnetz** *nt* COMP & DV message-switched network; **Nachrichtenweiterleitung** *f* COMP & DV message routing; **Nachrich-**

tenweitervermittlung *f* COMP & DV message transfer

Nachrüst- *pref* KONTROLL add-on

Nachrüsten *nt* NICHTFOSS ENERG retrofit

nachrüsten *vt* NICHTFOSS ENERG retrofit

Nachrüstung *f* COMP & DV retrofit

Nachsatz *m* COMP & DV tail, trailer, trailer record

Nachschaben *nt* FERTIG *Ziehen* shaving

nachschaben *vt* FERTIG *Ziehen*, MASCHINEN shave

Nachschieberfahrt *f* EISENBAHN pusher operation

Nachschlagetabelle *f* COMP & DV lookup table

Nachschleifen *nt* FERTIG regrinding, MASCHINEN re-sharpening

nachschleifen *vt* FERTIG *Freiwinkel* reback, *Ventilsitz* reface, KOHLEN regrind, MASCHINEN regrind, re-sharpen

Nachschliff *m* MASCHINEN resharpening

Nachschneider *m* FERTIG *Gewinde*, MASCHINEN master tap

Nachschub *m* LUFTTRANS reserves

Nachsetzlüfter *m* HEIZ & KÄLTE make-up fan

Nachsetzmaschine *f* KOHLEN cleaner jig

Nachsorge *f* ABFALL *einer Deponie* monitoring after site closure

Nachspannvorrichtung *f* EISENBAHN wire strainer

Nachsprechmikrofon *nt* AUFNAHME close-talking microphone

Nachspur *f* KFZTECH *Vorderräder* toe-out

nachstellbar: **~e Reibahle** *f* MASCHINEN expanding reamer

Nachstelleiste *f* FERTIG adjustable gib

Nachstellkeil *m* MASCHINEN tightening wedge

Nachstemmen *nt* FERTIG *Niet* recaulking

nachstemmen *vt* FERTIG *Niet* recaulk

Nachstrom *m* LUFTTRANS slipstream

Nachsynchronisieren *nt* AUFNAHME postsynchronization

nachsynchronisiert: **~es Halbbildaustastintervall** *nt* FERNSEH postsync field-blanking interval

Nachsynchronisierung *f* AKUSTIK postscoring

Nachtarbeit *f* SICHERHEIT night work

Nachtbelastung *f* ELEKTROTECH off-peak load

Nachtdienst *m* TELEKOM night service

nachteilig *adj* KERNTECH unfavourable

Nachtphase *f* RAUMFAHRT nocturnal phase

nachträglich:[1] **~ formatiert** *adj* COMP & DV postformatted

nachträglich:[2] **~e Hervorhebung** *f* AUFNAHME *von Tiefen* postemphasis; **~e Schutzeigenschaften** *f pl* SICHERHEIT corrective protective properties

Nachtreichweite *f* LUFTTRANS night range

Nachtrockner *m* PAPIER afterdryer

Nachtspeicherheizgerät *nt* HEIZ & KÄLTE night storage heater; **Nachtspeicherheizung** *f* HEIZ & KÄLTE, THERMOD night storage heating; **Nachtstromspeicherheizung** *f* THERMOD night storage heater; **Nachttarif** *m* ELEKTRIZ night tariff; **Nachtwelle** *f* LUFTTRANS night wave

Nachverarbeitung *f* ELEKTRONIK postprocessing

Nachverbrenner *m* KERNTECH afterburner

Nachverbrennung *f* THERMOD afterburning; **Nachverbrennungskammer** *f* KOHLEN postcombustion chamber

Nachvermessung *f* BAU resurvey

Nachverstärkung *f* FERNSEH postemphasis

Nachvertonen: **~ auf Videomagnetband** *nt* FERNSEH videotape dubbing

Nachvollziehbarkeit *f* QUAL traceability; **~ der Kalibrie-**

rung *f* QUAL, REGELUNG calibration traceability

Nachwahlkennstelle *f* COMP & DV suffix

Nachwärme *f* KERNTECH, LUFTTRANS afterheat

nachwärmen *vt* LEBENSMITTEL *Hartkäse* scald

Nachwärmeofen *m* METALL reheating furnace

Nachweis *m* QUAL evidence, STRAHLPHYS *von Radioaktivität* detection; **Nachweisbarkeit** *f* OPTIK detectivity

nachweisen *vt* QUAL verify; **neu ~** *vt* QUAL re-prove, re-test

Nachweis: **Nachweisgrenze** *f* GERÄT detection limit, limit of detection, OPTIK detection threshold

nachweispflichtig *adj* QUAL requiring verification

Nachweis: **Nachweispunkt** *m* QUAL witness point; **Nachweisschwelle** *f* OPTIK detection threshold; **Nachweisvermögen** *nt* TELEKOM detectivity; **Nachweiszeit** *f* GERÄT detection time

Nachwirkung *f* STRAHLPHYS aftereffect

Nachwuchten *nt* FERTIG rebalancing

nachzeichnen *vt* BAU trace

Nachziehen *nt* FERNSEH smearing, MASCHINEN tracing

nachzuweisend: **~e Qualifikation** *f* QUAL verifiable limit

Nackenschutz *m* SICHERHEIT neck shield

nackt[1] *adj* ELEKTROTECH, FERTIG *Elektrode* bare

nackt:[2] **~er Brand** *m* LEBENSMITTEL *Pflanzenkrankheitslehre* loose smut; **~er Lichtbogen** *m* ELEKTROTECH open arc; **~e Lichtbogen-Ionenquelle** *f* KERNTECH open arc ion source; **~er Reaktor** *m* KERNTECH bare reactor; **~es Teilchen** *nt* KERNTECH bare particle

Nadel *f* AUFNAHME *des Plattenspielers* stylus, GERÄT, KFZTECH *Vergaser* needle, LABOR pointer, MASCHINEN needle roller, PAPIER needle, pin, TEXTIL needle; **Nadelabweichung** *f* PHYS magnetic declination; **Nadelätzen** *nt* KER & GLAS needle etching; **Nadelbalken** *m* TEXTIL needle bar; **Nadelbett** *nt* TEXTIL needle bed; **Nadelbrecher** *m* KOHLEN pick breaker; **Nadeldrucker** *m* COMP & DV dot matrix printer, DRUCK matrix printer; **Nadeldüse** *f* KFZTECH *Vergaser* needle jet; **Nadeleinstell-Skale** *f* LABOR needle dial; **Nadelfeile** *f* MASCHINEN needle file; **Nadelfilz** *m* PAPIER needled felt

nadelförmig[1] *adj* FERTIG, METALL acicular

nadelförmig:[2] **~er Kristall** *m* METALL needle-shaped crystal; **~es Teilchen** *nt* METALL needle-shaped particle; **~e Zone** *f* METALL needle-shaped zone

Nadel: **Nadelgalvanometer** *nt* ELEKTRIZ moving-magnet galvanometer, needle galvanometer; **Nadelgeräusch** *nt* ELEKTRONIK surface noise; **Nadelhalter** *m* AUFNAHME needle holder; **Nadelholz** *nt* BAU softwood; **Nadelhülse** *f* MASCHINEN needle bush; **Nadelkäfig** *m* MASCHINEN needle cage; **Nadellager** *nt* MASCHINEN needle bearing, needle roller bearing; **Nadelloch** *nt* OPTIK pinhole; **Nadel-Nebengeräusch** *nt* AUFNAHME stylus crosstalk; **Nadelöler** *m* MASCHINEN needle lubricator; **Nadelrahmenspannmaschine** *f* TEXTIL pin stenter; **Nadelsteifheit** *f* AKUSTIK stiffness; **Nadelstich** *m* FOTO *auf Negativ oder Foto*, PAPIER pinhole; **Nadeltonquelle** *f* AKUSTIK pinpoint acoustic source; **Nadelventil** *nt* HEIZ & KÄLTE, KERNTECH, KFZTECH, LABOR *Gassteuerung*, MASCHINEN, NICHTFOSS ENERG needle valve; **Nadelventilführung** *f* KFZTECH needle valve guide; **Nadel-Wählscheibe** *f* LABOR needle dial; **Nadelwehr** *nt* WASSERVERSORG needle dam, pin weir; **Nadelzange** *f* MASCHINEN needle-nose pliers; **Nadelzunge** *f* TEXTIL latch

n-adrig: **~es Kabel** *nt* ELEKTROTECH n-core cable

Nagatelit *m* KERNTECH nagatelite

Nagel *m* BAU nail, MASCHINEN nail, spike, MECHAN nail;

~ mit runder Kuppe *m* MASCHINEN clout nail; **Nagelbohrer** *m* BAU gimlet; **Nageldachbinder** *m* BAU nail roof truss; **Nagelklaue** *f* BAU nail claw; **Nagelkopf** *m* MASCHINEN nail head; **Nagelmaschine** *f* VERPACK nailing machine; **Nageltreiber** *m* BAU nail punch; **Nagelzieheisen** *nt* BAU nail claw; **Nagelzieher** *m* BAU nail extractor, VERPACK nail puller

nah:[1] **am ~en Leitungsende** *adj* ELEKTROTECH, TELEKOM near-end

nah:[2] **~es Infrarot** *nt* STRAHLPHYS near infrared; **~es Ultraviolett** *nt* STRAHLPHYS near ultraviolet

Nahaufnahme *f* RAUMFAHRT close-up

Nahbereich *m* KONSTZEICH close-up range; **Nahbereichskabel** *nt* ELEKTROTECH short haul cable

Nahbesprechungs-Empfindlichkeit *f* AKUSTIK close-talking sensitivity

Nahbetrieb *m* TELEKOM local operation

nahebei: ~ angeordnete Spule *f* ELEKTRIZ adjacent coil

Naheinstellansatz *m* FOTO close-up attachment

Nähen *nt* TEXTIL sewing

nähen[1] *vt* TEXTIL sew, stitch

nähen[2] *vi* TEXTIL stitch

Näherei *f* TEXTIL sewing

nähern[1] *vt* GEOM approximate

nähern:[2] **sich ~** *v refl* MATH *einer Lösung oder einem Grenzwert* approximate to, WASSERTRANS *Navigation* approach

Näherung *f* MATH approximation; **durch ~ auftretender Fehler** *m* GERÄT approximative error; **Näherungsfehler** *m* TELEKOM error of approximation; **Näherungslithografie** *f* ELEKTRONIK proximity lithography; **Näherungsschalter** *m* ELEKTRIZ proximity switch, GERÄT approximating pick-up, KONTROLL proximity switch

Nahfeld *nt* OPTIK, TELEKOM near field; **Nahfeld-Abtastverfahren** *nt* OPTIK, TELEKOM near-field scanning technique; **Nahfeldanalyse** *f* TELEKOM near-field analysis; **Nahfeldbereich** *m* OPTIK, TELEKOM near-field region; **Nahfeldbeugungsdiagramm** *nt* TELEKOM near-field diffraction pattern; **Nahfeldbeugungsmuster** *nt* OPTIK near-field diffraction pattern; **Nahfeldbrechungsmethode** *f* TELEKOM refracted near-end method, refracted ray method; **Nahfelddiagramm** *nt* TELEKOM near-field pattern; **Nahfeldmaske aus vier konzentrischen Kreisen** *f* OPTIK four-concentric-circle refractive index template, *zur Bestimmung des Brechungsindex* four-concentric-circle near-field template; **Nahfeldmethode mit Brechung** *f* OPTIK refracted near-field method; **Nahfeldmuster** *nt* OPTIK *Lichtbeugung* near-field pattern; **Nahfeldrasterverfahren** *nt* OPTIK, TELEKOM near-field scanning technique; **Nahfeldstärke** *f* RAUMFAHRT *Weltraumfunk* near-field intensity; **Nahfeldstrahlungsdiagramm** *nt* TELEKOM near-field radiation pattern

Nahfrequenzsignal *nt* ELEKTRONIK, FERNSEH, RADIO close-frequency signal

Nähgarn *nt* TEXTIL sewing cotton

Nähmaschine *f* TEXTIL sewing machine

Nahnebensprechen *nt* ELEKTROTECH, TELEKOM NEXT, near-end crosstalk

nahrhaft *adj* LEBENSMITTEL nutritious, nutritive

Nährstoff *m* LEBENSMITTEL, MEERSCHMUTZ nutrient; **Nährstoffbedarf** *m* LEBENSMITTEL nutrient requirements; **Nährstoffgehalt** *m* LEBENSMITTEL nutrient content; **Nährstoffverlust** *m* LEBENSMITTEL nutrient loss

Nahrungsaufnahme *f* LEBENSMITTEL ingestion

Nahrungsbedarf *m* LEBENSMITTEL food requirements

Nährwert *m* LEBENSMITTEL nutritive value

Nähseide *f* TEXTIL sewing silk

Naht *f* BAU *Schweißen*, FERTIG *Nahtschweißen*, KER & GLAS, MASCHINEN, MECHAN, PAPIER, TEXTIL seam; **~ des Maschinensiebs** *f* PAPIER seam of the machine wire; **Nahtbasis** *f* MECHAN root; **Nahtbildung** *f* FERTIG *Gießen* finning; **Nahtdicke** *f* FERTIG throat thickness, *Schweißen* throat

Nahteil *nt* KER & GLAS short vision segment

Naht: Nahthöhe *f* FERTIG *Kehlnaht* actual throat of fillet weld; **Nahtlinie** *f* KER & GLAS seam line

nahtlos[1] *adj* FERTIG *Rohr*, MASCHINEN *Rohr* weldless, TEXTIL seamless; **~ gewalzt** *adj* MASCHINEN seamless rolled

nahtlos:[2] **~ gezogenes Stahlrohr** *nt* MASCHINEN solid-drawn steel tube

Naht: Nahtschweißung *f* FERTIG *Hammerschweißen* scarf weld, KERNTECH seam weld, MASCHINEN seam welding; **Nahtstellenüberwachung** *f* QUAL interface control; **Nahtvorbereitung** *f* METALL *Schweißarbeiten* joint preparation

Nahverkehr *m* EISENBAHN light rail transit (AmE), light rail transport (BrE), TRANS local traffic; **Nahverkehrsinformation** *f* TRANS local traffic information; **Nahverkehrszug** *m* EISENBAHN stopping train (AmE)

Name *m* COMP & DV name; **~ der Zeichenfolge** *m* COMP & DV string name; **Namensaufruf** *m* COMP & DV call by name; **Namenstaste** *f* TELEKOM name key; **Namensverzeichnis** *nt* TELEKOM name server

NAND: NAND-Funktion *f* (*UND-NICHT-Verknüpfung*) COMP & DV NAND operation *(NOT AND operation)*; **NAND-Gate** *nt* COMP & DV NAND gate, NOT AND gate; **NAND-Gatter** *nt* ELEKTRONIK NAND gate, PHYS NAND gate; **NAND-Gatter mit drei Eingängen** *nt* ELEKTRONIK three-input NAND gate; **NAND-Glied** *nt* ELEKTRONIK NAND circuit; **NAND-Tor** *nt* (*UND-Glied mit negiertem Ausgang*) COMP & DV NAND gate *(NOT AND gate)*; **NAND-Verknüpfung** *f* COMP & DV NAND operation

Nano- *pref* METROL nano-; **Nanosekunde** *f* COMP & DV, FERNSEH nanosecond

Napalm *nt* THERMOD napalm

Näpfchenziehversuch *m* FERTIG cupping test

Naphtha *f* CHEMIE, THERMOD naphtha

Naphthacen *nt* CHEMIE naphthacene

Naphthalen *nt* CHEMIE naphthalene; **Naphthalendisulfonsäure** *f* CHEMIE naphthalenedisulfonic acid (AmE), naphthalenedisulphonic acid (BrE)

Naphthalin *nt* CHEMIE naphthalene; **Naphthalin-** *pref* CHEMIE naphthalenic

Naphthan *nt* CHEMIE decahydronaphthalene, decalin, naphthane

Naphthen *nt* CHEMIE cyclane, cycloalkane, naphthene

Naphthenat *nt* CHEMIE naphthenate

naphthenisch *adj* CHEMIE naphthenic

Naphthion- *pref* CHEMIE naphthionic

Naphthochinon *nt* CHEMIE dihydrodiketonaphthalene, naphthoquinone

Naphthoe- *pref* CHEMIE naphthoic

Naphthol *nt* CHEMIE naphthol

Naphtholsulfon- *pref* CHEMIE naphtholsulfonic (AmE), naphtholsulphonic (BrE)

Naphthophenantren *nt* CHEMIE dibenzanthracene, naphthophenanthrene

Naphthoxazin *nt* CHEMIE naphtoxazine, phenoxazine

Naphthoyl- *pref* CHEMIE naphthoyl

Naphthyl- *pref* CHEMIE naphthyl; **Naphthylamin** *nt* CHEMIE naphthylamine

Naphthylen- *pref* CHEMIE naphthylene

Naphtylbenzoylester *m* CHEMIE benzonaphthol

narbig *adj* FERTIG pitted

Narbmaschine *f* PAPIER graining machine

Narbung *f* FERTIG grain, KER & GLAS pocking, PAPIER graining

Narcein *nt* CHEMIE narceine

Narcotin *nt* CHEMIE narcotine, opianine

Naringenin *nt* CHEMIE naringenin, trihydroxyflavanone

Naringin *nt* CHEMIE, LEBENSMITTEL naringin

NASA *abbr (Nordamerikanische Weltraumbehörde)* RAUMFAHRT NASA *(National Aeronautics and Space Administration)*

Nase *f* ELEKTROTECH *Röhre* aligning plug, FERTIG catch, cog, lug, KFZTECH stud, MASCHINEN catch, lug, RAUMFAHRT *Raumschiff* nose cone

nasenförmig: ~e **Kreuzung** *f* EISENBAHN swing nose crossing

Nase: Nasenkegel *m* LUFTTRANS nose cone; **Nasenkeil** *m* MASCHINEN gib, gib-head key, nose key; **Nasenklappe** *f* LUFTTRANS droop flap, leading-edge flap; **Nasenkonus** *m* AUFNAHME, LUFTTRANS nose cone; **Nasenring** *m* KERNTECH, KFZTECH *Motor* oil scraper ring; **Nasenstein** *m* KER & GLAS plate block; **Nasenwelle** *f* LUFTTRANS bow wave

Naß- *pref* KOHLEN, UMWELTSCHMUTZ, WASSERVERSORG wet; **Naß- und Trockenschleifen** *nt* KER & GLAS wet and dry polishing

naß[1] *adj* FERTIG *Verfahren* hydrometallurgical, PAPIER, TEXTIL, THERMOD wet; **~ anzufeuchtendes Etikett** *nt* VERPACK wet glue label; **~ in naß** *adj* KUNSTSTOFF wet on wet

naß:[2] **nasser saurer Niederschlag** *m* UMWELTSCHMUTZ wet acidic fallout

Naß-: Naßablagerung *f* UMWELTSCHMUTZ wet deposition; **Naßabscheider** *m* ABFALL wet scrubber, wet scrubbing device, CHEMTECH washer, UMWELTSCHMUTZ wet scrubber; **Naßabscheidung** *f* UMWELTSCHMUTZ wet precipitation; **Naßabsorber** *m* ABFALL wet scrubber, wet scrubbing device; **Naßaluminiumkondensator** *m* ELEKTROTECH wet aluminium capacitor (BrE), wet aluminum capacitor (AmE); **Naßausschuß** *m* PAPIER wet broke; **Naßbagger** *m* BAU grab dredger, MEERSCHMUTZ dredger, WASSERVERSORG river dredge; **Naßbehandlung** *f* KOHLEN, MASCHINEN wet treatment

naßbeständig *adj* THERMOD humidity-resistant

Naß-: Naßdampf *m* HEIZ & KÄLTE saturated steam, MASCHINEN, NICHTFOSS ENERG, THERMOD wet steam; **Naßdehnung** *f* PAPIER damping stretch

Nässe: vor ~ schützen *vt* VERPACK keep dry

Naß-: Naßelement *nt* ELEKTROTECH wet cell

nässen *vt* PHYS wet

Naß-: Naßentschwefelungsprozeß *m* UMWELTSCHMUTZ wet desulfurization process (AmE), wet desulphurization process (BrE); **Naßerdgas** *nt* ERDÖL wet natural gas; **Naßeruptionskreuz** *nt* ERDÖL wet tree; **Naßfäule** *f* BAU *Holz* wet rot

naßfest: ~es **Papier** *nt* PAPIER wet-strength paper

Naß-: Naßfestigkeit *f* KUNSTSTOFF wet strength; **Naßgas** *nt* ERDÖL wet natural gas; **Naßguß** *m* FERTIG green mold casting (AmE), green mould casting (BrE); **Naßgußsand** *m* FERTIG green sand

naßklassieren *vt* KOHLEN classify

Naß-: Naßkollodiumverfahren *nt* DRUCK, FOTO wet collodion process; **Naßkupplung** *f* MASCHINEN wet clutch; **Naßluftfilter** *nt* HEIZ & KÄLTE wet air filter

naßmachen *vt* THERMOD wet

Naß-: Naßmahlung *f* KOHLEN wet grinding; **Naßoxidation** *f* ABFALL WAO, wet air oxidation; **Naßpartie** *f* PAPIER wet end; **Naßperiode** *f* UMWELTSCHMUTZ wet period; **Naßplattenverfahren** *nt* DRUCK wet-plate process; **Naßpresse** *f* PAPIER wet press; **Naßprobe** *f* CHEMIE, KOHLEN wet assay; **Naßputzen** *nt* FERTIG liquid honing; **Naßradom** *m* TELEKOM wet radome; **Naßreiniger** *m* KERNTECH, KOHLEN scrubber; **Naßreinigung** *f* UMWELTSCHMUTZ wet scrubbing; **Naßschlamm** *m* ABFALL liquid sludge, slurry; **Naßschleifen** *nt* KER & GLAS wet polishing, MASCHINEN wet grinding; **Naßschleifmaschine** *f* FERTIG wet grinder, MASCHINEN wet-grinding machine; **Naßsieberei** *f* KOHLEN wet screening; **Naßspulen-Tantalkondensator** *m* ELEKTROTECH wet-slug tantalum capacitor; **Naßthermometer** *nt* HEIZ & KÄLTE wet-bulb thermometer; **Naßtreibstoff** *m* LUFTTRANS emulsified fuel; **Naßtrennverfahren** *nt* ABFALL *von Müll* wet sorting; **Naßwaschanlage** *f* SICHERHEIT wet washer; **Naßwäscher** *m* ABFALL wet scrubber, wet scrubbing device; **Naßzyklon** *m* CHEMTECH hydrocyclone; **Naßzylinderlaufbuchse** *f* KFZTECH wet cylinder liner

national: ~er **Code** *m* TELEKOM national code; ~es **Normal** *nt* QUAL national standard; ~es **Patent** *nt* PATENT national patent; ~es **Stromnetz** *nt* ELEKTRIZ, KERNTECH national grid

Nationalflagge *f* WASSERTRANS ensign

Nationalitätskennungsziffern *f pl* TELEKOM NID, nationality identification digits

Natrium *nt (Na)* CHEMIE sodium *(Na)*; **Natriumalginat** *nt* LEBENSMITTEL sodium alginate; **Natriumamid** *nt* CHEMIE sodamide; **Natrium-Ammonium-Hydrogenphosphat-Tetrahydrat** *nt* CHEMIE microcosmic salt

natriumarm: ~es **Salz** *nt* LEBENSMITTEL reduced sodium salt

Natrium: Natriumbicarbonat *nt* LEBENSMITTEL baking soda, bicarbonate of soda, sodium bicarbonate; **Natriumbogenlampe** *f* STRAHLPHYS sodium arc lamp; **Natriumcaseinat** *nt* LEBENSMITTEL sodium caseinate; **Natrium-D-Linie** *f* PHYS *Atomphysik* sodium D-line

natriumgekühlt: ~er **Reaktor** *m* KERNTECH sodium-cooled reactor; ~es **Ventil** *nt* KFZTECH sodium-cooled valve

Natrium: Natriumglutamat *nt* LEBENSMITTEL monosodium glutamate; **Natriumhydrogencarbonat** *nt* LEBENSMITTEL baking soda, bicarbonate of soda, sodium bicarbonate; **Natriumhydrosulfit** *nt* CHEMIE hydrosulfite (AmE), hydrosulphite (BrE); **Natriumlampe** *f* ELEKTRIZ sodium lamp; **Natriumpolyphosphat** *nt* LEBENSMITTEL sodium polyphosphate; **Natrium-Schwefel-Akkumulator** *m* TRANS sodium sulfur storage battery (AmE), sodium sulphur storage battery (BrE); **Natriumsulfat** *nt* KER & GLAS saltcake; **Natriumtetraborat** *nt* CHEMIE sodium borate

Natron *nt* KER & GLAS soda, LEBENSMITTEL baking soda, PAPIER soda; **Natronlauge** *f* FERTIG *Kunststoffinstallationen* caustic soda; **Natronsalpeter** *m* CHEMIE nitratine, KER & GLAS soda niter (AmE), soda nitre (BrE), sodium nitrate; **Natronzellstoff** *m* PAPIER soda pulp

Natur *f* BAU nature; **Naturasphalt** *m* BAU mineral pitch; **Naturbaustein** *m* BAU building stone

naturbelassen *adj* LEBENSMITTEL unrefined

Natur: **Natureckstein** *m* BAU *beidseitig sichtbar* perpend stone; **Naturfaser** *f* TEXTIL natural fiber (AmE), natural fibre (BrE); **Naturgasbus** *m* TRANS bus with pressurized natural gas; **Naturgasmotor** *m* KFZTECH natural gas engine; **Naturgröße** *f* KONSTZEICH full-scale representation, full-size representation; **Naturharz** *nt* FERTIG vegetable resin; **Natur-Hochtransparentpapier** *nt* KONSTZEICH natural high transparency paper; **Naturholzfarbe** *f* BAU oleoresinous paint

naturidentisch *adj* LEBENSMITTEL nature-identical

Natur: **Naturkautschuk** *m (NK)* KUNSTSTOFF natural rubber *(NR)*; **Naturkraft** *f* UMWELTSCHMUTZ physical agent

natürlich:[1] ~ **gealtert** *adj* THERMOD naturally-aged

natürlich:[2] ~**e Abdichtung** *f* ABFALL *einer Deponie* natural lining; ~**e Abnutzung** *f* MASCHINEN wear and tear; ~**es Altern** *nt* METALL natural ageing (BrE), natural aging (AmE); ~**e Alterung** *f* KUNSTSTOFF, THERMOD natural ageing (BrE), natural aging (AmE); ~**e Belüftung** *f* KERNTECH natural ventilation; ~ **bewegtes Kühlmittel** *nt* HEIZ & KÄLTE naturally-circulated coolant; ~**er Böschungswinkel** *m* BAU angle of repose; ~**e Breite** *f* KERNTECH *eines Energieniveaus* natural width; ~**e Entwässerung** *f* WASSERVERSORG natural drainage; ~**e Farben** *f pl* DRUCK true colours; ~**e Grundbelastung** *f* UMWELTSCHMUTZ background level; ~**e Grundwasserregenerierung** *f* WASSERVERSORG natural ground water recharge; ~**er Hafen** *m* WASSERTRANS natural harbor (AmE), natural harbour (BrE); ~**e Konvektion** *f* STRÖMPHYS natural convection; ~**e Konvektionskühlung** *f* HEIZ & KÄLTE, KERNTECH natural convection cooling; ~**e Koordinaten** *f pl* GEOM natural coordinates; ~**e Linienbreite** *f* STRAHLPHYS natural line width; ~**e Logarithmen** *m pl* MATH Naperian logarithms; ~**e Luftbewegung** *f* HEIZ & KÄLTE natural air circulation; ~**e Luftkühlung** *f* HEIZ & KÄLTE natural air cooling; ~**er Luftstrom** *m* HEIZ & KÄLTE natural draft (AmE), natural draught (BrE); ~**e Luftumwälzung** *f* HEIZ & KÄLTE natural air circulation; ~**er Luftzug** *m* HEIZ & KÄLTE natural draft (AmE), natural draught (BrE); ~**e Person** *f* PATENT natural person; ~**e Radioaktivität** *f* STRAHLPHYS natural radioactivity; ~**e Säuerung** *f* UMWELTSCHMUTZ natural acidification; ~**e Schwingung** *f* MASCHINEN natural oscillation; ~**e Sprache** *f* COMP & DV, KÜNSTL INT NL, natural language; ~**e Sprachverarbeitung** *f* KÜNSTL INT NLP, natural language processing; ~**e Umwelt** *f* UMWELTSCHMUTZ, WASSERVERSORG natural environment; ~ **vorkommendes Element** *nt* KERNTECH naturally occurring element; ~ **vorkommendes Radionuklid** *nt* STRAHLPHYS natural radionuclide; ~**e Zahl** *f* COMP & DV natural number; ~**er Zug** *m* HEIZ & KÄLTE natural draft (AmE), natural draught (BrE)

natürlichsprachlich: ~**e Schnittstelle** *f* KÜNSTL INT NLI, natural language interface

natursauer: ~**er See** *m* UMWELTSCHMUTZ naturally acid lake

Natursteinplatte *f* BAU flag

Natururan *nt* KERNTECH natural uranium; **Natururanblock** *m* KERNTECH *als Brennstoff* natural uranium slug; **Natururanbrennstoff** *m* KERNTECH natural uranium fuel; **Natururanreaktor** *m* KERNTECH uranium reactor

Nautik *f* WASSERTRANS navigation

Nautiker *m* WASSERTRANS navigator

nautisch[1] *adj* WASSERTRANS nautical

nautisch:[2] ~**es Instrument** *nt* WASSERTRANS navigational instrument; ~**es Jahrbuch** *nt* WASSERTRANS nautical almanac

Navier-Stokes: ~**sche Gleichung** *f* PHYS, STRÖMPHYS Navier-Stokes equation

Navigation *f* LUFTTRANS, WASSERTRANS navigation; ~ **nach Lotreihen** *f* WASSERTRANS navigation by sounding; **Navigationsgerät** *nt* WASSERTRANS navigational instrument; **Navigationsgerät für Horizontallage** *nt* LUFTTRANS horizontal situation indicator; **Navigationshilfe** *f* WASSERTRANS navigational aid; **Navigationsradar** *nt* WASSERTRANS navigation radar; **Navigationssatellitensystem** *nt (NNSS)* WASSERTRANS *der US-Marine* Navy Navigation Satellite System *(NNSS)*

Navigator *m* WASSERTRANS navigator

navigatorisch *adj* WASSERTRANS navigational

navigieren[1] *vt* WASSERTRANS navigate

navigieren[2] *vi* WASSERTRANS navigate

Naviplan *nt* WASSERTRANS naviplane

Nb *(Niobium)* CHEMIE Cb, Nb *(columbium)*

NC *abbr (numerische Steuerung)* COMP & DV, ELEKTRIZ, KONTROLL, MASCHINEN, MECHAN NC *(numerical control)*

NC-Maschine *f* MASCHINEN NC machine

Nd *(Neodymium)* CHEMIE Nd *(neodymium)*

Nebel *m* WASSERTRANS fog; **Nebelhorn** *nt* WASSERTRANS *Navigation* foghorn; **Nebelkammer** *f* TEILPHYS, WELLPHYS *um Strahlung nachzuweisen* cloud chamber; **Nebelleuchte** *f* KFZTECH, WASSERTRANS fog lamp; **Nebelsignal** *nt* WASSERTRANS fog signal; **Nebelwarnung** *f* WASSERTRANS fog warning

Neben- *pref* ERGON secondary, GEOM minor, MASCHINEN minor, secondary; **Neben- und Hauptwartungsleistung** *f* LUFTTRANS minor and major servicing operation; **Nebenachse** *f* GEOM *einer Ellipse* minor axis; **Nebenaufgabe** *f* ERGON secondary task; **Nebenausfall** *m* QUAL minor failure; **Nebencomputer** *m* COMP & DV slave; **Nebendarstellung** *f* KONSTZEICH secondary representation; **Nebeneffekt** *m* COMP & DV side effect

nebeneinander: ~ **geordnetes Fenster** *nt* COMP & DV tiled window

nebeneinanderliegend: ~**e Zylinder** *m pl* MASCHINEN side-by-side cylinders

Neben-: **Nebeneinanderschaltung** *f* ELEKTROTECH parallel arrangement; **Nebenfehler** *m* QUAL minor defect, minor non-conformance, minor non-conformity; **Nebenfluß** *m* WASSERTRANS *Geographie* tributary of river; **Nebengebäude** *nt* BAU outbuilding; **Nebengeräusch** *nt* AUFNAHME ambient noise, TELEKOM sidetone

nebengeschaltet *adj* ELEKTRIZ parallel, ELEKTROTECH parallel-connected

Neben-: **Nebengetriebe** *nt* FERTIG power takeoff; **Nebengleis** *nt* BAU spur track; **Nebengrundwasserspiegel** *m* WASSERVERSORG apparent water table; **Nebenkanalstörung durch Lagefehler** *f* FERNSEH positional crosstalk; **Nebenkeule** *f* PHYS, RAUMFAHRT *Weltraumfunk*, WASSERTRANS *Radar* side lobe; **Nebenlinie** *f* EISENBAHN branch line; **Nebenluft** *f* HEIZ & KÄLTE secondary air, KFZTECH air leak, MASCHINEN secondary air; **Nebenpleuelstange** *f* FERTIG auxiliary connecting rod; **Nebenprodukt** *nt* ERDÖL, KOHLEN, MASCHINEN, UMWELTSCHMUTZ by-product; **Nebenquelle** *f* ELEKTRONIK companion source; **Nebensammler** *m* WASSERVERSORG branch sewer

Nebenschluß *m* AKUSTIK shunt, ELEKTROTECH leakage path, shunt; **als ~ gewickelter Dynamo** *m* ELEKTROTECH shunt-wound dynamo; **als ~ gewickelter Motor** *m* ELEKTROTECH shunt-wound motor; **Nebenschlußdynamo** *m* ELEKTROTECH shunt dynamo; **Nebenschlußeinrichtung** *f* EISENBAHN shunter; **Nebenschlußelement** *nt* ELEKTRIZ shunting device; **Nebenschlußerregung** *f* ELEKTROTECH shunt excitation; **Nebenschlußkondensator** *m* GERÄT bypass capacitor; **Nebenschlußmotor** *m* ELEKTRIZ, ELEKTROTECH shunt motor; **Nebenschlußregler** *m* ELEKTROTECH shunt regulator; **Nebenschlußschalter** *m* ELEKTRIZ shunt switch, shunting switch; **Nebenschlußspule** *f* ELEKTROTECH shunt coil; **Nebenschlußstrom** *m* ELEKTROTECH shunt current; **Nebenschlußstromkreis** *m* ELEKTROTECH shunt circuit; **Nebenschlußwicklung** *f* ELEKTRIZ, ELEKTROTECH shunt winding; **Nebenschlußwiderstand** *m* ELEKTRIZ shunt, ELEKTROTECH shunt resistance, shunt resistor, shunt

Neben-: **Nebenschneide** *f* MASCHINEN minor cutting edge; **Nebenspannung** *f* KERNTECH secondary stress; **Nebenspeicher** *m* COMP & DV slave cache, slave store; **Nebensprechabstand** *m* ELEKTRONIK signal-to-crosstalk ratio; **Nebensprechdämpfung** *f* AUFNAHME crosstalk rejection, TELEKOM crosstalk attenuation; **Nebensprechdämpfungsmesser** *m* AUFNAHME crosstalk meter; **Nebensprecheinheit** *f* AUFNAHME crosstalk unit; **Nebensprechen** *nt* AKUSTIK, AUFNAHME, COMP & DV, FERNSEH, TELEKOM crosstalk

Nebenstelle *f* TELEKOM telephone extension; **Nebenstellenanlage mit Handvermittlung** *f* TELEKOM PMBX, private manual branch exchange; **Nebenstellenvermittlung** *f* TELEKOM PBX switchboard

Neben-: **Nebenstrahlung** *f* FERNSEH parasitic radiation; **Nebenstraße** *f* BAU byroad, byway, TRANS cross-country road; **Nebenstromluft** *f* RAUMFAHRT bypass air; **Nebenstromölfilter** *nt* KFZTECH bypass oil cleaner; **Nebenweganode** *f* ELEKTROTECH bypass anode; **Nebenzipfel** *m* ELEKTRONIK, PHYS side lobe; **Nebenzipfelunterdrückung** *f* ELEKTRONIK side lobe cancellation

Néel: **~scher Punkt** *m* PHYS Néel point; **~sche Temperatur** *f* ELEKTRIZ Néel temperature

Negation *f* COMP & DV NOT operation, negation

Negativ *nt* DRUCK, FOTO negative

negativ[1] *adj* ELEKTRIZ, MATH negative; **mit ~ em Lichtleitfähigkeits-Koeffizienten** *adj* FOTO light-negative

negativ:[2] **~e Anschlußklemme** *f* ELEKTRIZ, ELEKTROTECH, KFZTECH negative terminal; **~e Beschleunigung** *f* MASCHINEN minus acceleration; **~e Bildphase** *f* FERNSEH negative picture phase; **~e Charakteristik** *f* ELEKTROTECH negative resistance characteristic; **~ dotierte Zone** *f* PHYS negatively-doped region; **~e Elektrode** *f* ELEKTRIZ negative electrode, ELEKTROTECH cathode, negative electrode; **~e ganze Zahl** *f* MATH negative integer; **~ geerdete Anschlußklemme** *f* KFZTECH negative grounded terminal; **~ geerdeter Pol** *m* KFZTECH negative grounded terminal; **~ geladenes Ion** *nt* ELEKTRIZ, KOHLEN, PHYS, STRAHLPHYS negative ion; **~es Glimmlicht** *nt* PHYS negative glow; **~e Impedanz** *f* ELEKTROTECH negative impedance; **~e Konduktanz** *f* ELEKTRIZ negative conductance; **~e Kontaktbank** *f* KFZTECH negative bank; **~e Krümmung** *f* GEOM negative curvature; **~e Ladung** *f* ELEKTRIZ, ELEKTROTECH, PHYS negative charge; **~e Logik** *f* ELEKTRONIK negative logic; **~e Magnetostriktion** *f* ELEKTROTECH negative magnetostriction; **~e Mantelreibung** *f* KOHLEN negative skin friction; **~er Meniskus** *m* FOTO divergent meniscus; **~e Platte** *f* KFZTECH negative plate; **~er Pol** *m* ELEKTRIZ negative pole, ELEKTROTECH cathode, negative pole; **~e Profilverschiebung** *f* FERTIG *Getriebelehre* diameter decrease; **~e Quittung** *f* COMP & DV, TELEKOM NAK, negative acknowledgement; **~er Radsturz** *m* KFZTECH negative camber; **~e Reaktivität** *f* KERNTECH negative reactivity; **~er Reaktor** *m* KERNTECH negative reactor; **~e Rückkopplung** *f* AUFNAHME negative feedback, ELEKTRONIK inverse feedback, negative feedback, WELLPHYS negative feedback; **~e Rückmeldung** *f* COMP & DV, TELEKOM NAK, negative acknowledgement; **~e Spannung** *f* ELEKTROTECH negative voltage; **~e Spannungsgegenkopplung** *f* ELEKTROTECH voltage feedback; **~e Spannungsversorgung** *f* ELEKTROTECH negative voltage supply; **~er Spanwinkel** *m* FERTIG, MASCHINEN negative rake; **~e Speiseleitung** *f* ELEKTRIZ negative feeder; **~er Sprung** *m* WASSERTRANS *Schiffbau* reverse sheer; **~e Steigung** *f* LUFTTRANS *Propeller* reverse pitch; **~e Stromversorgung** *f* ELEKTROTECH negative power supply; **~es Videosignal** *nt* FERNSEH negative video signal; **~e Vorspannung** *f* ELEKTROTECH negative bias; **~e Vorspur** *f* KFZTECH *Vorderräder* toe-out; **~er Widerstand** *m* ELEKTRIZ, ELEKTROTECH negative resistance; **~er Winkel** *m* GEOM negative angle; **~e Zahl** *f* MATH negative number; **nicht ~e Zahlen** *f pl* MATH nonnegative numbers

Negativ: **Negativabtastung** *f* FERNSEH negative scanning; **Negativabzug** *m* FOTO negative print; **Negativbetrachter** *m* FOTO negative viewer; **Negativbild** *nt* FOTO negative image; **Negativecho** *nt* FERNSEH negative echo; **Negativfilm** *m* DRUCK negative film; **Negativfotolack** *m* ELEKTRONIK negative photoresist; **Negativfotoresist** *m* ELEKTRONIK negative photoresist; **Negativhalter** *m* FOTO negative carrier; **Negativlack** *m* ELEKTRONIK negative resist; **Negativlichtpausfilm** *m* KONSTZEICH negative diazotype film; **Negativlinse** *f* FOTO concave lens; **Negativluftkissen** *nt* KFZTECH negative air cushion; **Negativmodulation** *f* ELEKTRONIK negative modulation; **Negativstopfen** *nt* TELEKOM negative justification; **Negativtasche** *f* FOTO negative sleeve; **Negativwiderstandsdiode** *f* ELEKTRONIK negative resistance diode; **Negativwiderstandsoszillator** *m* ELEKTRONIK negative resistance oscillator; **Negativwiderstandsverstärker** *m* ELEKTRONIK negative resistance amplifier

Negator *m* COMP & DV negator

Negatron *nt* ELEKTRONIK negatron

Neger *m* FERNSEH caption stand, prompter

Negierung *f* COMP & DV negation

Nehmerzylinder *m* KFZTECH *Bremsen, Kupplung* slave cylinder

neigbar: **~er Mattscheibenrahmen** *m* FOTO swinging back

Neigekopf *m* FOTO *Vergrößerer* tilting head

neigen[1] *vt* BAU lean, sink

neigen:[2] **sich ~** *v refl* BAU lean

Neigung *f* BAU batter, falling gradient, inclination, incline, pitch, slant, *eines Daches* slope, FERTIG slant, splay, tilt, GEOM inclination, slope, MASCHINEN incline, MECHAN bevel, NICHTFOSS ENERG declination, PHYS inclination, RAUMFAHRT inclination, pitch; **Neigungsebene** *f* BAU inclined plane; **Neigungsmesser** *m* BAU clinometer, slope level, *Vermessung* batter level, KOHLEN clinometer, inclinometer, METROL clinometer; **Neigungsverhältnis** *nt* EISENBAHN gradient ratio; **Neigungswinkel** *m* FERTIG, GEOM angle of inclination, KER & GLAS angle of pitch, KFZTECH *Straße* camber, MECHAN bevel; **Neigungszeiger** *m* EISENBAHN gradient post

Nein-Schaltung *f* ELEKTRONIK inverter gate

nematisch: **~er Flüssigkristall** *m* ELEKTRONIK nematic liquid crystal

Nematode *f* LEBENSMITTEL eelworm

Nennabschaltstrom *m* ELEKTRIZ admissible interrupting current, rated interrupting current

Nennbedingungen *f pl* ELEKTROTECH rated conditions

Nennbelastbarkeit *f* ELEKTROTECH power rating

Nennbetriebsbedingungen *f pl* RAUMFAHRT *Raumschiff* nominal operating conditions

Nennbohrung *f* KERNTECH NB, nominal bore

Nenndaten *nt pl* PHYS rating

Nenndicke *f* WERKPRÜF *Glas* nominal thickness

Nenndruck *m* FERTIG *Kunststoffinstallationen* nominal pressure, MASCHINEN pressure rating

Nenndurchlauf *m* COMP & DV rated throughput

Nenndurchmesser *m* MASCHINEN nominal diameter

Nenndurchsatz *m* HEIZ & KÄLTE design water rate

Nenner *m* MATH denominator

Nennfrequenz *f* ELEKTRIZ rated frequency

Nenngehalt *m* VERPACK nominal content

Nenngröße *f* MASCHINEN, VERPACK nominal size

Nennheizleistung *f* HEIZ & KÄLTE rated heat output

Nennkapazität *f* ELEKTROTECH rating

Nennlast *f* ELEKTRIZ allowable load, full load, nominal load, ELEKTROTECH rated load, VERPACK effective load

Nennleistung *f* AUFNAHME power rating, COMP & DV rated output, ELEKTRIZ rated power, rating, ELEKTROTECH power rating, HEIZ & KÄLTE rating, KER & GLAS nominal capacity, KERNTECH *eines Reaktors* rated power capacity, KOHLEN rated capacity, MASCHINEN power rating, rated capacity, rated power, rating; **Nennleistungshöhe** *f* LUFTTRANS rated altitude

Nennlichtstärke *f* FOTO effective candle power

Nennmaß *nt* MASCHINEN nominal size, QUAL basic size

Nennmeßbereich *m* METROL rating

Nennmeßgenauigkeit *f* METROL rated accuracy

Nennöffnung *f* FOTO effective aperture; **~ eines Objektivs** *f* FOTO effective aperture of a lens

Nennschließstrom *m* ELEKTRIZ rated making capacity

Nennschub *m* RAUMFAHRT *im Vakuum* nominal thrust

Nennschweißstrom *m* BAU rated welding current

Nennspannung *f* ELEKTRIZ rated voltage, *eines Systems* nominal voltage, ELEKTROTECH full voltage, rated voltage, METALL nominal stress; **Nennspannungsfestigkeit der Isolierung** *f* ELEKTRIZ rated insulation level

Nennstärke *f* WERKPRÜF nominal thickness

Nennstrom *m* COMP & DV, ELEKTRIZ, ELEKTROTECH rated current

Nennweite *f* FERTIG *Kunststoffinstallationen* NB, nominal bore, HEIZ & KÄLTE nominal size, MASCHINEN nominal width

Nennwert *m* ELEKTRIZ nominal value, rated value, ELEKTROTECH rating; **~ des Durchflußstromes** *m* ELEKTRIZ rated through-current; **~ des kurzzeitigen Stromes** *m* ELEKTRIZ rated short-time current; **~ der Spannungsschritte** *m* ELEKTRIZ rated step voltage; **~ des Spannungsverhältnisses** *m* ELEKTRIZ rated voltage ratio

Nennwindgeschwindigkeit *f* NICHTFOSS ENERG rated wind speed

Neoabietin- *pref* CHEMIE neoabietic

Neodymium *nt (Nd)* CHEMIE neodymium *(Nd)*

Neodym-Laser *m* ELEKTRONIK neodymium laser

Neoergosterin *nt* CHEMIE neoergosterol

Neohexan *nt* CHEMIE neohexane, trimethylbutane, triptane

neoklassisch: **~er Pincheffekt** *m* KERNTECH neoclassical pinch effect

Neon- *pref* ELEKTRIZ, ELEKTROTECH neon; **Neonbeleuchtung** *f* ELEKTRIZ fluorescent lighting; **Neongasanzeiger** *m* ELEKTROTECH neon indicator; **Neonglimmlampe** *f* ELEKTRIZ neon glow-lamp; **Neonlampe** *f* ELEKTROTECH neon lamp; **Neonlicht** *nt* ELEKTROTECH fluorescent lighting, neon lamp; **Neonröhre** *f* ELEKTRIZ, ELEKTROTECH neon tube, PHYS neon fluorescent tube, neon tube

Neopren *nt* BAU, CHEMIE, KUNSTSTOFF, VERPACK neoprene; **Neopren-Weichdichtung** *f* KUNSTSTOFF neoprene molded seal (AmE), neoprene moulded seal (BrE)

Neper *nt* AKUSTIK, ELEKTRONIK neper, PHYS neper, TELEKOM neper

Nephelin *m* CHEMIE nepheline; **Nephelinsyenit** *m* KER & GLAS nepheline syenite

Neptunium *nt (Np)* CHEMIE neptunium *(Np)*

Nernst: **~scher Verteilungskoeffizient** *m* METALL partition coefficient

Nernst-Brücke *f* ELEKTROTECH Nernst bridge

Nerol *nt* CHEMIE dimethyloctadienol, nerol

nervig *adj* TEXTIL crisp

Netto- *pref* KERNTECH, METROL, UMWELTSCHMUTZ net; **Netto-Brutrate** *f* KERNTECH net breeding rate; **Nettodonator** *m* UMWELTSCHMUTZ net donator; **Nettofläche** *f* NICHTFOSS ENERG *eines Kollektores* net area; **Nettoflügelfläche** *f* LUFTTRANS net wing area; **Nettogewicht** *nt* VERPACK net weight; **Nettoladung** *f* ELEKTROTECH net charge; **Nettoregistertonnage** *f* WASSERTRANS net registered tonnage; **Nettoregistertonne** *f* METROL register ton; **Nettotonnage** *f* ERDÖL *Handel, Schiffahrt,* WASSERTRANS net tonnage; **Nettotonne** *f* METROL net ton; **Nettotonnengehalt** *m* WASSERTRANS net tonnage; **Nettowärmeverlust** *m* HEIZ & KÄLTE net heat loss; **Nettozeitintervall** *nt* TRANS net time interval

Netz *nt* BAU *Stromverteilung, Rohrleitungen* network, *von Rohren, Kabeln* system, COMP & DV net, network, ELEKTRIZ network, ELEKTROTECH *Radio, FERNSEH* mains (BrE), supply network (AmE), FERTIG grid, mains, *Kunststoffinstallationen* circuit, KONSTZEICH grid, KONTROLL, KUNSTSTOFF network, RAUMFAHRT *Sieb* mesh, TELEKOM, TRANS network; **~ zur gemeinsamen Nutzung von Betriebsmitteln** *nt* COMP & DV resource-sharing network; **~ mit Nachrichtenvermittlung** *nt* COMP & DV message-switched network; **~ mit Vermittlung** *nt* TELEKOM switched network; **Netzabschalter** *m* ELEKTRIZ power switch; **Netzabstand** *m* FERTIG *Raumgitter* interplanar spacing; **Netzabtrennschalter** *m* ELEKTRIZ line-isolating switch;

Netzanalysator *m* ELEKTRIZ network analyser (BrE), network analyzer (AmE); **Netzanalyse** *f* COMP & DV, ELEKTRIZ, ELEKTROTECH network analysis; **Netzanalysierer** *m* COMP & DV network analyser (BrE), network analyzer (AmE); **Netzanbieter** *m* TELEKOM network carrier; **Netzanlasser** *m* ELEKTRIZ line starter (AmE), starter (BrE); **Netzanschluß** *m* ELEKTRIZ connected to the electrical network (AmE), connected to the mains (BrE), line connection, mains supply, ELEKTROTECH power supply; **Netzanschlußfilter** *nt* ELEKTRONIK power supply filter; **Netzanschlußkabel** *nt* ELEKTROTECH mains lead; **Netzanschlußteil** *nt* ELEKTROTECH power pack; **Netzarchitektur** *f* COMP & DV, ELEKTROTECH network architecture

netzartig *adj* LUFTTRANS *Struktur* network-like

Netz: **Netzaufsicht** *f* TELEKOM network supervisor; **Netzausfall** *m* ELEKTROTECH line fault, power failure, TELEKOM network breakdown; **Netzausfallreserve mit Batterie** *f* RADIO battery backup; **Netzausläufer** *m* ELEKTROTECH network spur; **Netzbelastungsanalyse** *f* COMP & DV network load analysis

netzbetrieben *adj* ELEKTROTECH mains-operated

Netz: **Netzbetriebssystem** *nt* COMP & DV network operating system; **Netzbewehrung** *f* BAU mat reinforcement; **Netzbrummen** *nt* AKUSTIK hum, ELEKTRIZ mains hum; **Netzdatenbank** *f* COMP & DV network database; **Netzebene** *f* COMP & DV network level, ELEKTRIZ network sector, FERTIG *Kristall* face; **Netzeinwahl** *f* TELEKOM direct outward dialing (AmE), direct outward dialling (BrE); **Netz-Erde Spannung** *f* ELEKTRIZ line-to-earth voltage (BrE), line-to-ground voltage (AmE); **Netz-Erstanschluß** *m* KERNTECH first connection to grid; **Netzfilter** *nt* ELEKTRONIK line filter; **Netzflechtwerk** *nt* BAU *Draht* netting; **Netzfolgeverhalten** *nt* KERNTECH *eines Kernkraftwerkes* grid-following behaviour; **Netzfrequenz** *f* ELEKTRIZ mains frequency, ELEKTROTECH commercial power frequency; **Netzführung** *f* COMP & DV network management; **Netzführungszentrum** *nt* TELEKOM NMC, network management center (AmE), network management centre (BrE); **Netzgebiet** *nt* KONSTZEICH ruled area

netzgekoppelt *adj* ELEKTRIZ connected to the electrical network (AmE), connected to the mains (BrE), mains-linked

Netz: **Netzgerät** *nt* ELEKTRIZ power supply, ELEKTROTECH power pack, power supply unit; **Netzgerät mit einem Ausgang** *nt* ELEKTROTECH single output power supply; **Netzgeräusch** *nt* AUFNAHME current noise (AmE), mains noise

netzgespeist *adj* ELEKTRIZ mains-operated

Netz: **Netzgleichrichter** *m* ELEKTRIZ mains rectifier; **Netzkabel** *nt* ELEKTROTECH mains cable; **Netzkarte** *f* TELEKOM network map; **Netzklemme** *f* ELEKTRIZ line terminal; **Netzknoten** *m* COMP & DV, ELEKTRIZ, ELEKTRONIK, ELEKTROTECH, TELEKOM node; **Netzknotenprozessor** *m* COMP & DV node processor; **Netzkontrollzentrum** *nt* ELEKTRIZ net control station, TELEKOM NCC, network control center (AmE), network control centre (BrE); **Netzkoppler** *m* TELEKOM network gateway; **Netzkoppler auf Anwendungsebene** *m* TELEKOM application level gateway; **Netzkopplung** *f* ELEKTRIZ connection to mains; **Netzkupplung** *f* COMP & DV network interconnection, ELEKTROTECH interconnection; **Netzlinie** *f* KONSTZEICH ruled line; **Netzmantelelektronenschweißen** *nt* FERTIG fusarc

welding; **Netzmasche** *f* KOHLEN screening mesh; **Netzmittel** *nt* FOTO, KUNSTSTOFF, LEBENSMITTEL, MEERSCHMUTZ, PHYS, TEXTIL wetting agent; **Netzmodell** *nt* COMP & DV network model, ELEKTROTECH network analyser (BrE), network analyzer (AmE)

netzparallel: **~er Betrieb** *m* ELEKTRIZ mains parallel operation

Netz: **Netzplan** *m* COMP & DV network diagram, network map; **Netzplantechnik** *f* TEXTIL critical path analysis; **Netzregelung** *f* ELEKTROTECH line regulation; **Netzrißbildung** *f* BAU crazing; **Netzschalter** *m* COMP & DV line switch, ELEKTRIZ, ELEKTROTECH mains switch; **Netzschaltung** *f* ELEKTROTECH AC switching; **Netzschnittstellenkarte** *f* COMP & DV network interface card; **Netzschutz** *m* ELEKTRIZ network protection; **Netzspannung** *f* ELEKTRIZ line voltage, mains voltage, ELEKTROTECH, FERNSEH mains voltage, KONTROLL power mains; **Netzspannungsabfall** *m* ELEKTRIZ line drop; **Netzspannungsregler** *m* ELEKTROTECH voltage regulator; **Netzstation** *f* COMP & DV network station; **Netzsteckdose** *f* ELEKTROTECH mains socket; **Netzstecker** *m* ELEKTRIZ mains plug, power outlet, ELEKTROTECH mains plug, power plug; **Netzsteuerung** *f* TRANS network control; **Netzstrom** *m* ELEKTROTECH mains current, supply current; **Netzstromfrequenz** *f* ELEKTRIZ power frequency; **Netzstromstoß** *m* ELEKTRIZ line transient; **Netzstromversorgung** *f* ELEKTROTECH, PHYS mains supply; **Netzstruktur** *f* OPTIK reticle, reticule; **Netzsynchronisation** *f* FERNSEH locking; **Netzsynthese** *f* ELEKTRIZ network synthesis; **Netzteil** *nt* FERNSEH power supply, FOTO powerpack unit; **Netzton** *m* ELEKTRIZ mains hum; **Netzträger** *m* WASSERTRANS *Satellitenfunk* common carrier; **Netztransformator** *m* ELEKTRIZ, ELEKTROTECH current transformer (AmE), mains transformer (BrE), power transformer; **Netztrenner** *m* ELEKTRIZ power switch; **Netztrennschalter** *m* ELEKTRIZ line breaker; **Netzübergang** *m* TELEKOM gateway

netzüberschreitend: **~e Kommunikation** *f* TELEKOM internetwork communication

Netz: **Netzübertragungseinheit** *f* COMP & DV gateway; **Netzüberwacher** *m* COMP & DV network controller; **Netzüberwachung und- führung** *f* TELEKOM network supervision and management; **Netzverbund** *m* COMP & DV network interconnection, ELEKTROTECH interconnection; **Netzversorgung** *f* PHYS mains supply; **Netzverwaltung** *f* COMP & DV network management; **Netzverwaltungszentrale** *f* TELEKOM NMC, network management center (AmE), network management centre (BrE); **Netzverzögerung** *f* COMP & DV network delay

netzweit: **~e Erreichbarkeit** *f* TELEKOM anywhere call pickup

Netzwerk *nt* COMP & DV net, network, ELEKTROTECH mesh, KONTROLL network, RAUMFAHRT *Weltraumfunk* mesh network, TELEKOM network; **Netzwerkanalysator** *m* COMP & DV, ELEKTROTECH, TELEKOM network analyser (BrE), network analyzer (AmE); **Netzwerkanalyse** *f* COMP & DV, ELEKTRIZ, ELEKTROTECH network analysis; **Netzwerkarchitektur** *f* COMP & DV, ELEKTROTECH network architecture; **Netzwerkbetrieb** *m* COMP & DV networking; **Netzwerkbildner** *m* KER & GLAS network former; **Netzwerkentwurf** *m* COMP & DV network design; **Netzwerkkonstante** *f* ELEKTROTECH network constant; **Netzwerkmanager** *m* COMP & DV network manager;

Netzwerkmodell *nt* COMP & DV network model; **Netzwerkname** *m* COMP & DV network name; **Netzwerkplan** *m* COMP & DV network diagram; **Netzwerkprozessor** *m* COMP & DV network processor; **Netzwerksimulator** *m* COMP & DV network simulator; **Netzwerksteuerkanal** *m* COMP & DV network control channel; **Netzwerksteuerprogramm** *nt* COMP & DV network control program; **Netzwerksynthese** *f* ELEKTROTECH network synthesis; **Netzwerktheorie** *f* ELEKTROTECH network theory; **Netzwerktopologie** *f* COMP & DV network topology; **Netzwerkumwandlung** *f* RADIO network transformation; **Netzwerkverwaltung** *f* COMP & DV network management; **Netzwerkwandler** *m* KER & GLAS network modifier

Netz: **Netzzentrale** *f* ELEKTRIZ net control station; **Netzzug** *m* WASSERTRANS *Fischerei* haul; **Netzzugriffssteuerung** *f* COMP & DV network access control; **Netzzugriffsüberwachung** *f* COMP & DV network access control

Neu- *pref* QUAL new; **Neuanlauf** *m* COMP & DV restart; **Neuanzeige** *f* COMP & DV refresh

neuaufgebaut: ~es Bild *nt* ELEKTRONIK refreshed image

Neu-: **Neuaufladung** *f* ELEKTROTECH recharging; **Neuauflage** *f* DRUCK new edition; **Neuaufnahme** *f* BAU *Vermessung* releveling (AmE), relevelling (BrE); **Neuausstattung** *f* WASSERTRANS *Schiff* refit; **Neubearbeitung** *f* DRUCK revised edition; **Neubelag** *m* FERTIG relining; **Neubescheinigung** *f* QUAL recertification; **Neudruck** *m* DRUCK reprint; **Neueichung** *f* STRAHLPHYS recalibration; **Neueinspannung** *f* FERTIG *Werkstück* rechucking; **Neuformatierung** *f* COMP & DV reformatting; **Neugrad** *m* FERTIG centesimal degree, FOTO grad; **Neuheit** *f* PATENT novelty; **Neukalibrierung** *f* STRAHLPHYS recalibration; **Neukonditionierung** *f* RAUMFAHRT *Raumschiff* reconditioning; **Neulackieren** *nt* KUNSTSTOFF refinishing

Neuneck *nt* GEOM nonagon

Neunerkomplement *nt* COMP & DV nine's complement

90: um ~ Grad phasenverschoben *adj* PHYS in quadrature

90°: ~ Verschiebung *f* ELEKTRONIK *Phasenverschiebung* quadrature

Neu-: **Neuprofilieren** *nt* BAU reprofiling; **Neuqualifizierung** *f* QUAL requalification

neural: ~es Netz *nt* (*NN*) COMP & DV, KÜNSTL INT neural net, neural network (*NN*); **~es Netzwerk** *nt* (*NN*) COMP & DV, KÜNSTL INT neural net, neural network (*NN*)

Neuramin- *pref* CHEMIE neuraminic

Neurodin *nt* CHEMIE neurodine

Neuron *nt* COMP & DV neuron

Neu-: **Neusilber** *nt* METALL German silver, nickel silver; **Neustapelfähigkeit** *f* VERPACK restackability; **Neustart** *m* COMP & DV restart; **Neustart nach Netzausfall** *m* COMP & DV PFR, power fail restart

neutral[1] *adj* ELEKTRIZ, PHYS neutral

neutral:[2] **~e Achse** *f* BAU, MASCHINEN neutral axis; **~er Anker** *m* ELEKTRIZ neutral armature; **~es Atom** *nt* TEILPHYS neutral atom; **~es Element** *nt* MATH neutral element; **~es Gas** *nt* RAUMFAHRT neutral gas; **~es Polarrelais** *nt* ELEKTROTECH neutral polar relay; **~es Relais** *nt* ELEKTROTECH neutral relay, nonpolarized relay; **~er Strom** *m* PHYS *Elementarteilchen* neutral current; **~e Übertragung** *f* COMP & DV neutral transmission; **~es unpolarisiertes Relais** *nt* ELEKTROTECH nonpolarized relay; **~e Zone** *f* ELEKTROTECH neutral zone

Neutralfilter *nt* FOTO neutral density filter

Neutralglycerid *nt* CHEMIE triglyceride

Neutralisation *f* CHEMIE, ELEKTROTECH, KOHLEN, KUNSTSTOFF neutralization; **Neutralisationsmittel** *nt* ABFALL neutralizer, neutralizing agent, CHEMIE neutralizer

Neutralisator *m* CHEMIE neutralizer, METALL killing agent

Neutralisieren *nt* KUNSTSTOFF neutralization

neutralisiert: ~er Verstärker *m* ELEKTRONIK neutralized amplifier

Neutralisierung *f* ABFALL, ELEKTRIZ, RADIO neutralization; **Neutralisierungsmittel** *nt* SICHERHEIT neutralizing agent; **Neutralisierungswärme** *f* THERMOD heat of neutralization

Neutralsalzsprühnebeltest *m* ANSTRICH neutral salt spray test

Neutralsulfit *nt* PAPIER neutral sulfite (AmE), neutral sulphite (BrE); **Neutralsulfitzellstoff** *m* PAPIER neutral sulfite pulp (AmE), neutral sulphite pulp (BrE)

Neutralteilchen *nt* PHYS, TEILPHYS neutral particle; **Neutralteilchenstrahlinjektion** *f* KERNTECH neutral atom beam injection

Neutrino *nt* STRAHLPHYS *Elementartei¹chen*, TEILPHYS neutrino

Neutron *nt* (*n*) ELEKTRIZ, KERNTECH, STRAHLPHYS, TEILPHYS neutron (*n*); **Neutronenabschirmung** *f* KERNTECH neutron shield; **Neutronenabsorber** *m* KERNTECII neutron absorber

neutronenabsorbierend: ~e Reaktion *f* KERNTECH neutron-absorbing reaction

Neutron: **Neutronenabsorptionsquerschnitt Null** *m* KERNTECH zero neutron-absorption cross section; **Neutronenaktivierungsaufzeichnung** *f* KERNTECH neutron activation logging; **Neutronenaufzeichnung** *f* NICHTFOSS ENERG neutron log; **Neutronenausbeute** *f* STRAHLPHYS, TEILPHYS neutron yield; **Neutronenausbeute per Spaltereignis** *f* PHYS neutron field per fission; **Neutronenausbruch** *m* KERNTECH neutron burst; **Neutroneneinfang** *m* STRAHLPHYS, TEILPHYS neutron capture, neutron radiative capture; **Neutronenfluß** *m* KERNTECH neutron flux; **Neutronen-Gammalog** *nt* ERDÖL *Bohrlochmeßtechnik* neutron gamma log; **Neutronengift** *nt* KERNTECH nuclear poison; **Neutronenkonverter-Flußverstärker** *m* KERNTECH neutron converter donut (AmE), neutron converter doughnut (BrE); **Neutronenlethargie** *f* KERNTECH, PHYS lethargy; **Neutronenlog** *nt* ERDÖL *Bohrlochmeßtechnik* neutron log; **Neutronenmasse** *f* (*mn*) KERNTECH, STRAHLPHYS, TEILPHYS neutron mass (*mn*); **Neutronenmessung** *f* ERDÖL *Borlochmeßtechnik* neutron logging; **Neutronenmultiplikationskonstante** *f* (*k*) KERNTECH *Nuklearreaktor* neutron multiplication constant (*k*); **Neutronen-Neutronenlog** *nt* ERDÖL *Bohrlochmeßtechnik* neutron-neutron log; **Neutronenquelle** *f* KERNTECH neutron source; **Neutronenstern** *m* RAUMFAHRT neutron star; **Neutronenstrahl** *m* STRAHLPHYS, TEILPHYS neutron beam; **Neutronenstrahlreaktor** *m* KERNTECH beam reactor; **Neutronenstreuung** *f* STRAHLPHYS, TEILPHYS neutron scattering; **Neutronenüberschuß** *m* PHYS isotopic number, STRAHLPHYS, TEILPHYS neutron excess; **Neutronenzahl** *f* STRAHLPHYS, TEILPHYS neutron number; **Neutronenzählrohr** *nt* KERNTECH neutron counter tube

Neu-: Neuverdrahtung *f* ELEKTRIZ rewiring; **Neuversuch** *m* COMP & DV retry; **Neuverteilung** *f* ELEKTROTECH redistribution

neuzulassen *vt* QUAL recertify

Neuzündung *f* RAUMFAHRT *Raumschiff* reignition

Newton *nt (N)* ELEKTRIZ *Einheit,* HYDRAUL, METROL *Einheit,* STRÖMPHYS *Einheit* newton *(N);* **~sches Abkühlungsgesetz** *nt* STRÖMPHYS Newton's law; **~sches Fernrohr** *nt* PHYS Newtonian telescope; **~sche Flüssigkeit** *f* STRÖMPHYS Newtonian fluid; **~sche Mechanik** *f* PHYS Newtonian mechanics; **~sche Ringe** *m pl* FOTO, STRÖMPHYS Newton's rings; **~-Scheibe** *f* OPTIK Newton's disc, Newton's disk

Nf *abbr (Niederfrequenz)* AUFNAHME AF *(audio frequency),* LF *(low frequency),* ELEKTRONIK AF *(audio frequency),* LF *(low frequency),* FERNSEH, RADIO AF *(audio frequency),* LF *(low frequency),* TELEKOM LF *(low frequency)*

Nf: Nf-Generator *m* ELEKTRONIK AF oscillator; **Nf-Signalgenerator** *m* ELEKTRONIK AF signal generator; **Nf-Störung** *f (Niederfrequenzstörung)* ELEKTRONIK, RADIO, TELEKOM AFI *(audio-frequency interference);* **Nf-Weiche** *f* TELEKOM audio-frequency splitter; **Nf-Zwischenverstärker** *m* ELEKTRONIK booster amplifier

n-Halbleiter *m* ELEKTRONIK n-type semiconductor

n-Heptylaldehyd *m* CHEMIE oenanthal

Ni *(Nickel)* CHEMIE Ni *(nickel)*

Nialamid *nt* CHEMIE nialamide

Niccolit *m* CHEMIE *Mineralogie* niccolite, nickel arsenide

NiCd *abbr (Nickel-Cadmium)* FOTO, RADIO NiCd *(nickel-cadmium)*

Nichtaustastschaltung *f* FERNSEH unblanking circuit

Nicht-Bindungselektron *nt* KERNTECH nonbonding electron

Nicht-Draht-Potentiometer *nt* ELEKTRIZ nonwirewound potentiometer

Nichteigenzeit *f* PHYS improper time

Nichteisen- *pref* ELEKTRIZ, FERTIG nonferrous

Nichterfüllung *f* QUAL noncompliance

Nichterhaltung: ~ der Parität *f* PHYS nonconservation of parity

Nichtflüchtiges *nt* KUNSTSTOFF nonvolatile content

NICHT-Gatter *nt* COMP & DV NOT gate

Nicht-Gauß: ~sches Rauschen *nt* TELEKOM non-Gaussian noise

NICHT-Glied *nt* COMP & DV NOT circuit

nichtig: für ~ erklären *vt* PATENT revoke

Nichtigkeit *f* PATENT revocation; **Nichtigkeitsgründe** *m pl* PATENT grounds for revocation

Nichtleiter *m* ELEKTRIZ nonconductor, ELEKTROTECH *zwischen zwei Leitern* insulator

Nichtlöser *m* KUNSTSTOFF diluent

Nichtprimzahl *f* MATH composite number

Nichtsprachkommunikation *f* TELEKOM nonvoice communication

Nichtübereinstimmung *f* QUAL nonconformity

NICHT-UND-Schaltung *f (N-UND-Schaltung, NAND-Gatter)* PHYS NOT AND gate *(NAND gate)*

Nichtverbundhülle *f* RAUMFAHRT *Raumschiff* unbonded skin

Nichtverfügbarkeit *f* QUAL outage, unavailability; **Nichtverfügbarkeitsdauer** *f* QUAL outage duration; **Nichtverfügbarkeitsrate** *f* QUAL failure rate, outage rate

Nickachse *f* LUFTTRANS lateral axis, pitch axis, RAUM-FAHRT *Raumschiff* pitch axis

Nickdämpfer *m* LUFTTRANS pitch damper

Nickdüse *f* RAUMFAHRT *Raumschiff* pitch jet

Nickel *nt (Ni)* CHEMIE nickel *(Ni);* **Nickel-Cadmium** *nt (NiCd)* FOTO, RADIO nickel-cadmium *(NiCd);* **Nickel-Cadmium-Akku** *m* FOTO *Blitzlicht* NiCad battery; **Nickel-Cadmium-Akkumulator** *m* RAUMFAHRT *Raumschiff* nickel-cadmium battery; **Nickel-Cadmium-Batterie** *f* ELEKTROTECH, KFZTECH nickel-cadmium battery; **Nickel-Cadmium-Stahlakkumulator** *m* KFZTECH nickel-cadmium battery; **Nickel-Cadmium-Zelle** *f* ELEKTROTECH nickel-cadmium cell, RADIO NiCad cell, nickel-cadmium cell; **Nickel-Eisen-Akkumulator** *m* KFZTECH nickel-iron storage battery; **Nickel-Eisen-Batterie** *f* ELEKTROTECH nickel-iron battery

nickelhaltig *adj* FERTIG nickeliferous

Nickel: Nickelhydroxid *nt* RAUMFAHRT *Raumschiff* nickel-hydroxide; **Nickelin** *m* CHEMIE niccolite, nickel arsenide; **Nickellegierung** *f* ANSTRICH nickel alloy

nickelplattieren *vt* FERTIG nickel-clad

nickelplattiert *adj* FERTIG nickel-clad

Nickel: Nickelplattierung *f* ELEKTRIZ nickel plating

nickelreich: ~er Stahl *m* METALL high-nickel steel

Nickel: Nickelsilber *nt* ELEKTROTECH nickel silver; **Nickelstahl** *m* METALL high-nickel steel, nickel steel; **Nickel-Zink-Akkumulator** *m* KFZTECH nickel-zinc storage battery

Nicken *nt* LUFTTRANS pitching, RAUMFAHRT *Raumschiff* pitch

Nickkanal *m* LUFTTRANS pitch channel

Nickkreisel *m* RAUMFAHRT *Raumschiff* pitch gyro

Nicklage *f* RAUMFAHRT *Raumschiff* pitch attitude

Nickwinkel *m* LUFTTRANS pitch angle; **Nickwinkelgeschwindigkeitskreisel** *m* LUFTTRANS pitch rate gyro

Nicol-Prisma *nt* PHYS Nicol prism

Nicotinamid *nt* CHEMIE niacinamide, nicotinamide

Nicotinsäureamid *nt* CHEMIE niacinamide, nicotinamide

Nicotyrin *nt* CHEMIE nicotyrine

Nidridhärten *nt* CHEMIE *Metallurgie* nitridation

Niederbordwagen *m* EISENBAHN flatcar (AmE), platform wagon (BrE), gondola car, gondola wagon

niederbrennen *vt* THERMOD destroy by fire

Niederbringung: ~ einer Bohrung *f* ERDÖL *Bohrtechnik* well boring, well drilling, well sinking; **~ einer Förderbohrung** *f* ERDÖL *Fördertechnik* production drilling

Niederdruck *m* PHYS low pressure; **Niederdruckbrenner** *m* BAU low-pressure blowpipe, HEIZ & KÄLTE low-pressure burner

niederdrücken *vt* BAU weigh down

Niederdruck: Niederdruckgasbrenner *m* HEIZ & KÄLTE low-pressure gas burner; **Niederdruckheizung** *f* HEIZ & KÄLTE low-pressure heating; **Niederdruckkessel** *m* HEIZ & KÄLTE low-pressure boiler; **Niederdruckkolbenverdichter** *m* MASCHINEN low-pressure piston compressor; **Niederdruckkompressor** *m* MASCHINEN low-pressure compressor; **Niederdruckmanometer** *nt* GERÄT low-pressure gauge (BrE), low-pressure gage (AmE); **Niederdruckölbrenner** *m* HEIZ & KÄLTE low-pressure atomizer; **Niederdruckprüfung** *f* WERKPRÜF low-pressure test; **Niederdruck-Quecksilberdampflampe** *f* ELEKTRIZ low-pressure mercury lamp; **Niederdruckregler** *m* HEIZ & KÄLTE low-pressure controller; **Niederdruck-Schwimmerventil** *nt* HEIZ & KÄLTE low-pressure float valve; **Niederdruckspülen** *nt*

MEERSCHMUTZ low-pressure flushing; **Niederdruck-treibstofffilter** *nt* LUFTTRANS low-pressure fuel filter; **Niederdruckverdichter** *m* LUFTTRANS fan; **Niederdruckwarmwasseranlage** *f* HEIZ & KÄLTE low-pressure hot-water system; **Niederdruckwarmwasserkessel** *m* HEIZ & KÄLTE low-pressure hot-water boiler; **Niederdruckzylinder** *m* MASCHINEN low-pressure cylinder

nieder: **~e Dienstgüte** *f* TELEKOM lower quality of service; **~e Programmiersprache** *f* COMP & DV LLL, low-level language

niederenergetisch: **~er fokussierter Ionenstrahl** *m* STRAHLPHYS low-energy-focused ion beam

Niederenergie-Kernphysik *f* KERNTECH low-energy nuclear physics

Niederfrequenz *f* (*Nf*) AUFNAHME audio frequency *(AF)*, low frequency *(LF)*, ELEKTRONIK audio frequency *(AF)*, low frequency *(LF)*, FERNSEH audio frequency *(AF)*, RADIO audio frequency *(AF)*, low frequency *(LF)*, TELEKOM low frequency *(LF)*; **Niederfrequenzausgleich** *m* ELEKTRONIK, RADIO, TELEKOM low-frequency compensation; **Niederfrequenzfilter** *nt* ELEKTRONIK, RADIO, TELEKOM low-frequency filter; **Niederfrequenzgenerator** *m* ELEKTRIZ low-frequency generator, ELEKTRONIK, RADIO audio-frequency oscillator; **Niederfrequenzheizung** *f* ELEKTROTECH low-frequency heating; **Niederfrequenz-Induktionserwärmung** *f* ELEKTROTECH low-frequency induction heating; **Niederfrequenz-Induktionserwärmungsgerät** *nt* ELEKTROTECH low-frequency induction heater; **Niederfrequenzofen** *m* ELEKTROTECH low-frequency furnace; **Niederfrequenzoszillator** *m* ELEKTRONIK, RADIO, TELEKOM low-frequency oscillator; **Niederfrequenzsignal** *nt* ELEKTRONIK, RADIO audio-frequency signal, low-frequency signal, TELEKOM low-frequency signal; **Niederfrequenzsignalgenerator** *m* ELEKTRONIK, RADIO audio-frequency signal generator; **Niederfrequenz-Spektrometer** *nt* LABOR audio-frequency spectrometer; **Niederfrequenzstörung** *f* (*Nf-Störung*) ELEKTRONIK, RADIO, TELEKOM audio-frequency interference *(AFI)*; **Niederfrequenztrichterlautsprecher** *m* AUFNAHME low-frequency horn loudspeaker; **Niederfrequenzverstärker** *m* AUFNAHME audio-frequency amplifier, ELEKTRONIK audio-frequency amplifier, low-frequency amplifier, RADIO, TELEKOM low-frequency amplifier; **Niederfrequenzverstärkung** *f* ELEKTRONIK, RADIO, TELEKOM low-frequency amplification; **Niederfrequenzweiche** *f* TELEKOM audio-frequency splitter; **Niederfrequenz-Zwischenverstärker** *m* ELEKTRONIK booster amplifier

Niedergang *m* FERTIG downstroke, WASSERTRANS *Schiffbau* companionway; **Niedergangsluke** *f* WASSERTRANS *Schiffbau* companionway hatch; **Niedergangspfosten** *m* WASSERTRANS *Schiffbau* companionway post; **Niedergangstreppe** *f* WASSERTRANS *Schiffbau* companionway ladder

niederholen *vt* WASSERTRANS *Flagge, Segeln* haul down

Niederholer *m* WASSERTRANS *Tauwerk* downhaul

Niederhub *m* KFZTECH *Motor* downstroke

niederohmig[1] *adj* RADIO low-impedance

niederohmig:[2] **~er Widerstand** *m* PHYS low resistance

Niederohmigkeit *f* RADIO low impedance

Niederpegel *m* ELEKTRONIK low-logic level

Niederschlag *m* BAU precipitation, CHEMIE deposit, CHEMTECH, ERDÖL *Petrochemie* precipitate, FERTIG

deposit, LEBENSMITTEL bottoms, METALL precipitate, PHYS sedimentation, UMWELTSCHMUTZ *radioaktiv* fallout

niederschlagen[1] *vt* CHEMTECH precipitate, FERTIG *Galvanotechnik* deposit

niederschlagen:[2] **sich ~** *v refl* THERMOD condense

Niederschlag: **Niederschlagsammler** *m* UMWELTSCHMUTZ precipitation collector; **Niederschlagselektrode** *f* ABFALL, UMWELTSCHMUTZ collecting electrode; **Niederschlagsfront** *f* LUFTTRANS precipitation front; **Niederschlagsgebiet** *nt* WASSERVERSORG catchment area, drainage area, drainage basin, precipitation area, rainfall area; **Niederschlagsgefäß** *nt* CHEMTECH precipitation vessel; **Niederschlagsmenge** *f* NICHTFOSS ENERG rainfall; **Niederschlagsmesser** *m* BAU, LABOR, NICHTFOSS ENERG rain gage (AmE), rain gauge (BrE), WASSERVERSORG precipitation gage (AmE), precipitation gauge (BrE), rain gage (AmE), rain gauge (BrE); **Niederschlagsvorfall** *m* UMWELTSCHMUTZ precipitation event; **Niederschlagswasser** *nt* WASSERVERSORG storage level regulation, storm sewage

Niederschlagung *f* PHYS settling

Niederschraubabsperrventil *nt* BAU screw-down stop valve

Niederschraubhahn *m* BAU screw-down cock

Niederschraubventil *nt* BAU screw-down valve

Niederspannung *f* ELEKTRIZ, ELEKTROTECH low tension, low voltage, TELEKOM low voltage; **Niederspannungsanlage** *f* ELEKTROTECH low-voltage installation; **Niederspannungskabel** *nt* ELEKTRIZ low-voltage cable; **Niederspannungskreis** *m* ELEKTRIZ low-voltage network; **Niederspannungswicklung** *f* ELEKTRIZ low-voltage winding

Niedertemperaturprüfung *f* WERKPRÜF low-temperature test

Niedertor *nt* WASSERVERSORG *Schleusentor* aft gate

Niedervolt-Lautsprecher *m* AUFNAHME low-voltage electrostatic loudspeaker

niederwertig[1] *adj* COMP & DV low-order

niederwertig:[2] **~es Bit** *nt* COMP & DV low-order bit; **~e Position** *f* COMP & DV low-order position

niederwertigst[1] *adj* COMP & DV least significant

niederwertigst:[2] **~stes Bit** *nt* (*LSB*) COMP & DV least significant bit *(LSB)*; **~ste Ziffer** *f* COMP & DV LSD, least significant digit

niedrig:[1] **~e Auflösung** *f* COMP & DV low res, low resolution; **~e Dämpfung** *f* TELEKOM *Übertragung* low loss; **~e Drehzahl** *f* KFZTECH *Motor* slow speed, MASCHINEN low speed; **~er Druck** *m* PHYS low pressure; **~e Einfügungsdämpfung** *f* TELEKOM low-insertion loss; **~ste erreichbare Emissionsrate** *f* UMWELTSCHMUTZ lowest achievable emission rate; **~er Gang** *m* MASCHINEN low gear; **~e Geschwindigkeit** *f* KFZTECH *Motor* slow speed, MASCHINEN, TELEKOM low speed; **~e Kapazität** *f* ELEKTROTECH low capacitance; **~ster Niedrigwasserstand** *m* WASSERVERSORG minimum low water; **~ste nutzbare Frequenz** *f* (*NNF*) RADIO lowest usable frequency *(LUF)*; **~e Reynoldszahl** *f* STRÖMPHYS low Reynolds number; **~er Schwefelgehalt** *m* ERDÖL *Öl, Erdgas* low sulfur content (AmE), low sulphur content (BrE); **~er Signalpegel** *m* ELEKTRONIK low-signal level; **~es Überlaufwehr** *nt* HYDRAUL flat-crested weir; **~e Umlaufbahn** *f* RAUMFAHRT low-altitude orbit; **~er Widerstand** *m* TELEKOM low resistance

niedrig:[2] **~er einstufen** *vt* BAU *Gebäude* grade down

niedrigfest: **~er Bohrschlamm** *m* ERDÖL *Bohrtechnik* low-solid mud

niedriggekohlt *adj* FERTIG *Eisen* steely

Niedrig-Hoch-Übergang *m* ELEKTRONIK low-to-high transition

niedriglegiert[1] *adj* ANSTRICH *Stahl* low-alloy

niedriglegiert:[2] **~er Stahl** *m* METALL low-alloy steel

Niedrigpegelvideo *nt* FERNSEH low-level video

Niedrigschubtriebwerk *nt* RAUMFAHRT *Raumschiff* low-thrust motor

niedrigstabil: **~er Bohrschlamm** *m* ERDÖL low-solid mud

Niedrigwasser *nt* WASSERTRANS low tide, low water, *Gezeiten* ebb; **Niedrigwasserabfluß** *m* WASSERVERSORG low-water discharge; **Niedrigwasserlinie** *f* WASSERTRANS low-water mark; **Niedrigwassermarke** *f* BAU low-water mark; **Niedrigwasserstand** *m* WASSERVERSORG low-water level

Nierencharakteristik *f* RADIO cardioid pattern

nierenförmig: **~er Schlitz** *m* MASCHINEN kidney-shaped slot

Niet *m* BAU, MECHAN rivet; **Nietbolzenkette** *f* BAU pin chain

Niete *f* BAU, MECHAN rivet

Nieten *nt* BAU, MASCHINEN riveting

nieten *vt* FERTIG rivet, rivet up

Niete: **Nietenbefestigung** *f* MASCHINEN rivet fastening; **Nietendöpper** *m* MASCHINEN rivet header, rivet snap; **Nietenkaltpresse** *f* MASCHINEN rivet cold press; **Nietensetzkopf** *m* BAU set; **Nietentreiber** *m* MASCHINEN driver, rivet drift

Nieter *m* BAU riveter

Niet: **Niethammer** *m* BAU, MASCHINEN rivet hammer, riveting hammer; **Nietkopf** *m* BAU, MASCHINEN rivet head

Nietköpfe machen *vt* FERTIG snap

Niet: **Nietkopfsetzer** *m* BAU rivet set, FERTIG heading set; **Nietlochreibahle** *f* MASCHINEN bridge reamer, rivet-hole reamer; **Nietlochsenker** *m* MASCHINEN rivet countersink; **Nietmaschine** *f* BAU, MASCHINEN riveter, riveting machine; **Nietmutter** *f* MASCHINEN rivet nut; **Nietnaht** *f* MASCHINEN, VERPACK riveted seam; **Nietplatte** *f* BAU riveted plate; **Nietreihenabstand** *m* FERTIG back pitch

Nietrieren *nt* MASCHINEN nitriding

Niet: **Nietschaft** *m* MASCHINEN rivet shank; **Nietschaftdurchmesser** *m* MASCHINEN rivet shank diameter; **Nietstift** *m* MASCHINEN rivet pin

Nietung *f* BAU, MASCHINEN riveting

Niet: **Nietverbindung** *f* BAU, MASCHINEN rivet joint, riveted joint; **Nietverfahren** *nt* MASCHINEN riveting technique

Niobit *m* CHEMIE niobite

Niobium *nt* (*Nb*) CHEMIE columbium (AmE), niobium (BrE) (*niobium*)

Nippel *m* BAU, MASCHINEN, PAPIER nipple

Nipptide *f* NICHTFOSS ENERG, WASSERTRANS neap tide

Nirosta *m* ANSTRICH stainless steel

Nische *f* BAU housing, recess

Nit *nt* OPTIK *Einheit* nit

Nitramin *nt* CHEMIE nitramine

Nitrat *nt* CHEMIE, UMWELTSCHMUTZ nitrate; **Nitratcellulose** *f* KUNSTSTOFF cellulose nitrate

Nitrazin- *pref* CHEMIE nitrazine

Nitrid *nt* CHEMIE nitride; **Nitridreaktor** *m* KERNTECH nitride fueled reactor (AmE), nitride fuelled reactor (BrE); **Nitridstahl** *m* METALL nitriding steel

Nitrieren *nt* CHEMIE nitration

nitrieren[1] *vt* CHEMIE nitrate, nitride

nitrieren[2] *vi* CHEMIE nitrify

nitrierhärten *vt* CHEMIE *Metallurgie* nitride

Nitrierhärtung *f* MECHAN nitride hardening

Nitrierstahl *m* MECHAN nitrided steel

Nitrierung *f* CHEMIE nitration

nitrifizieren *vt* CHEMIE *Bakterien* nitrify

Nitril *nt* CHEMIE nitrile; **Nitrilkautschuk** *m* FERTIG *Kunststoffinstallationen*, KUNSTSTOFF nitrile rubber

Nitrin *nt* CHEMIE nitrine

Nitrit *nt* CHEMIE nitrite

Nitro- *pref* CHEMIE nitro-; **Nitroanilin** *nt* CHEMIE nitroaniline; **Nitrobenzen** *nt* CHEMIE nitrobenzene; **Nitrobenzol** *nt* CHEMIE nitrobenzene; **Nitrochloroform** *nt* CHEMIE chloropicrin, trichloronitromethane; **Nitroethan** *nt* CHEMIE nitroethane; **Nitrofilmunterlage** *f* FOTO nitrate base; **Nitroform** *nt* CHEMIE nitroforme; **Nitrogenium** *nt* (*N*) CHEMIE nitrogen (*N*); **Nitroglycerin** *nt* CHEMIE nitroglycerin; **Nitrolack** *m* BAU nitrocellulose lacquer; **Nitrometer** *nt* CHEMIE azotometer, nitrometer; **Nitromethan** *nt* CHEMIE nitromethane; **Nitronaphthalin** *nt* CHEMIE nitronaphthalene; **Nitrophenol** *nt* CHEMIE nitrophenol

nitros *adj* CHEMIE nitrous

Nitro-: **Nitrosat** *nt* CHEMIE nitrosate; **Nitrosierung** *f* CHEMIE nitrosation; **Nitrosit** *nt* CHEMIE nitrosite; **Nitrosyl-** *pref* CHEMIE nitrosyl; **Nitrosylhydrogensulfat** *nt* CHEMIE nitrosulfuric acid (AmE), nitrosulphuric acid (BrE); **Nitrotoluol** *nt* CHEMIE nitrotoluene; **Nitroweinsäure** *f* CHEMIE nitrotartaric acid

Nitryl- *pref* CHEMIE nitryl; **Nitrylchlorid** *nt* CHEMIE nitryl chloride

Niveau *nt* BAU grade, level, MECHAN, METROL, WASSERVERSORG level; **Niveauanzeige** *f* KERNTECH level indicator; **Niveauanzeiger** *m* GERÄT liquid level indicator

niveaugleich *adj* BAU at grade

Niveau: **Niveauhalten** *nt* KERNTECH level holding; **Niveaukonstanthalter** *m* GERÄT constant-level device; **Niveaumeßgerät** *nt* GERÄT level gage (AmE), level gauge (BrE); **Niveaumessung** *f* GERÄT level measurement; **Niveauschalter** *m* KONTROLL level switch; **Niveausteuerung** *f* KONTROLL level control system; **Niveauverschiebung** *f* KERNTECH level displacement, level shift; **Niveauwächter** *m* HEIZ & KÄLTE float switch

Nivellieren *nt* BAU *Vermessung* boning, FERTIG leveling (AmE), levelling (BrE)

nivellieren *vt* BAU *Straßenbau* grade, level, METROL bone in

Nivelliergerät *nt* BAU surveyor's level

Nivellierinstrument *nt* BAU leveling instrument (AmE), levelling instrument (BrE), level, transit, *Vermessung* A-1 level, GERÄT leveling instrument (AmE), levelling instrument (BrE)

Nivellierkreuz *nt* BAU *Vermessung* leveling rod (AmE), levelling rod (BrE)

Nivellierlatte *f* BAU leveling pole (AmE), levelling pole (BrE), sighting rod, *Vermessung* leveling staff (AmE), levelling staff (BrE), pole, EISENBAHN grade stake, *Vermessung* level indicator; **~ mit Anzeige** *f* BAU target leveling staff (AmE), target levelling staff (BrE), target leveling rod (AmE), target levelling rod (BrE)

Nivellierpunkt *m* BAU leveling point (AmE), levelling point (BrE)

Nivellierung *f* BAU leveling (AmE), levelling (BrE)

Nivellierwaage f BAU, METROL spirit level

Nivenit m KERNTECH nivenite

Nixie-Röhre f ELEKTRONIK Nixie tube (TM)

NK abbr (Naturkautschuk) KUNSTSTOFF NR (natural rubber)

N-Kanal m ELEKTRONIK n-channel; **N-Kanal FET** m RADIO N-channel FET; **N-Kanal-Filter** nt ELEKTRONIK n-channel filter; **N-Kanal-Gerät** nt ELEKTRONIK n-channel device; **N-Kanal-Metalloxid-Silizium** nt RADIO N-channel metal-oxide silicon; **N-Kanal Silikon-Gate MOS-Prozeß** m ELEKTRONIK n-channel silicon-gate MOS process; **N-Kanal-Technologie** f ELEKTRONIK n-channel technology

n-leitend[1] adj ELEKTRONIK n-type

n-leitend:[2] **~er Halbleiter** m PHYS n-type semiconductor; **~e Komponente** f ELEKTRONIK n-type component; **~es Silizium** nt ELEKTRONIK n-type silicon; **~er Störstoff** m ELEKTRONIK n-type impurity; **~es Trägermaterial** nt ELEKTRONIK n-type substrate

NLQ-Druckmodus m COMP & DV, DRUCK NLQ, near-letter quality

N-Methylglykokoll nt CHEMIE N-methylaminoacetic acid, sarcosine

NMOS[1] abbr ELEKTRONIK NMOS, n-channel metal-oxide semiconductor

NMOS:[2] **NMOS-Chip** m ELEKTRONIK NMOS chip; **NMOS-Integrationsschaltung** f ELEKTRONIK NMOS integrated circuit; **NMOS-Komponente** f ELEKTRONIK NMOS component; **NMOS-Logik** f ELEKTRONIK NMOS logic; **NMOS-Transistor** m ELEKTRONIK NMOS transistor

NMR abbr (magnetische Kernresonanz) ERDÖL, TEILPHYS NMR (nuclear magnetic resonance)

NN abbr COMP & DV (neurales Netz, neurales Netzwerk), KÜNSTL INT (neurales Netz, neurales Netzwerk) NN (neural network), WASSERTRANS (Normalnull) msl (mean sea level)

NNF abbr (niedrigste nutzbare Frequenz) RADIO LUF (lowest usable frequency)

NNSS abbr (Navigationssatellitensystem) WASSERTRANS NNSS (Navy Navigation Satellite System)

No (Nobelium) CHEMIE No (nobelium)

Nobelium nt (No) CHEMIE nobelium (No)

Nocke f FERTIG Getriebelehre disc cam (BrE), disk cam (AmE), Kunststoffinstallationen cam, KFZTECH, MECHAN cam

Nocken m KFZTECH cam, MASCHINEN cam, tappet; **~ und Stößel** m MASCHINEN cam and follower

nockenbetätigt adj MASCHINEN cam-operated

Nocken: Nockendrehen nt MASCHINEN cam turning; **Nockenerhebung** f FERTIG Getriebelehre, KFZTECH cam lobe; **Nockenform** f LUFTTRANS cam contour, MASCHINEN cam profile, MECHAN cam shape; **Nockenfräsmaschine** f FERTIG cam-milling machine

nockengesteuert[1] adj FERTIG Getriebelehre disc-cam-operated (BrE), disk-cam-operated (AmE)

nockengesteuert:[2] **~er Automat** m FERTIG disc-cam-operated screw machine (BrE), disk-cam-operated screw machine (AmE)

Nocken: Nockenprofil nt KFZTECH cam profile; **Nockenschalter** m ELEKTRIZ cam switch; **Nockenscheibe** f FERTIG plate cam, LUFTTRANS cam lobe, MASCHINEN disc cam (BrE), disk cam (AmE); **Nockenschleifmaschine** f MASCHINEN cam grinder; **Nockenschließwinkel** m KFZTECH cam angle; **Nockensteuerung** f FERTIG cam control, cam gear;

Nockenstößel m FERTIG Getriebelehre cam follower, KFZTECH cam following, LUFTTRANS cam follower, MASCHINEN cam follower, cam roller, MECHAN cam follower

nockenverriegelt adj FERTIG cam-lock

Nocken: Nockenvorsprung m KFZTECH cam lobe

Nockenwelle f KFZTECH, MASCHINEN, MECHAN camshaft; **Nockenwellenantrieb** m KFZTECH camshaft drive, camshaft drive chain; **Nockenwellenantriebsgehäuse** nt KFZTECH timing gear housing; **Nockenwellenbuchse** f KFZTECH camshaft bushing; **Nockenwellengehäuse** nt MASCHINEN camshaft box; **Nockenwellenhülse** f KFZTECH camshaft bushing; **Nockenwellenräder** nt pl MASCHINEN camshaft gears; **Nockenwellenschalter** m ELEKTRIZ camshaft controller; **Nockenwellenschleifmaschine** f MASCHINEN camshaft grinding machine; **Nockenwellenspiel** nt KFZTECH camshaft clearance

Nocken: Nockenwirkung f MASCHINEN cam action

nodular: ~e Korrosion f KERNTECH nodular corrosion

Nominalleistung f MASCHINEN rated capacity, rated power, rating

Nominalmerkmal nt QUAL nominal characteristic

nominell: ~er Meßbereich m LABOR rated range; **~e Musikleistung** f AUFNAHME music power rating

Nomogramm nt PHYS nomograph

Nonacosan nt CHEMIE nonacosane

Nonan nt CHEMIE nonane; **Nonan-** pref CHEMIE nonyl; **Nonansäure** f CHEMIE nonoic acid

Nonen nt CHEMIE nonene, nonylene

Nonius m FERTIG, MASCHINEN, MECHAN, METROL vernier; **Noniuseinstellung** f GERÄT vernier adjustment; **Noniuspotentiometer** nt ELEKTRIZ vernier potentiometer; **Noniusskale** f MASCHINEN vernier scale

Nonose f CHEMIE nonose

Nonstop: ~ Flug m LUFTTRANS nonstop flight; **Nonstop-Transportsystem** nt TRANS continuous transportation system

Nonwoven-Matte f KUNSTSTOFF nonwoven mat

Nonwoven-Scrim nt KER & GLAS nonwoven scrim

Nonyl- pref CHEMIE nonyl

NO-OP[1] abbr (Nulloperation, keine Operation) COMP & DV NO-OP (no-operation)

NO-OP:[2] **~ Befehl** m COMP & DV NO-OP instruction

Noppe f KER & GLAS knop, TEXTIL nep, slub

Noppen nt TEXTIL napping, picking

noppen vt TEXTIL nap

Noppenwerkzeuge nt pl KER & GLAS knob tools

Noradrenalin nt CHEMIE noradrenaline

Norator m PHYS elektrisches Bauelement norator

Norbornadien nt CHEMIE norbornadiene

Norbornan nt CHEMIE norbornane

Nord- pref WASSERTRANS north

Nordamerikanische Weltraumbehörde f (NASA) RAUMFAHRT National Aeronautics and Space Administration (NASA)

Norden[1] m WASSERTRANS north

Norden:[2] **nach ~ drehen** vi WASSERTRANS Wind veer northward

Nordhauser: ~sche Schwefelsäure f CHEMIE Nordhausen acid, oleum

nördlich[1] adj WASSERTRANS north, northerly

nördlich:[2] **~e Breite** f WASSERTRANS Navigation northern latitude

Nordlicht nt WASSERTRANS Wetterkunde aurora borealis, northern lights

Nordpol *m* PHYS north pole
nordstabilisiert *adj* WASSERTRANS *Radar* north-up
nordwärts[1] *adv* WASSERTRANS north, northerly
nordwärts:[2] ~ **anliegen** *vi* WASSERTRANS *Navigation* stand to the north
Nordwind *m* WASSERTRANS north wind
Norephedrin *nt* CHEMIE norephedrine
Norepinephrin *nt* CHEMIE noradrenaline
NOR-Gatter *nt* COMP & DV NOR gate
NOR-Glied *nt* COMP & DV NOR circuit
Norm *f* COMP & DV, FERNSEH, KONTROLL, MASCHINEN, METALL, TELEKOM standard
Normal *nt* QUAL measurement standard, standard, TELEKOM standard
normal[1] *adj* PHYS standard, *im rechten Winkel* normal
normal:[2] ~**e Abschaltung** *f* KERNTECH *eines Reaktors* proper shutdown; ~**e Arbeitsbedingungen** *f pl* MASCHINEN normal working conditions; ~**e Betriebsbedingungen** *f pl* KONTROLL normal operating conditions; ~**e Bremsbetätigung** *f* EISENBAHN normal brake application; ~**e Einsatzbedingungen** *f pl* MASCHINEN normal working conditions; ~**es Energieniveau** *nt* KERNTECH normal energy level; ~**er Fehler** *m* COMP & DV soft error; ~**e Hörfläche** *f* AKUSTIK normal auditory sensation area; ~**e Hör-Schmerzgrenze** *f* AKUSTIK normal threshold of painful hearing; ~**e Hörschwelle** *f* AKUSTIK normal hearing threshold; ~**e Leitung** *f* TELEKOM ordinary line; ~**e Prüfung** *f* QUAL normal inspection; ~**e Schwingung** *f* PHYS *linear polarisiert* normal mode; ~**er Sinkflugwinkel** *m* LUFTTRANS normal descent angle; ~**e Springzeitebbe** *f* NICHTFOSS ENERG low-water ordinary spring tides; ~**e Springzeitflut** *f* NICHTFOSS ENERG HWOST, high-water ordinary spring tide; ~**e Vakuumbremsbetätigung** *f* EISENBAHN normal vacuum brake application; ~**e Verbindung** *f* KERNTECH normal coupling; ~**er Verkehr** *m* TRANS normal traffic; ~**er Verkehrsfluß** *m* TRANS normal flow; ~**es Wasser** *nt* KERNTECH normal water, ordinary water; ~**er Zeeman-Effekt** *m* PHYS normal Zeeman effect
normal:[3] **auf ~en Druck bringen** *vt* KERNTECH depressurize
Normal: **Normalbatterie** *f* ELEKTROTECH standard cell; **Normalbaulänge** *f* FERTIG *Kunststoffinstallationen* standard overall length; **Normalbeanspruchung** *f* MASCHINEN normal stress; **Normalbedingungen** *f pl* MASCHINEN normal conditions; **Normalbenzin** *nt* KFZTECH regular gasoline (AmE), regular petrol (BrE); **Normalbereich** *m* COMP & DV normal range, GERÄT standard range; **Normalbeschleunigung** *f* MASCHINEN normal acceleration; **Normalbraunglas** *nt* KER & GLAS neutral amber glass; **Normalbruch** *m* METALL normal rupture; **Normaldatenfluß** *m* COMP & DV normal flow; **Normaldruck** *m* HEIZ & KÄLTE standard pressure
Normale *f* GEOM normal
Normal: **Normaleinstellung der Objektivstandarte** *f* FOTO front standard adjustment; **Normalelement** *nt* ELEKTRIZ, ELEKTROTECH, PHYS standard cell; **Normalfarben** *f pl* DRUCK standard inks; **Normalflamme** *f* BAU neutral flame; **Normalform** *f* COMP & DV normal form, MATH standard form; **Normalformat** *nt* COMP & DV normal format; **Normalfrequenz des Atomstrahls** *f* KERNTECH atomic beam frequency standard; **Normalfrequenzgenerator** *m* AUFNAHME mit *Frequenzsynthese* synthesizer, ELEKTRONIK, RADIO,

TELEKOM frequency synthesizer; **Normalfrequenz-Vergleichscharakteristik** *f* AKUSTIK standard frequency compensation characteristics; **Normalglas** *nt* KER & GLAS neutral glass
normalglühen *vt* MECHAN normalize
Normal: **Normalhöhe** *f* DRUCK standard height; **Normalhörender** *m* AKUSTIK normal listener
normalisiert: ~**e Bohrrate** *f* ERDÖL *Geologie* NDR, normalized drilling rate; ~**e Frequenz** *f* OPTIK, TELEKOM normalized frequency; ~**e Nachweisbarkeit** *f* OPTIK normalized detectivity
Normalisierung *f* COMP & DV normalization
Normal: **Normalkondensator** *m* ELEKTROTECH standard capacitor; **Normalkoordinaten** *f pl* PHYS normal coordinates; **Normalkraft** *f* FERTIG *Zahnrad* pressure load; **Normallehre** *f* MASCHINEN standard gage (AmE), standard gauge (BrE); **Normallichtquelle** *f* ELEKTROTECH standard light source, OPTIK standard source; **Normalmaß** *nt* MASCHINEN standard gage (AmE), standard gauge (BrE); **Normalmeßbereich** *m* GERÄT standard measuring range, standard range; **Normalmikrofon** *nt* AUFNAHME standard microphone; **Normalnull** *nt* (*NN*) WASSERTRANS mean sea level (*msl*); **über Normalnull** *nt* (*üNN*) WASSERTRANS above sea level (*asl*); **Normalobjektiv** *nt* FOTO medium-angle lens, standard lens; **Normalottokraftstoff** *m* KFZTECH regular gasoline (AmE), regular petrol (BrE); **Normalprobe** *f* QUAL standard size specimen; **Normalreflexion** *f* TELEKOM specular reflection; **Normalspannung** *f* ELEKTROTECH normal voltage, KOHLEN normal stress, MASCHINEN direct stress; **Normalspur** *f* BAU, EISENBAHN standard gage (AmE), standard gauge (BrE); **Normalspurbahn** *f* EISENBAHN standard gage railroad (AmE), standard gauge railway (BrE); **Normalstand** *m* KERNTECH normal level; **Normaltemperatur** *f* ERDÖL normal temperature, HEIZ & KÄLTE, PHYS standard temperature; **Normalverkehrszeit** *f* TRANS off-peak period; **Normalverteilung** *f* COMP & DV Gaussian distribution, normal distribution, ERGON normal distribution, MATH normal curve of distribution, PHYS, QUAL normal distribution; **Normalweißglas** *nt* KER & GLAS neutral white glass; **Normalzeit** *f* WASSERTRANS *Navigation* standard time; **Normalzelle** *f* ELEKTROTECH standard cell
Norm: **Normband** *nt* COMP & DV master tape; **Normblende** *f* HYDRAUL standard orifice; **Normdruck** *m* MASCHINEN, THERM normal pressure; **Normdüse** *f* GERÄT standard nozzle; **Normenfestlegung** *f* LUFTTRANS data convention; **Normenwandlung** *f* FERNSEH standards conversion; **Normfarbsignal** *nt* FERNSEH tristimulus signal
normgerecht *adj* KONSTZEICH conforming to standards
Norm: **Normgewicht** *nt* METROL standard weight
Normieren *nt* METROL gaging (AmE), gauging (BrE)
normieren *vt* COMP & DV scale
normiert: ~**er britischer Stecker** *m* ELEKTRIZ Home Office socket (BrE); ~**e Frequenz** *f* OPTIK, TELEKOM normalized frequency; ~**e Nachweisbarkeit** *f* TELEKOM normalized detectivity; ~**e Packung** *f* VERPACK package for standardization
Normierung *f* COMP & DV scaling, FERNSEH standardization; **Normierungsbit** *nt* COMP & DV noisy digit; **Normierungsfaktor** *m* COMP & DV scale factor
Norm: **Normkegel** *m* MASCHINEN standard taper
normkonform: **nicht ~** *adj* MASCHINEN bastard
Normorphin *nt* CHEMIE normorphine

Norm: **Normschrift** *f* KONSTZEICH standard lettering; **Normteil** *nt* MASCHINEN standard part; **Normtemperatur** *f* HEIZ & KÄLTE standard temperature; **Normtest** *m* LUFTTRANS certification test; **Normumformung** *f* FERNSEH standards conversion

Normung *f* COMP & DV, MASCHINEN standardization, METALL normalization, PHYS, TELEKOM standardization

Norm: **Normvorschrift** *f* MASCHINEN standard specification; **Normwahlschalter** *m* FERNSEH standards selector

Nornarcein *nt* CHEMIE nornarceine

Nornicotin *nt* CHEMIE nornicotine

Noropian- *pref* CHEMIE noropianic

Norton: **~scher Satz** *m* PHYS Norton's theorem; **Norton-Getriebe** *nt* FERTIG Norton-type mechanism, MASCHINEN Norton gearbox; **Nortongetriebekasten** *m* FERTIG Norton box; **Nortonschubgetriebe** *nt* FERTIG Norton-type feed box

Norvalin *nt* CHEMIE aminopentanoic acid, norvaline

NOR-Verknüpfung *f* COMP & DV NOR operation

NOS *abbr* (*Notrufortungssender*) TELEKOM ELT (*emergency locator transmitter*)

Noscapin *nt* CHEMIE narcotine, noscapine, opianine

Nose-In-Aufstellung *f* LUFTTRANS nose-in positioning

Nose-Out-Aufstellung *f* LUFTTRANS nose-out positioning

Not *f* FERTIG *Kunststoffinstallationen* emergency

notablassen *vt* LUFTTRANS jettison

Not: **Notabschalter** *m* SICHERHEIT *Maschinensicherheit* emergency stopping device; **Notabschaltknopf** *m* SICHERHEIT panic button; **Notabschaltstab** *m* KERNTECH emergency shutdown rod; **Notabschaltung** *f* COMP & DV emergency shutdown, KERNTECH emergency shutdown, scram; **Notabstieg** *m* LUFTTRANS emergency descent

notabwerfen *vt* LUFTTRANS jettison

Not: **Notaggregat** *nt* ELEKTROTECH stand-by set; **Notanlage** *f* TELEKOM emergency installation; **Notausgang** *m* LUFTTRANS escape lane, RAUMFAHRT *Raumschiff* emergency escape, SICHERHEIT emergency exit, fire escape, THERMOD fire exit; **Notausrüstung** *f* SICHERHEIT emergency equipment; **Notausstieg** *m* RAUMFAHRT escape hatch; **Notbake** *f* RAUMFAHRT *Sender* distress beacon; **Notbakensender** *m* RAUMFAHRT *Weltraumfunk* emergency beacon; **Notbatterie** *f* ELEKTRIZ, ELEKTROTECH emergency battery; **Notbehandlung** *f* SICHERHEIT emergency treatment; **Notbeleuchtung** *f* ELEKTRIZ emergency lighting; **Notbereitschaft** *f* TELEKOM emergency attention; **Notbetrieb** *m* RAUMFAHRT *Raumschiff* emergency mode; **Notbremse** *f* EISENBAHN emergency brake; **Notdecke** *f* SICHERHEIT rescue blanket; **Notdienst** *m* SICHERHEIT, TELEKOM emergency service; **Notdruckknopf** *m* ELEKTRIZ emergency button

Notfall *m* SICHERHEIT emergency, emergency case; **Notfallausrüstung** *f* LUFTTRANS emergency equipment; **Notfalleitung** *f* SICHERHEIT emergency control; **Notfallendschalter an Hebewerkzeugen** *m* SICHERHEIT emergency stop at end of hoist; **Notfallhilfe** *f* TRANS emergency aid; **Notfallmaßnahme** *f* SICHERHEIT emergency measure; **Notfallräumung** *f* SICHERHEIT *von Gebäuden* emergency evacuation; **Notfallspur** *f* LUFTTRANS escape lane; **Notfallzentrum** *nt* SICHERHEIT emergency center (AmE), emergency centre (BrE)

Not: **Notgerät** *nt* ELEKTROTECH stand-by unit;

Notglocke *f* ELEKTRIZ alarm bell; **Nothochwasserentlastungsanlage** *f* WASSERVERSORG emergency spillway

Notizblockspeicher *m* COMP & DV scratch pad memory

Not: **Notkompaß** *m* LUFTTRANS stand-by compass; **Notkühlung** *f* KERNTECH emergency cooling, *des Reaktorkerns* emergency core coolant; **Notlandung** *f* LUFTTRANS forced landing, *im Wasser* ditching, RAUMFAHRT *Raumschiff* emergency landing; **Notlasche** *f* EISENBAHN emergency fish-plating; **Notlaufeigenschaften** *f pl* FERTIG *Lagermetalle* resistance to galling; **Notluftschleuse** *f* KERNTECH emergency air lock; **Notoberflächenentlastungsanlage** *f* WASSERVERSORG emergency spillway

notorisch: **~ bekannte Marke** *f* PATENT well-known mark

Not: **Notortungsfeuer** *nt* LUFTTRANS, WASSERTRANS emergency location beacon; **Notplatzfeuer** *nt* LUFTTRANS, WASSERTRANS emergency location beacon; **Notrakete** *f* WASSERTRANS emergency rocket; **Notruder** *nt* WASSERTRANS jury rudder

Notruf *m* LUFTTRANS distress call, TELEKOM emergency call; **Notruffunkfeuer mit Standortmeldung** *nt* TELEKOM emergency position-indicating radio beacon; **Notrufortungssender** *m* (*NOS*) TELEKOM emergency locator transmitter (*ELT*); **Notrufsäule** *f* TRANS emergency telephone; **Notrufsystem** *nt* TRANS emergency call system; **Notruftelefon** *nt* TELEKOM emergency telephone

Not: **Notrutsche** *f* LUFTTRANS emergency slide, escape chute, SICHERHEIT rescue chute; **Notschalter** *m* LUFTTRANS crash switch, *Aufzug* emergency stop, **Notschwimmerfahrwerk** *nt* WASSERTRANS emergency flotation gear; **Notsignal** *nt* EISENBAHN danger signal, LUFTTRANS distress signal; **Notsignalfeuer** *nt* WASSERTRANS distress flare; **Notspeicherauszug** *m* COMP & DV rescue dump; **Notsteuerung** *f* LUFTTRANS emergency control; **Notstromaggregat** *nt* ELEKTRIZ emergency power supply, FERNSEH electric generator, MECHAN emergency power generator; **Notstrombatterie** *f* ELEKTROTECH floating battery; **Notstromdieselaggregat** *nt* KERNTECH emergency diesel generator; **Notstromumschaltung** *f* ELEKTROTECH battery backup; **Notstromversorgung** *f* ELEKTRIZ emergency power supply, FERNSEH emergency power supply, TELEKOM backup power supply; **Notventil** *nt* MECHAN safety valve; **Notverfahren** *nt* LUFTTRANS emergency procedure; **Notverschluß** *m* SICHERHEIT panic bolt; **Notversorgungstank** *m* LUFTTRANS emergency supply tank; **Notwasserung** *f* LUFTTRANS ditching; **Notzustand** *m* KERNTECH *eines Reaktors* emergency condition

Novain *nt* CHEMIE carnitine

Novocain *nt* CHEMIE novocaine

Novolak *m* KUNSTSTOFF novolac

Np[1] *abbr* (*Neper*) PHYS Np (*neper*)

Np[2] (*Neptunium*) CHEMIE Np (*neptunium*)

N-Phenylurethan *nt* CHEMIE N-phenyl urethane, phenylurea

npn-Transistor *m* ELEKTRONIK npn transistor

N-Ring *m* (*Nasenring*) KFZTECH *Motor* oil scraper ring

NRZ-Aufzeichnung *f* (*Aufzeichnung ohne Rückkehr zu Null*) COMP & DV NRZ recording (*nonreturn-to-zero recording*)

NRZ-Modulation *f* (*Modulation ohne Rückkehr zu Null*) TELEKOM NRZ modulation (*nonreturn-to-zero modulation*)

n-schrittig: **~er Anlasser** *m* ELEKTRIZ n-step starter

n-stellig: **~er Schalter** *m* ELEKTRIZ n-way switch

n-tes: ~ **Bündel** *nt* TELEKOM n-th choice group

NTSC *abbr (Amerikanischer Fernsehnormungsausschuß)* FERNSEH NTSC *(National Television Standards Committee)*

NTSC-Farbfernsehsystem *nt* FERNSEH NTSC color television system

Nuancierung *f* KUNSTSTOFF shading, tinting, TEXTIL shade

Nuclein *nt* CHEMIE nuclein; **Nuclein-** *pref* CHEMIE nucleic; **Nucleinsäure** *f* CHEMIE nucleic acid

Nucleohiston *nt* CHEMIE nucleohistone

Nucleon *nt* PHYS, TEILPHYS nucleon

nucleophil[1] *adj* CHEMIE nucleophilic

nucleophil:[2] ~**e Kraft** *f* CHEMIE nucleophilicity

Nucleophilie *f* CHEMIE nucleophilicity

Nü-Faktor *m* PHYS nu-factor

Nuklear- *pref* KERNTECH nuclear

nuklear[1] *adj* KERNTECH nuclear; ~ **betrieben** *adj* KERNTECH, RAUMFAHRT *Raumschiff* nuclear-powered

nuklear:[2] ~**er elektromagnetischer Impuls** *m* TELEKOM nuclear electromagnetic pulse; ~**e Spinquantenzahl** *f (I)* KERNTECH nuclear spin quantum number *(I)*; ~ **ungefährlicher Niederschlag** *m* UMWELTSCHMUTZ dry deposition

Nuklear-: Nuklearantrieb *m* RAUMFAHRT *Raumschiff* nuclear propulsion; **Nuklearaufklärungssatellit** *m* RAUMFAHRT nuclear detection satellite; **Nuklearbatterie** *f* ELEKTROTECH nuclear battery; **Nuklearlog** *nt* ERDÖL *Bohrlochmeßtechnik* nuclear log

nuklearmagnetisch: ~**er Resonanzlog** *nt* ERDÖL *Bohrlochmeßtechnik* nuclear magnetic resonance log

Nuklear-: Nuklearreaktor mit fossilem Brennstoff *m* KERNTECH fossil nuclear reactor; **Nuklearsicherheit** *f* KERNTECH, SICHERHEIT nuclear safety; **Nuklearstromversorgung** *f* KERNTECH, RAUMFAHRT *Raumschiff* nuclear power supply

Nukleierungsfaktor *m* KERNTECH nucleation factor

Nukleon: äußeres ~ *nt* KERNTECH peripheral nucleon

Nukleonenzahl *f (A)* TEILPHYS mass number *(A)*

Nukleonik *f* KERNTECH, PHYS nucleonics

Nukleus *m* COMP & DV nucleus

Nuklid *nt* PHYS, TEILPHYS nuclide

Null[1] *f* MATH naught, nil, zero

Null:[2] **mit** ~ **en auffüllen** *vt* COMP & DV zerofill; **auf** ~ **setzen** *vt* MATH zero; **auf** ~ **stellen** *vt* COMP & DV reset, zeroize, MASCHINEN reset to zero, set to zero

Null:[3] **zu** ~ **werden** *vi* PHYS become zero

Null: Nullabgleich *m* GERÄT *Brücke* null balance; **Nullachse** *f* BAU neutral axis; **Nulladreßbefehl** *m* COMP & DV zero-address instruction; **Nullanweisung** *f* COMP & DV null statement; **Nullanzeigegerät** *nt* GERÄT null instrument; **Nullanzeigeinstrument** *nt* GERÄT balance indicator; **Nullanzeiger** *m* COMP & DV null indicator

Nullator *m* PHYS *elektrisches Bauelement* nullator

Null: Nullauftriebswinkel *m* LUFTTRANS zero-lift angle; **Nullband** *nt* KERNTECH zero band; **Nullbefehl** *m* COMP & DV do-nothing instruction; **Nulldrehung** *f* TEXTIL zero twist; **Nulleinstellung** *f* FERTIG, KERNTECH zero setting, MASCHINEN zero adjustment, zero setting; **Nulleinsteuerung** *f* COMP & DV zero insert; **Nulleintrag** *m* COMP & DV null entry; **Nulleiter** *m* ELEKTROTECH *Verteilung* neutral conductor

nullen *vt* FERNSEH, MATH zero

Null: Nullenergiereaktor *m* KERNTECH zero-energy reactor, zero-power reactor; **Nullenunterdrückung** *f* COMP & DV zero elimination, zero suppression; **Nullenzirkel**

m FERTIG bow instrument, spring bow compass, MASCHINEN bow compass, spring bow compass; **Null-Fluß-Aufhängung** *f* KFZTECH null flux suspension; **Nullfolge** *f* COMP & DV null sequence; **Nullgalvanometer** *nt* ELEKTRIZ null galvanometer; **Null-Grad-Spanwinkel** *m* FERTIG zero rake angle; **Nullhubstellung** *f* FERTIG *Pumpe* no-stroke position; **Nullinie** *f* MASCHINEN zero line; **Nullinstrument** *nt* GERÄT balance meter, center-reading instrument (AmE), centre-reading instrument (BrE), central-zero instrument, null instrument; **Nulljustierung** *f* KERNTECH zero adjustment; **Null-Last-Prüfung** *f* ELEKTRIZ no-load test; **Null-Last-Testen** *nt* ELEKTRIZ no-load test; **Null-Lastwärmeverbrauch** *m* KER & GLAS no-load heat consumption; **Null-Leistungsfaktorprüfung** *f* ELEKTRIZ zero-power-factor test; **Null-Leistungsreaktor** *m* KERNTECH zero-energy reactor, zero-power reactor; **Null-Luminanz** *f* FERNSEH zero luminance; **Null-Luminanzebene** *f* FERNSEH zero-luminance plane; **Nullmethode** *f* ELEKTRIZ, PHYS null method; **Nulloperation** *f (NO-OP)* COMP & DV no-operation *(NO-OP)*; **Nulloperationsbefehl** *m* COMP & DV no-operation instruction; **Nullpegel** *m* AUFNAHME zero level

Nullpunkt *m* GEOM zero point, *von Koordinaten* origin, MATH zero point, *eines Grafs oder Koordinatensystems* origin, PHYS neutral point, THERMOD zero; **Nullpunkt-Amperemeter** *nt* GERÄT center zero ammeter (AmE), centre zero ammeter (BrE); **Nullpunktanhebung** *f* REGELUNG zero elevation; **Nullpunktdraht** *m* ELEKTRIZ neutral wire; **Nullpunktenergie** *f* KERNTECH zero-energy level, PHYS, STRAHLPHYS zero-point energy; **Nullpunktfehler** *m* COMP & DV zero error; **Nullpunktklemme** *f* ELEKTRIZ neutral terminal; **Nullpunktrelais** *nt* ELEKTRIZ neutral relay; **Nullpunktschwankungen** *f pl* STRAHLPHYS zero-point fluctuations; **Nullpunktverlagerung** *f* KER & GLAS zero displacement; **Nullpunktverschiebung** *f* COMP & DV zero shift; **Nullpunktverschiebungs-Spannung** *f* ELEKTRIZ neutral point displacement voltage

nullsetzen *vt* KONTROLL reset

Nullspannung *f* ELEKTRIZ no voltage, null voltage, zero potential, zero voltage; **Nullspannungsabgleich** *m* FERNSEH zero-volt adjustment; **Nullspannungsauslöserelais** *nt* ELEKTRIZ, ELEKTROTECH no-voltage release relay

nullspannungsgesichert *adj* COMP & DV nonvolatile

Null: Nullspant *m* WASSERTRANS *Schiffbau* midship section; **Nullstelle** *f* MATH *einer Funktion* zero

nullstellen *vt* AUFNAHME zero, COMP & DV zeroize

Nullstellung *f* COMP & DV reset, MASCHINEN zero adjustment, zero setting, zeroizing; ~ **eines Meßinstrumentes** *f* METROL zero of a measuring instrument

Null: Nullträger *m* FERNSEH zero carrier

nullwertig *adj* CHEMIE avalent, zerovalent

Null: Nullzeichen *nt* COMP & DV null character, null; **Nullzustand** *m* COMP & DV quiescent state

Numerierapparat *m* DRUCK numbering machine, VERPACK numbering apparatus

numeriert: ~**es Exemplar** *nt* DRUCK numbered copy

Numerierung *f* COMP & DV numeration, DRUCK, FOTO numbering; **Numerierungsart** *f* COMP & DV enumeration type

Numerierwerk *nt* DRUCK numbering machine

numerisch[1] *adj* COMP & DV, KONTROLL numeric, MATH

numerical; ~ **gesteuert** *adj* MECHAN numerically-controlled

numerisch:[2] **~e Analyse** *f* COMP & DV, MATH numerical analysis; **~e Apertur** *f* ELEKTROTECH, OPTIK, PHYS, TELEKOM NA, numerical aperture; **~e Apertur der Einkopplung** *f* TELEKOM launch numerical aperture; **~er Code** *m* COMP & DV numerical code; **~e Darstellung** *f* COMP & DV numeric representation; **~e Einkopplungsapertur** *f* OPTIK launch numerical aperture; **~es Feld** *nt* COMP & DV *COBOL* numeric item; **~ gesteuerte Lehrenbohrmaschine** *f* MASCHINEN NC jig borer; **~e gesteuerte Maschine** *f* MASCHINEN numerical control machine; **~es Literal** *nt* COMP & DV numeric literal; **~e Methode** *f* MATH numerical method; **~e Steuerung** *f* *(NC)* COMP & DV, ELEKTRIZ, KONTROLL, MASCHINEN, MECHAN numerical control *(NC)*; **~e Strömungsmechanik** *f* STRÖMPHYS computational fluid dynamics; **~e Tastatur** *f* COMP & DV numeric pad; **~er Tastenblock** *m* COMP & DV numeric keypad, numeric pad; **~er Wert** *m* METROL numerical value; **~er 10er-Block** *m* COMP & DV numeric keypad, numeric pad; **~es Zeichen** *nt* COMP & DV numeric character

Numerus *m* MATH antilogarithm

Nummer *f* COMP & DV number, TELEKOM code; **~ der Schiffsfunkstelle** *f* TELEKOM ship station number; **Nummerngeber** *m* TELEKOM call sender; **Nummernschalter** *m* TELEKOM dial; **Nummernscheibe** *f* TELEKOM dial; **Nummernschild** *nt* KFZTECH *Rechtsvorschriften* license plate (AmE), numberplate (BrE)

Nummerung *f* DRUCK numbering

N-UND-Schaltung *f* *(NICHT-UND-Schaltung)* PHYS NAND gate *(NOT AND gate)*

Nur-Frachtcharterflug *m* LUFTTRANS all-cargo charter flight

Nur-Frachtdienst *m* LUFTTRANS all-cargo service, all-freight service

Nur-Frachtfluglinie *f* LUFTTRANS all-cargo carrier

Nur-Frachtflugzeug *nt* LUFTTRANS all-cargo aircraft

Nur-Frachtlastfaktor *m* LUFTTRANS all-cargo load factor

Nur-Lese-Bit *nt* COMP & DV read-only bit

Nur-Lese-Speicher *m* *(ROM)* COMP & DV, ELEKTRIZ, ELEKTROTECH, RADIO read-only memory *(ROM)*

Nur-Postdienst *m* LUFTTRANS all-mail service

Nußabrieb *m* KOHLEN nutty slack

Nußklassiersieb *nt* KOHLEN nut-sizing screen

Nüstergatt *nt* WASSERTRANS *Schiffbau* limber hole

Nut *f* BAU flute, groove, housing, notch, quirk, rabbet, ELEKTROTECH slot, *Hohlleiter* gash, FERTIG gash, groove, rabbet, slot, *Kunststoffinstallationen* groove, MASCHINEN flute, groove; **Nut- und Federholz** *nt* BAU matchboard; **Nut- und Federverspundung** *f* BAU grooved and tongued joint; **Nutanker** *m* ELEKTROTECH slotted armature

Nutation *f* PHYS, RAUMFAHRT nutation; **Nutationdämpfung** *f* RAUMFAHRT *Raumschiff* nutation damper

Nute *f* KERNTECH groove

Nuteisen *nt* MECHAN groove-cutting chisel

Nuten *nt* BAU fluting, MASCHINEN grooving

nuten *vt* BAU channel, groove, rabbet, FERTIG keyway, match

Nute: **Nutenanker** *m* ELEKTRIZ slotted armature; **Nutenauslauf** *m* MASCHINEN flute run-out; **Nutendrehen** *nt* FERTIG grooving; **Nuteneinschleifen** *nt* FERTIG nicking; **Nutenfräsen** *nt* MASCHINEN keyway milling, keywaying, slot milling; **Nutenfräser** *m* MASCHINEN

T-slot cutter, keyway cutter; **Nutenfräsmaschine** *f* MASCHINEN keyway-milling machine, slot milling machine; **Nutenkeil** *m* MASCHINEN feather key, sunk key; **Nutenmeißel** *m* FERTIG cape chisel, half-round chisel, MASCHINEN grooving tool, slotting tool; **Nutenschaftfräser** *m* MASCHINEN slot mill; **Nutenscheibe** *f* FERTIG *Getriebelehre* disc cam (BrE), disk cam (AmE); **Nutenscheibenfräser** *m* MASCHINEN slotting side and face cutter; **Nutenstoßen** *nt* MASCHINEN keyway slotting; **Nutenstoßmeißel** *m* FERTIG slotting tool; **Nutenwalze** *f* MASCHINEN grooved roll

Nut: **Nuthobel** *m* BAU grooving plane, plough (BrE), plow (AmE), plough plane (BrE), plow plane (AmE), rabbet plane, rebate plane; **Nutkeil** *m* MASCHINEN key; **Nutmutter** *f* MASCHINEN slotted nut

NU-Ton *m* *(kein Anschluß unter dieser Nummer)* TELEKOM NUT *(number-unobtainable tone)*

Nut: **Nutringmanschette** *f* MASCHINEN chevron-type seal; **Nutrolle** *f* MASCHINEN grooved pulley; **Nutscheibe** *f* MASCHINEN grooved wheel; **Nutzarbeit** *f* MASCHINEN effective work; **Nutzaussendung** *f* TELEKOM wanted emission; **Nutzbandbreite** *f* AUFNAHME effective bandwidth

nutzbar[1] *adj* COMP & DV usable, MECHAN effective

nutzbar:[2] **~es Akustikzentrum** *nt* AUFNAHME effective acoustic center (AmE), effective acoustic centre (BrE); **~er Bereich** *m* GERÄT *unter einschränkenden Bedingungen* overrange; **~es Gefälle** *nt* NICHTFOSS ENERG effective head; **~e Leistung** *f* ELEKTRIZ available power; **~er Speicherraum** *m* WASSERVERSORG live storage

nutzbar:[3] **~ machen** *vt* WASSERVERSORG *Wasser* harness

Nutzbarmachung *f* METALL activation

Nutzbremsung *f* EISENBAHN regenerative braking

Nutzdampf *m* KERNTECH service steam

Nutzeffekt *m* HEIZ & KÄLTE useful effect

nutzen *vt* BAU occupy

Nutzenergie *f* ELEKTRIZ active current

Nutzfahrzeug *nt* KFZTECH utility vehicle, *Fahrzeugart* commercial vehicle; **Nutzfahrzeug-** *pref* KFZTECH utility

Nutzfläche *f* BAU floor space, MASCHINEN useful surface

Nutzförderhöhe *f* FERTIG operating head

Nutzholz *nt* BAU timber

Nutzladefaktor *m* TRANS *Transportflugzeuge* load factor

Nutzlast *f* BAU live load, ELEKTRIZ active load, KFZTECH live weight, payload, LUFTTRANS, MEERSCHMUTZ payload, RAUMFAHRT *Raumschiff* cargo, payload, TELEKOM payload, WASSERVERSORG service load; **Nutzlastbedienungsgerät** *nt* RAUMFAHRT *Raumschiff* payload manipulator arm

Nutzleistung *f* ELEKTRIZ effective power; **Nutzleistungsturbine** *f* LUFTTRANS free turbine

Nutzmachung *f* WASSERVERSORG harnessing

Nutzmasse *f* MEERSCHMUTZ payload

Nutzpferdestärke *f* MASCHINEN EHP, effective horsepower

Nutzschicht *f* TEXTIL top layer

Nutzsignal *nt* ELEKTRONIK wanted signal, TELEKOM desired signal

Nutzträger-Störträger-Abstand *m* TELEKOM wanted-to-unwanted carrier power ratio

Nutzungsdauer *f* KERNTECH, KOHLEN service life

nutzungsgemäß: **~e Zahlungsgrundlage** *f* TELEKOM pay-by-use basis

Nutzwärme *f* THERMOD available heat

Nutzzeit f COMP & DV *des Systems* uptime
Nutzzyklus m KONTROLL duty cycle
Nuvistor m RADIO nuvistor
Nydrazid nt CHEMIE nydrazid
Nylon nt DRUCK, KUNSTSTOFF nylon; **Nylonbuchse** f KUNSTSTOFF nylon bush; **Nylonseil** nt MASCHINEN nylon rope

nylonverstärkt adj VERPACK nylon-reinforced
Nyquist-Demodulator m FERNSEH Nyquist demodulator
Nyquist-Ortskurve f REGELUNG Nyquist plot
Nystagmus m ERGON nystagmus
Nystatin nt CHEMIE nystatin

O

OA *abbr (Operationsverstärker, Rechenverstärker)*
COMP & DV, ELEKTRONIK, PHYS, RADIO, TELEKOM op
amp *(operational amplifier)*

Obelisk *m* GEOM obelisk

oben:[1] **nach ~ gerichtete Winkelstellung der Rotorblätter** *f* LUFTTRANS *Hubschrauber* coning angle; **nach ~
gestellte Rotorblätter** *nt pl* LUFTTRANS *Hubschrauber*
coning; **obere Abdeckplatte** *f* KERNTECH roof shielding plate; **oberer Anschluß** *m* KERNTECH upper end
fitting, *eines Brennelementes* top fitting; **oberes Auffangbecken** *nt* KERNTECH upper containment pool;
oberer Druckraum *m* KERNTECH top plenum, upper
plenum; **obere Entscheidungsgrenze** *f* QUAL upper
control limit; **obere Grenzabweichung** *f* QUAL upper
limiting deviation; **obere Grenzwellenlänge** *f* ELEK-
TRONIK threshold wavelength; **oberes Hubende** *nt*
MASCHINEN top of stroke of piston; **obere Ionosphäre**
f TELEKOM upper ionosphere; **oberer Kompressionsring** *m* KFZTECH *Kolben* top compression ring; **obere
Kühltemperatur** *f* KER & GLAS upper annealing temperature; **oberer Mühlstein** *m* LEBENSMITTEL upper
millstone; **oberes Pleuelauge** *nt* KFZTECH connecting
rod small end, small end; **oberer Rand** *m* DRUCK head
margin; **oberes Raster** *nt* KERNTECH *in einem Bündelelement* upper grid; **obere Schleusenhaltung** *f*
WASSERVERSORG head bay, head crown; **oberes
Schleusentor** *nt* NICHTFOSS ENERG head gate, sluicegate, WASSERVERSORG up-stream water gate; **oberes
Seitenband** *nt (OSB)* ELEKTRONIK, RADIO, TELEKOM
upper sideband *(USB)*; **obere Spaltzone** *f* KERNTECH
upper core; **oberes Speicherbecken** *nt* NICHTFOSS
ENERG upper storage basin; **oberer Totpunkt** *m (OT)*
KFZTECH top dead center (AmE), top dead centre
(BrE) *(top dead center)*; **obere Tragrolle** *f* MASCHINEN
carrying idler; **oberer Türriegel** *m* BAU *Türrahmen* top
rail; **obere und untere Heftung** *f* VERPACK top and
bottom stapling; **obere Verbindungsplatte** *f* KERN-
TECH *eines Rasterelementes* upper tie plate; **oberer
Verdichtungsring** *m* KFZTECH *Kolben* top compression
ring; **oberer Verschluß eines Brennelements** *m* KERN-
TECH upper end plug; **obere Walze** *f* MASCHINEN
upper roll; **obere Zwischenstufe** *f* METALL upper
bainite

oben:[2] **nach ~ gehen** *vi* WASSERTRANS *Schiff* go above

obengesteuert: ~er Motor *m* KFZTECH overhead valve
engine, OHV engine; **~es Ventil** *nt* KFZTECH OHV,
overhead valve

obenliegend: ~e Nockenwelle *f* KFZTECH, MECHAN
OHC, overhead camshaft

Oben-Top: ~ Container *m* TRANS til-top container

o-Benzoesäuresulfimid *nt* CHEMIE saccharin

Oberantrieb *m* FERTIG overcrank action

Oberband *nt* FERNSEH high band

Oberbaumaterial *nt* BAU *Gleisbau* permanent-way
equipment

Oberbegriff *m* PATENT preamble

Oberbekleidung *f* TEXTIL outerwear

Oberdeck *nt* WASSERTRANS upper deck

Oberdominante *f* AKUSTIK submediant

Oberdruckpresse *f* KUNSTSTOFF downstroke press

Oberfläche:[1] **auf der ~ schwimmend** *adj* CHEMIE super-
natant

Oberfläche[2] *f* ANSTRICH finish, surface, BAU face, KER &
GLAS finish, LUFTTRANS *Luftfahrzeug* skin, PAPIER,
PATENT *eines Zeichnungsblattes* surface

Oberfläche:[3] **die ~ durchbrechen** *vt* WASSERTRANS
broach

Oberfläche: Oberflächenabfluß *m* BAU runoff; **Oberflä-
chenabtragung** *f* MASCHINEN surface removal

oberflächenaktiv[1] *adj* CHEMIE surface-active

oberflächenaktiv:[2] **~er Bohrschlamm** *m* ERDÖL *Bohrtechnik* surfactant mud; **~es Mittel** *nt* KOHLEN
surfactant; **~er Stoff** *m* LEBENSMITTEL surfactant,
MEERSCHMUTZ surface active agent, surfactant

Oberfläche: Oberflächenbehandlung *f* BAU *Straße* surface dressing, KER & GLAS surface treatment, PAPIER
surface application; **Oberflächenbereich** *m* UMWELT-
SCHMUTZ surface area; **Oberflächenberieselung** *f* HEIZ
& KÄLTE spray cooling; **Oberflächenbeschaffenheit** *f*
FERTIG, MASCHINEN surface finish, PAPIER appearance, surface finish

oberflächenbeschrieben: ~e CD *f* OPTIK surface-written
videodisc (BrE), surface-written videodisk (AmE)

Oberfläche: Oberflächenbewässerung *f* WASSERVER-
SORG surface irrigation; **Oberflächenbrecher** *m*
MEERSCHMUTZ breaker board; **Oberflächendruckkar-
te** *f* WASSERTRANS *Wetterkunde* surface pressure chart;
Oberflächeneffektfahrzeug *nt* KFZTECH surface effect
vehicle

oberflächenemittierend: ~e Leuchtdiode *f* OPTIK
surface-emitting light-emitting diode; **~e Lumineszenzdiode** *f* OPTIK surface-emitting light-emitting
diode

Oberfläche: Oberflächenenergie *f* PHYS surface energy;
Oberflächenentlastungsanlage *f* WASSERVERSORG
flood spillway; **Oberflächenentwässerung** *f* WASSER-
TRANS surface drainage; **Oberflächenerdungskontakt**
m ELEKTRIZ surface earthing connection (BrE), surface grounding connection (AmE);
Oberflächenfärbung *f* PAPIER surface coloring (AmE),
surface colouring (BrE); **Oberflächenfehler** *m* FERTIG
surface imperfection; **Oberflächenfestigkeit** *f* PAPIER
surface bonding strength; **Oberflächenform** *f* MASCHI-
NEN surface profile

oberflächengehärtet: ~e Schiene *f* EISENBAHN surface-
hardened rail; **~er Stahl** *m* MECHAN case-hardened
steel

oberflächengetrocknet *adj* FERTIG skin-dried

Oberfläche: Oberflächengüte *f* FERTIG, MASCHINEN finish, surface finish, surface quality, MECHAN finish,
PAPIER surface finish; **Oberflächenhärte** *f* MASCHINEN
surface hardness; **Oberflächenhärtung** *f* FERTIG surface hardening, MECHAN case hardening, METALL
surface hardening; **Oberflächenhöchsttemperatur** *f* SI-
CHERHEIT *für bestimmte Gerätetypen* surface
temperature limit; **Oberflächeninduktion** *f* FERNSEH

surface induction; **Oberflächenintegral** *nt* PHYS surface integral; **Oberflächenionisierung durch Laserstrahlung** *f* KERNTECH *Massenspektroskopie* laser impact surface ionization; **Oberflächenkanal** *m* ELEKTRONIK surface channel; **Oberflächenkühlung** *f* HEIZ & KÄLTE surface cooling; **Oberflächenladung** *f* ELEKTRIZ, PHYS surface charge; **Oberflächenladungsdichte** *f* ELEKTRIZ, PHYS surface charge density; **Oberflächenlängsriß** *m* FERTIG roke; **Oberflächenleimung** *f* PAPIER surface sizing; **Oberflächenmatte** *f* KUNSTSTOFF surfacing mat; **Oberflächenmeßgerät** *nt* METROL surface measuring instrument; **Oberflächenmethode** *f* ABFALL *Ablagerungstechnik* surface method; **Oberflächenmontage** *f* COMP & DV, ELEKTRIZ surface mounting

oberflächenmontiert: ~**es Element** *nt (SMD)* ELEKTRIZ surface mounting device *(SMD)*; ~**e Steckdose** *f* ELEKTRIZ surface socket, surface-mounted socket

Oberfläche: **Oberflächenporen** *f pl* KER & GLAS apparent porosity; **Oberflächenrauheit** *f* BAU, MASCHINEN surface roughness; **Oberflächenreibung** *f* MECHAN skin friction; **Oberflächenriß** *m* LABOR vent; **Oberflächenrost** *m* BAU surface rust; **Oberflächenschicht** *f* MEERSCHMUTZ surface layer; **Oberflächenschutzfilm** *m* VERPACK surface protection film; **Oberflächensensor** *m* GERÄT surface sensor; **Oberflächenspannung** *f* BAU, KOHLEN, KUNSTSTOFF, MASCHINEN, PHYS, STRÖMPHYS surface tension; **Oberflächenspannungsmesser** *m* LABOR surface tension meter; **Oberflächenspannungstank** *m* RAUMFAHRT *Raumschiff* surface tension tank; **Oberflächenstrom** *m* TELEKOM surface current; **Oberflächenströmung** *f* WASSERTRANS *Meer* surface current; **Oberflächenstruktur** *f* MASCHINEN surface texture; **Oberflächenthermometer** *nt* GERÄT contact thermometer, surface temperature sensor; **Oberflächenverbindung** *f* TELEKOM surface connection; **Oberflächenvergütung** *f* ANSTRICH finish, surface finish, KER & GLAS blooming; **Oberflächenverletzung** *f* ANSTRICH scratch; **Oberflächenvermarkung** *f* BAU *Vermessung* surface demarcation; **Oberflächenverschleiß** *m* MASCHINEN surface wear; **Oberflächenversiegelung** *f* ABFALL *einer Deponie* final cover; **Oberflächenvorbehandlung** *f* BAU surface preparation; **Oberflächenwasser** *nt* BAU, KOHLEN, UMWELTSCHMUTZ, WASSERVERSORG surface water; **Oberflächenwasserbewirtschaftung** *f* WASSERVERSORG surface water management; **Oberflächenwassererosion** *f* KOHLEN surface water erosion; **Oberflächenwelle** *f* OPTIK surface wave; **Oberflächenwellenbauelement** *nt* TELEKOM surface acoustic wave device; **Oberflächenwiderstand** *m* WERKPRÜF surface resistance

oberflächenwirksam: ~**e Substanz** *f* CHEMIE surfactant *Oberfläche*: **Oberflächenzeichen** *nt* KONSTZEICH surface symbol, systematic symbol

Oberflammofen *m* KER & GLAS top flame furnace

Obergautsche *f* PAPIER lumpbreaker

Obergerinne *nt* HYDRAUL headrace

Obergesenk *nt* FERTIG top die, MASCHINEN upper die

Obergrenze *f* TELEKOM upper limit

Obergurt *m* BAU top flange; **Obergurtplatte** *f* WASSERTRANS *Schiffbau* rider plate

oberhalb *adv* BAU upstream

Oberhaupt: ~ **einer Schleuse** *nt* WASSERVERSORG *Hangkanal oder Oberkanal* forebay

Oberhieb *m* MASCHINEN second cut

Oberholm *m* BAU head beam

oberirdisch[1] *adj* KOHLEN overground

oberirdisch:[2] ~**es Wasser** *nt* WASSERVERSORG surface water

Oberkasten *m* FERTIG *Getriebelehre* cope

Oberlage *f* TEXTIL top ply

Oberleitung *f* BAU, EISENBAHN, ELEKTRIZ, ELEKTROTECH overhead line; **Oberleitungsbus** *m* KFZTECH electric trolley, trolley bus; **Oberleitungsgelenkverbindung** *f* EISENBAHN overhead-line knuckle; **Oberleitungssystem** *nt (O-System)* TRANS trolley system

Oberlicht *nt* WASSERTRANS *Deckausrüstung* skylight; **Oberlichtaufbau** *m* EISENBAHN clerestory

Oberlinie *f* DRUCK cap line

Oberrinne *f* WASSERVERSORG *eines Wasserrads* headrace

oberschlächtig: ~**es Wasserrad** *nt* WASSERVERSORG overshot wheel

Oberschleusendrempel *m* WASSERVERSORG head miter sill (AmE), head mitre sill (BrE)

Oberschleusenschwelle *f* WASSERVERSORG head miter sill (AmE), head mitre sill (BrE)

Oberschlitten *m* MASCHINEN top slide

Oberschwingung *f* AKUSTIK, MECHAN, RADIO harmonic; **Oberschwingungsgehalt** *m* ELEKTRONIK relative harmonic content; **Oberschwingungsgenerator** *m* PHYS harmonic generator

Oberseite *f* DRUCK felt side, LUFTTRANS *eines Flügels* upper surface, PAPIER top side; **Oberseitenanschluß** *m* ELEKTROTECH face-up; **Oberseitenbandkanal** *m* FERNSEH channel using upper sideband

oberst: ~**e Rippe** *f* LUFTTRANS *des Seitenflossenansatzes* top rib; ~**es Stockwerk** *nt* KER & GLAS top floor

Oberstrichwert *m* AUFNAHME peak power output

Obersupport *m* MASCHINEN top slide rest

Oberteil *nt* TEXTIL top; ~ **des Spindelkastens** *nt* MASCHINEN barrel; **Oberteilkomplett** *nt* FERTIG *Kunststoffinstallationen* bonnet assembly

Oberton *m* ELEKTRONIK overtone

Obertor *nt* NICHTFOSS ENERG head gate, WASSERVERSORG sluicegate, upstream water gate, *einer Kanalschleuse* crown gate, *einer Schleuse* head gate

Oberwalze *f* KER & GLAS pressure roller, MASCHINEN, PAPIER top roll

Oberwasser *nt* HYDRAUL headwater, NICHTFOSS ENERG upstream head, WASSERVERSORG head bay, head crown, headwater

Oberwelle *f* AKUSTIK, ELEKTRONIK harmonic; **Oberwellendämpfung** *f* ELEKTRONIK harmonic attenuation; **Oberwellenfilter** *nt* ELEKTRONIK, RAUMFAHRT *Weltraumfunk* harmonic filter; **Oberwellengehalt** *nt* ELEKTRONIK harmonic content; **Oberwellengenerator** *m* PHYS, TELEKOM harmonic generator; **Oberwellenmeßgerät** *nt* GERÄT harmonic detector; **Oberwellenquarz** *m* ELEKTRONIK harmonic mode crystal; **Oberwellensperrung** *f* ELEKTRONIK harmonic rejection; **Oberwellenstrom** *f* ELEKTROTECH current ripple; **Oberwellenunterdrückung** *f* ELEKTRONIK harmonic rejection

Oberwerk *nt* WASSERTRANS *Schiffkonstruktion* upper works; **Oberwerkbau** *m* KOHLEN rise workings

Objekt *nt* COMP & DV object, object variable; **Objektcode** *m* COMP & DV object code; **Objekterzeugung** *f* COMP & DV object creation

Objektiv *nt* FOTO *mit Blendenvorwahl* lens, OPTIK objective, *Linsenkombination* lens, PHYS lens; ~ **mit großer**

Blende *nt* FOTO large-aperture lens; ~ **mit Vorsatz-Anamorphot** *nt* FOTO anamorphotic lens; **Objektivanschluß** *m* FOTO lens mount; **Objektivanschlußplatte** *f* FOTO lens mounting plate; **Objektivbrett** *nt* FOTO lens panel; **Objektivdeckel** *m* FOTO lens-cap; **Objektivdetektor** *m* TRANS objective detector

objektivgekoppelt: ~**er Belichtungsmesser** *m* FOTO lens-coupled exposure meter

Objektiv: **Objektivköcher** *m* FOTO lens case; **Objektivlinse** *f* LABOR *Mikroskop*, METALL objective lens; **Objektivmessung** *f* *(TTL-Messung)* FOTO through-the-lens metering *(TTL metering)*; **Objektivöffnung** *f* FOTO lens aperture; **Objektivrohr** *nt* OPTIK body tube; **Objektivsatz** *m* FOTO set of lenses; **Objektivträger** *m* FOTO camera front, KER & GLAS microscope slide; **Objektivtubus** *m* FOTO lens barrel, lens flange; **Objektiv-Verschluß** *m* FOTO lens shutter

Objekt: **Objektlautstärkepegel** *m* AKUSTIK loudness level of test sound; **Objektmodul** *nt* COMP & DV object module

objektorientiert: ~**e Architektur** *f* COMP & DV object-oriented architecture; ~**er Aufbau** *m* COMP & DV object-oriented architecture; ~**es Design** *nt* COMP & DV object-oriented design; ~**er Entwurf** *m* COMP & DV object-oriented design; ~**es Programmiersystem** *nt* COMP & DV object-oriented programming system; ~**e Programmierung** *f* *(OOP)* KÜNSTL INT object-oriented programming *(OOP)*

Objekt: **Objektprogramm** *nt* COMP & DV object program

objektseitig: ~**e Brennebene** *f* FOTO front focal plane

Objekt: **Objektsprache** *f* COMP & DV object language, target language; **Objektträger** *m* LABOR *Mikroskop* slide; **Objektvariable** *f* COMP & DV object, object variable

obligat: ~**er Aerobier** *m* LEBENSMITTEL obligate aerobe

Oblimak *m* KERNTECH oblate spheromak, oblimak

OBO *abbr* *(Erz-Schüttgut-Öl, Flüssigkeitsmassengut)* WASSERTRANS OBO *(ore-bulk oil)*

OBO-Frachter *m* WASSERTRANS *Schiff* OBO carrier

Obsidian *m* KER & GLAS obsidian

OC *abbr* *(Operationscharakteristik)* QUAL OC *(operating characteristic)*

Ochsengalle *f* DRUCK ox gall

Ockerton *m* KER & GLAS ochrey clay

OC-Kurve *f* QUAL operating characteristic curve

OCO *abbr* *(Erz-Kohle-Öl)* TRANS OCO *(ore-coal-oil)*

OCO-Frachter *m* TRANS OCO carrier

OCR *abbr* *(optische Zeichenerkennung)* COMP & DV OCR *(optical character recognition)*

OCR-Schriftart *f* COMP & DV OCR font

OCR-Zeichensatz *m* COMP & DV OCR font

Octacosan *nt* CHEMIE octacosane

Octadecadienat *nt* CHEMIE linoleate

Octadecan *nt* CHEMIE octadecane

Octadecyl- *pref* CHEMIE octadecyl

Octagon *nt* GEOM octagon

Octan *nt* CHEMIE octane; **Octan-** *pref* CHEMIE octane; **Octanal** *nt* CHEMIE octanal

Octanoyl- *pref* CHEMIE octanoyl

octavalent *adj* CHEMIE octavalent

Octen *nt* CHEMIE octene, octylene

Octin *nt* CHEMIE caprylidene, octyne

Octose *f* CHEMIE octose

Octylaldehyd *m* CHEMIE octanal

Octylen *nt* CHEMIE octene, octylene

ODER-Gatter *nt* PHYS OR circuit, OR gate

ODER-Glied *nt* COMP & DV, ELEKTRONIK OR circuit, OR gate

ODER-Schaltung *f* PHYS OR circuit, OR gate

ODER-Tor *nt* COMP & DV OR circuit, OR gate

ODER-Verknüpfung *f* COMP & DV OR operation

ODER-Zeichen *nt* ELEKTRONIK OR operator

Odometer *nt* BAU odometer

Odoriermittel *nt* ERDÖL *Petrochemie* odorant

OEM-Hersteller *m* MASCHINEN OEM, original equipment manufacturer

OEM-Modem *nt* ELEKTRONIK OEM modem

Oersted *nt* ELEKTROTECH oersted

Ofen[1] *m* ANSTRICH furnace, ELEKTROTECH heater, HEIZ & KÄLTE, LABOR, MASCHINEN furnace, METALL kiln, PAPIER kiln, oven, THERMOD oven; ~ **mit erzwungener Konvektion** *m* LABOR oven with forced convection; ~ **mit natürlicher Konvektion** *m* LABOR oven with natural convection

Ofen:[2] **im ~ trocknen** *vt* THERMOD kiln-dry

Ofen: **Ofenalterung** *f* KUNSTSTOFF oven ageing (BrE), oven aging (AmE); **Ofenauskleidung** *f* MASCHINEN furnace lining; **Ofenbär** *m* KER & GLAS bear; **Ofenbediener** *m* KER & GLAS teaser, top man; **Ofenbefüllung** *f* KER & GLAS furnace fill; **Ofenbruch** *m* METALL cadmia

ofenfest: ~**es Glas** *nt* THERMOD oven proof glass

ofengetrocknet *adj* THERMOD kiln-dried, oven-dried

Ofen: **Ofenherdgewebe** *nt* KER & GLAS bench cloth; **Ofenkoks** *m* KOHLEN oven coke; **Ofenkopf** *m* KER & GLAS port endwall; **Ofenkranz** *m* KER & GLAS port crown; **Ofenkuppel** *f* KER & GLAS crown; **Ofenleistung** *f* KER & GLAS furnace performance; **Ofenloch** *nt* KER & GLAS notch, porthole; **Ofenmantel** *m* KER & GLAS shell; **Ofenrast** *f* KER & GLAS bosh; **Ofenrost** *m* MASCHINEN furnace grate; **Ofenrückwand** *f* KER & GLAS port back wall; **Ofenruß** *m* KUNSTSTOFF furnace black; **Ofensau** *f* FERTIG sow; **Ofensohle** *f* KER & GLAS port sill

ofentrocken *adj* PAPIER bone-dry, oven-dry

ofentrocknend: ~**er Lack** *m* KUNSTSTOFF stoving finish, stoving varnish

Ofen: **Ofentrocknung** *f* BAU kiln drying; **Ofenwand** *f* KER & GLAS wicket wall, MASCHINEN furnace wall; **Ofenzug** *m* KER & GLAS port uptake

offen[1] *adj* COMP & DV open, ELEKTRONIK incomplete, TELEKOM uncoded, TEXTIL open-ended; **in** ~**er Bauart** *adj* MASCHINEN open-type; **auf** ~**er See** *adj* WASSERTRANS in the offing

offen:[2] ~**er Abzugsgraben** *m* ABFALL open drain, open sewer, WASSERVERSORG open drain; ~**e Blende** *f* FOTO full aperture; ~**er Brennstoffkreislauf** *m* KERNTECH once-through fuel cycle, open fuel cycle; ~**e Deltaschaltung** *f* ELEKTRIZ open delta connection; ~**e Dreieckschaltung** *f* ELEKTRIZ open delta connection; ~**es Gesenk** *nt* MASCHINEN open die; ~ **gewickelter Anker** *m* ELEKTRIZ open coil armature; ~**es Gitter** *nt* ELEKTRONIK *Elektronenröhre* free grid; ~**er Güterwagen** *m* EISENBAHN freight truck (AmE), goods lorry (BrE), gondola car, gondola wagon, TRANS truck; ~**e Haube** *f* PAPIER open hood; ~**es Intervall** *nt* MATH open interval; ~**er Kanal** *m* HYDRAUL open channel; ~**er Kern** *m* ELEKTRIZ open core; ~**er Kopfflunker** *m* FERTIG primary pipe; ~**er Kreis** *m* REGELUNG *in binären Schaltsystemen* open loop; ~**er Kreislauf** *m* LUFTTRANS open loop; ~**er Kühlkreis** *m* HEIZ & KÄLTE, KERNTECH open circuit cooling; ~**e Lage** *f* ELEKTRIZ open position; ~**er Leiter** *m* ELEKTROTECH open conductor; ~**er Lichtbogen** *m* ELEKTROTECH open arc; ~**es**

Meer *nt* WASSERTRANS high seas, open sea; **~e Misch-walze** *f* KUNSTSTOFF open mill; **~es Polygon** *nt* GEOM open polygon; **~er Propeller** *m* TRANS open propeller; **~er Resonator** *m* ELEKTRONIK open resonator; **~er Riemen** *m* FERTIG, PAPIER open belt; **~e Schleife** *f* ELEKTRIZ, LUFTTRANS open loop; **~es Schneideisen** *nt* MASCHINEN split die; **~e See** *f* WASSERTRANS offing; **~er Seekanal** *m* WASSERVERSORG lock and inland-lake canal; **~e Seite** *f* FERTIG mouth; **~er Selbstentlade-Drehgestellgüterwagen** *m* KFZTECH bogie open self-discharge wagon; **~e Sicherung** *f* ELEKTRIZ open fuse; **~e Spindeltreppe** *f* BAU open newel stairs; **~e Sprache** *f* TELEKOM *Mobiltelefon* clear speech; **~e Stirnseite** *f* HYDRAUL open front; **~e Stirnwand** *f* HY-DRAUL open front; **~er Stoffauflauf** *m* PAPIER open headbox; **~er Stromkreis** *m* ELEKTRIZ, ELEKTROTECH open circuit; **~es System** *nt* COMP & DV, THERMOD open system; **~e Tunnelbauweise** *f* BAU cut-and-cover method; **~e Unterlegscheibe** *f* MASCHINEN C-spacer; **~e Walzenstraße** *f* FERTIG looping mill; **~e Wartezeit** *f* KUNSTSTOFF open assembly time; **~es Wasser** *nt* WAS-SERTRANS open water; **~e Zelle** *f* KUNSTSTOFF open cell; **~er Zugriff** *m* COMP & DV open access
Offenbarung: **~ der Erfindung** *f* PATENT disclosure of the invention
Offenblendmessung *f* FOTO *Messen* full-aperture metering
offenkettig: **~er Kohlenwasserstoff** *m* KUNSTSTOFF aliphatic hydrocarbon
öffentlich: **~es bewegliches Landfunknetz** *nt* TELEKOM PAM network; **~es Bildschirmtelefon** *nt* ELEKTRONIK *zur Bedienung mit Telefonkarte* CRT-equipped public phone; **~es Datennetz** *nt* *(PDN)* COMP & DV public data network *(PDN)*; **~es Datenpaketvermittlungs-netz** *nt* *(CSPDN)* TELEKOM circuit-switched public data network *(CSPDN)*; **~es Fernsprechamt** *nt* TELE-KOM public telephone exchange; **~er Fernsprecher** *m* TELEKOM public telephone; **~es Fernsprechnetz** *nt* TELEKOM public switched telephone network, public telephone network; **~es Fernsprechwählnetz** *nt* TELE-KOM public switched telephone network; **~e Gesundheit** *f* WASSERVERSORG public health; **~es Mo-bilfunknetz** *nt* TELEKOM PLMN, public land mobile network; **~es Netz** *nt* TELEKOM public network; **~e Straße** *f* BAU public road; **~es Stromversorgungsnetz** *nt* ELEKTRIZ public supply network; **~es Telefon** *nt* TELEKOM public telephone; **~er Telefonanschluß im Flugzeug** *m* TELEKOM airphone (AmE); **~er Transport** *m* TRANS public transit (AmE), public transport (BrE); **~es Transportsystem mit ständigem Zugang** *nt* TRANS continuous access public transport system; **~e Versorgungsunternehmen** *nt pl* WASSERVERSORG pub-lic utilities; **~er Wählanschluß** *m* TELEKOM public dial-up port; **~e Wasserversorgung** *f* WASSERVERSORG public water supply
offenzellig: **~er Schaumstoff** *m* KUNSTSTOFF open cell cellular plastics
offiziell: **~er Fahrplan** *m* TRANS official timetable
Offline- *pref* COMP & DV, TELEKOM off-line; **Offline-Be-trieb** *m* TELEKOM off-line working; **Offline-Drucken** *nt* VERPACK printing off line; **Offline-Edieren** *nt* FERNSEH off-line editing; **Offline-Verarbeitung** *f* COMP & DV off-line processing
öffnen *vt* ELEKTROTECH *Stromkreis* break, FOTO *Blende*, PAPIER, TEXTIL *Faser* open
Öffnen *nt* ELEKTROTECH *Stromkreis* breaking, MASCHI-NEN opening
öffnend: **~er Kreis** *m* ELEKTROTECH opening circuit
Öffner *m* ELEKTRIZ closing contact, normally closed contact, ELEKTROTECH normally closed contact, TEX-TIL opener
Öffnung *f* ANSTRICH crack, BAU cutout, mouth, ELEK-TROTECH cutout, *Wellenleiter, Hohlleiter* port, *eines Kontaktes* break, FERTIG orifice, FOTO *Linse* aperture, HYDRAUL port, KOHLEN aperture, MASCHINEN mouth, opening, orifice, MECHAN aperture, port, PAPIER ope-ning, TELEKOM aperture; **Öffnungsanweisungen** *f pl* VERPACK instructions for opening, opening instruc-tions; **Öffnungskoeffizient** *m* *(m)* AKUSTIK flare coefficient of horn *(m)*; **Öffnungskontakt** *m* ELEKTRIZ normally closed contact, ELEKTROTECH break con-tact, normally closed contact; **Öffnungsmechanismus** *m* VERPACK opening mechanism; **Öffnungsring** *m* KER & GLAS orifice ring; **Öffnungsverhältnis** *nt* PHYS rela-tive aperture; **Öffnungswinkel** *m* ELEKTRONIK *Antennentechnik* beam angle, *Lichtwellenleiter* accep-tance angle, KERNTECH angular acceptance; **Öffnungswinkel eines Strahls** *m* KERNTECH accept-ance angle of beam; **Öffnungszeit** *f* ELEKTRIZ break time, opening time, ELEKTROTECH *eines Stromkreises* opening time
Offset- *pref* DRUCK, PAPIER, RAUMFAHRT, VERPACK off-set; **Offset-Antenne** *f* RAUMFAHRT *Weltraumfunk* offset antenna; **Offset-Betrieb** *m* ELEKTRONIK *Funk-technik* carrier offset; **Offset-Druck** *m* DRUCK offset, offset printing, PAPIER, VERPACK offset printing; **Off-set-Maschine** *f* DRUCK offset printing press; **Offset-Papier** *nt* PAPIER offset paper; **Offset-Presse** *f* DRUCK offset printing press, VERPACK offset press; **Offset-Reflektor** *m* RAUMFAHRT *Weltraumfunk* offset reflector; **Offset-Rollenrotationsmaschine** *f* DRUCK web-fed offset rotary press; **Offset-Rotationsdruck-maschine** *f* VERPACK offset rotary press; **Offset-Signalmethode** *f* FERNSEH offset signal method; **Off-set-Streichmaschine** *f* PAPIER offset coater; **Offset-Trägersystem** *nt* FERNSEH offset carrier system; **Off-set-Vorlage** *f* KONSTZEICH offset master; **Offset-Walze** *f* DRUCK offset roller
Offshore- *pref* ERDÖL, WASSERTRANS offshore; **Offshore-Bohrung** *f* ERDÖL offshore drilling, UMWELT-SCHMUTZ offshore well, WASSERTRANS offshore drilling; **Offshore-Feld** *nt* ERDÖL offshore field; **Offshore-Lagerstätte** *f* ERDÖL offshore field; **Offshore-Ölförderindustrie** *f* ERDÖL offshore oil in-dustry; **Offshore-Ölhafen** *m* WASSERTRANS offshore port; **Offshore-Plattform** *f* ERDÖL offshore platform
OFN *abbr* *(Ortsfernsprechnetz)* TELEKOM local ex-change area
Ohm *nt* ELEKTRIZ, ELEKTROTECH, METROL, PHYS, RADIO ohm
ohm: **~sche Belastung** *f* TELEKOM resistive load; **~sches Gesetz** *nt* ELEKTRIZ, ELEKTROTECH, PHYS Ohm's law; **~scher Kontakt** *m* ELEKTROTECH, PHYS ohmic contact; **~sche Last** *f* ELEKTROTECH resistive load **~scher Leiter** *m* PHYS ohmic conductor; **~scher Spannungsabfall** *m* ELEKTRIZ ohmic drop; **~scher Verlust** *m* ELEKTRIZ, ELEKTROTECH, PHYS ohmic loss; **~scher Wert** *m* ELEK-TROTECH ohmic value; **~scher Widerstand** *m* ELEKTRIZ ohmic resistance, ELEKTROTECH DC resi-stance, ohmic resistance, PHYS reactance;
ohmisch *adj* ELEKTRIZ ohmic, ELEKTROTECH resistive
Ohm: **Ohmmesser** *m* ELEKTROTECH resistance meter; **Ohm-**

meter nt ELEKTRIZ, ELEKTROTECH, PHYS, TELEKOM ohmmeter

ohne: ~ **Antrieb** adj FERTIG undriven; ~ **Ausladung** adj FERTIG throatless; ~ **Balligkeit** adj FERTIG Getriebelehre noncrowned; ~ **Durchschuß** adj DRUCK solid; ~ **Eisenkern** adj ELEKTROTECH Spule air core; ~ **Paginierung** adj DRUCK blind folio; ~ **Revolverkopf** adj FERTIG nonturret; ~ **Schablone** adj FERTIG jigless; ~ **Spannut** adj MASCHINEN fluteless; ~ **Spanwinkel** adj FERTIG neutral-rake; ~ **Überlappung** adj ANSTRICH unlapped; ~ **Werkstückträger** adj FERTIG nonpalletized; ~ **Zeildurchschuß gesetzt** adj DRUCK set solid; ~ **Zuckerzusatz** adj LEBENSMITTEL no added sugar

Ohr nt AKUSTIK ear

Öhr nt FERTIG Hammer eye, MASCHINEN ear, eye

Ohr: **Ohrenschutz** m SICHERHEIT ear protector, earmuff, hearing protector; **Ohrenstopfen** m pl SICHERHEIT earplug, noise-protective capsules and plugs; **Ohrharmonische** f AKUSTIK aural harmonic; **Ohrhörer** m RADIO earphone; **Ohrton** m AKUSTIK tinnitus

OHV-Motor m KFZTECH OHV engine

okkludieren vt CHEMIE occlude

okkludiert adj CHEMIE occluded

Okklusion f CHEMIE occlusion, WASSERTRANS Wetterkunde occluded front

Ökologie f UMWELTSCHMUTZ ecology

ökologisch: **~es Gleichgewicht** nt UMWELTSCHMUTZ ecological balance; **~e Pyramide** f UMWELTSCHMUTZ ecological pyramid; **~er Zusammenbruch** m UMWELTSCHMUTZ environmental collapse

Ökosystem nt UMWELTSCHMUTZ ecosystem

o-Kresol nt CHEMIE o-cresol

Oktaeder nt GEOM octahedron

oktaedrisch adj CHEMIE, GEOM octahedral

oktagonal adj GEOM octagonal

oktal adj COMP & DV octal

Oktalröhre f ELEKTRONIK octal tube

Oktalschreibweise f COMP & DV octal notation

Oktalsockel m MASCHINEN octal base

Oktan nt ERDÖL Petrochemie octane; **Oktanzahl** f ERDÖL Raffinerie, Erdölchemie octane number, KFZTECH octane index, octane number, octane rating; **Oktanzahlbestimmung** f KFZTECH ONR, octane number rating; **Oktanzahlwert** m KFZTECH ONR, octane number rating

Oktav nt DRUCK 8vo, octavo; **Oktavband** nt ELEKTRONIK, HEIZ & KÄLTE octave band; **Oktavbandfilter** nt ELEKTRONIK octave-band filter; **Oktavbandoszillator** m ELEKTRONIK octave-band oscillator; **Oktavbandpaßfilter** nt AUFNAHME octave filter; **Oktavbandpaßfiltersatz** m AUFNAHME octave filter set

Oktave f AKUSTIK, PHYS octave

Oktav: **Oktavformat** nt DRUCK 8vo, octavo; **Oktavmittenfrequenz** f HEIZ & KÄLTE octave mid-frequency; **Oktavschalldruckpegel** m HEIZ & KÄLTE octave sound-pressure level

Oktett nt CHEMIE, COMP & DV octet, ELEKTRONIK eight-bit byte; **Oktett-Ausgabe** f ELEKTRONIK eight-bit output

Oktode f ELEKTRONIK octode

oktogonal adj GEOM octagonal

Oktoidverzahnung f MASCHINEN octoid gear

Oktupol m ELEKTROTECH octupole

Okular nt FOTO eyepiece lens, LABOR Mikroskop eyepiece, OPTIK eyeglass, eyepiece, ocular, PHYS eyepiece; **~ mit Fadenkreuz** nt OPTIK webbed eyepiece

okular adj OPTIK ocular

Okular: **Okularmikrometer** nt OPTIK micrometer eyepiece

OK-Zeichen nt TELEKOM OK signal

Öl[1] nt ERDÖL, MASCHINEN, MEERSCHMUTZ, PAPIER oil

Öl:[2] ~ **entdecken** vi ERDÖL strike oil; **in ~ wirbeln** vi FERTIG Zahnrad churn

Öl: **Ölabdichtung** f MECHAN oil seal; **Ölabfall** m ABFALL residual oil, UMWELTSCHMUTZ oil waste

ölabgeschreckt adj FERTIG oil-quenched

Ölablaß m HEIZ & KÄLTE oil drain; **Ölablaßhahn** m HEIZ & KÄLTE oil drain valve; **Ölablaßöffnung** f KFZTECH oil drain hole; **Ölablaßschraube** f KFZTECH drain plug, Schmierung oil drain plug; **Ölablaßstopfen** m MECHAN oil drain plug; **Ölablaßventil** nt HEIZ & KÄLTE oil drain valve

Öl: **Ölablauf** m HEIZ & KÄLTE oil drain; **Ölabscheider** m ABFALL degreaser, oil separator, skimming tank, HEIZ & KÄLTE, MASCHINEN, PAPIER oil separator; **Ölabscheidering** m KFZTECH Motor oil scraper ring; **Ölabscheidung** f ABFALL de-oiling, oil removal, oil separation; **Ölabschöpfgerät** nt MEERSCHMUTZ recovery device; **Ölabschöpfsystem** nt MEERSCHMUTZ recovery system; **Ölabschreckung** f FERTIG, THERMOD oil quenching; **Ölabstreifer** m KERNTECH, KFZTECH Motor oil wiper; **Ölabstreifring** m KERNTECH oil scraper ring, oil wiper, KFZTECH oil control ring, Kolben oil control ring, Motor oil scraper ring; **Ölabziehstein** m MASCHINEN oilstone; **Ölanregung** f KERNTECH oil stimulation

ölanziehend adj CHEMIE oleophilic

Öl: **Ölaufbereitungsanlage** f ABFALL oil regeneration plant; **Ölaufnahme** f KUNSTSTOFF oil absorption; **Ölaufnahmeband** nt MEERSCHMUTZ oil mop

ölaufnehmend: **~es Band** nt MEERSCHMUTZ oleophilic belt; **~es Förderband-Abschöpfgerät** nt MEERSCHMUTZ oleophilic belt skimmer

Öl: **Ölaufsauger** m UMWELTSCHMUTZ skimmer; **Ölausbiß** m MEERSCHMUTZ seepage; **Ölausdehnungsgefäß** nt ELEKTROTECH oil conservator; **Ölausgleichsgefäß** nt ELEKTROTECH oil conservator; **Ölaustritt** m MEERSCHMUTZ oil leakage

Ölbad:[1] **im ~ abgeschreckt** adj THERMOD oil-quenched

Ölbad[2] nt LABOR oil bath

Ölbad:[3] **im ~ abschrecken** vt THERMOD oil-quench

Ölbad: **Ölbad-Anlassen** nt METALL oil tempering; **Ölbadluftfilter** nt KFZTECH oil-bath air filter; **Ölbadluftreiniger** m KFZTECH oil-bath air cleaner; **Ölbadschmierung** f MASCHINEN oil-bath lubrication

Öl: **Ölbecken** nt ERDÖL oil basin, petroleum basin

ölbefeuert adj ERDÖL Kessel, Öfen oilfired

Öl: **Ölbehälter** m ELEKTROTECH oil tank; **Ölbekämpfung** f MEERSCHMUTZ oil spill response; **Ölbekämpfungsschiff** nt MEERSCHMUTZ oil pollution combatting ship, UMWELTSCHMUTZ oil pollution fighter

ölbenetzt: **~e Luftfilterpatrone** f KFZTECH oil-moistened air filter cartridge

Öl: **Ölbergbau** m ERDÖL oil mining, petroleum mining; **Ölbeseitigung durch Trennmittel** f UMWELTSCHMUTZ removal of oil by separators; **Ölbeseitigungsschiff** nt UMWELTSCHMUTZ oil clearance vessel

ölbeständig adj KUNSTSTOFF oil-resistant

Öl: **Ölbohrung** f ERDÖL petroleum well, MASCHINEN oil hole; **Ölbremszylinder** m FERTIG oil dashpot; **Ölbrenner** m ERDÖL, HEIZ & KÄLTE, MASCHINEN, THERMOD oil burner; **Ölbunker** m ERDÖL Raffinerie, WASSER-

TRANS *Raffinerie* oil bunker

Oldham-Kupplung *f* MASCHINEN Oldham coupling

öldicht: ~**e Sicherheitshandschuhe** *m pl* SICHERHEIT oil-proof protective gloves

Öl: Öldichtung *f* MASCHINEN, MECHAN oil seal; **Öldruck-anzeige** *f* KFZTECH *Schmierung* oil pressure gage (AmE), oil pressure gauge (BrE); **Öldruckkontroll-leuchte** *f* KFZTECH oil pressure warning light; **Öldruckmesser** *m* KFZTECH *Schmierung* oil pressure gage (AmE), oil pressure gauge (BrE); **Öldruckpresse** *f* BAU hydraulic jack; **Öldruckstoßdämpfer** *m* MASCHINEN oil dashpot; **Öldruckverstärkerpumpe** *f* FERTIG booster pump; **Öldruckwächter** *m* HEIZ & KÄLTE oil pressure switch; **Öldurchflußmenge** *f* HEIZ & KÄLTE oil flow rate; **Öldüse** *f* KFZTECH oil jet

Oleat *nt* CHEMIE oleate

Olefin *nt* CHEMIE alkene, olefin, olefine, ERDÖL alkene, *Petrochemie* olefin; **Olefingehalt** *m* CHEMIE olefinic content

olefinisch *adj* CHEMIE olefinic

Olein *nt* CHEMIE olein

Öl: Öleinfüllstutzen *m* KFZTECH oil filler pipe, *Motor* oil filler; **Öleinfüllverschluß** *m* KFZTECH oil filler cap; **Öl-einlaßöffnung** *f* KFZTECH oil inlet

Olein-Palmitin-Gemisch *nt* CHEMIE oleo oil

Öl: Ölemulsion *f* MASCHINEN oil emulsion

Ölen *nt* TEXTIL oiling; **Ölentferner** *m* ANSTRICH degreaser

oleophil *adj* CHEMIE oleophilic

Oleoresin *nt* CHEMIE oleoresin

Öler *m* MASCHINEN oiler

Oleum *nt* CHEMIE Nordhausen acid, oleum, fuming sulfuric acid (AmE), fuming sulphuric acid (BrE)

Ölfang *m* WASSERVERSORG oil trap; **Ölfangblech** *nt* KERNTECH oil baffle; **Ölfangschale** *f* FERTIG sump

Öl: Ölfeld *nt* ERDÖL *Erdölgeologie* oilfield

ölfest[1] *adj* KUNSTSTOFF oil-resistant

ölfest:[2] ~**er Schlauch** *m* KUNSTSTOFF oil-resisting hose

Öl: Ölfeuerung *f* BAU oil firing, HEIZ & KÄLTE oilfired furnace; **Ölfeuerungsanlage** *f* MASCHINEN oilfired installation; **Ölfilm** *m* MEERSCHMUTZ oil film, oil slick; **Ölfilter** *nt* KFZTECH *Schmierung*, MASCHINEN, MECHAN oil filter; **Ölfilterdichtring** *m* KFZTECH oil filter gasket; **Ölfleck** *m* MEERSCHMUTZ oil patch, slick; **Öl-fluß** *m* ERDÖL flow of oil

ölfördernd *adj* ERDÖL oil-producing

ölfrei: ~**er Kompressor** *m* HEIZ & KÄLTE oil-free compressor

Öl: Ölfund *m* ERDÖL oil discovery; **Ölgas** *nt* ERDÖL oil gas

ölgefeuert[1] *adj* THERMOD oil-burning, oilfired

ölgefeuert:[2] ~**er Kessel** *m* HEIZ & KÄLTE oilfired boiler

ölgefüllt: ~**es Kabel** *nt* ELEKTRIZ oil-filled cable

Öl: Ölgehalt *m* KUNSTSTOFF oil length

ölgehärtet[1] *adj* THERMOD oil-hardened

ölgehärtet:[2] ~**es Sieb** *nt* PAPIER oil-tempered wire

ölgekapselt: ~**er Transformator** *m* ELEKTROTECH oil-immersed transformer

ölgekühlt[1] *adj* HEIZ & KÄLTE, THERMOD oil-cooled

ölgekühlt:[2] ~**er Transformator** *m* ELEKTRIZ, ELEKTROTECH oil-cooled transformer

ölgestreckt: ~**er Kautschuk** *m* KUNSTSTOFF oil-extended rubber

Öl: Ölhahn *m* MASCHINEN oil cock

ölhaltig: ~**es Abwasser** *nt* ABFALL oleiferous waste water, UMWELTSCHMUTZ oil-containing waste water

Öl: Ölhaltigkeit *f* KUNSTSTOFF oil length; **Ölhärtung** *f* METALL oil-hardening; **Ölharz-** *pref* CHEMIE oleoresinous; **Ölhaut** *f* TEXTIL oilskin; **Ölheizung** *f* ERDÖL, HEIZ & KÄLTE oil heating; **Ölheizungskessel** *m* HEIZ & KÄLTE oilfired boiler

ölig: ~**es Wasser** *nt* UMWELTSCHMUTZ black water

Oligomer *nt* CHEMIE, KUNSTSTOFF oligomer

oligomer *adj* CHEMIE oligomeric

Oligomeres *nt* CHEMIE oligomer

Oligomerisation *f* KUNSTSTOFF oligomerization

Oligomycin *nt* CHEMIE oligomycin

Öl: Ölindustrie *f* ERDÖL oil industry, petroleum industry; **Ölisolator** *m* ELEKTROTECH oil insulator

ölisoliert: ~**er Kondensator** *m* ELEKTRIZ oil-immersed capacitor

Olivenscharnier *nt* BAU *Verschluß* olive knuckle hinge

Öl: Ölkabel *nt* ELEKTROTECH oil-filled cable; **Ölkanal** *m* HEIZ & KÄLTE oil duct, KFZTECH, MASCHINEN oil channel; **Ölkännchen** *nt* FERTIG squirt oiler; **Ölkanne** *f* FERTIG hand oiler; **Ölkatastrophe** *f* MEERSCHMUTZ oil spill disaster; **Ölkessel** *m* HEIZ & KÄLTE oilfired boiler; **Ölkohlebelag** *m* KFZTECH oil-carbon deposit; **Ölkraftwerk** *nt* HEIZ & KÄLTE, THERMOD oilfired power station; **Ölkühler** *m* ELEKTRIZ, KFZTECH *Schmierung* oil cooler, MASCHINEN oil cooler, oil hole, THERMOD oil cooler; **Ölkühler-Wärmeaustauscher** *m* LUFTTRANS oil-cooler heat exchanger; **Ölkühlung** *f* ELEKTRIZ, MASCHINEN oil cooling; **Öllache** *f* MEERSCHMUTZ spill; **Öllagerstätte** *f* ERDÖL oilfield; **Ölleck** *nt* MEERSCHMUTZ oil leakage; **Ölleinwand** *f* VERPACK oiled canvas; **Ölleitblech** *nt* HEIZ & KÄLTE oil baffle; **Ölleitung** *f* ERDÖL *Ölindustrie* oil pipeline, KFZTECH oil line, MASCHINEN, TRANS oil pipeline; **Ölleitungsrohr** *nt* ERDÖL oil pipe

öllos: ~**es Lager** *nt* MASCHINEN oilless bearing

öllöslich *adj* KUNSTSTOFF oil-soluble

Öl: Ölmesser *m* ERDÖL oilometer, MASCHINEN oil gage (AmE), oil gauge (BrE), oilometer; **Ölmeßstab** *m* KFZTECH oil level stick, *Schmierung* dipstick; **Ölmotor** *m* ERDÖL *Dieselmotor, Schwerölmotor* oil engine; **Öl-Naturharz-** *pref* CHEMIE oleoresinous; **Ölnebelabscheider** *m* UMWELTSCHMUTZ oil aerosol separator; **Ölnebelkühlung** *f* FERTIG spray cooling; **Ölnebelschmierung** *f* MASCHINEN oil mist lubrication; **Ölnute** *f* MASCHINEN oil groove; **Ölpalme** *f* LEBENSMITTEL oil palm; **Ölpapier** *nt* VERPACK oil packing paper, oil-drenched paper; **Ölpauspapier** *nt* PAPIER oil tracing paper; **Ölpest** *f* UMWELTSCHMUTZ black tide, oil pollution; **Ölpier** *m* TRANS oil pier; **Ölpipeline** *f* ERDÖL, MASCHINEN, TRANS oil pipeline; **Ölprovinz** *f* ERDÖL petroleum province; **Ölpumpe** *f* HEIZ & KÄLTE, KFZTECH *Schmierung*, MASCHINEN oil pump; **Ölpumpendichtung** *f* HEIZ & KÄLTE oil pump gasket; **Ölraffinerie** *f* ERDÖL refinery; **Ölregenerat** *nt* ABFALL recovered oil; **Ölreservoir** *nt* ELEKTROTECH oil tank; **Ölring** *m* MASCHINEN oil control ring, oil ring

OLRT *abbr* (*Online-Echtzeit*) COMP & DV OLRT (*online real time*)

Ölrückgewinnung *f* MASCHINEN oil reclaiming; **Ölrück-gewinnungsschiff** *nt* UMWELTSCHMUTZ oil recovery vessel; **Ölrückgewinnungsschute** *f* UMWELTSCHMUTZ oil recovery barge; **Ölrückgewinnungsskimmer** *m* UMWELTSCHMUTZ oil recovery skimmer

Öl: Ölrückstände *m pl* ABFALL oil waste, residual oil; **Ölsaat** *f* LEBENSMITTEL oilseed; **Ölsand** *m* ERDÖL tar sand; **Ölsandform** *f* FERTIG *Gießen* oil mold (AmE), oil mould (BrE); **Ölsäure** *f* CHEMIE, LEBENSMITTEL oleic acid; **Ölsäureester** *m* CHEMIE oleate; **Ölschalter** *m* ELEKTRIZ oil switch, ELEKTROTECH oil circuit breaker, oil switch; **Ölschauglas** *nt* HEIZ & KÄLTE oil sight glass; **Ölschicht** *f* MEERSCHMUTZ oil film, oil slick; **Öl-schiefer** *m* ERDÖL *Erdölgeologie* oil shale; **Ölschlamm** *m* MEERSCHMUTZ chocolate mousse; **Ölschlamm-Öltanker** *m* WASSERTRANS oil-slurry oil tanker; **Ölschleuderring** *m* MASCHINEN oil slinger; **Ölschlitzring** *m* KFZTECH slotted oil control ring; **Ölsieb** *nt* KFZTECH oil strainer; **Ölspeichertank** *m* ERDÖL oil storage tank; **Ölsperre** *f* MEERSCHMUTZ jib boom, oil boom; **Ölsperrengebinde** *nt* MEERSCHMUTZ boom pack; **Ölspill-Identifikationssystem** *nt* MEERSCHMUTZ oil spill identification system; **Ölspreizring** *m* KFZTECH oil expander ring; **Ölspülung** *f* ERDÖL oil-base mud; **Ölspur** *f* ERDÖL *Erdölsuche* oil show; **Ölspurenanalysator** *m* ERDÖL *Erdölsuche* oil show analyser (BrE), oil show analyzer (AmE); **Ölstandanzeiger** *m* FERTIG contents gage (AmE), contents gauge (BrE), GERÄT oil level indicator, KFZTECH oil level stick; **Ölstandhahn** *m* FERTIG oil bleeder; **Ölstandsglas** *nt* HEIZ & KÄLTE oil sight glass; **Ölstandsmarkierung** *f* KFZTECH *Schmierung* oil level mark; **Ölstrahl** *m* KFZTECH oil jet; **Ölstrom** *m* HEIZ & KÄLTE oil flow rate; **Ölströmungsanzeiger** *m* HEIZ & KÄLTE oil flow indicator; **Ölströmungsmelder** *m* HEIZ & KÄLTE oil flow indicator; **Ölströmungswächter** *m* HEIZ & KÄLTE oil flow indicator; **Ölsumpfschmierung** *f* KFZTECH *Motorschmierung* sump-type lubrication; **Öltank** *m* ELEKTROTECH oil tank, ERDÖL *Raffinerie* oil storage tank, oil tank; **Öltanker** *m* ERDÖL *Schiffahrt* crude oil tanker, oil tanker, TRANS fuel tanker, UMWELTSCHMUTZ crude carrier, WASSERTRANS oil tanker; **Öltankerhaverie** *f* UMWELTSCHMUTZ average of an oil tanker; **Öltasche** *f* MASCHINEN oil pocket; **Öltemperaturanzeige** *f* LUFTTRANS *Flugwesen* oil temperature indicator; **Öltemperaturmeßfühler** *m* LUFTTRANS oil temperature probe

Ölteppich *m* MEERSCHMUTZ oil film, oil slick, spill; **Ölteppichbekämpfungsausrüstung** *f* MEERSCHMUTZ oil spill combatting equipment; **Ölteppichbeseitigung** *f* MEERSCHMUTZ oil slick sinking; **Ölteppichidentifikation** *f* MEERSCHMUTZ oil spill identification system

Öl: **Öltransformator** *m* ELEKTRIZ oil transformer, ELEKTROTECH oil-immersed transformer; **Öltrennschalter** *m* ELEKTRIZ oil circuit breaker; **Öltropfen** *m* PHYS oil drop; **Öltropfgefäß** *nt* MASCHINEN sight feed lubricator

ölverbrennend: **~es Kraftwerk** *nt* ELEKTRIZ oilfired power station

Öl: **Ölverdichtungsmittel** *nt* UMWELTSCHMUTZ oil-concentrating agent; **Ölvergasung** *f* ERDÖL *Gaserzeugung* oil gasification

ölverschmutzt: **~es Abwasser** *nt* UMWELTSCHMUTZ oil-polluted waste-water

Öl: **Ölverschmutzung des Meeres** *f* MEERSCHMUTZ, UMWELTSCHMUTZ oil spill; **Ölverschmutzungsnotfall** *m* MEERSCHMUTZ, UMWELTSCHMUTZ oil pollution emergency; **Ölverschüttung** *f* MEERSCHMUTZ spill

ölverseucht: **~e Gewässer** *nt pl* UMWELTSCHMUTZ oil-contaminated waters

Öl: **Ölversorgung** *f* KFZTECH *Schmierung* oil feed; **Ölverteiler** *m* MASCHINEN oil distributor; **Ölwaage** *f* METROL -oilometer; **Ölwanne** *f* KFZTECH oil sump, oilpan, LUFTTRANS oil sump, MECHAN oilpan; **Ölwannendichtung** *f*

KFZTECH oilpan gasket; **Ölwannenschutz** *m* KFZTECH *Motorschmierung* sump guard; **Ölwäsche** *f* ERDÖL *Gasaufbereitung* oil scrubbing; **Öl-Wasser-Berührungsfläche** *f* MEERSCHMUTZ oil-water interface; **Ölwechsel** *m* KFZTECH *Schmierung*, MASCHINEN oil change; **Ölzahl** *f* KUNSTSTOFF oil length; **Öl-Zentralheizung** *f* HEIZ & KÄLTE oilfired central heating system; **Ölzerstäubungsbrenner** *m* HEIZ & KÄLTE atomizing oil burner; **Ölzeug** *nt* TEXTIL, WASSERTRANS *wetterfeste Kleidung* oilskin; **Ölzufuhr** *f* KFZTECH *Schmierung* oil feed; **Ölzuführungskanal** *m* KFZTECH oil gallery

Ω *abbr (Volumen in Phase)* PHYS Ω *(volume in phase space)*

Omega-Minus-Teilchen *nt* PHYS *Elementarteilchen* omega minus particle

Omega-Schleife *f* FERNSEH omega loop

Omega-Umschlingung *f* FERNSEH omega wrap

Omnibuszug *m* KFZTECH passenger road train

OMR *abbr (optische Markierungserkennung)* COMP & DV OMR *(optical mark recognition)*

ON *abbr (Ortsnetz)* ELEKTRIZ distribution network, local network, TELEKOM local network

Önanth- *pref* CHEMIE oenanthic; **Önanthal** *nt* CHEMIE oenanthal

ONKz *abbr (Ortsnetzkennzahl)* TELEKOM area code

Online- *pref* COMP & DV online; **Online-Datenbank** *f* COMP & DV online database; **Online-Drucken** *nt* VERPACK printing on line; **Online-Echtzeit** *f (OLRT)* COMP & DV online real time *(OLRT)*; **Online-Messung** *f* KERNTECH online measurement; **Online-Testprogramm** *nt* COMP & DV OLT, online test program; **Online-Testsystem** *nt* COMP & DV OLTS, online test system; **Online-Verarbeitung** *f* COMP & DV online processing

Onshore- *pref* ERDÖL onshore; **Onshore-Basis** *f* ERDÖL

OOP *abbr (objektorientierte Programmierung)* KÜNSTL INT OOP *(object-oriented programming)*

opak: **~e Substanz** *f* STRAHLPHYS opaque substance

Opakglas *nt* KER & GLAS opaque glass

Opal *m* TEILPHYS Opal; **Opalglas** *nt* KER & GLAS opal glass; **Opalinglas** *nt* KER & GLAS opaline

Opazimeter *nt* PAPIER opacimeter

Opazität *f* CHEMIE, DRUCK, PAPIER, PHYS, WELLPHYS opacity

OPEC *abbr (Organisation ölexportierender Länder)* ERDÖL OPEC *(Organization of Petroleum-Exporting Countries)*

Open-Shop-Betrieb *m* COMP & DV hands-on operation

Open-Top-Container *m* TRANS open-top container

Open-Wall-Container *m* TRANS open wall container

Open-Wire-Feeder *nt* ELEKTROTECH open wire feeder

Operand *m* COMP & DV operand

Operation *f* COMP & DV, TELEKOM operation; **Keine ~** *f (NO-OP)* COMP & DV no-operation *(NO-OP)*; **Operationenrangfolge** *f* COMP & DV operator precedence; **Operationscharakteristik** *f (OC)* QUAL operating characteristic *(OC)*; **Operationscode** *m* COMP & DV op code, operation code; **Operationsfolge** *f* COMP & DV sequence of operations; **Operationsregister** *nt* COMP & DV operation register; **Operations-Research** *nt (OR)* COMP & DV operations research *(OR)*; **Operationsschlüssel** *m* COMP & DV op code, operation code; **Operationstabelle** *f* COMP & DV operation table; **Operationsverstärker** *m (OA)* COMP & DV, ELEKTRONIK, PHYS, RADIO, TELEKOM operational amplifier *(op amp)*; **Operationszyklus** *m* COMP & DV *Basissysteme*

memory cycle, *Mikroprozessoren* machine cycle
Operator *m* COMP & DV, MATH operator
operatorbedient: ~**er Betrieb** *m* COMP & DV hands-on operation
Operator: **Operatorenrechnung** *f* MATH operational calculus
Opferanode *f* ERDÖL *kathodischer Korrosionsschutz* sacrificial anode
opfern *vt* ANSTRICH sacrifice
opfernd *adj* ANSTRICH sacrificial
Opian- *pref* CHEMIE opianic
Opianyl *nt* CHEMIE meconin, opianyl
Oppositron *nt* ELEKTRONIK O-type tube
Optik *f* OPTIK optics; **Optiklithografie** *f* ELEKTRONIK optical lithography; **Optikmodulator** *m* ELEKTRONIK optical modulator; **Optikwerkzeug** *nt* KER & GLAS optical tool
optimal: ~**er Abbrand** *m* KERNTECH optimum burnup; ~**e Abtastung** *f* TELEKOM optimal sampling; ~**e Ballung** *f* ELEKTRONIK optimum bunching; ~**e Dämpfung** *f* ELEKTROTECH optimum damping; ~**e Lösung** *f* KÜNSTL INT optimal solution; ~**e Objektausleuchtung** *f* STRAHLPHYS optimum object illumination; ~**e Programmierung** *f* COMP & DV minimum-access programming; ~**es Regelmodell** *nt* ERGON optimal control model; ~**es Regelsystem** *nt* KERNTECH optimal control system; ~**e Regelung** *f* TELEKOM optimal control; ~**e Vormagnetisierung** *f* AUFNAHME optimal bias; ~**es Walzen** *nt* KOHLEN optimum grind; ~**er Wassergehalt** *m* BAU optimum moisture content; ~**er Weg** *m* TELEKOM optimal path; ~**er Wiedereintrittskorridor** *m* RAUMFAHRT *Landeanflug* optimum re-entry corridor
Optimalfilter *nt* ELEKTRONIK *Radar* analog matched filter
optimieren *vt* COMP & DV optimize
Optimierung *f* COMP & DV optimization
Option *f* COMP & DV, ERDÖL *Verträge* option; **Optionsfeld** *nt* COMP & DV option field; **Optionstabelle** *f* COMP & DV option table
optisch:[1] ~ **eben** *adj* FOTO optically-flat
optisch:[2] ~**e Aberration** *f* TELEKOM optical aberration; ~**er Abscheider** *m* ABFALL optical sorter; ~**e Absorption** *f* STRAHLPHYS optical absorption; ~**e Abstimmung** *f* TELEKOM optical tuning; ~**er Abtaster** *m* COMP & DV bar code scanner; ~**es Abtastgerät** *nt* FERNSEH optical scanning device; ~**e Achse** *f* FOTO, OPTIK optical axis, PHYS optic axis, TELEKOM fiber axis (AmE), fibre axis (BrE), optical axis; ~ **aktives Material** *nt* OPTIK, TELEKOM optically-active material; ~**e Aktivität** *f* PHYS optical activity; ~**er Alarm** *m* TELEKOM visual alarm; ~**es Anklopfen** *nt* TELEKOM optical call waiting indication; ~**es Archivierungssystem** *nt* OPTIK optical filing system; ~**er Aufheller** *m* KUNSTSTOFF optical brightener; ~**er Aufnehmer** *m* ELEKTRONIK optical sensor; ~**e Aufzeichnung** *f* AKUSTIK, AUFNAHME, TELEKOM optical recording; ~**er Ausgang** *m* ELEKTROTECH optical output; ~**e Ausgangsleistung** *f* ELEKTROTECH, TELEKOM optical output power, optical power output; ~**er Autofallendetektor** *m* TRANS optical speed trap detector; ~**es Band** *nt* OPTIK optical tape; ~**e Bank** *f* FOTO, METROL, PHYS optical bench; ~**er Belegleser** *m* COMP & DV, DRUCK optical character reader; ~**es Bild** *nt* ELEKTRONIK optical image; ~**e Bildplatte in ROM-Technik** *f* OPTIK laser optical disk; ~**e Bistabilität** *f* TELEKOM optical bistability; ~**e Brech-**

ung *f* TELEKOM optical refraction; ~**er Bus** *m* TELEKOM optical data bus; ~**es Dämpfungsglied** *nt* TELEKOM optical attenuator; ~**e Datenbank** *f* OPTIK optical database; ~**er Datenbus** *m* OPTIK, TELEKOM optical data bus; ~**e Datendiskette** *f* COMP & DV, OPTIK optical data disk; ~**e Datenerfassungsstation** *f* COMP & DV optical image unit; ~**er Datenträger** *m* COMP & DV optical medium; ~**er Detektor** *m* ELEKTRONIK, OPTIK, TELEKOM optical detector; ~**e Dichte** *f* (D) OPTIK optical density (D); ~**e Dicke** *f* OPTIK, TELEKOM optical thickness; ~**e Dispersion** *f* TELEKOM optical dispersion; ~**er Drehwinkel** *m* (α) OPTIK angle of optical rotation (α); ~**er Dünnschicht-Wellenleiter** *m* ELEKTRONIK thin film optical waveguide; ~**e Effekte** *m pl* FERNSEH visual effects; ~**e Eigenschaft** *f* TELEKOM optical characteristic; ~**er Eingang** *m* ELEKTROTECH optical input; ~**e Eingangsleistung** *f* ELEKTROTECH optical input power; ~**es Elektron** *nt* STRAHLPHYS optical electron; ~**er Empfänger** *m* TELEKOM optical receiver, receive fiberoptic terminal device (AmE), receive fibreoptic terminal device (BrE); ~**er Entfernungsmesser** *m* FOTO optical rangefinder; ~**e Erfassung** *f* ELEKTRONIK optical detection; ~**es Erholungsvermögen** *nt* OPTIK optical regenerative power; ~**e Erkennung** *f* ELEKTRONIK optical sensing; ~**e Faser** *f* ELEKTROTECH, PHYS optical fiber (AmE), optical fibre (BrE); ~**e Faser aus Allglas** *f* ELEKTROTECH all-glass optical fiber (AmE), all-glass optical fibre (BrE); ~**e Faser in Vollplastausführung** *f* ELEKTROTECH all-plastic optical fiber (AmE), all-plastic optical fibre (BrE); ~**es Fenster** *nt* OPTIK optical window; ~**er Festwertspeicher** *m* (OROM) COMP & DV optical ROM, optical read-only memory (optical ROM), OPTIK optical ROM, optical read-only memory (optical read-only memory); ~**es Filter** *nt* ELEKTRONIK, OPTIK, TELEKOM optical filter; ~**es Flintglas** *nt* KER & GLAS optical flint; ~**e Frequenz** *f* ELEKTRONIK optical frequency; ~ **gekoppeltes Festkörperrelais** *nt* ELEKTROTECH optically-coupled solid state relay; ~**es Gitter** *nt* OPTIK diffraction grating; ~**es Glas** *nt* FOTO optical glass; ~ **glatte Oberfläche** *f* PHYS optically-smooth surface; ~**er Hohlraum** *m* OPTIK optical cavity; ~**er Hohlraumresonator** *m* STRAHLPHYS, TELEKOM optical cavity; ~**e Hybridschaltung** *f* ELEKTRONIK optical hybrid circuit; ~**er IC** *m* ELEKTRONIK optical IC; ~**er Impuls** *m* ELEKTRONIK optical pulse; ~**e Informationsverarbeitung** *f* TELEKOM optical information processing; ~**es Instrument** *nt* PHYS optical instrument; ~**er integrierter Schaltkreis** *m* ELEKTRONIK, OPTIK integrated optical circuit, optical integrated circuit; ~**e Interferenz** *f* TELEKOM optical interference; ~**es Ionenstrahlsystem** *nt* STRAHLPHYS ion beam optical system; ~**er Isolator** *m* TELEKOM optical isolator; ~**e Isolierung** *f* ELEKTROTECH optical isolation; ~**es Isomer** *nt* CHEMIE enantiomer, optical isomer; ~**es Kabel** *nt* FERNSEH, OPTIK, TELEKOM optical cable; ~**e Karte** *f* OPTIK optical card; ~**e Kohärenz** *f* TELEKOM optical coherence; ~**er Kombinierer** *m* OPTIK optical combiner; ~**e Kommunikationstechnik** *f* TELEKOM optical communications; ~**er Komparator** *m* METROL optical comparator; ~**es Koppelfeld** *nt* TELEKOM OSN, optical switching network; ~**e Koppelmatrix** *f* TELEKOM optical switching matrix; ~**er Koppelpunkt** *m* TELEKOM optical switching crosspoint; ~**er Koppler** *m* ELEKTROTECH, OPTIK, TELEKOM optical coupler, optical fiber coupler (AmE), optical fibre coupler (BrE); ~**e Kopplung** *f* ELEKTROTECH op-

tical coupling; ~er **Korrelationsanalysator** m ELEK-
TRONIK optical correlator; ~er **Laseraufzeichner** m
ELEKTRONIK laser optical recorder; ~e **Leistung** f
ELEKTROTECH, OPTIK, TELEKOM optical power; ~e **Leistungsquelle** f ELEKTROTECH optical power source;
~er **Lesekopf** m OPTIK optical head; ~er **Leser** m COMP
& DV optical reader, optical scanner; ~es **Logikgatter**
nt ELEKTRONIK optical logic gate; ~es **Logikglied** nt
ELEKTRONIK optical logic gate; ~e **logische Schaltung**
f ELEKTRONIK optical logic circuit; ~e **Markierungserkennung** f *(OMR)* COMP & DV optical mark
recognition *(OMR)*; ~es **Markierungslesen** nt COMP
& DV OMR, optical mark reading; ~er **Markierungsleser** m COMP & DV optical mark reader; ~er **Maser** m
ELEKTRONIK *Laser* optical maser; ~e **Maske** f ELEK-
TRONIK optical mask; ~es **Medium** nt COMP & DV,
OPTIK optical medium; ~er **Melder** m RAUMFAHRT
optical sensor; ~es **Meßgitter** nt METROL optical graticule; ~e **Meßinstrument** nt METROL optical instrument
for dimensional measurement; ~er **Mittelpunkt** m
PHYS, TELEKOM optical center (AmE), optical centre
(BrE); ~e **Modulation** f ELEKTRONIK optical modulation; ~er **Modulator** m TELEKOM optical modulator;
~er **Multiplexer** m FERNSEH optical multiplexer; ~es
Multiplexing nt ELEKTRONIK optical multiplexing; ~es
Multiplexverfahren nt ELEKTRONIK optical multiplex;
~es **Muster** nt ELEKTRONIK optical pattern; ~e **Nachrichtentechnik** f TELEKOM optical communications;
~er **parametrischer Oszillator** m TELEKOM optical parametric oscillator; ~e **Platte** f COMP & DV optical disk;
~e **Polarisation** f TELEKOM optical polarization; ~e
Profilschleifmaschine f MASCHINEN optical profile
grinder; ~es **Publizieren** nt OPTIK optical publishing;
~es **Pumpen** nt ELEKTRONIK *Optoelektrik*, KERNTECH,
PHYS *Laser*, STRAHLPHYS optical pumping; ~es **Pyrometer** nt PHYS, STRAHLPHYS optical pyrometer; ~e
Qualitätskontrolle f QUAL optical quality control; ~e
Reflektrometrie f TELEKOM optical time domain reflectometry; ~e **Regenerierfähigkeit** f OPTIK optical
regenerative power; ~es **Relais** nt ELEKTROTECH optical relay, OPTIK optical repeater; ~er **Repeater** m
TELEKOM optical repeater; ~e **Resonanz** f ELEKTRONIK
optical resonance; ~er **Resonator** m STRAHLPHYS optical resonator, TELEKOM optical cavity, optical
resonator; ~e **Schablone** f ELEKTRONIK optical master; ~es **Schalten** nt ELEKTROTECH optical switching;
~er **Schalter** m ELEKTROTECH, TELEKOM optical
switch; ~es **Schrittschaltwerk** nt ELEKTRONIK optical
stepper; ~e **Schutzschicht** f ELEKTRONIK optical resist; ~e **Schwingung** f ELEKTRONIK optical oscillation;
~er **Seekabelverstärker** m TELEKOM submerged optical repeater; ~er **Sender** m TELEKOM transmit fiber
optic terminal device (AmE), transmit fibre optic
terminal device (BrE); ~er **Sensor** m OPTIK optical
detector; ~es **Servo** nt ELEKTROTECH optical servo;
~es **Signal** nt COMP & DV visual / audible signal, TELE-
KOM optical signal; ~e **Signalverarbeitung** f
ELEKTRONIK, STRAHLPHYS optical signal processing;
~e **Signalwandlung** f ELEKTROTECH optical signal conversion; ~er **Solarreflektor** m RAUMFAHRT *Raumschiff*
OSR, optical solar reflector; ~er **Speicher** m COMP &
DV optical storage, ELEKTROTECH optical memory,
OPTIK optic storage, optical memory; ~es **Speichermedium** nt OPTIK optical storage medium; ~e
Speicherung f OPTIK optical storage, TELEKOM optical
recording; ~e **Spektralanalyse** f ELEKTRONIK optical

spectral analysis; ~es **Spektrum** nt ELEKTRONIK, OP-
TIK, STRAHLPHYS optical spectrum; ~er
Spektrumsanalysator m ELEKTRONIK optical spectral
analyser (BrE), optical spectral analyzer (AmE); ~er
Spleiß m TELEKOM optical splice; ~e **Spleißstelle** f
OPTIK optical splice; ~er **Steckverbinder** m TELEKOM
optical connector, optical fiber connector (AmE),
optical fibre connector (BrE); ~e **Strahlung** f OPTIK,
TELEKOM optical radiation; ~es **System** nt ELEKTRO-
NIK optical system; ~es **Teleskop** nt RAUMFAHRT
optical telescope; ~es **Tonaufzeichnungsgerät** nt AUF-
NAHME optical sound recorder; ~er **Tonkopf** m
AUFNAHME optical sound head; ~e **Tonspur** f AUFNAH-
ME optical sound track; ~es **Tonwiedergabegerät** nt
AUFNAHME optical sound reproducer; ~er **Träger** m
ELEKTRONIK optical carrier; ~er **Übergang** m STRAHL-
PHYS optical transition; ~e **Übertragung** f COMP & DV
optical transmission; ~e **Übertragungsleitung** f ELEK-
TROTECH optical transmission line; ~es
Übertragungssystem nt OPTIK optical transmission
system; ~er **Verbinder** m OPTIK optical link; ~e **Ver-
mittlung** f COMP & DV optical switching, TELEKOM
optical exchange, optical switching; ~es **Vermittlungssystem** nt TELEKOM optical switching system; ~er
Verstärker m ELEKTRONIK, TELEKOM optical amplifier; ~e **Verstärkung** f ELEKTRONIK optical gain; ~e
Verzerrung f KER & GLAS optical distortion; ~e **Video-
diskette** f OPTIK optical videodisk; ~er **Weg** m OPTIK,
PHYS optical path; ~e **Weglänge** f OPTIK, TELEKOM
optical path length; ~e **Weiche** f TELEKOM optical
combiner; ~e **Welle** f ELEKTROTECH optical wave; ~er
Wellenleiter m ELEKTROTECH, OPTIK optical waveguide; ~e **Zeichenerkennung** f *(OCR)* COMP & DV
optical character recognition *(OCR)*; ~es **Zeichener-
kennungssystem** nt VERPACK optical character
reading system; ~er **Zeichenleser** m COMP & DV, VER-
PACK optical character reader; ~e **Zeitbereichs-
reflektrometrie** f OPTIK, TELEKOM optical time domain
reflectometry; ~e **Zielvorrichtung** f RAUMFAHRT optical sight; ~er **Zirkulator** m TELEKOM optical circulator;
~er **Zweig** m PHYS *Festkörpertheorie* optical branch;
~er **Zwischenregenerator** m TELEKOM optical regenerative repeater; ~er **Zwischenverstärker** m TELEKOM
optical repeater

Optocodierer m RAUMFAHRT *Weltraumfunk* optical encoder

Optoelektronik f COMP & DV, ELEKTROTECH, PHYS, TELE-
KOM optoelectronics

optoelektronisch[1] *adj* OPTIK, TELEKOM optoelectronic

optoelektronisch:[2] ~es **Bauelement** nt OPTIK optoelectronic device; ~er **Chip** m ELEKTRONIK optoelectronic
chip; ~er **Empfänger** m TELEKOM optoelectronic receiver; ~ **gekoppeltes Festkörperrelais** nt ELEKTROTECH
photocoupled solid-state relay; ~es **Gerät** nt ELEKTRO-
TECH optoelectronic device; ~e **Koppelmatrix** f
TELEKOM optoelectronic switching matrix; ~er **Koppelpunkt** m TELEKOM optoelectronic crosspoint; ~er
Koppler m ELEKTROTECH optoelectronic coupler; ~er
Schalter m ELEKTROTECH optoelectronic switch; ~er
Verstärker m ELEKTRONIK optoelectronic amplifier;
~er **Wandler** m ELEKTROTECH optoelectronic transducer

Optokoppler m ELEKTROTECH optocoupler, RADIO
optocoupler, optoisolator, TELEKOM optocoupler

OR *abbr (Operations-Research)* COMP & DV OR *(operations research)*

Orbit *m* RAUMFAHRT orbit
Orbital *nt* STRAHLPHYS orbital; **Orbitalarbeitsstation** *f* RAUMFAHRT orbital workshop
orbital: **~es Labor** *nt* RAUMFAHRT orbiting laboratory; **~es Observatorium** *nt* RAUMFAHRT orbiting astronomical observatory
Orbital: **Orbitalraumfahrzeug** *nt* RAUMFAHRT orbital vehicle; **Orbitalwinkelmomentzahl** *f (L)* KERNTECH total orbital angular momentum number *(L)*
Orbit: **Orbitänderung** *f* RAUMFAHRT orbit modification; **Orbitdauer** *f* RAUMFAHRT orbital period
Orbiter *m* RAUMFAHRT orbiter; **Orbiterstufe** *f* RAUMFAHRT orbiter stage
Orbit: **Orbitkorrektur** *f* RAUMFAHRT orbit correction; **Orbitnachführung** *f* RAUMFAHRT orbit tracking; **Orbitsteuerung** *f* RAUMFAHRT orbit control; **Orbittrimmen** *nt* RAUMFAHRT orbit trimming; **Orbitveränderung** *f* RAUMFAHRT *in andere Umlaufbahn* orbit transfer; **Orbitvorhersage** *f* RAUMFAHRT orbit prediction; **Orbitzähler** *m* RAUMFAHRT orbit counter
Orcein *nt* CHEMIE orcein
ordentlich: **~e Reflexion** *f* PHYS specular reflection
Ordinalmerkmal *nt* QUAL ordinal characteristic
Ordinalzahlen *f pl* GEOM ordinals
ordinär: **~er Strahl** *m* PHYS ordinary ray
Ordinate *f* COMP & DV ordinate, MATH ordinate, vertical axis, y-axis; **Ordinaten** *f pl* WASSERTRANS *Schiffbau* ordinates
Ordner *m* FERTIG *Knüppel* unscrambler
Ordnung: **~ der Interferenz** *f* PHYS order; **Ordnungsaxiom** *nt* METALL ordering axiom; **Ordnungsgütemaß** *nt* COMP & DV ordering bias; **Ordnungs-Unordnungsmodell** *nt* KERNTECH *eines Atomkerns* order-disorder model; **Ordnungszahl** *f* AKUSTIK *einer Harmonischen* order, KERNTECH atomic number, MATH ordinal number, PHYS, STRAHLPHYS atomic number; **Ordnungszahlen** *f pl* AKUSTIK, KERNTECH, MATH, PHYS, STRAHLPHYS ordinals; **Ordnung-Unordnung** *f* METALL order-disorder
Organ *nt* CHEMIE organ
Organisation ölexportierender Länder *f (OPEC)* ERDÖL Organization of Petroleum-Exporting Countries *(OPEC)*
Organisationskanal *m* TELEKOM set-up channel; organisatorisch: **~e Operation** *f* COMP & DV house-keeping operation
organisch[1] *adj* ANSTRICH, LEBENSMITTEL organic
organisch:[2] **~er Abfall** *m* ABFALL organic waste; **~e Bestandteile** *nt pl* ERDÖL *Erdölgeologie* organic matter; **~er Boden** *m* KOHLEN organic soil; **~er Flüssigkeitslaser** *m* ELEKTRONIK organic liquid laser; **~es Kühlmittel** *nt* MASCHINEN organic refrigerant; **~er Moderator** *m* KERNTECH organic moderator; **~es Polymer** *nt* ANSTRICH organic polymer; **~er Stoff** *m* UMWELTSCHMUTZ organic matter; **~es Sulfid** *nt* CHEMIE organic sulfide (AmE), organic sulphide (BrE), thioether; **~er Widerstand** *m* ELEKTROTECH organic resistor
organogen *adj* KOHLEN organogenous
Organomagnesium- *pref* CHEMIE organomagnesium; **Organomagnesiumverbindung** *f* CHEMIE organomagnesium compound
organometallisch *adj* CHEMIE organometallic
Organosol *nt* CHEMIE organosol
Organzin *nt* TEXTIL organzine
Orgelpfeifenanschlag *m* KER & GLAS organ stop

orientiert: **~e Kernbildung** *f* METALL oriented nucleation; **~es Wachstum** *nt* METALL oriented growth
Orientierungsfaktor *m* METALL orientation factor
Orientierungspunkt *m* BAU landmark
Original[1] *nt* AKUSTIK original, AUFNAHME master, COMP & DV first generation, magnetic master, master, DRUCK, FERNSEH original
Original:[2] **~ erstellen** *vi* AUFNAHME master
Original: **Originalausgabe** *f* DRUCK original edition; **Originalausstattung** *f* MASCHINEN original equipment; **Originalband** *nt* COMP & DV master tape; **Originalbearbeitung** *f* FERNSEH editing on original; **Originaldokument** *nt* COMP & DV source document
originalgetreu: **~e Darstellung der Druckausgabe am Bildschirm** *f (WYSIWYG)* COMP & DV what you see is what you get *(WYSIWYG)*
Original: **Originalmaßstab** *m* MASCHINEN full scale
originalsicher: **~er Verschluß** *m* VERPACK tamper-evident closure
Original: **Originalvorlagen** *f pl* KONSTZEICH original documents
O-Ring *m* FERTIG *Kunststoffinstallationen*, KFZTECH *(Runddichtring)* Schmierung, KUNSTSTOFF, MASCHINEN *(Runddichtring)*, MECHAN O-ring
Orizabin *nt* CHEMIE jalapin, orizabin
Orlean *m* LEBENSMITTEL anatto, annatto, bixin
Orlopdeck *nt* WASSERTRANS *Schiffbau* orlop deck
Ornamentglas *nt* KER & GLAS patterned glass
Ornamentierung *f* KER & GLAS figuring
Ornamentwalzglas *nt* KER & GLAS figured rolled glass
Ornithur- *pref* CHEMIE ornithuric
OROM *abbr (optischer Festwertspeicher)* COMP & DV, OPTIK OROM *(optical read-only memory)*
Orotron *nt* ELEKTRONIK orotron
Orsellin- *pref* CHEMIE orsellic
Ort:[1] **vor ~** *adv* BAU in situ, on the spot, KOHLEN in situ; **an ~ und Stelle** *adv* MECHAN in situ
Ort:[2] **vor ~ drucken** *vt* VERPACK print on site
Ortbeton *m* BAU in situ concrete, site concrete; **Ortbetonpfahl** *m* KOHLEN cast-in-place pile
orten *vt* ELEKTROTECH, WASSERTRANS *Schiff, Seezeichen* locate
Örterbau *m* KOHLEN stall working
Orthicon *nt* ELEKTRONIK *Bildaufnahmeröhre* orthicon
Orthit *m* KERNTECH orthite
Orthoameisensäure *f* CHEMIE orthoformic acid
Orthoborsäure *f* CHEMIE boric acid, orthoboric acid
orthochromatisch: **~e Emulsion** *f* FOTO orthochromatic emulsion
Orthodrombahn *f* RAUMFAHRT orthodromic track
Orthodromie *f* WASSERTRANS *Navigation* orthodromy
Orthodromprojektion *f* RAUMFAHRT orthodromic projection
orthogonal[1] *adj* MATH *Vektoren* orthogonal
orthogonal:[2] **~e Polarisation** *f* TELEKOM orthogonal polarization; **~e Signale** *nt pl* TELEKOM orthogonal signals; **~e Zerspanung** *f* FERTIG orthogonal cutting
Orthogonalebene *f* FERTIG orthogonal plane
Orthogonalfreiwinkel *m* FERTIG orthogonal clearance
orthogonalisieren *vt* GEOM orthogonalize
Orthogonalität *f* GEOM orthogonality
Orthogonalkeilwinkel *m* FERTIG orthogonal wedge angle
Orthogonalschnitt *m* FERTIG orthogonal cut
Orthokiesel- *pref* CHEMIE orthosilicic; **Orthokieselsäure** *f* CHEMIE orthosilicic acid, silicic acid, tetrasilicic acid

Orthokohlensäure f CHEMIE orthocarbonic acid
Orthonormalsystem nt GEOM orthonormal system
Ortho-Para-Umwandlung f KERNTECH orthopara conversion
Orthophosphat nt CHEMIE orthophosphate
Orthophosphor- pref CHEMIE orthophosphoric
Orthosilicat nt CHEMIE orthosilicate, tetraoxosilicate
orthotroph: ~e **Werkstoffe** m pl MASCHINEN orthotropic materials
Orthowasserstoff m CHEMIE orthohydrogen
Orthoxyol nt ERDÖL Petrochemie orthoxylene
örtlich: ~e **Ausrichtung** f ELEKTRONIK local alignment; ~e **Beanspruchung** f METALL local stress; ~e **Emissionsquelle** f UMWELTSCHMUTZ local emission, local emission source; ~e **Nachgiebigkeit** f METALL local yielding; ~e **Querschnittsvergrößerung** f FERTIG lateral swelling; ~ **starke Rotation** f STRÖMPHYS Wirbelstärke locally high vorticity
Orts- pref TELEKOM local; **Ortsamt** nt TELEKOM local exchange; **Ortsaufteilungskabel** nt TELEKOM local distribution cable; **Ortsbatterie** f (LB) COMP & DV local battery (LB); **Ortsbetrieb** m TELEKOM local operation; **Ortschaum** m KUNSTSTOFF foam-in-place compound; **Ortsfernsprechnetz** nt (OFN) TELEKOM local exchange area
ortsfest[1] adj TELEKOM landline
ortsfest:[2] ~e **Emissionsquelle** f UMWELTSCHMUTZ stationary emission source; ~e **Landfunkstelle** f TELEKOM Radio base station
Orts-: Ortsfrequenz f ELEKTRONIK, FERNSEH, RADIO, TELEKOM spacial frequency
ortsgebunden adj FERTIG Vektor localized, KOHLEN sedentary
Orts-: Ortsgespräch nt TELEKOM local call; **Ortskapazität** f TRANS local capacity; **Ortskurve des Frequenzganges** f ELEKTRONIK, RADIO frequency response locus, REGELUNG polar plot, TELEKOM frequency response locus; **Ortsleitungskonzentrator** m TELEKOM local line concentrator; **Ortsnetz** nt (ON) ELEKTRIZ distribution network, local network, TELEKOM local exchange area, local network; **Ortsnetzkennzahl** f (ONKz) TELEKOM area code; **Ortsteilnehmerendstelle** f TELEKOM LUT, local user terminal; **Ortsvektor** m GEOM, PHYS position vector; **Ortsverbindung** f TELEKOM local junction; **Ortsverbindungsleitung** f TELEKOM junction; **Ortsverkehr** m TRANS local traffic; **Ortsvermittlungsstelle** f (OVSt) TELEKOM local exchange, metropolitan switch; **Ortsverteilungsnetz** nt TELEKOM local distribution network
Ortungsboje f WASSERTRANS Seezeichen radio sonobuoy
Os (Osmium) CHEMIE Os (osmium)
Osazon nt CHEMIE osazone
OSB abbr (oberes Seitenband) ELEKTRONIK, RADIO, TELEKOM USB (upper sideband)
OSCAR abbr (Bahnsatellit für Amateurfunkzwecke) RADIO, RAUMFAHRT Weltraumfunk OSCAR (Orbiting Satellite Carrying Amateur Radio)
Öse f FERTIG ear, eye, ring, MASCHINEN ear, eye, lug, MECHAN lug, VERPACK eyelet, WASSERTRANS eye
ösen vt WASSERTRANS bail
Öse: Ösenschraube f MASCHINEN eye screw, MECHAN eyebolt
OSI abbr (Kommunikation offener Systeme) COMP & DV, TELEKOM OSI (open systems interconnection)

OSI-Schichten f pl TELEKOM OSI layers
Osmat nt CHEMIE osmate, tetraoxoosmate
Osmium nt (Os) CHEMIE osmium (Os)
Osmol nt CHEMIE osmole
Osmolarität f CHEMIE osmolarity
Osmondit m METALL osmondite
osmophor: ~e **Gruppe** f CHEMIE osmophore
Osmose f CHEMTECH, ERDÖL, PHYS osmosis; **Osmosevorgang** m CHEMTECH osmosis process
osmotisch[1] adj PHYS osmotic
osmotisch:[2] ~er **Druck** m ERDÖL, HEIZ & KÄLTE, PHYS osmotic pressure
OSO abbr (Erz-Schlamm-Öl) WASSERTRANS OSO (ore-slurry-oil)
Oson nt CHEMIE osone
OSO-Tanker m WASSERTRANS OSO tanker
Osotriazol nt CHEMIE osotriazole
Ossein nt CHEMIE ossein
Ost- pref WASSERTRANS east; **Osten** m WASSERTRANS east; **Ostlänge** f TRANS EL, east longitude
östlich adj WASSERTRANS east, easterly
Östradiol nt CHEMIE oestradiol
Östriol nt CHEMIE oestriol
Östron nt CHEMIE oestrone, theelin
Ostwald: ~sches **Viskosimeter** nt LABOR Ostwald viscometer
ostwärts adv WASSERTRANS east, easterly
O-System nt (Oberleitungssystem) TRANS trolley system
Oszillation f ELEKTRIZ, ELEKTRONIK oscillation, METALL vibration, RADIO, WELLPHYS oscillation
Oszillator m ELEKTRIZ, ELEKTRONIK, PHYS, RADIO, RAUMFAHRT Weltraumfunk, TELEKOM, WELLPHYS oscillator; ~ **im Frequenzsprungverfahren** m ELEKTRONIK, RADIO, TELEKOM frequency-hopping oscillator; ~ **mit negativem Widerstand** m PHYS negative resistance oscillator; ~ **mit offenem Schwingungskreis** m ELEKTRONIK open loop oscillator; ~ **mit Permeabilitätsabstimmung** m RADIO permeability-tuned oscillator; ~ **mit Spannungssteuerung** m ELEKTRONIK voltage-controlled oscillator; ~ **mit verlängerter Wechselwirkung** m ELEKTRONIK extended-interaction oscillator; ~ **mit Wien-Brücke** m ELEKTRONIK Wien bridge oscillator; ~ **mit YIG-abgestimmten Transistoren** m ELEKTRONIK YIG-tuned transistor oscillator; ~ **mit YIG-Abstimmung** m ELEKTRONIK YIG-tuned oscillator; **Oszillatorabstimmraum** m ELEKTRONIK oscillator cavity; **Oszillatorbatterie** f ELEKTRONIK bank of oscillators; **Oszillatordiode** f ELEKTRONIK diode oscillator; **Oszillatorkreis** m FERNSEH oscillating circuit; **Oszillatorquarz** m ELEKTRONIK oscillator crystal; **Oszillatorreihe** f ELEKTRONIK oscillator bank; **Oszillatorspule** f ELEKTROTECH oscillator coil
Oszillieren nt FERTIG rocking
oszillieren vt ELEKTRONIK oscillate, FERTIG rock
oszillierend[1] adj ELEKTRIZ, ELEKTRONIK Strom oscillating, FERTIG rocking, PAPIER oscillating, TELEKOM oscillatory
oszillierend:[2] ~es **Spritzrohr** nt PAPIER oscillating shower
Oszillogramm nt FERNSEH oscillogram, GERÄT oscilloscope presentation
Oszillograph m ELEKTRONIK, PHYS, WELLPHYS oscillograph
oszillographieren vt ELEKTRONIK display
Oszilloskop nt COMP & DV, ELEKTRIZ oscilloscope, ELEK-

TRONIK cathode-ray oscillograph, oscilloscope, FERNSEH, PHYS, RADIO, WELLPHYS oscilloscope; **Oszilloskopbild** *nt* GERÄT oscilloscope presentation; **Oszilloskopkurve** *f* ELEKTRONIK oscilloscope trace; **Oszilloskopröhre** *f* ELEKTRONIK oscilloscope tube

OT *abbr (oberer Totpunkt)* KFZTECH TDC *(top dead center)*

Otologie *f* ERGON otology

Ottogasmotor *m* KFZTECH liquefied petroleum gas engine

Ottokraftstoff *m* KFZTECH gas (AmE), gasoline (AmE)

Ottomotor *m* KFZTECH gas engine (AmE), gasoline engine (AmE), petrol engine (BrE), gas motor (AmE), gasoline motor (AmE), petrol motor (BrE), MASCHINEN spark ignition engine, THERMOD, WASSERTRANS *Verbrennungsmotor* gas engine (AmE), gasoline engine (AmE), petrol engine (BrE)

Ottoverfahren *nt* KFZTECH Otto cycle

Outsert-Technik *f* KUNSTSTOFF outsert molding (AmE), outsert moulding (BrE)

Oval[1] *nt* GEOM oval

oval[1] *adj* GEOM, METALL oval

oval:[2] **~er Boden** *m* KER & GLAS oval punt; **~e Scheibe** *f* MASCHINEN oval pulley

Oval: Ovaldrehmaschine *f* MASCHINEN oval-turning lathe; **Ovalfeile** *f* MASCHINEN oval file; **Ovalflansch** *m* MASCHINEN oval flange

ovalförmig *adj* GEOM oval-shaped

Oval: Ovalisierung *f* ERDÖL *Bohrproblem* ovalization; **Ovalradzähler** *m* GERÄT oval gear meter; **Ovalschleifmaschine** *f* FERTIG oval grinder; **Ovaltürknopf** *m* BAU oval knob; **Ovalzirkel** *m* MASCHINEN oval compass

Overdrive *m* KFZTECH *Getriebe, Motor* overdrive

Overhead *nt* TELEKOM overhead

Overlay *nt* FERNSEH overlay, overlaying

Overshot *m* ERDÖL *Bohrtechnik* overshot

Ovoglobulin *nt* CHEMIE ovoglobulin

OVSt *abbr (Ortsvermittlungsstelle)* TELEKOM local exchange

Owen-Brücke *f* ELEKTRIZ Owen bridge

OWN-Codierung *f* COMP & DV own coding

Oxalamid *nt* CHEMIE oxamide

Oxalat *nt* CHEMIE oxalate

Oxalessig- *pref* CHEMIE oxalacetic

Oxalsäure *f* FOTO, LEBENSMITTEL oxalic acid; **Oxalsäurediamid** *nt* CHEMIE oxamide; **Oxalsäuredianilid** *nt* CHEMIE oxanilide

Oxalur- *pref* CHEMIE oxaluric; **Oxalursäure** *f* CHEMIE oxaluric acid

Oxalyl- *pref* CHEMIE oxalyl; **Oxalylharnstoff** *m* CHEMIE oxalylurea, parabanic acid

Oxamid *nt* CHEMIE oxamide; **Oxamid-** *pref* CHEMIE oxamic

Oxanil- *pref* CHEMIE oxanilic; **Oxanilid** *nt* CHEMIE oxanilide

Oxazin *nt* CHEMIE oxazine

Oxazol *nt* CHEMIE oxazole

Oxeton *nt* CHEMIE oxetone

Oxid[1] *nt* AUFNAHME, CHEMIE, FERNSEH oxide

Oxid:[2] **in ~ verwandeln** *vt* CHEMIE oxidize

oxidabel *adj* CHEMIE oxidizable

Oxid: Oxidabfall *m* KOHLEN oxidic waste; **Oxidabschuppung** *f* FERNSEH oxide shedding

Oxidans *nt* CHEMIE oxidant

Oxidansammlung *f* FERNSEH oxide buildup

Oxidant *m* RAUMFAHRT *Raumschiff* oxidant

Oxidation *f* ANSTRICH corrosion, rust, CHEMIE, DRUCK, UMWELTSCHMUTZ oxidation; **~ zum Peroxid** *f* CHEMIE peroxidation; **Oxidation-Reduktion-Reaktion** *f* CHEMIE oxidation-reduction reaction; **Oxidation-Reduktionszelle** *f* LABOR oxidation-reduction cell

oxidationsfähig *adj* CHEMIE oxidable

Oxidation: Oxidationsfähigkeit *f* CHEMIE oxidizability; **Oxidationsflamme** *f* CHEMIE oxidizing flame; **Oxidationsgraben** *m* ABFALL, WASSERVERSORG oxidation ditch; **Oxidationsmittel** *nt* ANSTRICH oxidizer, CHEMIE oxidizer, oxidizing agent, LUFTTRANS oxydizer, THERMOD overtemperature, oxidant, UMWELTSCHMUTZ oxidizing agent; **Oxidationsschutzmittel** *nt* KUNSTSTOFF antioxidant; **Oxidationsteich** *m* ABFALL aerated lagoon, oxidation pond, sewage oxidation pond, WASSERVERSORG oxidation pond

oxidativ *adj* CHEMIE oxidizing

Oxidator *m* CHEMIE oxidant

Oxidbildung *f* AUFNAHME oxide buildup

Oxidchlorid *nt* CHEMIE chloride oxide

oxidierbar *adj* CHEMIE oxidable; **nicht ~** *adj* CHEMIE inoxidizable, unoxidizable

Oxidieren *nt* CHEMIE oxidation

oxidieren[1] *vt* ANSTRICH rust, CHEMIE oxygenate

oxidieren[2] *vi* CHEMIE oxidize

oxidierend[1] *adj* CHEMIE oxidizing

oxidierend:[2] **~e Flamme** *f* CHEMIE oxidizing flame; **~er Stoff** *m* SICHERHEIT oxidizing substance

oxidiert[1] *adj* CHEMIE oxidized; **nicht ~** *adj* CHEMIE unoxidized

oxidiert:[2] **~es Metall** *nt* METALL oxidized metal; **~e Zellulose** *f* CHEMIE oxidized cellulose

Oxidierung *f* ELEKTRIZ oxidation; **Oxidierungsmittel** *nt* THERMOD overtemperature, oxidant

oxidisch *adj* CHEMIE oxidic

Oxid: Oxidkatode *f* ELEKTROTECH oxide-coated cathode; **Oxidkeramik** *f* FERTIG oxide ceramics

oxidkeramisch: ~e Drehwerkzeuge *nt pl* MASCHINEN oxide ceramic lathe tools; **~er Schneidstoff** *m* FERTIG oxide ceramic cutting material; **~es Schneidwerkzeug** *nt* FERTIG oxide ceramic cutting tool

Oxid: Oxidsalz *nt* CHEMIE oxide salt; **Oxidschicht** *f* COMP & DV oxide layer

Oxidschicht: mit ~ *adj* FERTIG scummy

Oxid: Oxidseite *f* FERNSEH oxide side

Oxim *nt* CHEMIE oxime

Oxomanganat *nt* CHEMIE malonitrile

Oxonium *nt* CHEMIE oxonium

Oxopropan- *pref* CHEMIE pyruvic

Oxopyrazolin *nt* CHEMIE pyrazolone

Oxosabinan *nt* CHEMIE oxosabinane, thujone

Oxosalz *nt* CHEMIE oxysalt

Oxosäure *f* CHEMIE oxo acid

Oxosilan *nt* CHEMIE siloxane

Oxozon *nt* CHEMIE oxozone

Oxyarc-Schneiden *nt* FERTIG oxyarc cutting, oxygen arc cutting

Oxycellulose *f* CHEMIE oxidized cellulose

Oxyd *nt* AUFNAHME oxide

oxydationshemmend: ~es Mittel *nt* FERTIG anti-ager oxidant

Oxydationsteich *m* WASSERVERSORG maturation pond

Oxyd: Oxydoreduktion *f* CHEMIE oxidoreduction; **Oxydwandisolation** *f* ELEKTRONIK local oxidation

Oxygenase *f* CHEMIE oxygenase

oxygenieren *vt* CHEMIE oxygenate

Oxysäure *f* CHEMIE oxyacid

oxytozisch *adj* CHEMIE oxytocic

Ozalid® *nt* DRUCK Ozalid®; **Ozalidpapier®** *nt* DRUCK Ozalid® paper; **Ozalidverfahren®** *nt* DRUCK Ozalid® process

Ozean: **zum ~ entwässernd** *adj* WASSERVERSORG exorheic

ozeanisch: **~es Becken** *nt* WASSERTRANS oceanic basin

Ozeankabel *nt* TELEKOM submarine cable

Ozeanographie *f* WASSERTRANS oceanography

Ozon[1] *nt* CHEMIE ozone

Ozon:[2] **mit ~ anreichern** *vt* CHEMIE ozonize; **in ~ verwandeln** *vt* CHEMIE ozonize

Ozon: **Ozonabsorption** *f* STRAHLPHYS ozone absorption; **Ozonbeständigkeit** *f* KUNSTSTOFF ozone resistance

ozonfest: **~er Kautschuk** *m* KUNSTSTOFF ozone-resistant rubber

Ozon: **Ozonfestigkeit** *f* KUNSTSTOFF ozone resistance; **Ozonid** *nt* CHEMIE ozonide

ozonisieren *vt* CHEMIE ozonize

Ozon: **Ozonkonzentration** *f* UMWELTSCHMUTZ ozone concentration; **Ozonloch** *nt* RAUMFAHRT, UMWELTSCHMUTZ ozone hole

Ozonolyse *f* CHEMIE ozonolysis; **Ozonolyseprodukt** *nt* CHEMIE ozonide

Ozon: **Ozonoskop** *nt* CHEMIE ozonoscope; **Ozonosphäre** *f* RAUMFAHRT ozonosphere; **Ozonschaden** *m* UMWELTSCHMUTZ ozone damage

ozonschädlich *adj* UMWELTSCHMUTZ ozone-damaging

Ozon: **Ozonschicht** *f* RAUMFAHRT, UMWELTSCHMUTZ ozone layer; **Ozonspaltung** *f* CHEMIE ozonolysis

P

P [1] *abbr* ELEKTRIZ *(magnetischer Leitwert)* P *(permeance)*, ELEKTRIZ *(Leistung)* P *(power)*, KERNTECH *(Protonenzahl)* P *(proton number)*

P [2] *(Phosphor)* CHEMIE P *(phosphorus)*

p *abbr* AKUSTIK *(Schalldruck)* p *(sound pressure)*, AUFNAHME *(Schalldruck)* p *(acoustic pressure)*, KERNTECH *(Proton)* p *(proton)*, KERNTECH *(Resonanzfluchtwahrscheinlichkeit)* p *(resonance escape probability)*, METROL *(Piko-)* p *(pico-)*, PHYS *(Proton)* p *(proton)*, PHYS *(Schalldruck)* p *(sound pressure)*, RADIO *(Proton)* p *(proton)*, RAUMFAHRT *(Schalldruck)* p *(acoustic pressure)*, TEILPHYS *(Proton)* p *(proton)*

p⁻ ~ **Bereich** *m* ELEKTRONIK p⁻-region; ~ **Halbleiter** *m* ELEKTRONIK p⁻-semiconductor; ~ **Mangelhalbleiter** *m* ELEKTRONIK p⁻-semiconductor; ~ **Region** *f* ELEKTRONIK p⁻-region

PA *abbr* AUFNAHME *(Kraftverstärker, Leistungsverstärker)* PA *(power amplifier)*, CHEMIE *(Polyamid)* PA *(polyamide)*, ELEKTRONIK *(Leistungsverstärker)*, ELEKTROTECH *(Endstufe, Endverstärker, Leistungsverstärker)* PA *(power amplifier)*, KUNSTSTOFF *(Polyamid)* PA *(polyamide)*, PHYS *(Hauptverstärker, Leistungsverstärker)*, RADIO *(Endstufe, Leistungsverstärker)*, RAUMFAHRT *(Leistungsverstärker)*, TELEKOM *(Leistungsverstärker)* PA *(power amplifier)*, TEXTIL *(Polyamid)* PA *(polyamide)*

Pa *abbr (Pascal)* METROL, PHYS *Hydrostatik* Pa *(pascal)*

PAA *abbr (Polyacryl, Polyacrylat)* CHEMIE, KUNSTSTOFF PAA *(polyacrylate)*

Paar *nt* ELEKTROTECH, MASCHINEN couple; **Paarbildung** *f* ELEKTRIZ pairing; **Paarelektronen** *nt pl* STRAHLPHYS paired electrons

paaren *vt* ELEKTROTECH *Kabel* pair

Paar: **Paarerzeugung** *f* PHYS pair production

paariges: ~ **Kabel** *nt* ELEKTROTECH paired cable

Paar: **Paarproduktion** *f* TEILPHYS pair production; **Paarvernichtung** *f* KERNTECH pair annihilation; **Paarvernichtungsfoton** *nt* STRAHLPHYS annihilation photon; **Paarvernichtungs-Peak** *nt* STRAHLPHYS pair annihilation peak; **Paarvernichtungsstrahlung** *f* STRAHLPHYS annihilation radiation

paarverseilt: ~**es Kabel** *nt* ELEKTRIZ paired cable, ELEKTROTECH paired cable, twin cable, FERNSEH paired cable, TELEKOM twisted pair cable

paarweise: ~ **parallel schalten** *vt* ELEKTROTECH couple in parallel

Package-Kessel *m* HEIZ & KÄLTE packaged boiler

Packeis *nt* WASSERTRANS pack ice

packen *vt* COMP & DV pack

Packfong *nt* METALL German silver

Packhaus *nt* WASSERTRANS warehouse

Packmaschine: ~ **für Trays** *f* VERPACK tray packing machine

Packpapier *nt* ABFALL packaging paper, wrapping paper, PAPIER wrapping, VERPACK wrapping paper

Packpresse *f* PAPIER bundling press

Packstoff *m* ABFALL packaging material

Packung: ~ **mit Wiederversiegelung** *f* VERPACK resealable pack; **Packungsanteil** *m* OPTIK *Faserbündel*, PHYS, TELEKOM packing fraction; **Packungsattrappe** *f* VERPACK dummy; **Packungsdichte** *f* ELEKTRONIK *von Bauelementen* component density, KUNSTSTOFF packing density, OPTIK *Faserbündel*, PHYS, TELEKOM packing fraction; **Packungstransportvorrichtung** *f* VERPACK pack-handling equipment; **Packungstreiber** *m* KER & GLAS packing stick

Paddingmaschine *f* TEXTIL *Färben* pad

Pagina *f* DRUCK page number

paginieren *vt* COMP & DV, DRUCK paginate

Paginierung [1] *f* COMP & DV, DRUCK pagination

Paginierung [2] ~ **vornehmen** *vi* COMP & DV page, paginate

Paket *nt* COMP & DV packet, ELEKTROTECH *Bit bei Datenvermittlung* package, METALL, TELEKOM packet, TRANS parcel; **Paketanschlußstelle** *f* TELEKOM packet port; **Paketaufrechnung** *f* COMP & DV packet sequencing; **Paketbetriebsart** *f* COMP & DV packet mode; **Paketfunkverkehr** *m* RADIO *Datenfunk*, TELEKOM packet radio; **Paketgut** *nt* VERPACK parceled goods (AmE), parcelled goods (BrE)

Paketieranlage *f* VERPACK bundle-tying machine

Paketieren *nt* FERTIG piling

paketieren *vt* FERTIG packet, pile

Paketierer-Depaketierer *m* TELEKOM PAD, packet assembler-disassembler, packetizer/depacketizer

Paketiermaschine *f* VERPACK bundling machine, parcelling machine

Paketierungs-Depaketierungseinrichtung *f* COMP & DV PAD, packet assembler-disassembler

Paket: **Paketkarte** *f* TRANS parcel registration card; **Paketrundsendung** *f* TELEKOM packet broadcasting; **Paketrutsche** *f* TRANS parcels chute; **Paketschalter** *m* ELEKTROTECH gang switch, TRANS parcels counter

pakettiert *adj* VERPACK enclosed in a packet

Paket: **Paketübertragung** *f* COMP & DV, TELEKOM packet transmission

paketvermittelt: ~**es Netz** *nt* TELEKOM PSN, packet-switched network; ~**er Übermittlungsdienst** *m* TELEKOM packet-switched bearer service

Paketvermittlung *f* COMP & DV, ELEKTROTECH, TELEKOM packet switching; **Paketvermittlungsamt** *nt* TELEKOM packet-switching exchange; **Paketvermittlungseinrichtung** *f* ELEKTRIZ, TELEKOM PS, packet switch; **Paketvermittlungsknoten** *m* TELEKOM packet-switching node; **Paketvermittlungsnetz** *nt* TELEKOM packet-switching network; **Paketvermittlungsprozessor** *m* TELEKOM packet-switching processor

Paket: **Paketverzögerungszeit** *f* COMP & DV packet delay

paketweise: ~**er Datenservice** *m* COMP & DV PSN, packet-switched network

PAL *abbr (programmierbare logische Anordnung)* COMP & DV PAL *(programmable array logic)*

Paläodruck *m* ERDÖL *Geologie* palaeopressure (BrE), paleopressure (AmE)

paläogen: ~**er Druck** *m* ERDÖL *Geologie* palaeopressure

(BrE), paleopressure (AmE)

Paläomagnetismus *m* PHYS palaeomagnetism (BrE), paleomagnetism (AmE)

Paläozoikum *nt* ERDÖL *Erdgeschichte* Palaeozoic (BrE), Paleozoic (AmE)

Palette[1] *f* FERTIG, KER & GLAS *für Glasbehälter*, TRANS pallet; **~ mit abnehmbarer Seite** *f* TRANS pallet with loose partition

Palette:[2] **auf ~n packen** *vt* VERPACK palletize

Palette: **Palettenabstreifer** *m* ANSTRICH palette knife; **Palettenaufsetzrahmen** *m* TRANS pallet collar; **Palettenbelader** *m* VERPACK pallet loader; **Palettencontainer** *m* TRANS pallet container; **Palettenentlader** *m* VERPACK depalletizer; **Palettenentnahme** *f* VERPACK depalletization; **Palettenentnehmer** *m* VERPACK depalletizer; **Palettenhaube** *f* VERPACK pallet hood; **Palettenschiff** *nt* WASSERTRANS pallet ship, palletized cargo carrier; **Palettenschrumpfverpackung** *f* VERPACK pallet shrink-wrapping; **Palettenschrumpfverpackungsmaschine** *f* VERPACK pallet stretch-wrapping machine; **Palettenverpackungsbandmaterial** *nt* VERPACK pallet strapping material; **Palettenverpackungsmaschine** *f* VERPACK pallet wrapper

palettierbar *adj* TRANS palletizable

Palettieren *nt* VERPACK palletizing

palettieren *vt* TRANS, VERPACK palletize

Palettierklebstoff *m* VERPACK palletizing adhesive

Palettiermaschine *f* VERPACK palletizing machine

palettiert: **~er Karton** *m* VERPACK palletized board

Palettierung *f* TRANS palletization

Palettisierung *f* VERPACK palletization

PAL-Farbsystem *nt* FERNSEH PAL color system (AmE), PAL colour system (BrE)

Palisadenstein *m* KER & GLAS soldier block

Palisadenzaun *m* BAU palisade

Palladium *nt (Pd)* CHEMIE, METALL palladium *(Pd)*

Palmitat *nt* CHEMIE hexadecanoate, palmitate

Palmitin *nt* CHEMIE palmitin

Palmiton *nt* CHEMIE hentriacontanone, palmitone

Palmkernöl *nt* LEBENSMITTEL palm kernel oil

Palstek *m* WASSERTRANS *Knoten* bowline

PAL-System *nt* COMP & DV, FERNSEH PAL, phase alternation line

Palygorskit *nt* ERDÖL attapulgite

PAM *abbr (Pulsamplitudenmodulation)* COMP & DV, ELEKTRONIK, RADIO, TELEKOM PAM *(pulse amplitude modulation)*

PAN *abbr* UMWELTSCHMUTZ *(Peroxyacetylnitrat)* PAN *(peroxoacetylnitrate)*, UMWELTSCHMUTZ *(Polyacrylnitril)* PAN *(polyacrylonitrile)*

panchromatisch[1] *adj* CHEMIE, DRUCK, FOTO panchromatic

panchromatisch:[2] **~e Emulsion** *f* FOTO panchromatic emulsion

Paneel *nt* BAU panel; **Paneelvermittlungssystem** *nt* TELEKOM panel system

Panfilter *nt* KOHLEN pan filter

Panflavin *nt* CHEMIE panflavine

Pankreatin *nt* CHEMIE pancreatin

Panne[1] *f* COMP & DV, FERNSEH glitch, MECHAN flat, TELEKOM breakdown, TEXTIL panne, TRANS *Maschinenschaden* breakdown

Panne:[2] **eine ~ haben** *vt* KFZTECH break down

Panning *nt* COMP & DV panning

Panorama *nt* FERNSEH, FOTO, PHYS panorama; **Panora-**

maanzeige *f (PPI-Anzeige)* PHYS plan position indicator *(PPI)*; **Panoramaaufnahme** *f* FOTO panoramic photograph; **Panoramakamera** *f* FOTO panoramic camera; **Panoramakopf** *m* FOTO pan-and-tilt head; **Panoramaperiskop** *nt* KERNTECH panorama periscope

panschen *vt* LEBENSMITTEL adulterate

Pantograf *m* DRUCK, EISENBAHN pantograph; **Pantograf-Manipulator** *m* KERNTECH pantograph-type manipulator

Pantokarenen *f pl* WASSERTRANS *Schiffkonstruktion* cross-curves

pantonal: **~e Tonleiter** *f* AKUSTIK pantonal scale

Pantothenat- *pref* CHEMIE pantothenate

Panzer *m* ELEKTROTECH armor (AmE), armour (BrE); **Panzeraderleitung** *f* ELEKTROTECH metal-sheathed conductor; **Panzerbatterie** *f* TRANS armored battery (AmE), armoured battery (BrE); **Panzerblech** *nt* BAU armor plate (AmE), armour plate (BrE); **Panzerkabel** *nt* ELEKTROTECH armored cable (AmE), armoured cable (BrE), metal-sheathed cable, MASCHINEN, TELEKOM armored cable (AmE), armoured cable (BrE)

Panzern *nt* FERTIG hard-facing by welding

Panzer: **Panzerplatte** *f* MECHAN armor plate (AmE), armour plate (BrE); **Panzerplattenwalzwerk** *nt* FERTIG armor-plate mill (AmE), armour-plate mill (BrE); **Panzerung** *f* ELEKTROTECH armor (AmE), armour (BrE), *Kabeln, Adern* metal sheath; **Panzerventil** *nt* MASCHINEN armored valve (AmE), armoured valve (BrE)

Päonin *nt* CHEMIE peonine

Papain *nt* CHEMIE, LEBENSMITTEL papain

Papaverin *f* CHEMIE papaverine

Papayotin *nt* CHEMIE, LEBENSMITTEL papain

Paperback *nt* DRUCK paperback

Papier *nt* COMP & DV, DRUCK, PAPIER paper; **~ mit Wasserlinien** *nt* DRUCK, VERPACK *mit Egoutteurrippung* laid paper; **Papierabrißkante** *f* COMP & DV paper tear guide; **Papierauskleidung** *f* VERPACK *Karton* case-lining paper; **Papierbahn** *f* PAPIER web; **Papierband** *nt* ELEKTRIZ paper tape; **Papierbelichtungsmesser** *m* FOTO enlarging meter; **Papierbeutel** *m* VERPACK paper bag; **Papierbeutel- und Sackverschluß** *m* VERPACK paper bag and sack closure; **Papierbogen** *m* PAPIER sheet

Papierchromatographie *f* CHEMIE paper chromatography; **Papierchromatographiebehälter** *m* LABOR paper chromatography tank; **Papierchromatographiegerät** *nt* LABOR paper chromatography apparatus; **Papierchromatographietank** *m* LABOR paper chromatography tank

Papier: **Papierdichtung** *f* MASCHINEN paper gasket; **Papiereinlage** *f* VERPACK case-lining paper; **Papiereinzug** *m* COMP & DV paper feed, paper picker; **Papierende-Sensor** *m* COMP & DV form stop; **Papiererzeugung** *f* PAPIER papermaking; **Papierfabrik** *f* PAPIER paper mill, VERPACK board mill; **Papierfach** *nt* COMP & DV paper tray; **Papierfaser** *f* VERPACK paper fiber (AmE), paper fibre (BrE); **Papierfilter** *nt* MASCHINEN paper filter; **Papierformat** *nt* DRUCK, PAPIER paper size; **Papierfühler** *m* COMP & DV paper sensor; **Papiergewicht** *nt* PAPIER weight of paper; **Papiergröße** *f* DRUCK paper size; **Papierhäckselmaschine** *f* VERPACK shredding machine; **Papierhärtegrad** *m* FOTO paper grade; **Papierherstellung** *f* DRUCK papermaking; **Papierholz** *nt* ABFALL pulpwood papierisoliert: ~es Kabel *nt* ELEKTROTECH paper-insulated cable

Papier: Papierisolierung *f* ELEKTRIZ paper insulation; Papierkabel *nt* ELEKTROTECH paper-insulated cable; Papierkohle *f* KOHLEN paper coal, papyraceous lignite; Papierkondensator *m* ELEKTRIZ, ELEKTROTECH, RADIO paper capacitor; Papierkopie *f* COMP & DV hard copy; Papierlaminat *nt* VERPACK paper laminate; Papierlocher *m* PAPIER punch; Papiermangel *m* COMP & DV paper low; Papiermaschine *f* DRUCK, PAPIER paper machine; Papiermaschinenantrieb *m* PAPIER paper machine drive; Papiermaschinenausschuß *m* PAPIER machine broke; Papiermasse *f* DRUCK paper pulp; Papiernegativ *nt* FOTO paper negative; Papierpoliermaschine *f* KER & GLAS paper polisher; Papierrolle *f* PAPIER jumbo roll, reel of paper; Papiersack *m* VERPACK paper sack; Papierschneidemaschine *f* DRUCK, VERPACK guillotine, paper cutter; Papierschneider *m* DRUCK, VERPACK guillotine, paper cutter; Papierschnitzel *m pl* VERPACK paper chips; Papierspan *m* PAPIER shaving; Papierstapel *m* PAPIER stack of paper

papierstark: ~es Papier *nt* FOTO single weight paper

Papier: Papierstärke *f* VERPACK paper grade; Papierstoff *m* DRUCK paper pulp, PAPIER stock; Papierstreifentransport *m* GERÄT chart transport; Papiertransport *m* COMP & DV paper feed; Papiertüte *f* VERPACK paper bag; Papierverarbeitungsindustrie *f* VERPACK paper-converting industry; Papierverpackung *f* VERPACK paper wrapping; Papiervorschub *m* COMP & DV form feed, paper skip; Papierwalze *f* PAPIER *Superkalander* paper roll; Papierwolle *f* VERPACK paper chips; Papierzerreißmaschine *f* VERPACK shredding machine; Papierzug *m* PAPIER paper draw

Pappdeckel *m* PAPIER mill board

Pappe *f* DRUCK, PAPIER, VERPACK board, cardboard, paper board, paste board, pulp board; Pappenfilz *m* PAPIER board felt

Pappfaß *nt* VERPACK fiber drum (AmE), fibre drum (BrE)

Papptablett *nt* VERPACK cardboard tray

Paraban- *pref* CHEMIE parabanic; Parabansäure *f* CHEMIE oxalylurea, parabanic acid

Parabel *f* GEOM parabola; ~ dritten Grades *f* GEOM cubic parabola; Parabelgeschwindigkeit *f* RAUMFAHRT parabolic velocity; Parabelkriechen *nt* METALL parabolic creep

Parabol- *pref* RADIO parabolic, FERNSEH parabolic shading; Parabolantenne *f* RAUMFAHRT parabolic antenna, TELEKOM dish aerial; Parabolantenne mit Gitterreflektorschüssel *f* RAUMFAHRT parabolic mesh antenna

parabolisch[1] *adj* GEOM parabolic

parabolisch:[2] ~er Orbit *m* RAUMFAHRT parabolic orbit

Parabol-: Parabolprofil *nt* OPTIK, TELEKOM parabolic profile; Parabolreflektor *m* FERNSEH dishpan, FOTO parabolic reflector; Parabolspiegel *m* PHYS parabolic mirror; Parabolspiegelantenne *f* TELEKOM parabolic reflector antenna

Paracetaldehyd *m* CHEMIE paraldehyde

Parachor *m* CHEMIE parachor

Paracyan *nt* CHEMIE paracyanogen

Paradiazin *nt* CHEMIE pyrazine

Paradigma *nt* COMP & DV paradigm

Paraffin *nt* ERDÖL wax, *Petrochemie* paraffin (BrE)

Paraffinieren *nt* VERPACK paraffin coating

paraffiniert: ~es Papier *nt* VERPACK paraffin-impregnated paper

Paraffin: Paraffinkohlenwasserstoff *m* CHEMIE, ERDÖL alkane; Paraffinpapier *nt* VERPACK paraffin-waxed paper; Paraffinreihe *f* ERDÖL *Petrochemie* paraffin series; Paraffinwachs *nt* ELEKTRIZ paraffin wax

Paraldehyd *m* CHEMIE paraldehyde

Parallaxe *f* FOTO, MASCHINEN, PHYS parallax; Parallaxenausgleich *m* GERÄT parallactic compensation, *Ablesefehler* compensation of parallax

parallaxenfrei[1] *adj* GERÄT parallax-free

parallaxenfrei:[2] ~er Spiegel *m* GERÄT antiparallax mirror

Parallel- *pref* COMP & DV parallel

parallel[1] *adj* COMP & DV, ELEKTRIZ parallel, ELEKTROTECH shunt, GEOM, RADIO parallel; ~ gespeist *adj* LUFTTRANS parallel-fed

parallel:[2] ~e Analog-Digital-Umsetzung *f* ELEKTRONIK flash analog-to-digital conversion; ~es digitales Signal *nt* ELEKTRONIK parallel digital signal; ~e Ein-/Ausgabe *f* COMP & DV parallel input/output; ~e Verschiebung *f* GEOM translation

parallel:[3] ~ richten *vt* ELEKTRONIK *Strahlen* collimate; ~ schalten *vt* ELEKTROTECH connect in parallel

parallel:[4] ~ laufen *vi* GEOM run parallel

Parallel-: Parallelabfragespeicher *m* COMP & DV parallel-search storage; Paralleladdierer *m* COMP & DV parallel adder; Paralleladdierwerk *nt* ELEKTRONIK parallel adder; Parallelalgorithmus *m* COMP & DV parallel algorithm; Parallelanordnung *f* ELEKTRIZ parallel mounting; Parallelaufstellung *f* LUFTTRANS parallel positioning; Parallelband *nt* STRAHLPHYS parallel band; Parallelbetrieb *m* COMP & DV concurrent operation, DRUCK parallel operation; Parallelbewegung *f* MASCHINEN parallel motion; Paralleldrahtleitung *f* ELEKTROTECH parallel-wire line

Parallele *f* GEOM parallel line

Parallelendmaß *nt* FERTIG block, end block, MASCHINEN, MECHAN, METROL gage block (AmE), gauge block (BrE), slip gage (AmE), slip gauge (BrE)

Parallelepiped *nt* GEOM parallelepiped

Parallel-: Parallelflächner *m* GEOM parallelepiped; Parallelform *f* ELEKTROTECH parallel form; Parallelfräser *m* MASCHINEN parallel milling cutter; Parallelführung *f* MASCHINEN parallel guide; Parallelgegenkopplung *f* ELEKTROTECH shunt feedback; Parallelgerade *f* GEOM parallel line

parallelgeschaltet[1] *adj* ELEKTROTECH parallel-connected, GERÄT, PHYS connected in parallel

parallelgeschaltet:[2] ~e Funkenstrecken *f pl* ELEKTRIZ parallel spark gaps; ~e Widerstände *m pl* ELEKTRIZ parallel-connected resistances

parallelgespult: ~es Garn *nt* TEXTIL parallel-wound yarn

parallelgewickelt: ~er Dynamo *m* ELEKTROTECH shunt-wound dynamo; ~er Motor *m* ELEKTROTECH shunt-wound motor

Parallelisieren: ~ der Fasern *nt* TEXTIL parallelization of fibers (AmE), parallelization of fibres (BrE)

Parallel-: Parallelität *f* GEOM parallelism; Parallelkapazität *f* ELEKTROTECH shunt capacitance; Parallelkondensator *m* GERÄT bypass capacitor, PHYS bypass capacitor, shunt capacitor; Parallelkreis *m* ELEKTRIZ, TELEKOM parallel circuit; Parallelleitung *f* ELEKTRIZ butt contact; Parallellineal *nt* MASCHINEN parallel ruler; Parallelmanipulator *m* KERNTECH master-slave manipulator; Parallelmaus *f* COMP & DV parallel mouse; **Parallelmausadapter** *m* COMP & DV parallel mouse adaptor; **Parallelmausanschluß** *m* COMP & DV parallel mouse adaptor; **Parallelmultiplizierer** *m* ELEKTRONIK parallel multiplier; **Paralleloberflächenzeichnung** *f* ELEKTROTECH parallel lay; **Parallelogramm** *nt* GEOM, MECHAN parallelogram; **~ der Geschwindigkeiten** *nt* PHYS parallelogram of velocities; **~ der Kräfte** *nt* MASCHINEN, PHYS parallelogram of forces; **Parallelplattenkondensator** *m* ELEKTROTECH, PHYS parallel-plate capacitor; **Parallelprojektion** *f* GEOM, KONSTZEICH parallel projection; **Parallelprozessorkarte** *f* COMP & DV parallel card; **Parallelquerlenkerradaufhängung** *f* KFZTECH parallel-arm-type suspension; **Parallelrechnen** *nt* COMP & DV parallel arithmetic; **Parallelrechner** *m* (*SIMD-Rechner*) COMP & DV single instruction multiple-data machine *(SIMD machine)*; **Parallelreißer** *m* FERTIG marking gage (AmE), marking gauge (BrE), surface gage (AmE), surface gauge (BrE), scribing block, MASCHINEN marking gage (AmE), marking gauge (BrE), surface gage (AmE), surface gauge (BrE), MECHAN surface gage (AmE), surface gauge (BrE), METROL surface gage (AmE), surface gauge (BrE), surface geometry meter, vernier height gage (AmE), vernier height gauge (BrE); **Parallelresonanz** *f* AKUSTIK antiresonance, ELEKTRONIK, PHYS parallel resonance; **Parallelresonanzkreis** *m* ELEKTRONIK parallel resonant circuit, PHYS antiresonant circuit; **Parallelschallschluckwand** *f* AUFNAHME parallel absorbent baffle; **Parallelschaltung** *f* ELEKTROTECH parallel arrangement, parallel connection, shunt, PHYS parallel connection; **Parallelschere** *f* FERTIG guillotine plate shear, guillotine shear, guillotine shearing machine; **Parallelschnittstelle** *f* COMP & DV parallel interface, parallel port, DRUCK parallel interface; **Parallelschnittstellenanschluß** *m* COMP & DV parallel port; **Parallelschraubstock** *m* MASCHINEN parallel vice; **Parallelschwingfrequenz** *f* AKUSTIK, ELEKTRONIK *Schaltkreistechnik* antiresonant frequency; **Parallelschwingkreis** *m* ELEKTRONIK antiresonant circuit, parallel resonant circuit, rejector, RADIO rejector; **Parallel-Serien-Wandler** *m* ELEKTROTECH parallel-to-serial converter; **Parallel-Serien-Wandlung** *f* ELEKTROTECH parallel-to-serial conversion; **Parallelspeicher** *m* ELEKTROTECH parallel storage; **Parallelspeisung** *f* ELEKTRIZ parallel feeder, shunt feed, ELEKTROTECH shunt feed; **Parallelstrahl** *m* PHYS parallel beam; **Parallelstrahlenbündel** *nt* ELEKTRONIK parallel beam; **Parallelstreifenabschwächer** *m* ELEKTRONIK *Mikrowellen* parallel-vane attenuator; **Parallelstruktur** *f* REGELUNG parallel structure; **Parallelsynchronsystem** *nt* TELEKOM parallel synchronous system; **Parallelton** *m* AKUSTIK relative tone; **Paralleltonart** *f* AKUSTIK relative key; **Parallelübergabe** *f* COMP & DV parallel transmission; **Parallelübertrag** *m* COMP & DV carry lookahead, lookahead; **Parallelübertragung** *f* COMP & DV parallel transfer, parallel transmission, TELEKOM parallel transmission; **Parallelumsetzer** *m* ELEKTRONIK flash converter, parallel converter; **Parallelumsetzung** *f* ELEKTRONIK flash conversion, parallel conversion; **Parallelverarbeitung** *f* COMP & DV, ELEKTRONIK, TELEKOM parallel processing; **Parallelverbindung** *f* ELEKTRIZ parallel connection; **Parallelvierkantkeile** *nt pl* MASCHINEN square parallel keys; **Parallelwandler** *m* ELEKTRONIK flash converter; **Parallelwandlung** *f* ELEKTRONIK flash conversion;

Parallelwiderstand *m* ELEKTROTECH bleeder resistor, parallel resistance, PHYS shunt; **Parallelzahnräder** *nt pl* MASCHINEN parallel gears; **Parallelzange** *f* KERNTECH parallel-jaw tong; **Parallelzugriff** *m* COMP & DV parallel access

paramagnetisch[1] *adj* ELEKTRIZ, PHYS paramagnetic
paramagnetisch:[2] **~er Curiepunkt** *m* STRAHLPHYS paramagnetic Curie point; **~e Elektronenspinresonanz** *f* PHYS EPR, electron paramagnetic resonance; **~e Resonanz** *f* ELEKTRIZ, ELEKTRONIK, PHYS paramagnetic resonance; **~e Schienenbahn** *f* EISENBAHN paramagnetic rail; **~er Verstärker** *m* ELEKTRONIK paramagnetic amplifier

Paramagnetismus *m* PHYS paramagnetism
Parameter *m* COMP & DV, ELEKTRONIK, MATH, PHYS, RADIO parameter; **~ der Materialdispersion** *m* OPTIK material dispersion parameter; **Parameterempfindlichkeit** *f* ELEKTROTECH sensitivity; **Parametergleichungen** *f pl* MATH parametric equations; **Parameterprofil** *nt* OPTIK profile parameter, TELEKOM parameter profile; **Parameterprofildispersion** *f* OPTIK profile dispersion parameter; **Parametersubstitution** *f* COMP & DV parameter substitution; **Parameterübergabe** *f* COMP & DV parameter passing

parametrisch[1] *adj* COMP & DV parametric
parametrisch:[2] **~e Analyse** *f* ELEKTRONIK parametric analysis; **~er Elektronenstrahlverstärker** *m* ELEKTRONIK electron beam parametric amplifier; **~e Galliumarsenid-Verstärkerdiode** *f* ELEKTRONIK gallium arsenide parametric amplifier diode; **~er Laser** *m* ELEKTRONIK parametric laser; **~er Oszillator** *m* TELEKOM parametric oscillator; **~e Prüfung** *f* TELEKOM parametric test; **~er Verstärker** *m* ELEKTRONIK, PHYS, RADIO, RAUMFAHRT *Weltraumfunk*, TELEKOM parametric amplifier, paramp; **~e Verstärkung** *f* ELEKTROTECH parametric amplification

parametrisieren *vt* COMP & DV initialize
Parametrisierung *f* COMP & DV parameterization
Paramorphin *nt* CHEMIE *Pharmazie* paramorphine, thebaine

Parapepton *nt* CHEMIE parapeptone, syntonin
Paraphasenverstärker *m* FERNSEH paraphase amplifier
Pararosanilin *nt* CHEMIE pararosaniline
parasitär *adj* ELEKTRONIK parasitic
Parasitär- *pref* ELEKTRONIK, ELEKTROTECH, KERNTECH, PHYS, RADIO, TELEKOM parasitic; **Parasitärantenne** *f* PHYS parasitic aerial; **Parasitärantennenelement** *nt* PHYS parasitic element; **Parasitärdiode** *f* ELEKTRONIK parasitic diode; **Parasitärdrossel** *f* RADIO parasitic choke; **Parasitärinduktanz** *f* ELEKTROTECH parasitic inductance; **Parasitärkopplung** *f* ELEKTROTECH, TELEKOM parasitic coupling; **Parasitärneutroneneinfang** *m* KERNTECH parasitic capture; **Parasitärschwingung** *f* PHYS, RADIO, TELEKOM parasitic oscillation

paratypisch *adj* CHEMIE paratypical
Parawasserstoff *m* CHEMIE parahydrogen
paraxial: **~er Strahl** *m* PHYS paraxial ray
Paraxialstrahl *m* TELEKOM paraxial ray
Paraxylol *nt* ERDÖL *Petrochemie* paraxylene
Pardune *f* WASSERTRANS *Tauwerk* backstay
Parenthese *f* DRUCK parenthesis
Parität *f* COMP & DV, PHYS, STRAHLPHYS, TEILPHYS parity; **Paritätsanzeiger** *m* COMP & DV parity flag; **Paritätsbit** *nt* COMP & DV, RADIO parity bit; **Paritätserhaltung** *f* PHYS conservation of parity; **Paritätsfehler**

m COMP & DV parity error; **Paritätsprüfung** *f* COMP & DV odd-even check, parity check, TELEKOM parity control; **Paritätsprüfungsabbruch** *m* COMP & DV parity interrupt

Park: ~ **& Ride System** *nt* TRANS park and ride
Parkbremse *f* LUFTTRANS parking brake
Parkerisieren *nt* FERTIG parkerizing
parkerisieren *vt* FERTIG parkerize
Parkern *nt* METALL parkerizing
Parkettbodenbelag *m* BAU parquet flooring
Parkfläche *f* BAU parking area
Parkkralle *f* KFZTECH *Sperre zur Blockierung der Räder* boot, clamp
Parkleuchte *f* KFZTECH parking light, *Beleuchtung* position light
Parkorbit *m* RAUMFAHRT *Raumschiff* parking orbit
Parkplatz *m* BAU parking area
Parksperre *f* KFZTECH parking lock gear
Parksperrklinke *f* KFZTECH parking pawl
Parkstellung *f* KFZTECH parking gear
Parkuhr *f* TRANS parking meter; **Parkuhrladegerät** *nt* TRANS charger at parking meter
Parkway *m* TRANS parkway (AmE)
Parsec *nt* PHYS *astronomische Einheit* parsec
Parser *m* COMP & DV, KÜNSTL INT parser
Parsing *nt* COMP & DV, KÜNSTL INT parsing
Partialdruck *m* THERMOD partial pressure
Partial-Response-Code *m* TELEKOM partial response code
Partialwelle *f* TEILPHYS partial wave
Partie *f* QUAL batch; **Partiekontrolle durch Stichproben** *f* QUAL batch inspection by samples
partiell [1] *adj* MATH partial
partiell: [2] ~**e Ableitung** *f* MATH partial derivative; ~**e Faktorisierung** *f* MATH partial factorization; ~**e Kohärenz** *f* OPTIK, TELEKOM partial coherence
Partienstreuung *f* QUAL batch variation
Partikel *f* AKUSTIK, KOHLEN, TEILPHYS particle, UMWELTSCHMUTZ particulate material; **Partikelentfernung von Luftschadstoffen** *f* UMWELTSCHMUTZ particulate removal of air pollutants; **Partikelgröße** *f* CHEMTECH particle size
Partition *f* COMP & DV partition
partitionieren *vt* COMP & DV partition
partitioniert *adj* COMP & DV partitioned
Partitionierung *f* COMP & DV partitioning
Partitur *f* AUFNAHME score
Partner *m* COMP & DV peer; **Partnerinstanz** *f* COMP & DV peer entity
Parton *nt* TEILPHYS parton
Parvolin *nt* CHEMIE parvoline
Pascal *nt* (*Pa*) METROL *Einheit*, PHYS *Hydrostatik* pascal (*Pa*); ~**sches Dreieck** *nt* MATH Pascal's triangle
Paschen: ~**sches Gesetz** *nt* PHYS *Gasentladung* Paschen's law; ~**sche Serie** *f* PHYS *Atomphysik* Paschen series
Paschen-Back: ~**scher Effekt** *m* PHYS *Atomphysik* Paschen-Back effect
PA-Sprengstoff *m* CHEMIE ammonia dynamite
Passagier *n* LUFTTRANS, WASSERTRANS passenger; **Passagierdampfer** *m* WASSERTRANS ocean liner; **Passagierflugzeug ohne Service** *nt* LUFTTRANS skybus; **Passagiergroßflugzeug** *nt* LUFTTRANS air liner; **Passagierlinienschiff** *nt* WASSERTRANS passenger liner; **Passagierliste** *f* LUFTTRANS, TRANS, WASSERTRANS waybill; **Passagierschiff** *nt* WASSERTRANS

passenger ship; **Passagierschnellförderer** *m* KFZTECH high-speed passenger conveyor; **Passagiersitz** *m* LUFTTRANS passenger seat
Passatwinde *m pl* WASSERTRANS trade winds
Paßbohrung *f* MASCHINEN locating hole
passen *vi* MASCHINEN fit
Passepartout *nt* FOTO slip mount
Passer *m* DRUCK register mark, registration mark; **Passermarke** *f* DRUCK register mark, registration mark
Paßfeder *f* FERTIG key, KERNTECH feather key, MASCHINEN feather
Paßfläche *f* FERTIG faying surface; **Paßflächen** *f pl* MASCHINEN mating surfaces
Paßgenauigkeit *f* DRUCK register accuracy
passiv [1] *adj* ANSTRICH inert, COMP & DV, ELEKTRONIK passive
passiv: [2] ~**e Alarmierung** *f* TELEKOM passive alerting; ~**es Bandpaßfilter** *nt* ELEKTRONIK passive band-pass filter; ~**es Bandsperrfilter** *nt* ELEKTRONIK passive band-stop filter; ~**es Bauelement** *nt* ELEKTROTECH, TELEKOM passive component; ~**e Betriebsart** *f* ELEKTRONIK passive mode; ~**er Dipol** *m* ELEKTROTECH passive dipole; ~**e Elektrodynamikstoßdämpfung** *f* RAUMFAHRT *Raumschiff* passive electrodynamic snubber; ~**es Element** *nt* ELEKTRONIK passive element; ~**er Erddruck** *m* BAU, KOHLEN passive earth pressure; ~**es Filter** *nt* ELEKTRONIK, TELEKOM passive filter; ~**es Filtern** *nt* ELEKTRONIK passive filtering; ~**er Flachwagen** *m* KFZTECH passive flat car; ~**es Glied** *nt* REGELUNG passive element; ~**er Infrarotdetektor** *m* TRANS passive infrared detector; ~**es Insassenrückhaltesystem** *nt* KFZTECH passive occupant restraint system; ~**e Komponente** *f* ELEKTRONIK, KERNTECH passive component; ~**e Kraftfahrzeugsicherheit** *f* KFZTECH passive motor vehicle safety; ~**er Kreis** *m* TELEKOM passive circuit; ~**e Last** *f* ELEKTROTECH passive load; ~**es Netzwerk** *nt* ELEKTROTECH passive network; ~**er Satellit** *m* FERNSEH passive satellite; ~**e Schaltung** *f* PHYS passive circuit; ~**es Sicherheitsgurtsystem** *nt* KFZTECH passive seat belt system; ~**er Stern** *m* COMP & DV passive star; ~**e Steuerung** *f* RAUMFAHRT passive control; ~**er Strahler** *m* PHYS passive aerial; ~**er Stromkreis** *m* ELEKTRIZ passive network; ~**es System** *nt* AKUSTIK, NICHTFOSS ENERG passive system; ~**e Thermosteuerung** *f* (*PTC*) RAUMFAHRT passive thermal control (*PTC*); ~**es Trägermaterial** *nt* ELEKTRONIK passive substrate; ~**e Transporteinheit** *f* TRANS passive transport unit; ~**er Vierpol** *m* ELEKTROTECH passive quadripole; ~**er Wandler** *m* ELEKTROTECH passive transducer; ~**e Zielsuchlenkung** *f* LUFTTRANS homing passive guidance
passivieren *vt* ANSTRICH, ELEKTRONIK, PHYS, RAUMFAHRT *Raumschiff* passivate
passiviert: ~**er Transistor** *m* ELEKTRONIK passivated transistor
Passivierung *f* ELEKTRONIK, PHYS passivation; **Passivierungsglas** *nt* KER & GLAS passivation glass; **Passivierungsschicht** *f* ELEKTRONIK passivation layer
Passivität *f* ANSTRICH inertia
Paßkorrektur *f* DRUCK register adjustment
Paßlehre *f* ELEKTRIZ gage (AmE), gauge (BrE)
Paßscheibe *f* MASCHINEN locating disc (BrE), locating disk (AmE), shim
Paßschraube *f* FERTIG precision bolt, reamed bolt, MASCHINEN dowel screw
Paßstift *m* BAU dowel pin, MASCHINEN alignment pin,

dowel pin, locating pin, MECHAN alignment pin

Paßstück *nt* COMP & DV, ELEKTRIZ, ELEKTROTECH, FERTIG, LABOR, MASCHINEN, MECHAN, PHYS, RADIO, TELEKOM, TEXTIL adaptor

Paßteile *nt pl* MASCHINEN mating parts

Paßtoleranz *f* MASCHINEN tolerance of fit, MECHAN fitting tolerance

Passung *f* MASCHINEN fit, MECHAN seat; **Passungsflansch** *m* MECHAN mating flange

Paßwort *nt* COMP & DV, TELEKOM password

Paßzeichen *nt* DRUCK register mark, registration mark

Paßzugabe *f* MASCHINEN fitting allowance

Pasteurisieren *nt* THERMOD pasteurization

pasteurisieren *vt* THERMOD pasteurize

pasteurisiert *adj* THERMOD pasteurized

Pasteurisierung *f* THERMOD pasteurization

Pasteur-Pipette *f* LABOR Pasteur pipette

pastös: ~**er Abfall** *m* ABFALL pasty waste

Patent[1] *nt* PATENT patent

Patent:[2] **ein ~ benutzen** *vi* PATENT use a patent

patentfähig: ~**e Erfindung** *f* PATENT patentable invention

Patent: **Patentanker** *m* WASSERTRANS stockless anchor; **Patentanmeldung** *f* PATENT patent application; **Patentanspruch** *m* PATENT claim; **Patentanwalt** *m* PATENT patent agent; **Patentgebühren** *f pl* PATENT royalties; **Patentierbarkeit** *f* PATENT patentability

patentiert *adj* MASCHINEN patented

Patent: **Patentinhaber** *m* PATENT patent proprietor, proprietor of a patent; **Patentlog** *nt* WASSERTRANS patent log; **Patentschäkel** *m* WASSERTRANS *Beschläge* snap shackle; **Patentschrift** *f* PATENT patent specification, *gedruckt* specification; **Patenturkunde** *f* PATENT patent certificate; **Patentverletzer** *m* PATENT infringer

pathogen: ~**er Abfall** *m* ABFALL anatomical waste, infectious waste, pathological waste

pathogenetisch: ~**e Gefahr** *f* SICHERHEIT pathogenic hazard

Patina *f* FERTIG patina, verdigris

patinieren *vt* FERTIG patinate

Patio-Tür *f* KER & GLAS patio door

Patrize *f* FERTIG stamp

Patrone *f* ELEKTROTECH, FOTO *für 35mm Film* cartridge, MASCHINEN collet; **Patronenanlasser** *m* KFZTECH, LUFTTRANS, WASSERTRANS combustion starter; **Patronenfilter** *nt* KFZTECH *Schmierung* cartridge filter; **Patronensicherung** *f* ELEKTRIZ cartridge fuse, ELEKTROTECH enclosed fuse

patronieren *vt* TEXTIL *Weben* draft

Patrouillenboot *nt* MEERSCHMUTZ, WASSERTRANS patrol boat

Pattern: ~ **Matching** *nt* KÜNSTL INT pattern matching

Pauli: ~**sches Ausschließungsprinzip** *nt* PHYS, TEILPHYS Pauli exclusion principle; ~**sches Prinzip** *nt* STRAHLPHYS Pauli principle

Pauschalfrachtgeld *nt* ERDÖL *Handel, Schiffahrt* lump sum freight

Pauschalgebühr *f* PATENT flat-rate fee; **Pauschalgebührendienst** *m* TELEKOM flat-rate service

Pauschalpreis *m* BAU lumpsum price

Pauschaltarif *m* ELEKTRIZ flat-rate tariff, TELEKOM all-in tariff

Pause *f* AKUSTIK interval, rest, FERNSEH pause

pausen *vt* MASCHINEN trace

Pausenknopf *m* FERNSEH pause control

pausenlos: ~**es Fräsen** *nt* FERTIG index-base milling

Pause: **Pausensteuerung** *f* AUFNAHME pause control;

Pausenzeichen *nt* FERNSEH station identification

Pauspapier *nt* MASCHINEN tracing paper

Pawsey-Anpassungsglied *nt* RADIO *Antennen* Pawsey stub

Pay-TV *f* FERNSEH pay TV

PB *abbr* COMP & DV *(Pulsbreite)*, ELEKTRONIK *(Pulsbreite)*, FERNSEH *(Pulsbreite)* PW *(pulse width)*, KUNSTSTOFF *(Polybuten, Polybutylen)* PB *(polybutylene)*, PHYS *(Pulsbreite)*, TELEKOM *(Pulsbreite)* PW *(pulse width)*

Pb *(Blei)* CHEMIE Pb *(lead)*

P-Beiwert *m* REGELUNG proportional coefficient

PBT *abbr (Polybutylenterephthalat)* ELEKTRIZ, KUNSTSTOFF PBT *(polybutylene ephtalate)*

PBX *abbr (private Selbstwählnebenstelle)* TELEKOM PBX *(private branch exchange)*

PBX-Vermittlungsschrank *m* TELEKOM PBX switch-board

PC *abbr* COMP & DV *(Personal Computer)* PC *(personal computer)*, ELEKTRIZ *(Polycarbonat)*, KUNSTSTOFF *(Polycarbonat)* PC *(polycarbonate)*

PCB *abbr* COMP & DV *(Leiterplatte, Printplatte)*, ELEKTRIZ *(Leiterplatte)*, ELEKTRONIK *(Leiterplatte, gedruckte Schaltung)*, FERNSEH *(Leiterplatte)*, RADIO *(Leiterplatte)*, TELEKOM *(Leiterplatte)* PCB *(printed circuit board)*

PC-Karte *f* ELEKTRONIK PC board

PCM[1] *abbr (Pulscodemodulation)* AUFNAHME, COMP & DV, ELEKTRONIK, FERNSEH, RADIO, STRAHLPHYS, TELEKOM PCM *(pulse code modulation)*

PCM:[2] **PCM/FM-Modulation** *f* ELEKTRONIK PCM/FM modulation; **PCM-Filter** *nt* ELEKTRONIK PCM filter; **PCM-Multiplexer** *m* ELEKTRONIK PCM multiplexer; **PCM-Multiplexing** *nt* ELEKTRONIK PCM multiplexing; **PCM-System** *nt* TELEKOM PCM system; **PCM-Vermittlungssystem** *nt* TELEKOM PCM switching system

PCS-Faser *f (Plastic-Clad-Silika-Faser)* OPTIK, TELEKOM PCS fiber (AmE), PCS fibre (BrE) *(plastic-clad silica fiber)*

PCU *abbr (externe Steuereinheit, periphere Steuereinheit)* COMP & DV PCU *(peripheral control unit)*

PCV-Ventilation *f (Kurbelgehäusezwangsentlüftung, rückführende Kurbelgehäuseentlüftung)* KFZTECH PCV *(positive crankcase ventilation)*

Pd *(Palladium)* CHEMIE, METALL Pd *(palladium)*

PDAP *abbr (Polydiallyphthalat)* KUNSTSTOFF PDAP *(polydiallylphthalate)*

p-Diffusion *f* ELEKTRONIK p-type diffusion

PDM *abbr* COMP & DV *(Pulsdeltamodulation)* PDM *(pulse delta modulation)*, ELEKTRONIK *(Pulsdauermodulation)* PWM *(pulse width modulation)*

PDN *abbr (öffentliches Datennetz)* COMP & DV PDN *(public data network)*

p-dotierte: ~ **Basis** *f* ELEKTRONIK p-type base

PDR *abbr (vorläufige technische Prüfung)* RAUMFAHRT PDR *(preliminary design review)*

PD-Regelung *f (Proportional-Differential-Regelung)* LABOR PD control *(proportional plus derivative control)*

PD-Regler *m (Proportional-Differential-Regler)* LABOR PD controller *(proportional plus derivative controller)*

PD-Verhalten *nt (Proportional-Differential-Verhalten)* REGELUNG PD action *(proportional plus derivative action)*

Peak *m* KERNTECH peak

PE-C *abbr (chloriertes Polyethylen)* KUNSTSTOFF CPE *(chlorinated polyethylene)*

PEC *abbr (Fotozelle)* DRUCK, ELEKTRIZ, ELEKTRONIK, FERNSEH, FOTO, PHYS, STRAHLPHYS PEC *(photoelectric cell)*

Pech *nt* KER & GLAS, WASSERTRANS pitch; **Pechblende** *f* KERNTECH uranium black

pechen *vi* WASSERTRANS pitch

Pech: **Pechkohle** *f* KOHLEN pitch coal; **Pechpoliermaschine** *f* KER & GLAS pitch polisher; **Pechstein** *m* ERDÖL *Mineral* pitchstone

Pedal *nt* KFZTECH *Bremse, Kupplung* pedal, MASCHINEN treadle; **Pedalsteller** *m* KFZTECH *Bremse, Kupplung* pedal adjuster

Peer-zu-Peer- *adj* COMP & DV peer-to-peer

Pegel *m* AKUSTIK Schwellwert, AUFNAHME level, BAU gage (AmE), gauge (BrE), level, EISENBAHN *Flüssigkeit* level indicator, ELEKTRONIK *Geräusch, Flüssigkeit*, MASCHINEN level, MECHAN gage (AmE), gauge (BrE), METROL level, WASSERVERSORG water level gage (AmE), water level gauge (BrE); **Pegelabfall** *m* MASCHINEN level drop; **Pegelabgleichung** *f* ELEKTRONIK leveling (AmE), levelling (BrE); **Pegelanzeige** *f* MASCHINEN level indicator; **Pegelausgleich** *m* ELEKTRONIK level adjustment; **Pegeldifferenz** *f* AKUSTIK level difference; **Pegeldurchgangshäufigkeit** *f* TELEKOM level crossing rate; **Pegelhaltung** *f* AUFNAHME *durch Klemmschaltung* clamping; **Pegellatte** *f* BAU staff gage (AmE), staff gauge (BrE); **Pegelmarkierung** *f* KFZTECH *Schmierung* oil level mark; **Pegelmeßgerät** *nt* GERÄT decibel meter, level gage (AmE), level gauge (BrE), signal level meter; **Pegelmessung** *f* GERÄT level measurement; **Pegelregler** *m* VERPACK level control; **Pegelschreiber** *m* AUFNAHME level recorder; **Pegelstand** *m* NICHTFOSS ENERG water depth; **Pegelverschiebung** *f* ELEKTRONIK level shifting

Peilantenne *f* TRANS aural null loop (AmE), direction finder antenna (BrE)

Peilempfänger *m* RADIO, TELEKOM, WASSERTRANS DF receiver, direction-finding receiver

Peilen *nt* RADIO direction finding

peilen *vt* WASSERTRANS sound

Peilgerät *nt* GERÄT bearing instrument, LUFTTRANS direction finder

Peilkompaß *m* WASSERTRANS *Navigation* azimuth compass

Peillatte *f* WASSERTRANS *Deckausrüstung* sounding pole

Peilscheibe *f* WASSERTRANS *Navigation* pelorus, *Radar* bearing marker

Peilstrahl *m (PS)* WASSERTRANS *Radar* electronic bearing cursor, electronic bearing line

Peilung *f* RAUMFAHRT *Raumschiff* fix, heading, TELEKOM direction finding, WASSERTRANS sounding, *Navigation* bearing

Peitschenantenne *f* RADIO whip antenna

Peitschenhiebeffekt *m* TRANS whiplash effect

Pektin *nt* CHEMIE, LEBENSMITTEL pectin; **Pektingelee** *nt* LEBENSMITTEL pectin jelly; **Pektinose** *f* CHEMIE arabinose, pectinose

pektinsauer *adj* CHEMIE pectic

Pektin: **Pektinsubstanz** *f* CHEMIE pectin

Pektisation *f* CHEMIE pectization

pektisch *adj* CHEMIE pectic

pektisieren *vt* CHEMIE pectize

Pektose *f* CHEMIE pectose

Pelargonat *nt* CHEMIE pelargonate

pelargonsauer *adj* CHEMIE pelargonic

Pellet *nt* FERTIG, KERNTECH, KOHLEN, KUNSTSTOFF pellet; **Pelletieren** *nt* KUNSTSTOFF pelletizing; **Pelletierin** *nt* CHEMIE pelletierine, punicine; **Pelletiermaschine** *f* KUNSTSTOFF pelletizer; **Pelletisierung** *f* ABFALL pelletization; **Pelletizer** *m* KUNSTSTOFF *Kautschuk* pelletizer; **Pelletstapel** *m* KERNTECH *in Brennelementen* pellet stack

Pelorus *m* WASSERTRANS *Navigation* pelorus

Peltiereffekt *m* ELEKTRIZ, PHYS Peltier effect

Peltierkoeffizient *m* PHYS Peltier coefficient

Peltonrad *nt* NICHTFOSS ENERG Pelton wheel; **~ mit senkrechter Welle** *nt* NICHTFOSS ENERG vertical-shaft Pelton wheel; **~ mit waagerechter Welle** *nt* NICHTFOSS ENERG horizontal-shaft Pelton wheel; **Peltonradturbine** *f* NICHTFOSS ENERG Pelton wheel turbine

Pelz *m* TEXTIL lap

Pendel *nt* MECHAN pendulum; **Pendelachse** *f* KFZTECH full-floating axle, *Kraftübertragung* floating axle; **Pendelaufhängung** *f* TRANS pendulum suspension; **Pendelausschlag** *m* MECHAN pendulum deflection; **Pendelbecherwerk** *nt* TRANS tilt bucket elevator; **Pendelbedienung** *f* SICHERHEIT pendant switch control; **Pendelbewegung** *f* MASCHINEN, MECHAN pendulum motion; **Pendeleinlegevorrichtung** *f* KER & GLAS reciprocating charger; **Pendelfehler** *m* MECHAN pendulum error; **Pendelförderung** *f* KOHLEN shuttle haulage

pendelförmig *adj* MECHAN pendular

Pendel: **Pendelfräsen** *nt* MASCHINEN pendulum milling; **Pendelgewicht** *nt* MECHAN pendulum bob; **Pendelhalter** *m* MASCHINEN floating bush; **Pendelhärte** *f* KUNSTSTOFF pendulum hardness; **Pendelkugel** *f* MECHAN pendulum sphere; **Pendelkugellager** *nt* MASCHINEN self-aligning ball bearing; **Pendellager** *nt* KFZTECH self-aligning bearing, MASCHINEN self-aligning bearing, swivel bearing, swivel plummer block, MECHAN pendulum bearing; **Pendellänge** *f* MECHAN pendulum length; **Pendellinse** *f* MECHAN pendulum lenticle, PHYS pendulum bob; **Pendelmasse** *f* MECHAN pendulum mass; **Pendelmotor** *m* ELEKTRIZ swivel bearing motor; **Pendelmühle** *f* MECHAN pendulum mill

Pendeln *nt* ELEKTRIZ, ELEKTROTECH *Instrumentennadel* hunting, LUFTTRANS shuttle

pendeln *nt* RADIO hunt

pendelnahtschweißen *vt* FERTIG weave

pendelnd: **~er Werkzeughalter** *m* MASCHINEN floating tool holder

Pendel: **Pendelplatte** *f* HYDRAUL shuttle plate; **Pendelreibahle** *f* MASCHINEN floating reamer; **Pendelrollenlager** *nt* MASCHINEN self-aligning roller bearing; **Pendelsäge** *f* MECHAN pendulum saw; **Pendelscheibe** *f* PHYS pendulum bob; **Pendelschere** *f* MASCHINEN pendulum shears; **Pendelschwimmer** *m* KER & GLAS pendulum floater; **Pendelschwingung** *f* LUFTTRANS phugoid oscillation, MECHAN pendulum swing; **Pendelsignal** *nt* EISENBAHN wig-wag signal; **Pendeltor** *nt* BAU swing gate; **Pendeltrennschleifmaschine** *f* FERTIG oscillating-type abrasive cutting machine; **Pendeltür** *f* BAU swing door, swinging door

Pendelung *f* LUFTTRANS *Hubschrauber* cycling

Pendel: **Pendelverkehr** *m* LUFTTRANS shuttle service, shuttle traffic; **Pendelverkehr zwischen Flughäfen** *m* TRANS air shuttle; **Pendelversuch** *m* MECHAN pendulum test; **Pendelwirkung** *f* LUFTTRANS phugoid effect

Pendlerverkehr *m* TRANS commuter traffic, office-hour traffic

penetrant *adj* ANSTRICH penetrant

Penetrationsmeßgerät *nt* KUNSTSTOFF penetration tester

Penetrometer *nt* BAU penetrometer, KUNSTSTOFF penetration tester, LABOR penetrometer

Penizillin-Phiole *f* KER & GLAS penicillin phial (BrE), penicillin vial (AmE)

Pennyweight *nt* METROL pennyweight

Pentachlorid *nt* CHEMIE pentachloride

Pentacyanoferrat *nt* CHEMIE prussiate

Pentaeder *nt* GEOM pentahedron

Pentagon *nt* GEOM pentagon

pentagonal *adj* GEOM pentagonal

Pentagrid-Mischröhre *f* ELEKTROTECH pentagrid converter

Pentamethylen *nt* CHEMIE cyclopentane, pentamethylene; **Pentamethylendiamin** *nt* CHEMIE pentamethylenediamine; **Pentamethylenimin** *nt* CHEMIE pentamethyleneimide, piperidine

Pentan *nt* CHEMIE, ERDÖL *Petrochemie* pentane; **Pentandiamin** *nt* CHEMIE pentamethylenediamine; **Pentanol** *nt* CHEMIE amyl alcohol, pentanol; **Pentanon** *nt* CHEMIE pentanone

Penta-Prisma *nt* FOTO pentaprism

Pentaquin *nt* CHEMIE pentaquine

Pentasulfid *nt* CHEMIE pentasulfide (AmE), pentasulphide (BrE)

Pentathionat *nt* CHEMIE pentathionate

pentavalent *adj* CHEMIE pentavalent, quinquevalent

Pentavalenz *f* CHEMIE pentavalence, quinquevalence

Penten *nt* CHEMIE amylene, pentene

Penthiophen *nt* CHEMIE penthiophene

Pentin *nt* CHEMIE pentyne, valerylene

Pentit *nt* CHEMIE pentite, pentitol

Pentitol *nt* CHEMIE pentite, pentitol

Pentode *f* ELEKTRONIK, PHYS, RADIO pentode

Pentosan *nt* CHEMIE pentosan

Pentose *f* CHEMIE pentose; **Pentosenucleosid** *nt* CHEMIE pentoside

Pentosid *nt* CHEMIE pentoside

Pentyl- *pref* CHEMIE amyl, pentyl; **Pentylalkohol** *m* CHEMIE pentanol, pentyl alcohol; **Pentylentetrazol** *nt* CHEMIE pentylenetetrazol

Pepsin *nt* LEBENSMITTEL pepsin

Peptisation *f* LEBENSMITTEL peptization

peptisieren *vt* CHEMIE peptize

Peptisiermittel *nt* KUNSTSTOFF peptizer

Peptisierungsmittel: mit Peptisierungsmitteln abbauen *vt* CHEMIE *Gummi* peptize

Peptolyse *f* CHEMIE peptolysis

Perborat *nt* CHEMIE perborate

Percarbonat *nt* CHEMIE percarbonate

Perchlor- *pref* CHEMIE perchloric; **Perchlorat** *nt* CHEMIE perchlorate; **Perchlorethen** *nt* CHEMIE perchloroethylene, tetrachloroethylene; **Perchlorethylen** *nt* CHEMIE perchloroethylene, tetrachloroethylene

perchloriert *adj* CHEMIE perchlorinated

Perchrom- *pref* CHEMIE perchromic

Perchromat *nt* CHEMIE perchromate

Pereirin *nt* CHEMIE pereirine

Peressig- *pref* CHEMIE *Säure* peracetic

perfekt: ~es Dielektrikum *nt* ELEKTRIZ perfect dielectric

Perforation *f* ERDÖL *Bohrtechnik* casing perforation, FOTO perforation, sprocket hole, KER & GLAS perforation; **Perforationskanone** *f* ERDÖL *Bohrtechnik* gun perforator; **Perforationsloch** *nt* FOTO sprocket hole

Perforieren *nt* FERTIG piercing

perforieren *vt* FERTIG pierce

Perforiermaschine *f* VERPACK perforating machine

perforiert[1] *adj* COMP & DV perforated

perforiert:[2] **~e Beutel** *m pl* VERPACK perforated bags; **~es Spülrohr** *nt* LEBENSMITTEL sparge pipe

Perforierung *f* COMP & DV perforation

Perforierwerkzeug *nt* FERTIG puncher

Pergament *nt* DRUCK parchment; **Pergamentpapier** *nt* LEBENSMITTEL parchment paper, VERPACK greaseproof paper, parchment paper

Pergaminpapier *nt* LEBENSMITTEL glassine

Perhydrol *nt* CHEMIE perhydrol

Periastron *nt* RAUMFAHRT periastron

peridisch: ~es Rauschen *nt* AKUSTIK cyclic noise

Perigäum *nt* PHYS, RAUMFAHRT perigee; **Perigäumsschubtriebwerk** *nt* RAUMFAHRT perigee kick motor

Perihel *nt* NICHTFOSS ENERG, PHYS perihelion; **Periheldrehung** *f* PHYS advance

Periodat *nt* CHEMIE periodate

Periode *f* AKUSTIK period, ELEKTROTECH cycle, MATH, PHYS period; **~ einer Umlaufbahn** *f* RAUMFAHRT orbital period; **Periodenbereich** *m* KERNTECH period range; **Periodendauer** *f* AKUSTIK cycle, period; **Periodenmeßkanal** *m* KERNTECH period-measuring channel; **Periodenmischer** *m* LEBENSMITTEL batch mixer; **Periodensignal** *nt* ELEKTRONIK periodic signal; **Periodenzahl** *f* AKUSTIK, AUFNAHME, COMP & DV, ELEKTRONIK, PHYS, RADIO frequency; **Periodenzähler** *m* GERÄT cycle counter

periodisch[1] *adj* ELEKTRIZ, ELEKTRONIK periodic, ERDÖL cyclic, PHYS periodic

periodisch:[2] **~es Abschalten** *nt* KERNTECH *Reaktor* periodic shutdown; **~ arbeitendes Gefriergerät** *nt* HEIZ & KÄLTE batch-type freezer; **~e Blattverstellung** *f* LUFTTRANS *Hubschrauber* cyclic pitch control; **~e Dämpfung** *f* ELEKTROTECH periodic damping; **~e Dezimalzahl** *f* MATH recurring decimal, repeating decimal; **~e Funktion** *f* ELEKTRONIK periodic function; **~e Größe** *f* AKUSTIK, ELEKTRONIK periodic quantity; **~e Hilfstrimmeinrichtung** *f* LUFTTRANS *Hubschrauber* cyclic pitch servo trim; **~e Impulsgruppe** *f* ELEKTRONIK periodic pulse train; **~e Inspektion** *f* MASCHINEN periodic inspection; **~er Neuaufbau** *m* ELEKTRONIK *Bildschirm* periodic refresh; **nicht ~er Nickwinkel** *m* LUFTTRANS collective pitch angle; **~e Polaritätsinversion** *f* FERNSEH periodic polarity inversion; **~e Schallwelle** *f* WELLPHYS periodic sound wave; **~er Schlagwinkel** *m* LUFTTRANS *Hubschrauber* cyclic flapping angle; **~es Signal** *nt* ELEKTRONIK periodic signal, repetitive signal, TELEKOM periodic signal; **~e Steigung** *f* LUFTTRANS *Hubschrauber* cyclic pitch; **nicht ~e Steigung** *f* LUFTTRANS collective pitch; **nicht ~er Steigungsanzeiger** *m* LUFTTRANS collective pitch indicator; **nicht ~er Steigungseinstellhebel** *m* LUFTTRANS collective pitch lever; **nicht ~er Steigungsschalter** *m* LUFTTRANS collective pitch switch; **nicht ~e Steigungsservosteuerung** *f* LUFTTRANS collective pitch follow-up; **nicht ~e Steigungssteuerung** *f* LUFTTRANS collective pitch control; **nicht ~e Steigungssynchronisierung** *f* LUFTTRANS collective pitch synchronizer; **nicht ~e Steigungsvoreinstellung** *f* LUFTTRANS collective pitch anticipator; **nicht ~er Steigungswinkel** *m* LUFTTRANS collective pitch angle; ~e **Steuerstufe** f LUFTTRANS *Hubschrauber* cyclic control step; ~e **Strahlschwenkung** f TELEKOM *Antenne* scanning; ~er **Ton** m AKUSTIK periodic tone; ~e **Welle** f ELEKTROTECH periodic wave; ~e **Winde** m pl WASSERTRANS periodical winds; ~er **Wobbeldurchgang** m ELEKTRONIK repetitive sweep

Periodizität f ELEKTRONIK periodicity

peripher[1] *adj* COMP & DV peripheral

peripher:[2] ~e **Baugruppe** f TELEKOM peripheral module; ~es **Brennelement** nt KERNTECH peripheral fuel assembly; ~e **Einheit** f COMP & DV peripheral unit; ~er **Prozessor** m COMP & DV, TELEKOM peripheral processor; ~er **Schnittstellenadapter** m COMP & DV peripheral interface adaptor; ~er **Speicher** m COMP & DV backing storage (AmE), backing store (BrE), peripheral memory, peripheral storage; ~e **Steuereinheit** f *(PCU)* COMP & DV peripheral control unit *(PCU)*; ~es **Steuerelement** nt KERNTECH peripheral control element; ~e **Übertragung** f COMP & DV peripheral transfer

Peripherie:[1] **durch ~ in der Schnelligkeit eingeschränkt** *adj* COMP & DV peripheral-limited

Peripherie[2] f BAU periphery; **Peripherieführung** f TELEKOM peripheral management; **Peripheriegerät** nt COMP & DV peripheral equipment, peripheral, peripheral unit, ELEKTROTECH, TELEKOM peripheral device; **Peripherietechnik** f *(PPU)* COMP & DV peripheral processing units *(PPU)*

peripherisch *adj* TELEKOM peripheral

Periskop nt KERNTECH *Manipulator*, PHYS, RAUMFAHRT *Raumschiff*, WASSERTRANS *U-Boot* periscope; **Periskopantenne** f PHYS periscope aerial, periscope antenna

periskopisch[1] *adj* OPTIK periscopic

periskopisch:[2] ~es **Objektiv** nt FOTO periscopic lens

Periskopsextant m RAUMFAHRT *Raumschiff* periscopic sextant

Peristalsis-Pumpe f LABOR peristaltic pump

Peritektikum nt METALL peritectoid

peritektisch: ~e **Reaktion** f METALL peritectic reaction

Perkolation f CHEMIE, LEBENSMITTEL percolation

Perkussionsbohren nt ERDÖL percussion drilling

perlartig: ~er **Grat** m FERTIG *Brennschweißen* flash, ridge

Perle: ~ **im Flaschenhals** f KER & GLAS slug in neck

Perlglanzpigment nt KUNSTSTOFF nacreous pigment

Perlit m FERTIG, METALL pearlite

perlitisch *adj* FERTIG pearlitic

Perlitisieren nt METALL isothermal annealing

Perlmutperle f KER & GLAS mother-of-pearl bead

Perlmuttpigment nt KUNSTSTOFF nacreous pigment

Perlrohrdurchflußmeßgerät nt GERÄT bubble flow meter

Perlrohrfüllstandanzeigegerät nt GERÄT bubble-type level indicator

Perlrohrfüllstandmeßgerät nt GERÄT bubble pipe level meter

Perm nt ERDÖL *Geologie* Permian period

Permafrost m ERDÖL *Geographie*, KOHLEN permafrost

Permalloy nt ELEKTRIZ, PHYS permalloy

permanent: ~e **Datei** f COMP & DV permanent file; ~er **Fehler** m COMP & DV hard error, permanent error; ~e **Schwellwertverschiebung** f AKUSTIK permanent threshold shift; ~er **Speicher** m COMP & DV permanent memory; **nicht** ~er **Speicher** m COMP & DV, ELEKTROTECH volatile memory

permanenterregt: ~er **Generator** m ELEKTROTECH magnetoelectric generator

Permanentmagnet m ELEKTRIZ, ELEKTROTECH, MASCHINEN, PHYS, TELEKOM, TRANS permanent magnet

permanentmagnetisch: ~e **Fokussierung** f ELEKTROTECH permanent-magnet focusing; ~er **Generator** m ELEKTROTECH permanent-magnet generator; ~er **Kondensatormotor** m ELEKTROTECH permanent-magnet split-capacitor motor; ~er **Schrittmotor** m ELEKTROTECH permanent-magnet stepper motor; ~es **Schweben** nt TRANS levitation by permanent magnets; ~er **Synchronmotor** m ELEKTROTECH permanent-magnet synchronous motor

Permanentmagnet: **Permanentmagnet-Lautsprecher** m AKUSTIK permanent-magnet loudspeaker

Permanentmuster nt TEXTIL permanent patterning

Permanentspeicher m COMP & DV nonerasable storage, ELEKTROTECH permanent memory

Permangan- *pref* CHEMIE permanganic; **Permanganat** nt CHEMIE permanganate

permeabel *adj* CHEMIE permeable

Permeabilität f CHEMIE, ELEKTRIZ permeability, ERDÖL *Geologie*, KOHLEN, KUNSTSTOFF, NICHTFOSS ENERG, PHYS, RADIO, WERKPRÜF permeability; ~ **des Vakuums** f PHYS permeability of free space; **Permeabilitätsmesser** m KOHLEN permeameter; **Permeabilitätsmessung** f ERDÖL *Meßtechnik* permeability logging; **Permeabilitätszahl** f ELEKTROTECH relative permeability, KOHLEN permeability coefficient, PHYS relative permeability

Permeanz f ELEKTROTECH permeance

permissiv: ~er **Block** m EISENBAHN permissive block

Permittivität f ELEKTRIZ permittivity

Permutation f COMP & DV, MATH permutation

Peroxid nt CHEMIE, KUNSTSTOFF peroxide

peroxidieren vt CHEMIE peroxidize

Peroxidierung f CHEMIE peroxidation

Peroxoborat nt CHEMIE perborate

Peroxocarbonat nt CHEMIE *Bleichmittel* percarbonate

Peroxochromat nt CHEMIE perchromate

Peroxomonoschwefel m CHEMIE permonosulfur (AmE), permonosulphur (BrE)

Peroxonitrat nt CHEMIE pernitrate

Peroxophosphat nt CHEMIE peroxophosphate

Peroxosalpeter nt CHEMIE *Säure* pernitrat

Peroxosäure f CHEMIE peroxy acid, *anorganisch* peracid

Peroxosulfat nt CHEMIE persulfate (AmE), persulphate (BrE)

Peroxyacetylnitrat nt *(PAN)* UMWELTSCHMUTZ peroxoacetylnitrate *(PAN)*

Peroxydischwefel m CHEMIE *Säure* peroxydisulfur (AmE), peroxydisulphur (BrE)

Peroxysäure f CHEMIE peroxy acid, *organisch* peracid

Perpetuum: ~ **Mobile** nt THERMOD perpetual motion engine

Perrhenat nt CHEMIE perrhenate

Perrhenium- *pref* CHEMIE perrhenic

Persalz nt CHEMIE persalt

Persäure f CHEMIE peroxy acid, *anorganisch* peracid

Persenning f WASSERTRANS tarpaulin

Perseulose f CHEMIE perseulose

persistent: ~es **Öl** nt ABFALL persistent oil; ~e **Packstoffe** m pl ABFALL, VERPACK nonbiodegradable packaging

Person f EISENBAHN passenger; **Personalabteil** nt LUFTTRANS crew compartment; **Personal-Computer** m *(PC)* COMP & DV personal computer *(PC)*; **Personal-**

roboter *m* KÜNSTL INT personal robot
personell: ~ unterbesetzt *adj* TRANS undermanned
Person: Personenaufzug *m* TRANS passenger elevator (AmE), passenger lift (BrE); Personenaugenschutz *m* SICHERHEIT personal eye protector; Personenautofähre *f* WASSERTRANS passenger car ferry; Personenbeförderung *f* LUFTTRANS passenger service; Personendosimetrie *f* STRAHLPHYS personal dosimetry; Personenfähre *f* WASSERTRANS foot-passenger ferry, passenger ferry; Personenkilometer *m* TRANS passenger kilometer (AmE), passenger kilometre (BrE); Personenkraftwagen *m (PKW)* KFZTECH car, *Fahrzeugart* passenger car; Personenkraftwageneinheit *f (PKW-E)* KFZTECH passenger car unit *(PCU)*
Personenruf *m* TELEKOM paging; Personenrufanlage *f* SICHERHEIT staff calling installation; Personenrufdienst *m* TELEKOM paging service; Personenrufempfänger *m* TELEKOM pager; Personenrufempfänger für Mitteilungen *m* TELEKOM message pager
Personenschnellverkehr *m* TRANS personal rapid transport; Personenschnellverkehrssystem *nt* TRANS PRT, personal rapid transit, passenger rapid transit
Person: Personenschutz *m* SICHERHEIT personal protection; Personenschwebebahn *f* TRANS passenger ropeway
Personensicherheit beeinträchtigen *vt* SICHERHEIT endanger the safety of the person
Person: Personenverkehr *m* TRANS passenger transport; Personenwagenäquivalent *nt* TRANS passenger car equivalent; Personenzug *m* EISENBAHN slow train (BrE)
persönlich: ~er Mitteilungs-Übermittlungsdienst *m* TELEKOM interpersonal messaging system
Perspektive *f* GEOM perspective
perspektivisch: ~e Transformation *f* GEOM perspective transformation
Perspektivlinie *f* OPTIK line of direction, line of perspective, line of sight
Perspex® *nt* KUNSTSTOFF Perspex®
PERT *abbr (Programmbewertungs- und -überprüfungsverfahren)*, COMP & DV, RAUMFAHRT PERT *(program evaluation and review technique)*
Perveanz *f* ELEKTROTECH, TELEKOM perveance
Perylen *nt* CHEMIE perylene
Perzentil *nt* ERGON, QUAL percentile; Perzentilwert *m* QUAL percentile
Perzeption *f* KÜNSTL INT perception
PES *abbr (Polyester)* CHEMIE, ELEKTRIZ, KUNSTSTOFF, TEXTIL PES *(polyester)*
PET[1] *abbr (Polyethylen)* CHEMIE, ELEKTRIZ, ERDÖL, KUNSTSTOFF, TEXTIL, VERPACK PET *(polyethylene)*
PET:[2] PET-Container *m* VERPACK polyethylene container; PET-Film *m* VERPACK PET film; PET-Flasche *f* VERPACK PET bottle
PETP *abbr (Polyethylenterephthalat)* KUNSTSTOFF PETP *(polyethylene terephthalate)*
PET: PET-Palettenüberzüge *m pl* VERPACK polyethylene pallet covers
PETRIFIX-Verfahren *nt (Verfestigungsverfahren für Sonderabfälle)* ABFALL PETRIFIX process
Petri-Netz *nt* COMP & DV Petri net
Petri-Schale *f* LABOR Petri dish
Petrochemikalien *f pl* ERDÖL petrochemicals
petrochemisch[1] *adj* ERDÖL petrochemical
petrochemisch:[2] ~e Anlage *f* ERDÖL petrochemical

plant; ~es Zwischenprodukt *nt* ERDÖL *Raffinerie* intermediate chemical
Petrol- *pref* CHEMIE petrolic
Petrolat *nt* CHEMIE petrolatum, petroleum jelly
Petrolatum *nt* CHEMIE petrolatum, petroleum jelly
Petrologie *f* KOHLEN petrology
Pfad *m* COMP & DV, ELEKTROTECH, PHYS, TELEKOM path; Pfadangabe *f* COMP & DV path; Pfadname *m* COMP & DV path name
Pfahl *m* BAU pile, pole, stake, *Vermessung* peg, FERTIG, KOHLEN pile, WASSERTRANS *zum Festmachen* pile, *zum Festmachen* post; Pfahlabschnitt *m* KOHLEN pile segment; Pfahlabschnitthöhe *f* BAU, KOHLEN pile cut-off level; Pfahlanschluß *m* KOHLEN pile joint; Pfahlart *f* KOHLEN type of pile; Pfahlbau *m* BAU pilework; Pfahlbuhne *f* WASSERVERSORG pile groin (AmE), pile groyne (BrE); Pfahlgründung *f* ERDÖL *Tiefbautechnik* piling; Pfahlgruppe *f* KOHLEN pile group; Pfahlkopf *m* BAU, KOHLEN pile head; Pfahlkopfplatte *f* BAU, KOHLEN pile cap; Pfahllageplan *m* KOHLEN pile situation plan; Pfahllänge *f* KOHLEN pile length; Pfahlramme *f* BAU pile driver, piling frame, KOHLEN pile driver; Pfahlrammung *f* BAU, KOHLEN pile driving; Pfahlring *m* BAU pile ferrule; Pfahlschuh *m* BAU, KOHLEN pile shoe; Pfahlsockel *m* KOHLEN pile footing; Pfahlspitze *f* KOHLEN pile point, pile tip; Pfahlspleiß *m* KOHLEN pile splice; Pfahltreiben *nt* BAU, KOHLEN piling; Pfahlwerk *nt* HYDRAUL stockade, KOHLEN row of piles; Pfahlzieher *m* BAU pile drawer, pile extractor; Pfahlzwinge *f* BAU pile ferrule
Pfänden *nt* KOHLEN blocking
Pfandflasche *f* ABFALL deposit bottle, returnable bottle, waste bottle, VERPACK deposit bottle, returnable bottle
Pfandkasten *m* VERPACK reusable box
Pfanne *f* MASCHINEN pan; Pfannenbär *m* METALL button
Pfeffersandstrahlen *nt* KER & GLAS peppered sandblast
Pfeifboje *f* WASSERTRANS whistle buoy
Pfeifen *nt* AUFNAHME whistling, ELEKTRONIK whistle, *Verstärker* singing
Pfeifpunkt *m* ELEKTRONIK singing point
Pfeifton *m* AKUSTIK squealing
Pfeil *m* KONSTZEICH arrowhead, MATH arrow
Pfeiler *m* BAU pile, pillar, *Architektur* post, *Wände, Brücken* pier, KOHLEN cob, pillar, TELEKOM pillar, WASSERTRANS *Festmachen* pile; Pfeilerabbau *m* KOHLEN pillar drawing; Pfeilerkopf *m* BAU *Brücke* cutwater; Pfeilerstaumauer *f* BAU buttress dam
pfeilförmig: ~er Flügel *m* LUFTTRANS back-swept wing, swept wing, swept back wing
Pfeil: Pfeilflügel *m* LUFTTRANS arrowhead wing; Pfeillinie *f* KONSTZEICH arrow line; Pfeilrad *nt* MASCHINEN double helical gear, double helical gearwheel, herringbone gearwheel; Pfeilrädergetriebe *nt* MASCHINEN herringbone gear; Pfeilspitzenbohrer *m* MASCHINEN arrow-headed drill, arrowhead drill; Pfeilstellungswinkel *m* LUFTTRANS *Flugwerk* sweep angle; Pfeilstirnrad *nt* MASCHINEN herringbone gear; Pfeiltaste *f* COMP & DV cursor key
pfeilverzahnen *vt* MASCHINEN herringbone
pfeilverzahnt: ~es Getriebe *nt* MASCHINEN herringbone gear; ~es Rad *nt* FERTIG double helical gear, MASCHINEN double helical gear, double helical gearwheel, herringbone gearwheel
Pfeil: Pfeilverzahnung *f* MASCHINEN herringbone teeth; Pfeilwurzelmehl *nt* LEBENSMITTEL arrowroot

Pferdestärke f *(PS)* MASCHINEN horsepower *(hp)*

Pfette f BAU *Dach* purlin; **Pfettenstützholz** *nt* BAU purlin post

Pflanzeneiweiß *nt* LEBENSMITTEL vegetable protein

Pflanzengallerte f CHEMIE pectin

Pflanzenschutzgesetz *nt* ABFALL *in Deutschland* Plant Protection Act

pflanzentötend *adj* CHEMIE phytocidal

pflanzlich: **~er Abfall** *m* ABFALL vegetable waste

Pflaster *nt* BAU paving; **Pflasterbelag** *m* BAU pavement (BrE), sidewalk (AmE)

Pflasterer *m* BAU pavior (AmE), paviour (BrE)

Pflaster: **Pflasterglasbaustein** *m* KER & GLAS pavement light (BrE), sidewalk light (AmE); **Pflasterhammer** *m* BAU pavior's hammer (AmE), paviour's hammer (BrE), sledge hammer; **Pflasterklotz** *m* KER & GLAS paving block

pflastern *vt* BAU floor, pave

Pflaster: **Pflasterstein** *m* BAU paving stone, road stone, sett

Pflegekennzeichnung: **~ durch Etikett** f TEXTIL care labeling (AmE), care labelling (BrE)

pflegen *vt* BAU attend to

Pflichtbohrung f ERDÖL obligatory well

Pflichtenheft *nt* ELEKTRIZ specification

Pflock *m* FERTIG stake, MECHAN peg

pflocken *vt* FERTIG peg

Pflugbagger *m* KFZTECH loader

Pflugschar f WASSERTRANS *Festmachen* ploughshare (BrE), plowshare (AmE); **Pflugscharanker** *m* WASSERTRANS plough anchor (BrE), plow anchor (AmE)

PFM *abbr (Pulsfrequenzmodulation)* COMP & DV, ELEKTRONIK PFM *(pulse frequency modulation)*

Pforte f BAU portal

Pfosten *m* BAU pillar, stanchion, stile, EISENBAHN pillar, KOHLEN post, MASCHINEN upright, TRANS pillar, WASSERTRANS post; **Pfostenramme** f BAU post driver

Pfropfen *m* LEBENSMITTEL bung, WASSERTRANS plug

Pfropfpolymer *nt* KUNSTSTOFF graft polymer

Pfropfpolymerisat *nt* KUNSTSTOFF graft polymer

Pfropfpolymerisation f KUNSTSTOFF graft polymerization

Pfund *nt* METROL lb, pound, pound avoirdupois; **~ pro Kubikfuß** *nt* METROL pounds per cubic foot; **~ pro Quadratzoll** *nt* METROL pounds per square inch, psi

Pfund-Serie f PHYS Pfund series

Pfusch *m* FERTIG slipshod work

Pg *abbr (Gitterverlustleistung)* RADIO Pg *(grid dissipation power)*

P-Grad *m* REGELUNG proportional degree

pH-Abnahme f UMWELTSCHMUTZ pH drop

p-Halbleiter *m* PHYS p-type semiconductor

Phantomkanal-Lautsprecher *m* AUFNAHME phantom center channel loudspeaker (AmE), phantom centre channel loudspeaker (BrE)

Phantomkreis *m* ELEKTROTECH phantom circuit

Phantomleitung f ELEKTROTECH, TELEKOM phantom circuit

Phantomspule f ELEKTROTECH phantom coil

Phase:[1] **in ~** *adj* FERNSEH phased

Phase[2] f COMP & DV, ELEKTRIZ, ELEKTRONIK, METALL, PHYS, RADIO, THERMOD, TRANS phase; **~ einer Schallschwingung** f AKUSTIK phase of an acoustical vibration; **~ einer sinusförmigen Größe** f AKUSTIK phase of a sinusoidal quantity

Phase:[3] **in ~ nacheilen** *vt* PHYS lag in phase; **Phasen**

schieben *vt* ELEKTRONIK phase shift

Phase: **Phase-Erde-Schluß** *m* ELEKTRIZ phase-to-earth fault (BrE), phase-to-ground fault (AmE); **Phase-Locked-Loop** *m* TELEKOM phase-locked loop; **Phasenabgleich** *m* FERNSEH phase adjustment, TELEKOM phase alignment, phase tuning; **Phasenabgleich von Lautsprechern** *m* AUFNAHME phasing of loudspeakers; **Phasenabgleichsschalter** *m* AUFNAHME phasing switch; **Phasenabgleichsstecker** *m* AUFNAHME phasing plug; **Phasenabweichung** f ELEKTRONIK phase shift; **Phasenänderung** f ELEKTRIZ phase variation; **Phasenänderungsgeschwindigkeit** f TELEKOM phase change velocity; **Phasenanschluß** *m* ELEKTRIZ phase terminal; **Phasenausfall** *m* FERNSEH phase failure; **Phasenausgleich** *m* ELEKTRIZ phase compensation, phasing, TELEKOM phase compensation; **Phasenausgleicher** *m* ELEKTRIZ phase equalizer; **Phasenausgleichrelais** *nt* ELEKTRIZ phase balance relay; **Phasenbelag** *m* AKUSTIK phase change coefficient; **Phasendemodulation** f ELEKTRONIK, TELEKOM phase demodulation; **Phasendemodulator** *m* ELEKTRONIK phase demodulator; **Phasendetektor** *m* ELEKTRONIK, FERNSEH, RADIO, TELEKOM phase detector; **Phasendiagramm** *nt* KERNTECH, METALL, THERMOD phase diagram, TRANS phase diagram, phasing diagram

Phasendifferenz f AUFNAHME, ELEKTRONIK, PHYS, WELLPHYS phase difference; **Phasendifferenzmodulation** f *(DPSK)* ELEKTRONIK differential phase shift keying *(DPSK)*; **Phasendifferenzumtastung** f *(DPSK)* ELEKTRONIK differential phase shift keying *(DPSK)*; **Phasendifferenzwinkel** *m* ELEKTRIZ angle of phase difference

Phase: **Phasendiskriminator** *m* ELEKTRONIK phase detector, phase discriminator, RADIO phase discriminator

Phasen drehen *vi* ELEKTRONIK phase-shift

Phase: **Phasendreher** *m* PHYS gyrator; **Phasendrehung** f ELEKTRONIK phase shift; **Phaseneinsteller** *m* ELEKTRIZ phase changer; **Phaseneinstellungseinheit** f LUFTTRANS *Hubschrauber* phasing unit; **Phasenfehler** *m* ELEKTRONIK, FERNSEH phase error; **Phasenfolge** f ELEKTRIZ, ELEKTRONIK phase sequence; **Phasenfolgegleichrichter** *m* ELEKTRIZ phase sequence rectifier; **Phasenfrequenzgang** *m* AKUSTIK phase frequency response curve; **Phasenführungswinkel** *m* ELEKTRIZ angle of lead; **Phasengang** *m* ELEKTRONIK phase response; **Phasengang der Amplitude** *m* TELEKOM phase amplitude characteristic

phasengekoppelt: **~er Laser** *m* ELEKTRONIK mode-locked laser

Phase: **Phasengenerator** *m* ELEKTRONIK indirect frequency synthesizer, phase generator; **Phasengeschwindigkeit** f PHYS phase velocity

phasengespeist: **~e Antennengruppe** f RAUMFAHRT *Weltraumfunk* phased array antenna

phasengesteuert: **~e Gruppenantenne** f RADIO phased array; **~e Zündung** f RAUMFAHRT *Raumschiff* phased ignition

phasengleich[1] *adj* ELEKTRONIK, FERNSEH, PHYS in-phase

phasengleich:[2] **~e Antenne** f RAUMFAHRT broadside antenna

Phase: **Phasengleichgewicht** *nt* THERMOD phase equilibrium; **Phasengleichrichter** *m* ELEKTRONIK phase demodulator; **Phasengrenze** f METALL phase bound-

ary; **Phasenisolierung** *f* ELEKTRIZ phase insulation; **Phasenkettenoszillator** *m* ELEKTRONIK phase-shift oscillator; **Phasenklemme** *f* ELEKTRIZ phase terminal; **Phasenkoeffizient** *m* OPTIK phase coefficient; **Phasenkomparator** *m* FERNSEH phase comparator; **Phasenkonstante** *f* AKUSTIK *(β)*, ELEKTRIZ *(β)* phase constant *(β)*, OPTIK, PHYS phase constant, TELEKOM phase coefficient, phase constant
phasenkontinuierlich: **~e Frequenzumtastung** *f* *(CPFSK)* ELEKTRONIK, RADIO, TELEKOM continuous phase frequency shift keying *(CPFSK)*
Phase: **Phasenkontrastmikroskop** *nt* LABOR, PHYS contrasting phase microscope, phase contrast microscope; **Phasenkonverter** *m* FERNSEH phase converter; **Phasenkopplung** *f* ELEKTRONIK *Laser* mode locking; **Phasenmaß** *nt* FERNSEH phase constant; **Phasenmeßbrücke** *f* GERÄT phase bridge; **Phasenmodulation** *f (PM)* AUFNAHME, COMP & DV, ELEKTRONIK, FERNSEH, PHYS, RADIO, TELEKOM phase modulation *(PM)*; **Phasenmodulator** *m* ELEKTRONIK, TELEKOM phase modulator; **Phasennacheilung** *f* ELEKTRIZ, ELEKTRONIK phase lag; **Phasenquadratur** *f* FERNSEH quadrature; **Phasenrastung** *f* ELEKTRONIK phase locking; **Phasenraum** *m* PHYS, TEILPHYS phase space; **Phasenreferenzwert** *m* FERNSEH phase reference; **Phasenregel** *f* KERNTECH phase rule; **Phasenregelkreis** *m* *(PLL)* ELEKTRONIK, FERNSEH, RADIO, RAUMFAHRT, TELEKOM phase-locked loop *(PLL)*; **Phasenregelung** *f* TELEKOM phase control, phase regulation; **Phasenregler** *m* FERNSEH phaser; **Phasenreserve** *f* ELEKTRONIK phase margin; **Phasenresonanz** *f* PHYS velocity resonance; **Phasenschiebekette** *f* ELEKTRIZ phase-shifting network; **Phasenschiebekondensator** *m* ELEKTRIZ phase-shifting capacitor; **Phasenschieber** *m* ELEKTRIZ phase shifter, ELEKTRONIK phase changer, ELEKTROTECH synchronous capacitor, KERNTECH phase shifter, TELEKOM phase changer, phase shifter; **Phasenschieber der PIN-Diode** *m* ELEKTRONIK PIN diode phase shifter; **Phasenschieberschaltung** *f* ELEKTRIZ, PHYS phase-shifting network; **Phasenschnittfrequenz** *f* REGELUNG phase crossover frequency; **Phasenshift** *m* FERNSEH phase shift; **Phasensignal** *nt* FERNSEH phasing signal; **Phasenspalter** *m* AUFNAHME phase splitter; **Phasenspalteroszillator** *m* ELEKTRONIK phase splitter oscillator; **Phasenspannung** *f* ELEKTRIZ phase voltage; **Phasensprungmikrofon** *nt* AUFNAHME phase shift microphone; **Phasensprungtastung** *f (PSK)* COMP & DV phase shift keying *(PSK)*
phasenstabilisiert: **~er Demodulator** *m* RAUMFAHRT *Weltraumfunk* phase-locked demodulator
Phase: **Phasenstabilität** *f* ELEKTRIZ, TELEKOM phase stability
phasenstarr: **~e Quadratur** *f* ELEKTRONIK locked in-phase quadrature
Phase: **Phasensteuerung** *f* ELEKTRONIK, FERNSEH, TELEKOM phase control; **Phasenstrom** *m* ELEKTRIZ in-phase current, phase current, ELEKTROTECH phase current; **Phasensynchronisation** *f* TELEKOM phase locking; **Phasensynchronisationskreis** *m* TELEKOM phase-locked loop; **Phasensynthese** *f* ELEKTRONIK indirect frequency synthesis; **Phasenteiler** *m* ELEKTRIZ phase splitter; **Phasenteilung** *f* ELEKTRIZ phase splitting; **Phasentrenner** *m* RADIO phase splitter; **Phasentrennung** *f* ABFALL phase separation, ELEKTRONIK phase splitting; **Phasenübergang** *m* THERMOD phase

transformation; **Phasenübergangstemperatur** *f* PHYS transition temperature; **Phase-Nulleiter-Spannung** *f* ELEKTRIZ phase-to-neutral voltage; **Phasenumformer** *m* ELEKTRIZ phase converter, ELEKTRONIK phase changer, phase converter
phasenumgekehrt: **~e Sekundärströme** *m pl* ELEKTROTECH phase-reversed secondaries
Phase: **Phasenumkehr** *f* ELEKTRIZ, FERNSEH phase reversal; **Phasenumkehrer** *m* ELEKTRONIK phase inverter; **Phasenumkehrschalter** *m* ELEKTROTECH phase reversal switch; **Phasenumkehrung** *f* AUFNAHME, KOHLEN phase inversion; **Phasenumkehrverstärker** *m* ELEKTRONIK paraphase amplifier; **Phasenumtastung** *f* *(PSK)* ELEKTRONIK, RADIO, RAUMFAHRT, TELEKOM phase-shift keying *(PSK)*; **Phasenumtastung mit acht Phasen** *f* ELEKTRONIK eight-phase phase shift keying; **Phasenumtastungsmodulation** *f* ELEKTRONIK, RAUMFAHRT *Weltraumfunk* phase shift keyed modulation; **Phasenunterschied** *m* ELEKTRIZ, ELEKTRONIK, FERNSEH, TELEKOM phase difference; **Phasenvariation** *f* ELEKTRIZ phase variation; **Phasenverbesserung** *f* ELEKTROTECH power factor correction; **Phasenvergleicher** *m* ELEKTRONIK phase comparator; **Phasenverkettung** *f* FERNSEH phase lock, phase locking
phasenverschiebend: **~es Element** *nt* ELEKTRONIK phase-shifting element
Phase: **Phasenverschiebetransformator** *m* ELEKTRIZ phase-shifting transformer; **Phasenverschiebung** *f* ELEKTRIZ displacement of phase, phase displacement, phase shift, ELEKTRONIK phase lag, phase shift, KERNTECH, PHYS, RAUMFAHRT, TRANS phase shift, WELLPHYS phase-out; **Phasenverschiebung um neunzig Grad** *f* ELEKTRIZ quadrature; **Phasenverschiebungsinduktionsschleife** *f* TRANS phase displacement induction loop detector; **Phasenverschiebungsüberwachung** *f* RADIO phase-shift monitor; **Phasenverschiebungswinkel** *m* ELEKTROTECH angle of phase difference
phasenverschoben[1] *adj* ELEKTRIZ dephased, out-of-phase, ELEKTRONIK out-of-phase, phase-shifted, FERNSEH, WERKPRÜF out-of-phase
phasenverschoben:[2] **~e Abtastung** *f* FERNSEH quadruple scanning; **~es Signal** *nt* ELEKTRONIK quadrature signal
Phase: **Phasenverteilung** *f* METALL phase distribution; **Phasenverzerrung** *f* ELEKTRONIK, FERNSEH, RADIO, TELEKOM phase distortion; **Phasenverzögerung** *f* ELEKTRIZ, ELEKTRONIK phase lag, FERNSEH phase delay, PHYS phase lag; **Phasenvoreilung** *f* ELEKTRIZ phase advance, phase lead, ELEKTRONIK, PHYS phase lead; **Phasenvoreilwinkel** *m* ELEKTRIZ angle of lead; **Phasenvorschiebung** *f* ELEKTRIZ phase advance; **Phasenvorschub** *m* ELEKTRIZ phase lead; **Phasenwendungsrelais** *nt* ELEKTRIZ reverse phase relay; **Phasenwicklung** *f* ELEKTRIZ phase winding; **Phasenwinkel** *m* ELEKTRIZ, ELEKTRONIK, LUFTTRANS, NICHTFOSS ENERG, PHYS, WELLPHYS *Schwingung*, WERKPRÜF phase angle; **Phasenwinkeldifferenz** *f* TELEKOM phase difference; **Phasenzittern** *nt* RAUMFAHRT *Weltraumfunk* phase jitter
Phaseolunatin *nt* CHEMIE phaseolunatin
Phase-Phase-Spannung *f* ELEKTRIZ phase-to-phase voltage
Phellandren *nt* CHEMIE phellandrene
Phenacetin *nt* CHEMIE ethoxyacetanilide, phenacetin

Phenacetur- *pref* CHEMIE phenaceturic
Phenacyl *nt* CHEMIE phenacyl
Phenanthrachinon *nt* CHEMIE phenanthraquinone
Phenanthridin *nt* CHEMIE phenanthridine
Phenanthridon *nt* CHEMIE phenanthridone
Phenanthrol *nt* CHEMIE phenanthrol
Phenanthrolin *nt* CHEMIE phenanthroline
Phenat *nt* CHEMIE phenate, phenolate
Phenazin *nt* CHEMIE azophenylene, dibenzopyrazine, phenazine
Phenazon *nt* CHEMIE phenazone
Phenetidin *nt* CHEMIE ethoxyaniline, phenetidine
Phenetol *nt* CHEMIE ethoxybenzene, phenetole
Pheniramin- *pref* CHEMIE pheniramine
Phenol *nt* CHEMIE phenol
Phenolat *nt* CHEMIE phenate, phenolate, phenoxide
Phenol: Phenolharz *nt* ELEKTRIZ phenolic resin, FERTIG phenolic, phenolic resin, KUNSTSTOFF phenolic resin; Phenolharzschaumstoff *m* KUNSTSTOFF phenolic foam
phenolisch *adj* CHEMIE phenolic
Phenol: Phenolkunststoffleiste *f* FERTIG phenolic lining; Phenolphthalein *nt* CHEMIE phenolphthalein; Phenolsulfon *nt* CHEMIE phenolsulfon (AmE), phenolsulphon (BrE)
Phenoplast *m* KUNSTSTOFF phenolic plastic
Phenosafranin *nt* CHEMIE phenosafranine, safranin, safranine
Phenothiazin *nt* CHEMIE phenothiazine
Phenoxazin *nt* CHEMIE naphtoxazine, phenoxazine
Phenoxid *nt* CHEMIE phenate, phenoxide, phenolate
Phenoxybenzol *nt* CHEMIE diphenyl ether, phenoxybenzene
Phenthiazin *nt* CHEMIE phenothiazine
Phenyl- *pref* CHEMIE phenyl; Phenylacetaldehyd *m* CHEMIE phenylacetaldehyde; Phenylacetamid *nt* CHEMIE phenylacetamide; Phenylalanin *nt* CHEMIE phenylalanine; Phenylamin *nt* CHEMIE, DRUCK phenylamine; Phenylcarbinol *nt* CHEMIE phenylcarbinol; Phenylchromon *nt* CHEMIE flavone, phenylchromone; Phenylendiamin *nt* CHEMIE phenylenediamine; Phenylessig- *pref* CHEMIE phenylacetic; Phenylethylen *nt* CHEMIE phenylethylene; Phenylglycin *nt* CHEMIE phenylglycine; Phenylglycol- *pref* CHEMIE phenylglycolic; Phenylglykokoll *nt* CHEMIE phenylglycine; Phenylharnstoff *m* CHEMIE phenylurea; Phenylhydrazin *nt* CHEMIE phenylhydrazine; Phenylhydrazon *nt* CHEMIE phenylhydrazone; Phenylhydroxylamin *nt* CHEMIE phenylhydroxylamine
phenyliert *adj* CHEMIE phenylated
Phenyl: Phenyliodid *nt* CHEMIE iodobenzene, phenyl iodide; Phenylisocyanat *nt* CHEMIE carbanil, phenyl isocyanate; Phenylmercaptan *nt* CHEMIE penyl mercaptan, thiophenol; Phenylpropan *nt* CHEMIE cumene, cumol, phenylpropane; Phenylpropion- *pref* CHEMIE phenylpropiolic; Phenylsalicylat *nt* CHEMIE salol
φ *abbr* AKUSTIK *(Winkelverdrängung)* φ *(angular displacement)*, AKUSTIK *(Geschwindigkeitspotential)* φ *(velocity potential)*
Phiole *f* CHEMIE, KER & GLAS phial, vial
Phloretin *nt* CHEMIE phloretin; Phloretin- *pref* CHEMIE phloretic
Phloridzin *nt* CHEMIE phloridzin, phlorizin
Phlorol *nt* CHEMIE phlorol
Phloryhidzin *nt* CHEMIE phloryhizin
pH-Messer *m* KOHLEN, METROL pH meter

pH-Meßgerät *nt* LABOR pH meter
Phon *nt* AKUSTIK, PHYS *Einheit* phon
Phonem *nt* AKUSTIK phoneme
phonetisch: ~e Leistung *f* AKUSTIK phonetic power
Phonon *nt* PHYS phonon; Phonongasmodell *nt* PHYS phonon gas model
Phonovision *f* OPTIK phonovision
Phoron *nt* CHEMIE diisopropylidene acetone, dimethyl-heptadienone, phorone
phoronomisch *adj* FERTIG phoronomical
Phosgen *nt* CHEMIE phosgene
Phosphat *nt* ANSTRICH, CHEMIE phosphate
Phosphatase *f* CHEMIE phosphatase
Phosphatieren *nt* CHEMIE phosphatization, METALL parkerizing
Phosphat: Phosphat-Opalglas *nt* KER & GLAS phosphate-opal glass
Phosphid *nt* CHEMIE phosphide
Phosphit *nt* CHEMIE phosphite
Phosphoglycerin- *pref* CHEMIE phosphoglyceric
Phospholipid *nt* LEBENSMITTEL phospholipid
Phosphomonoesterase *f* CHEMIE phosphatase
Phosphonium *nt* CHEMIE phosphonium
Phosphor *m* CHEMIE *(P)* phosphorus *(P)*, ELEKTRONIK, PHYS *Element* phosphor; Phosphorbildschirm *m* FERNSEH phosphor screen; Phosphorbronze *f* ELEKTRIZ, ELEKTROTECH phosphor bronze; Phosphoreszenz *f* ELEKTRONIK, PHYS, STRAHLPHYS phosphorescence; Phosphoreszieren *nt* WASSERTRANS *Meer* phosphorescence
phosphoreszierend: ~es Material *nt* ELEKTRONIK phosphorescent material; ~es Sicherheitschild *nt* SICHERHEIT phosphorescent safety sign; ~ er Stoff *m* CHEMIE phosphor
phosphorigsauer: phosphorigsaures Salz *nt* CHEMIE phosphite
Phosphor: Phosphormolybdän- *pref* CHEMIE phosphomolybdic; Phosphorroheisen *nt* CHEMIE phosphoric pig iron; Phosphorsalz *nt* CHEMIE microcosmic salt; Phosphorsäure *f* CHEMIE phosphoric acid; Phosphorwolframat *nt* CHEMIE phosphatododecatungstate, phosphotungstate
Phosphoryl *nt* CHEMIE phosphoryl; Phosphorylase *f* CHEMIE phosphorylase
Photon *nt* OPTIK, PHYS, STRAHLPHYS, TEILPHYS photon; Photonenrauschen *nt* OPTIK, TELEKOM photon noise; Photonenvervielfachung *f* STRAHLPHYS photon amplification
pH-Regler *m* KOHLEN pH controller
pH-Regelung *f* KOHLEN pH control
Phthalat *nt* CHEMIE phthalate
Phthaldiamid *nt* CHEMIE phthalamide
Phthalein *nt* CHEMIE phthalein
Phthalid *nt* CHEMIE phthalide
Phthalin *nt* CHEMIE phthaline
Phthalocyanin *nt* KUNSTSTOFF phthalocyanine
phthalsauer *adj* CHEMIE phthalic
Phthalsäure- *pref* CHEMIE phthalic; Phthalsäureanhydrid *nt* KUNSTSTOFF phthalic anhydride; Phthalsäurediamid *nt* CHEMIE phthalamide
Phugoidbewegung *f* LUFTTRANS phugoid oscillation
Phugoidschwingung *f* LUFTTRANS phugoid oscillation
pH-Wert *m* UMWELTSCHMUTZ pH-value
physikalisch:[1] ~ trocknend *adj* FERTIG *Lack* air-drying
physikalisch:[2] ~-chemische Umgebung *f* UMWELTSCHMUTZ physio-chemical environment; ~e

Eigenschaften *f pl* PHYS physical properties; ~ **gelade-nes Teilchen** *nt* UMWELTSCHMUTZ charged particle; ~**e Optik** *f* OPTIK, PHYS, TELEKOM physical optics; ~**es Pendel** *nt* PHYS compound pendulum; ~**e Schicht** *f* TELEKOM *OSI* physical layer; ~**er Speicher** *m* ELEK-TROTECH physical memory; ~**e Übertragung** *f* COMP & DV physical transmission; ~**e Waage** *f* LABOR physical balance

physiologisch: ~**e Einwirkung** *f* SICHERHEIT physiologi-cal effect; ~**e Lautstärkeregelung** *f* AUFNAHME loudness control; ~**es Rauschen** *nt* AKUSTIK physiolo-gical noise

physisch[1] *adj* COMP & DV physical

physisch:[2] ~**e Datei** *f* COMP & DV physical file; ~**e Daten-bank** *f* COMP & DV physical database; ~**er Satz** *m* COMP & DV physical record; ~**e Steuereinheit** *f* COMP & DV physical control unit

Physostigmin *nt* CHEMIE eserine, physostigmine

Phytase *f* LEBENSMITTEL phytase

Phytin *nt* LEBENSMITTEL phytin; **Phytinsäure** *f* LEBENS-MITTEL phytic acid

phytotoxisch *adj* CHEMIE phytotoxic

PI *abbr (Polyimid)* ELEKTRIZ, ELEKTRONIK, KUNST-STOFF PI *(polyimide)*

Pi *nt* MATH pi

Piazin *nt* CHEMIE piazine, pyrazine

PIB *abbr (Polyisobutylen)* KUNSTSTOFF PIB *(polyisobu-tylene)*

Picaschrift *f* DRUCK pica

Pick-Up *m* KFZTECH pick-up, pick-up truck; ~ **Bahnab-nahme** *f* PAPIER pick-up; ~ **Filz** *m* PAPIER pick-up felt

Picosekunde f COMP & DV picosecond

PID-Regler *m (Proportional-Integral-Differential-Reg-ler)* LABOR PID controller *(proportional plus integral plus derivative controller)*

PID-Steuerung *f* ELEKTRIZ *(Differentialsteuerung)* deri-vative control, LABOR *(Proportional-Integral-Differential-Regler)* PID con-troller *(proportional plus integral plus derivative controller)*

PID-Verhalten *nt (Proportional-Integral-Differential-Verhalten)* REGELUNG PID action *(proportional plus integral plus derivative action)*

Piek *f* WASSERTRANS *Segeln* peak

Piepschalter *m* LUFTTRANS *Hubschrauber* beep switch

Pier *m* WASSERTRANS quay, *Hafen* pier

Pierce-Oszillator *m* ELEKTRONIK Pierce oscillator

Piezo- *pref* METROL piezo-; **Piezoeffekt** *m* ELEKTROTECH piezoelectric effect

piezoelektrisch[1] *adj* ELEKTROTECH, FERTIG, RADIO pie-zoelectric

piezoelektrisch:[2] ~ **abgestimmtes Magnetron** *nt* ELEK-TROTECH piezoelectric-tuned magnetron; ~**er Beschleunigungsaufnehmer** *m* HEIZ & KÄLTE piezo-electric acceleration sensor; ~**er Detektor** *m* TRANS piezoelectric detector; ~**er Effekt** *m* PHYS piezoelectric effect; ~**e Eigenschaften** *f pl* ELEKTROTECH piezoelec-tric properties; ~**es Element** *nt* ELEKTROTECH piezoelectric element; ~**er Kristall** *m* ELEKTROTECH piezoelectric crystal; ~**er Lautsprecher** *m* AUFNAHME piezoelectric loudspeaker; ~**er Meßfühler** *m* GERÄT piezoelectric sensing element; ~**es Mikrofon** *nt* AKU-STIK, AUFNAHME piezoelectric microphone; ~**er Oszillator** *m* ELEKTRIZ, ELEKTROTECH piezoelectric oscillator; ~**er Resonator** *m* ELEKTROTECH piezoelec-tric resonator; ~**er Stift** *m* OPTIK piezoelectric stylus;

~**es Substrat** *nt* ELEKTROTECH piezoelectric substrate; ~**er Transducer** *m* ELEKTROTECH piezoelectric trans-ducer; ~**er Wandler** *m* ELEKTROTECH piezoelectric transducer

Piezoelektrizität *f* ELEKTROTECH piezoelectricity

Piezometer *nt* KOHLEN piezometer

piezometrisch: ~**e Höhe** *f* ERDÖL piezometric head; ~**e Karte** *f* ERDÖL piezometric map

Pigment *nt* ANSTRICH, KUNSTSTOFF, TEXTIL pigment; **Pigmentfarbstoff** *m* TEXTIL pigment

pigmentieren *vt* TEXTIL pigment

pigmentiert: ~**e Anilinfarbe** *f* DRUCK pigmented aniline ink

Pigmentierung *f* TEXTIL pigmentation

Pigmentschlamm *m* ABFALL pigment sludge

Pikkolo-Brenner *m* KER & GLAS Piccolo burner

Piko- *pref (p)* METROL pico- *(p)*; **Pikolin** *nt* CHEMIE methylpyridine, pikoline

Pikrat *nt* CHEMIE picrate

Pikrin- *pref* CHEMIE picric

Pikrotin *nt* CHEMIE picrotin

Pikryl- *pref* CHEMIE picryl; **Pikrylmethyl** *nt* CHEMIE nitra-mine

Piktogramm *nt* COMP & DV icon, *bei grafischen Oberflä-chen* symbol, DRUCK pictograph, MATH pictogram, SICHERHEIT *Gefahrstoffe* pictorial symbol

Pilfer-Proof-Dichtung *f* VERPACK pilfer-proof seal

Pillbildung *f* TEXTIL pilling

pillen *vi* TEXTIL pill

Pilocarpidin *nt* CHEMIE pilocarpidine

Pilocarpin *nt* CHEMIE pilocarpine

Pilot *m* LUFTTRANS, TELEKOM pilot; **Pilotanlage** *f* KOH-LEN pilot plant; **Pilotballon** *m* LUFTTRANS pilot balloon; **Pilotdraht** *m* ELEKTROTECH *Meßtechnik* pilot wire; **Pilotenhandbuch** *nt* LUFTTRANS flight manual; **Pilotfrequenz** *f* TELEKOM pilot frequency; **Pilotprojekt** *nt* ERDÖL pilot project; **Pilotsignal** *nt* FERNSEH pilot signal; **Pilotton** *m* FERNSEH, RADIO pilot tone; **Pilotträ-ger** *m* TELEKOM pilot carrier

Pilzanker *m* WASSERTRANS *Festmachen* mushroom an-chor

Pilzdach *nt* BAU umbrella roof

pilzförmig: ~**er Kopf** *m* FERTIG mushroom head; ~**er Stopfen** *m* KER & GLAS mushroom stopper

Pilzisolator *m* ELEKTRIZ umbrella isolator, ELEKTRO-TECH mushroom insulator

Pilzkopflüfter *m* WASSERTRANS *Deckausrüstung* mushroom ventilator

Pilzstößel *m* MASCHINEN mushroom follower

Pilzventil *nt* KFZTECH mushroom valve

Pimar- *pref* CHEMIE pimaric

Pimelin- *pref* CHEMIE pimelic

Pi-Meson *nt* TEILPHYS pi meson

PIN *abbr (Positiv-Isolierend-Negativ)* ELEKTRONIK *(po-sitive-isolating-negative)*

PIN: **PIN-Dämpfungsdiode** *f* ELEKTRONIK PIN attenua-tor diode; **PIN-Diode** *f* ELEKTRONIK, PHYS, RADIO PIN diode; **PIN-Diodenabschwächer** *m* ELEKTRONIK PIN diode attenuator; **PIN-Diodenmodulation** *f* ELEKTRO-NIK PIN diode modulation

Pinakol *nt* CHEMIE pinacol, pinacone, tetramethylethy-leneglycol

Pinakon *nt* CHEMIE pinacol, pinacone, tetramethylethy-leneglycol

Pinch-Effekt *m* KERNTECH, PHYS pinch effect

Pi-Netz *nt* ELEKTROTECH pi network; **Pi-Netzwerk** *nt*

PHYS, RADIO pi network

PIN: **PIN-Fotodiode** *f* ELEKTRONIK PIN photodiode

Ping *m* RADIO *Meteorstreuung* ping

Pinkingeffekt *m* KUNSTSTOFF pinking effect

Pinksalz *nt* CHEMIE pink salt

Pinne *f* FERTIG pane, peen, KER & GLAS pip, MASCHINEN pane, peen

Pinning *nt* METALL pinning

Pinole *f* FERTIG quill, ram, KUNSTSTOFF mandrel, mandril, MASCHINEN quill, spindle sleeve

Pinonen *nt* CHEMIE pinonene

PIN: **PIN-Photodiode** *f* OPTIK, TELEKOM PIN photodiode

Pinsel *m* ANSTRICH paint brush, FERTIG *Formen* swab

Pinzette *f* KER & GLAS, LABOR tweezers

Pion *nt* PHYS *Teilchen*, TEILPHYS pion

Pipecolin *nt* CHEMIE methylpiperidine, pipecoline

Pipeline *f* COMP & DV, ERDÖL, MASCHINEN, TRANS, WASSERTRANS pipeline; **Pipelinestruktur** *f* KONTROLL pipelined architecture; **Pipelinesystem** *nt* TELEKOM pipeline system

Pipelinesystem: **im ~ verarbeiten** *vt* COMP & DV pipeline

Pipeline: **Pipelinetransport** *m* TRANS pipeline transportation; **Pipelineverarbeitung** *f* COMP & DV pipelining

Pipeliningmethode *f* COMP & DV pipelining

Piperazin *nt* CHEMIE diethylenediamine, hexahydropyrazine, piperazine

Piperidin *nt* CHEMIE piperidine

Piperin- *pref* CHEMIE piperic

Piperonal *nt* CHEMIE heliotropin, methylenedioxybenzaldehyde, piperonal

Piperonylaldehyd *m* CHEMIE heliotropin, methylenedioxybenzaldehyde, piperonal

Piperylen *nt* CHEMIE piperylene

Pipette *f* LABOR pipette; **Pipettenständer** *m* LABOR pipette stand

Pipettierkolben *m* LABOR pipetting bulb

Piping *nt* ERDÖL *Leitungen* piping

Pirani-Manometer *nt* PHYS Pirani gage (AmE), Pirani gauge (BrE)

Pirani-Vakuummeter *nt* LABOR Pirani vacuum gage (AmE), Pirani vacuum gauge (BrE)

Pirani-Wärmeleitungsvakuummeter *nt* LABOR Pirani vacuum gage (AmE), Pirani vacuum gauge (BrE)

PI-Regler *m* (*Proportional-Integral-Regler*) REGELUNG PI controller (*proportional plus integral controller*)

Piste *f* LUFTTRANS runway; **Pistenrichtung** *f* LUFTTRANS runway alignment; **Pistenrichtungsanzeiger** *m* LUFTTRANS runway alignment indicator

Pistonierkolben *m* ERDÖL swab

Pistonierung *f* ERDÖL swabbing

Pistophon *nt* AKUSTIK pistonphone

Pitotdruck *m* LUFTTRANS impact pressure

Pitot-Rohr *nt* PHYS Pitot tube

Pivalin- *pref* CHEMIE pivalic

PI-Verhalten *nt* (*Proportional-Integral-Verhalten*) REGELUNG PI action (*proportional plus integral action*)

Pi-Wicklung *f* ELEKTROTECH pi winding

Pixel *nt* COMP & DV pixel; **~ pro Inch** *nt pl* COMP & DV pixels per inch

P-Kanal *m* ELEKTRONIK P-channel; **P-Kanal-Feldeffekttransistor** *m* ELEKTRONIK P-channel FET; **P-Kanal-FET** *m* ELEKTRONIK, RADIO P-channel FET; **P-Kanal-Gerät** *nt* ELEKTRONIK P-channel device; **P-Kanal Metalloxid-Silizium** *nt* RADIO P-channel

metal-oxide silicon; **P-Kanal-MOS** *nt* COMP & DV PMOS, positive metal oxide semiconductor; **P-Kanal-MOS-Anreicherungstransistor** *m* ELEKTRONIK P-channel enhancement mode MOS transistor; **P-Kanal-MOS-Verarmungstransistor** *m* ELEKTRONIK P-channel depletion mode MOS transistor

p-Kollektor *m* ELEKTRONIK p-type collector

p-Kresol *nt* CHEMIE p-cresol

PKW *abbr* (*Personenkraftwagen*) KFZTECH car, passenger car

PKW-E *abbr* (*Personenkraftwageneinheit*) KFZTECH PCU (*passenger car unit*)

PL *abbr* (*Prädikatenlogik*) KÜNSTL INT PL (*predicate logic*)

PLA *abbr* (*programmierbare Logikanordnung*) COMP & DV PLA (*programmable logic array*)

Plakatschrift *f* DRUCK lettering style

Plan *m* BAU drawing, FERTIG *Geschwindigkeit* image, MECHAN layout, PHYS chart, WASSERTRANS plan

plan *adj* GEOM planar

planar: **~e Diffusion** *f* ELEKTRONIK planar diffusion; **~e integrierte Schaltung** *f* ELEKTRONIK planar integrated circuit; **~er Prozeß** *m* ELEKTRONIK planar process

Planardiode *f* ELEKTRONIK planar diode

Planar-Epitaxialdiode *f* ELEKTRONIK planar epitaxial diode

Planarhohlleiter *m* ELEKTROTECH planar waveguide

Planarleitung *f* ELEKTRONIK planar line

Planarprozeß *m* ELEKTRONIK *Transistoren* planar process

Planartransistor *m* RADIO planar transistor

Planartriode *f* ELEKTRONIK planar triode

Planarwellenleiter *m* ELEKTROTECH planar waveguide

planbearbeiten *vt* MASCHINEN face

Planbearbeitung *f* MASCHINEN facing

Planck: **~sche Konstante** *f* (*h*) PHYS, STRAHLPHYS, TEILPHYS Planck's constant (*h*); **~sche Quantenhypothese** *f* PHYS Planck's law; **~sche Strahlungsformel** *f* PHYS Planck's radiation formula; **~sches Strahlungsgesetz** *nt* PHYS, STRAHLPHYS, THERMOD Planck's radiation law; **~sches Wirkungsquantum** *nt* (*h*) PHYS, STRAHLPHYS, TEILPHYS Planck's constant (*h*)

Plandrehen *nt* MASCHINEN face turning, facing, surfacing

plandrehen *vt* FERTIG face, MASCHINEN surface

Plandrehfutter *nt* MASCHINEN facing head

Plandrehmaschine *f* FERTIG facing lathe, surfacing lathe, MASCHINEN surface lathe

Plandrehvorrichtung *f* MASCHINEN facing attachment

Plandrehwerkzeug *nt* MASCHINEN facing tool

Planen *nt* KÜNSTL INT planning

planen *vt* COMP & DV, EISENBAHN, FERNSEH schedule, FERTIG face, TELEKOM plan, schedule

Planencontainer *m* TRANS tilt container, tiltainer

Planer *m* BAU designer

Planet: **äußerer ~** *m* RAUMFAHRT outer planet

Planeten- *pref* MECHAN epicyclic, planetary; **Planetenbewegung** *f* FERTIG planetary movement; **Planetengetriebe** *nt* KFZTECH planet gear, MASCHINEN epicyclic gear, epicycloidal gear, planetary gear train, sun-and-planet gearing, MECHAN epicyclic gear train, WASSERTRANS *Motor* epicyclic gear; **Planetengetriebedifferential** *nt* KFZTECH planetary gear differential; **Planetengetriebesatz** *m* KFZTECH planetary gear set; **Planetengetriebesystem** *nt* KFZTECH planetary gear system; **Planeteninneres** *nt* RAUMFAHRT planetary interior; **Planetenmühle** f LABOR *Schleifen* planetary mill; **Planetenrad** nt FERTIG planetary gear, KFZTECH *Differential* pinion gear, MASCHINEN planet gear, planet wheel, planetary gear, planetary pinion; **Planetenrädersatz** m MASCHINEN epicyclic gear train, epicyclic train; **Planetenradgetriebe** nt FERTIG planetary gearing; **Planetenradträger** m MASCHINEN planet carrier; **Planetenritzel** nt KFZTECH planetary pinion; **Planetensonde** f RAUMFAHRT planetary probe; **Planetenspindel** f MASCHINEN planet spindle, planet-action spindle; **Planetenträger** m KFZTECH planet carrier; **Planetenzahnradgehäuse** nt LUFTTRANS *Hubschrauber* planet pinion cage

Planetoid m RAUMFAHRT planetoid
Planfilm m FOTO cut film
Planfräsen nt MASCHINEN plain milling
Planfräsmaschine f MASCHINEN planomilling machine
Planglasplatte f METROL optical flat
Planierarbeiten f pl BAU grading
Planieren nt BAU grading, planing, MASCHINEN planishing
planieren vt BAU grade, *Boden* skim, *Straße* trim, MASCHINEN flatten
Planiergerät nt BAU, MEERSCHMUTZ grader
Planierhammer m MASCHINEN dresser
Planiermaschine f BAU leveling machine (AmE), levelling machine (BrE), TRANS grader
Planierraupe f BAU, TRANS bulldozer; ~ **mit hebbarem Schild** f KFZTECH tiltdozer (BrE)
Planierschaufel f TRANS grader levelling blade
Planierstange f BAU leveling rod (AmE), levelling rod (BrE)
planiert adj BAU leveled (AmE), levelled (BrE)
Planierwerkzeug nt MASCHINEN planishing tool
Planimeter nt BAU, GEOM planimeter
Planimetrie f GEOM plane geometry, planimetry
Planke f BAU, WASSERTRANS *Schiffbau* plank
plankonkav[1] adj OPTIK plano-concave
plankonkav:[2] ~**e Linse** f PHYS plano-concave lens
plankonvex[1] adj OPTIK convexo-plane, plano-convex
plankonvex:[2] ~**e Linse** f PHYS plano-convex lens
Plankurvenfräsmaschine f FERTIG face cam milling machine
planmäßig: ~**e Betriebszeit** f TELEKOM scheduled operating time; ~**er Flug** m LUFTTRANS scheduled flight; ~**es Meldesignal** nt TELEKOM scheduled reporting signal; ~**e Unterbrechung** f TELEKOM foreseen interruption; ~**e Wartung** f COMP & DV, KERNTECH scheduled maintenance
Planoformat nt DRUCK broadside page
planometrisch: ~**e Projektion** f KONSTZEICH planometric projection
planparallel: ~**e Diode** f ELEKTRONIK planar diode
Planparallelfräsen nt MASCHINEN straddle milling, straddling
Planrad nt MASCHINEN crown gear
Planscheibe f FERTIG independent four-jaw chuck, MASCHINEN face chuck, face plate; **Planscheibenbefestigung** f MASCHINEN face plate mounting
Planschleifen nt FERTIG surface grinding, MASCHINEN face grinding, surface grinding
Planschleifer m MASCHINEN face grinder
Planschleifmaschine f MASCHINEN surface grinder, surface-grinding machine
Planschlitten m MASCHINEN cross slide, slide head, slide rest

Planschnitt m FERTIG facing cut
Planschverlust m FERTIG *Getriebelehre* churn loss
Plansenken nt MASCHINEN end facing, spot facing
Planung f KÜNSTL INT, TELEKOM planning
Planverzahnung f MASCHINEN crown gearing
Planvorschub m MASCHINEN cross feed
Planzug m FERTIG cross traverse
Plasma nt ELEKTRONIK, PHYS, RAUMFAHRT, TEILPHYS plasma
plasmaaktiviert: ~**es Chemical-Vapour-Deposition-Verfahren** nt ELEKTRONIK plasma-activated chemical vapor deposition process (AmE), plasma-activated chemical vapour deposition process (BrE); ~**e chemische Bedampfung** f OPTIK plasma-activated chemical vapor deposition (AmE), plasma-activated chemical vapour deposition (BrE); ~**e chemische Dampfabscheidung** f OPTIK plasma-activated chemical vapor deposition (AmE), plasma-activated chemical vapour deposition (BrE); ~**es CVD-Verfahren** nt ELEKTRONIK plasma-activated CVD process
Plasma: **Plasmaätzen** nt ELEKTRONIK plasma etching; **Plasmabehandlung** f ABFALL *Sonderabfall* thermoplastic solidification; **Plasmabildschirm** m COMP & DV plasma display
plasmaentwickelt: ~**er Fotolack** m ELEKTRONIK plasma-developed resist
Plasma: **Plasmalichtbogenschneiden** nt BAU, MASCHINEN plasma arc cutting; **Plasmalichtbogenstromkollektor** m TRANS plasma arc power collector; **Plasmaschneideanlage** f ELEKTRIZ plasma cutting machine; **Plasmaschneiden** nt BAU plasma cutting; **Plasmaschubtriebwerk** nt RAUMFAHRT *Raumschiff* plasma thruster; **Plasmaschweißanlage** f ELEKTRIZ plasma welder; **Plasmaschweißbrenner** m BAU torch for plasma welding; **Plasmatrennen** nt BAU plasma cutting; **Plasmatriebwerk** nt RAUMFAHRT *Raumschiff* plasma engine; **Plasmaumgebung** f RAUMFAHRT plasma environment
Plastbeschichtung f TELEKOM plastic coating
Plastfaser f OPTIK plastic fiber (AmE), plastic fibre (BrE)
Plastic-Clad-Silika-Faser f *(PCS-Faser)* OPTIK, TELEKOM plastic-clad silica fiber (AmE), plastic-clad silica fibre (BrE) *(PCS fiber)*
Plastifikator m FERTIG plasticizer
Plastifizieren nt BAU fluxing
plastifizieren vt FERTIG, KUNSTSTOFF plasticize
Plastifizierung f FERTIG plasticization
Plastikfaser f ELEKTROTECH plastic fiber (AmE), plastic fibre (BrE), TELEKOM all-plastic fiber (AmE), all-plastic fibre (BrE)
plastisch:[1] **nicht** ~ adj BAU nonplastic
plastisch:[2] ~**es Abstumpfen** nt METALL plastic blunting; ~**e Deformation** f KUNSTSTOFF plastic deformation; ~**e Eigenschaften** f pl STRÖMPHYS plastic properties; ~**e Fließeigenschaften** f pl KUNSTSTOFF plastic flow properties; ~**es Fließen** nt KUNSTSTOFF, METALL plastic flow; ~**e Instabililität** f METALL plastic instability; ~**es Nachgeben** nt KERNTECH plastic yield; ~**es Schutzelement** nt SICHERHEIT plastic protective element; ~**e Verformung** f BAU plastic deformation, KERNTECH plastic yield, KUNSTSTOFF, METALL, PHYS plastic deformation
plastisch:[3] ~ **verformen** vt FERTIG fail, overstrain

Plastisol *nt* KUNSTSTOFF plastisol

Plastizität *f* KOHLEN, KUNSTSTOFF, METALL plasticity; **Plastizitätsgrenze** *f* BAU, KOHLEN plastic limit; **Plastizitätsindex** *m* BAU, KOHLEN plasticity index

Plastomer *nt* CHEMIE, ERDÖL *Petrochemie* plastomer

Plastomeres *nt* CHEMIE plastomer

Plastometer *nt* KUNSTSTOFF plastimeter

plastummantelt: ~e Silikafaser *f* OPTIK plastic-clad silica fiber (AmE), plastic-clad silica fibre (BrE)

Plastummantelung *f* TELEKOM plastic coating

Plateau *nt* ERDÖL *Geologie* plateau; **Plateauhöhe** *f* ERDÖL *Geologie* plateau level; **Plateauniveau** *nt* ERDÖL *Geologie* plateau level

Plate-out *nt* KUNSTSTOFF *Formverschmutzung* plate-out

platieren *vt* FERTIG bond

Platierung *f* FERTIG bonding

Platin *nt* (*Pt*) CHEMIE platinum (*Pt*), ELEKTRIZ platinum; **Platin-** *pref* CHEMIE platinic

Platina *nt* CHEMIE platina

Platine *f* COMP & DV board, FERTIG blank, TEXTIL sinker; **Platinenbarre** *f* TEXTIL sinker bar

Platinieren *nt* METALL platinization

Platinotron *nt* PHYS platinotron

Platin: **Platintiegel** *m* LABOR platinum crucible; **Platinwiderstandsthermometer** *nt* PHYS platinum resistance thermometer

platonisch: ~er Körper *m* GEOM Platonic solid

Plättchen *nt* CHEMIE lamina, COMP & DV, ELEKTRONIK, ELEKTROTECH wafer, KER & GLAS split; **Plättchenschneidemaschine** *f* FERTIG dicing machine; **Plättchenverarbeitung** *f* ELEKTRONIK wafer processing; **Plättchenverzerrung** *f* ELEKTRONIK wafer distortion

Platte *f* AUFNAHME disc (BrE), disk (AmE), BAU slab, COMP & DV platform, *Daten* disk (AmE), DRUCK *Drucken* plate, printing plate, *Fotografie* plate, ELEKTRIZ, ELEKTROTECH *Elektroplattierung, Galvanisierung* plate, FERTIG *Kunststoffinstallationen* disc (BrE), disk (AmE), KER & GLAS slab, KFZTECH plate, KOHLEN panel, slab, KUNSTSTOFF platen, sheet, MASCHINEN plate, platen, MECHAN plate, sheet; ~ mit achtzig Spuren *f* COMP & DV eighty-track disk

Plätteisen *nt* KER & GLAS battledore

Platten: mit ~ überziehen *vt* ANSTRICH plate

Platte: **Plattenadresse** *f* COMP & DV disk address; **Plattenamalgamation** *f* KOHLEN plate amalgamation; **Plattenanschluß** *m* COMP & DV disk adaptor; **Plattenapplikator** *m* KER & GLAS apron applicator; **Plattenarchiv** *nt* AUFNAHME record library; **Plattenbalken** *m* BAU *Massivbau* T-beam; **Plattenbandförderer** *m* FERTIG apron conveyor, MASCHINEN apron conveyor, plate conveyor; **Plattenbearbeitungshalle** *f* WASSERTRANS *Schiffbau* platers' shop; **Plattenbelag** *m* BAU flagging; **Plattenbereich** *m* COMP & DV disk space; **Plattenbeschichtungsmaschine** *f* DRUCK plate-coating machine; **Plattendatei** *f* COMP & DV disk file; **Platteneinheit** *f* COMP & DV disk unit; **Plattenförderband** *nt* TRANS apron conveyor; **Plattenform** *f* KER & GLAS flag build; **Plattengang** *m* WASSERTRANS *Schiffbau* strake; **Plattengefrieranlage** *f* HEIZ & KÄLTE plate freezer; **Plattengußglas** *nt* KER & GLAS thick rough cast plate glass; **Plattenheizkörper** *m* HEIZ & KÄLTE panel-type radiator; **Platteninterferometrie** *f* OPTIK slab interferometry; **Plattenkamera** *f* FOTO plate camera; **Plattenkapazität** *f* COMP & DV disk space; **Plattenkas-**

sette *f* COMP & DV disk cartridge, FOTO dark slide, plate holder; **Plattenkondensator** *m* ELEKTRIZ plate capacitor, ELEKTROTECH disc capacitor (BrE), disk capacitor (AmE); **Plattenkopiereffekt** *m* AUFNAHME record crosstalk; **Plattenlaufwerk** *nt* COMP & DV disk drive; **Plattenpaar** *nt* ELEKTROTECH *Batterie* couple; **Plattenplatz** *m* COMP & DV disk space; **Plattenpresse** *f* KUNSTSTOFF platen press; **Plattenrecorder** *m* ELEKTRIZ disc recorder (BrE), disk recorder (AmE)

plattenresident *adj* COMP & DV disk-resident

Platte: **Plattensektor** *m* COMP & DV disk sector; **Plattenspeicher** *m* COMP & DV disk storage, TELEKOM disk store; **Plattenspieler** *m* AUFNAHME record player, OPTIK *Schallplatten, CD* disk player; **Plattenspielwerk** *nt* KONTROLL disk drive; **Plattenspur** *f* COMP & DV disk track; **Plattenstapel** *m* COMP & DV disk pack, KERNTECH *Brennelemente* slab pile; **Plattensteuereinheit** *f* COMP & DV disk controller; **Plattenstruktur** *f* METALL plate structure; **Plattenteller** *m* AKUSTIK, AUFNAHME turntable; **Plattenträger** *m* BAU plate girder; **Plattentrockner** *m* PAPIER slat dryer; **Plattenumdrehungsverzögerung** *f* COMP & DV rotational delay; **Plattenverbinder** *m* FERTIG *Riemen* plate fastener; **Plattenverlegen** *nt* BAU flagging; **Plattenvorsteven** *m* WASSERTRANS *Schiffbau* plate stem; **Plattenwärmeaustauscher** *m* HEIZ & KÄLTE plate heat exchanger; **Plattenwechsler** *m* AKUSTIK, AUFNAHME record changer; **Plattenwiedergabekopf** *m* AUFNAHME record playback head; **Plattenzugriff** *m* COMP & DV disk access; **Plattenzugriffsarm** *m* COMP & DV access arm

Plattform *f* BAU stage, COMP & DV, ERDÖL *Offshore* platform, FERTIG entablature, stillage, MASCHINEN platform; **Plattformausrüstung** *f* ERDÖL platform equipment; **Plattformwagen** *m* EISENBAHN flatcar (AmE), *Förderung* four-wheeled truck

Plattgatt *nt* WASSERTRANS *Schiffbau* flat stern, square transom stern

Platthammer *m* FERTIG *Schmieden* flatter

Plattheck *nt* WASSERTRANS *Schiffbau* flat stern

Plattieren *nt* ELEKTROTECH plating, FERTIG cast coating, MASCHINEN cladding

plattieren *vt* FERTIG clad

Plattierschicht *f* FERTIG clad plate

Plattierung *f* ELEKTROTECH, MASCHINEN plating

Platting *f* WASSERTRANS *Knoten* sennet

Platz *m* TELEKOM operator position; ~ für konzentrierte Abfrage *m* TELEKOM switched loop console; **Platzbedarf** *m* FERNSEH footprint; **Platzcode** *m* VERPACK site code

platzen[1] *vt* BAU burst

platzen[2] *vi* MASCHINEN burst

Platz: **Platzhalterzeichen** *nt* COMP & DV token, wildcard character; **Platzlampe** *f* ELEKTROTECH pilot lamp; **Platzreservierungssystem** *nt* TRANS passenger reservation system; **Platzrundenanflug** *m* LUFTTRANS circling approach; **Platzrundenführungsbefeuerung** *f* LUFTTRANS circling guidance light; **Platzsparen** *nt* VERPACK economy of space

platzsparend *adj* VERPACK space-saving

Playback *nt* FERNSEH audio playback, playback; **Playback-Charakteristika** *nt pl* FERNSEH playback characteristics; **Playback-Kopf** *m* FERNSEH playback head; **Playback-Verlust** *m* FERNSEH playback loss; **Playback-Videorecorder** *m* FERNSEH playback VTR

p-leitend: ~e Basis *f* ELEKTRONIK p-type base; ~e Dotierung *f* ELEKTRONIK p-type impurity; **~e Epitaxial-schicht** *f* ELEKTRONIK p-type epitaxial layer; **~e implantierte Schicht** *f* ELEKTRONIK p-type implanted layer; **~es Silizium** *nt* ELEKTRONIK p-type silicon; **~es Silizium-Trägermaterial** *nt* ELEKTRONIK p-type silicon substrate

p-Leitfähigkeit *f* ELEKTROTECH p-type conductivity

plesiochron: ~es Leitungsendgerät *nt* TELEKOM plesiochronous line terminal; **~e Übertragungseinrichtung** *f* TELEKOM plesiochronous transmission equipment

Pleuel *nt* LUFTTRANS connecting rod, MASCHINEN, MECHAN connecting rod, rod; **Pleuelaugenbuchse** *f* KFZTECH small end bush; **Pleuelbuchse** *f* KFZTECH piston-pin bushing, small end bushing; **Pleueldeckel** *m* KFZTECH connecting rod cap; **Pleuelende** *nt* MASCHINEN end; **Pleuelfuß** *m* KFZTECH connecting rod big end; **Pleuelfußlager** *nt* KFZTECH big end bearing; **Pleuelkopf** *m* KFZTECH connecting rod small end, small end; **Pleuellager** *nt* KFZTECH big end bearing, connecting rod bearing; **Pleuelschaft** *m* KFZTECH connecting rod shank; **Pleuelstange** *f* EISENBAHN piston rod, FERTIG conrod, KFZTECH con rod, connecting rod, piston rod, MASCHINEN connecting rod, rod, WASSERTRANS *Motor* piston rod, *Schiffantrieb* connecting rod; **Pleuelstangenfuß** *m* KFZTECH *Pleuel* big end

Plexiglas *nt* VERPACK acrylic plastic; **Plexiglasverkleidung** *f* LUFTTRANS plexiglass fairing

Plicht *f* WASSERTRANS *Schiff* cockpit

Plisseefalte *f* TEXTIL pleat

Plissieren *nt* TEXTIL pleating

plissieren *vt* TEXTIL pleat

Plissiermaschine *f* TEXTIL pleater, pleating machine

plissiert *adj* TEXTIL pleated

PLL *abbr* (*Phasenregelkreis*) ELEKTRONIK, FERNSEH, RADIO, RAUMFAHRT, TELEKOM PLL (*phase-locked loop*)

Plombe *f* BAU sealing, MECHAN seal; **Plombenzange** *f* VERPACK lead sealing pliers

plombieren *vt* FERTIG seal

Plot *m* COMP & DV, WASSERTRANS *Navigation* plot

Plotten *nt* COMP & DV plotting

plotten *vi* WASSERTRANS *Navigation* plot the position

Plotter *m* COMP & DV graph plotter, plotter, ELEKTRIZ plotter

Plott-Tisch *m* WASSERTRANS *Navigation* plotting table

plötzlich: ~er Ausfall *m* ELEKTROTECH catastrophic failure; **~e Querschnittskontraktion** *f* HYDRAUL sudden contraction of cross section; **~e Querschnittsvergrößerung** *f* HYDRAUL sudden enlargement of cross section; **~es Schlingern nach der Leeseite** *nt* WASSERTRANS lee lurch; **~er Übergang** *m* ELEKTRONIK *Halbleiter* abrupt junction

Plumbat *nt* CHEMIE plumbate

Plumbikon *nt* ELEKTRONIK *Bildaufnahmeröhre* plumbicon

Plumbit *nt* CHEMIE plumbite

Plunger *m* KER & GLAS plunger; **Plungerdorn** *m* KER & GLAS plunger spike; **Plungerfestsitz** *m* KER & GLAS plunger sticking; **Plungerhilfsmechanismus** *m* KER & GLAS plunger assist mechanism; **Plungerkolben** *m* KFZTECH *Bremsen, Kupplung* plunger, MASCHINEN plunger, plunger piston, ram; **Plungerpumpe** *f* WASSERVERSORG plunger pump

plus *adj* MATH plus

Plusplatte *f* KFZTECH positive plate

Pluspol *m* KFZTECH plus terminal, positive terminal

Pluszeichen *nt* MATH plus sign

Pluviometer *nt* BAU, LABOR, NICHTFOSS ENERG, WASSERVERSORG rain gage (AmE), rain gauge (BrE)

PM *abbr* (*Phasenmodulation*) AUFNAHME, COMP & DV, ELEKTRONIK, FERNSEH, PHYS, RADIO, TELEKOM PM (*phase modulation*)

Pm (*Promethium*) CHEMIE Pm (*promethium*)

PMC-Verfahren *nt* (*Pulverlack-Beschichtungstechnik*) KUNSTSTOFF PMC (*powder mould coating*)

p-Methoxypropenylbenzol *nt* CHEMIE anethole

PMMA *abbr* (*Polymethacrylat, Polymethylmethacrylat*) KUNSTSTOFF PMMA (*polymethyl methacrylate*)

Pneumatik *f* KFZTECH, PHYS pneumatics

pneumatisch[1] *adj* FERTIG air-actuated, air-operated, PHYS pneumatic

pneumatisch:[2] **~er Auslöser** *m* FOTO pneumatic release; **~ betätigter Schalter** *m* ELEKTRIZ pneumatically operated switch; **~er Bohrungsmeßdorn** *m* FERTIG, METROL air gage (AmE), air gauge (BrE); **~er Detektor** *m* TRANS pneumatic detector; **~es Dichtemeßgerät** *nt* GERÄT air bubble density meter; **~er Drehzahlregler** *m* KFZTECH suction-type governor; **~er Feinzeiger** *m* FERTIG, METROL air gage (AmE), air gauge (BrE); **~er Förderer** *m* FERTIG, MASCHINEN pneumatic conveyor; **~es Gerät** *nt* MASCHINEN pneumatic equipment; **~er Lautsprecher** *m* AKUSTIK pneumatic loudspeaker; **~e Meßvorrichtung** *f* MASCHINEN air gage (AmE), air gauge (BrE); **~er Plattenhalter** *m* DRUCK vacuum plate holder; **~er Röhrenförderer** *m* TRANS pneumatic pipe conveyor; **~e Sortieranlage** *f* ABFALL pneumatic sorter; **~es Sortieren** *nt* ABFALL pneumatic classification; **~es Ziehkissen** *nt* FERTIG air cushion

pneumohydraulisch: ~er Flüssigkeitsspeicher *m* FERTIG hydropneumatic accumulator

Pneumonik *f* FERTIG fluid technology

pn-Gleichrichter *m* ELEKTROTECH p-n rectifier

pn-Halbleiterdiode *f* ELEKTRIZ p-n junction diode

pnp *abbr* (*positiv-negativ-positiv*) ELEKTRONIK p-n-p (*positive-negative-positive*)

pnpn-Gerät *nt* ELEKTRONIK p-n-p-n device

pnpn-Komponente *f* ELEKTRONIK p-n-p-n component

pnp-Transistor *m* ELEKTRONIK, PHYS p-n-p transistor

pn-Übergang *m* ELEKTRONIK, PHYS p-n junction, RADIO *Halbleiter* junction

PO *abbr* KUNSTSTOFF (*Polyolefin*) PO (*polyolefin*), TEXTIL (*Polynosic-Faser*) PO (*polynosic fiber*), TEXTIL (*Polyolefin*) PO (*polyolefin*)

Po (*Polonium*) CHEMIE Po (*polonium*)

Pochholz *nt* MECHAN lignum vitae

pochieren *vt* LEBENSMITTEL poach

Pockennarben *f pl* KER & GLAS pockmarks

Pockholz *nt* WASSERTRANS lignum vitae

Podest *nt* KERNTECH pedestal; **Podeststufe** *f* BAU landing step; **Podestträger** *m* BAU bearer; **Podestwechselbalken** *m* BAU landing trimmer

Podocarpin- *pref* CHEMIE podocarpic

Podophyllin *nt* CHEMIE podophyllin

POGO-Effekt *m* RAUMFAHRT *Raumschiff* pogo effect

Pointkontakt-Gleichrichter *m* ELEKTRIZ point contact rectifier

Poiseuille: ~sches Gesetz *nt* PHYS Poiseuille's law; **~sche Strömung** *f* STRÖMPHYS Poiseuille flow

Poisson: ~sches Gesetz *nt* RAUMFAHRT *Raumschiff* Poisson's law; **~sche Gleichung** *f* PHYS Poisson's equation; **~sche Konstante** *f* (σ) PHYS Poisson's ratio;

~sches Verhältnis *nt* (σ) MECHAN Poisson's ratio (σ); ~scher Verkehr *m* TELEKOM Poisson traffic; ~sche Verteilung *f* COMP & DV, PHYS *Statistik*, QUAL Poisson distribution; ~sche Zahl *f* (σ) KOHLEN, KUNSTSTOFF Poisson's ratio (σ), MECHAN Poisson's ratio

Pökeln *nt* LEBENSMITTEL salting

pökeln *vt* LEBENSMITTEL *Fleisch* cure

Pol *m* ELEKTRIZ pole, ELEKTROTECH pole, terminal, KFZTECH terminal, METROL, PAPIER, PHYS, RADIO pole

Polaplexer *m* RADIO polaplexer

polar:[1] in ~er Umlaufbahn *adj* RAUMFAHRT polar-orbiting

polar:[2] ~es Dielektrikum *nt* PHYS polar dielectric; nicht ~es Dielektrikum *nt* PHYS nonpolar dielectric; ~es Molekül *nt* KUNSTSTOFF polar molecule

Polarbahn: in ~ *adj* RAUMFAHRT polar-orbiting

Polardiagramm *nt* PHYS, RADIO polar diagram

Polarimeter *nt* LABOR, OPTIK, PHYS, STRAHLPHYS polarimeter

Polarisation *f* ELEKTRIZ, ELEKTROTECH, FOTO, PHYS, RAUMFAHRT *Weltraumfunk*, STRAHLPHYS, TELEKOM polarization; ~ elektromagnetischer Wellen *f* ELEKTROTECH electromagnetic wave polarization; Polarisationsapparat *m* PHYS saccharimeter; Polarisationsbrille *f* FOTO polarizing spectacles; Polarisationsdiplexer *m* RAUMFAHRT *Weltraumfunk* polarization diplexer; Polarisationsebene *f* OPTIK, PHYS plane of polarization; Polarisationsfilter *nt* FOTO polarizing filter; Polarisationsgerät *nt* LABOR polarimeter; Polarisationsgitter *nt* RAUMFAHRT *Weltraumfunk* polarization grid; Polarisationsisolierung *f* RAUMFAHRT *Weltraumfunk* polarization isolation; Polarisationskopplungsdämpfung *f* TELEKOM polarization coupling loss; Polarisationsladung *f* PHYS polarization charge; Polarisationsmikroskop *nt* LABOR polarization microscope, polarizing microscope, PHYS polarizing microscope; Polarisationsprisma *nt* PHYS polarizer; Polarisationsreinheit *f* RAUMFAHRT *Weltraumfunk* polarization purity, Polarisationsstrom *m* PHYS polarization current; Polarisationswinkel *m* OPTIK angle of polarization, polarizing angle

Polarisator *m* METALL polarizer, PHYS polarizer, polaroid, RAUMFAHRT *Weltraumfunk*, TELEKOM polarizer

Polarisierbarkeit *f* PHYS polarizability

polarisieren *vt* OPTIK polarize

polarisierend *adj* OPTIK polarizing

polarisierend: ~e Substanz *f* LABOR polarizer

polarisiert[1] *adj* STRAHLPHYS polarized

polarisiert:[2] ~es Licht *nt* FOTO, PHYS, STRAHLPHYS polarized light; ~es Relais *nt* ELEKTRIZ, ELEKTROTECH polarized relay; ~er Stecker *m* ELEKTRIZ nonreversible plug; ~e Wellen *f pl* WELLPHYS polarized waves

Polarisierung *f* RADIO polarization

Polariskop *nt* OPTIK, PHYS polariscope

Polarität *f* ELEKTRIZ, ELEKTROTECH, PHYS polarity; Polaritätsprüfer *m* ELEKTRIZ polarity tester; Polaritätssteuerung *f* FERNSEH polarity control; Polaritätsumkehr *f* ELEKTRIZ polarity reversal; Polaritätswechsel *m* ELEKTRIZ polarity reversal; Polaritätswechsler *m* ELEKTRIZ polarity reverser; Polaritätszeichen *nt* ELEKTRIZ polarity sign

Polarkoordinaten *f pl* ELEKTRONIK *zweidimensional*, PHYS polar coordinates; Polarkoordinaten-Anzeigeinstrument *nt* GERÄT polar-coordinate-indicating instrument

Polarlicht *nt* WASSERTRANS *Wetterkunde* aurora polaris; Polarlichtzone *f* RADIO auroral zone

Polarographie *f* CHEMIE polarography

polarographische: ~ Analyse *f* CHEMIE polarography

Polaroid *nt* PHYS polaroid; Polaroidmaterial *nt* STRAHLPHYS polaroid

Polaron *nt* PHYS polaron

Polarorbit *m* RAUMFAHRT polar orbit

Pol: Polbahn *f* FERTIG centrode; Polbrücke *f* EISENBAHN, WASSERTRANS plate strap

Polder *m* ABFALL landfill cell, refuse cell; Polderverfahren *nt* ABFALL cell method

Polfläche *f* FERNSEH pole face

polfrei: ~es Filter *nt* ELEKTRONIK Chebyshev filter

Polierasche *f* BAU putty powder

Polieren *nt* BAU planing, KUNSTSTOFF polishing, MASCHINEN buffing, polishing, METALL burnishing, polishing

polieren *vt* ANSTRICH polish, BAU rub, KER & GLAS burnish, MECHAN polish, METALL burnish

Polierer *m* METALL burnisher

Polierkratzer *m* KER & GLAS sleek

Polierkugel *f* AKUSTIK advance ball

Polierleinwand *f* MASCHINEN crocus cloth

Poliermaschine *f* MASCHINEN polishing head, polishing lathe

Poliermittel *nt* ANSTRICH silica abrasive

Polierpaste *f* MECHAN grinding paste

Polierrot *nt* KER & GLAS rouge

Poliersand *m* ANSTRICH grit

Polierscheibe *f* FERTIG bob, polishing wheel, MASCHINEN buff, polishing wheel, MECHAN buffer, SICHERHEIT abrasive wheel

Polierstahl *m* KER & GLAS burnisher

poliert: ~e Steinoberfläche *f* BAU polished stone finish

Polierung *f* MECHAN burnishing

Polierwalze *f* MASCHINEN polishing roll

Politur *f* ANSTRICH polish, KER & GLAS burnishing; Politurmittel *nt* ANSTRICH polish

Polklemme *f* ELEKTROTECH binding post

Poller *m* WASSERTRANS bollard

Polling *nt* COMP & DV polling

polnisch: ~e Schreibweise *f* COMP & DV Polish notation, parenthesis-free notation

Polonium *nt* (Po) CHEMIE polonium (Po)

Pol: Polprüfer *m* GERÄT pole tester; Polschichtlänge *f* KOHLEN effective pile length; Polschlupf *m* ELEKTRIZ pole slip; Polschlüpfung *f* ELEKTRIZ pole slip; Polschuh *m* ELEKTROTECH pole piece, pole shoe, FERNSEH, PHYS pole shoe; Polspitzen *f pl* FERNSEH pole tips; Polstärke *f* PHYS pole strength; Polsteinkraft *f* ELEKTRIZ magnetic attraction

Polster *nt* BAU, KER & GLAS pad; Polsterbruch *m* KER & GLAS pad break; Polsterstoff *m* TEXTIL upholstery

Polsterung *f* MASCHINEN, PAPIER, TEXTIL padding, VERPACK cushioning product

Pol: Polstück *nt* AUFNAHME, ELEKTROTECH pole piece; Polumkehr *f* ELEKTROTECH polarity reversal

Polung *f* FERNSEH polarity

Pol: Polwechselschalter *m* ELEKTROTECH polarity-reversing switch; Polwechselranlasser *m* ELEKTRIZ pole-changing starter; Polwechslerschalter *m* ELEKTRIZ pole changer switch; Polwendeschalter *m* ELEKTROTECH reversing switch

Polyacetal *nt* CHEMIE polyacetal, polyoxymethylene, KUNSTSTOFF polyoxymethylene

Polyacryl *nt* *(PAA)* CHEMIE , KUNSTSTOFF polyacrylate *(PAA)*, TEXTIL acrylic

Polyacrylamid *nt* ERDÖL *Petrochemie* polyacrylamide

Polyacrylat *nt* *(PAA)* CHEMIE, KUNSTSTOFF polyacrylate *(PAA)*

Polyacrylnitril *nt* CHEMIE polyacrylonitrile, KUNSTSTOFF polyacrylonitrile, TEXTIL acrylic, UMWELTSCHMUTZ *(PAN)* polyacrylonitrile *(PAN)*

Polyalkohol *m* CHEMIE polyol

Polyamid *nt* *(PA)* CHEMIE, KUNSTSTOFF, TEXTIL polyamide *(PA)*

Polyamin *nt* KUNSTSTOFF polyamine

polyatomar *adj* CHEMIE polyatomic

Polybutadien *nt* RAUMFAHRT *Raumschiff* polybutadiene

Polybuten *nt* *(PB)* KUNSTSTOFF polybutene, polybutylene *(PB)*

Polybutylen *nt* *(PB)* KUNSTSTOFF polybutene, polybutylene *(PB)*; **Polybutylenterephthalat** *nt* *(PBT)* ELEKTRIZ, KUNSTSTOFF polybutylene ephtalate *(PBT)*

Polycarbonat *nt* *(PC)* ELEKTRIZ, KUNSTSTOFF polycarbonate *(PC)*

Polychloropren-Latex *m* KUNSTSTOFF polychloroprene latex

polychrom: ~es Glas *nt* KER & GLAS polychromatic glass

Poly-Cyanethylen *nt* CHEMIE poly-cyanoethylene, polyacrylonitrile

polycyclisch[1] *adj* CHEMIE polycyclic

polycyclisch:[2] **~e Aromaten** *nt pl* KUNSTSTOFF polynuclear aromatics

Polydiallyphthalat *nt* *(PDAP)* KUNSTSTOFF polydiallylphthalate *(PDAP)*

Polydimethylsiloxan *nt* CHEMIE polydimethylsiloxane

Polyeder *nt* GEOM, METALL polyhedron

polyedrisch *adj* GEOM polyhedral

Polyen *nt* CHEMIE polyene

Polyester *m* *(PES)* CHEMIE, ELEKTRIZ, KUNSTSTOFF, TEXTIL polyester *(PES)*; **Polyesterband** *nt* AUFNAHME polyester tape; **Polyesterbildung** *f* CHEMIE polyesterification; **Polyesterfarbe** *f* BAU polyester paint; **Polyesterharz** *nt* CHEMIE polyester resin; **Polyesterschaumstoff** *m* ABFALL polyester foam

Polyethersulfon *nt* ELEKTRIZ polyether sulfon

Polyethylen *nt* *(PET)* CHEMIE, ELEKTRIZ, ERDÖL, KUNSTSTOFF, VERPACK polyethylene (AmE), polythene (BrE) *(PET)*; **~ hoher Dichte** *nt* KUNSTSTOFF, VERPACK HDPE, high-density polyethylene; **Polyethylenschaumstoff** *m* KUNSTSTOFF polyether foam; **Polyethylenterephthalat** *nt* ELEKTRIZ polyethylene terephthalate, KUNSTSTOFF polyethylene terephthalate

Polyformaldehyd *m* CHEMIE polyacetal, polyoxymethylene

polyfunktionell *adj* CHEMIE multifunctional, polyfunctional

Polygon *nt* BAU traverse, FERTIG spherical triangle, GEOM polygon

polygonal[1] *adj* GEOM polygonal

polygonal:[2] **~e Laufzeitkette** *f* ELEKTRONIK polygonal delay line; **~er Spiegel** *m* OPTIK polygonal mirror

Polygon: **Polygonfläche** *f* GEOM polygon surface; **Polygonisieren** *nt* METALL polygonization **Polygonprofil** *nt* MASCHINEN spline profile; **Polygonschaltung** *f* ELEKTRIZ polygon connection; **Polygonversetzung** *f* METALL polygonal dislocation

Polyimid *nt* *(PI)* ELEKTRIZ, ELEKTRONIK, KUNSTSTOFF

polyimide *(PI)*; **Polyimid-Leiterplatte** *f* ELEKTRONIK polyimide printed circuit

Polyisobutylen *nt* *(PIB)* KUNSTSTOFF polyisobutylene *(PIB)*

Polyisocyanat *nt* KUNSTSTOFF polyisocyanate

Polyisopren *nt* CHEMIE, KUNSTSTOFF polyisoprene

Polykondensation *f* CHEMIE polycondensation

polykristallin: ~es Silizium *nt* ELEKTRONIK polycrystalline silicon

polymer *adj* CHEMIE polymeric

Polymer *nt* CHEMIE, ELEKTRIZ, ERDÖL *Petrochemie*, FERTIG, KUNSTSTOFF, TEXTIL polymer; **Polymerbeton** *m* KUNSTSTOFF polymer concrete; **Polymerdichtungsmasse** *f* ERDÖL sealant polymer; **Polymerfaser** *f* OPTIK polymer fiber (AmE), polymer fibre (BrE)

Polymerie *f* CHEMIE polymerism

Polymerisat *nt* CHEMIE, KUNSTSTOFF, TEXTIL polymer

Polymerisation *f* CHEMIE, ERDÖL *Petrochemie*, KUNSTSTOFF polymerization; **Polymerisationsgrad** *m* KUNSTSTOFF degree of polymerization; **Polymerisationskammer** *f* TEXTIL curing oven

Polymerisiereinrichtung *f* TEXTIL polymerizer

Polymerisieren *nt* CHEMIE polymerization

polymerisieren[1] *vt* CHEMIE, KUNSTSTOFF, PAPIER polymerize

polymerisieren[2] *vi* KUNSTSTOFF, PAPIER, TEXTIL polymerize

Polymer: **Polymermantel-Quarzglasfaser** *f* OPTIK, TELEKOM plastic-clad silica fiber (AmE), plastic-clad silica fibre (BrE); **Polymerweichmacher** *m* KUNSTSTOFF polymeric plasticizer

Polymethacrylat *nt* *(PMMA)* KUNSTSTOFF polymethacrylate, polymethyl methacrylate *(PMMA)*

Polymethakrylat *nt* KER & GLAS organic glass

Polymethylen *nt* CHEMIE polymethylene

Polymethylmethacrylat *nt* *(PMMA)* KUNSTSTOFF polymethacrylate, polymethyl methacrylate *(PMMA)*

Polymorphie *f* METALL polymorphism

Polynom *nt* COMP & DV polynomial, MATH multinomial, PHYS polynomial; **Polynomcode** *m* COMP & DV polynomial code

polynomisch: ~es Filter *nt* ELEKTRONIK polynomial filter

Polynosic-Faser *f* *(PO)* TEXTIL polynosic fiber (AmE), polynosic fibre (BrE) *(PO)*

Polynucleotid *nt* CHEMIE polynucleotide

Polyol *nt* CHEMIE, KUNSTSTOFF polyol

Polyolefin *nt* *(PO)* KUNSTSTOFF, TEXTIL polyolefin *(PO)*; **Polyolefincontainer** *m* VERPACK polyolefin container; **Polyolefinsperrfolie** *f* VERPACK polyolefin barrier film

Polyoxyethylen *nt* CHEMIE polyoxyethylene

Polyoxymethylen *nt* *(POM)* CHEMIE polyacetal, polyoxymethylene, KUNSTSTOFF polyoxymethylene *(POM)*

Polypeptid *nt* CHEMIE polypeptide

Polyphenol- *pref* CHEMIE polyphenol

Polypropylen *nt* *(PP)* CHEMIE, ELEKTRIZ, ERDÖL, KUNSTSTOFF, TEXTIL polypropylene *(PP)*

Polysilizium *nt* ELEKTRONIK polysilicon; **Polysiliziumgatter** *nt* ELEKTRONIK polysilicon gate; **Polysiliziumschicht** *f* ELEKTRONIK polysilicon layer

Polysiloxan *nt* KUNSTSTOFF polysiloxane

Polysolenoidmotor *m* KFZTECH tubular motor

Polystyren *nt* *(PS)* CHEMIE, KUNSTSTOFF polystyrene

(PS)
Polystyrol *nt (PS)* CHEMIE, ELEKTRIZ, KUNSTSTOFF polystyrene *(PS)*; **Polystyrol-Spritzgußetikett mit umgekehrter Lackierung** *nt* VERPACK polystyrene injection in-mould label
Polysulfid *nt* CHEMIE, KUNSTSTOFF polysulfide (AmE), polysulphide (BrE); **Polysulfidplast** *m* CHEMIE thioplast
Polyterpen *nt* CHEMIE polyterpene
Polytetrafluorethen *nt (PTFE)* FERTIG *Kunststoffinstallationen*, KUNSTSTOFF polytetrafluoroethylene *(PTFE)*
Polytetrafluorethylen *nt (PTFE)* FERTIG *Kunststoffinstallationen*, KUNSTSTOFF polytetrafluoroethylene *(PTFE)*
Polythermfrachter *m* TRANS polythermal cargo ship
Polythylen *nt* ERDÖL *Petrochemie* polythylene
Polyurethan *nt (PUR)* KUNSTSTOFF, TEXTIL polyurethane *(PUR)*; **Polyurethanschaum** *m* KUNSTSTOFF expanded polyurethane, polyurethane foam; **Polyurethanschaumstoff** *m* KUNSTSTOFF expanded polyurethane, polyurethane foam
polyvalent *adj* CHEMIE polyvalent
Polyvalenz *f* CHEMIE polyvalence, polyvalency
Polyveresterung *f* CHEMIE polyesterification
Polyvinyl *nt* CHEMIE, TEXTIL polyvinyl; **Polyvinylacetal** *nt* KUNSTSTOFF polyvinyl acetal; **Polyvinylacetat** *nt (PVAC)* KUNSTSTOFF polyvinyl acetate *(PVAC)*; **Polyvinylalkohol** *m (PVAL)* DRUCK, KUNSTSTOFF polyvinyl alcohol *(PVAL)*; **Polyvinylalkoholschlichte** *f* TEXTIL polyvinyl alcohol size; **Polyvinylbutyral** *nt (PVB)* KUNSTSTOFF polyvinyl butyral *(PVB)*; **Polyvinylchlorid** *nt (PVC)* BAU, ELEKTROTECH, FERTIG *Kunststoffinstallationen* polyvinyl chloride *(PVC)*; **Polyvinylether** *m (PVE)* KUNSTSTOFF polyvinyl ether *(PVE)*; **Polyvinylfluorid** *nt (PVF)* KUNSTSTOFF polyvinyl fluoride *(PVF)*; **Polyvinylidenchlorid** *nt (PVDC)* KUNSTSTOFF polyvinylidene chloride *(PVDC)*; **Polyvinylidenfluorid** *nt (PVDF)* KUNSTSTOFF polyvinylidene fluoride *(PVFD)*
polyzyklisch: **~er aromatischer Kohlenwasserstoff** *m* UMWELTSCHMUTZ polycyclic aromatic hydrocarbon
POM *abbr (Polyoxymethylen)* CHEMIE, KUNSTSTOFF POM *(polyoxymethylene)*
Pond *nt* FERTIG gram force
Ponton *m* BAU, WASSERTRANS pontoon; **Pontonbrücke** *f* WASSERTRANS pontoon bridge; **Pontondock** *nt* WASSERTRANS pontoon dock
Pool-Wagen *m* EISENBAHN pooling car
Poopdeck *nt* WASSERTRANS *Bootsbau* poop deck
Popcorn-Polymere *nt pl* KUNSTSTOFF popcorn polymers
Popelin *m* TEXTIL poplin
Populin *nt* CHEMIE benzoylsalicin, populin
Pore *f* BAU *Gewebe* interstice, KOHLEN interstice, pore, void, METALL void
Poren *f pl* METALL pitting; **Porendruck** *m* ERDÖL *Geologie*, KOHLEN pore pressure; **Porengasdruck** *m* KOHLEN pore gas pressure; **Porengrundwasser** *nt* WASSERVERSORG interstitial water; **Porenschließer** *m* KUNSTSTOFF sealer; **Porenvolumen** *nt* KOHLEN pore volume, VERPACK absorptive capacity; **Porenwasser** *nt* KOHLEN interstitial watèr, pore water; **Porenwasserdruck** *m* KOHLEN pore water pressure; **Porenwasserüberdruck** *m* KOHLEN pore overpressure; **Porenzeile** *f* BAU *Schweißen* linear porosity; **Porenzif-**

fer *f* KOHLEN void ratio
Porigkeit *f* METALL porosity
poromerbeschichtet: **~es Gewebe** *nt* KUNSTSTOFF poromeric coated fabric
Porometer *nt* CHEMTECH porometer
porös[1] *adj* ANSTRICH, NICHTFOSS ENERG porous
porös:[2] **~e Abdeckung** *f* ABFALL *einer Deponie* porous cover; **~er Absorber** *m* AKUSTIK porous absorber; **~er nichtreflektierender Körper** *m* AKUSTIK porous absorber
Porosimeter *nt* PAPIER porosimeter
Porosität *f* AKUSTIK, ANSTRICH, BAU, ERDÖL *Geologie*, KOHLEN, KUNSTSTOFF, METALL, NICHTFOSS ENERG, PAPIER, WASSERVERSORG porosity; **Porositätslog** *nt* ERDÖL *Meßtechnik* porosity log; **Porositätsprüfer** *m* PAPIER porosity tester
Porphin *nt* CHEMIE porphin
Porphyropsin *nt* CHEMIE porphyropsin
Port *m* COMP & DV, DRUCK port
Portal *nt* BAU portal, FERTIG *Hobelmaschine, Fräsmaschine*, MASCHINEN bridge, WASSERVERSORG gantry; **Portalkran** *m* BAU gantry crane, portal crane, EISENBAHN, KERNTECH, MASCHINEN, WASSERTRANS gantry crane; **Portalkranroboter** *m* KONTROLL gantry robot; **Portalmast** *m* WASSERTRANS portal mast
Portepee-Unteroffizier *m* WASSERTRANS *Marine* chief petty officer
Portioniervorrichtung *f* VERPACK portioning machine
portionsweise: **~ Zugabe** *f* ANSTRICH titration
Portraitlinse *f* FOTO portrait attachment
Porzellan *nt* KER & GLAS English china, china; **Porzellanabdampfschale** *f* KER & GLAS porcelain evaporating basin; **Porzellanbohrer** *m* KER & GLAS china borer, porcelain borer; **Porzellanbrennofen** *m* KER & GLAS porcelain calcining furnace; **Porzellandekor** *nt* KER & GLAS china decoration; **Porzellandekoration** *f* KER & GLAS porcelain decoration; **Porzellandreher** *m* KER & GLAS china thrower, porcelain thrower; **Porzellanerde** *f* KER & GLAS porcelain clay; **Porzellanfadenöse** *f* KER & GLAS porcelain thread guide; **Porzellanfarbe** *f* KER & GLAS porcelain colour; **Porzellanfilterplatte** *f* KER & GLAS porcelain filter plate; **Porzellangeräte** *nt pl* KER & GLAS porcelain utensils; **Porzellangießmaschine** *f* KER & GLAS china caster, porcelain caster; **Porzellanhersteller** *m* KER & GLAS porcelain maker; **Porzellanindustrie** *f* KER & GLAS porcelain industry; **Porzellanisolator** *m* ELEKTRIZ, ELEKTROTECH porcelain insulator, KER & GLAS china insulator, porcelain insulator; **Porzellanisolierung** *f* ELEKTROTECH porcelain insulation; **Porzellanjaspis** *m* KER & GLAS porcelain jasper; **Porzellanknopf** *m* KER & GLAS porcelain button; **Porzellanküvette** *f* KER & GLAS porcelain cell; **Porzellanlack** *m* KER & GLAS porcelain varnish; **Porzellanmalerei** *f* KER & GLAS china painting, painting on porcelain; **Porzellanrohr** *nt* KER & GLAS porcelain tube; **Porzellanscherben** *f pl* KER & GLAS pot sherds; **Porzellanschleifer** *m* KER & GLAS porcelain polisher; **Porzellantasse** *f* KER & GLAS porcelain cup; **Porzellantiegel** *m* KER & GLAS, LABOR porcelain crucible; **Porzellantrichter** *m* KER & GLAS porcelain funnel; **Porzellanvergolder** *m* KER & GLAS porcelain gilder; **Porzellanverteilerkasten** *m* KER & GLAS porcelain conduit box; **Porzellanverzierung** *f* KER & GLAS china ornamentation; **Porzellanwaren** *f pl* KER & GLAS porcelain goods; **Porzellanzahn** *m* KER

& GLAS porcelain tooth

POS-Anzeige *f (elektronische Kassenanzeige)* VERPACK POS display *(point of sale display)*

Position *f* WASSERTRANS *Navigation* position, *Radar* plot

positionieren *vt* KONTROLL, MASCHINEN position

Positionierfehler *m* FERTIG deviation

Positioniermagnet *m* FERNSEH beam-positioning magnet

Positionierung *f* FERNSEH registration, KONTROLL positioning, MASCHINEN location, positioning; **Positionierungsabweichung** *f* FERNSEH registration drift; **Positionierungsbewegung** *f* ERGON positioning movement; **Positionierungsgenauigkeit** *f* FERNSEH registration accuracy; **Positionierungsgeschwindigkeit** *f* MASCHINEN positioning speed; **Positionierungssteuerung** *f* FERNSEH registration control

Positioniervorrichtung *f* MASCHINEN positioner

Positionierzeit *f* COMP & DV seek time

Positionsanzeige *f* FERTIG position indication; **Positionsanzeiger** *m* COMP & DV cursor; **Positionsbestimmung** *f* COMP & DV rotation position sensing; **Positionsgeber** *m* ELEKTRIZ proximity switch; **Positionslampe** *f* LUFTTRANS navigation light; **Positionslaterne** *f* WASSERTRANS navigation light; **Positionslicht** *nt* RAUMFAHRT position light, WASSERTRANS navigation light; **Positionsschalter** *m* ELEKTROTECH position switch

Positiv *nt* DRUCK positive, FOTO *Bild, Abzug* positive, positive image

positiv[1] *adj* ELEKTRIZ, MATH positive; **mit positivem Lichtleitfähigkeits-Koeffizienten** *adj* FOTO light-positive; **~-negativ-positiv** *adj (pnp)* ELEKTRONIK positive-negative-positive *(p-n-p)*

positiv:[2] **~er Anschluß** *m* ELEKTRIZ positive terminal; **~e Anschlußklemme** *f* KFZTECH plus terminal, positive terminal; **~e Bewertung** *f* MATH plus factor; **~e Bildphase** *f* FERNSEH positive picture phase; **~ dotierter Bereich** *m* PHYS positively doped region; **~e Drehung** *f* ELEKTRIZ positive sequence; **~e Folge** *f* ELEKTRIZ positive sequence; **~er Fotolack** *m* ELEKTRONIK positive photoresist, positive resist; **~e ganze Zahl** *f* MATH positive integer; **~e Gaußsche Krümmung** *f* GEOM positive Gauss curvature; **~ geerdete Anschlußklemme** *f* KFZTECH positive-grounded terminal; **~ geerdeter Pol** *m* KFZTECH positive-grounded terminal; **~es Ion** *nt* ELEKTRIZ, PHYS positive ion; **~e Klemme** *f* ELEKTRIZ positive terminal; **~e Kontaktbank** *f* KFZTECH positive bank; **~e Krümmung** *f* GEOM positive curvature; **~e Ladung** *f* ELEKTRIZ, ELEKTROTECH, PHYS positive charge; **~e Logik** *f* ELEKTRONIK positive logic; **~e Magnetostriktion** *f* ELEKTROTECH positive magnetostriction; **~er Netzanschluß** *m* ELEKTROTECH positive power supply; **~e Phasendrehung** *f* ELEKTRIZ positive phase sequence; **~e Platte** *f* KFZTECH positive plate; **~er Pol** *m* ELEKTRIZ positive pole; **~e Profilverschiebung** *f* FERTIG *Getriebelehre* diameter enlargement; **~er Quadrant** *m* MATH positive quadrant; **~e Quadratwurzel** *f* MATH principal square root; **~e Quittung** *f* COMP & DV positive acknowledgement; **~er Radsturz** *m* KFZTECH positive camber; **~e Rückkopplung** *f* STRAHLPHYS positive feedback; **~e Rückmeldung** *f* COMP & DV positive acknowledgement; **~e Säule** *f* ELEKTRONIK, PHYS positive column; **~er Spanwinkel** *m* FERTIG, MASCHINEN positive rake; **~er Sprung** *m* WASSERTRANS *Bootbau*

normal sheer; **~es Stopfen** *nt* TELEKOM positive justification; **~e Vorspannung** *f* ELEKTROTECH keep-alive voltage, positive bias; **~er Winkel** *m* GEOM positive angle; **~e Zahl** *f* MATH positive number; **nicht ~e Zahlen** *f pl* MATH nonpositive numbers

Positiv: **Positivfilm** *m* DRUCK positive film; **Positiv-Isolierend-Negativ** *(PIN)* ELEKTRONIC positive-isolating negative *(PIN)*; **Positivkopie** *f* DRUCK positive print; **Positivmodulation** *f* ELEKTRONIK positive modulation

Positron *nt* PHYS *Teilchen*, TEILPHYS positron

Post- und Frachtterminal *m* LUFTTRANS mail and cargo terminal

Postambel *f* COMP & DV postamble

Posten *m* WASSERTRANS post; **Postenspeisung** *f* KER & GLAS gob feeding

POS-Terminal *nt (elektronische Kasse)* COMP & DV, VERPACK POS terminal *(point of sale terminal)*

Postfixschreibweise *f* COMP & DV postfix notation

Post-Mortem-Programm *nt* COMP & DV postmortem program

Postprozessor *m* COMP & DV postprocessor; **Postprozessorprogramm** *nt* COMP & DV postprocessor

Postulat *nt* MATH postulate

Postversand: **als ~ verpackt** *adj* LEBENSMITTEL mail-or-der-packed

Postzug *m* EISENBAHN mail train

Potential *nt* ELEKTRIZ, ELEKTROTECH potential, PHYS potential function, potential, RADIO potential; **~ der Schallschnelle** *nt* NICHTFOSS ENERG velocity potential; **Potentialabfall** *m* PHYS potential drop; **Potentialbarriere** *f* ELEKTROTECH, PHYS potential barrier; **Potentialdifferenz** *f* ELEKTRIZ, ELEKTROTECH, PHYS PD, potential difference

potentialfrei: **~er Ausgang** *m* ELEKTROTECH floating output; **~er Eingang** *m* ELEKTROTECH floating input

Potential: **Potentialfunktion** *f* PHYS potential function; **Potentialgefälle** *nt* ELEKTRIZ potential gradient; **Potentialgradient** *m* ELEKTRIZ potential gradient; **Potentialkoeffizienten** *m pl* PHYS coefficients of potential; **Potentialring** *m* PHYS guard ring; **Potentialschlinge** *f* ELEKTRIZ potential loop; **Potentialschranke** *f* ELEKTROTECH potential barrier; **Potentialschwelle** *f* ELEKTROTECH, PHYS potential barrier; **Potentialtopf** *m* PHYS potential well; **Potentialverschiebung** *f* ELEKTRONIK level shifting; **Potentialwall** *m* ELEKTROTECH potential barrier

potentiell[1] *adj* ANSTRICH potential

potentiell:[2] **~e Energie** *f* PHYS potential energy; **~e Evapotranspiration** *f* WASSERVERSORG potential evapotranspiration

Potentiometer *nt* AUFNAHME potentiometer, ELEKTRIZ adjustable voltage divider, adjustable resistor, potentiometer, ELEKTRONIK compensator, ELEKTROTECH, FERTIG *Kunststoffinstallationen*, LABOR *Elektrochemie* potentiometer, LUFTTRANS adjusting potentiometer, PAPIER potentiometer, PHYS compensator, potentiometer, RADIO potentiometer; **~ mit numerischer Anzeige** *nt* ELEKTRIZ read-out potentiometer; **Potentiometergeber** *m* GERÄT retransmitting slide wire; **Potentiometer-Gleitkontakt** *m* ELEKTRIZ potentiometer slider; **Potentiometerschleifer** *m* ELEKTRIZ potentiometer slider

potentiometrisch: **~e Ebene** *f* ERDÖL potentiometric level; **~e Höhe** *f* ERDÖL potentiometric head; **~e Karte** *f* ERDÖL potentiometric map; **~er Rheostat** *m* ELEKTRIZ potentiometer rheostat; **~e Titration** *f* CHEMIE electrometric titration

Potenz *f* MATH power; **Potenzgesetzindexfaser** *f* OPTIK power law index fiber (AmE), power law index fibre (BrE); **Potenzgesetzindexprofil** *nt* OPTIK power law index profile

Potenzieren *nt* MATH involution

Potenzierung *f* MATH involution

Potenzprofil *nt* TELEKOM power law index profile

Poti *nt* AUFNAHME pot

Pottasche *f* KER & GLAS potash

Pourpoint *m* KFZTECH *Öl* pour point

p-Oxytoluen *nt* CHEMIE p-cresol

Poynting: **~scher Satz** *m* PHYS Poynting's theorem; **~scher Vektor** *m (S)* ELEKTRIZ, PHYS Poynting vector *(S)*

PP *abbr (Polypropylen)* CHEMIE, ELEKTRIZ, ERDÖL, KUNSTSTOFF, TEXTIL PP *(polypropylene)*

PPI-Anzeige *f (Panoramaanzeige)* PHYS PPI *(plan position indicator)*

PPM *abbr (Pulsphasenmodulation)* COMP & DV, ELEKTRONIK *(Pulsphasenmodulation)* PPM *(pulse phase modulation)* ELEKTRONIK *(Pulslagenmodulation)* PPM *(pulse position modulation)*, TELEKOM *(Pulsphasenmodulation)* PPM *(pulse phase modulation)* TELEKOM *(Pulslagenmodulation)* PPM *(pulse position modulation)*

PP-Schnur *f* VERPACK polypropylene closure, polypropylene strap

PPU *abbr (Peripherietechnik)* COMP & DV PPU *(peripheral processing units)*

Präambel *f* COMP & DV preamble

Prädikat *nt* COMP & DV, KÜNSTL INT predicate; **Prädikatenlogik** *f (PL)* KÜNSTL INT predicate logic *(PL)*

Prädiktion *f* KÜNSTL INT prediction; **Prädiktionscodierung** *f* TELEKOM predictive coding

Präfix *nt* COMP & DV prefix; **Präfixschreibweise** *f* COMP & DV Polish notation, parenthesis-free notation, prefix notation

Präge- *pref* VERPACK, DRUCK imprint; **Präge- und Druckwerkzeug** *nt* VERPACK imprinter; **Prägedruck** *m* DRUCK blocking; **Prägedruck ohne Farbe** *m* DRUCK blind blocking, blind embossing; **Prägeetikett** *nt* VERPACK embossed label; **Prägeform** *f* MASCHINEN coining die, forming die; **Prägekalander** *m* VERPACK embossed calender; **Prägemaschine** *f* DRUCK stamping press

Prägen *nt* FERTIG sizing, KUNSTSTOFF embossing, MASCHINEN coining

prägen *vt* DRUCK mold (AmE), mould (BrE), FERTIG *Münzen* strike

Präge-: **Prägepapier** *nt* VERPACK embossed paper; **Prägepresse** *f* DRUCK stamping press, VERPACK embossing machine, embossing press; **Prägerillen-Aufnahme** *f* AUFNAHME embossed-groove recording; **Prägestempel** *m* FERTIG hob, MASCHINEN coining die, forming die

Pragmatik *f* COMP & DV pragmatics

Prägung *f* DRUCK embossing

Prahm *m* WASSERTRANS *Schifftyp* barge

Praktikum *nt* WASSERTRANS *Dokument* certificate of pratique, pratique

praktisch: **~e Erprobung** *f* MASCHINEN field test; **~e Leistungsfähigkeit** *f* TRANS practical capacity; **~e Leistungsfähigkeit unter ländlichen Bedingungen** *f* TRANS practical capacity under rural conditions; **~e Leistungsfähigkeit unter städtischen Beding-** ungen *f* TRANS practical capacity under urban conditions; **~e Prüfmethode** *f* OPTIK practical test method; **~e Prüfungsmethode** *f* TELEKOM practical test method

Prallblech *nt* FERTIG baffle breaker, KOHLEN impact plate, MASCHINEN baffle plate

Prallblechen: **mit ~ ausstatten** *vt* CHEMTECH baffle

Prallblechring *m* ERDÖL baffle ring

Prallbrecher *m* KOHLEN, MASCHINEN impact crusher

Prallschirm *m* CHEMTECH baffle plate

Prallzerfaserer *m* PAPIER fiberizer (AmE), fibrizer (BrE)

Prandtl: **~sche Grenzschichttheorie** *f* STRÖMPHYS Prandtl's boundary layer theory; **~sche Zahl** *f* STRÖMPHYS Prandtl number

Präparationsmittel *nt* TEXTIL lubricant

präparieren *vt* TEXTIL lubricate

Präpariernadel *f* LABOR dissection needle

Präsentationsgrafik *f* COMP & DV presentation graphics

Präsentierkarton *m* VERPACK display box

Prasseln *nt* AKUSTIK crackle

Pratica *f* WASSERTRANS *Dokument* pratique

Prävention: **~ von Gehörschäden** *f* ERGON hearing conservation

präventiv *adj* ANSTRICH preventive

praxisnah: **~er Versuch** *m* WERKPRÜF field trial

Präzession *f* PHYS, RAUMFAHRT precession; **Präzessionswert** *m* RAUMFAHRT precession rate; **Präzessionswinkel** *m* NICHTFOSS ENERG angle of precession; **Präzessionswinkelgeschwindigkeit** *f* FERTIG angle velocity of precession

Präzipitat *nt* CHEMTECH precipitate

Präzision *f* COMP & DV accuracy, precision, PHYS precision; **Präzisionsanflug** *m* LUFTTRANS precision approach; **Präzisionsanflugverfahren** *nt* LUFTTRANS precision approach procedure; **Präzisionsanzeigeinstrument** *nt* GERÄT precision indicating instrument; **Präzisionsbeschichtung** *f* ANSTRICH precision coating; **Präzisionsdrahtwiderstand** *m* ELEKTROTECH precision wirewound resistor

präzisionsgefertigt: **~e Unterlegscheibe** *f* MASCHINEN precision shim

Präzision: **Präzisionsgrad** *m* METROL class of accuracy; **Präzisionsinstrument** *nt* GERÄT high-accuracy instrument, precision instrument, PHYS precision instrument; **Präzisionslehre** *f* FERTIG precision gage (AmE), precision gauge (BrE); **Präzisionsmeßgerät** *nt* GERÄT high-accuracy instrument; **Präzisionsradareinstufung** *f* LUFTTRANS precision radar rating; **Präzisionsradarstufe** *f* LUFTTRANS precision radar rating; **Präzisionsschleifen** *nt* FERTIG, MASCHINEN precision grinding; **Präzisionsschlitten** *m* MASCHINEN precision slide; **Präzisionswaage** *f* GERÄT precision balance, LABOR balance, sensitive balance; **Präzisionswerkzeugmaschinen** *f pl* MASCHINEN precision machine tools; **Präzisionswiderstand** *m* ELEKTROTECH voltage multiplier; **Präzisionswiegen** *nt* VERPACK ultrahigh accuracy weighing

Preform *f* TELEKOM preform

P-Regler *m* REGELUNG proportional controller

Pregnan *nt* CHEMIE pregnane

Prehnit- *pref* CHEMIE prehnitic; **Prehnitol** *nt* CHEMIE prehnitene

Preis: **~ frei Küste** *m* ERDÖL *Handel* landed price; **Preisauszeichnung** *f* VERPACK prepricing, price marking; **Preisschild** *nt* VERPACK price tag; **Preistabelle** *f* BAU table of prices

Prellblock *m* EISENBAHN buffer stop block
Prellbock *m* EISENBAHN buffer, bumper (BrE), fender (AmE)
Prellplatte *f* BAU baffle
Prepreg *nt* KUNSTSTOFF prepreg
Preßbalken *m* MASCHINEN crosshead
Presse *f* DRUCK press, printing press, FERTIG gun, press, MASCHINEN, PAPIER press, SICHERHEIT power press, TEXTIL press; **~ mit verstellbarem Tisch** *f* FERTIG adjustable bed press
Pressen *nt* AUFNAHME *Schallplatten, CDs* pressing, FERTIG compression molding (AmE), compression moulding (BrE), molding (AmE), moulding (BrE), KER & GLAS, KUNSTSTOFF compression molding (AmE), compression moulding (BrE), MASCHINEN pressing, MECHAN extrusion, TEXTIL pressing, VERPACK compression molding (AmE), compression moulding (BrE)
pressen *vt* AUFNAHME press, FERTIG mold (AmE), mould (BrE), MASCHINEN press, MECHAN jam, PAPIER, TEXTIL press
Presse: **Pressenschleifer** *m* PAPIER pocket grinder; **Pressentisch** *m* KUNSTSTOFF platen; **Pressenwalze** *f* PAPIER press roll
Presser *m* AUFNAHME compressor
Presseur *m* KUNSTSTOFF impression roller
Preßfehler *m* FERTIG pit, KUNSTSTOFF molding defect (AmE), moulding defect (BrE)
Preßfettschmierung *f* FERTIG pressure grease lubrication
Preßfilter *nt* KOHLEN filter press
Preßfläche *f* FERTIG *Plaste* projected area
Preßform *f* KER & GLAS parison mold (AmE), parison mould (BrE), MASCHINEN compression mold (AmE), compression mould (BrE); **Preßformmaschine** *f* FERTIG squeezer
preßgeschweißt: **~es Schutzgitter** *nt* SICHERHEIT pressure-welded safety grating
Preßglas *nt* KER & GLAS molded glass (AmE), moulded glass (BrE), pressed glass; **Preßglasglimmer** *m* ELEKTROTECH *Isolator* glass-bonded mica
Preßgrat *m* KER & GLAS fin, KUNSTSTOFF flash
Pressiometer *nt* KOHLEN pressiometer
Pressionsmetermodul *nt* KOHLEN pressure meter modulus
Preßkammer *f* FERTIG gooseneck
Preßkohle *f* KOHLEN briquette
Preßkolben *m* KFZTECH *Brems- und Kupplungszylinder* plunger
Preßkraft *f* MASCHINEN pressing force
Preßling *m* AKUSTIK, ELEKTROTECH molding (AmE), moulding (BrE), KER & GLAS pressing, KUNSTSTOFF pellet
Preßluft *f* ERDÖL, FERTIG, MASCHINEN, PHYS air; **Preßluftbohren** *nt* ERDÖL air flooding; **Preßluftbohrer** *m* FERTIG, MECHAN, PHYS air drill; **Preßlufteinrichtung** *f* FERTIG air hydraulic unit; **Preßluftfutter** *nt* FERTIG air chuck, air-operated chuck; **Preßlufthammer** *m* FERTIG air hammer, *Schmieden* pneumatic hammer, MASCHINEN pneumatic hammer, MECHAN, PHYS air hammer; **Preßluftnietmaschine** *f* FERTIG pneumatic riveter; **Preßluftschalter** *m* ELEKTRIZ air breaker
Preßmaschine *f* KER & GLAS presser
Preßmassenfüllstoff *m* FERTIG *Schnitzel* macerate
Preßmatte *f* KER & GLAS blanket; **Preßmattenspeiser** *m* KER & GLAS blanket charger; **Preßmattenzuführung** *f*

KER & GLAS blanket feed
Preßmüllwagen *m* ABFALL compactor vehicle, compression vehicle, packer body
Preßnietmaschine *f* FERTIG compression riveter
Preßpappe *f* PAPIER, VERPACK molded board (AmE), moulded board (BrE)
Preßpassung *f* FERTIG press fit, MASCHINEN interference fit, press fit
Preßplatte *f* METALL squeeze head
Preßpulver *nt* KUNSTSTOFF molding powder (AmE), moulding powder (BrE)
Preßschiene *f* TEXTIL presser bar
Preßschweißen *nt* BAU, FERTIG pressure welding, MASCHINEN plastic welding
Preßschweißung *f* MASCHINEN pressure welding
Preßsintern *nt* CHEMTECH sintering under pressure
Preßsitz *m* MECHAN force fit
Preßstempel *m* FERTIG heading tool, KER & GLAS dolly, MASCHINEN die, extrusion die, stamper
Preßteil *nt* AKUSTIK molding (AmE), moulding (BrE), ELEKTROTECH molding (AmE), moulding (BrE), stamping
Pressung *f* MASCHINEN compression
Preßware *f* KER & GLAS pressware
Preßwerkzeug *nt* MASCHINEN press tool
Preßzyklus *m* KUNSTSTOFF molding cycle (AmE), moulding cycle (BrE)
Preventertau *nt* WASSERTRANS *Tauwerk* jumper stay
Priel *m* WASSERTRANS tideway
Primär- *pref* ABFALL, COMP & DV, ELEKTRIZ, ELEKTROTECH, ERDÖL, FERNSEH, FERTIG, HEIZ & KÄLTE, KER & GLAS, KFZTECH, METALL, OPTIK, PAPIER, STRAHLPHYS, TELEKOM, WASSERVERSORG primary
primär: **~er Anker** *m* ELEKTRIZ primary armature; **~er biologischer Schild** *m* KERNTECH primary biological shield; **~e Erdbebenwelle** *f* (*P-Welle*) PHYS P wave; **~e Induktanz** *f* ELEKTRIZ primary inductance; **~es Kältemittel** *nt* HEIZ & KÄLTE primary refrigerant; **~es Kühlmittel** *nt* HEIZ & KÄLTE primary coolant; **~er Mantel** *m* OPTIK *Faser* primary coating; **~er Speicher** *m* COMP & DV primary memory, primary storage, primary store; **~e Spule** *f* KFZTECH primary winding; **~e zyklische Verstellung** *f* LUFTTRANS *Hubschrauber* primary cyclic variation
Primär-: **Primärausdruck** *m* COMP & DV primary expression; **Primärbatterie** *f* ELEKTROTECH primary battery; **Primärbeschichtung** *f* TELEKOM primary coating; **Primärblau** *nt* FERNSEH blue primary; **Primärbremsbacke** *f* KFZTECH primary shoe; **Primärbrennstoffelement** *nt* KFZTECH primary fuel cell; **Primärdatei** *f* COMP & DV primary file; **Primäreinzellinearmotor** *m* KFZTECH single primary type linear motor; **Primärelektrode** *f* ELEKTROTECH initiating electrode; **Primärelement** *nt* ELEKTRIZ galvanic cell, voltaic cell; **Primäremission** *f* ELEKTRONIK primary emission; **Primärfarbe** *f* COMP & DV, DRUCK, OPTIK, PHYS primary color (AmE), primary colour (BrE), STRAHLPHYS prime colors (AmE), prime colours (BrE); **Primärfaser** *f* KER & GLAS primary fiber (AmE), primary fibre (BrE); **Primärfilter** *nt* WASSERVERSORG primary filter; **Primärförderung** *f* ERDÖL primary recovery; **Primärgrün** *nt* FERNSEH green primary; **Primärgruppe** *f* COMP & DV primary group, ELEKTROTECH, TELEKOM group; **Primärgruppenverteiler** *m* TELEKOM group distribution frame; **Primärindex** *m* COMP & DV primary index; **Primärioni-**

sierung *f* STRAHLPHYS primary ionization; **Primärkarbid** *nt* METALL primary carbide; **Primärkettenkasten** *m* KFZTECH *Motorradgetriebe* primary chaincase; **Primärkornbildung** *f* FERTIG ingotism; **Primärkriechen** *nt* METALL primary creep; **Primärkühlkreislauf** *m* KERNTECH primary coolant circuit; **Primärlichtquelle** *f* STRAHLPHYS illuminating source; **Primärluft** *f* HEIZ & KÄLTE primary air; **Primärmanschette** *f* KFZTECH primary cup; **Primärmantel** *m* OPTIK *Faser* primary coating; **Primärmultiplexanschluß** *m* TELEKOM PRA, primary rate access; **Primärratenanschluß** *m* TELEKOM *ISDN* PRA, primary rate access; **Primärrot** *nt* FERNSEH red primary; **Primärschlamm** *m* ABFALL primary sludge; **Primärschlüssel** *m* COMP & DV primary key; **Primärspannung** *f* ELEKTRIZ, ELEKTROTECH primary voltage; **Primärspeicher** *m* COMP & DV primary memory; **Primärspule** *f* ELEKTROTECH primary; **Primärstation** *f* COMP & DV primary station; **Primärstoffauflauf** *m* PAPIER primary headbox; **Primärstrahlung** *f* KERNTECH primary radiation; **Primärstrom** *m* ELEKTRIZ, ELEKTROTECH primary current; **Primärstromkreis** *m* ELEKTRIZ primary circuit; **Primärteilchen** *nt* ELEKTROTECH *Transformator* primary particle; **Primärwicklung** *f* ELEKTRIZ primary winding, ELEKTROTECH primary winding, *Transformator* primary, KFZTECH, PHYS primary winding, RADIO *Transformator* primary; **Primärwicklung mit Anzapfung** *f* ELEKTROTECH tapped primary winding; **Primärzelle** *f* ELEKTROTECH primary cell; **Primärzugriff** *m* TELEKOM primary access

Primer *m* KUNSTSTOFF primer
Primfaktor *m* MATH prime factor
Primulin *nt* CHEMIE primuline yellow
Primzahl *f* MATH prime number
Primzahligkeit *f* MATH primeness
Printplatte *f* (*PCB*) COMP & DV printed circuit board (*PCB*)
Prinzip *nt* PHYS principle; **~ von Addition und Teilen** *nt* ELEKTRONIK *Frequenzsynthese* add-and-divide principle; **~ der ergonomischen Entwicklung** *nt* SICHERHEIT ergonomic design principle; **~ des gefahrlosen Ausfalls** *nt* QUAL fail-safe; **~ der kleinsten Wirkung** *nt* PHYS principle of least action; **~ des kleinsten Zwanges** *nt* PHYS principle of least constraint; **~ der virtuellen Arbeit** *nt* PHYS principle of virtual work; **Prinzipschaltbild** *nt* FERTIG elementary circuit diagram

Priorität *f* COMP & DV precedence, priority, PATENT priority; **Prioritätplaner** *m* COMP & DV priority scheduler; **Prioritätrecht** *nt* PATENT priority right; **Prioritätsteuerung** *f* COMP & DV priority scheduling; **Prioritätstufe** *f* COMP & DV precedence level; **Prioritätventil** *nt* HYDRAUL priority valve; **Prioritätverkettung** *f* ELEKTRONIK daisy chain; **Prioritätverlust** *m* PATENT loss of priority; **Prioritätwarteschlange** *f* COMP & DV priority queue

Prisenkommando *nt* WASSERTRANS boarding party
Prisma *nt* FERTIG solid vee, vee, GEOM, KER & GLAS, LABOR, PHYS, TELEKOM prism
prismatisch *adj* GEOM prismatic
Prismenbinokular *nt* OPTIK prism binocular
Prismenblock *m* METROL vee block
Prismenfräser *m* FERTIG equal-angle cutter, MASCHINEN V-form cutter, double equal angle cutter
Prismenglas *nt* KER & GLAS prismatic glass
Prismenspektrograph *m* STRAHLPHYS prismatic spectrograph

Prismenspektrum *nt* STRAHLPHYS prismatic spectrum
Prismenstück *nt* FERTIG V-block
Pritschenwagen *m* KFZTECH pick-up, platform truck (AmE)
privat: **~e Datenleitung** *f* TELEKOM data private wire; **~es Fernsprechnetz** *nt* TELEKOM private telephone network; **~es Netz** *nt* TELEKOM private network; **~er Numerierungsplan** *m* TELEKOM private numbering plan; **~e Selbstwählnebenstelle** *f* (*PBX*) TELEKOM private branch exchange (*PBX*); **~er Wählanschluß** *m* TELEKOM private dial-up port
Privatfahrzeug *nt* KFZTECH private vehicle
Privatfernsehen *nt* FERNSEH commercial TV
Privatgüterwagen *m* EISENBAHN privately owned wagon
privilegiert: **~er Account** *m* COMP & DV privileged account; **~er Befehl** *m* COMP & DV privileged instruction; **~e Operation** *f* COMP & DV privileged operation
pro: **~ Einheitsfläche** *adj* PHYS per unit area; **~ Einheitslänge** *adj* PHYS per unit length; **~ Einheitsmasse** *adj* PHYS per unit mass; **~ Stunde** *adj* VERPACK *Ausgabe* hourly
probabilistisch *adj* KÜNSTL INT probabilistic
Probe[1] *f* GERÄT specimen, KOHLEN, KUNSTSTOFF sample, specimen, MASCHINEN specimen, test specimen, MECHAN specimen, METALL representative sample, sample, PHYS sample, QUAL sample, test, specimen, RAUMFAHRT, TELEKOM sample, TEXTIL trial, WASSERVERSORG sample, WERKPRÜF sampling; **~ mit Seiteneinschnitt** *f* METALL side-grooved specimen
Probe:[2] **~ nehmen** *vi* PHYS take a sample
Probe: Probeabzug *m* DRUCK prepress proof, proof, FOTO proof, test print; **Probeaufnahme** *f* FOTO test shot; **Probebelastung** *f* MASCHINEN test loading; **Probebohrung mit Spülung** *f* KOHLEN wash boring; **Probedrucke** *m pl* DRUCK prepress proofs; **Probedrukke für die Farbseparierung** *m pl* DRUCK separation proofs; **Probeentnahmen gleicher Menge** *f* UMWELTSCHMUTZ constant-volume sampling; **Probekörper** *m* KUNSTSTOFF sample; **Probelast** *f* MASCHINEN test loading; **Probelauf** *m* BAU trial run, COMP & DV dry run, KERNTECH proving run, proving trial, trial run, MASCHINEN test run; **Probelöffel** *m* BAU spoon auger; **Probenahme** *f* ABFALL, ERDÖL, LEBENSMITTEL, PHYS, QUAL, TELEKOM sampling; **Probenahme-Gerät** *nt* LABOR sampling device; **Probenbehälter** *m* KERNTECH sample holder, *Massenspektrometer* sample admission vessel; **Probenehmer** *m* COMP & DV sampler; **Probenentnahme** *f* ELEKTRONIK, RAUMFAHRT, WASSERVERSORG, WERKPRÜF sampling; **Probenentnahmeröhrchen** *nt* LABOR sampling tube; **Probenentnahmestelle** *f* KOHLEN sampling point; **Probengröße** *f* METROL sample size; **Probenhalter** *m* KERNTECH specimen holder; **Probenplan** *m* METROL sampling plan; **Probensatz** *m* GERÄT sampling theorem; **Probenschwenkarm** *m* KERNTECH sample swivel arm; **Probenstrom** *m* GERÄT *von Fluiden* sample stream; **Probenverkleinerung** *f* QUAL sample reduction; **Probenwechsler** *m* KERNTECH sample changer
Probe: Probepfahl *m* KOHLEN test pile; **Prober** *m* KOHLEN sampler; **Proberöhrchen** *nt* LABOR test tube; **Proberöhrchengestell** *nt* LABOR test tube rack; **Proberöhrchenhalter** *m* LABOR test tube holder; **Probeseiten** *f pl* DRUCK page proofs; **Probesilber** *nt* METALL standard silver; **Probestab** *m* MASCHINEN test bar;

Probestreifen *m* FOTO test strip; **Probestück** *nt* GERÄT, KOHLEN, KUNSTSTOFF, MASCHINEN, MECHAN, QUAL specimen; **Probetiegel** *m* FERTIG cupel

probeweise: ~ **Prüfung** *f* QUAL sampling test

Probe: **Probewürfel** *m* BAU test cube; **Probezylinder** *m* BAU test cylinder

probieren *vt* PHYS sample

Probierhahn *m* WASSERVERSORG gage cock (AmE), gauge cock (BrE), test cock, try cock

Probierofen *m* HEIZ & KÄLTE assay furnace

Probierstift *m* MASCHINEN touch needle

Problem *nt* COMP & DV, KÜNSTL INT problem; **Problembehebung** *f* COMP & DV problem recovery; **Problembeschreibung** *f* COMP & DV problem description; **Problembestimmung** *f* COMP & DV problem determination; **Problemdarstellung** *f* KÜNSTL INT problem representation; **Problemdefinition** *f* COMP & DV problem definition; **Problemdiagnose** *f* COMP & DV problem determination; **Problemlösen** *nt* KÜNSTL INT problem solving; **Problemlösungsstrategie** *f* KÜNSTL INT problem solving strategy; **Problemlösungsvorgang** *m* KÜNSTL INT problem solving

problemorientiert: ~**e Programmiersprache** *f* COMP & DV problem-oriented language; ~**e Programmiersprache für Geschäftsbetrieb** *f (COBOL)* COMP & DV common business oriented language *(COBOL)*; ~**e Software** *f* COMP & DV problem-oriented software

Procain *nt* CHEMIE procaine

Proctor-Prüfung *f* BAU Proctor test

Proctor-Versuch *m* KOHLEN Proctor compaction test

Produkt *nt* COMP & DV, MATH *einer Kalkulation* product; **Produktdetektor** *m* RADIO product detector; **Produktentwicklung** *f* COMP & DV product design

Produktion *f* COMP & DV production, KERNTECH output, MASCHINEN production, NICHTFOSS ENERG yield; ~ **pro Flächeneinheit** *f* KER & GLAS production per unit area; **Produktions- und Fertigungstechnik** *f* ERGON industrial engineering; **Produktionsabfall** *m* ABFALL process waste; **Produktionsausbeute** *f* ELEKTRONIK fabrication yield; **Produktionsband** *nt* KONTROLL line, production line; **Produktionsbericht** *m* COMP & DV production statement; **Produktionsbohrung** *f* ERDÖL *Fördertechnik* production well; **Produktionsdrehmaschine** *f* FERTIG manufacturing lathe, MASCHINEN production lathe; **Produktionseinrichtungen** *f pl* FERNSEH production facilities; **Produktionskolonne** *f* ERDÖL *Fördertechnik* production string; **Produktionskonsole** *f* FERNSEH production console; **Produktionsmenge** *f* PAPIER output; **Produktionsphase** *f* ERDÖL *Fördertechnik* production phase; **Produktionsplattform** *f* ERDÖL *Fördertechnik* production platform; **Produktionsregel** *f* KÜNSTL INT condition-action rule, if-then rule, production rule; **Produktionsregieraum** *m* FERNSEH production control room

produktionsspezifisch: ~**er Abfall** *m* ABFALL process waste

Produktion: **Produktionsstätte** *f* MECHAN fabricating shop; **Produktionssystem** *nt* KÜNSTL INT production system

Produktivzeit *f* COMP & DV productive time

produzieren *vt* FERNSEH produce

Profil *nt* ANSTRICH, COMP & DV profile, FERTIG form (AmE), KFZTECH *Reifen* tread, MASCHINEN outline, profile, section, PHYS profile; **Profil-** *pref* MASCHINEN sectional; **Profilbauch** *m* PHYS lower surface; **Profilbe-**

zugslinie *f* MASCHINEN pitch line; **Profildichtung** *f* KFZTECH gasket, MASCHINEN gasket, profiled gasket; **Profildispersion** *f* OPTIK, TELEKOM profile dispersion; **Profildispersionskoeffizient** *m* TELEKOM profile dispersion parameter; **Profileisenträger** *m* BAU beam; **Profilfräsen** *nt* MASCHINEN form milling, profile milling; **Profilfräsmaschine** *f* MASCHINEN profile-milling machine, profiler; **Profilglas** *nt* KER & GLAS bent glass; **Profilleiter** *m* ELEKTRIZ sector-shaped conductor; **Profilrolle mit ausgearbeitetem Profil** *f* FERTIG crusher roll; **Profilschleifen** *nt* MASCHINEN profile grinding, profiling; **Profilschleifer** *m* MASCHINEN profile grinder; **Profilschnitt** *m* KONSTZEICH removed section; **Profilsehne** *f* LUFTTRANS aerofoil chord (BrE), airfoil chord (AmE), chord; **Profilsehnenteil des Fachwerks** *nt* LUFTTRANS chord member of a truss; **Profilstahl** *m* MASCHINEN section steel, WASSERTRANS *Schiffbau* steel section; **Profiltiefe** *f* LUFTTRANS chord ratio; **Profiltiefenmesser** *m* KFZTECH *Reifen* tread depth gauge; **Profilton** *m* KER & GLAS tread clay; **Profilüberdeckung** *f* MASCHINEN transverse contact ratio; **Profilverschiebung** *f* FERTIG addendum correction, addendum modification, addendum shift, *Zahnrad* correction; **Profilverschiebung eines Diameters** *f* FERTIG *Getriebelehre* diameter increment; **Profilverschiebungsfaktor** *m* FERTIG addendum coefficient, addendum modification coefficient

profilwalzen *vt* FERTIG roll-form

Profil: **Profilwiderstand** *m* LUFTTRANS profile drag; **Profilziehverfahren** *nt* KUNSTSTOFF *Extrusion* pultrusion

Progesteron *nt* CHEMIE progesterone

Progestin *nt* CHEMIE progesterin

Prognose *f* COMP & DV forecasting, KÜNSTL INT prediction, WASSERVERSORG forecasting; **Prognosesystem** *nt* KÜNSTL INT prediction system

Prognostizierungsfähigkeit *f* KÜNSTL INT *Expertensystem* what-if capability

Programm[1] *nt* COMP & DV routine, software, FERNSEH program (AmE), programme (BrE), TELEKOM program; ~ **zur Ablaufverfolgung** *nt* COMP & DV trace program

Programm:[2] **ins** ~ **aufnehmen** *vt* FERNSEH program (AmE), programme (BrE)

Programm: **Programmabbruch** *m* COMP & DV program abort; **Programmablaufanlage** *f* COMP & DV object machine; **Programmablaufrechner** *m* COMP & DV object computer; **Programmablaufverfolgung** *f* COMP & DV trace; **Programmabsturz** *m* COMP & DV crash, program crash; **Programmänderung** *f* COMP & DV program patch; **Programmanforderung** *f* COMP & DV program request; **Programmanweisung** *f* COMP & DV program statement; **Programmaufruf** *m* COMP & DV program request; **Programmausführung** *f* COMP & DV program execution, run; **Programmausrüstung** *f* COMP & DV software; **Programmbaustein** *m* COMP & DV program unit; **Programmbefehl** *m* COMP & DV program instruction; **Programmbereich** *m* COMP & DV partition; **Programmbewertungs- und - Überprüfungsverfahren** *nt (PERT)* COMP & DV, RAUMFAHRT program evaluation and review technique *(PERT)*; **Programmbibliothek** *f* COMP & DV program library; **Programmdatei** *f* COMP & DV program file; **Programmdokumentation** *f* COMP & DV program documentation; **Programmdurchlauf** *m* COMP & DV program run; **Programmeinheit** *f* COMP & DV program unit; **Programmende** *nt* COMP & DV end of program; **Pro-**

grammentwicklung *f* COMP & DV program development; **Programmentwurf** *m* COMP & DV program design; **Programmfehler** *m* COMP & DV bug, *virtuelle Maschinen* program check; **Programmfolge** *f* COMP & DV suite of programs; **Programmfunktionssymbol** *nt* COMP & DV soft key; **Programmgeber** *m* ELEKTROTECH sequencer; **Programmgenerator** *m* COMP & DV program generator

Programme: alle ~ laufen *phr* COMP & DV all programs run

programmgesteuert[1] *adj* COMP & DV software-driven

programmgesteuert:[2] **~e Ausspeicherung** *f* COMP & DV memory dump; **~er Rechner** *m* TELEKOM stored program computer (AmE), stored programme computer (BrE); **~e Selbstwählnebenstelle** *f* TELEKOM stored program control PABX (AmE), stored programme control PABX (BrE); **~e Vermittlungsstelle** *f* TELEKOM stored program control exchange (AmE), stored programme control exchange (BrE)

Programm: **Programmgruppe** *f* COMP & DV suite of programs; **Programmhandbuch** *nt* COMP & DV documentation

programmierbar[1] *adj* KONTROLL programmable

programmierbar:[2] **nicht ~e Datenstation** *f* COMP & DV dumb terminal; **~er Doppelbasistransistor** *m* ELEKTRONIK programmable unijunction transistor; **~e Einheit** *f* COMP & DV programmable device; **~e Folgesteuerung** *f* TELEKOM programmable sequencer; **~es Gerät** *nt* COMP & DV, TELEKOM programmable device; **~er Lesespeicher** *m (PROM)* COMP & DV, RADIO programmable read-only memory *(PROM)*; **~e Logikanordnung** *f (PLA)* COMP & DV programmable logic array *(PLA)*; **~e logische Anordnung** *f (PAL)* COMP & DV programmable array logic *(PAL)*; **~es logisches Feld** *nt* COMP & DV programmable logic array; **~er logischer Schaltkreis** *m* TELEKOM programmable logic circuit; **~er Oszillator** *m* ELEKTRONIK programmable oscillator; **~er Regler** *m* LABOR programmable controller; **~er Signalgenerator** *m* ELEKTRONIK programmable signal generator; **~er Speicher** *m* COMP & DV programmable memory; **~e Speichersteuerung** *f* KONTROLL programmable memory control; **~es Steuergerät** *nt* LABOR programmable controller; **~e Steuerung** *f* COMP & DV, TELEKOM programmable control; **~e Taste** *f* COMP & DV programmable key

Programmieren *nt* COMP & DV programming

programmieren *vt* COMP & DV, TELEKOM program

Programmierentwicklungssystem *nt* COMP & DV software tool

Programmierer *m* COMP & DV programmer; **Programmierereinheit** *f* COMP & DV programmer unit

Programmiergerät *nt* COMP & DV programmer

Programmierhilfe *f* COMP & DV software tool

Programmiersprache *f* COMP & DV programming language

Programmierstandarten *m pl* COMP & DV programming standards

programmiert[1] *adj* COMP & DV programmed

programmiert:[2] **~e Anweisung** *f* ERGON programmed instruction; **~er Halt** *m* COMP & DV program stop; **~er Regler** *m* FERNSEH programmed control; **~es Servosystem** *nt* RAUMFAHRT *Weltraumfunk* programmed servosystem; **~er Verbrennungsmotor** *m* KFZTECH programmed combustion engine; **~e Werkzeuge** *nt pl (APT)* COMP & DV automatically programmed tools *(APT)*

Programmierung: ~ mit minimaler Zugriffszeit *f* COMP & DV minimum-access programming

Programmierwerkzeug *nt* COMP & DV software tool

Programm: **Programmkompatibilität** *f* COMP & DV program compatibility; **Programmkosten** *f pl* FERNSEH program cost (AmE), programme cost (BrE); **Programmlauf** *m* COMP & DV program run; **Programmliste** *f* COMP & DV program listing; **Programmodifikation** *f* COMP & DV preparation; **Programmpaket** *nt* COMP & DV package; **Programmparameter** *m* COMP & DV program parameter; **Programmpflege** *f* COMP & DV program maintenance; **Programmprüfung** *f* COMP & DV program testing, *Basissystem* program check; **Programmrumpf** *m* COMP & DV program body; **Programmsatz** *m* COMP & DV sentence; **Programmschalter** *m* COMP & DV sense switch; **Programmspeichersteuerung** *f* ELEKTRIZ *(SPS)* stored program control *(SPC)*, TELEKOM stored program control (AmE), stored programme control (BrE); **Programmspezifikation** *f* COMP & DV program specification; **Programmsprache** *f* COMP & DV language; **Programmstapel** *m* COMP & DV program stack; **Programmstatuswort** *nt* COMP & DV PSW, program status word; **Programmsteuerung** *f* COMP & DV program control; **Programmstruktur** *f* COMP & DV program structure; **Programmsynthese** *f* KÜNSTL INT program synthesis; **Programmteil** *m* COMP & DV program part; **Programmtest** *m* COMP & DV program testing; **Programmtesten** *nt* COMP & DV program checkout; **Programmtonspur** *f* FERNSEH programme audio track; **Programmumsetzer** *m* FERNSEH program repeater (AmE), programme repeater (BrE); **Programmunterlagen** *f pl* COMP & DV program documentation

Programmverbindung[1] *f* COMP & DV link editing

Programmverbindung:[2] **~ herstellen** *vi* COMP & DV link-edit

Programmverbindung: **Programmverbindungssoftware** *f* COMP & DV linkage software

Programm: **Programmverifikation** *f* COMP & DV program verification; **Programmverknüpfung** *f* COMP & DV linkage, program linking; **Programmverschiebung** *f* COMP & DV program relocation; **Programmverzahnung** *f* COMP & DV multiprogramming; **Programmverzahnungssystem** *nt* COMP & DV multiprogramming system; **Programmverzweigung** *f* COMP & DV branch; **Programmverzweigungspunkt** *m* ELEKTRONIK *Programmablauf* branch point; **Programmwähler** *m* TELEKOM programme selector; **Programmwiederaufnahme** *f* COMP & DV fall-back recovery; **Programmzähler** *m* COMP & DV program counter; **Programmzeituhr** *f* LABOR program timer (AmE), programme timer (BrE); **Programmzuführungskabel** *nt* TELEKOM *Kabelfernsehen* trunk cable; **Programmzweig** *m* COMP & DV program branch, ELEKTRONIK branch

progressiv: ~e Alterung *f* KUNSTSTOFF progressive ageing (BrE), progressive aging (AmE); **~e Zeilensprungabtastung** *f* FERNSEH progressive interlace

Progressivsystem *nt* TRANS progressive system

Projekt *nt* COMP & DV project; **Projektänderung** *f* BAU variation order; **Projektentwurf** *m* MASCHINEN project design

projektieren *vt* COMP & DV project

Projektion *f* BAU, DRUCK, PHYS *eines Vektors* projection;

Projektionsdiode *f* ELEKTRONIK projection diode; **Projektionsebene** *f* GEOM plane of projection, projection plane; **Projektionsfläche** *f* BAU projected area; **Projektionslampe** *f* FOTO projector lamp; **Projektionslänge** *f* BAU projection length; **Projektionslinie** *f* KONSTZEICH projection line; **Projektionslithografie** *f* ELEKTRONIK projection lithography; **Projektionsmethode** *f* KONSTZEICH first angle projection method, projection method; **Projektionsobjektiv** *nt* FOTO projection lens; **Projektionsrichtung** *f* GEOM direction of projection; **Projektionsskaleninstrument** *nt* GERÄT projected-scale instrument; **Projektionsskalenmeßgerät** *nt* GERÄT projected-scale instrument; **Projektionsstrahl** *m* GEOM projection ray;
projektiv: **~e Geometrie** *f* GEOM projective geometry
Projektor *m* FOTO projector
Projekt: **Projektsteuerung** *f* RAUMFAHRT *Raumschiff* project controller; **Projektstudie** *f* COMP & DV feasibility study; **Projektüberwacher** *m* RAUMFAHRT *Raumschiff* project controller; **Projektüberwachung** *f* BAU project monitoring; **Projektzeichnung** *f* KONSTZEICH project drawing
PROM *abbr (programmierbarer Lesespeicher)* COMP & DV, RADIO PROM *(programmable read-only memory)*
Promenadendeck *nt* WASSERTRANS hurricane deck, promenade deck
Promethium *nt (Pm)* CHEMIE promethium *(Pm)*
PROM: **PROM-Programmierer** *m* COMP & DV PROM programmer; **PROM-Programmiergerät** *nt* COMP & DV PROM burner
Prompt *nt* COMP & DV prompt
prompt: **~e Gammastrahlung** *f* KERNTECH, STRAHLPHYS prompt gamma radiation; **~es Neutron** *nt* PHYS prompt neutron; **~es Neutronen** *nt pl* KERNTECH, STRAHLPHYS prompt neutrons
prompt-kritisch *adj* KERNTECH prompt-critical
Pronation *f* ERGON pronation
Prontosil *nt* CHEMIE prontosil
Pronyscher: **~ Zaum** *m* KFZTECH, MASCHINEN Prony brake
Propadien *nt* CHEMIE allene, propadiene
Propagator *m* PHYS propagator
Propagierung *f* KÜNSTL INT propagation
Propan *nt* ERDÖL *Petrochemie* propane; **Propanamin** *nt* CHEMIE aminopropane, propylamine; **Propandiamid** *nt* CHEMIE malonamide, propanediamide; **Propanflasche** *f* SICHERHEIT propane cylinder; **Propanol** *nt* CHEMIE isopropanol, propanol; **Propanon** *nt* CHEMIE acetone, propanone; **Propantanker** *m* ERDÖL *Schiffahrt* propane tanker; **Propantankschiff** *nt* ERDÖL propane tanker
Propeller *m* LUFTTRANS airscrew, screw, MASCHINEN, MEERSCHMUTZ, PAPIER propeller, WASSERTRANS *Schiffbau* propeller, *Schiffantrieb* screw; **~ mit konstanter Drehzahl** *m* LUFTTRANS constant-speed propeller; **~ mit umkehrbarer Steigung** *m* WASSERTRANS reversible pitch propeller; **~ mit veränderlicher Steigung** *m* LUFTTRANS, WASSERTRANS variable-pitch air propeller; **Propellerantrieb** *m* LUFTTRANS propeller drive; **Propellernabe** *f* WASSERTRANS *Schiffbau* propeller hub; **Propellernuß** *f* WASSERTRANS *Schiffbau* propeller boss; **Propellerrelais** *nt* LUFTTRANS *Flugzeug* propeller relay unit; **Propellerschleppdrehmoment** *nt* LUFTTRANS windmill torque; **Propellerschub** *m* LUFTTRANS propeller thrust; **Propellersteigung** *f* LUFTTRANS propeller pitch; **Propellerturbine** *f* LUFT-

TRANS turbopropeller, MASCHINEN propeller turbine; **Propellerturbinenluftstrahlflugzeug** *nt* LUFTTRANS propeller turbine plane; **Propellerwelle** *f* LUFTTRANS, WASSERTRANS *Schiffbau* propeller shaft
Propen *nt* CHEMIE, ERDÖL *Petrochemie* propene, propylene
Propenyl- *nt* CHEMIE isopropenyl, propenyl
Propin *nt* CHEMIE allylene, methylacetylene, propyne
Propiol- *pref* CHEMIE propynoic
Proportion *f* GEOM, MATH proportion; **~ von Energie aus Kernkraftwerken** *f* ELEKTRIZ, KERNTECH nuclear tranche
proportional: **~e Kapazität** *f* ELEKTROTECH straight line capacitance; **~ wirkender Abschwächer** *m* FOTO proportional reducer
proportional: **~ zu** *adj* MATH in proportion to
Proportional- *pref* MATH proportional; **Proportionalabweichung** *f* ELEKTRONIK droop; **Proportionalarm** *m* ELEKTRIZ proportionate arm; **Proportionalbeiwert** *m* REGELUNG proportional coefficient; **Proportional-Differential-Regelung** *f* *(PD-Regelung)* LABOR proportional plus derivative control *(PD control)*; **Proportional-Differential-Regler** *m* *(PD-Regler)* LABOR proportional plus derivative controller *(PD controller)*; **Proportional-Differential-Verhalten** *nt* *(PD-Verhalten)* REGELUNG proportional plus derivative action *(PD action)*; **Proportionalglied** *nt* REGELUNG proportional element; **Proportional-Integral-Differential-Regler** *m* *(PID-Regler, PID-Steuerung)* LABOR proportional plus integral plus derivative controller *(PID controller)*; **Proportional-Integral-Differential-Verhalten** *nt* *(PID-Verhalten)* LABOR proportional plus integral plus derivative action *(PID action)*; **Proportional-Integral-Regler** *m* *(PI-Regler)* LABOR proportional plus integral controller *(PI controller)*; **Proportional-Integral-Verhalten** *nt* *(PI-Verhalten)* LABOR proportional plus integral action *(PI action)*; **Proportionalkammer** *f* TEILPHYS proportional chamber; **Proportionalzähler** *m* PHYS, TEILPHYS proportional counter
Propyl- *pref* CHEMIE propyl; **Propylamin** *nt* CHEMIE aminopropane, propylamine
Propylen *nt* CHEMIE, ERDÖL *Petrochemie* propene, propylene
Propylpiperidin *nt* CHEMIE conicine, coniine, propylpiperidine
Propynyl- *pref* CHEMIE propargyl, propynyl
Prospekt *m* FERTIG *Kunststoffinstallationen* brochure
Prospektion *f* ERDÖL *Lagerstättensuche* prospecting
Protease *f* CHEMIE protease
Proteinfasern *f pl* TEXTIL protein fibers (AmE), protein fibres (BrE)
proteinspaltend: **~es Enzym** *nt* CHEMIE protease
proteolytisch: **~es Enzym** *nt* CHEMIE protease
Protokoll *nt* COMP & DV log, protocol, trace, DRUCK protocol, KONTROLL record, RADIO, TELEKOM protocol; **Protokollausgabe** *f* COMP & DV recording output; **Protokollbereich** *m* COMP & DV bucket; **Protokollhierarchie** *f* COMP & DV protocol hierarchy
protokollieren *vt* COMP & DV log, KONTROLL record
Protokoll: **Protokollkonverter** *m* TELEKOM protocol converter; **Protokollumsetzer** *m* COMP & DV, TELEKOM protocol converter
Protolyse *f* CHEMIE protolysis
Proton *nt (p)* KERNTECH, PHYS *Elementarteilchen*, RADIO, TEILPHYS proton *(p)*;

Protonenabsorptionsfähigkeit *f* UMWELTSCHMUTZ proton-absorptive capacity; **Protoneneinstrahlung** *f* RAUMFAHRT proton irradiation; **Protonenmasse** *f (mp)* KERNTECH proton mass *(mp)*; **Protonenzahl** *f* KERNTECH *(P)* proton number *(P)*, TEILPHYS proton number

Protopektin *nt* CHEMIE pectose

Prototyp *m* COMP & DV, ELEKTRIZ, MASCHINEN, WASSERTRANS prototype; **Prototypenbau** *m* MASCHINEN prototype construction; **Prototypstadium** *nt* STRAHLPHYS prototype stage

Protuberanz *f* RAUMFAHRT solar flare

Proviant[1] *m* WASSERTRANS provisions

Proviant:[2] **mit ~ versehen** *vt* WASSERTRANS provision

Proximity-Log *nt* ERDÖL *Meßtechnik* proximity log

Prozedur *f* COMP & DV procedure; **Prozedurbibliothek** *f* COMP & DV procedure library; **Prozedurname** *m* COMP & DV procedure name; **Prozedurteil** *nt* COMP & DV procedure division; **Prozedurvereinbarungsanweisung** *f* COMP & DV declarative statement; **Prozedurvereinbarungssatz** *m* COMP & DV declarative sentence; **Prozedurvereinbarungsteil** *m* COMP & DV declarative section

Prozentrelais *nt* ELEKTROTECH biased relay

Prozentsatz *m* MATH percentage; **~ fehlerhafter Einheiten** *m* QUAL percent defective

prozentual: ~e Beeinträchtigung des Hörvermögens *f* AKUSTIK percent impairment of hearing; **~er Gehalt** *m* METALL percentage; **~es Kippen** *nt* FERNSEH percentage tilt; **~er Modulationsgrad** *m* ELEKTRONIK percentage modulation; **~e Synchronisation** *f* FERNSEH percentage synchronization; **~e Zusammensetzung** *f* KER & GLAS percentage composition

Prozeß *m* COMP & DV, KOHLEN, PAPIER process

prozeßabhängig: ~e Ablaufsteuerung *f* REGELUNG process-oriented sequential control

Prozeß: Prozeßaussetzung *f* COMP & DV process suspension; **Prozeßautomatisierung** *f* COMP & DV process automation; **Prozeßdatenverarbeitung** *f* COMP & DV process control; **Prozeßeintrag** *m* COMP & DV process entry; **Prozeßfarben** *f pl* DRUCK process colours; **Prozeßführung** *f* KONTROLL process management; **Prozeßgas** *nt* KOHLEN process gas

prozeßintegriert *adj* METROL in-process

Prozeß: Prozeßmeßgröße *f* GERÄT measured process quantity; **Prozeßmeßwert** *m* GERÄT process value

Prozessor:[1] **durch den ~ begrenzt** *adj* COMP & DV processor-limited

Prozessor[2] *m* COMP & DV, TELEKOM processor; **~ für Datenfernübertragung** *m* TELEKOM communications processor; **~ mit komplettem Befehlssatz** *m (CISC)* COMP & DV complex instruction set computer *(CISC)*

prozessorgesteuert: ~e Eingabe *f* COMP & DV processor-controlled keying

Prozessor: Prozessorspeicher *m* COMP & DV processor storage; **Prozessorstatuswort** *nt* COMP & DV PSW, processor status word; **Prozessorzwischenverbindung** *f* TELEKOM interprocessor link

Prozeß: Prozeßprüfung *f* QUAL process inspection; **Prozeßsignalformer** *m* REGELUNG receiver element; **Prozeßsteuerung** *f* COMP & DV, ELEKTRIZ, ELEKTROTECH, ERGON, KONTROLL, TELEKOM process control; **Prozeßunterbrechung** *f* COMP & DV process interrupt; **Prozeßvariable** *f* MASCHINEN process variable; **Prozeßwert** *m* GERÄT process value

Prüf- *pref* COMP & DV, ELEKTROTECH, GERÄT, QUAL inspection, test, VERPACK check, WERKPRÜF inspection, test; **~ und Kontrollpunkt** *m* QUAL inspection and test point; **~ und Meßmittel** *nt pl* QUAL measuring and test equipment; **Prüfablauf** *m* QUAL inspection and test sequence, test run, test sequence; **Prüfablaufplan** *m* QUAL inspection and test schedule, inspection and test sequence plan, inspection schedule; **Prüfanlage** *f* WERKPRÜF test rig; **Prüfanordnung** *f* GERÄT calibration set-up, QUAL test and examination sequence plan, test set-up; **Prüfanstalt** *f* QUAL testing laboratory; **Prüfanweisung** *f* QUAL inspection instruction, test instruction; **Prüfaufkleber** *m* QUAL inspection sticker; **Prüfaufzeichnung** *f* QUAL inspection and test records; **Prüfbeanspruchung** *f* MASCHINEN proof stress; **Prüfbecher** *m* LABOR flow cup; **Prüfbedingungen** *f pl* QUAL, VERPACK test conditions; **Prüfbericht** *m* METROL inspection record, QUAL inspection record, inspection report, test record, test report; **Prüfbescheinigung** *f* QUAL inspection certificate, test certificate; **Prüfbestätigung** *f* QUAL test certificate; **Prüfbetrieb** *m* QUAL testing shop; **Prüfbit** *nt* COMP & DV check bit, parity bit, ELEKTRONIK check bit; **Prüfblech** *nt* HYDRAUL test plate; **Prüfbrett** *nt* ELEKTRIZ test board; **Prüfcheckliste** *f* QUAL inspection checklist; **Prüfdaten** *nt pl* COMP & DV test data; **Prüfdatengenerator** *m* COMP & DV test data generator; **Prüfdraht** *m* ELEKTROTECH pilot wire; **Prüfdruck** *m* HYDRAUL test pressure, MASCHINEN proof pressure; **Prüfeinrichtung** *f* GERÄT calibration equipment, test equipment; **Prüfeinrichtungen** *f pl* QUAL inspection and test equipment

Prüfen *nt* COMP & DV testing; **~ mit induzierter Überspannung** *nt* ELEKTRIZ induced overvoltage test

prüfen *vt* BAU try, COMP & DV sense, verify, QUAL inspect, *Meßtechnik* test, SICHERHEIT approve

prüfend: zu ~e Einheit *f* QUAL unit under test

Prüfer *m* COMP & DV verifier, KONSTZEICH checker, PATENT examiner, QUAL inspector

Prüf-: Prüfergebnisse *nt pl* QUAL test results; **Prüfetikett** *nt* VERPACK control tag; **Prüffeld** *nt* TELEKOM test room; **Prüffolge** *f* QUAL test sequence; **Prüffolgeweg** *m* KONTROLL audit trail; **Prüffrequenz** *f* WERKPRÜF test frequency; **Prüfgerät** *nt* COMP & DV test equipment, ELEKTROTECH instrument, GERÄT calibration instrument, checking instrument, test equipment, test gage (AmE), test gauge (BrE), testing instrument, QUAL tester, testing apparatus, VERPACK inspection equipment

prüfgerecht: ~e Maßeintragung *f* KONSTZEICH inspection-oriented dimensioning

Prüf-: Prüfgeschwindigkeit *f* WERKPRÜF test speed; **Prüfglas** *nt* VERPACK inspection window; **Prüfinstrument** *nt* GERÄT calibration instrument, checking instrument, testing instrument; **Prüfintervall** *m* QUAL inspection interval; **Prüfkabel** *nt* ELEKTROTECH test lead; **Prüfklemme** *f* ELEKTROTECH test terminal; **Prüfklinke** *f* ELEKTROTECH test jack; **Prüflaboratorium** *nt* QUAL testing laboratory; **Prüflast** *f* LUFTTRANS *Lufttüchtigkeit* proof load, MASCHINEN proof load, test load; **Prüflauf** *m* COMP & DV test run; **Prüflehre** *f* GERÄT test gage (AmE), test gauge (BrE), MASCHINEN master gage (AmE), master gauge (BrE), reference gage (AmE), reference gauge (BrE); **Prüfleitung** *f* ELEKTROTECH patch cord, test lead

Prüfling *m* GERÄT, KOHLEN, KUNSTSTOFF, MASCHINEN,

MECHAN specimen, QUAL device under test, part under test, specimen

Prüf-: **Prüfliste** *f* COMP & DV audit trail, QUAL check list; **Prüflos** *nt* QUAL inspection lot, test lot; **Prüfluke** *f* RAUMFAHRT *Raumschiff* inspection door; **Prüfmanometer** *nt* GERÄT test gage (AmE), test gauge (BrE); **Prüfmaschine** *f* QUAL tester, testing apparatus, testing machine; **Prüfmenge** *f* QUAL test quantity; **Prüfmerkmal** *nt* QUAL inspection characteristic; **Prüfmethode** *f* QUAL test method; **Prüfmittelüberwachung** *f* QUAL control of inspection, measuring and test equipment; **Prüfmuster** *nt* QUAL sample; **Prüfnadel** *f* MASCHINEN test needle; **Prüfniveau** *nt* QUAL inspection level; **Prüfobjekt** *nt* QUAL device under test, unit under test; **Prüfort** *m* QUAL place of inspection; **Prüfoszillator** *m* ELEKTRONIK test oscillator; **Prüfpfad** *m* COMP & DV *Buchungskontrolle* audit trail

prüfpflichtig *adj* QUAL requiring approval, requiring official approval

Prüf-: **Prüfplakette** *f* QUAL inspection sticker; **Prüfplan** *m* QUAL inspection and test schedule, inspection plan; **Prüfplanung** *f* QUAL inspection and test planning, inspection planning; **Prüfplatz** *m* TELEKOM test position; **Prüfprisma** *nt* MASCHINEN V-block; **Prüfprobe** *f* QUAL test sample; **Prüfprogramm** *nt* COMP & DV test routine, MASCHINEN test schedule; **Prüfprotokoll** *nt* COMP & DV audit trail, QUAL inspection record, test record, test report; **Prüfpunkt** *m* COMP & DV checkpoint, QUAL inspection point, TELEKOM test point; **Prüfreihenfolge** *f* QUAL test sequence; **Prüfroutine** *f* QUAL test routine; **Prüfsachverständiger** *m* QUAL authorized inspector, *im Werk* factory-authorized inspector; **Prüfschalter** *m* ELEKTROTECH test switch; **Prüfschärfe** *f* ELEKTRIZ severity of testing, QUAL applicability, degree of inspection, severity of test, test item; **Prüfschild** *nt* KER & GLAS test plate; **Prüfschnur** *f* ELEKTROTECH patch cord; **Prüfschrank** *m* GERÄT test board; **Prüfsignal** *nt* WERKPRÜF test signal; **Prüfsignalgeber** *m* ELEKTRONIK test signal generator; **Prüfsonde** *f* GERÄT test probe; **Prüfspannung** *f* ELEKTRIZ proof voltage, test voltage; **Prüfspezifikation** *f* QUAL inspection specification; **Prüfspitze** *f* ELEKTRONIK sensing element, GERÄT probe, test prod; **Prüfspule** *f* ELEKTROTECH, FERTIG search coil; **Prüfspur** *f* COMP & DV parity track; **Prüfstab** *m* MASCHINEN test bar, test sieve; **Prüfstand** *m* ELEKTRIZ test bed, KERNTECH test stand, MASCHINEN test bed, test bench, MECHAN test bed, QUAL testing bed, testing bench, WERKPRÜF test rig; **Prüfstelle** *f* QUAL testing agency; **Prüfstempel** *m* QUAL inspection stamp; **Prüfstoff** *m* CHEMIE reagent; **Prüfstück** *nt* MASCHINEN test piece, test specimen, PHYS test piece, QUAL part under test, test sample, test specimen; **Prüfsumme** *f* COMP & DV, ELEKTRONIK *Datenverarbeitung* checksum; **Prüftest** *m* ELEKTRIZ proof test; **Prüfturnus** *m* QUAL inspection interval; **Prüfumfang** *m* QUAL amount of inspection, scope of inspection

Prüfung *f* COMP & DV check, test, verification, sense, testing, KOHLEN assay, trial, KONTROLL, MASCHINEN verification, PATENT examination, QUAL inspection, test, verification, TEXTIL test; **~ am Boden** *f* LUFTTRANS ground test; **~ gehärteter Zahnräder** *f* FERTIG *Getriebelehre* hard test; **~ auf gerade Bitzahl** *f* COMP & DV even parity; **~ bei Normalbetrieb** *f* METALL dynamic test; **~ bei Null-Leistungsfaktor** *f* ELEKTRIZ zero-power-factor test; **~ auf plötzlichen Kurzschluß** *f*

ELEKTRIZ sudden short-circuit test; **~ bei Sonneneinstrahlung** *f* WERKPRÜF solar radiation test; **~ auf ungerade Parität** *f* COMP & DV odd parity; **~ im Werk** *f* MECHAN factory inspection; **~ im Windkanal** *f* WERKPRÜF wind tunnel test; **Prüfungsabteilung** *f* QUAL test department; **Prüfungsanforderungen** *f pl* WERKPRÜF test requirements; **Prüfungsgrad** *m* QUAL degree of inspection; **Prüfungsklasse** *f* KOHLEN assay grade; **Prüfungsprotokolle** *nt pl* QUAL examination records; **Prüfungswert** *m* KOHLEN assay value

Prüf-: **Prüfunterlagen** *f pl* QUAL inspection and test documents; **Prüfverfahren** *nt* METROL audit procedure, inspection procedure, QUAL inspection and test procedure, inspection procedure, test procedure; **Prüfvermerk** *m* KONSTZEICH check note; **Prüfvorschrift** *f* METROL inspection procedure, QUAL test code, test specification; **Prüfweg** *m* KONTROLL audit trail; **Prüfwert** *m* GERÄT test value; **Prüfzeichen** *nt* COMP & DV check character, QUAL mark of conformity, TELEKOM check character; **Prüfzeichnung** *f* KONSTZEICH appraisal drawing; **Prüfzertifikat** *nt* QUAL inspection certificate; **Prüfzeugnis** *nt* ELEKTRIZ proof certificate, QUAL inspection report; **Prüfziffer** *f* COMP & DV check digit; **Prüfzustand** *m* QUAL inspection and test status, inspection status; **Prüfzuverlässigkeit** *f* QUAL test reliability

Prulaurasin *nt* CHEMIE prulaurasin

Prunetol *nt* CHEMIE genistein, prunetol

Prussiat *nt* CHEMIE prussiate

PS *abbr* CHEMIE *(Polystyren, Polystrol)*, ELEKTRIZ *(Polystrol)*, KUNSTSTOFF *(Polystyren, Polystrol)* PS *(polystyrene)*, MASCHINEN *(Pferdestärke)* hp *(horsepower)*, WASSERTRANS *(Peilstrahl)* EBL *(electronic bearing line)*

Pseudo- *pref* COMP & DV pseudo

pseudoakustisch: **~es Log** *nt* ERDÖL pseudosonic log; **~es Profil** *nt* ERDÖL pseudosonic profile

Pseudo-: **Pseudobefehl** *m* COMP & DV pseudoinstruction; **Pseudocode** *m* COMP & DV pseudocode

pseudo-elliptisch: **~es Filter** *nt* RAUMFAHRT *Weltraumfunk* pseudoelliptic filter

Pseudo-: **Pseudooperation** *f* COMP & DV pseudooperation

pseudopotentiometrisch: **~e Höhe** *f* ERDÖL pseudopotentiometric head

Pseudo-: **Pseudorauschcode** *m* TELEKOM pseudorandom noise code; **Pseudorauschen** *nt* TELEKOM PN, pseudonoise, pseudorandom noise; **Pseudosphäre** *f* GEOM pseudosphere; **Pseudosprache** *f* COMP & DV pseudolanguage; **Pseudostereophonie** *f* AUFNAHME pseudostereophony

pseudozufällig *adj* TELEKOM pseudorandom

Pseudozufalls- *pref* TELEKOM pseudorandom; **Pseudozufallssignal** *nt* TELEKOM pseudorandom signal; **Pseudozufallszahl** *f* COMP & DV pseudorandom number

PSK *abbr* COMP & DV *(Phasensprungtastung)* PSK *(phase shift keying)*, ELEKTRONIK *(Phasenumtastung)*, RADIO *(Phasenumtastung)*, RAUMFAHRT *(Phasenumtastung)*, TELEKOM *(Phasenumtastung)* PSK *(phase-shift keying)*

psophometrisch: **~er Gewichtungsfaktor** *m* RAUMFAHRT *Weltraumfunk* psophometric weighting factor

Psychoakustik *f* ERGON psychoacoustics

psychomotorisch[1] *adj* ERGON psychomotor

psychomotorisch:[2] **~es Training** *nt* ERGON psychomotor

training
psychophysisch: ~e **Methode** *f* ERGON psycho-physical method
Psychotrin *nt* CHEMIE psychotrine
Psychrometer *nt* LABOR psychrometer
Pt *(Platin)* CHEMIE Pt *(platinum)*
PTC *abbr (passive Thermosteuerung)* RAUMFAHRT PTC *(passive thermal control)*
Pterin *nt* CHEMIE pterin
PTFE *abbr (Polytetrafluorethen, Polytetrafluorethylen)* KUNSTSTOFF PTFE *(polytetrafluoroethylene)*
p-Toluolsulfonyl- *pref* CHEMIE tosyl-
Ptomain *nt* CHEMIE ptomaine
Puddeln *nt* METALL puddling
puddeln *vt* METALL puddle
Puddelstraße *f* FERTIG puddle train
Puddler *m* METALL puddler
Pudermittel *nt* KUNSTSTOFF powder
puffen *vt* LEBENSMITTEL *Mais, Reis, Hülsenfrüchte* puff
Puffer *m* BAU pad, COMP & DV buffer, push-down stack, EISENBAHN buffer, bumper (BrE), fender (AmE), ELEKTROTECH, FERNSEH, FERTIG *Spanung*, KUNSTSTOFF buffer, MASCHINEN buffer, bumper (BrE), fender (AmE), RADIO buffer; **Pufferanschlag** *m* EISENBAHN buffer stop; **Pufferarchitektur** *f* COMP & DV stack architecture; **Pufferbatterie** *f* EISENBAHN, ELEKTROTECH buffer battery; **Pufferberührung** *f* EISENBAHN buffer contact; **Pufferdynamo** *m* ELEKTRIZ buffer dynamo; **Pufferfaser** *f* OPTIK buffer fiber (AmE), buffer fibre (BrE); **Pufferfeder** *f* KFZTECH *Kupplung* cushion spring, MASCHINEN damping spring; **Pufferladegerät** *nt* ELEKTRIZ trickle charger; **Pufferladung** *f* ELEKTROTECH trickle charge; **Pufferlösung** *f* LEBENSMITTEL buffer solution
Puffern *nt* COMP & DV, OPTIK *Lichtleiter* buffering
puffern *vt* COMP & DV, RADIO buffer
Puffer: **Pufferregister** *nt* COMP & DV buffer register; **Pufferrohr** *nt* OPTIK buffer tube; **Pufferschaltung** *f* ELEKTRONIK buffer circuit; **Pufferspeicher** *m* COMP & DV buffer, ELEKTROTECH buffer memory, FERTIG in-process storage, TELEKOM buffer memory; **Pufferstück** *nt* COMP & DV pad; **Puffersubstanz** *f* LEBENSMITTEL buffering agent; **Pufferträger** *m* EISENBAHN buffer beam; **Pufferverstärker** *m* ELEKTRONIK, RADIO buffer amplifier
Pulegon *nt* CHEMIE pulegone
Pulfrich-Refraktometer *nt* PHYS Pulfrich refractometer
Pulldown-Menü *nt* COMP & DV pull-down menu
Pulpe *f* KOHLEN pulp
Pulper *m* PAPIER pulper
Puls *m* PHYS, WASSERTRANS *Radar* pulse; **Pulsamplitudenmodulation** *f (PAM)* COMP & DV, ELEKTRONIK, RADIO, TELEKOM pulse amplitude modulation *(PAM)*; **Pulsbetrieb** *m* ELEKTRONIK pulsed mode, pulsed operation; **Pulsbreite** *f (PB)* COMP & DV, ELEKTRONIK, FERNSEH, PHYS, TELEKOM pulse width *(PW)*; **Pulsbreitenfrequenz** *f* ELEKTRONIK pulse duration frequency; **Pulsbreitenmodulation** *f* ELEKTRONIK pulse width modulation, width coding; **Pulscode** *m* ELEKTRONIK pulse code; **Pulscodemodulation** *f (PCM)* AUFNAHME, COMP & DV, ELEKTRONIK, FERNSEH, RADIO, STRAHLPHYS, TELEKOM pulse code modulation *(PCM)*; **Pulscode-Sprachdaten** *nt pl* ELEKTRONIK PCVD, pulse code voice data; **Pulsdauer** *f* COMP & DV, ELEKTRONIK, FERNSEH, PHYS, TELEKOM pulse width; **Pulsdauermodulation** *f (PDM)* ELEKTRONIK pulse

width modulation *(PWM)*; **Pulsdehnung** *f* ELEKTRONIK expansion; **Pulsdeltamodulation** *f (PDM)* COMP & DV pulse delta modulation *(PDM)*; **Pulsfrequenz** *f* ELEKTRONIK pulse frequency, pulse rate; **Pulsfrequenzfaktor** *m* FERNSEH pulse rate factor; **Pulsfrequenzmodulation** *f* COMP & DV *(PFM)*, ELEKTRONIK *(PFM)* pulse frequency modulation *(PFM)*, RADIO pulse FM; **Pulsgenerator** *m* ELEKTRONIK pulse generator, pulser, PHYS pulse generator; **Pulsgenerierung** *f* ELEKTRONIK pulse generation; **Pulsgerät** *nt* PHYS pulse generator; **Pulshöhe** *f* ELEKTRONIK pulse height
pulsieren *vi* KONTROLL pulse
pulsierend: ~er **Fehler** *m* FERNSEH fluctuating error; ~es **Neutronenlog** *nt* ERDÖL pulsed neutron log; ~er **Staustrahlmotor** *m* LUFTTRANS pulsating jet engine, pulse jet; ~er **Strom** *m* ELEKTRIZ *unterbrochener Strom* pulsating current; ~e **Strömung** *f* STRÖMPHYS pulsating flow; ~e **Verbrennung** *f* THERMOD resonant burning
Puls: **Pulsintervall** *nt* ELEKTRONIK pulse interval; **Pulsintervallmodulation** *f* FERNSEH pulse interval modulation; **Pulsklipper** *m* FERNSEH pulse clipper; **Pulslage** *f* ELEKTRONIK pulse position; **Pulslagenmodulation** *f (PPM)* ELEKTRONIK, TELEKOM pulse position modulation *(PPM)*, **Pulslagenmodulator** *m* TELECOM pulse phase modulator; **Pulslänge** *f* ELEKTRONIK, WASSERTRANS *Radar* pulse length; **Pulslängencodierung** *f* ELEKTRONIK width coding; **Pulslaser** *m* ELEKTRONIK pulsed laser; **Pulsmodulation** *f* ELEKTRONIK pulse modulation; **Pulsmodulator** *m* ELEKTRONIK pulse modulator
pulsmoduliert *adj* ELEKTRONIK pulse-modulated
Puls: **Pulsmodulierung** *f* ELEKTRIZ pulse modulation; **Pulsneutronenlog** *nt* ERDÖL *Meßtechnik* pulsed neutron log
Pulsostrahltriebwerk *nt* LUFTTRANS athodyd
Pulsotriebwerk *nt* LUFTTRANS athodyd
Puls: **Pulsphase** *f* ELEKTRONIK pulse phase, FERNSEH pulse phasing; **Pulsphasenmodulation** *f (PPM)* COMP & DV, ELEKTRONIK, TELEKOM pulse phase modulation *(PPM)*; **Pulspolarität** *f* ELEKTRONIK pulse polarity; **Pulsrahmen** *m* TELEKOM frame; **Pulsrate** *f* ELEKTRONIK pulse rate; **Pulssynchronisierung** *f* FERNSEH pulse sync; **Pulsträger** *m* FERNSEH pulse carrier; **Pulstransformator** *m* PHYS pulse transformer; **Pulstrennung** *f* FERNSEH pulse separator; **Pulsübertrager** *m* PHYS pulse transformer; **Pulsverbesserung** *f* PHYS pulse regeneration; **Pulsverbreiterung** *f* TELEKOM pulse spreading; **Pulsweitenmodulation** *f (PWM)* ELEKTRONIK pulse width modulation *(PWM)*; **Pulswiederholfrequenz** *f* COMP & DV, ELEKTRONIK, PHYS, TELEKOM PRF, pulse repetition frequency; **Pulswiederholrate** *f* PHYS PRR, pulse repetition rate; **Pulszeitmodulation** *f* ELEKTRONIK PTM, pulse time modulation
Pult *nt* GERÄT desk, KONTROLL console; **Pultdach** *nt* BAU lean-to roof, pitch roof, shed roof
Pultrusion *f* KUNSTSTOFF pultrusion
Pulver *nt* KUNSTSTOFF, PAPIER powder; **Pulverabfüllanlage** *f* VERPACK powder filling machine; **Pulverbeschichten** *nt* KUNSTSTOFF powder coating; **Pulverbeschichtung** *f* KUNSTSTOFF powder coating; **Pulverbeugungskamera** *f* KERNTECH *Röntgenstrahlen* X-ray powder camera; **Pulverbrennschneiden** *nt* FERTIG powder cutting; **Pulverdiffraktometer** *nt* KERNTECH *Röntgenstrahlen* X-ray powder diffracto-

meter; **Pulverfeuerlöscher** *m* SICHERHEIT powder fire extinguisher

pulverförmig[1] *adj* CHEMTECH pulverized, FERTIG *Kunststoffinstallationen*, KOHLEN powdery, KUNSTSTOFF powdered

pulverförmig:[2] **~es Erz** *nt* KOHLEN fines

pulvergefüllt *adj* ELEKTROTECH powder-filled

pulverig *adj* FERTIG *Kunststoffinstallationen*, KOHLEN powdery

pulverisieren *vt* CHEMIE triturate, CHEMTECH grind, pulverize, FERTIG levigate, KOHLEN, MASCHINEN pulverize

Pulverisiermühle *f* CHEMTECH pulverizer

pulverisiert *adj* CHEMTECH pulverized, KUNSTSTOFF powdered

Pulver: **Pulverkautschuk** *m* KUNSTSTOFF powdered rubber; **Pulverkörnmaschine** *f* VERPACK granulating machine; **Pulverlack-Beschichtungstechnik** *f* (*PMC-Verfahren*) KUNSTSTOFF powder mold coating (AmE), powder mould coating (BrE) (*PMC*); **Pulververlöscher** *m* SICHERHEIT powder fire extinguisher; **Pulvermetall** *nt* MASCHINEN powder metal; **Pulvermühle** *f* CHEMTECH pulverizing equipment; **Pulverpreßteil** *nt* FERTIG compact; **Pulverraupe** *f* FERTIG accumulation of particles, particle pattern

pulvrig: **~e Formmasse** *f* KUNSTSTOFF molding powder (AmE), moulding powder (BrE)

Pumpe *f* MASCHINEN, MEERSCHMUTZ, WASSERTRANS, WASSERVERSORG pump; **~ mit beweglichem Widerlager** *f* FERTIG rotary abutment pump; **~ mit konstanter Fördermenge** *f* MASCHINEN constant flow pump

Pumpen *nt* RAUMFAHRT *Raumschiff* transfer, WASSERVERSORG pumping

pumpen *vi* MASCHINEN, WASSERTRANS, WASSERVERSORG pump

Pumpen: **Pumpenaggregat** *nt* WASSERVERSORG set; **Pumpenanlage** *f* WASSERVERSORG pump station, pumping plant; **Pumpenanschluß** *m* WASSERVERSORG pump connection; **Pumpenarmatur** *f* ERDÖL pump valve; **Pumpenbagger** *m* BAU pump dredger, WASSERTRANS pump dredge, pump dredger; **Pumpendruck** *m* ERDÖL pump pressure; **Pumpendüse** *f* KFZTECH acceleration jet, united injector; **Pumpeneinrichtung** *f* WASSERVERSORG pumping equipment; **Pumpengehäuse** *nt* WASSERTRANS pump housing, WASSERVERSORG *Schacht* pump compartment; **Pumpengetriebe** *nt* WASSERVERSORG pump gear; **Pumpenhaus** *nt* WASSERVERSORG pump house, pump room; **Pumpenkolben** *m* MECHAN plunger; **Pumpenrad** *nt* MASCHINEN impeller; **Pumpenraum** *m* WASSERVERSORG pump house, pump room; **Pumpensatz** *m* WASSERVERSORG set; **Pumpensaugbecken** *nt* ERDÖL sump; **Pumpenschacht** *m* WASSERVERSORG pump shaft, pumping shaft; **Pumpensonde** *f* ERDÖL pumping well; **Pumpenstand** *m* MEERSCHMUTZ pumping unit; **Pumpenstange** *f* MASCHINEN, WASSERVERSORG pump rod; **Pumpensteuerung** *f* KONTROLL pump control system; **Pumpensumpf** *m* FERTIG sump, WASSERVERSORG pump sump; **Pumpenturbine** *f* NICHTFOSS ENERG pump turbine; **Pumpenzylinder** *m* MASCHINEN, WASSERVERSORG pump barrel, pump cylinder

Pumpfotonen *nt pl* ELEKTRONIK pumping photons

Pumpfrequenz *f* RAUMFAHRT *Weltraumfunk* pump frequency

Pumplicht *nt* ELEKTRONIK pumping light; **Pumplichtla-**

ser *m* ELEKTRONIK optically-pumped laser

Pumpmaschine *f* WASSERVERSORG pumping engine

Pumpprüfung *f* KOHLEN pumping test

Pumpspeicherverfahren *nt* NICHTFOSS ENERG pumped storage scheme

Pumpspray *nt* VERPACK pump dispenser system

Pumpstange *f* MASCHINEN, NICHTFOSS ENERG sucker rod

Pumpstation *f* WASSERTRANS pumping station

Pumpversuch *m* WASSERVERSORG pumping test

Pumpwasser *nt* WASSERVERSORG pump water

Pumpwerk *nt* WASSERVERSORG pump station; **Pumpwerksumpf** *m* KOHLEN pumping pit

Punicin *nt* CHEMIE pelletierine, punicine

Punkt *m* COMP & DV point, DRUCK full point, point, GEOM, MATH, METROL point, PAPIER dot, PHYS point; **~ der Gleichzeitigkeit** *m* LUFTTRANS *Navigation* equal time point; **~ größter Annäherung** *m* WASSERTRANS *Navigation* closest point of approach; **Punktabsaugsystem** *nt* SICHERHEIT point vacuum cleaning system; **Punktanschnitt** *m* KUNSTSTOFF pin gate; **Punktbahn** *f* FERTIG *Getriebelehre* point path; **Punktberührung** *f* ELEKTROTECH point contact

punktförmig[1] *adj* FERTIG *Korrosion* localized

punktförmig:[2] **~e Abtastung** *f* COMP & DV scanning spot beam; **~ angreifende Einzellast** *f* FERTIG concavity, concentrated load; **~es Bild** *nt* FOTO point image; **~e Lichtquelle** *f* FOTO point source light; **~e Quelle** *f* FOTO point source; **~ verteilte Kapazität** *f* ELEKTRIZ, ELEKTROTECH lumped capacitance

Punkt: **Punktgenerator** *m* ELEKTRONIK dot generator; **Punktgröße** *f* DRUCK point size

Punktierung *f* KONSTZEICH dotting

Punktkontakt *m* ELEKTROTECH point contact; **Punktkontakt-Detektordiode** *f* ELEKTRONIK point contact detector diode; **Punktkontaktdiode** *f* ELEKTRONIK point contact diode; **Punktkontakt-Mischdiode** *f* ELEKTRONIK point contact mixer diode; **Punktkontakt-Siliziumdiode** *f* ELEKTRONIK point contact silicon diode; **Punktkontakttransistor** *m* ELEKTRONIK point contact transistor

Punkt: **Punktkoordinate** *f* GEOM point coordinate; **Punktladung** *f* ELEKTRIZ, PHYS point charge; **Punktlast** *f* FERTIG concavity, concentrated load, concentrated mass; **Punktleuchte** *f* ELEKTRIZ spotlight; **Punktmasse** *f* FERTIG particle mass; **Punktmatrix** *f* COMP & DV, ELEKTRONIK dot matrix; **Punktmatrixdrucker** *m* DRUCK dot matrix printer; **Punktmengentheorie** *f* MATH point set theory; **Punktquelle** *f* FOTO, UMWELTSCHMUTZ point source; **Punktquellenfunksender** *m* RADIO, TRANS point source radio transmitter; **Punktraster** *nt* COMP & DV raster, FERNSEH dot grating; **Punktschweißen** *nt* BAU, ELEKTRIZ spot welding, MASCHINEN resistance spot welding; **Punktschweißung** *f* MASCHINEN spot welding; **Punktsprungabtastung** *f* FERNSEH dot interlace scanning; **Punktstrahl** *m* RAUMFAHRT *Weltraumfunk* spot beam; **Punktstrahlbedeckung** *f* TELEKOM spot beam coverage; **Punktstrahlrichtantenne** *f* RAUMFAHRT *Weltraumfunk* spot beam antenna; **Punktsystem** *nt* DRUCK point system

punktuell: **~e Abbildung** *f* FOTO point image

punktweise: **~ Aufzeichnung** *f* COMP & DV plotting

Punkt: **Punktwert** *m* ERGON score; **Punktwiderstand** *m* KOHLEN point resistance; **Punktzahl für durchschnittliche Meinung** *f* TELEKOM MOS, mean opinion score

punktzentriert: ~er Strahl *m* PHYS homocentric beam

Punkt-zu-Mehrpunkt-Betrieb *m* TELEKOM point-to-multipoint operation

Punkt-zu-Punkt- *pref* COMP & DV peer-to-peer, point-to-point; **Punkt-zu-Punkt-Kopplung** *f* COMP & DV peer-to-peer link; **Punkt-zu-Punkt-Leitung** *f* COMP & DV point-to-point line; **Punkt-zu-Punkt-Transport** *m* TRANS point-to-point transport; **Punkt-zu-Punkt-Übertragung** *f* TELEKOM point-to-point transmission; **Punkt-zu-Punkt-Verbindung** *f* COMP & DV point-to-point connection, ELEKTROTECH point-to-point link; **Punkt-zu-Punkt-Verdrahtung** *f* ELEKTROTECH point-to-point wiring

Pupinisierung *f* ELEKTROTECH coil loading, loading

Pupinkabel *nt* ELEKTROTECH coil-loaded cable, loaded cable

Pupinspule *f* ELEKTRIZ, ELEKTROTECH, PHYS loading coil

Puppe *f* ERGON dummy

PUR *abbr* (*Polyurethan*) KUNSTSTOFF, TEXTIL PUR (*polyurethane*)

Purin *nt* CHEMIE purine

Purpur *nt* DRUCK magenta; **Purpurfiltereinstellung** *f* FOTO minus green filter adjustment

Purpurin *nt* CHEMIE purpurin

Push-Pull-Verstärker *m* ELEKTRONIK push-pull amplifier

Pütting *nt* WASSERTRANS *Segeln* chain plate

Putz *m* BAU *Innenputz* plaster; **Putzabstandshalter** *m* BAU furring; **Putzarbeiten** *f pl* BAU plaster work, plastering

Pütze *f* WASSERTRANS bucket

Putzen *nt* FERTIG rattling, rolling, scouring, *Guß* dressing, KER & GLAS, METALL dressing; **~ von Steingut** *nt* KER & GLAS fettling of earthenware

putzen *vt* FERTIG roll, snag, *Gießen* trim, *Guß* dress, rattle

Putzerei *f* FERTIG *Gießen* dressing

Putz: Putzkelle *f* BAU plastering trowel; **Putzleiste** *f* BAU counterlath; **Putzstern** *m* FERTIG star; **Putzträger** *m* BAU lathing

Puzzolanzement *m* BAU pozzolanic cement

PVAC *abbr* (*Polyvinylacetat*) KUNSTSTOFF PVAC (*polyvinyl acetate*)

PVAL *abbr* (*Polyvinylalkohol*) DRUCK, KUNSTSTOFF PVAL (*polyvinyl alcohol*)

PVB *abbr* (*Polyvinylbutyral*) KUNSTSTOFF PVB (*polyvinyl butyral*)

PVC *abbr* (*Polyvinylchlorid*) BAU, ELEKTROTECH, KUNSTSTOFF PVC (*polyvinyl chloride*)

PVC-C *abbr* (*chloriertes Polyvinylchlorid*) KUNSTSTOFF CPVC (*chlorinated polyvinyl chloride*)

PVC-U *abbr* KUNSTSTOFF U-PVC, unplasticized PVC

PVC: PVC-Band *nt* AUFNAHME PVC tape; **PVC-Einsatz** *m* VERPACK PVC insert fitment; **PVC-Flasche** *f* VERPACK PVC bottle; **PVC-hart** *nt* KUNSTSTOFF PVC rigid, U-PVC, unplasticized PVC; **PVC-Isolierung** *f* ELEKTRIZ PVC insulation;

PVDC *abbr* (*Polyvinylidenchlorid*) KUNSTSTOFF PVDC (*polyvinylidene chloride*)

PVDF *abbr* (*Polyvinylidenfluorid*) KUNSTSTOFF PVFD (*polyvinylidene fluoride*)

P/V-Diagramm *nt* (*Druck-Volumen-Diagramm*) THERMOD pressure volume diagram

PVE *abbr* (*Polyvinylether*) KUNSTSTOFF PVE (*polyvinyl ether*)

PVF *abbr* (*Polyvinylfluorid*) KUNSTSTOFF PVF (*polyvinyl fluoride*)

P-Welle *f* (*primäre Erdbebenwelle*) PHYS P wave

PWM *abbr* (*Pulsweitenmodulation*) ELEKTRONIK PWM (*pulse width modulation*)

p-Xylen *nt* CHEMIE p-xylene

Pyknometer *nt* ERDÖL *Dichtemeßgerät* pycnometer, LABOR density bottle, *Dichte* pycnometer, PHYS pycnometer

Pylon *m* BAU, ELEKTRIZ, LUFTTRANS pylon

Pyramide *f* GEOM pyramid; **Pyramidenebene** *f* METALL pyramidal plane; **Pyramidengleiten** *nt* METALL pyramidal slip; **Pyramidenhornspeisung** *f* RADIO pyramidal horn feeder

Pyran *nt* CHEMIE pyran

Pyranometer *nt* NICHTFOSS ENERG pyranometer

Pyranose *f* CHEMIE pyranose

Pyrazin *nt* CHEMIE piazine, pyrazine

Pyrazol *nt* CHEMIE pyrazole

Pyrazolin *nt* CHEMIE pyrazoline

Pyrazolon *nt* CHEMIE pyrazolone

Pyrheliometer *nt* NICHTFOSS ENERG pyrheliometer

Pyridazin *nt* CHEMIE pyridazine

Pyridin *nt* CHEMIE pyridine; **Pyridin-Carbonsäureamid** *nt* CHEMIE niacinamide, nicotinamide

Pyridon *nt* CHEMIE pyridone

Pyroarsenat *nt* CHEMIE pyroarsenate

Pyrocatechol *nt* CHEMIE pyrocatechol, pyrocatechin

Pyrogallol *nt* CHEMIE pyrogallol; **Pyrogallolphthalein** *nt* CHEMIE gallein

Pyrogallus- *pref* CHEMIE pyrogallic

pyrogallussauer *adj* CHEMIE pyrogallic

Pyrogallussäure *f* CHEMIE pyrogallol

pyrogen[1] *adj* THERMOD pyrogenic

pyrogen:[2] **~e Reaktion** *f* THERMOD pyrogenic reaction

pyrolitisch: ~e Beschichtung *f* KER & GLAS pyrolitic coating; **~e Zersetzung** *f* KERNTECH pyrolitic decomposition

Pyrolyse *f* ABFALL, CHEMIE, LEBENSMITTEL pyrolysis

pyrolytisch *adj* CHEMIE pyrolytic

Pyromekon- *pref* CHEMIE pyromeconic

Pyromellit- *pref* CHEMIE pyromellitic

Pyrometer *nt* ELEKTRIZ, GERÄT, KOHLEN, LABOR, STRAHLPHYS, THERMOD pyrometer; **Pyrometerschutzrohr** *nt* SICHERHEIT pyrometer protection tube; **Pyrometersonde** *f* ELEKTRIZ pyrometer probe

Pyrometrie *f* THERMOD pyrometry

pyrometrisch *adj* THERMOD pyrometric

Pyron *nt* CHEMIE pyrone

Pyrophosphat *nt* CHEMIE pyrophosphate

Pyrophyllit *nt* ERDÖL *Mineral* pyrophyllite

pyroschleimsauer *adj* CHEMIE pyromucic

Pyroskop *nt* PHYS pyroscope

Pyrostat *m* PHYS pyrostat

Pyrotechnik *f* RAUMFAHRT pyrotechnics

Pyrrol *nt* CHEMIE pyrrole

Pyrrolidin *nt* CHEMIE pyrrolidine, tetrahydropyrrol, tetramethyleneimine

Pyrrolin *nt* CHEMIE pyrroline

Pyruvat *nt* CHEMIE pyruvate

Pyruvin- *pref* CHEMIE pyruvic

Pythagoreisch: ~es Komma *nt* AKUSTIK Pythagorean comma; **~er Lehrsatz** *m* GEOM, MATH Pythagorean theorem

Q

QAM *abbr* COMP & DV *(Quadratur-Amplituden-modulation)*, ELEKTRONIK *(Quadratur-Amplitudenmodulation)* QAM *(quadrature amplitude modulation)*, ELEKTRONIK *(Quadratur-Amplitudenmodulator)* QAM *(quadrature amplitude modulator)*, TELEKOM *(Quadratur-Amplitudenmodulation)* QAM *(quadrature amplitude modulation)*

Q-Bit *nt (Unterscheidungsbit)* TELEKOM Q bit *(qualifier bit)*

QCD *abbr (Quantenchromodynamik)* TEILPHYS QCD *(quantum chromodynamics)*

QC-Flugzeug *nt (Quick-Change-Flugzeug)* LUFTTRANS QC aircraft *(quick-change aircraft)*

Q-Demodulator *m* ELEKTRONIK Q demodulator

QED *abbr (Quantenelektrodynamik)* PHYS QED *(quantum electrodynamics)*

Q-Elektron *nt* KERNTECH Q electron, Q shell electron

Q-Faktor *m (Gütefaktor, Qualitätsfaktor)* MECHAN, PHYS, QUAL, RADIO, UMWELTSCHMUTZ Q factor *(quality factor)*

Q-Kanal *m* ELEKTRONIK Q channel

Q-Kontrolle *f (Qualitätskontrolle)* DRUCK, LABOR, MASCHINEN, MECHAN, QUAL, VERPACK QC *(quality control)*

Q-Maschine *f* KERNTECH Q device

Q-Meter *nt (Gütefaktormesser)* PHYS Q meter

Q-Perzentil-Lebensdauer *f* QUAL Q percentile life

QP-Maschine *f* KERNTECH QP device

QPSK *abbr (Vierphasenumtastung)* ELEKTRONIK QPSK *(quaternary phase shift keying)*, TELEKOM QPSK *(quadriphase shift keying)*

QS *abbr (Qualitätssicherung)* KERNTECH, MASCHINEN, MECHAN, QUAL, VERPACK QA *(quality assurance)*

QSAM *abbr (erweiterte Zugriffsmöglichkeit für sequentielle Dateien)* COMP & DV QSAM *(queued sequential access method)*

Q-Schale *f* KERNTECH Q shell

QSG *abbr (Quasistellargalaxie)* RAUMFAHRT QSG *(quasi-stellar galaxy)*

QS: **QS-Handbuch** *nt* QUAL QA manual

Q-Signal *nt* ELEKTRONIK, FERNSEH Q signal

QSO *abbr (quasi-stellares Objekt)* RAUMFAHRT QSO *(quasi-stellar object)*

QS: **QS-Programmmodul** *nt* QUAL QA program module (AmE), QA programme module (BrE); **QS-Verfahrensanweisungen** *f pl* QUAL quality procedures; **QS-Verfahrenshandbuch** *nt* QUAL QA procedures manual

Quad-Antenne *f* RADIO cubical quad

Quader *m* GEOM cuboid; **Quaderstein** *m* BAU quarry

Quadrant *m* GEOM quadrant; **Quadranten-Elektrometer** *nt* ELEKTRIZ quadrant electrometer

Quadrat *nt* GEOM, MATH, METROL square; **Quadratdezimeter** *m* METROL square decimeter (AmE), square decimetre (BrE); **Quadratfuß** *m* METROL square foot

quadratisch[1] *adj* GEOM square, MATH quadratic; **~ abhängig** *adj* PHYS square-law

quadratisch:[2] **~es Entfernungsgesetz** *nt* KERNTECH square law; **~e Funktion** *f* MATH quadratic function; **~er Gleichrichter** *m* ELEKTROTECH square law detector; **~e Gleichung** *f* MATH quadratic equation; **~er Keil** *m* MASCHINEN square key; **~es Mittel** *nt (RMS)* AUFNAHME, ELEKTRIZ, ELEKTRONIK root mean square *(rms)*; **~er Mittelwert** *m* AUFNAHME, ELEKTRONIK, OPTIK, PHYS root mean square value; **~er Mittelwert der Abweichung** *m* ELEKTRIZ root mean square deviation; **~er Mittelwert der Geschwindigkeit** *m* PHYS mean square velocity; **~es Profil** *nt* OPTIK quadratic profile; **~er Wasserstandmittelwert** *m* NICHTFOSS ENERG root line mean square water level

Quadrat: **Quadratkeil** *m* MASCHINEN square key; **Quadratmaß** *nt* KONSTZEICH square dimension, METROL square measure; **Quadratmeile** *f* METROL square mile; **Quadratmeter** *m* METROL centiare, square meter (AmE), square metre (BrE)

Quadratur *f* COMP & DV, ELEKTRONIK, GEOM, NICHTFOSS ENERG, PHYS quadrature; **~ des Kreises** *f* GEOM squaring the circle; **Quadraturachse** *f* ELEKTRIZ quadrature axis; **Quadratur-Achsenkomponente** *f* ELEKTRIZ quadrature axis component; **Quadratur-Amplitudenmodulation** *f (QAM)* COMP & DV, ELEKTRONIK, TELEKOM quadrature amplitude modulation *(QAM)*; **Quadratur-Amplitudenmodulator** *m (QAM)* ELEKTRONIK quadrature amplitude modulator *(QAM)*; **Quadratur-Demodulator** *m* ELEKTRONIK quadrature demodulator; **Quadraturkomponente** *f* ELEKTRIZ quadrature component; **Quadraturleistung** *f* ELEKTRIZ quadrature power; **Quadratur-Modulator** *m* ELEKTRONIK quadrature amplitude modulator; **Quadraturspiegelfilter** *nt* TELEKOM quadrature mirror filter; **Quadratursteuerung** *f* ELEKTRIZ quadrature control

Quadrat: **Quadratwurzel** *f* MATH square root; **Quadratyard** *nt* METROL square yard; **Quadratzentimeter** *m* METROL square centimeter (AmE), square centimetre (BrE); **Quadratzoll** *m* METROL square inch

quadrieren *vt* MATH square

Quadrierschaltung *f* FERNSEH squaring circuit

Quadrophonie *f* AKUSTIK quadraphony

Quadruplex- *pref* FERNSEH quadruplex

Quadrupol *m* PHYS quadrupole; **Quadrupolanordnung** *f* KERNTECH quadrupolar configuration; **Quadrupolfeld** *nt* KERNTECH quadrupole field; **Quadrupolmoment** *nt* PHYS quadrupole moment; **Quadrupolpotential** *nt* KERNTECH quadrupole potential; **Quadrupolresonanz** *f* KERNTECH quadrupole resonance

Quakbox *f* AUFNAHME squawkbox

Qualifikationsanforderung *f* QUAL qualification requirement

Qualifikationsnachweis *m* QUAL qualification records

qualifiziert: **~er Name** *m* COMP & DV qualified name

Qualität *f* QUAL quality, VERPACK paper grade

qualitativ: **~e Analyse** *f* WASSERVERSORG qualitative analysis; **~e Autoradiographie** *f* KERNTECH qualitative autoradiography; **~es Merkmal** *nt* QUAL attribute, qualitative characteristic

Qualität: **Qualitätsaudit** nt QUAL quality audit; **Qualitätsaufzeichnungen** f pl QUAL quality records; **Qualitätsbeanstandung** f QUAL nonconformance report

qualitätsbeeinflussend: ~e **Tätigkeiten** f pl QUAL activities affecting quality

Qualität: **Qualitätsbericht** m QUAL quality report; **Qualitätsbeurteilung** f METROL quality assessment; **Qualitätsblech** nt FERTIG prime; **Qualitätseinbuße** f QUAL impairment of quality; **Qualitätselement** nt QUAL quality element; **Qualitätsfähigkeit** f QUAL quality capability; **Qualitätsfähigkeit des Lieferanten** f QUAL supplier's quality performance; **Qualitätsfähigkeits-Bestätigung** f QUAL quality verification; **Qualitätsfaktor** m (Q-Faktor) MECHAN, PHYS, QUAL, RADIO, UMWELTSCHMUTZ quality factor (Q factor); **Qualitätsförderung** f QUAL quality improvement; **Qualitätsingenieur** m QUAL quality assurance engineer; **Qualitätskontrolle** f (Q-Kontrolle) DRUCK, MASCHINEN, MECHAN, METROL, QUAL, VERPACK quality control (QC); **Qualitätskontrolle in der Fertigung** f QUAL process control; **Qualitätskosten** pl QUAL quality costs, quality-related costs; **Qualitätskreis** m QUAL quality loop; **Qualitätskriterien** nt pl MASCHINEN quality acceptance criteria; **Qualitätslage** f QUAL quality level; **Qualitätslenkung** f QUAL quality control; **Qualitätslenkung bei mehreren Merkmalen** f QUAL multivariate quality control; **Qualitätsmanagement** nt QUAL quality management; **Qualitätsmangel** m QUAL quality defect; **Qualitätsmarke** f VERPACK quality label; **Qualitätsmerkmal** nt QUAL quality characteristic, quality criterion; **Qualitätsminderung** f FERNSEH quality degradation, QUAL degradation of quality, impairment of quality; **Qualitätsnorm** f METROL standard of quality; **Qualitätsplanung** f QUAL quality planning; **Qualitätspolitik** f QUAL quality policy; **Qualitätsprodukt** nt MECHAN quality product; **Qualitätsprüfstelle** f QUAL quality inspection and test facility; **Qualitätsprüfung** f QUAL quality inspection and testing; **Qualitätsregelkarte** f QUAL control chart; **Qualitätsregelkarte für kumulierte Werte** f QUAL cusum chart; **Qualitätsregelung in der Fertigung** f QUAL in-process quality control

Qualitätssicherung f (QS) KERNTECH, MASCHINEN, MECHAN, QUAL, VERPACK quality assurance (QA); ~ **in Entwurf und Konstruktion** f QUAL design assurance; **Qualitätssicherungsabteilung** f QUAL quality assurance department; **Qualitätssicherungsauflagen** f pl QUAL quality assurance requirements; **Qualitätssicherungsbeauftragter** m QUAL QA representative, quality assurance representative; **Qualitätssicherungsbescheinigung** f MASCHINEN quality assurance certificate; **Qualitätssicherungsdokumentation** f QUAL quality documentation; **Qualitätssicherungshandbuch** nt QUAL quality assurance manual, quality manual; **Qualitätssicherungsprüfung** f KERNTECH quality assurance examination; **Qualitätssicherungssystem** nt QUAL quality management system, quality system; **Qualitätssicherungsverfahren** nt MASCHINEN quality assurance procedure

Qualität: **Qualitätsstand** m QUAL quality status; **Qualitätssteuerung** f QUAL quality control; **Qualitätssystem-Bescheinigungsmaterial** nt QUAL QSCM, quality system certificate material; **Qualitätstechnik** f QUAL quality engineering;

Qualitätsüberprüfung f KERNTECH QC, quality control; **Qualitätsüberwachung** f QUAL quality surveill-ance; **Qualitätsunterelement** nt QUAL quality subelement; **Qualitätsverbesserung** f QUAL quality improvement; **Qualitätsverlust** m KUNSTSTOFF deterioration; **Qualitätswesen** nt QUAL quality management; **Qualitätszahl** f QUAL quality number; **Qualitätsziel** nt QUAL quality objective

Quant nt COMP & DV, OPTIK, PHYS, TEILPHYS quantum

Quantelung f ELEKTRONIK quantization

Quant: **Quantenausbeute** f PHYS quantum yield, STRAHLPHYS quantum efficiency; **Quantenausbeute der Lumineszenz** f STRAHLPHYS quantum yield of luminescence

quantenbegrenzt: ~er **Betrieb** m OPTIK quantum-limited operation

Quant: **Quantenchromodynamik** f (QCD) TEILPHYS quantum chromodynamics (QCD); **Quantenelektrodynamik** f (QED) PHYS quantum electrodynamics (QED), TEILPHYS quantum electrodynamics; **Quantenfeldtheorie** f PHYS quantum field theory

Quanten-Hallscher Effekt m PHYS quantum Hall effect

Quant: **Quantenhydrodynamik** f PHYS quantum hydrodynamics; **Quantenmechanik** f PHYS, TEILPHYS quantum mechanics

quantenmechanisch: ~e **Linienform** f STRAHLPHYS quantum-mechanical line shape

quantenrauschbegrenzt: ~er **Betrieb** m TELEKOM quantum-limited operation

Quant: **Quantenrauschen** nt ELEKTRONIK, OPTIK quantum noise, RAUMFAHRT quantization noise, TELEKOM quantum noise; **durch Quantenrauschen begrenzter Betrieb** m OPTIK, TELEKOM quantum-noise-limited operation; **Quantensprung** m ELEKTRONIK quantum transition, TEILPHYS quantum leap; **Quantenstatistik** f PHYS quantum statistics; **Quantenstatus** m RAUMFAHRT quantum state; **Quantentheorie** f KERNTECH, RAUMFAHRT, TEILPHYS quantum theory; **Quantentheorie der Strahlung** f STRAHLPHYS quantum theory of radiation; **Quantenverzerrung** f ELEKTRONIK quantization distortion; **Quantenwirkungsgrad** m OPTIK, PHYS, STRAHLPHYS, TELEKOM quantum efficiency; **Quantenzahl** f KERNTECH (n) quantum number, LABOR (n) principal quantum number (n), PHYS, STRAHLPHYS, TEILPHYS quantum number; **Quantenzustand** m TEILPHYS quantum state

Quantil nt QUAL quantile; ~ **einer Wahrscheinlichkeitsverteilung** nt QUAL quantile of a probability distribution

quantisieren vt COMP & DV quantize, ELEKTRONIK digitize, quantize

Quantisierer m COMP & DV, ELEKTRONIK für DPCM-Methode, TELEKOM quantizer

quantisiert: ~e **Größe** f ELEKTRONIK quantized quantity; ~e **Pulslagemodulation** f ELEKTRONIK quantized pulse modulation; ~es **Signal** nt REGELUNG quantized signal; ~es **Zeichen** nt (QZ) ELEKTRONIK quantized signal (QS)

Quantisierung f COMP & DV quantization, MATH truncation, PHYS quantization; **Quantisierungsfehler** m COMP & DV, ELEKTRONIK, TELEKOM quantization error; **Quantisierungsgeräusch** nt COMP & DV, TELEKOM quantization noise; **Quantisierungsgröße** f COMP & DV quantization size; **Quantisierungsintervall** nt TELEKOM quantization interval; **Quantisierungspegel** m ELEKTRONIK quantization level; **Quantisierungsstufe**

_f_ COMP & DV quantization level

Quantität _f_ ELEKTRONIK, KONTROLL quantity, MATH amount

quantitativ:[1] **~e Analyse** _f_ WASSERVERSORG quantitative analysis; **~es Merkmal** _nt_ QUAL quantitative characteristic

quantitativ:[2] **~ bestimmen** _vt_ MATH quantify

Quantor _m_ MATH quantifier

Quantum _nt_ COMP & DV, PHYS quantum

Quarantäne _f_ WASSERTRANS quarantine; **Quarantäneflagge** _f_ WASSERTRANS quarantine flag, _Flagge_ yellow flag

Quark _nt_ PHYS _Teilchen_, TEILPHYS quark; **~ mit Eigenschaft Bottom** _nt_ PHYS bottom quark; **~ mit Eigenschaft Charm** _nt_ PHYS charmed quark; **~ mit Eigenschaft Down** _nt_ PHYS down quark; **~ mit Farbladung Blau** _nt_ PHYS blue quark; **~ mit Farbladung Rot** _nt_ PHYS red quark; **~ mit Topeigenschaft** _nt_ PHYS top quark; **~ mit Upeigenschaft** _nt_ PHYS up-quark; **Quark-Bag** _m_ TEILPHYS quark bag; **Quarkeinschluß** _m_ TEILPHYS quark confinement; **Quark-Gluon-Plasma** _nt_ TEILPHYS quark-gluon plasma; **Quarkteilchen** _nt_ PHYS _mit Farbladung grün_ green quark

Quart _nt_ AKUSTIK subdominant, METROL dry quart (AmE), liquid quart

Quartär _nt_ ERDÖL _Geologie_ Quaternary

quartär[1] _adj_ CHEMIE _Oniumverbindung_ quaternary

quartär:[2] **~e Spaltung** _f_ KERNTECH quaternary fission

Quartation _f_ CHEMIE quartation

Quarte _f_ AKUSTIK fourth, subdominant

Quarter _nt_ METROL quarter

Quartett _nt_ PHYS _Spektroskopie_ quartet; **Quartettmodell** _nt_ KERNTECH quartet model

Quart: **Quartformat** _nt_ _(Quarto)_ DRUCK 4to, quarto _(quarto)_

Quartiermeister _m_ WASSERTRANS quartermaster

Quartierung _f_ CHEMIE quartation, METALL inquartation

Quartil _nt_ MATH, QUAL quartile

Quarto _nt_ _(Quartformat)_ DRUCK 4to, quarto _(quarto)_; **Quartowalzwerk** _nt_ FERTIG four-high mill

Quartz _m_ METALL silica glass

Quarz _m_ ELEKTRONIK quartz, _Schaltungen_ crystal, PHYS quartz; **Quarzeichoszillator** _m_ RADIO crystal calibrator; **Quarzfilter** _nt_ ELEKTRONIK, STRAHLPHYS, TELEKOM quartz filter; **Quarzfrequenzquelle** _f_ ELEKTRONIK quartz frequency source

quarzgesteuert _adj_ ELEKTRONIK crystal-controlled

Quarzglas _nt_ KER & GLAS, OPTIK, TELEKOM vitreous silica; **Quarzglasbeschichtung** _f_ TELEKOM silica coating; **Quarzglasfaser** _f_ OPTIK, TELEKOM all-silica fiber (AmE), all-silica fibre (BrE), **Quarzglasprimärbeschichtung** _f_ TELEKOM silica coating

Quarz: Quarzhalter _m_ ELEKTRONIK crystal holder; **Quarzit** _m_ BAU quartzite; **Quarzkristall** _m_ COMP & DV, ELEKTRIZ quartz crystal; **Quarzlaufzeitkette** _f_ ELEKTRONIK quartz delay line; **Quarzmeßfühler** _m_ GERÄT piezoelectric sensing element; **Quarzoszillator** _m_ ELEKTRIZ crystal oscillator, quartz oscillator, ELEKTRONIK crystal oscillator, quartz oscillator; **Quarzoszillator mit Temperaturkompensation** _m_ ELEKTRONIK temperature-compensated crystal oscillator; **Quarzoszillator mit Temperaturregelung** _m_ ELEKTRONIK temperature-controlled crystal oscillator; **Quarzresonator** _m_ ELEKTRONIK quartz resonator, ELEKTROTECH piezoelectric resonator; **Quarzsand** _m_ KER & GLAS glassmaking sand; **Quarzschmelze** _f_ TELE-

KOM fused quartz; **Quarzschwinger** _m_ ELEKTRONIK quartz oscillator, KERNTECH quartz monochromator, PHYS piezoelectric oscillator, STRAHLPHYS crystal oscillator; **Quarzschwingquelle** _f_ ELEKTRONIK quartz frequency source; **Quarzsteuerung** _f_ AUFNAHME, LUFTTRANS crystal control; **Quarztaktsteuerung** _f_ ELEKTRIZ quartz crystal clock; **Quarzthermostat** _m_ RADIO crystal oven; **Quarzverzögerungsleitung** _f_ ELEKTRONIK, FERNSEH quartz delay line; **Quarzzeitbasis** _f_ ELEKTRONIK crystal time base

Quasi- _pref_ KERNTECH, PHYS quasi

quasi-adiabatisch: ~es Kalorimeter _nt_ KERNTECH quasi-adiabatic calorimeter

Quasi-: **Quasi-Albedo-Methode** _f_ KERNTECH quasi-albedo approach

quasi-binär _adj_ FERTIG quasi-binary

Quasi-: **Quasibrüter** _m_ KERNTECH quasi-breeder reactor

quasi-chemisch: ~e Annäherung _f_ METALL quasi-chemical approximation

quasi-konstant: ~es Gleiten _nt_ KERNTECH quasi-constant slip; **~e Zustandsverteilung** _f_ METALL quasi-steady-state distribution;

Quasi-: **Quasispitzenspannung** _f_ TELEKOM quasi-peak voltage

quasi-stabil: ~er Zustand _m_ PHYS quasi-steady state

quasi-statisch[1] _adj_ RAUMFAHRT quasi-statical

quasi-statisch:[2] **~e Ladung** _f_ RAUMFAHRT quasi-statical loading

quasi-stellar: ~e Entkopplung _f_ RAUMFAHRT quasi-stellar decoupling; **~es Objekt** _nt_ _(QSO)_ RAUMFAHRT quasi-stellar object _(QSO);_ **~e Radioquelle** _f_ RAUMFAHRT QSS, quasi-stellar radio source;

Quasi-: **Quasistellargalaxie** _f_ _(QSG)_ RAUMFAHRT quasi-stellar galaxy _(QSG);_ **Quasistreuung** _f_ KERNTECH quasi-scattering; **Quasiteilchen** _nt_ PHYS quasi-particle

quasi-unendlich: ~ langer Riß _m_ KERNTECH semi-infinite crack

Quassin _nt_ CHEMIE quassin

Quaste _f_ TEXTIL tuft

quaternär _adj_ CHEMIE _Legierung_, MATH quaternary

Quaternion _f_ MATH quaternion

Quecksilber _nt_ _(Hg)_ CHEMIE mercury _(Hg);_ **Quecksilber-** _pref_ CHEMIE mercuric; **Quecksilberamalgam** _nt_ METALL quicksilver amalgam; **Quecksilberbarometer** _nt_ PHYS mercury barometer; **Quecksilberbatterie** _f_ ELEKTROTECH mercury battery, mercury cell; **Quecksilber-benetztes Relais** _nt_ ELEKTRIZ mercury-wetted relay; **Quecksilberbogenlampe** _f_ PHYS mercury arc lamp; **Quecksilberbromid-Laser** _m_ ELEKTRONIK mercury-bromide laser; **Quecksilber-Chlorid** _nt_ CHEMIE calomel; **Quecksilberdampf** _m_ BAU, CHEMIE mercury vapor (AmE), mercury vapour (BrE); **Quecksilberdampfgleichrichter** _m_ ELEKTRIZ mercury arc converter, ELEKTROTECH mercury arc rectifier, mercury vapor rectifier (AmE), mercury vapour rectifier (BrE); **Quecksilberdampf-Gleichrichterröhre** _f_ ELEKTRIZ ignitron; **Quecksilberdampflampe** _f_ ELEKTRIZ mercury arc lamp, ELEKTROTECH mercury vapor lamp (AmE), mercury vapour lamp (BrE); **Quecksilberdampfstromrichter** _m_ ELEKTROTECH mercury arc converter; **Quecksilberdampfturbine** _f_ MASCHINEN mercury vapor turbine (AmE), mercury vapour turbine (BrE); **Quecksilberelement** _nt_ ELEKTROTECH mercury cell; **Quecksilber-Fulminat** _nt_ CHEMIE mercury fulminate; **Quecksilbergewinnung** _f_ CHEMIE mercurification; **Quecksilberkatode** _f_ ELEKTROTECH mercury pool cathode; **Quecksilberkippschalter** *m* ELEKTRIZ mercury tilt switch; **Quecksilberkontakte** *m pl* ELEKTROTECH mercury-wetted contacts; **Quecksilberkontaktthermometer** *nt* GERÄT mercury contact thermometer; **Quecksilberkugel** *f* CHEMIE mercury cup; **Quecksilber-Laser** *m* ELEKTRONIK mercury laser; **Quecksilberlichtbogen** *m* ELEKTROTECH mercury arc; **Quecksilberrelais** *nt* ELEKTRIZ mercury relay; **Quecksilberröhre** *f* ELEKTROTECH mercury pool tube; **Quecksilberschalter** *m* ELEKTRIZ, ELEKTROTECH mercury switch; **Quecksilberstrahlgleichrichter** *m* ELEKTROTECH mercury rectifier; **Quecksilberthermometer** *nt* HEIZ & KÄLTE, PHYS mercury thermometer; **Quecksilberunterbrecher** *m* ELEKTROTECH mercury interrupter; **Quecksilber-Verzögerungsleitung** *f* ELEKTRONIK mercury delay line

Quellbereich *m* UMWELTSCHMUTZ source area

Quelle *f* BAU spring, COMP & DV repository, source, ELEKTROTECH, HYDRAUL source; **~ der EMK** *f* PHYS source of emf

Quellelektrodenkontakt *m* ELEKTROTECH source contact

Quellen *nt* KUNSTSTOFF swelling, PAPIER bloating, TEXTIL swelling

quellen[1] *vt* FERTIG macerate

quellen[2] *vi* TEXTIL swell

Quelle: **Quellenadresse** *f* COMP & DV source address; **Quellenangabe** *f* PATENT indication of source; **Quellenbereich** *m* KERNTECH *Reaktor* source range; **Quellencode** *m* COMP & DV source code; **Quellendatei** *f* COMP & DV source file; **Quellendokument** *nt* COMP & DV source document; **Quellenelektrode** *f* ELEKTROTECH source; **Quellenfassung** *f* WASSERVERSORG tapping water; **Quellenimpedanz** *f* ELEKTROTECH source impedance; **Quellenprogramm** *nt* COMP & DV source program; **Quellensprache** *f* COMP & DV source language; **Quellenstärke** *f (S)* KERNTECH source strength *(S)*

Quellpunkt *m* KER & GLAS hot spot

Quellschweißen *nt* KUNSTSTOFF solvent welding

Quellton *m* ERDÖL *Mineral* swelling clay

Quellung *f* FERTIG *Beton* expansion, *Kunststoffinstallationen* swelling, KUNSTSTOFF swelling

Quellvolumen *nt* BAU bulking

Quellwasser *nt* LEBENSMITTEL, WASSERVERSORG spring water

Quellwiderstand *m* ELEKTROTECH source impedance

Quer- *pref* ANSTRICH, FERTIG *Bewegungsrichtung* lateral, WASSERTRANS *Schiffkonstruktion* transverse

quer: **~ zur Faserrichtung** *adv* FERTIG across the fiber grain (AmE), across the fibre grain (BrE)

querab *adv* WASSERTRANS abeam

Quer-: **Querabweichung** *f* RAUMFAHRT across track error; **Querachse** *f* LUFTTRANS lateral axis, pitch axis, MASCHINEN transverse axis; **Queranteil** *m* COMP & DV quadrature component; **Queraufzeichnung** *f* AUFNAHME, FERNSEH transverse recording; **Querbalken** *m* BAU crossbeam, traverse, FERTIG intertie, LUFTTRANS *Befeuerung* crossbar, MASCHINEN cross member; **Querbelastung** *f* MASCHINEN lateral load, transverse load; **Querbeschleunigungsanzeiger** *m* LUFTTRANS lateral accelerometer; **Querbespantung** *f* WASSERTRANS *Schiffbau* transverse framing; **Querbewegung** *f* MASCHINEN traverse motion; **Querbewehrungsstahl** *m* BAU distribution steel; **Querbrett** *nt* BAU *Gerüstbau* ledger; **Querbruch** *m* KER & GLAS cross break

Quercetin *nt* CHEMIE quercetin

Quercitrin *nt* CHEMIE quercitrin

Quer-: **Querdehnungszahl** *f* BAU Poisson's ratio

querelektrisch *adj* ELEKTROTECH transverse electric

querelektromagnetisch *adj* ELEKTROTECH, TELEKOM transverse electromagnetic

Quer-: **Querfaltung** *f* KONSTZEICH cross folding; **Querfeldkomponente** *f* COMP & DV quadrature component; **Querfeldvorspannung** *f* AUFNAHME cross-field bias; **Querfließpressen** *nt* MASCHINEN lateral extrusion, sideways extrusion; **Querflußlinearmotor** *m* TRANS transverse flux linear motor; **Querflußmaschine** *f* TRANS transverse flux machine; **Querformat** *nt* COMP & DV landscape format, DRUCK oblong size; **Querführung** *f* KFZTECH lateral guidance; **Quergefälle** *nt* BAU *Straßenbau* camber; **Quergleiten** *nt* METALL cross slip; **Querhaupt** *nt* MASCHINEN cross girth, top rail; **Querkeil** *m* FERTIG, MASCHINEN cotter; **Querkontraktionszahl** *f* KUNSTSTOFF Poisson's ratio; **Querkraft** *f* MASCHINEN, TRANS lateral force; **Querkugellager** *nt* MASCHINEN radial ball bearing; **Querlage** *f* LUFTTRANS *Flugzeug* bank; **Querlager** *nt* MASCHINEN, PAPIER radial bearing; **Querlenker** *m* KFZTECH *Radaufhängung* transverse control arm; **Querlenkerarm** *m* KFZTECH suspension arm

quermagnetisch *adj* ELEKTROTECH, TELEKOM transverse magnetic

Quer-: **Quermagnetisierungseffekt** *m* ELEKTRIZ cross-magnetizing effect; **Querneigung** *f* BAU crossfall, slope, TRANS *Straße* banking; **Querparität** *f* COMP & DV vertical parity; **Querparitätsprüfung** *f* COMP & DV VRC, vertical redundancy check; **Querprofil** *nt* BAU cross section; **Querrichtung** *f* PAPIER cross direction

Querrichtung: **in ~** *adv* FERTIG laterally

Quer-: **Querriegel** *m* BAU strap, *Holz* tie beam; **Querrippen** *f pl* TEXTIL crosswise ribs; **Querrippenglas** *nt* KER & GLAS cross reeded glass; **Querriß** *m* FERTIG *Gießen* head pull; **Querrollenlager** *nt* MASCHINEN radial roller bearing

Querruder *nt* LUFTTRANS aileron, wing flap; **Querruderausschlag** *m* LUFTTRANS aileron deflection; **Querrudernachsteuerung** *f* LUFTTRANS aileron follow-up; **Querruderstellungsanzeiger** *m* LUFTTRANS aileron position indicator; **Querrudersteuerung** *f* LUFTTRANS aileron control; **Querrudersteuerungsrad** *nt* LUFTTRANS aileron control wheel

Quer-: **Quersäge** *f* FERTIG crosscut saw; **Querschiene** *f* EISENBAHN crossbar

querschiffs *adv* WASSERTRANS aburton, athwartships

Quer-: **Querschlaghammer** *m* BAU cross-peen hammer; **Querschlitten** *m* FERTIG *Karusselldrehmaschine, Waagerechtstoßmaschine* saddle, MASCHINEN cross slide, saddle, slide head, slide rest; **Querschlitten des Tisches** *m* FERTIG *Waagrechtstoßmaschine* apron; **Querschlitz** *m* TELEKOM transverse slot; **Querschneide** *f* FERTIG *Spiralbohrer* chisel edge, dead center (AmE), dead centre (BrE); **Querschneider** *m* VERPACK sheet-cutting machine; **Querschneidewinkel** *m* FERTIG *Spiralbohrer* angle of point; **Querschnitt** *m* BAU cross section, FERTIG *Sägen* crosscut, MASCHINEN cross section, sectional view, METALL, PAPIER cross section, PHYS profile, TEXTIL cross section, WASSERTRANS *Schiffbau* cross section, *Schiffkonstruktion* transverse section; **Querschnitt des Luftschraubenblattes** *m* LUFTTRANS *Hubschrauber* blade cross section; **Querschnittsuntersuchung** *f* ERGON cross-sectional study;

Querschnittszeichnung *f* MASCHINEN cross-section drawing, WASSERTRANS *Schiffkonstruktion* cross-sectional drawing; **Querschott** *nt* WASSERTRANS *Schiffkonstruktion* transverse bulkhead; **Querschwingung** *f* MASCHINEN transverse vibration; **Quersee** *f* WASSERTRANS beam sea; **Quersieder** *m* HEIZ & KÄLTE cross tube boiler; **Quersiederrohrkessel** *m* HEIZ & KÄLTE cross tube boiler; **Querspanten** *nt pl* WASSERTRANS *Schiffbau* transverse framing; **Querspur-Aufzeichnung** *f* AUFNAHME cross track recording; **Querstabilisator** *m* KFZTECH antiroll bar; **Querstabilität** *f* KFZTECH lateral stability, WASSERTRANS *Schiffkonstruktion* transverse stability; **Querstrahler** *m* TELEKOM broadside array; **Querstrahlruder** *nt* WASSERTRANS *Schiffantrieb* side thruster; **Querstrebe** *f* BAU cross wall, KFZTECH antiroll bar; **Querstrich** *m* MATH bar

Querstrom *m* ELEKTRIZ leakage, leakage current, ELEKTROTECH wattless current, KER & GLAS transverse current, KFZTECH *Motor* cross flow; **Querstromgebläse** *nt* ELEKTRIZ radial fan; **Querstromkopfmotor** *m* *(DOHC-Motor)* KFZTECH direct-acting overhead camshaft engine *(DOHC engine)*; **Querstromkühler** *m* KFZTECH cross-flow radiator; **Querstromlüfter** *m* HEIZ & KÄLTE cross-flow fan; **Querstromofen** *m* KER & GLAS cross-fired furnace

Querströmung *f* KFZTECH cross flow

Querstrom: **Querstromventilator** *m* MASCHINEN cross flow fan; **Querstromverteiler** *m* PAPIER flow spreader; **Querstromwärmeaustauscher** *m* HEIZ & KÄLTE cross-flow heat exchanger

Quer-: **Quersumme** *f* MATH horizontal check sum; **Quersummenkontrolle** *f* COMP & DV parallel balance; **Quersupport** *m* FERTIG rail tool head (AmE), *Hobelmaschine* rail head, MASCHINEN cross slide; **Querträger** *m* BAU crossbar, wind brace, KFZTECH cross member, MASCHINEN cross girder, cross member, crossbeam, PHYS crosshead; **Querträgermaschine** *f* KER & GLAS x-arm machine; **Quertrimmung** *f* LUFTTRANS lateral trim; **Querverbandsteil** *nt* WASSERTRANS *Schiffbau* transverse member

Querverbindung *f* BAU interconnection, KFZTECH cross rail, KUNSTSTOFF cross link, TELEKOM interexchange (BrE), interoffice (AmE); **Querverbindungsleitung** *f* TELEKOM tie line; **Querverbindungsleitung zwischen Wählnebenstellen** *f* TELEKOM inter-PABX tie circuit; **Querverbindungsschnittstelle** *f* TELEKOM tie circuit interface

Quer-: **Quervergrößerung** *f* PHYS transverse magnification

querverlaufend *adv* WASSERTRANS *Schiffkonstruktion* transverse

Quer-: **Querverstrebung** *f* WASSERTRANS *Schiffbau* cross brace; **Quervorschub** *m* FERTIG lateral feed, MASCHINEN transverse feed; **Quervorschubleitung** *f*

LUFTTRANS cross-feed line; **Querwand** *f* BAU cross wall, MECHAN bulkhead; **Querzahl** *f* FERTIG rho ratio; **Querzusammenziehung** *f* METALL lateral contraction

Quetsch- *pref* BAU, FERTIG, MASCHINEN, SICHERHEIT, TEXTIL crushing

Quetsche *f* LEBENSMITTEL *Küchengerät* masher, TEXTIL squeezer

Quetschen *nt* PAPIER squeezing

quetschen *vt* ELEKTROTECH, RADIO crimp

Quetsch-: **Quetschfalte** *f* TEXTIL inverted pleat, knife pleat; **Quetschfestigkeit** *f* MASCHINEN ultimate crushing strength; **Quetschflüssigkeit** *f* FERTIG *Hydraulik* trapping; **Quetschgrenze** *f* MASCHINEN crushing yield point; **Quetschhahn** *m* BAU pinchcock; **Quetschleistung** *f* SICHERHEIT *Maschinen* crushing power; **Quetschmühle** *f* LEBENSMITTEL bruiser; **Quetschtube** *f* VERPACK collapsible tube; **Quetschung** *f* SICHERHEIT *Maschinen* crushing; **Quetschverbindung** *f* ELEKTROTECH crimped connection; **Quetschversuch** *m* WERKPRÜF compression test, crushing test; **Quetschwalze** *f* FOTO squeegee; **Quetschwalzwerk** *nt* KOHLEN chat roller; **Quetschwerk** *nt* TEXTIL squeezer; **Quetschwiderstand** *m* ELEKTROTECH pinched resistor; **Quetschzone** *f* KUNSTSTOFF pinch-off area

Quick-Change-Flugzeug *nt* *(QC-Flugzeug)* LUFTTRANS quick-change aircraft *(QC aircraft)*

Quicksand *m* KOHLEN quicksand

Quickton *m* KOHLEN quick clay

QUIL-Gehäuse *nt* ELEKTRONIK QUIP, quad-in-line package

Quint *nt* AKUSTIK fifth

Quintal *nt* METROL quintal (BrE)

Quinte *f* AKUSTIK fifth

Quintett *nt* PHYS *Spektroskopie* quintet

Quirl *m* LEBENSMITTEL agitator

quirlen *vt* CHEMTECH agitate

QUISAM *abbr (erweiterte indizierte Zugriffsmöglichkeit für sequentielle Dateien)* COMP & DV QUISAM *(queued unique index sequential access method)*

quittieren *vt* COMP & DV acknowledge

Quittierung *f* KONTROLL handshake

Quittung *f* COMP & DV, TELEKOM ACK, acknowledgement; **Quittungsbetrieb** *m* COMP & DV handshake, handshaking, TELEKOM handshaking; **Quittungszeichen** *nt* TELEKOM acknowledgement signal

Quotient *m* COMP & DV, MATH quotient; **Quotientenzweig** *m* GERÄT *Brückenschaltung* ratio arm

Q-Wert *m* PHYS *Kernphysik* Q value

QWERTY-Tastatur *f* COMP & DV *englischsprachiges Keyboard-Layout* QWERTY keyboard

QWERTZ-Tastatur *f* COMP & DV *deutschsprachiges Keyboard-Layout* QWERTZ keyboard

QZ *abbr (quantisiertes Zeichen)* ELEKTRONIK QS *(quantized signal)*

R

R *abbr* ELEKTRIZ *(Reluktanz)* R *(reluctance)*, ELEKTRIZ *(Widerstand)* R *(resistance)*, KERNTECH *(Rydberg-Konstante)* R *(Rydberg constant)*, KERNTECH *(Dosis)* R *(dose rate)*, KERNTECH *(linearer Bereich)* R *(linear range)*, PHYS *(Gaskonstante)* R *(gas constant)*, STRAHLPHYS *(Röntgen)* R *(röntgen)*, THERMOD *(Gaskonstante)* R *(gas constant)*

r *abbr* AKUSTIK *(Entfernung von der Schallquelle)* r *(distance from source)*, KERNTECH *(Kernradius)* r *(nuclear radius)*, OPTIK *(Brechungswinkel, Refraktionswinkel)* r *(angle of refraction)*, PHYS *(Brechungswinkel)* r *(angle of refraction)*

Ra *(Radium)* CHEMIE Ra *(radium)*

Rα *abbr (Rydberg-Konstante)* KERNTECH Rα *(Rydberg constant)*

Racah-Kopplung *f* KERNTECH Racah coupling

Racemat *nt* CHEMIE racemate

racemisch *adj* CHEMIE racemic

racemisieren *vt* CHEMIE racemize

Racemisierung *f* CHEMIE racemization

Rachen *m* FERTIG *Lehre* gap, MASCHINEN gap, jaws, throat; **Rachenlehre** *f* MASCHINEN, METROL caliper gage (AmE), calliper gauge (BrE), gap gage (AmE), gap gauge (BrE), snap gage (AmE), snap gauge (BrE)

Rad[1] *abbr (Einheit der Energiedosis)* STRAHLPHYS rad (dated), radiation absorbed dose (dated)

Rad[2] *nt* MASCHINEN wheel, WASSERTRANS radar; **~ mit Außenverzahnung** *nt* MASCHINEN external gear

rad GEOM radian

Rad: **Radabnutzung** *f* EISENBAHN wheel wear; **Radabweiser** *m* BAU spur post; **Radachse** *f* KFZTECH *eines Pferdewagens* axletree, MECHAN, PHYS axis of a wheel

Radar *nt* PHYS, RADIO, STRAHLPHYS radar; **Radarabdeckung** *f* RADIO radar dome, radome; **Radarabtaster** *m* LUFTTRANS, STRAHLPHYS, TRANS, WASSERTRANS radar scanner; **Radarabtastschema** *nt* LUFTTRANS, TRANS, WASSERTRANS radar scan pattern; **Radarabtastung** *f* LUFTTRANS, TRANS, WASSERTRANS radar scanning; **Radaranflug** *m* LUFTTRANS ground-controlled approach, radar approach; **Radaranflugkontrollzentrum** *nt* LUFTTRANS radar approach control center (AmE), radar approach control centre (BrE); **Radarantenne** *f* LUFTTRANS scanner, RADIO radar scanner, TRANS radar aerial, radar antenna, WASSERTRANS radar aerial, radar antenna, scanner; **Radarantennenverkleidung** *f* RAUMFAHRT radome; **Radarantwort** *f* LUFTTRANS, TRANS, WASSERTRANS radar response; **Radarantwortbake** *f* WASSERTRANS radar responding beacon, *Seezeichen* racon; **Radarauflösungsvermögen** *nt* RADIO radar resolution; **Radaraufzeichnung** *f* WASSERTRANS radar plotting; **Radarausrüstung** *f* LUFTTRANS, TRANS radar equipment; **Radarauswertung** *f* WASSERTRANS radar plotting; **Radarbake** *f* RADIO, STRAHLPHYS, TELEKOM radar beacon, WASSERTRANS *Seezeichen* radar beacon, radar marker beacon; **Radarbeobachtung** *f* RADIO radar picket; **Radarbeobachtungsstation** *f* TRANS, WASSERTRANS radar picket station; **Radarbild** *nt* RADIO image, WASSERTRANS radar image; **Radarbildschirm** *m* LUFTTRANS, TRANS, WASSERTRANS radar screen; **Radarboje** *f* WASSERTRANS radar marker float; **Radardrehantenne** *f* LUFTTRANS, TRANS, WASSERTRANS radar scanner; **Radarecho** *nt* LUFTTRANS radar echo, RADIO radar response, TRANS radar echo; **Radarechoanzeige** *f* LUFTTRANS radar blip; **Radareinstufung** *f* LUFTTRANS, TRANS, WASSERTRANS radar rating; **Radarerfassung** *f* TRANS radar contact; **Radarfeuer** *nt* STRAHLPHYS radar beacon; **Radarflugsicherungsdienst** *m* TRANS radar air traffic control; **Radarführung** *f* LUFTTRANS, TRANS, WASSERTRANS radar vectoring; **Radarfunkfeuer** *nt* LUFTTRANS, TELEKOM radar beacon; **Radargast** *m* WASSERTRANS *Besatzung* radar operator; **Radargeschwindigkeitsmesser** *m* TRANS radar speed meter

radargesteuert *adj* WASSERTRANS radar-controlled

Radar: **Radarhaube** *f* LUFTTRANS, WASSERTRANS radome; **Radarhöhenmesser** *m* LUFTTRANS radar altimeter; **Radarkennung** *f* LUFTTRANS, TRANS radar identification; **Radarkontrolle** *f* LUFTTRANS, TRANS radar control; **Radarkuppel** *f* LUFTTRANS radome, WASSERTRANS radar dome, radome; **Radarküstenbild** *nt* WASSERTRANS radar coast image; **Radarleitdienst** *m* TRANS radar surveillance; **Radarlotse** *m* LUFTTRANS, TRANS radar controller; **Radarmast** *m* WASSERTRANS radar mast; **Radarnase** *f* LUFTTRANS radome, *Hubschrauber* blister, RADIO, WASSERTRANS radome; **Radarnavigation** *f* LUFTTRANS radar navigation; **Radarortung** *f* WASSERTRANS radar detection; **Radarparabolreflektor** *m* LUFTTRANS, TRANS radar dish; **Radarpeilung** *f* WASSERTRANS radar bearing; **Radarpip** *nt* WASSERTRANS radar pip; **Radarreflektor** *m* LUFTTRANS, TRANS, WASSERTRANS radar reflector; **Radarreflektorboje** *f* WASSERTRANS radar reflector buoy; **Radarreichweite** *f* LUFTTRANS, TRANS, WASSERTRANS radar range; **Radarrelaisstation** *f* WASSERTRANS radar relay station; **Radarröhre** *f* ELEKTRONIK radar tube; **Radarrückstrahlvermögen** *nt* RADIO radar reflectivity; **Radarscanner** *m* STRAHLPHYS radar scanner; **Radarschirm** *m* LUFTTRANS, TRANS, WASSERTRANS radar screen; **Radarschirmbild** *nt* LUFTTRANS, TRANS radar display; **Radarschüssel** *f* LUFTTRANS, TRANS radar dish; **Radarsendebake** *f* WASSERTRANS *ohne Empfangsteil* ramark; **Radarsichtgerät** *nt* TRANS, WASSERTRANS radar scope; **Radarsonde** *f* STRAHLPHYS radar sensor; **Radarstation** *f* WASSERTRANS radar station; **Radarstelle** *f* LUFTTRANS, TRANS, WASSERTRANS radar unit; **Radarsteuerkurs** *m* LUFTTRANS, TRANS radar heading; **Radarstörung** *f* WASSERTRANS radar interference; **Radarstrahl** *m* WASSERTRANS radar beam; **Radartarnung** *f* RADIO radar camouflage; **Radarüberwachung** *f* LUFTTRANS radar monitoring, TRANS radar monitoring, radar surveillance; **Radarvorposten** *m* RADIO radar picket; **Radarwellen** *f pl* STRAHLPHYS radar waves; **Radarzeichnung** *f* LUFTTRANS radar plotting; **Radarzielansteuerung** *f* LUFTTRANS, TRANS radar homing; **Radarzielsuchkopf** *m* RADIO radar homing head; **Radarzielverfolgung** *f* LUFTTRANS, RADIO, TRANS RT, radar tracking

Rad: **Radaufhängung** *f* KFZTECH suspension system; **Radauswuchtung** *f* KFZTECH wheel balancing; **Radblende** *f* KFZTECH hub cap; **Radblockierer** *m* KFZTECH boot, wheel clamp; **Raddurchmesser** *m* FERTIG gear diameter; **Radeinstellung** *f* KFZTECH wheel alignment

Räder *nt pl* KFZTECH, MECHAN wheels; **Räderblock** *m* MASCHINEN cluster of gearwheels; **Räderfräsmaschine** *f* MASCHINEN gear milling machine; **Rädergetriebe** *nt* FERTIG gear unit, gearbox, gears, MASCHINEN gear train, train of gearing; **Räderkasten** *m* MASCHINEN, MECHAN gearbox; **Räderkegelwinkel** *m* MASCHINEN gear cone angle

räderlos *adj* MASCHINEN gearless

Räder: **Rädersatz** *m* KFZTECH set of wheels, MASCHINEN nest of gearwheels; **Räderschere** *f* FERTIG gear quadrant, quadrant plate, *Spanung* quadrant, MASCHINEN quadrant, quadrant plate; **Räderspindelkasten** *m* FERTIG gear head; **Rädervorgelege** *nt* FERTIG back gear; **Räderwerk** *nt* KFZTECH train of gears, MASCHINEN gear set, gear train, gearing, train of gears

Rad: **Radfahrweg** *m* BAU cycle track, TRANS cycle path; **Radfelge** *f* KFZTECH wheel rim; **Radflansch** *m* KFZTECH wheel flange; **Radflügelflugzeug** *nt* LUFTTRANS cyclogyro

radführend: **~er Lenker** *m* KFZTECH *Federung, Aufhängung* control arm

Rad: **Radgleitenanzeige** *f* EISENBAHN wheel-slide detection

Radial- *pref* FERTIG, MASCHINEN, MECHAN, PHYS radial

radial[1] *adj* ERGON, GEOM, MECHAN radial; **~ ausbaubar** *adj* FERTIG *Kunststoffinstallationen* with union ends

radial:[2] **~e Ablenkelektrode** *f* FERNSEH radial deflecting electrode; **~es Austauschen** *nt* KERNTECH *von Brennelementen* radial shuffling; **~e elektrische Felder** *nt pl* STRAHLPHYS radial electrical fields; **~e Leistungsverteilung** *f* KERNTECH radial power distribution; **~es Moment** *nt* LUFTTRANS annular momentum; **~er Neutronenfluß** *m* KERNTECH radial neutron flux; **~er Teil der Wellenfunktion** *m* STRAHLPHYS radial part of the wave function; **~er Tischvorschub** *m* FERTIG table infeed; **~es Umsetzen** *nt* KERNTECH *von Brennelementen* radial shuffling; **~e Verschiebung** *f* KERNTECH radial shift; **~e Verteilungsfunktion** *f* STRAHLPHYS radial distribution function; **~er Vorschub** *m* MASCHINEN radial feed

Radial-: **Radialanteil der Wellenfunktion** *m* STRAHLPHYS radial part of the wave function; **Radialbelastung** *f* FERTIG radial loading; **Radialbohrmaschine** *f* FERTIG, MASCHINEN radial drill, radial drilling machine, MECHAN radial drilling machine; **Radialbohrmaschine mit Höhenverstellung** *f* FERTIG adjustable radial drilling machine; **Radialdichtring** *m* MASCHINEN rotary shaft seal; **Radialflügelrad** *nt* HEIZ & KÄLTE radial vane wheel; **Radialgeschwindigkeit** *f* NICHTFOSS ENERG radial velocity; **Radialkolbenpumpe** *f* FERTIG radial piston pump; **Radialkomponente** *f* PHYS radial component; **Radialkraft** *f* FERTIG thrust force; **Radialkugellager** *nt* MASCHINEN radial ball bearing; **Radiallager** *nt* KFZTECH plain bearing, MASCHINEN journal bearing, radial bearing; **Radiallüfter** *m* ELEKTRIZ radial fan; **Radialreifen** *m* KFZTECH radial tire (AmE), radial tyre (BrE), KUNSTSTOFF radial ply tire

(AmE), radial ply tyre (BrE); **Radialschlag** *m* FERTIG, MASCHINEN radial run-out; **Radialspiel** *nt* FERTIG, MASCHINEN radial play; **Radialstrahl** *m* OPTIK *durch die Mitte der Apertur* direct radial; **Radialturbine** *f* MASCHINEN radial flow turbine; **Radialventilator** *m* HEIZ & KÄLTE radial fan, radial flow fan; **Radialverfahren** *nt* FERTIG *Schneckenfräsen* radial feed method; **Radialvorschub** *m* MASCHINEN radial feed; **Radialzylinderrollenlager** *nt* MASCHINEN parallel-roller journal bearing, radial cylindrical roller bearing

Radian *m* ELEKTRIZ, PHYS *Bogenmaß* radian

Radiant *m* ELEKTRONIK, GEOM radian

Radienschablone *f* FERTIG radius gage (AmE), radius gauge (BrE)

radieren *vt* FERTIG etch

Radierfestigkeit *f* KONSTZEICH resistance to erasure

Radikal *nt* KERNTECH, KUNSTSTOFF radical

radikalisch: **~e Polymerisation** *f* KUNSTSTOFF radical polymerization; **~e Reaktion** *f* KUNSTSTOFF free radical reaction

Radikal: **Radikalpolymerisation** *f* KUNSTSTOFF radical polymerization; **Radikalreaktion** *f* KUNSTSTOFF free radical reaction

Radikand *m* MATH *unter dem Wurzelzeichen* radicand

Radio *nt* PHYS, RADIO radio; **Radioactinium** *nt* STRAHLPHYS radioactinium

radioaktiv[1] *adj* ERDÖL, KERNTECH, PHYS, STRAHLPHYS, TEILPHYS radioactive

radioaktiv:[2] **~er Abfall** *m* ABFALL nuclear waste, radioactive waste, radwaste, KERNTECH effluent, nuclear waste, radioactive waste, STRAHLPHYS radioactive waste; **~e Altersbestimmung** *f* KERNTECH, STRAHLPHYS radioactive dating; **~es Cobalt** *nt* CHEMIE radiocobalt; **~es Element** *nt* KERNTECH, STRAHLPHYS radioactive element; **~es Gleichgewicht** *nt* KERNTECH, STRAHLPHYS radioactive equilibrium; **~e Halbwertszeit** *f* KERNTECH, STRAHLPHYS radioactive lifetime; **~es Isotop** *nt* CHEMIE radioisotope, KERNTECH radioactive isotope, PHYS radioisotope, STRAHLPHYS radioactive isotope, TEILPHYS radioisotope; **~er Kern** *m* PHYS radionuclide; **~er Kohlenstoff** *m* PHYS radiocarbon; **~ kontaminiertes Wasser** *nt* UMWELTSCHMUTZ contaminated water; **~e Kontaminierung** *f* KERNTECH, STRAHLPHYS radioactive contamination; **~er Körper** *m* KERNTECH, STRAHLPHYS radioactive body; **~es Log** *nt* ERDÖL radioactive log; **~es Markieren** *nt* KERNTECH, STRAHLPHYS radioactive labeling (AmE), radioactive labelling (BrE); **~ markiertes Atom** *nt* KERNTECH tagged atom; **~e Markierung** *f* KERNTECH, STRAHLPHYS radioactive tracer; **~es Material** *nt* ELEKTROTECH active material; **~er Niederschlag** *m* KERNTECH fallout, radioactive fallout, rainout, STRAHLPHYS, UMWELTSCHMUTZ radioactive fallout, rainout; **~es Nuklid** *nt* STRAHLPHYS radionuclide; **~es Präparat** *nt* KERNTECH radiation source; **~es Spurenelement** *nt* KERNTECH, STRAHLPHYS radioactive tracer; **~es Standardpräparat** *nt* KERNTECH radioactive standard, STRAHLPHYS radioactive standard, radioactivity standard; **~er Stoff** *m* SICHERHEIT, UMWELTSCHMUTZ radioactive substance; **~es Strontium** *nt* CHEMIE radiostrontium; **~er Übergang** *m* KERNTECH, STRAHLPHYS radioactive change; **~e Verschmutzung** *f* UMWELTSCHMUTZ radioactive pollution; **~e Verseuchung** *f* KERNTECH radioactive contamination, SICHERHEIT radioactive pollution, STRAHLPHYS radioactive contamination; **~er Zerfall** *m*

KERNTECH, STRAHLPHYS radioactive disintegration, radioactive decay; **~es Zerfallsgesetz** *nt* STRAHLPHYS law of radioactive decay; **~e Zerfallsrate** *f* KERNTECH, STRAHLPHYS radioactive decay rate; **~e Zerfallsreihe** *f* KERNTECH radioactive decay series, radioactive series, STRAHLPHYS radioactive series, radioactive decay series

Radioaktivität *f* KERNTECH, PHYS, STRAHLPHYS, TEIL-PHYS radioactivity; **Radioaktivitätslog** *nt* ERDÖL nuclear log; **Radioaktivitätsmeßgerät** *nt* STRAHLPHYS radioactivity meter

Radio: **Radioantenne** *f* KFZTECH radio aerial (BrE), *Zubehör* radio antenna (AmE), RADIO, TRANS radio aerial (BrE), radio antenna (AmE); **Radioastronomie** *f* PHYS, RAUMFAHRT radio astronomy; **Radioastronomieantenne** *f* TELEKOM radioastronomical antenna; **Radiochemie** *f* KERNTECH, STRAHLPHYS radiochemistry

radiochemisch: **~er Abzug** *m* KERNTECH radiochemical fume cupboard

Radio: **Radiofrequenz** *f (HF)* AUFNAHME, ELEKTRONIK, FERNSEH, RADIO, TELEKOM *Richtfunk*, WASSERTRANS radio frequency *(RF)*

radiofrequenzdurchlässig: **~er Bereich der Atmosphäre** *m* PHYS radio window

radiogen *adj* PHYS, STRAHLPHYS radiogenic

Radio: **Radiogoniometer** *nt* PHYS, STRAHLPHYS radiogoniometer; **Radiogoniometrie** *f* PHYS, ·RADIO, TRANS RDF, radio direction finding; **Radiographie** *f* PHYS radiography; **Radioisotop** *nt* CHEMIE radioisotope, KERNTECH, STRAHLPHYS radioactive isotope; **Radioisotopengenerator** *m* RAUMFAHRT radioisotope power generator; **Radiojod** *nt* CHEMIE radioiodine; **Radiokobalt** *m* STRAHLPHYS radiocobalt; **Radiokohlenstoff** *m* STRAHLPHYS radiocarbon; **Radiolog** *nt* ERDÖL *Meßtechnik* radioactive log; **Radiologie** *f* STRAHLPHYS radiology; **Radiolumineszenz** *f* STRAHLPHYS radioluminescence; **Radiolyse** *f* CHEMIE, KERNTECH, STRAHLPHYS radiolysis; **Radiolyse von Wasser** *f* KERNTECH water radiolysis

radiolytisch *adj* KERNTECH radiolytic

Radio: **Radiometer** *nt* NICHTFOSS ENERG radiometer; **Radiometrie** *f* CHEMIE radiometry

radiometrisch: **~e Analyse** *f* STRAHLPHYS radiometric analysis; **~e Bohrlochvermessung** *f* NICHTFOSS ENERG well logging

Radio: **Radiomimetikum** *nt* CHEMIE radiomimetic; **Radionuklid** *nt* STRAHLPHYS radionuclide; **Radionuklidreinheit** *f* KERNTECH, STRAHLPHYS radioactive purity; **Radiosonde** *f* TELEKOM radiosonde; **Radiospektrum** *nt* STRAHLPHYS radio spectrum; **Radiostern** *m* RAUMFAHRT *Weltraumfunk* radio star; **Radioteleskop** *nt* PHYS radio telescope; **Radiotoxizität** *f* STRAHLPHYS radiotoxicity; **Radiowelle** *f* ELEKTRIZ radio wave, ELEKTRONIK radio-wave, WELLPHYS radio wave

Radium *nt (Ra)* CHEMIE radium *(Ra)*; **Radium-Emanation** *f* STRAHLPHYS radium emanation

Radius *m* MASCHINEN, OPTIK, PHYS radius; **Radiusdrehmeißel** *m* MASCHINEN radius tool; **Radiusfräser** *m* MASCHINEN radius form cutter; **Radiuslehre** *f* MASCHINEN radius gage (AmE), radius gauge (BrE)

Radix *f* COMP & DV radix; **Radixkomplement** *nt* COMP & DV radix complement; **Radix-minus-eins-Komplement** *nt* COMP & DV radix-minus-one complement; **Radixpunkt** *m* COMP & DV radix point; **Radixschreib-**

weise *f* COMP & DV radix notation; **Radixschreibweise mit fester Notation** *f* COMP & DV fixed-base notation; **Radixschreibweise mit gemischter Basis** *f* COMP & DV mixed-base notation, mixed-radix notation

Radiziereinrichtung *f* METROL square root extracting device

Rad: **Radkappe** *f* KFZTECH hubcap; **äußerer Radkasten** *m* KFZTECH external wheel case; **Radkralle** *f* KFZTECH wheel clamp; **Radkranz** *m* EISENBAHN wheel flange, MASCHINEN wheel rim; **Radkurve** *f* GEOM cycloid; **Radlager** *nt* KFZTECH wheel bearing; **Radlagerspiel** *nt* KFZTECH wheel bearing clearance; **Radlast** *f* BAU, MASCHINEN wheel load; **Radmagnetron** *nt* PHYS cavity magnetron; **Radmittelpunkt** *m* FERTIG gear center (AmE), gear centre (BrE); **Radmutter** *f* KFZTECH wheel nut; **Radnabe** *f* FERTIG, TRANS hub, wheel hub; **Radnabenflansch** *m* KFZTECH hub flange; **Radnachlauf** *m* KFZTECH caster, castor

Radom *nt* LUFTTRANS *Hubschrauber* blister, TELEKOM radome

Radon *nt (Rn)* PHYS radon *(Rn)*

Rad: **Radpaar** *nt* LUFTTRANS dual wheel; **Radsatz** *m* EISENBAHN wheelset; **Radschacht** *m* LUFTTRANS *Fahrwerk* wheel well; **Radschlupf** *m* KFZTECH wheel slip; **Radschutz** *m* MASCHINEN wheel guard, SICHERHEIT guard; **Radschwingarm** *m* KFZTECH wheel suspension lever; **Radspur** *f* BAU rut; **Radstand** *m* EISENBAHN, KFZTECH wheelbase; **Radsteg** *m* EISENBAHN wheel web; **Radstern** *m* KFZTECH spoke wheel center (AmE), spoke wheel centre (BrE); **Radsturzwinkel** *m* KFZTECH camber angle; **Radtrommel** *f* HYDRAUL *Turbine* drum; **Radverbinder** *m* EISENBAHN wheel bond; **Radvorleger** *m* EISENBAHN scotch block; **Radzahnbahn** *f* EISENBAHN rack railroad (AmE), rack railway (BrE); **Radzahnbahnbeiwagen** *m* EISENBAHN rack railroad trailer (AmE), rack railway trailer (BrE); **Radzahnbahnschiene** *f* EISENBAHN rack track; **Radzapfen** *m* KFZTECH spindle; **Radzylinder** *m* KFZTECH wheel cylinder

raffen *vt* TEXTIL gather

Raffhalter *m* TEXTIL tie back

Raffination *f* FERTIG refining

Raffinerie *f* ERDÖL, FERTIG refinery; **Raffineriegas** *nt* ERDÖL *Destillationsprodukt* refinery gas; **Raffinerierückstände** *m pl* ABFALL refinery waste

raffinieren *vt* CHEMTECH clarify, METALL refine

Raffiniergas *nt* THERMOD refinery gas

Raffinierofen *m* THERMOD refining furnace

raffiniert[1] *adj* MEERSCHMUTZ refined

raffiniert:[2] **~es Produkt** *nt* MEERSCHMUTZ refined product

Raffinose *f* CHEMIE melicitose, raffinose

Rahmen[1] *m* BAU carrier, frame, *Tür, Fenster* frame, COMP & DV frame, DRUCK chase, EISENBAHN frame, FOTO *Foto oder Licht* mounting, *eines Fotos* frame, KFZTECH, MASCHINEN, MECHAN, PAPIER, RAUMFAHRT *Antenne* frame, TELEKOM bay, *Antenne* frame, loop, *digitale Übertragung* frame, VERPACK frame; **~ der Ansprüche** *m* PATENT scope of claims

Rahmen:[2] **im ~ von etwas liegen** *vt* PATENT fall within the scope of

rahmen *vt* FOTO frame

Rahmen: **Rahmenantenne** *f* RADIO frame aerial, frame antenna, TELEKOM loop, loop antenna; **Rahmenausrichtung** *f* RAUMFAHRT *Weltraumfunk* frame alignment; **Rahmenbildung** *f* TELEKOM frame generation; **Rahmenblechschere** *f* MECHAN guillotine shears; **Rahmencodierung** *f* COMP & DV skeletal coding, skeleton coding; **Rahmenfederung** *f* FERTIG arc spring; **Rahmenfehler** *m* COMP & DV frame error; **Rahmengestell** *nt* TELEKOM frame; **Rahmengleichlauf** *m* TELEKOM frame alignment; **Rahmenkennung** *f* TELEKOM frame marking; **Rahmenlänge** *f* RAUMFAHRT *Antenne* frame length; **Rahmenlängsträger** *m* KFZTECH chassis member; **Rahmenquerträger** *m* KFZTECH cross member, cross rail; **Rahmenspant** *nt* WASSERTRANS *Schiffbau* web frame; **Rahmenstiel** *m* BAU member; **Rahmensynchronisation** *f* TELEKOM frame alignment; **Rahmensynchronisierung** *f* RAUMFAHRT *Weltraumfunk*, TELEKOM frame synchronization; **Rahmensystem** *nt* KÜNSTL INT expert system shell; **Rahmenwirkungsgrad** *m* RAUMFAHRT *Weltraumfunk* frame efficiency

Rähmstück *nt* BAU breastsummer, summer beam
Rahnock *f* WASSERTRANS *Segeln* yardarm
Rainout *nt* UMWELTSCHMUTZ rainout
Rakel *f* DRUCK doctor blade, squeegee, KUNSTSTOFF, PAPIER doctor, TEXTIL knife, squeegee, VERPACK doctor blade; **Rakelmesser** *nt* DRUCK doctor blade; **Rakelstreichmaschine** *f* PAPIER blade coater, knife coater; **Rakelstreichverfahren** *nt* KUNSTSTOFF knife spreading, PAPIER blade coating; **Rakelwalze** *f* PAPIER doctor roll
Rakete *f* RAUMFAHRT rocket; **Raketenantrieb** *m* RAUMFAHRT rocket propulsion; **Raketenbasis** *f* RAUMFAHRT *Startplatz* launching base; **Raketenflugzeug** *nt* RAUMFAHRT rocketplane; **Raketenraumgleiter** *m* RAUMFAHRT orbital glider; **Raketenstart** *m* RAUMFAHRT JATO (AmE), RATO (BrE), jet-assisted takeoff (AmE), rocket-assisted takeoff (BrE); **Raketenstartanlage** *f* RAUMFAHRT rocket launching site; **Raketenstarter** *m* RAUMFAHRT rocket launcher; **Raketenstufe mit Fluchtgeschwindigkeit** *f* RAUMFAHRT escape rocket stage; **Raketentriebwerk** *nt* MASCHINEN, RAUMFAHRT rocket engine
RAM *abbr* COMP & DV *(Direktzugriffsspeicher, Lese-/Schreibspeicher, Schreib-/Lesespeicher)*, ELEKTRONIK *(Direktzugriffsspeicher, Schreib-/Lesespeicher)* RAM *(random access memory)*
Raman: **~scher Effekt** *m* PHYS, STRAHLPHYS Raman effect; **~sche Spektrometrie** *f* STRAHLPHYS Raman spectrometry; **~sche Spektroskopie** *f* PHYS Raman spectroscopy; **~sche Streuung** *f* PHYS Raman scattering
RAM: RAM-Bank *f* ELEKTROTECH bank of RAMs; **RAM-Laufwerk** *nt* OPTIK read-write drive
Rammarbeiten *f pl* BAU pile driving
Rammaufsatz *m* KOHLEN pileblock
Rammbär *m* BAU beetle head, pile driver, piling hammer, KOHLEN pile ram
Rammbug *m* TRANS, WASSERTRANS ram bow
Ramme *f* BAU rammer, ram, FERTIG hammer, monkey, rammer, *Gießen* punner, KOHLEN, MECHAN ram
Rammen *nt* BAU piling, *von Pfählen* spiling, PHYS ram
rammen *vt* BAU pile, ram, FERTIG *Gießen* pun, WASSERTRANS ram, *Schiff* run down
Rammgerüst *nt* BAU piling frame
Rammhammer *m* KOHLEN pile hammer
Rammhaube *f* BAU cap, pile cap
Rammprotokoll *nt* BAU penetration record
Rammtest *m* KOHLEN ram penetration test
Rammungsaufzeichnung *f* KOHLEN pile driving record

Rammungsformel *f* KOHLEN pile driving formula
Rampe *f* ELEKTROTECH, PAPIER ramp, RAUMFAHRT *für Raketen* pad; **Rampenbeleuchtung** *f* FOTO bank of lights
rampenförmig: ~er Lastanstieg *m* KERNTECH ramp change of load
Rampgewicht *nt* LUFTTRANS ramp weight
Rampstatus *m* LUFTTRANS ramp status
Ramsden-Kreis *m* OPTIK eye ring
Ramsdensches: ~ Okular *nt* PHYS Ramsden eyepiece
RAM-Speicher *m* COMP & DV memory random access
Rand[1] *m* BAU boundary, margin, skirt, *eines Abhangs* brow, COMP & DV edge, *Printout* margin, DRUCK margin, GEOM boundary, LABOR lip, MASCHINEN rim, PHYS fringe, TEXTIL, VERPACK edge
Rand:[2] **am ~ bündig ausrichten** *vt* COMP & DV justify
Rand: Randabstand *m* FERTIG *Punktschweißen*, MASCHINEN edge distance; **Randanleimmaschine** *f* VERPACK margin gluer; **Randausgleich** *m* COMP & DV justification; **Randbedingung** *f* COMP & DV constraint, ERGON, MATH boundary condition; **Randbemerkung** *f* DRUCK side note; **Randbeschnitt** *m* PAPIER trimmings; **Randdämpfung** *f* AUFNAHME surface damping, *Akustik* edge damping; **Randdetail** *nt* FERNSEH corner detail; **Randeffekt** *m* ELEKTROTECH, LUFTTRANS fringe effect; **Randeinstellung** *f* DRUCK margin settings
Rändelkopf *m* MASCHINEN milled head, milled knob
Rändelmeißel *m* FERTIG straight knurling tool
Rändelmutter *f* FERTIG hand nut, MASCHINEN knurled nut, milled nut
Rändeln *nt* FERTIG straight knurling, KER & GLAS, MASCHINEN knurling
rändeln *vt* FERTIG straight-knurl
Rändelschraube *f* MASCHINEN knurled screw
Rändelung *f* MASCHINEN knurl, knurling
Rändelwerkzeug *nt* FERTIG straight knurl, MASCHINEN, MECHAN knurling tool
Rand: Randentkohlung *f* FERTIG edge decarburization
Rändern *nt* KER & GLAS bead down
Rand: Randfaser *f* FERTIG outer fiber (AmE), outer fibre (BrE); **Randfeuer** *nt* LUFTTRANS boundary light; **Randkapazität** *f* KER & GLAS brim capacity; **Randkraft** *f* TRANS lateral force; **Randleiste** *f* DRUCK border, box rule; **Randlinie eines Zeichens** *f* COMP & DV character outline; **Randmode** *f* OPTIK bound mode; **Randnote** *f* DRUCK side note
Randomdatei *f* COMP & DV random file
Rand: Randperforation *f* COMP & DV running perforation; **Randplatte** *f* EISENBAHN bearing plate; **Randschicht** *f* OPTIK, TELEKOM barrier layer; **Randspritzer** *m* PAPIER trim shower; **Randstein** *m* BAU curb (AmE), kerb (BrE); **Randstreifen** *m* BAU margin; **Randverwerfung** *f* FERNSEH scallop, scalloping; **Randwasser** *nt* ERDÖL *Geologie* edge water; **Randwert** *m* MATH boundary value; **Randwertprüfung** *f* COMP & DV marginal check, marginal test; **Randwinkel** *m* FERTIG *Kappilarrohr* angle of contact, contact angle; **Randwirbel** *m* LUFTTRANS wing tip vortex; **Randwirbel am Luftschraubenblatt** *m* LUFTTRANS blade tip vortex; **Randwulst** *f* FERTIG bead; **Randzone** *f* LUFTTRANS fringe; **Randzonenverkehr** *m* TRANS suburban traffic
Rangfolgemethode *f* ERGON job-ranking method
Rangier- *pref* EISENBAHN shunting; **Rangieranzeigevorrichtung** *f* EISENBAHN classification detector; **Rangierbahngleis** *nt* EISENBAHN classification yard line; **Rangierbahnhof** *m* EISENBAHN classification

yard, marshalling yard (BrE), shunting yard, switching station (AmE), switchyard (AmE); **Rangiereinrichtung** *f* TELEKOM cross-connect unit; **Rangieren** *nt* EISENBAHN classification (BrE), shunting, switching (AmE); **Rangieren durch Umsetzen** *nt* EISENBAHN shunting on level tracks; **~er** *m* EISENBAHN *Person* pointsman (BrE), shunter, switchman (AmE); **Rangiergerät für Sattelanhänger** *nt* KFZTECH dolly; **Rangiergleis** *nt* EISENBAHN classification track (BrE), switching track (AmE), marshaling track (AmE), marshalling track (BrE), shunting siding, shunting track, sorting line; **Rangierleiter** *m* EISENBAHN foreman shunter, foreman switcher (AmE); **Rangierlok** *f* BAU shunting engine, switch engine; **Rangierlokomotive** *f* EISENBAHN, TRANS shunting engine, shunting locomotive, switch engine (AmE), switcher (AmE); **Rangierwinde** *f* BAU shunting winch, switching winch (AmE)

Rangordnung[1] *f* COMP & DV order of precedence
Rangordnung:[2] **in ~ bringen** *vt* ERGON rank
Rangreihenfolge: ~ für Unterbrechungen *f* REGELUNG daisy chain device priority
Rapidanalyse *f* CHEMIE proximate analysis
Rapportzahl *f* TEXTIL number of repeats
Rapsöl *nt* LEBENSMITTEL colza oil, rapeseed oil
rasch: ~ trennender Schalter *m* ELEKTRIZ quick-break switch
Raschel *f* TEXTIL raschel knitting machine; **Raschel-Kettenwirkmaschine** *f* TEXTIL raschel knitting machine; **Raschelmaschine** *f* TEXTIL raschel knitting machine
Raser-Tiefdruck *m* VERPACK intaglio printing
Raspe *f* BAU rasp
raspeln *vt* BAU rasp
Rast *f* FERTIG *Getriebelehre* dwell, *Hochofen* bosh, KER & GLAS *Schachtofen* belly; **Rastantrieb** *m* MECHAN rack-and-pinion; **Rastblende** *f* FOTO click stop; **Rastdeckel** *m* VERPACK snap-on lid
Raste *f* FERTIG, MASCHINEN notch, MECHAN catch
Raster *nt* BAU lattice, screen, COMP & DV raster, DRUCK screen, ELEKTRONIK graticule, pattern, *bei der Leiterplattenherstellung* grid, FERNSEH graticule, raster, MATH lattice, MECHAN screen
rasterabgetastet: ~er Strahl *m* ELEKTRONIK raster-scanned beam
Raster: Rasterabstand *m* FERNSEH raster pitch; **Rasterabtastung** *f* ELEKTRONIK, FERNSEH raster scanning; **Rasterabtastungs-Elektronenstrahl-Lithografie** *f* ELEKTRONIK raster scan electron beam lithography; **Rasterabtastungs-Kathodenstrahlröhre** *f* ELEKTRONIK raster scan cathode ray tube; **Rasteranzeige** *f* COMP & DV raster display; **Rasterätzung** *f* DRUCK halftone process; **Raster-Auger-Elektronenspektroskopie** *f* KERNTECH scanning Auger microscopy; **Rasterbild** *nt* DRUCK halftone, halftone image; **Rasterbildschirm** *m* COMP & DV raster screen; **Rastereinheit** *f* COMP & DV raster unit; **Rasterelektronenmikroskop** *nt* ELEKTRONIK, STRAHLPHYS scanning electron microscope; **Rasterelektronenstrahl** *m* ELEKTRONIK scanning electron beam; **Raster-Elektronenstrahl-Lithografie** *f* ELEKTRONIK scanning electron beam lithography; **Raster-Elektronenstrahlsystem** *nt* ELEKTRONIK scanning electron beam system; **Rasterelement** *nt* COMP & DV raster element; **Rasterfeld** *nt* COMP & DV raster
rasterförmig: ~e Abtastung *f* COMP & DV raster scanning
Raster: Rasterfrequenzteiler *m* FERNSEH field divider;

Rastergenerator *m* FERNSEH raster generator; **Rastergrafik** *f* COMP & DV, DRUCK raster graphics; **Rasterionenmikroskopie** *f* STRAHLPHYS scanning ion microscopy; **Rasterklischee** *nt* FOTO halftone block; **Rasterpunkt** *m* COMP & DV pixel, MATH lattice point; **Rasterschere** *f* FERTIG *Kunststoffinstallationen* ratchet; **Rastersonde** *f* KERNTECH grid probe; **Rasterstruktur der Spaltzone** *f* KERNTECH core grid structure; **Rastersystem** *nt* BAU bay system; **Rasterverriegelung** *f* FERNSEH locking; **Rasterwinkel** *m* DRUCK screen angle; **Rasterwinkelung** *f* DRUCK screen angle

Rast: Rastgetriebe *nt* FERTIG dwell mechanism; **Rastlinie** *f* FERTIG *Dauerbruch* mark; **Rastplatz** *m* TRANS lay-by; **Rastpolbahn** *f* FERTIG *Getriebelehre* body centrode; **Rastpolkegel** *m* FERTIG *Getriebelehre* herpolhode cone; **Rastrelais** *nt* ELEKTRIZ latching relay; **Raststift** *m* BAU, FERTIG latch pin; **Rastzahn** *m* MECHAN notch
Rate *f* COMP & DV rate
Ratenüberschreitung *f* KERNTECH burnout
rational: ~e Zahl *f* COMP & DV, MATH rational number
Rationalzahlen *f pl* MATH rational numbers
Ratsche *f* BAU ratchet, MASCHINEN ratchet spanner, ratchet stop, ratchet wrench
Rattenloch *nt* ERDÖL mousehole
Rätter *m* KOHLEN cribble, riddle, screen
Rattern *nt* FERTIG *Spanung*, MASCHINEN chatter
rattern[1] *vt* FERTIG *Spanung*, KER & GLAS chatter
rattern[2] *vi* MASCHINEN chatter
Raub: ~ von Transportgütern *m* LUFTTRANS hijack
rauben *vt* LUFTTRANS *Transportgut* hijack
Raubkopie *f* COMP & DV pirate copy, FERNSEH pirate recording
Rauch *m* KER & GLAS smoke; **Rauch- und Gasalarmanlage** *f* SICHERHEIT smoke and gas alarm installation; **Rauch- und Hitzeabzugsanlage** *f* SICHERHEIT smoke and heat exhaust installation; **Rauchabzug** *m* HEIZ & KÄLTE chimney; **Rauchalarm** *m* SICHERHEIT smoke alarm; **Rauchbegrenzung** *f* SICHERHEIT smoke control; **Rauchdiagramm** *nt* SICHERHEIT smoke chart
rauchdicht: ~er Helm *m* SICHERHEIT smoke helmet
rauchend: ~e Schwefelsäure *f* CHEMIE Nordhausen acid, oleum, fuming sulfuric acid (AmE), fuming sulphuric acid (BrE)
Räuchern *nt* LEBENSMITTEL smoking
Rauch: Rauchfahne *f* LUFTTRANS exhaust trail; **Rauchfang** *m* FERTIG *Schmieden* hood, HEIZ & KÄLTE smoke flue, MECHAN funnel
rauchfrei: ~er Bereich *m* SICHERHEIT smokeless zone
Rauchgas *nt* HEIZ & KÄLTE flue gas, smoke gas, PHYS, THERMOD, UMWELTSCHMUTZ flue gas; **Rauchgasanalyse** *f* MASCHINEN flue gas analysis; **~e** *nt pl* HEIZ & KÄLTE, UMWELTSCHMUTZ fumes; **Rauchgasentschwefelung** *f* UMWELTSCHMUTZ flue gas desulfurization (AmE), flue gas desulphurization (BrE); **Rauchgasentschwefelungsanlage** *f* SICHERHEIT flue gas desulfurization installation (AmE), flue gas desulphurization installation (BrE); **Rauchgasentstaubung** *f* ABFALL particulate collection; **Rauchgasreiniger** *m* HEIZ & KÄLTE flue gas dust collector; **Rauchgasreiniger** *m* THERMOD flue gas scrubber; **Rauchgasreinigung** *f* THERMOD flue gas scrubbing; **Rauchgasvorwärmer** *m* HEIZ & KÄLTE flue gas pre-heater
Rauch: Rauchglas *nt* KER & GLAS smoked glass; **Rauch-**

kammer *f* BAU, EISENBAHN smokebox; **Rauchkammer-rohrwand** *f* EISENBAHN smokebox tube plate; **Rauchkanal** *m* HEIZ & KÄLTE smoke duct

rauchlos *adj* SICHERHEIT smokeless

Rauch: **Rauchmaske** *f* LUFTTRANS smoke mask; **Rauch-melder** *m* SICHERHEIT smoke detector; **Rauchpilz** *m* STRÖMPHYS *thermische Strömungen* plume; **Rauch-rohr** *nt* HEIZ & KÄLTE smoke tube; **Rauchrohrkessel** *m* HEIZ & KÄLTE fire tube boiler, smoke tube boiler; **Rauchschieber** *m* HEIZ & KÄLTE slide damper; **Rauch-schutztür** *f* SICHERHEIT smoke protection door; **Rauchspiegelglas** *nt* KER & GLAS tint plate; **Rauchver-brauch** *m* KOHLEN consumption of smoke

rauchverzehrend *adj* CHEMIE fumivorous

Rauch: **Rauchzug** *m* THERMOD flue

rauh[1] *adj* ANSTRICH, PAPIER rough

rauh:[2] **mit ~em Wind** *adv* WASSERTRANS *Segeln* off the wind

rauh:[3] **~e Oberfläche** *f* MASCHINEN rough surface

Rauhdecke *f* BAU friction course

Rauheit *f* MASCHINEN, MECHAN roughness; **Rauheit-meßgerät** *nt* METROL surface measuring instrument; **Rauheitsnorm** *f* METROL surface roughness standard

Rauhen *nt* ELEKTROTECH brushing, FERTIG raising, KER & GLAS, KFZTECH, TEXTIL brushing

rauhen *vt* FERTIG raise, MASCHINEN roughen, TEXTIL *Wolle* card

Rauhgriffigkeit *f* TEXTIL harsh handle

Rauhhobel *m* BAU jack plane

Rauhigkeit *f* MASCHINEN, MECHAN, PAPIER roughness; **Rauhigkeitsprüfer** *m* PAPIER *der Papieroberfläche* roughness tester

Rauhmaschine *f* TEXTIL raising machine

Rauhputz *m* BAU roughcast

rauhschleifen *vt* BAU rough-down

Rauhschliff *m* KER & GLAS gray cutting (AmE), grey cutting (BrE)

Rauhtiefe *f* MASCHINEN maximum peak-to-valley height, peak-to-valley height, roughness height; **Rauhtiefenmesser** *m* METROL peak-to-valley height gage (AmE), peak-to-valley height gauge (BrE)

Raum *m* GEOM, MASCHINEN space, MECHAN chamber; **Raum-** *pref* HEIZ & KÄLTE ambient; **~ mit geringer Schallabsorption** *m* ERGON live room; **~ für Hilfsfall-schirme** *m* RAUMFAHRT auxiliary parachute bay; **Raumanzug** *m* RAUMFAHRT spacesuit; **Raumbedarf** *m* MASCHINEN space occupied, space taken up, MECHAN bulk

raumbeständig *adj* BAU *Beton* sound

Raum: **Raumbildbetrachter** *m* FOTO stereoscope

Räumbohrer *m* ERDÖL reaming bit

Raum: **Raumbreite** *f (b)* RAUMFAHRT galactic latitude *(b)*; **Raumdichte** *f* BAU density; **Raum-Dichte-Verhält-nis** *nt* TRANS volume-density relationship; **Raumeffekt** *m* AUFNAHME auditory perspective

Räumen *nt* MASCHINEN broaching

raumen *vi* WASSERTRANS *Wind* veer aft

räumen *vt* BAU vacate, MASCHINEN broach

Räumer *m* BAU, ERDÖL *Bohrtechnik* reamer

Raumfähre *f* RAUMFAHRT, TELEKOM space shuttle

Raumfahrttransportsystem *nt (STS)* RAUMFAHRT space transportation system *(STS)*; **Raumfahrtzen-trum** *nt* RAUMFAHRT astrodrome

Raumfahrzeug *nt* RAUMFAHRT spacecraft

Raum: **Raumfärbung** *f* AUFNAHME *Radio* acoustic coloring (AmE), acoustic colouring (BrE)

raumfest *adj* RAUMFAHRT space-bound

Raumflug *m* RAUMFAHRT space flight; **~ auf Umlaufbah-nen** *m* RAUMFAHRT circular flight; **Raumflugumsetzer** *m* RAUMFAHRT orbital transfer vehicle

Raum: **Raumformfräsen** *nt* FERTIG three-dimensional tracer milling

Räumfräsen *nt* MASCHINEN broach milling

Raum: **Raumfuge** *f* BAU expansion joint, running joint

raumgeteilt: **~e Vermittlung** *f* TELEKOM space division switching, space switch; **~e Vermittlungsstelle** *f* TELE-KOM space switch; **~es Vermittlungssystem** *nt* TELEKOM space division switching system

Raum: **Raumgitter** *nt* PHYS spatial grid; **Raumgleiter** *m* TRANS orbital glider; **Rauminhalt** *m* BAU content, GEOM volume, MECHAN, PHYS, WASSERTRANS *Ladung* cubic capacity; **Raumisomer** *nt* CHEMIE stereoisomer; **Raumkapsel** *f* RAUMFAHRT space capsule; **Raum-klangsystem** *nt* AUFNAHME binaural sound system; **Raumklimagerät** *nt* HEIZ & KÄLTE room air condi-tioner; **Raumkoordinate** *f* GEOM space coordinate

raumkrank *adj* RAUMFAHRT space-sick

Raum: **Raumkurve** *f* GEOM space curve

Raumladung *f* PHYS space charge; **Raumladungsimpuls** *m* ELEKTROTECH *bei Ladungsspeicherröhren* cloud pulse; **Raumladungskompensation** *f* PHYS space charge compensation; **Raumladungskonstante** *f* ELEKTROTECH, TELEKOM perveance

Raum: **Raumlast** *f* HEIZ & KÄLTE room load

räumlich[1] *adj* CHEMIE steric; **~ zentriert** *adj* METALL space-centered (AmE), space-centred (BrE)

räumlich:[2] **~e Anforderungen** *f pl* SICHERHEIT dimensio-nal requirements; **~e Auflösung** *f* KERNTECH spatial resolution; **~e Ausdehnung** *f* MECHAN, PHYS cubic expansivity, TELEKOM *Netzwerk* coverage; **~er Bereich** *m* ELEKTRONIK spatial domain; **~es Bild** *nt* TELEKOM three-dimensional image; **~e Entfernung** *f* PHYS di-stance; **~e Frequenz** *f* ELEKTRONIK, FERNSEH, RADIO, TELEKOM spacial frequency, spatial frequency; **~e Geometrie** *f* GEOM solid geometry; **~e Kohärenz** *f* PHYS spatial coherence, TELEKOM space coherence, spatial coherence; **~e Ladungsdichte** *f* PHYS volume charge density; **~e Lage** *f* KONSTZEICH location in space; **~e Modulation** *f* ELEKTRONIK spatial modulation; **~e Pe-riode** *f* ELEKTRONIK spatial period; **~e Quantisierung** *f* PHYS spatial quantization; **~e Relativität** *f* RAUMFAHRT spatial relativity; **~e Struktur** *f* UMWELTSCHMUTZ spa-tial pattern; **~e Tendenz** *f* UMWELTSCHMUTZ spatial trend; **~e Veränderlichkeit** *f* UMWELTSCHMUTZ spatial variability; **~es Verhalten** *nt* ELEKTRONIK spatial re-sponse; **~e Verteilung** *f* UMWELTSCHMUTZ spatial distribution; **~e Wahrnehmung** *f* ERGON space percep-tion; **~e Zuordnung** *f* KONSTZEICH correlation in space

räumlich-zeitlich: **~e Korrelation** *f* TELEKOM space-time correlation

Räumlöffel *m* BAU raker

Raum: **Raumlufttechnik** *f* HEIZ & KÄLTE ventilation and air conditioning

Räummaschine *f* FERTIG *Pilgerschrittwalze* broach, MA-SCHINEN broaching machine

Raum: **Raummasse** *f* KER & GLAS bulk density; **Raum-Multiplex-Betrieb** *m* COMP & DV space division multiplex; **Raumnachführung** *f* RAUMFAHRT space tracking

Räumnadel *f* MASCHINEN, MECHAN broach, broaching tool, internal broach; **Räumnadelziehmaschine** *f* ME-CHAN broaching machine

Räumpresse *f* FERTIG push-type broaching machine, MASCHINEN press-type vertical broaching machine

Raumschiff *nt* RAUMFAHRT spaceship; **Raumschiff mit Nuklearantrieb** *nt* RAUMFAHRT nuclear-powered spacecraft; **Raumschlepper** *m* RAUMFAHRT space tug

Räumschlitten *m* FERTIG broach ram, broach slide

raumschots: ~ **segeln** *vi* WASSERTRANS run free, sail free, sail on a broad reach, *Segeln* go free, sail on a close reach

Raum: **Raumschutz-Meldungsgeber** *m* TELEKOM intruder presence detector; **Raumsegment** *nt* RAUMFAHRT *Weltraumfunk* space segment; **Raumsimulator** *m* RAUMFAHRT space simulation chamber; **Raumstation** *f* RAUMFAHRT space station; **Raumstufe** *f* TELEKOM space stage; **Raumteilung** *f* BAU partitioning; **Raumtemperatur** *f* HEIZ & KÄLTE, METALL ambient temperature, THERMOD room temperature; **Raumtemperaturregler** *m* HEIZ & KÄLTE thermostat; **Raumthermostat** *m* HEIZ & KÄLTE, THERMOD room thermostat; **Raumtiefe** *f* WASSERTRANS *Schiffkonstruktion* registered depth; **Raumtoneffekt** *m* AKUSTIK binaural effect; **Raumverlust** *m* RAUMFAHRT *Weltraumfunk* free space loss; **Raumvielfachsystem** *nt* TELEKOM space division system

raumvoll: ~ **und auf Tiefgang** *adj* WASSERTRANS full and down

Raum: **Raumwelle** *f* PHYS, RADIO sky wave; **Raumwerkstatt** *f* RAUMFAHRT space workshop

Räumwerkzeug *nt* FERTIG helical broach, MASCHINEN broaching tool, broach, MECHAN broach, broaching tool

Raum: **Raumwinkel** *m* GEOM solid angle, METALL dihedral angle, PHYS solid angle

Räumzahn *m* FERTIG raked tooth

Raum: **Raum-Zeit-Beziehung** *f* PHYS space-time relation; **Raum-Zeit-Kontinuum** *nt* RAUMFAHRT space-time continuum; **Raum-Zeit-Raum-Koppelnetz** *nt* TELEKOM space-time-space network

Räumzug *m* MASCHINEN broaching pass

Raupe *f* MECHAN crawler; **Raupenfahrzeug** *nt* MASCHINEN crawler vehicle; **Raupenkette** *f* MASCHINEN crawler, crawler track; **Raupenrad** *nt* KFZTECH *Motorradgetriebe* sprocket; **Raupenschleifmaschine** *f* PAPIER caterpillar grinder

Rausch- *pref* RADIO noise; **Rauschabstand** *m* AKUSTIK, AUFNAHME, COMP & DV, ELEKTRONIK, FERNSEH, TELEKOM signal-to-noise ratio; **Rauschamplitudenverteilung** *f* TELEKOM NAD, noise amplitude distribution

rauscharm: ~**er Verstärker** *m* ELEKTRONIK, TELEKOM low-noise amplifier; ~**e Verstärkung** *f* ELEKTRONIK, TELEKOM low-noise amplification; ~**er Vorverstärker** *m* ELEKTRONIK, STRAHLPHYS low-noise preamplifier

Rausch-: **Rauschbild** *nt* FERNSEH noise field; **Rauschdiode** *f* ELEKTRONIK noise diode

Rauschen *nt* AKUSTIK, AUFNAHME noise, COMP & DV noise, static, ELEKTRONIK, FERNSEH, PHYS noise; **Rauschen kurzer Wellenlänge** *nt* ELEKTRONIK short wavelength noise; **Rauschen eines Störgenerators** *nt* ELEKTRONIK interference generator noise; **Rauschen der Wirbelstärke** *nt* STRÖMPHYS background vorticity

Rausch-: **Rauschfaktor** *m* PHYS noise factor

rauschfrei: ~**es Signal** *nt* GERÄT noise-free signal

Rausch-: **Rauschgenerator** *m* ELEKTRONIK, TELEKOM noise generator; **Rauschleistung** *f* (N) ELEKTRONIK, KERNTECH noise power (N); **Rauschmodulation** *f*

FERNSEH noise modulation; **Rauschpegel** *m* TELEKOM, WELLPHYS noise level; **Rauschquelle** *f* ELEKTRONIK noise generator, noise source; **Rauschsignal** *nt* FERNSEH noise signal; **Rauschsperre** *f* RADIO squelch, TELEKOM squelch, squelch circuit; **Rauschstörungsgenerator** *m* ELEKTRONIK random noise generator; **Rauschstörungsquelle** *f* ELEKTRONIK random noise source; **Rauschstörungssignal** *nt* ELEKTRONIK random noise signal; **Rauschstreifenbildung** *f* FERNSEH banding on noise; **Rauschtemperatur** *f* ELEKTROTECH noise temperature; **Rauschunterdrüker** *m* AUFNAHME noise reducer, noise suppressor, ELEKTROTECH noise suppressor, RADIO noise blanker; **Rauschunterdrückung** *f* AUFNAHME noise reduction, noise suppression, ELEKTROTECH noise suppression, GERÄT noise canceling (AmE), noise cancelling (BrE), RADIO noise blanking; **Rauschzahl** *f* ELEKTRONIK noise factor, ELEKTRONIK (F) noise figure (F), PHYS noise factor, RADIO (F) noise figure (F)

Raute *f* DRUCK, FERTIG *Walzen* diamond, GEOM lozenge, rhomb, rhombus; **Rautendrahtgitter** *nt* BAU diamond wire lattice; **Rautenschnitt** *m* KER & GLAS diamond cut pattern; **Rautenvorkaliber** *nt* FERTIG *Walzen* diamond pass

Rayleigh: ~**sche Auflösungsbedingung** *f* PHYS Rayleigh criterion; ~**sches Interferometer** *nt* PHYS Rayleigh interferometer; ~**sches Refraktometer** *nt* PHYS Rayleigh refractometer; ~**sche Scheibe** *f* AKUSTIK Rayleigh disc (BrE), Rayleigh disk (AmE); ~**scher Schwund** *m* TELEKOM Rayleigh fading; ~**sche Streuung** *f* OPTIK, PHYS, STRAHLPHYS, TELEKOM Rayleigh scattering; ~**sche Welle** *f* AKUSTIK Rayleigh wave

Rayleigh-Jeans: ~**sche Gleichung** *f* PHYS Rayleigh-Jeans formula

Rb (*Rubidium*) CHEMIE Rb (*rubidium*)

RBA *abbr* (*relative Byteadresse*) COMP & DV RBA (*relative byte address*)

RC[1] *abbr* ELEKTRONIK RC, resistor-capacitor

RC:[2] **RC-Abzweigfilter** *nt* ELEKTRONIK RC ladder filter; **RC-Filterschaltung** *f* ELEKTRONIK RC filter circuit; **RC-Generator** *m* ELEKTRONIK RC oscillator; **RC-Oszillator** *m* PHYS RC oscillator; **RC-Schaltklickfilter** *nt* RADIO snubber network

RCTL-Logik *f* (*Widerstands-Kondensator-Transistor-Logik*) ELEKTRONIK RCTL logic (*resistor-capacitor-transistor logic*)

RDB *abbr* (*relationale Datenbank*) TELEKOM RDB (*relational database*)

RDSS *abbr* (*Satellitenfunkortungssystem*) RADIO, TRANS, WASSERTRANS *Satellitenfunk* RDSS (*radio determination satellite system*)

Re[1] *abbr* (*Reynoldszahl*) HYDRAUL, LUFTTRANS, NICHTFOSS ENERG, PHYS, STRÖMPHYS Re (*Reynolds number*)

Re[2] (*Rhenium*) CHEMIE Re (*rhenium*)

re *abbr* (*Elektronenradius*) KERNTECH re (*electron radius*)

Reagens *nt* CHEMIE, FOTO, KOHLEN, KUNSTSTOFF reagent

Reagenz *nt* KUNSTSTOFF reagent; **Reagenzglas** *nt* LABOR test tube; **Reagenzglasgestell** *nt* LABOR test tube rack; **Reagenzglashalter** *m* LABOR test tube holder; **Reagenzienflasche** *f* LABOR reagent bottle

Reaktanz *f* AUFNAHME reactance, ELEKTRIZ (X) reactance (X), ELEKTROTECH reactance; **Reaktanzabfall** *m* ELEKTROTECH reactance drop; **Reaktanzdämpfer** *m* ELEKTRONIK reactance attenuator; **Reaktanz-**

diagramm *nt* RADIO reactance chart; **Reaktanzfrequenz-Vervielfacher** *m* ELEKTRONIK reactance frequency multiplier; **Reaktanzleitung** *f* ELEKTROTECH *Mikrowelle* adjustable short; **Reaktanzschaltung** *f* ELEKTRIZ reactance circuit; **Reaktanzspule** *f* ELEKTROTECH reactance coil; **Reaktanzstromkreis** *m* ELEKTRIZ reactance circuit; **Reaktanzverstärker** *m* ELEKTRONIK parametric amplifier; **Reaktanzverstärkerdiode** *f* ELEKTRONIK parametric amplifier diode

Reaktion *f* ANSTRICH *chemisch* reaction, ERGON response, PHYS reaction; ~ **auf eine Dosis** *f* ERGON dose response; **Reaktionsbereich** *m* KOHLEN reaction zone; **Reaktionsbombe** *f* LABOR reaction bomb; **Reaktionsenergie** *f (Q)* KERNTECH reaction energy *(Q)*; **Reaktionsgeschwindigkeit** *f* METALL reaction rate; **Reaktionsharzbeton** *m* KUNSTSTOFF polymer concrete; **Reaktionskleber** *m* KUNSTSTOFF two-pack adhesive; **Reaktionsmittel** *nt* ABFALL solidifying agent; **Reaktionsmotor** *m* ELEKTRIZ reaction motor; **Reaktionspartner** *m* CHEMIE reactant; **Reaktionsprimer** *m* KUNSTSTOFF wash primer; **Reaktionsrad** *nt* WASSERVERSORG reaction water wheel, reaction wheel; **Reaktionsreihenfolge** *f* METALL order of reaction; **Reaktionsschiene** *f* EISENBAHN reaction rail; **Reaktionsspektroskopie** *f* KERNTECH reaction spectroscopy; **Reaktionsstrahlschub** *m* LUFTTRANS reaction jet propulsion; **Reaktionsstrahlschubkraft** *f* LUFTTRANS reaction jet propulsion; **Reaktionsturbine** *f* MASCHINEN, MECHAN, NICHTFOSS ENERG reaction turbine; **Reaktionsverzögerer** *m* ABFALL retarder, retarding agent; **Reaktionswärme** *f* THERMOD heat of reaction; **Reaktionszeit** *f* ERGON reaction time, response time

reaktiv: ~**e Bewegung** *f* LUFTTRANS jet propulsion; **nicht** ~**e Last** *f* ELEKTRIZ nonreactive load; ~**es Lösemittel** *nt* KUNSTSTOFF reactive solvent; ~**e Plasmaätzung** *f* ELEKTRONIK reactive plasma etching; ~**er Schaltkreis** *m* ELEKTROTECH reactive circuit

Reaktivfarbstoff *m* TEXTIL reactive dye

reaktivieren *vt* CHEMIE reactivate

Reaktivierung *f* CHEMIE, KOHLEN reactivation

Reaktivität *f* KERNTECH, PHYS reactivity; **Reaktivitätsabnahme** *f* KERNTECH decrement in reactivity; **Reaktivitätsdefizit** *nt* KERNTECH deficit reactivity; **Reaktivitätselement** *nt* KERNTECH *beim Anfahren eines Reaktors* booster element; **Reaktivitätsrampe** *f* KERNTECH reactivity ramp; **Reaktivitätsrückkopplung** *f* KERNTECH reactivity feedback; **Reaktivitätssprung** *m* KERNTECH reactivity surge; **Reaktivitätsstab** *m* KERNTECH *beim Anfahren eines Reaktors* booster rod; **Reaktivitätsverlust** *m* KERNTECH reactivity loss

Reaktor *m* ELEKTROTECH pile, *Atomphysik* reactor, KERNTECH reactor; ~ **mit Beryllium-Reflektor** *m* - KERNTECH beryllium-reflected reactor; ~ **im Chargenbetrieb** *m* KERNTECH batch reactor; ~ **mit gasförmigem Reaktorkern** *m* KERNTECH gaseous core reactor; ~ **mit Lufteinblasung** *m* TRANS AIR, air injection reactor; ~ **mit luftisolierter Spule** *m* ELEKTRIZ nonencapsulated-winding dry type reactor; ~ **mit Naturkühlung** *m* KERNTECH natural nuclear reactor; ~ **mit nicht-gekapselter Trockenspule** *m* ELEKTRIZ nonencapsulated-winding dry type reactor; ~ **mit Plattenelementen** *m* KERNTECH slab reactor; **Reaktorabschaltung** *f* KERNTECH shutdown of a reactor; **Reaktorbau** *m* KERNTECH reactor art; **Reaktorbauteil** *nt* KERNTECH reactor component; **Reaktorbehälter** *m*

KERNTECH reactor vessel; **Reaktordruckbehälter** *m* KERNTECH pressure vessel; **Reaktordynamik** *f* KERNTECH reactor dynamics; **Reaktorformel** *f* KERNTECH reactor formula; **Reaktorgebäude** *nt* KERNTECH reactor hall; **Reaktorgift** *nt* KERNTECH nuclear poison; **Reaktorgitter** *nt* KERNTECH active lattice; **Reaktorkern** *m* KERNTECH core; **Reaktorkreislauf** *m* KERNTECH reactor loop; **Reaktorkühlmittel** *nt* KERNTECH reactor coolant; **Reaktormultiplikation** *f (M)* KERNTECH multiplication of a reactor *(M)*; **Reaktorperiode** *f* KERNTECH reactor period; **Reaktorplanung** *f* KERNTECH reactor design; **Reaktorsicherheit** *f* KERNTECH reactor safety; **Reaktorsinterung** *f* KERNTECH reaction sintering process; **Reaktortank** *m* KERNTECH reactor tank; **Reaktortechnik** *f* KERNTECH reactor engineering; **Reaktorunfall** *m* KERNTECH nuclear accident, reactor accident; **Reaktorverhalten** *nt* KERNTECH reactor behaviour; **Reaktorwand** *f* KERNTECH reactor wall; **Reaktorzelle** *f* KERNTECH reactor cell

real[1] *adj* COMP & DV real, FERTIG *Kristall* imperfect

real:[2] ~**e Adresse** *f* COMP & DV real address; ~**er Typ** *m* COMP & DV real type

realisierbar: ~**er Abbrand** *m* KERNTECH achievable burn-up

realisieren *vt* COMP & DV implement

Realspeicher *m* COMP & DV real memory

Real-Time-Umsetzersatellit *m* FERNSEH real-time repeater satellite

Rebe *f* LEBENSMITTEL vine

Reboiler *m* ERDÖL *Raffinerie* reboiler

Rechen *m* BAU, FERTIG rake; **Rechen-** *pref* COMP & DV arithmetic, computing, MATH arithmetic; **Rechenarten** *f pl* MATH arithmetic operations; **Rechenbefehl** *m* COMP & DV arithmetic instruction; **Rechenblatt** *nt* COMP & DV spreadsheet; **Rechendrehmelder** *m* GERÄT computing synchro; **Rechengeschwindigkeit** *f* COMP & DV computing speed; **Rechengröße** *f* COMP & DV operand; **Rechengut** *nt* CHEMIE *Abwasserbehandlung* screenings; **Rechenleistung** *f* COMP & DV computing power; **Rechenmaschine** *f* COMP & DV calculating machine; **Rechenmodell** *nt* COMP & DV mathematical model; **Rechenoperation** *f* COMP & DV arithmetic operation; **Rechenprüfung** *f* COMP & DV arithmetic check

rechenschaftspflichtig *adj* QUAL accountable

Rechen: **Rechenschaltung** *f* ELEKTRONIK arithmetic circuit; **Rechenscheibe** *f* MATH circular slide rule; **Rechenschieber** *m* COMP & DV, MASCHINEN, MATH slide rule; **Rechenstab** *m* MATH slide rule; **Rechenstreifen** *m* COMP & DV tally; **Rechensystem** *nt* TELEKOM data processing system; **Rechenverfahren nach der Methode der finiten Elemente** *nt* MECHAN finite element calculation method; **Rechenverstärker** *m (OA)* COMP & DV, ELEKTRONIK, PHYS, RADIO, TELEKOM operational amplifier *(op amp)*; **Rechenverstärker-Chip** *m* ELEKTRONIK operational amplifier chip; **Rechenverstärker-Komparator** *m* ELEKTRONIK operational amplifier comparator; **Rechenwerk** *nt* COMP & DV ALU, arithmetic and logic unit, arithmetic logic unit, arithmetic unit; **Rechenzeichen** *nt* COMP & DV arithmetic operator; **Rechenzentrum** *nt* COMP & DV DPC, data processing center (AmE), data processing centre (BrE), computing center (AmE), computing centre (BrE), TELEKOM DPC, data processing center (AmE), data processing centre (BrE)

Recherchenbericht *m* PATENT search report

Rechnen: ~ **mit einem Großrechner** *nt* COMP & DV supercomputing

Rechner *m* COMP & DV computer, computing device, computing facility, machine, ELEKTRIZ computer, ELEKTRONIK calculator; **~ der fünften Generation** *m* COMP & DV, KÜNSTL INT FGC, fifth generation computer; **~ mit variabler Wortlänge** *m* COMP & DV byte machine

rechnerabhängig: ~er Speicher *m* COMP & DV online storage

Rechner: **Rechnerfamilie** *f* COMP & DV computer family

rechnerisch: ~e Induktion *f* COMP & DV mathematical induction

Rechner: **Rechnernetz** *nt* COMP & DV, TELEKOM computer network

rechnerorientiert *adj* COMP & DV machine-oriented

Rechner: **Rechnerschnittstelle** *f* TELEKOM computer interface; **Rechnersicherheit** *f* COMP & DV computer security; **Rechnerstellwerk** *nt* EISENBAHN computer-controlled interlocking; **Rechnersystem** *nt* COMP & DV computer system

Rechnerverbund *m* COMP & DV, TELEKOM computer network; **im ~ arbeitendes Büro** *nt* COMP & DV integrated office system; **Rechnerverbundbetrieb** *m* COMP & DV multiprocessing; **Rechnerverbundsystem** *nt* COMP & DV multiprocessing system

Rechnung: in ~ stellen *vt* TELEKOM *Gespräch* charge

Rechnungssturzfluggeschwindigkeit *f* LUFTTRANS design-diving speed

Recht *nt* PATENT right; **~ auf ein Patent** *nt* PATENT right to a patent

recht:[1] **im rechten Winkel** *adj* GEOM *zu einer Geraden* at right angles

recht:[2] **am rechten Rand ausrichten** *vt* COMP & DV right justify

Rechteck *nt* GEOM oblong, rectangle; **Rechteckdeckleiste** *f* BAU square staff; **Rechteckferrit** *m* ELEKTROTECH square loop ferrite; **Rechteckgenerator** *m* FERNSEH square wave generator

rechteckig[1] *adj* GEOM rectangular

rechteckig:[2] **~e Hystereseschleife** *f* ELEKTROTECH rectangular hysteresis loop; **~er Keil** *m* MASCHINEN rectangular key; **~er Querschnitt** *m* BAU rectangular cross-section; **~e Verblattung** *f* BAU square splice

Rechteck: **Rechteckimpuls** *m* ELEKTRONIK rectangular pulse; **Rechteckoberwelle** *f* RAUMFAHRT tesseral harmonic; **Rechteckpotential** *nt* PHYS square potential; **Rechteckspannung** *f* FERNSEH square wave voltage; **Rechteckwelle** *f* AUFNAHME, ELEKTRONIK square wave, ELEKTROTECH rectangular wave, PHYS square wave, TELEKOM square waveform; **Rechteckwellengeber** *m* ELEKTRONIK square wave generator; **Rechteckwellengenerator** *m* AUFNAHME square wave generator; **Rechteckwellengenerierung** *f* ELEKTRONIK square wave generation

Rechte-Hand-Regel *f* ELEKTRIZ, ELEKTROTECH corkscrew rule, PHYS corkscrew rule, right-hand rule

Rechts:[1] **~ vor Links** *adj* TRANS priority to the right

Rechts-[2] *pref* MECHAN right-hand; **Rechtsabbiegerverkehr** *m* TRANS right-turning traffic; **Rechtsausrichtung** *f* COMP & DV right justification; **Rechtsmilch** *f* CHEMIE sarcolactic

rechts:[1] **~ flatternd** *adj* DRUCK ragged right

rechts:[2] **rechte Seite** *f* DRUCK recto; **rechte Seite einer Gleichung** *f* PHYS right-hand side of an equation; **rechter Rand** *m* DRUCK right margin; **rechter Stereokanal** *m* AUFNAHME right stereo channel; **rechter Winkel** *m* GEOM, PHYS right angle

rechts:[3] **~ ausrichten** *vt* COMP & DV right justify

rechtsbündig:[1] **~e Ausrichtung** *f* COMP & DV right justification

rechtsbündig:[2] **~ ausrichten** *vt* COMP & DV right justify

Rechtschreibüberprüfung *f* COMP & DV *in Textprogrammen* spelling checker

rechtsdrehen *vi* WASSERTRANS *Wind* veer

rechtsdrehend[1] *adj* LEBENSMITTEL clockwise-rotating, PHYS dextrorotatory

rechtsdrehend:[2] **~e Zirkularpolarisation** *f* RADIO, RAUMFAHRT *Weltraumfunk* right-hand circular polarization

Rechts-: **Rechtsdrehung** *f* TEXTIL Z-twist; **Rechtsflanke** *f* MASCHINEN right-hand tooth flank

rechtsgängig[1] *adj* MASCHINEN rh, right-hand, right-handed

rechtsgängig:[2] **~e Fräsmaschine** *f* MASCHINEN right-hand milling cutter; **~es Gewinde** *nt* MASCHINEN right-hand thread; **~e Spirale** *f* MASCHINEN right-handed spiral

rechtsgeschäftlich: ~e Übertragung *f* PATENT *der Patentanmeldung* assignment

Rechtsgewinde *nt* MASCHINEN right-hand thread; **Rechtsgewindeschraube** *f* MASCHINEN right-hand screw, right-handed screw

rechtshändig: ~es Koordinatensystem *nt* PHYS right-handed coordinate system

Rechts-: **Rechtshändigkeit** *f* ERGON dextrality

Recht: **Rechtsnachfolger** *m* PATENT successor in title; **Rechtspersönlichkeit** *f* PATENT legal personality

rechtsschief *adj* GEOM negatively-skewed

rechtsschneidend *adj* MASCHINEN right-hand, right-handed

Rechts-: **Rechtsübergang** *m* PATENT transfer; **Rechtsverkehr** *m* TRANS right-hand traffic; **Rechtsverschiebung** *f* COMP & DV right shift

Recht: **Rechtsvorgänger** *m* PATENT predecessor in title, *eines Patents* legal predecessor

Rechts-: **Rechtsweiche** *f* TRANS right-hand turnout

rechtweisend:[1] **~ Nord** *adj* WASSERTRANS *Navigation* true north

rechtweisend:[2] **~er Kurs** *m* WASSERTRANS *Navigation* true course

Rechtwinkelphase *f* ELEKTRONIK quadrature phase

rechtwinklig[1] *adj* GEOM orthogonal, rectangular, right-angled, PHYS right-angled; **nicht ~** *adj* MASCHINEN out of square

rechtwinklig:[2] **~e Abtastung** *f* FERNSEH rectilinear scanning; **~e axonometrische Projektion** *f* KONSTZEICH right-angled axonometric projection; **~e Bewegung** *f* PHYS rectilinear motion; **~es Dreieck** *nt* GEOM right-angled triangle; **~er Falzhobel** *m* BAU square rabbet plane; **~er Hohlleiter** *m* ELEKTROTECH, PHYS rectangular waveguide; **~es Knie** *nt* MASCHINEN right-angled bend; **~e Koordinaten** *f pl* PHYS normal coordinates; **~e Koordinatenachsen** *f pl* MATH rectangular axes; **~es Koordinatensystem** *nt* GEOM rectangular coordinate system; **~e Parallelprojektion** *f* KONSTZEICH right-angled parallel projection; **~es Prisma** *nt* OPTIK right-angled prism; **~e Verbindung** *f* BAU square joint; **~ versetzte Abknickung** *f* KONSTZEICH offset

rechtwinklig:[3] **~ schneiden** *vt* BAU *Holz* square

Rechtwinkligkeit *f* GEOM rectangularity

Rechtwinkligschneiden *nt* BAU squaring

Reckalterung *f* FERTIG strain ageing (BrE), strain aging (AmE)

Recken *nt* FERTIG preliminary drawing, *Rundformen* swaging, TEXTIL stretch

recken *vt* FERTIG forge down, rotary-swage, TEXTIL stretch, *Fasern* draw

Reckschmieden *nt* FERTIG hammering

Recorder *m* TELEKOM *für Magnetband* recorder

recyceln *vt* ABFALL, UMWELTSCHMUTZ *aus Altmaterial zurückgewinnen* recycle

recycliert: **~e Flasche** *f* VERPACK recycled bottle

Recycling *nt* ABFALL, ELEKTRIZ, KER & GLAS, MASCHINEN, UMWELTSCHMUTZ recycling; **~ von Multimaterialien** *nt* VERPACK multimaterial recycling; **Recyclinganlage** *f* ABFALL recycling plant

recyclingfähig *adj* ABFALL recyclable

Recycling: **Recyclingpapier** *nt* ABFALL recycled paper; **Recyclingprozeß** *m* ABFALL recycling process; **Recyclingquote** *f* ABFALL recycling rate

Redakteur *m* FERNSEH editor

Redaktionsschluß *m* DRUCK deadline

Redestillation *f* CHEMIE redistillation, rerun

Redistribution *f* ELEKTROTECH redistribution

Redoxelement *nt* TRANS redox cell

Redoxmeßzelle *f* GERÄT redox cell

Redoxpotential *nt* UMWELTSCHMUTZ oxidation-reduction potential

Redoxreaktion *f* CHEMIE oxidoreduction

Reduktion *f* KOHLEN reduction; **Reduktionsflamme** *f* THERMOD reducing flame; **Reduktionsgetriebe** *nt* MASCHINEN reducing gear, reduction gear, PAPIER speed reducer; **Reduktionskost** *f* LEBENSMITTEL reducing diet; **Reduktionsmittel** *nt* CHEMIE reducer, reducing agent, KOHLEN reducing agent; **Reduktionsprodukt** *nt* UMWELTSCHMUTZ reducing product; **Reduktionsröhre** *f* LABOR reduction tube; **Reduktionsventil** *nt* LABOR reduction valve

Reduktor *m* CHEMIE reducer, reducing agent

redundant[1] *adj* COMP & DV redundant

redundant:[2] **~er Code** *m* COMP & DV redundant code; **~e Zahl** *f* COMP & DV redundant number; **~es Zeichen** *nt* COMP & DV redundant character; **~e Ziffern** *f pl* COMP & DV redundant digitals

Redundanz *f* COMP & DV, RAUMFAHRT *Weltraumfunk* redundancy; **Redundanzprüfung** *f* COMP & DV redundancy check

reduzierbar: **~es Polynom** *nt* COMP & DV reducible polynomial

reduzieren *vt* KOHLEN reduce, MASCHINEN set down, METALL reduce

reduzierend: **~es Gas** *nt* THERMOD reducing gas

Reduziergas *nt* THERMOD reducing gas

Reduziermuffe *f* MASCHINEN reduction sleeve

Reduzierofen *m* THERMOD reduction furnace

Reduzierraum *m* AUFNAHME reduction room

Reduzierstück *nt* BAU reducer, reducing pipe fitting, MASCHINEN reducing socket

reduziert: **~er Betrieb** *m* COMP & DV graceful degradation; **~e Koordinaten** *f pl* PHYS reduced coordinates; **~e Masse** *f* PHYS reduced mass; **~e Prüfung** *f* QUAL reduced inspection

Reduzierung *f* KOHLEN reduction; **~ der Stromaufnahme** *f* ELEKTROTECH *Halbleiterspeicher* power down

Reduzierventil *nt* MASCHINEN reducing valve

Reduzierwiderstand *m* ELEKTROTECH dropping resistor

Reduzierzone *f* METALL reducing zone

Reede[1] *f* WASSERTRANS roads, roadstead

Reede:[2] **auf ~ vor Anker liegen** *vi* WASSERTRANS anchor in the roads; **auf ~ liegen** *vi* WASSERTRANS *Schiff* lie in the roads

Reeder *m* WASSERTRANS shipowner

Reederei *f* WASSERTRANS shipping company; **Reedereiflagge** *f* WASSERTRANS house flag

Reedlyte-Glas *nt* KER & GLAS reedlyte glass

Reed-Quecksilberrelais *nt* ELEKTROTECH mercury-wetted reed relay

Reed-Relais *nt* ELEKTRIZ reed contact relay, ELEKTROTECH, TELEKOM reed relay; **Reed-Relais-Koppelpunkt** *m* TELEKOM reed relay crosspoint; **Reed-Relais-Schalter** *m* ELEKTROTECH reed relay switch; **Reed-Relais-Schaltnetz** *nt* ELEKTROTECH *Fernmeldewesen* reed relay switching network; **Reed-Relais-Schaltung** *f* ELEKTROTECH reed relay switching

Reed-Schalter *m* ELEKTROTECH reed switch

Reedzunge *f* ELEKTRIZ reed

reell: **~es Bild** *nt* PHYS real image; **~e Komponente** *f* ELEKTROTECH real component; **~e Matrix** *f* MATH matrix of real numbers; **~e Zahl** *f* COMP & DV, MATH real number; **~e Zahlenebene** *f* MATH real plane

Referenz *f* COMP & DV reference; **Referenzachse** *f* AKUSTIK reference axis; **Referenzaufruf** *m* COMP & DV call by reference; **Referenzband** *nt* AKUSTIK, FERNSEH reference tape; **Referenzbandrand** *m* FERNSEH reference edge of tape; **Referenzebene** *f* COMP & DV reference level; **Referenzenergie** *f* ERDÖL *in Preisgleitklausel* reference fuel; **Referenzflächen-Toleranzbereich** *m* OPTIK reference surface tolerance field; **Referenzkante** *f* FERNSEH reference edge; **Referenzkondensator** *m* ELEKTRIZ reference capacitor; **Referenzleerband** *nt* AKUSTIK reference tape; **Referenzpegel** *m* ELEKTRONIK reference level; **Referenzphase** *f* FERNSEH reference phase

Referenzprogramm: **mit ~ testen** *vt* COMP & DV benchmark

Referenz: **Referenzschwarz** *nt* FERNSEH reference black; **Referenzsignal** *nt* RAUMFAHRT *Weltraumfunk* reference burst; **Referenzspannungsquelle** *f* ELEKTRIZ constant-voltage source; **Referenztabelle** *f* COMP & DV lookup table; **Referenztestmethode-Verfahren** *nt* (*RTM-Verfahren*) KUNSTSTOFF reference test method (*RTM*); **Referenztonpegel** *m* FERNSEH reference audio level; **Referenzweiß** *nt* FERNSEH reference white, white reference

Reff *nt* WASSERTRANS reef

reffen *vt* WASSERTRANS *Segeln* reef

Reff: **Reffkausch** *f* WASSERTRANS *Segeln* reef cringle; **Reffknoten** *m* WASSERTRANS *Knoten* reef knot

Refiner *m* PAPIER refiner; **Refinermahlung** *f* PAPIER refining

reflektieren *vt* OPTIK reflect

reflektierend[1] *adj* OPTIK reflecting

reflektierend:[2] **~e Flüssigkristallanzeige** *f* ELEKTRONIK reflective LCD; **~e Kleidung** *f* SICHERHEIT reflective clothing; **~e Rückwandbeschichtung** *f* ELEKTRONIK reflective back coating; **~e Schallwand** *f* AKUSTIK reflex baffle; **~e Scheibe** *f* OPTIK reflective disk

reflektiert: **~es Licht** *nt* OPTIK reflected light; **~er Strahl** *m* OPTIK reflected ray, PHYS reflected beam, *Licht, Röntgenstrahl* reflected ray, WELLPHYS reflected ray; **~e Wärme** *f* THERMOD reflected heat; **~e Welle** *f* ELEKTROTECH, PHYS, WELLPHYS reflected wave

Reflektion: **~ am Mond** *f* RADIO moonbounce; **Reflektionsabschirmung** *f* RAUMFAHRT antireflection coating; **Reflektionsbeschichtung** *f* RAUMFAHRT antireflection coating

Reflektometer *nt* KUNSTSTOFF, RADIO reflectometer

Reflektor *m* ELEKTRONIK reflector, ELEKTROTECH *bei Elektrode* repeller, FOTO, KERNTECH, KFZTECH *Sicherheitszubehör*, PHYS, RADIO *Antenne*, RAUMFAHRT reflector; **~ mit veränderlicher Brennweite** *m* FOTO variable focus reflector; **Reflektorantenne** *f* TELEKOM reflecting antenna; **Reflektorelektrode** *f* ELEKTROTECH, FERNSEH reflector electrode; **Reflektorprisma** *nt* OPTIK reflecting prism; **Reflektorspiegel** *m* OPTIK reflecting mirror; **Reflektorstativ** *nt* FOTO reflector stand

Reflex *m* MEERSCHMUTZ sheen; **Reflexebene** *f* OPTIK plane of reflection

Reflexion *f* AKUSTIK, ELEKTRONIK, GEOM, OPTIK, PHYS, RAUMFAHRT *Weltraumfunk*, TELEKOM, WELLPHYS *an der Ionosphäre* reflection; **durch ~ polarisiertes Licht** *nt* WELLPHYS polarized light by reflection; **~ von Röntgenstrahlen** *f* STRAHLPHYS X-ray reflection; **Reflexions-Brennkurve** *f* OPTIK caustic by reflection; **Reflexionsdichte** *f* OPTIK reflectance density; **Reflexionselektronenmikroskop** *nt* ELEKTRONIK reflection electron microscope; **Reflexionsfaktor** *m* ELEKTRONIK *Reflexionsgrad* reflection factor, PHYS reflectance, *Klystron* reflection factor

reflexionsfrei: ~er Raum *m* AKUSTIK anechoic room, PHYS anechoic room, dead room

Reflexion: Reflexionsgesetze *nt pl* PHYS laws of reflection; **Reflexionsgitter** *nt* PHYS, WELLPHYS reflection grating; **Reflexionsgrad** *m* ELEKTRONIK reflection coefficient, PHYS reflectance, *Klystron* reflection factor; **Reflexionskammer** *f* RAUMFAHRT reverberation chamber; **Reflexionskoeffizient** *m* OPTIK reflectance, PHYS, RADIO reflection coefficient, RAUMFAHRT reflectivity coefficient; **Reflexionsmeter** *nt* PAPIER reflection meter; **Reflexionsraum** *m* ELEKTRONIK *Klystron* reflector space; **Reflexionsschalldämpfer** *m* KFZTECH baffle muffler (AmE), baffle silencer (BrE); **Reflexionsspiegel** *m* FOTO reflex mirror; **Reflexionsstrahlungsheizung** *f* HEIZ & KÄLTE reflective radiant heating; **Reflexionsverfahren** *nt* KERNTECH reflection method; **Reflexionsverlust** *m* AUFNAHME, ELEKTRONIK reflection loss; **Reflexionsvermögen** *nt* ELEKTROTECH reflectance, HEIZ & KÄLTE, NICHTFOSS ENERG reflectivity, OPTIK, TELEKOM reflectance; **Reflexionswand** *f* AUFNAHME *eines Raums* live end; **Reflexionswinkel** *m* OPTIK, PHYS, WELLPHYS angle of reflection

Reflex: Reflexklystron *nt* ELEKTRONIK, PHYS reflex klystron; **Reflexkopiermethode** *f* FOTO reflex printing method; **Reflexlicht** *nt* FOTO reflected light

reflexmindernd: ~e Beschichtung *f* TELEKOM antireflective coating

Reflex: Reflexmodulation *f* ELEKTRONIK reflex bunching; **Reflexphasenfokussierung** *f* ELEKTRONIK reflex bunching; **Reflexstrahlfotodetektor** *m* TRANS reflected beam photo-electric detector; **Reflexsucher** *m* FOTO reflex viewfinder

Reformieren *nt* ERDÖL *Raffinerie* reforming

Reformkost *f* LEBENSMITTEL health food

Refraktärperiode *f* ERGON refractory period

Refraktion *f* WASSERTRANS refraction; **Refraktionsgitter** *nt* LABOR refraction grating; **Refraktionswinkel** *m (r)* OPTIK angle of refraction *(r)*

Refraktivität *f* OPTIK refractiveness, refractivity

Refraktometer *nt* LABOR, OPTIK, PHYS, STRAHLPHYS refractometer

Regal *nt* BAU, LABOR shelf; **Regalfach** *nt* KER & GLAS pigeonhole; **Regalmarkierungen** *f pl* KER & GLAS rack marks; **Regalplatz** *m* VERPACK shelf space

Regel *f* COMP & DV, KÜNSTL INT, METROL rule; **~ des gesunden Menschenverstands** *f* KÜNSTL INT commonsense rule; **Regelabweichungssignal** *nt* KERNTECH actuating signal; **Regelalgorithmus** *m* KONTROLL control algorithm; **Regelanlasser** *m* ELEKTROTECH starting rheostat

Regelation *f* PHYS regelation

regelbar [1] *adj* MASCHINEN variable, MECHAN adjustable

regelbar [2] **~e Geschwindigkeit** *f* MASCHINEN variable velocity; **~er Lüfter** *m* LUFTTRANS *mit verschiebbarer Schlitzplatte* fan, hit-or-miss governor, ventilator; **~er Motor** *m* MECHAN adjustable speed motor

regelbasiert [1] *adj* KÜNSTL INT rule-based

regelbasiert [2] **~es Expertensystem** *nt* KÜNSTL INT rule-based expert system; **~es System** *nt* COMP & DV, KÜNSTL INT rule-based system

Regel: Regelbasis *f* COMP & DV rule base; **Regelbereich** *m* REGELUNG control range; **Regelcharakteristik** *f* ELEKTROTECH control characteristic; **Regelcontainer** *m* TRANS standard container; **Regeldifferenz** *f* REGELUNG system deviation; **Regeleinrichtung** *f* MASCHINEN control unit, REGELUNG closed-loop controller; **Regelgenauigkeit** *f* KONTROLL control accuracy; **Regelgerät** *nt* ELEKTROTECH control unit

regelgesteuert: ~es System *nt* KÜNSTL INT rule-based system

regelgestützt *adj* KÜNSTL INT rule-based

Regel: Regelgröße *f* ELEKTROTECH, MASCHINEN controlled variable; **Regelkennlinie** *f* ELEKTROTECH control characteristic; **Regelklappe** *f* KFZTECH butterfly; **Regelkompaß** *m* WASSERTRANS standard compass; **Regelkompensator** *m* LUFTTRANS adjusting potentiometer; **Regelkreis** *m* ELEKTRIZ closed loop, ELEKTRONIK *Meß- und Regelungstechnik* feedback loop, *Regeltechnik* loop, ELEKTROTECH feedback control system, LUFTTRANS control system; **Regelkreisrückführsignal** *nt* ELEKTRONIK loop feedback signal

regellos: ~e Verteilung *f* METALL random distribution

regelmäßig: ~es Polygon *nt* GEOM regular polygon; **~e Wartung** *f* BAU scheduled service

Regeln *nt* MASCHINEN governing

regeln *vt* MECHAN adjust, RAUMFAHRT, TELEKOM control

Regel: Regelorgan *nt* MASCHINEN control device; **Regelpotentiometer** *nt* ELEKTROTECH control potentiometer; **Regelröhre** *f* ELEKTRONIK remote cutoff tube, *mit veränderlicher Steilheit* variable mu tube, variable mutual conductance tube; **Regelsatz in einem Expertensystem** *m* COMP & DV inference engine; **Regelschalter** *m* ELEKTROTECH control switch; **Regelschleife** *f* TELEKOM locked loop; **Regelsignal** *nt* ELEKTRONIK *zur Prozeßregelung* control signal; **Regelspur** *f* EISENBAHN standard gage (AmE), standard gauge (BrE); **Regelspurbahn** *f* EISENBAHN standard gage railroad (AmE), standard gauge railway (BrE); **Regelstab** *m* KERNTECH absorber rod, control rod; **Regelstange** *f* KFZTECH control rod; **Regelstrecke** *f* REGELUNG closed-loop controlled system; **Regeltechnik** *f* KONTROLL control technology; **Regeltrafo** *m* ELEKTROTECH variable ratio transformer, variable transformer; **Regeltransformator** *m* ELEKTROTECH control transformer, regulating transformer, variable ratio transformer, variable transformer, LABOR regulating transformer; **Regelumspanner** *m* ELEKTROTECH variable ratio transformer

Regelung *f* ELEKTRIZ control, ELEKTRONIK *einer Steuergröße* closed-loop control, *eines Prozesses* control, ELEKTROTECH regulation, KERNTECH regulating, KFZTECH, MASCHINEN control, REGELUNG *Einrichtung* closed-loop device, *Vorgang* closed-loop control, TELEKOM regulation; **~ mit Anzapfung** *f* ELEKTROTECH tapped control; **Regelungsbereich** *m* ELEKTROTECH regulation range; **Regelungshierarchie** *f* KONTROLL control hierarchy; **Regelungssystem** *nt* ELEKTRONIK closed-loop control system, KONTROLL control system; **Regelungssystem mit Rückkopplung** *nt* ELEKTROTECH feedback control system

regelungstechnisch: **~e Lösung** *f* REGELUNG solution from the control systems

Regel: **Regelventil** *nt* HEIZ & KÄLTE servo valve, HYDRAUL, KONTROLL control valve, LABOR *Flüssigkeitsregelung* regulating valve,-LUFTTRANS actuator control valve, MASCHINEN control valve, regulating valve, WASSERVERSORG flow-regulating valve; **Regelverstärker** *m* ELEKTRONIK variable gain amplifier; **Regelvorgang** *m* KONTROLL control action; **Regelvorrichtung** *f* ELEKTROTECH control gear, control unit; **Regelwehr** *nt* WASSERVERSORG level control weir; **Regelwiderstand** *m* ELEKTROTECH adjustable resistor, regulating resistance, rheostat, variable resistor, varistance

Regenbecken *nt* WASSERVERSORG rainwater catchment
Regenbogenquarz *m* METALL rainbow quartz
Regenerat *nt* KUNSTSTOFF reclaimed rubber, reclaim, regenerated rubber
Regeneration *f* ABFALL, COMP & DV, METALL regeneration
regenerativ[1] *adj* RAUMFAHRT *Weltraumfunk* regenerative
regenerativ:[2] **~e Energie** *f* NICHTFOSS ENERG renewable energy
Regenerativfeuerung *f* HEIZ & KÄLTE regenerative heating
Regenerativkühlung *f* HEIZ & KÄLTE, THERMOD regenerative cooling
Regenerativofen *m* KER & GLAS, MASCHINEN regenerative furnace, METALL regenerating furnace
Regenerativverfahren *nt* MASCHINEN regenerative system
Regenerativzelle *f* EISENBAHN, KFZTECH regenerative cell
Regenerator *m* ELEKTRONIK, MASCHINEN, METALL, TELEKOM regenerator
regenerieren *vt* CHEMIE reactivate, COMP & DV regenerate
regeneriert[1] *adj* ELEKTRONIK regenerated
regeneriert:[2] **~er Kautschuk** *m* KUNSTSTOFF reclaimed rubber, reclaim, regenerated rubber
Regenerierung *f* CHEMIE reactivation, ELEKTRONIK regeneration, KUNSTSTOFF, MEERSCHMUTZ recovery, RAUMFAHRT, TELEKOM, WASSERVERSORG regeneration
Regenfallrohr *nt* BAU downpipe, stack pipe
regenfrei: **~e Zeit** *f* UMWELTSCHMUTZ rain-free period
Regenleiste *f* EISENBAHN water guttering
Regenmeßgerät *nt* BAU, LABOR, NICHTFOSS ENERG, WASSERVERSORG rain gage (AmE), rain gauge (BrE)
Regentrübung *f* WASSERTRANS *Radar* rain clutter

Regenwasser *nt* KOHLEN storm water; **Regenwasserfallrohr** *nt* BAU rainwater downpipe; **Regenwassernutzung** *f* UMWELTSCHMUTZ utilization of rainwater
Regieanweisung: **~ für Tonmischung** *f* AUFNAHME dubbing cue sheet
Regieeinrichtung *f* FERNSEH cuer
Regieplan *m* FERNSEH cue sheet
Regieraum *m* FERNSEH control room, studio control room; **Regieraumfenster** *nt* FERNSEH control room window
Regiesignal *nt* FERNSEH cue; **Regiesignalschirm** *m* FERNSEH cue screen
Regiespur *f* FERNSEH cue track; **Regiespur-Zugriffscode** *m* FERNSEH cue track address code
Regiezeichen *nt* AUFNAHME cue
Regional- *pref* FERNSEH, LUFTTRANS, NICHTFOSS ENERG, RADIO regional
regional: **~e Verkehrsinformationen** *f pl* TRANS area traffic information
Regional-: **Regionalcarrier** *m* LUFTTRANS regional carrier; **Regionalflughafen** *m* LUFTTRANS regional airport; **Regionalfluglinie** *f* LUFTTRANS regional carrier; **Regionalmetamorphose** *f* NICHTFOSS ENERG regional metamorphism; **Regionalpatent** *nt* PATENT regional patent; **Regionalprogramm** *nt* FERNSEH, RADIO local program (AmE), local programme (BrE); **Regionalrundfunk** *m* RADIO local broadcasting; **Regionalrundfunksender** *m* RADIO local broadcasting station; **Regionalschienenverkehr** *m* EISENBAHN regional railroad traffic (AmE), regional railway traffic (BrE); **Regionalwarnfunknetz** *nt* RADIO, TRANS regional radio warning system
Register[1] *nt* COMP & DV index, register, ELEKTROTECH, KONTROLL, TELEKOM register; **~ mit Mehrfachzugriff** *nt* COMP & DV multiport register
Register:[2] **~ zusammenstellen** *vt* COMP & DV index
Register: **Registerauszug** *m* PATENT extract from the register; **Registerbezeichnung** *f* COMP & DV register name; **Registerbrief** *m* WASSERTRANS certificate of registration, *Dokumente* certificate of registry; **Registerdatei** *f* COMP & DV register file; **Registererstellung** *f* COMP & DV indexing; **Registerhafen** *m* WASSERTRANS port of registration, port of registry
registerhaltig[1] *adj* DRUCK in register; **nicht ~** *adj* DRUCK out of register
registerhaltig:[2] **~ machen** *vt* DRUCK register
Register: **Registerhaltigkeit** *f* DRUCK backing up, registration; **Registerhaltung** *f* DRUCK backing up, register, registration; **Registerlänge** *f* COMP & DV register length; **Registersystem** *nt* TELEKOM register-controlled system; **Registertonnengehalt** *m* METROL register tonnage; **Registerzuordner** *m* TELEKOM register translator
Registraturnummer *f* DRUCK file number
registrieren *vt* COMP & DV enroll, register, MECHAN index
registrierend: **~es Meßgerät** *nt* GERÄT recording instrument; **~es Temperaturmeßgerät** *nt* KERNTECH thermograph
Registriergerät *nt* GERÄT logging device, recording instrument
Registrierinstrument *nt* GERÄT recording instrument
Registrierkurve *f* GERÄT recorded curve, trace line
Registriermanometer *nt* GERÄT recording manometer
Registrierscheibe *f* AUFNAHME recording disk
Registrierstreifen *m* ELEKTRIZ strip chart, GERÄT chart,

continuous diagram, recording chart, *für Streifen-schreiber* strip chart; **Registrierstreifenantriebsmotor** *m* GERÄT chart motor; **Registrierstreifentransport** *m* GERÄT chart transport; **Registrierstreifenwalze** *f* GERÄT chart drum

Registrierthermometer *nt* PHYS thermograph, THERMOD recording thermometer

Registriertrommel *f* AUFNAHME recording drum

Registrierung *f* COMP & DV, LUFTTRANS registration, TELEKOM *Messen* recording, TRANS, WASSERTRANS registration

Registrierwaage *f* GERÄT recording balance

Regler *m* ELEKTROTECH control unit, controller, governor, regulator, KONTROLL controller, LABOR regulator, MASCHINEN control unit, governor, regulator, MECHAN governor, RAUMFAHRT control, TELEKOM *zur Einstellung* control, regulator, WASSERTRANS *Motor* governor; **Reglerdynamo** *m* ELEKTRIZ control dynamo, regulating dynamo; **Reglerschaltungs-Stangenanschlag** *m* LUFTTRANS governor control stop; **Reglerstange** *f* MASCHINEN governor rod; **Reglerventil** *nt* HYDRAUL governor valve, MECHAN check valve; **Reglerwiderstand** *m* KFZTECH rheostat

Reglette *f* DRUCK clump

Regression *f* COMP & DV regression; **Regressionsgleichung** *f* QUAL regression equation

Regularisation *f* WASSERVERSORG regularization

regulierbar[1] *adj* MASCHINEN adjustable

regulierbar:[2] **~es Grundwehr** *nt* UMWELTSCHMUTZ adjustable submersion weir

Reguliercharakteristik *f* FERTIG *Kunststoffinstallationen* flow characteristics

regulieren *vt* BAU *Instrument* adjust

Regulierschraube *f* MASCHINEN adjusting screw, regulating screw

Regulierung *f* ELEKTROTECH adjustment, regulation

Regulierventil *nt* KFZTECH check valve

Reib- *pref* CHEMIE triturating, MASCHINEN frictional; **Reibabnutzung** *f* ANSTRICH fretting wear

Reibahle *f* BAU, FERTIG, MASCHINEN, MECHAN reamer; **Reibahle mit Messereinstellung** *f* FERTIG adjustable blade reamer; **Reibahle mit Spiralnuten** *f* MASCHINEN reamer with spiral flutes; **Reibahle mit verstellbaren Messern** *f* MASCHINEN adjustable blade reamer; **Reibahlennutenfräser** *m* MASCHINEN reamer cutter

Reib-: **Reibbeiwert** *m* MASCHINEN coefficient of friction; **Reibbelag** *m* FERTIG, KFZTECH friction lining; **Reibbelagwerkstoff** *m* FERTIG friction material; **Reibbremse** *f* MASCHINEN friction brake; **Reibechtheit** *f* KUNSTSTOFF rub fastness, TEXTIL fastness to rubbing; **Reibeisen** *nt* BAU rasp

Reiben *nt* MASCHINEN galling, reaming, reaming-out

reiben *vt* MECHAN ream

Reiber *m* CHEMTECH pestle

Reib-: **Reibermüdung** *f* METALL fretting fatigue; **Reibgetriebe** *nt* MASCHINEN friction drive; **Reibkegelantrieb** *m* MASCHINEN friction cone drive; **Reibkorrosion** *f* ANSTRICH fretting corrosion; **Reibkorrosion durch Abrieb** *f* MECHAN abrasion-fretting corrosion; **Reibkugel** *f* MASCHINEN friction ball; **Reibmarkierung** *f* KER & GLAS scrub mark; **Reibrad** *nt* MASCHINEN friction wheel; **Reibradantrieb** *m* MASCHINEN friction wheel drive; **Reibrädergetriebe** *nt* MASCHINEN friction gear; **Reibradgetriebe** *nt* MASCHINEN friction gear, friction gearing; **Reibring** *m* MASCHINEN friction ring; **Reibsand** *m* MECHAN grit; **Reibschale** *f* CHEMTECH,

LABOR mortar; **Reibscheibe** *f* MASCHINEN friction disc (BrE), friction disk (AmE); **Reibschleifen** *nt* FERTIG lapping; **Reibschluß** *m* FERTIG *Getriebelehre* frictional grip, frictional resistance

reibschlüssig *adj* MASCHINEN frictional

Reib-: **Reibschweißen** *nt* FERTIG friction welding; **Reibspannung** *f* METALL friction stress; **Reibspindel** *f* MASCHINEN friction screw; **Reibspindelpresse** *f* FERTIG friction-driven screw press; **Reibspur** *f* FERTIG galling mark; **Reibstelle** *f* KER & GLAS rub

Reibung[1] *f* ANSTRICH, FERNSEH, KOHLEN, KUNSTSTOFF, MASCHINEN, MECHAN, PAPIER, PHYS, RAUMFAHRT, TEXTIL friction; **äußere ~** *f* MASCHINEN external friction; **~ der Ruhe** *f* MASCHINEN static friction

Reibung:[2] **durch ~ aufladen** *vt* PHYS *Reibungselektrizität* charge by friction

Reibungs- *pref* BAU frictional

Reibung: **Reibungsantrieb** *m* MASCHINEN friction drive; **Reibungsbahn** *f* EISENBAHN adhesion railroad (AmE), adhesion railway (BrE)

reibungsbehaftet: **~e inkompressible Strömung** *f* STRÖMPHYS viscous incompressible flow

Reibung: **Reibungsbeiwert** *m* BAU, ERGON coefficient of friction; **Reibungsbremse** *f* KFZTECH *Bremsanlage*, MASCHINEN friction brake; **Reibungsdämpfer** *m* MECHAN frictional damper; **Reibungsdrehmoment** *nt* RAUMFAHRT frictional torque

reibungselektrisch: **~er Detektor** *m* TRANS triboelectric detector

Reibung: **Reibungselektrizität** *f* BAU static electricity, ELEKTRIZ frictional electricity, PHYS triboelectricity, TEXTIL static electricity; **Reibungsfluß** *m* KERNTECH frictional flow

reibungsfrei[1] *adj* MASCHINEN, MECHAN frictionless, STRÖMPHYS inviscid; **~ gelagert** *adj* MASCHINEN mounted on frictionless bearings

reibungsfrei:[2] **~e Bewegung** *f* STRÖMPHYS inviscid motion; **~e Strömung** *f* STRÖMPHYS inviscid motion; **~e Strömungsverteilung** *f* STRÖMPHYS inviscid flow distribution

Reibung: **Reibungskoeffizient** *m* KUNSTSTOFF, MASCHINEN, MECHAN, METROL, PHYS, WASSERTRANS *Schiffkonstruktion* coefficient of friction; **Reibungskondensator** *m* ELEKTROTECH snubber capacitor; **Reibungskraft** *f* MASCHINEN force of friction, METALL friction force, PHYS frictional force; **Reibungskupplung** *f* KFZTECH friction clutch, MASCHINEN friction clutch, friction coupling; **Reibungsleistung** *f* FERTIG friction horsepower; **Reibungslokomotive** *f* EISENBAHN adhesion locomotive; **Reibungslumineszenz** *f* PHYS triboluminescence; **Reibungsmeßgerät** *nt* PHYS tribometer; **Reibungsmühle** *f* PAPIER attrition mill; **Reibungspfahl** *m* BAU, KOHLEN friction pile; **Reibungsschaltkreis** *m* ELEKTROTECH snubber circuit; **Reibungsschweißen** *nt* BAU friction welding; **Reibungsspannung** *f* STRÖMPHYS viscous stress; **Reibungsströmung** *f* LEBENSMITTEL, MASCHINEN, PHYS viscous flow; **Reibungstriebwagen** *m* EISENBAHN adhesion railcar

reibungsverhindernd *adj* MASCHINEN antifriction

Reibung: **Reibungsverlust** *m* MASCHINEN, NICHTFOSS ENERG friction loss; **Reibungsverschleiß** *m* MASCHINEN attrition; **Reibungswärme** *f* FERTIG, MASCHINEN frictional heat, THERMOD heat caused by friction; **Reibungswiderstand** *m* ELEKTROTECH snubber resistor, FERTIG frictional resistance, MASCHINEN friction resistance, MECHAN frictional drag, WASSERTRANS *Schiffkonstruktion* frictional resistance; **Reibungswinkel** *m* BAU, KOHLEN, MASCHINEN angle of friction; **Reibungszahl** *f* MASCHINEN, WASSERTRANS *Schiffkonstruktion* coefficient of friction

Reib-: **Reibzahl** *f* KUNSTSTOFF coefficient of friction

reichen: ~ **von** *vi* TELEKOM range from

Reichweite *f* ELEKTRONIK *eines Emitters* range, ERGON reachable space, GERÄT coverage, range, KFZTECH *Elektrofahrzeuge* cruising range, LUFTTRANS *eines Luftfahrzeugs* range, MASCHINEN reach, METALL working distance, PHYS, RAUMFAHRT range, TELEKOM coverage, range, WASSERTRANS *Funk* range; ~ **pro Ladung** *f* TRANS range of action per charge; **Reichweitenhüllkurve** *f* ERGON reach envelope

Reif *m* LEBENSMITTEL *gefrorene Lebensmittel* bloom, MECHAN hoop

Reifegradmesser *m* LEBENSMITTEL tenderometer

Reifen *m* EISENBAHN, KFZTECH tire (AmE), tyre (BrE), MECHAN hoop, ring, TRANS tire (AmE), tyre (BrE); ~ **ohne Profil** *m* KFZTECH bald tire (AmE), bald tyre (BrE), smooth tire (AmE), smooth tyre (BrE); **Reifengarn** *nt* TEXTIL tire yarn (AmE), tyre yarn (BrE); **Reifengrundgewebe** *nt* TEXTIL carcass; **Reifenlauffläche** *f* KFZTECH, KUNSTSTOFF tire tread (AmE), tyre tread (BrE); **Reifenmuster** *nt* KFZTECH tread design; **Reifenprofil** *nt* EISENBAHN tire profile (AmE), tyre profile (BrE), KFZTECH tread design, tread pattern; **Reifenrohling** *m* KUNSTSTOFF green tyre; **Reifenüberdruck** *m* KFZTECH over-inflation; **Reifenunterdruck** *m* KFZTECH under-inflation

Reifung *f* ERDÖL *Geologie* maturation, FOTO *Emulsion* ripening, LEBENSMITTEL ageing (BrE), aging (AmE); **Reifungstemperatur** *f* KER & GLAS maturing temperature

Reihe: [1] **in ~** *adj* COMP & DV serial; **in ~ geschaltet** *adj* ELEKTROTECH, GERÄT series-connected

Reihe [2] *f* COMP & DV series, GERÄT *von Einrichtungen* range, MATH series, TELEKOM *von Einrichtung* suite, TEXTIL course, range; **in ~ geschaltete Strecken** *f pl* TELEKOM series of links; **in ~ geschalteter Gleichstrommotor** *m* ELEKTROTECH series dc motor

Reihe: [3] **in ~ schalten** *vt* ELEKTROTECH connect in series

Reihen: in ~ *adj* PHYS in series

Reihe: **Reihenanlage** *f* TELEKOM key system; **Reihenanordnung** *f* ELEKTROTECH series arrangement; **Reihenbohrmaschine** *f* FERTIG gang drill, in-line multi drill, MASCHINEN gang drill; **Reiheneinspritzpumpe** *f* KFZTECH multicylinder injection pump

Reihenfolge *f* COMP & DV sequence; **Reihenfolgeplanung** *f* KONTROLL scheduling; **Reihenfolgeprüfung** *f* COMP & DV sequence check; **Reihenfolgezugriff** *m* COMP & DV sequential access

reihenförmig: ~ **angeordnete Zylinder** *m pl* KFZTECH in-line cylinders

Reihengegenkopplung *f* ELEKTROTECH series feedback

reihengeschaltet [1] *adj* ELEKTRIZ series

reihengeschaltet: [2] **~er Kondensator** *m* ELEKTRIZ series capacitor

reihengewickelt: **~er Dynamo** *m* ELEKTROTECH series-wound dynamo; **~er Motor** *m* ELEKTROTECH series-wound motor

Reihe: **Reihenklemme** *f* KFZTECH terminal block; **Reihenkondensator** *m* ELEKTROTECH series capacitor; **Reihen mit linken Maschen** *f pl* TEXTIL rows knitted in purl; **Reihenmotor** *m* KFZTECH, MASCHINEN, WAS-

SERTRANS in-line engine; **Reihenparallelschalter** *m* ELEKTROTECH series-parallel switch; **Reihenparallelschaltung** *f* ELEKTROTECH series-parallel circuit; **Reihenreaktanz** *f* ELEKTROTECH series reactance; **Reihen mit rechten Maschen** *f pl* TEXTIL wales of face stitches; **Reihenresonanzfrequenz** *f* ELEKTRONIK series resonance frequency, ELEKTROTECH series resonance, FERNSEH, RADIO, TELEKOM series resonance frequency; **Reihenresonanzkreis** *m* ELEKTROTECH series-resonant circuit; **Reihenschaltung** *f* ELEKTRIZ series connection, tandem connection, ELEKTROTECH series arrangement, series circuit, series connection, RADIO, TELEKOM series circuit; **Reihenschlußanlasser** *m* ELEKTRIZ series starter; **Reihenschlußanlaßschalter** *m* ELEKTRIZ series starter; **Reihenschlußdynamo** *m* ELEKTRIZ series-wound dynamo, ELEKTROTECH series dynamo; **Reihenschlußerregung** *f* ELEKTROTECH series excitation; **Reihenschlußmaschine** *f* ELEKTRIZ series-excited machine, series-wound machine; **Reihenschlußmotor** *m* ELEKTRIZ series motor, series-wound motor; **Reihenschlußwicklung** *f* ELEKTROTECH series winding; **Reihenspeisung** *f* ELEKTROTECH series feed; **Reihenstandmotor** *m* KFZTECH in-line engine; **Reihenstichprobenentnahme** *f* QUAL sequential sampling; **Reihenstichprobenprüfplan** *m* QUAL sequential-sampling plan; **Reihenwicklung** *f* ELEKTROTECH series winding; **Reihenwiderstand** *m* ELEKTROTECH series resistance

Rein- *pref* ABFALL, DRUCK, FERTIG, UMWELTSCHMUTZ cleaned

rein [1] *adj* MEERSCHMUTZ neat; ~ **darstellbar** *adj* CHEMIE isolable ~ **darstellen** *vt* CHEMIE isolate

rein: [2] **~es Auto- und LKW-Transportschiff** *nt* WASSERTRANS *Schifftyp* car and truck carrier; **~e Flüssigphase** *f* THERMOD liquid only phase; **~er Frachtcharterflug** *m* LUFTTRANS all-cargo charter flight; **~er Frachtdienst** *m* LUFTTRANS all-cargo service, all-freight service, all-freight; **~e Frachtfluglinie** *f* LUFTTRANS all-cargo carrier; **~er Frachtlastfaktor** *m* LUFTTRANS all-cargo load factor; **~es Frachttransportflugzeug** *nt* LUFTTRANS all-cargo aircraft; **~e gasförmige Phase** *f* THERMOD gas-only phase, gaseous phase only; **~er gasförmiger Zustand** *m* THERMOD gas-only phase, gaseous phase only; **~es Konnossement** *nt* WASSERTRANS *Dokumente* clean bill of lading; **~es Kupfer** *nt* METALL pure copper; **~e Mathematik** *f* MATH pure mathematics; **~er Postdienst** *m* LUFTTRANS all-mail service; **~e Quarte** *f* AKUSTIK perfect fourth; **~e Quinte** *f* AKUSTIK perfect fifth; **~es Spektrum** *nt* STRAHLPHYS pure spectrum

Rein-: **Reindarstellung** *f* FERTIG isolation; **Reingas** *nt* ABFALL cleaned gas, scrubbed gas; **Reinhadernpapier** *nt* DRUCK all-rag paper; **Reinhaltung** *f* UMWELTSCHMUTZ *Luft, Gewässer* pollution control

Reinigen *nt* PAPIER cleaning

reinigen *vt* BAU clarify, CHEMTECH purify, KOHLEN clarify, METALL purify, PAPIER clean, WASSERTRANS *Schiffinstandhaltung* grave, WASSERVERSORG cleanse, purify, *Schleusen* clean up

Reiniger *m* CHEMTECH purifier, SICHERHEIT cleaner; **Reinigerzelle** *f* KOHLEN cleaner cell

Reinigung *f* CHEMTECH defecation, ERDÖL purification, swabbing, KOHLEN clarification, MEERSCHMUTZ clean-up, SICHERHEIT cleaner, WASSERVERSORG cleansing; **Reinigungsahle** *f* KFZTECH *Werkzeug* reamer; **Reinigungsanlage** *f* WASSERVERSORG purification plant; **Reinigungsapparat** m CHEMTECH purifier, purifying apparatus; **Reinigungsbeginn** m KERNTECH *der Brennstoffaufbereitung* head end treatment; **Reinigungsbehälter** m WASSERVERSORG filtration vat; **Reinigungsbürste** f DRUCK cleaning brush; **Reinigungsfällung** f UMWELTSCHMUTZ below-cloud scavenging; **Reinigungsflüssigkeit** f ANSTRICH decontamination fluid; **Reinigungsgrad** m WASSERVERSORG degree of purification; **Reinigungshahn** m WASSERVERSORG purge cock, purging cock; **Reinigungskammer** f LABOR clean room; **Reinigungskolben** m ERDÖL swab; **Reinigungskraft** f CHEMIE detergency; **Reinigungsmittel** nt CHEMTECH purifying agent, TEXTIL detergent; **Reinigungsöffnung** f MASCHINEN inspection fitting; **Reinigungsvermögen** nt ABFALL purification capacity; **Reinigungswagen** m BAU cradle machine

Reinjektion f ERDÖL *Fördertechnik* reinjection

Rein-: **Reinkohle** f KOHLEN clean coal, cleans; **Reinluft** f HEIZ & KÄLTE filtered air; **Reinluftgebiet** nt UMWELTSCHMUTZ area of pure air; **Reinraum** m ELEKTRONIK, HEIZ & KÄLTE, VERPACK clean room; **Reinraumtechnik** f HEIZ & KÄLTE clean-room technology; **Reinregen** m UMWELTSCHMUTZ clean rain; **Reinstkohle** f KOHLEN super-clean coal; **Reinvorlage** f UMWELTSCHMUTZ net receiver; **Reinwasser** nt WASSERVERSORG clean water, pure water

Reise f KOHLEN *Ofen* campaign; **Reisecharter** m ERDÖL *Schiffahrt*, WASSERTRANS *Seehandel* voyage charter; **Reisedauer** f TRANS journey time; **Reisefluggeschwindigkeit** f LUFTTRANS cruising speed; **Reiseflughöhe** f LUFTTRANS cruising altitude; **Reiseflugleistung** f LUFTTRANS cruising power; **Reisegeschwindigkeit** f EISENBAHN schedule speed, WASSERTRANS cruising speed; **Reisekamera** f FOTO field camera; **Reisemikroskop** nt LABOR traveling microscope (AmE), travelling microscope (BrE); **Reisen im Weltall** nt RAUMFAHRT space travel; **Reiseomnibus** m KFZTECH motor coach; **Reiseroute** f WASSERTRANS *Navigation* itinerary; **Reisezug** m EISENBAHN passenger train; **Reisezugwagen** m EISENBAHN passenger car (AmE), passenger coach (BrE), railroad car (AmE), railway carriage (BrE); **Reisezugwagen mit schwenkbarem Wagenkasten** m EISENBAHN tilting body coach

Reismühle f LEBENSMITTEL rice mill

Reiß- pref BAU, LEBENSMITTEL, TEXTIL, VERPACK, WASSERTRANS drawing, tearing; **Reißband** nt VERPACK tear tape; **Reißbrett** nt BAU, TEXTIL, WASSERTRANS drawing board; **Reißdehnung** f KUNSTSTOFF elongation at break; **Reißdraht** m PAPIER tearing wire

Reißen nt FERNSEH tearing, WERKPRÜF *Glas* cracking

reißen[1] vt ANSTRICH crack, FERTIG fissure, scribe

reißen[2] vi BAU spring, KER & GLAS craze, KUNSTSTOFF tear

Reiß-: **Reißfeder** f FERTIG drawing pen; **Reißfestigkeit** f KUNSTSTOFF tear resistance, tear strength, MASCHINEN resistance to tearing, ultimate tensile strength, MEERSCHMUTZ resistance to tearing, METALL ultimate tensile strength, PHYS tensile strength, TEXTIL breaking strength, tear strength, VERPACK bursting strength, WASSERTRANS breaking load; **Reißkegelbildung** f FERTIG cupping; **Reißlack** m FERTIG brittle lacquer

Reißlänge f KUNSTSTOFF breaking length, PAPIER tensile strength; **Reißlängenprüfer** m PAPIER tensile strength tester; **Reißlängenprüfgerät** nt PAPIER breaking

strength tester

Reiß-: **Reißlehre** f BAU scribing gage (AmE), scribing gauge (BrE); **Reißleinengriff** m LUFTTRANS parachute release handle; **Reißnadel** f BAU scratch awl, FERTIG scriber; **Reißschiene** f MASCHINEN T-square; **Reißspitze** f BAU scribing awl; **Reißverschluß** m MECHAN fastener

Reißverschluß: sich mit ~ öffnen lassen v refl TEXTIL zip; **sich mit ~ schließen lassen** v refl TEXTIL zip

Reiß-: **Reißwerk** nt CHEMIE macerator; **Reißwolf** m VERPACK shredding machine; **Reißzwecke** f FERTIG thumbtack

Reiterchen nt LABOR *Waage* rider

Reiteretikett nt VERPACK header label

Reitergewölbe nt KER & GLAS rider arch

Reitstock m FERTIG tailstock, MASCHINEN back head, back puppet, deadhead, footstock, tailstock, MECHAN headstock; **Reitstockkörper** m FERTIG tailstock body; **Reitstockoberteil** nt FERTIG tailstock barrel; **Reitstockpinole** f FERTIG tailstock quill, MASCHINEN tail spindle, tailstock quill; **Reitstockspitze** f FERTIG tailstock center (AmE), tailstock centre (BrE), MASCHINEN back center (AmE), back center (AmE), back centre (BrE), dead center (AmE), dead centre (BrE), tailstock center (AmE), tailstock centre (BrE); **Reitstockunterteil** nt FERTIG tailstock base

Reizarmut f ERGON sensory deprivation

Reizstoff m SICHERHEIT irritant substance

Reizung f ERGON conditioning

Rekombination f ELEKTRONIK, KERNTECH, PHYS recombination; **Rekombinationsanlage** f KERNTECH recombination plant; **Rekombinationsbasisstrom** m ELEKTRONIK recombination base current; **Rekombinationskoeffizient** m PHYS recombination coefficient; **Rekombinationsrate** f ELEKTRONIK, PHYS recombination rate; **Rekombinationsvorgang** m ELEKTRONIK recombination process

rekonfigurierbar adj COMP & DV reconfigurable

rekonfigurieren vt COMP & DV reconfigure

Rekonfigurierung f COMP & DV reconfiguration

rekonstruieren vt BAU re-equip, COMP & DV reconstruct

Rekonstruktion f BAU reconstruction

Rekorder m ELEKTRIZ recorder

Rekristallisation f METALL recrystallization

Rektaszension f RAUMFAHRT *gerader Aufstieg* right ascension

rektifizieren vt ELEKTRIZ rectify

Rektifizierwalze f PAPIER rectifier roll

rekultivieren vt ABFALL revegetate

Rekultivierung f BAU land restoration, revegetation

Rekuperativkühlung f THERMOD regenerative cooling

Rekuperativofen m KER & GLAS recuperative furnace

Rekursion f COMP & DV recursion; **Rekursionsformel** f MATH recursion formula

rekursiv[1] adj COMP & DV recursive

rekursiv[2] **~es Digitalfilter** nt ELEKTRONIK recursive filter; **~ Digitalfilterung** f ELEKTRONIK recursive filtering; **~es Filter** nt TELEKOM IIR filter, recursive filter; **nicht ~es Filter** nt TELEKOM finite impulse response filter, nonrecursive filter; **~e Funktion** f COMP & DV recursive function; **~e Prozedur** f COMP & DV recursive procedure

Relais nt COMP & DV, ELEKTRIZ, KFZTECH *KFZ-Elektrik*, LABOR *Elektrizität*, PHYS, RADIO, TELEKOM relay; **~ mit mittlerer Ruhelage** nt ELEKTRIZ center stable relay (AmE), centre stable relay (BrE); **~ mit Zeitverriege-**

lung *nt* ELEKTRIZ time-locking relay; **Relaisanker** *m* ELEKTROTECH relay armature; **Relaiskern** *m* ELEKTROTECH relay core; **Relaiskontakt** *m* ELEKTRIZ break contact, ELEKTROTECH relay contact; **Relaismagnet** *m* ELEKTROTECH relay magnet; **Relaissatz** *m* TELEKOM relay set; **Relaisschaltsystem** *nt* ELEKTROTECH relay switching system; **Relaisspule** *f* ELEKTROTECH relay coil; **Relaisstelle Basisstation-Mobilteilnehmer** *f* TELEKOM base-to-mobile relay; **Relaisstelle Mobilteilnehmer-Basisstation** *f* TELEKOM mobile-to-base relay; **Relaisstellen-Frequenzplan** *m* RADIO *Frequenzzuweisung* repeater bandplan; **Relaissummen** *nt* ELEKTROTECH relay hum; **Relaissystem** *nt* TELEKOM relay system; **Relaiswicklung** *f* ELEKTRIZ relay winding; **Relaiszähler** *m* GERÄT magnetic counter

Relation *f* COMP & DV, MATH relation

relational[1] *adj* COMP & DV relational

relational:[2] ~**e Datenbank** *f* COMP & DV RDB, relational database, ~**er Graph** *m* KÜNSTL INT relation graph; ~**er Prozessor** *m* COMP & DV relational processor

Relationssymbol *nt* KÜNSTL INT relation symbol, relational operator

relativ: ~**e Adressierung** *f* COMP & DV relative addressing; ~**e Atommasse** *f* KERNTECH atomic weight, PHYS atomic weight, relative atomic mass, STRAHLPHYS atomic weight; ~**e Bezugsdämpfung** *f* AUFNAHME loudness volume equivalent; ~**er Brechungsindex** *m* OPTIK, PHYS relative refractive index; ~**e Byteadresse** *f* (*RBA*) COMP & DV relative byte address (*RBA*); ~**e Dichte** *f* KOHLEN relative density, KUNSTSTOFF relative density, specific gravity; ~**e Dielektrizitätskonstante** *f* ELEKTROTECH relative permittivity, specific inductive capacity, PHYS dielectric constant, relative permittivity; ~**e Empfindlichkeit** *f* GERÄT relative sensitivity; ~**er Fehler** *m* COMP & DV relative error; ~**e Feuchte** *f* HEIZ & KÄLTE, KUNSTSTOFF, TEXTIL relative humidity; ~**e Feuchtigkeit** *f* HEIZ & KÄLTE, MASCHINEN, PAPIER, TEXTIL relative humidity; ~**e Flughöhe** *f* LUFTTRANS relative altitude; ~**e Flußdichte** *f* ELEKTRIZ remanent flux density; ~**e Häufigkeit** *f* COMP & DV relative frequency, PHYS relative abundance, QUAL relative frequency; ~**e Leistung** *f* ELEKTROTECH relative power; ~**es lineares Bremsvermögen** *nt* PHYS relative linear stopping power; ~**e Luftfeuchte** *f* HEIZ & KÄLTE, PHYS relative humidity; ~**e Luftfeuchtigkeit** *f* WASSERTRANS, WASSERVERSORG relative humidity; ~**es Massenbremsvermögen** *nt* PHYS relative mass stopping power; ~**e Molekularmasse** *f* PHYS relative molecular mass; ~**e Öffnung** *f* PHYS relative aperture; ~**e Permeabilität** *f* ELEKTRIZ, ELEKTROTECH, PHYS relative permeability; ~**e Permittivität** *f* ELEKTRIZ relative permittivity; ~**e Profiltiefe** *f* LUFTTRANS chord ratio; ~**er Schlupf** *m* ELEKTRIZ relative slip; ~**e Signalamplitude** *f* ELEKTRONIK relative signal amplitude; ~**e Spannung** *f* ELEKTROTECH negative voltage, positive voltage; ~**e spektrale Strahlenverteilung** *f* NICHTFOSS ENERG spectral energy distribution; ~**e Steigung** *f* LUFTTRANS *Propeller* pitch diameter ratio; ~**er Trittschallpegel** *m* AKUSTIK normalized impact sound level; ~**e Unterschiedsschwelle** *f* AKUSTIK relative difference limit; ~**er Verdichtungsgrad** *m* PHYS relative pressure coefficient; ~**e Wassergeschwindigkeit** *f* NICHTFOSS ENERG relative water velocity; ~**er Winkelabweichungsgewinn** *m* AKUSTIK relative angular deviation gain; ~**er Winkelabweichungsverlust** *m* AKUSTIK relative angular deviation loss; ~**e Zähigkeit** *f* STRÖMPHYS relative viscosity

Relativbewegung *f* PHYS relative motion

Relativempfindlichkeit *f* GERÄT relative sensitivity; ~ **eines Wandlers** *f* AKUSTIK relative sensitivity of a transducer

Relativfilter *nt* ELEKTRONIK constant-percentage bandwidth filter

Relativgeschwindigkeit *f* FERNSEH head-to-tape speed, KOHLEN, PHYS relative velocity

relativistisch[1] *adj* RAUMFAHRT relativistic

relativistisch:[2] ~**e Mechanik** *f* PHYS, RAUMFAHRT relativistic mechanics; ~**es Partikel** *nt* RAUMFAHRT relativistic particle

Relativität *f* RAUMFAHRT relativity; **Relativitätseffekt** *m* RAUMFAHRT relativity effect; **allgemeine Relativitätstheorie** *f* PHYS general theory of relativity

Relaxation *f* KUNSTSTOFF relaxation; **Relaxationsschwingung** *f* ELEKTRIZ relaxation oscillation; **Relaxationszeit** *f* AKUSTIK relaxation time, ELEKTRIZ relaxation time

Release-Level *m* COMP & DV release level

Release-Papier *nt* DRUCK release paper

Reliabilität *f* ERGON *von psychologischen Tests*, METROL *Statistik* reliability

Relief *nt* FERTIG embossing; **Reliefdruck** *m* DRUCK relief printing; **Reliefgravur** *f* KER & GLAS engraving in relief; **Reliefwebart** *f* TEXTIL relief weave

Reling *f* WASSERTRANS handrail, *Schiffbau* rail; **Relingslog** *nt* WASSERTRANS *Meereskunde* Lagrangian drifter, *Navigation* Dutchman's log; **Relingsstütze** *f* WASSERTRANS railing stanchion; **Relingsstützenfuß** *m* WASSERTRANS stanchion deck fitting

Reluktanz *f* ELEKTRIZ (*R*) reluctance (*R*), ELEKTROTECH magnetic resistance, reluctance, PHYS reluctance; **Reluktanzmotor** *m* ELEKTRIZ, ELEKTROTECH, TRANS reluctance motor

Reluktivität *f* ELEKTRIZ, PHYS reluctivity

remanent: ~**e Feldstärke** *f* ELEKTRIZ remanent flux density; ~**e Ladung** *f* ELEKTROTECH remanent charge

Remanenz *f* AUFNAHME *Restmagnetisierung*, ELEKTRIZ, ELEKTROTECH remanence, PHYS remanence, retentivity; **Remanenzinduktion** *f* ELEKTROTECH remanent induction

Rendezvous[1] *nt* RAUMFAHRT rendezvous

Rendezvous:[2] **ein ~ durchführen** *vi* RAUMFAHRT rendezvous

Rendezvous: **Rendezvousbahn** *f* RAUMFAHRT rendezvous trajectory; **Rendezvousmanöver** *nt* RAUMFAHRT rendezvous maneuver (AmE), rendezvous manoeuvre (BrE); **Rendezvousradar** *m* RAUMFAHRT rendezvous radar; **Rendezvousverfahren** *nt* RAUMFAHRT rendezvous procedure

Renette *f* LEBENSMITTEL *Apfelsorte* rennet

Rennbahn-Mikrotron *nt* TEILPHYS race track microtron

Rennherd *m* METALL bloomery hearth

Rennin *nt* LEBENSMITTEL rennin

Rennkraftstoff *m* KERNTECH racing fuel

Reoxidation *f* CHEMIE reoxidation

Reparatur *f* WASSERTRANS repair; **Reparaturanleitung** *f* KFZTECH repair manual; **Reparaturdauer** *f* COMP & DV repair time; **Reparaturlack** *m* KUNSTSTOFF refinishing paint; **Reparaturwerkstatt** *f* KFZTECH garage with workshop, service station, TRANS garage

reparieren *vt* BAU make good, WASSERTRANS repair

Repertoire *nt* COMP & DV repertoire

Repetierbarkeit *f* MASCHINEN positioning repeatability

Replay *nt* FERNSEH replay
Repository *nt* COMP & DV repository
Reprise *f* TEXTIL, WERKPRÜF *Textil* moisture regain
Reproduktionskamera *f* DRUCK process camera, reproduction camera
reproduzierbar:[1] **nicht ~** *adj* VERPACK nonreproductible
reproduzierbar:[2] **~e Messung** *f* METROL repeatable measurement
Reproduzierbarkeit *f* GERÄT repeatability
reproduzieren *vt* AUFNAHME reproduce, FOTO duplicate
reprofähig: **~e Vorlage** *f* DRUCK CRC, camera ready copy
Reprografik *f* COMP & DV reprographics
Reprographie *f* DRUCK reprography
Reprokamera *f* DRUCK process camera, reproduction camera, FOTO copy camera
Reprostativ *nt* FOTO copying stand, copypod
Reprotechnik *f* KONSTZEICH reprographic technique
Repulsion *f* ELEKTROTECH repulsion; **Repulsionskraft** *f* METALL repulsive power; **Repulsionsmotor** *m* ELEKTRIZ, ELEKTROTECH repulsion motor
Resazurin *nt* CHEMIE resazurin
Reserpin *nt* CHEMIE reserpine
Reserve *f* COMP & DV stand-by, ERDÖL backup, MEERSCHMUTZ stand-by, RADIO *Batterie* backup, TELEKOM stand-by; **Reserveablaufteil** *nt* COMP & DV, TELEKOM backup supervisor; **Reserveanknotung** *f* TEXTIL magazine creeling; **Reserveausrüstung** *f* COMP & DV stand-by equipment; **Reservebatterie** *f* ELEKTROTECH reserve battery; **Reservefäden** *m pl* TEXTIL transfer tails; **Reservekanister** *m* KFZTECH jerrican, spare can; **Reservekapazität** *f* TRANS RC, reserve capacity; **Reservekessel** *m* HEIZ & KÄLTE stand-by boiler; **Reservekühleinrichtung** *f* KERNTECH stand-by cooling system; **Reserveleitung** *f* TELEKOM spare line; **Reservenummer** *f* TELEKOM spare number; **Reservepeilung** *f* RAUMFAHRT backup bearing; **Reserveprozessor** *m* TELEKOM stand-by processor; **Reservereaktor** *m* KERNTECH backup reactor; **Reserveseil** *nt* ERDÖL backup line, **Reservespur** *f* COMP & DV spare track; **Reservesystem** *nt* TELEKOM stand-by system; **Reservetreibstoffpumpe** *f* RAUMFAHRT fuel backup pump
reserviert: **nicht ~er Parkplatz** *m* TRANS nonreserved space; **~es Wort** *nt* COMP & DV reserved word
Reservoir *nt* HYDRAUL forebay, KFZTECH *Öl, Kraftstoff* reservoir, WASSERVERSORG reservoir, water tank
Reset *nt* COMP & DV reset; **Reset-Knopf** *m* FERNSEH reset knob
Reset-Set- *pref* ELEKTRONIK reset-set; **Reset-Set-Flipflop** *nt* (*RS-Flipflop*) ELEKTRONIK reset-set flip-flop (*RS flip-flop*); **Reset-Set-Kippschaltung** *f* (*RS-Kippschaltung*) ELEKTRONIK reset-set toggle (*RS toggle*)
Reset: **Reset-Taste** *f* COMP & DV reset button
resident[1] *adj* COMP & DV resident
resident:[2] **~es Programm** *nt* COMP & DV resident program; **~er Programmspeicher** *m* COMP & DV resident program storage
Residuum *nt* MEERSCHMUTZ residue; **Residuumarithmetik** *f* COMP & DV residue arithmetic
Resit *nt* FERTIG resite, KUNSTSTOFF C-stage resin, resite
Resitol *nt* FERTIG resitol, KUNSTSTOFF B-stage resin
Resol *nt* KUNSTSTOFF A-stage resin, resol
resonant[1] *adj* PHYS resonant
resonant:[2] **~e Energieübertragung** *f* STRAHLPHYS resonant energy transfer

Resonanz *f* AUFNAHME, ELEKTRIZ, ELEKTRONIK, PHYS, TEILPHYS, TELEKOM, WELLPHYS resonance; **Resonanzabsorption** *f* TELEKOM resonance absorption; **Resonanzanhebung** *f* ELEKTRONIK peaking; **Resonanzbrücke** *f* ELEKTRIZ resonance bridge; **Resonanzdämpfer** *m* SICHERHEIT resonance muffler (AmE), resonance silencer (BrE); **Resonanzeinfang** *m* KERNTECH *von Neutronen* resonance capture; **Resonanzfilter** *nt* AUFNAHME, STRAHLPHYS resonance filter; **Resonanzfluchtwahrscheinlichkeit** *f* (*p*) KERNTECH resonance escape probability (*p*); **Resonanzfrequenz** *f* AKUSTIK (*fR*), ELEKTRONIK (*fR*) resonant frequency (*fR*), STRAHLPHYS resonance frequency, TELEKOM (*fR*), WELLPHYS (*fR*) resonant frequency (*fR*); **Resonanzhohlraum** *m* OPTIK resonant cavity; **Resonanzkörper** *m* ELEKTRONIK resonant cavity, resonator; **Resonanzkreis** *m* ELEKTRONIK, TELEKOM resonant circuit; **Resonanzkreis-Induktionsschleifendetektor** *m* TRANS resonant-circuit induction loop detector; **Resonanzkurve** *f* FERNSEH resonance curve; **Resonanzleitung** *f* ELEKTRONIK resonant line; **Resonanzleitungsgenerator** *m* ELEKTRONIK resonant-line oscillator; **Resonanzlinie** *f* STRAHLPHYS resonance line; **Resonanzneutronenzähler** *m* STRAHLPHYS resonance neutron detector; **Resonanzpeak** *m* STRAHLPHYS resonance peak; **Resonanzschaltung mit Eisenkernspule** *f* ELEKTROTECH ferroresonance circuit; **Resonanzschärfe** *f* PHYS sharpness of resonance; **Resonanzschwingkreis** *m* PHYS resonant circuit; **Resonanzsieb** *nt* ABFALL, KOHLEN resonance screen; **Resonanzspektrum** *nt* WELLPHYS resonance spectrum; **Resonanzspitze** *f* AUFNAHME resonance peak; **Resonanzstrahlung** *f* STRAHLPHYS resonance radiation; **Resonanztransformator** *m* ELEKTROTECH tuned transformer; **Resonanzverbreiterung von Spektrallinien** *f* STRAHLPHYS resonance broadening of spectral lines; **Resonanzverstärker** *m* ELEKTRONIK tuned amplifier; **Resonanzwand** *f* AKUSTIK baffle; **Resonanzwellenmesser** *m* RADIO absorption wavemeter; **Resonanzzustände optischer Hohlraumresonatoren** *m pl* STRAHLPHYS resonant modes of optical cavities
Resonator *m* TELEKOM resonator; **Resonatorgitter** *nt* ELEKTRONIK resonator grid
Resorcin *nt* KUNSTSTOFF resorcinol, resorcin; **Resorcinharz** *nt* KUNSTSTOFF resorcinol resin, resorcinol formaldehyde resin
Resorcinol *nt* CHEMIE resorcin, resorcinol
Resorcinphthalein *nt* CHEMIE fluorescein
Resorcyl- *pref* CHEMIE resorcylic
Resorufin *nt* CHEMIE resorufine
respiratorisch *adj* SICHERHEIT respiratory
Ressource *f* COMP & DV, MEERSCHMUTZ resource
Rest *m* COMP & DV, MATH remainder; **Rest-** *pref* ANSTRICH residual, CHEMIE residuary; **Restabstand** *m* ELEKTROTECH residual gap
Re-Start *m* KONTROLL restart
Rest: **Restauftrieb** *m* WASSERTRANS *Schiffkonstruktion* reserve buoyancy; **Restaustenit** *m* METALL rest austenite; **Restbogenteile** *m pl* DRUCK oddments; **Restentladung** *f* ELEKTROTECH residual discharge; **Restfalte** *f* KONSTZEICH residual fold; **Restfehlerhäufigkeit** *f* COMP & DV residual error rate; **Restfehlerrate** *f* COMP & DV residual error rate; **Restfeuchte** *f* HEIZ & KÄLTE residual moisture; **Restfeuchtigkeit** *f* HEIZ & KÄLTE, VERPACK residual moisture; **Restflußdichte** *f*

ELEKTRIZ residual flux density; **Restfrequenzmodulation** *f* ELEKTRONIK *Rest-FM* residual frequency modulation; **Restgas** *nt* ELEKTRONIK, UMWELTSCHMUTZ residual gas; **Resthärte** *f* FERTIG *Kunststoffinstallationen* residual hardness; **Restkapazität** *f* ELEKTROTECH residual capacitance; **Restklassenrechnung** *f* MATH congruence arithmetic, modular arithmetic; **Restladung** *f* ELEKTRIZ, ELEKTROTECH, FERNSEH residual charge

restlich *adj* CHEMIE residuary, COMP & DV residual

Rest: **Restluftmenge** *f* HEIZ & KÄLTE residual air volume; **Restmagnetisierung** *f* PHYS remanence, STRAHLPHYS residual magnetization; **Restmagnetismus** *m* ELEKTRIZ residual magnetism; **Restmasse** *f* (m_0) KERNTECH rest mass (m_0); **Restmengenpumpe** *f* MEERSCHMUTZ stripping pump; **Restmüll** *m* ABFALL *nicht verwertbare Abfallstoffe* tailings; **Restschrumpf** *m* TEXTIL residual shrinkage; **Restseitenband** *nt* ELEKTRONIK *(RSB)* vestigial sideband *(VSB)*, FERNSEH vestigial sideband, TELEKOM residual sideband, vestigial sideband; **Restseitenbandfilter** *nt* ELEKTRONIK vestigial sideband filter; **Restseitenbandsignal** *nt* ELEKTRONIK vestigial sideband signal; **Restsignal** *nt* COMP & DV residual noise; **Restsilber** *nt* FOTO residual silver; **Restspannung** *f* BAU, KER & GLAS residual stress; **Reststoff** *m* ABFALL remainder; **Reststoffdeponie** *f* ABFALL residue landfill; **Reststrom** *m* ELEKTRIZ, ELEKTROTECH residual current; **Restwassergehalt** *m* OPTIK residual water content; **Restwiderstand** *m* ELEKTROTECH residual resistance

Resultante *f* MASCHINEN resultant

resultierend: ~er Schub *m* LUFTTRANS gross thrust

Resultierende *f* PHYS resultant; **~ einer Vektoraddition** *f* MATH vector resultant

resynchronisieren *vt* TELEKOM resynchronize

Retarder *m* KFZTECH, KUNSTSTOFF retarder

retardieren *vt* CHEMIE retard

retardiert: ~es Potential *nt* PHYS retarded potential

Reten *nt* CHEMIE methylisopropylphenanthrene, retene

Retention *f* CHEMIE, ELEKTROTECH retention; **Retentionsfähigkeit** *f* FERNSEH retentivity

Retikulum *nt* OPTIK reticle, reticule

Retorte [1] *f* CHEMTECH, ERDÖL, LABOR retort

Retorte [2] **in ~ destillieren** *vt* CHEMTECH retort

Retorte: **Retortenklemme** *f* LABOR retort clamp; **Retortenkohle** *f* KOHLEN retort coal; **Retortenschwelen** *nt* CHEMIE retorting

Retrieval *nt* TEXTIL retrieval

Retro-Abfolge *f* RAUMFAHRT retrosequence

retrograd: ~e Metamorphose *f* NICHTFOSS ENERG retrograde metamorphism

Retro-Gradation *f* LEBENSMITTEL retrogradation

Retro-Pack *nt* RAUMFAHRT retropack

Retro-Rakete *f* RAUMFAHRT retro-rocket

Retroschub *m* LUFTTRANS reverse thrust

retten *vt* PAPIER save, SICHERHEIT rescue

Rettung *f* LUFTTRANS recovery, rescue, WASSERTRANS recovery, *Notfall* rescue; **Rettungsaktion** *f* SICHERHEIT rescue operation; **Rettungsboje** *f* WASSERTRANS lifebuoy; **Rettungsboot** *nt* WASSERTRANS lifeboat; **Rettungsbootsmann** *m* WASSERTRANS lifeboatman; **Rettungsbootsstation** *f* WASSERTRANS lifeboat station; **Rettungsbootsübung** *f* WASSERTRANS boat drill; **Rettungsdienst** *m* SICHERHEIT rescue service; **Rettungsdienst und Feuerwehr** *m* LUFTTRANS rescue and firefighting service, WASSERTRANS rescue and fire

fighting service; **Rettungseinrichtung** *f* LUFTTRANS rescue apparatus, SICHERHEIT escape device, WASSERTRANS rescue apparatus; **Rettungsfahrzeug** *nt* KFZTECH rescue vehicle; **Rettungsfallschirm** *m* LUFTTRANS emergency parachute, escape parachute; **Rettungsfloß** *nt* SICHERHEIT, WASSERTRANS life raft; **Rettungsgerät** *nt* LUFTTRANS rescue apparatus, rescue equipment, SICHERHEIT rescue equipment, WASSERTRANS life-saving apparatus, rescue equipment; **Rettungsgerät für Brandeinsätze** *nt* SICHERHEIT fire rescue appliance; **Rettungsgürtel** *m* BAU life belt (BrE), WASSERTRANS life belt; **Rettungshubschrauber** *m* LUFTTRANS rescue helicopter; **Rettungsinsel** *f* WASSERTRANS life raft; **Rettungsleine** *f* WASSERTRANS lifeline; **Rettungsring** *m* SICHERHEIT life-saver, WASSERTRANS lifebuoy; **Rettungsschwimmer** *m* WASSERTRANS emergency flotation gear; **Rettungsstation** *f* SICHERHEIT rescue station; **Rettungstrupp** *m* SICHERHEIT rescue party; **Rettungsturm für Startphase** *m* RAUMFAHRT launch phase escape tower; **Rettungsübung** *f* WASSERTRANS emergency drill; **Rettungsweg bei Feuer** *m* LUFTTRANS fire rescue path; **Rettungsweste** *f* WASSERTRANS life jacket (BrE), life preserver (AmE), life vest (BrE)

Return *m* COMP & DV return

Retuschieren *nt* DRUCK, FOTO retouching

retuschieren *vt* FOTO retouch

Retuschierpinsel *m* DRUCK retouching brush

reversibel [1] *adj* THERMOD reversible

reversibel [2] **reversible Abschaltung** *f* KERNTECH reversible shutdown; **reversibler Transducer** *m* ELEKTROTECH reversible transducer; **reversibler Wandler** *m* ELEKTROTECH reversible transducer

reversierbar: nicht ~er Motor *m* ELEKTRIZ nonreversible motor; **nicht ~er Stecker** *m* ELEKTRIZ nonreversible plug

reversieren *vt* ELEKTRONIK reverse

Reversierwalzwerk *nt* FERTIG reversing mill

Reversion *f* KUNSTSTOFF reversion

Reversosmose *f* CHEMTECH reverse osmosis

revidieren *vt* DRUCK revise

Revision *f* MECHAN audit; **Revisionsabzug** *m* DRUCK press proof

Revolution *f* GEOM revolution

Revolver *m* MASCHINEN capstan; **Revolveranschlag** *m* MASCHINEN multiposition stop; **Revolverbank** *f* MECHAN lathe; **Revolverblende** *f* OPTIK revolving diaphragm; **Revolverbohrmaschine** *f* MASCHINEN turret-type drilling machine; **Revolverdrehbank** *f* MECHAN capstan lathe, turret lathe; **Revolverdrehen** *nt* MASCHINEN capstan turning; **Revolverdrehmaschine** *f* FERTIG capstan lathe, MASCHINEN turret lathe; **Revolverkopf** *m* FERTIG turret, MASCHINEN capstan tool head, turret, turret head, MECHAN turret; **Revolverkopfbohrmaschine** *f* MASCHINEN turret-type drilling machine; **Revolverkopfdrehmaschine** *f* MASCHINEN turret lathe; **Revolverkopfschaltstellung** *f* FERTIG turret head indexing position; **Revolverlochzange** *f* MASCHINEN revolving head punch; **Revolverschieber** *m* MASCHINEN turret slide; **Revolverschlitten** *m* MASCHINEN ram

Reynolds: **Reynoldsspannung** *f* STRÖMPHYS Reynolds stress; **Reynoldstransporttheorem** *nt* STRÖMPHYS Reynolds' transport theorem; **Reynoldszahl** *f* *(Re)* HYDRAUL, LUFTTRANS *Aerodynamik*, NICHTFOSS ENERG, PHYS, STRÖMPHYS Reynolds number *(Re)*;

Reynoldszahlbereich *m* STRÖMPHYS Reynolds number region
Reyon *nt* KUNSTSTOFF rayon
Rezension *f* DRUCK review
Rezeptierung *f* KUNSTSTOFF formulation
Rezeptor *m* ERGON receptor
Rezeptur *f* BAU mix design, KUNSTSTOFF formulation; **Rezepturänderung** *f* KUNSTSTOFF reformulation
Rezipientenglocke *f* CHEMIE bell jar
reziprok[1] *adj* COMP & DV, GEOM reciprocal, MASCHINEN converse, MATH reciprocal; **reziprok-quadratisch** *adj* PHYS inverse-square
reziprok:[2] ~**e Gleitzahl** *f* PHYS *Verhältnis von Auftrieb zu Widerstand* lift-drag ratio; ~**e Periode** *f* KERNTECH reciprocal period; ~**e Schaltung** *f* TELEKOM reciprocal circuit; **nicht ~e Schaltung** *f* TELEKOM nonreciprocal circuit; ~**e Steifigkeit** *f* AKUSTIK compliance; ~**er Wandler** *m* AKUSTIK reciprocal transducer; **nicht ~er Wellenleiter** *m* TELEKOM nonreciprocal wave guide; ~**er Wert** *m* GEOM reciprocal, MATH conjugate, inverse proportion, inverse ratio
Reziproke *f* MATH reciprocal
Reziprozitätssatz *m* ELEKTROTECH, PHYS reciprocity theorem
RF *abbr* (*Radiofrequenz*) AUFNAHME, ELEKTRIZ, ELEKTRONIK, FERNSEH, RADIO, TELECOM HF (*high frequency*), RF (*radio frequency*)
Rf (*Rutherfordium*) CHEMIE Rf (*rutherfordium*)
RG *abbr* (*elektronischer Rauschgenerator*) FERNSEH ENG (*electronic noise generator*)
RGB[1] *abbr* (*rot-grün-blau*) COMP & DV, FERNSEH RGB (*red-green-blue*)
RGB:[2] **RGB-Bildschirm** *m* COMP & DV RGB monitor; **RGB-Eingabe** *f* FERNSEH RGB input; **RGB-Monitor** *m* COMP & DV, FERNSEH RGB monitor; **RGB-System** *nt* COMP & DV RGB system
R-Gespräch *nt* TELEKOM collect call (AmE), reverse charge call (BrE), transferred charge call
R-Gespräch: ein ~ führen *vi* TELEKOM make a collect call (AmE), make a reverse charge call (BrE)
RH *abbr* (*Hallscher Koeffizient*) PHYS, RADIO RH (*Hall coefficient*)
Rh (*Rhodium*) CHEMIE Rh (*rhodium*)
Rhamnetin *nt* CHEMIE methylquercitin, rhamnetin
Rhamnit *m* CHEMIE rhamnite, rhamnitol
Rhamnose *f* CHEMIE rhamnose
Rhenat *nt* CHEMIE perrhenate
Rhenium *nt* (*Re*) CHEMIE rhenium (*Re*); **Rhenium-** *pref* CHEMIE rhenic
Rheologie *f* KOHLEN, KUNSTSTOFF, PHYS, STRÖMPHYS rheology
rheologisch: ~**e Eigenschaften** *f pl* STRÖMPHYS rheological properties; ~**e Variable** *f* METALL rheological variable
Rheostat *m* ELEKTRIZ, ELEKTROTECH, LABOR rheostat; **Rheostatgleitschieber** *m* ELEKTRIZ rheostat slider; **Rheostatkontaktschleifer** *m* ELEKTRIZ rheostat slider
RHIC *abbr* TEILPHYS RHIC, relativistic heavy ion collider
Rhodanid *nt* CHEMIE thiocyanate
Rhodeorhetin *nt* CHEMIE convolvulin, rhodeorhetin
Rhodium *nt* (*Rh*) CHEMIE rhodium (*Rh*)
Rhomboid *nt* GEOM rhomboid
rhomboidisch *adj* GEOM rhomboid, rhomboidal
Rhombus *m* GEOM rhomb, rhombus; **Rhombusantenne** *f* RADIO rhombic aerial (BrE), rhombic antenna

(AmE); **Rhombuswicklung** *f* ELEKTRIZ diamond winding
Rhumbatron *nt* ELEKTRONIK *Mikrowellen* rhumbatron
Rhythmus *m* AKUSTIK rhythm
RICH *abbr* (*ringbildender Tscherenkov-Zähler*) TEILPHYS RICH (*ring-imaging Cherenkov counter*)
Richtantenne *f* ELEKTRONIK beam aerial, beam antenna, FERNSEH directional antenna, RADIO beam aerial, beam antenna, directional array, RAUMFAHRT directional antenna, shaped beam antenna, TELEKOM directional antenna; ~ **mit passiven Strahlern** *f* RADIO parasitic array; **Richtantennengruppe mit kleinen Elementabständen** *f* RADIO close-spaced array; **Richtantennen-Öffnungswinkel** *m* RAUMFAHRT *am Half-Power Punkt* half-power beamwidth
Richtantrieb *m* RAUMFAHRT director
Richtapparat *m* MASCHINEN leveling machine (AmE), levelling machine (BrE)
Richtbake *f* WASSERTRANS *Navigation* guide beacon
Richtblei *nt* BAU plummet
Richtbohren *nt* ERDÖL *Bohrtechnik* directional drilling
Richtcharakteristik *f* AKUSTIK directivity pattern, ELEKTRONIK directional response, GERÄT directional diagram
Richtdiagramm *nt* AKUSTIK directivity pattern
Richten *nt* BAU straightening, ELEKTRONIK *von Signalen* directing, FERTIG *Blech* flattening, leveling (AmE), levelling (BrE), MASCHINEN leveling (AmE), levelling (BrE), straightening
richten *vt* BAU straighten, ELEKTRONIK *Signale* direct, FERTIG *Blech* flatten, level, MASCHINEN level, straighten
Richterskale *f* BAU Richter scale
Richtfaktor *m* AKUSTIK directivity factor
Richtfeuer *nt* WASSERTRANS *Navigation* guide light, range light
Richtfunk *m* RADIO microwave; **Richtfunkortungsgerät** *nt* TRANS directional detector; **Richtfunkstrahl** *m* TELEKOM *Relay* microwave beam; **Richtfunksystem** *nt* TELEKOM microwave system, radio relay system; **Richtfunkturm** *m* TELEKOM microwave tower; **Richtfunkverbindung** *f* TELEKOM microwave link; **Richtfunkverbindung innerhalb der Radiosichtweite** *f* TELEKOM line-of-sight radio relay link
Richtgeschwindigkeit *f* TRANS advisory speed, recommended speed
Richthöhe *f* MECHAN elevation
richtig: ~**es Heben von Hand** *nt* SICHERHEIT correct manual lifting techniques
Richtigkeit *f* METROL correctness, QUAL trueness
Richtkoppler *m* ELEKTROTECH, OPTIK, PHYS, TELEKOM directional coupler
Richtkopplung *f* ELEKTROTECH directional coupling
Richtkreisel *m* TRANS directional gyro
Richtlatte *f* BAU batten
Richtleiter *m* PHYS isolator
Richtlinie *f* ELEKTRIZ, KFZTECH guideline
Richtmaschine *f* MASCHINEN leveling machine (AmE), levelling machine (BrE), straightener, straightening machine
Richtmikrofon *nt* AKUSTIK, AUFNAHME directional microphone, unidirectional microphone
Richtplatte *f* MASCHINEN gib
Richtrelais *nt* ELEKTROTECH directional relay
Richtseezeichen *nt* WASSERTRANS guiding mark
Richtsender *m* FERNSEH directional-beam transmitter

Richtspannung *f* ELEKTROTECH rectified voltage

Richtstrahl *m* ELEKTRONIK directional beam, RADIO *Richtantenne*, RAUMFAHRT beam, TELEKOM directional beam; **Richtstrahlanzeige** *f* ELEKTRONIK directed-beam display

Richtstrahler¹ *m* PHYS reflector

Richtstrahler²: **mit ~ entsenden** *vt* RADIO beam

Richtstrahl: **Richtstrahlröhre** *f* ELEKTRONIK shaped beam tube; **Richtstrahlumschaltung** *f* RAUMFAHRT *Weltraumfunk* beam switching

Richtstrom *m* ELEKTROTECH rectified current

Richtung *f* COMP & DV route, sense, SICHERHEIT *Flaschenzug* direction; **Richtungsabhängigkeit** *f* FERTIG aelotropy, anisotropy

richtungsempfindlich: **~es Relais** *nt* ELEKTRIZ directional relay

Richtung: **Richtungsfahrbahn** *f* TRANS lane; **Richtungsfaktor** *m* AKUSTIK directivity factor; **Richtungsgleis** *nt* EISENBAHN sorting siding; **Richtungskommutator** *m* ELEKTRIZ *Stromwender* direction commutator; **Richtungskoppler** *m* OPTIK directional coupler; **Richtungskriterium** *nt* COMP & DV routing criterion; **Richtungsleitung** *f* TELEKOM *Mikrowellen* isolator; **Richtungsmaß** *nt* AKUSTIK directivity index; **Richtungspeilung** *f* PHYS direction finding; **Richtungspolarisation** *f* PHYS oriental polarization; **Richtungsschalter** *m* ELEKTRIZ direction switch; **Richtungsschaufel** *f* LUFTTRANS *Kompressor* compressor blade, stator vane; **Richtungsschild** *nt* BAU direction sign; **Richtungsspurkapazität** *f* TRANS tidal capacity; **Richtungsstabilität** *f* RAUMFAHRT directional stability; **Richtungstaktschrift** *f* COMP & DV PE, phase encoding; **Richtungsumkehr** *f* MASCHINEN reversing the motion; **Richtungswechsel** *m* TRANS tidal flow; **Richtungswechselbetrieb** *m* TRANS tidal flow system; **Richtungswechselspur** *f* TRANS reversible lane, tidal flow lane; **Richtungsweiche** *f* ELEKTRONIK *Richtfunkttechnik* branching filter, *Sende-Empfangsweiche* directional filter, TELEKOM directional filter; **Richtungswinkel** *m* BAU azimuth, *Kompaß* bearing

Richtverlust *m* RAUMFAHRT *Weltraumfunk* pointing loss

Richtwaage *f* FERTIG, METROL spirit level

Richtwalze *f* MASCHINEN planisher, planishing roll

Richtwert *m* QUAL standard value; **~e für das Flankenspiel** *m pl* FERTIG recommended backlash

Richtwirkung *f* FERNSEH directional selectivity, FERTIG directionality, RADIO, RAUMFAHRT directivity; **Richtwirkungsgrad** *m* ELEKTROTECH rectification efficiency; **Richtwirkungsindex** *m (Di)* AKUSTIK directivity index *(Di)*

RIC-Verfahren *nt* KUNSTSTOFF RIC molding (AmE), RIC moulding (BrE), runnerless injection compression molding (AmE), runnerless injection compression moulding (BrE)

riechstoffbildend *adj* UMWELTSCHMUTZ odorous

Riefe *f* FERTIG stria, *von Rad* wheel mark, KER & GLAS hackle mark, MASCHINEN flute, ridge, score, score mark

riefen *vt* FERTIG, MASCHINEN ridge

Riefe: **Riefenbildung** *f* FERTIG, MASCHINEN scoring; **Riefennachlauf** *m* FERTIG *Brennschneide* drag

Riefung *f* FERTIG striation

Riegel *m* BAU beam, lock bolt, shutter, *eines Schlosses* bar, KOHLEN wale, waling, MECHAN tie rod, SICHERHEIT lock, WASSERVERSORG *eines Schleusentors* crosspiece; **Riegelnut** *f* EISENBAHN locking notch;

Riegelwand *f* BAU framework wall

Riekediagramm *nt* ELEKTRONIK *Elektronenröhren* Rieke diagram

Riemann: **~ sche Geometrie** *f* GEOM Riemannian geometry

Riemen¹ *m* KFZTECH belt, MASCHINEN band, belt, MECHAN, PAPIER belt, WASSERTRANS *Rudern* oar

Riemen:² **einen ~ ausrücken** *vi* MASCHINEN throw a belt off; **die ~ einlegen** *vi* WASSERTRANS *Rudern* ship the oars; **einen ~ spannen** *vi* MASCHINEN tighten a belt

Riemen: **Riemenantrieb** *m* HEIZ & KÄLTE, MECHAN, PAPIER belt drive; **Riemenaufleger** *m* FERTIG belt mounter; **Riemenbeanspruchung** *f* MASCHINEN belt stress; **Riemendehnschlupf** *m* FERTIG belt creep; **Riemendehnung** *f* FERTIG belt stretch; **Riemenfett** *nt* MASCHINEN belt grease; **Riemengabel** *f* FERTIG belt fork, MASCHINEN strap fork; **Riemengetriebe** *nt* FERTIG belt drive, belt transmission

riemengetrieben *adj* FERTIG belt-driven

Riemen: **Riemenniet** *m* FERTIG belt rivet; **Riemenreibung** *f* MASCHINEN belt friction; **Riemenscheibe** *f* FERTIG belt pulley, MASCHINEN band pulley, pulley, sheave; **Riemenscheibendrehmaschine** *f* MASCHINEN pulley lathe, pulley turning lathe; **Riemenschlaufe** *f* SICHERHEIT belt-type sling; **Riemenschloß** *nt* PAPIER belt fastener; **Riemenschlupf** *m* MASCHINEN belt slip; **Riemenschutz** *m* MASCHINEN belt guard; **Riemenspannrolle** *f* FERTIG idler; **Riemenspannung** *f* MASCHINEN belt tension; **Riementrieb** *m* FERTIG belting, HEIZ & KÄLTE, MASCHINEN belt drive; **Riementrum** *nt* MASCHINEN end; **Riemenverbinder** *m* FERTIG belt lacer, fastener; **Riemenwerkstoff** *m* KUNSTSTOFF belting; **Riemenzug** *m* FERTIG belt tension

Ries *nt* DRUCK *500 Bogen Papier*, PAPIER ream

Rieselfeld *nt* ABFALL irrigation field, WASSERVERSORG sewage farm

Rieselhilfsmittel *nt* LEBENSMITTEL anticaking agent

Rieselkolonne *f* CHEMTECH washing tower

Rieselkühler *m* HEIZ & KÄLTE irrigation cooler

Rieselsieb *nt* KER & GLAS shower screen

Rieselturm *m* KERNTECH gas washer

Rieselwände *f pl* UMWELTSCHMUTZ scrubber walls

Riesenimpulslaser *m* ELEKTRONIK giant pulse laser

Riesenpulslaser *m* ELEKTRONIK Q-switch laser, Q-switched laser

Riet *nt* TEXTIL reed

Riff *nt* WASSERTRANS reef

Riffelglas *nt* BAU ribbed glass

Riffeln *nt* BAU fluting, FERTIG channelling (BrE)

riffeln *vt* BAU groove, FERTIG checker (AmE), chequer (BrE), serrate

Riffelprobenteiler *m* KOHLEN riffle sampler

Riffelung *f* BAU flute, FERTIG corrugation, KER & GLAS fluting, KONSTZEICH checkering (AmE), chequering (BrE)

Riffelwalze *f* KER & GLAS crimper, PAPIER fluter

Rille¹ *f* AKUSTIK groove, KER & GLAS flute, MASCHINEN groove, ridge, OPTIK groove

Rille:² **mit ~ versehen** *vt* KER & GLAS edge with a groove

Rillen *f pl* METALL striation

rillen *vt* DRUCK score

Rillen: **Rillenabstand** *m* FERTIG roughing width; **Rillenanordnung** *f* FERTIG ragging; **Rillenätzung** *f* ELEKTRONIK V-groove etching; **Rillenfehler** *m* AUFNAHME tracking error; **Rillengeschwindigkeit** *f* AKUSTIK, AUFNAHME groove speed; **Rillenkugellager** *nt* MASCHINEN deep-groove ball bearing, grooved ball bearing; **Rillenquerschnitt** *m* AKUSTIK groove shape; **Rillenscheibe** *f* MASCHINEN grooved wheel, sheave; **Rillenschiene** *f* EISENBAHN grooved rail; **Rillensicherung** *f* AKUSTIK groove guard; **Rillenverzerrung** *f* AKUSTIK tracing distortion; **Rillenwinkel** *m* AUFNAHME groove angle

RIM-Verfahren *nt* KUNSTSTOFF RIM, reaction injection molding (AmE), reaction injection moulding (BrE)

Rinde *f* PAPIER bark; **Rindenkessel** *m* PAPIER bark boiler; **Rindenpresse** *f* PAPIER bark press; **Rindenschälmaschine** *f* PAPIER barker

Ring *m* COMP & DV ring, ERDÖL *Bohrloch* annulus, FERTIG *Draht* bundle, GEOM torus, HYDRAUL *Kolben* ring, *Turbine* ring, KER & GLAS, KFZTECH *Kolben*, MASCHINEN, MECHAN ring, PHYS fringe, RAUMFAHRT annulus, ring; **Ringanker** *m* ELEKTRIZ ring armature; **Ringanschluß** *m* TELEKOM ring connection; **Ringantenne** *f* RAUMFAHRT halo; **Ringbalg** *m* FERTIG *Kunststoffinstallationen* liner

ringbildend: ~**er Tscherenkov-Zähler** *m* (*RICH*) TEILPHYS ring-imaging Cherenkov counter (*RICH*)

Ring: **Ringblitz** *m* FOTO ring flash; **Ringbolzen** *m* MASCHINEN lifting eyebolt, WASSERTRANS *Deckbeschläge* ring bolt; **Ringbrenner** *m* FERTIG ring burner; **Ringbuch** *nt* VERPACK binder; **Ring-Collider** *m* TEILPHYS ring collider; **Ringdehner** *m* FERTIG ring expander; **Ringdraht** *m* FERTIG bundle wire; **Ringdüse** *f* FERTIG ring nozzle; **Ringfeder** *f* FERTIG circlip, MASCHINEN annular spring

ringförmig[1] *adj* FERTIG annular, toroidal, GEOM ring-shaped, MECHAN, RAUMFAHRT *Raumschiff* annular

ringförmig:[2] ~**e Anlaufscheibe** *f* MASCHINEN ring-type thrust washer; ~**e Auskehlung** *f* FERTIG spool; ~**es Brennelement** *nt* KERNTECH annular fuel element; ~**er Collider** *m* TEILPHYS ring collider; ~**es Filmsieden** *nt* KERNTECH annular film boiling; ~**er Kohlelichtbogen** *m* KERNTECH tubular carbon arc; ~**er Luftspalt** *m* KERNTECH annular air gap; ~**er Reaktorkern** *m* KERNTECH ring core; ~**er Resonator** *m* ELEKTRONIK *Mikrowellentechnik* annular resonator; ~**er Riß** *m* KER & GLAS *Flaschenoberfläche* annular crack; ~**e Schweißnaht** *f* KERNTECH ring weld; ~**er Spalt** *m* KERNTECH annular gap; ~**e Spaltzone** *f* KERNTECH annular core; ~**e Ziehwanne** *f* KER & GLAS annular bushing

Ring: **Ringgehäuse der Brennkammer** *nt* KFZTECH, LUFTTRANS, WASSERTRANS combustion chamber annular case; **Ringkanal** *m* KERNTECH annular channel; **Ringkanone** *f* FERNSEH toroidal electron gun; **Ringkern** *m* ELEKTRIZ toroid, torus, ELEKTROTECH, KERNTECH *einer Spule* toroidal core; **Ringkernspule** *f* ELEKTRIZ toroidal coil; **Ringkolbenzähler** *m* GERÄT oscillating piston flowmeter; **Ringkopf** *m* AUFNAHME, FERNSEH ring head; **Ringkörper** *m* FERTIG torus; **Ringlehre** *f* MASCHINEN female gage (AmE), female gauge (BrE), ring gage (AmE), ring gauge (BrE); **Ringleitung** *f* COMP & DV loop, ELEKTRIZ ring main, ELEKTROTECH ring mains

Ringligkeit *f* TEXTIL barriness in the weft

Ring: **Ringmagnet** *m* FERNSEH, PHYS annular magnet, ring magnet; **Ringmaß** *nt* METROL ring gage (AmE), ring gauge (BrE); **Ringmeßkammer** *f* GERÄT *Normalblende* annular measuring chamber; **Ringmodulator** *m* AUFNAHME ring modulator; **Ringmühle** *f* CHEMTECH roller mill; **Ringmutter** *f* MASCHINEN ring nut; **Ring-**

netz *nt* COMP & DV loop network, ring network; **Ringnetzleitungssystem** *nt* ELEKTRIZ ring main system; **Ringnut** *f* FERTIG annular groove, MASCHINEN ring groove; **Ringofen** *m* FERTIG, KER & GLAS annular kiln; **Ringquetschung** *f* KERNTECH toroidal pinch effect; **Ringraum** *m* ERDÖL *Bohrloch* annular space; **Ringschieben** *nt* COMP & DV circular shift; **Ringschieber** *m* FERTIG, MASCHINEN annular slide valve; **Ringschlüssel** *m* KFZTECH *Werkzeug*, MASCHINEN, MECHAN box spanner (BrE), box wrench, ring spanner (BrE); **Ringschmieden** *nt* FERTIG saddling

ringschmieden *vt* FERTIG saddle

Ring: **Ringschmierung** *f* MASCHINEN ring lubrication; **Ringschraube** *f* KFZTECH *Kupplung* eyebolt, MASCHINEN lifting screw, ring bolt; **Ringspalt** *m* ERDÖL annulus, FERTIG annular clearance, radial clearance; **Ringspant** *m* LUFTTRANS *Rumpf des Luftfahrzeugs* ring frame, RAUMFAHRT annular rib; **Ringspeiseleitung** *f* ELEKTRIZ ring feeder; **Ringspinnerei** *f* TEXTIL ring spinning; **Ringspinngarn** *nt* TEXTIL ring spun yarn; **Ringspinnmaschine** *f* TEXTIL ring spinning frame; **Ringspule** *f* ELEKTRIZ ring winding, KERNTECH toroidal coil; **Ringsteg** *m* KFZTECH *Motor* piston land; **Ringstruktur** *f* TELEKOM ring configuration; **Ringtisch** *m* FERTIG *Werkzeugmaschine* annular table; **Ringtopologie** *f* COMP & DV ring topology; **Ringtransformator** *m* ELEKTROTECH toroidal transformer; **Ringventil** *nt* KFZTECH poppet valve, MASCHINEN annular valve; **Ringwaage** *f* GERÄT ring balance; **Ringwicklung** *f* ELEKTRIZ ring winding; **Ringzähler** *m* FERNSEH, GERÄT, RADIO ring counter

Rinne[1] *f* BAU channel, trench, *Rille* flute, FERTIG *Blechumformung* channel, MECHAN chute, flute

Rinne:[2] **Rinnen ziehen** *vi* LUFTTRANS gutter

Rinnenkasten *m* BAU rainwater head

Rinnstein *m* BAU gutter

Rippe[1] *f* BAU web, DRUCK rib, FERTIG stem, KOHLEN, LUFTTRANS *Luftfahrzeug* rib, MASCHINEN fin, MECHAN fin, rib, vane, PAPIER, TEXTIL rib; ~ **eines Gewebes** *f* TEXTIL wale

Rippe:[2] **mit Rippen versehen** *vt* RAUMFAHRT rib

rippen *vt* FERTIG *Rohr* fin, RAUMFAHRT *Raumschiff* rib

Rippe: **Rippenabstand** *m* HEIZ & KÄLTE fin spacing; **Rippenblech** *nt* METALL ribbed plate; **Rippenheizkörper** *m* HEIZ & KÄLTE ribbed radiator; **Rippenhülse** *f* KERNTECH finned can; **Rippenkühler** *m* HEIZ & KÄLTE ribbed cooler, ribbed radiator, KFZTECH ribbon cellular radiator; **Rippenkühlung** *f* KERNTECH fin cooling, rib cooling; **Rippenmarkierung** *f* KER & GLAS rib mark; **Rippenmuster** *nt* BAU reed; **Rippenrohr** *nt* FERTIG gilled tube, MASCHINEN, MECHAN finned tube; **Rippenröhrenkühler** *m* EISENBAHN tube and fin radiator; **Rippenrohrkühler** *m* HEIZ & KÄLTE finned-tube cooler, KFZTECH finned-tube radiator; **Rippenstich** *m* TEXTIL ribbed stitch; **Rippenwirkungsgrad** *m* HEIZ & KÄLTE fin efficiency

Rippmasche *f* TEXTIL ribbed stitch

Ripptide *f* WASSERTRANS *Gezeiten* rip tide

Riser *m* ERDÖL *Bohrung, Leitungsbau* riser

Risiko *nt* SICHERHEIT hazard, risk; **Risikoabschätzung** *f* MEERSCHMUTZ risk assessment; **Risikobewertung** *f* MEERSCHMUTZ risk assessment

Riß[1]: **einen ~ zukitten** *vi* KER & GLAS stop a crack

Riß[2] *m* ANSTRICH crack, BAU crack, fissure, *Holz* shake, *Vermessung* projection, *in Holz* break, FERTIG crevice, fissure, shake, KER & GLAS check, tearing, KOHLEN crack, MASCHINEN elevation, MECHAN, METALL crack, PAPIER flaw, RAUMFAHRT slit, TEXTIL breakage, break, burst, WASSERTRANS *Schiffbau* plan, WASSERVERSORG breach; **Rißauffangtemperatur** *f* METALL crack-arrest temperature; **Rißausbreitungsgeschwindigkeit** *f* KERNTECH crack propagation rate; **Rißausdehnungskraft** *f* METALL crack extension force; **Rißauslösung** *f* KERNTECH initiation of fracture; **Rißbeständigkeit** *f* KUNSTSTOFF crack resistance; **Rißbildung** *f* BAU, KUNSTSTOFF, MECHAN cracking, METALL crack formation; **Rißbreite** *f* METALL width of splitting; **Rißerweiterung** *f* KERNTECH crack-opening stretch; **Rißgeschwindigkeit** *f* METALL crack velocity; **Rißhaltetemperatur** *f* METALL ductile-brittle transition temperature

rissig: ~e Dämmplatte *f* AUFNAHME fissured acoustic tile

Riß: **Rißeingangsetzung** *f* METALL crack initiation; **Rißkernbildung** *f* METALL crack nucleation; **Rißlehre** *f* KONSTZEICH template, templet; **Rißlinie** *f* FERTIG scribed line; **Rißöffnungsverschiebung** *f* KERNTECH crack-opening displacement; **Rißspitze** *f* METALL crack tip; **Rißsucher** *m* KERNTECH, MASCHINEN crack detector; **Rißsuchgerät** *nt* KERNTECH crack detector; **Rißverzweigung** *f* METALL crack branching

RIT *abbr* *(Empfängerfeinabstimmung)* RADIO RIT *(receiver incremental tuning)*

Ritze *f* KOHLEN cut, MECHAN gap

Ritzel *nt* FERTIG *Getriebelehre*, KFZTECH *Getriebe* pinion, MASCHINEN pinion, pinion wheel; **Ritzelfräsmaschine** *f* MASCHINEN pinion-cutting machine; **Ritzelkopfhöhe** *f* FERTIG *Getriebelehre* pinion addendum; **Ritzelwälzfräsmaschine** *f* FERTIG pinion-hobbing machine; **Ritzelwelle** *f* MASCHINEN pinion shaft; **Ritzelwellenflansch** *m* KFZTECH *Triebstrang* pinion shaft flange

Ritzhärte *f* KUNSTSTOFF scratch resistance; **Ritzhärteprüfer** *m* PHYS sclerometer; **Ritzhärteprüfung** *f* FERTIG abrasion test

Ritz: ~ **sches Kombinationsprinzip** *nt* PHYS Ritz combination principle

Rizinusöl *nt* KUNSTSTOFF castor oil

RMS[1] *abbr* *(quadratischer Mittel)* AUFNAHME, ELEKTRIZ, ELEKTRONIK rms *(root mean square)*

RMS:[2] **RMS-Frequenzhub** *m* RAUMFAHRT *Weltraumfunk* rms frequency deviation

Rn *abbr* *(Radon)* PHYS Rn *(radon)*

Roadster *m* KFZTECH roadster

Roaming-Fähigkeit *f* TELEKOM roaming capability

Roaming-Teilnehmer *m* TELEKOM roaming subscriber

Roboter *m* COMP & DV, KONTROLL, KÜNSTL INT robot

Robotik *f* COMP & DV, KÜNSTL INT robotics

Robustheit *f* WERKPRÜF robustness

Rochellesalz *nt* ELEKTROTECH *piezoelektrisches Material*, LEBENSMITTEL Rochelle salt

Rock: ~ **& Roll-Aufnahme** *f* AUFNAHME rock-and-roll recording; ~ **& Roll-Ausrüstung** *f* AUFNAHME rock-and-roll equipment; ~ **& Roll-Mischung** *f* AUFNAHME rock-and-roll mixing

Rockwell-Härte *f* KUNSTSTOFF Rockwell hardness; **Rockwell-Härteprüfmaschine** *f* MASCHINEN Rockwell hardness testing machine; **Rockwell-Härteprüfung** *f* MASCHINEN Rockwell hardness test

Rod *nt* METROL perch, pole, rod

roden *vt* BAU clear, grub, stub

Roh- *pref* ABFALL, BAU, ERDÖL, FERNSEH, KOHLEN, KONSTZEICH, KUNSTSTOFF, LEBENSMITTEL, WASSER-

VERSORG crude, raw, rough

roh[1] *adj* ANSTRICH rough, LEBENSMITTEL unrefined, MASCHINEN unfinished

roh:[2] ~e **Unterlegscheibe** *f* MASCHINEN blank washer

Roh-: **Rohabwasser** *nt* WASSERVERSORG raw sewage; **Rohband** *nt* FERNSEH raw tape; **Rohbau** *m* BAU carcass, preliminary building works; **Rohbauarbeiten** *f pl* BAU rough work; **Rohbearbeitung** *f* KOHLEN roughing; **Rohbehauen** *nt* BAU *Stein* rough dressing; **Rohbenzin** *nt* ERDÖL light distillates, THERMOD naphtha; **Rohblatt** *nt* KONSTZEICH basic sheet; **Rohblei** *nt* FERTIG pig lead; **Rohblock** *m* FERTIG bloom; **Rohbrei** *m* ABFALL crude pulp; **Rohdichte** *f* BAU bulk density, bulk, KOHLEN apparent density

Roheisen *nt* FERTIG pig iron, METALL iron pig, pig iron; ~ **für das Windfrischverfahren** *nt* FERTIG Bessemer pig; **Roheisen-Erz-Verfahren** *nt* FERTIG pig-and-ore process

Roh-: **Roherz** *nt* FERTIG green ore, KOHLEN crude ore; **Rohessigsäure** *f* CHEMIE pyroacetic acid; **Rohfaser** *f* KER & GLAS basic fiber (AmE), basic fibre (BrE), LEBENSMITTEL crude fiber (AmE), crude fibre (BrE), dietary fiber (AmE), dietary fibre (BrE); **Rohfestigkeit** *f* KUNSTSTOFF green strength; **Rohform** *f* KER & GLAS body mold (AmE), body mould (BrE); **Rohgarn** *nt* TEXTIL feeder yarn; **Rohgewicht** *nt* PAPIER apparent specific gravity; **Rohgips** *m* BAU plaster rock, plaster stone; **Rohglas** *nt* KER & GLAS base glass; **Rohgrießkohle** *f* KOHLEN rough pea coal; **Rohgußglas** *nt* KER & GLAS rough-cast glass; **Rohgußmaß** *nt* KONSTZEICH rough-casting dimension; **Rohgußspiegelglas** *nt* KER & GLAS rough-cast plate; **Rohkante** *f* KER & GLAS edge as cut; **Rohkarosserie** *f* KFZTECH body shell; **Rohkautschuk** *m* KUNSTSTOFF crude rubber; **Rohkohle** *f* KOHLEN pit coal, raw coal, rough coal, unscreened coal; **Rohkollagen** *nt* CHEMIE ossein

Rohling *m* FERTIG solid bank, *Fließ- und Strangpressen* sludge, MASCHINEN blank; **Rohlingsrest** *m* FERTIG *Strangpressen* unextruded butt

Rohmaß: **auf ~ vorbearbeitet** *adj* MECHAN rough-machined

Rohmaterial *nt* KER & GLAS, KUNSTSTOFF raw material; **Rohmaterialien für Töpferwaren** *nt pl* KER & GLAS pottery raw materials

Roh-: **Rohmittelkohle** *f* KOHLEN unwashed coal; **Rohmüll** *m* ABFALL crude refuse, raw refuse, untreated refuse

Rohöl *nt* ERDÖL, KOHLEN, MEERSCHMUTZ, UMWELTSCHMUTZ crude, crude oil; **Rohölanalyse** *f* ERDÖL crude assay, crude oil analysis; **Rohöltanker** *m* WASSERTRANS crude carrier

Roh-: **Rohpapier** *nt* PAPIER base paper, raw paper; **Rohplatin** *nt* CHEMIE platina; **Rohprotein** *nt* LEBENSMITTEL crude protein

Rohr *nt* BAU pipe, tube, ERDÖL pipe, FERTIG conduit, MASCHINEN rigid pipe, tube, MECHAN pipe, NICHTFOSS ENERG tube, STRÖMPHYS pipe; **Rohr mit Doppelbogen** *nt* MASCHINEN gooseneck pipe; **Rohr mit Naht** *nt* MASCHINEN seamed pipe **Rohr aus nichtrostendem Stahl** *nt* MASCHINEN stainless steel tube; **Rohrabschneider** *m* MASCHINEN pipe cutter, tube cutter; **Rohrabzweigung** *f* MASCHINEN branch T; **Rohranheber** *m* ERDÖL elevator; **Rohranker** *m* ERDÖL tubing anchor; **Rohranschluß** *m* BAU pipe connection; **Rohranschlußstutzen** *m* MASCHINEN pipe nipple; **Rohraufhängungsteile** *nt pl* MASCHINEN pipe hanger fixtures; **Rohraufweiter** *m*

BAU tube expander; **Rohrbau** m BAU pipework; **Rohr-biegemaschine** f MASCHINEN pipe-bending machine; **Rohrboden** m KERNTECH tube plate; **Rohrbogen** m BAU pipe bend, MASCHINEN pipe bend, tube bend; **Rohrbruch** m MASCHINEN pipe burst; **Rohrbruchsicherung** f ERDÖL automatic shutoff valve; **Rohrbrücke** f ERDÖL pipe rack; **Rohrbündel** nt BAU tube nest, KERNTECH tube bundle

Röhrchen nt LABOR tube; **Röhrchenbürste** f LABOR tube brush; **Röhrchenhalter** m LABOR tube holder; **Röhrchenreinigungsbürste** f LABOR tube brush; **Röhrchenschneider** m LABOR tube cutter

Rohr: **Rohrdampfboiler** m HYDRAUL tubular furnace boiler; **Rohrdampfkessel** m HYDRAUL tubular furnace boiler; **Rohrdichter** m BAU casing expander; **Rohrdichtung** f BAU pipe gasket; **Rohrdiffusion** f METALL pipe diffusion; **Rohrdurchlaß** m BAU pipe culvert; **Rohrdurchmesser** m MASCHINEN pipe diameter

Rohre:[1] ~ **und Armaturen** nt pl BAU pipes and fittings

Rohre:[2] **durch ~ leiten** vt BAU pipe

Rohre:[3] ~ **verlegen** vi BAU pipe

Röhre f BAU, ELEKTRONIK tube, *Elektronenröhre* valve, ELEKTROTECH conduit, *Neonleuchte* bulb, MASCHINEN rigid pipe, tube, MECHAN duct, RADIO thermionic valve, tube (AmE), STRÖMPHYS pipe; ~ **mit automatischer Gittervorspannungserzeugung** f ELEKTRONIK self-biased tube; ~ **mit engem Bohrloch** f LABOR narrow-bore tube; ~ **mit kurzer Wechselwirkung** f ELEKTRONIK short interaction tube; ~ **mit Loktalsockel** f ELEKTRONIK *Elektronenröhren* loctal tube; ~ **ohne Regelkennlinie** f ELEKTRONIK sharp cut-off tube; ~ **mit verlängerter Wechselwirkung** f ELEKTRONIK extended-interaction tube; ~ **mit Zwillingselektronenkanone** f FERNSEH double-gun tube

Rohr: **Rohrelevator** m BAU casing elevator

Röhren[1]: **in ~** adj STRÖMPHYS in pipes

Röhren[2]: **aufeinander abgestimmte ~** f pl ELEKTRONIK matched tubes

Röhre: **Röhrenbahn** f EISENBAHN TVS, tube vehicle system; **Röhrenbahnfahrzeug** nt EISENBAHN tube vehicle; **Röhrendiode** f ELEKTRONIK, KERNTECH diode tube; **Röhrenfassung** f ELEKTROTECH tube socket; **Röhrenfedermanometer** nt ERDÖL Bourdon gage (AmE), Bourdon gauge (BrE); **Röhrenhals** m FERNSEH tube neck; **Röhrenkapazität** f PHYS internal capacity; **Röhrenkessel** m LEBENSMITTEL tubular boiler; **Röhrenkolben** m ELEKTRONIK envelope, ELEKTROTECH bulb; **Röhrenkühler** m KFZTECH tubular radiator, LEBENSMITTEL tubular cooler; **Röhrenleitungssystem** nt MASCHINEN ducting; **Röhrenlibelle** f FERTIG air level; **Röhrenluftvorwärmer** m HEIZ & KÄLTE tubular air heater; **Röhrenmodulator** m ELEKTRONIK vacuum tube modulator; **Röhrenoszillator** m ELEKTRONIK vacuum tube oscillator; **Röhrensender** m ELEKTROTECH thermionic generator; **Röhrentriode** f ELEKTRONIK *Dreielektronenröhre* triode tube; **Röhren-U-Bahn-Verkehr** m EISENBAHN tube transportation; **Röhren-U-Bahn-Zug** m EISENBAHN tube train; **Röhrenverstärker** m ELEKTRONIK vacuum tube amplifier, valve amplifier (BrE); **Röhrenwanddickenmesser** m KERNTECH tube thickness gage (AmE), tube thickness gauge (BrE); **Röhrenwärmeaustauscher** m HEIZ & KÄLTE, KERNTECH shell and tube heat exchanger, MASCHINEN tube heat exchanger; **Röhrenwicklung** f ELEKTRIZ cylindrical winding

Rohr: **Rohrfedermanometer** nt ERDÖL *Meßtechnik* Bourdon gage (AmE), Bourdon gauge (BrE), GERÄT Bourdon tube gage (AmE), Bourdon tube gauge (BrE), boundary tube gage (AmE), boundary tube gauge (BrE), spring tube manometer; **Rohrfitting** nt MASCHINEN tapped fitting; **Rohrformdorn** nt HYDRAUL boiler pipe shaping mandrel

rohrförmig adj FERTIG tubular

Rohr: **Rohrformstücke** nt pl MASCHINEN pipe fittings; **Rohrfräser** m MASCHINEN burring reamer; **Rohrgewinde** nt BAU pipe thread, FERTIG gas thread, MASCHINEN pipe thread; **Rohrgewindebohrer** m BAU pipe tap, MASCHINEN pipe tap, pipe-thread tap; **Rohrgewindeschneidbacke** f FERTIG pipe die; **Rohrglas** nt KER & GLAS tubing glass; **Rohrglocke** f FERTIG *Kunststoffinstallationen* pipe cover; **Rohrhaken** m BAU, ERDÖL *zur Montage von Rohrleitungen* pipe hook; **Rohrheizkörper** m KERNTECH tubular heating element; **Rohrklammer** f ERDÖL *Bohrtechnik* casing clamp; **Rohrklemmkeil** m ERDÖL slip; **Rohrkoje** f WASSERTRANS pipe cot; **Rohrkonstruktion** f ERDÖL *Offshore-Technik* jacket; **Rohrkopf** m BAU casing head; **Rohrkorrosionsschutz aus Bitumen** m MASCHINEN bitumen pipe coating; **Rohrkrümmer** m BAU pipe bend, pipe knee, MASCHINEN pipe bend; **Rohrkupplung** f MASCHINEN tube coupling; **Rohrleger** m MASCHINEN pipe layer

Rohrleitung f BAU conduit, pipe, pipeline, tubing, ELEKTROTECH conduit, ERDÖL pipeline, KOHLEN, MASCHINEN pipeline, piping, NICHTFOSS ENERG conduit, pipeline, tubing, TRANS, WASSERTRANS pipeline, WASSERVERSORG conduit; **Rohrleitungsbau** m FERTIG *Kunststoffinstallationen* pipeline construction; **Rohrleitungsnetz** nt BAU pipework; **Rohrleitungsplan** m WASSERTRANS *Schiffbau* piping plan; **Rohrleitungssystem** nt MASCHINEN pipework system; **Rohrleitungsverlegung** f BAU laying of pipes, pipe laying

Rohr: **Rohrmanschette** f BAU pipe collar; **Rohrmuffe** f BAU pipe joint, FERTIG pipe bell; **Rohrmühle** f KOHLEN tube mill; **Rohrnetz** nt BAU system of pipes, NICHTFOSS ENERG tubing; **Rohrniet** nt MASCHINEN tubular rivet; **Rohrnippel** m MASCHINEN barrel nipple; **Rohrplatte** f MASCHINEN tube plate; **Rohrplattform** f ERDÖL *Offshore-Technik* jacket platform; **Rohrpostanlage** f KERNTECH rabbit system; **Rohrrahmen** m KFZTECH *Motorrad* tubular frame; **Rohrreduzierstück** nt BAU pipe reducer; **Rohrreiniger** m MASCHINEN go-devil, pipe cleaner; **Rohrsatz** m KERNTECH tube nest; **Rohrschelle** f BAU casing clamp, pipe strap, tube clip, ERDÖL casing clamp, FERTIG pipe bracket, MASCHINEN clip, pipe clip; **Rohrschiebermotor** m KFZTECH sleeve valve engine; **Rohrschlange** f LABOR *Destillieren* serpent coil; **Rohrschlosser** m BAU, MASCHINEN pipe fitter; **Rohrschlüssel** m BAU, FERTIG pipe wrench, MASCHINEN tube wrench; **Rohrschlüssel mit Zähnen** m MASCHINEN alligator wrench; **Rohrschneider** m BAU casing cutter, pipe cutter, MASCHINEN pipe cutter; **Rohrschraubstock** m BAU pipe vice, MASCHINEN tube vice; **Rohrschweißung** f BAU tube welding; **Rohrspirale** f LABOR *Destillieren* serpent coil; **Rohrstahl** m METALL tube steel; **Rohrsteckverbindung** f BAU spigot joint; **Rohrstrang** m HEIZ & KÄLTE pipe run, MASCHINEN pipe conduit; **Rohrstrangpressen** nt MASCHINEN tube extrusion; **Rohrströmung** f STRÖMPHYS flow in pipes, pipe flow; **Rohrstutzen** m BAU, MASCHINEN socket; **Rohrträger** m ERDÖL *Tiefbohrtechnik* pipe rack; **Rohrverankerung** f ERDÖL *Bohrtechnik* tubing anchor; **Rohrverbindung** ƒ BAU pipe connection, pipe coupling, pipe joint, MASCHINEN pipe connection, pipe joint, pipe junction, pipe union; **Rohrverbindungsstück** nt BAU pipe union, MASCHINEN fitting, pipe coupling; **Rohrverleger** m ERDÖL lay barge; **Rohrverlegeschiff** nt ERDÖL *Offshore-Technik* lay barge, *Offshore-Leitungsbahn* pipe-laying barge; **Rohrverlegung** ƒ BAU pipe laying; **Rohrverschluß** m MASCHINEN pipe plug; **Rohrverschraubung** ƒ BAU pipe screwing, tube fitting, union, MASCHINEN screwed pipe coupling; **Rohrverschraubung mit Bolzen** ƒ MASCHINEN bolted pipe joint; **Rohrverschraubungsstück** nt MASCHINEN screwed fitting, tapped fitting, threaded fitting; **Rohrverzweigung** ƒ FERTIG, MASCHINEN manifold; **Rohrwelle** ƒ MASCHINEN tubular shaft; **Rohrwickler** m BAU pipe twister; **Rohrwiege** ƒ MECHAN cradle; **Rohrzange** ƒ BAU pipe tongs, pipe wrench, ERDÖL *Bohrtechnik* pipe tongs, MASCHINEN gas pliers; **Rohrziehdorn** m MASCHINEN tube-drawing mandrel

Roh-: **Rohschlamm** m ABFALL, WASSERVERSORG raw sludge; **Rohschmieröl** nt FERTIG black oil; **Rohschraube** ƒ FERTIG black bolt; **Rohstahl** m METALL crude steel; **Rohstoff** m ERDÖL raw material, FERTIG raw material, staple, KER & GLAS, KOHLEN, KUNSTSTOFF raw material, LEBENSMITTEL staple, MEERSCHMUTZ resource, PAPIER raw material; **Rohstoffrückgewinnung** ƒ ABFALL resource recovery; **Rohsulfat** nt LEBENSMITTEL salt cake; **Rohteil** nt FERTIG blank, part, MECHAN blank; **Rohtoluol** nt CHEMIE toluol; **Rohvaselin** nt CHEMIE petrolatum; **Rohvlies** nt KER & GLAS uncured mat; **Rohwasser** nt WASSERVERSORG raw water; **Rohzink** nt FERTIG spelter

Roll- *pref* LUFTTRANS, RAUMFAHRT rolling; **Rollachse** ƒ LUFTTRANS, RAUMFAHRT roll axis

Rolladen m BAU roller shutter, shutter; **Rolladenstab** m BAU reed; **Rolladentor** nt BAU rolling door; **Rolladentür** ƒ BAU rolling door

Roll-: **Rollage** ƒ RAUMFAHRT roll attitude; **Rollbacken** m FERTIG *Gewindewalzen* die plate

Rollbahn ƒ LUFTTRANS taxiway, TRANS moving carpet; **Rollbahnfeuer** nt LUFTTRANS taxiway light; **Rollbahnkreuzungsmarkierung** ƒ LUFTTRANS taxiway intersection marking; **Rollbahnmittellinienfeuer** nt LUFTTRANS taxiway centerline light (AmE), taxiway centreline light (BrE); **Rollbahnmittellinienmarkierung** ƒ LUFTTRANS taxiway centerline marking (AmE), taxiway centreline marking (BrE); **Rollbahnrandmarkierung** ƒ LUFTTRANS taxiway edge marker

Roll-: **Rollbalken** m COMP & DV scroll bar; **Rollband** nt TRANS moving floor, moving walkway; **Rollbewegung** ƒ MASCHINEN rolling motion; **Rollbord** nt FERTIG curl; **Rollbrücke** ƒ BAU roller bridge, rolling bridge

Rolle:[1] **von der ~ arbeitend** *adj* DRUCK reel-fed; **an der ~ perforiert** *adj* VERPACK perforated on the reel

Rolle[2] ƒ BAU *einer Walze* barrel, DRUCK, FERTIG reel, LUFTTRANS *Kunstflug* roll, MASCHINEN caster, castor, roll, roller, sheave, wheel, MECHAN roll, PAPIER reel, PHYS roll, WASSERTRANS *Tauwerk* coil

Roll-: **Rolleiste** ƒ COMP & DV scroll bar

Rollen nt COMP & DV scrolling, LUFTTRANS taxiing, MASCHINEN rolling

rollen[1] *vt* COMP & DV scroll, MASCHINEN roll

rollen[2] *vti* RAUMFAHRT bank

Rolle: **Rollen- und Rotationsstanzpresse** ƒ VERPACK roller and rotary cutting press; **Rollenaufnehmer** m VERPACK reel lifter; **Rollenbahn** ƒ MASCHINEN roller

path, roller track, VERPACK conveyor way; **Rollenbohrmeißel** m ERDÖL *Bohrtechnik* roller bit; **Rollenbreite** ƒ PAPIER reel width

rollend: **~es Material** nt EISENBAHN railroad vehicles (AmE), railway vehicles (BrE), KFZTECH rolling stock; **~er Schnitt** m FERNSEH wipe; **~er Start** m LUFTTRANS rolling takeoff

Rolle: **Rollendruckmaschine** ƒ DRUCK reel-fed press; **Rolleneinschlag- und Packmaschine** ƒ VERPACK reel wrapping and handling equipment; **Rollenetikettendruck** m VERPACK roll label printing; **Rollenförderer** m VERPACK conveyor way; **Rollenfreilaufkupplung** ƒ KFZTECH overrunning clutch; **Rollengegenführung** ƒ FERTIG roller box; **Rollengerüst mit Flaschenzug** nt KERNTECH gantry with hoist; **Rollengesperre** nt MASCHINEN roller clutch; **Rollenhebel** m MECHAN roller lever; **Rollenhülse** ƒ VERPACK core of spool; **Rollenkette** ƒ MASCHINEN bush-roller chain, roller chain; **Rollenkorb** m MASCHINEN roller cage; **Rollenkühlofen** m KER & GLAS *Flachglas* annealing lehr with rollers; **Rollenkupplung** ƒ KFZTECH, MECHAN roller clutch; **Rollenlager** nt KFZTECH, MASCHINEN, MECHAN roller bearing; **Rollenlagergehäuse** nt MASCHINEN roller-bearing box; **Rollenlippklampe** ƒ WASSERTRANS *Beschläge* roller fairlead; **Rollenlünette** ƒ MASCHINEN roller steady; **Rollenoffset** ƒ DRUCK web offset; **Rollenoffsetdruck** m DRUCK web offset printing; **Rollenpackmaschine** ƒ VERPACK reel overwrapper; **Rollenprobe** ƒ PAPIER reel sample; **Rollenquetscher** m FOTO squeegee; **Rollenrotationsmaschine** ƒ DRUCK web-fed rotary press; **Rollenrotationspresse** ƒ DRUCK web-fed rotary press; **Rollenschneidmaschine** ƒ PAPIER slitter-rewinder; **Rollensteuerkette** ƒ KFZTECH roller timing chain; **Rollenstößel** m KFZTECH roller shaft, roller tappet; **Rollenstromabnehmer** m TRANS trolley pole; **Rollentraglager** nt MECHAN angular roller bearing; **Rollenzuführung** ƒ MASCHINEN roller feed

Rollfeld nt LUFTTRANS airfield, landing field; **Rollfeldringstraße** ƒ LUFTTRANS perimeter track

Roll-: **Rollfilm** m FOTO roll film; **Rollgabelschlüssel** m FERTIG monkey wrench, MASCHINEN adjustable spanner (BrE), monkey wrench, screw wrench; **Rollgangsrahmen** m FERTIG *Walzen* table beam; **Rollgeld** nt TRANS cartage; **Rollglasschneider** m KER & GLAS glass cutting wheel; **Rollhalteort** m LUFTTRANS taxi holding position; **Rollkanal** m LUFTTRANS *Selbststeuerung* roll channel; **Rollkondensator** m ELEKTROTECH paper capacitor; **Rollkontakt** m MASCHINEN rolling contact; **Rollkreis** m GEOM rolling circle, MASCHINEN pitch circumference; **Rollkreisel** m RAUMFAHRT roll rate gyro; **Rollkugel** ƒ COMP & DV *Mausäquivalent beim Notebook* rolling ball, trackball, *Zeigereinheit bei grafischen Benutzeroberflächen* track ball; **Rollkurve** ƒ GEOM roulette; **Rollmembrane** ƒ FERTIG *Kunststoffinstallationen* cup seal; **Rollmenü** nt COMP & DV drop-down menu; **Rollmoment** nt LUFTTRANS *Luftfahrzeug*, MASCHINEN rolling moment; **Rollneigung** ƒ VERPACK curl

Roll-on-Roll-off nt *(Ro-Ro)* TRANS roll-on-roll-off *(ro-ro)*; **Roll-on-Roll-off-Anlage** ƒ *(Ro-Ro-Anlage)* WASSERTRANS roll-on roll-off dock *(ro-ro dock)*; **Roll-on-Roll-off-Frachter** m *(Ro-Ro-Frachter)* WASSERTRANS *Horizontalbeladung* roll-on roll-off vessel *(ro-ro vessel)*; **Roll-on-Roll-off-Hafen** m *(Ro-Ro-Hafen)* WASSERTRANS roll-on roll-off port *(ro-ro port)*; **Roll-on-Roll-off-Schiff** nt *(Ro-Ro-Schiff)* WASSERTRANS

roll-on roll-off ship, roll-on roll-off vessel *(ro-ro vessel)*; **Roll-on-Roll-off-System** *nt (Ro-Ro-System)* WASSERTRANS *Horizontalbeladung* roll-on roll-off system *(ro-ro system)*
Roll-: **Rollpalette** *f* TRANS roller pallet; **Rollreffbaum** *m* WASSERTRANS roller reefing boom; **Rollreibung** *f* MASCHINEN, PHYS rolling friction; **Rollreibungszahl** *f* MECHAN, PHYS coefficient of rolling friction
Rollschacht *m* KOHLEN chute
Roll-: **Rollschere** *f* FERTIG slitter; **Rollscheren** *nt* FERTIG slitting; **Rollschicht** *f* BAU *Mauerwerk* upright course; **Rollsichter** *m* KOHLEN roll screen; **Rollstabilität** *f* LUFTTRANS *Luftfahrzeug* rolling stability; **Rollstek** *m* WASSERTRANS *Knoten* rolling hitch; **Rolltreppe** *f* BAU escalator, moving staircase, moving stairway, TRANS moving staircase, moving stairway; **Rolltür** *f* KFZTECH roll-up door; **Rollwerk** *nt* LUFTTRANS landing gear; **Rollwiderstand** *m* MASCHINEN rolling resistance
Ro-Lo-Schiff *nt* WASSERTRANS rolo ship
ROM *abbr (Festwertspeicher, Nur-Lese-Speicher, ROM-Speicher)* COMP & DV, ELEKTRIZ, ELEKTROTECH, RADIO ROM *(read-only memory)*
Romandruckpapier *nt* DRUCK antique book paper
römisch: **~er Bogen** *m* BAU Roman arch, round arch; **~e Zahlen** *f pl* MATH Roman numerals; **~e Ziffern** *f pl* DRUCK, MATH Roman numerals
ROM: **ROM-Medium** *nt* OPTIK read-only medium
Rommeltrommel *f* FERTIG rumble
ROM: **ROM-Speicher** *m (ROM)* COMP & DV, ELEKTRIZ, ELEKTROTECH, RADIO read-only memory *(ROM)*
Ronde *f* FERTIG round blank
Röntgen *nt (R)* STRAHLPHYS röntgen *(R)*; **Röntgenabsorptionsanalyse** *f* STRAHLPHYS X-ray absorption analysis; **Röntgenabsorptionsspektrum** *nt* KERNTECH, PHYS X-ray absorption spectrum; **Röntgenanalyse** *f* GERÄT, STRAHLPHYS X-ray analysis; **Röntgenaufnahme** *f* STRAHLPHYS X-ray photograph; **Röntgenausbeute** *f* KERNTECH X-ray yield; **Röntgenbestrahlung** *f* KERNTECH X-ray irradiation; **Röntgenbeugung** *f* ELEKTRONIK X-ray diffraction; **Röntgenbeugungsanalyse** *f* STRAHLPHYS X-ray diffraction analysis; **Röntgenbeugungskamera** *f* KERNTECH X-ray diffraction camera; **Röntgenbild** *nt* FOTO X-ray photograph, KER & GLAS shadowgraph; **Röntgendiffraktometer** *nt* STRAHLPHYS X-ray diffractometer; **Röntgendosismesser** *m* GERÄT X-ray dosimeter; **Röntgendosismeßgerät** *nt* GERÄT X-ray dosimeter; **Röntgen-Escape-Peak** *m* STRAHLPHYS X-ray escape peak; **Röntgenfarberscheinung** *f* KERNTECH X-ray coloration (AmE), X-ray colouration (BrE); **Röntgenfluoreszenz** *f* STRAHLPHYS X-ray fluorescence; **Röntgenfluoreszenzanalyse** *f* STRAHLPHYS X-ray fluorescence analysis; **Röntgenfluoreszenz-Spektrometer** *m* STRAHLPHYS fluorescent X-ray spectrometer; **Röntgenhintergrundstrahlung** *f* STRAHLPHYS X-ray background radiation; **Röntgenkamera** *f* KERNTECH, STRAHLPHYS X-ray camera; **Röntgenkristallographie** *f* STRAHLPHYS X-ray crystallography; **Röntgenlaser** *m* ELEKTRONIK X-ray laser, KERNTECH X-raser, X-ray laser, STRAHLPHYS X-ray laser; **Röntgenlumineszenz** *f* KERNTECH roentgenoluminescence; **Röntgenluminiszenz** *f* KERNTECH X-ray luminescence; **Röntgenmetallographie** *f* KERNTECH X-ray metallography, roentgenometallography, STRAHLPHYS X-ray metallography; **Röntgenmikroskop** *nt* STRAHLPHYS X-ray microscope;

Röntgenographie *f* STRAHLPHYS radiography; **Röntgenphoton** *nt* KERNTECH X-ray photon; **Röntgenprüfung** *f* KERNTECH X-ray testing; **Röntgenquant** *nt* KERNTECH X-ray quantum; **Röntgenquelle** *f* KERNTECH X-ray source; **Röntgenröhre** *f* ELEKTRONIK, STRAHLPHYS X-ray tube; **Röntgenschutzglas** *nt* KER & GLAS, SICHERHEIT X-ray protective glass; **Röntgenspektrograph** *m* STRAHLPHYS X-ray diffractometer, X-ray spectrograph; **Röntgenspektrographie** *f* KERNTECH X-ray spectrography; **Röntgenspektrometer** *nt* STRAHLPHYS X-ray spectrometer; **Röntgenspektrometrie** *f* KERNTECH X-ray spectrometry; **Röntgenspektroskopie** *f* KERNTECH X-ray spectroscopy; **Röntgenspektrum** *nt* STRAHLPHYS X-ray spectrum
Röntgenstrahl *m* ELEKTRONIK X-ray beam
röntgenstrahlangeregt: **~ e Photoelektronenspektroskopie** *f (XPS)* PHYS X-ray photoelectron spectroscopy *(XPS)*
Röntgenstrahlen *m pl* ELEKTRIZ, METALL, RAUMFAHRT, STRAHLPHYS, WELLPHYS X-rays; **Röntgenstrahlenbrechung** *f* RAUMFAHRT, WELLPHYS X-ray diffraction; **Röntgenstrahlen-Näherungsdrucktechnik** *f* ELEKTRONIK X-ray proximity printing; **Röntgenstrahlen-Resist** *f* ELEKTRONIK X-ray resist
Röntgenstrahler *m* KERNTECH X-emitter
Röntgenstrahl: **Röntgenstrahlimpuls** *m* ELEKTRONIK X-ray pulse
röntgenstrahlinduziert: **~es Fotoelektronenspektrum** *nt* KERNTECH X-ray photoelectron spectrum
Röntgenstrahl: **Röntgenstrahllithographie** *f* ELEKTRONIK X-ray lithography; **Röntgenstrahlmaske** *f* ELEKTRONIK X-ray mask; **Röntgenstrahlmikroskop** *nt* KERNTECH X-ray microscope; **Röntgenstrahlprüfung** *f* MECHAN X-ray examination; **Röntgenstrahltest** *m* MECHAN X-ray examination
Röntgenstrahlung *f* PHYS X-rays, STRAHLPHYS X-radiation, X-rays
Röntgen: **Röntgentesten** *nt* KERNTECH X-ray testing; **Röntgentopographie** *f* METALL X-ray topography; **Röntgenuntersuchung** *f* KERNTECH *eines Gerätes*, RAUMFAHRT X-ray inspection
Roots-Gebläse *nt* MASCHINEN Roots blower; **Roots-Gebläseflügel** *m* FERTIG Roots-blower member
Roringstek *m* WASSERTRANS *Knoten* fisherman's bend
Ro-Ro[1] *abbr (Roll-on-Roll-off)* TRANS ro-ro *(roll-on-roll-off)*
Ro-Ro[2]: **Ro-Ro-Anlage** *f (Roll-on-Roll-off-Anlage)* WASSERTRANS ro-ro dock *(roll-on roll-off dock)*; **Ro-Ro-Frachter** *m (Roll-on-Roll-off-Frachter)* WASSERTRAN *Horizontalbeladung* ro-ro vessel *(roll-on roll-off vessel)*; **Ro-Ro-Hafen** *m (Roll-on-Roll- off-Hafen)* WASSERTRANS ro-ro port *(roll-on roll-off port)*; **Ro-Ro-Schiff** *nt (Roll-on-Roll-off-Schiff)* WASSERTRANS *Horizontalbeladung* ro-ro ship, ro-ro vessel *(roll-on roll-off vessel)*; **Ro-Ro-System** *nt (Roll-on-Roll-off-System)* WASSERTRANS *Horizontalbeladung* ro-ro system *(roll-on roll-off system)*
rosa: **~ Glas** *nt* KER & GLAS pink glass; **~ Rauschen** *nt* AKUSTIK, AUFNAHME pink noise
rösch: **~ gemahlener Zellstoff** *m* PAPIER free pulp
Rose *f* ELEKTROTECH rose; **Rosenkupfer** *nt* CHEMIE rose copper
Rosette *f* KER & GLAS rosette
Roßbreiten *f pl* WASSERTRANS horse latitudes
Rost *m* ANSTRICH, EISENBAHN rust, FERTIG aerugo,

stain, KER & GLAS grillage, KFZTECH, LEBENSMITTEL *Rostkrankheit des Getreides*, LUFTTRANS rust, MASCHINEN *Gitter* grate, grating, *Korrosion* rust, MECHAN, PAPIER rust, RAUMFAHRT *Raumschiff* lattice, TEXTIL grid, WASSERTRANS rust; **Rostanfressung** *f* BAU honeycombing

rostbeständig *adj* PAPIER rustproof

Rösten *nt* FERTIG calcination, KOHLEN, LEBENSMITTEL roasting, TEXTIL retting

rosten[1] *vt* ANSTRICH rust

rosten[2] *vi* EISENBAHN, LUFTTRANS, WASSERTRANS rust

rösten *vt* FERTIG calcine, LEBENSMITTEL fire, THERMOD scorch

rostend:[1] **nicht ~** *adj* ANSTRICH corrosion-resistant

rostend:[2] **nicht ~er Stahl** *m* ANSTRICH stainless steel

Rost: **Rostentferner** *m* MASCHINEN rust remover; **Rostfeuerung** *f* MASCHINEN grate firing; **Rostfläche** *f* BAU grate area; **Rostflocke** *f* ANSTRICH rust flake

rostfrei[1] *adj* ANSTRICH, FOTO, METALL stainless

rostfrei:[2] **~er Stahl** *m* KFZTECH, METALL, PAPIER stainless steel; **~er Stahlguß** *m* FERTIG *Kunststoffinstallationen* cast stainless steel

rostgeschützt *adj* MECHAN anticorrosive, antirust

Rost: **Rostinhibitor** *m* VERPACK rust preventive

rostlösend: ~es Öl *nt* KFZTECH penetrating oil

Röstofen *m* FERTIG calciner

Rostschutz *m* MASCHINEN rust protection, rustproofing, VERPACK rust protection; **Rostschutzanstrich** *m* KUNSTSTOFF antirust coating; **Rostschutzmittel** *nt* EISENBAHN, LUFTTRANS rust inhibitor, PAPIER antirust agent, rust inhibitor, VERPACK rust preventive, WASSERTRANS rust inhibitor; **Rostschutzverpackung** *f* VERPACK rust preventive packaging

Rost: **Roststab** *m* HEIZ & KÄLTE fire bar

rostverhindernd *adj* MECHAN anticorrosive

Rot *nt* PHYS *Rotation eines Vektorfeldes* curl

rot[1] *adj* METALL red

rot:[2] **~er Blutfarbstoff** *m* CHEMIE haemoglobin (BrE), hemoglobin (AmE); **~e Kante** *f* KER & GLAS red edge; **~er Laser** *m* ELEKTRONIK red laser; **~er Stab** *m* NICHTFOSS ENERG red rod; **~er Strahl** *m* ELEKTRONIK red beam

Rotamesser *m* ERDÖL rotameter

Rotameter *nt* LABOR, PAPIER rotameter

Rotarybohren *nt* ERDÖL, KOHLEN rotary drilling

Rotarybohrmeißel *m* ERDÖL rotary bit

Rotaryscheibenbohrmeißel *m* ERDÖL rotary disc bit (BrE), rotary disk bit (AmE)

Rotation *f* COMP & DV rotation, ELEKTRONIK *eines Vektors* curl, GEOM revolution, rotation, MASCHINEN, PHYS rotation, STRÖMPHYS *eines Vektors* curl; **~ im Gegenuhrzeigersinn** *f* MECHAN anticlockwise rotation, counterclockwise rotation; **~ im Uhrzeigersinn** *f* MECHAN clockwise rotation; **Rotationsabfüllmaschine** *f* VERPACK rotary filler; **Rotationsachse** *f* MASCHINEN, MECHAN, PHYS axis of rotation; **Rotationsauslenkung** *f* (*CR*) AKUSTIK rotational compliance (*CR*); **Rotationsdruck** *m* DRUCK rotary printing; **Rotationsdurchflußmesser** *m* PHYS rotameter; **Rotationsellipsoid** *nt* FERTIG, GEOM spheroid; **Rotationsfläche** *f* GEOM surface of revolution; **Rotationsform** *f* MASCHINEN rotational mould

rotationsfrei *adj* PHYS irrotational, nonkinking

Rotation: **Rotationskegel** *m* GEOM cone of revolution; **Rotationskolben** *m* MASCHINEN rotary piston; **Rotationskolbenmotor** *m* MASCHINEN rotary engine;

Rotationskompressor *m* HEIZ & KÄLTE rotary compressor; **Rotationskörper** *m* GEOM solid of revolution; **Rotationsmaschine** *f* DRUCK rotary press, rotary printing machine, rotary printing press; **Rotationsofen** *m* ABFALL rotary furnace, rotary kiln; **Rotationsoperation** *f* COMP & DV rotate operation; **Rotationspresse** *f* DRUCK rotary press, rotary printing machine, rotary printing press; **Rotationspumpe** *f* MASCHINEN, WASSERVERSORG rotary pump; **Rotationsquantenzahl** *f* PHYS rotational quantum number; **Rotationsschnellpresse für Tabletten** *f* VERPACK high-speed rotary tablet compression machine; **Rotationsspektrum** *nt* PHYS, STRAHLPHYS rotational spectrum; **Rotationsstabilisierung** *f* RAUMFAHRT stabilization of rotation; **Rotationstiefdruck** *m* DRUCK rotogravure, KUNSTSTOFF rotogravure printing; **Rotationsverdichter** *m* HEIZ & KÄLTE, MASCHINEN rotary compressor; **Rotationsvolumen** *nt* GEOM volume of rotation; **Rotationszerkleinerer** *m* ABFALL comminutor; **Rotationszerkleinerer mit Brechrollen** *m* ABFALL comminutor; **Rotationszylinder** *m* GEOM cylindrical solid of revolution

Rotenon *nt* CHEMIE *Insektizid* derrin, rotenone

Rot: **Rotfärbung** *f* ANSTRICH rust; **Rotgitter** *nt* FERNSEH red screen grid

rotglühend *adj* THERMOD red-hot

Rot: **Rotglut** *f* METALL red heat

rot-grün-blau *adj* (*RGB*) COMP & DV, FERNSEH red-green-blue (*RGB*)

Rot: **Rotguß** *m* FERTIG red brass, steam bronze, MECHAN gunmetal, METALL cannon metal, gunmetal

rotieren[1] *vt* COMP & DV rotate, MASCHINEN rotate, turn

rotieren[2] *vi* COMP & DV, MASCHINEN rotate, RAUMFAHRT spin

rotierend *adj* MASCHINEN rotating

rotierend: ~e Fluide *nt pl* STRÖMPHYS rotating fluids; **~e obere Feststufe** *f* (*SSUS*) RAUMFAHRT solid spinning upper stage (*SSUS*); **~e Pumpe** *f* PHYS rotary pump; **~er Ringspalt** *m* STRÖMPHYS rotating annulus; **~e Scheibe** *f* MASCHINEN rotating disc (BrE), rotating disk (AmE); **~e Siebbürste** *f* PAPIER rotary wire brush; **~es Spritzrohr** *nt* PAPIER rotating shower; **nicht ~er Stern** *m* LUFTTRANS *Hubschrauber* nonrotating star; **~er Umformer** *m* ELEKTRIZ dynamotor; **~er Verdampfungsapparat** *m* LABOR rotating evaporator; **~er Zuführ- und Sammeltisch** *m* VERPACK rotary feeder and collecting table

Rot: **Rotkanone** *f* FERNSEH red gun

Rotkupfer *nt* METALL red copper; **Rotkupfererz** *nt* CHEMIE, METALL red copper ore

rötlich: ~ verfärben *vt* ANSTRICH rust

Rot: **Rotmessing** *nt* METALL tombac; **Rotmischer** *m* FERNSEH red madder

Rotor *m* ELEKTROTECH rotor, KFZTECH trigger wheel, KOHLEN, KONTROLL, LUFTTRANS *Hubschrauber*, MASCHINEN, PHYS rotor, RADIO *für Antennen* rotator; **Rotorabwind** *m* LUFTTRANS *Hubschrauber* rotor inflow; **Rotorantriebswelle** *f* LUFTTRANS *Hubschrauber* rotor mast; **Rotorblatt** *nt* LUFTTRANS *Hubschrauber* rotor blade; **Rotorbock** *m* LUFTTRANS *Hubschrauber* rotor mast; **Rotordrehmoment** *nt* LUFTTRANS *Hubschrauber* rotor torque; **Rotordurchmesser** *m* NICHTFOSS ENERG rotor diameter; **Rotorfläche** *f* LUFTTRANS *Hubschrauber* disc area (BrE), disk area (AmE); **Rotorflächenbelastung** *f* LUFTTRANS disc loading (BrE), disk loading (AmE); **Rotorgewicht** *nt*

NICHTFOSS ENERG rotor weight; **Rotorkopf** *m* LUFT-
TRANS *Hubschrauber* rotor head; **Rotorkreis** *m*
LUFTTRANS *Hubschrauber* rotor disc (BrE), rotor disk
(AmE); **Rotorlamellierung** *f* ELEKTROTECH rotor lamination; **Rotornabe** *f* LUFTTRANS *Hubschrauber* rotor
hub; **Rotorplatte** *f* ELEKTROTECH rotor plate; **Rotorra-
dius** *m* LUFTTRANS *Hubschrauber* rotor radius;
Rotorschub *m* LUFTTRANS *Hubschrauber* rotor thrust;
Rotorstrahl *m* LUFTTRANS *Hubschrauber* rotor
stream; **Rotorüberdrehzahl** *f* LUFTTRANS *Hubschrauber* rotor overspeed; **Rotorwicklung** *f* ELEKTROTECH
rotor winding

Rot: **Rotphase** *f* TRANS red phase; **Rotröhre** *f* ELEKTRO-
NIK red tube; **Rotrost** *m* ANSTRICH red rust;
Rotschlamm *m* ABFALL red mud; **Rot-Schwarz-Pegel**
m FERNSEH red-black level

Rotsignal *nt* ELEKTRONIK red signal; **Rotsignaldauer** *f*
TRANS hour of red signal indication

Rot: **Rotspitzenpegel** *m* FERNSEH red peak level

Rotstrahl *m* ELEKTRONIK, FERNSEH red beam; **Rot-
strahlablenkmagnet** *m* FERNSEH red beam magnet

Rottedeponie *f* ABFALL digestion deposit

Rotten *nt* KER & GLAS rotting, PAPIER, TEXTIL *Flachs*
retting

Rottezelle *f* ABFALL composting drum

Rouleaudruck *m* TEXTIL roller printing

Route *f* WASSERTRANS route

Routine *f* COMP & DV, KONTROLL, QUAL routine; **Routin-
einspektion** *f* LUFTTRANS routine inspection;
Routineüberprüfung *f* LUFTTRANS routine inspection

Routing-Chart *nt* WASSERTRANS *Navigation* routeing
chart

Routing-System *nt* WASSERTRANS *Navigation* routeing
system

Roving *nt* KER & GLAS, KUNSTSTOFF *Glasseidenstrang
zur Verstärkung von Duroplasten* roving; **Roving-
Mikrofon** *nt* AUFNAHME roving mike; **Rovingtrommel** *f*
KER & GLAS roving winder

Rowland-Aufhängung *f* PHYS Rowland mounting

Rowland-Kreis *m* PHYS Rowland circle

Rowland-Versuch *m* PHYS Rowland's experiment

RP-1 *abbr* (*Kerosin*) ERDÖL, TRANS RP-1 (*kerosene*)

RSB *abbr* (*Restseitenband*) ELEKTRONIK VSB (*vestigial
sideband*)

RS-Flipflop *nt* (*Reset-Set-Flipflop*) ELEKTRONIK RS
flip-flop (*reset-set flip-flop*)

RS-Kippschaltung *f* (*Reset-Set-Kippschaltung*) ELEK-
TRONIK RS toggle (*reset-set toggle*)

RTG-Zug *m* EISENBAHN RTG train

RTM-Verfahren *nt* KUNSTSTOFF *GFK* resin transfer
moulding, KUNSTSTOFF (*Referenztestmethode-Verfahren*) *GFK* RTM (*reference test method*)

RTOL-Flugzeug *nt* (*verkürzt startendes und landendes
Flugzeug*) LUFTTRANS RTOL aircraft (*reduced takeoff and landing aircraft*)

RTTY *abbr* (*Funkfernschreiben*) RADIO RTTY (*radioteletype*)

Ru (*Ruthenium*) CHEMIE Ru (*ruthenium*)

Ruberythrin- *pref* CHEMIE ruberythric

Rubidium *nt* (*Rb*) CHEMIE rubidium (*Rb*)

Rubin *m* ELEKTRONIK ruby; **Rubinlaser** *m* ELEKTRONIK
ruby laser, STRAHLPHYS ruby crystal laser

Rüböl *nt* LEBENSMITTEL rapeseed oil

Rubrik *f* DRUCK column, head

Ruck *m* TRANS jolt

Rückanzeige *f* GERÄT back indication

Rückarbeitsbremsung *f* EISENBAHN regenerative
braking

ruckartig:[1] **~e Bewegung** *f* ERGON saccadic movement

ruckartig:[2] **~ ziehen** *vt* KFZTECH hitch

Rückassemblierer *m* COMP & DV disassembler

Rückbaukammer *f* BAU dismantling chamber

Rückbewegung *f* PHYS return stroke

Rückblick *m* BAU *Vermessung* back sight; **Rückblicksy-
stem** *nt* TRANS rearview system

Rückbremsung *f* TRANS reverse braking

Rückdampf *m* HYDRAUL reversing steam

Rückdiffusion *f* KERNTECH back diffusion

Rückdrehen *nt* WASSERTRANS *des Windes* backing

rückdrehend: **~es Moment** *nt* KFZTECH *Aerodynamik*,
LUFTTRANS *Aerodynamik*, WASSERTRANS *Aerodynamik* restoring moment

Rückdruck *m* HYDRAUL *Zylinder* back pressure, RAUM-
FAHRT drag; **Rückdruckventil** *nt* HYDRAUL
back-pressure valve

Rück-EMK *nt* PHYS back emf

Rücken[1] *m* BAU ridge, DRUCK back, spine, MASCHINEN
back, heel

Rücken:[2] **mit ~ versehen** *vt* DRUCK back

Rücken: **Rückenappretur** *f* TEXTIL *Beschichtung* back-
ing; **Rückenbeschichtung** *f* TEXTIL backcoating;
Rückenbeschichtungsmaterial *nt* TEXTIL backing;
Rückeneinlage *f* DRUCK back lining; **Rückenetikett** *nt*
VERPACK back label; **Rückenkante** *f* MASCHINEN heel;
Rückenlehne *f* ERGON backrest, KFZTECH backrest,
seat back; **Rückenspannung** *f* METALL back stress;
Rückenstütze *f* ERGON backrest

Rückentzerrung *f* ELEKTRONIK de-emphasis

rückenverstärkend: **~es Gewebe** *nt* TEXTIL backing
fabric

Rückenwindanteil *m* LUFTTRANS downwind leg

Rückerstattung *f* PATENT refund

Rückextraktionstank *m* KERNTECH backwash tank

Rückfahrkarte *f* TRANS return ticket

Rückfahrleuchte *f* KFZTECH backup light (AmE), reversing light (BrE)

Rückfahrscheinwerfer *m* KFZTECH backup light (AmE),
reversing light (BrE)

Rückfaltungsfrequenz *f* ELEKTRONIK *Signalverzerrung*
aliased frequency

rückfedern *vi* MASCHINEN rebound

Rückfederung *f* FERTIG elastic recovery, KUNSTSTOFF
rebound, MASCHINEN resilience, resiliency; **Rückfede-
rungsvermögen** *nt* KUNSTSTOFF resilience

Rückflankenverschiebung *f* ELEKTRONIK *von Start- und
Stoppsignalen bei Fernschreibern* end distortion

Rückfluß *m* CHEMTECH *Destillation* reflux, WASSERVER-
SORG backflow; **Rückflußkochen** *nt* CHEMTECH reflux
boiling; **Rückflußkühler** *m* KERNTECH, LABOR reflux
condenser; **Rückflußleitung** *f* FERTIG return line;
Rückflußlötung *f* RAUMFAHRT reflow soldering; **Rück-
flußstrom** *m* ELEKTROTECH return current;
Rückflußturbine *f* NICHTFOSS ENERG reverse flow turbine

Rückformung *f* KUNSTSTOFF recovery

Rückfracht *f* WASSERTRANS *Ladung* back freight, home
freight, reshipment, reshipping, return cargo

Rückfrage *f* TELEKOM consultation call, hold for inquiry; **Rückfragehäufigkeit** *f* TELEKOM repetition rate

rückfragen *vi* COMP & DV prompt

Rückfrage: **Rückfrageplatz** *m* TELEKOM inquiry position

Rückführen *nt* FERTIG recirculating; ~ **der Papierbahn** *nt* PAPIER *für Mehrfarbendruck* insetting

rückführend: ~**e Kurbelgehäuseentlüftung** *f (PCV-Ventilation)* KFZTECH *Motor* positive crankcase ventilation *(PCV)*

Rückführkreis *m* MASCHINEN feedback loop

Rückführsignal *nt* ELEKTRONIK *Meß- und Regelungstechnik* feedback signal

Rückführtaste *f* COMP & DV return key

Rückführung *f* COMP & DV, ELEKTRONIK feedback, KER & GLAS *der Ströme in Wannenofen* recirculation, KERNTECH, KONTROLL feedback, LUFTTRANS *Hubschrauber* follow-up, MECHAN, PHYS feedback, TELEKOM recycling, *Kontroll-Loop* feedback, UMWELTSCHMUTZ recycling, WELLPHYS feedback; ~ **von Spaltprodukten** *f* KERNTECH recirculation of fission products; **Rückführungskreis** *m* ELEKTRONIK, MASCHINEN feedback loop; **Rückführungsschleife** *f* ELEKTRONIK *bei Regelung im geschlossenen Kreis* feedback loop

Rückgabebehälter *m* VERPACK returnable container

Rückgabeflasche *f* VERPACK deposit bottle, returnable bottle

Rückgang *m* HYDRAUL *Niveau* fall; **Rückgangslinie** *f* WASSERVERSORG recession curve

rückgefaltet: ~**es Signal** *nt* ELEKTRONIK aliased signal

rückgewinnbar: ~**er Abfall** *m* ABFALL recoverable waste; **nicht** ~**e Abfälle** *m pl* ABFALL nonrecoverable waste

Rückgewinnung *f* ABFALL, KOHLEN recycling, KUNSTSTOFF, MEERSCHMUTZ recovery; **Rückgewinnungsanlage** *f* ABFALL reclamation plant, MASCHINEN recovery plant; **Rückgewinnungskessel** *m* ABFALL recovery boiler

rückgewonnen: ~**e Pulpe** *f* ABFALL recovered pulp; ~**e Wärme** *f* ABFALL recovered heat

Rückhalt *m* MECHAN backlog; **Rückhaltebecken** *nt* BAU retention basin, WASSERVERSORG detention basin, detention reservoir; **Rückhaltevermögen** *nt* KUNSTSTOFF hold-out

Rückholen *nt* TELEKOM call retrieval

Rückholfeder *f* KFZTECH, MASCHINEN return spring

Rückholmechanismus *m* KERNTECH *für Abschaltstab* return motion mechanism

rückhördämpfend *adj* TELEKOM antisidetone

Rückhördämpfungsschaltung *f* TELEKOM antisidetone circuit

Rückhörgeräusch *nt* TELEKOM *Telefon* sidetone

Rückkanal *m* AUFNAHME feedback channel, COMP & DV reverse channel, MASCHINEN return channel

Rückkehr *f* COMP & DV return; **Rückkehradresse** *f* COMP & DV return address; **Rückkehrbefehl** *m* COMP & DV return instruction; **Rückkehrcode** *m* COMP & DV return code; **Rückkehrkanal** *m* COMP & DV return channel; **Rückkehrkoeffizient** *m* MECHAN, PHYS coefficient of restitution

Rückkontrolle *f* BAU *Vermessung* back observation

Rückkopplung *f* AUFNAHME, COMP & DV, ELEKTRONIK, FERNSEH, KERNTECH, KONTROLL, MECHAN, PHYS, RADIO, TELEKOM, WELLPHYS feedback; **Rückkopplungsfaktor** *m* ELEKTRONIK feedback ratio

rückkopplungsfrei: ~**e Messung** *f* GERÄT open loop measurement; ~**e Relaisstation** *f* ELEKTRONIK *Radio* nonregenerative repeater; ~**er Verstärker** *m* ELEKTRONIK *Telefon* nonregenerative repeater

Rückkopplung: **Rückkopplungsgrad** *m* ELEKTRONIK feedback ratio; **Rückkopplungskreis** *m* ELEKTRONIK *Radio* regenerative circuit, FERNSEH feedback circuit;

Rückkopplungsoszillator *m* AUFNAHME, ELEKTRONIK feedback oscillator; **Rückkopplungsregelung** *f* ELEKTROTECH feedback control; **Rückkopplungsschaltung** *f* AUFNAHME feedback circuit; **Rückkopplungsschleife** *f* ELEKTRONIK, MECHAN feedback loop; **Rückkopplungsschneider** *m* AUFNAHME feedback cutter; **Rückkopplungsschwingung** *f* AUFNAHME feedback oscillation; **Rückkopplungsspannung** *f* ELEKTROTECH feedback voltage; **Rückkopplungsspule** *f* ELEKTROTECH feedback coil; **Rückkopplungsverstärker** *m* ELEKTRONIK feedback amplifier, *Radio* regenerative amplifier; **Rückkopplungsverstärkung** *f* ELEKTRONIK *Radio* regenerative amplification; **Rückkopplungswicklung** *f* ELEKTROTECH feedback winding; **Rückkopplungswiderstand** *m* ELEKTROTECH feedback resistor

Rückkühler *m* WASSERTRANS *Motor* heat exchanger

Rücklauf *m* CHEMTECH *Destillation* reflux, ELEKTRONIK *Kathodenstrahlröhren* retrace, FERNSEH back run, reverse motion, FERTIG *Gewindebohrer* withdrawing, HEIZ & KÄLTE return, HYDRAUL *Kesselwasser* backflow, *Kolben* back stroke, KERNTECH reverse motion, MASCHINEN noncutting stroke, return movement, return stroke, return travel, PHYS return stroke, WASSERVERSORG backflow; ~ **des Werkzeugs** *m* MASCHINEN noncutting return of the tool; **Rücklaufabtaststrahl** *m* FERNSEH return scanning beam; **Rücklaufachse** *f* KFZTECH reverse idler shaft; **Rücklaufaustastung** *f* FERNSEH flyback blanking

rücklaufend: ~**e Welle** *f* TELEKOM inward-propagating wave

Rückläufer *m* KER & GLAS runner back

Rücklauf: **Rücklaufgeschwindigkeit** *f* COMP & DV rewind speed

rückläufig: ~**e Skale** *f* GERÄT reversed scale

Rücklauf: **Rücklaufintervall** *nt* FERNSEH return interval; **Rücklaufkondensator** *m* LABOR reflux condenser

Rücklaufleitung: **zur** ~ **fließen** *vi* FERTIG pass to exhaust

Rücklauf: **Rücklauflücke** *f* FERNSEH back gap; **Rücklaufrad** *nt* KFZTECH *Getriebe* reverse idler gear; **Rücklaufrohr** *nt* HEIZ & KÄLTE return pipe; **Rücklaufschaltung** *f* ELEKTROTECH return circuit; **Rücklaufschlamm** *m* ABFALL recycle sludge, return sludge; **Rücklaufsperre** *f* BAU back stop, ELEKTRIZ reverse power flow protection; **Rücklaufspur** *f* ELEKTRONIK *Kathodenstrahlröhren* retrace; **Rücklauftaste** *f* COMP & DV return key; **Rücklauftransformator** *m* FERNSEH flyback transformer; **Rücklaufverhältnis** *nt* KERNTECH reflux ratio; **Rücklaufverlust** *m* ERDÖL *Bohrtechnik: Bohrschlamm* loss of returns; **Rücklaufzeitsteuerung** *f* FERNSEH back timing

Rückleiter *m* ELEKTRIZ return conductor, return wire

Rückleitung *f* ELEKTROTECH return wire, FERTIG *Hydraulik* shunt line; **Rückleitungsrohr** *nt* MASCHINEN return pipe

Rückleuchte *f* KFZTECH tail lamp

Rückmelder *m* FERTIG *Kunststoffinstallationen* checkback position indicator

Rückmeldesignal *nt* ELEKTRONIK repeater signal

Rückmeldung *f* COMP & DV ACK, acknowledgement, response, FERTIG *Kunststoffinstallationen* answerback signal, signaling unit (AmE), signalling unit (BrE), GERÄT back indication, TELEKOM ACK, acknowledgement; ~ **der Signalstellung** *f* EISENBAHN signal indication

Rückoxidation *f* CHEMIE, UMWELTSCHMUTZ reoxidation

Rückprallelastizität *f* KUNSTSTOFF rebound elasticity, resilience

Rückreaktion *f* KERNTECH back reaction

Rückreise:[1] **auf der ~ befindlich** *adj* WASSERTRANS homeward-bound

Rückreise[2] *f* WASSERTRANS homeward passage, return voyage

Rückruf *m* TELEKOM recall

Rückschaltzeichen *nt* COMP & DV SI character, shift-in character

Rückschlag *m* ELEKTROTECH kickback, HYDRAUL *Kolben* back stroke, MASCHINEN, MECHAN recoil, RAUMFAHRT backlash, WASSERVERSORG *Brunnen* kickback

rückschlagfrei: ~er Nylonhammer *m* SICHERHEIT recoilless nylon hammer

Rückschlag: Rückschlagklappe *f* FERTIG *Kunststoffinstallationen* swing-type check valve; **Rückschlagschutz** *m* SICHERHEIT *Ventile und Anschlüsse* flashback preventer; **Rückschlagsicherung** *f* BAU flame arrester; **Rückschlagventil** *nt* BAU nonreturn valve, FERTIG nonreturn valve, *Kunststoffinstallationen* check valve, HYDRAUL backpressure valve, KFZTECH check valve, *Schmierung* check valve, MASCHINEN check valve, nonreturn valve, retention valve, return valve, MECHAN check valve, NICHTFOSS ENERG nonreturn valve, RAUMFAHRT, WASSERVERSORG check valve; **Rückschlagzündung** *f* KFZTECH blowback

Rückschneidemethode *f* OPTIK, TELEKOM cutback technique

Rückseite *f* KER & GLAS *einer Glastafel* back surface, PAPIER back, rear

rückseitig: ~ bedruckt *adj* VERPACK reverse side printed

Rücksendungsetikett *nt* VERPACK return label

Rücksetzen *nt* COMP & DV reset, KFZTECH backing, reversing

rücksetzen *vt* KONTROLL reset

Rücksetzknopf *m* FERNSEH reset knob

Rücksetzung *f* COMP & DV reset

Rücksetzzeichen *nt* COMP & DV backspace character

Rücksignal *nt* ELEKTRONIK back signal

Rückspeicherung *f* COMP & DV restore

Rückspiegel *m* KER & GLAS rear-view mirror, KFZTECH driving mirror, rear-view mirror

Rücksprechmikrofon *nt* AUFNAHME interference microphone

Rücksprung *m* BAU recess, retreat, *Mauerwerk* offset; **Rücksprungadresse** *f* COMP & DV return address; **Rücksprunghärte** *f* FERTIG scleroscope hardness; **Rücksprunghärteprüfung** *f* FERTIG scleroscope method of determining hardness; **Rücksprungpalette** *f* TRANS stevedore-type pallet

Rückspulen *nt* FERNSEH rewinding

Rückspulgabel *f* FOTO rewind handle

Rückspulmitnehmer *m* FOTO rewind cam

Rückspulspannung *f* AUFNAHME *des Bandes* rewind tension

Rückspulvorrichtung *f* FOTO rewinder

Rückspulzeit *f* COMP & DV rewind time

Rückstand *m* ERDÖL, FERTIG, LEBENSMITTEL, MASCHINEN, MEERSCHMUTZ, UMWELTSCHMUTZ, WASSERVERSORG residue

Rückstände *m pl* BAU tailings, ERDÖL *Absetzung von Verunreinigungen* bottoms, *von Destillation* bottoms, LEBENSMITTEL bottoms, PAPIER tailings

Rückstand: Rückstandsammelbehälter *m* ERDÖL sump; **Rückstandsdeponie** *f* ABFALL residue landfill; **Rückstandsraffination** *f* ERDÖL *Raffinerie* residue refining process

Rückstau *m* ERDÖL, TRANS backup, WASSERVERSORG backwater; **Rückstauklappe** *f* BAU trap; **Rückstauwasser** *nt* WASSERVERSORG backwater; **Rückstauwirkung** *f* NICHTFOSS ENERG backwater effect

Rückstellelastizität *f* COMP & DV resilience

rückstellen *vt* COMP & DV restore

rückstellfähig *adj* KUNSTSTOFF resilient

Rückstellfähigkeit *f* KUNSTSTOFF rebound elasticity

Rückstellfeder *f* FERTIG *Kunststoffinstallationen* return action, KFZTECH return spring, MASCHINEN readjusting spring

Rückstellkraft *f* AUFNAHME *der Abspielnadel* stylus drag, ERGON, MASCHINEN restoring force

Rückstellmoment *nt* MASCHINEN righting moment

Rückstelltaste *f* COMP & DV reset button, reset key

Rückstellung *f* COMP & DV restore, FERTIG restoration, KUNSTSTOFF recovery

Rückstellzähler *m* GERÄT reset counter

Rücksteuerungssystem *nt* TELEKOM revertive control system

Rückstoß *m* ELEKTROTECH kickback, repulsion, ERDÖL kick, HYDRAUL *Kolben* back stroke, MASCHINEN, MECHAN recoil; **Rückstoßdüse** *f* LUFTTRANS propelling nozzle; **Rückstoßelektron** *nt* PHYS recoil electron; **Rückstoßenergie bei der Spaltung** *f* KERNTECH fission recoil; **Rückstoßkern** *m* PHYS recoil nucleus; **Rückstoßkraft** *f* ELEKTROTECH repulsion, repulsive force; **Rückstoßstromversorgung** *f* ELEKTROTECH kickback power supply

rückstrahlend: ~e Markierung *f* LUFTTRANS *Flughafen* retro-reflective marker

Rückstrahler *m* KFZTECH rear reflector, *Scheinwerfer* reflector

Rückstrahlung *f* AKUSTIK reflection; **Rückstrahlungsvermögen** *nt* NICHTFOSS ENERG reflectance

Rückstreueffekt *m* KERNTECH backscatter effect

rückstreuen *vt* OPTIK backscatter

rückstreuend: ~es Material *nt* KERNTECH backscatterer

Rückstreufehler *m* KERNTECH backscatter error

Rückstreumesser *m* KERNTECH backscatter gage (AmE), backscatter gauge (BrE)

Rückstreumethode *f* TELEKOM backscattering technique

Rückstreupeak *m* STRAHLPHYS backscatter peak

Rückstreuung *f* ELEKTRONIK, OPTIK backscattering, RADIO, RAUMFAHRT backscatter, STRAHLPHYS, TELEKOM backscattering

Rückstreuverfahren *nt* OPTIK backscattering technique

Rückstreuverlust *m* ELEKTROTECH spill

Rückstrom *m* ELEKTROTECH leakage current, return current, *Stromerzeuger* reverse current, HYDRAUL *Kesselwasser* backflow; **Rückstromauslösung** *f* ELEKTRIZ reverse current protection; **Rückstrombremsen** *nt* ELEKTRIZ reverse current circuit breaking; **Rückstromkoeffizient** *m* ELEKTROTECH return current coefficient; **Rückstromrelais** *nt* ELEKTRIZ reverse current relay

Rückströmung *f* HYDRAUL backset, KER & GLAS withdrawal current

Rücktitration *f* CHEMIE back titration

Rücktransformator *m* ELEKTRONIK reconverter

rücktreibend: ~e Kraft *f* MECHAN, PHYS restoring force;

~es Moment *nt* MECHAN restoring torque
Rücktrieb *m* NICHTFOSS ENERG *Hydraulik* drag
Rückübertrag *m* COMP & DV carry back
Rückverdampfer *m* ERDÖL reboiler
Rückverfolgbarkeit *f* QUAL traceability
rückverformen *vt* FERTIG recover
Rückverformung *f* KUNSTSTOFF rebound
Rückvergrößerung *f* KONSTZEICH re-enlargement; **Rückvergrößerungsverfahren** *nt* KONSTZEICH re-enlarging process
Rückwand *f* ELEKTRONIK *Gerätetechnik* backplate, *eines Computers* backplane, FOTO *einer Kamera* back, VERPACK end panel; **Rückwandleiterplatte** *f* ELEKTRONIK motherboard
rückwärtig: ~**er Raststift** *m* FERTIG back pin
Rückwärts- *pref* EISENBAHN, ELEKTRONIK, KFZTECH, MASCHINEN backward
rückwärts:[1] ~ **hobeln** *vt* FERTIG shape on the return stroke
rückwärts:[2] ~ **fahren** *vi* EISENBAHN *Zug* reverse
Rückwärts-: **Rückwärtsabtastung** *f* FERNSEH, GERÄT reverse scan; **Rückwärtsbestätigung** *f* COMP & DV reverse authentication
rückwärtsbewegend *adj* RAUMFAHRT retrograde
Rückwärts-: **Rückwärtsbewegung** *f* MASCHINEN backward motion, backward movement; **Rückwärtsdiode** *f* ELEKTRONIK backward diode; **Rückwärtsfahren** *nt* EISENBAHN reversing; **Rückwärtsfließpressen** *nt* MASCHINEN back extrusion, backward extrusion, inverted extrusion, reverse extrusion, **Rückwärtsflug** *m* LUFTTRANS backward flight; **Rückwärtsgang** *m* KFZTECH reverse gear, MECHAN reverse; **Rückwärtsgangzwischenwelle** *f* KFZTECH reverse idler shaft; **Rückwärtshub** *m* HYDRAUL *Kolben* back stroke, MASCHINEN return stroke; **Rückwärtsindikatorbit** *nt* TELEKOM backward indicator
rückwärtslaufend: ~**er Propeller** *m* LUFTTRANS blade pitch reversal
Rückwärts-: **Rückwärtsregelung** *f* TELEKOM feedback AGC, feedback automatic gain control; **Rückwärtsschweißen** *nt* MECHAN backhand welding; **Rückwärtssortierung** *f* COMP & DV backward sort; **Rückwärtsspülungswasser** *nt* WASSERVERSORG backwash water; **Rückwärtsstart** *m* LUFTTRANS *Hubschrauber* backward takeoff, rearward takeoff; **Rückwärtssuche** *f* KÜNSTL INT backward search; **Rückwärtssuchlauf** *m* COMP & DV backward search; **Rückwärtsverkettung** *f* KÜNSTL INT back chaining, backward chaining
Rückwärtswelle *f* ELEKTROTECH *Wanderfeldröhre* backward wave, *Übertragungsleitung* backward wave, TELEKOM backward wave; **Rückwärtswellenmagnetfeldröhre** *f* ELEKTRONIK O-type tube; **Rückwärtswellenoszillator** *m* ELEKTRONIK *Meßtechnik, Hochfrequenztechnik* carcinotron, ELEKTRONIK, PHYS backward-wave oscillator, TELEKOM carcinotron, TELEKOM backward-wave oscillator; **Rückwärtswellenoszillator Typ O** *m* ELEKTRONIK O-type carcinotron; **Rückwärtswellenoszillatorröhre** *f* ELEKTRONIK BWT, backward-wave tube; **Rückwärtswellenröhre** *f* ELEKTRONIK O-type tube, PHYS backward-wave tube; **Rückwärtswellenverstärker** *m* ELEKTRONIK BWA, backward-wave amplifier
Rückwärts-: **Rückwärtszähler** *m* ELEKTRONIK down counter, GERÄT backward counter, count-down counter; **Rückwärtszählimpuls** *m* ELEKTRONIK down pulse;

Rückwärtszeichen *nt* TELEKOM backward signal
Rückwasser *nt* HYDRAUL *Kesselwasser* backflow, NICHTFOSS ENERG tail water, PAPIER, WASSERVERSORG backwater; **Rückwasserstand** *m* NICHTFOSS ENERG tail water level
Rückweg *m* TELEKOM return path
Rückweisung *f* QUAL rejection; **Rückweisungswahrscheinlichkeit** *f* QUAL probability of rejection
rückwirkend: ~**e Elektrode** *f* ELEKTROTECH reflecting electrode
Rückwirkung *f* PHYS reaction; **Rückwirkungsfreiheit** *f* GERÄT absence of feedback; **Rückwirkungsimpedanz** *f* ELEKTROTECH reflected impedance; **Rückwirkungsleistung** *f* ELEKTROTECH reflected power; **Rückwirkungsspannung** *f* ELEKTROTECH reflected voltage; **Rückwirkungswiderstand** *m* ELEKTROTECH reflected resistance
Rückzahlung *f* PATENT reimbursement
Rückzugfeder *f* MASCHINEN drawback spring, pull-back spring, retractile spring
Rückzündung *f* ELEKTROTECH *Gleichrichter* arc back, KFZTECH backfire
rückzuweisend: ~**e Qualitätsgrenzlage** *f* QUAL limiting quality level, lot tolerance percentage of defectives; ~**e Qualitätslage** *f* QUAL rejectable quality level
Ruder[1] *nt* PHYS control surface, WASSERTRANS oar, *Steuerruder* rudder
Ruder:[2] ~ **mittschiffs legen** *vi* WASSERTRANS right the helm
Ruder: **Ruderanlage** *f* WASSERTRANS helm; **Ruderblatt** *nt* WASSERTRANS rudder blade; **Ruderboot** *nt* WASSERTRANS rowing boat; **Rudergänger** *m* WASSERTRANS helmsman; **Rudergängerin** *f* WASSERTRANS helmswoman; **Ruderhacke** *f* WASSERTRANS *Schiffbau* skeg; **Ruderhaken** *m* WASSERTRANS pintle; **Ruderhaus** *nt* WASSERTRANS wheel house; **Ruderkette** *f* WASSERTRANS steering chain; **Ruderkoker** *m* WASSERTRANS *Schiffbau* rudder trunk; **Ruderlagenanzeiger** *m* WASSERTRANS helm indicator, rudder angle indicator; **Ruderleine** *f* WASSERTRANS *Schiffbau* tiller rope; **Rudermaschine** *f* WASSERTRANS *Schiffantrieb* steering gear; **Rudermoment** *nt* LUFTTRANS hinge moment
rudern[1] *vt* WASSERTRANS row
rudern[2] *vi* WASSERTRANS row
Ruder: **Ruderöse** *f* WASSERTRANS rudder brace; **Ruderpfosten** *m* WASSERTRANS rudder post; **Ruderpinne** *f* WASSERTRANS *Bootbau* tiller, *Schiffbau* helm; **Ruderquadrant** *m* WASSERTRANS rudder quadrant; **Ruderschaden** *m* WASSERTRANS helm damage; **Ruderschaft** *m* WASSERTRANS rudder stock; **Ruderservoantrieb** *m* LUFTTRANS servo unit; **Rudersorgkette** *f* WASSERTRANS rudder chain; **Ruderstand** *m* WASSERTRANS *Schiffbau* helm
Ruf *m* TELEKOM *Läuten* call, ringing; **Rufabwicklung** *f* TELEKOM call handling; **Rufannahmezeichen** *nt* TELEKOM call acceptance signal; **Rufdauer** *f* TELEKOM ringing duration
rufend: ~**er Fernsprecher** *m* TELEKOM calling telephone; ~**e Leitung** *f* TELEKOM calling line; ~**er Teilnehmer** *m* TELEKOM caller; ~**es Telefon** *nt* TELEKOM calling telephone
Ruf: **Rufkanal** *m* TELEKOM calling channel, paging channel; **Rufkennung** *f* TELEKOM call identification; **Ruflampe** *f* TELEKOM calling lamp; **Rufmaschine** *f* TELEKOM ringing machine; **Rufnummer** *f* TELEKOM directory number; **Rufnummernanzeige** *f* TELEKOM

call indicating device

rufpflichtig: ~er Punkt m QUAL call point

Ruf: **Rufphase** f TELEKOM ringing period; **Rufportabilität** f TELEKOM call portability; **Rufsatz** m TELEKOM *Telefon* ringer; **Rufstrom** m TELEKOM ringing current; **Rufverzug** m TELEKOM postdialing delay (AmE), postdialling delay (BrE); **Rufweite** f WASSERTRANS hailing distance; **Rufzeichen** nt RADIO call sign, TELEKOM calling signal, WASSERTRANS *Funk* call sign

Ruhe- *pref* FERNSEH static; **Ruhefokussierung** f FERNSEH static focus; **Ruhehörschwelle** f AKUSTIK threshold in quiet; **Ruhekontakt** m ELEKTRIZ normally closed contact, resting contact, ELEKTROTECH break contact, normally closed contact; **Ruhekufen** f pl TRANS rest skids; **Ruhelage** f ELEKTRIZ, GERÄT *Zeiger* rest position; **Ruhemasse** f PHYS, STRAHLPHYS, TEILPHYS rest mass

ruhend: ~er Anker m ELEKTROTECH stationary armature; **~er Kontakt** m ELEKTRIZ fixed contact; **~e Luftschicht** f UMWELTSCHMUTZ static air layer; **~e Station** f COMP & DV dormant terminal; **~er Verkehr** m TRANS stationary traffic

Ruhe-: **Ruheperiode** f LUFTTRANS rest period; **Ruhepunkt** m MECHAN dead center (AmE), dead centre (BrE); **Ruhespannung** f ELEKTROTECH open circuit voltage; **Ruhestellung** f GERÄT *Zeiger* rest position, MASCHINEN neutral position; **Ruhestreifen** m AUFNAHME unmodulated track; **Ruhestrom** m COMP & DV *Datenfernverarbeitung* idle current, FERNSEH static current; **Ruheverlust** m ELEKTRIZ fixed loss; **Ruhewert** m ELEKTRIZ steady state value; **Ruhewinkel** m BAU angle of repose, PHYS angle of friction; **Ruhezustand** m COMP & DV stable state, ELEKTRIZ steady state, PHYS state of rest, TELEKOM idle state; **Ruhezustandsbetrieb** m KONTROLL standby mode

ruhig[1] *adj* COMP & DV quiescent, MASCHINEN smooth

ruhig:[2] **~er Lauf** m MASCHINEN quiet running, smooth running

Ruhofen m THERMOD batch furnace

Rührapparat m CHEMTECH agitator

Rührarm m ABFALL rabble arm

Rühren nt KER & GLAS stirring

rühren vt PAPIER agitate

Rührenzange f MECHAN long-nose pliers

Rührer m CHEMTECH agitator, KER & GLAS bubbler, *für im Hafen erschmolzenes optisches Glas* thimble, KUNSTSTOFF, LABOR stirrer, LEBENSMITTEL agitator

Rührflügel m PAPIER impeller

Rührfrischen nt FERTIG puddling

rührfrischen vt FERTIG puddle

Rührmaschine f CHEMTECH agitating machine, MASCHINEN agitator

Rührschaufel f LABOR stirrer blade, MASCHINEN paddle

Rührspatel m KER & GLAS paddle

Rührwerk nt ABFALL, ERDÖL *Kohlevergasung*, FERTIG agitator, KUNSTSTOFF mixer, MASCHINEN, PAPIER agitator; **Rührwerkskessel** m CHEMTECH agitating vessel

Rumpelfilter nt AUFNAHME rumble filter

Rumpelgeräusch nt AKUSTIK rumble

Rumpelpegel m AUFNAHME rumble level

Rumpf m ELEKTROTECH *eines Elektromotors* carcass, LUFTTRANS fuselage, hull, WASSERVERSORG *eines Baggers* hull; **~ ohne Zubehör** m LUFTTRANS bare fuselage, bare hull; **Rumpfatom** nt KERNTECH *nach Abspaltung von Elektronen* atomic trunk; **Rumpfnase** f RADIO

radar dome, radome; **Rumpfstufe** f LUFTTRANS hull step; **Rumpfverbindungsbeschlag** m RAUMFAHRT fuselage attachment

Rund- *pref* BAU, ELEKTROTECH, FERTIG, MASCHINEN, MECHAN, PHYS, TELEKOM circular, roll, round; **Rundbiegen** nt FERTIG roll bending; **Rundblickaufnahme** f FOTO panoramic photograph; **Rundbogen** m BAU Roman arch, round arch, semicircular arch; **Runddichtring** m *(O-Ring)* KFZTECH, MASCHINEN O-ring

Runde f ANSTRICH *beim Rennen* lap

Rundeisen nt MASCHINEN round bar, METALL round bar iron

Runden nt COMP & DV, MATH rounding; **~ und Binden** nt DRUCK rounding and binding; **~ und Rückenbildung** nt DRUCK rounding and backing

runden vt COMP & DV round, MASCHINEN radius, MATH round

Rund-: **Runderneuerung** f KFZTECH *eines Reifens* recapping (AmE), remolding (AmE), remoulding (BrE), retreading; **Rundfeile** f MASCHINEN round file, round-edge file; **Rundfräseinrichtung** f MASCHINEN circular milling attachment; **Rundfräsen** nt MASCHINEN circular milling; **Rundfräsmaschine** f MASCHINEN circular milling machine

Rundfunk[1] m FERNSEH, RADIO broadcasting, TELEKOM radio broadcasting

Rundfunk:[2] **durch ~ verbreiten** vt RAD broadcast

rundfunkbezogen: nicht ~e Rechte nt pl FERNSEH non-broadcast rights

Rundfunk: **Rundfunkgroßverstärker** m AUFNAHME PA amplifier, public address amplifier; **Rundfunknetz** nt FERNSEH broadcasting network; **Rundfunknorm** f FERNSEH broadcast standard; **Rundfunkqualität** f FERNSEH broadcast quality; **Rundfunksatellit** m FERNSEH broadcasting satellite; **Rundfunksatellit für Direktempfang** m RAUMFAHRT direct-broadcast satellite; **Rundfunksatellitendienst** m RAUMFAHRT broadcasting satellite service; **Rundfunksender** m RADIO broadcasting station, sound broadcast transmitter, TELEKOM broadcast transmitter

Rundfunksendung: als ~ ausstrahlen vt RADIO broadcast

Rundfunk: **Rundfunkstörung** f *(BCI)* RADIO broadcast interference *(BCI)*; **Rundfunkübertragung** f TELEKOM broadcasting, transmission; **Rundfunkumsetzer** m FERNSEH network broadcast repeater station; **Rundfunkvideografik** f FERNSEH broadcast videographics

Rund-: **Rundgesenkoberteil** nt MASCHINEN top rounding tool; **Rundgewinde** nt MASCHINEN round thread; **Rundgliederkette** f MASCHINEN round link chain; **Rundhaus** nt EISENBAHN roundhouse; **Rundheck** nt WASSERTRANS elliptical stern

Rundheit f MECHAN concentricity; **Rundheitsmeßgerät** nt METROL roundness measuring instrument

Rund-: **Rundhobel** m BAU compass plane; **Rundhobeln** nt MASCHINEN circular planing; **Rundhohlleiter** m ELEKTROTECH, PHYS, TELEKOM circular waveguide; **Rundhöhlung** f KOHLEN concave; **Rundholz** nt FERTIG spar; **Rundkämmaschine** f TEXTIL circular combing machine; **Rundkammstuhl** m TEXTIL circular combing machine; **Rundkeil** m MASCHINEN round key; **Rundkessel** m HYDRAUL plain cylindrical boiler; **Rundkolben** m LABOR round-bottomed flask; **Rundkopf** m MASCHINEN round head; **Rundkopfbolzen** m BAU button-head bolt; **Rundkopfschraube** f MASCHI-

NEN round-head bolt, round-head screw, MECHAN cheese-head screw; **Rundkopfschraube mit Schlitz** *f* MASCHINEN slotted round-head bolt; **Rundkörper** *m* KONSTZEICH round component; **Rundkuppe** *f* MASCHINEN rounded end; **Rundlauf** *m* FERTIG concentricity, MASCHINEN true running; **Rundlauffehler** *m* FERTIG runout, MASCHINEN eccentricity

rundlaufend *adj* MASCHINEN true, true-running

Rund-: **Rundläufer** *m* KER & GLAS rotating machine, KUNSTSTOFF rotary table machine; **Rundlaufsenkrechtfräsmaschine** *f* FERTIG vertical-spindle rotary-table miller; **Rundloch** *nt* FERTIG *Amboß* pritchel hole; **Rundlochperforation** *f* DRUCK round hole perforating; **Rundmagazin** *nt* FOTO *Diaprojektor* rotary magazine; **Rundmaulzange** *f* FERTIG hollow tongs; **Rundmeißel** *m* MASCHINEN round-nose chisel, round-nose tool; **Rundmutter** *f* MASCHINEN round nut; **Rundnaht** *f* FERTIG circumferential seam, KERNTECH *Schweißnaht* girth weld; **Rundnahtschweißen** *nt* MECHAN girth weld; **Rundofen** *m* KER & GLAS beehive kiln; **Rundprobe** *f* WERKPRÜF round specimen; **Rundprofil** *nt* BAU rounds; **Rundprofilinstrument** *nt* GERÄT round edgewise pattern instrument; **Rundregner** *m* WASSERVERSORG rotating sprayer; **Rundriß** *m* KERNTECH pennyshaped crack; **Rundschaltmaschine** *f* FERTIG index type of machine; **Rundschalttischmaschine** *f* FERTIG rotary; **Rundschieber** *m* HYDRAUL circular slide-valve; **Rundschleifen** *nt* MASCHINEN, MECHAN cylindrical grinding; **Rundschleifmaschine** *f* MECHAN cylindrical grinder; **Rundschnurring** *m* MASCHINEN toroidal sealing ring; **Rundschreiben** *nt* TELEKOM multiaddressing; **Rundschuppen** *m* EISENBAHN roundhouse; **Rundsenden** *nt* TELEKOM multiaddressing; **Rundsichtpeilanzeiger** *m* LUFTTRANS *Flugzeug* OBI, omnibearing indicator; **Rundsieb** *nt* PAPIER vat, *der Rundsiebpapiermaschine* cylinder; **Rundsiebpapiermaschine** *f* PAPIER cylinder machine; **Rundskale** *f* KFZTECH dial; **Rundspruch** *m* COMP & DV broadcast; **Rundspruchanlage** *f* LUFTTRANS PA system, public address system; **Rundspruchmodus** *m* COMP & DV broadcast mode; **Rundstab** *m* BAU astragal, rounds, *Holzbau* bead, MECHAN rod; **Rundstahl** *m* MASCHINEN round-nose tool, METALL round, runner; **Rundstrahlantenne** *f* RADIO, TELEKOM omnidirectional aerial, omnidirectional antenna; **Rundstrahlkursfunkfeuer** *nt* RADIO, TRANS omnidirectional radiorange; **Rundtaktmaschine** *f* MASCHINEN revolving transfer machine; **Rundtisch** *m* MASCHINEN rotary table; **Rundtischfräsmaschine** *f* MASCHINEN rotary table milling machine; **Rundtischschaltmaschine** *f* MASCHINEN rotary indexing machine; **Rundtörn mit zwei halben Schlägen** *m* WASSERTRANS *Knoten* round turn and two half-hitches

rundumerneuert: **~er Reifen** *m* KFZTECH recapped tire (AmE), recapped tyre (BrE), remolded tire (AmE), remoulded tyre (BrE), retreaded tire (ÅmE), retreaded tyre (BrE)

Rundumetikett *nt* VERPACK wraparound label

Rundumlicht *nt* WASSERTRANS *Signal* all-round light

Rundung *f* MATH truncation; **~ des Rands** *f* KER & GLAS rounding of the rim; **Rundungsfehler** *m* COMP & DV, MATH rounding error

Rund-: **Rundzange** *f* MASCHINEN round-nose pliers; **Rundzuführdüse** *f* HYDRAUL *Steuerung* rounded approach orifice

Runge *f* EISENBAHN stanchion, upright, FERTIG upright,

KFZTECH *zwischen Wagenseite und Radachse* post; **Rungenpalette** *f* TRANS post pallet

Run-up-Bereich *m* LUFTTRANS run-up area

Runzelbildung *f* KUNSTSTOFF silking

runzelig: **~e Oberfläche** *f* KER & GLAS cockled surface; **~e Oberfläche durch ungleichmäßige Kühlung** *f* KER & GLAS chill mark (BrE), chill wrinkle (AmE)

Runzelkorn *nt* FOTO *einer Emulsion* reticulation

Runzellack *m* KUNSTSTOFF wrinkle paint

Rupertstropfen *m* KER & GLAS Prince Rupert drop

Rupfen *nt* PAPIER picking, TEXTIL hessian

rupfen *vt* LEBENSMITTEL *Geflügel* pluck

rupfend: **~e Kupplung** *f* KFZTECH grabbing clutch

Rupffestigkeit *f* PAPIER picking resistance

Rüsche *f* TEXTIL ruffle

Rüschung *f* TEXTIL gathering

Rush-Hour *f* TRANS peak hour, rush hour

Ruß *m* KER & GLAS soot, KUNSTSTOFF carbon black

Russell-Saunders-Kopplung *f* (*L-S-Kopplung*) KERNTECH Russell-Saunders coupling (*l-s coupling*)

Ruß: **Rußpunkt** *m* MASCHINEN smoke point; **Rußschwarz** *nt* ERDÖL *Petrochemie* carbon black

Rüsteisen *nt* WASSERTRANS *Segeln* chain plate

Rüsten *nt* MASCHINEN *einer Maschine* setting up

rüsten *vt* MASCHINEN set-up

Rüster *m* WASSERTRANS *Bauholz* elm

Rüstzeit *f* COMP & DV, FERTIG *Maschine*, TEXTIL set-up time

Ruthenium *nt* (*Ru*) CHEMIE ruthenium (*Ru*); **Ruthenium-** *pref* CHEMIE ruthenic

Rutherfordium *nt* (*Rf*) CHEMIE rutherfordium (*Rf*)

Rutherford-Streuung *f* PHYS Rutherford scattering

Rutsche *f* BAU, KER & GLAS chute, MASCHINEN, MECHAN chute, slide

Rutschen *nt* BAU slippage, ELEKTROTECH slip, LUFTTRANS, TRANS skidding

rutschfest *adj* SICHERHEIT nonslip, TRANS nonskidding, WASSERTRANS nonslip

rutschfrei *adj* TRANS nonskidding

Rutschkupplung *f* MASCHINEN slip clutch

rutschsicher: **~er Bodenbelag** *m* SICHERHEIT antislip floor covering

Rutschsicherung *f* (*ASD*) KFZTECH *Bremsanlage* antiskid device, antislip device (*ASD*)

Rutschung *f* KOHLEN slide

Rüttelbeton *m* BAU vibrated concrete

Rüttelformmaschine *f* FERTIG bumper (BrE)

Rütteln *nt* TRANS jolting

Rüttelplatte *f* ABFALL tumbling station

Rüttelrost *m* FERTIG shake-out

Rüttelschaffußwalze *f* BAU vibrating sheepsfoot roller

Rüttelsieb *nt* CHEMIE vibrating screen; **Rüttelsiebrost** *m* KOHLEN vibrating grizzly

Rütteltisch *m* MASCHINEN concussion table, VERPACK jarring table

rüttelverdichten *vt* BAU *Beton* vibrate

Rüttler *m* BAU vibrator

Ruzahl *f* HEIZ & KÄLTE soot number

RWO *abbr* (*Rückwärtswellenoszillator*) ELEKTRONIK, PHYS, TELEKOM BWO (*backward-wave oscillator*)

R-Y-Achse *f* FERNSEH R-Y axis

Rydberg: **Rydberg-Energie** *f* PHYS Rydberg energy; **Rydberg-Konstante** *f* (*R, Rα*) KERNTECH Rydberg constant (*Rα*)

R-Y-Matrix *f* FERNSEH R-Y matrix

R-Y-Signal *nt* FERNSEH R-Y signal

S

S *abbr* ELEKTRIZ *(Poyntingscher Vektor)* S *(Poynting vector)*, HYDRAUL *(Gefälle)* S *(slope)*, KERNTECH *(Quellenstärke)* S *(source strength)*, KERNTECH *(spezifische Ionisierung)* S *(specific ionization)*, KERNTECH *(Anhaltleistung)* S *(stopping power)*, KERNTECH *(Spinquantengesamtzahl)* S *(total spin quantum number)*, METROL *(Siemens)* S *(siemens)*, PHYS *(Poyntingscher Vektor)* S *(Poynting vector)*

s *abbr* ELEKTRIZ *(Schlupf)* s *(slip)*, KERNTECH *(Spinquantenzahl)*, METROL *(Spinquantenzahl)*, PHYS *(Spinquantenzahl)* s *(spin quantum number)*

Saatelement *nt* KERNTECH seed assembly, seed element, spike; **Saatelementreaktor** *m* KERNTECH seed core reactor

Sabadillalkaloid *nt* CHEMIE cevadine

Sabinan *nt* CHEMIE sabinane, thujane

Sabine-Koeffizient *m* AKUSTIK Sabine coefficient

Sabinen *nt* CHEMIE sabinene, thujene

Saccharase *f* LEBENSMITTEL invertase, sucrase, *saccharosespaltendes Ferment* saccharase

Saccharat *nt* CHEMIE saccharate, sucrate

Saccharin *nt* CHEMIE saccharin

Saccharogenamylase *f* LEBENSMITTEL beta-amylase

Sachgebietswissen *nt* KÜNSTL INT domain knowledge

Sachverständigenabnahme *f* QUAL acceptance by an authorized inspector

Sack *m* KOHLEN, PAPIER bag, VERPACK sack; **Sackabfüllung** *f* VERPACK bag filling; **Sackeinsatz** *m* VERPACK insertable sack

sacken *vi* BAU *Untergrund* subside

Sack: **Sackfilter** *nt* KOHLEN bag filter; **Sackförderer** *m* TRANS bag conveyor; **Sackfüllmaschine** *f* VERPACK sack-filling machine; **Sackkammer** *f* UMWELTSCHMUTZ *Staubfilterkammer* baghouse; **Sackkarre** *f* VERPACK sack barrow; **Sackkleid** *nt* TEXTIL shift; **Sackleinwand** *f* TEXTIL hessian; **Sackloch** *nt* BAU *Bohren* blind hole; **Sackmesser** *nt* VERPACK sack knife; **Sacköffnungsmaschine** *f* VERPACK sack-opening machine; **Sackraum** *m* KOHLEN baghouse; **Sacktank** *m* LUFTTRANS *montierbar, nicht Teil des Rahmens* bladder tank

Sackung *f* ABFALL settlement, settling

Sack: **Sackverschließmaschine** *f* VERPACK sack sealer; **Sackwaage** *f* VERPACK sack scales; **Sackzunähmaschine** *f* VERPACK sack-closing sewing machine

Safranin *nt* CHEMIE safranin, safranine

Safrol *nt* CHEMIE allylmethylenedioxybenzene, safrole

Saftgehalt *m* LEBENSMITTEL juice content

Säge *f* MASCHINEN, MECHAN saw; **~ mit hin- und hergehender Schnittbewegung** *f* FERTIG reciprocating saw; **Sägeband** *nt* FERTIG saw band; **Sägebank** *f* BAU saw bench; **Sägeblatt** *nt* FERTIG saw blade, MASCHINEN blade, saw blade; **Sägeblatt mit grober Zahnteilung** *nt* FERTIG coarse-pitch blade; **Sägeblock** *m* BAU saw log; **Sägebock** *m* BAU buck (AmE), sawbuck, sawhorse; **Sägebügel** *m* MASCHINEN saw frame; **Sägefeile** *f* MASCHINEN saw file; **Sägegrat** *m* FERTIG saw burr; **Sägekerbe** *f* MASCHINEN saw kerf; **Sägemaschine** *f* BAU sawing machine, FERTIG bench saw, sawing machine, MASCHINEN sawing machine; **Sägemehl** *nt* BAU sawdust; **Sägemühle** *f* BAU sawmill;

Sägen *nt* BAU sawing

sägen *vt* BAU *Holz* cut, MECHAN saw

Säge: **Sägengewinde** *nt* FERTIG buttress screwthread, buttress thread, MASCHINEN buttress screwthread;- **Sägenut** *f* FERTIG saw groove, saw kerf; **Sägespannkluppe** *f* MASCHINEN saw clamp; **Sägeschärfmaschine** *f* MASCHINEN saw-sharpening machine; **Sägeschlitten** *m* FERTIG saw carriage; **Sägeschnitt** *m* BAU, FERTIG saw cut; **Sägeverzahnungswälzfräser** *m* FERTIG sawtooth hob; **Sägewelle** *f* MASCHINEN saw arbor (AmE), saw arbour (BrE); **Sägewerk** *nt* BAU, MASCHINEN sawmill

Sägezahn *m* FERTIG sawtooth; **Sägezahngenerator** *m* ELEKTRONIK *Kippgenerator* relaxation oscillator, ELEKTROTECH ramp generator, FERNSEH sawtooth generator; **Sägezahngewinde** *nt* BAU buttress thread, MASCHINEN buttress screwthread; **Sägezahnoszillator** *m* AUFNAHME sawtooth oscillator; **Sägezahnriß** *m* KER & GLAS serration hackle; **Sägezahnschwingungen** *f pl* ELEKTRIZ sawtooth oscillations; **Sägezahnsignale** *nt pl* ELEKTROTECH sawtooth signals; **Sägezahnspannung** *f* ELEKTRONIK linear time base, PHYS sawtooth voltage; **Sägezahnstrom** *m* FERNSEH sawtooth current; **Sägezahnteilung** *f* FERTIG saw pitch; **Sägezahnumsetzer** *m* GERÄT ramp encoder; **Sägezahnverschlüsseler** *m* GERÄT ramp encoder; **Sägezahnverschlüsselung** *f* GERÄT sawtooth conversion; **Sägezahnwellenform** *f* ELEKTROTECH ramp waveform, sawtooth waveform

saggital: **~e Brennlinie** *f* PHYS sagittal focal line; **~e Fokuslinie** *f* PHYS sagittal focal line

Saggitalebene *f* ERGON sagital plane

Saite *f* AKUSTIK chord; **Saitengalvanometer** *nt* ELEKTRIZ vibration galvanometer

sakkadisch: **~e Bewegung** *f* ERGON saccadic movement

Salacetol *nt* CHEMIE salacetol

Salantol *nt* CHEMIE salacetol, salantol

Salicin *nt* CHEMIE salicin, saligenin

Salicyl- *pref* CHEMIE salicyl; **Salicylacetol** *nt* CHEMIE salacetol, salantol; **Salicylaldehyd** *m* CHEMIE salicylaldehyde

Salicylat *nt* CHEMIE salicylate

Salicyl-: **Salicylsäurephenylester** *m* CHEMIE salol

Saligenin *nt* CHEMIE salicin, saligenin

Saline *f* LEBENSMITTEL saltern

Saling *f* WASSERTRANS *Takelage* crosstree

salinisch: **~e Quelle** *f* WASSERVERSORG saline spring

Salinität *f* CHEMIE, ERDÖL salinity

Salinometer *nt* KOHLEN salinometer

Salmanazar *f* KER & GLAS salmanazar

Salmiak *m* FERTIG *Kunststoffinstallationen* ammonium chloride; **Salmiakgeist** *m* THERMOD liquid ammonia

Salol *nt* CHEMIE salol

Salon *m* WASSERTRANS saloon; **Salondeck** *nt* WASSERTRANS saloon deck; **Salonwagen** *m* EISENBAHN club car, parlor car (AmE), saloon carriage (BrE)

Salpeter *m* KER & GLAS, LEBENSMITTEL saltpeter (AmE), saltpetre (BrE); **Salpeter-** *pref* CHEMIE nitrous; **Salpeterbildung** *f* CHEMIE nitrification

salpetersauer *adj* CHEMIE nitric

Salpetersäure[1] *f* CHEMIE, UMWELTSCHUTZ nitric acid

Salpetersäure:[2] **mit ~ behandeln** *vt* CHEMIE nitrate

Salpetrigsäureester *m* CHEMIE nitric ester

Salvarsan *nt* CHEMIE arsphenamine, salvarsan

Salz *nt* BAU, KERNTECH salt; **Salzagens** *nt* KERNTECH salting agent; **Salzbadlöten** *nt* BAU salt bath brazing; **salzbildend** *adj* CHEMIE salifiable

Salz: **Salzbildung** *f* CHEMIE salification

salzbildungsfähig *adj* CHEMIE salifiable

Salz: **Salzblase** *f* KER & GLAS salt bubble; **Salzdom** *m* ERDÖL *Geologie* salt dome; **Salzen** *nt* LEBENSMITTEL salting; **Salzgehalt** *m* CHEMIE, WASSERTRANS, WASSERVERSORG salinity

salzhaltig[1] *adj* WASSERVERSORG saline

salzhaltig:[2] **~e Luft** *f* HEIZ & KÄLTE salt-laden atmosphere; **~es Wasser** *nt* WASSERVERSORG saline water

Salz: **Salzhaltigkeit** *f* ERDÖL *Petrochemie*, NICHTFOSS ENERG, WASSERVERSORG salinity

salzig *adj* ANSTRICH saline

Salz: **Salzkissen** *nt* ERDÖL *Geologie* salt pillow; **Salzlösung** *f* KERNTECH saline solution, salt liquor; **Salzmutterlauge** *f* CHEMIE bittern; **Salznebel** *m* WERKPRÜF *Korrosionsprüfung* salt mist

salzsauer *adj* CHEMIE hydrochloric

Salz: **Salzsäure** *f* ANSTRICH, FERTIG *Kunststoffinstallationen* hydrochloric acid; **Salzschmelze** *f* FERTIG fused salt

salzschmelzengekühlt *adj* KERNTECH molten-salt-cooled

Salz: **Salzschmelzenreaktor** *m* KERNTECH molten-salt-cooled reactor; **Salzsprühnebel** *m* ANSTRICH salt spray; **Salzsprühnebelprüfung** *f* KUNSTSTOFF salt spray test; **Salzsprühnebeltest** *m* ANSTRICH salt spray test; **Salzsprühtest** *m* KER & GLAS salt spray test; **Salzsprühversuch** *m* KUNSTSTOFF salt spray test; **Salzstock** *m* ERDÖL *Geologie* salt diapir; **Salztektonik** *f* ERDÖL *Geologie* salt tectonics; **Salzton** *m* KER & GLAS saliferous clay; **Salzwasser** *nt* WASSERTRANS seawater, WASSERVERSORG saline water, salt water; **Salzwasserumwandlung** *f* WASSERVERSORG saline water conversion

Samarium *nt (Sm)* CHEMIE samarium *(Sm)*; **Samariumeffekt** *m* KERNTECH samarium effect

Sammelanschluß *m* TELEKOM collective line

Sammelaufruf *m* TELEKOM multipolling

Sammelbatterie *f* KFZTECH storage battery

Sammelbecken *nt* NICHTFOSS ENERG storage basin, upper storage basin

Sammelbehälter *m* BAU sump pan, ERDÖL *Raffinerie* receiver, UMWELTSCHUTZ storage tank

Sammelelektrode *f* ELEKTROTECH collector electrode

Sammelgefäß *nt* LABOR receiver

Sammelgleis *nt* EISENBAHN main track, recessing siding; **~ für Rangieren** *nt* EISENBAHN advance classification track

Sammelgraben *m* WASSERVERSORG collecting ditch

Sammelgrube *f* BAU catchpit, collecting pit

Sammelgüterzug *m* EISENBAHN pick-up goods train (BrE), way freight train (AmE)

Sammelgutverkehr *m* EISENBAHN groupage traffic

Sammelgutwagen *m* EISENBAHN groupage car (AmE),

groupage wagon (BrE)

Sammelherd *m* FERTIG recipient

Sammelkanal *m* ABFALL main collector, main sewer

Sammelleitung *f* ELEKTRIZ bus line, MASCHINEN manifold; **Sammelleitungsschalter** *m* ELEKTRIZ bus coupler switch

Sammellinse *f* FOTO convex lens, PHYS, WELLPHYS converging lens

sammelnd: ~es Aufschreiben *nt* COMP & DV gather write

Sammelpunkt *m* TRANS *Notfall* assembly area

Sammelreagens *nt* KOHLEN collecting reagent

Sammelrohr *nt* FERTIG header, MASCHINEN header, manifold, MECHAN header

Sammelschiene *f* COMP & DV, ELEKTRIZ busbar, ELEKTROTECH bus, busbar, MASCHINEN, TELEKOM busbar; **Sammelschienensystem** *nt* ELEKTRIZ busbar system; **Sammelschienen-Trennschalter** *m* ELEKTRIZ busbar-sectionalizing switch; **Sammelschienenverbinder** *m* ELEKTRIZ busbar coupler

Sammeltank *m* ABFALL collection tank, ERDÖL *Raffinerie, Bohrtechnik* accumulator tank

Sammelzeichnung *f* KONSTZEICH collection drawing

Sammler *m* BAU main line, ELEKTROTECH secondary cell, ERDÖL *Leitungsbau* manifold, pipe manifold, KOHLEN collecting agent, collector; **Sammlerzelle** *f* ELEKTRIZ accumulator cell, ELEKTROTECH storage cell

Sammlung *f* ELEKTROTECH *Elektronen, Strom* collection; **~ von Hausmüll** *f* ABFALL garbage disposal (AmE), refuse disposal (BrE)

Sampler *m* COMP & DV sampler

Sampling *nt* COMP & DV sampling; **Sampling-Oszilloskop** *nt* GERÄT sampling oscilloscope; **Sampling-Theorem** *nt* GERÄT sampling theorem; **Sampling-Verstärker** *m* ELEKTRONIK sampling amplifier

Samt *m* TEXTIL velvet; **Samtdichtung** *f* FOTO velvet trap

Sand[1] *m* KOHLEN sand

Sand:[2] **mit ~ abdecken** *vt* BAU sand; **mit ~ bestreuen** *vt* BAU grit

Sand: **Sandäquivalent** *nt* BAU sand equivalent; **Sandbad** *nt* LABOR *Erhitzen* sand bath; **Sandbelag auf Herdbank** *m* KER & GLAS breezing; **Sandboden** *m* WASSERTRANS sandy bottom; **Sandfalle** *f* ERDÖL *Geologie* sand trap; **Sandfang** *m* ABFALL sand filter, ERDÖL desander, WASSERVERSORG sand trap; **Sandfanganlage** *f* ABFALL detritor, grit chamber, sand trap; **Sandfänger** *m* ABFALL detritor, grit chamber, sand trap; **Sandfilter** *nt* ABFALL, KOHLEN sand filter; **Sandform** *f* FERTIG sand mold (AmE), sand mould (BrE)

sandfrei *adj* ERDÖL *Bohrung* free from sand

Sand: **Sandgrund** *m* WASSERTRANS sandy bottom; **Sandguß** *m* FERTIG *Zahnräder* sand casting

sandhaltig *adj* NICHTFOSS ENERG arenaceous

sandhydraulisch: ~es Naßgußputzverfahren *nt* FERTIG *Gießen* high-pressure water and sand cleaning; **~e Naßputzanlage** *f* FERTIG high-pressure water and sand cleaning plant, hydroblasting plant

sandig[1] *adj* NICHTFOSS ENERG arenaceous

sandig:[2] **~er Lehm** *m* BAU sandy loam

Sand: **Sandkruste** *f* FERTIG *Gießen* sand skin; **Sandleiste** *f* FERTIG *Gießen* lifter; **Sandpapier** *nt* DRUCK sandpaper, ELEKTRIZ abrasive paper, FERTIG, MECHAN sandpaper; **Sandpumpe** *f* ERDÖL *Seilbohren* sand pump; **Sandseil** *nt* ERDÖL *Seilbohren* sand line; **Sandseiltrommel** *f* ERDÖL *Seilbohren* sand reel; **Sandsieber** *m* FERTIG sand sifter; **Sandstein** *m* BAU, ERDÖL -Geologie sandstone

Sandstrahl *m* FERTIG sandblast; **Sandstrahlbehandlung** *f* MECHAN sandblasting; **Sandstrahldüse** *f* KER & GLAS sandblasting nozzle; **Sandstrahlen** *nt* BAU blasting, grit blasting, sandblasting, FERTIG, KER & GLAS sandblasting, MECHAN grit blasting, MEERSCHMUTZ, WASSERTRANS *Schiffinstandhaltung* sandblasting

sandstrahlen *vt* MECHAN sandblast

Sandstrahl: **Sandstrahlgebläse** *nt* KER & GLAS sandblast apparatus; **Sandstrahlmattierung** *f* KER & GLAS sandblast obscuring; **Sandstrahlreinigung** *nt* MEERSCHMUTZ sandblasting

Sand: **Sandstrak** *m* WASSERTRANS *Schiffbau* garboard strake; **Sandton** *m* BAU sandy clay; **Sand/Ton-Verhältnis** *nt* ERDÖL *Geologie* sand-shale ratio; **Sandwäsche** *f* ERDÖL sand washing

sanft: **auf ~en Ausfall konstruiert** *adj* KONTROLL fail-soft

Sanierungsmaßnahme *f* UMWELTSCHMUTZ measure of redevelopment

sanitär: **~e Einrichtungen** *f pl* WASSERVERSORG sanitation

Sanitärkeramik *f* KER & GLAS sanitary ware

Sanitärtechnik *f* WASSERVERSORG sanitary engineering

Sanitätswache *f* WASSERTRANS first-aid post

Santon- *pref* CHEMIE santonic; **Santonin** *nt* CHEMIE santonin; **Santoninlacton** *nt* CHEMIE santonin

Saphir *m* ELEKTRONIK sapphire; **Saphir-Trägermaterial** *nt* ELEKTRONIK sapphire substrate

Sapogenin *nt* CHEMIE sapogenine

Saponin *nt* CHEMIE saponin

SAR *abbr* (*Such- und Rettungsdienst*) WASSERTRANS *Notfall* SAR (*search and rescue*)

Sarcosin *nt* CHEMIE N-methylaminoacetic acid, sarcosine

Sarkin *nt* CHEMIE hypoxanthine, sarkine

SAR: **SAR-Leitstelle** *f* LUFTTRANS, WASSERTRANS RCC, rescue coordination center (AmE), rescue coordination centre (BrE)

Satcom *abbr* (*Satellitenfunk*) RADIO, TELEKOM, WASSERTRANS satcom (*satellite communication*)

Satellit *m* PHYS, TRANS satellite; **~ in Äquatorialumlaufbahn** *m* RAUMFAHRT equatorial orbiting satellite; **~ in Umlaufbahn** *m* RAUMFAHRT orbiting satellite; **~ zur Umweltuntersuchung** *m* RAUMFAHRT environment survey satellite; **Satellitenamt** *nt* TELEKOM satellite exchange; **Satellitenapogäumstriebwerksgruppe** *f* RAUMFAHRT satellite apogee motor combination; **Satellitenausleuchtungsbereich** *m* FERNSEH satellite coverage area; **Satellitendatenstation** *f* COMP & DV satellite terminal; **Satellitenfernmeßtechnik** *f* GERÄT satellite telemetry; **Satellitenfunk** *m* (*Satcom*) RADIO, TELEKOM, WASSERTRANS satellite communication, satellite radio (*satcom*); **Satellitenfunkortungssystem** *nt* (*RDSS*) RADIO, TRANS, WASSERTRANS radio determination satellite system (*RDSS*); **Satellitenfunkverbindung** *f* FERNSEH satellite link

satellitengeschaltet: **~er TDMA** *m* RAUMFAHRT *Weltraumfunk* satellite-switched TDMA

satellitengestützt: **~er Such- und Rettungsdienst auf See** *m* TELEKOM satellite-aided maritime search and rescue system

Satellit: **Satellitenkonstruktion** *f* RAUMFAHRT satellite design; **Satellitenlagerstätte** *f* ERDÖL moonpool; **Satelliten-Mehrdienstsystem** *nt* TELEKOM Satellite Multiservice System; **Satellitenmeteorologie** *f* RAUMFAHRT satellite meteorology; **Satelliten-Mobilfunk** *m* TELEKOM land mobile satellite service; **Satellitennavi-**

gation *f* (*Satnav*) WASSERTRANS satellite navigation (*satnav*); **Satellitennavigationsgerät** *nt* WASSERTRANS satellite navigator; **Satellitennetzwerk zur Ortung von Schiffen in Seenot** *nt* (*EPIRB*) WASSERTRANS emergency position-indicating radio beacon (*EPIRB*); **Satellitennotfunkbake mit Standortangabe** *f* TELEKOM satellite emergency position-indicating radio beacon; **Satellitennutzlast** *f* RAUMFAHRT satellite payload; **Satellitenrechner** *m* COMP & DV satellite computer; **Satellitenrundfunksendung** *f* FERNSEH satellite telecast; **Satellitenschaltung** *f* RAUMFAHRT satellite switching; **Satellitenschüssel** *f* FERNSEH satellite dish; **Satellitensystem-Betriebsanleitung** *f* (*SSOG*) RAUMFAHRT *Weltraumfunk* satellite system operation guide (*SSOG*); **Satellitentechnik** *f* RAUMFAHRT satellite design; **Satellitenübertragung** *f* TELEKOM satellite transmission; **Satellitenverbindung** *f* RAUMFAHRT satellite link

Satinage *f* PAPIER glazing

satinieren *vt* FOTO glaze

Satiniermaschine *f* VERPACK glazing machine

Satnav *abbr* (*Satellitennavigation*) WASSERTRANS satnav (*satellite navigation*)

satt *adj* DRUCK saturated, FERTIG *Auflage* tight

Sattdampf *m* HEIZ & KÄLTE, MASCHINEN saturated steam, NICHTFOSS ENERG wet steam, THERMOD saturated steam

sattdampfgekühlt[1] *adj* HEIZ & KÄLTE saturated steam-cooled

sattdampfgekühlt:[2] **~er Reaktor** *m* KERNTECH saturated steam-cooled reactor

Sattel *m* MASCHINEN saddle; **~ der Scheibenbremse** *m* EISENBAHN disc brake calliper (BrE), disk brake caliper (AmE); **Sattelauflieger** *m* KFZTECH *Sattelschlepper, Sattelzug* semitrailer, MECHAN trailer; **Sattelauflieger mit Plane** *m* TRANS tilt-type semitrailer; **Sattelbahn** *f* EISENBAHN monorail with straddling cars; **Sattelbahnfahrzeug** *nt* EISENBAHN vehicle straddling the guideway; **Sattelblech** *nt* BAU ridge plate; **Satteldach** *nt* BAU couple close roof, ridge roof, shed roof; **Satteleinschienenbahn** *f* EISENBAHN saddle bag monorail; **Sattelheftung** *f* DRUCK saddle stitching; **Sattelholz** *nt* BAU saddle; **Sattelkombination** *f* TRANS saddle mount combination; **Sattelkraftfahrzeug** *nt* KFZTECH semitrailer motor truck (AmE), semitrailer motor vehicle (BrE); **Sattelkupplung** *f* KFZTECH *Sattelschlepper* fifth wheel; **Sattelpunkt** *m* MATH saddle point, METALL node, saddle point; **Sattelrevolverdrehmaschine** *f* MASCHINEN capstan lathe, ram-type turret lathe; **Sattelschlepper** *m* BAU bogie (BrE), trailer (AmE), KFZTECH articulated vehicle, articulated lorry (BrE), articulated truck (AmE); **Sattelschlepperzug** *m* KFZTECH articulated lorry (BrE), articulated truck (AmE); **Satteltrichterwagen** *m* EISENBAHN hopper wagon; **Sattelverschluß** *m* KER & GLAS saddled finish; **Sattelwagen** *m* EISENBAHN saddle-bottomed car; **Sattelwange** *f* BAU cut stringer, *Treppe* open wall string; **Sattelzug** *m* EISENBAHN articulated train, KFZTECH articulated vehicle; **Sattelzugmaschine** *f* KFZTECH semitrailer towing truck (AmE), semitrailer towing vehicle (BrE), semitrailer lorry (BrE), semitrailer truck (AmE)

Sättigung *f* COMP & DV, ELEKTRIZ, ELEKTRONIK, ELEKTROTECH, FERNSEH, HEIZ & KÄLTE, KERNTECH, PAPIER, PHYS, RADIO saturation, RAUMFAHRT *Weltraumfunk* saturation point; **Sättigungs-Ausgangsleistung** *f*

ELEKTRONIK saturation output power; **Sättigungs-Ausgangsstatus** *m* ELEKTRONIK saturation output state; **Sättigungsbedingungen** *f pl* ELEKTROTECH saturation conditions; **Sättigungsbereich** *m* ELEKTRONIK saturation region; **Sättigungsbetriebsart** *f* ELEKTRONIK saturated mode; **Sättigungscharakteristik** *f* STRAHLPHYS saturation characteristic; **Sättigungsdampfdruck** *m* HEIZ & KÄLTE, PHYS saturated vapor pressure (AmE), saturated vapour pressure (BrE), saturation vapor pressure (AmE), saturation vapour pressure (BrE); **Sättigungsdrossel** *f* ELEKTROTECH saturable reactor; **Sättigungsdruck** *m* THERMOD saturation pressure

sättigungsfähig: ~e Drossel *m* PHYS *magnetischer Verstärker* saturable reactor

Sättigung: **Sättigungsgrad** *m* AUFNAHME saturation level, KOHLEN, MASCHINEN, TRANS degree of saturation; **Sättigungshärten** *nt* METALL saturation hardening; **Sättigungsinduktion** *f* ELEKTRIZ saturation magnetization, ELEKTROTECH saturation induction; **Sättigungskonzentration** *f* HEIZ & KÄLTE, THERMOD saturation concentration; **Sättigungskurve** *f* THERMOD saturation curve; **Sättigungslinie** *f* THERMOD saturation curve; **Sättigungslogik** *f* KONTROLL saturation logic; **Sättigungsmagnetisierung** *f* ELEKTROTECH saturation magnetization; **Sättigungsmittel** *nt* CHEMIE saturant; **Sättigungspunkt** *m* HEIZ & KÄLTE saturation point; **Sättigungssieden** *nt* KERNTECH saturated boiling; **Sättigungssignal** *nt* ELEKTRONIK saturation signal; **Sättigungsspannung** *f* ELEKTROTECH saturation voltage; **Sättigungsstörung** *f* COMP & DV saturation noise; **Sättigungsstreifenbildung** *f* FERNSEH banding on saturation; **Sättigungsstrom** *m* *(IS)* ELEKTRONIK, PHYS, RADIO saturation current *(IS)*; **Sättigungstemperatur** *f* HEIZ & KÄLTE saturation temperature; **Sättigungstest** *m* COMP & DV saturation testing; **Sättigungstransformator** *m* ELEKTROTECH saturable transformer; **Sättigungstransistor** *m* ELEKTRONIK saturated transistor; **Sättigungszeilenbildung** *f* FERNSEH saturation banding

Satz:[1] **zu einem ~ zusammengestellt** *adj* FERTIG ganged

Satz[2] *m* COMP & DV record, set, DRUCK composition, matter, typesetting, LEBENSMITTEL batch, MASCHINEN set; **~ von Ersatzlinsen** *m* FOTO set of supplementary lenses; **~ mit fester Länge** *m* COMP & DV fixed-length record; **~ Gewichte** *m* LABOR set of weights; **~ von Patentansprüchen** *m* PATENT set of claims; **~ des Pythagoras** *m* MATH Pythagoras' theorem; **~ mit variabler Länge** *m* COMP & DV variable-length record; **~ Wechselräder** *m* MASCHINEN set of change wheels; **~ Werkzeuge** *m* MASCHINEN tool set

Satz:[3] **zu einem ~ zusammenstellen** *vt* MASCHINEN gang

Satz: **Satzanordnung** *f* DRUCK layout; **Satzanweisung** *f* COMP & DV record line; **Satzanzahl** *f* COMP & DV record count; **Satzart** *f* COMP & DV record type; **Satzaufspannung** *f* FERTIG ganging; **Satzbetrieb** *m* CHEMTECH batch processing, batchwise operation, LEBENSMITTEL batchwise operation; **Satzbreite** *f* DRUCK measure; **Satzende** *nt* COMP & DV end of record; **Satzfahnen** *f pl* DRUCK typesetting galleys

satzfertig *adj* DRUCK ready for typesetting

Satz: **Satzfirma** *f* DRUCK typesetting company; **Satzfläche** *f* DRUCK live area, text area, type area; **Satzformat** *nt* COMP & DV record format, record layout; **Satzfortschreibung** *f* COMP & DV record updating; **Satzfräsen** *nt* FERTIG, MASCHINEN gang milling; **Satzfräser** *m*

MASCHINEN gang-milling cutter; **Satzfräsmaschine** *f* MASCHINEN gang-milling cutter; **Satzgruppe** *f* COMP & DV record set, TELEKOM circuit group; **Satzlänge** *f* COMP & DV record length; **Satzmodus** *m* COMP & DV record mode

satzreif *adj* DRUCK ready for typesetting

Satz: **Satzspiegel** *m* DRUCK live area, text area, type area; **Satztrennzeichen** *nt* COMP & DV record separator

satzweise: ~ ineinander anordnen *vt* FERTIG nest

Satz: **Satzzeichen** *nt pl* DRUCK punctuation marks; **Satzzeichnung** *f* KONSTZEICH set drawing

sauber[1] *adj* SICHERHEIT clean

sauber:[2] **~er Abzug** *m* DRUCK clean proof; **~er Schnee** *m* UMWELTSCHMUTZ clean snow; **~er Schnitt** *m* KER & GLAS clean cut; **~e Technologie** *f* ABFALL NWT, clean technology; **~e Umgebung** *f* HEIZ & KÄLTE clean situation

Sauberkeitsschicht *f* BAU subbase, *Tiefbau* base course

Säuberung *f* MEERSCHMUTZ clean-up; **~ der Küstenlinie** *f* MEERSCHMUTZ shoreline clean-up; **Säuberungsmethode** *f* MEERSCHMUTZ clean-up technique; **Säuberungsverfahren** *nt* MEERSCHMUTZ clean-up technique

sauer[1] *adj* LEBENSMITTEL sour; **~ zugestellt** *adj* FERTIG acid-lined

sauer:[2] **saurer Abfluß** *m* UMWELTSCHMUTZ acid runoff; **saures Abgas** *nt* ABFALL acid waste gas; **saure Ablagerung** *f* UMWELTSCHMUTZ acid deposit; **saures Aerosol** *nt* UMWELTSCHMUTZ acid aerosol; **saure Ausmauerung** *f* FERTIG acid bottom and lining, acid lining; **saures Bad** *nt* FOTO acid bath; **saurer Boden** *m* UMWELTSCHMUTZ acid soil; **saures Carbonat** *nt* CHEMIE hydrocarbonate; **saure Erde** *f* UMWELTSCHMUTZ acid earth; **saures Erdgas** *nt* ERDÖL sour gas; **saures Fixierbad** *nt* CHEMTECH, FOTO acid fixing bath; **saures Futter** *nt* FERTIG acid lining; **saure Lösung** *f* LEBENSMITTEL acid solution; **saurer Niederschlag** *m* UMWELTSCHMUTZ acid fallout, acid rain, acidic rain; **saurer Regen** *m* ANSTRICH acid rain, UMWELTSCHMUTZ acid rain, *spezifisch* acid fallout, *speziell* acidic rain; **saures Rohöl** *nt* ERDÖL sour crude; **saures Salz** *nt* LEBENSMITTEL acid salt; **saurer Schnee** *m* UMWELTSCHMUTZ acid snow; **saurer See** *m* UMWELTSCHMUTZ acid lake, acidified lake; **nicht saurer See** *m* UMWELTSCHMUTZ nonacidic lake; **saures Teilchen** *nt* UMWELTSCHMUTZ acid particle, acidic particle; **saure Umweltverschmutzung** *f* UMWELTSCHMUTZ acid pollution; **saures Verfahren** *nt* PAPIER acid process; **saures Wasser** *nt* UMWELTSCHMUTZ acid water; **~ zugestellter SM-Ofen** *m* FERTIG acid open-hearth furnace

sauer:[3] **~ werden** *vi* UMWELTSCHMUTZ acidify

Sauergas *nt* ERDÖL sour gas

säuerlich *adj* CHEMIE acidulous, sourish

Säuern *nt* CHEMIE acidulating

säuern[1] *vt* CHEMIE, LEBENSMITTEL, PAPIER, TEXTIL, UMWELTSCHMUTZ acidify

säuern[2] *vi* ANSTRICH acidify

säuernd *adj* PAPIER acidifying

Sauerstoff:[1] **mit ~ angereichert** *adj* CHEMIE oxidized

Sauerstoff[2] *m* CHEMIE oxygen

Sauerstoff:[3] **mit ~ anreichern** *vt* CHEMIE oxygenate

Sauerstoffversorgung bereitstellen *vi* SICHERHEIT provide an oxygen supply

Sauerstoff: **Sauerstoffalterung in der Druckkammer** *f* KUNSTSTOFF *Kautschuk* oxygen bomb ageing (BrE), oxygen bomb aging (AmE); **Sauerstoffanreicherung** f CHEMIE oxygenation, KER & GLAS oxygen boosting; **Sauerstoffatemgerät** *nt* RAUMFAHRT oxygen respirator, SICHERHEIT oxygen breathing apparatus; **Sauerstoffblasstahl** *m* METALL basic oxygen steel; **Sauerstoffbohren** *nt* BAU oxygen lancing; **Sauerstoffbrennschneiden** *nt* MASCHINEN oxycutting, oxygen cutting; **Sauerstofferzeuger** *m* BAU oxygen generator; **Sauerstoff-Flasche** f FERTIG, RAUMFAHRT oxygen cylinder

sauerstoff-frei: ~**e Säure** f CHEMIE hydracid

sauerstoffhaltig *adj* CHEMIE oxidic

Sauerstoff: **Sauerstoffhobeln** *nt* FERTIG gouging

sauerstoffhobeln *vt* FERTIG torch-gouge

Sauerstoff: **Sauerstoffindex** *m (LOI)* KUNSTSTOFF limiting oxygen index *(LOI)*; **Sauerstofflanze** f MASCHINEN oxygen lance; **Sauerstoff-Lichtbogenschneiden** *nt* BAU oxyarc cutting, oxygen arc cutting; **Sauerstoff-Lichtbogen-Schneidverfahren** *nt* FERTIG oxyarc cutting, oxygen arc cutting; **Sauerstoffmaske** f RAUMFAHRT, SICHERHEIT oxygen mask; **Sauerstoffofen** *m* KOHLEN oxygen furnace; **Sauerstoffschneiden** *nt* MECHAN oxycutting, oxygen cutting; **Sauerstoffträger** *m* ANSTRICH oxidizer, CHEMIE oxidant; **Sauerstoffvorrat** *m* RAUMFAHRT oxygen supply; **Sauerstoffzufuhrregler** *m* RAUMFAHRT oxygen regulator

Sauerteig *m* LEBENSMITTEL leaven, sour dough

Säuerung f ERDÖL *Bohrung* acidization, PAPIER acidification

säuerungsfähig *adj* CHEMIE, PAPIER acidifiable

Säuerungsmittel *nt* CHEMIE acidifier, TEXTIL acidifying agent

Saug- *pref* BAU, KER & GLAS, MEERSCHMUTZ, WASSERTRANS, WASSERVERSORG sucking; **Saug- und Druckpumpe** f WASSERVERSORG lift-and-force pump; **Saugabschöpfgerät** *nt* MEERSCHMUTZ *für Öl von der Wasseroberfläche* direct-suction skimmer; **Saugbagger** *m* BAU pump dredger, WASSERTRANS suction dredge, suction dredger, WASSERVERSORG suction dredge; **Saugbagger mit Laderaum** *m* WASSERTRANS *Baggern* suction hopper dredge, suction hopper dredger; **Saugbaggerlöffel** *m* WASSERTRANS dredger bucket; **Saug-Blas-Verfahren** *nt* KER & GLAS suck-and-blow process; **Saugbrenner** *m* BAU low-pressure blowpipe; **Saugdrosselventil** *nt* KFZTECH suction throttling valve

Saugen *nt* HEIZ & KÄLTE, TEXTIL suction

saugen *vt* WASSERVERSORG *Quellwasser* draw

Sauger *m* MECHAN exhauster

saugfähig[1] *adj* CHEMIE absorbent, PAPIER absorptive

saugfähig:[2] ~**er Beutel** *m* VERPACK moisture-absorbent bag

Saugfähigkeit f PAPIER absorptive capacity, VERPACK absorbency; **Saugfähigkeitswert** *m* PAPIER absorbency value

Saug-: **Saugfegmaschine** f ABFALL vacuum street sweeper; **Saugfilter** *nt* ABFALL suction filter, CHEMTECH suction strainer, FERTIG suction filter, KOHLEN vacuum filter, WASSERVERSORG suction filter; **Saugform** f KER & GLAS suction mold (AmE), suction mould (BrE); **Sauggautsche** f PAPIER suction couch roll; **Sauggebläse** *nt* HEIZ & KÄLTE exhaust fan, LABOR aspirator; **Saugheber** *m* BAU plunger elevator; **Saughöhe** f FERTIG *Pumpe* lift (BrE), KOHLEN capillary rise, WASSERVERSORG suction head, suction lift; **Saughöhenprüfgerät** *nt* PAPIER bibliometer;

Saughopperbagger *m* WASSERTRANS suction hopper dredge, suction hopper dredger; **Saughub** *m* FERTIG intake stroke; **Saugkammer** f FERTIG suction port, *Pumpe* inlet chamber, KFZTECH suction chamber; **Saugkasten** *m* PAPIER suction box, vacuum box; **Saugkastenbelag** *m* PAPIER suction box cover; **Saugkopf** *m* MEERSCHMUTZ *an Abschöpfgerät* skimming head; **Saugkorb** *m* FERTIG suction strainer, *Kunststoffinstallationen* screen assembly, MEERSCHMUTZ strainer, WASSERVERSORG rose, strainer; **Saugkreis** *m* ELEKTRIZ acceptor, acceptor circuit, RADIO acceptor circuit; **Saugleitung** f FERTIG suction line, MECHAN intake manifold, SICHERHEIT *Feuerwehr* suction hose, WASSERVERSORG suction pipe; **Saugluft** f HEIZ & KÄLTE suction air, MASCHINEN forced draft (AmE), forced draught (BrE); **Saugluftbremse** f EISENBAHN vacuum brake, MASCHINEN atmospheric brake, vacuum brake; **Sauglüfter** *m* MASCHINEN exhaust fan, extraction fan, extractor fan, suction fan; **Saugluftkühlung** f HEIZ & KÄLTE forced-draft cooling (AmE), forced-draught cooling (BrE); **Saugmaschine** f KER & GLAS suction machine; **Saugmotor** *m* KFZTECH unsupercharged engine; **Saugmund** *m* ABFALL *am Kehrfahrzeug* suction port; **Saugpapier** *nt* DRUCK absorbent paper; **Saugpumpe** f HYDRAUL aspiration pump, aspiring pump, suction pump, LEBENSMITTEL suction pump, MASCHINEN aspiration pump, drawing pump, double-acting pump, PAPIER, TEXTIL suction pump, WASSERVERSORG lift pump, suction pump; **Saugrohr** *nt* BAU tail pipe, KFZTECH, MASCHINEN suction pipe, NICHTFOSS ENERG draft tube (AmE), draught tube (BrE), WASSERTRANS suction pipe, WASSERVERSORG suction pipe, tail pipe; **Saugschlauch** *m* WASSERVERSORG suction hose; **Saugseite** f FERTIG *Pumpe* inlet side, MASCHINEN inlet side, suction side; **Saugspeisen** *nt* KER & GLAS suction feeding; **Saugstrahlpumpe** f LABOR syphon; **Saugventil** *nt* FERTIG *Pumpe* inlet valve, HEIZ & KÄLTE, HYDRAUL, KFZTECH, MASCHINEN suction valve; **Saugventilator** *m* MECHAN exhaust fan; **Saugwalzenfilz** *m* PAPIER suction roll felt

Saugzug *m* BAU forced draft (AmE), forced draught (BrE), HEIZ & KÄLTE, MASCHINEN induced draft (AmE), induced draught (BrE); **Saugzugbrenner** *m* HEIZ & KÄLTE induced-draft burner (AmE), induced-draught burner (BrE); **Saugzuglüfter** *m* HEIZ & KÄLTE induced-draft fan (AmE), induced-draught fan (BrE), suction fan; **Saugzugventilator** *m* MASCHINEN induced-draft fan (AmE), induced-draught fan (BrE)

Säule f BAU pillar, support, upright, *Wasser* head, EISENBAHN pillar, ELEKTROTECH *bei Batterie* pile, KER & GLAS, KOHLEN pillar, LABOR *eines Barometers* cup, MASCHINEN column, pillar, TRANS pillar; **Säulenbogen** *m* KER & GLAS pillar arch; **Säulenbohrmaschine** f MASCHINEN column-type drilling machine, pillar drill, pillar-drilling machine; **Säulenführung** f FERTIG die set, MASCHINEN pillar guide; **Säulengewölbe** *nt* KER & GLAS pillar arch; **Säulenhals** *m* BAU neck molding (AmE), neck moulding (BrE); **Säuleninsolator** *m* ELEKTROTECH post insulator; **Säulenkran** *m* BAU post crane; **Säulenpresse** f MASCHINEN pillar press; **Säulenschaft** *m* BAU shaft, shank; **Säulenwaage** f LABOR pillar scales

Saum *m* BAU *Stoff*, MECHAN seam, PHYS fringe, TEXTIL hem, seam

Säumen *nt* TEXTIL seaming

säumen *vt* TEXTIL seam

Säure:[1] durch ~ belastet *adj* UMWELTSCHMUTZ acid-stressed

Säure[2] *f* LEBENSMITTEL, PAPIER, TEXTIL acid

Säure:[3] mit ~ behandeln *vt* PAPIER acidize

Säure: **Säureabscheidebehälter** *m* ERDÖL *Raffinerie-technik* acid decantation drum; **Säureakzeptor** *m* KUNSTSTOFF acid acceptor; **Säureamid** *nt* LEBENSMITTEL acid amide; **Säureätzung** *f* MASCHINEN acid etching; **Säureauslaugung** *m* FERTIG acid leach; **Säurebad** *nt* PAPIER acid bath; **Säure-Basen-Gleichgewicht** *nt* LEBENSMITTEL *in Körpersäften* acid base balance; **Säurebehälter** *m* FERTIG acid reservoir; **Säurebeizung** *f* KERNTECH acid pickling; **Säurebelastung** *f* UMWELTSCHMUTZ acid loading, acid stress

säurebeständig[1] *adj* FERTIG acid-proof, acid-resistant, PAPIER acid-proof, UMWELTSCHMUTZ acid-proof, acid-resistant, VERPACK acid-resistant

säurebeständig:[2] ~e Schutzhandschuhe *m pl* SICHERHEIT acid-proof protective gloves

Säure: **Säurebeständigkeit** *f* KUNSTSTOFF, UMWELTSCHMUTZ acid resistance; **Säurebestimmung** *f* PAPIER acid determination

säurebildend *adj* CHEMIE acidic, FERTIG acid-forming

Säure: **Säurebildner** *m* FERTIG acid former, PAPIER acidifier; **Säurechlorid** *nt* LEBENSMITTEL acid chloride

säuredicht: ~e Batterie *f* KFZTECH *KFZ-Elektrik* non-spill battery

Säure: **Säuredichtemeßgerät** *nt* GERÄT acid density meter; **Säuredruckbehälter** *m* ERDÖL *Raffinerie* acid blow case; **Säuredruckvorlage** *f* CHEMTECH acid elevator

säureecht *adj* VERPACK acid-resistant

Säure: **Säureerhitzungsprobe** *f* ERDÖL *Raffinerie*, PAPIER acid heat test; **Säureester** *m* LEBENSMITTEL acid ester; **Säurefällung** *f* UMWELTSCHMUTZ acid precipitation; **Säurefarbstoff** *m* CHEMIE, TEXTIL acid dye

säurefest: ~e Farbe *f* BAU acid-resisting paint; ~er Lack *m* VERPACK acid-proof varnish; ~es Papier *nt* DRUCK acid-proof paper

säurefrei[1] *adj* PAPIER acid-free, VERPACK acidless

säurefrei:[2] ~er Kleber *m* FOTO acid-free glue; ~es Öl *nt* ERDÖL chemically neutral oil; ~es Papier *nt* DRUCK, VERPACK acid-free paper

Säuregehalt *m* PAPIER, UMWELTSCHMUTZ acidity, VERPACK acid content; **Säuregehaltsmeßgerät** *nt* PHYS hydrometer; **Säuregehaltsmessung** *f* PHYS hydrometry; **Säuregehaltsprüfer** *m* CHEMTECH acidimeter

Säuregrad *m* CHEMIE free acid, PAPIER acid value, UMWELTSCHMUTZ acidity level; **Säuregradmesser** *m* LEBENSMITTEL acidimeter; **Säuregradmessung** *f* CHEMIE, CHEMTECH, LEBENSMITTEL acidimetry

säurehaltig *adj* CHEMIE acidiferous, ERDÖL acidic, PAPIER acidiferous

Säure: **Säurehärter** *m* FERTIG acid catalyst, acid hardening; **Säurehydrazid** *nt* CHEMIE hydrazide; **Säurekennzeichnen** *nt* KER & GLAS acid badging; **Säurekitt** *m* FERTIG acid-proof cement; **Säurekonzentration** *f* UMWELTSCHMUTZ acid concentration; **Säuremarke** *f* KER & GLAS acid mark

säuremattiert: ~es Milchglas *nt* KER & GLAS acid-etched frosted glass

Säure: **Säuremattierung** *f* KER & GLAS acid etching; **Säuremesser** *m* PAPIER acidimeter

säuren *vt* PAPIER sour

Säure: **Säurenebel** *m* UMWELTSCHMUTZ acid fog; **Säureneutralisation** *f* UMWELTSCHMUTZ acid neutralizing;

Säureneutralisierungsvermögen *nt* UMWELTSCHMUTZ acid-neutralizing capacity; **Säurevorstufe** *f* UMWELTSCHMUTZ acidic precursor; **Säurepolitur** *f* KER & GLAS acid polishing; **Säureprägen** *nt* KER & GLAS acid embossing; **Säureprüfer** *m* PAPIER acid tester, PHYS hydrometer

Säure: **Säureradikal** *nt* LEBENSMITTEL acid radical

säureresistent: ~er Wand- und Fußbodenbelag *m* SICHERHEIT acid-resisting floor and wall covering

Säure: **Säurer** *m* ERDÖL acidizer; **Säurerest** *m* LEBENSMITTEL acid radical; **Säurerückgewinnung** *f* FERTIG acid recovery; **Säurerückgewinnungsanlage** *f* ERDÖL *Raffinerie* acid recovery plant; **Säureschock** *m* UMWELTSCHMUTZ acid shock; **Säurespaltung** *f* LEBENSMITTEL acidolysis; **Säurespiegel** *m* KFZTECH acid level; **Säuretauchbad** *nt* CHEMTECH acid dipping; **Säureturm** *m* PAPIER absorption tower; **Säureverträglichkeit** *f* UMWELTSCHMUTZ *des Bodens* acid tolerance; **Säurevorbeizung** *f* KERNTECH acid prepickling; **Säurewäsche** *f* PAPIER acid washing; **Säurewecker** *m* LEBENSMITTEL *bei Milchprodukten* starter; **Säurewert** *m (AV)* CHEMIE acid value *(AV)*; **Säurewiderstandsfähigkeit** *f* UMWELTSCHMUTZ acid tolerance; **Säurezahl** *f* ERDÖL *Petrochemie* acid number, KUNSTSTOFF *(SZ)*, LEBENSMITTEL *(SZ)* acid value

SAW-Bauelement *nt* ELEKTRONIK, TELEKOM SAW device

SAW-Expansionsfilter *nt* ELEKTRONIK SAW expansion filter

SAW-Filterung *f* ELEKTRONIK SAW filtering

SB *abbr (schneller Brutreaktor, schneller Brüter)* KERNTECH, PHYS FBR *(fast breeder reactor)*

Sb *(Antimon, Stibium)* CHEMIE Sb *(antimony)*

S-Bahn *f (Schnellbahn)* EISENBAHN regional express railroad (AmE), regional express railway (BrE)

S-Band *nt* ELEKTRONIK S-band; **S-Banddiode** *f* ELEKTRONIK S-band diode

SBFM *abbr (Schmalbandfrequenzmodulation)* ELEKTRONIK, RADIO, TELEKOM NBFM *(narrow-band frequency modulation)*

S-Bogen *m* FERTIG gooseneck

SBR *abbr (Styrol-Butadien-Kautschuk)* KUNSTSTOFF SBR *(styrene butadiene rubber)*

SB-Tankstelle *f (Selbstbedienungtankstelle)* TRANS self-service station

SBV *abbr (Sicherheitsabblasearmatur)* ERDÖL relief valve

Sc *(Scandium)* CHEMIE Sc *(scandium)*

Scandium *nt (Sc)* CHEMIE scandium *(Sc)*

Scannen *nt* COMP & DV, DRUCK, ELEKTRONIK, FERNSEH, STRAHLPHYS scanning

scannen *vt* COMP & DV, DRUCK, WELLPHYS *Radar* scan

Scanner *m* COMP & DV optical scanner, scanner, scanning device, DRUCK, ELEKTRONIK scanner, FERNSEH optical scanning device, scanner, KONTROLL, STRAHLPHYS scanner; **Scannerkopf** *m* DRUCK scanning head; **Scanner-Programm** *nt* COMP & DV scanning software; **Scanner-Software** *f* COMP & DV scanning software

Scatter *nt* RAUMFAHRT *Streuung* scatter

SCC *abbr* ABFALL *(Nachbrennkammer)*, MASCHINEN *(Nachbrennkammer, zweiter Brennraum)* SCC *(secondary combustion chamber)*

Schab *nt* BAU shave hook; **Schabeisen** *nt* MASCHINEN scraper

Schaben *nt* FERTIG scraping, *Zahnrad* shaving, MASCHI-

NEN shaving

schaben *vt* FERTIG *Zahnrad,* MASCHINEN shave, MEERSCHMUTZ scrape

Schaber *m* BAU scraper, DRUCK squeegee, LEBENSMITTEL, MASCHINEN, MEERSCHMUTZ scraper

Schabezahn *m* MASCHINEN shave tooth

Schablone *f* BAU strickle board, COMP & DV mask, template, templet, DRUCK stencil, ERDÖL template, FERTIG stencil, *Gießen* strickle, *Zahnradstoßmaschine* former, KER & GLAS stencil, KFZTECH *Werkzeug* template, templet, MASCHINEN gage (AmE), gauge (BrE), jig, pattern, template, templet, MECHAN, METROL jig; **Schablonenarm** *m* FERTIG loam board; **Schablonenbefehl** *m* COMP & DV template command, templet command; **Schablonenformen** *nt* FERTIG strickling

schablonenformen *vt* FERTIG strickle

Schablone: **Schablonenformerei** *f* FERTIG strickle molding (AmE), strickle moulding (BrE); **Schablonengrundplatte** *f* FERTIG *Lehmformerei* loam plate; **Schablonenkern** *m* FERTIG *Gießen* backup brickwork; **Schablonenseide** *f* KER & GLAS stencil silk; **Schablonenvergleich** *m* COMP & DV template matching, templet matching; **Schablonenwicklung** *f* KER & GLAS former winding

Schablonieren *nt* FERTIG sweeping

schablonieren *vt* FERTIG sweep

Schabotte *f* MASCHINEN anvil bed

Schachbrettmuster *nt* KER & GLAS checker pattern

Schacht *m* BAU stack, *Wasserbau* manhole, ERDÖL pit, FERTIG *Hochofen* stack, MECHAN chute, WASSERVERSORG shaft; **Schachtabdeckung** *f* BAU cowl, manhole cover; **Schachtausmauerung** *f* KOHLEN stone tubbing; **Schachtbrunnen** *m* KOHLEN sunk well

Schachtel *f* VERPACK carton; **Schachteleinheit** *f* VERPACK *aus einem Satz* nesting box

Schacht: **Schachtentlastungsanlage** *f* WASSERVERSORG shaft spillway; **Schachtleiter** *f* WASSERVERSORG shaft ladder; **Schachtofen** *m* ABFALL, FERTIG shaft furnace, KOHLEN shaft kiln; **Schachtring** *m* KOHLEN, NICHTFOSS ENERG well casing; **Schachttür** *f* BAU manhole door; **Schachtturbinenkammer** *f* WASSERVERSORG flume, open flume turbine chamber; **Schachtzimmerung** *f* KOHLEN timbering

Schaden[1] *m* PATENT damage; **~ an der Ruderanlage** *m* WASSERTRANS helm damage

Schaden:[2] **~ erleiden** *vi* PATENT suffer damage; **~ ersetzen** *vi* PATENT compensate for damage

Schaden: **Schadenermittlung** *f* SICHERHEIT extent of damage; **Schadenfeststellung** *f* WASSERTRANS *Versicherung* damage assessment; **Schadenlinie** *f* FERTIG damage curve

schadhaft[1] *adj* ELEKTRIZ faulty, TELEKOM damaged

schadhaft:[2] **~e Isolierung** *f* ELEKTRIZ faulty insulation

schädlich[1] *adj* CHEMIE noxious, KERNTECH unfavourable, SICHERHEIT injurious

schädlich:[2] **~e Substanz** *f* SICHERHEIT harmful substance; **~er Widerstand** *m* LUFTTRANS parasitic drag

Schädlichkeit *f* UMWELTSCHMUTZ harmfulness

Schädling *m* LEBENSMITTEL pest

Schadstoff *m* ABFALL contaminant, MEERSCHMUTZ, SICHERHEIT pollutant, UMWELTSCHMUTZ harmful substance, pollutant, toxic substance; **Schadstoffablagerung** *f* UMWELTSCHMUTZ pollutant deposition; **Schadstoffausbreitung** *f* UMWELTSCHMUTZ propagation of pollutant

schadstoffbelastet: **~es Erdreich** *nt* UMWELTSCHMUTZ pollutant-impacted ground

Schadstoff: **Schadstoffbelastung** *f* UMWELTSCHMUTZ pollution burden; **Schadstoffmessung** *f* GERÄT pollutant measurement; **Schadstoffregulierung bei Motoren** *f* MASCHINEN engine emission control; **Schadstoffvorstufe** *f* UMWELTSCHMUTZ precursor pollutant

Schadwirkung *f* UMWELTSCHMUTZ harmful effect

Schaffner *m* EISENBAHN sleeping car attendant, train conductor

Schaffung: **~ der Baufreiheit** *f* BAU clearing operations

Schaffußwalze *f* BAU sheep's foot roller

Schaft *m* BAU, DRUCK shank, FERTIG grip, rod (AmE), shank, MASCHINEN shaft, shank, stem, tang, MECHAN handle, shaft; **Schaftfräser** *m* MASCHINEN end mill, end-milling cutter

Schaftfräserumfang: **~ schleifen** *vi* FERTIG spiral

Schaft: **Schaftgewebe** *nt* TEXTIL dobby weave fabric; **Schafthülse** *f* FERTIG barrel; **Schaftlänge** *f* MASCHINEN shank length; **Schaftmaschine** *f* TEXTIL dobby; **Schaftmeißel** *m* FERTIG shank-type cutting tool; **Schaftschraube** *f* KFZTECH stud, MASCHINEN headless screw; **Schaftschraube mit Schlitz** *f* MASCHINEN slotted headless screw

Schäkel *m* BAU, KFZTECH *Schleppvorrichtung,* MASCHINEN, MEERSCHMUTZ shackle, WASSERTRANS *Beschläge* sextant altitude; **Schäkelbolzen** *m* MASCHINEN clevis bolt; **Schäkelisolator** *m* ELEKTROTECH shackle insulator

Schakengehänge *nt* EISENBAHN link suspension

Schalbretter *nt pl* BAU boarding

Schäldarm *m* LEBENSMITTEL cellulose casing

Schale *f* BAU layer, FOTO, KER & GLAS *für Walze bei der Herstellung von Walzflachglas* dish, KOHLEN *Bau* shell, LABOR basin, tray, LEBENSMITTEL skin, MASCHINEN insert liner, liner, pan, shell, PAPIER, RAUMFAHRT *Raumschiff* shell

Schäleisen *nt* BAU paring chisel

Schalen *nt* FERTIG molding (AmE), moulding (BrE)

Schälen *nt* LEBENSMITTEL shelling, *von Reis, Hafer* milling

schälen *vt* BAU peel, LEBENSMITTEL husk, peel

Schale: **Schalenbauweise** *f* BAU shell construction; **Schalenfehler** *m* LEBENSMITTEL *Obst* skin blemish; **Schalenfestigkeit** *f* LEBENSMITTEL shell strength; **Schalengußform** *f* MECHAN chill; **Schalenhartguß** *m* FERTIG chilled cast iron, METALL chill casting; **Schalenkreuzanemometer** *nt* GERÄT cup anemometer; **Schalenkupplung** *f* FERTIG *Kunststoffinstallationen* shell coupling; **Schalenmodell** *nt* PHYS *Kernphysik* shell model; **Schalenpackung** *f* VERPACK clam pack; **Schalenschaukel** *f* FOTO dish rocker; **Schalensitz** *m* KFZTECH bucket seat; **Schalenthermometer** *nt* FOTO dish thermometer; **Schalenwärmer** *m* FOTO dish heater

Schälfräser *m* FERTIG slab milling cutter

Schälholz *nt* BAU barked timber

Schalkleiste *f* WASSERTRANS *Segeln* batten

Schalklemme *f* BAU casing clamps

Schall[1] *m* AKUSTIK sound; **~~ und Vibrationsisolierung** *f* SICHERHEIT insulation against sound and vibration; **~~ und Vibrationsmesser** *m* SICHERHEIT noise and vibration measuring equipment

Schall:[2] **~ aussenden** *vi* WASSERTRANS sound; **Schallerzeuger betätigen** *vi* WASSERTRANS sound

Schall: **Schallabsorbierung** *f* AKUSTIK, AUFNAHME

sound absorption; **Schallanalysegerät** *nt* AKUSTIK sound analyser (BrE), sound analyzer (AmE); **Schallaufnehmer** *m* ACOUST acoustic sensor; **Schallaufzeichnung** *f* AKUSTIK sound recording; **Schallausbreitung** *f* AUFNAHME sound propagation; **Schallbelastungsmesser** *m* SICHERHEIT sound exposure meter; **Schallbeschleunigung** *f* AKUSTIK sound acceleration; **Schallbeschleunigungspegel** *m* AKUSTIK sound acceleration level

schalldämmend: ~es **Material** *nt* AUFNAHME sound-absorbing material; ~e **Weichgummibespannung** *f* SICHERHEIT antinoise soft rubber lining

Schall: **Schalldämmkoeffizient** *m* PHYS sound reduction index; **Schalldämmplatte** *f* SICHERHEIT acoustic board; **Schalldämmung** *f* AKUSTIK sound insulation, transmission loss, AUFNAHME, KFZTECH sound insulation, SICHERHEIT noise abatement; **Schalldämmwand** *f* SICHERHEIT noise-abating wall; **Schalldämmzahl** *f* PHYS sound reduction index; **Schalldämpfer** *m* AKUSTIK, BAU damper, muffler (AmE), silencer (BrE), HEIZ & KÄLTE attenuator, KFZTECH *Auspuffanlage* muffler (AmE), silencer (BrE), LUFTTRANS aerator muffler (AmE), aerator silencer (BrE), MECHAN exhaust muffler (AmE), exhaust silencer (BrE); **Schalldämpfer am Auspuff** *m* MECHAN exhaust muffler (AmE), exhaust silencer (BrE); **Schalldämpfer für Rohrleitungen** *m* SICHERHEIT muffler for pipelines (AmE), silencer for pipelines (BrE); **Schalldämpfung** *f* AKUSTIK sound absorption, ELEKTRONIK acoustic attenuation, HEIZ & KÄLTE sound attenuation; **Schalldämpfungskonstante** *f* ELEKTRONIK acoustic attenuation constant; **Schalldetektor** *m* TRANS sonic detector

schalldicht: ~e **Fliese** *f* SICHERHEIT soundproof tile; ~e **Kabine** *f* AUFNAHME sound booth, soundproofed booth; ~e **Kachel** *f* SICHERHEIT soundproof tile; ~e **Kammer** *f* SICHERHEIT noise protection booth; ~er **Raum** *m* AUFNAHME soundproof room; ~e **Tür** *f* SICHERHEIT sound-insulated door; ~e **Zwischenschicht** *f* BAU plugging

Schall: **Schalldichte** *f* AKUSTIK, PHYS sound-energy density; **Schalldichtepegel** *m* AKUSTIK sound-energy density level; **Schalldosen-Adapter** *m* AUFNAHME *für Empfänger* phono adaptor

Schalldruck *m* AKUSTIK pressure, AKUSTIK, AUFNAHME, PHYS, RAUMFAHRT *Raumschiff* acoustic pressure, sound pressure; **Schalldruckpegel** *m* AKUSTIK, ERGON, HEIZ & KÄLTE, PHYS, UMWELTSCHMUTZ sound pressure level; **Schalldruckspektrum** *nt* UMWELTSCHMUTZ sound pressure spectrum

Schall: **Schallehre** *f* AKUSTIK acoustics

Schalleistung *f* AKUSTIK acoustic power, PHYS sound power; **Schalleistungspegel** *m* AKUSTIK, HEIZ & KÄLTE, PHYS sound power level

Schall: **Schallenergie** *f* AKUSTIK, ELEKTROTECH sound energy; **Schallenergiedichte** *f* AKUSTIK, PHYS sound-energy density; **Schallenergiefluß** *m* (*J*) AKUSTIK, PHYS sound-energy flux (*J*); **Schallermüdung** *f* METALL sonic fatigue; **Schallerregung** *f* AKUSTIK sound excitation; **Schallfeld** *nt* AKUSTIK acoustical field, sound field; **Schallfilter** *nt* AKUSTIK acoustic filter; **Schallfluß** *m* AKUSTIK volume velocity; **Schallfühler** *m* ACOUST acoustic sensor; **Schallgeber** *m* AKUSTIK sound source; **Schallgenerator** *m* MASCHINEN acoustic generator; **Schallgeschwindigkeit** *f* AKUSTIK sound velocity, PHYS speed of sound, WELLPHYS *in Medium*

velocity of sound; **Schallgeschwindigkeitsprofil** *nt* NICHTFOSS ENERG acoustic velocity log; **Schallgewölbe** *nt* AUFNAHME acoustic vault

schallhart: ~er **Raum** *m* AUFNAHME echo chamber

Schall: **Schallhärte** *f* AKUSTIK acoustic stiffness; **Schallimpedanz** *f* AKUSTIK (*AI*), AUFNAHME (*ZA*), ELEKTROTECH (*ZA*), PHYS (*ZA*) acoustic impedance (*ZA*); **Schallimpuls** *m* AUFNAHME sound pulse, ELEKTRONIK acoustic pulse; **Schallintensität** *f* AKUSTIK, ERGON, PHYS sound intensity; **Schallintensitätsdichte** *f* AKUSTIK sound intensity density; **Schallintensitätspegel** *m* AKUSTIK, AUFNAHME sound intensity level; **Schallisolation** *f* AKUSTIK sound insulation, sound isolation; **Schallisolationsmaterial** *nt* UMWELTSCHMUTZ acoustic insulating materials; **Schallisolierung** *f* WASSERTRANS sound insulation; **Schallknall** *m* LUFTTRANS sonic boom, SICHERHEIT sonic bang; **Schallkörper** *m* ELEKTRONIK acoustic resonator; **Schallmachmeter** *nt* LUFTTRANS audible machmeter; **Schallmesser** *m* SICHERHEIT sound level meter; **Schallmeßgerät** *nt* WELLPHYS sonometer

schallnah[1] *adj* PHYS transonic

schallnah:[2] ~e **Geschwindigkeit** *f* PHYS, TRANS transonic speed

Schall: **Schalloch** *nt* MECHAN louver (AmE), louvre (BrE); **Schallöffnung** *f* AUFNAHME *eines Lautsprechers* louver (AmE), louvre (BrE); **Schallortung** *f* WELLPHYS sound ranging; **Schallortungsgerät** *nt* AKUSTIK sound locator; **Schallpegel** *m* AKUSTIK, HEIZ & KÄLTE sound level; **Schallpegelmesser** *m* AUFNAHME sound level meter; **Schallpegeldifferenz** *f* AKUSTIK sound-level difference; **Schallpegelmesser** *m* AKUSTIK, ERGON sound level meter; **Schallpegelmeßgerät** *nt* GERÄT sound level meter, volume unit meter; **Schallpegelverteilung** *f* AKUSTIK sound-level distribution; **Schallplatte** *f* AKUSTIK, AUFNAHME record, FERNSEH audio record; **Schallplattenaufnahmegerät** *nt* AKUSTIK disc recorder (BrE), AUFNAHME disk recorder (AmE), recorder; **Schallquelle** *f* UMWELTSCHMUTZ sound source; **Schallquellenleistung** *f* AKUSTIK sound power of a source; **Schallraum** *m* MASCHINEN acoustic testing room; **Schallreiz** *m* AKUSTIK acoustic stimulus; **Schallrückkopplung** *f* AUFNAHME acoustic feedback; **Schallschirm** *m* UMWELTSCHMUTZ baffle collector; **Schallschluckdecke** *f* SICHERHEIT sound-absorbing ceiling; **Schallschluckdekor** *m* AKUSTIK flat, AUFNAHME acoustic flat; **Schallschlucker** *m* AKUSTIK sound absorber; **Schallschluckglas** *nt* SICHERHEIT noise-protective insulating glass; **Schallschluckgrad** *m* AKUSTIK acoustical absorption coefficient; **Schallschluckhaube** *f* SICHERHEIT noise-protective hood; **Schallschlucktür** *f* SICHERHEIT noise abatement door; **Schallschnelle** *f* AKUSTIK sound particle velocity; **Schallschnellemesser** *m* AKUSTIK acoustic velocity meter; **Schallschnellepegel** *m* AKUSTIK acoustic velocity level; **Schallschutzwand** *f* AUFNAHME sound screen; **Schallschwächung** *f* ELEKTRONIK acoustic attenuation; **Schallschwingung** *f* AKUSTIK acoustic vibration; **Schallsender** *m* AKUSTIK sound source; **Schallsensor** *m* ACOUST acoustic sensor; **Schallsignal** *nt* AKUSTIK audio signal, EISENBAHN sound signal, ELEKTRONIK audio signal, WASSERTRANS *Signal* sound signal; **Schallspektrograph** *m* AKUSTIK sound spectrograph; **Schallspektrum** *nt* AKUSTIK acoustical spectrum; **Schallstärke** *f* AKUSTIK strength of single source, PHYS sound intensity; **Schallstärkepegel** *m*

PHYS sound intensity level; **Schalltechnik** *f* AKUSTIK acoustics

schalltot: **~er Raum** *m* AKUSTIK anechoic room, dead room, AUFNAHME dead room, ERGON dead room, free-field room, PHYS anechoic room, dead room; **~e Wand** *f* AUFNAHME *eines Raums* dead end; **~e Zone** *f* AUFNAHME dead zone

Schall: **Schalltransmissionslinie** *f* ELEKTROTECH acoustic transmission line; **Schalltrichter** *m* AKUSTIK foghorn, horn; **Schallübertragung** *f* ACOUST sound transmission; **Schallverzögerung** *f* ELEKTRONIK acoustic delay; **Schallwahrnehmung** *f* AKUSTIK auditory sensation; **Schallwand** *f* AKUSTIK, AUFNAHME baffle; **Schallwelle** *f* AKUSTIK acoustic wave, sound wave, ELEKTROTECH acoustic wave, PHYS, RADIO, TELEKOM, WELLPHYS sound wave; **Schallwellenwiderstand** *m* AKUSTIK *(AI)*, AUFNAHME *(ZA)*, ELEKTROTECH *(ZA)*, PHYS *(ZA)* acoustic impedance *(ZA)*

Schälmaschine *f* BAU paring machine, LEBENSMITTEL decorticator, husking machine

Schalöl *nt* BAU formwork oil

Schälrad *nt* FERTIG skiving wheel

Schalrohr *nt* BAU casing pipe

Schälschnitt *m* FERTIG slabbing cut

Schalt- *pref* COMP & DV, ELEKTRIZ, ELEKTROTECH, KFZTECH, MASCHINEN switch; **Schaltalgebra** *f* COMP & DV logic algebra; **Schaltanlage** *f* ELEKTRIZ, ELEKTROTECH switchgear; **Schaltanordnung** *f* ELEKTROTECH contact arrangement; **Schaltantrieb** *m* MASCHINEN ratchet motion; **Schaltautomatik** *f* KFZTECH *Getriebe* automatic gear change; **Schaltbalken** *m* FERNSEH switching bar

schaltbar[1] *adj* FERNSEH switchable

schaltbar:[2] **~e Kupplung** *f* MASCHINEN clutch; **nicht ~e Kupplung** *f* MASCHINEN coupling

Schalt-: **Schaltbefehl** *m* FERTIG indexability command; **Schaltbereichsanzeige** *f* KFZTECH *Automatikgetriebe* range indicator; **Schaltbild** *nt* ELEKTRIZ circuit diagram, wiring diagram, ELEKTROTECH circuit diagram, connection diagram, FERNSEH circuit diagram, FERTIG diagrammatic circuit, RADIO schematic diagram; **Schaltblock** *m* ELEKTROTECH contact block; **Schaltbogen** *m* ELEKTROTECH breaking arc; **Schaltbrett** *nt* ELEKTROTECH plugboard, KFZTECH dash, dashboard, MECHAN control panel; **Schaltdauer** *f* ELEKTROTECH switching time; **Schaltdifferenz** *f* REGELUNG differential gap; **Schaltdiode** *f* ELEKTRONIK, TELEKOM switching diode; **Schaltdraht** *m* RADIO, TELEKOM jumper, jumper wire; **Schalteingang** *m* REGELUNG gate input; **Schaltelement** *nt* COMP & DV gate, ELEKTRONIK circuit element, logic circuit, logic component, logic element, ELEKTROTECH circuit element, TELEKOM switching device; **Schaltelementmatrix** *f* ELEKTRONIK cellular array

Schalten *nt* ELEKTROTECH, RAUMFAHRT *Weltraumfunk* switching, MASCHINEN indexing, shifting

schalten *vt* COMP & DV switch, ELEKTROTECH *in Reihe, parallel* connect, KFZTECH put into gear, KONTROLL switch, PHYS trip, TELEKOM switch

Schalter *m* COMP & DV, ELEKTRIZ switch, ELEKTROTECH circuit breaker, switch, *Verzweigung* switch, FERNSEH switch, GERÄT selector, KONTROLL, PHYS, TELEKOM switch; **~ auf Schalterdeck** *m* ELEKTROTECH deck switch; **~ mit mehrfachen Kontakten** *m* ELEKTRIZ multiple-contact switch; **~ mit Sicherung** *m* ELEKTROTECH

switch fuse; **Schalterhalle** *f* EISENBAHN passenger hall; **Schaltersicherung** *f* ELEKTROTECH switch fuse; **Schaltertisch** *m* TELEKOM counter

Schalt-: **Schaltfehler** *m* ELEKTROTECH contact fault; **Schaltfeld** *nt* ELEKTROTECH switchboard; **Schaltfolge** *f* ELEKTRIZ switching sequence; **Schaltgabel** *f* KFZTECH *Getriebe* gearbox selector fork; **Schaltgenauigkeit** *f* FERTIG *Revolver* accuracy of indexing, indexability accuracy; **Schaltgerät** *nt* ELEKTROTECH switchgear, switching device, KFZTECH trigger box; **Schaltgeschwindigkeit** *f* ELEKTROTECH switching speed; **Schaltgetriebe** *nt* FERTIG intermittent gear, KFZTECH gearbox, manual transmission, *Getriebe* manual gearbox, MASCHINEN gearbox; **Schaltglied** *nt* MASCHINEN shifting link; **Schaltgriff** *m* ELEKTROTECH switch handle; **Schalthahn** *m* BAU switch cock; **Schalthäufigkeit** *f* FERTIG *Punktschweißen* interruption frequency; **Schalthebel** *m* ELEKTROTECH switch lever, FERTIG actuating arm, gear lever (BrE), gear shift (AmE), KERNTECH lever switch, LUFTTRANS control lever, MASCHINEN gear lever (BrE), gear shift (AmE); **Schalthysterese** *f* GERÄT dead spot; **Schaltjahr** *nt* PHYS leap year; **Schaltkette** *f* REGELUNG switching chain; **Schaltklinke** *f* FERTIG, MASCHINEN, MECHAN pawl; **Schaltknopf** *m* ELEKTROTECH contact button; **Schaltknüppel** *m* KFZTECH *Getriebe* gear lever (BrE), gear shift (AmE); **Schaltkontakt** *m* ELEKTROTECH make-and-break contact; **Schaltkraft** *f* FERTIG *Kupplung* operating force

Schaltkreis *m* ELEKTRONIK *Netzwerk mit einer oder mehreren Stromschleifen* circuit, ELEKTROTECH switching circuit, PHYS, RADIO circuit; **~ auf dem Chip** *m* ELEKTRONIK on-chip circuit; **~ mit mittlerem Integrationsgrad** *m* TELEKOM medium-scale integration circuit; **~ mit Übergroßintegration** *m* TELEKOM very large-scale integrated circuit; **~ zur Verhinderung von Stromspitzen** *m* ELEKTROTECH despiking circuit; **Schaltkreisanalyse** *f* ELEKTROTECH circuit analysis; **Schaltkreisentwurf** *m* ELEKTRONIK circuit design; **Schaltkreisintegration** *f* ELEKTRONIK circuit integration; **Schaltkreisparameter** *m pl* PHYS network parameters; **Schaltkreisverzögerung** *f* ELEKTRONIK circuit delay

Schalt-: **Schaltkulisse** *f* KFZTECH *Automatikgetriebe* gate; **Schaltkupplung** *f* MASCHINEN, WASSERTRANS *Motor* clutch; **Schaltkurve** *f* FERTIG index cam; **Schaltleistung** *f* ELEKTROTECH breaking capacity, making capacity; **Schaltmagnet** *m* FERNSEH solenoid; **Schaltmatrix** *f* FERNSEH, RAUMFAHRT *Weltraumfunk* switching matrix; **Schaltmotor** *m* ELEKTRIZ torque motor; **Schaltmultiplexer** *m* TELEKOM cross-connect multiplexer, switching multiplexer, switching mux; **Schaltnetz** *nt* COMP & DV, ELEKTRONIK *logische Schaltung ohne Speichervermögen* combinational circuit (AmE), combinatorial circuit (BrE), ELEKTROTECH switching network; **Schaltnetzgerät** *nt* ELEKTROTECH switching power supply; **Schaltnetzgerät mit nur einem Ausgang** *nt* ELEKTROTECH single output switching power supply; **Schaltnocke** *f* FERTIG *Kunststoffinstallationen* contact cam; **Schaltplan** *m* ELEKTROTECH circuit diagram, connection diagram, KONTROLL circuit diagram, TELEKOM wiring diagram; **Schaltplatte** *f* COMP & DV jack panel (BrE), patch panel (AmE); **Schaltpult** *nt* FERTIG inclined control panel, GERÄT desk, LUFTTRANS control panel; **Schaltrelais** *nt* ELEKTRIZ switch relay; **Schaltröhre** *f* ELEKTRONIK switching tube; **Schaltschema** *nt* ELEKTROTECH circuit diagram, FERTIG *Kunststoffinstallationen* electrical diagram; **Schaltschloß** *nt* FERNSEH switch lock; **Schaltschwelle** *f* KONTROLL switching threshold; **Schaltsignal** *nt* FERNSEH keying signal; **Schaltstange** *f* FERTIG actuating rod; **Schaltstellung** *f* FERTIG *Kunststoffinstallationen* setting position; **Schaltstromversorgung** *f* ELEKTROTECH switching power supply; **Schaltstück** *nt* ELEKTROTECH contact; **Schaltsystem** *nt* FERNSEH switching system

Schalttafel *f* BAU control panel, COMP & DV patch board, plugboard, ELEKTROTECH plugboard, switchboard, ERDÖL monkey board, FERNSEH switchboard, KONTROLL control panel, RADIO panel, RAUMFAHRT control panel, TELEKOM *Elektrik* switchboard, TEXTIL control panel, WASSERTRANS *Elektrik* switch panel; ~ des Bordingenieurs *f* LUFTTRANS flight engineer's panel; ~ **mit Steuerpult** *f* KERNTECH benchboard; **Schalttafelbuchse** *f* FERNSEH hub; **Schalttafelfeld** *nt* TELEKOM switchboard panel; **Schalttafelinstrument** *nt* GERÄT board-mounted instrument, panel-type instrument, switchboard panel instrument; **Schalttafelmeßgerät** *nt* GERÄT panel-type instrument; **Schalttafelmeßinstrument** *nt* GERÄT switchboard-type meter

Schalt-: **Schalttaste** *f* ELEKTROTECH contact button; **Schalttaster** *m* FERNSEH keyer; **Schalttemperatur** *f* THERMOD offset temperature; **Schalttisch** *m* MASCHINEN indexing table; **Schalttor** *nt* REGELUNG switching gate; **Schaltuhr** *f* ELEKTRIZ switch clock, FOTO timer, GERÄT clock relay, time switch, TELEKOM time switch

Schaltung *f* COMP & DV, ELEKTRIZ circuit, ELEKTROTECH circuit, switching, FERTIG actuation, index, MASCHINEN shift, PHYS circuit, TELEKOM switching; ~ **auf dem Chip** *f* ELEKTRONIK on-chip circuit; ~ **auf Platine** *f* ELEKTRONIK on-board circuitry; ~ **mit verzögerter Auslösung** *f* ELEKTROTECH delayed-action circuit breaking; **äußere ~** *f* ELEKTRIZ external circuit; **Schaltungsanalyse** *f* ELEKTROTECH circuit analysis; **Schaltungsaufbau** *m* ELEKTROTECH circuit design; **Schaltungsbeschreibung** *f* ELEKTROTECH circuit theory; **Schaltungsentwurf** *m* ELEKTRIZ circuit design; **Schaltungsnetz** *nt* ELEKTROTECH, TELEKOM network of circuit elements

Schalt-: **Schaltunterstation** *f* ELEKTROTECH switching substation; **Schaltventil** *nt* MASCHINEN on/off valve; **Schaltverbindung** *f* ELEKTROTECH interconnection; **Schaltverbindungsschicht** *f* ELEKTRONIK interconnection layer; **Schaltverlust** *m* ELEKTROTECH switching loss; **Schaltverzögerung** *f* COMP & DV gate delay, propagation delay, ELEKTRONIK time delay, KONTROLL switching delay, TELEKOM switching delay, *Relais, Schalter* time delay; **Schaltvorgang** *m* ELEKTROTECH switching; **Schaltvorrichtung** *f* ELEKTROTECH switchgear; **Schaltwalze** *f* FERTIG controller; **Schaltwarte** *f* HEIZ & KÄLTE, KERNTECH control room; **Schaltwerk** *nt* COMP & DV logic device, ELEKTRIZ switching station; **Schaltwerksentwurf** *m* COMP & DV logic design; **Schaltzeit** *f* ELEKTROTECH switching time; **Schaltzelle** *f* ELEKTROTECH cell; **Schaltzentrale** *f* ELEKTRIZ control room

Schalung *f* BAU formwork, shuttering, *Betonbau* formwork, FERTIG mold (AmE), mould (BrE); **Schalungsbrett** *nt* BAU shutter

Schaluppe *f* WASSERTRANS sloop

Schalwand *f* BAU plank partition

Schamfilen *nt* WASSERTRANS *Segeln, Tauwerk* chafing

Schamotte *f* KER & GLAS chamotte; **Schamottemanschette** *f* KER & GLAS *der Pfeife im Danner-Röhrenziehverfahren* collar; **Schamottestein** *m* BAU fire brick, HEIZ & KÄLTE firebrick, refractory brick, KER & GLAS fire brick, LABOR refractory brick, THERMOD firebrick; **Schamotteton** *m* KER & GLAS fireclay; **Schamottetonform** *f* KER & GLAS fireclay mold (AmE), fireclay mould (BrE); **Schamottetontiegel** *m* KER & GLAS fireclay crucible; **Schamotteziegel** *m* HEIZ & KÄLTE firebrick, refractory brick, LABOR *Ofen* fireclay brick

Schandeckel *m* WASSERTRANS *Schiffbau* covering board, *Schiffbau* gunnel, gunwale

Schanzkleid *nt* WASSERTRANS *Schiffbau* bulwark; **Schanzkleidreling** *f* WASSERTRANS *Schiffbau* bulwark rail

Schappenbohrer *m* KOHLEN auger

Schar *f* FERTIG *Kurven* group

scharf[1] *adj* MASCHINEN sharp; ~ **eingestellt** *adj* FOTO in focus; **mit ~ er Spitze** *adj* FERTIG cone point

scharf:[2] ~ **am Winde** *adv* WASSERTRANS *Segeln* full and by

scharf:[3] ~ **begrenzendes Filter** *nt* ELEKTRONIK sharp cut-off filter; ~ **begrenzte Linie** *f* KONSTZEICH sharply bounded line; ~ **begrenzter Impuls** *m* ELEKTRONIK sharp pulse; ~**e Kante** *f* BAU cutting edge (AmE), keen edge (BrE), KER & GLAS arris, sharp edge; ~**e Krümmung** *f* GEOM sharp curve; ~**e Kurve** *f* GEOM sharp curve; ~**e Oberfläche** *f* KER & GLAS sharp finish; ~**er Schiffsbug** *m* WASSERTRANS lean bow; ~**e Streckgrenze** *f* METALL sharp yield point

scharf:[4] ~ **einstellen** *vt* ELEKTRONIK, PHYS focus

Schärfe *f* AKUSTIK sharpness, BAU *Werkzeugschneide* keenness, ERGON acuity, FOTO, GEOM, MASCHINEN, OPTIK *Bild* sharpness, QUAL power; **Schärfeabfall** *m* FOTO decrease in definition; **Schärfeeinstellung** *f* FERNSEH sharpness control

Scharfeinstellfenster *nt* FOTO rangefinder window

Scharfeinstellung *f* FOTO focusing

Schärfemodulation *f* FERNSEH focus modulation

Schärfen *nt* FERTIG regrinding, MASCHINEN sharpening

schärfen *vt* MASCHINEN sharpen

Schärfentiefe *f* METALL depth of field, PHYS depth of focus, TELEKOM field depth

Schärferegler *m* FERNSEH focusing control

scharfkantig[1] *adj* MASCHINEN sharp, sharp-edged

scharfkantig:[2] ~**e Düse** *f* HYDRAUL sharp-edged orifice; ~**e Meßblendenbohrung** *f* HYDRAUL sharp-edged orifice; ~**e Mündung** *f* HYDRAUL sharp-edged orifice; ~**es Überlaufwehr** *nt* HYDRAUL sharp-crested weir; ~**es Wehr** *nt* HYDRAUL thin-edged weir, *Hydraulik* sharp-crested weir, WASSERVERSORG sharp-crested weir; ~**es Werkzeug** *nt* MASCHINEN sharp-edged tool

Schärfmaschine *f* MASCHINEN sharpening machine

Scharnier:[1] **mit ~** *adj* MASCHINEN hinged

Scharnier[2] *nt* BAU hinge, hinge joint, piano hinge, FERTIG articulation, hinge, MASCHINEN, MECHAN hinge; ~ **mit lösbaren Bolzen** *nt* BAU loose-pin hinge

Scharnier:[3] **mit ~ befestigen** *vt* BAU hinge; **mit ~ versehen** *vt* FERTIG hinge

Scharnier: **Scharnierband** *nt* BAU butt hinge, strap; **Scharnierbandkette** *f* MASCHINEN flat-top chain; **Scharnierbeschläge** *m pl* MASCHINEN hinge fittings; **Scharniergelenk** *nt* BAU knuckle; **Scharnierstift** *m* BAU hinge pin

Scharrieren *nt* BAU charring
Scharte *f* MASCHINEN nick
schartig *adj* MECHAN jagged
Schatten *m* DRUCK, FOTO shadow, OPTIK, PHYS umbra; **Schattenbereich** *m* FERNSEH shadow area; **Schattenbild** *nt* FERTIG *Profilprojektor* silhouette shadow; **Schattenbildung** *f* FERNSEH clouding; **Schattenfläche** *f* DRUCK shadow area; **Schattenkompensationssignal** *nt* FERNSEH shading compensation signal; **Schattenmaske** *f* FERNSEH shadow mask; **Schattenmaskenröhre** *f* FERNSEH shadow mask tube; **Schattensektor** *m* LUFTTRANS blind sector; **Schattenstreifen** *m* FERTIG ghost, ghost line; **Schattenwand** *f* KER & GLAS shadow wall
schattiert *adj* KER & GLAS shaded
Schattierung *f* DRUCK, FOTO, KER & GLAS shade
schätzen *vt* TEXTIL assess
Schätzfunktion *f* QUAL estimator
Schätzwert *m* QUAL estimate
Schaubild *nt* COMP & DV graph; **Schaubildaufzeichner** *m* LABOR chart recorder
Schauer *m* TEILPHYS shower; **Schauerteilchen** *nt* TEILPHYS shower particle
Schaufel:[1] **~ voll** *adj* BAU shovelful
Schaufel[2] *f* BAU blade, FERTIG *Turbine* blade, vane, HEIZ & KÄLTE vane, *eines Ventilators* blade, HYDRAUL paddle, LUFTTRANS *Turbomotoren* vane, MASCHINEN blade, bucket, paddle board, shovel, *des Ventilators, der Wasserturbine* paddle, MECHAN bucket, vane, MEERSCHMUTZ shovel, NICHTFOSS ENERG *Turbine*, WASSERVERSORG *eines Wasserrads* bucket; **Schaufelbagger** *m* BAU bucket dredger, KFZTECH shovel dredge, shovel dredger, WASSERVERSORG bucket dredger; **Schaufelblatt** *nt* HYDRAUL paddle; **Schaufelentnahmegerät** *nt* ABFALL scraper extractor; **Schaufelflügler** *m* LUFTTRANS cyclogyro; **Schaufelgeschwindigkeit** *f* NICHTFOSS ENERG blade speed, bucket velocity; **Schaufelkranz** *m* MASCHINEN blade ring; **Schaufelader** *m* MEERSCHMUTZ front-end loader; **Schaufelmenge** *f* NICHTFOSS ENERG blade quantity; **Schaufeln** *nt* BAU shovel work, MASCHINEN blades; **Schaufelrad** *nt* BAU bucket wheel, MASCHINEN bucket wheel, paddle wheel, MECHAN impeller, WASSERTRANS, WASSERVERSORG paddle wheel; **Schaufelradbagger** *m* MASCHINEN bucket wheel excavator; **Schaufelreihe** *f* BAU *Förderband* line of buckets; **Schaufelschrägstellung** *f* NICHTFOSS ENERG bucket angle; **Schaufelstiel** *m* BAU D-handle; **Schaufelteilung** *f* NICHTFOSS ENERG blade pitch; **Schaufelverjüngungsverhältnis** *nt* LUFTTRANS *Hubschrauber* blade taper ratio; **Schaufelwerkstoffe** *m pl* NICHTFOSS ENERG *Turbine* blade materials; **Schaufelzeilung** *f* LUFTTRANS *Hubschrauber* blade spacing system
Schauglas *nt* ERDÖL gage glass (AmE), gauge glass (BrE), HEIZ & KÄLTE sight glass, MASCHINEN sight feed glass
Schaukarton *m* VERPACK display box
Schaukel *f* MECHAN rocker; **Schaukelbewegung** *f* MASCHINEN seesaw motion, seesawing
Schaukeln *nt* MASCHINEN rocking, swinging
Schaukel: **Schaukelwelle** *f* NICHTFOSS ENERG seiche
Schauklappe *f* MECHAN inspection door; **~ für Ausfahrverriegelung beim Landen** *f* LUFTTRANS landing downlock optical inspection flap
Schauloch *nt* KER & GLAS observation hole
Schaum[1] *m* FERTIG, KER & GLAS, KOHLEN, KUNSTSTOFF, LEBENSMITTEL, METALL, PAPIER, WASSERTRANS foam, froth, scum
Schaum:[2] **~ bilden** *vi* CHEMTECH foam
Schaum: **Schaumabscheiden** *nt* CHEMTECH foam separation
schaumartig *adj* CHEMTECH foamy
schaumbedeckt *adj* CHEMTECH foamy, FERTIG scummy
Schaum: **Schaumbeständigkeit** *f* CHEMTECH foam persistence
schaumbildend *adj* SICHERHEIT intumescent
Schaum: **Schaumbildner** *m* CHEMTECH foamer, SICHERHEIT itumescence compound; **Schaumbildung** *f* CHEMTECH, ERDÖL foaming; **Schaumbildungshemmer** *m* ERDÖL defoaming agent; **Schaumbrecher** *m* CHEMTECH foam breaker; **Schaumdecke** *f* LUFTTRANS *Feuerschutzmaßnahme* foam blanket
Schäumen[1] *nt* FERTIG frothing, KER & GLAS foaming, KUNSTSTOFF frothing
Schäumen:[2] **zum ~ bringen** *vt* CHEMTECH foam
schäumen[1] *vt* BAU *Beton* aerate, TEXTIL foam
schäumen[2] *vi* FERTIG effervesce
schäumend *adj* LEBENSMITTEL effervescent
Schaum: **Schaumentwässerung** *f* CHEMTECH foam drainage; **Schaumfänger** *m* FERTIG *Gießen* skim bob; **Schaumfeuerlöscher** *m* LUFTTRANS foam extinguisher; **Schaumflotation** *f* CHEMTECH froth flotation
schaumgekrönt: **~e Welle** *f* WASSERTRANS *Seezustand* whitecap
Schaum: **Schaumglas** *nt* HEIZ & KÄLTE cellular glass, KER & GLAS foam glass, foamed glass; **Schaumgrenze** *f* KER & GLAS foam line; **Schaumgummi** *m* KUNSTSTOFF expanded rubber, foamed rubber, MECHAN expanded rubber
schaumig *adj* TEXTIL foamy
Schaum: **Schaumkunstmasse** *f* MECHAN expanded plastic; **Schaumkunststoff** *m* KUNSTSTOFF cellular plastic, expanded plastic; **Schaumlöffel** *m* FERTIG skimmer; **Schaumlöscher** *m* SICHERHEIT foam fire extinguisher; **Schaumlöschgerät** *nt* SICHERHEIT foam extinguishing apparatus; **Schaummittel** *nt* LEBENSMITTEL foaming agent, LUFTTRANS *Feuerschutzmaßnahme* foam compound; **Schaumprüfung** *f* LUFTTRANS foaming test; **Schaum-PS** *nt* (*geschäumtes Polysterol*) VERPACK ep (*expanded polystyrene*); **Schaumschalldämmplatte** *f* SICHERHEIT noise abating foam panel; **Schaumschicht** *f* SICHERHEIT *als Flammschutz* foam layer
schaumschichtbildend: **~er Anstrich** *m* KUNSTSTOFF intumescent paint; **~er Anstrichstoff** *m* KUNSTSTOFF intumescent paint
Schaum: **Schaumschichttrocknung** *f* LEBENSMITTEL foam mat drying
Schaumstoff *m* HEIZ & KÄLTE cellular plastic, KUNSTSTOFF foam, MECHAN expanded plastic, TEXTIL foam; **Schaumstoffkaschierung** *f* TEXTIL foam backing; **Schaumstoffschicht** *f* TEXTIL foam layer; **Schaumstoffverpackung** *f* VERPACK plastic foam packaging; **Schaumstoffverpackung und -auspolsterung** *f* VERPACK foam packaging and cushioning
Schaum: **Schaumtank** *m* PAPIER foam tank; **Schaumteppich** *m* LUFTTRANS *Feuerschutzmaßnahme* foam carpet; **Schaumverbesserer** *m* LEBENSMITTEL lather booster; **Schaumverdünnung** *f* CHEMTECH foam dilution; **Schaumverhinderungszusatz** *m* MASCHINEN antifoaming agent; **Schaumverhütungsmittel** *nt* CHEMTECH foam inhibitor, KUNSTSTOFF anti-

foaming agent
Schauöffnung *f* LUFTTRANS *Flugwerk* inspection panel
Schaupackung *f* VERPACK dummy
Schaustück *nt* VERPACK window packaging
Schautropföler *m* MASCHINEN sight feed lubricator
Schauverpackung *f* VERPACK display packaging, visual pack
Schauzeichen *nt* GERÄT annunciator
Scheduler *m* COMP & DV *Arbeit* scheduler
Scheibe *f* COMP & DV slice, wafer, ELEKTRIZ dial, ELEK-
TRONIK *Halbleiter* wafer, KER & GLAS *Tafelglas* piece,
MASCHINEN disc (BrE), disk (AmE), flat washer, pul-
ley, pulley wheel, sheave, washer, wheel, TEXTIL flange,
WASSERTRANS *Beschläge* sheave; **nur einmal
beschreibbare ~** *f* OPTIK write-once disc (BrE), write-
once disk (AmE); **~ mit hochdichter Aufzeichnung** *f*
FERNSEH video high-density disc (BrE), video high-
density disk (AmE); **~ mit konstanter Drehzahl** *f* OPTIK
constant-angular-velocity disc (BrE), constant-angular-velocity disk (AmE); **~ mit konstanter
Lineargeschwindigkeit** *f* OPTIK constant-linear-velocity disc (BrE), constant-linear-velocity disk (AmE);
~ mit konstanter Winkelgeschwindigkeit *f* OPTIK
constant-angular-velocity disc (BrE), constant-angular-velocity disk (AmE); **Scheiben- und Planfräser** *m*
MASCHINEN side-and-face milling cutter; **Scheiben-
abschöpfer** *m* UMWELTSCHMUTZ disc skimmer (BrE),
disk skimmer (AmE); **Scheibenabschöpfgerät** *nt*
MEERSCHMUTZ *für Öl von der Wasseroberfläche* disc
skimmer (BrE), disk skimmer (AmE); **Scheibenan-
guß** *m* KUNSTSTOFF diaphragm gate; **Scheibenanker**
m ELEKTRIZ, ELEKTROTECH disc armature (BrE), disk
armature (AmE); **Scheibenanode** *f* FERNSEH disc
anode (BrE), disk anode (AmE); **Scheibenantenne** *f*
TELEKOM disc antenna (BrE), disk antenna (AmE);
Scheibenbank *f* MASCHINEN bull block; **Scheiben-
bohrmeißel** *m* ERDÖL *Bohrtechnik* disc bit (BrE), disk
bit (AmE); **Scheibenbremsanlage** *f* BAU disc braking
system (BrE), disk braking system (AmE); **Scheibenbremse** *f* EISENBAHN, FERTIG, KFZTECH, MASCHINEN,
MECHAN disc brake (BrE), disk brake (AmE); **Schei-
benbremsenbelag** *m* KFZTECH disc brake pad (BrE),
disk brake pad (AmE); **Scheibenfeder** *f* FERTIG,
KFZTECH, MASCHINEN Woodruff key; **Scheiben-
federkupplung** *f* KFZTECH diaphragm clutch;
Scheibenfräser *m* MASCHINEN side mill, side milling
cutter; **Scheibengummi** *m* KFZTECH rubber weatherproof seal; **Scheibenherstellung** *f* ELEKTRONIK wafer
fabrication; **Scheibenklampe** *f* WASSERTRANS *Decksausrüstung* cheek block; **Scheibenkolben** *m* HYDRAUL
disc piston (BrE), disk piston (AmE), *Pumpe* solid
piston; **Scheibenkolbenpumpe** *f* HYDRAUL solid piston pump; **Scheibenkondensator** *m* ELEKTROTECH
disc capacitor (BrE), disk capacitor (AmE), OPTIK
capacitance electronic disc (BrE), capacitance electronic disk (AmE); **Scheibenkupfer** *nt* CHEMIE rose
copper; **Scheibenkupplung** *f* FERTIG, KFZTECH *Kupplung* disc clutch (BrE), disk clutch (AmE),
MASCHINEN disc clutch (BrE), disk clutch (AmE),
plate clutch, plate coupling, MECHAN disc clutch
(BrE), disk clutch (AmE); **Scheibenläufer** *m* ELEKTRO-
TECH disc armature (BrE), disk armature (AmE);
Scheibenmaske *f* ELEKTRONIK wafer mask; **Scheib-
enmotor** *m* ELEKTROTECH pancake motor;
Scheibenmühle *f* LEBENSMITTEL disc mill (BrE), disk
mill (AmE); **Scheibenpolieren** *nt* KER & GLAS disc

polishing (BrE), disk polishing (AmE); **Scheibenrad**
nt FERTIG disc (BrE), disk (AmE), KFZTECH disc centre wheel (BrE), disk center wheel (AmE),
MASCHINEN disc wheel (BrE), disk wheel (AmE);
Scheibenrekorder *m* ELEKTRIZ disc recorder (BrE),
disk recorder (AmE); **Scheibenrelais** *nt* EISENBAHN
vane relay; **Scheibenröhre** *f* ELEKTRONIK disc tube
(BrE), disk tube (AmE); **Scheibenschießen** *nt* EISEN-
BAHN target-shooting; **Scheibenschleifmaschine** *f*
MASCHINEN disc sanding machine (BrE), disk sanding
machine (AmE); **Scheibensignal** *nt* EISENBAHN disc
signal (BrE), disk signal (AmE); **Scheibenspeicher** *m*
FERTIG rotary magazine; **Scheibenspule** *f* ELEKTRO-
TECH pancake coil; **Scheibentriode** *f* ELEKTRONIK
disc-seal tube (BrE), disk-seal tube (AmE);
Scheibenunwucht *f* FERTIG wheel imbalance; **Schei-
benverdampfer** *m* HEIZ & KÄLTE tray evaporator;
Scheibenwaschanlage *f* KFZTECH *Glas* washer; **Schei-
benwicklung** *f* ELEKTROTECH disc winding (BrE), disk
winding (AmE); **Scheibenwischer** *m* KFZTECH wind-
screen wiper (BrE), windshield wiper (AmE)
Scheide *f* MECHAN sheath; **Scheidearbeit** *f* KOHLEN cul-
ling; **Scheidebürette** *f* CHEMTECH separating burette;
Scheideglas *nt* CHEMTECH refining glass; **Scheidemit-
tel** *nt* CHEMTECH separating agent; **Scheiden** *nt*
KOHLEN sorting; **Scheidepresse** *f* UMWELTSCHMUTZ
wringer; **Scheideschlamm** *m* CHEMIE *Zucker* scum;
Scheidetrichter *m* CHEMTECH separating funnel;
Scheidewand *f* MECHAN diaphragm
Scheidung *f* KOHLEN sorting, LEBENSMITTEL defecation,
liming
Schein- *pref* TEXTIL mock
scheinbar: **~es Bild** *nt* FOTO virtual image; **~e Höhe** *f*
WASSERTRANS *Navigation* apparent altitude; **~er Kör-
pergehalt** *m* KUNSTSTOFF false body; **~er Wind** *m*
WASSERTRANS *Navigation* apparent wind
Schein-: **Scheinenergie** *f* ELEKTRIZ apparent energy;
Scheinleistung *f* ELEKTRIZ, ELEKTROTECH, PHYS appa-
rent power; **Scheinleistungsmeßgerät** *nt* ELEKTRIZ
apparent-power meter; **Scheinleitwert** *m* ELEKTRO-
TECH, PHYS admittance; **Scheinvariable** *f* COMP & DV
dummy variable; **Scheinverriegelung** *f* FERNSEH
pseudolock
Scheinwerfer *m* ELEKTROTECH searchlight, FOTO spot-
light, KFZTECH *Beleuchtung* headlamp;
Scheinwerferabschwächungsschalter *m* ELEKTRIZ
dip selector switch; **Scheinwerferschalter** *m* ELEK-
TRIZ, KFZTECH headlight switch
Scheinwiderstand *m* AUFNAHME, ELEKTROTECH, PHYS,
TELEKOM impedance; **~ des Lautsprechers** *m*
AUFNAHME loudspeaker impedance; **Scheinwider-
standsanpassung** *f* AUFNAHME, PHYS impedance
matching; **Scheinwiderstandsausgleicher** *m* AUFNA-
HME impedance compensator; **Scheinwiderstands-
brücke** *f* GERÄT impedance measuring bridge;
Scheinwiderstandsmeßbrücke *f* GERÄT impedance
measuring bridge; **Scheinwiderstandsverhältnis** *nt*
AUFNAHME impedance ratio
Scheit *nt* FERTIG *Holz* billet
Scheitel *m* BAU crown, *eines Bogens* soffit, FERTIG apex,
crest, top, *Bogen* sagitta, GEOM, PHYS vertex, RAUM-
FAHRT apex; **Scheitelkanal** *m* WASSERVERSORG summit
canal; **Scheitelpunkt** *m* PHYS vertex; **Scheitelspan-
nungsmeßgerät** *nt* ELEKTRIZ, GERÄT peak voltmeter;
Scheitelwert *m* ELEKTRIZ, ELEKTRONIK peak value,
GERÄT crest value, TELEKOM peak value; **Scheitelwert-**

meßgerät *nt* GERÄT peak-reading instrument; **Scheitelwertmessung** *f* GERÄT peak value measurement; **Scheitelwinkel** *m pl* GEOM vertical angles

Schelf *nt* WASSERTRANS shelf

Schellack *m* BAU, ELEKTRIZ, FERTIG shellac

Schellbach-Rohr *nt* KER & GLAS schelbach tubing

Schelle *f* MASCHINEN, MECHAN clamp, clip; ~ **mit Schneckengewinde** *f* MASCHINEN worm drive clamp

Schema *nt* BAU sketch, COMP & DV schema, KÜNSTL INT *in der Wissensrepräsentation* frame, MASCHINEN scheme

schematisch: ~**es Schaltbild** *nt* KERNTECH schematic wiring diagram

Schenkel *m* BAU side, web, FERTIG grip, *Winkel* arm, side, *Zange* handle, GEOM leg, side, MASCHINEN, TELEKOM *Magnet* leg; **Schenkelpolläufer** *m* ELEKTROTECH salient pole rotor; **Schenkelpolstator** *m* ELEKTROTECH salient pole stator; **Schenkelrohr** *nt* MECHAN elbow, METALL bent pipe

Scher- *pref* AKUSTIK, FERTIG, KER & GLAS, MASCHINEN shear; **Scherbaum** *m* TEXTIL back beam

Scherbe *f* KER & GLAS cullet

Scher-: **Scherbeanspruchung** *f* MASCHINEN shearing strain, shearing stress, PHYS shear stress

Scherben: **aus ~ erschmolzenes Glas** *nt* KER & GLAS glass melted from cullet KER & GLAS body; **nur ~ Einlegen** *phr* KER & GLAS charging cullet only

Scherbe: **Scherbenbrechwerk** *nt* KER & GLAS cullet crusher; **Scherbenfänger** *m* KER & GLAS cullet catcher; **Scherbenrutsche** *f* KER & GLAS cullet chute; **Scherbenzerkleinerung** *f* KER & GLAS cullet crush

Scher-: **Scherblatt** *nt* MASCHINEN shear blade; **Scherbruch** *m* METALL shear fracture; **Scherdehnung** *f* PHYS shear strain

Schere *f* FERTIG metal shears, shears, KER & GLAS shears, MASCHINEN brace, scissors, shears, MECHAN shears

Scherebene *f* FERTIG shear plane

Scherelastizität *f (m)* AKUSTIK shear elasticity *(m)*

Scheren *nt* MASCHINEN shear, shearing

scheren *vt* MASCHINEN shear, METALL clip, TEXTIL crop, shear, warp

Scheren: **Scherenausrichtung** *f* KER & GLAS shear alignment; **Scherenbolzen** *m* FERTIG *Wechselräder* intermediate stud; **Scherenmarkierung** *f* KER & GLAS shear mark; **Scherenspray** *nt* KER & GLAS shear spray

Scher-: **Schererwärmung** *f* KUNSTSTOFF shear heating; **Scherfestigkeit** *f* FERTIG, KOHLEN, KUNSTSTOFF shear strength, MASCHINEN resistance to shearing, shearing strength, ultimate shearing strength, MECHAN, METALL shear strength; **Scherfläche** *f* METALL plane of shear; **Schergang** *m* WASSERTRANS *Schiffbau* sheerstrake; **Schergefälle** *nt* KUNSTSTOFF shear rate; **Schergeschwindigkeit** *f* KUNSTSTOFF rate of shear, shear rate

Schering: **Schering-Brücke** *f* ELEKTROTECH, PHYS Schering bridge

Scher-: **Scherkraft** *f* BAU shear force, FERTIG shear plane perpendicular force, MASCHINEN shear force, shearing force, MECHAN shear, PHYS shearing force; **Schermaschine** *f* KOHLEN, TEXTIL shearing machine; **Schermesser** *nt* KER & GLAS shear blade; **Schermodul** *nt* MASCHINEN *(G)* shear modulus *(G)*, PHYS rigidity modulus, PHYS *(G)* shear modulus *(G)*; **Scherschichten** *f pl* STRÖMPHYS *in rotierenden Fluiden* shear layers; **Scherschichtinstabilität** *f* STRÖMPHYS *an Grenzfläche zweier nicht mischbarer Fluide* shear flow instability;

Scherschnabel *m* METALL shear lip; **Scherschneidwerkzeug** *nt* FERTIG shear-action cutting tool; **Scherschnitt** *m* KER & GLAS shearcut; **Scherspannung** *f* BAU shearing stress, KUNSTSTOFF, PHYS, STRÖMPHYS shear stress; **Scherstahl** *m* METALL shear steel; **Scherstift** *m* MASCHINEN shear pin; **Scherströmung** *f* STRÖMPHYS shear flow

Scherung *f* KUNSTSTOFF, MECHAN, PHYS shear

Scher-: **Scherversuch** *m* MASCHINEN shear test; **Scherviskosität** *f* MASCHINEN shear viscosity; **Scherwiderstand** *m* FERTIG, MASCHINEN cohesive resistance; **Scherwinkel** *m* FERTIG shear plane angle, WASSERTRANS yaw angle; **Scherzone** *f* FERTIG zone of shear

Scheuerbesen *m* WASSERTRANS hog

Scheuerblech *nt* MASCHINEN chafing plate

Scheuerleiste *f* BAU baseboard (AmE), mopboard (AmE), skirting board (BrE), washboard, MASCHINEN wear strip

Scheuermittel *nt* MECHAN abrasive

Scheuern *nt* ANSTRICH fretting wear, FERTIG, MASCHINEN galling

scheuern *vt* ANSTRICH *durch Korrosion, durch Reiben* fret

Scheuersand *m* ANSTRICH silica abrasive

Scheuerstelle *f* KER & GLAS frigger

Schicht *f* ANSTRICH film, overlay, overlaying, BAU course, layer, COMP & DV, ELEKTRONIK layer, ERDÖL *Geologie* bed, FERTIG, KER & GLAS *Ziegel, Steine* course, KOHLEN bed, layer, stratum, KUNSTSTOFF layer, MASCHINEN ply, METALL layer, PAPIER *Papier* batch, RAUMFAHRT film, layer, ply, TEXTIL layer, VERPACK lamination, WASSERTRANS, WASSERVERSORG layer; **Schichtablagerung** *f* ELEKTRONIK layer deposition; **Schichtarbeit** *f* ERGON shiftwork; **Schichtband** *nt* AUFNAHME coated tape; **Schichtbildaufnahme** *f* KERNTECH tomography; **Schichtbildung** *f* ELEKTROTECH lamination; **Schichtbürste** *f* ELEKTROTECH laminated brush; **Schichtdicke** *f* KUNSTSTOFF coating thickness; **Schichtdickenmessung** *f* KERNTECH layer thickness gaging (AmE), layer thickness gauging (BrE)

Schichten:[1] **in ~ aufgebaut** *adj* MECHAN lamellar

Schichten:[2] *nt* KER & GLAS laying up

Schichten:[3] ~ **bilden** *vi* KOHLEN stratify

schichten *vt* ELEKTROTECH pile up

Schicht: **Schichtenanordnung** *f* KOHLEN coursing; **Schichtendetektor** *m* KOHLEN level detector; **Schichtenfolge** *f* KOHLEN layer sequence, *Geologie* bed sequence; **Schichtenkarte** *f* BAU *Vermessung* contour map; **Schichtenspaltung** *f* KUNSTSTOFF delamination; **Schichtentrennung** *f* FERTIG, KUNSTSTOFF delamination; **Schichtenwicklung** *f* ELEKTRIZ sandwich winding, ELEKTROTECH *bei Bürsten* layer winding; **Schichtfestigkeit** *f* KUNSTSTOFF interlaminar strength; **Schichtglas** *nt* KER & GLAS *Hohlglas* ply glass; **Schichtkern** *m* ELEKTROTECH laminated core; **Schichtkondensator** *m* ELEKTROTECH film capacitor; **Schichtkühlung** *f* RAUMFAHRT film cooling; **Schichtkunststoff** *m* WASSERTRANS laminated plastic; **Schichtlademotor** *m* KFZTECH stratified charge engine; **Schichtplatte** *f* AUFNAHME laminated record

schichtpressen *vt* BAU, FERTIG laminate

Schicht: **Schichtpreßstoff** *m* ELEKTRONIK laminate; **Schichtquelle** *f* WASSERVERSORG contact spring; **Schichtseite** *f* DRUCK emulsion side; **Schichtsieden** *nt*

KERNTECH sheet boiling; **Schichtspaltung** *f* KER & GLAS delamination; **Schichtstärke** *f* VERPACK lamination strength

Schichtstoff *m* KUNSTSTOFF laminate, laminated plastic; **Schichtstoffherstellung** *f* VERPACK laminating; **Schichtstofffolie** *f* BAU laminated sheet; **Schichtstoffprofil** *nt* KUNSTSTOFF laminated section; **Schichtstofftafel** *f* KUNSTSTOFF laminated sheet

Schicht: **Schichtträger** *m* FOTO film base; **Schichtumwandler** *m* RAUMFAHRT film transducer

Schichtung *f* ERDÖL *Geologie* bedding, stratification, QUAL stratification; **~ der Ladung** *f* WASSERTRANS charge stratification; **Schichtungsfestigkeit** *f* VERPACK lamination strength

Schicht: **Schichtwiderstand** *m* ELEKTROTECH film resis-tor, sheet resistance

Schiebebetrieb *m* KFZTECH *Motor* overrun

Schiebeboden *m* VERPACK sliding bottom

Schiebebühne *f* BAU traveling platform (AmE), travelling platform (BrE)

Schiebedach *nt* KFZTECH *Karosserie* sun roof

Schiebedeckel *m* VERPACK sliding lid

Schiebefenster *nt* BAU sash window, sliding sash, *Konstruktion mit Festverglasung und Hubfenster* Yorkshire light; **Schiebefensterbeschläge** *m pl* BAU sash hardware; **Schiebefensterfeststeller** *m* BAU sash fastener; **Schiebefensterrahmen** *m* BAU sash; **Schiebefensterverschluß** *m* BAU casement fastener

Schiebegelenk *nt* KFZTECH slip joint

Schiebegewicht *nt* MECHAN balancing weight

Schiebehülse *f* KFZTECH sliding sleeve

Schiebeimpuls *m* ELEKTRONIK shift pulse

Schiebekontakt *m* ELEKTROTECH sliding contact

Schiebekurve *f* LUFTTRANS *beim Trudeln* flat turn

Schiebelandung *f* LUFTTRANS crosswind landing

Schiebeleiter *f* BAU traveling ladder (AmE), travelling ladder (BrE)

Schiebelok *f* EISENBAHN booster locomotive, pusher locomotive (AmE)

Schiebelokomotive *f* EISENBAHN booster locomotive, pusher locomotive (AmE)

Schieben *nt* EISENBAHN banking

schieben *vt* MASCHINEN slip, MECHAN push, slide

Schiebenocken *m* MASCHINEN sliding cam

Schiebe-Potentiometer *nt* ELEKTRIZ slide rheostat

Schieber *m* BAU damper, FERTIG slide, *Kunststoffinstallationen* gate valve, *Meßschieber* movable head, HEIZ & KÄLTE register, slide, slide damper, valve, HYDRAUL *Absperrorgan von Rohrleitungen* valve, *Dampfmaschine, Hydraulik* slide valve, MASCHINEN gate valve, slide valve, slider, MATH slide, MECHAN slide, PAPIER bar, SICHERHEIT push stick

Schieberad *nt* KFZTECH *Getriebe*, MASCHINEN sliding gear

Schieberädergetriebe *nt* MASCHINEN sliding gear train

Schieberad: **Schieberadgetriebe** *nt* KFZTECH sliding gear transmission, MASCHINEN sliding gear drive

Schieberahmen *m* BAU window sash

Schieberdrosselventil *nt* HYDRAUL *Dampfmaschine* slide throttle valve

Schieberegister *nt* ELEKTRONIK, RADIO, TELEKOM shift register

Schieberiegel *m* MASCHINEN sliding bolt

Schiebering *m* MASCHINEN slider

Schieber: **Schieberkasten** *m* HYDRAUL steam chest, valve chest, *Dampfmaschine* slide box; **Schieber-**

klappe *f* HEIZ & KÄLTE slide damper

Schieberohr *nt* OPTIK *an optischem Gerät* sliding tube

Schieber: **Schieberstange** *f* HYDRAUL *Dampfmaschine* slide rod, *Kolbenschieber, Steuerschieber* stem, *Steuerkolben, Steuerschieber* rod; **Schiebersteuerung** *f* HYDRAUL slide valve gear; **Schiebersystem** *nt* RAUMFAHRT shutter system; **Schieberventil** *nt* HYDRAUL gate valve, KFZTECH slide valve

Schiebeschalter *m* ELEKTRIZ slide switch, ELEKTROTECH slide switch, sliding switch

Schiebesitz *m* *(SS)* MASCHINEN close sliding fit, push fit, sliding fit, MECHAN close-sliding fit, push fit, sliding fit

Schiebetor *nt* BAU sliding gate, WASSERVERSORG *einer Schleuse* sash gate

Schiebetür *f* BAU sliding door

Schiebevorrichtung *f* MECHAN slide

Schiebewelle *f* MASCHINEN sliding shaft

Schiebewiderstand *m* ELEKTRIZ slide rheostat

Schiebewinkel *m* LUFTTRANS crab angle

Schieblehre *f* MASCHINEN caliper square (AmE), calliper square (BrE), sliding calipers (AmE), sliding callipers (BrE), vernier gage (AmE), vernier gauge (BrE), METROL vernier caliper (AmE), vernier calliper (BrE)

schief[1] *adj* BAU slanting, *Turm* leaning, GEOM oblique, MASCHINEN out of plumb

schief:[2] **~ abgeschnittener Zylinder** *m* FERTIG *Kegel* ungula; **~e Biegung** *f* FERTIG bending in two planes; **~e Brücke** *f* BAU skew bridge; **~e Ebene** *f* BAU inclined plane; **~er Kegel** *m* GEOM oblique cone, scalene cone; **~er Strahl** *m* TELEKOM skew ray; **~e Umlaufbahn** *f* RAUMFAHRT drift orbit; **~e Verteilung** *f* QUAL skewed distribution; **~er Winkel** *m* GEOM oblique angle

Schiefbogen *m* BAU oblique arch

Schiefer *m* BAU slate, ERDÖL shale; **Schieferbedachung** *f* BAU slate roof cladding; **Schieferbruch** *m* METALL fibrous fracture; **Schieferdom** *m* ERDÖL *Geologie* shale dome; **Schieferkohle** *f* KOHLEN schistous coal; **Schiefernagel** *m* BAU slate nail; **Schieferplatte** *f* BAU slate; **Schieferschüttler** *m* ERDÖL shale shaker; **Schieferstock** *m* ERDÖL *Geologie* shale diapir; **Schieferton** *m* KER & GLAS schistous clay

schiefwinkelig *adj* BAU skew, FERTIG scalene

schiefwinklig: **~e axonometrische Projektion** *f* KONSTZEICH oblique axonometric projection; **~e Brücke** *f* BAU oblique bridge; **~es Dreieck** *nt* GEOM oblique triangle; **~e Parallelprojektion** *f* KONSTZEICH oblique parallel projection

Schiene *f* EISENBAHN rail, FERTIG *amerikanisches Schweißen* bar, MASCHINEN runner, TRANS road rail; **~ mit induktiver Rückkopplung** *f* EISENBAHN inductive reaction rail

Schienen *f pl* EISENBAHN metals

schienen *vt* FERTIG clout

Schiene: **Schienenauflager** *nt* EISENBAHN rail bed; **Schienenbeanspruchung** *f* EISENBAHN rail stress; **Schienenbiegepresse** *f* EISENBAHN rail-bending device; **Schienenbiegespannung** *f* EISENBAHN rail-bending stress; **Schienenbohrmaschine** *f* EISENBAHN rail-boring machine, rail-drilling machine; **Schienenbohrung** *f* EISENBAHN rail bore; **Schienenbruch** *m* EISENBAHN rail break; **Schienenbündel** *nt* EISENBAHN bundle of rails; **Schienenerhöhung** *f* EISENBAHN superelevation of the outer rail; **Schienenfahrzeug** *nt* EISENBAHN rail vehicle, TRANS railcar; **Schienenfuß** *m*

EISENBAHN rail flange, rail foot

schienengebunden *adj* TRANS rail-mounted

schienengleich: **~er Straßenübergang** *m* BAU, EISEN-BAHN grade crossing (AmE), level crossing (BrE)

Schiene: **Schienengleis** *nt* BAU tram track, EISENBAHN track; **Schienenhobelmaschine** *f* EISENBAHN rail-planing machine; **Schienenkabinensystem** *nt* EISENBAHN cabin system on rail; **Schienenkontakt** *m* EISENBAHN treadle; **Schienenkopf** *m* BAU, EISENBAHN, FERTIG rail head; **Schienenkopfausrundung** *f* EISEN-BAHN rail shoulder; **Schienenkran** *m* EISENBAHN rail crane; **Schienenlasche** *f* EISENBAHN fishplate, splice bar; **Schienenlegemaschine** *f* EISENBAHN track-laying machine; **Schienenlegen** *nt* EISENBAHN plate laying, rail laying, track laying; **Schienennagel** *m* EISENBAHN dog spike, MASCHINEN track spike; **Schienennetz** *nt* EISENBAHN railroad network (AmE), railway network (BrE); **Schienenomnibus** *m* EISENBAHN rail motor coach, railbus; **Schienenprofil** *nt* EISENBAHN rail profile, rail section; **Schienenquerschnitt** *m* EISEN-BAHN rail section; **Schienenräumer** *m* EISENBAHN cow catcher, pilot; **Schienenrücker** *m* EISENBAHN rail lifter, rail tongs; **Schienenschleifzug** *m* EISENBAHN rail-grinding train; **Schienenschwebebahn** *f* EISENBAHN suspended railroad (AmE), suspended railway (BrE); **Schienensteg** *m* EISENBAHN rail web; **Schienenstoß** *m* EISENBAHN rail joint; **Schienenstoßfutterblech** *nt* EI-SENBAHN shim; **Schienenstrang** *m* EISENBAHN rail track; **Schienenstromabnehmer** *m* EISENBAHN current collector; **Schienenstuhl** *m* EISENBAHN *für Doppelkopfschienen* chair; **Schienentankwagen** *m* EISENBAHN rail tank car; **Schienentragzange** *f* EISEN-BAHN rail tongs; **Schienenüberhöhung** *f* EISENBAHN superelevation of track; **Schienenuntersuchung** *f* EI-SENBAHN rail inspection; **Schienenverbinder** *m* EISENBAHN railbond; **Schienenverlegekran** *m* EISEN-BAHN rail-laying crane; **Schienenverschleißtoleranz** *f* EISENBAHN rail wear tolerance; **Schienenvorblock** *m* FERTIG rail bloom

Schiene-Straße- *pref* EISENBAHN rail-road; **Schiene-Straße-Sattelauflieger** *m* EISENBAHN, TRANS rail-road semitrailer; **Schiene-Straße-Verkehr** *m* EISENBAHN, TRANS rail-road-transport

schießen *vt* ERDÖL *Seismik* shoot

Schießhauer *m* KOHLEN blaster

Schiff:[1] **auf dem ~** *adj* WASSERTRANS on shipboard

Schiff[2] *nt* BAU *einer Halle, Kirche* bay, DRUCK galley, MEERSCHMUTZ vessel, WASSERTRANS boat; **~ mit geringem Tiefgang** *nt* WASSERTRANS shallow-draught vessel; **~ in Seenot** *nt* WASSERTRANS *Notfall* ship in distress; **~ mit Zellcontainern** *m* WASSERTRANS cellular container ship

Schiff:[3] **~ anhalten und durchsuchen** *vi* WASSERTRANS stop and examine a ship; **~ aufgeben** *vi* WASSERTRANS *Notfall* abandon ship; **~ in Dienst stellen** *vi* WASSER-TRANS put a ship into commission; **Schiffbruch erleiden** *vi* WASSERTRANS suffer shipwreck

Schiffahrt *f* WASSERTRANS shipping; **Schiffahrtskanal** *m* WASSERTRANS *künstliche Wasserstraße* ship canal; **Schiffahrtskunde** *f* WASSERTRANS navigation; **Schiffahrtslinie** *f* WASSERTRANS shipping line; **Schiffahrtsroute** *f* WASSERTRANS shipping lane, shipping route; **Schiffahrtswarnsignal** *nt* TELEKOM navigation warning signal

schiffbar *adj* WASSERTRANS *Gewässer* navigable; **nicht ~** *adj* WASSERTRANS innavigable

Schiff: **Schiffbarkeit** *f* WASSERTRANS navigability; **Schiffbau** *m* WASSERTRANS naval architecture, shipbuilding; **Schiffbauer** *m* WASSERTRANS shipbuilder, shipwright; **Schiffbauholz** *nt* WASSERTRANS timber; **Schiffbauingenieur** *m* WASSERTRANS marine architect, naval architect; **Schiffbauzeichnungen** *f pl* WASSERTRANS hull drawings; **Schiffbruch** *m* WASSERTRANS shipwreck

schiffbrüchig *adj* WASSERTRANS shipwrecked

Schiff: **Schiffsabfrage** *f* TELEKOM ship polling; **Schiffsartikel** *m* ERDÖL ship's article; **Schiffsausrüster** *m* WASSERTRANS ship chandler, ship chandlery; **Schiffsbedarfshändler** *m* WASSERTRANS ship chandler; **Schiffsbeladung** *f* WASSERTRANS ship loading; **Schiffsbergung** *f* WASSERTRANS salvaging; **Schiffsboden** *m* WASSERTRANS *Schiffbau* bottom; **Schiffsbreite** *f* WAS-SERTRANS breadth, *Schiffbau* beam; **Schiffsbrief** *m* WASSERTRANS ship's passport; **Schiffsdieselöl** *nt* WAS-SERTRANS marine diesel oil; **Schiffseigner** *m* WASSERTRANS shipowner; **Schiffsfracht** *f* VERPACK carriage by sea; **Schiffsführer** *m* WASSERTRANS *Handelsschiffahrt* shipmaster; **Schiffsführung** *f* WASSERTRANS ship handling; **Schiffskanal** *m* WASSER-TRANS ship canal; **Schiffskessel** *m* HEIZ & KÄLTE marine boiler; **Schiffskompaß** *m* WASSERTRANS *Navigation* mariner's compass; **Schiffskonstrukteur** *m* WASSERTRANS marine architect, ship designer; **Schiffskörper** *m* WASSERTRANS hull; **Schiffsküche** *f* WASSERTRANS galley; **Schiffskühlanlage** *f* HEIZ & KÄL-TE marine refrigeration plant; **Schiffsladung** *f* WASSERTRANS cargo, shipload; **Schiffsmakler** *m* WAS-SERTRANS ship broker; **Schiffsmannschaft** *f* WASSERTRANS *Besatzung* ship's hands; **Schiffsmaschinenbau** *m* WASSERTRANS marine engineering; **Schiffsmaschineningenieur** *m* WASSERTRANS marine engineer; **Schiffsmeldesystem** *nt* TELEKOM ship reporting system; **Schiffsnavigation** *f* WASSERTRANS navigation afloat; **Schiffsortung** *f* WASSERTRANS vessel location; **Schiffspapiere** *nt pl* WASSERTRANS ship's papers; **Schiffspoller** *m* WASSERTRANS *am Kai* bollard; **Schiffsposition** *f* WASSERTRANS ship's position; **Schiffspropeller** *m* MEERSCHMUTZ propeller; **Schiffsregister** *nt* WASSERTRANS ship's register; **Schiffsrumpf** *m* WASSERTRANS hull; **Schiffsschleuse** *f* WASSERVER-SORG lift lock; **Schiffsschleusung** *f* WASSERVERSORG *Schiff* locking; **Schiffsschraube** *f* MEERSCHMUTZ propeller, TRANS marine propeller, WASSERTRANS water propeller, water screw, *Schiffbau* propeller, *Schiffantrieb* screw; **Schiffsstandort** *m* WASSERTRANS ship's position; **Schiffstagebuch** *nt* WASSERTRANS ship's log, *Dokumente* logbook; **Schiffstaufe** *f* WASSERTRANS naming; **Schiffsträger** *m* WASSERTRANS *Schiffbau* hull girder, ship girder; **Schiffsverlader** *m* WASSERTRANS loader; **Schiffsvermietung** *f* WASSERTRANS *Schiff* charter; **Schiffsweg** *m* WASSERTRANS track; **Schiffswerft** *f* WASSERTRANS shipyard; **Schiffswinde** *f* MECHAN capstan; **Schiffszug** *m* WASSERTRANS bulk ship train

Schifter *m* BAU jack rafter

Schiftsparren *m* BAU jack rafter

Schikane *f* CHEMTECH *Wasserbehandlung* baffle

Schild *m* BAU, MASCHINEN shield, MECHAN plate, TRANS sign; **Schilderwärmung** *f* KERNTECH shield heat-up; **Schildkühlung** *f* KERNTECH shield cooling system; **Schildvortrieb** *m* EISENBAHN *Tunnelbau* shield tunneling (AmE), shield tunnelling (BrE); **Schildzapfen** *m* MECHAN trunnion

Schillern *nt* KER & GLAS iridescence, iridizing, MEER-SCHMUTZ iridescence, OPTIK irisation
Schimmel *m* LEBENSMITTEL mildew
schimmelfest *adj* VERPACK mold-resistant (AmE), mould-resistant (BrE)
Schimmer *m* MEERSCHMUTZ sheen
schimmernd *adj* TEXTIL lustrous
Schindel *f* BAU *Dach* shingle
Schirm *m* ELEKTRIZ screen, ELEKTRONIK screen, shield, ELEKTROTECH *für Lampe*, LABOR shield, MECHAN, OPTIK, PHYS screen; **Schirmanguß** *m* KUNSTSTOFF diaphragm gate; **Schirmbild** *nt* GERÄT screen image, TELEKOM *Radar* display; **Schirmgitter** *nt* ELEKTRONIK *Elektronenröhren* screen grid; **Schirmgitterröhre** *f* ELEKTRONIK screen grid tube; **Schirmhalter** *m* OPTIK screen holder; **Schirmraster** *nt* COMP & DV screen pattern; **Schirmträger** *m* ELEKTRONIK *Kathodenröhre* face plate
Schirmung *f* ELEKTRIZ shield; **Schirmungseffekt** *m* ELEKTRIZ screening effect
Schlachtausbeute *f* LEBENSMITTEL *Fleischerei* carcass dressing percentage, carcass yield
Schlachten *nt* LEBENSMITTEL *Schlachthaus* slaughtering
schlachten *vt* LEBENSMITTEL *Schlachthaus* slaughter, *Tiere* kill
Schlächter *m* LEBENSMITTEL slaughterer
Schlachthausabfall *m* ABFALL abattoir waste
Schlachtkreuzer *m* WASSERTRANS *Marine* battle cruiser
Schlacke *f* ABFALL clinker, BAU slag, FERTIG cinder, dross, scoria, slag, KER & GLAS *Glas, das auf Hafenofenherd spritzt* slag, KOHLEN scum, slag, METALL floss, slag, PAPIER slag; **Schlackebad** *nt* FERTIG molten slag
Schlacken *nt* FERTIG scumming; **Schlackenabzug** *m* FERTIG flushing; **Schlackenanhang** *m* FERTIG *Brennschneiden* adhering slag; **Schlackenlauf** *m* FERTIG skim gate; **Schlackenloch** *nt* FERTIG pit hole
schlacken *vt* FERTIG scum
schlackenrein *adj* THERMOD free from slag
Schlacken: **Schlackenschale** *f* METALL scorifier; **Schlackenstein** *m* METALL slag brick; **Schlackenwolle** *f* METALL slag wool
Schlaf *m* WASSERTRANS sleep; **Schlafkoje** *f* WASSERTRANS bunk; **Schlafwagen** *m* EISENBAHN sleeping car
Schlag:[1] **mit ~** *adj* TEXTIL flared
Schlag[2] *m* ANSTRICH impact, FERTIG eccentricity, MASCHINEN eccentricity, knock, lay, run-out, shock, MECHAN impact, WASSERTRANS leg
schlagartig: **~e Ausbreitung von Flammen** *f* THERMOD flashover
Schlag: **Schlagbeanspruchung** *f* FERTIG impact stress; **Schlagbelastung** *f* VERPACK impact stress; **Schlagbewegung** *f* LUFTTRANS *Hubschrauber* flapping; **Schlagbiegefestigkeit** *f* KFZTECH impact resistance; **Schlagbiegeprüfung** *f* MASCHINEN blow bending test; **Schlagbiegeversuch** *m* MASCHINEN impact bending test; **Schlagbohren** *nt* BAU boring by percussion, ERDÖL *Bohrtechnik*, KOHLEN percussion drilling; **Schlagbohrer** *m* BAU hammer drill, MASCHINEN percussion drill; **Schlagbohrmaschine** *f* MASCHINEN hammer drill, impact drill, percussion drill; **Schlagbohrschlamm** *m* ERDÖL spud mud; **Schlagbrecher** *m* KOHLEN impact crusher
Schlagen *nt* FERTIG *Walzen* chatter
schlagen[1] *vt* ANSTRICH agitate, FERTIG *Gießen* lash, *Seil* lay, MASCHINEN hammer, knock, lay

schlagen[2] *vi* BAU beat, FERTIG *Bohrer* wobble, *Walzen* chatter, MASCHINEN hammer, knock, run out of true
schlagfest[1] *adj* VERPACK shockproof
schlagfest:[2] **~es Polystyrol** *nt* KUNSTSTOFF impact polystyrene; **~e Preßmasse** *f* KUNSTSTOFF high-impact molding compound (AmE), high-impact moulding compound (BrE)
Schlag: **Schlagfestigkeit** *f* KERNTECH, KUNSTSTOFF, MECHAN, PHYS impact strength, VERPACK impact resistance, WERKPRÜF impact resistance, impact strength; **Schlagfestigkeit der Nabe** *f* LUFTTRANS *Hubschrauber* hub flapping stiffness; **Schlagfräsen** *nt* MASCHINEN fly cutting
schlagfrei *adj* FERTIG balanced
Schlag: **Schlaggalvanisierung** *f* ELEKTRONIK *elektronischer Niederschlag* striking; **Schlaggelenk** *nt* LUFTTRANS *Hubschrauber* flapping hinge; **Schlaggelenkbegrenzungsstift** *m* LUFTTRANS *Hubschrauber* flapping hinge pin; **Schlaghebel** *m* MECHAN ram lever; **Schlagknickversuch** *m* FERTIG impact buckling test; **Schlagkraft** *f* MASCHINEN percussive force; **Schlaglänge** *f* ELEKTROTECH, FERTIG *Drahtseil* lay; **Schlagloch** *nt* BAU, KFZTECH *Straße* pothole; **Schlagmeißel** *m* ERDÖL *zum Seilschlag bohren* cable drilling bit; **Schlagmeißel für Seilschlagbohren** *m* ERDÖL *Bohrtechnik* churn drill; **Schlagmikrofon** *nt* AUFNAHME impact microphone; **Schlagmoment** *nt* LUFTTRANS *Hubschrauber* flapping moment; **Schlagniet** *m* MASCHINEN percussion rivet; **Schlagnieten** *nt* FERTIG impact riveting, MASCHINEN percussion riveting
schlagnieten *vt* FERTIG impact-rivet
Schlag: **Schlagpressen** *nt* KUNSTSTOFF forging, MASCHINEN impact molding (AmE), impact moulding (BrE); **Schlagprobe** *f* VERPACK impact test; **Schlagprüfung** *f* PHYS impact test; **Schlagschere** *f* MASCHINEN guillotine shears; **Schlagschmieden** *nt* MASCHINEN impact forging; **Schlagschrauber** *m* MASCHINEN impact spanner (BrE), impact wrench (AmE); **Schlagseite** *f* WASSERTRANS list
Schlagseite: **~ haben** *vi* WASSERTRANS list
Schlag: **Schlagsieb** *nt* KOHLEN impact screen; **Schlagstrangpressen** *nt* MASCHINEN impact extrusion; **Schlagtonhöhe** *f* AKUSTIK strike note; **Schlagversuch** *m* ANSTRICH, KUNSTSTOFF, METALL, VERPACK, WERKPRÜF impact test; **Schlagwerk** *nt* MASCHINEN hammer mechanism; **Schlagwetter** *nt* SICHERHEIT explosive atmosphere, *Bergbau* flammable atmosphere
schlagwettergeschützt: **~er Motor** *m* ELEKTROTECH, THERMOD flameproof motor; **~er Schalter** *m* THERMOD flameproof switch
Schlag: **Schlagwetterschutz** *m* SICHERHEIT *Bergbau* flame protection; **Schlagwinkel** *m* LUFTTRANS flapping angle
schlagzäh: **~es Polystyrol** *nt* KUNSTSTOFF impact polystyrene
Schlagzähigkeit *f* KUNSTSTOFF impact strength
Schlag: **Schlagzahnfräsen** *nt* MASCHINEN fly cutting, thread whirling; **Schlagzeile** *f* DRUCK catchline; **Schlagzerreißversuch** *m* METALL tensile impact test; **Schlagzugversuch** *m* METALL tensile impact test
Schlamm *m* ABFALL sludge, slurry, KER & GLAS, KOHLEN slime, slurry, LEBENSMITTEL sludge, PAPIER slime, - WASSERVERSORG silt, slime, sludge; **Schlammablagerungen** *f pl* ABFALL alluvial deposits; **Schlammabscheider** *m* WASSERVERSORG silt trap; **Schlammabsetzvolumen** *nt* CHEMTECH *Abwasser* settled volu-

me; **Schlammanalyse** *f* BAU sedimentation test

Schlämmaschine *f* CHEMTECH decanting machine

Schlamm: **Schlammaufbereitung** *f* ABFALL sludge processing; **Schlammbecken** *nt* KOHLEN slurry pond; **Schlammbehandlung** *f* ABFALL sludge processing; **Schlammbelebung** *f* ABFALL activation of sludge; **Schlammbelebungsverfahren** *nt* WASSERVERSORG activated sludge process; **Schlammbeseitigung** *f* ABFALL sludge removal, WASSERVERSORG sludge disposal; **Schlammbildungsprüfung** *f* ELEKTRIZ sludge formation test; **Schlammbohrer** *m* ERDÖL *Bohrtechnik* mud bit

Schlämme *f* ANSTRICH slurry, BAU whitewash

Schlamm: **Schlammeindickung** *f* ABFALL sludge thickening, WASSERVERSORG sludge ripening, sludge thickening

Schlämmen *nt* BAU whitewashing

schlämmen *vt* FERTIG levigate

Schlamm: **Schlammentwässerung** *f* ABFALL dehydration of sludge, sludge dewatering

Schlämmeversiegelung *f* BAU slurry seal

Schlamm: **Schlammfang** *m* ABFALL sludge sump, WASSERVERSORG silt trap; **Schlammfaulbecken** *nt* ABFALL stabilization pond; **Schlammfaulbehälter** *m* ABFALL digestion sump, sludge digestion tank; **Schlammfaulung** *f* ABFALL sludge digestion; **Schlammfluid** *nt* ERDÖL *Bohrtechnik* mud fluid; **Schlammgehalt** *m* WASSERVERSORG mud content; **Schlammgewicht** *nt* ERDÖL *Tiefbohrtechnik* mud weight; **Schlammgrube** *f* ERDÖL *Bohrtechnik* mud pit; **Schlammkasten** *m* ERDÖL *Bohrtechnik* mud box; **Schlammkohle** *f* KOHLEN coal sludge, mud coal; **Schlammkompostierung** *f* ABFALL sludge composting; **Schlammkonditionierung** *f* WASSERVERSORG sludge bulking, sludge conditioning; **Schlammkonzentrat** *nt* KOHLEN concentrated sludge

Schlämmkreide *f* FERTIG whiting

Schlamm: **Schlammkuchen** *m* ABFALL sludge cake; **Schlammlagerraum** *m* WASSERVERSORG silt storage space; **Schlammlog** *nt* ERDÖL *Bohrtechnik* mud log; **Schlammraum** *m* KFZTECH *der untere Teil des Batteriegehäuses* sediment chamber, sediment space; **Schlammräumer** *m* ABFALL sludge rake; **Schlammring** *m* ERDÖL *Bohrtechnik* mud ring; **Schlammrückleitung** *f* ERDÖL *Bohrtechnik* mud return line; **Schlammsammelbehälter** *m* ABFALL silt container, sludge sump; **Schlammsäule** *f* ERDÖL *Bohrtechnik* mud column; **Schlammschwelle** *f* BAU mudsill; **Schlammseil** *nt* ERDÖL sand line; **Schlammsieb** *nt* KOHLEN slurry screen; **Schlammstabilisierung** *f* ABFALL sludge stabilization; **Schlammstapelteich** *m* WASSERVERSORG sump; **Schlammsystem** *nt* ERDÖL *Tiefbohrtechnik* mud system; **Schlammteich** *m* WASSERVERSORG sump; **Schlammteichverfahren** *nt* UMWELTSCHMUTZ *Eindämmen eines Wasserbeckens* lagooning; **Schlammtrockenbett** *nt* ABFALL sludge drying bed; **Schlammtrocknung** *f* ABFALL sludge drying

Schlämmung *f* CHEMTECH elution, KER & GLAS, LEBENSMITTEL elutriation

Schlamm: **Schlammverbrennung** *f* WASSERVERSORG sludge incineration; **Schlammverdickung** *f* ABFALL dehydration of sludge, sludge dewatering; **Schlammverlust** *m* ERDÖL *Bohrtechnik* mud losses

Schlämmversuch *m* BAU elutriation test

Schlamm: **Schlammverwertung** *f* ABFALL recycling of sludge; **Schlammvulkan** *m* ERDÖL *Geologie*, NICHTFOSS ENERG mud volcano; **Schlammwasser** *nt*

WASSERVERSORG sludge liquor; **Schlammzone** *f* WASSERTRANS *Geographie* mudflats

Schlange *f* KER & GLAS snake, KONTROLL queue, MASCHINEN coil; **Schlangenbildung** *f* KER & GLAS snaking; **Schlangenbohrer** *m* MASCHINEN screw auger

schlangenförmig *adj* BAU meandering

Schlange: **Schlangenrohr** *nt* BAU coil

schlankgenutet *adj* FERTIG slow-helix

Schlankheitsgrad *m* BAU slenderness ratio, LUFTTRANS *Stromlinienaufbau* fineness ratio

Schlauch *m* BAU flexible hose, hose, KFZTECH inner tube, LABOR *Verbindung* hose, MASCHINEN flexible pipe, flexible tube, hose, tube, MECHAN hose, NICHTFOSS ENERG tube, PAPIER, RAUMFAHRT hose, UMWELTSCHMUTZ bag, WASSERVERSORG hose; ~ **mit Gummieinlage** *m* WASSERVERSORG rubber-lined canvas hose; **Schlauchanschluß** *m* BAU hose coupler, MASCHINEN hose connection; **Schlauchboot** *nt* WASSERTRANS inflatable boat, inflatable dinghy, rubber boat, rubber dinghy; **Schlauchfilter** *nt* KOHLEN filter bag; **Schlauchfolienblasen** *nt* KUNSTSTOFF film blowing; **Schlauchhahn** *m* MASCHINEN hose tap; **Schlauchhaspel auf Wagen** *f* SICHERHEIT mobile hose reel; **Schlauchklemme** *f* MASCHINEN hose clip, MECHAN hose clamp; **Schlauchkupplung** *f* MASCHINEN, WASSERVERSORG *für einen Gartenschlauch* hose coupling; **Schlauchleitung** *f* MASCHINEN flexible tubing, tubing

schlauchlos: ~**er Reifen** *m* KFZTECH *Reifen* tubeless tire (AmE), tubeless tyre (BrE)

Schlauch: **Schlauchschelle** *f* MASCHINEN hose clamp; **Schlauchtrockenmaschine** *f* TEXTIL tubular dryer; **Schlauchtülle** *f* FERTIG connector, MASCHINEN hose nozzle; **Schlauchumflechtmaschine** *f* KUNSTSTOFF braiding machine; **Schlauchventil** *nt* FERTIG *Kunststoffinstallationen* pipe compression valve, KFZTECH valve

Schlaufe *f* VERPACK carrying handle

schlecht:[1] ~**e Dämmung** *f* ACOUST poor insulation; ~**er Eingriff** *m* FERTIG mismating; ~**e Isolation** *f* TELEKOM low insulation; ~**es Isoliermedium** *nt* ELEKTROTECH poor insulant; ~**e Isolierung** *f* ACOUST poor insulation; ~**er Kontakt** *m* ELEKTROTECH bad contact; ~**e Kühlung** *f* KER & GLAS bad annealing; ~**er Leiter** *m* ELEKTROTECH poor conductor; ~**e Lötverbindung** *f* ELEKTRIZ dry joint

schlecht:[2] ~ **werden** *vi* LEBENSMITTEL spoil, taint

Schlechtgrenze *f* QUAL limiting quality

Schlechtwetterausrüstung *f* WASSERTRANS foul weather gear

Schlegel *m* BAU beater, MECHAN mallet

Schleichen *nt* ELEKTROTECH crawling

schleichend: ~**e Bewegung** *f* STRÖMPHYS *zähe Strömungen* creeping motion; ~**e Verbrennung** *f* KFZTECH slow combustion

Schleichweg *m* TRANS rat run

Schleier *m* FOTO fog, KER & GLAS suspended curtain wall; **Schleierkühlung** *f* RAUMFAHRT film cooling

Schleif- *pref* ELEKTROTECH, GERÄT, MASCHINEN abrasion; **Schleifband** *nt* KER & GLAS *zum Schleifen von Glas*, MASCHINEN abrasive belt; **Schleifbandstandzeit** *f* FERTIG band life; **Schleifbarkeit** *f* CHEMTECH grindability; **Schleifbock** *m* MASCHINEN bench grinder; **Schleifdrahtmeßbrücke** *f* ELEKTROTECH, GERÄT slide wire bridge; **Schleifdruckbegrenzer** *m* PAPIER grinding-pressure limiter

Schleife *f* COMP & DV, ELEKTRIZ, ELEKTRONIK *geschlossener Stromweg* loop, FERTIG snarl, KER & GLAS, KONTROLL, PAPIER, RADIO, TELEKOM *Induktion* loop, TRANS *Straße* turning, WASSERTRANS *Tauwerk* loop

Schleifen *nt* ANSTRICH abrasion, KER & GLAS cutting, grinding, KUNSTSTOFF grinding, sanding, MASCHINEN grinding, sharpening, MECHAN, PAPIER grinding; **~ mit grobkörnigem Schleifkörper** *nt* FERTIG coarse-grain grinding; **~ und Polieren** *nt* KER & GLAS grinding and polishing

schleifen[1] *vt* ANSTRICH, BAU grind, FERTIG *Edelstein* cut, *Holz* sandpaper, *Werkzeug* grind, MASCHINEN grind, sharpen

schleifen[2] *vi* MASCHINEN grind

schleifend *adj* PAPIER abrasive; **nicht ~** *adj* FERTIG *Dichtung* nonrubbing

Schleife: **Schleifengalvanometer** *nt* ELEKTRIZ, ELEKTROTECH loop galvanometer

schleifengeschaltet *adj* ELEKTRIZ looped

Schleife: **Schleifenkopplung** *f* ELEKTROTECH loop coupling; **Schleifenmessung** *f* ELEKTRIZ loop test; **Schleifentrockner** *m* PAPIER loop drier, loop dryer; **Schleifenwicklung** *f* ELEKTROTECH lap winding

Schleifer *m* KER & GLAS *Arbeiter* polisher, *Gerät zum Glasschleifen* polisher, MASCHINEN grinder, sharpener; **Schleiferei** *f* KER & GLAS cutter's bay, cutting shop, polishing shop; **Schleifertrog** *m* PAPIER grinder pit

Schleif-: **Schleiffehler** *m* KER & GLAS bloach; **Schleifkohle** *f* KFZTECH brush; **Schleifkontakt** *m* ELEKTROTECH, PHYS sliding contact; **Schleifkörperabrichtung** *f* FERTIG wheel truing; **Schleifläufer** *m* KER & GLAS polishing runner; **Schleifleinen** *nt* MASCHINEN abrasive cloth; **Schleifleiste** *f* EISENBAHN pantograph wearing strip; **Schleifmaschine** *f* FERTIG disc grinder (BrE), disk grinder (AmE), KER & GLAS grinding unit, polishing unit, *für Spiegelglas* grinder, MASCHINEN grinder, grinding machine, sharpener, sharpening machine, MECHAN grinder, PAPIER grinding machine; **Schleifmaschinenbett** *nt* MASCHINEN grinding-machine bed; **Schleifmittel** *nt* ANSTRICH abrasive surface, FERTIG abrading medium, KER & GLAS grinding agent, polishing agent, KOHLEN abradant, MASCHINEN abrasive, PAPIER abrasive material; **Schleifmittel aus Aluminiumoxid** *nt* ANSTRICH alumina abrasive; **Schleifpapier** *nt* KER & GLAS polishing paper, MASCHINEN abrasive sheet, MECHAN abrasive paper; **Schleifpaste** *f* MASCHINEN, MECHAN grinding paste; **Schleifrad** *nt* KER & GLAS cutting wheel, grinding wheel, polishing wheel, MECHAN abrasive wheel, grinding wheel

Schleifring *m* CHEMTECH grinding cylinder, ELEKTROTECH rotor slip ring, KFZTECH, PHYS slip ring; **Schleifringanker** *m* ELEKTROTECH wound rotor; **Schleifringankermotor** *m* ELEKTROTECH slip ring induction motor; **Schleifringläufer** *m* ELEKTROTECH wound rotor; **Schleifringläufermotor** *m* HEIZ & KÄLTE slip ring motor; **Schleifringmotor** *m* ELEKTRIZ, HEIZ & KÄLTE slip ring motor; **Schleifringrotor** *m* ELEKTRIZ slip ring rotor, ELEKTROTECH wound rotor

Schleif-: **Schleifrohstoff** *m* FERTIG grinding raw material; **Schleifsand** *m* KER & GLAS grinding sand

Schleifscheibe *f* FERTIG abrasive wheel, grinding wheel, wheel dresser, MASCHINEN abrasive disc (BrE), abrasive disk (AmE), grinding wheel, wheel, MECHAN, SICHERHEIT abrasive wheel; **~ mit Harzbindung** *f* MASCHINEN resin-bonded wheel; **Schleifscheiben-**

abrichter *m* FERTIG grinding wheel dresser; **Schleifscheibenabrichtung** *f* FERTIG grinding wheel dressing; **Schleifscheibenabziehwerkzeug** *nt* MASCHINEN wheel dresser; **Schleifscheibenauswuchtung** *f* FERTIG grinding wheel balancing; **Schleifscheibenfutter** *nt* FERTIG grinding wheel chuck; **Schleifscheibenverschleißvolumen** *nt* FERTIG volume of wheel grain wear; **Schleifscheibenwuchtzustand** *m* FERTIG grinding wheel balance

Schleif-: **Schleifschiene** *f* KER & GLAS grinding runner; **Schleifsegment** *nt* FERTIG wheel segment, MASCHINEN grinding segment; **Schleifspäne** *m pl* FERTIG, MASCHINEN grindings

Schleifspindel *f* KER & GLAS grinder spindle, beim Schleifen von Hohlglas spindle, MASCHINEN grinding spindle, wheel spindle: **Schleifspindelschlitten** *m* FERTIG wheel head slide; **Schleifspindelstock** *m* FERTIG grinding head, wheel head

Schleif-: **Schleifspuren** *f pl* FERTIG wheel marks, MASCHINEN grinding marks; **Schleifstahl** *m* LEBENSMITTEL sharpening steel; **Schleifstaub** *m* FERTIG grit; **Schleifstein** *m* FERTIG grinding stone, grindstone, MECHAN grinding wheel; **Schleifstück** *nt* EISENBAHN *am Stromabnehmer* pantograph slipper; **Schleifsupport** *m* MASCHINEN wheel carriage; **Schleifverlust** *m* KER & GLAS cutting loss; **Schleifvermögen** *nt* FERTIG abrading capacity; **Schleifversuch** *m* FERTIG abrasion test; **Schleifvorrichtung** *f* FERTIG grinding fixture; **Schleifzylinder** *m* CHEMTECH, MASCHINEN grinding cylinder

Schleim *m* WASSERVERSORG slime

schleimbildend *adj* CHEMIE muciferous

Schleppboot *nt* MEERSCHMUTZ towboat, tug boat

Schleppbremse *f* KFZTECH drag brake

Schleppen *nt* TRANS haulage, towing, WASSERTRANS dredging, *Schiff* towage

schleppen *vt* MEERSCHMUTZ *Schiff* tow, TRANS haul, WASSERTRANS *Schiff* tow

Schlepper *m* KFZTECH tractor, LUFTTRANS prime mover, MEERSCHMUTZ towboat, tug boat, WASSERTRANS *Schifftyp* tug

Schleppflug *m* LUFTTRANS aerotow, areotow flight

Schleppgeschirr *nt* MEERSCHMUTZ towing gear

Schleppkahn *m* WASSERTRANS dumb barge

Schleppkante *f* PHYS trailing edge

Schleppkette *f* LUFTTRANS dragline

Schleppleine *f* MEERSCHMUTZ, WASSERTRANS *Tauwerk* towline

Schlepplift *m* TRANS drag lift

Schlepplöffelbagger *m* BAU dragline excavator

Schleppnetz[1] *nt* WASSERTRANS *Fischerei* dredge net, trawl, trawl net

Schleppnetz:[2] **mit ~ fischen** *vt* WASSERTRANS *Fischerei* haul, drag

Schleppnetz:[3] **mit ~ fischen** *vi* WASSERTRANS fish

Schleppnetzfischer *m* WASSERTRANS *Schifftyp* trawler

Schleppsaugbagger *m* WASSERTRANS trailing suction dredge, trailing suction dredger

Schleppschiff *nt* WASSERTRANS towboat; **Schleppschiffzug** *m* WASSERTRANS towed convoy

Schleppseil *nt* LUFTTRANS dragline

Schleppstange *f* MECHAN towbar

Schlepptrosse *f* WASSERTRANS towrope

Schleppung *f* ERDÖL *von Formationsschichten* drag

Schleppverband *m* WASSERTRANS tow train

Schleppversuchstank *m* WASSERTRANS *Schiffbau* ship

model test tank

Schleppwagen *m* TRANS tow car

Schleppwalze *f* FERNSEH idle roller

Schleppzange *f* FERTIG gripping jaws

Schleppzug *m* WASSERTRANS tug and tow

Schleuder *f* FERTIG *Schleuderguß* spinner, KUNSTSTOFF centrifuge; **Schleuderätzen** *nt* MASCHINEN spin etching; **Schleuderbeton** *m* BAU spun concrete

schleuderformgießen *vt* FERTIG centrifuge

Schleuder: **Schleuderformmaschine** *f* FERTIG *Gießen* slinger

Schleuderguß *m* FERTIG centrispinning, KER & GLAS, METALL centrifugal casting; **Schleudergußrohr** *nt* FERTIG spun pipe; **Schleudergußstück** *nt* FERTIG centrifugal casting; **Schleudergußteil** *m* FERTIG spun part

Schleudergußverfahren: **im ~ hergestellt** *adj* FERTIG spun

Schleuder: **Schleuderkopf** *m* FERTIG *Gießen: Sand-schleuderformmaschine* impeller head; **Schleuderkraft** *f* RAUMFAHRT *Raumschiff* ejection force; **Schleudermaschine** *f* CHEMTECH centrifugal machine; **Schleudermühle** *f* CHEMTECH centrifuge mill, LEBENS-MITTEL disintegrator

Schleudern *nt* CHEMTECH centrifugation, FERTIG *Bohrer* jolt, KOHLEN centrifuging, RAUMFAHRT *Beschleunigungsmanöver vom Orbit heraus durch Zentrifugalkraft* slingshot, TRANS skidding·

schleudern[1] *vt* FERTIG *Bohrer* jolt, *Formen* sling, KOHLEN, KUNSTSTOFF centrifuge

schleudern[2] *vi* KFZTECH skid

Schleuder: **Schleuderpumpe** *f* CHEMTECH centrifugal pump; **Schleuderschutzeinrichtung** *f* LUFTTRANS antitorque device; **Schleudersitz** *m* RAUMFAHRT ejection seat; **Schleudertrennung** *f* ABFALL ballistic separation; **Schleudertrockner** *m* CHEMTECH centrifugal hydroextractor, TEXTIL hydroextractor; **Schleuderziehverfahren** *nt* KER & GLAS centrifugal drawing

Schleuse[1] *f* BAU lock, HYDRAUL *Dampfturbine* gate, KERNTECH *an einem Handschuhkasten* transfer port, NICHTFOSS ENERG, WASSERVERSORG sluice

Schleuse:[2] **eine ~ passieren** *vi* WASSERTRANS pass through a lock

schleusen *vt* HYDRAUL gate, WASSERVERSORG *Schiff* lock

Schleuse: **Schleusenanlage** *f* WASSERVERSORG *eines Schiffs* lockage; **Schleusendeckel** *m* FERTIG manhole cover; **Schleusendrempel** *m* WASSERVERSORG lock sill, miter sill (AmE), mitre sill (BrE); **Schleusen-Füll- und Entleersystem** *nt* WASSERVERSORG drawgate; **Schleusengeld** *nt* WASSERTRANS *Binnenwasserstraßen* lock dues; **Schleusenhaupt** *nt* WASSERVERSORG head sluices; **Schleusenhaus** *nt* WASSERVERSORG lock house; **Schleusenkammer** *f* WASSERTRANS lock chamber, WASSERVERSORG gate chamber, lock chamber; **Schleusenkanal** *m* WASSERVERSORG sluiceway

schleusenlos: **~er Kanal** *m* WASSERVERSORG ditch canal

Schleuse: **Schleusenplattform** *f* WASSERVERSORG floatboard; **Schleusenrahmen** *m* WASSERVERSORG frame; **Schleusenschwelle** *f* WASSERVERSORG clap sill, lock sill, miter sill (AmE), mitre sill (BrE), sill; **Schleusensohle** *f* WASSERVERSORG floor; **Schleusentor** *nt* BAU gate, WASSERTRANS lock gate, sluicegate, WASSERVERSORG floodgate, gate, sluicegate; **Schleusentreppe** *f* WASSERVERSORG run of sluices; **Schleusenwärter** *m*

WASSERTRANS lock keeper

Schleusung *f* WASSERVERSORG sluicing

schlicht *adj* TEXTIL plain

Schlichtanlage *f* TEXTIL sizing machine

Schlichtaufnahme *f* TEXTIL size take-up

Schlichtband *nt* KER & GLAS finishing belt

Schlichtdrehmeißel *m* FERTIG finish turning tool

Schlichte *f* FERTIG slur, *Gießen* wash, KER & GLAS size, KUNSTSTOFF size, sizing agent, TEXTIL sizing, *Ausrüstung* size; **Schlichtebad** *nt* TEXTIL size bath; **Schlichtemittel** *nt* CHEMIE *Textil* sizing agent, TEXTIL size, sizing agent

Schlichten *nt* FERTIG finishing, KER & GLAS, TEXTIL sizing; **~ von Baum zu Baum** *nt* TEXTIL beam-to-beam sizing

schlichten *vt* FERTIG dress, MASCHINEN flat, plane, TEXTIL size

Schlichtfeile *f* FERTIG smooth-cut file

Schlichtfräsen *nt* MASCHINEN finish milling

Schlichthammer *m* FERTIG *Schmieden* flatter, MASCHINEN flat-face hammer, planisher, planishing hammer

Schlichthobel *m* FERTIG smooth plane

Schlichtmaschine *f* TEXTIL sizing machine

Schlichtsorte *f* FERTIG *Walzen* finishing grade

Schlichtwerkzeug *nt* MASCHINEN finishing tool

Schlichtzahn *m* MASCHINEN finishing tooth

Schlichtzugabe *f* FERTIG finish allowance

Schlick *m* KOHLEN slime, WASSERVERSORG silt; **Schlickablagerung** *f* ABFALL deposition of silt

Schlicker *m* FERTIG, KER & GLAS slip; **Schlickerguß** *m* KER & GLAS slip casting; **Schlickergußtiegel** *m* KER & GLAS slip-cast pot; **Schlickerofen** *m* KER & GLAS slip kiln

Schliere *f* FERTIG streak, stria, KER & GLAS ream, OPTIK streak; **Schlieren** *f pl* KER & GLAS cords; **Schlierenfotografie** *f* PHYS schlieren photography

schlierig *adj* KER & GLAS cordy

Schließbeschlag *m* BAU lock fitting

Schließblech *nt* BAU keeper, lock plate, striking plate, *eines Schlosses* box

Schließbolzen *m* MECHAN cotter pin

Schließdämpfer *m* KFZTECH dashpot

Schließdeckel *m* LUFTTRANS blanking cover; **~ für Kühlluftauslaß** *m* LUFTTRANS blanking cover for air-cooling-unit outlet

Schließdruck *m* ERDÖL *Lagerstättentechnik* shut-in pressure

Schließeffekt *m* LUFTTRANS blanking effect

Schließelement *nt* MASCHINEN closing element

Schließen *nt* EISENBAHN, ELEKTROTECH *eines elektrischen Stromkreises* closure, KÜNSTL INT inference, reasoning; **~ anhand von Standardvorgaben** *nt* KÜNSTL INT default reasoning; **~ der Form** *nt* DRUCK lock-up; **~ und Unterbrechen** *nt* ELEKTROTECH make and break

schließen *vt* BAU close, lock, shut, DRUCK lock up, ELEKTROTECH *Stromkreis, Kontakt*, FERTIG make

Schließer *m* ELEKTRIZ make contact, normally open contact, ELEKTROTECH normally open contact; **Schließer- und Öffnerelement** *nt* ELEKTRIZ make-and-break device; **Schließer- und Öffnerspule** *f* ELEKTRIZ make-and-break coil; **Schließerrelais** *nt* ELEKTRIZ make relay

Schließgeschwindigkeit *f* ELEKTRIZ closing speed

Schließkasten *m* BAU lock casing

Schließklappe *f* BAU box staple

Schließkontakt *m* ELEKTRIZ, ELEKTROTECH make contact, normally open contact, FERTIG maker
Schließkopf *m* FERTIG upset point
Schließnocken *m* MASCHINEN locking cam
Schließpfosten *m* BAU shutting post
Schließrahmen *m* DRUCK chase
Schließring *m* FOTO, MASCHINEN retaining ring
Schließtisch *m* DRUCK imposing table
Schließungsbelastbarkeit *f* ELEKTRIZ rated making capacity
Schließung-Schließung-Kontakt *m* ELEKTRIZ make-make contact
Schließungsimpuls *m* ELEKTROTECH make pulse
Schließungs-Öffnungszeit *f* ELEKTRIZ make-and-break time
Schließvorgang *m* ELEKTRIZ closing operation
Schließwinkel *m* KFZTECH dwell angle
Schließzeit *f* ELEKTRIZ closing time, make time
Schließzeug *nt* DRUCK quoins
Schliff *m* FERTIG grinding, grind, KER & GLAS cut, MECHAN finish; **Schliffbild** *nt* FERTIG grinding pattern; **Schliff-Fläche** *f* NICHTFOSS ENERG polished surface; **Schliffstopfen** *m* LABOR ground stopper, VERPACK ground-in stopper; **Schliffverbindung** *f* LABOR ground glass joint; **Schliffverbindungshalter** *m* LABOR ground glass joint clamp
Schlinge *f* AUFNAHME *des Tonbands* curl, FERTIG *Draht* snarl, KONTROLL, TEXTIL loop, WASSERTRANS *Tauwerk* loop, sling; **Schlingenbildung** *f* TEXTIL plucking; **Schlingenflor** *m* TEXTIL uncut pile; **Schlingenflorteppich** *m* TEXTIL loop pile carpet
Schlingerdämpfungsanlage *f* WASSERTRANS *Schiff* anti-rolling device
Schlingerkiel *m* WASSERTRANS bilge keel
Schlingerleiste *f* WASSERTRANS fiddle
Schlingern *nt* WASSERTRANS *Schiffbewegung* rolling; ~ **und Stampfen** *nt* WASSERTRANS *Schiffbewegungen* rolling and pitching
schlingern *vi* WASSERTRANS *Schiffbewegung* lurch
Schlingerstabilisierung *f* TRANS sway stabilization
Schlingerversuch *m* WASSERTRANS *Schiffkonstruktion* roll test
Schlitten *m* EISENBAHN carriage, MASCHINEN carriage, cradle, ram, slide rest, slide, MECHAN cradle, TRANS carrier; **Schlittendraht** *m* ELEKTRIZ skid wire; **Schlitteneinheit** *f* MASCHINEN slide unit; **Schlittenkufe** *m* MECHAN runner; **Schlittenrevolverdrehmaschine** *f* MASCHINEN combination lathe, saddle-type turret lathe; **Schlittenständer** *m* MASCHINEN integral way columns
Schlitz: [1] **mit ~** *adj* FERTIG *Schraube* recessed
Schlitz [2] *m* DRUCK, ELEKTROTECH, FERNSEH slot, HYDRAUL port, KERNTECH groove, *in einem Rotorblatt* slot, MASCHINEN recess, slot, PAPIER aperture, PHYS slit, RAUMFAHRT *Antenne* slit, slot, TELEKOM slot, WELLPHYS slit; **Schlitz- und Druckmaschine** *f* VERPACK slitting and printing machine; **Schlitzabtastung** *f* FERNSEH slit scanning; **Schlitzanodenmagnetron** *nt* ELEKTRONIK split anode magnetron; **Schlitzantenne** *f* TELEKOM slot antenna; **Schlitzblende** *f* FOTO slit diaphragm; **Schlitzdränung** *f* BAU *Tiefbau* mole drainage
Schlitzen *nt* FERTIG *Trennschleifen* slitting, MASCHINEN slitting, slotting
schlitzen *vt* BAU split, MASCHINEN slot, TEXTIL split
Schlitz: **Schlitzfeile** *f* MASCHINEN slot file, slotting file; **Schlitzflügel** *m* LUFTTRANS slotted wing; **Schlitzfräser**

m MASCHINEN keyway cutter, slot cutter, slotting cutter; **Schlitzkernkabel** *nt* OPTIK slotted core cable; **Schlitzklappe** *f* LUFTTRANS slot flap; **Schlitzkopf** *m* MASCHINEN slotted head; **Schlitzleitung** *f* PHYS slotline; **Schlitzmantelkolben** *m* KFZTECH split skirt piston; **Schlitzmaschine** *f* FERTIG slitter, KOHLEN nicking machine; **Schlitzmutter** *f* MASCHINEN slotted nut; **Schlitzmutterndreher** *m* MASCHINEN slotted-type screwdriver; **Schlitzmutternschlüssel** *m* MASCHINEN slotted-type screwdriver; **Schlitzniet** *m* BAU slotted rivet; **Schlitzprobe** *f* KOHLEN channel sample; **Schlitzrohr** *nt* BAU slot pipe; **Schlitzschraube** *f* MASCHINEN slotted head screw, slotted screw; **Schlitzschraube mit Zylinderkopf** *f* FERTIG fillister head; **Schlitzstrahlkathodenstrahlröhre** *f* FERNSEH split beam cathode-ray tube; **Schlitzsystem** *nt* RAUMFAHRT slit system; **Schlitzverschluß** *m* FERNSEH slit shutter, FOTO focal plane shutter, roller-blind shutter; **Schlitzwandverfahren** *nt* ABFALL slurry trenching
Schloß *nt* KFZTECH *Karosserie*, MASCHINEN, SICHERHEIT, WASSERTRANS lock; ~ **DIN rechts** *nt* BAU right-hand lock; ~ **ohne Klinke** *nt* BAU deadlock
Schlosser *m* MASCHINEN locksmith; **Schlosserhammer** *m* MASCHINEN fitter's hammer, locksmith's hammer; **Schlosserwerkstatt** *f* MASCHINEN fitting shop
Schloß: **Schloßgarnitur** *f* BAU lockset (AmE); **Schloßkasten** *m* BAU box staple, case, FERTIG apron housing, MASCHINEN apron; **Schloßmutter** *f* MASCHINEN clasp nut; **Schloßriegel** *m* BAU deadbolt; **Schloßschraube** *f* MASCHINEN coach bolt; **Schloßschutzblech** *nt* BAU finger plate
Schlot *m* BAU chimney stack, funnel, ERDÖL *Geologie* pipe
Schlotte *f* KOHLEN *Wasser, Kalk* cavity; **Schlotterventil** *nt* MASCHINEN puppet valve
Schluckbrunnen *m* WASSERVERSORG injection well
Schlucken *nt* BAU *Schall* absorption
Schlueter-Bewegungsgleichung *f* KERNTECH Schlueter equation of motion
Schluff *m* KOHLEN silt
Schlupf [1] *m* AKUSTIK drift, BAU slippage, ELEKTRIZ *(s)* slip, ELEKTROTECH, MASCHINEN slip, MECHAN backlash
Schlupf: [2] ~ **haben** *vi* MASCHINEN slip
schlupffrei: **~er Antrieb** *m* KFZTECH positive drive
Schluß *m* COMP & DV tail, KÜNSTL INT inference; **Schlußanstrich** *m* KUNSTSTOFF top coat; **Schlußbehandlung** *f* VERPACK final treatment; **Schlußflansch** *m* MASCHINEN end flange
Schlüssel *m* COMP & DV, DRUCK key, MASCHINEN key, screw wrench, spanner (BrE), wrench, RADIO, TELEKOM key; **Schlüsselbart** *m* BAU bit, keybit; **Schlüsselbrett** *nt* TELEKOM keyshelf; **Schlüsselfeile** *f* MASCHINEN key file, warding file; **Schlüsselfeld** *nt* COMP & DV key field
schlüsselfertig [1] *adj* BAU turnkey
schlüsselfertig: [2] **~er Einbau** *m* MASCHINEN turnkey installation; **~es Projekt** *nt* MASCHINEN turnkey project; **~es System** *nt* COMP & DV turnkey system
Schlüssel: **Schlüsselformblech** *nt* BAU ward; **Schlüsselloch** *nt* BAU keyhole, ERDÖL *Bohrtechnik* key seating; **Schlüssellochabdeckung** *f* BAU key drop; **Schlüsselschalter** *m* ELEKTRIZ key-operated switch, ELEKTROTECH keyswitch, TELEKOM key-operated switch; **Schlüsselschild** *nt* BAU drop, escutcheon, key plate, scutcheon; **Schlüsselstation** *f* FERNSEH key

station; **Schlüsselsystem** *nt* COMP & DV cryptographic system; **Schlüsselweite** *f* FERTIG across-flats dimensions, MASCHINEN across-flats dimension, diameter across flats, width across flats; **Schlüsselwort** *nt* COMP & DV *beim Durchsuchen einer Datenbank* keyword; **Schlüsselwortkontrolle** *f* COMP & DV password security; **Schlüsselwortparameter** *m* COMP & DV keyword parameter

Schluß: **Schlußfolgerung** *f* KÜNSTL INT inference

schlüssig: **~er Beweis** *m* PATENT conclusive evidence

Schluß: **Schlußlaterne** *f* EISENBAHN tail end marker lamp; **Schlußleuchte** *f* KFZTECH tail light; **Schlußpackwagen** *m* EISENBAHN caboose (AmE), guard's van (BrE); **Schlußstein** *m* BAU trap, *eines Gewölbes* capstone, keystone; **Schlußstrich** *m* KUNSTSTOFF finishing coat; **Schlußvignette** *f* DRUCK tailpiece; **Schlußzeichen** *nt* TELEKOM clearback signal

Schmack *f* WASSERTRANS *Fischerei* fishing smack

schmal: **~ gebündelter Strahl** *m* STRAHLPHYS pencil beam; **~er Impuls** *m* ELEKTRONIK narrow pulse; **~e Meeresbucht** *f* WASSERTRANS *Geographie* creek (BrE); **~e Rundfeile** *f* MASCHINEN rat-tail file

Schmalband *nt* COMP & DV, ELEKTRONIK, RADIO, TELEKOM narrow band; **Schmalband-** *pref* COMP & DV narrow-band; **Schmalband-Demodulation** *f* ELEKTRONIK narrow-band demodulation; **Schmalband-Einseitenband** *nt* RADIO narrow single sideband; **Schmalband-Einseitenbandmodulation** *f* RADIO narrow single sideband modulation; **Schmalbandempfänger** *m* TELEKOM narrow-band receiver; **Schmalbandfernsehen** *nt* (*SSTV*) FERNSEH slow scan television (*SSTV*); **Schmalbandfernsehen mit langsamer Abtastung** *nt* (*SSTV*) RADIO slow scan television (*SSTV*); **Schmalbandfernsehsystem** *nt* FERNSEH slow scan television system; **Schmalbandfilter** *nt* ELEKTRONIK narrow-band filter; **Schmalbandfiltern** *nt* ELEKTRONIK narrow-band filtering; **Schmalbandfrequenzmodulation** *f* (*SBFM*) ELEKTRONIK, RADIO, TELEKOM narrow-band frequency modulation (*NBFM*); **Schmalbandgeräusch** *nt* ELEKTRONIK narrow-band noise; **Schmalbandkoppelnetz** *nt* TELEKOM narrow-band switching network; **Schmalbandkoppler** *m* TELEKOM narrow-band switch; **Schmalband-Phasenumtastung** *f* TELEKOM NBPSK, narrow band phase shift keying; **Schmalbandrauschen** *nt* TELEKOM narrow-band noise; **Schmalband-Responsspektrum** *nt* KERNTECH narrow-band response spectrum; **Schmalbandröhre** *f* ELEKTRONIK narrow-band tube; **Schmalbandschaltung** *f* ELEKTRONIK narrow-band circuit; **Schmalbandsignal** *nt* ELEKTRONIK, TELEKOM narrowband signal; **Schmalband-Sperrfilter** *nt* ELEKTRONIK narrow-band rejection filter; **Schmalband-Sprachmodulation** *f* TELEKOM NBVM, narrow-band voice modulation; **Schmalband-SSB** *nt* RADIO narrow ssb; **Schmalband-SSB-Modulation** *f* RADIO narrow ssbmodulation; **Schmalbandstörung** *f* ELEKTRONIK narrow-band interference; **Schmalband-Tiefpaßfilter** *nt* ELEKTRONIK narrow-band low-pass filter; **Schmalband-Tiefpaßfiltern** *nt* ELEKTRONIK narrow-band low-pass filtering; **Schmalbandverstärker** *m* ELEKTRONIK narrow-band amplifier

Schmalbündel *nt* ELEKTRONIK pencil beam

Schmalgewebe *nt* TEXTIL narrow fabric

Schmalkeilriemen *m* MASCHINEN narrow V belt

Schmalseite *f* FERTIG end

Schmalspurbahn *f* EISENBAHN light railroad (AmE), light railway (BrE), narrow-gage railroad (AmE), narrow-gauge railway (BrE)

Schmalspurbefeuerung *f* LUFTTRANS *Start- und Landebahn* narrow-gage lighting system (AmE), narrow-gauge lighting system (BrE)

Schmalspurdiessellokomotive *f* EISENBAHN narrow-gage diesel locomotive (AmE), narrow-gauge diesel locomotive (BrE)

Schmalspurschienensystem *nt* EISENBAHN narrow-gage track system (AmE), narrow-gauge track system (BrE)

Schmalz *nt* LEBENSMITTEL lard

Schmälzeinrichtung *f* TEXTIL oiler

schmälzen *vt* TEXTIL lubricate

Schmälzmittel *nt* TEXTIL lubricant

Schmelz- *pref* KER & GLAS, MASCHINEN, PHYS, THERMOD melting; **Schmelzbad** *nt* FERTIG melt, *Schweißen* pool, THERMOD melting bath

schmelzbar *adj* THERMOD meltable

Schmelzbereich *m* THERMOD melting range

Schmelzbohren *nt* KOHLEN fusion drilling

Schmelzdauer *f* THERMOD melting period, melting time

Schmelzdraht *m* ELEKTRIZ, ELEKTROTECH fuse wire; **Schmelzdrahtsicherung** *f* ELEKTRIZ wire fuse

Schmelze *f* FERTIG fused metal, *Gießen* blow, METALL heat melting bath; **Schmelzeinsatz** *m* ELEKTROTECH fuse link

Schmelzen[1] *nt* ANSTRICH fusion, FERTIG *Glas* founding, KOHLEN smelting, KUNSTSTOFF fusion, PAPIER, TEXTIL melting, THERMOD fusing, fusion, melting

Schmelzen:[2] **zum ~ bringen** *vt* THERMOD fuse

schmelzen[1] *vt* LEBENSMITTEL thaw, METALL fuse, PAPIER, TEXTIL melt, THERMOD fuse, melt, melt down

schmelzen[2] *vi* ANSTRICH melt, ELEKTRIZ *Sicherung* blow, LEBENSMITTEL thaw

Schmelz-: **Schmelzenthalpie** *f* MECHAN, PHYS, THERMOD enthalpy of fusion; **Schmelzentropie** *f* MECHAN, PHYS, THERMOD entropy of fusion; **Schmelzerei** *f* FERTIG *Glas* foundry; **Schmelzfarben** *f pl* KER & GLAS vitrifiable colors (AmE), vitrifiable colours (BrE); **Schmelzfluß** *m* FERTIG coalescence, melting

schmelzflüssig *adj* THERMOD fusible

Schmelz-: **Schmelzformen** *nt* KER & GLAS fusion casting

schmelzgeschweißt *adj* MASCHINEN fusion-welded

Schmelz-: **Schmelzgießform** *f* KER & GLAS font mold (AmE), font mould (BrE); **Schmelzindex** *m* KUNSTSTOFF MFI, melt flow index; **Schmelzkegel** *m* FERTIG pyrometric cone; **Schmelzkernfänger** *m* KERNTECH melting core catcher; **Schmelzkessel** *m* THERMOD melting pot; **Schmelzkleber** *m* DRUCK hot-melt glue, KUNSTSTOFF hot-melt adhesive, VERPACK heat-sealing adhesive, hot-melt adhesive; **Schmelzkurve** *f* THERMOD melting-point curve; **Schmelzleiter** *m* ELEKTROTECH fuse element; **Schmelzlösen** *nt* PAPIER dissolving; **Schmelzlöser** *m* PAPIER dissolver; **Schmelzmittel** *nt* BAU flux; **Schmelzofen** *m* KOHLEN melting furnace, KUNSTSTOFF fusing oven, METALL smelter, smelting furnace, THERMOD melting furnace; **Schmelzperle** *f* KER & GLAS slug; **Schmelzprobe** *f* THERMOD melting test

Schmelzpunkt[1] *m* CHEMTECH, KUNSTSTOFF melting point, mp, METALL point of fusion, PAPIER, TEXTIL melting point, mp, THERMOD fusing point, melting point, mp

Schmelzpunkt:[2] **den ~ herabsetzen** *vi* FERTIG flux

Schmelzpunkt: **Schmelzpunktapparat nach Thiele** *m* LABOR Thiele melting-point tube, Thiele tube; **Schmelzpunkterniedrigung** *f* THERMOD lowering of the melting point; **Schmelzpunktkurve** *f* METALL melting-point curve

Schmelz-: **Schmelzrate** *f* STRÖMPHYS melt flow rate; **Schmelzschutzschild** *m* RAUMFAHRT *Raumschiff* ablation shield; **Schmelzschweißen** *nt* BAU, FERTIG, MASCHINEN, THERMOD fusion-welding; **Schmelzsicherung** *f* ELEKTRIZ nonrenewable fuse, ELEKTROTECH blowout fuse; **Schmelzsicherung für Dampfkessel** *f* HYDRAUL *Sicherheit* fusible plug for steam boiler; **Schmelzspleißung** *f* TELEKOM fusion splice; **Schmelzspleißverbindung** *f* OPTIK fusion splice

schmelztauchverzinken *vt* ANSTRICH galvanize by hot dipping

Schmelz-: **Schmelztiegel** *m* FERTIG, THERMOD melting crucible; **Schmelzton** *m* KER & GLAS fusible clay; **Schmelzung** *f* ELEKTROTECH smelting; **Schmelzverbindung** *f* OPTIK fusion splice; **Schmelzvorgang** *m* METALL smelting, THERMOD fusion, melting; **Schmelzwanne** *f* KER & GLAS tank; **Schmelzwärme** *f* THERMOD heat of fusion, melting heat; **Schmelzzone** *f* METALL melting zone

Schmerzgrenze *f* AKUSTIK threshold of pain

Schmerzschwelle *f* PHYS threshold of pain

Schmidt-Zahl *f* PHYS *Strömungslehre* Schmidt number

Schmied *m* MASCHINEN, METALL blacksmith

schmiedbar *adj* MECHAN malleable, METALL ductile

Schmiedbarkeit *f* METALL malleability

Schmiede *f* BAU smithy, MASCHINEN blacksmith's shop; **Schmiedearbeit** *f* BAU ironwork, smithery; **Schmiedebalg** *m* MASCHINEN blacksmith's bellows; **Schmiedeeisen** *nt* BAU wrought iron, MECHAN low-carbon steel, METALL iron

schmiedeeisern *adj* METALL wrought-iron

Schmiede: **Schmiedegesenk** *nt* MASCHINEN forging die, swage, MECHAN swage; **Schmiedehammer** *m* FERTIG forging hammer, MASCHINEN blacksmith's hammer, forging hammer; **Schmiedehandwerk** *nt* BAU smithery; **Schmiedeherd** *m* MASCHINEN blacksmith's forge; **Schmiedekonus** *m* FERTIG draft; **Schmiedemaschine** *f* MASCHINEN forging machine

Schmieden *nt* BAU hammering, FERTIG, KUNSTSTOFF, MASCHINEN forging

schmieden *vt* ANSTRICH, FERTIG forge

Schmiede: **Schmiedepresse** *f* FERTIG forging press; **Schmiedeschweißen** *nt* BAU forge welding; **Schmiedestahl** *m* MASCHINEN forged steel; **Schmiedestück** *nt* MECHAN, METALL forging; **Schmiedestück aus Titan** *nt* RAUMFAHRT titanium forging; **Schmiedestückzeichnung** *f* KONSTZEICH forging drawing; **Schmiedezange** *f* BAU smith's pliers, MASCHINEN blacksmith's tongs; **Schmiedezunder** *m* FERTIG forge scale, forging scale

Schmiegkreis *m* GEOM osculating circle

Schmierbohrung *f* MASCHINEN oil hole

Schmierbüchse *f* FERTIG grease box, MASCHINEN oil cup

schmieren[1] *vt* FERTIG lubricate, MASCHINEN grease, lubricate, MECHAN lubricate

schmieren[2] *vi* MASCHINEN grease

Schmierfett *nt* KFZTECH, MASCHINEN grease

Schmierfilm *m* FERTIG film, MASCHINEN lubricating film

Schmierkante *f* FERTIG oiler

Schmierkissen *nt* MASCHINEN oil pad, pad

Schmierlager *nt* MASCHINEN grease bearing

Schmierloch *nt* MASCHINEN oil hole

Schmierlötverbindung *f* FERTIG wiped joint

Schmiermittel *nt* BAU, ERDÖL lubricant, FERTIG sud, *Kunststoffinstallationen* lubricant, KFZTECH, MASCHINEN, MECHAN lubricant; **Schmiermittelpumpe** *f* MECHAN lubricating pump; **Schmiermittelrückstände** *m pl* ABFALL waste lubricants

Schmiernippel *m* KFZTECH *Motor* grease nipple, MASCHINEN grease nipple, lubricating nipple, lubrication fitting, MECHAN lubricating nipple

Schmieröl *nt* ERDÖL motor oil, FERTIG, KFZTECH lubricating oil; **Schmierölfleck** *m* KER & GLAS grease mark

Schmierpistole *f* BAU, KFZTECH *Werkzeug* grease gun

Schmierplan *m* MECHAN lubricating chart

Schmierstoff *m* ERDÖL, FERTIG, MASCHINEN lubricant, MECHAN grease

Schmiersystem *nt* KFZTECH, MASCHINEN lubricating system

Schmierung *f* FERTIG lubricating, KFZTECH, KONTROLL, MASCHINEN lubrication, PAPIER greasing; **~ von Hand** *f* MASCHINEN hand lubrication

Schmiervorrichtung *f* BAU lubricating unit

Schmirgel *m* FERTIG abrasive, emery, KER & GLAS, MECHAN emery; **Schmirgelleinen** *nt* FERTIG, MECHAN emery cloth; **Schmirgelpapier** *nt* ELEKTRIZ abrasive paper, FERTIG emery paper, MECHAN abrasive paper, emery paper, PAPIER rubber; **Schmirgelpulver** *nt* MASCHINEN emery powder, MECHAN abrasive powder; **Schmirgelscheibe** *f* FERTIG, MECHAN emery wheel

Schmitt-Trigger *m* PHYS Schmitt trigger

Schmorkontakt *m* FERTIG *Brennschweißen* flash

Schmutz *m* ABFALL, FERTIG, KFZTECH dirt; **Schmutzbehälter** *m* ABFALL *des Kehrfahrzeugs* dust collector; **Schmutzfänger** *m* FERTIG *Kunststoffinstallationen* line strainer, KER & GLAS catch pan, KFZTECH *Zubehör* mudflap; **Schmutzfestigkeit** *f* TEXTIL resistance to soiling; **Schmutzpunkt** *m* PAPIER speck; **Schmutzstoff** *m* MEERSCHMUTZ pollutant; **Schmutzwasser** *nt* ABFALL drain water, UMWELTSCHMUTZ wastewater; **Schmutzwasserpumpe** *f* KERNTECH dirty-water pump

Schnabel *m* LABOR lip, spout; **Schnabelkipper** *m* KFZTECH scoop tipper; **Schnabelrundkipper** *m* KFZTECH scoop dump car; **Schnabelwagen** *m* EISENBAHN Schnabel car (AmE), Schnabel wagon (BrE); **Schnabelzange** *f* MASCHINEN long-nose pliers

Schnalle *f* MASCHINEN buckle, clasp; **Schnallenriemen** *m* MASCHINEN buckle strap

Schnäpper *m* BAU *Türschloß* latch bolt; **Schnäpperschloß** *nt* BAU spring bolt lock

Schnappfassung *f* ELEKTROTECH snap-in socket

Schnappfeder *f* MASCHINEN catch spring

schnappig *adj* KUNSTSTOFF snappy

Schnappigkeit *f* KUNSTSTOFF snappiness

Schnappriegel *m* KFZTECH *Motorhaube* safety catch

Schnappschäkel *m* WASSERTRANS *Beschläge* snap shackle

Schnappschalter *m* ELEKTRIZ snap-action switch, ELEKTROTECH snap-action switch, snap-in switch

Schnappschloß *nt* BAU catch, latch lock

Schnappverschluß *m* VERPACK snap hinge closure, snap-on lid

Schnarchventil *nt* MASCHINEN air valve, air-snifting valve

Schnauze *f* FERTIG spout, MASCHINEN nozzle

Schnecke *f* BAU auger, FERTIG scroll, worm, *Kunststoff-*

installationen worm screw, *Schneckenpresse* pressure screw, KUNSTSTOFF screw, LABOR *Destillationsapparat* worm, MASCHINEN perpetual screw, screw, worm, MECHAN worm, PAPIER screw; **Schneckenantrieb** *m* KUNSTSTOFF screw drive; **Schneckenbohrer** *m* BAU gimlet; **Schneckenextender** *f* LEBENSMITTEL screw extruder; **Schneckenfeder** *f* MECHAN coil spring; **Schneckenfeder-Druckmeßelement** *nt* GERÄT helical pressure element; **Schneckenförderer** *m* FERTIG spiral conveyor, MASCHINEN screw conveyor, spiral conveyor, worm conveyor, PAPIER screw conveyor; **Schneckenfräser** *m* MASCHINEN worm milling cutter; **Schneckengetriebe** *nt* FERTIG *Kunststoffinstallationen* worm gearing, MASCHINEN worm gear pair, MECHAN worm gear; **Schneckenhandbohrer** *m* BAU shell gimlet; **Schneckenkanal** *m* KUNSTSTOFF screw channel; **Schneckenlinie** *f* GEOM, MASCHINEN helix; **Schnecken-Nenndurchmesser** *m* KUNSTSTOFF screw diameter; **Schneckenpumpe** *f* MASCHINEN spiral pump, MEERSCHMUTZ screw pump

Schneckenrad *nt* MASCHINEN screw wheel, spiral wheel, worm gear, worm wheel, WASSERTRANS worm gear; **Schneckenradachsantrieb** *m* KFZTECH worm gear final drive; **Schneckenradgetriebe** *nt* MASCHINEN worm gear pair; **Schneckenradwälzfräsen** *nt* FERTIG worm gear hobbing

Schnecke: **Schneckensegment** *nt* FERTIG *Kunststoffinstallationen* worm segment; **Schneckenspalt** *m* KUNSTSTOFF flight land clearance; **Schneckenspiel** *nt* KUNSTSTOFF radial screw clearance; **Schneckenspitze** *f* KUNSTSTOFF screw tip; **Schneckensteg** *m* KUNSTSTOFF screw flight; **Schneckenstrangpresse** *f* KUNSTSTOFF extruder; **Schneckentreppe** *f* BAU spiral stairs; **Schneckenverzahnung** *f* MASCHINEN worm gearing; **Schneckenwalze** *f* PAPIER worm roll; **Schneckenzahnstange** *f* MASCHINEN worm rack

Schnee *m* ELEKTRONIK *Bildstörung* grass, FERNSEH snow; **Schneebelastung** *f* BAU snow loading; **Schneedetektor** *m* TRANS snow detector; **Schneefanggitter** *nt* BAU snow guard; **Schneeflockenkurve** *f* GEOM snowflake curve; **Schneeflockentopologie** *f* COMP & DV snowflake topology; **Schneekufe** *f* LUFTTRANS tail skid; **Schneereifen** *m* KFZTECH snow tire (AmE), snow tyre (BrE); **Schneewasser** *nt* WASSERVERSORG snow water

Schneid: **-- und Wickelmaschine** *f* VERPACK slitting and rewinding machine

Schneidbacke *f* FERTIG screw die, MASCHINEN, MECHAN die

Schneidbrenner *m* BAU cutting blowpipe, flame cutter, FERTIG cutting blowpipe, MASCHINEN cutting torch, MECHAN flame cutter, THERMOD flame-cutting torch

Schneide[1] *f* BAU blade, cutting edge, FERTIG *Bohrer* cutting lip, *Waage* knife edge, MASCHINEN bit, edge, router, TEXTIL cutting edge

Schneide[2]: **eine ~ bilden** *vi* FERTIG take an edge

Schneideholz *nt* BAU saw timber

Schneideisen *nt* FERTIG *Gewinde* die, MASCHINEN die, screwing die, stock; **Schneideisenhalter** *m* MASCHINEN die holders, die stock holder

Schneide: **Schneidemaschine** *f* BAU cutter, DRUCK, FOTO trimmer, MASCHINEN cutting machine, shear, shears, VERPACK slit machine; **Schneidemaschinenbank** *f* KER & GLAS cutter's lathe; **Schneidemesser** *nt* MASCHINEN blade

Schneiden *nt* MASCHINEN cutting

schneiden *vt* BAU, DRUCK cut, GEOM intersect, MASCHINEN, MECHAN cut, PAPIER guillotine

schneidend:[1] **sich ~** *adj* GEOM, MATH intersecting secant

schneidend:[2] **sich ~e Ebenen** *f pl* GEOM intersecting planes; **~e Kante** *f* MECHAN cutting edge; **sich ~e Linien** *f pl* GEOM intersecting lines

Schneide: **Schneidenecke** *f* FERTIG tool corner; **Schneideneingriff** *m* FERTIG tool engagement point-of-cutting action; **Schneideneinsatz** *m* FERTIG insert, *Räumwerkzeug* section; **Schneidenkopf** *m* FERTIG bit, *Tieflochbohrer* drill tip; **Schneiden-Normalebene** *f* FERTIG tool edge normal plane; **Schneidenschaft** *m* FERTIG *Bohrer* body; **Schneidenteil** *m* FERTIG *Räumwerkzeug* active portion; **Schneidenteil und Hals** *m* FERTIG *Reibahle* body

Schneider *m* KER & GLAS birdcage, MASCHINEN cutter, shear, shears

Schneide: **Schneideritze** *f* KER & GLAS scratch; **Schneidestichel** *m* AKUSTIK cutting stylus

Schneidflüssigkeit *f* FERTIG *Spanung* coolant, MASCHINEN cutting fluid

Schneidgewinde *nt* MASCHINEN self-tapping thread

Schneidkante *f* BAU, KER & GLAS *des Glasschneiderdiamanten* cutting edge, MASCHINEN cutting edge, edge

Schneidkluppe *f* FERTIG *Gewinde* die stock, MASCHINEN screw plate stock, stock and dies

Schneidkopf *m* BAU *Tunnelbau*, MASCHINEN cutter head; **Schneidkopfbagger** *m* WASSERTRANS *Baggern* cutter dredge, cutter dredger

Schneidlippe *f* MASCHINEN cutting lip, lip

Schneidmaschine *f* LEBENSMITTEL slicer, MASCHINEN cutter, shearing machine

Schneidmühle *f* KUNSTSTOFF granulator

Schneidöl *nt* ERDÖL *Sonderöl* cut oil, FERTIG cutting fluid, MASCHINEN cutting oil

Schneidplatte *f* FERTIG insert

Schneidrad *nt* FERTIG *Schere* disc blade (BrE), disk blade (AmE), MASCHINEN cutter, rotary shear blade

Schneidrahmen *m* KER & GLAS cutting frame

Schneidrücken *m* MASCHINEN land

Schneidschaftlänge *f* FERTIG *Bohrer* body length

Schneidschraube *f* MASCHINEN self-cutting screw, self-tapping screw

Schneidstichel *m* AUFNAHME recording stylus

Schneidvorrichtung *f* KER & GLAS capper (AmE), cut-off man (BrE)

Schneidwerkzeug *nt* MASCHINEN cutter, cutting tool, die, MECHAN cutter, cutting tool; **Schneidwerkzeugwinkel** *m* MASCHINEN cutting angle

Schneidzähne *m pl* BAU cutting teeth

Schneidzange *f* BAU cutting pliers

Schnell- *pref* KERNTECH, LUFTTRANS fast

schnell:[1] **~ gefriergetrocknet** *adj* LEBENSMITTEL accelerated freeze-dried; **~ lyophilisiert** *adj* LEBENSMITTEL accelerated freeze-dried

schnell:[2] **~ ansprechende Sicherung** *f* ELEKTROTECH fast-acting fuse; **~er Brüter** *m (SB)* KERNTECH, PHYS accelerator breeder, fast breeder reactor; **~er Brutreaktor** *m (SB)* KERNTECH accelerator breeder, fast breeder reactor, PHYS fast breeder reactor *(FBR)*; **~e Diode** *f* ELEKTRONIK fast-recovery diode; **~es Entspannen** *nt* KER & GLAS rapid annealing; **~e Fourier-Transformation** *f* ELEKTRONIK fast Fourier transformation, ELEKTRONIK fast Fourier transform; **~es Frequenzsprungverfahren** *nt* ELEKTRONIK fast frequency hopping; **~e Frequenzumtastung** *f*

ELEKTRONIK fast frequency shift keying; ~es Gefrieren *nt* LEBENSMITTEL quick-freezing; ~e Gefriertrocknung *f* LEBENSMITTEL AFD, accelerated freeze-drying; ~es Herunterregeln *nt* FERNSEH fast pull-down; ~er Ionisationsstopp *m* KERNTECH fast burst; ~e Kapazitätsdiode *f* PHYS hyperabrupt varactor diode; ~er Kippvorgang *m* ELEKTRONIK fast sweep; ~e Leitungsvermittlung *f* TELEKOM fast circuit switch; ~e Logik *f* ELEKTRONIK fast logic, high-speed logic; ~ lösbare Befestigung *f* MASCHINEN quick-release fastener; ~ lösbare Rohrverbindung *f* MASCHINEN quick-release pipe coupling; ~e Luftkühlung *f* THERMOD rapid air cooling; ~e Lyophilisation *f* LEBENSMITTEL AFD, accelerated freeze-drying; ~e Maschenschaltung *f* ELEKTRONIK high-speed mesh; ~es Modem *nt* ELEKTRONIK high-speed modem; ~es Nachführen *nt* LUFTTRANS fast slaving; ~es Neutron *nt* PHYS fast neutron, prompt neutron; ~e Paketvermittlung *f (FPS)* TELEKOM fast packet server *(FPS)*; ~er Papiervorschub *m* COMP & DV paper slew; ~es Peripheriegerät *nt* COMP & DV fast peripheral; ~es Playback *nt* FERNSEH fast playback; ~er Pufferspeicher *m* COMP & DV cache memory; ~er Reaktor *m* KERNTECH fast reactor; ~es Richten *nt* LUFTTRANS fast slaving; ~er Rücklauf *m* MASCHINEN fast return; ~e Schaltdiode *f* ELEKTRONIK high-speed switching diode; ~ schaltender Leistungsgleichrichter *m* ELEKTROTECH fast-switching power rectifier; ~er Schalttransistor *m* ELEKTRONIK high-speed switching transistor; ~ spritzbarer Furnace-Ruß *m (FEF-Ruß)* KUNSTSTOFF fast extruding furnace carbon black *(FEF carbon black)*; ~es Teilchen *nt* KERNTECH fast particle; ~e Tonhöhenschwankungen *f pl* AKUSTIK flutter; ~ wechselndes Signal *nt* ELEKTRONIK fast-changing signal; ~er Wellenhohlleiter *m* ELEKTRONIK, TELEKOM fastwave tube; ~es Zählsystem für Mehrfachregale *nt* VERPACK high-speed multirack counting system

schnell:[3] ~ verschließen *vt* FERTIG scuff

Schnell-: Schnellablaß *m* KERNTECH *des Moderators im homogenen Reaktor* dump, LUFTTRANS *Treibstoff* dumping; Schnellabrollbahn *f* LUFTTRANS exit taxiway, high-speed exit taxiway, rapid exit taxiway; Schnellabschaltstab *m* KERNTECH scram rod; Schnellabschaltung eines Reaktors *f* KERNTECH reactor trip; Schnellabschaltungskontrolle *f* KERNTECH scram control; Schnellabstimmfilter *nt* ELEKTRONIK fast-tuned filter; Schnellabstimmoszillator *m* ELEKTRONIK fast-tuned oscillator; Schnelladesystem *nt* FOTO rapid loading system; Schnelladung *f* LUFTTRANS quick charge, TRANS boost charge; Schnellalterungsprüfung *f* FERTIG, KUNSTSTOFF accelerated ageing test (BrE), accelerated aging test (AmE); Schnellanschluß-Verbindungsstück *nt* LABOR quickfit connector; Schnelläufer *m* WASSERTRANS *Dieselmotor* high-speed engine; Schnelläufermotor *m* MECHAN high-speed engine; Schnellaufmotor *m* ELEKTRIZ high-speed motor; Schnellaufzughebel *m* FOTO single stroke lever; Schnellauslöser *m* MASCHINEN fast-acting trip; Schnellauslöseventil *nt* KERNTECH fast-acting trip valve; Schnellauslösung *f* ELEKTRIZ instantaneous release; Schnellbahn *f* EISENBAHN high-speed railroad (AmE), high-speed railway (BrE), EISENBAHN *(S-Bahn)* regional express railroad (AmE), regional express railway (BrE) *(regional express railroad)*; Schnellbahnsystem *nt* EISENBAHN rapid transit system; Schnellbahnwagen *m* EISEN-

BAHN rapid transit car; Schnellbewitterung *f* KUNSTSTOFF accelerated weathering test; Schnellbohrer *m* MECHAN high-speed drill; Schnellbrutreaktor *m* KERNTECH accelerator breeder; Schnelldrehmaschine *f* MASCHINEN speed lathe; Schnelldrehmeißel *m* MASCHINEN high-speed cutting tool; Schnelldrucker *m* DRUCK high-speed printer

Schnelle *f* AKUSTIK velocity

Schnell-: Schnelleinfrieren durch Eintauchen *nt* VERPACK dip freezing; Schnelleinschuß *m* KERNTECH *eines Steuerstabs* fast insertion; Schnelleitung *f* COMP & DV fast line; Schnellemesser *m* AKUSTIK velocity meter; Schnellentleerung *f* LUFTTRANS *Treibstoff* dumping; Schnellentwickler *m* FOTO fast developer; Schnellepotential *nt* AKUSTIK velocity potential; Schnellerhitzung *f* LEBENSMITTEL flash heating; Schnellessigbereiter *m* LEBENSMITTEL acetifier; Schnellfiltration *f* LEBENSMITTEL accelerated filtration; Schnellgang *m* MASCHINEN fast traverse, MECHAN overdrive; Schnellgangwelle *f* MASCHINEN quick-motion shaft; Schnellgefriereinrichtung *f* MASCHINEN quick-freezing installation; Schnellgefrieren *nt* HEIZ & KÄLTE quick-freezing

schnellhärtend *adj* KUNSTSTOFF fast-curing

Schnell-: Schnellheizelektrode *f* FERNSEH rapid heat-up cathode; Schnellkochtopf *m* LEBENSMITTEL autoclave, pressure cooker; Schnellkompostierung *f* ABFALL mechanical composting, rapid fermentation; Schnellkopie *f* FERNSEH dubbing; Schnellkühlen *nt* HEIZ & KÄLTE quick-chilling, rapid chilling; Schnellkühlung *f* THERMOD rapid cooling; Schnellkupplung *f* RAUMFAHRT quick coupler

Schnellnahverkehr *m* TRANS rapid transit (AmE); Schnellnahverkehrshochsystem *nt* EISENBAHN elevated rapid-transit system

Schnell-: Schnellösesystem *nt* MASCHINEN quick-release clamping system; Schnellösung *f* RAUMFAHRT *Raumschiff* quick release; Schnellpresse *f* DRUCK flatbed cylinder press, high-speed printing press; Schnellprüfung *f* VERPACK high-speed inspection; Schnellregelung *f* ERGON quickening; Schnellrelais *nt* ELEKTRIZ instantaneous relay; Schnellrichtrelais *nt* LUFTTRANS fast slaving relay; Schnellrücklauf *m* MASCHINEN quick return

schnellschaltend: ~er Leistungstransistor *m* ELEKTRONIK fast-switching power transistor

Schnell-: Schnellschalthebel *m* FOTO rapid film advance lever; Schnellschaltrelais *nt* ELEKTRIZ high-speed relay, ELEKTROTECH fast-acting relay

Schnellschluß *m* KERNTECH scram; Schnellschlußgriffstange *f* HYDRAUL throttle reach-rod; Schnellschlußklappenventil *nt* HYDRAUL clack valve, MASCHINEN clack valve, flap valve; Schnellschlußventil *nt* HYDRAUL throttle, MASCHINEN fast-closing valve, quick-action valve, WASSERVERSORG quick-closing valve

Schnell-: Schnellschnittstahl *m* MASCHINEN HSS, high-speed steel; Schnellschützen *m* TEXTIL fly shuttle; Schnellspaltfaktor *m* KERNTECH fast fission factor; Schnellspaltung *f* KERNTECH fast fission; Schnellspannhebel *m* FOTO rapid film advance lever, single stroke lever; Schnellspeicher *m* COMP & DV IAS, fast core, immediate access store; Schnellstahl *m* MASCHINEN HSS, high-speed steel, super high-speed steel, MECHAN HSS, high-speed steel; Schnellstraße *f* BAU thoroughfare (BrE), thruway (AmE); Schnellstraße mit **Mittelstreifen** *f* TRANS divided highway (AmE), dual carriageway (BrE); **Schnelltiefkühlen** *nt* HEIZ & KÄLTE quick-freezing; **Schnelltrennkupplung** *f* LUFT-TRANS *Hydraulik* quick disconnect

schnelltrocknen *vt* TEXTIL tumble

schnelltrocknend[1] *adj* TEXTIL, VERPACK quick-drying

schnelltrocknend:[2] **~es Öl** *nt* KUNSTSTOFF drying oil

Schnell-: **Schnellverbinder** *m* RAUMFAHRT *Raumschiff* quick coupler; **Schnellverdampfer** *m* THERMOD *in Dampfmotoren* flash boiler

schnellvergehend *adj* ELEKTROTECH transient

Schnellverkehr *m* TRANS rapid traffic; **Schnellverkehrsbusspur** *f* TRANS busway for rapid transit; **Schnellverkehrssystem ohne Zwischenhaltestation** *nt* TRANS nonstop rapid transit system

Schnell-: **Schnellversuch** *m* WERKPRÜF accelerated testing; **Schnellvorschub** *m* MASCHINEN quick feed; **Schnellwaage** *f* PHYS steelyard; **Schnellwechselbohrfutter** *nt* MASCHINEN quick-change drill chuck; **Schnellwechselfutter** *nt* MASCHINEN quick-action chuck; **Schnellwechselmeißel** *m* MASCHINEN quick-change tool; **Schnellwechselwerkzeughalter** *m* MASCHINEN rapid-change toolholder; **Schnellwelle** *f* ELEKTROTECH fast wave; **Schnellzerreißversuch** *m* WERKPRÜF high-speed tension test; **Schnellzug** *m* EISENBAHN express train, fast train, *mit Platzkartenzwang* limited train; **Schnellzugriff** *m* COMP & DV immediate access

Schnitt[1] *m* AKUSTIK dubbing, ERDÖL fraction, FERTIG die set, *Kunststoffinstallationen* sectional diagram, GEOM intersection, section, MASCHINEN cut, MATH intersection, MECHAN cut, TEXTIL style

Schnitt:[2] **im ~ darstellen** *vt* KONSTZEICH represent in section

Schnitt: **Schnittansicht** *f* MASCHINEN cutaway view; **Schnittbewegung** *f* MASCHINEN cutting stroke; **Schnittbildentfernungsmesser** *m* FOTO split image rangefinder; **Schnittbrenner** *m* LABOR flat-flame burner; **Schnittdarstellung** *f* KONSTZEICH sectional view, sectional representation; **Schnittteil** *nt* MASCHINEN blank, blanking; **Schnittfläche** *f* MASCHINEN cut surface; **Schnittflächenschraffurlinie** *f* FERTIG section line; **Schnittfuge** *f* FERTIG kerf; **Schnittgang** *m* MASCHINEN cutting stroke; **Schnittgerade** *f* GEOM intersection line; **Schnittgeschwindigkeit** *f* MASCHINEN cutting speed; **Schnittholz** *nt* BAU scantling; **Schnittiefe** *f* FERTIG working engagement, MASCHINEN, MECHAN depth of cut; **Schnittkante** *f* DRUCK cutting edge; **Schnittkantenzeichnung** *f* KONSTZEICH section indentification; **Schnittkraft** *f* MASCHINEN cutting force; **Schnittleistung** *f* MASCHINEN cutting capacity; **Schnittlinie** *f* GEOM intersection line; **Schnittmatte** *f* KUNSTSTOFF chopped-strand mat; **Schnittmenge** *f* COMP & DV, MATH intersection; **Schnitt-Modell** *nt* FERTIG *Kunststoffinstallationen* cutaway model; **Schnittplatte** *f* FERTIG die shoe, MASCHINEN blanking die, shearing die; **Schnittpresse** *f* FERTIG blanking press; **Schnittpunkt** *m* BAU intersection point, COMP & DV intersection, GEOM point of intersection

Schnittstelle *f* COMP & DV, ELEKTRIZ, ELEKTRONIK, KONTROLL, MASCHINEN, PHYS, TELEKOM *zwischen technischen Einheiten* interface; **~ der digitalen Verbindungsleitung** *f* TELEKOM DTI, digital trunk interface; **~ Rechner-Nebenstellenanlage** *f* TELEKOM computer-PBX interface; **Schnittstellen-Chip** *m* ELEKTRONIK interface chip; **Schnittstelleneinheit** *f* COMP & DV interface unit; **Schnittstellenkarte** *f* ELEKTRONIK interface card; **Schnittstellenleitung** *f* TELEKOM interface circuit; **Schnittstellenlogik** *f* ELEKTRONIK interface logic; **Schnittstellenmodul** *nt* TELEKOM IM, interface module; **Schnittstellenprogramm** *nt* COMP & DV interface routine; **Schnittstellenschaltung** *f* ELEKTRONIK interface circuit; **Schnittstellenstromkreis** *m* TELEKOM interface circuit; **Schnittstellenvoraussetzung** *f* COMP & DV interface requirement

Schnitt: **Schnittstempel** *m* FERTIG cutting punch; **Schnittweiten** *f pl* PHYS conjugate points; **Schnittwerkzeug** *nt* MASCHINEN cutter; **Schnittwinkel** *m* BAU intersection angle, FERTIG, LEBENSMITTEL cutting angle; **Schnittwunde** *f* SICHERHEIT cutter wound; **Schnittzeichnung** *f* MASCHINEN section drawing, WASSERTRANS *Schiffkonstruktion* sectional drawing

Schnüffelventil *nt* HYDRAUL blow valve

Schnur *f* DRUCK string, ELEKTRIZ, MASCHINEN cord

Schnürboden *m* WASSERTRANS *Schiffwerft* mold loft (AmE), mould loft (BrE); **Schnürbodenarbeiter** *m* WASSERTRANS *Schiffbau* loftsman; **Schnürbodenverfahren** *nt* WASSERTRANS *Schiffbau* lofting

Schnurgerüst *nt* BAU *Vermessung* batter board

schnurlos: **~er Fernsprechschrank** *m* TELEKOM cordless switchboard; **~er Klappenschrank** *m* TELEKOM cordless switchboard; **~es Telefon** *nt* TELEKOM cordless telephone; **~er Vermittlungsschrank** *m* TELEKOM cordless switchboard

Schnur: **Schnurlot** *nt* BAU plumb bob, plumb line; **Schnurnagel** *m* BAU line pin; **Schnurstromkreis** *m* TELEKOM cord circuit

Schnürverschluß *m* VERPACK tying closure

Schockgefrieren *nt* THERMOD quick-freezing

schockgefrieren *vt* THERMOD quick-freeze

schockgefroren *adj* THERMOD quick-frozen

Schockwelle: **~ nach Kernexplosion** *f* STRAHLPHYS nuclear shock waves

Schokoladenschaum *m* MEERSCHMUTZ *Öl-Wasser-Emulsion mit halbfesten Klumpen* chocolate mousse

Schön: **~ und Wiederdruckform** *f* DRUCK sheetwise form

Schoner *m* WASSERTRANS *Schifftyp* schooner

Schongang *m* KFZTECH *Getriebe, Motor* overdrive; **Schonganggetriebe** *nt* MASCHINEN overspeed gear, overspeeder

Schönheit *f* TEILPHYS *Quark-Geschmack* beauty

Schönschrift *f* COMP & DV letter-quality

Schönseite *f* PAPIER *des Papiers* felt side

Schönung *f* LEBENSMITTEL fining; **Schönungsmittel** *nt* LEBENSMITTEL fining agent

Schopf *m* FERTIG crop end

Schöpfbaum *m* WASSERTRANS *Fischerei* brailer boom

Schöpfbecher *m* LABOR scanning electron microscope

Schopfen *nt* FERTIG cropping

Schöpfen *nt* PAPIER dipping

schopfen *vt* FERTIG *Blöcke* crop

schöpfen *vt* KER & GLAS ladle, PAPIER dip

Schöpfform *f* PAPIER mold (AmE), mould (BrE)

Schöpfkelle *f* KER & GLAS, LEBENSMITTEL ladle

Schopfmaschine *f* FERTIG cropping shear

Schöpfrad *nt* WASSERVERSORG scoop wheel

Schöpfrahmen *m* PAPIER deckle

Schöpfschaufelrad *nt* TRANS scoop wheel elevator, scoop wheel feeder

Schöpfwasserrad *nt* WASSERVERSORG scoop water wheel

Schorf m LEBENSMITTEL *Schädlingsbekämpfung* scab
Schornstein m BAU chimney, funnel, stack, HEIZ & KÄLTE chimney, MECHAN funnel; **Schornsteinaufsatz** m BAU, HEIZ & KÄLTE cowl; **Schornsteinblechrinne** f BAU *kleine Rinne zwischen Dachschräge und Schornstein* fillet gutter; **Schornsteinkragen** m WASSERTRANS funnel bonnet; **Schornsteinzug** m BAU chimney flue
Schot f WASSERTRANS *Segeln* sheet; **Schothorn** nt WASSERTRANS *Segeln* clew; **Schotklemme** f WASSERTRANS *Beschläge* cam cleat; **Schotstek** m WASSERTRANS *Knoten* becket bend, *Knoten* sheet bend, sheet knot
Schott nt MECHAN, RAUMFAHRT *Raumschiff*, WASSERTRANS *Schiffbau* bulkhead
Schotte f BAU cross wall
Schottelpropeller m TRANS Schottel propeller
Schotter m BAU broken stone, crushed stone, gravel, *Tiefbau* metal, KOHLEN gravel, TRANS *Eisenbahn* ballast; **Schotterauftragmaschine** f BAU, TRANS macadam spreader; **Schotterbrecher** m BAU stone breaker, stone crusher; **Schotterdecke** f BAU, TRANS macadam; **Schotterschüttung** f BAU boxing; **Schottersteine** f pl BAU *übergroß* tailings; **Schotterstraße** f BAU metaled road (AmE), metalled road (BrE); **Schotterunterfütterung** f BAU hardcore; **Schotterverteilungsmaschine** f TRANS road metal spreading machine; **Schotterwagen** m EISENBAHN ballast wagon
Schottky: **Schottky-Barriere** f ELEKTRONIK, PHYS Schottky barrier; **Schottky-Bauelement** f ELEKTRONIK Schottky device; **Schottky-Diode** f ELEKTRONIK, PHYS, RADIO *Halbleiterdiode* Schottky barrier diode, Schottky diode, hot carrier diode; **Schottky-FET** m ELEKTRONIK Schottky barrier FET; **Schottky-Gleichrichterdiode** f ELEKTRONIK Schottky barrier rectifier diode; **Schottky-Klemmdiode** f ELEKTRONIK Schottky clamping diode; **Schottky-Klemmtransistor** m ELEKTRONIK Schottky clamped transistor; **Schottky-Mischdiode** f ELEKTRONIK Schottky barrier mixer diode; **Schottky-Rauschen** nt PHYS Schottky noise; **Schottky-TTL** f ELEKTRONIK Schottky TTL
Schott: **Schottplatte** f WASSERTRANS *Schiffbau* bulkhead plate; **Schottversteifung** f WASSERTRANS *Schiffbau* bulkhead stiffener
Schraffe f DRUCK serif
schraffieren vt FERTIG hachure, hatch
schraffiert[1] adj DRUCK shaded
schraffiert:[2] **~er Bereich** m KONSTZEICH hatched area
Schraffierung f FERTIG *technische Zeichnung* hachure
Schraffur f FERTIG hatching; **Schraffurmuster** nt KONSTZEICH hatching pattern; **Schraffurwinkel** m KONSTZEICH hatching angle
Schräg- pref BAU, FERTIG, LEBENSMITTEL, LUFTTRANS slant
schräg[1] adj BAU beveled (AmE), bevelled (BrE), slanting, FERTIG *Kante* bevel, GEOM oblique
schräg:[2] **~e Antriebswelle** f LUFTTRANS *Hubschrauber* inclined drive shaft; **~e Bahnkreuzung** f EISENBAHN diamond crossing, double diamond crossing; **~es Blatt** nt BAU splayed scarf; **~er Kanal** m KERNTECH inclined channel; **~es Licht** nt DRUCK oblique lighting; **~e Normschrift** f KONSTZEICH sloping-style standard lettering; **~e Serife** f DRUCK oblique serif; **~er Strahl** m OPTIK skew ray; **~e Strahlung** f KER & GLAS skew ray; **~e Verbindung** f BAU, MASCHINEN bevel joint
Schräg-: **Schrägagarkultur** f LEBENSMITTEL agar slant; **Schrägbalken** m BAU raker; **Schrägbruch** m METALL

slant fracture; **Schrägdach** nt BAU pitch roof
Schräge f BAU batter, cant, haunch, inclination, FERTIG draft, MASCHINEN incline, METROL bevel
Schräg-: **Schrägeingriff** m FERTIG *Getriebelehre*, MECHAN angular meshing; **Schrägeinstechschleifmaschine** f FERTIG angle head grinding machine
schrägen vt BAU chamfer
Schräg-: **Schrägfalte** f KONSTZEICH oblique fold; **Schrägfuge** f BAU bevel joint, chamfered joint
schräggeschliffen adj FERTIG *Schnitt* sheared
Schräg-: **Schrägheckfahrzeug** nt KFZTECH *Fahrzeugart* hatchback car, hatchback model; **Schrägkopfriegel** m BAU bevel-headed bolt; **Schrägkugellager** nt MASCHINEN angular contact ball bearing; **Schrägkurslinie** f LUFTTRANS slant course line
Schräglage[1] f DRUCK, GEOM slant, LUFTTRANS bank, banking
Schräglage:[2] **in ~ bringen** vt WASSERTRANS cant
Schräg-: **Schräglager** nt MASCHINEN angular contact bearing; **Schräglenker** m KFZTECH *Hinterachse* semi-trailing arm; **Schräglichtbeleuchtung** f METALL oblique illumination; **Schrägmotor** m KFZTECH slanter engine; **Schrägpolarisation** f ELEKTROTECH slant polarization; **Schrägrevolverkopf** m FERTIG tilted turret; **Schrägrinne** f FERTIG chute; **Schrägrohrmanometer** nt GERÄT inclined tube manometer; **Schrägschleifen** nt FERTIG oblique grinding; **Schrägschneidemaschine** f FERTIG angle-cutting machine; **Schrägschnitt** m FERTIG angle cut, MASCHINEN bevel cut
Schrägsitz m MASCHINEN inclined seat; **Schrägsitzmagnetventil** nt FERTIG *Kunststoffinstallationen* solenoid angle seat valve; **Schrägsitzrückschlagventil** nt FERTIG *Kunststoffinstallationen* angle seat check valve; **Schrägsitzventil** nt FERTIG *Kunststoffinstallationen* angle seat valve
Schrägspur- pref FERNSEH helical; **Schrägspurabtastung** f FERNSEH helical scan; **Schrägspuraufnahme** f FERNSEH helical recording; **Schrägspuredieren** nt FERNSEH physical helical editing; **Schrägspurverfahren** nt COMP & DV helical scan; **Schrägspurvideogerät** nt FERNSEH helical scan videotape recorder
schrägstellbar: **~e Stößelführung** f FERTIG *Senkrechtstoßmaschine* tilting body
schrägstellen vt BAU tilt
Schrägstellung f BAU skewing, COMP & DV skew
Schräg-: **Schrägstift** m MASCHINEN angle pin; **Schrägstirnrad** nt KFZTECH, MASCHINEN helical gear; **Schrägstrich** m GEOM oblique stroke, MATH solidus; **Schrägungsverhältnis am Luftschraubenblatt** nt LUFTTRANS *Hubschrauber* blade taper ratio; **Schrägungswinkel** m FERTIG *Zahnrad* lead angle; **Schrägverblattung** f BAU splayed joint
schrägverzahnt[1] adj FERTIG helix-toothed, MASCHINEN helical
schrägverzahnt:[2] **~es Getrieberad** nt FERTIG, KFZTECH helical gear
Schräg-: **Schrägverzahnung** f MASCHINEN helical teeth, spiral gearing; **Schrägverzerrung** f FERNSEH skew error; **Schrägwalzen** nt FERTIG rotary forging; **Schrägwand** f BAU batter wall; **Schrägzahnkegelrad** nt MASCHINEN helical bevel gear; **Schrägzahnrad** nt FERTIG helical gear, MASCHINEN helical gear, spiral gear, MECHAN helical gear
schralen vi WASSERTRANS *Wind* haul forward

Schramme *f* BAU kerbstone (BrE), KUNSTSTOFF scratch, TEXTIL scuffing

Schrammen *f pl* METALL striation

Schrammschutz: Schrammschutzplatte *f* RAUMFAHRT *Raumschiff* antifret plate

Schränkeisen *nt* MASCHINEN saw set, set

schränken *vt* FERTIG *Säge* set

Schränkmaschine: ~ für Sägen *f* MASCHINEN saw-setting machine

Schränkung *f* FERTIG *Säge*, MASCHINEN set

Schrapper *m* MEERSCHMUTZ scraper; **Schrappergefäß** *nt* UMWELTSCHMUTZ scoop

Schrappförderer *m* MASCHINEN scraper

Schraub- *pref* BAU, ELEKTROTECH, FERTIG, GERÄT, MASCHINEN, VERPACK screw

schraubbar: ~er Linsendeckel *m* FOTO screw-on lens cap

Schraub-: Schraubdeckel *m* VERPACK continuous thread cap, screw lid, screw top

Schraube[1] *f* BAU, EISENBAHN screw, FERTIG *Kunststoffinstallationen* bolt, KFZTECH bolt, screw, *Ablaßschraube, Ablaßstopfen* plug, LUFTTRANS screw, MASCHINEN bolt, propeller, screw, MECHAN, WASSERTRANS screw; **~ mit Bund** *f* MASCHINEN collar screw; **~ mit eingängigem Gewinde** *f* MASCHINEN single-threaded screw; **~ mit Flachgewinde** *f* MASCHINEN square thread screw, square-threaded screw; **~ mit Linksgewinde** *f* MASCHINEN left-hand screw, left-handed screw; **~ ohne Kopf** *f* MASCHINEN headless screw; **~ ohne Mutter** *f* MASCHINEN screw bolt; **~ mit Rechtsgewinde** *f* MASCHINEN right-hand screw, right-handed screw; **~ mit scharfgängigem Gewinde** *f* MECHAN angular thread screw; **~ mit Schlitz** *f* MASCHINEN slotted screw; **~ mit Spitzgewinde** *f* MASCHINEN V-threaded screw; **~ mit UN-Gewinde** *f* MASCHINEN unified bolt; **~ mit Vierkantansatz** *f* MASCHINEN square neck bolt; **~ mit zweigängigem Gewinde** *f* MASCHINEN double-threaded screw, two-start screw

Schraube:[2] **~ anziehen** *vi* MASCHINEN tighten a screw

Schrauben *nt* MASCHINEN bolting

schrauben *vi* MASCHINEN, MECHAN screw

Schraube: Schraubenautomat *m* MASCHINEN automatic screw machine, screw machine; **Schraubenbandfeder** *f* MASCHINEN volute spring; **Schraubenbewegung** *f* MASCHINEN screw motion; **Schraubenbock** *m* WASSERTRANS *Schiffbau* propeller bracket; **Schraubenbolzen** *m* KFZTECH threaded bolt, MASCHINEN bolt; **Schraubendrehautomat** *m* MASCHINEN screw machine; **Schraubendreher** *m* ELEKTROTECH, KFZTECH *Werkzeug* screwdriver, MASCHINEN screwdriver, turnscrew; **Schraubendrehereinsatz** *m* MASCHINEN screwdriver bit, turnscrew bit; **Schraubendrehmaschine** *f* MASCHINEN screw machine, screw-cutting lathe; **Schraubendruckfeder** *f* MASCHINEN helical compression spring; **Schraubenfeder** *f* KFZTECH coil spring, MASCHINEN helical spring, MECHAN coil spring, PHYS helical spring; **Schraubenfederkupplung** *f* KFZTECH coil-spring clutch; **Schraubenfedermanometer** *nt* GERÄT helical capsule manometer, helix capsule manometer; **Schraubenfläche** *f* GEOM helicoid

schraubenförmig[1] *adj* FERTIG helical, GEOM helical, helicoid, MASCHINEN helicoid, helicoidal

schraubenförmig:[2] **~e Bewegung** *f* MASCHINEN helicoidal motion, screw motion; **~e Nut** *f* FERTIG helical broaching; **~e Versetzung** *f* METALL helical dislocation

Schraube: Schraubenführungsklaue *f* MASCHINEN

screw dog; **Schraubenfutter** *nt* MASCHINEN screw chuck; **Schraubengang** *m* MASCHINEN convolution; **Schraubengewinde** *nt* FERTIG bolt thread, MASCHINEN screw thread; **Schraubengewinde in Zoll** *nt* MASCHINEN inch screw thread; **Schraubengewindelinie** *f* FERTIG helix; **Schraubengewindeprofil** *nt* MASCHINEN screw thread profile; **Schraubengewindetoleranzen** *f pl* MASCHINEN screw thread tolerances; **Schraubenkontakt** *m* ELEKTRIZ screw contact

Schraubenkopf *m* MASCHINEN bolt head, screw head, MECHAN bolt head; **Schraubenkopfanstauchen** *nt* FERTIG bolt heading; **Schraubenkopffeile** *f* MASCHINEN screw head file; **Schraubenkopfschlitzen** *nt* FERTIG screw head slotting; **Schraubenkopfstauchmaschine** *f* FERTIG bolt-forging machine

Schraube: Schraubenlehre *f* MASCHINEN, METROL screw gage (AmE), screw gauge (BrE); **Schraubenlinie** *f* FERTIG, GEOM helix, MASCHINEN helicoid, helix

Schraubenlinie: in ~ aufrollen *vt* FERTIG helix

Schraube: Schraubenlinie mit Linksdrall *f* FERTIG left-hand helical; **Schraubenlinienabtastung** *f* ELEKTRONIK helical scanning; **Schraubenlochkreis** *m* FERTIG *Flansch* bolt circle; **Schraubenlüfter** *m* HEIZ & KÄLTE propeller fan, LUFTTRANS *Propeller* propfan; **Schraubenmutter** *f* BAU nut bolt, MASCHINEN, MECHAN nut; **Schraubenpresse** *f* MASCHINEN screw press; **Schraubenpumpe** *f* BAU, FERTIG, MASCHINEN, MEERSCHMUTZ screw pump; **Schraubenrad** *nt* MASCHINEN spiral wheel, worm gear; **Schraubenrädergetriebe** *nt* MASCHINEN helical gear drive; **Schraubenradgetriebe** *nt* MASCHINEN spiral gearing; **Schraubenradpumpe** *f* MASCHINEN mixed-flow pump; **Schraubenrohling** *m* FERTIG, MASCHINEN screw blank; **Schraubenschaufler** *m* KFZTECH, MEERSCHMUTZ screw pump; **Schraubenschlüssel** *m* FERTIG spanner (BrE), wrench, KFZTECH *Werkzeug* spanner (BrE), MASCHINEN screw wrench, spanner (BrE), wrench, MECHAN spanner (BrE), wrench; **Schraubenspindelpumpe** *f* KFZTECH screw pump; **Schraubenstrahl** *m* LUFTTRANS propeller wash; **Schraubenumsteuerung** *f* MASCHINEN screw reversing gear; **Schraubenverbindung** *f* FERTIG bolt joint, bolted connection, bolted union, nipple, *Kunststoffinstallationen* assembly bolts, MASCHINEN bolted connection, bolted joint; **Schraubenverdichter** *m* MASCHINEN screw compressor; **Schraubenverschiebung** *f* METALL screw dislocation; **Schraubenwasser** *nt* MEERSCHMUTZ wake; **Schraubenwelle** *f* WASSERTRANS *Schiffbau* propeller shaft; **Schraubenwinde** *f* BAU screw jack; **Schraubenzieher** *m* ELEKTROTECH, KFZTECH *Werkzeug* screwdriver, MASCHINEN screwdriver, turnscrew; **Schraubenzwinge** *f* MASCHINEN holdfast

Schraub-: Schraubfitting *nt* MASCHINEN threaded fitting; **Schraubflansch** *m* MASCHINEN screwed flange; **Schraubflasche** *f* VERPACK screw cap bottle; **Schraubfräseinrichtung** *f* MASCHINEN spiral milling attachment; **Schraubfräsen** *nt* MASCHINEN spiral milling; **Schraubgewinde** *nt* MECHAN worm; **Schraubheftzwinge** *f* MASCHINEN G-clamp, G-cramp; **Schraubhülse** *f* MASCHINEN threaded bush; **Schraubkappe** *f* MASCHINEN, VERPACK screw cap; **Schraubklemme** *f* ELEKTROTECH terminal; **Schraubkopf** *m* ELEKTROTECH *bei Stöpselsicherung* fuse carrier; **Schraubkupplung** *f* MASCHINEN screw coupling; **Schraublehre** *f* FERTIG, GERÄT micrometer;

Schraubloch nt BAU screw hole; **Schraubmuffe** f BAU union, MASCHINEN screwed fitting; **Schraubölfilter** nt KFZTECH screw-type oil filter; **Schraubquetschung** f KERNTECH screw pinch; **Schraubring** m MASCHINEN screw ferrule; **Schraubsicherung** f VERPACK screw locking device; **Schraubsockel** m ELEKTROTECH bei Glühbirnen screw cap, für elektrische Lampen screw base; **Schraubspindel** f MASCHINEN jack screw, screw jack; **Schraubstempel** m BAU ratchet brace; **Schraubstock** m BAU, FERTIG, MASCHINEN, MECHAN vice (BrE), vise (AmE); **Schraubstockbacke** f MASCHINEN vice jaw (BrE), vise jaw (AmE); **Schraubstollen** m EISENBAHN screw spike; **Schraubstück** nt MASCHINEN screw piece; **Schraubstutzen** m MASCHINEN screw socket; **Schraubtrieb** m KFZTECH inertia drive; **Schraubtriebanlasser** m KFZTECH Bendix-type starter, inertia drive starting motor; **Schraubventil** nt LABOR Flüssgkeitsregler screw valve; **Schraubverbindung** f MASCHINEN screw joint, threaded joint; **Schraubverschluß** m FERTIG screw plug, VERPACK continuous thread closure, screw closure, twisting closure; **Schraubvorrichtung** f KERNTECH screwing device; **Schraubwerkzeug** nt MASCHINEN screw tool; **Schraubwinde** f MASCHINEN jack screw, lifting jack, screw jack, screw lifting jack; **Schraubzwinge** f BAU Klammer, joiner's clamp, FERTIG BWG, Birmingham Wire Gauge, C-clamp, MASCHINEN C-clamp, screw clamp

Schreckschicht f FERTIG chilling layer

Schrecksekunde f TRANS perception-reaction time, reaction time

Schredderanlage f ABFALL für Autos vehicle shredder

Schreibband nt GERÄT strip chart

Schreibbefehl m COMP & DV write instruction

Schreibdichte f COMP & DV pitch, recording density

schreiben vt COMP & DV type, write; **neu ~** vt COMP & DV rewrite

schreibend: ~er Drehschwingungsmesser m METROL torsiograph; **nicht ~e Taste** f COMP & DV nonprinting key

Schreiber m ELEKTRIZ plotter, recorder, GERÄT recording instrument, MASCHINEN, TELEKOM recorder; **Schreiberfeder** f GERÄT recording pen; **Schreiberstreifen** m GERÄT continuous diagram, recording chart

Schreibfehler m COMP & DV write error, DRUCK typo

schreibgeschützt[1] adj COMP & DV read-only

schreibgeschützt:[2] **~e Platte** f COMP & DV read-only disk

Schreibgeschwindigkeit f ELEKTRONIK writing speed, GERÄT Registriergerät tracing speed

Schreibimpuls m COMP & DV write pulse

Schreibkopf m COMP & DV head, magnetic head, record head, recording head, write head

Schreibkurve f GERÄT trace line

Schreib-/Lese- pref COMP & DV read/write; **Schreib-/Lesekopf** m COMP & DV read/write head; **Schreib-/Lesespeicher** m (RAM) COMP & DV, ELEKTRONIK random access memory (RAM)

Schreib-Lesespalt m COMP & DV im Schreib-/Lesekopf head gap

Schreibmarke f DRUCK cursor

Schreibmaschine f COMP & DV typewriter; **Schreibmaschinenpapier** nt DRUCK typewriter paper; **Schreibmaschinenschrift** f DRUCK typewriter face; **Schreibmaschinenzeilenabstand** m KONSTZEICH typewriter spacing

Schreibpapier nt PAPIER writing paper

Schreibring m COMP & DV write ring, write-enable ring, write-permit ring

Schreibröhrchen nt GERÄT recording pen

Schreib-Schlitzlocher: ~ für Wellpappe m VERPACK printer-slotter for corrugated board

Schreibschutz m COMP & DV write protect, write protection; **Schreibschutzetikett** nt COMP & DV write-protect label; **Schreibschutzkerbe** f COMP & DV write-protect notch

Schreibsperre f COMP & DV write ring; **Schreibsperreanzeiger** m COMP & DV read-only flag

Schreibspur f COMP & DV recording track

Schreibstift m AUFNAHME recording stylus

Schreibstrahlerzeuger m ELEKTRONIK Oszillatoren writing gun

Schreibtischtest m COMP & DV dry run

Schreibverfahren nt COMP & DV recording mode

Schreibverstärker m AUFNAHME record amplifier

Schreibwalze f COMP & DV platen

Schreibweise f COMP & DV notation

Schreibzeit f ELEKTROTECH magnetische Medien write time

Schrenzpapier nt CHEMIE screenings

Schrift f DRUCK face, font

Schriftart f COMP & DV font, typeface, typestyle, DRUCK font, typeface, KONSTZEICH style of lettering; **Schriftartänderung** f COMP & DV font change; **Schriftartplatte** f COMP & DV font disk

Schrift: Schriftbild nt COMP & DV typeface, typestyle, DRUCK face; **Schriftcassette** f COMP & DV cartridge font; **Schriftfahne** f KER & GLAS letter slip; **Schriftfamilie** f DRUCK type family; **Schriftfernübertrager** m COMP & DV, TELEKOM Teletype (TM), teleprinter (BrE), teletypewriter (AmE); **Schriftgarnitur** f DRUCK family of weights; **Schriftgießen** nt DRUCK type casting; **Schriftgießerei** f DRUCK type foundry; **Schriftgrad** m DRUCK type size; **Schriftgröße** f DRUCK type size, KONSTZEICH character height; **Schriftgutverfilmung** f KONSTZEICH filming of textual documents; **Schrifthobel** m DRUCK type planer

schrifthoch adj DRUCK type-high

Schrifthöhe f DRUCK height of type, height of typeface, type height, height-to-paper

Schrift: Schriftkasten m DRUCK case; **Schriftkegel** m DRUCK body

schriftlich: ~ belegte Überwachung f QUAL documented control

Schrift: Schriftlinie f DRUCK baseline; **Schriftmetall** nt DRUCK type metal; **Schriftpräge-Auftraggerät** nt VERPACK printer-applicator; **Schriftschablone** f KONSTZEICH lettering stencil; **Schriftsetzer** m DRUCK compositor, typesetter; **Schriftstärke** f DRUCK weight of face, weight of type, zinc plate; **Schrifttype** f DRUCK typeface

Schritt m COMP & DV iteration, step, LABOR Mikroskop stage, REGELUNG step; **Schrittabstimmung** f ELEKTRONIK incremental tuning; **Schrittfunktion** f COMP & DV step function

schritthaltend: ~e Verarbeitung f COMP & DV in-line processing

Schritt: Schrittmotor m COMP & DV stepper motor, ELEKTRIZ stepper motor, stepping motor, ELEKTROTECH stepper motor, KONTROLL stepper motor, stepper, MASCHINEN step motor, stepper motor, stepping motor; **Schrittnachführungssystem** nt RAUMFAHRT Weltraumfunk step track system; **Schrittschalter** m

ELEKTRIZ step switch, ELEKTROTECH selector switch, TELECOM stepping switch; **Schrittschaltsystem** *nt* TELEKOM step-by-step system; **Schrittwähler** *m* TELECOM stepping switch; **Schrittwählersystem** *nt* TELEKOM *Telefon* step-by-step system

schrittweise[1] *adj* KONTROLL step-by-step

schrittweise[2] *adv* KONTROLL step-by-step

schrittweise:[3] ~ **Abstimmung** *f* RADIO incremental tuning; ~ **Führung** *f* RAUMFAHRT iterative guidance; ~ **Näherung** *f* GERÄT successive approximation; ~ **Regelung** *f* ELEKTRIZ step-by-step control; **schrittweiser Betrieb** *m* KONTROLL step-by-step operation; **schrittweises Positionieren** *nt* KONTROLL stepping

Schritt: **Schrittweite** *f* ELEKTRONIK *einer Schleife* increment, ELEKTROTECH pitch, KONTROLL step size; **Schritt-Wiederholungs-Diode** *f* ELEKTRONIK step recovery diode; **Schrittzähler** *m* COMP & DV, KONTROLL step counter, PHYS pedometer; **Schrittzeit** *f* KONTROLL step time

Schrobteil *m* FERTIG sett

Schroedinger-Gleichung *f* PHYS Schrodinger's equation

schroff: ~**e Klippe** *f* WASSERTRANS *Geographie* bluff

Schröpfglas *nt* KER & GLAS cupping glass

Schrotbohren *nt* BAU boring by shot drills, ERDÖL shot drilling

schroten *vt* FERTIG chip, LEBENSMITTEL bruise, kibble

Schrotmeißel *m* FERTIG hot set, top chisel, MASCHINEN chipping hammer

Schrotmühle *f* LEBENSMITTEL bruiser

Schrotrauschen *nt* OPTIK, PHYS shot noise, TELEKOM granular noise, shot noise

Schrotrückstände *m pl* LEBENSMITTEL break tailings

Schrotstrahlen *nt* BAU grit blasting

Schrott *m* MECHAN junk, scrap, QUAL scrap; **Schrottballen** *m* ABFALL scrap bundle; **Schrotthändler** *m* ABFALL scrap dealer, scrap metal merchant; **Schrottmeißel** *m* FERTIG sett; **Schrottpaketierpresse** *f* ABFALL scrap baler, VERPACK baling press; **Schrottplatz** *m* ABFALL scrapyard; **Schrottpresse** *f* ABFALL junk press, scrap press, scrap-baling press; **Schrottsammlung** *f* ABFALL scrap collection; **Schrottschere** *f* ABFALL scrap shear; **Schrottschmelzverfahren** *nt* FERTIG all-scrap process; **Schrottsortierung** *f* ABFALL scrap sorting; **Schrotthüttung** *f* ABFALL scrap smelting; **Schrottverwertung** *f* ABFALL scrap processing, scrap re-use; **Schrottzusatz** *m* FERTIG admits of scrap

Schrotwalze *f* LEBENSMITTEL break roller

Schrubben *nt* KER & GLAS swabbing

Schrubber *m* KERNTECH, KOHLEN scrubber

Schrühware *f* KER & GLAS *Porzellan* biscuit ware

Schrumpf- *pref* THERMOD heat-shrinkable

schrumpfbar *adj* THERMOD *Folie* shrinkable

schrumpfecht *adj* PAPIER shrink-proof

Schrumpfen *nt* BAU shrinkage, shrinking, MASCHINEN shrinkage

schrumpfen *vi* KER & GLAS, PAPIER, TEXTIL shrink

Schrumpffolie *f* LEBENSMITTEL shrink-film, THERMOD heat-shrinkable film, shrink-film, VERPACK shrink-film; ~ **mit perforierter Überlappung** *f* VERPACK shrink-film with perforated overlap; **Schrumpffolien-Siegelmaschine** *f* VERPACK blister sealer; **Schrumpffolienverpackung** *f* VERPACK blister pack

Schrumpf-: **Schrumpfgrenze** *f* KOHLEN shrinkage limit; **Schrumpfpackung** *f* VERPACK shrink pack; **Schrumpfpalettenabdeckung** *f* VERPACK shrink-wrapped pallet cover; **Schrumpfpassung** *f* MASCHINEN shrink fit;

Schrumpfriß *m* FERTIG contraction crack, shrinkage crack; **Schrumpfrohr** *nt* PAPIER shrink sleeve; **Schrumpfschachtel** *f* VERPACK shrink capsule; **Schrumpfschlauchbeutel-Verpackungsmaschine** *f* VERPACK shrink sleeve wrapping machine; **Schrumpfsitz** *m* MASCHINEN, MECHAN shrink fit; **Schrumpfspannung** *f* MASCHINEN contraction strain; **Schrumpftoleranz** *f* MASCHINEN shrinkage, shrinkage allowance; **Schrumpftunnel für Schlauchverpackung** *m* VERPACK shrink tunnel for sleeving; **Schrumpftunnel für Schlauchverschweißung** *m* VERPACK shrink tunnel for sleeve sealing

Schrumpfung *f* FERTIG consolidation, *Kunststoffinstallationen* contraction, KUNSTSTOFF, MASCHINEN, PAPIER, PHYS shrinkage, TELEKOM shrinking, VERPACK after shrinkage; ~ **bei Verhärtung** *f* VERPACK shrinkage on solidification

schrumpfverpackt *adj* VERPACK *Produkt* shrink-wrapped

Schrumpf-: **Schrumpfverpackung** *f* LEBENSMITTEL *in Folie* shrink-wrap, VERPACK contract packaging; **Schrumpfverpackungsdienst** *m* VERPACK contract blister packaging service; **Schrumpfverpackungsmaschine** *f* VERPACK shrink overwrapping machine; **Schrumpfzugabe** *f* MASCHINEN shrinkage allowance

Schruppdrehen *nt* FERTIG rough turning

Schruppdurchgang *m* FERTIG *Spanung* roughing pass

Schruppen *nt* FERTIG roughing

schruppen *vt* FERTIG rough-cut, MASCHINEN rough-cut, rough

Schruppfeile *f* FERTIG coarse-cut file, rough-cut file, MASCHINEN rough-cut file, roughing file

Schruppfräsen *nt* MASCHINEN rough milling

Schruppfräser *m* MASCHINEN roughing cutter, roughing mill

Schruppmeißel *m* FERTIG rougher, MASCHINEN roughing tool

Schruppsorte *f* FERTIG *Werkstoff* roughing grade

Schruppwerkzeug *nt* MASCHINEN rougher

Schruppzahn *m* MASCHINEN roughing tooth

Schub[1] *m* FERTIG thrust, LEBENSMITTEL batch, LUFTTRANS thrust, MASCHINEN shear, thrust, MECHAN push, MEERSCHMUTZ thrust, PHYS thrust, RAUMFAHRT blast, thrust

Schub:[2] **auf ~ beanspruchen** *vt* BAU shear

Schub:[3] **Schubdruck ausüben** *vi* RAUMFAHRT boost

Schub: **Schubabnahme** *f* RAUMFAHRT thrust decay; **Schubabschaltung** *f* RAUMFAHRT thrust cut-off; **Schubachse** *f* RAUMFAHRT thrust axis; **Schubanlage** *f* LUFTTRANS power plant; **Schubbeanspruchung** *f* MASCHINEN shearing stress; **Schubbewegung** *f* MASCHINEN translation, translatory motion; **Schubboot** *nt* WASSERTRANS push tug, pusher tug; **Schubbug** *m* RAUMFAHRT thrust cone; **Schubdruck** *m* LUFTTRANS *Triebwerk*, RAUMFAHRT boost pressure; **Schubdüse** *f* LUFTTRANS exhaust nozzle, RAUMFAHRT thrust nozzle

Schuber *m* VERPACK slip case

Schub: **Schubfehleinstellung** *f* RAUMFAHRT thrust misalignment; **Schubfestigkeit** *f* KOHLEN shear strength, MASCHINEN shearing strength; **Schubgelenk** *nt* MASCHINEN prismatic joint; **Schubgewicht** *nt* LUFTTRANS power-weight ratio; **Schubkarre** *f* BAU wheelbarrow; **Schubkarren** *m* BAU barrow, FERTIG wheelbarrow, TRANS barrow, wheelbarrow; **Schubklauengetriebe** *nt*

KFZTECH *Getriebe mit ständigem Eingriff* constant-mesh gears; **Schubkoeffizient** *m* MASCHINEN reciprocal of shear modulus; **Schubkonus** *m* RAUM-FAHRT thrust nozzle; **Schubkraft** *f* BAU shear force, thrust, FERTIG longitudinal shear, MASCHINEN, MEER-SCHMUTZ thrust; **Schubkraftverstärker** *m* LUFTTRANS thrust augmenter; **Schubkugel** *f* KFZTECH torque ball; **Schubkurbel** *f* MASCHINEN slider crank; **Schublehre** *f* MASCHINEN caliper square (AmE), calliper square (BrE), sliding calipers (AmE), vernier gage (AmE), vernier gauge (BrE), MECHAN, PHYS vernier caliper (AmE), vernier calliper (BrE); **Schubmaschine** *f* EI-SENBAHN banking locomotive (BrE), pusher locomotive (AmE); **Schubmodul** *nt* KOHLEN rigidity modulus, KUNSTSTOFF shear modulus; **Schubmodulation** *f* RAUMFAHRT thrust modulation; **Schubriegel** *m* BAU tower bolt; **Schubrohrantrieb** *m* KFZTECH *Getriebe* torque tube drive; **Schubschiffahrt** *f* TRANS push-towing; **Schubschlepper** *m* WASSERTRANS *Schifftyp* pusher tug; **Schubschraubtriebanlasser** *m* KFZTECH screw push starter; **Schubschwinge** *f* FERTIG *Getriebelehre* oscillating slider; **Schubspannung** *f* BAU shearing stress, KUNSTSTOFF shear stress, MASCHINEN shearing stress; **Schubstange** *f* MASCHINEN connecting rod, rod, MECHAN connecting rod, push rod; **Schubsteuerprogramm** *nt* RAUMFAHRT thrust program (AmE), thrust programme (BrE); **Schubsteuerung** *f* RAUMFAHRT boosting regulator; **Schubstrebe** *f* KFZTECH *Radaufhängung* torque arm; **Schubsubsystem** *nt* RAUMFAHRT thrust subsystem; **Schubtriebwerk** *nt* RAUMFAHRT booster, thruster; **Schubumkehrer** *m* LUFTTRANS thrust reverser; **Schubumkehrvorrichtung** *f* LUFTTRANS thrust reverser; **Schubvektor** *m* RAUMFAHRT thrust vector; **Schubvektordüse** *f* RAUMFAHRT thrust vectoring nozzle; **Schubvektorsteuerung** *f* RAUMFAHRT thrust vector control; **Schubverband** *m* WASSERTRANS multiple-barge convoy set, push tow; **Schubvergrößerer** *m* LUFTTRANS thrust augmenter; **Schubwechselgetriebe** *nt* KFZTECH sliding gear transmission, straight-toothed gearbox; **Schubwelle** *f* AKUSTIK rotational wave, shear wave; **Schubwert der Luftschraube** *m* WAS-SERTRANS propeller thrust coefficient; **Schubzentrum** *nt* RAUMFAHRT center of thrust (AmE), centre of thrust (BrE)

Schuh *m* FERNSEH *Stromabnehmer* shoe

Schuhwerk: ~ **für Industrieeinsätze** *nt* SICHERHEIT industrial footwear

Schuilingit *m* KERNTECH schuilingite

Schulfunk *m* FERNSEH educational broadcasting

Schülpe *f* FERTIG *Gußstück* scab

Schulschiff *nt* WASSERTRANS *Marine* training ship

Schulter *f* FERNSEH porch, KER & GLAS shoulder, MA-SCHINEN collar, shoulder; **Schulterdecker** *m* LUFTTRANS high-wing plane; **Schulterdeckerflügel** *m* LUFTTRANS *Luftfahrzeug* shoulder wing; **Schulterhöhe** *f* DRUCK shoulder height; **Schulterkugellager** *nt* MASCHINEN separable ball bearing; **Schulterlager** *nt* MASCHINEN separable bearing; **Schulterpolster** *nt* TEXTIL pad, shoulder pad; **Schulterstativ** *nt* FOTO rifle grip

Schulungszeit: ~ **am Doppelsteuer** *f* LUFTTRANS dual-instruction time

Schuppen *m* BAU shed; **Schuppenbildung** *f* LUFTTRANS alligatoring; **Schuppenglas** *nt* KER & GLAS flake glass

schuppig *adj* FERTIG scaly

Schur *f* TEXTIL clip

Schürfe *f* BAU *Bodenuntersuchung* pit

Schürfgrube *f* KOHLEN test pit

Schürfraupe *f* TRANS bulldozer

Schürfschacht *m* ERDÖL *Lagerstättensuche* prospecting shaft

Schurre *f* FERTIG tip chute

Schürvorrichtung *f* HEIZ & KÄLTE mechanical stoker

Schürze *f* PAPIER, SICHERHEIT apron, WASSERTRANS skirt; ~ **mit veränderlicher Geometrie** *f* WASSERTRANS variable-geometry skirt; **Schürzensperre** *f* MEER-SCHMUTZ curtain boom

Schuß *m* ERDÖL *Erkundung von Lagerstätten* shot, FER-TIG roll-bent part, PAPIER weft, TELEKOM *Mastantenne* section; **Schußanschlag** *m* TEXTIL beat-up; **Schußbruch** *m* TEXTIL weft break; **Schußdichte** *f* TEXTIL beat-up, weft density; **Schußdraht** *m* FERTIG *Drahtweben* shute wire

Schüssel *f* KOHLEN, METROL bowl, RADIO *Antennenform* dish; **Schüsselklassierer** *m* KOHLEN bowl classifier

Schuß: **Schußfaden** *m* TEXTIL *Weben* pick; **Schußfäden je Zoll** *m pl* TEXTIL picks per inch; **Schußfadenwächter** *m* TEXTIL weft stop motion; **Schußgarn** *nt* PAPIER weft yarn; **Schußgewicht** *nt* KUNSTSTOFF shot weight; **Schußleistung** *f* TEXTIL pick rate; **Schußspulmaschine** *f* TEXTIL pirn-winding machine; **Schußstreifen** *m* TEX-TIL bar

Schusterjunge *m* DRUCK orphan

Schute *f* WASSERTRANS dumb barge, *Schifftyp* barge; **Schutenträger** *m* WASSERTRANS barge carrier

Schutt *m* BAU rubble, EISENBAHN excavated material; **Schuttabladeplatz** *m* BAU dump site

Schüttdichte *f* ERDÖL bulk density, KOHLEN apparent density, KUNSTSTOFF apparent density, bulk density, PHYS bulk density; **Schüttdichtemeßgerät** *nt* GERÄT bulk density meter

Schüttelapparat *m* LABOR shaker

Schüttelbewegung *f* MASCHINEN shake, shaking motion

Schüttelherd *m* KOHLEN oscillating table

Schütteln *nt* LUFTTRANS buffeting, MASCHINEN shaking, RAUMFAHRT *Raumschiff* buffet

Schüttelrutsche *f* FERTIG shaker conveyor

Schüttelsieb *nt* KOHLEN griddle, vibrating screen, VER-PACK vibratory sifter

Schütteltrichter *m* LABOR separating funnel

Schüttelzuführer *m* MECHAN vibratory feeder

Schüttgut *nt* BAU bulk material, FERTIG packing, KOH-LEN bulk material, VERPACK bulk goods, WASSERTRANS *Ladung* bulk cargo; **Schüttgutbehälter mit Gravitätsentladung** *m* WASSERTRANS bulk container with gravity discharge; **Schüttgutbehälter mit pneumatischer Entladung** *m* WASSERTRANS bulk container with pressure discharge; **Schüttgutcontainer** *m* WASSERTRANS dry-bulk container

Schüttkoeffizient *m (C)* NICHTFOSS ENERG discharge coefficient *(C)*

Schüttlage *f* BAU hardcore

Schüttsteine *m pl* BAU rip-rap

Schüttwasser *nt* LEBENSMITTEL make-up water

Schüttwinkel *m* PHYS angle of friction

Schutz[1] *m* ANSTRICH, COMP & DV protection, ELEKTRIZ, MASCHINEN guard, SICHERHEIT guard, protection, *an einer Maschine* guard; ~ **mit Auslöser** *m* SICHERHEIT trip guard; ~ **vor Einschaltspitzen** *m* ELEKTROTECH inrush current protection; ~~ **und Entschädigungsver-**

einigung *f* MEERSCHMUTZ Protection & Indemnity Association

Schutz:[2] ~ **gewähren** *vi* WASSERTRANS shelter; ~ **suchen** *vi* WASSERTRANS shelter

Schütz *nt* ELEKTRIZ contactor, electric relay, electrical relay, WASSERVERSORG *im Schleusentor* sash gate

Schutz: **Schutzabdeckung** *f* SICHERHEIT *Getriebegehäuse* cover; **Schutzabstand** *m* COMP & DV guard band, TELEKOM guard space

Schütz: **Schützabwehr** *f* WASSERVERSORG floodgate; **Schützanlasser** *m* ELEKTRIZ contactor starter

Schutz: **Schutzanstrich** *m* KER & GLAS protective paint, KUNSTSTOFF, PAPIER protective coating; **Schutzanzug** *m* SICHERHEIT protective suit; **Schutzanzug für Rettungsdienste** *m* SICHERHEIT protective clothing for rescue services; **Schutzbereich** *m* PATENT extent of protection; **Schutzbeschichtung** *f* KUNSTSTOFF protective coating; **Schutzbit** *nt* COMP & DV guard bit; **Schutzblech** *nt* FERTIG, MASCHINEN guard; **Schutzbrett** *nt* BAU baffle board; **Schutzbrille** *f* ERGON goggles, KER & GLAS eye-protection glasses, LABOR protective spectacles, SICHERHEIT goggles; **Schutzbrillenglas** *nt* SICHERHEIT glass for protective goggles; **Schutzdach** *nt* BAU shed, shelter; **Schutzdraht** *m* ELEKTRIZ, ELEKTROTECH guard wire; **Schutzeinrichtung** *f* FERTIG safety guard, MASCHINEN, SICHERHEIT guard

schützen *vt* COMP & DV protect, FERTIG guard, RAUMFAHRT shield; ~ **vor** *vt* SICHERHEIT guard against

schützend: **zu ~e Merkmale** *nt pl* PATENT features to be protected

Schütz: **Schützenschlag** *m* TEXTIL *Weben* picking; **Schützenspindel** *f* TEXTIL shuttle spindle

Schutz: **Schutzfilm** *m* VERPACK protective film; **Schutzfrequenzband** *nt* COMP & DV guard band; **Schutzfunkenstrecke** *f* ELEKTRIZ protective spark gap; **Schutzgamaschen** *f pl* SICHERHEIT protective gaiters

Schutzgas *nt* FERTIG inert gas, KERNTECH blanket gas, cover gas, MASCHINEN inert gas; **Schutzgasabfuhrleitung** *f* KERNTECH cover gas discharge line; **Schutzgasflammen** *nt* THERMOD annealing under gas; **Schutzgasglühen** *nt* THERMOD annealing under gas; **Schutzgas-Lichtbogenschweißen** *nt* FERTIG inert gas arc welding; **Schutzgasschweißen** *nt* MASCHINEN inert gas-shielded welding, MECHAN gas welding; **Schutzgasschweißgerät** *nt* SICHERHEIT protective gas welding machine; **Schutzgastrennanlage** *f* KERNTECH blanket gas separation plant

Schutz: **Schutzgefäß** *nt* KERNTECH guard vessel; **Schutzgeländer** *nt* BAU guard rail; **Schutzgitter** *nt* ELEKTRIZ guard, HEIZ & KÄLTE grille, SICHERHEIT guard rail, protective screen; **Schutzgitter für Kathodenstrahlröhren** *nt* SICHERHEIT protective screen for cathode ray tubes; **Schutzglas** *nt* SICHERHEIT protective glass, *Schweißarbeiten* filter; **Schutzhandschuhe** *m pl* SICHERHEIT protective gloves; **Schutzhandschuhe für Industrieeinsätze** *m pl* SICHERHEIT industrial gloves; **Schutzhaube** *f* HEIZ & KÄLTE *für Lüfter* fan hood, MECHAN cover, SICHERHEIT protective hood; **Schutzhelm** *m* SICHERHEIT helmet, protective helmet, safety helmet, TRANS safety helmet; **Schutzhülse** *f* MASCHINEN protection sleeve; **Schutzkäfig** *m* SICHERHEIT guard; **Schutzkappe** *f* BAU *am unteren Ende eines Fallrohres*, KFZTECH *am Bremszylinder* boot, MASCHINEN protective cap; **Schutzkiel** *m* WASSERTRANS rubbing strake; **Schutzkittel** *m* SI-

CHERHEIT protective gown; **Schutzklasse** *f* FERTIG *Kunststoffinstallationen* safety class; **Schutzkleidung** *f* SICHERHEIT protective clothing; **Schutzkleidung aus Kettenringen** *f* SICHERHEIT chainmail garment; **Schutzkleidung für Kühlräume** *f* SICHERHEIT cold-storage protective clothing; **Schutzklemme** *f* ELEKTRIZ armor clamp (AmE), armour clamp (BrE); **Schutzkontakte** *m pl* ELEKTRIZ sealed contacts; **Schutzkontaktkupplung** *f* MASCHINEN shrouded coupling; **Schutzkopie** *f* COMP & DV protected master; **Schutzkragen** *m* HEIZ & KÄLTE shroud; **Schutzlack** *m* KER & GLAS resist; **Schutzmanschette** *f* LUFTTRANS boot (BrE), trunk (AmE); **Schutzmanschettenhalter** *m* LUFTTRANS boot retainer; **Schutzmantel** *m* FERTIG shield, OPTIK protective coating; **Schutzmaßnahmen** *f pl* SICHERHEIT protective measures; **Schutzmittel** *nt* VERPACK protective agent; **Schutznetz** *nt* SICHERHEIT safety net, WASSERVERSORG guard net; **Schutzort** *m* KOHLEN blast shelter; **Schutzpapier** *nt* FOTO *Rollfilm* backing paper; **Schutzplane** *f* KFZTECH safety bonnet (BrE), safety hood (AmE); **Schutzraum** *m* BAU shelter; **Schutzring** *m* ELEKTRIZ, ELEKTROTECH, PHYS guard ring; **Schutzringelektrode** *f* ELEKTROTECH guard ring; **Schutzringkondensator** *m* ELEKTROTECH guard ring capacitor; **Schutzrohr** *nt* BAU, ELEKTROTECH conduit; **Schutzrohrkontakt** *m* ELEKTROTECH reed switch; **Schutzrohrkontaktrelais** *nt* ELEKTROTECH, TELEKOM reed relay; **Schutzrückhaltsystem** *nt* SICHERHEIT protective restraint system; **Schutzsalbe** *f* SICHERHEIT protective cream; **Schutzschaltung** *f* ELEKTRIZ protective circuit, ELEKTROTECH guard circuit, TELEKOM protection circuit; **Schutzschicht** *f* ANSTRICH protective film, BAU coating, KUNSTSTOFF resist coating, VERPACK protective layer; **Schutzschiene** *f* BAU check rail, EISENBAHN check rail, guard rail; **Schutzschild** *m* FERTIG *Schweißen* handscreen, MASCHINEN shield; **Schutzschirm** *m* RAUMFAHRT shield, SICHERHEIT protective screen; **Schutzschlauch** *m* FERTIG *biegsame Welle* shaft casing, MASCHINEN casing; **Schutzschürze** *f* SICHERHEIT protective apron; **Schutzspur** *f* AUFNAHME guard track; **Schutzstreckensignal** *nt* EISENBAHN dead-section warning signal; **Schutzstromstrecke** *f* ELEKTRIZ protective spark gap; **Schutzüberzug** *m* KUNSTSTOFF protective coating, VERPACK protective coat; **Schutzüberzug elektrochemisch aufgebracht** *m* ANSTRICH galvanized protective coating; **Schutzumhüllung** *f* PHYS *Lichtleiter* protective coating; **Schutzumschlag** *m* DRUCK dust cover, jacket, VERPACK *Buch* protective cover; **Schutzverpackung** *f* VERPACK protective wrapper; **Schutzvorrichtung** *f* MECHAN guard, WASSERVERSORG *Überlandssystem* guard net; **Schutzvorrichtung mit Fotozelle** *f* SICHERHEIT photoelectric guard; **Schutzwagen** *m* EISENBAHN match wagon, shock-absorbing wagon; **Schutzwand** *f* BAU screen; **Schutzweiche** *f* EISENBAHN catch points; **Schutzwiderstand** *m* ELEKTROTECH bleeder; **Schutzzone** *f* KERNTECH *im Heißlabor* safety zone

Schwabbel *f* METALL polishing wheel; **Schwabbeln** *nt* MASCHINEN buffing; **Schwabbelscheibe** *f* FERTIG buff, buffing wheel, rag buffing wheel, MASCHINEN buff, mop, rag wheel

schwach:[1] ~ **besetzte Matrix** *f* COMP & DV sparse matrix; ~ **führender Lichtwellenleiter** *m* TELEKOM weakly guiding fiber (AmE), weakly guiding fibre (BrE); **~e Kopplung** *f* KERNTECH weak coupling; **~e Kraft** *f* TEIL-

PHYS weak force, weak nuclear force; **~ leitende Faser** *f* OPTIK weakly guiding fiber (AmE), weakly guiding fibre (BrE); **~er Monofrequenzlaser** *m* STRAHLPHYS low-power single-frequency laser; **~er Positronen-übergang** *m* KERNTECH weak positron transition; **~e Quelle** *f* KERNTECH thin source; **~e Wechselrichtung** *f* ELEKTRONIK weak inversion; **~e Wechselwirkung** *f* KERNTECH, PHYS, TEILPHYS weak interaction

schwach:[2] **~ sieden** *vi* THERMOD boil slowly

Schwachpunktdesign *nt* RAUMFAHRT design to yield point

Schwachstellenanalyse *f* QUAL weak-point analysis

Schwachstrom *m* TELEKOM light current; **Schwach-strom-Netzschalter** *m* ELEKTRIZ light switch

Schwächung *f* ELEKTROTECH *Strahleneinwirkung* absorption, PHYS, WELLPHYS attenuation; **Schwä-chungsglied** *nt* AUFNAHME attenuator; **Schwächungskoeffizient** *m* ELEKTRONIK attenuation coefficient

Schwade *f* MEERSCHMUTZ swath

Schwaden *m* MEERSCHMUTZ swath

Schwalbennest *nt* BAU honeycomb; **Schwalbennestbil-dung** *f* BAU honeycombing

Schwalbenschwanz *m* BAU, MECHAN dovetail; **Schwal-benschwanzführung** *f* FERTIG dovetail; **Schwalbenschwanznut** *f* MASCHINEN dovetail groove; **Schwalbenschwanznutenfräser** *m* FERTIG dovetail cutter; **Schwalbenschwanzverbindung** *f* BAU dovetail joint, swallowtail joint, MECHAN dovetail joint

Schwammgummi *m* KUNSTSTOFF sponge rubber

Schwanenhals *m* BAU swan neck; **Schwanenhalsver-schluß** *m* BAU *Sanitär* S-trap

Schwanken *nt* GERÄT *Anzeigewert, Frequenz, Impuls-länge* jitter

schwanken *vi* ELEKTRIZ fluctuate

schwankend: **~es Echo** *nt* FERNSEH flutter echo; **~e Strömung** *f* KERNTECH unsteady flow

Schwankung *f* ELEKTRIZ drift, fluctuation; **~ innerhalb der Maschine** *f* KER & GLAS in-line variation

schwanzlastig: **~e Fluglage** *f* LUFTTRANS nose-up attitude

Schwanzlastigkeit *f* LUFTTRANS tail heaviness

Schwanzsporn *m* LUFTTRANS tail skid

Schwarz- *pref* DRUCK black

schwarz: **~es Brett** *nt* COMP & DV *bei E-Mail* bulletin board; **~er Fleck** *m* KER & GLAS black speck; **~er Körper** *m* FERNSEH, PHYS, RAUMFAHRT, STRAHLPHYS, THERMOD black body; **~es Loch** *nt* PHYS, RAUMFAHRT black hole; **~er Regelstab** *m* KERNTECH black absorber rod; **~er Strahler** *m* PHYS, STRAHLPHYS, THERMOD black body radiator

Schwarz-: **Schwarzblech** *nt* FERTIG black plate, METALL black iron plate, black sheet

Schwärze *f* DRUCK black, FERTIG *Gießen* black wash

schwärzen *vt* FERTIG *Gießen* black-wash, .THERMOD blacken

Schwarz-: **Schwarzfärbung** *f* KER & GLAS black staining; **Schwarzglühen** *nt* METALL black annealing; **Schwarz-guß** *m* FERTIG all-black malleable cast iron; **Schwarzklipper** *m* FERNSEH black clipper; **Schwarz-licht** *nt* DRUCK, OPTIK black light; **Schwarzlot** *nt* KER & GLAS black stain

schwarzrot *adj* METALL black red

Schwarz-: **Schwarzschild-Radius** *m* PHYS Schwarz-schild radius; **Schwarzschulter** *f* FERNSEH back porch; **Schwarzschulterklammerung** *f* FERNSEH back-

porch clamping; **Schwarzsender** *m* FERNSEH bootleg; **Schwarzsteuerdiode** *f* FERNSEH DC clamp diode; **Schwarzstraßenbau** *m* BAU flexible road construction

Schwärzung *f* AKUSTIK optical density, ELEKTRIZ *des Glaskolbens einer Glühlampe* blackening, KER & GLAS darkening, PHYS density; **Schwärzungseinstellung** *f* DRUCK darkness setting; **Schwärzungsindex** *m* KER & GLAS darkening index; **Schwärzungskurve** *f* FOTO characteristic curve; **Schwärzungsröhre** *f* ELEKTRO-NIK skiatron

Schwarzweiß- *pref* COMP & DV *Bildschirm* monochrome, DRUCK black and white, FOTO monochrome; **Schwarzweiß-Empfänger** *m* FERNSEH monochrome receiver; **Schwarzweiß-Fernsehen** *nt* FERNSEH black and white television; **Schwarzweiß-Überwachung** *f* FERNSEH black-white monitoring

Schwarz-: **Schwarzwertanhebung** *f* FERNSEH black lift; **Schwarzwertfrequenz** *f* FERNSEH black level fre-quency; **Schwarzwertpegel** *m* FERNSEH black level; **Schwarzwertspitze** *f* FERNSEH black peak; **Schwarz-wertunterdrückung** *f* FERNSEH black compression

Schwebebahn *f* TRANS cableway

Schwebebus *m* LUFTTRANS aerobus

Schwebefähigkeit *f* HYDRAUL buoyancy

Schwebeflugkupplung *f* LUFTTRANS *Hubschrauber* hover flight coupler

Schwebehöhe *f* TRANS hoverheight

Schwebekörper-Durchflußmesser *m* ERDÖL *Mengen-meßgerät* rotameter

Schwebekörper-Durchflußmeßgerät *nt* GERÄT variable area flowmeter

Schwebekörper-Füllstandsmessung *f* GERÄT suspen-ded-body level measurement

Schwebeladung *f* ELEKTROTECH floating charge

Schwebemittel *nt* KUNSTSTOFF antisettling agent

Schwebemotor *m* KFZTECH floating engine

Schweben *nt* LUFTTRANS *Hubschrauber* hovering; **~ eines Luftkissenfahrzeugs** *nt* TRANS height hovering

schwebend[1] *adj* ELEKTROTECH floating, ERDÖL *Geolo-gie* updip, MECHAN floating

schwebend:[2] **~es Grundwasser** *nt* WASSERVERSORG perched ground water; **~er Pfahl** *m* KOHLEN floating pile; **~er Schienenstoß** *m* BAU suspended joint; **~er Steueranschluß** *m* ELEKTRONIK floating gate; **~es Tröpfchen** *nt* UMWELTSCHMUTZ suspended liquid droplet

Schwebesandglühofen *m* KERNTECH fluid-bed furnace

Schwebesteuerung *f* LUFTTRANS *Hubschrauber* hover control

Schwebesystem *nt* EISENBAHN suspended system

Schwebeteilchenmessung *f* GERÄT *Luftverunreinigung* measurement of suspended particulate matter

Schwebevermögen *nt* LUFTTRANS *Hubschrauber* hovering capability

Schwebezustand *m* LUFTTRANS *Hubschrauber* hovering

Schwebstoff *m* UMWELTSCHMUTZ suspended particle; **Schwebstoff-Filter** *nt* CHEMTECH air filter; **Schweb-stoffteilchen** *nt* UMWELTSCHMUTZ particulate matter

Schwebung *f* AKUSTIK beat, ELEKTRONIK beating, PHYS beat; **Schwebungsfrequenz** *f* ELEKTRONIK, PHYS, RA-DIO beat frequency; **Schwebungsfrequenzoszillator** *m* *(BFO)* ELEKTRONIK, PHYS, RADIO beat frequency oscillator *(BFO)*; **Schwebungsnull** *f* FERNSEH zero beat; **Schwebungstondetektor** *m* ELEKTRONIK beat note detector

Schwefel[1] *m* ERDÖL, KUNSTSTOFF sulfur (AmE),

sulphur (BrE); **Schwefel-** *pref* CHEMIE sulfurous (AmE), sulphurous (BrE)

Schwefel:[2] **mit ~ behandeln** *vt* CHEMIE sulfurize (AmE), sulphurize (BrE)

schwefelarm: ~es Rohöl *nt* ERDÖL sweet crude

Schwefel: **Schwefelbad** *nt* FOTO sulfide toning (AmE), sulphide toning (BrE); **Schwefelchlorid** *nt* CHEMIE sulfur chloride (AmE), sulphur chloride (BrE); **Schwefeldioxid** *nt* CHEMIE, LEBENSMITTEL, UMWELT-SCHMUTZ sulfur dioxide (AmE), sulphur dioxide (BrE); **Schwefeldioxidreduktion** *f* UMWELTSCHMUTZ sulfur dioxide reduction (AmE), sulphur dioxide reduction (BrE); **Schwefelgehalt** *m* ERDÖL *Petrochemie* sulfur content (AmE), sulphur content (BrE)

schwefelhaltig[1] *adj* CHEMIE sulfurous (AmE), sulphurous (BrE)

schwefelhaltig:[2] **~er Boden** *m* KOHLEN sulfide soil (AmE), sulphide soil (BrE); **~er Brennstoff** *m* UM-WELTSCHMUTZ sulfurous combustible (AmE), sulphurous combustible (BrE); **~es Rohöl** *nt* ERDÖL sour crude

Schwefel: **Schwefelhaushalt** *m* UMWELTSCHMUTZ sulfur budget (AmE), sulphur budget (BrE); **Schwefelkoh-lenstoff** *m* CHEMIE carbon disulfide (AmE), carbon disulphide (BrE); **Schwefelkreislauf** *m* UMWELT-SCHMUTZ sulfur cycle (AmE), sulphur cycle (BrE); **Schwefelmonochlorid** *nt* CHEMIE disulfur dichloride (AmE), disulphur dichloride (BrE)

Schwefeln *nt* CHEMIE thionation

Schwefel: **Schwefeloxid** *nt* UMWELTSCHMUTZ sulfur oxide (AmE), sulphur oxide (BrE); **Schwefelrückge-winnungsanlage** *f* ABFALL sulfur recovery plant (AmE), sulphur recovery plant (BrE); **Schwefelsäure** *f* CHEMIE sulfuric acid (AmE), sulphuric acid (BrE), vitriolic acid, FERTIG *Kunststoffinstallationen*, UMWELTSCHMUTZ sulfuric acid (AmE), sulphuric acid (BrE); **Schwefelsäurediamid** *nt* CHEMIE sulfamide (AmE), sulphamide (BrE); **Schwefelsäurenanhydrid** *nt* UMWELTSCHMUTZ sulfuric anhydride (AmE), sulphuric anhydride (BrE); **Schwefel-Sepia-Tönung** *f* FOTO sepia toning; **Schwefeltrioxid** *nt* CHEMIE sulfur trioxide (AmE), sulphur trioxide (BrE)

Schwefelung *f* CHEMIE thionation, KOHLEN sulfuriza-tion (AmE), sulphurization (BrE)

Schwefelwasserstoff *m* CHEMIE hydrogen sulfide (AmE), hydrogen sulphide (BrE), LEBENSMITTEL hy-drogen sulfide (AmE), hydrogen sulphide (BrE), sulfurated hydrogen (AmE), sulphurated hydrogen (BrE), UMWELTSCHMUTZ hydrogen sulfide (AmE), hy-drogen sulphide (BrE)

schweflig: ~e Säure *f* UMWELTSCHMUTZ sulfurous acid (AmE), sulphurous acid (BrE); **~saures Salz** *nt* CHE-MIE sulfite (AmE), sulphite (BrE)

Schweif *m* RAUMFAHRT trail; **Schweifsäge** *f* MASCHINEN turning saw

Schweigezone *f* AUFNAHME zone of silence

Schweinsleder *nt* DRUCK pigskin

Schweiß- *pref* FERTIG, KERNTECH, MASCHINEN, MET-ALL, WERKPRÜF welding; **Schweißanzug** *m* SICHERHEIT welder's protective clothing; **Schweißauf-trag** *m* FERTIG *Schweißen* pad; **Schweißbad** *nt* FERTIG puddle, *Schweißen* molten pool, pool; **Schweißbarkeit** *f* MASCHINEN, METALL weldability; **Schweißbarkeits-versuch** *m* WERKPRÜF weldability test; **Schweißbereich** *m* KERNTECH weld region; **Schweiß-bogen** *m* MECHAN welding arc; **Schweißbrenner** *m*

BAU acetylene blowpipe, blowpipe, welding blowpipe, MASCHINEN welding torch, MECHAN welding blow-pipe, welding burner, welding torch, THERMOD welding torch; **Schweißbuckel** *m* FERTIG projection, projection weld; **Schweißdraht** *m* BAU welding wire, MASCHINEN filler wire, welding wire, MECHAN filler wire, welding rod, welding wire; **Schweißdüse** *f* ME-CHAN welding nozzle; **Schweißechtheit** *f* TEXTIL fastness to perspiration; **Schweißelektrode** *f* MASCHI-NEN welding electrode; **Schweißen** *nt* FERTIG welding, *Kunststoffinstallationen* fusion, KUNSTSTOFF, MA-SCHINEN, MECHAN, THERMOD welding; **~ von Flicken** *nt* FERTIG patching

schweißen *vt* ANSTRICH, MECHAN, PAPIER, THERMOD weld

Schweiß-: **Schweißerhandschirm** *m* BAU welding hand-shield; **Schweißerkennzeichen** *nt* QUAL welder identification; **Schweißerprüfung** *f* QUAL welder qualification; **Schweißfehler** *m* MECHAN welding de-fect; **Schweißflußmittel** *nt* ANSTRICH welding flux; **Schweißfolge** *f* BAU welding sequence; **Schweißform** *f* MECHAN welding die; **Schweißglut** *f* MECHAN welding heat; **Schweißgut** *nt* MECHAN welding stock; **Schweiß-gutausbringung** *f* FERTIG *Schweißen* deposition efficiency; **Schweißhandschutz** *m* SICHERHEIT welder's handshield; **Schweißhaube** *f* SICHERHEIT *mit automatischer Lichtdurchlässigkeitsanpassung* welder's hood; **Schweißhelm** *m* BAU welding helmet; **Schweißhitze** *f* MECHAN welding heat; **Schweißkon-struktion** *f* MECHAN weldment; **Schweißkrater** *m* FERTIG *Schweißen* crater; **Schweißlage** *f* MECHAN pass; **Schweißleistung** *f* MECHAN welding capacity; **Schweißlinse** *f* FERTIG *Punktschweißen* nugget; **Schweißmaschine** *f* MECHAN welding machine; **Schweißmetall** *nt* METALL weld metal; **Schweißmittel** *nt* ANSTRICH welding flux, MECHAN welding compound; **Schweißmuffe** *f* FERTIG *Kunststoffinstal-lationen* fusion socket; **Schweißnabe** *f* MECHAN hub

Schweißnaht *f* FERTIG weld, KERNTECH welding seam, MASCHINEN weld seam, welded body seam, MECHAN edge, seam, weld, welding seam, METALL, PAPIER wel-ded seam, THERMOD weld, VERPACK weight-filling machine; **Schweißnahtfestigkeit** *f* FERTIG weld strength; **Schweißnahtwurzel** *f* BAU root of weld

Schweiß-: **Schweißofen** *m* METALL balling furnace; **Schweißpaste** *f* MASCHINEN welding paste; **Schweiß-perle** *f* ANSTRICH weld spatter; **Schweißprogramm** *nt* BAU welding program (AmE), welding programme (BrE); **Schweißprozeß** *m* BAU welding process; **Schweißpulver** *nt* FERTIG unionmelt; **Schweißraupe** *f* FERTIG *Schweißen* bead, deposited metal, MASCHI-NEN, MECHAN bead; **Schweißrichtung** *f* FERTIG hand of welding; **Schweißschlacke** *f* MECHAN welding cinder; **Schweißschutzanzug** *m* SICHERHEIT welder's protective clothing; **Schweißschutzschild** *nt* SICHER-HEIT face shield, welder's shield; **Schweißschutzvorhang** *m* SICHERHEIT welder's pro-tective curtain; **Schweißspitze** *f* MECHAN welding tip; **Schweißspritzer** *m* ANSTRICH weld spatter; **Schweiß-stab** *m* MECHAN welding rod; **Schweißstahl** *m* BAU wrought iron, METALL weld steel; **Schweißstelle** *f* KERNTECH, MECHAN, METALL weld; **Schweißstrom** *m* MECHAN welding current; **Schweißstromkreis** *m* BAU, MECHAN welding circuit; **Schweißstutzen** *m* FERTIG *Kunststoffinstallationen* fusion spigot; **Schweißtakt** *m* BAU welding cycle; **Schweißtransformator** *m* ELEKTRO-

TECH welding transformer

Schweißung *f* KERNTECH, METALL, THERMOD weld; **~ an der Baustelle** *f* KERNTECH site weld; **~ vor Ort** *f* KERNTECH site weld

Schweiß-: **Schweißunterlagen** *f pl* QUAL welding material documentation; **Schweißverbindung** *f* FERTIG *Kunststoffinstallationen* fusion-welded joint, MASCHINEN weld joint; **Schweißverfahren** *nt* BAU welding procedure, MASCHINEN welding process; **Schweißverfahrensprüfung** *f* QUAL welding procedure qualification; **Schweißvorhang** *m* SICHERHEIT welder's protective curtain; **Schweißwärme** *f* MECHAN welding heat; **Schweißwurzel** *f* MECHAN root; **Schweißzusatz** *m* MECHAN filler metal; **Schweißzyklus** *m* BAU welding cycle

Schweizerisch: **~e Normenvereinigung** *f (SNV)* ELEKTRIZ Swiss Standards Association *(SSA)*

Schwelbrand *m* THERMOD smoldering fire (AmE), smouldering fire (BrE)

schwelen *vi* THERMOD smolder (AmE), smoulder (BrE)

schwelend: **~es Feuer** *nt* THERMOD smoldering fire (AmE), smouldering fire (BrE)

Schwelle *f* AKUSTIK threshold, BAU sole piece, threshold, COMP & DV threshold, EISENBAHN cross tie (AmE), sleeper (BrE), tie (AmE), ELEKTRONIK, ERGON threshold

schwellen *vt* WASSERVERSORG bulk

Schwelle: **Schwellenänderung** *f* ERGON threshold shift; **Schwellenbett** *nt* EISENBAHN sleeper-bed (BrE), tie bed (AmE); **Schwellenbohrmaschine** *f* EISENBAHN sleeper-drilling machine (BrE), tie-drilling machine (AmE); **Schwellendechselmaschine** *f* EISENBAHN sleeper-adzing machine (BrE), tie-adzing machine (AmE); **Schwellenenergie** *f* METALL, STRAHLPHYS threshold energy; **Schwellenerweiterungsdemodulator** *m* TELEKOM threshold extension demodulator; **Schwellenfeld** *nt* EISENBAHN distance between sleepers (BrE), distance between ties (AmE); **Schwellenkennzeichnung** *f* LUFTTRANS runway threshold marking; **Schwellenoperation** *f* COMP & DV threshold operation; **Schwellenschraube** *f* EISENBAHN sleeper screw (BrE), tie screw (AmE); **Schwellenschraubenausreißgerät** *nt* EISENBAHN spike puller; **Schwellenschraubeneindrehmaschine** *f* EISENBAHN sleeper screwdriver (BrE), tie screwdriver (AmE), spike driver; **Schwellenspannung** *f* ELEKTROTECH threshold voltage; **Schwellenstrom** *m* ELEKTROTECH threshold current, OPTIK *Laserdiode* threshold current laser diode, STRAHLPHYS, TELEKOM threshold current; **Schwellenüberschreitungszahl** *f* TELEKOM level crossing rate; **Schwellenwert** *m* COMP & DV threshold, ELEKTRONIK threshold value; **Schwellenwertsensor** *m* GERÄT threshold detector; **Schwellenwertsignal** *nt* GERÄT threshold signal

Schwellholz *nt* BAU sill plate

Schwellspannung *f* FERNSEH threshold voltage, FERTIG repeated cycle stress

Schwellwert *m* KONTROLL, RAUMFAHRT, SICHERHEIT threshold; **Schwellwertaudiometrie** *f* SICHERHEIT threshold audiometry; **Schwellwertoperation** *f* ELEKTRONIK thresholding; **Schwellwertschalter** *m* PHYS Schmitt trigger; **Schwellwertschaltung** *f* KONTROLL threshold circuit; **Schwellwertsensor** *m* GERÄT threshold detector; **Schwellwertsignal** *nt* ELEKTRONIK, GERÄT threshold signal; **Schwellwertsteuerung** *f* KONTROLL threshold control

Schwemmkegel *m* WASSERVERSORG alluvial cone

Schwemmland *nt* BAU alluvium; **Schwemmlandebene** *f* WASSERVERSORG alluvial plain

Schwengelbohrloch *nt* ERDÖL *Fördertechnik* beam well

Schwenk-: **~ und Neigekopf** *m* FOTO pan-and-tilt head

Schwenkachse *f* MASCHINEN swivel axis

Schwenkarm *m* MASCHINEN swinging arm, swivel arm

Schwenkarm: **am ~ hängender Drucktastenschalter** *m* FERTIG punchbutton pendant

schwenkbar[1] *adj* MECHAN hinged

schwenkbar:[2] **~es Brückenteil** *nt* TRANS turntable bridge; **~es Grundbrett** *nt* FOTO tilting baseboard; **~es Objektivbrett** *nt* FOTO swing front; **~er Reflektor** *m* FOTO swivel-mounted reflector; **~e Rückwand** *f* FOTO revolving back, swinging back

Schwenkbewegung *f* LUFTTRANS *Hubschrauber* flapping, *Rotor* hunting, MASCHINEN swinging movement

Schwenkbrücke *f* BAU swivel bridge

Schwenkdach *nt* WASSERTRANS swiveling roof (AmE), swivelling roof (BrE)

Schwenken *nt* BAU slewing (BrE), sluing (AmE), COMP & DV *seitliche Verschiebung der Ansicht auf Bildschirm* panning, FERNSEH pan and scan; **~ des Luftschraubenblattes** *nt* LUFTTRANS *Hubschrauber* hunting blade; **~ der Pfeife** *nt* KER & GLAS swinging of the pipe

schwenken[1] *vt* MASCHINEN slew (BrE), slue (AmE), swing, swivel, MECHAN slew (BrE), slue (AmE)

schwenken[2] *vi* MASCHINEN, MECHAN slew (BrE), slue (AmE)

Schwenkgelenk *nt* LUFTTRANS drag link; **~ des Luftschraubenblattes** *nt* LUFTTRANS blade-folding hinge; **Schwenkgelenkbegrenzungsstift** *m* LUFTTRANS *Hubschrauber* drag hinge pin

Schwenkgrube *f* KER & GLAS swinging pit

Schwenkhebel *m* MASCHINEN swiveling lever (AmE), swivelling lever (BrE)

Schwenkkörper *m* FERTIG *Axialkolbenpumpe* tilting yoke

Schwenkkran *m* BAU slewing crane (BrE), sluing crane (AmE), swing crane, KERNTECH slewing crane (BrE), sluing crane (AmE)

Schwenkmeißelhalter *m* MASCHINEN swivel toolholder

Schwenkradius *m* BAU *eines Kranes* swinging round

Schwenkrinne *f* BAU swinging chute

Schwenkrolle *f* FERTIG caster, castor

Schwenkrotorhubschrauber *m* LUFTTRANS tilting rotor helicopter

Schwenkscheibe *f* FERTIG *Pumpe* tilting box

Schwenkschildplanierraupe *f* BAU angledozer

Schwenkstein *m* KER & GLAS swinging brick

Schwenktisch *m* MASCHINEN swiveling table (AmE), swivelling table (BrE)

Schwenkwerk *nt* MASCHINEN slewing gear

Schwer- *pref* KFZTECH, PHYS, RAUMFAHRT heavy

schwer:[1] **~ entflammbar** *adj* SICHERHEIT flame-resistant; **~ zugänglich** *adj* BAU difficult to get at

schwer:[2] **~e Dünung** *f* WASSERTRANS *Seezustand* heavy swell; **~e Fraktionen** *f pl* ERDÖL *Raffinerietechnik* heavy fractions; **~e Gruppe** *f* KERNTECH *von Spaltprodukten* heavy group; **~es Heizöl** *nt* ERDÖL *Destillationsprodukt* residual fuel oil; **~er Hilfskran** *m* EISENBAHN heavy breakdown crane; **~er Holzhammer** *m* BAU maul; **~e Kohlenwasserstoff-Fraktionen** *f pl* ERDÖL *Raffinerie* heavy hydrocarbon fractions; **~e Masse** *f* PHYS gravitational mass; **~es Rohöl** *nt* ERDÖL heavy crude, heavy crude oil; **~e Schnitte** *m pl* ERDÖL heavy fractions; ~e See *f* WASSERTRANS rough sea, *Seezustand* heavy seas; ~ verarbeitbarer Kanalruß *m* *(HPC-Ruß)* KUNSTSTOFF hard-processing channel carbon black *(HPC carbon black)*; ~es Wasser *nt* PHYS heavy water; ~es Wasser D₂0 *nt* KERNTECH *Deuteriumoxid* heavy water; ~er Wasserstoff *m* CHEMIE deuterium; ~es Wetter *nt* WASSERTRANS heavy weather; ~er Zusammenstoß *m* TRANS primary collision

Schwer-: **Schwerbenzin** *nt* KFZTECH heavy gasoline (AmE), heavy petrol (BrE)

Schwere *f* KFZTECH, PHYS, RAUMFAHRT gravity; **Schwerefeld** *nt* PHYS gravitational field; **Schweregradientendrehmoment** *nt* RAUMFAHRT gravity gradient torque; **Schweregradientenspitze** *f* RAUMFAHRT gravity gradient boom; **Schweregradientenstabilisierung** *f* RAUMFAHRT gravity gradient stabilization

schwerelos: ~es Schweben *nt* TRANS air cushion levitation

Schwere: **Schwerelosigkeit** *f* RAUMFAHRT weightlessness

Schwer-: **Schwerentflammbarkeit** *f* KUNSTSTOFF flame resistance

Schwere: **Schwerewellen** *f pl* PHYS gravitational waves, gravity waves, STRAHLPHYS gravitational waves

Schwer-: **Schwerflintglas** *nt* KER & GLAS dense flint; **Schwerflüssigkeit** *f* KOHLEN dense liquid; **Schwerflüssigkeitsprüfung** *f* KOHLEN heavy-liquid test; **Schwergutbaum** *m* WASSERTRANS *Ladung* jumbo derrick; **Schwerhörigengerät** *nt* AKUSTIK hearing aid; **Schwerhörigkeit** *f* ERGON dysacusis, hearing disability; **Schwerionenfusion** *f* KERNTECH heavy ion fusion; **Schwerionensynchrotron** *nt (SIS)* TEILPHYS heavy-ion synchrotron *(HIS)*

Schwerkraft *f* BAU, MASCHINEN, PAPIER, PHYS, RAUMFAHRT gravity, UMWELTSCHMUTZ gravitational force; **Schwerkraftabscheider** *m* ABFALL gravity separator; **Schwerkraftfluß** *m* KERNTECH gravity flow; **Schwerkraftförderer** *m* MASCHINEN gravity conveyor, VERPACK conveyor way; **Schwerkraftfüllmaschine** *f* VERPACK gravity filling machine; **Schwerkraftfüllung** *f* RAUMFAHRT *Raumschiff* gravity filling; **Schwerkraftgießen** *nt* FERTIG gravity casting; **Schwerkraftguß** *m* FERTIG nonpressure casting; **Schwerkraftregelstab** *m* KERNTECH gravity drop absorber rod; **Schwerkraftsumlauf** *m* HEIZ & KÄLTE gravity circulation; **Schwerkrafttrenner** *m* ABFALL gravity separator; **Schwerkraftvakuum-Verkehrszug** *m* EISENBAHN gravity vacuum transit train; **Schwerkraftzusammenbruch** *m* RAUMFAHRT gravitation collapse

Schwer-: **Schwerkronglas** *nt* KER & GLAS dense crown

Schwerlast *f* KFZTECH, RAUMFAHRT heavy-lift; **Schwerlastfahrzeug** *nt* KFZTECH heavy lorry (BrE), heavy motor truck (AmE), heavy truck (AmE); **Schwerlastfahrzeugaufzug** *m* TRANS heavy-vehicle elevator (AmE), heavy-vehicle lift (BrE); **Schwerlasthubschrauber** *m* LUFTTRANS crane helicopter, heavy-lift helicopter; **Schwerlastkran** *m* BAU goliath crane; **Schwerlastraumträger** *m* RAUMFAHRT heavy-lift vehicle; **Schwerlastträgerrakete** *f (SL-Rakete)* RAUMFAHRT *zum Starten* heavy-lift launch vehicle *(HLLV)*; **Schwerlastverkehr** *m* TRANS HGV traffic, heavy goods vehicle traffic

Schwer-: **Schwermetall** *nt* KOHLEN, STRAHLPHYS, UMWELTSCHMUTZ heavy metal; **Schwermetall-Differenzenmethode** *f* KERNTECH heavy-metal difference technique; **Schwerölentschwefelung** *f* AB-

FALL heavy-oil desulfurization (AmE), heavy-oil desulphurization (BrE); **Schwerölmotor** *m* KFZTECH heavy-oil engine; **Schwerölrückstand** *m* ABFALL heavy-oil residue; **Schwerprofil** *nt* METALL heavy section

Schwerpunkt *m* BAU center of gravity (AmE), centre of gravity (BrE), FERTIG centroid, MECHAN, PHYS, RAUMFAHRT center of gravity (AmE), centre of gravity (BrE), TEILPHYS center of mass (AmE), centre of mass (BrE); ~ des Luftschraubenblattes *m* LUFTTRANS blade balance; ~ der Wasserlinienfläche *m* WASSERTRANS *Schiffkonstruktion* center of waterplane (AmE), centre of waterplane (BrE); **Schwerpunktenergie** *f* TEILPHYS collision energy; **Schwerpunktsystem** *nt* MECHAN, PHYS CMS, center-of-mass system (AmE), centre-of-mass system (BrE)

schwer: in ~er See laufen *vi* WASSERTRANS *Schiff* fight against heavy weather, labor (AmE), labour (BrE), make heavy weather

Schwer-: **Schwerspannstift** *m* FERTIG *Kunststoffinstallationen* spring cotter; **Schwerspat** *m* ERDÖL *Mineralogie*, KUNSTSTOFF baryte; **Schwerstange** *f* ERDÖL *Bohrtechnik* drill collar; **Schwerstoff** *m* KOHLEN dense medium

Schwert *nt* WASSERTRANS Schiffbau centerboard (AmE), centreboard (BrE); **Schwertfalzmaschine** *f* DRUCK blade folder

Schwerwasser *nt* KERNTECH *Deuteriumoxid* heavy water; **Schwerwasseranlage** *f* KERNTECH heavy-water plant; **Schwerwasserdampf** *m* KERNTECH heavy-water vapor (AmE), heavy-water vapour (BrE); **Schwerwasserentgaser** *m* KERNTECH heavy-water degasifier

schwerwassermoderiert: ~er Reaktor *m (SWR)* KERNTECH heavy-water-moderated reactor *(HWR)*; ~er Uranreaktor *m* KERNTECH uranium heavy-water reactor

Schwerwasser: **Schwerwasserreaktor** *m* KERNTECH heavy-water reactor; **Schwerwassersprühdüse** *f* KERNTECH heavy-water spray nozzle

schwerwiegend: ~er Fehler *m* COMP & DV fatal error

Schwimm-: ~ und Sinkanalyse *f* KOHLEN float-and-sink analysis

Schwimmaufbereitungsanlage *f* ABFALL flotation plant

Schwimmbadreaktor *m* KERNTECH underwater reactor

Schwimmbagger *m* BAU dredge, grab dredger, MEERSCHMUTZ dredger, WASSERTRANS *Baggern* dredge, dredger

Schwimmbohranlage *f* ERDÖL *Bohrtechnik* floating rig

Schwimmbrücke *f* WASSERTRANS floating bridge

Schwimmdock *nt* BAU, WASSERTRANS floating dock

Schwimmebene *f* WASSERTRANS *Schiffkonstruktion* waterplane

Schwimmen *nt* WASSERTRANS flotation

schwimmend[1] *adj* ELEKTROTECH, MASCHINEN, MECHAN floating, WASSERTRANS afloat

schwimmend:[2] ~es Gebirge *nt* KOHLEN running ground; ~er Kunststoffbehälter *m* MEERSCHMUTZ dracone; ~e Landungsbrücke *f* WASSERTRANS landing stage; ~er Pfahl *m* BAU friction pile; ~e Rückstände *m pl* ABFALL floating refuse; ~e Umschlagsanlage *f* WASSERTRANS offshore floating terminal

Schwimmer *m* KER & GLAS floater, KFZTECH float, *Vergaser* carburetor float (AmE), carburettor float (BrE), KOHLEN, MASCHINEN, MECHAN, WASSERTRANS, WASSERVERSORG float; **Schwimmerdichtemesser** *m* GERÄT float-type densitometer; **Schwimmerfahrwerk**

nt LUFTTRANS *Hubschrauber* floating gear; **Schwimmerflugzeug** nt LUFTTRANS float seaplane, TRANS floatplane, WASSERTRANS pontoon; **Schwimmerfüllstandsmesser** m GERÄT float-operated level meter; **Schwimmerfüllstandsmeßgerät** nt GERÄT buoyancy probe; **Schwimmergehäuse** nt KFZTECH *Vergaser* carburetor float chamber (AmE), carburettor float chamber (BrE), float chamber

schwimmergeregelt: **~e Alarmpfeife** f HYDRAUL float-controlled alarm whistle

Schwimmer: **Schwimmerhahn** m MASCHINEN ball cock; **Schwimmerkammer** f KFZTECH *Vergaser* carburetor float chamber (AmE), carburettor float chamber (BrE), float chamber; **Schwimmermesser** m ERDÖL rotameter; **Schwimmernadel** f KFZTECH float needle; **Schwimmeröffnung** f KER & GLAS floater notcher; **Schwimmerschalter** m ELEKTROTECH, HEIZ & KÄLTE float switch; **Schwimmerstütze** f KER & GLAS floater lug; **Schwimmerventil** nt HEIZ & KÄLTE float valve, HYDRAUL float trap, MASCHINEN float valve

schwimmfähig adj WASSERTRANS buoyant

Schwimmfähigkeit f WASSERTRANS *Schiff* buoyancy

Schwimmhaut f MEERSCHMUTZ webbing

Schwimmkammer f WASSERTRANS *Schiff* buoyancy tank

Schwimmkompaß m WASSERTRANS liquid compass

Schwimmkragen m RAUMFAHRT *aufblasbar zur Wasserung* flotation collar

Schwimmkran m WASSERTRANS floating crane, pontoon crane

Schwimmring m ERDÖL *Offshore-Technik* flotation collar; **Schwimmringdichtung** f MASCHINEN floating-ring oil seal

Schwimmsattel m KFZTECH floating caliper (AmE), floating calliper (BrE); **Schwimmsattelscheibenbremse** f KFZTECH floating caliper disk brake (AmE), floating calliper disc brake (BrE)

Schwimmschicht f CHEMIE *Wasser* scum

Schwimmschirm m UMWELTSCHMUTZ floating boom

Schwimmstoff m ABFALL floating matter

Schwimmtank m WASSERTRANS flotation tank

Schwimmweste f BAU life belt (BrE), life preserver (AmE), life vest (BrE), LUFTTRANS, SICHERHEIT, WASSERTRANS *Seenot* life jacket (BrE), life preserver (AmE), life vest (BrE)

Schwinden nt BAU, METALL, TELEKOM shrinkage, shrinking

schwinden vi AUFNAHME fade, BAU contract, KER & GLAS shrink

Schwindfuge f BAU contraction joint

Schwindmaß nt FERTIG shrinkage, MASCHINEN shrinkage, shrinkage allowance; **Schwindmaßstab** m FERTIG contraction rule, shrink rule

Schwindriß m BAU shrinkage crack

Schwindschutzzusatz m BAU antishrinkage admixture

Schwindung f HYDRAUL coefficient of contraction, KER & GLAS shrinkage, KUNSTSTOFF mold shrinkage (AmE), mould shrinkage (BrE); **Schwindungshohlraum** m FERTIG shrink hole

Schwingachse f KFZTECH swing axle

Schwingarm m FERTIG pawl arm, KFZTECH suspension arm

Schwingbalken m MASCHINEN walking beam

Schwingbeanspruchung f WERKPRÜF dynamic load

Schwingbereichsänderung f ELEKTRONIK *Magnetron* moding

Schwingdrossel f ELEKTROTECH swinging choke

Schwinge f FERTIG rocker, *Getriebelehre* lever, oscillating link, rocker arm; **Schwingen** nt AKUSTIK oscillation

Schwingen nt ELEKTRIZ hunting, MASCHINEN swinging, PAPIER swing

schwingen[1] vt FERTIG surge

schwingen[2] vi ELEKTRIZ hunt, ELEKTRONIK oscillate, MASCHINEN swing, WELLPHYS oscillate

schwingend[1] adj AUFNAHME rocking, ELEKTRIZ, ELEKTRONIK *Strom*, PAPIER oscillating, TELEKOM oscillatory

schwingend:[2] **~e Abtastung** f FERNSEH oscillatory scanning; **~es Filter** nt ELEKTRONIK free-bar filter; **~es Förderband** nt SICHERHEIT oscillating conveyor; **~er Kondensator** m ELEKTRIZ oscillating capacitor; **~e Kugelmühle** f LABOR *Schleifen* vibrating ball mill; **~e Saite** f PHYS vibrating string; **~er Stromkreis** m ELEKTRIZ oscillating circuit; **~es System** nt ELEKTRONIK oscillatory system

Schwingfestigkeit f FERTIG dynamic strength; **Schwingfestigkeitsprüfung** f WERKPRÜF fatigue test

Schwingförderer m LEBENSMITTEL vibration conveyor, MASCHINEN oscillating conveyor, vibrating conveyor, MECHAN push-bar conveyor

Schwinggröße f ELEKTRONIK oscillating quantity

Schwingkreis m ELEKTRONIK resonant circuit, *des Oszillators* oscillator circuit, TELEKOM resonant circuit

Schwingkristallmethode f STRAHLPHYS oscillating crystal method

Schwingloch nt GERÄT dead spot

Schwingmetallfeder f MASCHINEN rubber-metal spring

Schwingmühle f LABOR *Schleifen* vibrating ball mill

Schwingproben-Magnetometer nt KERNTECH vibrating sample magnetometer

Schwingquarz m ELEKTRIZ quartz crystal, ELEKTRONIK crystal resonator, quartz crystal, quartz crystal oscillator, PHYS quartz crystal oscillator; **Schwingquarzfilter** nt ELEKTRONIK quartz crystal filter

Schwingrahmen m MASCHINEN swing frame

Schwingrakel f PAPIER oscillating doctor

Schwingschalter m ELEKTROTECH rocker switch

Schwingschärfe f REGELUNG vibrational severity

Schwingschleifen nt FERTIG superfinish grinding

Schwingsieb nt KOHLEN swing sieve, vibrating screen

Schwingspeiser: **~ und Schwingförderer** m pl MASCHINEN vibrating feeders and conveyors

Schwingspule f ELEKTROTECH moving coil, oscillator coil; **Schwingspulenlautsprecher** m AUFNAHME moving-coil loudspeaker

Schwingstärke f NICHTFOSS ENERG amplitude of vibration

Schwingtisch m KER & GLAS rocking table

Schwingung f AKUSTIK cycle, oscillation, BAU, ELEKTRIZ, ELEKTRONIK oscillation, FERTIG jar, MASCHINEN oscillation, *eines Pendels* oscillation, MECHAN, METALL vibration, PHYS oscillation, vibration, RADIO, TELEKOM, WELLPHYS oscillation; **Schwingungsachse** f MECHAN, PHYS axis of oscillation; **Schwingungsamplitude** f MASCHINEN oscillation amplitude; **Schwingungsanalyse** f MECHAN vibration analysis; **Schwingungsart** f AKUSTIK mode; **Schwingungsausgleich** m AUFNAHME, ELEKTRONIK frequency compensation; **Schwingungsbauch** m AKUSTIK antinode, antinode of oscillation, antinode of vibration, loop, ELEKTRIZ, ELEKTROTECH antinode, FERTIG antinode, crest, vibration antinode; **Schwingungsbauch einer stehenden Welle** *m* WELLPHYS antinode of a stationary wave; **Schwingungsbreite** *f* AKUSTIK total oscillation amplitude; **Schwingungsbruch** *m* WERK-PRÜF fatigue fracture; **Schwingungsdämpfer** *m* HEIZ & KÄLTE vibration damper, KFZTECH damper, resonance damper, *Motor* vibration damper, MASCHINEN vibration damper; **Schwingungsdauer** *f* ELEKTRONIK oscillation period, MASCHINEN period of oscillation; **Schwingungsenergie** *f* KERNTECH vibrational energy; **Schwingungsentropie** *f* METALL vibrational entropy; **Schwingungserzeuger** *m* ELEKTRIZ, ELEKTRONIK oscillator, MASCHINEN vibrator, PHYS, RADIO, RAUMFAHRT *Weltraumfunk*, TELEKOM, WELLPHYS oscillator

schwingungsfähig: ~**es System** *nt* WELLPHYS vibrating system

Schwingung: **Schwingungsfestigkeit** *f* MASCHINEN fatigue strength; **Schwingungsform** *f* ELEKTRONIK *Wellenform* oscillation mode

schwingungsfrei: ~**e Befestigung** *f* HEIZ & KÄLTE antivibration mounting; ~**er Tisch** *m* LABOR antivibration table

Schwingung: **Schwingungsfrequenz** *f* ELEKTRONIK, TELEKOM oscillation frequency; **Schwingungsgeschwindigkeit** *f* HEIZ & KÄLTE velocity of vibration; **Schwingungsgesetze** *nt pl* WELLPHYS *einer eingespannten Saite* laws of vibration; **Schwingungsknoten** *m* ELEKTRONIK node of oscillation; **Schwingungslinie** *f* AKUSTIK antinodal line; **Schwingungsmeßeinrichtung** *f* GERÄT *mechanisch* vibration-measuring equipment; **Schwingungsmeßgerät** *nt* PHYS vibrometer; **Schwingungsmessung** *f* HEIZ & KÄLTE vibration measurement; **Schwingungsmittelpunkt** *m* MECHAN, PHYS center of oscillation (AmE), centre of oscillation (BrE); **Schwingungsperiode** *f* ELEKTRIZ period of oscillation, ELEKTROTECH cycle; **Schwingungsquantenzahl** *f* PHYS vibrational quantum number; **Schwingungs-Rotations-Spektrum** *nt* PHYS vibration rotation spectrum; **Schwingungsrührwerk** *nt* LABOR vibrating stirrer; **Schwingungsspektrum** *nt* PHYS vibrational spectrum; **Schwingungstest** *m* METROL vibration test; **Schwingungsverlauf** *m* COMP & DV waveform; **Schwingungsversuch** *m* WERKPRÜF vibration test; **Schwingungsweite** *f* MASCHINEN oscillation amplitude, NICHTFOSS ENERG amplitude of vibration; **Schwingungszahl** *f* AKUSTIK, AUFNAHME, COMP & DV, ELEKTRONIK, PHYS, RADIO frequency

Schwingverschluß *m* KER & GLAS swing stopper finish (BrE)

Schwingwelle *f* MASCHINEN rock shaft

Schwingzapfen *m* FERTIG *Kunststoffinstallationen* solenoid

Schwitzen *nt* HEIZ & KÄLTE sweating

schwitzen[1] *vt* LEBENSMITTEL *Gießerei* sweat

schwitzen[2] *vi* LEBENSMITTEL *Ofen* sweat

Schwitzkühlung *f* HEIZ & KÄLTE transpiration cooling

Schwitzung *f* HYDRAUL transpiration

Schwitzwasser *nt* HEIZ & KÄLTE condensate, WASSERTRANS sweat

schwojen *vi* WASSERTRANS *Schiff* swing

Schwund *m* AKUSTIK, RADIO, TELEKOM fade, fading; ~ **durch Mehrwegeausbreitung** *m* TELEKOM multipath fading; **Schwundausgleich** *m* ELEKTROTECH automatic volume control; **Schwundreserve** *f* TELEKOM link margins

Schwungkraftanlasser *m* MECHAN inertial starter

Schwungkugel *f* MASCHINEN ball; **Schwungkugelregler** *m* MASCHINEN ball governor

Schwungmasse *f* FERTIG gyrating mass, HEIZ & KÄLTE flywheel, KERNTECH centrifugal mass, gyrating mass

Schwungrad *nt* HEIZ & KÄLTE, KFZTECH *Motor*, MASCHINEN, MECHAN flywheel, RAUMFAHRT momentum wheel; ~ **zur Magnetpeilung** *nt* RAUMFAHRT magnetic-bearing momentum wheel; **Schwungradeffekt** *m* RADIO flywheel effect; **Schwungradgehäuse** *nt* KFZTECH *Motor* flywheel housing; **Schwungradzahnkranz** *m* KFZTECH *Motor* flywheel starter ring gear

Schwungring *m* HEIZ & KÄLTE flywheel

Schwungscheibe *f* HEIZ & KÄLTE flywheel, MASCHINEN inertia reel

SCN *abbr (Hinweis auf Spezifikationsänderungen)* TRANS SCN *(specification change notice)*

Scoop *nt* LABOR scanning electron microscope

Scopolamin *nt* CHEMIE hyoscine

Scorch *nt* KUNSTSTOFF scorch; **Scorchneigung** *f* KUNSTSTOFF scorching tendency

Scott-Schaltung *f* ELEKTRIZ Scott connection

SCPC[1] *abbr (Ein-Kanal-Träger)* RAUMFAHRT *Weltraumfunk*, TELEKOM SCPC *(single channel per carrier)*

SCPC:[2] **SCPC-System mit bedarfsorientierter Zuteilung** *nt* TELEKOM demand-assigned single-channel-per-carrier system

SCR[1] *abbr (siliziumgesteuerter Gleichrichter)* ELEKTRONIK, ELEKTROTECH SCR *(silicon-controlled rectifier)*

SCR:[2] **SCR-Abstimmtransformator** *m* ELEKTROTECH SCR trimmer transformer

Scram *m* KERNTECH scram

Scrambler *m* RAUMFAHRT *Verschlüsselungsgerät*, TELEKOM scrambler

Scraper *m* MEERSCHMUTZ scraper

Screening *nt* MEERSCHMUTZ screening

SCR: ~ **geregeltes Netzgerät** *nt* ELEKTROTECH *durch Thyristor geregelt* SCR-regulated power supply

Script *nt* COMP & DV script; **Scriptwriter** *m* FERNSEH scriptwriter

SCR: SCR-Konverter *m* ELEKTROTECH SCR converter; **SCR-Regelung** *f* ELEKTROTECH SCR regulation; **SCR-Regler** *m* ELEKTROTECH SCR regulator; **SCR-Verstärker** *m* ELEKTRONIK SCR amplifier; **SCR-Vorregelung** *f* ELEKTROTECH SCR preregulation; **SCR-Vorregler** *m* ELEKTROTECH SCR preregulator; **SCR-Wandler** *m* ELEKTROTECH SCR converter

SDLC *abbr (synchrone Datenübertragungssteuerung)* COMP & DV SDLC *(synchronous data link control)*

S-Draht *m* TEXTIL S-twist

S-Drehung *f* TEXTIL S-twist

Se *(Selen, Selenium)* CHEMIE Se *(selenium)*

Seabeeträgerschiff *nt* WASSERTRANS seabee carrier

SEALOSAFE-Verfahren *nt (Verfestigungsverfahren für Sonderabfälle)* ABFALL SEALOSAFE process

Sebacin- *pref* CHEMIE sebacic

sec *abbr* GEOM *(Sekans)*, GEOM *(Sekante) von Linie* sec *(secant)*

SECAM-Farbsystem *nt* FERNSEH SECAM system

Sechs *f* MATH six

Sechseck *nt* GEOM hexagon

sechseckig *adj* GEOM, KERNTECH hexagonal

Sechseck: **Sechseck-Maschengitter** *nt* KER & GLAS *in Drahtglas* hexagonal mesh

Sechs: **Sechsfachrevolverkopf** *m* MASCHINEN six-tool

capstan
sechsflächig *adj* GEOM, KERNTECH hexahedral
Sechs: **Sechsflächner** *m* GEOM hexahedron
Sechskant[1] *m* MASCHINEN hexagon, MATH hex, hexagon
Sechskant[2]: **Sechskant fräsen** *vi* FERTIG hex
Sechskant: **Sechskantkopf** *m* FERTIG hexagon head,
MASCHINEN hex head, hexagon head, hexagonal
head; **Sechskantmutter** *f* MASCHINEN hex nut, hexa-
gon nut, hexagonal nut, MECHAN hex nut;
Sechskantmutterkopf *m* MECHAN hexagon head;
Sechskantschlüssel *m* MASCHINEN spanner for hexa-
gon nuts (BrE), wrench for hexagon nuts;
Sechskantschneidmutter *f* MASCHINEN hexagonal die
nut; **Sechskantschraube** *f* MASCHINEN hex bolt, hexa-
gon bolt, hexagonal head bolt, MECHAN hexagon
head screw; **Sechskantschraubenschlüssel** *m* ME-
CHAN hex head wrench
Sechs: **Sechsphasengleichrichter** *m* ELEKTROTECH six-
phase rectifier; **Sechsphasenspannung** *f* ELEKTRIZ
hexagon voltage; **Sechsphasenstrom** *m* ELEKTRO-
TECH six-phase current; **Sechsspindelhalbautomat** *m*
FERTIG six-spindle automatic screw machine
sechste *adj* MATH sixth
Sechs: **Sechstel** *nt* MATH sixth; **Sechstonleiter** *f* AKU-
STIK hexatonic scale
sechswertig *adj* CHEMIE hexavalent
sechszählig *adj* CHEMIE hexad
Sechs: **Sechszylinder-V-Motor** *m* KFZTECH V-six engine
Sedezformat *nt* DRUCK sixteenmo
Sediment *nt* ERDÖL *Geologie*, KOHLEN, WASSERVERSORG
sediment; **Sedimentablagerung** *f* UMWELTSCHMUTZ
sedimentation, *Geologie* deposition, WASSERVERSORG
sediment discharge
Sedimentation *f* ERDÖL *Geologie*, KUNSTSTOFF, PHYS,
WASSERVERSORG sedimentation; **Sedimentations-
analyse** *f* KOHLEN sedimentation analysis;
Sedimentationsbecken *nt* ERDÖL *Geologie* sedimen-
tary basin, WASSERVERSORG sedimentation tank;
Sedimentationsbehälter *m* CHEMTECH settling tank;
Sedimentationsdauer *f* CHEMTECH settling time; **Sedi-
mentationsgeschwindigkeit** *f* ERDÖL *Geologie*
sedimentation rate; **Sedimentationspotential** *nt*
CHEMTECH sedimentation potential
Sediment: **Sedimentbecken** *nt* ERDÖL sedimentary ba-
sin; **Sedimentboden** *m* KOHLEN sedimentary soil;
Sedimentgestein *nt* ERDÖL *Geologie*, KOHLEN sedi-
mentary rock
sedimentieren[1] *vt* CHEMTECH settle
sedimentieren[2] *vi* CHEMTECH settle
Sedimentiergefäß *nt* CHEMTECH settling cone; **~ nach
Imhoff** *nt* LABOR Imhoff sedimentation cone
Sedimentzuwachs *m* WASSERVERSORG aggradation
See:[1] **~ auf ~** *adj* WASSERTRANS under way; **in ~** *adj* WASSER-
TRANS under way; **zur ~ fahrend** *adj* WASSERTRANS
seafaring; **von der ~ getragen** *adj* WASSERTRANS sea-
borne
See[2] *f* WASSERTRANS *Salzwasser* sea, *Süßwasser* lake;
See- *pref* WASSERTRANS marine, naval
See:[3] **zur ~ fahren** *vi* WASSERTRANS navigate; **zur ~ gehen**
vi WASSERTRANS go to sea; **eine ~ übernehmen** *vi*
WASSERTRANS ship a sea
See: **Seeanker** *m* WASSERTRANS *Schleppsack* drogue,
Schleppwiderstand sea anchor; **Seeaufklärungsradar**
nt WASSERTRANS *Marine* surface search radar
Seebeck: **Seebeck-Effekt** *m* ELEKTRIZ, ELEKTROTECH
thermoelektrische Wirkung, PHYS Seebeck effect; **See-**

beck-Koeffizient *m* PHYS Seebeck coefficient
See: **Seebedingungen** *f pl* WASSERTRANS sea conditions
seebeschädigt *adj* WASSERTRANS sea-damaged
See: **Seebrief** *m* WASSERTRANS ship's passport; **Seebrise**
f WASSERTRANS *Wind* sea breeze; **Seecontainer** *m*
WASSERTRANS overseas container; **Seedeich** *m* WAS-
SERTRANS sea wall, WASSERVERSORG sea dike; **Seedrift**
f WASSERTRANS flotsam; **See-Eigenschaften** *f pl* WAS-
SERTRANS seakeeping qualities; **See-Eis** *nt*
WASSERTRANS sea ice; **See-Erprobung** *f* WASSERTRANS
Schiffbau sea trials; **Seefähigkeitszeugnis** *nt* WASSER-
TRANS *Dokumente* certificate of seaworthiness;
Seefahrer *m* WASSERTRANS seafarer; **Seefracht** *f* WAS-
SERTRANS *Ladung* shipment; **Seefunkfeuer** *nt*
WASSERTRANS *Seezeichen* maritime radio beacon;
Seefunkvermittlungsstelle *f* TELEKOM MSC, maritime
switching center (AmE), maritime switching centre
(BrE)
Seegang *m* WASSERTRANS sea state; **Seegangsecho** *nt*
TELEKOM sea clutter; **Seegangsreflexe** *m pl* WASSER-
TRANS *Radar* sea clutter; **Seegangstrübung** *f*
WASSERTRANS *Radar* sea clutter
See: **Seegebiet** *nt* WASSERTRANS sea area
Seegerring *m* KFZTECH circlip; **Seegersicherung** *f* FER-
TIG circlip; **Seegersicherungsring** *m* MASCHINEN
circlip ring
See: **Seehafen** *m* WASSERTRANS seaport, trading port,
Hafen deep-water harbor (AmE), deep-water har-
bour (BrE); **Seehandbuch** *nt* WASSERTRANS sailing
directions; **Seehandel** *m* WASSERTRANS sea trade, se-
aborne trade, *Seehandel* shipping trade; **Seehöhe** *f*
WASSERTRANS sea level; **Seehorizont** *m* WASSERTRANS
sea line; **Seekabel** *nt* TELEKOM ocean cable, submarine
cable; **Seekabelverstärker** *m* TELEKOM submerged repeater; **Seekarte** *f* TRANS sea chart, WASSERTRANS
Navigation hydrographic chart; **Seeküste** *f* WASSER-
TRANS seaboard
Seele *f* ELEKTRIZ, ELEKTROTECH *eines Drahtseils oder
elektrischen Kabels*, FERTIG *Kabel* core, OPTIK *Licht-
leiter* central load-bearing element, TELEKOM *Kabel*,
WASSERTRANS *Tauwerk* core
See: **Seeleichter** *m* WASSERTRANS seagoing barge; **See-
lotse** *m* WASSERTRANS sea pilot; **Seemannsamt** *nt*
WASSERTRANS *Behörde* shipping office; **Seemann-
schaft** *f* WASSERTRANS seamanship; **Seemaschinist** *m*
WASSERTRANS marine engineer
seemäßig *adj* WASSERTRANS seaworthy; **~ verpackt** *adj*
VERPACK seaworthy packaging
See: **Seemeile** *f* METROL mile, WASSERTRANS nautical
mile
Seenot *f* WASSERTRANS *Notfall* distress at sea; **Seenot-
alarm** *m* TELEKOM distress alerting, WASSERTRANS
Notfall distress alert; **Seenotfunkbake** *f* WASSERTRANS
automatische Satellitenortung distress beacon; **See-
notrettungsboot** *nt* WASSERTRANS rescue boat;
Seenotrettungsleitstelle *f* LUFTTRANS, WASSERTRANS
RCC, rescue coordination center (AmE), rescue co-
ordination centre (BrE); **Seenotruf** *m* WASSERTRANS
Notfall distress signal; **Seenotsender mit kleiner Lei-
stung** *m* TELEKOM low-power distress transmitter;
Seenotzeichen *nt* WASSERTRANS *Notfall* distress signal
See: **Seeradar** *nt* WASSERTRANS *Radar* marine radar;
Seeradarfrequenz *f* WASSERTRANS *Radar* marine
radar frequency; **Seeräuberei** *f* WASSERTRANS piracy;
Seeraum *m* WASSERTRANS offing; **Seerecht** *nt* WASSER-
TRANS maritime law; **Seereise** *f* WASSERTRANS sea

voyage; **Seereling** *f* WASSERTRANS *Deckausrüstung* guardrail; **Seerisiko** *nt* WASSERTRANS *Versicherung* marine risk; **Seeroute** *f* WASSERTRANS sea route; **Seeschaden** *m* WASSERTRANS *Schiff* damage by sea, *Versicherung* sea damage; **Seeschiff** *nt* MEERSCHMUTZ seagoing vessel, WASSERTRANS sea vessel; **Seeschifffahrt** *f* WASSERTRANS ocean navigation, sea transport; **Seeschleuse** *f* WASSERTRANS sea lock

Seeseite: auf ~ *adj* WASSERTRANS seaward

See: **Seespediteur** *m* WASSERTRANS sea carrier; **Seestraße** *f* WASSERTRANS sea lane; **Seestreitkräfte** *f pl* WASSERTRANS naval forces; **Seetransport** *m* WASSERTRANS sea carriage, sea transport; **Seetransportrisiko** *nt* WASSERTRANS *Versicherung* maritime peril

seetüchtig[1] *adj* WASSERTRANS seagoing, seaworthy, *Schiff* navigable; **nicht ~** *adj* WASSERTRANS *Schiff* unseaworthy; **in seetüchtigem Zustand** *adj* WASSERTRANS *Schiff* in navigable condition

seetüchtig:[2] **~es Luftkissenfahrzeug** *nt* WASSERTRANS seagoing hovercraft

See: **Seetüchtigkeit** *f* MEERSCHMUTZ, WASSERTRANS seaworthiness

seeuntüchtig *adj* WASSERTRANS *Schiff* unseaworthy

See: **Seeventil** *nt* WASSERTRANS *Schiff* Kingston valve; **Seeverbindung** *f* WASSERTRANS maritime communication; **Seeverhältnisse** *nt pl* WASSERTRANS sea conditions; **Seeverkehr** *m* WASSERTRANS sea trade; **Seeverklappung** *f* ABFALL ocean dumping; **Seeverladung** *f* VERPACK carriage by sea; **Seevermessungsschiff** *nt* WASSERTRANS *Meereskunde* geodesic survey ship, hydrographic survey vessel; **Seeversand** *m* WASSERTRANS *Ladung* shipment; **Seeversicherung** *f* WASSERTRANS *Versicherung* marine insurance; **Seeversicherungsgeschäft** *nt* WASSERTRANS *Versicherung* underwriting; **Seewarte** *f* WASSERTRANS hydrographic office

seewärtig[1] *adj* WASSERTRANS seaward

seewärtig:[2] **~e Verbindung** *f* WASSERTRANS maritime communication

seewärts *adv* WASSERTRANS seawards

Seewasser *nt* UMWELTSCHMUTZ lake water, WASSERTRANS seawater; **Seewasser-in-Rohöl-Emulsion** *f* UMWELTSCHMUTZ seawater-in-crude-oil emulsion; **Seewassertemperatur** *f* WASSERTRANS sea temperature; **Seewassertemperatur an der Oberfläche** *f* WASSERTRANS sea surface temperature; **Seewasserwichte** *f* WASSERTRANS *Schiffkonstruktion* specific gravity of seawater

See: **Seeweg** *m* WASSERTRANS sea lane, sea route

Seeweg:[1] **auf dem ~ befördert** *adj* WASSERTRANS seaborne

Seeweg:[2] **auf dem ~** *adv* WASSERTRANS *Seehandel* by sea

See: **Seewind** *m* WASSERTRANS onshore wind; **Seewurf** *m* WASSERTRANS jetsam; **Seezeichen** *nt* WASSERTRANS mark, seamark; **Seezeichentender** *m* WASSERTRANS *Seezeichen* buoy tender; **Seezustand** *m* WASSERTRANS sea state

Segel[1] *nt* WASSERTRANS sail

Segel:[2] **die ~ setzen** *vi* WASSERTRANS set sail

Segel: **Segelboden** *m* WASSERTRANS sail loft; **Segelboot** *nt* WASSERTRANS sailboat (AmE), sailing boat (BrE); **Segelfläche** *f* WASSERTRANS sail area; **Segelflugzeug** *nt* LUFTTRANS glider; **Segeljolle** *f* WASSERTRANS sailing dinghy; **Segelkammer** *f* WASSERTRANS sail locker; **Segellatte** *f* WASSERTRANS batten; **Segelleinwand** *f* TEXTIL canvas; **Segelmacher** *m* WASSERTRANS sail-

maker; **Segelmacherwerkstatt** *f* WASSERTRANS *Segeln* sail loft

Segeln *nt* WASSERTRANS sailing

segeln *vi* WASSERTRANS sail

Segel: **Segelriß** *m* WASSERTRANS sail plan; **Segelschiff** *nt* WASSERTRANS sailing ship; **Segelsport** *m* WASSERTRANS sailing

Segelstellung:[1] **~ der Luftschraube** *f* LUFTTRANS feathered propeller; **~ der Luftschraubenblätter** *f* LUFTTRANS *Luftschraube* feathered pitch

Segelstellung:[2] **auf ~ bringen** *vt* LUFTTRANS *Luftschraube* feather

Segelstellung: **Segelstellungswinkel** *m* LUFTTRANS feathering angle; **Segelstellungswirkung** *f* LUFTTRANS feathering effect

Segel: **Segeltuch** *nt* BAU, TEXTIL canvas, WASSERTRANS sailcloth, *Segeln* canvas; **Segeltuchplane** *f* BAU tarpaulin

Segerkegel *m* FERTIG Seger cone, fusion cone, pyrometric cone, KER & GLAS Seger cone

Segler *m* WASSERTRANS *Schiff* sailing ship

Segment *nt* COMP & DV, GEOM, KERNTECH segment, MASCHINEN quadrant, segment; **Segmentbogen** *m* BAU segmental arch

segmentieren *vt* COMP & DV segment

segmentiert: ~e Abtastung *f* FERNSEH segmented scanning; **~e Aufzeichnung** *f* FERNSEH segmented recording; **~es Multiprozessorsystem** *nt* TELEKOM segmented multiprocessor system

Segmentierung *f* COMP & DV, KÜNSTL INT *von Bildern* segmentation

Segment: **Segmentkreissäge** *f* MASCHINEN segmental circular saw; **Segmentpfahl** *m* KOHLEN segmented pile; **Segmentrad** *nt* MASCHINEN segment gear; **Segmentsäge** *f* MASCHINEN segmented saw; **Segmentwehr** *nt* NICHTFOSS ENERG radial gate; **Segmentwelle** *f* KFZTECH sector shaft

Segner: ~sches Wasserrad *nt* WASSERVERSORG reaction water wheel

Sehachse *f* FOTO optical axis

Sehfeld *nt* ERGON visual field; **Sehfeldblende** *f* METALL field diaphragm, PHYS field stop

Sehne *f* GEOM, NICHTFOSS ENERG chord; **Sehnenlänge** *f* NICHTFOSS ENERG chord length; **Sehnenwicklung** *f* ELEKTROTECH fractional pitch winding

Sehrohr *nt* WASSERTRANS *U-Boot* periscope

Sehschärfe *f* ERGON vision acuity, visual acuity

Sehwinkel *m* TELEKOM angle of sight

Seiche *f* NICHTFOSS ENERG seiche

seicht *adj* WASSERTRANS *Wasser* shallow

Seide *f* KER & GLAS, TEXTIL silk; **Seidengewebe mit Ripseffekt** *nt* TEXTIL poult; **Seidengriff** *m* TEXTIL silk-like handle; **Seidenmattätzen** *nt* KER & GLAS satin etch; **Seidenpapier** *nt* VERPACK tissue paper; **Seidenraster** *nt* KER & GLAS silk screen; **Seidenspinnerei** *f* TEXTIL silk spinning; **Seidenstoff** *m* TEXTIL silk

Seife *f* CHEMIE soap; **Seifenerde** *f* CHEMIE smectite; **Seifenlauge** *f* CHEMIE suds; **Seifenlösung** *f* FERTIG *Kunststoffinstallationen* soap solution; **Seifenschaum** *m* CHEMIE suds; **Seifenton** *m* CHEMIE smectite; **Seifenwasser** *nt* SICHERHEIT soap and water solution

seigern *vt* FERTIG eliquate, sweat

Seigerung *f* FERTIG eliquation, liquation; **Seigerungsstreifen** *m* FERTIG ghost, ghost line

Seignettesalz *nt* ELEKTROTECH *piezoelektrisches Material*, LEBENSMITTEL Rochelle salt

Seil nt MASCHINEN, MECHAN, PAPIER, TEXTIL rope; **Seil-bahn** f TRANS cable railroad (AmE), cable railway (BrE), cableway; **Seilbahnwagen** m TRANS carrier; **Seilbremse** f MASCHINEN rope brake; **Seilfähre** f WASSERTRANS cable ferry; **Seilförderanlage** f TRANS cableway; **Seilförderung** f KOHLEN rope hauling; **Seilgarn** nt TEXTIL rope yarn; **Seilkinke** f MASCHINEN rope kink; **Seilkloben** m MASCHINEN rope block; **Seilöse** f WASSERTRANS Tauwerk becket; **Seilrettungsgerät** nt LUFTTRANS escape rope; **Seilrolle** f MASCHINEN rope pulley, rope wheel; **Seilrollenblock** m ERDÖL traveling block (AmE), travelling block (BrE); **Seilscheibe** f MASCHINEN pulley, sheave; **Seilschelle** f MASCHINEN rope clamp; **Seilschlagbohren** nt KOHLEN cable drilling, percussive rope boring; **Seilschlaufe** f SICHER-HEIT rope-type sling; **Seilschloß** nt MASCHINEN hook and eye; **Seilschrapper** m PAPIER drag scraper; **Seilschwebebahn** f EISENBAHN gondola cableway; **Seilträger** m PAPIER rope carrier; **Seiltrieb** m MASCHI-NEN rope drive; **Seiltrommel** f FERTIG rope barrel, MASCHINEN drum, rope drum, winding drum, VER-PACK cable reel; **Seilverspannung** f BAU guying; **Seilwinde** f ELEKTROTECH cable winch, MASCHINEN cable winch, rope winch, TRANS cable winch

Seismik f ERDÖL Meßtechnik seismic

seismisch[1] adj BAU seismic

seismisch:[2] **~er Aufschluß** m BAU seismic survey; **~e Erkundung** f ERDÖL, KOHLEN seismic exploration; **~e Exploration** f ERDÖL Lagerstättensuche seismic exploration

Seismograph m BAU, PHYS seismograph

Seismologie f PHYS seismology

Seite[1] f BAU side, COMP & DV, DRUCK, page, GEOM, MA-SCHINEN side; **~ im Querformat** f DRUCK oblong page

Seite:[2] **von der ~ beleuchten** vt FOTO sidelight

Seiten f pl (Sn) DRUCK pages (pp); **~ pro Minute** f pl COMP & DV pages per minute

Seite: **Seitenablagerung** f BAU von Bodenmaterial spoil area; **Seitenabrufmethode** f COMP & DV demand paging; **Seitenabstand** m MASCHINEN side clearance, TRANS lateral clearance; **Seitenabweichung** f LUFT-TRANS longitudinal divergence; **Seitenamt** nt TELEKOM dependent exchange; **Seitenanbau** m KER & GLAS side pocket; **Seitenaufbau** m ELEKTRONIK lateral structure; **Seitenaufprall** m TRANS side-on collision

Seitenband nt AUFNAHME, COMP & DV, ELEKTRONIK, FERNSEH, PHYS, RADIO, TELEKOM sideband; **Seitenbanddämpfung** f ELEKTRONIK sideband attenuation; **Seitenbandfrequenz** f (SF) ELEKTRONIK, FERNSEH, RADIO, TELEKOM sideband frequency (SF); **Seitenbandinterferenz** f ELEKTRONIK sideband interference; **Seitenbandlegierung** f METALL sideband alloy; **Seitenbandunterdrückung** f ELEKTRONIK sideband suppression

Seite: **Seitenbeplattung** f WASSERTRANS Schiffbau side plating; **Seitenblech** nt BAU side plate; **Seitendrehmeißel** m MASCHINEN knife tool; **Seitendriftlandung** f LUFTTRANS lateral drift landing; **Seitendrucker** m COMP & DV page printer; **Seiteneinfall** m WASSERTRANS Schiffbau tumblehome; **Seiteneinheit** f MASCHINEN wing base; **Seitenende** nt COMP & DV end of page; **Seitenfestigkeitsverband** m WASSERTRANS Schiffbau side construction; **Seitenfläche** f BAU cheek, flank, side, GEOM face, lateral face, MASCHINEN lateral face; **Seitenflosse** f LUFTTRANS keel, in den Rumpf überge-hend fuselage dorsal fin; **Seitenflossenansatzrahmen**

m LUFTTRANS fin stub frame; **Seitenfrequenz** f ELEK-TRONIK, FERNSEH, RADIO side frequency

seitengesteuert: **~er Motor** m KFZTECH L-head engine, KFZTECH (sv-Motor) side valve engine (sv engine)

Seite: **Seitenhöhe** f WASSERTRANS Schiffbau depth; **Seitenholm** m RAUMFAHRT fin post; **Seiteninversion** f FERNSEH lateral inversion; **Seitenkante** f FERTIG late-ral edge; **Seitenkeilwinkel** m MASCHINEN wedge angle; **Seitenkipper** m EISENBAHN side-dump car; **Seiten-klappen** f pl VERPACK folding sides, eines Kartons side panel; **Seitenkraft** f MASCHINEN lateral force; **Seiten-kraftkoeffizient** m LUFTTRANS lateral force coefficient; **Seitenlänge** f DRUCK length of page; **Seitenleitwerks-flosse** f LUFTTRANS keel, tail fin; **Seitenleuchte** f KFZTECH side light; **Seitenmeißel** m MASCHINEN side tool; **Seitenneigung** f LUFTTRANS Flugwesen bank; **Seitennumerierung** f DRUCK pagination; **Seitenpei-lung** f WASSERTRANS Navigation relative bearing; **Seitenplatte** f FERTIG end plate; **Seitenpufferschrau-benkupplung** f KFZTECH side buffer screw coupling; **Seitenrad** nt KFZTECH side gear; **Seitenrahmen** m COMP & DV page frame, VERPACK eines Containers side frame; **Seitenriß** m MASCHINEN side elevation, WASSER-TRANS Schiffkonstruktion sheer drawing, sheer plan

Seitenruder nt LUFTTRANS control surface, PHYS rudder; **Seitenruderausschlag** m LUFTTRANS control surface angle, rudder travel; **Seitenruderbewegung** f LUFT-TRANS rudder travel; **Seitenruderblockierung** f LUFTTRANS control surface locking; **Seitenruderfuß-hebel** m LUFTTRANS rudder bar; **Seitenruderhebel** m LUFTTRANS rudder bar; **Seitenruderholm** m LUFT-TRANS rudder post; **Seitenruderpedal** nt LUFTTRANS rudder pedal; **Seitenruderservoantrieb** m LUFTTRANS rudder power unit; **Seitenrudersteuerung** f LUFT-TRANS rudder control; **Seitenrudertrimmklappe** f LUFTTRANS rudder trim; **Seitenrudertrimmlicht** nt LUFTTRANS rudder trim light; **Seitenruderverriege-lung** f LUFTTRANS control surface locking

Seite: **Seitenrutsch** m PHYS side slip; **Seitenschneider** m MASCHINEN diagonal-cutting nippers, side-cutting nippers, side-cutting pliers, RAUMFAHRT Raumschiff cable cutter; **Seitenschrift** f AKUSTIK, AUFNAHME lateral recording; **Seitenschub** m NICHTFOSS ENERG side thrust; **Seitenschwert** nt WASSERTRANS leeboard; **Seitensichtradar** nt (SLAR) MEERSCHMUTZ side-ways-looking airborne radar (SLAR); **Seitenspiel** nt MASCHINEN side clearance, side play; **Seitenstabilität** f TRANS vertical stability; **Seitenstahl** m MASCHINEN cranked tool; **Seitenstrahlpropeller** m WASSERTRANS Schiffantrieb side thruster; **Seitenstraße** f BAU byroad, byway; **Seitentabelle** f COMP & DV page table; **Seiten-träger** m WASSERTRANS Schiffbau side girder; **Seitentransistor** m ELEKTRONIK lateral transistor; **Sei-tenumbruch** m COMP & DV page break, pagination, DRUCK make-up

Seitenumbruch: **~ erstellen** vi COMP & DV page

Seite: **Seitenverbandkonstruktion** f WASSERTRANS Schiffbau side construction; **Seitenvergrößerung** f PHYS lateral magnification; **Seitenverhältnis** nt ME-CHAN aspect ratio; **Seitenverkleidung** f KFZTECH Karosserie side panel; **Seitenverriegelung** f FERNSEH side lock; **Seitenversatz** m MASCHINEN lateral offset; **Seitenwand mit Lüftungsklappen** f KFZTECH sidewall with ventilation flaps; **Seitenwandluftkissenfahrzeug** nt LUFTTRANS sidewall hovercraft, TRANS sidewall-type hovercraft; **Seitenwechsel** m COMP & DV paging;

Seitenwechsel auf Anforderung *m* COMP & DV demand paging; **Seitenwind** *m* LUFTTRANS crosswind; **Seitenwinde** *f* BAU side pulley; **Seitenwindkomponente** *f* LUFTTRANS longitudinal wind component; **Seitenwinkel** *m* NICHTFOSS ENERG azimuth angle; **Seitenzahl** *f* DRUCK folio, page number; **Seitenzipfel** *m* WASSERTRANS *Radar* side lobe

Seitigkeit *f* ERGON left-right preference

seitlich:[1] ~ **versetzt** *adj* BAU off-center (AmE), off-centre (BrE)

seitlich:[2] ~**er Abstand** *m* MASCHINEN side clearance; ~ **angebrachte Anschlußklemme** *f* KFZTECH side-mounted terminal; ~ **angebrachter Pol** *m* KFZTECH side-mounted terminal; ~ **angepreßter Verschluß** *m* VERPACK crimp-on closure; ~**e Auslenkkraft** *f* AKUSTIK side thrust; ~**e Begrenzungsleuchte** *f* KFZTECH side marker light; ~**e Diffusion** *f* ELEKTRONIK lateral diffusion; ~**er Geräuschmeßpunkt** *m* LUFTTRANS lateral noise measurement point; ~**e Heftung** *f* DRUCK side stitching, stab stitching, VERPACK *mit Klammern* lateral stapling; ~**e Hitzeübertragung** *f* ANSTRICH lateral heat transfer; ~**es Nachgeben** *nt* KERNTECH lateral yielding; ~**es Spiel** *nt* MASCHINEN side play; ~**e Vertiefung** *f* OPTIK sidepit; ~ **zugeschnalltes Zusatzschubtriebwerk** *nt* RAUMFAHRT strap-on booster; ~**er Zusammenstoß** *m* TRANS side collision, sideswipe

Seitlichheftung *f* DRUCK side stitching, stab stitching

Sekans *m (sec)* GEOM secant *(sec)*

Sekante *f (sec)* GEOM secant *von Linie* secant *(sec)*

Sektion *f* TEXTIL, WASSERTRANS section; **Sektionsschären** *nt* TEXTIL section warping, sectional warping

Sektor *m* COMP & DV, ERDÖL *Geographie,* GEOM sector; **Sektordiagramm** *nt* MATH pie chart; **Sektorenfeuer** *nt* WASSERTRANS light with sectors; **Sektorschütz** *nt* NICHTFOSS ENERG sector gate; **Sektorwehr** *nt* WASSERVERSORG sector weir

Sekundär- *pref* STRAHLPHYS secondary

sekundär[1] *adj* RADIO, STRAHLPHYS secondary

sekundär:[2] ~**e Faser** *f* VERPACK secondary fiber (AmE), secondary fibre (BrE); ~**e Kernreaktion** *f* KERNTECH secondary nuclear reaction; ~**es Kriechen** *nt* METALL secondary creep; ~**es Maximum** *nt* OPTIK, PHYS secondary maxima; ~**e Rekristallisation** *f* METALL secondary recrystallization; ~**es Schnellabschaltsystem** *nt* KERNTECH secondary shutdown system; ~**e Wicklung** *f* ELEKTRIZ secondary winding

Sekundär-: **Sekundärabgriff** *m* ELEKTROTECH secondary tap; **Sekundärabzweigung** *f* ELEKTROTECH secondary tap; **Sekundäracetat** *nt* TEXTIL secondary acetate; **Sekundärakkumulator** *m* TRANS secondary storage battery; **Sekundärbatterie** *f* ELEKTRIZ storage battery, ELEKTROTECH secondary battery, storage battery; **Sekundärbeschichtung** *f* TELEKOM fiber jacket (AmE), fibre jacket (BrE), secondary coating; **Sekundärbremssystem** *nt* KFZTECH secondary brake system; **Sekundärbrennstoff** *m* ERDÖL derived fuel; **Sekundärbrennstoffelement** *nt* KFZTECH secondary fuel cell; **Sekundärbuchse** *f* KFZTECH secondary sleeve; **Sekundärdüse** *f* LUFTTRANS secondary nozzle

Sekundärelektron *nt* ELEKTRONIK, STRAHLPHYS secondary electron; **Sekundärelektronenvervielfacher** *m* STRAHLPHYS electron multiplier

Sekundär-: **Sekundärelement** *nt* ELEKTROTECH secondary cell

Sekundäremission *f* ELEKTRONIK, PHYS secondary emission; **Sekundäremissionsrauschen** *nt* ELEK-

TRONIK secondary emission noise; **Sekundäremissionsröhre** *f* ELEKTRONIK secondary emission tube; **Sekundäremissionsverhältnis** *nt* ELEKTRONIK secondary emission ratio; **Sekundäremissionsvervielfacher** *m* ELEKTRONIK photomultiplier, FERNSEH secondary emission multiplier

Sekundär-: **Sekundärenergie** *f* ERDÖL derived energy; **Sekundärfarben** *f pl* DRUCK secondary colors (AmE), secondary colours (BrE); **Sekundärförderung** *f* ERDÖL *Fördertechnik* secondary recovery; **Sekundärgitteremission** *f* ELEKTRONIK secondary grid emission; **Sekundärgittermauerwerk** *nt* KER & GLAS secondary checkers; **Sekundärgruppe** *f* COMP & DV, TELEKOM supergroup; **Sekundärindex** *m* COMP & DV secondary index; **Sekundärinduktanz** *f* ELEKTROTECH secondary inductance; **Sekundärionenemission** *f* TELEKOM secondary ionic emission; **Sekundärionenmassenspektrometrie** *f (SIMS)* PHYS secondary ion mass spectrometry *(SIMS)*; **Sekundärionisierung** *f* STRAHLPHYS secondary ionization; **Sekundärkältemittel** *nt* HEIZ & KÄLTE secondary refrigerant; **Sekundärkanal** *m* LUFTTRANS secondary duct; **Sekundärkern** *m* ERDÖL *Bohrtechnik* sidewall core; **Sekundärklemme** *f* ELEKTROTECH secondary terminal; **Sekundärkollision** *f* TRANS secondary collision; **Sekundärkreis** *m* ELEKTROTECH, HEIZ & KÄLTE secondary circuit; **Sekundärkrümmung** *f* KER & GLAS secondary curvature; **Sekundärkühlmittel** *nt* HEIZ & KÄLTE secondary coolant; **Sekundärlichtquelle** *f* STRAHLPHYS illuminated source; **Sekundärluft** *f* KFZTECH secondary air; **Sekundärmanschette** *f* KFZTECH secondary cup; **Sekundärnormal** *f* PHYS secondary standard; **Sekundärprozeß** *m* KERNTECH secondary process; **Sekundärquelle** *f* PHYS secondary source; **Sekundärreaktor** *m* KERNTECH secondary reactor; **Sekundärrelais** *nt* ELEKTRIZ secondary relay; **Sekundärrohstoff** *m* ABFALL secondary material, UMWELTSCHMUTZ waste product; **Sekundärseite** *f* KERNTECH secondary side; **Sekundärsetzung** *f* KOHLEN secondary settlement; **Sekundärspannung** *f* ELEKTRIZ, ELEKTROTECH secondary voltage; **Sekundärspeicher** *m* COMP & DV secondary memory, secondary storage, secondary store; **Sekundärspule** *f* ELEKTROTECH secondary coil, KFZTECH secondary winding; **Sekundärstoffauflauf** *m* PAPIER secondary headbox; **Sekundärstrahlung** *f* STRAHLPHYS secondary radiation

Sekundärstrom *m* ELEKTRIZ, ELEKTROTECH secondary current; **Sekundärstromkreis** *m* ELEKTROTECH secondary circuit

Sekundärteilchen *nt* KERNTECH secondary particle; **Sekundärteilchenradiographie** *f* KERNTECH, STRAHLPHYS, TEILPHYS charged-particle radiography

Sekundär-: **Sekundärtrennung** *f* KERNTECH secondary separation; **Sekundärwelle** *f (S-Welle)* PHYS secondary wave *(S-wave)*; **Sekundärwicklung** *f* ELEKTROTECH, KFZTECH, PHYS secondary winding; **Sekundärwicklung mit Anzapfung** *f* ELEKTROTECH tapped secondary winding; **Sekundärwiderstand** *m* ELEKTROTECH secondary resistance; **Sekundärzelle** *f* ELEKTRIZ secondary cell

Sekunde *f* AKUSTIK, METROL, PHYS *Zeiteinheit* second; **Sekundenzeiger** *m* MASCHINEN second hand

Selbstabgleich *m* GERÄT autobalance, self-balance

selbstabgleichend: ~**er Schalter** *m* ELEKTROTECH self-balancing switch

Selbstabnahmepapiermaschine ƒ PAPIER MG machine, machine-glazing machine

Selbstabschirmung ƒ KERNTECH self-shielding

selbstabsichernd: ~**e Pumpe** ƒ VERPACK self-sealing pump

Selbstabsorption ƒ KERNTECH self-absorption

Selbstalterung ƒ THERMOD natural ageing (BrE), natural aging (AmE)

selbständig[1] *adj* COMP & DV stand-alone; ~ **arbeitend** *adj* KONTROLL autonomous

selbständig:[2] ~**er Docksteuerstand** *m* WASSERTRANS off-line docking station; ~**e Emission** ƒ ELEKTRONIK spontaneous emission; **nicht** ~**e Regelung** ƒ REGELUNG manual control

selbstanlaufend: ~**er Synchronmotor** *m* ELEKTROTECH self-starting synchronous motor

selbstanpassend[1] *adj* COMP & DV self-adapting

selbstanpassend:[2] ~**e Abtastung** ƒ GERÄT adaptive sampling; ~**es Regelsystem** *nt* COMP & DV adaptive control system

Selbstanregung ƒ KERNTECH self-excitation

selbstansaugend: ~**e Pumpe** ƒ KFZTECH self-priming pump; ~**e Schmutzwasserpumpe** ƒ KERNTECH self-priming dirty-water pump

Selbstansteuerung ƒ RAUMFAHRT homing

Selbstantrieb: mit ~ *adj* TRANS self-propelling

selbstaufrichtend *adj* WASSERTRANS self-righting

Selbstauslöser *m* FOTO self-timer

Selbstbedienung ƒ VERPACK self-service; **Selbstbedienungstankstelle** ƒ (*SB-Tankstelle*) TRANS self-service station

selbstdiagnostisch *adj* COMP & DV self-diagnostic

selbstdichtend *adj* RAUMFAHRT self-sealing

Selbstdiffusion ƒ PHYS self-diffusion

selbstdokumentierend *adj* COMP & DV self-documenting

Selbsteinstellung ƒ GERÄT automatic adjustment

Selbstentladeeimer *m* BAU self-dumping bucket

Selbstentladegüterwagen *m* EISENBAHN self-discharge freight car (AmE), self-discharge freight wagon (BrE)

Selbstentladewagen *m* EISENBAHN self-discharging car (AmE), self-discharging wagon (BrE)

Selbstentladewaggon *m* EISENBAHN self-discharge car (AmE), self-discharge wagon (BrE)

Selbstentladewasserkübel *m* WASSERVERSORG self-discharging water bucket

Selbstentladung ƒ ELEKTROTECH self-discharge, self-sustained discharge, KFZTECH, RAUMFAHRT self-discharge; **Selbstentladungs-Zeitkonstante** ƒ ELEKTROTECH self-discharge time constant

Selbstentleerer: ~ **mit Sattelboden** *m* TRANS saddle-bottomed self-discharging car

Selbstentzündung ƒ RAUMFAHRT spontaneous ignition

Selbsterhitzung ƒ ELEKTROTECH self-heating; **Selbsterhitzungskoeffizient** *m* ELEKTROTECH self-heating coefficient

selbsterregend: ~**er Leistungsoszillator** *m* ELEKTRONIK self-excited power oscillator; ~**er Oszillator** *m* ELEKTRONIK self-excited oscillator

selbsterregt: ~**er Motor** *m* ELEKTRIZ self-excited motor; ~**e Schwingungen** ƒ *pl* FERTIG self-exited vibrations, self-induced vibrations

Selbsterregung ƒ ELEKTROTECH self-excitation

selbsterstarrend *adj* FERTIG *Kern* air-drying

selbstfahrend[1] *adj* KFZTECH automobile, automotive

selbstfahrend:[2] ~**er Kran** *m* KERNTECH self-propelled crane

Selbstfahrer *m* MEERSCHMUTZ self-propelled vessel, WASSERTRANS *Schifftyp* self-propelled barge

selbstgebacken *adj* LEBENSMITTEL home-baked

selbstgefertigt *adj* FERTIG engineered

Selbstglättung ƒ VERPACK automatic decurling

Selbstgreifer *m* KERNTECH *eines Krans* grab

selbsthaftend: ~**er Schmelzkleber** *m* VERPACK pressure-sensitive hot-melt adhesive

selbsthärtend *adj* FERTIG *Stahl* natural

Selbsthärtestahl *m* METALL self-hardening steel

selbstheilend: ~**er Kondensator** *m* ELEKTROTECH self-healing capacitor

Selbstheilung ƒ ELEKTROTECH self-healing

selbsthemmend *adj* FERTIG retained by friction

Selbstinduktion ƒ ELEKTROTECH, KFZTECH, PHYS self-induction; **Selbstinduktionskoeffizient** *m* ELEKTROTECH self-inductance; **Selbstinduktionsstrom** *m* ELEKTROTECH self-induction current

Selbstinduktivität ƒ ELEKTROTECH, PHYS self-inductance

selbstinduziert *adj* PHYS self-induced

Selbstionisierung ƒ PHYS, STRAHLPHYS autoionization

Selbstjustieren *nt* FERNSEH self-adjustment

selbstjustierend: ~**er Steueranschluß** *m* ELEKTRONIK SAG, self-aligned gate; ~**es System** *nt* FERNSEH self-controlling system; ~**er Transistor** *m* ELEKTRONIK self-aligned transistor

Selbstkipper *m* EISENBAHN self-tipping wagon

Selbstklebeband *nt* KUNSTSTOFF self-adhesive tape

Selbstklebeetikettiermaschine ƒ VERPACK pressure-sensitive labeller

selbstklebend[1] *adj* VERPACK self-sealing

selbstklebend:[2] ~**es Abziehschildchen** *nt* VERPACK easy-peel-off self-adhesive label; ~**es Band aus starkem Polyäthylen** *nt* VERPACK tough polyethylene self-adhesive tape; ~**er Briefumschlag** *m* VERPACK self-seal pocket envelope; ~**e Folie für kurzfristige Schutzabdeckung** ƒ VERPACK self-adhesive film for temporary surface protection; ~**es Isolierband** *nt* ELEKTROTECH adhesive insulating tape; ~**es Papier** *nt* VERPACK self-adhesive paper; ~**es PVC-Band** *nt* VERPACK PVC pressure-sensitive tape

selbstkommutierend: ~**er Umformer** *m* ELEKTRIZ self-commutated converter

selbstkorrigierend[1] *adj* COMP & DV self-correcting

selbstkorrigierend:[2] ~**er Code** *m* COMP & DV error-correcting code, self-correcting code, ELEKTRONIK error-correcting code

Selbstkühlung ƒ HEIZ & KÄLTE self-cooling, THERMOD natural cooling

Selbstladenbehälter *m* TRANS self-loading container

selbstlenzend *adj* WASSERTRANS self-draining

selbstlernend: ~**er Rechner** *m* COMP & DV self-learning machine

Selbstleuchten *nt* RAUMFAHRT self-luminosity

Selbstlockerung ƒ KERNTECH self-loosening

Selbstlöschung ƒ METALL volatility

Selbstlüftung ƒ HEIZ & KÄLTE natural ventilation; **Selbstlüftungssystem** *nt* VERPACK self-venting system

Selbstmitlauf *m* ELEKTRONIK *Filter* self-tracking

selbstmitlaufend: ~**es Bandpaßfilter** *nt* ELEKTRONIK self-tracking band-pass filter

Selbstnachführung ƒ ELEKTRONIK self-tracing

selbstnachstellend: ~**e Bremse** ƒ KFZTECH self-adjusting brake; ~**e Kupplung** ƒ KFZTECH self-adjusting clutch; ~**es Schwimmwehr** *nt* MEERSCHMUTZ self-adjusting floating weir selbstöffnend: **~er Gewindeschneidkopf** *m* MASCHINEN self-opening diehead, self-opening screwing head

selbstorganisierend: **~es System** *nt* COMP & DV self-organizing system

selbstprüfend: **~er Code** *m* COMP & DV, ELEKTRONIK error-detecting code

Selbstprüfung *f* COMP & DV automatic check, QUAL operator inspection

selbstregelnd: **~er Schalter** *m* ELEKTROTECH self-balancing switch; **~es System** *nt* ELEKTROTECH adaptive control system; **~es Wartungssystem** *nt* KFZTECH self-regulating maintenance system

Selbstregler *m* MASCHINEN automatic regulator

selbstreinigend[1] *adj* MASCHINEN self-cleaning

selbstreinigend:[2] **~es Luftfilter** *nt* HEIZ & KÄLTE self-cleaning air filter

Selbstreinigung *f* ABFALL natural purification, WASSERVERSORG self-purification; **Selbstreinigungskraft** *f* ABFALL assimilative capacity

Selbstrelativadresse *f* COMP & DV self-relative address

selbstrückfallend: **~es Relais** *nt* ELEKTRIZ self-resetting relay

selbstrücksetzend: **~e Schleife** *f* COMP & DV self-resetting loop

selbstrückstellend: **~er Zähler** *m* GERÄT self-resetting counter

Selbstschalttransistor *m* ELEKTRONIK latching transistor

selbstschließend[1] *adj* VERPACK self-closing

selbstschließend:[2] **~e Tür** *f* BAU self-closing door

Selbstschlußbatterie *f* BAU *Wasserhahn* self-closing faucet

selbstschmelzig *adj* PHYS self-fluxing

selbstschmierend *adj* MASCHINEN self-lubricating

Selbstschmierlager *nt* MASCHINEN self-lubricating bearing

selbstschneidend: **~es Gewinde** *nt* MASCHINEN self-tapping thread

Selbstschutzkohlenmonoxidfilter *nt* SICHERHEIT carbon monoxide filter for self-rescue

selbstschwingend: **~e Mischröhre** *f* ELEKTRONIK *Elektronenröhre*, ELEKTROTECH *bei elektrischen Röhren* converter

selbstsichernd[1] *adj* KFZTECH self-locking

selbstsichernd:[2] **~e Mutter** *f* MASCHINEN locknut, self-locking nut

selbstsperrend[1] *adj* KFZTECH self-locking

selbstsperrend:[2] **~es Ausgleichsgetriebe** *nt* KFZTECH nonslip differential

Selbstsperrung *f* FERTIG automatic interlock

Selbststabilisierungsgerät *nt* LUFTTRANS automatic stabilization equipment, TRANS automatic stabilizing equipment

Selbststarter *m* LUFTTRANS automatic starting unit

Selbststeueranlage *f* RAUMFAHRT, WASSERTRANS autopilot

Selbststeuerungsanlage *f* LUFTTRANS, WASSERTRANS gyropilot

selbsttätig[1] *adj* MASCHINEN self-acting

selbsttätig:[2] **~e Bremse** *f* KFZTECH self-acting brake; **~e Kupplung** *f* EISENBAHN automatic coupling; **~e Kupplung** *f* KFZTECH automatic clutch; **~e Kupplung** *f* KFZTECH automatic coupling; **~er Leistungsschalter** *m* ELEKTRIZ automatic circuit recloser; **~e Oxidation** *f* LEBENSMITTEL autoxidation; **~e Regelung** *f* REGELUNG automatic closed-loop control; **~er Regler** *m* MASCHINEN self-acting regulator; **~er Schalter** *m* ELEKTROTECH self-acting switch; **~ schließende Schleuse** *f* WASSERVERSORG balance bar

Selbsttönen *nt* AKUSTIK, AUFNAHME *bei Verstärkern* howling

selbsttragend[1] *adj* BAU self-contained, self-supporting, RAUMFAHRT self-supporting

selbsttragend:[2] **~e Karosserie** *f* KFZTECH *Karosserie* unit construction body

Selbstüberlagerer *m* ELEKTRONIK, RADIO autodyne

Selbstunterbrecher *m* ELEKTROTECH *Anker* trembler; **Selbstunterbrecherglocke** *f* ELEKTRIZ trembler bell

selbstverriegelnd *adj* VERPACK self-locking

selbstverschieblich: **~es Programm** *nt* COMP & DV self-relocating program

selbstverstärkend: **~es Polymer** *nt* KUNSTSTOFF self-reinforcing polymer

Selbstvulkanisation *f* KUNSTSTOFF self-vulcanization

Selbstwahl *f* TELEKOM automatic dialing (AmE), automatic dialling (BrE)

Selbstwählfernbetrieb *m* TELEKOM automatic trunk working

Selbstwählferndienst *m* *(SWFD)* TELEKOM direct distance dialing (AmE) *(DDD)*, subscriber trunk dialling (BrE) *(STD)*

Selbstwähllandzentrale *f* TELEKOM rural automatic exchange

Selbstwählnebenstelle *f* TELEKOM private branch exchange

selbstzentrierend: **~er Schraubstock** *m* MASCHINEN self-centering vise (AmE), self-centring vice (BrE); **~es Spannfutter** *nt* MASCHINEN concentric chuck, scroll chuck, self-centering chuck (AmE), self-centring chuck (BrE)

selbstzielsuchend *adj* RAUMFAHRT homing

Selbstzug *m* HEIZ & KÄLTE natural draft (AmE), natural draught (BrE)

Selbstzünder *m* KFZTECH compression-ignition engine

Selbstzündung *f* KFZTECH self-firing, self-ignition, *Motor* autoignition, *Zündanlage bei Dieselmotor* compression ignition, MASCHINEN self-ignition

Selbstzustellung *f* MASCHINEN automatic feed

SELCAL *abbr (Selektivrufsystem)* TELEKOM SELCAL *(selective calling system)*

selektieren *vt* DRUCK select

Selektion *f* ELEKTRONIK selectivity

selektiv: **~er Abschwächer** *m* FOTO selective reducer; **~e Beschichtung** *f* NICHTFOSS ENERG selective coating; **~er Bildschirmspeicher** *m* COMP & DV snapshot; **~es Bildschirmspeichern** *nt* COMP & DV snapshot; **~e Diffusion** *f* ELEKTRONIK selective diffusion; **~es Fading** *nt* TELEKOM selective fading; **~ galvanisierte Kontakte** *m pl* ELEKTROTECH selectively plated contacts; **~e Ionenelektrode** *f* LABOR *Elektrochemie* selective ion electrode; **~e katalytische Reduktion** *f* UMWELTSCHMUTZ selective catalytic reduction; **~es Löschen** *nt* COMP & DV selective erasure; **~e Oberfläche** *f* NICHTFOSS ENERG selective surface; **~ plattierte Kontakte** *m pl* ELEKTROTECH selectively plated contacts; **~es Protokollprogramm** *nt* COMP & DV snapshot; **~e Prüfung** *f* QUAL screening inspection, screening test; **~e Reflexion** *f* PHYS selective reflection; **~es Relais** *nt* ELEKTRIZ discriminating relay; **~e Rückkopplung** *f* ELEKTRONIK selective feedback; **~er Schrumpf** *m* TEXTIL differential shrinkage; **~es Schutzsystem** *nt* ELEKTRIZ discriminating protective system; **~er sequentieller**

Zugriff *m* COMP & DV selective sequential access; ~er Speicherauszug *m* COMP & DV selective dump; ~e Stromunterbrechung *f* ELEKTRIZ discriminating circuit-breaking; ~e Verkehrsumleitung *f* TRANS selective diversion of traffic; ~er Zugriff *m* COMP & DV selective access

Selektivität *f* PHYS selectivity; Selektivitätsschlange *f* AUFNAHME selectivity Q

Selektivruf *m* TELEKOM selective calling; Selektivrufsystem *nt* (*SELCAL*) TELEKOM selective calling system (*SELCAL*)

Selektivschwund *m* TELEKOM selective fading

Selektivsolvens *nt* ERDÖL selective solvent

Selektor *m* COMP & DV, ELEKTROTECH selector; Selektorkanal *m* COMP & DV selector channel; Selektorrelais *nt* ELEKTROTECH selector relay

Selen *nt* (*Se*) CHEMIE selenium (*Se*); Selen- *pref* CHEMIE selenic, selenious, selenous

Selenat *nt* CHEMIE selenate

Selencyan- *pref* CHEMIE selenocyanic

Selen: Selengleichrichter *m* ELEKTRIZ, ELEKTROTECH, PHYS selenium rectifier

Selenid *nt* CHEMIE selenide

selenig *adj* CHEMIE selenious, selenous

Selenit *m* CHEMIE selenite

Selenium *nt* (*Se*) CHEMIE selenium (*Se*)

Selen: Selen-Rubinglas *nt* KER & GLAS selenium ruby glass; Selenzelle *f* ELEKTROTECH electric eye, selenium cell, PHYS selenium cell

Sellersgewinde *nt* MASCHINEN Sellers thread, USS screw thread

Seltene-Erden-Glas *nt* KER & GLAS rare-earth glass

Seltsamkeit *f* TEILPHYS *spezielle Quantenzahl von Hadronen* strangeness

Semantik *f* COMP & DV semantics

semantisch: ~e Analyse *f* COMP & DV semantic analysis; ~er Fehler *m* COMP & DV semantic error

Semaphor *m* COMP & DV semaphore; Semaphorprogramm *nt* TRANS semaphoric program (AmE), semaphoric programme (BrE)

semiamphibisch: ~es Luftkissenfahrzeug *nt* WASSERTRANS semiamphibious air cushion vehicle, semiamphibious hovercraft

Semicarbazid *nt* CHEMIE semicarbazide

Semicarbazon *nt* CHEMIE semicarbazone

Semidin *nt* CHEMIE semidine

semihomogen: ~es Brennelement *nt* KERNTECH semihomogeneous fuel element

Semikundenchip *m* ELEKTRONIK *halbkundenspezifischer Chip* semicustom chip

Semikundenschaltung *f* ELEKTRONIK *halbkundenspezifische Schaltung* semicustom circuit

semipermeabel: semipermeable Membran *f* PHYS semipermeable membrane

Sendeantenne *f* FERNSEH transmitting antenna, PHYS transmitting aerial, TELEKOM transmit antenna

Sendeaufforderung *f* COMP & DV invitation to send, TELEKOM invitation to transmit

Sendeaufruf *m* COMP & DV invitation to send, polling, RADIO, TELEKOM polling; Sendeaufrufintervall *nt* COMP & DV polling interval; Sendeaufrufzeichen *nt* COMP & DV polling character

Sendebeginnzeichen *nt* FERNSEH, RADIO transmitter turn-on signal

Sendebeginnzeit *f* FERNSEH, RADIO transmitter turn-on time

Sendebereich *m* FERNSEH network coverage, range, station coverage, RADIO range

sendebereit *adj* COMP & DV clear-to-send, ready-to-send

Sendedatum *nt* FERNSEH air date

Sende-Empfangs- *pref* ELEKTRONIK TR, transmit-receive, transmitting-receiving

Sende-Empfangs-Gerät *nt* RADIO, TELEKOM transceiver

Sende-Empfangs-Weiche *f* ELEKTRONIK *Funktechnik* branching filter

Sendefernschreiber *m* TELEKOM transmit machine

Sendefrequenz *f* FERNSEH transmitting frequency

Sendeimpuls *m* RADIO pulse

Sendekettenkennung *f* FERNSEH network identification

Sendekettenzeichen *nt* FERNSEH network cue

Sendekopie *f* FERNSEH transmission copy

Sendeleistung *f* FERNSEH, RADIO transmitter power

Sendemikrofon *nt* AUFNAHME transmitting microphone

Sendemonitor *m* FERNSEH air monitor

Senden *nt* COMP & DV sending

senden[1] *vt* COMP & DV send, transmit, FERNSEH air, broadcast, transmit, RADIO broadcast, transmit

senden[2] *vi* RADIO broadcast

Sendepause *f* ELEKTROTECH off-air period

Sendeprüfung *f* FERNSEH air check

Sendequalität *f* FERNSEH air quality

Sender *m* FERNSEH, RADIO transmitter, TELEKOM sender, transmitter; Senderausfall *m* FERNSEH, RADIO transmitter failure

Senderecht[1] *nt* FERNSEH broadcasting right

Senderecht:[2] ~ anfordern *vt* COMP & DV bid

Senderecht: Senderechtanforderung *f* COMP & DV bid

Sender-Empfänger *m* COMP & DV sender-receiver, transceiver, FERNSEH transmitter-receiver, RADIO transceiver, transmitter-receiver; Sender-Empfänger-Zelle *f* FERNSEH, RADIO *Radar* transmitter-receiver cell

Sender: Senderfunkerkennungssignal *nt* FERNSEH, RADIO transmitter identification signal; Senderkennung *f* FERNSEH program identification signal (AmE), programme identification signal (BrE); Senderkette *f* FERNSEH network; Sendernetz *nt* ELEKTROTECH *Fernsehen*, FERNSEH network of transmitters; Senderöhre mit gekühlter Anode *f* (*CAT*) ELEKTRONIK cooled-anode transmitting valve (*CAT*); Sendersperröhre *f* ELEKTRONIK ATR-tube, antitransmit-receive tube; Senderzeit *f* FERNSEH station time; Senderzeitsteuerung *f* FERNSEH station timing

Sendestation *f* COMP & DV *Datenfernverarbeitung* master station

Sendesystem *nt* ELEKTROTECH transmission system

Sendetaste *f* TELEKOM *Telegrafie* key

Sendetermin *m* FERNSEH slot

Sendeüberwachungsband *nt* FERNSEH air check tape

Sendeweg *m* COMP & DV transmission path

Sendeweiche *f* TELEKOM combiner

Sendezeit *f* ELEKTROTECH on-air period, FERNSEH airtime, broadcasting time, TELEKOM airtime

Sendezentrale *f* FERNSEH network control room

Sendung:[1] auf ~ *adj* FERNSEH on-air; nicht auf ~ *adj* FERNSEH off-air

Sendung:[2] auf ~ gehen *vi* FERNSEH switch to air

Sendung[3] *f* FERNSEH, TELEKOM transmission; ~ mit hoher Leistung *f* TELEKOM high-power transmission

Sendung:[4] vor der ~ aufzeichnen *vt* FERNSEH prerecord

Senföl *nt* LEBENSMITTEL mustard oil, mustardseed oil

Sengen *nt* TEXTIL singeing

sengen *vt* TEXTIL singe

Sengmaschine *f* TEXTIL singeing machine

Senkblei *nt* BAU bob, plumb bob, FERTIG plumb, METROL bob

Senke *f* ELEKTROTECH, METALL sink

Senken *nt* KER & GLAS *Glas* sagging, MASCHINEN countersinking, recessing

senken *vt* ELEKTROTECH *Spannung* drop, lower

senkend: ~es Kissen *nt* TRANS height-off cushion

Senkenstrom *m* ELEKTROTECH drain current

Senker *m* MASCHINEN burr, counterbore, countersink, spot face cutter

Senkgrube *f* WASSERVERSORG cess pit, cess pool

Senkkasten *m* MASCHINEN, WASSERVERSORG caisson

Senkkopf *m* FERTIG flush head, MASCHINEN countersunk head, flat countersunk head; Senkkopfniet *nt* BAU countersunk button-head rivet, MASCHINEN flush-head rivet; Senkkopfschraube *f* MASCHINEN countersunk-head screw, flat-head bolt, flat-head screw; Senkkopfvernietung *f* BAU countersunk riveting

Senkkörper *m* LEBENSMITTEL sinker

Senklot *nt* FERTIG plummet

Senkniet *m* FERTIG flat countersunk head rivet, flush rivet, MASCHINEN countersunk-head rivet, countersunk rivet, flat countersunk rivet

Senkrecht- *pref* FERNSEH, MASCHINEN orthogonal

senkrecht[1] *adj* BAU upright, GEOM rectangular, vertical, PHYS *im rechten Winkel* normal; ~ auf *adj* GEOM perpendicular to; ~ aufeinander *adj* MATH orthogonal

senkrecht[2] *adv* BAU plumb

senkrecht:[3] ~er Abstand zur stillen Wasseroberfläche *f* NICHTFOSS ENERG distance perpendicular to still water surface; ~ arbeitende Vakuum-Siegelmaschine *f* VERPACK vertical vacuum sealer; ~e Beleuchtung *f* LUFTTRANS overhead light; ~e Ebenen *f pl* GEOM vertical planes; ~ eingebauter Motor *m* KFZTECH vertical engine; ~e Entwässerung *f* KOHLEN vertical drainage; ~e Falten *f pl* KER & GLAS brush marks; ~e Komponente *f* PHYS vertical component; ~e Rohrleitung *f* BAU stack; ~ startendes und landendes Flugzeug *nt* (*VTOL-Flugzeug*) LUFTTRANS vertical takeoff and landing aircraft (*VTOL aircraft*); ~e Welle *f* MASCHINEN upright shaft; ~ wirkende Reaktionskraft *f* PHYS normal reaction force; ~e Zugstange *f* EISENBAHN suspension rod

Senkrecht-: Senkrechtabtastung *f* FERNSEH orthogonal scanning; Senkrechtaußenräummaschine *f* MASCHINEN vertical surface-type broaching machine; Senkrechtbohrmaschine *f* MASCHINEN upright drilling machine, vertical boring machine, vertical boring mill, vertical drill press, vertical drilling machine; Senkrechtdrehmaschine *f* MASCHINEN vertical lathe

Senkrechte *f* BAU plumb, GEOM normal, perpendicular, vertical

Senkrechten: von der ~ abweichen *vi* MASCHINEN run out of the vertical

Senkrecht-: Senkrechtförderer *m* MASCHINEN elevator; Senkrechtförderschnecke *f* BAU screw elevator; Senkrechtfräsmaschine *f* FERTIG vertical-spindle milling machine, MASCHINEN vertical milling machine; Senkrechtfräsvorrichtung *f* MASCHINEN vertical milling attachment; Senkrechtgerüst *nt* FERTIG *Walzen* edging mill; Senkrechtmagnetisierung *f* FERNSEH perpendicular magnetization; Senkrechträummaschine *f* MASCHINEN vertical broaching machine;

Senkrechtschlitten *m* FERTIG *Hobelmaschine* head slide; Senkrechtschnitt *m* BAU vertical section; Senkrechtschnittkraft *f* FERTIG vertical tool thrust; Senkrechtstab *m* BAU stile, upright

senkrechtstehend: ~e Ebenen *f pl* GEOM vertical planes

Senkrecht-: Senkrechtstoßmaschine *f* FERTIG slotting machine, MASCHINEN vertical slotting machine; Senkrechttabulator *m* COMP & DV vertical tab; Senkrechtziehverfahren *nt* KER & GLAS up-draw process

Senkring *m* KER & GLAS settle ring

Senkschacht *m* BAU caisson

Senkschlitten *m* PAPIER lowering cradle

Senkschraube *f* FERTIG flat-head screw, MASCHINEN countersunk screw, countersunk-head screw, flat-head bolt, flat-head screw, MECHAN countersunk-head screw; ~ mit Schlitz *f* MASCHINEN slotted countersunk-head screw

Senkschraubenmutter *f* KERNTECH countersunk nut

Senkstange *f* KER & GLAS depression bar

Senkung *f* BAU slump, *Gebäude, Gelände* settling, KOHLEN settling, MASCHINEN counterbore, WASSERTRANS sinkage; Senkungsbecken *nt* ERDÖL *Stratigraphie* subsidence basin; Senkungskegel *m* WASSERVERSORG depression cone; Senkungsquelle *f* WASSERVERSORG depression spring

Senkwaage *f* LEBENSMITTEL densimeter, hydrometer

Senkwasser *nt* WASSERVERSORG percolating water

Sensibilisator *m* DRUCK sensitizer

sensibilisieren *vt* FOTO sensitize

Sensibilisierung *f* FOTO sensitization; Sensibilisierungsbad *nt* FOTO sensitizing bath

Sensitometrie *f* AKUSTIK sensitometry

Sensomotorik *f* ERGON sensorimotor system

sensomotorisch *adj* ERGON sensorimotor

Sensor *m* COMP & DV sensor, ELEKTRIZ pick-up, probe, ELEKTRONIK, ERGON sensor, GERÄT probe, KERNTECH, KFZTECH sensor, MASCHINEN detector, probe, sensor, PHYS, TELEKOM, WASSERTRANS *Meßinstrumente* sensor; Sensorbildschirm *m* COMP & DV touch-sensitive screen

sensorisch[1] *adj* ERGON sensory; sensorisch-neural *adj* ERGON sensorineural

sensorisch:[2] ~e Analyse *f* LEBENSMITTEL *zur Beurteilung sensorischer Merkmale von Lebensmitteln* tasting; ~e Schärfe *f* ERGON sensory acuity

Sensorsignal *nt* ELEKTRONIK sensor signal

Sente *f* WASSERTRANS *Schiffbau* ribband; Sentenriß *m* WASSERTRANS *Schiffkonstruktion* buttock lines, *Schiffbau* plan of diagonals

Sentlatte *f* WASSERTRANS *Schiffbau* ribband

separat: ~e Streichmaschine *f* PAPIER off-machine coater

Separator *m* MEERSCHMUTZ, TELEKOM separator; Separatorzentrifuge *f* CHEMTECH centrifugal separator

Separatstreichen *nt* PAPIER off-machine coating

Separierung *f* COMP & DV compartmentalization

Septime *f* AKUSTIK seventh

Septum *nt* ELEKTROTECH septum

Sequencer *m* COMP & DV sequencer

sequentiell[1] *adj* COMP & DV, KONTROLL sequential

sequentiell:[2] ~es Abtasten *nt* FERNSEH sequential scanning; ~e Arbeitsweise *f* COMP & DV sequential operation; ~er Computer *m* COMP & DV sequential computer; ~e Datei *f* COMP & DV sequential file; ~e Decodierung *f* TELEKOM sequential decoding; ~er

Modus *m* COMP & DV sequential mode; **~e Prüfung** *f* TELEKOM sequential test; **~es Sprungverfahren** *nt* FERNSEH sequential interlace; **~e Steuerung** *f* COMP & DV sequencing; **~e Suche** *f* COMP & DV sequential search; **~es Suchen** *nt* COMP & DV sequential search; **~e Verarbeitung** *f* COMP & DV sequential processing; **~er Zugriff** *m* COMP & DV sequential access

Sequenz *f* AKUSTIK, COMP & DV, KONTROLL sequence

Sequestiermittel *nt* CHEMIE sequestering agent

serialisieren *vt* COMP & DV serialize

Serie:[1] **in ~ geschaltet** *adj* GERÄT series-connected, PHYS connected in series

Serie[2] *f* FERTIG *Werkzeuge* gang, MASCHINEN series

seriell[1] *adj* COMP & DV, DRUCK serial, ELEKTRIZ series, KONTROLL, TELEKOM serial; **seriell-parallel** *adj* COMP & DV serial-parallel

seriell:[2] **~er A/D-Wandler** *m* ELEKTRONIK serial analog-digital converter; **~er Addierer** *m* COMP & DV ripple-carry adder; **~e Analog-Digital-Umsetzung** *f* ELEKTRONIK serial analog-digital conversion (AmE); **~er Anschluß** *m* COMP & DV serial connector; **~er Betrieb** *m* COMP & DV serial operation; **~er Computer** *m* COMP & DV serial computer; **~e Datei** *f* COMP & DV serial file; **~e digitale Ausgabe** *f* COMP & DV serial digital output; **~er Drucker** *m* COMP & DV, DRUCK serial printer; **~e Ein-/Ausgabe** *f* COMP & DV SIO, serial input/output; **~ erregte Maschine** *f* ELEKTRIZ series-excited machine, series-wound machine; **~ erregter Dynamo** *m* ELEKTRIZ series-wound dynamo; **~ erregter Motor** *m* ELEKTRIZ series-wound motor; **~e Form** *f* ELEKTROTECH serial form; **~es Kabel** *nt* ELEKTROTECH serial line; **~e Leitung** *f* ELEKTROTECH serial line; **~e Operation** *f* COMP & DV serial operation; **~-paralleler Umwandler** *m* ELEKTROTECH serial-to-parallel converter; **~-parallele Umwandlung** *f* ELEKTROTECH serial-to-parallel conversion; **~es Programmieren** *nt* COMP & DV serial programming; **~er Rechner** *m* (*SISD-Rechner*) COMP & DV single instruction single-data machine (*SISD machine*); **~e Schnittstelle** *f* COMP & DV, DRUCK, TELEKOM serial interface; **~er Speicher** *m* COMP & DV serial memory, serial storage, ELEKTROTECH serial memory; **~er Subtrahierer** *m* ELEKTRONIK serial subtracter; **~e Übertragung** *f* COMP & DV serial transfer, serial transmission; **~e Verarbeitung** *f* COMP & DV serial processing; **~e Wicklung** *f* ELEKTRIZ series winding; **~er Zugriff** *m* COMP & DV serial access

Serien- *pref* PHYS in series, TELEKOM serial; **Serienaddierer** *m* COMP & DV, ELEKTRONIK serial adder; **Serienarbeit** *f* FERTIG repetitive work; **Serienbetrieb** *m* COMP & DV serial operation; **Seriencode** *m* VERPACK batch code; **Serienfahrzeug** *nt* EISENBAHN production-type vehicle; **Serienfertigung** *f* FERTIG repetitive work; **Serienflugzeug** *nt* LUFTTRANS production aircraft; **Seriengegenkopplung** *f* ELEKTROTECH series feedback

seriengeregelt: ~e Stromversorgung *f* ELEKTROTECH series-regulated power supply

seriengeschaltet: ~e Spule *f* ELEKTRIZ series coil

seriengewickelt: ~er Dynamo *m* ELEKTROTECH series-wound dynamo; **~er Motor** *m* ELEKTROTECH series-wound motor

Serien-: Serienkapazität *f* ELEKTROTECH series capacitance; **Serienkollektorwiderstand** *m* ELEKTROTECH series collector resistance; **Serienkondensator** *m* ELEKTROTECH series capacitor; **Serienkonverter** *m*

ELEKTROTECH series converter; **Serienmarke** *f* PATENT associated mark

serienmäßig[1] *adj* FERTIG *Kunststoffinstallationen* standard

serienmäßig:[2] **~ hergestellter Leistungsreaktor** *m* KERNTECH series-produced power reactor; **~e Seitenruder** *nt pl* LUFTTRANS serial rudders

Serien-: Serienmotor *m* ELEKTROTECH series motor; **Seriennummer** *f* COMP & DV, FOTO, MASCHINEN serial number, VERPACK batch number; **Serienparallelschalter** *m* ELEKTROTECH series-parallel switch; **Serienparallelschaltung** *f* ELEKTROTECH series-parallel circuit; **Serienprüfung** *f* QUAL batch test; **Serienreaktanz** *f* ELEKTROTECH series reactance; **Serienresonanz** *f* PHYS series resonance; **Serienresonanzkreis** *m* ELEKTRIZ acceptor resonance circuit, ELEKTROTECH series-resonant circuit; **Serienschaltung** *f* ELEKTROTECH series circuit, series connection, PHYS series connection; **Serienspeisung** *f* ELEKTROTECH series feed; **Serienstörsignal** *nt* REGELUNG series mode signal; **Serienstörsignalunterdrückung** *f* REGELUNG series mode rejection; **Serienstörsignalunterdrückungsmaß** *nt* REGELUNG series mode rejection ratio; **Serienvergleichsumsetzer** *m* GERÄT level-at-a-time converter; **Serienwandler** *m* ELEKTROTECH series converter; **Serienwicklung** *f* ELEKTROTECH series winding; **Serienwiderstand** *m* ELEKTROTECH series resistance; **Serienzeichen** *nt* PATENT associated mark

Serife *f* DRUCK serif

serifenlos: ~e Linear-Antiqua *f* DRUCK, KONSTZEICH sans serif linear antiqua; **~e Schrift** *f* DRUCK, KONSTZEICH sans serif

Serifenschrift *f* DRUCK serif

Serigraphie *f* DRUCK serigraphy

Serotonin *nt* CHEMIE serotonin

Serpentinisierung *f* NICHTFOSS ENERG serpentinization

Server *m* COMP & DV, TELEKOM server

Service *m* MASCHINEN service; **Serviceoszillator** *m* ELEKTRONIK service oscillator; **Servicepersonal** *nt* LUFTTRANS crew

Servierwagen *m* LUFTTRANS *Flugzeug* service trolley

Servo *m* KFZTECH *Bremsen, Lenkung* servo; **~ zweiter Ordnung** *m* ELEKTROTECH second order servo; **Servoantrieb** *m* ELEKTRIZ servo drive, KFZTECH booster control; **Servobremse** *f* KFZTECH power brake, power-assisted brake, servo brake, MASCHINEN servo brake; **Servoeinrichtung** *f* MASCHINEN servomechanism

servogesteuert *adj* FERTIG *Kunststoffinstallationen* servo-acting

Servo: Servohöhenmesser *m* LUFTTRANS servo altimeter; **Servolenkgestängesystem** *nt* KFZTECH linkage power-steering system; **Servolenkpumpe** *f* KFZTECH power-steering pump; **Servolenkung** *f* KFZTECH power steering, power-assisted steering; **Servomanipulator** *m* KERNTECH servo manipulator; **Servomechanismus** *m* COMP & DV, ELEKTROTECH, FERNSEH, MASCHINEN, PHYS servomechanism; **Servomotor** *m* ELEKTROTECH, KERNTECH, KONTROLL, NICHTFOSS ENERG servomotor; **Servomotorsteuerung** *f* LUFTTRANS servo control; **Servopositionierer** *m* KONTROLL servo positioner; **Servorad** *nt* FERNSEH servo wheel; **Servoregelung** *f* ELEKTROTECH, KONTROLL servo control; **Servoregler** *m* KONTROLL servo controller; **Servoschleife** *f* FERNSEH servo loop; **Servostellglied** *nt* KONTROLL servo positioner; **Servo-**

steuerung f KONTROLL servo controller, LUFTTRANS servo control; **Servosteuerungssystem** nt LUFTTRANS *Hubschrauber* follow-up; **Servosystem** nt FERNSEH, KONTROLL servo system; **Servosystem mit Rückführung** nt KONTROLL closed-loop servo system; **Servosystemabweichung** f RAUMFAHRT *Weltraumfunk* servo system drift; **Servotonrolle** f FERNSEH servo capstan; **Servoventil** nt MASCHINEN pilot valve, servo valve; **Servoverstärker** m ELEKTRONIK servo amplifier

SES abbr *(Bordterminal für Satellitenfunk)* WASSERTRANS SES *(ship earth station)*

Sesamöl nt LEBENSMITTEL sesame oil

Sesselliftbahn f TRANS chair lift

Set nt TEXTIL set

Setzarbeit f KOHLEN jigging

Setzbecher m BAU *Ausbreitversuch* slump cone

Setzbett nt KOHLEN jig bed

Setzbord nt WASSERTRANS *Schiffbau* washboard

Setzeisen nt KER & GLAS flatter

Setzen nt DRUCK composition, typesetting, KOHLEN setting, settling, KUNSTSTOFF permanent set, set

setzen[1] vt BAU set, DRUCK compose, set, typeset, KONTROLL set

setzen[2] vi BAU *Untergrund* subside

Setzer m DRUCK compositor, typesetter

Setzkasten m KOHLEN jig, jig sieve, settling tank

Setzkopf m FERTIG *Nieten* die head, *Niet* preformed head, MASCHINEN set head, snap head

Setzlibelle f MASCHINEN striding level

Setzmaschine f DRUCK composing machine, KOHLEN jig, pan, settling tank; **Setzmaschinenzeile** f DRUCK slug

Setzmaß nt BAU slump

Setzprobe f BAU slump test

Setzpult nt DRUCK frame

Setzregal nt DRUCK frame

Setzschiff nt DRUCK galley

Setzstock m FERTIG end-support column, lathe steady, outer stay, MASCHINEN back rest, steady-rest

Setzstufe f BAU riser

Setzung f BAU subsidence, *Gebäude, Gelände* settlement, ERDÖL compaction, *Geologie* subsidence, KUNSTSTOFF permanent set, set; **Setzungsunterschied** m BAU differential settlement

Seuche f LEBENSMITTEL pest

Sext f AKUSTIK sixth

Sextant m PHYS, WASSERTRANS *Navigation* sextant

Sexte f AKUSTIK submediant

Sextett nt PHYS *Spektroskopie* sextet

Sezierbehälter m LABOR dissecting tray

Sezierschere f LABOR dissecting scissors

SF abbr BAU *(Sicherheitsfaktor)*, ELEKTRIZ *(Sicherheitsfaktor)* SF *(safety factor)*, ELEKTRONIK *(Seitenbandfrequenz)* SF *(sideband frequency)*, ELEKTRONIK *(Signalfrequenz)* SF *(signal frequency)*, ELEKTRONIK *(Sprachfrequenz)* VF *(voice frequency)*, SF *(speech frequency)*, FERNSEH *(Seitenbandfrequenz)* SF *(sideband frequency)*, FERNSEH *(Signalfrequenz)* SF *(signal frequency)*, KERNTECH *(Sicherheitsfaktor)*, KOHLEN *(Sicherheitsfaktor)*, MASCHINEN *(Sicherheitsfaktor)* SF *(safety factor)*, RADIO *(Seitenbandfrequenz)* SF *(sideband frequency)*, RADIO *(Signalfrequenz)* SF *(signal frequency)*, SICHERHEIT *(Sicherheitsfaktor)* SF *(safety factor)*, TELEKOM *(Seitenbandfrequenz)* SF *(sideband frequency)*, TELEKOM *(Signalfrequenz)* SF *(signal frequency)*, TELEKOM *(Sprachfrequenz)* SF *(speech frequency)*, VF *(voice frequency)*, TRANS *(Sicherheitsfaktor)* SF *(safety factor)*

S-förmig: **~er Geruchverschluß** m BAU *Sanitär* S-trap; **~er Haken** m MASCHINEN S-hook, S-shaped hook

SGML abbr *(Standardkorrekturzeichensatz)* COMP & DV, DRUCK SGML *(Standard Generalized Markup Language)*

Shapingmaschine f MASCHINEN shaping machine, shaping planer, MECHAN shaper

Shareware f COMP & DV shareware

Sheddach nt BAU sawtooth roof

Shell f COMP & DV, KÜNSTL INT *eines Expertensystems* shell

SHF[1] abbr *(superhohe Frequenz)* BAU, ELEKTRONIK, KOHLEN, KUNSTSTOFF, MECHAN, PHYS, THERMOD SHF *(superhigh frequency)*

SHF:[2] **SHF-Signalerzeuger** m ELEKTRONIK SHF signal generator; **SHF-Signalgenerator** m ELEKTRONIK SHF signal generator

Shippington f WASSERTRANS shipping ton

Shirting m TEXTIL shirting

Shockley-Diode f ELEKTRONIK Shockley diode

Shockley-Versetzung f METALL Shockley dislocation

Shoddygewebe nt TEXTIL shoddy fabrics

Shore-Härte f KUNSTSTOFF Shore hardness; **Shore-Härteprüfer** m LABOR Shore hardness tester

Shredder m PAPIER shredder, VERPACK shredding machine; **Shredderabfälle-Deponie** f ABFALL shredded refuse landfill

Shredding n ABFALL shredding

Shunt m AKUSTIK, ELEKTRIZ, ELEKTROTECH, PHYS shunt

Shuttle nt LUFTTRANS shuttle; **Shuttlehubschrauber** m ERDÖL *Transport* shuttle helicopter; **Shuttleplatte** f HYDRAUL shuttle plate; **Shuttletanker** m ERDÖL *Transport* shuttle tanker

Si *(Silizium)* CHEMIE Si *(silicon)*

sichelförmig: **~es Widerlager** nt FERTIG crescent

sicher: **~e Arbeitsbelastung** f SICHERHEIT safe working load; **~e Arbeitsweise** f SICHERHEIT safe method of working; **~e Belastung** f SICHERHEIT safe working load; **~er Einsatz** m SICHERHEIT safe use; **~er Einsatz von Sprengstoff** m SICHERHEIT *in Bauindustrie* safe use of explosive; **~e Geschwindigkeit** f EISENBAHN, KFZTECH, LUFTTRANS, TRANS, WASSERTRANS safety speed; **~es Gewässer** nt WASSERTRANS safe water; **~er Grund** m WASSERTRANS safe ground; **~e Höchstgeschwindigkeit** f LUFTTRANS maximum threshold speed; **~e Lagerung** f UMWELTSCHMUTZ safe keeping; **~e Mindestgeschwindigkeit** f LUFTTRANS minimum control speed; **~e Mindestvorführgeschwindigkeit** f LUFTTRANS minimum demonstrated threshold speed

Sicherheit f COMP & DV security, MECHAN, QUAL, RADIO safety; **~ auf See** f SICHERHEIT, WASSERTRANS marine safety; **~ beim Betrieb von Handgeräten** f SICHERHEIT safety of hand-operated machines; **~ im Haushalt** f SICHERHEIT safety in the home; **~ von Menschenmengen** f SICHERHEIT crowd safety; **~ im Straßenverkehr** f SICHERHEIT road safety; **Sicherheitsabblasearmatur** f *(SBV)* ERDÖL relief valve; **Sicherheitsabstand** m LUFTTRANS clearance, TRANS safe headway, safety headway, WASSERTRANS clearance; **Sicherheitsanschluß** m SICHERHEIT safety fitting, *für Heißwassersysteme* safety fitting; **Sicherheitsausleger** m ERDÖL containment boom; **Sicherheitsausschalter**

m EISENBAHN cutout switch, HEIZ & KÄLTE safety cutout; **Sicherheitsausschuß** *m* SICHERHEIT safety committee; **Sicherheitsautomat** *m* HEIZ & KÄLTE *elektrisch* safety cutout; **Sicherheitsband zwischen Frequenzbändern** *nt* FERNSEH guard band; **Sicherheitsbeauftragter** *m* SICHERHEIT safety officer; **Sicherheitsbehälter** *m* KERNTECH safety tank, LABOR safety container; **Sicherheitsbenzintank** *m* KFZTECH safety gasoline tank (AmE), safety petrol tank (BrE); **Sicherheitsberater** *m* BAU safety adviser; **Sicherheitsbericht** *m* KERNTECH *eines Reaktors* safety report; **Sicherheitsberstscheibe** *f* GERÄT safety disc (BrE), safety disk (AmE); **Sicherheitsbolzen** *m* SICHERHEIT security bolt; **Sicherheitsbrille** *f* LABOR safety glasses; **Sicherheitseinrichtung** *f* MASCHINEN safety appliance, SICHERHEIT safety appliance, *an Gebäuden* safety fitting; **Sicherheitseinrichtungen** *f pl* SICHERHEIT safety facilities; **Sicherheitserde** *f* ELEKTRIZ safety earth (BrE), safety ground (AmE); **Sicherheitsfaktor** *m (SF)* BAU, ELEKTRIZ, KERNTECH, KOHLEN, MASCHINEN, SICHERHEIT, TRANS safety factor *(SF)*; **Sicherheitsfarbe** *f* SICHERHEIT safety color (AmE), safety colour (BrE); **Sicherheitsfenster** *nt* SICHERHEIT security window; **Sicherheitsfilm** *m* DRUCK, FOTO safety film; **Sicherheitsfirma** *f* SICHERHEIT security firm

sicherheitsgeprüft *adj* SICHERHEIT approved

Sicherheit: **Sicherheitsgerät** *nt* RAUMFAHRT safety unit, SICHERHEIT safety apparatus, safety appliance; **Sicherheitsgeschirr** *nt* SICHERHEIT safety harness; **Sicherheitsglas** *nt* BAU, KER & GLAS safety glass, KFZTECH multilayer glass, safety glass, SICHERHEIT protective glass; **Sicherheitsgurt** *m* KFZTECH safety belt, safety harness, seat belt, LUFTTRANS safety harness, seat belt, RAUMFAHRT safety harness, SICHERHEIT safety belt, WASSERTRANS safety harness; **Sicherheitsgurtverankerung** *f* KFZTECH safety belt anchorage; **Sicherheitshahn** *m* MASCHINEN safety cock; **Sicherheitshaken** *m* MASCHINEN safety hook; **Sicherheitshinweisschild** *nt* SICHERHEIT safety sign; **Sicherheitskette** *f* MASCHINEN safety chain; **Sicherheitskopf** *m* FERNSEH video confidence head; **Sicherheitskopie** *f* COMP & DV security backup; **Sicherheitskupplung** *f* MASCHINEN safety coupling; **Sicherheitslampe** *f* KOHLEN Davy lamp; **Sicherheitsleitkegel** *m* TRANS road marker cone; **Sicherheitsleitplanke** *f* TRANS emergency crash barrier; **Sicherheitsluftventil** *nt* KFZTECH vacuum valve; **Sicherheitsmarge** *f* SICHERHEIT safety margin; **Sicherheitsmaßnahme** *f* SICHERHEIT safety measure; **Sicherheitsmeißelgriff** *m* SICHERHEIT safety handle for chisels; **Sicherheitsmindestgeschwindigkeit beim Start** *f* LUFTTRANS minimum takeoff safety speed; **Sicherheitsmindesthöhe** *f* LUFTTRANS minimum safe altitude; **Sicherheitsmotorhaube** *f* KFZTECH safety bonnet (BrE), safety hood (AmE); **Sicherheitsmutter** *f* MASCHINEN safety nut, self-locking nut; **Sicherheitsnetz** *nt* SICHERHEIT safety net; **Sicherheitsplakat** *nt* LABOR safety placard; **Sicherheitsprotokoll** *nt* BAU safety record; **Sicherheitsregel** *f* SICHERHEIT safety rule; **Sicherheitsrichtlinie** *f* EISENBAHN, KFZTECH, LUFTTRANS, TRANS, WASSERTRANS safety recommendation; **Sicherheitsrisiko** *nt* SICHERHEIT safety risk; **Sicherheitsrohr** *nt* LABOR safety tube; **Sicherheitssalbe** *f* SICHERHEIT occupational safety cream; **Sicherheitsschalter** *m* ELEKTRIZ, ELEKTROTECH safety

switch; **Sicherheitsschiene** *f* EISENBAHN safety rail; **Sicherheitsschirm** *m* LABOR safety screen; **Sicherheitsschloß** *nt* BAU safety lock; **Sicherheitsschlüssel** *m* COMP & DV security identification; **Sicherheitsschranke** *f* SICHERHEIT safety barrier; **Sicherheitsschuh** *m* SICHERHEIT safety boot; **Sicherheitsschuhe** *m pl* SICHERHEIT protective footwear; **Sicherheitssperre** *f* COMP & DV interlock; **Sicherheitsstiefel** *m* SICHERHEIT safety boot; **Sicherheitssystem** *nt* KERNTECH safety system, SICHERHEIT safety equipment; **Sicherheitstank** *m* SICHERHEIT safety storage tank; **Sicherheitstechnik** *f* SICHERHEIT safety engineering

sicherheitstechnisch: **~e Anforderungen** *f pl* ERGON safety requirements; **~e Anlage** *f* QUAL safety system

Sicherheit: **Sicherheitstor** *nt* BAU safety door; **Sicherheitstraining** *nt* SICHERHEIT safety education; **Sicherheitstrichter** *m* LABOR safety funnel; **Sicherheitstür** *f* BAU safety door, SICHERHEIT security door; **Sicherheitsumlenkrolle** *f* SICHERHEIT safety pulley block; **Sicherheitsventil** *nt* EISENBAHN overflow valve, HEIZ & KÄLTE relief valve, safety valve, HYDRAUL escape valve, *Dampfkessel* safety valve, KFZTECH *Schmierung* relief valve, MASCHINEN air valve, MECHAN safety valve, NICHTFOSS ENERG relief valve, SICHERHEIT safety valve; **Sicherheitsverankerung** *f* KFZTECH seat belt anchorage; **Sicherheitsverpackung** *f* VERPACK barrier packaging; **Sicherheitsverschluß** *m* SICHERHEIT safety clamp, VERPACK safety closure; **Sicherheitsvorhang** *m* SICHERHEIT safety curtain; **Sicherheitsvorkehrung** *f* SICHERHEIT safety precaution; **Sicherheitsvorrichtung** *f* MASCHINEN safety apparatus, safety device; **Sicherheitsvorschrift** *f* EISENBAHN, KFZTECH, LUFTTRANS safety specification, SICHERHEIT factory safety regulation, safety code, safety instruction, safety requirement, *behördlich* safety regulation, TRANS, WASSERTRANS safety specification; **Sicherheitsvorschrift und -überwachung** *f* SICHERHEIT safety requirement and supervision; **Sicherheitszone am Ende der Start- und Landebahn** *f* LUFTTRANS runway-end safety area

Sichern *nt* COMP & DV save

sichern *vt* BAU secure, COMP & DV save, *Daten* back up, MECHAN lock

Sicherung:[1] **durch ~ geschützt** *adj* ELEKTROTECH fuse-protected

Sicherung[2] *f* COMP & DV backup, ELEKTRIZ fuse, ELEKTROTECH backup, fuse, FERNSEH fuse, MASCHINEN locking device, RADIO fuse; **~ mit Alarm und Signalgeber** *f* ELEKTRIZ alarm fuse; **~ der mittleren Qualität** *f* QUAL average quality protection; **~ einer Qualität je Los** *nt* QUAL lot quality protection; **Sicherungsanordnung** *f* ELEKTROTECH fuse array; **Sicherungsautomat** *m* ELEKTRIZ expulsion fuse; **Sicherungsbereich** *m* COMP & DV save area; **Sicherungsblech** *nt* MASCHINEN lock plate, locking plate; **Sicherungsblech mit Nase** *nt* MECHAN tab washer; **Sicherungsbolzen** *m* WASSERTRANS *Decksausrüstung* safety pin; **Sicherungsboot** *nt* WASSERTRANS *Marine* seaward defence boat (BrE), seaward defense boat (AmE); **Sicherungsbrett** *nt* ELEKTROTECH fuseboard; **Sicherungsbrücke** *f* ELEKTRIZ link fuse; **Sicherungsbügel** *m* KFZTECH *Motor* circlip; **Sicherungsdatei** *f* COMP & DV save file; **Sicherungsdraht** *m* ELEKTRIZ, ELEKTROTECH fuse wire; **Sicherungseinsatz** *m* ELEKTRIZ fuse link; **Sicherungselement** *nt* ELEKTRIZ, ELEKTROTECH fuse link; **Sicherungsfach** *nt* KFZTECH *KFZ-Elektrik* fuse box;

Sicherungsfassung *f* ELEKTROTECH fuse holder; **Sicherungsfeder** *f* MASCHINEN retaining spring; **Sicherungsglied** *nt* ELEKTRIZ link fuse; **Sicherungsgriff** *m* ELEKTROTECH *bei Rohrpatronensicherung* fuse carrier; **Sicherungshalter** *m* ELEKTROTECH, FERNSEH fuse holder; **Sicherungskasten** *m* ELEKTRIZ, ELEKTROTECH, KFZTECH *KFZ-Elektrik* fuse box; **Sicherungskette** *f* SICHERHEIT safety chain; **Sicherungskopie** *f* COMP & DV backup, *auf Magnetband* back-up tape, security copy; **Sicherungslasche** *f* FERNSEH record defeat tab; **Sicherungsleiste** *f* ELEKTRIZ fuse strip; **Sicherungsmutter** *f* KFZTECH locknut, MASCHINEN locknut, pinch nut, MECHAN locknut; **Sicherungsnut** *f* KFZTECH lock groove; **Sicherungspatrone** *f* ELEKTROTECH enclosed fuse; **Sicherungsposten** *m* EISENBAHN flagman; **Sicherungsraste** *f* MASCHINEN safety catch; **Sicherungsring** *m* KFZTECH *Motor* circlip, MASCHINEN circlip, retaining ring, snap ring; **Sicherungsschaltung** *f* EISENBAHN signaling wiring diagram (AmE), signalling wiring diagram (BrE); **Sicherungsscheibe** *f* FERTIG retaining washer, MECHAN lock washer; **Sicherungsschicht** *f* TELEKOM data link layer; **Sicherungsschmelzstreifen** *m* ELEKTRIZ fuse strip; **Sicherungsspeicher** *m* COMP & DV backing storage (AmE), backing store (BrE); **Sicherungsstift** *m* MASCHINEN locking pin; **Sicherungstafel** *f* ELEKTROTECH fuseboard

Sicht *f* EISENBAHN, KFZTECH sight, LUFTTRANS sight, visibility, RAUMFAHRT optical sight, TRANS, WASSERTRANS sight, visibility; **~ am Boden** *f* LUFTTRANS ground visibility; **Sichtanflug** *m* RAUMFAHRT visual approach; **Sichtanflugpiste** *f* LUFTTRANS noninstrument runway; **Sichtanzeige** *f* COMP & DV readout, GERÄT visual display, PHYS visual display unit; **Sichtanzeige im Fahrzeug** *f* KFZTECH in-vehicle visual display

sichtbar: **~es Feld** *nt* OPTIK visual field; **~e Fläche** *f* PHYS face; **~es Gebiet** *nt* NICHTFOSS ENERG visible region; **~er Horizont** *m* WASSERTRANS *astronomische Navigation* visible horizon; **~e Laserlinien** *f pl* STRAHLPHYS visible laser lines; **~es Licht** *nt* TELEKOM visible light; **~e Seite** *f* GEOM visible face; **~es Spektrum** *nt* PHYS visible spectrum; **~e Strahlung** *f* OPTIK, TELEKOM visible radiation

Sicht: **Sichtbarkeit** *f* PHYS visibility; **Sichtbarmachung** *f* COMP & DV visualization

sichten *vt* CHEMTECH classify

Sicht: **Sichtentfernung** *f* RADIO line-of-sight distance

Sichter *m* KER & GLAS classifier

Sicht: **Sichtfeld** *nt* OPTIK visual field; **Sichtfenster** *nt* COMP & DV viewing window; **Sichtfläche** *f* BAU face, front; **Sichtflächen** *f pl* HEIZ & KÄLTE exposed surfaces; **Sichtflug** *m* LUFTTRANS contact flight; **Sichtfolie** *f* KONSTZEICH transparent film; **Sichtfunkpeiler** *m* TELEKOM cathode-ray direction finder; **Sichtgerät** *nt* COMP & DV display device, GERÄT display device, visual display, RADIO *Radar* display unit, RAUMFAHRT optical sight, TELEKOM visual display unit; **Sichtgitter** *nt* BAU screen; **Sichtglas** *nt* VERPACK inspection window, liquid level indicator; **Sichtglasöler** *m* MASCHINEN sight feed oiler; **Sichtgrenze** *f* LUFTTRANS, TRANS, WASSERTRANS visibility limit

sichtig: **~es Wetter** *nt* EISENBAHN, WASSERTRANS clear weather

Sicht: **Sichtkontrolle** *f* QUAL visual examination; **Sichtli-** nie *f* OPTIK line of sight, line of vision; **Sichtliniensignal** *nt* ELEKTRONIK line-of-sight signal; **Sichtlinienwinkel** *m* TELEKOM angle of sight; **Sichtloch** *nt* MASCHINEN sight hole; **Sichtmelder** *m* GERÄT annunciator; **Sichtprüfmenge** *f* QUAL inspection test quantity; **Sichtprüfung** *f* METROL visual inspection, QUAL VT, visual testing, visual examination, visual inspection, WERKPRÜF visual inspection; **Sichtprüfung der Fahrwerksausfahrverriegelung** *f* LUFTTRANS landing-gear downlock visual check; **Sichtscheibe** *f* COMP & DV viewing window; **Sichtschutz** *m* ABFALL *einer Deponie* screen; **Sichttafel** *f* GERÄT annunciator; **Sichtverhältnisse** *nt pl* EISENBAHN sighting; **Sichtvermerk** *m* KONSTZEICH endorsement; **Sichtweite** *f* BAU sight distance, EISENBAHN sight distance, sighting distance, KFZTECH sight distance, LUFTTRANS sight distance, visibility, visibility distance, OPTIK reach, TRANS, WASSERTRANS sight distance, visibility, visibility distance; **Sichtweitenmeßinstrument** *nt* LUFTTRANS, TRANS, WASSERTRANS visibility distance measuring equipment; **Sichtzeichengeber** *m* RAUMFAHRT annunciator

Sicke *f* BAU bead, FERTIG crease, dimple, reinforcing crease, MASCHINEN bead

Sicken *nt* MASCHINEN beading, crimping

sicken *vt* FERTIG crease, MASCHINEN bead, crimp

Sickenmaschine *f* FERTIG flanging machine

Sickerbecken *nt* ABFALL infiltration basin

Sickerbrunnen *m* WASSERVERSORG dry well

Sickern *nt* WASSERVERSORG seepage

Sickerschlitz *m* BAU weephole

Sickerstrahlung *f* ELEKTROTECH leakage radiation

Sickerwasser *nt* ABFALL leakage water, percolating water, seepage water, CHEMIE seepage water, KOHLEN gravitational water, METALL soakage water, WASSERVERSORG leak water, percolating water

siderisch: **~es Jahr** *nt* PHYS sidereal year; **~er Tag** *m* PHYS sidereal day; **~e Zeit** *f* RAUMFAHRT *Sternzeit* sidereal time

Siderit *m* METALL siderite

sideromagnetisch *adj* METALL sideromagnetic

Siderurgie *f* METALL siderurgy

Sieb *nt* ABFALL screening equipment, BAU screen, sieve, ELEKTRONIK *Netzwerk* filter, ERDÖL strainer, FERTIG ratter, screen, sifter, HEIZ & KÄLTE strainer, KER & GLAS silk screen, KFZTECH strainer, KOHLEN screen, sieve, LABOR sieve, MASCHINEN strainer, MECHAN screen, PAPIER wire, TEXTIL screen; **Siebanalyse** *f* CHEMTECH sieve analysis, *Minerale* sieve classification, KER & GLAS screen analysis, KERNTECH sieve analysis, KOHLEN screen analysis, sieve analysis; **Siebanlage** *f* KOHLEN screening plant; **Siebantriebswalze** *f* PAPIER wire drive roll; **Siebbereich** *m* BAU *Diagramm* grading envelope; **Siebblech** *nt* BAU punched-plate screen, KERNTECH perforated plate, KOHLEN screen plate; **Siebboden** *m* CHEMTECH sieve bottom, sieve plate, sieve tray; **Siebbohrloch** *nt* FERTIG *Kunststoffinstallationen* screen perforation; **Siebbüchse** *f* CHEMTECH sieve frame; **Siebdämpfung** *f* ELEKTRONIK filter attenuation; **Siebdrossel** *f* ELEKTROTECH filter choke, swinging choke; **Siebdruck** *m* DRUCK serigraphy, KER & GLAS screen printing, VERPACK silk screen printing; **Siebdruckmaschine** *f* VERPACK screen printing machine; **Siebdurchfall** *m* KOHLEN duff, underflow; **Siebdurchgang** *m* FERTIG sifting, KOHLEN screenings, MASCHINEN sieving; **Siebdurchlauf** *m* KOHLEN fines

Sieben *nt* ABFALL screening, BAU grading, screening, sieving, FERTIG, MEERSCHMUTZ screening

sieben *vt* BAU *Erde* screen, CHEMTECH sieve, FERTIG strain, LEBENSMITTEL sieve, sift, MEERSCHMUTZ sift, PAPIER screen

Sieben *f* MATH seven; **Siebeneck** *nt* FERTIG, GEOM heptagon

siebeneckig *adj* FERTIG, GEOM heptagonal

siebenflächig *adj* FERTIG heptahedral

Sieben: **Siebenflächner** *m* GEOM heptahedron; **Sieben-Schichten-Modell** *nt* TELEKOM *OSI* seven layer model; **Sieben-Schicht-Referenzmodell** *nt* COMP & DV *ISO/OSI* seven layer reference model; **Siebentonleiter** *f* AKUSTIK heptatonic scale

siebenwertig *adj* CHEMIE heptavalent, septivalent, FERTIG heptavalent

Siebereifeinkohle *f* KOHLEN duff

Sieb: **Siebfeines** *nt* KOHLEN fines; **Siebfilter** *nt* MEERSCHMUTZ strainer; **Siebfläche** *f* KOHLEN screening surface; **Siebfraktion** *f* KER & GLAS sieve fraction; **Siebgeflecht** *nt* KOHLEN sieve mesh; **Siebgeschwindigkeit** *f* CHEMTECH sieving rate; **Siebgewebe** *nt* CHEMTECH sieve cloth, KUNSTSTOFF filter screen, PAPIER wire cloth; **Siebglied** *nt* ELEKTRONIK filter element; **Siebkäfig** *m* FERTIG *Kunststoffinstallationen* screen cage; **Siebkette** *f* RADIO ladder filter

siebklassieren *vt* CHEMTECH *Erz* sieve

Sieb: **Siebklassierung** *f* CHEMTECH sieve classification; **Siebkohle** *f* KOHLEN sifted coal; **Siebkondensator** *m* ELEKTROTECH filter capacitor; **Siebkopf** *m* LABOR *Analyse* bolthead; **Siebkopfkolben** *m* LABOR *Analyse* bolthead flask (BrE), matrass (AmE); **Siebkurve** *f* KOHLEN grading curve; **Sieblaufregler** *m* PAPIER wire guide; **Siebleder** *nt* PAPIER apron; **Sieblederbrett** *nt* PAPIER apron board; **Sieblederlippe** *f* PAPIER apron lip; **Siebleitwalze** *f* PAPIER wire guide roll; **Sieblinie** *f* KOHLEN grading curve; **Siebmasche** *f* FERTIG mesh; **Siebpartie** *f* PAPIER wire end; **Siebrahmen** *m* CHEMTECH sieve frame, PAPIER wire frame; **Siebrest** *m* ABFALL screenings; **Siebrohr** *nt* FERTIG *Kunststoffinstallationen* screen; **Siebrost** *m* CHEMTECH sieve grate, KOHLEN grizzly; **Siebrückstand** *m* ABFALL, KOHLEN screenings; **Siebrückstände** *m pl* LEBENSMITTEL *Müllerei* tailings; **Siebsatz** *m* CHEMTECH sieve set; **Siebsaugwalze** *f* PAPIER suction roll; **Siebschaltung** *f* ELEKTRONIK ripple filter; **Siebscheuersand** *m* ANSTRICH mesh abrasive grit; **Siebschüttler** *m* LABOR sieve shaker; **Siebseite** *f* DRUCK, PAPIER wire side; **Siebspannvorrichtung** *f* PAPIER wire stretcher; **Siebtest** *m* CHEMTECH sieve test; **Siebtisch** *m* KOHLEN sieve table; **Siebtrockner** *m* CHEMTECH sieve drier, sieve dryer; **Siebtrommel** *f* BAU rotary screen, CHEMTECH sieve drum, KOHLEN revolving screen; **Siebtrommelzentrifuge** *f* KOHLEN basket centrifuge; **Siebtuch** *nt* KER & GLAS bolting cloth, PAPIER forming fabric, TEXTIL bolting fabric; **Siebumlenkwalze** *f* PAPIER wire return roll

Siebung *f* MEERSCHMUTZ, UMWELTSCHMUTZ sieving

Sieb: **Siebwalze** *f* PAPIER wire roll; **Siebweite** *f* PAPIER mesh; **Siebwirkungsgrad** *m* KOHLEN screening efficiency

Siedebarometer *nt* PHYS hypsometer

Siedebereich *m* ERDÖL *Destillation*, KUNSTSTOFF boiling range

Siedeblech *nt* CHEMTECH boiling plate

Sieden *nt* LEBENSMITTEL, THERMOD boiling; **~ im Behäl-** **ter** *nt* HEIZ & KÄLTE pool boiling

sieden *vi* THERMOD boil

siedend *adj* THERMOD boiling

Siedepunkt *m* KUNSTSTOFF, LEBENSMITTEL, MASCHINEN, PHYS, THERMOD boiling point; **Siedepunktkurve** *f* THERMOD liquid vapor equilibrium diagram (AmE), liquid vapour equilibrium diagram (BrE); **Siedepunktserhöhung** *f* MASCHINEN boiling point elevation

Siedereaktor *m* KERNTECH boiling reactor

Siederkessel *m* HYDRAUL elephant boiler

Siederohrkessel *m* HEIZ & KÄLTE water tube boiler

Siederrohrwalze *f* HYDRAUL boiler tube expander

Siedewasserreaktor *m (SWR)* KERNTECH, PHYS boiling light water moderated reactor, boiling water reactor; **~ mit Naturumlauf** *m* KERNTECH natural circulation boiling water reactor

Siedlungsabfall *m* ABFALL municipal waste, urban solid waste, urban waste

Siegel *nt* BAU sealing; **Siegelkappe** *f* VERPACK sealing cap; **Siegelmaschine** *f* VERPACK sealing machine; **Siegeltemperatur** *f* VERPACK heat seal temperature

SI-Einheit *f (internationales Einheitensystem)* ELEKTRIZ, METROL, PHYS SI unit *(international system of units)*

Siemens *nt (S)* METROL *Einheit der Leitfähigkeit* siemens *(S)*; **Siemens-Martin-Ofen** *m* FERTIG open hearth furnace; **Siemens-Martin-Stahl** *m* METALL Siemens-Martin steel, open hearth steel; **Siemens-Martin-Verfahren** *nt* METALL Siemens-Martin process

Sievert *m (Sv)* PHYS *Einheit*, STRAHLPHYS, TEILPHYS Sievert *(Sv)*

Sigma *nt* MATH sigma; **Sigmaschweißung** *f (SMAW)* KERNTECH shielded metal arc welding *(SMAW)*; **Sigmateilchen** *nt* PHYS sigma particle; **Sigmaverstärker** *m* KERNTECH sigma amplifier

σ *abbr* BAU σ, KOHLEN, KUNSTSTOFF, MECHAN σ, PHYS, THERMOD σ

Signal *nt* AKUSTIK signal, BAU *Vermessung* beacon, COMP & DV signal, EISENBAHN marker, signal, PHYS, WASSERTRANS signal; **~ für das Einphasen** *nt* ELEKTRONIK phasing signal; **~ mit hoher Amplitude** *nt* ELEKTRONIK high-amplitude signal; **~ mit kurzer Anstiegszeit** *nt* ELEKTRONIK fast-rise signal; **~ mit niedriger Amplitude** *nt* ELEKTRONIK low-amplitude signal; **~ mit scharfer Begrenzung** *nt* ELEKTRONIK hard-limited signal; **~ in Schleife** *nt* TELEKOM looped signal; **Signalabfall** *m* COMP & DV decay; **Signalabfallzeit** *f* COMP & DV decay time; **Signalabhängigkeit** *f* EISENBAHN signal interlocking; **Signalagilität** *f* ELEKTRONIK signal agility; **Signalamplitude** *f* ELEKTRONIK signal amplitude; **Signalanalysator** *m* STRAHLPHYS, TELEKOM signal analyser (BrE), signal analyzer (AmE); **Signalanalyse** *f* ELEKTRONIK, TELEKOM signal analysis; **Signalanalyseeinrichtung** *f* ELEKTRONIK signal analyser (BrE), signal analyzer (AmE); **Signalanlage** *f* EISENBAHN signal installation; **Signalantrieb** *m* EISENBAHN signal operating gear; **Signalaufbereitung** *f* ELEKTRONIK signal conditioning; **Signalauffrischung** *f* ELEKTRONIK signal regeneration; **Signalaufteiler** *m* FERNSEH signal splitter; **Signalausfall** *m* AUFNAHME, COMP & DV, ELEKTROTECH drop-out, RAUMFAHRT blackout; **Signalbandbreite** *f* ELEKTRONIK signal bandwidth; **Signalbegrenzung** *f* ELEKTRONIK signal clipping; **Signalbildung** *f* ELEKTRONIK signal generation; **Signalbuch** *nt* WASSERTRANS signal book; **Signalbuchflagge** *f* WAS-

SERTRANS code flag; **Signaldämpfung durch unkorrekte Lese-/Schreibkopfausrichtung** *f* COMP & DV gap loss; **Signaldehnung** *f* TELEKOM signal extension; **Signaldemodulator** *m* TELEKOM signal detector; **Signaldetektor** *m* TELEKOM signal detector; **Signal-Digitalisierer** *m* ELEKTRONIK signal digitizer; **Signaleinhüllende** *f* TELEKOM signal envelope; **Signaleinspeisung** *f* RADIO injection, signal injection; **Signaleinsteller** *m* REGELUNG signal adjuster; **Signalelektrode** *f* ELEKTRONIK signal electrode; **Signalerfassung** *f* TELEKOM signal detection; **Signalerzeuger** *m* PHYS signal generator; **Signalexpandierung** *f* TELEKOM signal expansion; **Signalflagge** *f* EISENBAHN signal flag; **Signalflanke** *f* ELEKTRONIK signal edge; **Signalformung** *f* COMP & DV, ELEKTRONIK signal shaping; **Signalformungsfilter** *nt* TELEKOM signal-shaping filter; **Signalfrequenz** *f* (*SF*) ELEKTRONIK, FERNSEH, RADIO, TELEKOM signal frequency (*SF*); **Signalgabe** *f* TELEKOM signaling (AmE), signalling (BrE); **Signalgabeentfernung** *f* TRANS signaling distance (AmE), signalling distance (BrE); **Signalgeber** *m* ELEKTRONIK signal generator, ELEKTROTECH transducer; **Signalgeber mit Frequenzaufbereitung** *m* ELEKTRONIK synthesized signal generator; **Signalgenerator** *m* PHYS, TELEKOM signal generator; **Signalgruppensteuerung** *f* TRANS master control; **Signalhorn** *nt* WASSERTRANS horn

Signalisieren *nt* WASSERTRANS signalling (BrE)

signalisieren *vt* WASSERTRANS signal

Signalisierung *f* COMP & DV, TELEKOM signaling (AmE), signalling (BrE); **Signalisierungsprotokoll** *nt* COMP & DV signaling protocol (AmE), signalling protocol (BrE)

Signal: **Signalkomplex** *m* FERNSEH signal complex; **Signalkompression** *f* TELEKOM signal compression; **Signalkomprimierungsausdehnung** *f* RAUMFAHRT companding; **Signallampe** *f* ELEKTROTECH pilot lamp, FERNSEH tally light, GERÄT annunciator, KONTROLL signal light; **Signallaterne** *f* EISENBAHN signal lamp; **Signallaufzeit** *f* TELEKOM signal delay; **Signalleistung** *f* ELEKTRONIK signal power; **Signalleitung** *f* ELEKTROTECH signal line; **Signalleuchte** *f* FERNSEH cue light, KONTROLL signal light; **Signalmeister** *m* WASSERTRANS *Marine* yeoman of signals; **Signalmittelung** *f* GERÄT signal averaging; **Signalmodellierung** *f* ELEKTRONIK signal modeling (AmE), signal modelling (BrE); **Signalpegel** *m* ELEKTRONIK, TELEKOM signal level; **Signalpegelmeßgerät** *nt* GERÄT signal level meter; **Signalpfeife** *f* MASCHINEN alarm whistle; **Signalphase** *f* ELEKTRONIK signal phase; **Signalplatte** *f* ELEKTRONIK signal plate; **Signalprozessor** *m* ELEKTRONIK, FERNSEH, TELEKOM signal processor; **Signal-Rausch-Abstand** *m* TELEKOM signal-to-noise ratio; **Signal-Rausch-Verhältnis** *nt* GERÄT, PHYS signal-to-noise ratio; **Signalregenerator** *m* ELEKTRONIK signal regenerator; **Signalschwankung** *f* RAUMFAHRT ripple; **Signalschwelle** *f* TELEKOM signal threshold; **Signalsimulierung** *f* ELEKTRONIK signal simulation; **Signalstation** *f* EISENBAHN signal station; **Signalstellung** *f* EISENBAHN position of a signal; **Signalstern** *m* WASSERTRANS Very light; **Signalstreuung an Meteoren** *f* RADIO meteor scatter; **Signalstruktur** *f* REGELUNG signal structure; **Signalsynthese** *f* ELEKTRONIK signal synthesis; **Signaltafel** *f* ELEKTROTECH annunciator; **Signaltechnik** *f* COMP & DV signaling system (AmE), signalling system (BrE); **Signalteilung** *f* EISENBAHN

signal spacing; **Signaltrommel** *f* AUFNAHME sound drum; **Signalübermittlung** *f* EISENBAHN signal transmission; **Signalübertragung** *f* TELEKOM signal transmission; **Signalübertragung außerhalb des Bandes** *f* RAUMFAHRT out-of-band signaling (AmE), out-of-band signalling (BrE); **Signalumsetzer** *m* COMP & DV, ELEKTRONIK, FERNSEH modulator, REGELUNG signal converter, TELEKOM modulator, signal converter; **Signalumsetzerwechsel** *m* COMP & DV, ELEKTRONIK modem interchange; **Signalumsetzung** *f* TELEKOM signal conversion; **Signalverarbeitung** *f* COMP & DV, ELEKTRONIK, KÜNSTL INT, REGELUNG, TELEKOM signal processing; **Signalverarbeitung auf Frequenzebene** *f* ELEKTRONIK, RADIO, TELEKOM frequency-domain signal processing; **Signalverarbeitung in der Zeitebene** *f* ELEKTRONIK time domain signal processing; **Signalverarbeitungschip** *m* ELEKTRONIK signal processing chip; **Signalverfolgung** *f* RADIO signal tracing; **Signalvergleich** *m* ELEKTRONIK signal comparison; **Signalvergleicher** *m* GERÄT comparing element; **Signalverstärker** *m* ELEKTRONIK low-level amplifier; **Signalverstärkung** *f* ELEKTRONIK low-level amplification; **Signalverteiler** *m* TELEKOM signal distributor; **Signalverzerrung** *f* ELEKTRONIK, TELEKOM signal distortion; **Signalverzögerung** *f* ELEKTRONIK, TELEKOM signal delay; **Signalverzögerung innerhalb des Chips** *f* ELEKTRONIK interchip signal delay; **Signalverzögerung im Schaltkreis** *f* ELEKTRONIK intercircuit signal delay; **Signalwandler** *m* ELEKTROTECH converter, REGELUNG, TELEKOM signal converter

Signatur *f* DRUCK nick; **Signaturnummer** *f* DRUCK signature number

signifikant: **~es Prüfergebnis** *nt* QUAL significant test result; **~e Ziffern** *f pl* MATH significant figures

Signifikanzprüfung *f* COMP & DV significance test

Signifikanztest *m* COMP & DV significance test, WERKPRÜF statistical test

Sikkativ *nt* CHEMIE desiccant, CHEMTECH desiccative, KUNSTSTOFF drier, dryer, drying agent, exsiccant, THERMOD desiccant, siccative

sikkativverpackt *adj* VERPACK packed with siccative

Silan *nt* CHEMIE monosilane, silicomethane, KUNSTSTOFF silane

Silbenkompandierung *f* TELEKOM syllabic companding

Silbentrennstrich *m* COMP & DV soft hyphen

Silbentrennungsprogramm *nt* DRUCK hyphenation program

Silbenverständlichkeit *f* TELEKOM logatom articulation; **Silbenverständlichkeitstest** *m* TELEKOM syllable articulation test

Silber *nt* (*Ag*) CHEMIE silver (*Ag*); **Silberbatterie** *f* ELEKTROTECH silver battery; **Silberbeizen** *nt* KER & GLAS silver staining; **Silberchlorid** *nt* ELEKTROTECH silver chloride; **Silberchloridemulsion** *f* FOTO silver chloride emulsion; **Silberelektrode** *f* LABOR *Elektrochemie* silver electrode; **Silberelement** *nt* ELEKTROTECH silver cell; **Silbergehalt** *m* FOTO silver content; **Silbergehäuse-Tantalkondensator** *m* ELEKTROTECH silver case tantalum capacitor; **Silbergeschirr** *nt* LEBENSMITTEL silverware; **Silber-Glimmer-Kondensator** *m* ELEKTROTECH silver mica capacitor; **Silberhalogenid** *nt* FOTO silver halide; **Silberhalogenidpapier** *nt* FOTO silver halide paper; **Silberhalogenidschicht** *f* FOTO silver halide emulsion

silberhell: **~e Stimme** *f* AKUSTIK silver voice

Silber: **Silberjodid** *nt* FOTO silver iodide; **Silber-Kadmium-Batterie** *f* ELEKTROTECH silver-cadmium battery; **Silber-Kadmium-Element** *nt* ELEKTROTECH silver-cadmium cell; **Silber-Kadmium-Zelle** *f* ELEKTROTECH silver-cadmium cell; **Silberkontakt** *m* ELEKTROTECH silver contact; **Silberlegierung** *f* FERTIG silver alloy; **Silberlot** *nt* FERTIG silver solder, MASCHINEN silver filler; **Silberlöten** *nt* ELEKTRIZ hard-soldering

Silberoxid *nt* ELEKTROTECH silver oxide; **Silberoxidakkumulator** *m* KFZTECH silver oxide storage battery; **Silberoxidbatterie** *f* ELEKTROTECH silver oxide battery; **Silberoxidelement** *nt* ELEKTROTECH silver oxide cell; **Silberoxidzelle** *f* ELEKTROTECH silver oxide cell

silberplattiert[1] *adj* FERTIG silver-clad

silberplattiert:[2] **~er Kontakt** *m* ELEKTROTECH silver-plated contact

Silber: **Silberrest** *m* FOTO residual silver; **Silberstahl** *m* MASCHINEN silver steel; **Silberzelle** *f* ELEKTROTECH silver cell; **Silber-Zink-Akkuelement** *nt* ELEKTROTECH silver-zinc storage cell; **Silber-Zink-Akkumulator** *m* ELEKTROTECH, KFZTECH silver-zinc storage battery; **Silber-Zink-Akkuzelle** *f* ELEKTROTECH silver-zinc storage cell; **Silber-Zink-Batterie** *f* ELEKTROTECH silver-zinc battery; **Silber-Zink-Element** *nt* ELEKTROTECH silver-zinc cell; **Silber-Zink-Primärbatterie** *f* ELEKTROTECH silver-zinc primary battery; **Silber-Zink-Primärelement** *nt* ELEKTROTECH silver-zinc primary cell; **Silber-Zink-Primärzelle** *f* ELEKTROTECH silver-zinc primary cell; **Silber-Zink-Zelle** *f* ELEKTROTECH silver-zinc cell

Silika *f* KER & GLAS silica; **Silikagel** *nt* VERPACK blue silica gel; **Silikaglas** *nt* KER & GLAS, OPTIK, TELEKOM vitreous silica; **Silikamasse** *f* CHEMIE silica; **Silikamaterial** *nt* CHEMIE *Keramik* silica; **Silikaschaum** *m* KER & GLAS silica scum; **Silikaschaumgrenze** *f* KER & GLAS batch-melting line (AmE), silica scum line (BrE); **Silikat** *nt* CHEMIE silicate

Silikatglas *nt* KER & GLAS, OPTIK, TELEKOM vitreous silica; **Silikatglasfaser** *f* OPTIK all-silica fiber (AmE), all-silica fibre (BrE), TELEKOM all-silica fiber (AmE), all-silica fibre (BrE), silica fiber (AmE), silica fibre (BrE); **Silikatglas-Lichtwellenleiter mit Kunststoffmantel** *m* TELEKOM plastic-clad silica fiber (AmE), plastic-clad silica fibre (BrE)

silikatisch *adj* CHEMIE siliceous

Silikatverbundfenster *nt* RAUMFAHRT *Raumschiff* fused silica window

Silikid *nt* CHEMIE silicide

Silikofluorid *nt* CHEMIE silicofluoride

Silikon *nt* ELEKTRIZ, ELEKTROTECH, KUNSTSTOFF, WASSERTRANS silicone; **Silikonauskleidung** *f* ELEKTROTECH silicone cladding; **Silikonelastomer** *nt* KUNSTSTOFF silicone elastomer; **Silikonflüssigkeit** *f* ELEKTRIZ silicone fluid; **Silikongummi** *nt* ELEKTRIZ silicone rubber

Silikonisieren *nt* KER & GLAS siliconing

Silikon: **Silikonkautschuk** *m* KUNSTSTOFF silicone rubber; **Silikonmasse** *f* WASSERTRANS silicone compound; **Silikonverkleidung** *f* ELEKTROTECH silicone cladding; **Silikonzelle** *f* NICHTFOSS ENERG silicon cell

Silizieren *nt* KER & GLAS siliconizing

Silizimoxid *nt* ELEKTRONIK silicon oxide

Silizium:[1] **mit ~ beruhigt** *adj* FERTIG silicon-killed

Silizium[2] *nt* CHEMIE *(Si)* silicon *(Si)*, COMP & DV, ELEKTRIZ, ELEKTRONIK, ELEKTROTECH, PHYS, WASSERTRANS silicon; **~ auf Saphir** *nt* *(SOS)* ELEKTRONIK silicon-on-sapphire *(SOS)*; **~ auf Saphir-Substrat** *nt* RADIO silicon on sapphire technology; **~ FET** *m* ELEKTRONIK silicon FET; **~ vom Typ n** *nt* ELEKTRONIK n-type silicon

Siliziumbauelement: **im ~ einspeichern** *vt* ELEKTRONIK commit to silicon

Silizium: **Silizium-Bipolartransistor** *m* ELEKTRONIK silicon bipolar transistor; **Siliziumbronze** *f* METALL silicon bronze; **Siliziumchip** *m* COMP & DV, ELEKTRIZ, ELEKTRONIK, STRAHLPHYS silicon chip; **Siliziumdetektor** *m* ELEKTRONIK silicon detector; **Siliziumdetektordiode** *f* ELEKTRONIK silicon detector diode; **Siliziumdiode** *f* ELEKTRONIK silicon diode; **Siliziumdioxid** *nt* CHEMIE silica

siliziumdioxidhaltig *adj* CHEMIE siliceous

Silizium: **Siliziumdotierung** *f* ELEKTRONIK silicon doping; **Silizium-Epitaxialschicht** *f* ELEKTRONIK silicon epitaxial layer; **Silizium-Flächendiode** *f* ELEKTRONIK silicon junction diode; **Silizium-Fotodiode** *f* ELEKTRONIK silicon photodiode; **Silizium-Fototransistor** *m* ELEKTRONIK silicon phototransistor; **Silizium-Gate-Transistor** *m* ELEKTRONIK silicon gate transistor; **Siliziumgatter** *nt* ELEKTRONIK silicon gate; **Siliziumgattertechnologie** *f* ELEKTRONIK silicon gate technology; **Siliziumgerät** *nt* ELEKTROTECH silicon device

siliziumgesteuert: **~er Gleichrichter** *m* *(SCR)* ELEKTRONIK, ELEKTROTECH silicon-controlled rectifier *(SCR)*

Silizium: **Silizium-Gießerei** *f* ELEKTRONIK silicon foundry; **Siliziumgleichrichter** *m* ELEKTRIZ, ELEKTROTECH silicon rectifier, PHYS silicon detector, silicon rectifier

Siliziumkarbid *nt* CHEMIE carborundum, silicon carbide, ELEKTROTECH, FERTIG, PHYS silicon carbide; **Siliziumkarbidvaristor** *m* ELEKTROTECH silicon carbide varistor

Siliziumkristall *m* ELEKTRONIK silicon crystal; **Siliziumkristallmischer** *m* ELEKTRONIK silicon crystal mixer

Silizium: **Silizium-Lawinenfotodiode** *f* ELEKTRONIK silicon avalanche diode, silicon avalanche photodiode; **Silizium-Miniaturschaltung** *f* COMP & DV silicon chip; **Silizium-Mischdiode** *f* ELEKTRONIK silicon mixer diode; **Silizium-Nachbeschleunigungs-Fangelektrode** *f* ELEKTRONIK silicon intensifier target; **Siliziumnitrid** *nt* ELEKTRONIK silicon nitride

Siliziumoxid *nt* CHEMIE silica, ELEKTRONIK silicon dioxide; **Siliziumoxidschicht** *f* ELEKTRONIK silicon dioxide layer

Silizium: **Siliziumschicht** *f* ELEKTRONIK silicon layer; **Siliziumsolarzelle** *f* ELEKTRONIK silicon solar cell

Siliziumstahl *m* ELEKTROTECH, METALL silicon steel; **Siliziumstahlbeschichtung** *f* ELEKTROTECH silicon steel lamination; **Siliziumstahlkern** *m* ELEKTROTECH silicon steel core

Silizium: **Silizium-Steuerelektronen-Technologie** *f* ELEKTRONIK silicon gate technology; **Silizium-Trägermaterial** *nt* ELEKTRONIK silicon substrate; **Siliziumvorrichtung** *f* ELEKTROTECH silicon device; **Siliziumwasserstoff** *m* CHEMIE monosilane, silicomethane; **Siliziumzähler** *m* STRAHLPHYS silicon checker (AmE), silicon counter (BrE), silicon detector; **Siliziumzelle** *f* ELEKTROTECH silicon cell

Silo *nt* BAU bunker, FERTIG bin; **Silodruck** *m* KOHLEN silo pressure

Siloxan *nt* CHEMIE siloxane

Silt *m* KOHLEN silt; **Siltfeld** *nt* KER & GLAS silt field; **Siltstein** *m* KER & GLAS silt block

SIMD-Rechner m *(Parallelrechner)* COMP & DV SIMD machine *(single instruction multiple-data machine)*
SIMM abbr *(einfaches schritthaltendes Speichermodul)* COMP & DV SIMM *(single in-line memory module)*
Simmerring m MASCHINEN shaft seal, shaft-sealing ring
Simplex- pref COMP & DV, TELEKOM simplex; **~ auf zwei Frequenzen** nt TELEKOM two-frequency simplex; **Simplexbetrieb** m COMP & DV simplex operation; **Simplexkarton** m PAPIER single ply board; **Simplexpumpe** f MASCHINEN simplex pump; **Simplexübertragung** f COMP & DV simplex transmission
SIMS abbr *(Sekundärionenmassenspektrometrie)* PHYS SIMS *(secondary ion mass spectrometry)*
Simsbrett nt BAU fascia board
Simshobel m BAU side rabbet plane
Simulation f COMP & DV, ELEKTRIZ, ELEKTRONIK, ERGON, WERKPRÜF simulation; **Simulationsanlage** f WERKPRÜF simulation equipment; **Simulationsprogramm** nt COMP & DV simulation program; **Simulationssprache** f COMP & DV simulation language
Simulator m COMP & DV, ELEKTRONIK, LUFTTRANS, TELEKOM simulator
simulieren vt COMP & DV simulate
simuliert: ~es Ereignis nt STRAHLPHYS simulated event
simultan[1] adj COMP & DV parallel, simultaneous, KONTROLL simultaneous; **~ verwendbar** adj COMP & DV re-entrant
simultan:[2] **~e Gleichungen** f pl MATH simultaneous equations; **~ verwendbarer Code** m COMP & DV re-entrant code; **~ verwendbares Programm** nt COMP & DV re-entrant program; **~ verwendbare Routine** f COMP & DV re-entrant routine
Simultanrechner m COMP & DV parallel computer
Simultanrundfunk m FERNSEH simulcast broadcasting
Simultanverarbeitung f COMP & DV multiprocessing; **Simultanverarbeitungssystem** nt COMP & DV multiprocessing system
sin abbr *(Sinus)* COMP & DV, GEOM sin *(sine)*
SINAD[1] abbr *(Störabstand einschließlich Verzerrungen)* TELEKOM SINAD *(signal-to-noise and distortion ratio)*
SINAD:[2] **SINAD-Abstand** m TELEKOM SINAD ratio
Sinapin nt CHEMIE sinapine; **Sinapin-** pref CHEMIE sinapic
Single-Jersey m TEXTIL single jersey
Single-Pair-Kabel nt ELEKTROTECH single pair cable
Singularität f PHYS singularity
Singulett nt PHYS *Spektroskopie* singlet
Sinken nt HYDRAUL *Niveau* fall
sinken vi BAU sink, WASSERTRANS go down, sink, *Schiff* founder
Sinkflug: ~ mit Reisefluggeschwindigkeit m LUFTTRANS cruise descent
Sinkgeschwindigkeit f KOHLEN settling speed, LUFTTRANS rate of descent; **~ des Wasserspiegels in der Wasserschicht** f NICHTFOSS ENERG drawdown of water in aquifer
Sinkgrenzwert: ~ des Flugzeugs m LUFTTRANS *Aufsetzen* limit rate of descent
Sinkgut nt MEERSCHMUTZ sinking agent, UMWELTSCHMUTZ deposited matter
Sinkmaterial nt MEERSCHMUTZ sinking agent
Sinkrate f LUFTTRANS rate of descent
Sinkstoff m UMWELTSCHMUTZ deposited matter
Sinkstoffe: m pl ABFALL settleable solids

Sinnenprüfung f LEBENSMITTEL tasting
Sinnesphysiologie f ERGON sensory physiology
sinnfrei: ~e Silbe f AKUSTIK logatom
Sinnverständlichkeit f AUFNAHME intelligibility
sinodisch adj FERTIG sinusoidal
Sinter- pref BAU, ELEKTROTECH, FERTIG, KER & GLAS sintering; **Sinteranode** f ELEKTROTECH sintered anode; **Sinterbeton** m BAU hooped concrete; **Sintererzeugnis** nt FERTIG agglomerate, KER & GLAS sintered refractory; **Sinterglas** nt KER & GLAS sintered glass; **Sinterkohle** f KOHLEN cherry coal, sintering coal; **Sinterkuchen** m KER & GLAS aggregate; **Sintermaterial** nt MASCHINEN sintered material; **Sintermetall** nt FERTIG hard carbide, MASCHINEN sintered metal; **Sintermetallwerkstoff** m MASCHINEN sintered metal material
Sintern nt FERTIG vitrification, KER & GLAS, KOHLEN, METALL sintering
sintern vt CHEMTECH cake, FERTIG bake, coalesce, slag, vitrify, MASCHINEN, METALL sinter
sinternd: ~e Sandkohle f KOHLEN sintering sand coal
Sinter-: Sinterstück nt FERTIG sintering; **Sintertechnik** f CHEMTECH sintering technique; **Sinterteil** nt FERTIG powder metal part; **Sinterung** f FERTIG caking, coalescence, TELEKOM sintering; **Sinterverfahren** nt CHEMTECH sintering technique
Sinus m COMP & DV sinusoid, COMP & DV *(sin)*, GEOM *(sin)* sine *(sin)*; **Sinusaufspannplatte** f METROL sine table; **Sinusbedingungen** f pl ELEKTROTECH sinusoidal conditions; **Sinusbussole** f METROL, PHYS sine galvanometer; **Sinusfeld** nt ELEKTROTECH sinusoidal field
sinusförmig[1] adj ELEKTRIZ, FERTIG sinusoidal
sinusförmig:[2] **~e Bewegung** f PHYS sinusoidal motion; **~es Signal** nt ELEKTRONIK sinusoidal signal; **~e Spannung** f PHYS sinusoidal voltage; **~er Strom** m PHYS sinusoidal current
Sinus: Sinusfunktion f ELEKTRONIK harmonic function, ELEKTROTECH sinusoidal function; **Sinusgröße** f ELEKTROTECH sinusoidal quantity; **Sinuskurve** f COMP & DV sine wave, sinusoid, MATH sine curve; **Sinuslineal** nt METROL sine bar; **Sinuslinie** f GEOM sinusoid; **Sinusmenge** f ELEKTROTECH sinusoidal quantity
Sinusoide f GEOM sinusoid
Sinus: Sinusoszillator m ELEKTRONIK harmonic oscillator; **Sinusquantität** f ELEKTROTECH sinusoidal quantity; **Sinussatz** m GEOM sine rule; **Sinusschwingung** f ELEKTRONIK sinusoidal oscillation; **Sinussignal** nt ELEKTRONIK, TELEKOM sinusoidal signal; **Sinussignalgeber** m ELEKTRONIK sinusoidal signal generator; **Sinusspannung** f ELEKTROTECH sinusoidal voltage; **Sinusstrom** m ELEKTROTECH sinusoidal current; **Sinustabelle** f GEOM, MECHAN sine table; **Sinustafel** f MECHAN sine table
Sinuswelle f AKUSTIK, ELEKTRIZ, ELEKTRONIK, GEOM, PHYS, RADIO, WELLPHYS sine wave; **Sinuswellenabstimmung** f ELEKTRONIK sine wave tuning; **Sinuswellenkonvergenz** f FERNSEH sine wave convergence; **Sinuswellenmodulation** f ELEKTRONIK sine wave modulation; **Sinuswellenoszillator** m ELEKTRONIK sine wave oscillator
Siphon m NICHTFOSS ENERG siphon, syphon; **~ für Vacuumpumpe** m LABOR trap for vacuum pump; **Siphonhöhe** f NICHTFOSS ENERG siphon crest; **Siphonüberlauf** m NICHTFOSS ENERG siphon spillway; **Siphonverschluß** m BAU *Sanitär* S-trap

SIP-Paket *nt (einfaches schritthaltendes Paket)* COMP &
DV, ELEKTRONIK SIP *(single in-line package)*
Sirene *f* SICHERHEIT *Alarm*, WASSERTRANS *Signal* siren;
~ **für die Räumung in Notfällen** *f* SICHERHEIT audible
emergency evacuation signal
SIS *abbr (Schwerionensynchrotron)* TEILPHYS HIS *(he-
avy-ion synchrotron)*
Sisalhanf *m* WASSERTRANS *Tauwerk* sisal hemp
Sisalseil *nt* MASCHINEN sisal rope
SISD-Rechner *m (serieller Rechner)* COMP & DV SISD
machine *(single instruction single-data machine)*
Sitosterin *nt* CHEMIE sitosterol
Sitosterol *nt* CHEMIE sitosterol
Situationskalkül *m* KÜNSTL INT situation calculus
Sitz *m* HYDRAUL *Ventil*, KFZTECH seat, MASCHINEN seat,
seating, MECHAN seat; **Sitzbank** *f* KFZTECH *Sitze*
bench seat; **Sitzbezug** *m* KFZTECH *Autositz* covering;
Sitzfläche *f* MASCHINEN face, seat, seating, seat; **Sitz-
kissen** *nt* KFZTECH seat cushion; **Sitzladefaktor** *m*
TRANS *Passagierflugzeuge* load factor; **Sitzpolster** *nt*
KFZTECH seat upholstery
Sitzung *f* COMP & DV session; **Sitzungsschicht** *f* COMP &
DV session layer
Sitz: **Sitzventil** *nt* FERTIG *Kunststoffinstallationen* globe
valve
Skalar *m* MATH, PHYS scalar; **Skalarfunktion** *f* COMP & DV
scalar function; **Skalarmessung** *f* ELEKTROTECH scalar measurement; **Skalarnetzanalyse** *f* ELEKTROTECH
scalar network analysis; **Skalarnetzanalysegerät** *nt*
ELEKTROTECH scalar network analyser (BrE), scalar
network analyzer (AmE); **Skalarprodukt** *nt* MATH
Vektoren, PHYS scalar product; **Skalartyp** *m* COMP & DV
scalar type
skalar[1] *adj* COMP & DV, MATH scalar
skalar:[2] **~es Potential** *nt* ELEKTROTECH, PHYS scalar potential; **~es Produkt** *nt* MATH scalar product; **~er
Widerstand** *m* ELEKTROTECH scalar resistor
Skale *f* AKUSTIK, COMP & DV, DRUCK scale, ELEKTRIZ
dial, scale, GEOM scale, GERÄT dial, METROL scale; ~
mit Nullpunkt links *f* GERÄT left margin zero scale; ~
mit Nullpunkt rechts *f* GERÄT right margin zero scale; ~
mit unterdrücktem Nullpunkt *f* GERÄT set-up scale,
suppressed zero scale; ~ **mit versetztem Nullpunkt** *f*
GERÄT displaced zero scale
Skalen: ~ **der Lautstärke** *f pl* AKUSTIK scales of loudness; ~ **der Tonhöhe** *f pl* AKUSTIK scales of pitch
Skale: **Skalenanzeige** *f* GERÄT scale indication; **Skalen-
bereich** *m* GERÄT range, scale range; **Skaleneinteilung**
f GERÄT scale, MASCHINEN index, scale division,
METROL scale spacing; **Skalenendausschlag** *m* RADIO
full-scale deflection; **Skalenendwert** *m* GERÄT full-
scale value, maximum scale value; **Skalengenauigkeit**
f GERÄT scale accuracy; **Skalenintervall** *nt* METROL
scale interval; **Skalenjustierung** *f* GERÄT dial adjustment; **Skalenlänge** *f* METROL scale length;
Skalenmarke *f* GERÄT hairline, memory pointer, scale
mark; **Skalenmarkierung** *f* METROL scale mark; **Ska-
lenmittenwert** *m* GERÄT midscale value;
Skalennumerierung *f* METROL scale numbering; **Ska-
lenscheibe** *f* GERÄT dial scale, MASCHINEN dial;
Skalenstrich *m* GERÄT hairline, MASCHINEN index,
scale division; **Skalenteilstrich** *m* GERÄT scale mark;
Skalenteilstrichabstand *m* METROL scale spacing;
Skalenteilung *f* ELEKTRIZ scale division, GERÄT scale,
scale division; **Skalenumschalter** *m* ELEKTRIZ scale
switch; **Skalenwert** *m* GERÄT scale value; **Skalenzeiger**

m GERÄT dial pointer
skalierbar: **~e Schrift** *f* DRUCK scalable font
Skalieren *nt* COMP & DV sizing
skalieren *vt* COMP & DV, DRUCK scale
Skalierfaktor *m* COMP & DV scale factor
Skalierung *f* COMP & DV scaling, ERGON rating, GERÄT
scale; **Skalierungsfaktor** *m* ELEKTRONIK, GEOM scaling
factor
Skalpell *nt* LABOR scalpel; **Skalpellklinge** *f* LABOR scalpel
blade
Skatol *nt* CHEMIE methylindole, skatole
Skelett *nt* BAU *Gebäude*, MASCHINEN skeleton; **Skelett-
Träger** *m* BAU skeleton girder
Skim-Kautschuk *m* KUNSTSTOFF skim rubber
Skimmer *m* ERDÖL *Umweltschutz*, MEERSCHMUTZ, UM-
WELTSCHMUTZ skimmer
Skimming *nt* KER & GLAS skimming
Skineffekt *m* ELEKTROTECH, PHYS, RADIO, WERKPRÜF
skin effect
Skinfolie *f* VERPACK skin film
Skinpack *nt* VERPACK skin pack
Skinpackung *f* VERPACK blister pack
Skizze *f* LUFTTRANS *Navigation* plot, MASCHINEN
outline
skizzieren *vt* BAU outline, sketch
Skleroprotein *nt* LEBENSMITTEL albuminoid, sclero-
protein
Skleroskopapparat *m* FERTIG scleroscope
Skleroskophärte *f* FERTIG scleroscope hardness
Skonto *m* COMP & DV CD, cash discount
Skrubber *m* CHEMTECH washing tower
Skullboot *nt* WASSERTRANS *Rudern* scull
skullen *vi* WASSERTRANS *Rudern* scull
Skullriemen *m* WASSERTRANS *Rudern* scull
SLAR *abbr (Seitensichtradar)* MEERSCHMUTZ SLAR
(sideways-looking airborne radar)
Slatis-Siegbahn-Spektrometer *nt* KERNTECH Slatis-
Siegbahn spectrometer
Slave *m* COMP & DV slave; **Slave-Anwendung** *f* COMP & DV
slave application
SLC *abbr (Stanford Linear Collider)* TEILPHYS SLC
(Stanford Linear Collider)
SLD *abbr (superlumineszierende Diode)* OPTIK SLD
(superluminescent LED), TELEKOM *(Superlumines-
zierende Diode)* SLD *(superluminescent LED)*, SRD
(superradiant diode)
Slice-Aufbau *m* COMP & DV slice architecture
Slick *m* UMWELTSCHMUTZ slick
Slipanlage *f* WASSERTRANS building slip
Slipkran *m* TRANS boat-launching crane
slippen *vt* WASSERTRANS *Bootbau* slip; ~ **lassen** *vt* WAS-
SERTRANS *Tauwerk* slip
Slipwagen *m* WASSERTRANS cradle
Slot *m* KÜNSTL INT *Schema* slot
Slotted-ALOHA-Zugriffssystem *nt* TELEKOM slotted
ALOHA system
Slow-Scan-Television *f (SSTV)* FERNSEH slow scan
television *(SSTV)*
Slow-Scan-Videokonferenz *f* TELEKOM slow scan video
conferencing
SLR *abbr (einäugige Spiegelreflexkamera)* FOTO SLR
(single lens reflex camera)
SL-Rakete *f (Schwerlastträgerrakete)* RAUMFAHRT
HLLV *(heavy-lift launch vehicle)*
Slug *nt* KOHLEN slug
Slurry-Tanker *m* KFZTECH slurry tanker, WASSERTRANS

oil-slurry oil tanker

Slush-Moulding *nt* KUNSTSTOFF *Gießverfahren* slush molding (AmE), slush moulding (BrE)

Sm *(Samarium)* CHEMIE Sm *(samarium)*

SMAW *abbr* *(Sigmaschweißung)* KERNTECH SMAW *(shielded metal arc welding)*

SMC *abbr* ELEKTRONIK *(SMD-Bauteil)*, TELEKOM *(Aufsetzbauelement)* SMC *(surface-mounted component)*

SMD) *abbr* *(Flachbauelement, oberflächenmontiertes Element)* ELEKTRIZ SMD *(surface mounting device)*

SMD-Bauteil *nt (SMC)* ELEKTRONIK surface-mounted component *(SMC)*

smektisch: ~e Flüssigkristalle *m pl* ELEKTRONIK smectic liquid crystals

Smektit *m* ERDÖL *Mineral*, KOHLEN smectite

S-Meter *nt* RADIO S-meter

Smiley-Männchen *nt* COMP & DV *Zeichen* smiley

Smith-Diagramm *nt* PHYS Smith chart

SM-Ofen *m* FERTIG open hearth furnace

Smog *m* UMWELTSCHMUTZ smog

SMPTE-Zeitcode *m (Zeitcode der Gesellschaft für Kino- und Fernsehtechniker)* FERNSEH SMPTE time code *(Society of Motion Pictures and Television Engineers time code)*

Sn *abbr (Seiten)* DRUCK pp *(pages)*

SNA *abbr (Systemnetzwerkarchitektur)* COMP & DV SNA *(systems network architecture)*

Snaking *nt* LUFTTRANS *Aerodynamik* snaking

SNA-Kommunikationskonzept *nt* COMP & DV systems network architecture

Snap-In-Fassung *f* ELEKTROTECH snap-in socket

Snellius: ~sches Gesetz *nt* PHYS Snell's law

SNG *abbr (Erdgasaustauschgas, synthetisch hergestelltes Gas)* ERDÖL SNG *(synthetic natural gas)*

Snubber-Kondensator *m* ELEKTROTECH snubber capacitor

Snubber-Schaltkreis *m* ELEKTROTECH snubber circuit

SNV *abbr (Schweizerische Normenvereinigung)* ELEKTRIZ SSA *(Swiss Standards Association)*

Sockel *m* BAU socket, ELEKTRIZ female connector, socket, ELEKTRONIK *Elektronikröhren* base, *Röhrenfassung* backplate, ELEKTROTECH *Lampe* cap, *Sicherung* fuse base, FERNSEH *Röhre* socket, KERNTECH header, MECHAN pedestal, socket, TELEKOM pad; **~ von Elektronenröhren** *m* ELEKTROTECH base; **Sockelleiste** *f* KER & GLAS washboard; **Sockelpegelregelung** *f* FERNSEH pedestal level control; **Sockelstift** *m* ELEKTROTECH *Bajonettfassung* pin; **Sockelwert** *m* FERNSEH pedestal; **Sockelwerteinstellung** *f* FERNSEH pedestal adjustment

Sofortanzeige *f* GERÄT instantaneous display

sofortig: ~e Auslösung *f* MASCHINEN instantaneous release

Soft-Copy *f* COMP & DV soft copy

Soft-Cover *m* DRUCK soft cover

Soft-Error *m* COMP & DV soft error

Soft-Fail *m* COMP & DV soft fail

Softstarteinrichtung *f* ELEKTRIZ soft start facility

Software *f* COMP & DV, ELEKTRIZ, FERNSEH, PHYS software; **~ zur Strukturanalyse** *f* RAUMFAHRT structural analysis software; **Softwareanpassung** *f* COMP & DV software adaptation; **Softwarebetriebsmittel** *nt* COMP & DV software resources; **Softwaredesign** *nt* COMP & DV software design; **Software-Engineering** *nt* COMP & DV software engineering; **Software-Entwicklung** *f* COMP & DV software development; **Software-Entwurf** *m* COMP & DV software design; **Softwarekonfiguration** *f* COMP & DV software configuration; **Softwaremethodik** *f* COMP & DV software methodology; **Softwarepaket** *nt* COMP & DV, PHYS software package; **Softwareprodukt** *nt* TELEKOM software product

Sog *m* MECHAN suction, MEERSCHMUTZ wake

Sohlbank *f* BAU sill

Sohldruck *m* BAU bearing pressure

Sohle *f* BAU *Becken* floor, *Rohrleitung, Tunnel* invert, *Tunnelbau* foot wall, FERTIG sole, *Herd* bed, MASCHINEN, METALL *Ofen* bed; **~ des Ofenmunds** *f* KER & GLAS base of neck; **Sohlenmaterial** *nt* KUNSTSTOFF soling material; **Sohlenplatte** *f* ERDÖL bed plate; **Sohlenschuß** *m* KOHLEN blasting from the bottom; **Sohlenversagen** *nt* KOHLEN base failure

Sohlplatte *f* BAU base plate, bottom, sole

Sohlpressungsmodul *m* KOHLEN subgrade reaction modulus

Sohn *m* AKUSTIK stamper; **Sohnplatte** *f* AKUSTIK stamper

Solanidin *nt* CHEMIE solanidine

Solar- *pref* ELEKTROTECH, RADIO solar; **Solarbatterie** *f* ELEKTROTECH solar cell panel; **Solardynamik** *f* NICHTFOSS ENERG solar dynamics; **Solarelektrizität** *f* ELEKTROTECH solar electricity; **Solarelement** *nt* ELEKTROTECH solar cell panel; **Solarenergie** *f* ELEKTROTECH, MASCHINEN, NICHTFOSS ENERG, PHYS solar energy; **Solarisation** *f* FOTO solarization

Solarenergie: Solarenergiekonversion *f* ELEKTROTECH solar energy conversion; **Solarenergieumwandlung** *f* ELEKTROTECH solar energy conversion

Solar-: Solargenerator *m* ELEKTRIZ solar cell, solar power generator, ELEKTROTECH, RAUMFAHRT solar generator; **Solarheizungssystem** *nt* NICHTFOSS ENERG solar heating system; **Solarimeter** *nt* NICHTFOSS ENERG solarimeter; **Solarkollektor** *m* MASCHINEN solar collector; **Solarkonstante** *f* NICHTFOSS ENERG solar constant; **Solarpond** *m* NICHTFOSS ENERG solar pond; **Solarstrom** *m* ELEKTROTECH solar electricity; **Solartechnik** *f* NICHTFOSS ENERG solar engineering, solar technology

solarthermisch: ~er Prozess *m* NICHTFOSS ENERG heliothermal process

Solarzelle *f* ELEKTROTECH solar cell panel, NICHTFOSS ENERG, PHYS, RAUMFAHRT, STRAHLPHYS, TELEKOM, THERMOD solar cell; **~ ohne Konzentrator** *f* ELEKTROTECH nonconcentrator solar cell; **Solarzellenausleger** *m* TELEKOM solar panel; **Solarzellenflügel** *m* RAUMFAHRT solar panel; **Solarzellengruppe** *f* RAUMFAHRT solar array; **Solarzellenlaken** *nt* NICHTFOSS ENERG array blanket; **Solarzellenplatte** *f* NICHTFOSS ENERG solar panel

Sole *f* KERNTECH brine; **Solekühlung** *f* LEBENSMITTEL brine cooling; **Solenkühlsystem** *nt* KERNTECH brine cooling system

Solenoid *nt* PHYS solenoid; **Solenoid-** *nt* FERTIG solenoid ELEKTRIZ, ELEKTROTECH *Elektromagnet*, KFZTECH *Anlasser* solenoid; **Solenoidbetätigung** *f* ELEKTROTECH solenoid actuation; **Solenoidfeld** *nt* PHYS solenoidal field; **Solenoidrelais** *nt* ELEKTRIZ, ELEKTROTECH solenoid relay; **Solenoidschrittmotor** *m* ELEKTROTECH solenoid stepper motor; **Solenoidventil** *nt* HYDRAUL solenoid valve

Soletröpfchen *nt* KERNTECH brine droplet

Solidstate *m* ELEKTRIZ solid state; **Solidstate-Relais** *nt*

ELEKTROTECH solid state relay; **Solidstate-Signal** *nt* ELEKTRONIK solid state signal; **Solidstate-Speicher** *m* ELEKTROTECH solid state memory device

Sollabbrand *m* KERNTECH target burn up

Sollbereich *m* GERÄT desired range

Sollbruchelement *nt* MASCHINEN breaking member

Sollbruchstelle *f* MASCHINEN breaking point

Sollflugbahn *f* LUFTTRANS required flightpath

Sollpegel *m* GERÄT desired level

Sollwert *m* GERÄT, KERNTECH desired value, MASCHINEN set value; **Sollwertabweichung** *f* REGELUNG deviation from the desired set point; **Sollwertanzeigeinstrument** *nt* GERÄT rated value indicating instrument; **Sollwertbereich** *m* GERÄT desired range; **Sollwerteinsteller für Fernbetätigung** *m* REGELUNG remote set-point adjuster

Sollzustand *m* GERÄT desired condition

Solvens *nt* CHEMIE dissolvent

Solventraffination *f* ERDÖL *Raffinerie* solvent refining

SOM *abbr (Anfang der Nachricht)* COMP & DV SOM *(start of message)*

Somatik *f* ERGON somatology

somatisch *adj* ERGON somatic

Somatotyp *m* ERGON somatotype

Sommerdeich *m* WASSERVERSORG overflow dam

Sommerfeld: **~sche Zahl** *f* NICHTFOSS ENERG Sommerfeld number

Sommertiefladelinie *f* WASSERTRANS *Schiffskonstruktion* summer load waterline

Sonargerät *nt* STRAHLPHYS, WASSERTRANS *Navigation* sonar

Sonde *f* FERNSEH electrode, FERTIG sound, GERÄT measuring head, probe, KOHLEN, PHYS, RADIO, RAUMFAHRT probe; **Sondenmikrofon** *nt* AKUSTIK, AUFNAHME probe microphone; **Sondenspule** *f* PHYS exploring coil, pick-up coil, search coil

Sonderabfall *m* ABFALL special waste; **Sonderabfallzwischenlager** *nt* ABFALL temporary deposit for hazardous waste

Sonder- *pref* DRUCK special; **Sonderausgabe** *f* DRUCK special edition; **Sonderausstattung** *f* MASCHINEN optional equipment

sonderberuhigt: **~er Stahl** *m* FERTIG abnormal steel

Sonder-: **Sonderfreigabe** *f* QUAL waiver; **Sondermaschine** *f* MASCHINEN special purpose machine

Sondermüll *m* ABFALL hazardous waste, special waste; **Sondermülldeponie** *f* ABFALL hazardous waste landfill; **Sondermülleinsammlung** *f* ABFALL hazardous waste collection

Sonder-: **Sonderstahl** *m* METALL special steel; **Sonderverfahren** *nt* QUAL special process; **Sondervermerk** *m* KONSTZEICH special note; **Sonderwagen** *m* EISENBAHN parlor car (AmE), saloon carriage (BrE); **Sonderweiche** *f* EISENBAHN special turnout; **Sonderzeichen** *nt* COMP & DV special character

sondieren *vt* KOHLEN sound

Sondierungsbericht *m* KOHLEN sounding record

Sone *nt* AKUSTIK, PHYS sone

Sonnen- *pref* BAU solar; **Sonnenabsorptionskoeffizient** *m* NICHTFOSS ENERG solar absorption coefficient; **Sonnenabsorptionsvermögen** *nt* NICHTFOSS ENERG solar absorption capacity; **Sonnenaktivität** *f* PHYS solar activity; **Sonnenazimut** *m* NICHTFOSS ENERG solar azimuth; **Sonnenbatterie** *f* FERNSEH, NICHTFOSS ENERG solar battery; **Sonnenbestrahlung** *f* HEIZ & KÄLTE, NICHTFOSS ENERG insolation; **Sonnenblende** *f*

FOTO hood, lens hood, KFZTECH *Zubehör* antidazzle visor; **Sonnendach** *nt* KFZTECH *Karosserie* sun roof; **Sonneneinstrahlung** *f* HEIZ & KÄLTE insolation

Sonnenenergie:[1] **mit ~ betrieben** *adj* ELEKTROTECH, NICHTFOSS ENERG solar-powered

Sonnenenergie[2] *f* ELEKTROTECH, MASCHINEN, NICHTFOSS ENERG, PHYS solar energy; **Sonnenenergiekonversion** *f* ELEKTROTECH solar energy conversion

Sonnen-: **Sonneneruption** *f* RAUMFAHRT solar flare; **Sonnenfarm** *f* NICHTFOSS ENERG solar farm; **Sonnenferne** *f* PHYS aphelion; **Sonnenfleck** *m* RADIO solar spot; **Sonnenfühler** *m* RAUMFAHRT sun sensor; **Sonnenhöhe** *f* NICHTFOSS ENERG solar altitude; **Sonnenkollektorplatte** *f* RAUMFAHRT solar panel; **Sonnenkraftanlage** *f* ELEKTROTECH solar power farm; **Sonnenkraftwerk** *nt* ELEKTROTECH solar power plant, solar power station; **Sonnenlichtabsorber** *m* RAUMFAHRT solar absorber; **Sonnennähe** *f* NICHTFOSS ENERG, PHYS perihelion; **Sonnenofen** *m* NICHTFOSS ENERG solar furnace; **Sonnenpaddel** *nt* TELEKOM solar panel; **Sonnenprotuberanz** *f* RADIO solar flare; **Sonnenrad** *nt* KFZTECH sun gear, MASCHINEN central gear, sun gear, sun wheel; **Sonnenradsperrverzahnung** *f* KFZTECH sun gear lockout teeth; **Sonnenradsteuerplatte** *f* KFZTECH sun gear control plate; **Sonnenschutz** *m* BAU screen; **Sonnenschutzfarbe** *f* KUNSTSTOFF shading paint; **Sonnenschutzglas** *nt* KER & GLAS dark glass, sunglass; **Sonnensegel** *nt* RAUMFAHRT solar sail, WASSERTRANS awning; **Sonnenstand** *m* NICHTFOSS ENERG solar altitude; **Sonnenstörung** *f* RAUMFAHRT sun interference; **Sonnenstrahlmagnetron** *nt* ELEKTRONIK rising sun magnetron; **Sonnenstrahlung** *f* NICHTFOSS ENERG, STRAHLPHYS, UMWELTSCHMUTZ solar radiation; **Sonnenstrahlungsdruck** *m* RAUMFAHRT solar radiation pressure

sonnensynchron: **~e Umlaufbahn** *f* RAUMFAHRT sun synchronous orbit

Sonnen-: **Sonnenturm** *m* NICHTFOSS ENERG solar tower; **Sonnenwärme** *f* NICHTFOSS ENERG solar heat; **Sonnenwärmekollektor** *m* NICHTFOSS ENERG solar collector; **Sonnenwärmekonzentrator** *m* NICHTFOSS ENERG solar concentrator; **Sonnenwende** *f* RAUMFAHRT solstice; **Sonnenwendepunkt** *m* RAUMFAHRT solstitial point; **Sonnenwind** *m* PHYS, RAUMFAHRT solar wind; **Sonnenzelle** *f* ELEKTROTECH solar cell panel

Sonometer *nt* PHYS sonometer

Sophorin *nt* CHEMIE cytisine, sophorine, ulexine

Sorbens *nt* MEERSCHMUTZ sorbent

Sorbinose *f* CHEMIE sorbose

Sorbit *m* METALL sorbite

Sorbose *f* CHEMIE sorbose

Sorption *f* WASSERVERSORG sorption; **Sorptionsmittel** *nt* MEERSCHMUTZ sorbent

Sortier- *pref* COMP & DV sorting; **~ und Sammelsystem** *nt* VERPACK *Buchbindereien* collating system

Sortierbegriff *m* COMP & DV sort key

Sortierdatei *f* COMP & DV sort file

Sortieren *nt* COMP & DV collation, sorting, KOHLEN grading

sortieren *vt* COMP & DV collate, sort, DRUCK sort, KOHLEN size

Sortierer *m* COMP & DV collator, ELEKTROTECH sequencer, PAPIER screen

Sortier-: **Sortierfeld** *nt* COMP & DV sort field; **Sortierfolge** *f* COMP & DV collating sequence, collation; **Sortiergene-**

rator *m* COMP & DV sort generator; **Sortiermaschine** *f* KER & GLAS sorter, MASCHINEN grading machine, VERPACK sorting machine; **Sortierprogramm** *nt* COMP & DV sort program; **Sortierprüfung** *f* QUAL screening inspection, screening test; **Sortierschlüssel** *m* COMP & DV sort key; **Sortiersteige für den Transport** *f* VERPACK collating transit tray; **Sortiertaste** *f* COMP & DV sort key

Sortierung *f* COMP & DV collation, sort, KER & GLAS grading; **~ von Abfällen** *f* ABFALL waste sorting; **~ im Druckluftstrom** *f* FERTIG *Pulvermetall* air classification; **~ von Hand** *f* ABFALL *Müll* manual separation

Sortiment *nt* TELEKOM, TEXTIL range

SOS *abbr (Silizium auf Saphir)* ELEKTRONIK SOS *(silicon-on-sapphire)*

SOS-Schaltkreis *m* RADIO SOS logic

Soundtrack *nt* FERNSEH soundtrack

Source *f* PHYS *Feldeffekttransistor* source; **Source-Elektrode** *f* ELEKTROTECH source; **Source-Impedanz** *f* ELEKTROTECH source impedance; **Source-Kontakt** *m* ELEKTROTECH source contact; **Source-Verstärker** *m* ELEKTRONIK common source amplifier

Soxhlet-Apparat *m* LABOR Soxhlet extractor

Soxhlet-Extraktor *m* LABOR Soxhlet extractor

Soziussitz *m* KFZTECH *Motorrad* pillion

Spacelab *nt* RAUMFAHRT spacelab

Spacewalk *m* RAUMFAHRT space walk

Spachtel *m* BAU trowel; **Spachtelmasse** *f* BAU filler, putty, KERNTECH filler; **Spachtelmasse für Karosseriereparaturen** *f* KFZTECH *Karosserie* body filler; **Spachtelmesser** *nt* BAU stopping knife

spachteln *vt* BAU putty, trowel, FERTIG prime, putty

Spachtelung *f* FERTIG priming

Spachtelverbindung *f* BAU putty joint

Spalier: mit ~ versehen *vt* BAU lath

Spalling *nt* KER & GLAS spalling

Spalt *m* BAU crack, fissure, ELEKTROTECH *Magnetkreisen* gap, *bei Relais* slot, FERTIG die clearance, HYDRAUL clearance, KER & GLAS, KERNTECH, MASCHINEN gap, MECHAN clearance, METALL crack, WELLPHYS slit; **äußerer ~** *m* HYDRAUL outside clearance; **Spaltauskleidung** *f* PHYS slot liner; **Spaltaxt** *f* BAU splitting ax (AmE), splitting axe (BrE); **Spalt-Azimuth** *m* AUFNAHME gap azimuth

spaltbar[1] *adj* FERTIG fissile, PHYS fissile, fissionable

spaltbar[2] **-es Isotop** *nt* PHYS fertile isotope, fissile isotope; **~es Material** *nt* STRAHLPHYS fissile material

Spalt: **Spaltblende** *f* FOTO slit diaphragm; **Spaltbreite** *f* AUFNAHME, ELEKTROTECH gap length, FERNSEH gap width; **Spaltbreitenhalter** *m* AUFNAHME gap spacer; **Spaltbruchstücke** *nt pl* PHYS fission fragments; **Spaltdämpfung** *f* OPTIK *Interferenz* gap loss

Spalte *f* ANSTRICH crack, COMP & DV, DRUCK column, KOHLEN crack, MASCHINEN gap

Spalteinstellung *f* FERNSEH gap setting

Spalten *nt* BAU cleaving, ripping

spalten *vt* FERTIG fissure, TEXTIL split; **mit einem Keil ~** *vt* BAU split with wedges

Spalte: **Spaltenabzug** *m* DRUCK galley, galley proof, slip proof; **Spaltensteller** *m* COMP & DV tabulator; **Spaltenwasser** *nt* KOHLEN joint water

Spalter *m* KOHLEN splitter

Spalt: **Spaltfestigkeit** *f* FERTIG interlaminar strength, KUNSTSTOFF interlaminar strength, *Klebstoff* adhesive shear strength; **Spaltfilter** *nt* MASCHINEN edge filter; **Spaltflügel** *m* LUFTTRANS slotted wing; **Spaltfragmente** *nt pl* PHYS fission fragments; **Spaltfuge** *f* BAU

Dachsparren split; **Spaltgasplenum** *nt* KERNTECH fission gas plenum; **Spaltgasspeicherraum** *m* KERNTECH fission gas plenum; **Spaltglas** *nt* KER & GLAS cleaved glass; **Spaltgröße** *f* KER & GLAS gap sizing; **Spalthammer** *m* BAU cleaver; **Spaltkammer** *f* KERNTECH fission ionization chamber; **Spaltklappe** *f* LUFTTRANS slot flap; **Spaltkohle** *f* KER & GLAS cracking coal; **Spaltlänge** *f* AKUSTIK gap length; **Spaltmesser** *nt* SICHERHEIT riving knife; **Spaltneutronen** *nt pl* STRAHLPHYS fission neutrons; **Spaltniet** *m* MASCHINEN bifurcated rivet; **Spaltölfilter** *nt* KOHLEN disc filter (BrE), disk filter (AmE); **Spaltphasenmotor** *m* ELEKTROTECH split phase motor; **Spaltpolmotor** *m* ELEKTROTECH shaded pole motor; **Spaltprodukt** *nt* ABFALL, KERNTECH fission product; **Spaltring** *m* MASCHINEN split ring; **Spaltriß** *m* BAU *Holz* split; **Spaltsäge** *f* BAU cleaving saw, MASCHINEN ripping saw; **Spaltstoffabbrand** *m (FIFA)* KERNTECH fissions per initial fissile atom *(FIFA)*; **Spaltstoffausnutzung** *f* KERNTECH nuclear fuel utilization; **Spaltstoffgitterabstand** *m* KERNTECH lattice pitch spacing; **Spaltstoffstruktur** *f* KERNTECH fuel assembly; **Spaltstoffverbrauch** *m (FIFA)* KERNTECH fissions per initial fissile atom *(FIFA)*; **Spaltstoffverhältnis** *nt* KERNTECH fissile inventory ratio; **Spalttiefe** *f* AKUSTIK, AUFNAHME, FERNSEH gap depth

Spaltung *f* BAU splitting, CHEMIE breakdown, METALL cleavage; **~ mit Thermoneutronen** *f* KERNTECH thermal neutron fission; **Spaltungsfläche** *f* METALL cleavage facet; **Spaltungsionisationskammer** *f* KERNTECH fission ionization chamber; **Spaltungsstörzone** *f* KERNTECH fission spike

Spalt: **Spaltverlust** *m* AKUSTIK, AUFNAHME, FERNSEH, OPTIK *Interferenz* gap loss; **Spaltversuch** *m* WERKPRÜF cleavage test; **Spaltwasser** *nt* KOHLEN cleft water; **Spaltzone** *f* KERNTECH *Reaktor* core; **äußere ~** *f* KERNTECH outer-fueled zone (AmE), outer-fuelled zone (BrE)

Span *m* BAU *Holz* splinter, FERTIG chip, fine, shaving, MASCHINEN, MECHAN chip; **Spanabflußrichtung** *f* FERTIG direction of chip flow

spanabhebend:[1] **~e Bearbeitung** *f* MASCHINEN cutting, machining

spanabhebend:[2] **~ bearbeiten** *vt* MASCHINEN machine

Span: **Spanabnahme** *f* FERTIG linear machining, MASCHINEN chip removal; **Spanabzug für Mühlen** *m* SICHERHEIT chips exhaust installation for milling machines; **Spanbrecher** *m* MASCHINEN chip breaker; **Spanbrecherplatte** *f* FERTIG breaker plate; **Spandicke** *f* MASCHINEN chip thickness

Späne *m pl* FERTIG swarf

Spanen *nt* FERTIG cutting, MASCHINEN chip removal, machining, metal cutting; **~ auf Gewicht** *nt* KER & GLAS chipping to the weight

spanen *vt* FERTIG machine

spanend:[1] **~ bearbeitbar** *adj* FERTIG machinable

spanend:[2] **~e Bearbeitbarkeit** *f* FERTIG machinability, machining property, machining quality; **~e Bearbeitung** *f* MASCHINEN machining, metal cutting

spanend:[3] **~ bearbeiten** *vt* MASCHINEN machine

Spänetrog *m* FERTIG *Spanung* trough

Spanfläche *f* FERTIG rake, tool face, top rake, *Werkzeug* face; **Spanflächen-Orthogonalebene** *f* FERTIG tool face orthogonal plane; **Spanflächen-Tangentialkraft** *f* FERTIG tool face tangential force

Span: **Spanfluß** *m* FERTIG flow of chips

Spange *f* BAU stay bolt, MECHAN clip

spanisch: ~**er Takling** *m* WASSERTRANS back splice

Spanleistung *f* FERTIG cutting capacity

spanlos[1] *adj* FERTIG nonchipping

spanlos:[2] ~**e Formgebung** *f* MASCHINEN noncutting shaping; ~**e Tragflügelbefestigung** *f* LUFTTRANS forged wing attachment

Span: **Spanlücke** *f* FERTIG gash; **Spanmenge** *f* FERTIG quantity of metal removed

Spann- *pref* spanning; **Spannbacke** *f* FERTIG *Stumpfschweißen* welding jaw, MASCHINEN chuck jaw, gripping jaw, jaw; **Spannbandmeßwerk** *nt* GERÄT tautband movement; **Spannbereich** *m* FERTIG holding capacity; **Spannbeton** *m* BAU prestressed concrete; **Spannbohle** *f* BAU strutting board; **Spannbolzen** *m* FERTIG clamping bolt; **Spannbüchse** *f* MASCHINEN spring collet; **Spannbuchse** *f* FERTIG holding bushing; **Spannbügel** *m* FERTIG clip, *Kunststoffinstallationen* clamp

Spanndorn *m* FERTIG *Fräsermaschine* arbor (AmE), arbour (BrE)

Spanndraht *m* BAU stretching wire

Spanne *f* MASCHINEN margin, METROL span

Spann-: **Spanneisen** *nt* FERTIG clamp, crossbar; ~ **mit Stift** *nt* FERTIG finger clamp

Spannen *nt* FERTIG *Blech* planishing, MASCHINEN tension; ~ **von Hand** *nt* FOTO manual cocking

spannen *vt* BAU tighten, FERTIG hold, stress, tauten, *Blech* planish, *Werkstück* secure, FOTO cock, TEXTIL stretch

Spanner *m* FERTIG clamping device, KFZTECH *Kette* tensioner, MASCHINEN tightener

Spann-: **Spannfaden** *m* TEXTIL tight pick; **Spannfeder** *f* MASCHINEN tension spring; **Spannfinger** *m* FERTIG toe dog; **Spannfutter** *nt* FERTIG chuck, MASCHINEN chuck, jaw chuck, MECHAN chuck; **Spanngitter** *nt* ELEKTRONIK *Elektronenröhre* frame grid; **Spannhebel** *m* FOTO cocking lever; **Spannhebel für Selbstauslöser** *m* FOTO self-time lever; **Spannhülse** *f* FERTIG adaptor sleeve, MASCHINEN clamping sleeve; **Spannhülsenlager** *nt* FERTIG adaptor bearing; **Spannhydraulik** *f* MASCHINEN hydraulic clamping; **Spannkette** *f* TEXTIL tight end; **Spannkettenrad** *nt* FERTIG idler sprocket; **Spannkloben** *m* MASCHINEN face chuck, face plate chuck, face plate dog, face plate jaw; **Spannkluppe** *f* MASCHINEN vice clamp (BrE), vise clamp (AmE); **Spannkraft** *f* VERPACK clamping force; **Spannmutter** *f* FERTIG *Kunststoffinstallationen* nut, MASCHINEN coupling nut; **Spannpatrone** *f* MASCHINEN draw-in collet; **Spannplatte** *f* MASCHINEN bolster plate; **Spannpratze** *f* FERTIG strap; **Spannrahmen** *m* BAU tenter, TEXTIL stenter frame (BrE), tenter frame (AmE); **Spannring** *m* FOTO cocking ring, MASCHINEN lock ring, MECHAN expansion ring; **Spannrolle** *f* FERNSEH idler, FERTIG, KFZTECH belt idler, MASCHINEN idler, tension roller, tightener, tightening pulley, MECHAN jockey pulley, PAPIER tension roller; **Spannsäule** *f* KOHLEN jack column; **Spannscheibe** *f* MASCHINEN tension pulley; **Spannschloß** *nt* BAU, FERTIG, MASCHINEN turnbuckle; **Spannschloßmutter** *f* MASCHINEN turnbuckle sleeve; **Spannschraube** *f* FERTIG clamping screw, MASCHINEN clamping screw, straining screw, tension screw, tightening screw, MECHAN turnbuckle, WASSERTRANS *Tauwerk* rigging screw, turnbuckle; **Spannseil** *nt* BAU stay, MASCHINEN tightening cord; **Spannstock** *m* MECHAN vice (BrE), vise (AmE); **Spannstockfutter** *nt* MASCHINEN vice chuck (BrE), vise chuck (AmE);

Spanntuch *nt* FOTO pressure cloth

Spannung:[1] *f* BAU tension, ELEKTRIZ potential, voltage, ELEKTRIZ voltage, ELEKTROTECH tension, ERDÖL *Werkstoff* stress, ERGON strain, FERTIG hold, stress, HYDRAUL *Dampf* pressure, KER & GLAS strain, stress, KFZTECH *Elektrik, Zündung* voltage, KOHLEN, KUNSTSTOFF *mechanisch* stress, MASCHINEN tension, MECHAN strain, METALL stress, tension, PAPIER stress, PHYS tension, voltage, RADIO, RAUMFAHRT *Weltraumfunk* potential, TELEKOM voltage, TEXTIL tension

Spannung:[2] **mit ~ schneiden** *vt* SICHERHEIT *fräsen* cut with a jig

Spannung: ~**anlegen** *vi* ELEKTROTECH apply a voltage; ~ **bei Belastung** *f* ELEKTROTECH *Klemmen* on-load voltage; ~ **gegen Erde** *f* ELEKTROTECH voltage to earth (BrE), voltage to ground (AmE); ~ **unter Last** *f* ELEKTROTECH closed-circuit voltage; ~ **zwischen Leiter und Erde** *f* ELEKTRIZ line-to-earth voltage (BrE), line-to-ground voltage (AmE); ~ **zwischen Leiter und Nullpunkt** *f* ELEKTRIZ line-to-neutral voltage; ~ **zwischen Leitern** *f* ELEKTRIZ line-to-line voltage; ~ **zum Nulleiter** *f* ELEKTRIZ voltage to neutral; ~ **zwischen Phasen** *f* ELEKTRIZ phase-to-phase voltage; **Spannung/Frequenz-Umwandlung** *f* ELEKTROTECH voltage-to-frequency conversion; **Spannung/Frequenz-Wandler** *m* ELEKTROTECH voltage-to-frequency converter

spannungführend *adj* ELEKTROTECH alive

Spannung: **Spannungsabbau** *m* KUNSTSTOFF relaxation of stress, stress relaxation

Spannungsabfall *m* ELEKTRIZ drop of potential, potential drop, voltage drop, ELEKTROTECH, FERTIG voltage drop, PHYS potential drop, voltage drop; ~ **an Induktanz** *m* ELEKTRIZ inductive drop; ~ **an einer Reaktanz** *m* ELEKTRIZ reactance drop; ~ **auf Impedanz** *m* ELEKTRIZ impedance voltage drop; ~ **durch Blindwiderstand** *m* ELEKTROTECH reactance drop; ~ **in Leitung** *m* ELEKTROTECH line drop; **Spannungsabfallwiderstand** *m* ELEKTROTECH voltage dropping resistor

spannungsabhängig: ~**er Widerstand** *m* ELEKTROTECH voltage-dependent resistor, PHYS varistor

Spannung: **Spannungsanstiegsrate** *f* ELEKTROTECH rate of voltage rise; **Spannungsanzeiger** *m* ELEKTROTECH voltage indicator, WASSERTRANS *Elektrik* charge indicator; **Spannungsausgleich** *m* ELEKTRIZ voltage balance; **Spannungsausgleichschaltung** *f* ELEKTROTECH equipotential connection; **Spannungsausgleichverbindung** *f* ELEKTROTECH equipotential connection; **Spannungsbauch** *m* ELEKTROTECH antinode, KERNTECH potential loop; **Spannungsbegrenzer** *m* ELEKTRIZ voltage limiter, ELEKTROTECH transient suppressor; **Spannungsbegrenzung** *f* ELEKTROTECH transient suppression; **Spannungsbegrenzungsstrecke** *f* ELEKTRIZ relief gap; **Spannungsbeobachter** *m* KER & GLAS strain viewer; **Spannungsbereich** *m* GERÄT voltage range; **Spannungsdehnung** *f* EISENBAHN stress expansion; **Spannungsdehnungsdiagramm** *nt* KUNSTSTOFF stress-strain curve; **Spannungsdehnungsschaubild** *nt* WASSERTRANS *Schiffbau* stress-strain diagram; **Spannungsdifferenz** *f* ELEKTRIZ, ELEKTROTECH, PHYS PD, potential difference; **Spannungsdurchschlag** *m* ELEKTRONIK puncture; **Spannungsentlastung** *f* WERKPRÜF stress relief; **Spannungserzeuger** *m* PHYS voltage generator; **Spannungsfernmeßgerät** *nt* GERÄT televoltmeter

spannungsfrei[1] *adj* ELEKTRIZ voltage-free
spannungsfrei:[2] **~ machen** *vt* FERTIG *Plaste* anneal
Spannung: **Spannungsfreiglühen** *nt* FERTIG lonealing, temper annealing
spannungsführend[1] *adj* ELEKTRIZ alive, ELEKTROTECH active, PHYS live
spannungsführend:[2] **~e Komponente** *f* ELEKTROTECH active component
Spannung: **Spannungsgefälle** *nt* ELEKTRIZ potential gradient, voltage gradient, PHYS potential gradient
spannungsgeregelt: **~er Eingang** *m* ELEKTROTECH voltage-controlled input; **~er Kondensator** *m* ELEKTROTECH voltage-controlled capacitor; **~es Netzgerät** *nt* ELEKTROTECH voltage-regulated power supply; **~er Oszillator** *m* RAUMFAHRT *Weltraumfunk* VCO, voltage-controlled oscillator; **~e Stromversorgung** *f* ELEKTRIZ voltage-stabilized power supply
spannungsgesteuert: **~er Oszillator** *m* ELEKTRONIK, TELEKOM VCO, voltage-controlled oscillator
Spannung: **Spannungsgleichhaltung** *f* ELEKTROTECH voltage regulation; **Spannungsgradient** *m* ELEKTRIZ voltage gradient, PHYS potential gradient; **Spannungsimpuls** *m* ELEKTRIZ voltage pulse; **Spannungsknoten** *m* ELEKTRONIK node; **Spannungskoeffizient** *m* THERMOD temperature pressure coefficient; **Spannungskonstanthalter** *m* ELEKTROTECH voltage regulator; **Spannungskorrosion** *f* WERKPRÜF stress corrosion
spannungslos[1] *adj* GERÄT dead
spannungslos:[2] **~e Freigabe** *f* ELEKTRIZ, ELEKTROTECH no-volt release
Spannung: **Spannungslosigkeit** *f* ELEKTROTECH no voltage, GERÄT absence of voltage; **Spannungsmeßbereich** *m* GERÄT voltage measuring range, voltage span; **Spannungsmeßgerät** *nt* ELEKTROTECH voltmeter, GERÄT voltage measuring instrument, PHYS voltmeter
spannungsoptisch[1] *adj* FERTIG photoelastic
spannungsoptisch:[2] **~er Koeffizient** *m* KER & GLAS stress optical coefficient
Spannung: **Spannungspolarität** *f* ELEKTROTECH voltage polarity; **Spannungsquelle** *f* ELEKTROTECH power supply, source, voltage source, PHYS voltage source; **Spannungsreferenz** *f* ELEKTROTECH voltage reference; **Spannungsreferenzdiode** *f* ELEKTRONIK voltage reference diode; **Spannungsreferenzröhre** *f* ELEKTROTECH voltage reference tube; **Spannungsregeltransformator** *m* ELEKTROTECH voltage-regulating transformer; **Spannungsregelung** *f* ELEKTRIZ voltage control, ELEKTROTECH voltage regulation; **Spannungsregler** *m* COMP & DV, ELEKTRIZ, FERNSEH, FERTIG, KFZTECH, KONTROLL voltage regulator, TEXTIL tension device; **Spannungsreglerdynamo** *m* ELEKTRIZ regulating dynamo; **Spannungsrelais** *nt* ELEKTROTECH voltage relay; **Spannungsrelaxation** *f* KUNSTSTOFF relaxation of stress, stress relaxation; **Spannungsresonanz** *f* ELEKTRONIK parallel resonance; **Spannungsriß** *m* WERKPRÜF stress crack
spannungsrißempfindlich *adj* FERTIG *Kunststoffinstallationen* prone to stress cracking
Spannung: **Spannungsscheibe** *f* KER & GLAS strain disc (BrE), strain disk (AmE); **Spannungsschlinge** *f* ELEKTRIZ potential loop; **Spannungsschwankung** *f* ELEKTRIZ voltage fluctuation; **Spannungsspitze** *f* ELEKTROTECH power surge, voltage spike, RADIO surge; **Spannungssprung** *m* ELEKTRIZ voltage jump,

TELEKOM voltage surge; **Spannungsstabilisator** *m* ELEKTROTECH voltage stabilizer; **Spannungsstabilisatordiode** *f* ELEKTRONIK voltage regulator diode; **Spannungsstabilisierung** *f* ELEKTROTECH voltage regulation; **Spannungsstoß** *m* ELEKTROTECH surge, voltage surge; **Spannungsstrommeßgerät** *nt* ELEKTROTECH voltmeter; **Spannungsstufe** *f* PHYS voltage step; **Spannungsteiler** *m* ELEKTRIZ voltage divider, ELEKTROTECH static balancer, voltage divider, FERNSEH voltage divider, PHYS potential divider, voltage divider, TELEKOM voltage divider; **Spannungsteilerschaltung** *f* GERÄT voltage divider network; **Spannungstensor** *m* PHYS stress tensor
spannungstragend[1] *adj* ELEKTRIZ live
spannungstragend:[2] **~e Leitung** *f* ELEKTRIZ live line
Spannung: **Spannungstransformator** *m* ELEKTRIZ potential transformer, ELEKTROTECH potential transformer, voltage transformer; **Spannung-Strom Charakteristik** *f* ELEKTROTECH voltage current characteristic; **Spannung-Strom Kennlinie** *f* ELEKTROTECH voltage current characteristic; **Spannungsübertragungsfaktor** *m* AKUSTIK response to voltage; **Spannungsumformer** *m* ELEKTRIZ voltage transformer; **Spannungsunterschied** *m* ELEKTRIZ voltage difference; **Spannungsverdoppler** *m* ELEKTRIZ, PHYS voltage doubler; **Spannungsverdreifachung** *f* RADIO tripling voltage; **Spannungsvergleich** *m* ELEKTROTECH voltage comparison; **Spannungsverlauf** *m* FERTIG flow of stress; **Spannungsverlust** *m* ELEKTRIZ voltage drop, voltage loss, ELEKTROTECH voltage drop, FERTIG line drop, voltage drop, PHYS voltage drop; **Spannungsverringerung** *f* MASCHINEN stress relief; **Spannungsversorgung** *f* AUFNAHME power supply, PHYS power supply, supply voltage; **Spannungsversorgungsuntersystem** *nt* RAUMFAHRT power subsystem; **Spannungsverstärker** *m* ELEKTRONIK voltage amplifier, ELEKTROTECH booster; **Spannungsverstärkung** *f* ELEKTRONIK voltage amplification, PHYS voltage gain; **Spannungsverstärkungsfaktor** *m* ELEKTROTECH voltage gain; **Spannungsverteiler** *m* RAUMFAHRT power bus; **Spannungsverteilersystem** *nt* RAUMFAHRT power distribution network; **Spannungsvervielfacher** *m* ELEKTRIZ, ELEKTROTECH voltage multiplier; **Spannungswähler** *m* ELEKTROTECH voltage selector; **Spannungswählschalter** *m* ELEKTROTECH voltage selector; **Spannungswandler** *m* ELEKTROTECH potential transformer, RAUMFAHRT power converter; **Spannungswandler Gleichstrom-Wechselstrom** *m* ELEKTROTECH DC-AC converter; **Spannungswandlung Gleichstrom-Wechselstrom** *f* ELEKTROTECH DC-AC conversion; **Spannungszone** *f* KER & GLAS stressed zone
Spann-: **Spannut** *f* MASCHINEN flute; **Spannutlänge** *f* MASCHINEN flute length; **Spannutsteigung** *f* MASCHINEN flute pitch; **Spannvorrichtung** *f* FERTIG workholding device, workholding fixture, MASCHINEN gripping device, jig, tensioning device, PAPIER stretcher; **Spannwalze** *f* PAPIER stretch roll, tightener; **Spannweite** *f* BAU span, GERÄT range, LUFTTRANS span, wing span, PHYS *einer Tragfläche* span, QUAL range; **Spannweitenachse des Luftschraubenblattes** *f* LUFTTRANS *Hubschrauber* blade span axis; **Spannweiten-Kontrollkarte** *f* QUAL range chart; **Spannwirbel** *m* MECHAN turnbuckle; **Spannzange** *f* MASCHINEN collet chuck; **Spannzeug** *nt* MASCHINEN chuck, chucking device

Spant *m* WASSERTRANS *Bootbau* rib, *Schiffbau* frame; **Spantabstand** *m* WASSERTRANS *Schiffbau* frame spacing; **Spantenriß** *m* WASSERTRANS *Schiffkonstruktion* body plan

Spantiefe *f* FERTIG depth of cut, rate of cut, MASCHINEN cut, depth of cut

Spantwinkel *m* WASSERTRANS *Schiffbau* frame angle

Spanumfangswinkel *m* FERTIG *Fräser* angle of approach

Spanungsbreite *f* FERTIG width of cut

Spanungsdicke *f* FERTIG thickness of cut

Spanwinkel *m* FERTIG *Räumwerkzeug* undercut angle, MASCHINEN angle of rake, rake

Sparbeize *f* FERTIG pickling inhibitor, restrainer

Spardeck *nt* WASSERTRANS spardeck

Spardiode *f* ELEKTRONIK efficiency diode

Spardüse *f* KFZTECH *Vergaser* economizer jet

Spargerät *nt* HEIZ & KÄLTE economizer

Späroguß *m* FERTIG *Kunststoffinstallationen* nodular cast iron

Sparpackung *f* VERPACK economy-size pack

Sparren *m* BAU rafter

sparsam: ~e Fahrt *f* WASSERTRANS economical speed

Spartein *nt* CHEMIE lupinidine, sparteine

Spartrafo *m* ELEKTROTECH autotransformer

Spartransformator *m* PHYS autotransformer

Spat *m* ERDÖL *Mineral* spar

Spätauslaßsteuerschieber *m* HYDRAUL *Dampf* late release slide valve

Späteinlaßsteuerschieber *m* HYDRAUL *Dampf* late admission slide valve

Spatel *m* LABOR spatula

Spatenruder *nt* WASSERTRANS spade rudder

Spatienkeil *m* DRUCK spaceband

Spatiieren *nt* DRUCK letter spacing

spatiieren *vt* DRUCK space

spationieren *vt* DRUCK space

Spationierung *f* DRUCK letter spacing

Spatium *nt* DRUCK space

Spatprodukt *nt* MATH triple scalar product

SPDT-Schalter *m* ELEKTRIZ *(einpoliger Wechselschalter)*, ELEKTROTECH *(einpoliger Umschalter)* SPDT switch *(single pole double-throw switch)*

Spediteur *m* TRANS forwarding agent

Spedition *f* WASSERTRANS shipping agency; **Speditionsauftrag** *m* WASSERTRANS shipping order; **Speditionsbüro** *nt* TRANS forwarding office; **Speditionsgebühren** *f pl* WASSERTRANS shipping charges

speerförmig *adj* KERNTECH *Brennstab* javelin-shaped

Speiche *f* MASCHINEN arm, spoke; **Speichenkreuz** *nt* FERTIG spider; **Speichenrad** *nt* KFZTECH spoke wheel

Speicher:[1] **im ~ abgelegt** *adj* COMP & DV memory-mapped

Speicher[2] *m* COMP & DV memory, store, storage device, ELEKTROTECH memory, FERTIG *Spanung* rack, RADIO memory, TELEKOM register, WASSERTRANS warehouse; **Speicher- und Adreßerweiterung** *f* COMP & DV storage expansion; **~ mit hoher Aufzeichnungsdichte** *m* COMP & DV high density storage; **~ mit hoher Dichte** *m* COMP & DV high-density storage; **~ mit indexsequentiellem Zugriff** *m* COMP & DV indexed sequential storage; **nur einmal beschreibbare ~** *f* OPTIK write-once optical storage; **~ mit seriellem Zugriff** *m* COMP & DV serial access memory, serial access storage; **~ mit veränderlichem Nachleuchten** *m* ELEKTRONIK variable-persistence storage; **Speicherabbild** *nt* COMP

& DV memory map; **Speicherabbildung** *f* COMP & DV storage map; **Speicherabgabe** *f* COMP & DV storage out; **Speicheradresse** *f* COMP & DV memory location, storage location; **Speicheradreßregister** *nt* COMP & DV MAR, memory address register; **Speicheraufbereitung** *f* COMP & DV memory edit; **Speicheraufteilungsübersicht** *f* COMP & DV storage usage map; **Speicherausnutzung** *f* COMP & DV storage efficiency, storage utilization

Speicherauszug[1] *m* COMP & DV dump, memory dump, storage dump; **~ der Änderungen** *m* COMP & DV change dump; **~ nach Störungen** *m* COMP & DV postmortem dump

Speicherauszug:[2] **~ erstellen** *vi* COMP & DV dump

Speicherauszug: **Speicherauszugsdatei** *f* COMP & DV dump data set; **Speicherauszugsprüfung** *f* COMP & DV dump check

Speicher: **Speicherbank** *f* COMP & DV memory bank; **Speicherbatterie** *f* PHYS storage battery; **Speicherbaustein** *m* COMP & DV memory chip; **Speicherbauteil** *nt* COMP & DV memory module; **Speicherbecken** *nt* NICHTFOSS ENERG storage basin, WASSERVERSORG reservoir basin; **Speicherbedarf** *m* COMP & DV storage requirement; **Speicherbelegung** *f* COMP & DV storage utilization; **Speicherbelegungsplan** *m* COMP & DV memory map; **Speicherbereich** *m* COMP & DV area; **Speicherbereinigung** *f* COMP & DV garbage collection (AmE), rubbish collection (BrE); **Speicherbereinigungsprogramm** *nt* COMP & DV garbage collector (AmE), rubbish collector (BrE); **Speicherbetrieb** *m* TELEKOM store-and-forward mode; **Speicherbildschirm** *m* ELEKTRONIK storage screen; **Speicherblase** *f* FERTIG bladder, sac; **Speicherchip** *m* COMP & DV memory chip; **Speicherdatenregister** *nt* (*MDR*) COMP & DV memory data register (*MDR*); **Speicherdatenübermittlung** *f* COMP & DV store-and-forward; **Speicherdichte** *f* COMP & DV bit density, packing density, storage density; **Speicherdirektzugriff** *m* RADIO DMA, direct memory access; **Speichereffekt** *m* ELEKTROTECH storage effect; **Speichereinheit** *f* COMP & DV storage device, TELEKOM SFU, SU, store-and-forward unit; **Speichereintrag** *m* COMP & DV storage entry; **Speicherelement** *nt* COMP & DV memory cell, storage element, ELEKTROTECH storage element; **Speichererweiterung** *f* COMP & DV processor storage, storage expansion; **Speicherfragmentierung** *f* COMP & DV storage fragmentation; **Speicherfunktion** *f* COMP & DV memory function; **Speichergerät** *nt* COMP & DV storage device; **Speicherheizkörper** *m* HEIZ & KÄLTE storage heater; **Speicherheizung** *f* HEIZ & KÄLTE storage heating, MASCHINEN storage heater; **Speicherhierarchie** *f* COMP & DV memory hierarchy, storage hierarchy; **Speicherkamera** *f* FOTO storage camera; **Speicherkapazität** *f* COMP & DV memory capacity, storage capacity, *Diskette* density, ELEKTROTECH memory capacity; **Speicherkarte** *f* COMP & DV memory card; **Speicherkomprimierung** *f* COMP & DV memory compaction; **Speicherkondensator** *m* ELEKTROTECH energy storage capacitor, reservoir capacitor, storage capacitor; **Speicherkonfiguration** *f* RAUMFAHRT *Raumschiff* storage configuration; **Speicherleistung** *f* COMP & DV memory capacity; **Speichermanagement** *nt* COMP & DV memory management; **Speichermasche** *f* ELEKTRONIK storage mesh; **Speichermedium** *nt* COMP & DV storage medium; **Speichermodul** *nt* COMP & DV memory module; **Speichermodum** *nt* COMP & DV memory module

Speichern: ~ und Befördern nt KONTROLL store-and-forward

Speichern nt COMP & DV save, store, storage, FERNSEH memory store

speichern vt COMP & DV save, store, ELEKTROTECH, KONTROLL store

Speicher: Speicherorganisation f COMP & DV file organization

speicherorientiert adj COMP & DV memory-mapped

Speicher: Speicherort m COMP & DV memory location; **Speicheroszilloskop** nt GERÄT, PHYS storage oscilloscope; **Speicherplatte** f COMP & DV storage disk; **Speicherplatz** m COMP & DV memory location, storage location; **Speicherplatzzuteilung** f COMP & DV storage allocation

speicherprogrammierbar: ~e Rechenanlage f COMP & DV stored program computer; **~e Steuerung** f (SPS) KONTROLL, REGELUNG programmable logic control (PLC)

speicherprogrammiert: ~e Rechenanlage f COMP & DV stored program computer; **~er Rechner** m KONTROLL stored program computer (AmE), stored programme computer (BrE); **~e Steuerung** f TELEKOM stored program control (AmE), stored programme control (BrE); **~e Vermittlungsstelle** f TELEKOM stored program control exchange (AmE), stored programme control exchange (BrE); **~es Vermittlungssystem** nt TELEKOM stored program switching system (AmE), stored programme switching system (BrE)

Speicher: Speicherprüfung f COMP & DV storage scan

speicherresident[1] adj COMP & DV memory-resident

speicherresident:[2] **~es Programm** nt COMP & DV resident software; **~e Software** f COMP & DV resident software

Speicher: Speicherring m TEILPHYS storage ring; **Speicherröhre** f COMP & DV storage tube, ELEKTRONIK memory tube, mesh; **Speicherröhre mit einem Elektronenstrahl** f ELEKTRONIK single gun storage tube; **Speicherröhre mit veränderlichem Nachleuchten** f ELEKTRONIK variable-persistence storage tube; **Speicherschaltdiode** f ELEKTRONIK snap-off diode; **Speicherschaltkreis** m TELEKOM memory circuit; **Speicherschema** nt NICHTFOSS ENERG storage scheme; **Speicherschreibsperre** f COMP & DV memory protection; **Speicherschutz** m COMP & DV memory protection, storage protection; **Speichersee** m WASSERVERSORG reservoir basin; **Speicherseite** f COMP & DV memory page; **Speichersicherung** f COMP & DV storage protection; **Speicherstapel** m COMP & DV storage stack; **Speicherstelle** f COMP & DV location, storage location; **Speichersteuerung** f COMP & DV memory control, ELEKTROTECH memory controller; **Speichersystem** nt FERNSEH memory system; **Speichertank für Aktivabfälle** m KERNTECH active effluent hold-up tank; **Speichertransistor** m ELEKTRONIK memory transistor; **Speichertrommel** f FERTIG magazine drum; **Speichertyp** m COMP & DV storage type

Speicherung f COMP & DV, MEERSCHMUTZ, TEILPHYS storage, WASSERVERSORG damming-up; **Speicherungsform** f COMP & DV file organization; **Speicherungsvermögen** nt WASSERVERSORG storage capacity

Speicher: Speicherverdichtung f COMP & DV memory compaction; **Speichervermittlung** f COMP & DV message switching, FERNSEH switching center (AmE), switching centre (BrE); **Speichervermittlungsnetz** nt

TELEKOM store-and-forward switching network; **Speichervermittlungsstelle** f TELEKOM message switching center (AmE), message switching centre (BrE); **Speicherverwaltung** f COMP & DV memory management, memory manager; **Speichervorgang** m COMP & DV storage; **Speicherzeit** f ELEKTRONIK decay time, ELEKTROTECH retention time, Daten, Ladung storage time; **Speicherzelle** f COMP & DV memory location, DRUCK storage cell, ELEKTROTECH cell, storage cell; **Speicherzugriff** m COMP & DV, ELEKTROTECH memory access; **Speicherzuordnung** f COMP & DV storage allocation; **Speicherzyklus** m COMP & DV memory cycle

Speigatt nt WASSERTRANS scupper

Speisebrei m LEBENSMITTEL Magen chyme

Speisebrücke f TELEKOM transmission bridge

Speisekabel nt ELEKTRIZ feeder cable, ELEKTROTECH feeder, FERNSEH feeder cable, RADIO feeder

Speisekopf m KERNTECH feeder head

Speiseleitung f ELEKTRIZ feeder, interconnecting line, ELEKTROTECH feeder, RADIO feeder line, RAUMFAHRT Weltraumfunk feeder

speisen vt ELEKTROTECH Strom feed

Speisepumpe f FERTIG, HEIZ & KÄLTE, MASCHINEN feed pump

Speiser m KER & GLAS feeder; **Speisereinlauf** m KER & GLAS feeder gate; **Speiserkolben** m KER & GLAS feeder plunger; **Speiseröffnung** f KER & GLAS feeder opening

Speiserohr nt FERTIG, MASCHINEN feed pipe

Speiseschüssel f KER & GLAS feeder nose

Speiseschaltung f ELEKTRIZ feed circuit

Speiseschiene f ELEKTRIZ feeder bar

Speisespannung f FERTIG Kunststoffinstallationen supply voltage

Speisestrom m ELEKTROTECH energizing current, supply current

Speisesystem nt FERTIG Gießen feeding head

Speisetransformator m ELEKTRIZ feeding transformer

Speiseverfahren nt KER & GLAS feeding process, method of feeding

Speisewalze f LEBENSMITTEL Walzenstuhl feed roll

Speisewasser nt HEIZ & KÄLTE, MASCHINEN, MECHAN, PAPIER, WASSERTRANS Motor, WASSERVERSORG feedwater; **Speisewasseranschluß** m KERNTECH feedwater inlet nozzle; **Speisewasseraufbereitung** f HEIZ & KÄLTE feedwater treatment; **Speisewasserenthärtung** f HEIZ & KÄLTE feedwater softening; **Speisewasserleitung** f MASCHINEN feedwater pipe; **Speisewasserpumpe** f MASCHINEN feedwater pump; **Speisewasserverteiler** m KERNTECH feedwater manifold; **Speisewasservorwärmer** m HYDRAUL Dampfkessel economizer

Speisung f ELEKTRIZ feed, ELEKTROTECH energization, Strom feed, HYDRAUL feed, TELEKOM power feed

Spektral- pref COMP & DV, GERÄT, METALL, PHYS spectral; **Spektralanalysator** m GERÄT spectral analyser (BrE), spectral analyzer (AmE); **Spektralanalyse** f COMP & DV spectral analysis, METALL spectographic analysis, PHYS spectral analysis, STRAHLPHYS spectrum analysis, TELEKOM spectral analysis; **Spektralansprechgeschwindigkeit** f OPTIK spectral responsivity; **Spektralbänder** nt pl WELLPHYS bands of the spectrum; **Spektralbelegungsgrad** m TELEKOM spectral occupancy; **Spektralbeleuchtungsstärke** f OPTIK, TELEKOM spectral irradiance; **Spektralbereich** m PHYS spectral range; **Spektralbestrahlungsstärke** f OPTIK, TELEKOM spectral irradiance; **Spektralbreite** f

TELEKOM spectral bandwidth, spectral width; **Spektraldarstellung** *f* AKUSTIK spectral distribution; **Spektraldichte** *f* AKUSTIK, ELEKTRONIK, PHYS spectral density; **Spektraldurchlaßgrad** *m* PHYS spectral transmittance; **Spektralemissionsvermögen** *nt* PHYS spectral emissivity; **Spektralempfindlichkeit** *f* TELEKOM spectral responsivity; **Spektralfarben** *f pl* STRAHLPHYS colors of the spectrum (AmE), colours of the spectrum (BrE); **Spektralfenster** *nt* OPTIK, TELEKOM spectral window; **Spektralfotometer** *nt* PHYS spectrophotometer; **Spektralfotometrie** *f* PHYS spectrophotometry; **Spektralleuchtvermögen** *nt* PHYS spectral luminance; **Spektrallichtausbeute** *f* PHYS spectral luminous efficiency; **Spektrallinie** *f* OPTIK line of spectrum, PHYS spectral line, STRAHLPHYS spectral line, TELEKOM spectral line; **Spektrallinienbreite** *f* OPTIK, STRAHLPHYS, TELEKOM spectral line width; **Spektrallinienprofil** *nt* STRAHLPHYS spectral line profile

Spektral-: **Spektralpyranometer** *nt* NICHTFOSS ENERG spectral pyranometer; **Spektralreflexionsgrad** *m* PHYS spectral reflectance; **Spektralstrahldichte** *f* TELEKOM spectral radiance; **Spektralterm** *m* PHYS spectral term; **Spektraltonhöhe** *f* AKUSTIK spectral pitch; **Spektraltransmissionsfenster** *nt* OPTIK spectral window; **Spektralverteilungscharakteristik** *f* ELEKTRONIK spectral characteristic; **Spektralverteilungskurve** *f* ELEKTRONIK spectral characteristic

Spektrograph *m* PHYS, STRAHLPHYS spectrograph

spektrographisch: **~e Analyse** *f* STRAHLPHYS spectrographic analysis

Spektrometer *nt* NICHTFOSS ENERG, PHYS, TELEKOM, WELLPHYS spectrometer

Spektrometrie *f* ERDÖL, TELEKOM spectrometry

spektrometrisch: **~e Analyse** *f* STRAHLPHYS spectrometric analysis

Spektroskop *nt* PHYS, WELLPHYS spectroscope

Spektroskopie *f* PHYS, STRAHLPHYS spectroscopy

Spektrum *nt* AUFNAHME, ELEKTRIZ, ELEKTRONIK, PHYS, RAUMFAHRT, STRAHLPHYS spectrum; **~ des sichtbaren Lichtes** *nt* WELLPHYS visible light spectrum; **~ der Turbulenz** *nt* STRÖMPHYS spectrum of turbulence; **Spektrumanalysator** *m* TELEKOM spectrum analyser (BrE), spectrum analyzer (AmE)

Spender *m* LABOR, LEBENSMITTEL, VERPACK dispenser

Spermidin *nt* CHEMIE spermidine

Spermin *nt* CHEMIE spermin, spermine

Sperr- *pref* ELEKTRONIK, FERTIG, MASCHINEN barrier; **Sperrad** *nt* FERTIG pawl wheel, ratchet, MASCHINEN dog wheel; **Sperrädchen** *nt* MASCHINEN click wheel; **Sperraste** *f* MASCHINEN lock pin, safety catch; **Sperrausgleichsgetriebe** *nt* KFZTECH limited slip differential; **Sperrband** *nt* KER & GLAS stop belt; **Sperrbecken** *nt* WASSERVERSORG catch basin, catchment basin; **Sperrbereich** *m* AUFNAHME filter attenuation band, ELEKTRONIK rejection band, FERNSEH guard band, RADIO filter attenuation band; **Sperrbeschichtung** *f* ANSTRICH barrier coating; **Sperrdifferential** *nt* KFZTECH limited slip differential

Sperre *f* BAU barricade, stop, COMP & DV lockout, ELEKTROTECH interlock, *Wellenleiter* choke, MASCHINEN catch, locking device, lock, stop, MEERSCHMUTZ boom, RADIO rejector, SICHERHEIT barricade, TELEKOM restriction

Sperr-: **Sperrelais** *nt* ELEKTROTECH lock-up relay; **Sperrschicht** *f* BAU barrier, damp-proof course, dpc, stop, waterproofing, ELEKTRONIK barrier layer, *Transistortechnik* depletion layer, RADIO junction, TELEKOM, UMWELTSCHMUTZ barrier layer; **Sperreingabe** *f* ELEKTRONIK inhibiting input; **Sperreingang** *m* COMP & DV, ELEKTRONIK inhibiting input; **Sperreinrichtung** *f* TELEKOM barring facility

Sperren *nt* ELEKTROTECH *Schalter* sticking, *Sperrelais* latching, FERNSEH blocking, METALL locking, TELEKOM blocking; **~ von Anrufen** *nt* TELEKOM call barring

sperren *vt* BAU lock, *Feuchtigkeit* insulate, stop, COMP & DV disable, inhibit, lock, ELEKTRONIK *Gatter* inhibit, ELEKTROTECH interlock, KONTROLL block, LUFTTRANS *Flugwesen* earth (BrE), ground (AmE), MASCHINEN inhibit, lock, QUAL hold, quarantine, WASSERTRANS *Schiffahrt, Hafen* blockade

Sperren: **Sperrenausbringkonfiguration** *f* MEERSCHMUTZ boom-laying configuration

sperrend: **nicht ~er Konzentrator** *m* ELEKTROTECH nonblocking concentrator; **nicht ~es Netzwerk** *nt* ELEKTROTECH nonblocking network; **nicht ~er Schalter** *m* ELEKTROTECH nonblocking switch

Sperren: **Sperrengebinde** *nt* MEERSCHMUTZ boom pack; **Sperrenrückgewinnung** *f* MEERSCHMUTZ *Wasser* boom retrieval; **Sperrenschleppe** *f* MEERSCHMUTZ boom towing

Sperr-: **Sperrfilter** *nt* ELEKTROTECH blocking network, RADIO block filter, TELEKOM blocking network; **Sperrfilterflansch** *nt* ELEKTROTECH choke flange; **Sperrgebiet** *nt* WASSERTRANS *Navigation* prohibited area; **Sperrgitter** *nt* ELEKTRONIK *Ladung* barrier grid; **Sperrgitter-Speicherröhre** *f* ELEKTRONIK barrier grid storage tube; **Sperrhaken** *m* BAU ratchet; **Sperrholz** *nt* BAU, KUNSTSTOFF, VERPACK, WASSERTRANS *Bootbau* plywood; **Sperrholzkiste** *f* VERPACK plywood case; **Sperrholzleim** *m* VERPACK plywood adhesive; **Sperrichtungsbetrieb** *m* ELEKTROTECH *Transistoren* reverse bias; **Sperrimpuls** *m* ELEKTRONIK inhibiting pulse; **Sperrklinke** *f* BAU catch, ratchet, FERTIG detent, dog, holding pawl, latch, locking pawl, pawl, retaining pawl, trip dog, MASCHINEN detent pawl, keeper, pawl, ratchet, MECHAN catch, pawl, ratchet; **Sperrkondensator** *m* ELEKTRIZ, ELEKTROTECH blocking capacitor; **Sperrkreis** *m* RADIO *Antennen* trap; **Sperrkreis für wilde Schwingungen** *m* ELEKTRONIK parasitic suppressor; **Sperrlager** *nt* QUAL hold store, quarantine store, restricted store, salvage store; **Sperrmauer** *f* BAU barrage, WASSERVERSORG dam

Sperrmüll *m* ABFALL bulky waste, dump for bulky waste; **Sperrmüllabfuhr** *f* ABFALL bulk collection; **Sperrmüllsammlung** *f* ABFALL bulk collection

Sperr-: **Sperr-Richtung** *f* ELEKTROTECH inverse direction; **Sperrscheibe** *f* LUFTTRANS blanking plate, MECHAN lock washer; **Sperrscheinwiderstand** *m* AKUSTIK blocked electrical impedance, ELEKTROTECH blocked impedance

Sperrschicht *f* ELEKTROTECH barrier; **Sperrschichteffekt** *m* ELEKTROTECH photovoltaic effect; **Sperrschichtelement** *nt* ELEKTROTECH photovoltaic cell; **Sperrschichtfeldeffekttransistor** *m* ELEKTRONIK, RADIO JFET, junction FET, junction field effect transistor; **Sperrschichtfolie** *f* VERPACK barrier film; **Sperrschichtfotodiode** *f* ELEKTRONIK depletion layer photodiode; **Sperrschichtfotoeffekt** *m* NICHTFOSS ENERG, PHYS, TELEKOM photovoltaic effect; **Sperrschichtfotozelle** *f* NICHTFOSS ENERG, PHYS photovoltaic cell; **Sperrschichtgenerator** *m* ELEKTRO-

TECH photovoltaic generator; **Sperrschichtkapazität** *f* ELEKTROTECH junction capacitance; **Sperrschichtkondensator** *m* ELEKTROTECH junction capacitor; **Sperrschichtpolymer** *nt* KUNSTSTOFF barrier resin; **Sperrschichtstoffe** *m pl* VERPACK barrier material; **Sperrschichtstrom** *m* ELEKTROTECH photovoltaic current; **Sperrschichtverpackung** *f* VERPACK barrier packaging; **Sperrschichtzelle** *f* ELEKTROTECH barrier layer cell, photovoltaic cell

Sperr-: **Sperrschrift** *f* COMP & DV spacing; **Sperrschwinger** *m* ELEKTRONIK, PHYS blocking oscillator; **Sperrsignal** *nt* ELEKTRONIK inhibiting signal; **Sperrspannung** *f* PHYS blocking voltage, sticking voltage; **Sperrstift** *m* MASCHINEN catch pin; **Sperrstrom** *m* ELEKTROTECH reverse current; **Sperrstromverstärkung** *f* ELEKTRONIK inverse gain; **Sperrung** *f* ELEKTRONIK *Gatter* inhibition, ELEKTROTECH suspension, *Leitfähigkeit* blocking, cutoff, HYDRAUL *der Dampfzufuhr* shutting off, LUFTTRANS interlock, MASCHINEN detent, QUAL holding, quarantining; **Sperrventil** *nt* RAUMFAHRT check valve; **Sperrverlust** *m* RAUMFAHRT *Weltraumfunk* blocking loss; **Sperrvermerk** *m* QUAL hold tag, stop note; **Sperrverzögerungszeit** *f* ELEKTRONIK reverse recovery time; **Sperrvorrichtung** *f* ELEKTRIZ locking device, ELEKTROTECH blocking device, MASCHINEN blocking device, catch, latch, lock, locking device, stop; **Sperrwand** *f* ABFALL slurry wall; **Sperrwandler** *m* ELEKTROTECH switching regulator; **Sperrwandlung** *f* ELEKTROTECH switching regulation; **Sperrwasser** *nt* KERNTECH seal water; **Sperrwerk** *nt* MASCHINEN pawl-and-ratchet motion, ratchet-and-pawl motion; **Sperrzeit** *f* ELEKTRONIK idle period, ELEKTROTECH *Gerät* off period, *Schaltstück* off period, QUAL quarantine period; **Sperrzeit bei positiver Anodenspannung** *f* ELEKTROTECH blocking period; **Sperrzustand** *m* ELEKTRONIK blocking state, ELEKTROTECH *Thyristoren* off-state

Spezial- *pref* COMP & DV, FERTIG, TELEKOM, VERPACK, WASSERTRANS special; **Spezialeffektbus** *m* FERNSEH special effects bus; **Spezialgummibeschichtung** *f* SICHERHEIT special rubber lining; **Spezialindizierung** *f* COMP & DV indexing; **Spezialkleber** *m* VERPACK purpose-formulated adhesive; **Spezialmutter** *f* FERTIG *Kunststoffinstallationen* special nut; **Spezialprozessor** *m* TELEKOM applications processor; **Spezialrechner** *m* COMP & DV special purpose computer; **Spezialsoftware** *f* COMP & DV, WASSERTRANS dedicated software

speziell:[1] **~ angefertigt** *adj* HEIZ & KÄLTE custom-made, purpose-made; **~ entworfen** *adj* VERPACK purpose-designed

speziell:[2] **~e Relativitätstheorie** *f* PHYS special theory

Spezifikation *f* BAU, COMP & DV, MASCHINEN spec, specification; **Spezifikations- und Beschreibungssprache** *f* TELEKOM specification and description language; **Spezifikationsblatt** *nt* FERNSEH specification sheet; **Spezifikationssprache** *f* COMP & DV specification language

spezifisch[1] *adj* ANSTRICH inherent, PHYS *auf Masseneinheit bezogen* specific

spezifisch:[2] **~e Aktivität** *f* PHYS specific activity; **~e Aktivität eines Elementes** *f* KERNTECH element-specific activity; **~e akustische Auslenkung** *f* AKUSTIK specific acoustic compliance; **~e Ausstrahlung** *f* PHYS radiant exitance, TELEKOM radiance; **~er Blindleitwert** *m* AKUSTIK specific acoustic susceptance; **~er Brennwert** *m* HEIZ & KÄLTE gross calorific value; **~e Bruchfestigkeit** *f* METALL ultimate tensile strength; **~er Brunnenkapazität** *m* NICHTFOSS ENERG specific capacity of a well; **~e Dämpfung** *f* RAUMFAHRT specific attenuation, TELEKOM attenuation coefficient; **~e Dichte** *f* PHYS relative density, specific gravity; **~es Drehvermögen** *nt* PHYS specific rotation; **~e Drehzahl** *f* NICHTFOSS ENERG specific speed; **~er Durchgangswiderstand** *m* ELEKTROTECH, KUNSTSTOFF volume resistivity; **~e elektrische Leitfähigkeit** *f* ELEKTROTECH conductivity; **~e Emission** *f* ELEKTROTECH specific emission; **~e Empfindlichkeit** *f* AKUSTIK specific sensitivity; **~e Enthalpie** *f* PHYS specific enthalpy; **~e Entropie** *f* PHYS specific entropy; **~es Gewicht** *nt* KOHLEN unit weight, PHYS relative density, specific gravity; **~e Gibbssche Funktion** *f* PHYS specific Gibbs function; **~e Haftkraft** *f* KUNSTSTOFF specific adhesion; **~er Halbleiter** *m* *(cf I-Halbleiter)* COMP & DV intrinsic semiconductor; **~e Heizleistung** *f* HEIZ & KÄLTE specific heat output; **~e Helmholtzfunktion** *f* PHYS specific Helmholtz function; **~er Impuls** *m* RAUMFAHRT specific impulse; **~e innere Energie** *f* PHYS specific internal energy; **~e Ionisierung** *f (S)* KERNTECH specific ionization *(S)*; **~e Kapazität** *f* ELEKTRIZ specific capacitance; **~e Ladung** *f* PHYS, STRAHLPHYS, TEILPHYS charge-mass ratio, specific charge; **~e Ladung eines Elektrons** *f* KERNTECH electron specific charge; **~e Lautheit** *f* AKUSTIK specific loudness; **~es Leistungsgewicht** *nt* MASCHINEN power-weight ratio; **~er Leitwert** *m* ELEKTRIZ conductivity, specific conductance; **~e Lichtausstrahlung** *f* PHYS luminous exitance, radiance, STRAHLPHYS radiance; **~er magnetischer Widerstand** *m* PHYS reluctivity; **~e Nachweisbarkeit** *f* OPTIK specific detectivity; **~e Nachweisfähigkeit** *f* TELEKOM specific detectivity; **~e Oberfläche** *f* KUNSTSTOFF specific surface area; **~er Oberflächenwiderstand** *m* ELEKTROTECH surface resistivity; **~e Schallimpedanz** *f* AKUSTIK, PHYS specific acoustic impedance; **~e Schmelzwärme** *f* PHYS specific latent heat; **~e spektrale Ausstrahlung** *f* TELEKOM spectral radiance; **~e Steife** *f* RAUMFAHRT specific stiffness; **~er Strömungswiderstand** *m* AKUSTIK flow resistivity; **~es Volumen** *nt* PHYS specific volume; **~er Volumenwiderstand** *m* ELEKTRIZ mass resistivity, ELEKTROTECH bulk resistivity; **~e Wärme** *f* HEIZ & KÄLTE, KUNSTSTOFF specific heat, PHYS *(c)* specific heat capacity *(c)*, RAUMFAHRT, THERMOD specific heat; **~e Wärmekapazität** *f (c)* THERMOD specific heat capacity *(c)*; **~er Wärmewiderstand** *m* PHYS, THERMOD thermal resistivity; **~er Widerstand** *m* ELEKTRIZ, ELEKTROTECH resistivity, specific resistance, ERDÖL, KOHLEN resistivity, KUNSTSTOFF electrical resistivity, resistivity

Spezifizierung *f* PATENT *Waren, Dienstleistungen* spec, specification

Sphäre *f* GEOM, PHYS sphere

sphärisch: **~e Aberration** *f* FOTO, OPTIK, PHYS, TELEKOM spherical aberration; **~e Dämmplatte** *f* AUFNAHME spherical baffle; **~es Dreieck** *nt* GEOM spherical triangle; **~e Geometrie** *f* GEOM spherical geometry; **~e Linse** *f* PHYS spherical lens; **~er Spiegel** *m* PHYS spherical mirror; **~es Zweieck** *nt* FERTIG spherical lune

Sphärizität *f* GEOM sphericity

Sphäroid *nt* GEOM, PHYS spheroid

sphärolithisch *adj* FERTIG spheroidal

Sphärometer *nt* PHYS spherometer

Sphingosin *nt* CHEMIE sphingosine

Spickelement *nt* KERNTECH spike
Spicken *nt* TEXTIL oiling
Spickungspräparat *nt* ELEKTRONIK *Radiologie* implant
Spiegel *m* KER & GLAS, PHYS mirror; **Spiegelbelegung** *f* FERTIG silvering; **Spiegelbild** *nt* GEOM mirror image; **Spiegelfrequenz** *f* ELEKTRONIK, FERNSEH image frequency; **Spiegelfrequenzstörung** *f* ELEKTRONIK, FERNSEH image frequency interference; **Spiegelgalvanometer** *nt* ELEKTRIZ light-spot galvanometer, mirror galvanometer, reflecting mirror galvanometer, GERÄT luminous pointer galvanometer, mirror galvanometer; **Spiegelglas** *nt* BAU plate glass, KER & GLAS plate; **Spiegelglasfehler durch unvollständiges Schleifen** *m* KER & GLAS short finish; **Spiegelheck** *nt* WASSERTRANS *Schiffbau* square transom stern, transom stern; **Spiegelherstellung** *f* KER & GLAS mirror making
spiegelig: **~e Oberfläche** *f* FERTIG glazing
Spiegel: **Spiegelkasten** *m* FOTO reflex housing; **Spiegelkerne** *m pl* PHYS mirror nuclei; **Spiegelnuklid** *nt* PHYS mirror nuclide; **Spiegelobjektiv** *nt* FOTO mirror lens; **Spiegelreaktor mit Feldumkehr** *m* KERNTECH field-reversed mirror reactor; **Spiegelreflexion** *f* PHYS, TELEKOM specular reflection; **Spiegelreflexionskoeffizient** *m* TELEKOM specular reflection coefficient; **Spiegelroheisen** *nt* METALL spiegel iron; **Spiegelschliff** *m* MECHAN mirror finish; **Spiegelskale** *f* GERÄT mirror scale; **Spiegelsymmetrie** *f* MATH dissymmetry; **Spiegelteleskop** *nt* PHYS reflecting telescope
Spiegelung *f* GEOM mirroring, reflection, WELLPHYS reflection; **Spiegelungsachse** *f* GEOM mirror line
spiegelverkehrt: **~e Darstellung** *f* GEOM mirrored representation
Spiel:[1] **mit ~** *adj* MASCHINEN loose
Spiel[2] *nt* HYDRAUL *Kolben* space, KERNTECH clearance, KFZTECH free travel, *Triebstrang* backlash, MASCHINEN allowance, backlash, clearance, play, slackness, MECHAN backlash, play; **äußeres ~** *nt* HYDRAUL clearance
Spiel:[3] **~ geben** *vi* MASCHINEN give clearance to
spielen *vt* FERNSEH, MECHAN play
spielfrei[1] *adj* FERTIG *Kunststoffinstallationen* no-play, GERÄT *Meßwerk* backlash-free
spielfrei:[2] **~e Paarung** *f* FERTIG zero-backlash mating
Spiel: **Spielpassung** *f* MASCHINEN clearance fit; **Spielraum** *m* COMP & DV *Zeit* margin, ELEKTROTECH, HYDRAUL clearance, MASCHINEN play, MECHAN clearance, play; **Spielsitz** *m* HYDRAUL *Ventil* loose seat; **Spieltheorie** *f* KÜNSTL INT, MATH game theory
Spiere *f* WASSERTRANS *Schiffbau* spar, *Seezeichen* perch; **Spierentonne** *f* WASSERTRANS *Seezeichen* pillar buoy, spar buoy
Spike *m* LUFTTRANS spike; **Spikereifen** *m* KFZTECH studded tire (AmE), studded tyre (BrE)
Spill *nt* ELEKTROTECH spill, MECHAN, WASSERTRANS *Schiffzubehör* capstan; **Spilltrommel** *f* WASSERTRANS *Schiffzubehör* capstan drum
Spin *m* PHYS, RAUMFAHRT, TEILPHYS spin; **Spinasterin** *nt* CHEMIE spinasterol; **Spind** *m* WASSERTRANS locker; **Spinnkabel** *nt* TEXTIL tow; **Spinnkuchen** *m* KER & GLAS *Glasfasern*, TEXTIL cake
Spinacen *nt* CHEMIE squalene
Spin: **Spinachse** *f* RAUMFAHRT spin axis; **Spinaustauschkraft** *f* KERNTECH spin exchange force; **Spin-Bahn-Kopplung** *f* PHYS spin orbit coupling
Spindel *f* BAU shaft, stem, *Drehbank* spindle, *Treppe*

newel, FERTIG mandrel, mandril, *Kunststoffinstallationen* spindle, stem, HYDRAUL *Schieber* rod, *Ventil* stem, KER & GLAS *Glasfasern*, KFZTECH spindle, MASCHINEN mandrel, mandril, screw, spindle, MECHAN shaft, spindle; **~ für Drehrichtungswechsel** *f* MASCHINEN reversing screw; **~ des Luftschraubenblattes** *f* LUFTTRANS *Hubschrauber* blade spindle; **Spindelaggregat** *nt* MASCHINEN spindle unit; **Spindelarm** *m* KFZTECH spindle arm; **Spindelbohrer** *m* FERTIG gun drill; **Spindelbremse** *f* EISENBAHN, KFZTECH, MASCHINEN screw brake; **Spindeldocke** *f* MASCHINEN headstock; **Spindeldrehmaschine** *f* MASCHINEN mandrel lathe, mandril lathe; **Spindelfräsmaschine** *f* BAU *Holzbau* spindle molding machine (AmE), spindle moulding machine (BrE); **Spindelkasten** *m* FERTIG gearbox, *Spanung* head assembly, MASCHINEN headstock; **Spindelkasten mit Reibungskupplung** *m* MASCHINEN friction headstock; **Spindelkopf** *m* MASCHINEN spindle head, spindle nose; **Spindellagerarm** *m* FERTIG adjustable arm; **Spindellagerplatte** *f* FERTIG *Spanung* pattern plate; **Spindelnase** *f* FERTIG nose, MASCHINEN mandrel nose, mandril nose; **Spindelpresse** *f* MASCHINEN fly press, screw press, PAPIER screw press; **Spindelstab** *m* BAU spindle; **Spindelstock** *m* FERTIG headstock, head, poppet, MASCHINEN head, headstock; **Spindelstockspitze** *f* FERTIG *Spanung* head center (AmE), head centre (BrE), MASCHINEN headstock center (AmE), headstock centre (BrE); **Spindeltreppe** *f* BAU solid newel stair; **Spindelung** *f* PHYS hydrometry; **Spindelvorgelege** *nt* FERTIG back gear; **Spindelvorlauf** *m* FERTIG advance of the spindle; **Spindelwange** *f* BAU *Treppe* outside string
Spin: **Spindrehimpuls** *m* PHYS spin angular momentum; **Spinellerzeugnis** *nt* KER & GLAS spinel refractory
Spinnaker *m* WASSERTRANS *Segeln* spinnaker; **Spinnakerbaum** *m* WASSERTRANS *Segeln* spinnaker boom
Spinndüse *f* KER & GLAS *Glasfasern* nozzle
Spinnen *nt* TEXTIL spinning
spinnen *vt* TEXTIL spin
Spinnereiabfall *m* TEXTIL trash
Spinnfasergarn *nt* TEXTIL spun yarn
spinngefärbt *adj* TEXTIL spun-dyed
Spinning-Reserve *f* NICHTFOSS ENERG spinning reserves
spinnkuchengefärbt *adj* TEXTIL cake-dyed
Spinnrad *nt* TEXTIL spinning wheel
Spinnseil *nt* ERDÖL spinning line
Spinnverfahren *nt* TEXTIL spinning system
Spinnvlies *nt* TEXTIL spunbonded fabric
spinodal: **~e Auflösung** *f* METALL spinodal decomposition
Spin: **Spinquantengesamtzahl** *f (S)* KERNTECH total spin quantum number *(S)*; **Spinquantenzahl** *f (s)* KERNTECH, LABOR, PHYS spin quantum number *(s)*; **Spinschubtriebwerk** *nt* RAUMFAHRT spin thruster; **Spinstabilisierung** *f* RAUMFAHRT spin stabilization; **Spintemperatur** *f* PHYS spin temperature; **Spinwelle** *f* PHYS spin wave
Spion *m* MASCHINEN feeler gage (AmE), feeler gauge (BrE)
Spionagesatellit *m* RAUMFAHRT spy satellite
Spiral- *pref* MASCHINEN spiral; **Spiralbewegung** *f* KERNTECH helicoidal motion; **Spiralbewegung von Teilchen** *f* KERNTECH particle spiraling; **Spiralbindung** *f* DRUCK spiral binding; **Spiralbohrer** *m* ERDÖL *Bohrtechnik* spiral bit, MASCHINEN jobber drill, twist bit, twist drill, MECHAN twist drill; **Spiralbohrer mit Morseke-**

gelschaft *m* MASCHINEN Morse taper shank twist drill; **Spiralbohrer mit Zylinderschaft** *m* MASCHINEN parallel-shank twist drill, straight shank twist drill, twist drill with parallel shank, twist drill with straight shank; **Spiralbohrerschleifmaschine** *f* MASCHINEN twist drill grinder; **Spiraldehnung** *f* FERTIG volution

Spirale *f* FERTIG scroll, volute, GEOM, MASCHINEN spiral; **~ für mehrteiligen Entwicklungsbehälter** *f* FOTO multiunit tank spiral

Spiral-: **Spiralfeder** *f* KFZTECH coil spring, MASCHINEN coil spring, spiral spring, MECHAN coil spring, helical spring

spiralförmig[1] *adj* GEOM spiral

spiralförmig:[2] **~er Bruch** *m* KER & GLAS spiral fracture

Spiral-: **Spiralfräseinrichtung** *f* MASCHINEN spiral milling attachment; **Spiralfräsen** *nt* MASCHINEN helical milling, spiral milling; **Spiralfräser** *m* MASCHINEN helical milling cutter, spiral milling cutter; **Spiralgehäuse** *nt* KFZTECH volute casing, MASCHINEN volute

spiralgenutet: **~er Gewindebohrer** *m* MASCHINEN spiral fluted tap

Spiral-: **Spiralhülse** *f* VERPACK spirally-wound tube

spiralig[1] *adj* FERTIG volute, GEOM, MASCHINEN spiral

spiralig:[2] **~e Turbulenz** *f* STRÖMPHYS spiral turbulence

Spiral-: **Spiralinstabilität** *f* KERNTECH helical instability; **Spiralkegelrad** *nt* MASCHINEN spiral bevel gear; **Spiralkegelradgetriebe** *nt* KFZTECH spiral bevel gearing; **Spiralkern** *m* ELEKTRIZ wound core; **Spiralklassierer** *m* KOHLEN spiral classifier; **Spirallaufschienen** *f pl* KER & GLAS nog plate spiral runner bars; **Spiralnut** *f* MASCHINEN helical groove; **Spiralschnecke** *f* MASCHINEN spiral worm; **Spiraltuner** *m* ELEKTRONIK continuous tuner; **Spiralwinkel** *m* MASCHINEN spiral angle; **Spiralzahnkegelrad** *nt* MASCHINEN spiral bevel gear

Spiran *nt* CHEMIE spiran; **Spiranverbindung** *f* CHEMIE spiran

Spirituosen *f pl* LEBENSMITTEL spirits

Spiritus *m* LEBENSMITTEL spirit; **Spirituslack** *m* BAU spirit lacquer; **Spirituslampe** *f* LABOR spirit lamp

spirozyklisch: **~e Verbindung** *f* CHEMIE spiran

spitz[1] *adj* MASCHINEN sharp, METROL *Winkel* acute

spitz:[2] **~er Maurerhammer** *m* BAU mattock; **~er Winkel** *m* GEOM acute angle

Spitzbogenkaliber *nt* FERTIG gothic pass

Spitzbohrer *m* FERTIG flat drill, spade drill, MASCHINEN flat drill

Spitze *f* ELEKTROTECH spike, FERNSEH peak, FERTIG *Gewinde* crest, *Kegelrad* apex, GEOM apex, vertex, *Kegel* apex, MASCHINEN bit, nose, nose, point, METALL cusp, RADIO peak, TEXTIL lace, WASSERTRANS *Festmachen* peak; **~ zu Spitze-Wert** *m* AKUSTIK peak-to-peak value

Spitzen *nt* FERTIG *Schmieden* end reduction

spitzen *vt* BAU point

Spitze: **Spitzenamplitude** *f* AUFNAHME, ELEKTRONIK peak amplitude; **Spitzenanhebungskreis** *m* FERNSEH peaking circuit; **Spitzenanhebungsschaltung** *f* FERNSEH peaking network; **Spitzenaufnahmepegel** *m* AUFNAHME peak recording level; **Spitzenbegrenzer** *m* FERNSEH peak limiter; **Spitzenbegrenzung** *f* AUFNAHME peak limitation, ELEKTRONIK peak clipping; **Spitzenbelastung** *f* ELEKTRIZ peaking capacity, ELEKTROTECH maximum demand; **Spitzenbelastungszeit** *f* TELEKOM peak busy hour

Spitzende *nt* BAU spigot

Spitze: **Spitzendefekt** *m* METALL point defect; **Spitzendiode** *f* ELEKTRONIK point contact diode; **Spitzendrehen** *nt* MASCHINEN turning between centers (AmE), turning between centres (BrE); **Spitzendrehmaschine** *f* FERTIG, MASCHINEN center lathe (AmE), centre lathe (BrE); **Spitzendrehmaschine mit Leitspindel** *f* MASCHINEN engine lathe; **Spitzendurchdringung** *f* FERNSEH tip penetration; **Spitzenfaktor** *m* ELEKTRONIK peak factor; **Spitzenfrequenzhub** *m* RAUMFAHRT, TELEKOM peak frequency deviation; **Spitzengebühr** *f* TELEKOM peak rate; **Spitzenhelligkeit** *f* FERNSEH peak brightness; **Spitzenherausragen** *nt* FERNSEH tip protrusion; **Spitzenhöhe** *f* FERNSEH tip height, MASCHINEN center height (AmE), centre height (BrE), height of centers (AmE), height of centres (BrE); **Spitzenimpuls-Amplitude** *f* ELEKTRONIK peak pulse amplitude; **Spitzenkegel** *m* LUFTTRANS nose cone; **Spitzenkontakt** *m* ELEKTROTECH point contact; **Spitzenkonzentration** *f* UMWELTSCHMUTZ peak concentration; **Spitzenlagerung** *f* MASCHINEN toe bearing; **Spitzenlast** *f* ELEKTRIZ maximum demand, peak load, ELEKTROTECH peak load; **Spitzenlastkraftwerk** *nt* ELEKTRIZ peak load power plant; **Spitzenlastpunkt** *m* KERNTECH hot spot; **Spitzenleistung** *f* BAU peak capacity, ELEKTROTECH, FERNSEH peak power, RADIO, TELEKOM PEP, peak envelope power

spitzenlos[1] *adj* MASCHINEN, MECHAN centerless (AmE), centreless (BrE)

spitzenlos:[2] **~e Rundschleifmaschine** *f* MECHAN centerless grinder (AmE), centreless grinder (BrE)

Spitze: **Spitzenmesser** *m* FERNSEH peak meter; **Spitzennadelkamm** *m* TEXTIL bearded needle frame; **Spitzenpegel** *m* AUFNAHME peak level; **Spitzenprojektion** *f* FERNSEH tip projection; **Spitzenregelung** *f* FERNSEH peaking control; **Spitzenschleifapparat** *m* FERTIG center grinder (AmE), centre grinder (BrE); **Spitzenschleifen** *nt* FERTIG on-center grinding (AmE), on-centre grinding (BrE); **Spitzensignal** *nt* FERNSEH peak signal; **Spitzensignalamplitude** *f* ELEKTRONIK peak signal amplitude; **Spitzenspannung** *f* ELEKTROTECH, FERNSEH, PHYS peak voltage; **Spitzenspannung eines Senders** *f* *(SS-Spannung)* RADIO peak envelope voltage *(PEV)*; **Spitzenspanwinkel** *m* FERTIG *Spanung* top rake; **Spitzensperrspannung** *f* ELEKTRIZ peak inverse voltage; **Spitzenspiel** *nt* FERTIG *Gewinde* crest clearance; **Spitzenstrahlungs-Laserstrahl** *m* ELEKTRONIK high-irradiance laser beam; **Spitzenstrom** *m* ELEKTRIZ, ELEKTROTECH, PHYS peak current; **Spitzenstundenfaktor** *m* EISENBAHN, TRANS peak hour factor; **Spitzenteilzirkel** *m* MASCHINEN spring bow divider; **Spitzenverkehr** *m* TRANS peak hour traffic, peak load traffic, peak period traffic; **Spitzenverkehrsaufkommen** *nt* TRANS peak traffic volume; **Spitzenverlust** *m* NICHTFOSS ENERG tip loss; **Spitzenverzerrung** *f* FERNSEH peak distortion; **Spitzenwasserbedarf** *m* WASSERVERSORG peak water demand; **Spitzenwasserdurchfluß** *m* WASSERVERSORG peak water flow; **Spitzenweite** *f* MASCHINEN distance between centers (AmE), distance between centres (BrE); **Spitzenwert** *m* ELEKTRIZ, ELEKTRONIK peak value, GERÄT crest value, KERNTECH maximum, PHYS peak value, RAUMFAHRT peak factor, TELEKOM peak value; **Spitzenwertbildung** *f* ELEKTRONIK ; **Spitzenwertmessung** *f* FERNSEH peak program meter (AmE), peak programme meter (BrE); **Spitzenwinkel** *m* FERTIG angle of point, *Bohrer* included angle; **Spitzenwirbel am Luftschraubenblatt** *m* LUFTTRANS *Hubschrauber* blade tip vortex; **Spitzenzähler** *m* ELEKTROTECH demand meter, GERÄT *Energieverbrauch* excess meter; **Spitzenzeit** *f* FERNSEH peak time; **Spitzenzuschaltung** *f* FERNSEH tip engagement

Spitze-Spitze- *pref (SS)* FERNSEH *Hüllkurve*, RADIO peak-to-peak *(pp)*; **Spitze-Spitze-Amplitude** *f* AUFNAHME, ELEKTRONIK peak-to-peak amplitude; **Spitze-Spitze-Signalamplitude** *f* FERNSEH peak-to-peak signal amplitude

Spitzformer *m* FERTIG *Gießen* pegging rammer
Spitzgewinde *nt* MASCHINEN V-thread, vee thread, sharp thread
Spitzheit *f* GEOM *Winkel* acuteness
Spitzigkeit *f* GEOM acuteness
Spitzkehre *f* EISENBAHN back shunt
Spitzkerbe *f* MASCHINEN V-notch
Spitzkolumne *f* DRUCK short page
Spitzkopfniet *m* BAU steeple head rivet
Spitzlicht *nt* DRUCK, FOTO highlight; **Spitzlichterabriß** *m* FERNSEH highlight tearing
Spitzlutte *f* KOHLEN hydraulic classifier
Spitzmarke *f* COMP & DV heading
Spitzsenken *nt* MASCHINEN countersinking
spitzsenken *vt* FERTIG sink
Spitzsenker *m* MASCHINEN countersink
Spitztonne *f* WASSERTRANS *Seezeichen* conical buoy
spitzwinkelig: **~es V-förmiges Unterwerkzeug** *nt* FERTIG acute angle die
spitzwinklig[1] *adj* FERTIG acute-angled, GEOM acute-angled, acute-angular
spitzwinklig:[2] **~es Dreieck** *nt* GEOM acute triangle
Spleiß *m* ELEKTRIZ joint, TELEKOM joint, splice, WASSERTRANS *Tauwerk* splice; **Spleißdämpfung** *f* TELEKOM splice loss; **Spleißdose** *f* ELEKTRIZ splice box
spleißen *vt* TELEKOM, TEXTIL *Seil* splice
Spleißer *m* TELEKOM jointer, splicer
Spleiß: **Spleißkasten** *m* ELEKTRIZ splice box; **Spleißstelle** *f* OPTIK splice; **Spleißstelle für Lichtleitfasern** *f* OPTIK optical fiber splice (AmE), optical fibre splice (BrE)
Spleißung *f* FERNSEH *Kabel* splice, TEXTIL splicing
Splint *m* BAU peg, ELEKTROTECH key, FERTIG cotter, MASCHINEN cotter pin, forelock, key bolt, split cotter pin, split pin, MECHAN cotter pin, spline, WASSERTRANS cotter pin; **Splintbolzen** *m* MASCHINEN cotter bolt; **Splintentreiber** *m* MASCHINEN driftpin, driver, key drift, rivet drift; **Splintloch** *nt* MASCHINEN cotter pin hole, split pin hole; **Splintverbindung** *f* BAU, MASCHINEN cottered joint; **Splintzieher** *m* MASCHINEN cotter pin extractor, pin extractor, split pin extracting tool
Splitt *m* ANSTRICH grit, BAU chip, crushed stone, stone chipping, KOHLEN chippings; **Splittelektrode** *f* FERNSEH splitting electrode
Splitter *m* BAU splinter, KER & GLAS chippings, sliver, MECHAN chip
splitterfrei: **~es Glas** *nt* KFZTECH shatter-proof glass
Splitterprüfung *f* WERKPRÜF *Glas* shatter test
splittrig: **~er Bruch** *m* KOHLEN splintery fracture
Splitt: **Splittstreuer** *m* TRANS grit spreader, stone spreader; **Splittstreumaschine** *f* TRANS gritter; **Splittzuschlag** *m* KOHLEN crushed aggregate
Spoiler *m* KFZTECH *Karosserie*, LUFTTRANS *Luftfahrzeug* spoiler

Spondeus *m* AKUSTIK spondee
Spongin *nt* CHEMIE spongin
spontan: **~e Anregung** *f* KERNTECH spontaneous excitation; **~e Bremsbetätigung** *f* EISENBAHN spontaneous brake application; **~e Emission** *f* PHYS spontaneous emission; **~e Emission von Strahlung** *f* STRAHLPHYS spontaneous emission of radiation; **~e Kernbildung** *f* METALL spontaneous nucleation; **~e Magnetisierung** *f* PHYS spontaneous magnetization; **~e Selbstentzündung** *f* RAUMFAHRT *Treibstoff* hypergolic ignition; **~e Spaltung** *f* PHYS, STRAHLPHYS spontaneous fission; **~e Spaltungswahrscheinlichkeit** *f* STRAHLPHYS spontaneous fission probability; **~e Strahlungsemission** *f* STRAHLPHYS spontaneous emission of radiation; **~e Übergänge** *m pl* STRAHLPHYS spontaneous transitions; **~e Verbrennung** *f* SICHERHEIT spontaneous combustion; **~er Zerfall** *m* STRAHLPHYS spontaneous decay
Spontanaktivität *f* AKUSTIK spontaneous activity
Spontanbruch *m* KER & GLAS spontaneous breaking
Spontanemission *f* TELEKOM spontaneous emission
Spontanmagnetisierung *f* STRAHLPHYS spontaneous magnetization
Sponung *f* WASSERTRANS rabbet
Spool-Betrieb *m* COMP & DV spooling
Spool-Einheit *f* COMP & DV spooling device
Spooler *m* COMP & DV spooler
Spooling *nt* COMP & DV spooling
Spool-Programm *nt (Ein-/Ausgabe parallel zu Rechenprogramm)* COMP & DV SPOOL *(simultaneous peripheral operations on-line)*
Sporn *m* FERTIG spur; **Spornrad** *nt* LUFTTRANS tail wheel
Sportsucher *m* FOTO *Kamera* sports finder
Sporttauchen *nt* WASSERTRANS scuba diving
Sportwagen *m* KFZTECH *Fahrzeugart* sports car; **~ mit offenem Verdeck** *m* KFZTECH *Fahrzeugart* cabriolet, convertible
Sprach- *pref* AKUSTIK, COMP & DV, TELEKOM speech; **~- und Daten-Nebenstellenanlage** *f* TELEKOM voice/data PBX; **~- und Datenpaketvermittlung** *f* TELEKOM voice/data packet switch
sprach: **~- und datenintegrierende Vermittlung** *f* TELEKOM integrated voice-data switch; **~- und datenintegrierende Wählnebenstelle** *f* TELEKOM integrated voice-data PABX
Sprach-: **Sprachanalyse** *f* TELEKOM speech analysis; **Sprachaudiogramm** *nt* AKUSTIK speech audiogram; **Sprachaudiometer** *nt* AKUSTIK speech audiometer; **Sprachaudiometrie** *f* AKUSTIK speech audiometry; **Sprachausgabe** *f* COMP & DV voice output, ELEKTRONIK audio output, TELEKOM voice response; **Sprachausgabe-Einheit** *f (ARU)* COMP & DV audio response unit *(ARU)*
sprachbeschreibend: **~e Sprache** *f* COMP & DV metalanguage
Sprach-: **Sprachbox** *f* TELEKOM voice mailbox; **Sprach-Chip** *m* COMP & DV speech chip; **Sprachcodierer** *m* TELEKOM voice coder; **Sprachcodierung** *f* RAUMFAHRT speech encoding, TELEKOM speech coding, speech encoding, vocoding; **Sprachdateneingabe** *f* COMP & DV voice data entry; **Sprach-Datennetz** *nt* TELEKOM speech data network; **Sprachdemodulation** *f* RAUMFAHRT speech detection; **Sprachdienst** *m* TELEKOM speech service
Sprache *f* COMP & DV language; **~ mit Blockstruktur** *f* COMP & DV block-structured language; **~ der fünften**

Generation *f* KÜNSTL INT fifth-generation language; **Spracheingabedaten** *nt pl* COMP & DV voice data entry; **Sprachenanweisung** *f* COMP & DV language statement; **Sprachenprozessor** *m* COMP & DV language processor

Sprach-: **Spracherkennung** *f* COMP & DV, KÜNSTL INT speech recognition; **Spracherzeugung** *f* TELEKOM speech generation; **Sprachfilter** *nt* AUFNAHME speech filter; **Sprachfrequenz** *f (SF)* ELEKTROTECH, TELEKOM speech frequency *(SF)*, voice frequency *(VF)*; **Sprachfrequenzen** *f pl* AKUSTIK conversational frequencies

sprachgesteuert: **~er Betrieb** *m* TELEKOM voice-controlled operation; **~es Relais** *nt* TELEKOM voice-operated relay; **~er Roboter** *m* KÜNSTL INT voice-operated robot; **~er Schalter** *m (VOX)* RADIO voice-operated switch *(VOX)*; **~er Sende-Empfangsumschalter** *m* TELEKOM voice-operated transmitter keyer; **~es Wählen** *nt* TELEKOM voice dialing (AmE), voice dialling (BrE)

Sprach-: **Sprachinterpolation** *f* RAUMFAHRT speech interpolation; **Sprachkanal** *m* COMP & DV speech channel, voice channel

sprachlich: **~es Gebilde** *nt* COMP & DV language construct

Sprach-: **Sprachmitteilungsprozessor** *m* TELEKOM voice message processor; **Sprachnetz** *nt* TELEKOM voice network; **Sprachschneidegerät** *nt* AUFNAHME speech clipper; **Sprachsignal** *nt* TELEKOM ˙speech signal; **Sprachspeicher** *m* TELEKOM speech memory; **Sprachspeicherdienst** *m* TELEKOM voice messaging; **Sprachsperre** *f* ELEKTROTECH *Telefon* guard circuit; **Sprachspitzenbegrenzung** *f* RADIO speech clipping; **Sprachspur** *f* AUFNAHME speech track, voice track; **Sprachsynthese** *f* COMP & DV, ELEKTRONIK, KÜNSTL INT speech synthesis; **Sprachsynthesizer** *m* COMP & DV speech synthesizer; **Sprachübersetzer** *m* COMP & DV language processor; **Sprachverarbeitung** *f* COMP & DV speech processing, KÜNSTL INT voice processing, RADIO, TELEKOM speech processing; **Sprachverschlüsseler** *m* COMP & DV vocoder; **Sprachverständlichkeit** *f* ERGON intelligibility; **Sprachverstehen** *nt (SU)* KÜNSTL INT language understanding, speech understanding

Spratzen *nt* RAUMFAHRT *Weltraumfunk* spurt

spratzen *vi* METALL spit

Spraydose *f* VERPACK aerosol container

Sprayschicht *f* BAU *Beton* curing membrane

Spreader *m* TRANS spreader

Spreadsheet *nt* COMP & DV spreadsheet

Sprechanlage *f* TELEKOM intercom

Sprechdaten: **Sprechdatenverarbeitung** *f* KÜNSTL INT speech processing

sprechend: **~es Straßenschild** *nt* TRANS talking road sign

Sprecherstudio *nt* AUFNAHME continuity studio

sprecherunabhängig: **~es Erkennungssystem** *nt* KÜNSTL INT speaker independent recognition system

Sprechfrequenzband *nt* COMP & DV voiceband; **Sprechfunkgerät** *nt* RADIO, WASSERTRANS radiotelephone; **Sprechgarnitur** *f* TELEKOM headset; **Sprechkanal** *m* TELEKOM working channel

sprechkanalfrei: **~er Verbindungsaufbau** *m* TELEKOM OACSU, off-air call setup

Sprechkopf *m* AUFNAHME, COMP & DV recording head; **Sprechkreis** *m* TELEKOM speech circuit; **Sprechkreisbündel** *nt* TELEKOM circuit group, group; **Sprechkreisverfügbarkeit** *f* TELEKOM circuit avail-

ability; **Sprechpegel** *m* AUFNAHME speech level; **Sprechpegeltest** *m* AUFNAHME voice level test; **Sprechspule** *f* ELEKTROTECH moving coil; **Sprechtaste** *f* AUFNAHME push-to-talk switch; **Sprechweg** *m* ELEKTROTECH channel; **Sprechwegenetzwerk** *nt* ELEKTROTECH switching network; **Sprechzeit** *f* TELEKOM airtime; **Sprechzeug** *nt* TELEKOM operator's telephone

spreizbar: **~er Gewindebohrer** *m* MASCHINEN expanding tap, expansion tap

Spreizbuchse *f* FERTIG split bushing

Spreizdorn *m* FERTIG expansion arbor (AmE), expansion arbour (BrE), MASCHINEN expanding arbor (AmE), expanding arbour (BrE), expanding mandrel

Spreizen: **~ zwischen Querbalken** *nt* BAU bridging

spreizen *vt* FERTIG straddle, MASCHINEN expand, MECHAN swage

Spreizkegel *m* FERTIG tapered plug

Spreizkörper *m* MECHAN spreader

Spreizmodulation *f* TELEKOM spread spectrum modulation

Spreizreibahle *f* FERTIG expansion reamer

Spreizringkupplung *f* FERTIG expanding band clutch

Spreizschraube *f* MASCHINEN expanding screw, expansion bolt

Spreizung *f* FERTIG *Dorn, Reibahle* expansion, METROL *Meßbereich, Skale* expanded scale

Spreizverfahren *nt* ELEKTRONIK *Halbbild-Trennung* additive method

Sprengbolzen *m* MECHAN explosion bolt, RAUMFAHRT explosive bolt

Sprengen *nt* KOHLEN blasting

sprengen *vt* BAU blast, shoot, ERDÖL shoot, KOHLEN blast, RAUMFAHRT blow up; **~ durch Erhitzung** *vt* KOHLEN blast by heating

Sprengfeder *f* MASCHINEN spring ring

Sprengführer *m* BAU blasting foreman

Sprenggerät *nt* ERDÖL sparger

Sprenglochbohren *nt* ERDÖL *Bohrtechnik* shot hole drilling

Sprenglochstopfen *m* ERDÖL *Bohrtechnik* shot hole plug

Sprengniet *nt* MASCHINEN explosive rivet, MECHAN explosive-type rivet

Sprengring *m* FERTIG circlip, MASCHINEN retainer, snap ring, spring clip, MECHAN circlip

Sprengscheibe *f* FERTIG bursting disc (BrE), bursting disk (AmE)

Sprengstoff *m* SICHERHEIT explosives

Sprengstrebe *f* BAU *Dachstuhl* straining beam, *Holzbau* strut

Sprengung *f* BAU blasting, ERDÖL shot

Sprengzünder *m* RAUMFAHRT, THERMOD detonator

sprenkeln *vt* TEXTIL speckle

Spreu *f* LEBENSMITTEL chaff

Springen *nt* WERKPRÜF *Glas* cracking

springen *vi* COMP & DV jump, *Programm* branch

Springer *m* ERDÖL gusher

Springflut *f* WASSERTRANS *Gezeiten* spring tide

Springleine *f* WASSERTRANS *Festmachen* spring line

Springnipptide-Zyklus *m* NICHTFOSS ENERG spring neap cycle

Springtide *f* NICHTFOSS ENERG spring tide

Springwalzwerk *nt* METALL jump mill

Sprinkler *m* SICHERHEIT, WASSERVERSORG sprinkler; **Sprinkleranlage** *f* LUFTTRANS *Notfall*, WASSERTRANS

Notfall fire sprinkler

Sprintmission *f* RAUMFAHRT sprint mission

Sprite *m* COMP & DV sprite

Spritz- *pref* BAU, FOTO, KUNSTSTOFF, VERPACK spray; **Spritzapparat** *m* FOTO airbrush; **Spritzauftrag** *m* BAU *Farbe* spray painting; **Spritzausblasgießmaschine** *f* VERPACK injection blow molding machine (AmE), injection blow moulding machine (BrE); **Spritzbeton** *m* BAU gunite, sprayed concrete; **Spritzblasen** *nt* KUNSTSTOFF injection blow molding (AmE), injection blow moulding (BrE); **Spritzblasformen** *nt* KUNSTSTOFF injection blow molding (AmE), injection blow moulding (BrE); **Spritzblasverfahren** *nt* KUNSTSTOFF injection blow molding (AmE), injection blow moulding (BrE); **Spritzdruck** *m* VERPACK injection molding pressure (AmE), injection moulding pressure (BrE); **Spritzdüse** *f* MASCHINEN sprayer nozzle, SICHERHEIT *Brandschutz* fire nozzle

Spritze *f* FERTIG gun, LABOR syringe

Spritzeinfüllung *f* VERPACK injection filling

Spritzen *nt* KER & GLAS gunning

Spritzer *m* BAU spatter, FERTIG *Schweißen* splash guard, PAPIER squirt

Spritz-: **Spritzflasche** *f* LABOR wash bottle; **Spritzform** *f* MASCHINEN injection mold (AmE), injection mould (BrE), mold for thermoplastics (AmE), mould for thermoplastics (BrE); **Spritzformen** *nt* KUNSTSTOFF injection molding (Ame), injection moulding (BrE)

spritzgegossen *adj* FERTIG *Plaste* die-cast

Spritz-: **Spritzgehäuse** *nt* LABOR *Spritzgerät* barrel; **Spritzgießen** *nt (IM)* FERTIG injection molding (AmE), injection moulding (BrE), pressure die-casting, KUNSTSTOFF, VERPACK injection molding (AmE), injection moulding (BrE) *(IM)*; **Spritzgießmaschine** *f (IM)* KUNSTSTOFF injection molding machine (AmE), injection moulding machine (BrE); **Spritzgießmasse** *f (IM)* KUNSTSTOFF injection molding compound (AmE), injection moulding compound (BrE); **Spritzgrat** *m* KUNSTSTOFF flash

Spritzguß:[1] **aus ~** *adj* MECHAN die-cast

Spritzguß[2] *m* FERTIG *Kunststoffinstallationen* injection molding (AmE), injection moulding (BrE), MECHAN extrusion, VERPACK injection moulding compound (AmE), injection moulding compound (BrE); **Spritzgußform** *f* KER & GLAS, MASCHINEN injection mold (AmE), injection mould (BrE); **Spritzgußmaschine** *f* FERTIG *Plaste* die-casting machine, SICHERHEIT injection molding machine (AmE), injection moulding machine (BrE); **Spritzgußteile mit Angußspritze** *n pl* FERTIG spray

Spritz-: **Spritzkabine** *f* ANSTRICH spray booth; **Spritzkappe** *f* WASSERTRANS spray hood; **Spritzkühlung** *f* KER & GLAS splat cooling; **Spritzlack** *m* KUNSTSTOFF spraying paint; **Spritzlackieren** *nt* ANSTRICH spray painting; **Spritzmetallisieren** *nt* FERTIG metal spraying; **Spritzpistole** *f* ANSTRICH spray gun, FERTIG blow gun, VERPACK airbrush; **Spritzprägeverfahren** *nt (IC-Verfahren)* KUNSTSTOFF injection compression process; **Spritzpressen** *nt* KUNSTSTOFF transfer molding (AmE), transfer moulding (BrE); **Spritzpreßform** *f* MASCHINEN transfer mold (AmE), transfer mould (BrE); **Spritzrohr** *nt* PAPIER shower; **Spritzschlauch** *m* WASSERVERSORG squirt hose; **Spritzschmierung** *f* EISENBAHN, KFZTECH, MASCHINEN splash lubrication; **Spritzschutz** *m* MASCHINEN splash guard; **Spritzschutzhaube** *f* LABOR *Destillation* antis-

plash head; **Spritzschutzmaske** *f* ANSTRICH spray mask; **Spritzsee** *f* WASSERTRANS *Meer* swash; **Spritzung** *f* FERTIG injection; **Spritzverdeck** *nt* WASSERTRANS spray hood; **Spritzverfahren** *nt* DRUCK airbrushing; **Spritzwand** *f* BAU splashback; **Spritzwasser** *nt* WASSERTRANS *Meer* spray

spritzwasserdicht *adj* FERTIG *Kunststoffinstallationen* splash-proof

spritzwassergeschützt: **~e Entlüftungskappe** *f* KFZTECH *Autobatterie* splash-proof vent cap

Sprödbruch *m* FERTIG nonplastic fracture, KERNTECH brittle failure, MECHAN brittle fracture, METALL brittle fracture, cleavage crack; **Sprödbruchbeständigkeit** *f* METALL brittle fracture resistance

spröde *adj* KUNSTSTOFF brittle, friable, MECHAN, METALL, PAPIER brittle

spröder-duktiler: **~ Übergang** *m* KERNTECH brittle-ductile transition

Sprödigkeit *f* KER & GLAS, KUNSTSTOFF, MECHAN, METALL brittleness; **Sprödigkeitsbruch** *m* KERNTECH brittle failure; **Sprödigkeitstemperatur** *f* FERTIG brittle point

Sprödriß *m* KERNTECH brittle crack

Sprosse *f* BAU tread, *Fenster* rail, COMP & DV *Matrix* row

Sprossen *f pl* BAU *Leiter* rungs; **Sprosseneisen** *nt* BAU sash bar; **Sprossenschrift** *f* AKUSTIK variable density recording; **Sprossenteilung** *f* COMP & DV row pitch

Spruchkopf *m* RAUMFAHRT *Weltraumfunk* preamble

Sprudelbohrung *f* ERDÖL gusher

Sprudeldichtemeßgerät *nt* GERÄT bubble-type density meter

sprudelnd: **~ kochen** *vi* THERMOD boil fast

Sprudelrohrfüllstandsmeßgerät *nt* GERÄT bubble pipe level meter

Sprüh- *pref* VERPACK spray; **Sprühausleger** *m* MEERSCHMUTZ spray boom; **Sprühbehälter** *m* VERPACK aerosol, aerosol container; **Sprühdüse** *f* CHEMTECH atomizer nozzle, PAPIER pulverizer, WASSERVERSORG *Abzweigrohr* spreader jet; **Sprühen** *nt* ELEKTROTECH sputtering, MASCHINEN spraying; **~er** *m* CHEMTECH atomizer; **Sprühentladung** *f* ELEKTRIZ brush discharge, ELEKTRIZ *(cf Glimmentladung)* corona discharge, ELEKTROTECH brown-out, brush discharge, PHYS brush discharge; **Sprühkanone** *f* MEERSCHMUTZ spray gun; **Sprühkühlung** *f* HEIZ & KÄLTE spray cooling; **Sprühöffnungen** *f pl* MEERSCHMUTZ *für Dispergatoren* spray aperture; **Sprühpfad** *m* MEERSCHMUTZ spray path; **Sprühstreichmaschine** *f* PAPIER spray coater; **Sprühwassersystem** *nt* KERNTECH water spray system

Sprung:[1] **~ hinten** *adj* WASSERTRANS *Schiffkonstruktion* sheer aft; **~ vorn** *adj* WASSERTRANS *Schiffkonstruktion* sheer forward

Sprung[2] *m* BAU *Fassade* break joint, COMP & DV jump, skip, *Programm* branch, MECHAN flaw, METALL jump, WASSERTRANS *Schiffbau* sheer, WASSERVERSORG breach; **Sprunganweisung** *f* COMP & DV branch instruction

sprungartig: **~e Änderung** *f* REGELUNG stepwise change

Sprung: **Sprungbefehl** *m* COMP & DV jump, jump instruction; **Sprungelastizität** *f* KUNSTSTOFF rebound elasticity; **Sprungentfernung** *f* RADIO skip distance; **Sprungfunktion** *f* COMP & DV jump function, ELEKTRONIK step function; **Sprungfunktionsgeber** *m* ELEKTRONIK step function generator; **Sprungfunktionsverhalten** *nt* ELEKTRONIK step function response

sprunghaft: **~ auftretender Vollausfall** *m* QUAL catastrophic failure

Sprung: **Sprunghöhe** *f* HYDRAUL *(j)* height of hydraulic jump *(j)*, REGELUNG *Eingangssignal* step height; **Sprungoperation** *f* COMP & DV jump operation; **Sprungrohr** *nt* BAU swan neck; **Sprungstart** *m* LUFT-TRANS *Hubschrauber* jump takeoff; **Sprungsuche** *f* FERNSEH shuttle search; **Sprungtemperatur** *f* KERN-TECH transition temperature; **Sprungtuch** *nt* SICHERHEIT *Feuerwehr* jumping sheet; **Sprungüber-deckung** *f* FERTIG *Zahnrad* face contact ratio; **Sprungverzerrung** *f* AUFNAHME transient distortion

sprungweise: ~ **Durchprüfung** *f* COMP & DV leapfrog test

SPS *abbr* COMP & DV *(Programmspeichersteuerung)* SPC *(stored program control)*, KONTROLL *(speicher-programmierbare Steuerung)*, LABOR *(speicherprogrammierbare Steuerung)* PLC *(pro-grammable logic control)*

SPST-Schalter *m* *(einpoliger Ein-/Ausschalter)* ELEK-TRIZ, ELEKTROTECH SPST switch *(single pole single-throw switch)*, KONTROLL SPST switch

Spuchstoffaustritt *m* PAPIER reject gate

Spuckstoff *m* CHEMIE *Papier* screenings

Spül- *pref* ERDÖL, WASSERTRANS wash; **Spülbecken** *nt* ERDÖL sump; **Spülbohren** *nt* ERDÖL *Bohrtechnik* wash boring; **Spülbohrverfahren** *nt* ERDÖL *Bohrtechnik* wash boring; **Spülbord** *nt* WASSERTRANS *Schiffbau* washboard

Spule *f* AKUSTIK *für Magnetband, Papierstreifen*, AUF-NAHME spool, COMP & DV reel, ELEKTRIZ coil, ELEKTROTECH bobbin, coil, FERNSEH reel, KER & GLAS bobbin, spool, KFZTECH *Zündung* coil, MECHAN coil, drum, PAPIER, RADIO coil, TELEKOM inductance, TEX-TIL bobbin, package; ~ **mit Wabenwicklung** *f* ELEKTROTECH lattice-wound coil

Spulen[1] *nt* ELEKTROTECH reeling, FERNSEH spooling

Spulen:[2] **aufstecken** *vi* TEXTIL *Gatter* place yarn containers

Spülen *nt* KERNTECH backflushing, MASCHINEN flushing

spulen *vt* BAU wind, FERNSEH spool, TEXTIL wind

spülen *vt* ERDÖL purging, MASCHINEN flush, WASSER-VERSORG blow off, scour

Spule: **Spulenabnahme** *f* TEXTIL doffing; **Spulengatter** *nt* TEXTIL creel, warping creel; **Spulenkern** *m* ELEK-TRIZ coil core, ELEKTROTECH *Abstimmung* slug, *Kondensatoren* slug, *bei Magnetrelais* core, MECHAN hub, TELEKOM core; **Spulenkörper** *m* ELEKTRIZ coil former, ELEKTROTECH bobbin, coil form, former; **Spu-lenrahmen** *m* ELEKTROTECH coil form; **Spulenwickeln** *nt* ELEKTRIZ coil winding

Spulfeld *nt* TEXTIL wind

Spül-: **Spülflüssigkeit** *f* ERDÖL drilling mud; **Spülkanal** *m* BAU water course; **Spülkante** *f* KER & GLAS fluxline; **Spülkantenangriff** *m* KER & GLAS fluxline attack; **Spül-kopf** *m* ERDÖL *Bohrtechnik* swivel

Spulkranz *m* TEXTIL uncollapsed cake

Spül-: **Spülleitung** *f* ERDÖL *Bohrtechnik* mud line; **Spül-mittel** *nt* FERTIG *Kunststoffinstallationen* cleansing agent; **Spülpumpe** *f* ERDÖL *Bohrtechnik* mud pump; **Spülpumpenarmatur** *f* ERDÖL *Bohrtechnik* mud pump valve; **Spülrohrtour** *f* ERDÖL *Tiefbohrtechnik* washover string; **Spülschlammanalyselog** *nt* ERDÖL *Bohrtechnik* mud analysis log

Spülung *f* ERDÖL *Bohrtechnik* drilling mud, mud, KER & GLAS washing, KERNTECH scavenging, MECHAN flus-hing, scavenging, MEERSCHMUTZ flushing, NICHTFOSS ENERG scour, PAPIER scouring, UMWELTSCHMUTZ flus-hing, WASSERTRANS *Motor* scavenging, WASSERVERSORG flush, scavenging, scour, scouring, *Spülwasserbohrung* flushing

Spulvorgang *m* FOTO spooling, TEXTIL winding process

Spund *m* BAU plug, spile, LEBENSMITTEL bung, MECHAN plug; **Spund- und Nutmaschine** *f* BAU matching ma-chine; **Spundbohle** *f* BAU pile plank, sheet pile, sheeting pile, KOHLEN sheet pile; **Spundbrett** *nt* BAU matchboard; **Spundeisen** *nt* BAU tonguing iron

spunden *vt* FERTIG match, spung

Spund: **Spundhobel** *m* BAU grooving plane, matching plane, plough plane (BrE), plow plane (AmE), tongue plane, tonguing plane; **Spundholzlage** *f* BAU mat-ching; **Spundloch** *nt* LEBENSMITTEL bunghole; **Spundmaschine** *f* BAU tonguing-and-grooving machi-ne; **Spundschalung** *f* BAU tight sheathing; **Spundung** *f* BAU tonguing-and-grooving; **Spundverbindung** *f* BAU ploughed and tongued joint (BrE), plowed and tongued joint (AmE), tongue-and-groove joint; **Spundwand** *f* BAU sheet piling, sheeting, steel piling, KOHLEN sheet piling

Spur *f* AUFNAHME toe, track, COMP & DV track, EISEN-BAHN gage (AmE), gauge (BrE), ELEKTROTECH *Leiter* trace, FERNSEH track, FERTIG *Lochstreifen* channel, KERNTECH, KONTROLL track, METROL gage (AmE), gauge (BrE), OPTIK track, TRANS gage (AmE), gauge (BrE); ~ **mit variabler Dichte** *f* FERNSEH variable den-sity track; **Spurabstand** *m* AUFNAHME track spacing, FERNSEH track pitch; **Spuraufzeichnung** *f* AUFNAHME toe recording; **Spurbenutzungshilfen** *f pl* TRANS direc-tional aids; **Spurbenutzungszählung** *f* TRANS directional census; **Spurbreite** *f* AUFNAHME track width; **Spurdichte** *f* OPTIK track density; **Spureinstel-lung** *f* FERNSEH track adjustment; **Spuren pro Inch** *f pl* COMP & DV TPI, tracks per inch; **Spurenanalyse** *f* WASSERVERSORG trace analysis; **Spurenelement** *nt* LE-BENSMITTEL, UMWELTSCHMUTZ trace element; **Spurerweiterung** *f* EISENBAHN, TRANS gage clearance (AmE), gauge clearance (BrE); **Spurfestlegung** *f* FERNSEH track configuration

spurgebunden: ~**es Luftkissenfahrzeug** *nt* WASSER-TRANS TACV, tracked air cushion vehicle, tracked hovercraft; ~**es Massentransportsystem** *nt* TRANS guided public mass transportation system

spurgeführt[1] *adj* EISENBAHN railborne

spurgeführt:[2] ~**es Fahrzeug** *nt* TRANS track-guided ve-hicle; ~**es Luftkissenfahrzeug** *nt* TRANS guided air cushion vehicle; ~**e Straße** *f* TRANS guided road; ~**es Transportsystem** *nt* TRANS track-guided transport system

spurgenau: ~ **laufen** *vi* COMP & DV track

Spur: **Spurhaltesystem** *nt* AUFNAHME sprocket hole control track system; **Spurkranz** *m* KFZTECH *Rad* flange; **Spurkranzreibung** *f* EISENBAHN wheel flange friction; **Spurkranzschmiermittel** *nt* EISENBAHN wheel flange lubricant; **Spurlager** *nt* MASCHINEN step bearing, step block; **Spurlinie** *f* ERDÖL *Bohrtechnik* spur line; **Spurmechanismus** *m* OPTIK tracking mechanism; **Spurrandbegrenzung** *f* FERNSEH edge of track banding; **Spurrille** *f* EISENBAHN flangeway; **Spurspiel** *nt* EISENBAHN flange-to-rail clearance; **Spurspreizung** *f* AUFNAHME track spreading; **Spur-stange** *f* EISENBAHN tie bar, KFZTECH tie rod, *Lenkung* track rod; **Spursteigung** *f* OPTIK track pitch; **Spur-strecke** *f* ERDÖL spur line; **Spurteilung** *f* AUFNAHME track pitch; **Spurverfolgung** *f* PHYS ray tracing; **Spurwähler** *m* FERNSEH track selector; **Spurwechselbahnhof** *m* EISENBAHN change-of-gage station (AmE), change-of-gauge station (BrE); **Spurweite** *f* BAU gage (AmE), gauge (BrE), EISENBAHN distance between rails, gage (AmE), gauge (BrE), rail gage (AmE), rail gauge (BrE), track gage (BrE), track gauge (BrE), KFZTECH track width, MECHAN, TRANS gage (AmE), gauge (BrE); **Spurzapfen** *m* BAU pintle

SQID *abbr (supraleitfähiger Quanteninterferenzmechanismus)* PHYS SQUID *(superconductive quantum interference device)*

Squalan *nt* CHEMIE squalane

Squalen *nt* CHEMIE squalene

Square *nt* METROL *Bauwesen* square

Sr *(Strontium)* CHEMIE Sr *(strontium)*

SRAM *abbr (statischer RAM)* COMP & DV SRAM *(static RAM)*

SRF-Ruß *m* KUNSTSTOFF SRF carbon black, semi-reinforcing carbon black

SR-Schaltung *f (Serienresonanzkreis)* ELEKTROTECH series-resonant circuit

SS *abbr* FERNSEH *(Spitze-Spitze-)* pp *(peak-to-peak)*, MASCHINEN *(Schiebesitz)* close sliding fit, push fit, MECHAN *(Schiebesitz)* close-sliding fit, push fit, sliding fit, RADIO *(Spitze-Spitze-)* pp *(peak-to-peak)*

SSB *abbr (Einseitenband)* ELEKTRONIK, FERNSEH, RADIO, TELEKOM, WASSERTRANS SSB *(single sideband)*

SSC *abbr (supraleitfähiges Supracollider)* TEILPHYS SSC *(superconducting super collider)*

SSI-Schaltung *f (Kleinintegration)* COMP & DV SSI, ELEKTRONIK SSI *(small-scale integration, single scale integration)*

SSM *abbr (Zweitflächenspiegel)* RAUMFAHRT SSM *(second surface mirror)*

SSMA *abbr (Breitbandmehrfachzugriff)* RAUMFAHRT SSMA *(spread spectrum multiple access)*

SSOG *abbr (Satellitensystem-Betriebsanleitung)* RAUMFAHRT SSOG *(satellite system operation guide)*

SS-Spannung *f (Spitzenspannung eines Senders)* RADIO PEV *(peak envelope voltage)*

SST *abbr (Überschalltransport)* LUFTTRANS SST *(supersonic transport)*

SSTV *abbr* FERNSEH *(Fernsehen mit langsamer Abtastung, Schmalbandfernsehen, Slow-Scan-Television)*, RADIO *(Schmalbandfernsehen mit langsamer Abtastung)* SSTV *(slow scan television)*

SSUS *abbr (rotierende obere Feststufe)* RAUMFAHRT SSUS *(solid spinning upper stage)*

Stab *m* BAU bar, member, rod, KER & GLAS rod, KOHLEN *Holz, Metall* b, bar, MASCHINEN bar, rod, MECHAN rod; **Stabanker** *m* ELEKTRIZ bar armature; **Stabantenne** *f* RADIO rod antenna; **Stabausdehnungs-Thermometer** *nt* GERÄT rod-and-tube thermometer, HEIZ & KÄLTE solid expansion thermometer

Stäbchenbakterie *f* LEBENSMITTEL bacillus

Stab: **Stabeisen** *nt* METALL merchant iron, rod iron; **Stabelektrode** *f* ELEKTRIZ rod electrode; **Staberder** *m* EISENBAHN earthing rod (BrE), grounding rod (AmE); **Stabfeder** *f* MECHAN rod spring; **Stabfilter** *nt* MECHAN filter cartridge; **Stabhalterung** *f* METALL *Pfahl* bar

stabil[1] *adj* MECHAN heavy; **nicht ~** *adj* ELEKTROTECH transient

stabil:[2] **~es Gleichgewicht** *nt* PHYS stable equilibrium; **~es Isotop** *nt* PHYS stable isotope

Stabilisator *m* ELEKTROTECH voltage regulator tube, voltage reference tube, voltage stabilizer tube, ERDÖL *Bohrtechnik*, FOTO, KER & GLAS stabilizer, KFZTECH stabilizer, *Aufhängung* stabilizer bar, KOHLEN, KUNSTSTOFF, LUFTTRANS *Luftfahrzeug*, WASSERTRANS stabilizer

stabilisieren *vt* BAU *Erdreich* grout, RAUMFAHRT *aus dem Trudeln* despin

Stabilisierkolonne *f* ERDÖL *Raffinerie* stabilizer tower

stabilisiert[1] *adj* RAUMFAHRT *Raumschiff* despun

stabilisiert:[2] **~er Latex** *m* KUNSTSTOFF stabilized latex

Stabilisierturm *m* ERDÖL stabilizer tower

Stabilisierung *f* ELEKTRIZ stabilization, ELEKTROTECH regulation, KOHLEN, KUNSTSTOFF stabilization, MASCHINEN steadying, RAUMFAHRT *Weltraumfunk* stabilization, TELEKOM *Spannung* regulation, WASSERTRANS *Schiffkonstruktion* stabilization; **Stabilisierungseinrichtung** *f* ELEKTRIZ stabilizer; **Stabilisierungsfläche** *f* LUFTTRANS *Luftfahrzeug* stabilizer; **Stabilisierungsflosse** *f* WASSERTRANS stabilizing fin; **Stabilisierungsflügel** *m* LUFTTRANS *Luftfahrzeug* stabilizer; **Stabilisierungsgardine** *f* WASSERTRANS stability curtain; **Stabilisierungskreisel** *m* PHYS gyrostat; **Stabilisierungsschiene** *f* EISENBAHN stabilization rail; **Stabilisierungsschürze** *f* WASSERTRANS stability skirt; **Stabilisierungssystem** *nt* RAUMFAHRT *Raumschiff* despin system; **Stabilisierungsvorrichtung** *f* ELEKTROTECH ballast, WASSERTRANS stabilization device; **Stabilisierungswicklung** *f* ELEKTRIZ stabilizing winding; **Stabilisierungswiderstand** *m* ELEKTROTECH ballast resistor

Stabilität *f* COMP & DV, KOHLEN, LUFTTRANS, RADIO, TELEKOM, WASSERTRANS stability; **~ einer Grenzschicht** *f* STRÖMPHYS boundary layer stability; **Stabilitätsdiagramm** *nt* STRÖMPHYS stability diagram; **Stabilitätskurve** *f* WASSERTRANS *Schiffkonstruktion* stability curve; **Stabilitätsuntersuchung** *f* STRÖMPHYS stability analysis

Stabilotron *nt* PHYS stabilotron

Stab: **Stabkristall** *nt* METALL columnar crystal; **Stabmagnet** *m* PHYS bar magnet; **Stabmühle** *f* KOHLEN rod mill, MASCHINEN bar mill, rod mill; **Stabprobe** *f* KER & GLAS rod proof; **Stab-Rohr-Methode** *f* TELEKOM rod-in-tube technique; **Stabschere** *f* MASCHINEN bar shears; **Stabschwingmühle** *f* KOHLEN vibrating rod mill; **Stabspannung** *f* FERTIG stress in the bar; **Stabstahl** *m* MASCHINEN bar stock, METALL merchant bar; **Stabstahlschere** *f* MASCHINEN bar-shearing machine; **Stabstahlwalzwerk** *nt* METALL merchant bar rolling mill; **Stabstahlwerk** *nt* FERTIG merchant mill; **Stabstraße** *f* FERTIG rod mill; **Stab-Temperaturregler** *m* HEIZ & KÄLTE immersion-type thermostat; **Stabtransformator** *m* ELEKTRIZ bar-type transformer; **Stabwicklung** *f* ELEKTRIZ *Motor* bar winding

Stachelbandführung *f* COMP & DV sprocket feed, tractor feed

Stachelrad *nt* COMP & DV tractor; **Stachelradwalze** *f* COMP & DV sprocket, sprocket wheel

Stachydrin *nt* CHEMIE stachydrine

Stachyose *f* CHEMIE stachyose

Stadiometer *nt* BAU *Vermessung* stadiometer

Stadt *f* EISENBAHN, TRANS, WASSERVERSORG town; **Stadt- und Regional-S-Bahn** *f* EISENBAHN urban and regional metropolitan railroad (AmE), urban and regional metropolitan railway (BrE); **Stadtbahn** *f* EI-

SENBAHN metropolitan railroad (AmE), metropolitan railway (BrE)

städteverbindend: **~er Transport** *m* TRANS intercity transport

Stadt: **Stadtgas** *nt* ERDÖL town gas

städtisch: **~es Einzugsgebiet** *nt* WASSERVERSORG urban catchment; **~es Netz** *nt* TELEKOM urban network; **~e Schnellstraße** *f* TRANS rapid urban artery; **~es Straßennetz** *nt* TRANS urban road network; **~es Transportsystem ohne Zwischenhaltestation** *nt* TRANS nonstop urban transportation; **~e Wasserbewirtschaftung** *f* WASSERVERSORG urban water management

Stadt: **Stadt-Land-Reifen** *m* KFZTECH town-and-country tire (AmE), town-and-country tyre (BrE); **Stadtmüll** *m* WASSERVERSORG municipal waste; **Stadtnetz** *nt* TELEKOM metropolitan network; **Stadtreinigung** *f* ABFALL public cleansing; **Stadtschnellbahn** *f* EISENBAHN rapid transit railroad (AmE), rapid transit railway (BrE); **Stadtstraßenbahn** *f* EISENBAHN streetcar metro (AmE), tramway metro (BrE); **Stadtverkehr** *m* EISENBAHN light rail transit (AmE), light rail transport (BrE), KFZTECH *Fahrbetrieb* urban cycle, TRANS urban traffic; **Stadtviertel** *nt* BAU block; **Stadtwasser** *nt* WASSERVERSORG town water; **Stadtwerke** *nt pl* WASSERVERSORG public works

Staffel *f* TELEKOM progressive grading; **Staffelleitung** *f* TELEKOM series circuit; **Staffelwalze** *f* METALL stepped roll

Stag[1] *nt* WASSERTRANS *Tauwerk* stay

Stag:[2] **über ~ gehen** *vi* WASSERTRANS *Segeln* go-about

Staggarnat *nt* WASSERTRANS *Tauwerk* Spanish burton

stagnierend: **~es Gewässer** *nt* WASSERVERSORG stagnant water

Stag: **Stagreiter** *m* WASSERTRANS *Segeln* jib hank, *Tauwerk* hank; **Stagsegel** *nt* WASSERTRANS *Segeln* fore staysail

Stahl *m* MASCHINEN, METALL steel; **Stahl-** *pref* METALL steel; **Stahlanreißlineal** *nt* METROL steel straightedge; **Stahlbandförderer** *m* MASCHINEN steel band conveyor; **Stahlbandkette** *f* BAU *Vermessung* steel band chain; **Stahlbandumreifung** *f* VERPACK steel band strapping; **Stahlbau** *m* BAU steel construction; **Stahlbeton** *m* BAU reinforced concrete, WASSERTRANS *Schiffbau* ferroconcrete; **Stahlblech** *nt* FERTIG iron plate, KFZTECH *Karosserie*, MASCHINEN, METALL sheet steel; **Stahlblock** *m* METALL steel ingot; **Stahlbolzenkette** *f* MASCHINEN pintle chain; **Stahldraht** *m* WASSERTRANS *Schiffbau* steel wire; **Stahldrahtseil** *nt* MASCHINEN steel wire rope; **Stahlenformung** *f* ELEKTRONIK beam shaping; **Stahlfeder** *f* MASCHINEN steel spring; **Stahlflechter** *m* BAU *Stahlbeton* steelfixer; **Stahlgießerei** *f* METALL steel foundry; **Stahlgittermast** *m* BAU lattice tower; **Stahlguß** *m* FERTIG cast steel, METALL cast steel, steel casting, PAPIER cast steel; **Stahlgußstück** *nt* WASSERTRANS *Schiffbau* steel casting; **Stahlhalter** *m* MASCHINEN tool post; **Stahlkappe** *f* SICHERHEIT *Schuhwerk* steel toe cap; **Stahlkern** *m* FERTIG *Kunststoffinstallationen* steel core; **Stahlkonstruktion** *f* BAU steel construction; **Stahlmantelwalze** *f* BAU smooth roller; **Stahlmaßband** *nt* METROL steel measuring tape; **Stahl-Mehrwegcontainer zu Demontagezwecken** *m* VERPACK steel re-usable CKD container; **Stahlmörser** *m* LABOR *Schleifen* percussion mortar; **Stahlpfahl** *m* BAU, KOHLEN steel pile; **Stahl-**

plattform *f* ERDÖL *Offshore-Technik* steel platform; **Stahlrad** *nt* EISENBAHN steel wheel; **Stahlrohrblock** *m* FERTIG steel ingot; **Stahlrohrgerüst** *nt* BAU tubular scaffolding; **Stahlschalung** *f* BAU steel forms; **Stahlschienensystem** *nt* EISENBAHN steel rail system; **Stahlschiff** *nt* WASSERTRANS *Schiffbau* steel vessel; **Stahlschmieden** *nt* METALL steel forging; **Stahlschrank** *m* LABOR steel locker; **Stahlschrot** *m* FERTIG shot; **Stahlschrott** *m* ABFALL steel scrap; **Stahlseilfördergurt** *m* MASCHINEN steel cord conveyor belt; **Stahlstichdruck** *m* MECHAN die-stamping; **Stahlstichprägung** *f* DRUCK die-stamping; **Stahlstreifenkolben** *m* KFZTECH autothermic piston; **Stahlstütze** *f* BAU stanchion; **Stahlträger** *m* BAU steel beam; **Stahlverbundplatte** *f* BAU bonded steel plate; **Stahlvorspannglied** *nt* KERNTECH steel tendon; **Stahlwerk** *nt* FERTIG steel works; **Stahlwinkel** *m* FERTIG structural angle

Stähne *f* FERTIG rap

Stakuleiter *m* RADIO copperweld wire

Stall: **~ am Luftschraubenblatt** *m* LUFTTRANS *Hubschrauber* blade stall; **~ am rücklaufenden Blatt** *m* LUFTTRANS *Hubschrauber* retreating blade stall; **~ an der Luftschraubenblattspitze** *m* LUFTTRANS *Hubschrauber* blade tip stall

Stamm *m* BAU stem, ELEKTROTECH physical circuit, TELECOM side circuit; **Stamm-** *pref* COMP & DV master; **Stammabfluß** *m* UMWELTSCHMUTZ stemflow; **Stammband** *nt* AUFNAHME, COMP & DV master tape; **Stammblatt** *nt* FERTIG disc (BrE), disk (AmE), *Säge* body; **Stammbruch** *m* MATH unit fraction; **Stammdatei** *f* COMP & DV master file; **Stammdateisatz** *m* COMP & DV master record; **Stammdaten** *nt pl* COMP & DV master data, UMWELTSCHMUTZ historical data

stammen *vi* WASSERTRANS *Hafen* hail

Stamm: **Stammholz** *nt* BAU standing timber; **Stammkarte** *f* COMP & DV master card; **Stammleitung** *f* ELEKTROTECH physical circuit, TELECOM side circuit; **Stammplatte** *f* COMP & DV master disk; **Stammsatz** *m* COMP & DV master record; **Stammsäure** *f* CHEMIE parent acid; **Stammzeichnung** *f* KONSTZEICH parent drawing

Stampf- *pref* CHEMIE tamped

stampfbar *adj* FERTIG rammable

Stampfbarkeit *f* FERTIG rammability

Stampf-: **Stampfbewegung** *f* PHYS pitching, WASSERTRANS pitch; **Stampfdichte** *f* KUNSTSTOFF tamped density

Stampfen *nt* BAU, FERTIG ramming, WASSERTRANS *Schiffbewegung* pitching

stampfen[1] *vt* BAU puddle, ram, tamp, EISENBAHN tamp

stampfen[2] *vi* WASSERTRANS pitch

Stampfer *m* BAU rammer, FERTIG punner, rammer, tamper, tamp, *Gießen* pummel, KOHLEN pneumatic ram

Stampf-: **Stampfmasse** *f* KER & GLAS tamping clay; **Stampfstange** *f* BAU tamping rod; **Stampfwinkel** *m* WASSERTRANS *Schiffbewegung* angle of pitch

Stand:[1] **auf den neuesten ~ bringen** *vt* MASCHINEN bring up to date, update

Stand[2] *m* KONTROLL, PATENT state; **~ der Technik** *m* KONTROLL state of the art, state of technology, PATENT prior art, state of the art

Stand:[3] **neuester technischer ~** *adj* KONTROLL state-of-the-art

Standard *m* COMP & DV default, standard, KONTROLL standard; **~ Ohm** *nt* ELEKTRIZ standard ohm; **Stan-**

dardabweichung *f* COMP & DV, ERGON, MATH, PHYS, QUAL standard deviation; **Standardabweichung des Mittelwerts** *f* COMP & DV mean square error; **Standardband** *nt* FERNSEH standard tape; **Standardbaugruppe** *f* KONTROLL standard assembly; **Standardblende** *f* HYDRAUL standard orifice; **Standarddokument** *m* COMP & DV standard document; **Standarddurchmesser** *m* MASCHINEN standard diameter; **Standardelement** *nt* PHYS standard cell; **Standardfehler** *m* QUAL standard error; **Standardflottengewicht** *nt* LUFTTRANS fleet weight; **Standardformat** *nt* COMP & DV master format; **Standardfunktion** *f* COMP & DV standard function; **Standardhöhenmessereinstellung** *f* LUFTTRANS standard altimeter setting

standardisiert: ~e Hörschwelle *f* AKUSTIK standardized threshold hearing; **~e Pegeldifferenz** *f* AKUSTIK standardized level difference; **nicht ~e Steuerspur** *f* FERNSEH nonstandard control track; **~er Trittschall** *m* AKUSTIK standardized impact sound

Standardisierung *f* COMP & DV normalization, standardization, MASCHINEN, PHYS, TELEKOM standardization

Standard: **Standardkorrekturzeichensatz** *m (SGML)* COMP & DV, DRUCK Standard Generalized Markup Language *(SGML)*; **Standardlaufwerk** *nt* COMP & DV default drive; **Standardlautstärkeanzeige** *f* AUFNAHME standard volume indicator; **Standardlautstärkepegel** *m* AKUSTIK loudness level of reference sound; **Standardlichtquelle** *f* ELEKTROTECH standard light source; **Standardmaßeinheit** *f* METROL standard measure

standardmäßig *adj* COMP & DV standard

Standard: **Standardmehrfachmeßelement** *nt* METROL standard multigaging element (AmE), standard multigauging element (BrE); **Standardmenü** *nt* COMP & DV default menu; **Standardmeßsignal** *nt* FERNSEH standard measuring signal; **Standardmodell** *nt* TEILPHYS standard model; **Standardmodus** *m* COMP & DV native mode; **Standardmuster** *nt* FERNSEH standard pattern; **Standardmutter** *f* MASCHINEN standard nut; **Standardprotokoll** *nt* KONTROLL standard protocol; **Standardschall** *m* AKUSTIK standard sound; **Standardschnittstelle** *f* COMP & DV standard interface; **Standardverdichtung** *f* KOHLEN laboratory compaction; **Standardweltzeit** *f (UT, UTC)* RADIO, RAUMFAHRT universal time, universal time coordinated *(UTC)*

Standarte *f* FOTO camera front; **Standarteneinstellung** *f* FOTO *Balgeneinheit* back standard adjustment; **Standartenverstellung** *f* FOTO lens movement

Stand: **Standbeutel** *m* VERPACK flat-end sack; **Standbild** *nt* FERNSEH freeze frame, still frame, FOTO still picture; **Standbildübertragung** *f* TELEKOM static picture transmission; **Standbremse** *f* EISENBAHN, LUFTTRANS parking brake; **Standbybetrieb** *m* KONTROLL stand-by; **Standbymodus** *m* KONTROLL, RAUMFAHRT stand-by mode

Stander *m* WASSERTRANS *Flaggen* burgee

Ständer *m* BAU *Holz* timber pillar, ELEKTRIZ bearing, ELEKTROTECH stator, FERTIG standard, upright, KFZTECH stator, *Motorrad* stand, MASCHINEN column, frame, holder, housing, pedestal, post, standard, support, upright; **Ständerblech** *nt* ELEKTROTECH stator lamination; **Ständerbohrmaschine** *f* FERTIG vertical box-column drill, vertical box-column

drilling machine, MASCHINEN column-type drilling machine; **Ständerführung** *f* MASCHINEN column guideway; **Ständerplatte** *f* ELEKTROTECH stator plate; **Ständerverbindung** *f* BAU stud union; **Ständerwand** *f* BAU stud partition; **Ständerwicklung** *f* ELEKTROTECH stator winding

Stand: **Standfestigkeit** *f* FERTIG *Sandmischung* air-dried strength, KOHLEN stability; **Standfläche** *f* MASCHINEN footstep; **Standgerät** *nt* HEIZ & KÄLTE upright unit; **Standguß** *m* MASCHINEN gravity casting

ständig:[1] ~ **vorhanden** *adj* COMP & DV resident

ständig:[2] **~er Belegungsdetektor** *m* TRANS continuous presence detector; **~es Echo** *nt* RAUMFAHRT permanent echo; **~er Fehler** *m* COMP & DV permanent error; **~er Fluß** *m* PHYS steady flow; **~ mitlaufende Reserve** *f* NICHTFOSS ENERG spinning reserves

Stand: **Standkühler** *m* KFZTECH upright radiator; **Standleitung** *f* COMP & DV, TELEKOM dedicated line; **Standmesser** *m* VERPACK liquid level indicator; **Standmeßgerät** *nt* GERÄT level gage (AmE), level gauge (BrE); **Standmessung** *f* GERÄT level measurement

Standort[1] *m* BAU, COMP & DV, ELEKTRIZ location, LUFTTRANS radio fix, RAUMFAHRT fix, TRANS radio fix, WASSERTRANS radio fix, *Navigation* position; **~ der Deponie** *m* ABFALL tip

Standort:[2] ~ **festlegen** *vi* BAU locate

standortabhängig: **~e Streuung** *f* RAUMFAHRT site diversity

Standort: **Standortaktualisierung** *f* TELEKOM location update; **Standortbestimmung** *f* WASSERTRANS *Navigation* positioning; **Standortdatei** *f* TELEKOM LR, location register; **Standortkriterien** *nt pl* KERNTECH, UMWELTSCHMUTZ site criteria; **Standortlöschung** *f* TELEKOM LCP, location cancellation procedure; **Standortwahl** *f* KERNTECH siting

Stand: **Standplatte** *f* ERDÖL bed plate; **Standreibung** *f* PHYS static friction; **Standrohr** *nt* ERDÖL *Flüssigkeitsniveau*, RAUMFAHRT standpipe; **Standrohrstopfen** *m* FERTIG *Kunststoffinstallationen* standpipe adaptor, standpipe plug; **Standschub** *m* LUFTTRANS static thrust; **Standseilbahn** *f* EISENBAHN funicular, funicular railroad (AmE), funicular railway (BrE), TRANS cable railroad (AmE), cable railway (BrE), underground cable railroad (AmE), underground cable railway (BrE)

standsicher: **~e Leichtmetalleiter** *f* SICHERHEIT fall-safe light metal ladder

Stand: **Standspur** *f* BAU, KFZTECH hard shoulder; **Standvermögen** *nt* KUNSTSTOFF nonslump properties; **Standversuch** *m* METALL creep test; **Standzeit** *f* ANSTRICH *Lacken* pot life, FERTIG cutting-edge life, edge life, endurance, useful life, MASCHINEN endurance, life; **Standzeitversuch** *m* MASCHINEN tool life testing

Stanford: ~ **Linear Collider** *m (SLC)* TEILPHYS Stanford Linear Collider *(SLC)*

Stange *f* BAU rod, ERDÖL bar, HYDRAUL *Schieber* rod, *Ventil* stem, LABOR *Rührer* rod, MASCHINEN bar, rod, rod, METROL pole, WASSERVERSORG rod; **Stangenanguß** *m* KUNSTSTOFF sprue gate; **Stangenautomat** *m* MASCHINEN bar automatic lathe; **Stangenbohrer** *m* MASCHINEN auger bit; **Stangenmagazin** *nt* FERTIG bar magazine; **Stangenmaterial** *nt* MASCHINEN bar stock; **Stangenriegel** *m* BAU bar bolt; **Stangenrißprüfgerät** *nt* FERTIG rod crack-test instrument; **Stangenrost** *m* MASCHINEN bar screen; **Stangenschwefel** *m* CHEMIE roll sulfur (AmE), roll sulphur (BrE); **Stangensystem** *nt*

MECHAN rod system

Stangenvorschub *m* MASCHINEN bar feed; **Stangenvorschubvorrichtung** *f* MASCHINEN bar feed mechanism

Stangenzirkel *m* FERTIG beam trammel, METROL beam compasses; **~ mit Stellschraube** *m* METROL beam compasses with adjusting screw

Stangenzuführung *f* FERTIG stock feeding device

Stangpressen *nt* METALL extrusion

Stanniol *nt* FERTIG tinfoil; **Stanniolverpackungsmaschine** *f* VERPACK tinfoiling machine

Stantonzahl *f* KERNTECH Stanton number

Stanzabfall *m* COMP & DV chad, FERTIG punching

Stanze *f* FERTIG stamping press, MASCHINEN blanking press, MECHAN punch, punch press, VERPACK punch

Stanzen *nt* FERTIG blanking, stamping

stanzen *vt* BAU, MASCHINEN, MECHAN punch

Stanzer *m* BAU punch

Stanzgewindebohrer *m* FERTIG serial hand tap

Stanzmaschine *f* MASCHINEN punch, punching machine

Stanzpresse *f* MASCHINEN blanking press, MECHAN punch press

Stanzteil *nt* MASCHINEN stamping

Stanzwerkzeug *nt* MASCHINEN blanking die, punching tool, stamping tool

Stapel[1] *m* BAU stack, COMP & DV batch, pack, stack, DRUCK, FERTIG pile, KER & GLAS *Flachglas* stack, *Platten* stack, MASCHINEN stack, MECHAN file

Stapel:[2] **vom ~ lassen** *vt* BAU launch; **vom ~ laufen lassen** *vt* WASSERTRANS *Schiff* launch

Stapel: **Stapeladresse** *f* COMP & DV stack address

stapelbar *adj* VERPACK stackable

Stapel: **Stapelcontainer** *m* TRANS stackable container; **Stapelfalte** *f* KONSTZEICH stacking fold; **Stapelfaser** *f* KER & GLAS, TEXTIL staple fiber (AmE), staple fibre (BrE); **Stapelfasergewebe** *nt* KER & GLAS staple tissue; **Stapelferneingabe** *f* COMP & DV remote batch entry; **Stapelfernverarbeitung** *f* COMP & DV remote batch processing, remote batch teleprocessing; **Stapelförderer** *m* VERPACK stacking conveyor; **Stapelgarn** *nt* TEXTIL stapled yarn; **Stapelglasseide** *f* KER & GLAS chopped strand; **Stapelhöhe** *f* VERPACK stacking height; **Stapeljobverarbeitung** *f* COMP & DV stack job processing; **Stapelkasten** *m* VERPACK stacking box; **Stapellänge** *f* TEXTIL staple length; **Stapellauf** *m* WASSERTRANS launch, *Schiff, Boot* launching

Stapeln *nt* BAU piling, COMP & DV, KER & GLAS *Kühlofen, Lagerraum*, PAPIER stacking

stapeln *vt* BAU pile, stack, stockpile, COMP & DV stack, PAPIER stack up, VERPACK stack

Stapel: **Stapelpalette** *f* LUFTTRANS pallet, TRANS, VERPACK stacking pallet; **Stapelsäule** *f* KER & GLAS stack plume; **Stapelspeicher** *m* COMP & DV nesting store, stack, VERPACK nesting magazine; **Stapelspeicherüberlauf** *m* COMP & DV stack overflow; **Stapelstütze** *f* WASSERTRANS shore; **Stapelung von Anforderungen** *f* COMP & DV request batching; **Stapelverarbeitung** *f* COMP & DV batch processing; **Stapelverarbeitungsmodus** *m* COMP & DV batch mode

Staphisagrin *nt* CHEMIE delphinine

Stapler *m* FERTIG piler, KER & GLAS stacker; **Staplerarm** *m* KER & GLAS stacker arm

stark[1] *adj* OPTIK *Linse* strong; **~ dotiert** *adj* ELEKTRONIK heavily-doped

stark:[2] **~ fehlerhafte Sekunde** *f* TELEKOM SES, severely errored second; **~e Injektion** *f* ELEKTRONIK

Halbleiter high-level injection; **~e Kraft** *f* TEILPHYS strong force, strong nuclear force; **~es Negativbild** *nt* ELEKTRONIK strong inversion; **~er Seegang** *m* WASSERTRANS *Seezustand* heavy seas; **~e Strömung** *f* WASSERTRANS *Meer* race; **~e Wechselwirkung** *f* KERNTECH, TEILPHYS strong interaction; **~er Weichmacher** *m* BAU *Beton* superplasticizer

Stärke *f* AKUSTIK *(I)* intensity *(I)*, DRUCK weight of type, FERTIG amylum, LEBENSMITTEL starch, MASCHINEN power, METALL strength, PAPIER staple, starch, PHYS strength, TEXTIL starch; **~ des ausfädelnden Verkehrs** *f* TRANS diverging volume

Stark-Effekt *m* PHYS Stark effect

Stärke: **Stärkegranulose** *f* TEXTIL amylopectin; **Stärkegummi** *nt* CHEMIE, LEBENSMITTEL dextrin

stärkehaltig *adj* LEBENSMITTEL starchy, PAPIER amylaceous

Starkstrom-: *pref* ELEKTRIZ, ELEKTROTECH power; **Starkstromgleichrichter** *m* ELEKTRIZ power rectifier; **Starkstrominduktor** *m* ELEKTROTECH power inductor; **Starkstromkabel** *nt* ELEKTROTECH power cable; **Starkstromleitung** *f* ELEKTROTECH power transmission line, *Überland* overhead power line; **Starkstromleitungsarmaturen** *f pl* ELEKTROTECH *Überland* overhead power line fittings; **Starkstromnetz** *nt* ELEKTROTECH high-tension power supply, power system, power transmission network

starr[1] *adj* MASCHINEN rigid

starr:[2] **~er Flügel** *m* LUFTTRANS fixed wing; **~es freitragendes Fahrzeug** *nt* TRANS self-supporting rigid vehicle; **~er Fuß** *m* FOTO *Stativ* rigid leg; **~e Koaxialleitung** *f* ELEKTROTECH rigid coaxial line; **~er Körper** *m* MECHAN rigid body; **~e Kupplung** *f* HEIZ & KÄLTE, MASCHINEN rigid coupling; **~e Motoraufhängung** *f* LUFTTRANS pylon; **~e Motorhalterung** *f* LUFTTRANS pylon; **~er Reflektor** *m* RAUMFAHRT rigid reflector; **~er Rotor** *m* LUFTTRANS *Hubschrauber* rigid rotor

Starrachse *f* KFZTECH rigid axle

Starrflügelluftfahrzeug *nt* MEERSCHMUTZ fixed-wing aircraft

Starrflügler *m* MEERSCHMUTZ fixed-wing aircraft

Start:[1] **vor dem ~** *adv* RAUMFAHRT preflight

Start[2] *m* COMP & DV start, KONTROLL start-up, LUFTTRANS takeoff, RAUMFAHRT blast, launch; **~ mit Gas** *m* LUFTTRANS power takeoff; **~ mit Hilfsrakete** *m* RAUMFAHRT JATO (AmE), RATO (BrE), jet-assisted takeoff (AmE), rocket-assisted takeoff (BrE); **Start- und Landebahn** *f* LUFTTRANS runway; **Start- und Landebahnbezeichnung** *f* LUFTTRANS runway designator; **Start- und Landebahnendbefeuerung** *f* LUFTTRANS runway end light; **Start- und Landebahnkreuzungsfeuer** *nt pl* LUFTTRANS runway crossing lights; **Start- und Landebahnmittellinie** *f* LUFTTRANS runway centerline (AmE), runway centreline (BrE); **Start- und Landebahnmittellinienbefeuerung** *f* LUFTTRANS runway centerline light (AmE), runway centreline light (BrE); **Start- und Landebahnmittellinienmarke** *f* LUFTTRANS runway centerline marking (AmE), runway centreline marking (BrE); **Start- und Landebahnneigung** *f* LUFTTRANS runway gradient; **Start- und Landebahnnummer** *f* LUFTTRANS runway number; **Start- und Landebahnränder** *m pl* LUFTTRANS runway shoulders; **Start- und Landebahnschwelle** *f* LUFTTRANS runway threshold; **Start- und Landebahnschwellenmarkierung** *f* LUFTTRANS runway threshold marking; **Start- und Landebahnstreifen**

m pl LUFTTRANS *Flughafen* runway strips; **Start- und Landebereich** *m* LUFTTRANS *Flugplatz* landing area; **Start- und Landestreifen** *m* LUFTTRANS strip; **Start- und Zielort-Gleichung** *f* TRANS O-D equation, origin-destination equation; **Start- und Zielortübersicht** *f* TRANS O-D survey, origin-destination survey

Start:[3] **zum ~ freigegeben** *vt* LUFTTRANS cleared for takeoff; **für den ~ vorbereiten** *vt* HYDRAUL *Dampfkessel* prime

Start: **Startabbruch** *m* LUFTTRANS aborted takeoff; **Startabbruchstrecke** *f* LUFTTRANS accelerate-stop distance; **Startautomatik** *f* KFZTECH automatic choke; **Startazimuth** *m* RAUMFAHRT launch azimuth

Startbahn *f* LUFTTRANS takeoff flight path; **Startbahnmarkierung** *f* LUFTTRANS *Vorfeld* hold-short line (AmE), lead-out line (BrE)

Start: **Startband** *nt* AKUSTIK leader; **Startbedingung** *f* RAUMFAHRT launch window; **Startbereich** *m* LUFTTRANS takeoff area; **Startbit** *nt* COMP & DV start bit, start element; **Startbrummen** *nt* FERNSEH starting hum

Starten *nt* COMP & DV triggering, MASCHINEN starting

starten[1] *vt* BAU launch, COMP & DV start, trigger, KONTROLL start up, start, RAUMFAHRT launch; **neu~** *vt* COMP & DV, KONTROLL restart

starten[2] *vi* COMP & DV start, KONTROLL start up

Starter *m* KFZTECH, RAUMFAHRT starter; **Starterbatterie** *f* KFZTECH starter battery; **Starterfolgswahrscheinlichkeit** *f* RAUMFAHRT launch success probability; **Starterklappe** *f* KFZTECH choker plate, *Vergaser* choke; **Starterknopf** *m* KFZTECH *Motor* starter button; **Starterritzel** *nt* KFZTECH *Motor* starter motor pinion; **Starterzahnkranz** *m* KFZTECH *Motor* flywheel starter ring gear

Start: **Startfähigkeit** *f* LUFTTRANS takeoff ability; **Startfenster** *nt* RAUMFAHRT launch window; **Startflugbahn** *f* LUFTTRANS takeoff flight path; **Startfunke** *m* PHYS streamer; **Startfunkenkammer** *f* PHYS streamer chamber; **Startgeschwindigkeit** *f* LUFTTRANS liftoff speed, takeoff speed; **Startgewicht** *nt* RAUMFAHRT liftoff weight; **Starthilfekabel** *nt* BAU jumper cable, KFZTECH *Elektrik* jump lead; **Startinstruktion** *m* COMP & DV initial instruction; **Startkapazität** *f* LUFTTRANS takeoff ability; **Startkonfiguration** *f* RAUMFAHRT launching configuration; **Startkontrollsystem** *nt* LUFTTRANS takeoff monitoring system; **Startladedruck** *m* LUFTTRANS manifold pressure; **Startlufttrichter** *m* LUFTTRANS takeoff funnel; **Startmasse** *f* LUFTTRANS *Flugzeug* gross weight; **Startnennleistung** *f* LUFTTRANS takeoff power rating; **Startphase** *f* LUFTTRANS takeoff phase; **Startprogramm** *nt* COMP & DV initial program header, KONTROLL start routine; **Startrampe** *f* RAUMFAHRT launching pad; **Startrettungssystem** *nt* RAUMFAHRT launch escape system; **Startrollstrecke** *f* LUFTTRANS takeoff run; **Startsignal** *nt* FERNSEH start mark

Start-Stopp-Betrieb *m* KONTROLL start-stop operation

Startturm *m* RAUMFAHRT launching tower; **Startumgebung** *f* RAUMFAHRT launch environment; **Startunfall** *m* KERNTECH start-up accident; **Startvermögen** *nt* COMP & DV log in, logon, KFZTECH pick-up; **Startvorbereitung** *f* HYDRAUL priming; **Startwinkel** *m* RAUMFAHRT launch azimuth; **Startzeit** *f* COMP & DV start time, *Datenverarbeitung* acceleration time

Statik *f* BAU structural analysis, ELEKTROTECH, PHYS static; **Statikbetrieb** *m* ELEKTROTECH static operation;

Statiktransformator *m* ELEKTROTECH static transformer

Station *f* EISENBAHN, ELEKTROTECH, WASSERTRANS *Schiff* station

stationär: **~er Anker** *m* ELEKTRIZ fixed armature; **~es Aufladegerät** *nt* TRANS stationary charger; **~er Betrieb** *m* COMP & DV local mode; **~es Feld** *nt* ELEKTROTECH stationary field; **~er Flug** *m* LUFTTRANS steady flight; **~es Kriechen** *nt* METALL steady state creep; **~e Lichtwellen** *f pl* WELLPHYS stationary light waves; **~e Longitudinalwellen** *f pl* WELLPHYS stationary longitudinal waves; **~e Modenleistungsverteilung** *f* TELEKOM steady state condition; **~e Modenverteilung** *f* TELEKOM equilibrium mode distribution, steady state condition; **nicht ~e Modenverteilung** *f* TELEKOM nonequilibrium mode distribution; **~e Phase** *f* TELEKOM stationary phase; **~er Punkt** *m* RAUMFAHRT stationary point; **~er Satellitendienst** *m* RAUMFAHRT fixed satellite service; **~e Spule** *f* ELEKTRIZ fixed coil; **~e Strömung** *f* LUFTTRANS *Aerodynamik*, STRÖMPHYS steady flow; **~e Transversalwellen** *f pl* WELLPHYS stationary transversal waves; **~e Umlaufbahn** *f* RAUMFAHRT stationary orbit; **~e Welle** *f* AKUSTIK, AUFNAHME, ELEKTROTECH, PHYS, TELEKOM, WELLPHYS standing wave, stationary wave (dated); **~e Wellen in der Luft** *f pl* WELLPHYS stationary aerial waves; **~es Wellenmuster** *nt* WELLPHYS stationary wave pattern; **~er Zustand** *m* ELEKTROTECH steady state condition, PHYS, STRAHLPHYS stationary state, TELEKOM steady state, steady state condition, THERMOD stationary state

Stationaritätsbedingung *f* TELEKOM steady state condition

Station: **Stationsauffindungszeichen** *nt* COMP & DV enquiry character; **Stationsaufforderung** *f* COMP & DV query; **Stationsnetz** *nt* ELEKTROTECH network of stations

statisch[1] *adj* COMP & DV, ELEKTROTECH static

statisch:[2] **~e Aufladung** *f* ELEKTROTECH static charge; **~er Auftrieb** *m* WASSERVERSORG static head, static lift; **~es Auswuchten** *nt* MASCHINEN static balancing; **~e Beanspruchung** *f* MASCHINEN static strain; **~e Bedingungen** *f pl* ELEKTROTECH static conditions; **~er Druck** *m* AKUSTIK, HEIZ & KÄLTE static pressure; **~er Eintrag** *m* COMP & DV static input; **~e Elektrizität** *f* BAU, TEXTIL static electricity; **~es Elektrizitätsfeld** *nt* ELEKTROTECH static electric field; **~er Elutionstest** *m* ABFALL static leaching test; **~es Feld** *nt* ELEKTROTECH, TELEKOM static field; **~e Förderhöhe** *f* WASSERVERSORG static discharge head; **~es Gleichgewicht** *nt* MASCHINEN static balance; **~e Höhe** *f* HYDRAUL *Hydraulik* static head; **~e Kennlinie** *f* ELEKTROTECH static characteristic; **~er Konverter** *m* RAUMFAHRT static inverter; **~es Moment** *nt* MASCHINEN static moment, PHYS moment; **~e Prüfung** *f* WERKPRÜF static test; **~er RAM** *m* *(SRAM)* COMP & DV static RAM *(SRAM)*; **~e Reibung** *f* MASCHINEN, PHYS static friction; **~es Relais** *nt* TELEKOM static relay; **~e Saughöhe** *f* WASSERVERSORG stem; **~er Schub** *m* LUFTTRANS static thrust; **~es Schweben** *nt* WASSERTRANS static hovering; **~er Speicher** *m* COMP & DV static memory, static storage, ELEKTROTECH static memory; **~er Speicherauszug** *m* COMP & DV static dump; **~e Stabilität** *f* LUFTTRANS *Lufttüchtigkeit* static stability; **~e Störung** *f* AUFNAHME static; **~er Umformer** *m* ELEKTRIZ static converter, static inverter; **~es Unterprogramm** *nt* COMP & DV static subroutine; **~er Wechselrichter** *m* ELEKTROTECH static inverter; **~e Zuordnung** *f* COMP & DV static allocation

statisch:[3] **~ und dynamisch auswuchten** *vt* HEIZ & KÄLTE balance statically and dynamically

Statistik *f* COMP & DV, MATH statistics; **Statistikdaten** *nt pl* COMP & DV statistical data

statistisch: ~e Analyse *f* COMP & DV statistical analysis; **~e Daten** *nt pl* COMP & DV statistical data; **~er Fehler** *m* COMP & DV, GERÄT random error; **~er Gesamtfehler** *m* COMP & DV mean square error; **~es Gewicht** *nt (g)* PHYS statistical weight *(g)*; **~er Multiplexer** *m* COMP & DV, TELEKOM statistical multiplexer, statmux; **~e Physik** *f* PHYS statistical physics; **~e Prüfung** *f* METROL statistical check, WERKPRÜF statistical test; **~e Qualitätslenkung** *f* QUAL statistical quality control; **~e Qualitätsprüfung** *f* QUAL statistical quality inspection; **~es Rauschen** *nt* ELEKTRONIK random noise; **~e Sicherheit** *f* COMP & DV confidence level, QUAL confidence; **~e Streuung** *f* KERNTECH random scattering; **~e Verteilung** *f* QUAL statistical distribution

Stativ[1] *nt* FERTIG, FOTO tripod, LABOR retort stand, stand; **~ mit Panoramakopf** *nt* FOTO pan head tripod

Stativ:[2] **mit ~ arbeiten** *vi* FOTO work with a tripod

Stativ: Stativanschluß *m* FOTO tripod bush; **Stativbein** *nt* FOTO tripod leg; **Stativgewinde** *nt* FOTO tripod bush; **Stativkompaß** *m* BAU surveyor's compass; **Stativkopf** *m* FOTO tripod head; **Stativscheinwerfer** *m* FOTO spotlight; **Stativverlängerung** *f* FOTO tripod extension

Stator *m* ELEKTRIZ stator, ELEKTROTECH stator, *Elektromotor* frame, KFZTECH *Generator*, PHYS stator; **Statorgehäuse** *nt* ELEKTROTECH stator frame; **Stator-Rotor-Anlassermotor** *m* ELEKTRIZ stator rotor starter motor; **Statorspule** *f* ELEKTROTECH stator coil

Status *m* COMP & DV state, status, KONTROLL status; **Statusbit** *nt* COMP & DV status bit; **Statusdiagramm** *nt* COMP & DV state diagram; **Statusregister** *nt* COMP & DV status register; **Statuswort** *nt* COMP & DV status word; **Statuszeichen** *nt* COMP & DV status character

Stau *m* ERDÖL *Bohrtechnik* backup, TRANS road jam (AmE), tailback (BrE), traffic jam (BrE), WASSERVERSORG backwater, damming-up; **Stauanlage** *f* WASSERVERSORG barrage

Stauben von gestrichenem Papier *nt* PAPIER powdering of coated paper

Staufferbuchse *f* MASCHINEN grease cup

Staufferbüchse *f* FERTIG grease cup

Staufferfett *nt* FERTIG grease

Staub *m* KOHLEN, SICHERHEIT, UMWELTSCHMUTZ dust; **~ in der Luft** *m* SICHERHEIT airborne dust; **Staub- und Sprühschutzhaube** *f* SICHERHEIT dust and spray protective hood; **Staubabdeckung** *f* MASCHINEN dust cover; **Staubabgabevorrichtung** *f* VERPACK dust-exhausting device; **Staubabsaugungsventilator** *m* KOHLEN dust exhaust fan; **Staubabscheider** *m* ABFALL dust separator, KOHLEN dust chamber, KUNSTSTOFF dust collector; **Staubabscheidung** *f* ABFALL particulate collection; **Staubabzug** *m* SICHERHEIT dust exhaust fan; **Staubabzugshaube** *f* SICHERHEIT dust hood

Stau: **Staubalken** *m* BAU stop log

Staub: **Staubanteil** *m* UMWELTSCHMUTZ dust content; **Staubaustritt** *m* VERPACK dust-exhausting device; **Staubbekämpfung** *f* CHEMTECH dust control; **Staubbindeanlage** *f* BAU dust suppression system

staubdicht *adj* ELEKTRIZ dustproof, FERTIG dust-tight, SICHERHEIT dustproof, VERPACK dust-tight, dust-

proof

Stau: **Staubecken** *nt* WASSERVERSORG catch basin, catchment basin, reservoir

Staub: **Staubentsorgung für Essengase** *f* SICHERHEIT dust-removal plant for flue gas; **Staubexplosion** *f* KOHLEN dust explosion; **Staubfangbeutel** *m* SICHERHEIT *Staubsauger, Lüfter* dust bag; **Staubfänger** *m* KOHLEN dust catcher; **Staubfilter** *nt* KOHLEN dust collector, dust filter, UMWELTSCHMUTZ fabric filter; **Staubflocke** *f* PAPIER fluff

staubfrei: ~e Konditionen *f pl* SICHERHEIT asceptic area conditions; **~e Müllabfuhr** *f* ABFALL controlled emptying, enclosed emptying; **~er Raum** *m* HEIZ & KÄLTE, SICHERHEIT clean room

staubgeladen: ~e Atmosphäre *f* KOHLEN dust-laden atmosphere; **~e Umgebung** *f* KOHLEN dust-laden atmosphere

staubgeschützt[1] *adj* MASCHINEN dustproof

staubgeschützt:[2] **~er Motor** *m* ELEKTRIZ dustproof motor

staubhaltig *adj* FERTIG *Luft* dust-laden

staubig: ~e Luft *f* SICHERHEIT dust-laden atmosphere

Staub: **Staubkappe** *f* FERTIG dust seal, MASCHINEN dust cap; **Staubkern** *m* ELEKTROTECH powdered iron core; **Staubkohle** *f* KOHLEN dust coal, fine coal; **Staubkonzentration in der Luft** *f* SICHERHEIT airborne dust concentration

Stau: **Staublech** *nt* CHEMTECH baffle plate

Staub: **Staubmaske** *f* FERTIG dust respirator; **Staubmehl** *nt* LEBENSMITTEL mill dust; **Staubmühle** *f* CHEMTECH pulverizer

Stau: **Staubohle** *f* WASSERVERSORG *Wehr, Schleusentor* flash board

Staub: **Staubpinsel** *m* FOTO dusting brush; **Staubsauggebläse** *nt* VERPACK dust aspirator; **Staubschutz** *m* KOHLEN, VERPACK dust guard; **Staubschutzbalg** *m* KFZTECH *Gangschalthebel* dust boot (BrE), dust trunk (AmE); **Staubschutzhaube** *f* SICHERHEIT dust cover; **Staubschutzmaske** *f* SICHERHEIT dust mask; **Staubteilchen** *nt* UMWELTSCHMUTZ dust particle; **Staubtrenner** *m* SICHERHEIT dust separator

Stauchautomat *m* FERTIG automatic header

Stauchdraht *m* FERTIG heading wire

Stauchdruckprüfung *f* WERKPRÜF crushing test

Stauchen *nt* FERTIG forging, metal gathering, shrinking

stauchen *vt* FERTIG forge, gather, *Umformung* upset, *Walzen* edge, PAPIER *Festigkeitsprüfung* crush

Stauchfalzmaschine *f* DRUCK buckle folder machine

Stauchkaliber *nt* FERTIG *Walzen* edging pass

Stauchmatrize *f* FERTIG forging machine die

Stauchpresse *f* MASCHINEN upsetting press

Stauchschlitten *m* FERTIG *Druckschweißen* moving platen, traveling platen (AmE), travelling platen (BrE)

Stauchstempel *m* FERTIG header, MASCHINEN header die, heading die

Stauchung *f* FERTIG linear compression, upset, KUNSTSTOFF compression, MECHAN compressive strain, WASSERTRANS strain; **~ des Fahrwerkfederbeins** *f* LUFTTRANS landing-gear shock strut compression

Stauchversuch *m* MECHAN compression test

Stauchwiderstand *m* PAPIER crushing resistance

Stau: **Staudamm** *m* WASSERVERSORG barrage, dam, retaining dam, river dam

Staudruck *m* FERTIG dynamic head, KER & GLAS, KUNSTSTOFF back pressure, LUFTTRANS dynamic pressure, impact pressure, STRÖMPHYS stagnation pressure;

Staudruckluft *f* HEIZ & KÄLTE ram air; **Staudruckmesser** *m* REGELUNG Pitot tube
Stauen *nt* WASSERVERSORG catching
stauen *vt* BAU *Wasser* retain, FERTIG baffle, WASSERVERSORG dam
Stauer *m* WASSERTRANS *Hafen* stevedore;
Stau: **Staufläche** *f* UMWELTSCHMUTZ surface area; **Stauhöhe** *f* BAU head of water; **Stauinformationen** *f pl* TRANS backup service; **Staukörper** *m* BAU gate; **Staumauer** *f* BAU retaining wall, WASSERVERSORG retaining structure; **Staumauer aus übergroßen Schottersteinen** *f* BAU tailings dam; **Staumenge** *f* WASSERVERSORG catchment; **Staupunkt** *m* ERDÖL flounder point, LUFTTRANS *Aerodynamik*, STRÖMPHYS stagnation point; **Stauscheibe** *f* FERTIG baffle plate, baffle sheet; **Stauscheibendurchflußmesser** *m* GERÄT baffle disc flow meter (BrE), baffle disk flow meter (AmE); **Stauscheiben-Durchflußmeßumformer** *m* REGELUNG target flow transducer; **Stauschwelle** *f* WASSERVERSORG drowned weir; **Stausee** *m* WASSERVERSORG artificial lake, impounding reservoir; **Staustrahltriebwerk** *nt* LUFTTRANS aero-thermodynamic duct, ramjet, THERMOD, TRANS ramjet engine
Stauung *f* KOHLEN congestion, NICHTFOSS ENERG dike (AmE), dyke (BrE), WASSERTRANS hold, *Ladung* stowage
Stau: **Stauwarngerät** *nt* TRANS queue warning sign; **Stauwarnsystem** *nt* TRANS congestion-warning system; **Stauwarnzeichen** *nt* TRANS queue warning sign; **Stauwasser** *nt* NICHTFOSS ENERG tail water, WASSERTRANS *Gezeiten* slack water, stand of tide, WASSERVERSORG perched ground water, *Kanal* backwater; **Stauwehr** *nt* BAU barrage, WASSERVERSORG retaining dam; **Stauwiderstand** *m* TRANS ram drag
Steamkracken *nt* ERDÖL *Raffinerie* steam cracking
Stearin *nt* CHEMIE glyceryl tristeate, stearin, tristearin, LEBENSMITTEL stearin
Stearyl- *pref* CHEMIE stearyl
Stechbeitel *m* MECHAN chisel
Stechdrehmeißel *m* MASCHINEN parting tool
Stecheisen *nt* MECHAN broaching
Stechfase *f* BAU *Tischlerarbeiten* chamfer stop
Stechmeißel *m* FERTIG *Spanung* necking tool, MASCHINEN cutoff tool
Stechwerkzeug *nt* FERTIG *Blech* louvring die
Stechzirkel *m* FERTIG divider, MASCHINEN pair of dividers, MATH, METROL, WASSERTRANS *Navigation* dividers
Steckanschluß *m* ELEKTRIZ plug-in termination
steckbar[1] *adj* ELEKTROTECH pluggable
steckbar:[2] **~e Verbindungsleitung** *f* COMP & DV patch cord
Steckblende *f* MECHAN push plug
Steckbrücke *f* ELEKTRIZ jumper
Steckbuchse *f* BAU lock bush, ELEKTRIZ plug receptacle, KFZTECH *Elektrik* plug socket, RADIO receptacle
Steckdorn *m* BAU pin spanner (BrE), pin wrench
Steckdose *f* COMP & DV outlet, ELEKTRIZ plug receptacle, socket, ELEKTROTECH connector socket, mains socket, plug box, plug connector, FERTIG receptacle, KFZTECH *Elektrik* plug socket, LABOR electric socket, MECHAN socket, TELEKOM outlet, socket outlet; **Steckdosenleiste** *f* ELEKTROTECH socket board
Steckelwalzwerk *nt* FERTIG Steckel mill
steckenbleiben *vi* NICHTFOSS ENERG stall
Stecker[1] *m* COMP & DV jack, ELEKTRIZ plug, ELEKTROTECH connector, coupler, male connector, plug, FERNSEH plug, FERTIG connector, RADIO plug, TELEKOM connector, male plug, plug
Stecker:[2] **~ herausziehen** *vi* ELEKTRIZ, RADIO, TELEKOM unplug
Stecker: **Steckeradapter** *m* ELEKTROTECH plug adaptor; **Steckeranschluß** *m* ELEKTROTECH plug connection; **Steckerbuchse** *f* ELEKTRIZ female connector; **Steckerdraht** *m* ELEKTROTECH plug wire; **Steckerfeld** *nt* FERTIG pin board; **Steckerkabel** *nt* ELEKTROTECH patch cord
steckerkompatibel[1] *adj* ELEKTROTECH plug-compatible
steckerkompatibel:[2] **steckerkompatibler Hersteller** *m* ELEKTRONIK plug-compatible manufacturer
Stecker: **Steckerkompatibilität** *f* ELEKTROTECH plug compatibility; **Steckerleitung** *f* ELEKTROTECH patch cord; **Steckermaß** *nt* METROL plug gage (AmE), plug gauge (BrE); **Steckerschalter** *m* ELEKTROTECH plug switch; **Steckerschnur** *f* ELEKTROTECH patch cord; **Steckerstift** *m* ELEKTROTECH contact pin, pin; **Steckertyp für Koaxkabeln** *m* RADIO connector type for coaxial cables
Steckfeld *nt* FERNSEH patch panel
Steckfilterfassung *f* FOTO sliding filter drawer
Steckglied *nt* ELEKTRIZ jumper
Steckkarte *f* TELEKOM board; **Steckkartenplatz** *m* COMP & DV card slot
steckkraftlos: **~es Bauelement** *nt* ELEKTRONIK zero insertion force connector
Steckmuffe *f* FERTIG *Kunststoffinstallationen* push-fit fitting
Steckschlüssel *m* FERTIG socket spanner (BrE), socket wrench, MASCHINEN box spanner (BrE), box wrench, socket spanner (BrE), socket wrench, MECHAN box spanner (BrE), box wrench; **Steckschlüsselsatz im Kasten** *m* KFZTECH *Zubehör* case of box spanners (BrE), case of box wrenches
Steckschuh *m* FOTO accessory shoe
Steckschwert *nt* WASSERTRANS *Schiff* daggerboard, drop keel
Stecksicherung *f* FERTIG *Kunststoffinstallationen* retaining pin
Steckstift *m* BAU peg
Stecktafel *f* ELEKTROTECH plugboard, FERNSEH patch board
Steckverbinder *m* ELEKTRIZ plug, ELEKTROTECH connector, plug, TELEKOM plug-type connector, *elektrisch* connector; **~ aus einem Stück** *m* ELEKTROTECH one-piece connector; **~ für Lichtleitfasern** *m* OPTIK optical fiber connector (AmE), optical fibre connector (BrE); **~ für Lichtleitkabel** *m* OPTIK optical fiber connector (AmE), optical fibre connector (BrE); **~ ohne spannungsführende Teile auf der Vorderseite** *m* ELEKTROTECH dead-front connector
Steckverbindung[1] *f* ELEKTRIZ plug-type connection, *Stecker und Buchse* coupler, ELEKTROTECH plug connection, *gasgefüllte Leitung* pressurized connection, MECHAN socket joint, TELEKOM plug and socket
Steckverbindung:[2] **~ unterbrechen** *vi* ELEKTRIZ unplug
Steckverschluß *m* KER & GLAS socket cap
Steckvorrichtung *f* ELEKTROTECH coupler
Stefan-Boltzmann: **~sche Konstante** *f* (σ) PHYS, THERMOD Stefan-Boltzmann constant (σ); **~sches Gesetz** *nt* PHYS Stefan-Boltzmann law, THERMOD fourth power law; **~sches Strahlungsgesetz** *nt* FERNSEH fourth power law, STRAHLPHYS Stefan's law

Steg *m* AUFNAHME land, BAU stud link, web, *Träger* stem, KERNTECH catwalk, KONSTZEICH ligament, KUNSTSTOFF land, MASCHINEN bridge, stud, MECHAN *Balken* web; **Stegblech** *nt* WASSERTRANS *Schiffbau* tripping bracket

Stege *m pl* DRUCK furniture

Steg: **Steghohlleiter** *m* ELEKTROTECH, RADIO ridge waveguide; **Stegkette** *f* BAU stud link cable chain, studded link cable chain, MASCHINEN stud chain, studded chain; **Stegplatten** *f pl* KUNSTSTOFF cellular sheet

Stehbildkamera *f* FOTO still camera

Stehbolzen *m* BAU, EISENBAHN stay bolt, FERTIG dowel pin, KFZTECH stud, MASCHINEN stay bolt; **Stehbolzengewindebohrer** *m* FERTIG boiler tap, stay bolt tap, MASCHINEN boiler stay screwing tap

Stehenbleiben *nt* MASCHINEN stalling

stehend[1] *adj* BAU upright

stehend:[2] **~e Bake** *f* WASSERTRANS *Seezeichen* fixed beacon; **~es Gut** *nt* WASSERTRANS *Tauwerk* standing rigging; **~er Motor** *m* KFZTECH, MASCHINEN vertical engine; **~e Peilung** *f* WASSERTRANS *Navigation* steady bearing; **~es Tauwerk** *nt* WASSERTRANS *Tauwerk* standing rigging; **~e Welle** *f* AKUSTIK, AUFNAHME, ELEKTROTECH, PHYS, TELEKOM, WELLPHYS standing wave, stationary wave (dated)

stehengeblieben: **~e Mantelfläche** *f* FERTIG land surface

stehenlassen *vt* METALL allow to stand

Stehkolben *m* LABOR flat-bottomed flask

Stehlager *nt* MASCHINEN pedestal bearing, pillow, pillow block, plummer block, plummer block bearing

Stehleiter *f* SICHERHEIT standing step ladder

Stehsatz *m* DRUCK alive matter, live matter, standing matter, standing type

Stehsetzstock *m* MASCHINEN steadyrest follower

Stehwelle *f* AKUSTIK, AUFNAHME, ELEKTROTECH, PHYS, TELEKOM, WELLPHYS standing wave, stationary wave (dated); **Stehwellenverhältnis** *nt* (*SWV*) PHYS standing-wave ratio (*SWR*), voltage standing wave ratio (*VSWR*), RADIO standing-wave ratio (*SWR*), TELEKOM standing-wave ratio (*SWR*), voltage standing wave ratio (*VSWR*)

Steif-: **~ und Faltkartons** *m pl* VERPACK rigid and folding cartons

steif[1] *adj* TEXTIL stiff

steif:[2] **~e Einlage** *f* TEXTIL stiffener; **~er Karton** *m* VERPACK rigid box; **~e Konstruktion** *f* BAU rigid construction; **~er Wind** *m* WASSERTRANS moderate gale

Steifappretur *f* TEXTIL stiff finish

Steife *f* FERTIG prop, TEXTIL stiffness; **Steifezahl** *m* KOHLEN compressibility coefficient

Steifheit *f* AKUSTIK stiffness, MASCHINEN rigidity, rigidness, stiffness, PHYS *Feder* stiffness

steifholen *vt* WASSERTRANS *Tauwerk* haul taut

Steifigkeit *f* MASCHINEN rigidity, rigidness, stiffness, PAPIER stiffness, PHYS rigidity, TEXTIL stiffness

Steifleinen *nt* TEXTIL interlining canvas

Steifmittel *nt* TEXTIL stiffening agent

steifsetzen *vt* WASSERTRANS *Tauwerk* set taut

Steigeaufrichter *m* VERPACK tray erector

Steigeisen *nt* BAU spur, step iron

steigen *vi* RAUMFAHRT *Raumschiff* climb, WASSERTRANS *Wasser* rise

Steigenabdichtung *f* VERPACK tray sealer

steigend: **~e Bemaßung** *f* KONSTZEICH rising dimensioning sequence; **~er Bogen** *m* BAU rampant arch, rising arch; **~er Guß** *m* FERTIG uphill casting

Steigendgießen *nt* FERTIG bottom casting

Steiger *m* ERDÖL riser, FERTIG *Gießen* rising gate

steigern *vt* ELEKTROTECH boost

Steigerohr *nt* ELEKTRIZ rising main

Steigersystem *nt* FERTIG *Gießen* risering

Steigfilmverdampfer *m* LEBENSMITTEL climbing film evaporator

Steigflug *m* LUFTTRANS climb, climb cruise; **~ mit Reisefluggeschwindigkeit** *m* LUFTTRANS cruise climb; **Steigflugbeginn** *m* LUFTTRANS climb out; **Steigfluggeschwindigkeit** *f* LUFTTRANS climb speed; **Steigflugkorridor** *m* LUFTTRANS climb corridor; **Steigflugkurve** *f* LUFTTRANS climb turn; **Steigflugphase** *f* LUFTTRANS climb phase

Steiggeschwindigkeit *f* RAUMFAHRT *Raumschiff* climb rate

Steiggradient *m* LUFTTRANS climb gradient

Steigleistung *f* LUFTTRANS climb performance

Steigleitung *f* BAU riser, rising main, ELEKTRIZ riser, ERDÖL riser, *Offshore* marine riser, FERTIG ascending main, riser

Steignahtschweißen *nt* MECHAN uphand welding

Steigrate *f* LUFTTRANS rate of climb; **Steigratenanzeige** *f* LUFTTRANS indicator of the rate of climb

Steigrohr *nt* BAU riser pipe, ELEKTRIZ rising main, ERDÖL *Bohrlochausrüstung* tubing, *Fördertechnik* production tubing

Steigstromvergaser *m* KFZTECH updraft carburetor (AmE), updraught carburettor (BrE)

Steigung *f* BAU gradient, inclination, incline, pitch, rising gradient, slope, upgrade, EISENBAHN gradient, ELEKTRONIK *Gewinde* lead, LUFTTRANS pitch, MASCHINEN lead, MATH gradient, MECHAN *Gewinde* pitch, PHYS slope, WASSERTRANS pitch; **~ einer Geraden** *f* GEOM gradient of a straight line; **Steigungsänderung des Luftschraubenblattes** *f* LUFTTRANS *Hubschrauber* blade pitch variation; **Steigungsanzeiger für die Luftschraube** *m* LUFTTRANS *Hubschrauber* blade pitch indicator; **Steigungsdrehmelder** *m* LUFTTRANS pitch synchro; **Steigungseinstellung** *f* LUFTTRANS climb setting, *Propeller* pitch setting; **Steigungsfehler** *m* FERTIG error from backlash, error of pitch; **Steigungsgenauigkeit** *f* FERTIG pitch accuracy; **Steigungsgeschwindigkeit** *f* LUFTTRANS rate of climb; **Steigungsgeschwindigkeitsanzeige** *f* LUFTTRANS rate-of-climb indicator; **Steigungshöhe** *f* BAU *Stufen* rise; **Steigungsinformation** *f* LUFTTRANS pitch information; **Steigungskompensierung** *f* LUFTTRANS *Hubschrauber* pitch compensation; **Steigungskorrekturvorrichtung** *f* LUFTTRANS *Flugkontrolle* pitch correcting unit; **Steigungsradius** *m* LUFTTRANS pitch radius; **Steigungsrate** *f* LUFTTRANS rate of climb; **Steigungssinn** *m* FERTIG hand of helix; **Steigungssteuerung** *f* LUFTTRANS *Hubschrauber* pitch control; **Steigungssteuerungskompensator des Luftschraubenblattes** *m* LUFTTRANS *Hubschrauber* blade pitch control compensator; **Steigungssynchro** *nt* LUFTTRANS pitch synchro; **Steigungsumkehr** *f* LUFTTRANS *Propeller* pitch reversing; **Steigungsverhältnis** *nt* LUFTTRANS *Propeller* advance diameter ratio; **Steigungsverstellachse** *f* LUFTTRANS *Hubschrauber* pitch change axis; **Steigungsverstelldrehkreuz** *nt* LUFTTRANS *Hubschrauber* pitch change spider; **Steigungsverstellholm**

m LUFTTRANS *Hubschrauber* pitch change beam; **Steigungsverstellstange** *f* LUFTTRANS *Hubschrauber* pitch change rod; **Steigungswinkel** *m* GEOM angle of elevation, KER & GLAS angle of pitch, LUFTTRANS climb angle, *Hubschrauber* pitch angle, MASCHINEN helix angle, lead angle, NICHTFOSS ENERG pitch angle; **Steigungszunahme** *f* LUFTTRANS *Hubschrauber* pitch increase

Steigzeit *f* ELEKTRONIK rise time

steil[1] *adj* KER & GLAS steep

steil:[2] **~er Abhang** *m* BAU steep gradient; **~es Einfallen** *nt* ERDÖL *Geologie* high-angle dip; **~er Filter** *nt* ELEKTRONIK sharp cutting filter; **~es Flöz** *nt* KOHLEN edge seam; **~ gelagerte Kohle** *f* KOHLEN edge coal; **~e Kehrkurve** *f* LUFTTRANS steep turn; **~e Straße** *f* BAU steep road

Steilanschnitt *m* KER & GLAS steep bevel

Steilböschung *f* BAU steep slope

Steildach *nt* BAU steep roof

Steilförderer *m* TRANS bag conveyor

steilgängig *adj* FERTIG *Gewinde* coarse-pitch

Steilheit *f* BAU steepness, PHYS *Elektronenröhre* transconductance

Steilkantenvorbereitung *f* BAU *Schweißen* square edge preparation

Steilufer *nt* WASSERTRANS *Geographie* bluff

Stein *m* BAU stone; **~ mit runder Ecke** *m* KER & GLAS edger block (AmE), jamb block (BrE); **Steinbearbeitung** *f* BAU stoneworking

steinbesetzt *adj* MECHAN jeweled (AmE), jewelled (BrE)

Stein: Steinbettung *f* KOHLEN stone bed, WASSERVERSORG rock layer; **Steinbohrung** *f* KOHLEN jumper boring; **Steinbrecher** *m* BAU crusher, rock breaker; **Steinbruch** *m* BAU cut stone quarry, quarry, stone pit; **Steindübel** *m* BAU, KOHLEN rock dowel; **Steinfräse** *f* BAU stone mill; **Steinfrucht** *f* LEBENSMITTEL stone fruit

Steingut *nt* KER & GLAS earthenware; **Steingutdekorationsmaler** *m* KER & GLAS earthenware decorator; **Steingutglasur** *f* KER & GLAS earthenware glazing; **Steingutrohr** *nt* BAU earthenware pipe

steinig[1] *adj* BAU stony

steinig:[2] **~er Untergrund** *m* BAU stony ground

Steinkohle *f* KOHLEN coal; **Steinkohlenasche** *f* KOHLEN coal ash; **Steinkohlenaufbereitung** *f* KOHLEN coal dressing; **Steinkohlenflöz** *nt* KOHLEN coal bed; **Steinkohlengas** *nt* KOHLEN coal gas; **Steinkohlennaphtha** *f* KOHLEN coal naphtha; **Steinkohlenschicht** *f* KOHLEN coal bed; **Steinkohlenteer** *m* KOHLEN coal tar, gas tar; **Steinkohlenteernaphtha** *f* KOHLEN coal-tar naphtha

Stein: Steinmeteorit *m* RAUMFAHRT *Raumfahrt* aerolite

Steinmetz *m* BAU stone dresser, stonemason; **~sches Gesetz** *nt* PHYS *Elektrotechnik* Steinmetz law; **~scher Koeffizient** *m* PHYS Steinmetz coefficient

Stein: Steinobst *nt* LEBENSMITTEL stone fruit; **Steinramme** *f* BAU beetle; **Steinsalz** *nt* CHEMIE, LEBENSMITTEL rock salt; **Steinschotter** *m* TRANS *Straße* ballast; **Steinschraube** *f* BAU rag bolt, MASCHINEN stone bolt; **Steinschüttung** *f* BAU rip-rap, rock fill, rubble, WASSERVERSORG rock fill; **Steinsetzer** *m* BAU pavior (AmE), paviour (BrE); **Steinsetzerhammer** *m* BAU pavior's hammer (AmE), paviour's hammer (BrE); **Steinwand** *f* KOHLEN stonewall; **Steinzeug** *nt* KER & GLAS stoneware

Stek *m* WASSERTRANS *Knoten* knot

Stell- *pref* MASCHINEN adjusting; **Stellantrieb** *m* COMP &

DV servomechanism, FERTIG *Kunststoffinstallationen* actuator unit, KONTROLL *Positioniersystem* actuator

stellar *adj* RAUMFAHRT stellar

Stellaratorröhre: ~ in Achterform *f* KERNTECH figure eight stellarator tube

Stell-: Stellaufgabe *f* ERGON control task; **Stellbereich** *m* FERTIG *Kunststoffinstallationen* control range, setting range, MASCHINEN regulating range; **Stellbewegung** *f* FERTIG *Kunststoffinstallationen* actuation, function; **Stellbogen** *m* MASCHINEN quadrant

Stelle *f* MATH digit

Stelleiste *f* MASCHINEN adjustable gib, gib

Stellen: ~ hinter dem Komma *f pl* COMP & DV fractional part

stellen *vt* KONTROLL position, PAPIER set

Stell-: Stellenschreibimpuls *m* COMP & DV enable pulse; **Stellenverschiebung** *f* COMP & DV shift; **Stellenwert** *m* MATH place value; **Stellgetriebe** *nt* ELEKTROTECH control gear; **Stellglied** *nt* ELEKTROTECH actuator, KONTROLL servo positioner, *Positioniersystem* actuator, MASCHINEN control element, MECHAN vane, REGELUNG active element, final controlling element, TRANS *KFZ, Flugzeug* actuator; **Stellgröße** *f* MASCHINEN control variable; **Stellgrößensprung** *m* REGELUNG stepwise change of the manipulated variable

Stelling *f* WASSERTRANS gangway

Stellitventil *nt* KFZTECH stellite valve

Stell-: Stellkeil für Schrauben *m* MASCHINEN screw key; **Stellknopf** *m* GERÄT adjustment knob; **Stellkraft** *f* ELEKTRIZ positioning force; **Stellmechanismus** *m* FERTIG *Kunststoffinstallationen* operating mechanism, GERÄT adjusting mechanism; **Stellmotor** *m* KONTROLL servomotor, MECHAN actuator; **Stellmutter** *f* MASCHINEN adjusting nut, check nut, checking nut, regulating nut; **Stellnocke** *f* FERTIG *Kunststoffinstallationen* adjusting cam; **Stellorgan** *nt* FERTIG *Kunststoffinstallationen* regulating unit; **Stellort** *m* REGELUNG control point, regulating point; **Stellpotentiometer** *nt* GERÄT adjustable potentiometer; **Stellring** *m* GERÄT adjustment ring, MASCHINEN adjusting ring, set collar, setting ring, MECHAN collar; **Stellschraube** *f* GERÄT adjustable screw, MASCHINEN adjusting screw, regulating screw, set bolt, set screw, temper screw; **Stellstab** *m* KERNTECH absorber rod; **Stellteil** *nt* ERGON control; **Stelltisch** *m* EISENBAHN driving desk

Stellung *f* ERGON posture, KONTROLL positioning; **Stellungsanzeige** *f* FERTIG *Kunststoffinstallationen* position indicator; **Stellungsbegrenzungsschalter** *m* FERTIG *Kunststoffinstallationen* position limiter switch; **Stellungsmeßgerät** *nt* GERÄT position measuring instrument; **Stellungsschalter** *m* ELEKTRIZ proximity switch

Stell-: Stellventil *nt* HEIZ & KÄLTE servo valve; **Stellvertreterzeichen** *nt pl* COMP & DV *bei Angabe von Dateinamen* wildcard characters; **Stellwerk** *nt* EISENBAHN signal box (BrE), signal tower (AmE); **Stellwerk des Rangierbahnhofs** *nt* EISENBAHN classification yard tower (AmE); **Stellwiderstand** *m* ELEKTROTECH rheostat, variable resistor, GERÄT adjustable resistor; **Stellwinkel** *m* FERTIG *Kunststoffinstallationen* operating angle; **Stellwirkung** *f* REGELUNG regulating action; **Stellzeit** *f* FERTIG *Kunststoffinstallationen* control time

Stelzbogen *m* BAU stilted arch

Stemmaschine *f* BAU mortising machine, FERTIG mortise machine, MASCHINEN mortising machine

Stemmeisen *nt* BAU chisel, mortise chisel, MECHAN chisel, crowbar

Stemmeißel *m* BAU mortise chisel

Stemmen *nt* FERTIG chiseling (AmE), chiselling (BrE)

stemmen *vt* BAU chisel

Stemmloch *nt* BAU chisel

Stemmnaht *f* FERTIG caulk weld, WASSERTRANS *Schiffbau* caulked joint

Stempel *m* BAU punch, KOHLEN strut, KUNSTSTOFF ram, MASCHINEN die, punch, ram, MECHAN punch, QUAL stamp; **Stempelätzpaste** *f* KER & GLAS stamp etching paste; **Stempelaufnahmeplatte** *f* KOHLEN punched plate; **Stempelberechtigter** *m* QUAL stamp holder; **Stempelberechtigung** *f* QUAL stamp authorization; **Stempelfarbe** *f* KONSTZEICH stamp pad ink; **Stempelhalteplatte** *f* MASCHINEN punch plate; **Stempelhalter** *m* MASCHINEN punch holder; **Stempelüberwachung** *f* QUAL stamp control

Stengelglas *nt* KER & GLAS stemware

Stengelkristall *m* METALL columnar crystal

Steppdecke *f* TEXTIL comforter, continental quilt, quilt

steppen *vt* TEXTIL quilt

Ster *nt* METROL stere

Steradiant *m* ELEKTRONIK *Einheit*, PHYS *Einheit* steradian

Stereo *nt* DRUCK stereotype plate; **Stereoabstimmgerät** *nt* AUFNAHME stereo tuner; **Stereoaufnahme** *f* AUFNAHME stereo recording, stereophonic recording; **Stereobandaufnahme** *f* AUFNAHME stereo tape recording; **Stereobetrachter** *m* FOTO stereo viewer, stereoscope; **Stereobildpaar** *nt* FOTO stereoscopic pair; **Stereodecoder** *m* AUFNAHME stereo decoder; **Stereoeffekt** *m* AUFNAHME stereo effect; **Stereofernsehen** *nt* FERNSEH stereovision

stereo *adj* AUFNAHME stereo

stereographisch: ~e **Projektion** *f* METALL stereographic projection

Stereo: **Stereohilfsträger** *m* AUFNAHME stereo subcarrier; **Stereoisomer** *nt* CHEMIE stereoisomer; **Stereokamera** *f* FOTO stereoscopic camera; **Stereokompaktanlage** *f* AUFNAHME three-in-one stereo component system; **Stereokopfhörer** *m* AUFNAHME stereo headphone; **Stereokopierrahmen** *m* FOTO transposing frame; **Stereomer** *nt* CHEMIE stereoisomer; **Stereomikroskop** *nt* LABOR stereomicroscope

stereophon: ~e **Tonwiedergabe** *f* AUFNAHME stereophonic reproduction

Stereo: **Stereophonie** *f* AKUSTIK, AUFNAHME stereophony

stereophonisch: ~e **Aufnahme** *f* AKUSTIK stereophonic recording; ~e **Mikrorille** *f* AUFNAHME stereophonic microgroove

Stereo: **Stereoschallplatte** *f* AUFNAHME stereophonic record; **Stereositzplatz** *m* AUFNAHME stereo seat; **Stereoskopie** *f* FOTO stereoscopy; **Stereoton** *m* AUFNAHME stereophonic sound; **Stereotonabnehmer** *m* AKUSTIK stereophonic pick-up; **Stereotonbandgerät** *nt* AUFNAHME stereo tape recorder; **Stereotrennung** *f* AUFNAHME stereo separation

Stereotypie *f* DRUCK stereotyping; **Stereotypieplatte** *f* DRUCK stereotype plate

Stereo: **Stereounterkanal** *m* AUFNAHME stereo subchannel; **Stereovideorecorder** *m* FERNSEH stereo VCR

steril *adj* KOHLEN sterile, LEBENSMITTEL aseptic

sterilisiert *adj* LEBENSMITTEL sterilized

Sterilverband *m* SICHERHEIT sterile dressing

Sterin *nt* CHEMIE sterol

sterisch *adj* CHEMIE steric

Stern:[1] ~e **betreffend** *adj* RAUMFAHRT stellar

Stern[2] *m* RAUMFAHRT star; **Sternanker** *m* ELEKTRIZ spider-type armature; **Sternanordnung** *f* FERTIG *Zylinder* radial arrangement; **Sternbohrmeißel** *m* ERDÖL *Bohrtechnik* star bit; **Sternbruch** *m* KER & GLAS star fracture

Sterndreieck *nt* ELEKTRIZ, ELEKTROTECH, PHYS star delta; **Sterndreieckanlasser** *m* ELEKTRIZ Y-delta starter, star delta starter, ELEKTROTECH star delta starter; **Sterndreieckanlasserschalter** *m* ELEKTRIZ star delta starting switch; **Sterndreieckanlaßschalter** *m* ELEKTRIZ Y-delta starting switch; **Sterndreieckschalter** *m* ELEKTROTECH star delta starter, star delta switch; **Sterndreieckschaltung** *f* ELEKTROTECH star delta connection; **Sterndreiecktransformation** *m* PHYS star delta transformation; **Sterndreiecktransformierung** *f* ELEKTRIZ star-to-delta transformation; **Sterndreieckumformung** *f* ELEKTRIZ star-to-delta conversion

Stern: **Sterndurchgangsdetektor** *m* RAUMFAHRT star transit detector

sternförmig: ~es **Netzwerk** *nt* COMP & DV active star; ~er **Riß im Porzellan** *m* KER & GLAS spider; ~es **Speisesystem** *nt* ELEKTRIZ radial feeder system; ~es **System** *nt* ELEKTRIZ radial system; ~es **Verteilungssymbol** *nt* COMP & DV switched star

Stern: **Sternfühler** *m* RAUMFAHRT star sensor; **Stern-Gerlach-Versuch** *m* PHYS Stern-Gerlach-experiment

sterngeschaltet: ~er **Anker** *m* ELEKTRIZ star-connected armature

Stern: **Sterngriff** *m* FERTIG *Kunststoffinstallationen* locking handle, MASCHINEN star wheel; **Sternhaufen** *m* RAUMFAHRT diffuse nebula; **Sternkarte** *f* WASSERTRANS *Navigation* star chart; **Sternkeilwelle** *f* MASCHINEN multispline shaft; **Sternkompaß** *m* RAUMFAHRT astrocompass; **Sternkonfiguration** *f* TELEKOM star configuration; **Sternkoppler** *m* OPTIK, TELEKOM star coupler; **Sternmotor** *m* KFZTECH radial engine; **Sternnähe** *f* RAUMFAHRT periastron; **Sternnetz** *nt* COMP & DV, TELEKOM star network; **Sternnetzwerk** *nt* COMP & DV star network; **Sternpeilung** *f* RAUMFAHRT astro fix; **Sternpunkt** *m* PHYS *Dreiphasenstrom* neutral point; **Sternpunktdraht** *m* ELEKTRIZ neutral wire; **Sternrad** *nt* KFZTECH star wheel, MASCHINEN Geneva wheel, spoke wheel, star gear, star wheel; **Sternrevolver** *m* MASCHINEN star turret; **Sternriß** *m* BAU *Holz* star shake, KER & GLAS star crack; **Sternschaltung** *f* COMP & DV star connection, ELEKTRIZ Y-connection, star connection, wye connection, ELEKTROTECH star connection, PHYS Y-connection, star connection, RAUMFAHRT *Weltraumfunk* star network; **Sternspannung** *f* ELEKTRIZ star voltage; **Stern-Stern-Schaltung** *f* ELEKTRIZ star-star connection; **Sternstruktur** *f* TELEKOM star structure; **Sterntopologie** *f* COMP & DV star topology; **Sternverfolger** *m* RAUMFAHRT star tracker; **Sternverteilung** *f* TELEKOM star distribution; **Sternvierer** *m* ELEKTROTECH star quad; **Sternviererkabel** *nt* ELEKTROTECH, PHYS star quad cable; **Sternwalze** *f* PAPIER starred roll

Steroid *nt* CHEMIE steroid

Sterol *nt* CHEMIE sterol

stetig[1] *adj* MATH *Funktion* continuous; ~ **durchstimmbar** *adj* GERÄT continuously tunable

stetig:[2] ~e **Kurve** *f* GEOM continuous curve; ~es **Merkmal**

nt QUAL continuous characteristic; ~e **Regeleinrichtung** *f* REGELUNG continuous controlling system; ~er **Regler** *m* ELEKTRONIK *Steuer- und Regelungstechnik* continuous action controller, continuous beam; ~ **wirkende Regeleinrichtung** *f* REGELUNG continuous controlling system; ~ **wirkendes Glied** *nt* REGELUNG continuously acting element

Stetigförderer *m* MASCHINEN continuous flow conveyor; ~ **für Fußgänger** *m* TRANS passenger conveyor

Stetigkeit *f* MATH continuity

Stetigpoliermaschine *f* KER & GLAS continuous polisher

Stetigschleifer *m* PAPIER continuous grinder; ~ **und -polierer** *m* KER & GLAS continuous grinder and polisher

Steuer- *pref* COMP & DV, ELEKTRIZ, HEIZ & KÄLTE, KERNTECH, KOHLEN, KONTROLL, RAUMFAHRT control; **Steuer- und Anzeigegerät** *nt* RAUMFAHRT CDU, control and display unit; **Steuer- und Sicherheitseinrichtung** *f* HEIZ & KÄLTE control and safety device; **Steueralgorithmus** *m* KONTROLL control algorithm; **Steueranlage** *f* ELEKTRIZ control gear, WASSERTRANS steering system; **Steueranlage eines Reaktors** *f* KERNTECH reactor control board; **Steuerantrieb** *m* KOHLEN control driving; **Steueranweisung** *f* COMP & DV control statement; **Steuerarm** *m* FERNSEH control arm; **Steuerbandgerät** *nt* FERNSEH control deck

steuerbar: ~e **Drossel** *f* PHYS transductor; ~er **Siliziumschalter** *m* ELEKTROTECH silicon-controlled switch

Steuer-: **Steuerbarkeit** *f* KERNTECH *Kraftniveau* maneuverability (AmE), manoeuvrability (BrE), LUFTTRANS controllability, maneuverability (AmE), manoeuvrability (BrE); **Steuerbefehl** *m* COMP & DV control command, control instruction, KONTROLL control instruction; **Steuerbit** *nt* COMP & DV control bit; **Steuerblock** *m* COMP & DV control block; **Steuerbord** *nt* WASSERTRANS right, starboard

steuerbord *adv* RAUMFAHRT starboard

Steuer-: **Steuerbus** *m* COMP & DV control bus; **Steuercode** *m* COMP & DV control sequence; **Steuercodes** *m pl* COMP & DV control codes; **Steuerdaten** *nt pl* COMP & DV control data; **Steuerdiagramm** *nt* MASCHINEN distribution diagram; **Steuerdrossel** *f* ELEKTROTECH saturable reactor; **Steuerdruck** *m* FERTIG *Kunststoffinstallationen* control pressure, RAUMFAHRT feel; **Steuerdruckmechanismus** *m* RAUMFAHRT feel mechanism; **Steuerdruckventil** *nt* LUFTTRANS feel simulator valve; **Steuerebene** *f* LUFTTRANS control plane; **Steuereinheit** *f* COMP & DV control unit, controller, ELEKTROTECH control unit, RADIO controller, TELEKOM control unit, TRANS driving unit; **Steuereinrichtung** *f* REGELUNG open loop control system, TELEKOM control equipment; **Steuerelektrode** *f* ELEKTROTECH control electrode, PHYS *Thyristor* gate; **Steuerfeld** *nt* COMP & DV control field; **Steuerfläche** *f* LUFTTRANS control surface, rudder, PHYS control surface; **Steuerfluß** *m* COMP & DV control flow; **Steuerfrequenz** *f* ELEKTRONIK, FERNSEH, RADIO control frequency

Steuergehäuse *nt* EISENBAHN control housing, KFZTECH timing gear housing, MASCHINEN control box; **Steuergehäusedeckel** *m* KFZTECH timing gear cover

Steuer-: **Steuergerät** *nt* ELEKTRIZ control unit, ELEKTROTECH control gear, controller, KFZTECH trigger box; **Steuergestänge** *nt* HYDRAUL valve gear; **Steuergetriebe** *nt* ELEKTROTECH control gear; **Steuergitter** *nt* AKUSTIK driving grid, ELEKTROTECH *Elektronenkanone* control grid; **Steuerhebelquadrant** *m* LUFTTRANS control lever quadrant; **Steuerkennlinie** *f* ELEKTROTECH control characteristic; **Steuerkette** *f* KFZTECH timing chain, *Steuerung, Spritzverstellung, Triebstrang* chain, WASSERTRANS steering chain; **Steuerknopf** *m* GERÄT control button

Steuerknüppel *m* COMP & DV joystick, LUFTTRANS control column, control stick, RAUMFAHRT joystick; ~ **für periodische Steigungssteuerung** *m* LUFTTRANS cyclic control pitch stick; ~ **für zyklische Blattverstellung** *m* LUFTTRANS *Hubschrauber* cyclic control pitch stick, cyclic pitch stick; **Steuerknüppelbesatz** *m* LUFTTRANS control column whipping; **Steuerknüppelumwicklung** *f* LUFTTRANS control column whipping

Steuer-: **Steuerkolben** *m* FERTIG *Hydraulik* actuating piston, HYDRAUL *Dampfmaschine* slide valve, MASCHINEN control piston; **Steuerkolbenstange** *f* HYDRAUL valve rod; **Steuerkolbenventil** *nt* HYDRAUL slide valve; **Steuerkompaß** *m* WASSERTRANS steering compass; **Steuerkonsole** *f* COMP & DV control panel; **Steuerkräfteausfallanzeiger** *m* LUFTTRANS artificial feel failure detector; **Steuerkreis** *m* COMP & DV, TELEKOM control circuit; **Steuerkreisel** *m* LUFTTRANS *Hubschrauber* control gyro

Steuerkurs *m* LUFTTRANS compass heading, heading, WASSERTRANS compass heading; **Steuerkursfernanzeige** *f* LUFTTRANS heading remote indicator; **Steuerkurshalten** *nt* LUFTTRANS heading hold; **Steuerkursinformation** *f* LUFTTRANS heading information; **Steuerkurs-Synchronisiereinrichtung** *f* LUFTTRANS heading synchronizer; **Steuerkurs-Übermittlungsumsetzer** *m* LUFTTRANS heading repeater; **Steuerkurswähler** *m* LUFTTRANS heading selector

Steuer-: **Steuerkurve** *f* FERTIG operating cam; **Steuerleitung** *f* ELEKTROTECH *Fahrstuhl* trailing cable, *bei E-Antrieb* pilot wire, TELEKOM control circuit; **Steuerlochband** *nt* COMP & DV control tape; **Steuermann** *m* WASSERTRANS *Handelsmarine* mate; **Steuermembrane** *f* FERTIG *Kunststoffinstallationen* control diaphragm; **Steuermodus** *m* COMP & DV control mode

Steuern *nt* REGELUNG open loop controlling

steuern[1] *vt* COMP & DV control, KONTROLL control, *Richtung* steer, LUFTTRANS, TRANS steer, WASSERTRANS steer, *Schiffbau* helm

steuern[2] *vi* KONTROLL *Richtung*, LUFTTRANS, TRANS, WASSERTRANS *Navigation* steer

steuernd: ~es **Basissignal** *nt* ELEKTRONIK base drive signal; ~er **Basisstrom** *m* ELEKTRONIK *Transistoren* current base drive; ~er **Taktgeber** *m* TELEKOM master clock

Steuer-: **Steueröffnung** *f* PHYS port; **Steueroszillator** *m* ELEKTRONIK master oscillator; **Steuerpodest** *nt* LUFTTRANS control pedestal; **Steuerprogramm** *nt* COMP & DV MCP, control routine, master control program, TRANS control program (AmE), control programme (BrE); **Steuerpult** *nt* BAU control panel, EISENBAHN control desk, ELEKTRIZ console, control console, FERNSEH control console, GERÄT console, KONTROLL console, control console, control panel, operator console, LUFTTRANS console, control panel, WASSERTRANS *Schiff* console; **Steuerquarz** *m* ELEKTRONIK oscillator crystal; **Steuerrad** *nt* ASSERTRANS *Bootbau* steering wheel, KFZTECH wheel; **Steuerrakete**

f RAUMFAHRT control rocket; **Steuerrechner für Vermittlungssysteme** *m* TELEKOM switching system processor; **Steuerregister** *nt* COMP & DV control register; **Steuerrelais** *nt* ELEKTRIZ control relay; **Steuerriemen** *m* MECHAN timing belt; **Steuerrotor** *m* LUFTTRANS control rotor; **Steuerroutine** *f* COMP & DV control routine; **Steuerruder** *nt* LUFTTRANS rudder; **Steuerschalter** *m* ELEKTRIZ control switch, ELEKTROTECH control switch, controller, RAIL *handgesteuert* master controller; **Steuerschaltung** *f* ELEKTRIZ control circuit; **Steuerschaltventil** *nt* LUFTTRANS actuator control valve; **Steuerschieber** *m* HYDRAUL *Dampfmaschine, Hydraulik* slide valve; **Steuerschiebergehäuse** *nt* HYDRAUL valve chest; **Steuerschieberstange** *f* HYDRAUL valve rod; **Steuerschieberventil** *nt* HYDRAUL slide valve; **Steuerschlitz** *m* KFZTECH *Motor* port; **Steuerschrank** *m* EISENBAHN control box, GERÄT console; **Steuerseil** *nt* MASCHINEN control cable; **Steuersender** *m* AKUSTIK driver; **Steuersignal** *nt* ELEKTRONIK, FERNSEH control signal; **Steuersprache** *f* COMP & DV CL, control language; **Steuerspule** *f* ELEKTROTECH drive coil; **Steuerspur** *f* AKUSTIK, AUFNAHME, FERNSEH control track; **Steuerspursignal** *nt* AUFNAHME, FERNSEH control track signal; **Steuerspurzeitcode** *m* AUFNAHME, FERNSEH control track time code; **Steuerstab** *m* PHYS *Kernreaktion* control rod; **Steuerstange** *f* LUFTTRANS control rod; **Steuerstangenresonanz** *f* LUFTTRANS *Hubschrauber* control rod resonance; **Steuerstreifen** *m* AKUSTIK control track; **Steuerstrich** *m* RAUMFAHRT, WASSERTRANS *Kompaß* lubber's line; **Steuerstufe** *f* ELEKTRONIK master oscillator, LUFTTRANS control stage; **Steuersystem** *nt* ELEKTRIZ, TELEKOM control system; **Steuersystem mit festverdrahtetem Programm** *nt* TELEKOM wired program control system (AmE), wired programme control system (BrE); **Steuertafel** *f* ELEKTRIZ control board; **Steuertaste** *f* *(Strg-Taste)* COMP & DV control key *(Ctrl key)*; **Steuerteil** *m* FERTIG *Kunststoffinstallationen* control unit; **Steuertriebwagen** *m* KFZTECH driving motor car; **Steuertriebwerk** *nt* RAUMFAHRT vernier motor; **Steuertrommel** *f* KER & GLAS timing drum

Steuerung *f* COMP & DV, ELEKTRIZ, ELEKTRONIK *Ein/Ausstellung* control, ELEKTROTECH control unit, FERNSEH biasing, pilot, HYDRAUL *Dampflokomotive* valve gear, *Turbine* guide, KFZTECH control, KONTROLL controller, control, LUFTTRANS control system, MASCHINEN, RAUMFAHRT control, REGELUNG open loop control, TELEKOM control, steering; **~ auf hell** *f* ELEKTRONIK positive modulation; **~ mittels Elektronenstrahl** *f* ELEKTRONIK electronic beam steering; **Steuerungs- und Anzeigegeräte** *nt pl* LUFTTRANS controls and indicating devices; **Steuerungsabfolge** *f* KONTROLL control sequence; **Steuerungsart** *f* LUFTTRANS control system; **Steuerungsaufwand** *m* TELEKOM overhead; **Steuerungsball** *m* COMP & DV track ball; **Steuerungsdämpfer** *m* LUFTTRANS control damper; **Steuerungsdiagramm** *nt* COMP & DV timing diagram; **Steuerungseinheit** *f* MASCHINEN control unit; **Steuerungsfolge** *f* KONTROLL control sequence

steuerungsführend: **~e Betriebsart** *f* KONTROLL master mode

Steuerung: **Steuerungsführung** *f* SICHERHEIT jig; **Steuerungshebel** *m* COMP & DV joystick; **Steuerungshierarchie** *f* KONTROLL control hierarchy; **Steuerungskasten des Motoranlassers** *m* LUFTTRANS engine starting control box; **Steuerungssystem** *nt* KONTROLL control system; **Steuerungstechnik** *f* REGELUNG control engineering; **Steuerungsübergabe** *f* KONTROLL control transfer, passing of control

Steuer-: **Steuerventil** *nt* HYDRAUL control valve, governor valve, KONTROLL control valve, MASCHINEN control valve, distribution valve, MECHAN control valve; **Steuerverhalten** *nt* LUFTTRANS controllability, RAUMFAHRT *Raumschiff* handling; **Steuerverschlußstein** *m* KER & GLAS control tweel; **Steuervolumen** *nt* FERTIG *Kunststoffinstallationen* swept volume; **Steuervorgang** *m* KONTROLL control action; **Steuerwagen** *m* EISENBAHN driving trailer car; **Steuerwalze** *f* FERTIG controller; **Steuerwarte** *f* ELEKTRIZ console, KERNTECH control room; **Steuerwelle** *f* KFZTECH camshaft; **Steuerwerk** *nt* ELEKTROTECH, TELEKOM control unit; **Steuerwinkel** *m* WASSERTRANS *Navigation* steering angle; **Steuerwort** *nt* COMP & DV control word; **Steuerzeichen** *nt* COMP & DV control character, DRUCK functional character; **Steuerzentrale** *f* ELEKTRIZ control room, FERNSEH control center (AmE), control centre (BrE)

Stevenanlauf *m* WASSERTRANS *Schiffbau* forefoot
Stevenrohr *nt* WASSERTRANS *Schiffbau* stern tube
Stibium *nt (Sb)* CHEMIE stibium *(Sb)*
Stibnit *m* CHEMIE stibnite
Stich[1] *m* BAU camber, *Bogen* rise, TEXTIL stitch; **Stichbalken** *m* BAU tail beam; **Stichbogen** *m* BAU flat arch, segmental arch; **Sticheinreißfestigkeit** *f* KUNSTSTOFF puncture resistance
Stichel *m* AKUSTIK rake, stylus; **Stichelkraft** *f* AKUSTIK stylus force
stichfest *adj* ABFALL semisolid
Stich: **Stichflamme** *f* THERMOD darting flame; **Stichflammentest** *m* KER & GLAS dart impact test; **Stichkabel** *nt* BAU branch cable; **Stichleitung** *f* ELEKTROTECH, RADIO *Antennen* stub; **Stichloch** *nt* KER & GLAS tapping hole
Stichprobe *f* COMP & DV sample, KOHLEN random sampling, spot check, MASCHINEN, QUAL, TELEKOM *Qualität* sample; **Stichprobenahme** *f* ERGON sampling, KOHLEN random sample; **Stichprobenauswahlsatz** *m* QUAL sampling fraction; **Stichprobenentnahme** *f* TELEKOM *Qualität* sampling; **Stichprobenplan** *m* ERGON sampling plan, QUAL sampling scheme; **Stichprobenprüfung** *f* QUAL batch test, sampling inspection, WERKPRÜF random sample test; **Stichprobensystem nach einem quantitativen Merkmal** *nt* QUAL attribute sampling system; **Stichprobenumfang** *m* ELEKTRONIK, QUAL sample size
Stich: **Stichsäge** *f* BAU compass saw, keyhole saw, MASCHINEN alternating saw, compass saw
Stichwort *nt* ELEKTRIZ keyword
Stichwort: **~ geben** *vi* AUFNAHME cue
Stichwort: **eine Stichwortanalyse** *f* COMP & DV KWIC, keyword in context; **Stichwortanalyse mit Text** *f* *(KWOC-Index)* COMP & DV keyword out of context *(KWOC)*; **Stichwortmikrofon** *nt* AUFNAHME cue mike
Stickdioxid *nt* SICHERHEIT *Luft* nitrogen dioxide
Stickoxid *nt* ABFALL nitrogen oxide, UMWELTSCHMUTZ nitric oxide
Stickstoff *m* CHEMIE nitrogen; **~ als Schutzgas** *m* KERNTECH nitrogen cover gas; **Stickstoffbestimmungsapparat nach Kjeldahl** *m* LABOR Kjeldahl digestion apparatus; **Stickstoffdioxid** *nt* CHEMIE nitrogen dioxide, UMWELTSCHMUTZ nitrogen dioxide,

nitrogen peroxide

stickstoffgekühlt: ~er Reaktor *m* KERNTECH nitrogen-cooled reactor

stickstoffhaltig *adj* CHEMIE nitrogenous

Stickstoff: **Stickstoffoxid** *nt* CHEMIE nitrous oxide; **Stickstoffpentoxid** *nt* UMWELTSCHMUTZ nitrogen pentoxide; **Stickstoffspülung** *f* RAUMFAHRT *Raumschiff* nitrogen purging; **Stickstoffwasserstoff-** *pref* CHEMIE hydrazoic

Stiefel *m* FERTIG *Pumpe* barrel, penstock, KER & GLAS boot, MASCHINEN barrel

Stiel *m* BAU *Pfettendach* strut, KER & GLAS stem, MASCHINEN handle, MECHAN handle, shaft; **Stielhammer** *m* FERTIG helve; **Stielpfanne** *f* MASCHINEN bull ladle; **Stielträger** *m* KER & GLAS stem carrier

Stift *m* BAU brad, dowel, pin, plug, ELEKTROTECH pin, FERTIG pintle, *Kunststoffinstallationen* pin, KFZTECH stud, MASCHINEN finger, peg, pin, spike, tack, MECHAN peg, pin, stud; ~ **mit Bund** *m* MASCHINEN collared pin; **Stiftbolzen** *m* FERTIG stud; **Stiftbüchse** *f* FERTIG pin barrel; **Stiftfassung** *f (cf Bajonettfassung)* ELEKTRIZ bayonet socket; **Stiftisolator** *m* ELEKTRIZ pin insulator; **Stiftkolben** *m* BAU pin vice (BrE), pin vise (AmE); **Stiftkontakt** *m* ELEKTRIZ plug pin; **Stiftlampenfassung** *f* ELEKTRIZ bayonet lamp holder; **Stiftloch** *nt* MASCHINEN pinhole; **Stiftplotter** *m* COMP & DV pen plotter; **Stiftschlüssel** *m* BAU pin spanner (BrE), pin wrench; **Stiftschraube** *f* MASCHINEN stud, tap bolt; **Stiftsicherung** *f* FERTIG pin lock; **Stiftsockel** *m* ELEKTRIZ bayonet cap, FERTIG pin base; **Stiftstecker** *m* ELEKTROTECH pin plug; **Stiftventil** *nt* BAU pin valve

Stigmasterin *nt* CHEMIE stigmasterol

Stigmasterol *nt* CHEMIE stigmasterol

stigmatisch: ~e Linse *f* FOTO stigmatic lens

Stilben *nt* CHEMIE stilbene, toluylene

still: ~e Verbrennung *f* KFZTECH slow combustion; ~es Wasser *nt* LEBENSMITTEL still water, WASSERVERSORG quiet water

Stillebenfotografie *f* FOTO still life photography

stillegen *vt* BAU put out of service, COMP & DV quiesce, KOHLEN deactivate, TELEKOM

Stillegung *f* COMP & DV quiescing, KERNTECH *Reaktor* decommissioning

stillgelegt: ~er Teilnehmer *m* TELEKOM ceased subscriber

stilliegen *vi* MASCHINEN lie idle

Stillstand[1] *m* FERTIG *Getriebelehre* dwell, KER & GLAS shutdown, KFZTECH stop, LUFTTRANS rest period, MASCHINEN standstill, stop; ~ der Gezeiten *m* WASSERTRANS stand of tide

Stillstand:[2] zum ~ kommen *vi* MASCHINEN come to a standstill

Stillstand: **Stillstandsgetriebe** *nt* FERTIG dwell mechanism; **Stillstandsheizung** *f* HEIZ & KÄLTE anticondensation heater; **Stillstandspause** *f* FERTIG dwelling; **Stillstandsstellung** *f* FERTIG dwell position; **Stillstandzeit** *f* ERDÖL downtime

stillstehend: ~er Anker *m* ELEKTRIZ stationary armature; ~es Gewässer *nt* WASSERVERSORG still water; ~e Luft *f* NICHTFOSS ENERG still air; ~er Verkehr *m* TRANS stationary traffic

Stillwasser *nt* WASSERTRANS *Gezeiten* slack water

Stimmaufzeichnung *f* TELEKOM voice recorder

Stimme *f* COMP & DV voice

Stimmen *nt* AKUSTIK, ELEKTRONIK tuning

stimmen *vt* AKUSTIK, ELEKTRONIK tune

Stimmerkennung *f* RAUMFAHRT voice detector

Stimmgabel *f* AKUSTIK, AUFNAHME, PHYS, WELLPHYS tuning fork; **Stimmgabeloszillator** *m* ELEKTRONIK fork oscillator

Stimmskale *f* AUFNAHME tuning dial

Stimmton *m* AKUSTIK pitch

Stimmung *f* AKUSTIK pitch

stimuliert: ~e Emission *f* OPTIK, TELEKOM stimulated emission; ~e Strahlungsabsorption *f* STRAHLPHYS stimulated absorption of radiation; ~e Strahlungsemission *f* STRAHLPHYS stimulated emission of radiation

Stinger *m* ERDÖL *Offshore* stinger

Stinkbrand *m* LEBENSMITTEL *Getreidekrankheit* bunt

Stippe *f* KUNSTSTOFF fish eye

Stippen *nt* KER & GLAS stippling

Stirlingmotor *m* MASCHINEN Stirling engine

Stirn *f* MASCHINEN end; **Stirnabschreckversuch** *m* FERTIG end quench test; **Stirnbrett** *nt* BAU side board; **Stirndrehmeißel** *m* FERTIG end-cut turning tool, MASCHINEN facing tool

Stirnfläche[1] *f* BAU butt end, FERTIG end, MASCHINEN end face

Stirnfläche:[2] Stirnflächen bearbeiten *vi* MASCHINEN face

Stirnfläche: **Stirnflächenbearbeitung** *f* MASCHINEN facing; **Stirnflächenbreite** *f* FERTIG face width

Stirn: **Stirnfräsen** *nt* MASCHINEN end milling, face milling; **Stirnfräser** *m* MASCHINEN face cutter, face mill, face-milling cutter, facing cutter; **Stirnkantenplatte** *f* KER & GLAS front lip tile; **Stirnkurbel** *f* MASCHINEN outside crank; **Stirnmauer** *f* BAU face wall, *Durchlaß* head wall

Stirnrad *nt* MASCHINEN cylindrical gear, spur gear, spur wheel; **Stirnradgetriebe** *nt* KFZTECH cylindrical gear pair, MASCHINEN spur gear

Stirnrädergetriebe *nt* MASCHINEN spur gear

Stirn: **Stirnreibahle** *f* FERTIG bottoming reamer; **Stirnschneidenfreiwinkel** *m* MASCHINEN front clearance; **Stirnseite** *f* MASCHINEN end, face; **Stirnseite des Kühlofens** *f* KER & GLAS end of lehr

stirnseitig: ~ schneidend *adj* FERTIG end-cutting

Stirn: **Stirnradpaar** *nt* MASCHINEN cylindrical gear pair; **Stirnradverzahnungsmaschine** *f* MASCHINEN spur gear cutting machine; **Stirnsenken** *nt* MASCHINEN end facing; **Stirnsenker** *m* MASCHINEN counterbore, end mill reamer; **Stirnteilung** *f* FERTIG *Getriebelehre* real circular pitch; **Stirnwalzenfräsen** *nt* MASCHINEN shell-end milling; **Stirnwandtür** *f* KER & GLAS end door; **Stirnzahn** *m* FERTIG *Fräser* radial tooth

stochastisch[1] *adj* COMP & DV, ERGON, MATH stochastic

stochastisch:[2] ~e Abtastung *f* TELEKOM random sampling; ~e Anregung *f* TELEKOM random excitation; ~e Belastung *f* METALL stochastic loading; ~e Kühlung *f* TEILPHYS stochastic cooling; ~er Prozess *m* PHYS stochastic process

Stöchiometrie *f* CHEMIE stoichiometry

stöchiometrisch[1] *adj* CHEMIE stoichiometric

stöchiometrisch:[2] ~e Zusammensetzung *f* METALL stoichiometric composition

Stock *m* FERTIG *Amboß* body; **Stockanker** *m* WASSERTRANS stock anchor; **Stockblender** *m* KUNSTSTOFF *Kautschuk* stock blender

Stöckel *m* FERTIG anvil stake

Stocken *nt* RADIO *Yagi-Antennen* stacking

stocken *vt* BAU point

stocklos: ~er Anker *m* WASSERTRANS stockless anchor

Stock: **Stockpunkt** m FERTIG pour point, HEIZ & KÄLTE solidification point, KFZTECH Öl pour point, KUNST-STOFF, MASCHINEN solidification point; **Stockschaltung** f KFZTECH *Getriebe* floor shift
Stockung f FERTIG *Plaste* hang-up
Stockwerk nt BAU floor, storey; **Stockwerkschalter** m ELEKTRIZ landing switch
Stockzwinge f MECHAN ferrule
Stoff m TEXTIL cloth, fabric, woven fabric; ~ **mit elektrischem Verlust** m ELEKTRIZ lossy material; **Stofffänger** m PAPIER pulp saver, save-all; **Stofffängertrog** m PAPIER save-all tray; **Stoffaufbereitung** f PAPIER stock preparation; **Stoffauflauf** m PAPIER flow box, headbox; **Stoffauflauflippe** f PAPIER slice; **Stoffbahn** f TEXTIL panel; **Stoffballen** m TEXTIL roll; **Stoffbespannung** f RAUMFAHRT *Raumschiff* cloth; **Stoffbreite** f TEXTIL fabric width; **Stoffbütte** f PAPIER stock chest, stuff; **Stoffdichte** f PAPIER consistency; **Stoffdichteregler** m PAPIER consistency regulator; **Stoffeinlauf** m PAPIER stock inlet; **Stoffgewicht** nt TEXTIL fabric weight; **Stoffgrund** m TEXTIL blotch; **Stofffilter** nt ABFALL fabric filter; **Stoffkasten** m PAPIER drainer; **Stoffleimung** f PAPIER stuff sizing; **Stoffmenge** f PHYS amount of substance; **Stoffmengenkonzentration** f CHEMIE molarity; **Stoffmuster** nt TEXTIL fabric sample, strike off sample, swatch
stofffrei adj FERTIG immaterial
Stoff: **Stoffrezeptur** f PAPIER furnish
stoffspezifisch: ~**e Haftung** f KUNSTSTOFF specific adhesion
Stoff: **Stofftrennprozeß** m ABFALL material separation operation; **Stoffverteilung** f PAPIER approach flow
Stoffwechsel: m ERGON, LEBENSMITTEL metabolism; **Stoffwechselschlacken** f pl ABFALL metabolic waste; **Stoffwechselstörung** f LEBENSMITTEL metabolic disorder
Stokes: ~**sches Gesetz** nt PHYS Stokes' law; **Stokes-Geschwindigkeit** f KER & GLAS Stokes' velocity; ~**sche Theorie** f STRÖMPHYS Stokes' theory
STOL-Flugzeug nt *(Fastsenkrechtstarter, Kurzstart-Kurzlande-Flugzeug, Kurzstartflugzeug)* LUFTTRANS STOL aircraft *(short takeoff and landing aircraft)*
Stollen m MASCHINEN cleat; **Stollenholz** nt KOHLEN timber
Stone nt METROL *Körpergewicht* stone
Stop-and-Go-Verkehr m TRANS stop-and-go traffic
Stopf- pref EISENBAHN, TELEKOM, TEXTIL stuffing; **Stopfaggregat** nt EISENBAHN tamping unit; **Stopfbit** nt TELEKOM stuffing digit
Stopfbüchse f ERDÖL *Rohrleitung* gland, FERTIG stuffing box, HEIZ & KÄLTE gland, packing gland, LEBENSMITTEL stuffing box, MASCHINEN gland, packing gland, stuffing box, MECHAN gland; **Stopfbüchsenabdichtung** f RAUMFAHRT *Raumschiff* gland; **Stopfbüchsenbrille** f MASCHINEN stuffing box gland, MECHAN, WASSERTRANS gland; **Stopfbüchsendeckel** m KERNTECH stuffing box lid
stopfbüchsenlos adj FERTIG *Kunststoffinstallationen* glandless
Stopf-: **Stopfeinrichtung** f TELEKOM stuffing device
Stopfen m BAU plug, COMP & DV padding, ERDÖL *Rohrleitungen, Bohrloch* plug, FERTIG bott, iron plug, stoppage, stopper, *Kunststoffinstallationen* cap, HYDRAUL, KFZTECH *Ablaß* plug, MASCHINEN plug, stopper, TELEKOM justification, stuffing, TEXTIL darning, mending, plugging, WASSERTRANS plug

stopfen[1] vt BAU tamp, *Fugen* caulk, *Schotter* pack, FERTIG stop, TEXTIL darn
stopfen[2] vti TEXTIL mend
Stopfen: **Stopfendichtung** f FERTIG *Kunststoffinstallationen* standpipe adaptor seal
Stopf-: **Stopfgeschwindigkeit** f TELEKOM stuffing rate; **Stopfmaschine** f EISENBAHN tamping machine; **Stopfnadel** f TEXTIL darning needle; **Stopfrate** f TELEKOM stuffing rate; **Stopfstelle** f TEXTIL darn; **Stopfstich** m TEXTIL darning stitch; **Stopfwolle** f TEXTIL darning wool; **Stopfzeichen** nt TELEKOM stuffing character
Stopp m COMP & DV halt, stop, KFZTECH stop, MASCHINEN check; **Stoppanweisung** f COMP & DV halt instruction; **Stoppbad** nt FOTO stop bath; **Stoppbahn** f LUFTTRANS stopway; **Stoppbahnfeuer** nt LUFTTRANS stopway light; **Stoppbit** nt COMP & DV stop bit, stop element; **Stoppcode** m COMP & DV stop code; **Stoppelement** nt COMP & DV stop element
Stoppen nt PHYS stop
stoppen vi COMP & DV stop
Stopperknoten m WASSERTRANS stopper knot
Stopp: **Stoppliste** f COMP & DV stoplist; **Stoppover** m LUFTTRANS stopover; **Stopptaste** f FERNSEH stop key; **Stoppuhr** f LABOR, PHYS stopwatch; **Stoppzeit** f KONTROLL stop time; **Stoppzylinderpresse** f DRUCK stop cylinder press
Stöpsel m KER & GLAS plug, LABOR bung, MASCHINEN plug, stopper, MECHAN, TELEKOM *Telefon* plug; **Stöpselfeld** nt ELEKTROTECH plugboard
stöpseln vt ELEKTROTECH plug
Stöpsel: **Stöpselschalter** m ELEKTROTECH plug switch; **Stöpselsicherung** f ELEKTRIZ cartridge fuse; **Stöpselverbindung** f ELEKTROTECH plug connection
Störablaufprotokollierung f COMP & DV postmortem review
Störabstand m AKUSTIK, FERNSEH signal-to-noise ratio; ~ **einschließlich Verzerrungen** m *(SINAD)* TELEKOM signal-to-noise and distortion ratio *(SINAD)*
Störaustaster m FERNSEH interference eliminator
Störaustastungsfaktor m RAUMFAHRT interference reduction factor
Störbeeinflussung f ELEKTRONIK interference
Störbegrenzer m AUFNAHME noise limiter
Störecho nt TELEKOM clutter
Störeinbruch m TELEKOM breakthrough
Stören nt RADIO jamming
stören vt ANSTRICH disrupt, BAU disturb, RAUMFAHRT *Weltraumfunk* jam
störend[1] adj ELEKTRONIK parasitic
störend:[2] ~**e Beeinflussung** f FERNSEH *Funk* interference; ~**e Beeinflussung des Kabelfernsehdienstes** f *(CATVI)* RADIO cable television interference *(CAT-VI)*
Störer m ELEKTRONIK jammer
Störfall m KERNTECH abnormal occurrence, QUAL accident condition, TRANS incident; **Störfallanalyse** f QUAL accident analysis
störfest adj ELEKTRIZ interference-proof
Störfestigkeit f COMP & DV interference immunity, noise immunity, TELEKOM immunity to interference; **Störfestigkeitsprüfung** f ELEKTRIZ interference resistance test
Störfilter nt RAUMFAHRT interference filter
Störfleck m ELEKTRONIK *Radar* clutter
Störfunkstelle f ELEKTRONIK jammer
Störgenerator m ELEKTRONIK interference generator

Störgerät *nt* ELEKTRONIK jammer
Störgeräusch *nt* WERKPRÜF interference noise
Störgrößenaufschaltung *f* REGELUNG disturbance variable feedforward
Störhäufigkeit *f* QUAL failure frequency
Störklappe *f* LUFTTRANS *Luftfahrzeug* spoiler
Störort *m* REGELUNG point of disturbance
Störoszillator *m* ELEKTRONIK jammer oscillator
Störpegel *m* AUFNAHME noise floor, noise level, GERÄT disturbance level; **Störpegelmeßgerät** *nt* GERÄT interference level meter; **Störpegelmeßplatz** *m* GERÄT transmission impairment measuring set
Störrauschpegel *m* UMWELTSCHMUTZ background level
Störschutzfilter *nt* AUFNAHME noise filter
Störschutzschirm *m* AUFNAHME noise shield
Störsender *m* ELEKTRONIK jammer
Störsignal *nt* COMP & DV drop-in, ELEKTRONIK incident signal, interference signal, jamming signal, ELEKTROTECH drop-in, GERÄT perturbation signal; **Störsignalpaket** *nt* ELEKTROTECH drop-in package
Störspannung *f* ELEKTROTECH noise voltage
Störstelle *f* ELEKTRONIK impurity, ELEKTROTECH defect; **Störstellenausbreitung** *f* ELEKTRONIK impurity diffusion; **Störstellendichte** *f* ELEKTRONIK impurity concentration, impurity density, *Halbleiter* defect density; **Störstellenelement** *nt* RADIO impurity element; **Störstellen-Fotoleitfähigkeit** *f* ELEKTROTECH extrinsic photoconductivity; **Störstellenhalbleiter** *m* COMP & DV extrinsic semiconductor; **Störstelleninversionszone** *f* ELEKTRONIK, PHYS p-n junction; **Störstellenleitfähigkeit** *f* ELEKTROTECH extrinsic conductivity; **Störstellenleitung** *f* ELEKTROTECH defect conduction; **Störstellenniveau** *nt* ELEKTRONIK impurity level; **Störstellenstreuung** *f* ELEKTRONIK impurity scattering
Störstrahlung *f* FERNSEH parasitic radiation; **Störstrahlungspegel** *m* RAUMFAHRT spurious emission level
Störung *f* ANSTRICH disruption, AUFNAHME interference, BAU breakdown, COMP & DV failure, interference, malfunction, noise, ELEKTRIZ interference, ELEKTROTECH interruption, FERNSEH interference, KERNTECH *Störfall* disturbance, MASCHINEN interference, malfunctioning, METALL disorder, obstacle, PHYS distortion, QUAL deficiency, malfunction, RADIO, RAUMFAHRT interference, STRÖMPHYS disturbance, perturbation, TELEKOM fault, interference, noise; **äußere ~** *f* ELEKTRIZ *von außen verursachte Störung* external disturbance; **~ durch Industriegeräte** *f* ELEKTROTECH industrial interference; **~ durch Nachbarkanal** *f* AUFNAHME adjacent channel interference; **~ in Niederfrequenzgeräten** *f* RADIO audio equipment interference; **~ im Rundfunkempfänger** *f* RADIO broadcast receiver interference; **Störungsannahme** *f* TELEKOM FRC, fault reception center (AmE), fault reception centre (BrE); **Störungsaufzeichnung** *f* COMP & DV failure logging; **Störungsbereich** *m* FERNSEH interference area; **Störungsbeseitigung** *f* TELEKOM fault clearance; **Störungsdatenkarte** *f* LUFTTRANS failure data card; **Störungsdauer** *f* LUFTTRANS downtime, QUAL malfunction time; **Störungsfilter** *nt* ELEKTRIZ interference filter, ELEKTRONIK *Radar* clutter filter; **Störungsmeldung** *f* LUFTTRANS error signal
störungssicher *adj* ELEKTROTECH fail-safe
Störung: **Störungssignal** *nt* LUFTTRANS error signal; **Störungssucher** *m* MASCHINEN troubleshooter

Störunterdrückung *f* ELEKTRONIK interference rejection, RADIO, TELEKOM interference suppression; **Störunterdrückungssignal** *nt* ELEKTRONIK interference rejection signal
Störursache *f* RAUMFAHRT perturbation
Störwellenmethode *f* KERNTECH distorted wave method
Stoß *m* ANSTRICH impact, BAU abutment, butt, meeting, *Holz* stack, ELEKTRIZ, ERDÖL *Strömung* surge, FERTIG joint, LUFTTRANS blast, MASCHINEN shock, MECHAN impulse, push, METALL jog, PHYS collision, RAUMFAHRT shock, TRANS jolt; **Stoßanregung** *f* STRAHLPHYS impact excitation
stoßartig *adj* MASCHINEN impulsive
Stoß: **Stoßaufhängung** *f* RAUMFAHRT shock mount; **Stoßbau-Kohlenschrämmaschine** *f* KOHLEN short wall coal-cutting machine; **Stoßbelastung** *f* LUFTTRANS impact load, VERPACK impact stress; **Stoßbetrieb** *m* COMP & DV burst mode; **Stoßbohren** *nt* KOHLEN percussion drilling; **Stoßbohrmaschine** *f* KOHLEN piston drill; **Stoßbremse** *f* KERNTECH dashing vessel, dashpot; **Stoßbrenner** *m* TRANS aeropulse; **Stoßdämpfer** *m* BAU, FERTIG shock absorber, KERNTECH dashing vessel, dashpot, KFZTECH damper, *Federung* shock absorber, MASCHINEN dashpot, shock absorber, MECHAN shock absorber, RAUMFAHRT snubber, SICHERHEIT resilient isolator, shock absorber; **Stoßdämpfung** *f* AKUSTIK transition loss; **Stoßdichte** *f* STRAHLPHYS collision density
Stößel *m* BAU ram, FERTIG ram, *Presse* slide, KFZTECH tappet, KUNSTSTOFF ram, LABOR *Schleifen* pestle, MASCHINEN tappet, tool ram, MECHAN ram; **~ und Mörser** *m* LABOR pestle and mortar
Stoß: **Stoßelastizität** *f* KUNSTSTOFF resilience
Stößel: **Stößelführung** *f* FERTIG *Senkrechtstoßmaschine* body; **Stößelkopf** *m* FERTIG *Waagerechtstoßmaschine* head; **Stößelschaft** *m* KFZTECH tappet stem; **Stößelschutz** *m* FERTIG ram guard; **Stößelstange** *f* KFZTECH push rod; **Stößelsteuerung** *f* PAPIER *Spindelpresse* follower trainer
Stoßen *nt* FERTIG *Zahnräder* shaping
stoßen *vt* BAU ram, FERTIG *Zahnräder* plane, shape, MECHAN push
Stoß: **Stoßerregung** *f* STRAHLPHYS impact excitation, TELEKOM impulse excitation, shock excitation; **Stoßexperiment** *nt* TEILPHYS collision experiment; **Stoßfängerhorn** *nt* KFZTECH *Karosserie* overrider
stoßfest *adj* METROL resistant to impact
Stoß: **Stoßfestigkeit** *f* KUNSTSTOFF shock resistance, MASCHINEN resistance to shock, resistance to impact, shock resistance, VERPACK impact resistance; **Stoßfläche** *f* FERTIG abutting end, abutting surface, MASCHINEN abutting surface; **Stoßfuge** *f* BAU butt joint, straight joint; **Stoßfunktion** *f* ELEKTRONIK impulse function; **Stoßgalvanometer** *nt* ELEKTRIZ ballistic galvanometer; **Stoßgenerator** *m* ELEKTRIZ impulse generator, pulse generator; **Stoßgeräusch-Analysator** *m* AUFNAHME impact noise analyser (BrE), impact noise analyzer (AmE)
stoßgeschützt: **~er Wagen** *m* EISENBAHN cushion car (AmE), cushion wagon (BrE)
Stoß: **Stoßintegral** *nt* STRAHLPHYS *Boltzmann-Gleichung* collision integral; **Stoßionisation** *f* STRAHLPHYS impact ionization, ionization by collision, TEILPHYS ionization by collision; **Stoßionisierung** *f* STRAHLPHYS impact ionization; **Stoßkante** *f* FERTIG *Blech* abutting edge, MECHAN edge, TEXTIL hem; **Stoßkopf** *m* MASCHI-

NEN shaper head; **Stoßkraft** *f* MASCHINEN drive; **Stoßlasche** *f* EISENBAHN rail splice, MASCHINEN butt strap; **Stoßlast** *f* BAU dynamic loading; **Stoßmaschine** *f* FERTIG vertical push-cut shaper, vertical shaper, MASCHINEN slotter, slotting machine; **Stoßmeißel** *m* MASCHINEN shaper tool, shaping tool, slotting tool; **Stoßmittelpunkt** *m* MECHAN, PHYS center of percussion (AmE), centre of percussion (BrE); **Stoßnaht** *f* ERDÖL *Schweißen* abutting joint; **Stoßparameter** *m* PHYS impact parameter; **Stoßplatte** *f* MECHAN butt plate; **Stoßprüfung** *f* WERKPRÜF impact test; **Stoßratendichte** *f* STRAHLPHYS collision density; **Stoßräumen** *nt* MASCHINEN push-broaching; **Stoßregler** *m* RAUMFAHRT bucking regulator; **Stoßring** *m* KFZTECH thrust washer; **Stoßschubregler** *m* RAUMFAHRT buck-boost regulator; **Stoßschweißen** *nt* MECHAN butt welding; **Stoßspannung** *f* ELEKTROTECH impulse voltage; **Stoßspannungsgenerator** *m* ELEKTROTECH impulse generator; **Stoßspannungsprüfung** *f* ELEKTROTECH impulse test; **Stoßstange** *f* EISENBAHN *Karosserie*, KFZTECH *Karosserie* bumper (BrE), fender (AmE), MASCHINEN push rod; **Stoßstelle** *f* FERTIG junction; **Stoßstrom** *m* ELEKTRIZ impulse current; **Stoßtest** *m* PHYS ram; **Stoßtheorie der Linienverbreiterung** *f* STRAHLPHYS impact theory of line broadening; **Stoßverstärker** *m* ELEKTRONIK burst amplifier; **Stoßvorrichtung** *f* EISENBAHN buffing gear; **Stoßwelle** *f* PHYS, WELLPHYS shock wave; **Stoßwellenauslöser** *m* RAUMFAHRT shock-wave initiator

Strafe *f* QUAL penalty

straff:[1] ~ **gespannt** *adj* FERTIG taut

straff:[2] **~es Trumm** *nt* MECHAN *Riemenantrieb* driving end

Strafpunkte *m pl* QUAL penalty

Strahl *m* ELEKTRONIK ray, FERTIG half-line, jet, KERNTECH *Flüssigkeit*, MASCHINEN, METALL jet, OPTIK ray, STRÖMPHYS jet, TELEKOM ray; **Strahlablenkung** *f* MASCHINEN deflection of beams; **Strahlablenkungsröhre** *f* RADIO deflection beam valve; **Strahlabschaltung** *f* FERNSEH beam cut-off; **Strahlabschwächer** *m* ELEKTRONIK beam attenuator; **Strahlabschwächung** *f* ELEKTRONIK beam attenuation; **Strahlabtastung** *f* ELEKTRONIK beam scanning; **Strahlaufspaltung** *f* ELEKTRONIK beam splitting; **Strahlaufteiler** *m* OPTIK beam splitter; **Strahlausrichtung** *f* FERNSEH beam alignment; **Strahlaustastung** *f* FERNSEH beam blanking, GERÄT blanking; **Strahlbohren** *nt* ERDÖL *Bohrtechnik* jet bit drilling; **Strahlbohrer** *m* ERDÖL *Bohrtechnik* jet bit; **Strahlbreite** *f* ELEKTRIZ, ELEKTRONIK, OPTIK beamwidth; **Strahlbündeldichte** *f* ELEKTRONIK beam power density; **Strahldichte** *f* OPTIK, PHYS, TELEKOM radiance; **Strahldivergenz** *f* OPTIK, TELEKOM beam divergence; **Strahldurchmesser** *m* OPTIK beam diameter; **Strahldüse** *f* MECHAN injector, WASSERVERSORG jet; **Strahldüsenbohren** *nt* KOHLEN jet piercing; **Strahlemittanz** *f* OPTIK *Punktgröße* radiant emittance

strahlen[1] *vt* ANSTRICH *etwa mit Sand* blast

strahlen[2] *vi* FERNSEH, STRAHLPHYS radiate

Strahlenarbeitern: von ~ akkummulierte Dosis *f* STRAHLPHYS dose accumulated by workers

Strahl: **Strahlenbehandlung** *f* STRAHLPHYS radiation treatment; **Strahlenbelastung** *f* KERNTECH, SICHERHEIT radiation exposure; **Strahlenbrechung** *f* OPTIK refringence, WASSERTRANS refraction; **Strahlenbündel** *nt* ELEKTRONIK, FERTIG beam, OPTIK beampencil of light, TELEKOM beam; **Strahlenbündelung** *f* ELEKTRO-

NIK beam focusing, beam forming; **Strahlenbüschel** *nt* OPTIK beampencil of light, pencil of rays; **Strahlenchemie** *f* KERNTECH radiation chemistry, STRAHLPHYS radiochemistry

strahlenchemische: ~ Zersetzung *f* CHEMIE radiolysis

Strahl: **Strahlenchromatographie** *f* STRAHLPHYS radiochromatography

strahlend[1] *adj* PHYS, THERMOD radiant

strahlend:[2] **~er Kreis** *m* FERNSEH radiating circuit

Strahl: **Strahlendetektor** *m* LABOR radiation detector, PHYS Golay cell; **Strahlendiagnose** *f* STRAHLPHYS radio diagnosis; **Strahlendosimeter mit akustischem Alarm** *nt* STRAHLPHYS sound alarm radiation dosimeter; **Strahlendosis** *f* UMWELTSCHMUTZ radiation dose; **Strahlendurchlässigkeitsgrad** *m* OPTIK transmittance; **Strahlenempfindlichkeit** *f* STRAHLPHYS radio sensitivity; **Strahlenexponierung** *f* KERNTECH radiation exposure; **Strahlenexposition** *f* PHYS radiant exposure; **Strahlengang** *m* TELEKOM optical path; **Strahlengefährdung** *f* KERNTECH radiation hazard

strahleninduziert[1] *adj* STRAHLPHYS radiation-induced

strahleninduziert:[2] **~e Reaktion** *f* STRAHLPHYS radiation-induced reaction

Strahl: **Strahlenkonzentration** *f* ELEKTRONIK beam forming; **Strahlenkrankheit** *f* KERNTECH, STRAHLPHYS radiation sickness; **Strahlenladen** *nt* FERNSEH beam loading; **Strahlenmeßgerät** *nt* PHYS radiometer, STRAHLPHYS actinometer; **Strahlenoptik** *f* OPTIK geometric optics, ray optics, PHYS geometrical optics, TELEKOM ray optics; **Strahlenphysik** *f* KERNTECH, STRAHLPHYS radiation physics; **Strahlenquelle** *f* STRAHLPHYS radiation source, radio source; **Strahlenschaden** *m* KERNTECH, STRAHLPHYS radiation damage

Strahlenschutz *m* KERNTECH, STRAHLPHYS, UMWELTSCHMUTZ radiation protection; **Strahlenschutzbeauftragter** *m* KERNTECH radiation protection officer; **Strahlenschutzglas** *nt* KER & GLAS radiation shielding glass; **Strahlenschutzraum** *m* KERNTECH fallout shelter; **Strahlenschutzzelle** *f* KERNTECH hot cell

strahlensicher *adj* KERNTECH, STRAHLPHYS radiation-proof

Strahl: **Strahlentherapie** *f* KERNTECH radiotherapy; **Strahlenvernetzung** *f* KUNSTSTOFF radiation cross-linking; **Strahlenweg** *m* OPTIK path of rays; **Strahlenzählrohr** *nt* ELEKTRONIK radiation counter tube

Strahler *m* ELEKTROTECH emitter, HEIZ & KÄLTE, MECHAN radiator, RADIO driven element, radiator, RAUMFAHRT radiator, STRAHLPHYS emitter, THERMOD radiator

Strahl: **Strahlfokussierung** *f* FERNSEH beam focusing; **Strahlhinlauf** *m* FERNSEH sweep; **Strahlkabine** *f* ANSTRICH blast cabinet; **Strahlkegel** *m* OPTIK cone of rays; **Strahlkies** *m* FERTIG grit; **Strahlkondensator** *m* HYDRAUL ejector condenser; **Strahlkühlung** *f* TEILPHYS cooling; **Strahlläppen** *nt* FERTIG vapor blasting (AmE), vapour blasting (BrE)

strahlläppen *vt* FERTIG vapor-blast (AmE), vapour-blast (BrE)

Strahl: **Strahllärm** *m* LUFTTRANS aerodynamic noise, airframe noise; **Strahllärmdämpfer** *m* LUFTTRANS jet noise suppressor; **Strahlmischer** *m* MASCHINEN jet mixer; **Strahlmittel** *nt* ANSTRICH blast medium; **Strahlmittelkorn** *nt* FERTIG abrasive grain for blasting;

Strahlöffnung *f* OPTIK beamwidth; **Strahlpositionier-system** *nt* FERNSEH beam-positioning system; **Strahlpositionierzeit** *f* OPTIK radial positioning time; **Strahlpulser** *m* KERNTECH beam pulser; **Strahlpumpe** *f* KERNTECH, WASSERVERSORG jet pump; **Strahlreinigen** *nt* BAU shot blasting; **Strahlreinigung** *f* FERTIG impact cleaning

Strahlrichtung: in ~ *adv* FERNSEH downstream

Strahl: **Strahlrohr** *nt* BAU tail pipe, KERNTECH *Reaktor* beam hole; **Strahlrücklauf** *m* FERNSEH beam return, GERÄT *Oszilloskop* retrace; **Strahlschärfung** *f* ELEKTRONIK beam sharpening; **Strahlsignal** *nt* ELEKTRONIK beam signal; **Strahlspanen** *nt* FERTIG vapor-blast cutting (AmE), vapour-blast cutting (BrE); **Strahlstärke** *f* ELEKTRONIK beam power; **Strahlsteuerung** *f* OPTIK radial control; **Strahlstrom** *m* LUFTTRANS jet stream; **Strahlteiler** *m* FERNSEH, OPTIK beam splitter; **Strahltetrode** *f* ELEKTRONIK beam power tube; **Strahltilt** *nt* FERNSEH beam tilt; **Strahltriebwerk** *nt* MECHAN jet engine; **Strahlturbine** *f* LUFTTRANS jet turbine, turbojet

strahlumlenkend: ~e **Düse** *f* LUFTTRANS *Luftfahrzeug* thrust vectoring nozzle

Shrahl: **Strahlumschalter** *m* GERÄT *Elektronen* electron beam switch

Strahlung[1] *f* ELEKTRIZ, ELEKTRONIK, FERNSEH, HEIZ & KÄLTE, KERNTECH radiation, LABOR *(N)* radiance *(N)*, MASCHINEN radiation, OPTIK irradiance, radiation, OPTIK *(N)* radiance *(N)*, PHYS, RADIO, RAUMFAHRT, STRAHLPHYS, TEILPHYS, TELEKOM, THERMOD radiation; ~ **des schwarzen Körpers** *f* PHYS, STRAHLPHYS, THERMOD black body radiation; ~ **mit hoher Energie** *f* STRAHLPHYS high-energy radiation; ~ **mit kleinem Pegel** *f* STRAHLPHYS low-level radiation

Strahlung:[2] ~ **aussetzen** *vi* RAUMFAHRT *Weltraumfunk* irradiate

Strahlungs- *pref* STRAHLPHYS radiative, THERMOD radiant, *Energie* radiative

Strahlung: **Strahlungsabschirmung** *f* SICHERHEIT radiation shield; **Strahlungsabsorption** *f* WELLPHYS absorption of radiation; **Strahlungsabsorptionsanalyse** *f* KERNTECH radiation absorption analysis; **Strahlungsanregung** *f* ELEKTRONIK radiation excitation; **Strahlungsaufbereitung** *f* KERNTECH radiation processing; **Strahlungsausbeute** *f* PHYS radiant efficiency; **Strahlungsbeiwert** *m* HEIZ & KÄLTE radiation coefficient; **Strahlungsbeständigkeit** *f* TELEKOM radiation hardness; **Strahlungsbündler** *m* NICHTFOSS ENERG solar concentrator; **Strahlungsdetektor** *m* GERÄT, STRAHLPHYS radiation detector; **Strahlungsdiagramm** *nt* FERNSEH *Richtantenne* beam pattern, RADIO *Antenne* antenna pattern, radiation pattern, TELEKOM radiation pattern; **Strahlungsdichte** *f* PHYS radiant energy denisty rate, radiant flux density, STRAHLPHYS radiant density, TELEKOM radiant intensity; **Strahlungsdosimetrie** *f* STRAHLPHYS radiation dosimetry; **Strahlungsdosis** *f* RAUMFAHRT, STRAHLPHYS radiation dose; **Strahlungsdruck** *m* AKUSTIK, PHYS, STRAHLPHYS, TEILPHYS radiation pressure; **Strahlungseinfang** *m* PHYS radiative capture; **Strahlungseinheit** *f* STRAHLPHYS radiation unit; **Strahlungsemission** *f* TELEKOM radiant emittance; **Strahlungsempfänger** *m* GERÄT radiation detector

strahlungsempfindlich: ~es **Papier** *nt* KONSTZEICH radiation-sensitive paper

Strahlung: **Strahlungsenergie** *f* OPTIK radiant power,

OPTIK *(U)* radiant energy *(U)*, PHYS, STRAHLPHYS, TELEKOM radiant energy; **Strahlungsenergiedichte** *f* PHYS radiant energy density; **Strahlungserwärmung** *f* STRAHLPHYS radiation heating

strahlungserzeugt *adj* PHYS, STRAHLPHYS radiogenic

Strahlung: **Strahlungsfestigkeit** *f* KERNTECH radiation resistance; **Strahlungsfläche** *f* STRAHLPHYS *einer Antenne* radiation field; **Strahlungsfluß** *m* OPTIK, PHYS radiant flux, STRAHLPHYS flux of radiation, radiant flux, TELEKOM radiant flux; **Strahlungsflußdichte** *f* KERNTECH radiation flux density, OPTIK, STRAHLPHYS radiant flux density, TELEKOM radiant flux density, *Stromdichte* irradiance; **Strahlungsfrequenz** *f* KERNTECH frequency of radiation; **Strahlungsfunktion** *f* NICHTFOSS ENERG spectral energy distribution; **Strahlungsgefahr** *f* SICHERHEIT radiation hazard

strahlungsgefährdet: ~er **Bereich** *m* KERNTECH radiation danger zone

Strahlung: **Strahlungsgesetze** *nt pl* STRAHLPHYS radiation laws; **Strahlungsgürtel** *m* RAUMFAHRT, STRAHLPHYS radiation belt; **Strahlungshärtung** *f* KERNTECH radiation hardening; **Strahlungsheizkörper** *m* HEIZ & KÄLTE radiant heater, radiant panel; **Strahlungsheizung** *f* HEIZ & KÄLTE radiant heater, radiant panel heating, radiant-heating system, THERMOD radiant heating

strahlungsinduziert[1] *adj* STRAHLPHYS radiation-induced

strahlungsinduziert:[2] ~e **Aktivierung** *f* STRAHLPHYS radiation-induced activation; ~e **Mutation** *f* STRAHLPHYS radiation-induced mutation

Strahlung: **Strahlungsintensität** *f* NICHTFOSS ENERG irradiance, OPTIK radiant intensity, PHYS R, dose rate, radiant intensity, RAUMFAHRT *Weltraumfunk* radiation intensity, TELEKOM radiant intensity; **Strahlungskaskade** *f* STRAHLPHYS radiative cascade; **Strahlungskatalyse** *f* STRAHLPHYS radiation catalysis; **Strahlungskessel** *m* HEIZ & KÄLTE radiant boiler; **Strahlungskeule** *f* RADIO, RAUMFAHRT *Weltraumfunk* lobe; **Strahlungskollision** *f* STRAHLPHYS radiative collision; **Strahlungskonstante** *f* HEIZ & KÄLTE radiation constant; **Strahlungskontrolle** *f* STRAHLPHYS radiation monitoring; **Strahlungskraft** *f* ERGON emissivity; **Strahlungskühler** *m* THERMOD radiant cooler; **Strahlungskühlung** *f* THERMOD radiant cooling; **Strahlungslänge** *f* TEILPHYS radiation length; **Strahlungsleistung** *f* FERNSEH radiated power, TELEKOM radiant power; **Strahlungslichtbogenofen** *m* FERTIG indirect arc furnace

strahlungslos: ~er **Übergang** *m* STRAHLPHYS radiationless transition

Strahlung: **Strahlungsmesser** *m* PHYS actinometer; **Strahlungsmeßfühler** *m* GERÄT radiation detector; **Strahlungsmeßgerät** *nt* RAUMFAHRT bolometer, STRAHLPHYS radioactivity meter; **Strahlungsmeßkanal** *m* KERNTECH radiation channel; **Strahlungsmeßstift** *m* KERNTECH pocket dosemeter; **Strahlungsmessung** *f* PHYS actinometry, STRAHLPHYS actinometry, radiation measurements; **Strahlungsmode** *f* OPTIK radiation mode; **Strahlungsmodus** *m* TELEKOM radiation mode; **Strahlungsmuster** *nt* OPTIK *Lichtleiter*, PHYS, RAUMFAHRT *Weltraumfunk* radiation pattern; **Strahlungsmuster im stationären Zustand** *nt* OPTIK equilibrium radiation pattern; **Strahlungsnormal** *nt* OPTIK standard source; **Strahlungspotential** *nt* STRAHLPHYS radiation potential;

Strahlungspyrometer nt GERÄT, LABOR, PHYS radiation pyrometer; **Strahlungspyrometer mit Thermoelement** nt GERÄT thermocouple pyrometer; **Strahlungsquelle** f ELEKTRONIK radiation source, ELEKTROTECH source, HEIZ & KÄLTE radiator, KERNTECH, STRAHLPHYS radiation source; **Strahlungsrekombination** f ELEKTRONIK radiative recombination; **Strahlungsschutz** m SICHERHEIT radiation protection

strahlungssicher adj KERNTECH radiation-proof

Strahlung: **Strahlungsspektrum** nt RAUMFAHRT emission spectrum; **Strahlungstemperaturmesser** m LABOR pyrometer; **Strahlungsthermometer** nt GERÄT pyrometer; **Strahlungstrockner** m PAPIER radiant drier, radiant dryer; **Strahlungsübergang** m STRAHLPHYS radiative transition; **Strahlungsüberhitzer** m HEIZ & KÄLTE radiant superheater; **Strahlungsübertragung** f STRAHLPHYS radiative transfer; **Strahlungsüberwachung** f RAUMFAHRT Raumschiff, STRAHLPHYS radiation monitoring; **Strahlungsverbrennungen** f pl STRAHLPHYS radiation burns; **Strahlungsverlust** m TEILPHYS radiation loss; **Strahlungsvermögen** nt PHYS radiant power; **Strahlungsvernetzen** nt KUNSTSTOFF radiation cross-linking; **Strahlungsvernetzung** f KUNSTSTOFF radiation cross-linking; **Strahlungswärme** f STRAHLPHYS, THERMOD radiant heat; **Strahlungswärmegewinn** m HEIZ & KÄLTE radiant heat gain; **Strahlungswiderstand** m KERNTECH, PHYS Antenne, RADIO radiation resistance; **Strahlungswinkel** m OPTIK, TELEKOM radiation angle; **Strahlungswirkungsgrad** m PHYS radiant efficiency; **Strahlungszahl** f THERMOD unit conductance; **Strahlungszähler** m STRAHLPHYS radiation counter

Strahl: **Strahlverbreiterung** f TELEKOM beam divergence; **Strahlverdichter** m MASCHINEN jet compressor; **Strahlverdunkelung** f ELEKTRONIK Kathodenstrahlröhren beam blanking; **Strahlverfolgung** f FERNSEH ray tracing; **Strahlwasserhahn** m WASSERVERSORG jet cock; **Strahlwiedereintrittsröhre** f ELEKTRONIK re-entrant beam tube; **Strahlwinkel** m ELEKTRONIK beam angle; **Strahlzittern** nt FERNSEH beam jitter; **Strahlzufuhr** f KERNTECH beam injection

Strainer m ERDÖL strainer

Strak m WASSERTRANS Schiffbau strake

Stramin m TEXTIL Stickereien canvas

Strand: **auf den ~ setzen** vt WASSERTRANS haul on the beach

Stranden nt WASSERTRANS stranding

stranden vi WASSERTRANS Schiff get stranded

Strandgut nt WASSERTRANS jetsam

Strandlinie f KER & GLAS shoreline

Strandmauer f BAU sea wall

Strang m FERTIG looping mill, MASCHINEN leg, string, MECHAN, PAPIER rope; **Strangaufweitung** f KUNSTSTOFF die swell; **Strangbruchdetektor** m KER & GLAS strand break detector;

Strangeness f TEILPHYS spezielle Quantenzahl von Hadronen strangeness

stranggepreßt[1] adj FERTIG extrusion molded (AmE), extrusion moulded (BrE), MASCHINEN extruded

stranggepreßt:[2] **~e Isolierung** f ELEKTRIZ extruded insulation

Strang: **Stranggießen** nt MECHAN continuous casting; **Strangpresse** f MASCHINEN extruder, extrusion press, METALL extrusion press, PAPIER extruder

Strangpressen nt FERTIG extrusion molding (AmE),

extrusion moulding (BrE), MASCHINEN extrusion

strangpressen vt MASCHINEN, METALL extrude

Strang: **Strangpreßprofil** nt MECHAN extrusion; **Strangpreßteil** nt MASCHINEN extruded part; **Strangpreßverfahren** nt MASCHINEN extrusion process; **Strangpreßwerkzeug** nt FERTIG Plaste die head, MASCHINEN extrusion die; **Strangrohrpresse** f VERPACK extrusion machine for tubes

strapazierfähig adj VERPACK wear-resistant

Strapazierfähigkeit f TEXTIL wear resistance

Straße[1] f TRANS road, road rail, WASSERTRANS Geographie strait; **~ mit jeweils zwei Fahrbahnen getrennt in jede Fahrtrichtung** f TRANS dual carriageway; **~ in Tieflage** f BAU sunken road; **wenig befahrene ~** f BAU low-traffic road

Straße:[2] **auf ~ und Schiene transportieren** vt TRANS transport by rail and road

Straße: **Straßenablauf** m BAU Regenwasser storm drain; **Straßenabwasser** nt BAU surface water; **Straßenarbeiten** f pl TRANS road works; **Straßenaufreißer** m TRANS road ripper

Straßenbahn f EISENBAHN streetcar (AmE), tramway (BrE); **Straßenbahnfahrplan** m EISENBAHN streetcar schedule (AmE), tram schedule (BrE); **Straßenbahnhaltestelle** f EISENBAHN streetcar stop (AmE), tram stop (BrE); **Straßenbahnschienen** f pl EISENBAHN streetcar tracks (AmE), tram tracks (BrE); **Straßenbahntriebwagen** m EISENBAHN streetcar motor coach (AmE), tramway motor coach (BrE); **Straßenbahnverkehr im Expreßbetrieb** m TRANS express streetcar (AmE), express tramway (BrE); **Straßenbahnwagen** m EISENBAHN streetcar (AmE), tram (BrE), TRANS trolley car (AmE)

Straße: **Straßenbankett** nt BAU shoulder; **Straßenbau** m TRANS road building, road making; **Straßenbaumaschine** f BAU road making machine, TRANS road building machinery; **Straßenbezeichnungsschild** nt TRANS road identification sign; **Straßenbrücke** f BAU, TRANS road bridge; **Straßendamm** m BAU bank; **Straßendecke** f BAU sheeting, **Straßendeckenbelag** m BAU carpet, coat; **Straßendeckenbeton** m BAU pavement-quality concrete (BrE), sidewalk-quality concrete (AmE); **Straßenfahrzeugwaage** f TRANS road vehicle weighing machine; **Straßenfertiger** m BAU finisher, TRANS road finishing machine; **Straßengabelung** f TRANS bifurcation, road junction

straßengestützt: **~er Sender** m TRANS road-based transmitter

Straße: **Straßenglätte** f TRANS skidding conditions; **Straßenhobel** m BAU grader; **Straßenkarte** f TRANS road map; **Straßenkehricht** m ABFALL litter; **Straßenkehrmaschine** f ABFALL mechanical sweeper; **Straßenkreuzungspunkt** m BAU road crossing; **Straßenmeisterei** f TRANS traffic management; **Straßenneigung** f TRANS road camber; **Straßennetz** nt TRANS road system; **Straßenperle** f KER & GLAS road bead; **Straßenpflug** m TRANS road plough; **Straßenplanierer** m TRANS motor grader, road grader; **Straßenplatte** f BAU pad; **Straßenschienenbus** m TRANS bimodal bus, road-rail bus; **Straßenschotter** m BAU road metal; **Straßentankfahrzeug** nt TRANS RTC, road tank car; **Straßenteermaschine** f TRANS road tarring machine; **Straßenverbindung** f TRANS road communication; **Straßenverkehr** m TRANS road traffic; **Straßenverkehrskontrolle** f TRANS road traffic control; **Straßenwalze** f BAU compactor, roller, TRANS

roadroller; **Straßenzugmaschine** f KFZTECH road tractor, trailer towing machine; **Straßenzustandsbericht**
m TRANS road news
stratifizieren vt KOHLEN stratify
Stratigraphie f KOHLEN stratigraphy
stratigraphisch: ~e Falle f ERDÖL *Geologie* stratigraphic
trap
Stratocumulus m LUFTTRANS *Meteorologie* stratocumulus
Streamer m COMP & DV streaming tape drive, *zur Datensicherung* streamer; **Streamerkammer** f TEILPHYS
streamer chamber
Streb m KOHLEN bank; **Strebbau** m KOHLEN straining
work; **Strebbausystem** nt KOHLEN longwall system
Strebe f BAU brace, prop, shore, spur, stay, FERTIG spur,
HYDRAUL brace, KFZTECH strut, MASCHINEN brace,
MECHAN brace, strut, tie rod; **Strebenkopf** m BAU
strutting head
strebenlos: ~er Balken m BAU unsupported beam
Strebepfeiler m BAU *Wand, Brücke* buttress
Streb: **Strebfront** f KOHLEN breast; **Strebstrecke** f KOH-
LEN gate road
Streckbalken m BAU binding beam, string piece
streckbar adj MASCHINEN tensile
Streckbarkeit f KUNSTSTOFF extensibility
Streckbereich m TEXTIL draft zone
Streckblasformen nt KUNSTSTOFF stretch blow molding
(AmE), stretch blow moulding (BrE)
Streckdehnung f KUNSTSTOFF elongation
Strecke¹ f GEOM line segment, KOHLEN adit, TELEKOM
path, range, route, TRANS route
Strecke:² ~ **zurücklegen** vi TRANS run
Strecken nt FERTIG drawing-out, KER & GLAS flatting,
Zylinder flattening, TEXTIL drawing, stretch; ~ **des**
Zylinders nt KER & GLAS elongation of the cylinder
strecken vt BAU stretch, MASCHINEN flatten, stretch,
TEXTIL draw, stretch
Strecke: **Streckenabschnitt zwischen zwei Flughäfen** m
LUFTTRANS mileage; **Streckenaufseher** m EISENBAHN
lineman; **Streckenbelastung** f RAIL traffic density;
Streckenbeschreibung f LUFTTRANS route descrip-
tion; **Streckenbilanz** f RADIO *Satellitenfunk* link
budget; **Streckenblock** m EISENBAHN block system;
Streckeneinweisungsflug m LUFTTRANS route fami-
liarization flight; **Streckenfahrdienstleiter** m
EISENBAHN dispatcher; **Streckenforschungspro-
gramm** nt TRANS shortest route program (AmE),
shortest route programme (BrE); **Streckenhöchst-
geschwindigkeit** f EISENBAHN speed limit;
Streckenlizenz f LUFTTRANS route licence (BrE), route
license (AmE), route licensing; **Streckenlokomotive** f
EISENBAHN road locomotive (AmE); **Streckenprüfzug**
m EISENBAHN spot train; **Streckenrelais** nt ELEKTRIZ
distance relay; **Streckenschalter** m ELEKTRIZ distance
switch; **Streckenüberlastung** f TELEKOM route congestion; **Streckenwärter** m TRANS *Rohrleitungen*,
WASSERTRANS pipeliner
Strecker m BAU *Mauerwerk* binder
Streckfolie f KUNSTSTOFF stretch wrapping film, VER-
PACK stretch film
Streckformen nt MASCHINEN stretch forming
streckformen vt FERTIG stretch-form
Streckgesenk nt MASCHINEN fuller
Streckgrenze f ANSTRICH, KUNSTSTOFF yield strength,
MASCHINEN limit of elasticity, MECHAN elastic limit,
yield point, yield strength, METALL yield point, yield

stress, WERKPRÜF yield strength
Streckmaschine f TEXTIL drawing frame
Streckmetall nt MECHAN, METALL expanded metal
Streckmittel nt CHEMTECH diluting agent, FERTIG *Plaste*
filler, KUNSTSTOFF extender, LEBENSMITTEL adul-
terant
Streckofen m KER & GLAS flattening kiln
Streckspannung f KUNSTSTOFF, PHYS yield stress
Strecktisch m KER & GLAS flattening table
Streckung f MASCHINEN extension
Streckverpackung f VERPACK stretch wrapping
Streckvorrichtung f MASCHINEN strainer, stretcher
Streckwalze f FERTIG cogging roll, cogging-down roll
Streckwalzwerk nt FERTIG elongator
Streckwerk nt TEXTIL drafting system, drawing frame
Streckwerkzeug nt KER & GLAS flattening tool
Streckziehen nt FERTIG metal stretching
streckziehen vt FERTIG stretch-form
Strehlen nt MASCHINEN chasing
strehlen vt MASCHINEN chase
Strehler m MASCHINEN chaser; **Strehlerkluppe** f MASCHI-
NEN chaser die stock
Strehlmaschine f MASCHINEN chasing lathe, chasing
machine
Streichanlage f VERPACK coating machine
Streichbalken m BAU head plate, trimmer, trimmer
beam
Streichblech nt FERTIG *Formen* sleeker
Streicheisen nt KER & GLAS crack-off iron (AmE), wet-
ting-off iron (BrE)
Streichen nt PAPIER coating, TEXTIL *Spinnen* carding
streichen vt ANSTRICH paint, BAU coat, COMP & DV
delete, RADIO cancel
Streichgarnspinnerei f TEXTIL woollen spinning
Streichgießverfahren nt PAPIER cast coating
Streichlinien f pl STRÖMPHYS streaklines
Streichmaschine f KUNSTSTOFF coating machine, PA-
PIER coater, coating machine; ~ **mit Abquetschwalze** f
PAPIER squeeze roll coater
Streichmaß nt BAU scratch gage (AmE), scratch gauge
(BrE)
Streichmasse f PAPIER coating color (AmE), coating
colour (BrE), coating mixture, VERPACK coating com-
pound
Streichmesser nt PAPIER doctor blade
Streichrohpapier nt PAPIER coating base paper
Streichung f COMP & DV deletion
Streichverfahren nt KUNSTSTOFF spread coating
Streichwehr nt WASSERVERSORG spillway
Streifen m COMP & DV strip, stripe, tape, GERÄT *für
Registriergerät* chart, KER & GLAS segregation, MET-
ALL strip, METROL ribbon, PAPIER streak, PHYS fringe,
gleicher Neigung fringes, TEXTIL crack, strip, stripe;
Streifenabreißstab m GERÄT *Registriergerät* chart pa-
per tear-off bar; **Streifenabstand** m PHYS *Interferenz*
fringe separation; **Streifenantriebsmotor** m GERÄT
chart motor; **Streifenauslenkung** f FERTIG *Interferenz*
band deviation; **Streifenberieselung** f WASSERVER-
SORG border irrigation; **Streifenbildung** f FERNSEH
banding, fringing, KER & GLAS banding
streifend: ~er Einfall m PHYS grazing incidence; ~er Stoß
m KERNTECH glancing collision; ~er Strahl m AKUSTIK
grazing ray
Streifen: **Streifendetektor** m RAUMFAHRT *Raumschiff*
strip-type detector; **Streifenformat** nt KONSTZEICH
strip size; **Streifenfüllung** f KER & GLAS strip filling;

Streifengummierung *f* DRUCK strip gumming; **Streifenleiter** *f* ELEKTROTECH strip line; **Streifenleitung** *f* PHYS strip line; **Streifenlocher** *m* COMP & DV tape punch; **Streifenmarkierung** *f* TEXTIL rope marking; **Streifenschneider** *m* KER & GLAS slitter; **Streifenschreiber** *m* ELEKTRIZ strip chart recorder; **Streifentransport** *m* GERÄT *Registriergerät* chart feed, chart transport; **Streifenversilberung** *f* KER & GLAS striped silvering; **Streifenvorschub** *m* GERÄT chart feed; **Streifenwalze** *f* GERÄT *Registriergerät* chart drum; **Streifenware** *f* TEXTIL striped fabric; **Streifenzuführung** *f* GERÄT chart feed

streifig[1] *adj* PAPIER striped

streifig:[2] **~er Perlit** *m* METALL lamellar pearlite

Streifigkeit *f* TEXTIL barriness in the weft

streng: **~e Überwachung** *f* SICHERHEIT close supervision

Stretch *m* TEXTIL stretch

Stretcherring *m* TEILPHYS stretcher ring

Stretchfolie *f* KUNSTSTOFF stretch film

Streu- *pref* AKUSTIK, ELEKTRONIK, ELEKTROTECH, KERNTECH, PHYS scattering, stray; **Streubaumwolle** *f* KUNSTSTOFF cotton linters; **Streubeleuchtung** *f* ELEKTRIZ floodlighting

streuend *adj* PHYS straying

Streu-: **Streufaktor** *m* CHEMTECH dispersion coefficient; **Streufeld** *nt* FERTIG *Magnetpulververfahren*, TELEKOM leakage field; **Streufeld-Methode** *f* AUFNAHME diffuse-field method; **Streufluß** *m* PHYS leakage flux; **Streufluß über der Fehlstelle** *m* FERTIG crack leakage flux; **Streufolie** *f* KERNTECH scattering foil; **Streuglas** *nt* KER & GLAS diffusing glass; **Streugrenze** *f* QUAL dispersion limit; **Streugrenzen** *f pl* QUAL limits of variation; **Streukapazität** *f* PHYS stray capacitance; **Streukoeffizient** *m* AKUSTIK *(m)* flare coefficient of horn *(m)*, TELEKOM scattering coefficient; **Streukopplung** *f* ELEKTROTECH stray coupling; **Streukörper** *m* OPTIK *Licht*, TELEKOM diffuser; **Streulicht** *nt* OPTIK, STRAHLPHYS scattered light; **Streumedium** *nt* KERNTECH scattering medium; **Streuneutron** *nt* KERNTECH scattered neutron; **Streuquerschnitt** *m* PHYS cross section, scattering cross section; **Streusand** *m* FERTIG *Gießen* parting sand; **Streuschwingung** *f* PHYS stray oscillation; **Streusignalaufnahme** *f* GERÄT stray signal pick-up; **Streuspektrum-Modulation** *f* ELEKTRONIK spread spectrum modulation; **Streuspektrum-Modulator** *m* ELEKTRONIK spread spectrum modulator; **Streustrahlung** *f* ELEKTROTECH leakage radiation, STRAHLPHYS scattered radiation, stray radiation; **Streustrom** *m* ELEKTROTECH stray current; **Streutransformator** *m* ELEKTROTECH constant-current transformer

Streuung *f* AKUSTIK scattering, COMP & DV scatter, ELEKTROTECH leakage, spill, FERTIG *Strom* leak, KERNTECH, METALL, NICHTFOSS ENERG, OPTIK scattering, QUAL dispersion, RADIO *Verluststrom* leak, scatter, STRAHLPHYS dispersion, scattering, TELEKOM dispersion, leakage, scattering; **~ mit großen Streuwinkeln** *f* KERNTECH wide-angle scattering; **~ im Lichtwellenleiter** *f* TELEKOM fiber scattering (AmE), fibre scattering (BrE); **~ durch Regen** *f* RAUMFAHRT *Weltraumfunk* rain scatter; **~ der Verteilung** *f* QUAL variance of distribution

streuungsfrei: **~es Medium** *nt* PHYS nondispersive medium

Streuung: **Streuungshalo** *m* KERNTECH halo of dispersion

Streu-: **Streuverlust** *m* AKUSTIK *Wandler* transducer dissipation loss, FERTIG leakage; **Streuvermögen** *nt* PHYS dispersive power; **Streuwerte** *m pl* GERÄT scattered data; **Streuwinkel** *m* PHYS scattering angle; **Streuwirkungsquerschnitt** *m* PHYS scattering cross section

Strg-Taste *f (Steuertaste)* COMP & DV Ctrl key *(control key)*

Strich *m* DRUCK line, rule, FERTIG prime, MASCHINEN stroke, OPTIK *Beugungsgitter* groove, TEXTIL *Gewebe* pile

Strichcode *m* COMP & DV, TELEKOM, VERPACK bar code; **Strichcode-Lesegerät** *nt* VERPACK bar code reader; **Strichcode-Leser** *m* COMP & DV bar code slot reader, bar code scanner; **Strichcode-Markendrucker** *m* VERPACK bar code label printer

Strich: **Strichdiagramm** *nt* COMP & DV line graph; **Strichdichte** *f* DRUCK stroke density

Striche: **~ der Kompaßrose** *m pl* WASSERTRANS points of the compass

Strich: **Strichendmaß** *nt* FERTIG hair gageblock (AmE), hair gaugeblock (BrE); **Strichlehre** *f* METROL length gage (AmE), length gauge (BrE); **Strichlinie** *f* FERTIG dashed line; **Strichlistendiagramme** *nt pl* MATH tally diagrams; **Strichmarkierung** *f* VERPACK bar code; **Strichmarkierungssystem** *nt* VERPACK bar code labeling system (AmE), bar code labelling system (BrE); **Strichplan** *m* ELEKTRIZ single line diagram

strichpunktiert: **~er Kreis** *m* KONSTZEICH chain-like circle

Strich: **Strichpunktlinie** *f* KONSTZEICH chain line; **Strichskalenwaage** *f* METROL line-graduated master scales; **Strichstärke** *f* DRUCK weight of face, weight of type, zinc plate; **Strichvorlage** *f* DRUCK line artwork, KONSTZEICH line master; **Strichzeichnung** *f* DRUCK line drawing, ELEKTRIZ single line diagram, GEOM line drawing

Strick *m* TEXTIL rope

Strick: **Strickschlauch** *m* TEXTIL circular knitted fabric

String *m* DRUCK string

Stringer *m* RAUMFAHRT *Raumschiff*, WASSERTRANS *Bootbau* stringer; **Stringerwinkel** *m* WASSERTRANS *Schiffbau* stringer angle

Stringkonstruktion *f* STRAHLPHYS string construction

Striping *nt* AUFNAHME striping

Strippen *nt* DRUCK stripping

Stroboskop *nt* PHYS, WELLPHYS stroboscope; **Stroboskopband** *nt* AUFNAHME stroboscopic tape

stroboskopisch: **~er Impuls** *m* TELEKOM strobe pulse

Stroboskoplicht *nt* RAUMFAHRT strobe light

Stroh *nt* PAPIER straw; **Strohpappe** *f* DRUCK, VERPACK strawboard; **Strohzellstoff** *m* PAPIER straw pulp; **Strohzellstoffpappe** *f* VERPACK strawboard

Strom *m* COMP & DV stream, ELEKTRIZ current, ELEKTROTECH current, electric power, power, PHYS current, RADIO current, WASSERTRANS *Navigation* current; **außer ~ setzen** *vt* ELEKTROTECH de-energize **~ in Durchlaßrichtung** *m* ELEKTROTECH forward current; **~ in Sperrichtung** *m* ELEKTROTECH reverse current; **durch ~ verursachter Unfall** *m* SICHERHEIT electrical accident; **Stromabgabe** *f* ELEKTROTECH current output

Stromabnehmer *m* EISENBAHN pantograph, ELEKTROTECH current collector; **Stromabnehmergestell** *nt* EISENBAHN pantograph frame; **Stromabnehmersignal** *nt* EISENBAHN pantograph signal; **Stromabnehmer-**

system *nt* TRANS power collection system
stromabwärterig: ~er Pfeilerkopf *m* WASSERVERSORG downstream cutwater
stromabwärts:[1] **~ gelegen** *adj* PHYS, STRÖMPHYS downstream
stromabwärts[2] *adv* MECHAN, RAUMFAHRT, STRÖMPHYS, WASSERTRANS downstream
Strom: **Stromanstiegsrate** *f* ELEKTROTECH rate of current rise; **Stromanzeige** *f* GERÄT current reading; **Stromanzeigewert** *m* GERÄT current reading
Stromaufnahme[1] *f* ELEKTROTECH power consumption; **~ eines blockierten Läufers** *f* ELEKTRIZ locked rotor current
Stromaufnahme:[2] **~ reduzieren** *vi* ELEKTROTECH *Halbleiterspeicher* power down
Stromaufnahme: **Stromaufnahmebürste** *f* ELEKTROTECH current-collecting brush
stromaufwärts[1] *adj* BAU, NICHTFOSS ENERG, STRÖMPHYS upstream
stromaufwärts[2] *adv* NICHTFOSS ENERG, RAUMFAHRT, STRÖMPHYS, WASSERTRANS upstream
stromaufwärts:[3] **~ gelegenes Totwasser** *nt* STRÖMPHYS upstream wake
Strom: **Stromausfall** *m* ELEKTROTECH power failure; **Stromausgang** *m* ELEKTROTECH electrical output; **Stromauswanderung** *f* TELEKOM current drift; **Strombahn** *f* ELEKTROTECH current path; **Strombauch** *m* ELEKTROTECH current antinode
Strombauch: im ~ gespeist *adj* RADIO current-fed
strombegrenzend: ~e Drosselspule *f* ELEKTROTECH current-limiting reactor; **~e Schmelzsicherung** *f* ELEKTRIZ current-limiting fuse link; **~er Unterbrecher** *m* ELEKTRIZ current-limiting circuit breaker
Strom: **Strombegrenzer** *m* ELEKTRIZ, ELEKTROTECH current limiter; **Strombegrenzung** *f* ELEKTROTECH current limiting; **Strombegrenzungsdrossel** *f* ELEKTRIZ current-limiting inductor, ELEKTROTECH current-limiting reactor; **Strombegrenzungsreaktanz** *f* ELEKTRIZ current-limiting reactor; **Strombegrenzungsspule** *f* ELEKTRIZ current-limiting reactor; **Strombegrenzungswiderstand** *m* ELEKTRIZ limiting resistor; **Strombereich** *m* GERÄT current range; **Strombetriebslogik** *f* ELEKTROTECH current mode logic; **Stromdichte** *f* ELEKTRIZ ampere density, current density, ELEKTROTECH current density, current intensity, METALL, PHYS current density; **Stromdifferenzsschutz** *m* ELEKTRIZ current differential protection; **Stromeingang** *m* ELEKTROTECH current input, electrical input, power input; **Stromelement** *nt* PHYS current element
Strömen *nt* ELEKTROTECH flow
strömen *vi* NICHTFOSS ENERG, STRÖMPHYS, WASSERTRANS *Fluß*, Gezeiten flow
Strom: **Stromerhitzung** *f* KERNTECH joule heating
stromerzeugend[1] *adj* ELEKTROTECH generating
stromerzeugend:[2] **~e Anlage** *f* ELEKTROTECH generating plant
Strom: **Stromerzeuger** *m* BAU generator, ELEKTROTECH current generator, electric generator, generator, WASSERTRANS *Elektrik* generator; **Stromerzeugung** *f* ELEKTROTECH electricity generation, KERNTECH electroproduction; **Stromerzeugungskapazität** *f* ELEKTRIZ generating capacity; **Stromfernmessung** *f* GERÄT current telemetering
Strom: **Stromfluß im Schaltkreis** *m* PHYS flux through a circuit; **Stromflußplan** *m* ELEKTRIZ circuit diagram
stromführend[1] *adj* ELEKTROTECH active, alive, live, PHYS

live
stromführend:[2] **~er Draht** *m* ELEKTROTECH live wire; **~e Komponente** *f* ELEKTROTECH active component; **~er Kreis** *m* ELEKTROTECH live circuit; **~e Leitung** *f* ELEKTROTECH live wire; **~es Mikrofon** *m* AUFNAHME live microphone; **~e Spule** *f* PHYS current-carrying coil
Strom: **Stromführungskapazität** *f* ELEKTRIZ current-carrying capacity; **Stromfunktion** *f* STRÖMPHYS stream function; **Stromgebiet** *nt* WASSERTRANS *Fluß* water system; **Stromgenerator** *m* FERNSEH, KERNTECH electric generator, PHYS current generator; **Stromgeneratoraggregat** *nt* ELEKTRIZ generating set; **Stromgeschwindigkeit** *f* WASSERTRANS *Meer* current rate
stromgesteuert: ~er Oszillator *m* ELEKTRONIK current-controlled oscillator; **~e Vorrichtung** *f* ELEKTROTECH current-controlled device
Strom: **Stromimpuls** *m* ELEKTROTECH current pulse; **Stromintensität** *f* ELEKTRIZ intensity of current; **Stromkabelung** *f* WASSERTRANS *Gezeiten* rip tide; **Stromkarte** *f* WASSERTRANS *Navigation* current chart; **Stromkompensator** *m* GERÄT current compensator; **Stromkörper** *m* ELEKTROTECH current sink; **Stromkreis** *m* ELEKTRIZ circuit, electric circuit, ELEKTROTECH *bei Druckschaltungsleiter* line
Stromkreis:[1] **einen ~einschalten** *vi* ELEKTROTECH close a circuit; **einen ~schließen** *vi* ELEKTROTECH close a circuit
Stromkreis:[2] **im ~** *adj* ELEKTRIZ in circuit
Strom: **Stromkreis für den Leerlauf und für niedrige Drehzahlen** *m* KFZTECH idle and low speed circuit; **Stromkreisunterbrecher** *m* ELEKTRIZ *Luftisolierung* air interrupter; **Stromlauf** *m* ELEKTROTECH circuit diagram; **Stromlaufplan** *m* KFZTECH wiring diagram; **Stromleiter** *m* ELEKTROTECH conductor; **Stromleiterdraht** *m* ELEKTROTECH conductor wire; **Stromleiterschiene** *f* ELEKTRIZ conductor rail; **Stromleitung** *f* BAU transmission line, ELEKTROTECH conduction, electrical transmission line; **Stromlieferung ans Verbrauchernetz** *f* KERNTECH delivery into the mains
Stromlinie *f* PHYS streamline, *Flüssigkeit* filament, STRÖMPHYS *Flüssigkeiten, Gasen* streamline; **Stromlinienbild** *nt* STRÖMPHYS streamline pattern, WASSERVERSORG flow pattern; **Stromlinienform** *f* MASCHINEN streamlined form
stromlinienförmig[1] *adj* KFZTECH *Karosserie* streamlined, LUFTTRANS faired, MASCHINEN, PHYS, RAUMFAHRT, STRÖMPHYS streamlined
stromlinienförmig:[2] **~e Verkleidung** *f* LUFTTRANS fairing
stromlos *adj* GERÄT dead; **~ geschlossen** *adj* FERTIG *Kunststoffinstallationen* de-energized closed
Strom: **Stromlosigkeit** *f* GERÄT absence of current; **Strommeßbereich** *m* GERÄT current range; **Strommesser** *m* ELEKTROTECH, LABOR ammeter, NICHTFOSS ENERG, WASSERTRANS *Ozeanographie*, WASSERVERSORG current meter; **Strommeßgerät** *nt* GERÄT ammeter, amperemeter, current-measuring instrument; **Strommeßinstrument** *nt* GERÄT current-measuring instrument; **Strommessung** *f* ELEKTROTECH current sensing; **Strommeßwiderstand** *m* ELEKTROTECH current-sensing resistor; **Strommodulation** *f* ELEKTRONIK current modulation; **Stromnetz** *nt* ELEKTRIZ mains (BrE), supply network (AmE), mains supply, ELEKTROTECH mains (BrE), supply network (AmE), power supply circuit, power system,

FERTIG electric mains; **Strompfad** *m* ELEKTROTECH current path, path; **Stromquelle** *f* ELEKTROTECH current source, power source, source, PHYS current source; **Stromrauschen** *nt* AUFNAHME current noise (AmE), mains noise; **Stromregelung** *f* ELEKTRIZ current regulation, ELEKTROTECH current control, current regulation; **Stromregler** *m* ELEKTRIZ current regulator, ELEKTROTECH barretter, current regulator; **Stromrelais** *nt* ELEKTRIZ current relay, ELEKTROTECH current relay, electric relay, electrical relay, electrical relay

Stromrichter *m* ELEKTROTECH static converter; **Stromrichteranlage** *f* ELEKTROTECH static converter; **Stromrichtergruppe** *f* ELEKTROTECH static converter; **Stromrichterlokomotive** *f* EISENBAHN thyristor-controlled locomotive

Stromrichtung: in ~ *adv* PHYS, STRÖMPHYS downstream

Strom : **Stromrichtung** *f* ELEKTROTECH current direction

Strom: **Stromrückkopplung** *f* ELEKTROTECH current feedback; **Stromsammlerring** *m* ELEKTRIZ collector ring; **Stromsammlerschuh** *m* EISENBAHN collector shoe; **Stromsättigung** *f* ELEKTRONIK current saturation; **Stromschiene** *f* EISENBAHN conductor rail, contact rail, live rail, third rail, ELEKTRIZ conductor rail, ELEKTROTECH busbar, bus, conductor rail, TELEKOM busbar; **Stromschlag** *m* ELEKTROTECH, SICHERHEIT electric shock; **Stromschleife** *f* PHYS, RADIO current loop; **Stromschließer** *m* ELEKTROTECH circuit closer; **Stromschnelle-Überlauf** *m* NICHTFOSS ENERG chute spillway; **Stromschreiber** *m* GERÄT current recorder; **Stromschritt** *m* RADIO *Telegrafie* mark pulse, TELEKOM marking; **Stromschutz** *m* ELEKTRIZ *Luftisolierung* air break switch, air interrupter; **Stromschutzvorschrift** *f* SICHERHEIT electrical safety requirement; **Stromschwankung** *f* ELEKTRIZ current fluctuation; **Strom-Spannungs-Charakteristik** *f* ELEKTROTECH current-voltage characteristic; **Strom-Spannungs-Kennlinie** *f* ELEKTROTECH, RAUMFAHRT *Raumschiff* current-voltage characteristic; **Strom-Spannungs-Kurve** *f* ELEKTROTECH current-voltage characteristic; **Stromspeicheraggregat** *nt* KFZTECH, WASSERTRANS battery; **Stromspitze** *f* ELEKTRIZ current peak, ELEKTROTECH power surge; **Stromstärke** *f* ELEKTRIZ amperage, intensity of current, ELEKTROTECH amperage, current strength, current, current intensity; **Stromstecker** *m* ELEKTRIZ power outlet

Stromstoß *m* ELEKTROTECH current pulse, current surge; **Stromstoßgenerator** *m* ELEKTRIZ surge generator; **Stromstoßrelais** *nt* ELEKTRIZ latching relay; **Stromstoßrelais mit Doppelspule** *nt* ELEKTROTECH dual-coil latching relay

Strom: **Stromstreckentrennung** *f* ELEKTRIZ sectionalization; **Stromsystem mit fest geerdetem Nulleiter** *nt* ELEKTRIZ solidly earthed neutral system (BrE), solidly grounded neutral system (AmE); **Stromsystem mit durch Impedanz geerdetem Mittelleiter** *nt* ELEKTRIZ impedance earthed neutral (BrE), impedance grounded neutral (AmE); **Stromtankstelle** *f* ELEKTRIZ electric power filling station; **Stromteiler** *m* ELEKTRIZ current divider; **Stromtor-Inverter** *m* ELEKTRONIK thyratron inverter; **Stromtransformationsverhältnis** *nt* ELEKTRIZ current transformation ratio; **Stromtransformator** *m* ELEKTRIZ, ELEKTROTECH current transformer (AmE), mains transformer (BrE); **Stromübergang** *m* NICHTFOSS ENERG ohmic contact;

Stromübertragung *f* PHYS electricity transmission; **Stromübertragungsfaktor** *m* AKUSTIK response to current

Strömung *f* BAU, ELEKTROTECH flow, ERDÖL *Flüssikeiten, Gasen* fluid flow, HYDRAUL, NICHTFOSS ENERG, PHYS flow, STRÖMPHYS flow, stream, *durch Blenden* flow, WASSERTRANS *Navigation* current; **~ in offenen Gerinnen** *f* STRÖMPHYS flow in open channels, open channel flow; **~ in offenen Kanälen** *f* STRÖMPHYS flow in open channels, open channel flow

Strömungsabriß: ~ am Luftschraubenblatt *m* LUFTTRANS *Hubschrauber* blade stall; **~ an der Luftschraubenblattspitze** *m* LUFTTRANS *Hubschrauber* blade tip stall, mean aerodynamic chord; **~ am rücklaufenden Blatt** *m* LUFTTRANS retreating blade stall

Strömung: **Strömungsbild** *nt* HEIZ & KÄLTE, WASSERVERSORG flow pattern; **Strömungsbremse** *f* KFZTECH hydro-kinetic brake; **Strömungsdurchsatz** *m* KUNSTSTOFF flow rate, rate of flow; **Strömungsdüse** *f* MASCHINEN flow nozzle, PHYS jet; **Strömungsförderer** *m* MASCHINEN flow conveyor; **Strömungsgeschwindigkeit** *f* HEIZ & KÄLTE flow velocity, velocity of flow, STRÖMPHYS flow speed, WASSERTRANS *Meer* current rate, WASSERVERSORG flow rate; **Strömungsgeschwindigkeitmeßgerät** *nt* GERÄT anemometer; **Strömungsgetriebe** *nt* MASCHINEN fluid transmission; **Strömungsinstabilität** *f* STRÖMPHYS flow instability; **Strömungskanal** *m* LUFTTRANS, WASSERTRANS wind tunnel, WASSERVERSORG calibration flume, flume; **Strömungskupplung** *f* KFZTECH *Kraftübertragung* fluid coupling, MASCHINEN hydraulic coupling; **Strömungslehre** *f* MASCHINEN fluid mechanics, STRÖMPHYS fluid dynamics; **Strömungslinien** *f pl* TELEKOM flow lines; **Strömungsmechanik** *f* STRÖMPHYS fluid dynamics, fluid mechanics; **Strömungsmengenmeßgerät** *nt* GERÄT rate-of-flow meter; **Strömungsmeßgerät** *nt* HYDRAUL current meter; **Strömungsmessung** *f* GERÄT flow measurement; **Strömungsmuster** *nt* STRÖMPHYS flow pattern, THERMOD gas flow; **Strömungsregler** *m* MECHAN control valve

Strömungsrichtung[1] *f* COMP & DV flow direction

Strömungsrichtung[2]: **in ~** *adv* FERNSEH upstream

Strömung: **Strömungsrohr** *nt* HYDRAUL flow pipe; **Strömungssichtbarmachung** *f* STRÖMPHYS flow visualization; **Strömungstechnik** *f* STRÖMPHYS fluid engineering; **Strömungsventil** *nt* LUFTTRANS flux valve; **Strömungsvisualisierung** *f* STRÖMPHYS flow visualization; **Strömungswächter** *m* HEIZ & KÄLTE flow indicator; **Strömungswiderstand** *m* AKUSTIK flow resistance, HEIZ & KÄLTE drag, HYDRAUL *(DD)* coefficient of drag *(DD)*, MASCHINEN flow resistance, PHYS drag, STRÖMPHYS resistance to flow, TRANS captation drag, WASSERTRANS *Schiffkonstruktion* drag

Strom: **Stromunterbrecher** *m* ELEKTRIZ circuit breaker, switch, ELEKTROTECH circuit breaker; **Stromverdrängungseffekt** *m* ELEKTROTECH skin effect; **Stromversetzung** *f* WASSERTRANS *Navigation* current set

Stromversorgung *f* BAU electricity supply, EISENBAHN, ELEKTRIZ power supply, ELEKTROTECH electrical power supply, power supply, PHYS, TELEKOM power supply; **~ der Heizung** *f* ELEKTROTECH heater power supply; **~ mit nur einem Ausgang** *f* ELEKTROTECH single output power supply; **Stromversorgungsanlage**

f TELEKOM power plant; **Stromversorgungsnetz** *nt* ELEKTRIZ mains (BrE), supply network (AmE), ELEKTROTECH electric power system, mains (BrE), supply network (AmE), power grid, power supply circuit; **Stromversorgungssystem mit geerdetem Nulleiter** *nt* ELEKTRIZ earthed-neutral system (BrE), grounded-neutral system (AmE); **Stromversorgungsunternehmen** *nt* ELEKTRIZ *EVU* electric power supply company; **Stromversorgungswerk** *nt* ELEKTROTECH electric power station

Strom: **Stromverstärker** *m* ELEKTRIZ, ELEKTRONIK current amplifier; **Stromverstärkung** *f* AUFNAHME current amplification, ELEKTRONIK current amplification, current gain, PHYS current gain; **Stromverstimmung** *f* ELEKTRONIK, RADIO, TELEKOM frequency pushing; **Stromverteilung** *f* ELEKTRIZ current distribution, distribution of electricity; **Stromverteilungsgeräusch** *nt* ELEKTRONIK partition noise; **Stromverteilungsrauschen** *nt* RADIO partition noise; **Stromverteilungssystem** *nt* ELEKTRIZ distribution system; **Stromwaage** *f* ELEKTRIZ ampere balance, current balance, GERÄT ampere balance, PHYS current balance; **Stromwaage-Relais** *nt* ELEKTRIZ current balance relay; **Stromwächter** *m* ELEKTROTECH current relay; **Stromwandler** *m* ELEKTROTECH current transformer (AmE), mains transformer (BrE); **Stromwandlung** *f* ELEKTRIZ conversion; **Stromwärmeverlust** *m* ELEKTRIZ ohmic loss; **Stromweg** *m* ELEKTROTECH current path; **Stromwelle** *f* ELEKTROTECH current ripple; **Stromwender** *m* ELEKTRIZ current reverser, ELEKTROTECH commutator, *dynamoelektrische Maschine* collector; **Stromwendermotor** *m* ELEKTROTECH collector motor, KFZTECH commutator motor; **Stromzähler** *m* ELEKTROTECH electricity meter, electricity supply meter; **Stromzange** *f* GERÄT current probe; **Stromzangeninstrument** *nt* ELEKTRIZ tong test instrument; **Stromzapfsäule** *f* ELEKTRIZ electric power filling station; **Stromzufuhr** *f* BAU electricity supply; **Stromzuführung** *f* TELEKOM power feeding; **Stromzuleitung** *f* ELEKTROTECH current lead; **Stromzweig** *m* ELEKTROTECH path

Strontium *nt (Sr)* CHEMIE strontium *(Sr)*; **Strontiumpref** CHEMIE strontic; **Strontiumoxid** *nt* CHEMIE strontium oxide; **Strontium-90** *nt* CHEMIE radiostrontium

Strophanthin *nt* CHEMIE strophanthin

Stropp *m* MEERSCHMUTZ *Anschlagmittel*, WASSERTRANS *Tauwerk* sling

Strouhalzahl *f* STRÖMPHYS Strouhal number

Strudel *m* KOHLEN vortex, WASSERTRANS *Wasser* eddy

Struktur *f* COMP & DV pattern, structure, EISENBAHN structure, FERTIG *Öl* body, KONTROLL structure, PAPIER formation; **~ der Blattunterseite** *f* LUFTTRANS *Hubschrauber* bottom structure; **~ der Flügeldruckseite** *f* LUFTTRANS bottom structure; **~ der Flügelunterseite** *f* LUFTTRANS bottom structure

strukturell: **~e Falle** *f* ERDÖL *Geologie* structural tap

Struktur: **Strukturerkennung** *f* COMP & DV pattern recognition

strukturiert[1] *adj* COMP & DV patterned

strukturiert:[2] **nicht ~er Baum** *m* COMP & DV unordered tree; **~e Entwicklung** *f* COMP & DV structured design; **~es Programmieren** *nt* COMP & DV structured programming; **~e Programmierung** *f* COMP & DV structured programming; **~e Suche** *f* COMP & DV tree search; **~er Typ** *m* COMP & DV structured type

Struktur: **Strukturindex** *m* RAUMFAHRT structure index;

Strukturmodell *nt* RAUMFAHRT structural model; **Strukturmodell aus finiten Elementen** *nt* RAUMFAHRT finite element structural model; **Strukturschaumstoff** *m* KUNSTSTOFF integral foam, integral skin foam; **Strukturspeicher** *m* COMP & DV NVM, nonvolatile memory; **Strukturteppich** *m* TEXTIL textured carpet

Strumpf *m* MECHAN hose; **Strumpfformen** *nt* TEXTIL boarding; **Strumpfwirkerei** *f* TEXTIL hose knitting

STS *abbr* *(Raumfahrttransportsystem)* RAUMFAHRT STS *(space transportation system)*

Stubben *m* BAU stump

Stück:[1] **aus einem ~** *adj* MASCHINEN in one piece; **in einem ~** *adj* MASCHINEN in one piece, integral

Stück:[2] **in einem ~ färben** *vt* TEXTIL dye in the piece

stückgefärbt *adj* TEXTIL piece-dyed

Stuckgips *m* BAU plaster of Paris

Stückgut *nt* EISENBAHN less-than-carload freight, part load, part-load good, TRANS break bulk

Stückgüterladung *f* TRANS package freight

Stückgut: **Stückgutfrachter** *m* WASSERTRANS *Schifftyp* mixed cargo ship; **Stückgutfrachtschiff** *nt* WASSERTRANS break bulk ship, general cargo ship; **Stückgutkurswagen** *m* TRANS station wagon; **Stückgutsendung** *f* EISENBAHN less-than-carload freight shipment, part-load consignment; **Stückgutverkehr** *m* EISENBAHN part-load traffic

Stück: **Stückkohle** *f* KOHLEN best coal; **Stückliste** *f* BAU piece list, MASCHINEN parts list; **Stücknummer** *f* VERPACK part number; **Stückware** *f* TEXTIL piece goods

Studio: **~ mit Reflexions- und schalltoter Wand** *nt* AUFNAHME live-end dead-end studio; **Studioansprechsystem** *nt* AUFNAHME studio address system; **Studioauskleidung** *f* AUFNAHME studio lining; **Studioeinrichtung** *f* FERNSEH studio facilities; **Studiokamera** *f* FOTO studio camera; **Studioleiter** *m* FERNSEH studio manager; **Studiomonitor** *m* FERNSEH studio monitor; **Studiorecorder** *m* FERNSEH transverse scanning recorder; **Studiosendung** *f* FERNSEH studio broadcast

Stufe *f* COMP & DV level, KER & GLAS step, KONTROLL stage, MASCHINEN, METALL step, PAPIER stage; **~ des Umlaufgetriebes** *f* LUFTTRANS first-stage planet gear; **Stufenausbeute** *f* ELEKTRONIK stage efficiency; **Stufenbohrer** *m* FERTIG stepped drill, MASCHINEN multidiameter drill, step drill; **Stufenbohrmeißel** *m* ERDÖL *Bohrtechnik* step bit; **Stufenbreite** *f* BAU going, length of step; **Stufenformplotter** *m* COMP & DV incremental plotter; **Stufenfräsen** *nt* MASCHINEN step milling

stufenfrei: **~e Regelung** *f* ELEKTRIZ stepless control

Stufe: **Stufengesenk** *nt* FERTIG multistage die; **Stufengitter** *nt* PHYS echelette grating; **Stufenhärten** *nt* FERTIG marquenching, martempering; **Stufenhöhe** *f* BAU rise; **Stufenindexfaser** *f* OPTIK graded index fiber (AmE), graded index fibre (BrE), step index fiber (AmE), step index fibre (BrE), PHYS, TELEKOM step index fiber (AmE), step index fibre (BrE); **Stufenindex-Lichtwellenleiter** *m* TELEKOM step index fiber (AmE), step index fibre (BrE); **Stufenindex-LWL** *m* TELEKOM step index fiber (AmE), step index fibre (BrE); **Stufenindexprofil** *nt* OPTIK graded index profile, step index profile, TELEKOM step index profile; **Stufenindexprofil im stationären Zustand** *nt* OPTIK equivalent step index profile; **Stufenkantenlinie** *f* BAU nosing line; **Stufenkeil** *m* FOTO step wedge; **Stufenkolben** *m* MASCHINEN differential piston, step piston; **Stufenkopplung** *f* ELEKTROTECH stage coupling

stufenlos:[1] **~ einstellbar** *adj* ELEKTRONIK continuously adjustable; **~ regulierbar** *adj* MASCHINEN infinitely variable

stufenlos:[2] **~ abstimmbarer Oszillator** *m* ELEKTRONIK continuously tunable oscillator; **~ einstellbares Dämpfungsglied** *nt* ELEKTRONIK continuously variable attenuator; **~e Einstellung** *f* ELEKTRONIK continuous adjustment; **~es Getriebe** *nt* MASCHINEN infinitely variable drive; **~e Regelung** *f* AUFNAHME slide control

Stufe: **Stufenpresse** *f* MASCHINEN gang press; **Stufenprofil** *nt* TELEKOM step index profile; **Stufenrad** *nt* MASCHINEN step tooth gear, stepped gear; **Stufenrädergetriebe** *nt* MASCHINEN step cone drive; **Stufenregelung** *f* ELEKTRIZ step-by-step control; **Stufenschalter** *m* ELEKTROTECH multiple-contact switch, tap changer; **Stufenscheibe** *f* FERTIG speed cone, MASCHINEN cone pulley, cone sheave, cone wheel, speed cone, step cone pulley, stepped pulley; **Stufenscheibenantrieb** *m* MASCHINEN cone pulley drive; **Stufenskale** *f* GERÄT step scale; **Stufensprung** *m* FERTIG progressive ratio; **Stufentrenn-Retrorakete** *f* RAUMFAHRT stage separation retro-rocket; **Stufenumsetzer** *m* GERÄT *AD-Umsetzung* digit-at-a-time converter; **Stufenverschlußler** *m* GERÄT *AD-Umsetzung* digit-at-a-time converter

stufenweise: ~ Reinigung *f* COMP & DV stepwise refinement

Stuffing-Bit *nt* TELEKOM stuffing digit

stuhlfertig *adj* TEXTIL loomstate

stuhlroh: ~es Gewebe *nt* TEXTIL loomstate weft

Stuhlschiene *f* EISENBAHN bull-headed rail

Stulpe *f* MASCHINEN sleeve

Stülpen *nt* FERTIG *Ziehen* inside-out redrawing

stülpen *vt* FERTIG *Ziehen* clinch

Stulpmanschette *f* MASCHINEN sleeve packing

Stummabstimmung *f* TELEKOM muting device

Stummel *m* KOHLEN stump, MASCHINEN stub; **Stummelwelle** *f* LUFTTRANS *Hubschrauber* stub shaft

Stummheit *f* AKUSTIK muteness

Stumpf *m* BAU stub, FERTIG frustum, *Schweißen* stub, GEOM *Pyramide* frustum, KOHLEN stump, PHYS stub; **Stumpffuge** *f* BAU *Holzbau* header joint

stumpf[1] *adj* FERTIG *Winkel*, GEOM obtuse, MASCHINEN blunt, METROL *Winkel* obtuse

stumpf:[2] **~ beginnender Absatz** *m* DRUCK flush paragraph; **~er Bohrmeißel** *m* ERDÖL *Tiefbohrtechnik* dull bit; **~es Ende** *nt* BAU butt; **~er Stoß** *m* MASCHINEN butt joint, straight joint; **~er Winkel** *m* GEOM obtuse angle

stumpf:[3] **~ stoßen** *vt* FERTIG bustle-joint

stumpf:[4] **~ werden** *vi* MASCHINEN blunt

Stumpfheit *f* GEOM obtuseness

Stumpf: **Stumpfnaht** *f* FERTIG groove joint, MASCHINEN butt seam; **Stumpfsägenfeile** *f* MASCHINEN blunt saw file

Stumpfschweißen *nt* BAU butt welding, FERTIG *Kunststoffinstallationen* butt fusion jointing, MASCHINEN, MECHAN, METALL butt welding

stumpfschweißen *vt* FERTIG jump-weld

Stumpfstoß *m* BAU butt joint, scarf joint, *Schweißen* abutting joint, FERTIG abutting joint

Stumpfstoßen *nt* BAU scarf jointing

stumpfstoßen *vt* BAU butt-joint

Stumpftonne *f* WASSERTRANS *Seezeichen* can buoy

stumpfwinklig[1] *adj* GEOM obtuse-angled, obtuse-angular

stumpfwinklig:[2] **~es Dreieck** *nt* GEOM obtuse triangle

Stumpfzahn *m* FERTIG, MASCHINEN stub tooth

Stunde *f (h)* METROL hour *(h)*; **Stundenkreis** *m* METROL hour circle; **Stundenlohnarbeiten** *f pl* BAU dayworks; **Stundenzeiger** *m* METROL hour hand

stürmisch: ~e Überfahrt *f* WASSERTRANS rough crossing

Sturmklappe *f* ERDÖL storm choke

Sturmlaterne *f* BAU, WASSERTRANS hurricane lamp

Sturmschutzverglasung *f* KER & GLAS antistorm glazing

Sturmsegel *nt* WASSERTRANS storm sail

Sturz *m* BAU head; **~ eines Rades** *m* KFZTECH *Rad* camber; **Sturzbalken** *m* BAU bressumer, summer beam

stürzen[1] *vt* KOHLEN dump

stürzen:[2] **nicht ~** *phr* COMP & DV keep upright

Sturzflug[1] *m* LUFTTRANS, RAUMFAHRT dive

Sturzflug:[2] **in ~ übergehen** *vi* RAUMFAHRT *Raumschiff* dive

Sturzflug: **Sturzflugbremse** *f* LUFTTRANS diving brake

Sturz: **Sturzrinne** *f* FERTIG tip chute; **Sturzsee** *m* ERDÖL surge; **Sturzspirale** *f* LUFTTRANS spiral dive; **Sturzwelle** *f* WASSERTRANS *Seezustand* breaker; **Sturzwinkel** *m* KFZTECH camber angle

Stützbalken *m* BAU principal, stringer, supported beam, KOHLEN brace

Stützbock *m* BAU jack

Stützdorn *m* FERTIG *Biegen* arbor (AmE), arbour (BrE), mandrel, mandril

Stütze *f* BAU pillar, post, prop, shore, spur, stay, strut, FERTIG prop, HYDRAUL bracket, KER & GLAS jamb, KFZTECH *Motorrad* stand, KOHLEN pillar, MASCHINEN bracket, prop, rest, support, MECHAN brace, bracket, WASSERTRANS *Schiffbau* pillar

Stützeinrichtung *f* TRANS *Sattelschlepper* landing gear

Stutzen *m* BAU stub, union, FERTIG *Kunststoffinstallationen* end connector, HEIZ & KÄLTE collar, gland, KFZTECH neck, MASCHINEN connection, muff, PHYS stub

Stützen *nt* BAU shoring

stützen *vt* BAU bear, buttress, carry, lean, shore, stay, FERTIG, MECHAN buttress, WASSERTRANS *Schiffbau* shore up

stützend *adj* BAU supporting

Stützgleis *nt* EISENBAHN supporting rack

Stützholz *nt* BAU propwood

Stützhülse *f* FERTIG carrying bracket

Stützisolator *m* ELEKTROTECH cap-and-pin insulator, pin insulator

Stützklappe *f* MECHAN tab

Stützkraft *f* BAU bearing pressure

Stützlager *nt* FERTIG back rest

Stützlänge *f* BAU span

Stützmauer *f* BAU breast wall, retaining wall, revetment, supporting wall, KER & GLAS breast wall

Stützpfahl *m* BAU prop

Stützpfähle *m pl* BAU shoring

Stützpfeiler *m* BAU buttress, *Holzbau* abutment

Stützpunkt *m* GEOM checkpoint

Stützrad *f* TRANS stabilizing wheel

Stützrippe *f* FERTIG stiffening rib

Stützrolle *f* MASCHINEN supporting roller

Stützsäule *f* BAU strut

Stützschiene *f* EISENBAHN supporting rail

Stützstange *f* ELEKTRIZ stay pole, LUFTTRANS backing bar

Stützwalze *f* FERTIG idle roll, PAPIER antideflection roll, backing roll

Stützwinkel *m* FERTIG support bracket, MASCHINEN angle bracket, bracket, WASSERTRANS *Schiffbau* strut angle

Stützzylinder *m* FERTIG *Sinuslineal* plug

STX *abbr (Textanfang)* COMP & DV STX *(start of text)*

Styphninsäure *f* CHEMIE styphnic acid, trinitroresorcinol

Styracit *m* CHEMIE styracitol

Styren *m* CHEMIE phenylethylene, styrene, styrolene

Styrol *nt* CHEMIE phenylethylene, styrene, styrolene, vinylbenzene, ERDÖL *Petrochemie* styrene; **Styrol-Butadien-Kautschuk** *m (SBR)* KUNSTSTOFF styrene butadiene rubber *(SBR)*; **Styrol-Copolymer** *nt* ELEKTRIZ styrol copolymer

SU *abbr (Sprachverstehen)* KÜNSTL INT SU *(speech understanding)*

Subadresse *f* TELEKOM *ISDN* subaddress

Subadressierung *f* TELEKOM subaddressing

Subchlorid *nt* CHEMIE subchloride

Subdominante *f* AKUSTIK subdominant

Subduktion *f* ERDÖL subduction

Suberat *nt* CHEMIE suberate

Suberin *nt* CHEMIE suberin; **Suberin-** *pref* CHEMIE suberic

Suberon *nt* CHEMIE cycloheptanone, suberone

Suberyl- *pref* CHEMIE suberyl

Subharmonische *f* AKUSTIK, ELEKTRONIK subharmonic

subjektiv: ~ empfundene Lautheit *f* AKUSTIK subjective loudness; ~er Fehler *m* GERÄT personal error; ~er Meßfehler *m* GERÄT personal error; ~er Test *m* TELEKOM subjective test; ~er Ton *m* AKUSTIK subjective tone

subkritisch[1] *adj* KERNTECH subcritical

subkritisch:[2] ~e Reaktion *f* STRAHLPHYS subcritical reaction

subletal: ~e Dosis *f* UMWELTSCHMUTZ sublethal dose; ~er Effekt *m* UMWELTSCHMUTZ sublethal effect

Sublimat *nt* CHEMIE, ERDÖL sublimate

Sublimation *f* PHYS, THERMOD sublimation; **Sublimationswärme** *f* THERMOD sublimation heat

Sublimat: **Sublimatverstärkung** *f* FOTO mercury intensification

Sublimieren *nt* THERMOD sublimation

sublimieren *vi* THERMOD sublimate

Sublimiergefäß *nt* CHEMIE sublimating vessel

sublimiert: ~es Zinkoxid *nt* METALL sublimated oxide of zinc

subliminal *adj* ERGON subliminal

Subnitrat *nt* CHEMIE subnitrate

Subnormale *f* GEOM subnormal

Subreflektor *m* RAUMFAHRT *Weltraumfunk* subreflector

Subroutine *f* COMP & DV subroutine

Subsatellitenpunkt *m* RAUMFAHRT subsatellite point

Subschalter *m* FERNSEH subswitcher

Subsegment *nt* COMP & DV subsegment

Substandardschiff *nt* WASSERTRANS substandard ship

Substantivfarbstoff *m* TEXTIL direct dyestuff

Substanz *f* KER & GLAS substance, TEXTIL body of the fabric

Substitution *f* MATH *einer Gleichung* substitution; **Substitutionszeichen** *nt* COMP & DV SUB character, substitute character, substitution character

Substrat *nt* CHEMIE *Enzyme* reactant, COMP & DV, KUNSTSTOFF, TELEKOM substrate; **Substrat-Transistor** *m* ELEKTRONIK parasitic transistor

subsynchron: ~er Satellit *m* RAUMFAHRT subsyn-

chronous satellite

Subsystem *nt* COMP & DV, RAUMFAHRT, TELEKOM subsystem

Subtangente *f* GEOM subtangent

Subtask *nt* COMP & DV subtask

subthermisch: ~es Neutron *nt* KERNTECH ultracold neutron

Subträger *m* RAUMFAHRT *Weltraumfunk* subcarrier

Subtrahend *m* COMP & DV subtrahend

subtrahieren *vt* COMP & DV, MATH subtract

Subtrahierer *m* COMP & DV subtracter

Subtrahierglied *nt* COMP & DV subtracter

Subtraktion *f* COMP & DV, MATH subtraction

subtraktiv: ~e Farbmischung *f* FOTO subtractive synthesis; ~e Primärfarben *f pl* FERNSEH subtractive primaries

Subtraktivmethode *f* ELEKTRONIK subtractive method

Subtyp *m* COMP & DV subtype

Subvorwahlschalter *m* FERNSEH subpreset switch

Subvorwahlsteuerung *f* FERNSEH subpreset master

Subziel *nt* KÜNSTL INT subgoal

Such: ~- und Rettungsdienst *m (SAR)* WASSERTRANS search and rescue *(SAR)*

Suchalgorithmus *m* KÜNSTL INT search algorithm

Sucharm *m* COMP & DV seek arm

Suchbaum *m* KÜNSTL INT search tree

Suchbegriff *m* COMP & DV search key, search pattern

Suchbereich *m* COMP & DV seek area

Suche *f* COMP & DV, KÜNSTL INT search; ~ in Rückwärtsrichtung *f* KÜNSTL INT backward search; ~ in verknüpfter Liste *f* COMP & DV chaining search; ~ in Vorwärtsrichtung *f* KÜNSTL INT forward search

Suchen *nt* COMP & DV searching

suchen *vt* COMP & DV seek

Sucher *m* FOTO finder, viewfinder, RAUMFAHRT viewfinder; ~ mit aufrechtem Bild *m* FOTO erect image viewfinder; ~ mit einem unter 45° geneigten Spiegel *m* FOTO right-angle finder; **Sucherokular** *nt* FOTO viewfinder eyepiece; **Sucherokular mit Korrekturlinse** *nt* FOTO viewfinder eyepiece with correcting lens; **Sucherokularabdeckung** *f* FOTO finder hood;

Suchfehler *m* COMP & DV seek error

Suchkriterium *nt* COMP & DV search key

Suchlauf *m* COMP & DV browsing

Suchmuster *nt* COMP & DV search pattern

Suchprogramm *nt* COMP & DV search program

Suchscheinwerfer *m* KFZTECH spotlight

Suchspule *f* ELEKTRIZ exploring coil, search coil, ELEKTROTECH search coil, PHYS exploring coil, pick-up coil, search coil

Suchstrategie *f* KÜNSTL INT search strategy

Suchtiefe *f* KÜNSTL INT search depth

Suchwort *nt* COMP & DV search word

Suchzeit *f* COMP & DV, OPTIK seek time

Süd:[1] ~ zu Ost *adv* WASSERTRANS *Kompaß* south by east; ~ zu West *adv* WASSERTRANS *Kompaß* south by west

Süd-[2] *pref* WASSERTRANS south; **Süden** *m* WASSERTRANS south

südlich[1] *adj* WASSERTRANS south, southerly

südlich:[2] ~e Breite *f* WASSERTRANS *Navigation* southern latitude

Südlicht *nt* WASSERTRANS *Wetterkunde* aurora australis

Südost:[1] ~ zu Ost *adv* WASSERTRANS *Kompaß* southeast by east; ~ zu Süd *adv* WASSERTRANS *Kompaß* southeast by south

Südost-[2] *pref* WASSERTRANS southeast

Südosten *m* WASSERTRANS *Kompaß* southeast
Sudoster *m* WASSERTRANS southeaster
südöstlich *adj* WASSERTRANS southeast
südostwärts *adv* WASSERTRANS southeast, southeasterly
Südost-: **Südostwind** *m* WASSERTRANS southeast wind
Südpol *m* PHYS South Pole
Südsüdosten *m* WASSERTRANS *Kompaß* south-south-east
südsüdöstlich *adj* WASSERTRANS south-southeast
Südsüdwesten *m* WASSERTRANS *Kompaß* south-south-west
südsüdwestlich *adj* WASSERTRANS south-southwest
südwärts *adv* WASSERTRANS south, southerly
Südwest:[1] **~ zu Süd** *adv* WASSERTRANS *Kompaß* southwest by south; **~ zu West** *adv* WASSERTRANS *Kompaß* southwest by west
Südwest-[2] WASSERTRANS southwest *m* WASSERTRANS *Kompaß* southwest
Südwester *m* WASSERTRANS southwester
südwestlich *adj* WASSERTRANS southwest
südwestwärts *adv* WASSERTRANS southwest, southwesterly
Südwest-: **Südwestwind** *m* WASSERTRANS southwest wind
Suffix *nt* COMP & DV suffix; **Suffixnotation** *f* COMP & DV suffix notation; **Suffixschreibweise** *f* COMP & DV suffix notation
Sugkopf *m* WASSERVERSORG strainer
sukzessiv[1] *adj* KONTROLL successive
sukzessiv:[2] **~e Approximation** *f* GERÄT successive approximation
Sulfaguanidin *nt* CHEMIE sulfaguanidine (AmE), sulphaguanidine (BrE)
Sulfamat *nt* CHEMIE sulfamate (AmE), sulphamate (BrE)
Sulfamid *nt* CHEMIE sulfamide (AmE), sulphamide (BrE); **Sulfamid-** *pref* CHEMIE sulfamic (AmE), sulphamic (BrE); **Sulfamidat** *nt* CHEMIE sulfamate (AmE), sulphamate (BrE)
Sulfanil- *pref* CHEMIE sulfanilic (AmE), sulphanilic (BrE); **Sulfanilamid** *nt* CHEMIE sulfanilamide (AmE), sulphanilamide (BrE); **Sulfanilguanidin** *nt* CHEMIE sulfaguanidine (AmE), sulphaguanidine (BrE)
Sulfapyridin *nt* CHEMIE p-aminobenzenesulfamidopyridine (AmE), p-aminobenzenesulphamidopyridine (BrE), sulfapyridine (AmE), sulphapyridine (BrE)
Sulfat *nt* CHEMIE, UMWELTSCHMUTZ sulfate (AmE), sulphate (BrE); **Sulfatangriff** *m* BAU *Beton* sulfate attack (AmE), sulphate attack (BrE)
sulfatbeständig: ~er Portlandzement *m* BAU Portland sulfate-resisting cement (AmE), Portland sulphate-resisting cement (BrE)
Sulfat: **Sulfathiazol** *nt* CHEMIE sulfathiazole (AmE), sulphathiazole (BrE); **Sulfatzellstoff** *m* PAPIER sulfate pulp (AmE), sulphate pulp (BrE)
Sulfenamidbooohlouniger *m* KUNSTSTOFF sulfene amide accelerator (AmE), sulphene amide accelerator (BrE)
Sulfhydryl- *pref* CHEMIE sulfhydryl (AmE), sulphhydryl (BrE)
Sulfidglas *nt* KER & GLAS sulfide glass (AmE), sulphide glass (BrE)
Sulfin- *pref* CHEMIE sulfinic (AmE), sulphinic (BrE)
Sulfinyl- *pref* CHEMIE sulfinyl (AmE), sulphinyl (BrE), thionyl
Sulfit *nt* CHEMIE sulfite (AmE), sulphite (BrE)

Sulfocyanat *nt* CHEMIE thiocyanate
Sulfohydrat *nt* CHEMIE sulfhydrate (AmE), sulphydrate (BrE)
Sulfolan *nt* CHEMIE, ERDÖL *Petrochemie* sulfolane (AmE), sulpholane (BrE)
Sulfolen *nt* ERDÖL *Petrochemie* sulfolene (AmE), sulpholene (BrE)
Sulfon *nt* CHEMIE sulfone (AmE), sulphone (BrE); **Sulfonamid** *nt* CHEMIE sulfonamide (AmE), sulphonamide (BrE); **Sulfonamidpräparat** *nt* CHEMIE sulfa drug (AmE), sulpha drug (BrE)
Sulfonat *nt* CHEMIE sulfonate (AmE), sulphonate (BrE)
sulfoniert *adj* CHEMIE sulfonated (AmE), sulphonated (BrE)
Sulfonierung *f* CHEMIE sulfonation (AmE), sulphonation (BrE)
Sulfon: **Sulfonsäureamid** *nt* CHEMIE sulfonamide (AmE), sulphonamide (BrE); **Sulfonsäureester** *m* CHEMIE sulfonate (AmE), sulphonate (BrE)
Sulfonyl- *pref* CHEMIE sulfonyl (AmE), sulfuryl (AmE), sulphonyl (BrE), sulphuryl (BrE)
Sulfurierung *f* CHEMIE sulfonation (AmE), sulphonation (BrE)
Sulfuryl- *pref* CHEMIE sulfonyl (AmE), sulfuryl (AmE), sulphonyl (BrE), sulphuryl (BrE)
Süll *nt* WASSERTRANS *Schiffbau* coaming; **Süllrahmen** *m* LUFTTRANS coaming
Sumatrol *nt* CHEMIE sumatrol
Summand *m* COMP & DV addend
Summe *f* COMP & DV sum
Summen *nt* AUFNAHME hum; **~ des Transformators** *nt* AUFNAHME transformer hum
Summe: **Summen-Differenz-Technik** *f* AUFNAHME sum-and-difference technique; **Summenganglinie** *f* NICHTFOSS ENERG summation hydrograph; **Summenhäufigkeit** *f* QUAL cumulative frequency; **Summenhäufigkeitspolygon** *nt* QUAL cumulative frequency polygon; **Summenkurve** *f* QUAL cumulative curve; **Summenlinie** *f* QUAL cumulative frequency polygon; **Summensignal** *nt* TELEKOM aggregate signal; **Summenstanzen** *nt* COMP & DV summary punching; **Summenstanzer** *m* COMP & DV summary punch; **Summenverteilung** *f* QUAL cumulative distribution; **Summenwahrscheinlichkeit** *f* QUAL cumulative probability; **Summenzeichen** *nt* MATH sigma
Summer *m* ELEKTRIZ, ELEKTROTECH, TELEKOM, TRANS buzzer
summierend: ~er Verstärker *m* LUFTTRANS integrator amplifier; **~er Volumenmesser** *m* LUFTTRANS integrating flowmeter; **~er Zähler** *m* ELEKTRONIK accumulating counter
Summierer: ~ mit bewerteten Eingängen *m* REGELUNG weighted summing unit
Summierglied *nt* ELEKTRONIK *Schaltkreistechnik* adder
Summierstelle *f* REGELUNG summing point
Summierstufe *f* ELEKTRONIK mixer stage
Sumpf *m* ERDÖL *Bohrtechnik* sump, KOHLEN bog, WASSERVERSORG sump; **Sumpfboden** *m* BAU swampy soil
sumpfig *adj* KOHLEN boggy
Sumpftorf *m* KOHLEN bog peat
Sund *m* WASSERTRANS sound
Superaustastimpuls *m* FERNSEH super-blanking pulse
Superbenzin *nt* ERDÖL *Destillation* premium gasoline (AmE), premium petrol (BrE), premium grade gasoline (AmE), premium grade petrol (BrE), KFZTECH four-star gasoline (AmE), four-star petrol (BrE), pre-

mium fuel, premium gasoline (AmE), premium petrol (BrE), premium grade gasoline (AmE), premium grade petrol (BrE)

Superbrechung f RAUMFAHRT *Weltraumfunk* superrefraction

Supercomputer m COMP & DV number cruncher

Supercooling nt PHYS supercooling

Superdominante f AKUSTIK submediant

Superfinieren nt MASCHINEN superfinishing

Supergroßraumcontainer m TRANS SHC, super high cube

Superhochtonlautsprecher m AUFNAHME supertweeter loudspeaker

superhohe: ~ **Frequenz** f *(SHF)* BAU, ELEKTRONIK, KOHLEN, KUNSTSTOFF, MECHAN, PHYS, THERMOD superhigh frequency *(SHF)*

Superikonoskop nt ELEKTRONIK image iconoscope

Superkalander m PAPIER supercalender

Superkargo m WASSERTRANS *Handelsmarine* supercargo

superkavitierend: ~**er Propeller** m WASSERTRANS supercavitating propeller

Superleiter m ELEKTRIZ superconductor

Superlumineszenz f OPTIK superluminescence, TELEKOM superluminescence, superradiance

superlumineszierend: ~**e Diode** f *(SLD)* OPTIK superluminescent LED *(SLD)*, TELEKOM superluminescent LED *(SLD)*, superradiant diode *(SRD)*; ~**e Leuchtdiode** f OPTIK superluminescent LED

Superminicomputer m COMP & DV supermini

Supernova f RAUMFAHRT supernova

Superorthikon nt ELEKTRONIK image orthicon

Super-Ottokraftstoff m ERDÖL premium gasoline (AmE), premium petrol (BrE), KFZTECH four-star gasoline (AmE), four-star petrol (BrE), premium fuel, premium gasoline (AmE), premium petrol (BrE)

Superoxid nt RAUMFAHRT peroxide; **Superoxid-Ion** nt CHEMIE hyperoxide

Superphosphat nt CHEMIE superphosphate

Superpositionsprinzip nt PHYS, WELLPHYS principle of superposition

Superrechner m COMP & DV supercomputer

superschwer: ~**er Kern** m PHYS superheavy nucleus

superstark: ~**er faserarmierter Wellkarton** m VERPACK heavy duty corrugated fiber board (AmE), heavy duty corrugated fibre board (BrE)

superstrahlend: ~**e Diode** f OPTIK SRD, superradiant diode

Superstrahlung f OPTIK superradiance

Superstrings m pl STRAHLPHYS superstrings

supersymmetrisch: ~**e Teilchen** nt pl STRAHLPHYS supersymmetrical particles

Supertanker m ERDÖL very large crude carrier, WASSERTRANS mammoth tanker, supertanker

Supervisor m COMP & DV executive, supervisor; **Supervisoraufruf** m COMP & DV supervisor call

Superzentrifuge f CHEMIE, LABOR ultracentrifuge

supin adj ERGON supine

Supination f ERGON supination

Supplementärwinkel m pl GEOM supplementary angles

Support m FERTIG *Hobelmaschine* head, MASCHINEN saddle, slide rest, tool rest; **Supportdrehmaschine** f MASCHINEN slide lathe, slide rest lathe

Suprafluidität f CHEMIE, PHYS superfluidity

Supraflüssigkeit f CHEMIE superfluidity, PHYS superfluid

supraleitend[1] adj TEILPHYS superconducting

supraleitend:[2] ~**es Bauteil** nt ELEKTRONIK superconducting device; ~**er Magnet** m TRANS superconducting magnet; ~**er Speicher** m COMP & DV cryogenic memory, superconducting memory; ~**e Spule** f TRANS superconducting coil

Supraleiter m ELEKTRIZ, ELEKTRONIK, PHYS, TELEKOM superconductor; **Supraleiterkabel** nt TELEKOM superconductor cable

supraleitfähig: ~**er Quanteninterferenzmechanismus** m *(SQID)* PHYS superconductive quantum interference device *(SQUID)*; ~**es Supracollider** nt *(SSC)* TEILPHYS superconducting super collider *(SSC)*

Supraleitfähigkeit f COMP & DV, ELEKTRIZ, ELEKTRONIK, STRAHLPHYS superconductivity; **Supraleitfähigkeitsleitung** f TELEKOM superconductor line

Supraleitmagnetschwebesystem nt TRANS superconducting magnet levitation

Supraleitrolle f TRANS superconducting coil

Supraleitung f COMP & DV, PHYS, STRAHLPHYS, TEILPHYS superconductivity

supraliminal adj ERGON supraliminal

Surfactant m CHEMIE surfactant, PHYS surface tension

suspendiert: ~**er Rotor** m NICHTFOSS ENERG teetered rotor

Suspension f KUNSTSTOFF suspension; **Suspensionspolymerisation** f KUNSTSTOFF suspension polymerization; **Suspensionstechnik** f CHEMIE mull technique

süß: ~ **es Rohöl** nt ERDÖL sweet crude

Süßholzzucker m CHEMIE glycyrrhizine

Süßstoff m LEBENSMITTEL sweetener

Süßwasser nt WASSERTRANS, WASSERVERSORG freshwater; **Süßwasserbohrschlamm** m ERDÖL *Bohrtechnik* freshwater mud; **Süßwasservorrat** m WASSERVERSORG freshwater stock

Suszeptanz f ELEKTROTECH, PHYS susceptance

Suszeptibilität f ELEKTRIZ susceptibility

Sutton: ~**sche Gleichung** f KERNTECH Sutton equation

Sv abbr *(Sievert)* PHYS, STRAHLPHYS, TEILPHYS Sv *(Sievert)*

SVA abbr *(gemeinsam benutzbarer virtueller Bereich)* COMP & DV SVA *(shared virtual area)*

S-Verzerrung f FERNSEH S-distortion

sv-Motor m *(seitengesteuerter Motor)* KFZTECH sv engine *(side valve engine)*

Sward-Härteprüfung f KUNSTSTOFF Sward hardness test, Sward rocker hardness test

S-Welle f *(Sekundärwelle)* PHYS S-wave *(secondary wave)*

SWFD abbr *(Selbstwählferndienst)* TELEKOM DDD (AmE) *direct distance dialing*, STD (BrE) *(subscriber trunk dialling)*

SWR abbr KERNTECH *(Siedewasserreaktor)* BWR *(boiling water reactor)*, KERNTECH *(schwerwassermoderierter Reaktor)* HWR *(heavy-water-moderated reactor)*, PHYS *(Siedewasserreaktor)* BWR *(boiling water reactor)*

SWV abbr *(Stehwellenverhältnis)* PHYS SWR *(standing-wave ratio)*, VSWR *(voltage standing-wave ratio)*, RADIO SWR *(standing-wave ratio)*, TELEKOM SWR *(standing-wave ratio)*, VSWR *(voltage standing-wave ratio)*

Syenit m CHEMIE syenite

Sylvestren nt CHEMIE sylvestrene

Symbiose f ERGON symbiosis

Symbol *nt* COMP & DV *grafische Oberflächen* symbol, *in grafischer Benutzeroberfläche* icon

symbolisch: ~e **Adresse** *f* COMP & DV symbolic address; ~e **Adressierung** *f* COMP & DV symbolic addressing; ~er **Befehl** *m* COMP & DV symbolic code, symbolic instruction; ~er **Code** *m* COMP & DV symbolic code; ~e **Logik** *f* MATH mathematical logic, symbolic logic; ~er **Name** *m* COMP & DV symbolic name; ~e **Programmiersprache** *f* COMP & DV symbolic language; ~es **Testen** *nt* COMP & DV symbolic debugging; ~e **Verarbeitung** *f* COMP & DV symbolic processing

Symbol: **Symbolsatz** *m* COMP & DV symbol set; **Symboltabelle** *f* COMP & DV symbol table; **Symboltaste** *f* COMP & DV symbol key

Symmetrie *f* GEOM symmetry; ~ **bezüglich Anströmung und Abströmung** *f* STRÖMPHYS upstream-downstream symmetry; **Symmetrieachse** *f* GEOM axis of symmetry, MASCHINEN symmetry axis; **Symmetrieebene** *f* GEOM plane of symmetry, symmetry plane, MASCHINEN symmetry plane, METALL plane of symmetry; **Symmetriezentrum** *nt* GEOM center of symmetry (AmE), centre of symmetry (BrE)

symmetrisch[1] *adj* COMP & DV symmetric, symmetrical, GEOM symmetrical, symmetric; ~ **gegen Erde** *adj* ELEKTROTECH balanced to earth; ~ **gegen Masse** *adj* ELEKTROTECH balanced to earth

symmetrisch:[2] ~er **Anastigmat** *m* FOTO symmetric anastigmat, symmetrical anastigmat; ~e **Anordnung** *f* ELEKTROTECH symmetrical arrangement; ~e **Belastung** *f* ELEKTROTECH balanced load; ~e **doppelte Gleisverbindung** *f* EISENBAHN scissors crossing; ~er **Eingang** *m* ELEKTROTECH, GERÄT balanced input; ~er **Fehler** *m* COMP & DV balanced error; ~e **Leitung** *f* AUFNAHME balanced line, ELEKTRIZ balanced line, balancing coil, ELEKTROTECH balanced line; ~e **Matrix** *f* COMP & DV symmetric matrix, symmetrical matrix; ~e **Meßleitung** *f* GERÄT balanced measuring line; ~es **Netzwerk** *nt* ELEKTROTECH balanced network; ~e **Schaltung** *f* AUFNAHME balanced circuit, ELEKTRIZ balanced network; ~es **Schutzrelais** *nt* ELEKTRIZ symmetrical protective relay; ~e **Ströme** *m pl* ELEKTROTECH balanced currents; ~e **Teilgruppe** *f* TELEKOM balanced grading group; ~es **T-Glied** *nt* ELEKTROTECH H-network; ~e **Tonspur** *f* AKUSTIK symmetrical soundtrack; ~er **Wandler** *m* ELEKTROTECH symmetrical transducer; ~e **Wellenfunktion** *f* PHYS symmetric wave function

Synanthrose *f* CHEMIE levulin, synanthrose

Synärese *f* KUNSTSTOFF, LEBENSMITTEL syneresis

Synchro- *pref* COMP & DV, ELEKTRONIK synchronous; **Synchrocompurverschluß** *m* FOTO synchro compur shutter; **Synchrodrehmomentempfänger** *m* GERÄT synchro torque receiver

Synchron- *pref* COMP & DV, ELEKTRONIK synchronous; **Synchronalternator** *m* ELEKTRIZ synchronous alternator; **Synchronantrieb** *m* FERNSEH synchronous drive

Synchronisation *f* COMP & DV synchronization, FERNSEH dubbing, MASCHINEN synchronization

synchron: ~e **Datenübertragungssteuerung** *f (SDLC)* COMP & DV synchronous data link control *(SDLC)*; ~er **Port** *m* TELEKOM synchronous port; ~e **Übertragung** *f* COMP & DV isochronous transmission, TELEKOM synchronous transmission

Synchron-: **Synchrongenerator** *m* ELEKTRIZ, ELEKTROTECH synchronous generator, FERNSEH station sync generator, sync generator; **Synchrongeschwindigkeit** *f*

ELEKTRIZ, NICHTFOSS ENERG synchronous speed; **Synchrongetriebe** *nt* KFZTECH synchromesh, synchromesh transmission, *Getriebe* constant mesh; **Synchroninput** *m* FERNSEH sync input

Synchronisation *f* FERNSEH, COMP & DV synchronization; **Synchronisationsaustastung** *f* FERNSEH sync blanking; **Synchronisationsbit** *nt* COMP & DV flag bit, sync bit; **Synchronisationsdemodulation** *f* COMP & DV synchronous detection; **Synchronisationsglied** *nt* ELEKTROTECH synchronizer; **Synchronisationsimpuls** *m* COMP & DV, KONTROLL sync pulse; **Synchronisationsleerzeichen** *nt* COMP & DV synchronous idle; **Synchronisationsmechanismus** *m* COMP & DV interlock; **Synchronisationsnetz** *nt* TELEKOM synchronization network; **Synchronisationsstörung** *f* ELEKTRONIK jitter noise, *Fernsehen* jitter; **Synchronisationszeichen** *nt* COMP & DV SYN, synchronous idle character

Synchron-: **Synchronisator** *m* ELEKTROTECH, KFZTECH synchronizer; **Synchronisieraufstellung** *f* FERNSEH sync line-up; **Synchronisiereinheit** *f* COMP & DV timing generator

Synchronisieren *nt* COMP & DV synchronization

synchronisieren *vt* FERNSEH dub, sync, synchronize

Synchronisierer *m* COMP & DV, ELEKTROTECH synchronizer

Synchron-: **Synchronisierimpulse** *m pl* FERNSEH synchronization pulses; **Synchronisierleitung** *f* KONTROLL sync line, synchronizing line; **Synchronisierrelais** *nt* ELEKTRIZ synchronizing relay; **Synchronisierrückkoppelung** *f* FERNSEH sync feedback

synchronisiert[1] *adj* FERNSEH in sync; **nicht** ~ *adj* FERNSEH nonsync

synchronisiert:[2] ~es **Getriebe** *nt* KFZTECH synchronized transmission; ~er **Induktionsmotor** *m* ELEKTROTECH synchronous induction motor

Synchronisierung *f* AUFNAHME synchronization, COMP & DV SYN, synchronous idle character, FERNSEH dub, KFZTECH, KONTROLL synchronization, TELEKOM alignment, synchronization; **Synchronisierungsbit** *nt* COMP & DV sync bit; **Synchronisierungsfenster** *nt* RAUMFAHRT synchronization window; **Synchronisierungsimpuls** *m* COMP & DV, KONTROLL sync pulse; **Synchronisierungsverlust** *m* ELEKTRIZ loss of synchronism; **Synchronisierungsvorrichtung** *f* KFZTECH synchronizer; **Synchronisierungszeichen** *nt* COMP & DV SYN, synchronous idle character

Synchron-: **Synchronisiervorrichtung** *f* ELEKTRIZ synchronizer; **Synchronismus** *m* AUFNAHME, ELEKTRONIK synchronism; **Synchronität** *f* MASCHINEN synchronism; **Synchronklappe** *f* AUFNAHME clapper; **Synchronkondensator** *m* ELEKTROTECH synchronous capacitor; **Synchronkontaktgeber** *m* ELEKTROTECH synchronizer; **Synchronleichrichtung** *f* ELEKTRONIK synchronous detection; **Synchronmaschine** *f* ELEKTRIZ, ELEKTROTECH synchronous machine; **Synchron-Modem** *nt* ELEKTRONIK synchronous modem; **Synchronmodus** *m* COMP & DV synchronous mode; **Synchronmotor** *m* ELEKTRIZ, ELEKTROTECH, PHYS, TRANS synchronous motor; **Synchronmotor auf Asynchronprinzip** *m* ELEKTRIZ synchronous induction motor; **Synchronpulsgenerator** *m* FERNSEH sync pulse generator; **Synchronrechner** *m* COMP & DV synchronous computer; **Synchronriemen** *m* KFZTECH *Nockenwellenantrieb* timing belt, MASCHINEN synchronous belt, timing belt; **Synchronriemenantrieb** *m*

MASCHINEN synchronous belt drive; **Synchronsatellit** *m* RAUMFAHRT synchronous satellite, TELEKOM geosynchronous satellite; **Synchronschaltung** *f* TELEKOM synchronous circuit; **Synchronsignal** *nt* COMP & DV clocked signal; **Synchronsteuerung** *f* FERNSEH genlock, genlocking; **Synchronsystem** *nt* TRANS simultaneous system; **Synchronteiler** *m* FERNSEH sync separator; **Synchronton** *m* AUFNAHME sync sound; **Synchronübertragung** *f* COMP & DV synchronous transmission; **Synchronuhr** *f* ELEKTRIZ electric synchronous clock; **Synchronumformer** *m* ELEKTRIZ synchronous converter; **Synchronverfahren** *nt* COMP & DV synchronous mode; **Synchronverlust** *m* FERNSEH sync loss; **Synchronverstärker** *m* FERNSEH sync amplifier; **Synchronwort** *nt* TELEKOM syncword; **Synchronzähler** *m* GERÄT synchronous counter

Synchro-: **Synchroton** *nt* PHYS synchroton; **Synchrotransformator** *m* ELEKTROTECH synchro transformer; **Synchrotron** *nt* TEILPHYS synchrotron; **Synchrotronstrahlung** *f* PHYS synchrotron radiation, STRAHLPHYS synchrotron emission, TEILPHYS synchrotron radiation; **Synchrozentralverschluß** *m* FOTO synchro compur shutter; **Synchrozyklotron** *nt* PHYS synchrocyclotron

Synergismus *m* UMWELTSCHMUTZ synergetic effect, synergy

Synergist *m* LEBENSMITTEL synergist

synergistisch: **~er Effekt** *m* KUNSTSTOFF synergism effect, synergistic effect

Synklinale *f* ERDÖL *Geologie* syncline

synoptisch: **~ e Schalttafel** *f* ELEKTRIZ synoptical switchboard

syntaktisch[1] *adj* CHEMIE syntactic

syntaktisch:[2] **~er Analysator** *m* TELEKOM syntactic analyser (BrE), syntactic analyzer (AmE); **~e Analyse** *f* TELEKOM syntactic analysis

syntaktisch:[3] **~ analysieren** *vt* COMP & DV parse

Syntax *f* COMP & DV syntax; **Syntaxanalyse** *f* COMP & DV parsing, syntax analysis; **Syntaxanalyseprogramm** *nt* COMP & DV syntax analyser (BrE), syntax analyzer (AmE); **Syntaxfehler** *m* COMP & DV grammatical error, syntax error; **Syntaxprüfung** *f* COMP & DV syntax checking

Syntheseelastomer *nt* ERDÖL synthetic elastomer

Synthesegenerator *m* TELEKOM synthesizer

Synthesekautschuk *m* ERDÖL, KUNSTSTOFF synthetic rubber

Syntheseöl *nt* ERDÖL synthetic crude oil

synthetisch: **~es Benzin** *nt* KFZTECH synthetic gasoline (AmE), synthetic petrol (BrE); **~es Elastomer** *nt* ERDÖL synthetic elastomer; **~e Faser** *f* TEXTIL synthetic fiber (AmE), synthetic fibre (BrE); **~ hergestelltes Gas** *nt (SNG)* ERDÖL synthetic natural gas *(SNG)*; **~er Latex** *m* KUNSTSTOFF synthetic latex; **~es Öl** *nt* ERDÖL synthetic crude, MASCHINEN synthetic oil; **~e Schlichte** *f* TEXTIL synthetic size; **~e Sprache** *f* KÜNSTL INT synthetic speech

synthetisiert: **~e Musik** *f* ELEKTRONIK synthesized music

Synthol *nt* CHEMIE synthol

Syntonin *nt* CHEMIE parapeptone, syntonin

syntonisch: **~es Komma** *nt* AKUSTIK syntonous comma

Sypersynchro-Signal *nt* FERNSEH supersync signal

Syringa- *pref* CHEMIE syringic

System *nt* BAU *Rohren, Kabeln,* COMP & DV, EISENBAHN, TELEKOM system, TRANS system with intermediate stops; **~ für Aktivabfälle** *nt* KERNTECH active effluent system; **~ mit Bereitschaftsbetrieb** *nt* TELEKOM hot stand-by system; **~ mit digitaler Modulation** *nt* TELEKOM digital modulation system; **~ mit einfachem Anruf** *nt* TELEKOM combined local/toll system; **~ mit Ersatzschaltung** *nt* TELEKOM *Radio* stand-by system; **~ mit erweiterter Bandbreite** *nt* RADIO extended-bandwidth system; **~ mit festverdrahteter Logik** *nt* TELEKOM wired logic system; **~ mit Funktionsteilung** *nt* TELEKOM function division system; **~ mit heißer Reserve** *nt* TELEKOM hot stand-by system; **~ zur Informationsabfrage** *nt* COMP & DV information retrieval system; **~ mit künstlicher Intelligenz** *nt* KÜNSTL INT artificial intelligence system; **~ für künstliche Verzögerung** *nt* AUFNAHME artificial delay system; **~ mit Mehrfachzugriff** *nt* COMP & DV multiaccess system; **~ mit Motorantrieb** *nt* TELEKOM motor-driven system; **~ mit Registersteuerung** *nt* TELEKOM register-controlled system; **~ zur Rettung von Menschenleben bei Seenotfällen** *nt (GMDSS)* WASSERTRANS global marine distress and safety system *(GMDSS)*; **~ mit unterdrücktem Träger** *nt* FERNSEH suppressed carrier system; **~ für verteilte Dateien** *nt* COMP & DV distributed file system; **~ mit verteilter Steuerung** *nt* TELEKOM distributed control system; **~ vorbestimmter Zeiten** *nt* ERGON predetermined motion time system; **~ der vorlaufenden Luftschraubenblätter** *nt* LUFTTRANS advancing blade concept; **~ zum Wiederauffinden von Informationen** *nt* COMP & DV information retrieval system; **~ mit Zeitschlitzen** *nt* TELEKOM slotted system; **~ mit Zentralsteuerung** *nt* TELEKOM common control system; **Systemabschluß** *m* COMP & DV closedown; **Systemabsturz** *m* COMP & DV system crash; **Systemanalyse** *f* COMP & DV system analysis; **Systemanalyseprogramm** *nt* COMP & DV system analyser program (BrE), system analyzer program (AmE); **Systemanbieter** *m* TELEKOM system provider; **Systemantwort** *f* COMP & DV response; **Systemanzeige** *f* COMP & DV prompt; **Systemarchitektur** *f* ELEKTRIZ system configuration; **Systemarchitektur mit Funktionsteilung** *f* TELEKOM function-division system architecture

systematisch: **~e Ergebnisabweichung** *f* QUAL bias of result, systematic error of result; **~er Fehler** *m* ELEKTROTECH bias, GERÄT *Meßwesen* bias error, PHYS systematic error; **~er Fehler des Meßgeräts** *m* GERÄT instrumental error; **~e Probenentnahme** *f* COMP & DV systematic sampling; **~e Stichprobe** *f* QUAL systematic sample; **~e Stichprobenentnahme** *f* QUAL systematic sampling

System: **Systemausfall** *m* KONTROLL system failure; **Systembau** *m* BAU systems building

systembedingt: **~er Fehler** *m* METROL systematic error

System: **Systembelastung** *f* COMP & DV processing load, TELEKOM system load; **Systembibliothek** *f* COMP & DV system library, systems library; **Systembilanz** *f* TELEKOM *Mikrowellen* link power budget; **Systemblockade** *f* COMP & DV deadlock; **Systemdesigner** *m* COMP & DV system designer; **Systementwurfsingenieur** *m* TELEKOM system designer; **Systemerde** *f* ELEKTRIZ system earth (BrE), system ground (AmE); **Systemfehler** *m* KONTROLL system error; **Systemfunktionsbild** *nt* ELEKTRIZ system operational diagram; **Systemfunktionsplan** *m* ELEKTRIZ system operational diagram; **Systemgenerierung** *f* COMP & DV sysgen, system generation; **Systemgestaltung** *f* ERGON system design; **Systemkern** *m* COMP & DV nucleus; **Systemkonfiguration** *f*

COMP & DV system configuration; **Systemkonsole** *f* COMP & DV *Basissystem* master console; **Systemkonstante** *f (Gx)* AKUSTIK system-rating constant *(Gx)*; **Systemmeldung** *f* COMP & DV message; **Systemmeldungskopf** *m* COMP & DV message header; **Systemnetzwerkarchitektur** *f (SNA)* COMP & DV systems network architecture *(SNA)*; **Systemplan** *m* ELEKTRIZ system diagram; **Systemplanung** *f* COMP & DV system design; **Systemplatte** *f* COMP & DV system disk; **Systemplattform** *f* COMP & DV platform; **Systemprogrammierung** *f* COMP & DV systems programming; **Systemprotokoll** *nt* COMP & DV system log; **Systemprüfung** *f* COMP & DV system check, system testing, QUAL system check; **Systemsicherheit** *f* COMP & DV system security; **Systemsoftware** *f* COMP & DV system software, systems software; **Systemsteuerkonsole** *f* COMP & DV system control panel; **Systemsteuerung** *f* KONTROLL system control; **Systemsynthese** *f* ELEKTROTECH network synthesis; **Systemtechnik** *f*

COMP & DV systems engineering; **Systemüberlastung** *f* COMP & DV thrashing; **Systemurband** *nt* COMP & DV master tape; **Systemverklemmung** *f* COMP & DV deadlock; **Systemverwaltung** *f* COMP & DV housekeeping; **Systemverwaltungsprozedur** *f* COMP & DV housekeeping procedure

systolisch: ~**e Architektur** *f* TELEKOM systolic architecture; ~**e Matrix** *f* COMP & DV systolic array

Syzygie *f* NICHTFOSS ENERG syzygy

SZ *abbr (Säurezahl)* KUNSTSTOFF, LEBENSMITTEL acid value

Szenenanalyse *f* KÜNSTL INT scene analysis

Szintillation *f* PHYS, TELEKOM scintillation; **Szintillationskoinzidenz-Spektrometer** *nt* KERNTECH scintillation coincidence spectrometer; **Szintillations-Spektrometer** *nt* STRAHLPHYS scintillation spectrometer; **Szintillationszähler** *m* GERÄT, PHYS, STRAHLPHYS scintillation counter

Szintillator *m* STRAHLPHYS scintillator

T

T ^{1} *abbr* AKUSTIK *(Nachhallzeit)*, AUFNAHME *(Nachhallzeit)* T *(reverberation time)*, ELEKTRIZ *(Drehmoment)*, ELEKTROTECH *(Drehmoment)*, ERDÖL *(Drehmoment)* T *(torque)*, FERTIG *(Drehmoment)* T, *Kunststoffinstallationen* T *(torque)*, HYDRAUL *(Transpiration)* T *(transpiration)*, KFZTECH *(Drehmoment)* T *(torque)*, LABOR *(Tesla)* T *(Tesla)*, MASCHINEN *(Drehmoment)*, MECHAN *(Drehmoment)* T *(torque)*, METROL *(absolute Temperatur)* T *(absolute temperature)*, METROL *(Tera-)* T *(tera-)*, PHYS *(Tesla)* T *(Tesla)*, PHYS *(thermodynamische Temperatur)* T *(thermodynamic temperature)*

T ^{2} *(Tritium)* CHEMIE T *(tritium)*

t *abbr* HYDRAUL *(Tiefe)* d *(depth)*, TEILPHYS *(Triton)* t *(triton)*

Ta *(Tantal)* CHEMIE Ta *(tantalum)*

TAA *abbr (Technische Anleitung Abfall)* ABFALL Technical Instruction on Waste Management

Tab *m* COMP & DV tab

Tabakin-Potential *nt* KERNTECH Tabakin potential

tabellarisch ^{1} *adj* COMP & DV tabular

tabellarisch: ^{2} **~e Aufstellung** *f* COMP & DV tabulation

Tabelle *f* COMP & DV table, *in der Tabellenkalkulation* spreadsheet, PHYS chart

Tabellen *f pl* RAUMFAHRT ephemerides; **Tabellenausgabe** *f* COMP & DV table output; **Tabellenbereich** *m* COMP & DV table space

Tabellenform: **in ~** *adv* COMP & DV in tabular form

Tabellen: **Tabellenkalkulation** *f* COMP & DV spreadsheet; **Tabellenkopf** *m* DRUCK boxed head; **Tabellenmaß** *nt* KONSTZEICH tabular dimension, tabulator dimension; **Tabellensatz** *m* DRUCK tabular work; **Tabellensuche** *f* COMP & DV table search; **Tabellensuchoperation** *f* COMP & DV table lookup; **Tabellenüberschrift** *f* COMP & DV table header; **Tabellenzeichnung** *f* KONSTZEICH tabular drawing

Tabellieren *nt* COMP & DV tabulation

tabellieren *vt* COMP & DV tabulate

Tablett *nt* COMP & DV *Grafikverarbeitung* tablet, *zur Grafikeingabe* data tablet, VERPACK food tray

Tablette *f* KUNSTSTOFF pellet; **Tablettenfläschchen** *nt* KER & GLAS tablet bottle; **Tablettensortier- und Kontrollmaschine** *f* VERPACK tablet sorting and inspection machine; **Tablettenzählvorrichtung** *f* VERPACK missing pill equipment

Tablettieren *nt* FERTIG pelleting, KUNSTSTOFF pelletizing

Tablettiermaschine *f* FERTIG pelleter, KUNSTSTOFF pelletizer

Tabulator *m* COMP & DV tabulator; **Tabulatorgitter** *nt* COMP & DV tab rack; **Tabulatorstopp** *m* COMP & DV tab stop; **Tabulatortaste** *f* COMP & DV tabulator key

tabulieren *vt* COMP & DV tabulate

Tabuliertaste *f* COMP & DV tabulator key

T-Abzweig *m* BAU T-junction

Tacheometrie *f* BAU *Vermessung* tacheometry

Tachometer *nt* FERNSEH tachometer, GERÄT speed indicator, KFZTECH tachometer, *Zubehör* speedometer, MASCHINEN speedometer, PHYS tachometer; **Tachometerantrieb** *m* KFZTECH speedometer drive gear; **Tachometereinrastung** *f* FERNSEH tachometer lock

tachometrisch: **~e Vermessung** *f* BAU stadia surveying

Tachymeter *nt* BAU *Vermessung* tacheometer

Tachyon *nt* PHYS tachyon

Tafel *f* BAU *einer Wand*, DRUCK plate, ELEKTRIZ panel, KERNTECH *dünne Platte* sheet, KOHLEN panel, KÜNSTL INT blackboard, MASCHINEN plate, PHYS chart, RADIO panel; **Tafel-Abriebmaschine** *f* KUNSTSTOFF Taber abrader; **Tafelblei** *nt* BAU sheet lead; **Tafelglas** *nt* KER & GLAS sheet glass; **Tafelglaszuschnitte** *m pl* KER & GLAS cut sizes; **Tafelmontage** *f* ELEKTRIZ panel mounting

täfeln *vt* BAU pane, panel, *Decke* ceil

Tafel: **Tafelschere** *f* FERTIG guillotine shearing machine, guillotine plate shear, MASCHINEN plate shears, sheet shears

Täfelung *f* BAU panel

Taft *m* TEXTIL taffeta

Tag *m* ELEKTRIZ, ERGON, FOTO, KUNSTSTOFF, LUFTTRANS day; **Tagebau** *m* COAL open-pit mining; **Tagebaubergwerk** *nt* KOHLEN daylight colliery; **Tagebücher** *nt pl* RAUMFAHRT ephemerides; **Tageskilometerzähler** *m* KFZTECH odometer, trip mileage indicator, *Instrument* trip counter; **Tagesleuchtfarbe** *f* KUNSTSTOFF Day-Glo® paint; **Tageslichtaufnahme** *f* FOTO daylight exposure; **Tageslichtfotografie** *f* FOTO daylight photography; **Tageslichtquotient** *m* ERGON daylight factor; **Tageslichttank** *m* FOTO daylight loading tank; **Tagesreichweite** *f* LUFTTRANS day range; **Tagesrückenlast** *f* ELEKTRIZ daily base rate; **Tagesverbrauch** *m* WASSERVERSORG daily consumption; **Tagesverkehr** *m* TRANS day traffic; **Tageswanne** *f* KER & GLAS day tank; **Tageswasserfluß** *m* WASSERVERSORG daily water flow

täglich ^{1} *adj* ERGON, RAUMFAHRT diurnal

täglich: ^{2} **~e Änderung** *f* WASSERTRANS *Luftdruck* diurnal variation; **~e Druckverteilung** *f* WASSERTRANS *Luftdruck* diurnal variation

Tagwasser *nt* KOHLEN surface water

Taillenabnäher *m* TEXTIL waist dart

Takelage *f* WASSERTRANS *Segeln*, *Tauwerk* rigging

Takelplan *m* WASSERTRANS *Tauwerk* rigging drawing

Takelriß *m* WASSERTRANS *Tauwerk* rigging drawing

Takler *m* WASSERTRANS rigger

Takling *m* WASSERTRANS *Tauwerk* whipping

Takt *m* AKUSTIK beat, rhythm, time, ELEKTRONIK clock, KONTROLL clock, timing, KUNSTSTOFF cycle, PHYS stroke; **Taktableitung** *f* TELEKOM clock extraction; **Taktdiagramm** *nt* COMP & DV timing diagram

takten ^{1} *vt* COMP & DV clock, pace, ERGON pace, FERTIG, GERÄT clock

takten ^{2} *vi* ELEKTRONIK pulse

Takt: **Taktfolge** *f* ELEKTRONIK clocking sequence; **Taktfrequenz** *f* ELEKTRONIK, FERNSEH clock frequency, GERÄT clock rate, RADIO clock frequency; **Taktgabe** *f* KONTROLL clocking; **Taktgeber** *m* COMP & DV clock, clock generator, real-time clock, ELEKTRONIK master oscillator, timing generator, KONTROLL clock, clock generator, timer, TELEKOM clock generator, clock, timer; **Taktgebermaß** *nt* GERÄT clock rate; **Taktgebung** *f* ELEKTRONIK timing; **Taktgeschwindigkeit** *f* COMP & DV clock speed

taktgesteuert: **~es Flipflop** *nt* ELEKTRONIK clocked flip-flop

taktgleich *adj* ELEKTRONIK synchronous

taktil *adj* ERGON tactile

Takt: **Taktimpuls** *m* COMP & DV clock pulse, ELEKTRONIK clock pulse, timing pulse, KONTROLL clock pulse; **Taktintervall** *nt* ELEKTRONIK clock period; **Taktizität** *f* KUNSTSTOFF tacticity; **Taktrate** *f* COMP & DV, GERÄT clock rate; **Taktrelais** *nt* ELEKTRIZ clock relay; **Taktsignal** *nt* COMP & DV clock pulse, clock signal, ELEKTRONIK clock signal, timing signal; **Taktsignalverzögerung** *f* ELEKTRONIK clock signal skew; **Taktspur** *f* AUFNAHME clock track, timing track, COMP & DV clock track

taktsteuern *vt* GERÄT clock

Takt: **Taktumschaltung** *f* KONTROLL clock changeover; **Taktunterbrechungseinstellung** *f* TRANS cycle split adjustment

taktzustandsgesteuert: **nicht ~e Kippschaltung** *f* ELEKTRONIK unclocked flip-flop

Takt: **Taktzyklus** *m* COMP & DV, ELEKTRONIK, GERÄT, KONTROLL clock cycle, timing cycle

Talg *m* CHEMIE, FERTIG, TEXTIL tallow

talgig *adj* LEBENSMITTEL tallowy

Talg: **Talgöl** *nt* CHEMIE tallow oil

Talje *f* WASSERTRANS *Tauwerk* purchase, tackle; **Taljereep** *nt* WASSERTRANS *Tauwerk* reefing pennant

Talkum *nt* KER & GLAS talc

Tallöl *nt* CHEMIE, KUNSTSTOFF tall oil

Talon- *pref* CHEMIE talonic

Talsohle *f* BAU bottom

Talsperre *f* WASSERVERSORG barrage, dam, river dam

Talstation *f* TRANS valley station

Tambour *m* PAPIER reel spool; **Tambourwalze** *f* PAPIER reel drum

tan *abbr* GEOM *(Tangens)*, GEOM *(Tangente)* tan *(tangent)*

Tandem *nt* KFZTECH tandem; **Tandemachse** *f* KFZTECH *LKW* tandem axle; **Tandembauart** *f* MASCHINEN tandem construction; **Tandembeschleuniger** *m* KERNTECH tandem accelerator, PHYS tandem generator; **Tandemhubschrauber** *m* LUFTTRANS dual tandem helicopter, tandem rotor helicopter; **Tandemmaschine** *f* MASCHINEN tandem engine; **Tandemmotor** *m* KONTROLL tandem motor; **Tandem-Potentiometer** *nt* ELEKTRIZ dual-ganged potentiometer; **Tandemschaltung** *f* ELEKTRIZ tandem connection; **Tandemvibrationswalze** *f* BAU *Straßenbau* tandem vibrating roller

Tangens *m* *(tan)* GEOM *an eine Funktion* tangent *(tan)*

Tangente *f* *(tan)* GEOM *Linie, Kurve* tangent, MATH *Linie, Kurve* tangent *(tan)*; **Tangentenbussole** *f* ELEKTROTECH tangent galvanometer, PHYS tangent compass, tangent galvanometer; **Tangenten-Galvanometer** *nt* ELEKTRIZ tangent galvanometer; **Tangentengleichung** *f* GEOM equation of the tangent

Tangential- *pref* MASCHINEN, PHYS tangential; **Tangentialbeanspruchung** *f* MASCHINEN tangential stress; **Tangentialbelastung** *f* MASCHINEN tangential strain; **Tangentialbeschleunigung** *f* MASCHINEN, MECHAN tangential acceleration; **Tangentialdrehmeißel** *m*

FERTIG, MASCHINEN tangential turning tool; **Tangentialgeschwindigkeit** *f* NICHTFOSS ENERG tangential velocity; **Tangentialkomponente** *f* PHYS tangential component; **Tangentialschneidbacke** *f* MASCHINEN tangential threading die; **Tangentialschneidplatte** *f* FERTIG on-end insert; **Tangentialschnitt** *m* PHYS tangential focal line; **Tangentialsteuerung** *f* OPTIK tangential control; **Tangentialwälzfräsen** *nt* FERTIG tangential hobbing

tangential[1] *adj* GEOM, MECHAN, PHYS tangential

tangential:[2] **~er Vorschub** *m* MASCHINEN tangential feed

Tangentkeil *m* MASCHINEN tangent key, tangential key; **Tangentkeilnut** *f* MASCHINEN tangent keyway

tangierend: **~e Kreise** *m pl* GEOM tangent circles

Tank *m* ERDÖL, HEIZ & KÄLTE tank, KFZTECH *Kraftstoff* gas tank (AmE), gasoline tank (AmE), petrol tank (BrE), *Öl* reservoir, MECHAN, RAUMFAHRT, UMWELTSCHMUTZ tank, WASSERVERSORG cistern; **~ mit Elastomermembran** *m* RAUMFAHRT elastomer membrane tank; **Tankcontainer** *m* KFZTECH tank container; **Tankdecke** *f* WASSERTRANS *Schiffbau* tank top; **Tankdeckel** *m* KFZTECH filler cap, tank cap

Tanken *nt* KFZTECH, WASSERTRANS refueling (AmE), refuelling (BrE)

tanken *vt* TRANS fill up

Tank: **Tankentlüftung** *f* RAUMFAHRT tank vent; **Tankentwicklung** *f* FOTO tank development

Tanker *m* ERDÖL *Schiffahrt*, WASSERTRANS tanker; **Tanker-Terminal** *m* WASSERTRANS tanker terminal

Tank: **Tankfahrzeug** *nt* KFZTECH tank lorry (BrE), tank truck (AmE), tanker, MEERSCHMUTZ tanker; **Tankflugzeug** *nt* KFZTECH refueller; **Tankfrachtkran** *m* WASSERTRANS tank barge; **Tankklappe** *f* KFZTECH filler compartment flap; **Tankluke** *f* WASSERTRANS tank hatch; **Tankreaktor** *m* KERNTECH tank reactor; **Tanksattelanhänger** *m* KFZTECH tank semi-trailer; **Tankstelle** *f* TRANS filling station, gas station (AmE), gasoline station (AmE), petrol station (BrE), road petrol station (BrE); **Tankventil** *nt* HYDRAUL tank valve; **Tankverbindungsstück** *nt* RAUMFAHRT *Raumschiff* intertank connector; **Tankwagen** *m* KFZTECH tanker, MEERSCHMUTZ road tanker, WASSERTRANS tanker lorry (BrE); **Tankwaggon** *m* WASSERTRANS tanker lorry (BrE), tanker truck (AmE); **Tankwall** *m* ERDÖL *Raffinerie* fire wall; **Tankwärmer** *m* FOTO tank heater; **Tankzwischenstück** *nt* RAUMFAHRT *Raumschiff* intertank connector

Tannat *nt* CHEMIE tannate

Tannenbaumkristall *m* FERTIG fir tree crystal, pine crystal

Tannenbaumprofil *nt* FERTIG fir tree profile

Tannin *nt* CHEMIE tannin; **Tanningerbstoff** *m* CHEMIE tannin

T-Anschluß *m* BAU T-piece union

Tantal *nt* *(Ta)* CHEMIE tantalum *(Ta)*; **Tantal-** *pref* CHEMIE tantalic, tantalum; **Tantalanode** *f* ELEKTROTECH tantalum anode; **Tantalat** *nt* CHEMIE tantalate; **Tantalfestkondensator** *m* ELEKTROTECH tantalum solid capacitor; **Tantalfilmkondensator** *m* ELEKTROTECH tantalum foil capacitor; **Tantalkern** *m* ELEKTROTECH tantalum slug; **Tantalkernkondensator** *m* ELEKTROTECH tantalum slug capacitor; **Tantalkondensator** *m* ELEKTROTECH tantalum capacitor; **Tantalnaßkondensator** *m* ELEKTROTECH tantalum wet capacitor; **Tantaloxid** *nt* ELEKTROTECH tantalum oxide; **Tantaloxidkondensator** *m* ELEKTROTECH tantalum oxide capacitor; **Tantalschichtkondensator** *m* ELEKTROTECH tantalum foil capacitor

Tantiemen *f pl* DRUCK royalties

tapezieren *vt* BAU paper

Tapeziererleim: ~ **auf Wasserbasis** *m* VERPACK water-based backing adhesive

Tapeziernagel *m* MASCHINEN tintack

Tara *nt* TEXTIL, TRANS *Leergewicht*, VERPACK *Verpak-kungsgewicht* tare

Target *nt* TEILPHYS target; **Targetbestrahlung** *f* KERNTECH target irradiation

Tarieren *nt* LUFTTRANS calibration

Tarif *m* TELEKOM charge rate, tariff; ~ **für Telefondienst** *m* TELEKOM call charge rate; **Tarifstruktur** *f* TELEKOM tariff structure

Tarnverpackung *f* VERPACK deceptive packaging

Tartrat *nt* CHEMIE tartrate

Tartron- *pref* CHEMIE tartronic

Tartronoylharnstoff *m* CHEMIE dialuric acid, hydroxybarbituric acid, tartronoylurea

Tasche *f* KOHLEN, PAPIER *des Holzschleifers* pocket; **Taschendosimeter** *nt* STRAHLPHYS pocket dosemeter; **Taschendosimeter mit Skale** *nt* STRAHLPHYS graduated pocket dosimeter; **Taschenentlüftungsleitung** *f* PAPIER pocket-ventilating duct; **Taschenentlüftungswalze** *f* PAPIER pocket-ventilating roll; **Taschenlampe** *f* ELEKTRIZ flashlight, pocket lamp, ELEKTROTECH inspection lamp; **Taschenrechner** *m* COMP & DV calculator, pocket calculator, MATH, TELEKOM pocket calculator; **Taschenterminal** *nt* TELEKOM pocket terminal

Tasksteuerung *f* COMP & DV task management

Tast- *pref* FERNSEH, KONTROLL, TELEKOM touch

Tastatur *f* AUFNAHME *elektronische Orgel oder Synthesizer*, COMP & DV, DRUCK, ELEKTRIZ, FERNSEH, RADIO, TELEKOM keyboard; **Tastaturbelegung** *f* COMP & DV keyboard layout; **Tastaturbeschriftung** *f* COMP & DV keyboard overlay; **Tastaturcodierer** *m* COMP & DV keyboard encoder; **Tastatureingabe** *f* COMP & DV, TELEKOM keying; **Tastaturfolie** *f* COMP & DV keyboard overlay; **Tastaturmaskierung** *f* COMP & DV keyboard mask; **Tastaturschablone** *f* COMP & DV keyboard mask, keyboard overlay, keyboard template; **Tastatursende-Empfangsmodus** *m* COMP & DV *Datenstation und serieller Drucker mit Bildschirmfunktion* KSR, keyboard send-receive; **Tastatursperre** *f* COMP & DV keyboard lock

tastbar *adj* ERGON tactile

Tast-: **Tastbügelregler** *m* GERÄT chopper bar controller

Taste *f* AKUSTIK key, AUFNAHME push button, COMP & DV *einer Tastatur* button, key, DRUCK, ELEKTROTECH, FERNSEH key, TELEKOM button, key; **Taste-Entf** *f* (*Entfernungstaste*) COMP & DV delete key (*DEL key*)

tasten *vt* DRUCK keyboard, FERNSEH, RADIO key

Taste: **Tastenanordnung** *f* COMP & DV keyboard layout; **Tastenanschlag** *m* COMP & DV keystroke; **Tastenblock** *m* COMP & DV keypad; **Tastenfeld** *nt* AUFNAHME, COMP & DV, FERNSEH, TELEKOM keyboard, keypad; **Tastengeber** *m* TELEKOM keyboard sender

tastengesteuert *adj* COMP & DV key-driven

Taste: **Tastenknopf** *m* KONTROLL button; **Tastenkürzel** *nt* COMP & DV keyboard shortcut; **Tastennummer** *f* COMP & DV key number; **Tastensperre** *f* COMP & DV keyboard locking, EISENBAHN lock and block; **Tastenwahl** *f* TELEKOM push-button dial; **Tastenweg** *m* COMP & DV key travel; **Tastenwiderstand** *m* COMP & DV

key force

Taster *m* ELEKTRIZ push button, LABOR calipers (AmE), callipers (BrE), MASCHINEN calipers (AmE), callipers (BrE), feeler, METROL feeler pin, *Zirkel* caliper (AmE), calliper (BrE); **Tasterzirkel** *m* METROL caliper compasses (AmE), calliper compasses (BrE)

Tast-: **Tastfehler** *m* TELEKOM keying error; **Tastfeld** *nt* COMP & DV, KONTROLL touchpad; **Tastfernsprecher** *m* TELEKOM key-operated telephone; **Tastflächen** *f pl* BAU points; **Tastimpuls** *m* FERNSEH gating pulse; **Tastklick** *m* COMP & DV, RADIO, TELEKOM key click; **Tastknopf-Befehlstafel** *f* ELEKTRIZ push-button control panel; **Tastknopf-Steuertafel** *f* ELEKTRIZ push-button control panel; **Tastkopf** *m* GERÄT sensing head, PHYS probe; **Tastlehre** *f* MASCHINEN, MECHAN caliper (AmE), calliper (BrE); **Tastnase** *f* FERTIG *Spanung* follower; **Tastpegel** *m* FERNSEH key level; **Tastrelais** *nt* RADIO keyer relay; **Taströhre** *f* RADIO *Senderbau* keyer valve; **Tastschalterbetätigung** *f* FOTO push-button operation; **Tastspule** *f* FERTIG probe coil, surface probe coil, PHYS exploring coil, pick-up coil, search coil; **Taststift** *m* MASCHINEN tracer pin

Tastung *f* COMP & DV modulation

Tast-: **Tastverhältnis** *nt* PHYS mark space ratio

Tastwahl *f* TELEKOM push-button dial; **Tastwahlapparat** *m* TELEKOM key telephone set, push-button telephone; **Tastwahlfernsprechsystem** *nt* TELEKOM key telephone system; **Tastwahltelefon** *nt* TELEKOM key telephone set, push-button telephone

Tast-: **Tastzirkel** *m* FERTIG morphy caliper (AmE), morphy calliper (BrE), MASCHINEN caliper compasses (AmE), calliper compasses (BrE), calipers (AmE), callipers (BrE), external and internal calipers (AmE), external and internal callipers (BrE)

Tätigkeit *f* ERGON job, LUFTTRANS agency; **Tätigkeits-und Fehlerbericht** *m* QUAL status report; **Tätigkeitsanforderung** *f* ERGON job demand; **Tätigkeitsbeschreibung** *f* ERGON job description; **Tätigkeitsnachweis** *m* QUAL proof of action

tatsächlich[1] *adj* MECHAN effective, TEXTIL actual

tatsächlich:[2] ~**e Fahrgeschwindigkeit** *f* MECHAN actual running speed; ~**er Flugweg** *m* LUFTTRANS actual flight path; ~**er Parameter** *m* COMP & DV actual parameter; ~**e Spaltlänge** *f* FERNSEH real gap length; ~**e Umlaufgeschwindigkeit** *f* MECHAN actual running speed; ~**er Zustand** *m* KERNTECH actual state

Tau *m* PAPIER dew, WASSERTRANS rope

τ *abbr* (*Relaxationszeit*) AKUSTIK τ (*relaxation time*)

Taubheit *f* AKUSTIK deafness

Taubstummheit *f* AKUSTIK deaf-muteness

Tau: **Taubucht** *f* WASSERTRANS *Tauwerk* fake

Tauch- *pref* FERTIG, KUNSTSTOFF, WASSERTRANS dip; **Tauchbad** *nt* FERTIG immersing bath; **Tauchbeschichten** *nt* FERTIG, KUNSTSTOFF dip coating; **Tauchbeschichtung** *f* KUNSTSTOFF dip coating; **Taucheinfrieren** *nt* VERPACK immersion freezing; **Tauchelektrode** *f* FERTIG dipped electrode

Tauchen *nt* VERPACK immersion coating

tauchen[1] *vt* TEXTIL dip

tauchen[2] *vi* WASSERTRANS dive

Taucher *m* WASSERTRANS diver; **Taucherglocke** *f* WASSERTRANS diving bell; **Taucherkrankheit** *f* WASSERTRANS bends

Tauch-: **Tauchfräsen** *nt* MASCHINEN plunge cutting, plunge milling, plunge-cut milling; **Tauchgerät** *nt* WASSERTRANS scuba; **Tauchglocke** *f* ERDÖL *Tieftauch-*

technik diving bell, METALL bell plunger; **Tauchglokkendurchflußmesser** *m* GERÄT bell flowmeter; **Tauchglocken-Manometer** *nt* FERTIG inverted-bell manometer, GERÄT bell pressure gage (AmE), bell pressure gauge (BrE), bell-type manometer; **Tauchglockenwirkdruckgeber** *m* GERÄT bell-type difference pressure transmitter; **Tauchhärtung** *f* FERTIG liquid hardening; **Tauchheizkörper** *m* ELEKTROTECH immersion heater; **Tauchkammer** *f* FERTIG *Druckguß* gooseneck; **Tauchkern** *m* ELEKTROTECH *bei Relais* plunger; **Tauchkern-Relais** *nt* ELEKTROTECH plunger relay

Tauchkolben *m* BAU, ELEKTROTECH, KFZTECH *Bremsund Kupplungszylinder* plunger, MASCHINEN plunger, plunger piston, ram; **Tauchkolbenmotor** *m* KFZTECH, WASSERTRANS trunk piston engine; **Tauchkolbenpumpe** *f* MASCHINEN, WASSERVERSORG plunger pump

Tauch-: **Tauchlackierung** *f* VERPACK dipping process, immersion painting; **Tauchlöten** *nt* BAU *Hartlötung*, FERTIG dip brazing; **Tauchlötung** *f* MASCHINEN dip soldering; **Tauchmuffel** *f* KER & GLAS immersion muffle; **Tauchöl** *nt* METALL immersion oil; **Tauchprobeverfahren** *nt* METALL dip test technique; **Tauchpumpe** *f* HEIZ & KÄLTE submersible pump; **Tauchschaben** *nt* MASCHINEN plunge shaving; **Tauchschmierung** *f* EISENBAHN, KFZTECH, MASCHINEN splash lubrication; **Tauchsieder** *m* ELEKTRIZ, ELEKTROTECH, HEIZ & KÄLTE, LABOR, MASCHINEN, MECHAN immersion heater

Tauchspule *f* ELEKTROTECH *bei Lautsprecher* moving coil; **Tauchspulenmikrofon** *nt* AKUSTIK, AUFNAHME, PHYS moving-coil microphone

Tauch-: **Tauchstreichverfahren** *nt* VERPACK dip coating; **Tauchteiler** *m* ELEKTRONIK *Mikrowellen* flap attenuator; **Tauchüberziehen** *nt* VERPACK hot-dipping; **Tauchverfahren** *nt* BAU dipping method; **Tauchzählrohr** *nt* HEIZ & KÄLTE liquid flow counter tube; **Tauchzelle** *f* GERÄT immersion cell, WASSERTRANS *U-Boot* ballast tank

tauen *vt* MEERSCHMUTZ *Schiff* tow

Taumelkolbenzähler *m* GERÄT nutating-piston meter

taumeln[1] *vt* FERTIG gyrate

taumeln[2] *vi* MASCHINEN wobble

Taumelscheibe *f* FERTIG Z-crank, swash plate, wabbling disc (BrE), wabbling disk (AmE), wobble plate, MASCHINEN swash plate, wobble plate; **Taumelscheibenmotor** *m* MASCHINEN wobble plate engine; **Taumelscheibenpumpe** *f* FERTIG Z-crank pump

Tau-Neutrino *nt* PHYS *Elementarteilchen* tauon neutrino, TEILPHYS tau neutrino

Tauon *nt* PHYS *Elementarteilchen* tauon

Taupunkt *m* HEIZ & KÄLTE dew point, LEBENSMITTEL dew point, thawing point, LUFTTRANS, MASCHINEN, PAPIER, PHYS dew point; **Taupunkt-Hygrometer** *nt* THERMOD dew-point hygrometer; **Taupunktmessung** *f* KER & GLAS dew-point measurement; **Taupunkttemperatur** *f* HEIZ & KÄLTE, KERNTECH, THERMOD dew-point temperature

Taurin *nt* CHEMIE aminoethionic acid, taurine

Taurochol- *pref* CHEMIE taurocholic

Taurocholat *nt* CHEMIE taurocholate

Tauröste *f* TEXTIL dew retting

Täuschung: **~ durch Nachahmung** *f* ELEKTRONIK imitative deception; **Täuschungssignal** *nt* ELEKTRONIK, RADIO deception signal

Tausend *nt* MATH thousand

tausendfach *adj* MATH thousandfold

Tausend: **Tausendstel** *nt* MATH thousandth

Tau-Teilchen *nt* TEILPHYS tau particle

Tautomer *nt* CHEMIE tautomer

tautomer *adj* CHEMIE tautomeric

Tautomeres *nt* CHEMIE tautomer

Tautomerisierung *f* CHEMIE tautomerization

Tautropfenglas *nt* KER & GLAS dewdrop glass

Tauwasser *nt* HEIZ & KÄLTE condensate

Tauwerk *nt* WASSERTRANS cordage

Taylor: **~sche Entwicklung** *f* MATH Taylor expansion; **~scher Kegel** *m* STRAHLPHYS Taylor cone; **~sche Reihe** *f* MATH Taylor expansion; **~sche Zahl** *f* STRÖMPHYS Taylor number

Tb *(Terbium)* CHEMIE Tb *(terbium)*

TBKZ *abbr (Technisches- und Betriebskontrollzentrum)* RAUMFAHRT TOCC *(Technical and Operational Control Center)* (AmE)

TBP *abbr (Tributylphosphat)* KERNTECH TBP *(tributylphosphate)*

TBP-Verfahren *nt* KERNTECH TBP process

Tc *(Technetium)* CHEMIE Tc *(technetium)*

TCR *abbr (Telemetriesteuer- und Meßsystem)* RAUMFAHRT TCR *(telemetry command and ranging subsystem)*

TD *abbr (theoretische Dichte)* KERNTECH TD *(theoretical density)*

TDI *abbr (Toluendiisocyanat, Toluoldiisocyanat)* KUNSTSTOFF TDI *(toluyene diisocyanate)*

TDM *abbr (Multiplexen mit Zeitteilung, Zeitmultiplexmethode, Zeitmultiplexverfahren)* COMP & DV, ELEKTRONIK, TELEKOM TDM *(time division multiplex)*

TDMA *abbr (Mehrfachzugriff im Zeitmultiplex, nicht gleichzeitiger Mehrfachzugriff)* COMP & DV, ELEKTRONIK, RAUMFAHRT *Weltraumfunk*, TELEKOM TDMA *(time division multiple access)*

TDMA-Terminal *nt* RAUMFAHRT *Weltraumfunk* TDMA terminal

TE *abbr (transversal elektrisch)* ELEKTROTECH, TELEKOM TE *(transverse electric)*

Te *(Tellur)* CHEMIE Te *(tellurium)*

Technetium *nt* *(Tc)* CHEMIE technetium *(Tc)*

Technik *f* MASCHINEN engineering; **neuester Stand der ~** *m* BAU state-of-the-art technique, KONTROLL state of technology

Technisch: **~e Anleitung Abfall** *f* *(TAA)* ABFALL Technical Instruction on Waste Management

technisch: **~e Abteilung** *f* MASCHINEN engineering department; **~e Anforderung** *f* METROL technical requirement; **~er Bericht** *m* FERNSEH technical report; **~e Beschreibung** *f* COMP & DV physical description, EISENBAHN technical instructions; **~e Daten** *nt pl* WASSERTRANS specifications; **~e Daten eines Triebwerks** *nt pl* LUFTTRANS engine ratings; **~es Datenblatt** *nt* KFZTECH specifications sheet; **~e Dichtmasse** *f* KUNSTSTOFF engineering sealant; **~e Einrichtung** *f* BAU equipment; **~e Einschränkung** *f* RAUMFAHRT technological restriction; **~er Fehler** *m* COMP & DV malfunction; **~e Gebäudeausrüstung** *f* BAU building services; **~er Gesichtspunkt** *m* TELEKOM technical viewpoint; **~e Harze** *nt pl* KUNSTSTOFF industrial resins; **~e Kunststoffe** *m pl* KUNSTSTOFF engineering plastics; **~es Modell** *nt* RAUMFAHRT engineering model; **~es Natriumsulfat** *nt* LEBENSMITTEL salt cake; **~e Normen** *f pl* MASCHINEN engineering standards; **~e**

Produktdokumentation *f* SICHERHEIT technical product documentation; ~**e Sicherheitsanforderung** *f* SICHERHEIT technical safety requirement; ~**e Sicherheitsvorschrift** *f* SICHERHEIT technical safety requirement; ~**e Störung** *f* TELEKOM technical breakdown; ~**e Zeichnung** *f* MASCHINEN engineering drawing; ~**e Zwischenlandung** *f* LUFTTRANS technical stop; ~**e Zwischenüberprüfung** *f* RAUMFAHRT intermediate design review

Technisches und Betriebskontrollzentrum *nt (TBKZ)* RAUMFAHRT *Weltraumfunk* Technical and Operational Control Center (AmE) *(TOCC)*

Technologie: ~ **des schnellen Brüters** *f* KERNTECH fast breeder reactor technology; **Technologiestand** *m* KONTROLL state of technology

technologisch: ~**er Durchbruch** *m* RAUMFAHRT technological breakthrough

Teer *m* BAU pitch, tar, KUNSTSTOFF, WASSERTRANS tar; **Teer- und Bitumenkocher** *m* BAU binder heater; **Teeranstrich** *m* KUNSTSTOFF tar coating

teeren *vt* BAU, WASSERTRANS tar

Teer: **Teerkessel** *m* BAU tar boiler; **Teerklumpen** *m* MEERSCHMUTZ tarball; **Teerleinwand** *f* BAU tarpaulin; **Teermakadam** *m* BAU *Tiefbau* tarmac, tarmacadam; **Teerpapier** *nt* VERPACK tarred board; **Teerpappe** *f* BAU tarred felt, VERPACK tarred board; **Teerpech** *nt* KOHLEN coal-tar pitch; **Teersand** *m* ERDÖL *Geologie* tar sand; **Teerspritzgerät** *nt* BAU tar sprinkler; **Teerspritzmaschine** *f* BAU tar sprayer

Teerung *f* BAU tarring

Teflon® *nt* CHEMIE, KUNSTSTOFF Teflon®

Teich *m* KOHLEN, WASSERVERSORG pond

Teiglösung *f* KUNSTSTOFF skimming dough

Teigpreßverfahren *nt* KER & GLAS dough molding (AmE), dough moulding (BrE)

Teil *nt* COMP & DV part, MASCHINEN member, part, MECHAN component; ~ **der Ummantelung** *m* KERNTECH shell section; **Teilabschaltung** *f* KERNTECH *eines Reaktors* partial trip; **Teilamt mit Überbrückungsverkehr** *nt* TELEKOM discriminating satellite exchange; **Teilansicht** *f* KONSTZEICH partial plan, partial view; **Teilantrieb** *m* PAPIER sectional drive; **Teilapparat** *m* FERTIG divider, MASCHINEN dividing apparatus, dividing heads; **Teilaufzeichnung** *f* AUFNAHME half-track recording; **Teilausschnitt** *m* KONSTZEICH cut; **Teilbandcodierung** *f* TELEKOM subband coding

teilbar[1] *adj* MATH divisible

teilbar:[2] ~**e Zahl** *f* MATH composite number

Teil: **Teilbaum** *m* TEXTIL section beam

Teilbild *nt* FERNSEH field; **Teilbildflackern** *nt* FERNSEH field rate flicker; **Teilbildkonvergenz** *f* FERNSEH field convergence; **Teilbildneigung** *f* FERNSEH field tilt; **Teilbildrücklauf** *m* FERNSEH field flyback; **Teilbildschaltung** *f* FERNSEH field gating circuit; **Teilbildselektierung** *f* COMP & DV panning; **Teilbildsynchronisierung** *f* FERNSEH field sync; **Teilbildzentrierungsregelung** *f* FERNSEH field-centering control (AmE), field-centring control (BrE)

Teilchen *nt* AKUSTIK, ELEKTRONIK, KOHLEN, PHYS, TEILPHYS, TEXTIL particle, UMWELTSCHMUTZ particulate material; ~ **kleiner als Atome** *nt* PHYS subatomic particle; ~ **mit kurzer Reichweite** *nt* KERNTECH short range particle; **Teilchenbeschleuniger** *m* KERNTECH accelerator, PHYS, TEILPHYS particle accelerator; **Teilchenbeschleunigung** *f* AKUSTIK particle acceleration; **Teilchenbewegung** *f* PHYS motion of a particle; **Teil-**

chendynamik *f* KERNTECH particle dynamics; **Teilchenfamilie** *f* TEILPHYS particle family; **Teilchenfluß** *m* PHYS particle flux; **Teilchenflußrate** *f* PHYS particle fluence rate; **Teilchengeschwindigkeit** *f* AKUSTIK particle velocity; **Teilchengröße** *f* KERNTECH *in Pulvern,* KUNSTSTOFF, METALL particle size; **Teilchengrößenanalysator** *m* CHEMTECH, KERNTECH PSA, particle size analyser (BrE), particle size analyzer (AmE); **Teilchengrößenmessung** *f* KUNSTSTOFF particle size measurement; **Teilchenklassierung** *f* CHEMTECH particle classification; **Teilchennachweis** *m* TEILPHYS particle detection; **Teilchenpaket** *nt* PHYS bunch; **Teilchenphysik** *f* TEILPHYS particle physics; **Teilchenschnelle** *f* AKUSTIK particle velocity; **Teilchenschwund** *m* KERNTECH *durch Leck* particle leakage; **Teilchenstoß** *m* TEILPHYS particle collision; **Teilchenstoßbereich** *m* KERNTECH range collision; **Teilchenstrahl** *m* TEILPHYS beam of particles; **Teilchenstrahlung** *f* STRAHLPHYS corpuscular radiation; **Teilchenstreuung** *f* TEILPHYS particle scattering; **Teilchentrennung** *f* TEILPHYS particle separation; **Teilchenverstärkung** *f* METALL particle reinforcement; **Teilchenzahl** *f* METALL particle number

Teil: **Teilcontainerschiff** *nt* WASSERTRANS semicontainer ship; **Teildatei** *f* COMP & DV member; **Teildruck** *m* PHYS partial pressure; **Teileherstellung** *f* FERTIG component manufacture; **Teileliste** *f* MASCHINEN parts list; **Teil-Ellipse** *f* GEOM partial ellipsis

Teilen *nt* MASCHINEN dividing, indexing

teilen *vt* BAU split, FERTIG *Teilkopf* index, MATH divide

Teil: **Teilentladung** *f* ELEKTRIZ paramagnetism, partial discharge; **Teilenummer** *f* VERPACK part number

Teiler *m* MATH divisor, METROL *Einheit* submultiple, TELEKOM divider; **Teilerdose** *f* ELEKTRIZ splitter box

Teil: **Teilezuführrutsche** *f* FERTIG loading chute; **Teilezuführung** *f* MASCHINEN hopper; **Teilfarb-Andrucke** *m pl* DRUCK progressive proofs, progressives; **Teilflächenbeschichtung** *f* KUNSTSTOFF pattern coating, strip coating; **Teilfunktion** *f (Z)* PHYS partition function *(Z)*; **Teilgenauigkeit** *f* FERTIG accuracy of indexing; **Teilgesamtheit** *f* QUAL subpopulation; **Teilgraph** *m* KÜNSTL INT subgraph

teilhärten *vt* THERMOD flash-harden

Teil: **Teilkammerkessel** *m* HEIZ & KÄLTE sectional boiler; **Teilkammersystem mit elastischen Schürzen** *nt* WASSERTRANS multiple-skirted plenum chamber; **Teilkanal** *m* ELEKTRONIK subchannel; **Teilkegel** *m* FERTIG *Kegelrad,* MASCHINEN pitch cone; **Teilknoten** *m* AKUSTIK, ELEKTROTECH partial node; **Teilknstrukteur** *m* FERTIG detailer; **Teilkopf** *m* MASCHINEN dividing head, indexing head; **Teilkreis** *m* MASCHINEN dividing circle, pitch circle, MATH limb; **Teilkreisdurchmesser** *m* FERTIG circle diameter, LUFTTRANS pitch circle diameter, pitch diameter; **Teilkurbel** *f* FERTIG index crank; **Teilladung** *f* EISENBAHN part load; **Teillast** *f* KFZTECH part load; **Teillinie** *f* MASCHINEN pitch line; **Teilmaschine** *f* MASCHINEN dividing machine; **Teilmenge** *f* COMP & DV, MATH subset; **Teilmeßbereich** *m* GERÄT partial measuring range; **Teilmodul** *nt* KONTROLL submodule; **Teilmontage** *f* FERTIG subassembling

teilmultiplexen *vt* TELEKOM submultiplex

Teilnehmer[1] *m* COMP & DV, ELEKTRIZ subscriber, TELEKOM Fernmeldnetz user, subscriber; ~ **an Bord** *m* TELEKOM on-board subscriber

Teilnehmer:[2] ~ **erreichen** *vi* TELEKOM obtain a

subscriber

Teilnehmer: Teilnehmeradresse *f* TELEKOM party address; **Teilnehmeranschlußleitung** *f (TNL)* TELEKOM subscriber's line; **Teilnehmerbetrieb** *m* ELEKTRONIK, TELEKOM time slicing; **Teilnehmerbetriebsklasse** *f* TELEKOM class of service; **Teilnehmerdienst** *m* TELEKOM subscriber service

teilnehmereigen: ~e Fernsprech-Handvermittlung *f* TELEKOM private manual exchange

Teilnehmer: Teilnehmerentstörung *f* TELEKOM subscriber service; **Teilnehmergesprächsdichte** *f* TELEKOM subscriber calling rate; **Teilnehmerleitung** *f* TELEKOM loop; **Teilnehmer-Netz-Schnittstelle** *f* TELEKOM user-network interface; **Teilnehmersatz** *m (TNS)* TELEKOM subscriber line circuit *(SLC)*; **Teilnehmerschaltung** *f* TELEKOM line circuit; **Teilnehmersprechstelle** *f* TELECOM substation; **Teilnehmer-Teilnehmer-Information** *f (TNI)* TELEKOM user-to-user information *(UUI)*; **Teilnehmer-Teilnehmer-Zeichengabe** *f* TELEKOM UUS, user-to-user signaling (AmE), user-to-user signalling (BrE); **Teilnehmervermittlungsstelle** *f (TVSt)* TELEKOM access exchange; **Teilnehmer-Zeichengabe-Übermittlungsdienst** *m* TELEKOM user-signaling bearer service (AmE), user-signalling bearer service (BrE)

Teil: Teilnetz *nt* TELEKOM subnetwork; **Teilpipette** *f* LABOR graduated pipette; **Teilproblem** *nt* KÜNSTL INT subproblem; **Teilpunkt** *m* MASCHINEN division point; **Teilrad** *nt* MASCHINEN dividing wheel, division wheel; **Teil-RAM** *m* COMP & DV partial RAM; **Teilraster** *m* FERNSEH field; **Teilreflexion** *f* WELLPHYS *von Lichtwellen* partial reflection; **Teilrute** *f* TEXTIL split rod; **Teilsatz** *m* COMP & DV subset; **Teilschären** *nt* TEXTIL section warping, sectional warping; **Teilschärmaschine** *f* TEXTIL sectional warping machine; **Teilscheibe** *f* MASCHINEN dividing plate, division plate, index dial, index plate; **Teilschere** *f* MASCHINEN dividing shears; **Teilschnecke** *f* MASCHINEN dividing screw, indexing worm screw; **Teilschnitt** *m* KONSTZEICH local section; **Teilschritt** *m* MASCHINEN fractional pitch; **Teilseitenanzeige** *f* COMP & DV part-page display; **Teilsperre** *f* TELEKOM restricted service; **Teilsteigung** *f* MASCHINEN divided pitch; **Teilstrahlungs-Pyrometer** *nt* GERÄT spectrally selective pyrometer; **Teilstrecke** *f* EISENBAHN section; **Teilstreckenübertragung** *f* TELEKOM store-and-forward transmission; **Teilstrich** *m* GERÄT scale division, scale mark, LABOR graduation mark; **Teilstrichabstand** *m* PHYS *Beugungsgitter* spacing; **Teilstromentnahme nach Verdünnung** *f (CVS)* UMWELTSCHMUTZ constant volume sampling *(CVS)*; **Teilsystem** *nt* TELEKOM subsystem; **Teilton** *m* AKUSTIK partial tone; **Teilübertrag** *m* COMP & DV partial carry

Teilung *f* FERTIG *Zahnrad*, MASCHINEN pitch, PHYS *der Wellenfront* division; **Teilungsfehler** *m* FERTIG error of pitch; **Teilungsfläche** *f* BAU jointing plane; **Teilungskorngröße** *f* KOHLEN partition size

Teil: Teilverbrennungsraum *m* KFZTECH antechamber; **Teilverfahren** *nt* MASCHINEN indexing method; **Teilvermittlungsleitung** *f* TELEKOM store-and-forward line; **Teilversetzung** *f* METALL partial dislocation; **Teilvorrichtung** *f* MASCHINEN index center (AmE), index centre (BrE)

teilweise:[1] ~ konstanter Druckveränderer *m* LUFTTRANS cryptosteady pressure exchanger; ~ verkehrsabhängiges Signal *nt* TRANS semitraffic-actuated signal; ~es Öffnen der Vorform *nt* KER & GLAS blank cracking

teilweise:[2] ~ löschen *vt* MEERSCHMUTZ lighten

Teil: Teilwelle *f* TEILPHYS partial wave; **Teilwinkelverhältnis** *nt* LUFTTRANS angular pitch rate; **Teilzeichenfolge** *f* COMP & DV substring; **Teilzeichnung** *f* KONSTZEICH detail drawing; **Teilziel** *nt* KÜNSTL INT subgoal; **Teilzirkel** *m* MASCHINEN, MATH, METROL dividers; **Teilzusammenbau** *m* MASCHINEN subassembly; **Teilzylinder** *m* MASCHINEN pitch cylinder; **Teilzylindermantel** *m* FERTIG *Stirnrad* pitch surface

T-Eisen *nt* METALL T-iron

Tektogenese *f* ERDÖL *Geologie* tectogenesis

Tektonik *f* ERDÖL tectonics

tektonisch[1] *adj* ERDÖL *Geologie* tectonic

tektonisch:[2] ~er Prozeß *m* ERDÖL *Geologie* tectonic process

Tele- *pref* TELEKOM tele; **Telearbeit** *f* TELEKOM tele-working; **Telecine-Maschine** *f* FERNSEH telecine machine; **Teledienst** *m* TELEKOM teleservice

teledynamisch *adj* MASCHINEN teledynamic

Telefax *nt* COMP & DV facsimile, RADIO *(Fax)*, TELEKOM *(Fax)* facsimile *(fax)*; **Telefaxgerät** *nt* COMP & DV, TELEKOM facsimile machine

Telefon *nt* TELEKOM telephone; ~ für MFC- und Impulswahl *nt* TELEKOM dual-signaling telephone (AmE), dual-signalling telephone (BrE); ~ für Wählbetrieb *nt* TELEKOM dial telephone; **Telefonanlage** *f* ELEKTROTECH telephone switchgear; **Telefonanrufbeantworter** *m* TELEKOM answering machine; **Telefonbeamter** *m* TELEKOM telephone operator (AmE), telephonist (BrE); **Telefonbrummer** *m* ELEKTRIZ *erzeugt Störton zur Warnung* growler; **Telefonbuch** *nt* TELEKOM telephone directory; **Telefondienst für Flugzeugpassagiere** *m* TELEKOM skyphone; **Telefondraht** *m* ELEKTROTECH telephone wire; **Telefongespräch** *nt* TELEKOM call, telephone call; **Telefonhörkapsel** *f* AKUSTIK telephone earphone; **Telefoninduktionsspule** *f* ELEKTROTECH telephone induction coil

Telefonist *m* TELEKOM operator, switchboard operator (AmE)

Telefon: Telefonkabel *nt* ELEKTROTECH telephone cable, telephone line; **Telefonkabelpaar** *nt* ELEKTROTECH telephone cable pair; **Telefonkarte** *f* TELEKOM phone card; **Telefonklingel** *f* TELEKOM telephone bell; **Telefonkonferenz** *f* TELEKOM telephone conference; **Telefonleitung** *f* ELEKTROTECH telephone line, telephone wire; **Telefonnetz** *nt* TELEKOM telephone network; **Telefonnummernverzeichnis** *nt* TELEKOM telephone number list; **Telefonrelais** *nt* ELEKTROTECH telephone relay; **Telefonschalter** *m* ELEKTROTECH telephone switch; **Telefonsonderdienst** *m* TELEKOM custom calling service; **Telefonsprechkapsel** *f* AKUSTIK telephone transmitter; **Telefonumschalter** *m* ELEKTROTECH telephone switch; **Telefonvermittlungsschrank** *m* ELEKTROTECH telephone switchgear; **Telefonzelle** *f* TELEKOM telephone box; **Telefonzentrale** *f* ELEKTROTECH telephone switchgear

Telegraf *m* TELEKOM telegraph; **Telegrafenamt** *nt* ELEKTROTECH telegraph exchange; **Telegrafenanlage** *f* TELEKOM telegraph installation; **Telegrafendrähte** *m pl* FOTO *Fehlergebnisse* tram lines; **Telegrafengleichung** *f* PHYS propagation equation; **Telegrafenkabel** *nt* ELEKTROTECH telegraph cable

Telegrafie *f* RADIO telegraphy; **Telegrafierstromschritt** *m* TELEKOM unit

Telegraf: Telegrafleitung *f* ELEKTROTECH telegraph line

Telegramm *nt* ELEKTROTECH telegram, cablegram **Tele-**

grammwähldienst *m (Gentex)* TELEKOM general telegraph exchange *(gentex)*

Tele-: **Teleinformatik** *f* TELEKOM teleinformatics; **Telekonferenz** *f* COMP & DV, TELEKOM teleconference; **Telemarketing** *nt* TELEKOM telemarketing; **Telematik** *f* TELEKOM telematics; **Telemechanik** *f* MASCHINEN telemechanics; **Telemetrie** *f* KERNTECH, MASCHINEN, PHYS, RAUMFAHRT, TELEKOM telemetry; **Telemetriesteuer- und Meßsystem** *nt (TCR)* RAUMFAHRT *Weltraumfunk* telemetry command and ranging subsystem *(TCR)*; **Teleobjektiv** *nt* FOTO narrow-angle lens, tele-lens, telephoto lens; **Telepoint**® *m* TELEKOM *öffentliches Funktelefonsystem von BT* Telepoint®; **Teleschreiben** *nt* TELEKOM telewriting; **Teleshopping** *nt* COMP & DV electronic shopping

Teleskop *nt* RAUMFAHRT, WASSERTRANS telescope; **Teleskopbrücke** *f* LUFTTRANS jetway; **Teleskopgabeln** *f pl* KFZTECH *Motorradfederung* telescopic forks; **Teleskopheber** *m* MASCHINEN telescope jack; **Teleskopmontagearm** *m* MASCHINEN telescopic erector arm; **Teleskopschutz** *m* SICHERHEIT telescopic guard; **Teleskopstoßdämpfer** *m* KFZTECH *Federung, Aufhängung* telescopic shock absorber; **Teleskopverbindung** *f* MASCHINEN telescope joint; **Teleskopwelle** *f* MASCHINEN telescopic shaft; **Teleskopzylinder** *m* MASCHINEN telescopic cylinder

Tele-: **Telesoftware** *f* COMP & DV *BTX* telesoftware; **Teletext**® *m* FERNSEH, TELEKOM Teletext®; **Teletext-Dienst** *m* COMP & DV teletext; **Televertrieb** *m* TELEKOM telesales

Telex *nt* COMP & DV, TELEKOM telex; **Telexplatz** *m* TELEKOM telex position; **Telexvermittlungsstelle** *f* TELEKOM telex exchange

Teller *m* KER & GLAS *Keramik* plate; **Teller- und Kegelradgetriebe** *nt* KFZTECH *Differential* ring and pinion gearing; **Tellerbeschicker** *m* FERTIG disc feeder (BrE), disk feeder (AmE); **Tellerbürste** *f* ABFALL *an Straßenkehrmaschine* circular broom; **Tellerfeder** *f* MASCHINEN disc spring (BrE), disk spring (AmE); **Tellerfederkupplung** *f* KFZTECH diaphragm clutch; **Tellerfederpaket** *nt* FERTIG *Kunststoffinstallationen* spring washer set; **Tellermembrane** *f* FERTIG *Kunststoffinstallationen* plate diaphragm; **Tellermesser** *nt* PAPIER slitter; **Tellermühle** *f* KOHLEN disc mill (BrE), disk mill (AmE); **Tellerrad** *nt* KFZTECH *Triebstrang* crown wheel, *des Ausgleichsgetriebes* ring gear, MASCHINEN crown wheel, face gear, ring gear; **Tellerrad und Ritzel** *nt* KFZTECH ring and pinion; **Tellerschleifer** *m* MASCHINEN disc sanding machine (BrE), disk sanding machine (AmE); **Tellerstößel** *m* KFZTECH flat-bottom tappet; **Tellerventil** *nt* FERTIG poppet valve, HYDRAUL disc valve (BrE), disk valve (AmE), KFZTECH mushroom valve, poppet valve, MASCHINEN disc valve (BrE), disk valve (AmE)

Tellur *nt (Te)* CHEMIE tellurium *(Te)*; **Tellur-** *pref* CHEMIE telluric, tellurium, tellurous

tellur *adj* NICHTFOSS ENERG telluric

Tellurat *nt* CHEMIE tellurate

Tellurid *nt* CHEMIE telluride

tellurig *adj* CHEMIE tellurous

Tellur: **Tellurit** *m* CHEMIE tellurite; **Tellurmesser** *nt* BAU tellurometer; **Tellurnitrit** *nt* CHEMIE tellurium nitrate, ELEKTROTECH tellurium nitride; **Tellurnitrit-Widerstand** *m* ELEKTROTECH tellurium nitride resistor; **Tellurocker** *m* CHEMIE *Mineralogie* tellurite

TEM[1] *abbr (transversal elektromagnetisch)* ELEKTRO-

TECH, TELEKOM TEM *(transverse electromagnetic)*

TEM:[2] **TEM-Mode** *f* ELEKTROTECH, TELEKOM TEM mode

TE-Modus *m* ELEKTROTECH H-mode, TE mode, TELEKOM TE mode

Temperafarbe *f* KUNSTSTOFF distemper

Temperatur[1] *f* AKUSTIK temperament, ERDÖL, PHYS, TEXTIL, THERMOD temperature; **~ von Berührungsflächen** *f* SICHERHEIT *von Maschinen* temperature of touchable surfaces; **~ des schwarzen Körpers** *f* PHYS black body temperature, STRAHLPHYS, THERMOD black body temperature; **~ unterhalb Umgebungstemperatur** *f* MASCHINEN subambient temperature

Temperatur:[2] **~ halten** *vi* KER & GLAS, METALL soak

Temperatur: **Temperaturabfall** *m* THERMOD heat drop, temperature drop

temperaturabhängig[1] *adj* THERMOD temperature-dependent

temperaturabhängig:[2] **~er Widerstand** *m* ELEKTROTECH temperature-dependent resistor

Temperatur: **Temperaturabhängigkeit** *f* THERMOD temperature response; **Temperaturanstieg** *m* PHYS rise in temperature, THERMOD, UMWELTSCHMUTZ temperature rise; **Temperaturanzeige** *f* GERÄT temperature indication; **Temperaturausgleich** *m* THERMOD temperature balance, temperature compensation, temperature equalization, temperature equalizing; **Temperaturausgleichkondensator** *m* ELEKTROTECH temperature-compensating capacitor; **Temperaturausgleichnetz** *nt* ELEKTROTECH temperature-compensating network; **Temperaturbereich** *m* THERMOD temperature range; **Temperaturblitz** *m* KERNTECH thermal flash; **Temperaturcharakteristik** *f* TELEKOM thermal characteristic; **Temperaturdifferenz** *f* THERMOD difference in temperature, offset temperature, temperature difference; **Temperaturdiffusionsverfahren** *nt* KERNTECH temperature cycle; **Temperaturerhöhung** *f* PHYS raising of temperature; **Temperaturerniedrigung** *f* PHYS lowering of temperature; **Temperaturfernüberwachung** *f* THERMOD remote temperature monitoring

temperaturfest *adj* HEIZ & KÄLTE heat-resistant

Temperatur: **Temperaturfühler** *m* GERÄT temperature sensor, THERMOD temperature probe; **Temperaturgefahrenkurve** *f* PHYS, THERMOD critical temperature curve; **Temperaturgefälle** *nt* THERMOD temperature difference, temperature gradient, thermal gradient

temperaturgeregelt[1] *adj* THERMOD temperature-controlled

temperaturgeregelt:[2] **~er Quarzoszillator** *m* ELEKTRONIK temperature-controlled crystal; **~er Schalter** *m* ELEKTROTECH temperature-controlled switch

Temperatur: **Temperaturgrad** *m* PHYS, THERMOD degree of temperature; **Temperaturgradient** *m* THERMOD thermal gradient; **Temperaturkoeffizient** *m* THERMOD temperature coefficient; **Temperaturkoeffizient der Kapazität** *m* THERMOD temperature coefficient of capacitance; **Temperaturkoeffizient des Widerstandes** *m* THERMOD temperature coefficient of resistance; **Temperaturkompensation** *f* GERÄT thermal compensation, THERMOD temperature compensation

temperaturkompensierend: **~er Kondensator** *m* ELEKTROTECH temperature-compensating capacitor; **~es Netzwerk** *nt* ELEKTROTECH temperature-compensating network

temperaturkompensiert: **~e Schattenmaskenaufhän-**

gung *f* FERNSEH temperature-compensated shadow mask mount

Temperatur: **Temperaturkurve** *f* THERMOD temperature curve; **Temperaturleitfähigkeit** *f* STRÖMPHYS diffusivity; **Temperaturleitzahl** *f* HEIZ & KÄLTE, STRÖMPHYS thermal diffusivity; **Temperaturlogging** *nt* THERMOD *Bohrlochmeßtechnik* temperature logging; **Temperaturmesser** *m* THERMOD pyrometer; **Temperaturmeßgerät** *nt* GERÄT pyrometer, temperature measuring instrument, thermal instrument; **Temperaturmeßgerät mit Thermoelement** *nt* GERÄT thermocouple thermometer, thermoelectric thermometer; **Temperaturmeßinstrument** *nt* GERÄT temperature measuring instrument; **Temperaturmeßkreis mit Thermoelement** *m* GERÄT thermocouple-type temperature measurement system; **Temperaturmessung** *f* THERMOD pyrometry; **Temperaturmeßverfahren** *nt* THERMOD temperature logging; **Temperaturmodell** *nt* RAUMFAHRT thermal model; **Temperaturprofil** *nt* THERMOD temperature profile; **Temperaturregelung** *f* THERMOD temperature control; **Temperaturregler** *m* HEIZ & KÄLTE attemperator; **Temperaturschock** *m* ANSTRICH thermal shock; **Temperaturschockprüfung** *f* WERKPRÜF temperature shock test; **Temperaturschockresistenz** *f* ANSTRICH thermal shock resistance; **Temperaturschreiber** *m* GERÄT recording pyrometer, temperature recorder, LABOR thermograph; **Temperaturschwankung** *f* THERMOD temperature fluctuation; **Temperatursicherung** *f* THERMOD thermal link; **Temperaturskale** *f* GERÄT temperature scale

temperaturstabil *adj* THERMOD temperature-stable

Temperatur: **Temperaturtasche** *f* ERDÖL, METROL thermowell; **Temperaturumkehr** *f* THERMOD temperature inversion, UMWELTSCHMUTZ meteorological inversion; **Temperaturunterschied** *m* THERMOD difference in temperature; **Temperaturverhältnis** *nt* THERMOD temperature ratio; **Temperaturverteilung** *f* THERMOD temperature distribution; **Temperaturwechselbeständigkeit** *f* THERMOD resistance to thermal shock; **Temperatur-Zeit-Test** *m* THERMOD *in der Materialprüfung* thermal cycle

Temperguß *m* FERTIG, MECHAN malleable cast iron

temperiert: **~e Tonleiter** *f* AKUSTIK major scale of equal temperament

Temperit *m* METALL sorbite

Tempern *nt* ELEKTRONIK anneal, FERTIG malleablizing, MASCHINEN tempering

tempern *vt* ANSTRICH *Legierungen*, BAU temper, MECHAN anneal, METALL temper, PHYS anneal

Temperofen *m* MECHAN annealing furnace

Tempo *nt* AKUSTIK tempo; **Tempolimit** *nt* TRANS speed limit; **Tempomat** *m* KFZTECH cruise control device

temporär: **~er Staudamm** *m* WASSERVERSORG temporary dam

TEM: **TEM-Welle** *f* ELEKTROTECH, TELEKOM TEM wave

Tender *m* EISENBAHN, MEERSCHMUTZ tender, WASSERTRANS supply vessel, tender

Tensid *nt* CHEMIE, KUNSTSTOFF, LEBENSMITTEL *Seifen und seifenartige Substanzen* surfactant, MEERSCHMUTZ surface active agent, surfactant

Tensor *m* MATH tensor; **Tensorrechnung** *f* MATH tensor calculus

Teppich *m* ERDÖL, MEERSCHMUTZ slick; **Teppichgarn** *nt* TEXTIL carpet yarn; **Teppichgrund** *m* TEXTIL backing; **Teppichgrundgewebe** *nt* TEXTIL backing for carpet;

Teppichunterlage *f* TEXTIL underlay

Tera- *pref* *(T)* METROL tera- *(T)*; **Terabyte** *nt* OPTIK terabyte; **Teraelektronenvolt** *nt* *(TeV)* TEILPHYS tera electron volt *(TeV)*

Terbium *nt* *(Tb)* CHEMIE terbium *(Tb)*

Terephthal- *pref* CHEMIE terephthalic

Terephthalat *nt* CHEMIE terephthalate

Term *m* COMP & DV, MATH term, METROL level, PHYS energy level, term

Termin *m* FERNSEH deadline

Terminal *nt* COMP & DV, ERDÖL *Schiffahrt*, TELEKOM terminal; **~ im Ruhezustand** *nt* COMP & DV dormant terminal; **Terminalbereich** *m* LUFTTRANS terminal area; **Terminaleinheit** *f* COMP & DV terminal device; **Terminalknoten** *m* KÜNSTL INT *eines Baumes* end node, terminal node; **Terminalserver** *m* COMP & DV terminal server

Terminierung *f* KONTROLL *eines Prozesses* termination

Termin: **Terminplaner** *m* COMP & DV dater; **Terminprogramm** *nt* COMP & DV dating program

termolekular *adj* CHEMIE termolecular, trimolecular

ternär[1] *adj* CHEMIE ternary, triple, MATH ternary

ternär[2]: **~e Legierung** *f* METALL ternary alloy

Terpentin *nt* KUNSTSTOFF turpentine; **Terpentinsäure** *f* CHEMIE terebic acid

Terpinen *nt* CHEMIE terpinene

Terpineol *nt* CHEMIE terpineol

Terpinolen *nt* CHEMIE terpinolene

Terpolymer *nt* CHEMIE, KUNSTSTOFF terpolymer

Terpolymeres *nt* CHEMIE terpolymer

Terrainaufnahme *f* BAU land surveying

Terramycin *nt* CHEMIE *Pharmazie* oxytetracycline

tert-Butylalkohol *m* CHEMIE trimethylcarbinol

Tertiär *nt* ERDÖL *Geologie* Tertiary era

tertiär: **~es Brechen** *nt* KOHLEN tertiary crushing; **~e Förderung** *f* ERDÖL tertiary recovery; **~e Rekristallisation** *f* METALL tertiary recrystallization

Tertiär: **Tertiärförderung** *f* ERDÖL EOR, enhanced oil recovery; **Tertiärgruppe** *f* *(TG)* TELEKOM mastergroup; **Tertiärkraftstoff** *m* KFZTECH tertiary fuel; **Tertiärkriechen** *nt* METALL tertiary creep; **Tertiärwicklung** *f* ELEKTRIZ tertiary winding

tervalent *adj* CHEMIE trivalent

Terylene® *nt* CHEMIE, WASSERTRANS *Segeln* Dacron® (AmE), Terylene® (BrE)

Terz *f* AKUSTIK third

Tesla *nt* *(T)* METROL, PHYS Tesla *(T)*; **Teslaspule** *f* ELEKTROTECH Tesla coil

Test *m* AUFNAHME, COMP & DV, FERNSEH, HYDRAUL, KERNTECH, LUFTTRANS, QUAL, RAUMFAHRT test; **~ auf Dauerfestigkeit** *m* LUFTTRANS fatigue test; **~ bei Nullast** *m* KERNTECH zero-power test; **~ ohne Last** *m* KERNTECH zero-power test; **Testabbrand** *m* RAUMFAHRT test firing; **Testanforderung** *f* RAUMFAHRT test specification; **Testanlage** *f* RAUMFAHRT test rig; **Testband** *nt* AUFNAHME test tape; **Testbedingung** *f* QUAL test condition; **Testbild** *nt* FERNSEH test pattern; **Testblech** *nt* HYDRAUL test plate; **Testdruck** *m* HYDRAUL test pressure; **Testeinrichtung** *f* MASCHINEN test rig; **Testelement** *nt* KERNTECH test assembly

Testen: **~ unter Betriebsbedingungen** *nt* MECHAN *Gerät* environmental testing

testen *vt* QUAL test

Tester *m* QUAL tester, testing apparatus

Test: **Testfenster** *nt* COMP & DV test box; **Testflug** *m* LUFTTRANS, RAUMFAHRT test flight; **Testgelände** *nt*

LUFTTRANS test ground; **Testgerüst** *nt* RAUMFAHRT test bed; **Testhubschrauber** *m* LUFTTRANS experimental helicopter; **Test-Isotop** *nt* KERNTECH isotopic tracer; **Testkunde** *m* QUAL test customer; **Testliner** *m* VERPACK *für Wellpappe* test liner board; **Testmaterial für Acryl** *nt* VERPACK acrylic tester; **Testmuster** *nt* COMP & DV, ELEKTRONIK *zur Verwendung bei Logikanalysatoren* test pattern; **Testpilot** *m* LUFTTRANS test pilot; **Testplatte** *f* AUFNAHME test record; **Testprogramm** *nt* COMP & DV benchmark, test program, MASCHINEN test schedule; **Testprotokoll** *nt* QUAL test log; **Testschuß** *m* RAUMFAHRT test firing; **Testsendung** *f* FERNSEH test transmission; **Teststrecke** *f* TRANS test section; **Teststreifen** *m* FOTO test strip; **Testumgebung** *f* COMP & DV test bed; **Testverfahren** *nt* MASCHINEN *für Bremsanlagen* test procedure; **Testwert** *m* GERÄT test value

TE/TM-Schwingungsmodus *m* PHYS TE/TM mode

Tetra- *pref* CHEMIE tetra-

Tetrabor- *pref* CHEMIE *Säure* pyroboric

Tetra-: **Tetrabromethan** *nt* CHEMIE tetrabromoethane; **Tetrabromethylen** *nt* CHEMIE tetrabromoethylene; **Tetrabromid** *nt* CHEMIE tetrabromide; **Tetracen** *nt* CHEMIE naphthacene, tetrazene; **Tetrachlorethylen** *nt* CHEMIE perchloroethylene, tetrachloroethylene; **Tetrachlorid** *nt* CHEMIE tetrachloride; **Tetrachlorkohlenstoff** *m* CHEMIE tetrachloromethane; **Tetrachlormethan** *nt* CHEMIE carbon tetrachloride, tetrachloromethane; **Tetrachloroplatinat** *nt* CHEMIE tetrachloroplatinate; **Tetrachord** *m* AKUSTIK tetrachord; **Tetradecan-** *pref* CHEMIE *Säure* tetradecanoic; **Tetraeder** *nt* GEOM tetrahedron

Tetraethyl- *pref* CHEMIE tetraethyl; **Tetraethylblei** *nt* CHEMIE lead tetraethyl, tetraethyl lead, tetraethylplumbane, KFZTECH tetraethyl lead

tetragonal: **~es System** *nt* METALL tetragonal system

Tetra-: **Tetrahydrid** *nt* CHEMIE pyrrolidine, tetrahydropyrrol, tetrahydride; **Tetrahydrooxazin** *nt* CHEMIE morpholine, tetrahydrooxazine; **Tetrahydropyrrol** *nt* CHEMIE pyrrolidine, tetrahydropyrrol

Tetraiod- *pref* CHEMIE tetraiod; **Tetraiodfluorescein** *nt* CHEMIE iodeosin, tetraiodofluorescein; **Tetraiodoaurat** *nt* CHEMIE iodoaurate, tetraiodoaurate; **Tetraiodthyronin** *nt* CHEMIE thyroxine

Tetra-: **Tetrakistriwolframatophosphat** *nt* CHEMIE phosphatododecatungstate, phosphotungstate; **Tetralin** *nt* CHEMIE tetralin

tetramer *adj* CHEMIE tetrameric

Tetramethyl- *pref* CHEMIE tetramethyl; **Tetramethylenimin** *nt* CHEMIE pyrrolidine, tetramethylenimine; **Tetramethylethylenglycol** *nt* CHEMIE pinacol, pinacone, tetramethylethyleneglycol

Tetra-: **Tetramin** *nt* CHEMIE tetramine; **Tetranitro-N-Methylanilin** *nt* CHEMIE tetryl; **Tetraoxomolybdat** *nt* CHEMIE molybdate, tetraoxomolybdate; **Tetraoxygen** *nt* CHEMIE oxozone; **Tetra Pak®** *m* LEBENSMITTEL, VERPACK Tetra Pak®; **Tetrasulfid** *nt* CHEMIE tetrasulfide (AmE), tetrasulphide (BrE); **Tetrathion-** *pref* CHEMIE tetrathionic

tetravalent *adj* CHEMIE quadrivalent, tetravalent

Tetra-: **Tetravalenz** *f* CHEMIE quadrivalence, tetravalence, tetravalency; **Tetrazin** *nt* CHEMIE tetrazine; **Tetrazol** *nt* CHEMIE tetrazole

Tetrode *f* ELEKTRONIK tetrode tube, tetrode, PHYS, RADIO tetrode; **~ ohne Kennlinienknick** *f* RADIO kinkless tetrode

Tetrol- *pref* CHEMIE tetrolic

Tetrose *f* CHEMIE tetrose

Tetroxid *nt* CHEMIE tetroxide

Tetroxo- *pref* CHEMIE silicic; **Tetroxokieselsäure** *f* CHEMIE orthosilicic acid, silicic acid, tetrasilicic acid; **Tetroxoosmat** *nt* CHEMIE osmate, tetraoxoosmate; **Tetroxosilicat** *nt* CHEMIE orthosilicate, tetraoxosilicate

Tetryl *nt* CHEMIE tetralite

TeV *abbr* *(Teraelektronenvolt)* TEILPHYS TeV *(tera electron volt)*

TE-Welle *f* ELEKTROTECH, TELEKOM H-wave, TE wave

Text *m* COMP & DV *auch E-Mail*, DRUCK text; **Textanfang** *m (STX)* COMP & DV start of text *(STX)*; **Textanwendung** *f* COMP & DV text management; **Textaufbereitung** *f* COMP & DV, DRUCK text editing; **Textaufbereitungsprogramm** *nt* COMP & DV, DRUCK text editor; **Textbaustein** *m* COMP & DV, DRUCK text segment; **Textbearbeitung** *f* COMP & DV, DRUCK text editing, text manipulation; **Textbildschirm** *m* COMP & DV, DRUCK text screen; **Textdatei** *f* COMP & DV, DRUCK text file; **Texteditor** *m* COMP & DV, DRUCK text editor; **Textende** *nt* COMP & DV end of text; **Textformatierer** *m* COMP & DV, DRUCK text formatter

Textil- *pref* TEXTIL textile; **Textilabfall** *m* ABFALL textile waste; **Textiletikettierung** *f* TEXTIL textile labeling (AmE), textile labelling (BrE); **Textilglasfaser** *f* TEXTIL textile glass fiber (AmE), textile glass fibre (BrE); **Textilgurt** *m* MASCHINEN fabric belt; **Textilriemen** *m* FERTIG woven fabric belt, MASCHINEN fabric belt; **Textilstaubsammler** *m* SICHERHEIT fabric dust collector; **Textilverbundstoffe** *m pl* TEXTIL nonwovens

textilverstärkt: **~es Papier** *nt* PAPIER reinforced paper

Text: **Textkomprimierung** *f* COMP & DV, DRUCK text compression; **Textpostfach** *nt* TELEKOM text mailbox; **Textspeicher** *m* COMP & DV, DRUCK text storage; **Textspur** *f* AUFNAHME narration track

Textur *f* KÜNSTL INT *eines Objekts oder Bildes* texture; **Texturgarn** *nt* KER & GLAS textured yarn

texturiert: **~es Pflanzeneiweiß** *nt* LEBENSMITTEL textured vegetable protein; **~es Pflanzenprotein** *nt (TPP)* LEBENSMITTEL textured vegetable protein *(TVP)*

Text: **Textverarbeitung** *f* COMP & DV, DRUCK WP, word processing, text processing; **Textverarbeitungsprogramm** *nt* COMP & DV word processing package; **Textverarbeitungssystem** *nt* COMP & DV, DRUCK word processor; **Textzeiger** *m* COMP & DV pointer, *Cursor in Form von senkrechtem Strich* text pointer, DRUCK pointer, text pointer

Tf *abbr* AUFNAHME *(Tonfrequenz)* AF *(audio frequency)*, AUFNAHME *(Trägerfrequenz)* CF *(carrier frequency)*, ELEKTRONIK *(Tonfrequenz)* AF *(audio frequency)*, ELEKTRONIK *(Trägerfrequenz)* CF *(carrier frequency)*, FERNSEH *(Tonfrequenz)* AF *(audio frequency)*, FERNSEH *(Trägerfrequenz)* CF *(carrier frequency)*, RADIO *(Tonfrequenz)* AF *(audio frequency)*

TFEL *abbr* *(Dünnschicht-Elektrolumineszenz)* ELEKTRONIK TFEL *(thin film electroluminescence)*

TFEL-Anzeigetechnik *f* ELEKTRONIK TFEL display technology

T-Flipflop *nt* ELEKTRONIK T-flip-flop

T-förmig: **~er Koppler** *m (T-Koppler)* OPTIK, TELEKOM tee coupler *(T-coupler)*; **~e Nut** *f (T-Nut)* FERTIG, MASCHINEN tee slot *(T-slot)*; **~e Nutenschraube** *f* MASCHINEN tee bolt; **~es Spleiß** *nt* ELEKTRIZ tee joint; **~es Stück** *nt* MASCHINEN T, T-piece; **~es Teil** *nt* MA-

SCHINEN tee; ~e **Verbindung** f (T-Verbindung) BAU tee piece union (T-piece union)
TF-Störung f ELEKTRONIK, RADIO, TELEKOM AFI (audio-frequency interference)
TG abbr (Tertiärgruppe) TELEKOM mastergroup
T-Glied nt TELEKOM T-network
Tg-Wert m KUNSTSTOFF glass transition temperature
Th (Thorium) CHEMIE Th (thorium)
T^1/$_2$ abbr (Halbwertszeit) KERNTECH, PHYS, STRAHLPHYS, TEILPHYS T^1/$_2$ (half-life)
Thallium nt (Tl) CHEMIE thallium (Tl); **Thallium-** pref CHEMIE thallic, thallium
Thebain nt CHEMIE dimethylmorphine, paramorphine, thebaine
Theobromin nt CHEMIE dimethylxanthine, theobromine
Theodolit m BAU transit, Vermessung theodolite
Theophyllin nt CHEMIE theophylline
Theorem nt MATH, PHYS theorem
theorembeweisend: ~es **Programm** nt KÜNSTL INT theorem prover
Theorem: Theorembeweiser m KÜNSTL INT theorem prover
theoretisch: ~e **Bedingungen** f pl TRANS ideal conditions; ~e **Dichte** f (TD) KERNTECH theoretical density (TD); ~e **Grenzfrequenz** f ELEKTRONIK theoretical cut-off frequency; ~es **Kraftstoff-Luft-Verhältnis** nt KFZTECH ideal mixture ratio; ~e **maximale numerische Apertur** f OPTIK, TELEKOM maximum theoretical numerical aperture; ~es **Mischungsverhältnis** nt KFZTECH ideal mixture ratio, perfect mixture ratio
Theorie: ~ **der elektroschwachen Wechselwirkung** f TEILPHYS electroweak theory; ~ **der großen Vereinigung aller Kräfte** f PHYS GUT, grand unified theory; ~ **laminarer Strömungen** f STRÖMPHYS laminar flow theory; ~ **transzendenter Zahlen** f MATH theory of transcendental numbers
thermalisieren vt CHEMIE thermalize
Thermalisierung: ~ **von Neutronen** f STRAHLPHYS, TEILPHYS neutron thermalization
Thermalquelle f THERMOD thermal spring
Thermalruß m KUNSTSTOFF thermal black, thermal carbon black
Thermion nt THERMOD thermion; **Thermionen-Elektronenröhre** f ELEKTRONIK hot-cathode tube; **Thermionenröhre** f ELEKTRONIK hot-cathode tube
thermionisch[1] adj THERMOD thermionic
thermionisch:[2] ~e **Emission** f STRAHLPHYS thermionic emission; ~e **Strahlung** f STRAHLPHYS thermionic emission; ~e **Umwandlung** f KERNTECH thermionic conversion
thermisch[1] adj THERMOD thermal, thermic; ~ **stabil** adj THERMOD heat-stable
thermisch:[2] ~e **Alterung** f KUNSTSTOFF heat ageing (BrE), heat aging (AmE); ~ **angeregte Strömungen** f pl STRÖMPHYS thermal flows; ~er **Ausdehnungskoeffizient** m MECHAN, PHYS coefficient of thermal expansion; ~e **Behaglichkeitszone** f ERGON thermal comfort zone; ~e **Behandlung** f TEXTIL baking; ~e **Diffusion** f THERMOD thermodiffusion; ~e **Eigenschaften** f pl THERMOD thermal properties; ~e **Emission** f ELEKTROTECH thermionic emission; ~es **Empfängerrauschen** nt TELEKOM thermal noise ratio; ~e **Ersatzschaltung** f THERMOD equivalent thermal network; ~ **erzeugter Auftrieb** m UMWELTSCHMUTZ thermally-induced buoyancy; ~er **Generator** m ELEKTROTECH thermionic generator; ~ **gepumpter Laser** m

ELEKTRONIK thermally-pumped laser; ~er **Gleichrichter** m ELEKTROTECH thermionic rectifier; ~e **Gleichrichtung** f ELEKTROTECH thermionic rectification; ~e **Indifferenzzone** f ERGON thermal indifference zone; ~e **Kontraktion** f THERMOD contraction due to cold; ~e **Konversion** f ELEKTROTECH thermionic conversion; ~er **Konverter** m ELEKTROTECH thermionic converter; ~e **Nachverbrennung** f KFZTECH thermal post-combustion; ~e **Neutralzone** f ERGON thermal neutral zone; ~es **Neutron** nt PHYS slow neutron; ~er **Nutzfaktor** m PHYS thermal utilization factor; ~e **Schneidspitze** f THERMOD thermic lance; ~e **Stabilität** f KUNSTSTOFF, VERPACK heat stability; ~es **Telefon** nt AKUSTIK thermophone; ~e **Trennung von ^{2}He und ^{3}He** f KERNTECH in flüssigem Helium heat flush; ~es **Ungleichgewicht** nt THERMOD thermal imbalance; ~es **Verbrennungsverfahren** nt ABFALL incineration train; ~e **Wandlung** f ELEKTROTECH thermionic conversion; ~e **Wechselbeanspruchung** f KUNSTSTOFF thermal cycling; ~ **wirksame Masse** f THERMOD thermal mass; ~e **Zersetzung** f ABFALL pyrolysis, THERMOD decomposition by heat; ~e **Zufallsbewegung** f STRAHLPHYS strahlender Atome random thermal motion
Thermistor m ELEKTROTECH, PHYS, TELEKOM thermistor; **Thermistorbrücke** f ELEKTROTECH thermistor bridge; **Thermistormeßkopf** m ELEKTROTECH thermistor mount; **Thermistorregler** m ELEKTROTECH thermistor control
Thermit nt CHEMIE, METALL thermite; **Thermit-Schienenschweißung** f EISENBAHN thermal rail welding; **Thermitschmelzschweißen** nt FERTIG aluminothermic fusion welding, nonpressure thermic welding; **Thermitschweißen** nt FERTIG, MECHAN aluminothermic welding
Thermo- pref ELEKTRONIK, RAUMFAHRT, THERMOD thermal; **Thermoabbau** m ABFALL, KUNSTSTOFF thermal decomposition; **Thermoabschalten** nt ELEKTRONIK thermal shutdown; **Thermoabstimmung** f ELEKTRONIK thermal tuning; **Thermoanalyse** f THERMOD thermal analysis, thermoanalysis; **Thermoausblühen** nt ELEKTRONIK thermal blooming; **Thermobatterie** f ELEKTROTECH thermal battery, RAUMFAHRT thermopile; **Thermobehälter** m THERMOD insulated container; **Thermobild** nt THERMOD thermal imaging sight; **Thermobrutreaktor** m KERNTECH thermal breeding reactor; **Thermochemie** f CHEMIE thermochemistry; **Thermodifferentialmelder** m THERMOD rate-of-rise detector
Thermodiffusion f PHYS thermal diffusion; **Thermodiffusionsfaktor** m PHYS thermal diffusion ratio; **Thermodiffusions-Koeffizient** m PHYS thermal diffusion coefficient; **Thermodiffusionskonstante** f (aT) PHYS thermal diffusion constant (aT); **Thermodiffusionsverfahren** nt PHYS thermal diffusion process; **Thermodiffusionszahl** f PHYS thermal diffusion factor
Thermo-: Thermodiffusivität f HEIZ & KÄLTE thermal diffusivity; **Thermodiode** f ELEKTRONIK thermal diode; **Thermodissoziation** f THERMOD thermal decomposition, thermal dissociation; **Thermodrucker** m COMP & DV electrothermal printer, DRUCK thermal printer, VERPACK thermal transfer printer; **Thermodurchbruch** m ELEKTRONIK Halbleiter thermal breakdown; **Thermodynamik** f THERMOD thermodynamics
thermodynamisch[1] adj THERMOD thermodynamic
thermodynamisch:[2] ~e **Funktion** f THERMOD thermody-

namic function; ~es **Potential** nt THERMOD thermodynamic potential; ~es **System** nt THERMOD thermodynamic system; ~e **Temperatur** f HYDRAUL (θ) absolute temperature (θ), PHYS (T), THERMOD (θ) absolute temperature, empirical temperature, thermodynamic temperature; ~er **Vorgang** m THERMOD thermodynamic process; ~e **Wahrscheinlichkeit** f THERMOD thermodynamic probability; ~e **Zustandsänderung** f THERMOD thermodynamic transformation; ~e **Zustandsgleichung** f THERMOD equation of thermal state, thermodynamic equation of state

thermoelastisch: ~er **Martensit** m METALL thermoelastic martensite; ~e **Verzerrung** f RAUMFAHRT thermoelastic distortion

thermoelektrisch[1] adj ELEKTRIZ thermoelectrical, ELEKTROTECH, PHYS, THERMOD thermoelectric

thermoelektrisch:[2] ~er **Effekt** m ELEKTRIZ thermoelectric effect; ~er **Generator** m ELEKTRIZ thermoelectric generator; ~e **Kälteerzeugung** f HEIZ & KÄLTE thermoelectric cooling; ~e **Konversion** f ELEKTROTECH thermoelectric conversion; ~e **Kraft** f ELEKTRIZ thermoelectric power, thermoelectromotive force; ~es **Kraftwerk** nt ELEKTROTECH thermal-electric power plant, thermal-electric power station; ~es **Kühlelement** nt HEIZ & KÄLTE thermoelectric cooling couple; ~e **Kühlung** f HEIZ & KÄLTE thermoelectric cooling; ~e **Säule** f ELEKTROTECH thermopile; ~e **Sonnenenergieumwandlung** f NICHTFOSS ENERG solar thermoelectric conversion; ~e **Wandlung** f ELEKTROTECH thermoelectric conversion

Thermo-: **Thermoelektrizität** f ELEKTRIZ, PHYS thermoelectricity

Thermoelement nt ELEKTRIZ, KERNTECH, LABOR thermocouple, MASCHINEN thermoelement, PHYS, THERMOD thermocouple; **Thermoelementanschluß-Kompensator** m GERÄT thermocouple potentiometer; **Thermoelementinstrument** nt GERÄT thermocouple instrument; **Thermoelement-Thermometer** nt GERÄT thermocouple thermometer, thermoelectric thermometer

Thermo-: **Thermoemission** f PHYS thermal emission; **Thermofixieren** nt TEXTIL heat setting; **Thermoformen** nt KUNSTSTOFF thermoforming; **Thermoform-Maschine** f VERPACK thermoform machinery; **Thermoform-Verpackungssystem** nt VERPACK thermoforming packaging system; **Thermofühler** m GERÄT temperature sensor, THERMOD temperature probe; **Thermofusionsfaser** f TEXTIL thermobonding fiber (AmE), thermobonding fibre (BrE); **Thermogeschwindigkeit** f PHYS thermal velocity; **Thermogleichgewicht** nt THERMOD thermal equilibrium; **Thermoglühbirne** f KFZTECH thermal bulb

Thermograph m KERNTECH, LABOR thermograph; **Thermographie** f PHYS thermal imaging, THERMOD thermal imaging, Bild thermograph

Thermo-: **Thermogravimetrie** f KUNSTSTOFF thermogravimetry, THERMOD thermal gravimetric analysis

thermogravimetrisch: ~es **Analysiergerät** nt LABOR thermogravimetric analyser (BrE), thermogravimetric analyzer (AmE)

Thermo-: **Thermoinstabilität** f THERMOD thermal instability, thermal runaway; **Thermokapazitanz** f NICHTFOSS ENERG thermal capacitance; **Thermokette** f ELEKTROTECH thermopile; **Thermokomponente** f METALL thermal component; **Thermokonverter** m

ELEKTRIZ, KERNTECH, LABOR, PHYS, THERMOD thermocouple converter; **Thermokopierverfahren** nt KONSTZEICH thermocopying process; **Thermokracken** nt ERDÖL Raffinerie thermal cracking

thermolumineszent adj THERMOD thermoluminescent

Thermolumineszenz f STRAHLPHYS, THERMOD thermoluminescence; **Thermolumineszenz-Dosimeter** nt STRAHLPHYS thermoluminescent dosimeter

Thermo-: **Thermolyse** f THERMOD thermal decomposition, thermal dissociation, thermolysis

thermomagnetisch adj THERMOD thermomagnetic

Thermo-: **Thermomagnetismus** m THERMOD thermomagnetism

thermomechanisch: ~er **Effekt** m THERMOD thermomechanical effect

Thermometer nt GERÄT pyrometer, HEIZ & KÄLTE, LABOR thermometer; ~ **mit Fernablesung** nt HEIZ & KÄLTE remote-reading thermometer; ~ **mit Fernanzeige** nt HEIZ & KÄLTE remote-reading thermometer; **Thermometerglas** nt LABOR thermometer glass; **Thermometerröhre** f PHYS stem

Thermo-: **Thermometrie** f THERMOD thermometry

thermometrisch adj THERMOD thermometric

Thermo-: **Thermoneutron** nt KERNTECH, PHYS, STRAHLPHYS thermal neutron

thermonuklear[1] adj KERNTECH thermonuclear

thermonuklear:[2] ~e **Reaktion** f KERNTECH thermonuclear reaction; ~e **Stromerzeugung** f KERNTECH thermonuclear power generation

Thermo-: **Thermopaar** nt PHYS couple; **Thermophon** nt AKUSTIK thermophone; **Thermophosphoreszenz** f THERMOD thermophosphorescence

thermoplastisch[1] adj FERTIG heat-deformable, KUNSTSTOFF, MECHAN, WASSERTRANS Schiffbau thermoplastic

thermoplastisch:[2] ~er **Kautschuk** m KUNSTSTOFF thermoplastic rubber

Thermo-: **Thermoplastizität** f KUNSTSTOFF thermoplasticity; **Thermoplastkunststoff** m KUNSTSTOFF, SICHERHEIT thermoplastic; **Thermoreaktor** m KFZTECH thermal exhaust manifold reactor; **Thermoreformierung** f ERDÖL Raffinerie thermal reforming; **Thermorelais** nt ELEKTROTECH thermal relay; **Thermosäule** f ELEKTROTECH thermopile, KERNTECH thermal column, PHYS, RAUMFAHRT thermopile, THERMOD thermoelectric pile; **Thermosbehälter** m THERMOD heat-insulated container; **Thermoschalter** m ELEKTROTECH thermal switch; **Thermoschild** m KERNTECH thermal shield; **Thermoschutzschalter** m THERMOD thermal circuit breaker; **Thermosegelflug** m LUFTTRANS thermal soaring; **Thermosicherung** f THERMOD thermal link; **Thermosiphon** m NICHTFOSS ENERG thermosiphon; **Thermospaltung** f ERDÖL thermal cracking; **Thermospannung** f ELEKTRIZ contact potential; **Thermospannungskompensator** m GERÄT thermocouple potentiometer

thermostabil adj THERMOD thermostable

Thermo-: **Thermostabilität** f THERMOD thermal stability; **Thermostat** nt HEIZ & KÄLTE, KFZTECH, PHYS, THERMOD thermostat

thermostat: ~ **gesteuertes Bad** nt LABOR thermostatically-controlled bath

Thermo-: **Thermostatik** f THERMOD thermostatics

thermostatisch[1] adj THERMOD thermostatic

thermostatisch:[2] ~e **Drossel** f LUFTTRANS antisurge baffle; ~ **geregeltes Ventil** nt HEIZ & KÄLTE thermostatically-controlled valve; **~ gesteuerte Ent-wicklungsschale** *f* FOTO thermostatically-controlled developing dish

Thermo-: Thermostatregelung *f* HEIZ & KÄLTE thermostat control; **Thermostatventil** *nt* MASCHINEN thermostatic valve; **Thermosteuerung** *f* RAUMFAHRT thermal control

Thermostrom *m* KERNTECH thermocurrent; **Thermostrommeßgerät** *nt* ELEKTRIZ thermoamperemeter

Thermoumformer *m* ELEKTROTECH bolometer; **Thermoumformerinstrument** *nt* GERÄT thermocouple instrument

Thermo-: Thermoventil *nt* MASCHINEN thermovalve, THERMOD temperature valve; **Thermowaage** *f* CHEMIE thermobalance; **Thermowandler** *m* ELEKTRIZ, KERNTECH, LABOR, PHYS, THERMOD thermocouple converter; **Thermozersetzung** *f* ABFALL, KUNSTSTOFF thermal decomposition

θ *abbr* HYDRAUL *(Wärmewiderstand, absolute Temperatur, thermodynamische Temperatur)* θ *(absolute temperature)*, PHYS *(Wärmewiderstand)* θ *(thermal resistance)*, THERMOD *(absolute Temperatur, thermodynamische Temperatur)* θ *(absolute temperature)*, THERMOD *(Wärmewiderstand)* θ *(thermal resistance)*

θD *abbr (Debyesche Temperatur)* PHYS, THERMOD θD *(Debye temperature)*

θK *abbr (Einsteinsche Temperatur)* THERMOD θK *(Einstein temperature)*

Thévenin: ~scher Satz *m* PHYS Thévenin's theorem

Thevetin *nt* CHEMIE thevetin

Thialdin *nt* CHEMIE thialdine

Thiamin *nt* CHEMIE aneurin, thiamin

Thiazin *nt* CHEMIE thiazine

Thiazol *nt* CHEMIE thiazole

Thiazolin *nt* CHEMIE dihydrothiazole, thiazoline

Thiele: ~ Rohr *nt* LABOR *Schmelzpunkt* Thiele melting-point tube

Thio- *pref* CHEMIE thio-; **Thioaldehyd** *m* CHEMIE thioaldehyde; **Thioalkohol** *m* CHEMIE hydrosulfide (AmE), hydrosulphide (BrE), thiol; **Thioamid** *nt* CHEMIE thioamide; **Thioarsen-** *pref* CHEMIE *Säure* thioarsenic; **Thiocarbamid** *nt* CHEMIE thiocarbamide, thiourea; **Thiocarbanilid** *nt* CHEMIE N, N-diphenylthiourea, thiocarbanilide; **Thiocarbonat** *nt* CHEMIE sulfocarbonate (AmE), sulphocarbonate (BrE), thiocarbonate; **Thiocarbonyldichlorid** *nt* CHEMIE thiophosgene

Thiocyan- *pref* CHEMIE thiocyanic; **Thiocyanat** *nt* CHEMIE thiocyanate

Thio-: Thiodiphenylamin *nt* CHEMIE phenothiazine, thiodiphenylamine; **Thioessig-** *pref* CHEMIE *Säure* thioacetic; **Thioether** *m* CHEMTECH organic sulfide (AmE), organic sulphide (BrE), thioether; **Thioflavin** *nt* CHEMIE thioflavin; **Thiofuran** *nt* CHEMIE thiophene; **Thioglycol-** *pref* CHEMIE mercaptoacetic, thioglycolic; **Thioharnstoff** *m* CHEMIE thiocarbamide, thiourea

Thioindigo *nt* CHEMIE thioindigo; **Thioindigorot** *nt* CHEMIE thioindigo

Thio-: Thioketon *nt* CHEMIE thioketone; **Thiokohlen-** *pref* CHEMIE *Säure* thiocarbonic; **Thiol** *nt* CHEMIE hydrosulfide (AmE), hydrosulphide (BrE), thiol

Thiolat *nt* CHEMIE mercaptide

Thion- *pref* CHEMIE *Säure* thionic; **Thionaphthen** *nt* CHEMIE benzothiophene, thionaphthene; **Thionin** *nt* CHEMIE thionine

Thio-: Thionyl- *pref* CHEMIE thionyl; **Thiopental-** *pref*

CHEMIE thiopental; **Thiophen** *nt* CHEMIE thiophene; **Thiophenol** *nt* CHEMIE penyl mercaptan, thiophenol; **Thiophosgen** *nt* CHEMIE thiophosgene; **Thiosäure** *f* CHEMIE thioacid

Thioschwefel- *pref* CHEMIE *Säure* thiosulfuric (AmE), thiosulphuric (BrE)

Thio-: Thiosulfat *nt* CHEMIE thiosulfate (AmE), thiosulphate (BrE); **Thioxanthon** *nt* CHEMIE thioxanthone; **Thioxen** *nt* CHEMIE thioxene

thixotrop *adj* CHEMIE, KUNSTSTOFF, PHYS thixotropic

Thixotropie *f* CHEMIE, KOHLEN, PHYS thixotropy

Thomas: Thomasbirne *f* FERTIG basic Bessemer converter, basic converter; **Thomasroheisen** *nt* FERTIG basic Bessemer pig; **Thomas-Schlacke** *f* METALL Thomas's slag; **Thomasstahl** *m* FERTIG basic Bessemer steel, basic converter steel, METALL basic Bessemer steel; **Thomasverfahren** *nt* FERTIG basic Bessemer process

Thomson: ~sche Brücke *f* ELEKTRIZ, ELEKTROTECH Kelvin bridge, Thomson bridge; **~sche Doppelbrücke** *f* ELEKTRIZ double Thomson bridge; **~scher Effekt** *m* PHYS Thomson effect; **~scher Koeffizient** *m* PHYS Thomson coefficient; **~sche Meßbrücke** *f* ELEKTROTECH Kelvin bridge; **~sche Streuung** *f* PHYS Thomson scattering; **~scher Wirkungsquerschnitt** *m* PHYS Thomson cross-section

Thorianit *m* CHEMIE thorianite

thoriert: ~er Wolframfaden *m* ELEKTROTECH thoriated tungsten filament

Thorit *m* KERNTECH thorite

Thorium *nt (Th)* CHEMIE thorium *(Th)*; **Thorium-** *pref* CHEMIE thoric; **Thoriumdioxid** *nt* CHEMIE thoria; **Thoriumreaktor** *m* KERNTECH thorium-fueled reactor (AmE), thorium-fuelled reactor (BrE); **Thoriumreihe** *f* STRAHLPHYS thorium series

Thread *m* COMP & DV thread

Threose *f* CHEMIE threose

Thujan *nt* CHEMIE sabinane, thujane

Thujen *nt* CHEMIE sabinene, thujene

Thujenol *nt* CHEMIE sabinol, thujenol, thujol

Thujon *nt* CHEMIE oxosabinane, thujone

Thujylalkohol *m* CHEMIE thujyl alcohol

Thulium *nt (Tm)* CHEMIE thulium *(Tm)*

Thymiancampher *m* CHEMIE thymol

Thymol *nt* CHEMIE thymol; **Thymolphthalein** *nt* CHEMIE thymolphthalein

Thyratron *nt* CHEMIE, PHYS thyratron

Thyristor *m* ELEKTRIZ, ELEKTRONIK, ELEKTROTECH, PHYS, TELEKOM thyristor; **Thyristor-Abstimmtransformator** *m* ELEKTROTECH SCR trimmer transformer; **Thyristordiode** *f* ELEKTRONIK diode thyristor; **Thyristor-Koppelpunkt** *m* TELEKOM SCR crosspoint, silicon-controlled rectifier crosspoint; **Thyristor-Regelung** *f* ELEKTROTECH SCR regulation; **Thyristor-Regler** *m* ELEKTROTECH SCR regulator; **Thyristor-Vorregelung** *f* ELEKTROTECH SCR preregulation; **Thyristor-Vorregler** *m* ELEKTROTECH SCR preregulator; **Thyristorwandler** *m* ELEKTROTECH SCR converter; **Thyristor-Wechselrichter** *m* ELEKTRIZ thyristor inverter

Thyronin *nt* CHEMIE *Biochemie* thyronine

Thyroxin *nt* CHEMIE thyroxine

Ti *(Titan)* CHEMIE Ti *(titanium)*

Tide *f* WASSERTRANS tide; **Tideablauf** *m* NICHTFOSS ENERG ebb tide; **Tidenanstieg** *m* WASSERTRANS *Gezeiten* rise of tide; **Tidenbecken** *nt* WASSERTRANS tidal dock; **Tidenfall** *m* WASSERTRANS fall of the tide; **Tiden-**

gebiet *nt* MEERSCHMUTZ *Zone zwischen Hoch- und Niedrigwasser* intertidal zone; **Tidenhub** *m* WASSERTRANS tidal range, *Gezeiten* range of tide; **Tidenniedrigwasser** *nt* WASSERTRANS low tide; **Tidensignale** *nt pl* WASSERTRANS tidal signals, tide signals; **Tidenstrich** *m* WASSERTRANS tide gate; **Tidentafeln** *f pl* WASSERTRANS tide tables

Tief *nt* NICHTFOSS ENERG fairway, WASSERTRANS *Wetterkunde* low; **Tief-** *pref* DRUCK, WASSERTRANS deep

tief: **~es Fehlerfach** *nt* ELEKTRONIK *Sortiergerät* deep rejection trap; **~es Grundwasser** *nt* WASSERVERSORG deep groundwater; **~-inelastischer Stoß** *m* KERNTECH deep inelastic collision; **~er kosmischer Raum** *m* RAUMFAHRT deep space; **~er Polierkratzer** *m* KER & GLAS deep sleek; **~es Probenschälchen** *nt* KERNTECH well-type planchet; **~er Spannungseinbruch** *m* ELEKTRONIK *Hochfrequenztechnik* deep fading; **~ ultraviolette Strahlung** *f* ELEKTROTECH deep ultraviolet radiation; **~e Wassersäule** *f* NICHTFOSS ENERG low head; **~er Wasserstollen** *m* WASSERVERSORG deep adit; **~er Weltraum** *m* RAUMFAHRT far space

Tief-: **Tiefätzbad** *nt* KER & GLAS deep-etching bath

tiefätzen *vt* FERTIG deep-etch

Tief-: **Tiefätzpaste** *f* KER & GLAS deep-etching paste; **Tiefbagger** *m* MEERSCHMUTZ backhoe; **Tiefbauingenieur** *m* BAU civil engineer; **Tiefbaukohle** *f* KOHLEN deep-mining coal; **Tiefbettfelge** *f* KFZTECH *Rad* drop center rim (AmE), drop centre rim (BrE); **Tiefbettlader** *m* BAU low-bed trailer, low-boy trailer; **Tiefbettrahmen** *m* KFZTECH *Fahrgestell* drop bed frame

tiefbohren *vt* FERTIG deep-bore

Tief-: **Tiefbohrloch** *nt* KOHLEN well drill hole; **Tiefbrunnen** *m* WASSERVERSORG deep well; **Tiefdecker** *m* LUFTTRANS low-wing plane

Tiefdruck *m* DRUCK gravure, intaglio, intaglio printing, KER & GLAS intaglio; **Tiefdruckätzung** *f* DRUCK intaglio etching; **Tiefdruckgebiet** *nt* WASSERTRANS low-pressure area; **Tiefdruckrinne** *f* WASSERTRANS *Wetterkunde* trough

Tiefe *f* HYDRAUL *(t)* depth *(d)*, WASSERTRANS *Schiff, See* depth

Tief-: **Tiefeinbrandelektode** *f* FERTIG *Schweißen* deep-penetration electrode

Tiefe: **Tiefenanschlag** *m* FERTIG depth-control stop, MASCHINEN depth stop; **Tiefenauslösung** *f* FERTIG depth trip; **Tiefendosis** *f* STRAHLPHYS depth dose; **Tiefenkarte** *f* WASSERTRANS *Navigation* bathymetric chart; **Tiefenlehre** *f* MASCHINEN, MECHAN depth gage (AmE), depth gauge (BrE); **Tiefenlinie** *f* WASSERTRANS isobath; **Tiefenlot** *nt* WASSERTRANS *Navigation* depth sounder; **Tiefenmaß** *nt* FERTIG, METROL depth gage (AmE), depth gauge (BrE); **Tiefenmeßapparat** *m* MECHAN depth gage (AmE), depth gauge (BrE); **Tiefenmesser** *m* PHYS bathometer, WASSERTRANS *Navigation* depth sounder; **Tiefenmeßlehre** *f* WASSERTRANS *Navigation* bathymetry; **Tiefenmeßschieber** *m* MASCHINEN, METROL vernier depth gage (AmE), vernier depth gauge (BrE); **Tiefenmeßschraube** *f* FERTIG metal depth gage (AmE), metal depth gauge (BrE); **Tiefenmessung** *f* GERÄT depth measurement, METROL depth gage (AmE), depth gauge (BrE), NICHTFOSS ENERG bathymetry; **Tiefenruder** *nt* WASSERTRANS hydroplane, *U-Boot* diving rudder; **Tiefenschärfe** *f* FERNSEH depth of focus, FOTO depth of field, depth of focus; **Tiefenschärfenskale** *f* FOTO depth-of-field

scale, depth-of-focus scale; **Tiefenschrift** *f* AKUSTIK vertical recording; **Tiefensehen** *nt* ERGON depth perception

tiefensichtig *adj* PHYS orthoscopic

Tiefe: **Tiefenskale** *f* FERTIG depth dial; **Tiefensperre** *f* AUFNAHME bass cut; **Tiefensperrfilter** *nt* AUFNAHME bass-cut filter; **Tiefensuche** *f* KÜNSTL INT depth-first search; **Tiefentaster** *m* METROL depth gage (AmE), depth gauge (BrE)

Tief-: **Tiefentladung** *f* ELEKTROTECH deep depletion

Tiefe: **Tiefenwahrnehmung** *f* ERGON depth perception

Tief-: **Tiefgang** *m* WASSERTRANS *Schiff* draft (AmE), draught (BrE); **Tiefgangsmarken** *f pl* WASSERTRANS *Schiffkonstruktion* draft marks (AmE), draught marks (BrE); **Tiefgefrieranlage** *f* HEIZ & KÄLTE quick-freezer; **Tiefgefrieren** *nt* HEIZ & KÄLTE, THERMOD deep-freezing

tiefgefrieren *vt* THERMOD deep-freeze

Tief-: **Tiefgefriergerät** *nt* THERMOD quick-freezer; **Tiefgefrierschrank** *m* HEIZ & KÄLTE upright freezer

tiefgefroren *adj* THERMOD deep-frozen

tiefgehen *vi* WASSERTRANS *Schiff: bestimmter Tiefgang* draw

tiefgekühlt *adj* HEIZ & KÄLTE refrigerated, LEBENSMITTEL deep-frozen

tiefgestellt: **~es Zeichen** *nt* COMP & DV subscript

tiefgezogen *adj* FERTIG deep-drawn, dished

tiefgezogen:[2] **~e Folie** *f* VERPACK deep-drawing foil; **~e Klarsichtfolie** *f* VERPACK deep-drawing film; **~er Verschluß** *m* VERPACK embossing closure

Tief-: **Tiefgründung** *f* KOHLEN deep foundation; **Tiefkühlen** *nt* HEIZ & KÄLTE deep-freezing, freezing, THERMOD deep-freezing

tiefkühlen *vt* HEIZ & KÄLTE refrigerate, *von Lebensmitteln* freeze, THERMOD deep-freeze, freeze

Tief-: **Tiefkühlfahrzeug** *nt* HEIZ & KÄLTE freezing trawler; **Tiefkühlgerät** *nt* HEIZ & KÄLTE domestic freezer, freezer, frozen-food cabinet; **Tiefkühlkonzentration** *f* HEIZ & KÄLTE cryoconcentration; **Tiefkühlkost** *f* LEBENSMITTEL quick-frozen food, VERPACK deep-frozen food; **Tiefkühlmittel** *nt* HEIZ & KÄLTE freezing medium; **Tiefkühlprodukt** *nt* VERPACK frozen product; **Tiefkühltechnik** *f* HEIZ & KÄLTE cryoengineering; **Tiefkühltruhe** *f* HEIZ & KÄLTE chest freezer, THERMOD deep freeze; **Tiefkühlung** *f* HEIZ & KÄLTE superchilling; **Tiefkühlverfahren** *nt* HEIZ & KÄLTE freezing process; **Tiefkühlzerkleinerung** *f* ABFALL cryogenic process; **Tiefladelinie** *f* WASSERTRANS *Schiff* deep-waterline; **Tiefladewagen** *m* EISENBAHN float, well wagon; **Tieflochbohren** *nt* FERTIG deep-hole drilling, MASCHINEN deep-hole boring, deep-hole drilling; **Tieflochbohrer** *m* FERTIG deep-hole drill, drill bit, gun drill; **Tieflöffelbagger** *m* MEERSCHMUTZ backhoe, TRANS backhoe loader; **Tiefofen** *m* KOHLEN low kiln, METALL soaking pit

Tiefpaß *m* ELEKTRONIK, LUFTTRANS, TELEKOM low-pass; **Tiefpaß-Abtastfilter** *nt* ELEKTRONIK low-pass sampled-data filter; **Tiefpaßfilter** *nt* AUFNAHME, COMP & DV, ELEKTRIZ, ELEKTRONIK, PHYS, TELEKOM low-pass filter; **Tiefpaßfilter zweiter Ordnung** *nt* ELEKTRONIK second order low-pass filter; **Tiefpaßfiltern** *nt* ELEKTRONIK low-pass filtering; **Tiefpaßteil** *m* ELEKTRONIK low-pass section; **Tiefpaß-Verhalten** *nt* ELEKTRONIK low-pass response

Tief-: **Tiefpegel-Gerät** *nt* ELEKTRONIK low-level device; **Tiefpegel-Modulation** *f* ELEKTRONIK low-level modulation; **Tiefpegeltransistor** *m* ELEKTRONIK low-level transistor

tiefrot *adj* METALL bright red

Tief-: Tiefschachtofen *m* KOHLEN low-shaft furnace; **Tiefschnitt** *m* KER & GLAS deep cut

Tiefsee *f* WASSERTRANS *Meer* deep-sea; **Tiefseedock** *nt* BAU deep-water dock; **Tiefseegraben** *m* MEERSCHMUTZ trench; **Tiefseekabel** *nt* WASSERTRANS deep-sea cable, submarine cable; **Tiefseetaucher** *m* WASSERTRANS deep-sea diver; **Tiefseewellen** *f pl* PHYS deep-water waves

tiefst: ~ zulässige Betriebsstellung *f* KERNTECH *von Trimmstäben* lowest permitted operating position

Tief-: Tiefstabilisierung *f* KOHLEN deep stabilization

tiefstehend: ~es Zeichen *nt* DRUCK subscript

Tieftemperatur *f* PHYS low temperature; **Tieftemperaturbeständigkeit** *f* KUNSTSTOFF low-temperature resistance; **Tieftemperaturbrechen** *nt* ABFALL *von Festabfällen* cyrogenic crushing; **Tieftemperaturchemie** *f* HEIZ & KÄLTE cryochemistry; **Tieftemperaturphysik** *f* HEIZ & KÄLTE cryophysics; **Tieftemperaturtechnik** *f* COMP & DV, HEIZ & KÄLTE, PHYS, RAUMFAHRT, THERMOD cryogenics; **Tieftemperatur-Thermometer** *nt* THERMOD low-temperature thermometer; **Tieftemperaturverfahren** *nt* THERMOD low-temperature techniques; **Tieftemperaturzerkleinern** *nt* ABFALL *von Festabfällen* cyrogenic crushing; **Tieftemperaturzerkleinerung** *f* ABFALL cryogenic process, cryogrinding, freeze-grinding

Tief-: Tieftonlautsprecher *m* AUFNAHME woofer; **Tiefungswert** *m* FERTIG cupping ductility value; **Tiefziehblech** *nt* FERTIG deep-drawing sheet; **Tiefziehen** *nt* AUFNAHME cupping, FERTIG, MASCHINEN, MECHAN deep drawing

tiefziehen *vt* FERTIG dish

Tief-: Tiefziehstanze *f* VERPACK deep-drawing machine; **Tiefziehversuch** *m* FERTIG cupping test; **Tiefziehwerkzeug** *nt* MASCHINEN deep-drawing die

Tiegel *m* FERTIG *Gießen* crucible, KER & GLAS pan, LABOR crucible, pan, THERMOD crucible; **Tiegeldruck** *m* DRUCK platen printing; **Tiegeldruckpresse** *f* DRUCK platen press

tiegelfrei: ~es Schmelzen *nt* KERNTECH floating zone melting method

Tiegel: Tiegelkühlofen *m* KER & GLAS pan lehr; **Tiegelofen** *m* FERTIG, LABOR, THERMOD crucible furnace; **Tiegelzange** *f* LABOR crucible tongs

tierisch: ~er Abfall *m* ABFALL animal waste; **~es Fett** *nt* LEBENSMITTEL animal fat; **~e Stärke** *f* LEBENSMITTEL animal starch

Tierleim *m* KUNSTSTOFF, PAPIER animal glue

Tierseuchengesetz *nt* ABFALL Epizootic Diseases Act

Tiglin- *pref* CHEMIE *Säure* tiglic

TIG-Schweißbrenner *m* BAU torch for TIG welding

Tilgungsfähigkeit *f* FERTIG *Schwingen* absorbability

Tilgungszeichen *nt* DRUCK deletion mark

Timbre *nt* AKUSTIK timbre

Timesharing *nt* COMP & DV time-sharing

Timing *nt* KONTROLL timing

Tinnitus *m* AKUSTIK tinnitus

Tinte *f* PAPIER ink; **Tintenfestigkeit** *f* PAPIER ink hold-out

tintenlos: ~es Strahlsystem *nt* VERPACK inkless ink jet system

Tinte: Tintenschreiber *m* COMP & DV pen recorder; **Tintenstrahldrucker** *m* COMP & DV, VERPACK ink jet printer

tippen *vti* COMP & DV type

Tippfehler *m* COMP & DV typo (colloq); **Tippfehlerquote** *f* COMP & DV keying error rate

Tisch *m* FERTIG *Hobelmaschine* platen, *Presse* bed, MASCHINEN platen, table; **~ mit Teileinrichtung** *m* MASCHINEN indexing table; **Tischanschlag** *m* FERTIG table dog; **Tischbewegung** *f* FERTIG working traverse; **Tischbohrer** *m* MASCHINEN bench drill; **Tischbohrer mit Schraubstock** *m* MASCHINEN bench drill with vice (BrE), bench drill with vise (AmE); **Tischbohrmaschine** *f* FERTIG, MASCHINEN bench drilling machine, MECHAN bench drill; **Tischbohrmaschine mit Rundsäule** *f* MASCHINEN bench pillar drilling machine; **Tischcomputer** *m* COMP & DV desktop computer; **Tischdrehbank** *f* BAU, MECHAN bench lathe; **Tischgerät** *nt* COMP & DV desktop computer; **Tischgußverfahren** *nt* KER & GLAS table casting; **Tischhobel** *m* BAU bench plane

Tischlerleim *m* BAU joiner's glue

Tisch: Tischmaschine *f* FERTIG bench-mounted machine; **Tischmikrofon** *nt* AUFNAHME table mike; **Tischrechner** *m* COMP & DV desktop computer; **Tisch-Reproduktionsgerät** *nt* FOTO copy stand **Tischstativ** *nt* FOTO table tripod; **Tischvorschubbewegung** *f* FERTIG table feed motion

Tissue *nt* VERPACK tissue paper; **Tissuepapier** *nt* PAPIER tissue paper; **Tissuepapiermaschine** *f* PAPIER tissue machine

Titan *nt (Ti)* CHEMIE titanium *(Ti)*; **Titanat** *nt* CHEMIE titanate; **Titandioxid** *nt* CHEMIE, KUNSTSTOFF titanium dioxide; **Titandioxidabfall** *m* ABFALL *roter Schlamm* titanium dioxide waste; **Titanium-** *pref* CHEMIE titanic; **Titanlegierung** *f* ANSTRICH, RAUMFAHRT titanium alloy; **Titanoxid** *nt* CHEMIE titanium dioxide; **Titansäureanhydrid** *nt* CHEMIE titanium dioxide; **Titanschmieden** *nt* RAUMFAHRT titanium forging

Titanyl *nt* CHEMIE titanyl

Titel *m* DRUCK title; **Titelblatt** *nt* DRUCK title page; **Titelei** *f* DRUCK front matter, prelims; **Titelfeld** *nt* FERNSEH safe title area; **Titelschalter** *m* FERNSEH title keyer; **Titelschrift** *f* DRUCK display face, display type, titling font; **Titelzeile** *f* DRUCK header

Titer *m* CHEMIE titre, TEXTIL count

Titration *f* ANSTRICH, CHEMIE titration

titrieren *vt* CHEMIE, KOHLEN titrate

Titrierung *f* CHEMIE, KOHLEN titration

Titrimeter *nt* CHEMIE titremeter

Titrimetrie *f* GERÄT titrimetry

T-Koppler *m (T-förmiger Koppler)* OPTIK, TELEKOM T-coupler *(tee coupler)*

Tl *(Thallium)* CHEMIE Tl *(thallium)*

T-Leitwerk *nt* LUFTTRANS *Luftfahrzeug* T-tail

TL-Triebwerk *nt (Turbostrahltriebwerk)* LUFTTRANS turbojet

TM *abbr (transversal magnetisch)* ELEKTROTECH, TELEKOM TM *(transverse magnetic)*

Tm *(Thulium)* CHEMIE Tm *(thulium)*

TM: TM-Modus *m* ELEKTROTECH E mode, TM mode, OPTIK E Mode, TM mode, TELEKOM E mode, TM mode

T-Muffe *f* BAU *Sanitär* T-joint

TMUX *abbr (Transmultiplexer)* TELEKOM TMUX *(transmultiplexer)*

TM: TM-Welle *f* ELEKTROTECH, PHYS, TELEKOM E wave, TM wave

T-Netz *nt* ELEKTROTECH T-network

TNI *abbr (Teilnehmer-Teilnehmer-Information)* TELE-KOM **UUI** *(user-to-user information)*

TNL *abbr (Teilnehmeranschlußleitung)* TELEKOM subscriber's line

TNR *abbr (gesteuerter Thermonuklearreaktor)* KERN-TECH CTR *(controlled thermonuclear reactor)*

TNS *abbr (Teilnehmersatz)* TELEKOM SLC *(subscriber line circuit)*

TNT *abbr (Trinitrotoluol)* CHEMIE TNT *(trinitrotoluene)*

T-Nut *f (T-förmige Nut)* FERTIG, MASCHINEN T-slot *(tee slot)*; **T-Nutenschraube** *f* MASCHINEN T-bolt

Tochter- *pref* STRAHLPHYS daughter; **Tochtergerät** *nt* FERNSEH slave unit; **Tochterkern** *m* STRAHLPHYS daughter nucleus; **Tochterkompaß** *m* LUFTTRANS, WASSERTRANS compass repeater, compass repeater indicator, repeater compass, repeating compass; **Tochterprodukt** *nt* STRAHLPHYS daughter product; **Tochtervideorecorder** *m* FERNSEH slave VCR

Tocopherol *nt* LEBENSMITTEL tocopherol

tödlich: ~e **Konzentration** *f* UMWELTSCHMUTZ lethal concentration; ~e **radioaktive Dosis** *f* KERNTECH, STRAHLPHYS lethal radioactive dose; ~er **Unfall** *m* SICHERHEIT fatal accident; ~e **Wirkung** *f* UMWELTSCHMUTZ lethal effect

Tokamak *m* PHYS tokamak

Token *nt* COMP & DV token; **Token-Bus** *m* COMP & DV token bus; **Token-Ring** *m* COMP & DV token ring; **Token-Ring-Netz** *nt* COMP & DV token ring network, token-passing ring network

Toleranz *f* AKUSTIK, ANSTRICH tolerance, MASCHINEN, MECHAN allowance, tolerance, METROL, QUAL tolerance; **allgemeine** ~ *f* MASCHINEN general tolerance; ~ **des Kerndurchmessers** *f* OPTIK *Lichtleiter* core diameter tolerance; ~ **des Manteldurchmessers** *f* OPTIK *Lichtleiter* cladding diameter tolerance; ~ **der Mittenabweichung** *f* MECHAN concentricity tolerance; **Toleranzbereich** *m* QUAL tolerance zone; **Toleranzgrenze** *f* MASCHINEN tolerance limit, METROL limit of tolerance, QUAL tolerance limit; **Toleranzklasse** *f* MASCHINEN tolerance class; **Toleranzprüfung** *f* COMP & DV MC, marginal check, marginal test

toleriert: ~es **Maß** *nt* KONSTZEICH toleranced dimension

Toluchinolin *nt* CHEMIE toluquinoline

Toluendiisocyanat *nt (TDI)* KUNSTSTOFF toluyene diisocyanate *(TDI)*

Toluidin *nt* CHEMIE aminotoluene, toluidine

Toluonitril *nt* CHEMIE cyanotoluene, toluonitrile

Toluol *nt* CHEMIE, ERDÖL *Petrochemie* toluene; **Toluoldiisocyanat** *nt (TDI)* KUNSTSTOFF toluene diisocyanate *(TDI)*

Toluyl- *pref* CHEMIE toluic

Toluyliden *nt* CHEMIE toluylene

Tolyl- *pref* CHEMIE tolyl

Tomographie *f* KERNTECH, MASCHINEN tomography

Ton *m* AKUSTIK sound, tone, AUFNAHME sound, BAU argil, clay, DRUCK, FOTO tone, HYDRAUL pug, KER & GLAS clay, *Material* adobe, KOHLEN clay, RADIO sound, TELEKOM tone; **Ton-** *pref* AUFNAHME, COMP & DV, RADIO audio

Tonabnehmer *m* AKUSTIK reproducer, AUFNAHME pick-up; **Tonabnehmerarm** *m* AUFNAHME pick-up arm, *beim Plattenspieler* tone arm; **Tonabnehmerkopf** *m* AKUSTIK pick-up; **Tonabnehmerstecker** *m* AUFNAHME phono plug

Ton: Tonabschaltung *f* RAUMFAHRT tone disabler; **Tonabschwächer** *m* ELEKTRONIK audio attenuator;

Tonabstufung *f* FOTO tonal gradation

tonal: ~er **Klang** *m* AKUSTIK tonal note

Ton: Tonalität *f* AUFNAHME tonality; **Tonarchiv** *nt* AUFNAHME sound archive; **Tonarm** *m* AKUSTIK pick-up arm; **Tonart** *f* AKUSTIK key

tonartig *adj* NICHTFOSS ENERG argillaceous

Ton: Tonaufnahme *f* AUFNAHME, TELEKOM sound recording; **Tonaufnahmesystem** *nt* AUFNAHME sound recording system; **Tonaufzeichnung** *f* TELEKOM sound recording; **Tonaufzeichnungsgerät im Cockpit** *nt* LUFTTRANS cockpit voice recorder; **Tonausfall** *m* AUFNAHME audio dropouts; **Tonbalken** *m* AUFNAHME sound bar

Tonband *nt* AKUSTIK magnetic tape, AUFNAHME tape, ELEKTRIZ magnetic tape; ~ **mit Klebestellengeräusch** *nt* AUFNAHME blooping tape; **Tonbandaufnahmegerät** *nt* AUFNAHME recording tape deck; **Tonbanddeck** *nt* AKUSTIK tape deck; **Tonband-Frequenzschallplatte** *f* AUFNAHME tone band frequency record; **Tonbandgerät** *nt* AKUSTIK tape recorder, AUFNAHME magnetic tape recorder, tape deck, FERNSEH audio tape machine; **Tonbandgerät mit zwei Rollen** *nt* AUFNAHME reel-to-reel taperecorder

Ton: Tonbehälter *m* KER & GLAS earthenware tank; **Tondecke** *f* AUFNAHME sound blanket; **Tondreieck** *nt* LABOR *Tiegelhalter* pipeclay triangle; **Toneffekt** *m* AUFNAHME sound boom

Toner *m* DRUCK, KONSTZEICH toner

Tonerde *f* FERTIG alumina

tonerdehaltig *adj* PAPIER aluminiferous

Ton: Tonerdeschleifmittel *nt* ANSTRICH alumina abrasive; **Tonfilter** *nt* ELEKTRONIK audio filter

tonfrequent *adj* ELEKTRONIK audio

Tonfrequenz *f (Tf)* AUFNAHME, ELEKTRONIK audio frequency *(AF)*, sound frequency, FERNSEH audio frequency *(AF)*, sound frequency, RADIO audio frequency *(AF)*, sound frequency; **Tonfrequenzband** *nt* AUFNAHME audio band, COMP & DV voiceband; **Tonfrequenzgenerator** *m* ELEKTRONIK audio oscillator, audio-frequency oscillator, RADIO audio-frequency oscillator; **Tonfrequenzkanal** *m* AUFNAHME audio channel; **Tonfrequenz-Leistungsverstärker** *m* ELEKTRONIK audio power amplifier; **Tonfrequenzmesser** *m* AUFNAHME audio-level meter; **Ton- frequenzrelais** *nt* ELEKTRIZ tuned relay; **Tonfrequenz-Rückkopplung** *f* AUFNAHME audio feedback; **Tonfrequenzsignal** *nt* ELEKTRONIK, RADIO audio-frequency signal; **Tonfrequenz-Signalgenerator** *m* ELEKTRONIK, RADIO audio-frequency signal generator; **Tonfrequenz-Spektrometer** *nt* GERÄT audio- frequency spectrometer; **Tonfrequenzspektrum** *nt* AUFNAHME audible spectrum; **Tonfrequenzstörung** *f* ELEKTRONIK audio-frequency interference, RADIO, TELEKOM audio-frequency interference; **Tonfrequenzstrom zur Aufnahme** *m* AUFNAHME recording audio-frequency current; **Tonfrequenzverstärker** *m* AUFNAHME audio-frequency amplifier, ELEKTRONIK audio amp; **Tonfrequenzverstärkung** *f* ELEKTRONIK, RADIO, TELEKOM low-frequency amplification

Ton: Tongehalt *m* KOHLEN clay content; **Tongemisch** *nt* AKUSTIK complex sound, complex tone; **Tongenerator** *m* AUFNAHME, TELEKOM tone generator; **Tongewinnungsmaschine** *f* KER & GLAS clay-working machine; **Tongrube** *f* KER & GLAS clay works

tonhaltig[1] *adj* NICHTFOSS ENERG argillaceous

tonhaltig:[2] ~er **Bohrschlamm** *m* ERDÖL *Bohrtechnik* clay-base mud

Tonheit f AKUSTIK critical band rate; **Tonheitsmuster** nt AKUSTIK critical band-rate pattern; **Tonheitszeitmuster** nt AKUSTIK critical band-rate time pattern

Ton: **Tonhobel** m KER & GLAS clay cutter

Tonhöhe f AKUSTIK, PHYS, WELLPHYS pitch; **Tonhöhenempfindung** f AKUSTIK pitch sensation; **Tonhöhenfrequenz** f ELEKTRONIK, RADIO, TELEKOM frequency corresponding to pitch; **Tonhöhenschwankung** f AUFNAHME *Jaulen* wow; **Tonhöhen-Unterschiedsschwelle** f AKUSTIK differential threshold of frequency; **Tonhöhenverschiebung** f AKUSTIK pitch shift

tonig adj NICHTFOSS ENERG argillaceous

Ton: **Tonimpuls** m AKUSTIK tone burst; **Tonindustrie** f KER & GLAS clay industry; **Toningenieur** m AUFNAHME audio control engineer; **Tonintervall** nt WELLPHYS *zwischen zwei Noten* musical interval; **Tonkanal** m AUFNAHME, FERNSEH sound channel; **Tonklebestelle** f AUFNAHME blooping patch; **Tonkneter** m KER & GLAS clay kneader; **Tonknetmaschine** f KER & GLAS clay-kneading machine; **Tonkopf** m AUFNAHME audio head, FERNSEH sound head; **Tonkrug** m KER & GLAS earthenware jar; **Tonlage** f AKUSTIK pitch; **Tonlehm** m BAU clay loam; **Tonlehre** f AUFNAHME sonics; **Tonleiter** f AKUSTIK musical scale, scale; **Tonlosung** f WASSERVERSORG clay suspension; **Tonlösung** f FOTO toning solution; **Tonmaskierung** f AKUSTIK aural masking; **Tonmasse** f KER & GLAS clay mass; **Tonmergel** m WASSERVERSORG clay marl, marly clay; **Tonmineral** nt KOHLEN clay mineral; **Tonmischapparatur** f AUFNAHME rerecording machine; **Tonmischer** m KER & GLAS clay mixer; **Tonmischmaschine** f KER & GLAS clay-mixing machine; **Tonmischpult** nt AUFNAHME dubbing console, sound console; **Tonmischraum** m AUFNAHME dubbing room, sound control room; **Tonmischsitzung** f AUFNAHME rerecording session; **Tonmischstudio** nt AUFNAHME dubbing studio; **Tonmischung** f AKUSTIK dubbing; **Tonmodulation** f ELEKTRONIK audio modulation; **Tonmodulierung** f AKUSTIK, AUFNAHME sound modulation; **Tonmühle** f KER & GLAS clay mill

Tonnage f METROL, WASSERTRANS tonnage; **Tonnagegebühr** f METROL tonnage

Tonne f LEBENSMITTEL, MECHAN barrel, METROL gross ton, long ton, metric ton, ton, PHYS, TRANS barrel, WASSERTRANS *Seezeichen* buoy; **Tonnenfeder** f MASCHINEN barrel spring

tonnenförmig: ~e Verzeichnung f FOTO barrel distortion, FOTO, OPTIK *(cf kissenförmige Verzeichnung) einer Linse* barrel-shaped distortion, PHYS barrel distortion, barrel-shaped distortion

Tonne: **Tonnengewölbe** nt BAU barrel vault, tunnel vault, wagon vault; **Tonnenlager** nt MASCHINEN barrel roller bearing, barrel-shaped roller bearing, spherical roller bearing; **Tonnentragfähigkeit** f WASSERTRANS dead-weight tons; **Tonnenverzeichnung** f MECHAN barrel distortion

Ton: **Tonperspektive** f AUFNAHME sound perspective; **Tonplatte** f KER & GLAS earthenware slab; **Tonplattenpresse** f KER & GLAS clay plate press; **Tonqualität** f TELEKOM sound quality; **Tonquelle** f ELEKTRONIK sound source; **Tonregiesystem** nt AUFNAHME *Mischpult* audio console; **Tonrohr** nt BAU earthenware pipe, KER & GLAS clay pipe; **Tonröhre** f KER & GLAS earthenware pipe; **Tonrolle** f AKUSTIK, FERNSEH capstan; **Tonrollenantrieb** m FERNSEH capstan drive; **Tonrück-**

koppelungskreis m FERNSEH audio feedback circuit; **Tonsäule** f AKUSTIK, AUFNAHME sound column; **Tonschlamm** m WASSERVERSORG clay silt; **Tonschleife** f AUFNAHME sound loop; **Tonschneider** m AKUSTIK cutter; **Tonsieb** nt KER & GLAS earthenware sieve; **Tonsignal** nt AKUSTIK audio signal, ELEKTRONIK audio signal, tone signal, FERNSEH, RADIO audio signal, TELEKOM audio signal, sound signal; **Tonsignalisierung** f ELEKTRONIK tone signaling (AmE), tone signalling (BrE); **Tonspur** f AKUSTIK soundtrack, AUFNAHME soundtrack, squeeze track, FERNSEH audio track; **Tonstaub** m KER & GLAS clay dust; **Tonsteuerungsverstärker** m AUFNAHME gating amplifier; **Tonstudio** nt AUFNAHME audio control room, sound studio; **Tonstufe** f AUFNAHME sound stage; **Tonsuspension** f WASSERVERSORG clay suspension; **Tonsystem** nt AUFNAHME sound system; **Tontechnik** f MASCHINEN acoustic engineering; **Tontiegel** m KER & GLAS clay crucible; **Tonträger** m *(TT)* AUFNAHME, FERNSEH sound carrier; **Tonträgerdienst** m TELEKOM audio bearer service; **Tonübertragung** f ACOUST sound transmission; **Tonumfang** m AKUSTIK scale; **Tonung** f FOTO toning; **Tonverstärker** m AUFNAHME audio amplifier; **Tonverteilung** f AUFNAHME sound distribution; **Tonwahl** f *(TW)* TELEKOM multifrequency dialing (AmE), multifrequency dialling (BrE) *(MFD)*; **Tonwalzen** f pl KER & GLAS clay rollers; **Tonwarnanlage** f GERÄT audio alarm system; **Tonwelle** f AKUSTIK capstan; **Tonwert** m FOTO tonal value; **Tonwertwiedergabe** f FOTO reproduction of tonal values

Tonwiedergabe f AUFNAHME tone reproduction; **Tonwiedergabegerät** nt AKUSTIK reproducer; **Tonwiedergabesystem** nt AUFNAHME sound reproduction system

Ton: **Tonziegel** m KER & GLAS clay brick; **Tonzusammensetzung** f KER & GLAS clay composition

Tool nt COMP & DV software tool, tool; **Toolkit** m COMP & DV toolkit

TOP abbr *(Bürokommunikationsprotokoll)* TELEKOM TOP *(technical and office protocol)*

Top-Down- pref COMP & DV top-down; **Top-Down-Methode** f COMP & DV top-down methodology; **Top-Down-Programmierung** f COMP & DV top-down programming; **Top-Down-Strategie** f KÜNSTL INT top-down strategy; **Top-Down-Verfahren** nt COMP & DV top-down methodology

Töpfer m KER & GLAS crockery maker; **Töpfererde** f KER & GLAS potter's earth; **Töpfergeschirr** nt KER & GLAS coarse pottery; **Töpferhammer** m KER & GLAS potter's beetle; **Töpferofen** m THERMOD pottery kiln; **Töpferscheibe** f KER & GLAS potter's wheel; **Töpferton** m ERDÖL *Mineral* ball clay; **Töpfertongewinnung** f KER & GLAS potter's clay extraction; **Töpferwarendekorator** m KER & GLAS pottery decorator

topfförmig: ~er Feldwiderstand m ELEKTRIZ pot-type field rheostat

Topfkern m RADIO pot core

Topfkreis m ELEKTRONIK coaxial resonator, FERNSEH cavity resonator, RAUMFAHRT *Weltraumfunk* cavity

Topfofen m THERMOD pot furnace

Topfschleifscheibe f FERTIG cup wheel

Topfschraube f WASSERTRANS *Takelage, Beschläge* bottle screw

Topfzeit f KUNSTSTOFF pot life

Topologie f COMP & DV, GEOM topology

topologisch: ~e **Eigenschaften** f pl GEOM topological properties

topotaktisch adj KERNTECH topotactical

Topp[1] m WASSERTRANS masthead

Topp:[2] **vor ~ und Takel legen** vt WASSERTRANS Schiff lay ahull

Topp: **Topplicht** nt WASSERTRANS Navigation masthead light; **Toppnant** f WASSERTRANS Tauwerk topping lift; **Toppzeichen** nt WASSERTRANS Seezeichen topmark

Topzementierung f ERDÖL Bohrtechnik top cementing plug

Torbernit m KERNTECH torbernite

Torf m KOHLEN peat; **Torfkohle** f KOHLEN peat coal

Torflügelpfosten m WASSERVERSORG meeting post

torgesteuert: ~e **Diode** f ELEKTRONIK gated diode

Torimpuls m ELEKTRONIK gating pulse

Tor-Kathoden-Widerstand m ELEKTROTECH gate-to-cathode resistor

Torkretbeton m BAU gunite

Torkretieren nt BAU guniting

Törn m WASSERTRANS Tauwerk turn

Tornister m FERNSEH portapack

Törnvorrichtung f WASSERTRANS Motor turning gear

Toroid nt ELEKTRIZ ring winding, KERNTECH toroid

Torpedo m FERTIG Extruder muller, KUNSTSTOFF Extruder, Spritzgießmaschine, WASSERTRANS torpedo; **Torpedoboot** nt WASSERTRANS torpedo boat

Torpfosten m BAU swinging post

Torriegel m BAU gate latch

Torschiff nt WASSERTRANS caisson

Torschließbolzen m BAU barrel bolt

Torsion f MASCHINEN, METALL, PHYS torsion; **Torsionsbeanspruchung** f MASCHINEN torsional strain, torsional stress; **Torsionsfaden** m ELEKTROTECH torsion string; **Torsionsfaden-Galvanometer** nt ELEKTRIZ torsion string galvanometer; **Torsionsfeder** f MASCHINEN spring subjected to torsion, torsion spring; **Torsionsfestigkeit** f MASCHINEN torsion resistance; **Torsionsfestigkeitsprüfer** m PAPIER torsional strength tester; **Torsionskabel** nt COMP & DV twisted pair cable; **Torsionskonstante** f PHYS torsional constant; **Torsionsmesser** m LABOR, MASCHINEN torsion meter; **Torsionsmodul** m PHYS modulus of rigidity; **Torsionsmoment** nt MASCHINEN torsional moment; **Torsionspendel** nt PHYS torsional pendulum; **Torsionsschwingung** f PHYS torsional oscillation; **Torsionssteifigkeit** f MASCHINEN torsion resistance; **Torsionsstrebe** f KFZTECH torque arm; **Torsionsversuch** m MASCHINEN torsion test, torsional test; **Torsionswaage** f MASCHINEN, METROL, PHYS torsion balance; **Torsionswinkel** m MASCHINEN angle of torsion

Torschaltung f PHYS logischer Schaltkreis gate

Torsteuerung f ELEKTRONIK gating; **Torsteuerungssignal** nt ELEKTRONIK gating signal

Tortendiagramm nt COMP & DV pie chart

Torus m ELEKTRIZ ring winding, toroid, torus, GEOM, STRAHLPHYS torus; **~ mit drei Öffnungen** m GEOM three-hole torus; **Torusantenne** f TELEKOM toroidal antenna

Tosyl- pref CHEMIE tosyl-

Tot- pref PHYS, THERMOD, WASSERTRANS dead

tot: ~e **Bewegung** f FERTIG Walzen idle pass; ~es **Ende** nt MASCHINEN dead end; ~er **Raum** m KERNTECH stagnant space; ~es **Werk** nt WASSERTRANS Schiffkonstruktion deadworks; ~er **Winkel** m LUFTTRANS blind angle; ~e **Zone** f COMP & DV dead zone, ELEKTROTECH Regler dead band

total: ~e **Wärmesenke** f KERNTECH ultimate heat sink

Totalreflexion f KER & GLAS total internal reflection, OPTIK, PHYS, TELEKOM total reflection; **Totalreflexionswinkel** m OPTIK angle of total reflection

Totem-Pole-Aufbau m ELEKTRONIK Verstärker totem pole arrangement

Tot-: **Totenflaute** f WASSERTRANS Wind dead calm; **Totgang** m KFZTECH Triebstrang MECHAN backlash

totgebrannt adj THERMOD dead burned

Tot-: **Totholz** nt WASSERTRANS Schiffbau deadwood; **Totlage** f PHYS stagnation point; **Totmahlen** nt KOHLEN overgrinding; **Totmannsteuerung** f TRANS dead man's control

totpumpen vt ERDÖL Bohrtechnik kill

Totpunkt m KFZTECH Motor, Kolben dead center (AmE), MECHAN dead center (AmE), dead centre (BrE); **Totrösten** nt METALL dead roasting; **Totseilanker** m ERDÖL Ankertechnik dead line anchor; **Totspeicher** m COMP & DV nonerasable storage; **Tötung ~ durch Stromschlag** f RADIO electrocution

Totwasser nt STRÖMPHYS wake

totweich: ~er **Stahl** m METALL dead soft steel

Tot-: **Totweichglühen** nt THERMOD dead soft anneal; **Totzeit** f COMP & DV, ELEKTRONIK, KONTROLL dead time, MECHAN downtime, PHYS dead time

Touch-Downbereich: **~ der Start- und Landebahn** m LUFTTRANS Aufsetzen bei Landung runway touchdown zone

Touchscreen nt COMP & DV touch screen

Touren: **auf ~ bringen** vt KFZTECH Motor rev up

Tourenzähler m GERÄT revolution counter

Townsend-Entladung f ELEKTRONIK Townsend discharge

Toxikologie f SICHERHEIT toxicology

toxisch[1] adj ERDÖL, KOHLEN toxic

toxisch:[2] ~e **Abfälle** m pl ABFALL toxic waste; ~es **Abfallprodukt** nt UMWELTSCHMUTZ toxic degradation product; ~e **Gesamtwirkung** f UMWELTSCHMUTZ cumulative toxic effect; ~e **Wirkung** f UMWELTSCHMUTZ toxic effect

Toxizität f CHEMIE, ERDÖL, KERNTECH, KUNSTSTOFF, MEERSCHMUTZ toxicity

TPP abbr (texturiertes Pflanzenprotein) LEBENSMITTEL TVP (textured vegetable protein)

TQMS abbr (abteilungsübergreifendes Qualitätssicherungssystem) QUAL TQMS (Total Quality Management System)

Tracer m KERNTECH tracer; **Tracer-Isotop** nt KERNTECH isotopic tracer

Trackball m COMP & DV Laptop track ball

Trafostation f ELEKTRIZ substation

Trafostufenschalter m ELEKTROTECH tap changer

Trag- pref TEXTIL carrying

Tragant nt LEBENSMITTEL tragacanth; **Tragantgummi** nt LEBENSMITTEL gum tragacanth

Trag-: **Tragarm** m BAU bracket; **Tragbahre** f SICHERHEIT stretcher; **Tragbalken** m MECHAN girder, PAPIER carrying bar

tragbar[1] adj COMP & DV portable, transportable, SICHERHEIT hand-held

tragbar:[2] ~e **Bodenstation** f RAUMFAHRT Weltraumfunk transportable Earth station; ~e **Bohrmaschine** f MASCHINEN portable drilling machine; ~er **Computer** m COMP & DV laptop, laptop computer, portable; ~er **Empfänger** m TELEKOM portable receiver; ~es **Haus-**

gerät *nt* ELEKTRIZ portable appliance; ~er **Lötofen** *m* FERTIG devil; ~e **Masse** *f* LABOR portable pulp; ~er **Sender** *m* FERNSEH portable transmitter; ~es **Terminal** *nt* COMP & DV, WASSERTRANS *Satellitenfunk* portable terminal; ~er **Umsetzer** *m* FERNSEH portable relay

Trag-: Tragbeutel *m* VERPACK carrier bag; **Tragbild** *nt* MASCHINEN contact pattern; **Tragblock** *m* TRANS carrying block

Trage *f* BAU handbarrow

träge[1] *adj* ANSTRICH inert, RAUMFAHRT inertial

träge:[2] ~ **Masse** *f* PHYS inertial mass; ~ **Sicherung** *f* ELEKTROTECH delayed-action fuse, slow blow fuse

Trage: Tragebalken *m* MASCHINEN beam, WASSERTRANS *Schiffbau* girder

tragen *vt* BAU bear, carry, COMP & DV support, MASCHINEN bear, PAPIER carry, TEXTIL carry, wear

tragend *adj* BAU bearing, supporting, MASCHINEN bearing

tragend: ~e **Achse** *f* MASCHINEN carrying axle; ~es **Bauteil** *nt* LUFTTRANS primary structure; ~e **Fläche** *f* LUFTTRANS *Luftfahrzeug* mainplane; **nicht** ~e **Mauerverkleidung** *f* BAU veneer; ~e **Wand** *f* BAU bearing wall, load-bearing wall; ~e **Wände** *f pl* BAU *eines Gebäudes* main walls; ~e **Zahnflanke** *f* FERTIG *Getriebelehre* active profile

Träger *m* AUFNAHME carrier, BAU girder, COMP & DV, ELEKTRONIK *Nachrichten übermittelndes System oder Organisation*, FERNSEH carrier, HYDRAUL bracket, KUNSTSTOFF substrate, MASCHINEN arm, beam, girder, holder, support, MECHAN bracket, girder, RADIO, RAUMFAHRT *Weltraumfunk*, TELEKOM carrier, TEXTIL backing for carpet, VERPACK joist, WASSERTRANS *Schiffbau* girder; ~ **für Frachtbehälter** *m* LUFTTRANS *Hubschrauber* cargo carrier support; **Trägerabfrage** *f* ELEKTRONIK CS, carrier sense; **Trägerabfragesignal** *nt* TELEKOM carrier sense signal; **Trägerabgleich** *m* FERNSEH carrier balance; **Trägerabtastsignal** *nt* TELEKOM carrier sense signal; **Trägeranalyse** *f* KERNTECH carrier analysis; **Trägerauffüllung** *f* ELEKTRONIK carrier replenishment; **Trägerbandbreite** *f* ELEKTRONIK carrier bandwidth; **Trägerdetektion** *f (CD)* COMP & DV, ELEKTRONIK, TELEKOM carrier detection *(CD)*; **Trägerdienst** *m* TELEKOM bearer service; **Trägerdienst im Paketmodus** *m* TELEKOM packet mode bearer service; **Trägerdifferenzsystem** *nt* FERNSEH carrier difference system; **Trägereinspeisungsoszillator** *m* RADIO carrier insertion oscillator; **Trägererfassung** *f* ELEKTRONIK carrier acquisition; **Trägererkennung** *f (CD)* COMP & DV, ELEKTRONIK, TELEKOM carrier detection *(CD)*; **Trägererzeugung** *f* ELEKTRONIK carrier generation; **Trägerflansch** *m* BAU flange; **Trägerflüssigkeit** *f* FERTIG carrying agent

Trägerfrequenz *f (Tf)* AUFNAHME, ELEKTRONIK, FERNSEH, RADIO carrier frequency *(CF)*; **Trägerfrequenzerzeuger** *m* ELEKTRONIK, FERNSEH, RADIO carrier frequency oscillator; **Trägerfrequenzoffset** *nt* ELEKTRONIK, FERNSEH, RADIO carrier frequency offset; **Trägerfrequenzpegel** *m* ELEKTRONIK carrier level; **Trägerfrequenzsystem** *nt* COMP & DV carrier system; **Trägerfrequenzversatz** *m* ELEKTRONIK, FERNSEH, - RADIO carrier frequency offset; **Trägerfrequenzverstärker** *m* ELEKTRONIK carrier repeater

Träger: Trägergas *nt* KERNTECH, UMWELTSCHMUTZ carrier gas; **Träger-Geräuschabstand** *m* TELEKOM carrier-to-noise density ratio; **Trägergewebe** *nt* TEXTIL backing fabric; **Trägerimpuls** *m* ELEKTRONIK pulse carrier; **Trägerkörper** *m* TELEKOM substrate; **Trägerleistung** *f* RADIO carrier power; **Trägermast** *m* ELEKTRIZ supply pylon

Trägermaterial *nt* ANSTRICH, ELEKTRONIK substrate, ELEKTROTECH base; ~ **für Dickschicht-Hybridschaltung** *nt* ELEKTRONIK thick film hybrid circuit substrate; ~ **für Dünnschicht-Hybridschaltung** *nt* ELEKTRONIK thin film hybrid circuit substate; ~ **vom Typ n** *nt* ELEKTRONIK n-type substrate

Träger: Trägermodulation *f* ELEKTRONIK carrier modulation; **Trägerplatte** *f* FERNSEH backplate, FERTIG *Lumineszenzschirm* screen base, RAUMFAHRT support plate; **Trägerrauschen** *nt* ELEKTRONIK carrier noise; **Träger-Rauschprüfgerätschaft** *f* ELEKTRONIK carrier noise test set; **Träger-Rauschverhältnis** *nt* AUFNAHME carrier-to-noise ratio; **Trägerschicht** *f* BAU base; **Trägerschiff** *nt* WASSERTRANS barge carrier; **Trägerschiffleuchter** *m* TRANS shipborne lighter; **Trägerschwelle** *f* BAU summer; **Trägerschwingung** *f* COMP & DV carrier; **Trägersignal** *nt* COMP & DV carrier signal; **Trägersignal für mehrere Empfänger** *nt* RAUMFAHRT multidestination carrier; **Trägersteuerungsmodulation** *f* ELEKTRONIK controlled carrier modulation, *Radio* variable carrier modulation; **Trägerunterdrückung** *f* ELEKTRONIK, TELEKOM carrier suppression; **Trägerunterseite** *f* LUFTTRANS lower surface; **Trägerverstärker** *m* TELEKOM carrier amplifier

Trägerwelle *f* FERNSEH, PHYS, RADIO, WELLPHYS carrier wave, cw; **Trägerwellengenerator** *m* PHYS, WELLPHYS carrier-wave generator; **Trägerwellenmodulation** *f* PHYS, WELLPHYS carrier-wave modulation

Träger: Trägerwiederbelegungsoperator *m* ELEKTRONIK carrier reinsertion operator

Trag: Tragetasche *f* VERPACK carrier bag

tragfähig[1] *adj* TEXTIL wearable

tragfähig:[2] ~er **Boden** *m* KOHLEN footing

Tragfähigkeit *f* BAU bearing capacity, capacitance, *eines Kranes* lift, ERDÖL *Gesamtzuladung* dead weight, KOHLEN bearing capacity, MASCHINEN carrying capacity, load rating, load-bearing capacity, MECHAN, NICHTFOSS ENERG carrying capacity, TRANS loading capacity, WASSERTRANS *Schiffkonstruktion* dead weight; **Tragfähigkeitsversuch** *m* BAU bearing test

Tragfahrzeug: ~ **mit berührungsloser Aufhängung** *nt* TRANS support vehicle with non-contact suspension

Trag-: Tragfeder *f* MASCHINEN suspension spring; **Tragfestigkeit** *f* KOHLEN bearing strength

Tragfläche *f* LUFTTRANS aerofoil chord (BrE), airfoil chord (AmE), MASCHINEN bearing surface, NICHTFOSS ENERG aerofoil (BrE), airfoil (AmE), PHYS wing, WASSERTRANS hydrofoil; **Tragflächenbelastung** *f* LUFTTRANS wing loading; **Tragflächenboot** *nt* WASSERTRANS hydrofoil; **Tragflächenende** *nt* LUFTTRANS wing tip

Tragflügel *m* LUFTTRANS aerofoil (BrE), aerofoil chord (BrE), airfoil (AmE), airfoil chord (AmE), *Luftfahrzeug* mainplane, WASSERTRANS aerofoil (BrE), airfoil (AmE); **Tragflügelansatz** *m* LUFTTRANS wing root; **Tragflügelbehälter** *m* LUFTTRANS wing tank; **Tragflügelenteisung** *f* LUFTTRANS aerofoil de-icing (BrE), airfoil de-icing (AmE); **Tragflügelenteisungsklappe** *f* LUFTTRANS aerofoil de-icing valve (BrE), airfoil de-icing valve (AmE); **Tragflügelentfrostung** *f* LUFTTRANS aerofoil de-icing (BrE), airfoil de-icing (AmE); **Tragflügelmittelstück** *nt* LUFTTRANS center of wing section (AmE), centre of wing section (BrE); **Tragflü-**

gelrumpf *m* WASSERTRANS aerofoil hull (BrE), airfoil hull (AmE); **Tragflügelwurzel** *f* LUFTTRANS wing root

Trag-: **Traggriff** *m* MECHAN, VERPACK carrying handle

Trägheit *f* ANSTRICH, HEIZ & KÄLTE, MASCHINEN, MECHAN, PHYS, UMWELTSCHMUTZ inertia; **Trägheits-** *pref* RAUMFAHRT inertial; **Trägheitsabscheider** *m* KERNTECH inertial separator; **Trägheitsachse** *f* MECHAN, PHYS axis of inertia; **Trägheits-Beschleunigungsmesser** *m* RAUMFAHRT inertial accelerometer; **Trägheitseinschluß** *m* PHYS inertial confinement; **Trägheitsellipse** *f* MECHAN ellipse of inertia; **Trägheitshalbmesser** *m* MASCHINEN radius of gyration; **Trägheitskraft** *f* KERNTECH, MASCHINEN, PHYS inertial force; **Trägheitsmelder** *m* RAUMFAHRT inertial sensor; **Trägheitsmittelpunkt** *m* MECHAN, PHYS center of inertia (AmE), centre of inertia (BrE); **Trägheitsmoment** *nt* BAU, ERGON moment of inertia, FERTIG inertia moment, HEIZ & KÄLTE inertial torque, MASCHINEN, WASSERTRANS *Schiffbau* moment of inertia; **Trägheitsmoment des Blattes** *nt* LUFTTRANS *Hubschrauber* blade moment of inertia; **Trägheitsnavigation** *f* RAUMFAHRT inertial navigation; **Trägheitsnavigationssystem** *nt* LUFTTRANS, RAUMFAHRT *Raumschiff*, WASSERTRANS INS, inertial navigation system; **Trägheitsplattform** *f* MASCHINEN inertial platform; **Trägheitsprodukt** *nt* PHYS product of inertia; **Trägheitsradius** *m* BAU radius of gyration; **Trägheitsrahmen** *m* RAUMFAHRT inertial frame; **Trägheitsschalter** *m* ELEKTROTECH inertia switch; **Trägheitssteuerung** *f* RAUMFAHRT inertial guidance; **Trägheitssystem** *nt* RAUMFAHRT inertial system; **Trägheitszentrum** *nt* MECHAN, PHYS center of inertia (AmE), centre of inertia (BrE)

Trag-: **Traghülse** *f* FERTIG carrying sleeve; **Tragkettenförderer** *m* PAPIER arm elevator; **Tragkonstruktion** *f* BAU supporting structure; **Tragkraft** *f* MASCHINEN load-bearing capacity; **Traglager** *nt* FERTIG *Fräsdorn* yoke, MASCHINEN journal bearing, journal box; **äußeres ~** *nt* FERTIG *Främaschine* outer arbour support; **Traglast** *f* FERTIG collapse load, KOHLEN ultimate load; **Tragleiter** *f* SICHERHEIT portable ladder; **Tragöse** *f* MASCHINEN lifting lug; **Tragplatte** *f* MASCHINEN, PAPIER base plate; **Tragriemen** *m* FOTO strap; **Tragring** *m* KFZTECH thrust collar, MASCHINEN thrust block; **Tragring für Schaltdrähte** *m* TELEKOM jumper ring; **Tragrolle** *f* KER & GLAS carrying roller; **Tragrumpf-Schwebekörper-Flugzeug** *nt* LUFTTRANS lifting-body aircraft; **Tragschere** *f* KER & GLAS shank; **Tragschicht** *f* BAU base course, *Geologie* bearing bed; **Tragschichtmaterial** *nt* BAU base material; **Tragschraube** *f* LUFTTRANS *Hubschrauber* lifting rotor; **Tragschraubenblatt** *nt* LUFTTRANS *Hubschrauber* rotor blade; **Tragschrauber** *m* LUFTTRANS autogyro; **Tragseil** *nt* BAU supporting rope, EISENBAHN track cable, MASCHINEN supporting cable, TRANS carrier rope, carrying rope; **Tragtiefe** *f* FERTIG *Gewinde* engagement depth; **Tragtrommelroller** *m* PAPIER pope reel; **Tragvermögen** *nt* NICHTFOSS ENERG, VERPACK carrying capacity; **Tragwagen** *m* EISENBAHN rail carrier wagon; **Tragwalze** *f* KER & GLAS carrying roll, PAPIER king roll; **Tragwerk** *nt* BAU frame, framework; **Tragzapfen** *m* MECHAN trunnion

tragzellenförmig *adj* LUFTTRANS cellular

Traktion *f* EISENBAHN, MASCHINEN traction; **Traktionsnetz** *nt* ELEKTRIZ traction network

Traktor *m* COMP & DV tractor, KFZTECH traction engine, tractor; **Traktorzuführung** *f* DRUCK tractor feed

Tränenblech *nt* METALL bulb plate

Trangwalze *f* KER & GLAS trang roll

Tränken *nt* PAPIER soaking, TEXTIL impregnation, soaking

tränken *vt* BAU saturate, temper

Tränklack *m* ELEKTRIZ impregnating varnish

Tränkung *f* BAU *Holz*, FERTIG *Sinterpreßteil* impregnation

Transaktion *f* COMP & DV transaction; **Transaktionsdatei** *f* COMP & DV transaction file; **Transaktionssatz** *m* COMP & DV transaction record; **Transaktionsverarbeitung** *f* COMP & DV transaction processing; **Transaktionsverwaltungssoftware** *f* COMP & DV transaction management software

Transcoder *m* FERNSEH, TELEKOM transcoder

Transcontainer *m* TRANS transcontainer

Transducer *m* ELEKTRIZ, ELEKTROTECH, GERÄT transducer

Transduktor *m* ELEKTROTECH magamp, magnetic amplifier, transductor, PHYS magnetic amplifier, transductor

Transfer *m* KER & GLAS decal (AmE), transfer (BrE), TELEKOM transfer; **Transfer-Gate-Schaltung** *f* ELEKTROTECH transfer gate; **Transferglas** *nt* KER & GLAS transfer glass; **Transfermaschine** *f* MASCHINEN transfer machine; **Transferreaktion** *f* KERNTECH transfer reaction; **Transferstraße** *f* MASCHINEN transfer line; **Transfersystemteil** *nt* TELEKOM message transfer agent

transfinit *adj* MATH transfinite

Transformation *f* ELEKTROTECH, GEOM transformation; **Transformationen** *f pl* MATH transforms; **Transformationsbereich** *m* KER & GLAS transformation range; **Transformationstemperatur** *f* KER & GLAS transformation point

Transformator *m* ELEKTRIZ, ELEKTROTECH, PHYS, RADIO, TELEKOM transformer; **~ mit Abzapfpunkten** *m* ELEKTRIZ tapped transformer; **~ mit Anzapfungen** *m* ELEKTROTECH tapped transformer; **~ mit luftisolierter Spule** *m* ELEKTRIZ nonencapsulated-winding dry-type transformer; **~ mit nicht-gekapselter Trockenspule** *m* ELEKTRIZ nonencapsulated-winding dry-type transformer; **~ mit offenem Kern** *m* ELEKTRIZ open core transformer; **~ mit separater Wicklung** *m* ELEKTRIZ separate winding transformer; **~ zur Spannungserhöhung** *m* ELEKTROTECH step-up transformer; **Transformatoranzapfung** *f* ELEKTROTECH transformer tap; **Transformatorblech** *nt* ELEKTROTECH core lamination; **Transformator-EMK** *f* ELEKTRIZ, PHYS transformer emf; **Transformatorenöl** *nt* ELEKTRIZ transformer oil; **Transformatorenstation** *f* ELEKTRIZ, ELEKTROTECH transformer substation

transformator-gekoppelt *adj* ELEKTRIZ transformer-coupled

Transformator: **Transformatorisolierung** *f* ELEKTROTECH transformer isolation; **Transformatorkern** *m* ELEKTRIZ, ELEKTROTECH transformer core; **Transformatorkopplung** *f* ELEKTROTECH transformer coupling, TELEKOM mutual coupling; **Transformator-Leistungsfaktor** *m* ELEKTRIZ transformer efficiency; **Transformator-Umspannwerk** *nt* ELEKTRIZ, ELEKTROTECH transformer substation; **Transformatorverlust** *m* ELEKTROTECH transformer loss

transformerlos: **~e Stromversorgung** *f* ELEKTRIZ transformerless power supply

transformieren *vt* COMP & DV transform
Transformierung *f* ELEKTROTECH transformation
Transfusionsflasche *f* KER & GLAS transfusion bottle
transient: ~e Bedingungen *f pl* ELEKTROTECH transient conditions
Transistor *m* COMP & DV, ELEKTRIZ, PHYS transistor; ~ in Basisschaltung *m* ELEKTRONIK common-base transistor; ~ auf Chip *m* ELEKTRONIK on-chip transistor; ~ in Drainschaltung *m* ELEKTRONIK common-drain transistor; ~ in Emitterschaltung *m* ELEKTRONIK common-emitter transistor; ~ in Gateschaltung *m* ELEKTRONIK common-gate transistor; ~ in Overlaytechnik *m* RADIO overlay transistor; ~ in Source-Schaltung *m* ELEKTRONIK common source transistor; Transistorbasisschaltung *f* ELEKTRONIK transistor base circuit; Transistor-Charakteristik *f* ELEKTRONIK transistor characteristics; Transistorchip *m* ELEKTRONIK transistor chip
Transistoren: aufeinander abgestimmte ~ *m pl* ELEKTRONIK matched transistors
transistorisiert *adj* KONTROLL solid state
Transistor: Transistor-Leistungsverstärker *m* ELEKTRONIK transistor power amplifier; Transistor-Leistungsverstärkung *f* AUFNAHME transistor power gain; Transistor-Modulator *m* ELEKTRONIK transistor modulator; Transistor-Oszillator *m* ELEKTRONIK transistor oscillator; Transistorpaar *nt* ELEKTRONIK transistor pair; Transistorregler *m* KFZTECH transistorized regulator; Transistorsättigung *f* ELEKTRONIK transistor saturation; Transistorschaltgerät *nt* KFZTECH transistor control unit; Transistor-Tetrode *f* ELEKTRONIK *Triac* tetrode transistor; Transistor-Transistor-Logik *f (TTL)* COMP & DV, ELEKTRONIK transistor-transistor logic *(TTL)*; Transistorverstärker *m* ELEKTRONIK transistor amplifier; Transistorverstärkung *f* ELEKTRONIK transistor amplification; Transistorvorspannung *f* ELEKTRONIK transistor bias; Transistorzündanlage *f* KFZTECH transistor ignition unit, transistorized ignition system
Transit *m* TELEKOM, TRANS transit; Transitamt *nt* TELEKOM transit exchange; Transitfernamt *nt* TELEKOM trunk transit exchange; Transitpassagier *m* TRANS transit passenger; Transitverkehr *m* TELEKOM transit traffic
Translation *f* GEOM translation; Translationsbewegung *f* MASCHINEN translation, translatory motion; Translationsfläche *f* METALL gliding plane
Transliteration *f* COMP & DV transliteration
transliterieren *vt* COMP & DV transliterate
Transmission *f* FERTIG shafting, MASCHINEN, MECHAN transmission; Transmissionsdichte *f* OPTIK transmittance density; Transmissions-Elektronenmikroskop *nt* ELEKTRONIK, KERNTECH, LABOR, PHYS transmission electron microscope; Transmissions-Elektronenmikroskopie *f* STRAHLPHYS transmission electron microscopy; Transmissionsfähigkeit *f* PHYS transmission power; Transmissionsfenster *nt* OPTIK transmission window; Transmissions-Fotometer *nt* GERÄT haze meter; Transmissionsgitter *nt* OPTIK transmission grating; Transmissionsgrad *m* OPTIK transmittance; Transmissionskette *f* MASCHINEN transmission chain; Transmissionsriemen *m* MASCHINEN driving belt, PAPIER transmission belting; Transmissionswelle *f* LUFTTRANS connecting shaft, MASCHINEN shafting
transmissiv: ~e LCD-Anzeige *f* ELEKTROTECH transmissive LCD
Transmultiplexer *m (TMUX)* TELEKOM transmultiplexer *(TMUX)*
Transomplatte *f* WASSERTRANS *Schiffbau* transom plate
Transparent- *pref* COMP & DV, TELEKOM transparent
transparent: ~es Kabinendach *nt* LUFTTRANS *Flugzeug* canopy; ~e Scheibe *f* OPTIK transparent disk (AmE); ~er Trägerdienst *m* TELEKOM transparent bearer service; nicht ~er Trägerdienst *m* TELEKOM nontransparent bearer service
Transparent-: Transparentemail *nt* KER & GLAS transparent enamel; Transparentetikett *nt* VERPACK *durch Wärmeübertragung aufgetragen* heat transfer label; Transparentglasur *f* KER & GLAS transparent glaze; Transparentpapier *nt* KONSTZEICH transparent paper; Transparentvordruck *m* KONSTZEICH preprint
Transparenz *f* DRUCK, KUNSTSTOFF, TELEKOM *Netzwerk* transparency
Transpiration *f (T)* HYDRAUL transpiration *(T)*; Transpirationskühlung *f* HEIZ & KÄLTE transpiration cooling
Transplutonium-Element *nt* KERNTECH transplutonium element
Transponder *m* RADIO, RAUMFAHRT *Weltraumfunk*, TELEKOM transponder
transponieren *vt* MATH *Matrix* transpose
transponierend: ~es Instrument *nt* AKUSTIK transposing instrument
Transport *m* COMP & DV transport, FERTIG handling, TRANS conveyance, haulage, transport, VERPACK *verschiedener Werkstücke* work handling; Transport- und Installationsanweisungen *f pl* TRANS handling and installation instructions; ~ in Niedrigdruckröhren *m* TRANS transport in low-pressure tube; Transport- und Rettungshubschrauber *m* LUFTTRANS transport and rescue helicopter; Transport- und Verbindungsflugzeug *nt* LUFTTRANS transport and communications aircraft; Transportanlage *f* TRANS conveying plant; Transportband *nt* MECHAN conveyor belt, VERPACK band conveyor, belt conveyor; Transportbehälter *m* TRANS, VERPACK container; Transportbeton *m* BAU ready-mixed concrete; Transporteur *m* FERTIG protractor; Transportfaktor *m* ELEKTROTECH transfer efficiency; Transporthubschrauber *m* LUFTTRANS transport helicopter
transportierbar¹ *adj* COMP & DV portable, transportable
transportierbar:² ~e Gasflasche *f* SICHERHEIT transportable gas container; ~e Steckdose *f* ELEKTRIZ portable socket outlet
transportieren *vt* TEXTIL carry, TRANS transport, WASSERTRANS ship
Transport: Transportkasten *m* FERTIG tote box; Transportkette *f* MASCHINEN conveyor chain; Transportkiste *f* VERPACK carrier box; Transportkran *m* VERPACK material-handling crane; Transportleitung *f* ERDÖL *Erdgas* transmission main; Transportmakler *m* TRANS forwarding agent; Transportmechanismus *m* FERNSEH transport mechanism; Transportmischer *m* BAU mixer truck; Transportmodell *nt* UMWELTSCHMUTZ transport model; Transportprotokoll *nt* COMP & DV transport protocol; Transportquelle *f* UMWELTSCHMUTZ transportation source; Transportraupe *f* COMP & DV tractor; Transportrolle *f* MASCHINEN caster, castor; Transportschnecke *f* VERPACK screw conveyor; Transportsicherheit *f* SICHERHEIT transportation safety; Transportsystem *nt* BAU transportation

system; **Transportsystem mit mehreren Betriebsarten** *nt* TRANS multiple-mode transportation system; **Transportunternehmen** *nt* TRANS common carrier, haulage contractor; **Transportvorrichtungen** *f pl* VERPACK handling equipment; **Transportwagen** *m* BAU carrier car (AmE), carrier wagon (BrE), KERNTECH trolley, KFZTECH dolly

Transposition *f* AKUSTIK transposition

Transputer *m* COMP & DV transputer, KONTROLL transputer

transreflektierend: ~e Flüssigkristallanzeige *f* ELEKTRONIK reflective LCD

Transsonikflugzeug *nt* LUFTTRANS transonic aircraft

Transtainer *m* TRANS transtainer

Transuran *nt* KERNTECH transuranic nuclide; **Transuranabfall** *m* KERNTECH TRU, transuranic waste; **~e** *nt pl* STRAHLPHYS transuranic elements

Transversal- *pref* TELEKOM, OPTIK transversal

transversal:[1] **~ elektrisch** *adj (TE)* ELEKTROTECH, TELEKOM transverse electric *(TE)*; **~ elektromagnetisch** *adj (TEM)* ELEKTROTECH, TELEKOM transverse electromagnetic *(TEM)*; **~ magnetisch** *adj (TM)* ELEKTROTECH, TELEKOM transverse magnetic *(TM)*

transversal:[2] **~e chromatische Aberration** *f* PHYS *senkrecht zur optischen Achse* transverse chromatic aberration; **~er elektrischer Modus** *m* ELEKTROTECH, TELEKOM transverse electric mode; **~e elektrische Welle** *f* ELEKTROTECH, TELEKOM transverse electric wave; **~er elektromagnetischer Modus** *m* ELEKTROTECH, TELEKOM transverse electromagnetic mode; **~e elektromagnetische Welle** *f* ELEKTROTECH, TELEKOM transverse electromagnetic wave; **~e Energieverteilung** *f* STRAHLPHYS transverse energy distribution; **~e Interferometrie** *f* OPTIK, TELEKOM transverse interferometry; **~er magnetischer Modus** *m* ELEKTROTECH, TELEKOM transverse magnetic mode; **~e magnetische Welle** *f* ELEKTROTECH, TELEKOM transverse magnetic wave; **~e Magnetisierung** *f* AKUSTIK transverse magnetization

Transversale *f* GEOM transversal

Transversal-: Transversalfilter *nt* TELEKOM transverse filter; **Transversalglied** *nt* TELEKOM transversal section; **Transversal-Interferometrie** *f* OPTIK transverse interferometry; **Transversalkomponente** *f* PHYS transverse component; **Transversal-Spurvideorecorder** *m* FERNSEH quadruplex videotape recorder; **Transversaltonspur** *f* AUFNAHME variable area sound track; **Transversalwelle** *f* AKUSTIK, ELEKTROTECH, PHYS, TELEKOM, WELLPHYS transverse wave

Transverter *m* RADIO transverter

transzendental: ~e Zahl *f* MATH transcendental number

Transzendenz *f* MATH *von Zahlen* transcendence

Trap *m* COMP & DV *nichtprogrammierter Sprung* trap

Trapatt-Diode *f* ELEKTRONIK trapatt diode, trapped plasma avalanche time transit diode, PHYS trapatt diode, trapped plasma avalanche time transit diode

Trapez *nt* GEOM trapezoid; **Trapezfeder** *f* MASCHINEN trapezoidal spring; **Trapezflügel** *m* LUFTTRANS tapered wing

trapezförmig *adj* GEOM trapezoidal

Trapez: Trapezgewinde *nt* MASCHINEN acme thread, trapezoidal thread; **Trapezgewindeschneider** *m* MASCHINEN acme thread tap; **Trapezquerlenkeraufhängung** *f* KFZTECH trapezoid arm-type suspension; **Trapezquerlenker-Radaufhängung** *f* KFZTECH doublewishbone suspension; **Trapezverzeichnung** *f* FERNSEH keystone distortion; **Trapezverzerrung** *f* ELEKTRONIK

trapezoidal distortion, FERNSEH keystone distortion

trassieren *vt* BAU locate, route

Trassierung *f* BAU location, TELEKOM *von Leitungen* routing

Traubenkernöl *nt* LEBENSMITTEL grapeseed oil

Traubenzucker *m* LEBENSMITTEL grape sugar

Trauerflagge *f* WASSERTRANS mourning flag

Traufbohle *f* BAU eaves board

Traufbrett *nt* BAU fascia board

Traufe *f* BAU eaves

Traverse *f* BAU crossbar, crossbeam, suspension bracket, FERTIG crosshead, top beam, MASCHINEN crossbeam, crosshead, top rail, WASSERTRANS *Schiffbau* cross tie (AmE), sleeper (BrE)

traversenartig: ~es Aufnahmegestell *nt* KERNTECH bartype pick-up base

Travertin *m* NICHTFOSS ENERG travertine

Trawl *nt* MEERSCHMUTZ trawl net

trawlen *vi* WASSERTRANS *Fischerei* trawl

Trawler *m* WASSERTRANS *Schifftyp* trawler

Trayaufrichter: ~ und -belader *m* VERPACK tray erector and loader

Treber *m pl* LEBENSMITTEL pomace

Treffer *m* COMP & DV hit; **Trefferliste** *f* COMP & DV hit list

Treffgenauigkeit *f* QUAL accuracy of the mean

Treffpunkt *m* GEOM *von drei oder mehr Linien* point of concurrence

Trehalose *f* CHEMIE trehalose

Treibanker *m* WASSERTRANS *Notfall* drogue, sea anchor

Treibbake *f* WASSERTRANS *Seezeichen* floating beacon

Treibboje *f* WASSERTRANS *Wetter* drifting buoy

Treibeis *nt* WASSERTRANS drift ice

Treiben *nt* WASSERTRANS flotation

treiben[1] *vt* FERTIG hollow, MASCHINEN, RADIO drive; **~ lassen** *vt* WASSERTRANS float

treiben[2] *vi* WASSERTRANS drift

treibend[1] *adj* ELEKTRIZ, MASCHINEN driving, WASSERTRANS *Schiff* adrift

treibend:[2] **~e Kraft** *f* METALL driving force; **~es Ölfeld** *nt* MEERSCHMUTZ spill

Treiber *m* AKUSTIK, COMP & DV driver, KONTROLL *Plattenspielwerk* drive, RADIO *Senderstufe* driver; **Treiberimpuls** *m* FERNSEH driving pulse; **Treiberprogramm** *nt* COMP & DV driver; **Treiberroutine** *f* COMP & DV peripheral driver; **Treibersignale** *nt pl* FERNSEH driving signals; **Treiberspannung** *f* FERNSEH booster voltage, drive voltage; **Treiberstufe** *f* KFZTECH, RAUMFAHRT *Sendeverstärker* driver stage

Treibgut *nt* ABFALL floating refuse, WASSERTRANS flotsam

Treibhammer *m* MASCHINEN beating hammer

Treibhauseffekt *m* HEIZ & KÄLTE, NICHTFOSS ENERG, PHYS, UMWELTSCHMUTZ greenhouse effect

Treibholz *nt* WASSERTRANS driftwood

Treibkette *f* MASCHINEN transmission chain

Treibkörper *m* WASSERTRANS *Meereskunde* surface float

Treibmittel *nt* KUNSTSTOFF blowing agent, foaming agent, LEBENSMITTEL *Hefe, Backpulver* raising agent, UMWELTSCHMUTZ propellant, propellent

Treibnetz *nt* WASSERTRANS *Fischerei* drift net

Treibofen *m* FERTIG cupel, cupellation furnace

Treiböl *nt* MEERSCHMUTZ bunkers

Treibrad *nt* MASCHINEN driving wheel

Treibriemen *m* MASCHINEN belt, drive belt, driving belt, transmission belt; **Treibriemenabdeckung** *f* SICHERHEIT belt guard

Treibsand *m* KOHLEN quicksand

Treibscheibe *f* KFZTECH *Drehstromlichtmaschine* drive pulley

Treibschraube *f* MASCHINEN hammer-drive screw

Treibsitz *m* *(TS)* MASCHINEN drive fit

Treibstange *f* EISENBAHN connecting rod

Treibstoff *m* KFZTECH fuel, gas (AmE), gasoline (AmE), RAUMFAHRT fuel, propellant, propellent, WASSERTRANS fuel; **~ für Düsentriebwerk** *m* LUFTTRANS jet engine fuel; **Treibstoffablassen** *nt* RAUMFAHRT fuel dumping; **Treibstoffablaßsystem** *nt* RAUMFAHRT fuel-dumping system; **Treibstoffabsperrhahn** *m* LUFTTRANS fuel shut-off cock; **Treibstoffabsperrhahnsteuerung** *f* LUFTTRANS fuel shut-off cock control link

treibstoffaufwendig *adj* RAUMFAHRT fuel-costly

Treibstoff: **Treibstoffausgleichsbehälter** *m* LUFTTRANS fuel ullage box; **Treibstoffdruck** *m* RAUMFAHRT fuel pressure; **Treibstoffhahn** *m* LUFTTRANS fuel cock; **Treibstofffilter** *nt* LUFTTRANS fuel filter; **Treibstoffkühler-Wärmeaustauscher** *m* LUFTTRANS fuel coolant heat exchanger; **Treibstoffleitungsschacht** *m* RAUMFAHRT fuel line duct; **Treibstoffmangel** *m* THERMOD lack of fuel; **Treibstoffmasse** *f* RAUMFAHRT fuel mass, propellant mass, propellent mass; **Treibstoffmassendurchsatz** *m* LUFTTRANS mass fuel rate of flow; **Treibstoffmesser** *m* RAUMFAHRT fuel-measuring unit; **Treibstoff-Oxidant-Mischungsverhältnis** *nt* RAUMFAHRT fuel-oxidizer mixture ratio; **Treibstoffpumpe** *f* LUFTTRANS, MECHAN, RAUMFAHRT fuel pump; **Treibstoffreglereinheit** *f* LUFTTRANS fuel control unit; **Treibstoffreserve** *f* LUFTTRANS fuel reserve; **Treibstoffschnellablaß** *m* LUFTTRANS fuel jettison; **Treibstoff-Schnellablassventil** *nt* LUFTTRANS jettison valve; **Treibstoffsorte** *f* LUFTTRANS fuel grade

treibstoffsparend *adj* RAUMFAHRT fuel-efficient

Treibstoff: **Treibstoffstandgeber** *m* LUFTTRANS fuel level transmitter; **Treibstoffstandsensor** *m* RAUMFAHRT fuel level sensor; **Treibstoffsystem** *nt* KFZTECH, LUFTTRANS fuel system; **Treibstofftank** *m* LUFTTRANS fuel tank; **Treibstofftankwahlschalter** *m* LUFTTRANS fuel tank selector switch; **Treibstofftemperaturfühler** *m* LUFTTRANS fuel temperature probe; **Treibstoffventil** *nt* LUFTTRANS fuel cock; **Treibstoffverbrauch** *m* KFZTECH fuel consumption; **Treibstoffversorgung** *f* KFZTECH fueling (AmE), fuelling (BrE), LUFTTRANS fuelling (BrE); **Treibstoff-Vorratsprogrammsteuerung** *f* LUFTTRANS fuel level pre-setting controls; **Treibstoffvorrat-Wahlschalter** *m* LUFTTRANS fuel level selector; **Treibstoffvorschubventil** *nt* LUFTTRANS fuel cross-feed valve; **Treibstoffzelle** *f* RAUMFAHRT fuel cell; **Treibstoffzufuhr** *f* KFZTECH fueling (AmE), fuelling (BrE), LUFTTRANS fuelling (BrE); **Treibstoffzufuhrsteuerung** *f* LUFTTRANS fuel control; **Treibstoffzuladung** *f* LUFTTRANS fuel load

Treibwageneinheit *f* EISENBAHN rail motor unit

Treibzapfen *m* MASCHINEN drive pin

Treidelroute *f* TRANS bridletrack

Treidelweg *m* TRANS bridleroad, *Schiff* bridleway

Treisegel *nt* WASSERTRANS *Segeln* trysail

Tremolo *nt* AKUSTIK tremolo

Trend *m* TEXTIL trend; **Trendschreiber** *m* GERÄT trend recorder

Trennautomat *m* COMP & DV burster, decollator, MECHAN burster

Trennbarkeit *f* KERNTECH separability

Trennbruch *m* FERTIG rupture, METALL cleavage crack

Trenndichte *f* KOHLEN separation density

Trenndiode *f* ELEKTRONIK isolation diode

Trenneinsätze *m pl* VERPACK partitioning inserts

Trennelement *nt* OPTIK isolator

Trennen *nt* BAU ripping, ELEKTROTECH partitioning, *des Stromkreises* breaking, FERTIG disc cutting (BrE), disk cutting (AmE); **~ und Ausschließen** *nt* DRUCK h&j, hyphenation and justification

trennen *vt* COMP & DV decollate, ELEKTRIZ *der Leitung* disconnect, ELEKTROTECH isolate, *der Leitung* disconnect, *galvanisch* isolate, KFZTECH break, MASCHINEN disconnect, disjoint, TELEKOM *der Verbindung* disconnect

Trennfestigkeit *f* KUNSTSTOFF bond strength

Trennfilter *nt* ELEKTRONIK, FERNSEH separation filter

Trennflüssigkeit *f* CHEMTECH separation liquid

Trennfuge *f* FERTIG parting line

Trenngatter *nt* ELEKTROTECH partition gate

trenninduziert: **~er Strom** *m* ELEKTROTECH break-induced current

Trennkasten *m* ELEKTRIZ dividing box

Trennkolonne *f* LABOR *Destillieren* fractionation column

Trennkondensator *m* ELEKTRIZ, ELEKTROTECH blocking capacitor

Trennkontakt *m* ELEKTROTECH break contact

Trennkreis *m* FERNSEH separation circuit

Trennladung *f* ELEKTROTECH partitioned charge

Trennmanöver *nt* RAUMFAHRT separation maneuver (AmE), separation manoeuvre (BrE)

Trennmaschine *f* FERTIG cutting-off machine

Trennmesser *nt* MASCHINEN parting blade

Trennmethode *f* CHEMTECH separation process

Trennmittel *nt* KUNSTSTOFF mold release agent (AmE), mould release agent (BrE), release agent

Trennölfleck *m* KER & GLAS dope mark

Trennpapier *nt* VERPACK *Fleischereierzeugnisse* absorbents

Trennprogramm *nt* DRUCK hyphenation program

Trennrakete *f* RAUMFAHRT separation rocket

Trennrelais *nt* ELEKTROTECH disconnect relay

Trennrohr *nt* KERNTECH calandria tube

Trennsäule *f* CHEMTECH separating column, GERÄT *Gaschromatographie* capillary column

Trennschalter *m* BAU circuit breaker, ELEKTRIZ circuit breaker, disconnecting switch, isolating switch, *mit Luftisolierung* air break switch, ELEKTROTECH disconnecting switch, single pole switch, PHYS, TELEKOM isolator; **~ mit magnetischer Löschung** *m* ELEKTRIZ magnetic blowout circuit breaker

Trennschärfe *f* COMP & DV, ELEKTRONIK selectivity, QUAL power, RADIO selectivity

Trennscheibe *f* KER & GLAS slitting disc (BrE), slitting disk (AmE), MASCHINEN cutoff wheel, cutter wheel, cutting wheel, cutting-off wheel

Trennschichtpapier *nt* PAPIER release-coated paper

Trennschleifen *nt* FERTIG abrasive friction cutting, abrasive wheel cutting-off, KER & GLAS disc grinding (BrE), disk grinding (AmE), MASCHINEN abrasive cutting, parting-off

Trennschleifmaschine *f* FERTIG abrasive wheel cutting-off machine, KER & GLAS disc grinder (BrE), disk grinder (AmE), MASCHINEN parting-off grinder

Trennschleifscheibe *f* MASCHINEN parting-off wheel

Trennschleuder *f* CHEMTECH centrifuge, KER & GLAS

spinner
Trennschneiden *nt* FERTIG splitting
Trennschritt *m* TELEKOM *Doppelstrom* marking
Trennschutzschalter *m* ELEKTROTECH isolating switch
Trennseite *f* COMP & DV file separator
Trennstelle *f* EISENBAHN sleeper station (BrE), tie station (AmE), ELEKTROTECH break
Trennstufe *f* ELEKTROTECH buffer, TELEKOM *Radio* separator
Trenntransformator *m* COMP & DV, ELEKTROTECH isolation transformer
Trenntrichter *m* CHEMTECH, LABOR separating funnel
Trenntriebwerk *nt* RAUMFAHRT separation motor
Trennung *f* ABFALL separation, ELEKTROTECH cutoff, disconnection, ERDÖL separation, FERNSEH cutoff, KERNTECH *von Isotopen* partition, KOHLEN separation, MASCHINEN disconnection, parting, TELEKOM cutoff, *Telefonist* interruption, TRANS diverging; ~ **des Luftstroms** *f* LUFTTRANS *Vergaser* airstream separation; ~ **nach Korngröße** *f* CHEMTECH particle sizing; **Trennungsblech** *nt* FERTIG baffle sheet; **Trennungsmarke** *f* COMP & DV group mark, group marker; **Trennungsschicht** *f* CHEMTECH separation layer; **Trennungsstrich** *m* DRUCK hyphen
Trennverfahrenprozeß *m* ERDÖL *Raffinerie, Gasaufbereitung* extraction process
Trennvermögen *nt* KERNTECH separating power; ~ **eines Anlagenteils** *nt* KERNTECH unit separative power
Trennverstärker *m* AUFNAHME buffer amplifier, ELEKTRONIK isolation amplifier
Trennversuch *m* KERNTECH separative effort, KUNSTSTOFF peel test
Trennwand *f* ABFALL slurry wall, BAU partition wall, partition, FERTIG baffle, MASCHINEN bulkhead
Trennwerkzeug *nt* MASCHINEN parting tool
Trennwichte *f* KOHLEN partition density
Trennwiderstand *m* FERTIG cohesive resistance
Trennzeichen *nt* COMP & DV separator
Trennzentrifuge *f* LEBENSMITTEL separator
Treppe *f* BAU stairs, WASSERTRANS *Schiff* ladder; **Treppenabsatz** *m* BAU half pace; **Treppenboden** *m* BAU landing
treppenförmig: ~**e Steinanordnung im Ofen** *f* KER & GLAS corbel
Treppe: **Treppenlauf** *m* BAU flight of stairs; **Treppenlochwange** *f* BAU face string; **Treppenpfosten** *m* BAU newel; **Treppenpodest** *nt* BAU landing; **Treppenschacht** *m* BAU well; **Treppenstufe** *f* BAU step; **Treppenwange** *f* BAU string, stringer
Tresse *f* TEXTIL braid
Trester *m pl* CHEMIE *Rückstände bei Obstsäften, Wein* residue, LEBENSMITTEL *Rückstände beim Keltern, Bierbrauen* pomace
Tri *nt* CHEMIE trilene
Triac *nt* ELEKTRIZ triac, ELEKTRONIK *Halbleitertetrode* tetrode thyristor, ELEKTROTECH triac
Triacetat *nt* TEXTIL triacetate
Triacetin *nt* CHEMIE triacetin
Triacetonamin *nt* CHEMIE triacetonamin, triacetonamine
Triade *f* CHEMIE triad
Triamyl- *pref* CHEMIE triamyl
Triangulation *f* GEOM, RAUMFAHRT triangulation; **Triangulationspunkt** *m* BAU triangulation point
triangulieren *vt* GEOM triangulate
Triangulierung *f* GEOM triangulation
Triazol *nt* CHEMIE triazole

Tribokorrosion *f* CHEMIE *mechanisch-chemischer Verschleißprozeß* tribo-corrosion
Tribromacetaldehyd *nt* CHEMIE bromal
Tribromethanal *nt* CHEMIE bromal
Tribrommethan *nt* CHEMIE bromoform
Tributylphosphat *nt* *(TBP)* KERNTECH tributyl phosphate *(TBP)*
Tributyrin *nt* CHEMIE tributyrin
Tricarballyl- *pref* CHEMIE *Säure* tricarballylic
Trichloressig- *pref* CHEMIE *Säure* trichloroacetic
Trichlorethen *nt* CHEMIE trichloroethylene
Trichlorethylen *nt* CHEMIE trichloroethylene
Trichlorid *nt* CHEMIE trichloride
Trichlornitromethan *nt* CHEMIE chloropicrin, trichloronitromethane
Trichroismus *m* PHYS trichroism
trichroitisch *adj* PHYS trichroic
Trichter *m* BAU, CHEMIE, ELEKTRONIK, FERTIG, KER & GLAS, LABOR, LEBENSMITTEL, MECHAN funnel, PAPIER hopper; **Trichterantenne** *f* LUFTTRANS *Funkwesen* horn
trichterförmig: ~**e Ausweitung** *f* FERTIG bell
Trichter: **Trichterfüllgerät** *nt* KUNSTSTOFF hopper; **Trichterlautsprecher** *m* AKUSTIK, AUFNAHME horn loudspeaker
trichterlos: ~**er Lautsprecher** *m* AKUSTIK direct loudspeaker, radiator loudspeaker
Trichter: **Trichtermühle** *f* KOHLEN conical mill; **Trichteröffnung** *f* AKUSTIK horn mouth; **Trichterrohr** *nt* LABOR thistle funnel
Trickeinblendung *f* FERNSEH electronic inlay
Trickgenerator *m* FERNSEH special effects generator
Trickschieber *m* MASCHINEN Allan valve, trick valve
Tricosan *nt* CHEMIE tricosane
Tricresol *nt* CHEMIE tricresol
Tricresyl- *pref* CHEMIE tricresyl
Tricyansäuretriamid *nt* CHEMIE melamine
tricyclisch *adj* CHEMIE tricyclic
Trieb *m* LEBENSMITTEL *Teiglockerung* rising power; **Triebdrehgestell** *nt* EISENBAHN motor bogie (BrE), motor truck (AmE); **Triebdrehgestell mit einem Antriebsmotor** *nt* EISENBAHN monomotor bogie (BrE), monomotor truck (AmE); **Triebfahrzeug** *nt* EISENBAHN tractive unit; **Triebfahrzeugpark** *m* EISENBAHN fleet; **Triebfahrzeugpersonal** *nt* KFZTECH driving crew; **Triebkraft** *f* MASCHINEN propulsive force, TEXTIL agency; **Triebrad** *nt* KFZTECH *Getriebe* pinion; **Triebseite** *f* ELEKTROTECH drive end; **Triebspule** *f* ELEKTROTECH drive coil; **Triebstange** *f* MASCHINEN pitman; **Triebstock** *m* FERTIG driving pin wheel, round; **Triebstockgetriebe** *nt* MASCHINEN lantern gear; **Triebstockverzahnung** *f* MASCHINEN lantern gearing; **Triebstockzahnrad** *nt* FERTIG trundle wheel; **Triebstrang** *m* KFZTECH transmission, *Kraftübertragung* drive train; **Triebwagen** *m* EISENBAHN power car; **Triebwagenende** *nt* TRANS rear of the railcar; **Triebwasser** *nt* HYDRAUL headwater; **Triebwasserkanal** *m* HYDRAUL headrace
Triebwerk *nt* KFZTECH power unit, train of gears, LUFTTRANS engine, motor, MASCHINEN engine; ~ **ohne Nachbrenner** *nt* LUFTTRANS dry engine; **Triebwerkabstellen im Flug** *nt* LUFTTRANS engine shut-down in flight; **Triebwerkdrehzahl** *f* LUFTTRANS engine speed; **Triebwerkleistung** *f* LUFTTRANS *bei Reisegeschwindigkeit* cruising power; **Triebwerksabschaltung** *f* LUFTTRANS engine flame-out; **Triebwerksanlage** *f*

LUFTTRANS power plant; **Triebwerksausfall** m LUFT-
TRANS engine flame-out; **Triebwerksbefestigungen** f
pl LUFTTRANS engine mountings; **Triebwerksblock** m
KFZTECH power unit

Triebwerkschub: ~ **erhöhen** vi LUFTTRANS advance
throttle

Triebwerk: **Triebwerksdrehmoment** nt KFZTECH, LUFT-
TRANS engine torque; **Triebwerksdüse** f LUFTTRANS
engine nozzle cluster; **Triebwerksgondel** f LUFTTRANS
engine nacelle, engine pod, nacelle; **Triebwerksgon-
delstutzen** m LUFTTRANS engine nacelle stub;
Triebwerkshalterung f LUFTTRANS engine mount;
Triebwerkskonus m RAUMFAHRT jet nozzle; **Trieb-
werkskörper** m LUFTTRANS engine body;
Triebwerksluft-Ansaugstutzen m LUFTTRANS engine
air-intake extension; **Triebwerksnebenluftstrom** m
LUFTTRANS engine bypass air; **Triebwerksprüfstand** m
LUFTTRANS engine test stand; **Triebwerksrahmen** m
LUFTTRANS engine mount; **Triebwerkstarter** m LUFT-
TRANS *Anlasser* crank switch; **Triebwerkstrahlsog** m
LUFTTRANS engine jet wash; **Triebwerksunter-
brechung** f LUFTTRANS engine flame-out;
Triebwerksuntersatz m LUFTTRANS engine stand;
Triebwerkswiderlager und Schubgerüst nt LUFTTRANS
engine mount-and-thrust structure; **Triebwerkswin-
kelsteuerung** f RAUMFAHRT engine angle command;
Triebwerkverkleidung f LUFTTRANS cowling; **Trieb-
werkwellenlager** nt LUFTTRANS engine shaft bearing

Trieder nt GEOM trihedron

Trifluormethan nt CHEMIE fluoroform

Trifokalglas nt KER & GLAS *Brille* trifocal glass

Triftraum m ELEKTRONIK *Klystron* drift space

Triftröhre f ELEKTRONIK drift tube

Trigger m COMP & DV, ELEKTRIZ trigger; **Triggerdiode** f
ELEKTRONIK trigger diode; **Triggerimpuls** m ELEKTRO-
NIK trigger pulse, FERNSEH triggering pulse, TELEKOM
triggering lead pulse; **Triggerkreis** m ELEKTRIZ trigger
circuit

triggern vt ELEKTRIZ, PHYS trigger

Trigger: **Triggerschaltung** f ELEKTRIZ, ELEKTRONIK,
PHYS trigger circuit; **Triggerspannung** f FERNSEH triggering voltage; **Triggersysteme** nt pl STRAHLPHYS
triggering systems

Triglycerid nt CHEMIE triglyceride

Trigonometrie f GEOM trigonometry

trigonometrisch[1] adj GEOM trigonometric, trigonometrical

trigonometrisch:[2] ~**e Funktionen** f pl GEOM, MATH trigonometrical functions

Trihydrat nt CHEMIE trihydrate

Trihydroxyflavon nt CHEMIE naringenin, trihydroxyflavanone

Triiodid nt CHEMIE triiodide

Triiodmethan nt CHEMIE iodoform, triiodomethan

triklin[1] adj CHEMIE triclinic

triklin:[2] ~**es System** nt METALL triclinic system

Triller m AKUSTIK trill

Trimellith- pref CHEMIE trimellitic

Trimer nt CHEMIE, KUNSTSTOFF trimer

Trimerisat nt CHEMIE, KUNSTSTOFF trimer

trimerisieren vt CHEMIE trimerize

Trimesin- pref CHEMIE trimesic

Trimetallplatte f DRUCK trimetallic plate

Trimethylbenzol nt CHEMIE trimethylbenzene

Trimethylen nt CHEMIE cyclopropane, trimethylene

trimetrisch: ~**e Projektion** f KONSTZEICH trimetric pro-

jection

Trimm- pref ELEKTROTECH, KERNTECH trimming;
Trimm-Abschaltstab m KERNTECH shim safety rod;
Trimmauflösung f ELEKTROTECH trimming resolution;
Trimmelement nt KERNTECH shim assembly, shim ele-
ment, shim member

trimmen vt MECHAN, RAUMFAHRT, WASSERTRANS *Schiff*
trim

Trimmer m ELEKTRIZ preset pot, ELEKTROTECH adjustable capacitor, RADIO padder; **Trimmerkondensator** m
ELEKTROTECH trimmer capacitor, RADIO padder capacitor

Trimm-: **Trimmlage** f WASSERTRANS *Schiff* trim; **Trimm-
Nachfolge-Element** nt KERNTECH automatic control
assembly; **Trimm-Nachfolgesteuerung** f KERNTECH
automatic control assembly; **Trimmpotentiometer** nt
ELEKTRIZ, ELEKTROTECH trimming potentiometer;
Trimmruder nt LUFTTRANS trimming tab; **Trimmruder
des Luftschraubenblattes** nt LUFTTRANS *Hubschrauber* blade trim tab; **Trimmstab** m KERNTECH shim rod;
Trimmstab mit Feinantrieb m KERNTECH differential
control rod; **Trimmstabblock** m KERNTECH shim rod
bank; **Trimmstabilität** f LUFTTRANS trim stability;
Trimmsteuerung f LUFTTRANS trim control

Trimmung f LUFTTRANS trimming, RAUMFAHRT trim

trimolekular adj CHEMIE termolecular, trimolecular

trimorph adj CHEMIE trimorphic, trimorphous

Trimorphie f CHEMIE *Kristallchemie* trimorphism

Trinatrium- pref CHEMIE trisodium

Trinitrat nt CHEMIE ternitrate, trinitrate

trinitriert adj CHEMIE trinitrated

Trinitrobenzol nt CHEMIE trinitrobenzene

Trinitrotoluol nt *(TNT)* CHEMIE trinitrotoluene *(TNT)*

trinkbar adj WASSERVERSORG potable

Trinkwasser nt LEBENSMITTEL, WASSERVERSORG drinking water; **Trinkwasserqualität** f WASSERVERSORG
drinking water quality; **Trinkwasserversorgung** f WAS-
SERVERSORG drinking water supply

Trinom nt MATH trinomial

Triode f CHEMIE three-electrode valve, triode, ELEKTRO-
NIK, PHYS triode; **Triode-Hexode** f ELEKTRONIK
triode-hexode; **Trioden-Oszillator** m ELEKTRONIK triode oscillator; **Triodenverhalten** nt ELEKTRONIK triode
action

Triol nt CHEMIE trihydric acid, triol

Triose f CHEMIE triose

Triowalzwerk nt MASCHINEN three-high mill, three-high
rolls, three-high train

Trioxid nt CHEMIE teroxide, trioxide

Trioxoborsäure f CHEMIE boric acid, orthoboric acid

Trioxosilicat nt CHEMIE bisilicate, metasilicate

Tripalmitin nt CHEMIE tripalmitin

Tripelkarton m PAPIER three-layer board

Tripelpunkt m METALL, PHYS, THERMOD triple point

Triphenylmethan nt CHEMIE triphenylmethane

Triphenylmethyl nt CHEMIE trityl

Triplett nt KERNTECH, PHYS *Spektroskopie* triplet; **Tri-
plettlinse** f FOTO triplet lens

Triptan nt CHEMIE neohexane, trimethylbutane, triptane

Trisecschiff nt TRANS TRISEC ship, planing-hull-type
ship

Trisilikat nt CHEMIE trisilicate

Tristate-Ausgang m ELEKTRONIK three-state output

Tristearin nt CHEMIE glyceryl tristeate, tristearin

trisubstituiert adj CHEMIE trisubstituted

Tritan nt CHEMIE triphenylmethane

Trithion- *pref* CHEMIE trithionic
Tritium *nt (T)* CHEMIE tritium *(T)*; **mit ~ markiertet**
Verbindung *f* KERNTECH tritiated compound; **Tritium-**
trennung *f* KERNTECH *aus schwerem Wasser* tritium
extraction
Triton *nt (t)* TEILPHYS triton *(t)*
Trittbrett *nt* EISENBAHN step
Trittplattenbremsventil *nt* KFZTECH treadle brake valve
Trittschall *m* AKUSTIK impact sound; **Trittschall reduzie-**
rendes Material *nt* AKUSTIK impact sound-reducing
material; **Trittschall-Übertragungspegel** *m* AKUSTIK
impact sound transmission level
Trittstufe *f* BAU tread
trivalent *adj* CHEMIE ternary, triple, trivalent
Trivalenz *f* CHEMIE tervalence, trivalence, trivalency
Trochoide *f* GEOM trochoid; **Trochoiden-Massenspek-**
trometer *nt* KERNTECH trochoidal mass spectrometer
Trocken- *pref* ANSTRICH, DRUCK, THERMOD dry
trocken[1] *adj* ANSTRICH, PAPIER, THERMOD dry
trocken:[2] **~e Abscheidung** *f* ABFALL dry gas cleaning;
~er adiabatischer Temperaturgradient *m* UMWELT-
SCHMUTZ *der Atmosphäre* dry adiabatic lapse rate;
~es Ammoniak *nt* ERDÖL anhydrous ammonia; **~er**
Bohrschlamm *m* ERDÖL *Bohrtechnik* dry mud; **~e De-**
position *f* UMWELTSCHMUTZ dry deposition; **~es**
Erdgas *nt* ERDÖL dry natural gas, nonassociated gas;
~es Eruptionskreuz *nt* ERDÖL *Bohrlochkopfabsperrsy-*
stem dry tree; **~es Präzisionsschleifen** *nt* MASCHINEN
dry precision grinding; **~ saurer Fallout** *m* UMWELT-
SCHMUTZ dry acid deposit; **~ saurer Niederschlag** *m*
UMWELTSCHMUTZ dry acidic fallout
trocken:[3] **~ aufbewahren** *vt* VERPACK keep dry
trocken:[4] **~ laufen** *vi* WASSERVERSORG run dry
Trocken-: **Trockenabteil** *nt* LEBENSMITTEL drying sec-
tion; **Trockenakku** *m* ELEKTRIZ dry-storage battery;
Trockenakkumulator *m* ELEKTRIZ dry-storage battery;
Trockenanschluß *m* ELEKTROTECH dry connection;
Trockenanschlußklemme *f* ELEKTROTECH dry connec-
tor; **Trockenapparat** *m* VERPACK drying machine;
Trockenaufziehen *nt* FOTO dry mount; **Trocken-**
aufziehpresse *f* FOTO dry mounting press;
Trockenausschuß *m* PAPIER dry broke; **Trockenbat-**
terie *f* ELEKTROTECH dry battery, PHYS dry cell;
Trockenbatterie für Glocke *f* ELEKTRIZ bell battery;
Trockenbett *nt* ABFALL drying bed; **Trockenbohrer** *m*
ERDÖL *Bohrtechnik* claying bar; **Trockendampf** *m* HEIZ
& KÄLTE, NICHTFOSS ENERG dry steam; **Trockendampf-**
anteil *m* HEIZ & KÄLTE dryness fraction of steam;
Trockendock *nt* BAU dry dock, WASSERTRANS dry
dock, graving dock
Trockendock: ins ~ gehen *vi* WASSERTRANS *Schiff*
drydock
Trocken-: **Trockenei** *nt* LEBENSMITTEL powdered egg;
Trockeneis *nt* HEIZ & KÄLTE carbon dioxide snow, dry
ice, LEBENSMITTEL, THERMOD dry ice; **Trockenelektro-**
abscheidung *f* UMWELTSCHMUTZ dry precipitation;
Trockenelektrolyt *nt* ELEKTROTECH dry electrolyte;
Trockenelement *nt* ELEKTROTECH dry cell; **Trocken-**
entschwefelungsprozess *m* UMWELTSCHMUTZ dry
desulfurization process (AmE), dry desulphurization
process (BrE); **Trockenfäule** *f* WASSERTRANS dry rot;
Trockenfilter *nt* MASCHINEN dry filter; **Trockenfilz** *m*
DRUCK drying felt, PAPIER dry felt; **Trockenfläche** *f*
LEBENSMITTEL drying area; **Trockenfrachter** *m* WAS-
SERTRANS dry-bulk carrier; **Trockengehalt** *m* PAPIER
dry content; **Trockengestell** *nt* FOTO drying frame,

LABOR draining rack; **Trockengewicht** *nt* LUFTTRANS
Triebwerk und Motor, RAUMFAHRT, VERPACK dry
weight; **Trockenhaus** *nt* KOHLEN drying kiln; **Trocken-**
heit *f* KOHLEN, TEXTIL dryness; **Trockenhitze** *f* TEXTIL
dry heat
trockenhitzefixieren *vt* TEXTIL dry-heat-set
Trocken-: **Trockenkammer** *f* KUNSTSTOFF, MASCHINEN
drying cabinet, THERMOD drying chamber; **Trocken-**
klebefolie *f* FOTO dry mounting tissue; **Trockenkruste** *f*
KOHLEN dry crust; **Trockenkupplung** *f* KFZTECH, MA-
SCHINEN dry clutch; **Trockenlager** *nt* MASCHINEN dry
bearing; **Trockenlaufen** *nt* MASCHINEN dry running;
Trockenlaufkompressor *m* HEIZ & KÄLTE oil-free compressor, MASCHINEN dry-running compressor;
Trockenlaufzeit *f* KUNSTSTOFF dry-cycle time; **Trok-**
kenlegen *nt* BAU *Tiefbau* dewatering, WASSERVERSORG
drainage
trockenlegen *vt* WASSERVERSORG drain
Trocken-: **Trockenmaschine** *f* TEXTIL drier, dryer; **Trok-**
kenmasse *f* ABFALL dry matter, RAUMFAHRT dry mass;
Trockenmatte *f* DRUCK dry mat; **Trockenmauer** *f* BAU
dry wall, dry-stone wall; **Trockenmedium** *nt* CHEMIE
desiccant; **Trockenmilch** *f* LEBENSMITTEL dried milk,
milk powder; **Trockenmittel** *nt* CHEMTECH dehydrating agent, dehydrator, desiccative, KERNTECH
dehumidifier, KUNSTSTOFF drier, dryer, drying agent,
LEBENSMITTEL siccative, THERMOD desiccant, drying
agent, siccative, VERPACK desiccant, drying agent;
Trockenmittelbeutel *m* VERPACK desiccant bag;
Trockenmühle *f* KOHLEN dryer mill; **Trockennetztrans-**
formator *m* ELEKTROTECH dry-type power
transformer; **Trockenofen** *m* FERTIG *Formen* drying
stove, KOHLEN drying oven, LABOR vacuum oven,
LEBENSMITTEL drying kiln, drying oven, MASCHINEN
drying furnace, PAPIER drying oven, TEXTIL baking
stove, drying oven, drying stove, oven, VERPACK drying oven; **Trockenoffset** *nt* DRUCK dry offset, letterset;
Trockenoffsetdruck *m* VERPACK dry offset printing;
Trockenöl *nt* KUNSTSTOFF drying oil; **Trockenpartie** *f*
PAPIER dryer section; **Trockenpresse** *f* FOTO print
dryer; **Trockenpulverfeuerlöscher** *m* SICHERHEIT
dry-powder fire extinguisher; **Trockenraum** *m* KUNST-
STOFF drying cabinet; **Trockenreibung** *f* MASCHINEN
dry friction; **Trockenrohdichte** *f* BAU, KOHLEN dry
density; **Trockensäule** *f* LABOR drying column;
Trockenschale *f* FERTIG *Gießen* core plate; **Trocken-**
schaltkreis *m* ELEKTROTECH dry circuit;
Trockenschlammdeponie *f* UMWELTSCHMUTZ dry-
sludge disposal site
trockenschleifen *vt* KER & GLAS polish till dry
Trocken-: **Trockenschleuder** *f* CHEMTECH, FERTIG, KOH-
LEN centrifugal drier, centrifugal dryer;
Trockenschrank *m* KUNSTSTOFF drying cabinet, TEX-
TIL oven; **Trockenschrank mit gleichbleibender**
Temperatur *m* LABOR constant-temperature oven;
Trockenschrumpfung *f* BAU drying shrinkage; **Trok-**
kenschwund *m* BAU drying shrinkage; **Trockenstaub-**
Beseitigungsanlage *f* SICHERHEIT dry-dust removal
installation; **Trockenstoff** *m* KUNSTSTOFF exsiccant;
Trockensubstanz *f* ABFALL dry matter; **Trockensumpf**
m KFZTECH *Motor* dry sump; **Trockensumpf-**
schmierung *f* KFZTECH dry-sump lubrication;
Trockentemperatur *f* HEIZ & KÄLTE dry-bulb temperature; **Trockenthermometer** *nt* HEIZ & KÄLTE, THERMOD
dry-bulb thermometer; **Trockentransformator** *m*
ELEKTRIZ dry-type transformer; **Trockentrennung** *f*

ABFALL von *Müll* dry sorting; **Trockentrommel** *f* BAU drying drum; **Trockentunnel** *m* LEBENSMITTEL, VERPACK drying tunnel; **Trockenturm** *m* LEBENSMITTEL drying tower; **Trocken-Überschlagspannung** *f* ELEKTRIZ dry flashover voltage; **Trockenverbinder** *m* ELEKTROTECH dry connector; **Trockenvermahlung** *f* KOHLEN dry crushing; **Trockenwand** *f* BAU dry-stone wall; **Trockenzelle** *f* ELEKTRIZ *Batterie*, ELEKTROTECH, PHYS dry cell; **Trockenzentrifuge** *f* CHEMTECH centrifugal drier, centrifugal dryer; **Trockenziehen** *nt* FERTIG dry drawing; **Trockenzylinder** *m* PAPIER dryer cylinder, TEXTIL drying cylinder; **Trockenzylinder der Selbstabnahmepapiermaschine** *m* PAPIER yankee cylinder

Trockne: zur ~ eindampfen *vt* CHEMTECH evaporate to dryness

Trocknen *nt* BAU *Holz* seasoning, CHEMIE, ERDÖL desiccation, KOHLEN, KUNSTSTOFF, PAPIER, TEXTIL drying, THERMOD desiccation, drying, VERPACK desiccation

trocknen *vti* ANSTRICH dry, BAU bake, CHEMIE, HEIZ & KÄLTE desiccate, KOHLEN dry, LEBENSMITTEL desiccate, *Tee* fire, THERMOD desiccate, dry

trocknend[1] *adj* THERMOD siccative

trocknend:[2] **~es Öl** *nt* LEBENSMITTEL drying oil

Trockner *m* HEIZ & KÄLTE desiccator, KFZTECH receiver-dryer, *Flüssigkeitsbehälter mit Filtertrockner im Wärmekreislauf einer Klimaanlage* receiver-dehydrator, KOHLEN, MASCHINEN, TEXTIL, THERMOD drier, dryer, VERPACK drying machine

Trocknung *f* CHEMTECH desiccation, ERDÖL dehydration, drying, *Bohrtechnik* desiccation, KUNSTSTOFF drying, LEBENSMITTEL desiccation, TEXTIL drying, THERMOD, VERPACK desiccation; **Trocknungsgrad** *m* BAU degree of drying; **Trocknungskammer** *f* THERMOD drying chamber; **Trocknungsleistung** *f* THERMOD *eines Trockners* rate of drying; **Trocknungsmesser** *m* PAPIER drying meter; **Trocknungsmittel** *nt* HEIZ & KÄLTE, LEBENSMITTEL desiccant

Trog *m* KER & GLAS tray, LABOR tray, trough, MASCHINEN trough; **Trogbandförderer** *m* MASCHINEN trough conveyor; **Trogbrücke** *f* BAU trough bridge; **Troggurtförderer** *m* MASCHINEN trough conveyor; **Trogmischer** *m* KER & GLAS trough mixer; **Trogstange** *f* KER & GLAS tray bar

Trommel *f* FERNSEH drum, FERTIG roll, *Automat* carrier, HYDRAUL, KOHLEN drum, MASCHINEN barrel, pulley, MECHAN, MEERSCHMUTZ, PAPIER, RADIO *Fax*, VERPACK drum; **Trommelabschöpfgerät** *nt* MEERSCHMUTZ drum skimmer; **Trommelabtaster** *m* FERNSEH drum scanner; **Trommelanker** *m* ELEKTRIZ, ELEKTROTECH drum armature; **Trommelanlasser** *m* ELEKTRIZ drum starter; **Trommelantrieb** *m* MASCHINEN drum drive; **Trommelblattdiagramm** *nt* GERÄT drum chart diagram; **Trommelbohrmaschine** *f* MASCHINEN drum-type drilling machine; **Trommelbremse** *f* KFZTECH drum brake; **Trommeldrucker** *m* COMP & DV barrel printer (BrE), drum printer (AmE); **Trommelfilter** *nt* KOHLEN drum filter; **Trommelfräsmaschine** *f* MASCHINEN drum milling machine; **Trommelgeschwindigkeit** *f* RADIO *Fax* drum speed; **Trommelhöhenmesser** *m* LUFTTRANS drum altimeter; **Trommelkessel** *m* HYDRAUL cylinder boiler; **Trommelkiln** *m* THERMOD drum kiln; **Trommelkurve** *f* FERTIG drum cam; **Trommelmischer** *m* BAU drum mixer, LEBENSMITTEL barrel mixer

Trommeln *nt* KUNSTSTOFF tumbling

Trommel: **Trommelplotter** *m* COMP & DV drum plotter; **Trommelrevolver** *m* FERTIG horizontal axis turret, MASCHINEN drum turret; **Trommelschalter** *m* ELEKTRIZ drum controller, drum switch; **Trommelscheider** *m* KOHLEN trommel washer; **Trommelschütze** *f* NICHTFOSS ENERG drum gate; **Trommelsieb** *nt* KOHLEN drum separator; **Trommelspeicher** *m* COMP & DV drum, TELEKOM drum store; **Trommeltrocknen** *nt* KERNTECH in-drum drying; **Trommeltrockner** *m* MASCHINEN, THERMOD drum drier, drum dryer; **Trommelwascher** *m* BAU drum washer; **Trommelwelle** *f* MASCHINEN drum shaft; **Trommelwicklung** *f* ELEKTROTECH drum winding; **Trommelwinde** *f* MASCHINEN drum winch

Trompete *f* WASSERTRANS *Knoten* sheepshank

trompetenförmig: ~e Ausweitung *f* MASCHINEN bell mouth

Troostit *m* METALL troostite

Tropenverpackung *f* VERPACK tropical packaging

Tropf *m* KER & GLAS, LABOR drip; **Tropfbecher** *m* BAU drip cup; **Tropfblech** *nt* MASCHINEN drip plate

Tröpfchen *nt* UMWELTSCHMUTZ droplet

Tropfen *m* KER & GLAS drop, tear, LEBENSMITTEL, PAPIER drop; **Tropfenabscheider** *m* ABFALL demister unit, mist eliminator; **Tropfenbewässerung** *f* FERTIG *Kunststoffinstallationen* drip irrigation; **Tropfenbildung** *f* STRÖMPHYS drop formation; **Tropfenwasserzeichen** *nt* PAPIER drop watermark; **Tropfenzähler** *m* LABOR dropper, dropping bottle, PHYS stalagmometer, VERPACK drop counter; **Tropfenzählröhrchen** *nt* LABOR dropper tube, dropping tube

tropfen *vi* PAPIER drop

Tropf: **Tropfflasche** *f* LABOR dropping bottle; **Tropfkörper** *m* ABFALL percolating filter, sprinkling filter, trickling filter, UMWELTSCHMUTZ trickling filter; **Tropfkörperanlage** *f* CHEMTECH *Abwässer* biological filter; **Tropföler** *m* FERTIG drip oiler, MASCHINEN drip-feed lubricator; **Tropfölschmierung** *f* FERTIG, MASCHINEN drip-feed lubrication; **Tropfpunkt** *m* FERTIG drop point; **Tropfpunktapparat** *m* LABOR *Schmierfette* drop-point apparatus; **Tropfschale** *f* HEIZ & KÄLTE drip tray; **Tropftrichter** *m* LABOR tap funnel; **Tropfwasser** *nt* HEIZ & KÄLTE drip water; **Tropfwasserbildung** *f* HEIZ & KÄLTE dripping moisture

tropfwassergeschützt *adj* MASCHINEN drip-proof

Tropf: **Tropfzylinder** *m* BAU drip cup

Tropin *nt* CHEMIE tropine

tropisch: ~er Wirbelsturm *m* WASSERTRANS tropical revolving storm

Troposphäre *f* RAUMFAHRT troposphere

troposphärisch[1] *adj* RADIO tropospheric

troposphärisch:[2] **~e Streuung** *f* TELEKOM tropospheric scatter

Trosse[1] *f* MASCHINEN hawser, WASSERTRANS cable, cluster, *schweres Tau oder Drahtseil* hawser

Trosse:[2] **~ nachschleppen** *vi* WASSERTRANS *Festmachen* stream a warp

Trotyl *nt* CHEMIE trotyl

Troy-Gewicht *nt* METROL troy weight

Trub *m* LEBENSMITTEL *bei Wein oder Bier* sludge

trüb[1] *adj* TEXTIL hazy

trüb:[2] **~e Atmosphäre** *f* NICHTFOSS ENERG turbid atmosphere; **~es Wasser** *nt* UMWELTSCHMUTZ turbid water

Trübglas *nt* KER & GLAS opalescent glass

Trübheit *f* NICHTFOSS ENERG turbidity, TEXTIL cloudiness

Trübstoffe *m pl* CHEMIE *Wasserbehandlung* turbidity
Trübung *f* KUNSTSTOFF haze, turbidity, NICHTFOSS ENERG turbidity, TEXTIL cloudiness, WASSERTRANS *Radar* clutter; **Trübungsanalyse** *f* CHEMIE turbidimetry; **Trübungskoeffizient** *m* NICHTFOSS ENERG turbidity coefficient; **Trübungsmesser** *m* GERÄT haze meter, LABOR nephelometer, turbidity meter; **Trübungsmittel** *nt* KER & GLAS opacifier, LEBENSMITTEL cloudifier; **Trübungspunkt** *m* HEIZ & KÄLTE cloud point
Truck-to-Truck-System *nt* WASSERTRANS truck-to-truck system (AmE)
Trudelflugerprobung *f* LUFTTRANS spin flight testing
Trudeln *nt* LUFTTRANS spin
True: ~ **Motion Radar** *nt* RADIO true motion radar
Truffel *f* FERTIG sprue cutter, *Gießen* trowel
Trum *nt* MASCHINEN end
Trümmer *nt pl* BAU ruins; **Trümmergestein** *nt* BAU, KOHLEN fragmented rocks
Truxill- *pref* CHEMIE truxillic
Truxillin *nt* CHEMIE truxilline
tryptisch *adj* CHEMIE tryptic
Trysegel *nt* WASSERTRANS *Segeln* trysail
TR-Zelle *f* FERNSEH, RADIO TR cell
TS *abbr* (*Treibsitz*) MASCHINEN drive fit
T-Schaltung *f* PHYS T-network
Tschebyscheff: ~**sches Filter** *nt* PHYS Chebyshev filter; ~**sches Filter achter Ordnung** *nt* ELEKTRONIK *polfrei* eighth-order Chebyshev filter
Tscherenkow: ~**scher Detektor** *m* STRAHLPHYS, TEILPHYS Cerenkov detector; ~**scher Effekt** *m* STRAHLPHYS, TEILPHYS Cerenkov effect; ~**sche Strahlung** *f* STRAHLPHYS, TEILPHYS Cerenkov radiation; ~**scher Zähler** *m* STRAHLPHYS, TEILPHYS Cerenkov counter
T-Spleiß *nt* ELEKTRIZ T-joint
T-Stoß *m* BAU *Sanitär* T-joint
T-Stück *nt* BAU union-T, FERTIG branch tee, MASCHINEN T, T-piece
TT *abbr* (*Tonträger*) AUFNAHME, FERNSEH sound carrier
TTL *abbr* (*Transistor-Transistor-Logik*) COMP & DV, ELEKTRONIK TTL (*transistor-transistor logic*)
TTL-Messung *f* (*Objektivmessung*) FOTO TTL metering (*through-the-lens metering*)
TT-Logik *f* COMP & DV, ELEKTRONIK transistor-transistor logic
T-Träger *m* BAU T-beam
Tubenfüll-: ~ **und-Ausspritzmaschine** *f* VERPACK tube filling and cleaning machine
Tubenverschließmaschine *f* VERPACK tube-closing machine
Tubing *nt* ERDÖL production tubing, tubing
Tuch *nt* TEXTIL cloth, fabric, woven fabric; **Tuchfilter** *nt* UMWELTSCHMUTZ fabric filter; **Tuchpolierer** *m* KER & GLAS cloth polisher; **Tuchscheren** *nt* TEXTIL cropping
Tufting-Teppich *m* TEXTIL tufted carpet
Tülle *f* MASCHINEN grommet
Tumblerschalter *m* ELEKTROTECH tumbler switch
Tünche *f* BAU whitewash
Tuner *m* FERNSEH, RADIO *Frequenzabstimmvorrichtung*, TELEKOM tuner
Tunnel *m* EISENBAHN subway (AmE), underground (BrE), NICHTFOSS ENERG tunnel; **Tunnelanguß** *m* KUNSTSTOFF tunnel gate; **Tunnelbau** *m* BAU tunneling (AmE), tunnelling (BrE); **Tunnelbaumaschine** *f* BAU tunneling machine (AmE), tunnelling machine (BrE); **Tunnelbauverfahren** *nt* BAU tunneling technique (AmE), tunnelling technique (BrE); **Tunnelbohrmaschine** *f* BAU tunnel-boring machine; **Tunneldiode** *f* ELEKTRONIK, PHYS Esaki diode, tunnel diode; **Tunneldiodenverstärker** *m* RAUMFAHRT *Weltraumfunk* tunnel diode amplifier; **Tunneleffekt** *m* ELEKTRONIK, PHYS tunnel effect; **Tunnelkühlofen** *m* KER & GLAS tunnel lehr; **Tunnelmode** *f* OPTIK tunneling mode (AmE), tunnelling mode (BrE); **Tunnelstoß** *m* BAU face; **Tunnelstrahl** *m* OPTIK tunneling ray (AmE), tunnelling ray (BrE)
Tunnelung *f* ELEKTRONIK *Halbleiter*, TELEKOM tunneling (AmE), tunnelling (BrE)
Tunnelvorgang *m* TELEKOM tunneling (AmE), tunnelling (BrE)
Tüpfelplatte *f* LABOR spotting plate
Tür *f* BAU, KFZTECH *Karosserie* door; **Türangel** *f* BAU garnet hinge, hinge; **Türband** *nt* BAU door hinge
Turbidimetrie *f* CHEMIE turbidimetry
Turbine *f* ELEKTRIZ, KFZTECH, MASCHINEN, MECHAN, NICHTFOSS ENERG, WASSERTRANS turbine; ~ **mit innerer Beaufschlagung** *f* HYDRAUL outward-flow turbine; **Turbinenabschlußventil** *nt* KERNTECH turbine stop valve; **Turbinenantrieb** *m* KFZTECH, WASSERTRANS turbine propulsion; **Turbinenblatt** *nt* HYDRAUL blade; **Turbinenbohranlage** *f* ERDÖL *Bohrtechnik* turbodrill; **Turbinenbohren** *nt* ERDÖL *Bohrtechnik* turbine drilling; **Turbinendeckband** *nt* LUFTTRANS *Turbinentriebwerk* shroud ring; **Turbinendurchflußmesser** *m* GERÄT turbine flow meter; **Turbinenfundament** *nt* KFZTECH, WASSERTRANS turbine seating; **Turbinengebäude** *nt* KERNTECH turbine building; **Turbinengehäuse** *nt* KFZTECH, WASSERTRANS turbine casing; **Turbinengrube** *f* HYDRAUL turbine pit; **Turbinenhaus** *nt* KERNTECH turbine building, turbine house; **Turbinenkammer** *f* HYDRAUL turbine chamber; **Turbinenkammer des geschlossenen Typs** *f* HYDRAUL turbine chamber of the closed system; **Turbinenlagerung** *f* KFZTECH, WASSERTRANS turbine seating
Turbinenläufer mit Schaufeln ausrüsten *vi* HYDRAUL *Montage* provide a turbine wheel with vanes
Turbine: **Turbinenlaufschaufel** *f* FERTIG turbine blade; **Turbinenleistung** *f* NICHTFOSS ENERG turbine output; **Turbinenleistungsvermögen** *nt* NICHTFOSS ENERG turbine efficiency; **Turbinenluftstrahltriebwerk** *nt* LUFTTRANS jet turbine engine; **Turbinenmotor** *m* KFZTECH, WASSERTRANS turbine engine; **Turbinenpumpe** *f* HYDRAUL, MASCHINEN turbine pump, NICHTFOSS ENERG pump turbine, WASSERVERSORG turbopump; **Turbinenrad** *nt* HYDRAUL *Dampf-, Wasserturbine*, KFZTECH turbine wheel, MASCHINEN runner, turbine wheel, WASSERTRANS turbine wheel; **Turbinenschaufel** *f* FERTIG turbine blade, HYDRAUL blade, KFZTECH turbine blade, MASCHINEN turbine blade, turbine vane, NICHTFOSS ENERG, WASSERTRANS turbine blade; **Turbinenstaustrahltriebwerk** *nt* LUFTTRANS turboramjet; **Turbinenstufe** *f* MASCHINEN turbine stage; **Turbinentreibstoff** *m* LUFTTRANS jet engine fuel; **Turbinenzähler** *m* GERÄT turbine flow meter, vane meter; **Turbinenzug** *m* EISENBAHN turbotrain
Tür: **Türblatt** *nt* BAU leaf; **Türblattquerholz** *nt* BAU middle rail; **Türblocken** *nt* EISENBAHN door blocking
Turbo- *pref* ELEKTRIZ, LUFTTRANS, PHYS turbo; **Turboabscheidung** *f* LEBENSMITTEL turboseparation;

Turbo-Alternatorsatz m ELEKTRIZ turbo-alternator; **Turbobohranlage** f ERDÖL turbodrill; **Turbobohren** nt ERDÖL turbine drilling

turboelektrisch: **~er Triebwagen** m EISENBAHN turbo-electric motor coach

Turbo-: **Turbogebläse** nt MASCHINEN turboblower; **Turbogenerator** m ELEKTROTECH, PHYS turbogenerator; **Turbojet-Flugzeug** nt LUFTTRANS turbojet; **Turbokammzug** m TEXTIL turbotop; **Turbokompressor** m KFZTECH, WASSERTRANS turbocompressor; **Turbokreuzer** m WASSERTRANS turbocruiser; **Turbolader** m KFZTECH turbocharger, turbocompressor, MASCHINEN turbocharger, WASSERTRANS turbocharger, turbocompressor; **Turboluftstrahltriebwerk** nt THERMOD turbojet engine; **Turbomolekularpumpe** f MASCHINEN turbo-molecular pump, PHYS molecular pump; **Turbomotor** m KFZTECH turbine engine, THERMOD turboshaft engine, WASSERTRANS turbine engine; **Turbopropflugzeug** nt LUFTTRANS turboprop; **Turboproptriebwerk** nt LUFTTRANS propjet engine; **Turbopumpe** f MASCHINEN, RAUMFAHRT, WASSERVERSORG turbopump; **Turbostapler** m TEXTIL turbostapler; **Turbostrahltriebwerk** nt *(TL-Triebwerk)* LUFTTRANS turbojet; **Turboverdichter** m KFZTECH centrifugal supercharger, MASCHINEN turbocompressor; **Turbo-Wechselstromgenerator** m ELEKTROTECH turbo-alternator

turbulent[1] *adj* STRÖMPHYS turbulent

turbulent:[2] **~e Ablösung** f STRÖMPHYS turbulent separation; **~e Diffusion** f KERNTECH turbulent diffusion; **~e Energie** f STRÖMPHYS turbulent energy; **~er Fleck** m STRÖMPHYS turbulent spot; **~e Grenzschicht** f STRÖMPHYS turbulent boundary layer; **~e Nachströmung** f PHYS wake; **~e Strömung** f FERTIG sinuous flow, HEIZ & KÄLTE eddy flow, PHYS, STRÖMPHYS turbulent flow; **~es Wiederanlegen** nt STRÖMPHYS turbulent re-attachment

Turbulenz f KFZTECH, NICHTFOSS ENERG, RAUMFAHRT, STRÖMPHYS turbulence; **Turbulenzballen** m STRÖMPHYS turbulent plug

turbulenzerzeugend: **~es Gitter** nt STRÖMPHYS turbulence-generating grid

Tür: **Türdrücker** m BAU door opener; **Türfalle** f KFZTECH door catch; **Türflügel** m BAU leaf, wing; **Türfüllung** f BAU door panel, panel; **Türfutter** nt BAU door case, jamb lining; **Türgitter** nt EISENBAHN deadlight

Turgordruck m LEBENSMITTEL *Pflanzenwellen: Gewebespannung* turgor

Tür: **Türgriff** m BAU, KFZTECH *Tür* door handle

Turingmaschine f COMP & DV Turing machine; **Turingtest** m COMP & DV Turing test

Tür: **Türkantenschoner** m BAU edge plate; **Türklinke** f BAU door, handle; **Türknauf** m BAU door knob; **Türkontakt** m ELEKTROTECH gate contact; **Türlüftungsöffner** m SICHERHEIT ventilation door opener

Turm m WASSERTRANS *U-Boot* conning tower

Turmalin nt PHYS tourmaline

Turm: **Turmansatz** m BAU stump; **Turmbereich** m KER & GLAS tower section; **Turmdrehkran** m BAU tower crane, MASCHINEN tower slewing crane; **Turmgerüst** nt BAU tower; **Turmkran** m BAU, MASCHINEN tower crane; **Turmpfeiler** m BAU tower pier; **Turmseilrollenblock** m ERDÖL *Hebetechnik* crown block; **Turmsystem** nt AB-FALL *Kompostierungsverfahren* tower system; **Turmtür** f KER & GLAS tower door; **Turmverbindung** f BAU derrick girt; **Turmwäscher** m CHEMTECH washer

Tür: **Türöffnung** f BAU doorway; **Türpfosten** m BAU door post, jamb, post; **Türquerriegel** m BAU *in Schloßhöhe* lock rail; **Türrahmen** m BAU door frame; **Türriegel** m BAU bolt, latch, door bolt; **Türsäule** f KFZTECH door pillar; **Türscharnier** nt KFZTECH door hinge; **Türschließmechanismus** m KFZTECH door-locking mechanism; **Türschloß** nt KFZTECH door lock; **Türschwelle** f BAU doorsill, sill, threshold; **Türstange** f BAU door bar; **Türstock** m KER & GLAS goal post; **Türsturz** m BAU browpiece, lintel; **Türverkleidung** f BAU door panel; **Türverriegelung** f KFZTECH door locking; **Türzarge** f BAU buck (AmE), door case, door casing, door frame

Tuschieren nt FERTIG marking

tuschieren vt FERTIG mark

Tüten: **in ~ verpacken** vt LEBENSMITTEL, VERPACK bag

Tütennähmaschine f VERPACK bag-stitching machine

TV abbr *(Fernsehen)* FERNSEH TV *(television)*

T-Verbindung f BAU T-piece union, ELEKTRIZ, MASCHINEN T-joint

T-Verbindungsstück nt LABOR T-piece, T-piece connector

T-Verschraubung f BAU T-piece union

TVI abbr *(Fernsehempfangsstörung, Fernsehstörung)* FERNSEH TVI *(television interference)*

TV-Kabel nt FERNSEH television cable

TVSt abbr *(Teilnehmervermittlungsstelle)* TELEKOM access exchange

TW abbr *(Tonwahl)* TELEKOM MFD *(multifrequency dialling)*

Twill m TEXTIL twill

Twisted-Pair nt ELEKTROTECH twisted pair; **~ Flachkabel** nt ELEKTROTECH twisted pair flat cable

Tyndall-Effekt m PHYS Tyndall effect

Typ m COMP & DV type; **Typanweisung für ganzzahlige Daten** f COMP & DV *Fortran* integer type

Type f COMP & DV type; **Typenabnahme** f RAUMFAHRT type approval; **Typenfreigabe** f RAUMFAHRT type approval; **Typenhöhe** f DRUCK height of type, height of typeface; **Typenkopf** m COMP & DV print head; **Typenprüfung** f LUFTTRANS *Turbomotor*, RAUMFAHRT type test; **Typenrad** nt COMP & DV, DRUCK daisywheel, print wheel; **Typenraddrucker** m COMP & DV barrel printer (BrE), daisywheel printer, drum printer (AmE), DRUCK daisywheel printer; **Typenreihe** f MASCHINEN series; **Typenschild** nt MECHAN nameplate; **Typenwalzendrucker** m COMP & DV barrel printer (BrE), drum printer (AmE)

typisiert: **~e Variable** f KÜNSTL INT tagged variable

Typ n adj ELEKTRONIK n-type

Typographie f DRUCK typography

typographisch: **~er Punkt** m DRUCK typographic point

Typometer m DRUCK line gage (AmE), line gauge (BrE), type scale

Typ: **Typprüfbericht** m QUAL type test report; **Typprüfmenge** f QUAL type test quantity; **Typprüfmuster** nt QUAL type test sample; **Typprüfung** f QUAL type test; **Typprüfungen** f pl QUAL type verifications and tests; **Typprüfungsprotokoll** nt QUAL type test report

Tyrosin nt CHEMIE tyrosine

U

U[1] *abbr* AKUSTIK *(Volumengeschwindigkeit, Volumenstrom)* U *(volume current)*, ELEKTRIZ *(Spannung)* V *(voltage)*, OPTIK *(Strahlungsenergie)* U *(radiant energy)*, THERMOD *(Wärmeübertragungskoeffizient)* U *(overall heat transfer coefficient)*

U[2] *(Uran)* CHEMIE U *(uranium)*

û *abbr (wahrscheinlichste Geschwindigkeit)* PHYS û *(most probable speed)*

U-Ablauf *m* FERNSEH U-wrap

U-Bahn *f* EISENBAHN tube, (BrE) underground, subway (AmE)

Überarbeitung *f* ERDÖL workover

überbeanspruchen *vt* BAU, MASCHINEN overstress

Überbeanspruchung *f* BAU, MASCHINEN overstress

Überbelastung *f* AUFNAHME, ELEKTROTECH overload, FERTIG overtensioning, METALL overstressing, TRANS *Straße* overloading

Überbelegung *f* TELEKOM congestion, VERPACK overload

überbelichten *vt* FOTO overexpose

überbelichtet: ~es Bild *nt* FOTO overexposed picture; ~er Film *m* FOTO overexposed film

Überbelichtung *f* FOTO overexposure

Überblattung *f* BAU overleap joint

Überbleibsel *nt* ANSTRICH residue

Überblendbild *nt* FERNSEH cut slide

überblenden *vt* COMP & DV cross-fade

Überblendregler *m* AUFNAHME, ELEKTRONIK *Film* fader

Überblendung *f* AKUSTIK dissolve

Überbringer *m* TRANS carrier

überbrücken *vt* BAU bridge, EISENBAHN bridge over, PHYS bypass, shunt

überbrückt: ~es H-Netzwerk *nt* ELEKTROTECH *vierpolig* bridged-H network; ~es T-Netzwerk *nt* ELEKTROTECH *vierpolig* bridged-T network

Überbrückung *f* BAU *von Rissen* bridging, ELEKTRIZ butt contact, bypassing, GERÄT, KFZTECH, PHYS, RADIO bypassing; **Überbrückungsdraht** *m* ELEKTROTECH jumper; **Überbrückungskondensator** *m* GERÄT, PHYS bypass capacitor, shunt capacitor; **Überbrückungskontakt** *m* ELEKTROTECH bridging contact; **Überbrückungsschalter** *m* ELEKTRIZ bypass switch

überchlorsaures: ~ Salz *nt* CHEMIE perchlorate

überdacht:[1] nicht ~ *adj* BAU open

überdacht:[2] ~e Anlage *f* HEIZ & KÄLTE sheltered installation

Überdachung *f* BAU roofing

überdecken *vt* ANSTRICH lap, BAU overcoat, *Ziegel* lap

überdeckt: ~er Abzugsgraben *m* ABFALL covered drain

Überdeckung *f* BAU overlap, shelter, GERÄT coverage, MASCHINEN overlap, profile overlap; **äußere ~** *f* HYDRAUL outside lap, *Steuerschieber* outside lap; **~ durch Geräusch** *f* TELEKOM noise masking; **Überdeckungsgrad** *m* FERTIG *Getriebelehre* engagement factor; **Überdeckungswinkel** *m* ELEKTRIZ angle of overlap, MASCHINEN overlap angle

überdimensionieren *vt* BAU, MASCHINEN oversize

Überdimensionierung *f* BAU oversizing, MASCHINEN overdimensioning, oversizing

Überdosierung *f* TEXTIL overfeed, UMWELTSCHMUTZ overdosage

Überdosis *f* UMWELTSCHMUTZ OD, overdose

überdrehen *vt* FERTIG *Gewinde* strip

Überdrehungsgrad *m* FERTIG overlap

Überdrehzahl *f* MASCHINEN, MECHAN overspeed; **Überdrehzahlkontrolle** *f* NICHTFOSS ENERG overspeed control; **Überdrehzahlschutz** *m* MASCHINEN overspeed brake

Überdruck *m* ERDÖL *Geologie* overpressure, HEIZ & KÄLTE excess pressure, LUFTTRANS overpressure, MASCHINEN excess pressure;

Überdrucken *nt* VERPACK overprinting;

Überdruck: **Überdruckkammer** *f* ERDÖL *Tauchtechnik* hyperbaric chamber; **Überdruck-Klimaanlage** *f* HEIZ & KÄLTE plenum system; **Überdruckkühlkreislauf** *m* KFZTECH sealed cooling system; **Überdruckmanometer** *nt* GERÄT overpressure gage (AmE), overpressure gauge (BrE); **Überdruckpumpe für Kraftstoff** *f* LUFTTRANS booster pump; **Überdruck-Schnellschlußventil** *nt* MASCHINEN pop valve; **Überdruck-Staubabzugshaube** *f* SICHERHEIT positive-pressure-powered dust hood; **Überdruck-Staubabzugsschürze** *f* SICHERHEIT positive-pressure-powered dust blouse; **Überdruckturbine** *f* NICHTFOSS ENERG reaction turbine; **Überdruckventil** *nt* EISENBAHN, FERTIG, HEIZ & KÄLTE, HYDRAUL, KFZTECH *Schmierung*, MASCHINEN, MECHAN pressure relief valve, relief valve

Übereckmaß *nt* MASCHINEN across corner dimension, width across corners

übereinander:[1] ~ angeordnete Pressen *f pl* PAPIER stacked presses

übereinander:[2] ~ lagern *vt* FERNSEH superimpose

Übereinstimmung *f* COMP & DV conformance, GERÄT fit, MASCHINEN accordance; **Übereinstimmungsgrad** *m* TRANS degree of compliance

überendlich *adj* MATH transfinite

überentwickeln *vt* FOTO overdevelop

Überernährung *f* LEBENSMITTEL overnutrition

Überfahrt *f* WASSERTRANS passage, *Navigation* crossing

Überfall *m* HYDRAUL nappe; **Überfallfischgerinne** *nt* NICHTFOSS ENERG overfall-type fish pass; **Überfallwehr** *nt* NICHTFOSS ENERG spillway, WASSERVERSORG spillway, waste weir

Überfalz *m* DRUCK over fold

überfalzt: ~e Fuge *f* BAU rebated joint

Überfang *m* KER & GLAS flash; **Überfangen** *nt* KER & GLAS flashing; **Überfangglas** *nt* KER & GLAS flashed glass; **Überfangnoppe** *f* KER & GLAS flashing knob; **Überfangopalglas** *nt* KER & GLAS flashed opal; **Überfangrubinglas** *nt* KER & GLAS flash ruby

überfärben *vt* TEXTIL cross-dye, overdye

Überfärben *nt* KER & GLAS overstriking

Überfärbung *f* TEXTIL double dyeing

Überflur- *pref* MASCHINEN floor-mounted; **Überflurhydrant** *m* BAU pillar hydrant, SICHERHEIT pillar fire hydrant

Überflußverlust *m* RAUMFAHRT *Weltraumfunk* spillover loss

überfluten[1] *vt* MECHAN flood, WASSERVERSORG submerge

überfluten[2] *vi* WASSERTRANS *Flut* flood

überflutet: **~e Düse** *f* LUFTTRANS flooded jet

Überflutung *f* WASSERVERSORG inundation, overflow

Überform *f* FERTIG mantle, *Gießen* coat

überführen *vt* BAU *Straße* pass over

Überführen *nt* RAUMFAHRT *von Tank* transfer

Überführung *f* BAU overbridge, KER & GLAS carry-over; **Überführungsflug** *m* LUFTTRANS ferry flight; **Überführungsisolator** *m* ELEKTROTECH terminal insulator

Überfunktion *f* METALL excess function

Übergabe *f* KERNTECH handover, KONTROLL transfer; **Übergabeanweisung** *f* KONTROLL transfer instruction; **Übergabesignal** *nt* FERNSEH change-over cue

Übergang *m* EISENBAHN crossover, *von Steg zum Schienenkopf* fillet radius, LUFTTRANS *während des Fluges* in-flight transition, OPTIK *Halbleiter* joint, TELEKOM *Hableiter* junction; **~ erster Ordnung** *m* PHYS first-order transition; **~ in Grundzustand** *m* TEILPHYS ground state transition; **~ zu neuer Serie** *m* FERTIG job changeover; **~ zur Turbulenz** *m* STRÖMPHYS transition to turbulence; **~ während des Fluges** *m* LUFTTRANS flight transition; **~ zweiter Ordnung** *m* PHYS second order transition; **Übergangsabschnitt** *m* LUFTTRANS *Landung* transition segment; **Übergangsarmatur** *f* FERTIG transition fitting; **Übergangsbahnhof** *m* EISENBAHN interchange track; **Übergangsbereich** *m* COMP & DV transient area; **Übergangsbogen** *m* TRANS flareout; **Übergangsbohrung** *f* KFZTECH bypass bore; **Übergangsbrücke** *f* EISENBAHN gangway; **Übergangselement** *nt* METALL transition element; **Übergangsenthalpie** *f* KERNTECH transition enthalpy; **Übergangsfehler** *m* COMP & DV transient error; **Übergangsfläche** *f* METALL *zwischen Medien* interface; **Übergangsfunktion** *f* ELEKTRONIK indicial response, step function, ELEKTROTECH *Prozeßsteuerung* transient response; **Übergangsgleichgewicht** *nt* PHYS transient equilibrium; **Übergangsimpedanz** *f* ELEKTRIZ transition impedance; **Übergangskriechen** *nt* METALL transient creep; **Übergangskurve** *f* TRANS transition curve; **Übergangsmetall** *nt* METALL transition metal; **Übergangsmuffe** *f* MASCHINEN reducing socket; **Übergangsorbit** *m* RAUMFAHRT interim orbit, transfer orbit; **Übergangspassung** *f* MASCHINEN transition fit; **Übergangsphase** *f* METALL transient phase; **Übergangspunkt** *m* KERNTECH transition point; **Übergangsreibstelle** *f* KER & GLAS transit rub; **Übergangsrohrstück** *nt* MASCHINEN reducing pipe; **Übergangssee** *m* UMWELTSCHMUTZ transition lake; **Übergangsstecker** *m* ELEKTROTECH plug adaptor; **Übergangsstelle** *f* COMP & DV flowchart connector; **Übergangsstück** *nt* BAU, MASCHINEN reducer; **Übergangsverhalten** *nt* FERNSEH transient response, REGELUNG transient behavior (AmE), transient behaviour (BrE); **Übergangsverschraubung** *f* FERTIG adaptor union; **Übergangsvorgang** *m* KONTROLL transient; **Übergangswahrscheinlichkeit** *f* PHYS transition probability; **Übergangswiderstand** *m* ELEKTRIZ transition impedance; **Übergangszeit** *f* PHYS transit time; **Übergangszone** *f* ERDÖL *Lagerstättentechnik* transition zone

übergeben *vt* KONTROLL transfer

übergehen *vt* FERTIG *Form* blend

übergeordnet *adj* HEIZ & KÄLTE upstream

Übergeschwindigkeit *f* MECHAN overspeed

übergesetzt: **~er Akzent** *m* DRUCK piece accent

Übergewicht *nt* METROL overweight, VERPACK excess weight

übergewichtig *adj* VERPACK overweight

Überglasung *f* KER & GLAS glaze

übergroß *adj* MASCHINEN oversize

Übergröße *f* KOHLEN oversize, MASCHINEN overdimension, oversize

Übergroßintegration *f* (*VLSI*) COMP & DV, ELEKTRONIK, TELEKOM very large-scale integration (*VLSI*)

Übergruppe *f* COMP & DV super group, supergroup, TELEKOM supergroup

Überhandknoten *m* WASSERTRANS overhand knot

Überhang *m* BAU overhang, DRUCK kern, KFZTECH *Karosserie*, MASCHINEN overhang

überhängend: **~er Vorsteven** *m* WASSERTRANS *Schiffbau* raking stem; **~e Welle** *f* MASCHINEN overhanging shaft

Überhang: **Überhangwand** *f* BAU overhanging wall; **Überhangzeit** *f* RAUMFAHRT hangover time

Überhärten *nt* KUNSTSTOFF overcure

Überhärtung *f* KUNSTSTOFF overcure

Überheizen *nt* ELEKTROTECH overheating

Überhitzen *nt* ELEKTROTECH, KFZTECH *des Motors*, THERMOD overheating

überhitzen[1] *vt* HEIZ & KÄLTE superheat, THERMOD overheat

überhitzen:[2] **sich ~** *v refl* THERMOD overheat

Überhitzer *m* HEIZ & KÄLTE, KERNTECH superheater; **Überhitzerelement** *nt* KERNTECH superheat assembly; **Überhitzerschlange** *f* HEIZ & KÄLTE superheater coil

überhitzt: **~er Dampf** *m* HEIZ & KÄLTE, MASCHINEN, PHYS, THERMOD superheated steam

Überhitzung *f* ELEKTROTECH, MASCHINEN overheating, METALL, PHYS superheating; **Überhitzungsthermresistor** *m* LUFTTRANS overheat thermoresistor

Überhitzungswärme abführen *vi* HEIZ & KÄLTE desuperheat

überhöhen *vt* BAU bank

überhöht[1] *adj* FERTIG leptokurtic

überhöht:[2] **~er Druck** *m* LUFTTRANS overpressure

Überhöhung *f* AKUSTIK camber, BAU superelevation, EISENBAHN cant, FERTIG leptokurtosis, step; **~ der Abluftfahne** *f* UMWELTSCHMUTZ plume rise; **Überhöhungsfaktor** *m* KERNTECH advantage factor

Überholen *nt* TRANS passing, WASSERTRANS *Schiffbewegung* lurch

Überholhilfen *f pl* TRANS passing aids

Überholklauenkupplung *f* EISENBAHN override clutch

Überholkupplung *f* LUFTTRANS *Flugwesen* overrunning clutch, MASCHINEN freewheel clutch, overrunning clutch

Überholsichtweite *f* TRANS passing sight distance

Überholspur *f* BAU passing lane, *Straße* acceleration lane, TRANS overtaking lane, passing lane

überholt *adj* FERTIG obsolete

Überholung *f* KFZTECH *eines Motors*, LUFTTRANS *Gerätschaften*, WASSERTRANS *Instandsetzung* overhaul

Überhörfrequenz *f* ELEKTRONIK, STRAHLPHYS supersonic frequency

Überhub *m* RAUMFAHRT *Weltraumfunk* overdeviation

Überkapazität *f* KER & GLAS wrong capacity, LUFTTRANS *Lufttransport* overcapacity

überkleben *vt* KONSTZEICH mark

überkochen *vi* THERMOD boil over

Überkompoundierung *f* ELEKTROTECH overcompounding

Überkopfförderband *nt* VERPACK overhead conveyor

Überkopfschutzgitter *nt* SICHERHEIT *für Gabelstapler* overhead guards

Überkragung *f* FERTIG overhang

Überkreuzungsbereich *m* ELEKTRONIK crossover area

Überkreuzverzerrung *f* AUFNAHME crossover distortion

überkritisch: **~e Ballung** *f* ELEKTRONIK overbunching; **~e Dämpfung** *f* PHYS overdamping; **~e Reaktion** *f* STRAHLPHYS supercritical reaction

Überladebrücke *f* WASSERTRANS gantry crane

überladen *adj* ELEKTRIZ overloaded

Überladung *f* ELEKTRIZ, ELEKTROTECH overcharge, MASCHINEN overload

überlagern[1] *vt* FERNSEH overlay

überlagern:[2] **sich ~** *v refl* RADIO *Hochfrequenztechnik* beat

überlagert: **~e Funkzone** *f* TELEKOM overlaid cell

Überlagerung *f* ANSTRICH overlay, overlaying, COMP & DV interference, superimposition, overlay, overlaying, ELEKTRONIK *von Sendern* blanking, FERNSEH heterodyning, PHYS interference; **Überlagerungsanalysator** *m* AUFNAHME heterodyne sound analyser (BrE), heterodyne sound analyzer (AmE); **Überlagerungsempfang** *m* TELEKOM heterodyne reception; **Überlagerungsempfänger** *m* RADIO superheterodyne receiver; **Überlagerungsfrequenzumsetzer** *m* ELEKTROTECH heterodyne conversion transducer; **Überlagungsoszillator** *m* RADIO local oscillator; **Überlagerungspermeabilität** *f* ELEKTRONIK *mit Vorpolarisierung* incremental permeability; **Überlagerungsprinzip** *nt* ELEKTRONIK *synthetische Prüfung*, PHYS superposition principle; **Überlagerungsstörung** *f* FERNSEH superimposed interference; **Überlagerungsumsetzung** *f* ELEKTROTECH heterodyne conversion; **Überlagerungswellenmesser** *m* RADIO heterodyne wavemeter

Überland- *pref* KFZTECH overhead; **Überlandleitung** *f* ELEKTROTECH overhead cable, overhead power line; **Überlandstraße** *f* TRANS arterial safety road

Überlappen *nt* METALL overlapping

überlappen *vt* ANSTRICH, BAU lap

überlappend anordnen *vt* COMP & DV cascade

überlappend: **~ geschweißte Hülse** *f* KERNTECH weld overlay cladding; **~e Klappen** *f pl* VERPACK overlapping flaps; **~e Schweißnaht** *f* KERNTECH lap weld; **~er Stoß** *m* MECHAN lap joint; **~e Tonhöhen** *f pl* AKUSTIK conjoined pitches; **nicht ~e Tonhöhen** *f pl* AKUSTIK disjoined pitches

Überlappnaht *f* FERTIG lap weld, *Schweißen* overlapping spot-weld

Überlappnietung *f* FERTIG lap riveting

Überlappschweißung *f* VERPACK lap weld

Überlappstoß *m* FERTIG shear joint

überlappt: **~e Isolierung** *f* ELEKTRIZ lapped insulation; **~e Nahtschweißung** *f* FERTIG lap seam-welding; **~e Teilfuge** *f* BAU lap joint; **~e Verbindung** *f* BAU lapped scarf; **~e Wicklung** *f* ELEKTRIZ lap winding

Überlappung *f* ANSTRICH lap, BAU lap, overlap, step joint, COMP & DV interleaving, overlap, DRUCK overlap, EISENBAHN *von Blockabschnitten* overlapping, ELEKTRONIK *Datenverarbeitung* pipelining, ELEKTRONIK overlapping, FERNSEH overlap, FERTIG *Schweißen* cold shut, HYDRAUL *Steuerschieber und -kolben*, KER & GLAS lap, MASCHINEN overlap, PHYS *von Spektrallinien*

overlapping; **Überlappungs- und Voreilsteuerschwinge** *f* HYDRAUL *Dampfsteuergetriebe* lap and lead lever

überlappungsfrei: **~es Ventil** *nt* HYDRAUL lapless valve

Überlappung: **Überlappungsnietung** *f* VERPACK lap riveting; **Überlappungsschweißung** *f* MASCHINEN lap welding; **Überlappungsstoß** *m* BAU lap joint, overlapping joint; **Überlappungsventil** *nt* HYDRAUL lap valve

Überlast *f* ELEKTRIZ, ELEKTROTECH overload, KOHLEN surcharge load, PHYS, TELEKOM overload; **Überlastabwehr** *f* TELEKOM *Verkehrskontrolle* flow control; **Überlastanzeiger** *m* ELEKTRIZ overload indicator; **Überlastbarkeit** *f* FERTIG *Kunststoffinstallationen* overload capacity; **Überlastbündel** *nt* TELEKOM high-usage circuit group

überlasten *vt* BAU overstress, FERNSEH overload, MASCHINEN overstrain, RADIO, TELEKOM overload

überlastet *adj* PHYS, TELEKOM overloaded

Überlast: **Überlastfaktor** *m* ELEKTRIZ overload factor; **Überlastfeder** *f* MASCHINEN overload spring; **Überlastgrenze** *f* REGELUNG overrange limit; **Überlastkupplung** *f* MASCHINEN overload coupling; **Überlastrelais** *nt* ELEKTRIZ overload relay; **Überlastschutz** *m* ELEKTRIZ overload protection; **Überlastspannung** *f* ELEKTRIZ overload voltage; **Überlaststrom** *m* ELEKTRIZ overload current

Überlastung *f* COMP & DV overload, trashing, MASCHINEN overload, overstrain, RADIO, RAUMFAHRT *Weltraumfunk* overload, TELEKOM overload, *Netzwerke* congestion; **Überlastungsfeder** *f* MASCHINEN overload spring; **Überlastungsprüfung** *f* ELEKTRIZ overload test; **Überlastungsrelais** *nt* ELEKTROTECH overload relay; **Überlastungsschutz** *m* ELEKTROTECH overload protection, overload protection device, RADIO overload protection; **Überlastungsschutzvorrichtung** *f* ELEKTROTECH overload protection device; **Überlastungsstrom** *m* ELEKTROTECH overload current

Überlast: **Überlastverhältnis** *nt* ELEKTRIZ overload factor

Überlauf *m* BAU spillway, COMP & DV overflow, FERTIG overtravel, *Kunststoffinstallationen* overflow, KER & GLAS weir, KFZTECH *Kühlanlage* overflow pipe, KOHLEN overflow, MASCHINEN overflow, MECHAN overflow; **Überlaufanzeiger** *m* COMP & DV overflow flag; **Überlaufbereich** *m* COMP & DV overflow area; **Überlaufbit** *nt* COMP & DV overflow bit; **Überlaufecho** *nt* WASSERTRANS *Radar* second trace echo

Überlaufen *nt* MASCHINEN overflow

überlaufen[1] *vt* FERTIG overtravel

überlaufen[2] *vi* MASCHINEN overrun, WASSERVERSORG run over

Überlauf: **Überlaufkanal** *m* HYDRAUL spillway canal, NICHTFOSS ENERG spillway channel; **Überlaufkante** *f* BAU lip; **Überlauföffnung** *f* KFZTECH overflow hole; **Überlaufverfahren** *nt* KER & GLAS overflow process; **Überlaufverkehr** *m* TELEKOM overflow traffic; **Überlaufwehr** *nt* HYDRAUL weir, KERNTECH leaping weir; **Überlaufwehrmessung** *f* HYDRAUL notch gaging (AmE), notch gauging (BrE)

überlegen: **sich ~** *v refl* WASSERTRANS *Schiff* cant over

Überleitrille *f* AKUSTIK, AUFNAHME lead-over groove

Überliegegeld *nt* WASSERTRANS demurrage

Übermaß *nt* MASCHINEN interference, overdimension, overmeasure, oversize, MECHAN oversize; **~ durch Losschlagen des Modells** *nt* FERTIG *Gießen* rappage

übermäßig: **~e Bestrahlung** *f* STRAHLPHYS

overexposure; **~es Entladen** *nt* ELEKTROTECH over-discharging

Übermaßzeichnung *f* KONSTZEICH drawing dealing with oversize parts

Übermittler: **~ mit unterdrücktem Träger** *m* ELEKTRONIK suppressed carrier transmitter

Übermittlung *f* TELEKOM *von daten* transfer; **Übermittlungsdienst** *m* TELEKOM bearer service; **Übermittlungsdienst über virtuelle Verbindung** *m* TELEKOM virtual-circuit bearer service; **Übermittlungsschicht** *f* TELEKOM data link layer; **Übermittlungssystem** *nt* COMP & DV communication system; **Übermittlungsträger** *m* TELEKOM transmission bearer; **Übermittlungsvorschrift** *f* COMP & DV link protocol

Übermodulation *f* AUFNAHME, RADIO overmodulation

Übernahme *f* COMP & DV inheritance, MECHAN acceptance

übernommen: **~er Fehler** *m* COMP & DV inherited error

überoxidieren *vt* CHEMIE overoxidize

Überpotentialschutz *m* ELEKTROTECH overpotential protection

überprüfen *vt* KONTROLL inspect, VERPACK check

Überprüfung *f* MECHAN, QUAL examination, RAUM-FAHRT review, VERPACK check; **~ vor Inbetriebnahme** *f* KERNTECH precommissioning checks; **~ nach meldepflichtigen Unfällen** *f* SICHERHEIT inspection following notifiable accidents; **~ durch Rundgang** *f* RAUMFAHRT *Raumschiff* walkaround inspection; **~ durch die Unternehmensführung** *f* QUAL management audit

überreif *adj* LEBENSMITTEL overripe

Überrollbügel *m* KFZTECH roll bar, rollover bar

Überrollen *nt* LUFTTRANS overrun

übersättigen *vt* CHEMIE supersaturate, THERMOD *Dampf* oversaturate

übersättigt *adj* UMWELTSCHMUTZ supersaturated

Übersättigung *f* FERNSEH oversaturation

übersäuern *vt* CHEMIE peroxidize

Übersäuerung *f* LEBENSMITTEL hyperacidity; **~ des Wassers** *f* UMWELTSCHMUTZ aquatic acidification

Überschall- *pref* WELLPHYS supersonic

Überschallbereich: **im ~** *adj* WELLPHYS supersonic

Überschall-: **Überschallflugzeug** *nt* LUFTTRANS hypersonic aircraft, supersonic aircraft, transonic aircraft; **Überschallfrequenz** *f* AKUSTIK ultrasonic frequency, ELEKTRONIK supersonic frequency, PHYS ultrasonic frequency, STRAHLPHYS supersonic frequency; **Überschallgeschwindigkeit** *f* FERTIG hypersonic speed, PHYS supersonic speed; **Überschallknall** *m* PHYS sonic boom; **Überschalltransport** *m (SST)* LUFTTRANS supersonic transport *(SST)*

überschalten *vt* FERTIG override

Überschiebmuffe *f* FERTIG *Kunststoffinstallationen* slide coupling, MASCHINEN collar

Überschiebung *f* ERDÖL *Geologie* overthrust

Überschlag *m* ELEKTRIZ flashover, sparkover voltage, ELEKTROTECH arc-over, FERTIG arcing, PHYS breakdown, TELEKOM discharge

Überschlagen *nt* KFZTECH overturning, WASSERTRANS roll-over

Überschlag: **Überschlagprüfung** *f* ELEKTROTECH flash test; **Überschlagspannung** *f* ELEKTRIZ withstand voltage, ELEKTROTECH flash-over voltage; **Überschlagspannungsprüfung** *f* ELEKTRIZ withstand-voltage test; **Überschlagsrechnung** *f* BAU rough calculation

überschneiden *vt* AUFNAHME overdub, BAU intersect

Überschneiden *nt* AKUSTIK overcutting

Überschneidungsfrequenz *f* ELEKTRONIK, FERNSEH, RADIO crossover frequency

Überschreiben *nt* COMP & DV overwriting

Überschreibung *f* COMP & DV destructive addition

Überschreiten *nt* ELEKTROTECH overshoot

Überschrift *f* COMP & DV heading, DRUCK caption, head, headline, title; **Überschriftzeile** *f* DRUCK header, headline

Überschuß *m* ANSTRICH excess; **Überschußhalbleiter** *m* ELEKTRONIK n-semiconductor

überschüssig[1] *adj* PAPIER odd

überschüssig:[2] **~er Aushubboden** *m* BAU *Tiefbau* spoil; **~er Boden** *m* BAU spoil; **~e Energie** *f* THERMOD excess energy

Überschuß: **Überschußreaktivität** *f* KERNTECH excess reactivity; **Überschußstrom** *m* ELEKTRIZ excess current

überschwellig *adj* ERGON supraliminal

Überschwemmung *f* STRÖMPHYS drowned flow, WASSER-TRANS *Hochwasser, Fluß* flood, WASSERVERSORG overflow; **Überschwemmungsgebiet** *nt* WASSERVERSORG flood plain

überschwer: **~er Wasserstoff** *m* CHEMIE, PHYS tritium

Überschwing- *pref* ELEKTROTECH, GERÄT overshooting

überschwingen *vt* MECHAN overshoot

Überschwingen *nt* ELEKTROTECH overshoot

Überschwing-: **Überschwingfaktor** *m* GERÄT *Meßgerät* ballistic factor; **Überschwingspitze** *f* ELEKTROTECH spike; **Überschwingweite** *f* REGELUNG transient overshoot

Übersee- *pref* WASSERTRANS *Seehandel* overseas; **Überseedampfer** *m* WASSERTRANS *Schiff* transatlantic liner; **Überseefracht- und Fahrgastschiff** *nt* WASSER-TRANS combined cargo and passenger liner

überseeisch *adj* WASSERTRANS overseas

Übersee-: **Überseepassagierschiff** *nt* WASSERTRANS liner; **Überseetelegramm** *nt* WASSERTRANS cable; **Überseeverpackung** *f* VERPACK overseas packaging

Übersegler *m* WASSERTRANS track chart

Übersender *m* TRANS *Person* consignor

übersetzen *vt* COMP & DV compile, interpret, translate

Übersetzer *m* COMP & DV interpreter, processor; **Übersetzerprogramm** *nt* COMP & DV interpreter, translator; **Übersetzersprache** *f* COMP & DV interpretative language

übersetzt: **~es Programm** *nt* COMP & DV object program

Übersetzung *f* COMP & DV translation, MASCHINEN gear ratio, multiplication, MECHAN gear ratio; **~ ins Langsame** *f* KFZTECH transmission reduction; **Übersetzungsanlage** *f* COMP & DV source machine; **Übersetzungsanweisung** *f* COMP & DV directive; **Übersetzungsgetriebe** *nt* MASCHINEN step-up gear; **Übersetzungsrad** *nt* MASCHINEN translating wheel; **Übersetzungsverhältnis** *nt* ELEKTROTECH turns ratio, FERTIG increasing ratio, KFZTECH transmission ratio, *Getriebe* gear ratio, MASCHINEN gear ratio; **Übersetzungsverhältnis der Steuerung** *nt* LUFTTRANS control gearing ratio

Übersicht *f* BAU survey, KERNTECH general drawing, KONSTZEICH general plan; **Übersichtsschalttafel** *f* ELEKTRIZ synoptical switchboard; **Übersichtszeichnung** *f* KERNTECH general drawing, MECHAN general arrangement drawing

überspannen *vt* BAU *Tal* bridge, FERTIG overtension

Überspannung *f* ELEKTRIZ excess voltage, overvoltage, ELEKTROTECH overvoltage, FERTIG *Kette* overtensioning, PHYS overvoltage; **Überspannungsableiter** *m* ELEKTRIZ surge arrester, surge diverter, ELEKTROTECH arrester, surge arrester; **Überspannungsausfall** *m* ELEKTROTECH overvoltage breakdown; **Überspannungsauslöser** *m* GERÄT overvoltage trip; **Überspannungsauslösung** *f* ELEKTRIZ overvoltage release; **Überspannungsblitz** *m* FOTO photoflood bulb; **Überspannungsrelais** *nt* ELEKTRIZ, ELEKTROTECH overvoltage relay; **Überspannungsschutz** *m* ELEKTRIZ excess voltage protection, overvoltage protection, surge absorber, ELEKTROTECH overvoltage protection, surge protection; **Überspannungsschutzvorrichtung** *f* ELEKTROTECH overvoltage protection device

überspielen *vt* AUFNAHME dub

Überspielen: ~ **von Film auf Band** *nt* FERNSEH film-to-tape transfer; ~ **von Filmen** *nt* FERNSEH film transfer

Überspielung *f* AKUSTIK dubbing

Übersprechdämpfung *f* AKUSTIK crosstalk

Übersprechen *nt* AKUSTIK, AUFNAHME, COMP & DV, FERNSEH, PHYS crosstalk

Überspringbefehl m COMP & DV skip instruction

Überspringen [1]*nt* COMP & DV skip

überspringen[2] *vt* COMP & DV skip

überspringen[3] *vi* ELEKTRIZ jump

überspült *adj* WASSERTRANS awash, flooded

Überstand *m* BAU projection, DRUCK bleed

Überstaubewässerung *f* WASSERVERSORG flood irrigation

Überstauung *f* WASSERTRANS overstowage, WASSERVERSORG flood irrigation

überstehen *vt* DRUCK bleed

übersteuern:[1] **übersteuernd** *adj* MECHAN overriding

übersteuern[2] *vt* ELEKTROTECH, FERTIG override

Übersteuerung *f* FERTIG override, KFZTECH oversteering, *Lenkung* oversteer, LUFTTRANS override control; **Übersteuerungsschalter** *m* ELEKTRIZ override switch

Überstrahlung *f* FOTO blooming

überstreichen *vt* BAU top

Überstrom *m* ELEKTRIZ, ELEKTROTECH overcurrent

Überström- *pref* ELEKTROTECH, MASCHINEN overflowing

Überstrom: **Überstromauslöser** *m* ELEKTROTECH overcurrent trip; **Überstromausschalter** *m* ELEKTROTECH overcurrent circuit breaker; **Überstromblockiereinrichtung** *f* ELEKTRIZ overcurrent blocking device

Überströmen *nt* MASCHINEN overflow

Überström-: **Überströmkanal** *m* KFZTECH *Zweitaktmotor* transfer port

Überström-: **Überstromleistungsschalter** *m* ELEKTROTECH overcurrent power switch

Überström-: **Überströmöffnung** *f* KFZTECH overflow port

Überstrom: **Überstromrelais** *nt* ELEKTRIZ overcurrent relay

Überström-: **Überströmrohr** *nt* KFZTECH *Kühlanlage* overflow pipe

Überström-: **Überstromschalter** *m* ELEKTRIZ excess current switch, overcurrent switch; **Überstromschutz** *m* ELEKTRIZ, ELEKTROTECH overcurrent protection; **Überstromschutzschalter** *m* ELEKTROTECH overcurrent circuit breaker; **Überstromunterbrecher** *m* ELEKTRIZ overcurrent circuit breaker

Überström-: **Überströmventil** *nt* HYDRAUL, KFZTECH, MASCHINEN overflow valve

Überstruktur *f* FERTIG superlattice, superlattice structure

überstumpf: ~**er Winkel** *m* GEOM reflex angle

übertage *adv* KOHLEN above ground

Übertastung *f* FERNSEH overscan

Übertemperaturrelais *nt* ELEKTROTECH thermal relay

Übertemperatur-Stromunterbrecher *m* ELEKTRIZ thermal circuit breaker

Übertönen *nt* ELEKTRONIK *Transmitter* capture effect

Übertrag *m* COMP & DV, ELEKTRONIK carry

übertragen:[1] ~**e Wärme** *f* THERMOD convected heat

übertragen[2] *vt* AUFNAHME, BAU transfer, COMP & DV carry, transfer, KONTROLL transfer, MASCHINEN *Kraft* convey, MATH *beim Rechnen* carry, RADIO transmit, THERMOD *Energie* impart

Übertrager *m* PHYS, TELEKOM transformer; **Übertragerspule** *f* ELEKTROTECH repeating coil

Übertragung *f* COMP & DV, ELEKTRIZ, KONTROLL, MASCHINEN, MECHAN, PHYS, TELEKOM transfer, translation, transmission; ~ **aus dem Speicher** *f* COMP & DV copy-out; ~ **im Klartext** *f* TELEKOM clear transmission; ~ **zwischen mehreren Stationen** *f* COMP & DV multidrop transmission; ~ **mittels Lichtleitkabel** *f* OPTIK fiberoptic transmission (AmE), fibreoptic transmission (BrE); ~ **in den Speicher** *f* COMP & DV copy-in; ~ **über Lichtleitfasern** *f* OPTIK optical fiber transmission (AmE), optical fibre transmission (BrE); ~ **mit unterdrücktem Träger** *f* ELEKTRONIK suppressed carrier transmission; **Übertragungsanweisung** *f* KONTROLL transfer instruction; **Übertragungsart** *f* COMP & DV mode of transmission; **Übertragungsbeiwert** *m* REGELUNG *der Regelstrecke* transfer coefficient; **Übertragungsbeiwert einer Wanderwellenröhre** *m* RAUMFAHRT *Weltraumfunk* TWT transfer coefficient; **Übertragungsbereich** *m* COMP & DV frequency response; **Übertragungsblock** *m* COMP & DV transmission block; **Übertragungscharakteristik** *f* PHYS transfer characteristic, TELEKOM transmission characteristic; **Übertragungscode** *m* COMP & DV transmission code, TELEKOM line code; **Übertragungsdämpfung** *f* COMP & DV, TELEKOM SRI, Sound Reduction Index, TL, transmission loss; **Übertragungsende** *nt* COMP & DV end of transmission; **Übertragungsfaktor** *m* AKUSTIK response; **Übertragungsfehler** *m* COMP & DV, TELEKOM transmission error; **Übertragungsfenster** *nt* OPTIK, TELEKOM transmission window; **Übertragungsfolge** *f* COMP & DV transmission sequence; **Übertragungsfrequenzgang** *m* AKUSTIK magnitude frequency response; **Übertragungsfunktion** *f* COMP & DV transmission function, OPTIK, TELEKOM transfer function; **Übertragungsfunktion für das Grundfrequenzband** *f* OPTIK baseband response function, baseband transfer function; **Übertragungsgeschwindigkeit** *f* COMP & DV bit rate, data rate, line speed, transfer rate, transmission rate, TELEKOM data signaling rate (AmE), data signalling rate (BrE), transmission rate; **Übertragungsgüte** *f* TELEKOM transmission quality; **Übertragungs-Highway** *m* TELEKOM transmission highway; **Übertragungskanal** *m* COMP & DV communication channel, transmission channel, TELEKOM transmission channel; **Übertragungskennlinie** *f* ELEKTRONIK transfer characteristic; **Übertragungskonstante** *f* AKUSTIK propagation coefficient; **Übertragungskopf** *m* COMP & DV transmission header; **Übertragungsleitung** *f* COMP & DV communication line, transmission line, ELEKTRONIK,

ELEKTROTECH, PHYS, RADIO transmission line; **Übertragungsleitung mit mehreren Stationen** *f* COMP & DV multidrop circuit; **Übertragungsleitungsverluste** *m pl* ELEKTRIZ line losses; **Übertragungsleitweg** *m* TELEKOM transmission line; **Übertragungslimit** *nt* COMP & DV transmission limit; **Übertragungsmaß** *nt* AKUSTIK image transfer exponent; **Übertragungsmatrix** *f* PHYS *Netzwerktheorie* transfer matrix; **Übertragungsmedium** *nt* COMP & DV, OPTIK transmission medium; **Übertragungsmodus** *m* COMP & DV mode of transmission; **Übertragungsnetz** *nt* ELEKTRIZ transmission line network, TELEKOM transmission network; **Übertragungsnetzknoten** *m* TELEKOM transmission node; **Übertragungsnetzwerk** *nt* KONTROLL communication network; **Übertragungsphase über Aufwärtsstrecke** *f* TELEKOM uplink transmission phase; **Übertragungsprotokoll** *nt* COMP & DV transmission control protocol, transport protocol; **Übertragungsrate** *f* COMP & DV bit rate, ELEKTROTECH transmission rate; **Übertragungsschicht** *f* TELEKOM transmission layer; **Übertragungsserver** *m* COMP & DV communication server; **Übertragungssicherheit** *f* COMP & DV transmission security; **Übertragungssicherung** *f* ELEKTRONIK error protection; **Übertragungsstange** *f* MASCHINEN transmission rod; **Übertragungssteuerung** *f* COMP & DV transmission control; **Übertragungsstörung** *f* TELEKOM transmission breakdown; **Übertragungssystem** *nt* ELEKTROTECH transmission system; **Übertragungsverfahren** *nt* ELEKTRONIK transmission mode; **Übertragungsverhältnis** *nt* FERNSEH transfer ratio; **Übertragungsverlust** *m* OPTIK, RAUMFAHRT *Weltraumfunk*, TELEKOM *Transducer* TL, transmission loss; **Übertragungswagen** *m* FERNSEH mobile control unit; **Übertragungsweg** *m* COMP & DV bus (BrE), channel, highway, transmission path, trunk (AmE), TELEKOM channel, transmission path; **Übertragungswiderstand** *m* ELEKTRIZ coupling impedance; **Übertragungszeit** *f* PHYS transit time; **Übertragungsziffer** *f* COMP & DV carry digit

übertrocknen *vt* PAPIER overdry

Über- und Unterstromrelais *nt* ELEKTRIZ over-and-under current relay

Überverbrauchszähler *m* ELEKTRIZ excess energy meter, GERÄT excess meter

Übervergüten *nt* METALL overageing (BrE), overaging (AmE)

Überwachen *nt* FERNSEH monitoring

überwachen *vt* AUFNAHME monitor, BAU attend to, COMP & DV, MEERSCHMUTZ, RADIO, TEXTIL monitor

Überwacher *m* KONTROLL *Person* supervisor

überwacht: **~es Abladen von Schutt** *nt* UMWELTSCHMUTZ controlled dumping; **~er Ablauf** *m* COMP & DV attended operation; **~er Betrieb** *m* COMP & DV attended operation

Überwachung *f* AUFNAHME monitoring, BAU observation, COMP & DV monitoring, KFZTECH control, RAUMFAHRT monitoring, SICHERHEIT surveillance, TELEKOM monitoring, supervision, TEXTIL monitoring; **von Arbeitern in Risikobereichen** *f* SICHERHEIT *Gesundheitsschutz* surveillance of workers exposed to health risks; **~ von gesundheitsgefährdenden Stoffen** *f* SICHERHEIT *Vorschriften* COSHH, control of substances hazardous to health; **~ und Instandhaltung** *f* TELEKOM monitoring and maintenance; **~ an Ort und Stelle** *f* KERNTECH in situ monitoring; **~ von Prüf- und Meßmitteln** *f* QUAL control of inspection, measuring

and test equipment; **~ der Prüfung** *f* QUAL monitor the review; **~ von Qualitätsmaßnahmen** *f* QUAL control of quality measures; **~ der Qualitätssicherung des Lieferanten** *f* QUAL quality assurance surveillance; **~ der Unterlagen** *f* QUAL document control; **~ der Unterlagen und ihrer Änderungen** *f* QUAL documentation and change control; **~ von Verfahren** *f* QUAL control of processes; **~ der Wasserbeschaffenheit** *f* WASSERVERSORG water quality monitoring; **Überwachungs- und Leitsystem im Flugzeug** *nt* (*AWACS*) LUFTTRANS airborne warning and control system (*AWACS*); **Überwachungsanlage** *f* TEXTIL control system; **Überwachungsarmatur** *f* FERTIG process control; **Überwachungsfernsehen** *nt* (*CCTV*) FERNSEH closed-circuit TV (*CCTV*); **Überwachungshilfe** *f* TELEKOM supervisory aid; **Überwachungskopf** *m* AUFNAHME monitor head; **Überwachungslampe** *f* ELEKTROTECH pilot lamp; **Überwachungsleitung** *f* TELEKOM guard circuit; **Überwachungsmeldung** *f* TELEKOM supervisory message; **Überwachungsnachweis** *m* QUAL evidence of control; **Überwachungsraum** *m* AUFNAHME control room; **Überwachungsrelais** *nt* ELEKTRIZ pilot relay; **Überwachungssatellit** *m* RAUMFAHRT surveillance satellite; **Überwachungsschaltung des eigenen Amts** *f* TELEKOM own-exchange supervisory circuit; **Überwachungsstelle** *f* QUAL inspection agency; **Überwachungssystem** *nt* KONTROLL supervising system, QUAL, STRAHLPHYS monitoring system, supervising system, supervisory system; **Überwachungston** *m* TELEKOM supervisory tone; **Überwachungsverfahren** *nt* QUAL monitoring procedure; **Überwachungszeit** *f* COMP & DV monitor time, RAUMFAHRT *Weltraumfunk* guard time; **Überwachungszeitgeber** *m* COMP & DV watchdog timer, TELEKOM supervisory timer

überwalzen *vt* FERTIG rebate

Überwasser *nt* WASSERVERSORG surplus water; **Überwassergeschwindigkeit** *f* WASSERTRANS *U-Boot* surface speed; **Überwasserteile** *nt pl* WASSERTRANS *Schiffbau* topsides

überwendlich: **~ nähen** *vt* TEXTIL oversew

Überwindung *f* FERTIG override

Überwucht *f* FERTIG amount of overbalance; **Überwuchtmasse** *f* FERTIG amount of overbalance

Überwurf *m* BAU lock bush; **Überwurfkrümmer** *m* BAU union elbow; **Überwurfmutter** *f* FERTIG clamping nut, *Kunststoffinstallationen* valve nut, MASCHINEN box nut, sleeve nut, union nut

überziehen *vt* BAU *Material* surface, KUNSTSTOFF, LEBENSMITTEL coat, MECHAN plate

Überziehen *nt* KER & GLAS overlay, overlaying, KUNSTSTOFF coating, LUFTTRANS *Strömungsabriß eines Flugzeugs* stall, MASCHINEN, PHYS cladding; **~ von Stahlblech** *nt* FERTIG *Tauchverfahren* terne coating

Überzug *m* ANSTRICH overlay, overlaying, protective film, BAU overlay, overlaying, ELEKTROTECH sheathing, LEBENSMITTEL *für Süßwaren, Kuchen* topping, MECHAN film; **Überzugsdicke** *f* VERPACK coating thickness; **Überzugsmaterial** *nt* MASCHINEN coating material, VERPACK coating compound

Überzwirnung *f* TEXTIL snarl

Ubitron *nt* ELEKTRONIK ubitron, undulating beam interaction electron tube

üblich: **~es Reparaturwerkzeug** *nt* MASCHINEN common repair tool

U-Bolzen *m* KFZTECH *Federung, Blattfeder*, WASSER-

TRANS *Schiffbau* U-bolt
U-Boot *nt* (*Unterseeboot*) WASSERTRANS submarine; **U-Boot-Abwehr** *f* WASSERTRANS *Marine* antisubmarine defence (BrE), antisubmarine defense (AmE); **U-Boot-Bekämpfungshubschrauber** *m* LUFTTRANS antisubmarine helicopter; **U-Boot-Bunker** *m* WASSERTRANS *Marine* submarine pen
U-Bügel *m* MASCHINEN stirrup, stirrup bolt
Übungsflug *m* LUFTTRANS training flight
Übungskurve *f* ERGON learning curve
U-Eisen *nt* BAU channel iron, METALL U-iron
Ufer:[1] **über die ~ getreten** *adj* WASSERTRANS *Fluß* in flood
Ufer[2] *nt* BAU bank, WASSERTRANS shore, waterfront; **Uferlinie** *f* MEERSCHMUTZ, WASSERTRANS shoreline
Ufer:[3] **über die ~ treten** *vi* WASSERTRANS *Fluß* flood
UFH *abbr* (*Harnstoff-Formaldehydharz*) ELEKTRIZ, FERTIG, KUNSTSTOFF UFR (*urea formaldehyde resin*)
UFO *abbr* (*nicht identifiziertes Flugobjekt*) RAUMFAHRT UFO (*unidentified flying object*)
U-förmig:[1] TRANS U-shaped track girder
U-förmig:[2] **~e Grundplatte** *f* MASCHINEN U-shaped base, stirrup-shaped bed; **~er Fahrbalken** *m* TRANS U-shaped track girder; **~er Zughaken** *m* MASCHINEN clevis
U-Formstahl *m* METALL channel section
UF6 *abbr* (*Uranhexafluorid*) KERNTECH UF6 (*uranium hexafluoride*)
UHF[1] *abbr* (*Ultrahochfrequenz*) ELEKTRONIK, FERNSEH, RADIO, TELEKOM, WELLPHYS UHF (*ultrahigh frequency*)
UHF:[2] **UHF-Konverter** *m* FERNSEH UHF converter; **UHF-Rundfunk** *m* FERNSEH UHF broadcasting; **UHF-Signal** *nt* ELEKTRONIK UHF signal; **UHF-Signalgenerator** *m* ELEKTRONIK UHF signal generator; **UHF-Tuner** *m* FERNSEH UHF tuner
Uhr *f* COMP & DV *Symbol* clock, PHYS chronometer; **Uhrgang** *m* METROL rate of clock; **Uhrglas** *nt* LABOR watch glass; **Uhrwerk** *nt* MECHAN clockwork
Uhrzeigersinn: **im ~ drehend** *adj* LEBENSMITTEL clockwise-rotating
UHT *abbr* (*Ultrahochtemperatur*) LEBENSMITTEL UHT (*ultrahigh temperature*)
UIC *abbr* (*Internationaler Eisenbahnverband*) EISENBAHN UIC (*International Railway Union*)
UJT *abbr* (*Zweizonentransistor*) ELEKTRONIK UJT (*unijunction transistor*)
U-Klammer *f* MECHAN clevis
UKW[1] *abbr* (*Ultrakurzwelle*) RADIO, WELLPHYS USW, VSW (*ultrashort wave*)
UKW:[2] **UKW-Drehfunkfeuer** *nt* (*Ultrakurzwellen-Drehfunkfeuer*) LUFTTRANS VHFO (*very-high-frequency omnirange*); **UKW-Radio** *nt* FERNSEH VHF radio; **UKW-Rundstrahlkursfunkfeuer** *nt* TRANS VHF omnidirectional radio range; **UKW-Sprechfunk** *m* RADIO VHF radio telephone; **UKW-Sprechfunkgerät** *nt* RADIO VHF radio telephone
Ulexin *nt* CHEMIE cytisine, ulexine
Ulme *f* WASSERTRANS *Bauholz* elm
Ulmin *nt* CHEMIE ulmin; **Ulmin-** *pref* CHEMIE ulmic
ulnar *adj* ERGON ulnar
ULSI[1] *abbr* (*Ultragroßintegration*) ELEKTRONIK ULSI (*ultralarge-scale integration*)
ULSI:[2] **ULSI-Schaltkreis** *m* TELEKOM ULSI circuit
Ultra- *pref* CHEMIE, KERNTECH ultra; **Ultrafeinfokus** *m* KERNTECH ultrafine focus; **Ultrafilter** *nt* CHEMIE ultrafilter, CHEMTECH membrane filter; **Ultrafiltrat** *nt*

CHEMIE ultrafiltrate; **Ultrafiltration** *f* CHEMIE, CHEMTECH ultra filtration; **Ultrafiltrieren** *nt* CHEMIE *Vorgang* ultra filtration; **Ultragroßintegration** *f* (*ULSI*) ELEKTRONIK ultralarge-scale integration (*ULSI*); **Ultragroßintegration-Schaltkreis** *m* TELEKOM ultralarge-scale integration circuit
Ultrahoch- *pref* ELEKTRONIK, TELEKOM, TRANS ultrahigh; **Ultrahochfrequenz** *f* (*UHF*) ELEKTRONIK, FERNSEH, RADIO, TELEKOM, WELLPHYS ultrahigh frequency (*UHF*); **Ultrahochfrequenzwelle** *f* WELLPHYS ultrahigh frequency wave; **Ultrahochgeschwindigkeitsverkehr** *m* TRANS ultrahigh speed traffic; **Ultrahochtemperatur** *f* (*UHT*) LEBENSMITTEL ultrahigh temperature (*UHT*); **Ultrahochvakuum** *nt* HEIZ & KÄLTE, PHYS ultrahigh vacuum, THERMOD ultravacuum
Ultrakurzwelle *f* (*UKW*) RADIO, WELLPHYS ultrashort wave, very short wave (*USW*); **Ultrakurzwellen-Drehfunkfeuer** *nt* LUFTTRANS (*UKW-Drehfunkfeuer*) very-high-frequency omnirange (*VHFO*), RADIO very-high-frequency omnidirectional radio range; **Ultrakurzwellen-Rundstrahlkursfunkfeuer** *nt* TRANS very-high-frequency omnidirectional radio range; **Ultrakurzwellen-Sprechfunkgerät** *m* RADIO very-high-frequency radio telephone
Ultra-: **Ultraleichtlegierung** *f* RAUMFAHRT ultralight alloy; **Ultramarin** *nt* CHEMIE *Farbe* ultramarine; **Ultramikroanalyse** *f* KERNTECH ultramicroanalysis; **Ultramikroskop** *nt* CHEMIE ultramicroscope; **Ultramikroskopie** *f* CHEMIE ultramicroscopy
ultramikroskopisch *adj* CHEMIE ultramicroscopic
Ultra-: **Ultrapasteurisierung** *f* LEBENSMITTEL uperization, THERMOD ultrapasteurization
Ultraschall *m* ELEKTRIZ ultrasonics, PHYS, STRAHLPHYS ultrasound; **Ultraschallabtragung** *f* MASCHINEN ultrasonic removal; **Ultraschallbad** *nt* ELEKTRIZ, LABOR ultrasonic bath; **Ultraschallbearbeitung** *f* KERNTECH *von Materialien*, MASCHINEN, STRAHLPHYS *von Werkstücken* ultrasonic machining; **Ultraschallbohren** *nt* MASCHINEN ultrasonic drilling; **Ultraschallbohrmaschine** *f* FERTIG ultrasonic drilling machine; **Ultraschalldetektor** *m* TRANS ultrasonic detector; **Ultraschalldickenmeßgerät** *nt* GERÄT ultrasonic thickness gage (AmE), ultrasonic thickness gauge (BrE); **Ultraschallfrequenz** *f* AKUSTIK, PHYS ultrasonic frequency; **Ultraschallgenerator** *m* LABOR ultrasound generator, STRAHLPHYS ultrasonic generator; **Ultraschallgeschwindigkeit** *f* PHYS hypersonic speed; **Ultraschallkraftstoffzerstäuber** *m* TRANS ultrasonic fuel atomizer; **Ultraschall-Lötung** *f* MASCHINEN ultrasonic soldering; **Ultraschallmaterialprüfung** *f* MASCHINEN ultrasonic materials testing; **Ultraschallortung** *f* WELLPHYS ultrasonic sounding; **Ultraschallprüfung** *f* EISENBAHN ultrasonic probe, KERNTECH ultrasonic testing, ultrasonic examination, MASCHINEN, MECHAN ultrasonic examination, ultrasonic testing; **Ultraschallreinigung** *f* AUFNAHME, FERNSEH ultrasonic cleaning; **Ultraschallschweißen** *nt* ELEKTRIZ, KUNSTSTOFF ultrasonic welding, THERMOD ultrasonic welding, ultrasonic sealing; **Ultraschallsonde** *f* BAU ultrasonic probe; **Ultraschalltechnik** *f* MASCHINEN ultrasonic engineering, WELLPHYS ultrasonics; **Ultraschalltransducer** *m* ELEKTRIZ ultrasonic transducer; **Ultraschalluntersuchung** *f* KERNTECH, MECHAN ultrasonic examination, STRAHLPHYS ultrasound scan, WELLPHYS ultrasonic inspection;

Ultraschallwelle *f* ELEKTRIZ, WELLPHYS ultrasonic wave; **Ultraschallzerspanung** *f* FERTIG ultrasonic machining
ultrasonisch *adj (US)* ELEKTRIZ supersonic, ultrasonic *(SS)*
Ultra-: **Ultra-Supertanker** *m* ERDÖL ULCC, ultralarge crude carrier
ultraviolett[1] *adj (UV)* OPTIK, PHYS ultraviolet *(UV)*
ultraviolett:[2] **~es Licht** *nt* KUNSTSTOFF, STRAHLPHYS ultraviolet light; **~ sichtbares Spektrofotometer** *nt* LABOR ultraviolet-visible spectrophotometer
Ultraviolett *nt* RAUMFAHRT ultraviolet; **Ultraviolettfilter** *nt* FOTO, SICHERHEIT ultraviolet filter; **Ultraviolettfotografie** *f* STRAHLPHYS ultraviolet photography; **Ultraviolettkatastrophe** *f* PHYS ultraviolet catastrophe; **Ultraviolettlampe** *f* LABOR ultraviolet lamp; **Ultraviolettlöschen** *nt* COMP & DV ultraviolet erasing; **Ultraviolett-Mikroskop** *nt* STRAHLPHYS ultraviolet microscope; **Ultraviolettspiegel** *m* STRAHLPHYS ultraviolet mirror; **Ultraviolettstrahlen** *m pl* OPTIK, WELLPHYS ultraviolet rays; **Ultraviolettstrahlung** *f* NICHTFOSS ENERG, OPTIK, PHYS, RAUMFAHRT, STRAHLPHYS, UMWELTSCHMUTZ ultraviolet radiation
Ultra-: **Ultrazentrifuge** *f* CHEMIE, KERNTECH, LABOR, PHYS ultracentrifuge; **Ultrazentrifugieren** *nt* CHEMIE *Vorgang*, KERNTECH ultracentrifugation
umarbeiten *vt* BAU redesign
Umbau *m* BAU reconstruction, MASCHINEN conversion
Umbauen *nt* BAU rebuilding
umbauen *vt* BAU rebuild, reconstruct
Umbausatz *m* MASCHINEN conversion kit
Umbell- *pref* CHEMIE umbellic
umbiegen *vt* MECHAN crimp, PAPIER angle
Umbilden: ~ eines Zuges *nt* EISENBAHN reforming of a train
umbördeln *vt* BAU bead over
umbrechen *vt* DRUCK make up
umbrochen: ~e Korrekturfahnen *f pl* DRUCK page proofs
Umbruch *m* DRUCK make-up; **Umbruchprogramm** *nt* DRUCK page make-up program
Umbuchantrag *m* TELEKOM cell change request
Umbuchnachricht *f* TELEKOM roaming indication
Umcodierung *f* COMP & DV transform, TELEKOM transcoding
Umdrehen *nt* SICHERHEIT overturning
Umdrehung *f* LUFTTRANS *eines Luftfahrzeugs* turnaround (AmE), turnround (BrE), MASCHINEN, PAPIER, PHYS, RAUMFAHRT revolution, turn; **~ pro Minute** *f* KFZTECH, PHYS revolution per minute; **Umdrehungsgeschwindigkeit** *f* NICHTFOSS ENERG rotational speed; **Umdrehungskegel** *m* GEOM cone of revolution; **Umdrehungszähler** *m* GERÄT revolution counter; **Umdrehungszählgerät** *nt* GERÄT revolution counter
Umdruck *m* DRUCK transfer
umdrucken *vt* DRUCK transfer
umfahren *vt* WASSERTRANS round
Umfahrgleis *nt* EISENBAHN loop line
Umfahrung *f* BAU bypass; **Umfahrungsstrecke** *f* KOHLEN bypass
Umfang[1] *m* BAU perimeter, periphery, GEOM circumference, perimeter, MECHAN bulk, PATENT *Umfang eines Schutzes* scope
Umfang:[2] **~ eines Werks berechnen** *vi* DRUCK cast off
Umfang: **Umfangsbeanspruchung** *f* METALL circumferential stress; **Umfangsgeschwindigkeit** *f* LUFTTRANS circumferential speed, NICHTFOSS ENERG peripheral velocity; **Umfangsschleifen** *nt* FERTIG peripheral grinding; **Umfangsspannung** *f* FERTIG *Kunststoffinstallationen* circumferential stress; **Umfangteilung** *f* MECHAN circular pitch
umfassen *vt* MASCHINEN encompass
umfassend *adj* COMP & DV global
Umfassung *f* ERGON enveloping grip; **Umfassungsmauer** *f* BAU enclosing wall
umflochten[1] *adj* ELEKTRIZ braided, ELEKTROTECH covered
umflochten:[2] **~e Leitung** *f* ELEKTRIZ braided wire; **~er Schlauch** *m* KUNSTSTOFF braided hose
Umformen *nt* KUNSTSTOFF forming, MASCHINEN forming, pressing, shaping
umformen *vt* ELEKTROTECH convert
umformend: ~e Bearbeitung *f* MASCHINEN forming, shaping
Umformer *m* ELEKTRIZ, ELEKTRONIK, ELEKTROTECH, GERÄT, KONTROLL converter, inverter, transducer; **Umformergruppe** *f* ELEKTROTECH motor generator set; **Umformersatz** *m* ELEKTROTECH motor generator set
Umformstation *f* ELEKTRIZ converter station, converting station
Umformung *f* FERTIG metal working
Umformwerk *nt* ELEKTRIZ converter station, converting station
Umformwerkzeug *nt* MASCHINEN forming tool, shaping die
Umführungsstraße *f* TRANS diversion
Umführungsventil *nt* LABOR bypass valve
Umgang *m* ELEKTRONIK *der Wicklung* convolution, KERNTECH gallery; **Umgangsleitung** *f* ERDÖL bypass
umgebend[1] *adj* HEIZ & KÄLTE ambient
umgebend:[2] **~e Luft** *f* UMWELTSCHMUTZ ambient air
Umgebung *f* ANSTRICH, COMP & DV *des Systems*, ERGON environment, PHYS surroundings; **~ für Sprachenunterstützung** *f* COMP & DV language support environment; **Umgebungsbedingungen** *f pl* METROL, QUAL environmental conditions; **Umgebungsdrehmoment** *nt* RAUMFAHRT environmental torque; **Umgebungsgas** *nt* KERNTECH peripheral gas; **Umgebungsgeräusch** *nt* TELEKOM ambient noise; **Umgebungsgeräuschpegel** *m* GERÄT ambient noise level; **Umgebungslärm** *m* ERGON ambient noise; **Umgebungsluft** *f* HEIZ & KÄLTE ambient air; **Umgebungsluftfeuchte** *f* GERÄT ambient humidity; **Umgebungsluftüberwachung** *f* SICHERHEIT quality monitoring of ambient air; **Umgebungsprüfkammer** *f* RAUMFAHRT environmental test chamber; **Umgebungsradioaktivität** *f* STRAHLPHYS environmental radioactivity; **Umgebungstemperatur** *f* FERTIG, HEIZ & KÄLTE, KONTROLL, METALL, METROL, PHYS, THERMOD ambient temperature; **Umgebungsvariable** *f* COMP & DV environment variable
umgehen *vt* ELEKTRIZ, GERÄT, KFZTECH, KONTROLL bypass
Umgehung *f* BAU, HYDRAUL bypass; **Umgehungsgleis** *nt* EISENBAHN loop line; **Umgehungskanal** *m* WASSERVERSORG diversion canal; **Umgehungsleitung** *f* HYDRAUL, MASCHINEN bypass; **Umgehungsstraße** *f* BAU bypass, TRANS bypass road; **Umgehungsventil** *nt* LUFTTRANS antisurge valve, MASCHINEN bypass valve
umgekehrt[1] *adj* MATH inverse, PHYS reversible; **~ proportional** *adj* GEOM inversely proportional; **in ~ em**

Verhältnis *adj* MASCHINEN in inverse ratio

umgekehrt[2] *adv* TEXTIL contrariwise

umgekehrt:[3] **~er Carnotscher Kreisprozeß** *m* THERMOD vapor compression cycle (AmE), vapour compression cycle (BrE); **~e Polnische Notation** *f (UPN)* COMP & DV reverse Polish notation *(RPN)*; **~es Steuerwerk** *nt* LUFTTRANS reversed controls; **~e V-Antenne** *f* RADIO inverted-V dipole; **~es Verhältnis** *nt* MASCHINEN inverse ratio, reciprocal ratio

umgeschrieben: **~er Kreis** *m* GEOM circumcircle, circumscribed circle

umgewälzt: **~e Luft** *f* HEIZ & KÄLTE recirculated air

umgießen *vt* CHEMTECH decant

Umgipserei *f* KER & GLAS jointing yard

umgraben *vt* BAU spade

Umgreifen *nt* ERGON side changing

Umhaspeln *nt* TEXTIL rewinding

umherlavieren *vi* WASSERTRANS cast about

Umhüllen *nt* BAU coating

umhüllen *vt* BAU clad, coat, sheathe, ELEKTROTECH *Kabel* sheathe, FERTIG clad, *Elektrode* coat

umhüllt[1] *adj* ELEKTRIZ, ELEKTROTECH covered

umhüllt:[2] **~e Stabelektrode** *f* ELEKTRIZ coated rod electrode

Umhüllung *f* DRUCK wrapping, ELEKTRIZ jacket, ELEKTROTECH jacket, sheathing, FERTIG *Elektrode* shielding, KERNTECH *der Stäbe* cladding, MASCHINEN shrouding, shroud, MECHAN jacket, RAUMFAHRT *Raumschiff* casing, shroud, TEXTIL wrapping; **äußere ~** *f* ELEKTRIZ oversheath; **Umhüllungsmaschine** *f* VERPACK envelope machine

Umkehr *f* MASCHINEN reversing, *der Drehrichtung* reversing; **Umkehranzeige** *f* COMP & DV inverse video, reverse image, reverse video; **Umkehrbad** *nt* FOTO reversing bath

umkehrbar[1] *adj* THERMOD reversible; **nicht ~** *adj* PHYS, THERMOD irreversible; **~ eindeutig** *adj* GEOM bijective

umkehrbar:[2] **~e Abschaltung** *f* KERNTECH reversible shutdown; **nicht ~e Abschaltung** *f* KERNTECH irreversible shutdown; **~er Wandler** *m* ELEKTROTECH reversible transducer; **~er Zähler** *m* GERÄT reversible counter

Umkehr: **Umkehrbarkeit** *f* PHYS reversibility; **Umkehrbeschichten** *nt* KUNSTSTOFF reverse roll coating; **Umkehrbild** *nt* PHYS inverted image; **Umkehrbildschalter** *m* FERNSEH reverse image switch; **Umkehrdampf** *m* HYDRAUL reversing steam; **Umkehrdarstellung** *f* COMP & DV inverse video; **Umkehreingang** *m* ELEKTRONIK inverting input; **Umkehremission** *f* ELEKTRONIK reverse emission

umkehren[1] *vt* COMP & DV invert, ELEKTRONIK, MASCHINEN reverse

umkehren[2] *vi* MASCHINEN reverse

umkehrend: **nicht ~** *adj* ELEKTROTECH noninverting

Umkehr: **Umkehrentwicklung** *f* FOTO reversal processing **Umkehrer** *m* COMP & DV inverter

Umkehr: **Umkehrfilm** *m* FOTO reversal film; **Umkehrfunktion** *f* MATH inverse function; **Umkehrgetriebe** *nt* MASCHINEN reverse gear, reversing gear; **Umkehrgrenzpunkt** *m* LUFTTRANS point of no return; **Umkehrkompatibilität** *f* FERNSEH reverse compatibility; **Umkehrkopieren** *nt* FOTO reverse printing; **Umkehrlinse** *f* FERNSEH beam-reversing lens; **Umkehrliste** *f* COMP & DV push-down list; **Umkehrluftschraube** *f* LUFTTRANS reversible pitch propeller; **Umkehrmotor** *m* ELEKTRIZ reversing motor,

ELEKTROTECH, TRANS reversible motor; **Umkehrosmose** *f* ABFALL, BAU reverse osmosis; **Umkehroszillator** *m* ELEKTRONIK inverter oscillator; **Umkehrpunkt** *m* FERTIG dead center (AmE), dead centre (BrE), MATH reversal point, METALL *einer Kurve* cusp; **Umkehrreaktion** *f* KERNTECH reverse reaction; **Umkehrrichtung** *f* ELEKTRONIK reverse direction; **Umkehrring** *m* FOTO reversing ring; **Umkehrrolle** *f* MASCHINEN return pulley; **Umkehrschalter** *m* ELEKTROTECH reversible switch, reversing switch; **Umkehrspanne** *f* GERÄT dead spot; **Umkehrstapel** *m* COMP & DV push-down stack; **Umkehrsteuerwelle** *f* EISENBAHN reversing shaft; **Umkehrsucher** *m* FOTO reversal finder; **Umkehrtemperatur** *f* ELEKTRIZ inversion temperature; **Umkehrtransistor** *m* ELEKTRONIK inverting transistor

Umkehrung *f* DRUCK reversal, ELEKTRONIK inversion, TELEKOM reversal; **~ des Luftschraubengangs** *f* LUFTTRANS reversal of the propeller pitch; **~ des Steuerungsmomentes** *f* LUFTTRANS control reversal

Umkehr: **Umkehrventil** *nt* HYDRAUL *Dampfstrom* reversing valve; **Umkehrverfahren** *nt* DRUCK reversal process; **Umkehrverstärker** *m* ELEKTRONIK differential amplifier, inverting amplifier; **Umkehrwalzenschalter** *m* ELEKTRIZ reversing drum switch

Umkippen *nt* BAU tipping

umkippen *vi* BAU tilt, tip, tip up

umklappbar: **~es Bein** *nt* FOTO *eines Stativs* fold-over leg

Umklappen *nt* FERNSEH flopover

Umklappvorgang *m* KERNTECH rotating process

Umkleideraum *m* BAU changing room, locker room

Umkleidung: **äußere ~** ELEKTRIZ *Armierung* oversheath

Umklöppelung *f* FERTIG, TEXTIL braiding

umkonfigurierbar *adj* COMP & DV reconfigurable

umkonfigurieren *vt* COMP & DV reconfigure

Umkoppelungsvorgang *m* COMP & DV routing

Umkreis *m* BAU perimeter, periphery, GEOM circumcircle

umkreisen *vt* RAUMFAHRT orbit

Umkreis: **Umkreismittelpunkt** *m* FERTIG, GEOM circumcenter (AmE), circumcentre (BrE); **Umkreisradius** *m* GEOM long radius

Umkristallisierung *f* METALL recrystallization

Umladegleis *nt* EISENBAHN transfer track, transshipment track

umladen *vt* WASSERTRANS *Ladung* transship

Umladung *f* WASSERTRANS transshipment

Umlage *f* ELEKTROTECH *Spule, Wicklung* turn

Umlauf *m* ERDÖL, MASCHINEN circulation; **Umlaufabwicklung** *f* ELEKTRONIK deconvolution

Umlaufbahn *f* PHYS, RADIO, RAUMFAHRT orbit, STRAHLPHYS orbital; **Umlaufbahnberechnung** *f* RAUMFAHRT orbit determination; **Umlaufbahneinschuß** *m* RAUMFAHRT orbital injection; **Umlaufbahnflug** *m* RAUMFAHRT orbital flight; **Umlaufbahninklination** *f* RAUMFAHRT orbit inclination; **Umlaufbahnradiusverringerung** *f* RAUMFAHRT orbital decay; **Umlaufbahnsteuerung** *f* RAUMFAHRT orbital maneuvering system (AmE), orbital manoeuvering system (BrE); **Umlaufbahnverkleinerung** *f* RAUMFAHRT orbit trimming

Umlauf: **Umlaufbiegetorsionsprüfung** *f* WERKPRÜF rotary bending and torsion fatigue test; **Umlaufbiegeversuch** *m* METALL rotating bending test; **Umlaufdurchmesser** *m* MASCHINEN swing; **Umlaufdurchmesser über Bett** *m* MASCHINEN swing of the bed, swing-over bed; **Umlaufdurchmesser über Kröpfung**

m MASCHINEN swing-over gap; **Umlaufdurchmesser über Schlitten** *m* MASCHINEN swing of the rest, swing-over saddle

Umlaufen *nt* DRUCK overrun

umlaufen *vt* HEIZ & KÄLTE circulate, RADIO orbit

umlaufend: ~**es Ende** *nt* PAPIER tail end; ~**e Kante** *f* KONSTZEICH circumferential edge; ~**e Nut** *f* OPTIK groove; ~**es Teil** *nt* MASCHINEN rotating part

Umlauf: **Umlauffrequenz** *f* PHYS frequency of gyration; **Umlaufgebläse** *nt* FERTIG rotary blower

umlaufgeschmiert *adj* FERTIG pressure-lubricated

Umlauf: **Umlaufgeschwindigkeit** *f* AUFNAHME running speed, FERTIG rate of circulation, MASCHINEN rotating speed; **Umlaufgetriebe** *nt* FERTIG epicyclic gear, KFZTECH angle transmission, planetary gears, MASCHINEN epicyclic gear, epicycloidal gear, sun-and-planet gearing; **Umlaufintegral** *nt* PHYS *eines Vektorfeldes* circulation; **Umlaufkessel** *m* HYDRAUL circulating boiler; **Umlaufkühlung** *f* HEIZ & KÄLTE refrigeration by circulation; **Umlaufmotor** *m* KFZTECH rotary engine; **Umlaufpumpe** *f* HEIZ & KÄLTE circulation pump; **Umlaufrad** *nt* FERTIG planetary gear; **Umlaufreinigung** *f* LEBENSMITTEL CIP, cleaning in place; **Umlaufschlange** *f* HEIZ & KÄLTE run-around coil; **Umlaufschmierung** *f* FERTIG circulation lubrication, MASCHINEN recirculating lubrication, recirculation lubrication; **Umlaufsystem** *nt* MASCHINEN circulating system, RAUMFAHRT *Weltraumfunk* circulator; **Umlaufzeit** *f* EISENBAHN turnaround time (AmE), turnround time (BrE)

Umlegung *f* TELEKOM transfer

umleiten *vt* BAU divert, ELEKTRIZ, GERÄT, KFZTECH, KONTROLL bypass, TELEKOM redirect, TRANS *Verkehr* divert, WASSERTRANS *Seehandel* reroute, WASSERVERSORG *Fluß* deflect

Umleitung *f* BAU bypass, TELEKOM alternative routing, rerouting, TRANS bypass, diversion; **Umleitungsempfehlung** *f* TRANS advisory diversion; **Umleitungskanal** *m* WASSERVERSORG diversion canal

Umlenkblech *nt* BAU baffle plate

Umlenkhebel *m* KFZTECH relay arm

Umlenkplatte *f* BAU baffle plate

Umlenkprisma *nt* TELEKOM deviation prism

Umlenkrinne *f* KER & GLAS deflector chute, *Glas* deflector

Umlenkrolle *f* FERTIG tail sheave, SICHERHEIT pulley block

Umlenkscheibe *f* MASCHINEN return pulley

Umlenkung *f* LUFTTRANS deflection

Umlenkwalze *f* KER & GLAS *Libbey-Owens Verfahren* bending roller

Umluft *f* HEIZ & KÄLTE circulating air, recirculated air; **Umluftgerät** *nt* HEIZ & KÄLTE circulating air unit

Ummanteln *nt* KUNSTSTOFF sheathing

ummanteln *vt* ANSTRICH encapsule, BAU case, sheathe, *mit Beton* encase, ELEKTROTECH *Kabel* sheathe, FERTIG jacket

ummantelt[1] *adj* FERTIG *Kunststoffinstallationen* coated, MECHAN jacketed, lagged

ummantelt:[2] ~**es Hohlglas** *nt* KER & GLAS cased hollow ware; ~**e Schraube** *f* LUFTTRANS shrouded propeller, MASCHINEN shrouded screw; ~**es Thermoelement** *nt* KERNTECH sheathed thermocouple

Ummantelung *f* ELEKTRIZ jacket, sheath, ELEKTROTECH envelope, jacket, *eines Kabels* sheathing, KER & GLAS casing, KERNTECH jacketing, shell, LUFTTRANS *Flug-*

wesen case, MASCHINEN jacket, MECHAN casing, MEERSCHMUTZ skirt; **Ummantelungsring** *m* LUFTTRANS *Turbinentriebwerk* shroud ring

ummauert: ~**er Raum** *m* BAU walled enclosure

Umordnungsstoß *m* KERNTECH rearrangement collision

U-Motor *m* KFZTECH U-type engine, underfloor engine

umplanen *vt* BAU redesign

Umpolarisierung *f* RAUMFAHRT polarity reversal

Umpolung *f* ELEKTROTECH polarity reversal; **Umpolungsschalter** *m* ELEKTROTECH polarity-reversing switch

Umrahmung *f* BAU *Trennwand* framing; **Umrahmungsleiste** *f* DRUCK box rule

Umrandung *f* DRUCK border

Umrechnung *f* FERTIG *Kunststoffinstallationen* conversion; **Umrechnungstabelle** *f* MATH conversion table

Umreifungsgeräte *nt pl* VERPACK strapping equipment

Umreifungsstahl *nt* VERPACK strapping steel

umreißen *vt* BAU outline

Umrichter *m* ELEKTRIZ inverter, ELEKTROTECH converter

Umriß[1] *m* BAU, FERTIG contour, MASCHINEN outline

Umriß:[2] **im** ~ **fräsen** *vt* FERTIG contour

Umriß: **Umrißfräsen** *nt* MASCHINEN contour milling; **Umrißprojektor** *m* METROL profile projector; **Umrißzeichnung** *f* MASCHINEN outline drawing

Umrollen *nt* PAPIER rewind

Umroller *m* PAPIER rewinder

Umrüstanlage *f* VERPACK conversion machinery

Umrüstsatz *m* MASCHINEN conversion kit

Umrüstung *f* MASCHINEN conversion, retooling

Umschalt-: *pref* MASCHINEN, HEIZ & KÄLTE reversing

umschaltbar: ~**es blockierungsfreies Netz** *nt* TELEKOM rearrangeable nonblocking network

umschalten *vt* COMP & DV shift, toggle, KONTROLL switch over, REGELUNG *Signalfluss* redirect

Umschalter *m* COMP & DV toggle, ELEKTROTECH change-over switch, double-throw switch, selector switch, *Änderung* switch, WASSERTRANS *Elektrik* change-over switch; ~ **mit beweglicher Faser** *m* TELEKOM moving-fiber switch (AmE), moving-fibre switch (BrE)

Umschalt-: **Umschalthebel** *m* MASCHINEN reversing lever; **Umschaltklappe** *f* HEIZ & KÄLTE change-over damper; **Umschaltkontakt** *m* ELEKTROTECH double-throw contact; **Umschaltrelais** *nt* ELEKTRIZ, ELEKTROTECH change-over relay; **Umschalttor** *nt* REGELUNG change-over gate

Umschaltung *f* COMP & DV shift, toggle, TELEKOM transfer; ~ **auf Bereitschaft** *f* TELEKOM change-over to stand-by; ~ **auf Reserve** *f* TELEKOM change-over to stand-by

Umschalt-: **Umschaltventil** *nt* HYDRAUL switch valve; **Umschaltzeichen** *nt* COMP & DV shift character; **Umschaltzeichen für Dauerumschaltung** *nt* COMP & DV SO character, shift-out character; **Umschaltzeit** *f* COMP & DV turnaround time (AmE), turnround time (BrE)

umschiffen *vt* WASSERTRANS double

Umschlag *m* ERDÖL *Schiffahrt* transshipment; **Umschlaganlagen** *f pl* TRANS transship facilities

Umschlagen *nt* DRUCK work and turn, VERPACK overwrap

Umschlag: **Umschlagklappe** *f* VERPACK tuck-in flap; **Umschlagplatz** *m* TRANS terminal; **Umschlagpumpe** *f* MEERSCHMUTZ transfer pump; **Umschlagpunkt** *m* KERNTECH transition point; **Umschlagverpackung** *f*

VERPACK overwrapping packaging; **Umschlagzeit** *f* ELEKTRIZ, ELEKTROTECH *Relais* transit time

umschließend: **~es Gehäuse** *nt* HYDRAUL *Turbine* enclosed casing

Umschlingen *nt* TEXTIL overcasting

Umschlingung *f* FERTIG contact; **Umschlingungsbogen** *m* FERTIG *Getriebelehre, Riemenantrieb* arc of conduct; **Umschlingungswinkel** *m* FERTIG angle of contact, contact angle

umschlossen *adj* MASCHINEN enclosed

Umschmelzen *nt* METALL refusion, remelting

umschmelzen *vt* FERTIG recast

Umschmelzmaschine *f* KER & GLAS burning-off and edge-melting machine (BrE), remelting machine (AmE)

Umschmelzwerk *nt* METALL smelting and refining works

Umschnitt *m* AKUSTIK rerecording

umschreiben *vt* COMP & DV transcribe, GEOM circumscribe

umschrieben: **~er Kreis** *m* GEOM circumscribed circle

umsegeln *vt* WASSERTRANS round

umsetzen *vt* COMP & DV convert, translate, ELEKTROTECH convert

Umsetzer *m* COMP & DV converter, FERNSEH translator station, GERÄT converter, RAUMFAHRT *Weltraumfunk* repeater, TELEKOM converter, *Kanal* translator; **Umsetzerchip** *m* ELEKTRONIK converter chip; **Umsetzerfunkstelle** *f* FERNSEH relay station; **Umsetzergehäuse** *nt* TELEKOM converter cabinet; **Umsetzersatellit** *m* FERNSEH relay satellite, RAUMFAHRT relay satellite, repeater satellite; **Umsetzersender** *m* FERNSEH relay transmitter

Umsetzung *f* COMP & DV conversion, encoding, transform, ELEKTROTECH transformation; **Umsetzungsprodukt** *nt* ABFALL CFS-processed waste, CFS-treated waste, solidified waste, solidified product, solidified material; **Umsetzungsprogramm** *nt* COMP & DV translator

umspannen *vt* FERTIG *Werkstück* rechuck

Umspannung *f* ELEKTROTECH transformation, FERTIG rechucking

Umspannwerk *nt* ELEKTROTECH distribution station

umspinnen *vt* TEXTIL wrap

Umspringen: **~ des Wellentyps** *nt* ELEKTRONIK *Mikrowellen* mode jump; **~ des Windes** *nt* WASSERTRANS sudden change of wind direction

umspringen *vi* WASSERTRANS *Wind* come-to, shift

umspringend: **~e Winde** *m pl* WASSERTRANS baffling winds

umspritzt *adj* FERTIG *Kunststoffinstallationen* molded (AmE), moulded (BrE)

Umspulen *nt* TEXTIL packaging, rewinding

umspulen *vt* TEXTIL rewind

Umstechen *nt* TEXTIL overcasting

umstechen *vt* TEXTIL *Nähen* overcast

Umstecken *nt* FERTIG *Räder* changing

umstecken *vt* FERTIG *Räder* change

Umsteckrad *nt* FERTIG pick-off change gear, pick-off gear

Umsteckwalzwerk *nt* METALL looping mill

Umsteigeaufenthalt *m* LUFTTRANS stopover

Umsteigen *nt* EISENBAHN *für Passagiere* crossover

Umstellbahnhof *m* EISENBAHN shunting yard

Umstellen: **~ von Formeln** *nt* MATH transposition of formulae

Umstellungsverfahren *nt* VERPACK changeover procedure

umsteuerbar: **~er Zähler** *m* GERÄT reversible counter

Umsteuerdampf *m* HYDRAUL reversing steam

Umsteuerknagge *f* FERTIG reverse dog

Umsteuermöglichkeit *f* EISENBAHN reversibility

umsteuernd *adj* ELEKTRONIK reversing

Umsteuerpropeller *m* WASSERTRANS reversible pitch propeller, *Bootsbau* reversible pitch propeller

Umsteuerung *f* MASCHINEN reversing gear, reversing motion; **~ des Propellers** *f* LUFTTRANS reversal of the propeller; **Umsteuerungsvorrichtung** *f* MASCHINEN reversing gear; **Umsteuerungswelle** *f* MASCHINEN reversing shaft

Umsteuerventil *nt* HYDRAUL *Dampfstrom*, MASCHINEN reversing valve

Umströmung *f* WASSERVERSORG circulation

umstürzen[1] *vt* MASCHINEN overturn

umstürzen[2] *vi* MASCHINEN overturn

Umverpackung *f* ABFALL overpackaging, secondary packaging, LEBENSMITTEL packaging

umwälzen *vt* HEIZ & KÄLTE circulate, *Luft* circulate

Umwälzheizlüfter *m* SICHERHEIT regenerative airheater

Umwälzpumpe *f* FERTIG circulating pump, circulation pump, recirculating pump, HEIZ & KÄLTE circulation pump, HYDRAUL circulating pump, LEBENSMITTEL circulating pump, circulation pump, recirculating pump, MASCHINEN recirculating pump

Umwälzung *f* FERTIG circulation, MASCHINEN recirculation

Umwälzventilator *m* HEIZ & KÄLTE ventilating fan

umwandeln *vt* COMP & DV convert, transform, translate, *Programmiersprache* assemble, ELEKTROTECH convert

Umwandler *m* KONTROLL transducer

Umwandlung *f* COMP & DV transform, *von Zeichencodes* conversion, ELEKTROTECH transformation, KERNTECH conversion, transmutation, PAPIER converting, PHYS transmutation, RADIO conversion; **~ von Abfallstoffen** *f* ABFALL waste processing; **~ von Fahrbahnen in Fußgängerbereiche** *f* TRANS pedestrianization; **Umwandlungsöl** *nt* ERDÖL conversion oil; **Umwandlungsoszillator** *m* ELEKTRONIK conversion oscillator; **Umwandlungsrate** *f* UMWELTSCHMUTZ transformation rate; **Umwandlungstemperatur** *f* HEIZ & KÄLTE, METALL transition temperature

Umweglenkung *f* TELEKOM alternative routing, rerouting

Umwelt *f* UMWELTSCHMUTZ environment; **Umweltbedingungen** *f pl* ELEKTRIZ, METROL environmental conditions; **Umweltbelastung** *f* UMWELTSCHMUTZ environmental impact; **Umweltbewußtsein** *nt* UMWELTSCHMUTZ ecological awareness; **Umweltfaktor** *m* UMWELTSCHMUTZ ecological factor

umweltfreundlich[1] *adj* VERPACK environmentally friendly

umweltfreundlich:[2] **~es Auto** *nt* KFZTECH clean air car; **~e Technologie** *f* ABFALL NWT, clean technology

Umwelt: **Umweltgefahr** *f* UMWELTSCHMUTZ ecological menace; **Umweltgesetz** *nt* UMWELTSCHMUTZ environmental law; **Umweltgesundheit** *f* SICHERHEIT environmental health; **Umweltimpulse** *m pl* ERGON exteroceptive impulses; **Umweltkatastrophe** *f* UMWELTSCHMUTZ environmental disaster; **Umweltkontrolle** *f* GERÄT environment monitoring; **Umweltlärm** *m* SICHERHEIT environmental noise; **Umweltplanung** *f* UMWELTSCHMUTZ environmental planning,

planned environment; **Umweltsauberkeit** *f* SICHER-
HEIT *in geschlossenen Räumen* environmental
cleanliness

umweltschädlich *adj* UMWELTSCHMUTZ harmful to the
environment

Umwelt: **Umweltschadstoff** *m* MEERSCHMUTZ
pollutant; **Umweltschutz** *m* UMWELTSCHMUTZ environmental protection, UMWELTSCHMUTZ environ-
mentalism; **Umweltschutzbehörde** *f* environmental
protection agency; **Umweltstress** *m* RAUMFAHRT environmental stress; **Umwelttestverfahren** *nt* SICHERHEIT
environmental testing procedure; **Umweltüberwa-
chung** *f* GERÄT environment monitoring; **Umweltverschmutzung durch Wärme** *f* UMWELTSCHMUTZ
heat pollution; **Umweltverschmutzungsforschung** *f*
UMWELTSCHMUTZ pollution research; **Umweltver-
träglichkeit** *f* UMWELTSCHMUTZ environmental com-
patability; **Umweltverträglichkeitsprüfungsbericht** *m*
UMWELTSCHMUTZ environmental impact statement

Umwerter *m* TELEKOM translator

Umwertespeicher *m* TELEKOM translation store

umwickeln *vt* ELEKTRIZ rewind, TEXTIL rewind, wrap

umwickelt: **~es Garn** *nt* TEXTIL wrapped yarn; **~er Verschluß** *m* VERPACK taped closure

Umwindefaser *f* TEXTIL wrap fiber (AmE), wrap fibre
(BrE)

Umwindungsgarn *nt* TEXTIL covered yarn .

Umzäunung *f* BAU boundary fence, enclosure

umzeichnen *vt* KONSTZEICH redraw

Umziehgerüst *nt* BAU traveling cradle (AmE), travelling
cradle (BrE)

umzwirnt: **~es Garn** *nt* TEXTIL covered yarn

unabgeglichen: **~e Brücke** *f* GERÄT *Meßbrücke* unbalanced bridge

unabgesättigt *adj* CHEMIE unsaturated

unabhängig[1] *adj* HEIZ & KÄLTE self-contained

unabhängig[2] **~e Erregung** *f* ELEKTROTECH independent
excitation; **~es Gerät** *nt* COMP & DV self-contained
equipment; **~e Hinterradaufhängung** *f* KFZTECH independent rear suspension; **~e Navigationshilfe** *f*
LUFTTRANS self-contained navigational aid; **~er Patentanspruch** *m* PATENT independent claim; **~es
Seitenband** *nt (ISB)* RADIO independent sideband
(ISB); **~e Steuerung** *f* KERNTECH independent control; **~es System** *nt* KONTROLL stand-alone system;
~es Teilchenmodell *nt* KERNTECH independent particle model; **~e Variable** *f* MATH independent variable

unangreifbar: **~ machen** *vt* PHYS *Korrosion* passivate

unannehmbar *adj* QUAL unacceptable

unär[1] *adj* COMP & DV monadic, unary

unär[2] **~e Operation** *f* COMP & DV monadic operation,
unary operation

unaufbereitet: **~e Daten** *nt pl* ELEKTRONIK raw data

unausgeglichen: **~er Kanal** *m* AUFNAHME unbalanced
channel

unausgewuchtet *adj* FERTIG unbalanced

unbeabsichtigt: **~es Bremsen** *nt* TRANS accidental
braking

unbeantwortet: **~er Anruf** *m* TELEKOM no-reply call,
unanswered call

unbearbeitet[1] *adj* MASCHINEN unfinished

unbearbeitet[2] **~e Scheibe** *f* MASCHINEN blank washer;
~es Teil *nt* MASCHINEN blank; **~es Werkstück** *nt* FER-
TIG rough work, unmachined work

unbeaufsichtigt: **~er Betrieb** *m* KONTROLL unattended
operation

Unbedenklichkeitsschwelle *f* UMWELTSCHMUTZ limit of
absolute safety

unbedingt[1] *adj* COMP & DV imperative, unconditional

unbedingt[2] **~e Anweisung** *f* COMP & DV unconditional
statement; **~e Instruktion** *f* COMP & DV imperative
instruction; **~er Sprungbefehl** *m* COMP & DV unconditional jump; **~e Verzweigung** *f* COMP & DV
unconditional branch

unbefugt[1] **~er Zugang** *m* KONTROLL unauthorized access; **~er Zugriff** *m* KONTROLL unauthorized access

unbefugt[2] **~ eingreifen in** *vt* SICHERHEIT tamper with

unbegrenzt: **~es Ansprechen auf Impuls** *nt (IIR)* ELEK-
TRONIK infinite impulse response *(IIR)*

unbehauen *adj* FERTIG unhewn

unbehebbar: **~er Fehler** *m* COMP & DV irrecoverable error

unbeladen: **~es Schiff** *nt* WASSERTRANS lightship; **~es
Schiff ohne Antriebsmaschine** *nt* WASSERTRANS lightvessel

unbelastet[1] *adj* LUFTTRANS no-load

unbelastet[2] **~e Gleichspannung** *f* ELEKTRIZ no-load
direct voltage

unbelegt *adj* TELEKOM idle

unbelichtet: **~er Film** *m* FOTO unexposed film

unbemannt[1] *adj* RAUMFAHRT unattended, unmanned

unbemannt[2] **~es Amt** *nt* TELEKOM unattended exchange, unmanned exchange; **~e Ausweichstelle** *f*
EISENBAHN unmanned turnout; **~es Landefahrzeug** *nt*
RAUMFAHRT unmanned lander; **~er Zug** *m* EISENBAHN
unmanned train

unbemaßt *adj* KONSTZEICH undimensioned

unbenannt: **~er Koeffizient** *m* METALL undefined coefficient

unberuhigt[1] **~ vergossen** *adj* FERTIG *Stahl* open, rim-
med, unkilled

unberuhigt[2] **~es Vergießen** *nt* FERTIG rimming; **~ ver-
gossener Stahl** *m* FERTIG open steel

unberuhigt[3] **~ vergießen** *vt* FERTIG rim

unbeschichtet *adj* ANSTRICH uncoated

unbeschränkt: **~er Dienst mit 64 kbit/s** *m* TELEKOM
ISDN sixty-four kbps unrestricted service; **~e Mode** *f*
OPTIK unbound mode

unbeschriftet[1] *adj* COMP & DV blank

unbeschriftet[2] **~er Datenträger** *m* COMP & DV blank
medium, empty medium

unbesetzt *adj* TELEKOM idle

unbespielt[1] *adj* COMP & DV virgin

unbespielt[2] **~er Datenträger** *m* COMP & DV virgin
medium

unbespult: **~es Kabel** *nt* TELEKOM unloaded cable

unbeständig: **~er Verkehrsfluß** *m* TRANS unstable flow

unbestimmt: **~er Befehl** *m* COMP & DV undefined statement; **~es Integral** *nt* MATH indefinite integral

Unbestimmtheitsprinzip *nt* PHYS uncertainty principle

Unbestimmtheitsrelation *f* TEILPHYS uncertainty
relation

unbewehrt: **~er Beton** *m* BAU mass concrete, plain concrete

unbewertet: **~er Rauschpegel** *m* AUFNAHME un-
weighted noise level

unbrennbar *adj* SICHERHEIT nonflammable

Unbrennbarkeitstest *m* SICHERHEIT noncombustibility
test

UNC-Grobgewinde *nt* MASCHINEN UNC, Unified
National Coarse screw thread (AmE), Unified
coarse thread

Undecan- *pref* CHEMIE *Säure* undecanoic

Undecen- *pref* CHEMIE undecylenic

Undecylen- *pref* CHEMIE undecylenic

undefiniert: ~**e Anweisung** *f* COMP & DV undefined statement; ~**er Fehler** *m* COMP & DV undefined error; ~**er Satz** *m* COMP & DV undefined record; ~**e Taste** *f* COMP & DV undefined key

undeutlich: ~ **machen** *vt* KONSTZEICH *Darstellung* detract from the clarity of

UND-Funktion *f* COMP & DV conjunction, equivalence function, equivalence operation

UND-Gatter *nt* PHYS AND gate

UND-Glied *nt* COMP & DV, ELEKTRONIK *logisch* AND gate; ~ **mit negiertem Ausgang** *nt* (*NAND-Tor*) COMP & DV NOT AND gate (*NAND gate*)

undicht¹ *adj* WASSERTRANS leaky

undicht:² ~**es Brennelement** *nt* KERNTECH leaking fuel assembly; ~**e Stelle** *f* WASSERTRANS *Schiff* leak

Undichtheitserkennung *f* VERPACK leakage detection

Undichtheitsprüfung *f* VERPACK leakage test

Undichtigkeit *f* BAU leak, ELEKTROTECH, NICHTFOSS ENERG leakage, PHYS, WASSERTRANS leak

undissoziiert: ~**e Versetzung** *f* METALL undissociated dislocation

UND-Knoten *m* KÜNSTL INT AND node

UND-NICHT-Verknüpfung *f* (*NAND-Funktion*) COMP & DV NOT AND operation (*NAND operation*)

UND/ODER-Graph *m* KÜNSTL INT AND/OR graph

UND-Schaltung *f* COMP & DV *exklusive NOR-Verknüpfung,* ELEKTRONIK *exklusive NOR-Verknüpfung,* PHYS *exklusive NOR-Verknüpfung* AND circuit, AND gate

undurchdringlich *adj* ANSTRICH solid

undurchlässig¹ *adj* ERDÖL, MECHAN, PAPIER impervious, SICHERHEIT impermeable, VERPACK impervious, WASSERVERSORG impermeable

undurchlässig:² ~**es Bohrloch** *nt* ERDÖL tight hole

Undurchlässigkeit *f* BAU, PAPIER, TELEKOM impermeability

undurchsichtig: ~**es Medium** *nt* PHYS opaque medium

UND-Verknüpfung *f* COMP & DV AND operation, conjunction

Und-Zeichen *nt* DRUCK ampersand

uneben: ~**er Rand** *m* KER & GLAS wrinkled rim

Unebenheit *f* KER & GLAS bruise

unedel¹ *adj* FERTIG *Metall* base, ignoble

unedel:² **unedles Metall** *nt* FERTIG, METALL base metal; ~ **unedles Thermoelement** *nt* GERÄT base-metal thermocouple

uneffektiv: ~**e Sendezeit** *f* TELEKOM ineffective air-time

uneingeschränkt: ~**er Informationsübermittlungsdienst** *m* TELEKOM unrestricted information transfer service; ~**er Übermittlungsdienst** *m* TELEKOM unrestricted bearer service

unelastisch: ~**e Neutronenstreuung** *f* PHYS inelastic neutron scattering; ~**er Stoß** *m* PHYS inelastic collision; ~**e Streuung** *f* PHYS inelastic scattering

Unempfindlichkeit *f* WERKPRÜF robustness; **Unempfindlichkeitsfehler** *m* REGELUNG dead band error

unempfindlichst: ~**er Meßbereich** *m* GERÄT least sensitive range

unendlich¹ *adj* MATH infinite

unendlich:² ~**e Dezimalzahl** *f* MATH nonterminating decimal; ~ **dicke Schicht** *f* STRAHLPHYS infinitely thick layer; ~**e Reihe** *f* MATH infinite series; ~ **starke Dämpfung** *f* ELEKTRONIK *eines Filters* infinite attenuation

unendlich:³ **auf ~ einstellen** *vt* FOTO focus for infinity

Unendlichkeit *f* MATH infinity

unentflammbar *adj* ELEKTRIZ flameproof

unentwickelt *adj* MATH implicit

unerwünscht¹ *adj* ELEKTRONIK parasitic, RADIO spurious

unerwünscht:² ~**e Amplitudenmodulation** *f* ELEKTRONIK incidental amplitude modulation; ~**e Aussendung** *f* TELEKOM unwanted emission; ~**e Frequenzmodulation** *f* ELEKTRONIK, FERNSEH, RADIO incidental frequency modulation; ~**e Modulation** *f* ELEKTRONIK incidental modulation

Unfall *m* MECHAN emergency, TRANS accident; ~ **beim Heben** *m* SICHERHEIT lifting accident; ~ **beim Laufen** *m* SICHERHEIT running accident

unfallanfällig *adj* SICHERHEIT accident-prone

Unfall: Unfallberichterstattung *f* SICHERHEIT accident reporting; **Unfalldatenmeldung** *f* TRANS accident date reporting; **Unfalldetektor** *m* TRANS accident detector; **Unfallneigung** *f* ERGON accident proneness; **Unfallverhütung** *f* SICHERHEIT accident prevention; **Unfallverhütungsvorsorgemaßnahmen** *f pl* SICHERHEIT precautions to be taken to prevent accidents; **Unfallwarnsignal** *nt* TRANS accident advisory sign, incident warning sign; **Unfallwarnzeichen** *nt* TRANS accident advisory sign

unfertig *adj* ANSTRICH unfinished

UNF-Feingewinde *nt* MASCHINEN UNF, Unified National Fine screw thread (AmE), Unified fine thread

unformatiert: ~**e Daten** *nt pl* COMP & DV raw data

unfreiwillig: ~**er Reflex** *m* ERGON involuntary reflex

ungebrannt¹ *adj* KER & GLAS, THERMOD unfired

ungebrannt:² ~**er Tiegel** *m* KER & GLAS green pot; ~**er Ziegel** *m* THERMOD unburnt brick

ungebunden: ~**e Mode** *f* OPTIK unbound mode

ungedämpft: ~**e Schwingung** *f* ELEKTRONIK continuous oscillation, sustained oscillation, PHYS maintained oscillation; ~**e Welle** *f* (*CW*) AUFNAHME, ELEKTRONIK, ELEKTROTECH, FERNSEH continuous wave (*CW*)

ungeerdet *adj* ELEKTROTECH floating

ungefähr *adj* MATH approximate

Ungefährmaß *nt* KONSTZEICH approximate dimension

ungefärbt *adj* TEXTIL undyed

ungefedert: ~**es Gewicht** *nt* KFZTECH *Räder, Reifen, Bremsen* unsprung weight

ungeformt *adj* KER & GLAS unmolded (AmE), unmoulded (BrE)

ungeglättet¹ *adj* ANSTRICH rough

ungeglättet:² ~**e Seite** *f* PAPIER backside

ungehärtet *adj* KUNSTSTOFF uncured

ungekürzt: ~**e Länge** *f* TELEKOM uncut length

ungeladen *adj* ELEKTRIZ uncharged

ungelagert: ~**e Schrumpfverpackung** *f* VERPACK unsupported shrink wrapping

ungelocht: ~**er Streifen** *m* TELEKOM unperforated tape

ungelöscht¹ *adj* CHEMIE *Kalk* unslaked

ungelöscht:² ~**er Kalk** *m* KER & GLAS quicklime

ungelöst *adj* FERTIG quick

ungemustert *adj* TEXTIL plain

ungenau: ~**es Fluchten** *nt* FERTIG malalignment

Ungenauigkeitsauflösung *f* RAUMFAHRT ambiguity resolution

ungenehmigt: ~**e Deponie** *m* ABFALL phantom dump

ungenießbar *adj* LEBENSMITTEL inedible

ungenutzt: ~**e Stauung** *f* NICHTFOSS ENERG dead dike (AmE), dead dyke (BrE)

ungeordnet: ~**e Ablagerung** *f* ABFALL uncontrolled dumping, uncontrolled disposal; ~**e Deponie** *f* ABFALL fly tipping, open dump, uncontrolled tipping

ungepaart: ~es **Elektron** *nt* PHYS unpaired electron; ~es **Neutron** *nt* KERNTECH unpaired neutron; ~es **Proton** *nt* KERNTECH unpaired proton

ungepackt *adj* COMP & DV unpacked

ungepolt: ~er **Elektrolytkondensator** *m* ELEKTROTECH nonpolarized electrolytic capacitor

ungerade[1] *adj* DRUCK odd

ungerade:[2] ~ **harmonische Schwingungen** *f pl* PHYS odd harmonic vibrations; ~ **Parität** *f* COMP & DV odd parity; ~ **Seite** *f* DRUCK recto; ~ **Zahl** *f* MATH odd number

Ungerade-Gerade: Ungerade-Gerade-Drehung *f* KERNTECH odd-even spin; **Ungerade-Gerade-Kern** *m* STRAHLPHYS odd-even nucleus; **Ungerade-Gerade-Spin** *m* KERNTECH odd-even spin

Ungerade-Ungerade: Ungerade-Ungerade-Drehung *f* KERNTECH odd-odd spin; **Ungerade-Ungerade-Kern** *m* STRAHLPHYS odd-odd nucleus; **Ungerade-Ungerade-Spin** *m* KERNTECH odd-odd spin

ungeradzahlig: ~e **Harmonische** *f* RADIO odd harmonic; ~e **Parität** *f* PHYS odd parity

ungeregelt: ~es **Bussystem** *nt* RAUMFAHRT unregulated bus system; ~e **Kreuzung** *f* TRANS unsignalized junction; ~e **Spannung** *f* ELEKTROTECH unregulated voltage

ungerichtet: ~e **Endlosfasern** *f pl* KUNSTSTOFF nondirectional filaments; ~e **Fasern** *f pl* KUNSTSTOFF randomly distributed fibers (AmE), randomly distributed fibres (BrE); ~er **Graph** *m* KÜNSTL INT nondirected graph, nonoriented graph, undirected graph; ~es **Mikrofon** *nt* AKUSTIK omnidirectional microphone

ungesättigt[1] *adj* CHEMIE unsaturated

ungesättigt:[2] ~er **Dampf** *m* THERMOD unsaturated steam; ~es **Fett** *nt* LEBENSMITTEL unsaturated fat; ~e **Kohlenstoff-Kohlenstoff-Bindung** *f* ERDÖL unsaturated carbon-to-carbon bond; ~er **Kohlenwasserstoff** *m* ERDÖL alkene, *Petrochemie* unsaturated hydrocarbon; ~e **Logik** *f* ELEKTRONIK nonsaturated logic; ~er **Polyester** *m (UP)* KUNSTSTOFF unsaturated polyester *(UP)*; ~er **Stoff** *m* CHEMIE unsaturate

ungeschichtet: ~e **Zufallsstichprobe** *f* QUAL simple random sample

ungeschützt:[2] ~e **Datei** *f* COMP & DV scratch file, work file; ~e **Einzeltonnenvertänung** *f (ELSBM)* ERDÖL exposed location single buoy mooring *(ELSBM)*

ungesiebt: ~e **Kohle** *f* KOHLEN run of mine coal, unscreened coal

ungesintert: ~er **Preßling** *m* FERTIG green compact

ungespannt: ~es **Grundwasser** *nt* KOHLEN unconfined ground water, WASSERVERSORG unconfined water

ungesponnen: ~e **Fasern** *f pl* TEXTIL raw materials

ungestört: ~e **Probe** *f* KOHLEN undisturbed sample

ungestrichen *adj* ANSTRICH uncoated

ungetaktet: ~e **Arbeit** *f* ERGON self-paced work

ungeteilt: ~es **Lager** *nt* MASCHINEN bushed bearing; ~e **Lagerbüchse** *f* MASCHINEN unsplit bush; ~es **Schneideisen** *nt* MASCHINEN solid die

ungewaschen: ~e **Kohle** *f* KOHLEN unwashed coal

ungiftig *adj* ANSTRICH nontoxic

unglasiert *adj* CHEMIE unglazed

ungleich[1] *adj* MATH unequal; ~ **Null** *adj* MATH *Zahl* nonzero

ungleich:[2] ~e **Ladungen** *f pl* ELEKTRIZ opposite charges; ~e **Pole** *m pl* ELEKTRIZ unlike poles

ungleichförmig: ~e **Bewegung** *f* PHYS nonuniform motion

Ungleichgewicht *nt* MASCHINEN unbalance

Ungleichheitszeichen *nt* MATH chevron

Ungleichlauf *m* PHYS asynchronism

ungleichlaufend *adj* PHYS asynchronous

ungleichmäßig: ~er **Boden** *m* KER & GLAS slugged bottom; ~e **Härtung** *f* KER & GLAS uneven temper; ~e **Setzung** *f* BAU differential settlement; ~e **Verkehrsbelastung** *f* TELEKOM traffic load imbalance; ~e **Verkehrsverteilung** *f* TELEKOM traffic distribution imbalance

ungleichnamig: ~e **Pole** *m pl* PHYS unlike poles

ungleichseitig[1] *adj* FERTIG scalene

ungleichseitig:[2] ~es **Dreieck** *nt* GEOM scalene triangle

Ungleichung *f* COMP & DV inequality

Ungültigkeitszeichen *nt* COMP & DV ignore character

ungünstig[1] *adj* KERNTECH unfavourable

ungünstig:[2] ~er **Wind** *m* WASSERTRANS foul wind

unidirektional *adj* TELEKOM unidirectional

unifarben *adj* TEXTIL plain

Unifikation *f* KÜNSTL INT *von Variablen* unification

Unifilaraufhängung *f* ELEKTRIZ unifilar suspension

Unifining *nt* CHEMIE unifining

Unifizierung *f* KÜNSTL INT *von Variablen* unification

uniform *adj* CHEMIE *Struktur* uniform

Unikat *nt* KONSTZEICH unique record

Unipolar- *pref* COMP & DV, ELEKTROTECH unipolar

unipolar: ~e **Leitung** *f* ELEKTROTECH unidirectional conduction; ~er **Transistor** *m* ELEKTRONIK unipolar transistor

Unipolar-: Unipolardynamo *m* ELEKTRIZ unipolar dynamo; **Unipolargenerator** *m* ELEKTROTECH homopolar generator; **Unipolar-IC** *m* ELEKTRONIK unipolar IC, unipolar integrated circuit; **Unipolarmaschine** *f* ELEKTROTECH homopolar machine

Unipolgenerator *m* ELEKTRIZ homopolar generator

unisoliert[1] *adj* FERTIG *Rohr* unlagged

unisoliert:[2] ~er **Stromleiter** *m* ELEKTRIZ plain conductor

universal *adj* ELEKTROTECH GP, general-purpose

Universal- *pref* COMP & DV, ELEKTROTECH GP, general-purpose; **Universalantenne** *f* PHYS multiband antenna; **Universalbohrmeißel** *m* FERTIG universal boring tool; **Universalbrücke** *f* ELEKTRIZ, GERÄT universal bridge; **Universalchip** *m* ELEKTRONIK general-purpose chip; **Universalcomputer** *m* COMP & DV GP computer, general-purpose computer; **Universaldrehmaschine** *f* MASCHINEN universal lathe; **Universalentwicklungstank** *m* FOTO universal developing tank; **Universalfräsmaschine** *f* MASCHINEN universal milling machine; **Universalfutter** *nt* MASCHINEN combination chuck; **Universalgelenk** *nt* KFZTECH *Triebstrang*, MASCHINEN universal joint; **Universalgerät** *nt* GERÄT general-purpose instrument; **Universalhobelmaschine** *f* MASCHINEN universal planer; **Universalinstrument** *nt* GERÄT general-purpose instrument; **Universal-Leiterplatte** *f* ELEKTRONIK general-purpose board; **Universalmanipulator** *m* KERNTECH universal manipulator; **Universalmenge** *f* COMP & DV, MATH universal set; **Universalmeßbrücke** *f* GERÄT universal bridge; **Universalmeßgerät** *nt* GERÄT general-purpose instrument, universal measuring instrument; **Universalmeßinstrument** *nt* GERÄT universal measuring instrument; **Universalmotor** *m* ELEKTRIZ all-current motor (AmE), all-mains motor (BrE), universal motor, ELEKTROTECH universal motor; **Universalne-**

benwiderstand *m* ELEKTRIZ universal shunt; **Universalprogramm** *nt* COMP & DV general-purpose program; **Universalrechner** *m* COMP & DV GP computer, general-purpose computer; **Universalreißer** *m* MASCHINEN scribing block; **Universalrelais** *nt* ELEKTROTECH general-purpose relay; **Universalrundschleifmaschine** *f* FERTIG universal cylindrical grinder; **Universalschalter** *m* ELEKTRIZ universal switch; **Universalschleifmaschine** *f* KER & GLAS, MASCHINEN universal grinder; **Universalschlüssel** *m* KFZTECH *Werkzeug* adjustable spanner (BrE); **Universalschneider** *m* MASCHINEN universal cutter; **Universalschraubstock** *m* MASCHINEN universal vice (BrE), universal vise (AmE); **Universalselbstentlader** *m* KFZTECH all-round dumping wagon; **Universal-Shunt** *m* ELEKTRIZ universal shunt; **Universalspannfutter** *nt* MASCHINEN scroll chuck, self-centering chuck (AmE), self-centring chuck (BrE), universal chuck; **Universalsprache** *f* COMP & DV general-purpose language; **Universalsucher** *m* FOTO universal viewfinder; **Universalwerkzeugschleifmaschine** *f* FERTIG universal cutter and tool grinding machine; **Universalwiderstand** *m* ELEKTROTECH general-purpose resistor; **Universalwindeisen** *nt* MASCHINEN universal tap wrench; **Universalwinkelmesser** *m* METROL universal bevel protractor; **Universalzeichensatz** *m* COMP & DV universal character set

universell: **~er S-Anschluß** *m* TELEKOM S-universal access; **~e S-Schnittstelle** *f* TELEKOM S-universal interface; **~e S-Schnittstellenkarte** *f* TELEKOM S-universal interface card; **~es Wandgesetz** *nt* STRÖMPHYS *in turbulenter Grenzschicht* universal motion

Univibrator *m* ELEKTRONIK monostable multivibrator

unklar:[1] **~er Anker** *m* WASSERTRANS *Festmachen* fouled anchor

unklar:[2] **~ kommen** *vi* WASSERTRANS *Festmachen, Tauwerk* foul

unklassifiziert: **~e Zuschlagstoffe** *m pl* BAU all-in ballast

unkollidiert: **~es Neutron** *nt* KERNTECH uncollided neutron

unkontrolliert: **~e Aufzeichnung** *f* AUFNAHME wild recording

unkorrigierbar: **~er Abbruchfehler** *m* COMP & DV fatal error

unkorrigiert: **~es Ergebnis** *nt* METROL uncorrected result

unkristallin *adj* FERTIG amorphous

unlauter: **~er Wettbewerb** *m* PATENT unfair competition

unlegiert: **~er Kohlenstoffstahl** *m* METALL plain carbon steel; **~ Stahl** *m* FERTIG ordinary steel, KOHLEN carbon steel, METALL ordinary steel

unleserlich *adj* DRUCK illegible

unlogarithmiert: **~er Sinus** *m* GEOM natural sine

unlösbar:[1] *adj* MASCHINEN permanent

unlösbar:[2] **~e Verbindung** *f* MASCHINEN permanent joint

unlösbar:[3] **~ verbinden** *vt* KONSTZEICH connect together non-detachably

unlöslich *adj* ERDÖL *Petrochemie* insoluble

Unlöslichkeit *f* TEXTIL insolubility

unmagnetisch *adj* PHYS nonmagnetic

unmaßstäblich *adj* KONSTZEICH not to scale

unmischbar *adj* LEBENSMITTEL immiscible

unmittelbar[1] *adj* TELEKOM, WASSERVERSORG direct

unmittelbar:[2] **~e Adresse** *f* COMP & DV immediate address, zero-level address; **~e Adressierung** *f* COMP & DV immediate addressing; **~e Litzenleitung** *f* OPTIK direct strand cable; **~e manuelle Wartung** *f* KERNTECH direct

maintenance; **~e Schallaufzeichnung** *f* AUFNAHME direct recording; **~e Schienenbefestigung** *f* EISENBAHN direct rail fastening; **~e Verarbeitung** *f* COMP & DV demand processing, immediate processing; **~er Zugriff** *m* COMP & DV immediate access

Unmittelbar-Lese-nach-Schreib-Platte *f* OPTIK direct read-after-write

unmodifiziert: **~e Adresse** *f* COMP & DV presumptive address; **~er Befehl** *m* COMP & DV presumptive instruction

unmoduliert[1] *adj* RAUMFAHRT unmodulated

unmoduliert:[2] **~e Rille** *f* AKUSTIK blank groove

üNN *abbr* (*über Normalnull*) WASSERTRANS asl (*above sea level*)

Unordnung *f* METALL disorder

unperiodisch: **~er Impuls** *m* ELEKTRONIK nonrecurrent pulse

unplastifiziert *adj* KUNSTSTOFF unplasticized

unpolar: **~es Lösemittel** *nt* KUNSTSTOFF nonpolar solvent

unregelmäßig: **~es Garn** *nt* TEXTIL irregular yarn; **~e Kante** *f* KER & GLAS irregular edge; **~es Polyeder** *nt* GEOM irregular polyhedron

unrein: **~er Grund** *m* WASSERTRANS foul bottom, foul ground

unrund[1] *adj* KFZTECH, MASCHINEN out of round

unrund:[2] **~er Verschluß** *m* KER & GLAS out-of-round finish

Unrunddrehen *nt* MASCHINEN cam turning

Unrundheit *f* MASCHINEN out-of-roundness, OPTIK *des Mantels, Kerns*, TELEKOM *des Mantels, Kerns* noncircularity

unrundkopieren *vt* FERTIG profile

unrundlaufen *vi* MASCHINEN run out of true

unscharf[1] *adj* ELEKTRIZ fuzzy, FOTO out of focus, KER & GLAS blurred, KÜNSTL INT fuzzy

unscharf:[2] **~es Bild** *nt* FOTO fuzzy image, out of focus image; **~ eingestellter Verstärker** *m* ELEKTRONIK flat amplifier; **~er Hintergrund** *m* FOTO background blur; **~e Logik** *f* COMP & DV, KÜNSTL INT fuzzy logic; **~e Menge** *f* COMP & DV, KÜNSTL INT fuzzy set

Unschärfe *f* FERTIG flatness; **Unschärferelation** *f* PHYS uncertainty principle

unselbständig: **~e Entladung** *f* ELEKTROTECH nonself-sustained discharge

unsicher: **~e Umweltbedingung** *f* SICHERHEIT unsafe environmental condition

Unsicherheit *f* COMP & DV uncertainty

unsichtbar: **~e Kante** *f* KONSTZEICH hidden edge

unspezifisch: **~er Transistor** *m* ELEKTRONIK uncommitted transistor

unstabil[1] *adj* PHYS unstable

unstabil:[2] **~er Bruch** *m* METALL unstable fracture

Unstabilität *f* VERPACK instability

unstetig: **~er Verstärker** *m* ELEKTRONIK discontinuous amplifier

unstreifig: **~er Perlit** *m* METALL nonlamellar pearlite

Unsymmetrie *f* CHEMIE, GEOM dissymmetry

unsymmetrisch[1] *adj* ELEKTRIZ unbalanced, GEOM asymmetrical, dissymmetrical, dissymmetric, unsymmetrical, RAUMFAHRT unbalanced

unsymmetrisch:[2] **~e Anordnung** *f* ELEKTROTECH unsymmetrical arrangement; **~er Ausgang** *m* ELEKTROTECH unbalanced output, *bei Vierpol* single-ended output, RAUMFAHRT unbalanced output; **~es Drehstromsystem** *nt* ELEKTRIZ unbalanced three-phase system; **~er Eingang** m ELEKTROTECH unbalanced input; **~es Filter** nt AUFNAHME unbalanced filter; **~e Leitung** f ELEKTROTECH unbalanced line; **~es System** nt TELEKOM unbalanced system

untätig adj WASSERTRANS inactive

unten:[1] **nach ~** adv WASSERTRANS below

unten:[2] **nach ~ gehen** vi WASSERTRANS Schiff go below

unter:[1] **~ Dampf** adj MASCHINEN under steam; **~ Deck** adj WASSERTRANS below deck, below decks, below; **Druck gesetzt** adj MECHAN pressurized; **~ Druck verformbar** adj FERTIG malleable; **Kontrolle** adj MASCHINEN under control; **~ Last** adj KFZTECH Motor, MASCHINEN under load; **~ Planungshöhe** adj BAU below grade; **~ Spannung stehend** adj ELEKTROTECH alive, live **~ Strom** adj ELEKTROTECH alive; **~ Vakuum** adj PHYS, THERMOD under vacuum; **~ weißer Flagge** adj WASSERTRANS under White Ensign

unter:[2] **~er Anschluß** m KERNTECH bottom fitting; **~er Behälter** m KFZTECH lower tank; **~e Drehpfanne** f EISENBAHN center casting (AmE), centre casting (BrE); **~er Durchlaßbereich** m TELEKOM low-pass band; **~es Gelenk** nt LUFTTRANS Hubschrauber lower link; **~e Grenzabweichung** f QUAL lower limiting deviation; **~e Grenzfrequenz** f ELEKTRONIK, RADIO, TELEKOM low-frequency cutoff; **~e Gurtplatte** f BAU sole plate; **~e Heizleistung** f ABFALL LCV, lower calorific value; **~e Kontrollgrenze** f QUAL lower control limit; **~e Kühltemperatur** f KER & GLAS lower annealing temperature; **~ Last kommutierbarer Umformer** m ELEKTRIZ load-commutated converter; **~ Last laufende Maschine** f MASCHINEN loaded machine; **~er Mühlstein** m LEBENSMITTEL bottom millstone; **~e Nachweisbarkeitsgrenze** f UMWELTSCHMUTZ lower limit of detectability; **~e Nachweisgrenze** f GERÄT detection limit; **~es Pleuelauge** nt KFZTECH connecting rod big end; **~er Querfries** m BAU bottom rail; **~es Sammelbecken** nt NICHTFOSS ENERG lower storage basin; **~es Seitenband** nt (LSB) ELEKTRONIK, RADIO Sprechfunk, TELEKOM lower sideband (LSB); **~er Seitenrand** m DRUCK tail; **~es Speicherbecken** nt NICHTFOSS ENERG lower storage basin; **~e Streckgrenze** f METALL lower yield point; **~er Totpunkt** m FERTIG Hammer pick-up point, KFZTECH Motor, Zündung bottom dead center (AmE), bottom dead centre (BrE), MECHAN BDC, bottom dead center (AmE), bottom dead centre (BrE); **~e Treppenwange** f BAU rough string; **~e Welle** f KFZTECH lower shaft; **~es Zwischenstufengefüge** nt METALL lower bainite

unter:[3] **~ Druck halten** vt HEIZ & KÄLTE pressurize; **~ Druck setzen** vt HEIZ & KÄLTE pressurize; **~ Kontrolle bringen** vt ERDÖL Bohrung nach Eruption bring under control; **~ Luftabschluß anlassen** vt THERMOD pot-anneal; **~ Putz legen** vt BAU conceal; **~ Quarantäne stellen** vt WASSERTRANS quarantine; **~ Spannung setzen** vt ELEKTROTECH apply a voltage; **~ Vakuum setzen** vt PAPIER apply vacuum to

unter:[4] **~ Last laufen** vi MASCHINEN run under load; **~ Segel gehen** vi WASSERTRANS set sail

Unteradresse f TELEKOM subaddress

Unteramboß m MASCHINEN anvil bed

Unteramt nt TELEKOM dependent exchange

Unterband nt TELEKOM lower band; **Unterbandaufnahme** f FERNSEH low-band recording; **Unterbandnorm** f FERNSEH low-band standard

Unterbau m BAU base course, foundation, subbase, Straßenbau substructure, ERDÖL substructure, KOH-

LEN foundation

Unterbauen nt FERTIG shimming

unterbauen vt FERTIG, MASCHINEN shim

Unterbaugrube f LUFTTRANS jig-pit

Unterbelastung f PHYS unloading

unterbelichten vt FOTO underexpose

unterbelichtet: **~es Bild** nt FOTO underexposed picture

Unterbelichtung f FOTO underexposure

Unterbeton m BAU blinding concrete

Unterboden m KFZTECH underbody; **Unterbodenholm** m LUFTTRANS floor beam; **Unterbodenschutz** m KFZTECH underbody protection, Karosserie undersealant

Unterbrechen nt FERNSEH cutoff

unterbrechen vt ANSTRICH disrupt, COMP & DV interrupt, ELEKTROTECH isolate, Stromkreis break, KONTROLL interrupt

Unterbrecher m ELEKTRIZ air interrupter, interrupter, ELEKTROTECH break, circuit breaker, cutout, interrupter, make and break, mit Kontaktzunge trembler, KFZTECH breaker, Motor contact breaker, SICHERHEIT elektrische Sicherheit cutout device, TELEKOM interrupter; **Unterbrecherbad** nt FOTO stop bath; **Unterbrecherfeder** f KFZTECH breaker spring; **Unterbrecherklappe** f LUFTTRANS Luftfahrzeug spoiler; **Unterbrecherkontakt** m ELEKTROTECH break contact, KFZTECH Zündung breaker contact, point; **Unterbrecherkontaktsteuerung** f KFZTECH breaker triggering; **Unterbrecherschließwinkel** m KFZTECH dwell angle

Unterbrechung f ANSTRICH disruption, COMP & DV break, interrupt, ELEKTROTECH break, cutoff, cutout, disconnection, interruption, FERTIG isolation, KERNTECH der Kettenreaktion disruption, MASCHINEN check, PHYS breakdown, RADIO Sprechfunk break-in, TELEKOM interruption; **~ der Stromversorgung** f COMP & DV power supply interrupt; **Unterbrechungsanforderung** f COMP & DV interrupt request

unterbrechungsfrei: **~e Stromversorgung** f (USV) KONTROLL stand-by battery power supply

unterbrechungsgesteuert: **~es System** nt KONTROLL interrupt-driven system

Unterbrechung: **Unterbrechungshalt** m COMP & DV dead halt

unterbrechungslos[1] adj TELEKOM break-free

unterbrechungslos[2] **~e Stromversorgung** f RAUMFAHRT no-break power supply

Unterbrechung: **Unterbrechungsmaske** f COMP & DV interrupt mask; **Unterbrechungspriorität** f COMP & DV interrupt priority; **Unterbrechungspunkt** m COMP & DV breakpoint; **Unterbrechungspunktbetrieb** m KONTROLL breakpoint operation; **Unterbrechungsserviceprogramm** nt COMP & DV interrupt service routine; **Unterbrechungssignal** nt COMP & DV interrupt signal; **Unterbrechungstaste** f COMP & DV attention key; **Unterbrechungszeit** f TELEKOM down-time; **Unterbrechungszielsteuerung** f COMP & DV interrupt vectoring

unterbreiten vt PATENT submit

unterbringen vt EISENBAHN stable

Unterbringungsplan m WASSERTRANS accommodation plan

unterbrochen[1] adj TELEKOM broken

unterbrochen:[2] **~e Ankerwicklung** f ELEKTRIZ open coil armature; **~es Bewegen** nt FOTO Entwickler intermittent agitation; **~es Feuer** nt WASSERTRANS Seezeichen occulting light; **~ gezeichnetes Teil** nt KONSTZEICH interrupted view of a part, interrupted view of a compound; **~es Gruppenfeuer** *nt* WASSERTRANS *Seezeichen* group-occulting light; **~e Linie** *f* GEOM broken line; **~er Strom** *m* ELEKTRIZ pulsed current; **~er Stromkreis** *m* ELEKTRIZ open circuit; **~er Träger** *m* BAU tailpiece; **~er Verkehrsfluß** *m* TRANS interrupted traffic flow; **~e Wicklung** *f* ELEKTRIZ open circuit winding, open winding

unterdämpft *adj* GERÄT *Meßwerk* underdamped

Unterdeck *nt* WASSERTRANS lower deck

unterdimensionieren *vt* BAU underdesign

unterdimensioniert: ~er Durchmesser *m* NICHTFOSS ENERG nondimensional diameter

Unterdruck *m* KFZTECH, MASCHINEN depression, negative pressure, underpressure, vacuum, MECHAN vacuum, PHYS depression, negative pressure, underpressure, vacuum; **Unterdruckbremse** *f* KFZTECH vacuum brake; **Unterdruckbremskraftverstärker** *m* KFZTECH vacuum-assisted power brake

unterdrücken *vt* COMP & DV suppress

Unterdruck: **Unterdruckförderpumpe** *f* KFZTECH vacuum fuel pump; **Unterdruckhinweis** *m* SICHERHEIT negative pressure sign; **Unterdruckmesser** *m* MASCHINEN vacuum gage (AmE), vacuum gauge (BrE); **Unterdruckregler** *m* KFZTECH suction-type governor, *Zündung* vacuum advance mechanism; **Unterdruckregulierventil** *nt* KFZTECH vacuum check valve; **Unterdruckschlauch** *m* MASCHINEN vacuum hose; **Unterdruckseite** *f* LUFTTRANS *eines Flügels* upper surface

unterdrückt: ~er Strahl *m* ELEKTRONIK blanked beam

Unterdrückung *f* COMP & DV, ELEKTROTECH suppression; **~ von Einschaltstößen** *f* ELEKTROTECH transient suppression; **~ der Nummernanzeige des gerufenen Teilnehmers** *f* TELEKOM connected-line identification restriction; **Unterdrückungsfaktor** *m* ELEKTRONIK *bei Differentialverstärkern* rejection, RAUMFAHRT suppression factor

Unterdruck: **Unterdruckventil** *nt* KFZTECH vacuum valve; **Unterdruckversteller** *m* KFZTECH *Zündung* vacuum advance mechanism; **Unterdruckzündverstellung** *f* KFZTECH vacuum advance mechanism

Untereinheit *f* KONTROLL subunit

unterentwickeln *vt* FOTO underdevelop

Unterfahrschutz *m* KFZTECH under-run guard

Unterfahrstoßstange *f* KFZTECH under-run bar, under-run bumper

Unterfangung *f* BAU underpinning, vertical shoring; **Unterfangungsschalung** *f* KOHLEN interpit sheeting

Unterflansch *m* BAU bottom flange

Unterflosse *f* LUFTTRANS *Flugzeug* lower surface

Unterflurbelüftung *f* HEIZ & KÄLTE underfloor ventilation

Unterflurbewässerung *f* WASSERVERSORG subsurface irrigation

Unterflurkondensator *m* KERNTECH underfloor condenser

Unterflurmotor *m* KFZTECH underfloor engine

unterführen *vt* BAU pass under

Unterführung *f* BAU underbridge, underpass, EISENBAHN *für Fußgänger* subway (AmE), underground (BrE)

Unterfütterung *f* BAU bed

untergärig: ~e Hefe *f* LEBENSMITTEL bottom yeast

untergehen *vi* WASSERTRANS *Schiff* founder, *Schiff* go down, sink

untergeordnet[1] *adj* HEIZ & KÄLTE downstream

untergeordnet:[2] **~e Anwendung** *f* COMP & DV slave application; **~es Bussystem** *nt* COMP & DV bus slave; **~er Computer** *m* COMP & DV slave; **~e Datenstation** *f* COMP & DV slave station; **~er Prozessor** *m* COMP & DV slave processor; **~er Typ** *m* COMP & DV subtype

Untergesenk *nt* FERTIG bottom die, bottom swage, MASCHINEN bottom die, lower die

Untergestell *nt* BAU bogie (BrE), trailer (AmE), carrier, EISENBAHN frame, underframe, FERTIG base, KERNTECH underframe, MASCHINEN foot, undercarriage, underframe, RAUMFAHRT undercarriage, VERPACK skid base

untergliedert[1] *adj* COMP & DV partitioned

untergliedert:[2] **~e Datei** *f* COMP & DV partitioned file

Untergraph *m* KÜNSTL INT subgraph

Untergrenze *f* TELEKOM lower limit

Untergröße *f* KOHLEN undersize

Untergrund *m* PHYS, STRAHLPHYS, TEILPHYS background; **Untergrundabdichtung** *f* ABFALL bottom sealing; **Untergrundbedingungen** *f pl* ERDÖL *Geologie* subsurface conditions; **Untergrundbus** *m* TRANS underground bus; **Untergrundmuster** *nt* DRUCK mechanical tint; **Untergrundrauschen** *nt* PHYS background noise

Untergruppentrennzeichen *nt* COMP & DV RS, record separator

Untergruppen: ~ zusammenbauen *vi* FERTIG subassemble

Untergurt *m* BAU bottom flange, girt

unterhalb *adv* BAU downstream; **~ der Taille** *adv* TEXTIL below the waist

unterhalten *vt* MASCHINEN, MECHAN *Werkzeuge* maintain

Unterhaltungselektronik *f* ELEKTROTECH consumer electronics, domestic electronic equipment

Unterhaupt *nt* WASSERVERSORG *eines Durchlasses oder Schleuse* tail bay

Unterhitze *f* KER & GLAS bottom heat

Unterhörfrequenz *f* AKUSTIK, ELEKTRONIK infrasonic frequency

unterirdisch: ~e Ausbreitung *f* TELEKOM subterranean propagation; **~e Bewässerung** *f* WASSERVERSORG subsurface irrigation; **~e Dränage** *f* WASSERVERSORG underground drainage; **~e Erosion** *f* WASSERVERSORG subsurface erosion; **~e Lagerung** *f* THERMOD underground storage; **~e Leitung** *f* TELEKOM underground line; **~e Speicherung** *f* WASSERVERSORG underground storage; **~es Wasser** *nt* UMWELTSCHMUTZ underground water, WASSERVERSORG ground water, subterranean water

Unterkasten *m* FERTIG nowel, *Formen* lower box, *Gießen* drag, WASSERVERSORG tail box

Unterkette *f* COMP & DV substring

Unterkolbenpresse *f* KUNSTSTOFF upstroke press

Unterkonstruktion *f* BAU substructure, *für Putzauftrag* furring

Unterkorn *nt* KOHLEN undersize

unterkritisch[1] *adj* KERNTECH subcritical; **~ gedämpft** *adj* GERÄT *Meßwerk* underdamped

unterkritisch:[2] **~e Ballung** *f* ELEKTRONIK underbunching; **~e Menge** *f* KERNTECH off-critical amount; **~e Reaktion** *f* STRAHLPHYS subcritical reaction

unterkühlen *vt* THERMOD *Dampf* undercool, *Flüssigkeit* subcool

Unterkühler *m* HEIZ & KÄLTE subcooler

unterkühlt *adj* HEIZ & KÄLTE subcooled, PHYS super-cooled

Unterkühlung *f* METALL, PHYS supercooling, WASSERTRANS hypothermia

Unterlage *f* BAU backing, ballast, base, bed, support, FERTIG *Kunststoffinstallationen* base, KOHLEN precoating, LUFTTRANS backing bar, MASCHINEN bolster, PHYS substrate, TEXTIL, VERPACK backing

unterlagernd: ~es Gestein *nt* WASSERVERSORG bedrock

Unterlagsblech *nt* BAU backplate

Unterlängen *f pl* DRUCK descenders

Unter-Last: ~ Abzapfwechsel *m* ELEKTRIZ load-tapchanger

Unterlast *f* KERNTECH, MASCHINEN underload; **Unterlastprüfung** *f* ELEKTRIZ load test; **Unterlastrelais** *nt* ELEKTRIZ underload relay

Unterlastung *f* ELEKTROTECH, QUAL derating; **Unterlastungsgrad** *m* QUAL derating factor

Unterlauf *m* COMP & DV, WASSERVERSORG underflow

Unterlegblech *nt* MASCHINEN packing piece

Unterlegbrett *nt* FERTIG *für Stampfen und Stürzen* oddside

Unterlegen *nt* FERTIG shimming; **~ von Scheiben** *nt* MASCHINEN shimming

unterlegen *vt* FERTIG, MASCHINEN shim

Unterlegscheibe *f* BAU, FERTIG washer, KERNTECH shim, KFZTECH plain washer, KFZTECH *Schraube, Bolzen* washer, MASCHINEN flat washer, plain washer, shim, washer

unterlegt: ~es Fenster *nt* COMP & DV tiled window

Unterlieferant *m* QUAL subcontractor

Unterliek *nt* WASSERTRANS *Segeln* foot

Unterlizenz *f* PATENT sublicence (BrE), sublicense (AmE)

Untermaß *nt* KOHLEN, MASCHINEN undersize

Untermenge *f* COMP & DV subset

Untermesser *nt* PAPIER *Querschneider* bed knife

untermoderiert[1] *adj* KERNTECH *Reaktor* undermoderated

untermoderiert:[2] **~es Schutzgas** *nt* KERNTECH undermoderated blanket

Untermodulation *f* AUFNAHME, ELEKTRONIK undermodulation

Unternahtriß *m* KERNTECH underbead crack

Unternehmensforschung *f* COMP & DV operational research, operations research

Unterniveau *nt* PHYS sublevel

Unterpflaster-Omnibus *m* TRANS underground trolley bus

Unterpflasterstraßenbahn *f* TRANS underground tramway

unterphosphorisch *adj* CHEMIE hypophosphorous

Unterproblem *nt* KÜNSTL INT subproblem

Unterprogramm *nt* COMP & DV subprogram, subroutine; **Unterprogrammaufruf** *m* COMP & DV subroutine call; **Unterprogrammbibliothek** *f* COMP & DV program library, subroutine library

Unterpulverschweißen *nt* BAU submerged arc-welding

Unterputz *m* BAU rendering; **Unterputzschicht** *f* BAU undercoat

Unterraum *m* PHYS subspace

Unterreaktivität *f* KERNTECH deficit reactivity

Unterrichtsreaktor *m* KERNTECH training reactor

Untersattel *m* FERTIG anvil pallet, bottom pallet

Untersättigung *f* METALL undersaturation

Untersatz *m* FERTIG *Kokille* stool

Unterschale *f* PHYS subshell

Unterschall- *pref* ELEKTRONIK, LUFTTRANS subsonic, PHYS infrasonic, STRAHLPHYS subsonic; **Unterschallfrequenz** *f* ELEKTRONIK, STRAHLPHYS subsonic frequency; **Unterschallgeschwindigkeit** *f* PHYS infrasonic speed; **Unterschall-Luftfahrzeug** *nt* LUFTTRANS subsonic aircraft

unterscheidend *adj* PATENT distinctive

Unterscheidung *f* ERGON discrimination; **Unterscheidungsbit** *nt (Q-Bit)* TELEKOM qualifer bit *(Q bit)*; **Unterscheidungskraft** *f* PATENT distinctiveness

unterscheidungskräftig *adj* PATENT distinctive

Unterscheidung: Unterscheidungsvermögen *nt* ERGON discrimination, sensory discrimination

Unterschicht *f* TEXTIL sublayer

Unterschied *m* COMP & DV difference

unterschiedlich: ~es Gelände *nt* TELEKOM mixed terrain

Unterschiedsschwelle *f* AKUSTIK differential threshold, just noticeable difference, AUFNAHME difference limen

Unterschlackeschweißen *nt* MECHAN electroslag welding

Unterschleusendrempel *m* WASSERVERSORG tail mitre sill

Unterschleusenwelle *f* WASSERVERSORG tail mitre sill

Unterschneiden *nt* DRUCK kerning, MASCHINEN undercut

unterschneiden *vt* DRUCK kern, MASCHINEN undercut

Unterschneidung *f* MASCHINEN undercut; **Unterschneidungswerte** *m pl* DRUCK kerning values

Unterschnitt *m* KER & GLAS undercut, MASCHINEN interference, undercut; **Unterschnittsfreiheit** *f* FERTIG absence of undercutting

Unterschrift *f* COMP & DV signature

unterschwellig *adj* ERGON subliminal

Unterschwingen *nt* FERNSEH underswing

unterschwingen *vt* ELEKTRONIK *unter Bezugswert* undershoot

Untersee- *pref* WASSERTRANS submarine; **Unterseeboot** *nt (U-Boot)* WASSERTRANS submarine

unterseeisch[1] *adj* WASSERTRANS submarine

unterseeisch:[2] **~e Rohrleitung** *f* TRANS undersea pipeline

Untersee-: Unterseekabel *nt* ELEKTROTECH, PHYS submarine cable; **Unterseetanker** *m* WASSERTRANS submarine tanker

Unterseite *f* BAU soffit, *eines Hobels* sole, DRUCK wire side; **~ des Luftschraubenblattes** *f* LUFTTRANS *Hubschrauber* blade lower surface; **Unterseitenanschluß** *m* ELEKTROTECH face-down; **Unterseitenbandkanal** *m* FERNSEH channel using lower sideband

untersetzend: ~er Multivibrator *m* ELEKTRONIK dividing multivibrator

Untersetzer *m* COMP & DV binary circuit, ELEKTRONIK divider; **Untersetzerschaltung** *f* ELEKTRONIK dividing circuit

Untersetzung *f* MASCHINEN demultiplication, gear reduction, reduction ratio; **Untersetzungsgetriebe** *nt* KFZTECH *Getriebe* reduction gear, MASCHINEN reduction gear, step-down gear; **Untersetzungsverhältnis** *nt* KFZTECH *Getriebe* gear ratio, MASCHINEN reduction ratio

Untersicht *f* BAU *eines Gewölbes* intrados, *eines Balkens* soffit

unterspannt: ~er Balken *m* BAU trussed beam

Unterspannung *f* METALL minimum stress

Unterspülung *f* BAU undermining

Unterstation *f* TELECOM substation

Untersteuerung *f* KFZTECH *Lenkung* understeer

unterstreichen *vt* DRUCK underline

Unterstrom *m* NICHTFOSS ENERG undercurrent, WASSERTRANS *Seezustand* undertow; **Unterstromrelais** *nt* ELEKTRIZ undercurrent relay

Unterströmung *f* NICHTFOSS ENERG undercurrent, WASSERTRANS *Seezustand* undercurrent, undertow, WASSERVERSORG undercurrent

unterstützen *vt* BAU back, COMP & DV support, MECHAN boost

Unterstützung *f* BAU *Pfettendach* strutting, COMP & DV support, SICHERHEIT assistance; **Unterstützungselement** *nt* COMP & DV support element; **Unterstützungsmannschaft** *f* LUFTTRANS relief crew; **Unterstützungsprogramm** *nt* COMP & DV support program

untersuchen *vt* KOHLEN sound, KONTROLL inspect

Untersuchung *f* ANSTRICH analysis, KOHLEN assay, WERKPRÜF examination; **~ des Kornaufbaus** *f* KER & GLAS granulometric analysis; **~ von Mikrostrukturen mit Röntgenstrahlen** *f* KERNTECH X-ray microstructure investigation; **Untersuchungsabschnitt** *m* PHYS test section; **Untersuchungsergebnisse** *nt pl* METROL results of the inspection

Untersystem *nt* COMP & DV subsystem

Untertagedeponie *f* ABFALL *UTD* subsurface repository, underground depot

Untertage-Sicherheitsventil *nt* ERDÖL *Bohrtechnik* downhole safety valve

untertägig[1] *adj* ERDÖL *Bohrtechnik* downhole

untertägig:[2] **~e Bedingungen** *f pl* ERDÖL *Bohrtechnik* downhole conditions

Unterteil *nt* ELEKTROTECH *einer Sicherung* fuse base, FERTIG *Kunststoffinstallationen* body, KONTROLL module

unterteilen *vt* BAU partition, split into

unterteilt: **~e Anflugbahn** *f* LUFTTRANS segmented approach path; **~e Klappe** *f* LUFTTRANS *Luftfahrzeug* split flap

Unterteilung *f* LABOR graduation; **~ eines Schiffes in wasserdichte Abteilungen** *f* WASSERTRANS *Schiffbau* compartmentation; **~ in Teilbänder** *f* TELEKOM band splitting

Untertitel *m pl* FERNSEH subtitles; **Untertitelerzeuger** *m* FERNSEH subtitler; **Untertitelgenerator** *m* FERNSEH caption generator; **Untertitelscanner** *m* FERNSEH caption scanner; **Untertitelung** *f* FERNSEH subtitling

Unterton *m* AKUSTIK, ELEKTRONIK lower harmonic

Untertor *nt* WASSERVERSORG aft gate, *einer Schleuse* tail gate, tail sluice

Unterträger *m* FERNSEH subcarrier; **Unterträgerabstand** *m* FERNSEH subcarrier offset; **Unterträgereinrastung** *f* FERNSEH subcarrier lock; **Unterträgerfrequenz** *f* ELEKTRONIK, FERNSEH, RADIO, TELEKOM subcarrier frequency; **Unterträgergleichrichtung** *f* FERNSEH subcarrier rectification; **Unterträgerkomponente** *f* FERNSEH subcarrier component; **Unterträgermodulation** *f* FERNSEH subcarrier modulation; **Unterträgeroszillator** *m* FERNSEH subcarrier oscillator; **Unterträgerphase** *f* FERNSEH subcarrier phase

untertrocknen *vt* FERTIG underbake

Untertunnelung *f* BAU tunneling (AmE), tunnelling (BrE)

unterverdichtet[1] *adj* ERDÖL *Geologie* undercompacted

unterverdichtet:[2] **~e Zone** *f* ERDÖL *Geologie* undercompacted zone

Unterverdichtung *f* ERDÖL *Geologie* undercompaction

Unterwalze *f* FERTIG *Blechbiegen* low roll, MASCHINEN lower roll

Unterwanten *nt pl* WASSERTRANS *Tauwerk* lower shrouds

Unterwaschung *f* BAU undermining

Unterwasser *nt* HYDRAUL tail water, KOHLEN underflow, WASSERVERSORG tail water; **Unterwasser-Atomexplosion** *f* UMWELTSCHMUTZ underwater atomic explosion; **Unterwasserausbreitung** *f* TELEKOM underwater propagation; **Unterwasserbeton** *m* BAU submerged concrete; **Unterwasserblende** *f* HYDRAUL submerged orifice; **Unterwasserbohranlage** *f* BAU marine-drilling rig; **Unterwasserbohrloch** *nt* UMWELTSCHMUTZ subsea well; **Unterwasserbohrlochkopf** *m* ERDÖL *Offshore-Technik* subsea wellhead; **Unterwasserdüse** *f* HYDRAUL submerged orifice; **Unterwasserfotografie** *f* FOTO underwater photography; **Unterwassergehäuse** *nt* FOTO underwater housing; **Unterwassergeschwindigkeit** *f* WASSERTRANS *U-Boot* submerged speed; **Unterwassergraben** *m* WASSERVERSORG mill tail; **Unterwasserhöhe eines Wehrs** *f* HYDRAUL degree of submergence; **Unterwasserkabel** *nt* WASSERTRANS submarine cable; **Unterwasserkamera** *f* FOTO underwater camera; **Unterwasserkanal** *m* WASSERVERSORG aft bay race; **Unterwasserkomplettierung** *f* ERDÖL *Offshore-Technik* subsea completion; **Unterwasserkondensator** *m* HEIZ & KÄLTE submerged condenser; **Unterwasserlautsprecher** *m* AUFNAHME underwater loudspeaker; **Unterwassermündung** *f* HYDRAUL submerged orifice; **Unterwasserpumpe** *f* WASSERVERSORG subaqueous pump, submerged pump; **Unterwasserquelle** *f* WASSERVERSORG submerged spring; **Unterwasserschiff** *nt* WASSERTRANS underwater hull; **Unterwasserschneidbrenner** *m* BAU underwater cutting blowpipe; **Unterwasserschweißen** *nt* THERMOD underwater welding; **Unterwassertragflügel** *m* WASSERTRANS hydrofoil; **Unterwasserturbine** *f* HYDRAUL submerged turbine

Unterweisung *f* QUAL indoctrination

Unterwerk *nt* ELEKTRIZ, TELECOM substation

Unterzeichenkette *f* COMP & DV substring

Unterziel *nt* KÜNSTL INT subgoal

Unterzug *m* BAU beam, bearer, girder, joist, main beam, sill, transom, trussing, HEIZ & KÄLTE bottom flue; **Unterzugbalken** *m* BAU bridging piece

Unterzustand *m* PHYS sublevel

Untiefe *f* WASSERTRANS *Geographie* shoal

Untiefen *f pl* WASSERTRANS shallows

Untiefenmarkierung *f* WASSERTRANS isolated danger mark

unüberwacht: **~es Drucken** *nt* COMP & DV unattended printing; **~es Empfangen** *nt* COMP & DV unattended receive; **~er Modus** *m* COMP & DV unattended mode; **~es Senden** *nt* COMP & DV unattended transmit

ununterbrochen: **~er Fluß** *m* TRANS uninterrupted flow; **~er Strahl** *m* ELEKTRONIK continuous beam

Ununterscheidbarkeit: **~ identischer Partikel** *f* PHYS indistinguishability of identical particles

unverbleit: **~es Benzin** *nt* KFZTECH unleaded gasoline (AmE), unleaded petrol (BrE)

unverbrennbar *adj* FERTIG incombustible

Unverbrennbarkeit *f* FERTIG incombustibility

unverdaulich *adj* LEBENSMITTEL indigestible

unverdichtet: **~e Entladung** *f* ELEKTROTECH noncondensed discharge

unverdünnt *adj* CHEMIE undiluted, MEERSCHMUTZ neat

unvergütet *adj* ANSTRICH unfinished

unverklebt: ~e Außenhaut *f* RAUMFAHRT *Raumschiff* unbonded skin

unverkleidet: ~er Ventilator *m* LUFTTRANS *Motor, Triebwerk* unducted fan

unverkokt *adj* KOHLEN noncoking

unverletzt *adj* ANSTRICH intact

unverlierbar: ~e Mutter *f* MASCHINEN captive nut; ~e Schraube *f* MASCHINEN captive screw

unverlötet *adj* RADIO solderless

unvermischt *adj* MEERSCHMUTZ neat

unvernetzt *adj* KUNSTSTOFF uncured

unverpackt *adv* KOHLEN in bulk

unverschlüsselt: ~e Sprache *f* TELEKOM clear speech

Unversehrtheit *f* COMP & DV integrity

unverstellbar[1] *adj* MECHAN fixed

unverstellbar:[2] ~e Luftschraube *f* LUFTTRANS fixed-pitch propeller; ~er Magnetkopf *m* COMP & DV fixed head

unverzerrt *adj* COMP & DV unbiased, ELEKTRONIK undistorted

unverzwirnt: ~es Roving *nt* KER & GLAS no-twist roving

unvollkommen: ~e Elastizität *f* METALL anelasticity; ~er Isolationsstoff *m* ELEKTRIZ imperfect dielectric

unvollständig: ~e Füllung *f* HYDRAUL cavitation

unvorhergesehen: ~e Unterbrechungen *f pl* TELEKOM unforeseen interruptions

Unwucht *f* FERTIG imbalance, KFZTECH unbalance, MASCHINEN out-of-balance force, out-of-balance, run-out, MECHAN unbalance

unwuchtig *adj* MASCHINEN out of balance, unbalanced

Unze *f* METROL ounce avoirdupois, ounce, ounce troy

unzerbrechlich[1] *adj* VERPACK resistance to shattering

unzerbrechlich:[2] ~es Glas *nt* KER & GLAS unbreakable glass

unzersetzt *adj* CHEMIE undecomposed

unzulässig: ~er Befehl *m* COMP & DV illegal instruction; ~e Instruktion *m* COMP & DV illegal instruction; ~e Operation *f* COMP & DV illegal operation; ~e Verformung *f* FERTIG failure; ~es Zeichen *nt* COMP & DV illegal character

unzureichend *adj* KONTROLL unsatisfactory

UP *abbr (ungesättigter Polyester)* KUNSTSTOFF UP *(unsaturated polyester)*

Uperisation *f* LEBENSMITTEL uperization

UP-Harz *nt* CHEMIE UP resin

Uplink-Frequenz *f* RAUMFAHRT *Weltraumfunk* uplink frequency

Uplink-Verbindung *f* RAUMFAHRT uplink

UPN *f (umgekehrte Polnische Notation)* COMP & DV RPN *(reverse Polish notation)*

U-Profil *nt* BAU channel, METALL U-section

Uracil *nt* CHEMIE pyrimidinedione, uracil; **Uracil-D-Ribosid** *nt* CHEMIE uridine

Uran *nt (U)* CHEMIE uranium *(U)*; **Uran-** *pref* CHEMIE uranic, uranium, uranium, uranous; ~ **ohne Tochternuklide** *nt* KERNTECH uranium free from its daughters; **Uranabfall** *m* KERNTECH uranium scrap; **Uranat** *nt* CHEMIE uranate; **Uranbarren** *m* KERNTECH uranium ingot; **Uranblock** *m* KERNTECH uranium slug; **Uranbrennelement** *nt* KERNTECH uranium fuel element; **Urandikarbid** *nt* KERNTECH uranium dicarbide; **Urandioxid-Brennstoff** *m* KERNTECH uranium

dioxide fuel; **Urandioxid-Pellet** *nt* KERNTECH uranium dioxide pellet; **Uranfluorid** *nt* KERNTECH uranic fluoride

uranführend *adj* CHEMIE, STRAHLPHYS uranium-bearing

Uran: **Uran-Gadolinit-Pellet** *nt* KERNTECH urania-gadolinia pellet; **Uran-Galinit** *nt* KERNTECH uranium-galena

uranhaltig: ~es Mineral *nt* KERNTECH uranium-bearing mineral

Uran: **Uranhexafluorid** *nt* KERNTECH uranic fluoride, KERNTECH *(UF6)* uranium hexafluoride *(UF6)*; **Uraninit** *m* KERNTECH uraninite; **Urankern** *m* KERNTECH uranium nucleus; **Urankonversionsanlage** *f* KERNTECH uranium conversion plant; **Urankonzentrat** *nt* KERNTECH *für homogene Reaktoren* uranium concentrate; **Uranoid** *nt* CHEMIE uranide; **Uranoxid** *nt* CHEMIE uranium oxide; **Uranoxid-Brennstoff** *m* KERNTECH uranium oxide fuel; **Uranoxidgemisch nach Kalzinierung** *nt* KERNTECH yellow cake (colloq); **Uranpechblende** *f* KERNTECH pitchblende; **Uranpecherz** *nt* KERNTECH pitchblende; **Uran-Plutonium-Kreislauf** *m* KERNTECH U-Pu cycle, uranium-plutonium cycle; **Uranreinigung** *f* KERNTECH uranium refining; **Uranverbindung** *f* KERNTECH uranium compound; **Uranvorkonzentrat** *nt* KERNTECH uranium preconcentrate; **Uranzerkleinern** *nt* KERNTECH uranium milling

Urazol *nt* CHEMIE urazole

Urband *nt* COMP & DV master tape

Ureid *nt* CHEMIE ureide

Ureido- *pref* CHEMIE ureido-; **Ureidoessigsäure** *f* CHEMIE hydantoic acid; **Ureidohydantoin** *nt* CHEMIE allantoin

ureotel *adj* CHEMIE ureotelic

Urethan *nt* ANSTRICH urethane

Urform *f* KER & GLAS block

Urformen *nt* KUNSTSTOFF molding (AmE), moulding (BrE)

urgeformt: ~er Schlauch *m* KUNSTSTOFF molded hose (AmE), moulded hose (BrE)

Uridin *nt* CHEMIE uridine

Urknalltheorie *f* PHYS big bang theory

Urladen *nt* COMP & DV bootstrapping

urladen *vt* COMP & DV bootstrap

Urladeprogramm *nt* COMP & DV bootstrap

Urlader *m* COMP & DV initial program loader

Urmaß *nt* PHYS primary standard

Urmeter *m* PHYS standard meter (AmE), standard metre (BrE)

Urmuster *nt* PHYS standard

Urnormal *nt* PHYS primary standard

Urobilin *nt* CHEMIE hydrobilirubin, urobilin; **Urobilinogen** *nt* CHEMIE urobilinogen

U-Rohr *nt* LABOR U-tube; **~-Manometer** *nt* HEIZ & KÄLTE U-tube manometer

Uron- *pref* CHEMIE uronic

Urotropin *nt* CHEMIE methenamine, urotropine

Uroxan- *pref* CHEMIE uroxanic

Urspannungsquelle *f* ELEKTROTECH constant-voltage source

Ursprung *m* COMP & DV, ELEKTROTECH source, GEOM origin, HYDRAUL source, MATH *eines Grafs oder Koordinatensystems* origin; ~ **der EMK** *m* PHYS source of emf

ursprünglich[1]**:** **in der ~en Lage** *adv* KOHLEN in situ

ursprünglich[2]**:** ~es Feld *nt* COMP & DV parent field

Ursprung: **Ursprungsadresse** *f* COMP & DV source address; **Ursprungsamt** *nt* TELEKOM originating exchange; **Ursprungsformat** *nt* COMP & DV native format; **Ursprungsknoten** *m* TELEKOM originating junctor; **Ursprungsmodus** *m* COMP & DV native mode; **Ursprungsregister** *nt* TELEKOM originating register; **Ursprungsvermittlungsstelle** *f* TELEKOM originating exchange

Urushinsäure *f* CHEMIE laccol

US *abbr (ultrasonisch)* ELEKTRIZ SS, US *(supersonic)*

U-Schäkel *m* WASSERTRANS *Beschläge* D-shackle

U-Scheibe *f* FERTIG *Kunststoffinstallationen*, KFZTECH *(Unterlegscheibe) Schraube, Bolzen*, MASCHINEN washer

US-Schweißen *nt* ELEKTRIZ, KUNSTSTOFF, THERMOD US welding

US-Standard-Schraubengewinde *nt* MASCHINEN US standard thread

U-Stab *m* METALL U-bar

U-Stahl *m* FERTIG structural channel, MASCHINEN channel section

UST-Gewinde *nt* MASCHINEN UST, Unified Screw Thread (AmE)

US-Transducer *m* ELEKTRIZ US transducer

USV *abbr (unterbrechungsfreie Stromversorgung)* KON-TROLL stand-by battery power supply

UT *abbr (Standardweltzeit)* RADIO, RAUMFAHRT UT *(universal time)*

UTC *abbr (Standardweltzeit)* RADIO, RAUMFAHRT UTC *(universal time coordinated)*

UV *abbr (ultraviolett)* OPTIK, PHYS UV *(ultraviolet)*

UV: **UV-absorbierendes Glas** *nt* KER & GLAS UV-absorbing glass; **UV-durchlässiges Glas** *nt* KER & GLAS UV-transmitting glass

U-Verschluß *m* BAU running trap

UV: **UV-Filter** *nt* FOTO, SICHERHEIT UV filter; **UV-Fotografie** *f* STRAHLPHYS UV photography

Uvitin- *pref* CHEMIE uvitic

UV: **UV-Katastrophe** *f* PHYS UV catastrophe; **UV-Lampe** *f* LABOR UV lamp; **UV-Licht** *nt* KUNSTSTOFF, STRAHLPHYS UV light; **UV-Löschen** *nt* COMP & DV UV erasing; **UV-Mikroskop** *nt* STRAHLPHYS UV microscope; **UV-sichtbares Spektrofotometer** *nt* LABOR UV-visible spectrophotometer; **UV-Spiegel** *m* STRAHLPHYS UV mirror; **UV-Strahlen** *m pl* OPTIK, WELLPHYS UV rays; **UV-Strahlung** *f* NICHTFOSS ENERG, PHYS, RAUMFAHRT, STRAHLPHYS, UMWELTSCHMUTZ UV radiation

Ü-Wagen *m* FERNSEH OB van, OB vehicle

UZ *abbr (Zenerspannung)* ELEKTRONIK BDV *(breakdown voltage)*

V

V [1] *abbr* AUFNAHME *(Verstärkung)* A *(amplification)*, AUFNAHME *(Volt)* V *(volt)*, ELEKTRIZ *(Verstärkung)* A *(amplification)*, ELEKTRIZ *(Volt)* V *(volt)*, ELEKTRONIK *(Verstärkung)* A *(amplification)*, ELEKTRONIK *(Volt)* V *(volt)*, METROL *(Verstärkung)* A *(amplification)*, METROL *(Volt)* V *(volt)*, OPTIK *(Verstärkung)* A *(amplification)*, OPTIK *(Volt)* V *(volt)*, RADIO *(Verstärkung)* A *(amplification)*, RADIO *(Volt)* V *(volt)*

V [2] *(Vanadium)* CHEMIE V *(vanadium)*

v *abbr* COMP & DV *(Volumen)* v *(volume)*, KERNTECH *(Vibrationsquantenzahl)* v *(vibrational quantum number)*, PHYS *(Volumen)*, TEXTIL *(Volumen)*, THERMOD *(Volumen)* v *(volume)*

VAD *abbr (Axialabscheideverfahren aus Dampfphase)* OPTIK, TELEKOM VAD *(vapor phase axial deposition technique AmE)*, *(vapour phase axial deposition technique BrE)*

vados: **~es Grundwasser** *nt* WASSERVERSORG vadose water

vage *adj* KÜNSTL INT fuzzy

Vakuole *f* CHEMIE *Zellplasma*, KUNSTSTOFF void

Vakuum *nt* ERDÖL, FERNSEH, KFZTECH, MASCHINEN, MECHAN, PAPIER, PHYS, RAUMFAHRT vacuum; **im ~ aufgedampfte Schicht** *f* ELEKTRONIK vacuum-deposited film; **Vakuum-Abfüllmaschine** *f* VERPACK vacuum filling machine; **Vakuumabfüllung** *f* LEBENSMITTEL vacuum filling; **Vakuumaufdampfung** *m* ELEKTRONIK vacuum deposition; **Vakuumaufhängung** *f* TRANS vacuum suspension

vakuumbedampfen *vt* FERTIG vacuum-deposit

Vakuum: **Vakuumbedampfung** *f* KER & GLAS vapor deposition (AmE), vapour deposition (BrE); **Vakuumblase** *f* KER & GLAS vacuum bubble; **Vakuumbremse** *f* EISENBAHN, MASCHINEN vacuum brake; **Vakuumdestillation** *f* CHEMTECH, LEBENSMITTEL, PHYS vacuum distillation

vakuumdicht *adj* FERTIG *Kunststoffinstallationen* leakproof under vacuum

Vakuum: **Vakuumdichtung** *f* MASCHINEN vacuum seal; **Vakuumdiode** *f* ELEKTRONIK vacuum diode; **Vakuum-Entladung** *f* ELEKTROTECH vacuum discharge; **Vakuumexsikkator** *m* LABOR vacuum desiccator; **Vakuumfaktor** *m* ELEKTRONIK gas ratio, KERNTECH vacuum factor; **Vakuumfilter** *nt* ABFALL, KOHLEN, WASSERVERSORG vacuum filter; **Vakuumfiltration** *f* ABFALL, KOHLEN, LABOR, LEBENSMITTEL vacuum filtration; **Vakuum-Folientransportsystem** *nt* VERPACK vacuum film transport system; **Vakuumform** *f* MASCHINEN vacuum mold (AmE), vacuum mould (BrE); **Vakuumformen** *nt* KER & GLAS vacuum blowing, KUNSTSTOFF vacuum forming; **Vakuumführung** *f* FERNSEH vacuum guide; **Vakuumführungssystem** *nt* FERNSEH vacuum guide system; **Vakuumgefäß** *nt* KER & GLAS vacuum flask

vakuumgeformt [1] *adj* VERPACK vacuum-formed

vakuumgeformt: [2] **~e Verpackung** *f* VERPACK vacuum-formed package

Vakuum: **Vakuum-Gefriertrockner** *m* VERPACK vacuum freeze-dryer

vakuumgekapselt *adj* ELEKTROTECH vacuum-encapsulated

Vakuum: **Vakuumgießen** *nt* KERNTECH vacuum casting; **Vakuumgitterspektrograph** *m* WELLPHYS vacuum grating spectrograph; **Vakuumglühanlage** *f* METALL vacuum annealing plant; **Vakuumhartlöten** *nt* BAU vacuum brazing; **Vakuum-Hitzeversiegler** *m* VERPACK vacuum heat sealer

vakuumisoliert *adj* ELEKTROTECH vacuum-insulated

Vakuumisolierung *f* ELEKTROTECH vacuum insulation

Vakuum: **Vakuumkammer** *f* FERNSEH vacuum chamber; **Vakuumkolben** *m* LABOR vacuum flask; **Vakuum-Kondensator** *m* ELEKTROTECH vacuum capacitor; **Vakuum-Kontaktplattenverfahren** *nt* LEBENSMITTEL vacuum contact plate process; **Vakuumkühlung** *f* HEIZ & KÄLTE vacuum cooling; **Vakuumleitung** *f* LEBENSMITTEL vacuum line; **Vakuum-Lichtbogen** *m* ELEKTROTECH vacuum arc; **Vakuumluftpumpe** *f* LEBENSMITTEL vacuum air pump; **Vakuummeßgerät** *nt* METROL vacuum gage (AmE), vacuum gauge (BrE); **Vakuummeßinstrument** *nt* LEBENSMITTEL vacuum gage (AmE), vacuum gauge (BrE); **Vakuummeßzelle** *f* PHYS vacuum gage (AmE), vacuum gauge (BrE); **Vakuummetallisierung** *f* KER & GLAS vacuum metalizing (AmE), vacuum metallizing (BrE); **Vakuummeter** *nt* LEBENSMITTEL, MASCHINEN vacuum gage (AmE), vacuum gauge (BrE); **Vakuumofen** *m* MASCHINEN vacuum furnace; **Vakuumpfanne** *f* LEBENSMITTEL *Zuckerfabrikation* vacuum pan; **Vakuumplattentrockner** *m* LEBENSMITTEL vacuum shelf dryer; **Vakuumpolarisierung** *f* KERNTECH vacuum polarization; **Vakuumpumpe** *f* LABOR, LEBENSMITTEL, MASCHINEN, MEERSCHMUTZ, PHYS vacuum pump; **Vakuumröhre** *f* COMP & DV, ELEKTRONIK vacuum tube, KFZTECH vacuum valve, PHYS vacuum tube; **Vakuumröhrenverstärkung** *f* ELEKTRONIK vacuum tube amplificaton; **Vakuumsaugwagen** *m* MEERSCHMUTZ vacuum truck; **Vakuumschalter** *m* ELEKTRIZ vacuum switch; **Vakuumschaumtrocknung** *f* LEBENSMITTEL foam vacuum drying; **Vakuumschmelzen** *nt* METALL vacuum melting; **Vakuumschub** *m* RAUMFAHRT vacuum thrust; **Vakuum-Siegelmaschine** *f* VERPACK vacuum sealing machine; **Vakuumsintern** *nt* METALL vacuum sintering; **Vakuumsystem** *nt* KFZTECH evacuated system; **Vakuumtechnik** *f* MASCHINEN vacuum engineering, vacuum technology; **VakuumThermoformungsmaschine** *f* VERPACK vacuum thermoforming machine; **Vakuumtiefziehen** *nt* KUNSTSTOFF vacuum forming; **Vakuumtonrolle** *f* AUFNAHME, FERNSEH vacuum capstan; **Vakuumtriode** *f* ELEKTRONIK vacuum triode; **Vakuumtrockenofen** *m* LEBENSMITTEL vacuum drying oven; **Vakuumtrockenschrank** *m* MASCHINEN vacuum drying cabinet; **Vakuumtrockner** *m* KOHLEN, LEBENSMITTEL vacuum dryer; **Vakuumtrocknung** *f* LEBENSMITTEL vacuum drying; **Vakuumultraviolett** *nt* RAUMFAHRT vacuum ultraviolet; **Vaku-**

um-Umhüllung *f* KERNTECH vacuum jacket; **Vakuum-verdampfer** *m* LEBENSMITTEL, WASSERVERSORG vacuum evaporator; **Vakuumverdampfung** *f* HEIZ & KÄLTE vacuum evaporation

vakuumverpackt *adj* LEBENSMITTEL vacuum-packed

Vakuum: **Vakuumverpackung** *f* MASCHINEN vacuum packaging, VERPACK vacuum pack, vacuum packaging; **Vakuumverpackungsmaschine** *f* VERPACK vacuum packaging machine; **Vakuum-Verschluß-maschine** *f* VERPACK vacuum closing machine; **Vakuum-Wärmebehandlung** *f* METALL vacuum heat treatment

Valenz *f* CHEMIE valence, valency, COMP & DV valency, METALL, PHYS valence; **Valenzband** *nt* PHYS *Halbleiterphysik* valence band; **Valenzelektron** *nt* PHYS *Atomphysik* valence electron; **Valenzelektronenkonzentration** *f* KERNTECH valence electron concentration; **Valenzzustand** *m* KERNTECH valence state

Valeramid *nt* CHEMIE valeramide

Valerat *nt* CHEMIE valerate

Valerian- *pref* CHEMIE valeric

Valeryl- *pref* CHEMIE valeryl

Valerylen *nt* CHEMIE pentyne, valerylene

validieren *vt* RAUMFAHRT validate

VAN *abbr (Mehrwertdienstnetz, Mehrwertnetz)* COMP & DV, TELEKOM VAN *(value-added network)*

Vanadat *nt* CHEMIE vanadate, vanadiate

Vanadium *nt* CHEMIE *(V)* vanadium *(V)*, METALL vanadium

vanadiumhaltig *adj* CHEMIE vanadic, vanadiferous

Vanadiumstahl *m* METALL vanadium steel

Vanadyl- *pref* CHEMIE vanadyl

Van-Allen- : ~scher Gürtel *m* PHYS, RAUMFAHRT van Allen belt

Van-de-Graaff- : ~scher Beschleuniger *m* PHYS van de Graaff generator; ~scher Generator *m* ELEKTRIZ, ELEKTROTECH, PHYS van de Graaff generator

Van-der-Waals- : ~sche Gleichung *f* PHYS van der Waals equation; ~scher Radius *m* PHYS van der Waals radius

V-Antenne *f* TELEKOM V-shaped antenna

Vapotron *nt* ELEKTRONIK *Dampfkühlungsverfahren für Leistungsröhren* Vapotron

var *abbr (Blindleistungseinheit)* LABOR var *(volt-amperes reactive)*

Varactor *m* ELEKTRONIK *Kapazitätsdiode* varactor

varactorabgestimmt : ~er Oszillator *m* ELEKTRONIK varactor-tuned oscillator

Varactor: **Varactorabstimmung** *f* ELEKTRONIK varactor tuning; **Varactorchip** *m* ELEKTRONIK varactor chip; **Varactordiode** *f* FERNSEH, PHYS varactor diode

variabel[1] *adj* KONTROLL, MATH variable

variabel:[2] **variabler Amplitudentest** *m* METALL variable amplitude test; **variables Dämpfungsglied** *nt* ELEKTRONIK variable attenuator, PHYS piston attenuator; **variable Dämpfung** *f* ELEKTRONIK variable attenuation; **variable Daten** *nt pl* COMP & DV variable data; **variabel einstellbare Einlaßschieber** *m pl* KERNTECH variable-pitch inlet vanes; **variable Flächenaufzeichnung** *f* FERNSEH variable area recording; **variables Format** *nt* COMP & DV variable format; **variable Geschwindigkeit** *f* MASCHINEN variable velocity; **variabler Geschwindigkeitsregler** *m* FERNSEH variable speed control; **variabler Hörfrequenzpegel** *m* AUFNAHME variable audio level; **variabler Koaxialdämpfer** *m* ELEKTRONIK variable coaxial attenuator; **variables**

Mikrowellen-Dämpfungsglied *nt* ELEKTRONIK variable microwave attenuator; **variabler Quarzoszillator** *m (VCO)* RADIO variable crystal oscillator *(VXO)*; **variabler Reluktanzmotor** *m* KFZTECH variable reluctance motor; **variable Steuerzeiteinstellung** *f* TRANS *Ventil* variable valve timing; **variable Ventileinstellung** *f* TRANS variable valve timing; **variabler Venturi-Vergaser** *m (VV-Vergaser)* KFZTECH variable venturi carburetor (AmE), variable venturi carburettor (BrE) *(VV-carburetor)*; **variable Zeitlupe** *f* FERNSEH variable slow motion; **variabler Zwischenraum** *m* DRUCK variable space

Variabilitätsindex *m* ELEKTRONIK standard deviation

Variable *f* COMP & DV, KONTROLL, MATH, QUAL variable; **Variablenbindung** *f* KÜNSTL INT variable binding; **Variablenfeld** *nt* COMP & DV, ELEKTROTECH variable field; **Variablenformat** *nt* COMP & DV variable format; **Variablenlänge** *f* COMP & DV variable length; **Variablenname** *m* COMP & DV variable name; **Variablenprüfung** *f* QUAL inspection by variables; **Variablensammlung** *f* COMP & DV heap

Variantenzeichnung *f* KONSTZEICH variant drawing

Varianz *f* MATH, PHYS, QUAL variance; ~ **einer Wahrscheinlichkeitsverteilung** *f* QUAL variance of a variate

Variation *f* MATH variation; **Variationskoeffizient** *m* QUAL coefficient of variation; **Variationsrechnung** *f* MATH variational calculus

variiert : ~es Uranpecherz *nt* KERNTECH varied pitchblende

Variokoppler *m* ELEKTROTECH variocoupler

Variometer *nt* ELEKTROTECH inductometer, variometer

Varistor *m* ELEKTRIZ, PHYS varistor

VAR-Meter *nt* ELEKTRIZ apparent energy meter

Vasopressin *nt* CHEMIE vasopressin

Vater *m* AKUSTIK, AUFNAHME *Original einer Plattenaufnahme* master; **Vaterdatei** *f* COMP & DV father file; **Vaterplatte** *f* AKUSTIK master, AUFNAHME metal master; **Vaterstecker** *m* ELEKTROTECH male connector; **Vatersteckverbinder** *m* ELEKTROTECH male connector; **Vaterstück** *nt* FERNSEH master

Vauxhall-Facette *f* KER & GLAS Vauxhall bevel

VCO *abbr (variabler Quarzoszillator)* RADIO VXO *(variable crystal oscillator)*

VCR *abbr* FERNSEH *(Videorecorder)* VCR *(video cassette recorder)*, FERNSEH *(Videomagnetbandgerät)* VTR *(video tape recorder)*

VD *abbr (Viskositäts-Dichteverhältnis)* NICHTFOSS ENERG kinematic viscosity

VDE *abbr (Verein Deutscher Elektrotechniker)* ELEKTRIZ Association of German Electrical Engineers

VDI *abbr (Verein Deutscher Ingenieure)* ELEKTRIZ Association of German Engineers

Vegetation *f* METALL vegetation

vegetieren *vi* METALL vegetate

Veitch-Diagramm *nt* COMP & DV Veitch diagram

Vektor *m* COMP & DV, ELEKTRIZ, ELEKTROTECH, GEOM, MATH vector; **Vektorabtastung** *f* ELEKTRONIK vector scanning; **Vektoranalysis** *f* MATH vector analysis; **Vektorbild** *nt* COMP & DV vector graphics; **Vektorbildschirm** *m* ELEKTRONIK vector-scan cathode-ray tube; **Vektor-Boson** *nt* PHYS intermediate boson; **Vektor-Elektronenstrahl-Lithographie** *f* ELEKTRONIK vector-scan electron-beam lithography

Vektoren : in ~ umgesetzt *adj* RAUMFAHRT vectored

Vektor: **Vektorenrechner** *m* COMP & DV pipeline processor; **Vektorfeld** *nt* ELEKTRIZ, ELEKTROTECH vector field; **Vektorgrafik** *f* COMP & DV vector graphics; **Vektorgruppe** *f* ELEKTRIZ vector group

vektoriert *adj* RAUMFAHRT vectored

Vektor: **Vektorkomponente** *f* PHYS component of vector; **Vektorkopplung** *f* STRAHLPHYS vector coupling; **Vektormeson** *nt* TEILPHYS vector meson; **Vektormodell des Atoms** *nt* PHYS vector model of the atom; **Vektornetzanalysator** *m* ELEKTROTECH vector network analyser (BrE), vector network analyzer (AmE); **Vektornetzanalyse** *f* ELEKTROTECH vector network analysis; **Vektorpotential** *nt* ELEKTROTECH vector potential; **Vektorprodukt** *nt* GEOM cross product, MATH, PHYS vector product; **äußeres ~** *nt* MATH, PHYS vector product; **Vektorprozessor** *m* COMP & DV array processor, pipeline processor, vector processor; **Vektorraum** *m* MATH vector space; **Vektorrechner** *m* COMP & DV array processor; **Vektorschub** *m* RAUMFAHRT vectored thrust; **Vektorschubtriebwerk** *nt* RAUMFAHRT vectored-thrust engine; **Vektorskop** *nt* FERNSEH vectorscope; **Vektorstrahl** *m* ELEKTRONIK vector-scanned beam; **Vektorsumme** *f* MATH vector resultant, vector sum; **Vektorunterbrechung** *f* COMP & DV vectored interrupt; **Vektorverarbeitung** *f* COMP & DV vector processing

Velinpapier *nt* DRUCK wove paper, PAPIER wove

Velourieren *nt* TEXTIL napping

velourieren *vt* TEXTIL raise

Velourisieren *nt* TEXTIL raising

Venn-Diagramm *nt* COMP & DV Venn diagram

Ventil *nt* AKUSTIK key, BAU cock, valve, FERTIG valve, *Kunststoffinstallationen* valve, HYDRAUL *Absperrorgan von Rohrleitungen*, KERNTECH, KFZTECH valve, MASCHINEN air valve, valve, MECHAN, MEERSCHMUTZ, RAUMFAHRT valve; **~ mit konischem Sitz** *nt* HYDRAUL valve with conical seat; **Ventilabdichtring** *m* KFZTECH valve shaft seal

Ventilator *m* BAU fan, ventilating fan, HEIZ & KÄLTE fan, ventilator, KFZTECH cooling fan, fan, LEBENSMITTEL blower, LUFTTRANS turbofan, MASCHINEN ventilating fan, MECHAN, PHYS fan, SICHERHEIT ventilator, THERMOD fan; **~ mit Motor** *m* SICHERHEIT motor-driven fan; **Ventilatorflügel** *m* HEIZ & KÄLTE, KFZTECH, MECHAN, THERMOD fan blade; **Ventilatorgebläse** *nt* MASCHINEN fan blower; **Ventilatorläufer** *m* SICHERHEIT fan wheel; **Ventilatorleistung** *f* HEIZ & KÄLTE fan performance; **Ventilatorleistungskennlinie** *f* HEIZ & KÄLTE fan performance curve; **Ventilatorlüftung** *f* MASCHINEN fan ventilation; **Ventilatorpumpe** *f* PAPIER fan pump; **Ventilatorrad** *nt* HEIZ & KÄLTE fan impeller; **Ventilatorriemen** *m* HEIZ & KÄLTE, KFZTECH *Kühlsystem*, MECHAN, THERMOD fan belt; **Ventilatorriemenscheibe** *f* KFZTECH *Kühlsystem* fan pulley; **Ventilatorverkleidung** *f* KFZTECH fan shroud

Ventil: **Ventilaufsatz** *m* HYDRAUL cap of a valve; **Ventilbewegung** *f* HYDRAUL valve gear, valve motion; **Ventildeckel** *m* HYDRAUL cap of a valve; **Ventildiagramm** *nt* MASCHINEN valve diagram; **Ventildichtfläche** *f* KFZTECH valve mating surface; **Ventildrehvorrichtung** *f* KFZTECH valve rotator; **Ventilexzenter** *m* HYDRAUL valve eccentric; **Ventilfeder** *f* KFZTECH, MASCHINEN valve spring; **Ventilführung** *f* KFZTECH valve guide, *Motor* collet; **Ventilgang** *m* HYDRAUL valve motion; **Ventilgehäuse** *nt* HYDRAUL valve chest, KFZTECH valve body, MASCHINEN valve box; **Ventilgetriebe** *nt* HYDRAUL valve gear; **Ventilhahn** *m* HYDRAUL, MASCHINEN valve cock; **Ventilhub** *m* HY-

DRAUL valve motion, valve travel, MASCHINEN valve lift; **Ventilhubstange** *f* KFZTECH valve push rod

ventilieren *vt* BAU, HEIZ & KÄLTE, THERMOD ventilate

ventiliert *adj* HEIZ & KÄLTE, THERMOD ventilated

Ventil: **Ventilkammer** *f* MASCHINEN valve chamber; **Ventilkappe** *f* HYDRAUL cap of a valve; **Ventilkegel** *m* MASCHINEN valve cone; **Ventilklappe** *f* KERNTECH flap, valve flap, KFZTECH *Reifen* valve cap; **Ventilkolben** *m* HYDRAUL bucket; **Ventilkolbenpumpe** *f* HYDRAUL bucket pump; **Ventilkörper** *m* HYDRAUL valve chest, MASCHINEN valve body; **Ventillauf** *m* HYDRAUL valve gear, valve motion

ventillos: **~er Motor** *m* KFZTECH valveless engine

Ventil: **Ventilnachschleifen** *nt* FERTIG refacing; **Ventilneueinschleifen** *nt* FERTIG reseating; **Ventilöffnung** *f* MASCHINEN valve outlet; **Ventilschaft** *m* KFZTECH valve shaft, valve stem; **Ventilschaftabdeckung** *f* KFZTECH valve shaft seal; **Ventilschaftführung** *f* KFZTECH *Motor* collet; **Ventilschiebersitz** *m* HYDRAUL *Steuerkolben, Steuerschieber* valve seat; **Ventilschleifmaschine** *f* FERTIG valve seat grinder; **Ventilschlüssel** *m* BAU cock key; **Ventilsitz** *m* HYDRAUL valve seat, KERNTECH seat, KFZTECH valve seat; **Ventilsitzfläche** *f* KFZTECH valve face, valve mating surface; **Ventilsitzring** *m* KFZTECH insert, MASCHINEN valve seat ring; **Ventilsitzringfeder** *f* KFZTECH insert spring; **Ventilspiel** *nt* KFZTECH, MASCHINEN valve clearance; **Ventilspieleinstellung** *f* KFZTECH valve setting; **Ventilspindel** *f* HYDRAUL valve rod, valve stem; **Ventilstange** *f* EISENBAHN valve rod, HYDRAUL valve rod, valve stem; **Ventilstellungsregler** *m* REGELUNG positioner; **Ventilsteuerung** *f* EISENBAHN valve train, HYDRAUL valve gear, KFZTECH valve control, MASCHINEN trip gear; **Ventilsteuerung beim Motor mit T-förmigem Verbrennungsraum** *f* KFZTECH T-head valve train; **Ventilsteuerung beim OHV-Motor** *f* KFZTECH I-head valve train; **Ventilsteuerzeitendiagramm** *nt* KFZTECH valve timing diagram; **Ventilstößel** *m* KFZTECH tappet, valve lifter, valve tappet, MECHAN cam follower; **Ventilstößelstange** *f* KFZTECH valve push rod; **Ventilteller** *m* KFZTECH valve disc (BrE), valve disk (AmE), valve head; **Ventilteller mit Dichtungsring** *m* FERTIG *Kunststoffinstallationen* disc and seating (BrE), disk and seating (AmE); **Ventiltrieb** *m* KFZTECH valve gear mechanism, valve gear; **Ventiltriebsritzel** *nt* KFZTECH timing gear; **Ventilüberdeckung** *f* KFZTECH valve lap; **Ventilüberschneidung** *f* KFZTECH valve lap

Ventimeter *nt* WASSERTRANS ventimeter

ventral *adj* ERGON ventral

Venturi: **Venturi-Düse** *f* MECHAN venturi nozzle; **Venturi-Meßdüse** *f* MASCHINEN venturi meter; **Venturi-Meßrohr** *nt* MASCHINEN venturi tube; **Venturi-Rohr** *nt* KFZTECH *Vergaser* venturi, MASCHINEN venturi tube, PHYS venturi meter; **Venturi-Schlamm** *m* KOHLEN venturi sludge; **Venturi-Schrubber** *m* KOHLEN venturi scrubber; **Venturi-Wäscher** *m* UMWELTSCHMUTZ venturi scrubber

Verabredungs-Bridge *f* TELEKOM meet-me bridge

Verabredungskonferenz *f* TELEKOM meet-me conference call

Veracevin *nt* CHEMIE cevadine

verallgemeinert: **~e Koordinaten** *f pl* PHYS generalized coordinates

veraltet *adj* FERTIG obsolete

veränderbar: **~e Nachleuchtdauer** *f* ELEKTRONIK *Kathodenstrahlröhre* variable persistence

veränderlich¹ *adj* KONTROLL, MATH variable, WASSER-TRANS *Wetter* changeable

veränderlich:² **~e Brennweite** *f* FOTO variable focal length; **~es Dämpfungsglied** *nt* ELEKTRONIK *Telefontechnik* fader; **~e Geometrie** *f* (VG) LUFTTRANS variable geometry (VG); **~e Induktanz** *f* ELEKTRIZ, ELEKTROTECH variable inductance; **~er Kondensator** *m* ELEKTRIZ, ELEKTROTECH, PHYS variable capacitor; **~e Kopplungsspule** *f* ELEKTROTECH variocoupler; **~e Menge** *f* ELEKTROTECH variable quantity; **~e Mischung** *f* KFZTECH variable mixture; **~e Quantität** *f* ELEKTROTECH variable quantity; **~e Tragflügelgeometrie** *f* (VG) LUFTTRANS variable geometry (VG); **~er Widerstand** *m* ELEKTRIZ variable resistor, ELEKTROTECH variable resistance, variable resistor, PHYS variable resistor

Veränderliche *f* MATH variable

verändern *vt* COMP & DV modify

Veränderung *f* MATH variation; **~ der Metalloberfläche** *f* ANSTRICH passivation

Verankern *nt* BAU anchoring, MEERSCHMUTZ mooring

verankern *vt* BAU anchor, stay, KOHLEN brace, MEERSCHMUTZ moor, RAUMFAHRT *Raumschiff* anchor, WASSERTRANS *Festmachen* moor

verankert: **~e Boje** *f* WASSERTRANS *Seezeichen* moored buoy

Verankerung *f* BAU anchorage, KER & GLAS *der Wannensteine*, KOHLEN bracing, RAUMFAHRT *Raumschiff* anchoring, WASSERTRANS anchorage; **Verankerungsbolzen** *m* MASCHINEN anchor bolt; **Verankerungskette** *f* MEERSCHMUTZ mooring chain; **Verankerungsmast** *m* ELEKTRIZ anchoring tower; **Verankerungsnetz** *nt* LUFTTRANS mooring harness; **Verankerungsplatte** *f* BAU anchoring plate; **Verankerungsstrebe** *f* MASCHINEN brace strut; **Verankerungssystem** *nt* KERNTECH anchorage system

veranschlagen *vt* TEXTIL assess

veranschlagt: **~e normale Nutzlast** *f* LUFTTRANS estimated normal payload

verantwortlich *adj* QUAL accountable, responsible

Verantwortlichkeit *f* QUAL accountability

Verantwortung *f* QUAL accountability, authority, responsibility, SICHERHEIT care; **~ für Lager mit Brennbarem** *f* SICHERHEIT care of inflammable stores

Verarbeitbarkeit *f* BAU workability

verarbeiten *vt* COMP & DV, LEBENSMITTEL, RADIO process

verarbeitet: **~es Erdöl** *nt* ERDÖL *Raffinerie* refined petroleum

Verarbeitung *f* BAU workmanship, COMP & DV computation, processing, ERDÖL processing, *Raffinerie* refining, KONTROLL, TELEKOM processing; **~ auf dem Chip** *f* ELEKTRONIK on-chip processing; **~ im Direktzugriff** *f* COMP & DV random processing; **~ von Meldungen** *f* COMP & DV message handling; **~ natürlicher Sprache** *f* KÜNSTL INT natural language processing; **~ von nur einem Glasposten** *f* KER & GLAS single gob processing; **Verarbeitungsart** *f* COMP & DV *COBOL* processing mode; **Verarbeitungsbereich** *m* KER & GLAS working range; **Verarbeitungseinheit** *f* TELEKOM processor

verarbeitungsfähig *adj* BAU workable

Verarbeitung: **Verarbeitungsfolge** *f* COMP & DV processing sequence; **Verarbeitungsleistung** *f* TELEKOM processing power; **Verarbeitungsmodus** *m* COMP & DV processing mode; **Verarbeitungsschaltkarte** *f* TELEKOM processing card; **Verarbeitungsschicht** *f* TELEKOM application layer; **Verarbeitungsspielraum**

m KUNSTSTOFF pot life; **Verarbeitungsstatus** *m* COMP & DV process state; **Verarbeitungsteil** *m* COMP & DV procedure division; **Verarbeitungstemperatur** *f* KER & GLAS working temperature; **Verarbeitungsvorgang** *m* COMP & DV task; **Verarbeitungszeit** *f* COMP & DV processing time

verarmen *vt* KERNTECH deplete

verarmt: **~er Kernbrennstoff** *m* KERNTECH depleted nuclear fuel

Verarmung *f* ELEKTRONIK *Mikroelektronik* depletion, KERNTECH depletion, *von Erzen* impoverishment; **Verarmungsschicht** *f* RADIO depletion layer; **Verarmungstyp** *m* ELEKTRONIK depletion mode; **Verarmungszone** *f* PHYS depletion layer

veraschen *vt* THERMOD incinerate

Veraschungsofen *m* THERMOD incinerator

verästelt: **~es Wasserleitungsnetz** *nt* WASSERVERSORG arterial system

Verästelungsrohrnetz *nt* WASSERVERSORG arterial system

Veratramin *nt* CHEMIE veratramine

Veratrin *nt* CHEMIE cevadine, veratrine; **Veratrin-** *pref* CHEMIE veratric; **Veratrinum** *nt* CHEMIE veratrine

Veratrol *nt* CHEMIE veratrole

Verb *nt* COMP & DV verb

Verband¹ *m* BAU *Mauerwerk* bond

Verband:² **im ~ legen** *vt* BAU bond

Verbandskasten *m* SICHERHEIT *KFZ* first-aid kit

Verbau *m* BAU lining

Verbesserer *m* ERDÖL *Wirkstoff zur Geruchs- oder Fließverbesserung* improver

verbessert: **~er Brennstoffkreislauf** *m* KERNTECH advanced fuel cycle; **~er Dieselmotor** *m* KFZTECH improved diesel engine

Verbesserung *f* LEBENSMITTEL, PATENT, SICHERHEIT improvement; **Verbesserungsbenachrichtigung** *f* SICHERHEIT improvement notice; **Verbesserungsmittel** *nt* LEBENSMITTEL improver; **Verbesserungspatent** *nt* PATENT improvement patent

Verbeulung *f* KERNTECH *in einem Brennelement* buckling

verbiegen *vt* MECHAN deform

Verbinden *nt* ANSTRICH fusion, BAU joining, TELEKOM jointing

verbinden¹ *vt* ANSTRICH weld, BAU bond, connect, joint, join, tail, tie, *zu fester Masse* concrete, COMP & DV connect, *Programme* bind, combine, ELEKTROTECH *mit Verbindungsleitung*, FERNSEH patch, FERTIG agglutinate, PHYS, TELEKOM connect, VERPACK *Verschweißen von Plastik* bond to; **miteinander ~** *vt* BAU interlock

verbinden:² **sich ~** *v refl* CHEMIE coalesce

Verbinder *m* ELEKTROTECH connector, RAUMFAHRT binder; **~ für gedruckte Schaltungen** *m* ELEKTRONIK printed circuit connector; **~ für Lichtleitfasern** *m* OPTIK optical fiber link (AmE), optical fibre link (BrE)

verbindlich¹ *adj* QUAL mandatory

verbindlich:² **~er Standard** *m* BAU mandatory standard

Verbindung¹ *f* ANSTRICH compound, BAU connection, joint, COMP & DV link, linkage, ELEKTRIZ interconnection, joint, junction, ELEKTROTECH coupling, *von Stromleitern* connection, FERNSEH bearding, KERNTECH joining, linkage, *zwischen Brennmaterial und Hülle* bond, KONTROLL link, KUNSTSTOFF compound, KÜNSTL INT *Graph* arc, *zwischen Knoten in Graph* edge, link, MASCHINEN connection, junction, linking, tie,

MECHAN coupling, OPTIK joint, PHYS coupling, RADIO junction, TELEKOM connection, joint, link, linking, WASSERTRANS *Schiffbau* bonding; **~ mit digitaler Modulation** *f* TELEKOM digital modulation link; **nicht zur ~ führender Ruf** *m* TELEKOM lost call

Verbindung:[2] **eine ~ halten** *vi* TELEKOM put a call on hold; **~ lösen** *vi* MASCHINEN unmake a joint

Verbindung: **Verbindungs- und Trennungszeichengabe** *f* TELEKOM connect and disconnect signaling (AmE), connect and disconnect signalling (BrE); **Verbindungsabbau** *m* TELEKOM connection tear-down; **Verbindungsablauf** *m* TELEKOM call flow, call sequence; **Verbindungsableitstrom** *m* ELEKTROTECH junction leakage current; **Verbindungsableitung** *f* ELEKTROTECH junction leakage

Verbindungsaufbau *m* TELEKOM call set-up, connection set-up; **Verbindungsaufbaudauer** *f* TELEKOM call set-up time, connecting delay; **Verbindungsaufbauphase** *f* TELEKOM call set-up phase; **Verbindungsaufbauverzug** *m* TELEKOM call set-up delay

Verbindung: **Verbindungsbahn** *f* EISENBAHN interchange track; **Verbindungsband** *nt* RAUMFAHRT *Raumschiff* bonding strap; **Verbindungsbearbeitung** *f* TELEKOM call handling; **Verbindungsbogen** *m* MASCHINEN bend coupling; **Verbindungsbolzen** *m* BAU bat bolt, gudgeon; **Verbindungsbrücke** *f* ELEKTROTECH bonding jumper; **Verbindungscomputer** *m* COMP & DV gateway computer; **Verbindungsdauer** *f* COMP & DV connect time, TELEKOM call duration; **Verbindungsdoppelbrücke** *f* LUFTTRANS *Fahrwerk* connecting twin yoke; **Verbindungsdoppelgabel** *f* LUFTTRANS connecting twin yoke; **Verbindungsdraht** *m* ELEKTROTECH connecting wire, jumper; **Verbindungselement** *nt* COMP & DV link, FERTIG fastener, MASCHINEN fastener, link, MECHAN link; **Verbindungsfestigkeit** *f* VERPACK joint strength; **Verbindungsflansch** *m* MASCHINEN, RAUMFAHRT connecting flange; **Verbindungsfuge** *f* FERTIG joint clearance; **Verbindungsfugenbreite** *f* FERTIG joint clearance; **Verbindungsgefäße** *nt pl* LABOR communicating vessels; **Verbindungsgleis** *nt* EISENBAHN interchange track; **Verbindungsglied** *nt* MASCHINEN connecting link, coupling link, shackle, MEERSCHMUTZ shackle; **Verbindungskabel** *nt* BAU interconnecting cable, COMP & DV feeder cable, patch cable, patch cord, ELEKTROTECH connecting cable, interconnection cable, junction cable; **Verbindungsklemme** *f* ELEKTROTECH binding post; **Verbindungskriechstrom** *m* ELEKTROTECH junction leakage current; **Verbindungskristall** *m* METALL compound crystal; **Verbindungslasche** *f* BAU backplate; **Verbindungsleitung** *f* ELEKTRIZ interconnecting feeder, interconnecting line, trunk line, ELEKTROTECH patch cord, LUFTTRANS interconnection, *Flugwerk* airframe bonding lead, TELEKOM *Telegrafie* junction; **Verbindungsleitungskabel** *nt* ELEKTROTECH trunk cable; **Verbindungslinie** *f* METALL tie line

verbindungslos: ~er Trägerdienst *m* TELEKOM connectionless bearer service

Verbindung: **Verbindungsmaterial** *nt* KERNTECH bonding material; **Verbindungsmuffe** *f* FERTIG joint sleeve, MASCHINEN connector, coupling sleeve, TELEKOM cable joint; **Verbindungspfad** *m* COMP & DV linkage path; **Verbindungsplatte** *f* ELEKTROTECH junction plate, KERNTECH tie plate; **Verbindungsprotokoll** *nt* COMP & DV *Datenfernverarbeitung* link protocol; **Verbindungs-**

punkt *m* ELEKTROTECH junction point; **Verbindungsrechner** *m* COMP & DV gateway computer; **Verbindungsschicht** *f* TELEKOM link layer; **Verbindungsschnur** *f* FOTO connecting cord, TELEKOM *Zentrale* cord; **Verbindungsschraube** *f* MASCHINEN connecting screw; **Verbindungsschürze** *f* RAUMFAHRT connecting skirt; **Verbindungsspeiseleitung** *f* ELEKTRIZ trunk feeder; **Verbindungsstange** *f* LUFTTRANS connecting rod, MASCHINEN link rod, tie bar, tie rod; **Verbindungsstelle** *f* KER & GLAS splice, KERNTECH joint, MASCHINEN junction; **Verbindungssteuerung** *f* COMP & DV end-to-end control; **Verbindungsstoß** *m* WASSERTRANS *Schiffbau* butt; **Verbindungsstück** *nt* ELEKTROTECH coupling, LABOR connector; **Verbindungstopologie** *f* COMP & DV interconnection topology; **Verbindungstunnel** *m* RAUMFAHRT connecting tunnel; **Verbindungsumschaltung** *f* TELEKOM hand-off, intercell switching, *bei Zellenwechsel* intercell hand-off; **Verbindungsursprung** *m* TELEKOM call origin; **Verbindungsverlust** *m* ELEKTROTECH junction leakage; **Verbindungsverlustberechnung** *f* RAUMFAHRT *Weltraumfunk* link budget; **Verbindungsverluststrom** *m* ELEKTROTECH junction leakage current; **Verbindungsversuch** *m* TELEKOM call attempt; **Verbindungswärme** *f* THERMOD heat of combination; **Verbindungswertigkeit** *f* METALL *Schweißarbeit* joint efficiency; **Verbindungszone zwischen Gewölbe und Widerlager** *f* KER & GLAS spring zone; **Verbindungszusammenstoß** *m* TELEKOM clashing

verblassen[1] *vt* TEXTIL fade

verblassen[2] *vi* BAU fade

verbleibend: ~er Abstand *m* ELEKTROTECH residual gap; **~e Ladung** *f* ELEKTROTECH residual charge; **~er Widerstand** *m* ELEKTROTECH residual resistance

verbleien *vt* BAU plumb, FERTIG lead

verbleit *adj* FERTIG lead-coated, leaded

verblenden *vt* BAU face, *Fenster* screen, *mit Ziegeln* brick

Verblendstein *m* KER & GLAS facing block

Verblendung *f* BAU facing

Verblitzen: ~ des Films *nt* FOTO *elektrostatisch* static on film

verblocken *vt* MASCHINEN interlock

Verblockung *f* MASCHINEN interlocking

verbolzen *vt* FERTIG pin, MECHAN bolt

verbolzt *adj* FERTIG pinned

Verbolzung *f* FERTIG pinning, MASCHINEN, SICHERHEIT bolting

verborgen:[1] **~e Barcode-Identifikation** *f* VERPACK hidden bar code identification; **~e Schicht** *f* KÜNSTL INT *in einem neuralen Netz* hidden layer; **~e Wärme** *f* BAU, ERDÖL *Thermodynamik*, HEIZ & KÄLTE, PHYS, THERMOD latent heat; **~e Wärmelast** *f* HEIZ & KÄLTE latent heat load

verborgen:[2] **sich ~ halten** *vt* WASSERTRANS *U-Boot* shelter

Verbot *nt* SICHERHEIT prohibition notice

verboten: ~es Band *nt* STRAHLPHYS forbidden band; **~es Energieband** *nt* KERNTECH forbidden energy band; **~er Übergang** *m* KERNTECH, STRAHLPHYS forbidden transition; **~e Zerfallsart** *f* STRAHLPHYS forbidden decay mode

Verbot: **Verbotsschild** *nt* SICHERHEIT prohibition sign

verbrannt[1] *adj* METALL burnt, THERMOD burned, burnt, incinerated

verbrannt:[2] **nicht ~es Uran** *nt* KERNTECH unburned

uranium

Verbrauch *m* ELEKTROTECH dissipation, KFZTECH, MECHAN consumption; **~ pro Kopf** *m* WASSERVERSORG per capita consumption

verbrauchen *vt* MASCHINEN dissipate

Verbrauch: **Verbraucherstromkreis** *m* TELEKOM load circuit; **Verbrauchsdatum** *nt* VERPACK use by date; **Verbrauchsleitung** *f* BAU supply pipe; **Verbrauchsspitze** *f* ELEKTRIZ consumption peak, load peak; **Verbrauchszähler** *m* GERÄT demand meter

verbraucht: **~e Luft** *f* HEIZ & KÄLTE vitiated air

Verbrechensverhütung *f* SICHERHEIT crime prevention

verbreiten *vt* RAD broadcast

verbreiterbar: **~e Antenne** *f* RAUMFAHRT deployable aerial, deployable antenna

Verbreitung *f* MEERSCHMUTZ spreading, RAUMFAHRT spread; **~ von Schallwellen** *f* ELEKTROTECH acoustic-wave propagation

Verbrennen *nt* CHEMIE, THERMOD combustion

verbrennen[1] *vt* KOHLEN char, THERMOD burn, destroy by fire, incinerate

verbrennen[2] *vi* METALL burn away

Verbrennung *f* CHEMIE, FERTIG *von Gas*, KUNSTSTOFF, MASCHINEN combustion, METALL burning, SICHERHEIT combustion, *Verletzung* burn, THERMOD burning, combustion; **~ durch Chemikalien** *f* SICHERHEIT chemical burn; **~ ersten Grades** *f* SICHERHEIT first-degree burn; **Verbrennungsanalyse** *f* THERMOD combustion analysis; **Verbrennungsenergie** *f* THERMOD combustion energy; **Verbrennungsgas** *nt* RAUMFAHRT *Raumschiff* combustion gas, UMWELTSCHMUTZ flue gas; **Verbrennungsgeschwindigkeit** *f* MASCHINEN combustion speed, THERMOD rate of combustion; **Verbrennungsinstabilität** *f* THERMOD combustion instability; **Verbrennungskammer** *f* HYDRAUL *Dampfkessel*, KFZTECH *Motor*, LUFTTRANS, THERMOD, WASSERTRANS combustion chamber; **Verbrennungskraftmaschine** *f* ERDÖL, MASCHINEN internal combustion engine, MECHAN internal combustion machine, TRANS combustion engine; **Verbrennungsluft** *f* THERMOD combustion air; **Verbrennungsmittel** *nt* MEERSCHMUTZ *für Öl* burning agent; **Verbrennungsmotor** *m* ELEKTROTECH, FERTIG internal combustion engine, KFZTECH explosion engine, explosion motor, internal combustion engine, motor, *Motor* combustion engine, LUFTTRANS, MASCHINEN, WASSERTRANS combustion engine; **Verbrennungsofen** *m* MASCHINEN combustion furnace, THERMOD incinerator; **Verbrennungsrückstand** *m* ABFALL combustion residue, incineration residue, incineration ash; **Verbrennungsrückstände** *m pl* THERMOD combustion deposits; **Verbrennungsschiffchen** *nt* LABOR combustion boat; **Verbrennungsschlacke** *f* ABFALL incineration slag; **Verbrennungssteuerung** *f* WASSERTRANS *Motor* combustion control; **Verbrennungstechnik** *f* THERMOD combustion engineering; **Verbrennungswärme** *f* MASCHINEN combustion heat, THERMOD burning heat, combustion heat, heat of combustion; **Verbrennungswirkungsgrad** *m* RAUMFAHRT *Raumschiff* combustion efficiency; **Verbrennungszahl** *f* THERMOD combustion index; **Verbrennungszone** *f* METALL combustion zone

verbrühen *vt* SICHERHEIT scald, *Hand* scald

Verbrühung *f* SICHERHEIT scald

Verbund *m* BAU bond, bonding, COMP & DV bonding, group, RAUMFAHRT *Raumschiff* bonding; **Verbund-**

pref ANSTRICH composite, RAUMFAHRT *Raumschiff* bonded

verbunden[1] *adj* BAU jointed, COMP & DV *Programme* linked, ELEKTRIZ connected, interconnected, ELEKTROTECH coupled, MASCHINEN, PHYS connected; **miteinander ~** *adj* TELEKOM linked together

verbunden:[2] **~es Mauerwerk** *nt* BAU bonded masonry; **~e Netze** *nt pl* ELEKTRIZ connected networks; **~e Steuerorgane** *nt pl* LUFTTRANS interconnected controls; **~e Stromkreise** *m pl* ELEKTRIZ linked circuits

Verbund: **Verbundfestigkeit** *f* KERNTECH bonding strength; **Verbundfolie** *f* KUNSTSTOFF multilayer film; **Verbundgas** *nt* ERDÖL connection gas; **Verbundglas** *nt* KFZTECH multilayer glass; **Verbundglaswindschutzscheibe** *f* KFZTECH *Karosserie* laminated windscreen (BrE), laminated windshield (AmE); **Verbundgruppenbezeichnung** *f* KONSTZEICH composite assembly drawing; **Verbundhubschrauber** *m* LUFTTRANS compound helicopter; **Verbundkern** *m* PHYS compound nucleus; **Verbundkompressor** *m* KERNTECH compound compressor; **Verbundlager** *nt* MASCHINEN composite bearing; **Verbundlenkerachse** *f* KFZTECH dead beam axle; **Verbundmaschine** *f* MASCHINEN compound engine; **Verbundmotor** *m* ELEKTRIZ compound motor, compound-wound motor, ELEKTROTECH compound motor, MASCHINEN composite engine; **Verbundnetz** *nt* ELEKTROTECH interconnection; **Verbundpapier** *nt* (*BDP*) PAPIER bonded double paper (*BDP*); **Verbundpfahl** *m* KOHLEN composite pile; **Verbundplatte** *f* FERTIG sandwich panel; **Verbundröhre** *f* ELEKTRONIK multiple-unit tube; **Verbundstoff** *m* FERTIG *Plaste*, KUNSTSTOFF, VERPACK composite; **Verbundstoffbehälter** *m* VERPACK composite container; **Verbundstück** *nt* MECHAN fitting; **Verbundsystem** *nt* COMP & DV distributed system; **Verbundträger** *m* BAU built-up girder, composite girder, compound girder; **Verbundverpackung** *f* ABFALL composite packaging; **Verbundwerkstoff** *m* KUNSTSTOFF composite, RAUMFAHRT *Raumschiff* composite material; **Verbundwicklung** *f* ELEKTRIZ, ELEKTROTECH compound winding

Verchromung *f* KFZTECH, METALL chromium plating

Verdampfen *nt* CHEMTECH vaporization

verdampfen[1] *vt* CHEMIE vaporize, volatize, CHEMTECH, THERMOD vaporize; **~ lassen** *vt* THERMOD vaporize

verdampfen[2] *vi* HEIZ & KÄLTE evaporate

Verdampfer *m* CHEMTECH *Trennen von Stoffgemischen* vaporizer, HEIZ & KÄLTE evaporator, KERNTECH vaporizer, KFZTECH *Klimaanlage*, LABOR evaporator, THERMOD vaporizer; **Verdampferschlange** *f* HEIZ & KÄLTE evaporator coil; **Verdampferteil** *m* HEIZ & KÄLTE evaporator section

Verdampfschale *f* CHEMTECH vaporization dish

verdampft *adj* THERMOD vaporized

Verdampfung *f* CHEMIE volatilization, DRUCK, ERDÖL *Physik*, HEIZ & KÄLTE, HYDRAUL evaporation, KFZTECH vaporization, MASCHINEN, NICHTFOSS ENERG evaporation, PHYS vaporization, THERMOD evaporation; **~ mit Laser** *f* PHYS, STRAHLPHYS laser vaporization; **Verdampfungsapparat** *m* CHEMIE *Kältemaschine* vaporizer; **Verdampfungsbrenner** *m* THERMOD vaporizing burner; **Verdampfungsenthalpie** *f* CHEMTECH evaporation enthalpy; **Verdampfungsentropie** *f* MECHAN, PHYS, THERMOD entropy of vaporization; **Verdampfungsfähigkeit** *f* CHEMTECH evaporative capacity; **Verdampfungsgeschwindigkeit**

f HEIZ & KÄLTE evaporation rate; **Verdampfungskessel** *m* WASSERVERSORG evaporation pan; **Verdampfungskühlung** *f* CHEMTECH evaporation cooling, HEIZ & KÄLTE evaporative cooling, MASCHINEN evaporation cooling, THERMOD evaporative cooling; **Verdampfungsleistung** *f* HEIZ & KÄLTE evaporative capacity, evaporative power; **Verdampfungsmethode** *f* KERNTECH atomic vapor method (AmE), atomic vapour method (BrE); **Verdampfungspunkt** *m* CHEMTECH, HEIZ & KÄLTE evaporating point; **Verdampfungsratenmeßgerät** *nt* CHEMTECH evaporation rate meter; **Verdampfungstemperatur** *f* HEIZ & KÄLTE evaporating temperature; **Verdampfungsverlust** *m* CHEMTECH, HEIZ & KÄLTE, WASSERVERSORG evaporation loss; **Verdampfungsvermögen** *nt* HEIZ & KÄLTE evaporative capacity; **Verdampfungswärme** *f* THERMOD heat of vaporization

Verdaulichkeit *f* LEBENSMITTEL digestibility
Verdauungsenzym *nt* LEBENSMITTEL digestive enzyme
Verdeck *nt* KFZTECH *Karosserie, Cabrio* bonnet (BrE), hood (AmE)
Verdecken *nt* AUFNAHME *eines Geräuschs* masking; ~ **von Daten** *nt* COMP & DV information hiding
verdecken *vt* BAU conceal, WASSERVERSORG blind
Verdeckriegel *m* KFZTECH *Motorhaube* hood catch
verdeckt[1] *adj* FERTIG *Lichtbogenschweißen* shielded
verdeckt:[2] ~**es Lichtbogenschweißen** *nt* BAU submerged arc-welding
Verdeckung: ~ **durch Rauschen** *f* AKUSTIK masking by noise; ~ **durch Töne** *f* AKUSTIK masking by tones; **Verdeckungseffekt** *m* AKUSTIK masking effect; **Verdeckungsmaß** *nt* AKUSTIK masking index
verderben[1] *vt* BAU mar
verderben[2] *vi* LEBENSMITTEL spoil, *Fleisch* taint
verdichtbar[1] *adj* FERTIG rammable
verdichtbar:[2] ~**er Abfall** *m* ABFALL compressible waste
Verdichtbarkeit *f* BAU compactibility, FERTIG compactibility, rammability, HEIZ & KÄLTE compressibility
Verdichten *nt* FERTIG ramming, *Formsand* jarring, METALL shingling, TELEKOM condensing
verdichten *vt* BAU compact, *Straße* pack, COMP & DV pack, *Daten* compress, FERTIG ram, *Formsand* jar, *Gießen* pack, METALL shingle, PAPIER agglomerate, VERPACK condense
verdichtend *adj* PAPIER agglomerative
Verdichter *m* BAU compressor, vibrator, ERDÖL, HEIZ & KÄLTE, KFZTECH *Motor*, MASCHINEN compressor, PAPIER condenser; **Verdichterleistung** *f* HEIZ & KÄLTE compressor rating; **Verdichterleitrad** *nt* LUFTTRANS compressor stator; **Verdichterrotor** *m* LUFTTRANS *Hubschrauber* compressor rotor; **Verdichterschaufel** *f* LUFTTRANS compressor blade; **Verdichterwirkungsgrad** *m* PHYS pressure coefficient
verdichtet[1] *adj* PAPIER agglomerated
verdichtet:[2] ~**e Impulsbreite** *f* ELEKTRONIK compressed pulse width; **nicht** ~**e Deponie** *f* ABFALL uncompacted tip
Verdichtung *f* ABFALL compaction, compression, BAU compaction, condensation, *Boden* compression, COMP & DV, ELEKTRONIK, ERDÖL *Geologie*, FERTIG, HEIZ & KÄLTE, HYDRAUL, KERNTECH, KOHLEN, KUNSTSTOFF compaction, compression, MECHAN packing, PAPIER agglomeration, PHYS, THERMOD compaction, compression, WELLPHYS compression; **Verdichtungsanlage** *f* ABFALL compacting machine, landfill compactor, packer unit; **Verdichtungsdeponie** *f* AB-

FALL tipping with compaction; **Verdichtungsdruck** *m* MASCHINEN discharge pressure; **Verdichtungsgerät** *nt* BAU compactor; **Verdichtungsgrad** *m* BAU, KOHLEN degree of compaction; **Verdichtunghub** *m* KFZTECH *Motor* compression stroke; **Verdichtungskurve** *f* THERMOD compressibility curve; **Verdichtungslinie** *f* KOHLEN compression curve; **Verdichtungsraum** *m* KFZTECH compression chamber; **Verdichtungsring** *m* KFZTECH *Motor, Kolben* compression ring; **Verdichtungsstoß** *m* FERTIG shock; **Verdichtungsstufe** *f* MASCHINEN compression stage; **Verdichtungstakt** *m* KFZTECH *Motor*, THERMOD compression stroke; **Verdichtungstrend** *m* ERDÖL *Geologie* compaction trend; **Verdichtungsverhältnis** *nt* AUFNAHME, ELEKTRONIK *Mikrowellen*, HEIZ & KÄLTE, KFZTECH *Motor*, MASCHINEN, THERMOD compression ratio; **Verdichtungswärme** *f* THERMOD heat of combustion, heat of compression; **Verdichtungswelle** *f* AKUSTIK compressional wave

Verdicken *nt* LEBENSMITTEL *einer Flüssigkeit* thickening
verdickt: ~**er Rand** *m* KUNSTSTOFF fat edge
Verdickungsmittel *nt* CHEMTECH *viskositätserhöhend*, KUNSTSTOFF, LEBENSMITTEL thickener, thickening agent
verdoppeln *vt* DRUCK double, TEXTIL *Strümpfe* splice
Verdopplung *f* AKUSTIK doubling
verdrahten *vt* FERNSEH wire
Verdrahtung *f* ELEKTRIZ, ELEKTROTECH, RAUMFAHRT wiring; **Verdrahtungsfeld** *nt* COMP & DV platter; **Verdrahtungsplan** *m* ELEKTRIZ, TELEKOM wiring diagram; **Verdrahtungsplatte** *f* ELEKTRONIK wiring board
verdrängen *vt* BAU displace
Verdränger *m* FERTIG *Pumpe* impeller; **Verdrängerkolben** *m* MASCHINEN displacement piston; **Verdrängerpumpe** *f* HYDRAUL positive-displacement pump
verdrängt: ~**es Flüssigkeitsvolumen** *nt* FERTIG displacement
Verdrängung *f (D)* MASCHINEN, WASSERTRANS *Schiffkonstruktion*, WASSERVERSORG displacement *(D)*; ~ **auf Spanten** *f* WASSERTRANS *Schiffkonstruktion* molded displacement (AmE), moulded displacement (BrE); **Verdrängungsfaktor** *m* RAUMFAHRT *Raumschiff* displacement coefficient; **Verdrängungsfehler** *m* LUFTTRANS *Instrumentenlandesystem* displacement error; **Verdrängungskühlung** *f* HEIZ & KÄLTE cooling by relative displacement; **Verdrängungspumpe** *f* MASCHINEN displacement pump, positive-displacement pump; **Verdrängungsschwerpunkt** *m* WASSERTRANS *Schiffbau* center of buoyancy (AmE), centre of buoyancy (BrE); **Verdrängungsstrom** *m* ELEKTRIZ displacement current; **Verdrängungstonne** *f* METROL *Schiffe* displacement ton, WASSERTRANS *Seezeichen* ton of displacement; **Verdrängungsvakuumpumpe** *f* MASCHINEN positive-displacement vacuum pump; **Verdrängungszähler** *m* GERÄT displacement meter, positive-displacement meter, volumetric displacement flow meter

Verdrehen *nt* BAU winding, MASCHINEN twisting
verdrehen *vt* BAU twist
Verdrehfestigkeit *f* MASCHINEN resistance to twisting
Verdrehflankenspiel *nt* FERTIG *Getriebelehre* circumferential backlash
Verdrehmoment *nt* MASCHINEN twisting moment; ~ **des Luftschraubenblattes** *nt* LUFTTRANS *Hubschrauber*

blade twisting moment
Verdrehrohr *nt* KFZTECH torque tube
Verdrehung *f* MASCHINEN twist, METALL torsion; ~ **durch ungebrannte Stellen** *f* KER & GLAS green patch distortion; ~ **der Feldlinien** *f* KERNTECH twist of the field lines; ~ **mit Scherung** *f* KERNTECH twist with shear; **Verdrehungsfeder** *f* MASCHINEN spring subjected to torsion, torsion spring; **Verdrehungsmesser** *nt* FERTIG troptometer, MASCHINEN torsion meter; **Verdrehungswinkel** *m* MASCHINEN angle of twist
Verdrehverformung *f* METALL twisting strain
verdrillen *vt* BAU twist
verdrillt[1] *adj* COMP & DV twisted pair
verdrillt:[2] ~**es Adernpaar** *nt* COMP & DV twisted pair cable; ~**er Hohlleiter** *m* ELEKTROTECH twisted waveguide
Verdrillung *f* MASCHINEN twist
Verdrückungsfalle *f* ERDÖL *Lagerstätten* pinch-out trap
verdübeln *vt* BAU dowel, key, peg, FERTIG peg
Verdübelung *f* BAU plugging
Verdunklungsvorhang *m* TEXTIL blackout curtain
verdünnbar *adj* FERTIG rarefiable
Verdünnen *nt* BAU reducing, CHEMTECH *Vorgang* dilution
verdünnen *vt* BAU thin, CHEMTECH dilute, FERTIG rarefy, KOHLEN, KUNSTSTOFF, PAPIER dilute
Verdünner *m* CHEMIE thinner, KUNSTSTOFF diluent
verdünnt[1] *adj* FERTIG rarefied; **in ~er Form** *adj* ANSTRICH slurried
verdünnt:[2] ~**e Legierung** *f* METALL dilute alloy; ~**e Lösung** *f* CHEMTECH dilution, METALL dilute solution
Verdünnung *f* CHEMIE thinning, *einer Flüssigkeit* dilution, ERDÖL dilution, FERTIG rarefaction, KER & GLAS attenuation, KERNTECH thindown, PHYS, WELLPHYS rarefaction; **Verdünnungsmittel** *nt* CHEMTECH diluting agent, KUNSTSTOFF, PAPIER diluent
verdunsten[1] *vt* CHEMIE volatize; ~ **lassen** *vt* HEIZ & KÄLTE evaporate
verdunsten[2] *vi* FOTO *im Vakuum*, HEIZ & KÄLTE evaporate
Verdunster *m* KFZTECH *Klimaanlage* evaporator
Verdunstung *f* CHEMIE *unterhalb des normalen Siedepunktes* volatilization; **Verdunstungsapparat** *m* CHEMTECH evaporating apparatus; **Verdunstungskälte** *f* PHYS, THERMOD latent heat of evaporation; **Verdunstungsmesser** *m* CHEMTECH evaporimeter
veredeln *vt* METALL fine, refine, PAPIER convert
Veredelung *f* BAU *Leichtmetall* ageing (BrE), aging (AmE), FERTIG *Stahl* refining, PAPIER converting
Verein: ~ **Deutscher Elektrotechniker** *m* (*VDE*) ELEKTRIZ Association of German Electrical Engineers; ~ **Deutscher Ingenieure** *m* (*VDI*) ELEKTRIZ Association of German Engineers
Vereinbarung *f* COMP & DV declaration, declarative, declarative statement
Vereindeutigung *f* KÜNSTL INT disambiguation
vereinen *vt* GEOM join
vereinfachen *vt* MATH simplify
vereinfacht: ~**e Ansicht** *f* KONSTZEICH simplified view
vereinigen *vt* GEOM join
Vereinigung *f* ERDÖL *Bergrecht* unitization, TRANS merging; **Vereinigungsmenge** *f* MATH union of sets
vereint: ~**er Antrieb** *m* RAUMFAHRT unified propulsion
vereisen *vt* THERMOD freeze
Vereisung *f* LUFTTRANS, WASSERTRANS icing, WASSERVERSORG ice accretion; **Vereisungsanzeigerelais** *nt* LUFTTRANS, WASSERTRANS ice detector relay; **Vereisungsmeßfühler** *m* LUFTTRANS, WASSERTRANS icing probe; **Vereisungswarngerät** *nt* LUFTTRANS, WASSERTRANS ice detector
verengen *vt* FERTIG neck
verengt: ~**er Flaschenhals** *m* KER & GLAS choke
Verengung *f* MASCHINEN contraction, MECHAN gooseneck, neck
Vererbung *f* COMP & DV *objekt-orientierte Programmierung* inheritance; **Vererbungsgraph** *m* KÜNSTL INT inheritance graph
verestern *vt* CHEMIE esterify
Veresterung *f* LEBENSMITTEL esterification
Verfahren *nt* COMP & DV procedure, process, ELEKTRIZ, KOHLEN process, MASCHINEN procedure, TEXTIL process; ~ **vor dem europäischen Patentamt** *nt* PATENT proceedings before the EPO; ~ **zur Sammlung meteorologischer und ozeanographischer Daten** *nt* WASSERTRANS oceanographic and environmental research; ~ **mit Trägerabtastung** *nt* TELEKOM carrier sense system; **Verfahrenseignungsbericht** *m* QUAL *Schweißen* procedure qualification record; **Verfahrensfehler** *m* COMP & DV truncation error; **Verfahrenshandbuch** *nt* QUAL procedures manual
verfahrensorientiert: ~**e Programmiersprache** *f* COMP & DV procedural language, procedure-oriented language; **nicht ~e Programmiersprache** *f* COMP & DV nonprocedural language
Verfahren: **Verfahrensprüfung** *f* QUAL process inspection and testing; **Verfahrenssteuerung** *f* ELEKTROTECH process control; **Verfahrenstechnik** *f* ERDÖL, MASCHINEN process engineering; **Verfahrenstechniker** *m* MASCHINEN methods engineer
Verfalldatum *nt* RAUMFAHRT decay date
verfälschen *vt* COMP & DV corrupt, LEBENSMITTEL adulterate
Verfälschung *f* COMP & DV corruption; **Verfälschungsmittel** *nt* LEBENSMITTEL adulterant
verfälschungssicher[1] *adj* VERPACK tamper-proof
verfälschungssicher:[2] ~**er Verschluß** *m* VERPACK tamper-proof closure
Verfalzung *f* BAU *Metallbau* bead
Verfangen *nt* SICHERHEIT entanglement, *von Kleidung und Haaren* entanglement
verfangen[1] *vi* SICHERHEIT entangle
verfangen:[2] **sich ~** *v refl* SICHERHEIT become entangled
verfärben[1] *vt* KUNSTSTOFF stain
verfärben:[2] **sich ~** *v refl* BAU color (AmE), colour (BrE)
verfärbend: nicht ~ *adj* KUNSTSTOFF nonstaining
Verfärbung *f* KUNSTSTOFF discoloration (AmE), discolouration (BrE)
Verfasserkorrektur *f* DRUCK author's alterations
Verfaulen: zum ~ bringen *vt* LEBENSMITTEL putrefy
verfaulen *vi* LEBENSMITTEL putrefy
verfaulend *adj* LEBENSMITTEL putrescent
verfault *adj* LEBENSMITTEL putrid
verfertigen *vt* MECHAN fabricate
Verfestigen *nt* BAU grouting
verfestigen *vt* ABFALL solidify
verfestigt: ~**es Kieselgeröll** *nt* BAU conglomerate; ~**es Material** *nt* BAU stabilized material
Verfestigung *f* BAU compaction, MASCHINEN hardening, PHYS solidification; ~ **von Abfällen** *f* ABFALL solidifying waste; **Verfestigungsgrad** *m* KOHLEN degree of consolidation; **Verfestigungsmittel** *nt* ABFALL fixative, solidifying agent, MEERSCHMUTZ solidifier; **Verfesti-**

gungsprodukt *nt* ABFALL CFS-processed waste, CFS-treated waste, solidified waste, solidified product, solidified material; **Verfestigungsverfahren** *nt* ABFALL fixation technique, solidification technique, stabilization technique; **Verfestigungsverfahren für Sonderabfälle** *nt (PETRIFIX-Verfahren, SEALOSAFE-Verfahren, VRS-Verfahren)* ABFALL WPC-VRS process; **Verfestigungszeit** *f* KUNSTSTOFF setting time

Verfilzbarkeit *f* PAPIER felting power

Verfilzen *nt* PAPIER felting

verfilzen *vi* TEXTIL mat

verflanschen *vt* ERDÖL flange up

verflechten *vt* COMP & DV, ELEKTRONIK, TEXTIL interlace

Verflechtung *f* TEXTIL interlacing, TRANS weaving; **Verflechtungsfaktor** *m* TRANS weaving factor; **Verflechtungssteuerung** *f* TRANS merging control

verflüchtigen[1] *vi* TEXTIL volatilize

verflüchtigen:[2] **sich ~** *v refl* CHEMTECH *unterhalb des normalen Siedepunktes* evaporate

Verflüssigen *nt* BAU fluxing

verflüssigen[1] *vt* PAPIER fluidify

verflüssigen:[2] **sich ~** *v refl* THERMOD liquefy

Verflüssiger *m* HEIZ & KÄLTE condenser, liquefier, PAPIER fluidizer

verflüssigt *adj* THERMOD liquefied

Verflüssigung *f* BAU *Gase*, HEIZ & KÄLTE condensation, THERMOD liquefaction

Verfolgbarkeit *f* METROL traceability

Verfolgen *nt* RADIO *Signale* tracing

verfolgen *vt* COMP & DV monitor, trace

Verfolgung *f* RAUMFAHRT *Raumschiff*, TELEKOM *Satellit* tracking; **Verfolgungsantenne** *f* RAUMFAHRT tracking antenna; **Verfolgungsfilterdemodulator** *m* RAUMFAHRT *Weltraumfunk* tracking filter demodulator; **Verfolgungsradar** *nt* RAUMFAHRT tracking radar; **Verfolgungsstation** *f* RAUMFAHRT tracking station; **Verfolgungstelemetrie und -steuerung** *f* RAUMFAHRT *Weltraumfunk* TTC, tracking telemetry and command

verformbar: **~er Frontbereich** *m* KFZTECH deformable front section; **~er Heckbereich** *m* KFZTECH deformable rear section

Verformbarkeit *f* FERTIG plasticity, KER & GLAS workability; **~ unter Druckbeanspruchung** *f* FERTIG malleability

verformen *vt* MECHAN deform, METALL bend

verformt: **~er Stab** *m* METALL bent rod

Verformung *f* KERNTECH, KOHLEN, KUNSTSTOFF, MASCHINEN, MECHAN, METALL, PHYS, STRAHLPHYS deformation, distortion; **~ des Blattes** *f* LUFTTRANS *Hubschrauber* blade distortion; **~ unter Last** *f* MASCHINEN strain; **Verformungsbruch** *m* METALL ductile fracture; **Verformungsenergie** *f* FERTIG resilience; **Verformungsfestigkeit** *f* KERNTECH yield strength; **Verformungsmodul** *m* KOHLEN compressibility modulus, deformation modulus; **Verformungsriß** *m* METALL ductile crack

Verfrachter *m* WASSERTRANS carrier, *Seehandel* shipper

verfügbar: **~e Benutzerzeit** *f* COMP & DV available time; **~e Landestrecke** *f* LUFTTRANS landing distance available; **~e Leistung** *f* AUFNAHME *eines Verstärkers*, ELEKTRIZ, MASCHINEN, TELEKOM available power; **~e Leistungsverstärkung** *f* AUFNAHME available power gain; **~e Startabbruchstrecke** *f* LUFTTRANS accelerate-stop distance available; **~e Startstrecke** *f* LUFTTRANS takeoff distance available

Verfügbarkeit *f* COMP & DV, QUAL, RAUMFAHRT availability; **Verfügbarkeitskonzept** *nt* QUAL availability concept; **Verfügbarkeitszeit** *f* QUAL uptime

Verfugen *nt* BAU *Material* pointing

verfugen *vt* BAU point, *Mauerwerk* point; **neu ~** *vt* BAU repoint

Verfugung *f* KERNTECH grouting

Verfügung *f* QUAL disposition

Verfüllbeton *m* BAU packing

Verfüllboden *m* UMWELTSCHMUTZ *Erdbau* backfill

verfüllt: **~e Deponie** *f* ABFALL complete fill

Verfüllung *f* ABFALL backfilling, filling, BAU backfill

Vergabe: **~ gegen Höchstgebot** *f* ERDÖL *Konzession* blind auction

Vergärung *f* CHEMIE *Tätigkeit* fermentation

vergasen *vt* PHYS gasify

Vergaser *m* KER & GLAS carburetor (AmE), carburettor (BrE), KFZTECH carburetor (AmE), carburettor (BrE), *Kraftstoffversorgung* carburetor (AmE), carburettor (BrE), MASCHINEN, MECHAN carburetor (AmE), carburettor (BrE), WASSERTRANS carburetor (AmE), carburettor (BrE), carburettor (BrE); **Vergasergestänge** *nt* KFZTECH *Vergaser* carburetor linkage (AmE), carburettor linkage (BrE); **Vergaserglocke** *f* KFZTECH suction chamber; **Vergaserheizmantel** *m* KFZTECH carburetor jacket (AmE), carburettor jacket (BrE); **Vergaserknallen** *nt* KFZTECH blowback; **Vergaserkraftstoff** *m (VK)* ERDÖL gas (AmE), gasoline (AmE), petrol (BrE), KFZTECH fuel, gas (AmE), gasoline (AmE), petrol (BrE), THERMOD gas (AmE), gasoline (AmE), petrol (BrE), TRANS motor spirit; **Vergaserluftdüse** *f* MECHAN choke; **Vergaserluftklappe** *f* KFZTECH choker plate; **Vergasermischkammer** *f* KFZTECH carburetor barrel (AmE), carburettor barrel (BrE); **Vergasermotor** *m* KFZTECH carburetor engine (AmE), carburettor engine (BrE), MASCHINEN spark ignition engine, THERMOD gas engine (AmE), gasoline engine (AmE), petrol engine (BrE); **Vergasernadel** *f* KFZTECH carburetor needle (AmE), carburettor needle (BrE); **Vergaserpatschen** *nt* KFZTECH blowback; **Vergasersaugkanal** *m* KFZTECH carburetor barrel (AmE), carburettor barrel (BrE); **Vergaserschwimmer** *m* KFZTECH carburetor float (AmE), carburettor float (BrE); **Vergaserseilzug** *m* KFZTECH carburetor control cable (AmE), carburettor control cable (BrE)

Vergasung *f* ABFALL, ERDÖL *Umwandlung von Kohle oder Öl in Gas*, THERMOD gasification

vergeben *vt* BAU *Auftrag*, FERTIG place

Vergießen *nt* FERTIG teeming, KUNSTSTOFF embedding, encapsulation, potting

vergießen *vt* BAU grout, mold (AmE), mould (BrE), FERTIG, KER & GLAS teem

Vergiftung *f* KERNTECH *eines Reaktors*, UMWELTSCHMUTZ poisoning

Vergilben *nt* PAPIER yellowing

vergilben[1] *vt* PAPIER age

vergilben[2] *vi* TEXTIL yellow

vergilbend: **nicht ~** *adj* KUNSTSTOFF nonyellowing

vergilbungsbeständig *adj* KUNSTSTOFF nonyellowing

vergittern *vt* BAU *Fenster* screen

Verglasen *nt* BAU, KER & GLAS *Fenster* glazing

verglasen *vt* BAU pane, FERTIG vitrify, KER & GLAS *mit Glas versehen* glaze

verglast: **~e Tür** *f* BAU glazed door

Verglasung *f* FERTIG, KER & GLAS vitrification, KFZTECH

Kühler blind, NICHTFOSS ENERG glazing; **Verglasungsindustrie** *f* KER & GLAS glazing industry

Vergleich *m* COMP & DP, GERÄT comparison; **~ über verschiedene Sinnesorgane** *m* ERGON cross-sensory matching

vergleichbar *adj* MATH *Größen* commensurable; **nicht ~** *adj* MATH incommensurable

Vergleich: **Vergleichbarkeit** *f* QUAL reproducibility

vergleichen *vt* COMP & DV compare

vergleichend: **~er Versuch** *m* PHYS comparative test

Vergleicher *m* COMP & DV, ELEKTRONIK, KONTROLL, METROL *EDV*, TELEKOM comparator

Vergleich: **Vergleichsabstimmfrequenz** *f* AKUSTIK standard tuning frequency; **Vergleichsausdruck** *m* COMP & DV relational expression; **Vergleichsbedingungen** *f pl* QUAL reproducibility conditions; **Vergleichseinrichtung** *f* METROL, PHYS comparator; **Vergleichselektrode** *f* LABOR *Elektrochemie* reference electrode; **Vergleichsfrequenz** *f* AKUSTIK SF, standard frequency; **Vergleichsglied** *nt* GERÄT comparing element; **Vergleichsgrenze** *f* QUAL reproducibility limit; **Vergleichsgröße** *f* KOHLEN control size; **Vergleichslehre** *f* MASCHINEN master gage (AmE), master gauge (BrE), reference gage (AmE), reference gauge (BrE); **Vergleichsmesser** *m* METROL *Maschinenbau* comparator; **Vergleichsmessung** *f* GERÄT comparative measurement, comparison measurement, reference measurement; **Vergleichsmeßwert** *m* GERÄT reference measurement; **Vergleichsmodell** *nt* COMP & DV relational model; **Vergleichsnormal** *nt* QUAL reference standard; **Vergleichsoberfläche** *f* TELEKOM reference surface; **Vergleichsoperator** *m* COMP & DV relational operator; **Vergleichsprüfmethode** *f* OPTIK reference test method; **Vergleichspunkt** *m* COMP & DV benchmark; **Vergleichsschall** *m* AKUSTIK reference sound; **Vergleichsschaltung** *f* TELEKOM comparison circuit; **Vergleichsspannung** *f* KOHLEN effective stress; **Vergleichsstelle** *f* GERÄT *beim Thermoelement* comparison junction, REGELUNG reference junction; **Vergleichsstellentemperatur** *f* GERÄT *Thermoelement* reference junction temperature; **Vergleichsstrecke** *f* KONSTZEICH comparative length; **Vergleichsstück** *nt* WERKPRÜF reference piece; **Vergleichssystem** *nt* ERGON benchmark system

Vergleichstest durchführen *vi* COMP & DV benchmark

Vergleich: **Vergleichston** *m* AKUSTIK reference tone; **Vergleichswerte** *m pl* AKUSTIK comparison values

Vergolden *nt* FERTIG gilding

vergolden *vt* FERTIG gild, METALL gold-plate

vergoldet: **~er Übergang** *m* RAUMFAHRT gold flashing

Vergoldung *f* KER & GLAS gilding

vergoren: **~er Abfall** *m* ABFALL fermented waste

Vergraben *nt* ABFALL *von Müll* land burial

vergrößern *vt* FERTIG coarsen

Vergrößern *nt* COMP & DV zooming, FOTO enlargement process

vergrößern *vt* COMP & DV zoom in, FOTO enlarge, *Foto* blow up, PHYS magnify

vergrößert:[1] **~es Bild** *nt* PHYS enlarged image; **~e Spurweite** *f* EISENBAHN wide track gage (AmE), wide track gauge (BrE); **~es Sucherbild** *nt* FOTO magnified viewfinder image

vergrößert:[2] **~ zeichnen** *vt* KONSTZEICH draw to a larger scale

Vergrößerung *f* COMP & DV zoom-in, DRUCK enlargement, FOTO enlargement, enlargement print, OPTIK

magnification, power, PHYS magnification; **~ in Längsrichtung** *f* PHYS longitudinal magnification; **Vergrößerungsabdeckrahmen** *m* FOTO masking frame; **Vergrößerungsapparat** *m* FOTO enlarger; **Vergrößerungsglas** *nt* KER & GLAS glass, LABOR, MECHAN, PHYS magnifying glass; **Vergrößerungskamera** *f* DRUCK enlarging camera, FOTO enlarger camera, enlarging camera; **Vergrößerungsmaßstab** *m* KONSTZEICH enlargement scale; **Vergrößerungspapier** *nt* FOTO enlarging paper; **Vergrößerungsrahmen** *m* FOTO masking frame; **Vergrößerungssäule** *f* FOTO enlarger column; **Vergrößerungsunterlage** *f* FOTO enlarger support; **Vergrößerungsvermögen** *nt* PHYS magnifying power

Vergußmasse *f* FERTIG compound, KERNTECH grouting

vergütbar *adj* FERTIG *Stahl*, THERMOD heat-treatable

Vergütbarkeit *f* FERTIG *Stahl* heat treatability

Vergüten *nt* FERTIG quenching and tempering, THERMOD *Glas* anneal

vergüten *vt* ANSTRICH finish, BAU *Stahl* temper, METALL age, THERMOD *Glas* anneal

vergütet[1] *adj* THERMOD heat-treated, *Glas* annealed

vergütet:[2] **~e Linse** *f* FOTO, PHYS bloomed lens, coated lens; **~es Objektiv** *nt* PHYS coated lens; **~er Stahl** *m* PAPIER annealed steel

Vergütung *f* BAU ageing (BrE), aging (AmE), FERTIG ageing (BrE), aging (AmE), quench ageing (BrE), quench aging (AmE), FOTO, PHYS coating, THERMOD heat treatment; **Vergütungsdiagramm** *nt* THERMOD heat treatment diagram; **Vergütungsriß** *m* THERMOD heat treatment crack; **Vergütungsstahl** *m* FERTIG heat-treatable steel

Verhalten *nt* BAU, ERGON, MEERSCHMUTZ *eines Ölteppichs* behavior (AmE), behaviour (BrE), TEXTIL properties; **~ mit fester Stellgeschwindigkeit** *nt* REGELUNG single speed floating action; **~ im niederfrequenten Bereich** *nt* ELEKTRONIK, RADIO, TELEKOM low-frequency response; **~ eines Schiffes im Seegang** *nt* WASSERTRANS sea keeping; **Verhaltensmuster** *nt* ERGON behavior pattern (BrE), behaviour pattern (BrE)

Verhältnis *nt* GEOM proportion, HEIZ & KÄLTE ratio, MATH proportion, ratio, PHYS ratio; **~ Flotte zu Ware** *nt* TEXTIL liquor-to-goods ratio; **~ zwischen Förderhöhe und Widerstand** *nt* NICHTFOSS ENERG lift-to-drag ratio; **~ zwischen Geschwindigkeit und Verkehrsdichte** *nt* TRANS speed density relationship; **~ zwischen Geschwindigkeit und Verkehrsfluß** *nt* TRANS speed flow diagram, speed flow relationship; **~ Gewinn zu Rauschtemperatur** *nt* RAUMFAHRT *Weltraumfunk* G/t, gain-to-noise temperature ratio; **~ Kern-Mantel** *nt* TELEKOM core-cladding ratio; **~ Länge/Breite** *nt* ELEKTROTECH aspect ratio; **~ Reaktanz/Widerstand** *nt* (Q) AKUSTIK ratio of reactance to resistance (Q); **~ Schub/Gewicht** *nt* RAUMFAHRT thrust-to-weight ratio; **~ von Seitenhöhe zu Tiefgang** *nt* WASSERTRANS *Schiffkonstruktion* depth-to-draft ratio (AmE), depth-to-draught ratio (BrE); **~ Signal zu Rauschen** *nt* GERÄT *meist Spannungsverhältnis* signal-to-noise ratio; **~ der spezifischen Wärmen** *nt* PHYS ratio of specific heats; **Verhältniskondensatoren** *m pl* ELEKTROTECH ratioed capacitors; **Verhältnislautheit** *f* AKUSTIK relative loudness; **Verhältnismessung** *f* GERÄT ratio measurement; **Verhältnisoperator** *m* COMP & DV relational operator; **Verhältnisschabotte** *f* FERTIG anvil ratio; **Verhältnistonhöhe** *f* AKUSTIK relation pitch; **Verhältniswerte** *m pl* AKUSTIK ratio values; **Verhältniszahl** *f* MATH ratio

verhärten[1] *vt* FERTIG indurate, METALL harden

verhärten[2] *vi* BAU set

Verhärtung: **~ durch Neutronenausfluß** *f* KERNTECH leakage hardening

verharzen *vt* FERTIG *Öl* gum up

Verharzung *f* FERTIG gumming up, gummy deposit

Verholen *nt* WASSERTRANS *Tauwerk* warping

verholen *vt* WASSERTRANS *Schiff* warp

Verholkopf *m* WASSERTRANS *Deckausrüstung* warping head, *Deckausrüstung* gipsy, gypsy

Verholleine *f* WASSERTRANS *Tauwerk* warp

Verholtrommel *f* WASSERTRANS *Deckbeschläge* warping drum

Verhütung: **~ von Luftverschmutzung** *f* UMWELT-SCHMUTZ prevention of atmospheric pollution; **~ der unbeabsichtigten Zündung brennbarer Luft** *f* SICHER-HEIT prevention of inadvertent ignition of flammable atmospheres; **~ der Wasserverschmutzung** *f* UMWELT-SCHMUTZ prevention of water pollution

Verifizierung *f* COMP & DV, KONTROLL, MASCHINEN, QUAL verification; **~ mittels Grenzlehren** *f* MASCHINEN verification by means of limit gages (AmE), verification by means of limit gauges (BrE)

verjüngen[1] *vt* BAU batter, reduce

verjüngen:[2] **sich ~** *v refl* FERTIG contract, taper

verjüngt[1] *adj* BAU beveled (AmE), bevelled (BrE), *Holzbau* splayed

verjüngt:[2] **~er Abschnitt** *m* ELEKTROTECH tapered section

Verjüngung *f* FERTIG conicity, draft, MASCHINEN back taper, *konisch* tapering, MECHAN taper

verkabelt: **~er Haushalt** *m* FERNSEH cabled home

Verkabelung *f* ELEKTRIZ, ELEKTROTECH, TELEKOM cabling

verkalkt *adj* METALL calcified

Verkalkung *f* METALL calcification

verkämmt: **~e Zeilenabtastung** *f* FERNSEH line-interlaced scanning

verkanten *vt* BAU bend out of line

Verkantungsvorrichtung *f* LUFTTRANS leveling unit (AmE), levelling unit (BrE)

verkatten *vt* WASSERTRANS *Anker* back

Verkauf *m* ERDÖL *Konzessionsbeteiligung* farming-out; **Verkaufsdatum** *nt* VERPACK sell-by date

Verkehr *m* TRANS traffic

verkehrsabhängig: **~ gesteuertes Signal** *nt* TRANS traffic-actuated signal; **~e Signale** *nt pl* TRANS vehicle-actuated traffic signals; **~e Signalgebung** *f* TRANS vehicle-actuated signalization; **~e Signalsteuerung** *f* TRANS vehicleactuated control

Verkehr: **Verkehrsablauf** *m* TRANS traffic flow; **Verkehrsabschnitt** *m* TRANS traffic cut; **Verkehrsabwicklung** *f* TELEKOM traffic flow; **Verkehrsampel** *f* TRANS traffic lights; **Verkehrsampelanlage** *f* ELEKTRONIK traffic signal; **Verkehrsanalysator** *m* TRANS traffic analyser (BrE), traffic analyzer (AmE); **Verkehrsanalysedetektor** *m* TRANS traffic analysis detector; **Verkehrsangebot** *nt* TELEKOM traffic offered

verkehrsangepaßt: **~es Steuergerät** *nt* TRANS traffic-adjusted controller

Verkehr: **Verkehrsaufkommen** *nt* TRANS service volume, traffic volume; **Verkehrsaufteilungsmodell** *nt* TRANS traffic assignment model; **Verkehrsaufteilungsprogramm** *nt* TRANS traffic assignment program (AmE),

traffic assignment programme (BrE); **Verkehrsaufteilungssystem** *nt* TELEKOM traffic division system; **Verkehrsausscheidungszahl** *f* TELEKOM *Telefon* prefix; **Verkehrsbedingungen** *f pl* TRANS traffic conditions; **Verkehrsbelastungsplan** *m* TRANS traffic flow diagram

verkehrsberuhigt: **~e Zone** *f* TRANS traffic restraint area

Verkehr: **Verkehrsdetektor** *m* TRANS traffic detector; **Verkehrsdichte** *f* RAIL traffic density, TRANS density of traffic; **Verkehrsdurchsage** *f* TRANS road message; **Verkehrserhebung** *f* TRANS traffic survey; **Verkehrsflugzeug** *nt* LUFTTRANS passenger plane; **Verkehrsfluß** *m* TELEKOM, TRANS traffic flow; **Verkehrsfunk** *m* RADIO, TRANS roadside radio transmitter; **Verkehrsfunksender** *m* RADIO, TRANS traffic radio transmitter; **Verkehrsgüte** *f* TELEKOM grade of service; **Verkehrsinformation** *f* TRANS traffic information; **Verkehrsinformationserkennungszeichen** *nt* TRANS traffic information identification signal; **Verkehrskapazität** *f* TELEKOM traffic-handling capability; **Verkehrsknotenpunkt** *m* EISENBAHN rail junction, TRANS rail junction, traffic center (AmE), traffic centre (BrE); **Verkehrskontrollanlage** *f* TRANS traffic control installation; **Verkehrskontrolle** *f* TRANS traffic control; **Verkehrskontrollprogramm** *nt* TRANS traffic control program (AmE), traffic control programme (BrE); **Verkehrskonzentration** *f* TRANS traffic concentration; **Verkehrskreisel** *m* TRANS rotary (AmE), roundabout (BrE), traffic circle (AmE); **Verkehrslage** *f* TRANS traffic situation; **Verkehrslast** *f* BAU rolling load, traveling load (AmE), travelling load (BrE), *Tiefbau* live load, TELEKOM, TRANS traffic load; **Verkehrsleitungsprogramm** *nt* TRANS traffic-routing program (AmE), traffic-routing programme (BrE); **Verkehrslenkung** *f* TELEKOM traffic control, TRANS guidance, WASSERTRANS channelization; **Verkehrslenkungsstrategie** *f* TELEKOM traffic-routing strategy; **Verkehrsleuchtnagel** *m* BAU *auf der Straße* reflecting stud; **Verkehrsnachfrage** *f* TRANS traffic demand; **Verkehrsparameter** *m* TRANS traffic parameter; **Verkehrsplanung** *f* TRANS traffic planning, traffic schedule; **Verkehrspolizei** *f* TRANS traffic police; **Verkehrsprognose** *f* TRANS traffic forecast; **Verkehrsprognoseprogramm** *nt* TRANS traffic-forecasting program (AmE), traffic-forecasting programme (BrE); **Verkehrsqualität** *f* TRANS level of service; **Verkehrsradar** *m* TRANS road traffic radar; **Verkehrsrechner** *m* TRANS traffic computer

Verkehrsregelung *f* TRANS traffic regulation; **~ mit geschlossener Schleife** *f* LUFTTRANS closed-loop traffic control system

Verkehr: **Verkehrsregion** *f* TRANS traffic region; **Verkehrsrichtung** *f* EISENBAHN direction of traffic; **Verkehrsschild** *nt* TRANS marker

verkehrsschwach: **~e Zeit** *f* TELEKOM slack traffic period, TRANS light hours (AmE), lowest hourly traffic

Verkehr: **Verkehrssicherheit** *f* TRANS road safety; **Verkehrssicherheitsprogramm** *nt* TRANS road safety programme; **Verkehrssignal** *nt* TRANS traffic signal; **Verkehrssignalprogramm** *nt* TRANS traffic signals program (AmE), traffic signals programme (BrE); **Verkehrssignalsteuereinheit** *f* TRANS traffic signal controller; **Verkehrssimulation** *f* TRANS simulation of traffic, traffic simulation; **Verkehrssimulationsprogramm** *nt* TRANS traffic simulation program (AmE), traffic simulation programme (BrE); **Verkehrssimula-**

tor *m* TRANS traffic simulator; **Verkehrsstau** *m* TRANS traffic jam (BrE); **Verkehrssteuerung** *f* TRANS control of flow; **Verkehrsstrom** *m* TRANS traffic stream; **Verkehrstechnik** *f* TRANS traffic engineering; **Verkehrsteilnehmer** *m* TRANS road user; **Verkehrstrennungsgebiet** *nt* WASSERTRANS *Navigation* traffic separation scheme

verkehrstüchtig *adj* KFZTECH roadworthy

Verkehr: **Verkehrsüberwachung** *f* TELEKOM traffic supervision, TRANS traffic surveillance; **Verkehrsumlegung** *f* TRANS traffic assignment; **Verkehrsumleitung** *f* TRANS diversion, diversion of traffic, traffic diversion; **Verkehrsunfall** *m* TRANS traffic accident; **Verkehrsverstoß** *m* TRANS traffic violation; **Verkehrsvolumenzähler** *m* TRANS traffic volume meter; **Verkehrsvorhersage** *f* TRANS traffic forecasting; **Verkehrsvorschrift** *f* TRANS traffic regulations; **Verkehrsweg** *m* WASSERTRANS *Navigation* traffic lane; **Verkehrswert** *m* TELEKOM traffic carried; **Verkehrszähler** *m* TRANS traffic counter; **Verkehrszählung** *f* TRANS traffic census; **Verkehrszählung am Querschnitt** *f* TRANS traffic count; **Verkehrszeichen** *nt* TRANS road sign, sign, traffic sign

verkehrt: ~ **bombiert** *adj* FERTIG *Walzen* concave; ~ **konisch** *adj* FERTIG *Gießen* inverted

Verkeilen *nt* FERTIG, MASCHINEN keying

verkeilen *vt* BAU block, key, FERTIG chock, key, wedge, MASCHINEN cotter, key, MECHAN wedge

verkeilt *adj* FERTIG keyed, MECHAN splined

Verkeilung *f* BAU keying, MASCHINEN wedging

Verketten *nt* TELEKOM concatenation

verketten *vt* COMP & DV, KONTROLL concatenate

verkettet: ~**e Busstruktur** *f* COMP & DV daisy chain bus; ~**e Dateien** *f pl* COMP & DV concatenated data sets

Verkettung *f* COMP & DV, ELEKTRONIK concatenation, ELEKTROTECH concatenation, connection, KÜNSTL INT chaining, MECHAN linkage, TELEKOM concatenation

verkitten *vt* BAU cement, putty, seal, stuff, FERTIG lute

verkittet: ~**es Glas** *nt* KER & GLAS cemented glass; ~**e Linsen** *f pl* KER & GLAS cemented lenses

verklammern *vt* BAU joggle, FERTIG cramp

Verklappung: ~ **auf See** *f* MEERSCHMUTZ, UMWELTSCHMUTZ discharge at sea

Verklarung *f* WASSERTRANS *Versicherung* ship's protest

Verkleben *nt* BAU bonding, cementing, KUNSTSTOFF bonding

verkleben *vt* BAU cement, stick

Verklebung *f* CHEMTECH agglutination, KUNSTSTOFF bond, MECHAN bonding; ~ **des Bootskörpers mit dem Deck** *f* WASSERTRANS *Schiffbau* deck-hull bonding

verkleiden *vt* BAU board, box up, clad, face, line, *Material* surface

verkleidet: ~**er Träger** *m* BAU cased beam

Verkleidung *f* BAU facing, *Gebäude* revetment, ELEKTRIZ reinforcement, ELEKTROTECH envelope, ERDÖL lagging, HEIZ & KÄLTE fairing, HYDRAUL ·cladding, clothing, *Dampfmaschine* lagging, KFZTECH *Karosserie* panel, LUFTTRANS case, *Flugzeug* fairing, MECHAN casing, RAUMFAHRT *aerodynamisch* cladding, fairing; ~ **der Luftschraubenblattspitze** *f* LUFTTRANS *Hubschrauber* blade tip fairing; **Verkleidungsblech** *nt* HYDRAUL clothing plate; **Verkleidungsmaterial** *nt* BAU sheeting; **Verkleidungsübergang** *m* LUFTTRANS *Flugwerk* fillet

verkleinern *vt* COMP & DV zoom out

verkleinert: ~**er Maßstab** *m* KONSTZEICH reduced scale; ~**es Modell** *nt* TELEKOM reduced model

Verkleinerung *f* FOTO reduction print; **Verkleinerungsgrenze** *f* KER & GLAS diminishing stop level; **Verkleinerungsmaske** *f* FOTO reduction mask

verklemmt *adj* RAUMFAHRT jammed

Verklumpung *f* LEBENSMITTEL agglutination

Verknüpfbarkeit *f* COMP & DV, TELEKOM *Teile eines Systems* connectivity

verknüpfen *vt* COMP & DV combine, *Programme* bind, concatenate

verknüpft[1] *adj* COMP & DV *Programme* interlaced

verknüpft:[2] ~**e Dateien** *f pl* COMP & DV concatenated data sets

Verknüpfung *f* COMP & DV concatenation, ELEKTRONIK *Schaltkreistechnik* conjunction, ELEKTROTECH connection; **Verknüpfungsanweisung** *f* COMP & DV logic instruction; **Verknüpfungsbefehl** *m* COMP & DV logic instruction; **Verknüpfungsglied** *nt* COMP & DV logic element, logic gate, ELEKTRONIK gate, logic gate; **Verknüpfungsschaltung** *f* COMP & DV logic circuit, FERNSEH combiner circuit; **Verknüpfungstransistor** *m* ELEKTRONIK gating transistor

Verkohlen *nt* KOHLEN carbonization

verkohlen[1] *vt* KOHLEN coal

verkohlen[2] *vi* THERMOD get blackened with heat

verkohlt *adj* KOHLEN carbonized

verkokbar *adj* KOHLEN coking

Verkoken *nt* KOHLEN coking

verkoken *vt* KOHLEN carbonize, coke, THERMOD carbonize

Verkokung *f* KOHLEN carbonization

Verkorkung *f* CHEMIE suberification, KER & GLAS bore (BrE), corkage (AmE); **Verkorkungsmaschine** *f* VERPACK corking machine

verkratzen *vt* ANSTRICH scratch

verkratzt: ~**e Form** *f* KER & GLAS scratched mold (AmE), scratched mould (BrE)

verkupfert *adj* BAU coppered, METALL copper-plated

Verkupferung *f* KER & GLAS, METALL copper-plating, coppering

verkürzen *vt* PHYS contract

verkürzt: ~**er Bogen** *m* BAU diminished arch, skeen arch, skene arch; ~**e Gleitwinkelbefeuerung** *f* LUFTTRANS abbreviated visual approach slope indicator system; ~**e Präzisionsanflugswinkelbefeuerung** *f* LUFTTRANS abbreviated precision approach path indicator; ~ **startendes und landendes Flugzeug** *nt* (*RTOL-Flugzeug*) LUFTTRANS reduced takeoff and landing aircraft (*RTOL aircraft*)

Verkürzung *f* KONSTZEICH shortening, *durch ungünstige Projektion* foreshortening, PHYS contraction; **Verkürzungsvorsatz** *m* FOTO portrait attachment

Verladeband *nt* TRANS loading conveyor

Verladebrücke *f* EISENBAHN, TRANS, WASSERTRANS loading bridge

verladen *vt* WASSERTRANS *Ladung* ship

Verladeschein *m* WASSERTRANS shipping note

Verlag *m* DRUCK publishing company, publishing house

Verlagerung *f* WASSERTRANS *Schiffbau* shifting

Verlag: **Verlagswesen** *nt* DRUCK publishing industry

verlängern *vt* BAU stretch

verlängert[1] *adj* GEOM prolate, MECHAN elongated

verlängert:[2] ~**e Doppel-Zeppelinantenne** *f* RADIO extended double Zepp; ~**es Flugzeug** *nt* LUFTTRANS stretched aircraft; ~**er Sattelpunkt** *m* METALL extended node; **~e Standzeit** *f* MASCHINEN extended tool life; **~e Viertelwellenantenne mit Gegengewicht** *f* RADIO extended ground plane

Verlängerung *f* TELEKOM *Zeit* extension; **~ von Fristen** *f* PATENT extension of time limits; **Verlängerungskabel** *nt* ELEKTROTECH extension cable; **Verlängerungsrohr** *nt* LABOR expansion tube, extension tube, MASCHINEN lengthening tube; **Verlängerungsspule** *f* RADIO loading coil; **Verlängerungsstange** *f* MASCHINEN lengthening rod; **Verlängerungsstößel** *m* KOHLEN *Pfahlgründung* follower; **Verlängerungsstück** *nt* MASCHINEN extension piece, lengthening bar, lengthening piece; **Verlängerungsstutzen** *m* MASCHINEN extension socket; **Verlängerungstubus** *nt* FOTO extension tube

Verlangsamung *f* RAUMFAHRT deceleration, TRANS slowing down; **Verlangsamungsmesser** *m* RAUMFAHRT decelerometer; **Verlangsamungsvorrichtung** *f* TRANS deceleration device

Verlaschen *nt* FERTIG fishing, jointing

verlaschen *vt* BAU joint, FERTIG fish, strap

verlascht: ~er Schienenstoß *m* EISENBAHN fishplated rail joint

verlassen *vt* COMP & DV *Programm* exit

Verläßlichkeit *f* ELEKTRIZ reliability

Verlauf *m* BAU *einer Straße* course, KUNSTSTOFF flow

Verlaufen *nt* FERTIG *Bohrer* deviation, drift, run-out, MASCHINEN drift, running out of center (AmE), running out of centre (BrE), wandering

verlaufen[1] *vt* FERTIG *Bohrer* divert

verlaufen[2] *vi* BAU spread, *Farbe* run

verlaufend: ~es Weiß *nt* FERNSEH bleeding whites

Verläufer *m* ERDÖL *Bohrmeißel* diverter

Verlauf: Verlauffilter *nt* FOTO graduated filter; **Verlaufhilfsmittel** *nt* KUNSTSTOFF coalescing agent; **Verlaufmittel** *nt* KUNSTSTOFF coalescing agent; **Verlaufschreiber** *m* ELEKTRIZ event recorder

verlegbar: ~e Steckdose *f* ELEKTRIZ portable socket outlet

Verlegelänge *f* TELEKOM laying length

Verlegen *nt* BAU setting; **~ von Elektroleitungen** *nt* BAU electric wiring

verlegen *vt* BAU pave, place, *Leitungen* lay, *Rohre* lay, FERTIG install, TELEKOM lay

Verleger *m* DRUCK publisher

Verlegung *f* BAU laying, FERTIG *Rohre* installation

Verleimen *nt* BAU bonding

verleimen *vt* BAU, MECHAN bond

Verleimung *f* MECHAN bonding

Verletzer *m* PATENT infringer

Verletzung[1] *f* PATENT infringement, SICHERHEIT injury; **~ am Arbeitsplatz** *f* SICHERHEIT injury in the work-place; **~ durch Stromschlag** *f* RADIO electrocution **~ in der Industrie** *f* SICHERHEIT industrial injury; **~ der Sicherheitsvorschriften** *f* SICHERHEIT breach of safety rules

Verletzung:[2] **~ darstellen** *vi* PATENT constitute infringement

Verletzungen: ~ verursachend *adj* SICHERHEIT injurious

verlitzen *vt* FERTIG strand

Verlitzung *f* FERTIG stranding

verloren: ~e Betonschalung *f* BAU permanent concrete shuttering; **~er Kopf** *m* FERTIG shrink head, *Gießen* feeding head, sinkhead; **~e Schalung** *f* BAU permanent shuttering

verlöschen *vi* ELEKTRIZ *Lichtbogen* blow out

Verlötungsgefahr *f* SICHERHEIT brazing hazard

Verlust *m* ELEKTROTECH leakage, ERDÖL *an Bohrschlamm*, MASCHINEN, OPTIK, TELEKOM loss; **~ durch Antennenausrichtungsfehler** *m* TELEKOM antenna-pointing loss; **~ durch falsche Kopfausrichtung** *m* AUFNAHME head misalignment loss; **~ durch Längsversatz** *m* OPTIK longitudinal offset loss; **~ durch Rückdiffusion** *m* KERNTECH back diffusion loss; **~ durch seitlichen Versatz** *m* OPTIK lateral offset loss; **~ durch transversalen Versatz** *m* OPTIK transverse offset loss; **~ im Koppelelement** *m* OPTIK *zwischen Lichtleitern* coupler loss; **~ im Koppler** *m* TELEKOM coupler loss; **~ im Kühlsystem** *m* HEIZ & KÄLTE ventilating and cooling loss; **~ im Ruhezustand** *m* ELEKTRIZ no-load loss; **~ auf See** *m* WASSERTRANS marine loss; **~ im unbelasteten Zustand** *m* ELEKTRIZ no-load loss; **~ des Unterscheidungsvermögens** *m* ERGON discrimination loss; **~ an äußerer Verbindungsstelle** *m* OPTIK extrinsic joint loss, extrinsic junction loss;

verlustarm[1] *adj* ELEKTRIZ low loss

verlustarm:[2] **~es Dielektrikum** *nt* ELEKTRIZ low-loss dielectric; **~e Diode** *f* ELEKTRONIK low-leakage diode; **~e Faser** *f* OPTIK low-loss fiber (AmE), low-loss fibre (BrE); **~es Glas** *nt* KER & GLAS low-loss glass; **~er Isolator** *m* ELEKTROTECH low-loss insulator; **~es Kabel** *nt* ELEKTRIZ low-loss cable

verlustbehaftet[1] *adj* ELEKTROTECH lossy

verlustbehaftet:[2] **~e Leitung** *f* PHYS lossy line; **~e Mode** *f* OPTIK *Lichtleiter* leaky mode; **~er Strahl** *m* OPTIK leaky ray

Verlust: Verlustbetrieb *m* TELEKOM loss mode working; **Verlustdämpfung** *f* GERÄT loss attenuation; **Verlustenergie zerstreuendes Medium** *nt* PHYS dissipative medium; **Verlustfaktor** *m* ELEKTRIZ dissipation factor, loss factor, LUFTTRANS alleviating factor

verlustfrei *adj* ELEKTRIZ loss-free, ELEKTROTECH lossless

Verlust: Verlustleistung *f* ELEKTROTECH dissipation, HEIZ & KÄLTE heat loss, RADIO dissipation; **Verlustleitung** *f* ELEKTROTECH lossy line

verlustlos[1] *adj* ELEKTROTECH lossless

verlustlos:[2] **~es Dielektrikum** *nt* ELEKTRIZ perfect dielectric; **~e Leitung** *f* TELEKOM zero-loss circuit

Verlust: Verlustmessung *f* GERÄT loss measurement; **Verlustraum** *m* HYDRAUL waste space

verlustreich[1] *adj* ELEKTROTECH lossy

verlustreich:[2] **~es Dielektrikum** *nt* ELEKTRIZ absorptive dielectric

Verlust: Verlustschmierung *f* MASCHINEN total loss lubrication; **Verluststrom** *m* ELEKTROTECH leakage current; **Verlustverkehr** *m* TELEKOM lost traffic; **Verlustwärme** *f* HEIZ & KÄLTE heat loss; **Verlustwiderstand eines Dielektrikums** *m* ELEKTRIZ dielectric leakage resistance; **Verlustwinkel** *m* ELEKTRIZ, PHYS loss angle; **Verlustzeit** *f* COMP & DV dead time

Vermahlung *f* KERNTECH comminution

vermascht[1] *adj* ELEKTRIZ interconnected

vermascht:[2] **~e Netzwerke** *nt pl* ELEKTRIZ connected networks; **~es Netzwerk** *nt* ELEKTRIZ meshed network

Vermaschung *f* ELEKTRIZ, FERTIG interconnection

Vermeidung: ~ von Lärmbelästigung *f* UMWELTSCHMUTZ prevention of noise pollution

vermengen *vt* TEXTIL blend

vermessen *vt* MEERSCHMUTZ survey, METROL measure

Vermesser *m* BAU surveyor

vermessingen *vt* FERTIG, METALL brass

Vermessung *f* BAU survey, surveying, topographical survey, METROL, WASSERTRANS survey, surveying; **Ver-**

messungsgrundlinie *f* BAU transit line; **Vermessungs-instrument** *nt* BAU surveyor's transit, *mit portablem Dreibockständer* Y-level; **Vermessungsstange** *f* BAU stadia; **Vermessungsstation** *f* WASSERTRANS geodesic station; **Vermessungstiefe** *f* WASSERTRANS *Schiffkonstruktion* registered depth; **Vermessungswesen** *nt* WASSERTRANS surveying

vermieten: ~ **an** *vt* WASSERTRANS *Schiff* charter to

vermindern *vt* COMP & DV decrement

vermindert: ~**es Intervall** *nt* AKUSTIK diminished interval

vermischen *vt* ANSTRICH agitate, compound, BAU, TEXTIL blend

vermischt: ~**e Abwasserbehandlung** *f* WASSERVERSORG mixed sewage treatment; ~**e Synchronsignale** *nt pl* FERNSEH mixed syncs

Vermitteln *nt* COMP & DV switching

vermitteln *vt* TELEKOM *Telefon* switch

vermittelt: ~**e Leitung** *f* TELEKOM switched circuit

Vermittlung:[1] **über ~ hergestellt** *adj* TELEKOM switched

Vermittlung[2] *f* COMP & DV switching, TELEKOM exchange, *Telefon* switching; ~ **über virtuelle Verbindung** *f* TELEKOM VCS, virtual-circuit switch; **Vermittlungsablauf** *m* TELEKOM call processing; **Vermittlungsamt** *nt* TELEKOM central office switch (AmE); **Vermittlungseinheit** *f* TELEKOM *ISDN* switching unit; **Vermittlungseinrichtung** *f* COMP & DV switching equipment, TELEKOM *Telefon* switching device; **Vermittlungsknoten über virtuelle Verbindung** *m* TELEKOM virtual-circuit switching node; **Vermittlungsnetz** *nt* TELEKOM switched network; **Vermittlungsplatz** *m* TELEKOM operating position, operator position; **Vermittlungsprogramm** *nt* TELEKOM switching program; **Vermittlungsrechner** *m* TELEKOM switching processor, switching system; **Vermittlungsschicht** *f* COMP & DV network layer, TELEKOM switched network layer; **Vermittlungsschrank** *m* ELEKTROTECH switchboard, TELEKOM board, switchboard, telephone switchboard; **Vermittlungsschrank-Querverbindungsleitung** *f* TELEKOM interswitchboard tie circuit; **Vermittlungsschrankreihe** *f* TELEKOM suite of switchboards; **Vermittlungsstelle** *f* TELEKOM switch, switching center (AmE), switching centre (BrE); **Vermittlungsstelle mit Handbetrieb** *f* TELEKOM manual exchange; **Vermittlungsstelle mit Zeitteilung** *f* TELEKOM *Telefon* time switch; **Vermittlungssystem** *nt* COMP & DV, TELEKOM switching system; **Vermittlungssystem für mehrere Bitraten** *nt* TELEKOM multirate switching system; **Vermittlungssystem mit Reed-Relais** *nt* TELEKOM reed relay system; **Vermittlungssystem mit Zentralsteuerung** *f* TELEKOM common-control switching system; **Vermittlungstheorie** *f* COMP & DV switching theory; **Vermittlungszentrale mit Zeitteilung** *f* TELEKOM time division exchange

Vermodern *nt* BAU rotting

vermodern *vi* BAU *Holz* rot

Vermoderung *f* CHEMIE decomposition

vermörteln *vt* BAU grout

Vermörtelung *f* BAU cement stabilization

Vernadelung *f* TEXTIL needling

Vernetzen *nt* KUNSTSTOFF cure

vernetzen *vt* KUNSTSTOFF cross-link, cross-linking, cure

Vernetzer *m* KUNSTSTOFF cross-linking agent, curing agent

vernetzt: ~**es Polyethylen** *nt* (*VPE*) KUNSTSTOFF cross-linked polyethylene (*XPE*)

Vernetzung *f* COMP & DV network, KUNSTSTOFF cross-linking, curing; **Vernetzungsgeschwindigkeit** *f* KUNSTSTOFF cure rate, rate of cure; **Vernetzungsmittel** *nt* KUNSTSTOFF cross-linking agent, curing agent; **Vernetzungsstelle** *f* KUNSTSTOFF cross link

Verneuil-Methode *f* OPTIK *Aufdampfung nach Verneuil* vapor phase verneuil method (AmE), vapour phase verneuil method (BrE)

Vernichtung *f* TEILPHYS annihilation; **Vernichtungsstrahlung** *f* STRAHLPHYS annihilation radiation

vernickeln *vt* FERTIG nickelize

vernieten *vt* FERTIG rivet, rivet up

Vernin *nt* CHEMIE vernine

vernuten *vt* FERTIG tongue

veröffentlichen *vt* DRUCK, PATENT publish

Verordnung *f* TELEKOM *Regel* regulation; **Verordnungsstrategie** *f* TRANS regulation strategy

verpacken *vt* PAPIER wrap

verpackt: ~**e Waren** *f pl* VERPACK parceled goods (AmE), parcelled goods (BrE)

Verpackung: ~ **in geregelter Atmosphäre** *f* (*CA-Verpackung*) VERPACK controlled-atmosphere packaging (*CAP*); **für Mikrowellen geeignete** ~ *n* VERPACK microwaveable packaging; ~ **aus verschäumtem Kunststoff** *f* VERPACK plastic foam packaging; **Verpackungs- und Entpackungsmaschine** *f* VERPACK *für Ampullen* case packing and unpacking; **Verpackungsabfall** *m* ABFALL packaging waste; **Verpackungsband für Ballen** *nt* VERPACK bale hoop; **Verpackungsbandeisen** *nt* METALL, VERPACK hoop iron; **Verpackungsbereich** *m* KER & GLAS packer's bay; **Verpackungslinie** *f* VERPACK packaging line; **Verpackungslinie für Flüssigstoffe** *f* VERPACK liquid packaging line; **Verpackungsmaschine** *f* TEXTIL packer, VERPACK boxing machine; **Verpackungsmaterial** *nt* ABFALL packaging material; **Verpackungsmüll** *m* ABFALL packaging waste; **Verpackungsprofil** *nt* VERPACK packaging profile; **Verpackungsprüfung** *f* VERPACK package test; **Verpackungsstation** *f* VERPACK packaging station, packing station; **Verpackungstablett** *nt* VERPACK *für Obst, Kuchen* punnet tray; **Verpackungszeichnung** *f* KONSTZEICH packing drawing

verpuffen *vt* SICHERHEIT deflagrate

Verpuffungsstrahlrohr *nt* TRANS aeropulse

Verputz *m* BAU coating, plaster

Verputzen *nt* BAU coating, plaster work, plastering

verputzen *vt* BAU torch

Verrauchung: ~ **der Umwelt** *f* UMWELTSCHMUTZ fumigation

verrauscht: ~**e Schwarzwerte** *m pl* FERNSEH noisy blacks; ~**es Signal** *nt* ELEKTRONIK signal buried in noise, FERNSEH degraded signal; ~**e Synchronisierung** *f* FERNSEH degraded sync

Verrauschtsein *nt* FERNSEH degradation

Verreibwalze *f* DRUCK distributing roller mechanism

verrichten *vt* TELEKOM perform

verriegelbar: ~**er Steckverbinder** *m* ELEKTROTECH lockable connector

verriegeln *vt* BAU block, bolt, COMP & DV interlock, latch, lock, ELEKTROTECH interlock, FERTIG interconnect, KONTROLL block, MASCHINEN lock, MECHAN bolt, SICHERHEIT lock

verriegelt: ~**e Weiche** *f* EISENBAHN locked switch

Verriegelung *f* BAU keeper, COMP & DV interlock, latch, ELEKTROTECH interlock, latching, HYDRAUL shutter,

KERNTECH locking, *eines Steuerstabes* latch, LUFT-TRANS, MECHAN interlock, SICHERHEIT *feuerbeständiger Türen* locking device; **Verriegelungsbolzen** *m* BAU locking bolt; **Verriegelungseinrichtung** *f* BAU lock staple; **Verriegelungskontakt** *m* ELEKTROTECH interlock contact; **Verriegelungsrelais** *nt* ELEKTRIZ interlock relay, interlocking relay, ELEKTROTECH interlock relay; **Verriegelungsschalter** *m* ELEKTROTECH interlock switch; **Verriegelungsschaltung** *f* ELEKTROTECH interlock circuit, FERNSEH interlock; **Verriegelungssignal** *nt* ELEKTRONIK inhibiting signal; **Verriegelungssystem** *nt* AUFNAHME interlocking system; **Verriegelungsventil** *nt* LUFTTRANS *Flugwesen* lock-out valve; **Verriegelungsvorrichtung** *f* VERPACK interlocking device
verringern *vt* COMP & DV decrement
Verringerung: ~ **des Jojo-Effekts** *f* RAUMFAHRT *Raumschiff* yoyo despin
verrippen *vt* FERTIG rib
verrohren *vt* ERDÖL *Bohrung* tube
Verrohrung *f* BAU piping, tubing; **Verrohrungsbühne** *f* ERDÖL *Bohrtechnik* stabbing board; **Verrohrungskopf** *m* ERDÖL *Bohrung* bradenhead; **Verrohrungsseil** *nt* BAU casing line
verrottbar: ~**er Stoff** *m* ABFALL putrescible matter
verrotten *vi* BAU rot
verrücken *vt* BAU *Gebäude* dislodge
verrühren *vt* ANSTRICH agitate
Versagen *nt* ELEKTROTECH, MECHAN failure, TELEKOM *Stromversorgung* breakdown; **versagen** *vi* BAU break down, MECHAN fail, PHYS break down **versagen ~ des Reziprozitätsgesetztes** *nt* FOTO reciprocity failure; **Versagenskriterium** *nt* MECHAN criterion of failure
Versalhöhe *f* DRUCK capital height, height of capital letters
Versand *m* WASSERTRANS shipping; **Versandaktion** *f* COMP & DV mailing; **Versandbedingungen** *f pl* WASSERTRANS shipping terms; **Versandfaß für Einzelelemente** *nt* KERNTECH *für Brennelemente* single element shipping cask; **Versandhülle** *f* VERPACK mailing sleeve; **Versandkiste** *f* TEXTIL packing case; **Versandkontrolle** *f* QUAL shipping inspection; **Versandpapiere** *nt pl* WASSERTRANS shipping documents; **Versandprobe** *f* QUAL shipping sample; **Versandrolle** *f* VERPACK mailing tube, postal tubes; **Versandtasche** *f* VERPACK wallet-type envelope; **Versandzeichnung** *f* KONSTZEICH dispatch drawing
Versatz *m* BAU break joint, FERNSEH staggering, MASCHINEN displacement, misalignment, offset; **Versatzsatz** *m* KONSTZEICH parallel offset
versauern *vi* CHEMIE *Boden* acidify
Versauerung *f* UMWELTSCHMUTZ *des Bodens* acidification
Verschachteln *nt* COMP & DV nesting, FERNSEH interleaving
verschachteln *vt* COMP & DV interlace, interleave, nest, ELEKTRONIK interleave
verschachtelt[1] *adj* COMP & DV nested
verschachtelt:[2] ~**er Makroaufruf** *m* COMP & DV nested macrocall; ~**e Prozedur** *f* COMP & DV nested procedure; ~**e Schleife** *f* COMP & DV nested loop; ~**es Sendesignal** *nt* FERNSEH interleaved transmission signal; ~**e Struktur** *f* COMP & DV nested structure; ~**e Wicklung** *f* ELEKTROTECH banked winding
Verschachtelung *f* COMP & DV nesting; **Verschachtelungsebene** *f* COMP & DV nesting level;

Verschachtelungsgrad *m* COMP & DV nesting level; **Verschachtelungsspeicher** *m* COMP & DV nesting store
verschalen *vt* BAU board, timber, *mit Leisten* batten
verschalken *vt* WASSERTRANS *Luken* batten down
Verschalung *f* BAU timbering, *mit Bohlen* planking
verschärft: ~**er AQL-Wert** *m* QUAL reduced AQL value; ~**e Inspektion** *f* KERNTECH tightened inspection; ~**e Prüfung** *f* QUAL increased inspection, tightened inspection
Verschicken *nt* COMP & DV mailing
verschiebbar[1] *adj* COMP & DV relocatable, FERTIG traveling (AmE), travelling (BrE)
verschiebbar:[2] ~**e Adresse** *f* COMP & DV relocatable address; ~**er Ausdruck** *m* COMP & DV relocatable expression; ~**e Daten** *nt pl* COMP & DV relocatable data; ~**es Format** *nt* COMP & DV relocatable format; ~**er Kern** *m* ELEKTRIZ movable core; ~**es Programm** *nt* COMP & DV relocatable program
Verschiebebahnhof *m* EISENBAHN classification yard, marshalling yard (BrE), switchyard (AmE), shunting yard, switching station (AmE)
Verschiebedienst *m* EISENBAHN shunting
Verschiebegleis *nt* EISENBAHN classification yard line, sorting line
Verschiebelok *f* EISENBAHN shunter
Verschieben *nt* EISENBAHN switching (AmE), FERTIG traversing
verschieben[1] *vt* BAU displace, COMP & DV relocate, shift, ELEKTROTECH *Bürsten* displace
verschieben:[2] **sich ~** *v refl* WASSERTRANS *Ladung* shift
Verschieberegister *nt* COMP & DV shift register
Verschiebewiderstand *m* MASCHINEN resistance to motion
Verschiebung *f* BAU *räumlich, zeitlich* offset, COMP & DV relocation, COMP & DV *(D)*, ELEKTRIZ *(D)*, ELEKTROTECH *(D)* displacement *(D)*, FERNSEH shift, KERNTECH shift, travel, KONTROLL *(D)* displacement *(D)*, PHYS displacement, translation, RADIO drift, RAUMFAHRT *Raumschiff* drift, *Weltraumfunk* shift; **Verschiebungsstörzone** *f* KERNTECH displacement spike; **Verschiebungsstrom** *m* ELEKTROTECH, PHYS displacement current
verschiefern *vt* BAU split into thin sheets
verschießen *vt* TEXTIL *Farbe* fade
Verschiffung *f* WASSERTRANS shipment; **Verschiffungsgewicht** *nt* WASSERTRANS *Ladung* shipping weight; **Verschiffungskosten** *m pl* WASSERTRANS shipping; **Verschiffungsspediteur** *m* WASSERTRANS shipping agent
Verschlackung *f* KERNTECH *Akkumulation von Spaltprodukten* slagging
verschlämmen *vt* WASSERVERSORG blind
Verschlammung *f* ABFALL sludge accumulation, CHEMIE silting, WASSERVERSORG silting-up
verschlechtern: **sich ~** *v refl* VERPACK deteriorate
verschlechtert: ~**e Betriebsbedingungen** *f pl* RAUMFAHRT degraded operating conditions
Verschlechterung *f* COMP & DV degradation, VERPACK deterioration
Verschleiß[1] *m* BAU attrition, ELEKTRIZ wearout, FERTIG *durch Auswaschung* cavitation, KER & GLAS scuffing, KERNTECH *durch Reibung* galling, KUNSTSTOFF abrasive wear, MASCHINEN wear, MECHAN abrasion, compensation for wear, wear, MEERSCHMUTZ wear, PAPIER wear, TEXTIL wear and tear; **durch ~ bedingte Formabweichung vom Kreis** *f* KFZTECH out of round wear

Verschleiß:[2] ~ **ausgleichen** *vi* MECHAN compensate for wear; ~ **kompensieren** *vi* MECHAN compensate for wear

Verschleiß: **Verschleißanzeige** *f* MASCHINEN wear indicator; **Verschleißausgleich** *m* MECHAN compensation for wear

verschleißbeständig *adj* MASCHINEN hardwearing, wear-resistant

Verschleiß: **Verschleißbeständigkeit** *f* MASCHINEN wear resistance; **Verschleißblech** *nt* MASCHINEN wear plate, wearing plate

verschleißen *vt* MASCHINEN wear, wear down, wear off, wear out

verschleißend[1] *adj* FERTIG abrasive

verschleißend:[2] ~ **wirken** *vt* FERTIG wear

Verschleiß: **Verschleißfaktor** *m* MECHAN abrasion factor; **Verschleißfehler** *m* KERNTECH wearout defect

verschleißfest *adj* FERTIG wear-resistant, MASCHINEN hardwearing, resistant to wear, wear-resistant

Verschleiß: **Verschleißfestigkeit** *f* BAU *Beton* abrasion resistance, FERTIG abrasion resistance, wear resistance, KUNSTSTOFF abrasion resistance, MASCHINEN resistance to wear, wear resistance; **Verschleißfestigkeitskennzahl** *f* KUNSTSTOFF abrasion resistance index; **Verschleißfortschritt** *m* FERTIG amount of wear

verschleißfrei *adj* FERTIG free from wear, wearless, MASCHINEN no-wear

Verschleiß: **Verschleißgrenze** *f* MASCHINEN wear limit; **Verschleißkehle** *f* EISENBAHN hollow tread; **Verschleißkomponente** *f* KERNTECH wearing element

verschleißlos *adj* MASCHINEN no-wear

Verschleiß: **Verschleißmarke** *f* FERTIG wear mark; **Verschleißmarkenbreite** *f* FERTIG wear land value, width of wear mark; **Verschleißmessung** *f* FERTIG wear measurement; **Verschleißplatte** *f* FERTIG wearing plate; **Verschleißprozeß** *m* MASCHINEN wear process; **Verschleißprüfmaschine** *f* MECHAN abrasion tester; **Verschleißschicht** *f* BAU surface dressing, veneer, wearing course, MASCHINEN wearing surface; **Verschleißteil** *nt* FERTIG *Kunststoffinstallationen* worn part, KERNTECH wearing detail, working part, KOHLEN wearing part, MASCHINEN wear part, wearing part; **Verschleißteilzeichnung** *f* KONSTZEICH drawing dealing with wearing parts; **Verschleißverhalten** *nt* FERTIG wear behavior (AmE), wear behaviour (BrE); **Verschleißvolumen** *nt* FERTIG volume of metal worn away; **Verschleißwert** *m* BAU wear rate; **Verschleißwiderstand** *m* KUNSTSTOFF abrasion resistance

Verschlickung *f* CHEMIE silting

Verschließen *nt* BAU sealing, ERDÖL plugging

verschließen *vt* ANSTRICH seal, BAU cap, lock, SICHERHEIT lock

Verschließmaschine *f* VERPACK closing machine

verschlissen: ~ **er Bohrmeißel** *m* ERDÖL *Tiefbohrtechnik* worn bit

verschlossen[1] *adj* MEERSCHMUTZ sealed

verschlossen:[2] ~ **er Kanal** *m* WASSERVERSORG locked canal

Verschluß *m* BAU shutter, ERDÖL plug, FOTO *Kamera*, HYDRAUL shutter, KER & GLAS *einer Flasche* finish, LUFTTRANS interlocking, MECHAN blind, seal, VERPACK closure; ~ **mit Außengewinde** *m* KER & GLAS external-screw-thread finish; ~ **mit B-Einstellung** *m* FOTO shutter with B setting; **Verschlußauslöser** *m* FOTO shutter release; **Verschlußauslösung** *f* FOTO shutter release; **Verschlußdecke** *f* BAU *Straßenbau* seal

coat; **Verschlußdeckel** *m* KFZTECH filler cap, MECHAN cover

Verschlüssel-Fertigungslinie *f* VERPACK closure production line

verschlüsseln *vt* COMP & DV encode, ELEKTRONIK encipher, encrypt

verschlüsselt[1] *adj* RAUMFAHRT *Weltraumfunk* cryptographic

verschlüsselt:[2] ~ **e Sprache** *f* TELEKOM encrypted speech

Verschlüsselung *f* COMP & DV encryption, ELEKTRONIK encipherment, encryption, RADIO encryption, RAUMFAHRT cryptography, encryption, TELEKOM coding, encoding; **Verschlüsselungschip** *m* COMP & DV, ELEKTRONIK encryption chip; **Verschlüsselungsgerät** *nt* FERNSEH encryption; **Verschlüsselungsmuster** *nt* RAUMFAHRT filter template; **Verschlüsselungsschema** *nt* ELEKTRONIK coding scheme; **Verschlüsselungsvorlage** *f* RAUMFAHRT filter mask

Verschluß: **Verschlußhaken** *m* EISENBAHN locking hook; **Verschlußhülse** *f* VERPACK strapping seal; **Verschlußkappe** *f* KER & GLAS screw cap; **Verschlußlamelle** *f* FOTO shutter blade

Verschlüssler *m* FERTIG encoder

Verschluß: **Verschlußloch** *nt* BAU plughole; **Verschlußmutter** *f* FERTIG *Kunststoffinstallationen* valve nut; **Verschlußspannknopf** *m* FOTO shutter-cocking knob; **Verschlußstein** *m* KER & GLAS tweel block; **Verschlußstopfen** *m* MASCHINEN obturating plug, sealing plug, stopper; **Verschlußstück** *nt* MASCHINEN cap; **Verschlußzeit** *f* FOTO shutter speed; **Verschlußzeiteinstellknopf** *m* FOTO shutter speed setting knob; **Verschlußzeiteinstellung** *f* FOTO shutter speed setting; **Verschlußzeitkontrolle** *f* FOTO shutter speed control

verschmelzen *vt* FERTIG coalesce

Verschmelzung *f* ERGON, PHYS fusion

verschmieden *vt* FERTIG *Schmieden* cog

verschmieren *vt* FERTIG lute

verschmiert: ~ **er Kopf** *m* FERNSEH clogged head

verschmolzen: ~ **e Bifokallinsen** *f pl* KER & GLAS fused bifocals; ~ **es Bündel** *nt* KER & GLAS fused bundle

verschmutzen *vt* KOHLEN contaminate, SICHERHEIT pollute

verschmutzt[1] *adj* UMWELTSCHMUTZ polluted

verschmutzt:[2] ~ **er Buchstabe** *m* DRUCK pick; ~ **es Regenwasser** *nt* UMWELTSCHMUTZ polluted rainwater; ~ **es Wasser** *nt* WASSERVERSORG polluted water

Verschmutzung *f* KOHLEN contamination; ~ **durch Feststoffe** *f* UMWELTSCHMUTZ material pollution; **Verschmutzungsgrad** *m* HEIZ & KÄLTE fouling factor, UMWELTSCHMUTZ degree of pollution; **Verschmutzungsgrad des Wassers** *m* UMWELTSCHMUTZ pollutional index; **Verschmutzungsüberwachung** *f* GERÄT contamination monitoring

Verschneiden *nt* LEBENSMITTEL blending

verschneiden *vt* BAU mix, FERTIG *Flüssigkeiten* blend, LEBENSMITTEL adulterate, TEXTIL blend

Verschnitt *m* TEXTIL blend, VERPACK offcut; **Verschnittbitumen** *nt* BAU cut back; **Verschnittmittel** *nt* CHEMIE, KUNSTSTOFF diluent; **Verschnittöl** *nt* ERDÖL extender oil

verschoben: ~ **es Atom** *nt* KERNTECH displaced atom; ~ **e Oberfläche** *f* KER & GLAS shifted finish

verschränken *vi* TEXTIL interlock

Verschrauben *nt* MASCHINEN screwing

verschrauben *vt* FERTIG bolt, MASCHINEN screw

Verschraubung *f* BAU bolting, union, ERDÖL screwing,

FERTIG *Kunststoffinstallationen* union, MASCHINEN bolted joint, bolting, screw joint, SICHERHEIT bolting; **Verschraubungsteile** *nt pl* MASCHINEN threaded components

verschrotten *vt* QUAL scrap

Verschwelung *f* CHEMIE charring

Verschwindungspunkt *m* GEOM, KONSTZEICH vanishing point

verschwommen: **~es Bild** *nt* PHYS blurred image

Verscrambelungssteuerung *f* TELEKOM scrambling control

versehen: **~ mit** *adj* TELEKOM fitted with

Verseifbarkeit *f* FERTIG saponifiability

verseifen *vt* FERTIG saponify

Verseifung *f* CHEMIE, FERTIG saponification; **Verseifungsmittel** *nt* CHEMIE saponifier; **Verseifungszahl** *f* LEBENSMITTEL *Fettkennzahl* saponification number

Verseilen *nt* FERTIG cabling

verseilt: **~es Kabel** *nt* ELEKTROTECH stranded cable

Versenden *nt* COMP & DV mailing

versenden *vt* COMP & DV send

Versendung *f* TRANS consignment

versengen *vt* KOHLEN char, THERMOD scorch

versengt *adj* THERMOD scorched

versenkbar: **~e Antenne** *f* LUFTTRANS flush aerial; **~e Linse** *f* FOTO flush lens

Versenken *nt* BAU plunging, MECHAN *Schraubenkopf* counterboring

versenken *vt* WASSERTRANS scuttle, *Schiff* sink

versenkt: **~e Antenne** *f* TELEKOM flush antenna; **~es Einsetzen** *nt* FOTO sunk mount, sunk setting; **~e Fassung** *f* FOTO countersunk mount, countersunk setting, *Objektiv* sunk mount, sunk setting; **~er Kanal** *m* ELEKTRONIK buried channel, *Transistortechnik* buried channel; **~es Schloß** *nt* BAU dormant lock

versetzt[1] *adj* MASCHINEN offset, staggered; **mit ~er Bewegungsebene** *adj* FERTIG drunken

versetzt:[2] **~e Fuge** *f* BAU broken joint; **~e Köpfe** *m pl* AUFNAHME, FERNSEH staggered heads; **~e Schwelle** *f* LUFTTRANS *Start- und Landebahn* displaced threshold

versetzt:[3] **~ zeichnen** *vt* KONSTZEICH draw staggered

Versetzung *f* AKUSTIK transposition, ELEKTROTECH *(D)*, FERTIG *(D) Kristall* displacement *(D)*, MASCHINEN offset, PHYS *(D)* displacement *(D)*, WASSERTRANS drift; **Versetzungsannihilation** *f* METALL dislocation annihilation; **Versetzungsdichte** *f* METALL dislocation density; **Versetzungsgeschwindigkeit** *f* METALL dislocation velocity; **Versetzungskern** *m* METALL dislocation core; **Versetzungsknickung** *f* METALL dislocation kink; **Versetzungsmast** *m* ELEKTRIZ transposition tower; **Versetzungsschutt** *m* METALL dislocation debris; **Versetzungsverbindung** *f* METALL dislocation junction; **Versetzungsverlust** *m* OPTIK misalignment loss

verseuchen *vt* KERNTECH, SICHERHEIT contaminate

Verseuchung *f* KERNTECH, RAUMFAHRT, SICHERHEIT contamination, UMWELTSCHMUTZ contamination, *radioaktiv* contamination; **Verseuchungsmesser** *m* SICHERHEIT contamination meter

Versickern *nt* MEERSCHMUTZ seepage

Versickerung *f* ABFALL *Abwasserreinigung* infiltration, KOHLEN, WASSERVERSORG seepage; **Versickerungsbecken** *nt* WASSERVERSORG infiltration gallery; **Versickerungsbrunnen** *m* WASSERVERSORG injection well

versiegeln *vt* ANSTRICH, BAU seal

versiegelt: **~er Kühlkreislauf** *m* KFZTECH sealed cooling system; **~es Präparat** *nt* KERNTECH sealed source

Versiegelung *f* SICHERHEIT tamper-proof seal; **Versiegelungsmittel** *nt* ANSTRICH sealant

Versiegler *m* VERPACK sealing machine

Versilbern *nt* FERTIG *Galvanostegie* silver plating

versilbert[1] *adj* FERTIG silver-plated

versilbert:[2] **~e Gegenstände** *m pl* METALL *nur in England gebräuchlich* electroplated nickel silver *(EPNS)*

Versilberung *f* FERTIG silvering; **Versilberungsförderband** *nt* KER & GLAS conveyor for silvering

Version *f* COMP & DV *eines Programms* release, version, MASCHINEN version; **neueste ~** *f* COMP & DV update *eines Programms* current version

versorgen *vt* BAU, ELEKTRIZ supply

versorgend: **~es Amt** *nt* TELEKOM serving exchange

Versorger *m* WASSERTRANS *Schifftyp* supply vessel, support vessel

Versorgung *f* RADIO coverage; **Versorgungsanschluß** *m* RAUMFAHRT umbilical connector; **Versorgungsbasis** *f* ERDÖL *Offshore-Technik* supply base; **Versorgungsbehälter** *m* KFZTECH supply tank; **Versorgungsbereich** *m* LUFTTRANS service area, RADIO coverage area; **Versorgungsbereich einer Relaisstelle** *m* RADIO repeater coverage area; **Versorgungseinrichtung** *f* BAU, RAUMFAHRT utility; **Versorgungsfahrzeug** *nt* LUFTTRANS service vehicle; **Versorgungsgrad** *m* TELEKOM degree of coverage; **Versorgungshauptleitung** *f* ELEKTROTECH supply main; **Versorgungskanal** *m* WASSERVERSORG delivery race; **Versorgungsleitung** *f* BAU supply pipe, utility line, ELEKTROTECH feeder, RAUMFAHRT umbilical cable; **Versorgungsluft-Manometer** *nt* GERÄT air supply gage (AmE), air supply gauge (BrE); **Versorgungsmast** *m* RAUMFAHRT umbilical mast; **Versorgungspumpe** *f* MEERSCHMUTZ supply pump; **Versorgungsraumfahrzeug** *nt* RAUMFAHRT cargo vehicle; **Versorgungssatellit** *m* RAUMFAHRT utility satellite; **Versorgungsschaltung** *f* ELEKTRIZ feed circuit; **Versorgungsschiff** *nt* WASSERTRANS replenishing ship, supply boat, support vessel, tender, *Schifftyp* supply vessel, support vessel; **Versorgungsspannungs-Überwachung** *f* REGELUNG power fail circuit; **Versorgungstelemetrie** *f* RAUMFAHRT housekeeping telemetry

Verspachteln *nt* BAU stopping

verspannen *vt* FERTIG rig

Verspannung *f* EISENBAHN *von Laschen* application

verspannungslos: **~er Flügel** *m* LUFTTRANS cantilever wing

Verspannung: **Verspannungs-Meßgerät** *nt* LABOR strain gage (AmE), strain gauge (BrE)

verspätet: **~e Ausstrahlung** *f* FERNSEH delayed broadcast

versperren *vt* BAU barricade

verspiegelt: **~e Lampe** *f* FOTO mirror-coated lamp

Verspiegelung *f* KER & GLAS mirror plating, silvering

Verspinnen *nt* KER & GLAS, TEXTIL spinning

Verspleißung *f* EISENBAHN splice joint

Versplinten *nt* MASCHINEN cottering

versplinten *vt* MASCHINEN cotter

Versprödung[1] *f* KERNTECH, METALL embrittlement

Versprödung:[2] **~ beseitigen** *vi* ANSTRICH de-embrittle

Versprühen *nt* MEERSCHMUTZ *von Dispersionsmitteln* dispersant spraying; **~ eines Wasserstrahls** *nt* WASSERVERSORG spout hole

versprühen *vt* WASSERVERSORG spread
Versprüher *m* LABOR atomizer
Verstählen *nt* FERTIG acierage, METALL acierage, steeling
verstählen *vt* METALL acierate, steel
Verständigung: **~ durch Läuterwerk** *f* EISENBAHN bell communication
Verständlichkeit *f* AKUSTIK, RADIO intelligibility; **Verständlichkeitsfaktor** *m* AKUSTIK articulation index, intelligibility index, TELEKOM articulation index
Verstärken *nt* BAU reinforcing
verstärken *vt* AUFNAHME fade up, BAU brace, COMP & DV amplify, ELEKTRONIK amplify, boost, *Licht* intensify, ELEKTROTECH boost, LEBENSMITTEL enhance, OPTIK amplify, TEXTIL splice, WASSERVERSORG *Damm, Stausee* reinforce, WELLPHYS amplify
verstärkend[1] *adj* ELEKTRIZ amplifying, OPTIK amplificatory, amplifying
verstärkend:[2] **~er Füllstoff** *m* KUNSTSTOFF reinforcing filler; **~es Zweitgefüge** *nt* RAUMFAHRT secondary structure
Verstärker *m* AUFNAHME amplifier, COMP & DV amplifier, repeater, ELEKTRIZ amplifier, *mit hohem Verstärkungsgrad* booster, ELEKTRONIK amplifier, repeater, ELEKTROTECH *in Gegenschaltung* booster, PHYS amplifier, repeater, RADIO amplifier, TELEKOM amplifier, repeater, WELLPHYS amplifier; **~ auf dem Chip** *m* ELEKTRONIK on-chip amplifier; **~ in Basisschaltung** *m* ELEKTRONIK common-base amplifier; **~ mit geringem Rauschen** *m* RAUMFAHRT *Weltraumfunk* low-noise amplifier; **~ mit hohem Verstärkungsgrad** *m* ELEKTRONIK high-gain amplifier; **~ in Kollektorschaltung** *m* ELEKTRONIK common-collector amplifier; **~ mit Lautstärkebegrenzung** *m* ELEKTRONIK volume-limiting amplifier; **~ mit niedriger Verstärkung** *m* ELEKTRONIK low-gain amplifier; **~ mit niedriger Verstärkungsleistung** *m* ELEKTRONIK small-gain amplifier; **~ für selektive Rückkopplung** *m* ELEKTRONIK selective feedback amplifier; **~ für zweite ZF** *m* ELEKTRONIK second IF amplifier; **Verstärkerbaugruppe** *f* ELEKTRONIK amplifier module; **Verstärker-Chip** *m* ELEKTRONIK amplifier chip; **Verstärkerelektrode** *f* FERNSEH intensifier electrode; **Verstärkergestell** *nt* TELEKOM repeater deck; **Verstärkergrundschaltung** *f* ELEKTRONIK basic amplifier circuit; **Verstärkerklasse** *f* ELEKTRONIK amplifier class; **Verstärkermaschine** *f* ELEKTROTECH rotary amplifier; **Verstärkerrauschen** *nt* ELEKTRONIK amplifier noise; **Verstärkerring** *m* FERNSEH intensifier ring; **Verstärkerröhre** *f* ELEKTRONIK amplifier tube, *Bildverstärker* intensifier tube; **Verstärkersäule** *f* CHEMTECH concentration column; **Verstärkerschaltung** *f* ELEKTRONIK amplifier circuit; **Verstärkerstation** *f* FERNSEH booster station; **Verstärkerstufe** *f* AUFNAHME amplifying stage, ELEKTRONIK amplifier stage; **Verstärker-Vidikon** *nt* ELEKTRONIK *Bildaufnahmeröhre* intensifier vidicon; **Verstärkerzugang** *m* RADIO repeater access
verstärkt[1] *adj* FERTIG *Bohrerkern* heavy
verstärkt:[2] **~er Kunststoff** *m* KUNSTSTOFF reinforced plastic; **~es Passagierabteil** *nt* TRANS strengthened passenger compartment; **~er Rand** *m* KER & GLAS reinforced rim; **~er Zug** *m* BAU forced draft (AmE), forced draught (BrE)
Verstärkung *f* AKUSTIK *eines Übertragungssystems* amplification, gain, transmission gain, AUFNAHME gain, AUFNAHME *(V)* amplification *(A)*, BAU haunch, reinforcement, stiffening, ELEKTRIZ gain, ELEKTRIZ *(V)*

amplification *(A)*, ELEKTRONIK gain, ELEKTRONIK *(V)* amplification *(A)*, ERDÖL backup, FOTO intensification, HYDRAUL *Unterwasser* backing up, KER & GLAS thickening, MASCHINEN backing, METROL *(V)* amplification *(A)*, OPTIK *(V)* amplification, gain, PAPIER backing, RADIO *(V)* amplification, gain *(G)*, RADIO (μ) *einer Elektronenröhre* amplification factor (μ), RAUMFAHRT *Weltraumfunk* amplification, gain, TELEKOM amplification, gain, *Absorption* enhancement, TEXTIL backing, splicing, VERPACK backing; **~ auf dem Chip** *f* ELEKTRONIK on-chip amplification; **~ der Eingangsstufe** *f* ELEKTRONIK input stage gain; **~ des geschlossenen Regelkreises** *f* GERÄT closed-loop gain; **~ für Hängedisplays** *f* VERPACK tape hanging display reinforcement; **Verstärkungsabgleich** *m* ELEKTRONIK gain trimming; **Verstärkungsbogen** *m* BAU safety arch; **Verstärkungsdrift** *f* ELEKTRONIK gain drift, gain droop; **Verstärkungseinstellung** *f* ELEKTRONIK gain adjustment, gain setting; **Verstärkungsfaktor** *m* AUFNAHME amplification factor, ELEKTRONIK amplification factor, amplifier gain, PHYS amplifier gain, TELEKOM gain; **Verstärkungs-Gewichtungsfaktor** *m* ELEKTRONIK gain weighting factor; **Verstärkungsgrad** *m* COMP & DV gain; **Verstärkungskurve** *f* ELEKTRONIK gain curve; **Verstärkungsmaß** *nt* ELEKTRONIK *Logarithmus des Verstärkungsfaktors* gain; **Verstärkungsmaß-Änderung** *f* ELEKTRONIK gain change; **Verstärkungsmessung** *f* GERÄT gain measurement; **Verstärkungsmittel** *nt* KUNSTSTOFF reinforcing agent; **Verstärkungspfosten** *m* ERDÖL backup post; **Verstärkungspumpen** *nt* AUFNAHME gain pumping; **Verstärkungsregelung** *f* AUFNAHME, COMP & DV, ELEKTRONIK gain control; **Verstärkungsschaltung** *f* ELEKTRONIK amplifying circuit; **Verstärkungsseil** *nt* ERDÖL backup line; **Verstärkungsstütze** *f* ERDÖL backup post; **Verstärkungstransistor** *m* ELEKTRONIK amplifying transistor; **Verstärkungsüberhöhung** *f* ELEKTRONIK peaking; **Verstärkungsveränderung** *f* ELEKTRONIK gain change; **Verstärkungsverhältnis** *nt* AUFNAHME amplification ratio; **Verstärkungsverschiebung** *f* RAUMFAHRT *Weltraumfunk* emphasis; **Verstärkungszug** *m* EISENBAHN relief train
verstauen *vt* RAUMFAHRT, WASSERTRANS *Ladung* stow
Verstehen: **~ einer zusammenhängenden Rede** *nt* KÜNSTL INT discourse understanding
Versteifen *nt* BAU strutting, RAUMFAHRT stiffening
versteifen *vt* FERTIG strut, MASCHINEN brace
versteifend: **~e Ausfütterung** *f* LUFTTRANS *eines Sitzes* backing
Versteifung *f* BAU web, *von Außenwänden* lining, FERTIG web, KERNTECH boom, MASCHINEN backing, stiffening; **Versteifungsblech** *nt* FERTIG stiffening sheet, MASCHINEN stiffening plate; **Versteifungselement** *nt* HEIZ & KÄLTE stiffening member, MASCHINEN stiffener; **Versteifungsmaterial** *nt* VERPACK reinforced packaging material; **Versteifungsprofil** *nt* WASSERTRANS *Schiffbau* stiffener; **Versteifungsrippe** *f* FERTIG rib; **Versteifungsspreize** *f* LUFTTRANS horizontal strut
Versteinerung: **~ von Schlämmen** *f* ABFALL sludge petrification
Verstell- *pref* FERTIG, MASCHINEN adjustable; **Verstellarm** *m* FERTIG *Bohrspindel* adjustable arm
verstellbar[1] *adj* MASCHINEN, PAPIER adjustable; **nicht ~** *adj* FERTIG *Pumpe* constant-flow
verstellbar:[2] **~er Abgriff** *m* GERÄT adjustable strap; **~er Anschlag** *m* MASCHINEN adjustable stop; **~er Antrieb**

m MASCHINEN variable-speed drive; **~er Dreifuß** *m* LABOR adjustable tripod; **~e Düse** *f* MASCHINEN adjustable nozzle; **~er Innenspiegel** *m* KFZTECH *Zubehör* adjustable rear-view mirror; **~er Meßring** *m* WASSERTRANS *Radar* variable range marker; **~er Metallsägebogen** *m* MASCHINEN adjustable hacksaw frame; **~es Mikrofon** *nt* AUFNAHME rifle microphone; **~es Okular** *nt* FOTO adjustable eyepiece; **~e Reibahle** *f* MASCHINEN adjustable reamer; **~e Schaufeln** *f pl* MASCHINEN adjustable blades; **~e Schelle** *f* GERÄT *an Widerstand* adjustable strap; **~es Schleusentor** *nt* HYDRAUL shuttle; **~er Schraubenschlüssel** *m* FERTIG monkey wrench, MASCHINEN adjustable spanner (BrE), coach wrench, monkey wrench, shifting spanner (BrE); **~e Skalenmarke** *f* GERÄT memory pointer; **~es Spanneisen** *nt* FERTIG offset clamp; **~e Spindel** *f* FERTIG *Mehrspindelbohrmaschine* adjustable arm **~e Spule** *f* ELEKTRIZ adjustable inductance, adjustable inductance coil; **~es Stativ** *nt* METROL *Vermessung* adjustable tripod; **~es Strichmaß** *nt* METROL caliper gage (AmE), calliper gauge (BrE); **~er Tiefenanschlag** *m* MASCHINEN adjustable stop; **~er Transformator** *m* ELEKTRIZ adjustable transformer; **~e Verdrängungspumpe** *f* GERÄT variable displacement pump; **~e Vorhangwand** *f* KER & GLAS adjustable curtain wall; **~es Windeisen** *nt* MASCHINEN adjustable tap wrench

verstellen *vt* FERTIG *Kunststoffinstallationen* displace

Verstell-: **Verstellmutter** *f* MASCHINEN regulating nut; **Verstellpropeller** *m* LUFTTRANS variable-pitch propeller, variable-pitch air propeller, MEERSCHMUTZ variable-pitch propeller, WASSERTRANS variable-pitch air propeller, variable-pitch propeller, *Schiffantrieb* controllable-pitch propeller; **Verstellpumpe** *f* FERTIG variable delivery pump; **Verstellschraube** *f* WASSERTRANS variable-pitch propeller; **Verstellstange** *f* MASCHINEN adjusting rod; **Verstellluftschraube** *f* MEERSCHMUTZ variable-pitch propeller; **Verstellungsgestänge** *nt* LUFTTRANS *Hubschrauber* blade pitch change rod

Verstemmen *nt* FERTIG *Niet,* MASCHINEN caulking

verstemmen *vt* FERTIG hammer-tighten, MASCHINEN caulk

Verstemmhammer *m* MASCHINEN caulking hammer

Verstickstahl *m* MECHAN nitrided steel

Verstiften *nt* FERTIG *Reparaturschweißung* studding

verstiften *vt* BAU dowel, peg, FERTIG dowel pin, *Reparaturschweißung* stud, MASCHINEN dowel, pin

verstiftet *adj* FERTIG pinned, *Reparaturschweißung* studded

verstimmen *vt* ELEKTRONIK detune

verstimmt: **~e Frequenz** *f* ELEKTRONIK off-tune frequency

Verstimmung *f* ELEKTRONIK detuning

Verstopfen *nt* ERDÖL *Rohrleitungen, Bohrloch* plugging, FERTIG choking, tamping, MASCHINEN clogging, plugging

verstopfen[1] *vt* BAU block, FERTIG *Schleifscheibe,* MASCHINEN clog, MECHAN pack, PAPIER clog, RAUMFAHRT *Raumschiff* retard, WASSERVERSORG clog

verstopfen[2] *vi* MECHAN jam

verstopft[1] *adj* HEIZ & KÄLTE choked, MASCHINEN clogged

verstopft:[2] **~e Düse** *f* LUFTTRANS choked nozzle; **~er Filz** *m* KER & GLAS clogged felt

Verstopfung *f* BAU obstruction, KOHLEN, PAPIER clogging, TRANS road jam (AmE), traffic jam (BrE),

Verkehr tailback (BrE), WASSERVERSORG clogging, stoppage of a water pipe; **Verstopfungsgrad** *m* TRANS *Verkehr* level of congestion

verstöpselt: **~e Flasche** *f* LABOR stoppered bottle; **~er Kolben** *m* LABOR stoppered flask; **~er Meßzylinder** *m* LABOR stoppered measuring cylinder

Verstreben *nt* BAU strutting

verstreben *vt* BAU brace, shore, strut, MASCHINEN brace

Verstrebung *f* EISENBAHN pantograph tie-bar, HYDRAUL, MASCHINEN brace; **Verstrebungsbalken** *m* BAU straining beam, straining piece

Verstrecken *nt* TEXTIL drawing

verstrecken *vt* TEXTIL *Spinnen* draw

Verstreckung *f* TEXTIL *Spinnen* draft

verstümmeln *vt* ELEKTROTECH clip

Verstümmelung *f* AUFNAHME *von Signalen* clipping, COMP & DV corruption

Versuch *m* GERÄT, KOHLEN trial, PHYS test, TEXTIL trial; **Versuchsablaufkanal** *m* WASSERVERSORG test flume; **Versuchsabschnitt** *m* BAU experimental section; **Versuchsanlage** *f* KONTROLL trial equipment; **Versuchsanstalt** *f* LABOR laboratory; **Versuchsaufbau** *m* COMP & DV breadboard; **~ eines Schaltungsmodells** *m* ELEKTROTECH breadboard model; **Versuchsaufnahme** *f* FOTO test shot; **Versuchsbecken** *nt* WASSERVERSORG experimental basin, tapping; **Versuchsbedingungen** *f pl* QUAL test conditions; **Versuchsbeschreibung** *f* RAUMFAHRT test specification; **Versuchsbohrung** *f* ERDÖL *Erdölsuche* trial boring; **Versuchseinrichtung** *f* KONTROLL trial equipment, MASCHINEN try-out facility; **Versuchshafen** *m* KER & GLAS monkey pot; **Versuchshubschrauber** *m* LUFTTRANS experimental helicopter; **Versuchslast** *f* LUFTTRANS *Lufttüchtigkeit* proof load; **Versuchslauf** *m* COMP & DV test run, KONTROLL trial run; **Versuchsmodell** *nt* MECHAN experimental model, WERKPRÜF test model; **Versuchsplanung** *f* QUAL experimental design; **Versuchsplatz** *m* KERNTECH test rig; **Versuchspumpe** *f* WASSERVERSORG test pump; **Versuchsraum** *m* LEBENSMITTEL proving cabinet; **Versuchsreihen** *f pl* RAUMFAHRT experiment package; **Versuchsstadium** *nt* STRAHLPHYS prototype stage; **Versuchsstand** *m* KERNTECH test bay, test stand; **Versuchsstrecke** *f* BAU experimental section, KFZTECH test track; **Versuchswerkstatt** *f* FERTIG *Kunststoffinstallationen* test center (AmE), test centre (BrE); **Versuchszug** *m* EISENBAHN test train

Vertäuboje *f* MEERSCHMUTZ mooring buoy

Vertäubung *f* ERGON masking

vertäuen *vt* WASSERTRANS *Festmachen* moor

Vertäuklampe *f* WASSERTRANS *Bootsbau, Deckzubehör* mooring cleat

Vertäuplatz *m* WASSERTRANS *Hafen* mooring berth

Vertäupoller *m* WASSERTRANS *Hafen* mooring bitts

Vertauschen: **~ der Stecker über Kreuz** *nt* AUFNAHME cross-plugging

Vertauschung *f* MATH commutation

Vertäuung: **~ loswerfen** *vi* WASSERTRANS *Festmachen* unmoor

verteilen *vt* BAU distribute, spread

Verteiler *m* COMP & DV switch, ELEKTRIZ distributor, KERNTECH manifold, KFZTECH distributor, LEBENSMITTEL dispenser, LUFTTRANS manifold, MASCHINEN distributor, MECHAN distributor, manifold, TELEKOM distribution frame, distribution board, VERPACK distributor; **~ für E-Mail** *m* COMP & DV e-mail distribution

list; **Verteilerantrieb** *m* KFZTECH *Zündung* distributor drive; **Verteilerdose** *f* ELEKTRIZ, ELEKTROTECH, RAUMFAHRT conduit box, distribution box, junction box; **Verteilereinspritzpumpe** *f* KFZTECH distributor injection pump; **Verteiler-Entstörstecker** *m* KFZTECH *Zündung* distributor suppressor; **Verteilerfinger** *m* KFZTECH distributor finger, distributor rotor, *Zündung* rotor arm; **Verteilerkabel** *nt* ELEKTRIZ distribution cable; **Verteilerkappe** *f* KFZTECH distributor cap; **Verteilerkasten** *m* ELEKTRIZ distribution box, joint box (BrE), ELEKTROTECH conduit box, distribution box, junction box, terminal box; **Verteilerklemmschraube** *f* KFZTECH distributor clamp bolt; **Verteilerläufer** *m* ELEKTROTECH rotor, KFZTECH distributor finger, distributor rotor, rotor, *Zündung* rotor arm; **Verteilerleitung** *f* KERNTECH distributed digital processing; **Verteilernetz** *nt* BAU distribution network, VERPACK distribution chain; **Verteilerring** *m* KERNTECH distribution ring; **Verteilerrohr** *nt* MASCHINEN header, MECHAN manifold, WASSERVERSORG distributing pipe; **Verteilerschaltdraht** *m* TELEKOM *Telefon* jumper; **Verteilerscheibe** *f* KFZTECH distributor cap; **Verteilerschiene** *f* ELEKTRIZ distributing busbar, distribution bus, - ELEKTROTECH bus; **Verteilerservice** *m* VERPACK distribution chain; **Verteilerstück** *nt* FERTIG spreader; **Verteilerstufe** *f* TELEKOM distribution stage; **Verteilertafel** *f* ELEKTRIZ distributing board, ELEKTROTECH distribution board; **Verteilertechnik** *f* VERPACK distribution technique; **Verteilerwelle** *f* KFZTECH distributor shaft; **Verteilerzentrale** *f* TELEKOM *Telefon* distribution center (AmE), distribution centre (BrE)
Verteilfernamt *nt* TELEKOM *Telefon* distribution center (AmE), distribution centre (BrE)
verteilt[1] *adj* COMP & DV distributed
verteilt:[2] **~es Betriebssystem** *nt* COMP & DV distributed operating system; **~e Datenbank** *f* COMP & DV distributed database; **~e Datenverarbeitung** *f* COMP & DV DDP, distributed data processing, distributed processing; **~e digitale Datenverarbeitung** *f* COMP & DV distributed digital processing; **~e Induktivität** *f* ELEKTROTECH distributed inductance; **~e Kapazität** *f* ELEKTROTECH distributed capacitance; **~es Mehrfachantennensystem** *nt* TELEKOM distributed multi-antenna system; **~e Nebenstellenanlage** *f* TELEKOM distributed PBX; **~es Netz** *nt* COMP & DV distributed network; **~es System** *nt* TELEKOM dispersed system; **~e Systeme** *nt pl* COMP & DV distributed systems; **~e Verarbeitung** *f* COMP & DV distributed processing
Verteilung *f* ELEKTRIZ, HYDRAUL, KER & GLAS, KFZTECH *Zündung*, MASCHINEN distribution, PATENT apportionment, QUAL distribution; **~ der Ausfallhäufigkeit** *f* QUAL failure frequency distribution; **~ mit Baumstruktur** *f* TELEKOM tree distribution; **~ von festen Partikeln in der Flüssigkeit** *f* ANSTRICH dispersion; **Verteilungschromatographie** *f* CHEMIE partition chromatography; **Verteilungsfehler** *m* KER & GLAS defect in distribution
verteilungsfrei *adj* QUAL distribution-free
Verteilung: **Verteilungsfunktion** *f* PHYS *Quantenoptik* Q function, QUAL distribution function; **Verteilungskabel** *nt* ELEKTROTECH distribution cable; **Verteilungskurve** *f* MATH, QUAL distribution curve; **Verteilungsnetz** *nt* ELEKTROTECH distribution system, distribution network, TELEKOM distribution network,

WASSERVERSORG distribution system; **Verteilungsrohr** *nt* MECHAN intake manifold; **Verteilungssicherungskasten** *m* ELEKTRIZ distribution fuse board; **Verteilungssystem** *nt* ELEKTROTECH distribution system; **Verteilungstafel** *f* TELEKOM *Stromversorgung* distribution board; **Verteilungsunterwerk** *nt* ELEKTRIZ distribution substation
Verteilverstärker *m* FERNSEH distribution amplifier
Vertiefen *nt* BAU recessing
vertiefen *vt* BAU deepen, recess, hollow, MASCHINEN recess
vertieft: **~e Form** *f* FERTIG intaglio
Vertiefung *f* BAU hollow, FERTIG dimple, recess, *Schraubenkopf* seating, KER & GLAS impression, MASCHINEN cavity, depression, pit, recess
Vertikal- *pref* ELEKTRONIK, FERNSEH, PHYS vertical; **Vertikalablenkplatte** *f* ELEKTRONIK *Kathodenstrahlröhre*, PHYS vertical deflection plate; **Vertikalablenkung** *f* FERNSEH vertical deflection; **Vertikalablenkungsspule** *f* ELEKTROTECH vertical deflection coil; **Vertikalabtastung** *f* FERNSEH vertical scanning; **Vertikalachse** *f* (*Y-Achse*) MATH vertical axis (*y-axis*); **Vertikalamplitude** *f* FERNSEH vertical amplitude; **Vertikalamplitudenregler** *m* FERNSEH vertical-amplitude control; **Vertikalanflugsführung** *f* LUFTTRANS approach elevation guidance; **Vertikalanordnung** *f* BAU vertical alignment; **Vertikalaufnahme** *f* AUFNAHME perpendicular recording; **Vertikalaustastimpuls** *m* FERNSEH vertical blanking pulse; **Vertikalaustastlücke** *f* FERNSEH vertical blanking interval; **Vertikalaustastung** *f* ELEKTRONIK, FERNSEH vertical blanking; **Vertikalbezugssystemeinheit** *f* RAUMFAHRT vertical reference unit; **Vertikalbildlageregelung** *f* ELEKTRONIK vertical centering (AmE), vertical centring (BrE); **Vertikalbipolartransistor** *m* ELEKTRONIK vertical bipolar transistor; **Vertikalblättern** *nt* COMP & DV vertical scrolling
vertikal[1] *adj* GEOM vertical
vertikal:[2] **~ e Axe** *f* PHYS vertical axis; **~ er MOS-Leistungstransistor** *m* ELEKTRONIK vertical power MOS transistor; **~er MOS-Transistor** *m* ELEKTRONIK vertical MOS transistor; **~ es seismisches Profil** *nt* (*VSP*) ERDÖL vertical seismic profile (*VSP*)
Vertikale *f* GEOM, MATH vertical
Vertikal-: **Vertikalempfindlichkeit** *f* GERÄT *Oszilloskop* Y-sensitivity, vertical sensitivity; **Vertikalendstufe** *f* ELEKTRONIK vertical output stage; **Vertikal-FET** *m* ELEKTRONIK vertical field-effect transistor; **Vertikalflosse** *f* LUFTTRANS keel, tail fin; **Vertikalformat** *nt* COMP & DV vertical format; **Vertikalfräsmaschine** *f* MASCHINEN vertical milling machine; **Vertikalführung** *f* LUFTTRANS elevation guidance; **Vertikalgeschwindigkeit** *f* RAUMFAHRT vertical speed; **Vertikalgeschwindigkeitsanzeige** *f* RAUMFAHRT vertical-speed indicator; **Vertikalitätstoleranz** *f* KER & GLAS verticality tolerance; **Vertikalkartoniermaschine** *f* VERPACK vertical cartoner; **Vertikalkonvergenz** *f* ELEKTRONIK vertical convergence; **Vertikalkreisel** *m* LUFTTRANS vertical gyro, RAUMFAHRT gyroscopic verticant, vertical gyro; **Vertikallinearitätsregler** *m* FERNSEH vertical linearity control; **Vertikallücke** *f* FERNSEH vertical interval; **Vertikalmagnetisierung** *f* AKUSTIK perpendicular magnetization; **Vertikalmaßeinteilung** *f* MATH vertical scale; **Vertikalmittenabgleich** *m* FERNSEH vertical centering control (AmE), vertical centring control (BrE); **Ver-**

tikalmodus *m* FERNSEH vertical mode; **Vertikalpausenzeichen** *nt* FERNSEH vertical interval test signal; **Vertikalpolarisation** *f* ELEKTROTECH, PHYS *Antenne*, TELEKOM vertical polarization; **Vertikalrohrpost** *f* KERNTECH vertical rabbit; **Vertikalstab** *m* FERTIG column, strut; **Vertikalstabilität** *f* TRANS vertical stability; **Vertikalsteuerung** *f* OPTIK vertical control; **Vertikalsynchronisierimpuls** *m* FERNSEH vertical sync pulse; **Vertikalsynchronisierung** *f* COMP & DV vertical tab, FERNSEH vertical lock; **Vertikaltabulator** *m* COMP & DV vertical tabulator; **Vertikaltragsäule** *f* EISENBAHN supporting column; **Vertikalunterdrückung** *f* COMP & DV vertical blanking; **Vertikalversetzung** *f* NICHTFOSS ENERG *der Boje* heaving displacement

Vertikalverstärker *m* ELEKTRONIK VA, vertical amplifier; **Vertikalverstärkerausgang** *m* ELEKTRONIK vertical-amplifier output; **Vertikalverstärker-Eingang** *m* ELEKTRONIK vertical-amplifier input

Vertikal-: **Vertikalverteilung** *f* UMWELTSCHMUTZ vertical dispersion; **Vertikalzylinderschleifmaschine** *f* MASCHINEN vertical cylinder-grinding machine

Vertonung *f* FERNSEH sound on vision

Vertrag *m* BAU, PATENT contract

Verträglichkeit *f* AKUSTIK, KUNSTSTOFF, MASCHINEN compatibility; **Verträglichkeitsprüfung** *f* UMWELTSCHMUTZ impact statement, WASSERVERSORG impact study

Vertrag: **Vertragsänderung** *f* BAU contract modification; **Vertragspflichtenheft** *nt* BAU specifications; **Vertragsstaat** *m* PATENT contracting state

Vertrauen *nt* QUAL confidence; **Vertrauensbereich** *m* QUAL confidence interval, confidence range, confidence region; **Vertrauensgrenze** *f* QUAL confidence limit; **Vertrauensgrenze der Erfolgswahrscheinlichkeit** *f* QUAL assessed reliability; **Vertrauensgrenze eines Lebensdauer-Perzentils Q** *f* QUAL assessed Q-percentile life; **Vertrauensgrenze der mittleren Lebensdauer** *f* QUAL assessed mean life; **Vertrauensniveau** *nt* QUAL confidence coefficient, confidence level

Vertraulichkeit *f* COMP & DV privacy

Vertriebsmethoden *f pl* VERPACK distribution technique

vertrimmt *adj* LUFTTRANS out-of-trim

Vertrimmung *f* LUFTTRANS *Luftfahrzeug* out-of-trim

verunreinigen *vt* ANSTRICH contaminate, FERTIG vitiate, KOHLEN contaminate, UMWELTSCHMUTZ pollute

verunreinigt:[1] **nicht ~** *adj* SICHERHEIT clean

verunreinigt:[2] **~er Bohrschlamm** *m* ERDÖL *Bohrtechnik* contaminated mud

Verunreinigung *f* ANSTRICH contaminant, CHEMIE contamination, ELEKTRONIK impurity, KER & GLAS tramping, KOHLEN contamination, METALL impurity; **~ des Grundwassers** *f* ABFALL ground water contamination, ground water pollution; **Verunreinigungsquelle** *f* UMWELTSCHMUTZ pollution source; **Verunreinigungssubstanz** *f* ABFALL contaminant

Verursacherprinzip *nt* UMWELTSCHMUTZ polluter-pays principle

vervielfachen *vt* COMP & DV multiply

Vervielfacher *m* ELEKTRONIK *multipliziert Eingangssignalkurve mit Konstante*, TELEKOM multiplier; **Vervielfacherelement** *nt* COMP & DV multiplexer

Vervielfachung *f* COMP & DV multiplication

vervielfältigen *vt* COMP & DV multiply

Vervielfältigung *f* AKUSTIK duplicating, duplication; **Vervielfältigungsgetriebe** *nt* MASCHINEN multiplying gear; **Vervielfältigungsversuch** *m* KONSTZEICH duplicating trial

verwachsen: **~e Versetzung** *f* METALL grown-in dislocation

Verwachsenes *nt* KOHLEN true middlings

Verwählen *nt* TELEKOM dialing error (AmE), dialling error (BrE)

Verwaltungsbereich *m* BAU administrative area

Verwaltungseinheit *f* TELEKOM management unit

Verwandlung: **~ in Stahl** *f* METALL acieration; **Verwandlungshubschrauber** *m* LUFTTRANS convertiplane

Verwaschungsdüse *f* LUFTTRANS confusion cone

verwechslungsfrei: **~ gekennzeichnet** *adj* QUAL unambiguously marked

Verweil- *pref* COMP & DV, FERTIG residence; **Verweildauer** *f* ABFALL residence time, retention time, MECHAN dwell time, TEXTIL dwelling time; **Verweiltank** *m* KERNTECH delay tank; **Verweilzeit** *f* ABFALL, COMP & DV residence time, KER & GLAS dwell time, MASCHINEN dwell

Verweis: **~ nach vorne** *m* COMP & DV forward reference

verwendbar[1] *adj* COMP & DV usable

verwendbar:[2] **~e Nebenprodukte** *nt pl* UMWELTSCHMUTZ usable by-products

Verwendbarkeitsdauer *f* MASCHINEN working life

verwenden *vt* COMP & DV use

Verwerfen *nt* BAU, ELEKTRONIK *unbrauchbarer Daten* warping, QUAL final rejection, refusal

verwerfen[1] *vt* MASCHINEN discard, QUAL reject

verwerfen:[2] **sich ~** *v refl* MASCHINEN warp

Verwerfung *f* ERDÖL *Geologie* fault, PATENT rejection; **~ aufwärts** *f* WASSERVERSORG uptake; **Verwerfungsbecken** *nt* ERDÖL *Geologie* fault basin; **Verwerfungsfalle** *f* ERDÖL *Geologie* fault trap; **Verwerfungsquelle** *f* WASSERVERSORG fault spring

verwertbar[1] *adj* ABFALL recyclable

verwertbar:[2] **nicht ~er Rückstand** *nt* ABFALL waste product

Verwertungsquote *f* ABFALL recycling rate

verwesen *vi* LEBENSMITTEL putrefy

verwesend *adj* LEBENSMITTEL putrescent

Verwinden *nt* STRÖMPHYS *der Wirbelstärke* twisting

Verwindung *f* MASCHINEN torsion

verwindungsfrei *adj* FERTIG distortion-free

Verwindung: **Verwindungssteifigkeit** *f* MASCHINEN torsional strength; **Verwindungsversuch** *m* MASCHINEN torsion test, torsional test

verwirbelt: **~es Garn** *nt* TEXTIL comingle yarn

Verwirbelung *f* PHYS vorticity

Verwirrung *f* ERGON disorientation

verwittern *vi* BAU weather

verwittert: **~es Öl** *nt* MEERSCHMUTZ weathered oil

Verwitterung *f* ERDÖL *Geologie* decomposition, KOHLEN, MEERSCHMUTZ weathering; **Verwitterungsfläche** *f* BAU area of deep weathering

verwölben *vt* FERTIG warp

Verwölbung *f* FERTIG warping

verworfen: **~es Holz** *nt* BAU warped timber

verwunden[1] *adj* MECHAN warped

verwunden:[2] **~es Rad** *nt* TRANS buckled wheel

Verwurf *m* QUAL refusal

Verwürfler *m* TELEKOM scrambler

Verzahnen *nt* MASCHINEN gear cutting, gear-tooth generating, toothing; **~ von Schneckenrädern** *nt* MECHAN worm wheel cutting

verzahnen *vt* BAU interlock, joggle, key, MASCHINEN gear

verzahnt[1] *adj* COMP & DV interleaved
verzahnt:[2] ~e **Verarbeitung** *f* ELEKTRONIK concurrent processing
Verzahnung[1] *f* BAU joggle, keying, *Mauerwerk* toothing, COMP & DV interleaving, FERTIG indentation, MASCHINEN toothing;
Verzahnung:[2] ~ **auflösen** *vi* COMP & DV, ELEKTRONIK de-interleave
Verzahnung: ~ **von Schneckenrädern** *f* MASCHINEN worm cutting; **Verzahnungsmaschine** *f* MASCHINEN gear-cutting machine; **Verzahnungstoleranz** *f* MASCHINEN gearing tolerance
verzapft *adj* MECHAN cogged
Verzapfung *f* BAU tenon joint
verzehren *vt* MASCHINEN absorb, dissipate
Verzehrung *f* MASCHINEN absorption
Verzeichnis *nt* COMP & DV catalog (AmE), catalogue (BrE), dictionary, directory, record; **Verzeichnisspeicher** *m* TELEKOM directory store; **Verzeichnissteuersystem** *nt* TELEKOM directory control system
Verzeichnung *f* FERNSEH *Bild* distortion
verzeichnungsfrei *adj* PHYS orthoscopic
verzerrt[1] *adj* KER & GLAS out-of-shape
verzerrt:[2] ~es **Signal** *nt* ELEKTRONIK distorted signal; ~e **Wellenmethode** *f* KERNTECH distorted wave method
Verzerrung *f* AKUSTIK, ELEKTRIZ, ELEKTRONIK *Abweichung vom Ursprungssignal*, FERNSEH *Signal*, PHYS *Bild* distortion, QUAL bias, RADIO, TELEKOM distortion; ~ **durch die dritte Harmonische** *f* ELEKTRONIK third harmonic distortion; ~ **durch Hüllkurvenverzögerung** *f* RAUMFAHRT *Weltraumfunk* envelope delay distortion; ~ **durch Überregelung** *f* FERNSEH overshoot distortion; ~ **der zweiten Harmonischen** *f* ELEKTRONIK second harmonic distortion; **Verzerrungsanalysator** *m* ELEKTRONIK harmonic analyser (BrE), harmonic analyzer (AmE), GERÄT distortion analyser (BrE), distortion analyzer (AmE)
verzerrungsarm: ~e **Modulation** *f* ELEKTRONIK low-distortion modulation
verzerrungsbegrenzt: ~er **Betrieb** *m* TELEKOM distortion-limited operation
Verzerrung: **Verzerrungsfalle** *f* AUFNAHME bias trap
verzerrungsfrei[1] *adj* ELEKTRONIK distortion-free
verzerrungsfrei:[2] ~e **Modulation** *f* ELEKTRONIK linear modulation
Verzicht *m* PATENT waiving
Verziehen *nt* BAU warping, winding, MASCHINEN distortion, TEXTIL drafting
verziert: ~er **Sturz** *m* BAU platband
Verzierungsarbeiten *f pl* WASSERTRANS fancywork
verzinken *vt* ANSTRICH galvanize, BAU zinc, FERTIG galvanize, METALL zinc
verzinkt: ~es **Stahlblech** *nt* HEIZ & KÄLTE galvanized sheet steel
Verzinkung *f* KUNSTSTOFF zinc coating
Verzinnen *nt* BAU, KER & GLAS, METALL tinning
verzinnen *vt* FERTIG tin, wet, METALL tin
verzinnt[1] *adj* CHEMIE, LEBENSMITTEL canned (AmE), tinned (BrE)
verzinnt:[2] ~es **Blech** *nt* FERTIG, METALL sheet tin; ~er **Draht** *m* ELEKTROTECH tinned wire; ~er **Leiter** *m* ELEKTRIZ tinned conductor
Verzinnung *f* ELEKTRIZ tinning
verzogen[1] *adj* LUFTTRANS *Hubschrauber* out-of-track, MASCHINEN out-of-true, MECHAN warped
verzogen:[2] ~e **Antrittsstufe** *f* BAU commode step; ~e

Stufe *f* BAU dancing step
Verzögerer *m* ELEKTROTECH *Relais* slug, KUNSTSTOFF retarder, LEBENSMITTEL inhibitor, PAPIER retarder, TEXTIL retarding agent
verzögern *vt* ANSTRICH, BAU retard, ELEKTRIZ, ELEKTRONIK *in der Ausführungsfolge*, KONTROLL, RADIO delay
verzögernd: ~e **Zeitablenkung** *f* ELEKTRONIK *Oszillograph* delaying sweep; ~e **Zeitbasis** *f* ELEKTRONIK delaying time base
verzögert[1] *adj* KONTROLL deferred
verzögert:[2] ~e **Abtastung** *f* FERNSEH delayed scanning; ~e **Adressierung** *f* COMP & DV deferred addressing; ~es **Austastsignal** *nt* FERNSEH DBS, delayed blanking signal; ~e **automatische Verstärkungsregelung** *f* AUFNAHME delayed automatic gain control; ~e **Belegung** *f* TELEKOM delayed call; ~e **Bewegung** *f* MASCHINEN retarded motion; ~es **Brechen** *nt* METALL delayed fracture; ~er **Fluß** *m* KERNTECH delayed flux; ~e **Geschwindigkeit** *f* MASCHINEN retarded velocity; ~es **Härten** *nt* THERMOD delayed hardening; ~er **Kippvorgang** *m* ELEKTRONIK *Oszillograph* delaying sweep; ~e **Koinzidenzspektren** *nt pl* STRAHLPHYS delayed coincidence spectra; ~~**kritischer Reaktor** *m* KERNTECH delayed critical reactor ~e **modifizierte Phasenumtastung** *f* ELEKTRONIK delayed modified phase shift keying; ~e **modulierte Phasenumtastung** *f* ELEKTRONIK MPSK, modulated phase shift keying; ~es **Neutron** *nt* KERNTECH, PHYS *Kernphysik*, STRAHLPHYS delayed neutron; ~e **Regelschleife** *f* TELEKOM delay lock loop; ~es **Relais** *nt* TELEKOM delay mode relay; ~e **selbsttätige Verstärkungsregelung** *f* ELEKTRONIK *für Empfänger* delayed automatic gain control; ~e **Strahlung** *f* KERNTECH delayed emission; ~er **Trennschalter** *m* ELEKTRIZ slow break switch; ~es **Verkoken** *nt* THERMOD delayed coking;
Verzögerung *f* COMP & DV delay, ELEKTRIZ, ELEKTRONIK delay, lag, ELEKTROTECH, FERNSEH delay, FERTIG lag, GERÄT, KERNTECH delay, KFZTECH deceleration, *Motor* offset, KONTROLL delay, LUFTTRANS *Hubschrauber* lag, MASCHINEN deceleration, retardation, retarded acceleration, retarded motion, MECHAN braking, RADIO, TELEKOM, TRANS delay, WASSERVERSORG lag; ~ **durch Konkurrenzbetrieb** *f* COMP & DV contention delay ~ **höherer Ordnung** *f* ELEKTRONIK high-order delay;
verzögerungsarm: ~e **Regelstrecke** *f* REGELUNG low-lag closed-loop-controlled system
Verzögerung: **Verzögerungsbad** *nt* FOTO *Entwicklung* restraining bath; **Verzögerungseinheit** *f* REGELUNG lag module; **Verzögerungsfreiheit** *f* REGELUNG *des Reglers* absence of lag; **Verzögerungsglied** *nt* PHYS lag element; **Verzögerungsglieder mit Abgriffen** *nt pl* ELEKTRONIK tapped delay elements; **Verzögerungskabel** *nt* FERNSEH delay cable; **Verzögerungskette** *f* GERÄT delay network; **Verzögerungskette mit konstanter Laufzeit** *f* ELEKTRONIK constant delay line; **Verzögerungskomponente** *f* ELEKTRONIK *Bauteil* delay component, KERNTECH delay component, delay unit; **Verzögerungsleitung** *f* COMP & DV, FERNSEH, PHYS delay line, TELEKOM delay circuit; **Verzögerungsleitung mit Abgriffen** *f* ELEKTRONIK tapped delay line; **Verzögerungsmittel** *nt* BAU *Beton, Zement* retarding agent, KUNSTSTOFF retarder; **Verzögerungsmultivibrator** *m* ELEKTRONIK delay multivibrator; **Verzögerungsrelais** *nt* ELEKTRIZ delay relay, slow-act-

ing relay, time delay relay, time lag relay, ELEKTRO-
TECH delay relay; **Verzögerungsröhre** *f* ELEKTRONIK
slow wave tube, RAUMFAHRT transit time tube; **Verzö-
gerungsschalter** *m* ELEKTRIZ delay switch;
Verzögerungsschaltkreis *m* FERNSEH delay circuit;
Verzögerungsschaltung *f* ELEKTRIZ delay circuit,
ELEKTRONIK time delay circuit, *Laufzeitnetzwerk* de-
lay circuit, GERÄT delay network; **Verzögerungsspur** *f*
BAU deceleration lane; **Verzögerungssystem** *nt* LUFT-
TRANS lagging system; **Verzögerungstank** *m*
KERNTECH delay tank; **Verzögerungsventil** *nt* MASCHI-
NEN delay valve; **Verzögerungsverzeichnung** *f*
FERNSEH delay distortion; **Verzögerungsvorrichtung** *f*
TRANS deceleration device; **Verzögerungswicklung** *f*
ELEKTRIZ retardation coil; **Verzögerungswinkel** *m*
ELEKTRIZ angle of lag, LUFTTRANS lag angle;
Verzögerungszeit *f* COMP & DV deceleration time,
ELEKTRIZ delay time, ELEKTRONIK time lag, ERDÖL
Bohrtechnik lagtime, TELEKOM delay time

Verzug *m* KUNSTSTOFF warpage, MASCHINEN distortion;
Verzugszeit *f* ELEKTRONIK dead time
Verzundern *nt* FERTIG scaling
verzweigen[1] *vt* COMP & DV branch, FERTIG ramify
verzweigen:[2] **sich ~** *v refl* BAU branch
verzweigt: **~es Polymer** *nt* KUNSTSTOFF branched polymer
Verzweigung *f* COMP & DV switch, EISENBAHN junction,
FERTIG ramification, KERNTECH manifold, PHYS
branching; **Verzweigungsfilter** *nt* ELEKTRONIK
branching filter; **Verzweigungskabel** *nt* ELEKTROTECH
distribution cable; **Verzweigungskasten** *m* ELEKTRIZ
junction box; **Verzweigungspunkt** *m* COMP & DV
branch point, ELECTRONIK node; **Verzweigungsstück**
nt OPTIK Y-coupler; **Verzweigungsverhältnis** *nt* PHYS
branching ratio
Vestibularapparat *m* ERGON vestibular mechanism
VF *abbr* FERNSEH *(Videofrequenz)* VF *(video frequency)*, FERNSEH *(Videofrequenzwandler)* VF
(video-frequency converter)
V-Form *f* LUFTTRANS dihedral
V-förmig[1] *adj* MASCHINEN V-shaped
V-förmig:[2] **~e Rille** *f* ELEKTRONIK V-groove
VG *abbr (veränderliche Geometrie, veränderliche Trag-
flügelgeometrie)* LUFTTRANS VG *(variable geometry)*
VHD *abbr (sehr hohe Dichtigkeit)* OPTIK VHD *(very
high density)*
VHF[1] *abbr (Meterwellen-Hochfrequenz)* RADIO, TELE-
COM VHF *(very high frequency)*
VHF:[2] **VHF-Band** *nt* FERNSEH VHF band; **VHF-Signal** *nt*
ELEKTRONIK VHF signal; **VHF-Signalgeber** *m* ELEK-
TRONIK VHF signal generator; **VHF- und UHF-Tuner** *m*
FERNSEH VHF and UHF tuner;
VHS *abbr (Heimvideosystem)* FERNSEH VHS *(video
home system)*
VHS-C *abbr (Heimvideo-Aufzeichnungssystem)* FERN-
SEH VHS-C *(video home system-compact)*
VI *abbr (Viskositätsindex, Viskositätszahl)* KFZTECH,
MASCHINEN, STRÖMPHYS, THERMOD VI *(viscosity in-
dex)*
Vibration *f* ELEKTRONIK oscillation, PHYS, SICHERHEIT
vibration; **Vibrationsdämpfer** *m* LUFTTRANS *Luft-
fahrzeug*, SICHERHEIT vibration damper;
Vibrationsförderer *m* FERTIG vibratory feeder, vib-
ratory hopper, VERPACK vibratory feeder;
Vibrations-Galvanometer *nt* ELEKTRIZ, PHYS vibration
galvanometer; **Vibrationsgefahr** *f* SICHERHEIT vibra-

tion hazard; **Vibrationsgefahr durch Hand** *f* SICHER-
HEIT *Elektrobohrer* hand-transmitted vibration
hazard; **Vibrationsgenerator** *m* RAUMFAHRT vibration
generator; **Vibrationsgeräusch** *nt* LUFTTRANS buzz;
Vibrationsprüfung *f* WERKPRÜF vibration test; **Vibrationsquantenzahl** *f (v)* KERNTECH vibrational
quantum number *(v)*; **Vibrationsrost** *m* FERTIG shake-
out; **Vibrationsrührwerk** *nt* LABOR vibrating stirrer;
Vibrationssieb *nt* CHEMIE vibrating screen; **Vibrations-
stärke** *f* SICHERHEIT vibration severity; **Vibrationstest**
m VERPACK jarring test; **Vibrationstisch** *m* KER & GLAS
vibrating table; **Vibrationsverdichtung** *f* KERNTECH
vibrocompaction; **Vibrationswalze** *f* BAU vibrating
roller
Vibrato *nt* AKUSTIK vibrato
Vibrator *m* ELEKTROTECH, MASCHINEN vibrator; **Vibra-
toraufgeber** *m* VERPACK filling vibrator
Vibrieren *nt* FERTIG jarring
vibrieren[1] *vt* FERTIG jar
vibrieren[2] *vi* ELEKTRONIK oscillate
vibrierend *adj* ELEKTRIZ, ELEKTRONIK *Strom*, PAPIER
oscillating
Vibriersieb *nt* ABFALL vibrator screen
Vibrometer *nt* PHYS vibrometer
Vickershärte *f* FERTIG *Walzen* diamond-pyramid hardness, diamond-pyramid hardness number,
MASCHINEN Vickers hardness; **Vickershärtetestgerät**
nt MASCHINEN Vickers hardness testing machine
Video *nt* FERNSEH video; **Videoaufzeichnung** *f* FERNSEH
video recording; **Videoausgabe** *f* FERNSEH video
output; **Videoband** *nt* FERNSEH video; **Videobandab-
spielgerät** *nt* FERNSEH videotape player;
Videobandbreite *f* FERNSEH video bandwidth; **Video-
cassette** *f* FERNSEH video cassette; **Video-Clip** *nt*
FERNSEH videoclip; **Videoeingabe** *f* FERNSEH video
input; **Videofrequenz** *f (VF)* FERNSEH video frequency *(VF)*; **Videofrequenzwandler** *m (VF)* FERNSEH
video-frequency converter *(VF)*; **Videogerät mit Tuner** *nt* FERNSEH telerecorder; **Videographie** *f* FERNSEH
videography; **Videokabel** *nt* FERNSEH video cable; **Vi-
deokamera mit Bandaufzeichnung** *f* FERNSEH
camcorder; **Videokarte** *f* COMP & DV video card; **Video-
konferenz** *f* FERNSEH video conference; **Videokopf** *m*
FERNSEH video head; **Videokopfbaugruppe** *f* FERNSEH
video head assembly; **Videokopfjustierung** *f* FERNSEH
video head alignment; **Videokopfoptimierer** *m* FERN-
SEH video head optimizer; **Video-Langspiel** *nt (VLP)*
FERNSEH video long play *(VLP)*, long-playing video
Videomagnetband *nt* FERNSEH videotape; **Videoma-
gnetbandeinrichtungen** *f pl* FERNSEH videotape
facilities; **Videomagnetbandgerät** *nt (VCR)* FERNSEH
video tape recorder *(VTR)*; **Videomagnetbandrecor-
der** *m* FERNSEH videotape recorder
Video: **Videopegel** *m* FERNSEH video level; **Videorecorder** *m (VCR)* FERNSEH video cassette recorder, video
recorder; **Videorückkoppelungskreis** *m* FERNSEH video feedback circuit; **Videoschaltverteiler** *m* FERNSEH
video switch; **Videosignal** *nt* FERNSEH picture signal,
video signal, PHYS, TELEKOM video signal; **Videospur** *f*
FERNSEH video track; **Videospurhinterflanke** *f* FERN-
SEH trailing edge video track; **Videoterminal** *nt*
FERNSEH video terminal
Videotex *nt* FERNSEH videotex; **Videotex-Gateway** *m*
FERNSEH videotex gateway; **Videotex-Server** *m* FERN-
SEH videotex server

Video: **Videotext** *m* FERNSEH, TELEKOM teletext

Video: **Videothek** *f* FERNSEH video tape library; **Videoübertragung** *f* FERNSEH video transmission; **Videoverstärker** *m* FERNSEH video amplifier; **Videoverstärkung** *f* FERNSEH video amplification; **Videozubehör** *nt* FERNSEH videoware

Vidikon *nt* ELEKTRONIK vidicon; **Vidikon-Kamera** *f* FERNSEH vidicon camera

vielatomig[1] *adj* CHEMIE polyatomic

vielatomig:[2] **~e Transferreaktion** *f* KERNTECH many-nuclear transfer reaction

Vieleck *nt* GEOM polygon

vieleckig *adj* GEOM polygonal

Vielfach *nt* TELEKOM multiplex

vielfach[1] *adj* MATH multiple

vielfach:[2] **~e Entwicklung** *f* NICHTFOSS ENERG multiple development

vielfach:[3] **~ nutzen** *vt* COMP & DV multiplex

Vielfach: **Vielfachecho** *nt* AUFNAHME multiple echo; **Vielfachelektromessung** *f* ERDÖL *Bohrlochmessung* multiple special electrical logging; **Vielfaches** *nt* MATH multiple; **~ einer Einheit** *nt* METROL multiple of a unit

Vielfachleitung *f* COMP & DV bus (BrE), highway, trunk (AmE); **Vielfachmeßinstrument** *nt* FERNSEH, RADIO multimeter; **Vielfachschrank** *m* TELEKOM multiple switchboard; **Vielfachstreuung** *f* TEILPHYS multiple scattering; **Vielfachübertrager** *m* COMP & DV multiplexer; **Vielfachübertragung** *f* COMP & DV multiplexing, multiplex; **Vielfachübertragungskanal** *m* COMP & DV multiplexor channel; **Vielfachzugriff** *m* TELEKOM multiple access; **Vielfachzugriff im Zeitmultiplex** *m* TELEKOM time division multiple access

vielflächig *adj* GEOM polyhedral

Vielflächner *m* GEOM polyhedron

Vielkammerklystron *nt* PHYS multicavity klystron

Vielkanal-Impulshöhenanalysator *m* PHYS multichannel analyser (BrE), multichannel analyzer (AmE)

Vielkanalprotokoll *nt* COMP & DV multichannel protocol

Vielkeilverzahnung *f* FERTIG multiple splining

Vielkörperzerfall *m* TEILPHYS multibody decay

vielphasig *adj* ELEKTROTECH polyphase

Vielpunkt- *pref* COMP & DV multiplex

Vielschlitzmagnetron *nt* ELEKTRONIK multisegment magnetron

Vielschnittdrehmaschine *f* FERTIG multiple-tool lathe

Vielseitigkeit *f* RAUMFAHRT versatility

Vielsprecher *m* TELEKOM high-calling-rate subscriber

Vielstoffmotor *m* KFZTECH, THERMOD multifuel engine

Vielstrahl-Kathodenstrahlröhre *f* ELEKTRONIK multibeam CRT

Vielzweckdrehmaschine *f* FERTIG general-purpose lathe

Vielzweckfaser *f* PHYS multimode fiber (AmE), multimode fibre (BrE)

Vier *f* MATH four

vier:[1] **mit ~ Seiten** *adj* GEOM four-sided

vier:[2] **vierte Dimension** *f* MATH fourth dimension; **vierte Generation** *f* COMP & DV fourth generation; **vierter Virialkoeffizient** *m* (*D*) THERMOD fourth virial coefficient (*D*)

vieradrig: **~es Kabel** *nt* PHYS quad cable

Vier: **Vieratomigkeit** *f* CHEMIE tetratomicity; **Vierbackenfutter** *nt* MASCHINEN four-jaw chuck

vierbasig *adj* CHEMIE quadribasic, tetrabasic

Vier: **Vier-Bit-Byte** *nt* COMP & DV nibble, nybble

4-D: **~ Verstärkung** *f* RAUMFAHRT 4-D reinforcement

vierdimensional *adj* PHYS four-dimensional

Vierdraht- *pref* TELEKOM four-wire; **Vierdraht-Drehstromsystem** *nt* ELEKTRIZ three-phase four-wire system; **Vierdrahtdurchschaltung** *f* TELEKOM four-wire switch; **Vierdrahtkoppelpunkt** *m* TELEKOM four-wire crosspoint; **Vierdrahtvermittlung** *f* TELEKOM four-wire switch; **Vierdraht-Vermittlungssystem** *nt* TELEKOM four-wire switching system; **Vierdrahtverstärker** *m* ELEKTRONIK four-wire repeater

Vier: **Viereck** *nt* GEOM quadrangle, quadrilateral, tetragon

viereckig[1] *adj* GEOM quadrangular

viereckig:[2] **~er Dipolrahmen** *m* ELEKTROTECH square loop

Vier: **Vierende-Elträger** *m* BAU open-web girder; **Vieranschluß** *m* TELEKOM four-party line with selective ringing; **Viererleitung** *f* ELEKTROTECH, TELEKOM phantom circuit; **Vierervektor** *m* PHYS four-vector

Vierfach- *pref* FOTO, KFZTECH fourfold; **Vierfach-Expansionsmaschine** *f* MASCHINEN quadruple-expansion engine; **Vierfachmeißelbohrer** *m* ERDÖL *Bohrtechnik* four-way bit; **Vierfachmeißelhalter** *m* MASCHINEN four-stud tool post, four-tool turret; **Vierfach-Stativgestell** *nt* FOTO fourfold tripod stand; **Vierfachvergaser** *m* KFZTECH four-barrel carburetor (AmE), four-barrel carburettor (BrE); **Vierfach-Verstärker** *m* ELEKTRONIK quad-operational amplifier

vierfädig: **~e Wicklung** *f* RADIO quadrifilar winding

Vier: **Vier-Faktorenformel** *f* KERNTECH four-factor formula

Vierfarben- *pref* DRUCK four-color (AmE), four-colour (BrE); **Vierfarbendruck** *m* DRUCK four-color process (AmE), four-colour process (BrE), printing with four colors (AmE), printing with four colours (BrE); **Vierfarbendruckfarbe** *f* DRUCK four-color process ink (AmE), four-colour process ink (BrE); **Vierfarbenseparation** *f* DRUCK four-color separation (AmE), four-colour separation (BrE); **Vierfarbentheorem** *nt* GEOM four-color theorem (AmE), four-colour theorem (BrE)

vierflächig *adj* GEOM tetrahedral

Vier: **Vierflächner** *m* GEOM tetrahedron; **Vierflankenmethode** *f* GERÄT quad-slope method; **Vierflügelbohrmeißel** *m* ERDÖL four-wing bit; **Vierfrequenz-Duplex-Telegraphie** *f* TELEKOM four-frequency duplex telegraphy; **Vierkanal-Verstärker** *m* ELEKTRONIK four-channel amplifier

Vierkant *m* FERTIG *Kunststoffinstallationen* square end; **Vierkantendrehmeißel** *m* FERTIG square cutting tool; **Vierkantfeile** *f* MASCHINEN square file; **Vierkantformmeißel** *m* FERTIG square forming tool; **Vierkantkopf** *m* MASCHINEN square head; **Vierkantkopfschraube** *f* BAU coach screw; **Vierkantmutter** *f* MASCHINEN square nut; **Vierkantscheibe** *f* MASCHINEN square washer; **Vierkantschlüssel** *m* MASCHINEN square spanner (BrE), square wrench (AmE); **Vierkantschraube** *f* BAU square bolt, MASCHINEN square head bolt; **Vierkantstahl** *m* METALL square; **Vierkantventil** *nt* BAU cock with square head

Vierkurbelgetriebe *nt* MASCHINEN four-crank mechanism

Vierleiter- *pref* ELEKTROTECH four-wire; **Vierleiteranlage** *f* ELEKTROTECH four-wire system; **Vierleiternetz** *nt* ELEKTROTECH four-wire system

Vier: **Viermaster** *m* WASSERTRANS *Segeln* four-master; **Vierniveau-Maser** *f* ELEKTRONIK four-level maser

Vierphasen- *pref* ELEKTRONIK, TELEKOM four-phase;

Vierphasenmodulator *m* TELEKOM four-phase modulator; **Vierphasenumtastung** *f (QPSK)* ELEKTRONIK, TELEKOM quadriphase shift keying, quaternary phase shift keying *(QPSK)*; **Vierphasenumtastung mit geglättetem Phasenverlauf** *f* TELEKOM phase-shaped QPSK

vierphasig *adj* ELEKTRONIK four-phase

Vierpol *m* ELEKTROTECH two-port network, PHYS Schaltungstheorie quadripole; **~ in H-Schaltung** *m* ELEKTROTECH H-network; **Vierpolanordnung** *f* KERNTECH quadrupolar configuration; **Vierpolfeld** *nt* KERNTECH quadrupole field; **Vierpolfilter** *nt* ELEKTRONIK four-pole filter; **Vierpolgenerator** *m* ELEKTRIZ four-pole generator

vierpolig [1] *adj* ELEKTRIZ four-polar, four-pole

vierpolig: [2] **~er Ausschalter** *m* ELEKTROTECH 4 PST switch, four-pole single-throw switch; **~e Ausschaltkontakte** *m pl* ELEKTROTECH 4 PST contacts; **~es Ausschaltrelais** *nt* ELEKTROTECH 4 PST relay; **~er magnetischer Lautsprecher** *m* AUFNAHME balanced-armature loudspeaker; **~er Umschalter** *m* ELEKTROTECH 4 PDT switch, four-pole double-throw switch; **~e Umschaltkontakte** *m pl* ELEKTROTECH 4 PDT contacts; **~es Umschaltrelais** *nt* ELEKTROTECH 4 PDT relay

Vierpol: **Vierpolkreuzglied** *nt* ELEKTROTECH lattice network; **Vierpolschaltung** *f* ELEKTRIZ quadripole, ELEKTROTECH four-terminal network; **Vierpolübertragungsmaß** *nt* AKUSTIK image transfer exponent

Vier-: **Vierpunktlager** *nt* MASCHINEN four-point support; **Vierquadrantenbetrieb** *m* ELEKTRIZ four-quadrant operation; **Vierquadranten-Multiplizierer** *m* ELEKTRONIK four-quadrant multiplier; **Vierradantrieb** *m* KFZTECH four-wheel drive; **Vierradbremsanlage** *f* KFZTECH *Bremsanlage* four-wheel brake system; **Vierschichtdiode** *f* ELEKTRONIK four-layer diode; **Vierschichtzelle** *f* ELEKTRONIK *Halbleiter* p-n-p-n device; **Vierschneidenbohrmeißel** *m* ERDÖL *Bohrtechnik* four-wing bit; **Vierschraubenfutter** *nt* MASCHINEN bell chuck, cup chuck

vierseitig [1] *adj* GEOM four-sided, quadrilateral

vierseitig: [2] **~e Fläche** *f* KONSTZEICH four-sided area; **~e Skizze** *f* VERPACK four-sided sketch

Vier-: **Vierspindelbohrmaschine** *f* FERTIG four-spindle drilling machine; **Vierspur-Aufnahme** *f* AUFNAHME quarter-track recording

vierspurig: **~es Aufzeichnen** *nt* AUFNAHME four-track recording; **~er Recorder** *m* AUFNAHME four-track recorder

Vier-: **Vierspur-Tonaufzeichnung** *f* AKUSTIK tetraphonic recording; **Vierstoff-** *pref* CHEMIE quaternary; **Viertakter** *m* MASCHINEN four-stroke engine; **Viertakthub** *m* KFZTECH *Motor* four-stroke cycle; **Viertaktmotor** *m* KFZTECH *Motor*, MASCHINEN, MECHAN, WASSERTRANS *Motor* four-stroke engine

Viertel *nt* MATH fourth, quarter, METROL quarter; **Viertelabsatz** *m* BAU *Treppe* quarter space; **Viertelansicht** *f* KONSTZEICH quarter view; **Viertelelliptikfeder** *f* MASCHINEN quarter-elliptic spring; **Viertelgallone** *f* METROL quart (BrE); **Vierteljahr** *nt* MATH quarter;

Viertelkreis *m* GEOM, MECHAN quadrant; **Viertelkreisfräser** *m* MASCHINEN corner-rounding cutters, quarter-round milling cutter; **Viertelkreissims** *m* BAU ovolo

Viertel: **Viertelmaske** *f* SICHERHEIT quarter mask; **Viertelscheffel** *nt* METROL peck; **Viertelstab** *m* BAU astragal, quarter round; **Viertelwellenlänge** *f* ELEKTRONIK quarter wavelength; **Viertelwellenleitung** *f* PHYS quarter-wave line; **Viertelwellen-Peitschenantenne** *f* TELEKOM quarter-wave whip antenna; **Viertelwellen-Vertikalantenne mit Gegengewicht** *f* RADIO ground plane; **Viertelwert** *m* MATH quartile

Vier-: **Vierwegehahn** *m* WASSERVERSORG four-way cock; **Vierwege-Palette** *f* VERPACK four-way pallet; **Vierwegeventil** *nt* MASCHINEN four-way valve

vierwertig *adj* CHEMIE quadribasic, quadrivalent, tetravalent

Vier-: **Vierwertigkeit** *f* CHEMIE quadrivalence, tetravalence, tetravalency; **Vierzahnbohrer** *m* ERDÖL *Bohrtechnik* quadricone bit; **Vierzylinderboxermotor** *m* TRANS flat-four engine; **Vierzylinder-Motorrad** *nt* KFZTECH four-cylinder motorcycle; **Vierzylinder-V-Motor** *m* KFZTECH V-four engine

Vignettierung *f* FOTO vignetting

Vinyl- *pref* CHEMIE vinyl; **Vinylacetylen** *nt* CHEMIE vinylacetylene; **Vinylation** *f* CHEMIE vinylation; **Vinylbenzen** *nt* CHEMIE vinylbenzene; **Vinylbenzol** *nt* CHEMIE styrene, styrolene; **Vinylethen** *nt* CHEMIE divinyl; **Vinylethin** *nt* CHEMIE vinylacetylene; **Vinylethylen** *nt* CHEMIE divinyl

vinylhomolog *adj* CHEMIE vinylogous

Vinyl-: **Vinylhomologes** *nt* CHEMIE vinylog; **Vinyliden-** *pref* CHEMIE vinylidene; **Vinylierung** *f* CHEMIE vinylation; **Vinyllack** *m* BAU vinyl lacquer

vinylog *adj* CHEMIE vinylogous

Vinyl-: **Vinyloges** *nt* CHEMIE vinylog; **Vinylpyridin** *nt* CHEMIE vinylpyridine

Violinblock *m* WASSERTRANS *Deckbeschläge* fiddle block

Violur- *pref* CHEMIE violuric

Virial- *pref* PHYS virial; **Virialsatz** *m* PHYS virial theorem; **Virialtheorem** *nt* PHYS virial theorem

Viridin *nt* CHEMIE viridine

virtuell [1] *adj* COMP & DV virtual

virtuell: [2] **~e Adresse** *f* COMP & DV virtual address; **~es Bild** *nt* FOTO, OPTIK, WELLPHYS *eines Hologramms* virtual image; **~e Datenstation** *f* COMP & DV virtual terminal; **~e Dauerschaltung** *f* COMP & DV permanent virtual circuit; **~e Maschine** *f* COMP & DV virtual machine; **~e Netzwerkdatenstation** *f* COMP & DV network virtual terminal; **~e Platte** *f* COMP & DV virtual disk; **~er Rufdienst** *m* COMP & DV virtual call service; **~e Schallquelle** *f* AKUSTIK virtual sound source; **~er Speicher** *m* COMP & DV virtual memory, virtual storage; **~es Speichersystem** *nt* COMP & DV virtual memory system; **~e Speicherverwaltung** *f (VMS)* COMP & DV virtual memory specification *(VMS)* **~es Teilchen** *nt* TEILPHYS virtual particle; **~es Terminal** *nt* COMP & DV virtual terminal; **~e Tonhöhe** *f* AKUSTIK virtual pitch; **~e Verbindung** *f* COMP & DV virtual circuit, virtual connection, TELEKOM virtual circuit; **~e Verbindung des D-Kanals** *f* TELEKOM D-channel virtual circuit; **~er Verbindungsdienst des B-Kanals** *m* TELEKOM B-channel virtual circuit service

Viscin *nt* CHEMIE viscin

Viscokupplung *f* KFZTECH *Getriebe* viscous clutch

Viscose *f* CHEMIE viscose

Visier [1] *nt* OPTIK hole, SICHERHEIT visor

Visier: [2] **~ schaffen** *vi* OPTIK hole sight

Visier: **Visiereinrichtung** *f* BAU sight; **Visierfernrohr** *nt* BAU sighting telescope; **Visiergerät** *nt* RAUMFAHRT diopter; **Visiertafel** *f* BAU *Vermessung* boning rod

Viskoelastizität *f* KUNSTSTOFF viscoelasticity

Viskometer *nt* STRÖMPHYS viscometer

viskos[1] *adj* CHEMIE, LEBENSMITTEL, MASCHINEN, PHYS viscous

viskos:[2] **~e Flüssigkeit** *f* LEBENSMITTEL, MASCHINEN, PHYS viscous fluid; **~e Strömung** *f* LEBENSMITTEL, MASCHINEN, PHYS viscous flow; **~e Unterschicht** *f* STRÖMPHYS viscous sublayer; **~er Zustand** *m* FERTIG *Plaste* treacle stage

Viskosefilament *nt* TEXTIL rayon; **Viskosefilamentfaser** *f* TEXTIL rayon

Viskosimeter *nt* FERTIG viscosimeter, KUNSTSTOFF viscometer, viscosimeter, LABOR, MASCHINEN viscometer, STRÖMPHYS viscosimeter, THERMOD viscosity meter

Viskosität *f* CHEMIE, ERDÖL *Petrochemie*, FERTIG, KOHLEN, KUNSTSTOFF, MASCHINEN, PHYS, STRÖMPHYS, THERMOD viscosity; **Viskositäts-Dichte-Konstante** *f* THERMOD viscosity gravity constant; **Viskositäts-Dichteverhältnis** *nt* (*VD*) NICHTFOSS ENERG *Kunststoffe* kinematic viscosity; **Viskositätsindex** *m* (*VI*) KFZTECH *Öl*, MASCHINEN, STRÖMPHYS, THERMOD viscosity index (*VI*); **Viskositätskoeffizient** *m* PHYS, STRÖMPHYS coefficient of viscosity, THERMOD viscosity coefficient; **Viskositätsmeßgerät** *nt* KUNSTSTOFF viscometer, viscosimeter; **Viskositäts-Temperatur-Koeffizient** *m* THERMOD viscosity temperature coefficient; **Viskositäts-Temperaturverhalten** *nt* THERMOD viscosity temperature characteristics; **Viskositätsverbesserer** *m* ERDÖL *Petrochemie* viscosity index improver; **Viskositätszahl** *f* (*VI*) KFZTECH *Öl*, MASCHINEN, STRÖMPHYS, THERMOD viscosity index (*VI*)

Visualisierung *f* COMP & DV visualization

visuell[1] *adj* OPTIK ocular

visuell:[2] **~er Störabstand** *m* AUFNAHME weighted signal-to-noise ratio; **~e Wahrnehmung** *f* ERGON visual perception; **~es Zeichenlesesystem** *nt* VERPACK character-reading vision system

Vitellin *nt* CHEMIE vitellin

Viterbi-Decodierung *f* TELEKOM Viterbi decoding

Vitrifikation *f* CHEMIE vitrification

Vitriolbildung *f* CHEMIE vitriolization

VK *abbr* (*Vergaserkraftstoff*) ERDÖL, KFZTECH, THERMOD fuel, gas (AmE), gasoline (AmE), petrol (BrE)

V-Kerbe *f* KERNTECH V-shaped notch

VLCC *abbr* (*Supertanker*) ERDÖL VLCC (*very large crude carrier*)

V-Leitwerk *nt* LUFTTRANS V-tail

Vlies *nt* PAPIER mat; **Vliesbildung** *f* KER & GLAS mat formation

VLP[1] *abbr* (*Video-Langspiel*) FERNSEH VLP (*video long play*)

VLP:[2] **VLP-Bildplatte** *f* COMP & DV optical memory

VLSI[1] *abbr* (*Höchstintegration, Übergroßintegration*) COMP & DV, ELEKTRONIK, TELEKOM VLSI (*very large-scale integration*)

VLSI:[2] **VLSI-Chip** *m* COMP & DV VLSI chip; **VLSI-Schaltkreis** *m* PHYS, TELEKOM VLSI circuit

V-Meißel *m* BAU double-beveled chisel (AmE), double-bevelled chisel (BrE)

VMOS-Transistor *m* ELEKTRONIK VMOS transistor

V-Motor *m* KFZTECH V-engine, V-type engine, MASCHINEN V-cylinder engine, V-engine

VMS *abbr* (*virtuelle Speicherverwaltung*) COMP & DV VMS (*virtual memory specification*)

V-Null-Getriebe *nt* FERTIG *Getriebelehre* long-and-short addendum gears

Vocoder *m* AUFNAHME *Sprachverschlüsselungsgerät*, COMP & DV, TELEKOM vocoder; **~ mit linearer Prädiktionscodierung** *m* TELEKOM linear predictive coding vocoder; **~ mit Pitch-Anregung** *m* TELEKOM pitch-excited vocoder

Vogelkäfigantenne *f* RADIO birdcage aerial

Vogelnest *nt* KER & GLAS bird's nest

Vogelschlaggefahr *f* LUFTTRANS bird strike hazard

Void *nt* CHEMIE void

Voile *m* TEXTIL voile

volatil *adj* CHEMIE volatile

Voll- *pref* COMP & DV, ELEKTRIZ, WASSERTRANS full

voll:[1] **~ betriebsbereit** *adj* MASCHINEN in full working order; **mit ~ lem Bug** *adj* WASSERTRANS bluff-bowed; **~ im Eingriff** *adj* FERTIG fully meshed

voll:[2] **~e Bohrung** *f* MASCHINEN full bore; **~e Drehung** *f* LUFTTRANS *Kunstflug* roll; **~e Größe** *f* MASCHINEN full scale; **~es Rohr** *nt* HYDRAUL full pipe; **~e Rundkante** *f* KER & GLAS full round edge; **~e Schleife** *f* LUFTTRANS *Kunstflug* closed loop; **~er Schub** *m* RAUMFAHRT full thrust; **~er Ton** *m* AUFNAHME round tone; **~e Wasserdruckhöhe** *f* HYDRAUL full head of water

voll:[3] **mit ~er Auslastung arbeiten** *vi* MASCHINEN work to full capacity; **~ durchkentern** *vi* WASSERTRANS turn turtle

Voll-: **Volladdierer** *m* COMP & DV full adder; **Vollautomat** *m* MASCHINEN fully automatic lathe

vollautomatisch: **~e Blende** *f* FOTO fully automatic diaphragm; **~e Etikettiermaschine** *f* VERPACK *für selbstklebende Etiketten* fully automatic self-adhesive labeling machine (AmE), fully automatic self-adhesive labelling machine (BrE); **~es Landesystem** *nt* TRANS autoland system; **~e Landung** *f* LUFTTRANS autoland; **~e Streckverpackung** *f* VERPACK fully automatic stretch-wrapper pack

Voll-: **Vollbahn** *f* EISENBAHN standard gage railroad (AmE), standard gauge railway (BrE); **Vollbereichslautsprecher** *m* AUFNAHME full-range loudspeaker; **Vollbildabzug** *m* FOTO full-frame print; **Vollbinder** *m* BAU perpend stone; **Volldraht** *m* ELEKTRIZ solid wire

Volldruck *m* LUFTTRANS impact pressure; **Volldruckmaschine** *f* MASCHINEN nonexpansion engine

Voll-: **Vollduplex** *nt* COMP & DV fault-tolerant system, RADIO full duplex; **Volleinschlag** *m* KFZTECH *Lenkung* steering lock

vollelastisch: **~er Stoß** *m* KERNTECH billiard ball collision

vollfett: **~e Schrift** *f* DRUCK full-face type

vollfarbig *adj* BrE DRUCK full-color (AmE), full-colour

vollflächig *adj* FERTIG holohedral

vollfliegend: **~e Achse** *f* KFZTECH full-floating axle

Voll-: **Vollgas** *nt* LUFTTRANS full-open throttle

vollgebunden *adj* DRUCK full-bound, whole-bound

vollgelaufen *adj* WASSERTRANS waterlogged

Voll-: **Vollgestängebohren** *nt* BAU boring by percussion with rods

völlig:[1] **nicht ~ abgesättigt** *adj* CHEMIE *Valenz* unsaturated

völlig:[2] **~ absorbierendes Target** *nt* STRAHLPHYS total absorption target; **~ blockierungsfreies Netz** *nt* TELEKOM strictly non-blocking network; **~e Windstille** *f* WASSERTRANS dead calm

Völligkeit *f* WASSERTRANS *Schiffbau* fineness; **Völligkeitsgrad** *m* WASSERTRANS *Schiffkonstruktion* coefficient of fineness

vollimprägnieren *vt* BAU saturate

***Voll-*: Vollinie** *f* KONSTZEICH continuous line; **Vollinjektionsturbine** *f* HYDRAUL full-injection turbine

vollisoliert: **~er Schalter** *m* ELEKTRIZ all-insulated switch

***Voll-*: Vollkammerluftkissensystem** *nt* TRANS plenum chamber air cushion system; **Vollkegel** *m* FERTIG external taper; **Vollkeilriemen** *m* FERTIG solid vee-belt; **Vollkernisolator** *m* ELEKTROTECH solid core-type insulator

vollkommen:[1] **~ trocken** *adj* TEXTIL bone-dry

vollkommen:[2] **~er Kristall** *m* METALL perfect crystal; **~e Schmierung** *f* MASCHINEN thick film lubrication

***Voll-*: Vollkreis** *m* GEOM, KONSTZEICH full circle; **Vollkundenschaltung** *f* ELEKTRONIK *voll kundenspezifischer Schaltkreis* full-custom circuit; **Vollkurzschluß** *m* ELEKTROTECH dead short; **Voll-Last** *f* ELEKTRIZ full load, WASSERTRANS full power; **Voll-Lastbündel** *nt* TELEKOM high-usage circuit group; **Voll-Lastkonfiguration** *f* RAUMFAHRT full-load configuration **Voll-Leimen** *nt* VERPACK full gluing; *m* ELEKTRIZ solid conductor; **Voll-Leiter** *m* ELEKTRIZ solid conductor; **Vollmacht** *f* PATENT authorization; QUAL authority; **Vollmantelkorb** *m* KOHLEN *Zentrifuge* bowl centrifuge; **Vollmaterial** *nt* ANSTRICH solid; **Vollniet** *m* MASCHINEN full rivet

Vollpappe *f* VERPACK solid fiber board (AmE), solid fibre board (BrE); **Vollpappenkiste** *f* VERPACK container board box

***Voll-*: Vollpolläufer** *m* KFZTECH smooth-core armature; **Vollprüfung** *f* QUAL one-hundred-percent inspection; **Vollrad** *nt* EISENBAHN solid wheel; **Vollrohr** *nt* HYDRAUL full pipe

vollsaugen: sich ~ *v refl* LEBENSMITTEL soak

***Voll-*: Vollschalenbauweise** *f* RAUMFAHRT monocoque structure; **Vollscheibe** *f* FERTIG arborless wheel, MASCHINEN solid pulley; **Vollschmierung** *f* MASCHINEN thick film lubrication; **Vollschnitt** *m* KONSTZEICH full section

vollschwarz: **~er Pfeil** *m* KONSTZEICH blackened arrowhead

***Voll-*: Vollsperrung** *f* EISENBAHN complete track load

Vollspur *f* AKUSTIK, AUFNAHME full track, EISENBAHN standard gage (AmE), standard gauge (BrE); **Vollspur-Aufnahme** *f* AUFNAHME full-track recording; **Vollspur-Aufnahmegerät** *m* AUFNAHME full-track recorder

vollständig:[1] **~ in Halbleiter-Technik** *adj* ELEKTRONIK *Ausführung* all-solid state

vollständig:[2] **~ es Höhenleitwerk** *nt* LUFTTRANS empennage **~e Induktion** *f* MATH mathematical induction; **~es Quadrat** *nt* MATH perfect square; **~e Reinigung** *f* KERNTECH complete purification; **~er Schutz** *m* PATENT full protection; **~e Verkehrsverlagerung** *f* TRANS complete diversion

***Voll-*: Vollständigkeit** *f* COMP & DV integrity; **Vollstromölfilter** *nt* KFZTECH *Schmierung* full-flow oil filter; **Vollsubtrahierer** *m* COMP & DV full subtractor

volltanken *vt* TRANS fill up

vollverstreckt: **~es Garn** *nt* TEXTIL fully drawn yarn

vollverteilt: **~es Steuersystem** *nt* TELEKOM fully distributed control system

vollwandig: **~er Träger** *m* BAU I-girder

***Voll-*: Vollwandrippe** *f* RAUMFAHRT rib; **Vollwandträger** *m* BAU plate girder

Vollweg *m* ELEKTRIZ, ELEKTROTECH full wave; **Vollweg-**brückenschaltung *f* ELEKTRIZ full bridge; **Vollweggleichrichten** *nt* ELEKTROTECH full-wave rectification; **Vollweggleichrichter** *m* ELEKTRIZ, ELEKTROTECH full-wave rectifier; **Vollweggleichrichtung** *f* ELEKTRIZ full-wave rectification

***Voll-*: Vollwelle** *f* MASCHINEN solid shaft; **Vollwertkost** *f* LEBENSMITTEL wholefood; **Vollzapfen** *m* BAU through tenon; **Vollziegel** *m* BAU solid brick

Volt *nt* *(V)* AUFNAHME, ELEKTRIZ *Einheit der Spannung*, ELEKTRONIK, METROL, OPTIK, RADIO volt *(V)*; **Voltameter** *nt* CHEMIE voltameter, ELEKTROTECH coulometer, voltameter, voltameter, PHYS coulometer, voltameter; **Voltampere** *nt* ELEKTRIZ voltampere

Volta: **~sche Säule** *f* ELEKTROTECH voltaic pile; **~sche Zelle** *f* ELEKTROTECH voltaic cell

Volterra: Volterra-Versetzung *f* METALL Volterra dislocation

***Volt*: Voltmeter** *nt* ELEKTROTECH, PHYS voltmeter

Volumeinheit *f* AKUSTIK VU, volume unit

Volumen *nt* COMP & DV volume, GEOM volume, MASCHINEN capacity, MECHAN bulk, METROL cubage, cubic measure, PHYS volume, TEXTIL bulk, TEXTIL, THERMOD volume; **~ von Feststoffen** *nt* METROL solid measure; **~ in Phase** *nt* (Ω) PHYS volume in phase space (Ω); **Volumenausdehnungskoeffizient** *m* THERMOD expansion coefficient; **Volumendiffusion** *f* METALL volume diffusion; **Volumendosierung** *f* VERPACK volume dosing; **Volumendurchflußmeßgerät** *nt* GERÄT volumetric flow meter; **Volumenelastizitätsmodul** *m* *(B)* THERMOD modulus of volume elasticity *(B)*; **Volumenemissions- und Absorptionskoeffizient** *m* STRAHLPHYS volume emission and absorption coefficient

volumenerhaltend: **~e Strömungen** *f pl* STRÖMPHYS isochoric flows

***Volumen*: Volumenfraktion** *f* METALL volume fraction; **Volumenfraktion von Teilchen** *f* METALL volume fraction of particles; **Volumenfüllung** *f* VERPACK volume filling; **Volumengeometrie** *f* GEOM CSG, constructive solid geometry; **Volumengeschwindigkeit** *f* *(U)* AKUSTIK volume current *(U)*; **Volumengrößenfaktor** *m* METALL volume size factor; **Volumenintegral** *nt* PHYS volume integral; **Volumen-Kapazitätsverhältnis** *nt* TRANS V-C ratio, volume-capacity ratio; **Volumenkraft** *f* FERTIG body force; **Volumenmessung** *f* METROL cubic measurement; **Volumenmodell** *nt* GEOM volume model; **Volumenoszillator** *m* ELEKTRONIK *Mikrowellentechnik* bulk-wave oscillator; **Volumenschallwelle** *f* ELEKTROTECH bulk acoustic wave; **Volumenstrom** *m* AKUSTIK *(U)* volume current *(U)*, HEIZ & KÄLTE volume flow, volume flow rate, volumetric flow; **Volumenstrommeßgerät** *nt* GERÄT volumetric flow meter; **Volumenstromrechner** *m* GERÄT volumetric flow calculator; **Volumenveränderung** *f* METALL volume change; **Volumenverdrängung** *f* *(X)* AKUSTIK volume displacement *(X)*; **Volumenwellen-Resonator** *m* ELEKTRONIK bulk-wave resonator; **Volumenzähler** *m* GERÄT volumetric flow meter

Volumeter *nt* AKUSTIK volumeter

volumetrisch: **~e Effizienz** *f* ELEKTROTECH *Platte in Kommutatoren* volumetric efficiency; **~e Gleichung** *f* METALL volumetric equation; **~er Wirkungsgrad** *m* KFZTECH, MASCHINEN, NICHTFOSS ENERG volumetric efficiency

voluminös *adj* PAPIER bulky

Von-Neumann: Von-Neumann-Maschine *f* COMP & DV

von Neumann machine

Vor: ~- **und Rückwärtssuche** *f* KÜNSTL INT bidirectional search

Vor-/Rückwärtszähler *m* ELEKTRONIK increment/decrement counter

Vorabaufnahme *f* FERNSEH off-air pick-up

Vorabaufzeichnung *f* FERNSEH off-air recording

Vorab-Beurteilung *f* QUAL initial evaluation

Vorabdruck *m* DRUCK preprint

Vorabfühlschleife *f* AUFNAHME presence loop

vorabspeichern *vt* COMP & DV prestore

Voralterung *f* TELEKOM preageing (BrE), preaging (AmE)

Vorankündigung *f* TRANS advance information; **Vorankündigungszeichen** *nt* TRANS advance direction sign

Voranmeldungsgespräch *nt* TELEKOM personal call

Voranode *f* ELEKTROTECH first anode

Voranstrich *m* BAU prime coat, KUNSTSTOFF primer

Vorarbeiten *nt* FERTIG roughing-down

Vorarbeiter *m* KER & GLAS gaffer

Voraufbereitung *f* CHEMIE *Trinkwasser, Abwasser* pre-treating

voraufgezeichnet *adj* COMP & DV prerecorded

voraus[1] *adv* WASSERTRANS ahead

voraus:[2] **im ~ bezahlter Sondertarif** *m* (*APEX*) LUFTTRANS advance purchase excursion fare (*APEX*)

Vorausanzeige *f* WASSERTRANS *Radar* heading marker

vorausberechnet: ~**es Lebensdauer-Perzentil Q** *nt* QUAL predicted Q-percentile life; ~**e mittlere Instandhaltungsdauer** *f* QUAL assessed mean active maintenance time; ~**e mittlere Lebensdauer** *f* QUAL predicted mean life

Vorausexemplar *nt* DRUCK advance copy

Vorausfahrt *f* WASSERTRANS *Schiffbewegung* headway

Vorauslaugen *nt* KOHLEN preleaching

vorausplanen *vt* COMP & DV project

voraussichtlich: ~**e Abflugszeit** *f* (*ETD*) LUFTTRANS, WASSERTRANS estimated time of departure (*ETD*); ~**e Ankunftszeit** *f* (*ETA*) LUFTTRANS, WASSERTRANS estimated time of arrival (*ETA*); ~**es Ausfallperzentil** *nt* QUAL predicted Q-percentile life; ~**e Flugzeit** *f* LUFTTRANS estimated flight time; ~**e mittlere Instandhaltungsdauer** *f* QUAL predicted failure rate; ~**e Offblockzeit** *f* LUFTTRANS estimated off-block time

vorausstabilisiert *adj* WASSERTRANS *Radar* head-up

Vorausströmung *f* HYDRAUL exhaust lead

Voraustritt *m* HYDRAUL exhaust lead

Vorbad *nt* FOTO preliminary bath

Vorband *nt* AUFNAHME leader tape

Vorbau *m* WASSERTRANS *Schiffbau* prototype;

Vorbaum *m* TEXTIL back beam

vorbearbeiten *vt* COMP & DV pre-edit

Vorbearbeitung *f* ELEKTRONIK preprocessing

Vorbecken *nt* HYDRAUL forebay

vorbehandeln *vt* ANSTRICH pretreat

Vorbehandlung *f* ABFALL, ANSTRICH, KOHLEN pretreatment, KUNSTSTOFF conditioning, MASCHINEN pretreatment, WASSERVERSORG preliminary treatment

vorbeifahren *vt* EISENBAHN *am Signal* pass

Vorbeiflug *m* RAUMFAHRT fly-by; **Vorbeiflugeinwirkung** *f* RAUMFAHRT fly-by effect

Vorbeipendeln *nt* RAUMFAHRT swing-by

Vorbelastung *f* ELEKTROTECH, KOHLEN *mechanisch* bias, UMWELTSCHMUTZ *des Wassers* initial level of water pollution; **Vorbelastungsdruck** *m* KOHLEN preconsolidation pressure; **Vorbelastungswiderstand** *m*

ELEKTROTECH *für Gleichrichter* bleeder resistor

Vorbenutzung *f* PATENT prior use

Vorbereiten *nt* MASCHINEN setting, setup

vorbereiten *vt* COMP & DV initialize, MASCHINEN set-up

vorbereitet *adj* LEBENSMITTEL prepared

Vorbereitung *f* ANSTRICH pretreatment, COMP & DV, LEBENSMITTEL preparation

vorbespielt: ~**es Magnetband** *nt* AUFNAHME prerecorded magnetic tape

Vorbestellung *f* TELEKOM advance booking

vorbetrieblich: ~**e Überprüfung** *f* KERNTECH precommissioning checks

vorbeugend: ~**e Instandhaltung** *f* BAU preventive maintenance; ~**e Prüfung** *f* QUAL preventive inspection; ~**e Wartung** *f* COMP & DV, MASCHINEN, TELEKOM preventive maintenance

vorbildlich *adj* COMP & DV model

Vorblasen *nt* KER & GLAS blow back, preblowing, puff

Vorblick *m* BAU *Vermessung* minus sight

Vorblock *m* FERTIG *Profil* beam blank, METALL bloom

vorblocken *vt* FERTIG *Luppen* bloom

Vorblock-Putzerei *f* METALL bloom yard

vorbohren *vt* BAU hole, MASCHINEN predrill

Vorbohrer *m* BAU gimlet

Vorbohrloch *nt* NICHTFOSS ENERG mousehole

Vorbohrschlamm *m* ERDÖL *Flachbohrtechnik* spud mud

Vorbrecher *m* KOHLEN primary crusher

Vorbrennen: ~ **des Glashafens** *nt* KER & GLAS pot arching

Vordach *nt* BAU canopy, porch roof

vordefiniert *adj* COMP & DV predefined

Vordehnung *f* METALL prestrain

Vorder- *pref* WASSERTRANS *Schiff* forward, *am Schiff* fore-

vorder: ~**e Einzelradaufhängung** *f* KFZTECH independent front suspension; ~**e Hafenöffnung** *f* KER & GLAS front arch; ~**er Kolben** *m* KFZTECH front piston, primary piston; ~**es Lot** *nt* WASSERTRANS *Schiffkonstruktion* forward perpendicular; ~**e Schwarzschultertastung** *f* FERNSEH front porch switch; ~**er Spalt** *m* AUFNAHME front gap; ~**er Verschlußstein** *m* KER & GLAS front tweel; ~**er Zellenring** *m* RAUMFAHRT forward frame section

Vorder-: **Vorderabtastung** *f* FERNSEH front scanning; **Vorderachse** *f* KFZTECH *Räder, Kraftübertragung*, MASCHINEN front axle; **Vorderdeck** *nt* WASSERTRANS foredeck; **Vorderflanke** *f* ELEKTRONIK *eines Impulses*, FERTIG, PHYS *eines Impulses*, TELEKOM leading edge; **Vorderflankenimpulszeit** *f* FERNSEH leading-edge pulse time; **Vorderglied** *nt* FOTO *eines Objektivs* front element

Vordergrund:[1] **im ~** *adj* COMP & DV foreground

Vordergrund[2] *m* COMP & DV foreground; **Vordergrundpref** COMP & DV foreground; **Vordergrundjob** *m* COMP & DV foreground job; **Vordergrundprogramm** *nt* COMP & DV foreground program; **Vordergrundverarbeitung** *f* COMP & DV foregrounding, foreground processing

Vorder-: **Vorderkante** *f* DRUCK *eines Buches* fore edge, ELEKTRONIK *von Belegen*, FERTIG, LUFTTRANS, PHYS *Impuls*, TELEKOM leading edge; **Vorderkante des Luftschraubenblattes** *f* LUFTTRANS *Hubschrauber* blade leading edge; **Vorderplatte** *f* GERÄT *an Gerät* front panel

Vorderrad *nt* TRANS front wheel; **Vorderradantrieb** *m* KFZTECH front-wheel drive; **Vorderradaufhängung** *f* KFZTECH front suspension; **Vorderradeinstellung** *f*

KFZTECH front-wheel alignment

Vorder-: **Vorderrahmen** *m* FOTO front frame; **Vorderseite** *f* BAU face, front, COMP & DV front end, MASCHINEN face, front, PAPIER front side

Vorderwand *f* KER & GLAS front wall; **Vorderwandzelle** *f* ELEKTROTECH front-wall photovoltaic cell

Vorder-: **Vorderzapfen der Kurbelwelle** *m* KFZTECH crankshaft front end

Vordrossel *f* KFZTECH *Vergaser* choke

Vordruck *m* COMP & DV form, DRUCK printed form, PATENT form; **Vordruckwalze** *f* DRUCK dandy roll; **Vordruckzeichnung** *f* KONSTZEICH preprinted drawing

Voreilen *nt* FERTIG leading

voreilen *vi* MASCHINEN advance

Voreilung *f* ELEKTRIZ *Phase* advance, FERTIG *Phase* lead, HYDRAUL *Dampf* preadmission, *Steuerschieber* lead, KONTROLL speed-up, MASCHINEN advance, lead, TEXTIL overfeed

Voreilwinkel *m* ELEKTRIZ *Phase* advance angle, KFZTECH angle of advance, MASCHINEN angle of advance, angle of lead

Voreinflugzeichen *nt* LUFTTRANS outer marker

voreingestellt: **~e Frequenz** *f* ELEKTRONIK preset frequency; **~es Potentiometer** *nt* ELEKTRIZ preset pot

Voreinstellen *nt* ELEKTRONIK presetting

voreinstellen *vt* AUFNAHME, COMP & DV, MASCHINEN preset

Voreinstellung *f* COMP & DV presetting

Voreinstellzähler *m* GERÄT preselection counter, preset counter

Voreinströmung *f* HYDRAUL *Dampf* preadmission, *Steuerschieber* lead; **äußere ~** *f* HYDRAUL outside lead

Vorentflammung *f* KFZTECH *Zündung* advance

Vorentwurf *m* BAU preliminary design

Vorfahre *m* *semantische Netze* ancestor node, antecedent node

Vorfahrt *f* TRANS right of way; **Vorfahrtsrecht** *nt* LUFTTRANS *Flughafen* right of way, TRANS priority, right of way, WASSERTRANS right of way

Vorfalldatenmeldung *f* LUFTTRANS incident date reporting

Vorfeld *nt* LUFTTRANS ramp, TRANS apron; **Vorfelddienst** *m* LUFTTRANS apron management service, ramp services; **Vorfeldrollbahn** *f* LUFTTRANS, TRANS apron taxiway; **Vorfeldwartebereich** *m* LUFTTRANS *Flughafen* holding apron, holding bay

vorfertigbearbeiten *vt* FERTIG semifinish

vorfertigen *vt* BAU precast

Vorfilter *nt* ELEKTRONIK prefilter, RADIO input filter; **~ zweiter Ordnung** *nt* ELEKTRONIK second order prefilter

Vorfiltern *nt* ELEKTRONIK prefiltering

Vorflügel *m* LUFTTRANS slat of the leading edge

Vorflugsrecht *nt* LUFTTRANS *Flughafen* right of way

Vorflutdrän *m* BAU main drain

Vorfluter *m* ABFALL receiving water, WASSERVERSORG drainage ditch, receiving water

Vorform *f* KER & GLAS *der Hohlglasfertigungsmaschine* blank, OPTIK, TELEKOM preform; **Vorformabdruck** *m* KER & GLAS baffle mark; **Vorformdeckel** *m* KER & GLAS *Hohlglasfertigung* baffle

Vorformen *nt* FERTIG *Walzen* edging, KUNSTSTOFF preforming

Vorformen *nt* FERTIG *Hämmern* saddening, *Schmieden* fillering

vorformen *vt* FERTIG sadden, *Schweißen* filler

Vorformling *m* KER & GLAS, KUNSTSTOFF preform

Vorform: **Vorformriß** *m* KER & GLAS blank tear; **Vorformspeiseöffnung** *f* KER & GLAS baffle hole; **Vorformtisch** *m* KER & GLAS blank table

Vorfräsen von Zahnlücken *nt* FERTIG gashing

Vorfräser *m* MASCHINEN rougher

Vorgabe *f* COMP & DV default, QUAL handicap; **Vorgabepref** COMP & DV default; **Vorgabewert** *m* COMP & DV default value

Vorgalvanisierbad *nt* FERTIG strike

Vorgang *m* HYDRAUL *Drehung* event, *Hub* event, *Steuerschieber* event, QUAL function

Vorgänger *m* COMP & DV ancestor, KÜNSTL INT *in semantischen Netzen* predecessor, *semantischen Netzen* ancestor node, antecedent node; **Vorgängerknoten** *m* KÜNSTL INT *in semantischen Netzen* predecessor, *semantischen Netzen* ancestor node, antecedent node

Vorgarn *nt* TEXTIL rove, roving

Vorgebirge *nt* WASSERTRANS *Geographie* promontory

vorgebohrt: **~er Pfahl** *m* KOHLEN prebored pile

vorgedruckt *adj* VERPACK preprinted

vorgefertigt *adj* BAU precast

vorgeformt: **~e Faser** *f* TELEKOM preformed fiber (AmE), preformed fibre (BrE); **~es Material** *nt* FERTIG dummy; **~er Spritzwascher** *m* UMWELTSCHMUTZ preformed spray scrubber

vorgegeben: **~e Flugbahn** *f* LUFTTRANS assigned flight path; **~er Widerstand** *m* RADIO preset resistor

vorgegossen *adj* FERTIG roughcast

vorgehängt: **~e Wand** *f* BAU curtain wall

Vorgehensweise *f* COMP & DV procedure

vorgekocht *adj* LEBENSMITTEL precooked

vorgekühlt *adj* LEBENSMITTEL precooled

Vorgelege *nt* MASCHINEN countershafting, transmission; **Vorgelegegetriebe** *nt* FERTIG intermediate gearbox; **Vorgelegerad** *nt* MASCHINEN countergear; **Vorgelegewelle** *f* FERTIG jack shaft, KFZTECH countershaft, countershaft gear, MASCHINEN countershaft, intermediate shaft, layshaft

Vorgerüst *nt* FERTIG *Walzen* roughing stand

vorgeschaltet[1] *adj* HEIZ & KÄLTE, MASCHINEN upstream

vorgeschaltet:[2] **~es Filter** *nt* ELEKTRONIK prefilter

vorgeschliffen *adj* FERTIG preground

vorgeschmiedet[1] *adj* FERTIG *Bohrung* punched

vorgeschmiedet:[2] **~es Material** *nt* FERTIG dummy

vorgeschrieben[1] *adj* QUAL mandatory

vorgeschrieben:[2] **~er Haltepunkt** *m* QUAL mandatory hold point; **~es Schild** *nt* SICHERHEIT *Sicherheitshinweise* mandatory sign

Vorgesenk: **im ~ vorformen** *vt* FERTIG rough-stamp

vorgespannt[1] *adj* PHYS biased

vorgespannt:[2] **~es Glas** *nt* KER & GLAS toughened glass, TRANS prestressed glass, toughened glass; **~es Lager** *nt* MASCHINEN preloaded bearing

vorgesteuert: **~es Ventil** *nt* HEIZ & KÄLTE servo-assisted valve

vorgewalzt: **~er Block** *m* FERTIG cogged ingot, KER & GLAS rough rolled

vorgezeichnet: **~es Wetterverhalten** *nt* RAUMFAHRT weather pattern

Vorgießen *nt* FERTIG rough-casting; **~ von Bohrungen** *nt* FERTIG *Spanung* coring

vorgießen *vt* FERTIG rough-cast

Vorglüheinrichtung *f* KFZTECH *Dieselmotor* preheater

Vorgriff *m* COMP & DV lookahead

Vorhafen *m* WASSERTRANS offshore terminal

Vorhalteinheit *f* REGELUNG lead module

Vorhaltverstärkung *f* REGELUNG derivative action gain

Vorhang *m* KER & GLAS *Abtrennung im Fourcault-Verfahren zum Ziehen von Tafelglas* curtain; **Vorhangantenne** *f* RADIO curtain; **Vorhangbeschichter** *m* KUNSTSTOFF curtain coater; **Vorhangbeschichtung** *f* KER & GLAS curtain coating; **Vorhangbildung** *f* KUNSTSTOFF curtaining

Vorhängeschloß *nt* BAU padlock

vorheizen *vt* HEIZ & KÄLTE, THERMOD preheat

vorher: ~ aufnehmen *vt* AUFNAHME prerecord

Vorherd *m* FERTIG *Kupolofen*, KER & GLAS forehearth; **Vorherdeingang** *m* KER & GLAS forehearth entrance

vorhergesagt: ~e Zuverlässigkeit *f* RAUMFAHRT predicted reliability

Vorher-Nachher-Untersuchung *f* TRANS before-and-after study

vorherrschend: ~e Winde *m pl* WASSERTRANS prevailing winds

Vorhersage *f* KÜNSTL INT prediction; **Vorhersagefähigkeit** *f* UMWELTSCHMUTZ predictive capability; **Vorhersagesystem** *nt* KÜNSTL INT prediction system

vorhobeln *vt* MECHAN rough-plane

Vorimprägnieren *nt* KER & GLAS prepregging

Vorkammer *f* KFZTECH antechamber, *Dieselmotor* prechamber, precombustion chamber, THERMOD *eines Verbrennungsmotors* precombustion chamber

Vorkehrung *f* SICHERHEIT precaution

Vorklärbecken *nt* ABFALL preliminary settling basin, primary settling basin, primary settlement tank

Vorklassierrost *nt* FERTIG grizzly

Vorkommnis: ~ während des Fluges *nt* RAUMFAHRT flight occurrence

Vorkompilierer *m* COMP & DV preprocessor

vorkompiliert: ~er Code *m* COMP & DV precompiled code

vorkontrollieren *vt* FERNSEH preview

Vorkonzentrat *nt* KOHLEN preconcentrate

Vorkühler *m* HEIZ & KÄLTE precooler

Vorlage *f* KONSTZEICH master; **Vorlagestück** *nt* FERTIG abutting piece

Vorlast *f* FERTIG *Werkstoffe* initial load

vorlastig[1] *adj* WASSERTRANS trimmed by the head

vorlastig[2] *adv* WASSERTRANS *Schiff* down by the head

Vorlauf *m* ELEKTROTECH pretravel, FERNSEH preroll, FERTIG lead, HEIZ & KÄLTE advance, LEBENSMITTEL first running, *Destillation* fore-running, MASCHINEN advance, approach, forward motion

vorlaufen: ~e Welle *f* ELEKTROTECH forward wave

Vorlauffaser *f* TELEKOM launching fiber (AmE), launching fibre (BrE)

vorläufig: ~er Kostenvoranschlag *m* BAU preliminary cost estimate; **~e Lagerung** *f* ABFALL *von Müll* temporary storage; **~e Prüfung** *f* PATENT preliminary examination; **~e technische Prüfung** *f (PDR)* RAUMFAHRT preliminary design review *(PDR)*

Vorlauf: Vorlaufrohr *nt* HEIZ & KÄLTE flow pipe; **Vorlauftemperatur** *f* HEIZ & KÄLTE flow temperature; **Vorlaufzeit** *f* ELEKTRONIK *Zeit zwischen Produktentwurf und Fertigung* lead time, FERNSEH preroll time, FERTIG, MASCHINEN lead time

Vorlegescheibe *f* FERTIG dummy block; **Vorlegezahnrad** *nt* MECHAN idler

vorlich: ~er als dwars *adv* WASSERTRANS forward of the beam; **~er als querab** *adv* WASSERTRANS forward of the beam

vormagnetisiert: nicht ~ *adj* COMP & DV unbiased

Vormagnetisierung *f* AUFNAHME bias, biasing, premagnetization, COMP & DV bias, ELEKTROTECH bias, magnetic bias, FERTIG bias; **Vormagnetisierungsfrequenz** *f* AUFNAHME bias frequency; **Vormagnetisierungsoszillator** *m* AUFNAHME, ELEKTRONIK *Tonbandgeräte* bias oscillator; **Vormagnetisierungsquelle** *f* ELEKTROTECH bias source

Vormauerziegel *m* BAU facing brick

Vormischen *nt* AUFNAHME rough mix

Vormischerstufe *f* RADIO premixer

Vormischung *f* KUNSTSTOFF batch, master batch

Vormittagsspitze *f* TRANS a.m. peak

Vormontage *f* FERTIG, MASCHINEN preassembly, WASSERTRANS *Schiffbau* prefabrication

vormontieren *vt* FERTIG preassemble, *Kunststoffinstallationen* preassemble

vormontiert *adj* FERTIG preassembled

vorn[1] *adv* WASSERTRANS fore; **nach ~** *adv* WASSERTRANS forward

vorn:[2] **nach ~ gepfeilter Flügel** *m* LUFTTRANS forward-swept wing

vorn:[3] **von ~ beleuchten** *vt* FOTO front-light

Vornutenfräser *m* MASCHINEN roughing slot-mill

vorordnen *vt* COMP & DV prestore

Vorort *pref* TRANS urban; **Vor-Ort-Einsatzleiter** *m* MEERSCHMUTZ OSC, on-scene commander; **Vorortmischen** *nt* BAU mix in place; **Vorortpendlerzug** *m* EISENBAHN commuter rail system; **Vorortzug** *m* EISENBAHN interurban train (AmE), local train

Vorpiek *f* WASSERTRANS *Schiffbau* forepeak

Vorplastifizieren *nt* KUNSTSTOFF preplasticizing

vorpolieren *vt* MECHAN rough-polish

Vorpresse *f* PAPIER baby press

Vorpressen *nt* KUNSTSTOFF preforming

Vorpreßling *m* KUNSTSTOFF preform

vorprogrammiert *adj* COMP & DV preprogrammed

Vorprozessor *m* COMP & DV preprocessor

Vorprüfung *f* QUAL preacceptance inspection; **Vorprüfungsprotokoll** *nt* QUAL preacceptance inspection report

Vorrang *m* COMP & DV priority

vorrangig: ~e Unterbrechungsebene *f* COMP & DV priority interruption level

Vorrang: Vorrangunterbrechung *f* COMP & DV priority interrrupt; **Vorrangventil** *nt* HYDRAUL priority valve; **Vorrangverarbeitung** *f* COMP & DV priority processing

Vorrat *m* COMP & DV repertoire

vorrätig: ~er Durchmesser *m* TELEKOM stock diameter

Vorrat: Vorratsbehälter *m* STRÖMPHYS *für Flüssigkeit* reservoir, VERPACK bin; **Vorratsglas** *nt* KER & GLAS dispensing glass; **Vorratskathode** *f* ELEKTROTECH dispenser cathode; **Vorratslänge** *f* TELEKOM slack; **Vorratsschrank** *m* LABOR storage cupboard; **Vorratstank** *m* LUFTTRANS feeder tank; **Vorratswasserheizer** *m* HEIZ & KÄLTE storage water heater

vorraussichtlich: ~e Anflugzeit *f* LUFTTRANS expected approach time

Vorreaktanz *f* ELEKTROTECH series reactance

Vorrechner *m* TELEKOM front-end processor

Vorreibahle *f* MASCHINEN roughing reamer

Vorreiber *m* BAU casement fastener, *Jalousie* turnbuckle

Vorreibzahn *m* MASCHINEN semifinishing tooth

Vorrichtung *f* MASCHINEN apparatus, appliance, contrivance, device, fixture, jig, MEERSCHMUTZ, TELEKOM device, TEXTIL appliance

Vor-Rücklauf-Schalter *m* FERNSEH normal-reverse

switch

Vor-Rückverhältnis *nt* RADIO *Antennengewinn* front-to-back ratio

Vor-Rückwärtszähler *m* ELEKTRONIK bidirectional counter

Vorsatz *m* MASCHINEN attachment; **Vorsatzbalgengerät** *nt* FOTO extension bellows; **Vorsatzblatt** *nt* DRUCK end sheet; **Vorsatzgerät** *nt* MASCHINEN attachment; **Vorsatzgerät für Auflicht** *nt* FOTO incident light attachment; **Vorsatzkuchen** *m* KER & GLAS stopper

vorsätzlich: ~**e Einleitung** *f* UMWELTSCHMUTZ *Abwässer* intentional discharge

Vorsatz: **Vorsatzlinse** *f* FOTO supplementary lens

Vorschalldämpfer *m* KFZTECH premuffler (AmE), presilencer (BrE)

Vorschaltfaser *f* TELEKOM launching fiber (AmE), launching fibre (BrE)

Vorschaltgerät *nt* ELEKTROTECH ballast, control gear

Vorschaltwiderstand *m* ELEKTROTECH ballast resistor, voltage multiplier, *bei Gleichrichter, Anschluß* series resistance

Vorschau *f* FERNSEH preview; **Vorschaumonitor** *m* FERNSEH preview monitor

vorschieben *vt* ELEKTRIZ *Bürsten* advance, MASCHINEN feed

Vorschlaghammer *m* BAU slater's hammer, sledge, sledge hammer, MASCHINEN sledge hammer

Vorschleifen *nt* FERTIG pregrinding, KER & GLAS rough grinding

vorschleifen *vt* FERTIG pregrind, KER & GLAS *erste Phase des Schleifprozesses* polish

Vorschleuse *f* WASSERVERSORG head sluices

Vorschlichten *nt* FERTIG blocking

Vorschmelzer *m* KER & GLAS foremelter

Vorschmiede: **Vorschmiedegesenk** *nt* FERTIG blanker, blocker, blocking die, MASCHINEN blocking die; **Vorschmieden** *nt* FERTIG blocking

vorschmieden *vt* FERTIG *Schmieden* edge

Vorschneiden *nt* KER & GLAS rough cutting

Vorschneider *m* FERTIG first-cut tap, tap No1, taper tap, *Werkzeug* head, MASCHINEN *Gewinde* first-cut tap, tap No1

Vorschneidzahn *m* MASCHINEN nicker

Vorschnell-Gießöffnung *f* VERPACK flip spout closure

Vorschriften *f pl* BAU, WASSERTRANS specifications; **Vorschriften über Nichteisenmetalle** *f pl* SICHERHEIT nonferrous metals regulations; **Vorschriften zu Polierscheiben** *f pl* SICHERHEIT abrasive wheels regulations; **Vorschriften zu Schleifscheiben** *f pl* SICHERHEIT abrasive wheels regulations; **Vorschriften zur Überwachung von gesundheitsgefährdenden Stoffen** *f pl* SICHERHEIT COSHH, control of substances hazardous to health

Vorschub[1] *m* COMP & DV carriage, KOHLEN feed, MASCHINEN feed, feeding, MECHAN, PAPIER feed

Vorschub:[2] ~ **geben** *vi* MECHAN feed

Vorschub: **Vorschubbegrenzer** *m* MASCHINEN feed limiter; **Vorschubbereich** *m* FERTIG range of feeds; **Vorschubgeschwindigkeit** *f* MASCHINEN feed rate, feed speed; **Vorschubgetriebe** *nt* MASCHINEN feed gear; **Vorschubgetriebekasten** *m* FERTIG feed box; **Vorschubkasten** *m* FERTIG, MASCHINEN, PAPIER feed box; **Vorschubkomponente** *f* KERNTECH feed component; **Vorschubkraft** *f* MASCHINEN feed force; **Vorschubkugelumlaufspindel** *f* FERTIG recirculating ball feed screw; **Vorschublochband** *nt* COMP & DV con-

trol tape; **Vorschubmechanismus** *m* FERTIG advance mechanism, MASCHINEN feed mechanism; **Vorschubmotor** *m* MASCHINEN feed motor; **Vorschubmutter** *f* FERTIG feed nut; **Vorschubpatrone** *f* FERTIG collet, feeding collet; **Vorschubrad** *nt* FERTIG *Fräsmaschine* feed gear; **Vorschubschieber** *m* FERTIG *Stangenvorschub* pusher; **Vorschubschlitten** *m* MASCHINEN feed slide; **Vorschubsperrgetriebe** *nt* FERTIG feed-pawl mechanism; **Vorschubspindel** *f* MASCHINEN feed screw; **Vorschubsteuerung** *f* COMP & DV carriage control; **Vorschubumschaltgetriebe** *nt* MASCHINEN feed reversing gear; **Vorschubwalze** *f* PAPIER feed roll; **Vorschubwechselhebel** *m* FERTIG feed-change lever; **Vorschubzahl** *f* KOHLEN feed rate; **Vorschubzahnstange** *f* FERTIG, MASCHINEN feed rack

Vorserienflugzeug *nt* LUFTTRANS preproduction aircraft

Vorsicht *f* ERGON alertness

Vorsignal *nt* EISENBAHN distant signal; **Vorsignalabstand** *m* EISENBAHN presignaling distance (AmE), presignalling distance (BrE), warning distance, LUFTTRANS, TRANS, WASSERTRANS warning distance; **Vorsignalankündigung** *f* EISENBAHN outer distant signal

Vorsilbe *f* COMP & DV prefix

Vorsitzender: ~ **der Konferenzverbindung** *m* TELEKOM conference call chairman

Vorsorge *f* SICHERHEIT precaution; **Vorsorgemaßnahme** *f* SICHERHEIT precautionary measure; **Vorsorgeplanung** *f* MEERSCHMUTZ contingency plan

vorsorglich *adj* ANSTRICH preventive

Vorspann *m* COMP & DV log, logarithm, prefix, tape header, tape leader, FERNSEH leader; **Vorspannband** *nt* AKUSTIK leader

Vorspannen *nt* KER & GLAS tempering

vorspannen *vt* MASCHINEN preload, pretension

Vorspann: **Vorspannglied** *nt* KERNTECH tendon

Vorspannung:[1] **mit** ~ *adj* FERTIG *Feder* compressed

Vorspannung[2] *f* ELEKTROTECH, FERNSEH, FERTIG bias, MASCHINEN initial tension, preload, PHYS bias voltage, RADIO *Transistor* bias; **Vorspannungsbatterie** *f* ELEKTROTECH bias; **Vorspannungskreis** *m* ELEKTROTECH bias circuit; **Vorspannungsstrom** *m* FERNSEH biasing current; **Vorspannungswicklung** *f* ELEKTROTECH bias winding; **Vorspannungswiderstand** *m* ELEKTROTECH bias resistor

Vorspann: **Vorspannverschluß** *m* FOTO preset shutter

vorspeichern *vt* COMP & DV prestore

Vorspinnmaschine *f* TEXTIL roving frame

Vorspring *f* WASSERTRANS bow spring

vorspringend[1] *adj* FERTIG *Winkel* salient

vorspringend:[2] ~**er Teil** *m* KFZTECH *Karosserie* overhang

Vorsprung *m* BAU nose, *Wand* break, MASCHINEN boss, nose, shoulder, MECHAN *eines Nockens* load; ~ **an Gußteil** *m* KER & GLAS *verursacht durch Schmelze in der Entlüftungsöffnung der Form* riser

vorspulen *vt* FERNSEH fast-forward

Vorspur *f* KFZTECH *Vorderräder* toe-in

Vorstag *nt* WASSERTRANS forestay

Vorstecker *m* FERTIG forelock

Vorsteckbolzen *m* FERTIG cotter bolt, MASCHINEN forelock bolt; **Vorsteckkeil** *nt* FERTIG splint pin

vorstehen *vi* BAU project

Vorsteuerdruckkammer *f* LUFTTRANS pilot pressure chamber; **Vorsteuerventil** *nt* FERTIG *Kunststoffinstallationen* servo valve

Vorsteven *m* WASSERTRANS *Bootsbau* stem; **Vorsteven-beschlag** *m* WASSERTRANS *Bootsbau* stem head fitting

Vorstreichen *nt* PAPIER precoating

Vorstreichmaschine *f* KUNSTSTOFF bar coater

Vorstrich *m* FERTIG cogging pass, *Walzen* breaking-down pass

Vorstrom *m* LUFTTRANS inflow

Vorteiler *m* ELEKTRONIK scaler, RADIO prescaler

Vortreiben *nt* BAU *Tunnelbau* forcing

Vortrieb *m* KOHLEN advance; **Vortriebskraft** *f* MASCHI-NEN propelling force; **Vortriebsschild** *m* BAU *Tunnelbau* shield

Vortrockenzylinder *m* PAPIER baby dryer, predryer

vorübergehend[1] *adj* KONTROLL, PHYS transient; **~ nicht erreichbar** *adj* TELEKOM *Vermittlungsplatz* temporarily unavailable

vorübergehend:[2] **~e Abweichung** *f* REGELUNG transient deviation; **~e Kohärenz** *f* OPTIK, PHYS, TELEKOM temporal coherence; **~e Sollwertabweichung** *f* REGELUNG transient deviation from desired set point; **~er Vorgang** *m* FERTIG transient; **~e Zusammenschaltung** *f* ELEKTROTECH patching

Vorvakuum *nt* PHYS prevacuum

vorverarbeiten *vt* COMP & DV preprocess

vorverarbeitet[1] *adj* ELEKTRONIK preprocessed

vorverarbeitet:[2] **~e Lebensmittel** *nt pl* LEBENSMITTEL convenience food

Vorverarbeitung *f* ELEKTRONIK preprocessing; **Vorverarbeitungsprozessor** *m* TELEKOM front-end processor

Vorverbrennung *f* THERMOD precombustion; **Vorverbrennungskammer** *f* KFZTECH, LUFTTRANS, WASSERTRANS combustion prechamber

Vorverdichterdruckstutzen *m* LUFTTRANS *Klimatisierung* pressure inlet

Vorverdichtung *f* KFZTECH supercharging, LUFTTRANS supercharge, MECHAN supercharger

Vorverstärker *m* AUFNAHME, ELEKTRONIK, PHYS, RA-DIO, TELEKOM preamplifier

vorverstärkt *adj* ELEKTRONIK preamp

Vorverstärkung *f* ELEKTRONIK preamplification, FERNSEH, RAUMFAHRT pre-emphasis; **Vorverstärkungsfaktor** *m* RAUMFAHRT pre-emphasis improvement factor

Vorversuch *m* KOHLEN pilot test

Vorverzerrung *f* AKUSTIK pre-emphasis, pre-equalization, predistortion, AUFNAHME, ELEKTRONIK, PHYS pre-emphasis; **Vorverzerrungstechnik** *f* TELEKOM predistortion technique

vorvulkanisiert: **~er Latex** *m* KUNSTSTOFF prevulcanized latex

Vorwahl:[1] **mit ~** *adj* FERTIG preoptive

Vorwahl:[2] *f* KFZTECH preselection

Vorwähler *m* ELEKTRONIK, HEIZ & KÄLTE, KFZTECH *Getriebe*, TELEKOM preselector; **Vorwahlgangschaltung** *f* KFZTECH *Getriebe* preselection gear change

Vorwählgerät *nt* HEIZ & KÄLTE preselector

Vorwahl: **Vorwahlkennziffer** *f* TELEKOM prefix number; **Vorwahlmeßgerät** *nt* METROL presetting gage (AmE), presetting gauge (BrE); **Vorwahlschalter** *m* GERÄT preselection switch

Vorwählschalter *m* HEIZ & KÄLTE preselector

Vorwahl: **Vorwahlzähler** *m* GERÄT batching counter, predetermining counter, preselection counter, preset counter

Vorwalze *f* FERTIG bloom roll, cogging-down roll, roughing roll, MASCHINEN blooming roll, breaking-down roll

Vorwalzen *nt* FERTIG rough rolling

vorwalzen *vt* BAU rough-down, FERTIG rough-roll, rough, KOHLEN rough

Vorwalzer *m* KOHLEN rougher

Vorwalzgerüst *nt* FERTIG cogging-down stand

Vorwalzwerk *nt* FERTIG cogging mill, MASCHINEN blooming mill

Vorwärmen *nt* EISENBAHN, KUNSTSTOFF, METALL preheating

vorwärmen *vt* FERTIG recuperate, HEIZ & KÄLTE preheat

Vorwärmer *m* ERDÖL *Raffinerietechnik* preheater, FER-TIG economizer, HEIZ & KÄLTE economizer, recuperator, KERNTECH, KFZTECH *Dieselmotor* preheater

Vorwärts- *pref* GERÄT, MASCHINEN forward; **Vorwärts-und Rückwärtsbewegung** *f* MASCHINEN backward-and-forward motion; **Vorwärtsauslösung** *f* TELEKOM forward release; **Vorwärtsfehlerkorrektur** *f* COMP & DV, TELEKOM forward error correction; **Vorwärtsfließpressen** *nt* MASCHINEN direct extrusion, forward extrusion; **Vorwärtsführung** *f* COMP & DV feedforward control; **Vorwärtsgeschwindigkeit** *f* LUFTTRANS translation speed; **Vorwärtskennlinie** *f* ELEKTRONIK forward characteristic

vorwärtslaufend: **~es Blatt** *nt* LUFTTRANS *Luftschraube* advancing blade

Vorwärts-: **Vorwärtsregelung** *f* TELEKOM feedforward AGC, feedforward automatic gain control; **Vorwärtsrichtung** *f* ELEKTRIZ forward-conducting direction; **Vorwärts-Rückwärtsbewegung** *f* MASCHINEN back-and-forth motion; **Vorwärts-Rückwärtszähler** *m* ELEKTRONIK up-down counter, FERNSEH forward-backward counter, GERÄT bidirectional counter, forward-backward counter, up-down counter; **Vorwärtsstart** *m* LUFTTRANS *Hubschraub* forward takeoff; **Vorwärtsstreuung** *f* AUFNAHME forward scattering, RADIO forward scatter; **Vorwärtsstrom** *m* ELEKTRIZ forward current; **Vorwärtssuche** *f* KÜNSTL INT forward search; **Vorwärtsverkettung** *f* KÜNSTL INT forward chaining; **Vorwärtsverstärker** *m* ELEKTRONIK forward amplifier; **Vorwärtsvorspannung** *f* ELEKTRO-TECH forward bias; **Vorwärtswellenbeschleuniger** *m* STRAHLPHYS progressive wave accelerator; **Vorwärtswiderstand** *m* ELEKTRIZ forward resistance; **Vorwärtszähler** *m* GERÄT count-up counter, up counter; **Vorwärtszeichen** *nt* TELEKOM forward signal; **Vorwärtszweig** *m* ELEKTROTECH, REGELUNG *des Regelkreises* forward path

Vorwaschen *nt* TEXTIL scouring

vorwaschen *vt* TEXTIL scour

Vorwiderstand *m* ELEKTROTECH dropping resistor, voltage multiplier, GERÄT additional resistor, RADIO bias resistance

vorwiegend: **~ zum Lesen geeigneter Speicher** *m* COMP & DV read-mostly memory

Vorzeichen *nt* COMP & DV, MATH sign; **Vorzeichenbit** *nt* COMP & DV sign bit; **Vorzeichenziffer** *f* COMP & DV sign digit

Vorzeichnung *f* AKUSTIK key signature

vorzeitig:[1] **~e Beendigung** *f* COMP & DV abnormal termination

vorzeitig:[2] **~ beenden** *vt* COMP & DV abend, abort

Vorzerkleinerung *f* ABFALL prior crushing, KOHLEN pre-crushing

Vorziehen *nt* FERTIG precupping

vorziehen *vt* FERTIG precup

Vorzimmeranlage *f* TELEKOM manager/secretary station

Vorzug *m* COMP & DV, FERTIG, LEBENSMITTEL, QUAL, RAUMFAHRT advantage; **Vorzugs-AQL-Werte** *m pl* QUAL preferred acceptable quality levels; **Vorzugsbetrieb** *m* COMP & DV privileged operation; **Vorzugsliste** *f* RAUMFAHRT preferential list; **Vorzugsmilch** *f* LEBENSMITTEL certified milk; **Vorzugsreihe** *f* FERTIG *Kunststoffinstallationen* preferential range; **Vorzugswert** *m* RADIO preference value; **Vorzugszahlenreihe** *f* MATH preferred numbers

Vorzündung *f* KFZTECH advanced ignition, premature ignition, *Zündung* advance, preignition

Votatoranlage *f* LEBENSMITTEL *für kontinuierliche Margarineherstellung* votator

Voute *f* BAU haunch

VOX *abbr* (*sprachgesteuerter Schalter*) RADIO VOX (*voice-operated switch*)

VPE *abbr* (*vernetztes Polyethylen*) KUNSTSTOFF XPE (*cross-linked polyethylene*)

V-Rad *nt* MASCHINEN V-gear

VRS-Verfahren *nt* (*Verfestigungsverfahren für Sonderabfälle*) ABFALL WPC-VRS process

V-Schaltung *f* ELEKTRIZ V-connection

V-Scheibe *f* MASCHINEN V-pulley

VSP *abbr* (*vertikales seismisches Profil*) ERDÖL VSP (*vertical seismic profile*)

V-Stellung *f* LUFTTRANS dihedral; **~ des Blattes** *f* LUFTTRANS *Hubschrauber* blade tilt

VSWR *abbr* (*Welligkeitsfaktor*) RADIO VSWR (*voltage standing wave ratio*)

VTOL-Flugzeug *nt* (*senkrecht startendes und landendes Flugzeug*) LUFTTRANS VTOL aircraft (*vertical take-off and landing aircraft*)

V-Tragflächenboot *nt* WASSERTRANS VEE foil craft

Vulkanfiberscheibe *f* MASCHINEN vulcanized fiber disk (AmE), vulcanized fibre disc (BrE)

Vulkanit *m* ELEKTRIZ vulcanite, NICHTFOSS ENERG extrusive rocks, igneous rocks

Vulkanisation *f* KUNSTSTOFF, MASCHINEN, THERMOD vulcanization; **Vulkanisationsgeschwindigkeit** *f* KUNSTSTOFF rate of cure; **Vulkanisationsverzögerer** *m* KUNSTSTOFF antiscorching agent, retarder

vulkanisch *adj* ERDÖL *Geologie* volcanic

vulkanisieren *vt* THERMOD vulcanize, *im Ofen* heat-cure

vulkanisiert *adj* THERMOD vulcanized

Vulkanisierung *f* MASCHINEN, THERMOD vulcanization; **Vulkanschlot** *m* NICHTFOSS ENERG *Geologisch* conduit

VU-Meter *nt* GERÄT VU-meter

VV-Vergaser *m* (*variabler Venturi-Vergaser*) KFZTECH VV-carburetor (AmE), VV-carburettor (BrE) (*VV-carburetor*)

V-Zahl *f* OPTIK V-number

W

W^1 *abbr* ELEKTRIZ *(elektrische Energie)* W *(electric energy)*, ELEKTROTECH *(Watt)* W *(watt)*, HYDRAUL *(Webersche Zahl)* W *(Weber number)*, KERNTECH *(durchschnittliche Energie)* W *(average energy)*, METROL *(Watt)* W *(watt)*, OPTIK *(Abstrahlung)* W *(radiant emittance)*

W^2 *(Wolfram)* CHEMIE W *(tungsten)*

Waage:^{1} in ~ *adj* FERTIG level

Waage^2 *f* ELEKTRIZ, LABOR balance, MASCHINEN scales, METROL balance, scale, PAPIER *Vorrichtung*, PHYS balance

Waagebalken *m* GERÄT balance beam, LUFTTRANS balance arm, MASCHINEN scale beam, METROL balance beam, beam; **Waagebalkenachse** *f* KFZTECH *Anhänger* pivot axle; **Waagebalkenaufleger** *m* METROL knife edge; **Waagebalkenaufleger auf Achatplanlager** *m pl* METROL knife edges of balance beam resting in agate

Waage: Waagebürste *f* LABOR balance brush; **Waagelagerung** *f* METROL bearings; **Waagengenauigkeit** *f* METROL accuracy of a balance

waagerecht^1 *adj* BAU, FERTIG, GEOM, MASCHINEN horizontal

waagerecht:^{2} ~er Seitenschub *m* BAU horizontal thrust; ~e Stiefe *f* BAU *temporär* flying shore

Waagrecht- *pref* MASCHINEN horizontal; **Waagrechtbohr- und Fräsmaschine** *f* MASCHINEN horizontal drilling, boring and milling machine; **Waagrechtbohrmaschine** *f* MASCHINEN horizontal boring machine, horizontal drilling machine; **Waagrechtbohrwerk** *nt* FERTIG horizontal boring and milling machine; **Waagrechte** *f* GEOM horizontal; **Waagrechtfräsmaschine** *f* MASCHINEN horizontal milling machine; **Waagrechtfrässpindel** *f* MASCHINEN horizontal milling spindle; **Waagrechtjustierschraube** *f* MASCHINEN leveling screw (AmE), levelling screw (BrE); **Waagrechträummaschine** *f* MASCHINEN horizontal broaching machine; **Waagrechtschleifscheibe** *f* KER & GLAS horizontal grinding disc (BrE), horizontal grinding disk (AmE); **Waagrechtstoßen** *nt* MASCHINEN shaping; **Waagrechtstoßmaschine** *f* MASCHINEN shaping machine, shaping planer; ~ mit zwei Supporten *f* MASCHINEN double-headed shaping machine; **Waagrechtziehverfahren** *nt* KER & GLAS horizontal drawing process

Waagschale *f* LABOR scale pan, weighing boat, weighing dish, MASCHINEN scale, scale pan, METROL scale

Wabe *f* LUFTTRANS honeycomb; **Wabenbauweise** *f* LUFTTRANS honeycomb construction; **Wabengebilde für den Güterschutz** *nt* VERPACK *Hohlraumfüller aus Papier und Pappe* honeycomb protection system; **Wabengitter** *nt* LUFTTRANS *aerodynamisch* honeycomb filler, honeycomb grill; **Wabenkonstruktion** *f* VERPACK honeycomb structure; **Wabenkühler** *m* KFZTECH honeycomb radiator; **Wabenmaterial** *nt* VERPACK honeycomb material; **Wabenstruktur** *f* BAU honeycomb structure; **Wabenwicklung** *f* ELEKTROTECH honeycomb winding

Wache: ~ halten *vi* WASSERTRANS keep watch

Wachkanal *m* COMP & DV guard channel

Wachs *nt* ERDÖL *Bestandteil der Erdöle*, KER & GLAS, MASCHINEN, TEXTIL, VERPACK wax

Wachsamkeit *f* EISENBAHN vigilance, ERGON alertness, vigilance; **Wachsamkeitskontrolle** *f* EISENBAHN vigilance control

Wachs: Wachsausschmelzguß *m* KER & GLAS lost wax; **Wachsen** *nt* FERTIG *Grauguß* growth, LEBENSMITTEL waxing; **Wachsgießformen** *f pl* MASCHINEN wax investment molds (AmE), wax investment moulds (BrE); **Wachspapier** *nt* VERPACK impregnated paper, wax paper; **Wachsplatte** *f* AUFNAHME wax master; **Wachsschutzschicht** *f* KER & GLAS wax resist; **Wachstuch** *nt* TEXTIL, VERPACK oilcloth

Wachstum *nt* KERNTECH, METALL growth; **Wachstumsmodell** *nt* METALL growth pattern; **Wachstumsspirale** *f* METALL growth spiral; **Wachstumsstufe** *f* METALL growth step; **Wachstumszwilling** *m* METALL growth twin

Wackeln *nt* RAUMFAHRT wobble

wackeln *vi* RAUMFAHRT *in der Drehachse* wobble

Wade *f* WASSERTRANS *Fischerei* seine net

Wafer *m* COMP & DV, ELEKTRONIK, ELEKTROTECH wafer; **Wafer-Ausbeute** *m* ELEKTRONIK wafer yield; **Wafer-Integration** *f (WS-Integration)* COMP & DV, ELEKTRONIK wafer scale integration *(wsi)*; **Waferschalter** *m* ELEKTROTECH wafer switch

Wägefläschen *nt* LABOR density bottle, *Dichtemessung* pycnometer

Wägeglas *nt* CHEMIE, LABOR weighing bottle

Wägemaschine *f* VERPACK checkweighing machine

Wagen *m* DRUCK carriage, EISENBAHN car (AmE), carriage (BrE), coach (BrE), KFZTECH car, passenger car, MECHAN car; ~ A mit Motor *m* KFZTECH carriage A containing the motor; ~ mit Hecktür *m* KFZTECH hatchback car, hatchback model; ~ für Krankenbahre *m* SICHERHEIT stretcher cart; ~ mit Pendelaufhängung *m* KFZTECH car with pendulum suspension; **Wagenablauf** *m* EISENBAHN wagon humping; **Wagenausbesserungswerkstatt** *f* KFZTECH car shop; **Wagendeck** *nt* WASSERTRANS car deck; **Wagenguß** *m* FERTIG bogie casting

Wagenheber *m* KFZTECH *Werkzeug*, MECHAN jack; **Wagenheberansatzpunkt** *m* KFZTECH jacking point; **Wagenheberauflage** *f* KFZTECH jacking pad

Wagen: Wagenhebewerk *nt* EISENBAHN wagon hoist, wagon lift; **Wagenherdofen** *m* FERTIG bogie furnace; **Wagenkasten** *m* EISENBAHN body, TRANS *Fahrzeug* box; **Wagenkipper** *m* BAU tip, EISENBAHN dumper; **Wagenladung** *f* EISENBAHN car load (AmE), wagon load (BrE), TRANS cart load; **Wagenpark** *m* KFZTECH fleet; **Wagenrad** *nt* KFZTECH lorry wheel (BrE), truck wheel (AmE); **Wagenrücklauf** *m* TELEKOM carriage return; **Wagenschuppen** *m* EISENBAHN wagon shed; **Wagenverfügung** *f* EISENBAHN car distribution; **Wagenzug** *m* EISENBAHN train set

Waggonkippanlage *f* EISENBAHN car dumper

Wahl *f* TELEKOM dialing (AmE), dialling (BrE)

Wähl- *pref* COMP & DV, TELEKOM dialing (AmE), dialling (BrE); **Wählanschluß** *m* TELEKOM dial-up port

Wahl: **Wahlaufforderungszeichen** *nt* TELEKOM proceed-to-select signal

wählbar[1] *adj* COMP & DV random, ELEKTRONIK, ELEKTROTECH selectable

wählbar:[2] **~er Impuls** *m* ELEKTRONIK random pulse; **~e Leiterbahn** *f* ELEKTRONIK *Wafer* chooseable wiring; **~e Verarbeitung** *f* COMP & DV random processing

Wähl-: **Wählcode** *m* TELEKOM dialing code (AmE), dialling code (BrE)

Wahl: **Wahldatei** *f* COMP & DV optional file

Wählen *nt* TELEKOM dialing (AmE), dialling (BrE)

wählen[1] *vt* COMP & DV poll

wählen[2] *vti* TELEKOM dial

Wählen: **~ bei aufliegendem Hörer** *nt* TELEKOM on-hook dialing (AmE), on-hook dialling (BrE)

Wähler *m* COMP & DV, ELEKTROTECH, TELEKOM selector

Wähl-: **Wählfehler** *m* TELEKOM dialing error (AmE), dialling error (BrE)

wahlfrei[1] *adj* COMP & DV optional, random

wahlfrei:[2] **~e Verarbeitung** *f* COMP & DV random processing; **~er Zugriff** *m* COMP & DV random access

Wähl-: **Wählhebel** *m* KFZTECH *Automatikgetriebe* selector

Wahl-: **Wahlmöglichkeit beim Einstellen** *f* COMP & DV set-up option

Wähl-: **Wählnetz** *nt* COMP & DV switched network

Wahl-: **Wahlreaktion** *f* ERGON choice reaction

Wähl-: **Wählrelais** *nt* ELEKTROTECH selector relay; **Wählschalter** *m* ELEKTROTECH selector switch, GERÄT, TELEKOM selector; **Wählscheibe** *f* RADIO, TELEKOM dial; **Wählsterneinrichtung** *f* TELEKOM line concentrator, *Fernsprechnetz* concentrator

Wahl: **Wahlstufe** *f* TELEKOM selection stage, switching stage

Wähl-: **Wähltonverzug** *m* TELEKOM dial tone delay; **Wählvermittlungsstelle** *f* TELEKOM automatic switchboard

wahlweise[1] *adj* COMP & DV optional

wahlweise:[2] **~ anwendbare Prüfmethode** *f* OPTIK alternative test method; **wahlweiser Halt** *m* COMP & DV optional stop

Wahl: **Wahlwiederholung** *f* TELEKOM last number recall, last number redial; **Wahlwort** *nt* COMP & DV optional wor

Wähl: **Wählzeit** *f* TELEKOM dialing period (AmE), dialling period (BrE)

wahr[1] *adj* COMP & DV, ELEKTRIZ, KERNTECH, LUFTTRANS, METALL, RAUMFAHRT true

wahr:[2] **~e Anomalie** *f* RAUMFAHRT true anomaly; **~e Beanspruchung** *f* METALL true stress; **~e Bruchspannung** *f* METALL true fracture stress; **~e Dehnung** *f* METALL true strain; **~e Dichte** *f* KERNTECH true density; **~e Eigengeschwindigkeit** *f* LUFTTRANS TAS; **~e Fluggeschwindigkeit** *f* LUFTTRANS TAS, true air speed; **~e Impedanz** *f* ELEKTRIZ intrinsic impedance; **~e Ladungen** *f pl* PHYS conduction charges; **~er Wind** *m* WASSERTRANS *Navigation* true wind

Wahrheit *f* COMP & DV truth; **Wahrheitstabelle** *f* COMP & DV truth table; **Wahrheitswert** *m* COMP & DV *COBOL* logical value

Wahrnehmung *f* ERGON cognition, perception, KÜNSTL INT perception; **Wahrnehmungsgeschwindigkeit** *f* ERGON speed of perception

wahrscheinlich: **~ste Geschwindigkeit** *f (û)* PHYS most probable speed *(û)*; **~e Reserven** *f pl* ERDÖL *Lagerstätten* probable reserves

Wahrscheinlichkeit *f* COMP & DV, ERGON, KÜNSTL INT, MATH, PHYS, QUAL, TELEKOM probability; **~ der Wartezeitüberschreitung** *f* TELEKOM probability of excess delay; **Wahrscheinlichkeitsdichte** *f* PHYS probability density; **Wahrscheinlichkeitsfunktion** *f* QUAL probability function; **Wahrscheinlichkeitskurve** *f* MATH probability curve; **Wahrscheinlichkeitsrechnung** *f* KÜNSTL INT probability calculus

wahrscheinlichkeitstheoretisch *adj* GEOM, KÜNSTL INT probabilistic

Wahrscheinlichkeit: **Wahrscheinlichkeitstheorie** *f* MATH probability theory; **Wahrscheinlichkeitsverteilung** *f* COMP & DV probability distribution, MATH probability curve, QUAL probability density, probability distribution

Walken *nt* TEXTIL fulling, *Leder* milling

Walm *m* BAU hip; **Walmdach** *nt* BAU hip roof, hipped roof; **Walmziegel** *m* BAU hip tile

Walz- *pref* FERTIG, MASCHINEN rolling

Wälz- *pref* FERTIG, MASCHINEN rolling; **Wälzachse** *f* FERTIG rolling axis; **Wälzbahn** *f* MASCHINEN pitch line

Walz-: **Walzbarren** *m* FERTIG slab; **Walzbart** *m* MECHAN burr; **Walzblock** *m* METALL bloom; **Walzdoppelung** *f* FERTIG lamination

Walze *f* BAU shaft, COMP & DV drum, platen, DRUCK cylinder, roller, platen, FERTIG cylinder, drum, roll, HYDRAUL *Dampfdruckindikator* drum, KOHLEN drum, ring, roller, KUNSTSTOFF cylinder, mill, roller, roll, LEBENSMITTEL drum, roller, MASCHINEN platen, roll, MECHAN drum, roll, roller, PAPIER roll, roller, TEXTIL roller

Walzen *nt* BAU, KER & GLAS, MASCHINEN, PAPIER rolling

walzen *vt* KOHLEN mill, MASCHINEN roll

Walze: **Walzenanlasser** *m* ELEKTRIZ drum starter; **Walzenanpreßdruck** *m* PAPIER nip pressure; **Walzenbeschichten** *nt* KUNSTSTOFF roll coating; **Walzenbiegemaschine** *f* FERTIG bending roll; **Walzenbrecher** *m* KOHLEN roller crusher; **Walzendrehmaschine** *f* MASCHINEN roll lathe, roll-turning lathe; **Walzendruck** *m* DRUCK cylinder printing, TEXTIL roller printing; **Walzendruckmaschine** *f* DRUCK cylinder printing machine, VERPACK rotary printing press; **Walzeneinstellung** *f* TEXTIL roller setting; **Walzenfräser** *m* FERTIG cylindrical cutter, MASCHINEN plain-milling cutter; **Walzengußeisen** *nt* METALL chilled roll iron; **Walzenhals** *m* PAPIER neck; **Walzenkleeblattzapfen** *m* FERTIG roll wobbler; **Walzenkopf** *m* PAPIER roll head; **Walzenmarkierung** *f* KER & GLAS roller mark; **Walzenmühle** *f* CHEMTECH, MECHAN roller mill; **Walzenpuffer** *m* KER & GLAS roller bump; **Walzenringmühle** *f* KOHLEN ring-roll crusher; **Walzensatz** *m* PAPIER set of rolls; **Walzenschalter** *m* ELEKTRIZ drum controller, drum switch; **Walzenscheider** *m* KOHLEN drum cobber; **Walzenschüsselmühle** *f* KOHLEN bowl mill crusher; **Walzenschütze** *f* NICHTFOSS ENERG drum gate; **Walzenspalt** *m* PAPIER nip; **Walzenständer** *m* FERTIG holster, roll housing, MASCHINEN bearer, standard; **Walzenstirnfräser** *m* FERTIG end-face mill, MASCHINEN shell-end mill; **Walzenstoffauflauf** *m* PAPIER roll headbox; **Walzenstraße** *f* MASCHINEN train of rolls; **Walzenstreichverfahren** *nt* PAPIER roller coating; **Walzenstuhl** *m* LEBENSMITTEL *mit Walzen als Mahlkörper* roller mill; **Walzentasche** *f* PAPIER roll pocket; **Walzenträger** *m* PAPIER roller beam; **Walzentrockner** *m*

KOHLEN, LEBENSMITTEL drum drier, drum dryer; **Walzentrog** *m* KER & GLAS roller tray; **Walzenvorschub** *m* MASCHINEN roll feed; **Walzenwehr** *nt* WASSERVERSORG roller weir

Walz-: **Walzfehler** *m* FERTIG cobble

Wälz-: **Wälzfehler** *m* FERTIG *Getriebelehre* overall variation, total composite error; **Wälzfläche** *f* MASCHINEN pitch surface

Wälzfräs- *pref* FERTIG, MASCHINEN generating; **Walzfräsen** *nt* FERTIG peripheral milling, MASCHINEN roll milling

Wälzfräsen *nt* FERTIG gear hobbing, generating, hobbing, MASCHINEN hobbing; **~ im Gleichlauf** *nt* FERTIG climb hobbing

walzfräsen *vt* FERTIG slab-mill

wälzfräsen *vt* FERTIG, MASCHINEN hob

Walzfräser *m* FERTIG slab milling cutter

Wälzfräser *m* FERTIG, MASCHINEN gear hob, generating cutter, hob, hobbing cutter

Wälzfräs-: **Wälzfräsmaschine** *f* FERTIG generator, MASCHINEN gear hobber, gear hobbing machine, hob, hobber, hobbing machine; **Wälzfrässchichten** *nt* FERTIG finish hob

wälzgefräst *adj* FERTIG hobbed

wälzgelagert *adj* FERTIG anti-ager friction-bearing

Wälz-: **Wälzgelenk** *nt* MASCHINEN rolling contact joint

Wälz-: **Walzgeschmiedet** *adj* FERTIG roll-forged

Walz-: **Walzglas** *nt* KER & GLAS rolled glass; **Walzglattglas** *nt* KER & GLAS plain-rolled glass; **Walzgrat** *m* FERTIG flash, *Walzen* cold shut

walzhart *adj* FERTIG as-rolled

Wälz-: **Wälzhobelmaschine** *f* MASCHINEN gear planer; **Wälzkolbenzähler** *m* GERÄT oval gear meter, rod piston meter/element; **Wälzkörper** *m* MASCHINEN rolling meter/element; **Wälzkreis** *m* MASCHINEN circle of contact, pitch circle, pitch line, rolling circle; **Wälzlager** *nt* KFZTECH roller bearing, MASCHINEN antifriction bearing, rolling bearing, rolling contact bearing

Walz-: **Walzlegierung** *f* MECHAN rolled alloy; **Walzmarkierung** *f* KER & GLAS roll mark; **Walzmaschine** *f* MASCHINEN rolling machine; **Walznast** *f* FERTIG roller burr; **Walzplattierdeckmetall** *nt* FERTIG liner; **Walzprofil** *nt* WASSERTRANS *Schiffbau* rolled section; **Walzprofilieren** *nt* MASCHINEN profile rolling, shape rolling

Wälz-: **Wälzpunkt** *m* FERTIG *Zahnrad*, MASCHINEN pitch point

Walz-: **Walzpuppe** *f* FERTIG *Extruder* billet

Wälz-: **Wälzradius** *m* MASCHINEN pitch radius; **Wälzreibung** *f* MASCHINEN sliding and rolling friction

Walzrichtung: in ~ trennen *vt* FERTIG fishmouth

Wälz-: **Wälzschälen** *nt* FERTIG skiving; **Wälzschleifen** *nt* FERTIG, MASCHINEN grinding-generating; **Wälzschleifmaschine** *f* MASCHINEN gear-grinding machine

Walz-: **Walzschmieden** *nt* MASCHINEN roll forging; **Walzsinter** *m* FERTIG mill scale; **Walzstirnfräsen** *nt* MASCHINEN shell-end milling

Wälz-: **Wälzstoßmaschine** *f* MASCHINEN shaper

Walz-: **Walzstraße** *f* FERTIG roll line, roll train, rolling mill train

Wälz-: **Wälztrommel** *f* FERTIG *Spanung* cradle

Walz-: **Walzverfahren** *nt* KER & GLAS rolling process

Wälz-: **Wälzverfahren** [1] *nt* FERTIG generative process

Wälzverfahren: [2] **im ~ herstellen** *vt* FERTIG generate

Wälzverzahnen *nt* MASCHINEN gear generating, genera-

ting

Walz-: **Walzwerk** *nt* FERTIG rolling mill, section mill; **~ für Massenfertigung** *nt* FERTIG merchant mill

Wälz-: **Wälzwinkel** *m* MASCHINEN rolling angle

Walz-: **Walzzunder** *m* FERTIG mill scale, roll coating

WAN *abbr* COMP & DV, TELEKOM *(breites Bereichsnetzwerk)* WAN *(wide area network)*

Wand *f* BAU, ELEKTRIZ, FERTIG, LABOR wall, LUFTTRANS *eines Holms* web, MASCHINEN, STRÖMPHYS *eines Kanals oder Rohres* wall; **Wandanschlußleiste** *f* BAU fillet; **Wandarm** *m* MECHAN angle bracket; **Wandbaustoffe** *m pl* BAU walling; **Wanddicke** *f* MASCHINEN wall thickness; **Wanddickenmessung** *f* KERNTECH wall thickness gaging (AmE), wall thickness gauging (BrE); **Wanddurchführung** *f* BAU wall duct, FERTIG *Kunststoffinstallationen* wall inlet fitting; **Wandeffekt** *m* KOHLEN wall effect; **Wandeinfluß** *m* STRÖMPHYS wall effect; **Wandeinführungsisolator** *m* ELEKTROTECH wall entrance insulator; **Wandeinsteckholz** *nt* BAU needle

Wandel *m* AKUSTIK alteration; **Wandelflugzeug** *nt* LUFTTRANS compound helicopter, convertiplane

Wander- *pref* BAU, TELEKOM traveling (AmE), travelling (BrE)

Wanderfeld *nt* ELEKTRONIK traveling field (AmE), travelling field (BrE); **Wanderfeldlinearmotor** *m* TRANS traveling field motor (AmE), travelling field motor (BrE); **Wanderfeldmagnetfeldröhre** *f* ELEKTRONIK traveling wave magnetron (AmE), travelling wave magnetron (BrE); **Wanderfeldmagnetron** *nt* ELEKTRONIK multicavity magnetron; **Wanderfeldmaser** *m* ELEKTRONIK TWM, traveling wave maser (AmE), travelling wave maser (BrE); **Wanderfeldröhre** *f* RADIO, TELEKOM TWT, traveling wave tube (AmE), travelling wave tube (BrE); **Wanderfeldröhre für X-Band** *f* ELEKTRONIK X-band traveling wave tube (AmE), X-band travelling wave tube (BrE); **Wanderfeldverstärker** *m* AUFNAHME traveling wave acoustic amplifier (AmE), travelling wave acoustic amplifier (BrE), TELEKOM traveling wave amplifier (AmE), travelling wave amplifier (BrE)

Wander-: **Wanderkontrolle** *f* QUAL patrol inspection; **Wanderlast** *f* BAU moving load

Wandern *nt* TELEKOM traveling (AmE), travelling (BrE)

wandernd: ~er Lichtpunkt *m* FERNSEH flying spot

Wander-: **Wanderprüfung** *f* QUAL patrol inspection; **Wanderrost** *m* ABFALL traveling grate (AmE), travelling grate (BrE)

Wanderung *f* KUNSTSTOFF migration

wanderungsbeständig: ~er Weichmacher *m* KUNSTSTOFF nonmigratory plasticizer

Wanderwelle *f* AKUSTIK, ELEKTRONIK, PHYS, TELEKOM traveling wave (AmE), travelling wave (BrE); **Wanderwellenantenne** *f* FERNSEH traveling wave aerial (AmE), travelling wave aerial (BrE), TELEKOM traveling wave antenna (AmE), travelling wave antenna (BrE); **Wanderwellenleiter** *m* TELEKOM traveling waveguide (AmE), travelling waveguide (BrE); **Wanderwellenmotor** *m* ELEKTRIZ traveling wave motor (AmE), travelling wave motor (BrE)

Wanderwellenröhre *f* RAUMFAHRT TWT, traveling wave tube (AmE), travelling wave tube (BrE); **Wanderwellenröhrenverstärker** *m* *(WWRV)* ELEKTRONIK, RAUMFAHRT *Weltraumfunk* traveling wave tube amplifier (AmE), travelling wave tube amplifier (BrE) *(TWTA)*

Wand: **Wandhalterung** *f* BAU wall holdfast; **Wandhei-**

zung f THERMOD *Gerät* panel heater, *Verfahren* panel heating; **Wandinstrument** nt GERÄT wall-mounted instrument; **Wandkonsole** f BAU, TELEKOM wall bracket; **Wandkran** m BAU wall crane; **Wandlampe** f ELEKTRIZ wall lamp

Wandler m AKUSTIK transducer, ELEKTRIZ converter, ELEKTRONIK sensing element, ELEKTROTECH converter, GERÄT converter, transducer, KFZTECH converter, KONTROLL transducer, MASCHINEN converter, PHYS converter, transducer, TELEKOM transducer; **~ zur Erzeugung negativer Widerstandskennlinien** m ELEKTROTECH negative impedance converter; **Wandlerempfindlichkeit** f AKUSTIK transducer sensitivity; **Wandlerverlustfaktor** m AKUSTIK transducer loss factor

Wandlung: **~ des optischen Signals** f ELEKTROTECH optical signal conversion

Wand: **Wandnetzstecker** m ELEKTRIZ wall outlet; **Wandreibung** f MASCHINEN wall friction, MECHAN skin friction; **Wandschale** f BAU leaf; **Wandschrank** m LABOR wall cupboard; **Wandstärke** f MASCHINEN wall thickness; **Wandsteckdose** f ELEKTRIZ wall outlet, wall socket; **Wandsystem** nt BAU walling; **Wandtafel** f KÜNSTL INT blackboard; **Wandtemperatur** f STRÖMPHYS wall temperature

Wandung f FERTIG, MASCHINEN wall

Wand: **Wandwange** f BAU wall string

Wange f BAU cheek, side plate, FERTIG cheek, *Bett* bearer, shears, KFZTECH *Kurbelwelle* web, MASCHINEN cheek, shears, web; **~ mit eingestemmten Stufen** f BAU housed string

Wankelmotor m KFZTECH, MASCHINEN, THERMOD Wankel engine

Wanne f BAU sump pan, KER & GLAS *Glaswannenofen* bath, *bei der Herstellung von Behälterglas* trough, LABOR trough, MASCHINEN pan, tray; **Wannenatmosphäre** f KER & GLAS bath atmosphere; **Wannenauskleidungsglas** nt KER & GLAS tank lining glass; **Wannendichtung** f BAU tanking; **Wannenofen** m KER & GLAS tank, tank furnace; **Wannenofenmund** m KER & GLAS tank neck; **Wannenposition** f FERTIG *Schweißen* downhand position; **Wannenstein** m KER & GLAS tank block

Want nt WASSERTRANS *Takelage* shroud; **Wantspanner** m WASSERTRANS *Tauwerk* rigging screw

Ward-Leonard-Satz m ELEKTROTECH Ward-Leonard set

Ware f QUAL commodity

Waren: **~ unter Zollverschluß** f pl WASSERTRANS bonded goods

Ware: **Wareneingangsprüfung** f QUAL incoming inspection, receiving inspection; **Warenfluß** m VERPACK flow of goods; **Warengruppe** f VERPACK commodity group; **Warenstrang** m TEXTIL rope; **Warentransport** m VERPACK handling, handling of goods; **Warentransportsystem** nt VERPACK conveyor handling system; **Warenzeichen** nt PATENT trademark

Warfarin nt CHEMIE warfarin

Warm- *pref* KUNSTSTOFF, THERMOD warm

Wärm- *pref* THERMOD warm

warm[1] *adj* THERMOD warm

warm:[2] **~e Zündkerze** f KFZTECH hot spark plug

warm:[3] **~ härten** vt THERMOD heat-harden; **~ verbinden** vt THERMOD hot-bond; **~ ziehen** vt THERMOD hot-draw

warmabbindend: **~er Kleber** m KUNSTSTOFF hot-setting adhesive

warmaushärten vt FERTIG age artificially, age with increased temperature

Warmbadhärten nt FERTIG austempering, marquenching, martempering, stepped hardening

Wärme:[1] **in ~ aushärtend** *adj* MECHAN, THERMOD thermosetting; **durch ~ dehnbar** *adj* KOHLEN dilatable

Wärme-[2] *pref* THERMOD caloric, thermal

Wärme[3] f HEIZ & KÄLTE, KERNTECH, PAPIER, PHYS, TEXTIL, THERMOD heat

Wärme:[4] **~ abstrahlen** vi BAU radiate

Wärme: **sich durch ~ ausdehnende Erde** f KOHLEN dilatant soil; **Wärmeabfall** m THERMOD heat drop; **Wärmeabfuhr** f HEIZ & KÄLTE heat rejection, heat removal, KERNTECH *in Watt pro Stunde* heat rejection rate, THERMOD heat emission; **Wärmeabführleistung** f HEIZ & KÄLTE heat-removal capacity; **Wärmeabführvermögen** nt HEIZ & KÄLTE heat-removal property; **Wärmeabgabe** f HEIZ & KÄLTE heat emission, heat release, KERNTECH heat release, THERMOD heat emission; **Wärmeableitung** f HEIZ & KÄLTE heat dissipation, heat removal, RADIO heat dissipation; **Wärmeabschirmung** f KERNTECH thermal shield

wärmeabsorbierend *adj* THERMOD heat-absorbing

Wärme: **Wärmeabsorption** f THERMOD heat absorption; **Wärmeabstrahlung** f HEIZ & KÄLTE heat radiation; **Wärmeaktivierung** f METALL thermal activation; **Wärmealterung** f KUNSTSTOFF heat ageing (BrE), heat aging (AmE); **Wärmeanstieg** m THERMOD heat rise; **Wärmeäquivalent** nt THERMOD thermal equivalent; **Wärmeätzen** nt METALL thermal etching; **Wärmeaufnahme** f HEIZ & KÄLTE heat absorption; **Wärmeausbreitung** f HEIZ & KÄLTE heat propagation; **Wärmeausbreitungsvermögen** nt PHYS thermal diffusivity; **Wärmeausdehnung** f GERÄT heat dilatation, LABOR heat expansion, thermal expansion, MASCHINEN, THERMOD heat dilatation, heat expansion, thermal expansion; **Wärmeausdehnungskoeffizient** m MASCHINEN, THERMOD thermal expansion coefficient; **Wärmeausdehnungssonde** f GERÄT thermal expansion measuring element; **Wärmeausgleich** m THERMOD heat compensation; **Wärmeausstoß** m PHYS caloric output, THERMOD caloric output, heat output; **Wärmeaustausch** m ERGON, FERTIG, HEIZ & KÄLTE heat exchange, KONTROLL thermal exchange, MASCHINEN, THERMOD heat exchange; **Wärmeaustauscher** m HEIZ & KÄLTE heat exchanger, recuperator, KERNTECH, LEBENSMITTEL, MECHAN, NICHTFOSS ENERG heat exchanger, THERMOD heat economizer, heat exchanger; **Wärmeaustauscher mit Spiralwindungen** m KERNTECH helical coil-type heat exchanger; **Wärmeaustauschmedium** nt THERMOD heat-exchanging medium; **Wärmeaustauschrohr** nt MASCHINEN heat exchanger tube; **Wärmebad** nt PHYS heat reservoir; **Wärmebeanspruchung** f THERMOD thermal stress; **Wärmebedarf** m HEIZ & KÄLTE, THERMOD heat demand

wärmebehandeln vt THERMOD heat-treat

Wärme-: **Wärmebehandlung** f KOHLEN, MASCHINEN, THERMOD heat treatment; **Wärmebelästigung** f THERMOD, UMWELTSCHMUTZ thermal pollution; **Wärmebelastung** f THERMOD heat load, rate of heat release, thermal pollution, UMWELTSCHMUTZ thermal load, thermal pollution; **Wärmebelastungsplan** m UMWELTSCHMUTZ heat load plan

wärmebeständig *adj* ERDÖL thermostable, HEIZ & KÄL-

TE, PHYS heat-resistant, THERMOD heat-resisting, heat-resistant, heatproof, thermostable, VERPACK heatproof

Wärme: **Wärmebeständigkeit** *f* KUNSTSTOFF heat resistance, PHYS thermal resistivity, THERMOD heat resistance, heat resisting, resistance to heat, thermal resistivity; **Wärmebewegung** *f* METALL thermal agitation; **Wärmebilanz** *f* ERGON, HEIZ & KÄLTE heat balance, THERMOD thermal balance; **Wärmebild** *nt* THERMOD heat image; **Wärmebildröhre** *f* ELEKTRONIK thermal-imaging tube; **Wärmeblitz** *m* KERNTECH thermal flash; **Wärmebrücke** *f* HEIZ & KÄLTE, THERMOD heat bridge; **Wärmedamm** *m* KFZTECH heat dam

wärmedämmend *adj* THERMOD heat-insulating

Wärme: **Wärmedämmfähigkeit** *f* THERMOD heat insulation effectiveness, heat insulation power; **Wärmedämmfaktor** *m* PHYS coefficient of thermal insulation; **Wärmedämmung** *f* HEIZ & KÄLTE thermal insulation, THERMOD heat insulation, *Material* thermal lagging, *Verfahren* thermal insulation, VERPACK heat insulation; **Wärmedämmzahl** *f* THERMOD heat insulation factor; **Wärmedehnung** *f* KOHLEN dilatancy, THERMOD thermal expansion; **Wärmedehnungsfuge** *f* THERMOD thermal expansion joint; **Wärmedichte** *f* THERMOD heat density; **Wärmediffusion** *f* THERMOD thermodiffusion; **Wärmedissipation** *f* THERMOD heat dissipation; **Wärmedunst** *m* THERMOD heat haze; **Wärmedurchbiegungstemperatur** *f* WERKPRÜF *Kunststoffe* heat deflection temperature; **Wärmedurchgang** *m* HEIZ & KÄLTE, THERMOD heat transition; **Wärmedurchgangszahl** *f* HEIZ & KÄLTE heat transition coefficient, thermal transmittance; **Wärmedurchlaß** *m* THERMOD heat carrying, heat conductivity

wärmedurchlässig: ~**e Wand** *f* PHYS diathermal wall

Wärme: **Wärmedurchsatz** *m* HEIZ & KÄLTE *BrE* heat throughput, heat thruput (AmE), THERMOD heat throughput (BrE), heat thruput (AmE); **Wärmeeinflußbereich** *m* THERMOD heat-affected zone; **Wärmeeinflußzone** *f* THERMOD heat-affected zone; **Wärmeeinheit** *f* THERMOD heat unit, thermal unit

wärmeempfindlich[1] *adj* KUNSTSTOFF, THERMOD heat-sensitive

wärmeempfindlich[2] *f* PHYS heat-sensitive; ~**e Farbe** *f* THERMOD heat-sensitive paint; ~**es Material** *nt* VERPACK heat-sensitive material

Wärme: **Wärmeempfindlichkeit** *f* KUNSTSTOFF heat sensitivity; **Wärmeenergie** *f* HEIZ & KÄLTE thermal energy, THERMOD heat energy, thermal emissivity, thermal energy; **Wärmeenergiespeichersystem** *nt* THERMOD thermal energy storage system; **Wärmeentbindung** *f* HEIZ & KÄLTE heat release; **Wärmeentwicklung** *f* THERMOD development of heat, heat build-up; **Wärmeermüdung** *f* THERMOD thermal fatigue

wärmeerzeugend *adj* THERMOD heat-generating

Wärme: **Wärmeerzeuger** *m* HEIZ & KÄLTE, THERMOD heat generator; **Wärmeerzeugung** *f* THERMOD heat generation; **Wärmefalle** *f* KERNTECH heat trap

wärmefest *adj* VERPACK heat-resistant

Wärmefestigkeit *f* KUNSTSTOFF heat resistance; **Wärmefestigkeitsgrenze** *f* FERTIG heat distortion point

Wärmefluß *m* HEIZ & KÄLTE, LABOR, THERMOD heat flow; **Wärmeflußbild** *nt* THERMOD heat balance chart, heat balance diagram; **Wärmeflußdiagramm** *nt* THERMOD heat flow diagram; **Wärmeflußmeßgerät** *nt* GERÄT heat flow meter

Wärme: **Wärmeformbeständigkeit** *f* KUNSTSTOFF heat distortion temperature; **Wärmefortleitung** *f* HEIZ & KÄLTE thermal conduction

wärmefreisetzend *adj* HEIZ & KÄLTE heat-released

Wärme: **Wärmefreisetzung** *f* HEIZ & KÄLTE, KERNTECH heat release; **Wärmefühler** *m* THERMOD heat detector, heat sensor; **Wärmefunktion** *f* HEIZ & KÄLTE, KOHLEN, MECHAN, NICHTFOSS ENERG, PHYS, RAUMFAHRT, THERMOD enthalpy

wärmegedämmt *adj* HEIZ & KÄLTE insulated against heat

Wärme: **Wärmegefälle** *nt* THERMOD thermal head; **Wärmegehalt** *m* THERMOD caloric content, heat content, thermal content; **Wärmegerät** *nt* HEIZ & KÄLTE heating appliance; **Wärmegewinn** *m* HEIZ & KÄLTE heat gain; **Wärmegleiche** *f* LUFTTRANS isotherm; **Wärmegleichgewicht** *nt* THERMOD thermal balance; **Wärmegleichrichter** *m* ELEKTROTECH thermionic rectifier; **Wärmegrad** *m* PHYS, THERMOD degree of heat

wärmehärtbar[1] *adj* DRUCK, MECHAN, THERMOD thermosetting

wärmehärtbar:[2] ~**e Farbe** *f* DRUCK thermosetting ink

Wärme: **Wärmehaushalt** *m* HEIZ & KÄLTE, PAPIER heat balance, PHYS calorific balance, THERMOD caloric balance, heat balance, thermal balance; **Wärmeinhalt** *m* PHYS water equivalent, THERMOD thermal content; **Wärmeinstabilität** *f* THERMOD thermal instability; **Wärmeisolation** *f* MECHAN heat insulation

wärmeisolieren:[1] **wärmeisolierend** *adj* LUFTTRANS, PHYS, THERMOD heat-insulating

wärmeisolieren[2] *vt* FERTIG lag

wärmeisolierend: ~**e Wand** *f* LUFTTRANS, PHYS, THERMOD heat-insulating wall

wärmeisoliert *adj* HEIZ & KÄLTE, MECHAN, THERMOD heat-insulated

Wärme: **Wärmeisolierung** *f* HEIZ & KÄLTE thermal insulation, THERMOD thermal insulation, *Material* lagging, *Vorgang* heat insulation, *angebrachte Schutzschicht* heat-insulating jacket; **Wärmekapazität** *f* HEIZ & KÄLTE heat capacity, thermal capacity, THERMOD heat capacity, thermal bonding, thermal capacity; **Wärmekapazität bei konstantem Druck** *f* (Cp) LABOR heat capacity at constant pressure (Cp); **Wärmekapazität bei konstantem Volumen** *f* THERMOD heat capacity at constant volume; **Wärmekonstante** *f* THERMOD heat constant; **Wärmekontraktion** *f* THERMOD thermal contraction; **Wärmekonvektion** *f* THERMOD heat convection; **Wärmekraftmaschine** *f* MASCHINEN, MECHAN heat engine; **Wärmekraftwerk** *nt* ELEKTROTECH thermal-electric power station, thermal-electric power plant, KERNTECH thermal power plant, thermal power station; **Wärmekreislauf** *m* HEIZ & KÄLTE heat cycle; **Wärmelagerung** *f* KUNSTSTOFF heat ageing (BrE), heat aging (AmE); **Wärmelast** *f* HEIZ & KÄLTE heat load; **Wärmelehre** *f* THERMOD thermodynamics; **Wärmeleistung** *f* HEIZ & KÄLTE, KERNTECH *eines Reaktors* thermal output, THERMOD caloric power, thermal output

wärmeleitend[1] *adj* KER & GLAS, TEXTIL, THERMOD heat-conducting

wärmeleitend:[2] ~**es Glas** *nt* KER & GLAS heat-conducting glass

Wärmeleitfähigkeit *f* HEIZ & KÄLTE, LABOR thermal conductivity, PHYS thermal conductance, THERMOD caloric conductibility, heat conductivity, thermal conductibility, thermal diffusivity; **Wärmeleitfähigkeits-Analysengerät** *nt* GERÄT thermal conductivity gas analyzer; **Wärmeleitfähigkeits-Analysenmeßgerät** *nt* GERÄT thermal conductivity gas analyzer; **Wärmeleitfähigkeitsdetektor** *m* GERÄT thermal-conductivity detector; **Wärmeleitfähigkeitskoeffizient** *m* MECHAN coefficient of thermal conduction

Wärme: **Wärmeleitung** *f* HEIZ & KÄLTE thermal conduction, THERMOD caloric conductibility, heat conductivity, thermal conduction; **Wärmeleitungsmesser** *m* THERMOD heat conductivity meter; **Wärmeleitvermögen** *nt* HEIZ & KÄLTE, THERMOD thermal conductivity; **Wärmeleitweg** *m* HEIZ & KÄLTE heat path; **Wärmeleitwert** *m* HEIZ & KÄLTE thermal conductance; **Wärmeleitwiderstand** *m* THERMOD temperature lag; **Wärmeleitzahl** *f* ERGON heat transfer coefficient, HEIZ & KÄLTE thermal conductance, thermal conductivity coefficient, KUNSTSTOFF thermal conductivity coefficient; **Wärmemaschine** *f* THERMOD heat engine, thermal engine; **Wärmemauer** *f* KERNTECH, THERMOD heat barrier; **Wärmemelder** *m* THERMOD heat detector; **Wärmemenge** *f* PHYS quantity of heat, THERMOD amount of heat, q-gas, quantum of heat; **Wärmemengenzähler** *m* GERÄT heat meter, HEIZ & KÄLTE calorimetric meter; **Wärmemesser** *m* HEIZ & KÄLTE calorimeter; **Wärmemessung** *f* HEIZ & KÄLTE calorimetry, THERMOD thermometry; **Wärmemischung** *f* KERNTECH thermal mixing; **Wärmemitführung** *f* HEIZ & KÄLTE, THERMOD thermal convection; **Wärmeofen** *m* METALL, THERMOD heating furnace; **Wärmepumpe** *f* HEIZ & KÄLTE, MASCHINEN, THERMOD heat pump; **Wärmequelle** *f* HEIZ & KÄLTE heat source; **Wärmerauschen** *nt* ELEKTRONIK, PHYS thermal noise; **Wärmerauschgenerator** *m* ELEKTRONIK thermal noise generator; **Wärmerelais** *nt* ELEKTROTECH thermal relay; **Wärmeriß** *m* FERTIG heat check; **Wärmerißbildung** *f* FERTIG heat checking; **Wärmerückgewinnung** *f* ABFALL heat recovery, HEIZ & KÄLTE heat reclamation, heat recovery, THERMOD heat rate, heat rate curve, heat recovery; **Wärmeschaltbild** *nt* THERMOD heat flow chart, heat flow diagram; **Wärmeschalter** *m* ELEKTROTECH thermal switch; **Wärmeschild** *m* THERMOD heat shield; **Wärmeschluckvermögen** *nt* THERMOD heat-absorbing power; **Wärmeschockprüfung** *f* THERMOD heat shock test; **Wärmeschrumpfen** *nt* THERMOD heat shrinking

wärmeschrumpfen *vt* THERMOD heat-shrink

Wärmeschutz:[1] **mit ~ versehen** *adj* HEIZ & KÄLTE insulated against heat

Wärmeschutz[2] *m* FOTO, KER & GLAS heat absorbing, THERMOD thermal lagging, VERPACK heat insulation; **Wärmeschutzfilter** *nt* FOTO heat-absorbing filter; **Wärmeschutzglas** *nt* KER & GLAS heat-absorbing glass; **Wärmeschutzschirm** *m* ELEKTROTECH heat shield; **Wärmeschutzverglasung** *f* KER & GLAS heat-absorbing glazing; **Wärmeschutzwert** *m* THERMOD thermal insulation index

Wärme: **Wärmespannung** *f* THERMOD *mechanische* thermal stress; **Wärmespeicher** *m* THERMOD heat accumulator

wärmespeichernd *adj* THERMOD heat-retaining

Wärme: **Wärmespeicherung** *f* ERGON heat storage; **Wärmespeichervermögen** *nt* HEIZ & KÄLTE, THERMOD thermal capacity; **Wärmespektrum** *nt* THERMOD heat spectrum, thermal spectrum; **Wärmesperre** *f* HEIZ & KÄLTE thermal barrier; **Wärmespiegel** *m* NICHTFOSS ENERG heat mirror; **Wärmespritzen** *nt* FERTIG flame spraying

wärmestabil *adj* THERMOD heat-stable

wärmestabilisiert *adj* THERMOD heat-stabilized

Wärme: **Wärmestabilität** *f* KUNSTSTOFF heat stability, THERMOD heat stability, thermal stability, VERPACK heat stability; **Wärmestau** *m* THERMOD heat accumulation; **Wärmestauung** *f* THERMOD heat accumulation; **Wärmesteigrohr** *nt* KFZTECH heat riser tube; **Wärmestoß** *m* THERMOD thermal shock; **Wärmestrahlung** *f* HEIZ & KÄLTE heat radiation, KERNTECH, LABOR, PHYS thermal radiation, THERMOD heat radiation, thermal radiation, VERPACK heat radiation; **Wärmestrahlungdetektor** *m* GERÄT thermal radiation detector

Wärmestrom *m* ERGON, LABOR, THERMOD heat flow; **Wärmestromdichte** *f* KERNTECH surface heat flux; **Wärmestromlinie** *f* THERMOD heat flow line; **Wärmestrommeßgerät** *nt* GERÄT heat flow meter

Wärme: **Wärmeströmung** *f* HEIZ & KÄLTE heat flow, THERMOD heat convection

wärmesuchend *adj* THERMOD heat-seeking

Wärme: **Wärmesystem** *nt* KFZTECH heater system; **Wärmetauscher** *m* ERDÖL, HEIZ & KÄLTE, PAPIER, WASSERTRANS heat exchanger; **Wärmetechnik** *f* MASCHINEN heat engineering; **Wärmetod** *m* THERMOD heat death; **Wärmeträger** *m* FERTIG coolant, HEIZ & KÄLTE heat carrier, THERMOD heat transfer medium; **Wärmeträgheit** *f* HEIZ & KÄLTE, THERMOD thermal inertia; **Wärmetransport** *m* ERDÖL, HEIZ & KÄLTE, PHYS, STRÖMPHYS, THERMOD convection; **Wärmetrennabziehbild** *nt* KER & GLAS heat-release decal; **Wärmeturbine** *f* KERNTECH heat turbine

Wärmeübergang *m* HEIZ & KÄLTE, KUNSTSTOFF, THERMOD *zwischen verschiedenen Körpern* heat transfer, heat transmission; **Wärmeübergangsleistung** *f* HEIZ & KÄLTE heat transfer efficiency; **Wärmeübergangszahl** *f* ERGON, THERMOD heat transfer coefficient

Wärmeübertragung *f* BAU convection, HEIZ & KÄLTE heat transfer, heat transmission, PHYS heat transfer, THERMOD heat transfer, heat transmission; **Wärmeübertragungsfläche** *f* HEIZ & KÄLTE, THERMOD heat transfer surface; **Wärmeübertragungskoeffizient** *m* PHYS heat transfer coefficient, THERMOD *(U)* overall heat transfer coefficient *(U)*; **Wärmeübertragungsmittel** *nt* HEIZ & KÄLTE heat transfer medium; **Wärmeübertragungszahl** *f* THERMOD heat transfer coefficient

Wärme: **Wärmeumhüllung** *f* OPTIK thermal wrap; **Wärmeumsatz** *m* THERMOD heat transformation; **Wärmeumwandlung des Meeres** *f* NICHTFOSS ENERG ocean thermal conversion; **Wärmeundurchlässigkeit** *f* PHYS athermancy

Wärmeverbrauch *m* LABOR, THERMOD heat consumption; **Wärmeverbrauchsmeßgerät** *nt* GERÄT heat consumption meter; **Wärmeverbrauchszähler** *m* GERÄT heat consumption meter, HEIZ & KÄLTE calorimetric meter

Wärme: **Wärmeverdampfung** *f* METALL thermal evaporation; **Wärmeverhalten** *nt* THERMOD thermal properties

Wärmeverlust *m* ELEKTRIZ, MASCHINEN, NICHTFOSS ENERG, THERMOD heat loss, loss of heat; **Wärmeverlustleistung** *f* ELEKTRIZ dissipated power; **Wärmeverlustmode** *f* OPTIK heat ablation mode

Wärme: **Wärmeverschiebung** *f* THERMOD heat displacement; **Wärmeversorgung** *f* THERMOD heat supply; **Wärmewandler** *m* ELEKTROTECH thermal converter; **Wärmewert** *m* ERDÖL calorific value, THERMOD calorific value, thermal value; **Wärmewiderstand** *m* (θ)

HYDRAUL, PHYS, THERMOD thermal resistance (θ)

Wärmewirkung *f* THERMOD heat effect; **Wärmewirkungsgrad** *m* PHYS, THERMOD heat efficiency, thermal efficiency

Wärme: **Wärmezähler** *m* GERÄT heat meter; **Wärmeziffer** *f* HEIZ & KÄLTE heat transfer factor; **Wärmezufuhr** *f* THERMOD heat input

warmfest: ~**e Legierung** *f* MECHAN high-temperature alloy

wärmfest *adj* VERPACK heatproof

Warm-: **Warmformen** *nt* KUNSTSTOFF thermoforming, MECHAN hot-forming

warmgehärtet *adj* THERMOD heat-hardened

warmgeschmiedet *adj* THERMOD hot-forged

warmgewalzt[1] *adj* MECHAN, THERMOD *Metall* hot-rolled

warmgewalzt:[2] ~**es Stahlblech** *nt* FERTIG latten

warmgezogen *adj* THERMOD hot-drawn

Warm-: **Warmhärtung** *f* THERMOD heat hardening; **Warmkalandrieren** *nt* THERMOD hot-rolling

warmkalandrieren *vt* THERMOD hot-roll

warmkalandriert *adj* THERMOD hot-rolled

Warm-: **Warmkautschuk** *m* KUNSTSTOFF hot rubber

Wärm-: **Wärmkurve** *f* THERMOD heating temperature curve

Warm-: **Warmlabor** *nt* KERNTECH semihot laboratory, warm laboratory; **Warmlaufbereich** *m* LUFTTRANS *Flughafen* run-up area; **Warmlaufen** *nt* FERTIG *Lager* heat exchange

warmlaufen:[1] ~ **lassen** *vt* THERMOD warm up

warmlaufen[2] *vi* LUFTTRANS *Motor und Triebwerk* run-up

Warmluft *f* HEIZ & KÄLTE warm air; **Warmlufterzeuger** *m* HEIZ & KÄLTE fan-assisted air heater, warm-air heater; **Warmluftfront** *f* WASSERTRANS *Wetterkunde* warm front; **Warmluftgebläse** *nt* HEIZ & KÄLTE hot-air blower; **Warmluftkorridor** *m* LUFTTRANS hot-air corridor, hot-air gallery; **Warmluftleitung** *f* LUFTTRANS hot-air duct; **Warmluftregler** *m* KFZTECH heater control; **Warmluftvorhang** *m* HEIZ & KÄLTE hot-air curtain

warmnieten *vt* MASCHINEN hot-rivet

Warm-: **Warmnietung** *f* MASCHINEN hot-riveting; **Warmprägefolie** *f* VERPACK hot-stamping foil; **Warmprägen** *nt* VERPACK hot-stamping; **Warmriß** *m* MASCHINEN heat crack, thermal crack; **Warmschmiedegesenk** *nt* MASCHINEN hot-forging die; **Warmschmieden** *nt* THERMOD hot forging

warmschmieden *vt* THERMOD hot-forge

Warm-: **Warmstart** *m* COMP & DV soft reset, warm start, LUFTTRANS hot start; **Warmstauchversuch** *m* WERKPRÜF hot-compression test; **Warmumformen** *nt* MASCHINEN hot forging, warm forming

Warm: **Warmverarbeitung** *f* KER & GLAS hot working; **Warmverbindung** *f* THERMOD hot bonding

warmverformbar *adj* WASSERTRANS *Schiffbau* thermoplastic

warmverformen *vt* THERMOD heat-form

warmverformt *adj* THERMOD heat-formed

Warm-: **Warmverformung** *f* THERMOD heat distortion, heat forming

warmverschweißbar *adj* THERMOD heat fusible

Warm-: **Warmwalzen** *nt* THERMOD hot-rolling

warmwalzen *vt* THERMOD hot-roll

Warmwasser *nt* HEIZ & KÄLTE hot-water; **Warmwasserboiler der Heizung** *m* HEIZ & KÄLTE calorifier; **Warmwasserheizung** *f* HEIZ & KÄLTE hot-water

heating system; **Warmwasserheizungsanlage** *f* HEIZ & KÄLTE hot-water heating system; **Warmwasserspeicher** *m* HEIZ & KÄLTE hot-water tank; **Warmwasserzähler** *m* GERÄT *Thermo-Hydrometer* hot-water meter

Wärm-: **Wärmzeit** *f* THERMOD heating time

Warm-: **Warmziehen** *nt* MASCHINEN, THERMOD hot-drawing; **Warmzyklon** *m* KOHLEN hot cyclone

Warn- *pref* ELEKTROTECH, KFZTECH, SICHERHEIT alarming; **Warnanzeige** *f* ELEKTROTECH warning light, MASCHINEN alarm; **Warnblinkanlage** *f* KFZTECH hazard-warning system; **Warnblinkleuchte** *f* KFZTECH hazard-warning lamp; **Warndreieck** *nt* SICHERHEIT warning triangle; **Warngrenzen** *f pl* QUAL warning limits; **Warnlampe** *f* MASCHINEN, SICHERHEIT warning light; ~ **für niedrigen Pegelstand** *f* MASCHINEN low-level warning light; **Warnleuchte** *f* ELEKTROTECH warning light, LUFTTRANS indicator light, SICHERHEIT warning light; **Warnlicht** *nt* EISENBAHN, LUFTTRANS, TRANS, WASSERTRANS warning light; **Warnmeldung** *f* EISENBAHN, LUFTTRANS, TRANS, WASSERTRANS warning message; **Warnrelais** *nt* ELEKTRIZ alarm relay; **Warnschild** *nt* SICHERHEIT warning sign, VERPACK caution label; **Warnsignal** *nt* EISENBAHN caution signal, warning signal, LUFTTRANS warning signal, MASCHINEN alarm, alarm signal, TRANS, WASSERTRANS warning signal; **Warnthermometer** *nt* MASCHINEN alarm thermometer

Warnung *f* SICHERHEIT warning label

Warpanker *m* WASSERTRANS *Festmachen* kedge anchor

Warpen *nt* WASSERTRANS *Tauwerk* warping

warpen *vt* WASSERTRANS *Schiff* kedge

Warren-Motor *m* KFZTECH Warren engine

Warte- *pref* LUFTTRANS, TELEKOM holding; **Wartebereich für die Gepäckaufbereitung** *m* LUFTTRANS racetrack holding pattern; **Warteeinrichtung** *f* TELEKOM queueing device; **Warteflugbahn** *f* LUFTTRANS holding path; **Wartefluggeschwindigkeit** *f* LUFTTRANS holding speed; **Wartegleis** *nt* EISENBAHN holding track; **Wartehalle** *f* TRANS shelter

warten[1] *vt* COMP & DV service, MASCHINEN service, *Werkzeuge und Geräte* maintain, MECHAN *Werkzeuge und Geräte* maintain

warten[2] *vi* ELEKTRIZ delay

wartend: ~**e Belegung** *f* TELEKOM waiting call

Warte-: **Warteordner** *m* TELEKOM call store; **Wartepunkt** *m* LUFTTRANS holding point

Warteschlange *f* COMP & DV, KONTROLL, TELEKOM queue; ~ **mit einer Bedieneinheit** *f* TELEKOM single server queue; **Warteschlangenbetrieb** *m* TELEKOM call holding, callqueueing; **Warteschlangenblock** *m* COMP & DV queue block; **Warteschlangenelement** *nt* COMP & DV queue element; **Warteschlangengröße** *f* COMP & DV queue size; **Warteschlangennetz** *nt* TELEKOM queueing network; **Warteschlangensteuerung** *f* TELEKOM queue control; **Warteschlangentheorie** *f* COMP & DV, ERGON queueing theory; **Warteschlangenverwaltung** *f* COMP & DV queue management

Warte-: **Warteschleife** *f* COMP & DV wait loop, LUFTTRANS flight-holding pattern, holding, holding pattern; **Wartestapel** *m* LUFTTRANS holding stack; **Wartestation** *f* COMP & DV passive station; **Wartestatus** *m* COMP & DV wait condition, wait state; **Wartesteuerung** *f* KONTROLL wait control; **Wartesystem** *nt* TELEKOM call queueing facility; **Warteverfahren** *nt* LUFTTRANS holding procedure; **Wartezeit** *f* COMP & DV

latency, queueing time, queue time, ELEKTRIZ delay
time, FERNSEH queueing time, TELEKOM delay,
queueing time; **Wartezeitzähler** *m* COMP & DV quiesce
counter

Warte-: **Wartezustand** *m* KONTROLL wait condition;
Wartezyklus *m* KONTROLL wait cycle

Wartung *f* BAU, COMP & DV maintenance, service, EISEN-
BAHN, ELEKTRIZ, FERNSEH, KFZTECH, LUFTTRANS
maintenance, MASCHINEN service, MECHAN, PAPIER,
TELEKOM maintenance; **allgemeine ~** *f* KERNTECH general maintenance; **~ am Ort** *f* TELEKOM local
maintenance; **Wartungsaufzeichung** *f* LUFTTRANS
maintenance recorder; **Wartungsdauer** *f* QUAL active
preventive maintenance time

wartungsfrei *adj* ELEKTRIZ, FERTIG *Kunststoffinstallationen*, KFZTECH *Batterie* maintenance-free

Wartung: **Wartungsintervall** *nt* COMP & DV mean time
between maintenance, MASCHINEN maintenance interval; **Wartungslogbuch** *nt* LUFTTRANS maintenance
recorder; **Wartungsprogramm** *nt* COMP & DV service
program; **Wartungstunnel** *m* BAU service tunnel; **War-
tungsvorschrift** *f* LUFTTRANS maintenance manual;
Wartungswerkstatt *f* BAU maintenance shop; **War-
tungswerkzeug** *nt* MASCHINEN service tool

Warze *f* FERTIG projection, *Schweißen* embossment,
METALL *Defekt* button; **Warzenblech** *nt* FERTIG war-
ted plate; **Warzendurchmesser** *m* FERTIG *Schweißen*
diameter of projection

Wasch- *pref* KOHLEN, TEXTIL washing; **Waschanleitung**
f TEXTIL washing instructions; **Waschbarkeit** *f* TEXTIL
washability; **Waschbord** *nt* WASSERTRANS *Schiffbau*
washboard; **Waschbühne** *f* KOHLEN strake

Wäsche *f* ERDÖL *Gasreinigungsverfahren* scrubbing,
KOHLEN dressing, PAPIER washup, TEXTIL washing,
UMWELTSCHMUTZ *Brennstoffaufbereitung* scrubbing
(AmE), stripping (BrE)

waschecht *adj* CHEMIE *Farbstoff*, TEXTIL *Farbstoff*
washfast

Wasch-: **Waschechtheit** *f* TEXTIL fastness to washing

Waschen *nt* TEXTIL laundering, washing

waschen[1] *vt* KOHLEN clean, PAPIER wash, TEXTIL scour

waschen[2] *vi* TEXTIL wash

Wäscher *m* CHEMTECH washer, KOHLEN dresser

Wasch-: **Waschflasche** *f* LABOR wash bottle, PHYS
bubbler; **Waschflüssigkeit** *f* CHEMTECH *verbraucht*
washings; **Waschgrieß** *m* KOHLEN washed smalls;
Waschmaschine *f* TEXTIL washer, washing machine;
Waschmittel *nt* TEXTIL detergent; **Waschout-Rate** *f*
UMWELTSCHMUTZ washout rate; **Waschprodukte** *nt pl*
KOHLEN clean coal, cleans; **Waschröhrchen** *nt* LABOR
washing tube; **Waschtrommel** *f* PAPIER washing drum;
Waschturm *m* CHEMTECH washing column

Washout *nt* UMWELTSCHMUTZ washout

Washprimer *m* KUNSTSTOFF wash primer

Wasser:[1] **in ~ löslich** *adj* VERPACK soluble

Wasser:[2] **zu ~** *adv* WASSERTRANS by water

Wasser[3] *nt* PHYS, TEXTIL water; **~ entziehendes Mittel** *nt*
CHEMTECH dehydrating agent; **zum Verbrauch be-
stimmtes ~** *nt* WASSERVERSORG consumption water

Wasser:[4] **zu ~ lassen** *vt* WASSERTRANS *Schiff* launch; **mit
~ versorgen** *vt* WASSERVERSORG supply with water

Wasser:[5] **~ absondern** *vi* BAU *Beton absondern* bleed; **~
entziehen** *vi* CHEMIE dehydrate; **~ machen** *vi* WASSER-
TRANS *Schiff* make water; **auf ~ notlanden** *vi* LUFT-
TRANS ditch; **~ übernehmen** *vi* WASSERTRANS take on
water; **ein ~ übernehmen** *vi* WASSERTRANS ship a water

Wasser: **Wasserabdichtung** *f* BAU waterproofing; **Was-
serabgabe** *f* WASSERVERSORG water delivery;
Wasserablaßhahn *m* WASSERVERSORG priming cock;
Wasserablenkplatte *f* KERNTECH water baffle; **Was-
serabscheidebauwerk** *nt* BAU water extraction
structure; **Wasserabscheider** *m* MASCHINEN, WASSER-
VERSORG water separator; **Wasserabschrecken** *nt*
METALL water quenching; **Wasserabspaltung** *f* CHE-
MIE dehydration

wasserabweisend[1] *adj* CHEMIE *Ionen, Atomgruppen* hydrophobic, TEXTIL water-repellent

wasserabweisend:[2] **~e Imprägnierung** *f* TEXTIL water-
repellent finish

wasseraktiviert: **~e Batterie** *f* ELEKTROTECH water-acti-
vated battery

Wasser: **Wasseranalyseausrüstung** *f* LABOR water analysis kit; **Wasserangebot** *nt* WASSERVERSORG water
supply; **Wasseranlagerung** *f* CHEMIE hydration; **Was-
seranschluß** *m* BAU tap (BrE); **Wasseraufbereitung** *f*
ABFALL *bei Abwässern* water purification, KERNTECH
water treatment, water-conditioning process, KOHLEN
water treatment, WASSERVERSORG water conditioning,
water purification; **Wasseraufbereitungsanlage** *f* BAU,
WASSERVERSORG water treatment plant; **Wasserauf-
nahme** *f* WERKPRÜF water absorption

wasseraufnehmend *adj* BAU hygroscopic

Wasser: **Wasseraustritt** *m* HEIZ & KÄLTE water outlet;
Wasseraustrittsöffnung *f* HEIZ & KÄLTE water outlet;
Wasserbad *nt* LABOR water bath; **Wasserbadver-
dampfer** *m* KERNTECH water bath evaporator

wasserbasiert *adj* ANSTRICH aqueous-based, water-
based

Wasser: **Wasserbehälter** *m* EISENBAHN water tank, TEX-
TIL water container, WASSERTRANS water tank,
WASSERVERSORG cistern, water tank; **Wasserbehand-
lungsanlage** *f* WASSERVERSORG water treatment plant;
Wasserbehörde *f* WASSERVERSORG water authority;
Wasserbelieferung *f* WASSERVERSORG water delivery,
water supply; **Wasserbeschaffenheit** *f* WASSERVER-
SORG water quality

wasserbeständig[1] *adj* TEXTIL, VERPACK water-resistant

wasserbeständig:[2] **~es Schleifpapier** *nt* MASCHINEN waterproof abrasive paper

Wasser: **Wasserbeständigkeit** *f* WERKPRÜF *Glas* hydro-
lytic resistance; **Wasserbewirtschaftung** *f* WASSERVER-
SORG integral water management; **Wasserbilanz** *f* WAS-
SERVERSORG water balance; **Wasserbindung** *f*
WASSERVERSORG water retention; **Wasserbohr-
schlamm** *m* ERDÖL *Bohrtechnik* water-based mud;
Wasserbohrung *f* WASSERVERSORG bore, boring; **Was-
serbus** *m* WASSERTRANS *auf Flüssen* river bus;
Wasserdampf *m* CHEMTECH, HEIZ & KÄLTE, HYDRAUL,
NICHTFOSS ENERG, PAPIER, PHYS, TEXTIL steam; **Was-
serdampfdestillation** *f* CHEMTECH steam distillation;
Wasserdampfhemmung *f* VERPACK water vapor bar-
rier (AmE), water vapour barrier (BrE)

wasserdicht[1] *adj* HEIZ & KÄLTE waterproof, watertight,
KUNSTSTOFF, PAPIER waterproof, PHYS watertight,
TEXTIL waterproof, watertight, WASSERTRANS water-
tight

wasserdicht:[2] **~e Bitumenisolierung eines Kellerge-
schosses** *f* BAU asphalt tanking; **~e Folie** *f* TEXTIL
waterproof sheet; **~er Stecker** *m* ELEKTRIZ watertight
socket outlet; **~er Steckkontakt** *m* ELEKTRIZ watertight socket outlet; **~ versiegelte Kamera** *f* FOTO
waterproof-sealed camera

wasserdicht:[3] ~ **machen** *vt* HEIZ & KÄLTE waterproof
Wasser: **Wasserdichtmachen** *nt* TEXTIL waterproofing, WASSERVERSORG coffering; **Wasserdruck** *m* BAU, HEIZ & KÄLTE water pressure, HYDRAUL *resultierend aus Standhöhe oder Bewegung* head of water pressure, NICHTFOSS ENERG hydraulic thrust, TEXTIL, WASSERVERSORG water pressure; **Wasserdruckbehälter** *m* HYDRAUL hydraulic reservoir; **Wasserdurchlässigkeit** *f* KUNSTSTOFF water permeability; **Wasserdurchprüfung** *f* MECHAN hydrotests; **Wasserdüse** *f* FERTIG water nozzle; **Wassereinbruch** *m* KERNTECH water ingress; **Wassereinlaß** *m* HEIZ & KÄLTE water inlet, WASSERVERSORG water inflow; **Wassereinspritzung** *f* ERDÖL water injection; **Wassereintritt** *m* NICHTFOSS ENERG water intake, WASSERVERSORG water inlet; **Wassereintrittsöffnung** *f* HEIZ & KÄLTE water inlet; **Wasserenthärten** *nt* CHEMTECH water softening; **Wasserenthärter** *m* BAU, CHEMTECH, TEXTIL water softener; **Wasserenthärtungsanlage** *f* FERTIG water-softening plant; **Wasserenthärtungsmittel** *nt* TEXTIL water softener; **Wasserentnahme** *f* WASSERVERSORG draw-off; **Wasserentziehung** *f* HEIZ & KÄLTE dehydration; **Wasserentzug** *m* PAPIER anhydration; **Wassererschließung** *f* UMWELTSCHMUTZ water reclamation; **Wasserfahrzeug** *nt* WASSERTRANS boat, vessel; **Wasserfallhöhe** *f* HYDRAUL waterfall height; **Wasserfarbe** *f* BAU water-based paint; **Wasserfaß** *nt* BAU water butt
wasserfest *adj* TEXTIL water-resistant, VERPACK watertight
Wasser: **Wasserfilter** *nt* MASCHINEN, WASSERTRANS, WASSERVERSORG water filter; **Wasserflugzeug** *nt* LUFTTRANS, WASSERTRANS hydroplane, seaplane; **Wasserförderschnecke** *f* MEERSCHMUTZ screw pump; **Wasserfracht** *f* WASSERTRANS *Seehandel* waterage
wasserfrei[1] *adj* CHEMIE, ERDÖL *Petrochemie* anhydrous, LEBENSMITTEL anhydrous, desiccated, PAPIER anhydrous, UMWELTSCHMUTZ waterless
wasserfrei:[2] ~**es Ammoniak** *nt* ERDÖL *Petrochemie* anhydrous ammonia; ~**es Natriumkarbonat** *nt* PAPIER soda ash
Wasser: **Wasserfreimachung** *f* ERDÖL *einer Rohrleitung* dewatering
wasserführend[1] *adj* WASSERVERSORG aquiferous
wasserführend:[2] ~**e Schicht** *m* WASSERVERSORG shaft water-bearing ground
Wasser: **Wassergang** *m* WASSERTRANS boot topping; **Wassergehalt** *m* BAU, KOHLEN, OPTIK water content; **Wassergehaltsprüfung** *f* FERTIG *Form* moisture content test
wassergehärtet *adj* THERMOD water-hardened
wassergekühlt[1] *adj* ELEKTRIZ, ELEKTRONIK, HEIZ & KÄLTE, KERNTECH, KFZTECH, THERMOD water-cooled
wassergekühlt:[2] ~**es Klimagerät** *nt* HEIZ & KÄLTE water-cooled air conditioning unit; ~**er Motor** *m* KFZTECH water-cooled engine; ~**er Reaktor** *m* KERNTECH water-cooled reactor; ~**e Röhre** *f* ELEKTRONIK water-cooled tube; ~**es System** *nt* MASCHINEN water-cooled system; ~**er Transformator** *m* ELEKTRIZ water-cooled transformer
wassergelöst[1] *adj* ANSTRICH aqueous-based, water-based
wassergelöst:[2] ~**er Feststoff** *m* ANSTRICH water-borne slurry
Wasser: **Wassergewinnung** *f* UMWELTSCHMUTZ water reclamation, WASSERVERSORG water catchment; **Wasserglas** *nt* KER & GLAS water glass; **Wasserglätte** *f*

KFZTECH aquaplaning; **Wassergüte** *f* WASSERVERSORG water quality; **Wasserhahn** *m* BAU bibcock, spigot, water cock, LABOR water tap, MASCHINEN bib tap, bibcock, WASSERVERSORG water tap
wasserhaltig[1] *adj* CHEMIE, ERDÖL, PAPIER aqueous
wasserhaltig:[2] ~**es Silicat** *nt* CHEMIE hydrosilicate
Wasser: **Wasserhammer** *m* STRÖMPHYS water hammer; **Wasserhärte** *f* WASSERVERSORG water hardness; - **Wasserhärten** *nt* METALL water tempering; **Wasserhaushaltsgesetz** *nt* WASSERVERSORG water law; **Wasserhaushaltung** *f* WASSERVERSORG integral water management; **Wasserheizvorrichtung** *f* LABOR water heater; **Wasserhose** *f* WASSERTRANS waterspout
wässerig *adj* CHEMIE, FERTIG *Kunststoffinstallationen*, STRÖMPHYS, WASSERVERSORG aqueous
Wasser: **Wasserinhalt** *m* PHYS water content; **Wasserinjektion** *f* ERDÖL *Sekundärfördertechnik* water injection; **Wasserkasten** *m* KER & GLAS water box
Wasserkraft *f* ELEKTRIZ, NICHTFOSS ENERG, THERMOD, WASSERVERSORG hydroelectric power, hydroelectricity, water power; **Wasserkraftgenerator** *m* ELEKTRIZ hydroelectric generator; **Wasserkraftprojekt** *nt* BAU hydroelectric project; **Wasserkraftwerk** *nt* ELEKTRIZ hydroelectric generating station, hydroelectric power plant, hydroelectric power station, water power station, ELEKTROTECH hydroelectric generating station, hydroelectric power station, hydroelectric power plant, water power station, NICHTFOSS ENERG hydroelectric generating station, hydroelectric power plant, hydroelectric power station, water power station
Wasser: **Wasserkühler** *m* HEIZ & KÄLTE water cooler; **Wasserkühlung** *f* HEIZ & KÄLTE hydrocooling, KFZTECH, MASCHINEN water cooling; **Wasserkunde** *f* KOHLEN hydrology; **Wasserlandung** *f* LUFTTRANS landing on water; **Wasserlauf** *m* BAU, UMWELTSCHMUTZ water course; **Wasserleitung** *f* BAU aqueduct, water line, WASSERVERSORG conduit; **Wasserleitungsrohr** *nt* WASSERVERSORG water pipe
Wasserlinie *f* DRUCK wire mark, MEERSCHMUTZ water line, WASSERTRANS water line, *Schiffbau* floating line; **Wasserlinienebene** *f* WASSERTRANS *Schiffskonstruktion* waterplane; **Wasserlinienriß** *m* WASSERTRANS *Schiffkonstruktion* half-breadth plan; **Wasserlinienschwerpunkt** *m* WASSERTRANS *Schiffkonstruktion* center of flotation (AmE), centre of flotation (BrE)
Wasser: **Wasserlöscher** *m* SICHERHEIT water fire extinguisher
wasserlöslich[1] *adj* BAU, LEBENSMITTEL, MASCHINEN, TEXTIL water-soluble
wasserlöslich:[2] ~**es Flußmittel** *nt* BAU water-soluble flux
Wassermangel *m* WASSERVERSORG water deficiency; **Wassermangelsicherung** *f* HYDRAUL *Dampfkessel* plug, safety plug; **Wassermangelsicherung für Dampfkessel** *f* HYDRAUL *Sicherheit* fusible plug for steam boiler
Wasser: **Wassermantel** *m* THERMOD *zum Kühlen oder Heizen* water jacket; **Wassermesser** *m* WASSERVERSORG instant flowmeter
Wässern *nt* PAPIER, TEXTIL soaking
wässern *vt* BAU water, LEBENSMITTEL macerate
Wasser: **Wassernase** *f* BAU gorge; **Wasseroberfläche** *f* WASSERTRANS *Meer* surface; **Wasseroberflächenbreite** *f* HYDRAUL water surface width; **Wasserpaß** *m* WASSERTRANS boot topping; **WasserprobeEntnahmevorrichtung** *f* LABOR water sampler; **Wasserpumpe** *f* KFZTECH water pump; **Wasserpumpengehäuse** *nt*

KFZTECH water pump housing; **Wasserpumpenzange** *f* MASCHINEN multigrip pliers, pipe wrench; **Wasserputzstrahlen** *nt* FERTIG liquid honing; **Wasserqualität** *f* NICHTFOSS ENERG, UMWELTSCHMUTZ, WASSERVERSORG water quality; **Wasserquelle** *f* HYDRAUL hydraulic pressure source; **Wasserquerschnitt** *m* WASSERVERSORG *eines Kanals oder Flusses* cross section; **Wasserquotient** *m* KOHLEN water ratio; **Wasserrad** *nt* MASCHINEN water wheel; **Wasserreiniger** *m* TEXTIL water purifier; **Wasserreinigung** *f* CHEMTECH, WASSERVERSORG water purification; **Wasserreinigungsfilter** *nt* CHEMTECH water purification filter; **Wasserrohr** *nt* HEIZ & KÄLTE, WASSERTRANS water tube; **Wasserröhrenkühler** *m* KFZTECH flanged-tube radiator; **Wasserrohrkessel** *m* HEIZ & KÄLTE water tube boiler; **Wasserrückkühler** *m* HEIZ & KÄLTE water-cooled heat exchanger; **Wassersand-Abschneider** *m* ABFALL, ERDÖL, KOHLEN hydrocyclone; **Wassersäule** *f* BAU, HYDRAUL, NICHTFOSS ENERG head of water, UMWELTSCHMUTZ *Unterwasser-Atomexplosion* plume; **Wassersäulenhöhe** *f* HYDRAUL *Wasserdruck resultierend aus statischer Höhe* head; **Wasserscheide** *f* WASSERVERSORG watershed; **Wasserschenkel** *m* BAU throat; **Wasserschicht** *f* NICHTFOSS ENERG aquifer, WASSERTRANS aquifier; **Wasserschlag** *m* FERTIG *Kunststoffinstallationen*, WASSERTRANS water hammer; **Wasserschlämme** *f* ANSTRICH water-borne slurry; **Wasserschlauch** *m* WASSERVERSORG garden hose; **Wasserschleuse** *f* WASSERTRANS sluice; **Wasserschloß** *nt* HYDRAUL, WASSERTRANS surge tank; **Wasserspeicher** *m* HYDRAUL, KERNTECH water accumulator, WASSERVERSORG reservoir

wassersperrend: ~**e Rohrtour** *f* ERDÖL *Bohrtechnik* water string

Wasser: **Wasserspiegel** *m* ERDÖL *Bohrtechnik*, WASSERTRANS water table; **Wasserstag** *nt* WASSERTRANS *Tauwerk* bob stay

Wasserstand: **Wasserstandsanzeiger** *m* MASCHINEN water gage (AmE), water gauge (BrE), WASSERVERSORG water level gage (AmE), water level gauge (BrE), water level indicator; **Wasserstandshahn** *m* WASSERVERSORG gage cock (AmE), gauge cock (BrE), try cock; **Wasserstandsmarke** *f* KER & GLAS watermark, WASSERVERSORG water level gage (AmE), water level gauge (BrE); **Wasserstandsmesser** *m* WASSERVERSORG water level gage (AmE), water level gauge (BrE), water level indicator; **Wasserstandsregler** *m* WASSERVERSORG constant level regulator

Wasser: **Wasserstock** *m* WASSERVERSORG water hydrant
Wasserstoff[1] *m (H)* CHEMIE hydrogen *(H)*
Wasserstoff:[2] ~ **abspalten** *vi* CHEMIE dehydrogenate
Wasserstoff: **Wasserstoffabspaltung** *f* CHEMIE dehydrogenation; **Wasserstoffemissionslinie** *f* STRAHLPHYS hydrogen emission line; **Wasserstoffentschwefelung** *f* UMWELTSCHMUTZ hydrodesulfurization (AmE), hydrodesulphurization (BrE); **Wasserstoffgas** *nt* CHEMIE hydrogen gas; **Wasserstofflinie** *f* STRAHLPHYS hydrogen emission line; **Wasserstoffperoxid** *nt* CHEMIE hydrogen peroxide, FERTIG *Kunststoffinstallationen*, RAUMFAHRT peroxide; **Wasserstoffsäure** *f* CHEMIE hydracid; **Wasserstoffsulfid** *nt* CHEMIE hydrogen sulfide (AmE), hydrogen sulphide (BrE); **Wasserstoffsuperoxid** *nt* CHEMIE, RAUMFAHRT hydrogen peroxide; **Wasserstofftank** *m* RAUMFAHRT hydrogen tank; **Wasserstoffthyratron** *nt* ELEKTRONIK hydrogen thyratron

Wasser: **Wasserstollen** *m* WASSERVERSORG water adit
Wasserstrahl *m* WASSERVERSORG water jet, *Ausströmen einer Flüssigkeit* jet; **Wasserstrahlantrieb** *m* TRANS water jet propulsion, WASSERTRANS hydrojet, hydrojet propulsion; **Wasserstrahlpumpe** *f* MASCHINEN, WASSERTRANS water jet pump; **Wasserstrahl-Verwirbelungsverfahren** *nt* KUNSTSTOFF hydraulic entanglement process, hydroentanglement process

Wasser: **Wasserstraße** *f* WASSERTRANS waterway; **Wasserstratifikation** *f* NICHTFOSS ENERG stratification of waters; **Wasserströmungsgeschwindigkeit** *f* HEIZ & KÄLTE water flow rate; **Wassertank** *m* EISENBAHN, WASSERTRANS water tank; **Wassertanker** *m* BAU water tanker; **Wasserthermostat** *m* THERMOD water thermostat; **Wassertiefe** *f* NICHTFOSS ENERG water depth; **Wassertransport** *m* WASSERTRANS water transport; **Wassertrieb** *m* ERDÖL *Erdöl- und Erdgasförderung* water drive; **Wasserturbine** *f* MASCHINEN, NICHTFOSS ENERG, THERMOD hydroturbine, water turbine; **Wasserturm** *m* BAU water tower

Wasserung *f* LUFTTRANS landing on water;
wasserundurchlässig *adj* BAU impermeable, watertight, HEIZ & KÄLTE waterproof, watertight, KUNSTSTOFF, PAPIER, TEXTIL waterproof

Wasser: **Wasserundurchlässigkeit** *f* BAU watertightness
Wässerungstank *m* FOTO wash tank
wasserunlöslich *adj* TEXTIL insoluble in water

Wasser: **Wasserventil** *nt* BAU water valve; **Wasserverhältnis** *nt* KOHLEN water ratio; **Wasserverlust** *m* WASSERVERSORG leakage; **Wasserversorger** *m* UMWELTSCHMUTZ, WASSERTRANS water supplier

Wasserversorgung *f* UMWELTSCHMUTZ, WASSERVERSORG water supply; ~ **im ländlichen Raum** *f* WASSERVERSORG rural water supply; **Wasserversorgungsleitung** *f* WASSERVERSORG water supply pipe; **Wasserversorgungssystem** *nt* WASSERVERSORG water supply system

Wasser: **Wasserverteilung** *f* BAU, WASSERVERSORG water distribution

wasserverunreinigend: ~**er Stoff** *m* UMWELTSCHMUTZ water pollutant
Wasserverunreinigung *f* UMWELTSCHMUTZ water pollution

Wasser: **Wasservorwärmer** *m* HEIZ & KÄLTE water preheater; **Wasserwaage** *f* BAU air level, water level, MASCHINEN spirit level, MECHAN, METROL level; **Wasserwagen** *m* BAU water truck; **Wasser-Wasser-Wärmeaustauscher** *m* HEIZ & KÄLTE water-to-water heat exchanger; **Wasserzähler** *m* FERTIG *Kunststoffinstallationen*, TEXTIL, WASSERVERSORG water meter; **Wasserzapfstelle** *f* WASSERVERSORG water outlet, water outlet port; **Wasserzeichen** *nt* DRUCK, PAPIER watermark; **Wasserzeichenzylinder** *m* PAPIER watermark roll; **Wasser-Zement-Faktor** *m* BAU water-cement ratio; **Wasserzerstäuber** *m* WASSERVERSORG water atomizer; **Wasserzufluß** *m* MASCHINEN water inlet; **Wasserzulauf** *m* BAU, NICHTFOSS ENERG water intake, WASSERVERSORG feed, water intake; **Wasserzurückhaltung** *f* WASSERVERSORG water retention; **Wasserzwischenraum** *m* KERNTECH water gap

wäßrig: ~**er Ausfluß** *m* UMWELTSCHMUTZ aqueous effluent; **nicht ~e Elektrolysebatterie** *f* KFZTECH nonacqueous electrolyte battery; ~**e Phase** *f* KOHLEN aqueous phase; ~**e Suspension** *f* KERNTECH water suspension

Watt *nt* ELEKTRIZ watt, ELEKTROTECH, METROL watt,

WASSERTRANS *Geographie* mudflats; **~sches Fissions-spektrum** *nt* KERNTECH Watt's fission spectrum

Watte *f* TEXTIL wad; **~ in Lagen** *f* TEXTIL batting; **Wattenmeer** *nt* WASSERTRANS *Geographie* shoal

wattieren *vt* TEXTIL wad

Wattierung *f* TEXTIL padding, wadding, VERPACK air bubble cushioning, wadding

wattlos[1] *adj* ELEKTRIZ wattless

wattlos:[2] **~e Energie** *f* ELEKTRIZ apparent energy; **~e Komponente** *f* ELEKTRIZ wattless component; **~er Strom** *m* ELEKTRIZ idle current, wattless current

Watt: **Wattmesser** *m* ELEKTRIZ wattmeter; **Wattmeßgerät** *nt* PHYS wattmeter; **Wattmeter** *nt* ELEKTRIZ wattmeter; **Wattsekunde** *f* ELEKTRIZ wattsecond

Wattstunde *f* ELEKTRIZ, ELEKTROTECH, PHYS watt-hour; **Wattstundenmeßgerät** *nt* PHYS watt-hour meter; **Wattstundenzähler** *m* GERÄT active energy meter

Watt: **Wattzahl** *f* CHEMIE wattage

Waugelb *nt* CHEMIE luteolin

Wavelet *nt* WELLPHYS wavelet

WB *abbr* (*Wissensbasis*) COMP & DV, KÜNSTL INT KB (*knowledge base*)

Wb *abbr* (*Weber*) ELEKTRIZ, ELEKTROTECH, METROL Wb (*weber*)

W-Boson *nt* PHYS *Elementarteilchen* W particle, TEILPHYS W boson

WBS *abbr* (*wissensbasiertes System*) COMP & DV KBS (*knowledge-based system*)

WDM *abbr* (*Wellenlängenmultiplex*) OPTIK, TELEKOM WDM (*wavelength division multiplexing*)

Web- *pref* TEXTIL weaving; **Webbaum** *m* TEXTIL beam; **Webbing** *nt* MEERSCHMUTZ webbing; **Webblatt** *nt* TEXTIL reed

Weben *nt* TEXTIL weaving

weben *vti* TEXTIL weave

Weber *m* ELEKTRIZ (*Wb*), ELEKTROTECH (*Wb*) *Einheit des magnetischen Flußes*, METROL (*Wb*) weber (*Wb*), PHYS *Einheit des magnetischen Flusses* weber; **~sche Zahl** *f* (*W*) HYDRAUL Weber number (*W*) **Weberschiffchen** *nt* TEXTIL shuttle

Web-: **Webfach** *nt* TEXTIL shed; **Webkante** *f* BAU, PAPIER, TEXTIL selvage, selvedge; **Webkette** *f* TEXTIL warp; **Webleinenstek** *m* WASSERTRANS *Knoten* clove hitch; **Webmaschine** *f* TEXTIL loom; **Webschützen** *m* TEXTIL shuttle; **Webstuhl** *m* TEXTIL loom; **Webstuhldrehzahl** *f* TEXTIL loom speed; **Webteppich** *m* TEXTIL woven carpet; **Webwarenstückanfang** *m* TEXTIL head end

Wechsel *m* BAU, ELEKTROTECH, FERNSEH, FERTIG, WERKPRÜF alternation; **Wechselbalken** *m* BAU trimmer, trimmer beam; **Wechselbeanspruchung** *f* WERKPRÜF alternating stress, cyclic loading; **Wechselburst** *m* FERNSEH alternating burst; **Wechselfeld** *nt* ELEKTROTECH alternating field; **Wechselfestigkeit** *f* FERTIG alternate strength; **Wechselfeuer** *nt* WASSERTRANS *Signal* alternating colored lights (AmE), alternating coloured lights (BrE); **Wechselfluß** *m* ELEKTRIZ alternating flux; **Wechselgetriebe** *nt* MASCHINEN change gear, change-speed gear; **Wechselinduktion** *f* ELEKTRIZ, ELEKTROTECH mutual induction; **Wechselinduktivität** *f* ELEKTROTECH mutual inductance; **Wechsellichtfotometer** *nt* GERÄT chopped-light photometer

Wechseln *nt* FERNSEH change-over

wechselnd[1] *adj* ELEKTRIZ alternating

wechselnd:[2] **~e Ladung** *f* METALL varying loading

Wechsel: **Wechselobjektiv** *nt* FOTO interchangeable

lens; **Wechselplatte** *f* COMP & DV exchangeable disk, removable disk

wechselpolar *adj* ELEKTROTECH heteropolar

wechselpolig *adj* ELEKTROTECH heteropolar

Wechsel: **Wechselrad** *nt* MASCHINEN change gear, change gear wheel; **Wechselrädergetriebe** *nt* MASCHINEN change gear drive; **Wechselräderkasten** *m* MASCHINEN change gear box; **Wechselrelais** *nt* ELEKTRIZ, ELEKTROTECH change-over relay; **Wechselrichten** *nt* ELEKTRONIK inversion; **Wechselrichter** *m* ELEKTRIZ static converter, ELEKTRONIK (*WR*), ELEKTROTECH (*WR*), PHYS (*WR*), RADIO (*WR*) inverter; **Wechselsack** *m* FOTO changing bag; **Wechselschalter** *m* ELEKTROTECH alternate action switch, change-over switch, double-throw switch; **Wechselschalter mit Unterbrechung** *m* FERNSEH break-before-make switch; **Wechselspannung** *f* ELEKTROTECH alternating voltage, FERTIG alternate stress; **Wechselstraßenzeichen** *nt* TRANS variable route sign

Wechselstrom *m* (*AC, WS*) ELEKTROTECH alternating current (*AC*); **Wechselstromdiodenschalter** *m* ELEKTRONIK diode alternating-current switch

wechselstromgekoppelt *adj* KONTROLL AC-coupled

Wechselstrom: **Wechselstromgenerator** *m* ELEKTRIZ, ELEKTROTECH, PHYS alternator; **Wechselstrom-Gleichstrom** *m* (*AC-GS, WS-GS*) ELEKTROTECH AC-DC (*alternating current-direct current*); **Wechselstrom-Gleichstrom Umformer-Lok** *f* EISENBAHN locomotive with AC/DC motor converter set; **Wechselstromlichtmaschine** *f* KFZTECH alternator; **Wechselstrommaschine** *f* NICHTFOSS ENERG alternator; **Wechselstromversorgung** *f* ELEKTRIZ alternating-current supply

Wechsel: **Wechselumformer** *m* ELEKTRIZ inverted rotary converter; **Wechselventil** *nt* MASCHINEN shuttle valve; **Wechselverkehrszeichen** *nt* TRANS variable message sign, *Geschwindigkeitsanzeige* variable-speed message sign

wechselweise *adj* MASCHINEN alternating

Wechselwinkel: **äußere ~** *m pl* GEOM alternate exterior angles

wechselwirken *vi* STRAHLPHYS interact

Wechselwirkung *f* ANSTRICH reaction, ELEKTRONIK, KERNTECH, LABOR, MASCHINEN, METALL, STRAHLPHYS interaction; **~ mit endlicher Reichweite** *f* KERNTECH finite range interaction; **~ zwischen Strahl und Plasma** *f* KERNTECH beam-plasma interaction; **Wechselwirkungseffekt** *m* LUFTTRANS coupling; **Wechselwirkungsenergie** *f* METALL interaction energy; **Wechselwirkungsfreiheit** *f* GERÄT absence of interaction

wechselwirkungslos *adv* STRAHLPHYS without interacting

Wechselwirkung: **Wechselwirkungsraum** *m* ELEKTRONIK *Querfeldröhren* interaction space; **Wechselwirkungsspalt** *m* ELEKTRONIK *bei Elektronenstrahlröhren* interaction gap

Wechsler *m* FERTIG *Kunststoffinstallationen* variator; **Wechslerschalter** *m* ELEKTRIZ two-way switch

Wecker *m* *Telefon* ringer; **Weckeruhr** *f* LABOR alarm clock

Weckglas *nt* VERPACK glass jar

Weg *m* AKUSTIK displacement, ELEKTROTECH path, ERDÖL seismic path, MASCHINEN daylight, deflection, stroke, travel, PHYS, RADIO, TELEKOM *Ausbreitung* path, TRANS route; **~ in Gegenrichtung** *m* TELEKOM return path; **Wegamplitude** *f* AKUSTIK displacement; **Wegebesetzt-Zustand** *m* TELEKOM *Fernsprechverkehr* congestion; **Wegerecht** *nt* WASSERTRANS right of way

wegführend: **~es Gleis** *nt* EISENBAHN *von der Hauptstadt weg* down line

Weg: **Weglänge** *f* KERNTECH path length, LUFTTRANS, TRANS distance covered; **Wegleitstrahl** *m* LUFTTRANS glide path beam; **Wegmeßsystem** *nt* GERÄT *numerische Steuerung* path-measuring system; **Wegplatte** *f* BAU pad; **Wegpunkt** *m* WASSERTRANS *Navigation* waypoint

wegräumen *vt* BAU clear away

wegschmelzen *vi* CHEMIE deliquesce

Weg: **Wegschrittgröße** *f* FERTIG *Programmieren* bit size; **Wegspeicher** *m* TELEKOM path memory; **Wegstreckenzähler** *m* KFZTECH odometer; **Wegunterführung** *f* BAU undergrade crossing; **Wegunterschied** *m* PHYS path difference

Wegwerf- *pref* ABFALL expendable; **Wegwerfartikel** *m* MASCHINEN expendable item; **Wegwerfölfilter** *nt* KFZTECH throw-away oil filter; **Wegwerfprodukt** *nt* ABFALL throw-away product; **Wegwerfspritze** *f* LABOR disposable syringe; **Wegwerfverpackung** *f* ABFALL one-way pack, LEBENSMITTEL nonreturnable packaging

wehenerregend *adj* CHEMIE oxytocic

Wehnelt-Zylinder *m* PHYS Wehnelt cylinder

Wehr *nt* HYDRAUL nappe, weir, MEERSCHMUTZ dam, weir, NICHTFOSS ENERG weir, UMWELTSCHMUTZ, WASSERVERSORG dam, weir; **Wehrabschöpfer** *m* UMWELTSCHMUTZ weir skimmer; **Wehrabschöpfgerät** *nt* MEERSCHMUTZ weir skimmer; **Wehrkrone** *f* WASSERVERSORG crest of a weir; **Wehrnadel** *f* WASSERVERSORG *eines Wehres oder Schleuse* stop plank; **Wehrölsperre** *f* MEERSCHMUTZ weir boom; **Wehrverschluß** *m* WASSERVERSORG floodgate

Weich- *pref* BAU, FERTIG, FOTO, KER & GLAS, TEXTIL soft

weich[1] *adj* COMP & DV, ELEKTRONIK, FOTO, METALL, PAPIER, PHYS, STRAHLPHYS, WASSERTRANS soft

weich:[2] **-er Boden** *m* BAU bad ground; **~e Bremsung** *f* EISENBAHN smooth braking; **~es Bromsilberpapier** *nt* FOTO soft bromide paper; **~er Fehler** *m* COMP & DV soft fail; **~er Grauguß** *m* METALL soft cast iron; **~er Griff** *m* TEXTIL soft handle; **~e Röhre** *f* ELEKTRONIK soft tube; **~e Röntgenstrahlen** *m pl* PHYS, STRAHLPHYS soft X-rays; **~e Röntgenstrahlung** *f* PHYS, STRAHLPHYS soft X-rays; **~e Seite** *f* PAPIER tender side; **~e Strahlen** *m pl* STRAHLPHYS soft radiation; **~e Strahlung** *f* STRAHLPHYS soft radiation; **~er Supraleiter** *m* ELEKTRONIK soft superconductor; **~e Trennfuge** *f* COMP & DV soft hyphen; **~es Wasser** *nt* WASSERVERSORG soft water

weich:[3] **~ machen** *vt* PAPIER soften

weicharbeitend: **~er Entwickler** *m* FOTO soft contrast developer, soft effect developer

Weich-: **Weichdichtung** *f* MASCHINEN flexible gasket

Weiche *f* EISENBAHN points (BrE), switch (AmE), switch rail, turnout, ELEKTRONIK band separation; **Weichen und Kreuzungen** *f pl* EISENBAHN switchgear

Weicheisen *nt* ELEKTRIZ moving iron, ELEKTROTECH, LABOR, METALL, PHYS soft iron; **Weicheiseninstrument** *nt* GERÄT soft iron instrument; **Weicheisenkern** *m* ELEKTROTECH soft iron core; **Weicheisenstrommeßgerät** *nt* ELEKTRIZ moving-iron ammeter

weich-elastisch: **~e Verpackung** *f* VERPACK flexible package

Weiche: **Weichenhebel** *m* EISENBAHN switch lever; **Wei-**

chenheizgerät *nt* EISENBAHN point heater; **Weichenkreuz** *nt* EISENBAHN double crossover, scissors crossing; **Weichenlaterne** *f* EISENBAHN indicator lamp, switchpoint light; **Weichenseite** *f* EISENBAHN turnout side; **Weichenstange** *f* EISENBAHN throw rod; **Weichenstellstange** *f* EISENBAHN point-operating stretcher; **Weichenstellwerk** *nt* EISENBAHN signal box (BrE), signal tower (AmE); **Weichenzugstange** *f* EISENBAHN point rod

Weich-: **Weichfäule** *f* LEBENSMITTEL *bei Früchten* soft rot; **Weichfeuer** *nt* KER & GLAS soft fire

weichgemacht: **nicht ~** *adj* KUNSTSTOFF unplasticized

Weich-: **Weichglas** *nt* KER & GLAS soft glass; **Weichglühen** *nt* FERTIG spheroidize annealing, METALL soft annealing, softening, THERMOD dead anneal, soft anneal

weichglühen *vt* FERTIG spheroidize

Weich-: **Weichgummi** *nt* KUNSTSTOFF soft rubber; **Weichharz** *nt* CHEMIE oleoresin; **Weichhaut** *f* FERTIG bark; **Weichheit** *f* PAPIER softness; **Weichholz** *nt* BAU, WASSERTRANS softwood; **Weichkohle** *f* KOHLEN soft coal; **Weichlot** *nt* BAU, ELEKTRIZ soft solder, FERTIG ordinary solder, MASCHINEN soft solder; **Weichlöten** *nt* BAU, ELEKTRIZ, MASCHINEN soft soldering, soldering

weichlöten *vt* BAU solder, METALL sweating

Weich: **Weichmachen** *nt* METALL softening, work softening

weichmachend *adj* FERTIG emollient

Weichmacher *m* BAU, FERTIG plasticizer, KUNSTSTOFF plasticizer, softener, TEXTIL softener, softening agent; **äußerer ~** *m* KUNSTSTOFF external plasticizer

weichmacherfrei[1] *adj* KUNSTSTOFF unplasticized

weichmacherfrei:[2] **~es PVC** *nt* FERTIG *Kunststoffinstallationen* PVC rigid, U-PVC

Weichmacher: **Weichmacherlösung** *f* PAPIER softener water; **Weichmachermigration** *f* KUNSTSTOFF plasticizer migration; **Weichmacherwanderung** *f* KUNSTSTOFF plasticizer migration

weichmagnetisch: **~es Material** *nt* ELEKTROTECH, PHYS soft magnetic material

Weich-: **Weichmetall** *nt* METALL soft metal; **Weichpackung** *f* MASCHINEN soft packing seal; **Weichplastikradierer** *m* KONSTZEICH soft plastic eraser; **Weichporzellan** *nt* KER & GLAS soft porcelain; **Weichroheisen** *nt* METALL soft pig iron; **Weichrückstellung** *f* COMP & DV soft reset; **Weichschaum** *m* KUNSTSTOFF flexible foam

weichsektoriert[1] *adj* COMP & DV soft-sectored

weichsektoriert:[2] **~e Platte** *f* COMP & DV soft-sectored disk

Weich-: **Weichsektorierung** *f* COMP & DV soft sectoring; **Weichspülmittel** *nt* TEXTIL *Waschen* softener; **Weichstahl** *m* METALL mild steel

weichstellen *vt* KUNSTSTOFF plasticize

Weich-: **Weichstoffpackung** *f* MASCHINEN soft packing seal; **Weichüberspannung** *f*: **~ mit kreuzender Fahrleitung** *f* EISENBAHN overhead junction crossing; **Weichweizen** *m* LEBENSMITTEL soft wheat

Weichzeichner *m* FOTO diffuser scrim; **Weichzeichnerlinse** *f* FOTO soft-focus lens

Weinhold: **~sches Gefäß** *nt* CHEMTECH, LABOR *Isolierung* Dewar flask

Weinhold-Dewar: **~sches Gefäß** *nt* CHEMTECH, LABOR *Isolierung* Dewar flask

Weinstein *m* CHEMIE tartar, LEBENSMITTEL cream of

tartar

Weinstock *m* LEBENSMITTEL vine

weiß[1] *adj* DRUCK, FOTO white;

weiß:[2] **~es Arsenik** *nt* KER & GLAS *Arsentrioxid* arsenic trioxide; **~er Glimmer** *m* KUNSTSTOFF white mica; **~es Licht** *nt* PHYS white light; **~es Phosphat-Opalglas** *nt* KER & GLAS white phosphate opal; **~es Rauschen** *nt* AKUSTIK white noise, AUFNAHME random noise, white noise, COMP & DV Gaussian noise, white noise, ELEKTRONIK, PHYS, RAUMFAHRT white noise, TELEKOM random noise, white noise; **~e Strahlung** *f* RAUMFAHRT white radiation

Weiß *nt* DRUCK, FOTO white; **~scher Bezirk** *m* PHYS Weiss domain; **Weißabgleich** *m* FERNSEH white balance; **Weißanlaufen** *nt* KUNSTSTOFF blushing; **Weißaufnahme** *f* AUFNAHME white recording; **Weißblech** *nt* METALL tin plate; **Weißblechabfall** *m* ABFALL tin plate waste; **Weißblechdose** *f* ABFALL tin-plated can, VERPACK *Konserven* metal can; **Weißbleche** *nt pl* FERTIG menders

Weißen *nt* BAU whitewashing

weißglühend *adj* FERTIG, STRAHLPHYS incandescent, THERMOD white hot: **~er Festkörper** *m* STRAHLPHYS incandescent solid

Weiß: Weißglut *f* METALL, THERMOD white heat; **Weißgrad** *m* PAPIER whiteness

Weissit *nt* CHEMIE telluride

weißkaschiert: ~e Pappe *f* VERPACK white-lined board

Weiß: Weißlichtinterferenz *f* PHYS white light fringe

Weißmetall *nt* MASCHINEN babbitt metal, white metal, METALL antifriction metal, bearing metal; **Weißmetallausguß** *m* METALL antifrictionning; **Weißmetall-futterlager** *nt* FERTIG babbitt-lined bearing; **Weißmetall-Lagerausguß** *m* FERTIG babbitting

Weißpegel *m* FERNSEH white level; **Weißpegelfrequenz** *f* FERNSEH white level frequency; **Weißpegelkompression** *f* FERNSEH white compression

Weiß: Weißrauschen *nt* AUFNAHME random noise, white noise, ELEKTRONIK white noise; **Weißrauschgenerator** *m* AUFNAHME random noise generator, ELEKTRONIK white noise generator; **Weißrauschquelle** *f* ELEKTRONIK white noise source; **Weißrauschsignal** *nt* ELEKTRONIK white noise signal; **Weißspitze** *f* FERNSEH peak white, white peak; **Weißwäsche** *f* TEXTIL linen; **Weißwertbegrenzung** *f* FERNSEH white clip, white limiter

Weit- *pref* FOTO, REGELUNG, TELEKOM broad, wide

weit:[1] **~er Flaschenhals** *m* VERPACK wide-mouth neck; **~er Laufsitz** *m* (*WL*) MASCHINEN loose fit

weit:[2] **~ abhalten von** *vti* WASSERTRANS *Schifführung* give a wide berth

Weite *f* KOHLEN cavity

Weiter- *pref* TELEKOM widee

weiterleiten *vt* TELEKOM redirect

Weiter-: Weiterleitung *f* COMP & DV routing

Weiterreiß- *pref* KUNSTSTOFF tearing; **Weiterreißbarkeitsprüfer** *m* PAPIER tearing tester; **Weiterreißen** *nt* KUNSTSTOFF tear propagation; **Weiterreißprüfung** *f* KUNSTSTOFF tearing test; **Weiterreißversuch** *m* KUNSTSTOFF tearing test

Weiter-: Weiterschaltbedingung *f* REGELUNG step-enabling condition; **Weiterschaltimpuls** *m* GERÄT advance pulse

weitersenden *vt* TELEKOM retransmit

Weiter-: Weiterübertragung *f* REGELUNG *des Signals* onward transmission; **Weiterverarbeitung** *f* REGEL-

UNG *des Signals* processing

weiterverfolgen *vt* PATENT *Anmeldung* prosecute

Weiter-: Weiterverteilung *f* COMP & DV *von E-Mail* redistribution; **Weiterverwertung** *f* ABFALL reclamation

Weithals- *pref* LABOR wide mouth; **Weithalsflasche** *f* LABOR wide-mouth bottle; **Weithalskolben** *m* LABOR wide-necked flask; **Weithalspackung** *f* KER & GLAS wide-mouth container; **Weithalsröhrchen** *nt* LABOR wide-bore tube

weitreichend: ~er Lautsprecher *m* AUFNAHME extended-range loudspeaker; **~er Transport** *m* UMWELTSCHMUTZ *von Luftschadstoffen* long-range transport

Weitung *f* KOHLEN cavity

Weit-: Weitverkehrsrichtfunk *m* TELEKOM backbone radio relay; **Weitwinkelobjektiv** *nt* FOTO panoramic lens, wide-angle lens; **Weitwinkelvorsatz** *m* FOTO wide-angle converter

Weizen *m* LEBENSMITTEL wheat; **Weizenflugbrand** *m* LEBENSMITTEL *Pflanzenkrankheitslehre* loose smut of wheat; **Weizenfuttermehl** *nt* LEBENSMITTEL wheatmeal; **Weizensteinbrand** *m* LEBENSMITTEL *Getreidekrankheit* bunt

welk *adj* LEBENSMITTEL withered

Well- *pref* KER & GLAS, PAPIER, VERPACK corrugated

Wellblech *nt* BAU, MASCHINEN corrugated iron, corrugated sheet iron

Welle *f* AKUSTIK wave, BAU axle, shaft, *Rolladen* roller, COMP & DV mode, ELEKTRIZ, ELEKTRONIK, ELEKTROTECH wave, FERTIG shaft, KER & GLAS buckle, KFZTECH *Motor, Triebstrang* shaft, MASCHINEN arbor (AmE), arbour (BrE), shaft, MECHAN shaft, PAPIER axle, *der Wellpappe* flute, PHYS, TELEKOM wave, WASSERTRANS wave, *Schiffantrieb, Motor* shaft; **~ im Hörbereich** *f* ELEKTRONIK acoustic wave

Wellen *nt* FERTIG shafting, *Zahnreihe* setting, MASCHINEN shafting

Welle: Wellen in Fluiden *f pl* STRÖMPHYS fluid waves; **Wellen in Flüssigkeiten** *f pl* STRÖMPHYS fluid waves; **Wellenabschattungseffekte** *m pl* TELEKOM wave-shadowing effects; **Wellenantenne** *f* RADIO Beverage aerial; **Wellenantrieb** *m* KFZTECH *Triebstrang*, MASCHINEN shaft drive; **Wellenausbreitung** *f* NICHTFOSS ENERG, PHYS, RADIO, WELLPHYS wave propagation; **Wellenausbreitungsgeschwindigkeit** *f (c)* HYDRAUL wave celerity *(c)*; **Wellenausgleichskupplung** *f* MASCHINEN resilient shaft coupling; **Wellenband** *nt* STRAHLPHYS, WELLPHYS waveband; **Wellenbauch** *m* AKUSTIK wave loop, ELEKTROTECH, WELLPHYS antinode; **Wellenbereich** *m* RADIO waveband, TELEKOM range; **Wellenberg** *m* NICHTFOSS ENERG wave crest; **Wellenbeugung** *f* TELEKOM wave diffraction

Wellenbewegung *f* WELLPHYS wave motion; **Wellenbewegungsenergie pro Meter Woge** *f* NICHTFOSS ENERG wave momentum per meter of crest (AmE), wave momentum per metre of crest

Welle: Wellenbrecher *m* BAU, WASSERTRANS, WASSERVERSORG breakwater; **Wellenbund** *m* MASCHINEN shaft collar; **Wellendämpfungskoeffizient** *m* ELEKTRONIK image attenuation coefficient; **Wellendichtring** *m* MASCHINEN shaft seal, shaft-sealing ring; **Wellendichtung** *f* MASCHINEN shaft seal, shaft sealing; **Wellendrahtglas** *nt* KER & GLAS corrugated-wired glass; **Wellenende** *nt* MASCHINEN shaft end; **Wellenenergie** *f* WELLPHYS wave energy, wave power; **Wellenerzeuger**

m WASSERTRANS *Schiffkonstruktion* wave generator; **Wellenerzeugung** *f* TELEKOM wave generation; **Wellenfilter** *nt* ELEKTRIZ, WELLPHYS wave filter; **Wellenfolge** *f* AKUSTIK wave train; **Wellenform** *f* COMP & DV, ELEKTRIZ, ELEKTROTECH, PHYS waveform, TELEKOM waveshape, WELLPHYS waveform; **Wellenformsynthese** *f* ELEKTRONIK waveform synthesis; **Wellenfortpflanzung** *f* NICHTFOSS ENERG wave propagation; **Wellenfront** *f* AKUSTIK, COMP & DV, ELEKTROTECH, OPTIK, PHYS, TELEKOM, WELLPHYS wavefront; **Wellenfrontbereich** *m* COMP & DV wavefront array; **Wellenfunktion** *f* PHYS, TEILPHYS, WELLPHYS wave function; **Wellengenerator** *m* WELLPHYS wave generator; **Wellengeschwindigkeit** *f* WELLPHYS wave velocity; **Wellenglas** *nt* KER & GLAS corrugated glass; **Wellengleichung** *f* PHYS, STRAHLPHYS wave equation; **Wellengruppe** *f* AKUSTIK wave train, PHYS wave group; **Wellenhöhe** *f* WASSERTRANS wave height; **Welleninterferenz** *f* AKUSTIK, TELEKOM wave interference; **Wellenkamm** *m* NICHTFOSS ENERG wave crest; **Wellenkeil** *m* MASCHINEN shaft key; **Wellenkohärenz** *f* TELEKOM wave coherence; **Wellenkonstante** *f (k)* AKUSTIK wave constant *(k)*; **Wellenkopf** *m* AKUSTIK wavefront; **Wellenkopplung** *f* ELEKTROTECH shaft coupling, TELEKOM wave coupling; **Wellenkuppelung** *f* MASCHINEN shaft coupling; **Wellenlager** *nt* MASCHINEN shaft bearing; **Wellenlänge** *f* AKUSTIK, ELEKTRIZ, ELEKTRONIK, METALL, OPTIK, PHYS, RADIO, STRAHLPHYS, TELEKOM, WASSERTRANS *Seezustand*, WELLPHYS wavelength; ~ **höchster Strahlungsintensität** *f* TELEKOM peak intensity wavelength; ~ **der maximalen Helligkeit** *f* OPTIK peak intensity wavelength; **Wellenlängen der Spektrallinien** *f pl* STRAHLPHYS wavelengths of spectral lines; **Wellenlängenmultiplex** *nt (WDM)* OPTIK, TELEKOM wavelength division multiplexing *(WDM)*; **Wellenlängenumschaltung** *f* TELEKOM wavelength switching

Welle: **Wellenläppmaschine** *f* MASCHINEN shaft-lapping machine; **Wellenleiter** *m* ELEKTRONIK waveguide, ELEKTROTECH wave duct, waveguide, PHYS, RADIO, TELEKOM, WELLPHYS waveguide; **Wellenleiterdispersion** *f* OPTIK, TELEKOM waveguide dispersion; **Wellenleiterfilter** *nt* ELEKTRONIK waveguide filter; **Wellenleitermodus** *m* TELEKOM waveguide mode; **Wellenleitwert** *m* ELEKTROTECH, PHYS admittance; **Wellenmechanik** *f* ELEKTROTECH, PHYS, WELLPHYS wave mechanics; **Wellenmesser** *m* PHYS, WASSERTRANS *Funk*, WELLPHYS wavemeter; **Wellenoberfläche** *f* ELEKTROTECH wave surface; **Wellenoptik** *f* OPTIK physical optics, wave optics, TELEKOM wave optics; **Wellenpaket** *nt* PHYS wave packet; **Wellenparameterfilter** *nt* AUFNAHME composite filter; **Wellenperiode** *f* WASSERTRANS *Schiffkonstruktion* wave period; **Wellenpferdestärke** *f (WPS)* MASCHINEN shaft horse power; **Wellenpolarisation** *f* TELEKOM wave polarization; **Wellenreiten** *nt* WELLPHYS surfing; **Wellensieb** *nt* WELLPHYS wave filter; **Wellenspektrum** *nt* WELLPHYS wave spectrum; **Wellenstrang** *m* MASCHINEN line, line of shafting, line shaft, shafting; **Wellenstreuung** *f* TELEKOM wave dispersion; **Wellental** *nt* WASSERTRANS *Meer* trough; **Wellentheorie des Lichtes** *f* WELLPHYS wave theory of light; **Wellentrennlänge** *f* FERTIG *Rauheit* cutoff

Wellentyp *m* COMP & DV *Datenübertragung*, ELEKTRONIK *Mikrowellen* mode; **Wellentypfilter** *nt* ELEKTRONIK mode filter; **Wellentypumwandlung** *f* COMP & DV mode conversion

Wellenübertragung *f* TELEKOM wave transmission; **Wellenübertragungsmaß** *nt* AKUSTIK image transfer exponent, ELEKTRONIK image transfer coefficient

Welle: **Wellenvektor** *m* ELEKTROTECH, PHYS wave vector; **Wellenverbindung** *f* MASCHINEN connection between two shafts; **Wellenverstärkung** *f* TELEKOM wave amplification; **Wellenwicklung** *f* ELEKTROTECH series winding; **Wellenwiderstand** *m* AKUSTIK image impedance, ELEKTRIZ characteristic admittance, surge impedance, ELEKTROTECH characteristic impedance, image impedance, iterative impedance, LUFTTRANS wave drag, PHYS characteristic impedance, image impedance, WASSERTRANS *Schiffkonstruktion* wave resistance; **Wellenwiderstand im Vakuum** *m* PHYS characteristic vacuum impedance, impedance of free space; **Wellenzahl** *f* AKUSTIK, WELLPHYS wave number; **Wellenzapfen** *m* KFZTECH journal of a shaft; **Wellenzug** *m* AKUSTIK, PHYS, WELLPHYS wave train; **Welle-Teilchen-Dualismus** *m* WELLPHYS wave particle duality; **Welle-Teilchen-Dualität** *f* PHYS wave particle duality

Well-: **Wellfaserplatte** *f* VERPACK corrugated fiber board (AmE), corrugated fibre board (BrE); **Wellglas** *nt* KER & GLAS corrugated glass

wellig[1] *adj* FERTIG undulating, KER & GLAS wavy, TELEKOM undulating

wellig:[2] ~**e Oberfläche** *f* TELEKOM undulating surface; ~**e Schliere** *f* KER & GLAS wavy cord

Welligkeit *f* AKUSTIK, ELEKTRIZ, ELEKTRONIK ripple, KER & GLAS settle mark, MASCHINEN waviness; **Welligkeitsdämpfung** *f* ELEKTRONIK ripple attenuation; **Welligkeitsfaktor** *m* PHYS standing-wave ratio, voltage standing wave ratio, RADIO standing-wave ratio, - RADIO voltage standing wave ratio, TELEKOM standing-wave ratio, voltage standing wave ratio; **Welligkeitsmeßgerät** *nt* GERÄT ripple measuring equipment

Well-: **Wellpapier** *nt* VERPACK corrugated paper

Wellpappe *f* PAPIER, VERPACK corrugated board, corrugated cardboard; **Wellpappenkarton** *m* VERPACK corrugated board box; **Wellpappenmaschine** *f* PAPIER corrugator; **Wellpappenprodukt** *nt* VERPACK corrugated product

Wellrohr *nt* GERÄT pressure bellows, MASCHINEN corrugated pipe; **Wellrohrmanometer** *nt* GERÄT bellows gage (AmE), bellows gauge (BrE)

Wellung *f* FERTIG, KER & GLAS, PAPIER corrugation

Welt *f* RAUMFAHRT space; **Weltall** *nt* RAUMFAHRT outer space, space; **Weltentstehungslehre** *f* RAUMFAHRT cosmogony; **Weltfernmeldewesen** *nt* TELEKOM worldwide communications; **Weltmeer** *nt* WASSERTRANS ocean

Weltraum *m* RAUMFAHRT outer space, space, TELEKOM space; **Weltraumbahnhof** *m* RAUMFAHRT spaceport; **Weltraumbeschreibung** *f* RAUMFAHRT cosmography; **Weltraumdruckanzug** *m* RAUMFAHRT extra-vehicular pressure garment; **Weltraumeignung** *f* RAUMFAHRT space qualification; **Weltraumfahrer** *m* RAUMFAHRT cosmonaut; **Weltraumfahrtbehörde** *f* RAUMFAHRT space agency; **Weltraumforschung** *f* RAUMFAHRT space research; **Weltraumhafen** *m* RAUMFAHRT spaceport; **Weltraumkapsel** *f* RAUMFAHRT space capsule; **Weltraumkrankheit** *f* RAUMFAHRT space sickness; **Weltraumnachrichtentechnik** *f* TELEKOM space communications; **Weltraumobjekt** *nt* RAUMFAHRT object in space; **Weltraumprogramm** *nt* RAUMFAHRT space program; **Weltraumrendezvous** nt RAUMFAHRT space rendezvous; **Weltraumschlepper** m RAUMFAHRT space tug; **Weltraumschuß** m RAUMFAHRT space shot; **Weltraumsonde** f RAUMFAHRT deep-space probe, space probe; **Weltraumstart** m RAUMFAHRT space launch; **Weltraumtechnik** f RAUMFAHRT space engineering, space technology; **Weltraumtelekommunikation** f TELEKOM space communications; **Weltraumtransponder** m RAUMFAHRT deep-space transponder; **Weltraumumgebung** f RAUMFAHRT space environment; **Weltraumzeitalter** nt RAUMFAHRT space age; **Weltraumzentrum** nt RAUMFAHRT space center (AmE), space centre (BrE)

Welt: **Weltschwefelhaushalt** m UMWELTSCHMUTZ global sulfur budget (AmE), global sulphur budget (BrE)

weltumspannend: ~es **Funknetz** nt RAUMFAHRT worldwide network

weltweit: ~e **Abdeckung** f WASSERTRANS *Satellitensysteme* global coverage; ~e **Emissionen** f pl UMWELTSCHMUTZ global emissions; ~e **Überdeckung** f TELEKOM global coverage

Wende[1] f WASSERTRANS *Segeln* tack

Wende:[2] **eine ~ segeln** vi WASSERTRANS *Segeln* make a tack

Wende: **Wendebecken** nt WASSERTRANS *Hafen* turning basin; **Wendeformblasverfahren** nt KER & GLAS turn mold blowing (AmE), turn mould blowing (BrE); **Wendegenauigkeit** f FERTIG indexability; **Wendegetriebe** nt FERTIG *Vorschub* feed-drive reverse, MASCHINEN reverse gear, reversing gear; **Wendeherz** nt MASCHINEN tumbler gear; **Wendekette** f FERTIG *Schmieden* sling chain; **Wendeklappe** f HYDRAUL flap valve

Wendel f ELEKTROTECH filament, MASCHINEN spiral, MECHAN coil; **Wendelabtastung** f ELEKTRONIK helical scanning; **Wendelantenne** f RADIO helix, TELEKOM corkscrew antenna, helical antenna, spiral antenna; **Wendelfeder** f MASCHINEN spiral coiled spring

wendelförmig: ~er **Wellenleiter** m ELEKTROTECH helix waveguide

wendelgekoppelt: ~e **Wanderwellenröhre** f ELEKTRONIK helix-traveling wave tube (AmE), helix-travelling wave tube (BrE)

Wendel: **Wendelhohlleiter** m ELEKTROTECH helix waveguide, TELEKOM spiral waveguide

Wendeln nt ELEKTROTECH helixing

Wendel: **Wendelresonatorfilter** nt RADIO helical filter

Wendelspan bilden vi FERTIG helix

Wendel: **Wendelspur** f OPTIK spiral track; **Wendelstufe** f BAU winder; **Wendeltreppe** f BAU corkscrew stairs, spindle stairs, spiral stairs

Wende: **Wendemotor** m ELEKTROTECH reversible motor

Wenden[1] nt FERTIG rolling, rolling over, KER & GLAS turnover, LUFTTRANS *eines Luftfahrzeugs* turnaround (AmE), turnround (BrE), TRANS *Fahrzeug* turning; ~ **der Vorform** nt KER & GLAS blank mold turnover (AmE), blank mould turnover (BrE)

Wenden:[2] **im ~ begriffen sein** vi WASSERTRANS *Segeln* be in stays

wenden[1] vt MASCHINEN reverse, WASSERTRANS cant, *Schiff* turn

wenden[2] vi MASCHINEN reverse, WASSERTRANS *Schifführung* come-to, *Schiff* turn, *Segeln* go-about, tack

wenden:[3] **sich ~ an** v refl MECHAN apply for

Wende: **Wendepol** m ELEKTRIZ commutating pole; **Wendepresse** f PAPIER reversed press; **Wendepressen-**

filz m PAPIER reversed press felt; **Wendepunkt** m BAU turning point, GEOM point of inflection, MATH *einer Funktion* reversal point; **Wendeschalter** m ELEKTROTECH reversing switch; **Wendeschiene** f EISENBAHN reversing rail; **Wendeschneidplatte** f MASCHINEN indexable insert; **Wendeschütz** nt ELEKTRIZ reversing contactor; **Wendezug** m EISENBAHN push-pull train

Wendung f FERTIG *Schneidplatte* index, TRANS *Straßen* turning

Wenigsprecher m TELEKOM low-calling-rate subscriber

Wenn-Dann-Regel f KÜNSTL INT condition-action rule, if-then rule

Werbeblock m FERNSEH advertising slot

Werbefotografie f FOTO advertising photography

werben vt DRUCK advertise

Werbeplakat: ~ **zur Unfallverhütung** nt SICHERHEIT accident prevention advertising sign

Werbung f FERNSEH commercial

Werfen nt FOTO *Emulsion* buckling

Werft f WASSERTRANS dockyard

Werg nt FERTIG oakum, TEXTIL tow, WASSERTRANS *Tauwerk* oakum

Werk:[1] **im ~ justiert** adj MECHAN factory-adjusted

Werk[2] nt FERTIG work, MASCHINEN mill; **Werkstoff** m ABFALL, MASCHINEN, QUAL, TEXTIL, WERKPRÜF materials

Werkbank f BAU, FERTIG, MASCHINEN bench, workbench; **Werkbank-Waagrechtstoßmaschine** f MASCHINEN bench-type shaping machine; **Werkbankzwinge** f MASCHINEN holdfast

Werk: **Werkblei** nt FERTIG raw lead; **Werkkanal** m NICHTFOSS ENERG, WASSERVERSORG headrace canal; **Werkprüfung** f QUAL manufacturer's inspection, shop test; **Werksatz** m DRUCK book composition; **Werksbescheinigung** f QUAL certificate of compliance with order; **Werkschrift** f DRUCK body type, composition sizes; **Werkschutzbeauftragter** m SICHERHEIT security officer; **Werkshilfstransformator** m KERNTECH unit auxiliary transformer; **Werkskontrolle** f QUAL manufacturer's quality control; **Werksprüfprotokoll** nt QUAL work test report; **Werksprüfung** f WERKPRÜF factory test; **Werksprüfzeugnis** nt QUAL work certificate; **Werkssachverständiger** m QUAL factory-authorized inspector

Werkstatt[1] f FERTIG, KER & GLAS *Arbeitsplatz*, MASCHINEN shop, MECHAN factory, workshop, shop

Werkstatt:[2] **eine ~ belüften** vi SICHERHEIT ventilate a workshop

Werkstatt: **Werkstattabnahme** f MECHAN factory acceptance; **Werkstattabnahmelehre** f MASCHINEN factory acceptance gage (AmE), factory acceptance gauge (BrE); **Werkstattgleis** nt EISENBAHN repair track, rip track; **Werkstatthandbuch** nt KFZTECH overhaul manual; **Werkstattluft** f SICHERHEIT workplace air; **Werkstattmikroskop** nt METROL toolmaker's microscope; **Werkstattniet** m MASCHINEN shop rivet; **Werkstattprüfgerät** nt PHYS work standard; **Werkstattprüfung** f QUAL shop test; **Werkstattzeichnung** f KONSTZEICH workshop drawing

Werkstein m BAU cut stone

Werkstoff: **Werkstoffehler** m WERKPRÜF materials flaw; **Werkstoffeigenschaft** f WERKPRÜF materials characteristic; **Werkstoffkenngröße** f WERKPRÜF materials characteristic; **Werkstoffnachweis** m QUAL materials verification; **Werkstoffnutzungszyklus** m ABFALL utilization cycle of materials; **Werkstoffprüfprotokoll** nt

QUAL materials test certificate; **Werkstoffprüfsystem** *nt* TEXTIL materials-testing system; **Werkstoffprüfung** *f* QUAL materials inspection, materials testing, WERK-PRÜF materials testing; **Werkstoffspezifikation** *f* QUAL materials specification; **Werkstoffsteifigkeit** *f* WERK-PRÜF materials stiffness

werkstofftechnisch: ~es Qualitätsmerkmal *nt* QUAL materials quality feature

Werkstoff: **Werkstoffvorschub** *m* FERTIG bar feed; **Werkstoffzugabe** *f* MASCHINEN materials allowance; **Werkstoffzylinder** *m* FERTIG wad

Werkstück *nt* FERTIG, MASCHINEN, MECHAN workpiece; **Werkstückabmessungen** *f pl* MASCHINEN workpiece dimensions; **Werkstückaufnahme** *f* MASCHINEN workholding; **Werkstückbewegung** *f* FERTIG workpiece motion; **Werkstückdurchmesser** *m* FERTIG workpiece diameter; **Werkstücknocken** *m* FERTIG workpiece cam contour; **Werkstückspannvorrichtung** *f* MASCHINEN workholding device; **Werkstückstange** *f* FERTIG bar stock; **Werkstückträger** *m* FERTIG *Fertigungsstraße* pallet, *Transferstraße* platen

Werk: **Werksuhr** *f* SICHERHEIT work recording clock; **Werktisch** *m* MASCHINEN work table; **Werkzeichnung** *f* MASCHINEN working drawing

Werkzeug *nt* BAU utensil, COMP & DV tool, FERTIG chase, tool, die, KER & GLAS *mit flacher Klinge* tool, KUNST-STOFF mold (AmE), mould (BrE), MASCHINEN, MECHAN implement, tool, TEXTIL appliance; ~ aus gekohltem Stahl *nt* MASCHINEN carbon steel tool; ~ zum Drehen von der Stange *nt* MASCHINEN bar-turning tool; ~ mit Hartmetallschneide *nt* MECHAN carbide-tipped tool; ~ mit Zylinderschaft *nt* MASCHI-NEN parallel-shank tool; **Werkzeugatmung** *f* KUNSTSTOFF mold breathing (AmE), mould breathing (BrE); **Werkzeugauflage** *f* MASCHINEN tool rest; **Werkzeugausgabe** *f* FERTIG tool crib; **Werkzeugbasisfreiwinkel** *m* FERTIG tool base clearance; **Werkzeugbestimmungsgröße** *f* FERTIG tool element; **Werkzeugbohrung** *f* FERTIG tool bore; **Werkzeugeckenwinkel** *m* FERTIG tool-included angle; **Werkzeugeinsatz** *m* KUNSTSTOFF mold insert (AmE), mould insert (BrE), MASCHINEN tool bit; **Werkzeug-Einstellergänzungswinkel** *m* FERTIG tool approach angle; **Werkzeugeinstellung** *f* FERTIG tooling; **Werkzeugeinstellwinkel** *m* FERTIG tool cutting-edge angle; **Werkzeugfreiwinkel** *m* FERTIG tool clearance; **Werkzeugführung** *f* FERTIG die set; **Werkzeugfutter** *nt* FERTIG tool chuck; **Werkzeuggeometrie** *f* FERTIG tool geometry; **Werkzeuggriff** *m* BAU shank; **Werkzeughalter** *m* MASCHINEN cutter bar, tool carrier, tool holder, tool post; **Werkzeugkasten** *m* MASCHINEN tool box; **Werkzeugmacher** *m* MASCHINEN toolmaker; **Werkzeugmacherdrehmaschine** *f* MASCHINEN toolmaker's lathe

Werkzeugmaschine *f* FERTIG machine tool, KONTROLL machine tool, MASCHINEN, MECHAN machine tool; **Werkzeugmaschinenhydraulik** *f* FERTIG machine tool circuit; **Werkzeugmaschinensteuerung** *f* KONTROLL machine tool control

Werkzeug: **Werkzeugneigungswinkel** *m* FERTIG tool cutting-edge angle, tool cutting-edge inclination;

Werk: **Werkzeugnis** *nt* QUAL work test report;

Werkzeug: **Werkzeugrückebene** *f* FERTIG tool back plane; **Werkzeugrückfreiwinkel** *m* FERTIG tool back clearance; **Werkzeugrückkeilwinkel** *m* FERTIG tool back wedge angle; **Werkzeugrückspanwinkel** *m* FER-TIG tool back rake; **Werkzeugsatz** *m* MASCHINEN kit,

tool set; **Werkzeugschaft** *m* MASCHINEN tool shank; **Werkzeugschleifen** *nt* MASCHINEN tool grinding, tool sharpening; **Werkzeugschleifmaschine** *f* MASCHINEN tool grinder, tool sharpener; **Werkzeugschlitten** *m* MASCHINEN carriage, tool carriage, tool holding slide, tool slide, MECHAN carriage; **Werkzeugschneide** *f* FERTIG tool tip, MASCHINEN tool edge; **Werkzeugschneidenebene** *f* FERTIG tool cutting-edge plane; **Werkzeugspannvorrichtung** *f* MASCHINEN tool holding fixture; **Werkzeugstahl** *m* METALL tool steel; **Werkzeugstandzeit** *f* MASCHINEN tool life; **Werkzeugteil** *nt* FERTIG tool element; **Werkzeugträger** *m* MASCHINEN tool box; **Werkzeugwechsel** *m* MASCHI-NEN retooling; **Werkzeugwechseleinrichtung** *f* MASCHINEN tool changing system; **Werkzeugwinkel** *m* FERTIG, MASCHINEN tool angle

Wert *m* COMP & DV, ERGON, LABOR, TELEKOM value; **Wertanalyse** *f* ERGON value analysis engineering; **Wertaufruf** *m* COMP & DV call by value; **Wertebereich** *m* COMP & DV, GERÄT range, MATH *bei Variablen* domain; **Wertereihe** *f* GERÄT range; **Werteverlauf** *m* REGELUNG value band, value pattern; **Wertigkeit** *f* PHYS valence, valency

wertlos: ~e Daten *nt pl* COMP & DV garbage

Wertstoff *m* ABFALL *verwertbarer Bestandteil des Abfalls* valuable substance; **Wertstoffelement** *nt* KERNTECH valuable element; **Wertstoffrückgewinnung** *f* ABFALL resource recovery

Wert: **Wertziffer** *f* MECHAN quality index

wesentlich: ~e Abweichung *f* QUAL significant nonconformance, significance; ~es Merkmal *nt* PATENT essential feature

West- *pref* WASSERTRANS west

Westcott-Modell *nt* KERNTECH Westcott model

Westen:[1] **nach** ~ *adv* WASSERTRANS west

Westen[2] *m* WASSERTRANS west

Westeuropäisch: ~e Zeit *f* (*WEZ*) MECHAN Greenwich Mean Time (*GMT*)

westlich *adj* WASSERTRANS west, westerly, westward

Weston-Element *nt* ELEKTRIZ, ELEKTROTECH Weston standard cell

westwärts *adv* WASSERTRANS west, westerly, westward

Westwind *m* WASSERTRANS westerly wind; **Westwindgürtel** *m* WASSERTRANS roaring forties

Wetter:[1] **vom** ~ **mitgenommen** *adj* WASSERTRANS *beschädigt* weather-beaten

Wetter[2] *nt* WASSERTRANS *Meteorologie* weather; **Wetterbeobachtungsschiff** *nt* WASSERTRANS weather ship

Wetterbericht *m* WASSERTRANS weather report; **Wetterbericht für Landung** *m* LUFTTRANS weather report for landing; **Wetterbericht für Start** *m* LUFTTRANS weather report for takeoff

Wetter: **Wetterdrosseltür** *f* KOHLEN air regulator; **Wetterdüse** *f* KOHLEN air nozzle; **Wettereinzugstrecke** *f* KOHLEN air intake; **Wetterfahne** *f* BAU vane

wetterfest[1] *adj* PAPIER weatherproof

wetterfest:[2] ~e Gummidichtung *f* KFZTECH rubber weatherproof seal

Wetter: **Wetterfestigkeit** *f* MASCHINEN weathering resistance, weatherproofness

wetterhart *adj* WASSERTRANS weather-beaten

Wetter: **Wetterlage** *f* WASSERTRANS atmospheric conditions; **Wettermuster** *nt* RAUMFAHRT weather pattern; **Wettersatellit** *m* RAUMFAHRT meteorological satellite

Wetterschutz *m* WASSERTRANS shelter; **Wetterschutzabdeckung** *f* BAU weathering; **Wetterschutzdach** *nt* BAU hood

Wetter: **Wetterseite** *f* WASSERTRANS weather side; **Wetterstationsschrank** *m* WASSERTRANS weather station cabinet; **Wetterwechsel** *m* KOHLEN circulation of the air

wetzen *vt* MASCHINEN sharpen

Wetzstein *m* FERTIG oilstone, whetstone

WEZ *abbr* (*Westeuropäische Zeit*) MECHAN GMT (*Greenwich Mean Time*)

Wheatstone: **~sche Brücke** *f* ELEKTRIZ, ELEKTROTECH, PHYS Wheatstone bridge

Whipstock *m* ERDÖL whipstock

Whisker *m* KUNSTSTOFF whisker

White: **~ Room** *m* RAUMFAHRT *Einstiegskammer am Startturm* white room

Whitworth-Gewinde *nt* MASCHINEN BSW thread, British Standard Whitworth thread, Whitworth screw thread

Wichtekurve *f* KOHLEN specific gravity curve

Wichtestufe *f* KOHLEN specific gravity fraction

wichtig: **~stes Zeichen** *nt* COMP & DV most significant character, most significant digit; **~ste Ziffer** *f* COMP & DV most significant digit

Wickel- *pref* DRUCK, PAPIER, VERPACK wraparound; **Wickelfeder** *f* MASCHINEN coil spring, coiled spring; **Wickelkern** *m* COMP & DV hub, ELEKTRIZ wound core; **Wickelkondensator** *m* ELEKTROTECH paper capacitor; **Wickelkörper** *m* TEXTIL package

Wickeln *nt* MASCHINEN winding, wrapping

wickeln *vt* BAU wind, FERTIG *Feder* coil, MASCHINEN wind, wrap, PHYS wind

Wickel-: **Wickelpappenmaschine** *f* PAPIER intermittent board machine, wet-board machine; **Wickelplatte** *f* DRUCK wraparound plate; **Wickelrohr** *nt* VERPACK laminated tube; **Wickelwalze** *f* PAPIER winding drum; **Wickelwatte** *f* TEXTIL lap; **Wickelwerk** *nt* TEXTIL wind-up

Wicklung *f* ELEKTRIZ turn, winding, ELEKTROTECH winding, FERTIG *Kunststoffinstallationen* coil, KFZTECH *Generator* winding, MECHAN coil, PAPIER, PHYS winding; **~ mit Anzapfung** *f* ELEKTROTECH tapped winding; **~ für drei Nuten** *f* ELEKTRIZ three-slot winding; **~ mit Schrittverlängerung** *f* ELEKTROTECH long-pitch winding; **Wicklungsdrahtabstand** *m* ELEKTRIZ winding pitch; **Wicklungseinführung** *f* ELEKTRIZ feed-in of winding; **Wicklungsisolierung** *f* ELEKTRIZ winding insulation; **Wicklungskapazität** *f* ELEKTRIZ, ELEKTROTECH winding capacitance; **Wicklungsschritt** *m* ELEKTRIZ winding pitch; **Wicklungsverhältnis** *nt* KFZTECH turns ratio

Widerdruck *m* DRUCK backup, perfecting

Widerhaken *m* MASCHINEN barb; **Widerhakenbolzen** *m* BAU barbed bolt

Widerhall *m* AKUSTIK echo, AUFNAHME echo, reverberation, COMP & DV, ELEKTRONIK, PHYS, RADIO, WELLPHYS echo

Widerlager *nt* BAU thrust, *Architektur* abutment, FERTIG abutment, KER & GLAS skewback, MECHAN dolly; **Widerlagerdruck** *m* FERTIG abutment pressure; **Widerlagerstein** *m* KER & GLAS skewback block

Widerspruchsfreiheit *f* QUAL consistency

Widerstand:[1] **mit ~ versehen** *adj* ELEKTROTECH resistive

Widerstand[2] *m* ANSTRICH resistance, ELEKTRIZ (*R*), ELEKTROTECH resistance, resistor, KFZTECH resistor, KUNSTSTOFF, MASCHINEN resistance, MECHAN drag, PHYS resistance, RADIO *Bauteil* resistor, *Wert* resistan-

ce, STRÖMPHYS *Kraft in Strömungsrichtung* drag, *bei niedrigen Reynoldszahlen* drag on a sphere, TELEKOM, TEXTIL resistance, THERMOD *gegen Hitze oder Kälte* temperature resistance, TRANS *gegen Forwärtsbewegung* resistance; **~ mit Anzapfung** *m* ELEKTROTECH tapped resistor; **~ bei positiver Phasenfolge** *m* ELEKTRIZ positive phase sequence reactance; **~ gegen Metallverbindung** *m* ANSTRICH refractory metal; **~ von Körpern** *m* FERTIG *Strömungslehre* drag; **~ pro Einheitslänge** *m* PHYS resistance per unit length; **Widerstandsabfall** *m* ELEKTRIZ resistance drop; **Widerstandsabgleich** *m* ELEKTROTECH resistor trimming; **Widerstandsachse** *f* LUFTTRANS drag axis; **Widerstandsanlasser** *m* ELEKTROTECH rheostat starter; **Widerstandsanpassungs-Schaltkreis** *m* PHYS impedance matching network; **Widerstandsaufzeichnung** *f* NICHTFOSS ENERG resistivity log; **Widerstandsbeiwert** *m* LUFTTRANS coefficient of drag, drag coefficient, NICHTFOSS ENERG (*DD*) coefficient of drag, drag coefficient (*DD*), STRÖMPHYS, WASSERTRANS *Schiffkonstruktion* coefficient of drag, drag coefficient; **Widerstandsbremse** *f* EISENBAHN dynamic brake, TRANS rheostatic brake; **Widerstandsbremsung** *f* EISENBAHN rheostatic braking; **Widerstandsbrücke** *f* GERÄT resistance bridge; **Widerstandsbrücke aus Ohmschen Widerständen** *f* GERÄT resistive bridge; **Widerstandsdehnungsmeßstreifen** *m* GERÄT resistor gauge (BrE), resistor gage (AmE); **Widerstandsdraht** *m* ELEKTRIZ, ELEKTROTECH, METALL resistance wire; **Widerstandsdrehmoment** *nt* KFZTECH resisting torque; **Widerstandsdünnschicht** *f* ELEKTRONIK resistive thin film; **Widerstandselement** *nt* ELEKTROTECH resistive element

widerstandsfähig *adj* KUNSTSTOFF resistant

Widerstand: **Widerstandsfähigkeit** *f* ANSTRICH durability, resistance, COMP & DV robustness, KUNSTSTOFF resistance; **Widerstandsfähigkeit gegen Temperaturschock** *f* ANSTRICH thermal shock resistance; **Widerstandsferngeber** *m* GERÄT retransmitting slide wire; **Widerstandsgeber** *m* GERÄT retransmitting slide wire; **Widerstandsheizung** *f* ELEKTRIZ, THERMOD resistance heating; **Widerstandsjustierung** *f* ELEKTROTECH resistor trimming; **Widerstandskapazität** *f* ELEKTRONIK resistance capacity; **Widerstandskapazitätskopplung** *f* ELEKTROTECH resistance capacity coupling; **Widerstandskasten** *m* ELEKTROTECH resistance box; **Widerstandskennlinie** *f* ELEKTROTECH load line; **Widerstandskern** *m* ELEKTROTECH resistor core; **Widerstandskette** *f* ELEKTROTECH resistor string; **Widerstands-Kondensator-Transistor-Logik** *f* (*RCTL-Logik*) ELEKTRONIK resistor-capacitor-transistor logic (*RCTL logic*); **Widerstandskopplung** *f* ELEKTROTECH resistive coupling; **Widerstandskörper** *m* ELEKTROTECH resistor; **Widerstandskraft** *f* FERTIG stamina, METALL, NICHTFOSS ENERG *Aerodynamik* drag; **Widerstandslast** *f* ELEKTRIZ, ELEKTROTECH resistive load; **Widerstandsleiter** *f* ELEKTROTECH resistance ladder; **Widerstandslog** *nt* ERDÖL *Bohrlochvermessung* resistivity log; **Widerstandslötung** *f* FERTIG electrode soldering; **Widerstandsmanometer** *nt* GERÄT resistance gauge (BrE), resistance gage (AmE); **Widerstandsmaterial** *nt* ELEKTROTECH resistance material; **Widerstandsmeßbrücke** *f* GERÄT resistance bridge; **Widerstandsmesser** *m* ELEKTRIZ resistance meter, RADIO ohmmeter; **Widerstandsmeßgerät** *nt* ELEKTROTECH, PHYS ohmmeter; **Widerstandsmoment**

nt FERTIG section modulus; **Widerstandsnaht-schweißen** *nt* BAU resistance seam welding; **Widerstandsnetz** *nt* ELEKTROTECH resistor network; **Widerstandsofen** *m* ELEKTROTECH resistance furnace; **Widerstandspunktschweißen** *nt* ELEKTRIZ resistance spot welding; **Widerstandsregler** *m* ELEKTROTECH rheostat; **Widerstandsschaltung** *f* ELEKTROTECH, TELEKOM resistive circuit; **Widerstandsschleifkontakt** *m* KFZTECH rheostat-sliding contact; **Widerstandsschweißen** *nt* BAU, ELEKTRIZ, THERMOD resistance welding; **Widerstandsschweißung** *f* MASCHINEN, THERMOD resistance welding; **Widerstandsspannungsteiler** *m* ELEKTRIZ resistive voltage divider, ELEKTROTECH resistor voltage divider; **Widerstandsspule** *f* ELEKTROTECH resistance coil; **Widerstandsstumpfschweißen** *nt* BAU resistance butt welding, THERMOD upset welding; **Widerstandstemperaturmeßfühler** *m* GERÄT resistance temperature detector; **Widerstandsthermometer** *nt* HEIZ & KÄLTE resistance thermometer; **Widerstandsträger** *m* ELEKTROTECH resistor core; **Widerstandsverminderung** *f* STRÖMPHYS drag reduction; **Widerstandszelle** *f* ELEKTRONIK photoconductive cell; **Widerstandszündkerze** *f* KFZTECH resistor-type spark plug
widerstehen *vt* ANSTRICH resist
Widmannstätten: ~ **Platte** *f* METALL Widmannstätten plate; ~ **Struktur** *f* METALL Widmannstätten structure
Wiedemann-Franz: ~**sches Gesetz** *nt* PHYS Wiedemann-Franz law
Wieder- *pref* COMP & DV, ELEKTROTECH, KERNTECH, KONTROLL, MASCHINEN, METALL re-
wiederabgleichen *vt* GERÄT rebalance
wiederandocken *vi* RAUMFAHRT redock
Wiederanlassen *nt* METALL retempering
wiederanlassen *vt* ANSTRICH retemper, KFZTECH, LUFTTRANS *Motor und Triebwerk*, WASSERTRANS restart
Wiederanlauf *m* COMP & DV, KONTROLL restart; **Wiederanlaufbefehl** *m* COMP & DV restart instruction; **Wiederanlaufen lassen** *nt* MASCHINEN *die Maschinen* restart
wiederanlaufen *vi* COMP & DV restart
Wiederanlauf: **Wiederanlaufroutine** *f* COMP & DV fallback routine
Wiederanlegen: ~ **von Wirbeln** *nt* STRÖMPHYS reattachment of eddies
wiederanschließen *vt* ELEKTROTECH reconnect
Wiederanschluß *m* ELEKTROTECH, TELEKOM reconnection
Wiederaufarbeitung *f* MASCHINEN regeneration
Wiederaufbauen *nt* BAU rebuilding, reconstruction
wiederaufbauen *vt* BAU rebuild, reconstruct
wiederaufbereiten *vt* FERTIG *Formsand* recondition
wiederaufbereitet: ~**er Altsand** *m* FERTIG reconditioned sand
Wiederaufbereitung *f* KERNTECH reprocessing, MASCHINEN reconditioning, MEERSCHMUTZ recovery
Wiederauffindbarkeit *f* QUAL retrieval
Wiederauffinden *nt* COMP & DV retrieval; ~ **von Informationen** *nt (IR)* COMP & DV information retrieval *(IR)*; ~ **von Nachrichten** *nt* COMP & DV message retrieval; ~ **von Systemmeldungen** *nt* COMP & DV message retrieval
wiederauffinden *vt* COMP & DV, KONTROLL retrieve
Wiederauffindung: ~ **von Gepäck** *f* LUFTTRANS baggage retrieval; **Wiederauffindungssystem** *nt* COMP & DV reference retrieval system
Wiederaufheizzeit *f* THERMOD comeback

Wiederaufkohlung *f* CHEMIE *Metallurgie*, METALL recarburization
wiederaufladbar[1] *adj* ELEKTROTECH, FOTO, RADIO rechargeable
wiederaufladbar:[2] ~**e Batterie** *f* ELEKTROTECH rechargeable battery
wiederaufladen *vt* ELEKTROTECH recharge
Wiederaufladezeit *f* FOTO *Blitz* recycle time, recycling time
Wiederaufladung *f* ELEKTROTECH recharging
wiederauflebend *adj* WASSERVERSORG resurgent
Wiederaufnahme *f* AUFNAHME rerecording, COMP & DV recovery; ~ **nach Programmstopp** *f* COMP & DV checkpoint recovery
Wiederauftauchen *nt* WASSERTRANS *U-Boot* return to surface
Wiederaufwärmen: ~ **von Glas zur Weiterverarbeitung** *nt* KER & GLAS warming-in
wiederausbrechen *vi* SICHERHEIT *Feuer* break out again
Wieder-: **Wiederausgießen** *nt* FERTIG relining
Wiederausrichten *nt* BAU *Mauer* throwing back into alignment
wiederausstrahlen *vt* FERNSEH rebroadcast
Wiederbeatmer *m* SICHERHEIT resuscitator
Wiederbeatmungsgerät *nt* SICHERHEIT resuscitation equipment
Wiederbelegungsentfernung *f* TELEKOM reuse distance
Wiederbelüftung *f* WASSERVERSORG reaeration
wiederbenutzbar *adj* COMP & DV reusable
wiedereinkuppeln *vt* MASCHINEN reengage
wiedereinrichten *vt* MASCHINEN reset
wiedereinschalten *vt* COMP & DV restart
wiedereinschiffen *vt* WASSERTRANS *Passagiere* re-embark
Wiedereinschiffung *f* WASSERTRANS *Passagiere* re-embarkation
Wiedereinstiegspunkt *m* COMP & DV restart point
Wiedereintritt: ~ **in die Atmosphäre** *m* RAUMFAHRT atmospheric re-entry; **Wiedereintrittshöhe** *f* RAUMFAHRT earth reentry altitude
wiedererhitzen *vt* KER & GLAS reheat
Wiedererhitzer *m* WASSERTRANS reheat
Wiedergabe *f* AKUSTIK reproducing, AUFNAHME playback, replay, reproduction, COMP & DV image, FERNSEH playback, reproducing, FOTO reproducing; ~ **der Tonwerte** *f* FOTO reproduction of tonal values; **Wiedergabecharakteristik** *f* AKUSTIK reproducing characteristic, AUFNAHME playback characteristics, replay characteristic; **Wiedergabeeigenschaft** *f* FERNSEH reproduction characteristic; **Wiedergabegerät** *nt* AUFNAHME sound reader; **Wiedergabegeschwindigkeit** *f* AUFNAHME playback speed; **Wiedergabegüte** *f* AKUSTIK, ERGON fidelity; **Wiedergabekette** *f* FERNSEH reproducing chain; **Wiedergabekopf** *m* FERNSEH reproducing head; **Wiedergabemagnetkopf** *m* AKUSTIK reproducing magnetic head; **Wiedergabepegel** *m* AUFNAHME playback level; **Wiedergabesteuerung** *f* AUFNAHME playback control; **Wiedergabesystem** *nt* AUFNAHME playback system; **Wiedergabetreue** *f* ERGON fidelity; **Wiedergabeverlust** *m* AKUSTIK reproducing loss, AUFNAHME playback loss, FERNSEH reproduction loss; **Wiedergabeverstärker** *m* AUFNAHME playback amplifier
wiedergeben *vt* AUFNAHME reproduce
Wiedergefrieren *nt* PHYS regelation
wiedergewinnen *vt* ABFALL *Rohstoffe*, KOHLEN, TELE-

KOM recover, TEXTIL retrieve

Wiedergewinnung *f* ABFALL recycling, *von Rohstoffen* recovery, KOHLEN re-extraction, recovery, KUNST-STOFF, THERMOD recovery, WASSERVERSORG backflow; **~ von Wärme** *f* THERMOD heat rate, heat rate curve, heat recovery; **Wiedergewinnungsanlage** *f* AB-FALL reclamation plant, resource recovery plant; **Wiedergewinnungssystem** *nt* KERNTECH recovery system

wiedergewonnen: ~e Ladung *f* ELEKTROTECH recovered charge; **~es Öl** *nt* ABFALL recovered oil; **~er Rohstoff** *m* ABFALL secondary material

Wiederherstellen der ursprünglichen Form *nt* TELEKOM regeneration

wiederherstellen *vt* ANSTRICH, COMP & DV restore

Wiederherstellung *f* ANSTRICH restoration, COMP & DV recovery, restore, RAUMFAHRT *Raumschiff* reconditioning, TELEKOM restore; **Wiederherstellung des Signals** *f* TELEKOM signal restoration; **Wiederherstellungsmodus** *m* RAUMFAHRT restoration mode

wiederholbar: ~er Ablauf *m* KONTROLL routine; **nicht ~e Messung** *f* METROL nonrepeatable measurement

Wiederholbarkeit *f* GERÄT repeatability

Wiederholbedingungen *f pl* QUAL repeatability conditions

wiederholen *vt* COMP & DV iterate, rerun

Wiederholgenauigkeit *f* METROL repeating accuracy

Wiederholgrenze *f* QUAL repeatability limit

Wiederholpräzision *f* QUAL repeatability

wiederholt:[1] **~er Flugplan** *m* LUFTTRANS repetitive flight plan; **~es Signal** *nt* ELEKTRONIK repeated signal; **~er Start mit durch Fahrtwind angetriebenem Propeller** *m* LUFTTRANS windmilling restart; **~er Verbindungsversuch** *m* TELEKOM repeated call attempt; **~er Zündversuch** *m* KFZTECH continual relight

wiederholt:[2] **~ überprüfen** *vt* METROL recheck

Wiederholung *f* AKUSTIK duplication, COMP & DV rerun, retry, FERNSEH repeat, rerun; **Wiederholungsanlauf** *m* COMP & DV fall-back; **Wiederholungslauf** *m* COMP & DV rerun; **Wiederholungsprobe** *f* QUAL retest specimen; **Wiederholungsprüfung** *f* QUAL renewal of qualification, repeat test, retest; **Wiederholungssignal** *nt* EISENBAHN repeating signal; **Wiederholungstaste** *f* FERNSEH repeat key

Wiederholungsprüfung: einer ~ unterziehen *vt* QUAL retest

Wiederinbetriebnahme *f* TELEKOM return to service

wiederkehrend: ~e Impulse *m pl* ELEKTRONIK recurrent pulses; **~e Kosten** *f pl* RAUMFAHRT recurrent cost

Wiederkehrspannung *f* ELEKTRIZ recovery voltage

Wiedernutzbarmachung *f* UMWELTSCHMUTZ rehabilitation

Wiedersynthese *f* KÜNSTL INT resynthesis

wiederurbar: ~ gemachtes Gebiet *nt* UMWELTSCHMUTZ reclaimed area

Wiederurbarmachung *f* UMWELTSCHMUTZ *von Land oder Wasser* recultivation

Wiedervereinigungskoeffizient *m* PHYS recombination coefficient;

Wiederverladung *f* WASSERTRANS *Ladung* reshipment, reshipping

wiederverwendbar[1] *adj* COMP & DV re-entrant, reusable; **nicht ~** *adj* COMP & DV nonreusable

wiederverwendbar:[2] **~e Datei** *f* COMP & DV reusable file; **~er Datenbestand** *m* COMP & DV reusable data set; **~er Karton** *m* VERPACK reusable box; **~es Programm** *nt*

COMP & DV reusable routine; **~es Verpackungsmaterial** *nt* VERPACK reusable packaging

Wiederverwendung *f* ABFALL *einer Pfandflasche* recycling, reuse, KOHLEN recycling; **~ gewerbliche Abfälle** *f* ABFALL reuse of industrial waste

wiederverwendungsfähig: ~es Raumschiff *nt* RAUMFAHRT recoverable orbiter

wiederverwertbar[1] *adj* UMWELTSCHMUTZ recyclable, reusable

wiederverwertbar:[2] **~es Abfallprodukt** *nt* ABFALL, UMWELTSCHMUTZ reusable waste product; **~er Treibsatz** *m* RAUMFAHRT *Raumschiff* recoverable thruster; **~e Verpackung** *f* VERPACK returnable packaging

wiederverwertet: ~e Flasche *f* VERPACK recycled bottle

Wiederverwertung *f* ABFALL *von Abfallstoffen*, TELEKOM recycling, UMWELTSCHMUTZ recovery

wiedervorstellen[1] *vt* QUAL *Prüflos* resubmit

wiedervorstellen[2] *vi* QUAL *Prüflos* resubmit

Wiederzündspannung *f* ELEKTROTECH reignition voltage

Wiege *f* EISENBAHN bolster; **~ des Drehgestells** *f* EISENBAHN bogie bolster

Wiegen *nt* PAPIER weighing; **Wiegenfederung** *f* EISENBAHN secondary suspension

Wien: ~ sche Brücke *f* ELEKTRONIK, PHYS Wien bridge; **~sches Strahlungsgesetz** *nt* STRAHLPHYS Wien law; **~sches Verschiebungsgesetz** *nt* PHYS Wien displacement law

Wigner: ~ -Effekt *m* PHYS Wigner effect

WIG-Schweißen *nt* FERTIG inert arc welding with nonconsumable electrode

wild: ~e Ablagerung *f* ABFALL, WASSERVERSORG illegal dumping; **~e Müllablagerung** *f* ABFALL fly tipping, open dump, uncontrolled tipping; **~e Schwingung** *f* PHYS, RADIO, TELEKOM parasitic oscillation; **~e See** *f* WASSERTRANS *Seezustand* confused sea

Wildzaun *m* ABFALL *einer Deponie* fence

Willison-Kupplung *f* KFZTECH Willison coupling

willkürlich: ~e Konstante *f* PHYS arbitrary constant; **~ verteilte Wicklung** *f* ELEKTRIZ random winding

Wilson: ~sche Nebelkammer *f* PHYS Wilson cloud chamber

Wimpel *m* WASSERTRANS *Flagge* pennant

Wimshurst: Wimshurstmaschine *f* ELEKTROTECH Wimshurst machine

Winchesterplatte *f* COMP & DV Winchester disk

Wind:[1] **dem ~ abgekehrt** *adj* NICHTFOSS ENERG downwind

Wind:[2] **mit dem ~** *adv* NICHTFOSS ENERG, UMWELTSCHMUTZ, WASSERTRANS *Segeln* downwind

Wind:[3] *m* WASSERTRANS, LUFTTRANS wind

Wind:[4] **in den ~ drehen** *vt* LUFTTRANS decrab, WASSERTRANS bear down

Wind:[5] **vom ~ abfallen** *vi* WASSERTRANS *Segeln* pay off; **vor dem ~ drehen** *vi* WASSERTRANS *Segeln* wear; **vor dem ~ laufen** *vi* WASSERTRANS *Segeln* run before the wind; **vor dem ~ segeln** *vi* WASSERTRANS *Segeln* run before the wind

windbetrieben: ~er Generator *m* ELEKTROTECH wind-driven generator

Wind: Wind- und Seetauglichkeit *f* WASSERTRANS wind-and-sea state capability handling; **Windbrett** *nt* BAU side board; **Winddruck** *m* LUFTTRANS, WASSERTRANS wind pressure; **Winddruckschwerpunkt** *m* WASSERTRANS *Schiffkonstruktion* center of wind pressure (AmE), centre of wind pressure (BrE)

Winde *f* BAU gin, jack, winch, LUFTTRANS hoist, MASCHI-NEN capstan, lifting jack, winch, windlass, MECHAN hoist, jack, WASSERTRANS *Deckbeschläge* winch

Windeisen *nt* MASCHINEN tap wrench

Winden *nt* BAU, MASCHINEN winding

winden[1] *vt* MASCHINEN wind

winden:[2] **sich ~** *v refl* MASCHINEN coil, wind

Winden: **Windenbohrer** *m* FERTIG bit brace

Wind: **Windenergie** *f* NICHTFOSS ENERG, PHYS wind energy

Winden: **Windenkopf** *m* WASSERTRANS *Deckzubehör* gipsy head; **Windentrommel** *f* WASSERTRANS *Deckbeschläge* winch drum

Wind: **Winderhitzer** *m* HEIZ & KÄLTE, THERMOD Cowper stove, blast preheater; **Windflügel** *m* BAU vane, HEIZ & KÄLTE, MECHAN, THERMOD fan blade

Windfrischen *nt* FERTIG *Gießen* converting

windfrischen *vt* FERTIG bessemerize

Windfrischstahl *m* FERTIG blown metal, FERTIG Bessemer steel

Windfrischverfahren *nt* FERTIG Bessemer process

Wind: **Windgenerator** *m* ELEKTRIZ wind generator, wind-driven generator, wind-powered generator, ELEKTROTECH wind generator, wind-driven generator, wind-powered; **Windgeschwindigkeit** *f* LUFTTRANS wind speed, NICHTFOSS ENERG wind velocity, WASSER-TRANS wind speed; **Windgeschwindigkeitsmesser** *m* NICHTFOSS ENERG wind gage (AmE), wind gauge (BrE), PHYS anemometer; **Windgeschwindigkeitsmessung** *f* PHYS anemometry

windgetrieben: **~er Generator** *m* ELEKTRIZ wind-powered generator; **~er Stromgenerator** *m* ELEKTRIZ wind-powered generator

Wind: **Windhose** *f* WASSERTRANS *Wetterkunde* vortex

Windkanal *m* BAU, LUFTTRANS, MASCHINEN, PHYS, RAUMFAHRT, WASSERTRANS wind tunnel; **~ mit geschlossener Meßstrecke** *m* PHYS closed-throat wind tunnel; **Windkanaleinfluß** *m* LUFTTRANS tunnel effect; **Windkanaltest** *m* RAUMFAHRT wind tunnel testing; **Windkanalwaage** *f* LUFTTRANS, WASSERTRANS wind tunnel balance

Wind: **Windkarte** *f* WASSERTRANS wind chart; **Windkasten** *m* FERTIG air box, MASCHINEN blast box; **Windkessel** *m* FERTIG air dome, dashpot, tank, ME-CHAN, PHYS air cylinder; **Windkraft** *f* NICHTFOSS ENERG wind power; **Windkraftanlage** *f* ELEKTRIZ wind generator; **Windkraftwerk** *nt* ELEKTROTECH wind-electric power station; **Windmesser** *m* LABOR, NICHTFOSS ENERG, WASSERTRANS anemometer; **Windmotorpumpe** *f* NICHTFOSS ENERG windmill pump; **Windmühle** *f* NICHTFOSS ENERG windmill; **Windmühlenflügel** *m* NICHTFOSS ENERG windmill vane; **Windmühlenrad** *nt* LUFTTRANS *Hubschrauber* engine windmilling, NICHT-FOSS ENERG windmill; **Windpressung** *f* FERTIG blast pressure; **Windrad** *nt* NICHTFOSS ENERG windmill

windrecht *adj* WASSERTRANS *Festmachen* wind-rode

Wind: **Windringleitung** *f* FERTIG bustle pipe; **Windrose** *f* NICHTFOSS ENERG wind rose; **Windsack** *m* LUFTTRANS wind cone, wind sock, WASSERTRANS wind cone, wind sock, wind sail; **Windschatten** *m* WASSERTRANS lee

windschief: **~er Flug** *m* LUFTTRANS drifting flight

windschlüpfrig *adj* LUFTTRANS faired

windschnittig *adj* MASCHINEN streamlined

Windschutz *m* AUFNAHME windshield; **Windschutzscheibe** *f* EISENBAHN, KER & GLAS, KFZTECH windscreen (BrE), windshield (AmE); **Windschutz-**

scheibengebläse *nt* KFZTECH *Zubehör* demister system

Wind: **Windseite** *f* WASSERTRANS weather side; **Windsichten** *nt* LEBENSMITTEL air classification, air separation; **Windsichter** *m* ABFALL air classifier, air separator, air separation plant; **Windsichtung** *f* AB-FALL airstream sorting; **Windstärke** *f* LUFTTRANS, WASSERTRANS wind speed; **Windstille** *f* NICHTFOSS ENERG still air, WASSERTRANS calm, lull; **Windstoß** *m* LUFTTRANS blast, RAUMFAHRT, WASSERTRANS gust; **Windstrebe** *f* BAU wind brace; **Windsurfingbrett** *nt* WASSERTRANS sailboard; **Windturbine** *f* MASCHINEN, NICHTFOSS ENERG wind turbine; **Windturbinengenerator** *m* NICHTFOSS ENERG wind turbine generator; **Windturbinenpumpe** *f* NICHTFOSS ENERG windmill pump

Windung *f* ELEKTRIZ turn, FERTIG *Feder* coil, MASCHI-NEN coil, spire, thread, turn, winding, PHYS, WASSERTRANS *Tauwerk* turn; **Windungsabstand** *m* ELEKTRIZ coil pitch; **Windungsrichtung** *f* FERTIG *Feder* hand of coils; **Windungsübersetzung** *f* PHYS turns ratio; **Windungsverhältnis** *nt* ELEKTRIZ, PHYS turns ratio; **Windungszahl** *f (N)* ELEKTRIZ number of turns in a winding *(N)*; **Windungszahl pro Längeneinheit** *f (n)* ELEKTRIZ turns per unit length *(n)*; **Windungszahlverhältnis** *nt* ELEKTROTECH, KFZTECH turns ratio

Wind: **Windverband** *m* BAU wind bracing; **Windversetzung** *f* WASSERTRANS leeway

windwärtig *adj* WASSERTRANS windward

windwärts *adv* WASSERTRANS windward

Wind: **Windwiderstand** *m* STRÖMPHYS wind resistance; **Windwinkel** *m* WASSERTRANS yaw angle; **Windwirbel** *m* LUFTTRANS, WASSERTRANS wind eddy

Winkel *m* FERTIG set square, vortex, *Kunststoffinstallationen* elbow, GEOM angle, MASCHINEN elbow joint, square, PAPIER, PHYS, WASSERTRANS angle; **äußerer ~** *m* GEOM outward angle; **~ der magnetischen Inklination** *m* PHYS angle of magnetic inclination; **~ mit der reellen Achse** *m* MATH *einer komplexen Zahl* argument; **~ der Totalreflexion** *m* OPTIK angle of total reflection; **Winkelabhängigkeit** *f* FERTIG angle dependence; **Winkelabrichteeinrichtung** *f* FERTIG angle-dressing fixture; **Winkelabstand** *m* TELEKOM angular separation; **Winkelabweichung** *f* ELEKTROTECH angular deviation; **Winkelantrieb** *m* MECHAN angle drive; **Winkelband** *nt* BAU, FERTIG angle brace, angle tie; **Winkelbeschleunigung** *f (α)* MECHAN angular acceleration *(α)*; **Winkelbohrung** *f* FERTIG *Kunststoffinstallationen* ninety-degree bore; **Winkeldämpfung** *f* TELEKOM corner loss; **Winkeldurchmesser** *m* RAUMFAHRT *Raumfahrt* angular diameter; **Winkeleckleiste** *f* BAU nosing; **Winkeleisen** *nt* BAU angle bar, angle iron, EISENBAHN angle bar, MASCHINEN angle iron, MECHAN angle bracket; **Winkeleisengelenk** *nt* BAU angle iron joint; **Winkelendmaß** *nt* METROL angle gage (AmE), angle gauge (BrE); **Winkelfehler** *m* GE-RÄT, METROL angle error; **Winkelfenster** *nt* BAU splayed window; **Winkelfräsen** *nt* MASCHINEN angle milling; **Winkelfräser** *m* FERTIG angle cutter, angular milling cutter, MASCHINEN angle cutter, angular milling cutter, dovetail cutter, dovetail-milling cutter, inverse dovetail cutter, single angle cutter, MECHAN angle cutter, angular milling cutter; **Winkelfrequenz** *f* AKUSTIK, ELEKTRONIK, PHYS angular frequency; **Winkelfunktionen** *f pl* GEOM trigonometrical functions; **Winkelgelenk** *nt* BAU angle joint; **Winkelgeschwindig-**

keit *f* ELEKTROTECH, FERTIG angular velocity, LUFT-TRANS rate of turn, MASCHINEN, NICHTFOSS ENERG, PHYS, RAUMFAHRT *Raumschiff* angular velocity; **Winkelgeschwindigkeit der Präzession** *f* NICHTFOSS ENERG angular velocity of precession

winkelgetreu *adj* GEOM isogonal

Winkel: **Winkelgetriebe** *nt* BAU miter gear (AmE), mitre gear (BrE), KFZTECH angle transmission, ring and pinion gearing, MASCHINEN angle transmission; **Winkelhaken** *m* DRUCK composing stick, setting stick; **Winkelhalbierende** *f* GEOM bisectrix; **Winkelhebel** *m* MASCHINEN bell crank lever, METALL bent lever; **Winkelhebelsystem** *nt* MECHAN bell crank system

winkelig[1] *adj* FERTIG, MASCHINEN, PAPIER angled

winkelig:[2] **~e Biegung** *f* FERTIG, MASCHINEN angle of bend

Winkel: **Winkelkaliber** *nt* FERTIG *Werkstoffe* angle pass; **Winkelkonsole** *f* BAU, MECHAN angle bracket; **Winkelkonstante** *f* TELEKOM phase coefficient; **Winkelkopf** *m* BAU cross-staff head; **Winkelkreuz** *nt* BAU *Vermessung* cross staff; **Winkelkurbel** *f* MASCHINEN bell crank; **Winkellasche** *f* BAU knee brace, EISENBAHN angle fishplate (BrE), applying of angle joint bar (AmE), FERTIG angle fishplate; **Winkellehre** *f* FERTIG, METROL angle gage (AmE), angle gauge (BrE); **Winkelmaß** *nt* KONSTZEICH angular dimension, MASCHINEN engineer's square, METROL bevel square; **Winkelmesser** *nt* FERTIG protractor, GEOM goniometer, protractor, MECHAN quadrant, METROL angle meter, protractor; **Winkelmesserskale** *f* MECHAN quadrant scale; **Winkelmeßinstrument** *nt* METROL protractor; **Winkelmeßsystem** *nt* GERÄT *Steuerungstechnik* angular position measuring system; **Winkelmessung** *f* METROL angle measurement; **Winkelmodulation** *f* ELEKTRONIK angle modulation; **Winkelmomentquantenzahl** *f (J)* KERNTECH total angular momentum quantum number *(J)*; **Winkelplatte** *f* MASCHINEN angle plate; **Winkelprofil** *nt* ELEKTRONIK L-section, MECHAN angle section; **Winkelreflektorantenne** *f* RADIO corner reflector aerial; **Winkelreibahle** *f* MASCHINEN angled reamer; **Winkelrotorgeschwindigkeit** *f* LUFTTRANS angular rotor speed; **Winkelsäule** *f* FOTO *Vergrößerungsgerät* angled column; **Winkelschälversuch** *m* KUNSTSTOFF T-peel test, angle-peeling test; **Winkelschiene** *f* FERTIG set square; **Winkelschleifer** *m* FERTIG angle grinder; **Winkelschnitt** *m* PAPIER angle cut; **Winkelschraubendreher** *m* MASCHINEN angular screwdriver, offset screwdriver; **Winkelsekunde** *f* PHYS second of arc; **Winkelstahl** *m* MECHAN angle steel; **Winkelstirnfräser** *m* FERTIG single angle cutter; **Winkelstoß** *m* BAU angle joint; **Winkelstoß mit Nut und Feder** *m* BAU angular grooved-and-tongued joint; **Winkelstrahl** *m* FERTIG angle bar; **Winkelstreichwalze** *f* PAPIER angle spread roll; **Winkelstück** *nt* LABOR elbow, MASCHINEN bracket, MECHAN elbow; **Winkelstütze** *f* BAU angle bracket; **Winkelstützmauer** *f* BAU cantilevered wall, cantilever retaining wall; **Winkelträger** *m* BAU L-beam; **Winkeltrieb** *m* MASCHINEN V drive; **Winkelverdrängung** *f (φ)* AKUSTIK angular displacement *(φ)*; **Winkelvergrößerung** *f* PHYS angular magnification; **Winkelversatzverlust** *m* OPTIK angular misalignment loss; **Winkelverschiebung** *f* ELEKTRIZ, GERÄT, LUFTTRANS angular displacement; **Winkelverschiebungsanfälligkeit** *f* LUFTTRANS angular displacement sensitivity; **Winkelverschraubung** *f* MASCHINEN elbow screw joint; **Winkelverstärkung** *f* FERTIG

angle bracket; **Winkelvoreilung** *f* FERTIG angle advance; **Winkelzahn** *m* MASCHINEN straight back tooth; **Winkelzahngetriebe** *nt* MECHAN herringbone gear

Winkligbiegen *nt* FERTIG angled bending

Winsch *f* MEERSCHMUTZ *Winde* winch

Winston-Kollektor *m* NICHTFOSS ENERG Winston collector

Winterlagerung *f* WASSERTRANS *Schiff* winter storage

Winterreifen *m* KFZTECH *Reifen* snow tire (AmE), snow tyre (BrE)

Wippenbank *f* MASCHINEN pole lathe

Wippenfederung *f* EISENBAHN bow suspension

Wipper *m* KOHLEN tipper

Wippkran *m* BAU luffing crane

Wippsäge *f* BAU jig saw

Wippschalter *m* ELEKTROTECH rocker switch

Wipptisch *m* KER & GLAS tilt table

Wirbel *m* EISENBAHN, ELEKTRIZ, FERNSEH, KERNTECH, KOHLEN, LABOR, MASCHINEN, MECHAN, PHYS, RAUMFAHRT, STRÖMPHYS eddy, swirl, vortex, WASSERTRANS *Beschläge* swivel, *Wasser, Wind* eddy, swirl, vortex, WERKPRÜF eddy, swirl, vortex; **~ bei Strahlinstabilität** *m pl* STRÖMPHYS vortices in jet instability; **Wirbelabschöpfgerät** *nt* MEERSCHMUTZ vortex skimmer

wirbelbehaftet *adj* STRÖMPHYS vortical

Wirbel: **Wirbelbettvergasung** *f* CHEMTECH fluidized-bed gasification; **Wirbeldehnung** *f* STRÖMPHYS vortex stretching; **Wirbeldiffusion** *f* KERNTECH eddy diffusion; **Wirbeldurchflußmesser** *m* REGELUNG vortex-shedding device; **Wirbelerzeuger** *m* WASSERTRANS vortex generator

wirbelfrei[1] *adj* GEOM, PHYS, RADIO, STRÖMPHYS irrotational

wirbelfrei:[2] **~es Feld** *nt* PHYS irrotational field; **~e Strömung** *f* PHYS irrotational flow

Wirbel: **Wirbelgarn** *nt* TEXTIL intermingled yarn; **Wirbelhaken** *m* WASSERTRANS *Takelage, Beschläge* swivel hook; **Wirbelkammer** *f* KFZTECH turbulence chamber, turbulence combustion chamber; **Wirbelkern** *m* STRÖMPHYS vortex core; **Wirbellinie** *f* STRÖMPHYS vortex line; **Wirbelmeißel** *m* FERTIG whirling tool

Wirbeln *nt* FERTIG whirling

wirbeln *vi* WASSERTRANS eddy

Wirbel: **Wirbelpaar** *nt* STRÖMPHYS vortex pair; **Wirbelring** *m* STRÖMPHYS vortex ring; **Wirbelröhre** *f* STRÖMPHYS vortex tube; **Wirbelscheibe** *f* LUFTTRANS actuator disc (BrE), actuator disk (AmE)

Wirbelschicht *f* HEIZ & KÄLTE fluidized bed; **Wirbelschichtgefrieren** *nt* HEIZ & KÄLTE fluidized-bed freezing; **Wirbelschichtofen** *m* CHEMTECH fluidized-bed furnace; **Wirbelschichtröstofen** *m* CHEMTECH fluidized-bed roasting furnace; **Wirbelschichttrockner** *m* HEIZ & KÄLTE fluidized-bed drier (AmE), fluidized-bed dryer (BrE), LEBENSMITTEL fluidized bed drier (AmE), fluidized bed dryer (BrE); **Wirbelschichtverbrennung** *f* UMWELTSCHMUTZ fluidized-bed combustion; **Wirbelschichtverbrennungsanlage** *m* ABFALL fluidized-bed incinerator; **Wirbelschichtvergasung** *f* CHEMTECH fluidized-bed gasification

Wirbel: **Wirbelschleppe** *f* STRÖMPHYS vortex trailing; **Wirbelseil** *nt* ERDÖL spinning line; **Wirbelsintern** *nt* CHEMTECH fluidized bed coating; **Wirbelsinterverfahren** *nt* KUNSTSTOFF fluidized-bed coating; **Wirbelstärke** *f* STRÖMPHYS *Rotation in Strömungsgleichungen entspricht Wirbelstärke* vorticity; **Wirbelstraße** *f* STRÖMPHYS *im Nachlauf einer ebenen*

Platte vortex street; **Wirbelstreckung** *f* STRÖMPHYS vortex stretching

Wirbelstrom *m* ELEKTRIZ, FERNSEH, PHYS, STRÖMPHYS, WERKPRÜF eddy current; **Wirbelstrombereich** *m* KERNTECH wake area; **Wirbelstrombremse** *f* EISEN-BAHN, ELEKTRIZ, FERNSEH eddy current brake, FERTIG disc brake (BrE), disk brake (AmE), MASCHINEN, MECHAN eddy current brake; **Wirbelstromdämpfung** *f* ELEKTROTECH magnetic damping; **Wirbelstromdurch-flußzähler** *m* KERNTECH eddy current flowmeter; **Wirbelstromgehäuse** *nt* MASCHINEN vortex chamber; **Wirbelstromgleisbremse** *f* EISENBAHN eddy current rail brake; **Wirbelstromleistungsbremse** *nt* WERK-PRÜF eddy current dynamometer; **Wirbelstromraum** *m* KERNTECH wake space; **Wirbelstromschaltung** *f* ELEKTRIZ eddy current circuit

Wirbel: **Wirbelströmung** *f* HEIZ & KÄLTE, KOHLEN eddy flow, NICHTFOSS ENERG turbulence

Wirbelstrom: **Wirbelstromuntersuchung** *f* EISENBAHN eddy current inspection; **Wirbelstromverlust** *m* FERN-SEH, PHYS, STRÖMPHYS eddy current loss

Wirbel: **Wirbelsturm** *m* WASSERTRANS whirlwind; **Wirbel-transportgleichung** *f* STRÖMPHYS vorticity equation

Wirbelung *f* FERTIG rabbling

Wirbel: **Wirbelverteilung** *f* STRÖMPHYS vortex distribution; **Wirbelzerfall** *m* STRÖMPHYS vortex decay; **Wirbelzug** *m* STRÖMPHYS vortex train

Wireline-Log *nt* ERDÖL *Bohrlochmessung* wireline log

Wire-Wrap-Verfahren *nt* MASCHINEN wire wrap technique

Wirkanteil *m* TELEKOM active component

Wirkbezugebene *f* FERTIG working reference plane

Wirkdruck *m* LABOR, MASCHINEN differential pressure; **Wirkdruckdurchflußmesser** *m* GERÄT differential pressure flowmeter; **Wirkdruckgeber** *m* GERÄT differential transducer; **Wirkdruckmeßumformer** *m* GERÄT differential pressure transducer

Wirkeinstellergänzungswinkel *m* FERTIG working approach angle, working lead angle (AmE)

Wirkeinstellwinkel *m* FERTIG working cutting-edge angle, working minor cutting edge angle

wirken *vi* TEXTIL knit

wirkend[1] *adj* ELEKTROTECH active

wirkend:[2] **~e Kraft** *f* TEXTIL agency

Wirkenergie *f* ELEKTRIZ active energy, FERTIG working energy

Wirkfreiwinkel *m* FERTIG working clearance

Wirkhauptschneide *f* FERTIG working major cutting edge

Wirkkeilwinkel *m* FERTIG working wedge angle

Wirkkomponente *f* ELEKTROTECH, TELEKOM active component

Wirkkraft *f* FERTIG working force

Wirklagewinkel *m* FERTIG working orientation angle

Wirklänge: **~ des Windes** *f* WASSERTRANS *Seezustand* fetch

Wirklast *f* ELEKTRIZ, ELEKTROTECH active load

Wirkleistung *f* ELEKTRIZ active power, ELEKTROTECH real power, *Halbleiterspeicher* active power, *WS-Kreis* active power, FERTIG working power, LABOR active power, MASCHINEN effective power, PHYS active power; **Wirkleistungsrelais** *nt* GERÄT active power relay

wirklich[1] *adj* COMP & DV physical

wirklich:[2] **~er Flugweg** *m* LUFTTRANS actual flight path

Wirknebenschneide *f* FERTIG working minor-cutting edge

Wirkneigungswinkel *m* FERTIG working cutting-edge inclination

Wirknormalfreiwinkel *m* FERTIG working normal clearance

Wirknormalkraft *f* FERTIG working perpendicular force

Wirknormalspanwinkel *m* FERTIG working normal rake

Wirkorthogonalebene *f* FERTIG working orthogonal plane

Wirkorthogonalfreiwinkel *m* FERTIG working orthogonal clearance

Wirkorthogonalkeilwinkel *m* FERTIG working orthogonal wedge angle

Wirkpaar *nt* FERTIG working pair

Wirkrückebene *f* FERTIG working back plane

Wirkrückfreiwinkel *m* FERTIG working back clearance

Wirkrückkeilwinkel *m* FERTIG working back wedge angle

Wirkrückspanwinkel *m* FERTIG working back rake

wirksam[1] *adj* COMP & DV, ELEKTRIZ, ELEKTROTECH, FER-TIG *Federwindung* active, MASCHINEN, MECHAN effective, PHYS efficient

wirksam:[2] **~es Bildsignal** *nt* FERNSEH effective picture signal; **~er Druck** *m* MECHAN active pressure; **~e Kes-selkühlfläche** *f* HEIZ & KÄLTE effective tank-cooling surface; **~e Leistung** *f* ELEKTRIZ active power; **~es Mittel** *nt* TEXTIL agent; **~e Querschnittsfläche** *f* ME-CHAN effective cross-sectional area; **~e Spannung** *f* ERDÖL *geologie* effective stress; **~er Widerstand** *m* ELEKTRIZ active impedance; **~e Windung** *f* FERTIG active coil

wirksam:[3] **~ werden** *vi* MASCHINEN become effective

Wirksamkeit *f* ANSTRICH *Mehrkomponentenlacken* pot life, LUFTTRANS agency, MEERSCHMUTZ effectiveness

Wirkschneidenebene *f* FERTIG working cutting-edge plane

Wirkschneidennormalebene *f* FERTIG working cutting-edge normal plane

Wirkseitenfreiwinkel *m* FERTIG working side clearance

Wirkseitenkeilwinkel *m* FERTIG working side wedge angle

Wirkspannung *f* ELEKTRIZ active potential, active voltage, effective electromotive force, ELEKTROTECH, PHYS active voltage

Wirkstoff *m* MASCHINEN, TEXTIL agent

Wirkstrom *m* ELEKTRIZ, PHYS active current

Wirktemperatur *f* THERMOD effective temperature; **Wirktemperaturbereich** *m* THERMOD effective temperature range

Wirkung *f* ANSTRICH *auf oder gegen etwas* reaction, MECHAN action; **~ der Corioliskraft** *f* STRÖMPHYS *auf rotierende Fluide* Coriolis effect; **Wirkungsablauf** *m* REGELUNG sequence of action; **Wirkungsbereich** *m* RAUMFAHRT *Weltraumfunk* effective area

Wirkungsgrad *m* AUFNAHME *eines Verstärkers*, ELEK-TRIZ, HEIZ & KÄLTE, KERNTECH, LUFTTRANS, MASCHINEN efficiency, MECHAN coefficient of efficiency, effect, efficiency, PHYS coefficient of efficiency, *einer Wärmekraftmaschine* efficiency, RADIO, RAUM-FAHRT *Weltraumfunk*, TELEKOM, THERMOD efficiency; **~ des Blattes** *m* LUFTTRANS *Hubschrauber* blade efficiency factor; **~ des Rotors** *m* LUFTTRANS *Hubschrauber* rotor efficiency; **~ der Quelle** *m* OPTIK, TELEKOM source power efficiency; **~ der Verbrennung** *m* THERMOD combustion efficiency

Wirkung: **Wirkungslinie** *f* FERTIG *Kraft*, REGELUNG line of action

WORM

wirkungsmäßig: ~e Abhängigkeit f REGELUNG von Signalen action-related dependence; ~e Betrachtung f
REGELUNG von Regelung, Steuerung action-oriented
consideration
Wirkung: Wirkungsquantum nt PHYS quantum of ac-
tion; Wirkungsquerschnitt m PHYS, STRAHLPHYS,
TEILPHYS cross section; Wirkungsrichtung f REGEL-
UNG direction of action
wirkungsvoll¹ adj MECHAN effective
wirkungsvoll:² ~e Verpackung f VERPACK efficient pack-
aging
Wirkung: Wirkungsweg m REGELUNG path of action,
signal flow path; Wirkungsweise f ELEKTROTECH ope-
rating mode, MASCHINEN action; Wirkungszone f
WASSERVERSORG area of influence
Wirkverbrauchsrelais nt ELEKTRIZ active power relay
Wirkverbrauchszähler m ELEKTRIZ active power meter
Wirkwaren f pl TEXTIL hosiery
Wirkwert m ELEKTROTECH real component
Wirkwinkel m FERTIG, MASCHINEN working angle
wirtschaftlich: ~ abbaubare Lagerstätte f ERDÖL Förde-
rung commercial field; ~ genutzte Kernenergie f
KERNTECH industrial nuclear power; ~es Projekt nt
ERDÖL economic project
Wischer m FERTIG squeegee, KFZTECH, MASCHINEN wi-
per; Wischerarm m KFZTECH wiper arm; Wischerblatt
nt KFZTECH wiper blade; Wischerwelle f MASCHINEN
wiper shaft
Wischkontakt m ELEKTRIZ wiping contact
Wisch-Waschanlage f KFZTECH windscreen washer
(BrE), windshield washer (AmE)
Wismutdraht m FERTIG bismuth wire
Wismutlot nt FERTIG bismuth solder
Wissen nt COMP & DV knowledge, ERGON cognition,
KÜNSTL INT knowledge; Wissensakquisition f KÜNSTL
INT knowledge acquisition
wissensbasiert¹ adj COMP & DV, KÜNSTL INT knowledge-
based
wissensbasiert:² ~es System nt (WBS) COMP & DV
knowledge-based system (KBS), KÜNSTL INT
knowledge-based system
Wissen: Wissensbasis f (WB) COMP & DV, KÜNSTL INT
knowledge base (KB)
wissenschaftlich: ~e Bezeichnung f MATH scientific notation; ~e Schreibweise f MATH scientific notation
Wissen: Wissensdarstellung f COMP & DV, KÜNSTL INT
knowledge representation; Wissensdarstellungsspra-
che f COMP & DV KRL, knowledge representation
language; Wissensengineering nt KÜNSTL INT KE,
knowledge engineering; Wissenserwerb m KÜNSTL
INT knowledge acquisition; Wissensrepräsentation f
(WR) COMP & DV, KÜNSTL INT knowledge representation (KR); Wissenstechnik f COMP & DV KE,
knowledge engineering; Wissensverarbeitung f KÜN-
STL INT knowledge processing
witterungsbedingt adj WASSERTRANS Auslaufen eines
Schiffes weather-bound
Witterungseinflüssen aussetzen vt BAU weather
Witterungsspiegel m UMWELTSCHMUTZ meteorological
data
Witterungsverhältnisse nt pl UMWELTSCHMUTZ atmos-
pheric conditions, meteorological conditions
WL abbr (weiter Laufsitz) MASCHINEN loose fit
W-Motor m KFZTECH W-type engine
WOB abbr (Bohrmeißelauflast) ERDÖL WOB (weight on
bit)

Wobbelbetrieb m ELEKTRONIK sweep mode
Wobbelfrequenz f ELEKTRONIK, FERNSEH, LABOR sweep
frequency, TELEKOM sweep frequency, sweep rate
Wobbeln nt ELEKTRONIK sweep, TELEKOM warble
wobbeln vt RAUMFAHRT wobble
Wobbelton m AKUSTIK warble tone
Wobbler m ELEKTRONIK Meßtechnik wobbler
Woge f ERDÖL Ozeanographie surge, WELLPHYS auf See
wave
wogen vi WASSERTRANS heave
Wöhlerkurve f FERTIG SIN curve, stress-number curve
Wohlklang m AKUSTIK consonance, harmony
wohltemperiert: ~e Tonleiter f AKUSTIK just scale, major
scale of just temperament
Wohn/Bohr-Plattform f ERDÖL Offshore-Betrieb hotel
rig
Wohnmobil nt KFZTECH Fahrzeugart camper (AmE),
caravan (BrE), motor caravan (BrE)
Wohnplattform f ERDÖL Offshore-Technik accommodation platform, flotel, Offshore-Betrieb hotel platform
Wohnraum m WASSERTRANS accommodation, quarter
Wohnung f BAU flat; Wohnungsbau m BAU house
building; Wohnungsnetzinstallation f ELEKTROTECH
domestic electric installation; Wohnungstrennwand f
BAU partition
Wohnwagen m KFZTECH caravan (BrE), mobile home,
trailer (AmE); Wohnwagenanhänger m KFZTECH caravan (BrE), trailer (AmE)
wölben¹ vt BAU vault, FERTIG camber, crown
wölben:² sich ~ v refl BAU camber
Wölbung f BAU arch, crowning, vault, FERTIG Riemenscheibe camber, crowning, KER & GLAS warpage,
MASCHINEN camber, PAPIER arch, QUAL kurtosis; Wöl-
bungsklappe f LUFTTRANS wing flap; Wölbungs-
meßgerät m PHYS spherometer
Wolfram nt (W) CHEMIE tungsten, wolfram (W); Wol-
fram- pref CHEMIE wolframic; Wolframat nt CHEMIE
tungstate, wolframate; Wolframatosilicat nt CHEMIE
tungstosilicate; Wolframglühdraht m STRAHLPHYS glowing tungsten filament; Wolframglühfaden m
STRAHLPHYS glowing tungsten filament; Wolfram-
heizfaden m ELEKTRIZ tungsten filament;
Wolframinertgasschweißen nt MECHAN tungsten
inert-gas welding; Wolframinertschweißen nt BAU
TIG welding; Wolframit m CHEMIE wolframite; Wol-
framkarbid nt ERDÖL Hartmetall, MASCHINEN
tungsten carbide; Wolframspritzer m BAU Schweißen
tungsten spatter; Wolframstahl m METALL tungsten
steel, wolfram steel
Wolkenbruch m WASSERTRANS cloudburst
Wolkenhöhenmesser m LUFTTRANS ceilograph, ceilo-
meter
Wolkenuntergrenze f LUFTTRANS, WASSERTRANS cloud
base
wolkig: ~er Anlauf m KER & GLAS paper hum
wollartig adj TEXTIL woolly
Wolle f PAPIER, TEXTIL wool
wollig adj TEXTIL woolly
Wolligkeit f TEXTIL woolliness
Wollkammzug m TEXTIL combed top
Wollwaren f pl TEXTIL woollens
Wood-Glas nt KER & GLAS Wood's glass
Woodruff-Keil m KFZTECH, MASCHINEN Woodruff key
Workstation f COMP & DV, KONTROLL work station
WORM¹ abbr (Einmalbeschreibung-Mehrfachlesen) OP-
TIK WORM (write once read many times)

WORM[2]: **WORM-Platte** *f* COMP & DV write-once disk, write-once read many times disk

Wort *nt* COMP & DV word; **Wortabstand** *m* COMP & DV spacing; **Wortangaben** *f pl* KONSTZEICH verbal notes; **Wortbegrenzungszeichen** *nt* COMP & DV word delimiter; **Wortebene** *f* COMP & DV word plane; **Worterkennung** *f* KÜNSTL INT word recognition; **Worterzeugung** *f* ELEKTRONIK word generation; **Wortgenerator** *m* ELEKTRONIK *Meßtechnik* word generator; **Wortlänge** *f* COMP & DV word length, word size

wortorientiert *adj* COMP & DV word-oriented

Wort: **Wortübertragungszeit** *f* COMP & DV word time; **Wortumbruch** *m* COMP & DV word wrap; **Wortzeichen** *nt* PATENT word mark; **Wortzeit** *f* COMP & DV word time

WPS *abbr* (*Wellenpferdestärke*) MASCHINEN shaft horse power

WR *abbr* COMP & DV (*Wissensrepräsentation*) KR (*knowledge representation*), ELEKTRONIK (*Wechselrichter*), ELEKTROTECH (*Wechselrichter*) inverter, KÜNSTL INT (*Wissensrepräsentation*) KR (*knowledge representation*), PHYS (*Wechselrichter*), RADIO (*Wechselrichter*) inverter

Wrack *nt* WASSERTRANS wreck

Wracker *m* WASSERTRANS wrecker

Wraparound-Banderolemaschine *f* VERPACK wraparound sleeving machine

Wringen *nt* PAPIER wringing

wringen *vt* TEXTIL wring

Wringwalze *f* PAPIER wringer roll

WS[1] *abbr* (*Wechselstrom*) ELEKTROTECH AC (*alternating current*)

WS:[2] **WS-Adapter** *m* ELEKTROTECH AC adaptor; **WS-Animeter** *nt* ELEKTROTECH AC animeter; **WS-Ausgang** *m* ELEKTROTECH AC output; **WS-Beschichten** *nt* CHEMTECH AC bed coating; **WS-Betrieb** *m* ELEKTROTECH AC operation; **WS-Brücke** *f* ELEKTROTECH AC bridge; **WS-Dickfilm-Elektrolumineszenzanzeige** *f* ELEKTRONIK AC thick-film electroluminescent display; **WS-Eingang** *m* ELEKTROTECH AC input; **WS-Entladung** *f* ELEKTROTECH AC discharge; **WS-Erregung** *f* ELEKTROTECH AC excitation; **WS-Erzeugung** *f* ELEKTROTECH AC current generation, AC generation; **WS-Feld** *nt* ELEKTRIZ AC field

WS-gekoppelt *adj* KONTROLL AC-coupled

WS: **WS-Generator** *m* ELEKTRIZ, PHYS AC generator

WS-GS[1] *abbr* (*Wechselstrom-Gleichstrom*) ELEKTROTECH AC-DC (*alternating current-direct current*)

WS-GS:[2] **WS-GS-Umsetzer** *m* ELEKTROTECH AC-DC converter; **WS-GS-Umsetzung** *f* ELEKTROTECH AC-DC conversion; **WS-GS-Wandler** *m* ELEKTROTECH AC-DC converter; **WS-GS-Wandlung** *f* ELEKTROTECH AC-DC conversion

WS: **WS-Integration** *f* (*Wafer-Scale-Integration*) COMP & DV, ELEKTRONIK WSI (*wafer scale integration*); **WS-Josephson-Effekt** *m* ELEKTRONIK AC Josephson effect; **WS-Kompensator** *m* ELEKTRIZ AC potentiometer; **WS-Komponente** *f* ELEKTRIZ AC component; **WS-Kondensator** *m* ELEKTROTECH AC capacitor; **WS-Koppler** *m* TELEKOM AC coupler; **WS-Kraft** *f* ELEKTROTECH AC electromotive force; **WS-Kreis** *m* ELEKTRIZ AC circuit, AC network; **WS-Last** *f* ELEKTROTECH AC load; **WS-Leistung** *f* ELEKTROTECH AC power; **WS-Leitung** *f* ELEKTROTECH AC line; **WS-Lichtbogen** *m* ELEKTROTECH AC arc; **WS-Lichtbogenschweißen** *nt* ELEKTROTECH AC arc welding; **WS-Marker** *m* WASSERTRANS AC marker;

WS-Maschine *f* ELEKTROTECH AC machine; **WS-Meßbrücke** *f* ELEKTRIZ AC bridge; **WS-Meßinstrument** *nt* ELEKTRIZ AC meter; **WS-Motor** *m* ELEKTRIZ, ELEKTROTECH, FERTIG, PHYS AC motor; **WS-Netz** *nt* ELEKTRIZ AC network, ELEKTROTECH AC network, AC power line; **WS-Netzausfall** *m* ELEKTROTECH AC power failure; **WS-Netzleitung** *f* ELEKTROTECH AC power line; **WS-Quelle** *f* ELEKTROTECH AC current source; **WS-Relais** *nt* ELEKTRIZ AC relay, ELEKTROTECH AC armature relay, AC relay; **WS-Schaltkreis** *m* ELEKTROTECH AC circuit; **WS-Schaltung** *f* ELEKTROTECH AC switching; **WS-Schweißlichtbogen** *m* FERTIG AC welding arc; **WS-Servomotor** *m* ELEKTROTECH AC servomotor; **WS-Spannung** *f* ELEKTRIZ AC voltage; **WS-Stellmotor** *m* ELEKTROTECH AC servomotor; **WS-Übertragungsleitung** *f* ELEKTRIZ AC transmission line; **WS-Versorgung** *f* ELEKTRIZ AC supply, ELEKTROTECH AC current source; **WS-Versorgungssystem** *nt* RAUMFAHRT *Raumschiff* AC power system; **WS-Verstärker** *m* ELEKTROTECH AC amplifier; **WS-Voltmeter** *nt* ELEKTRIZ, ELEKTROTECH AC voltmeter; **WS-Vorspannung** *f* AUFNAHME AC bias; **WS-Widerstand** *m* ELEKTROTECH AC resistance

W-Teilchen *nt* TEILPHYS W particle

Wuchtbaum *m* BAU lifter

Wuchten *nt* MASCHINEN balancing, counterbalancing

Wuchtfehler *m* FERTIG amount of unbalance, unbalance

Wuchtgewichte *nt pl* MASCHINEN balancing weights

Wuchtmaschine *f* MASCHINEN balancing machine

Wuchtzustand *m* FERTIG balance

Wulcherblock *m* KER & GLAS shaping block

Wulchereisen *nt* KER & GLAS shaping tool

Wulst *m* BAU bead, bulge, collar, flange, FERTIG ring, KER & GLAS *Flasche* bead, KFZTECH *Reifen* bead, *der Radnabe* boss, MASCHINEN bead, MECHAN pad, METALL, WASSERTRANS bulb; **Wulstband** *nt* TEXTIL *Reifen* chafer; **Wulstblech** *nt* METALL bulb plate; **Wulstbug** *m* WASSERTRANS bulbous bow; **Wulsteisen** *nt* METALL bulb iron; **Wulstfacette** *f* KER & GLAS beaded bevel

wulstig *adj* MECHAN padded

Wulst: **Wulstkante** *f* KER & GLAS bulb edge; **Wulstkern** *m* KFZTECH bead core

Wurfanker *m* WASSERTRANS *Festmachen* grappling hook, kedge anchor

Würfel *m* GEOM cube

würfeln *vt* LEBENSMITTEL dice

Wurfförderer *m* MASCHINEN throw conveyor

Wurfkette *f* ERDÖL throwing chain

Wurfleine *f* WASSERTRANS *Tauwerk* heaving line

Würze *f* LEBENSMITTEL flavor (AmE), flavoring (AmE), flavour (BrE), flavouring (BrE)

Wurzel *f* COMP & DV radix, root, MATH radical, root; **Wurzelfehler** *m* KERNTECH incomplete root penetration; **Wurzel-Nyquist-Filter** *nt* ELEKTRONIK matched filter; **Wurzelzeichen** *nt* MATH radical sign; **Wurzelziehen** *nt* MATH *aus einem beliebigen Ausdruck oder Potenz* evolution

würzen *vt* LEBENSMITTEL flavor (AmE), flavour (BrE)

WWRV *abbr* (*Wanderwellenröhrenverstärker*) ELEKTRONIK TWTA (*traveling wave tube amplifier AmE*), RAUMFAHRT TWTA (*travelling wave tube amplifier BrE*)

WYSIWYG *abbr* (*originalgetreue Darstellung der Druckausgabe am Bildschirm*) COMP & DV WYSIWYG (*what you see is what you get*)

X

X *abbr* AKUSTIK *(Volumenverdrängung)* X *(volume displacement)*, ELEKTRIZ *(Blindwiderstand, Reaktanz)* X *(reactance)*, KERNTECH *(Belastung)* X *(exposure)*

X-Ablenkplatte *f* ELEKTRONIK horizontal deflection plate

X-Ablenkung *f* ELEKTRONIK *Kathodenstrahlröhre* horizontal deflection, FERNSEH X-deflection

X-Ablenkverstärker *m* GERÄT *Oszilloskop* sweep deflection amplifier

X-Achse *f* BAU, FERNSEH, GEOM x-axis, MATH x-axis, PHYS, RAUMFAHRT *Raumschiff* x-axis, TELEKOM time base

Xanthat *nt* CHEMIE xanthate

Xanthein *nt* CHEMIE xanthein

Xanthen *nt* CHEMIE xanthene; **Xanthenol** *nt* CHEMIE xanthydrol; **Xanthenon** *nt* CHEMIE xanthone; **Xanthenyl** *nt* CHEMIE xanthyl; **Xanthin** *nt* CHEMIE dihydroxypurine, xanthine

Xanthogen- *pref* CHEMIE xanthic, xanthogenic; **Xanthogenat** *nt* CHEMIE xanthate

Xanthon *nt* CHEMIE xanthone

Xanthophyll *nt* CHEMIE lutein, xanthophyll

Xanthoprotein- *pref* CHEMIE xanthoproteic

Xanthosin *nt* CHEMIE xanthosine

Xanthotoxin *nt* CHEMIE xanthotoxin

Xanthoxylen *nt* CHEMIE xanthoxylene

Xanthoxylin *nt* CHEMIE xanthoxylin

Xanthydrol *nt* CHEMIE xanthydrol

Xanthyl *nt* CHEMIE xanthyl

X-Band *nt* ELEKTRONIK X-band; **X-Band-Magnetron** *nt* ELEKTRONIK X-band magnetron; **X-Band-Wanderfeldröhre** *f* ELEKTRONIK X-band TWT, X-band traveling wave tube (AmE), X-band travelling wave tube (BrE)

XC *abbr (kapazitiver Blindwiderstand)* ELEKTRIZ XC *(capacitive reactance)*

Xe *(Xenon)* CHEMIE Xe *(xenon)*

Xenon *nt (Xe)* CHEMIE xenon *(Xe)*; **Xenon-Chloridlaser** *m* ELEKTRONIK xenon chloride laser; **Xenoneffekt** *m*

KERNTECH xenon effect; **Xenongipfel** *m* KERNTECH xenon peak; **Xenon-Reaktivität** *f* KERNTECH xenon reactivity; **Xenonspitze** *f* KERNTECH xenon peak; **Xenonspitze nach Abschaltung** *f* KERNTECH xenon buildup after shutdown; **Xenonvergiftung** *f* KERNTECH xenon poisoning effect

Xerographie *f* COMP & DV, ELEKTRIZ, ELEKTRONIK xerography

xi-Teilchen *nt* PHYS *Elementarteilchen* xi particle

X-Koordinate *f* PHYS x-coordinate

XL *abbr (induktiver Blindwiderstand)* ELEKTRIZ XL *(inductive reactance)*

XLR-Anschluß *m* FERNSEH XLR connector

X-Motor *m* KERNTECH *eines Manipulators* X-motor, KFZTECH X-type engine

XMS *abbr (Erweiterungsspeicher)* COMP & DV XMS *(extended memory specification)*

XM-synchronisiert: ~er Verschluß *m* FOTO XM synchronized shutter

XM-Synchroverschluß *m* FOTO XM synchronized shutter

X-Naht *f* FERTIG double-V groove weld; **X-Nahtverbindung** *f* FERTIG double-V butt joint

XPS *abbr* COMP & DV *(Expertensystem)*, KÜNSTL INT *(Expertensystem)* XPS *(expert system)*, PHYS *(röntgenstrahlangeregte Photoelektronenspektroskopie)* XPS *(X-ray photoelectron spectroscopy)*

X-Stoß *m* FERTIG double-V butt joint

X-Y: ~ Abgleich *m* FERNSEH X-Y alignment; **~ Schreiber** *m* ELEKTRIZ X-Y recorder, GERÄT graph plotter, GERÄT two-axis plotter

Xylen *nt* KUNSTSTOFF xylene

Xylenol *nt* CHEMIE hydroxydimethylbenzene, xylenol

Xylidin *nt* CHEMIE xylidine

Xylit *nt* CHEMIE, LEBENSMITTEL *Zuckeralkohol* xylitol

Xylitol *nt* CHEMIE xylitol

Xylol *nt* CHEMIE dimethylbenzene, xylene, xylol, ERDÖL *Petrochemie*, KUNSTSTOFF xylene

Xylyl- CHEMIE xylyl *pref* CHEMIE xylylene

Y

Y *(Yttrium)* CHEMIE Y *(yttrium)*

YA *abbr (akustische Admittanz)* AKUSTIK, ELEKTRO-TECH YA *(acoustic admittance)*

Y-Ablenkung *f* ELEKTRONIK vertical deflection, FERN-SEH Y-deflection

Y-Achse *f* BAU, FERNSEH, GEOM y-axis, MATH y-axis, PHYS y-axis

Y-Ader *f* AUFNAHME Y-lead

Y-Admittanzschaltung *f* PHYS Y-network

YAG *abbr (Yttrium-Aluminium-Granat)* CHEMIE YAG *(yttrium-aluminium garnet)*

Yagein *nt* CHEMIE harmine, yageine

Yagi-Antenne *f* TELEKOM Yagi antenna

YAG: **YAG-Laser** *m* ELEKTRONIK *Neodym-Laser* YAG laser

Y-Anschluß *m* ELEKTROTECH Y-connection

Yard *nt* METROL, TEXTIL yard

Yawl *f* WASSERTRANS *Schifftyp* yawl

Yb *(Ytterbium)* CHEMIE Yb *(ytterbium)*

YIG[1] *abbr (Yttrium-Eisen-Granat)* CHEMIE YIG *(yttrium-iron garnet)*

YIG[2]: **YIG-Abstimmung** *f* ELEKTRONIK YIG tuning; **YIG-Bandpaßfilter** *nt* ELEKTRONIK YIG band-pass filter; **YIG-Filter** *nt* ELEKTRONIK YIG filter

Y-Kabel *nt* FERNSEH Y-cable

Y-Koordinate *f* PHYS y-coordinate

Y-Koppler *m* OPTIK, TELEKOM Y-coupler

Young: **~scher Doppelspalt** *m* PHYS Young's slits; **~scher Modul** *m* *(E)* ERDÖL *Elastizität*, HYDRAUL *Elastizität*, KOHLEN *Elastizität*, KUNSTSTOFF *Elastizität*, METALL *Elastizität*, PHYS *Elastizität* Young's modulus *(E)*

Yrast-Strahlung *f* KERNTECH yrast radiation

Y-Schaltung *f* PHYS Y-network

Y-Signal *nt* FERNSEH Y-signal, luminance signal

Ytterbium *nt* *(Yb)* CHEMIE ytterbium *(Yb)*; **Ytterbium-oxid** *nt* CHEMIE ytterbium oxide

Yttrium *nt* *(Y)* CHEMIE yttrium *(Y)*; **Yttrium-Aluminium-Granat** *nt* *(YAG)* CHEMIE yttrium-aluminium garnet (BrE), yttrium-aluminum garnet (AmE) *(YAG)*; **Yttrium-Eisen-Granat** *nt* *(YIG)* CHEMIE yttrium-iron garnet *(YIG)*; **Yttriumoxid** *nt* CHEMIE yttrium oxide

Yukawa-Potential *nt* PHYS Yukawa potential; **Yukawa-Potentialtopf** *m* KERNTECH Yukawa well

Y-Verbindung *f* ELEKTRIZ forked connection, ELEKTRO-TECH Y-connection; **Y-Verbindungsstück** *nt* LABOR *Zwischenstück* Y-piece

Y-Vierpolparameter *m pl* ELEKTRONIK Y-parameters

Z

Z *abbr* ELEKTRIZ *(Impedanz)* Z *(impedance)*, KERN-TECH *(Atomzahl)* Z *(atomic number)*, PHYS *(Teilfunktion, Zustandsfunktion)* Z *(partition function)*

z *abbr (Kompressibilitätsfaktor)* THERMOD z *(compressibility factor)*

ZA *abbr (Schallimpedanz, Schallwellenwiderstand, akustische Impedanz, akustischer Scheinwiderstand)* AUFNAHME, ELEKTROTECH, PHYS ZA *(acoustic impedance)*

Z-Achse *f* GEOM z-axis

Zacke *f* BAU tine, ELEKTROTECH spike, FERTIG jag, TELEKOM *CRT* pip

zackig *adj* FERTIG ragged

zäh *adj* STRÖMPHYS viscid

Zähfestigkeit *f* TEXTIL toughness

zähflüssig *adj* CHEMIE viscous, FERTIG syrupy, LEBENSMITTEL, MASCHINEN, PHYS viscous

Zähflüssigkeit *f* CHEMIE viscosity

Zähigkeit *f* ANSTRICH tenacity, ERDÖL, FERTIG viscosity, KERNTECH toughness, KOHLEN viscosity, KUNSTSTOFF toughness, viscosity, MASCHINEN tenacity, toughness, viscosity, METALL toughness, PHYS toughness, viscosity, STRÖMPHYS *Widerstand gegenüber Bewegung* viscidity, viscosity, THERMOD viscosity; **Zähigkeitsdämpfung** *f* MECHAN viscous damping; **Zähigkeitskoeffizient** *m* PHYS, STRÖMPHYS coefficient of viscosity; **Zähigkeitskraft** *f* LEBENSMITTEL, MASCHINEN, PHYS viscous force; **Zähigkeitsdraft bezogen auf Volumeneinheit** *f* LEBENSMITTEL, MASCHINEN, PHYS viscous force per unit volume; **Zähigkeitsmessgerät** *nt* STRÖMPHYS viscometer; **Zähigkeitsmessung** *f* STRÖMPHYS viscosity measurement; **Zähigkeitsverhalten** *nt* FERTIG tenacity behavior (AmE), tenacity behaviour (BrE); **Zähigkeitswirkung** *f* STRÖMPHYS action of viscosity, viscous action

Zahl *f* COMP & DV number, DRUCK figure, MATH approximation, number

Zählautomat *m* VERPACK counting device; **~ für neun Ziffern** *m* VERPACK nine digit counter

Zählcodierer *m* GERÄT *AD-Umsetzung* counting coder

Zähldetektor *m* TRANS passage detector

Zahl: **Zahlenbereich** *m* COMP & DV number range; **Zahlendarstellung** *f* COMP & DV number representation; **Zahlenrollenwerk** *nt* GERÄT counter; **Zahlensystem** *nt* COMP & DV number system; **Zahlentheorie** *f* MATH number theory, theory of numbers; **Zahlenwert** *m* METROL numerical value

Zähler *m* COMP & DV counter, *summe* tally, ELEKTRIZ, ELEKTRONIK, GERÄT, KONTROLL counter, MASCHINEN counter, meter, MATH numerator, RADIO counter, TELEKOM counter, *Telefon* meter (AmE), metre (BrE); **Zählergebnis** *nt* GERÄT counting result; **Zählergehäuse** *nt* GERÄT meter case; **Zählerschaltuhr** *f* GERÄT time switch; **Zählerschaltung** *f* ELEKTRONIK counter circuit; **Zählerstand** *m* GERÄT count

Zählfrequenzmeßgerät *nt* GERÄT counter frequency meter

Zählgerät *nt* GERÄT counting instrument

Zählgeschwindigkeit *f* ELEKTRONIK counting rate; **Zählgeschwindigkeitsmesser** *m* GERÄT count rate meter

Zählimpuls *m* GERÄT count; **Zählimpulsgeber** *m* GERÄT counting pulse generator

Zählmagnet *m* GERÄT magnetic counter

Zahlmeister *m* WASSERTRANS *Handelsmarine* purser

Zählmethode: **nach ~ arbeitender Analog-Digital-Umsetzer** *m* GERÄT analog-digital counter-type converter

Zählregister *nt* GERÄT counter

Zählrelais *nt* GERÄT magnetic counter

Zählrohr *nt* ELEKTRONIK, GERÄT counter tube, STRAHLPHYS counting tube

Zählröhre: **~ mit kalter Kathode** *f* ELEKTRONIK cold-cathode counter tube

Zählrohrsonde *f* KERNTECH counter tube probe

Zählschaltung *f* ELEKTRONIK *Schaltkreistechnik* counter

Zählschritt *m* GERÄT count; **~ rückwärts** *m* ELEKTRONIK decrement

Zählstatistik *f* COMP & DV tabulation

Zählstelle *f* TRANS counting station

Zählstrich *m* COMP & DV, MATH *auf Strichliste* tally

Zählumsetzer *m* GERÄT *AD-Umsetzer* level-at-a-time converter

Zahlung: **~ im Einzugsverfahren** *f* TELEKOM direct-debit payment

Zählung *f* GERÄT count, MATH enumeration, TELEKOM *telephone* metering

Zählvorgang *m* GERÄT *counting* count

Zählwerk *nt* COMP & DV register, ELEKTRIZ, ELEKTRONIK *Register*, FERTIG counter, GERÄT counter, counter mechanism, TELEKOM *Zählgerät* counter, register

Zahlzeichen *nt* DRUCK numeral

Zahn *m* MASCHINEN cog, sprocket, tooth, MECHAN *beim Zahnrad* cog; **~ eines Zahnrads** *m* MASCHINEN gear tooth

Zahn: **Zahnanlage** *f* FERTIG bearing; **Zahnbogen** *m* KFZTECH sector gear, MASCHINEN sector gear, sector wheel, segmental wheel; **Zahnbreite** *f* FERTIG *Kinematik* face width; **Zahndicke** *f* LUFTTRANS *Getriebe* chordal thickness, MASCHINEN tooth thickness; **Zahndicke als Bogen** *f* FERTIG *Getriebelehre* arc thickness; **~ Teilkreis** *f* MASCHINEN circular thickness

Zähne *m pl* MASCHINEN teeth, *eines Zahnrads* teeth; **~ ohne Kopfkürzung** *m pl* FERTIG *Getriebelehre* long-addendum teeth

Zahn: **Zahneingriff** *m* MASCHINEN tooth contact, tooth engagement

Zähnen: **mit ~ versehen** *vt* MASCHINEN cog

zahnen *vt* MECHAN dent

Zahn: **Zahnflanke** *f* MASCHINEN tooth flank

Zahnform *f* MASCHINEN tooth form; **Zahnformfräsen** *nt* MECHAN gear cutting; **Zahnformfräser** *m* MASCHINEN gear cutter

Zahnfuß *m* FERTIG *Getriebelehre* dedendum, MASCHINEN dedendum, tooth root, MECHAN dedendum; **Zahnfußhöhe** *f* MASCHINEN dedendum, depth below pitch line

Zahn: **Zahngesperre** *nt* MASCHINEN ratchet-and-pawl mechanism; **Zahngrund** *m* FERTIG gullet; **Zahnhobel** *m* BAU tooth plane, toothing plane; **Zahnhöhe** *f* FERTIG *Fräser* depth of cut, MASCHINEN tooth height; **Zahnhöhenkürzung** *f* FERTIG addendum reduction; **Zahnkanten-Abrundmaschine** *f* FERTIG gear-tooth rounding and chamfering machine; **Zahnkeilriemen** *m* MASCHINEN toothed V-belt; **Zahnkette** *f* FERTIG gear chain, MASCHINEN tooth-type chain, TEXTIL *Reißverschluß* chain

Zahnkopf *m* FERTIG *Getriebelehre* crest, MASCHINEN tooth crest, MECHAN addendum; **~ mit Stumpfverzahnung** *m* FERTIG addendum-corrected gear; **~ mit Zahnkopfkorrektur** *m* FERTIG addendum-corrected gear; **Zahnkopfhöhe** *f* FERTIG *Getriebelehre*, MASCHINEN addendum; **Zahnkopfwinkel** *m* FERTIG *Kegelrad* addendum angle

Zahn: **Zahnkranz** *m* KFZTECH *auf Schwungrad, in das das Anlasserritzel einspurt*, MASCHINEN ring gear; **Zahnkreisteilung** *f* MECHAN circular pitch; **Zahnlücke** *f* MASCHINEN tooth gap

Zahnlücken vorfräsen *vi* FERTIG gash

Zahn: **Zahnlückengrund** *m* MASCHINEN bottom land; **Zahnprofil** *nt* MASCHINEN tooth profile

Zahnrad *nt* FERTIG toothed wheel, wheel, KFZTECH *Getriebe* pinion, MASCHINEN cogwheel, gearwheel, gear, toothed wheel, MECHAN gear ratio, WASSERTRANS gear; **~ mit geraden Flanken** *nt* MASCHINEN straight flank gear; **~ und Sperrklinke** *nt* MASCHINEN ratchet and pawl; **~ mit Zykloidenverzahnung** *nt* MECHAN cycloidal gear; **Zahnradabzieher** *m* KFZTECH *Werkzeug* gear puller; **Zahnradachsverlagerung** *f* FERTIG gear center-distance variation (AmE), gear centre-distance variation (BrE); **Zahnradantrieb** *m* MASCHINEN gear drive; **Zahnradbahn** *f* EISENBAHN cog railroad (AmE), cog railway (BrE), rack railroad (AmE), rack railway (BrE), rack-and-pinion railroad (AmE), rack-and-pinion railway (BrE); **Zahnradbahnlokomotive** *f* EISENBAHN rack engine, TRANS rack locomotive

Zahnräder *nt pl* FERTIG gears

Zahnrad: **Zahnradfräser** *m* FERTIG gear cutter, MASCHINEN cutter, gear cutter; **Zahnradfräser Evolventenverzahnung** *f* MASCHINEN involute gear cutter; **Zahnradfräsmaschine** *f* MASCHINEN gear milling machine, gear-cutting machine; **Zahnradgebirgsbahn** *f* TRANS rack mountain railroad (AmE), rack mountain railway (BrE); **Zahnradgetriebe** *nt* MASCHINEN gearing, gears, MECHAN gear drive; **Zahnradherstellung** *f* MASCHINEN ; **Zahnradhobelmaschine** *f* MASCHINEN gear planer; **Zahnradmeßzylinder** *m* METROL gear measuring cylinder; **Zahnradnabe** *f* FERTIG gear hub; **Zahnradölpumpe** *f* KFZTECH gear-type oil pump; **Zahnradpaar** *nt* FERTIG equal gearing; **Zahnradprüfgerät** *nt* METROL gear testing machine; **Zahnradpumpe** *f* FERTIG double helical pump, gear pump, HEIZ & KÄLTE, KFZTECH, KUNSTSTOFF gear pump, MASCHINEN gear pump, gear-type pump, gearwheel pump; **Zahnradrohling** *m* FERTIG wheel blank, MASCHINEN gear blank; **Zahnradrollmaschine** *f* MASCHINEN gear rolling machine; **Zahnradschabmaschine** *f* MASCHINEN gear shaving machine; **Zahnradschneidmaschine** *f* MASCHINEN gear-cutting machine; **Zahnradstange** *f* EISENBAHN rack rail; **Zahnradstoßmaschine** *f* FERTIG shaper, MASCHINEN gear shaper, gear shaping machine; **Zahnradvorgelege** *nt*

MASCHINEN back gear, back gearing; **Zahnradwälzfräser** *m* FERTIG gear hob; **Zahnradwechselgetriebe** *nt* KFZTECH straight-toothed gearbox; **Zahnradzahn** *m* FERTIG gear tooth

Zahn: **Zahnriemen** *m* KFZTECH *Zündverstellung* cog belt, cogged belt, notched belt, MASCHINEN cog belt, cogged belt; **Zahnriemeneinstellung** *f* KFZTECH cogged belt timing, notched belt timing; **Zahnring** *m* MASCHINEN annular gear; **Zahnringanker** *m* ELEKTRIZ toothed ring armature; **Zahnscheibe** *f* MASCHINEN antiturn washer, tooth lock washer, toothed lock washer

Zahnsegment *nt* KFZTECH sector gear, MASCHINEN segmental wheel, toothed segment; **Zahnsegmenthebel** *m* FERTIG quadrant lever, quadrant level

Zahn: **Zahnspiel** *nt* KFZTECH *Getriebe* backlash

Zahnstange *f* FERTIG *Getriebelehre* rack, KERNTECH toothed rack, KFZTECH *Lenkung* rack, MASCHINEN rack, ratch, MECHAN rack, rack-and-pinion; **Zahnstangenantrieb** *m* MASCHINEN rack-and-pinion drive; **Zahnstangenfräseinrichtung** *f* MASCHINEN rack milling attachment; **Zahnstangenfräser** *m* MASCHINEN rack cutter, rack milling cutter; **Zahnstangenfräsmaschine** *f* MASCHINEN rack milling machine; **Zahnstangengetriebe** *nt* MASCHINEN rack-and-pinion drive, rack-and-pinion gear; **Zahnstangenlenkung** *f* KFZTECH rack-and-pinion steering; **Zahnstangenritzel** *nt* KFZTECH rack pinion; **Zahnstangenteilebene** *f* FERTIG *Getriebelehre* datum plane; **Zahnstangentrieb** *m* FERTIG rack-and-pinion drive, MECHAN rack-and-pinion; **Zahnstangentriebrad** *nt* MASCHINEN rack wheel; **Zahnstangenvorschub** *m* MASCHINEN rack feed; **Zahnstangenwinde** *f* MASCHINEN lifting jack, rack-and-pinion jack

Zahn: **Zahnstein** *m* BAU *Mauerwerk* toothing stone; **Zahnteilung** *f* FERTIG pitch, *Reibahle* spacing; **Zahnteilung im Teilkreis** *f* MASCHINEN CP, circular pitch; **Zahntrieb** *m* TRANS rack gearing; **Zahntrommel** *f* MASCHINEN sprocket drum; **Zahnweite** *f* MASCHINEN tooth distance

zäh-spröde: **~ Umwandlung** *f* METALL tough-brittle transition

Zange *f* BAU *Holz zum Zusammenhalten von Holzkonstruktionen* brace, *Holzbau* horizontal timber, ELEKTRIZ pliers, FERTIG *Drahtzug* clamp, KFZTECH *Werkzeug* pliers, MASCHINEN pliers, tongs; **~ mit gebogenem Kopf** *f* MASCHINEN bent-nose pliers; **~ für Sicherungsringe** *f* MASCHINEN circlip pliers; **Zangenbremse** *f* EISENBAHN clasp brake (AmE); **Zangenfutter** *nt* MASCHINEN collet chuck; **Zangengreifer** *m* MASCHINEN pince gripper; **Zangenmarkierungen** *f pl* KER & GLAS tong marks; **Zangenseil** *nt* ERDÖL *Bohrtechnik* tong line; **Zangenspannfutter** *nt* FERTIG spring collet chuck; **Zangenstromwandler** *m* GERÄT current probe; **Zangenwagen** *m* FERTIG *Rohrziehen* gripping jaw carriage

Zapfen[1] *m* BAU gudgeon, pintle, tenon, *eines Hahns* spigot, FERTIG neck, spigot, trunnion, *Kunststoffinstallationen* stem, KFZTECH neck, MASCHINEN gudgeon, journal, neck, spigot, tenon, MECHAN cog, faucet (AmE), journal, lug, METALL *Walzwerke* neck; **~ der Kurbelwelle** *m* KFZTECH *Motor* crankpin

Zapfen[2]: **mit ~ versehen** *vt* FERTIG tang

Zapfen[3]: **sich um einen ~ drehen** *v refl* FERTIG pivot

zapfen *vt* LEBENSMITTEL tap

Zapfen: **Zapfenbüchse** *f* FERTIG *Kunststoffinstallatio-*

nen stem sleeve; **Zapfendichtung** *f* FERTIG *Kunststoff-installationen* stem seal; **Zapfendüse** *f* KFZTECH *Dieselmotor* pintle-type nozzle; **Zapfenerweiterung** *f* FERTIG *Getriebelehre* pin enlargement; **Zapfenhals** *m* FERTIG *Kunststoffinstallationen* stem neck; **Zapfen-kreuz** *nt* MECHAN journal cross; **Zapfenlager** *nt* EISENBAHN axle box (BrE), journal box (AmE), FER-TIG pillow, MASCHINEN pin bearing; **Zapfenlagerung** *f* FERTIG pivoting, MASCHINEN trunnion mounting; **Zapfenlänge** *f* FERTIG pilot length; **Zapfenloch** *nt* BAU mortice, mortise; **Zapfenlochverbindung** *f* BAU slot mortise joint; **Zapfenring** *m* KFZTECH pivot ring; **Zap-fenschaltung unter Last** *f* ELEKTRIZ on-load tap changing; **Zapfenschlitz** *m* BAU through mortice; **Zap-fenschlüssel** *m* MASCHINEN pin spanner (BrE), pin wrench; **Zapfenschneidemaschine** *f* MASCHINEN te-noning machine; **Zapfensenker** *m* FERTIG piloted counterbore; **Zapfenspannglied** *nt* BAU shouldered te-non; **Zapfenstreichmaß** *nt* BAU mortise gage (AmE), mortise gauge (BrE); **Zapfenturbine** *f* HYDRAUL jour-nal turbine; **Zapfenverbindung** *f* BAU mortise and tenon joint

Zapfhahn *m* MASCHINEN faucet (AmE), tap (BrE)

Zapfluftventil *nt* LUFTTRANS air bleed valve

Zapfstelle *f* BAU tap (BrE)

Zaponfolie *f* KERNTECH zapon foil

Zaponlack *m* KERNTECH zapon lacquer

Zarge *f* BAU frame, FERTIG can body (AmE), tin body (BrE); **Zargenblech** *nt* FERTIG body stock; **Zargenrun-dung** *f* FERTIG body forming

Zartmacher *m* LEBENSMITTEL tenderizer

Zäsium *nt* CHEMIE caesium (BrE), cesium (AmE)

zäsiumdotiert: **~es Glas** *nt* RAUMFAHRT *Raumschiff* cae-sium-doped glass (BrE), cesium-doped glass (AmE)

Zäsium: **Zäsiumfotoröhre** *f* ELEKTRONIK caesium phototube (BrE), cesium phototube (AmE); **Zäsium-kathode** *f* ELEKTROTECH caesium cathode (BrE), cesium cathode (AmE); **Zäsiumstrahlresonator** *m* ELEKTRONIK caesium-beam resonator (BrE), cesium-beam resonator (AmE); **Zäsiumuhr** *f* RAUMFAHRT *Weltraumfunk* caesium clock (BrE), cesium clock (AmE)

Zaunlatte *f* BAU pale; **Zaunölsperre** *f* MEERSCHMUTZ fence boom

Z-Boson *nt* PHYS *Elementarteilchen* Z-particle, TEIL-PHYS Z-boson

ZB-Vermittlungsschrank *m* TELEKOM common battery switchboard

Z-Diode *f* ELEKTRIZ Z-diode, PHYS Zener diode; **~ mit Temperaturkompensation** *f* ELEKTRONIK temperat-ure-compensated Zener diode

Z-Draht *m* TEXTIL Z-twist

Z-Drehung *f* TEXTIL Z-twist

Z-Durchbruch *m* ELEKTRONIK Zener breakdown

Zeaxanthin *nt* CHEMIE zeaxanthin

Zebrastreifen *m* TRANS pedestrian crossing

Zeche *f* KOHLEN pit; **Zechenabraum** *m* ABFALL colliery waste

Zeeman-Effekt *m* KERNTECH, PHYS Zeeman effect

Zeeman-Komponente *f* PHYS Zeeman component

Zehneck *nt* GEOM decagon

Zehnerlogarithmus *m* COMP & DV common logarithm

Zehnertastatur *f* KONTROLL ten digit keyboard

zehnflächig *adj* GEOM decagonal, decahedral

Zehnflächner *m* GEOM decahedron

zehnpolig: **~es Filter** *nt* ELEKTRONIK ten pole filter

Zeichen[1] *nt* AUFNAHME signal, COMP & DV character, mark, KONTROLL character; **~ mit höchster Wertigkeit** *nt* COMP & DV high-order bit; **~ in Kursivdarstellung** *nt* COMP & DV italic character; **~ für Notfall** *nt* SICHERHEIT emergency sign; **~ pro Sekunde** *nt pl* (*Z/sec*) COMP & DV characters per second, cps (*characters per second*), DRUCK characters per second (*cps*); **~ pro Stunde** *nt pl* (*Z/Std*) DRUCK characters per hour, cph (*characters per hour*); **~ pro Zoll** *nt pl* COMP & DV pitch, DRUCK characters per inch, cpi

Zeichen[2]: **~ geben** *vt* WASSERTRANS signal

Zeichen: **Zeichenabfühlung** *f* COMP & DV mark scanning; **Zeichenabstand** *m* DRUCK character pitch; **Zeichen-abtastung** *f* COMP & DV mark scanning; **Zeichenanzeigeröhre** *f* GERÄT symbol indicator tube; **Zeichenarbeit** *f* KONSTZEICH drawing work; **Zeichen-art** *f* COMP & DV character type; **Zeichenbit** *nt* COMP & DV sign bit; **Zeichenbreite** *f* DRUCK character width; **Zeichenbrett** *nt* BAU, TEXTIL, WASSERTRANS *Schiffs-konstruktion* drawing board; **~ mit Zusatzfläche** *nt* KONSTZEICH drawing board with free margin; **Zei-chenbüro** *nt* BAU drawing office; **Zeichencode** *m* COMP & DV character code; **Zeichendichte** *f* COMP & DV bit density, character density, DRUCK character width; **Zeichendreieck** *nt* MASCHINEN set square, triangle; **Zeichendrucker** *m* COMP & DV character printer; **Zei-chenelement** *nt* ELEKTRONIK *Telefon* signal component; **Zeichenempfänger** *m* TELEKOM signal receiver; **Zeichenerkennung** *f* COMP & DV character recognition; **Zeichenerklärung** *f* FERTIG *Kunststoffin-stallationen* abbreviation; **Zeichenfehlerhäufigkeit** *f* TELEKOM character error rate; **Zeichenfläche** *f* KONST-ZEICH drawing area

Zeichenfolge *f* COMP & DV character string, string; **~ der Länge Null** *f* COMP & DV null string; **Zeichenfolgenbe-arbeitung** *f* COMP & DV string manipulation; **Zeichenfolgenfunktion** *f* COMP & DV string function; **Zeichenfolgenoperation** *f* COMP & DV string operation; **Zeichenfolgenvariable** *f* COMP & DV string variable; **Zeichenfolgenverkettung** *f* COMP & DV string concate-nation

Zeichen: **Zeichenfolie** *f* KONSTZEICH white drawing film

Zeichengabe *f* TELEKOM *telephone* signaling (AmE), signalling (BrE); **~ mit gemeinsamem Zeichenkanal** *f* TELEKOM common channel signaling (AmE), com-mon channel signalling (BrE); **~ innerhalb der Zeitlagen** *f* TELEKOM in-slot signaling (AmE), in-slot signalling (BrE); **Zeichengabe-Generator** *m* ELEKTRO-TECH signaling generator (AmE), signalling generator (BrE); **Zeichengabeinformation** *f* TELEKOM signaling information (AmE), signalling information (BrE); **Zeichengabekanal** *m* TELEKOM signaling channel (AmE), signalling channel (BrE); **Zeichengabenetz** *nt* TELEKOM signaling network (AmE), signalling net-work (BrE); **Zeichengabesystem** *nt* TELEKOM signaling system (AmE), signalling system (BrE)

Zeichengebung *f* TELEKOM marking; **~ innerhalb des Bandes** *f* RAUMFAHRT *Weltraumfunk* in-band signa-ling (AmE), in-band signalling (BrE)

Zeichen: **Zeichengenauigkeit** *f* COMP & DV plotting accu-racy; **Zeichengenerator** *m* COMP & DV, ELEKTRONIK *Datenverarbeitung* character generator; **Zeichenkette** *f* COMP & DV, DRUCK string; **Zeichenkontrollgerät** *nt* ELEKTRONIK *Telegrafie* signal comparator; **Zeichenli-neal** *nt* METROL ruler; **Zeichenmittel** *nt* KONSTZEICH drawing instrument

zeichenorientiert *adj* COMP & DV character-oriented
Zeichen: **Zeichenpapier** *nt* BAU plotting paper, GEOM drawing paper; **Zeichenplatte** *f* COMP & DV plotting board; **Zeichenquantisierung** *f* TELEKOM signal quantization; **Zeichenrohr** *nt* KONSTZEICH tubular tip; **Zeichensatz** *m* COMP & DV *ASCII*, DRUCK character set; **Zeichenschiene** *f* KONSTZEICH T-square, tee square; **Zeichenstiftplotter** *m* COMP & DV pen plotter; **Zeichentablett** *nt* FERNSEH graphic tablet; **Zeichenteilmenge** *f* COMP & DV character subset; **Zeichentisch** *m* COMP & DV plotting board; **Zeichentusche** *f* DRUCK drawing ink; **Zeichentyp** *m* COMP & DV character type; **Zeichenumriß** *m* COMP & DV character outline; **Zeichenumschalter** *m* TELEKOM character switch; **Zeichenumschaltung** *f* COMP & DV figures shift; **Zeichenumsetzung** *f* TELEKOM signal conversion; **Zeichenverzerrung** *f* TELEKOM *Telegrafie* signal distortion; **Zeichenvorrat** *m* COMP & DV character repertoire, DRUCK character set; **Zeichenwiederherstellung** *f* TELEKOM signal restoration; **Zeichenwinkel** *m* MASCHINEN set square; **Zeichenzuordnung** *f* COMP & DV character assignment
zeichnen *vti* WASSERTRANS draw
Zeichner *m* BAU draftsman (AmE), draughtsman (BrE)
Zeichnung *f* COMP & DV plot, GEOM, MASCHINEN drawing, MATH graph; **~ in den Schatten** *f* FOTO shadow detail; **~ mit vorgedruckten Darstellungen** *f* KONSTZEICH drawing containing preprinted representations; **Zeichnungsänderung** *f* KONSTZEICH amendment of drawing; **Zeichnungsänderungsdienst** *m* KONSTZEICH drawing amendment service; **Zeichnungsaustausch** *m* KONSTZEICH exchange of drawings; **Zeichnungsblatt** *nt* KONSTZEICH drawing sheet, PATENT sheet of a drawing; **Zeichnungsersteller** *m* KONSTZEICH originator of the drawing; **Zeichnungserstellung** *f* KONSTZEICH preparation of drawing; **Zeichnungsfeld** *nt* KONSTZEICH drawing area, drawing panel
zeichnungsgeprüft *adj* KONSTZEICH drawing-checked
Zeichnung: **Zeichnungsmaßstab** *m* KONSTZEICH scale of the drawing; **Zeichnungsnorm** *f* KONSTZEICH drawing practice standard; **Zeichnungsrichtlinien** *f pl* KONSTZEICH principles for the preparation of drawings; **Zeichnungssatz** *m* KONSTZEICH set of drawing; **Zeichnungsschriftfeld** *nt* KONSTZEICH title block; **Zeichnungssystematik** *f* KONSTZEICH systematic arrangement of drawings; **Zeichnungsunterlage** *f* KONSTZEICH preprinted drawing; **Zeichnungsverfilmung** *f* KONSTZEICH filming of drawings; **Zeichnungsvordruck** *m* KONSTZEICH preprinted drawing sheet; **Zeichnungswesen** *nt* KONSTZEICH drawing practice
Zeiger *m* BAU hand, COMP & DV, EISENBAHN, ELEKTRIZ, ELEKTROTECH *im Instrument* pointer, GERÄT needle, LABOR pointer, MASCHINEN arm, finger, index, needle, pointer; **~ des Belichtungsmessers** *m* FOTO exposure meter needle; **Zeigerarm** *m* WASSERTRANS *Navigation* index bar; **Zeigerausschlag** *m* GERÄT *Meßgerät* amplitude of movement; **Zeigerdarstellung** *f* ELEKTROTECH phasor representation
zeigergesteuert: **~e Unterbrechung** *f* COMP & DV vectored interrupt
Zeiger: **Zeigerinstrument** *nt* GERÄT pointer instrument; **Zeigerkette** *f* COMP & DV pointer chain; **Zeigermanometer** *nt* GERÄT, HEIZ & KÄLTE indicating pressure gage (AmE), indicating pressure gauge (BrE); **Zeiger-**

thermometer *nt* HEIZ & KÄLTE dial thermometer; **Zeigerwaage** *f* METALL bent-lever balance
Zeile *f* AUFNAHME line, COMP & DV line, row, DRUCK, FERNSEH line, FERTIG *Gießen* band; **Zeilen pro Minute** *f pl (LPM)* COMP & DV lines per minute *(LPM)*; **Zeilenablenkung** *f* ELEKTRONIK horizontal deflection, FERNSEH line output; **Zeilenabriß** *m* FERNSEH line tear; **Zeilenabstand** *m* COMP & DV line spacing, row pitch, spacing, DRUCK line spacing; **Zeilenabtastdauer** *f* FERNSEH trace interval; **Zeilenabtastgerät** *nt* COMP & DV raster scan device; **Zeilenabtastung** *f* COMP & DV line scanning, raster scan, ELEKTRONIK line scanning; **Zeilenamplitudenregelung** *f* FERNSEH line amplitude control; **Zeilenaustastpegel** *m* FERNSEH line-blanking level; **Zeilenaustastung** *f* FERNSEH line blanking; **Zeilencode** *m* VERPACK line code; **Zeilendichte** *f* COMP & DV line increment, scanning density; **Zeilendiffusion** *f* FERNSEH line diffusion; **Zeilendrucker** *m* COMP & DV line printer; **Zeilenende** *nt* COMP & DV end of line; **Zeilenfräsen** *nt* FERTIG parallel-stroke milling, straight milling; **Zeilenfräsmethode** *f* FERTIG *Spanung* line-by-line technique; **Zeilenfrequenz** *f* FERNSEH line frequency; **Zeilenfrequenzteiler** *m* FERNSEH line divider; **Zeilengefüge** *nt* METALL banded structure; **Zeilengießmaschine** *f* DRUCK line caster; **Zeilenkippen** *nt* FERNSEH line tilt; **Zeilenkriechen** *nt* FERNSEH line crawl; **Zeilenlauf** *m* FERNSEH line sweep; **Zeilenlinearitätsregelung** *f* FERNSEH line linearity control; **Zeilenmaß** *nt* DRUCK line gage (AmE), line gauge (BrE), type scale; **Zeilenmodell** *nt* METALL band model; **Zeilennummer** *f* COMP & DV line number; **Zeilenpaarung** *f* FERNSEH pairing; **Zeilenpegel** *m* FERNSEH line level; **Zeilenrücklauf** *m* ELEKTRONIK, FERNSEH line flyback; **Zeilenschärfe** *f* FERNSEH line focus; **Zeilenschlupf** *m* FERNSEH line slip
Zeilensprung *m* KONSTZEICH line spacing; **Zeilensprungabtastung** *f* FERNSEH interlace scanning; **Zeilensprungsequenz** *f* FERNSEH interlace sequence; **Zeilensprungverfahren** *nt* COMP & DV interlacing
Zeile: **Zeilenteilung** *f* COMP & DV scanning pitch; **Zeilentreibersignal** *nt* FERNSEH line drive signal; **Zeilenumbruch** *m* COMP & DV line folding, word wrap; **Zeilenvorschub** *m* COMP & DV line feed, line skipping, TELEKOM line feed; **Zeilenzwischenraum** *m* DRUCK leading, line spacing
Zein *nt* CHEMIE, KUNSTSTOFF zein
Z-Eisen *nt* METALL Z-iron
Zeising *nt* WASSERTRANS seizing
Zeit[1] *f* AKUSTIK, COMP & DV time, HYDRAUL duration, PHYS time; **~ bis zur Berührungstrockenheit** *f* KUNSTSTOFF touch dry time; **~ vor Entdecken eines Fehlers** *f* KERNTECH undetected failure time; **~ zwischen Flugsteig zu Flugsteig** *f* LUFTTRANS ramp-to-ramp time; **~ zwischen Sonnenwenden** *f* RAUMFAHRT solstitial period;
Zeit:[2] **~ nehmen** *vi* ELEKTRONIK clock
zeitabhängig: **~es Filter** *nt* ELEKTRONIK time-varying filter; **~es Signal** *nt* ELEKTRONIK time-varying signal
Zeitablauf: **~ beim Start** *m* RAUMFAHRT chronology of launching; **Zeitablaufdiagramm** *nt* KFZTECH timing diagram; **Zeitablaufplanung** *f* COMP & DV scheduling; **Zeitablaufsteuereinrichtung** *f* KONTROLL time schedule controller
Zeit: **Zeitableitung** *f* PHYS time derivative; **Zeitablenkgenerator** *m* ELEKTRONIK *Kathodenstrahloszillograph* time base generator; **Zeitablenkschaltung** *f* PHYS time

base circuit, TELEKOM *circuit* time base; **Zeitablenk-signal** *nt* GERÄT time base signal; **Zeitablenkspannung** *f* ELEKTROTECH sawtooth voltage; **Zeitablenkungs-frequenz** *f* ELEKTRIZ time base frequency; **Zeitablenkverstärker** *m* GERÄT *Oszilloskop* sweep deflection amplifier; **Zeitabschnitt** *m* AKUSTIK period; **Zeitachse** *f* ELEKTRONIK time base; **Zeitansage** *f* TELEKOM speaking clock

zeitaufgelöst: **~es Spektrum** *nt* STRAHLPHYS time-resolved spectrum

Zeit: **Zeitaufnahme** *f* FOTO time exposure; **Zeitauslösung** *f* COMP & DV time-out

Zeitbasis *f* ELEKTRONIK, PHYS, TELEKOM time base; **Zeit-basisspreizung** *f* ELEKTRONIK *Oszilloskop* expanded sweep; **Zeitbasisumsetzer** *m* GERÄT *AD-Umsetzer* ramp encoder; **Zeitbasisverschlüsselung** *f* GERÄT *AD-Umsetzung* sawtooth conversion

Zeit: **Zeitberechnung** *f* COMP & DV timing; **Zeitbereich** *m* ELEKTRONIK *Fourieranalyse* time domain, FERNSEH time slot; **Zeitbereichsfilterung** *f* GERÄT time averaging; **Zeitbereichs-Reflektometer** *nt* GERÄT time domain reflectometer; **Zeitbestimmung** *f* PHYS dating; **Zeitblock während der Hauptsendezeit** *m* FERNSEH prime time slot; **Zeitbruchkurve** *f* KUNSTSTOFF time to fracture curve; **Zeitcharter** *f* ERDÖL *Schiffahrt*, WAS-SERTRANS *Seehandel* time charter

Zeitcode *m* AUFNAHME, FERNSEH time code; **Zeitcode der Gesellschaft für Kino- und Fernsehtechniker** *f* *(SMPTE-Zeitcode)* FERNSEH Society of Motion Pictures and Television Engineers time code (AmE) *(SMPTE time code)*; **Zeitcode der Mittelspur** *m* AUF-NAHME center track time code (AmE), centre track time code (BrE)

Zeit: **Zeitdauer** *f* ELEKTRONIK time period, HYDRAUL duration; **Zeitdehngrenze** *f* METALL creep strain limit; **Zeitdehnlinie** *f* KUNSTSTOFF creep curve; **Zeitdehn-spannung** *f* KUNSTSTOFF creep stress; **Zeitdehnung** *f* GERÄT time scaling, PHYS time dilation; **Zeit-Demulti-plextechnik** *f* ELEKTRONIK time division demultiplexing; **Zeitdiagrammessung** *f* COMP & DV timing analysis; **Zeitdifferenz** *f* RAUMFAHRT hangover time; **Zeitdifferenz zwischen Kanälen** *f* AUFNAHME interchannel time difference; **Zeit-Diversity-Empfang** *m* TELEKOM time diversity reception; **Zeitdrift** *f* ELEK-TRONIK *Abweichung* time drift; **Zeitdrucker** *m* EISENBAHN time indicator; **Zeitedieren** *nt* FERNSEH time code editing; **Zeiteinheit je Tarifeinheit** *f* TELEKOM metering rate

Zeiten: **~ niedriger Verkahrsbelastung** *f pl* TELEKOM nonbusy hours

Zeit: **Zeitfehler** *m* FERNSEH time base error; **Zeitfehler-korrektur** *f* FERNSEH time base error correction; **Zeitfenster** *nt* RAUMFAHRT time slot; **Zeitfestigkeit** *f* ANSTRICH limited life fatigue, FERTIG endurance limit; **Zeitfolge** *f* COMP & DV time series, MECHAN elapsed time; **Zeitgeber** *m* COMP & DV clock register, interval timer, timing equipment, ELEKTRONIK timing generator, PHYS, TELEKOM timer

zeitgesteuert: **~es Magnetventil** *nt* KONTROLL timer-controlled magnet valve

zeitgeteilt: **~e Vermittlung** *f* TELEKOM time switching

Zeit: **Zeitimpuls** *m* FERNSEH timing pulse; **Zeitintervall** *m* ELEKTRONIK time interval, *Telefon* period, TELEKOM time slot; **Zeitintervallgeber** *m* REGELUNG interval timer; **Zeitintervallmeßgerät** *nt* GERÄT time interval measuring instrument

zeitinvariant: **~es Signal** *nt* ELEKTRONIK time-invariant signal

Zeit: **Zeitkanal** *m* TELEKOM time slot; **Zeitkohärenz** *f* TELEKOM time coherence; **Zeitkompression** *f* TELE-KOM time compression; **Zeitkonstante** *f* ELEKTRIZ, PHYS time constant; **Zeitkoordinate** *f* PHYS time coordinate; **Zeitkorrekturschaltung** *f* FERNSEH time-base corrector; **Zeitkorrelation** *f* TELEKOM time correlation; **Zeitlage** *f* TELEKOM time slot; **Zeitlagenwechsler** *m* TELEKOM time slot interchanger

zeitlich: **~ aufgelöste Radiographie** *f* KERNTECH time-resolved radiography; **~e Auflösung** *f* UMWELTSCHMUTZ temporal resolution; **~es Auflösungsvermögen** *nt* UMWELTSCHMUTZ temporal resolution; **~e Dosis-verteilung** *f* UMWELTSCHMUTZ temporal dose distribution; **~ festgelegte Hauptverkehrsstunde** *f* TE-LEKOM time-consistent busy hour; **~e Kohärenz** *f* OPTIK temporal coherence, time coherence, PHYS, TE-LEKOM temporal coherence; **~e Korrelationsanalyse** *f* KERNTECH time correlation analysis; **~er Lösungsab-lauf** *m* COMP & DV machine time; **~e Mittelwertbildung** *f* GERÄT time averaging; **~e Programmplanung** *f* COMP & DV program scheduling; **~e Schwankung** *f* UMWELT-SCHMUTZ temporal fluctuation, temporal variation; **~e Schwellwertverschiebung** *f* AKUSTIK temporary threshold shift; **~es Zittern** *nt* ELEKTRONIK time jitter

Zeit: **Zeit-Licht-Leistungskurve** *f* FOTO *Blitz* time/light-output curve; **Zeitlimit** *nt* COMP & DV time-out; **Zeitlimitüberschreitung** *f* COMP & DV watchdog time-out; **Zeitlupendisk** *f* FERNSEH slow motion disc (BrE), slow motion disk (AmE); **Zeitmarkengeber** *m* ELEK-TRONIK time marker, GERÄT time mark generator; **Zeitmarkengenerator** *m* GERÄT time mark generator; **Zeitmarkenimpuls** *m* GERÄT time marker pulse

Zeitmarkierung: **mit ~ versehen** *vt* TELEKOM time-tag

Zeit: **Zeitmaß** *nt* AKUSTIK tempo, GERÄT time clock rate; **Zeitmaßstab** *m* GERÄT timescale; **Zeitmesser** *m* LABOR chronometer, timer; **Zeitmeßgerät** *nt* GERÄT chrono-meter, time interval measuring instrument; **Zeitmessung** *f* COMP & DV timing; **Zeitmittelung** *f* GERÄT time averaging; **Zeitmodulation** *f* ELEKTRONIK time modulation

Zeitmultiplex *m* FERNSEH time multiplex; **Zeitmultiplex-abtastregelung** *f* REGELUNG time-shared control; **Zeitmultiplexdurchschaltung** *f* COMP & DV time divi-sion switching

Zeitmultiplexer *m* ELEKTRONIK time division multi-plexer

Zeitmultiplex: **Zeitmultiplexleitung** *f* TELEKOM highway; **Zeitmultiplexmethode** *f* *(TDM)* COMP & DV, ELEKTRO-NIK, TELEKOM time division multiplex *(TDM)*; **Zeitmultiplexnetz** *nt* TELEKOM time division network; **Zeitmultiplexsignal** *nt* ELEKTRONIK time division mul-tiplexed signal; **Zeitmultiplexverfahren** *nt* *(TDM)* COMP & DV, ELEKTRONIK time division multiplex *(TDM)*, TELEKOM time division multiplex, time mul-tiplexing; **Zeitmultiplexvermittlung** *f* TELEKOM time division switching; **Zeitmultiplexvermittlungssystem** *nt* TELEKOM time division switching system

Zeit: **Zeitnehmer** *m* COMP & DV timer

zeitperiodisch: **~es Feld** *nt* ELEKTROTECH time periodic field

Zeit: **Zeitplan** *m* COMP & DV, FERNSEH schedule; **Zeitpla-nung** *f* FERNSEH scheduling; **Zeitplanungsprogramm** *nt* COMP & DV scheduler

zeitraffend: **~e Prüfung** *f* QUAL accelerated test, WERK-

PRÜF accelerated testing

Zeit: **Zeitraffer** *m* FERNSEH fast motion; **Zeitrafferübersicht** *f* TRANS time lapse survey; **Zeitraffung** *f* COMP & DV fast time scale, GERÄT time scaling; **Zeitraffungsfaktor** *m* QUAL acceleration factor; **Zeitraster** *m* KERNTECH time slot pattern; **Zeitrasterung** *f* REGELUNG interval timing; **Zeit-Raum-Diagramm** *nt* TRANS time-space diagram; **Zeit-Raum-Zeit-Koppelnetz** *nt* TELEKOM time-space-time network; **Zeitregelung** *f* ELEKTRONIK timing; **Zeitregulierband** *nt* AUFNAHME timing tape; **Zeitreihenanalyse** *f* ELEKTRONIK time series analysis; **Zeitschachtelung** *f* COMP & DV time slicing; **Zeitschalter** *m* ELEKTRIZ, ELEKTROTECH time switch, GERÄT clock relay, time switch, TELEKOM time switch; **Zeitschaltrelais** *nt* GERÄT clock relay; **Zeitscheibe** *f* COMP & DV, ELEKTRONIK time slice; **Zeitscheibenverfahren** *nt* COMP & DV time slicing

Zeitschlitz *m* ELEKTRONIK time slot, TELEKOM time slot, *PCM* slot; **Zeitschlitzeinblendung** *f* TELEKOM blankburst mode

Zeit: **Zeitschreiber** *m* GERÄT time recorder; **Zeitschriftensatz** *m* DRUCK magazine typesetting; **Zeitsetzung** *f* KONTROLL timing; **Zeitsignal** *nt* WASSERTRANS time signal; **Zeitskale** *f* GERÄT timescale; **Zeitspanne** *f* ELEKTRONIK periodic time; **Zeitsperre** *f* COMP & DV time-out; **Zeitstandfestigkeit** *f* KUNSTSTOFF creep strength; **Zeitstandsfestigkeitslinie** *f* KUNSTSTOFF time to fracture curve; **Zeitstandversuch** *m* KUNSTSTOFF, WERKPRÜF creep test; **Zeitsteuertakt** *m* ELEKTRONIK period pulse; **Zeitsteuertakte** *m pl* ELEKTRONIK periodic pulses; **Zeitsteuerung** *f* KFZTECH timing, KONTROLL time control, timing; **Zeitsteuerungseinstellung** *f* KFZTECH timing adjustment; **Zeitstufe** *f* TELEKOM time stage; **Zeitsynthese** *f* ELEKTRONIK time synthesis; **Zeitsynthesizer** *m* ELEKTRONIK time synthesizer; **Zeittakt** *m* FERNSEH time base, TELEKOM clock, metering rate

Zeittakt: nach ~ steuern *vt* GERÄT clock

Zeit: **Zeittaktgeber** *m* FERNSEH time code generator; **Zeittaktgenerator** *m* FERNSEH time-base generator; **Zeitteilung** *f* ELEKTRONIK time division; **Zeittrend** *m* UMWELTSCHMUTZ time trend; **Zeitüberwachung** *f* TELEKOM time-out; **Zeituhr** *f* LABOR timer

Zeitung *f* DRUCK newspaper; **Zeitungsdruck** *m* DRUCK newsprint; **Zeitungsdruckpapier** *nt* PAPIER newsprint; **Zeitungsformat** *nt* DRUCK *etwa 300 x 400 mm* tabloid format; **Zeitungsspalte** *f* DRUCK newspaper column

Zeit: **Zeitverhalten** *nt* FERNSEH transient response, TELEKOM time characteristic; **Zeitverlust** *m* TRANS delay

zeitverschachtelt: ~e Struktur *f* KONTROLL pipelined architecture

Zeit: **Zeitverschiebung** *f* ELEKTRONIK time shift; **Zeitverschlüsseler** *m* GERÄT *AD-Umsetzer* ramp encoder

zeitversetzt *adj* KONTROLL deferred

Zeit: **Zeitverzögerung** *f* ELEKTRONIK, KONTROLL time lag; **Zeitverzögerungsrelais** *nt* ELEKTROTECH time delay relay; **Zeitvielfachsystem** *nt* TELEKOM time division system; **Zeitvielfachzugriff** *m* ELEKTRONIK time division multiple access

zeitweilig: ~e Belastung *f* KOHLEN temporary load; ~er Vorgang *m* FERTIG transient

Zeit: **Zeitzählung** *f* ELEKTRONIK timing; **Zeitzeichen** *nt* ELEKTRONIK, WASSERTRANS time signal; **Zeitzone** *f* WASSERTRANS time zone; **Zeitzyklus** *m* GERÄT timing cycle

Zelle *f* COMP & DV cell, ELEKTRIZ battery, ELEKTROTECH *Batterie*, KOHLEN, LABOR cell, LUFTTRANS nacelle, TELEKOM *land mobile* cell, WASSERTRANS *Schiffbau* tank; **Zellenbündel** *nt* TELEKOM *C-Netz* cluster; **Zellendoppelboden** *m* WASSERTRANS *Schiffbau* cellular double bottom; **Zellenfiltersaugtrockner** *m* HEIZ & KÄLTE filter drier, filter dryer; **Zellengleichrichter** *m* LUFTTRANS honeycomb filler, honeycomb grill; **Zellenkühler** *m* KFZTECH honeycomb radiator; **Zellenladung** *f* RADIO cell charge; **Zellenpolarisation** *f* ELEKTROTECH cell polarization; **Zellenschalter** *m* ELEKTROTECH multiple-contact switch

Zellglas *nt* KUNSTSTOFF cellulose film

Zellgrenze *f* TELEKOM *land mobile* cell boundary

Zellgummi *nt* HEIZ & KÄLTE cellular rubber

Zellhorn *nt* VERPACK celluloid

Zellophan *nt* VERPACK cellophane

Zellspannung *f* ELEKTROTECH *Batterie* closed-circuit voltage, *offener Stromkreis* open circuit voltage; ~ bei Stromfluß *f* ELEKTROTECH *Batterie* on-load voltage

Zellstoff *m* ABFALL paper pulp, DRUCK, PAPIER chemical pulp, VERPACK cellulose, woodpulp, WASSERVERSORG pulp; **Zellstoffentwässerungsmaschine** *f* PAPIER wet machine; **Zellstoffkocher** *m* PAPIER digester; **Zellstoffpreßsystem** *nt* VERPACK pulp molding system (AmE), pulp moulding system (BrE); **Zellstoffwatte** *f* CHEMIE artificial cotton, PAPIER wadding

zellular[1] *adj* ELEKTRONIK cellular

zellular:[2] ~es Funktelefon *nt* TELEKOM cellular radiotelephone; ~es Netz *nt* TELEKOM cellular network; ~e Struktur *f* TELEKOM cellular structure

Zellularsystem *nt* TELEKOM cellular system

Zellularverfahren *nt* TELEKOM cellular technique

Zelluloid *nt* VERPACK celluloid; **Zelluloidaugenschutz** *m* SICHERHEIT eyeshade

Zellulose *f* VERPACK cellulose; **Zellulosefasern** *f pl* ABFALL cellulose fibers (AmE), cellulose fibres (BrE)

zellulosehaltig: ~er Abfall *m* ABFALL cellulose waste

zellulosisch *adj* TEXTIL cellulosic

Zeltleinwand *f* TEXTIL canvas

Zeltstoff *m* BAU canvas

Zement *m* BAU, KER & GLAS, KUNSTSTOFF cement; **Zementabbindungslog** *nt* ERDÖL *Bohrtechnik* cement bond log

Zementation *f* ERDÖL cementing, METALL cementation; **Zementationszone** *f* METALL cementation zone

Zement: **Zementbeton** *m* BAU cement concrete; **Zementbrennerei** *f* KER & GLAS cement works

Zementieren *nt* FERTIG converting

zementieren *vt* BAU, METALL cement

zementierend *adj* ELEKTROTECH cementing

Zement: **Zementierofen** *m* METALL cementation furnace, cementing furnace; **Zementierstrang** *m* ERDÖL cementing string; **Zementiertour** *f* ERDÖL *Bohrtechnik* cementing string

Zementierung *f* BAU cementation, cementing, ERDÖL *Bohrtechnik* cementing, KERNTECH cementation

Zement: **Zementit** *m* CHEMIE *Metall* carbide of iron, cementite; **Zementkupfer** *nt* METALL cement copper; **Zementmilch** *f* BAU cement slurry, laitance; **Zementschachtofen** *m* KER & GLAS cement kiln; **Zementschlämme** *f* BAU cement slurry, grout; **Zementstahl** *m* METALL blister steel, cement steel, cementation steel, cemented steel; **Zementstaub** *m* BAU cement dust; **Zementstopfen** *m* ERDÖL *Bohrtechnik* cement plug, cementing plug; **Zementverdämmung** *f* ERDÖL cement plug, cementing plug;

Zementverfestigung *f* BAU cement stabilization; **Zementverpressung** *f* BAU cement injection; **Zementwerk** *nt* BAU cement mill, cement plant, cement works; **Zementwinden** *nt* BAU shrinkage in cement

Zener- *pref* PHYS Zener; **Zenerdiode** *f* PHYS, TELEKOM Zener diode; **Zenereffekt** *m* ELEKTRONIK Z-effect; **Zener-Hollomonsches Parameter** *m* METALL Zener-Hollomon parameter; **Zenerspannung** *f* (*UZ*) ELEKTRONIK breakdown voltage (*BDV*)

Zenit *m* WASSERTRANS *astronomische Navigation* zenith; **Zenitalpunkt** *m* RAUMFAHRT zenith point; **Zenitentfernung** *f* RAUMFAHRT zenith distance; **Zenitfernrohr** *nt* RAUMFAHRT zenith telescope; **Zenitvergaser** *m* KFZTECH zenith carburetor (AmE), zenith carburettor (BrE); **Zenitreduktion** *f* RAUMFAHRT zenith reduction; **Zenitwinkel** *m* NICHTFOSS ENERG zenith angle

Zenti- *pref* (*c*) METROL centi (*c*); **Zentigramm** *nt* METROL centigram; **Zentiliter** *m* METROL centiliter (AmE), centilitre (BrE)

Zentimeter *m* METROL centimeter (AmE), centimetre (BrE); **Zentimeter-Gramm-Sekunde-System** *nt* (*CGS-System*) METROL centimeter-gram-second system (AmE), centimetre-gram-second system (BrE) (*CGS system*); **Zentimeterwellen** *f pl* PHYS centimeter waves (AmE), centimetre waves (BrE)

Zentner *m* METROL cwt, hundredweight, cwt, metric centner, hundredweight

Zentral- *pref* COMP & DV, MASCHINEN central

zentral[1] *adj* COMP & DV centralized

zentral:[2] ~e Ladevorrichtung *f* TELEKOM central charging equipment; ~es lasttragendes Element *nt* OPTIK *Lichtleiter* central load-bearing element; ~e Operation *f* COMP & DV centralized operation; ~e Rechnereinheit *f* (*CPU*) COMP & DV, TELEKOM central processing unit (*CPU*); ~es Staubsaugersystem *nt* SICHERHEIT central vacuum cleaning system; ~es Steuersystem *nt* TELEKOM centralized control system; ~e Steuerung *f* TELEKOM central control, centralized control; ~e Tendenz *f* ERGON central tendency; ~es tragendes Glied *nt* OPTIK *Lichtleiter* central strength member; ~er Zeichengabekanal *m* TELEKOM common signaling channel (AmE), common signalling channel (BrE)

Zentrale *f* WASSERTRANS *Schiff* control room

Zentral-: **Zentraleinheit** *f* (*CPU*) COMP & DV central processing unit, central processor, TELEKOM central processing unit, central processor (*CPU*)

zentralgesteuert: ~e Einrichtung *f* TELEKOM common control equipment; ~es System mit Einzelprozessor *nt* TELEKOM single processor common-control system; ~es Vermittlungssystem *nt* TELEKOM common-control switching system

Zentral-: **Zentralkanalzeichengabe** *f* TELEKOM common channel signaling (AmE), common channel signalling (BrE); **Zentralkathode** *f* ELEKTROTECH common cathode; **Zentralkraft** *f* MASCHINEN, PHYS central force; **Zentralnervensystem** *nt* ERGON central nervous

system; **Zentralprojektion** *f* GEOM central projection; **Zentralprozessor** *m* COMP & DV, TELEKOM central processor; **Zentralrechner** *m* COMP & DV mainframe computer; **Zentralschmierung** *f* KFZTECH centralized lubrication, MASCHINEN central lubrication, centralized lubrication, centralized lubricating system; **Zentralspeicher** *m* COMP & DV CM, central memory, main memory, main store; **Zentralverbindung** *f* COMP & DV backbone; **Zentralvermittlungsstelle** *f* TELEKOM central switching unit; **Zentralverriegelung** *f* KFZTECH *Türen* central locking; **Zentralwert** *m* AKUSTIK, COMP & DV, MATH, QUAL median

Zentrieransatz *m* FERTIG spigot

Zentrierbohren *nt* MASCHINEN center drilling (AmE), centre drilling (BrE)

zentrierbohren *vt* MASCHINEN center-drill (AmE), centre-drill (BrE)

Zentrierbohrer *m* FERTIG center drill (AmE), centre drill (BrE), MASCHINEN center drill (AmE), centre drill (BrE), centering drill (AmE), centring drill (BrE), combination drill

Zentrierbohrung *f* FERTIG center hole (AmE), centre hole (BrE), MASCHINEN centering hole (AmE), centring hole (BrE)

Zentrierbuchse *f* MASCHINEN centering bush (AmE), centring bush (BrE), centering sleeve (AmE), centring sleeve (BrE)

Zentrieren *nt* MASCHINEN centering (AmE), centring (BrE)

zentrieren *vt* MASCHINEN center (AmE), centre (BrE)

Zentrierer *m* ERDÖL centralizer

Zentrierlinse: ~ mit Fadenkreuz *f* KER & GLAS centering lens with ruled cross (AmE), centring lens with ruled cross (BrE)

Zentriermaschine *f* MASCHINEN centering lathe (AmE), centring lathe (BrE)

Zentriermutter *f* MASCHINEN centering nut (AmE), centring nut (BrE)

Zentrierring *m* FERNSEH centering ring (AmE), centring ring (BrE)

Zentrierschraube *f* MASCHINEN centering screw (AmE), centring screw (BrE)

Zentrierspitze *f* MASCHINEN center point (AmE), centre point (BrE)

Zentrierstift *m* MASCHINEN, MECHAN centering pin (AmE), centring pin (BrE)

zentriert: ~es System *nt* OPTIK centered system (AmE), centred system (BrE)

Zentrierung *f* MASCHINEN location, MECHAN centering (AmE), centring (BrE); ~ der Bremsscheibe *f* KFZTECH *Bremsanlage* brake disc alignment (BrE), brake disk alignment (AmE)

Zentriervorrichtung *f* ERDÖL *Bohrtechnik* centralizer

Zentrifugal-: *pref* CHEMTECH centrifugal

zentrifugal *adj* MECHAN, PHYS centrifugal

Zentrifugal-: **Zentrifugalabschöpfgerät** *nt* MEERSCHMUTZ *für Öl* centrifugal skimmer; **Zentrifugalextraktor** *m* KERNTECH centrifugal extractor; **Zentrifugalfilter** *nt* KOHLEN centrifugal filter; **Zentrifugalhubgebläse** *nt* LUFTTRANS centrifugal flow lift fan; **Zentrifugalkompressor** *m* MASCHINEN centrifugal compressor; **Zentrifugalkraft** *f* CHEMTECH, MASCHINEN, PHYS, RAUMFAHRT, STRÖMPHYS, UMWELTSCHMUTZ centrifugal force; **Zentrifugalmoment** *nt* PHYS product of inertia; **Zentrifugalpumpe** *f* CHEMTECH, MASCHINEN, MEERSCHMUTZ centrifugal pump;

Zentrifugalregler m NICHTFOSS ENERG governor; **Zentrifugalreiniger** m CHEMTECH centrifugal cleaner, PAPIER cleaner

Zentrifugation f CHEMTECH centrifugation

Zentrifuge f CHEMTECH centrifugal, centrifuge, KUNSTSTOFF, LABOR, MECHAN, PHYS centrifuge; **Zentrifugengarn** nt TEXTIL boxspun yarn; **Zentrifugenglas** nt LABOR centrifuge tube; **Zentrifugentrommel** f LABOR centrifuge rotor

Zentrifugieren nt ABFALL centrifugation, centrifuging, KOHLEN centrifuging

zentrifugieren vt CHEMTECH, KOHLEN, KUNSTSTOFF centrifuge

zentrifugiert: ~er Latex m KUNSTSTOFF centrifuged latex

Zentrifugierung f WASSERVERSORG centrifugation

zentrifugisch: ~ kontrollierte Schaufelteilung f NICHTFOSS ENERG centrifugally-operated blade pitch control

zentripetal adj PHYS centripetal

Zentripetalbeschleunigung f FERTIG centripetal acceleration, LUFTTRANS centrifugal acceleration, centripetal acceleration

Zentripetalkraft f MASCHINEN, PHYS centripetal force

zentrisch adj FERTIG Schubkurbelgetriebe radial

Zentrum nt TELEKOM center (AmE), centre (BrE); ~ für Linearbeschleunigung in Stanford nt TEILPHYS Stanford Linear Accelerator Center; **Zentrumsbohrer** m MASCHINEN center bit (AmE), centre bit (BrE); **Zentrumswicklerrolle** f PAPIER center wind reel (AmE), centre wind reel (BrE); **Zentrumswicklung** f PAPIER center winding (AmE), centre winding (BrE)

Zerbrechen nt FERTIG Kunststoffinstallationen fracture

zerbrechen[1] vt BAU break, break up

zerbrechen[2] vi BAU spring, KOHLEN crush

zerbrechlich adj VERPACK fragile

Zerbrechlichkeit f MECHAN brittleness

zerbröckeln vt KOHLEN grind

zerbröckelt: ~e Kohle f KOHLEN coal slake

zerdrücken vt BAU, LEBENSMITTEL, PAPIER crush

Zerdrückfestigkeit f MASCHINEN resistance to crushing

Zerfall m ERDÖL decomposition, KERNTECH, PHYS, STRAHLPHYS, TEILPHYS decay

zerfallen[1] vt CHEMIE Kohle slake

zerfallen[2] vi MASCHINEN come apart, VERPACK disintegrate

Zerfall: Zerfallsarten f pl KERNTECH, PHYS, STRAHLPHYS, TEILPHYS decay modes; **Zerfallsenergie** f (Q) KERNTECH disintegration energy (Q); **Zerfallsgeschwindigkeit** f KERNTECH, PHYS, STRAHLPHYS, TEILPHYS decay rate; **Zerfallshohlraum** m KERNTECH decay cavity; **Zerfallskette** f KERNTECH, PHYS, STRAHLPHYS, TEILPHYS decay chain; **Zerfallskonstante** f KERNTECH, PHYS, STRAHLPHYS, TEILPHYS decay constant; ~ bei Gammazerfall f STRAHLPHYS, TEILPHYS, WELLPHYS gamma constant; **Zerfallskurve** f PHYS, STRAHLPHYS, TEILPHYS decay curve; **Zerfallsrate** f KERNTECH, PHYS, STRAHLPHYS, TEILPHYS decay rate; **Zerfallsteilchen** nt KERNTECH, PHYS, STRAHLPHYS, TEILPHYS decay particle; **Zerfallswahrscheinlichkeit** f KERNTECH decay constant; **Zerfallszeit** f ELEKTROTECH decay time

Zerfaserer m PAPIER pulp machine

Zerfließbarkeit f LEBENSMITTEL deliquescence

Zerfließen nt CHEMIE deliquescence

zerfließen vi CHEMIE deliquesce

zerfließend adj CHEMIE deliquescent

Zerhacken nt ELEKTRONIK von Gleichstrom chopping, FERNSEH scrambling

zerhacken vt FERNSEH scramble

Zerhacker m ELEKTRONIK chopper, ELEKTROTECH vibrator, RADIO alternator, RAUMFAHRT DC-AC converter; **Zerhackermodus** m ELEKTRONIK chopped mode; **Zerhackerschaltung** f RAUMFAHRT Raumschiff chopper circuitry; **Zerhackerverstärker** m ELEKTRONIK wandelt Gleichspannung in Rechteckwechselspannung um chopper amplifier

zerhackt: ~es Signal nt ELEKTRONIK chopped signal

zerkeilen vt BAU split with wedges

Zerkleinerer: m ABFALL crusher, BAU pulverizer, MASCHINEN grinding machine KOHLEN milling

Zerkleinern nt ABFALL shearing, KUNSTSTOFF crushing

zerkleinern vt ABFALL crush, BAU crush, pulverize, KOHLEN mill

zerkleinert: ~er Abfall m ABFALL crushed waste

Zerkleinerung f ABFALL grinding, (der Abfälle) crushing, KUNSTSTOFF crushing; **Zerkleinerungsanlage** f ABFALL crusher unit, CHEMTECH crushing plant; **Zerkleinerungsgerät** nt LEBENSMITTEL disintegrator, grinder; **Zerkleinerungsgrad** m KOHLEN reduction ratio; **Zerkleinerungsmaschine** f CHEMTECH crushing machine, grinding mill, MASCHINEN crushing machine; **Zerkleinerungsverfahren** nt ABFALL crushing system; **Zerkleinerungswerk** nt ABFALL crusher unit

Zerklüftung f ERDÖL Geologie fracturing

zerknittern vt PAPIER crumple

zerknittert adj PAPIER crumpled

Zerlegen nt MASCHINEN disassembly, taking to pieces

zerlegen vt BAU break down, COMP & DV parse, KERNTECH strip, MASCHINEN decompose, disassemble, dismount, strip, take down

Zerlegung f AKUSTIK resolution, KERNTECH eines Brennelemenes dismantling, PHYS breakdown; ~ in Abschnitte f KERNTECH sectioning technique; ~ in Faktoren f MATH factorization; **Zerlegungsgleis** nt EISENBAHN siding for splitting up trains

zermahlen vt ABFALL grind, BAU mill, LEBENSMITTEL crush

zermalmen vt KOHLEN crush

Zer-Polierrot nt KER & GLAS ceri-rouge

zerquetschen vt LEBENSMITTEL bruise

Zerreiben nt KOHLEN, PAPIER attrition, TEXTIL grinding

Zerreiß- pref MASCHINEN tensile

Zerreißen nt ABFALL von Abfällen crushing, PAPIER tearing

zerreißen vt BAU break, PAPIER tear

Zerreiß-: Zerreißfestigkeit f KUNSTSTOFF tear resistance, tensile strength, MASCHINEN tensile strength, ultimate strength, MECHAN breaking strength, tensile strength, TEXTIL tear strength, tensile strength; **Zerreißgrenze** f MASCHINEN ultimate strength, MECHAN breaking point; **Zerreißprobe** f MASCHINEN tensile specimen, tensile test piece, MECHAN breaking test, PHYS tensile test; **Zerreißprüfgerät** nt MASCHINEN tensile test equipment; **Zerreißprüfmaschine** f MASCHINEN tension testing machine; **Zerreißprüfstück** nt MASCHINEN tensile specimen, tensile test piece; **Zerreißprüfung** f MASCHINEN tensile test, WERKPRÜF breaking test; **Zerreißversuch** m METALL tensile test

Zerrspiegel m KER & GLAS distorting mirror

Zerschmelzen nt CHEMIE deliquescence

Zerschneideblattsystem nt KONSTZEICH sheet dissection system

Zerschneiden nt ABFALL shearing
zersetzen vt MEERSCHMUTZ foul, VERPACK disintegrate
Zersetzung f ABFALL digestion, CHEMIE, COMP & DV decomposition, KUNSTSTOFF degradation, LEBENS-MITTEL decomposition, VERPACK deterioration; **~ von Wasser durch Bestrahlung** f KERNTECH water decomposition under irradiation; **Zersetzungsbereich** m FERTIG *Kunststoffinstallationen* decomposition zone; **Zersetzungsmittel** nt CHEMIE decomposing agent; **Zersetzungstemperatur** f KUNSTSTOFF, VERPACK *warme Lagerung* decomposition temperature
zerspalten vt BAU split
zerspanbar adj FERTIG machinable
Zerspanbarkeit f FERTIG machinability, machinability rating
zerspanend: ~ feinstbearbeiten vt FERTIG superfinish
Zerspangröße f FERTIG cutting variable, machining variable
Zerspankraft f MASCHINEN cutting force
zerspant: ~es Volumen nt FERTIG volume of metal removed
Zerspanung f FERTIG cutting; **Zerspanungsbedingung** f FERTIG cutting condition; **Zerspanungsleistung** f FERTIG cutting efficiency; **Zerspanungsvolumen** nt FERTIG volume of metal removed by cutting
Zerspanvorgang m FERTIG machining operation
Zersprühung f FERTIG *Funkenbild* fork burst, *Schleiffunkenversuch* explosion
zerstampfen vt LEBENSMITTEL pound
zerstäuben vt BAU pulverize, PAPIER atomize
Zerstäuber m LABOR atomizer, PAPIER atomizer, sprayer; **Zerstäuberdüse** f CHEMTECH atomizer nozzle, FERTIG diffuser jet, LEBENSMITTEL atomizing nozzle
Zerstäubung f ABFALL *von Abfällen* grinding, ELEKTRO-TECH sputtering, ERDÖL *Ölverbrennung* atomization; **~ durch Glimmentladung** f KERNTECH glow discharge sputtering; **Zerstäubungsbrenner** m HEIZ & KÄLTE, THERMOD atomizing burner
zerstörend: nicht ~e Prüfung f MASCHINEN, PHYS nondestructive test; **~es Prüfverfahren** nt WERKPRÜF destructive testing; **~er Versuch** m MASCHINEN, WERK-PRÜF destructive test
Zerstörfestigkeit f ELEKTRIZ destruction resistance
Zerstörung: ~ durch Stoß f STRAHLPHYS collisional destruction
zerstörungsfrei: ~es Prüfsystem nt MASCHINEN nondestructive testing system; **~e Prüfung** nt MASCHINEN, PHYS nondestructive testing, RAUMFAHRT NDT, nondestructive testing; **~e Prüfverfahren** nt MASCHINEN NDT, nondestructive testing; **~e Werkstoffprüfung** f KERNTECH nondestructive materials testing
Zerstrahlung f TEILPHYS annihilation; **Zerstrahlungsfoton** nt STRAHLPHYS annihilation photon
zersträuben vt FERTIG reduce
Zerstreuen: ~ von Elektronenballungen nt ELEKTRONIK debunching
zerstreuen vt FOTO, OPTIK *Licht* diffuse
zerstreut: ~e Reflexion f ELEKTROTECH diffuse reflection
Zerstreuung f ELEKTROTECH dissipation, KOHLEN dispersion; **Zerstreuungskreis** m FOTO circle of confusion; **Zerstreuungslinse** f PHYS diverging lens; **Zerstreuungsscheibchen: am wenigsten wahrnehmbares ~** nt FOTO circle of least confusion; **Zerstreuungsvermögen** nt PHYS dispersive power
Zerstückeln nt ABFALL crushing

Zerstückelung f COMP & DV fragmentation
Zerteilung f CHEMIE deflocculation
Zertifikat: ~ der Werft nt WASSERTRANS builder's certificate
Zertifizierung f COMP & DV, QUAL certification; **Zertifizierungsstelle** f QUAL certification body; **Zertifizierungssystem** nt QUAL certification system
zertrümmern vt KOHLEN fragment
Zertrümmerung f METALL fragmentation
Zetteln nt TEXTIL beaming, warping
zetteln vt TEXTIL warp
Zf[1] abbr *(Zwischenfrequenz)* ELEKTRONIK, RADIO, TELEKOM IF *(intermediate frequency)*
Zf[2]: **Zf-Durchschlag** m RADIO IF breakthrough
Zfm abbr *(Zwischenfrequenzmodulation)* ELEKTRONIK, RADIO, TELEKOM IFM *(intermediate frequency modulation)*
Zf: Zf-Oberwelle f RADIO IF harmonic; **Zf-Signal** nt ELEKTRONIK IF signal; **Zf-Stufe** f ELEKTRONIK IF stage; **Zf-Unterdrückung** f ELEKTRONIK IF rejection; **Zf-Verstärker** m ELEKTRONIK IF amplifier; **Zf-Verstärkung** f ELEKTRONIK IF amplification
Zibeton nt CHEMIE cibetone, civetone
Zickzackkerbe f KERNTECH chevron notch
Zickzacklaufschienen f pl KER & GLAS nog plate chevron runner bars
Zickzackpackung f KER & GLAS staggered packing
Zickzackverbindung f ELEKTRIZ zigzag connection
Zickzackversetzung f METALL zigzag dislocation
Ziegel m KER & GLAS tile; **Ziegelbogen** m BAU brick arch; **Ziegelbrand** m KER & GLAS batch; **Ziegelbrenner** m KER & GLAS tile burner; **Ziegeldraht** m KER & GLAS sling; **Ziegelei** f KER & GLAS brick works; **Ziegelerde** f BAU brick earth; **Ziegelfabrik** f KER & GLAS tile factory; **Ziegelhersteller** m KER & GLAS tile maker; **Ziegelherstellungsmaschine** f KER & GLAS brick and tile machine; **Ziegelklammer** f KER & GLAS tile cramp; **Ziegelmauer** f BAU brick wall; **Ziegelmauerwerk** nt BAU brickwork
Ziegeln: mit ~ mauern vt BAU brick
Ziegel: Ziegelofen m BAU brick kiln; **Ziegelpflaster** nt BAU brick pavement (BrE), brick sidewalk (AmE); **Ziegelpflasterung** f BAU brick paving; **Ziegelpresse** f KER & GLAS brick molding machine (AmE), brick moulding machine (BrE), tile press; **Ziegelrohling** m KER & GLAS cob brick; **Ziegelstein** m BAU, KER & GLAS brick; **Ziegelton** m BAU brick clay, loam, KER & GLAS common clay; **Ziegelwand** f BAU brick wall
Ziehbank f FERTIG *Ziehen* rack
Ziehbrettformen nt FERTIG striking
Ziehdorn m KER & GLAS mandrel, mandril
Ziehdüse f FERTIG drawing die, *Draht* die plate, *Drahtzug* hole, KER & GLAS debiteuse; **Ziehdüsenblase** f KER & GLAS debiteuse bubble; **Ziehdüsenschlitz** m KER & GLAS slot
Zieheisen nt FERTIG drawing die, drawing plate, drawplate, *Ziehen* die plate
Ziehen nt KUNSTSTOFF drawing, MASCHINEN pulling, PAPIER draw, pull, TRANS haulage;
ziehen[1] vt BAU *Schrauben* drive, FERTIG *Nuten* cut, MATH extract, PAPIER draw, pull, TRANS haul
ziehen[2] vi BAU draw; **~ lassen** vi LEBENSMITTEL infuse
Ziehen: ~ von Blechgefäßen nt FERTIG cupping; **~ eines Nagels** nt MASCHINEN pulling out of a nail; **~ von Schlüssen** nt KÜNSTL INT inference, reasoning
Ziehfaden m TEXTIL snag

Ziehfähigkeit *f* FERTIG drawability
Ziehfett *nt* FERTIG drawing grease
Ziehglas *nt* KER & GLAS drawn glass
Ziehgrenze *f* FERTIG drawing limit
Ziehkeil *m* MASCHINEN draw key; **Ziehkeilgetriebe** *nt* MASCHINEN draw-key transmission
Ziehkissen *nt* FERTIG *Presse* cushion, die cushion
Ziehklinge *f* BAU spokeshave
Ziehkopf *m* FERTIG *Räummaschine* draw head
Ziehmittel *nt* FERTIG drawing compound
Ziehräumen *nt* FERTIG, MASCHINEN pull-broaching
Ziehräumnadel *f* FERTIG, MASCHINEN pull broach
Ziehring *m* FERTIG drawing ring, *Tiefziehen* die
Ziehschleifen *nt* FERTIG, MASCHINEN honing
ziehschleifen *vt* FERTIG, MASCHINEN, MECHAN hone
Ziehschleifmaschine *f* MECHAN honing machine
Ziehschleifwerkzeug *nt* FERTIG hone
Ziehschütze *f* NICHTFOSS ENERG sliding sluice
Ziehstab *m* KER & GLAS draw rod
Ziehstange *f* FERTIG drawing clamp
Ziehstein *m* FERTIG *Ziehen* flatter
Ziehstempel *m* FERTIG deep-drawing punch, drawing punch, *Tiefziehen* punch, MASCHINEN drawing punch
Ziehstufe *f* FERTIG *Ziehen* reduction
Ziehtrichter *m* MECHAN die
Ziehtrommel *f* FERTIG drawing block
Ziehturm *m* KER & GLAS drawing tower
Ziehverpackung *f* VERPACK deep-drawn packaging
Ziehvorgang *m* TELEKOM drawing process
Ziehvorrichtung *f* ELEKTRONIK *Halbleitertechnik* active pull-up device, KER & GLAS drawing machine
Ziehwanne *f* KER & GLAS bushing assembly; **Ziehwannengebläse** *nt* KER & GLAS bushing blower
Ziehwerkzeug *nt* FERTIG cupping tool
Ziehzange *f* FERTIG gripping jaws; **~ zur Entfernung von Heftklammern** *f* VERPACK stapling pliers
Ziehzwiebel *f* KER & GLAS onion
Ziel:[1] **mit ~ Weltraum** *adj* RAUMFAHRT space-bound
Ziel[2] *nt* COMP & DV, ERGON, FERNSEH, QUAL target
Ziel:[3] **über das ~ hinausgehen** *vt* MECHAN overshoot
Ziel: ~ der Sekundäremission *nt* ELEKTRONIK secondary emission target; **Zielansteuerung** *f* WASSERTRANS *Navigation* homing
zielbeleuchtend: ~er Laser *m* ELEKTRONIK target-illuminating laser
Ziel: Zielcomputer *m* COMP & DV target computer; **Zielebene** *f* COMP & DV target level; **Zielelektrode** *f* ELEKTROTECH, FERNSEH target electrode; **Zielen** *nt* BAU sighting; **Zielerkennung** *f* ERGON target detection; **Zielfahrt** *f* WASSERTRANS *Navigation* homing; **Zielfenster** *nt* RAUMFAHRT firing window; **Zielfernrohr** *nt* BAU sighting telescope; **Zielführung per Radio** *f* TRANS route guidance by radio
zielgesteuert: ~es System *nt* KÜNSTL INT goal-driven system
Ziel: Zielgitter *nt* FERNSEH target mesh; **Zielprogramm** *nt* COMP & DV object program; **Zielrechner** *m* COMP & DV target computer; **Zielscheibe** *f* TEILPHYS target; **Zielschicht** *f* FERNSEH target layer; **Zielsignal** *nt* ELEKTRONIK target signal; **Zielsprache** *f* COMP & DV object language, target language; **Zielsuchkopf** *m* RAUMFAHRT homing head; **Zielsuchlenkung** *f* RAUMFAHRT homing; **Zielverfolgungsstation** *f* TRANS radar tracking station; **Zielverkehr** *m* TRANS terminating traffic; **Zielvermittlungsstelle** *f* TELEKOM destination exchange; **Zielweg** *m* WASSERTRANS track

Zierbuchstabe *m* DRUCK swash letter
Zierleiste *f* BAU batten, molding (AmE), moulding (BrE), DRUCK ornamental border, KFZTECH *Karosserie* chrome strip
Zierlinie *f* DRUCK ornamental rule
Zierscheibe *f* KFZTECH wheel cover
Ziffer *f* COMP & DV digit, DRUCK figure, numeral, MATH digit, numeral; **Ziffern- oder Zeichenfeld** *nt* COMP & DV figures case; **Ziffernanzeige** *f* GERÄT digital display, digital readout; **Ziffernblatt** *nt* MASCHINEN dial, dial plate; **Ziffernradschalter** *m* ELEKTRIZ thumb wheel switch; **Zifferntaste** *f* COMP & DV numeric key; **Ziffernumschaltung** *f* TELEKOM figure shift
Zigarrenantenne *f* RAUMFAHRT cigar antenna
Zimmer *nt* BAU room; **Zimmerantenne** *f* ELEKTROTECH indoor antenna; **Zimmerei** *f* BAU carpentry; **Zimmerhandwerk** *nt* BAU carpentry
Zimmermann *m* BAU carpenter; **Zimmermannshammer** *m* BAU claw hammer; **Zimmermannsstek** *m* WASSERTRANS *Knoten* timber hitch
Zimmer: Zimmertemperatur *f* PHYS, THERMOD room temperature
Zimtblütenöl *nt* LEBENSMITTEL cassia oil
Zimtsäurebenzylester *m* LEBENSMITTEL benzyl cinnamate
Zimtsäureethylester *m* LEBENSMITTEL ethyl cinnamate
Zingiberen *nt* CHEMIE zingiberene
Zink *nt* CHEMIE zinc
Zinkat *nt* CHEMIE zincate
Zink: Zinkätzung *f* DRUCK zinc etching; **Zinkblech** *nt* FERTIG sheet zinc; **Zinkblume** *f* FERTIG spangle; **Zinkdampf** *m* KOHLEN zinc vapor (AmE), zinc vapour (BrE)
Zinke *f* BAU tine, MASCHINEN prong; **Zinkenfräser** *m* FERTIG dovetail cutter
Zink: Zinkkondensation *f* KOHLEN zinc condensation; **Zink-Luft-Akkumulator** *m* KFZTECH zinc-air storage battery; **Zinkoxid** *nt* KUNSTSTOFF zinc oxide; **Zinkplatte** *f* DRUCK zinc plate; **Zinkschutzüberzug** *m* ANSTRICH galvanized protective coating; **Zinküberzug** *m* KUNSTSTOFF zinc coating
Zinkung *f* FERTIG *Holz* dovetail
Zinn *nt* (*Sn*) CHEMIE tin (*Sn*); **Zinn-** *pref* CHEMIE stannic; **Zinndioxid** *nt* CHEMIE stannic oxide; **Zinnfolie** *f* METALL tinfoil; **Zinngießerei** *f* FERTIG pewtery; **Zinnlöten** *nt* BAU soldering; **Zinnoxid** *nt* CHEMIE stannic oxide; **Zinnsäureanhydrid** *nt* CHEMIE stannic oxide; **Zinnstreifen** *m* KER & GLAS tin streak
Zipfel *m* FERTIG *Tiefziehen* scallop; **Zipfelkante** *f* TEXTIL wavy selvedge; **Zipfelziehen** *nt* FERTIG *beim Tiefziehen* earing
Zirconat *nt* CHEMIE zirconate
Zirconium *nt* (*Zr*) CHEMIE zirconium (*Zr*); **Zirconium-** *pref* CHEMIE zirconic; **Zirconiumdioxid** *nt* CHEMIE zirconia; **Zirconiumoxid** *nt* CHEMIE *Mineralogie* zirconia
Zirconyl- *pref* CHEMIE zirconyl
Zirkaloy *nt* KERNTECH zircaloy, zirconium base alloy; **Zirkaloy-Hülse** *f* KERNTECH zircaloy cladding, zircaloy hull
Zirkel *m* BAU compass, GEOM compasses, pair of compasses, MASCHINEN compasses
Zirkon *m* KER & GLAS zircon; **Zirkonerde** *f* KER & GLAS zirconia; **Zirkonerzeugnis** *nt* KER & GLAS zircon refractory; **Zirkonoxiderzeugnis** *nt* KER & GLAS zirconia refractory; **Zirkonschwamm** *m* KERNTECH zirconium sponge

zirkular: ~ **polarisierte Welle** *f* AKUSTIK circularly-polarized wave; PHYS circular-polarized wave; ~ **polarisierte Wellen** *f pl* WELLPHYS circular waves
zirkulär *adj* GEOM circular
zirkularisieren *vt* RAUMFAHRT *Umlaufbahn* circularize
Zirkularisierung: ~ **der Umlaufbahn** *f* RAUMFAHRT *Änderung in kreisförmige Umlaufbahn* circularization of orbit
Zirkularpolarisation *f* PHYS, TELEKOM circular polarization; ~ **des Lichtes** *f* STRAHLPHYS circular polarization of light
zirkularpolarisierte Hornspeisung *f*; ~ *f* RADIO circular horn feed
Zirkularpolarisierung *f* RADIO circular polarization
Zirkulation *f* ERDÖL *Bohrschlamm*, MASCHINEN circulation; **Zirkulationskessel** *m* HYDRAUL circulating boiler; **Zirkulationspumpe** *f* HYDRAUL circulating pump; **Zirkulationsverlust** *m* ERDÖL *Bohrschlamm* lost circulation
Zirkulator *m* TELEKOM *Wellenleiter* circulator
Zirpen *nt* OPTIK *vogelstimmenähnliche Frequenz* chirping
Zischen *nt* AUFNAHME *Mikrofon* sibilance
Zischfilter *nt* AUFNAHME hiss filter
Zischventil *nt* HYDRAUL pet valve
Ziselierung *f* KONSTZEICH chasing
Zisterne *f* WASSERVERSORG cistern
Zitat *nt* DRUCK quotation
Zitieren *nt* PATENT citation
zitieren *vt* PATENT cite
Zitronensäure *f* LEBENSMITTEL citric acid
Zitterbewegung *f* ELEKTRONIK *Überwindung von Reibung durch periodische Erregung des zu bewegenden Teils* dither
zitterfrei *adj* ELEKTRONIK *Fernsehen* jitter-free
Zittern *nt* GERÄT *Zeiger* jitter
Zitteroszillator *m* ELEKTRONIK dither oscillator
Zivilflugvorschriften *f pl (CAR)* RAUMFAHRT Civil Air Regulations *(CAR)*
Zivilisationsmüll *m* ABFALL waste products of civilization
Z-Koordinate *f* PHYS z-coordinate
Zoll *m* FERTIG *Kunststoffinstallationen* in, inch, METALL inch, METROL in, inch, TRANS customs; ~ **pro Sekunde** *m pl* AUFNAHME, COMP & DV IPS, inches per second; **Zollabfertigung** *f* LUFTTRANS clearance, TRANS customs clearance, WASSERTRANS clearance; **Zollflughafen** *m* LUFTTRANS airport of entry; **Zollfreischein** *m* WASSERTRANS shipping bill; **Zollfreizone** *f* WASSERTRANS *Hafen* bonded area; **Zollgewinde** *nt* MASCHINEN inch thread; **Zollgut** *nt* ERDÖL *Handel* bonded goods; **Zollkutter** *m* WASSERTRANS *Zoll* revenue cutter; **Zollmaß** *nt* FERTIG imperial measure; **Zollschranke** *f* TRANS turnpike (AmE); **Zollschraubengewinde** *nt* MASCHINEN inch screw thread; **Zollspeicher** *m* WASSERTRANS *Zoll* bonded warehouse; **Zollstock** *m* BAU carpenter's gage (AmE), carpenter's gauge (BrE), TEXTIL yardstick; **Zollstreifenboot** *nt* WASSERTRANS *Zoll* customs patrol boat
Zone *f* COMP & DV, KOHLEN, METALL, RADIO zone, TELEKOM cell; ~ **gleichmäßiger Beanspruchung** *f* MASCHINEN section of uniform strength; ~ **stärkster Beanspruchung** *f* MASCHINEN section of maximum intensity of stress; **Zonenbit** *nt* COMP & DV zone bit; **Zonenformation** *f* METALL zone formation
zonengehärtet: ~**es Glas** *nt* KER & GLAS zone-toughened glass

Zone: **Zonenhärtung** *f* KER & GLAS zone toughening; **Zonenreinigung** *f* METALL zone refining; **Zonenschmelzverfahren** *nt* KERNTECH, METALL zone melting; **Zonenzeit** *f* WASSERTRANS zone time, *Navigation* standard time
Zoom *nt* COMP & DV zoom; **Zoomaufnahme** *f* FOTO zoom picture
Zoomen *nt* COMP & DV, *Vergrößerung/Verkleinerung der Bildschirmdarstellung* zoom, zooming
Zoom: **Zoomhebel** *m* FERNSEH zoom lever; **Zoomobjektiv** *nt* FOTO zoom lens
Zoosterin *nt* CHEMIE zoosterine, zoosterol
Zr *(Zirconium)* CHEMIE Zr *(zirconium)*
Z/Sek *abbr (Zeichen pro Sekunde)* DRUCK cps *(characters per second)*
Z-Spannung *f* PHYS Zener voltage
Z-Stab *m* METALL Z-bar
Z-Stahl *m* METALL zees
Z/Std *abbr (Zeichen pro Stunde)* DRUCK cph *(characters per hour)*
Z-Teilchen *nt* TEILPHYS Z-particle
Zubehör *nt* GERÄT attachment, MECHAN component, TEXTIL appliance; **Zubehörtasche** *f* FOTO gadget bag; **Zubehörteile** *nt pl* TEXTIL appliance parts
zubereitet *adj* LEBENSMITTEL *Speise* dressed
Zubereitung *f* KUNSTSTOFF formulation
Zubringen *nt* FERTIG loading
zubringen *vt* FERTIG *Räumwerkzeug* handle
Zubringer *m* EISENBAHN feeder line, feeder train; ~ **Erde-Orbit** *m* RAUMFAHRT earth-to-orbit shuttle; **Zubringer-Airline** *f* LUFTTRANS *Lufttransport* feeder airline; **Zubringerbesen** *m* ABFALL *am Kehrfahrzeug* feeder broom; **Zubringerkabel** *nt* COMP & DV feeder cable; **Zubringerluftverkehrslinie** *f* LUFTTRANS feeder line; **Zubringerschiff** *nt* WASSERTRANS feeder ship; **Zubringerstraße** *f* TRANS collector road; **Zubringerverkehr** *m* LUFTTRANS shuttle service
Zubringung *f* FERTIG handling
Zubruchbauen: ~ **des Hangenden** *nt* KOHLEN broken working
züchten *vt* FERTIG *Kristalle* grow
Züchtung *f* FERTIG growing
Zucker *m* LEBENSMITTEL sugar; **Zuckerguß** *m* LEBENSMITTEL frosting, icing; **Zuckern** *nt* LEBENSMITTEL sugaring; **Zuckerrohrabfallwalze** *f* LEBENSMITTEL bagasse roller; **Zuckerrohrsaft** *m* LEBENSMITTEL *Zuckerraffination* cane juice
zudruckumformen *vt* FERTIG stretch-squeeze form
zuerst: ~ **Abgelegtes wird als erstes bearbeitet** *phr (FIFO-Prinzip)* COMP & DV first-in-first-out *(FIFO)*
Zufahrt *f* BAU approach; **Zufahrtdosierung** *f* LUFTTRANS ramp metering; **Zufahrtsrampe** *f* BAU, TRANS access ramp; **Zufahrtsrinne** *f* WASSERTRANS *Navigation* approach channel; **Zufahrtssperrsignal** *nt* LUFTTRANS ramp closure sign; **Zufahrtstraße** *f* BAU access road
Zufall- *pref* COMP & DV, ELEKTROTECH, METALL, QUAL random
zufällig[1] *adj* COMP & DV, ERGON, GEOM stochastic, METROL random
zufällig:[2] ~**er Ausfluß** *m* UMWELTSCHMUTZ accidental discharge; ~**e Ergebnisabweichung** *f* QUAL random error of result; ~**er Fehler** *m* GERÄT, PHYS random error; ~**er Impuls** *m* TELEKOM random pulse; ~**e Phasenfehler** *m pl* FERNSEH random phase errors; ~**e Stichprobenauswahl** *f* MATH random sampling; ~**e**

Stichprobenentnahme f MATH random sampling
zufallsabhängig: ~es Signal nt GERÄT accidental signal
Zufall-: **Zufallsabtastung** f COMP & DV random scan;
Zufallsanordnung f METALL random arrangement;
Zufallsausfall m COMP & DV, ELEKTROTECH, TELEKOM
random failure; **Zufallsbelastung** f METALL random
loading; **Zufallseinflüsse** m pl QUAL chance causes;
Zufallsergebnis nt ELEKTRONIK random event; **Zu-
fallsfehler** m COMP & DV random error, ELEKTROTECH
random failure, GERÄT, KOHLEN, METROL, TELEKOM
random error
zufallsgestreut: ~es **Stichprobenverfahren** nt CHEMIE
random sampling
Zufall-: **Zufallsgröße** f QUAL random variable, variate;
Zufallslogik f ELEKTRONIK random logic; **Zufallslö-
sung** f METALL random solution; **Zufallsmodell** nt
COMP & DV stochastic model; **Zufallsmodulation** f AKU-
STIK accidental inflection; **Zufallsnummer** f COMP & DV
random number; **Zufallsprobenahme** f QUAL random
sampling; **Zufallssignal** nt ELEKTRONIK, TELEKOM,
WASSERTRANS Radar random signal; **Zufallsspannung**
f ELEKTROTECH random voltage; **Zufallsstichprobe** f
LEBENSMITTEL, QUAL random sample; **Zufallsstich-
probenuntersuchung** f QUAL random sampling;
Zufallsstreubereich m QUAL random dispersion inter-
val; **Zufallsstreuung** f KERNTECH random scattering,
QUAL chance variation; **Zufallsvariable** f COMP & DV,
ELEKTRONIK, QUAL random variable; **Zufallsverkehr**
m TELEKOM pure chance traffic; **Zufallsverteilung** f
COMP & DV probability distribution; **Zufallswicklung** f
ELEKTRIZ, ELEKTROTECH random winding; **Zufalls-
zahl** f COMP & DV random number;
Zufallszahlengenerator m COMP & DV, TELEKOM ran-
dom number generator
Zufassung f ERGON seize grip
Zufluß m WASSERVERSORG inflow, von Wasser influx of
water
Zufrieren nt THERMOD freeze-up
Zuführapparat m VERPACK feeder
zuführen vt BAU supply, COMP & DV, ELEKTROTECH Strom
feed; ~ **und entlüften** vt KERNTECH feed and bleed
Zuführkabel nt ELEKTRIZ lead-in cable
Zuführleitung f KERNTECH feedline
Zuführrollgang m FERTIG Walzen feed roller table
Zuführtisch m VERPACK feeding table
Zufuhrtrichter m VERPACK feed hopper
Zuführung f COMP & DV, ELEKTROTECH Strom, HY-
DRAUL, KFZTECH feed, PAPIER feeding; ~ **in
Längsrichtung** f KONTROLL endwise feed; **Zuführungs-
bewegung** f FERTIG Spanung feed motion; **Zuführungs-
walze** f MASCHINEN feed roll, feed roller,
PAPIER leading-in roll
Zuführwalze f LEBENSMITTEL feed roller
Zug:[1] **auf ~ wirkend** adj FERTIG drawback
Zug[2] m BAU Festigkeitslehre tension, FERTIG Schweißen
run, KER & GLAS pull, MASCHINEN draft (AmE),
draught (BrE), pull, tension, OPTIK draw, RAUMFAHRT
pull; ~ **mit beschränkter Platzzahl** m EISENBAHN limited train; ~ **mit Postbeförderung** m EISENBAHN mail
train; ~~ **und Tragseil** nt TRANS hauling and carrying
rope
Zugabe f FERTIG introduction, MASCHINEN allowance
Zug: **Zugabstand** m EISENBAHN train spacing; **Zugabteil**
nt EISENBAHN Im Zug passenger compartment; **Zug-
achse** f METALL tensile axis
Zugang m BAU approach, COMP & DV Datenkommunika-

tion KOHLEN, RAUMFAHRT Raumschiff access, TELE-
KOM access, data port, port
zugänglich: ~e **Reservenquelle** f NICHTFOSS ENERG ac-
cessible resource base
Zugänglichkeit f MECHAN accessibility, ease of access
Zugang: **Zugangsberechtigung** f COMP & DV password;
Zugangsburstzeichen nt TELEKOM access burst signal;
Zugangsgebühr f TELEKOM access charge rate;
Zugangskanal m TELEKOM access channel; **Zugangs-
konzentrator** m TELEKOM access concentrator;
Zugangsleitung f TELEKOM access circuit; **Zugangs-
netz** nt TELEKOM access network; **Zugangsnummer** f
TELEKOM access number; **Zugangspunkt** m TELEKOM
access port, data port, Netzwerk port; **Zugangsrampe**
f RAUMFAHRT walkway; **Zugangsstollen** m BAU Tun-
nelbau adit; **Zugangstafel** f RAUMFAHRT Raumschiff
access panel; **Zugangstür** f LUFTTRANS access door
Zug: **Zuganker** m BAU stay, tie bar, tie rod, FERTIG tie,
MASCHINEN tension rod, MECHAN connecting rod,
WASSERTRANS tie rod; **Zugarm** m COMP & DV tension
arm; **Zugauflösung** f EISENBAHN splitting up trains;
Zugbalken m BAU stretcher, tie beam; **Zugband** nt
FERTIG tie rod
zugbeansprucht: ~es **Element** nt MASCHINEN tension
member; ~es **Glied** nt MEERSCHMUTZ tension member
Zug: **Zugbeanspruchung** f MASCHINEN, MECHAN, MET-
ALL tensile stress
zugbedient: ~e **Wegübergangssicherungsanlage** f EI-
SENBAHN automatic level crossing safety installation
Zug: **Zugbeförderungsverfahren** nt EISENBAHN method
of routing; **Zugbegleiter** m EISENBAHN pilot; **Zug-
belastung** f MASCHINEN, METALL tensile strain;
Zugbildung f EISENBAHN marshaling (AmE), marshalling (BrE); **Zugbinder** m BAU through binder;
Zugbrücke f BAU drawbridge; **Zugdeichsel** f BAU
tongue; **Zugdrahtseil** nt TRANS haulage cable; **Zug-
Druck-Wechselversuch** m WERKPRÜF ten-
sion/compression testing
zugehörig: ~e **Verstärkung** f ELEKTRONIK associated
gain
Zugehörigkeit f COMP & DV membership; **Zugehörig-
keitskennzeichnung** f QUAL match marking
zugelassen[1] adj TRANS approved; **nicht ~** adj TELEKOM
nonapproved
zugelassen:[2] ~e **Sicherheitslampe** f KOHLEN approved
safety lamp
zugeordnet: ~e **Frequenz** f COMP & DV assigned frequency
zugerichtet: ~e **Ecke** f KER & GLAS dubbed corner
zugeschärft: ~e **Kante** f BAU feather edge
zugesetzt adj MASCHINEN clogged
zugespitzt: ~e **Faser** f OPTIK tapered fiber (AmE), tapered fibre (BrE)
zugewiesen: ~e **Frequenz** f FERNSEH allocated frequency; ~er **Kanal** m FERNSEH dedicated channel
Zug: **Zugfahrer** m EISENBAHN train driver; **Zugfahrplan**
m EISENBAHN schedule (AmE), timetable (BrE), train
schedule; **Zugfalten** f pl PAPIER ribbing; **Zugfeder** f
FERTIG helical tension spring, MASCHINEN extension
spring, tension spring
Zugfestigkeit f ANSTRICH tenacity, FERTIG Kunststoffinstallationen tensile strength, KUNSTSTOFF tensile
strength, ultimate tensile strength, MASCHINEN resistance to tension, tensile strength, ultimate tensile
strength, MECHAN tensile strength, ultimate tensile
strength, PHYS, TELEKOM, TEXTIL tensile strength; ~ **in**

ofentrockenem Zustand *f* TEXTIL oven-dry tensile strength; **Zugfestigkeitsprüfgerät** *nt* MASCHINEN tensile test equipment; **Zugfestigkeitsprüfmaschine** *f* MASCHINEN tension testing machine; **Zugfestigkeitstest** *m* ANSTRICH tensile test

Zug: **Zugfolgeabstand** *m* EISENBAHN headway; **Zugförderung** *f* EISENBAHN traction; **Zuggabel** *f* KFZTECH *Anhänger* drawbar; **Zuggeschirr** *nt* MECHAN harness; **Zuggewölbe** *nt* KER & GLAS uptake crown; **Zugglied** *nt* MASCHINEN, MEERSCHMUTZ tension member; **Zughaken** *m* EISENBAHN draw hook, KFZTECH *Anhänger* tow hook; **Zugkasten** *m* HYDRAUL draft box (AmE), draught box (BrE); **Zugkette** *f* SICHERHEIT lifting chain; **Zugklappe** *f* HEIZ & KÄLTE slide damper, RAUMFAHRT shutter; **Zugkraft** *f* BAU traction, MASCHINEN tensile force, traction, METROL tractive force, PHYS tensile force; **Zugleiter** *m* EISENBAHN traffic controller; **Zugluft** *f* HEIZ & KÄLTE draft (AmE), draught (BrE); **Zugmaschine** *f* EISENBAHN hauling engine, KFZTECH tow vehicle, traction engine, tractor, tractor unit, LUFTTRANS prime mover, MASCHINEN traction engine; **Zugnummernmelder** *m* EISENBAHN train describer; **Zugorgan** *nt* FERTIG *Keilriemen* core; **Zugöse** *f* MASCHINEN coupling ring; **Zugpersonal** *nt* EISENBAHN train crew; **Zugpropeller** *m* LUFTTRANS tractor propeller; **Zugprüfmaschine** *f* KUNSTSTOFF tensile tester; **Zugprüfung** *f* WERKPRÜF tensile test; **Zugramme** *f* MECHAN drop pile hammer; **Zugraupe** *f* FERTIG string bead; **Zugregister** *nt* HEIZ & KÄLTE slide damper; **Zugregistriereinrichtung** *f* EISENBAHN train describer; **Zugregler** *m* HEIZ & KÄLTE draft regulator (AmE), draught regulator (BrE)

zugreifen:[1] **~ auf** *vt* COMP & DV access
zugreifen[2] *vi* COMP & DV seek
Zugriff *m* COMP & DV, RADIO, TELEKOM *Speicher, Dokument* access; **~ nach der Warteschlangenmethode** *m* COMP & DV queued access method; **Zugriffsarm** *m* COMP & DV *Diskette* actuator; **Zugriffsart** *f* COMP & DV, TELEKOM access mode; **Zugriffsautorisierung** *f* COMP & DV access authority; **Zugriffsbefugnis** *f* COMP & DV access authority; **Zugriffscode** *m* COMP & DV privacy; **Zugriffsgeschwindigkeit** *f* ELEKTROTECH *Rechner* access speed; **Zugriffsliste** *f* COMP & DV access list; **Zugriffsmethode** *f* COMP & DV access method; **Zugriffsöffnung** *f* KERNTECH access port; **Zugriffspfad** *m* COMP & DV access path; **Zugriffsrecht** *nt* COMP & DV privilege; **Zugriffsschlüssel** *m* COMP & DV access key; **Zugriffstafel** *f* RAUMFAHRT *Raumschiff* access panel; **Zugriffsverfahren** *nt* TELEKOM access mode; **Zugriffszeit** *f* COMP & DV, DRUCK, ELEKTROTECH, OPTIK access time

Zug: **Zugrohr** *nt* OPTIK drawtube; **Zugsattelzapfen** *m* KFZTECH *Sattelschlepper* fifth-wheel kingpin; **Zugschaffner** *m* EISENBAHN guard; **Zugschalter** *m* ELEKTRIZ pull switch; **Zugscherversuch** *m* KUNSTSTOFF lap shear test; **Zugschraube** *f* LUFTTRANS tractor propeller; **Zugseil** *nt* BAU stay, EISENBAHN traction cable, traction rope, MASCHINEN pulling rope, traction rope, TRANS hauling rope; **Zugsicherung** *f* EISENBAHN train protection; **Zugspannung** *f* FERTIG *Kunststoffinstallationen* tensile strength, MECHAN, PHYS tensile stress; **Zugspannungsempfindlichkeit** *f* AKUSTIK tension sensitivity; **Zugspindel** *f* MASCHINEN feed shaft; **Zugspindeldrehmaschine** *f* MASCHINEN sliding lathe; **Zugstab** *m* BAU tie bar, tie rod, EISENBAHN *zur Streckensicherung* single line token

Zugstange *f* BAU anchor bar, EISENBAHN draft bar (AmE), draught bar (BrE), drawbar, KER & GLAS tie rod, KFZTECH *Anhänger* drawbar, towbar, LUFTTRANS *Hubschrauber* dog bone, tie bar, MASCHINEN drawbar, pitman, pull rod, TEXTIL tension bar, WASSERTRANS tie rod; **Zugstangenbolzen** *m* KFZTECH *Anhänger* drawbar bolt; **Zugstangenfeder** *f* EISENBAHN drawgear spring; **Zugstangenführung** *f* EISENBAHN drawbar guide

Zug: **Zugstrom** *m* KER & GLAS pull current; **Zug-Torsionsversuch** *m* WERKPRÜF tension/torsion testing; **Zugtrum** *nt* FERTIG *Riemen* driving side; **Zugüberwacher** *m* EISENBAHN traffic controller; **Zugverband** *m* EISENBAHN train rake

zugverformbar *adj* FERTIG ductile
Zug: **Zugverformungsrest** *m* KUNSTSTOFF tension set; **Zugversuch** *m* MASCHINEN, METALL tensile test; **Zugvorrichtung** *f* KFZTECH hitch; **Zugwalze** *f* KER & GLAS pull roll, PAPIER draw roll; **Zugwinkel** *m* MECHAN angle of traction; **Zugzerlegung durch Abstoß** *f* EISENBAHN fly shunting

zuhaken *vt* MASCHINEN clasp
Zuhaltung *f* BAU *Türschloß* tumbler; **Zuhaltungsschloß** *nt* BAU tumbler lock
Zukurzkommen *nt* LUFTTRANS undershoot
Zulage *f* HEIZ & KÄLTE allowance
zulassen *vt* QUAL approve
zulässig: **~es Abmaß** *nt* MASCHINEN tolerance; **~e Abweichung** *f* ANSTRICH tolerance; **~e Beanspruchung** *f* MASCHINEN safe stress; **~e Belastung** *f* KOHLEN permissible load, TRANS safe load; **~e Biegebeanspruchung** *f* MASCHINEN safe stress under bending; **~e Bügeltemperatur** *f* TEXTIL safe ironing temperature; **~e Fahrzeugfolgezeit** *f* TRANS tolerable gap between vehicles; **~es Gesamtgewicht** *nt* KFZTECH permitted gross vehicle weight, total permissible laden weight, *Rechtsvorschriften* total permissible weight; **~e Geschwindigkeit** *f* TRANS posted speed; **~e Höchstleistung** *f* TELEKOM maximum admissible power; **~e Kontaktbelastung** *f* ELEKTROTECH contact rating; **~e Landemasse** *f* LUFTTRANS allowable landing mass; **~e Last** *f* ELEKTRIZ allowable load, FERTIG design load; **~e Maßabweichung** *f* FERTIG amount of variation permitted; **~er Patentanspruch** *m* PATENT admissible claim; **~e Spannung** *f* ELEKTRIZ *Nennspannung eines Gerätes* highest voltage, ELEKTROTECH permissible current, permissible voltage; **~e Spannung an einer Wicklung** *f* ELEKTRIZ rated voltage of a winding; **~es Spektrum** *nt* KERNTECH allowed spectrum; **~e Startmasse** *f* LUFTTRANS allowable landing mass; **~er Störpegel** *m* RAUMFAHRT *Weltraumfunk* permissible level of interference; **~er Strom** *m* ELEKTROTECH permissible current; **~es Verfahren** *nt* QUAL qualified procedure; **~er Wert** *m* ELEKTRIZ rated value

Zulassung *f* ELEKTRIZ approval, KFZTECH *Rechtsvorschriften* certification, homologation, LUFTTRANS registration, QUAL approval, TRANS approval, registration, WASSERTRANS registration; **Zulassungsbescheinigung** *f* LUFTTRANS certificate of registration, QUAL certificate of accredition, TRANS approval certificate; **Zulassungsprüfung** *f* WERKPRÜF approval test; **Zulassungsüberwachung** *f* QUAL certification review; **Zulassungszeichen** *nt* QUAL certification mark
Zulauf *m* FERTIG *Gießen* runner, MECHAN intake; **Zulaufkanal** *m* WASSERVERSORG inflow canal, intake canal;

Zulaufschleuse *f* WASSERVERSORG intake sluice
Zulegierung *f* FERTIG *Elektrodenumhüllung* introduction of alloying elements
zuleiten *vt* MECHAN feed
Zuleitung *f* ELEKTRONIK lead, ELEKTROTECH feeder, *Strom* feed, *Stromdrahtversorgung* lead, *an Gerät befestigt* lead; **Zuleitungsdraht** *m* ELEKTROTECH lead wire, lead-in wire; **Zuleitungskabel** *nt* ELEKTROTECH feed cable; **Zuleitungswellenleiter** *m* ELEKTROTECH feed waveguide
Zulieferer *m* QUAL subcontractor
Zulieferpreis *m* FERTIG *Kunststoffinstallationen* cost price
Zuluft *f* HEIZ & KÄLTE fresh air, incoming air, supply air; **Zuluftkanal** *m* HEIZ & KÄLTE supply duct; **Zuluftrohr** *nt* MASCHINEN air inlet pipe; **Zuluftventilator** *m* HEIZ & KÄLTE supply air fan
zumessen *vt* BAU meter
Zumeßventil *nt* KFZTECH proportioning valve
Zumischen *nt* STRÖMPHYS entrainment
Zunahme *f* FERTIG increment
Zünddynamo *m* LUFTTRANS ignition generator
Zündeinstellmarke *f* KFZTECH timing mark
Zündeinstellung *f* KFZTECH ignition setting, ignition timing
Zündelektrode *f* ELEKTROTECH starter, starter electrode
Zünden *nt* FERTIG *Schweißen* drawing
zünden *vt* FERTIG *Lichtbogen* draw, strike, KERNTECH *Plasma*, RAUMFAHRT ignite
Zunder *m* ANSTRICH rust flake, FERTIG cinder, iron scale, metal scale, scale
Zünder *m* ELEKTRIZ igniter, FERTIG detonator, MASCHINEN, RAUMFAHRT igniter
zunderverhütend *adj* FERTIG anti-ager scale
Zündexperiment *nt* KERNTECH ignition experiment
zündfähig[1] *adj* KFZTECH, THERMOD explosive
zündfähig:[2] **~es Gemisch** *nt* KFZTECH explosive mixture
Zündflamme *f* MASCHINEN pilot flame
Zündfolge *f* KFZTECH *Motor* firing order
Zündfunke *m* ELEKTROTECH, KFZTECH spark
Zündimpuls *m* ELEKTROTECH *Gasröhren-Doppelwegthyristor* firing pulse
Zündkerze *f* ELEKTRIZ spark plug, ELEKTROTECH plug, KFZTECH spark plug, sparker, *Motor* sparking plug, *Zündung* ignition plug, plug, MECHAN ignition plug; **~ mit niedrigem Wärmewert** *f* KFZTECH hot spark plug; **Zündkerzendichtung** *f* KFZTECH spark plug gasket; **Zündkerzenelektrode** *f* KFZTECH spark plug electrode; **Zündkerzengehäuse** *nt* KFZTECH spark plug body, spark plug shell; **Zündkerzenkabel** *nt* KFZTECH spark plug cable, spark plug wire; **Zündkerzenklemmschraube** *f* KFZTECH spark plug terminal; **Zündkerzenloch** *nt* KFZTECH spark plug hole; **Zündkerzenspitze** *f* KFZTECH spark plug point
Zündkondensator *m* KFZTECH ignition capacitor
Zündkontakt *m* KFZTECH *Zündung* point
Zündkreis *m* RAUMFAHRT ignition circuit
Zündmagnet *m* ELEKTRIZ magneto, KFZTECH *Zündung* ignition magneto, magneto
Zündpunkt *m* ERDÖL *Physik*, PHYS ignition point
zundrig *adj* FERTIG scaly
Zündschalter *m* KFZTECH ignition starter switch, *Zündung* ignition switch
Zündschlüssel *m* KFZTECH ignition key
Zündspannung *f* ELEKTROTECH *Gasröhren-Doppelwegthyristor*, KFZTECH firing voltage

Zündspule *f* ELEKTRIZ, ELEKTROTECH ignition coil, KFZTECH ignition coil, *Zündung* coil, LUFTTRANS ignition coil; **Zündspulenprimärwicklung** *f* KFZTECH primary winding
Zündstecker *m* KFZTECH *Zündung* ignition plug
Zündstellwinkel *m* KFZTECH *Zündung* timing angle
Zündstift *m* ELEKTROTECH ignitor; **Zündstiftröhre** *f* ELEKTROTECH ignitron
Zündtemperatur *f* MASCHINEN ignition temperature
Zündtransformator *m* ELEKTROTECH ignition transformer
Zündung *f* ELEKTRIZ ignition, ELEKTRONIK *Magnetron* firing, ELEKTROTECH *Gasröhren-Doppelwegthyristor* firing, *Gasröhre* ignition, *Lichtbogen* striking, FERTIG striking, KFZTECH, LUFTTRANS, MASCHINEN, RAUMFAHRT ignition, TRANS sparking
Zündunterbrecher *m* KFZTECH *Motor* contact breaker; **Zündunterbrecherkontakt** *m* KFZTECH contact breaker point (BrE), points; **Zündunterbrechernocken** *m* KFZTECH distributor cam
Zündversteller *m* KFZTECH *Zündung* advance mechanism
Zündverstellung *f* KFZTECH timing
Zündverteiler *m* KFZTECH, MASCHINEN ignition distributor; **Zündverteileranlage** *f* LUFTTRANS ignition harness
Zündverteilung *f* KFZTECH *Zündung* distribution
Zündvorrichtung *f* FERTIG primer, HEIZ & KÄLTE ignition device
Zündwinkel *m* ELEKTROTECH *Gasentladungsröhre* blocking period
Zündzeit *f* ELEKTROTECH *Gasröhren-Doppelwegthyristor* firing time
Zündzeitpunkt *m* KFZTECH ignition point, *Zündung* point, MECHAN ignition point; **Zündzeitpunkteinstellung** *f* KFZTECH spark timing, timing of ignition; **Zündzeitpunktmarke** *f* KFZTECH timing mark
zunehmend: **~e Erwärmung** *f* UMWELTSCHMUTZ incremental heating; **~e Polarisation** *f* ELEKTROTECH mounting polarization; **~e Steigung** *f* LUFTTRANS *Hubschrauber* pitch increase
Zunge *f* BAU tongue, FERTIG *Schieblehre* blade, LABOR hand, pointer, MASCHINEN tongue, MATH *des Rechenschiebers* cursor; **~ der Glasmacherpfeife** *f* KER & GLAS tongue; **Zungenband** *nt* BAU T-hinge, cross-garnet hinge, cross-garnet hinge; **Zungenfrequenzmesser** *m* GERÄT vibration reed frequency meter, LABOR vibrating-reed frequency meter; **Zungenfrequenzmeßgerät** *nt* GERÄT *für die Netzfrequenz, Zunge unter Schutzgas* reed frequency meter, LABOR vibrating-reed frequency meter, vibration reed frequency meter; **Zungenhorn** *nt* WASSERTRANS *Navigation* reed horn; **Zungenkontakt** *m* TELEKOM reed contact; **Zungennadel** *f* TEXTIL latch needle; **Zungenschalter** *m* PHYS reed switch; **Zungenspitze** *f* EISENBAHN *Weiche* tip of switch tongue; **Zungenverschluß** *m* EISENBAHN point lock; **Zungenweiche** *f* EISENBAHN point switch
zuordnen *vt* COMP & DV allocate, assign, translate, *Datenverarbeitung* allocate
Zuordner *m* KONTROLL sequencer, TELEKOM translator
Zuordnung *f* COMP & DV, ELEKTROTECH, RADIO allocation; **~ nach Anforderung** *f* RAUMFAHRT *Weltraumfunk* demand assignment; **Zuordnungsanweisung** *f* COMP & DV *Programmiersprache* assignment statement; **Zuordnungsbefehl** *m* COMP & DV reference instruction; **Zuordnungsdatei** *f* COMP & DV reference file

Zupfen *nt* KER & GLAS pluck, TEXTIL plucking
Zurichtebogen *m* DRUCK makeready sheet
Zurichten *nt* BAU *von Holz* dressing
zurichten *vt* BAU size, *Holz* trim, DRUCK make ready
Zurichthammer *m* BAU maul
Zurichtungsbogen *m* DRUCK makeready sheet
Zurring *f* WASSERTRANS *Ladung* lashing
Zurrungsplan *m* WASSERTRANS *Ladung* lashing plan
zurück:[1] ~ **zur Ausgangsgröße** *adj* RAUMFAHRT *Gyroskop* anisoelastic
zurück[2] *adv* WASSERTRANS *Fahrt/Motor* astern
zurückbleibend[1] *adj* KOHLEN residual
zurückbleibend:[2] ~**e Magnetisierung** *f* ELEKTROTECH remanence, PHYS remanent magnetization
Zurückfedern *nt* FERTIG resilience
zurückfedern *vi* MASCHINEN spring back
zurückgeben *vt* COMP & DV return
zurückgelegt: ~**e Fahrtstrecke** *f* LUFTTRANS mileage
zurückgewiesen: ~**er Verkehr** *m* TELEKOM lost traffic
zurückgewinnen *vt* ABFALL *Rohstoffe*, KOHLEN, UMWELTSCHMUTZ recover
Zurückgewinnung *f* KOHLEN recovery
zurückgewonnen: ~**es Öl** *nt* UMWELTSCHMUTZ *Altölregenerierung* recovered oil
zurückgeworfen: ~**es Signal** *nt* ELEKTRONIK reflected signal
zurückhalten *vt* BAU retain
Zurückhaltung *f* ELEKTROTECH, WASSERVERSORG retention
zurückkehren *vi* COMP & DV return
Zurückklappen *nt* AUFNAHME foldback; ~ **des Luftschraubenblattes** *nt* LUFTTRANS *Hubschrauber* blade folding
zurücklaufen: ~ **lassen** *vt* COMP & DV rewind
zurücknehmen *vt* PATENT *Registrierung* abandon
zurückrollen *vi* LUFTTRANS backtrack
Zurückschieben *nt* LUFTTRANS push-back
zurückschieben *vt* LUFTTRANS push back
Zurückschwenken: ~ **des Luftschraubenblattes** *nt* LUFTTRANS blade folding
zurücksenden *vt* PHYS reflect
zurückspeichern *vt* COMP & DV restore
zurückspringen *vi* COMP & DV return
zurückspulen *vt* AUFNAHME, COMP & DV rewind
zurückstellen *vt* COMP & DV reset
Zurückverfolgung *f* COMP & DV backtracking
zurückweisen *vt* QUAL reject
Zurückweisung *f* COMP & DV rejection, PATENT refusal, QUAL final rejection, rejection; **Zurückweisungsfehler** *m* COMP & DV rejection error; **Zurückweisungszahl** *f* QUAL rejection number
zurückwerfen *vt* PHYS reflect
zurückziehen *vt* KOHLEN retreat
zurückzuweisend: ~**e Qualitätsgrenzlage** *f* QUAL rejectable quality level
Zusammenarbeit *f* TELEKOM *zwischen Netzen* interworking
Zusammenbacken *nt* KUNSTSTOFF, LEBENSMITTEL caking
zusammenbacken *vi* LEBENSMITTEL cake
Zusammenballen *nt* FOTO *von Körnern* grain clumping, KOHLEN, METALL balling
zusammenballen[1] *vt* KOHLEN agglomerate, METALL *Reifen* ball up
zusammenballen:[2] **sich** ~ *v refl* CHEMIE flocculate
zusammenbändeln *vt* WASSERTRANS tie up

Zusammenbau *m* BAU *Balkenträger* framing, MASCHINEN, MECHAN assembly
zusammenbauen *vt* BAU assemble, mount; **wieder** ~ *vt* BAU reassemble
Zusammenbau: **Zusammenbauwerkzeuge** *nt pl* MASCHINEN assembly tools; **Zusammenbauzeichnung** *f* KONSTZEICH, MASCHINEN, MECHAN assembly drawing
zusammenbinden *vt* MASCHINEN band
zusammenblatten *vt* BAU *Holzbau* halve
zusammenbrechen[1] *vt* BAU break down
zusammenbrechen[2] *vi* BAU break down
Zusammenbruch *m* BAU breakdown, failure, ELEKTRIZ, PHYS breakdown
Zusammendrücken *nt* FERTIG *Rohr* flattening, KUNSTSTOFF, MASCHINEN compression
Zusammenfallen *nt* UMWELTSCHMUTZ subsidence
zusammenfassen *vt* COMP & DV abstract
Zusammenfassung *f* COMP & DV summary, DRUCK *eines wissenschaftlichen Artikels*, PATENT abstract
Zusammenfluß *m* WASSERVERSORG confluence
Zusammenfügen *nt* BAU, KER & GLAS joining, KERNTECH jointing
zusammenfügen *vt* BAU join on to, MASCHINEN join
Zusammenfügung *f* KERNTECH joining, RADIO junction
Zusammenführen *nt* COMP & DV merging, *von Daten* merge
zusammenführen *vt* COMP & DV *Daten* merge
Zusammenführung *f* COMP & DV *von Leitungen* junction, ELEKTROTECH fan-in, TELEKOM junction
zusammengebaut: ~ **gezeichnete Teile** *nt pl* KONSTZEICH parts drawn in the assembled condition
zusammengedreht *adj* TELEKOM twisted together
zusammengefaßt *adj* COMP & DV ganged
zusammengeschaltet: ~**e Steuerungen** *f pl* LUFTTRANS interconnected controls
zusammengesetzt[1] *adj* METALL composite
zusammengesetzt:[2] ~**er Absorber** *m* KERNTECH composite absorber; ~**e Anweisung** *f* COMP & DV compound statement; ~**e Bewegung** *f* MECHAN compound motion; ~**es Farbsignal** *nt* FERNSEH composite color signal (AmE), composite colour signal (BrE); ~**er Graph** *m* KÜNSTL INT composite graph; ~**er Klang** *m* AKUSTIK complex sound; ~**e Kurbelwelle** *f* MASCHINEN built-up crank; ~**es logisches Element** *nt* COMP & DV compound logical element; ~**e Mikroschaltung** *f* COMP & DV microassembly; ~**es Mikroskop** *nt* PHYS compound microscope; ~**es Objektiv** *nt* OPTIK compound lens; ~**es Okular** *nt* OPTIK compound eyepiece; ~**er Schall** *m* AKUSTIK combination sound; ~**es Signal** *nt* ELEKTRONIK, FERNSEH composite signal; ~**es Synchronisierungssignal** *nt* FERNSEH composite sync signal; ~**er Ton** *m* AKUSTIK complex tone; ~**es Videosignal** *nt* FERNSEH composite video signal; ~**e Welle** *f* TELEKOM complex wave, composite wave; ~**e Zahl** *f* MATH composite number, compound number; ~**es Zeichen** *nt* PATENT *aus gleichartigen Bestandteilen* composite mark
Zusammenhang *m* COMP & DV context
zusammenhängend[1] *adj* COMP & DV contiguous
zusammenhängend:[2] **nicht** ~**es Gleiten** *nt* METALL discontinuous glide; ~**e Grafiken** *f pl* COMP & DV contiguous graphics
zusammenkitten *vti* MECHAN bond
zusammenklammern *vt* MATH bracket together
zusammenklappbar *adj* BAU collapsible
Zusammenkleben *nt* CHEMTECH agglutination

zusammenkleben vt CHEMTECH, FERTIG agglutinate
zusammenklumpen vt CHEMTECH, FERTIG agglutinate
zusammenkneifen vt BAU punch
Zusammenlaufen nt KONSTZEICH *von Rastern* merging
zusammenlegbar[1] adj MASCHINEN collapsible
zusammenlegbar:[2] ~e **Faltflasche** f FOTO *für Entwickler* collapsible bottle; ~er **Frachtcontainer** m WASSERTRANS collapsible freight container; ~es **Teil** nt TRANS collapsible section
Zusammennähen nt TEXTIL gathering
Zusammenpassen nt MASCHINEN mating
zusammenpassen[1] vt BAU match; ~ **mit** vt MASCHINEN fit with
zusammenpassen[2] vi MASCHINEN mate
zusammenschaltbar adj TRANS *Behälter* joinable
zusammenschalten vt RADIO interconnect
Zusammenschaltung f FERTIG connection, LUFTTRANS interconnection
zusammenschiebbar[1] adj MASCHINEN telescoping
zusammenschiebbar:[2] ~es **Bein** nt FOTO *Stativ* sliding leg; ~e **Lenksäule** f KFZTECH collapsible steering column; ~es **Stativ** nt FOTO extension tripod, folding tripod; ~es **Stativbein** nt FOTO telescopic leg; ~er **Tubus** m FOTO telescopic tube
zusammenschnüren vt MASCHINEN contract, VERPACK bind
Zusammenschweißen nt MECHAN welding
Zusammensetz-Edit nt FERNSEH assemble edit
Zusammensetzen: ~ **von Kräften** nt MECHAN composition of forces
zusammensetzen vt BAU build up, COMP & DV *Datenverarbeitung* assemble
Zusammensetzung f EISENBAHN structure, KERNTECH composition, TEXTIL analysis
Zusammensintern nt EISENBAHN sintering
zusammensintern vt FERTIG agglomerate
Zusammenstoß m EISENBAHN, KFZTECH, KOHLEN collision, PHYS collision, impact, RAUMFAHRT, SICHERHEIT, WASSERTRANS collision; ~ **in der Luft** m LUFTTRANS aerial collision
zusammenstoßen: ~ **mit** vt TRANS collide with, run into, WASSERTRANS *Schiff* come into collision with
Zusammentragen nt DRUCK gathering
Zusammentragmaschine f DRUCK gathering machine
Zusammentreibeffekt m MEERSCHMUTZ herder effect
Zusammentreibmittel nt MEERSCHMUTZ *für Öl auf Wasseroberfläche* herding agent
zusammenziehbar[1] adj TEXTIL contractile
zusammenziehbar:[2] ~er **Boden** m KOHLEN contractant soil
Zusammenziehen nt TEXTIL *Falten* gathering
zusammenziehen vt PHYS contract
Zusammenziehung f KOHLEN contractancy, PHYS contraction; **Zusammenziehungskoeffizient** m NICHTFOSS ENERG contraction coefficient
Zusatz m DRUCK additive, KER & GLAS admix, MASCHINEN addition, MECHAN additive; **Zusatz-** pref COMP & DV peripheral, KONTROLL, RAUMFAHRT *Raumschiff* ancillary; **Zusatzantrieb** m LUFTTRANS accessory drive; **Zusatzausrüstung** f MECHAN ancillary equipment; **Zusatzbatterie** f KFZTECH booster battery; **Zusatzbauteil** nt RAUMFAHRT *Raumschiff* added on component; **Zusatzbits** nt pl TELEKOM overhead bits; **Zusatzdämpfung** f TELEKOM excess attenuation; **Zusatzdienst** m TELEKOM enhanced service, supplementary service; **Zusatzdraht** m FERTIG *Schweißen*

filler rod; **Zusatzdüse** f KFZTECH high-speed auxiliary jet, *Vergaser* auxiliary jet; **Zusatzdynamo** m ELEKTRIZ booster dynamo; **Zusatz-Edit** nt FERNSEH add-on edit; **Zusatzfeld** nt COMP & DV option field; **Zusatzfläche** f KONSTZEICH free margin; **Zusatzgenerator** m ELEKTRIZ booster generator; **Zusatzgerät** nt KOHLEN, MASCHINEN attachment; **Zusatzgeräte** nt pl FERTIG ancillary equipment, *Kunststoffinstallationen* secondary equipment; **Zusatzheizungssystem** nt NICHTFOSS ENERG booster heating system; **Zusatzkontakt** m ELEKTROTECH auxiliary contact; **Zusatzleiterplatte** f ELEKTRONIK daughter board
zusätzlich[1] adj MASCHINEN additional, PATENT supplementary
zusätzlich:[2] ~e **Induktanz** f ELEKTRIZ incremental inductance; ~e **Kapazität** f ELEKTRIZ incremental capacitance; ~e **Leistungen** f pl BAU auxiliary work; ~es **Merkmal** nt PATENT additional feature; ~e **Wicklung** f GERÄT additional winding
Zusatz: **Zusatzlinse** f FOTO supplementary lens; **Zusatzluft** f KFZTECH secondary air; **Zusatzmaschine in Gegenschaltung** f ELEKTROTECH negative booster; **Zusatzmaschine für Zu- und Gegenschaltung** f ELEKTROTECH reversible booster; **Zusatzmetall** nt FERTIG *Schweißen* filler metal; **Zusatzmittel** nt BAU *Beton* admixture, CHEMIE dope; **Zusatzmühle** f NICHTFOSS ENERG booster mill; **Zusatzpermeabilität** f WERKPRÜF incremental permeability; **Zusatzplatte** f COMP & DV auxiliary disk; **Zusatzprüfung** f QUAL penalty test; **Zusatzrakete** f RAUMFAHRT booster, kick rocket; **Zusatzreinigung** f UMWELTSCHMUTZ supplementary purification; **Zusatzschub** m LUFTTRANS reheat; **Zusatzschuh** m FOTO auxiliary shoe; **Zusatzspeicher** m COMP & DV add-on memory, auxiliary memory, auxiliary storage (AmE), auxiliary store (BrE), secondary memory; **Zusatzspiegel** m FOTO auxiliary mirror; **Zusatzstab** m FERTIG *Schweißen* filler rod; **Zusatzstoff** m FERTIG *Kunststoffinstallationen* admixture, LEBENSMITTEL additive, METALL addition
zusatzstofffrei adj LEBENSMITTEL additive-free
Zusatz: **Zusatztank** m RAUMFAHRT additional tank; **Zusatztastatur** f DRUCK additional keyboard; **Zusatztransformator** m ELEKTRIZ auxiliary transformer, booster transformer, ELEKTROTECH booster transformer, *in Gegenschaltung* booster transformer; **Zusatzwasser** nt HEIZ & KÄLTE, LEBENSMITTEL make-up water; **Zusatzwecker** m TELEKOM extension bell; **Zusatzwicklung** f GERÄT additional winding; **Zusatzwiderstand** m GERÄT additional resistor; **Zusatzziffer** f TELEKOM extra digit
zuschalten vt COMP & DV connect, ELEKTROTECH power up, *Schaltkreis schließen* switch in, FERTIG make
Zuschaltung f ELEKTROTECH switching in
Zuschaltventil nt MASCHINEN sequence valve
zuschärfen vt FERTIG scarf
Zuschauer m FERNSEH viewer; **Zuschauerbewertung** f FERNSEH rating; **Zuschauerzahlen** f pl FERNSEH audience rating
Zuschlag m BAU acceptance of tender, HEIZ & KÄLTE allowance, METALL addition; **Zuschlagablöseversuch** m BAU aggregate stripping test; **Zuschlagablösung** f BAU aggregate stripping; **Zuschlagabnutzungswert** m BAU aggregate abrasion value; **Zuschlagbüro** nt EISENBAHN excess fare office; **Zuschlagdruckfestigkeit** f BAU aggregate crushing value
Zuschläger m FERTIG *Schmieden* striker

Zuschlag: **Zuschlagstoff** *m* ABFALL additive, BAU, FERTIG aggregate

Zuschnappklappe *f* VERPACK flap snap

zuschneiden *vt* BAU *Holz* lumber

Zuschnitt *m* TEXTIL cutting

Zusetzen *nt* MASCHINEN plugging

zuspitzen *vt* BAU tip

Zuspitzung *f* MECHAN taper

Zustand *m* COMP & DV condition, state, status, KONTROLL status; **~ vor der Bearbeitung** *m* MASCHINEN premachined condition

zustandegekommen: **~er Anruf** *m* TELEKOM completed call; **nicht ~es Weiterreichen** *nt* TELEKOM missed handover

zuständig *adj* QUAL appropriate, responsible

Zuständigkeit *f* QUAL responsibility; **Zuständigkeitsgrenzen** *f pl* QUAL jurisdictional boundaries

Zustand: **Zustandsänderung** *f* PHYS, THERMOD change of state; **Zustandsanzeigelampe** *f* TELEKOM status lamp; **Zustandsbit** *nt* COMP & DV status bit; **Zustandsdaten** *nt pl* TELEKOM status data; **Zustandsdiagramm** *nt* THERMOD phase diagram; **Zustandsfunktion** *f (Z)* PHYS function of state, partition function; **Zustandsgleichung** *f* MECHAN, PHYS equation of state, THERMOD state equation; **Zustandsgleichung des Atomkerns** *f* STRAHLPHYS nuclear equation of state; **Zustandsgröße** *f* THERMOD state quantity; **Zustandsschaubild** *nt* FERTIG alloy diagram; **Zustandsübergang** *m* KONTROLL state transition; **Zustandsübergangsdiagramm** *nt* TELEKOM state transition diagram; **Zustandswechsel** *m* KONTROLL state change

Zustellgetriebe *nt* FERTIG *Spanung* feeding-in mechanism

Zustellung *f* MASCHINEN in-feed, PATENT notification

Zustimmungsblock *m* EISENBAHN permissive block

Zustöpseln *nt* BAU plugging

Zustrom *m* STRÖMPHYS *turbulenter Grenzschicht* inrush, WASSERVERSORG inflow

Zuströmverhältnis *nt* LUFTTRANS inflow ratio

Zustromwinkel *m* LUFTTRANS inflow angle

Zutat *f* LEBENSMITTEL ingredient

zuteilen *vt* COMP & DV allocate, *Datenverarbeitung* allocate

Zuteilung *f* COMP & DV, ELEKTROTECH, RADIO allocation

zutreffend: **nicht ~er Fehler** *m* COMP & DV false error

zuverlässig [1] *adj* COMP & DV fault-tolerant

zuverlässig [2]: **~er Transfer-Server** *m* TELEKOM reliable transfer server

Zuverlässigkeit *f* COMP & DV, ELEKTROTECH, ERGON, MASCHINEN, MEERSCHMUTZ, METROL, QUAL, TELEKOM reliability; **~ der Zeichengabe** *f* TELEKOM signaling reliability (AmE), signalling reliability (BrE); **Zuverlässigkeitsanalyse** *f* RAUMFAHRT *Raumschiff* reliability analysis; **Zuverlässigkeitsmerkmal** *nt* QUAL reliability characteristic; **Zuverlässigkeitsprüfung** *f* ELEKTROTECH reliability test, reliability testing; **Zuverlässigkeitssicherung** *f* QUAL reliability assurance

Zuwachs *m* MATH increment, WASSERVERSORG accretion; **Zuwachs-** *pref* FERTIG incremental; **Zuwachsbemaßung** *f* KONSTZEICH *von unterbrochenen Nähten* progressive dimensioning; **Zuwachsfaktor** *m* KERNTECH advantage factor, build-up factor; **Zuwachspermeabilität** *f* WERKPRÜF incremental permeability

zuweisen *vt* COMP & DV allocate, assign, *Datenverarbeitung* allocate

Zuweisung *f* COMP & DV, ELEKTROTECH, RADIO *Frequenzband* allocation; **~ eines Frequenzspektrums** *f* RADIO spectrum allocation; **Zuweisungsanweisung** *f* COMP & DV *Programmiersprache* assignment statement

zuwiderhandeln *vt* SICHERHEIT *Vorschriften* contravene

Z-Vierpolparameter *m pl* ELEKTRONIK *Widerstandsparameter* Z-parameters

Zwang *m* HEIZ & KÄLTE, HYDRAUL, KERNTECH compulsion; **Zwangsabschaltung** *f* KERNTECH emergency shutdown, scram; **Zwangsdurchlaufkessel** *m* HEIZ & KÄLTE forced-circulation boiler, once-through boiler, HYDRAUL flash boiler, flasher; **Zwangskonvektion** *f* HEIZ & KÄLTE forced convection; **Zwangskonvektionskühlofen** *m* KER & GLAS forced-convection lehr; **Zwangskraft** *f* MASCHINEN constraining force; **Zwangskühlung** *f* MASCHINEN forced cooling

zwangsläufig [1] *adj* FERTIG positive

zwangsläufig [2]: **~er Antrieb** *m* KFZTECH positive drive

Zwang: **Zwangslizenz** *f* PATENT compulsory licence (BrE), compulsory license (AmE); **Zwangsluftkühlung** *f* MASCHINEN ducted cooling, forced-air cooling; **Zwangslüftung** *f* MASCHINEN forced ventilation; **Zwangsschmierung** *f* MASCHINEN forced lubrication; **Zwangsumlauf** *m* MASCHINEN forced circulation, forced flow; **Zwangsumlaufkessel** *m* HEIZ & KÄLTE forced-circulation boiler; **Zwangsumlaufreaktor** *m* KERNTECH forced-circulation reactor; **Zwangsumschaltung** *f* TELEKOM forced handoff; **Zwangswasserkühlung** *f* MASCHINEN forced-water cooling

zwanzigflächig: *adj* GEOM icosahedral

Zwanzigflächner *m* GEOM icosahedron

zweckbestimmt: **~e Anlage für Klarsichtfolie** *f* VERPACK *zur Verpackung von Lebensmitteln* dedicated food grade film plant

Zwecke *f* MASCHINEN tack

Zweckforschung *f* UMWELTSCHMUTZ applied research

zweckgebunden: **~er Chip** *m* ELEKTRONIK dedicated chip

zweckgestaltet *adj* VERPACK purpose-designed

zweckmäßig *adj* MECHAN efficient

Zwei *f* MATH two

zwei [1]: **in ~ Richtungen arbeitend** *adj* COMP & DV bidirectional; **zweites** *adj* MATH second

zwei [2]: **von ~ Ebenen gebildeter Winkel** *m* GEOM dihedral angle; **zweiter Brennraum** *m (SCC)* MASCHINEN afterburner chamber, secondary combustion chamber; **zweites Deck** *nt* WASSERTRANS *Schiffskonstruktion* second deck; **zweiter Hauptsatz der Thermodynamik** *f* PHYS second law of thermodynamics; **zweiter Ingenieur** *m* WASSERTRANS *Besatzung* second engineer; **zweites Ionisationspotential** *nt* PHYS second ionization potential; **zweiter Korrekturabzug** *m* DRUCK second proof; **zweiter Offizier** *m* WASSERTRANS *Besatzung* second mate; **zweiter Reduktionsbrand** *m* KER & GLAS second reducing firing; **zweiter Überlagerungsoszillator** *m* ELEKTRONIK second local oscillator; **zweiter Vergaserlufttrichter** *m* KFZTECH secondary barrel

zweiachsig [1] *adj* METALL biaxial

zweiachsig [2]: **~es Drehgestell** *nt* EISENBAHN four-wheel bogie

Zwei: **Zweiadreßbefehl** *m* COMP & DV two-address

instruction

zweiarmig: ~**er Hebel** *m* MASCHINEN lever of the first kind

zweiatomig[1] *adj* CHEMIE biatomic, diatomic

zweiatomig:[2] ~**es Gas** *nt* PHYS diatomic gas; ~**es Molekül** *nt* PHYS, STRAHLPHYS diatomic molecule

zweiäugig: ~**e Spiegelreflexkamera** *f* FOTO twin-lens reflex, twin-lens reflex camera

Zwei: **Zweibackenfutter** *nt* FERTIG, MASCHINEN two-jaw chuck; **Zweibadtonung** *f* FOTO two-bath toning; **Zweibadverfahren** *nt* DRUCK two-bath process; ~ **der Dekontaminierung** *nt* KERNTECH two-bath method of decontamination; **Zweibandkabel** *nt* KFZTECH twin-ribbon cable; **Zweibein** *nt* FERTIG bipod; **Zweibereichsinstrument** *nt* GERÄT double-range instrument, dual-range instrument; **Zweibereichsmeßgerät** *nt* GERÄT double-range instrument, dual-range instrument; **Zweibrennstoffsystem** *nt* KFZTECH, LUFTTRANS dual-fuel system

zweidimensional[1] *adj* COMP & DV, GEOM, PHYS two-dimensional

zweidimensional:[2] ~ **nachformen** *vt* FERTIG contour, profile

zweidrähtig: ~**es Dreieck-Stromnetz** *nt* ELEKTRIZ two-wire delta network; ~**es Stromnetz** *nt* ELEKTRIZ two-wire network

Zweidraht- *pref* TELECOM two wire; **Zweidrahtkoppelpunkt** *m* TELEKOM two-wire crosspoint; **Zweidrahtleitung** *f* COMP & DV two-wire circuit; **Zweidrahtsystem** *nt* ELEKTRIZ double-wire system, two-wire system, ELEKTROTECH, TELEKOM two-wire system; **Zweidrahtvermittlung** *f* TELEKOM two-wire switch; **Zweidraht-Vermittlungssystem** *nt* TELEKOM two-wire switching system

Zwei: **Zwei-Elektronen-Problem** *nt* KERNTECH two-electron problem; **Zweieranschluß** *m* TELEKOM dual party line; **Zweierkomplement** *nt* COMP & DV two's complement; **Zweietagen-Kuppelofen** *m* KER & GLAS double-deck crown furnace

Zweifach- *pref* ELEKTRONIK, KER & GLAS, KFZTECH double

zweifach:[1] ~ **wirkend** *adj* MASCHINEN double-acting

zweifach:[2] ~ **diffundierter Transistor** *m* ELEKTRONIK double-diffused transistor

Zweifach-: **Zweifachdiffusion** *f* ELEKTRONIK double diffusion; **Zweifachform** *f* KER & GLAS double-cavity mold (AmE), double-cavity mould (BrE); **Zweifachkette** *f* KFZTECH *Kraftübertragung* duplex chain; **Zweifachregler** *m* LUFTTRANS dual control; **Zweifachrollenkette** *f* KFZTECH double roller chain

Zweifarbe- *pref* DRUCK, ELEKTRONIK, OPTIK two-color (AmE), two-colour (BrE); **Zweifarbendruckmaschine** *f* DRUCK two-color press (AmE), two-colour press (BrE); **Zweifarbenfilter** *nt* ELEKTRONIK, OPTIK dichroic filter; **Zweifarbenspiegel** *m* OPTIK dichroic mirror

zweifarbig[1] *adj* DRUCK two-color (AmE), two-colour (BrE)

zweifarbig:[2] ~**e Flüssigkristalle** *nt pl* ELEKTRONIK dichroic liquid crystals; ~**es Glas** *nt* KER & GLAS dichroic glass

Zweiflach *nt* FERTIG dihedron

zweiflächig[1] *adj* FERTIG, GEOM dihedral

zweiflächig:[2] ~**e Antenne** *f* TELEKOM dihedral antenna

zweiflutig: ~**er Kessel** *m* HEIZ & KÄLTE double-pass boiler; ~**er Kühler** *m* HEIZ & KÄLTE double-pass heat exchanger; ~**es Luftstrahltriebwerk** *nt* LUFTTRANS dual-flow jet engine

Zweifrequenz- *pref* RADIO, TELEKOM two-frequency; **Zweifrequenzkanalbelegungsplan** *m* TELEKOM two-frequency channeling plan (AmE), two-frequency channelling plan (BrE); **Zweifrequenzrichtfunksystem** *nt* TELEKOM two-frequency radio relay system; **Zweifrequenztonwahl** *f* TELEKOM two-frequency signaling (AmE), two-frequency signalling (BrE)

Zweig *m* ELEKTRIZ, ELEKTROTECH *eines Netzwerkes* branch, GERÄT *Brückenschaltung* ratio arm, MECHAN, PHYS branch; **Zweigangabfüllung** *f* VERPACK two-speed filling; **Zweigangachsantrieb** *m* KFZTECH two-speed final drive

zweigängig[1] *adj* MASCHINEN double-threaded

zweigängig:[2] ~**es Gewinde** *nt* MASCHINEN double thread, two-start thread

Zweig: **Zweigleitung** *f* BAU *Rohrleitung*, ELEKTRIZ branch line, ELEKTROTECH branch, WASSERVERSORG branch pipe; **Zweigverbindung** *f* ELEKTRIZ parallel connection

zweihäusig: ~**e Wanne** *f* KER & GLAS wasp-waisted tank

Zwei: **Zweihöhendotierungsprofil** *nt* ELEKTRONIK low-high-low doping profile

zweiholmig: ~**e Seitenflosse** *f* RAUMFAHRT *Raumschiff* twin-spar vertical fin

Zwei: **Zweihüllendesign** *nt* WASSERTRANS *Schiffbau* double-skin design

zweijährlich *adj* MATH biennial

Zwei: **Zweikanalanlage** *f* HEIZ & KÄLTE dual-conduit system; **Zweikanalsichtfunkpeilung** *f* TELEKOM dual-carrier visual direction finding

Zweikomponenten- *pref* KUNSTSTOFF, RAUMFAHRT two-pack; **Zweikomponenten-Primer** *m* KUNSTSTOFF two-pack primer; **Zweikomponententreibstoff** *m* RAUMFAHRT bipropellant; **Zweikomponententreibstoffantrieb** *m* RAUMFAHRT *Raumschiff* liquid bipropellant propulsion

Zwei: **Zweikontaktregler** *m* KFZTECH two-contact regulator

Zweikreis- *pref* ELEKTRONIK double-tuned; **Zweikreisbremse** *f* KFZTECH double-circuit brake, dual-circuit brake, LUFTTRANS dual-circuit brake; **Zweikreisbremssensystem** *nt* TRANS separated braking circuits; **Zweikreisfilter** *nt* ELEKTRONIK double-tuned circuit; **Zweikreishohlraum** *m* ELEKTRONIK double-tuned cavity; **Zweikreis-TL-Triebwerk** *nt* LUFTTRANS ducted-fan turbo engine, THERMOD bypass engine; **Zweikreistriebwerk** *nt* LUFTTRANS ducted-fan engine, THERMOD turbofan engine; **Zweikreisverstärker** *m* ELEKTRONIK double-tuned amplifier; **Zweikreiszündanlage** *f* KFZTECH two-circuit ignition system

Zwei: **Zweikristall-Spektrometer** *nt* KERNTECH two-circle instrument; **Zweileitungsbremse** *f* KFZTECH twin-line brake; **Zweimeißeldrehmaschine** *f* MASCHINEN duplex lathe

zweimotorig *adj* MASCHINEN twin-engined

Zwei: **Zwei-Nukleonen-System** *nt* KERNTECH two-nucleon system

zweiohrig[1] *adj* AKUSTIK binaural

zweiohrig:[2] ~**es Hören** *nt* AKUSTIK binaural audition

Zweiphasen- *pref* ELEKTROTECH, KERNTECH, LUFTTRANS, TRANS two-phase; **Zweiphasen-Jet** *m* LUFTTRANS diaphasic jet; **Zweiphasenkontrollgerät** *nt* TRANS two-phase controller; **Zweiphasenkühlung** *f* KERNTECH two-phase cooling; **Zweiphasenläufer** *m* ELEKTROTECH two-phase rotor; **Zweiphasenma-**

schine *f* ELEKTROTECH two-phase machine; **Zweiphasenmotor** *m* ELEKTRIZ, ELEKTROTECH two-phase motor; **Zweiphasenreaktor** *m* KERNTECH two-phase reactor; **Zweiphasenrotor** *m* ELEKTROTECH two-phase rotor; **Zweiphasenrotorwicklung** *f* ELEKTROTECH two-phase rotor winding; **Zweiphasenstator** *m* ELEKTROTECH two-phase stator; **Zweiphasenstatorwicklung** *f* ELEKTROTECH two-phase stator winding; **Zweiphasenstrom** *m* ELEKTROTECH two-phase current; **Zweiphasenströmung** *f* STRÖMPHYS two-phase flow; **Zweiphasensystem** *nt* ELEKTROTECH two-phase system; **Zweiphasenumtastung** *f (BPSK)* TELEKOM binary phase shift keying *(BPSK)*

zweiphasig[1] *adj* ELEKTRIZ biphase, two-phase, ELEKTROTECH diphase, two-phase

zweiphasig:[2] ~**er Alternator** *m* ELEKTRIZ two-phase alternator; ~**es Netz** *nt* ELEKTRIZ two-phase network; ~**er Strom** *m* ELEKTRIZ biphase current; ~**es System** *nt* ELEKTRIZ two-phase system

Zwei: **Zwei-plus-Eins-Adreßbefehl** *m* COMP & DV two-plus-one address instruction

Zweipol *m* PHYS two-terminal network

zweipolig[1] *adj* ELEKTRIZ bipolar

zweipolig:[2] ~**er Ein/Aus-Schalter** *m (DPST)* ELEKTROTECH double-pole single-throw *(DPST)*; ~**es Ein/Aus-Schaltrelais** *nt* ELEKTRIZ DPST relay, double-pole single-throw relay; ~**er Kippschalter** *m* ELEKTRIZ double-pole snap switch; ~**e Maschine** *f* ELEKTRIZ bipolar machine; ~**er Schalter** *m* ELEKTRIZ double-pole switch, ELEKTROTECH double-pole switch; ~**er Stecker** *m* ELEKTROTECH two-pin plug; ~**e Stromversorgung** *f* ELEKTROTECH bipolar power supply; ~**er Umschalter** *m (DPDT)* ELEKTROTECH double-pole double-throw *(DPDT)*; ~**es Umschaltrelais** *nt* ELEKTRIZ double-pole double-throw relay; ~**er Verstärker** *m* ELEKTRONIK bipolar amplifier; ~**er Wechselschalter** *m (DPDT)* ELEKTROTECH double-pole double-throw *(DPDT)*; ~**es Wechselschaltrelais** *nt* ELEKTRIZ double-pole double-throw relay

Zweipol: **Zweipolmotor** *m* ELEKTRIZ two-pole motor; **Zweipolstecker** *m* ELEKTROTECH two-pin plug; **Zweipolsystem** *nt* ELEKTRIZ two-pole system; **Zweipolwicklung** *f* ELEKTRIZ bipolar winding

Zweipunkt- *pref* KFZTECH, REGELUNG two-step; **Zweipunktglied** *nt* REGELUNG two-step action element; **Zweipunktgurt** *m* KFZTECH *Sicherheitszubehör* safety belt; **Zweipunktregelung** *f* REGELUNG two-step control; **Zweipunktregler** *m* REGELUNG two-position controller; **Zweipunktsignal** *nt* REGELUNG two-step signal; **Zweipunktverhalten** *nt* REGELUNG two-step action

zweirädrig *adj* MASCHINEN two-wheeled

zweireihig: ~**es Kugellager** *nt* MASCHINEN double-row ball bearing

Zweirichtungs- *pref* TELEKOM bidirectional; **Zweirichtungsanzeige** *f* GERÄT bidirectional read-out; **Zweirichtungshobelmaschine** *f* MASCHINEN double-cutting planing machine; **Zweirichtungs-Thyristordiode** *f* ELEKTROTECH triac; **Zweirichtungszähler** *m* GERÄT bidirectional counter, reversible counter

Zweirollen- *pref* AUFNAHME reel-to-reel; **Zweirollen-Abspielgerät** *nt* AUFNAHME reel-to-reel player

zweisäurig *adj* CHEMIE *Basen* diacidic

Zweischeiben- *pref* FERTIG, KFZTECH two-disc (BrE), two-disk (AmE); **Zweischeibenkupplung** *f* KFZTECH two-disc clutch (BrE), two-disk clutch (AmE), two-

plate clutch; **Zweischeibenschleifmaschine** *f* FERTIG duplex grinder, MASCHINEN two-wheel grinding machine; **Zweischeibentrockenkupplung** *f* KFZTECH double-plate dry clutch

zweischenklig: ~**es Manometer** *nt* GERÄT two-leg manometer

Zwei: **Zweischneidenschleifmaschine** *f* KER & GLAS double-edge grinder

zweischneidig[1] *adj* MASCHINEN double-edge, double-edged

zweischneidig:[2] ~**er Bohrer** *m* MASCHINEN fiddle drill

Zwei: **Zweischnurklappenschrank** *m* TELEKOM double-cord switchboard; **Zweischraubflansch** *m* MASCHINEN two-bolted flange

Zweiseitenband *nt* ELEKTRONIK, RADIO double sideband; **Zweiseitenband-Modulation** *f* ELEKTRONIK double-sideband modulation; **Zweiseitenband-Modulator** *m* ELEKTRONIK double-sideband modulator

zweiseitig:[1] ~ **arbeitend** *adj* MECHAN double-acting

zweiseitig:[2] ~**e Belüftung** *f* HEIZ & KÄLTE double-ended ventilation; ~**e Brennstoffbeschickung** *f* KERNTECH bidirectional refueling (AmE), bidirectional refuelling (BrE); ~ **gerichteter Datenfluß** *m* COMP & DV bidirectional flow; ~ **gerichtetes Mikrofon** *nt* AKUSTIK, AUFNAHME bidirectional microphone; ~ **geschliffenes Tafelglas** *nt* KER & GLAS twin-ground plate; ~**er Koppler** *m* ELEKTROTECH bidirectional coupler; ~**e Leiterplatte** *f* ELEKTRONIK double-sided printed circuit, double-sided printed circuit board; ~**er Pflasterhammer** *m* BAU double-ended sledgehammer; ~**er Spundhobel** *m* BAU double-ended match plane; ~**er Verstärker** *m* ELEKTRONIK bilateral amplifier

Zwei: **Zweiseitigkeit** *f* PAPIER two sidedness; **Zweispindeldrehmaschine** *f* MASCHINEN twin-screw lathe, twin-spindle lathe; **Zweispitzniet** *m* FERTIG bifurcated rivet; **Zweiständerhobelmaschine** *f* MASCHINEN double-column planing machine, double-housing planing machine; **Zweiständerpresse** *f* MASCHINEN arch press

Zweistoff- *pref* CHEMIE, KFZTECH, METALL binary; **Zweistofflegierung** *f* METALL binary alloy; **Zweistoffmotor** *m* KFZTECH, LUFTTRANS dual-fuel engine

zweistrahlig: ~**e Einspritzdüse** *f* KFZTECH twin-jet injection nozzle

Zwei: **Zweistrahlkathodenstrahlröhre** *f* ELEKTRONIK dual-beam cathode-ray tube

Zweistrom- *pref* EISENBAHN, LUFTTRANS dual-current; **Zweistromlokomotive** *f* EISENBAHN dual-current locomotive; **Zweistromtriebwerk** *nt* LUFTTRANS bypass engine, fan jet, turbofan; **Zweistromtriebwerkturbine** *f* LUFTTRANS fan jet turbine

Zweistufen- *pref* ELEKTRIZ, TELEKOM dual-level; **Zweistufenplan** *m* TELEKOM dual-level plan; **Zweistufenrelais** *nt* ELEKTRIZ two-stage relay; **Zweistufenvergaser** *m* KFZTECH two-phase carburetor (AmE), two-phase carburettor (BrE)

zweistufig: ~**er Betrieb** *m* ELEKTROTECH bilevel operation; ~**e Funktion** *f* ELEKTROTECH bilevel operation; ~**er Kompressor** *m* MASCHINEN two-stage compressor; ~**er Verdichter** *m* MASCHINEN two-stage compressor

Zwei: **Zweisystemkontaktunterbrecher** *m* KFZTECH two-system contact breaker

Zweit- *pref* FERNSEH, KUNSTSTOFF, WASSERTRANS second

Zwei: **Zweitakter** *m* MASCHINEN twin-stroke engine, MECHAN two-stroke engine
zweite *adj* AKUSTIK second
zweit: **~e Ableitung** *f* MATH second differential coefficient; **~e Freifläche** *f* FERTIG second flank; **~e Gärung** *f* LEBENSMITTEL secondary fermentation; **~e Generation** *f* COMP & DV second generation; **~e Harmonische** *f* ELEKTRONIK second harmonic; **~e harmonische Einspeisung** *f* ELEKTRONIK second harmonic injection; **~e Ionisationsstufe** *f* PHYS second ionization potential; **~e Spanfläche** *f* FERTIG second face; **~e Stufe** *f* AKUSTIK *Tonleiter* supertonic; **~e Zwischenfrequenz** *f* ELEKTRONIK, FERNSEH, RADIO, TELEKOM second intermediate frequency
Zweitakt- *pref* KFZTECH two-stroke; **Zweitaktgemisch** *nt* KFZTECH *Zweitaktmotor* gas-oil mixture (AmE), gasoline-oil mixture (AmE), petrol-oil mixture (BrE); **Zweitaktmotor** *m* KFZTECH two-stroke engine, MASCHINEN twin-stroke engine, MECHAN, WASSERTRANS two-stroke engine; **Zweitaktöl** *nt* KFZTECH two-stroke oil
Zweit-: **Zweitanode** *f* FERNSEH second anode; **Zweitauslenkungsecho** *nt* WASSERTRANS *Radar* second trace echo; **Zweitbeschleunigereffekt** *m* KUNSTSTOFF synergism effect, synergistic effect; **Zweitdestillation** *f* CHEMIE redistillation, rerun
zweiteilig: **~e Antriebswelle** *f* KFZTECH ·two-piece drive shaft; **~e Instabilität** *f* KERNTECH two-stream instability; **~e Kardanwelle** *f* KFZTECH two-piece propeller shaft; **~er Steckverbinder** *m* ELEKTROTECH two-piece connector; **~er Verbinder** *m* ELEKTROTECH two-piece connector
Zweit-: **Zweitflächenspiegel** *m* *(SSM)* RAUMFAHRT *Raumschiff* second surface mirror *(SSM)*; **Zweitluft** *f* HEIZ & KÄLTE, MASCHINEN secondary air; **Zweitmantel** *m* OPTIK secondary coating
Zwei: **Zweitonvorlagen** *f pl* DRUCK bi-tones; **Zweitourenmaschine** *f* DRUCK two-revolution press; **Zweitourenpresse** *f* DRUCK two-revolution press; **Zweitträgerübertragung** *f* TELEKOM dual-carrier transmission
zweitürig: **~e Limousine** *f* KFZTECH coach (AmE)
Zweit-: **Zweitweg** *m* TELEKOM second choice route
32-Bit-Busarchitektur *f* ELEKTRONIK MCA, microchannel architecture
Zwei: **Zweiunddreißigerformat** *nt* DRUCK thirty-two-mo; **Zweiwalz-Entrockner** *m* LEBENSMITTEL double-drum drier, double-drum dryer
Zweiweg- *pref* KFZTECH, MASCHINEN, PHYS, WASSERVERSORG two-way; **Zweiwegdämpfungsventil** *nt* KFZTECH two-way damper valve; **Zweiweggleichrichter** *m* PHYS full-wave rectifier; **Zweiweghahn** *m* LABOR two-way tap, MASCHINEN, WASSERVERSORG two-way cock; **Zweiwegpalette** *f* TRANS two-way pallet; **Zweiwegspiegel** *m* KER & GLAS two-way mirror; **Zweiwegventil** *nt* HEIZ & KÄLTE two-way valve
zweiwertig: **~e Modulation** *f* TELEKOM binary modulation
Zwei: **Zweiwertigkeit** *f* CHEMIE bivalence, divalence; **Zweizonenreaktor** *m* KERNTECH two-zone reactor; **Zweizonentransistor** *m* *(UJT)* ELEKTRONIK programmable unijunction transistor, unijunction transistor; **Zweizweckfahrzeug** *nt* KFZTECH *Fahrzeugart* dual-purpose vehicle
Zweizylinder- *pref* KFZTECH, MASCHINEN two-cylinder; **Zweizylinderboxermotor** *m* KFZTECH flat twin engine,

flat twin; **Zweizylinderdruckmaschine** *f* DRUCK two-cylinder press; **Zweizylindermotor** *m* MASCHINEN double-cylinder engine, duplex-cylinder engine; **Zweizylinderspinnerei** *f* TEXTIL cotton condenser spinning
Zwergstern *m* RAUMFAHRT dwarf star
Zwickel *m* BAU spandrel, ELEKTRIZ filler
Zwilling *m* METALL twin; **Zwillingsbildung** *f* METALL twinning; **Zwillingsfläche** *f* METALL twinning plane; **Zwillingsflugssteuerungssystem** *nt* LUFTTRANS dual flight control system; **Zwillingsflugzeug** *nt* LUFTTRANS composite aircraft; **Zwillingsgrenze** *f* METALL twin boundary; **Zwillingshahn** *m* WASSERVERSORG twin cock; **Zwillingskabel** *nt* ELEKTROTECH twin cable; **Zwillingslamelle** *f* METALL twin lamella; **Zwillingsmotor** *m* MASCHINEN twin engines; **Zwillingsparadoxon** *nt* PHYS twin paradox; **Zwillingspumpe** *f* MASCHINEN two-throw pump; **Zwillingsräder** *nt pl* LUFTTRANS *Fahrgestell* twin wheels; **Zwillingsräumen** *nt* MASCHINEN twin broaching; **Zwillingsreaktoranlage** *f* KERNTECH twin-reactor station; **Zwillingsscheren** *nt* METALL twinning shear; **Zwillingssystem** *nt* METALL twinning system; **Zwillingstriebwerk** *nt* LUFTTRANS twin engine; **Zwillingstriebwerksdüsenjet** *m* LUFTTRANS· twin-engine jet aircraft; **Zwillingstunnel** *m* EISENBAHN twin tunnel
Zwinge *f* FERTIG holdfast, LABOR clamp, MASCHINEN clamp, collar, collet, cramp, ferrule, MECHAN clamp, vice (BrE), vise (AmE), OPTIK ferrule
Zwirn *m* TEXTIL thread, twist
Zwirnen *nt* KER & GLAS *von Glasfasern* twisting, TEXTIL throwing
Zwirn: **Zwirnmaschine** *f* TEXTIL twister
Zwischen- *pref* ABFALL, DRUCK, KFZTECH, LUFTTRANS, PHYS intermediate; **Zwischenabdeckung** *f* ABFALL *einer Deponie* intermediate cover; **Zwischenabzüge** *m pl* DRUCK interim proofs, intermediate proofs; **Zwischenanflug** *m* LUFTTRANS intermediate approach; **Zwischenanflugsposition** *f* LUFTTRANS intermediate approach fix; **Zwischenbild** *nt* PHYS intermediate image; **Zwischenbildcodierung** *f* TELEKOM interframe coding; **Zwischenbildikonoskop** *nt* ELEKTRONIK image iconoscope; **Zwischenbildorthikon** *nt* ELEKTRONIK image orthicon; **Zwischenboden** *m* HEIZ & KÄLTE false floor; **Zwischendatei** *f* COMP & DV intermediate file; **Zwischendeck** *nt* WASSERTRANS *Schiff* between deck, *Schiffbau* tweendeck
Zwischendeck: **im ~** *adv* WASSERTRANS *Schiff* betweendecks
Zwischen-: **Zwischendecke** *f* BAU intermediate ceiling, HEIZ & KÄLTE false ceiling; **Zwischendichtungsglas** *nt* KER & GLAS intermediate sealing glass (BrE), solder glass (AmE); **Zwischenfalte** *f* KONSTZEICH intermediate fold; **Zwischenfassung** *f* ELEKTROTECH *für elektronische Röhren* socket adaptor
Zwischenfrequenz *f* *(Zf)* ELEKTRONIK, RADIO, TELEKOM intermediate frequency *(IF)*; **Zwischenfrequenzmodulation** *f* *(Zfm)* ELEKTRONIK, RADIO, TELEKOM intermediate frequency modulation *(IFM)*; **Zwischenfrequenzsignal** *nt* ELEKTRONIK, RADIO, TELEKOM intermediate frequency signal; **Zwischenfrequenzverstärker** *m* ELEKTRONIK, RADIO, TELEKOM intermediate frequency amplifier
Zwischen-: **Zwischenfutter** *nt* MASCHINEN cat head, spider; **Zwischengehäuse** *nt* LUFTTRANS intermediate case

zwischengelagert *adj* ERDÖL *Geologie* interlayer
zwischengeschaltet *adj* FERTIG interposed
Zwischen-: **Zwischengeschoß** *nt* BAU intermediate storey
zwischengespeichert: ~e Eingabe/Ausgabe *f* COMP & DV buffered input/output
Zwischen-: **Zwischengetriebe** *nt* MASCHINEN transmission gear; **Zwischengitterplatz** *m* PHYS interstitial place; **Zwischenglühen** *nt* FERTIG *Blech* process annealing, MASCHINEN intermediate annealing, process annealing; **Zwischenglühung** *f* FERTIG intermediate softening, METALL process annealing; **Zwischengut** *nt* KOHLEN middlings; **Zwischenholm** *m* LUFTTRANS false spar; **Zwischenhülse** *f* FERTIG socket; **Zwischenkammer** *f* MASCHINEN receiver; **Zwischenkern** *m* KERNTECH compound nucleus; **Zwischenkopierpapier** *nt* KONSTZEICH intermediate copying paper; **Zwischenkühler** *m* HEIZ & KÄLTE intercooler; **Zwischenlage** *f* KFZTECH *Reifen* ply, PAPIER interleaving; **Zwischenlagen** *f pl* VERPACK cushioning product, padding
Zwischenlager *nt* FERTIG *Fließstraße* bank, MASCHINEN intermediate bearing; **Zwischenlagerplatz** *m* ABFALL refuse transfer station; **Zwischenlagerung** *f* ABFALL *von Müll* intermediate storage; **Zwischenlagerung in Kühlanlagen** *f* HEIZ & KÄLTE cold storage
Zwischenlandung: ~ aus technischen Gründen *f* LUFTTRANS technical stop
Zwischen-: **Zwischenleitung** *f* TELEKOM link; **Zwischenleitungsanordnung** *f* TELEKOM link system; **Zwischenlinsenverschluß** *m* FOTO between the lens shutter; **Zwischenmauer** *f* BAU party wall; **Zwischenmodenverzerrung** *f* OPTIK intramodal distortion; **Zwischenmodulation** *f* AUFNAHME, ELEKTRONIK intermodulation; **Zwischenmodulationsprodukt** *nt* ELEKTRONIK intermodulation product; **Zwischenmodulationsverzerrung** *f* (IMD) ELEKTRONIK intermodulation distortion (IMD)
zwischenmolekular *adj* CHEMIE, METALL intermolecular
zwischenphasig: ~er Kurzschluß *m* ELEKTRIZ interphase short circuit
Zwischen-: **Zwischenplatte** *f* FERTIG *Kunststoffinstallationen* spacer, MECHAN diaphragm; **Zwischenpodest** *nt* BAU half pace; **Zwischenpol** *m* ELEKTRIZ interpole; **Zwischenpolmaschine** *f* ELEKTRIZ interpole machine; **Zwischenprodukt** *nt* FERTIG in-process product, LEBENSMITTEL *Grieß, Dunst* middlings, MATH partial product; **Zwischenproduktcontainer** *m* VERPACK intermediate bulk container; **Zwischenprüfung** *f* QUAL in-process inspection; **Zwischenpumpe** *f* MASCHINEN booster pump; **Zwischenrad** *nt* FERTIG idle gear, idler gear, idler wheel, KFZTECH *Getriebe* idle gear, MASCHINEN idle wheel, idler wheel, idler, intermediate gear, intermediate wheel, stud wheel; **Zwischenrädergetriebe** *nt* LUFTTRANS *eines Hubschraubers* intermediate gearbox; **Zwischenraum** *m* COMP & DV gap, spacing, DRUCK space, FERTIG interstice, HYDRAUL clearance, KERNTECH gap, KOHLEN compartment, LUFTTRANS *von Propeller, Flügel*, WASSERTRANS clearance; **Zwischenraum zwischen zwei Bandblöcken** *m* COMP & DV IBG, interblock gap
Zwischenraum: ~ herausnehmen *vi* DRUCK close up
Zwischen-: **Zwischenregenerator** *m* TELEKOM intermediate regenerator; **Zwischenregister** *nt* COMP & DV temporary register

zwischenschalten *vt* FERTIG interpose
Zwischen-: **Zwischenschaltung** *f* FERTIG interposition; **Zwischenschicht** *f* LUFTTRANS *Lufttransport* interlining, TELEKOM interface; **Zwischenschichtisolierung** *f* ELEKTRIZ layer insulation; **Zwischenschneide** *f* FERTIG *Spanung* drag; **Zwischensetzen** *nt* FERTIG insertion; **Zwischensockel** *m* ELEKTROTECH socket adaptor; **Zwischenspannungswicklung** *f* ELEKTRIZ intermediate-voltage winding; **Zwischensparren** *m* BAU common rafter; **Zwischenspeicher** *m* COMP & DV intermediate storage, temporary storage, ELEKTROTECH temporary memory, TELEKOM buffer memory; **Zwischenspeicherbibliothek** *f* COMP & DV staging library
Zwischenspeichern *nt* COMP & DV buffering, staging
zwischenspeichern *vt* COMP & DV buffer
zwischenstädtisch: ~er Fluglinienverkehr *m* TRANS intercity air service
Zwischen-: **Zwischenstecker** *m* ELEKTROTECH plug adaptor; **Zwischenstellenmodem** *nt* TELEKOM repeater modem; **Zwischenstellung** *f* FERTIG *Kunststoffinstallationen* intermediate position; **Zwischenstück** *nt* BAU spacer block, COMP & DV, ELEKTRIZ, ELEKTROTECH adaptor, FERTIG adaptor, *Kunststoffinstallationen* adaptor, transition piece, LABOR, MASCHINEN, MECHAN, PHYS, RADIO, TELEKOM, TEXTIL adaptor; **äußeres ~** *nt* RAUMFAHRT *Raumschiff* external interface; **~ mit Außengewinde** *nt* MASCHINEN male adaptor; **~ mit Innengewinde** *nt* MASCHINEN female adaptor; **Zwischenstufen-Dampfmaschine** *f* HYDRAUL *Dampfmaschine* intermediate cylinder steam engine; **Zwischenstufengefüge** *nt* FERTIG, METALL bainite; **Zwischenstufenzylinder** *m* HYDRAUL *Dampfmaschine* intermediate pressure cylinder; **Zwischensumme** *f* COMP & DV *pro Stapel* batch total; **Zwischensumme pro Stapel** *f* COMP & DV batch total; **Zwischentransformator** *m* ELEKTROTECH interstage transformer
zwischenüberhitzen *vt* HEIZ & KÄLTE reheat, superheat
Zwischen-: **Zwischenüberhitzer** *m* HEIZ & KÄLTE reheater; **Zwischenüberhitzung** *f* HEIZ & KÄLTE reheating; **Zwischenverbindung** *f* BAU interconnection; **Zwischenverdichterplattform** *f* ERDÖL *Offshore-Technik; Leitungstransport* booster platform; **Zwischenverstärker** *m* RADIO repeater, TELEKOM regenerator; **Zwischenverteiler** *m* TELEKOM IDF, intermediate distribution frame; **Zwischenvorgelege** *nt* MASCHINEN transmission gear; **Zwischenwand** *f* BAU baffle, partition, KER & GLAS midfeather; **Zwischenwelle** *f* FERTIG jack shaft, MASCHINEN intermediate shaft, jack shaft; **Zwischenzeilenabtastung** *f* ELEKTRONIK *Fernsehen* interlaced scanning; **Zwischenzeilenflimmern** *nt* FERNSEH interline flicker; **Zwischenzeilenverfahren** *nt* FERNSEH scanning interlace system; **Zwischenzelle** *f* RAUMFAHRT *Raumschiff* interstage section
Zwitschern *nt* RADIO *Morsefunk* chirp, RAUMFAHRT *Weltraumfunk* chirp modulation
Zwitterion *nt* CHEMIE zwitterion
Zwitterkontakt *m* ELEKTROTECH hermaphroditic contact
Zwittersteckverbinder *m* ELEKTROTECH hermaphroditic connector
Zwölfeck *nt* GEOM dodecagon
zwölfeckig *adj* GEOM dodecagonal
zwölfflächig *adj* GEOM dodecahedral
Zwölfflächner *m* GEOM dodecahedron
Zyklenteilverfahren *nt* COMP & DV cycle stealing

zyklisch: ~e Abtragung *f* ANSTRICH cyclical erosion; ~e Aufeinanderfolge *f* COMP & DV wraparound; ~e Bitverschiebung *f* COMP & DV cyclic shift; ~e Blattverstellung *f* LUFTTRANS *Hubschrauber* cyclic pitch control; ~e Blockcodes *m pl* TELEKOM cyclic block codes; ~e Blockprüfung *f (CRC)* COMP & DV, ELEKTRONIK, REGELUNG, TELEKOM cyclic redundancy check *(CRC)*; ~e Blocksicherung *f (CRC)* COMP & DV, ELEKTRONIK, LABOR, TELEKOM cyclic redundancy check *(CRC)*; ~e Codes *m pl* TELEKOM cyclic codes; ~er Einstellwinkel *m* LUFTTRANS cyclic pitch; ~e Erosion *f* ANSTRICH cyclical erosion; ~er Graph *m* KÜNSTL INT cyclic graph; ~e Hilfstrimmeinrichtung *f* LUFTTRANS *Hubschrauber* cyclic pitch servo trim; ~er Konuswinkel *m* LUFTTRANS *Hubschrauber* cyclic flapping angle; ~e Längssteuerungsknüppelbelastung *f* LUFTTRANS *Hubschrauber* longitudinal cyclic stick load; ~e Quersteuerungshilfe *f* LUFTTRANS *Hubschrauber* lateral cyclic control support; ~er Schlagwinkel *m* LUFTTRANS *Hubschrauber* cyclic flapping angle; ~er Seitensteigungswinkel *m* LUFTTRANS *Hubschrauber* lateral cyclic pitch; ~e Stellenverschiebung *f* COMP & DV cyclic shift; ~er Steuerknüppel *m* LUFTTRANS *Hubschrauber* cyclic stick; ~e Steuerstufe *f* LUFTTRANS *Hubschrauber* cyclic control step

Zykloide *f* FERTIG, GEOM cycloid; Zykloidenverzahnung *f* FERTIG *Getriebelehre* cycloidal gear teeth, cycloidal teeth, cycloidal-profile teeth

Zyklon *m* ERDÖL *Abscheidetechnik*, KOHLEN, UMWELTSCHMUTZ, WASSERTRANS *tropischer Wolkensturm* cyclone; Zyklonabscheider *m* MASCHINEN cyclone separator; Zyklonabscheidung *f* ABFALL cyclone separation, cyclone; Zyklonabschneider *m* ERDÖL cyclone

Zyklone *f* WASSERTRANS *Wettertief* cyclone

Zyklon: Zyklonentstauber *m* UMWELTSCHMUTZ cyclone; Zyklonfilter *nt* MASCHINEN cyclone filter; Zyklonofen *m* KER & GLAS cyclone furnace

zyklop: ~er Staudamm *m* WASSERVERSORG cyclopic barrage

Zyklopenbeton *m* BAU cyclopean concrete

Zyklotron *nt* ELEKTROTECH, PHYS, STRAHLPHYS, TEILPHYS cyclotron; Zyklotronfrequenz *f* KERNTECH electron cyclotron frequency, STRAHLPHYS, TEILPHYS cyclotron frequency; Zyklotronresonanz *f* TELEKOM cyclotronic resonance; Zyklotronsicherheit *f* PHYS, STRAHLPHYS, TEILPHYS cyclotron safety; Zyklotronstrahlung *f* PHYS, STRAHLPHYS, TEILPHYS cyclotron radiation

Zyklus *m* AKUSTIK, COMP & DV, ELEKTRIZ, ELEKTROTECH, KONTROLL, KUNSTSTOFF, MASCHINEN cycle; ~ von Intervallen *m* AKUSTIK cycle of intervals; Zykluszähler *m* GERÄT cycle counter; Zykluszeit *f* COMP & DV cycle time

Zylinder *m* COMP & DV *Festplatte*, DRUCK cylinder, ELEKTROTECH *Spule* solenoid, FERTIG drum, *Extruder, Plastherstellung* barrel, GEOM cylinder, HYDRAUL *Dampfmaschine* barrel, *Dampfdruckindikator* drum, KER & GLAS *zur Produktion von gewalztem Flachglas*, KFZTECH *Motor* cylinder, KUNSTSTOFF, MASCHINEN, MECHAN, PAPIER cylinder, VERPACK drum, WASSERTRANS *Motor* cylinder; ~ in V-Anordnung *m pl* KFZTECH V-shaped cylinders; Zylinderauflager *nt* FERTIG *Extruder* barrel support; Zylinderblock *m* KFZTECH *Motor* cylinder block; Zylinderbohrung *f* KFZTECH bore, MASCHINEN cylinder bore; Zylinder-

bohrwerk *nt* FERTIG, MASCHINEN cylinder boring mill; Zylinderbuchse *f* KFZTECH *Motor* cylinder liner; Zylinderdeckel *m* EISENBAHN cylinder head, HYDRAUL *frontseitig* cylinder cover, *hinten* cylinder head, *rückseitig* cylinder cover, KFZTECH, MASCHINEN, WASSERTRANS *Motor* cylinder head; Zylindereinspritzmotor *m* TRANS direct injection engine; Zylinderfläche *f* GEOM cylinder surface; Zylinderflansch *m* KFZTECH *Motor* cylinder flange; Zylinderglas *nt* KER & GLAS blown sheet (AmE), cylinder glass (BrE); Zylinderheizraum *m* HYDRAUL steam jacket; Zylinderinhalt *m* KFZTECH cylinder capacity, MASCHINEN capacity of a cylinder; Zylinderkondensator *m* PHYS cylindrical capacitor; Zylinderkoordinaten *f pl* PHYS cylindrical coordinates

Zylinderkopf *m* EISENBAHN, HYDRAUL *vorn* cylinder head, KFZTECH *Motor* cylinder head, head cylinder, MASCHINEN cheese head, cylinder head, WASSERTRANS *Motor* cylinder head; ~ mit Innensechskant *m* MASCHINEN hexagon socket head; Zylinderkopfdichtung *f* KFZTECH *Motor* cylinder head gasket, head gasket, MASCHINEN cylinder head gasket; Zylinderkopfniete *f* BAU cheese-head rivet; Zylinderkopfschraube *f* KFZTECH cylinder head bolt, MASCHINEN cheese-head screw, fillister-head screw

Zylinder: Zylinderkörper *m* MASCHINEN cylinder barrel; Zylinderlaufbahn *f* KFZTECH *Motor* cylinder barrel; Zylinderlaufbuchse *f* KFZTECH cylinder sleeve, *Motor* cylinder liner, MECHAN cylinder liner; Zylindermantel *m* FERTIG cylinder barrel; Zylindermaß *nt* FERTIG roller; Zylinderöffnung *f* KER & GLAS opening of the cylinder; Zylinderreflektorantenne *f* TELEKOM cylindrical reflecting antenna; Zylinderreibahle *f* FERTIG parallel reamer; Zylinderring *m* KFZTECH *Motor* cylinder ring; Zylinderrollenlager *nt* MASCHINEN cylindrical roller bearing; Zylinderschaft *m* MASCHINEN parallel shank, plain shank, straight shank; Zylinderschloß *nt* BAU cylinder lock, pin tumbler, MASCHINEN cylinder lock; Zylinderschnecke *f* MASCHINEN cylindrical worm; Zylinderschraube *f* FERTIG cheese-head screw, fillister head, *Kunststoffinstallationen* bolt, securing screw, MASCHINEN cheese-head screw; ~ mit Schlitz *f* MASCHINEN slotted cheese-head screw (BrE); Zylinderstift *m* FERTIG parallel pin, MASCHINEN cylindrical pin, straight pin

zylindersymmetrisch: ~e Couetteströmung *f* STRÖMPHYS rotating Couette flow; ~e Couetteströmung im Ringspalt *f* STRÖMPHYS rotating Couette flow in an annulus

Zylinder: Zylindertrockenmaschine *f* TEXTIL cylinder drying machine; Zylindertrockenschlichtmaschine *f* TEXTIL cylinder-sizing machine; Zylindertrockner *m* TEXTIL cylinder drying machine; Zylinderverfahren *nt* KER & GLAS cylinder process; Zylindervolumen *nt* KFZTECH cylinder capacity; Zylinder-V-Winkel *m* KFZTECH *von zwei Zylinderreihen in V-Motor* cylinder bank angling; Zylinderwand *f* KFZTECH *Motor*, MASCHINEN cylinder wall; Zylinderwandung *f* KFZTECH *Motor* cylinder wall; Zylinderwelle *f* AKUSTIK cylindrical wave; Zylinderwicklung *f* ELEKTRIZ cylindrical winding; Zylinderzange *f* KER & GLAS straight pincers; Zylinderziehverfahren *nt* KER & GLAS cylinder drawing process

zylindrisch[1] *adj* FERTIG *Schaft* parallel

zylindrisch:[2] ~es Ausgleichsventil *nt* NICHTFOSS ENERG cylindrical balanced valve; ~e Bohrung *f* FERTIG parallel hole, MASCHINEN cylindrical bore; ~e **Druckform** *f* DRUCK plate cylinder; ~er **Flammrohrkessel** *m* HYDRAUL cylindrical flue boiler; ~e **Hülle** *f* RAUMFAHRT *Raumschiff* cylindrical shell; ~e **Kreuzspule** *f* TEXTIL cheese; ~es **Mundstück** *nt* HYDRAUL cylindrical mouthpiece; ~es **Rohr-Innengewinde** *nt* FERTIG *Kunststoffinstallationen* BSP parallel thread; ~er **Rotationskörper** *m* GEOM cylindrical solid of revolution; ~e **Schraubenfeder** *f* MASCHINEN cylindrical helical spring; ~e **Spaltzone** *f* KERNTECH annular core; ~e **Strahlungsquelle** *f* KERNTECH cylindrical irradiator; ~es **System** *nt* ABFALL *ein Kompostierungsverfahren* drum system

Zymase *f* CHEMIE zymase

Zymologie *f* CHEMIE zymology

zymotisch *adj* CHEMIE zymotic

Abbreviations/Abkürzungen

A AKUSTIK *(Amplitude)*, AUFNAHME *(Amplitude)* A *(amplitude)*, CHEMIE *(Affinität)* A *(affinity)*, COMP & DV *(Amplitude)* A *(amplitude)*, ELEKTRIZ *(Ampere)* A *(ampere)*, ELEKTRIZ *(Amplitude)* A *(amplitude)*, ELEKTRIZ *(lineare Stromdichte)* A *(linear current density)*, ELEKTRONIK *(Amplitude)* A *(amplitude)*, ELEKTROTECH *(Ampere)* A *(ampere)*, ELEKTROTECH *(Anode)*, FERNSEH *(Anode)* A *(anode)*, FERTIG *(Ampere)* A *(ampere)*, KERNTECH *(Aktivität)* A *(activity)*, KERNTECH *(Massenzahl)* A *(mass number)*, METROL *(Ampere)* A *(ampere)*, PHYS *(Aktivität, Schallstärke)* A *(activity)*, PHYS *(Ampere)* A *(ampere)*, PHYS *(Amplitude)* A *(amplitude)*, PHYS *(Anode)* A *(anode)*, PHYS *(Isotopenmasse, Massenzahl)* A *(mass number)*, RADIO *(Ampere)* A *(ampere)*, RADIO *(Amplitude)* A *(amplitude)*, RADIO *(Anode)* A *(anode)*, TEILPHYS *(Massenzahl, Nukleonenzahl)* A *(mass number)*, WASSERTRANS *(Amplitude)* A *(amplitude)*, WASSERTRANS *(Anode)* A *(anode)*, WELLPHYS *(Amplitude)* A *(amplitude)*

a AKUSTIK *(akustische Absorption)* a *(total acoustic absorption)*, METROL *(Ar)* a *(are)*

Å *(Angström)* METROL Å *(angstrom)*

AACS *(Luftfahrtfunkdienst)* RAUMFAHRT AACS *(airways and air communications service)*

AADT *(durchschnittliches Tagesverkehrsaufkommen pro Jahr)* TRANS AADT *(annual average daily traffic)*

AAP *(akustischer Akzeptanzpegel)* AKUSTIK ACI *(acoustic comfort index)*

AB *(akustischer Blindleitwert)* AKUSTIK BA *(acoustic susceptance)*

ABC *(automatische Helligkeitsregelung)* FERNSEH ABC *(automatic brightness control)*

AbfG *(Abfallgesetz)* ABFALL Waste Avoidance and Management Act, Waste Disposal Act

ABS KFZTECH *(Antiblockiersystem)* ABS *(antiblocking system)*, KUNSTSTOFF *(Acrylnitril-Butadien-Styrol) Copolymer* ABS *(acrylonitrile butadiene styrene)*

AC ELEKTROTECH *(Wechselstrom)* AC *(alternating current)*, FERTIG *(Adaptivsteuerung)* AC *(adaptive control)*

AC-GS ELEKTROTECH *(Wechselstrom-Gleichstrom)* AC-DC *(alternating current-direct current)*

ACR *(Anflugradar)* RAUMFAHRT ACR *(approach control radar)*

ACSR *(Einseitenband mit kompandierter Amplitude)* RADIO ACSS *(amplitude-compandered single sideband)*

ACC *(automatische Chrominanzregelung)* FERNSEH ACC *(automatic chrominance control)*

ACIA *(Asynchron-übertragungs-Schnittstellenanpasser, asynchronischer Übertragungs-schnittstellenanpasser)* KONTROLL ACIA *(asynchronous communications interface adaptor)*

ACN *(automatische Himmelsnavigation)* RAUMFAHRT ACN *(automatic celestial navigation)*

ACNA *(Analogrechner für Netzabgleich)* COMP & DV ACNA *(analog computer for net adjustment)*

ACO *(Anpassungssteuerung mit Optimierung)* LABOR ACO *(adaptive control optimization)*

ACU *(automatisches Rufgerät)* RAUMFAHRT, TELEKOM ACU *(automatic calling unit)*

A/D *(Analog-Digital-)* ELEKTRONIK, FERNSEH, FERTIG A/D *(analog-digital)*

ADF *(Funkpeilgerät, automatischer Funkkompaß)* LUFTTRANS, RADIO, TELEKOM ADF *(automatic direction finder)*

ADI *(duldbare tägliche Aufnahmemenge)* LEBENSMITTEL ADI *(acceptable daily intake)*

ADPCM *(adaptive Differenz-Pulscodemodulation)* TELEKOM ADPCM *(adaptive differential pulse code modulation)*

ADU *(Analog-Digital-Umsetzer)* COMP & DV, ELEKTRONIK, FERNSEH, FERTIG ADC *(analog-digital converter)*

ADV *(automatische Datenverarbeitung)* COMP & DV ADP *(automatic data processing)*

AE *(astronomische Einheit)* LABOR AU *(astronomical unit)*

AEC *(Amerikanischer Atomenergieverband)* KERNTECH AEC *(Atomic Energy Commission)*

AES *(Augersche Elektronenspektroskopie)* PHYS, STRAHLPHYS AES *(Auger electron spectroscopy)*

AFGC *(automatische Frequenz- und Verstärkungsregelung)* ELEKTRONIK, FERNSEH, RADIO AFGC *(automatic frequency and gain control)*

AFI *(automatische Fahrzeugidentifikation)* TRANS AVI *(automatic vehicle identification)*

AFO *(automatische Fahrzeugortung)* TRANS AVL *(automatic vehicle location)*

AFR *(automatische Frequenzregelung)* ELEKTRONIK, FERNSEH, RADIO AFC *(automatic frequency control)*

AFS *(fester Flugfunkdienst)* LUFTTRANS AFS *(aeronautical-fixed service)*

AFT *(automatische Scharfabstimmung)* RADIO AFT *(automatic fine tuning)*

AFTN *(festes Flugfunknetz)* LUFTTRANS AFTN *(aeronautical-fixed telecommunication network)*

AG *(amerikanisches Maß)* MASCHINEN AG *(American gage)*

AGCA *(automatische Anflugsteuerung vom Boden)* RAUMFAHRT AGCA *(automatic ground-controlled approach)*

AGCL *(automatische Landesteuerung vom Boden)* RAUMFAHRT AGCL *(automatic ground-controlled landing)*

AGE *(Allylglycidether)* KUNSTSTOFF AGE *(allyl glycidyl ether)*

AGR *(fortgeschrittener Gas-Graphit-Reaktor)* KERNTECH AGR *(advanced gas-cooled reactor)*

AI *(Schallimpedanz, Schallwellenwiderstand, akustische Impedanz, akustischer Scheinwiderstand)* AKUSTIK ZA *(acoustic impedance)*

AIA *(Amerikanischer Luft- und Raumfahrtverband)* RAUMFAHRT AIA *(Aerospace Industries Association)*

AIS *(aeronautischer Informationsdienst)* RAUMFAHRT AIS *(aeronautical information service)*

AK *(akustische Kapazität)* AKUSTIK AC *(acoustic capacitance)*

AL AKUSTIK *(akustischer Leitwert)* GA *(acoustic conductance)*, TELEKOM *(Anschlußleitung)* subscriber's line

ALC KFZTECH *(automatischer Niveauausgleich)*, RADIO *(automatische Pegelregelung)* ALC *(automatic level control)*

α AKUSTIK *(Absorptionskoeffizient)* α *(absorption coefficient)*, GEOM *(Alpha)* α *(alpha)*, MECHAN *(Winkelbeschleunigung)* α *(angular acceleration)*, OPTIK *(Absorptionsfaktor)* α *(absorption factor)*, OPTIK *(optischer Drehwinkel)* α *(angle of optical rotation)*, PHYS *(Absorptionskoeffizient)*, RADIO *(Absorptionskoeffizient)*, STRAHLPHYS *(Absorptionskoeffizient)* α *(absorption coefficient)*

ALR *(automatische Lautstärkeregelung)* ELEKTROTECH, FERNSEH, MECHAN, RADIO AVC *(automatic volume control)*

AM AKUSTIK *(akustische Masse)* AM *(acoustic mass)*, AUFNAHME *(Amplitudenmodulation)*, COMP & DV *(Amplitudenmodulation)*, ELEKTRIZ *(Amplitudenmodulation)*, ELEKTRONIK *(Amplitudenmodulation)*, FERNSEH *(Amplitudenmodulation)*, PHYS *(Amplitudenmodulation)*, RADIO *(Amplitudenmodulation)*, TELEKOM *(Amplitudenmodulation)*, WELLPHYS *(Amplitudenmodulation)* AM *(amplitude modulation)*

AME *(Atommasseneinheit)* KERNTECH AWU *(atomic weight unit)*

AMI *(bipolare Schrittinversion)* TELEKOM AMI *(alternate mark inversion)*

AMS *(aeronautische Werkstoffnorm)* RAUMFAHRT AMS *(aeronautical material standard)*

amu *(atomare Masseneinheit)* KERNTECH amu *(atomic mass unit)*

ANC *(Luftfahrt-Navigationsausschuß)* LUFTTRANS ICAO *(International Civil Aviation Organization)*

a₀ *(Bohrscher Radius)* PHYS a₀ *(Bohr radius)*

AOCS *(Fluglage- und Umlaufbahnkontrollsystem)* RAUMFAHRT AOCS *(attitude and orbit control system)*

AOQ *(durchschnittliche Fertigproduktqualität)* QUAL AOQ *(average outgoing quality)*

AOQL *(durchschnittlicher Fertigproduktqualitätsgrenzwert)* QUAL AOQL *(average outgoing quality limit)*

AOS *(automatisches Signal zur Mikrofonübergabe)* TELEKOM AOS *(automatic over signal)*

AOW *(akustische Oberflächenwelle)* ELEKTRONIK, TELEKOM SAW *(surface acoustic wave)*

APD *(Avalanchefotodiode)* ELEKTRONIK, OPTIK APD *(avalanche photodiode)*

APEX *(im voraus bezahlter Sondertarif)* LUFTTRANS APEX *(advance purchase excursion fare)*

API *(Amerikanisches Erdölinstitut)* ERDÖL API *(American Petroleum Institute)*

APR ELEKTRONIK *(automatische Phasenregelung)*, FERNSEH *(automatische Phasensteuerung)* APC *(automatic phase control)*

APT *(programmierte Werkzeuge)* COMP & DV APT *(automatically programmed tools)*

AQL *(akzeptabler Qualitätspegel, annehmbare Qualitätsgrenzlage, annehmbare Qualitätslage)* QUAL AQL *(acceptable quality level)*

AR *(Ausgangsregister)* TELEKOM HLR *(home location register)*

ARGOS *(automatische Satellitenerfassung von geomagnetischen Daten)* WASSERTRANS ARGOS *(Automatic Remote Geomagnetic Observatory System)*

ARL *(akzeptabler Zuverlässigkeitspegel)* QUAL ARL *(acceptable reliability level)*

ARPA *(automatische Radaraufnahmehilfe)* WASSER-TRANS ARPA *(automatic radar plotting aid)*

ARQ *(automatische Wiederholanforderung)* RADIO, TELEKOM ARQ *(automatic repeat request)*

ARRL *(Amerikanischer Amateurdachverband)* RADIO ARRL *(American Radio Relay League)*

ARSR *(Flugüberwachungsradar)* RAUMFAHRT ARSR *(air route surveillance radar)*

ARU COMP & DV *(Sprachausgabe-Einheit)* ARU *(audio response unit)*, RADIO *(automatische Rauschunterdrückung)* ANL *(automatic noise limiter)*

asb *(Apostilb)* OPTIK asb *(apostilb)*

ASCII *(Amerikanische Datenübertragungs-Codenorm)* COMP & DV, DRUCK ASCII *(American Standard Code for Information Interchange)*

ASD *(Rutschsicherung)* KFZTECH ASD *(antiskid device)*

ASE KÜNSTL INT *(automatische Spracherkennung)* ASR *(automatic speech recognition)*, TRANS *(Selbststabilisierungsgerät)* ASE *(automatic stabilizing equipment)*

ase *(Flugnormwirkungsgrad)* RAUMFAHRT ase *(air standard efficiency)*

ASG *(Flugnormengruppe)* RAUMFAHRT ASG *(aeronautical standards group)*

ASI LUFTTRANS *(Eigengeschwindigkeitsanzeiger, Geschwindigkeitsmesser)*, RAUMFAHRT *(Geschwindigkeitsanzeiger)* ASI *(airspeed indicator)*

ASK *(Amplitudenumtastung)* ELEKTRONIK ASK *(amplitude-shift keying)*

ASL *(atomare Sicherheitslinie)* KERNTECH ASL *(atomic safety line)*

ASLT *(fortschrittliche Festkörperlogik)* ELEKTRONIK ASLT *(advanced solid logic technology)*

ASME *(Amerikanische Gesellschaft der Maschinenbau-Ingenieure)* QUAL ASME *(American Society of Mechanical Engineers)*

ASR COMP & DV *(automatischer Sender-Empfänger)* ASR *(automatic send-receive)*, LUFTTRANS *(Flughafen-Überwachungsradar)* ASR *(airport surveillance radar)*

ASTM *(Amerikanische Gesellschaft für Werkstoffprüfung)* MASCHINEN, QUAL ASTM *(American Society for Testing Materials)*

AT *(fortschrittliche Technologie)* COMP & DV AT *(advanced technology)*

aT *(Thermodiffusionskonstante)* PHYS aT *(thermal diffusion constant)*

ATC EISENBAHN *(automatische Zugsteuerung)* ATC, ATO *(automatic train operation)*, METALL *(automatischer Werkzeugwechsler)* ATC *(automatic tool changer)*, RADIO *(kapazitive Antennenanpassung)* ATC *(aerial-tuning capacitor)*

ATE *(automatische Prüfeinrichtung)* COMP & DV ATE *(automatic test equipment)*

ATF *(Automatikgetriebeöl)* KFZTECH ATF *(automatic transmission fluid)*

ATI *(Antennenabstimmspule)* RADIO ATI *(aerial-tuning inductance)*

ATM *(Azimutal-Transversal-Mode)* OPTIK optische Fasern ATM *(azimuthal transversal mode)*

ATP *(Adenosintriphosphat)* LEBENSMITTEL ATP *(adenosine triphosphate)*

ATU *(Antennenanpassung)* RADIO ATU *(aerial-tuning unit)*

ATV *(Amateurfernsehen)* FERNSEH ATV *(amateur television)*

AUTOPROMT *(automatisierte Maschinenwerkzeugpro-grammierung)* FERTIG AUTOPROMT *(automated programming of machine tools)*

AUTOSPOT *(automatisierte Werkzeugpositionierung)* FERTIG AUTOSPOT *(automated system for positioning tools)*

AV *(Säurewert)* CHEMIE AV *(acid value)*

AVR *(automatische Verstärkungsregelung)* ELEKTRO-NIK, RADIO, TELEKOM AGC *(automatic gain control)*

AWACS *(Überwachungs- und Leitsystem im Flugzeug)* LUFTTRANS AWACS *(airborne warning and control system)*

AWG *(Amerikanische Einheit für Drahtdurchmesser)* METROL AWG *(American wire gage)*

B AKUSTIK *(Bel)* B *(bel)*, AUFNAHME *(magnetischer Scheinwiderstand)*, ELEKTRIZ *(Magnetinduktion)* B *(magnetic induction)*, ELEKTROTECH *(Bel)* B *(bel)*, ELEKTROTECH *(Magnetinduktion)* B *(magnetic induction)*, KERNTECH *(Bindungsenergie)* B *(binding energy)*, PHYS *(Bel)* B *(bel)*, PHYS *(Magnetinduktion)* B *(magnetic induction)*, STRAHLPHYS *(Bindungsenergie, Kernbindungsenergie)*, TEILPHYS *(Bindungsenergie, Kernbindungsenergie)* B *(binding energy)*, TELEKOM *(Magnetinduktion)* B *(magnetic induction)*, THERMOD *(Volumenelastizitätsmodul)* B *(modulus of volume elasticity)*

b KOHLEN *(Bar)*, LABOR *(Bar)* Luftdruckeinheit b *(bar)*, RAUMFAHRT *(Raumbreite)* b *(galactic latitude)*

BASIC *(Beginner's All-purpose Symbolic Instruction Code)* DRUCK Programmiersprache BASIC *(beginner's all-purpose symbolic instruction code)*

BB *(Basisband)* ELEKTROTECH BB *(baseband)*

BBD ELEKTROTECH *(Eimerkettenspeicher)*, TELEKOM *(Eimerkettenschaltung)* BBD *(bucket brigade device)*

BBL *(Blindlandung mit Bakeunterstützung)* RAUM-FAHRT BBL *(beacons and blind landing)*

BBV *(Breitbandverstärker)* ELEKTRONIK wideband amplifier

BCC *(Blockprüfzeichen)* TELEKOM BCC *(block check character)*

BCD COMP & DV *(binärcodierte Dezimalzahl, binärcodierte Drehzahl)*, RADIO *(binärcodierte Dezimalzahl)* BCD *(binary-coded decimal)*

BCI *(Rundfunkstörung)* RADIO BCI *(broadcast interference)*

BCS *(Bardeen-Cooper-Schrieffer)* COMP & DV BCS *(Bardeen-Cooper-Schrieffer)*

B/d *(Barrel pro Tag)* ERDÖL BCD *(barrels per calendar day)*

BDP *(Verbundpapier)* PAPIER BDP *(bonded double paper)*

BE ELEKTRIZ *(elektrischer Blindleitwert)* BE *(electric susceptance)*, TELEKOM *(Basiseinheit)* BU *(base unit)*

BEG *(Bodeneffektgerät)* KFZTECH GEM *(ground effect machine)*

BEPC *(Beijing Electron Positron Collider)* TEILPHYS BEPC *(Beijing Electron Positron Collider)*

BER *(Bitfehlerquote, Bitfehlerrate)* COMP & DV BER *(bit error rate)*

β AKUSTIK *(Phasenkonstante)*, ELEKTRIZ (Phasenkonstante) β *(phase constant)*, GEOM *(Beta)* β

BFO *(Schwebungsfrequenzoszillator)* ELEKTRONIK, PHYS, RADIO BFO *(beat frequency oscillator)*

Bg *(geometrisches Buckling)* KERNTECH Bg *(geometric*

buckling)

BHA *(Butylhydroxyanisol)* LEBENSMITTEL BHA *(butylated hydroxyanisole)*

BHT *(Butylhydroxytoluol)* LEBENSMITTEL BHT *(butylated hydroxytoluene)*

BIGFET *(Feldeffekttransistor mit bipolarisoliertem Gatter)* ELEKTRONIK BIGFET *(bipolar-insulated gate field-effect transistor)*

BMOSFET *(Halbleiter-Feldeffekttransistor mit Rückgatter)* ELEKTRONIK BMOSFET *(back-gate metal-oxide semiconductor field-effect transistor)*

BOP *(Blowout-Preventer)* ERDÖL BOP *(blowout preventer)*

BOT *(Bandanfang)* COMP & DV BOT *(beginning of tape)*

BPF *(Bandpaßfilter)* AUFNAHME, ELEKTRONIK, FERN-SEH, PHYS, RADIO BPF *(band-pass filter)*

bpi *(Bits pro Zoll)* COMP & DV bpi *(bits per inch)*

BPS *(Bremspferdestärke)* FERTIG, KFZTECH, MECHAN BHP *(brake horsepower)*

bps *(Bits pro Sekunde)* COMP & DV bps *(bits per second)*

BPSK *(Zweiphasenumtastung, binäre Phasenumtastung)* TELEKOM BPSK *(binary phase shift keying)*

Bq *(Becquerel)* METROL, PHYS Bq *(becquerel)*

BS FERTIG *(Windfrischstahl)*, MASCHINEN *(Bessemerstahl)* BS *(Bessemer steel)*

BSA *(Bohrlochsohlenausrüstung)* ERDÖL BHA *(bottom hole assembly)*

BSB *(biologischer Sauerstoffbedarf)* ABFALL, LEBENS-MITTEL, UMWELTSCHMUTZ BOD *(biological oxygen demand)*

BSS *(Britische Normenspezifikation, Britische Normvorschrift)* MASCHINEN BSS *(British Standard Specification)*

BThU *(Britische Wärmeeinheit)* MASCHINEN, METROL Energie BThU *(British Thermal unit)*

BTU *(Britische Wärmeeinheit)* LABOR, MASCHINEN BTU (AmE) *(British Thermal unit)*

Btx *(Bildschirmtext)* FERNSEH Videotex, TELEKOM Teletext®

BV *(Bildverstehen, Bildverständnis)* KÜNSTL INT IU *(image understanding)*

BW *(Bandbreite, Bandweite)* AUFNAHME, COMP & DV, ELEKTRONIK, FERNSEH, OPTIK, RADIO, TELEKOM BW *(bandwidth)*

BZ *(Betriebszentrum)* TELEKOM operations center (AmE), operations centre (BrE)

C BAU *(Kapazität)*, ELEKTRIZ *(Kapazität)* C *(capacity)*, ELEKTRIZ *(Coulomb)* C *(coulomb)*, ELEKTROTECH *(Kapazität)* C *(capacity)*, ELEKTROTECH *(Coulomb)* C *(coulomb)*, ERDÖL *(Kapazität)*, HEIZ & KÄLTE *(Kapazität)* C *(capacity)*, HYDRAUL *(Cauchysche Zahl)* C *(Cauchy coefficient)*, HYDRAUL *(Chezy-Koeffizient)* C *(Chezy coefficient)*, HYDRAUL *(Ausflußkoeffizient, Durchflußkoeffizient)* C *(discharge coefficient)*, LABOR *(Celsius)* C *(centigrade)*, METROL *(Coulomb)* C *(coulomb)*, NICHTFOSS ENERG *(Schüttkoeffizient)* C *(discharge coefficient)*, PHYS *(Kapazität)* C *(capacitance)*, PHYS *(Coulomb)* C *(coulomb)*, RADIO *(Kapazität)*, TELEKOM *(Kapazität)* C *(capacitance)*

c ELEKTRONIK *(Konzentration)*, ELEKTRIZ *(Konzentration)* c *(concentration)*, HYDRAUL *(Wellenausbreitungsgeschwindigkeit)* c *(wave celerity)*, KOHLEN *(Konzentration)*, KUNSTSTOFF *(Konzentration)* c *(concentration)*, METROL *(Zenti-)*

c *(centi)*, METROL *(Lichtgeschwindigkeit)* c *(velocity of light)*, OPTIK *(Lichtgeschwindigkeit)* c *(speed of light in empty space)*, PHYS *(spezifische Wärme)* c *(specific heat capacity)*, PHYS *(Schallgeschwindigkeit)* c *(speed of sound)*, TELEKOM *(Konzentration)* c *(concentration)*, THERMOD *(spezifische Wärmekapazität)* c *(specific heat capacity)*, UMWELTSCHMUTZ *(Konzentration)* c *(concentration)*

CA HEIZ & KÄLTE *(kontrollierte Atmosphäre)* CA *(controlled atmosphere)*, KUNSTSTOFF *(Celluloseacetat)*, TEXTIL *(Celluloseacetat)* CA *(cellulose acetate)*

CAD *(computergestützte Konstruktion, computergestützter Entwurf)* COMP & DV, ELEKTRIZ, KONTROLL, MECHAN, TELEKOM, TRANS CAD *(computer-aided design)*

CADCAM *(computergestützte Konstruktion und Anfertigung)* COMP & DV CADCAM *(computer-aided design and manufacturing)*

CAL COMP & DV *(computergestützter Unterricht)* CAI *(computer-aided instruction)*, COMP & DV *(computergestütztes Lernen)* CAL *(computer-aided learning)*

CAM COMP & DV *(computergestützte Fertigung, computergestützte Produktion)* CAM *(computer-aided manufacturing)*, COMP& DV *(Assoziativspeicher, inhaltsadressierbarer Speicher)* CAM *(content-addressable memory)*, ELEKTRIZ *(computergestützte Fertigung, computergestützte Produktion)* CAM *(computer-aided manufacturing)*, KÜNSTL INT *(Assoziativspeicher, inhaltsadressierbarer Speicher)* CAM *(content-addressable memory)*

CAP *(computergestütztes Publizieren)* DRUCK CAP *(computer-aided publishing)*

CAR *(Zivilflugvorschriften)* RAUMFAHRT CAR *(Civil Air Regulations)*

CASE *(computergestützte Softwareentwicklung)* COMP & DV CASE *(computer-aided software engineering)*

CAT COMP & DV *(computerunterstützte Übersetzung)* CAT *(computer-assisted translation)*, ELEKTRONIK *(Senderöhre mit gekühlter Anode)* CAT *(cooled-anode transmitting valve)*, LUFTTRANS *(Kaltluftturbulenzen)* CAT *(cold air turbulence)*

CATV *(Fernsehen über Gemeinschaftsantenne)* FERNSEH CATV *(community antenna television system)*

CATVI FERNSEH *(Kabelfernsehstörung)*, RADIO *(störende Beeinflussung des Kabelfernsehdienstes)* CATVI *(cable television interference)*

CAV *(computerunterstütztes Sehen)* KÜNSTL INT CAV *(computer-aided vision)*

CCD *(Ladungsverschiebeelement, ladungsgekoppeltes Bauelement)* ELEKTRONIK, PHYS, TELEKOM CCD *(charge-coupled device)*

CCITT *(Internationaler Fernmeldeberatungsausschuß)* TELEKOM CCITT *(International Telegraph and Telephone Consultative Committee)*

CCTV *(Kabelfernsehen zu Überwachungszwecken)* FERNSEH CCTV *(closed-circuit television)*

CD COMP & DV *(Trägerdetektion, Trägererkennung)* CD *(carrier detection)*, COMP & DV *(Kollisionserkennung)* CD *(collision detection)*, COMP & DV *(Compact Disk)* CD *(compact disk)*, ELEKTRONIK *(Trägerdetektion, Trägererkennung)* CD *(carrier detection)*, OPTIK *(Compact Disk)* CD *(compact disk)*, TELEKOM *(Trägerdetektion, Trägererkennung)* CD *(carrier detection)*, TELEKOM *(Kollisionserkennung)* CD *(collision detection)*

cd *(Candela)* ELEKTROTECH, METROL, OPTIK, PHYS cd *(candela)*

CD-i *(beschreibbare CD)* OPTIK CD-I *(compact disk-interactive)*

CDM *(kompandierte Deltamodulation)* TELEKOM CDM *(companded delta modulation)*

CD-ROM COMP & DV *(Compact-Disk ohne Schreibmöglichkeit)*, OPTIK *(Compact-Disk-Speicher ohne Schreibmöglichkeit)* CD-ROM *(compact disk read-only memory)*

CE *(elektrische Kapazität)* AKUSTIK CE *(electric capacitance)*

CEBAF *(Gleichstromelektronenbeschleuniger)* TEILPHYS CEBAF *(continuous electron beam facility)*

CERN *(Europäisches Kernforschungszentrum)* TEILPHYS CERN *(European Organization for Nuclear Research)*

CGA *(Farbgrafikadapter)* COMP & DV CGA *(colour graphics adaptor)*

Ci *(Curie)* PHYS, STRAHLPHYS Ci *(curie)*

CIM COMP & DV *(CompuServe Information Manager®)* CIM *(CompuServe Information manager®)*, COMP & DV *(computerintegrierte Fertigung)* CIM *(computer-integrated manufacture)*

cim *(Kubikzoll pro Minute)* LABOR cim *(cubic inches per minute)*

CISC *(Prozessor mit komplettem Befehlssatz, konventioneller Rechner)* COMP & DV CISC *(complex instruction set computer)*

CL COMP & DV *(Befehlssprache, Betriebssprache)* CL *(command language)*, HYDRAUL *(Auftriebsbeiwert, Auftriebszahl)*, LUFTTRANS *(Auftriebszahl)*, NICHTFOSS ENERG *(Auftriebsbeiwert, Auftriebszahl)*, PHYS *(Auftriebsbeiwert, Auftriebszahl)*, WASSERTRANS *(Auftriebsbeiwert, Auftriebszahl)* CL *(lift coefficient)*

cl *(Geschwindigkeit von Längswellen)* AKUSTIK cl *(velocity of longitudinal waves)*

CM *(mechanische Auslenkung)* AKUSTIK CM *(mechanical compliance)*

CMC *(Carboxymethylcellulose)* KUNSTSTOFF, LEBENSMITTEL CMC *(carboxymethylcellulose)*

CMOS *(Komplementär-Metalloxid-Halbleiter)* COMP & DV, ELEKTRONIK CMOS *(complementary metal oxide semiconductor)*

CNC *(computernumerische Steuerung)* MASCHINEN CNC *(computerized numeric control)*

coax *(koaxial)* RADIO coax *(coaxial)*

COBOL *(problemorientierte Programmiersprache für Geschäftsbetrieb)* COMP & DV COBOL *(common business oriented language)*

COR *(Druckausgabeverkleinerung)* COMP & DV COR *(character output reduction)*

COSMOS *(Komplementär-Symmetrischer Metalloxid-Halbleiter)* ELEKTRONIK COSMOS *(complementary-symmetrical metal oxide semiconductor)*

cot *(Kotangens)* GEOM cot *(cotangent)*

Cp *(Wärmekapazität bei konstantem Druck)* LABOR Cp *(heat capacity at constant pressure)*

CPFSK *(phasenkontinuierliche Frequenzumtastung)* ELEKTRONIK, RADIO, TELEKOM CPFSK *(continuous phase frequency shift keying)*

CPK *(Chloroprenkautschuk)* KUNSTSTOFF CR *(chloroprene rubber)*

CPM *(Methode des kritischen Weges)* COMP & DV CPM *(critical path method)*

CPU *(Zentraleinheit, zentrale Rechnereinheit)* COMP & DV, TELEKOM CPU *(central processing unit)*

CR *(Rotationsauslenkung)* AKUSTIK CR *(rotational compliance)*

CRC *(zyklische Blockprüfung, zyklische Blocksicherung)* COMP & DV, ELEKTRONIK, LABOR, TELEKOM CRC *(cyclic redundancy check)*

CRCA *(kalt gewalzt und ausgeglüht)* METALL CRCA *(cold-rolled and annealed)*

CS *(Durchschaltevermittlung)* COMP & DV, TELEKOM CS *(circuit switching)*

CSB *(chemischer Sauerstoffbedarf)* UMWELTSCHMUTZ COD *(chemical oxygen demand)*

CSI *(Chlorschwefelisocyanat)* UMWELTSCHMUTZ CSI *(chlorosulfonyl isocyanate)*

CSM *(Kommando- und Servicemodul)* RAUMFAHRT Raumschiff CSM *(command and service module)*

CSMA *(Mehrfachzugriff durch Trägerprüfung)* COMP & DV CSMA *(carrier sense multiple access)*

CSMA/CD *(CSMA/CD-Verfahren)* COMP & DV CSMA/CD *(carrier sense multiple access with collision detection)*

CSN *(Durchschalte-Vermittlungsnetz)* COMP & DV, TELEKOM CSN *(circuit-switched network)*

CSPDN *(öffentliches Datenpaketvermittlungsnetz)* TELEKOM CSPDN *(circuit-switched public data network)*

ct *(Geschwindigkeit von Transversalwellen)* LABOR ct *(velocity of transversal waves)*

CTA *(Cellulosetriacetat)* KUNSTSTOFF CTA *(cellulose triacetate)*

CTCSS *(Hilfsträgergeräuschsperre)* RADIO CTCSS *(continuous tone-coded squelch system)*

CTD ELEKTROTECH *(Ladungsverschiebeschaltung)* Halbleiter, PHYS *(ladungsgekoppeltes Bauelement)*, RAUMFAHRT *(Ladungsübertragungsgerät)*, TELEKOM *(Ladungstransferelement)* CTD *(charge transfer device)*

CTS *(Containerschiff)* WASSERTRANS CTS *(container ship)*

CUG *(geschlossene Benutzergruppe, geschlossener Benutzerkreis)* COMP & DV, TELEKOM CUG *(closed user group)*

CVD *(Gasphasenabscheidung)* ELEKTRONIK, TELEKOM CVD *(chemical vapour deposition)*

CVS *(Teilstromentnahme nach Verdünnung)* UMWELTSCHMUTZ CVS *(constant volume sampling)*

CW *(Dauerstrich, ungedämpfte Welle)* AUFNAHME, ELEKTRONIK, ELEKTROTECH, FERNSEH CW *(continuous wave)*

D AKUSTIK *(Schwärzung)* D *(optical density)*, ELEKTRIZ *(Verschiebung)* D *(displacement)*, ELEKTRONIK *(Diffusionskoeffizient)* D *(diffusion coefficient)*, FERTIG *(Durchmesser)* D *(diameter)*, FERTIG *(Versetzung)* D *(displacement)*, GEOM *(Durchmesser)* D *(diameter)*, KERNTECH *(Absorptionsdosis)* D *(absorbed dose)*, MASCHINEN *(Durchmesser)* D *(diameter)*, OPTIK *(optische Dichte)* D *(optical density)*, PHYS *(Diffusionskoeffizient)* D *(diffusion coefficient)*, PHYS *(Versetzung)* D *(displacement)*, RADIO *(Diffusionskoeffizient)* D *(diffusion coefficient)*, STRAHLPHYS *(absorbierte Dosis)* D *(absorbed dose)*, THERMOD *(vierter Virialkoeffizient)* D *(fourth virial coefficient)*

d CHEMIE *(Deuteron)* d *(deuteron)*, LABOR *(Dezi-)* d

(deci-), PHYS *(Deuteron)*, TEILPHYS *(Deuteron)* d *(deuteron)*

D/A *(Digital-Analog-)* AUFNAHME, COMP & DV, ELEKTRONIK, FERNSEH, LABOR, TELEKOM D/A *(digital-analog)*

DA *(direkter Zugriff)* COMP & DV DA *(direct access)*

da *(Deka-)* LABOR da *(deca-)*

DAMA *(bedarfsgesteuerter Vielfachzugriff)* TELEKOM DAMA *(demand-assigned multiple access)*

DAT *(Digital-Audio-Tape)* AUFNAHME DAT *(digital audio tape)*

DAU *(Digital-Analog-Umsetzer)* COMP & DV, ELEKTRONIK, FERNSEH, TELEKOM DAC *(digital-analog converter)*

dB *(Dezibel)* AKUSTIK, AUFNAHME, ELEKTRONIK, PHYS, RADIO, STRAHLPHYS, UMWELTSCHMUTZ dB *(decibel)*

DBA *(Datenbankadministrator, Datenbankverwalter)* COMP & DV DBA *(database administrator)*

dBi *(Dezibel über Isotropstrahler)* STRAHLPHYS dBi *(decibels over isotropic)*

DCC *(Datenübermittlungskanal)* TELEKOM DCC *(data communication channel)*

DCD *(Datenträgerdetektor)* TELEKOM DCD *(data carrier detector)*

DCTL *(direktgekoppelte Transistorlogik)* ELEKTRONIK DCTL *(direct-coupled transistor logic)*

DD HYDRAUL *(Strömungswiderstand)*, NICHTFOSS ENERG *(Luftwiderstandsbeiwert, Widerstandsbeiwert)* DD *(coefficient of drag)*

DDE *(direkte Dateneingabe, direkter Dateneintrag)* COMP & DV DDE *(direct data entry)*

DDP *(Doppeldiodenpentode)* ELEKTRONIK DDP *(double diode pentode)*

DDT *(Dichlordiphenyltrichlorproäthan)* CHEMIE DDT *(dichlordiphenyltrichlorproethane)*

DEE *(Datenendeinrichtung)* COMP & DV, TELEKOM DTE *(data terminal equipment)*

DESY *(Deutsches Elektronensynchroton)* TEILPHYS DESY

DFT *(diskrete Fourier-Transformation)* ELEKTRONIK DFT *(discrete Fourier transform)*

DFV *(Datenfernverarbeitung)* COMP & DV TP *(teleprocessing)*

DGPS *(Differential-GPS)* WASSERTRANS Satellitennavigation DGPS *(differential global positioning system)*

Di *(Richtwirkungsindex)* AKUSTIK Di *(directivity index)*

Diac *(bidirektionale Triggerdiode)* ELEKTRONIK, RADIO diac *(diode alternating-current switch)*

DIN *(Deutsches Institut für Normung)* MASCHINEN DIN, German Standards Institution

DIP *(Doppelreihenanschluß gehäuse)* ELEKTROTECH DIP *(dual-in-line package)*

dl *(Deziliter)* LABOR dl *(deciliter)*

DM *(Deltamodulation)* ELEKTRONIK, RAUMFAHRT, TELEKOM DM *(delta modulation)*

DMA *(Direkt-Speicherzugriff, Direktzugriffsspeicher)* COMP & DV DMA *(direct memory access)*

DMC *(kittartige Formmasse)* KUNSTSTOFF DMC *(dough-moulding compound)*

D₂O *(Deuteriumoxid)* CHEMIE D_2O *(deuterium oxide)*

DOP *(Dioctylphthalat)* KUNSTSTOFF DOP *(dioctylphthalate)*

DP *(Diametral-Pitch)* MASCHINEN DP *(diametral pitch)*

DPCM *(Differenz-Pulscodemodulation)* ELEKTRONIK

DPCM *(differential pulse code modulation)*

DPDT *(zweipoliger Umschalter, zweipoliger Wechselschalter)* ELEKTROTECH DPDT *(double-pole double-throw)*

DPSK *(Phasendifferenzmodulation, Phasendifferenzumtastung)* ELEKTRONIK DPSK *(differential phase shift keying)*

DPST *(zweipoliger Einl Aus-Schalter)* ELEKTROTECH DPST *(double-pole single-throw)*

dpt *(Dioptrie)* OPTIK dpt *(dioptre)*

DRAM *(dynamischer RAM)* COMP & DV DRAM *(dynamic random access memory)*

3-D *(dreidimensional)* MASCHINEN , PHYS 3-D *(three-dimensional)*

DSB *(Doppelseitenband)* ELEKTRONIK, RADIO DSB *(double sideband)*

DSI *(digitale Sprachinterpolation)* RAUMFAHRT, TELEKOM DSI *(digital speech interpolation)*

DSV *(Digitalsignalverbindung)* TELEKOM digital connection

DT *(Dichtigkeitstest)* ERDÖL LOT *(leak-off test)*

DTA *(Differentialthermoanalyse)* KUNSTSTOFF, THERMOD, UMWELTSCHMUTZ DTA *(differential thermal analysis)*

DTL *(Dioden-Transistor-Logik)* ELEKTRONIK DTL *(diode transistor logic)*

DTP *(Desktop-Publishing)* COMP & DV, DRUCK DTP *(desktop publishing)*

DÜE *(Datenübertragungseinrichtung)* COMP & DV DCE *(data communication terminating equipment)*, TELEKOM DCE *(data circuit terminating equipment)*

DV *(Datenverarbeitung)* COMP & DV, ELEKTRONIK, KONTROLL, TELEKOM DP *(data processing)*

E DRUCK *(Evaporation, Verdampfung)* E *(evaporation)*, ELEKTRIZ *(elektrische Feldstärke)* E *(electric field strength)*, ELEKTRIZ *(Energie)* E *(energy)*, ELEKTROTECH *(elektrischer Feldvektor)* E *(electric field vector)*, ELEKTROTECH *(elektrische Feldstärke)* E *(electric field strength)*, ELEKTROTECH *(Energie)* E *(energy)*, ERDÖL *(Evaporation, Verdampfung)* E *(evaporation)*, ERDÖL *(Youngscher Modul)* Elastizität E *(Young's modulus)*, HEIZ & KÄLTE *(Evaporation, Verdampfung)*, HYDRAUL *(Evaporation, Verdampfung)* E *(evaporation)*, HYDRAUL *(Youngscher Modul)* Elastizität E *(Young's modulus)*, KERNTECH *(Energie)* E *(energy)*, KOHLEN *(Youngscher Modul)* Elastizität, KUNSTSTOFF *(Youngscher Modul)* Elastizität E *(Young's modulus)*, MASCHINEN *(Evaporation, Verdampfung)* E *(evaporation)*, MECHAN *(Energie)* E *(energy)*, METALL *(Youngscher Modul)* Elastizität E *(Young's modulus)*, METROL *(Energie)* E *(energy)*, NICHTFOSS ENERG *(Evaporation, Verdampfung)* E *(evaporation)*, OPTIK *(Energie)* power, PHYS *(elektrische Feldstärke)* E *(electric field strength)*, PHYS *(Energie)* E *(energy)*, PHYS *(Evaporation, Verdampfung)* E *(evaporation)*, PHYS *(Youngscher Modul)* Elastizität E *(Young's modulus)*, THERMOD *(Energie)* E *(energy)*, THERMOD *(Evaporation, Verdampfung)* E *(evaporation)*

e *(Elektron)* ELEKTRIZ, ELEKTROTEC, PHYS, RADIO, TEILPHYS e *(electron)*

E/A COMP & DV *(Eingabel Ausgabe)*, ELEKTRIZ *(Eingabel Ausgabe, Eingangl Ausgang)* I/O *(input/output)*

EAS *(äquivalente Fluggeschwindigkeit)* LUFTTRANS EAS *(equivalent airspeed)*

EC *(Ethylcellulose)* KUNSTSTOFF EC *(ethyl cellulose)*

ECL *(emittergekoppelte Logik)* COMP & DV, ELEKTRONIK ECL *(emitter-coupled logic)*

EDTV *(hochauflösendes Fernsehen)* FERNSEH EDTV *(extended definition television)*

EDV *(elektronische Datenverarbeitung)* COMP & DV, ELEKTRIZ, ELEKTRONIK, KONTROLL EDP *(electronic data processing)*

EEB *(elektroerosive Bearbeitung)* MASCHINEN EDM *(electro-discharge machining)*

EEPROM *(elektrisch löschbarer programmierbarer Lesespeicher)* ELEKTRONIK EEPROM *(electrically-erasable programmable read-only memory)*

EEROM *(elektronisch löschbarer Festwertspeicher, elektronisch löschbarer Lesespeicher)* COMP & DV EEROM *(electronically erasable read-only memory)*

EFS *(essentielle Fettsäure)* LEBENSMITTEL EFA *(essential fatty acid)*

EFuRD *(Europäischer Funkrufdienst)* TELEKOM European radio-paging system

EHF *(Millimeterwellen)* RADIO EHF *(extremely high frequency)*

E.h.t. *(Hochspannung, Höchstspannung)* FERNSEH EHT *(extremely high tension)*

EIRP *(äquivalente Isotropenstrahlungsleistung)* RADIO, RAUMFAHRT EIRP *(effective isotropically-radiated power)*

EL *(Elektrolumineszenz-Anzeige)* ELEKTRONIK EL *(electroluminescent display)*

ELED *(Kantenemitter-Lumineszenzdiode, kantenstrahlende Lumineszenzdiode)* TELEKOM ELED *(edge-emitting light-emitting diode)*

ELSBM *(ungeschützte Einzeltonnenvertäuung)* ERDÖL ELSBM *(exposed location single buoy mooring)*

EMK *(elektromotorische Kraft)* BAU, EISENBAHN, ELEKTRIZ, ELEKTROTECH, FERNSEH, PHYS, RADIO EMF *(electromotive force)*

EMS *(Expansionsspeicher-Spezifikation)* COMP & DV EMS *(expanded memory specification)*

EMV *(elektromagnetische Verträglichkeit)* ELEKTRIZ, RADIO, RAUMFAHRT Raumfahrt EMC *(electromagnetic compatibility)*

EN *(Europäische Norm)* ELEKTRIZ European Standard

ENF *(extrem niedrige Frequenz)* RADIO ELF *(extremely low frequency)*

EOB *(Blockende)* COMP & DV EOB *(end of block)*

EOD *(Datenende)* COMP & DV EOD *(end of data)*

EOF *(Dateiende)* COMP & DV EOF *(end of file)*

EOM *(Nachrichtenende)* COMP & DV EOM *(end of message)*

EOT *(Bandende)* COMP & DV EOT *(end of tape)*

EP *(Höchstdruck)* MASCHINEN EP *(extreme pressure)*

EPIRB *(Satellitennetzwerk zur Ortung von Schiffen in Seenot)* WASSERTRANS Funk EPIRB *(emergency position-indicating radio beacon)*

EPM *(Äquivalent je Million)* UMWELTSCHMUTZ EPM *(equivalent per million)*

EPNS *(versilberte Gegenstände)* METALL EPNS *(electroplated nickel silver)*

EPROM *(löschbarer programmierbarer Lesespeicher)* COMP & DV, RADIO EPROM *(erasable programmable read-only memory)*

ε HYDRAUL *(kinematische Wirbelzähigkeit)* ε *(kinematic eddy viscosity)*, PHYS *(durchschnittliche kinetische Molekularenergie)* ε *(average molecular kinetic energy)*

Erl *(Erlang)* TELEKOM Erl *(Erlang)*

ES ELEKTRONIK *(Elektronenstrahl)*, KERNTECH *(Elektronenstrahl)* EB *(electronic beam)*, KÜNSTL INT *(Expertensystem)* ES *(expert system)*

Es *(Einsteinium)* CHEMIE, STRAHLPHYS Es *(einsteinium)*

ESA RAUMFAHRT *(Europäische Raumfahrtbehörde)* ESA *(European Space Agency)*, UMWELTSCHMUTZ *(elektrostatischer Staubabscheider)* ESP *(electrostatic precipitator)*

ESCA *(Fotoelektronenspektroskopie)* PHYS ESCA *(electron spectroscopy for chemical analysis)*

ESPRIT ELEKTRIZ ESPRIT, European Semiconductor Production Research Initiative

ESR *(Elektronenspinresonanz)* PHYS, STRAHLPHYS, TEILPHYS ESR *(electron spin resonance)*

ETA *(voraussichtliche Ankunftszeit)* LUFTTRANS, WASSERTRANS ETA *(estimated time of arrival)*

ETD *(voraussichtliche Abflugszeit)* LUFTTRANS, WASSERTRANS ETD *(estimated time of departure)*

EURATOM *(Europäische Atomgemeinschaft)* TEILPHYS EURATOM *(European Organization for Nuclear Research)*

eV *(Elektronenvolt)* ELEKTRIZ, ELEKTROTECH, PHYS, STRAHLPHYS, TEILPHYS eV *(electronvolt)*

EVA *(Ethylenvinylacetat)* KUNSTSTOFF EVA *(ethylene vinyl acetate)*

EVS *(Endvermittlungsstelle)* TELEKOM terminating exchange

EVU *(Elektrizitätsversorgungsunternehmen)* ELEKTRIZ electricity supply company

F AKUSTIK *(Frequenz)*, AUFNAHME *(Frequenz)*, COMP & DV *(Frequenz)* f *(frequency)*, ELEKTRIZ *(Farad)* F *(farad)*, ELEKTRONIK *(Rauschzahl)* F *(noise figure)*, ELEKTRONIK *(Frequenz)* f *(frequency)*, ELEKTROTECH *(Farad)* F *(farad)*, HYDRAUL *(Froudensche Zahl)* F *(Froude number)*, KERNTECH *(hyperfeine Quantenzahl)* F *(hyperfine quantum number)*, METALL *(Kraft)* F *(force)*, METALL *(freie Energie)* F *(free energy)*, METROL *(Fahrenheit)* F *(Fahrenheit)*, METROL *(Farad)* F *(farad)*, METROL *(Femto-)* f *(femto-)*, PHYS *(Froudensche Zahl)* F *(Froude number)*, PHYS *(Farad)* F *(farad)*, PHYS *(Kraft)* F *(force)*, PHYS *(freie Energie)* F *(free energy)*, PHYS *(Frequenz)* f *(frequency)*, RADIO *(Rauschzahl)* F *(noise figure)*, RADIO *(Frequenz)* f *(frequency)*

fA *(Antiresonanzfrequenz)* AKUSTIK, ELEKTRONIK fA *(antiresonant frequency)*

fas *(frei Längsseite Schiff)* WASSERTRANS fas *(free alongside ship)*

FB *(Flughafenbake)* LUFTTRANS, RAUMFAHRT ABn *(aerodrome beacon BrE, airdrome beacon AmE)*

FCKW *(Fluorchlorokohlenwasserstoff)* UMWELTSCHMUTZ, VERPACK CFC *(chlorofluorocarbon)*

FCNE *(Flugüberwachungs- und Navigationsausrüstung)* LUFTTRANS FCNE *(flight control and navigational equipment)*

FEM *(Finite-Elemente-Methode)* MASCHINEN FEM *(finite elements method)*

FET *(Feldeffekttransistor)* COMP & DV, ELEKTRONIK, OPTIK, PHYS, RADIO, RAUMFAHRT FET *(field effect transistor)*

FFS *(flexibles Fertigungssystem)* KÜNSTL INT FMS *(flexible manufacturing system)*

FFT *(schnelle Fourier-Transformation)* ELEKTRONIK

FFT *(fast Fourier transform)*

FHV *(Fernleitungshauptverteiler)* TELEKOM TDF *(trunk distribution frame)*

FIFA *(Spaltstoffabbrand, Spaltstoffverbrauch)* KERNTECH FIFA *(fissions per initial fissile atom)*

FIR *(begrenztes Ansprechen auf einen Impuls)* ELEKTRONIK FIR *(finite impulse response)*

FKO *(Fließkommaoperation)* COMP & DV FLOP *(floating-point operation)*

FKP *(Fließkommaprozessor)* COMP & DV FPP *(floating-point processor)*

FM *(Frequenzmodulation)* COMP & DV, ELEKTRONIK, PHYS, RADIO, TELEKOM FM *(frequency modulation)*

FMR *(Flüssigmetallreaktor)* KERNTECH FSR *(flowable solids reactor)*

fob *(frei an Bord)* ERDÖL, WASSERTRANS fob *(free on board)*

FPS *(schnelle Paketvermittlung)* TELEKOM FPS *(fast packet server)*

fR *(Resonanzfrequenz)* AKUSTIK, ELEKTRONIK, TELEKOM, WELLPHYS fR *(resonant frequency)*

FS COMP & DV *(Fernschreiber)* TTY *(teletypewriter)*, LUFTTRANS *(Flugsicherung)* ATC *(air traffic control)*, MASCHINEN *(Festsitz)* force fit, TELEKOM *(Fernschreiber)* TTY *(teletypewriter)*

FSK *(Frequenzumtastung)* COMP & DV, ELEKTRONIK, RADIO, TELEKOM FSK *(frequency shift keying)*

FSTV *(Breitbandfernsehen)* FERNSEH FSTV *(fast-scan television)*

FVSt *(Fernvermittlungsstelle)* TELEKOM toll exchange (AmE), trunk exchange (BrE), trunk switching center (AmE), trunk switching centre (BrE)

G AUFNAHME *(Gauß)*, ELEKTRIZ *(Gauß)* G *(gauss)*, ELEKTRONIK *(Gewinn)*, ERGON *(Gewinn)*, FERNSEH *(Gewinn)* G *(gain)*, MASCHINEN *(Schermodul)* G *(shear modulus)*, METROL *(Giga-)* G *(giga)*, PHYS *(Gibbssche Funktion)* G *(Gibbs function)*, PHYS *(Schermodul)* G *(shear modulus)*, RADIO *(Gewinn)*, RAUMFAHRT *(Gewinn)*, TELEKOM *(Gewinn)* G *(gain)*, THERMOD *(Gibbssche Funktion)* G *(Gibbs function)*

g CHEMIE *(Gramm)* g *(gram)*, KERNTECH *(gyromagnetisches Verhältnis)* g *(gyromagnetic ratio)*, LABOR *(Gramm)*, PHYS *(Gramm)* g *(gram)*, PHYS *(gyromagnetisches Verhältnis)* g *(gyromagnetic ratio)*, PHYS *(statistisches Gewicht)* g *(statistical weight)*, RAUMFAHRT *(Erdbeschleunigung)* g *(gravitational acceleration)*

GaAs *(Galliumarsenid)* ELEKTRONIK, OPTIK, PHYS, RADIO GaAs *(gallium arsenide)*

GAU *(größter anzunehmender Unfall)* KERNTECH MCA *(maximum credible accident)*

GB *(Gigabyte)* COMP & DV, OPTIK GB *(gigabyte)*

GFK KUNSTSTOFF *(Glasfaserkunststoff, glasfaserverstärkter Kunststoff)*, VERPACK *(glasfaserverstärkter Kunststoff)*, WASSERTRANS *(glasfaserverstärkter Kunststoff)* Schiffbau GRP *(glass fiber-reinforced plastic, glass fibre-reinforced plastic)*

ggT *(größter gemeinsamer Teiler)* MATH HCF *(highest common factor)*

GIGO *(Müll rein, Müll raus)* COMP & DV GIGO *(garbage in, garbage out)*

GII *(globale Informations-Infrastruktur)* COMP & DV GII *(Global Information Infrastructure)*

GMDSS *(System zur Rettung von Menschenleben bei Seenotfällen)* WASSERTRANS GMDSS *(global marine *distress and safety system)*

g/m² *(Gramm pro Quadratmeter)* DRUCK gsm *(grams per square metre)*

GÖV *(Gas-Öl-Verhältnis)* ERDÖL *Lagerstättentechnik* GOR *(gas-to-oil ratio)*

GP *(Glühpunkt)* METALL AP *(annealing point)*

GPC *(Gel-Permeations-Chromatographie)* KUNST-STOFF, LABOR GPC *(gel permeation chromatography)*

GPG *(Grundprimärgruppe)* TELEKOM basic group

GPS *(globales Positionsbestimmungssystem)* WASSER-TRANS *Satellitennavigation* GPS *(global-positioning system)*

GrVST *(Gruppenvermittlungsstelle)* TELEKOM GSC *(group-switching centre)*

GS *(Gleichstrom)* AUFNAHME, COMP & DV, EISENBAHN, ELEKTRIZ, ELEKTROTECH, FERNSEH, FERTIG, PHYS, RA-DIO, TELEKOM DC *(direct current)*

GSZ *(Gesamtsäurezahl)* CHEMIE TAN *(total acid number)*

Gx *(Systemkonstante)* AKUSTIK Gx *(system-rating constant)*

gy *(Gray)* PHYS *Einheit der Energiedosis,* TEILPHYS *Einheit der Strahlendosis* gy *(gray)*

H ELEKTRIZ *(Henry)* H *(henry)*, ELEKTRIZ *(magnetische Feldstärke)* H *(magnetic field strength)*, ELEKTROTECH *(Henry)* H *(henry)*, ELEKTROTECH *(magnetische Feldstärke)* H *(magnetic field strength)*, HEIZ & KÄLTE *(Enthalpie)* H *(enthalpy)*, HYDRAUL *(Hamiltonsche Funktion)* H *(Hamiltonian function)*, KOHLEN *(Enthalpie)*, MECHAN *(Enthalpie)* H *(enthalpy)*, METROL *(Henry)* H *(henry)*, NICHT-FOSS ENERG *(Enthalpie)* H *(enthalpy)*, OPTIK *(Bestrahlungsstärke)* H *(irradiance)*, PHYS *(Enthalpie)* H *(enthalpy)*, PHYS *(Henry)* H *(henry)*, PHYS *(Magnetfeldstärke)* H *(magnetic field strength)*, RA-DIO *(Henry)* H *(henry)*, RAUMFAHRT *(Enthalpie)*, THERMOD *(Enthalpie)* H *(enthalpy)*

h COMP & DV *(Höhe)*, GEOM *(Höhe)* h *(height)*, METROL *(Hekto-)* h *(hecto-)*, METROL *(Stunde)* h *(hour)*, PHYS *(Plancksche Konstante, Plancksches Wirkungsquantum)* h *(Planck's constant)*, RADIO *(Höhe)* h *(height)*, STRAHLPHYS *(Plancksche Konstante, Plancksches Wirkungsquantum)*, TEILPHYS *(Plancksche Konstante, Plancksches Wirkungsquantum)* h *(Planck's constant)*

ha *(Hektar)* LABOR ha *(hectare)*

HADES *(Dielektronen-Spektrometer mit hoher Akzeptanz)* TEILPHYS HADES *(high acceptance di-electron spectrometer)*

HC *(Großraumcontainer)* TRANS HC *(High Cube)*

HD COMP & DV *(Festplatte)* HD *(hard disk)*, COMP & DV *(halbduplex)* HDX *(half-duplex)*, MASCHINEN *(Hochleistung)* HD *(heavy duty)*, TELEKOM *(Festplatte)* HD *(hard disk)*

HDTV *(hochauflösendes Fernsehen, hochzeiliges Fernsehverfahren)* FERNSEH HDTV *(high-definition television)*

HERA *(Hadron-Elektron-Ring-Anlage)* TEILPHYS HERA *(hadron-electron ring collider)*

HEX COMP & DV *(hexadezimal)*, GEOM *(hexadezimal)* hex *(hexadecimal)*, GEOM *(Hexagon)* hex *(hexagon)*

HF AUFNAHME *(Funkfrequenz, Hochfrequenz)* HF *(high frequency)*, RF *(radio frequency)*, ELEKTRIZ *(Hochfrequenz)* HF *(high frequency)*, ELEKTRONIK *(Funkfrequenz, Hochfrequenz)*, FERNSEH *(Funkfre-*

quenz, Hochfrequenz) HF *(high frequency)*, RF *(radio frequency)*, RADIO *(Hochfrequenz)* HF *(high frequency)*, RADIO *(Funkfrequenz)* RF *(radio frequency)*, TELEKOM *(Funkfrequenz, Hochfrequenz)* HF *(high frequency)*, RF *(radio frequency)*, WASSER-TRANS *(Hochfrequenz)* HF *(high frequency)*, RF *(radio frequency)*

hl *(Hektoliter)* LABOR hl *(hectoliter)*

HNF *(höchste nutzbare Frequenz)* RADIO MUF *(maximum usable frequency)*

HPLC *(Hochdruckflüssigchromatographie)* LABOR, LE-BENSMITTEL HPLC *(high-pressure liquid chromatography)*

HPS *(höhere Programmiersprache)* COMP & DV, TELE-KOM HLL *(high-level language)*

HTR *(Hochtemperaturreaktor)* KERNTECH HTR *(high-temperature reactor)*

HVSt *(Hauptvermittlungsstelle)* TELEKOM main exchange

HVStd *(Hauptverkehrsstunde)* TELEKOM busy hour

HVt *(Hauptverteiler)* TELEKOM MDF *(main distribution frame)*

HWZ *(Halbwertszeit)* KERNTECH, PHYS, STRAHLPHYS, TEILPHYS T^1/$_2$ *(half-life)*, TELEKOM FDHM *(full duration half maximum)*

Hz *(Hertz)* ELEKTRIZ, ELEKTROTECH, FERNSEH, METROL, PHYS, RADIO Hz *(hertz)*

HZK *(höchstzulässige Konzentration)* UMWELT-SCHMUTZ MAC *(maximum allowable concentration)*, TLV *(threshold limit value)*

I AKUSTIK *(Intensität, Stärke)* I *(intensity)*, ELEKTRIZ *(elektrischer Strom)* I *(electric current)*, ELEKTRIZ *(Intensität)* I *(intensity)*, KERNTECH *(Energiefluß-dichte)* I *(energy flux density)*, KERNTECH *(nukleare Spinquantenzahl)* I *(nuclear spin quantum number)*, OPTIK *(Intensität)* I *(intensity)*, PHYS *(elektrischer Strom)*, TELEKOM *(elektrischer Strom)* I *(electric current)*

ICAS *(Kommerzieller und Amateurfunkdienst)* RADIO ICAS *(Intermittent Commercial and Amateur Services)*

ICRP *(Internationale Strahlenschutzkommission)* STRAHLPHYS ICRP *(International Commission on Radiological Protection)*

ID *(Identifikation, Kennung)* COMP & DV identification

IFR *(Instrumentenflugregeln)* LUFTTRANS IFR *(instrument flight rules)*

IFRB *(Internationale Frequenz-Zuweisungsbehörde)* RAUMFAHRT IFRB *(International Frequency Registration Board)*

IGFET *(Isolierschicht-Feldeffekttransistor)* ELEKTRO-NIK, RADIO IGFET *(insulated gate field-effect transistor)*

IIR *(unbegrenztes Ansprechen auf Impuls)* ELEKTRONIK IIR *(infinite impulse response)*

ILS *(Blindfluglandesystem durch Eigenpeilung, Instrumentenlandesystem)* LUFTTRANS, RAUMFAHRT ILS *(instrument landing system)*

IM FERTIG *(Injection-Moulding, Spritzgießen)*, KUNST-STOFF *(Injection-Moulding, Spritzgießen, Spritzgießmasse)*, KUNSTSTOFF *(Spritzgießmaschine)*, VERPACK *(Injection-Moulding, Spritzgießen)* IM *(injection molding, injection moulding)*

IMD AUFNAHME *(Intermodulationsverzerrung)*, ELEK-TRONIK *(Zwischenmodulationsverzerrung)*, RADIO

(Intermodulationsverzerrung) IMD *(intermodulation distortion)*

IMO *(Internationale Schifffahrtorganisation)* WASSER-TRANS *Behörde* IMO *(International Maritime Organization)*

IOS ELEKTRONIK *(integrierter optischer Schaltkreis)*, OPTIK *(integrierter optischer Schaltkreis)*, TELEKOM *(integrierte optische Schaltung)* IOC *(integrated optical circuit)*

IP *(Eingabe)* COMP & DV IP *(input)*

IPL *(Initialprogrammlader)* COMP & DV IPL *(initial program loader)*

IR COMP & DV *(Wiederauffinden von Informationen)* IR *(information retrieval)*, KUNSTSTOFF *(Infrarot)*, OPTIK *(Infrarot)*, PHYS *(Infrarot)*, STRAHLPHYS *(Infrarot)* IR *(infrared)*

IRPTC *(Internationales Verzeichnis für potentiell toxische Chemikalien)* UMWELTSCHMUTZ IRPTC *(International Register of Potentially Toxic Chemicals)*

IRS *(Internationales Referenzsystem)* UMWELT-SCHMUTZ IRS *(International Referral System)*

IS COMP & DV *(Integrierschaltung, integrierte Schaltung, integrierter Schaltkreis)*, ELEKTRIZ *(Integrierschaltung, integrierte Schaltung, integrierter Schaltkreis)*, ELEKTRONIK *(Integrierschaltung, integrierte Schaltung, integrierter Schaltkreis)* IC *(integrated circuit)*, ELEKTRONIK *(Sättigungsstrom)* IS *(saturation current)*, KONTROLL *(Integrierschaltung, integrierte Schaltung, integrierter Schaltkreis)*, PHYS *(Integrierschaltung, integrierte Schaltung, integrierter Schaltkreis)* IC *(integrated circuit)*, PHYS *(Sättigungsstrom)* IS *(saturation current)*, RADIO *(Integrierschaltung, integrierte Schaltung, integrierter Schaltkreis)* IC *(integrated circuit)*, RADIO *(Sättigungsstrom)* IS *(saturation current)*, TELEKOM *(Integrierschaltung, integrierte Schaltung, integrierter Schaltkreis)* IC *(integrated circuit)*

ISB *(unabhängiges Seitenband)* RADIO ISB *(independent sideband)*

ISDN *(integriertes digitales Fernmeldenetz)* TELEKOM ISDN *(integrated service digital network)*

ISM *(Betriebsüberwachung)* TELEKOM ISM *(in-service monitoring)*

ISO *(Internationale Normungsorganisation)* ELEKTRIZ, MASCHINEN ISO *(International Standards Organization)*

ISW *(internationale Selbstwahl)* TELEKOM IDD *(international direct dialling)*, IDDD *(international direct distance dialling)*

ITA *(internationales Telegraphenalphabet)* LUFTTRANS, WASSERTRANS ITA *(international telegraph alphabet)*

ITU *(Internationale Fernmeldeunion)* RADIO, WASSER-TRANS ITU *(International Telecommunications Union)*

IUC *(Meß- und Regeltechnik)* ELEKTRONIK IUC *(instrumentation and control)*

J AKUSTIK *(Schallenergiefluß)* J *(sound-energy flux)*, ELEKTRIZ *(Joule)* J *(joule)*, KERNTECH *(Winkelmomentquantenzahl)* J *(total angular momentum quantum* number*)*, LEBENSMITTEL *(Joule)*, MECHAN *(Joule)* J *(joule)*, MECHAN *(mechanisches Wärmeäquivalent)* J *(mechanical equivalent of heat)*, METROL *(Joule)*, PHYS *(Joule)* J *(joule)*, PHYS *(Schallenergiefluß)* J *(sound-energy flux)*, THERMOD *(Joule)* J

(joule), THERMOD *(mechanisches Wärmeäquivalent)* J *(mechanical equivalent of heat)*

j *(Sprunghöhe)* HYDRAUL j *(height of hydraulic jump)*

JET STRAHLPHYS JET, Joint European Torus

K AKUSTIK *(Magnetostriktionskonstante)* K *(magnetostriction constant)*, ELEKTRIZ *(Kelvin)* K *(kelvin)*, HYDRAUL *(Kompressionsmodul)* K *(bulk modulus of compression)*, HYDRAUL *(Elastizitätsmodul)* K *(bulk modulus of elasticity)*, KERNTECH *(Kerma)* K *(kerma)*, METROL *(Kelvin)*, PHYS *(Kelvin)* K *(kelvin)*, PHYS *(freigesetzte kinetische Energie geladener Teilchen in Materie)* K *(kerma)*, THERMOD *(Gleichgewichtskonstante)* K *(equilibrium constant)*, THERMOD *(Kelvin)* K *(kelvin)*

k AKUSTIK *(Wellenkonstante)* k *(wave constant)*, ELEKTRIZ *(Kopplungskoeffizient)* k *(coupling coefficient)*, KERNTECH *(Multiplikationskonstante für infinite Systeme)* k *(multiplication constant for an infinite system)*, KERNTECH *(Neutronenmultiplikationskonstante)* k *(neutron multiplication constant)*, LABOR *(Kilo, Kilogramm)* k *(kilo)*, PHYS *(Boltzmannsche Konstante, Boltzmannsche Zahl)* k *(Boltzmann constant)*, PHYS *(Kopplungskoeffizient)* k *(coupling coefficient)*, THERMOD *(Boltzmannsche Konstante, Boltzmannsche Zahl)* k *(Boltzmann constant)*

KARS *(kohärente Antistokes-Raman-Streuung)* STRAHLPHYS, WELLPHYS CARS *(coherent anti-Stokes Raman scattering)*

KAW *(Kanaladreßwort)* COMP & DV CAW *(channel address word)*

KB *(Kilobyte)* COMP & DV, TELEKOM KB *(kilobyte)*

kcal *(Kilokalorie)* LEBENSMITTEL kcal *(kilocalorie)*

keff *(effektive Neutronen-Multiplikationskonstante)* KERNTECH keff *(effective neutron multiplication constant)*

keV *(Kilo-Elektronenvolt)* TEILPHYS keV *(kilo electronvolt)*

KF *(Konfidenzfaktor)* KÜNSTL INT CF *(confidence factor)*

kfG *(kontextfreie Grammatik)* KÜNSTL INT CFG *(context-free grammar)*

Kfz *(Kraftfahrzeug)* KFZTECH MC *(motorcar)*

kg *(Kilo, Kilogramm)* LABOR, PHYS kg *(kilogram)*

kgN *(kleinster gemeinsamer Nenner)* MATH LCD *(least common denominator)*

kgT *(kleinster gemeinsamer Teiler)* GEOM LCD *(least common denominator)*

kgV *(kleinstes gemeinsames Vielfaches)* COMP & DV LCM *(least common multiple)*, GEOM LCM *(lowest common multiple)*

kHz *(Kilohertz)* ELEKTRIZ, RADIO kHz *(kilohertz)*

KNN *(künstliches neuronales Netzwerk)* KÜNSTL INT ANN *(artificial neural network)*

KPK *(kritische Pigmentvolumenkonzentration)* KUNST-STOFF cpvc *(critical pigment volume concentration)*

KS *(Kerbstift)* FERTIG, MASCHINEN grooved pin, splined pin

ksG *(kontextsensitive Grammatik)* KÜNSTL INT CSG *(context-sensitive grammar)*

KSR *(Kathodenstrahlröhre)* COMP & DV, DRUCK, ELEKTRIZ, ELEKTRONIK, FERNSEH, RADIO CRT *(cathode-ray tube)*

KV *(kombinierter Verteiler)* TELEKOM CDF *(combined distribution frame)*

kV *(Kilovolt)* ELEKTROTECH kV *(kilovolt)*

kW *(Kilowatt)* ELEKTRIZ kW *(kilowatt)*

kWh *(Kilowattstunde)* ELEKTRIZ, ELEKTROTECH, PHYS kWh *(kilowatt hour)*

KZG *(Kurzzeitgedächtnis)* ERGON, KÜNSTL INT STM *(short-term memory)*

L AKUSTIK *(Lautstärke)* L *(loudness)*, AUFNAHME *(Induktivität)*, ELEKTRIZ *(Induktivität)*, ELEKTROTECH *(Induktivität)* L *(inductance)*, KERNTECH *(Diffusionslänge)* L *(diffusion length)*, KERNTECH *(lineare Energieübertragung)* L *(linear energy transfer)*, KERNTECH *(Orbitalwinkelmomentzahl)* L *(total orbital angular momentum number)*, MECHAN *(Lagrangesche Funktion)* L *(Lagrangian function)*, METROL *(Induktivität)* L *(inductance)*, OPTIK *(Luminanz)* L *(luminance)*, PHYS *(Induktivität)* L *(inductance)*, RADIO *(Induktivität)* L *(inductance)*, STRAHLPHYS *(lineare Energieübertragung)* L *(linear energy transfer)*, TELEKOM *(Induktivität)* L *(inductance)*, THERMOD *(Lorenzsche Einheit)* L *(Lorenz unit)*

l COMP & DV *(Länge)*, GEOM *(Länge)* l *(length)*, KERNTECH l, KERNTECH *(effektive Neutronenlebensdauer)* l *(effective neutron lifetime)*, PHYS *(Länge)*, TELEKOM *(Länge)* l *(length)*

LAGA *(Länderarbeitsgemeinschaft Abfall)* ABFALL *in Deutschland* Federal States Working Group on Waste

LAN *(lokales Netz)* COMP & DV, TELEKOM LAN *(local area network)*

LB COMP & DV *(Ortsbatterie)*, ELEKTROTECH *(lokale Batterie)* LB *(local battery)*

LC *(Flüssigkristall)* COMP & DV, ELEKTRIZ LC *(liquid crystal)*

LCD *(Flüssigkristallanzeige)* COMP & DV, ELEKTRIZ, ELEKTRONIK, FERNSEH, LABOR, TELEKOM, THERMOD LCD *(liquid crystal display)*

LD₅₀ *(mittlere letale Dosis)* STRAHLPHYS LD_{50} *(median lethal dose)*

LEAR *(Antiprotonenring mit geringer Energie)* TEILPHYS LEAR *(Low-Energy Antiproton Ring)*

LED *(Leuchtdiode, Lumineszenzdiode, lichtemittierende Diode)* COMP & DV, ELEKTRIZ, ELEKTRONIK, FERNSEH, OPTIK, PHYS, TELEKOM LED *(light-emitting diode)*

LEM *(Mondlandefahrzeug, Mondlandefähre)* RAUMFAHRT LEM *(lunar excursion module)*

LEP *(Elektronen-Positronen-Kollideranlage)* TEILPHYS LEP *(large electron-positron collider)*

LHC *(Hadronkollideranlage)* PHYS LHC *(large hadron collider)*

LIFO *(Last-in First-out)* COMP & DV LIFO *(last-in-first-out)*

LINEAC *(Linearbeschleuniger)* ELEKTROTECH, PHYS LINAC *(linear accelerator)*, TEILPHYS LINEAC *(linear accelerator)*

LISP *(Listenprogrammiersprache)* COMP & DV LISP *(list-programming language)*

LKF *(Luftkissenfahrzeug)* KFZTECH SEV *(surface effect vehicle)*, TRANS ACV, *(air cushion vehicle)*, WASSERTRANS hovercraft (BrE), hydroskimmer (AmE), surface effect ship

LKT *(luftgekühlte Triode)* ELEKTRONIK ACT *(air-cooled triode)*

Lkw *(Lastkraftwagen)* KFZTECH HGV *(heavy goods vehicle)*

LM *(Lunar-Modul)* RAUMFAHRT *Raumschiff* LM *(lunar module)*

lm *(Lumen)* FERNSEH, METROL, PHYS lm *(lumen)*

LNG *(Flüssigerdgas)* ERDÖL, THERMOD LNG *(liquefied natural gas)*

LOI *(Sauerstoffindex)* KUNSTSTOFF LOI *(limiting oxygen index)*

LORAN *(Langstreckennavigationskette)* LUFTTRANS, WASSERTRANS loran *(long-range navigation)*

LOX *(Flüssigsauerstoff)* RAUMFAHRT, THERMOD lox *(liquid oxygen)*

LP *(Langspielplatte)* AUFNAHME EP *(extended-play record)*, LP *(long-playing record)*

LPC *(lineare Prädiktionscodierung)* ELEKTRONIK, TELEKOM LPC *(linear predictive coding)*

LPG *(Flüssiggas)* ERDÖL, HEIZ & KÄLTE, KFZTECH, THERMOD, WASSERTRANS LPG *(liquefied petroleum gas)*

LPM *(Zeilen pro Minute)* COMP & DV LPM *(lines per minute)*

LQ *(Korrespondenzqualität)* COMP & DV, DRUCK LQ *(letter quality)*

LS *(Laufsitz)* MASCHINEN running fit

LSB COMP & DV *(niederwertigstes Bit)* LSB *(least significant bit)*, ELEKTRONIK *(unteres Seitenband)*, RADIO *(unteres Seitenband)*, TELEKOM *(unteres Seitenband)* LSB *(lower sideband)*

LSI *(Großintegration, hoher Integrationsgrad)* COMP & DV, ELEKTRONIK, PHYS, TELEKOM LSI *(large-scale integration)*

LUT *(Bodenstation)* WASSERTRANS *Satellitennavigation* LUT *(local user terminal)*

LW *(Langwelle)* RADIO LW *(long wave)*

lx *(Lux)* FOTO, LABOR, OPTIK, PHYS lx *(lux)*

LZG *(Langzeitgedächtnis)* ERGON, KÜNSTL INT LTM *(long-term memory)*

M ERDÖL *(Molekulargewicht)* M *(molecular weight)*, HYDRAUL *(Machzahl)* M *(Mach number)*, KERNTECH *(Reaktormultiplikation)* M *(multiplication of a reactor)*, LUFTTRANS *(Machzahl)* M *(Mach number)*, METROL *(Mega-)* M *(mega-)*, PHYS *(Machzahl)* M *(Mach number)*, PHYS *(Molekulargewicht)*, THERMOD *(Molekulargewicht)* M *(molecular weight)*

m AKUSTIK *(Streukoeffizient, Öffnungskoeffizient)* m *(flare coefficient of horn)*, AKUSTIK *(Scherelastizität)* m *(shear elasticity)*, MASCHINEN *(Masse)* m *(mass)*, METROL *(Meter)* m *(meter)*, METROL *(Milli-)* m *(milli-)*, PHYS *(Masse)* m *(mass)*, PHYS *(Molekularmasse)* m *(molecular mass)*, PHYS *(Gegeninduktivität)* m *(mutual inductance)*, THERMOD *(Masse)* m *(mass)*

MA *(Mittabstand)* FERTIG, KFZTECH, MASCHINEN CD *(center distance, centre distance)*

Ma *(Atommasse)* KERNTECH Ma *(atomic mass)*

MAC *(magnetisches Kalorimeter)* TEILPHYS MAC *(magnetic calorimeter)*

MAP *(Manufacturing Automation Protocol)* KONTROLL *Standard für Fabrikautomatisierungsgeräte* MAP *(manufacturing automation protocol)*

MB *(Mbyte, Megabyte)* COMP & DV MB *(megabyte)*

MBE *(Molekularstrahlepitaxie)* ELEKTRONIK, STRAHLPHYS MBE *(molecular-beam epitaxy)*

MDI *(Diphenylmethandiisocyanat)* KUNSTSTOFF MDI *(diphenylmethane diisocyanate)*

MDR *(Speicherdatenregister)* COMP & DV MDR *(memory data register)*

me *(Elektronenmasse)* CHEMIE, KERNTECH, TEILPHYS me *(electron mass)*

MEA *(Means-End-Analyse, Mittel-Zweck-Analyse)* KÜNSTL INT MEA *(means-end analysis)*

MEK KUNSTSTOFF *(Methylethylketon)* MEK *(methyl ethyl ketone)*, UMWELTSCHMUTZ *(maximale Emissionskonzentration)* maximum emission concentration

MEP *(mittlerer Nutzdruck)* LUFTTRANS, MASCHINEN mep *(mean effective pressure)*

MESFET *(Metallhalbleiter-Feldeffekttransistor)* ELEKTRONIK MESFET *(metal semiconductor field effect transistor)*

MeV *(Million Elektronenvolt)* TEILPHYS MeV *(million electron volts)*

MF ELEKTRIZ *(Melamin-Formaldehydharz, Melaminharz)* MF *(melamine resin)*, ELEKTRONIK *(Mittelfrequenz)* MF *(medium frequency)*, ELEKTRONIK *(Mehrfachfrequenz)* MF *(multiple frequency)*, KUNSTSTOFF *(Melamin-Formaldehydharz, Melaminharz)* MF *(melamine formaldehyde resin)*, RADIO *(Mittelfrequenz)* MF *(medium frequency)*, RADIO *(Mehrfachfrequenz)* MF *(multiple frequency)*, TELEKOM *(Mittelfrequenz)* MF *(medium frequency)*, TELEKOM *(Mehrfachfrequenz)* MF *(multiple frequency)*

MFC *(Multifrequenzcode)* TELEKOM MFC *(multifrequency code)*

MFM *(modifizierte Frequenzmodulation)* ELEKTRONIK, RADIO, TELEKOM MFM *(modified frequency modulation)*

MFW *(Mehrfrequenzwahl)* RADIO DTMF *(dual-tone multifrequency)*, TELEKOM MFD *(multifrequency dialling)*

Mg *(Magnesium)* CHEMIE Mg *(magnesium)*

MGD *(Magnetogasdynamik)* KERNTECH MGD *(magnetogasdynamics)*

MHz *(Megahertz)* ELEKTRIZ, ELEKTROTECH, FERNSEH, RADIO MHz *(megahertz)*

MIC *(integrierter Mikrowellenschaltkreis)* ELEKTRONIK, WELLPHYS MIC *(microwave integrated circuit)*

MICR *(Magnetschrifterkennung, Magnetschriftzeichenerkennung)* COMP & DV MICR *(magnetic ink character recognition)*

MIPS *(Millionen Befehle pro Sekunde)* COMP & DV MIPS *(millions of instructions per second)*

MIS COMP & DV *(Management-Informationssystem)* MIS *(management information system)*, ELEKTRONIK *(Metallisolator-Halbleiter)* MIS *(metal insulator semiconductor)*

MISFET *(Metallisolator-Feldeffekttransistor)* ELEKTRONIK MISFET *(metal insulator semiconductor field effect transistor)*

MLIPS *(Millionen logischer Inferenzen pro Sekunde)* KÜNSTL INT MLIPS *(millions of logical inferences per second)*

MMI *(Mensch-Maschine-Interface, Mensch-Maschine-Schnittstelle)* COMP & DV, KONTROLL, KÜNSTL INT, RAUMFAHRT MMI *(man-machine interface)*

MMK *(magnetomotorische Kraft)* ELEKTRIZ, PHYS, STRÖMPHYS mmf *(magnetomotive force)*

MN *(Kernmasse)* KERNTECH MN *(nuclear mass)*

mn *(Neutronenmasse)* KERNTECH, STRAHLPHYS, TEILPHYS mn *(neutron mass)*

m₀ *(Restmasse)* KERNTECH m_0 *(rest mass)*

mol *(Mole)* CHEMIE, LABOR, mol *(mole)*

MOS COMP & DV *(Metalloxid-Halbleiter)*, ELEKTRONIK *(Metalloxid-Halbleiter, Metalloxid-Transistor)* MOS *(metal oxide semiconductor)*

MOSFET *(Metalloxid-Silizium-Feldeffekttransistor)* RADIO MOSFET *(metal oxide silicon field effect transistor)*

MP COMP & DV *(Mikroprozessor)*, ELEKTRIZ *(Mikroprozessor)*, MASCHINEN *(Mikroprozessor)* MP *(microprocessor)*, VERPACK *(Metallpapier)* MP *(metallic paper)*

mp *(Protonenmasse)* KERNTECH mp *(proton mass)*

MS TELEKOM *(Mitteilungsspeicherung)* MS *(message storing)*, TELEKOM *(Mobilstation)* MS *(mobile station)*

MSC *(Funkvermittlungsstelle)* TELEKOM MSC *(mobile switching centre)*

MSI *(mittlere Integrationsdichte, mittlere Integrationstechnik, mittlerer Integrationsgrad)* COMP & DV, ELEKTRONIK, TELEKOM MSI *(medium-scale integration)*

MSK COMP & DV *(Minimalphasenumtastung)*, ELEKTRONIK *(kleinste Umtastung)*, RADIO *(Minimalphasenumtastung)*, TELEKOM *(Minimalphasenumtastung)* MSK *(minimum-shift keying)*

MTR *(Materialprüfreaktor)* KERNTECH MTR *(materials-testing reactor)*

MTTR COMP & DV *(mittlere Reparaturdauer)*, ELEKTROTECH *(mittlere Zeit bis zur Reparatur)*, MECHAN *(mittlere Instandsetzungszeit)*, QUAL *(mittlere Reparaturdauer)*, RAUMFAHRT *(mittlere Reparaturdauer)* MTTR *(mean time to repair)*

MÜ *(Maschinenübersetzung)* KÜNSTL INT MT *(machine translation)*

mu *(Atommassenkonstante)* KERNTECH mu *(unified atomic mass constant)*

μ ELEKTRIZ *(Permeabilität)* μ *(permeability)*, RADIO *(Verstärkung)* μ *(amplification factor)*, THERMOD μ

μH *(Hallsche Mobilität)* RADIO μH *(Hall mobility)*

μV *(Mikrovolt)* ELEKTRIZ, ELEKTROTECH μV *(microvolt)*

MUX *(Multiplexer)* COMP & DV, ELEKTRONIK, FERNSEH, TELEKOM MUX *(multiplexer)*

MVA *(Müllverbrennungsanlage)* ABFALL garbage incineration plant (AmE), refuse incineration plant (BrE), waste incineration plant, waste incinerator, VERPACK garbage incinerator (AmE), refuse incinerator (BrE)

MW *(Mittelwelle)* FERNSEH, RADIO MW *(medium wave)*

Mx *(Maxwell)* ELEKTRIZ, ELEKTROTECH Mx *(maxwell)*

N ELEKTRIZ *(Newton)* N *(newton)*, ELEKTRIZ *(Windungszahl)* N *(number of turns in a winding)*, ELEKTRONIK *(Rauschleistung)* N *(noise power)*, HYDRAUL *(Newton)* N *(newton)*, KERNTECH *(Rauschleistung)* N *(noise power)*, LABOR *(Newton)* N *(newton)*, METROL *(Strahlung)*, OPTIK *(Strahlung)* N *(radiance)*, PHYS *(Molekülzahl)* N *(number of molecules)*, STRÖMPHYS *(Newton)* N *(newton)*

n ELEKTRIZ *(Neutron)* n *(neutron)*, ELEKTRIZ *(Windungszahl pro Längeneinheit)* n *(turns per unit length)*, KERNTECH *(Neutron)* n *(neutron)*, KERNTECH *(Quantenzahl)*, METROL *(Quantenzahl)* n *(principal quantum number)*, PHYS *(Molekulardichte)* n *(molecular density)*, STRAHLPHYS *(Neutron)*, TEILPHYS *(Neutron)* n *(neutron)*, THERMOD *(Molekulardichte)* n *(molecular density)*

N_A *(Avogadrosche Zahl, Loschmidtsche Zahl)* PHYS,

THERMOD N_A *(Avogadro's number, Loschmidt number)*

NASA *(Nordamerikanische Weltraumbehörde)* RAUM-FAHRT NASA *(National Aeronautics and Space Administration)*

NC *(numerische Steuerung)* COMP & DV, ELEKTRIZ, KONTROLL, MASCHINEN, MECHAN NC *(numerical control)*

Nf *(Niederfrequenz)* AUFNAHME, ELEKTRONIK, FERNSEH, RADIO AF *(audio frequency)*, LF *(low frequency)*, TELEKOM LF *(low frequency)*

NiCd *(Nickel-Cadmium)* FOTO, RADIO NiCd *(nickel-cadmium)*

NK *(Naturkautschuk)* KUNSTSTOFF NR *(natural rubber)*

NMOS ELEKTRONIK NMOS, n-channel metal-oxide semiconductor

NMR *(magnetische Kernresonanz)* ERDÖL, TEILPHYS NMR *(nuclear magnetic resonance)*

NN COMP & DV *(neurales Netz, neurales Netzwerk)*, KÜNSTL INT *(neurales Netz, neurales Netzwerk)* NN *(neural network)*, WASSERTRANS *(Normalnull)* msl *(mean sea level)*

NNF *(niedrigste nutzbare Frequenz)* RADIO LUF *(lowest usable frequency)*

NNSS *(Navigationssatellitensystem)* WASSERTRANS NNSS *(Navy Navigation Satellite System)*

NO-OP *(Nulloperation, keine Operation)* COMP & DV NO-OP *(no-operation)*

NOS *(Notrufortungssender)* TELEKOM ELT *(emergency locator transmitter)*

Np *(Neper)* PHYS Np *(neper)*

NTSC *(Amerikanischer Fernsehnormungsausschuß)* FERNSEH NTSC *(National Television Standards Committee)*

OA *(Operationsverstärker, Rechenverstärker)* COMP & DV, ELEKTRONIK, PHYS, RADIO, TELEKOM op amp *(operational amplifier)*

OBO *(Erz-Schüttgut-Öl, Flüssigkeitsmassengut)* WASSERTRANS OBO *(ore-bulk oil)*

OC *(Operationscharakteristik)* QUAL OC *(operating characteristic)*

OCO *(Erz-Kohle-Öl)* TRANS OCO *(ore-coal-oil)*

OCR *(optische Zeichenerkennung)* COMP & DV OCR *(optical character recognition)*

OFN *(Ortsfernsprechnetz)* TELEKOM local exchange area

OLRT *(Online-Echtzeit)* COMP & DV OLRT *(online real time)*

Ω *(Volumen in Phase)* PHYS Ω *(volume in phase space)*

OMR *(optische Markierungserkennung)* COMP & DV OMR *(optical mark recognition)*

ON *(Ortsnetz)* ELEKTRIZ distribution network, local network, TELEKOM local network

ONKz *(Ortsnetzkennzahl)* TELEKOM area code

OOP *(objektorientierte Programmierung)* KÜNSTL INT OOP *(object-oriented programming)*

OPEC *(Organisation ölexportierender Länder)* ERDÖL OPEC *(Organization of Petroleum-Exporting Countries)*

OR *(Operations-Research)* COMP & DV OR *(operations research)*

OROM *(optischer Festwertspeicher)* COMP & DV, OPTIK OROM *(optical read-only memory)*

OSB *(oberes Seitenband)* ELEKTRONIK, RADIO, TELEKOM USB *(upper sideband)*

OSCAR *(Bahnsatellit für Amateurfunkzwecke)* RADIO, RAUMFAHRT Weltraumfunk OSCAR *(Orbiting Satellite Carrying Amateur Radio)*

OSI *(Kommunikation offener Systeme)* COMP & DV, TELEKOM OSI *(open systems interconnection)*

OSO *(Erz-Schlamm-Öl)* WASSERTRANS OSO *(ore-slurry-oil)*

OT *(oberer Totpunkt)* KFZTECH TDC *(top dead center)*

OVSt *(Ortsvermittlungsstelle)* TELEKOM local exchange

P ELEKTRIZ *(magnetischer Leitwert)* P *(permeance)*, ELEKTRIZ *(Leistung)* P *(power)*, KERNTECH *(Protonenzahl)* P *(proton number)*

p AKUSTIK *(Schalldruck)* p *(sound pressure)*, AUFNAHME *(Schalldruck)* p *(acoustic pressure)*, KERNTECH *(Proton)* p *(proton)*, KERNTECH *(Resonanzfluchtwahrscheinlichkeit)* p *(resonance escape probability)*, METROL *(Piko-)* p *(pico-)*, PHYS *(Proton)* p *(proton)*, PHYS *(Schalldruck)* p *(sound pressure)*, RADIO *(Proton)* p *(proton)*, RAUMFAHRT *(Schalldruck)* p *(acoustic pressure)*, TEILPHYS *(Proton)* p *(proton)*

PA AUFNAHME *(Kraftverstärker, Leistungsverstärker)* PA *(power amplifier)*, CHEMIE *(Polyamid)* PA *(polyamide)*, ELEKTRONIK *(Leistungsverstärker)*, ELEKTROTECH *(Endstufe, Endverstärker, Leistungsverstärker)* PA *(power amplifier)*, KUNSTSTOFF *(Polyamid)* PA *(polyamide)*, PHYS *(Hauptverstärker, Leistungsverstärker)*, RADIO *(Endstufe, Leistungsverstärker)*, RAUMFAHRT *(Leistungsverstärker)*, TELEKOM *(Leistungsverstärker)* PA *(power amplifier)*, TEXTIL *(Polyamid)* PA *(polyamide)*

Pa *(Pascal)* METROL, PHYS Hydrostatik Pa *(pascal)*

PAA *(Polyacryl, Polyacrylat)* CHEMIE, KUNSTSTOFF PAA *(polyacrylate)*

PAL *(programmierbare logische Anordnung)* COMP & DV PAL *(programmable array logic)*

PAM *(Pulsamplitudenmodulation)* COMP & DV, ELEKTRONIK, RADIO, TELEKOM PAM *(pulse amplitude modulation)*

PAN UMWELTSCHMUTZ *(Peroxyacetylnitrat)* PAN *(peroxoacetylnitrate)*, UMWELTSCHMUTZ *(Polyacrylnitril)* PAN *(polyacrylonitrile)*

PB COMP & DV *(Pulsbreite)*, ELEKTRONIK *(Pulsbreite)*, FERNSEH *(Pulsbreite)* PW *(pulse width)*, KUNSTSTOFF *(Polybuten, Polybutylen)* PB *(polybutylene)*, PHYS *(Pulsbreite)*, TELEKOM *(Pulsbreite)* PW *(pulse width)*

PBT *(Polybutylenterephthalat)* ELEKTRIZ, KUNSTSTOFF PBT *(polybutylene ephtalate)*

PBX *(private Selbstwählnebenstelle)* TELEKOM PBX *(private branch exchange)*

PC COMP & DV *(Personal Computer)* PC *(personal computer)*, ELEKTRIZ *(Polycarbonat)*, KUNSTSTOFF *(Polycarbonat)* PC *(polycarbonate)*

PCB COMP & DV *(Leiterplatte, Printplatte)*, ELEKTRIZ *(Leiterplatte)*, ELEKTRONIK *(Leiterplatte, gedruckte Schaltung)*, FERNSEH *(Leiterplatte)*, RADIO *(Leiterplatte)*, TELEKOM *(Leiterplatte)* PCB *(printed circuit board)*

PCM *(Pulscodemodulation)* AUFNAHME, COMP & DV, ELEKTRONIK, FERNSEH, RADIO, STRAHLPHYS, TELEKOM PCM *(pulse code modulation)*

PCU *(externe Steuereinheit, periphere Steuereinheit)* COMP & DV PCU *(peripheral control unit)*

PDAP *(Polydiallyphthalat)* KUNSTSTOFF PDAP *(polydiallylphthalate)*

PDM COMP & DV *(Pulsdeltamodulation)* PDM *(pulse delta modulation)*, ELEKTRONIK *(Pulsdauermodulation)* PWM *(pulse width modulation)*

PDN *(öffentliches Datennetz)* COMP & DV PDN *(public data network)*

PDR *(vorläufige technische Prüfung)* RAUMFAHRT PDR *(preliminary design review)*

PE-C *(chloriertes Polyethylen)* KUNSTSTOFF CPE *(chlorinated polyethylene)*

PEC *(Fotozelle)* DRUCK, ELEKTRIZ, ELEKTRONIK, FERNSEH, FOTO, PHYS, STRAHLPHYS PEC *(photoelectric cell)*

PERT *(Programmbewertungs- und Überprüfungsverfahren)* COMP & DV, RAUMFAHRT PERT *(program evaluation and review technique)*

PES *(Polyester)* CHEMIE, ELEKTRIZ, KUNSTSTOFF, TEXTIL PES *(polyester)*

PET *(Polyethylen)* CHEMIE, ELEKTRIZ, ERDÖL, KUNSTSTOFF, TEXTIL, VERPACK PET *(polyethylene)*

PETP *(Polyethylenterephthalat)* KUNSTSTOFF PETP *(polyethylene terephthalate)*

PFM *(Pulsfrequenzmodulation)* COMP & DV, ELEKTRONIK PFM *(pulse frequency modulation)*

Pg *(Gitterverlustleistung)* RADIO Pg *(grid dissipation power)*

φ AKUSTIK *(Winkelverdrängung)* φ *(angular displacement)*, AKUSTIK *(Geschwindigkeitspotential)* φ *(velocity potential)*

PI *(Polyimid)* ELEKTRIZ, ELEKTRONIK, KUNSTSTOFF PI *(polyimide)*

PIB *(Polyisobutylen)* KUNSTSTOFF PIB *(polyisobutylene)*

PIN *(Positiv-Isolierend-Negativ)* ELEKTRONIK pin *(positive-isolating-negative)*

PKW *(Personenkraftwagen)* KFZTECH car, passenger car

PKW-E *(Personenkraftwageneinheit)* KFZTECH PCU *(passenger car unit)*

PL *(Prädikatenlogik)* KÜNSTL INT PL *(predicate logic)*

PLA *(programmierbare Logikanordnung)* COMP & DV PLA *(programmable logic array)*

PLL *(Phasenregelkreis)* ELEKTRONIK, FERNSEH, RADIO, RAUMFAHRT, TELEKOM PLL *(phase-locked loop)*

PM *(Phasenmodulation)* AUFNAHME, COMP & DV, ELEKTRONIK, FERNSEH, PHYS, RADIO, TELEKOM PM *(phase modulation)*

PMMA *(Polymethacrylat, Polymethylmethacrylat)* KUNSTSTOFF PMMA *(polymethyl methacrylate)*

pnp *(positiv-negativ-positiv)* ELEKTRONIK p-n-p *(positive-negative-positive)*

PO KUNSTSTOFF *(Polyolefin)* PO *(polyolefin)*, TEXTIL *(Polynosic-Faser)* PO *(polynosic fiber)*, TEXTIL *(Polyolefin)* PO *(polyolefin)*

POM *(Polyoxymethylen)* CHEMIE, KUNSTSTOFF POM *(polyoxymethylene)*

PP *(Polypropylen)* CHEMIE, ELEKTRIZ, ERDÖL, KUNSTSTOFF, TEXTIL PP *(polypropylene)*

PPM COMP & DV *(Pulsphasenmodulation)*, ELEKTRONIK *(Pulsphasenmodulation)* PPM *(pulse phase modulation)*, ELEKTRONIK *(Pulslagenmodulation)* PPM *(pulse position modulation)*, TELEKOM *(Pulsphasenmodulation)* PPM *(pulse phase modulation)* TELEKOM *(Pulslagenmodulation)* PPM *(pulse position modulation)*

PPU *(Peripherietechnik)* COMP & DV PPU *(peripheral processing units)*

PROM *(programmierbarer Lesespeicher)* COMP & DV,

RADIO PROM *(programmable read-only memory)*

PS CHEMIE *(Polystyren, Polystyrol)*, ELEKTRIZ *(Polystyrol)*, KUNSTSTOFF *(Polystyren, Polystyrol)* PS *(polystyrene)*, MASCHINEN *(Pferdestärke)* hp *(horsepower)*, WASSERTRANS *(Peilstrahl)* EBL *(electronic bearing line)*

PSK COMP & DV *(Phasensprungtastung)*, ELEKTRONIK *(Phasenumtastung)*, RADIO *(Phasenumtastung)*, RAUMFAHRT *(Phasenumtastung)*, TELEKOM *(Phasenumtastung)* PSK *(phase-shift keying)*

PTC *(passive Thermosteuerung)* RAUMFAHRT PTC *(passive thermal control)*

PTFE *(Polytetrafluorethen, Polytetrafluorethylen)* KUNSTSTOFF PTFE *(polytetrafluoroethylene)*

PUR *(Polyurethan)* KUNSTSTOFF, TEXTIL PUR *(polyurethane)*

PVAC *(Polyvinylacetat)* KUNSTSTOFF PVAC *(polyvinyl acetate)*

PVAL *(Polyvinylalkohol)* DRUCK, KUNSTSTOFF PVAL *(polyvinyl alcohol)*

PVB *(Polyvinylbutyral)* KUNSTSTOFF PVB *(polyvinyl butyral)*

PVC *(Polyvinylchlorid)* BAU, ELEKTROTECH, KUNSTSTOFF PVC *(polyvinyl chloride)*

PVC-C *(chloriertes Polyvinylchlorid)* KUNSTSTOFF CPVC *(chlorinated polyvinyl chloride)*

PVC-U KUNSTSTOFF U-PVC, unplasticized PVC

PVDC *(Polyvinylidenchlorid)* KUNSTSTOFF PVDC *(polyvinylidene chloride)*

PVDF *(Polyvinylidenfluorid)* KUNSTSTOFF PVFD *(polyvinylidene fluoride)*

PVE *(Polyvinylether)* KUNSTSTOFF PVE *(polyvinyl ether)*

PVF *(Polyvinylfluorid)* KUNSTSTOFF PVF *(polyvinyl fluoride)*

PWM *(Pulsweitenmodulation)* ELEKTRONIK PWM *(pulse width modulation)*

QAM COMP & DV *(Quadratur-Amplitudenmodulation)*, ELEKTRONIK *(Quadratur-Amplitudenmodulation)* QAM *(quadrature amplitude modulation)*, ELEKTRONIK *(Quadratur-Amplitudenmodulator)* QAM *(quadrature amplitude modulator)*, TELEKOM *(Quadratur-Amplitudenmodulation)* QAM *(quadrature amplitude modulation)*

QCD *(Quantenchromodynamik)* TEILPHYS QCD *(quantum chromodynamics)*

QED *(Quantenelektrodynamik)* PHYS QED *(quantum electrodynamics)*

QPSK *(Vierphasenumtastung)* ELEKTRONIK QPSK *(quaternary phase shift keying)*, TELEKOM QPSK *(quadriphase shift keying)*

QS *(Qualitätssicherung)* KERNTECH, MASCHINEN, MECHAN, QUAL, VERPACK QA *(quality assurance)*

QSAM *(erweiterte Zugriffsmöglichkeit für sequentielle Dateien)* COMP & DV QSAM *(queued sequential access method)*

QSG *(Quasistellargalaxie)* RAUMFAHRT QSG *(quasistellar galaxy)*

QSO *(quasi-stellares Objekt)* RAUMFAHRT QSO *(quasistellar object)*

QUISAM *(erweiterte indizierte Zugriffsmöglichkeit für sequentielle Dateien)* COMP & DV QUISAM *(queued unique index sequential access method)*

QZ *(quantisiertes Zeichen)* ELEKTRONIK QS *(quantized signal)*

R ELEKTRIZ *(Reluktanz)* R *(reluctance)*, ELEKTRIZ *(Widerstand)* R *(resistance)*, KERNTECH *(Rydberg-Konstante)* R *(Rydberg constant)*, KERNTECH *(Dosis)* R *(dose rate)*, KERNTECH *(linearer Bereich)* R *(linear range)*, PHYS *(Gaskonstante)* R *(gas constant)*, STRAHLPHYS *(Röntgen)* R *(röntgen)*, THERMOD *(Gaskonstante)* R *(gas constant)*

r AKUSTIK *(Entfernung von der Schallquelle)* r *(distance from source)*, KERNTECH *(Kernradius)* r *(nuclear radius)*, OPTIK *(Brechungswinkel, Refraktionswinkel)*, PHYS *(Brechungswinkel)* r *(angle of refraction)*

Rad STRAHLPHYS rad (dated), radiation absorbed dose (dated)

Rα *(Rydberg-Konstante)* KERNTECH Rα *(Rydberg constant)*

RAM COMP & DV *(Direktzugriffsspeicher, Lese-/Schreibspeicher, Schreib-/Lesespeicher)*, ELEKTRONIK *(Direktzugriffsspeicher, Schreib-/Lesespeicher)* RAM *(random access memory)*

RBA *(relative Byteadresse)* COMP & DV RBA *(relative byte address)*

RC ELEKTRONIK RC, resistor-capacitor

RDB *(relationale Datenbank)* TELEKOM RDB *(relational database)*

RDSS *(Satellitenfunkortungssystem)* RADIO, TRANS, WASSERTRANS *Satellitenfunk* RDSS *(radio determination satellite system)*

Re *(Reynoldszahl)* HYDRAUL, LUFTTRANS, NICHTFOSS ENERG, PHYS, STRÖMPHYS Re *(Reynolds number)*

re *(Elektronenradius)* KERNTECH re *(electron radius)*

RF *(Radiofrequenz)* AUFNAHME, ELEKTRIZ, ELEKTRONIK, FERNSEH, RADIO, TELEKOM HF *(high frequency)*, RF *(radio frequency)*

RG *(elektronischer Rauschgenerator)* FERNSEH ENG *(electronic noise generator)*

RGB *(rot-grün-blau)* COMP & DV, FERNSEH RGB *(red-green-blue)*

RH *(Hallscher Koeffizient)* PHYS, RADIO RH *(Hall coefficient)*

RHIC TEILPHYS RHIC, relativistic heavy ion collider

RICH *(ringbildender Tscherenkov-Zähler)* TEILPHYS RICH *(ring-imaging Cherenkov counter)*

RIT *(Empfängerfeinabstimmung)* RADIO RIT *(receiver incremental tuning)*

RMS *(quadratischer Mittel)* AUFNAHME, ELEKTRIZ, ELEKTRONIK rms *(root mean square)*

Rn *(Radon)* PHYS Rn *(radon)*

ROM *(Festwertspeicher, Nur-Lese-Speicher, ROM-Speicher)* COMP & DV, ELEKTRIZ, ELEKTROTECH, RADIO ROM *(read-only memory)*

Ro-Ro *(Roll-on-Roll-off)* TRANS ro-ro *(roll-on-roll-off)*

RP-1 *(Kerosin)* ERDÖL, TRANS RP-1 *(kerosene)*

RSB *(Restseitenband)* ELEKTRONIK VSB *(vestigial sideband)*

RTTY *(Funkfernschreiben)* RADIO RTTY *(radioteletype)*

RWO *(Rückwärtswellenoszillator)* ELEKTRONIK, PHYS, TELEKOM BWO *(backward-wave oscillator)*

S ELEKTRIZ *(Poyntingscher Vektor)* S *(Poynting vector)*, HYDRAUL *(Gefälle)* S *(slope)*, KERNTECH *(Quellenstärke)* S *(source strength)*, KERNTECH *(spezifische Ionisierung)* S *(specific ionization)*, KERNTECH *(Anhaltleistung)* S *(stopping power)*, KERNTECH *(Spinquantengesamtzahl)* S *(total spin quantum number)*, METROL *(Siemens)* S *(siemens)*, PHYS *(Poyntingscher Vektor)* S *(Poynting vector)*

s ELEKTRIZ *(Schlupf)* s *(slip)*, KERNTECH *(Spinquantenzahl)*, METROL *(Spinquantenzahl)*, PHYS *(Spinquantenzahl)* s *(spin quantum number)*

SAR *(Such- und Rettungsdienst)* WASSERTRANS *Notfall* SAR *(search and rescue)*

Satcom *(Satellitenfunk)* RADIO, TELEKOM, WASSERTRANS satcom *(satellite communication)*

Satnav *(Satellitennavigation)* WASSERTRANS satnav *(satellite navigation)*

SB *(schneller Brutreaktor, schneller Brüter)* KERNTECH, PHYS FBR *(fast breeder reactor)*

SBFM *(Schmalbandfrequenzmodulation)* ELEKTRONIK, RADIO, TELEKOM NBFM *(narrow-band frequency modulation)*

SBR *(Styrol-Butadien-Kautschuk)* KUNSTSTOFF SBR *(styrene butadiene rubber)*

SBV *(Sicherheitsabblasearmatur)* ERDÖL relief valve

SCC ABFALL *(Nachbrennkammer)*, MASCHINEN *(Nachbrennkammer, zweiter Brennraum)* SCC *(secondary combustion chamber)*

SCN *(Hinweis auf Spezifikationsänderungen)* TRANS SCN *(specification change notice)*

SCPC *(Ein-Kanal-Träger)* RAUMFAHRT *Weltraumfunk*, TELEKOM SCPC *(single channel per carrier)*

SCR *(siliziumgesteuerter Gleichrichter)* ELEKTRONIK, ELEKTROTECH SCR *(silicon-controlled rectifier)*

SDLC *(synchrone Datenübertragungssteuerung)* COMP & DV SDLC *(synchronous data link control)*

sec GEOM *(Sekans)*, GEOM *(Sekante)* von Linie sec *(secant)*

SELCAL *(Selektivrufsystem)* TELEKOM SELCAL *(selective calling system)*

SES *(Bordterminal für Satellitenfunk)* WASSERTRANS SES *(ship earth station)*

SF BAU *(Sicherheitsfaktor)*, ELEKTRIZ *(Sicherheitsfaktor)* SF *(safety factor)*, ELEKTRONIK *(Seitenbandfrequenz)* SF *(sideband frequency)*, ELEKTRONIK *(Signalfrequenz)* SF *(signal frequency)*, ELEKTRONIK *(Sprachfrequenz)* SF *(speech frequency)*, VF *(voice frequency)*, FERNSEH *(Seitenbandfrequenz)* SF *(sideband frequency)*, FERNSEH *(Signalfrequenz)* SF *(signal frequency)*, KERNTECH *(Sicherheitsfaktor)*, KOHLEN *(Sicherheitsfaktor)*, MASCHINEN *(Sicherheitsfaktor)* SF *(safety factor)*, RADIO *(Seitenbandfrequenz)* SF *(sideband frequency)*, RADIO *(Signalfrequenz)* SF *(signal frequency)*, SICHERHEIT *(Sicherheitsfaktor)* SF *(safety factor)*, TELEKOM *(Seitenbandfrequenz)* SF *(sideband frequency)*, TELEKOM *(Signalfrequenz)* SF *(signal frequency)*, TELEKOM *(Sprachfrequenz)* SF *(speech frequency)*, VF *(voice frequency)*, TRANS *(Sicherheitsfaktor)* SF *(safety factor)*

SGML *(Standardkorrekturzeichensatz)* COMP & DV, DRUCK SGML *(Standard Generalized Markup Language)*

SHF *(superhohe Frequenz)* BAU, ELEKTRONIK, KOHLEN, KUNSTSTOFF, MECHAN, PHYS, THERMOD SHF *(super-high frequency)*

σ *abbr* COAL TECH *(Poisson's ratio)* σ *(Poissonsche Zahl)*, CONST *(Poisson's ratio)* σ MECHANICS *(Poisson's ratio)* σ *(Poissonsches Verhältnis)*, PHYS *(Stefan-Boltzmann constant)* σ *(Stephan-Boltzmannsche-Konstante)*, PLAS *(Poisson's ratio)* σ *(Poissonsche Zahl)*, THERMODYN *(Stephan-Boltz-*

mann constant) σ (*Stephan-Boltzmannsche- Konstante*)

SIMM (*einfaches schritthaltendes Speichermodul*) COMP & DV SIMM (*single in-line memory module*)

SIMS (*Sekundärionenmassenspektrometrie*) PHYS SIMS (*secondary ion mass spectrometry*)

sin (*Sinus*) COMP & DV, GEOM sin (*sine*)

SINAD (*Störabstand einschließlich Verzerrungen*) TELEKOM SINAD (*signal-to-noise and distortion ratio*)

SIS (*Schwerionensynchrotron*) TEILPHYS HIS (*heavy-ion synchrotron*)

SLAR (*Seitensichtradar*) MEERSCHMUTZ SLAR (*sideways-looking airborne radar*)

SLC (*Stanford Linear Collider*) TEILPHYS SLC (*Stanford Linear Collider*)

SLD (*superlumineszierende Diode*) OPTIK SLD (*superluminescent LED*), TELEKOM SLD (*superluminescent LED*), SRD (*superradiant diode*)

SLR (*einäugige Spiegelreflexkamera*) FOTO SLR (*single lens reflex camera*)

SMAW (*Sigmaschweißung*) KERNTECH SMAW (*shielded metal arc welding*)

SMC ELEKTRONIK (*SMD-Bauteil*), TELEKOM (*Aufsetzbauelement*) SMC (*surface-mounted component*)

SMD (*Flachbauelement, oberflächenmontiertes Element*) ELEKTRIZ SMD (*surface mounting device*)

Sn (*Seiten*) DRUCK pp (*pages*)

SNA (*Systemnetzwerkarchitektur*) COMP & DV SNA (*systems network architecture*)

SNG (*Erdgasaustauschgas, synthetisch hergestelltes Gas*) ERDÖL SNG (*synthetic natural gas*)

SNV (*Schweizerische Normenvereinigung*) ELEKTRIZ SSA (*Swiss Standards Association*)

SOM (*Anfang der Nachricht*) COMP & DV SOM (*start of message*)

SOS (*Silizium auf Saphir*) ELEKTRONIK SOS (*silicon-on-sapphire*)

SPS COMP & DV (*Programmspeichersteuerung*) SPC (*stored program control*), KONTROLL (*speicherprogrammierbare Steuerung*), LABOR (*speicherprogrammierbare Steuerung*) PLC (*programmable logic control*)

SQID (*supraleitfähiger Quanteninterferenzmechanismus*) PHYS SQUID (*superconductive quantum interference device*)

SRAM (*statischer RAM*) COMP & DV SRAM (*static RAM*)

SS FERNSEH (*Spitze-Spitze-*) pp (*peak-to-peak*), MASCHINEN (*Schiebesitz*) close sliding fit, push fit, MECHAN (*Schiebesitz*) close-sliding fit, push fit, sliding fit, RADIO (*Spitze-Spitze-*) pp (*peak-to-peak*)

SSB (*Einseitenband*) ELEKTRONIK, FERNSEH, RADIO, TELEKOM, WASSERTRANS SSB (*single sideband*)

SSC (*supraleitfähiges Supracollider*) TEILPHYS SSC (*superconducting super collider*)

SSM (*Zweiflächenspiegel*) RAUMFAHRT SSM (*second surface mirror*)

SSMA (*Breitbandmehrfachzugriff*) RAUMFAHRT SSMA (*spread spectrum multiple access*)

SSOG (*Satellitensystem-Betriebsanleitung*) RAUMFAHRT SSOG (*satellite system operation guide*)

SST (*Überschalltransport*) LUFTTRANS SST (*supersonic transport*)

SSTV FERNSEH (*Fernsehen mit langsamer Abtastung, Schmalbandfernsehen, Slow-Scan-Television*), RADIO (*Schmalbandfernsehen mit langsamer Abtastung*)

SSTV (*slow scan television*)

SSUS (*rotierende obere Feststufe*) RAUMFAHRT SSUS (*solid spinning upper stage*)

STS (*Raumfahrttransportsystem*) RAUMFAHRT STS (*space transportation system*)

STX (*Textanfang*) COMP & DV STX (*start of text*)

SU (*Sprachverstehen*) KÜNSTL INT SU (*speech understanding*)

Sv (*Sievert*) PHYS, STRAHLPHYS, TEILPHYS Sv (*Sievert*)

SVA (*gemeinsam benutzbarer virtueller Bereich*) COMP & DV SVA (*shared virtual area*)

SWFD (*Selbstwählferndienst*) TELEKOM DDD (AmE) (*direct distance dialing*), STD (BrE) (*subscriber trunk dialling*)

SWR KERNTECH (*Siedewasserreaktor*) BWR (*boiling water reactor*), KERNTECH (*schwerwassermoderierter Reaktor*) HWR (*heavy-water-moderated reactor*), PHYS (*Siedewasserreaktor*) BWR (*boiling water reactor*)

SWV (*Stehwellenverhältnis*) PHYS SWR (*standing-wave ratio*), VSWR (*voltage standing-wave ratio*), RADIO SWR (*standing-wave ratio*), TELEKOM SWR (*standing-wave ratio*), VSWR (*voltage standing-wave ratio*)

SZ (*Säurezahl*) KUNSTSTOFF, LEBENSMITTEL acid value

T AKUSTIK (*Nachhallzeit*), AUFNAHME (*Nachhallzeit*) T (*reverberation time*), ELEKTRIZ (*Drehmoment*), ELEKTROTECH (*Drehmoment*), ERDÖL (*Drehmoment*) T (*torque*), FERTIG (*Drehmoment*) T, *Kunststoffinstallationen* T (*torque*), HYDRAUL (*Transpiration*) T (*transpiration*), KFZTECH (*Drehmoment*) T (*torque*), LABOR (*Tesla*) T (*Tesla*), MASCHINEN (*Drehmoment*), MECHAN (*Drehmoment*) T (*torque*), METROL (*absolute Temperatur*) T (*absolute temperature*), METROL (*Tera-*) T (*tera-*), PHYS (*Tesla*) T (*Tesla*), PHYS (*thermodynamische Temperatur*) T (*thermodynamic temperature*)

t HYDRAUL (*Tiefe*) d (*depth*), TEILPHYS (*Triton*) t (*triton*)

TAA (*Technische Anleitung Abfall*) ABFALL Technical Instruction on Waste Management

tan GEOM (*Tangens*), GEOM (*Tangente*) tan (*tangent*)

τ (*Relaxationszeit*) AKUSTIK τ (*relaxation time*)

TBKZ (*Technisches- und Betriebskontrollzentrum*) RAUMFAHRT TOCC (*Technical and Operational Control Center*)

TBP (*Tributylphosphat*) KERNTECH TBP (*tributyl phosphate*)

TCR (*Telemetriesteuer- und Meßsystem*) RAUMFAHRT TCR (*telemetry command and ranging subsystem*)

TD (*theoretische Dichte*) KERNTECH TD (*theoretical density*)

TDI (*Toluendiisocyanat, Toluoldiisocyanat*) KUNSTSTOFF TDI (*toluyene diisocyanate*)

TDM (*Multiplexen mit Zeitteilung, Zeitmultiplexmethode, Zeitmultiplexverfahren*) COMP & DV, ELEKTRONIK, TELEKOM TDM (*time division multiplex*)

TDMA (*Mehrfachzugriff im Zeitmultiplex, nicht gleichzeitiger Mehrfachzugriff*) COMP & DV, ELEKTRONIK, RAUMFAHRT *Weltraumfunk*, TELEKOM TDMA (*time division multiple access*)

TE (*transversal elektrisch*) ELEKTROTECH, TELEKOM TE (*transverse electric*)

TEM (*transversal elektromagnetisch*) ELEKTROTECH, TELEKOM TEM (*transverse electromagnetic*)

TeV *(Teraelektronenvolt)* TEILPHYS TeV *(tera electron volt)*

Tf AUFNAHME *(Tonfrequenz)* AF *(audio frequency)*, AUFNAHME *(Trägerfrequenz)* CF *(carrier frequency)*, ELEKTRONIK *(Tonfrequenz)* AF *(audio frequency)*, ELEKTRONIK *(Trägerfrequenz)* CF *(carrier frequency)*, FERNSEH *(Tonfrequenz)* AF *(audio frequency)*, FERNSEH *(Trägerfrequenz)* CF *(carrier frequency)*, RADIO *(Tonfrequenz)* AF *(audio frequency)*

TFEL *(Dünnschicht-Elektrolumineszenz)* ELEKTRONIK TFEL *(thin film electroluminescence)*

TG *(Tertiärgruppe)* TELEKOM mastergroup

T¹/₂ *(Halbwertszeit)* KERNTECH, PHYS, STRAHLPHYS, TEILPHYS T¹/₂ *(half-life)*

θ HYDRAUL *(Wärmewiderstand, absolute Temperatur, thermodynamische Temperatur)* θ *(absolute temperature)*, PHYS *(Wärmewiderstand)* θ *(thermal resistance)*, THERMOD *(absolute Temperatur, thermodynamische Temperatur)* θ *(absolute temperature)*, THERMOD *(Wärmewiderstand)* θ *(thermal resistance)*

θD *(Debyesche Temperatur)* PHYS, THERMOD θD *(Debye temperature)*

θK *(Einsteinsche Temperatur)* THERMOD θK *(Einstein temperature)*

TM *(transversal magnetisch)* ELEKTROTECH, TELEKOM TM *(transverse magnetic)*

TMUX *(Transmultiplexer)* TELEKOM TMUX *(transmultiplexer)*

TNI *(Teilnehmer-Teilnehmer-Information)* TELEKOM UUI *(user-to-user information)*

TNL *(Teilnehmeranschlußleitung)* TELEKOM subscriber's line

TNR *(gesteuerter Thermonuklearreaktor)* KERNTECH CTR *(controlled thermonuclear reactor)*

TNS *(Teilnehmersatz)* TELEKOM SLC *(subscriber line circuit)*

TNT *(Trinitrotoluol)* CHEMIE TNT *(trinitrotoluene)*

TOP *(Bürokommunikationsprotokoll)* TELEKOM TOP *(technical and office protocol)*

TPP *(texturiertes Pflanzenprotein)* LEBENSMITTEL TVP *(textured vegetable protein)*

TQMS *(abteilungsübergreifendes Qualitätssicherungssystem)* QUAL TQMS *(Total Quality Management System)*

TS *(Treibsitz)* MASCHINEN drive fit

TT *(Tonträger)* AUFNAHME, FERNSEH sound carrier

TTL *(Transistor-Transistor-Logik)* COMP & DV, ELEKTRONIK TTL *(transistor-transistor logic)*

TV *(Fernsehen)* FERNSEH TV *(television)*

TVI *(Fernsehempfangsstörung, Fernsehstörung)* FERNSEH TVI *(television interference)*

TVSt *(Teilnehmervermittlungsstelle)* TELEKOM access exchange

TW *(Tonwahl)* TELEKOM MFD *(multifrequency dialling)*

U AKUSTIK *(Volumengeschwindigkeit, Volumenstrom)* U *(volume current)*, ELEKTRIZ *(Spannung)* V *(voltage)*, OPTIK *(Strahlungsenergie)* U *(radiant energy)*, THERMOD *(Wärmeübertragungskoeffizient)* U *(overall heat transfer coefficient)*

û *(wahrscheinlichste Geschwindigkeit)* PHYS û *(most probable speed)*

UFH *(Harnstoff-Formaldehydharz)* ELEKTRIZ, FERTIG, KUNSTSTOFF UFR *(urea formaldehyde resin)*

UFO *(nicht identifiziertes Flugobjekt)* RAUMFAHRT

UFO *(unidentified flying object)*

UF₆ *(Uranhexafluorid)* KERNTECH UF₆ *(uranium hexafluoride)*

UHF *(Ultrahochfrequenz)* ELEKTRONIK, FERNSEH, RADIO, TELEKOM, WELLPHYS UHF *(ultrahigh frequency)*

UHT *(Ultrahochtemperatur)* LEBENSMITTEL UHT *(ultrahigh temperature)*

UIC *(Internationaler Eisenbahnverband)* EISENBAHN UIC *(International Railway Union)*

UJT *(Zweizonentransistor)* ELEKTRONIK UJT *(unijunction transistor)*

UKW *(Ultrakurzwelle)* RADIO, WELLPHYS USW *(ultrashort wave)*, VSW *(very short wave)*

ULSI *(Ultragroßintegration)* ELEKTRONIK ULSI *(ultra-large-scale integration)*

üNN *(über Normalnull)* WASSERTRANS asl *(above sea level)*

UP *(ungesättigter Polyester)* KUNSTSTOFF UP *(unsaturated polyester)*

US *(ultrasonisch)* ELEKTRIZ SS *(supersonic)*, US *(ultrasonic)*

USV *(unterbrechungsfreie Stromversorgung)* KONTROLL stand-by battery power supply

UT *(Standardweltzeit)* RADIO, RAUMFAHRT UT *(universal time)*

UTC *(Standardweltzeit)* RADIO, RAUMFAHRT UTC *(universal time coordinated)*

UV *(ultraviolett)* OPTIK, PHYS UV *(ultraviolet)*

UZ *(Zenerspannung)* ELEKTRONIK BDV *(breakdown voltage)*

V AUFNAHME *(Verstärkung)* A *(amplification)*, AUFNAHME *(Volt)* V *(volt)*, ELEKTRIZ *(Verstärkung)* A *(amplification)*, ELEKTRIZ *(Volt)* V *(volt)*, ELEKTRONIK *(Verstärkung)* A *(amplification)*, ELEKTRONIK *(Volt)* V *(volt)*, METROL *(Verstärkung)* A *(amplification)*, METROL *(Volt)* V *(volt)*, OPTIK *(Verstärkung)* A *(amplification)*, OPTIK *(Volt)* V *(volt)*, RADIO *(Verstärkung)* A *(amplification)*, RADIO *(Volt)* V *(volt)*

v COMP & DV *(Volumen)* v *(volume)*, KERNTECH *(Vibrationsquantenzahl)* v *(vibrational quantum number)*, PHYS *(Volumen)*, TEXTIL *(Volumen)*, THERMOD *(Volumen)* v *(volume)*

VAD *(Axialabscheideverfahren aus Dampfphase)* OPTIK, TELEKOM VAD *(vapor phase axial deposition technique, vapour phase axial deposition technique)*

VAN *(Mehrwertdienstnetz, Mehrwertnetz)* COMP & DV, TELEKOM VAN *(value-added network)*

var *(Blindleistungseinheit)* LABOR var *(volt-amperes reactive)*

VCO *(variabler Quarzoszillator)* RADIO VXO *(variable crystal oscillator)*

VCR FERNSEH *(Videorecorder)* VCR *(video cassette recorder)*, FERNSEH *(Videomagnetbandgerät)* VTR *(video tape recorder)*

VD *(Viskositäts-Dichteverhältnis)* NICHTFOSS ENERG kinematic viscosity

VDE *(Verein Deutscher Elektrotechniker)* ELEKTRIZ Association of German Electrical Engineers

VDI *(Verein Deutscher Ingenieure)* ELEKTRIZ Association of German Engineers

VF FERNSEH *(Videofrequenz)* VF *(video frequency)*, FERNSEH *(Videofrequenzwandler)* VF *(video-frequency converter)*

VG *(veränderliche Geometrie, veränderliche Tragflügel-*

geometrie) LUFTTRANS VG *(variable geometry)*

VHD *(sehr hohe Dichtigkeit)* OPTIK VHD *(very high density)*

VHF *(Meterwellen-Hochfrequenz)* RADIO VHF *(very high frequency)*

VHS *(Heimvideosystem)* FERNSEH VHS *(video home system)*

VHS-C *(Heimvideo-Aufzeichnungssystem)* FERNSEH VHS-C *(video home system-compact)*

VI *(Viskositätsindex, Viskositätszahl)* KFZTECH, MASCHINEN, STRÖMPHYS, THERMOD VI *(viscosity index)*

VK *(Vergaserkraftstoff)* ERDÖL, KFZTECH, THERMOD fuel, gas (AmE), gasoline (AmE), petrol (BrE)

VLCC *(Supertanker)* ERDÖL VLCC *(very large crude carrier)*

VLP *(Video-Langspiel)* FERNSEH VLP *(video long play)*

VLSI *(Höchstintegration, Übergroßintegration)* COMP & DV, ELEKTRONIK, TELEKOM VLSI *(very large-scale integration)*

VMS *(virtuelle Speicherverwaltung)* COMP & DV VMS *(virtual memory specification)*

VOX *(sprachgesteuerter Schalter)* RADIO VOX *(voice-operated switch)*

VPE *(vernetztes Polyethylen)* KUNSTSTOFF XPE *(cross-linked polyethylene)*

VSP *(vertikales seismisches Profil)* ERDÖL VSP *(vertical seismic profile)*

VSWR *(Welligkeitsfaktor)* RADIO VSWR *(voltage standing wave ratio)*

W ELEKTRIZ *(elektrische Energie)* W *(electric energy)*, ELEKTROTECH *(Watt)* W *(watt)*, HYDRAUL *(Webersche Zahl)* W *(Weber number)*, KERNTECH *(durchschnittliche Energie)* W *(average energy)*, METROL *(Watt)* W *(watt)*, OPTIK *(Abstrahlung)* W *(radiant emittance)*

WAN *(breites Bereichsnetzwerk)* COMP & DV, TELEKOM WAN *(wide area network)*

WB *(Wissensbasis)* COMP & DV, KÜNSTL INT KB *(knowledge base)*

Wb *(Weber)* ELEKTRIZ, ELEKTROTECH, METROL Wb *(weber)*

WBS *(wissensbasiertes System)* COMP & DV KBS *(knowledge-based system)*

WDM *(Wellenlängenmultiplex)* OPTIK, TELEKOM WDM *(wavelength division multiplexing)*

WEZ *(Westeuropäische Zeit)* MECHAN GMT *(Greenwich Mean Time)*

WL *(weiter Laufsitz)* MASCHINEN loose fit

WOB *(Bohrmeißelauflast)* ERDÖL WOB *(weight on bit)*

WORM *(Einmalbeschreibung-Mehrfachlesen)* OPTIK WORM *(write once read many times)*

WPS *(Wellenpferdestärke)* MASCHINEN shaft horse power

WR COMP & DV *(Wissensrepräsentation)* KR *(know-ledge representation)*, ELEKTRONIK *(Wechselrichter)*, ELEKTROTECH *(Wechselrichter)* inverter, KÜNSTL INT *(Wissensrepräsentation)* KR *(knowledge representation)*, PHYS *(Wechselrichter)*, RADIO *(Wechselrichter)* inverter

WS *(Wechselstrom)* ELEKTROTECH AC *(alternating current)*

WS-GS *(Wechselstrom-Gleichstrom)* ELEKTROTECH AC-DC *(alternating current-direct current)*

WWRV *(Wanderwellenröhrenverstärker)* ELEKTRONIK, RAUMFAHRT TWTA *(traveling wave tube amplifier, travelling wave tube amplifier)*

WYSIWYG *(originalgetreue Darstellung der Druckausgabe am Bildschirm)* COMP & DV WYSIWYG *(what you see is what you get)*

X AKUSTIK *(Volumenverdrängung)* X *(volume displacement)*, ELEKTRIZ *(Blindwiderstand, Reaktanz)* X *(reactance)*, KERNTECH *(Belastung)* X *(exposure)*

XC *(kapazitiver Blindwiderstand)* ELEKTRIZ XC *(capacitive reactance)*

XL *(induktiver Blindwiderstand)* ELEKTRIZ XL *(inductive reactance)*

XMS *(Erweiterungsspeicher)* COMP & DV XMS *(extended memory specification)*

XPS COMP & DV *(Expertensystem)*, KÜNSTL INT *(Expertensystem)* XPS *(expert system)*, PHYS *(röntgenstrahlangeregte Photoelektronenspektroskopie)* XPS *(X-ray photoelectron spectroscopy)*

YA *(akustische Admittanz)* AKUSTIK, ELEKTROTECH YA *(acoustic admittance)*

YAG *(Yttrium-Aluminium-Granat)* CHEMIE YAG *(yttrium-aluminium garnet)*

YIG *(Yttrium-Eisen-Granat)* CHEMIE YIG *(yttrium-iron garnet)*

Z ELEKTRIZ *(Impedanz)* Z *(impedance)*, KERNTECH *(Atomzahl)* Z *(atomic number)*, PHYS *(Teilfunktion, Zustandsfunktion)* Z *(partition function)*

z *(Kompressibilitätsfaktor)* THERMOD z *(compressibility factor)*

ZA *(Schallimpedanz, Schallwellenwiderstand, akustische Impedanz, akustischer Scheinwiderstand)* AUFNAHME, ELEKTROTECH, PHYS ZA *(acoustic impedance)*

Zf *(Zwischenfrequenz)* ELEKTRONIK, RADIO, TELEKOM IF *(intermediate frequency)*

Zfm *(Zwischenfrequenzmodulation)* ELEKTRONIK, RADIO, TELEKOM IFM *(intermediate frequency modulation)*

Z/sek *(Zeichen pro Sekunde)* COMP & DV, DRUCK cps *(characters per second)*

Z/Std *(Zeichen pro Stunde)* DRUCK cph *(characters per hour)*

Conversion tables/
Umrechnungstabellen

1 Length / Längenmaße

		metre *Meter*	inch† *Zoll*	foot*† *Fuß*	yard*† *Yard*	rod*† *Rod*	mile*† *Meile*
1 metre *Meter*	=	1	39.37	3.281	1.093	0.1988	6.214×10^{-4}
1 inch *Zoll*	=	2.54×10^{-2}	1	0.083	0.02778	5.050×10^{-3}	1.578×10^{-5}
1 foot *Fuß*	=	0.3048	12	1	0.3333	0.0606	1.894×10^{-4}
1 yard *Yard*	=	0.9144	36	3	1	0.1818	5.682×10^{-4}
1 rod *Rod*	=	5.029	198	16.5	5.5	1	3.125×10^{-3}
1 mile *Meile*	=	1609	63360	5280	1760	320	1

1 imperial standard yard† = 0.914 398 41 metre / 1 Yard (gesetzlicher Standard) = 0,914 398 41 Meter
1 yard (scientific)† = 0.9144 metre (exact) / 1 Yard (wissenschaftlich) = 0,9144 Meter (genau)
1 US yard† = 0.914 401 83 metre / 1 Yard US = 0,914 401 83 Meter
1 English nautical mile† = 6080 ft = 1853.18 metres / 1 englische Seemeile = 6080 Fuß = 1853,18 Meter
1 international nautical mile† = 1852 metres = 6076.12 ft / 1 internationale Seemeile = 1852 Meter = 6076,12 Fuß

† = not a SI-unit / keine SI-Einheit
* = not used in German-speaking countries / im deutschen Sprachraum nicht gebräuchlich

2 Area / Flächenmaße

		sq. metre m^2	sq. inch† $(Zoll)^2$	sq. foot*† $(Fuß)^2$	sq.yard*† $(Yard)^2$	acre*† $Acre$	sq. mile*† $(Meile)^2$
1 sq. metre m^2	=	1	1550	10.76	1.196	2.471×10^{-4}	3.861×10^{-7}
1 sq. inch $(Zoll)^2$	=	6.452×10^{-4}	1	6.944×10^{-3}	7.716×10^{-4}	1.594×10^{-7}	2.491×10^{-10}
1 sq. foot $(Fuß)^2$	=	0.0929	144	1	0.1111	2.296×10^{-5}	3.587×10^{-8}
1 sq. yard $(Yard)^2$	=	0.8361	1296	9	1	2.066×10^{-4}	3.228×10^{-7}
1 acre $Acre$	=	4.047×10^3	6.273×10^6	4.355×10^4	4840	1	1.563×10^{-3}
1 sq. mile $(Meile)^2$	=	259.0×10^4	4.015×10^9	2.788×10^7	3.098×10^6	640	1

1 are† = 100 sq. metres = 0.01 hectare / 1 Ar = 100 m² = 0,01 Hektar
1 circular mil†* = 5.067×10^{-10} sq. metre / 1 runder Querschnitt von $1/1000$ Zoll Durchmesser = $5,067 \times 10^{-10}$ m²
        = 7.854×10^{-7} sq. in / = $7,854 \times 10^{-7}$ $(Zoll)^2$
1 acre†* (statute) = 0.4047 hectare / 1 Acre (gesetzlicher Standard) = 0,4047 Hektar

3 Volume / Raummaße

		cubic metre m^3	cubic inch*† $(Zoll)^3$	cubic foot*† $(Fuß)^3$	UK gallon*† $Gallone\ UK$	US gallon*† $Gallone\ US$
1 cubic metre m^3	=	1	6.102×10^4	35.31	220.0	264.2
1 cubic in $(Zoll)^3$	=	1.639×10^{-5}	1	5.787×10^{-4}	3.605×10^{-3}	4.329×10^{-3}
1 cubic ft $(Fuß)^3$	=	2.832×10^{-2}	1728	1	6.229	7.480
1 UK gallon[1] $Gallone\ UK$	=	4.546×10^{-3}	277.4	0.1605	1	1.201
1 US gallon[2] $Gallone\ US$	=	3.785×10^{-3}	231.0	0.1337	0.8327	1

[1] volume of 10 lb of water at 62 ° F / Volumen von 10 britischen Pfund H_2O bei 62 ° F
[2] volume of 8.328 28 lb of water at 60 ° F / Volumen von 8,328 britischen Pfund H_2O bei 60 ° F
1 cubic metre = 1000 litres / 1 m³ = 1000 Liter
1 acre foot† = 271 328 UK gallons = 1233 cubic metres / 1 Acre-Fuß = 271 328 Gallonen UK = 1233 m³ (Kubikmeter)
Until 1976 the litre was equal to 1000.028 cm³ (the volume of 1 kg of water at maximum density) but then it was revalued to be 1000 cm³ exactly.
Bis 1976 war der Liter als 1000,028 cm³ definiert (das Volumen von 1 kg H_2O bei maximaler Dichte), wurde dann aber als exakt 1000 cm³ umdefiniert.

† = not a SI-unit / keine SI-Einheit
* = not used in German-speaking countries / im deutschen Sprachraum nicht gebräuchlich

4 Angle / Winkelmaße

		degree *Grad*	minute *Minute*	second *Sekunde*	radian *Radian*	revolution *Undrehung*
1 degree *Grad*	=	1	60	3600	1.745×10^{-2}	2.778×10^{-3}
1 minute *Minute*	=	1.677×10^{-2}	1	60	2.909×10^{-4}	4.630×10^{-5}
1 second *Sekunde*	=	2.778×10^{-4}	1.667×10^{-2}	1	4.848×10^{-6}	7.716×10^{-7}
1 radian *Radian*	=	57.30	3438	2.063×10^{5}	1	0.1592
1 revolution *Umdrehung*	=	360	2.16×10^{4}	1.296×10^{6}	6.283	1

1 mil†* = 10^{-3} radian / 1 Mil (Artilleriemaß) = $^1/_{64,000}$ von 360° = 10^{-3} Radian.

5 Time / Zeit

		year *Jahr*	solar day *mittlerer (Sonnen)tag*	hour *Stunde*	minute *Minute*	second *Sekunde*
1 year *Jahr*	=	1	365.24[1]	8.766×10^{3}	5.259×10^{5}	3.156×10^{7}
1 solar day *mittlerer (Sonnen)tag*	=	2.738×10^{-3}	1	24	1440	8.640×10^{4}
1 hour *Stunde*	=	1.141×10^{-4}	4.167×10^{-2}	1	60	3600
1 minute *Minute*	=	1.901×10^{-6}	6.944×10^{-4}	1.667×10^{-2}	1	60
1 second *Sekunde*	=	3.169×10^{-8}	1.157×10^{-5}	2.778×10^{-4}	1.667×10^{-2}	1

1 year = 366.24 sidereal days / 1 Jahr = 366,24 siderische Tage
1 sidereal day = 86 164.090 6 seconds / 1 siderischer Tag= 86 164,090 6 Sekunden
[1] exact figure = 365.242 192 64 in AD 2000 /genaue Zahl =365,242 192 64 im Jahr 2000 A.D.

† = not a SI-unit / keine SI-Einheit
* = not used in German-speaking countries / im deutschen Sprachraum nicht gebräuchlich

6 Mass / Masse

		kilogram *Kilogramm*	pound*† *britisches Pfund*	slug*† *Slug*	metric slug*† *metrisches Slug*	UK ton*† *UK-Tonne*	US ton*† *US-Tonne*	u*† *u*
1 kilogram *Kilogramm*	=	1	2.205	6.852×10^{-2}	0.1020	9.842×10^{-4}	11.02×10^{-4}	6.024×10^{26}
1 pound *britisches Pfund*	=	0.4536	1	3.108×10^{-2}	4.625×10^{-2}	4.464×10^{-4}	5.000×10^{-4}	2.732×10^{26}
1 slug *Slug*	=	14.59	32.17	1	1.488	1.436×10^{-2}	1.609×10^{-2}	8.789×10^{27}
1 metric slug *metrisches Slug*	=	9.806	21.62	0.6720	1	9.652×10^{-3}	1.081×10^{-2}	5.907×10^{27}
1 UK ton *UK-Tonne*	=	1016	2240	69.62	103.6	1	1.12	6.121×10^{29}
1 US ton *US-Tonne*	=	907.2	2000	62.16	92.51	0.8929	1	5.465×10^{29}
1 u *u*	=	1.660×10^{-27}	3.660×10^{-27}	1.137×10^{-28}	1.693×10^{-28}	1.634×10^{-30}	1.829×10^{-30}	1

1 imperial standard pound† = 0.453 592 338 kilogram / 1 britisches Pfund (gesetzlicher Standard) = 0,453 592 338 Kilogramm
1 US pound† = 0.453 592 427 7 kilogram / 1 US-Pfund= 0,453 592 427 7 Kilogramm
1 international pound† = 0.453 592 37 kilogram / 1 internationales Pfund = 0,453 592 37 Kilogramm
1 ton† = 10^3 kilograms / 1 Tonne = 10^3 Kilogramm
1 troy pound = 0.373 242 kilogram / 1 Troypfund = 0,373 242 Kilogramm

7 Force / Kraft

		dyne *Dyn*	newton *Newton*	pound force*† *Pound-Force*	poundal*† *Poundal*	gram force*† *Gram-Force*
1 dyne *Dyn*	=	1	10^{-5}	2.248×10^{-6}	7.233×10^{-5}	1.020×10^{-3}
1 newton *Newton*	=	10^5	1	0.2248	7.233	102.0
1 pound force *Pound-Force*	=	4.448×10^5	4.448	1	32.17	453.6
1 poundal *Poundal*	=	1.383×10^4	0.1383	3.108×10^{-2}	1	14.10
1 gram force *Gram-Force*	=	980.7	980.7×10^{-5}	2.205×10^{-3}	7.093×10^{-2}	1

† = not a SI-unit / keine SI-Einheit
* = not used in German-speaking countries / im deutschen Sprachraum nicht gebräuchlich

8 Power /Leistung

		Btu per hr*	ft lb s^{-1}*	kg metre s^{-1}	cal s^{-1}*	HP*†[1]	watt
		Btu/h	*Fuß-Pfund/s*	*Kg m/s*	*Kalorie/s*	*PS*[2]	*Watt*
1 Btu per hour *Btu/h*	=	1	0.2161	2.987 x 10^{-2}	6.999 x 10^{-2}	3.929 x 10^{-4}	0.2931
1 ft lb per second *Fuß-Pfund/s*	=	4.628	1	0.1383	0.3239	1.818 x 10^{-3}	1.356
1 kg metre per second *Kg m/s*	=	33.47	7.233	1	2.343	1.315 x 10^{-2}	9.807
1 cal per second *Kalorie/s*	=	14.29	3.087	4.268 x 10^{-1}	1	5.613 x 10^{-3}	4.187
1 HP *PS*	=	2545	550	76.04	178.2	1	745.7
1 watt *Watt*	=	3.413	0.7376	0.1020	0.2388	1.341 x 10^{-3}	1

1 international watt = 1.000 19 absolute watt / 1 Watt international = 1,000 19 Watt absolut
[1] HP (Horsepower) = British unit. 1 HP = 745.7 watt / HP = britische Einheit. 1HP = 745,7 Watt
[2] PS (Pferdestärke) = European unit. 1 PS = 735.498 watt / PS = europäische Einheit. 1 PS = 735,498 Watt

† = not a SI-unit / keine SI-Einheit
* = not used in German-speaking countries / im deutschen Sprachraum nicht gebräuchlich

9 Energy, work, heat / Energie, Arbeit, Wärme

		Btu*† Btu	joule $Joule$	ft lb*† $Fuß\text{-}Pfund$	cm⁻¹ cm^{-1}	cal*† $Kalorie$	kW h $Kilowattstunde$	electron volt $Elektronenvolt$
1 Btu Btu	=	1	1.055×10^{3}	778.2	5.312×10^{25}	252	2.930×10^{-4}	6.585×10^{21}
1 joule $Joule$	=	9.481×10^{-4}	1	7.376×10^{-1}	5.035×10^{22}	2.389×10^{-1}	2.778×10^{-7}	6.242×10^{18}
1 ft lb $Fuß\text{-}Pfund$	=	1.285×10^{-3}	1.356	1	6.828×10^{22}	3.239×10^{-1}	3.766×10^{-7}	8.464×10^{18}
1 cm⁻¹ cm^{-1}	=	1.883×10^{-26}	1.986×10^{-23}	1.465×10^{-23}	1	4.745×10^{-24}	5.517×10^{-30}	1.240×10^{-4}
1 cal 15°C $Kalorie\ bei\ 15°C$	=	3.968×10^{-3}	4.187	3.088	2.108×10^{23}	1	1.163×10^{-6}	2.613×10^{19}
1 kW h $Kilowattstunde$	=	3412	3.600×10^{6}	2.655×10^{6}	1.813×10^{29}	8.598×10^{5}	1	2.247×10^{25}
1 electron volt $Elektronenvolt$	=	1.519×10^{-22}	1.602×10^{-19}	1.182×10^{-19}	8.066×10^{3}	3.827×10^{-20}	4.450×10^{-26}	1

† = not a SI-unit / keine SI-Einheit
* = not used in German-speaking countries / im deutschen Sprachraum nicht gebräuchlich

10 Pressure / Druck

	=	standard atmosphere† / Normal-atmosphäre	kg force cm⁻²† / Kg/cm^{-2}	dyne cm⁻² / Dyn/cm^{-2}	pascal / Pascal	pound force in⁻²*† / $Fuß\text{-}Pfund/(Zoll)^{-2}$	pound force ft⁻²*† / $Fuß\text{-}Pfund/(Fuß)^{-2}$	millibar† / Millibar	torr† / Torr	barometric in. Hg†[1] / Zoll Quecksilbersäule
1 standard atmosphere / Normalatmosphäre	=	1	1.033	1.013×10^6	1.013×10^5	14.70	2116	1013	760	29.92
1 kg force cm⁻² / Kg/cm^{-2}	=	0.9678	1	9.804×10^5	9.804×10^4	14.22	2048	980.7	735.6	28.96
1 dyne cm⁻² / Dyn/cm^{-2}	=	9.869×10^{-7}	10.20×10^{-7}	1	0.1	14.50×10^{-6}	2.089×10^{-3}	10^{-3}	750.1×10^{-6}	29.53×10^{-6}
1 pascal / Pascal	=	9.869×10^{-6}	10.20×10^{-6}	10	1	14.50×10^{-5}	2.089×10^{-2}	10^{-2}	750.1×10^{-5}	29.53×10^{-5}
1 pound force in⁻² / $Fuß\text{-}Pfund/(Zoll)^{-2}$	=	6.805×10^{-2}	7.031×10^{-2}	6.895×10^4	6.895×10^3	1	144	68.95	51.71	2.036
1 pound force ft⁻² / $Fuß\text{-}Pfund/(Fuß)^{-2}$	=	4.725×10^{-4}	4.882×10^{-4}	478.8	47.88	6.944×10^{-3}	1	47.88×10^{-2}	0.3591	14.14×10^{-3}
1 millibar / Millibar	=	0.9869×10^{-3}	1.020×10^{-3}	10^3	10^2	14.50×10^{-3}	2.089	1	0.7500	29.53×10^{-3}
1 torr / Torr	=	1.316×10^{-3}	1.360×10^{-3}	1.333×10^2	1.333×10^3	1.934×10^{-2}	2.784	1.333	1	3.937×10^{-2}
1 barometric in. Hg / Zoll Quecksilbersäule	=	3.342×10^{-2}	3.453×10^{-2}	3.386×10^4	3.386×10^3	4.912×10^{-1}	70.73	33.87	25.40	1

1 torr = 1 barometric mmHg density 13.5951 g cm⁻³ at 0° C and acceleration due to gravity 980.665 cm/s – 2v / 1 Torr = 1mm Quecksilber Zu Normalbedingungen bei 13,5951 g/cm⁻³ Dichte, bei 0° C und Schwerebeschleunigung von 980,665 cm /s⁻²

1 dyne cm⁻² = 1 barad / 1 Dyn cm⁻² = 1 Barad /

[1] normally, only the HG unit is given / normalerweise wird nur die Hg-Säule angegeben

† = not a SI-unit / keine SI-Einheit

* = not used in German-speaking countries / im deutschen Sprachraum nicht gebräuchlich

11 Magnetic flux / Magnetfluß

		maxwell †[1] Maxwell (Line)	kiloline †[1] Kiloline	weber Weber
1 maxwell (1 line) Maxwell (Line)	=	1	10^{-3}	10^{-8}
1 kiloline Kiloline	=	10^3	1	10^{-5}
1 weber Weber	=	10^8	10^5	1

[1] obsolete/veraltet

12 Magnetic flux density / Magnetische Flußdichte

		gauss Gauß	weber m^{-2} (tesla) Weber / m^{-2} (Tesla)	gamma Gamma	maxwell cm^{-2}† Maxwell / cm^{-2}
1 gauss (line cm^{-2}) Gauß	=	1	10^{-4}	10^5	1
1 weber m^{-2} (tesla) Weber / m^{-2} (Tesla)	=	10^4	1	10^9	10^4
1 gamma Gamma	=	10^{-5}	10^{-9}	1	10^{-5}
1 maxwell cm^{-2} Maxwell / cm^{-2}	=	1	10^{-4}	10^5	1

13 Magnetomotive force / Magneto-EMK

		abamp turn†* Ab-Amperewicklung	amp turn Amperewindung AW	gilbert†[2] Gilbert
1 abampere turn Ab-Amperewicklung	=	1	10	12.57
1 ampere turn Amperewindung AW	=	10^{-1}	1	1.257
1 gilbert Gilbert	=	7.958×10^{-2}	0.7958	1

[2] obsolete/veraltet

† = not a SI-unit / keine SI-Einheit
* = not used in German-speaking countries / im deutschen Sprachraum nicht gebräuchlich

14 Magnetic field strength / Magnetische Feldstärke

		amp turn cm^{-1} *Amperewindung / cm^{-1}*	amp turn m^{-1} *Amperewindung / m^{-1}*	oersted *Oersted*
1 amp turn cm^{-1} *Amperewindung / cm^{-1}*	=	1	10^2	1.257
1 amp turn m^{-1} *Amperewindung / m^{-1}*	=	10^{-2}	1	1.257×10^{-2}
1 oersted *Oersted*	=	0.7958	79.58	1

15 Illumination / Ausleuchtung

		lux *Lux*	phot†* *Phot*	foot-candle*† *Footcandle*
1 lux (1 lm m^{-2}) *Lux lm / m^{-2}*	=	1	10^{-4}	9.29×10^{-2}
1 phot (1 lm cm^{-2}) *Phot lm / an^{-2}*	=	10^4	1	929
1 foot-candle (1 lm ft^{-2}) *Footcandle lm / Fuß$^{-2}$*	=	10.76	10.76×10^{-4}	1

† = not a SI-unit / keine SI-Einheit
* = not used in German-speaking countries / im deutschen Sprachraum nicht gebräuchlich

16 Luminance / Leuchtdichte

		nit†*[1] Nit	stilb†*[1] Stilb	$cd\,ft^{-2}$† Candela / $Fuß^{-2}$	apostilb* Apostilb	lambert Lambert	foot-lambert† Foot-Lambert
1 nit ($cd\,m^{-2}$) Nit (Candela / m^{-2})	=	1	10^{-4}	9.29×10^{-2}	π	$\pi \times 10^{-4}$	0.292
1 stilb ($cd\,cm^{-2}$) Stilb (Candela / cm^{-2})	=	10^{4}	1	929	$\pi \times 10^{4}$	π	2920
1 $cd\,ft^{-2}$ (Candela / $Fuß^{-2}$)	=	10.76	1.076×10^{-3}	1	33.8	3.38×10^{-3}	π
1 apostilb ($1m\,m^{-2}$) Apostilb ($1m / m^{-2}$)	=	$1/\pi$	$1/(\pi \times 10^{4})$	2.96×10^{-2}	1	10^{-4}	9.29×10^{-2}
1 lambert ($1m\,cm^{-2}$) Lambert ($1m / cm^{-2}$)	=	$1/(\pi \times 10^{-4})$	$1/\pi$	296	10^{4}	1	929
1 foot lambert or equivalent foot candle Foot-Lambert	=	3.43	3.43×10^{-4}	$1/\pi$	10.76	1.076×10^{-3}	1

Luminous intensity of candela = 98.1% that of international candle / Leuchtkraft Candela = 98,1% der internationalen Candela
1 lumen = flux emitted by 1 candela into unit solid angle / 1 Lumen = Lichtstrom, der von 1 Candela Leuchtkraft in den Einheitsraumwinkel abgegeben wird.
[1] obsolete/veraltet

† = not a SI-unit / keine SI-Einheit
* = not used in German-speaking countries / im deutschen Sprachraum nicht gebräuchlich

Chemical elements/Chemische Elemente

Symbol/Symbol	Element	Element	Ordnungszahl Atomic number/
Ac	Actinium	Actinium	89
Ag	Silver	Silber	47
Al	Aluminium	Aluminium	13
Am	Americium	Americium	95
Ar	Argon	Argon	18
As	Arsenic	Arsen	33
At	Astatine	Astatin	85
Au	Gold	Gold	79
B	Boron	Bor	5
Ba	Barium	Barium	56
Be	Beryllium	Beryllium	4
Bi	Bismuth	Wismut	83
Bk	Berkelium	Berkelium	97
Br	Bromine	Brom	35
C	Carbon	Kohlenstoff	6
Ca	Calcium	Kalzium	20
Cd	Cadmium	Cadmium	48
Ce	Cerium	Cerium	58
Cf	Californium	Californium	98
Cl	Chlorine	Chlor	17
Cm	Curium	Curium	96
Co	Cobalt	Kobalt	27
Cr	Chromium	Chrom	24
Cs	Caesium	Caesium	55
Cu	Copper	Kupfer	29
Dy	Dysprosium	Dysprosium	66
Er	Erbium	Erbium	68
Es	Einsteinium	Einsteinium	99
Eu	Europium	Europium	63
F	Fluorine	Fluor	9
Fe	Iron	Eisen	26
Fm	Fermium	Fermium	100
Fr	Francium	Francium	87
Ga	Gallium	Gallium	31
Gd	Gadolinium	Gadolinium	64
H	Hydrogen	Wasserstoff	1
He	Helium	Helium	2
Hf	Hafnium	Hafnium	72
Hg	Mercury	Quecksilber	80
Ho	Holmium	Holmium	67
I	Iodine	Iod	53
In	Indium	Indium	49
Ir	Iridium	Iridium	77
K	Potassium	Kalium	19

Kr	Krypton	Krypton	36
La	Lanthanum	Lanthan	57
Li	Lithium	Lithium	3
Lr	Lawrencium	Lawrencium	103
Lu	Lutetium	Lutetium	71
Md	Mendelevium	Mendelevium	101
Mg	Magnesium	Magnesium	12
Mn	Manganese	Mangan	25
Mo	Molybdenum	Molybden	42
N	Nitrogen	Stickstoff	7
Na	Sodium	Natrium	11
Nb	Niobium	Niob	41
Nd	Neodymium	Neodym	60
Ne	Neon	Neon	10
Ni	Nickel	Nickel	28
No	Nobelium	Nobelium	102
Np	Neptunium	Neptunium	93
O	Oxygen	Sauerstoff	8
Os	Osmium	Osmium	76
P	Phosphorus	Phosphor	15
Pa	Protactinium	Protactinium	91
Pb	Lead	Blei	82
Pd	Palladium	Palladium	46
Pm	Promethium	Promethium	61
Po	Polonium	Polonium	84
Pr	Praseodymium	Praseodym	59
Pt	Platinum	Platin	78
Ra	Radium	Radium	88
Rb	Rubidium	Rubidium	37
Re	Rhenium	Rhenium	75
Rh	Rhodium	Rhodium	45
Rn	Radon	Radon	86
Ru	Ruthenium	Ruthenium	44
S	Sulphur	Schwefel	16
Sb	Antimony	Antimon	51
Sc	Scandium	Scandium	21
Se	Selenium	Selen	34
Si	Silicon	Silicium	14
Sm	Samarium	Samarium	62
Sn	Tin	Zinn	50
Sr	Strontium	Strontium	38
Ta	Tantalum	Tantal	73
Tb	Terbium	Terbium	65
Tc	Technetium	Technetium	43
Te	Tellurium	Tellur	52
Th	Thorium	Thorium	90
Ti	Titanium	Titan	22
Tl	Thallium	Thallium	81
Tm	Thulium	Thulium	69
U	Uranium	Uran	92
V	Vanadium	Vanadium	23
W	Tungsten	Wolfram	74
Xe	Xenon	Xenon	54
Y	Yttrium	Yttrium	39

Yb	Ytterbium	Ytterbium	70
Zn	Zinc	Zink	30
Zr	Zirconium	Zirkon	40